THE
CHRISTIAN BAPTIST

Edited by

Alexander Campbell

Revised by

D.S. Burnet in 1835

From the second edition, with Mr. Campbell's last corrections

THE CHRISTIAN BAPTIST
BACKGROUND AND INDEX

Compiled by

Gary L. Lee

SEVEN VOLUMES IN ONE

College Press Publishing Co., Inc., Joplin, Missouri

Library of Congress Catalog Card Number: 83-71986
International Standard Book Number: 0-89900-232-3

Chapter I

BIOGRAPHY OF ALEXANDER CAMPBELL

Ancestry and Early Life

The home in which Alexander was reared influenced his life and actions throughout his years. His home life was the source of much of the preparation and education which he drew upon all his life. His parents were godly people. His father, Thomas, was born in County Down, Ireland, on February 1, 1763. He was deeply religious in nature. Early in his life he decided to enter the ministry of the Seceeder Presbyterian Church. Thomas' education included three years at Glasgow University and completion of a course of study at the Anti-Burgher Theological School. After completing this phase of his education, he was licensed as a probationer by the Seceeder Presbyterian Church in Ireland.

Thomas married Jane Corneigle, a twenty-four year old girl of French Huguenot background, on June 1, 1787. The first of their eight children, Alexander, was born some fifteen months later, September 12, 1788, in Ballymena, County Antrim, Ireland.[1] After the birth of Alexander, Thomas continued to teach at Sheepbridge and Market Hill to augment his income as well as to preach as a probationer.

In 1798, the Thomas Campbell family moved to a place near Rich Hill, where they lived on a farm while Thomas preached at Ahorey. The year 1805 brought the opening of a private academy with Thomas as the headmaster and his seventeen year old son, Alexander, as his assistant. Later, as the family finances improved, the family moved from the farm to the town of Rich Hill.

Thomas Campbell was concerned about the divisions in the religious world, particularly in his own communion, the Seceeder Presbyterian Church. Thomas was a member of the Old Light, Anti-Burgher, Seceeder Presbyterian group. He was so concerned about the divisions in the Presbyterian Church that he tried to effect a union between the Burgher and Anti-Burgher factions.[2] The General Associate Synod in Scotland, after hearing the proposal, expressed disapproval of the measure and it was pursued no further. The union was accomplished two decades later in 1820.

While preaching at Ahorey and Rich Hill, Thomas and Alexander would often exercise the privilege of "occasional hearing." This was simply an opportunity afforded by the Seceeder Church to its ministers and members to hear preachers from other denominations. This gave the Campbells the opportunity to hear men like Roland Hill, James Haldane, Alexander Carson, and John Walker. These men were called "independents," because they did not belong to the established Presbyterian bodies.

The strain of the years of preaching and teaching began to take its toll on the industrious Thomas Campbell. His physician told him that if he continued his present pace his life would be in jeopardy, and recommended a sea voyage. So, at the age of forty-four, Thomas set sail for America on April 8, 1807. He spent thirty-five days on the ship *Brutus*.

Alexander's education was largely under the tutelage of his family members. He spent most of his youthful years on the farm near Rich Hill, attending several schools in the area. He spent some time at the elementary school in Market Hill, where he was a boarder with a local merchant. Two or three years were spent under the instruction of his uncles, Archibald and Enos, who had an academy in Newry. Later, he was taught by his father in the academy Thomas established at Rich Hill.

---

1. For a more complete discussion concerning the birth date of Alexander Campbell, see Robert Richardson, *Memoirs of Alexander Campbell*, 2 vols. in one; reprint ed., (Indianapolis, Indiana: Religious Book Service, n.d.), 1:28-29.

2. The background for understanding the divisions in the Presbyterian Church may be found in Richardson's *Memoirs of Alexander Campbell*, 1:56-57.

Alexander's love of sports and lack of attention to his studies prompted his father to engage him in field labor for some years. As he matured, so did his love of books and learning. He determined to become "one of the best scholars in the kingdom."[3] His father endeavored to give him a broad preparatory education.

> He managed to perfect his son in the preliminary English branches, and to give him such instruction in Latin and Greek as would enable him, should opportunity ever present itself to enter the classes of the university.[4]

Alexander's spiritual life was influenced greatly by his home life. Spiritual matters were of supreme importance in the Thomas Campbell household and were not to be treated lightly. "It was their rule that every member should memorize, during each day, some portion of the Bible, to be recited at evening worship."[5] In his later years, Alexander recalls the influence of his parents in his life.

> I can but gratefully add, that to my mother as to my father, I am indebted for having memorized in early life almost all the writings of Solomon—his Proverbs, his Ecclesiastes and many of the Psalms of his father David. They have not only been written on the tablet of my memory, but incorporated with my modes of thinking and speaking.[6]

Alexander's observance of the actions and attitudes of the organized religions with which he had contact also shaped his spiritual growth. In his own denomination, he often encountered a narrow-minded, legalistic view of the Scriptures and religious life. Appeals for church reform were ignored; observance of the church sacraments were neglected.

The Campbells were also affected by the Independents, such as J. A. Haldane, Robert Haldane, and Greville Ewing, whose teachings were in sharp contrast to the Calvinistic doctrines of the Presbyterian Church. Many of the Independent churches were simply congregations under the leadership of an individual, with no strong religious organization for the group. The people were pious and hard working. Bible study and private interpretation of the Scriptures were encouraged. The weekly observance of the Lord's Supper and offerings were attended to. These and many other concepts would lead Thomas and Alexander to break from the Presbyterian Church and attempt to bring about the religious union both dreamed about.

His Father's Early American Experiences, 1807-1809

Thomas Campbell stepped off the *Brutus* and first set foot on American soil on May 13, 1807. After landing in Philadelphia, he presented his credentials to the Associate Synod of North America and was assigned to the Presbytery of Chartiers.[7] This presbytery had jurisdiction over Washington County, Western Pennsylvania, where Thomas settled in order to be with some of his former friends from Ireland who had come to America some time before.

In the session of the Presbytery of Chartiers held on June 30, and July 1, 1807, at the Harmony Meeting House, Thomas was assigned his ministerial duties. He was to be an itinerant minister, traveling to many different churches during the remainder of the year. It was the policy of the Presbytery to require an explanation from any minister for failure to meet his appointed meeting. There is no record of Thomas failing to carry out his duties.

Thomas Campbell's trouble with the Presbytery of Chartiers arose when John Anderson was required to give the Presbytery an explanation as to why he failed to assist Thomas in the celebration of the Lord's Supper at Buffaloe at its meeting on October 27, 1807. Anderson

---

3. Thomas W. Grafton, *Alexander Campbell* (St. Louis: Christian Publishing Company, 1897), p. 23.

4. *Ibid.,* p. 25.

5. Richardson, *Memoirs of Alexander Campbell,* 1:35.

6. *Ibid.,* 1:37.

7. William H. Hanna, *Thomas Campbell, Seceder and Christian Union Advocate* (Cincinnati: Standard Publishing Co., 1935), pp. 28-29.

replied that he had refused to assist Thomas because of testimony he had heard concerning Campbell's beliefs. The meeting revealed that Anderson had acted upon the testimony of William Wilson, who stated that he had heard Thomas express publicly opinions which he felt were contrary to the Presbyterian confession of faith. It was upon Wilson's testimony that Anderson decided to neglect his appointment.[8] The Presbytery accepted Anderson's reason. The opinions which Thomas had expressed dealt with his disagreement with certain church doctrines and customs. The Presbytery investigated the charges against Thomas, and decided to suspend him temporarily from his ministerial duties.

Thomas appealed his case to the higher church court, the Associate Synod of North America. The Synod investigated the charges against Campbell, which resulted in three major actions. The action of the Presbytery of Chartiers was judged irregular. The suspension of Thomas was reversed by the Synod. The third action taken by the Synod was that it decided to review the case. In its subsequent investigation, the Synod found Thomas' answers "unsatisfactory and highly equivocal" concerning the charges about faith in Christ and confession of faith.[9] Discipline was rendered on May 27, 1808, when Thomas was rebuked and admonished by the moderator.

The Presbytery was angered because its decision had been reversed by the Synod for its improper proceedings in the matter. Thomas returned to the Presbytery after two months' absence but found no preaching appointments waiting. The Presbytery would not allow the matter to drop and tried to inflict a higher censure upon Thomas than the discipline meted out by the Synod.

On September 14, 1808, Thomas submitted a letter to the Presbytery in which he declined their authority over him. This letter had been originally submitted to the Synod on May 27, 1808, in which Thomas renounced their authority concerning him, but he withdrew the letter. This statement of disclamation of the Presbyterian's authority was accepted by the Presbytery. The letter was a formal statement of his actions taken toward the Presbytery on September 13, 1808, the previous day. The Presbytery accepted the letter and voted for his suspension.

The Synod was informed of the actions of both parties by the officials of the Presbytery. The Synod during its meeting on May 23, 1809, instructed the Presbytery to take Campbell's name off its roll. It was also noted in the meeting that Thomas had returned the fifty dollars given to him by the Synod when he came to America in 1807.

The Presbytery continued to summon Campbell to appear before it but no reply was made by Campbell until April 17, 1810. The substance of his reply is not known. On April 18, 1810, the Presbytery finally and formally deposed Campbell from his offices and privileges as a minister of the Gospel.

The defrocked Thomas Campbell continued to preach. He began preaching in the home of his friends "General" Thomas Acheson, James Foster, Thomas Hodgens, and Abraham Altars. His preaching acquired enough of a following that on August 17, 1809, the Christian Association of Washington was formed, and Campbell became the guiding force of a society organized for the propagation of the simple gospel. The purpose of the Association was stated in the following terms:

> That we form ourselves into a religious association under the denomination of the Christian Association of Washington, for the sole purpose of promoting simple evangelical Christianity, free from all mixture of human opinions and inventions of men.[10]

The Association built a meeting house on the Sinclair farm near Mt. Pleasant, Pennsylvania. In the home of Mr. Welch, Thomas Campbell penned a most remarkable document. In order to explain to the religious world the actions of the Association, the

---

8. *Ibid.*, pp. 33-34.

9. *Ibid.*, p. 83.

10. *Declaration and Address of the Christian Association of Washington* (Washington: Brown and Sample, 1809; reprint ed., Lincoln: Lincoln Christian College and Seminary Press), p. 2.

Declaration and Address of the Christian Association of Washington was written. This document has been called "the Magna Carta of the new religious movement,"[11] and "one of the immortal documents of religious history."[12]

The *Declaration and Address* is a call for unity in the religious world. The organizational and spiritual goals were set forth in the beginning pages of the document. The spiritual goals were as follows:

> That this society by no means consider itself a Church, nor does it assume to itself that powers peculiar to such a society; nor do the members, as such consider themselves as standing connected in that relation; nor as at all associated for the peculiar purposes of Church association; but merely as voluntary advocates for Church reformation; and, as possessing the powers common to all individuals, who may please to associate in a peaceable and orderly manner, for any lawful purpose, namely, the disposal of their time, counsel and property, as they may see cause.[13]

Turbulent Years, 1811-1830

Thomas' family in Ireland received a letter from him in March, 1808, stating that he was sufficiently settled for them to come to America. Preparations were made, and on October 1, 1808, his family set sail on the *Hibernia* for the United States. On October 7, 1808, the ship hit a submerged rock and sank. The ship's company and passengers made it safely to the Island of Islay. It was during the shipwreck that Alexander resolved to give himself wholly to the ministry of Christ.

After deciding that it was too late in the year to attempt another voyage, Alexander and the other members of the family made their way to Glasgow, where Alexander enrolled in Glasgow University. During his studies at the University, he met several Independent preachers of the city and adopted many of their teachings. Greville Ewing, particularly, had a great influence on him. His changing religious sentiment caused him to refuse to participate in the semi-annual communion service just before leaving Scotland. By not partaking of the communion, but instead returning the token (a symbol of his worthiness as a communicant) he broke from the Seceeder Presbyterian Church.

The University closed its session in May 1809. These eight months were the only university education Alexander received. In late summer the American journey was resumed. The Thomas Campbell family arrived in the United States on September 29, 1809. On October 19, 1809, the Campbells were reunited. During the family separation, Thomas and Alexander had severed their relations with the Seceeder Presbyterian Church and acquired similar religious views.

In 1810, Thomas Campbell was approached by some Presbyterians who urged him to seek affiliation with the Presbyterian Church for himself and the Christian Association of Washington. The Christian Association had no formal ecclesiastical affiliation, but many of the members were from a Presbyterian background. Application was made to the Synod of Pittsburg for admittance and it was rejected. The Synod decided that the plan of the Association would have a negative and harmful effect on religion, and that the Synod did not agree with Thomas' personal religious beliefs.

The rejection of the Association by the Synod of Pittsburg caused an action by the Association which Thomas wanted to avoid. He realized that the Association could not remain a loosely-organized group of people. The ministerial and spiritual needs of the members were not being met. So, on May 4, 1811, the Christian Association of Washington was organized

---

11. Frederick D. Kershner, *The Restoration Handbook,* Series I (San Antonio, Texas: Southern Christian Press, 1960), p. 14.

12. Frederick D. Kershner, *The Christian Union Overture* (St. Louis: The Bethany Press, 1923), pp. 13-14.

13. *Declaration and Address,* p. 3.

into an independent congregation called the Brush Run Church.[14] Three church members, Joseph Bryant, Margaret Fullerton, and Abraham Altars, did not partake of the weekly communion service. When questioned about the reason for their refusal, these individuals stated that they had not been baptized in any form and thus felt unauthorized to join in the observance of the ordinance. After much discussion with the members of the church, Thomas agreed that immersion was the proper baptismal mode. Thus, these persons were immersed in Buffaloe Creek by Thomas Campbell on July 4, 1811. However, the matter was not pressed nor was immersion made a requirement for church membership. Those persons who wished to be immersed were, and the majority of the church eventually followed suit. Those who did not desire to be immersed left, leaving Brush Run composed of immersed persons. Thomas, Alexander, and their families were among those who were immersed. It was after this action that Alexander emerged as the dominant force in the Brush Run Church.

This action aligned the church more closely with the Baptists than with the Presbyterians. In 1815, the Brush Run Church applied for membership in the Redstone Baptist Association. Many historians give the date as 1813, but the minutes of the Redstone Baptist Association show the following action on September 2, 1815:

> [Item] 5. A Letter from a Church in Washington was read, requesting union with this Association, which was unanimously granted.
>
> [Item] 6. Likewise a letter was received, making a similar request from a church at Brush Run; —which was also granted.[15]

The union with the Redstone Association was a conditional one.

> The church of Brush Run did finally agree to unite with that Association on the ground that no terms of union or communion other than the Holy Scriptures should be required. On this ground, after presenting a written declaration of our belief (always distinguishing betwixt making a declaration of our faith for the satisfaction of others, and binding that declaration on others as a term of communion) we united with the Redstone Association.[16]

This union was not without opposition. William Brownfield, Secretary of the Redstone Association, opposed the union unless the Brush Run Church adopted the *Philadelphia Confession of Faith* as an authoritative creed.[17] Pressure within the Association toward the church caused it to be disfellowshiped by the Association in 1824.

Tensions were strained in 1816 when Alexander preached his *Sermon on the Law* at Cross Creek, Virginia, August 30, at the regular meeting of the Baptist Association. In spite of opposition to his preaching, Alexander proclaimed the message which "afterwards involved me in a seven years' war with some members of said association, and became a matter of much

---

14. See Richardson, *Memoirs of Alexander Campbell*, 1:365-367; Lester G. McAllister and William E. Tucker, *Journey in Faith, A History of the Christian Church (Disciples of Christ)* (Saint Louis: The Bethany Press, 1975), p. 117 and Enos Dowling, *The Restoration Movement* (Cincinnati: Standard Publishing Company, 1964), p. 53.

15. *Minutes of the Redstone Baptist Association*, (September 1-3, 1815) (Denver: M. F. Cottrell, 1964), [p. 47]. The 1813 date stated in the *Christian Baptist* and the *Millennial Harbinger* was accepted as correct in subsequent histories. See Alexander Campbell, *Christian Baptist* (Va.: Buffaloe Printing Office, 1825),, 2:41. (All quotations of the *Baptist* in this dissertation are taken from the first or original edition.) See also Alexander Campbell, *Millennial Harbinger* (Bethany, Va.; reprint ed., Joplin: College Press, n.d.), 1832:3, 1839:165 and 1848:346 in which the 1813 date is given. See also Earl West, *Search for the Ancient Order*, 1:61; W. T. Moore, *A Comprehensive History of the Disciples of Christ* (New York: Fleming H. Revell Co., 1909), p. 154; Errett Gates, *The Early Relation and Separation of the Baptists and Disciples* (Chicago: R. R. Dunnelley & Sons Company, 1904), p. 20. Campbell gives the correct date of 1815, some thirty-nine years later in his *Memoirs of Elder Thomas Campbell* (Cincinnati: H. S. Bosworth, 1861), p. 123, as does Lester G. McAllister and William E. Tucker, *Journey in Faith, A History of the Christian Church (Disciples of Christ)*, p. 120.

16. Campbell, *Christian Baptist*, 2:41. See also the *Millennial Harbinger*, 1832:3.

17. Campbell, *Millennial Harbinger*, 1832:4.

debate."[18] The sermon was not in harmony with the accepted Baptist doctrine of the day. Alexander preached that both the Old and New Testaments were inspired of God, but only the New Testament was binding upon and the authoritative rule for the Christian. The official response is found in the minutes of the Association dated September 2-4, 1817.

> Having received several charges and complaints against the doctrines maintained by the Church of Brush Run and more especially against a sermon preached before the last association by Alex'r Campbell one of the elders. Resolved that having heard a written declaration of their faith as well as verbal explanations relative to the charges made against him, we are fully satisfied with the declarations of said Church.[19]

His sermon did not cause Alexander or his father to be totally ostracized from the body, for in the following years, both men held official positions within the Association. Alexander served as the clerk in 1817, 1818, 1819, and moderator in 1820. Thomas held the position as moderator in 1822. Both men wrote associational letters for the Association to the members which were published in the minutes. Alexander wrote the circular letter in 1817 and the corresponding letters in 1819 and 1821. Thomas wrote the circular letter in 1816.

In 1818, Alexander opened "a classical and mercantile academy,"[20] Buffaloe Seminary, in his home at Bethany, West Virginia, to educate young men for the ministry. Buffaloe Seminary existed for four years until in 1822 Alexander was forced to close the school due to a failure to attract a significant number of students to keep it open. During these years, the Campbells' opponents in the Redstone Association would not forget Alexander's tenets preached in his *Sermon on the Law* and strove to cause trouble for them.[21] The opposition to the Campbells in the Association came to the forefront in 1823. In August of 1823, Alexander learned that his opposers were trying to secure messengers who were hostile toward the Campbells to attend the next Redstone Association meeting. The Campbells' antagonists were intent on excommunicating them from the Association at the September meeting. In order to foil the plan of exclusion, Alexander Campbell and thirty-two members of the Brush Run Church withdrew from the church on August 31, 1823. These individuals then established a church at Wellsburg, Virginia. Alexander Campbell in the second volume of the *Baptist*, related the event in these words,

> I should have observed that a church was organized in the town of Wellsburg in 1823, which was composed for the most part of members dismissed from the church at Brush Run, of which I was appointed a bishop.[22]

Richardson, in his *Memoirs of Alexander Campbell*, reproduced the letter issued by the Brush Run Church which testified to the good standing of the out going members.[23] Alexander attended the September meeting of the Redstone Association but not as a messenger from the Brush Run Church. As he was no longer a member of the Brush Run Church, and not under the jurisdiction of the Association, the plot to disfellowship him was not successful.

In 1824, the Wellsburg Church requested admittance into the Mahoning Baptist Association in Ohio. The church was accepted into the Association and continued in its fellowship until the Association's dissolution at Austintown, Ohio, in August, 1830. The Association became an annual meeting for worship and to hear reports of the progress of the churches.

Thomas and the remaining members of the Brush Run Church continued in the fellowship of the Redstone Association until their exclusion from it in 1824. The official reason for the exclusion was an informality in their church letter.

---

18. *Ibid.*, 1846:493. Also see Alexander Campbell, *Sermon on the Law* (Reprint ed., Lincoln, Illinois: Lincoln Christian College Press, 1971), p. 1.
19. Cottrell, (September 2-4, 1817), p. [64].
20. Campbell, *Christian Baptist*, 2:41.
21. *Ibid.*, 7:16.
22. *Ibid.*, 2:42.
23. Richardson, *Memoirs of Alexander Campbell*, 2:69.

[Item] 7th. The representatives of the church at Brush Run; not able to give satisfactory reasons for the informality in their letter, were objected to.

[Item] 9th. Resolved, that this Association have no fellowship with the Brush Run Church.

[Item] 10th. Resolved that the 11th. article of business in the Minutes of 1816, be null and void.[24]

The informality was the failure of the church to affirm their acceptance of the *Philadelphia Confession of Faith* as the authoritative creed of the congregation.

In 1826, thirteen sister churches were disfellowshipped by the Association for the same reason.[25] The excluded churches met together in Washington, Pennyslvania, on September 7, 1827, and formed the Washington Baptist Association.

As late as 1830, the Association's actions pertaining to the Brush Run Church were still being dealt with. In the minutes of the September, 1830 meeting, the actions of the 1824 meeting were explained and rendered binding.

> Whereas the items of business of the Association contained in the minutes for the year 1824, and numbered 7 and 9, concerning the exclusion of the Church at Brush Run, (of which Thos. Campbell and his son Alexander were members,)[26] are indefinite as to the cause of exclusion: And this Association having received some communication from a distance, requesting more specific information as to the cause of their exclusion: Therefore unanimously, Resolved, that for the satisfaction of all concerned, we now further state, that their exclusion was on account of being erroneous in doctrine, maintaining namely, the essential derivation and (---)[27] of the true and proper Deity of Christ and the Spirit; that faith in Christ is only a belief of historical facts, recorded in the Scriptures, rejecting and deriding what is commonly called christian experience; that there is no operation of the Spirit on the hearts of men, since the days of pentecost, &c.[28]

Later Significant Developments, 1830-1866

Alexander published the *Christian Baptist* from 1823-1830. It will be discussed in another part of this paper. On July 5, 1830, he ceased publishing this periodical and continued publishing the *Millennial Harbinger,* which he had begun in January, 1830. It was published for four years after his death in 1866. The *Harbinger* was instrumental in shaping the thought and goals of the movement.

The passing of 1831 and the beginning of 1832 brought a major change to the followers of the Campbells and B. W. Stone. The new development was the merger of the Disciples and Christian congregations into one religious communion. Such a union was not uncommon. Disciple and Christian congregations had worshiped informally together prior to the consolidation in 1831, but the occasions were not common. The emphasis and support of the leaders of both groups plus the encouragement of the periodicals, *The Millennial Harbinger* and the *Christian Messenger* were major factors in the move toward union.

The impetus toward the union effort of 1831 was the friendship of John T. Johnson, minister of the Disciples church at Great Crossings, Kentucky, and Barton Stone, minister of the neighboring Christian church in Georgetown, Kentucky. These two men also shared a mutual goal in the promotion of Christian unity. Under the leadership of these two men, the two congregations began to worship together as one body.

---

24. Cottrell, (September 3 5, 1824), p. [99].

25. Campbell, *Christian Baptist,* 3:91-96 and 4:55-63 for Alexander Campbell's and James Phillip's account of the events. See also *Minutes of the Redstone Baptist Association,* (September 3-5, 1826) for the specific accounts of the exclusion of the Pigeon Creek, Washington, and Somerset churches, [p. 104].

26. The minutes are in error at this point. Alexander Campbell was not a member of the Redstone Association, when the Brush Run Church was disfellowshipped. Thomas Campbell was a member. See page (6) of this paper.

27. The word in the text is not decipherable.

28. Cottrell, (September 3-5, 1830), p. [128].

These men were encouraged by the response of their respective congregations and began to broaden the opportunities for union. Joint meetings of interested individuals from both groups were held in Georgetown, Kentucky, during December 25-29, 1831, and Lexington, Kentucky, during January 1-4, 1832. These gatherings were mass meetings in which the possibilities of union were discussed. The Lexington meeting was held in the Hill Street Church. "Raccoon" John Smith and Barton Stone were two of the speakers during this meeting. Both men preached and urged the union of the two groups. Smith spoke first and Stone followed with his address. Barton Stone, as he concluded his sermon, offered Smith his hand as a sign of friendship and concurring desire and commitment to the union. Following the two addresses, the persons in attendance who were in favor of the union, expressed the desire by offering to one another their hands in friendship and fellowship. These individuals then agreed to such a merger of the two groups. The next day, the Lord's Day, was marked by a union communion service in which both groups once more affirmed the union.

These meetings were the mergering of the desires and goals of these particular individual Christians. The merger did not necessitate the automatic merger of the two separate groups beyond those individuals present in the two meetings in Georgetown and Lexington. Union between the individual congregations of the Reformers and Christians was a matter of choice, although such an action was urged by the leaders of the two groups.

An elder from each group, John Smith from the Disciples and John Rogers of the Christians, rode together to the churches of Kentucky, exhorting both groups to follow the union meetings at Georgetown and Lexington.[29] The successful union of the two groups was shown in the fact that Johnson became the co-editor with Stone in the publishing of the *Christian Messenger* in 1831. The road to consolidation of these two groups was not an easy one. There were times when the subsequent united groups would divide over various issues but generally would reunite into one body. Ultimately, most of the congregations of the two groups in the state came together. There were some churches which did not join the union and became part of the Congregational churches which in 1931 formed the Congregational Christian Church. This body in 1957-1961, merged with the Evangelical and Reformed Churches to form the United Church of Christ.

Alexander continued to take an active role in the leadership of the movement. During his lifetime, he engaged in numerous debates, both oral and written. He began two educational ventures, Buffaloe Seminary (1818-1822) and Bethany College (1841), which were two pioneer institutions among the Disciples in the nineteenth century.

He conducted many tours of the country, visiting and encouraging the brethren. He continued to edit and publish the *Harbinger* until one year before his death, when W. K. Pendleton took over. Campbell's son, William, handled the labor of managing his property while his father was in ill health.

Alexander's health continued to decline. He died at 11:45 p.m. on March 4, 1866. His biographer, Robert Richardson, conducted the funeral services. Alexander was laid to rest at Bethany in the family cemetery.

---

29. Barton W. Stone, The *Christian Messenger* (Georgetown, Ky.: reprint ed., Fort Worth, Texas: Star Bible Publications, 1978), 1832:6-8.

Chapter II

THE *CHRISTIAN BAPTIST*, 1823-1830

"Restoration" Publications

Herald of Gospel Liberty

Thomas Grafton states in his biography of Alexander Campbell that the *Christian Baptist* was "a veritable John the Baptist in religious journalism."[1] While the *Christian Baptist* was a pioneer in the field of religious journalism, it was not the first. The distinction of being "the first religious newspaper in America" is claimed by Elias Smith, editor of the *Herald of Gospel Liberty*. This paper had a short life, 1808-1817, under the editorship of Smith.

Elias Smith was born on June 17, 1769, in Lyme, Connecticut. At the age of eleven years, his scanty education was completed in Hebron, Connecticut. As a child, he was concerned about religion and seriously studied the Scriptures. In May of 1779, Smith began to give much thought to the subject of baptism. After studying the matter, he concluded that adults should be baptized by immersion. Consequently, he was immersed and sought fellowship among the Baptists. In the summer of 1789, he was ordained as a Baptist minister.

When Smith moved to Salisbury, New Hampshire in 1791, he was disenchanted with the Baptist doctrine and began an intensive study concerning it. In May, 1802, he preached a sermon on Acts 11:26, in which he advocated the abandoning of religious party names and taking the name Christian. As Smith began to preach his views, opposition by the Baptist clergy grew.

Smith's disenchantment with the teachings of Calvinism continued. Although he was considered by many of his fellow Baptists as a Baptist minister in good standing, he had "mental reservations" concerning the message he preached.[2]

He decided that the doctrine of election was wrong and embraced the doctrine of universalism. His younger brother was a primary influence in Elias' initial fifteen day acceptance of the doctrine of universalism.[3] Throughout his ministerial career, Smith accepted and renounced the doctrine of universalism several times.

In 1802, he organized a church in Portsmouth, New Hampshire, based solely on the teachings of the New Testament. On September 1, 1808, Smith published the first issue of the *Herald of Gospel Liberty*. It was through the pages of this periodical that he proclaimed such teachings as immersion as the only Scriptural mode of baptism, that creeds should not be made a term of communion, and a return to the Bible as man's sole authority in religion.

His subscription list was small, (only 274 subscribers for the first issue), but it swelled to 1,500 subscribers in later years. The first issue carried a reprint of the *Last Will and Testament of the Springfield Presbytery,* with an endorsement of the work of Barton W. Stone and other men in the West.[4] The financial situation of the paper caused Smith to change it from a weekly to a monthly paper in 1816. His financial burdens finally forced him in 1817 to suggest discontinuing the paper unless the subscription notes were paid. The last issue of the paper was printed on October 1, 1817, with a notice that Smith had accepted the doctrine of universalism.

The *Herald of Gospel Liberty* was succeeded in May of 1818 by the *Christian Herald*. This paper was not published long. Some seventeen years later, on January 15, 1835, the *Christian Herald* reported that it had been bought by the Eastern Publishing Association. The *Christian Journal* became the successor of the *Christian Herald*.[5]

Many of the teachings of Elias Smith were echoed again by another young man who came to

---

1. Grafton, *Alexander Campbell*, p. 109.
2. J. Pressley Barrett, *The Centennial of Religious Journalism* (Dayton: Christian Publishing Association, 1908), p. 306.
3. *Ibid.,* p. 306.
4. James DeForrest Murch, *Christians Only* (Cincinnati: Standard Publishing, 1962), p. 90.
5. Barrett, The Centennial of Religious Journalism, pp. 50, 53.

a similar religious position by his personal study of the Bible. Alexander Campbell would, some six years later, proclaim many of these same sentiments to his Baptist brethren in the East.

Alexander Campbell's Earliest Writings
"Clarinda"

Although the publication of the *Christian Baptist* was the first attempt of Alexander Campbell in the field of religious journalism, it was not his first attempt at writing for publication. As early as 1810, his views were published concerning various social conditions prevalent in the surrounding area of Washington, Pennsylvania.

His first essay appeared in May 14, 1810, issue of the *Reporter,* a weekly newspaper published by Mr. William Sample, Washington, Pennsylvania. He wrote under the pen name of "Clarinda." The purpose was to "attempt to reform the general conduct of our and the opposite sex, in what particularly relates to forming of connections for life."[6]

The occasion for the essays were some of the social customs prevalent at the time. Due to the small population, the harshness of the life and the vast distances between families, social gatherings were not frequent. Various duties would bring the families together for work and social communication. The actions of the young men and women at such occasions as a "husking frolic," or "a quilting party," or an "apple-paring," were a shock to Alexander. To correct these abuses, "Clarinda" was created.

The issues were discussed in a series of ten essays which were published from May 14 to July 23, 1810. "Clarinda" was praised and criticized in replies from interested parties such as "J. C.," "Eusebia Anxious," and "Observator." The discussion did have a positive effect. The public discussion of such issues resulted in the cessation of the offensive activities.

Campbell's beginning literary activities were not without significance. It showed that he was not hesitant to speak out on matters which he felt needed correction. As he had been in the United States for only ten months, the newness of the culture and surroundings could have deterred him from speaking out. Campbell not only spoke out against abuses but he strove to provide the means of improving the situations. Thus, early in his writing career, he not only identified the areas of concern but tried to show the way of improving the conditions.

"Bonus Homo"

His second series of essays for the *Reporter* appeared under the name of "Bonus Homo." the series ran from October, 1810, to December 3, 1810. These articles were a response to a program sponsored by Washington College in which virtue and morality were mocked. The ethnic backgrounds of the Scotch and Irish immigrants were also made sport of.

Other articles appeared in the paper defending the actions of the students and criticizing "Bonus Homo" for his displeasure concerning the program. Many years later, the aged college principal, Mr. Brown, admitted to Alexander that he was correct in his chastisement of the college for its action in the program.

"Candidus"

Under the pseudonym of "Candidus," in the April 27, 1820, edition of the *Washington Reporter,* Campbell challenged the Moral Society of Middletown. This was one of the many moral societies appearing at that time in that section of the country. These societies were "organized for the reputable purpose of suppressing vice and immorality."[7] These self-styled moral committees were attentive to every infraction against their private codes of conduct. Campbell

---

6. Richardson, *Memoirs of Alexander Campbell,* 1:285.
7. *Ibid.,* 1:516.

picked up the gauntlet and battled the repressive societies. His essays continued until February 25, 1822. His journalistic efforts caused many individuals to realize that such societies for the private regulation of the community were wrong and the societies waned. Later, Campbell used "The Reformed Clergyman" as a pseudonym in his discussion of Mr. McCorkle's essays on the millennium in the *Millennial Harbinger.*[8]

The *Christian Baptist* (1823-1830)

Thomas Campbell in the "Postscript" of the *Declaration and Address* recommends to the Christian Association of Washington two actions by which the interests of the body could be promoted. He urges the preparation and publication of a "catechetical exhibition of the fulness and precision of the holy scriptures upon the entire subject of christianity," to which would be prefixed a dissertation on the perfection and sufficiency of the Scriptures. He also proposed a "periodical publication, for the express purpose of detecting and exposing the various anti-christian enormities, innovations and corruptions, which infect the christian church."[9]

The periodical was to be called *"The Christian Monitor,"* and was to appear monthly, beginning in 1810, if five hundred subscribers could be obtained. Unfortunately, a sufficient number of subscribers was not secured, so the periodical was never published. Alexander Campbell does not say that *The Christian System* and the *Christian Baptist* are his response to the call for a catechism and monthly periodical as expressed by his father. But there are several similiarities between the wishes of the Association and the writings of Alexander Campbell which suggest that this may be so. Alexander implied that the *Christian Baptist* was the logical expression of the principles set forth in the *Declaration and Address*, in the "Preface" of *The Christian System.*[10] Garrison and DeGroot maintain in their book, *The Disciples of Christ, A History*, that another person had to write in the phrase found in the "Postscript" of the *Declaration and Address* concerning the anti-christian enormities which "The Christian Monitor" was to expose.[11] They believe that Thomas' temperament would have not allowed him to edit such a periodical with such a narrow religious purpose.

Garrison and DeGroot maintain also that Thomas' viewpoint toward differences in opinion was more conciliatory than the phrase in the "Postscript" would allow. His emphasis on christian unity and his toleration of differing beliefs on non-biblical tenets would have kept him from writing the phrase or editing the paper. Thus, the phrase would have been added by a person other than Thomas Campbell.

The writer disagrees with the conclusion that Thomas could not have written the phrase in the "Postscript" for two reasons. The first reason is that as far as the writer knows, there is no evidence to suggest that Thomas Campbell did not write the entire document. Secondly, the writer feels that such a statement would not be out of character for Thomas Campbell. He had experienced such anti-christian behavior and attitudes from the Presbytery of Chartiers and the Associate Synod of North America. Thomas had been disciplined by these two religious courts because of his disagreement with them in non-biblical areas. He had experienced first hand the division which can occur when conformity in non-biblical matters was insisted upon. As this type of attitude would destroy the basis for any biblical union for the divided churches in Christendom, it would most readily be contended. It was such divisions on non-biblical matters which had kept Christian union from being realized. Before union could be accomplished,

---

8. Moore, *A Comprehensive History of the Disciples of Christ,* p. 304.

9. *Declaration and Address,* pp. 88-89.

10. Alexander Campbell, *The Christian System* (Reprint ed., Nashville: Gospel Advocate Company, 1970), pp. xii-xiv.

11. Winfred Ernest Garrison and Alfred T. DeGroot, *The Disciples of Christ, A History* (St. Louis: The Bethany Press, 1948), p. 152.

these divisions would have to be eliminated from church life. In accordance with his dream of Christian union, such drastic measures would be necessary.

There are two additional similarities in the two papers which are interesting but do not prove conclusively that the *Baptist* is the response to the Association's desire for a periodical. The frequency of publication and the length of the periodicals are the same. Both papers were monthly publications and were twenty-four pages long.[12] Thus, while there is no conclusive evidence that the *Christian Baptist* is a response to the proposed, but unpublished, "Christian Monitor," such a conclusion may have some proponents.

Inception of the *Baptist*

The inception of the *Christian Baptist* was largely caused by the acceptance and circulation of the printed form of his debate with John Walker in 1820. The first and second printings of the debate which totaled four thousand volumes were published between 1820 and 1822. In the concluding article of the last volume of the *Baptist,* Campbell related the circumstances that caused the periodical to begin.

> It was not until after I discovered the effects of that discussion, [debate with Walker] that I began to hope that something might be done to rouse this generation from its supineness and spiritual lethargy. About two years afterwards I conceived the plan of this work, and thought I should make the experiment. I did so, and the effects are now before the public.[13]

Such publishing ventures, unlike the many available five or six decades later, were not common. Grafton calls the *Christian Baptist* a "veritable John the Baptist in religious journalism."[14] Grafton made this analogy because like John the Baptist, the forerunner of Christ, preparing the way for the coming of the Messiah by preaching repentance and reformation of life to the Jewish nation, the *Baptist* gave a clarion call to return to the Christianity and church of the New Testament by the abandonment of all unscriptural teachings and practices. It was the independent nature of the paper that Campbell claimed set it apart from the other contemporary periodicals. Campbell boldly exposed the doctrinal errors and the unscriptural practices of the Baptist communion of which he was a part, rather than support the sectarian causes or spirits he perceived prevalent in the Baptist churches of his day. Thus, in the independent nature of the periodical, seeking to promote truth instead of party causes, the *Baptist* was a pioneer and model for later papers.

Many historians and biographers of Alexander Campbell and Walter Scott give credit to the naming of the paper to Walter Scott, a close friend of the Campbell family.[15] The accepted version of the account was that Alexander wanted to call the paper the "Christian" and Walter Scott suggested the title "Christian Baptist." Scott added the name "Baptist" to gain a wider acceptance among the Baptists. Apparently this account was the accepted version in Campbell's day. However, he took exception to it in the 1839 *Millennial Harbinger.*

> When we drew up our Prospectus for our publication, we headed it "The Christian"; and had it not been that we found ourselves anticipated we should have adhered to the title. I hesitated between the title "Baptist Christian" and "Christian Baptist," and on my suggesting my embarrassment to a friend, who had since given himself due credit for the hint, as an original idea; he thought the latter was a better passport into favor than either of the others. We never fully approved, but from expediency adopted it.[16]

---

12. *Declaration and Address,* p. 89. See also the *Christian Baptist,* 1:[6].

13. Campbell, *Christian Baptist,* 7:284.

14. Grafton, *Alexander Campbell,* p. 109.

15. See Richardson, *Memoirs of Alexander Campbell,* 2:49-50; Murch, *Christians Only,* p. 70; Dwight E. Stevenson, *Walter Scott, Voice of the Golden Oracle* (St. Louis: Christian Board of Publication, 1946), p. 42; William Baxter, *Life of Elder Walter Scott* (Cincinnati: Bosworth, Chase & Hall, 1874), p. 73; and H. Leo Boles, *Biographical Sketches of Gospel Preachers* (Nashville: Gospel Advocate Company, 1932), pp. 74-75.

16. Campbell, *Millennial Harbinger,* 1839:338.

This misunderstanding concerning the name of the paper did not affect Alexander's relationship with Walter Scott. Scott contributed many articles to the *Baptist* and later to the *Millennial Harbinger.* Walter Scott signed many of his articles with the pen name of "Phillip." This signature indicated his relationship to Alexander.

> All articles were signed 'Phillip' for he was conscious of being on the threshold of a new religious reformation, in which he thought of his friend Alexander Campbell as the Luther and himself the Melanchthon.[17]

The first issue of the monthly periodical was published on August 3, 1823. It continued for seven years, terminating in July, 1830. As most papers in those early days, the *Baptist* was quite small. It had a type face measuring 3¼ by 5¾ inches. In order that he would not be dependent upon another publisher, Campbell bought all the necessary equipment and printed the paper himself. This was an accomplishment, as he had no training in the field of printing.

Significant Articles

Campbell provided many topics in the *Baptist* for his readers to enjoy. He not only dealt with the religious issues, but also provided interesting comments and reports on a variety of subjects. Some of the major issues discussed in the paper related to the clergy, missionary societies, church associations, baptism, creeds, etc. The titles of some of the articles are listed so as to familiarize the reader with the wide scope of the subjects included in the periodical. Articles on the clergy included "The Christian Religion," "The Third Epistle of Peter to the Preachers and Rulers of Congregations," and "A Familiar Dialogue between the Editor and a Clergyman." Creeds were discussed in such articles as "The Casting Vote, or the Creed Triumphant over the Bible," and "Parable of the Iron Bedstead." Other major topics discussed were the mode and significance of baptism. The essays entitled "The Ancient Gospel," numbered one through ten, explored this subject. Subjects such as creeds, nomenclature, the Lord's Supper, the office of elders and deacons, discipline, and order in the early church were discussed in "A Restoration of the Ancient Order of Things." Socialism and the philosophy of Robert Owen were examined in such articles as "Mr. Robert Owen and the Social System" and "To Mr. D., A Sceptic." Political issues were discussed when their ramifications affected the church or christian society.

When a religious body sought to control a state supported college, "A Presbyterian University at Danville, Ky.!!!" appeared, in which Campbell spoke out against sectarian authority. "Acts of Incorporation" and "Chartered College & Legalized Priestcraft; or, Notes on an Oration" discussed whether a religious college should be chartered by the state. The controversial bill faced by the Congressional Committee of Post Offices and Post Roads, which debated the proposal of allowing mail to be delivered on Sunday, was addressed in the articles "Sabbath Mail Report," "Sunday Mails," and "What Next?."[18]

Alexander Campbell solicited articles from others. He did not try to carry the entire editorial load himself, but published articles and essays from other individuals when he felt they would be instructive to his readers. These articles did not have to agree with his teaching or beliefs to be published in the paper. He published these articles so that his readers could get both sides of the question or issue being discussed.

Tone of the Paper

The spirit of the work was one which did not endear him to his opponents. The attitude of the paper was often strong, caustic, and dogmatic. It was the tone of the paper which caused

---

17. Stevenson, *Walter Scott, Voice of the Golden Oracle,* pp. 42-43.
18. This section will be treated more extensively in Part I, Chapter 3.

the majority of the students of theology in the Philomathesean Society of Hamilton Seminary in New York to ask him that they no longer be sent the *Baptist.* The letter stated that although Campbell personally had been kind and courteous to them, his attitude in the paper was repugnant to them. The students agreed with him in the fact that there were many practices in the church which needed to be changed, but questioned whether the changes would be accomplished by "a confirmed course of ridicule and sarcasm, or by a dignified, argumentative, and candid exposition of error, and a mild and persuasive invitation to amendment?"[19]

Campbell suggested that the reason the students objected to the *Baptist* was because he did not patronize their beliefs.[20] A minority of the students in the Society also sent Campbell a letter requesting that the paper be continued. They asked for the paper as individuals and not as members of the society.

Robert Semple, likewise, sent Campbell a letter and asked that he be not so strong and extreme in the paper. Semple accused him of having a Sandemanian or Haldanian attitude because Campbell was so uncompromising in the pages of the *Baptist.* He stated that Campbell was actually two personalities, one when writing and another in the social circle. Semple stated that like the Haldanians and Sandemanians, Campbell was harsh and sarcastic in his writing. The forbearance which Campbell exhibited towards persons with opposing views was narrow and inadequate. Semple continued to state that when Campbell was not writing for publication, he was a pleasant, kind man, loved by many. Campbell was encouraged to take a milder tone in the paper. Semple felt that such a move would be of more benefit to any reform within the church, in contrast to Campbell's present course. Mr. Semple pointed out that it was this same lack of forbearance and gentleness which marred his book *Debate on Baptism.* Semple affirmed that the teaching was correct, but the spirit in which the book was written did it much harm.[21]

Campbell replied to Semple, stating that he had read some of the books written by James and Robert Haldane and Robert Sandeman but had been influenced by them only in a small way. His lack of forbearance was not due to any influence of their writings, but was evident because of the scope of the *Baptist* and the opposition he had received.

> There are many topics which would lead to the exhibition of what would appear in the fullest sense, and in your own sense, of the words, "A New Testament spirit," which I would have gladly introduced into this work; but owing to its circumscribed dimensions and the force of opposition, I have had to withhold, or to cause them to yield to those topics which are the least conducive to what, in the estimation of the majority, is the spirit you would wish to see more strikingly exhibited.[22]

Some five years later, Campbell once more explained the reason for the severity of the *Baptist* in the *Millennial Harbinger* for 1831.

> In a word, and without a figure, he regarded the so called christian community as having lost all healthy excitability; and his first volume of the "Christian Baptist," the "most uncharitable," the severe, sarcastic, and ironical he ever wrote, was an experiment to ascertain whether society could be moved by fear or rage—whether it could be made to feel at all the decisive symptoms of the moral malady which was consuming the last spark of moral life and motion. It operated favorably upon the whole, though very unfavorably to the reputation of its author as respected his "christian spirit."[23]

Although Campbell faced opposition and criticism from the clergy in and out of the Baptist fellowship to which he belonged, he continued undaunted. The *Baptist* made an unprecedented

---

19. Campbell, *Christian Baptist,* 4:85.
20. *Ibid.,* 4:87.
21. *Ibid.,* 3:197-200.
22. *Ibid.,* 3:206.
23. Campbell, *Millennial Harbinger,* 1831:19-20.

offer by giving a fair hearing to all who read the paper. His allies and opponents could have their articles and letters printed in the paper without fear of censure, but usually, not without reply. Campbell continued this policy for the duration of the paper, even though he was not accorded the same courtesy by his fellow editors.

Influence of the Paper

The influence of the *Baptist* was a major factor in shaping and spreading the views of the Reformers. When one considers the nature of the times, the uncertainty of the postal system, the publication of such a periodical was quite remarkable. As with any venture, there were many people who praised the work and many who condemned it. Thomas Grafton probably overstates the influence of the *Baptist* when he writes,

> The effect of the "Christian Baptist" was almost magical. It, of course, met with the most bitter denunciation from those whose authority it attacked. Pastors forbade their flocks reading it, and it was treated as an incarnation of evil. But it found a wide reading and ready acceptance among another class. Many there were, who, wearied with denominational strife, and restive under ecclesiastical denomination, awaited a prophet whose aim was spiritual emancipation, and whose strong and fearless leadership they could trust. To such the "Christian Baptist" was a welcome visitor.[24]

The influence of the paper is reflected in the many letters received from his readers. Many thanked him for the instruction given through his periodical. In an unsigned letter from a reader from West Port, Kentucky, the *Christian Baptist* was credited with bringing the reader to a more perfect understanding of the Scriptures.[25] "J. W." wrote from the state of Louisiana concerning the *Baptist*,

> that your publication has been the greatest source of information that I ever enjoyed, except the Bible; and to me is worth more than all the commentaries and systems of divinity that I have any knowledge of.[26]

"W." wrotes these positive words about the periodical, "this same Christian Baptist has stripped me of my 'call,' my 'ambassadorship,' etc. and has taught me that the treasure which the Apostles had in earthen vessels I have in the Bible."[27]

The *Baptist* was not only widely praised for the instruction rendered in teaching the Bible more perfectly, but was credited in being a catalyst in the conversion of several individuals to Christ. "A Friend to the Restoration of the Ancient Order of Things" wrote Campbell of such an instance. He stated that a deist, after reading Campbell's third number addressed to a sceptic, had his former arguments against the Bible defeated. Thus, he began to read the Bible and became a Christian.[28] Colonel J. Mason, of Kentucky, wrote of the influence of the *Baptist* and Campbell's edition of the New Testament in the counties of Montgomery and Bath, Kentucky.

> I am constrained to believe that the few copies of your first edition [of the New Testament] which have been scattered among us, together with the light issuing from the *Christian Baptist*, have been the instruments, in the hands of God, of doing more good and producing happier times in Montgomery and Bath counties than was ever before witnessed.[29]

He added a personal testimony stating that for twenty years he was a member of the Baptist Church and did not doubt the teachings of the church until he read Campbell's "Essay on Experimental Religion" in the *Baptist*.[30]

---

24. Grafton, *Alexander Campbell*, pp. 115-116.
25. Campbell, *Christian Baptist*, 5:203.
26. *Ibid.*, 6:55.
27. *Ibid.*, 5:162.
28. *Ibid.*, 4:273.
29. *Ibid.*, 5:249.
30. *Ibid.*, 5:249-250.

The *Baptist* was influential in the proclamation of the gospel and the teaching of the New Testament to a number of the pioneer preachers in the state of Indiana. John Philips Thompson began to preach the gospel in Kentucky in August, 1819, in several Baptist churches. In the fall of 1819, while traveling to the Friends of Humanity Baptist Association meeting held in Ohio, he first set foot in Indiana. He returned to Indiana in the fall of 1820 to visit relatives who urged him to settle near them. Thompson heeded their invitation and settled in Rush County in 1821.

Thompson's vocation was that of a carpenter, but he also preached as a supply preacher for other neighboring churches. In the fall of 1821, he traveled as a delegate from the Flat Rock church to the White River Association meeting at Franklin, Indiana. At the meeting, he aligned himself with one of the two opposing factions which comprised the body. He sided with and became a primary voice in the so-called Arminian group. He also became a popular member of the White River Association.

In June, 1826, he became a subscriber of the *Christian Baptist*. He read the evangelistic reports in the paper by such men as Walter Scott and John Smith with interest. It was not until he had learned that the reformation had reached his old home community in Kentucky and that many of his friends and neighbors had embraced the new teaching, that he decided to go to Kentucky and investigate the situation himself. He found that the reports were true, and listened as his friends told of their new faith. He was not moved in his religious views. It was a remark of elder John Smith which prompted him to begin a private investigation of the new religious movement. The study convinced him of the doctrinal errors in his beliefs and he embraced the cause of New Testament Christianity. He did not pronounce his new faith to the Flat Rock church until a meeting in the home of Elias Stone. The effect of the sermon was such that the congregation began to study the Bible and sought biblical proof for every tenet which had been proclaimed.

Persons who sought the truth continued to increase as Thompson preached at Flat Rock church and in the community. The number of adherents continued to grow. About sixty members withdrew from the Flat Rock church, with the church's consent, and started a new congregation in Fayette County, Indiana.

Thompson's preaching met with opposition by the leading Baptist preachers in the area. When the opposing ministers realized that they could not dissuade him from his views, a more stringent measure was taken. Thompson was brought before the Flat Rock church so that the church could decide whether his teachings were heretical. After considering the matter, the church absolved Thompson of any heretical teaching.

After these proceedings, the Baptists and the Reformers decided to use the church building alternately for one year. Thompson and his followers formed a separate body called the Church of Christ and continued an amicable relationship with the Flat Rock Baptist Church. The Church of Christ continued to grow in members and influence in the community. In 1832, John O'Kane and John Thompson traveled in eastern Indiana and preached the gospel, to which many persons responded. In a meeting in Greensburg, Indiana, the first gospel sermon was preached and the first disciple was made in eastern Indiana. Thus through the pages of the *Christian Baptist* and the testimony of pious friends and preachers, John Thompson accepted the reformation and became a major influence in evangelizing eastern Indiana.[31]

Ryland T. Brown was another pioneer preacher in Indiana influenced by the *Christian Baptist*. He arrived with his parents to Rush County, Indiana, in 1821. In the spring of 1822, he accepted Christ as Savior and, being from a Baptist heritage, united with the "Clifty Church." In 1826, he learned the existence of the *Christian Baptist* and became a subscriber to the periodical.

His first overt action as a member of the New Testament church occurred as the Flat Rock Association tried to bind new articles of faith on the Clifty church. A motion was made to recind the old articles of faith on the Clifty church and to adopt the new rules. Brown recommended that the single motion be divided into two separate ones. The recommendation

31. Madison Evans, *Biographical Sketches of the Pioneer Preachers of Indiana* (Philadelphia: James Challen and Sons, 1862), pp. 126-138.

was accepted and two separate motions were created. The motion to recind the old articles of faith was carried. At this point, Brown proposed an amendment which stated that only the New Testament would be considered binding upon the church. The motion was carried. From 1826 to the spring of 1829, Brown studied medicine, pursuing his studies at the Ohio Medical College in Cincinnati, Ohio. After he graduated in the spring of 1829, he returned home to Rush County, Indiana. The area was alive with the discussions concerning the preaching of John P. Thompson. After investigating the matter, Brown embraced the message preached by Thompson and became a disciple.

Brown's actions aroused the ire of the local clergy and he was charged with being a Campbellite and brought before the Clifty church. He was excluded from the church.[32] Brown wrote a letter to the *Christian Baptist* in which he related the incident. Campbell replied that such a spirit which was manifested by Brown's accusers was not a christian spirit but a divisive one. Such persons who cause divisions by setting up their own ideas as standards must be excluded, not because of their differing opinions, but because their opinions have become an idol to them and that homage was demanded to their opinions.[33] Brown became a member of the Church of Christ at Little Flat Rock, which John P. Thompson organized, and became an active member.[34]

In 1832, Brown moved to Connersville, Indiana, with wife, Mary, to practice medicine. He soon became respected in the community as a doctor and as a preacher. He was not ashamed of nor afraid to share his new-found faith. As a result of his preaching, he immersed many people in the community. He was prohibited from preaching in the church buildings of the established churches in the town. So he preached in the court house at Milton, Wayne County, Indiana. He was assisted by John O'Kane, and many people accepted Christ as Savior. John O'Kane then went to Connersville and preached. The church of Christ was organized there in 1833.

From 1833 to 1842, Brown preached extensively throughout the White Water county area and identified with many of the counties. In June, 1842, in Connersville, at the state meeting of the churches, Brown and three other men were appointed to labor with the other churches in Indiana for a year. He had to resign his post because of ill health and spent a year in manual labor. He returned to his practice of medicine and the preaching of the gospel in 1844.

In his later years, Brown studied at Wabash College in Crawfordsville, Indiana, and served as Indiana State geologist, and instructor at Northwestern Christian University. He also was a leader in the temperance movement and active in politics. Throughout all these activities, he continued to preach the gospel and remained true to the principles he loved so much.[35]

The mixed reactions of the Flat Rock and Clifty churches were typical of the responses given by the Baptists to the Reformers. The variety of responses were primarily dependent upon the attitudes of the persons involved in situations in which the reformers became vocal in their views. The different responses are further illustrated in the ministries of reformer Philip S. Fall. While Fall was preaching for the Baptist church in Louisville, Kentucky, in 1825, several members of the church accepted his views. The fellow believers along with Fall left the established church and formed an independent congregation. The separation was a friendly one and the division of the church property was accomplished without any malice by either side. P. S. Fall had a similar experience with the Baptist church in Nashville, Tennessee.[36]

A negative response was recorded in the *Baptist* by "S. E. S.---." When this correspondent protested against the Northumberland Particular Baptist Association using creeds as a test of fellowship, the response was hostile. He was pressured to retract his protest by members of

32. The letter Brown wrote to Campbell is found in Evans, *Biographical Sketches of Pioneer Preachers in Indiana*, pp. 305-307, and the *Christian Baptist*, 7:[239-240] which are misnumbered 243-244 in the periodical.

33. Campbell's reply to Brown's letter is found in the *Christian Baptist*, 7:242-243.

34. See biographical sketch of John P. Thompson in Evan's *Biographical Sketches of Pioneer Preachers in Indiana*, pp. 126-128.

35. *Ibid.*, pp. 300-314.

36. McAllister and Tucker, *Journey in Faith, A History of the Christian Church (Disciples of Christ)*, p. 142.

the association. In his account of the association's proceedings against him, he stated that some of his fellow Baptists blamed the *Christian Baptist* and Alexander Campbell for his departure from the faith. Yet, as the proceedings continued and he stood his ground, a member of the Shamokin church took a similar stand against creeds.[37]

The reaction by the Baptist community involved more than just a few isolated cases or a small number of individuals. John Smith in reviewing the results of his preaching over a certain number of months in 1828, made this statement to his wife, Nancy: "I have baptized seven hundred sinners, and capsized fifteen hundred Baptists. . . ."[38]

In June, 1828 issue of the *Baptist*, extracts of letters received from the field evangelists were published. Jeremiah Vardeman reported that from November 1, 1827, to May 1, 1828, he had immersed about 550 persons. John Smith also reported that from the first weeks in February till April, 1828, he had immersed some 339 persons. Evangelists Walter Scott, Sidney Rigdon, and Adamson Bentley reported immersing about eight hundred persons in the first six months of 1828 in Ohio. The report also listed other successful revival statistics.[39] Such large numbers of conversions would have made an impact on any religious body. As Campbell's teachings continued to be preached and taught, the effect upon the Baptist churches continued to be felt.

In the article "A Good Omen," Campbell reported that in Virginia, the Goshen Baptist Association broke away from the General association over the question of the validity of the associational structure and authority. The Goshen Association, led by Uriah Higgason, determined "that money was the bond of union of that association, and that it was an unlawful amalgamation of the world and the church."[40] But the separation was a peaceful and friendly one.[41]

"A Subscriber," in the article "Reformed Baptist Churches," related the actions of several dissenting churches in three Baptist associations. The actions of these churches were in opposition to current Baptist missionary programs and methods. It was stated that nine Baptist churches withdrew from the Raleigh Baptist Association, North Carolina, because of the congregations dissatisfactions over Baptist missions. Fifteen churches were reported to have withdrawn from the Neuse Baptist Association and one church withdrew from the Kehuke Association for the same reason.[42]

In order to preserve its membership and to maintain their doctrine, Baptist churches and associations which were opposed to the teaching of the Reformers began to take strong counter measures against them. "N. H." told of a man in Louisa county, Virginia, who was rebaptized by Baptist minister Timothy T. Swift because the man had previously been immersed by a minister using the "new way." The initial preacher immersed the man using the words "I immerse thee into the name," etc. instead of saying "I baptize thee in the name," etc. The individual wanted to join the Fork church but was refused until the man could relate his Christian experience before the church once more and be reimmersed. These conditions were met and the man was accepted into the church.[43]

"Epaphras" stated in his letter to Campbell, that "some have gone so far as to pass resolutions to prohibit those who are advocates for the *Ancient Gospel from the privilege of proclaiming the gospel in their meeting houses, to the people, that they might be saved!!*"[44] Some Baptist churches, such as the North Elkton and Mount Pleasant churches, in their letter to the Elkhorn Baptist Association in Kentucky, urged the association to oppose any doctrine contrary to the *Philadelphia Confession of Faith*.[45]

---

37. Campbell, *Christian Baptist*, 4:224-225.
38. John A. Williams, *Life of Elder John Smith* (Cincinnati: Standard Publishing Company, 1904), p. 208.
39. *Christian Baptist*, 5:263-264.
40. *Ibid.*, 6:119.
41. *Ibid.*, 4:117-118.
42. *Ibid.*, 6:192.
43. *Ibid.*, 7: [79]-80. Page 79 is misnumbered page 84 in the periodical.
44. *Ibid.*, 7:158.
45. *Ibid.*, 6:83-84.

More drastic measures were taken by the Beaver Baptist Association, of Pennsylvania, in 1829. This association condemned and anathematized Campbell and the Mahoning Baptist Association of Ohio because "the Mahoning Association disbelieve and deny many of the doctrines of the Holy Scriptures."[46] The effect of the Beaver Anathema was recounted in a report by Walter Scott concerning the Youngstown, Palmyra, Achor, and Salem churches in Ohio.[47] These four churches were members of the Mahoning Association and were accused in the Beaver Anathema of "having left their former connexion (sic), because of 'damnable heresy.'"[48] The heresy of which these churches were convicted was their adherence to the teachings of the Reformers. In the years 1828-1829, Scott had preached at the established though declining Baptist church in Youngstown and William Hayden at the Baptist church in Palmyra. The preaching was successful in both of the churches. The new Christians in the Youngstown church determined to adhere to the Scriptures only as their guide in religion, and constituted a separate church. The older members of the established church were invited to join the new church, and many did. The church numbered about one hundred and fifty persons with elders and five deacons.

The new church was opposed by a group numbering between eleven to sixteen persons who called themselves the Church of Youngstown. This group appealed to the Beaver Association for assistance in excommunicating the new church. The judgment was rendered by the Beaver Association and the new church was stricken from the Baptist Associational lists throughout the nation.[49] The opposition of the new church in Palmyra which numbered about eleven persons took a similar action. They called themselves the Palmyra Church and joined the Beaver Association.[50]

The Anchor church had been a growing congregation in past years but had declined after a Baptist minister, a Mr. Winters, helped eject some of its best members. When Scott preached at the church in 1828, he was so opposed that he had to quit and go elsewhere.

While preaching at the Salem church, Scott immersed forty-one persons in ten days. Yet, by the time the monthly meeting occurred when the new Christians would have been admitted into the church, none of the new members were accepted. The opposition to Scott and his preaching had determined that some of the new Christians were really unconverted and sought to keep them from being admitted to the church. Their efforts were successful, and none of those converts thought suspect were admitted to the church. Scott had to leave the church for five weeks absence to preach revivals in other places. When he returned, he found that twenty-one of the new converts were "cajoled" into the church, while the remainder had organized a church outside of town.[51]

So it can be seen that as the Reformers became more vocal and active concerning their beliefs, confrontation with the opposing Baptists grew. As they continued to move away from the Baptists in the later 1820's, they found that they had more in common with Stone and the group known as "Christians." In the 1830's they eventually merged with the Stone's "Christians" and formed one religious body.

In keeping with his editorial policy of giving anyone who wished a hearing, Campbell published letters and reports which stated a negative view of the *Baptist.* Robert B. Semple in a letter to Silas M. Noel, expresses his feelings toward the influence of the paper in these words:

> The 'Christian Baptist' has doubtless exhibited many valuable pieces and principles; but, taken as a whole, I am persuaded it has been more mischievous than any publication I have ever known. The ability of the editor, joined to the plausibility of his plans or doctrines, has

---

46. *Ibid.,* 7:185.
47. *Ibid.,* 7:269-272.
48. *Ibid.,* 7:269.
49. *Ibid.,* 7:270.
50. *Ibid.,* 7:270-271.
51. *Ibid.,* 7:271-272.

succeeded in sowing the seeds of discord among brethren to an extent in many places alarming.[52]

It was also labeled "A religious incendiary, and will do a world of mischief," and a "disorganizer" and "dangerous to our children."[53]

There are several interesting instances reported in the *Baptist* concerning the methods of the opposing clergy in attacking the paper. It was reported that Rev. Abner Clopton attacked the periodical in his November 19, 1828, sermon in Virginia. "Aristarchus" who heard his sermon reported that

> His method of opposing, however, is not by any serious argument or criticism; but by assertions and misrepresentations, insinuations and detractions, imbittering [sic] the minds of opposers, and filling with prejudice those who have never read the 'Christian Baptist.'[54]

In a letter to the editor, "A Constant Reader" reported that many clergymen use their opposition to the *Baptist* as the basis for their sermons.

> Many of the 'ministry' (as they call themselves,) are in the habit of abusing you and the Christian Baptist every time they "preach." And yet every one [sic] who reads the Christian Baptist may clearly see that they have obtained a great part of what they preach from it. It is, indeed, said of the Elkton clergymen, that 'two thirds' of his *sermons* are sometimes made up of extracts from the Christian Baptist and that the other third is employed in abusing it.[55]

So, as with any venture, there were many supporters and detractors. Although the opposition was at times quite vehement, Campbell continued spreading the Gospel through this periodical.

Circulation of the Paper

The subscription and circulation figures were not given in yearly totals. The agents for the *Baptist* were not listed in the periodical until December 5, 1825, in the third volume. The only other list of agents in the third volume is found at the end of the July 3, 1826, issue. Thereafter, the list of agents is given at the end of each monthly issue.

An examination of the lists of agents indicates a large circulation, as shown by this representative survey of states: the New England states, Vermont, Massachusetts, New Jersey, and Maryland; the Southern states, Georgia, Kentucky, and Tennessee; the Middle western states, Indiana, Illinois, and Ohio. There were agents outside the United States in Canada and Ireland.[56]

Although no circulation figures are given in the paper, it is credited with a respectable circulation by its editor. Campbell wrote in 1826 of its growing circulation, "The *Christian Baptist* continues to receive a considerable accession of respectable patrons, most of whom wish to obtain the work from its commencement."[57]

In 1827, the *Baptist Recorder* charged the *Christian Baptist* with losing one hundred per cent of its readers in Kentucky. Campbell defended the circulation of the paper by saying:

> The fact is, that the Christian Baptist is more generally read, and has more subscribers this year in Kentucky than it has ever had before. In Virginia, too, where it is represented as declining fast, it has gained in the last two years, more than a hundred per cent, per annum.

---

52. *Ibid.*, 5:199.
53. *Ibid.*, 1:174.
54. *Ibid.*, 6:146.
55. *Ibid.*, 6:150.
56. See Robert M. Hall, "The Christian Baptist (1823-1830): A Study of the Periodical's Influence as Reflected by Internal Evidences and a Complete Index" (Bachelor of Divinity Thesis, School of Religion, Butler University, 1947), p. 49, for the geographical distribution of new agents for the *Christian Baptist*, volumes three to seven.
57. Campbell, *Christian Baptist*, 4:168.

And for the past three months, since the commencement of the present volume, our regular increase has been about seventy new subscribers per month.[58]

An examination of the chart in Hall's thesis, listing the source of monthly receipts in the *Baptist,* volumes six and seven, show a substantial increase each year. Volume six showed a yearly income of $345.00. The receipts for volume seven showed nearly a four-fold increase, ending with a total of $1,200.00.[59] These figures show that, while there was opposition to the paper, it did not hamper the interest in and circulation of the *Baptist.*

The *Christian Baptist* ceased publication with the July 5, 1830, issue of the paper. In the last article entitled "Concluding Remarks," Campbell gave his reasons for ending the periodical:

> Hating sects and sectarian names, I resolved to prevent the name of *Christian Baptists* from being fixed on us, to do which, efforts were making. It is true, men's tongues are their own, and they may use them as they please; but I am resolved to give them no just occasion for nicknaming advocates for the ancient order of things.[60]

One hundred and fifty years have passed since the cessation of the *Baptist.* Yet, as one picks up a volume and reads it, he will find the material to be as fresh and relevant as it was in 1830. Many of the problems, attitudes, and situations in the contemporary religious world are similar to those Campbell faced. Alexander Campbell has a great deal to teach us. We may not agree with all that he says, but he deserves a hearing.

---

58. *Ibid.,* 5:111.
59. Hall, "The Christian Baptist (1823-1830): A Study of the Periodical's Influence as Reflected by Internal Evidences and a Complete Index," p. 50.
60. Campbell, *Christian Baptist,* 7:285 misnumberd 281 in the periodical.

Chapter III

AIMS OF THE CHRISTIAN BAPTIST

Alexander Campbell set forth four major aims in his "Prospectus" of the *Baptist* pertaining to its purpose. His goals for the paper were:

> THE "CHRISTIAN BAPTIST" shall espouse the cause of no religious sect, excepting that Ancient Sect, called "CHRISTIANS FIRST AT ANTIOCH." Its sole object shall be the eviction of truth, and the exposure of error in doctrine and practice. The Editor acknowledging no standard of religious faith or works, other than the Old and New Testaments, and the latter as the only standard of the religion of Jesus Christ will, intentionally at least, oppose nothing which it contains, and recommend nothing which it does not enjoin. Having no worldly interest at stake from the adoption or reprobation of any article of faith or religious practice—having no gift nor religious office of any worldly emolument to blind his eyes or to pervert his judgment—he hopes to manifest that he is an impartial advocate of truth.[1]

A shortened statement of the aims can be found in the "Dedication" of the periodical.[2] Following these four aims, Campbell listed seven items which are to be implemented to achieve these goals. The seven items are:

> I. Animadversions of the moral of Professors of the Christain (sic) religion.
> II. Strictures of the religious systems of the present day, and the leading measures of the religious sects of our country.
> III. Essays on man's primitive state, on the Patriarchal, Jewish, and Christian dispensations.
> IV. Religious News, or a record of the passing events of our time, accompanied with such remarks as they may naturally excite.
> V. Historical Sketches, or retrospective views of the origin and progress of the most reputable opinions and practices of modern times.
> VI. Biographical notices, and religious anecdotes.
> VII. General Views of the religious and political state of nations not professing the Chriatian [sic] religion.[3]

This section of the paper will examine these aims and determine if Alexander Campbell reached them.

The impetus behind these aims is Campbell's perception of the state of the contemporary religious world. His "worldview" is summed up in his "Prefatory Remarks" in volume four.

> "God made man upright; but he has sought out many inventions." To restore man to uprightness and happiness is the grand end of the whole remedial government of God. To be instrumental in introducing that state of things which God instituted, and which was once exhibited; of leading the disciples to see that they need but one bond of union, one prophet, priest and king, one Bible, one book on the science of religion, and one treatise on the art of living well, is the supreme object of all our efforts.[4]

Thus, these four aims were to be one of the means of restoring man to his proper relationship with God.

Espouse Only the Doctrines Set Forth in Scripture

The first aim of the *Baptist* was that it would espouse the cause of no religious sect, but seek only to maintain the doctrines set forth in the Scriptures. Prior to the proclamation of these

---

1. *Ibid.*, 1: [3].
2. *Ibid.*, 1: [5].
3. *Ibid.*, 1: [3].
4. *Ibid.*, 4:2-3.

(22)

doctrines, it must be determined what doctrines the Bible teaches. To determine these doctrines, Campbell set forth the basic and fundamental teachings of the New Testament. He strove to determine which doctrines were divine and which were man-made. He consistently urged a thorough study of the New Testament as the touchstone for such a determination.

It was in these seven volumes that he tried to point out what the Bible taught on such issues as the church, the role of the clergy, the eldership, etc. In realizing the biblical standard and purpose for these matters, the departures from this standard become apparent and a reconciliation to the divine standard can be accomplished.

The series of essays in which the New Testament pattern of the church is discussed is entitled "A Restoration of the Ancient Order of Things." This is one of the better known series, in which he discusses the early pattern of the church: creeds, nomenclature, the order of worship, the Lord's Supper, elders, deacons, hymns, fellowship, and the discipline of the church. But, the mere description of the teachings and life of the early church is not sufficient to restore man to his proper relationship with God. Christians must be motivated to incorporate these practices into their lives.

> Now, in attempting to accomplish this, it must be observed, that it belongs to every individual, and to every congregation of individuals, to discard from their faith and their practice every thing that is not found written in the New Testament of the Lord and Saviour; and to believe and practise [sic] whatever is there enjoined.[5]

> But to come to the things to be discarded, we observe that, in the ancient order of things, there were no creeds or compilations of doctrine in abstract terms, nor in any terms, other than the terms adopted by the Holy Spirit in the New Testament. *Therefore, all such are to be discarded.*[6]

Such a restoration of man's proper relationship with God is crucial for the church, the reason being that "*a RESTORATION of the ancient order of things* is all that is necessary to the happiness and usefulness of Christians."[7] Campbell explained what he meant by the term "ancient order of things" in the second volume of the *Baptist.*

> To bring the societies of Christians *up* to the New Testament, is just to bring the disciples, individually and collectively, to walk in the faith, and in the commandments of the Lord and Saviour, as presented in that blessed volume; and this is to *restore* the ancient order of things.[8]

Campbell believed that the inception and progress of the millennium would proceed in direct relation with the restoration of the church. "Just in so far as the ancient order of things, or the religion of the New Testament, is restored, just so far has the Millennium commenced, and so far has its blessings been enjoyed."[9] It was the emphasis of the restoration of the church rather than the reformation of it, that labeled his efforts "The Restoration Movement." The reasoning behind such an emphasis was discussed in the first number of "A Restoration of the Ancient Order of Things." Campbell stated "all the famous reformations in history have rather been reformations of creeds and of clergy, than of religion" and "though called reformations of religion, they have always left religion where it was."[10]

> Human systems, whether of philosophy or of religion, are proper subjects of reformation; but Christianity cannot be reformed. Every attempt to reform Christianity is like an attempt to create a new sun, or to change the revolutions of the heavenly bodies—unprofitable and vain.[11]

---

5. *Ibid.,* 2:176.
6. *Ibid.,* 2:176-177.
7. *Ibid.,* 2:156.
8. *Ibid.,* 2:156.
9. *Ibid.,* 2:156.
10. *Ibid.,* 2:154-155.
11. *Ibid.,* 2:156.

No attempt "to reform the doctrine, discipline, and government of the church," (a phrase too long in use), can promise a better result than those that have been attempted and languished unto death. We are glad to see, in the above extract, that the thing proposed, is to bring the Christianity and the church of the present day up to the standard of the New Testament.[12]

Campbell discussed the nature and work of the Holy Spirit in his "Essays on the Work of the Holy Spirit in the Salvation of Men." He concluded that no man could have believed the biblical revelation without the work of the Holy Spirit in his attestation of the gospel by miracles.[13] Miracles were defined as the displays of power whose purpose was to confirm that Jesus was risen from the dead. They were also given to fill believers with knowledge and light.[14] The miracles performed by the Holy Spirit in his attestation of the testimony of the apostles were "*numerous, public,* and *beneficent*," and "the cures were *always instantaneous, always complete,* and *always permanent.*"[15]

In commenting upon the second definition of a miracle, Campbell referred to Ephesians 4:8-13. He stated that the persons mentioned in this passage were Christ's gifts to the church upon his ascension; that these men were given to the church for a limited time, for the purpose of building up and teaching the infant church. Once this task was accomplished, the gifts would cease. The time for the cessation of these supernaturally gifted teachers would come when the church was able to defend and direct itself without supernatural aid.[16] The pastors and teachers mentioned in Ephesians 4:8-13 were not of the local church, but, rather, men who were instantaneously equipped for their offices by the Holy Spirit. These men were converts to the Christian religion and by the supernatural gifts of the Holy Spirit qualified to teach the whole religion.[17] These supernaturally equipped teachers and pastors were distinguished from the church's elders and deacons who were qualified to serve by ordinary means, namely, selection from among their own brethren for the work of their office.

The character of the Holy Spirit was characterized by Campbell as the Spirit of Wisdom, Power, and Goodness.

As the *Spirit of Wisdom,* he bestowed those gifts of wisdom, of the word of knowledge, of prophecy, and of tongues to the ambassadors of Messiah, to qualify them to reveal, in words adapted to every ear, the character and achievements of *God's only Son,* and the benevolent purposes of the Father, through him, towards the human race. As the *Spirit of Power,* he clothed them with all those magnificent gifts of power over the bodies of men, by which they were always able to prove their mission and demonstrate their authority, as the plenipotentiaries of the Son of God. What remains is to notice, with the same brevity, what the scriptures teach us of him as the *Spirit of all Goodness.* The Apostle saith, "The fruit of the Spirit is in all *goodness,* and righteousness and truth." This fruit, on another occasion, he particularized thus: "The *fruit* of the Spirit is love, joy, peace, long suffering, gentleness, goodness, *fidelity,* meekness, temperance."[18]

The time limits on the manifestations of power of the Holy Spirit as given to the early church were also discussed by Campbell.

While his distributions, as the *Spirit of Wisdom and of Power,* were confined to the Apostolic age, and to only a portion of the saints that lived in that age, his influences, as the *Spirit of all Goodness,* were *felt* and *realized* by *all* the primitive saints, and are *now* felt by all the subjects of the *New Reign,* or by *all* the citizens of that *new* kingdom which the God of Heaven *set up* in the reign of the Cesars [*sic*]. [19]

---

12. *Ibid.*, 2:156.
13. *Ibid.*, 2:16, also see 2:121-125.
14. *Ibid.*, 2:33.
15. *Ibid.*, 2:37.
16. *Ibid.*, 2:58.
17. *Ibid.*, 2:57.
18. *Ibid.*, 2:145-146.
19. *Ibid.*, 2:146.

The Holy Spirit was shown to be the Spirit of Goodness, in that his revelation of God was suited to the nature of man. "There is a *moral fitness* in the word of reconciliation to become the means of the impartation of the Spirit of Goodness."[20] In his discussion of the impartation of the Holy Spirit, Campbell defined the phrase as the renewal of the Holy Spirit. This definition was in contrast to the popular Calvinistic doctrines of the day. Campbell stated that renewal of the Holy Spirit was not some irresistible grace or an overwhelming influence of the Holy Spirit as Calvinism taught. But rather, the scriptures authorize us in declaring, that it consists in presenting *new objects* to the faculties, volitions, and affections of men; which *new objects* apprehended, engage the faculties or powers of the human understanding, captivate the affections and passions of the human soul, and, consequently, direct or draw the whole man into new aims, pursuits, and endeavors.[21]

Thus, the renewal of the Spirit was the acceptance of Christ, after the gospel had been presented to the individual. The individual was converted, not by a deluge of supernatural power, but by the acceptance of the gospel message as true and the appropriate response to the message.

Campbell also discussed the grace of Christ in this series on the Holy Spirit. The term grace was simply defined as the favor of God toward sinners. This grace was shown in Jesus Christ and is exhibited by his Spirit.

> But to conclude, we commenced this essay with the intention of exhibiting the import of the grace of God, in the fixed style of the New Testament, regardless of the spurious dialect, or new nomenclature of modern divinity. The prominent ideas intended to be exhibited are, that the Gospel of Jesus Christ is emphatically the grace of God; that this Gospel received is the grace of God received; that this grace of God when received, works in the hearts of them that believe, that the Spirit of grace therein dwells in the hearts of men, and teaches them to deny ungodliness and worldly lusts, to live soberly, righteously, and Godlily [sic] in this present world; that they have "received the grace of God in vain" who do not exhibit its fruits; that Christians continue in the grace of God" while they abound in these fruits; and that while men hold fast the Gospel as delivered by the Apostles, they "stand in the true grace of God."[22]

The series was summed up in these words in the last article.

> Thus we see that the whole work of the spirit of God in the salvation of men, as the spirit of wisdom, the spirit of power, and the spirit of grace or goodness, is inseparably [sic] connected with, and altogether subservient to, the Gospel or glad tidings of great joy unto all people, of the love God exhibited in the humiliation unto death of his only begotten Son.[23]

God's work through the ages was examined in the series of essays entitled, "Essays on Man in his Primitive State, and under the Patriarchal, Jewish and Christian Dispensations." The development of God's redemptive plan for mankind was traced, beginning with the creation of man. Adam and Eve were placed in the garden of Eden so that they could care for it. Their relationship with God was one of intimacy. God spoke with them and they were not afraid. But Adam and Eve sinned and were cast out of the garden. Campbell reflected upon the consequences of their transgression.

> Man lost by his fall his personal glory as above described; he lost a true idea of the image of his Creator; and the actual moral likeness he before had to him; with this he lost his favor also, and was thereby not only become obnoxious to all the punishment annexed to his original transgression; but was, as far as in him lay; utterly disqualified to regain either a true idea of God's moral character, conformity to him, or the enjoyment of his favor.[24]

20. *Ibid.*, 2:175.
21. *Ibid.*, 2:171.
22. *Ibid.*, 2:198.
23. *Ibid.*, 2:198.
24. *Ibid.*, 6:64.

In order to allow man the opportunity of restoration to his former relationship with God, the scheme of redemption was set in motion. This plan of redemption climaxed in the resurrection of Christ and the establishment of the church. Campbell divided the time frame associated with God's plan into four dispensations.

> Thus the patriarchal age was the star-light of the moral world; the Jewish age was the moonlight; the ministry of the harbinger the twilight; and the christian age the sun-light of the moral world.[25]

The Patriarchal Age was marked by the simplicity of worship and divine revelation. God communicated with man through angelic messengers, signs, and dreams. Man's extreme sinfulness caused God to flood the earth as punishment. After the flood, man once more repopulated the earth and God continued with the scheme of redemption. The rudimentary systems of the priesthood and worship were developed.

The Jewish Age was noted for the enlargement of the scope of religious worship to God. Prior to this dispensation, the worship of God was on an individual basis, each family worshiped God with the father of the family acting as priest. In the Jewish age, the worship was on a national scale. God had entered into a covenant relationship with Israel and gave his law to the nation. Although the Jewish age was more advanced in its worship and relationship to God, the dispensation had its shortcomings.

> We are warrented in saying that the enjoyment of eternal salvation was not derived to the Jews from anything in their religion but what was prospective in it; and that it was not instituted for that purpose.[26]

In the concluding years of the Jewish age, John the Baptist appeared as God's harbinger to the Jews. He preached remission of sins and reformation of life under this second dispensation. He proclaimed the coming of Christ and anticipated the coming of the sunlight age.

The Christian Age was the consummation of God's scheme of redemption. "Something that was wanting in every previous dispensation is supplied in this—a rational and certain pledge of the forgiveness of all sins."[27] "When the proclamation of the Reign of God was first made, reformation and remission of sins, or faith and immersion went hand in hand."[28] One of the distinguishing characteristics of the Christian age from the former dispensations was that it was a reign of favor.[29] The followers of Christ obey him out of love and devotion. Theirs was not a system of laws and rules, but rather, in the areas where the Scriptures are silent, discretion of the believers was to be exercised. Whatever action or exercise was done, it was to be done in decency and order. Thus, in the Christian age, the believers were considered capable of living godly lives without the stringent rules of the previous eras. Campbell concluded the series by stating

> that a hearty and unreserved submission to the authority of Jesus Christ, will generally, and, perhaps, universally, issue in a uniformity of practice as respects even those discretionary matters which we have seen to result from the fact of our being treated as men rather than as children.[30]

It is through writings such as these, that Campbell sought to show what God's church was as revealed in the New Testament.

In the series, the "Ancient Gospel," Campbell discussed the proper mode and purpose for the act of Baptism. He stated that immersion was the "gospel in water"[31]; that immersion

---

25. *Ibid.*, 6:90. Also see 7:222.
26. *Ibid.*, 7:173.
27. *Ibid.*, 7:254.
28. *Ibid.*, 7:256.
29. *Ibid.*, 7:265.
30. *Ibid.*, 7:269.
31. *Ibid.*, 5:158.

was the medium which God had set apart for the remission of sins. In the act of immersion, our past sins are forgiven and "through confession, reformation, and petition, the blood of Christ will cleanse them from this also."[32]

Immersion is a positive command not only for the remission of sins, but also for the reception of the Holy Spirit.

> Before the Holy Spirit can be received, the heart must be purified; before the heart can be purified, guilt must be removed from the conscience; and before guilt can be removed from the conscience, there must be a sense, a feeling, or an assurance than [sic] sin is pardoned and transgression covered. For obtaining this, there must be some appointed way—and that means or way, is immersion into the name of the Father, Son, and Holy Spirit.[33]

Prior to immersion, certain conditions must be present. Faith in Christ, and repentance are necessary prerequisites to be manifested by the believer before his immersion into Christ.[34]

> In the natural order of the evangelical economy the items stand thus:—1. Faith; 2. Reformation; 3. Immersion; 4. Remission of sins; 5. Holy Spirit; and 6. Eternal Life. We do not teach that one of these precedes the other, as cause and effect; but that they are all naturally connected, and all, in this order, embraced in the glad tidings of salvation. In the apostolic age these items were presented in this order.[35]

Any effort to change this order of spiritual growth was to change the divine plan set forth in the Scriptures. The reordering of these Scriptural truths was to cause another gospel to be preached. Thus, in order to restore the doctrine and faith as revealed in the New Testament, immersion as the proper mode of baptism, preceded by faith in Christ, and the removal of sin, and the gift of the Holy Spirit after immersion, must be proclaimed. Other essays which pointed out the positive teachings of the Scriptures were articles such as "Christian Morality," and "Conscience."[36]

Preach the Truth and Expose Errors in Doctrine and Practice

His second aim was to preach the truth and to expose errors in doctrine and practice. It was in pursuit of this aim that some of his well known essays were written. Campbell sought to point out the abuses which would rob the church of its proper role with God and man. In trying to show this relationship, he insisted that many of the schemes and actions of his contemporary religious leaders and organizations were not consistent with the teachings of the New Testament.

Some of the areas of emphasis will be discussed along with his response to the abuse of them. In the early volumes of the *Baptist*, his opposition to Bible and missionary societies is noted. "Robert Cautious" questioned him on this matter in a letter to the editor. He pointed out that missionary and Bible societies had done a good work and should be supported by the editor. Campbell's reply to his contention revealed his opposition to such societies.

> With regard to Bible Societies, they are the most specious and plausible of all the institutions of this age. No man who loves the Bible can refrain from rejoicing at its increasing circulation. But every Christian who understands the nature and design, the excellence and glory of the institution called the Church of Jesus Christ, will lament to see its glory transferred to a human corporation—The Church is robbed of its character by every institution, merely human, that would ape its excellence and substitute itself in its place.[37]

---

32. *Ibid.*, 5:174.
33. *Ibid.*, 5:223.
34. *Ibid.*, 5:245-248. Also see 6:13-16.
35. *Ibid.*, 6:66.
36. *Ibid.*, 3:101-103, 161-165, 193-197, 254-257; 4:18-19, 112-114.
37. *Ibid.*, 1:129. Also see 1:20.

He not only perceived that such societies could usurp the position and authority of the church but also could serve as a means of perpetuating sectarian causes. In answering a letter which sought his views on missions, Campbell stated another reason for his opposition.

> But, my dear sir, how can I, with the New Testament before my face, approve the Catholic, the Episcopalian, the Presbyterian, &c. missionary schemes. Are they not evidently mere sectarian speculations, for enlarging their sects, and finding appointments for their supernumerary clergy. Look again at the sums of money squandered, at home and abroad, under the pretext of converting the world; and again, wherein is the heathen world benefited by such conversions?[38]

He continued to state that he is not against missions, only the abuses of them.

> My opponents, . . . do represent me, as opposing the means of converting the world, not wishing to discriminate, in my case at least, between a person's opposing the abuses of a good cause, and the cause itself. I did contribute my mite and my efforts to the popular missionary cause, until my conscience forbade me, from an acquaintance with the abuses of the principle.[39]

Campbell also opposed missionary societies on the basis of the divisions that such societ[] caused in the church. In contrasting the early church with the church of his day, he observ[] a sharp contrast in the two. He stated that the early church possessed a unity which th[] church in his day did not possess. The early church was not

> fractured into missionary societies, Bible societies, Education societies: nor did they dream of organizing snch [sic] in the world. The head of a believing household was not in those days a president, or manager of a board of foreign missions; his wife, the president of some female Education Society; his eldest Son, the recording secretary of some domestic Bible Society; his eldest daughter, the corresponding secretary of a mite Society; his servant maid, the vice-president af [sic] a rag Society; and his little daughter, a tutoress of a sunday school. They knew nothing of the *hobbies* of modern times. *In their church capacity alone they moved.*[40]

Many of the prevalent missionary ventures and efforts for the raising of money were reported in the *Baptist.* Such efforts as the missionary wheel[41] and the missionary box[42] were used to raise money. The raising and selling of flowers and vegetables for missionary causes was a[] other popular method.[43] It was reported in the *Reformer* that there was even a missionary[] Ohio who was involved in land speculation as he traveled throughout the state.[44] It was[] abuses of such various support schemes as these that caused Campbell to oppose societ[]

Another means of raising money for the support of missionaries was direct contributior[] the Baptist Board of Foreign Missions. The *Minutes of the Redstone Baptist Associa*[] record that the Brush Run Church supported missions in this manner from 1816-1820.[] comparison of mission giving of the Brush Run Church to two other congregations in t[] Redstone Association indicated that the Brush Run church gave quite well to missions. Th[] mission giving of the member churches of the Redstone Association was listed in the *Minutes* for the years 1816-1820. These figures are not entirely accurate because the list of amounts given is partially blacked out in the 1818 listing, but enough of the 1818 list can be read to give a general idea of the various mission offerings given during this four year period. The Brush Run Church gave an approximated total of $69.50 from 1816 to 1820 to missions. Two

---

38. *Ibid.,* 1:272. Also see 2:4-5.
39. *Ibid.,* 1:272-273.
40. *Ibid.,* 1:20.
41. *Ibid.,* 1:81-82.
42. *Ibid.,* 1:82.
43. *Ibid.,* 1:82-83.
44. *Ibid.,* 1:226-227.

sister congregations, Connellsville, and Pigeon Creek gave approximately $90.37½ and $19.87½ to missions respectively.[45]

Campbell also felt that the methodology of the missionary societies was in error. The evangelistic task of winning the world to Christ by sending missionaries to the heathen sustained by missionary societies was considered by Campbell to be wrong. The evangelistic task was considered hopeless by Campbell because the enterprise lacked the biblical qualifications for success. The missionaries in the Scriptures were always equipped with supernatural powers in which the testimony given could be confirmed. Such Old Testament personages as Moses and Joshua were cited as proof. When these men were given their specific tasks by God, they were equipped and empowered for the task by the ability to perform miracles. The seventy disciples of Jesus and later, the disciples at Pentecost, were given miraculous gifts to confirm their word. These signs and miracles continued till the gospel was preached unto both Jew and Gentile, and until churches were planted in all nations, then the gifts ceased. Accordingly, Campbell's view of the association between the missionaries and miracles of the first century church was that

> all the missioneionaries [sic], sent from heaven, were authorised [sic] and empowered to confirm their doctrine with signs and wonders, sufficient to awe opposition, to subdue the deepest rooted prejudices, and to satisfy the most inquisitive of the origin of their doctrine.[46]

"The Bible, then, gives us no idea of a Missionary without the power of working miracles.— Miracles and Missionaries are inseperably [sic] connected in the New Testament."[47]

Consequently, the missionary societies were violating the Scriptural norm by sending forth missionaries who were not endued with the supernatural power from God. This was the capital mistake of modern missions in Campbell's thinking as revealed in the article "Remarks on Missionaries."

> From these plain and obvious facts and considerations it is evident, that it is a *Capital mistake* to suppose, that Missionaries, in heathen lands, without the power of working miracles, can succeed in establishing the Christian religion. If it was necessary for the first missionaries to posses [sic] them, it is as necessary for those of our time who go to pagan lands, to possess them.[48]

"Is then the attempt to convert the heathen by means of modern Missionaries, an unauthorized and a hopeless one? It seems to be unauthorized, and, if so, then it is a hopeless one."[49] If modern missions were engaged in a hopeless venture to win the world to Christ because they unscripturally equipped for the task, how then shall the world be won? The New Testament teaches us that the association, called the Church of Jesus Christ is, in *propria forma*, the only institution of God left on earth to illuminate and reform the world."[50] The illumination and reformation of the world would be accomplished by the church by its doctrine and example.[51] The Scriptural missionary method would operate in the following terms.

> If, in the present day, the amongst all those who talk so much of a Missionary spirit, there could be found such a society, though it were composed of but twenty: willing to emigrate to some heathen land, where they would support themselves like the natives, wear the same garb, adopt the country as their own, and profess nothing like a Missionary project,—Should such a society sit down and hold forth in word and deed the saving truth, not deriding the gods nor the religion of the natives, but allowing their own works and example to speak for

---

45. Cottrell, *Minutes of the Redstone Baptist Association*, pp. 53, 65, 73, 77, 81.
46. Campbell, *Christian Baptist*, 1:53.
47. *Ibid.*, 1:54.
48. *Ibid.*, 1:54.
49. *Ibid.*, 1:54.
50. *Ibid.*, 1:55.
51. *Ibid.*, 1:55.

their religion, and practising as above hinted; we are persuaded that, in process of time, a more solid foundation for the conversion of the natives would be laid, and more actual success resulting, than from all the Missionaries employed for 25 years. Such a course would have some warrant from scripture but the present has proved itself to be all human.[52]

David S. Burnet, in an article entitled "The Christian Baptist, and Missionary and Bible Societies," included in the "Preface" to the fifteenth edition of the *Christian Baptist*, 1889, explained Campbell's opposition to missionary societies. He also offered an apology for any misunderstandings caused by Campbell in his attacks on the societies. Burnet stated that there were many abuses of such societies in the area of raising support for missions. He explained the actions taken by the editor in those early days. The first action was that many of the terms employed by the editor were too harsh. Burnet assured his readers that Campbell had matured and would not use such language against the societies in the years since the *Baptist.* Secondly, he regretted that at times, the institutions themselves were confused with the abuses of them. Thirdly, Burnet regretted that the churches at that time were also antagonistic toward societies. He concluded that the times had changed and such feelings were no longer felt by the churches. He further stated that the movement had Bible, tract, and missionary societies, and that Campbell himself was the president of one of them. The churches were supporting these societies and greatly appreciated them.[53]

The American Christian Bible Society which was organized on January 27, 1845, in Cincinnati, Ohio, by David Burnet and other local supporters was not supported by Campbell. Campbell's objections to such an organization were similar to those of "S. A." and Aylett Raines.[54] Four objections were voiced by Campbell toward the new enterprise. The four objections were that such an organization should not be created without the support and agreement of the entire brotherhood; that such a society would duplicate the work already done by existing Bible societies; that such an independent society would further breach the movement's already widening relationship with the Baptists; and that the brotherhood would not financially support such a venture. Burnet suggested another reason why Campbell was against the Bible Society—that it might take away support from Bethany College.

David Burnet replied to Campbell's objections, but Alexander remained unconvinced.[55] The opposing views of Campbell and his attitude toward the Bible society were expressed in the concluding remarks of his answer to David Burnet.

> Whenever they remove my objections already stated, and show that the expenses of a new establishment,—the outlay of a new set of officers to manage it, and of solicitors to support it,—with all the deductions of various agencies,—will give more, and cheaper, and better Bibles to the *heathen*, than we could have bestowed, in connexion with the "American and Foreign Bible Society,"—I will become a member of it, and do all in my power to further the benevolent objects of the institution.[56]

In spite of Campbell's objections concerning the society, he was elected as one of its nine vice presidents, although he was not present at the organizational meeting.[57]

The shortcomings of the clergy were exposed and discussed in such articles as his "The Christian Religion—The Clergy," "The Origin of the Christian Clergy," "Splendid Meeting House, and Fixed Salaries, exhibited from Ecclesiastical History," "The Third Epistle of

---

52. *Ibid.,* 1:56-57.

53. Alexander Campbell, *The Christian Baptist*, ed. by D. S. Burnet, 15th edition (St. Louis: Christian Publishing Company, 1889), p. vi.

54. For a comparison of views concerning the American Bible Society, see the *Millennial Harbinger*, 1845:366-369, 372-373, and 455-460 for the objections to it. See also the *Harbinger*, 1845:369-372, and 452-455 for the supporting views.

55. *Ibid.,* 1845:452-455.

56. *Ibid.,* 1845:459-460.

57. Dowling, *The Restoration Movement*, p. 77. Also see Stone, *Christian Messenger*, 1844:359-362.

Peter to Preachers and Rulers of Congregations," and "A Sermon upon Goats." There is one tenet concerning the clergy attributed to Campbell which had been distorted throughout the years. It has been claimed that Campbell was opposed to ministers receiving a salary in return for their ministerial services. Such an allegation must have been popular early in Campbell's ministry, for he answered it in a reply to a letter in the first volume of the *Baptist* published in 1823-1824.

Two issues need clarification in order to understand where he stood on the matter of ministerial salaries. First, there was his distinction between the "clergy" and the legitimate leadership of the local congregation. Second, there was his personal view on receiving remuneration for ministerial services. Campbell viewed the elders and deacons of the local congregation as its spiritual leaders. These men were chosen from within the congregation for its oversight. The duties of this oversight were carried on out of love for Christ and his church.[58]

The clergy, on the other hand, were viewed as a corruption of the divinely authorized leadership. The clergy, or "hireling preachers," were defined as

> Those who are trained for the precise purpose of teaching religion as their calling, please the mass of people, establish themselves into a distinct order, from which they exclude all who are not so trained, and, for hire, affect to be the only legitimate interpreters of revelation.[59]

> A hireling is one who prepares himself for the office of 'a preacher' or 'minister,' as a mechanic learns a trade, and who obtains a license from a congregation, convention, presbytery, pope, or diocesan bishop, as a preacher or minister, and agrees by the day, or sermon, month or year, for a stipulated reward.[60]

Campbell also considered "hireling preachers" men who, under the supposed inward moving of the Holy Spirit, preach sermons based upon their supposed spiritual impressions for money. The conclusion Campbell drew concerning such men as this:

> Upon the whole, I do not think we will err very much in making it a general rule, that every man who receives money for *preaching the gospel*, or for *sermons*, by the day, month, or year, is a hireling in the language of truth and soberness—whether he preaches out of his saddlebags, or from the *immediate suggestions* of the Holy Spirit.[61]

Campbell realized that not every minister would fit into this category and said that he was talking about the whole of the clerical order rather than in regard to specific individuals.[62]

Campbell stated that he did not object to the leadership of the local congregation receiving compensation for their help and labor.[63] But the clergy were not entitled to such compensation because,

> they have put themselves into an office which heaven never gave them, trample upon the rights of the people, keep them in ignorance, and *practically* deny that heavenly aphorism of our Lord, which saith, '*It is more blessed to give than to receive.*' They practically say, 'It is more blessed to receive than to give.'[64]

Alexander stressed that his personal view of preaching without receiving a salary began while a student at the University of Glasgow, Scotland. In order to do so, he pursued another vocation to provide a livelihood; however, he did not enjoin his philosophy on others.[65]

Alexander Campbell in his adherence to the second aim, that of exposing error in doctrine and practice, investigated religious groups other than his own. His views towards the Baptist

58. Campbell, *Christian Baptist*, 1:70-71. Also see 3:213-214.
59. *Ibid.*, 1:168-169.
60. *Ibid.*, 3:212.
61. *Ibid.*, 3:213.
62. *Ibid.*, 1:63. Also see 1:274.
63. *Ibid.*, 1:274. Also see 3:214.
64. *Ibid.*, 1:274.
65. *Ibid.*, 1:273-274.

and Paido-baptist communions were expressed in his "Address to the Public" in volume two of the *Baptist*.

> The Baptist views of the church of Jesus Christ are constitutionally correct; the Paido-Baptist views are unconstitutional. To make myself more intelligible—there are to be found in the Baptist system such views of the Christian church, as, if carried out to their legitimate issue, will place them on Apostolic grounds; but the (---)[66] of the views found in all the numerous sects of Paido-Baptists would, if carried out, place them in the bosom of the Roman pontiff. Yes, the one system would place the church upon the foundation of the apostles and prophets, Jesus Christ himself the chief cornerstone. The other system would place it upon St. Peter as the rock. The Baptist system is capable of being reformed or brought back again to the constitution of the kingdom of heaven; the Paido-Baptist cannot. It must be destroyed. The one system carries in its bosom the means of its purification; the other, the fire that must consume it. The foundation of the former needs but to have the rubbish cleared away; the foundation of the latter must be totally razed. The constitution of the one is essentially of Divine construction; the constitution of the other is altogether human. The good confession of the King of Martyrs before Pontius Pilate, is received by the Baptist and rejected by the Paido-Baptist system.[67]

Although Campbell felt that the Baptist church was the closest in form and doctrine to the apostolic church, he had to leave it when the Baptist church departed from the practice of the early church.[68] Campbell acknowledged that there were Christians in the churches whose doctrines and practices he opposed. In a letter to Robert Semple, he wrote, "I love all christians, of whatever name; and if there is any diversity in my affection, it is predicated upon, or rather graduated by, the scale of their comparative conformity to the will of my Sovereign."[69]

The efforts of reform by Barton W. Stone and the "Christians" were applauded by Campbell. He credited them with growing numbers and influence. Their beliefs were generally endorsed by Campbell. But there were several aspects of their doctrine that he disagreed with, such as their name.

> No objections can be made either against the *name* which they have chosen, against their *creed* or *form of discipline*, except *one*, and this may become a very serious one. It is this: Should they not be the same sort of people which were first called *Christians at Antioch*, and who doubtless had no other creed or rules of discipline than the apostolic writings—in that case their assumption of the name, and their adoption of an inspired creed, will be more injurious to the *"Restoration of the Ancient Order of Things"* than the assumption of any other name and the adoption of any other creed.[70]

Another area of concern for Campbell was about the "Christians" views concerning Christ.

> I am truly sorry to find that certain opinions, called Arian or Unitarian, or something else, are about becoming the sectarian badge of a people who have assumed the sacred name *Christian*; and that some peculiar views of atonement or reconciliation are likely to become characteristic of a people who have claimed the high character and dignified relation of *"the Church of Christ."* I do not say that such is yet the fact; but things are, in my opinion, looking that way; and if not suppressed in the bud, the name *Christian* will be as much a *sectarian name* as *Lutheran*, *Methodist*, or *Presbyterian*.[71]

Stone countered the charge with this explanation in the second volume of the *Christian Messenger*.

---

66. Two words in the text are not decipherable.
67. *Ibid.*, 2:51.
68. *Ibid.*, 5:180.
69. *Ibid.*, 5:180.
70. *Ibid.*, 4:263.
71. *Ibid.*, 5:66. Also see Stone, *Christian Messenger*, 1827:10.

You express your fears lest the name *christian*, will become as much a sectarian name as any other, because of certain opinions received by them, called Arian, Unitarian, &c. We thank you for your friendly, warning hints; but we cannot prevent our opposers from attaching what names they please on us and our opinions. We do not believe that our opinions are either Arian, or Unitarian in the present acceptation of the latter term. I confine this observation to us in the West. The *Christians* in the East, we are sorry to say, have admitted the name *Unitarian*. This has caused much sorrow to some of us in the West, and has excited in us the same fears, which you have expressed as felt by yourself. I have no doubt that they admitted the term without due consideration of the consequence, and that they will retract it on mature reflection.[72]

The occasion for this concern on Campbell's part for the Christians was Stone's response to some correspondence between Campbell and "Timothy." "Timothy" wrote Campbell about Campbell's views concerning the trinity. Campbell's response to the inquiry aroused Stone's attention in the matter.[73]

Campbell's views on the trinity centered around Christ's relationship to God. He believed that the key to understanding this relationship was found in his interpretation of John 1:1. Campbell believed that

As a word is an exact image of an idea, so is "*The Word*" an exact image of the invisible God. As a word cannot exist without an idea, nor an idea without a word; so God never was without "*The Word*," nor "*The Word*" without God; or as a word is of equal age or co-etaneous with its idea, so "*The Word*" and God are co-eternal. And as an idea does not create its word, nor a word its idea; so God did not create "*The Word*," nor "*The Word*" God.[74]

The relationship between God and Christ was marked by two time frames. Prior to the incarnation, Christ was equal and eternal with God. The subsequent relationship of Christ to God, as expressed in the terms Father and Son, was not manifested until the advent of Christ as man. Consequently, Jesus was not the Messiah or Savior, nor the Son of God until his birth.[75]

Stone responded to Campbell's reply to "Timothy" in two letters.[76] Campbell defended his views in a letter to Stone printed in the *Baptist* and the *Christian Messenger*.[77] Stone's concept of Christ was summed up in his criticism of Campbell for his assumption of what Stone believed about Christ. Stone upbraided Campbell for addressing him as a brother because Campbell thought that Stone prayed to Christ as there was no other God in the universe. Stone told Campbell that he did not regard Christ as the only God in the universe. His view of Christ was that Christ was not the Word, the co-existing deity with God. But, that the Word was "but a person that existed with the only true God before creation began; not from eternity, else he must be the only true God; but long before the reign of Augustus Cesar [*sic*]."[78]

Stone agreed with Campbell that Jesus was not the Savior or the Son of God until his incarnation. Stone disagreed that such titles as Jesus Christ, Messiah, and Son of God belonged to Christ alone. To prove his point, Stone cited examples of Joshua, Cyrus, and Adam, as being addressed by these terms.[79] Stone believed that Campbell's views created three equal but separate beings, a concept which he could not accept.

Campbell's reply to Stone's views stated that Stone knew nothing of the existence of the spirits.

---

72. Stone, *Christian Messenger*, 1827:13.
73. See Campbell, *Christian Baptist*, 4:230-231, for Timothy's letter and Campbell's response.
74. *Ibid.*, 4:233.
75. *Ibid.*, 4:231-234.
76. Campbell, *Christian Baptist*, 5:60-64. Also see Stone, *Christian Messenger*, 1827:10-13.
77. Campbell, *Christian Baptist*, 5:64-67. Also see Stone, *Christian Messenger*, 1827:[6]-10.
78. Campbell, *Christian Baptist*, 5:63.
79. *Ibid.*, 5:63-64.

All bodies you know any thing of occupy both time and space; consequently it would be absurd to suppose that three beings, whose modes of existence are such as to be governed by time and space, could be one being. But inasmuch as we do know *nothing* about the mode of existence of spirits, we cannot say that it would be incompatible with their nature, or modes of existence, that three might be one, and that one being might exist in three beings.[80]

Stone replied with the argument that such a doctrine was not a "doctrine of revelation," and "that the three beings, the Father, Word and Spirit, are but one being, appears to my weak mind too metaphysical to produce conviction."[81]

Stone was criticized by Campebll for making an issue of his reply to "Timothy" concerning the trinity. Campbell stated that he believed Stone had told him he was forced into the controversy and that Stone had regretted it.[82] Campbell said that if Stone found his exposition of John 1:1 objectionable, he should have said so and left the matter alone.[83] But because of Stone's objections, Campbell found himself in an unsatisfactory position of contending for a speculation which no living man could fully understand.[84]

Campbell rejoiced when Walter Scott was appointed the evangelist for the Mahoning Baptist Association throughout the Western Reserve, (Northeastern Ohio),[85] in 1827. Scott was to serve one year, traveling to the various churches of the Association, seeking to revive them.[86] Alexander Campbell had first met Scott in 1822. Scott began to revitalize the churches with clear biblical preaching which ended with an invitation to accept Christ as Savior. The Mahoning Association increased greatly that year, with over a thousand additions to the churches reported.

When the Campbells heard the reports of the great evangelistic successes being obtained through Scott's labors on the Western Reserve, Thomas went to investigate the situation. He observed Scott for five months and approved of what he saw and heard.[87] Thomas wrote Alexander this account of Scott's teachings.

We have long known the former (the theory), and have spoken and published many things correctly concerning the ancient gospel, its simplicity and perfect adaptation to the present state of mankind, for the benign and gracious purposes of his immediate relief and complete salvation; but I must confess that, in respect to the direct exhibition and application of it for that blessed purpose, I am present for the first time upon the ground where the thing has appeared to be practically exhibited to the proper purpose.[88]

Upon the receipt of these words, Alexander's concern for Scott's teaching was resolved and he supported Scott overwhelmingly.

Preach Only What the Bible Taught

His third goal was to preach only what the Bible taught. This goal was the culmination of the first and second goals. After discerning what was the message of the ancient gospel and the abuses and corruptions of it, one was able to preach the pure message of the Scriptures. In order for the gospel to be communicated effectively, the message must be scriptural and orderly. It was on the subject of proclaiming the gospel properly that Campbell wrote his "Sermons to Young Preachers." Two aspects of preaching were emphasized in the *Baptist*. The first, was

---

80. *Ibid.,* 5:66.
81. Stone, *Christian Messenger*, 1827:12.
82. Campbell, *Christian Baptist*, 5:64.
83. *Ibid.,* 5:64-65.
84. *Ibid.,* 5:64-65.
85. McAllister and Tucker, *Journey in Faith, A History of the Christian Church (Disciples of Christ)*, p. 132.
86. Campbell, *Christian Baptist*, 5:70-71.
87. Garrison and DeGroot, *The Disciples of Christ, A History*, p. 191.
88. Baxter, *Life of Walter Scott*, pp. 158-159.

the proper and correct manner to preach and what the message was. The second aspect was the misuse or abuse of the pulpit by some of his contemporary preachers.

The proper way to study the Bible was given in an "Address to readers of the Christian Baptist—No. I." Following his instructions, the reader would read the New Testament through three times. He encouraged that the study be done in a group so that all the readers might profit from the study. He also warned against the use of commentaries for the explanation of Bible passages before personal study was done. Campbell reminded the reader that constant prayer to God for wisdom and understanding of His revelation was necessary. "Theophilus" submitted a similar plan for Bible study in his "Proper Use of the Sacred Writings" in volume two.

In "Sermons to Young Preachers," the young minister was warned against noisy and unseemly habits and gestures in the pulpit, and urged to speak in his natural voice. The preachers were encouraged to have a clear idea in mind on what they intended to present when they entered the pulpit. Their attitude in the pulpit was to be one of humility. They were also told to remember the audience to be addressed in the preparation and delivery of the message. Extracts of sermons were presented in the periodical as examples of good and bad preaching. These were printed even though Campbell may not have agreed with the sermon's content. Sermons from William Guthrey; James Madison, President and professor of moral and natural philosophy at the University of William and Mary, Virginia; Gideon Blackburn, Minister of the Presbyterian church in Louisville, Kentucky; and Dr. Chalmer were printed.

Campbell also discussed the misuse of the Scriptures and the poor preaching of his day. "J. T.," in a letter to Campbell, revealed the homiletic method of some of the contemporary preachers. "For I was in hopes your remarks would have the effect of causing some to abandon the absurd custom of preaching sermons three hours on three words."[89] Examples of this type of sermon were shown in "Texts and Textuary Divine." Campbell related a sermon he read when he was fourteen years old, given by a minister to a congregation of beer drinkers on the word MALT.[90] Another example of a sermon in which the scriptural context was ignored by the minister dealt with the exposition of Revelation 12:1.

> "And there appeared a great wonder in heaven, a woman." He omitted her description, and raised his doctrine on those insulated words. He amused his hearers with a rare exhibition of pulpit eloquence; though some of the ladies were not so well pleased with "the doctrinal part."[91]

A sermon entitled "The Textuaries," was based upon the words of the wicked servant, when he was reprimanded by the master for not investing the one talent entrusted to him. The servant accused his master of being an austere man. The preacher could not spell well and read the word as being an "oyster man." Thus his sermon was built upon the words, "Thou art an oyster man," and preached a five point sermon upon this text.[92] The misuse of Scriptural passages, in which the context of the passage was ignored, was discussed in the article, "Scripture Quotations," in which the context of Psalm 145:9, I Samuel 13:14, and Revelation 10:6 were discussed.

Another abuse which Campbell addressed was the use of "canned" sermons. In the article, "A True Anecdote," he related an incident in which some children found a collection of thirteen or fifteen manuscript sermons which had been preached continually over a nine to ten year span. A similar instance was recorded in "A Dropped Letter." In place of Bible study and adequate preparation, old sermons were reused or new ones purchased from various individuals. It was a steady diet of such preaching to which Campbell pointed out as a major factor in the spiritual decline of the churches.

---

89. Campbell, *Christian Baptist,* 7:32.
90. *Ibid.,* 2:218-219.
91. *Ibid.,* 2:218.
92. *Ibid.,* 3:115.

An Impartial Advocate of Truth

The fourth aim was his desire to be an impartial advocate of truth. In the "Preface" of the first volume of the *Baptist,* he stated that he strove to be impartial because he was free from various entanglements which could color his judgment. He was free from religious bias because the paper was pledged to no religious sect. He was free from financial interest as the price of the paper was only one dollar per year. He was also free to admit error if any fact was later proven to be false. The editorial policy of the paper was a testimony of his desire to seek the truth.

> We have only to add, in this place that we shall thankfully receive such essays, as are accordant with the Bible, and suitable to the peculiar design of this paper; and if any essays, short, and well composed, written in opposition to our views, should be forwarded, they shall be inserted, accompanied with appropriate remarks. The author's name must accompany all communications.[93]

The editorial policy did exclude essays and reports of such matters which Campbell considered to be transitory in their nature and edification of his readers.

> Besides, this work is not intended to be filled with long accounts of revivals, ordinations, baptisms, reports of Bible and missionary societies, the constitutions and proceedings of cent societies, the election of presidents, vice-presidents and managers, secretaries and treasurers of mite societies, and all such splendid and glorious things as fill the pages of most of the religious publications of the day. We wish to publish such things as will bear to be read a year or two hence as far as the subject matter is concerned.[94]

As the volumes of the periodical are examined, it will be noticed that Campbell did not consider himself the sole advocate of truth. The essays and articles which are published testify to this fact. His father, Thomas, often wrote essays under the pseudonym of "T. W." Walter Scott penned articles under the name "Phillip." Over seventy-nine different periodicals are mentioned in the *Baptist.* Campbell gleaned many articles and reports from these papers and reprinted them in his paper because he felt the articles would be instructive to his readers. In his response to the many essays and articles sent to the editor, Campbell tried not to allow his personal feelings and differences to color his judgment. He strove to respond to the issue addressed and not the man who had written him.

Given the religious situation in which he wrote, and the religious sentiments of the time, his aims for the *Baptist* were remarkably broad in their scope. These aims became the pattern for many periodicals which followed the *Baptist.* While these aims may not have been completely and perfectly met, certainly credit must be given to Campbell for trying to do so. We must not expect more from him than we do from ourselves. He did not try or intend to set himself up as the sole interpreter of the faith. He was a seeker after truth. Everything he expressed may not be agreed with, but his last request in the "Preface" of the *Christian Baptist* should be granted. The request was that he be given an impartial and patient hearing.

---

93. *Ibid.,* 1:13.
94. *Ibid.,* 1:36.

THE

CHRISTIAN BAPTIST;

EDITED

BY ALEXANDER CAMPBELL.

"WHAT a glorious freedom of thought do the Apostles recommend! and how contemptible in their account is a blind and implicit faith! May all christians use this liberty of judging for themselves in matters of religion, and allow it to one another, and to all mankind."   *Benson.*

"PROVE all things: hold fast that which is good."   *Paul the Apostle.*

REVISED

BY D. S. BURNET,

FROM THE SECOND EDITION, WITH MR. CAMPBELL'S LAST CORRECTIONS.

SEVEN VOLUMES IN ONE.

CINCINNATI:
PUBLISHED BY D. S. BURNET.
STEREOTYPED BY J. A. JAMES
1835.

Printed by James and Gazlay,
No. 1, Baker Street,
Cincinnati, Ohio.

PREFACE

TO THE STEREOTYPE EDITION.

EXPERIENCE is an effectual teacher. By the trial, persevered in amidst many difficulties, we have seen that effected, which was deemed impracticable,—an extensive religious reformation, founded upon the scriptural knowledge, personal holiness, and the constant sacrifice of all its abettors. Such an abiding, extensive and personal reformation, consisting in the knowledge and obedience of the sacred writings, differs largely from those hasty excitements of popular interest, which issue in an ephemeral association, whose bond of union is some sectarian peculiarity. But this is not all. The reformation alluded to, and which this book pleads, differs from others in this important respect: it contemplates not the change of any one sect or system, nor the amalgamation of any number or all of them; but it claims as a right, and labors to attain as its object, the reformation of society by a *restoration* of primitive christianity, *i. e.* christianity itself, in its gospel, institutions and laws. A creed reformed is a dividing barrier patched, and a sect remodelled is but a daughter of the mother of abominations in a new dress. This reformation aims at the demolition of the creed and the sect, genera and species, reformed or unreformed, as purity is incompatible with corruption.

The happiest illustration of the justness of their cause, attempted by the apologists for modern degeneracy, fractured into "names and denominations," is most infelicitous. They would harmonize around the Lord as sects, like Jacob's sons around their father, and the tribes of Israel about the ark, while marching in the wilderness, or when settled in Canaan, about the temple in the city of peace. But they are strangely insensible of the truth, that the twelve tribes had the same priests, subordinate and chief, the same altar, laver and table, offered the same incense and approached the mercy seat on one day, by a common intercessor; and that when they abandoned the one worship, God forsook them. They have forgotten that Jesus, in his death, grasped the towers, and bowed himself in the gate-way of the "wall of partition"—the two tables of the fleshly covenant, and in his resurrection demolished them forever. They are not aware that "the disciples were first called christians at Antioch," when this imperishable name arose upon the ruins of all religious distinctions, in the first union of Jews and Gentiles in one corporate body. This name in its origin and object, designating the subjects of the one Lord Messiah, who is the Prince of Peace, is the most anti-sectarian of any applied to man; but when coupled with the surname Papist or Protestant, Presbyterian, Baptist or Methodist, &c., becomes dead in law, prophets and gospel, the signal of interminable divisions, and the war-cry of the bitterest persecution. Never was there a more complete misnomer than "Christian sect."

But has such a resuscitation of the ancient religion, but just now quite forgotten, been effected? Yes! and perhaps one hundred thousand persons in these United States now rejoice in its light and life. If we may believe the sectarian press, the millennium is just coming in upon our coasts, upon the tide of modern schemes, and by the united or disunited efforts of modern schemists. Such is the burden of every song in praise of the misguided benevolent operations of the day, while the truth that the growth of the army of the sects bears no proportion to the increase of population, stares them in the face. But this is studiously concealed from the blinded multitude, until it is thought that the Romanists are likely to have a majority in the entire republic. In the meantime, (think it not incredible,) the energies of this large number have been put forth in earnest to meet the Lord with oil and light furnished and prepared. Churches of the primitive stamp, subjects of the Prince of Peace, with their officers, his faithful and self-denying servants have, as by magic, sprung up from the seed of the word cast upon some of the good ground in the bosom of corrupt society; and to the admiration of thousands, have exhibited the ancient gospel, the ancient ordinances and the ancient laws of Christ; and though these institutions are yet in their infancy, God providentially indicates that they shall have a glorious harvest, if they betray not his cause.

But what has been the signal instrumentality? It is conceded universally that this book, more than any other means, has consolidated and extended the number and influence of those who have found in the scriptures " him of whom Moses in the law, and the prophets did write." It is now near twelve years since the Christian Baptist first lifted its warning voice, and displayed the light of its counsel. It claimed none of its discoveries as original; and if its distinguished editor had genius and talent, and erudition, and if from the hills of Western Virginia, he succeeded in wielding an influence which is felt in every corner of the Union, and waged a warfare with sectaries and sceptics, the fame and dread of which have passed the Atlantic, he aspired only to be the humble director of the public attention to the oracles of God and the order of his house! The Christian Baptist was the trumpet which was blown throughout the length and breadth of the land; and Mr. Campbell was not alone—some were already " waiting for the consolation of Israel," and others were roused by the first blast; and upon every onset of the opposers, some high spirits were captured, who, taking their places in the ranks, at the price of liberty, hurried the progress of the reformation; all these, through its columns, spoke fearlessly, terror to the aliens, and encouragement to the loyal in all the dominions of Prince Messiah. In this peculiar train of events this work became in many respects, the most remarkable of the age. The French revolution can never occur again, neither can the power of Napoleon ever be revived. In all antiquity Noah's family alone inhabited two worlds, and Adam, the progenitor of all the race, was the only man born an adult. This reformation has taken the highest ground which ever can be assumed among men; and in renouncing all alliance with politics, all creeds, systems and sects, except the inspired writings, and the one sect of christians, which, in the days of the Cesars, was every where spoken against, is as far before the politico-ecclesiastic revolutions of Luther and Calvin, as they were before the pollutions which they only modified and afterwards rendered perpetual, reformed corruptions by those engines of impurity and oppression, creeds and ecclesiastic power. But this is conceding too much. We cannot compromise the value of a reformation, which cannot be mended, as far as these grounds are concerned. It is obvious that the Christian Baptist can never be reproduced by the same or greater talents; for the events will be wanting—events, the occasions which make men and originate all great and abiding interests. The work is now scarce, and I have ventured a new and improved edition for the following reasons:

1. The restoration of primitive christianity in each community, is a new and distinct reformation. Consequently, in every place the means must essentially be the same; and past experience recommends this volume as the best possible to effect the object.

2. Since it ceased being published, great numbers have been converted; old churches have been reformed and new ones established, the organization of which is frequently imperfect, if they are organized at all. They should profit by the experience of others, as detailed on these pages.

3. The scepticism of this age, so diversified in its character, has received a large share of attention, and has been foiled in a masterly manner in this work, which is proposed for extensive circulation in society, now alarmingly affected with this leprosy, to remove which, perhaps no other miscellaneous work is better calculated.

4. The Christian Baptist is admirably contrived to annihilate the existence, and to remove the evils and remembrance of sectarianism, by the accuracy of its calculations, the extent of its developments, and most of all, by its clear and forcible statement, illustration and defence of the christian religion.

5. The Romanists are determined upon the conquest of this country; and at this time the wishes of the Pope are nearer being realized than most imagine; and it is confidently believed, that the principles herein set forth are a sure defence against the man of sin and the mother of abominations.

6. Tired of filing reasons for this undertaking, we observe lastly, that it is republished because having attained, and being now better than ever prepared to attain, these objects, it is but right that the scarcity of the first edition should be remedied by this improved, correct, neat and portable volume.

Those long interested in the success of the reformation, will recognize an old acquaintance in this edition, now more venerable and none the less captivating by age. To them no apology is necessary for its appearance, and there should be none to all those who wish to see the apostles of Jesus Christ restored to their rightful dominion. Let these pages but be circulated and read by a candid and enlightened public, and we fear not the fate of the principles maintained, or the practices defended by them.

For the satisfaction of the curious inquirer, it may not be amiss to give him a glance at its general contents, which we will do in the form of

A SYNOPSIS OF DIVINE REVELATION.

DISPENSATIONS.

PATRIARCHAL, (*Adam.*) **JEWISH, (*Moses.*)** **CHRISTIAN, (*Messiah.*)**

EACH of these "dispensations" had its gospel, ordinances, laws, priesthood, &c. The gospel proclaimed by God to Adam is found, *Genesis* iii. 15, the gospel proclaimed by Moses to the Israelites, *Exodus,* iii. chap, and the gospel of Jesus the Messiah, preached by the apostles to the world, *Acts,* ii. chap.

Christianity contains a Gospel—Ordinances—Laws.

Scheme of the Gospel of Jesus Christ our Lord to the World.

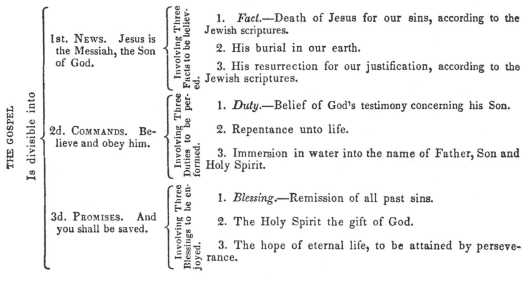

THE GOSPEL Is divisible into

1st. NEWS. Jesus is the Messiah, the Son of God. — Involving Three Facts to be believed.
1. *Fact.*—Death of Jesus for our sins, according to the Jewish scriptures.
2. His burial in our earth.
3. His resurrection for our justification, according to the Jewish scriptures.

2d. COMMANDS. Believe and obey him. — Involving Three Duties to be performed.
1. *Duty.*—Belief of God's testimony concerning his Son.
2. Repentance unto life.
3. Immersion in water into the name of Father, Son and Holy Spirit.

3d. PROMISES. And you shall be saved. — Involving Three Blessings to be enjoyed.
1. *Blessing.*—Remission of all past sins.
2. The Holy Spirit the gift of God.
3. The hope of eternal life, to be attained by perseverance.

Concerning the above table, which might have been extended to many times its length, let the reader notice:

1. That all things in the departments of nature, society and religion, are divisible into original elements; so that we must have light, heat, moisture, &c., to produce vegetation—intelligence and law as well as human beings to produce good society; and we must have all the items which were originally proclaimed for immediate salvation, to assure us that we have the gospel. Light and heat alone, can by no ingenuity produce an apple or a pear; masses of men, subordinated to authority, but devoid of intelligence, will be but enslaved savages; and a religion called christian, wanting either the gospel, the ordinances or the laws of Christ, though it have the other items, is a false religion; for all false religions of all ages and all nations, are but perversions of one or all of the revealed systems. Likewise, any gospel deficient in any of the nine items of the foregoing scheme, is not the gospel of Christ, but should be surnamed after its modern inventor.

2. The elements of any system being determined, it is then equally necessary to ascertain the order in which they are properly associated. We have the natural, social and evangelical order. God, the author of all things, is the author of order, and in disregarding it we are sinning against him. Now, it is impossible to prove the bible divine if we precede the patriarchal age by the christian, or succeed the christian by the Jewish. So the christian scheme becomes a humanized-sectarian thing, if in its operation we make it commence in ordinances, succeeded by laws, and consummated by the gospel, as do some. The evangelical order is gospel for the rebellious sinner—baptism for him, believing and penitent, and the King's table and all his laws for him, when, by regular naturalization, he becomes a true subject.

Again, if in this degenerate age we would be assured that we have the original gospel, after having ascertained to whom it was committed, when and where it was promulged, we must repair to the person, at the time and place, by the aid of the scriptures, and assemble all the items of the proclamation in the precise order in which they were delivered. Now, in the foregoing *scheme* we have the gospel divided into *news, commands* and *promises.* Who does not see that were the promises, the third item in this division, made the first, they would thereby be effectually separated from the gospel, while the gospel without them would be useless? Interfere with this order in any other way, and the consequences are equally disastrous.— Once more, each of these three items is divided into other three; the first into three facts. Can we, by any effort of imagination, place the resurrection of Christ before his death? Would not such a gospel be anathematized by all good sense? But it is as great an infraction of good order to put baptism, the third duty, before faith, the first. And who would think of placing eternal life precedent to remission of sins? But this is not the place to pursue this subject. It may not, however, be amiss to observe that this scheme can be sustained, and is largely sustained in this volume, item by item, and position by position, in the light of reason and revelation.

I have devoted several months to the revision and correction of this work, and it is sanguinely hoped that, aided by the corrections of Mr. Campbell, it will now meet public expectation as to style of execution and accuracy. Some of the ephemeral matter, embracing notices, correspondence of local interest, personalities, &c., has been omitted; but with the concurrence of Mr. Campbell, to whom the list of omissions was submitted. The style has been modernized, and in several respects improved; but not being a literary work, and embracing in its correspondence, composition of every variety, it must, like all other miscellaneous periodicals, in many instances, ask the indulgence of the critical. But the work speaks only for the sentiment it contains, and it is presumed that men of all diversities of intellect and learning can understand it.

In reference to manner and means of propagating the christian religion, some things are said in the first pages of this volume, which, to be properly understood, the following facts should be before the mind. The great obstacle to the success of every reformation of religious society, has been the dominant priesthood. They have, *en masse*, always opposed the rights of the people. There are but a few honorable exceptions to this remark. There were *two* bishops that stood up with a large minority of noblemen, in favor of the recent English reform. This clerical grasping after power would be harmless, were it not for the lethargy which has overspread the public mind upon the subject. The people think the priesthood a necessary constituent of society. They do not understand that all christians are priests. Now, to break this spell it was needful that the unscripturality and unrighteousness of these clerical claims be made manifest. So necessarily engrossing was this topic, many had like to have overlooked the office of evangelist. So often was the new testament bishop contrasted with the popular clergyman, the presiding officer of one congregation with the circuit riding superintendant of many, that they began to think that no other officer, evangelist or messenger, was requisite to the extension of the church. Experience, however, has corrected and supplied what was wanting; and the few hints upon the subject in this volume have been acted upon largely. Many scores of evangelists and messengers of the churches, are now going to and fro, and the knowledge of the Lord has increased. Thousands have bowed to King Messiah. Thus the bishop's office has been preserved, and the office of the evangelist not lost to a generation which needed it as much as the people of the apostolic age.

I cannot better conclude these prefatory remarks, than by expressing my unfeigned thanks to the Giver of all mercies, that I have the opportunity to contribute my mite to his great treasury of means, in sending forth this edition. To him I commend the undertaking; and to him be glory in the church by Christ Jesus, during the endless successions of ages: Amen.

D. S. BURNET

MARCH 2, 1835.

CONTENTS.

CONTENTS.

CONTENTS.

CONTENTS.

ORIGINAL DEDICATION.

To ALL those, without distinction, who acknowledge the Scriptures of the Old and New Testaments to be a Revelation from God; and the New Testament as containing the Religion of JESUS CHRIST:—

Who, willing to have all religious tenets and practices tried by the Divine Word; and who feeling themselves in duty bound to search the Scriptures for themselves, in all matters of Religion, are disposed to reject all doctrines and commandments of men, and to obey the truth, holding fast the faith once delivered to the Saints—this work is most respectfully and affectionately dedicated by

THE EDITOR.

PREFACE TO THE FIRST EDITION.

No MAN can reasonably claim the attention of the public, unless he is fully persuaded that he has something of sufficient importance to offer. When so many writers are daily addressing the religious community, it may perhaps be demanded why another should solicit a reading? When so many religious papers are daily issuing from the press, why add another to the number? To these and similar queries it may be answered—that, of all the periodical religious papers of this day, with which we have any acquaintance, but a very few are of an independent character. They are generally devoted to the interest of some one or other of the religious sects which diversify the devout community; so much so, at least, that, being under the control of the leading members of the respective sects, under whose auspices they exist and to whose advancement they are destined, they are commonly enlisted in the support of such views and measures as are approbated by the leaders of each sect. And such must every sectarian paper be. It is a rarity, seldom to be witnessed, to see a person boldly opposing either the doctrinal errors or the unscriptural measures of a people with whom he has identified himself, and to whom he looks for approbation and support. If such a person appears in any party, he soon falls under the frowns of those who either think themselves wiser than the reprover, or would wish so to appear. Hence it usually happens that such a character must lay his hand upon his mouth, or embrace the privilege of walking out of doors. Although this has usually been the case, we would hope that it would not always continue so to be.

If this, however, had not usually happened, we should have had no Episcopalians, Presbyterians, Methodists, &c. If the party from which these sects sprang had received the admonitions and attended to the remonstrances of those bold and zealous men who first began to reprove and testify against it for alledged errors and evils existing in it, no separation would have taken place. Had the well-meant remonstrances of Luther, Calvin and Wesley, been acknowledged and received by the sects to which they belonged, the mother would have been reformed, and the children would have lived under the same roof with her. But she would not. They were driven out of doors, and were compelled either to build a house for themselves or to lodge in the open air. As it has happened to those called teachers of religion, so it has often happened to religious papers. Hence it is generally presumed that a paper will soon fall into disrepute if it dare to oppose the views or practices of the leaders of the people addressed. Editors generally, too sensible of this, are very cautious what they publish. Some of them are very conscientiously attentive to avoid giving offence; insomuch, that when an article is presented for insertion, the first objection to it sometimes is, "The people will not like this, and you know a man must please his customers." All this may do very well when a writer proposes to please his readers, or when he pledges himself to support the tenets or practices of any people. But when the exhibition of truth and righteousness is proposed, neither the passions nor prejudices of men—neither the reputation nor pecuniary interest of the writer, should be consulted.

To this course we have heard it objected, that, "should a writer on religious subjects assert the truth, oppose error, and reprove unrighteousness, with christian fidelity, regardless of pleasing or displeasing men, he might expect to starve to death if he seek his living thereby, or to be imprisoned and perhaps beheaded as John the Baptist was, should circumstances permit." We shall not, in the mean time, oppose or assert the truth of this objection. We shall submit the principle to the test of experience, and practically prove its truth or falsehood.

We now commence a periodical paper, pledged to no religious sect in christendom, the express and avowed object of which is the eviction of truth and the exposure of error, as stated in the Prospectus. We expect to prove whether a paper perfectly independent, free from any controling jurisdiction except the bible, will be read; or whether it will be blasted by the poisonous breath of sectarian zeal and of an aspiring priesthood. As far as respects ourselves, we have long since afforded such evidence as would be admitted in most cases, of the disinterested nature of our efforts to propagate truth, in having always declined every pecuniary inducement that was offered, or that could have been expected,

A   1 in adopting a course of public instruction suited to the times, the taste and prejudices of men. Of this an apostle once boasted, that he had deprived his enemies of an occasion to say, that he had made a gain of them. Yea, he affirms that, " as the truth of Christ is in me, no man shall stop me of this boasting in the regions of Achaia" But, adds he, "what I do, I will do that I may cut off occasion from them that desire occasion." So say we.

The price of this paper is such as must convince all who reflect, that it cannot be a lucrative scheme. We know however, that there is no course of conduct which can be adopted, against which carping envy and prating malevolence may not devise ill-natured objections. A striking instance of this we have in the life of John the Baptist, and in that of the Messiah. It reads thus: "John the Baptist is come, abstaining from bread and wine, and you say, "He has a demon." The Son of Man is come, using both, and you say, " He is a lover of banquets and wine, an associate of publicans and sinners."

We have often heard the leaders of devotion in popular assemblies confessing their ignorance, praying for more light, and anxiously looking for a more desirable time, when knowledge, truth, and holiness should abound. This circumstance clearly argues that every thing is not right amongst them, themselves being judges. Yet we have often heard those same leaders of devotion vindicate themselves from error, and attempt to justify themselves and all their measures as soon as any reprover presented himself. This, though a common occurrence, is a singular proof that many deceive themselves, as well as their simple hearers, " by good words and fair speeches."

We are very certain that to such as are praying for illumination and instruction in righteousness, and not availing themselves of the means afforded in the Divine Word to obtain an answer to their prayers, our remarks on many topics will appear unjust, illiberal, and even heretical; and as there are so many praying for light, and inattentive to what God has manifested in his word, there must be a multitude to oppose the way of truth and righteousness. This was the case when God's Messiah, the mighty Redeemer of Israel, appeared. Ten thousand prayers were daily offered for his appearance, ten thousand wishes expressed for his advent, ten thousand orations pronounced respecting the glory of his character and reign; and, strange to tell! when he appeared the *same* ten thousand tongues were employed in his defamation! Yea, they were praying for his coming when he stood in the midst of them, as many now are praying for *light* when it is in their hands, and yet they will not look at it.

There is much less diversity in the views, passions, prejudices, and circumstances of mankind, as respects the true religion in the different ages of the world, than at first thought we would willingly admit. Who is there that has attentively considered the history of Cain and Abel, of Noah and his contemporaries, of the twelve patriarchs, of Moses and the Egyptian magicians, of the Lord's prophets and the prophets of Baal, of Israel's true and false prophets, of the Lord of Life and his disciples, with that of the religious sects of that day, of the present advocates of primitive christianity in Europe and America, and of the supporters of the popular systems of this age—I say, who is there that having considered such histories, will not be astonished at their remarkable coincidences; their striking similarities, and their concurrent contexture of events.

This paper shall embrace a range of subjects and pursue a course not precisely similar to those of any other periodical work which we have seen. Of this, however, the work itself will give the plainest and most intelligible exhibition. In introducing facts and documents in support of assertion or demonstration, there is a possibility of adducing such as are not true or genuine, owing to a variety of causes. Of this indeed, we shall be always on our guard. If, however, on any occasion any thing should be exhibited as fact which is not fact, we pledge ourselves to give publicity to any statement, decently written, tending to disprove any such alledged facts. The truth of God and the religion of the bible never yet gained advantage, but, on all occasions, sustained injury, from falsehood and lies employed in their defence.

From the subscription we have already received to this work, having subscribers from almost all sects, we would at once despair were it our intention to please them all—if the support of their peculiarities, or of the party to which they belong, were expected. We are happy to say that this circumstance so accords with our design of maintaining the Apostles' doctrine only, in opposition to every system, how specious soever, that it will serve as a new impulse to keep us in the course intended. We must also keep in mind the fable of the man and his ass, who strove to please every body, but finally pleased neither himself nor any one else, and lost his ass into the bargain. Besides, when there are so many accommodating themselves to the bias of the people, and endeavoring to conciliate their good opinion, we might suppose that they would be able to endure one that might be disposed not to smile at their mistakes and countenance them in error.

Amongst so many panegyrists, one monitor might be endured. These things, however, we say when viewing the subject through the medium of public opinion. We are assured that there are many who will approve of what is truth, and the course adopted, and that many will know that we are not alone in the views to be exhibited, but that there are many who heartily accord with them.

We know from acquaintance that there is a goodly number of sensible and intelligent persons, at this day, entirely disgusted with many things *called* religious; and that, upon the whole, it is an age of inquiry. We are therefore, somewhat sanguine that a fair opportunity presents itself for a work of this nature. We have learned that to make truth the sole object of our inquiries, and to be disposed to obey it when known, serves more to guide us into it than all commentators. We have been taught that we are liable to err; we have found ourselves in many errors; we candidly acknowledge that we have changed our views on many subjects, and that our views have changed our practice. If it be a crime to change our views and our practice in religious concerns, we must certainly plead guilty. If it be a humiliating thing to say we have been wrong in our belief and practice, we must abase ourselves thus far. We were once trained and disciplined in the popular religion, and were then steady and uniform in one course for a time. But the foundation of our assent to, and accordance with, the popular religion was destroyed, and down came the edifice about our ears. We are thankful that we were not buried in the ruins. We have learned one lesson of great importance in the pursuit of truth; one that acts as a pioneer to prepare the way of knowledge—one that cannot be adopted and acted upon, but the result must be salutary. It is this: Never to hold any sentiment or proposition as more certain than the evidence on which it rests; or, in other words, that our assent to any proposition should be precisely proportioned to the evidence on which it rests.* All beyond this we esteem enthusiasm—all short of it, incredulity. In this place I must cite the words of the justly celebrated Dr. George Campbell, author of the best translation of the four gospels which ever yet appeared in our language. They are from the conclusion of his preface to the "Preliminary Dissertations," volume 1, page 59. They accord with our own experience, and breathe our sentiments. He says, "The language of our Lord to his hearers was, If any man *will* come under my guidance. Nothing is obtruded or forced upon the unwilling. Now, as the great source of the infidelity of the Jews was a notion of the temporal kingdom of the Messiah, we may justly say, that the great source of the corruptions of christians, and of their general defection foretold by the inspired writers, has been an attempt to render it in effect a temporal kingdom, and to support and extend it by earthly means. This is that spirit of Antichrist which was so early at work as to be discoverable even in the days of the Apostles." In the same page he says, "If to make proselytes by the sword is tyranny in rulers, to resign our understanding to any man, and receive implicitly what we ought to be rationally convinced of, would be, on our part, the lowest servility.—Every thing, therefore, here is subjected to the test of scripture and sound criticism. I am not very confident of my own reasonings. I am sensible that, on many points, I have changed my opinion, and found reason to correct what I had judged formerly to be right. The consciousness of former mistakes proves a guard to preserve me from such a presumptuous confidence in my present judgment, as would preclude my giving a patient hearing to whatever may be urged, from reason or scripture, in opposition to it. Truth has been in all my inquiries, and still is, my great aim. To her I am ready to sacrifice every personal consideration; but am determined not, knowingly, to sacrifice her to any thing." These are the sentiments and determination of my heart, as though they had been indited there.

We have only to add in this place, that we shall thankfully receive such essays as are accordant with the Bible and suitable to the peculiar design of this paper; and if any essays, short and well composed, written in opposition to our views, should be forwarded, they shall be inserted, accompanied with appropriate remarks. The author's name must accompany all communications.

It is very far from our design to give any just ground of offence to any, the weakest of the disciples of Christ, nor to those who make no pretensions to the christian name; yet we are assured that no man ever yet became an advocate of that faith which cost the life of its founder and the lives of so many of the friends and advocates of it, that did not give offence to some. We are also assured that in speaking plainly and accordant to fact, of many things of high esteem at present, we will give offence. In all such cases we esteem the reasoning of Peter unanswerable. It is better to hearken unto God, in his word, than to men, and to please him than all the world beside. There is another difficulty of which we are aware, that, as some objects are manifestly good, and the means attempted for their accomplishment manifestly evil, speaking against the means employed we may be sometimes understood as opposing the object abstractly,

---

*Much is couched in this rule, and it deserves to be written in characters of gold upon the walls of every man's study, upon the door of every place of instruction, and inscribed upon the title page of every book. Let the amount of evidence be the measure of our confidence, and we will be more careful in forming and more modest in expressing our opinions; our zeal and our knowledge would not be so disproportioned; and at the same time, we would not be wanting in zeal for the truth, which alone can justly claim our reverence, and command our obedience.

Reader! commit this rule to memory, and treasure it in your heart, if you would have the assurance of certainty in your conclusions, and the consciousness of the divine approbation of your conduct. PUBLISHER.

especially by those who do not wish to understand, but rather to misrepresent. **For** instance—that the conversion of the heathen to the christian religion is an object manifestly good all christians will acknowledge; yet every one acquainted with the history of the means employed, and of the success attendant on the means, must know that these means have not been blessed; and every intelligent christian must know that many of the means employed have been manifestly evil. Besides, to convert the heathen to the popular christianity of these times would be an object of no great consequence, as the popular christians themselves, for the most part, require to be converted to the christianity of the New Testament. We have only one request to make of our readers—and that is, an impartial and patient hearing; for which we shall make them one promise, viz. that we shall neither approve nor censure any thing without the clearest and most satisfactory evidence from reason and revelation.

A. CAMPBELL.

Buffaloe, July 4, 1823.

CHRISTIAN BAPTIST.

VOL. I, NO. I. BUFFALOE, (BETHANY) BROOKE CO. VA., AUGUST 3, 1823.

Style no man on earth your Father: for he alone is your Father who is in heaven; and all ye are brethren. Assume not the title of Rabbi; for ye have only One Teacher: neither assume the title of Leader; for ye have only One Leader, the Messiah. *Messiah*

THE CHRISTIAN RELIGION.

CHRISTIANITY is the perfection of that divine philanthropy which was gradually developing itself for four thousand years. It is the bright effulgence of every divine attribute, mingling and harmonizing, as the different colors in the rainbow, in the bright shining after rain, into one complete system of perfections—the perfection of GLORY to God in the highest heaven, the perfection of PEACE on earth, and the perfection of GOOD WILL among men.

The eyes of patriarchs and prophets, of saints and martyrs, from Adam to John the Baptist, with longing expectation, were looking forward to some glorious age, indistinctly apprehended, but ardently desired. Every messenger sent from heaven, fraught with the communications of the Divine Spirit, to illuminate, to reprove, and to correct the patriarchs and the house of Israel, was brightening the prospect and chastening the views of the people, concerning the glory of the COMING AGE. The "FOUNDER OF THE FUTURE AGE," as one of Israel's prophets calls the Messiah, was exhibited, in the emblems of the prophetic style, as rising, expanding and brightening to view; from the glistening "Star of Jacob," to the radiating "Sun of Righteousness," with salutiferous and vivifying rays.

The person, character and reign of Messiah the Prince, exhausted all the beauties of language, all the grandeur and resplendencies of creation, to give some faint resemblances of them. In adumbrating Emmanuel and his realm, "Nature mingles colors not her own." She mingles the brighter splendors of things celestial, with things terrestrial, and kindly suits the picture to our impaired faculties. She brings the rose of Sharon and the lily of the vales—the mild lustre of the richest gems, and the brightest radiance of the choicest metals. She makes the stars of heaven sparkle in his hand, and the brightness of the sun shine in his face. She causes the mountains to flow down at his presence; his advent to gladden the solitary place; before him the deserts to rejoice and blossom as the rose. To the desert, at his approach, she gives the glory of Lebanon, the excellency of Carmel and Sharon.

Under his peaceful banner and gracious sceptre, the wolf dwells with the lamb; the leopard lies down with the kid; the calf, the young lion, and the fatling in harmony follow the mandates of a child; the cow and bear feed together; their young ones lie down in concord; and the lion eats straw like the ox. The sucking child plays on the hole of the asp; and the weaned child puts its hand on the cockatrice's den. Under his munificent government the wilderness becomes a fruitful field; and the field once esteemed fruitful is counted for a forest. He makes the eyes of the blind to see; the ears of the deaf to hear; and the tongue of the dumb to speak. The stammerer becomes eloquent, and the wise men of other times become as babes. He brings the captive from the prison, and those that sit in darkness out of the prison house. His people march forth with joy; they are led forth with peace. The mountains and the hills break forth into singing, and all the trees of the field clap their hands.

"He shall judge the poor of the people; he shall save the children of the needy, and shall break in pieces the oppressor. They shall fear him as long as the sun and moon endure, throughout all generations. He shall come down like rain upon the mown grass; as showers that water the earth. In his days shall the righteous flourish, and abundance of peace as long as the moon endureth. He shall have dominion from sea to sea, and from the river unto the ends of the earth. They that dwell in the wilderness shall bow before him, and his enemies shall lick the dust. The kings of Tarshish and of the Isles shall bring presents: the kings of Sheba and Seba shall offer gifts. Yea, all kings shall fall down before him: all nations shall serve him. For he shall deliver the needy when he crieth, the poor also, and him that hath no helper. He shall spare the poor and the needy, and shall save the souls of the needy. He shall redeem their souls from deceit and violence; and precious shall their blood be in his sight. There shall be, in his day, a handful of corn in the earth upon the top of the mountains; the fruit thereof shall shake like Lebanon: and they of the city shall flourish like grass of the earth. His name shall endure forever; his name shall be continued as long as the sun; and men shall ever be blessed in him: all nations shall call him blessed." *Psalm* lxxii. 4—17. Such were the glorious things spoken of Zion and her King, by holy kings and ancient seers, fired with prophetic impulse. These are but a taste of the sweetness which flows in the stream of prophecy, which revived, cheered and animated the drooping, disconsolate and afflicted hearts of the righteous ancients. Such things they uttered who saw his glory and spake of him. These prospective views of Messiah and his institution, prepare us to expect the brightest exhibition of glory in himself, and the highest degree of moral excellence and felicity in the subjects of his reign.

The fulness of time is come. Messiah appears. But lo! he has no form nor comeliness. He comes forth as a languishing shoot from a

5

dry and sterile soil. He comes to his own, and his own receive him not. He comes to the people who had the visions of the Almighty, and who heard the prophecies of the Spirit concerning him; yet they reject him as an impostor. They recognize no charms in his person—no glory in his purposed reign. Their hearts are infatuated with worldly notions, and they view him with a prejudiced eye. They see no diadem upon his head—no sceptre in his hand. They see no gorgeous apparel upon his person—no nobles nor princes in his train. They hear no sound of the trumpet—no confused sound of mighty warriors preparing for battle. They see no garments rolled in blood, nor captives led in chains. They are offended at the meanness of his parentage; at the humble birth and character of his attendants, and at his own insignificant appearance. His glories, and their views of glory, correspond in no one instance. His glory was that of unparalleled condescension, incomparable humility, meekness and love. The most resplendent gems in his crown were his abject poverty, his patient endurance of the grossest indignities, and the unreserved devotion of his whole soul, as the righteous servant of Jehovah. His victories were not those of a mighty chieftain, at the head of many thousands, marching through opposing ranks, demolishing citadels, devastating countries, causing iron gates to open at his approach, and leading bound to his triumphal chariot his captive enemies. No! his victories were the conquest of all temptations, of death, and of him that had the power of death. He triumphed over all principalities and powers of darkness, error and death. In his death and resurrection he gained the greatest conquest ever won: he vanquished death and the grave; he obtained eternal redemption; he opened the gates of Paradise, and procured an inheritance incorruptible, undefiled and unfading, for all them that look for deliverance. Such were the personal achievements of the Captain of our Salvation.

The precepts of his institution correspond with his appearance and deportment among men. He inculcates a morality pure as himself, and such as must render his disciples superior to all the world besides. He gives no scope to any malignant passions, and checks every principle that would lead to war, oppression or cruelty. His precepts respect not merely the overt act, but the principles from which all overt acts of wickedness proceed. Ambition, pride, avarice, lust, malevolence, are denounced as really criminal, as the actions to which they give rise. His precepts are no dry, lifeless system of morality, to be forced upon his disciples, or to be worn as an outside garment; but they are inculcated by arguments and considerations which when apprehended, engrave them upon the heart, and render them of easy practice. The reason, the nature, and the import of his death, afford, to those who understand it, an argument that gives life and vigor to all his precepts, and that makes his yoke easy and his burthen light. When we turn our attention to the character and exploits of his first disciples, his *ambassadors to the world*, what an illustrious exhibition of the excellency of his doctrine, and of the purity of his morals do they afford! In them how conspicuous faith, hope, and love! What zeal, what patience, what self-denial, what deadness to the world! How gladly they spend and are spent in the good work of faith, labor of love, and patience of hope! They glory in reproaches, in privations, in stripes, in imprisonments, in all manner of sufferings; yea, in death itself, for the Son of Man's sake. How freely, how cheerfully, how laboriously they performed the ministry which they had received! They look for no applause, for no stipend, no fixed salary, no lucrative office, no honorable title among men. They have continually in their eye the example of their Chief, "looking off *from the ancients* to Jesus the Captain and Finisher of the Faith, who, for the joy set before him, endured the cross, despising the shame, and sat down on the right hand of God." Amidst their enemies and false friends, how calm, how meek, how prudent, how resolute, how persevering! They exhibit virtues, in comparison of which, the virtues of all other religionists appear either as splendid sins, or as meagre empty names. Such was the character of the ambassadors and subordinate ministers of the New Institution.

The societies called churches, constituted and set in order by those ministers of the New Testament, were of such as received and acknowledged Jesus as Lord Messiah, the Saviour of the World, and had put themselves under his guidance. The ONLY BOND OF UNION among them was faith in him and submission to his will. No subscription to abstract propositions framed by synods; no decrees of councils sanctioned by kings; no rules of practice commanded by ecclesiastical courts were imposed on them as terms of admission into, or of continuance in this holy brotherhood. In the "apostles' doctrine" and in the "apostles' commandments" they steadfastly continued. Their fraternity was a fraternity of love, peace, gratitude, cheerfulness, joy, charity, and universal benevolence. Their religion did not manifest itself in public fasts nor carnivals. They had no festivals—no great and solemn meetings. Their meeting on the first day of the week was at all times alike solemn, joyful and interesting. Their religion was not of that elastic and porous kind, which at one time is compressed into some cold formalities, and at another expanded into prodigious zeal and warmth. No—their piety did not at one time rise to paroxysms, and their zeal to effervescence, and, by and by, languish into frigid ceremony and lifeless form. It was the pure, clear, and swelling current of love to God, of love to man, expressed in all the variety of doing good.

The *order* of their assemblies was uniformly the same. It did not vary with moons and seasons. It did not change as dress nor fluctuate as the manners of the times. Their devotion did not diversify itself into the endless forms of modern times. They had no monthly concerts for prayer; no solemn convocations, no great fasts, nor preparation, nor thanksgiving days. Their churches were not fractured into missionary societies, bible societies, education societies; nor did they dream of organizing such in the world. The head of a believing household was not in those days a president or manager of a board of foreign missions; his wife, the president of some female education society; his eldest son, the recording secretary of some domestic bible society; his eldest daughter, the corresponding secretary of a mite Society; his servant maid, the vice-president of a rag society; and his little daughter, a tutoress of a Sunday school. They knew nothing of the hobbies of modern times. In their church capacity alone they moved. They neither transformed themselves into any other kind of association, nor did they fracture and sever themselves into divers societies. They viewed the church of Jesus Christ as the scheme of Heaven to ameliorate the world; as members of it, they considered themselves bound to do all they could for the glory of God and the good of men. They dare not transfer to a missionary society, or bible society, or education society, a cent or a prayer, lest in so doing they should rob the church of its glory, and exalt the inventions of men above the wisdom of God. In their church capacity alone they moved. The church they considered "the pillar and ground of the truth;" they viewed it as the temple of the Holy Spirit; as the house of the living God. They considered if they did all they could in this capacity, they had nothing left for any other object of a religious nature. In this capacity, wide as its sphere extended, they exhibited the truth in word and deed. Their good works, which accompanied salvation, were the labors of love, in ministering to the necessities of saints, to the poor of the brotherhood. They did good to all men, but especially to the household of faith. They practiced that pure and undefiled religion, which, in overt acts, consists in "taking care of orphans and widows in their affliction, and in keeping one's self unspotted by (the vices of) the world."

In their church capacity they attended upon every thing that was of a social character, that did not belong to the closet or fireside. In the church, in all their meetings, they offered up their joint petitions for all things lawful, commanded or promised. They left nothing for a missionary prayer meeting, for seasons of unusual solemnity or interest. They did not at one time abate their zeal, their devotion, their gratitude or their liberality, that they might have an opportunity of showing forth to advantage or of doing something of great consequence at another. Such things they condemned in Jews and Pagans. No, gentle reader, in the primitive church they had no Easter Sunday, Thanksgiving Monday, Shrove Tuesday, Ash Wednesday, Holy Thursday, Good Friday, nor Preparation Saturday. All days were alike good—alike preparation—alike thanksgiving. As soon as some Pharisees that believed began to observe days and months, and times, and years; so soon did the apostle begin to stand in doubt of them.

Having taken a cursory view of some of the leading features of the christian religion, exhibited in *prospective*, and in actual existence at its first institution, we shall in the last place advert to its present appearance. But alas! "how is the fine gold become dim!" Instead of the apostles' doctrine, simply and plainly exhibited in the New Testament, we have got the sublime science of theology, subdivided into scholastic, polemic, dogmatic and practical divinity. Instead of the form of sound words given by the Spirit to be held fast, we have countless creeds, composed of terms and phrases, dogmas and speculations, invented by whimsical metaphysicians, christian philosophers, rabbinical doctors, and enthusiastic preachers. Instead of the divinely established order of bishops and deacons, or as they are sometimes called, elders and deacons, which remained when the age of "spiritual gifts" and "spiritual men" passed away, we have popes, cardinals, archbishops, metropolitan bishops, diocesan bishops, rectors, prebendaries, deans, priests, arch deacons, presiding elders, ruling elders, circuit preachers, local preachers, licentiates, class leaders, abbots, monks, friars, &c. &c.

Our devotion exhibits itself in prayers, in the set phrase of pompous oratory; in singing choirs; in long sermons, modelled after Grecian and Roman orations, logical themes and metaphysical essays; in revivals, camp-meetings,

praying societies, theological schools, education societies, missionary societies, Sunday schools, and in raising large sums of money by every way that ingenuity can devise, for propagating the gospel.

Our zeal burns brightest in contending for orthodox tenets, and a sort of technical language rendered sacred, and of imposing influence by long prescription. Such as the covenant of works, the covenant of grace; the active and passive obedience of Christ; legal repentance; the terms and conditions of the gospel; the gospel offer; the holy sacraments; ministerial, sacramental and catholic communion; the mediatorial kingdom of Christ; the millennium; historic faith, temporary faith, the faith of miracles, justifying faith, the faith of devils, the faith of assurance, and the assurance of faith; the direct act of faith, the reflex act of faith; baptismal vows; kirk sessions; fencing the tables; metallic tokens; &c. &c. Thus to speak in clerical dignity, anagogically, more than half the language of Ashdod is mingled with less than half the language of Canaan; and the people are generally zealous about such confounding, misleading and arrogant distinctions, which all result in divesting christianity of its glorious simplicity, which adapts it to boys and girls, as well as to philosophers, and which distort it into a mystery fit to employ linguists, philosophers, doctors of divinity, all their leisure hours, at a handsome per annum, in studying and then in giving publicity to their own discoveries, or in retailing those of others.

But into how diverse and opposite extremes and absurdities have many run, in their wild, superstitious, and chimerical views of the christian religion. Inquisitive reader, turn your eyes to yonder monastery, built in that solitary desert, filled with a religious order of monks, and an abbot at their head. Why have they shut themselves out from the world in that solitary recluse? It is for the purpose of becoming more abstemious, more devout, more devoted to the study of mystic theology. Hear them contending whether the Solitaires, the Cœnabites or the Sarabaites have chosen the course most congenial to the gospel. See these poor, gloomy, lazy set of mortals, habited in their awful black, their innocent white, or their spiritual grey, according to their order, forsaking all the business and enjoyments of society, spending their days in penury and affliction for the sake of sublimer contemplations of God and of the heavenly world; and say have they ever seen a bible! Again, see this sacred gloom, this holy melancholy, this pious indolence, becoming so popular as to affect all the seminaries of christendom for a time! See it command the respect of the highest dignitaries of the church; and hear them call those haunts of gloom and superstition, as some of the reformed orders of modern times call our colleges, "fountains and streams that make glad the city of God" by qualifying pious divines! Yes, these monasteries became so famous for piety and solemnity, that the church looked to them for her most useful ministers. And, indeed, much of the gloomy aspect, dejected appearance, and holy sighing of modern times, and especially of the leaders of devotion, sprang from those monasteries.

Next, consider for a moment, yon sobbing anchorite, with his amulet round his neck, his beads solemnly moving through his fingers, bent upon his naked knees in yon miserable cell, muttering his "Ave Maria," and invoking St. Andrew to intercede in his behalf; and say has he a bible? O yes! It lies mouldering and moth eaten on his shelves.

From this scene of infatuation turn your eyes to yonder dismal edifice, with iron gates and massy bars. Within its merciless apartments view the "*minister of religion,*" the "*ambassador of Christ,*" attired in his sacred robes, with holy aspect and flaming zeal for "divine honor" and that of his church, exhorting the vile heretic on pain of the most excruciating torments here, and eternal damnation hereafter, to abjure his heresy. As an argument to enforce his pious exhortations, observe the red hot pincers in hand, pointing to the boiling lead, the piles of fagots, the torturing wheels, and all the various engines of horrid vengeance. Do you ask who is he? I answer, It is the *Reverend* Inquisitor. On the most solemn AUTO DA FE, see this incorrigible heretic brought forward, arrayed in his *santo benito,* or sleeveless yellow coat, flowered to the border with the resemblance of flames, of red serge, decorated with his own picture, surrounded with devils, as doomed to destruction for the good of his soul. Then declare of what use is reason or revelation to many called christians!

But leaving the dungeon and that quarter of the globe, visit the group of reformed christians, and see another order of "teachers of the christian faith," "ministers of religion," having prepared themselves by the study of Grecian and Roman languages, laws, history, fables, gods, goddesses, debaucheries, wars, and suicides; having studied triangles, squares, circles, and ellipses, algebra and fluxions, the mechanical powers, chemistry, natural philosophy, &c. &c. for the purpose of becoming teachers of the christian religion; and then going forth with their saddlebags full of scholastic divinity in quest of a call to some eligible living; then ask again, Where is the bible?

And, stranger still, see that christian general, with his ten thousand soldiers, and his chaplain at his elbow, preaching, as he says, the gospel of good will among men; and hear him exhort his general and his christian warriors to go forth with the bible in one hand and the sword in the other, to fight the battles of God and their country; praying that the Lord would cause them to fight valiantly, and render their efforts successful in making as many widows and orphans as will afford sufficient opportunity for others to manifest the purity of their religion by taking care of them!!! If any thing is wanting to finish a picture of the most glaring inconsistencies, add to this those christians who are daily extolling the blessings of civil and religious liberty, and at the same time, by a system of the most cruel oppression, separating the wife from the embraces of her husband, and the mother from her tender offspring; violating every principle, and rending every tie that endears life and reconciles man to his lot; and that, forsooth, because "*might gives right,*" and a man is held guilty because his skin is a shade darker than the standard color of the times. Adverting to these signs of the times, and many others to which these reflections necessarily lead, will you not say that this prophecy is now fulfilled—2 *Tim.* iv. 3, 4—"There will be a time when they will not endure wholesome teaching; but having itching ears, they will, according to their own lusts, heap up to themselves teachers. And from the truth, indeed, they will turn away their ears and be turned aside to fables." Chap. iii. 1—5. "This also know, that in latter days perilous times will come. For men will be self-

lovers, money-lovers, boasters, proud, blasphemers, disobedient to parents, ungrateful, unholy, without natural affection, covenant-breakers, slanderers, having a form of godliness, but denying the power of it. Now FROM THESE TURN AWAY." Christian reader, remember this command—and "from such turn away."

The Origin of the "Christian Clergy," splendid Meeting Houses, and Fixed Salaries, exhibited from Ecclesiastical History.

Nota Bene.—IN our remarks upon the "Christian Clergy," we never include the Elders or Deacons of a Christian Assembly, or those in the New Testament called the overseers and servants of the Christian Church. These we consider as very different offices, and shall distinguish them in some future number.

Mosheim, vol. i. p. 73, Charlestown edition. "Another circumstance that irritated the Romans against the christians, was the simplicity of their worship, which resembled in nothing the sacred rites of any other people. The Christians had neither sacrifices, nor temples, nor images, nor oracles, nor sacerdotal robes; and this was sufficient to bring upon them the reproaches of an ignorant multitude, who imagined that there could be no religion without these. Thus they were looked upon as a sort of Atheists; and by the Roman laws, those who were chargeable with Atheism, were declared the pest of human society. But this was not all. The sordid interests of a multitude of lazy and selfish priests were immediately connected with the ruin and oppression of the christian cause. The public worship of such an immense number of deities was a source of subsistence, and even of riches, to the whole rabble of priests and augurs, and also to a multitude of merchants and artists. And the progress of the gospel threatened the ruin of this religious traffic and the profits it produced. This raised up new enemies to the christians, and armed the rage of mercenary superstition against their lives and their cause."

"The places in which the first christians assembled to celebrate divine worship, were, no doubt, the houses of private persons." p. 124.

"In these assemblies the holy scriptures were publicly read, and for that purpose were divided into certain portions or lessons. This part of divine service was followed by a brief exhortation to the people, in which eloquence and art gave place to the natural and fervent expressions of zeal and charity." p. 124, 125.

Haweis' Church History, volume i. p. 150. "Nothing could be more unadorned than the primitive worship. A plain man, chosen from among his fellows, in his common garb, stood up to speak, or sat down to read the Scriptures to as many as chose to assemble in the house appointed. A back room, and that probably often a mean one, or a garret, to be out of the way of observation, was their temple."

"As pride and worldly mindedness must go hand in hand, assumed pomp and dignity require a sort of maintenance very different from the state when the pastor wrought with his own hands to minister to his necessities, and labored by day that he might serve the church by night. The idea of priesthood had yet scarcely entered into the christian sanctuary, as there remained no more sacrifice for sin, and but one high-priest of our profession, Jesus Christ. But, on the dissolution of the whole Jewish economy under Adrian, when the power of the associated clergy began to put forth its bud, the ambitious and designing suggested, what many of the rest received in their simplicity, that the succession to these honors now devolved upon them, and that the bishop stood in the place of the high-priest; the presbyters were priests; and the deacons, Levites: and so a train of consequences followed. Thus a new tribe arose, completely separated from their brethren, of clergy distinct from laity—men sacred by office, exclusive of a divine call and real worth. The altar, indeed, was not yet erected, nor the unbloody sacrifice of the eucharist perfected; but it approached by hasty strides to add greater sanctity to the priesthood, and the not unpleasant adjunct of the divine right of tithes, attached to the divine right of episcopacy." p. 181, 182.

"The simplicity of the primitive worship, contrasted with the pomp of paganism, was striking. It was concluded by the heathen, that they who had neither altar, victim, priest, or sacrifice, must be Atheists, and without God in the world. Those who were now rising into self-created eminence, had therefore little difficulty to persuade that it would be for the interest and honor of christianity to remove these objections of the Gentiles, by very harmless but useful alterations. Though magnificent temples had not yet risen, the names of things began to change. There were already *priests;* and *oblations* were easily rendered *sacrifices*. The separation of the clergy, as a body, became more discriminated by their habits. *High-Priests* must have more splendid robes than the simple tunic of linen. A variety of new ceremonies were invented to add dignity to the mysteries of christianity and obviate the objections to its meanness and simplicity. And as the populace were particularly attached to their idolatry by the festivals in honor of their heroes and their gods, and delighted with the games and pastimes on these occasions, the great Gregory Thaumaturgus shortly afterward contrived to bilk the devil, by granting the people the indulgence of all the same pleasures of feasting, sporting, and dancing at the tombs, and on the anniversary of the martyrs, as they had been accustomed to in the temples of their gods; very wisely and christianly supposing that thus, *sua sponte ad honestiorem et accuratiorem vitæ rationem transirent*—of their own accord they would quit their idolatry, and return to a more virtuous and regular course of life. I must be exceedingly hard drove for a christian, before I can put such men as Gregory Thaumaturgus into the number." p. 182, 183.

"Constantine having become the conqueror of Maxentius, and, as it seems, chiefly by the support of christians, his favor to them increased in great munificence to build them churches, and in abounding liberality to their poor. Their bishops were honored by him and caressed, and their synods held and supported by his authority." p. 246, 247.

"Having now no longer a competitor, Constantine resolved to take the most decided part with the christians. He prohibited the heathen sacrifices and shut up the temples, or converted them to the purposes of christian worship. He universally established christianity, and tolerated no other religion openly throughout the bounds of the empire; the justice of which I doubt, and even the policy. I see no right to compel even an idolater, contrary to his conscience." p. 247.

"The bounties he bestowed, the zeal he displayed, his liberal patronage of episcopal men, the pomp he introduced into worship, and the power invested with general councils, made the church appear great and splendid, but I discern not a trace in Constantine of the religion of the Son of God." p. 248.

"I am persuaded that his establishment of christianity, and of those bishops whom particularly at last he most espoused and favored, contributed beyond any thing to the awful debasement and declension of true religion, and from him and his son Constantius evangelical truth suffered in the spirit of christian professors, as much as their persons had undergone from Dioclesian or Galerius." p. 249.

"The church now in esteem of some, was exalted to the highest pinnacle of prosperity, invested with vast authority, and the episcopal order collected in synods and councils, with almost sovereign dominion. The churches vied in magnificence with palaces; and the robes and pomp of service, imitating imperial splendor, eclipsed paganism itself, with mitres, tiaras, tapers, crosiers, and processions. If outward appearances could form a glorious church, here she would present herself; but these meretricious ornaments concealed beneath them all the spirit of the world—pride, luxury, covetousness, contention, malignity, and every evil word and work. Heresy and schism abounded, and wickedness of every kind, like a flood, deluged the christian world; whilst the heads of the church more engaged in controversy, and a thousand times more jealous about securing and increasing their own wealth and pre-eminence, than presenting examples of humility, patience, deadness to the world and heavenly mindedness, were, like gladiators, armed in all their councils, and affected imperial power and pomp in the greater dioceses." p. 261.

The statements made by these two historians, we are able to confirm from a great variety of documents. If there be a fact, more clear than any other established upon the page of ecclesiastical history, it is the following, viz: that the confounding of the Jews' religion with the christian religion, or the viewing of the latter as an improvement of the former, has been the fountain of error which has, since the apostolic age, corrupted the doctrine, changed the order, and adulterated the worship of the christian church. This, together with the influence of pagan priests and pagan philosophers, proselyted to the christian religion, has been the Pandora's box to the professing christian community. We happened upon the truth, when we published as our opinion, about seven years ago, that "the present popular exhibition of the christian religion is a compound of judaism, heathen philosophy and christianity." From this unhallowed commixture sprang all political ecclesiastical establishments, a distinct order of men called clergy or priests, magnificent edifices as places of worship, tithes or fixed salaries, religious festivals, holy places and times, the christian circumcision, the christian passover, the christian Sabbaths, &c. &c. These things we hope to exhibit at full length in due time.

From the extracts already adduced from these eminent historians, it appears clear as the morning that the distinction betwixt *clergy* and *laity*, originated by degrees, and widened into all the extreme points of dissimilarity in the lapse of a few generations. But behold the mighty difference! and in it see the arrogance of the clergy and the abject servility of the laity—when the high-priest, the head of the clergy mounts his horse, the king (as layman) holds his stirrup, and in obeisance, kisses his toe. A respectable portion of this high-priest's spirit has fallen upon all the clergy, and a becoming share of servility even yet exists amongst those who admire them most. Happy they who know the truth! for it makes them free! How blissful the words of the Saviour of the world! and how true! "If the son shall make you free, you shall be free indeed!"   Editor.

Dr. Beattie's opinion of the Christian Religion.

"The Christian Religion, according to my creed, is a very simple thing, intelligent to the meanest capacity; and what, if we are at pains to join practice to knowledge, we may make ourselves acquainted with without turning over many books. It is the distinguished excellence of this religion that it is entirely popular and fitted, both in its doctrines and its evidences, to all conditions and capacities of reasonable creatures—a character which does not belong to any other religious or philosophical system that ever appeared in the world. I wonder to see so many men eminent both for their piety and for their capacity, laboring to make a *mystery* of this divine institution. If God vouchsafe to reveal himself to mankind, can we suppose that he chooses to do it in such a manner that none but the learned and contemplative can understand him? The generality of mankind can never, in any possible circumstances, have leisure or capacity for learning or profound contemplation. If, therefore, we make christianity a mystery, we exclude the greater part of mankind from the knowledge of it; which is directly contrary to the intention of its author, as is plain from his explicit and reiterated declarations. In a word, I am perfectly convinced that an intimate acquaintance with the SCRIPTURE, particularly the Gospels, is all that is necessary to our accomplishment in true christian knowledge. I have looked into some systems of theology, but I never read one of them to an end, because I found I could never reap any instruction from them. To darken what is clear, by wrapping it up in a veil of system and science, was all the purpose that the best of them seems to me to answer."

No. 2.]   September 1, 1823.

The following essay, from the pen of a close and constant student of the Bible, is most worthy of the attention and examination of those engaged in teaching the christian religion. It is the first of an intended series of essays on one of the most desirable subjects, viz. to point out a divinely authorized plan of teaching the christian religion. We earnestly entreat our readers to give these essays a fair, full, and strict examination.   Editor.

On Teaching Christianity.—No. I.

Our exertions for increasing the number of copies of the Scriptures are now multiform and great; societies for effectuating this object are to be found almost every where. Towns, cities, villages, and even the wilderness, are forward in endeavors to make the number of bibles in the world as great as possible; and though it cannot be said that the bible is even now a scarce book, yet the day is anticipated when the number of copies shall be greatly multiplied, and when the blessed volume shall be found in the possession of every family, perhaps of every individual. The object of the present paper, however, is not to enlarge either on the benevolence or the extent of the present or probable success of those societies formed for multiply-

ing copies of the bible; but only to lend assistance to those societies or churches formed for understanding it, to present christians with an authorized plan of studying the scriptures, and to furnish the christian teacher with a certain method by which he ought to proceed in making known the great salvation to his hearers.

Were a vision vouchsafed us for the single purpose of revealing one uniform and universal plan of teaching the christian religion, would not every christian admire the goodness of God in determining a matter on which scarce two, calling themselves christian teachers, now agree? Would not every teacher feel himself bound in duty to abandon his own plan, and to adopt the plan of God—to study it, to teach by it, and, in short, to maintain its superiority and authority against all other schemes, how plausible soever in their configuration, how apparently suitable soever in their application? The writer has not been favored with any vision on this matter; moreover, as he deems it unnecessary, he of course does not expect any. And surely if his plan be authorized by the example of God himself—by the Lord Jesus Christ—by the Holy Spirit, in his method of presenting the truth to all men in the scriptures; if the apostles taught the truth on this plan, and if missionaries in teaching idolaters feel themselves forced to the adoption of it; then there is no need of angel or vision. The path of duty is before us, and we ought to pursue it. What shall we say of the present babel-like confusion among those calling themselves teachers of christianity? The champions of each sect forming schemes for themselves of teaching as chance, or whim, or interest directs, and all employing themselves in confirming certain factional dogmas—in making merchandize of the people, or in propagating damnable heresies. Timothy had known the holy scriptures from a child, and the apostle assured him that they alone were able to make him wise unto salvation; that they were profitable for doctrine, for reproof, for correction, and instruction in righteousness; conjuring him at the same time, as he hoped to account for his conduct before God and the Lord Jesus Christ, to be instant in season and out of season, in teaching the word of God; asserting for it as a reason that the time was approaching when the professors of the religion, having itching ears, would, after their own lusts, (the love of novelty and of eloquence,) become disgusted with the scriptures, and make for themselves teachers, who would turn away people's ears from the truth and entertain them with fables.

Passing by, for the present, the various stupid schemes, all different and all wrong, pursued by Roman Catholics, Socinians, Arians, Covenanters, Seceders, Presbyterians, High-Churchmen, Baptists, Independents, and so forth, let us attend to the plan of teaching the truth pursued by God—by the Lord Jesus Christ—by the Holy Spirit, in presenting it to all men in the scriptures, and by the apostles and all who first preached it—a plan founded in the very nature of the saving truth itself, and into which ignorant missionaries feel themselves driven when every human scheme has failed. But what is the truth? Times out of number we are told in scripture that the grand saving truth is, that "Jesus is the Christ." This is the bond of union among christians—the essence—the spirit of all revelation. All the scriptures testify and confirm this simple truth, that "he that believeth that Jesus is the Christ, is begotten by God." *John* v. 2. For he who believeth it, sets to his seal that God is true. Such a one, John says, loveth God and Christ and the brethren, keepeth his commands, and is purified from all his sins, and overcometh the world, and shall be saved. Christ declared when departing into heaven, that he that believeth not shall be damned. The grand truth, then, being that "Jesus is the Christ" let us attend to those scriptures which are written for the express purpose of establishing this proposition; these are the writings of the four evangelists, which at once show us in what manner God would have us to learn this truth; in what manner the Lord Jesus taught it; how the Holy Spirit has been pleased to present it to mankind; how the apostles wrote of it, and of course taught it to the world. This is the beginning of the plan authorized of heaven; and every teacher of the christian religion should commence by unfolding to his hearers the matter of the four evangelists. "These things, says John, are written that ye might believe that Jesus is the Christ; and that believing, ye might have life through his name." Now, what definition soever the holy scripture has given of one evangelist, that is the definition of them all; for each of them contain a history of that marvellous evidence by which Jesus proved that he was the Christ; by which his pretensions to the Messiahship were so amply confirmed among the Jews.

The perfection of christian intelligence is a knowledge of the holy scriptures, and no christian is intelligent but as he knows the scriptures. The desideratum, then, is a plan for teaching them to the people. By commencing with the four evangelists and abiding by them until they are relished and understood, we learn, chief of all things, that Jesus is the Christ; and while the number, magnitude, variety, sublimity and benignity of his miracles delight, astonish and instruct us, they, at the same time, carry irresistable conviction to the heart, purge it, elevate it, and fix our faith in the mighty power of God. By and by, as we become familiarized to the miraculous evidence, we become reconciled, and even strongly attached to it; losing all suspicion of its reality, and of course of the reality of our holy religion; because we come to perceive that these things were not done in a corner, but in public, and under the inspection of men who were both able and forward to decide upon their truth and certainty; men who, in point of intellect, reason, and character, might have vied with the choicest of our modern sceptics; men, in short, whose abilities to detect were equalled only by their readiness to pervert. In the writings of the evangelists we behold that power which created man and all things, exerting itself with all possible unaffected pomp and majesty, tempering, uniting, and clothing itself with all goodness and philanthropy; and so entirely at the will of the Holy One, that it accompanies those who accompany him. It sparkles, it flashes, it shines, it heals, it renovates, it creates, it controls, it rests, it leaps, it flies, it kindly raises up the bowed down, or hushes into silence the swelling and reluctant storm; it flies forth with the breath of his mouth, it operates at the tuft of his mantle, at the tip of his finger, or at the distance of a hundred leagues; now it is in the air with a voice like thunder; it shakes open the nodding tombs, or it rends the crashing mountains around Jerusalem; always marvellous, it is always harmless, and mostly benevolent. True, there is nothing conciliating or winning in power abstractly considered; apart from goodness, we always choose to inspect it at a distance; but if joined with malevolence, we fly from it with horror and affright. Power is formidable and even terrifying in the tiger, because in him it is a mere instrument of cruelty; but the same power becomes amiable in the horse, because all the thunder of his neck, all the glory of his nostrils, the strength of his limbs, and the fierceness of his attitude, are continually held in check by that beautiful docility which so eminently characterizes this noble animal, and by which his very will is identified with that of his rider. In the evangelists we behold the everlasting, the unexpended power itself, revealed in the form of a servant, and with more than a servant's humility, the strength of the Lion of the tribe of Judah, and harmlessness of the Lamb, dwelling together in the same one.

In short, we see that the Lord our Saviour is unweariedly and everlastingly employed in supplying, comforting, and saving the unfortunate creatures whom he had originally made upright.

PHILIP.

To the Editor of the Christian Baptist.

Sir—FROM the nature and design of this work, as stated in your proposals to the public, and from the character of those who may be supposed desirous to patronize it, as a work not devoted to the interests of any party, but merely and exclusively to the evolution and exhibition of christianity in its primitive simplicity and native excellence; it is presumed that an essay on the proper and primary intention of the gospel, with its proper and immediate effects in those that received it, would be a suitable introduction to such a work, as it would not only furnish an interesting and radical criterion, whereby to judge between the present and primitive state of christianity; but also would serve to show the grievous and incalculable privation of blissful and efficacious privileges, occasioned by a long and almost universal departure from the original apostolic exhibition of it; and thus tend to excite a general and just concern in the public mind, to repair the incalculable loss, by strictly adverting to the pure original gospel as exhibited by the apostles, and thus to contend earnestly for the faith as it was once delivered to the saints. If you, sir, think with the writer, that such a subject would be a suitable commencement; and that the following will, in some good measure, answer that purpose, you will please accept it as a token of sincere desire for the utility and success of your undertaking, and as a pledge on the part of the writer, of his hearty determination to contribute any assistance in his power, to the accomplishment of so worthy an object.

Yours respectfully, T. W.

Essay on the proper and primary intention of the gospel, and its proper and immediate effects.

THAT the reconciliation of a guilty world, in order to complete and ultimate salvation, was the proper and primary intention of the gospel, is evident from the uniform tenor of the gospel testimony, as recorded in the New Testament. The gospel itself is called the word of reconciliation, 2 *Cor.* v. 19. The work of preaching it, as at first enjoined upon the apostles, and afterwards executed by them, is styled the ministry of reconciliation, 2 *Cor.* v. 18, 19. Their manner of proceeding in it was to this effect: "As though God did beseech you by us, we pray you in Christ's stead, be ye (sinners) reconciled to God," 2 *Cor.* v. 20, 21. The instruction under which they proceeded to the execution of their office, was, "that repentance and remission of sin should be preached, in the name of Christ, to all nations,' *Luke* xxiv. 47. Their commencement at Jerusalem, in addressing the multitude, that appeared convinced of the truth of their testimony concerning Jesus, was, "Repent and be baptized every one of you in the name of Jesus Christ," *Acts* ii. 38. The immediate effect of their preaching, in all that were suitably affected by it, was reconciliation, *Rom.* v. 10. when we were enemies, we were reconciled to God by the death of his Son; and *Col.* i. 19—21, "For it pleased the Father by him to reconcile all things unto himself; and you that were some time alienated, and enemies in your mind by wicked works, yet now hath he reconciled," in the body of his flesh through death, 2 *Cor.* v. 18, "God was in Christ reconciling the world unto himself, not imputing their trespasses unto them. Therefore, if any man be in Christ, he is a new creature; old things are passed away; behold all things are become new;" and "all things are of God, who hath reconciled us to himself by Jesus Christ," v. 17, 18. From these, and a multitude of passages that might be adduced, it is evident that the proper and immediate intention of God in the publication of the gospel to the nations, whether Jews or Gentiles, was reconciliation to himself by Jesus Christ; and also, that the proper and immediate effect of this publication on all on whom it had its proper effect, that is, on all that understood and believed it, was reconciliation to God; and that in order to their complete and final salvation, according to *Rom.* v. 10. "For if, when we were enemies, we were reconciled to God by the death of his Son, much more, being reconciled, we shall be saved by his life."

Moreover, from the above cited scriptures, and many others, it is equally evident that the immediate and reconciling effect of the gospel, in all that were reconciled by it, was the belief of a full and free pardon of all their sins through Christ, and for his sake, on account of the propitiatory sacrifice which he voluntarily made of himself upon the cross; which is therefore called the atonement or reconciliation. Indeed, when we contemplate the state of the world in the light of divine revelation, we find that all, both Jews and Gentiles, had sinned and come short of the glory of God; that the whole world was become guilty before him; there was none righteous— no, not one; none that practiced good and sinned not. And that, except a very few spiritual characters amongst the Jews, whose minds were supported by the hopes of a promised Messiah, all mankind were alienated from the life of God, through the blindness of ignorance; and were become enemies in their minds by wicked works. Such, then, being the actual state of mankind, considered as the object of divine benevolence, we see the indispensable necessity of the means which infinite wisdom and goodness devised to effect a change for the better among such guilty creatures; namely, the proclamation of a general and everlasting amnesty, a full and free pardon of all offences, to all, without respect of persons; and this upon such terms as brought it equally near to, equally within the reach of *all;* which was effectually done by the preaching of the gospel; see *Acts* xiii. 16—19, and x. 34—43, and ii. 14—35, with many other scriptures. In the passages above referred to, we have a sufficient and satisfactory specimen of the truly primitive and apostolic gospel, as preached both to Jews and Gentiles, by the two great Apostles, Peter and Paul; in each of which we have most explicitly, the same gracious proclamation of pardon to every one that received their testimony

concerning Jesus. Repent, said Peter to the convinced and convicted Jews, (Acts ii. 38,) and be baptized every one of you in the name of Jesus Christ, for the *remission of sins.* And again, *Acts* x. 43, to him give all the prophets witness that through his name, whosoever believeth in him shall receive *remission of sins.* To the same effect, Paul, in his sermon at Antioch, in the audience both of Jews and Gentiles, *Acts* xiii. 38, 39. Be it known unto you, therefore, men and brethren, that through this man is preached unto you the *forgiveness of sins,* and by him, all that believe are justified from all things. God, by the gospel, thus avowing his love to mankind, in giving his only begotten Son for the life of the world; and through him, and for his sake, a full and free remission of all sins; and all this in a perfect consistency with his infinite abhorrence of sin, in the greatest possible demonstration of his displeasure against it, in the death of his Son, (which he has laid as the only and adequate foundation for the exercise of sin-pardoning mercy;) has at once secured the glory of his character, and afforded effectual relief and consolation to the perishing guilty, by a full and free pardon of sin. "And you being dead in your sins, and in the uncircumcision of your flesh, hath he quickened together with him, having forgiven you all trespasses," *Col.* ii. 13. Such being the gospel testimony concerning the love of God, the atonement of Christ, and the import of baptism for the remission of sins; all, therefore, that believed it, and were baptized for the remission of their sins, were as fully persuaded of their pardon and acceptance with God, through the atonement of Christ, and for his sake, as they were of any other article of the gospel testimony. It was this, indeed, that gave virtue and value to every other item of that testimony, in the estimation of the convinced sinner; as it was this alone that could free his guilty burthened conscience from the guilt of sin, and afford him any just ground of confidence towards God. Without this justification, which he received by faith in the divine testimony, could he have had peace with God through the Lord Jesus Christ, or have rejoiced in hope of his glory, as the apostle testifies concerning the justified by faith? *Rom.* v. 1, 2. Surely no; or how could he have been reconciled to God by the death of his Son, had he not believed, according to the testimony, that he had redemption through his blood, even the forgiveness of sins, according to the riches of the divine grace, thus most graciously manifested? Or why could he have received baptism, the import of which to the believer was the remission of his sins, had he not believed the divine attestation to him in that ordinance, concerning the pardoning of his sins upon his believing and being baptized? Every one, then, from the very commencement of christianity, who felt convinced of the truth of the gospel testimony, and was baptized, was as fully persuaded of the remission of his sins, as he was of the truth of the testimony itself. Indeed, how could it be otherwise, seeing the testimony held forth this as the primary and immediate privilege of every one that believed it? "For to him gave all the prophets witness, that through his name, whosoever believeth in him, shall receive remission of sins." Likewise Ananias to Saul of Tarsus, after he was convinced of the truth concerning Jesus of Nazareth, saying, "Why tarriest thou; arise, and be baptized, and wash away thy sins," &c. &c. But the fulness of evidence with which the scriptures attest this blissful truth, will abundantly appear to all that search them for obtaining a full discovery of it. In the mean time, from what has been produced we may see with what great propriety the pure and primitive preaching of the gospel was called the ministry of reconciliation, and how admirably adapted it was to that gracious purpose. Indeed, how could it possibly fail of producing that blissful and happy effect in every one that believed it? Was it not a divinely attested declaration of the love of God to a guilty, perishing world, to such a degree as to give his only begotten Son to become a sacrifice and ransom for the sins of men; and that through him, whosoever believeth in him, has remission of sins; is justified from all things; shall not come unto condemnation, but shall have everlasting life; and all this immediately upon his believing, figuratively, that is typically, declared and confirmed to him by his baptism, a solemn rite of divine appointment for this very purpose, as the apostles have explained it. See *Rom.* 6th chapter, &c. &c. Hence, also, we may see a just and adequate reason of the great joy, consolation and happiness that universally accompanied the primitive preaching and belief of the gospel amongst all sorts of people; as also, of the very singular and eminent fruits of universal benevolence, of zeal, of brotherly kindness, of liberality, of fortitude, of patience, of resignation, of mutual forbearance and forgiveness; in a word, of universal self-denying obedience in conformity to Christ; contentedly, nay, even joyfully, suffering the loss of all things for his sake; so that the apostle John could boldly and confidently challenge the world, saying, "Who is he that overcometh the world, but he that believeth that Jesus Christ is the Son of God?"

Such was the virtue of the primitive faith; and such faith the just and genuine effect of the apostolic gospel; for it could produce no other correspondent faith, if it produced any at all. In fine, from the premises before us, that is, from the whole apostolic exhibition of the gospel, and its recorded effects upon all who professed to believe it, many of whom, it is certain, did not truly understand the gospel, and therefore could not truly believe it; nevertheless, from the whole of the premises, it is evident that the professing world is far gone, yea, very far indeed, from original ground; for such was the import of the gospel testimony, as we have seen, that all who professed to believe it, whether they were intelligent persons or not, understood at least so much by it, that it gave assurance of pardon and acceptance with God to every one that received it; that is, to every baptized believer; consequently, every one that was baptized, making the same profession, he both thought himself, and was esteemed by his professing brethren, a justified and accepted person. Hence we do not find a single instance, on the sacred record, of a doubting or disconsolate christian; nor a single hint dropped for the direction or encouragement of such; but, on the contrary, much said to detect and level presumptuous confidence. How different this from the present state of the professing world, the discreet and judicious reader need not be informed. Now, surely, if similar causes uniformly produce similar effects, the same preaching would as uniformly produce the same faith that it did in the beginning in all them that believed it; and even in all them that *thought* they believed it; namely, of the person's justification and acceptance with God; and, of course, the same faith would produce the same peace and joy in the believer, and in him that

thought himself to be such, as it did in the days, and under the preaching, of the apostles and of their faithful coadjutors.   T. W.

Remarks on Missionaries.

FOR two centuries the "christian nations," emperors, kings, princes, priests and laity, were uniting their efforts to rescue the "holy land," in which the Saviour lived and died, from the hands of the infidels. A superstitious veneration for the city of Bethlehem, the place of the nativity; for the villages of Judea, the theatre of the miracles; and for Jerusalem, the place of the crucifixion, and the sepulchre of the Messiah, was the cause of innumerable pilgrimages to Palestine. These pilgrimages were, for many years, performed with safety. But, in the year 1065, this land fell into the hands of the Turks, and pilgrimages to it became extremely dangerous. The merit and indispensable necessity of these pilgrimages increased, in popular estimation, with the dangers attendant on them. The hard usage of the pilgrims, from the tyranny of the Turks, filled all Europe with complaints. In a council of four thousand ecclesiastics and thirty thousand seculars, it was determined to be meritorious in the sight of God, to be a great and pious design, and to be "the will of God," that all christians should engage in one grand system of hostilities against the Turks; that great and powerful expeditions should be fitted out against the infidels who possessed the "holy land;" that the soldiers should all wear a cross on their right shoulders, and, with swords in their hands, open the way into the holy city. These expeditions were called croisades, from the circumstance of the soldiers wearing the cross. All Europe was engaged in this project. Buck tells us in his compend of history, that "all ranks of men, now deeming the croisades the only road to heaven, were impatient to open the way, with their swords, to the holy city. Nobles, artisans, peasants, even priests enrolled their names, and to decline this service, was branded with the reproach of impiety and cowardice. The nobles were moved by the romantic spirit of the age to hope for opulent establishments in the East, the chief seat of arts and commerce at that time. In pursuit of these chimerical projects, they sold at low prices, their ancient castles and inheritances, which had now lost all value in their eyes. The infirm and aged contributed to the expedition by presents and money, and many of them attended it in person, being determined, if possible, to breathe their last in sight of that city where their Saviour died for them. Even women, concealing their sex under the disguise of armour, attended the camp." The first croisade consisted of three hundred thousand undisciplined and about seven hundred thousand disciplined men. No less than eight croisades were undertaken in something less than two hundred years. Upwards of two millions were destroyed in these croisades—and yet the Holy Land is still retained by the infidels. "If," says the same Charles Buck, "the absurdity and wickedness of this conduct can be exceeded by any thing, it must be by what follows. In 1204 the frenzy of croisading seized the children, who are ever ready to imitate what they see their parents engaged in; their childish folly was encouraged by the monks and schoolmasters, and thousands of those innocents were conducted from the houses of their parents, on the superstitious interpretation of these words: "Out of the mouths of babes and sucklings hast thou perfected praise." Their base conductors sold a part of them to the Turks, and the rest perished miserably."

We are all prepared to call those croisades chimerical and wicked projects, and to compliment ourselves as elevated above such wild enthusiasm and debasing superstition; yet, perhaps some of the great and popular undertakings of our era may be pronounced by posterity as absurd and superstitious, as enthusiastic and unscriptural as those we so cheerfully censure. The collecting of money by the hands of a constable, to pay a "divine" for teaching us righteousness, mercy, and the love of God; the incorporating of a christian society by the act of a legislative body, often composed of men of no religion, of sceptics in the christian revelation, and of men of different religious sects; the asking and receiving money from those who have not received the gospel as the gospel of their salvation, to send the word to the heathen which they themselves have not obeyed; the selling of pews for hundreds of dollars to defray the expenses of building a house of worship, decorated like a theatre, to gratify the pride of life; the taxing of those pews to collect a revenue to support the reverend incumbent, who weekly from the rostrum sells his prayers and his sermons; the consecrating of grave-yards; the laying the foundation stones of cathedrals and meeting-houses with masonic and clerical honors; the making of holy water, or the consecrating a few drops from a common to a special use; and many other pranks of protestant priests, will, no doubt, be viewed by those that come after us as superstitious, as enthusiastic, as anti-christian as the croisades; though, perhaps, inferior in magnitude and not so palpably wicked.

For three hundred years great exertions have been made to convert the whole world to the christian religion. Much zeal has been exhibited, many privations have been endured, and great dangers have been braved by missionaries to heathen lands. In this laudable object the most ignorant and most superstitious sect in christendom has been the most active, and, if we can credit its reports, by far the most successful. The Portuguese and Spaniards of the holy see of Rome, in the sixteenth century, spread (what they call) the gospel, through large districts in Asia, Africa, and America. Different orders of monks, particularly, the Dominicans, Franciscans, and, above all, the Jesuits, displayed astonishing zeal, and spent immense sums in reclaiming African, Asian, and American Pagans. The great missionary Xavier spread the Romish gospel through the Portuguese settlements in the East Indies, through most of the India continent, and of Ceylon. In 1549, he sailed to Japan and founded a church there, which soon amounted to six hundred thousand Roman christians. Others penetrated into China, and founded churches that continued one hundred and seventy years. In 1580, other Catholic missionaries penetrated into Chili and Peru, and converted the natives. Others labored with ardent zeal and unwearied industry among the Greeks, Nestorians, Abysinians and Egyptian Copts. In 1622, the pope established a congregation of cardinals, *de propaganda fide*, and endowed it with ample revenues for propagating the faith. In 1627, Urban, the pope, added a college, in which the languages of pagans were taught. France copied the example of Rome, and formed establishments for the same purposes. Amongst all the religious orders there was "a holy ambition," which should do most. "The Jesuits claimed the first

rank as due to their zeal, learning, and devotedness to the holy see. The Dominicans, Franciscans, and others, disputed the palm with them. The new world and the Asiatic regions were the chief field of their labors. They penetrated into the uncultivated recesses of America. They visited the untried regions of Siam, Tonkin, and Cochin China. They entered the vast empire of China itself, and numbered millions among their converts. They dared to confront the dangers of the tyrannical government of Japan. In India they assumed the garb and austerities of the Brahmins, and boasted, on the coast of Malabar, of a thousand converts baptized in one year by a single missionary. Their sufferings were, however, very great; and in China and Japan they were exposed to the most dreadful persecutions, and many thousands were cut off, with, at last, a final expulsion from the empires."—*Buck's Theological Dictionary, vol.* 1, *p.* 147.

We all, who call ourselves protestants, hesitate not to say, that those missionaries, notwithstanding their zeal, their privations, and their sufferings in the missionary cause, left the heathen no better than they found them; nay, in some instances, they left them much worse; and, that there is as much need for their conversion from the religion of those missionaries, as there was from the religion of idols. It may be worthy of the serious consideration of many of the zealous advocates of the various sectarian missions in our day, whether, in a few years, the same things may not be said of their favorite projects which they themselves affirm of the Catholic missions and missionaries. They should also remember that it was once as unpopular and as *impious* to speak against the missionary undertakings of the "mother church," as it can possibly be now to even call in question the schemes of any of her daughters. It might not be amiss also to consider, that a Dominican or a Jesuit *did* appeal to the privations and sufferings of their missionaries as a proof of their sincerity and piety, and to their great success, as a proof that the Lord of Hosts was with them. These reflections suggest the necessity of great caution in forming opinions on the measures of the religionists of our time. We pass over the Moravian, the Episcopalian, the Presbyterian, the Methodist, and the Baptist missionaries of this age, and proceed to suggest, in the most respectful manner, to the religious community, a few thoughts on what appears to us the capital mistake of all the missionary schemes of our time.

The capital mistake of modern missionary schemes.

IN order that this may appear as plain as possible, we shall take a brief view of the two grand missions instituted by God. The first was that of Moses and Joshua. Moses was the great apostle from God to the Israelites in Egypt. Before he became God's missionary, from his own benevolence, to his brethren the Jews, and from a sense of the tyranny of the Egyptians, he became a revenger of the wrongs of his people, and delivered one of them from the hands of an Egyptian. In this period of his history he very much resembled one of our best missionaries: he was a benevolent, zealous, and bold man; felt himself called to a good work; but not being commissioned by God, his efforts were unavailing, and he was obliged to fly his country for his ill-timed zeal. After forty years, the Lord appeared to him and commissioned him as his missionary to Egypt. Moses, from his own experience on a former occasion, discovered that something more was necessary to his success than good professions and good speeches; he, therefore, answered and said, "But, behold, they will not believe me, nor hearken to my voice; for they will say, the Lord hath not appeared unto thee." The Lord immediately authorized and empowered him to work miracles. He now goes forth, in conjunction with his brother Aaron, clothed with proper authority, confirming his testimony with signs and wonders, and effects the deliverance of the Israelites from ignorance and bondage. (See an account of this mission, *Exodus*, 3d and 4th chapters.) The success of his mission Stephen compendiously relates in these words, *Acts* vii. 35, 36. "This Moses whom they refused, saying, who made thee a ruler and a judge? the same did God *send* to be a ruler and a deliverer by the hand of the angel that appeared unto him in the bush. He brought them out, after that he had shewn wonders and signs in the land of Egypt, and in the Red Sea, and in the wilderness forty years."

Joshua becomes, after the death of Moses, the second missionary in this mission, and is thus authorized, *Joshua*, i. 5. "There shall not any man be able to stand before thee all the days of thy life: as I was with Moses, so I will be with thee; I will not fail thee nor forsake thee." 9. "Have not I commanded thee? Be strong and of a good courage; be not afraid, neither be thou dismayed; for the Lord thy God is with thee whithersoever thou goest." Signs and wonders accompanied the ministry of Joshua until he placed the tribes of Israel in their own land and divided it to them by lot. In this manner the first grand mission commenced, progressed, and terminated. Without pausing on the mission of John the Baptist, to introduce the christian era, which was also authenticated by signs and wonders attendant on his conception and birth, and which were noised abroad throughout all Judea, whereby his testimony was confirmed to the people; we proceed to the second in order of time, but in fact the first grand mission to which all others were subservient— we mean the Father's sending his own Son into the world as his great apostle or missionary, and the Son's sending his missionaries to perfect this grand mission. We need scarcely stop here to shew that signs and wonders accompanied his preaching, as every christian, on the evidence of those signs and wonders, receives him as God's Messiah, the Saviour of the world. But how did he send forth his missionaries? He tells them, "As the Father sent me, so also I send you." Matthew informs us, chap. x., that "Jesus called unto him his twelve disciples, and gave them power against unclean spirits, to cast them out, and to heal all manner of sickness and disease." These he commanded to go to the lost sheep of the house of Israel, and to preach the approaching reign of heaven, and to confirm it by miracles—"Heal the sick, cleanse the lepers, raise the dead, cast out demons: freely you have received, freely give."

The seventy disciples, who were sent out by the Messiah to go before his face, and to announce the approaching reign, were sent, in the same manner, empowered to confirm their testimony by signs and wonders. See *Luke* x. The apostles, in the last commission, were sent to all the world; but were prohibited, in the accompanying instructions, from commencing their operations, until they should be endued with a power from on high. Thus all the missionaries, sent from heaven, were authorized and empowered to confirm their doctrine with signs and wonders sufficient to awe opposition, to subdue the deepest rooted prejudices, and to satisfy the most inquisitive of the origin of their doctrine.

After Pentecost their powers were enlarged and new signs added. So sensible are they of the vast importance of those miracles, that their prayers ran in the following style, *Acts* iv. 29. "Lord, behold their threatenings; and grant unto thy servants, that, with all boldness, they may speak thy word, by stretching forth thy hand to *heal*, and that signs and wonders may be done by the name of thy holy son Jesus." Those spiritual gifts continued until the gospel was preached to all the world, Jews and Gentiles, and until churches were planted in all nations. Then they ceased. Why? Doubtless, because, in the eyes of Omniscience, they were no longer necessary. The missionary work was done. The gospel had been preached to all nations before the end of the apostolic age. The bible, then, gives us no idea of a missionary without the power of working miracles. Miracles and missionaries are inseparably connected in the New Testament. Nor can it be considered an objection to this fact, should it appear that some persons in the train of the true missionaries wrought no miracles, seeing those that led the van performed every thing of this kind that was necessary. Just as if a missionary were sent to India, with powers equal to those of Paul, with a score of attendants and fellow-laborers, his spiritual gifts or miraculous powers accredit the mission as of divine origin, and are as convincing to the witnesses as though they all wrought miracles. From these plain and obvious facts and considerations, it is evident that it is a capital mistake to suppose that missionaries in heathen lands, without the power of working miracles, can succeed in establishing the christian religion. If it was necessary for the first missionaries to possess them, it is as necessary for those of our time who go to pagan lands, to possess them. Every argument that can be adduced to show that those signs and wonders, exhibited in Judea, were necessary to the success of that mission, can be turned to show that such signs and wonders are necessary at this day in China, Japan, or Burmah, to the success of a missionary.

The success of all modern missionaries is in accordance with these facts. They have, in some instances, succeeded in persuading some individuals to put on a sectarian profession of christianity. As the different philosophers, in ancient nations, succeeded in obtaining a few disciples to their respective systems, each new one making some inroads upon his predecessors; so have the modern missionaries succeeded in making a few proselytes to their systems, from amongst the disciples of the different pagan systems of theology. But that any thing can be produced, of a credible character, resembling the success of the divine missionaries, narrated in the New Testament, is impossible; or, that a church, resembling that at Jerusalem, Samaria, Cesarea, Antioch, or Rome, has been founded in any pagan land, by the efforts of our missionaries, we believe incapable of proof. Is, then, the attempt to convert the heathen by means of modern missionaries, an unauthorized and a hopeless one? It seems to be unauthorized, and, if so, then it is a hopeless one.

How, then, is the Gospel to spread through the World?

The New Testament is the only source of information on this topic. It teaches us that the association, called the church of Jesus Christ is, in *propria forma*, the only institution of God left on earth to illuminate and reform the world. That is, to speak in the most definitive and intelligible manner, a society of men and women, having in their hands the oracles of God; believing in their hearts the gospel of Jesus Christ; confessing the truth of Christ with their lips; exhibiting in their lives the morality of the gospel, and walking in all the commandments and ordinances of the Lord, blamelessly, in the sight of all men. When spiritual men, i. e. men having spiritual gifts, or, as now termed, miraculous gifts, were withdrawn, this institution was left on earth, as the grand scheme of Heaven, to enlighten and reform the world. An organized society of this kind, modelled after the plan taught in the New Testament, is the consummation of the manifold wisdom of God to exhibit to the world the civilizing, the moralizing, the saving light, which renovates the human heart, which elevates human character, and which prostrates in the dust all the boasted expedients of ancient and modern times. The church of the living God is therefore styled the pillar and ground of the truth; or, as Macknight more correctly renders it, the pillar and support of the truth.

The christian religion is a social religion, and cannot be exhibited to the full conviction of the world, only when it appears in this social character. An individual or two, in a pagan land, may talk about the christian religion, and may exhibit its morality as far as respects mankind in general; but it is impossible to give a clear, a satisfactory, a convincing exhibition of it, in any other way than by exhibiting a church, not on paper, but in actual existence and operation, as divinely appointed. The ambassadors of Christ, or his missionaries to the world, were commissioned to go to all nations in quest of materials to build this pillar of truth, this house of the living God; and then to place and cement these materials in such a way as to bear the inscription of the blessed gospel, and to exhibit it in such conspicuous and legible characters, as to be known and read by all men. This work the apostles accomplished in having made of twain one new man, i. e. of Jew and Gentile one new institution, or associated body, the church; and having placed this in all nations, in the most conspicuous and elevated situations; in the most populous countries, the most commercial states, and in the most renowned cities, they were taken to heaven, and left the church, by its doctrine and example, to christianize the world. All that has been necessary ever since was to hold fast the apostles' doctrine and commandments. If this had been faithfully done, there would have been no need, at this moment, to talk of converting the heathen. But it has happened, by the woeful departure of ambitious and ignorant men, from the ancient simplicity of the new religion, that the same awful crime is justly preferred against the people called Christians, that was, by an apostle, charged upon the Jews, viz. "The christian name has been, through your crimes, blasphemed among the heathen." Yes, indeed, so blasphemed, so disgraced, so vilified, that amongst those pagans that have heard of it, the term *christian* denotes every thing that is hateful and impious. If the channel of the vast Atlantic were filled with tears of the deepest contrition, they would not suffice to wash the "christian nations" from the odium and turpitude of crime with which they have debased themselves, so as to appear worthy

of the approbation of the pagans that know them best. Nothing can be done worthy of admiration by the christians of this age, with any reference to the conversion of the pagan nations, until the christians separate themselves from all the worldly combinations in which they are swallowed up, until they come out from amongst them that have a form of godliness, but deny the power of it; until they cast out all the selfish, money-lovers, boasters, proud, blasphemers, drunkards, covenant-breakers, disobedient to parents, ungrateful, without natural affection, slanderers, incontinent, fierce, betrayers, headstrong, puffed up, and lovers of pleasures more than lovers of God; until they form themselves into societies independent of hireling priests and ecclesiastical courts modelled after the forum, the parliament, or national conventions; until they cast to the moles and to the bats the Platonic speculations, the Pythagorean dreams and Jewish fables they have written in their creeds; until they return to the ancient model delineated in the New Testament; and until they keep the ordinances as delivered to them by the apostles. Then suppose a christian church were to be placed on the confines of a heathen land, as some of them must inevitably be, the darkness of paganism will serve, as a shade in a picture, to exhibit the lustre of christianity. Then the heathen around them will see their humility; their heavenly-mindedness, their hatred of garments spotted with the flesh, their purity, their chastity, their temperance, their sobriety, their brotherly love; they will observe the order of their worship, and will fall down in their assemblies, as Paul affirms, and declare that God is in them of a truth. Then will be verified anew the words of the Saviour—"If ye love one another, all men will know that you are the disciples of the Saviour of the world." They will say to one another, and proclaim to their countrymen on every occasion, "These christians are peaceful, benevolent, humane, forgetful, and forgiving of injuries; they hate war, oppression, theft, falsehood, detraction; they are always talking of the hope of a glorious resurrection from the dead, and are looking for the coming of him whom they call their Lord. In their assemblies there is order, peace, love, and harmony. Their chief guide is not distinguished by his dress, as our priests, nor does he, like them, live upon the sweat and sacrifices of the people. He works with his own hands as those who meet with him in their assembly. They repay the curses of wicked pagans with blessings, and their benevolence is not confined to themselves. They are as benevolent to all our people as to themselves—come, see if their religion is not better than ours—better than all others." When the christian church assumes such a character, there will be no need of missionaries. She will shine forth in the doctrine and in the practice of her members, as the sun in the firmament, and the brightness of her radiance will cheer the region and shadow of death.

If, in the present day, and amongst all those who talk so much of a missionary spirit, there could be found such a society, though it were composed of but twenty, willing to emigrate to some heathen land, where they would support themselves like the natives, wear the same garb, adopt the country as their own, and profess nothing like a missionary project; should such a society sit down and hold forth in word and deed the saving truth, not deriding the gods nor the religion of the natives, but allowing their own works and example to speak for their religion, and practicing as above hinted; we are persuaded that, in process of time, a more solid foundation for the conversion of the natives would be laid, and more actual success resulting, than from all the missionaries employed for twenty-five years. Such a course would have some warrant from scripture; but the present has proved itself to be all human.

We do not intend to dwell much on this topic. We have thought the above remarks were due to the great interest manifested by many in those enterprizes. We know many of the well disposed are engaged in these projects; nay, it is not long since we ourselves were enthusiastic in the missionary spirit. Let the reader remember our motto—let him "prove all things, and hold fast that which is good."   EDITOR.

Missionaries to Burmah.

ON Wednesday, the 11th of June, at Utica, New York, the Rev. Jonathan Wade and his consort were set apart as missionaries to the Burman empire, by a committee of the board of managers of the Baptist General Convention. An interesting sermon was delivered on the occasion by the Rev. Nathaniel Kendrick, from 2 *Tim.* ii. 10. "Therefore I endure all things for the elect's sake, that they also may obtain the salvation which is in Christ Jesus with eternal glory." Rev. Alfred Bennett led in offering up the consecrating prayer. Rev. Daniel Hascall gave Mr. Wade an appropriate charge, and the Rev. Joel W. Clark gave him the right hand of fellowship, "that he should go to the heathen;" Rev. John Peck addressed Mrs. Wade, and Rev. Elon Galusha gave her the right hand of fellowship. Rev. Elijah F. Willey offered the concluding prayer. The services were performed in Rev. Mr. Atkin's meeting-house. The day was fine, and the assemblage was very large, and proved, by their fixed and silent attention to the services, how much they felt for the world that lieth in wickedness; and by a collection of $86. 23 taken on the spot, they showed a willingness to share in the pleasure and expense of spreading the gospel in all the earth.

Mr. Wade is a young man, and a native of the state of New York. He received his classical and theological education in the theological seminary at Hamilton. He appeared before the committee a man of good sense, of ardent piety, and understandingly led by the spirit of God to the work in which he has now engaged. Mrs. Wade is from a respectable family in Hamilton, Madison county, daughter of deacon Lapham. Her early piety and active zeal in the cause of her Redeemer, has encouraged the hope that she will be eminently useful in the cause of missions with her husband.—[*Latter Day Luminary.*

Note by the Editor.—How accordant is the language and spirit of the above to the following passage from the 13th chapter of the Acts of the Apostles:—"On Wednesday, the 11th of June, A. D. 44, the Rev. Saulus Paulus and the Rev. Joses Barnabas were set apart as missionaries to the Gentiles dispersed throughout the world, by a committee of the board of managers of the Baptist General Convention, met in the city of Antioch. An interesting sermon was delivered on the occasion by the Rev. Simon Niger, from *Isaiah* xlii. 4. "The isles shall wait for his law." Rev. Lucius of Cyrene led in offering up the consecrating prayer. Rev. Manaen gave Mr. Paulus and his companion (Mr. Barnabas) an appropriate charge; and the Rev. John Mark

gave them the right hand of fellowship, "that they should go to the heathen." The Rev. Lucius of Cyrene offered up the concluding prayer. The services were performed in the Rev. Mr. Simeon Niger's meeting-house. The day was fine, and the assemblage was very large, and proved, by their fixed and silent attention to the services, how much they felt for the world that lieth in wickedness; and by a collection of $86 25 cents, they shewed a willingness to aid the Rev. Mr. Paulus and the Rev. Mr. Barnabas in carrying the gospel to the heathen.

Mr. Paulus is a young man, and a native of the city of Tarsus; he received his classical and theological education in the theological seminary in Jerusalem. He appeared before the committee a man of good sense, of ardent piety, and understandingly led by the spirit of God to the work in which he has now engaged."

It is then plain that the above notification is just in the spirit and style of this passage from the 13th chapter of the *Acts*. But in the common translation the original loses much of its aptitude and beauty; for, lo! it reads thus: "Now there was in the church that was at Antioch certain prophets and teachers; as, Barnabas, and Simon that was called Niger, and Lucius of Cyrene, and Manaen, which had been brought up with Herod the tetrarch, and Saul. As they ministered to the Lord, and fasted, the Holy Ghost said, separate me Barnabas and Saul for the work whereunto I have called them. And when they had fasted and prayed, and laid their hands on them, they sent them away."

It is much to be desired that the Baptists in the western country will not imitate these precedents of pompous vanity, so consecrated in the east; and that they will rather cherish the spirit and copy the style of that much despised little volume called the New Testament. Then we know they will remember that it is spoken by our Lord, "Be not called Rabbi," or Reverend. Then they will confess that many things of high reputation in this age are an abomination in the sight of God.

The Boston Recorder.

THE editor of the Boston Recorder, in a late address to his subscribers and to the public in general, has made a very generous proposal to the American Education Society, that if, by any means, he can get a thousand names added to his subscription list, (which at present amounts to 3500,) who will *pay* as well as subscribe, he will give a thousand dollars to the Education Society; and so in proportion for a greater or smaller number above the present 3500, in each succeeding year. As an inducement to their liberality, he gives a nearly correct list of the annual income of all the principal missionary and charitable societies of the day, which is as follows, viz:—

English Education Society for propagating the gospel, annual income, 253,080 dollars.

Society of the United Brethren, 32,000 dollars.

Wesleyan Missionary Society, 119,360 dollars.

English Baptist Missionary Society, 58,666 dollars.

London Missionary Society, 130,708 dollars.

Edinburgh Missionary Society, 14,715 dollars.

Church Missionary Society, 146,000 dollars.

London Jews' Society, 50,000 dollars.

American Board of Foreign Missions, 59,397 dollars.

American Baptist Board for Foreign Missions, 18,000 dollars.

United Foreign Mission Society, 11,948 dollars.
British and Foreign Bible Society, 460,884 dollars.
American Bible Society, 38,682 dollars.
London Religious Tract Society, 41,000 dollars.
New England Tract Society, 3,691 dollars.
Besides these there are Domestic Missionary and Education Societies in nearly all the United States.

Thus one million four hundred and thirty-eight thousand one hundred and thirty-one dollars, or about one million and a half per annum, is spent in the various schemes of the day. He represents the great need of more learned divines, and of more readers of religious newspapers, such as the Recorder, from various considerations. Among others we find the lamentable condition of the New England states and the state of New York adduced, amounting to about four hundred thousand families, "and of these one hundred thousand may be supposed to be christian families," and but few of these, for want of religious intelligence (for want of his paper and others like it) "take any deep interest in these mighty movements which are now making for the conversion of the world." Yet, with all the "mighty movements," he supposes that three hundred thousand families in the above states are not christianized, i. e. three-fourths of his own people! Religious newspapers, learned divines, and missionaries are much wanted in New England on this writer's hypothesis!

He then suggests to his present readers the necessity of regarding as a "sacred duty" which they owe God and their country, to persuade their neighbors and friends to take his paper; to "ministers of the gospel," the necessity of recommending it from the pulpit; to "enterprizing females," the excellence of persuading others; to "students of colleges," especially the beneficiaries, to spend a part of their vacations; to "teachers of schools," to extend their usefulness; to parents, and "persons travelling," "having a commission from the publisher," to do good by circulating religious newspapers in their respective spheres.

The Boston Recorder casts his mite into the treasury of the American Education Society. To make learned teachers of christianity is his grand object, next to enlarging his subscription list. "The reasons," he says, "why the Education Society was formed, may be found in the following facts: One hundred and forty-six towns in Maine; forty-five towns in two counties of New Hampshire; one hundred and thirty-nine towns in Vermont; fifty-three congregations in Massachusetts; three hundred and eighty-nine congregations in the Presbyterian church in New York, Pennsylvania, and Ohio; forty-six counties containing three hundred and four thousand inhabitants, in Virginia; three hundred and thirty-two churches of different denominations in South Carolina, all Indiana, Illinois, Missouri, and Michigan, except so far as a few ministers can supply a population of three hundred thousand scattered over a territory almost three times as large as New England; one thousand churches in the Baptist, and four hundred and fifty-one churches in the Presbyterian connexion, are destitute of educated ministers. Add to these appalling facts, the unparalleled increase of our population and the disproportionate increase of our religious institutions, and to these the deep darkness that covers vast portions of our globe, and truly "the

harvest is great and the laborers are few." Hence, then, the necessity of the American Education Society."

How very different the course recommended by the Recorder to enlighten the world, and that recommended by the Saviour and his apostles! The scheme of a learned priesthood chiefly composed of beneficiaries, has long since proved itself to be a grand device to keep men in ignorance and bondage; a scheme, by means of which the people have been shrewdly taught to put out their own eyes, to fetter their own feet, and to bind the yoke upon their own necks. From this iniquitous scheme, a knowledge of the New Testament is the only means that can set the people free.

No. 3.]   OCTOBER 6, 1823.

The Clergy.—No. 1.

NO CLASS or order of men that ever appeared on earth have obtained so much influence, or acquired so complete an ascendency over the human mind, as the clergy. The christian clergy have exercised, for about fifteen hundred years, a sovereign dominion over the bible, the consciences, and the religious sentiments of all nations professing christianity. Even kings and emperors bowed with deference to their authority, acknowledging their supremacy, and not daring to wield the sceptre until consecrated and crowned by a minister of religion.—Though vials of wrath have been poured from heaven upon the kingdom of the clergy; though many of them have gnawed their tongues and bit their lips with pain, at the loss of their former magnificent and mighty sway—yet, still their dominion, though much impaired, exists to an alarming extent; and their eagerness to have an unrivalled control over public sentiment, in all religious affairs, remains unabated. Behold the arrogance of their claims! and the peerless haughtiness of their pretensions! They have said, and of them many still say, they have an exclusive right, an official right to affix the proper interpretation to the scriptures; to expound them in public assemblies; insomuch, that it would be presumptuous in a layman to attempt to exercise any of those functions which they have assumed. They must "christen" the new born infant; they must catechise and conform the tender stripling; they must celebrate the rites of matrimony; they must dispense all ordinances in religion; they must attend the corpse to its grave, preach a funeral sermon, and consecrate the very ground on which it is laid. This dominion they at first obtained by slow degrees; but from its great antiquity and general prevalence, it is almost universally acquiesced in, approved, yea, even admired by the devout community. From this dominion over the feelings and consciences of mankind, it was not difficult to slide the hand into the purse of the superstitious. The most artful, and, indeed, the most effectual way, to get hold of the purse, is to get a hold of the conscience. The deeper the impression is made on the one, the deeper the draft on the other. Thus it came to pass that the clergy obtained worldly establishments, enriched themselves, and became an order as powerful in the state as in the church. The history of France before the Revolution, and of Spain until the establishment of the Constitution and the Cortes, is a convincing proof of the truth of these positions. Niles, in his "Weekly Register," informs us, that in Spain, before the Revolution, "the number of secular clergy, monks and friars, &c., was one hundred and forty-eight thousand, two hundred and forty-two. Nuns and religious women, thirty-two thousand; total, one hundred and eighty thousand, two hundred and forty two. These persons occupied three thousand convents." "The property," adds the same writer, "belonging to the clergy, in lands and buildings, amounted to the enormous sum of eight hundred and twenty-nine millions of dollars! exclusive of tithes and various other taxes and dues."

In the kingdom of the clergy there are many ranks and degrees, as respects influence, authority, wealth, and dignity. From the haughty pontiff that sits upon the throne of an imaginary St. Peter, down to the poor curate who sells his fifty-two sermons per annum, for a starving advance of twenty per cent. on the first cost; what a diversity of rank, of authority, of wealth, and dignity!! Perhaps it may be said, that the kingdom of the clergy was designed to bear a resemblance to the kingdom of nature, which exhibits an endless variety, that it may please, delight and instruct us. Thus, from the mighty elephant, down to the oyster that clings to its native rock, what a variety! And from the gorgeous majesty and wide dominion of his holiness, down to the humble class-leader, marching at the head of twelve "candidates for immortality," what a diversity! But with all this diversity, what a unity of spirit, of aim, and of pursuit!! The class-leader would become a local preacher; the local preacher, a circuit-rider; the circuit-rider, a presiding elder; and the presiding elder, a bishop. Then the highest round of the ladder is possessed. No further exaltation; no higher preferment in one province of the kingdom of the clergy. But in another province of the same kingdom, there is a greater diversity of gifts, honors and emoluments; but still the spirit, and temper, and aim, are one and the same. The bishop is an inferior dignitary in another province of this realm; he views with envious eyes the superior dignity of the lord archbishop, and when promoted to this honor, his ambition is circumscribed by his circumstances. Every member, then, of this kingdom of priests is aiming for one and the same object; and though, in other provinces, the ranks may be fewer, and the honors less, the desires, and aims, and pursuits of the priesthood are specifically the same. To say that every individual of this nation of clergy is actuated by such motives, and such only, is very far from our intention. There have been good and pious kings, and there are good and pious clergy. Yet we confess it is much easier to be a good and pious king, than a good and pious clergyman. There are, in the christian religion, constitutional principles that must be trampled upon, before a man becomes a priest: but none that impede his advancement to the throne as a president or as a king. The exceptions to the general spirit and aim of the clergy, are, however, so few, that we may safely ascribe to them, as an order of men, the above views, aims, and pursuits.

But, to descend from general to particular remarks on the kingdom of the clergy, let us inquire how they came to invest themselves with such authority and dominion? If we mistake not, they acquired their authority and dominion by the use of two grand means; the first is, that of an alledged special call of God to what is commonly called the work of the ministry; the other, the necessity of a consociation of these called ones, for the better administration of their government, and the securing what were called the interests of the church. Many sermons have been delivered on the necessity and importance of a special call to the ministry; on the necessity and importance of the confederation of the ministry, in the form of general councils, synods, assemblies, associations, and conferences; in order to their securing the interests of religion, which seem so completely identified with the interests of the clergy, that many have been tempted to think that the phrase, "the interests of religion," means, the interests of the clergy.

Now, although I feel myself as able to demonstrate and prove that both the one and the other of these positions is false, as I am to prove that there is a God, the creator of heaven and earth; yet, I cheerfully admit that there are now, and there were formerly, many good men who have advocated the necessity, and expatiated on the importance, of a special call of the Holy Spirit to the work of teaching the christian religion, and, also, who have earnestly contended for that confederation of the ministers of religion as above stated. Nay, that many good and eminent men have really thought such things indispensable to the promotion of christianity. But shall we be deterred from examining any principle because good and great men have espoused it? Nay, verily! Should we adopt this course, all examination of principles is at an end. We shall then venture to ask one of these called ones to furnish us with the evidences of his having been specially called by the Holy Spirit, to the preaching and teaching of the christian religion. The purposes to be answered by such a call, it is replied, render it necessary. What then are the purposes to be answered by such a call? It is answered, that they are two; first, the qualification of the preacher himself; and secondly, the regard to be paid to the instructions which he communicates. Doubtless, then, it is necessary that the call be evidenced to those to whom he is sent. For if the instructions are the more to be regarded, because of the preacher's call by the Holy Spirit, it is absolutely necessary that his call be well authenticated, that his instructions may be well received. It must either be criminal or not criminal to disregard the instruction of a teacher of the christian religion. On the supposition of its being criminal, the criminality must arise from the neglect or despite of his authority to instruct; but his authority to instruct must be rendered apparent and manifest before it is criminal to neglect or despise it; therefore, it is necessary that he demonstrate his authority, to render it criminal to neglect or despise his instructions. How then does he demonstrate his authority? By producing a license, or a certificate, from Papists, Episcopalians, Presbyterians, Methodists, or Baptists, that they considered him competent and authorized to preach and teach christianity. Does this prove that he is called by God. No, assuredly; for then God calls men to preach different gospels and to teach different kinds of christianity!! This will not satisfy the conscientious. Will his saying or his swearing that he is moved by the Holy Spirit to preach and teach christianity, prove that he is so moved? No; for many have thought that they were so moved, who afterwards declared and exhibited that they were mistaken. And many have said that they were so moved by the Holy Spirit, who were conscious at the moment that they were not so moved, but sought the office for filthy lucre's sake. Nothing of this kind will be admitted as evidence that any man is specially moved by the Holy Spirit to preach or teach the christian religion. Neither a license from any established sect, nor his own saying or swearing that he is specially moved by the Holy Spirit to the preaching or teaching of the christian religion, is a proof sufficient to render it criminal in any to neglect or despise his instructions. Nothing short of divine attestations or miracles can evince that any man is especially called by the Spirit of God to instruct us in the christian religion. Can those who say they are moved by the Holy Spirit to teach the christian religion, produce this sort of evidence? No, no. It is then in vain to say they are so moved. Who is called to believe any thing without evidence? Does God command any man to believe without evidence? No, most assuredly. When, then, I hear a modern preacher, either with or without his diploma in his pocket saying that he is an ambassador of Christ, sent by God to preach the gospel, moved by the Holy Ghost to take upon him the work of the ministry; I ask him to work a miracle, or afford some divine attestation of his being such a character. If he cannot do this, I mark him down as a knave or an enthusiast; consequently, an impostor, either intentionally or unintentionally.

But again—It was said that a special call of the Divine Spirit is necessary to qualify a preacher of the gospel. Let it be asked, in what respect to qualify him? Doubtless to give him the knowledge of the christian religion, and the faculty of communicating it. But do those who say they are moved by the Holy Spirit to assume the work of the ministry, possess this gift of knowledge, and this gift of utterance? If they do, let them show it. Have they not, for the most part after they profess to be thus called, to go to study the religion, and to study languages in order to communicate their ideas intelligibly? Then, indeed, their call does not qualify them! The meaning of this call, then, is, "Go and learn the religion, and learn the use and meaning of words, that you may communicate your knowledge of it; and then I will send you to preach, and lay you under a woful necessity of declaring the religion." This is the special call of the Holy Spirit contended for. What an abuse of language! nay, rather, what an abuse of principle!!! This man is especially called to do a work, or to go a warfare at his own expense! But did this called clergyman hear a voice? He answers, Yes, or No. If he heard a voice, how does he know whose voice it was? If the voice of God, how is it proved to be such? If he says he heard no voice, why then does he say that he is called? Suppose this same man who contends for a call, without a voice, had a son ploughing in his field, and his son leaves the plough and goes to visit his friend. After some time he sends a message for his son. His son appears; and when asked why he forsook the plough, and went about riding and feasting with his friends, he answers, Father, you called me from the plough, and commanded me to visit your and my friends. Nay, son, replies the father, did you hear my voice calling or commanding you to such a course of conduct? No, father, replies the son, I did not hear your voice specially calling or commanding me, but I had a deep impression on my mind that it was your wish and my duty to leave the plough and go a visiting. Go, sir, answers the irritated father, to your plough, and remember it is time enough to consider yourself called when your hear my voice. I say, suppose one of those who contend for a call, without a voice, were thus addressed, would they not be

constrained to condemn themselves? But to test this mode of reasoning, let us see how it applies to those who said, in holy writ, that they were called to the work of the ministry. The Lord, we are told, called twelve men of the Jews during his life time, to be eye and ear witnesses of all that he said and did. These he afterwards called to be apostles, or ambassadors, or ministers of the New Testament, as they are equally distinguished by any of these names or titles of office. These he called by his own voice, and qualified them to preach and teach infallibly the whole scope of their commission. Their instructions always extended to their commission. In other words, their instructions or qualifications, and their commission were co-extensive. In their first call and commission they were sent only to the lost sheep of the house of Israel, and were commanded to announce the approaching reign, saying, "Repent, for the kingdom of heaven is at hand." And to despise or neglect their instruction was criminal in the highest degree. He that despised them, despised him that sent them. But this could not have been the case, had they had no means of convincing their hearers that they were so called and sent. For this purpose they healed the sick, they cast out demons, they cleansed the lepers, they raised the dead; and as they received these powers without money or price, they freely, without money or price, imparted their benefits. In their second commission, and in the special commission of Peter to open the door of faith to the Gentiles, as "the keys" had been committed to him; and in the call of Saul of Tarsus to become an apostle to, and a preacher and a teacher of the truth among the Gentiles, the same circumstances accompanied their call. A voice was heard, the gift of wisdom, the gift of knowledge, the gift of utterance, and the gift of working miracles, were communicated and exhibited. It is evident that all who were called to the ministry by God or by his Spirit, possessed every thing that has been contemplated as necessary in the antecedent remarks. When other persons called in question Paul's call to the work of the ministry or to become an ambassador of Christ, how did he contend for it? By referring to the wonders he had wrought, as well as to the labors he had endured. See 2 Cor. xii. 12. "Truly," says he, "the signs of an apostle were fully wrought among you with all patience; by signs, and wonders, and powers." Again he tells them, chap. xiii. 6. "But I trust when I make you a visit, that ye shall know that we are not without proof"—"of Christ's speaking by me."

From these premises we may conclude, that every one moved by the Holy Spirit, or specially called to the preaching or teaching of christianity, is possessed of these three requisites—

1st. He has heard the voice of God calling him.

2d. He is qualified to speak infallibly.

3d. He is capable of confirming his testimony by divine attestations, or by the working of miracles.

Every ambassador of Christ, mentioned in the New Testament, possessed these three requisites. It is absurd, vain and presumptuous for any now to call themselves ambassadors of Christ, or to say that they are specially called to the ministry of the New Testament, who possess not these three essential attributes of the called ministers of the New Testament.

But some, unable to resist the evidence of the preceding facts and reasons, will exclaim, What! have we no men among us called and sent by

God? Stop, my friend. What use have we for such men? Do we need any new message from the skies? No. Divine messages require divine messengers. If there be no need of a new message from God, or a new revelation of the Spirit, then there is no need of new ambassadors, of new revealers, or new prophets. If the message of the twelve apostles, or if the revelation of the New Testament is incomplete, is imperfect, is inadequate, then we have need of a new message and new messengers from the skies. But until some bold genius undertakes to prove that there is need for a new revelation or a new message from God, we shall fearlessly declare, that while we have the writings of the four evangelists, the writings of Paul, of Peter, of James, of Jude and John, we want no new message from the skies—no ambassadors from Christ. In short, there is no *need* to have men among us professing to be " called and sent by God." In the natural world we might as reasonably look for, and expect a new sun, a new moon, and new stars; as, in the kingdom of Christ, to expect new ambassadors, new messages from God, new revelations of the Spirit. On this subject we have much to say; but in the mean time, we shall simply add, to prevent misapprehensions, that, as we have a revelation developing all the mysteries of the love and benevolence of God towards sinners through Christ, a revelation clear, simple, full and complete; it is the duty of every one who acknowledges it to be such, to devote his mind to it, and study it for himself.

Amongst those who believe and understand the christian religion, there are individuals called, in the subordinate sense of the phrase, to sundry good works, of much profit to men. Those that are rich in this world, professing the faith, are called by the word of God, written and read by all men, to communicate of their substance to the wants of the poor, to be ready to distribute, to be willing to communicate to the wants of the brotherhood, and to the wants of others. When a brother in distress appears in the presence of a brother rich in this world, the brother of high degree is called by the word of God and the providence of God, or the circumstances of the case call upon him to put his hand into his pocket and to communicate to his distress. Just in the same sense, a brother who is well instructed into the doctrine of the kingdom of heaven who has attained to the full assurance of understanding of what Paul, and Peter, and James, and John, and the other writers of the New Testament have taught concerning the way of life and salvation; when he finds persons ignorant or unbelieving, either in public or private, is called by the word of God, and the circumstances of the case, to teach and preach Christ, or to show the things that the ambassadors have taught and authenticated; these things he may urge on their authority who confirmed their testimony with signs and wonders. And as it would be absurd and vain for the rich man to say that he was specially called and sent by God, or moved by the Spirit of God to give alms; so it would be absurd and vain for the person possessed of the knowledge of the New Testament, to say that he was moved by the Holy Spirit, or specially called by its operations and sent by God to preach.

Besides this there is another fact to which we would advert, viz. that when there is a voluntary association of any number of disciples of Christ, met in any one place to attend to the duties and privileges of a church, should they call any one of their own number, who possesses the qualifications belonging to the bishop or overseer, laid down by the Holy Spirit in the written word; and should they appoint him to office, as the Holy Spirit has taught them in the same written word—then it may be said to such a person, " Take heed to yourself and to the flock over which the Holy Spirit has made you overseer." But this bishop, of whom we have now spoken, is neither priest, ambassador, minister of religion, clergyman, nor a reverend divine; but simply one that has the oversight of one voluntary society, who, when he leaves that society, has no office in any other in consequence of his being an officer in that. His discharge of the work of a bishop is limited by, and confined to, the particular congregation which appointed him to office. If he should travel abroad and visit another congregation, even of the same views with that of which he was or is bishop, he is then no bishop; he is then in the capacity of an unofficial disciple. To suppose the contrary is to constitute different orders of men, or to divide the church into the common classes of clergy and laity, than which nothing is more essentially opposite to the genius and spirit of christianity. We have seen some bishops, ignorant of the nature of the office, acting very much out of character, placing themselves in the bishop's office, in a church which they might occasionally visit, and assuming to act officially in an assembly over which they had no bishopric. They acted as absurdly and as unconstitutionally as the president of the United States would do, if, when on a visit to London, he should enter the English parliament and place himself on the throne, either *solus*, or in conjunction with his majesty George IV. and that, forsooth, because he is, or was president of the United States. But of this more afterwards. In the meantime, we conclude that one of those means used to exalt the clergy to dominion over the faith, over the consciences, and over the persons of men, by teaching the people to consider them as specially called and moved by the Holy Spirit, and sent to assume the office of ambassadors of Christ, or ministers of the christian religion, is a scheme unwarranted by God, founded on pride, ignorance, ambition, and impiety; and, as such, ought to be opposed and exposed by all them that love our Lord Jesus Christ in sincerity.   EDITOR.

———

PHILIP, No. II., on teaching the christian religion, not having come to hand, we will insert an article written by him on the resurrection of Jesus Christ from the dead. This article furnishes us with an argument in proof of the fact, which we have never seen noticed by any writer on this most important of all the facts recorded by the four evangelists. The whole *machina evangelica* turns on this pivot, or the whole christian religion rests upon this fact. If Christ be not risen from the dead, the preaching of Christ and the faith of christians are in vain. No historic fact was ever so well proved as this, and no fact was ever pregnant with such marvellous and exhilarating consequences. It is not only the highest proof of the truth of all Messiah's pretensions; it is not only a pledge to us of the divine acceptance of the atonement of the Redeemer; but, it is to us the surest earnest, and most convincing demonstration of the hope of christians, viz. a glorious resurrection to eternal life. The objects of the christian's hope are the grandest and most exalted in the whole range of human conception. A new heaven and a new earth; a new body, spiritual, incorruptible, and immortal; a society transcendantly pure, entertaining, and exalted; transporting joys, unmingled with sorrow, and increasing bliss, unalloyed with doubt, or fear, or pain, constitute the glorious hopes of every true disciple of Christ; which, when reduced to a unit, consist in being made like the Son of God. This glorious hope immediately germinates or springs from the fact, that the Lord is risen indeed. This article, then, will be, not only edifying, but ineffably cheering, to every one that has this hope in him.

As this argument was derived from no other source than an intimate acquaintance with the four evangelists, it will form a new incentive to those who presume to read the New Testament, without the spectacles of any system before their eyes, and will furnish a new proof of the entertainment, edification, assurance, and comfort to be obtained from a diligent, humble, and persevering perusal of the blissful volume. Oh! that all who acknowledge it to be the volume of salvation, the word of the living God, would read it! and, conscious of their need of that wisdom which comes from above, would ask of God, who gives liberally and upbraids not!

[Editor.

RESPECTING Jesus of Nazareth, the Jewish nation seems to have been divided into two principal parties—that which favored, and that which rejected his pretensions. That the views of his scheme too, entertained by both, were not almost, but altogether political, we have all the reason, I think, in the world, to believe. The opposition party regarded the whole as a political cabal, and its abettors as reformers of the state. Radical's, whose ultimate objects were to put down the prevailing party; to abandon allegiance to the Romans; to assert the independence of the Jewish nation; and, under the conduct of Jesus as their general, or, as his own party would have it, their king, to maintain it sword in hand. This is the only view that accords with the warlike spirit of the times, the popular belief respecting Messiah's reign and kingdom, and with what we read in the four evangelists. Now, it was to check the spirit of that enterprize that the leaders of the opposite party voted the destruction of Jesus, who was looked upon by the great men as the life's blood of this conspiracy. From the moment when Caiphas delivered his sentiments on the grand question, "what was to be done for the safety of the state!" the death of Jesus was eagerly desired by them all. These princes, preferring rank and honor with their present inglorious ease under foreign masters, to the distant and uncertain advantages of a noble and magnanimous declaration of the nation's independence—these lordlings, conceived power and pomp to be the chief good and the only thing worthy of ambition. They conceived that to form the object of the Lord's ambition also, and endeavored by mean arts to draw from him this secret. The views of his followers were nothing different in kind from those of his opposers; they were equally worldly and political; and both parties, contemplating the destinies of the Lord Jesus under this mistaken and degraded point of view, it is not wonderful that his resurrection from the dead should be an event equally distant from the expectations of all. Both parties, too, seem to have considered his decease as an unequivocal refutation of his pretensions—as an event which at once reflected the greatest discredit on the party, and great apparent ponderosity and

importance to those who had slain him, and who, during the whole of his public ministry, had steadily persisted in rejecting and disproving his pretensions. Had the Lord then not appeared to some of his followers on that day on which he arose, the dispute of the two parties would not have been whether he had risen from the dead, but only which of them had stolen the body from the sepulchre. This is evident from the easy assent which the two disciples gave to the hasty suggestions of Mary Magdalene. They believed that the opposite faction had stolen the body; John alleging for it as a reason, that the disciples knew not yet that he must rise from the dead. The anticipation of such an event was equally foreign from the conceptions of his murderers, who barricaded the tomb, and sealed it with the seal of the state, not to prevent his resurrection, but, as they themselves said, to prevent his followers from taking the body by stealth. I think too, that the rulers really and sincerely believed his followers to have taken away the body, and that, in the first instance, they regarded the wonders told them by the soldiers, of earthquakes and angels, to be nothing more than cunningly devised fables, trumped up by his disciples for the safety of the guards, who, as they believed, had permitted them (the disciples) undisturbedly, perhaps for a sum of money, to bear away the body in the dark. But their bribing the soldiers again, may seem to contradict this opinion. Well then, suppose, for argument's sake, that the rulers did believe the reports of the guards, viz. that the Lord had risen. If they did, then they must have believed that he would also immediately appear among them again in person, to assert the reality of his claims, and maintain the certainty of the confession, for which he had been put to death; for of his ascent into heaven they had no conceptions. If they believed him to be risen, to have said that his disciples had stolen him, would have been a miserable invention, and nowise suited to the exigency of the case. Such an invention would never have counterbalanced one single well attested appearance of the Lord; and we have seen that they, having no just notions of his reign and kingdom, would have expected to see him again in person, if so be they believed the reports of the soldiers. After all, if the Pharisees expected him to rise, why did they put him to death? The rulers, then, believed the guards to be telling a falsehood, and they bribed them to report what the Pharisees themselves conceived to be the true state of the case. As the opposing faction all along regarded the enterprize as a political one, they foresaw that if once its abettors should get the dead body into their possession, they might make it the instrument of greater mischief to the nation than it had been when alive. They foresaw that one of the reformers might personate their former leader, exhibit himself at a distance, and set up for Messiah on the grounds of having risen from the dead. Such an evidence they foresaw would be altogether irresistible; the Jews would flock to his standard, and the cause would derive accessions from all quarters of the land—such accessions, too, as nothing but the arm of the imperial government would be able to break or dissolve. If once the Romans had engaged in the quarrel, their rulers would have seen a realization of all their former fears. The temple and the city, they foresaw, would ultimately have become the grand bone of contention, and this whole enterprize, or, as they called it, last error, issue in consequences more fatal to their place and nation than the first, under the conduct of Jesus of Nazareth. All these forebodings of the rulers seem to have arisen out of what the Lord said or dropt concerning his resurrection. The Pharisees then suspected his followers of having stolen the body, and his followers, with the exception of those who saw him on the first day, seem to have suspected the Pharisees or rulers; a circumstance which in itself indeed proves that neither party had done it; for if either party had stolen the body it never could have conscientiously blamed the other, as we have seen it did; if the rulers had it, the disciples would not have dared to say that it was alive; and if the disciples had it under their control, and said it was alive, they would have embraced the first opportunity of exhibiting him in order to refute the calumny of the rulers, who said the body was in the possession of the party, but it was not alive. These things show us, at all events, that on the first day the body was not where it had been originally laid, and where both parties hoped to find it; they show us that both parties agree in this, viz. that the body was missing from the sepulchre, and now there seems to be only two possible ways of accounting for its departure. Seeing, then, it was not removed by any of the parties concerned, it must either have been taken off by some unconcerned party, or have departed itself; which last opinion, indeed, is the more probable of the two; for to suppose that any unconcerned party would endanger themselves, or bribe the guards for a dead person, about whose fate they had been altogether unconcerned whilst alive, would be nonsense. But to suppose that there was any unconcerned party in the capital where Jesus was crucified, would argue great ignorance of the spirit of the times. He was not stolen by any party, either concerned or unconcerned about his fate; and the only conclusion remaining is, that the body departed itself, that "the Lord Jesus has arisen indeed." He has also ascended up on high; he led captivity captive, and has given gifts to men, who have announced to us by the Holy Spirit, the things which are given to us by God without any cause.   PHILIP.

———

No. 4.]   NOVEMBER 3, 1823.
On teaching Christianity.—No. II.

READER, you observe that this piece is entitled "An essay on teaching christianity." Perhaps you are at a loss to know what it means. You will understand it better by and by. My last paper was intended simply to intimate to christian bishops or pastors, that, in spite of the discrepant and inapt schemes of sermonizing that now prevail by means of learned and popular establishments, there yet exists a certain, uniform, authorized plan of preaching Jesus, a plan consecrated by the high examples of all the heavens, and the holy apostles and prophets.

I should immediately proceed to develope it, were I not thoroughly convinced that a recognition of a few preliminaries is absolutely necessary to the adoption of this authorized plan, and even to the understanding of it. These preliminaries, indeed, are neither very numerous nor very remote from vulgar apprehension—they are only two, and a very superficial glance at scripture will put the reader in possession of all that is necessary for understanding the writer of these papers. The first of these prefatory articles is, that the members of a church of Christ

are united to one another by the belief of a matter of fact, viz. that "Jesus is the Christ, the Son of God," and not by any attribute of government, catholic or sectarian. The second is, that the scriptures propose the belief of this fact, that "Jesus is the Christ," as the only means for increasing the body or church of God. Hence the didactical labors of a bishop or elder who would wish to edify and increase the body of Christ, divide themselves into two several sorts. In order to increase the body, he proves to the world by means of these ancient and venerable monuments which God has put into his hands, the four gospels, that "Jesus is the Christ, the Son of God;" and, in order to edify the church, he points out in all the scriptures, as these holy and sublime interpretations which the Spirit has every where given of this illustrious fact. But if it is true (as we shall immediately see from scripture it is,) that the body of Christ is united in its several members by the belief of this matter of fact, viz. that Jesus is the Son of God, and that it is increased by the confession and belief of it—then a number of very important corollaries are deducible from these two revealed propositions: First, the peace and union of a church of Christ are not the result of any sort of ecclesiastical government. Secondly, the increase of Christ's body is not predicated on any thing so exceedingly exceptionable as modern confessions of faith; but on the confession of the first truth. Thirdly, the worshipping establishments now in operation throughout christendom, increased and cemented by their respective voluminous confessions of faith, and their ecclesiastical constitutions, are not churches of Jesus Christ, but the legitimate daughters of that Mother of Harlots, the Church of Rome. In these establishments a breach of canon is punished with ejection, and to nauseate their vitiated creeds is a certain bar to induction, unless a man is rich, and then he may do or deny anything. But, in order that the reader may entertain no doubt respecting the above mentioned propositions, let us attend to the scriptures—let us attend to the voice of the beloved Saviour, speaking in *Matthew* xvi. 13. "When he came into the coasts of Cesarea, he asked his disciples, saying, who do men say that I the Son of Man am? And they said, some say that you are John the Baptist; some, Elias; and others, Jeremias, or one of the prophets. He said unto them, but whom say you that I am? And Simon Peter answered and said, you are the Christ, the Son of the living God. And Jesus answered and said to him, blessed are you, Simon Barjona; for flesh and blood has not revealed it to you, but my Father who is in heaven. And I say also to you, that you are Peter, and upon this rock I will build my church, and the gates of hell shall not prevail against it." In this beautiful, interesting, and highly significant passage, four things are particularly remarkable: First, the name, Christ, Son of the living God, which Simon gives to Jesus. Second, the name *Petros*, stone, which Jesus gives to Simon. Third, the truth itself, which Simon confesses. And fourth, the name *Petra*, rock, by which the Saviour, figuratively, in allusion to Simon's name, *Petros*, stone, designates this eternal truth, that he is the Christ the Son of the living God. On the belief of this fact, then, his church is founded, and by it is held together. I do not remember to have seen it remarked, but it is very much in our Lord's manner to reply in the very same words in which he is addressed. For instance, the leper says, "if you will;" Jesus replies, "I will." Thomas says, "how can we know the way?" The Lord answers, "I am the way." "Why do your disciples transgress?" say the Pharisees; and "why do you also transgress?" says the Saviour. From want of attending to this, the vivacity of our Lord's reply to Simon is not felt, and the spirit of the whole passage, indeed, almost vanishes—you are the Christ—and you are stone, *Petros.* The Lord Jesus was very apt to speak in metaphor too. He styles Herod a fox; he calls his own body a temple, in allusion to the temple in which he at that time was. When he is on Mount Olivet among the vines, he styles himself the vine; he calls death a sleep; his own death a baptism; Simon a stone, *Cephas:* and in the above passage he calls the grand truth that he was the Son of the living God, a *Petra,* Rock, in allusion to Simon's name, Stone, and on account of its stedfast and indestructible certainty; and he adds, that "the gates of hell shall not prevail against it;" i. e. as I suppose, his death, which was soon to be effected by the wicked Jews, should not disprove his pretensions to the Messiahship; or perhaps he means that the grave should not interrupt the fellowship of his church, which was to be founded on this imperishable fact, that he was the Christ. This passage sufficiently shows us what is the bond of union among the despised people; and it shows us even more, for it lets us know that the confession and belief of this bare fact, (Peter at this moment knowing nothing more, nothing as yet of his crucifixion for sin,) is attended with certain blessing and salvation— "Blessed are you, Simon," &c. To the same purpose Paul says, "if you confess with your mouth the Lord Jesus, and believe in your heart that God has raised him from the dead, you shall be saved." Now, if modern confessions of faith had such blessing and such salvation appended to them by such authorities, their abettors might well boast. But they who bow down to such idols shall go down to the grave with a lie in their right hand. The sword of the Lord's mouth is unsheathed against the man of sin, nor will it kiss the scabbard until his enemies are consumed. O Gamaliel! O Socrates! O Satan! save your sinking disciples whose judgment now of a long time lingers not, and their damnation slumbers not!

But that the glorious truth, and nothing else, holds the saints together in particular churches, is evident from the holy epistles which are addressed to them in their individual capacities. Paul, in writing to the Corinthians, who were beginning to name themselves by their respective favorites, as the moderns do, informs that church, that, when he had first come among them, he had determined to know nothing among them but the bare gospel fact, that Jesus was the Christ, and had been crucified; nor did he attempt to ornament it with the eloquence of words, thinking, as I suppose, that a truth so supremely magnificent in itself, was perfectly insusceptible of extrinsic ornament, and in its own native excellency defied the united pens and tongues of men and angels. His only aim was to demonstrate its reality by the spirit and power of God which filled him, that the disciple's faith might not stand in his word, but in the power of God—the miracles. Knowing that if this great argument, supported as it was with miracles, failed to reduce men to union and to Christ, he had nothing of equal importance to propose for this purpose. The apostle, therefore, in order to reduce them to unity,

reminds them of the fundamental bond of union by which they had been originally congregated, thus: "according to the grace (apostleship) of God to me, as a wise master-builder, I have laid the foundation and another builds thereon; but let every man take heed how he builds thereon, for other foundation (of union) can no man lay than that is laid, which is, Jesus is the Christ." These things may suffice to show that the bond of union among christians is the belief of a matter of fact, viz. that Jesus of Nazareth is the Son of God. The reader may consult *Ephesians*, ii., iii. and iv. chapters, all the *Galatians,* epistles to the *Colossians, Romans, Timothy,* &c. &c., where the apostles lay it down as a universal maxim, that this truth or word of salvation works effectually in all them that believe it!

But our second proposition, viz. that the body of Christ is increased by belief of the bare truth that Jesus is the Son of God, and our Saviour, is a scripture doctrine, which the populars nauseate, if possible, more than our first. It is so simple, so manifestly foolish, that the sons of Gamaliel and Socrates are equally scandalized and ashamed of it. Yet, says Paul, it saves them that believe it. But it is chiefly abhorrent to modern establishments on account of the consequences of which it is pregnant—it sets aside all canon, all confession, every thing indeed which opposes and exalts itself against Christ and the New Testament. Nevertheless, this second prefatory article, that the body is increased by the confession and belief of the truth, is perfectly obvious from scripture. "Whosoever shall confess me before men, says the Redeemer, him will the Son of Man confess before the angels of God." Peter, we have seen, confessed him to be the Son of the living God, though apparently a mere man; and the blessed Saviour honored his confession with a most gracious benediction—"blessed are you Simon, son of Jonas, for flesh and blood has not revealed this to you, but my Father who is in heaven." Now Peter at this moment was perfectly ignorant of every thing besides this truth, which he had learned from the Father, by the miraculous evidence which he had vouchsafed in support of it. It is wonderful the honor which the scripture writers every where do this single truth, that "Jesus was the Son of God." Paul would not dare to use learned words in speaking it, cautions the Hebrews against letting it slip out of their minds, and says to the Corinthians, that they are saved by it if they keep it in mind! *John,* 1st epistle, chap. v. declared that the man who believed it is born of God; and wrote and recorded all the miracles in his gospel to prove this illustrious fact. "These things are written," says he, "that you might believe that Jesus is the Christ, the Son of God, and that believing you might have life through his name." In John's days there were many antichrists; but this holy man did not dare to use any unlawful means for securing the disciples against their deleterious influence. He did not write to them that they should covenant like the Covenanters, form any sort of ecclesiastic government, make confessions of faith, liturgy, rubric, &c. &c. No—these things, says he, I have written concerning them that (would) seduce you—these things I have written to you who believe in the name of the Son of God, that you may know that you have eternal life, and that you may (continue to) believe in the name of the Son of God. One has only to believe in this name, and his is eternal life. The body of

Christ, thus, then, is also increased by the belief of this excellent truth; and to be convinced of this, the reader has only to turn to any page of the New Testament, and he will read it in every line.

We have glanced at the vast honor every where in scripture put upon this majestic truth, that Jesus is the Son of Almighty God; we have seen how Paul and John exalted it, and also that it is the foundation and bond of union in the church of God, and how that the body of Christ is increased by the belief of it. But look at the marvellous evidence vouchsafed in support of it; the amazing concatenation of miracles drawn out to identify the person of the Christ; miracle after miracle follows each other in rapid succession, surprisingly diversified in manner, kind, and form; until the mighty chain terminates in that amazing and inscrutable wonder, his resurrection from the dead; a miracle which, for its transcendant peculiarities, the apostle, (*Eph.* i. 19,) singles out as affording the most illustrious display of the mighty power of God. But the Holy Spirit also, in all his diversified working of gifts and graces, in wisdom and knowledge, and miracles, and healings, discoursing of spirits, tongues, prophecy, and interpretation, was given to prove that Jesus was the Christ. And Peter makes this use of them on the day of Pentecost, when pointing to the multitude of separated tongues that crowned the heads of the apostles, he said, let all the house of Israel therefore know assuredly, that God has made that Jesus whom ye have crucified both Lord and Christ. It was to preach and prove this that all the apostles were sent to the nations. But greater reverence could not be paid to any truth than the Lord Jesus himself pays to this, that he was the Son of God; when he bids all men worship him as they would the Father, he says, it is eternal life to know him; and in the moment of quitting this world enforces the belief of the truth with the sanctions of eternal life and death—"he that believes (that he is the Son of God) shall be saved; he that believes not shall be damned." The philosophers indeed have stolen away these sanctions from the faith of Jesus, and have pinned them to their jejune, pretended science of moral philosophy, where the name of the Saviour is perhaps never once mentioned. But 'they had better confine themselves to their own baubles, and let the truth of God alone, otherwise believe it; for if they do not, he will philosophize them when he comes to be glorified in his saints, when he shall be revealed from heaven with his mighty angels, taking vengeance on them that obey not God, and believe not the gospel of our Lord Jesus Christ.   PHILIP.

The Clergy.—No. II.

WE observed in our last number, that one of those means by which the clergy obtained so complete a dominion over the bible, the consciences and the religious sentiments of mankind, was the pretence of a divine call to the work of the christian ministry. We now proceed to notice the second grand means employed to effectuate this object, viz. the confederation of themselves into associated bodies, called councils, synods, general assemblies, associations or conferences. Though the organized bodies distinguished by those names do not all claim the same powers or the same extent of dominion, yet they all agree in one essential characteristic, which is, that they all profess to

D

have some divine warrant, which authorizes them to have control over the members, whether considered as individuals or as churches, which comprise the religious community, over the faith, the practices, or destinies of which they preside. The systems of what is called "church government," which the respective sects have adopted, though differing in many respects, all agree in this, that whomsoever they will, they kill; and whomsoever they will, they save alive—not their bodies we mean, but their reputation for "piety and orthodoxy." Few of those confederations, now-a-days, even of those who propose authoritatively to determine matters of faith, cases of conscience and rules of practice, literally kill those whom they condemn to suffer the vengeance of their censures. But there is a species of robbery which is worse than taking a man's property; and there is a species of murder worse than taking a man's life; and of both of these ecclesiastical courts are, even in this age, often guilty. But of this more hereafter.

Now although the forms of "church government" adopted by the respective sects, differ, as was said, in many respects, there is another grand point of coincidence, which fixes upon them all, one and the same general character. This point of coincidence is, that they are all modelled after, and assimilated to the different forms of civil government which have obtained in the nations of the earth, and often according to the government of the state in which the sect originated. Thus we have an ecclesiastic monarchy, an ecclesiastic aristocracy, an ecclesiastic democracy, an ecclesiastic mixed government. Yet, after all that has been said upon the subject of church government, lodged in human hands; after all the angry contests, whether an episcopacy similar to a monarchy; whether a presbytery similar to an aristocracy, or an independency similar to a democracy, be the government instituted by God, or authorized in the New Testament—it might perhaps appear, upon an impartial examination of the scriptures, that the whole controversy is a mere "*vox et preterea nihil*"—a sound and nothing else; that there is no such a thing as "church government," in the popular sense of the terms. But if we must, from the imperial power of custom, still retain the terms "church government" in our vocabulary, we will attach to the words the following meaning: we will say, that the government of the church is an absolute monarchy, and the Lord Jesus Christ is the absolute monarch, on whose shoulders is the government and in whose hands are the reins. That his will, published in the New Testament, is the sole law of the church; and that every society or assembly, meeting once every week in one place, according to this law, or the commandments of this king, requires no other head, king, lawgiver, ruler, or lord, than this Mighty One; no other law, rule, formula, canon or decrees, than his written word; no judicatory, court or tribunal, other than the judgment seat of Christ. That every such society, with its bishops and deacons, is the highest tribunal on earth to which an individual christian can appeal; that whosoever will not hear it, has no other tribunal to which he can look for redress. To suppose that two churches have more power than one, that one hundred have more power than one, or that the bishops of one hundred churches, with any other delegates sent from the churches, have more power than one church, is to place the power or authority in men, and not in the one king or head. For if numbers create greater power, it is the power of men—it is human authority, and not the authority of God.

That ecclesiastical authority which is capable of increase, which accumulates with the numbers that combine, is not the authority of God, nor of his word; for his authority and that of his word are one and the same in all circumstances. Now if one church has not the right or authority to make any law for the government of itself, all the churches on earth combined have not a right nor authority to make a law to govern it. If they have no right to make laws, they have no right to dictate doctrinal sentiments; and if they have no right to dictate doctrinal sentiments, they have no right to impose on it interpretations of scripture; and if they have no right to do any of these things, they have no control, no jurisdiction, no authority over it whatever. So that in fact there is no other authority recognized, allowed, or regarded, by a society of christians, meeting in one place as a church of Jesus Christ, than the authority of its king or head. The king appointed twelve men, to whom he gave authority to act in his name, and when his kingdom came he authorized them to sit on thrones, pronouncing statutes and judgments to the Israel of God. The remnant of the twelve tribes that believed in the Messiah, immediately yielded to the mission of those apostles, because of his authority commissioning them. Therefore, they continued steadfast in the apostles' doctrine, and in the apostles' commandments. And thus the apostles spake, saying, We are authorized by God; "he that is of God hears us; he that hears us not, is not of God." From this it is evident that the authority of the apostles is the authority of God, and that their commandments are the commandments of the Lord and Saviour. But the modern clergy have often placed themselves upon this throne which was given to the apostles only; and they have, if possible, in some instances, been still more impious—they have placed themselves upon the throne of God, and dealt damnation with a liberal hand to all their foes, judging, as they thought, correctly, that whosoever opposed them, opposed God. But they have combined their energies and augmented their sway, by confederating in one holy alliance, by which they carry their decisions into more powerful and speedy effects. Then let us ask, whence is the divine warrant for such confederations. The 15th chapter of the *Acts* of the apostles is appealed to. The incidental meeting of the apostles at Jerusalem, and their being called together with the elders and the whole church on one question, is converted into a warrant for an ecclesiastical council by Romanists and Episcopaleans. It is converted into a presbytery, a synod, or general assembly by Presbyterians. It is converted into an association by Baptists. It becomes a conference in the hands of a Methodist. This is a flexible and pliant passage, if it answers all these purposes. But, strange as it may appear at the first glance, this meeting of the apostles and the church at Jerusalem, was not a Catholic nor Episcopalean council, summoned by a prince, king, or an emperor; it was not composed of the bishops of two, ten, or a hundred churches: nor was it a Presbyterian synod, for they were not the preaching and ruling elders of two or three congregations, nor of any plurality convened; nor was it a Baptist association, for they were not the ministers and messengers of a number of churches meeting annually or biennially to

hear the state of the churches and to give their advice in difficult cases. Nor was it a Methodistic conference composed of preachers of a certain grade, without a layman among them. And what renders it a meeting *per se—sui generis*, a meeting of its own kind, is that its decisions were the decisions of the Holy Spirit, and became a part of holy writ, or of the law of Christ. It was adjourned *sine die*, never to meet again. But we have said it was incidental, or as some would say, accidental. The circumstances of the case were these: Certain brethren of the Jews, zealous of the law, went down from Judea to Antioch, where Paul and Barnabas were teaching, saying that they had a commandment from the apostles who happened to be at Jerusalem at that time, authorizing them to command the Gentile converts to be circumcised, and to keep the law of Moses, in order to salvation. After that, Paul and Barnabas had no small dissension and disputation with them, the Judaizers persisting that they had a commandment from the apostles in Jerusalem, to this effect, the church at Antioch sent Paul and Barnabas and certain others with them to Jerusalem, to see the apostles, who happened to be all there; thither they came and were all received by the apostles, and elders, and church. They told their errand; the apostles, and elders, and the whole church came together, called a meeting to consider this matter. The subject was the greatest ever agitated in the world, since the christian era. It lay at the very basis of making of twain one new man, i. e. of uniting Jews and Gentiles in one associated body—the church. The question itself respected, too, the law of Moses, its perpetuity and universal obligation. This was a most delicate point. Moreover, the recent calling of the Gentiles astonished all the apostles, as an event they had not been looking for. It was the last evolution and developement of the manifold wisdom and goodness of God to their minds; it was the discovery of the last secret in the admirably gracious plan of God, with respect to the whole human race. From all these considerations it was not wonderful that it should have produced so much excitement in the minds of all. It was consequently necessary that the minds of all the apostles, or the revelation of the Spirit communicated to them all, should be fully and publicly expressed and recorded. It was also necessary that this should be done in the first and grandest church of the Jews, and in the metropolis of the Jewish nation, while the nation yet existed; so that the reception of the Gentiles, and the renunciation of the Jewish system, might be first approved and recommended by the Jews themselves: and that the most public refutation of the errors of the Judaizers might be afforded, and the whole scheme denounced by the very persons from whom, and in the very place from which, they said they had their instructions. It is a most precious fact to us Gentiles, that all the apostles who were Jews; all the elders of the church who were Jews, and the whole church of Christ in the metropolis, composed of Jews, should thus, by the revelation of the Spirit, publicly renounce the whole system, and declare that, with all their birthright and natural privileges and religion, "they expected to be saved by the grace of the Lord Jesus just as the Gentiles." And thus they exhilarated the Gentiles by telling them in their decrees, that it not only seemed good to the Holy Spirit, but "also to us" Jews, that those decrees should be established and proclaimed. Such was the nature, design and utility of the interview at Jerusalem, like which there never was, and like which there shall never be another. This occurrence correctly viewed, and the whole scheme of a confederated priesthood appears in its naked deformity, unsupported by the most distant allusion to any scriptural warrant, a worldly scheme, the wickedness of which we hope to make fully appear.

We are at this moment called from home for some time, and deprived of the opportunity of bringing this article to a close. Hoping to resume it again, we must dismiss it for the present.   EDITOR.

Abuses of Christianity.

THE following is an extract from a work of modern date, which, though it may in some respects be exceptionable, is nevertheless deserving of the candid investigation of every advocate of primitive christianity.—EDITOR.

IT will be allowed that the best human institutions, through the lapse of time and the gradual encroachments of corrupt society, become changed in their nature and tendency, though they may retain their original names and pretensions. The art of building is architecture still; but from the difference in materials, plan, and construction, very different fabrics result. An African's hut is not a Solomon's temple. If, then, it fares thus with the institutions of men, was it to be expected that christianity, the supreme excellency of which no man can know only by the special teaching of heaven, should share a better fate, and be mocked with no spurious imitations. Surely no. Let it not here be understood that man is void of sufficient intellectual faculties; were it so, he would be excusable in rejecting the oracles of God, and blameless in making him a liar. From man's perverseness and depravity alone, his religious errors spring; it is hence that his views are perverted and corrupt, and he is said to be spiritually dead in trespasses and sins, alienated from the life of God, through the ignorance that is in him.

Christianity was first propagated by apostolic agency. Their doctrine was a stream of pure grace, issuing from the throne of God. The light which first irradiated the earth was but a faint figure of the light held forth by the apostles; for they exhibited the Deity himself in all the grandeur and excellency of his character. The focus of this light was the resurrection of Jesus; hence whatever might be the exordium of their discourses, they always made haste to testify this fact. It was this which demonstrated Jesus to be the Son of God. It was this which showed the design of his death accomplished; that death was virtually abolished, and "life and immortality" brought to light. The effect, in those that believed their testimony, was life; they were quickened by it; begotten, or born again; entering a life of friendship with God which they did not previously possess. The resurrection of Jesus implies his previous death, an event which shows the peculiar character of Deity, as "the just God and the Saviour;" hence Jesus is called "the image of the invisible God." To such a character all "baptized infidels" and professed deists are entire strangers; they worship another god, a god corresponding with their own imaginations.

By this statement may be seen the rock, the foundation on which the primitive churches were built. We may see what it was which

gave them life, and animated with a boldness and confidence that often astonished and confounded their adversaries, who imagining their gods to be offended by christians refusing to do them honor, made no scruple to sacrifice them. At what period of time the teachers of christianity turned aside from primitive simplicity is not necessary to say; but early as the days of Constantine, we see them engrossed with very different things. In his days was the great uproar with the Unitarians, which did not subside with his reign; for his successors being some unitarian and others orthodox, continued to convulse the religious world till orthodoxy finally prevailed. In those commotions the teachers of both parties appeared more like greedy wolves than imitators of the Lamb of God. Their rage for victory over each other seemed to be animated by the love of power and emolument. Church livings began then to be rich, particularly that of Rome, which, when it became vacant, set in motion all the clerical chariots in the empire, rolling towards Rome to obtain the fat living. As these things were too disgusting to christianity, some spoke boldly against them. But soon the arm of power was stretched out against all whose love of truth led them to oppose reigning abuses, and those of them who could not escape felt the vengeance of christianity, so called. Those who escaped took refuge in the mountains and vallies of the Alps, and in those wintry regions subsisted for ages by mechanical trades. Often were they invaded, harassed, and nearly destroyed, but never exterminated till Louis XIV. of France sent an army to assist his son-in-law, the duke of Savoy, in accomplishing it. About the same time Louis had converted France into a complete slaughter house, that if he enjoyed the title of "Beloved Son of the Church," he showed himself worthy of it by his zeal in what he no doubt imagined to be her interests.[*]

Thus history shows us, that, instead of converting men by the plain apostolic truth, concerning "Jesus and the resurrection," simply, they were more zealous to improve upon Nebuchadnezzar's plan, who, in his zeal for the worship of God represented by the image on the plain of Dura, heated a tremendous furnace, and hurled the impious into it. He had music to draw and fire to drive, and imagined, no doubt, that the heart must be hard, stubborn, and rebellious, which would not be melted by the influence of one, nor softened by the allurements of the other.

But since the great furnace is no more, our moderns have recourse to means somewhat different in appearance, though not in effect. They make very little use of the tale concerning "Jesus and the resurrection;" this is too stale for the improved ears of their audience; and what gave life to the dead in sins nearly eighteen centuries past, might seem (to them) to have lost its effect, and will, by no means, answer their purpose. Their plan is briefly this: First, they set man to judge in his own cause— man, whose heart the scripture declares "is deceitful above all things and desperately wicked; who can know it?" is set to judge of himself; not, indeed, by the rules of justice, but by certain marks and signs, to distinguish

[*] To allude to all the historic evidence contained in the volumes of Mosheim, Gibbon, and others, would be too tedious. For a concentration of historical information upon the subject, from the most credible authors of various parties, and writers of different ages, see Jones' History of the Waldenses.

himself from other men as converted, or partly converted; a believer, or desiring to believe; religious, or seeking to be religious. Those who are of neither class; but hardened to heedlessness, they endeavor to melt down by pouring upon them fire and brimstone, feeding them with the thunderbolts of heaven, answerable to Nebuchadnezzar's furnace. Those who imagine themselves distinguished from other men, are fed with very different things; the scriptures are cut up into piecemeal, and the very best given to the first rates; while those who are a kind of half converts, wanting something to complete their happiness, as decided favorites of heaven, receive every encouragement, and are set diligently to work, in one shape or other, to obtain the *ultimatum* of their wishes. In this manner Paul is despised when he says, " If by grace, then it is no more of works, otherwise grace is no more grace; but if it be of works, then is it no more of grace, otherwise work is no more work."

Now, as those whose life springs from "Jesus and the resurrection" alone are never tired of this grand subject, but dwell upon it with sweet delight; so those whose life springs from another source, never make it the soul of their discourse, but are ever harping upon experimental faith, vital godliness, inherent holiness, and the like; and though they swell their mouth with the word gospel five hundred times in a single discourse, yet they never hold the thing forth from the pulpit only in such manner as to have a very different effect to that which it produced in the days of Paul. Hence the striking difference between primitive christians and those of modern times, the latter being as zealous for the doctrines and commandments of men as the former were for the precepts of the Christian Lawgiver. The close attachment of professed christians to the traditions and precepts of men, is not matter of wonder, if we consider again the high pretensions with which teachers array themselves. They speak of themselves in the words which apply only to the apostles. Instead of being content with the simple title, TEACHER, they swell themselves into all the importance of *ambassadors* from the court of heaven, "stewards of the mysteries of God," and the channel through which God conveys salvation. They seem "willingly ignorant of this," that the apostles can have no successors, seeing that none after Paul were witnesses of the resurrection of Jesus, not having seen him alive after that event. This was the first grand requisite in an apostle. "As stewards of the mysteries of God," the apostles too were guided into all truth; but can our moderns say this of themselves? In fact, the apostles need no successors; for, as "the law and the prophets prophesied until John," so Christ and the apostles continue to preach and to testify in all ages. There is no new edition of the gospel, and, strictly speaking, no new preachers; for a preacher is a publisher, and a publisher is a preacher.

As for the office of pastor, very few possess the requisite qualifications laid down in the scriptures; and to give that title to whom the scriptures do not, would be doing violence to those scriptures: the bare appellation of teacher is all that such can claim. Now the word pastor is equivalent to that of shepherd, or bishop; and the word elder is often used in reference to the same office, as will be seen by comparing the scriptures of Peter and Paul.

Thus we see the extravagant pecuniary claims, as well as the high-sounding titles of reverend gentlemen, fall to the ground by the touch of the scriptures. But as questions opposing the scripture plan never cease, it will be asked, when are teachers to study? I answer, when they walk by the way, when they lie down, and when they rise up, as every saint does; and if they be taught of God, the word of Christ will dwell in them richly; so that with natural abilities for communication, they will be "apt to teach" and ready on all occasions. If, indeed, teachers cannot be prepared for want of time to study, why do they make a monopoly of teaching: for by attending to Paul's instructions to the churches at Rome, Corinth, Ephesus, and others, it will be seen that teaching is a thing not to be restricted to an individual of an assembly, but that every man in an assembled body of christians, possessing in a great or less degree the gifts for teaching or exhortation, should not be obstructed, but allowed opportunity to exercise the same. But this is not permitted where one man engrosses all, and drinks up too, the resources of the congregation, which ought to be appropriated to the use of the poor, as Paul enjoins. "Upon the first day of the week let every one of you lay by him in store as God has prospered him," that is, to form a "collection for the saints" in want. It will be said that inferior teachers must exercise their gifts at other times, and not when the whole church is assembled. I answer that the scripture knows nothing of such plan. The gifts of the saints ought to be exercised in love for edification of the whole body; but how can this be done except when they are come together? As for appointing other days besides the "Lord's day, the first day of the week," no man who trembles at the word of God, would presume to "bind upon the disciples" any such thing: it would be legislating for Christ, changing his "times and laws."

"The first day of the week" is the day on which primitive christians came together, and their example is as the law to christians of all ages; for they acted under the eye and instruction of the apostles, to whom the Lord Jesus said, "He that hears you hears me." The pulpits of the present day call "the first day of the week" sabbath; but the New Testament does not speak so. As they please to call it sabbath, so they legislate as to the manner in which it must be observed; for, instead of obeying the injunction relative to the seventh day sabbath, that they should make no fire in all their dwellings, nor cook their victuals, they enjoin what they please, and very frequently enforce their precepts by the civil power. Thus the fear of man is substituted for the fear of God. Such proceedings can answer only one purpose—by compelling people to be at leisure, they will be more likely to attend before the pulpits.

As our moderns do not keep the "first day of the week" as sabbath, so neither do they observe it as the "Lord's day." Upon "the first day of the week the disciples came together to break bread" in remembrance of the Lord's death; and as the "first day of the week" comes once in seven, the plain christian, whose inquiry is, "Lord, what would you have me to do?" needs not the finger of some great divine to point out his duty or privilege in respect to partaking of the "Lord's supper" every "Lord's day." But the customs or traditions of men have made void this institution. The same contempt of his authority who commanded his apostles to teach believers " to observe all things whatsoever he had commanded them," is often manifested in respect to baptism. The scripture very significantly places that ordinance between a confession of "the truth as it is in Jesus," and admission into the churches as members of the faithful body: but the authority of men has transferred that ordinance, or something under its name, to the speechless infant, making of "none effect" the ordinance of God.

It is tiresome to follow the steps of corruption. Another instance wherein the authority of God is supplanted by the will of man, shall suffice. It will be recollected that "the author and finisher" of the christian faith manifested an utter aversion to ostentation; hence he spoke against the practice of praying standing at the corners of the streets, and commanded his disciples to keep within doors when they wished to pray; and not only so, but to enter into the closet, praying in secret. The reverse of this is commanded by the pulpits, not indeed that men should attend to it in the streets; it is sufficient for their purpose that the devotee be seen or heard, praying in his family.*

These, out of many specimens of departure from primitive simplicity, are enough to show that the authority of the christian lawgiver is not more regarded now than it was in the twelfth or fourteenth century; for though a great part of the professing world may reject this, that, and the other abuse; yet, whilst they do what they please, obey what they like, and cherish whatever abuses may suit their taste, prejudices, or circumstances, how can it be said that they recognize the King of Zion? And, indeed, what better could be expected, when such is the purity and sublimity of the christian faith, that none can know or appreciate its excellency but by the teaching of God—whilst such is the perversity and depravity of the human heart, that it seems to pervert or contaminate whatever does not correspond with its corrupt principles. Besides, a man might seem to be born to his religion as to his father's inheritance—it forms, as it were, a great part of his patrimony. And whatever it might be that induced some of our forefathers to suffer so nobly in opposing some abuses of christianity, yet they could not communicate their spirit to their children, and so posterity cease to advance in the work of reform. They prefer the *ipse dixit* of man to the labor of thinking for themselves. It is thus their prejudices become firm as the foundations of the mountains, and their abhorrence of change is in proportion.

But some will say that these are hard sayings, harsh and uncharitable, and seem like judging. I answer, that nothing is hard to him whose foundation is eternal truth; even the "wrath which is to come" he views with fearless countenance. No coming storm can move him to dismay. As for the harshness of truth, it will be harsh to the ear fostered and fed by flattery. But if it be uncharitable to speak truth, surely it is more uncharitable to poison with deceit and falsehood. And where is charity when the love of truth is absent? Charity rejoices not in iniquity, but "rejoices in the truth." Charity regards the truth as its true mother, and will pine and die under a step-mother. As respects judging, no judging can be wrong which is measured by the truth on which we stand, and hope to stand in judgment yet to come. Nay, further—a measure of judging is absolutely

* The remainder of this sentence, which is highly objectionable, is excluded. The author errs. Family worship is as old as society, and has been, in the wisdom of God, essential to every dispensation.   PUBLISHER.

necessary to every christian. Is he not to discriminate and recognize the brethren of his Lord? Yes, verily, or he would be neglecting the "new commandment," that peculiar precept, by the observance of which He will distinguish his sheep from the goats, who said, "Love one another as I have loved you." This love, says John, is "for the truth's sake as it is in Jesus," dwelling in those that believe it. This love cannot exist where the views of the professing body are not simplified as respects the truth being the sole ground of their only hope, joy, and peace. When, therefore, the plain christian looks for "the love of the truth" and brotherly charity in the gay and pompous assemblies of the professing world, he is constrained to say, they are not here.

No. 5.]   DECEMBER, 1, 1823.
                 The Clergy.—No. III.

IN our last article under this head, we had got so far in the exposure of the means employed by the clergy to establish their dominion over the bible, the consciences, the sentiments, and over the persons of men, as to show that their confederation into councils, synods, &c., was entirely destitute of any divine warrant in the New Testament. The only passage adduced from the New Testament, in support of such consociations, is the 15th of the *Acts of the Apostles;* and this we considered in our last, and, as we think, demonstrated to be no warrant for ecclesiastical courts or church judicatories. Indeed, the present holy alliance of the crowned potentates of Europe, for the purpose of sustaining the assumptions of kings against the rights of the people, is just as accordant to the genius and spirit of christianity, as the councils of priests, or the confederation of the clergy now existing among us. There is, in fact, a much greater resemblance between the holy alliance of kings and the holy alliance of clergy than at first thought would appear. In the first place, kings and clergymen of this day find themselves pretty much alike. They have both got upon thrones by the common consent of the people. The king upon a golden throne, or a gilded one—the priest upon a wooden one, sometimes gilded, and sometimes crimson-cushioned too. The king wears a crown, and the priest a mitre. The king from his throne publishes his speeches and proclaims the laws of the state—the priest from his pulpit, or wooden throne, publishes his sermons and proclaims the canons of the church. The king is high in honor and lives upon the toils of his people—the priest is high in honor too, and lives upon the sweat and sacrifices of his people. The king pleads his divine right to rule, to be supported, and to be honored by the people of his realm—the priest pleads his divine right to instruct his people into the meaning of the bible, and to be supported and honored by the people over whom he reigns. The king pleads the antiquity of his order, and goes back to Genesis to show that his order is there mentioned and dignified in the person of Nimrod, Amraphel, Tidal, and Chedorlaomer. The priest is equally fond of antiquity, and turns over to Genesis in support of his order, and pleads that his order is found in the person of Melchisedec and the priests of Egypt. The king pleads his right to peculiar immunities from immemorial usage—the priest pleads the same right from usage as ancient; he quotes *Genesis,* xlii. 22. "The land of the priests Joseph would not buy, for the priests had a portion assigned them by Pharoah, and did eat the portion which Pharoah gave them." The kings of ancient and modern times united in leagues offensive and defensive for the better management of their affairs, the securing of their interests, dominion, and rule. Of this sort was the confederation of the vale of Siddim nearly four thousand years ago. The priests of ancient and modern times have united in synods and councils, "ministerially to determine controversies of faith and cases of conscience, to set down rules and direction3 for the better ordering of the public worship and government of the church." Of this sort was the confederation of priests in all ancient nations, in Egypt, in Chaldea, in Greece and Rome. The Jewish sanhedrim, that condemned the Son of God to death, and that excommunicated the apostles, and would have silenced them, was of this complexion. In all these items we discover remarkable coincidences between the kings and the priests of ancient and modern times.

But in the nature and object of their alliances or consociations there are the most remarkable analogies. We shall take the existing holy alliance of kings in Europe and the existing holy alliance of American clergy, and examine their respective aspects. The holy alliance of monarchs have sworn and subscribed to certain articles of common faith, necessary, essentially necessary, to their salvation. They have pledged themselves to inculcate and support the same by all means and at every risk. Have not the confederated clergy of America done the same? Have not the respective ecclesiastical councils solemnly vowed and subscribed to certain articles of faith, deemed essential to salvation? Have not they pledged themselves to inculcate the same at the risk of their livings and sacred honor?

Again, the object of the holy alliance and that of the allied priests is one and the same, ostensibly and really. The ostensible object of the allied monarchs is the peace and prosperity of Europe; the ostensible object of the allied priests is the peace and prosperity of Zion. But the *real* object of most of the allied monarchs is their crowns, their thrones, and their revenues: and the *real* object of most of the allied priests is their mitres, their pulpits, and their stipends. The allied monarchs call those who write or speak against their schemes, "traitors, rebels, or enthusiastic demagogues," whose object it is to sow discord, and to revolutionize that they may reign: the allied clergy represent those who speak or write against them as infidels, schismatics, heretics, or bewildered enthusiasts, who oppose them from some sinister motives. The allied monarchs have amongst their subjects such as they have honored with more than usual respect, and these plead their cause, defend their measures, and denounce those who plead for reform; these kiss the tyrant's rod, and lick the dust on which he walks—just so, the allied priests have amongst those over whom they reign, certain ones whom they honor with more than ordinary respect; these plead the cause of the priests, defend their proceedings, and denounce those who plead for reform; these kiss the priest's toe and hold his stirrup; these are the veriest bigots; these are the ass on which Balaam rides. When one of the allied monarchs is likely to become too powerful, or to be too strong for the others, the other sovereigns become jealous, begin to explain away the obligation of the alliance, and prepare themselves for his exclusion; when one of the allied priests becomes too popular or too powerful in the dio-

cess, the others say it is better that one man perish, or be destroyed, than that the whole priesthood suffer. But in fact the analogy appears perfect in every instance; the allied monarchs and the allied clergy resemble a monstrous production of nature which we once saw, two bodies united, and but one soul. Thus, though allied monarchs and allied clergy are two apparently distinct bodies, they possess but one and the same soul and spirit.

In this country we have no kings, and no king craft. We are not, therefore, afraid to laugh at the impious and vain pretensions of the allied sovereigns. But in this country we have priests and priestcraft, and therefore may tremble to lisp a word against priests and priestcraft. But while we pity the condition, cordially pity the vassalage and privations of those under the despotic sway of the allied sovereigns of Europe, we see the approach, we hail the approach of their deliverance. Light travels with immeasurable force, with incalculable velocity. A fire is kindled that will burn and burn—that will, in proportion to the restraints imposed on it, burst forth with unquenchable violence, and consume the allied heads and hands that oppress Europe and the world. And as we sit and condole over the spiritual wickedness in high places; while we mourn for the blinded, the deluded, the oppressed, the robbed, and murdered subjects of the allied clergy, we lift up our eyes from the mournful and appalling picture with a hope that HE who has for some time been consuming with the spirit of his mouth the works of the Man of Sin, will continue with accumulated force to destroy and to consume, until iniquity ashamed shall hide its face; until allied priests shall be driven to confusion; or rather, as we would earnestly desire, led to repent and become obedient to the truth.

EDITOR.

A Review of an " Extract of a Narrative of the State of Religion within the Bounds of the Synod of Kentucky;" published in the Pittsburgh Recorder of November 6th.

THIS narrative of the state of religion, if we may judge of the whole from the specimen presented in the Recorder, is, as respects style, matter, and spirit, one of the poorest things we have ever seen from a body of men professing to be learned and religious. What renders it worthy of notice is its extraordinary character of imbecility, incongruity, superciliousness, and ignorance of christianity. But let it speak for itself. The first paragraph reads—

" It is with pleasure the synod presents to the people a view of the state of religion within our bounds. From some points this view is dark; from others, encouraging."

Reader, observe: the synod with *pleasure* presents a view from some points of the compass *dark*, from other points of the compass encouraging, i. e. *light*. The synod are of a happy turn of mind; they have pleasure in presenting a view, dark or light. But stranger still, the synod have *pleasure* in *lamenting!* for after telling us that it is with *pleasure* the synod presents to the people a view, &c., they utter seven lamentations. They lament the ravages of disease; they lament the death of four ministers of their communion; they lament that " in some places infidelity prevails;" they lament that " intemperance, profane swearing, and indeed vice of every kind, prevails" in certain parts of their bounds; they lament, or rather " deeply deplore, that in many places the Sabbath is greatly profaned;" they lament the " prevalency of lukewarmness in many of our churches, accompanied with a sinful conformity to the world;" and in the seventh place, " they are sorry to state, that there are still many vacancies within our bounds. From these vacancies we hear the pitiable Macedonian cry, Help us!"

The Macedonian cry is become weak and curtailed in these vacancies! Amongst all the synods whose narratives we have heard, we never heard one that could with *pleasure* utter seven such lamentations. This narrative of the synod reminds us of a speech of king George IV. to the citizens of Dublin. The king was telling the citizens with what heart-rending grief he had just heard of the death of his beloved spouse, queen Caroline; and, in the same breath, while the crocodile tears were streaming down his cheeks, he expresses the great pleasure he then felt to be surrounded with his Irish subjects.

The synod presents a view of the state of religion within its bounds. Is it the state of Presbyterianism, or the state of religion? or are the words Presbyterianism and religion synonymous? The synod must identify the terms assuredly; for they never mention the state of any other sect. The synod of Kentucky, then, must possess within its bounds all the religion in the state. But it may be said, that it only speaks of its own communion. Then, I ask, why does it mention the prevalence of infidelity in Lexington, Frankfort? &c. Is this within the bounds of its communion? Does infidelity prevail within its communion? The bounds of the synod must mean the whole state, or else infidelity and universalism prevail in some parts of its communion. The state of religion within its *bounds* is a most equivocal and deceitful sentence. And the synod must either arrogate to itself all the religion in the state, or it gives a false representation of the state of religion in the state. We are assured that the representation of the state of religion within Lexington is not correct, if it mean any thing more than the synod's communion; for having been in Lexington immediately after the publication of this narrative, and having observed a little of the astonishment which it excited, I was led to inquire into the state of other religious sects in that town; and, from the best authority, ascertained that other religious sects had increased much more during the last year than for some years past. But the fact is, that the prevalence of infidelity in Lexington, means, that the synod having lost the management of the Transylvania University, and this seminary having, since it was by the state put under the management of others, flourished exceedingly, it has become exceedingly mortifying to the synod, which is about trying to get up another, for synods have always aimed at the sovereignty of colleges as subservient to their designs; consequently, whenever they lose the sway in any seminary, infidelity begins to rear its odious brow in that place.

And the first of the joyful things mentioned by the synod is, that "several churches within our bounds which were vacant," A vacant church! O for a new dictionary! "and almost without the means of grace," i. e. a learned priest, "have within the last year been supplied with faithful pastors."

Let it be remembered that the synod of Kentucky represent, and consequently consider, a faithful pastor, the means of grace; for every church is almost without the means of grace who has not a faithful pastor. O you poor! who

are not able to hire a faithful pastor, pray to be *rich* that you may be saved! O Matthew, Mark, Luke and John! O Paul and Peter! James and Jude! what shall we say to you! You did not free yourselves from the blood of all men! Nay, you shunned to declare unto us the whole counsel of God! You kept back many things, and you spake so darkly, that, having you all, and wanting a faithful pastor from a theological school, we are almost destitute of the means of grace!! The synod adds:

" Thus your prayers have been answered, and God has sent some of you the desire of your hearts: men to break to you and to your children, the bread of life."

Without this faithful pastor the bread of life would not have been broken! You must have starved to death, or eat it whole! O you faithful pastors! O you self-importants! if the people starve, alas for you!

The synod answers the weak and faultering Macedonian cry thus:

" We have it not in our power to answer their call. We have not laborers equal to the harvest. Do these vacant congregations say, what must we do? Must we and our children perish for want of the bread of life? The synod would say, two things at least they must do: they must look, by fervent prayer, to God. But this is not all; they, in conjunction with our churches that have regular pastors, must cheerfully and liberally engage in the support of our Theological Seminary. They must cheerfully and liberally contribute to the support of poor and pious youth in their preparatory studies. Were these two things perseveringly attended to, our vacant churches would soon be supplied and new churches formed."

Yes, yes, support the Theological Seminary, contribute money, give money to make faithful pastors, and then tell them, freely you have received, now freely give. No, that will not obtain them. Give money to make poor pious youths learned clergy, or vain pretenders to erudition; and then pray that they may preach to you; yes, and pay them too. Was there ever such a craft as priestcraft? No, it is the craftiest of all crafts! It is so crafty that it obtains by its craft the means to make craftsmen, and then it makes the deluded support them! The synod rejoices at last, that there is a growing reverence for the Sabbath; that Sabbath schools have been organized; that in some congregations monthly concerts for prayer are well attended; that the principle of inter-communion is recognized and acted upon; that parochial visitations have been attended to in some churches with most encouraging results; and that though no revivals had taken place, yet in many places there are encouraging appearances. Such is the dark and light view which it presents to the people. Oh that the people would read the scriptures and think and act for themselves, and then the people who fear God would learn his statutes, walk in his commandments, enjoy an intelligent mind, a comfortable hope, and would grow in grace and in the knowledge of our Lord and Saviour Jesus Christ. Then they would shine as lights in the world, they would live as the salt of the earth, and many would be reclaimed from the error of their way. Then they would choose from among themselves such as they had proved to be faithful men, and "apt to teach," for bishops, who would take the oversight, not for the sake of filthy lucre, but of a ready mind; not as lords over God's heritage, but examples to the flock.   EDITOR.

Address to readers of the Christian Baptist.—No. I.

My Friends :—In the different articles presented to your perusal in this paper, you will find some that you approve, and some likely that you disapprove. We need scarcely inform you that we approve of every item yet presented from our own pen, or those of our correspondents. There was a sentence or two, in an extract on the "*Abuses of Christianity,*" published during our absence, which, perhaps, we would have either not inserted, or have noted with a remark, had we been present at its insertion; but the general spirit and purport of the extract we approve. Our views of christianity differ very materially from the popular views. This we fearlessly and honestly avow. But while we remember our own mistakes, and the systems and teachings of our time, we must acknowledge many to be christians who are led away and corrupted from the simplicity of Christ. These cannot enjoy christian health. They resemble those who live in an unwholesome climate and inhale a sickening air—they live, but they do not enjoy health or life. It is one thing to live, and another to enjoy life. One may be a christian, and yet a babe, and yet carnal. It is, however, the privilege, the happiness, and glory of christians, to be men in Christ—to be free men too, and to stand fast in, and enjoy the liberty, the glorious liberty of sons and heirs of God, is the grand desirable—the high aim of all the sons and daughters of the Lord God Almighty. To see christians enjoy their privileges, and to see sinners brought from darkness to light, are the two great objects for which we desire to live, to labor, and to suffer reproach. In endeavoring to use our feeble efforts for these glorious objects, we have found it necessary, among other things, to attempt to dethrone the reigning popular clergy from their high and lofty seats, which they have for ages been building for themselves. While we attempt to dethrone them, it is solely for this purpose, that we might enthrone the holy apostles in those thrones which Christ promised them; or rather, that we might turn the attention of the people to them placed upon thrones by the Great and Mighty King. Many will, from various motives, decry the clergy, as indeed they have rendered themselves odious to all who dare think for themselves, in every age and nation. They have made more deists or sceptics than christians, in every country, and amongst all people. In opposing and exposing them, and their kingdom, it is not to join the infidel cry against priests or priestcraft; it is not to gratify the avaricious, or the licentious; but it is to pull down their babel, and to emancipate those whom they have enslaved, to free the people from their unrighteous dominion and unmerciful spoliation. We have no system of our own, nor of others, to substitute in lieu of the reigning systems. We only aim at substituting the New Testament in lieu of every creed in existence; whether Mahometan, Pagan, Jewish, or Sectarian. We wish to call christians to consider that Jesus Christ has made them kings and priests to God. We neither advocate Calvinism, Arminianism, Arianism, Socinianism, Trinitarianism, Unitarianism, Deism, or Sectarianism, but *New Testamentism*. We wish, cordially wish, to take the New Testament out of the abuses of the clergy, and put it into the hands of the people. And to do this is no easy .ask, as the clergy have formed the opinions of nine-tenths of christendom before they could form an opinion of their own. They have, in order to raise the people's admiration of them,

for their own advantage, taught them in creeds, in sermons, in catechisms, in tracts, in pamphlets, in primers, in folios, that they alone can expound the New Testament; that without them, people are either almost, or altogether destitute of the means of grace. They must lead in the devotion of the people; they must consecrate their prayers, their praises; and latterly they must even open a cattle-show or an exhibition of manufactures with prayers and religious pageantry!

Such readers of this paper as believe that Jesus is the Messiah, the Son of God, and consequently desire to understand his word, to do, and to enjoy his will—we address, in a subserviency to our grand design, in the following words:—

That you may relish and understand the New Testament, and all the revelation of God, is our ardent desire. We will, therefore, suggest to you a plan of reading the blessed volume which reason, common sense, and the experience of all who have tried it, recommend and enforce. We will only premise one sentence, viz. that as God kindly revealed himself, his will, and our salvation in human language, the words of human language, which he used for this purpose, must have been used by his spirit in the commonly received sense amongst mankind generally; else it could not have been a revelation; for a revelation in words not understood in the common sense, is no revelation at all. You will then take, say, a New Testament, and sit down with a pencil or pen in your hand. Begin with Matthew's gospel; read the whole of it at one reading, or two; mark on the margin every sentence you think you do not understand. Turn back again; read it a second time, in less portions at once than in the first reading; cancel such marks as you have made which noted passages, that, on the first reading appeared to you dark or difficult to understand, but on the second reading opened to your view. Then read Mark, Luke, and John, in the same manner, as they all treat upon the same subject. After having read each evangelist in this way, read them all in succession a third time. At this time you will no doubt be able to cancel many of your marks. Thus read the Acts of the Apostles, which is the key to all the Epistles; then the Epistles in a similar manner; always before reading an epistle, read every thing said about the people addressed in the epistle, which you find in the Acts of the Apostles. This is the course which we would take to understand any book. You will no doubt see, from what you read, the necessity of accompanying all your readings with supplications to the Father of Lights, for that instruction which he has graciously promised to all that ask him; praying that "the God of our Lord Jesus Christ, the Father of Glory, may give to you the spirit of wisdom and revelation in the knowledge of him; the eyes of your understanding being enlightened; that you may know what is the hope of his calling, and what the riches of the glory of his inheritance in the saints, and what is the exceeding greatness of his power toward us who believe, according to the working of his mighty power, which he wrought in Christ when he raised him from the dead, and set him at his own right hand in the heavenly places." *Ephesians*, i. 17—20. "That Christ may dwell in your hearts by faith; that you being rooted and grounded in love, may be able to comprehend with all saints what is the breadth, and length, and depth, and height, and to know the love of Christ which passes knowledge, that you might be filled with all the fullness of God." *Ephesians*, iii. 17—19.

In pursuing this plan, we have no doubt, in getting even three times through the New Testament, that you will understand much more of the christian religion than a learned divine would teach you in seven years. It will add, however, exceedingly to your advantage, should you find two, three, ten, or a dozen similarly disposed, who will meet and read, and converse and pray with you, and you with them once a-week; or should you be the member of a church walking in all the commandments and ordinances of the Lord: Do, we entreat you, make the experiment, and if it prove not as useful as we have hinted, remind us of it; tell us of your disappointment, and then we will be deservedly worthy of blame. Beware of having any commentator or system before your eyes or your mind. Open the New Testament as if mortal man had never seen it before. Your acquaintance with the Old Testament will incalculably facilitate your proficiency in the New. The time requisite will be redeemed time. It will not interfere with your ordinary duties. Oh remember that this knowledge is better than all acquisitions! "that happy is the man that finds wisdom, and the man that gets understanding! For the merchandize of it is better than the merchandize of silver, and the gain thereof than fine gold! she is more precious than rubies; and all the things you can desire are not to be compared to her. Length of days is in her right hand; and in her left hand riches and honor. Her ways are the ways of pleasantness, and all her paths are peace. She is a tree of life to them that lay hold upon her; and happy is every one that retains her." *Prov.* iii. 13—18.   EDITOR.

Mr. Editor:—

SIR: HAVING read with considerable attention the numbers of the Christian Baptist already published, and approving of the general spirit and tendency of your work, I take the liberty of suggesting to you the necessity of avoiding extremes. I have, for some years, lamented that so many who have opposed prevailing errors with considerable ability and commendable zeal, have defeated their own good efforts by outstepping the fixed boundaries of truth; and thus introducing schemes and opinions, as subversive of the religion of the New Testament, and as fraught with mischief, in their ultimate operations, as the schemes, which they opposed. In hastening out of Babylon they ran past Jerusalem. I would, with due respect, suggest to you, that I think your opposition to bible societies savors a little of this error. You have classed these most benevolent and useful institutions with schemes, as unwarranted of God as enthusiastic, as they are irrational and absurd. In this one instance, I honestly think, you have erred; you will please reconsider this matter. Consider only one fact, that it is owing to these benevolent institutions, that so many of the poor have the word of life at this moment in their hands. I readily allow that it is difficult, very difficult to keep within the limits of propriety, within the limits of truth, in taking up the pen against a world of errors. It is also possible to fall short of the proper bounds, as Luther and Calvin very plainly have done. These men were reformers of popery, not advocates of the religion of the bible. They brought the pope's chair with them, and established a religion as political as that of Rome. The very essential principles of popery are to be found in the works

of these reformers. As for instance, these words of Calvin, "the church did grant liberty to herself since the beginning to change the rites (ordinances) somewhat, excepting the substance." (*Calvin's Com. on Acts* viii. 38.) This principle recognized and acted upon, re-establishes popery on its proper basis. And the present appearance of Lutherism and Calvinism shows how trifling the difference between the great mother and her elder daughters. Hoping that you will keep close to the grand model, I am your well-wisher,   ROBERT CAUTIOUS.

P—, Va. November 6th, 1823.

Mr. Robert Cautious:—

SIR: Yours of the 6th instant came duly to hand. I am obliged to you for its contents. You think that it was rather going to an extreme to rank bible societies with other popular schemes. Perhaps a more intimate acquaintance with our views of christianity would induce you to think as we do upon this subject. We are convinced, fully convinced, that the whole head is sick, and the whole heart faint of modern fashionable christianity—that many of the schemes of the populars resemble the delirium, the wild fancies of a subject of fever, in its highest paroxysms—and that these most fashionable projects deserve no more regard from sober christians, christians intelligent in the New Testament, than the vagaries, the febrile flights of patients in an inflammatory fever. We admit that it is quite as difficult to convince the populars of the folly of their projects, as it generally is to convince one in a febrile reverie, that he is not in the possession of his reason. Some of the actions, however, of these subjects of disease, approximate very nigh to the actions of those in perfect health, while others are extravagantly wild. The course pursued by physicians in such cases as we have alluded to, for the cure of the body, is analogous to the proper course to be pursued by those who would reduce the minds of the populars to views and practices consistent with scripture. It is not the administration of stimulants, but a system of depletion, that will effect a cure. It is not the recommendation of the popular schemes, it is not the prescription of zealously engaging in all the projects of converting the world, recommended by the popular clergy, that will heal the diseases of the people; but it is an abandonment of every human scheme, and a submission to learn and study christianity as developed in the bible. This is the course, and the only course, that will effect a cure and renovate the constitution. Every other course resembles the palliatives, and sedatives, and stimulants of quackery.

With regard to bible societies, they are the most specious and plausible of all the institutions of this age. No man who loves the bible can refrain from rejoicing at its increasing circulation. But every christian who understands the nature and design, the excellence and glory of the institution called the Church of Jesus Christ, will lament to see its glory transferred to a human corporation. The church is robbed of its character by every institution, merely human, that would ape its excellence and substitute itself in its place. Should a physician of extraordinary skill exhibit a medicine as an infallible remedy of consumption, in all its stages, when administered according to his prescription; should he represent it as perfectly adapted, without any commixture, or addition, to the patient in every stage; should he also be

E   3

a person of unbounded benevolence, what would be his feelings when some ignorant quack would bring himself into notice by recommending the grand specific as infallible, should a little sage tea or some innocent anodyne be added? Would not the physician feel his skill insulted, his character traduced, and would not his benevolence provoke him to anger at the impudent or ignorant quack who would thus strive to creep into notice at his expense, and at the same time, partially, if not altogether, defeat the real utility of his medicine? The case is parallel, at least sufficiently so, to illustrate our meaning. The infallible physician has exhibited an infallible remedy for sinners; he has also established a society to which he has committed it, to be preserved and exhibited in purity. This society he has called the house of the living God, the temple of the Holy Spirit. The honor and glory of this society, of this institution, and the honor and glory of its founder, require, that in its own character, not in that of a heterogeneous association of Calvinists, Arminians, Mammonites, Socinian Philosophers, and Philosophical Sceptics, it present and disseminate, in their purity the oracles of God. Let every church of Christ, then, if it can only disseminate twenty bibles or twenty testaments in one year, do this much. Then it will know into what channel its bounty flows; it will need no recording secretary, no president, no managers of its bounty. It will send all this pageantry, this religious show, to the regions of pride and vanity, whence they came. Then the church and its king will have all the glory. The limits of my sheet command me to come to an abrupt close. Your friend,

THE EDITOR.

B——, November 20th, 1823.

THE following language from an English protestant, where hereditary political prejudices give greater force to the religious, may be considered liberal, and indicates the prevalence of more benign and tolerant feeling than has, until lately, existed towards the Roman Catholic Church in that country.—[*Nat. Int.*

"AMONGST all grave and religious men, the ancient hostility to the church of Rome has entirely passed away, and has been succeeded by a kind of tenderness, a species of reverence, for what, in a historical point of view, is unquestionably the mother church. We avow, that we ourselves feel this tenderness and reverence, and we know that in this feeling we agree with some of the best and most learned men of every age and country. The late Dr. Johnson used to stop at once all invectives against the Roman Catholics, by saying, "Nay, sir, do not abuse a church from which we all spring." The bishops of Rome are men, and have fallen in process of time into gross errors and vices; but still they are the successors of St. Peter. Barrow, Clarke, and a hundred more of our most learned prelates and sages had the same feelings; and we have reason to believe, indeed to know, that they prevail very extensively in the present day. It is, in truth, a vulgar and most mischievous bigotry, to confound the papal power of the present times with the popes of the dark and middle ages, and to treat all the existing Catholics of the present day as if they shared in the guilt and sanguinary persecutions of those of that dark period."—[*Bell's London Weekly Mess.*

This is liberal, charitable, just, and honest. It is honest; for assuredly every sect that holds a human creed and an ecclesiastical court, is a legitimate daughter of the holy mother; and it is no more than common honesty to own the relationship. But, indeed, we did not know, that "amongst all grave and religious men, the ancient hostility to the church of Rome had entirely passed away, and that it had been succeeded by a kind of tenderness, a species of reverence, for what, in a historical point of view, is unquestionably the mother church." Nor did we know that dissenters from the mother church would "avow" that they feel a "reverence" for the old mother of harlots, the scarlot whore, drunken with the blood of the saints of the Most High. Indeed, we have long seen a most striking family likeness between the numerous progeny of this crimsoned queen in their religious establishments and religious proceedings; but never before this "era of good feelings," did we hear that almost all grave and religious men reverence this venerable nurse of an adulterous brood. As every thing of English manufacture is so highly esteemed in this country, it is presumed that the style and sentiment of the above extract will be quite fashionable amongst us.   EDITOR.

Debate.

A DEBATE took place in Washington, Mason county, Kentucky, between the Rev. *W. L. Maccalla*, of Kentucky, and *A. Campbell*, of Virginia, which commenced on the 15th and ended on the 22d of October, on BAPTISM. This debate continued seven days, owing to Mr. Maccalla having collected documents and written notes, which he said, before the debate commenced, would require eight days to discuss. As this debate is about being put to press, we forbear making any remarks upon it. It excited great interest, and was patiently heard by a very numerous and respectable assembly, to its close. It is expected that it will make its appearance next spring.   EDITOR.

No. 6.]   JANUARY 5, 1824.

The Clergy.—No. IV.

AS THE clergy have occupied a most conspicuous place in the Egyptian, Chaldean, Persian, Grecian, Roman, and anti-Christian empires, common courtesy requires that we should pay them more than common attention. Our present number shall be devoted to their training and consecration.

A lad, sometimes of twelve or fourteen years, is, by his parents, destined for "holy orders." To the grammar school he hies away. In the course of two or three years he is initiated into the Latin tongue. The fables of Æsop, the *Viri Romæ*, the wars of Cæsar, the metamorphoses of Ovid, the conspiracy of Catiline, the wars of Jugurtha, the pastoral songs of Virgil, with his Georgics and Æneid; the amorous and bacchanalian odes of Horace, his satires and epistles; the sapient invectives of Juvenal and Perseus; the amours, the debaucheries, the lecherous intrigues, the murders, and suicides of real and fictitious heroes and heroines; the character and achievements of Jupiter, Juno, Bacchus, and Venus, well relished and well understood, prepare him for introduction to the Grecian tongue. Now subjects of a similar character, written in a different alphabet, but written by men of the same religion and morals, command his attention for a year or two longer. He now enters college, perfects his knowledge in the pantheon, admires the beauties of Anacreon, is charmed with the sublimity of Homer, reveres the mythology of

Hesiod, and scans with rapture the flights of Pindar. From the inspiration of the Muses, from the summit of Parnassus, he descends to the frigid contemplation of triangles, squares, and curves. For this he acquires a taste also. The demonstrations of Euclid, the algebraic process, and Newton's principia captivate his powers of ratiocination. The logic of Aristotle, the rhetoric of Longinus and Quintilian, the ethics of Plato, and the metaphysics of the Gnostics, elevate him to very high conceptions of himself. So far the candidates for law, physic, and divinity accompany each other. Each of these, having got his diploma of Bachelor of all these Arts, shakes hands with his classmates, and enters into a department of preparation consentaneous to his future destiny. One puts himself under a doctor of law, another under a doctor of physic, and the pupil with whom we set out, puts himself under a doctor of divinity. His former classmates, with whom he was once so jovial, retain their former jocularity or sobriety,—there is no alteration of their visage. But my young priest gradually assumes a sanctimonious air, a holy gloom overspreads his face, and a pious sedateness reigns from his eyebrows to his chin. His very tone of voice participates of the deep devotion of his soul. His words flow on with a solemn slowness, and every period ends with a heavenly cadence. There is a kind of angelic demeanor in his gait, and a seraphic sweetness in all his movements. With his sunday coat, on a sabbath morn, he puts on a mantle of deeper sanctity, and imperceptibly learns the three grand tones—the sabbath tone, the pulpit tone, and the praying tone—these are the devout, the more devout, and the most devout.

Meantime he reads volumes of scholastic divinity, and obtains, from sermon books and skeletons of sermons, models for future practice. Bodies of divinity, adapted to the sect to whom he looks for maintenance, are closely studied; and the bible is sometimes referred to as a book of proofs for the numerous articles of his creed. A partial acquaintance with church history is formed, and a minute attention is paid to the rules and manner of proceeding in ecclesiastical courts. Now he can descant upon "natural" and "revealed" religion; now the mysteries of scholastic divinity, viz. "eternal generation," "filiation," "the origin of moral evil," "the eternal compact," "the freedom of the human will," "eternal, unconditional election and reprobation," "the generality or speciality of the atonement," &c. &c. are, to him, as common place topics. After being a year or two at the feet of this Gamaliel, he appears before the presbytery or some other ecclesiastical tribunal: he delivers a sermon on which he has spent two or three months first, in collecting or inventing documents, then in writing, and lastly, in memorizing the whole. When he has it well committed, the only thing preparatory yet remaining, is to fix upon the proper attitudes of body, tones and gestures suited to the occasion; and, above all, he endeavors to conceal all art, that it may appear to flow from unfeigned sincerity. The sermon is pronounced and approbated, with a small exception or two. On the whole, it was a finished piece of mechanism. He lifts his indentures, and after another specimen or two, receives a license, which places him on a footing with those of other trades called journeymen. Indeed he is for a time hired by the day, and sent hither or thither at the will of his superiors. This, however, contributes to his ease, inasmuch as it saves him the toil of preparing new sermons, the same discourses being always new to a strange congregation.

Such is the common training of a clergyman. It may not be so extensive, or it may be more extensive; he may commence his studies at an earlier or later period; he may be sent by his parents or by others, or he may go of his own accord; he may be a beneficiary, or he may be able to pay his way. These circumstantial differences may and do exist, yet the training of a clergyman is specifically the same in all cases.

To this course, which is, with some very small differences, the course pursued by Romanists, Episcopalians, Presbyterians of every grade, Congregationalists, and, perhaps, by some others; it has been objected that there is not much dependence upon grace in this plan. This is, perhaps, a futile objection; for what need is there of grace, or what cause for dependence upon the grace of God, in a person so well qualified by art for this reverend office? A clergyman, thus qualified, can deliver a very popular and orthodox sermon without any grace; as easily too as a lawyer can plead the cause of his client without grace. If a lawyer can be so much interested in the cause of his client as to be warmly eloquent; if his soul can be so moved by sympathy, as it often is, even to seek relief in copious tears, without the influence of grace or supernatural aid, why may not a clergyman be elevated to the same degree, or to a higher degree of zeal, of warmth, of sympathy, of deep distress, in his pathetic addresses from the pulpit? Again, if one so well versed in theology, as to be able to comprehend, in one view, all the divinities, from the crocodiles, the gods of Egypt, up to Olympic Jove, or the venerable Saturn, as any clergyman from his youthful studies is; if a competent acquaintance with the sublimities of natural religion, and with the philosophical mysteries of scholastic divinity, cannot be eloquent, animated, and orthodox, without grace, he must, indeed, be as stupid as an ass.

But there are some who think that there is some kind of an almost inseparable connexion between clerical acquisitions and the grace of God—that none can be eminently possessed of the former, that does not possess a competent portion of the latter. How can this be? If a parent who has three sons, A, B, and C, educates A for a divine, B for a carpenter, and C for a doctor of medicine; why should A possess the grace of God or the faith of the gospel rather than B or C? If such were the case, how could it be accounted for? Has the parent any divine promise that A shall possess the heavenly gift rather than B or C? Is there any reason in the nature of things, that the training of A, B, and C, will secure grace to A rather than to B and C? If so, then there is a connexion between Latin and Grecian languages, mythology, science, and the grace of God, that does not exist between the education of a carpenter or a medical doctor, and that grace. If the education of A secures the boon of heaven, then it becomes the imperious duty of every father thus to educate his sons. But this is impossible. He has not the means. Then the gift of God is purchased with money!!! It is, then, unreasonable to suppose that the training of a clergyman can, in any respect, contribute to his possessing the grace of God, even in the popular sense of that grace. Indeed, we would cheerfully undertake to prove that the training of a carpenter or mason is more *innocent* and less *injurious* to the human mind, than the training of a clergyman in the popular course, and that there is more in the education of the latter to disqualify him to enter into the kingdom of God, than there is in the education of the former to unfit for admission into this kingdom. From these considerations the most favorable opinion which we could form of the regular clergy, is, that if there be, say, for the sake of precision, five thousand of them in the United States, five thousand carpenters, and five thousand doctors; there is an equal number of christian carpenters, of christian doctors, or of any other trade, proportionally according to their aggregate number, as there is of christian clergy. If we err in this opinion, our error is on the side of charity for the clergy. For we conceive it would be much easier to prove from the bible and from reason, that in five thousand carpenters, masons, tailors, farmers, there is a larger proportion, in each, of members of the kingdom of God, than in the same number of regularly educated ministers. If we were to form our opinions on this subject alone from the history of the regular orthodox clergy in the time of the Jewish prophets, or in the era of Christ and his apostles, alas! alas! for the regular orthodox divines of this time!

An objector asks, "Must our clergy, then, be ignorant and unlettered men?"—"is ignorance the mother of devotion?" Ignorance is often the mother of enthusiasm or superstition, either of which is, with many, equivalent to devotion. Many of those unlettered divines who are supposed to speak entirely from the Spirit, for every one knows it is not from a fund of knowledge or from literary attainments which they possess, are indeed as evidently without the grace of God as his *holiness* the pope or his *grace* the duke of York. They speak from the spirit, but it is from the spirit of enthusiasm. Enthusiasm is frequently accompanied with a remarkable volubility of speech and pathos of expression. There are none more eloquent or more ungrammatical than the enthusiastic. Indeed, some writers on eloquence of the highest order, say that this kind of eloquence is the creature of enthusiastic ardor. Thousands of ignorant unlettered men, not fettered by the rules of grammar, not circumscribed by the restraints of reason, not controled by the dictates of common sense, nor limited by the written word of God, are nevertheless both fluent, and, though incorrect, eloquent speakers: they are elevated by enthusiasm, and, like the meteors of the night, shine with more resplendence than the real stars. But to answer the above objector I would say, Let us have no clergy at all, learned or unlearned—let us have bishops and deacons, such as Paul appoints, such as he has described 1st *Tim.* iii. 1—14. *Titus* i. 5—9.

But, to resume the young clergyman where we left him, working by the day as a licentiate: he preaches, he travels, he explores "vacant churches," he receives his per diem, his daily compensation. Like a young gentleman in quest of a wife, who visits the "vacant" ladies; forms an acquaintance with the most charming, the best accomplished, until he finds one to whom he can give his heart and hand; the nuptial engagements are formed, and the ceremonies of marriage are completed; he settles down into domestic life and builds up his house. So the young priest, in quest of a "vacant church," forms as extensive an acquaintance as possible with all the unmarried establishments of this character, pays court to the most charming, i. e. the most opulent and honorable, if he be a young gentleman of high standing, until he find one that answers his expectations. A "call" is

presented and accepted. His reverend seniors come to the celebration of his nuptials—with holy hands they consecrate him—he vows to be a faithful teacher of the doctrines of the sect; a loving pastor of the flock, and they vow to be to him a faithful congregation, to support him according to promise, to *love* him for the work's sake, and to be obedient to his authority until God separate them—by death—no, but until he gets another and a louder call from some "vacant church" who falls in love with him, and for whom he is known to possess feelings incompatible with his present married state. Thus he is consecrated a priest for life or good behavior, and then he sets about building up his cause and interest, which is ever afterwards represented and viewed as the cause and interest of Christ. Here we shall leave him for the present.

EDITOR.

On Teaching Christianity.—No. III.

"You are the Christ, the Son of the living God," said Simon, and "you are Stone," replied Jesus to the son of Jonas. Both the speakers were human apparently, and had been introduced to each other by Andrew, on the banks of the Jordan, about the commencement of the Saviour's ministry, when Simon had the name of Stone given to him, &c. To such an acquaintance the introduction of Andrew was sufficient, common civility seldom requiring more on such occasions, than "this is such a one, and this is such another one." Simon, with others, seems to have had no higher views of the Lord Jesus in the first instance, than the popular sect of our own day, called Socinians. Philip expresses these views to Nathaniel, "We have found him of whom Moses in the law and the prophets did write, Jesus of Nazareth, the Son of Joseph." But though Peter in the first instance conceived of him as the son of Joseph, yet afterwards, as is evident, he had his views corrected, and was introduced to him as the son of one infinitely august; not, indeed, by flesh and blood, not by his brother Andrew, but by God the Father. "Blessed are you, Simon, son of Jonas, for flesh and blood has not revealed this to you, but my Father who is in Heaven."— All the Jews regarded Jesus as the son of Joseph. As such, they rejected his pretensions to the Messiahship; and, as such, he was reputed poor and vile by the rich and great of his own nation. If I am not wofully deceived, however, the noblest peculiarity of the christian books consists in their disproving the false conceptions of the Jews on this point, by showing that he was the son of the living God. "*God manifest in the flesh*," is the grand arcanum of christianity —the sublime mystery it divulges to those who are initiated! But I must stop, for this would clash with the paradox of the Socinians, who are both gentlemen and philosophers, and Jews and saints.

I think, and perhaps, too, the reader thinks, that in my last paper it was showed by a series of New Testament quotations, that this peerless fact, that "*Jesus is the Christ*," forms the sole bond of union among the holy brethren, and is also the means through faith for increasing the body of Christ in the earth.

Hence it may be affirmed, without fear of being disproved, that the church of Christ is something essentially different from the popular establishments, that are maintained and increased by money, and their respective ecclesiastical constitutions and confessions. Let

Mammon withhold his support from these schemes and they would instantly be dissolved. The church of Christ, however, is founded on a rock, and its union and fellowship are as indestructible as the eternal and imperishable fact by which it is knit together; yea, it could exist if there were no such things as silver and gold in the world, and, indeed, the church of Jesus is fast passing into a world where there are no such things. A spark of common sense might teach any of us that God and Mammon can have no communion, even in this world; and this circumstance may well teach every person who has large annual contributions to make for the support of clergymen, that the society to which he belongs is not the church of Christ, that society requiring no such support.

But has the Son of God indeed visited our benighted planet? Has the Creator of the ends of the earth really stretched forth a human hand? Has the great God for certainty strode across the stage of this ephemeral existence, and acted so mighty a part? Why then, O Emmanuel! why should we for a moment be in wonder if this matchless truth be made the bond of union among them that believe it! and the fact by which the sinful sons of men are born again into the everlasting kingdom! Reader, have your eyes been opened to this illustrious truth? The scriptures disclose this secret and lift it high above all the other revelations of God. It is the very sun of the spiritual system. Shut your eyes to it, and christianity is a most dark and perplexing scheme. Once behold it, and you behold the most certain and substantial argument for love to God and men. This same Holy One died for sin, and if the knowledge of it fails to influence our hope, and love, and joy, it may safely be said that the scriptures have nothing of equal weight to propose for this purpose. That man is, or is not a christian, who is, or is not constrained by this grand truth to abandon sin and live unto God; and this is all the scriptures mean by the word *gospel* in the noblest sense of that term. This is the grace and philanthropy of God, which, having appeared to all men, teaches us to deny all ungodliness, and to live soberly, righteously, and godly, in the present evil world. The word "gospel," I am bold to say, is a term more abused than any other in our language.

The religious public devoutly reckon a pulpit man to be explaining this term, and to preach the glad tidings of heaven, if he be but deducing some grave spiritual secret from such scraps of Holy Writ as the following—"Naphtali is a hind let loose"—"Ephraim is a cake unturned" —"Remember Lot's wife"—"Judas went and hanged himself"—"We took sweet counsel together," &c. &c. Such texts, "for Antichrist has made the word of God a mere text-book," such texts, I say, may afford the learned, subtle, and seraphic preacher an opportunity of exhibiting his own pretty talents before a polite and fashionable assembly; but they were never written by the Holy Spirit to establish the gospel fact, but for quite a different purpose; and the dry heathenish harangues spun from them are as dissimilar from the grand, certain, and divine evangelical narration, as the fabulous cosmogony of Epicurus is from the Mosaic history of the creation. In the mouth of the popular preachers, the gospel is quite a fugitive thing—rapid, flitting, retiring, uncertain—it eludes the grasp of the most expert and attentive hearer; accordingly few or none of all who attend the heptdomidal levees of these spiritual courtiers, can ever tell, in precise terms, what the gospel of the New Testament means. I have heard of several pious presbyterians who would not accept of an excellent property in the western country, because they could not think of leaving the gospel; so that the bible, which records the gospel, was to them a mere plaything of their preachers. *Apropos:* Two popular christians have this moment called to quarrel with me for saying, in my last paper, that the peerless gospel fact is the sole bond of union among the holy children; and that the testimony of the Father, Son, and Holy Spirit for this fact is recorded in the four evangelists. These two gentlemen will probably see this paper, and I here appeal to them whether the drift of their conversation with me was not to show that the writings of the evangelists were intended for the Jews only, and that the Gentiles had no need of these four books to support the grand fact that Jesus is the Son of the living God.

The gospel is a question of fact. Is Jesus the Son of the living God, or is he not? If it is false, the popular preachers cannot make it true —if it is true, the four evangelists have the honor of recording the evidence for its truth; and this brings us at once to their writings. Let us look at the circumstance of this fact as found in Matthew, Luke, &c. and we shall at once see whether any thing the pulpit men can strip from texts like those quoted above, can afford the shadow of an opportunity for preaching, i. e. proving that Jesus is the Christ. The evangelists tell us that this same personage was born in a stable, of a poor, but a religious female, at a moment, too, when she seems to have been exhausted by a long and fatiguing journey; accordingly, he was cradled in a manger, until the king of the country getting intelligence of his birth, obliged his guardians to seek for safety in a flight by night to Egypt. On his return misfortune still seemed to pursue him, and the family were compelled to pass their native canton and to seek a wretched security in Zabulon. At the age of thirty, he preferred his claims to the Messiahship, i. e. to be the Son of the living God. His pretensions were instantly rejected, and his fellow citizens *en masse* conspired against him, and drove him from the city. From this time he lived a wandering life, without a place to repose his head. His own tribe did not receive him; his own brethren disbelieved him; the people who heard him, pronounced him mad; and the priests who argued with him, and who are never behind in reprehending the good, declared him possessed. He more than twice escaped being stoned, and was actually scourged publicly. He was a known friend to sinners; and so excessively poor, that when he wanted to see Cæsar's head he had to ask for a penny. Thus he lived, insulted and abused, until an intimate acquaintance of his own betrayed him for the paltry sum of thirty shillings. When he was seized in a garden by a banditti of soldiers in the dark, and accused by many of seditions and blasphemy before the national senate, the petty officer of that court smote him on the cheek, and when afterwards brought before the Roman tribunal, it was only to receive the same contumely afresh. They dressed him like a puppet, spit in his face, and struck him with the palms of their hands. He was adjudged to be crucified, and departed for the place of execution bearing his own cross. He was immediately nailed to it, and the malicious clergymen continued to persecute him with their pious scoffs, until, as if the world was in danger while the enemy to their power was alive, they sent a ruffian soldier to pierce his side with a spear. But these doctors of divinity shall look on him whom they pierced. Thus he lived without a place to repose his head in life; and thus he died, without a grave to hide his murdered form in death. Now all this is intended to humble us in the dust. And it is the history of one pretending to be the Son of Almighty God; and to believe him to be the Son of God, is to believe the gospel; and to preach the gospel, is to show by the writings of the evangelists that this same suffering was all voluntary, and that he was the only begotten Son of God. But the writings of Matthew, &c. bear no resemblance to a popular preacher's gospel, which, too generally, is little better than a song of logic or metaphysics.

Dear Lord, when I reflect that I have spent twenty years of my life under the noisy verbosity of a Presbyterian clergyman, without receiving the least degree of light from the holy word of God; when I see others led the same dark dance by the same blind leaders, I am prompted to address myself to the bishops and deacons of the church of Christ. Brethren, you are not numerous in N. America, and you see the religion of our Lord and Saviour is still in the hands of schoolmen—boys brought from colleges and sworn to maintain schemes that maintain them; as I suppose you to have adopted no system, permit me therefore to beseech you by your affection for the flock of God, by that great mystery which holds it together, by that dear name Jesus, by your fear of death and hope of life, by your bowels of love for a perishing world, throw wide open the boards of the bible, and abandon the popular scheme of teaching our holy religion by scraps. O Jesus! let me ever lay hold of you through the medium of the bible, your holy word which defies all extrinsic ornament, and is the faithful compass which ever points to heaven. Your pretended preachers have abandoned the holy commandment; they have adopted worldly schemes; they have usurped your authority, and turned the people's ears away to fables. They have no guide. Methinks I see afar, tossed upon the billows of the never sleeping Atlantic, a slender bark; the treacherous breezes have seduced her from the shore; the pilot, unable to retrace his course, stands upon the poop, and in an agony of fearful anticipation, gazes on the wide and pathless ocean: around him the bewildered crew are seized with pale affright. But why this distraction—why this horror and dismay? An angel whispers me they have no compass; and already the winds are up, the sky lowers, and no friendly star appears to point them to their much loved port. How gladly would they hie them away, but they have seen the spirit of the storm to flit athwart the heavens, and the rush of waters is in every soul. At last the tempest, the whole heaven descends, and the unbefriended bark sinks amid the tumult of conflicting waters. The mystery of this is manifest; the popular assemblies are without the bible; and may be divided generally into the superstitious, the unintelligently devout, the enthusiastic, and the philosophic or Socinian.

Now, reader, in preaching the gospel or in arguing for the truth of this illustrious fact, that Jesus is indeed the Lord of heaven, do you think that, upon the whole, it is common among the pulpit men to argue from the same topics from which the Lord himself argued? After reading the above sketch of the life of Jesus, perhaps you may think that there is no topic from which any probable argument can be drawn in support of his claims. You will probably say, what in

the world can a preacher have to say in proof of this, for all human testimony seems to be in array against it? You will ask, what has he to oppose to the decisions of a Roman judicature, so famed for the inflexibility of its justice? What mighty argument to counterbalance the adjudication of the Jewish sanhedrim, the most ancient and most authoritative council that ever sat? And if it could be shown that these erred in condemning him, how is he to obviate the difficulty about the priest and the people who thought him a madman, and the testimony of his brethren who discredited him and his fellow-citizens? &c. &c. Dear reader, the modern preachers of christianity could prove any thing if you only give them a pulpit, on the terms, that not a soul of all who listen shall have the right of questioning a single word they say; accordingly they will preach up the cross and the gospel from any text between Genesis and Revelations. The two popular christians, above alluded to, averred that the gospel could be preached at any time in five minutes; yet our Lord on his plan taught only very few, though he preached for three years, and his followers had all the glory of the miraculous evidence laid right before them. It took the Bereans two whole years before they could decide upon the reality of the report. But popular preachers can teach this truth, and nobody, even the taught, can tell how. This fact, by which we are saved, is nevertheless greatly proved; the testimony, the united testimony of the Father, Son, and Holy Spirit has set it to rest; and though Jews and antichristian preachers have done all in their power to disprove and obscure it, yet we are all taught by God, and he that receives his testimony sets to his seal that God is true.   PHILIP.

Address to the readers of the Christian Baptist. No. II.

It is presumable, that some of you, my friends, read this paper with a prejudiced mind. If this were not the case, it would be, to us, matter of astonishment. Good men have their prejudices as well as others. Nathaniel, an Israelite indeed, in whom there was no guile, was so prejudiced, that when Philip told him that "he had found him, of whom Moses in the law and the prophets did write, Jesus of Nazareth the son of Joseph," he said, "Can any good thing come out of Nazareth!" To our prejudiced readers we would say, as Philip said to Nathaniel, "Come and see." Come and search the scriptures, and see whether these things are so; whether the popular schemes, or what we oppose to them, is founded on the divine word. This is all the favor we ask of you; and neither your candor, your honor, nor your interest will allow you to do otherwise. Philip said, come see this Jesus, this son of Joseph, and judge for yourself. He came, and saw, and heard. From a very short acquaintance, he received this Jesus, not as the son of Joseph, as Philip had designated him; but he received him as the Son of God. He, convinced from his interview, exclaims, "Rabbi, you are the Son of God, you are the King of Israel."

The apostles themselves were long under the dominion of prejudice concerning Messiah's death, resurrection and kingdom. The teaching of the scribes, and the traditions of the elders; the popular notions of the times bewildered them. When plainly informed of his death, Peter exclaims, "That be far from you, Lord, it shall not be so done to you." When they were told of his resurrection from the dead by those to whom he appeared alive, "they were astonished," and the words of their informants "appeared unto them as idle tales, and they believed them not." Of his reign and kingdom they had no correct ideas until Pentecost. Till that day they looked for temporal rule and dominion to be given to Israel according to the flesh. They expected Messiah's kingdom to be a continuation of the old Jewish, enlarged and improved. The citizens of Berea are represented by the inspired Luke as more noble than the citizens of Thessalonica. And why? Because they heard the word with all readiness of mind, and "searched the scriptures daily whether these things were so." My friends, be thus noble, and go and do likewise. Perhaps the consequence may be similar to the history of the Bereans, marked with an emphatic *therefore*: "THEREFORE, many of them believed."

"Good has been often called evil, and evil good. Truth has been piously called error, and error truth. Pure religion has frequently been called heresy, and heresy pure religion. Paul had to confess that he worshipped God in the way which the populars called heresy. So we frankly confess, that some of our views have been by the populars called heretical and blasphemous. Because we have said, that we christians are not under Moses, but under Christ; not under the law as a rule of life, but under the gospel, we are said to have spoken "blasphemous words against Moses and the law." Because we have said that the Jewish sabbath is no more, we are represented as without religion, profane and impious; and, because we have called much of what is called *warm* preaching, and warm feelings, and great revivals, enthusiasm; we are said to deny "experimental religion" or the influence of the Holy Spirit, by the word, upon the minds of believers. "Yes," say our enemies, "you deny the moral law, the christian Sabbath and experimental religion."

To the first of these charges we shall, in the present address, call your attention, reserving the others for a future day.

The "moral law," or decalogue, is usually plead as the rule of life to believers in Christ, and it is said that it ought to be preached "as a means of conviction of sin." The scriptures never divide the law of Moses into moral, ceremonial, and judicial. This is the work of schoolmen, who have also divided the invisible world into heaven, hell, and purgatory; who have divided the obedience of Christ into active, passive, and both; who have divided the members of the church into speechless babes, seekers of religion and regenerated saints; who have divided the kingdom of heaven, or christian kingdom, into clergy, ruling elders, and laity; and who have philosophized, allegorized, and mysticized christianity into an incomprehensible and ineffable jargon of christianized paganism and judaism.

We published, seven years ago, a speech pronounced to an association on this subject, in which we objected to this division of the law; the substance of which, if we recollect right, was this: we objected to this division of the law, First, because it was unauthorized by either the Old or New Testament, i. e. neither God by Moses, his Son Jesus Christ, nor his apostles, had ever made such a division. They always spoke of the law as one grand whole. "The law was given by Moses, but the grace and the truth by Jesus Christ." "The law and the prophets continued until John the Baptist." "You are not under the law," &c. &c. Here is no moral, ceremonial or judicial law, but "the law." Secondly, because this division of the law perplexes the mind of a student of the bible, who, while he meets the words "the law," is puzzled to know which of the three is meant; whereas, if he would always view the phrase "the law," when not otherwise defined, as the one and undivided law of Moses, he would never be perplexed. Because, in the third place, this division is illogical or incorrect, as respects the moral and judicial laws. All writers and speakers we have either heard or seen, blend, in their expositions, moral and judicial precepts, making the latter as moral as the former. They have no palpable or distinguishable criteria of distinction. Because, in the fourth place, they represent the ten commands as the moral law: whereas they tell us that the law contained two tables: the former teaching religion, or our duty to God; the second teaching morality, or our duty to our neighbor. This moral law, then, is both moral and religious; for these same divines distinguish religion and morality. In the fifth place, because one precept of this moral law was as ceremonial as any item in their ceremonial law, viz: the fourth commandment. For these reasons and others, we objected then to this division of the law. We have never heard any thing said, though much has been said on that subject, of the least weight to change our views delivered at that time.

But, without going further into the detail on this part of the subject, we proceed to observe, that Moses, the great lawgiver to the Jews, delivered this law as a rule of life to the Jews only; and it was all equally important to them, and binding upon them. It was all holy, just, and good, as respected its design; and was equally divine and authoritative. He that touched the ark died the death, as well as he who stole the golden wedge. He that offered strange fire upon the altar was consumed, as well as he that cursed his father. He that gathered fuel on the Sabbath, and he that blasphemed the God of Israel, were devoted to the same destruction. But the law of Moses was given for a limited time. The world was about twenty-five hundred years old before it was given; "for until the law sin was in the world," and this law was designed only to continue till the promised seed should come, the great Lawgiver. Moses pointed Israel to this great Lawgiver. Malachi told the Jews to remember this law until Elias should come. The Messiah said plainly, "that the law and the prophets preached till John." But, "since that time, the kingdom of God was preached." Paul repeatedly affirms that christians are not under the law, but under the gospel, as a rule of life. In teaching the Jews he compared the law to a school-master until Christ came; but since faith or Christ came, he assured them they were no longer under the school-master. He declared they "were delivered from the law"—"they were free from it"—"they were dead to it." He says, "it is done away"—"it is abolished"—"it is disannulled."

Moses had a brother of great dignity, of illustrious fame, whose name was Aaron. This brother of the lawgiver was divinely ordained a high priest, and divine laws ordained concerning him and his successors. In process of time the son of Jesse was crowned king over Israel, under God, who still retained the sovereignty. Concerning this David and his successors divine laws were published. Israel were under Moses as a lawgiver, under Aaron as high priest, under

David as king. These three were types of Christ as lawgiver, priest, and king. Now the populars and we agree in one grand point on this topic. They say that "Jesus Christ is our only prophet, priest, and king." To this we cordially and fully agree. Therefore, we will not submit to Moses as our prophet or lawgiver, to Aaron as our high priest, to David as our king. If we would yield to Moses as our lawgiver, we would yield to his brother Aaron as our high priest, and to the son of Jesse as our king. We honor Moses, Aaron, and David. We study their history, their offices, and their deeds. We revere them as Messiah's types. We will treat them with every due respect; but will not put ourselves under them. While we acknowledge Jesus to be the great lawgiver, the great prophet, the great high priest, David's son, and David's king, we are assured that every part of Moses' law worthy of our regard has been republished and reenacted under more glorious circumstances and with more illustrious sanctions by him—that every item of Aaron's priesthood has been fulfilled by him—that every excellent trait in the character and government of David has been exhibited by him, free from imbecility and imperfection. Messiah, you are my only prophet, priest, and king; for you are worthy!

"Then," say the populars, "you have no moral law as a rule of life—no preaching of the law as a means of conviction of sin; you may live as you list—your doctrine is licentious—it is antinomian—it is dangerous to morals—to piety —to all good."

Blessed Jesus! are you thus insulted by pretended friends? Are your laws an inadequate rule of life? Guided by your statutes, will our lives be licentious, our morals loose, ourselves abandoned to all crime? Was Moses a more consummate lawgiver than you? Did his commandments more fully or more clearly exhibit the moral, the godly course of life, than yours? Were the sanctions of his law of more solemn import, of more restraining authority, than your precepts? Is there no means of conviction of sin, of its evil and demerit, in your doctrine, manner of life, or in your death? What argument, what inducement, to cease to do evil and to learn to do well, in all the laws of Moses, in all the statutes of Israel, in all the examples of patriarchs, saints, and martyrs, speaks such language, exhibits such motives, conciliates such regard, denounces such vengeance, attracts so much reverence, inspires with so much awe, wins by so much goodness, and reconciles with so much power, as your death? That heart, O Lord! that feels not the force of this argument, this omnipotent argument, to cease to do evil and to learn to do well, in vain will be assailed by moral suasion or by moral law. The thunders of Sinai—the flashing fluid of unmeasured force—the rending echoes of the celestial trumpet—the nodding summit—the crashing rocks— and the trembling base of the smoking mount, veiled in the blackest darkness, cannot constrain nor allure it to righteousness, humanity, and the love of God. Philosophy, marching forth in all her imaginary strength, clad in all her fancied charms, is perfect impotence compared to your doctrine. The example of patriarchs, of prophets, of saints, and martyrs, from Abel to Noah, from Abraham to David, from David to John the Baptist, is inefficacious compared with yours. Moses and his fiery law, his statutes and his judgments, as the body without the spirit is dead, are lifeless and inoperative compared with your new commandment, your piercing law, animated and quickened by your life, confirmed and sanctioned by your death. No; the statutes and ordinances commanded in Horeb, the meekness of Moses, the patience of Job, the zeal of Elijah, the piety of Daniel, the pathos of David, and the wisdom of Solomon, will not, cannot illumine that understanding, captivate those affections, purify those desires, purge those motives, subdue those lusts, which your doctrine, your example, your law, your love, your sufferings, your death, your resurrection, your exaltation, fail to accomplish. But did your character, your doctrine, your life, your death, your resurrection and your exaltation ever fail, when fully apprehended, ever fail to purify, to renovate, to reform? No! never! never! Who can know you and not love righteousness, and not hate iniquity? When the dying thief, in his day, saw your character and heard your fame, he entrusted his soul to you, and preached righteousness to his companion. When the persecuting Saul saw you, O Saviour of the world! enthroned in glory—when he heard your winning voice, he fell beneath the rays of your majesty, and from a lion put on the meekness of the lamb.

Yet having your New Testament, ratified by your blood, are we without a rule of life? are we authorized to live as we list? The thought is impious! O Sun of Righteousness! your salutiferous rays were long expected to enlighten, to cheer, and to quicken those sitting in darkness, in the region and shadow of death. Yet you have risen, and more glory shines from the clouded face of Moses than from yours!! Great Lawgiver, the Gentiles long waited for your law, and have you left them without law, to live as they list? Moses and Elias waited on you on the holy mount—they laid their honors and their commission at your feet. When they ascended to the skies, your Father's voice commanded your disciples to hear your law, to yield exclusively to you—and shall we not? Forbid it Heaven!

Lord Jesus, may your character open to our view as depicted in your doctrine, your miracles, your sufferings, your death, your resurrection, and your glory; and then we shall not fear to put ourselves exclusively under you, as our lawgiver, our prophet, our priest, and our king!

EDITOR.

The conversion of the world.

MAN has been often considered as a creature of circumstances. Diversified by climate, by language, by religion, by morals, by habit, he presents a most varied aspect to the contemplative mind. Betwixt "the frozen Icelander and the sun-burned Moor," the wandering Indian and the polished cit, the untutored savage and the sage philosopher, the superstitious pagan and the intelligent christian, what a difference! To the sceptic reasoner the human race presents an insoluble enigma. The questions, what am I? whence came I? and whither do I go? are questions which philosophy in its boasted powers, deism in its bold excursions, infidelity in its daring enterprizes, attempts in vain. The bible alone answers them with satisfaction and certainty. To the disbeliever of it the world has neither beginning, middle, nor end. The sceptic feels himself a speck of matter, floating down the stream of time into a region of impenetrable darkness, alike ignorant of his origin and his destiny. Whether there is in him a spark of immortality, or whether he is all annihilated in the grave, are, to him, things unknown and unknowable. The reptile, encased in its kindred shell, the oyster clinging to its native rock, could as easily calculate the rapidity of the particles of light, or measure, by its powers, the orbit of a comet, as the most gigantic genius, by its own vigor, unaided by the bible, could prove that there is a God, that there was a creation, that there is an immortal spirit in man, or that there will be an end of this mundane state of things. We know what deism, philosophy, and natural religion arrogate to themselves: but their pretensions are as vain as their efforts to give assured hope are impotent and unavailing. Deism steals from the bible the being of a God, the immortality of the soul, the future state of rewards, and shutting the volume of light, impudently arrogates to itself that it has originated those ideas from its own ingenerate sagacity. But we are insensibly falling into a disquisition foreign to our present purpose.

The world, as respects religion, is divided into four grand divisions—the Pagan, the Mahometan, the Jewish, and the Christian. In the first of these there are some fragments of divine revelation mutilated and corrupted. The knowledge of God once communicated to Noah, was transmitted to his descendants; and although many of them were never favored with any other revelation than that committed to him; and although that revelation was vitiated and corrupted with thousands of the wildest fancies and most absurd notions, yet it never has been completely lost. Hence the most ignorant savages have some idea of a God, and offer him some kind of worship. They endeavor to propitiate him by sacrifice, and consider themselves under some kind of moral obligation to one another. They view certain actions as pleasing, and others as displeasing to him.

The Jewish religion, though once enjoined by divine authority, as exhibited in the Old Testament, has, by the same authority, been set aside as having answered its design. In the best form in which it could now appear on earth, it would be as dry and useless as a shell when the kernel is extracted. The good things once in it are no longer to be found; and, as corrupted by the modern Jews, it is quite another religion than that instituted by Moses. There is no salvation in it.

The Mahometan religion recognizes three hundred and thirteen apostles, of whom six brought in new dispensations, viz. Adam, Noah, Abraham, Moses, Jesus, and Mahomet. The last vacated or rendered obsolete all the preceding. It consequently contains many items of divine revelation; but these are like the fragments of revelation found in the pagan establishments, so perverted as to be darkness instead of light. The Mahometans have, like the modern christians, their different sects, their orthodox and heterodox teachers and opinions.

The "christian nations" have the bible, but many of them have, like the Jews, rendered it of little or no effect by their traditions. Dividing the whole family of man into thirty parts, five parts are professed Christians; six parts are Mahometans and Jews; and nineteen parts Pagans. This is the mournful state of the world according to the most correct statements. Add the Mahometans, Jews, and Pagans together, and they amount to twenty-five thirtieths of the whole human race. So that but one-sixth of Adam's offspring possess, and but few of these enjoy, the revelation of God.

F

To what is this doleful state of the world attributable is a question that deserves the attention of every christian. If there were no hereafter, the temporal wretchedness of ignorance and superstition presents an object that must awaken the sympathies of every benevolent mind. And if there be a hereafter, and if future happiness were attainable to those immersed in pagan and Mahometan gloom, wretchedness, and crime, still the amelioration of their earthly condition, the rational and christian enjoyment of this present life are objects of such vast importance as to excite all that is within us to consider whether those possessing the light of heaven are, in any sense, chargeable with the crimes and miseries of the heathen world.

If, as some affirm, every man is accountable not only for what he has done, but for what he might have done, the question would not be of difficult determination. But as we would wish to see this point established on more solid and convincing ground than abstruse speculations, we shall appeal to the New Testament. The Saviour of the world charged the scribes and pharisees of that age with having "shut up the kingdom of heaven against men," with having "neither gone in themselves, nor suffered those that were entering to go in." He charged the lawyers or doctors of divinity with having taken away the key of knowledge from the people. The apostle Paul taught the christians that it was possible for them so to walk as to give occasion to the adversaries of their cause to speak reproachfully of it and them; that they might so walk as that the name of God, of Jesus, and his doctrine might be blasphemed. And Peter declared that, in consequence of false teachers and disciples, "the way of truth should be evil spoken of." He also teaches that christians may so conduct themselves as that those who behold their conduct may be allured to the belief of the gospel. [See *Matt.* xxiii. 13., *Luke* xi. 52., 1st *Tim.* v. 14. vi. 1., 1st *Pet.* iii. 1., 2d *Pet.* ii. 1, 2.] Those records show that professed disciples may, both by omitting to do their duty, and by committing faults, prevent and greatly retard the spread of the gospel, the enlargement of Messiah's kingdom. We are convinced that the character of the "christian communities" is the greatest offence or stumbling block in the way of the conversion of the world. And that therefore the only hopeful course to convert the world is to reform the professors of christianity.

But what kind of a reformation is requisite to this end? It is not the erection of a new sect, the inventing of new *shibboleths*, or the setting up of a new creed, nor the adopting of any in existence save the New Testament, in the form in which it pleased the Spirit of God to give it. It is to receive it as it stands, and to make it its own interpreter, according to the ordinary rules of interpreting all books. It is not to go back to primitive Calvinism, or primitive Methodism, or primitive Lutherism, but to primitive Christianity. The history of the church for many centuries has proved, the history of every sect convinces us, that it is as impossible for any one sect to gain such an ascendance as to embrace as converts the others, and thus unite in one grand phalanx the christians against the allied powers of darkness, as it is to create a world. Every sect, with a human creed, carries in it, as the human body, the seeds of its own mortality. Every sect has its infancy, its childhood, its manhood, and its dotage. Some die as soon as they are born, and others live to a good old age, but their old age is full of grief and trouble. And die they must. As it is appointed unto all men once to die, and after that the judgment, so it is ordained by God that all sects must die, and that because their bond of union is under the curse. Where are the hundreds of sects that have already existed? They only live in history as beacons to posterity.

It need not be objected that some sects have already taken the New Testament and run into the wildest extremes; for either they interpreted it according to the reveries of Swedenburg, the fanaticism of Shakerism, or the enthusiasm of New Lightism, or they apostatized from a good profession. Recollect, we say, that the scriptures are to be their own interpreter, according to the common rules of interpreting other writings.

Christians, as you honor the Saviour and the Father that sent him; as you love the peace and prosperity of the kingdom of the Holy One; as you love the souls of your children, your relatives, your fellow-citizens; as you deeply deplore the reign of darkness, of paganism, of horrid cruelty over such multitudes of human beings; as you desire and pray for the salvation of the world, the downfall of Antichrist, of Mahometan delusion, of Jewish infidelity, of pagan superstition;—return, return to the religion of our common Lord, as delivered unto us by his holy apostles! Model your churches after the primitive model, erected under the agency of the Holy Spirit—and then the churches of the saints will have rest and will be edified, "and walking in the fear of the Lord and in the comfort of the Holy Spirit, they will be multiplied" with accessions until all flesh shall see the salvation of our God.   EDITOR.

THE first Baptist church in America was founded at Providence in 1639. Their sentiments spreading into Massachusetts, in 1651, the general court passed a law against them, inflicting banishment for persisting in the promulgation of their doctrines. In 1656, Quakers making their appearance in Massachusetts, the legislature of that colony passed several laws against them. No master of a vessel was allowed to bring any one of this sect into its jurisdiction on penalty of £100. Other still severer penalties were inflicted upon them in 1657, such as cutting their ears and boring their tongues with a red hot iron. They were at length banished on pain of death; and four, refusing to go, were executed in 1656.

[Plain Truth.

No. 7.]   FEBRUARY 2, 1824.

The Clergy—No. V.

WE left the young clergyman in the arms of his lately espoused congregation, living upon the dowry of his spiritual consort; duly trained, divinely consecrated, formally wedded, and actively employed in building up the cause of God, in which his own cause is deeply interested. Here again we find him, and hear him teaching that "they that preach the gospel should live by the gospel." With great eloquence he remonstrates against "muzzling the ox that treads out the corn;" and with zeal for justice and righteousness, he exclaims, "the laborer is worthy of his hire." That his congregation may not consider themselves doing him a favor when they pay him five hundred or a thousand a year, he argues with great pathos:

"Our debtors you are, for if we impart to you our spiritual things, it is a matter of poor return if you impart to us your carnal things."

Indeed, money is of vital consequence in the kingdom of the clergy. Without it a clergyman could not be made, nor a congregation supplied with a "faithful pastor." O Mammon, you wonder-working god! well did Milton sing of thee—

There stood a hill not far, whose grisly top
Belch'd fire and rolling smoke; the rest entire
Shone with a glossy scurf, undoubted sign
That in his womb was hid metallic ore,
The work of sulphur. Thither wing'd with speed
A numerous brigade hasten'd; as when bands
Of pioneers, with spade and pickaxe arm'd,
Forerun the royal camp to trench a field
Or cast a rampart. Mammon led them on;
Mammon, the least erected spirit that fell
From heaven; for e'en in heav'n his looks and thoughts
Were always downward bent, admiring more
The riches of heav'n's pavement, trodden gold,
Than aught divine or holy else enjoyed
In vision beatific: by him first
Men also, and by his suggestion taught,
Ransack'd the centre, and with impious hands
Rifled the bowels of their mother earth
For treasures better hid. Soon had his crew
Open'd into the hill a spacious wound,
And digg'd out ribs of gold. Let none admire
That riches grow in hell; that soil may best
Deserve the precious bane.
Mammon thus speaks—
          ——This desert soil
Wants not her hidden lustre, gems and gold;
Nor want we skill or art from whence to raise
Magnificence; and what can heaven show more?

Yes, Mammon, you have "skill" and "art," and treasure. You lead the stripling to the grammar school, and for years you give him skill, and art, and science; and when you have fed and clothed, and educated him with books and pedagogues, you teach him divinity, and crown him master of every art, and, chief of all, the art of winning you. God of this world, who is insensible to your charms! Your brilliant countenance sheds a charming lustre on every thing! You distil into the souls of priests and people an animating sweetness, and when every other "call" is disregarded, your voice wakens into ecstacy, zeal, and piety, the slumbering ear—it wakes obsequious to your nod.

Money is the bond of union, the associating principle in all popular establishments. There is a "christian congregation." I think it is christened Associate Reformed, or, perhaps, Episcopalian, or General Assembly, or some other name. It has not met for three months. Why? It is "vacant." What do you mean by "vacant?" It has not the bread of life broken to it by a faithful pastor. Why? It is "weak"— not able to hire a pastor. It is not able to pay "supplies." Whenever they can "raise" four or six dollars, this sum brings them all together, and a faithful pastor with his mouth full of the bread of life. The little flock sit sweetly entertained under the "droppings of the sanctuary" for a few hours. He bids them God speed. They go home, and in the course of some time a similar sum brings them together a second time. May be they get so "strong" as to be a sixth or a fourth part of the "support" of one of "the watchmen of Zion." He is half his time in one congregation, a fourth in another, and a fourth in a third. Three churches, one pastor— one husband, three wives! Married to the three! To one congregation he gives half his time and half his divinity, and receives half his living, half his stipends for it. To the other two, share and share alike, because they are alike weak. Thus the strong becomes stronger, and the weak, weaker. Now who is so blind as not to see that money is the cause of this mystery. It is another proof of the old text, "no pay, no preach."

But let us look at this matter again. A young gentleman of fine talents comes forward; and from the same "divinity school" another one of slender talents, but he is "a well meaning man," a pious soul, humble and plain. They both push their fortune. The one is placed on the frontiers over a charge of three hundred dollars; the other in the city over a charge of two thousand. What is the cause of this mystery? Another text explains it. It is found in the chronicles of the British parliament. It reads thus: "every man has his price." Yes, and every congregation has its own taste. A wealthy and a polite congregation sits very uneasy under the pious efforts of a homespun, coarse, and awkward mechanic. His sing-song monotony, and sawing gesticulation, animated by the zeal of Elijah, freezes the genial current of their souls. It will not do. He tries it again. The pews are empty. Worse than ever. To the west he goes. In the wilderness he is like John the Baptist. His disgusting elocution, his awkward figure, and his frightful gestures, are all unsullied sanctity, unfeigned devotion. The rural saint is full of his praise. Of his whole performance and appearance he says—

> Behold the picture! Is it like? Like whom?
> The things that mount the rostrum with a skip,
> And then skip down again; pronounce a text;
> Cry hem! and, reading what they never wrote,
> Just thirty minutes, huddle up their work,
> And with a well-bred whisper close the scene.—*Cowper.*

The young divine of fine talents is admired, is adored, where his class-mate would not be heard; not because of his supposed want of piety, but his want of talent and politeness. But when the fashionable orator places himself in the pulpit, the house is crowded, the galleries are full.

> Forth comes the pocket-mirror. First he strokes
> An eyebrow; composes next a straggling lock;
> Then, with an air most gracefully performed,
> Falls back into his seat, extends an arm,
> And lays it at his ease with gentle care,
> With handkerchief in hand depending low.
> The better hand, more busy, gives the nose
> Its bergamot, or aids the indebted eye
> With opera glass, to watch the moving scene,
> And recognize the slow-retiring fair.—*Cowper.*

And yet, with all his reputed talents, he is often a mere retailer, a mere reader:

> He grinds divinity of other days
> Down into modern use; transforms old print
> To zigzag manuscript, and cheats the eyes
> Of gallery critics by a thousand arts.—*Cowper.*

Money, I think, may be considered not merely as the bond of union in popular establishments, but it is really the rock on which the popular churches are built. Before church union is proposed, the grand point to ascertain is, are we able to support a church? Before we give a call, let us see, says the prudent saint, what we can "make up." A meeting is called—the question is put, "how much will you give?" It goes round. Each man writes his name or makes his mark. A handsome sum is subscribed. A petition is sometimes presented to the legislature for an act of incorporation to confirm their union and to empower them to raise by the civil law, or the arm of power, the stipulated sum. All is now secure. The church is founded upon this rock. It goes into operation. The parson comes. Their social prayers, praises, sacraments, sermons and fasts commence; every thing is put into requisition. But what was the *primum mobile?* What the mov-

ing cause? Money. As proof of this, let the congregation decrease by emigration or death; the money fails; the parson takes a missionary tour; he obtains a louder call; he removes. Money failed is the cause; and when this current freezes, social prayers, praises, "sacraments," sermons, and congregational fasts all cease. Money, the foundation, is destroyed, and down comes the superstructure raised upon it. Reader, is not this fact? And dare you say that money is not the basis of the modern religious establishments? It begins with money; it goes on with money, and it ends when money fails. Money buys Æsop's fables for the destined priest; money consecrates him to office, and a moneyed contract unites him and his parish. The church of Jesus Christ is founded upon another basis, nourished by other means, is not dissolved by such causes, and will survive all the mines of Peru, all the gold of Ophir. The modern clergy say they do not preach for money. Very well; let the people pay them none, and they will have as much of their preaching still. Besides, there will be no suspicion of their veracity.   EDITOR.

Address to the Readers of the Christian Baptist.
No. III.

THE subject of our present address is the sabbath day and the Lord's day. Either christians are bound to observe the sabbath day, or they are not. If they are, let us see what the nature of that observance is, which was prescribed for the sabbath day. The law reads thus: "Remember the sabbath day, to keep it holy. Six days shall you labor and do *all* your work: the seventh day is the sabbath of the Lord your God: In it you shall not do *any work*, you, nor your son, nor your daughter, nor your man servant, nor your maid servant, nor your cattle, nor the stranger that is within your gates. For in six days the Lord made heaven and earth, the sea and all that is in them, and rested the seventh day; wherefore the Lord blessed the sabbath day and hallowed it." You will observe that, in this command, God positively prohibits all manner of work or labor on this day. Son, daughter, servant, cattle, stranger, are commanded to be exempted from all manner of work. In examining the particular precepts originating from this law, recorded in the Old Testament, we find the following specifications:—

1. "You shall kindle no fire throughout your habitations on the sabbath day." *Ex.* xxxv. 3.

2. "Abide you every man in his place, (house or tent;) let no man go out of his place, (house or tent,) on the sabbath day. *Ex.* xvi. 29.

3. "He gives you on the sixth day the bread of two days. Bake that which you will bake this day, and seethe what you will seethe, and that which remains over, lay up for you to be kept until the morning." *Ex.* xvi. 29. 23.

4. "Bear no burden on the sabbath day, nor bring it in by the gates of Jerusalem; neither carry forth a burden out of your houses on the sabbath day." *Jer.* xvii. 21. 22.

5. "Not doing your own ways, nor finding your own pleasure, nor speaking your own words." *Is.* lxii. 13.

6. "From evening unto evening shall you celebrate your sabbath." *Lev.* xxiii. 32.

7. "Whoever does any work on the sabbath day, he shall surely be put to death. Every one that defiles it shall surely be put to death." *Ex.* xxxi. 14. 15.

"And while the children of Israel were in the wilderness, they found a man that gathered sticks upon the sabbath day. And they that found him gathering sticks brought him to Moses and Aaron, and to all the congregation. And they put him in ward, because it was not declared what should be done to him. And the Lord said unto Moses, The man shall be surely put to death; all the congregation shall stone him with stones without the camp. And all the congregation brought him without the camp, and stoned him with stones, and he died, as the Lord commanded Moses." *Numbers*, xv. 32—36.

The above items are a few of many that might be selected out of the Old Testament on this subject. We believe them to be a fair specimen of the law given by Moses, as explained and enforced upon the nation of Israel.

Now the question is, are we under this law? If we are, we pay little or no respect to it. For who is there that does not *habitually* violate *the rest* enjoined on this day? Those who make the most ado about sabbath breakers are themselves, according to the above law, worthy of death. They kindle fire in their houses. They go out of their houses, and travel on their cattle miles. Their sons and their daughters do some kind of work. They bring in burdens of water, wood, and prepare food. They celebrate it not from evening to evening, but from morning to evening they violate it. They speak their own words, and do many things worthy of death. Why then is not the penalty enforced? Assuredly their observance of this law is mere mockery. It is an insult on the Lawgiver!

We know that some of the clergy have given, if not sold them indulgences to violate it. They have told them that certain "works of necessity and mercy" are allowable. But who told *them* so? They tell them they may prepare food, bring in fuel and water. But God forbade those under this law to do so. So far was he from countenancing such "works of necessity," that he wrought three miracles to prevent the necessity of doing a "work of necessity." He sent two days' portion of manna from heaven the sixth day; he sent none the seventh; he preserved that gathered on the sixth from putrefaction until the close of the seventh: all of which were special miracles for the space of forty years. If he wrought *three miracles* to prevent an Israelite from crossing his threshold to gather up a little manna for his daily food, how dare any give a dispensation, in his name, to do that which is tenfold more laborious!!!

Because the Saviour of the world put to silence those who accused him of breaking the sabbath, by appealing to their own conduct in relieving animals in distress, this doctrine of "works of necessity and mercy," has been represented as of divine origin. What a perversion! An *argumentum ad hominem* converted into a general maxim!! But such a perversion shows consummate inattention to the laws of Israel. While Israel kept the law there never would occur an opportunity for a work of necessity or of mercy, such as these lawgivers tolerate. For while they kept the law, they should be blessed in their basket, stores, fields, houses, children, flocks, herds; no house would take fire; no ox would fall into a pit, &c. And if they transgressed the law, they should be cursed in all these respects, and no toleration of a violation of the law was granted as a means of mitigating the curse.

Again: Let me ask, Was there ever a law published relaxing that rigid observance of rest enjoined upon the sabbath? Was there a law published, saying, You must or you may observe the sabbath with less care, with less respect; you may now speak your own words, kindle fire in your houses, and prepare victuals? &c. &c. I say, Was there ever such a law published? No, indeed—either the law remains in all its force, to the utmost extent of its literal requirements, or it is passed away with the Jewish ceremonies. If it yet exist, let us observe it according to law. And if it does not exist, let us abandon a mock observance of another day for it.

"But," say some, "it was *changed* from the seventh to the first day." Where? when? and by whom? No man can tell. No, it never was changed, nor could it be, unless creation was to be gone through again: for the reason assigned must be changed before the observance, or respect to the reason, can be changed!! It is all old wives' fables to talk of the change of the sabbath from the seventh to the first day. If it be changed, it was that august personage changed it who changes times and laws *ex officio* —I think his name is DOCTOR ANTICHRIST.

But was not the sabbath given to the Jews only? And again, Was it not a shadow or type? This deserves attention.

The preface to the law, of which it was a part, says, "I am the Lord your God who brought you out of the land of Egypt, out of the house of bondage; therefore, remember the sabbath day," &c. The preface to this law, as the inscription or address upon a letter, ascertains whose property it was. It was the property of the Jews. But Moses tells them this, not leaving it to an inference, *Deut.* v. 15. "Remember that you were a servant in the land of Egypt, and the Lord your God brought you out thence, through a mighty hand, and by a stretched out arm; therefore, the Lord your God commanded you to keep the sabbath day." Ezekiel says the same, or rather the Lord by the prophet says, chap. xx. 12. "Moreover, also, I gave them my sabbath, to be a sign between me and them." Yes, said the Lord by Moses, "The sabbath is a sign between me and the children of Israel for ever." *Ex.* xxxi. 17. It is worthy of note in this place, that of all the sins in the long black catalogue of sins specified against the gentiles, in all the New Testament, the sin of sabbath-breaking is never once preferred against them!! We conclude, then, that the sabbath day was as exclusively the property of the Jews as circumcision.

But was it not a shadow and a type? Let us hear Paul. "Let no man judge you (condemn you for not observing) in meats and drinks, (for eating and drinking,) or in respect of a holy day, or of a new moon, or of the sabbath, which are a shadow of things to come; but the body is of Christ," or, according to Macknight, "the body is Christ's body." Paul, then, says it was a *shadow*. In the Epistle to the Hebrews, 4th chapter, he makes *it* and Canaan "types of that *rest* which remained for the people of God." The sabbath then was a shadow—a type given to the Jews only.

Since beginning this article, we noticed, for the first time, a very correct note of Dr. Macknight's, the celebrated translator of the apostolic epistles, which expresses our view of this matter. With many, we know, his views will be received with more readiness of mind than ours. He was, strange as it may appear, a dignitary in the presbyterian church; yet he expresses himself in the following manner, on Colossians ii. 16. "The *whole* of the law of

Moses being abrogated by Christ, (*Col.* ii. 14.) christians are under no obligation to observe any of the Jewish holy days, not even the seventh day sabbath. Wherefore, if any teacher made the observance of the seventh day a necessary duty, the Colossians were to resist him. But though the brethren, in the first age, paid no regard to the Jewish seventh day sabbath, they set apart the first day of the week for public worship, and for commemorating the death and resurrection of their master by eating his supper on that day; also, for private exercises of devotion. This they did, either by the precept or by the example of the apostles, and not by virtue of any injunction in the law of Moses. Besides, they did not sanctify the first day of the week in the Jewish manner, by a total abstinence from bodily labor of every kind. That practice was condemned by the council of Laodicea as *judaizing*. Lec. Suiceri Thes. Eccl. *voce Sabbaton.*"

The sabbath was, by the Lord of the sabbath, set aside, as well as every other part of the law of Moses, as stated in our last address. The learned Macknight is with us also in this instance. His words on Col. ii. 14. " It is evident," says he, " that the law of Moses, *in all its parts*, is now abolished and taken away. Consequently, that christians are under no obligation to obey even the moral precepts of that law, on account of their being delivered by Moses to the Jews. For if the obligations of the moral precepts of his law are still continued, mankind are still under its curse." I would just observe, on this item, that the Lord Jesus Christ observed the last sabbath that was obligatory on any of the human race, by lying in the grave from evening to evening. In the silence of death and the grave he celebrated it literally, " *not going out of his place*," until the sabbath was past. Then, very early in the morning, when the sabbath was past, the Jewish religion being consummated, he rises and becomes the beginning of the new creation.

Christians, by apostolic *example*, which to them is the same as *precept*, are, in honor of the commencement of the new creation, constrained by Christ's authority and grace to meet on the first day of the week, to show forth his death and to commemorate his resurrection. When they assemble they are to be instructed and to admonish one another; they are to learn his statutes, and " to continue *stedfastly* in the apostles' doctrine, in breaking bread, in fellowship, and in prayers, praising God." Such was the practice of the primitive church, as the epistles demonstrate. The first day of the week is *not regarded to the Lord* when these things are not done. For if professors of christianity were to keep in their houses from morning to evening and celebrate this day as the Jews did the sabbath, instead of honoring they are dishonoring Christ. No two days are more unlike in their import and design, than the Sabbath and *the first day.* The former commemorated the consummation of the old creation, the cessation of creation work; the latter commemorates the beginning of the new creation. The former was to Israel, a memorial that they were once slaves in Egypt—the latter assures us that the year of release has come. The former looked back, with mournful aspect, to the toils and sorrows entailed upon the human body, from an evil incident to the old creation—the latter looks forward, with an eye beaming with hope, to perpetual exemption from toil, and pain, and sorrow. The sabbath was a day of awful self-denial and

profound religious gloom—the resurrection day is a day of triumph, of holy joy, and religious festivity. The Jew, on a sabbath morn, from his casement surveyed the smokeless chimneys and the bolted doors of the silent tribes of Israel. A solemn stillness holds the streets of the city and the hamlet, and not a vagrant foot disturbs the grassy field. The flowers breathe forth their fragrance to the gentle breeze—no hand plucks the blooming rose—no ear is charmed with the mellifluous notes of the tenants of the groves. The banks of the limpid streams are not frequented by the noisy youths, nor does their clamor mingle with the murmurs of the vocal rills. Striking emblems of the silent rest allotted to the tenants of the grave. The christian welcomes the dawn of the triumphant morn. The new heavens and the new earth open to his view. The incorruptible, the immortal bodies of the saints, rising from the ashes of the grave, in all the vigor and beauty of immortal youth, fill his soul with unutterable admiration of the wondrous victory of the all-conquering chief. While he surveys his mortal frame and feels the sentence of death in every department of his earthly house, his soul forgets the infirmities of its partner, and soars on the pinions of faith and hope to the resurrection morn; it is lost in the contemplation of millions of every tribe and tongue clothed in the indescribable beauties of immortality. While overwhelmed in the extatic admiration of the glorious bodies around him, his eye ultimately fixes on the FIRST BORN of many brethren. While he adores him at the head of the innumerable host of ransomed immortals, his memory musters up the recollections of Gethsemane, Pilate and his judgment seat, Mount Calvary, and the sepulchre in the garden. To the assembly of the saints with eagerness he hastens, and, anxious to share in the praises of his glorious chief, to join in the recollection of his humiliation unto death, and to participate in the triumph of his resurrection, his soul is feasted with the abundance of his house and with the communion of those whom he hopes to embrace in his immortal arms on the day of the resurrection to eternal life.

Christians, what a difference between the Jewish sabbath, and this day of triumph! They have much to learn of the glory of christianity who think that going to a synagogue, and hearing a harangue, and returning to their firesides, is suitable to the design or expressive of the import of this joyful and triumphant day. On this day Messiah entered Jerusalem as son of David, as King of Judah. On this day he rose from the dead. On this day, after his resurrection, he generally met with his disciples in their assemblies. On this day, he sent the Holy Spirit down from heaven and erected the first christian church. "On this day the disciples came together to break bread." On this day the christians joined in the fellowship of the saints, or in making contributions for the saints. And, on this day, the Spirit finished its work of revelation on the Isle of Patmos, in giving to John the beloved the last secrets of the divine plan ever to be uttered in human language while time endures. If no authoritative precedent enforced the assembly of saints on this day, and the observance of the order of the Lord's house, the very circumstance of such a coincidence of glorious wonders would point it out as the Lord's day; and love to him, the most powerful principle that ever impelled to action, would constrain all saints not to forsake the assembling of themselves on this day; but to meet, to animate and to be animated; to remember, to admire, to adore, to hymn in songs divine, the glorious and mighty king. Christians, could you say, no?

Editor.

Queries.

AGAINST whom did the holy prophets of the Jews, the Saviour of the world and his apostles inveigh with the utmost severity?

Ans. The popular clergy. Never were any things spoken by the Saviour of the world, or by the holy apostles with so much keenness, with so much severity, as their reproofs of, as their denunciations against, the popular clergy.

Who were the popular clergy in those days?

Ans. Those who pleased the people, taught for hire and established themselves into an order distinct from the people.

Who are the popular clergy now?

Ans. Those who are trained for the precise purpose of teaching religion as their calling, please the mass of the people, establish themselves into a distinct order, from which they exclude all who are not so trained, and, for hire, affect to be the only legitimate interpreters of revelation.

What are the most effectual means to diminish the power and dominion of the popular clergy?

Ans. The same means which the Lord and his apostles used in their day against those of that time: chiefly to persuade the people to hold fast the holy commandments of the apostles, and to build themselves up in the christian faith. *Jude. 2 Pet.* iii. 2.

On Teaching Christianity.—No. IV.

THE ultimate design of these papers on christianity is, to exhibit a plan of preaching Christ to mankind, having for its authority the example of the Father, the Son, and the Holy Spirit, together with that of the apostles and others, who, in the beginning, were commissioned to promulgate the new doctrine. The design, indeed, may at first sight seem as adventurous as it is novel; but what of that? Christian pastors, for whom these sheets are more immediately designed, are not to be startled at the apparent presumption or novelty of my attempt. Their principal concern must be about the reality of what I propose. Is there one way, and only one, of preaching Christ to sinners; and is that one way supported by the above authorities? I answer in the affirmative; there is but one authorized way of making Christ known to men, in order that they may believe and be saved. And now it is my business to show, by scripture, that this is the case. The reader will remember that it has been shown in a former paper, that Jesus having died for sin and arisen again to introduce the hope of immortality, the great fact to be believed in order to be saved, is, that he is the Son of God; and this being a matter-of-fact question, the belief of it as necessarily depends upon the evidence by which it is accompanied, as the belief of any other fact depends upon its particular evidence. No one thinks of accrediting a mere assertion. Our blessed Saviour scrupled not to tell those among whom he alleged his divine authority; that if he alone said "he was the Messiah," his testimony was not to be regarded, and then reminded them of the testimony given by John the Baptist, whom they held to be a prophet; the testimony of the Father too, and of the Holy Spirit, and of the scriptures; and we shall see by and by that to preach the gospel is just to propose this glorious truth to sinners, and support it by its proper evidence. We shall see that the heavens and the apostles proposed nothing more in order to convert men from the error of their ways, and to reduce them to the love and obedience of Christ.

I am not ignorant that there are thousands, who, like a certain able divine in Canonsburg, stupidly suppose that there is something else far more necessary than this. They are ready to say that every body believes Jesus to be the Son of God, and to have been put to death for sin. To this it may be proper to reply, that not a single soul who attends the popular preachers has ever been convinced of this fact, that "Jesus is the Saviour," by its proper evidences. Clergymen do not preach the gospel with its proper evidences. They proceed in their annual round of sermonizing on this capital mistake, that the audience have believed Jesus to be the Saviour; so that their very best harangues, generally denominated gospel sermons, seldom deserve a better name than rants about the everlasting fire that shall consume the despisers of the offered salvation. But every body who has read the New Testament must have observed that the scriptures never propose the rewards and punishments which are appended to the belief and rejection of the gospel as a proof of its truth; and every one who knows how the apostles preached the gospel, must know also that they never did so; that they never produced the sanctions of everlasting burning in order to secure the faith and obedience of their hearers. If, indeed, their hearers were sometimes refractory, and would even dare to despise the gospel when set before them with its proper evidences, the gifts, the miracles, and the prophecies, then, indeed, the apostles made known the terrors of the Lord—not the terrors of the law. Then, indeed, they made it known that the Lord should be revealed from heaven to take vengeance by fire on them that obeyed not God, i. e. believed not the gospel of the Lord Jesus Christ; but this, not to prove the truth of their gospel, not to prove that Jesus had been put to death for sin, and was the Son of God; but only to warn those who might be disposed to despise or neglect that splendid evidence of gifts, miracles, &c. which proved their gospel to be true, which proved Jesus to have been crucified for sin, and to be the Son of God. In short, the apostles proceed thus: they first proposed the truth to be believed; and secondly, they produced the evidences necessary to warrant belief; and thirdly, if any seemed to despise the gospel, or resist the Holy Spirit, i. e. the evidence afforded by the Holy Spirit in gifts, miracles, and prophecy, then they warned these despisers of the consequences, and thus freed themselves from the blood of all men.

But let us see if this be the method of making the truth known, pursued by the Father, the Son, and the Holy Spirit, and the apostles; and to begin with the last, the apostles. Did the apostles begin to preach Christ on a plan of their own; or at the time when, and the place where, they themselves judged most proper? By no means! In every thing that regarded time, place and manner, they acted in entire subjection to the commandments of the Saviour; and this we learn from the first chapter of the Acts. Our blessed Saviour did not treat mankind as modern ministers do—scold and insult them for not believing or having faith in a proposition, for which they are no way careful to adduce the proper evidence. He well knew that such a wonder as his being the Son of God, crucified for sin, and raised from the dead, could not be believed without the most transcendent testimony; and, therefore not permitting the apostles immediately to blaze abroad his resurrection, he ordered them to remain in Jerusalem until they should be endowed with power from on high, i. e. until the Holy Spirit should descend and furnish these unlettered preachers with proper evidences to establish the gospel fact! With regard to place, the Lord Jesus was very precise, telling them to begin at Jerusalem, then to proceed to the country of Judea; then to Samaria, and lastly to the Gentiles, the uttermost parts of the earth. Now if we would ascertain the apostles' plan of preaching Christ, we must follow them to these several places, and examine, in train, their sermons in Jerusalem, in Judea, in Samaria, and among the Gentiles, and to begin with them in Jerusalem. The day of Pentecost was fully come, and the apostles were in Jerusalem, when the Spirit of the Almighty, moving as he lists, blew athwart this valley of dry bones, and lo! a noise from heaven as of a mighty rushing wind—in a moment blazing tongues like fire shone upon the heads of the disciples of Jesus; they were all filled with the Holy Spirit, and began to speak in languages as the Spirit gave them utterance. Great was the shaking in Jerusalem. The dry bones came together to be clothed with sinews, flesh and skin, and to receive breath; to repent, believe and be baptized, and receive the Holy Spirit! Parthians and Medes, Elamites and the dwellers in Mesopotamia, in Judea, in Cappadocia, in Pontus and Asia, Phrygia, and Pamphylia, in Egypt, in the parts of Lybia about Cyrene, and strangers of Rome, all, either Jews or proselytes, Cretes and Arabians, rushed to the place where the apostles stood, in all the grandeur of this fiery spectacle. They beheld and were amazed. They listened and were in doubt, exclaiming: "What means this? Do we hear them speak in our own tongues the wonderful works of God? Are not all they who speak Galileans? Others mocking, said, these men are full of new wine." Illustrious crisis! Great and glorious day! The moment destined by heaven for proclaiming the mystery of Christ, was now arrived; the Spirit was already poured from on high; the apostles were now constituted able ministers of the new covenant; the truth and its evidences were now both in their possession; and men, devout men from every nation under heaven, stood calling for an explanation of the surprising phenomena before them—What means this? The apostle Peter, (*Acts* ii.) standing up, addressed them solemnly; and having showed them that all they saw and heard was agreeable to the prediction of their own prophet, Joel, he takes occasion to introduce the truth, the saving truth, viz. that Jesus was arisen from the dead. "Men of Israel," says he, "hear these words: Jesus of Nazareth," &c. Will the reader please to read the second chapter of the Acts? "Him," says the apostle, "being delivered by the determined counsel and foreknowledge of God, you have taken and by wicked hands have crucified and slain. Him God has raised up from the dead," &c. The apostle then shows that this fact also was according to prophecy; and having cleared both the truth to be believed and its evidences from all suspicion, by showing that they had been plainly foretold by their own prophets, he tells them that Christ was in heaven, and having received the promised Spirit from the Father, he had shed down what they all saw and heard—the multitude of separated tongues that blazed on the apostles' heads, and the gifts of languages, concluding thus, "Therefore, let all the house of Israel know assuredly, that God has made that same Jesus whom you have crucified both Lord and Christ."

The first of all christian addresses merits a more than ordinary share of our attention, if we would preach Jesus as the apostles did; moreover, the reader ought to watch Philip very closely here. He says that there is but one authorized method of proposing the saving truth in order that men may believe it. Now he must have learned this from an induction of particulars, i. e. from an examination of particular addresses, or preachings, found in the New Testament. And if Philip's scheme is true, it follows that all samples of apostolic preaching, recorded in the Acts of the Apostles, or in the Evangelists, or any other where, are essentially the same. The truth to be believed and its evidences will form the spirit of every gospel address made by the apostles. Is there any thing else in the Pentecostian address? Does Peter speak for any other purpose than to convince them that he who had been slain was now in heaven? or does he employ any other means for convincing the crowd of this fact, but the testimony of the Holy Spirit, the power of miracles, and the gifts of tongues, with which he and his fellows had been endowed from on high? The apostle, (verse 36,) in the conclusion of his address, makes use of the illative conjunction, *therefore.* "Therefore," says he, "let all the house of Israel know," &c. The word "therefore" has reference to the evidence which was then before the multitude; and the apostle pointing to what they saw and heard, told them from these things to know assuredly that Jesus was the Lord and the Christ. The evidence was so obvious that it pierced them to the heart; and, in agony of terror, they exclaimed, "Men and brethren, what shall we do?" And now we see that in this most primitive of all christian speeches, there are just two things that are essentially obvious: the fact of the Saviour's resurrection, and the testimony of God which proves it. That is what all men are called to believe in order to be saved; and this is what warrants their belief, the gifts, the miracles, and the prophecies. And now it will be necessary to compare with this the other apostolic addresses delivered in Jerusalem, to see whether they are essentially the same; this, however, must be the business of some future paper. At present I shall only remark, that if Heaven intends that the belief of this glorious fact shall save the world, it has certainly afforded a most glorious evidence in support of it. In furnishing the christian with such accounts of our Saviour's miracles and the miracles of the apostles, Heaven has certainly put it in a preacher's power to proclaim the truth with success; and he who contrary to all scripture examples, would select a scrap, and prefer this to preach Christ from, instead of displaying before his hearers that glorious chain of miracles recorded for the very purpose of preaching Christ, must certainly have a very bad taste. And let no one think that any thing more is necessary to our salvation than to believe this fact—it is perfectly operative in all who receive it in the love of it. The three thousand Pentecostian converts had nothing else proposed for their belief; and when they received it, gladly they lived together, had all things common, sold their possessions and goods, and distributed to all as every one had need. The belief of this same fact caused them to continue in the apostles' doctrine, and to praise God in public and private; and we may well say that if the belief of this glorious fact fails to make a man obey the Lord Jesus, every thing else must fail.   PHILIP.

Tithes.

A certain woman found by the way side a lamb perishing with cold and hunger. She had pity upon the lamb, and took it to her house and nursed it, and brought it again to life.— And it came to pass, that the lamb grew up and was a goodly ewe, and had a large fleece. And the poor woman sheared the ewe; when, lo! the priest came to the woman and said, "The first fruits of every thing belong to the Lord— and I must have the wool." The woman said, "It is hard;" the priest said, "It is written"— and so he took the wool. And it came to pass, that soon after the ewe yeaned and brought forth a lamb; when lo! the chief priest came again to the woman and said, "The firstling of every flock belongs to the Lord—I must have the lamb." The woman said, "It is hard;" the priest said, "It is written"—and he took the lamb. And when it came to pass that the woman found that she could make no profit from the ewe, she killed and dressed it; when lo! the chief priest came again to her, and took a leg, a loin, and a shoulder, for a burnt offering. And it came to pass that the poor woman was exceeding wroth because of the robbery; and she said to the chief priest, "Curse on the ewe! Oh! that I had never meddled therewith!" And the chief priest straightway said to her, "Whatsoever is cursed belongs to the Lord"—so he took the remainder of the mutton, which he and the Levites ate for their supper.

[*Plain Truth.*

No. 8.]   MARCH 1, 1824.
Address to the readers of the Christian Baptist.
No. IV.

WE have, in the two preceding numbers, presented our views on two charges that have been very generally rumored against us. There yet remains another which we have promised to notice. On these points we wish to be clearly understood. The charge now before us, is, that we deny "experimental religion." Before we plead "guilty," or "not guilty," of this impeachment, we should endeavor to understand the subject matter of it. Not having been in the use of the phrase "experimental religion," I could neither affirm nor deny any thing about it. The question, then, is, what is the thing? The name we have not in our vocabulary; and, therefore, could only deny the thing constructively. We will first ask, what does the bible say about it? Upon examination, I found it says not one word about "experimental religion." The bible is as silent upon this topic as upon the "Romish mass." I then appealed to the Encyclopedia. The only thing like it, which I could find, was "experimental philosophy," which is a philosophy that can be proved by experiment. I then looked into the theological dictionaries, and soon found different kinds of religion, such as "natural," "revealed," &c. but not a word about "experimental." I then applied to a friend, who had once been deeply initiated into the modern sublimities of the refined popular doctrine. I was then informed that there were two kinds of religion much

talked of in the pulpit and amongst the people— the one called "heart religion," and the other "head religion"—the latter dwelling exclusively in the head, and the former in the heart. I also learned that the former was sometimes called "christian experience," and this was presumed to be the thing intended by the words "experimental religion." As the New Testament is my religious creed, I appealed to it again. But it was as silent as the grave on all these distinctions. I then began to philosophize, in the popular way, on the head and the heart, with a design of deciding which of these two religions was the better one. I had heard that "head religion" consisted in *notions,* and "heart religion" in *feelings.* Finding that all the learned agreed that the spirit of a man dwells in his head, and not in his heart, I had well nigh concluded that "head religion" must be the better of the two, as the human spirit is concerned more immediately with what takes place in its habitation than elsewhere. I reasoned in this way—that if the spirit of a man dwells in his head, then head religion must be better than heart religion, and heart religion better than hand religion, &c.* Being unwilling to conclude too hastily on this subject, I thought of examining the phrase "christian experience." On reflection, I found that this phrase represented a very comprehensive idea. Every christian has considerable experience, and some have experienced a thousand times more than others. Paul experienced many perils by land and by sea—by his own countrymen—by the heathen—in the city, in the wilderness—among false brethren. He experienced weariness, painfulness, watchings often, hunger, thirst, fastings, cold, and nakedness, stripes and imprisonments. From the Jews, he experienced five whippings, each of forty stripes, save one. He was thrice beaten with rods— once stoned—thrice shipwrecked—a day and a night in the deep. Besides this, he experienced all the anxieties and griefs, all the sorrows and joys that arose from the care of the churches. This was, indeed, the experience of a christian, and this I never denied. Many christians can tell of similar experiences, but none can give a narrative so long, so varied, and entertaining, as that of Paul. Even Peter the apostle, was not able to detail such an experience.

But on reading this to a friend, I am told that I have not yet hit upon the point in question; that the christian experience of which the populars speak, is, "the inward experience of grace upon the heart." What is the meaning of this grace upon the heart, said I? I know that the glad tidings is sometimes called the grace of God. Thus says Paul, "the grace of God that brings salvation, has appeared to all men, teaching us," &c. Here the gospel is called "the grace of God appearing to all men." Again, says Paul, he who seeks to be justified by the law, is fallen from grace; or has renounced the gospel. Indeed, nothing is so worthy of the name "grace of God" as the gospel. Now if this gospel, which is sometimes called "the

---

* To prevent mistakes, let it be understood that, in speaking of the head and heart, in the above connexion, we speak after the manner of vain philosophy. The term heart is often met with in the scriptures, and it has ascribed to it every exercise of the understanding, will, and affections. The moderns suppose it to have respect to the affections and dispositions only. But in scripture it is said, "to know, to understand, to study, to discern, to devise, to meditate, to reason, to indite, to ponder, to consider, to believe, to doubt, to be wise," &c. See Deut. iv. 39. Ps. xlv. 1. xlix. 3. Prov. x. 8. xv. 28. xvi. 9. xix. 21. Eccl. viii. 5. Jer. xxiv. 7. Matt. xiii. 15. Mark ii. 6—8. xi. 23. Luke ii. 19. 35.

word of God," "the spirit," "the grace," and "the truth," dwell in a man, that is, be believed sincerely, like a fruitful vine it yields in his heart and in his life the heavenly cluster of love, joy, peace, long suffering, gentleness, goodness, fidelity, meekness, temperance. These are the fruits of the Spirit. Like precious ointment it diffuses in his heart heavenly odors, and the sweetness of its perfume exhales in his life, in the work of faith, the labor of love, and the patience of hope. This, said I, is just what I contend for. If you call this "christian experience," I never denied it; yea, I have always taught it. But I cannot approve of the name, since it is altogether an ambiguous name.

My friend replied, "This is not precisely the popular use of the phrase. It denotes, amongst most of the populars, a certain mental experience to becoming a christian, an exercise of mind, a process through which a person must pass before he can esteem himself a true christian; and until we know from his recital of it that he has been the subject of it, we cannot esteem him a christian."

Then it is some invisible, indescribable energy exerted upon the minds of men in order to make them christians; and that, too, independent of, or prior to, the word believed. I read in the New Testament of many who were the subjects of energies and diverse gifts of the Holy Spirit, but it was "after they had believed." The gifts of the Holy Spirit by which the gospel was confirmed, by which it was demonstrated to be of God, were conferred on the Jews and Samaritans after they had believed. Even the apostles themselves did not receive those powers and gifts of the Holy Spirit until they became disciples of Christ. On the Gentiles was poured out the Holy Spirit, or his gifts, while they heard Peter preaching the glad tidings, which they believed; for they came to hear Peter in such circumstances as to dispose them to believe every word he said. The age of those gifts has passed away, and now the influence of the Holy Spirit is only felt in and by the word believed. Hence says Peter, "You are born again, not of corruptible, but of incorruptible seed, by the word of God, which lives and abides for ever"—and "this is the word which by the gospel is preached to you."

This descriptive preaching, of which we hear so much, is the most insipid and useless thing in the world. An orthodox divine of my acquaintance spends about one-fourth of every year in preaching up the necessity, nature, and importance of regeneration. He usually tells the people his own story; that is, the history of his own regeneration. He sometimes comes to "visions and revelations." He tells the people that they are "as spiritually dead as a stone;" "there is not one spark of life in unregenerate sinners;" nor can they, "in the state of nature," do any thing that can contribute to their regeneration. "It depends entirely upon the Spirit of God, which, as the wind blows where it lists, works when, and upon whom it pleases. If there were not a thousand preachers like him, I would not disturb his mind by thus noticing the burden of his message. The spirit by which he speaks is doubtless not that Spirit which was promised the apostles; for that Spirit, Messiah said, would not speak of himself, but of *him*. But this preacher's spirit speaks of himself, and not of Christ. It is worthy of notice that the twelve apostles, in all their public addresses, on record, delivered not one sentence of this kind of preaching; no, not one.—And

G

suppose it were as true as the gospel, that such is the state of mankind, we can conceive of no possible good which could result from such descriptive harangues. They resemble a physician, who, instead of administering a remedy to his patient, delivers him a lecture on the nature of his disease. Miserable comforters are such preachers! They have no glad tidings of great joy to all people. Methinks I see a poor unfortunate sinner, lying in a slough, up to the neck in the mire, perishing with cold and hunger; and one of the orthodox divines riding along observes him. Methinks I hear him tell him, fellow sinner, you are in a miserable condition—mired from head to foot. Believe me, you are both cold and hungry; and I can assure you that you are unable to help yourself out of this calamity. You could as easily carry one of these hills upon your shoulders as extricate yourself from your present circumstances. Perish with cold and hunger you must; it is in vain for you to attempt an escape. Every effort you make to get out only sinks you deeper in distress. Your Creator could, if he pleased, bring you out; but whether he lists or not, is uncertain. Fare you well!—The unfortunate sinner exclaims, What good is in your address?—He is assured that it is an article of precious truth, worthy to be believed. But when believed, what good is in the faith of it? The gospel is glad tidings of great joy to all people; and whatever is called "gospel," that is not good news and worthy of all acceptation, is not gospel. —But I have wandered from my subject.

The popular belief of a regeneration previous to faith, or a knowledge of the gospel, is replete with mischief. Similar to this is a notion that obtains among many of a "*law work*," or some terrible process of terror and despair through which a person must pass, as through the pious Bunyan's slough of *Despond*, before he can believe the gospel. It is all equivalent to this; that a man must become a desponding, trembling infidel, before he can become a believer. Now, the gospel makes no provision for despondency, inasmuch as it assures all who believe and obey it, upon the veracity of God, that they are forgiven and accepted in the Beloved.

A devout preacher told me, not long since, that he was regenerated about three years before he believed in Christ. He considered himself "as born again by a physical energy of the Holy Spirit, as a dead man would be raised to life by the mighty power of the Eternal Spirit." Upon his own hypothesis, (metaphysical, it is true,) he was three years a "godly unbeliever." He was pleasing and acceptable to God "without faith;" and if he had died during the three years, he would have been saved, though he believed not the gospel.* Such is the effect of metaphysical theology.

* We would observe, that we conceive the great error of the modern philosophers, concerning the operations of the Holy Spirit, to be, that they are the same physical operations now, which were exhibited in those days when men spake with tongues, healed diseases, and wrought every species of miracles, by the immediate agency of the Holy Spirit, for the confirmation of their testimony; when they spake, prophesied, discerned spirits, and interpreted oracles, by the immediate impulse of the Spirit.— We do not suppose that they contend for an agency to the same degree, but only of the same species. But we are taught that since those gifts have ceased, the Holy Spirit now operates upon the minds of sinners only by the word. With respect to pagans and all those incapable of hearing the word, the scriptures do not teach us what Plato has taught thousands of modern divines. The re-

I read, some time since, of a revival in the state of New York, in which the Spirit of God was represented as being abundantly poured out on Presbyterians, Methodists, and Baptists. I think the converts in the order of the names were about three hundred Presbyterians, three hundred Methodists, and two hundred and eighty Baptists. On the principles of Bellamy, Hopkins, and Fuller, these being all regenerated without any knowledge of the gospel, there is no difficulty in accounting for their joining different sects. The Spirit did not teach the Presbyterians to believe that "God had foreordained whatsoever comes to pass;" nor the Methodists to deny it. He did not teach the Presbyterians and the Methodists that infants were members of the church, and to be baptized; nor the Baptists to deny it. But on the hypothesis of the Apostle James, viz. "Of his own will begat he us by the word of truth." I think it would be difficult to prove that the Spirit of God had any thing to do with the aforesaid revival.

Enthusiasm flourishes, blooms under the popular systems. This man was regenerated when asleep, by a vision of the night. That man heard a voice in the woods, saying, "Your sins be forgiven you." A third saw his Saviour descending to the tops of the trees at noonday. A thousand form a band, and sit up all night to take heaven by surprise. Ten thousand are waiting in anxiety for a power from on high to descend upon their souls; they frequent meetings for the purpose of obtaining this power.— Another class, removed so far south, by special illumination, have discovered that there is no hell; that the Devil and his angels will ultimately ascend to the skies; and that Judas himself, Herod and Pontius Pilate, will shine like stars forever and ever. And, to encourage the infatuation, the preacher mounts the rostrum, and with his sermon, either in notes or committed to memory, he " prays to God for his spirit to guide his tongue, and to send a message that he will bless to the salvation of that dear congregation." Thus the people lay themselves out for operations and new revelations. Like the Phœnix in the fable, they and the preacher have gathered a bundle of dry sticks, and they set about clapping their wings with one accord, that they may fan them into a flame—which sometimes actually happens, if our faith could be so strong as to believe it.

From all this scene of raging enthusiasm, be admonished, my friends, to open your Bibles and to hearken to the voice of God, which is the voice of reason. God now speaks to us only by his word. By his Son, in the New Testament, he has fully revealed himself and his will. This is the only revelation of his Spirit which we are to regard. The popular preachers, and the popular systems, alike render the word of God of none effect. Some of them are so awfully bold as to represent it as "a dead letter." According to them it ought never to have been translated; for the reading of it in an unknown tongue, if accompanied with some supernatural power,

generation of pagans without the word, is a dogma not quite so rational as the dogmas of a regeneration after death in purgatory. In spite of all our efforts, the vortex of metaphysical jargon will draw us in. I wrote this to prevent mistakes—perhaps it may create some. But, " to the testimony," believe us not if we speak not its dogmas. We doubt not, but in the above we speak a mixed dialect; perhaps half the language of Ashdod and half the language of Canaan. We are positive on one point, that the scriptures teach us not the modern doctrine, nor the ancient philosophical doctrine of " physical operations of the Divine Spirit," in order to faith.

with some new revelation of the Spirit, would have been as suitable to the salvation of men, as though read in our own tongue. The jarring elements of which their systems are composed, do, however, by the necessary laws of discordant principles, in the act of combustion reflect so much light as to convince us that the written word is the last appeal. Let us make it the first and the last. It comes to us in the demonstration of the Holy Spirit, and with the power of miraculous evidence. The word of Jesus Christ is, "spirit and life." "The word of God is quick and powerful, sharper than any two-edged sword;" yea, it is the sword of the Spirit, it is the spirit of his mouth. "The entrance of thy word, O Lord, gives light, and makes the simple wise."   EDITOR.

In a work so small as the present, we should aim at brevity and variety in the articles inserted. This has always been our intention, though we have not been able to conform to it. The following article requires an apology on account of its length, but this we have in its importance. The argument may be called a new one, as far as any thing that is now discovered in the scriptures can be called new. We know that Mr. Wardlaw in his reply to Mr. Yates, and other writers, have urged the same passages in support of their views; but not in the same manner, nor with half the effect. We think it is unanswerable. Small as our work is, we would not hesitate to allow half a dozen of pages to any writer that will attempt to answer it, provided that the reply be exclusively confined to this one argument. On this condition alone could we admit it. We publish it on two accounts: the one, its own intrinsic merit; the other, as proof positive of our innocence of a recent charge brought against us, as favoring the Socinian hypothesis. While we renounce the metaphysical jargon found in creeds, on what is called the doctrine of the " trinity," such as " eternal generation," "filiation," &c. we regard both Arianism, semi-Arianism, and Socinianism, as poor, miserable, blind, and naked nonsense and absurdity.   EDITOR.

THE presumptuous Socinians call themselves christians. Alas! poor men! they are drivelling philosophers. The polite and the stupid may, indeed, suppose that on their heretical paradox these doctors reason divinely. Well, be it so. "Jesus," say they, "is the son of Joseph." Excellent christians! If you, gentlemen, interpret nature as you do religion; if you unlock the mysteries of the material world with the same adroitness and perspicacity with which you usher into the open day the spiritual abortions of your own disordered brains, indeed you are divine philosophers. I have always thought the paradox of the Socinians a little too barefaced even for the vulgar. The devotees of the popular religion are very stupid, because their teachers generally leave them, in point of information, just where they find them, prodigiously ignorant of the holy scriptures; nevertheless, if they should at all look into the sacred volume, they will not be apt, I should think, to gather up Socinianism.

We have got a nest of these little creatures in our good city, where, with the incredible industry of pismires, they have succeeded in throwing up an earthen shell over their heads; and this they call a church!

Let us hear them in religion. "Jesus," say they, "is the son of Joseph." Now the twelve apostles, and all whom they taught the religion, worshipped Jesus; *ergo,* the apostles and all whom they taught worshipped the son of Joseph: *ergo,* the apostles and all whom they taught were idolaters!

But now, beloved, if we should show that the Socinian sect fails of a peculiarity which distinguished the first christian church, and those by whom it was gathered and instructed, the apostles, from all other worshippers besides, even from those who held many other things in common with them, what then? Again, if we should show that it was this very peculiarity which the Socinians have wiped from their creed that procured the disciples of Jesus the name of Christians at Antioch; and, lastly, if we should make it appear from reason and scripture that the Socinian paradox is a mere quibble, what then? Will it not inevitably follow that these little bigots, act very fondly when they assume the name of christians?

To our first proposition, then. But let not the reader suppose that I go out of my way to break my lance over the steel cap of the poor Socinians. I am no churchman militant—but a layman, as Antichrist would call me, because I reckon a New Testament a better tutor in the kingdom of the Saviour than all the doctors of divinity in christendom. From my heart I pity the Socinians—I compassionate their temerity—and would not, the bible being in my hand, rush into the presence of the Judge of quick and dead with their sentiments, for twice the value of the universe. But this only by the way.

And now to discover that peculiarity in the sentiments of the first christians, which then distinguished them from their own infidel countrymen, the Jews; and now from our own countrymen the Socinians; let us away to the New Testament and rummage in it in search of the mighty cause of that dreadful persecution which commenced with the death of Stephen. *Acts* vii.

To find out this, let it be noted that the two great prevailing parties in Jerusalem, at the moment of publishing the new institution were the Pharisean and Sadducean. Now what were the more prominent doctrines of these two sects? The scriptures, and I desire no better authority, the scriptures inform us that the Sadducees denied the resurrection, and the existence of angels and human spirits; but that the Pharisees maintained both. These two sects divided between them the inhabitants of the capital; and, as the Pharisaic party was at all times vastly more numerous than the Sadducean, it follows that a very large proportion of the citizens of Jerusalem held the resurrection of the dead and the existence of angels and spirits. Now what aspect did the apostles' doctrine bear to the respective sentiments of these sectaries? Why it confirmed, in the most illustrious manner, the dogmas of the Pharisees; it set the doctrine of the resurrection on an entire new footing; and, at the same time, covered with shame and contempt the sentiments of the Sadducean materialists. The apostles first delivering with great power of miracles their testimony concerning the resurrection of Jesus, they immediately grounded the general doctrine of a resurrection on that splendid and well attested event, and gave such a blow to the pretensions of the Sadducees, as completely excited the *odium theologicum* of these incomparable doctors. But here it is but reasonable to suppose that the apostles' doctrine would irritate. This supposition, indeed, agrees well with the fact, for the chief priest (Caiaphas) and all his party, the sect

of the Sadducees, were filled with zeal, and laid their hands on the apostles and put them in the common prison. *Acts* v. The reader may perhaps wish to know why the Sadducees liked the doctrine of a resurrection so ill from the mouths of the apostles, and yet made this tenet a matter of forbearance in the case of the Pharisees. St. Paul says that we suffer fools gladly when we know that we ourselves are wise. The Sadducees well knew that the doctrine of a resurrection was not appended to the law of Moses, and these five books were all that these men held sacred; consequently, the Pharisaic arguments in proof of a resurrection must always have appeared very impotent and unsatisfactory to the Sadducees, because they were drawn chiefly from the lesser prophets' writings, which that party did not recognize as canonical. But the apostles grounded the general doctrine on the specific certainty of Christ's resurrection, and this was what irritated the Sadducees; they were grieved that the apostles preached "through Christ" the resurrection from the dead, *Acts* iv. 2. But now as this particular in the apostles' doctrine incurred the resentment of the Sadducees, whose sentiments it condemned: so it is but reasonable to suppose that it would conciliate the favor and protection of the Pharisees, whose sentiments it confirmed. This in fact was the case; for when the Sadducees, who had imprisoned the apostles, consulted about putting them to death, as the sharpest and surest refutation of their hated argument for a general resurrection, there stood up a man in the sanhedrim, a Pharisee, named Gamaliel, a teacher of the law, in great esteem among all the people, (*Acts* v.) and this divine plead the cause of the christian teachers with such moderation and eloquence, that "to him they agreed." The apostles were dismissed, but charged by the Sadducees to teach the doctrine no more by the resurrection of Jesus, though, indeed, they had already filled the city with it. Now here it is wonderful and entertaining to behold the workings and contortions of religious bigotry! The Sadducees thought they saw in the apostles their last worst enemies, and they could have worried them. On the other hand the crafty Gamaliel saw in the apostles' doctrine the most certain argument for a resurrection, the favorite tenet of his own party, and with what art does he procure them their dismission. However, all this had occurred at the moment of publishing the new religion, before either party, Sadducean or Pharisaic, could well determine what was the grand peculiarity. I dare say that both these sects, in the first instance, were induced to think christianity nothing more than some modification of Pharisaism; for the great tumult and conversion which the new doctrine at its first appearance excited in the city, together with the confusion of feeling caused by the preaching of the resurrection of Jesus, which was always very prominent in the public addresses of the apostles, had prevented these sectaries from inquiring more minutely into the faith and practice of the apostles.

The church must have already consisted of many thousands by this time. The first address of Peter, on the day of Pentecost, proselyted three thousand; and we are told that the Lord continued to add to the church daily the cured. Afterwards it amounted to five thousand, and still multitudes, both of men and women, were the more added to the Lord; myriads of the priests were obedient to the faith, and the word or doctrine of the Lord increased mightily in

Jerusalem. Now all these had hitherto enjoyed the favor and protection of Gamaliel and his sect, and had been, perhaps, chiefly Pharisees themselves. We have seen how the Sadducees opposed them, and how artfully Gamaliel procured the release of the apostles who were at the head of the church. These things bring us to the end of the fifth chapter. The death of Stephen and a horrible persecution of the church generally, are the very next events which follow in the order of the Acts of the Apostles. And here a reader, awake to what the author of this treatise recounted, must pause in astonishment—must be confounded at the fickleness of religious favor. Stephen is murdered by the sectaries, and the disciples of that very Gamaliel, who had, but this moment, employed all his eloquence in the defence of the Nazarenes, are now imbruing their hands in their blood, entering into houses and dragging out both men and women. Paul, the scholar of Gamaliel, committed them to prison. What was their crime? By what unheard of practice did the brethren forfeit the favor and protection of the people, for hitherto they were in favor with them all? Were they still only the Sadducees who persecuted the disciples? Alas! the Pharisees were turned against them also, and had now discovered a peculiarity in the christian doctrine, which made them as much the enemies of the apostles as the Sadducees had been before. But did not both parties just now agree to let the christians go on unmolested? Did not Gamaliel say, "let them alone?" resolving all into this pious conclusion, that if this counsel, or this work, were of men, it would come to nought; but if it were of God it could not be overcome. What had the christians done? Why all this horrible persecution? It was not because they had violated any legal institute—any of the external Mosaic observances. For though the word of God increased mightily in Jerusalem, though multitudes of men and women were the more added to the Lord, and myriads of the priests were obedient to the faith; yet were they all zealous of the law. The new doctrine, however Pharisees and Sadducees may have rated it, seemed only to make those who received it better men, for they were daily with one accord in the temple praising God and having favor with all the people. Now if the brethren were not persecuted for abandoning the law, for this they carried with them into the new religion, then they must have been persecuted for the apostles' doctrine, and yet not for all the several points in that doctrine; for we have seen that the Pharisees favored their method of preaching the resurrection, and protected them on account of it from the outrages of the Sadducees. Indeed, it was formally agreed by both these parties to let the christians alone; to let them proceed unmolested, as long as nothing worse than the doctrine of a resurrection marked their religious creed. But this they did at a time when they had not as yet thought that the apostles' doctrine merited a more minute investigation. Still, however, the question returns, what had the christians done to excite the united fury of these two sects? Is there no scriptural answer to this important question? Is there nothing which might serve as a clue to bring us to the bottom of this persecution? We have seen who inflicted the punishment, and who had to endure it. But the cause—what was that? Not the doctrine of the resurrection. What then? Let us follow the scholar of Gamaliel to Damascus; let us accompany this pious student of divinity to the place of his destination; the place whither he was commissioned by letters (no doubt clerically patent) for the godly and religious purpose of hunting up the poor innocents of the Lord of Glory. The time was come when those who slew them thought they offered an acceptable service to God. Alas! mistaken men! they shall give an account to Him who is ready to judge the quick and the dead. Paul tells us that in this affair he carried with him to Damascus letters of authority from the high priests, but he does not himself mention the very crime which characterized a christian; the peculiarity which distinguished a follower of Jesus from other Jews, that made him obnoxious to the persecutors, and liable to be carried off by Paul to Jerusalem. And this leaves us as much in the dark as ever concerning the particular point in the apostles' doctrine, which lay at the root of this persecution. However, the apostle was converted on his way to Damascus, and the surprising phenomena which accompanied his conversion were obvious to those who accompanied him. The whole party was struck to the earth by the splendor of the Saviour's glory. And the change in Paul's sentiments—his conversion from judaism to christianity, was soon blazed throughout the city. Paul (Acts ix.) immediately associated with those whom he had come to persecute and to carry bound to Jerusalem; and had even the courage to enter the Jewish synagogue, and to preach Jesus that he was the "Son of God;" at which all the Jews and proselytes of Damascus who heard his address, who listened to his arguments and were as yet unsuspecting of the change, were surprized, were confounded! The young scholar of the great Gamaliel, the famous zealot, who had carried it against the christians with such a high hand at Jerusalem, was now an abettor of the supposed heresy of the Nazarenes—in short, was, in the pious estimation of the synagogue people, lost! an apostate! an idolater! What were the reflections of those who witnessed all this—who heard him speak, who heard him argue, who knew the tenor of his commission, and the particular crime of those whom he persecuted in Jerusalem and had come hither to seize? Reader, attend! the following are their very words: "Is not this he who made havoc of them at Jerusalem who call on (invoke) this name, and came hither to carry such bound to the chief priests?" Surprising sentence! "Carry such." Carry whom? All who invoked the name of "the Son of God." We have hit at last, then, on the particular point in the apostles' doctrine which made the church so obnoxious to the Pharisees and Sadducees after they had discovered it. The brethren, then, it was found, lived in the idolatrous practice, as the Socinians would call it, of "invoking the Lord Jesus." Now, then, we can see the full import of that passage in the ninth chapter, where Ananias manifests such reluctance to visit Paul, even after the Lord Jesus bade him. Ananias, poor man, was guilty; he was one of those who invoked the name of Jesus, and was probably doing so at the hour of prayer, when the Lord Jesus vouchsafed him this vision. Reader, hear his own words. When the Lord desired him to go visit Paul in the house of one Judas, "Lord," says he, "I have heard from many concerning this man, how much evil he has done to your saints in Jerusalem, and he is here with authority from the chief priests to bind all who invoke your name." Acts ix. 13. Now, in these two quotations, the church in Jerusalem, and the brethren in Damascus, are alike obnoxious, and are guilty of the same crime—the invocation of Jesus. Yet the church of Jerusalem was gathered and instructed by the apostles; nay, it was the first of all christian churches, and is to be imitated by all. Is christianity really a system of idolatry? Is the Son of God, whom christians have been taught by the apostles to adore, the son of Joseph, the carpenter? Take these words of the apostle *John*, 1st epistle, v. 13. "These things I have written to you who believe in the name of the Son of God, that you may know that you have everlasting life," &c. "This also is the confidence which we have in him, that if we ask any thing according to his will, he hearkens to us. Now if we know that he hearkens to us in whatever we ask, we know that we obtain from him the petitions which we have asked." This is a very odd sort of sentence on the Socinian scheme. John says that he had entire confidence in being heard: perhaps the reader does not know what the apostle alludes to in this expression. The allusion, reader, is to an expressive declaration made by the Saviour himself whilst on earth; (*John's gospel,* chapter xiv.) The apostles were dreadfully alarmed at the idea of his leaving them, being ignorant of the nature of his kingdom; so, in order to comfort them, he tells them that though he must leave them, yet he would return, and then whatever they would ask in his name he would do it for them—I am going away, i. e. to heaven; but, reader, mark the Lord's own words—"but whatever you ask in my name that I will do." Again, "that the Father may be glorified in the Son, if you ask any thing in my name I will do it." Amen! It was this promise that made John confident that Christ would hear us. Thus Jesus corrupted the apostles, and they corrupted the church of Jerusalem, and all others who would wish to shape their faith and practice by their example and teaching in the New Testament. And thus we see the origin of Stephen's dying prayer, "Lord Jesus receive my spirit—Lord, lay not this sin to their charge." And now the Socinians may themselves query whether this characteristic of the first of all christians, and christian churches, belongs to them. No man, however, can triumph over these little creatures. I know them well. A Socinian is a little mortal—

> "Destroy his fib and sophistry. In vain!
> "The creature's at his dirty work again."   O.

To the editor of the *Christian Baptist.*

Sir—Your having received with so much candor the few lines I sent you some time since, emboldens me to be so intrusive as to address you again. I have carefully read seven numbers of the "Baptist," and I can assure you that the work, taken as a whole, merits my unfeigned approbation. To say that it has no defects, would be saying more than I dare say of any work of fallible authors. Your remarks in reply to my few lines of the 6th November last were satisfactory upon the item on which I addressed you; so far as this, that you advocate the circulation of the bible only on principles, or in a manner, different from the present popular plan. Your plan is no doubt more accordant to the genius of the christian religion; however, as Paul rejoiced that Christ was preached, whether in pretence or sincerity, so I rejoice that the bible is widely diffused by bible societies, whether in pretence or in sincerity. You will not, however, understand me as disagreeing with your plan; for I can assure you I think

well of it, and would wish to see the churches of Christ all doing so. I would much rather see the bible disseminated in this way than the present; as I have no doubt but the apostle would rather have seen Christ preached sincerely, than in pretence. But until I see your plan carried into effect, I will aid the present plan of distributing the bible.

I have thought much on the missionary plan since I read the first number of your paper, and I have read a good deal on the subject; and your views, as far as I understand them, appear to accord with mine. I have sent you, some time since, by a friend, Brown's History of Missions, which I wish you to read if you have not. I would, were I disposed to expose the missionary mistakes, desire no other documents than what come from the pens of missionary men and their advocates, to show their folly and the ignorance of christianity which appear in this popular project. I hope you will kindly receive these few hints from the pen of a friend, whose heart desires the success of truth, and who wishes you all success in opposing Antichrist in the various forms which he assumes. The plainness of these remarks forbids their appearance in your magazine; but I know you will respect the motives which dictated them.

Your sincere friend,
ROBERT CAUTIOUS.
P——, Va. Feb. 23, 1824.

—

To Mr. Robert Cautious.

Dear Sir—The "plainness of your remarks," as respects myself, should not, in my judgment, preclude their insertion in this work. I thankfully receive them, and in general acquiesce in their correctness. They are, indeed, such as had occurred to my own mind, and your statement of them confirmed me in the truth of them. I thank you for Brown's History. I will read it carefully, as soon as I find leisure. I have but partially read it, and at considerable intervals.

Our objections to the missionary plan originated from the conviction that it is unauthorized in the New Testament; and that, in many instances, it is a system of iniquitous peculation and speculation. I feel perfectly able to maintain both the one and the other of these positions. What charity, what lawless charity would it require to believe that a Reverend Divine, for instance, coming to the city of Pittsburgh some time since, under the character of a missionary, and after "preaching four sermons" of scholastic divinity to a few women and children in the remote corners of the city, called on the treasurer of the missionary fund in that place, and actually drew forty dollars for the four sermons: I say, what lawless charity would it require to consider such a man a servant of Jesus Christ, possessed of the spirit of Paul, or Peter, or any of the true missionaries!! My informant is a very respectable citizen of Pittsburgh. He assured me he had the intelligence from the treasurer's own lips. Ten dollars for a sermon one hour long! preached to the heathen in the city of Pittsburgh by a regularly educated, pious missionary!! How many widows' mites, how many hard earned charities were swallowed in one hour by this gormandizer!! Tell it not in Gath, publish it not in the streets of Askelon! "But," says an apologist, "it required the good man a week to study it; besides, he gave them prayers into the bargain." A week to study a sermon! for a graduate at college too!! Why his sermon was not worth a cent! There is not a lawyer in Pittsburgh who could not prepare an orthodox sermon in a week, and deliver it handsomely too for ten dollars. From the prayers and sermons of such missionaries, may the pagans be long preserved!

Not questioning the piety and philanthropy of many of the originators, and present abettors of the missionary plan, we must say that the present scheme is not authorized by our King. This, I think, we proved some time ago; and no man that we have heard of, has come forward publicly to oppose our views. Indeed, I think we have few men of any information who would come forward openly to defend the plan of saving the world by means of money and science; of converting pagans by funds raised indirectly from spinning wheels, fruit stalls, corn fields, melon patches, potatoe lots, rags, children's play things, and religious newspapers, consecrated to missionary purposes; and from funds raised directly by begging from every body, of every creed, and of no creed whatever. By sending out men to preach begging sermons, and to tell the people of A's missionary patch of potatoes producing twice as much per acre, as those destined for himself and children; of B's uncommon crop of missionary wheat, a part of which he covetously alienated from the missionary to himself, and, as a judgment upon him, his cow broke into his barn and ate of it until she killed herself; of E's missionary sheep having each yeaned two lambs a piece, while his own only yeaned him one a piece, and a variety of other miracles wrought in favor of the missionary fund. I say, what man of good common sense and of a reasonable mind would come forward to defend a scheme of converting the world by such means, and by the means of that very "vain philosophy" and "science falsely so called," condemned by the apostles. Hoping always to hear from you when you have any thing deemed worthy of my attention, I remain your friend,   A. Campbell.

When the Messiah was crowned Lord of All, he sent out missionaries, called and qualified to proclaim salvation to the ends of the earth, and to set up his kingdom in the world. Behold their success in the following abstract from Paley's Evidences, p. 235.   Ed.

"The institution, which properly began only after its author's removal from the world, before the end of thirty years has spread itself throughout Judea, Galilee, and Samaria; almost all the numerous districts of the Lesser Asia, through Greece, and the islands of the Ægean Sea, the sea coast of Africa, and had extended itself to Rome and into Italy. At Antioch in Syria, at Joppa, Ephesus, Corinth, Thessalonica, Berea, Iconium, Derbe, Antioch in Pisidia, at Lydia, Saron, the number of converts is intimated by the expressions "a great number," "great multitudes," "much people." Converts are mentioned, without any designation of their number, at Tyre, Cesarea, Troas, Athens, Philippi, Lystra, Damascus. During all this time, Jerusalem continued not only the centre of the mission, but a principal seat of the religion; for when saint Paul returned thither, at the conclusion of the period of which we are now considering the accounts, the other apostles pointed out to him, as a reason for a compliance with their advice, "how many thousands [myriads, ten thousands] there were in that city who believed." Thus the work goes on in which the Lord has a hand."

Numbers of our neighboring clergy read the Christian Baptist, and having read it, as public censors of the press, tell their people, on "the Sabbath," that they ought not to read it: that it is dangerous to families to admit it within their walls. (Because it recommends the scriptures as their own interpreter, and exposes the tricks of the clergy.) This is like themselves. On all occasions, when the craft has been in danger, they have acted thus. The clergy once obtained a decree that every man's goods should be confiscated, who admitted into his house the writings of a monk, who opposed the priesthood, and recommended the bible. But, to save the clergy from the sin of "sabbath breaking," we will give any of them an opportunity of publishing in this paper, *literatim et punctuatim*, any thing they have to offer in their own defence, or against us. We shall give them page for page. Do, then, gentlemen, come forward manfully, and speak out against us. We speak openly. Come and do likewise.   Editor.

Queries.

Did God ever *call* a man to any work for which he was not fully qualified, and in the performance of which he was not successful?

Ans. No, if we except the modern preachers at home, and those called missionaries abroad. They say they are *specially called*, but neither their qualifications nor their success warrant the belief of these professions. With an open bible in my hand, I must say that God never called a man to any work for which he was not fully qualified, and in the performance of which he was not successful.

If you believed yourself specially called by God to preach the gospel to the Birmans, what would you do?

Ans. I would not ask the leave of any Board of Missions, nor their support; but, confiding in the power and faithfulness of him that called me, I would, without conferring with flesh and blood, depart, and look to Heaven for every provision, protection, and support, by land and sea, necessary for safe conduct thither, and also for success when I arrived. If I could not thus act, I could not believe myself called, nor expect success in the undertaking. This, reason requires. But enthusiasm, superstition, or covetousness would prompt one to apply to flesh and blood for patronage and support, and at the same time to profess to be called by God and to rely upon him for protection and success. Editor.

No. 9.]   April 5, 1824.

Essays on ecclesiastical characters, councils, creeds, and sects.—No. I.

Having paid a little attention to the clergy of our time, we shall now examine the principles, views and circumstances, that gave rise to such an order of men. The modern clergy are much indebted to those who laid the foundation of their empire. Other men have labored, and they have entered into their labors. Little do many think, and indeed little do they know, that the modern clergy are indebted to Pythagoras, Socrates, Plato, Aristotle, Zeno, Epicurus, and a thousand Pagan philosophers, Jewish and Christian theorists, for the order of things which they found ready to their hand, soon as they put on the sacerdotal robes. Philosophers originated opinions, opinions obtained disciples, disciples made sects, sects adopted creeds,

creeds required councils, councils published canons; and all these created and required priests to illustrate, to approbate and to fulminate their decisions. The consolidation of systems of measures for establishing and perpetuating a flourishing spiritual commonwealth, required a thousand ingredients that escape public notice, because not submitted to public inspection.

Our plan requires us to notice the ancient philosophers and the sects which they established, as many of their opinions were early imbibed by most of the christian teachers, and were soon an element of their creeds. We shall begin with Pythagoras.

This philosopher flourished about five hundred and fifty years before Christ. He travelled extensively, and spent twenty-five years in Egypt in quest of knowledge. He opened a school at Croton in Italy, which was much frequented by Grecian and Italian youths. He was the first man that called himself a philosopher, and gave currency to the name. He inculcated on his pupils the austerities of the Egyptian priests. He obliged them all to put their property into a common stock, and thus to have all things in common. He used the three sorts of style adopted by the Egyptians in teaching their mysteries: the simple, the hieroglyphical, and the symbolical. He preferred the last. He first called the world *kosmos*, from its order and beauty; and became famous for his skill in geometry, astronomy and arithmetic. But his theological principles are those which we have in view. He taught that,

"All mankind lived in some pre-existent state, and that for the sins committed by them in that state, some of their souls were sent into human bodies, and others into brutes, to be punished for, and to be purged from, their former sins. Viewing the whole brutal creation to be animated by human souls, he held it unlawful to kill any animal, and to eat animal food. In order to purge themselves from sins committed in a pre-existent state, he taught his disciples to practise long fastings, and other severities, to subdue their bodily appetites, and to subordinate all desires to the soul. These were the grand peculiarities of his system."

Socrates flourished four hundred years before Christ. He is said to have taught (for he left nothing in writing behind him) that,

"The soul of man is immortal, because immaterial; that there is but one supreme God; that there are demons that superintend the affairs of this world; that men ought not to pursue riches or worldly honors, but to cultivate their minds and to practise virtue. It is believed that he borrowed some of his ideas from the Jewish scriptures."

Plato, the scholar of Socrates, flourished three hundred and forty-eight years before Christ. It is chiefly from his writings that we learn the sentiments of Socrates. He improved upon the principles of Socrates, and his fame transcended that of all other philosophers, in the department of religion and morality. He taught that,

"The universe was governed by a being of glorious power and wisdom, possessed of perfect liberty, and independence. That there were a certain invincible malignity and corruption in matter, insuperable by the power of God. That the human soul is an emanation from God, so, necessarily immortal; that evil must necessarily exist from the union of matter and mind in the human person; that demons were an order of beings inferior to the Deity, but superior to men, and that they governed the world; consequently, that they should be worshipped because of their agency in human affairs. Some of them he viewed as mediators, "carrying men's prayers to God and his answers to men." In his Timæus he declares, that "it is neither easy to find the parent of the universe, nor safe to discover him to the vulgar when found." He therefore taught that, in matters of worship, his disciples ought to govern themselves by the laws of their country (*nomo poleos*.) This was the maxim of Socrates, and to it Plato agreed. In his book viii. De Rep. he orders "worship and rites to be performed to the gods, and to demons, and to Esculapius, lest he should too much shock the prejudices of the vulgar."

Aristotle, the disciple of Plato, flourished three hundred and thirty-two years before Christ. He taught that,

"Matter was eternal; that the world, by powers natural to matter, has continued from all eternity the same as we see it, and that there exists nothing in the universe distinct from matter; that the present course of things, consisting of the motions of the heavens, and of the successive generations and corruptions of animals and vegetables, can neither be interrupted nor destroyed by any thing extraneous, but must continue forever. As for the Deity, if there were any, he taught that it is a nature happy in the contemplation of itself, and entirely regardless of human affairs."

Epicurus, founder of the Epicurean system of philosophy in Greece, flourished two hundred and seventy years before Christ. The Epicureans maintained that,

"The world arose from chance; that the gods whose existence they did not dare to deny, neither did nor could extend their providential care to human affairs; that the soul was mortal; that pleasure was to be regarded as the ultimate end of man, and that virtue was neither worthy of esteem nor choice but with a view to the attainment of pleasure."*

Zeno, the first teacher of the Stoic system, flourished in Greece two hundred and sixty four years before Christ.

"The god of the Stoics is described as a corporeal being, united to matter by a necessary connexion, and subject to the determination of an immutable fate. This fate is, however, explained by the Stoics to be the wise counsels of their sovereign, to which he is obliged to conform, and from which he can never depart. When the Stoics say Jupiter is subject to fate, they mean he is subject to the wisdom of his own counsels, and must act in conformity with his supreme perfections. They said that the existence of the soul was confined to a certain period of time. They looked with indignant contempt upon effeminate vices. Simplicity and moderation were carried to the extreme of austerity, and external good and evil were viewed with haughty contempt."

The Cynic philosophy, taught first by Antisthenes, was so similar in its moral discipline to that of the Stoics, that we shall subjoin the sum of moral doctrine of Antisthenes and the Cynic sect:

"Virtue alone is a sufficient foundation for a

---

* Pleasure is supposed by some to mean, in this system, not only sensual, but to comprehend moral and intellectual pleasures. "If so," says a learned writer, "in what does the scheme of Epicurus, as respects virtue, differ from the opinion of those christian philosophers, who maintain that self-love is the only spring of all human affections and actions."

happy life. Virtue consists, not in a vain ostentation of learning, or an idle display of words, but in a steady course of right conduct. Wisdom and virtue are the same. A wise man will always be contented with his condition, and will live rather according to the precepts of virtue, than according to the laws or customs of his country. Wisdom is a secure and impregnable fortress—virtue, armor which cannot be taken away. Whatever is honorable is good—whatever is disgraceful is evil. Virtue is the only bond of friendship. It is better to associate with a few good men against a vicious multitude, than to join the vicious, however numerous, against the good. The love of pleasure is a temporary madness." The following maxims and apothegms are also ascribed to Antisthenes: "As rust consumes iron, so does envy consume the heart of man. That state is hastening to ruin, in which no difference is made between good and bad men. The harmony of brethren is a stronger defence than a wall of brass. A wise man converses with the wicked, as a physician with the sick, not to catch the disease, but to cure it. A philosopher gains at least one thing from his manner of life—a power of conversing with himself. The most necessary part of learning is, to unlearn our errors. The man who is afraid of another, whatever he may think of himself, is a slave. Antisthenes, being told that a bad man had been praising him, said, What foolish thing have I been doing?"

The Academics, who, with the Epicureans, were the most numerous of the Grecian sects at the christian era, despaired of finding truth in such a variety of opinions, and therefore taught that,

"It was uncertain whether the gods existed or not; whether the soul was mortal or immortal; whether virtue was preferable to vice, or vice to virtue."

The Eclectics supposed that many things were unreasonable and absurd in all the systems of philosophy, and therefore set about forming a new system, comprising, what they supposed, the most reasonable tenets and doctrines of all the sects. This eclectic philosophy was taught with great success in Alexandria in Egypt, when the Messiah was born. And Philo the Jew, who was a member of this sect, represents it as very flourishing at that time. The Eclectics held Plato in the highest esteem, yet they made no scruple to join with his doctrines whatever they thought conformable to reason in the tenets and opinions of other philosophers.

Hitherto we have mentioned only the systems of philosophy that obtained first among the Greeks, and afterwards among the Romans. We shall just, in the same brief manner, notice the oriental philosophy, denominated by orientalists, not philosophy, but science. The votaries of the oriental science were numerous in Persia, Syria, Chaldea, and Egypt. Of this science there were many sects. It is worthy of remark, that, while "the Grecian and Roman sects of philosophy were much divided about the first principles of science, all the sects of the oriental science deduced their tenets from one fundamental principle." This science supposed that,

"The origin of evils, with which the universe abounds, was to be found not in God, whom they viewed as essentially good and benevolent; but as there was nothing beyond or without the Deity but matter, therefore matter is the centre and source of all evil, of all vice. That matter was eternal and derived its present form, not

from the will of the supreme God, but from the creating power of some inferior intelligence, to whom the world and its inhabitants owed their existence. Some imagined two eternal principles from whence all things proceeded, the one presiding over light and the other over matter; and by their perpetual conflict, explained the mixture of good and evil that appears in the universe. Others maintained that the being that presided over matter was not an eternal principle, but a subordinate intelligence, one of those whom the supreme God produced from himself. They supposed that this being was moved by a sudden impulse to reduce to order the rude mass of matter, and to create the human race. A third sort fell upon another system, and said that there was a triple divine principle, or a triumvirate of beings, in which the Supreme Deity was distinguished from the material, and from the creator of this world. The Supreme Being they supposed to be as a radiant light, most pure, diffused through the immensity of space, called the pleroma. The eternal nature, having dwelt long in solitude, produced from itself two minds of a different sex, which resembled the Supreme Parent in the most perfect manner. In process of time, from these two proceeded a celestial family. These were called Æons. How many of these there were was not decided. The Creator of this world they called Demiurge.

"Man, they considered a compound of terrestrial and celestial nature—of the evil principle of matter, and of the divinity. Those who subdue the evil principle that propels them to sin against the Supreme ascend directly to the Pleroma. Those yielding to the evil principle shall be sent after death into other bodies until they awake from their sinful lethargy. In the end the Supreme God shall come forth victorious, and, having delivered from their servitude the greatest part of those enslaved souls, shall dissolve the frame of this visible world and involve it in ruin. After this, primitive tranquility will be restored in the universe, and God shall reign with happy spirits in undisturbed felicity through endless ages."

Such were the prominent features of the oriental philosophy. Among the Jews, prior to the birth of the Messiah, there was also a variety of opinions and sects. They imbibed many of the opinions popular among the sects of philosophers, and even some of the superstitious notions of the Egyptians, Syrians and Arabians who lived in their neighborhood. In Palestine, the Jewish and Samaritan religions flourished at the christian era. The Samaritans originated in the time of king Rehoboam. Shalmanesser, king of Assyria, having besieged Samaria, the capital of the kingdom of Israel, contradistinguished from the capital of the kingdom of Judah, carried the people captive and filled their place with Babylonians, Cutheans, and other idolators. These having obtained an Israelitish priest, to instruct them in the ancient religion of the land, embraced the Jews' religion, with which they mixed a great part of their own idolatry. After the return of the Jews from their captivity, they entirely quitted the worship of idols. They, though united in religion with the Jews, quarrelled with them about the rebuilding of the temple; and when they could not prevail, they erected a temple on Mount Gerizim, in opposition to that at Jerusalem. The Jews and Samaritans, like many sects in our time, who approximate very nigh to each other, but go not the whole length, cherished a cordial antipathy against each other; so much so, as to have no dealings with one another. The Jews were divided into three principal sects, besides many subordinate ones, at the christian epoch—the Essenes, the Pharisees, and the Sadducees. The Essenes dwelt generally in solitude, and maintained that,

"Religion consisted, wholly in contemplation and silence. They practised a most religious abstinence. Many of them lived in celibacy, and observed a variety of penitential exercises and mortifications, borrowed from Egypt where many of them dwelt. The Essenes of Syria thought it possible to appease God by sacrifices, though in a manner quite different from the Jewish. Others maintained that a serene and composed mind, addicted to the contemplation of divine things, was the only sacrifice acceptable to God. They viewed the law of Moses as an allegorical system of spiritual and mysterious truths, and renounced all regard to its letter in the explication of it. They held absolute predestination, and that only the soul would be punished in a future state."

The Sadducees maintained that,

"Only the written law was of divine authority; that neither the oral law nor the prophets were to be regarded as of divine authority; that the written law was to be interpreted literally; that there was no resurrection, nor future state, angel, nor human spirit; that there was no predestination; that man was an absolute master of all his actions."

The Pharisees taught that,

"The law of Moses, the prophets, and the oral law, or the traditions of the elders, were of equal authority; that there was a resurrection of the dead, a future state, angels and spirits; that the children of Abraham alone should be raised from the dead and enter into future happiness; that there should be eating and drinking in a future state; and that every man would be reunited to his former wife. They held absolute predestination, and at the same time, with the Sadducees, they held free will. They separated from all they deemed sinners, and would not so much as eat or drink with them. They held that the words of the Old Testament had a double sense—the one *literal*, the other *mysterious*. They were strict observers of all the traditions of the elders, and cultivated a very sanctified appearance in the presence of the people."

Such were the leading moral and religious philosophical sects that were flourishing when the Messiah was born. Besides these there was an endless variety of subdivisions. Nearly three hundred different opinions were entertained amongst the Romans concerning the *summum bonum*, or chief good. Thus the Messiah found the world with respect to opinion; and as respected the worship of idols in all its variety, volumes could do no more than give their names. Their gods, their temples, their priests, their sacrifices, and their festivals, would require an age to unfold.

The use we intend to make of the preceding documents in the course of this work, demanded this brief notice of them. We hope our readers will ultimately agree with us in the necessity of giving this abstract.—EDITOR.

———

Extracts from my Sentimental Journal.
No. I.
The Nature and Power of Faith illustrated.

IN approaching the city we met multitudes of men and women flying in every direction, some

H

of them having literally forsaken all that they had; husbands had left their wives, parents their children, and children their parents. I asked every one who would stop to hear me, what was the matter. I always heard in reply, "The barbarian foes, the ruthless band, the merciless Scythians are approaching our city." Have they yet entered it? replied I. "No," said they. Are they yet in sight? I rejoined. I was again answered in the negative. Why then do you hasten? was the last question their trepidation would afford me time to ask. The answer which I received was pronounced with uncommon vehemence. Every feature in their face, and every tone corresponded with the import of their reply. It was this: "Twelve heralds of undoubted veracity gave the intelligence that they were just at hand, arrayed in all the vengeance of savage ferocity, stimulated to furious excess, from the ills they had received from our nation." I joined the fugitives, and, after retiring to a cave, fell into the following reflections:—

What an advantage to mankind that they have received from their Creator the capacity or faculty of being so certain of what they have not seen, of that for which they have not the evidence of sense, as to be moved, excited, and impelled to every kind of exertion, suited to the nature of the case, from what they have believed, as though they had seen it. The uncultivated citizen, as well as the sage philosopher, is equally certain, and equally moved by the belief of testimony. It is a blessing, thought I, an inexpressible favor, that we have this capacity of being assured of what we have not seen, of what we have not felt, upon the testimony of others; and that this is as common to all mankind as instinct is to brutes, and so perfect at first that it is not capable of improvement; for a child believes as firmly, what it can apprehend, as a hoary-headed sage. This people, thought I, have been saved by faith—saved from the jaws of destruction, by believing what the twelve heralds reported. I could not but reflect with surprise at the stupidity of those rabbinical doctors who have made so many nonsensical distinctions about the way and manner of believing, and the different kinds of faith. I found those people saved their lives by faith, without ever stopping to inquire of what kind their faith was; the only inquiry was about the evidence—about the number, character, ability, and faithfulness of the witnesses. Being satisfied upon these points, they never thought of consulting their own feelings upon the occasion. But the fact which they believed operated upon all that was within them, just according to its own nature. It produced all its natural results; for every fact believed has its natural or necessary results, and from the nature of all things it must necessarily be so. It was not their belief or their faith, abstract from the fact, that saved them; but the fact believed, that produced such a change upon them and upon their conduct. In one word, these people were saved by the belief of one fact, and that fact was of so great importance as to change their views and practice.

Leaving the cave, and making my retreat into the interior of the country, I met, after a few days, an old acquaintance, Timothy Stedfast, who used to be rather of a melancholy temperament, when employed as a menial servant in the service of Lord A. His countenance, attire, and gait, astonished me. Instead of that downcast aspect, and evil-boding, melancholic appearance, a peculiar cheerfulness overspread his countenance, and an eye beaming with joy, indicated that some marvellous change had taken place in the views and circumstances of Timothy.— His raiment, too, was not of that rough and homespun texture as that in which he formerly performed his services in the fields and gardens of his former master. He was sumptuously apparelled, and even his style of address and demeanor participated in the general elevation and improvement in his aspect. What! said I, so far from home, friend Timothy! "Yes," said he, "and I must be farther yet; I am just going to the sea coast to embark for Jamaica."— What! to Jamaica? "O yes, and I would go much farther on the same errand." Pray can you inform me of the nature of your errand? "Yes, with pleasure, and no doubt it will give you joy to know it." Say on. "You know I had an old uncle, of whom I once told you, living in Jamaica, who was very rich; his children being all dead, he has left me his vast estate, and now I am going to possess it. It is said to be worth half a million, and the old gentleman having lately departed this life, has bequeathed the whole of it to your humble servant." Indeed! said I. But how do you know that such is the fact? He replied, that three persons whom he once knew, men of undoubted veracity, had written to him informing him of the fact; "besides," said he, "a copy of his last will and testament has been forwarded to me, to which the seal of the chief magistrate is appended.— I am certain, I am certain," exclaimed he. "It is a fact." O then, said I, I wish you all possible happiness; but be mindful that you were once poor. We parted.

I began to muse again on the excellency and power of faith. Truly I thought it was the "confidence of things hoped for, and the conviction of things not seen." And what first struck me with irresistible force, was, that the fact believed always operates according to its own nature. What a change in the views, feelings, appearance, and pursuits of Timothy!— Once a rough, unpolished, downcast, desponding servant; now he possesses a smooth and polished exterior, a cheerful countenance, and a joyful heart; rich in faith, though not yet in actual possession of the inheritance. How powerful the principle! What an impulse to activity, industry, and perseverance! He forsakes the land of his nativity, his father's house, his kindred, and the companions of his youth; he encounters the toils of a long journey, perils by land and dangers by sea, from the influence of faith.— This is the cause, the sole cause, of this extraordinary change. He cultivates the manners, the style, the demeanor, suitable to his anticipated circumstances; and though yet not in possession of the inheritance, rejoices in hope of realizing all his expectations. And what still astonishes me, the belief of one fact thus converts the man—not the way and manner of believing, but the fact believed is the whole mystery.

I was roused from my meditations upon this striking instance of the nature and power of faith, by meeting a friend whom I had met a few days ago, in all the cheerfulness and joy of good health, of good circumstances, of the finest animal spirits, light, gay, buoyant; but now clothed in mourning, and of a sad and dejected appearance. A heavy sigh and a cheek washed with tears indicated the bitterness of her grief. With querulous accents she told me that two friends, of great respectability of character, had written to her that her aged father,

her younger brothers, and sisters, had perished by the victorious barbarians in the late invasion; that her father did not hear the tidings in time to effect an escape. I told her not to faint in the day of adversity; besides, said I, it may not be so bad as you expect; perhaps your informants were not assured of the fact. "Oh!" exclaimed she, "I could wish I could not believe their testimony; but I know their character and their competency to give certain information; and I am certain, yes, undoubtingly certain, that such is the fact." I dismounted and retired to an inn, where I spent the evening in meditating upon the simplicity, the power, and excellency of faith. The following conclusions were the necessary results of the scenes through which I had recently passed:—

1. In the first place the singular power of faith is manifested in all places and amongst all people. It demonstrates itself to be one of the common, the most common, and intelligible principles of action; and produces the greatest changes in human character, in the views and pursuits of mankind. It overcomes the greatest difficulties, and impels men to the highest achievements known in the world.

2. It always operates according to the fact believed. Joy and sorrow, love and hatred, fear and hope, are the effects of the fact believed, and not of the manner of believing, so much talked of.

3. Evidence alone produces faith, or testimony is all that is necessary to faith. This is demonstrably evident in every case; and therefore the certainty felt is always proportioned to the character of the testimony produced. Faith is capable of being greatly increased in many instances; but only in one way, and that is, either by affording additional evidence, or by brightening the evidences already produced.— To exhort men to believe, or to try to scare them into faith by loud vociferations, or to cry them into faith by effusions of natural or mechanical tears, without submitting evidence, is as absurd as to try to build a house or plant a tree in a cloud.

4. Faith, abstract from facts, produces no substantial, no real effect. Faith and opinions have nothing to do with each other—there is no consanguinity between them. A man might as reasonably expect to support animal life by the simple act of chewing, as to be saved by the mere act of believing. It is not a man's eating that keeps him alive, but what he does eat; so it is not a man's believing that saves his soul, but what he does believe.

5. All controversies about the nature of faith, about the different kinds of modern faith, are either learned or unlearned nonsense, calculated to deceive and bewilder the superstitious multitudes that hang upon the lips of spiritual guides. The only, the grand question with every man is, What is fact, or truth? This ascertained, let there be no inquiries about how a man believes, or whether his faith be of the right kind. If a man really believes any fact, his faith soon becomes apparent by the influence of the fact upon him.

6. No person can help believing when the evidence of truth arrests his attention. And without evidence it is as impossible to believe, as to bring something out of nothing.

7. The term *faith* is used in the Bible in the commonly received sense of mankind, and the faith which we have in the testimony of God differs from that we have in the testimony of men in this one respect only—that as men may

be deceived, and may deceive others, so the confidence we repose in their testimony, in some instances, may be very limited; but as God cannot be deceived himself, neither can deceive others, so the confidence we have in his testimony is superior to that we repose in the testimony of men; and as the word comes to us in demonstration of the Holy Spirit, or attested to us by the supernatural gifts which accompanied the testimony of the original witnesses; so it affords the highest possible evidence, and therefore produces the greatest confidence. If we receive the testimony of men, says John, and act upon it in the most important concerns, the testimony of God is greater, and is capable of producing greater certainty, and infinitely worthy of being acted upon in the all-important concerns of the world to come.   EDITOR.

That Jesus is the Christ.

GEORGE KING is the name of a man; but that George is king, is a proposition that expresses what either is, or is not true. And that George is the king is a proposition not only more definite than George is king, but it expresses something more. It expresses that he is either the chief of kings, or that he is the king spoken of or referred to by the speaker. This, we presume, is apprehended by all. Now, Jesus Christ is the name of a person; but that Jesus is Christ, or that Jesus is the Christ, is a proposition that is either true or false. In the four gospels, or during the lifetime of the Messiah, the term Christ was never applied to him as a proper name, but as an appellative. After some time it was used as a proper name, and frequently without the name Jesus attached to it, it designated the Saviour. Thus, when Matthew wrote "the lineage of Jesus Christ," he used the word as a proper name; but it is obvious to all, from the perusal of the four gospels, especially in the original, or in Campbell's improved translation, that the term Christ was never addressed to the Saviour, while on earth, as a proper name, but as an appellative. The use of the article in the Greek is lost in many places in the English by the negligence or misapprehensions of king James' translators. Dr. Campbell observes in his Preliminary Dissertations, vol. i. p. 223: "If we were to judge by the common version, or even by most versions into modern tongues, we should consider the word as rather a proper name than an appellative, or name of office, and should think of it only as a surname given to our Lord. Our translators have contributed greatly to this mistake, by very seldom prefixing the article before Christ, though it is rarely wanting in the original. The word Christ was at first as much an appellative as the word baptist was, and the one was as regularly accompanied with the article as the other. Yet our translators, who always say *the* baptist, have, one would think, studiously avoided saying *the* Christ. This may appear, to superficial readers, an inconsiderable difference; but the addition of the article will be found, when attended to, of real consequence for conveying the meaning in English, with the same perspicuity and propriety with which it is conveyed in Greek. So much virtue there is in the article, which, in our idiom, is never prefixed to the name of a man, though it is invariably prefixed to the name of office, unless where some pronoun or appropriating expression renders it unnecessary; that, without it, the sense is always darkened, and sometimes marred. Thus, in such expressions as these, "this Jesus whom I preach unto you is Christ—Paul testified to the Jews that Jesus was Christ—showing by the scriptures that Jesus was Christ"—the unlearned reader forms no distinct apprehension, as the common application of the words leads him uniformly to consider Jesus and Christ, as no other than the name and surname of the same person. It would have conveyed to such a reader precisely the same meaning to have said, "Paul testified to the Jews that Christ was Jesus;" and so of the rest. The article alone, therefore, in such cases, adds considerable light to the expression; yet no more than what the words of the historian manifestly convey to every reader who understands his language. It should be, therefore, "Paul testified to the Jews that Jesus was the Christ, or the Messiah," &c. Many other examples might be brought to the same purpose; but these are sufficient."

That Jesus is the Christ is proposed to us as a truth in the New Testament. But what is implied in the term Christ? John tells us that it is a correct translation of the word Messiah. Now both terms denote one and the same thing; for Messiah in Hebrew, and Christ in Greek, signify anointed. That Jesus is the anointed, is, in our tongue, equivalent to "Jesus is the Christ." But still a question may occur, What is the meaning or peculiar import of the term "anointed" in this connexion? To this we answer from the bible, that persons designed for the office of king, for the office of high priest, and, sometimes, for the office of prophet, were, by a divine command, anointed with oil, and thus empowered and consecrated by God to the office for which they were designated. Thus Saul was called the Lord's anointed, and this consideration prevented David from taking away his life when obnoxious to his wrath and in his power. David also, and the kings of Judah were thus consecrated and empowered to act as kings, as viceroys, under God, over Israel. In allusion to this ceremony of inauguration, Paul applies to our King these words: "your God has anointed you with the oil of gladness above your associates in office," above all the prophets, priests, and kings that were ever sent to Israel.

Three eminent prophets, David, Isaiah, and Daniel, represent the promised Deliverer as an anointed prophet, an anointed priest, and an anointed king. Isaiah represents him as an anointed prophet, chap. lxi. 1. "The Lord has anointed me to preach good tidings to the poor." Daniel represents him as an anointed priest, chap. ix. 25. 26. "And after threescore and two weeks shall the anointed, Messiah the Prince, be cut off, but not for himself," &c. David, in the second psalm, represents him as an anointed king. He represents the alliance of the kings of the earth against the Lord's anointed, and sings his coronation upon Zion the hill of his holiness. The whole of the salvation which sinful men require is comprised in the performance of these three offices. We are ignorant, guilty, and enslaved. To remove ignorance is the office of a prophet; to remove guilt, the office of a priest; and to emancipate and lead to victory, to defend and protect, the office of a king. Now, to believe that "Jesus is the Christ," is to receive him as the only prophet, the only priest, and the only king, qualified and empowered by our heavenly Father to instruct us, to atone and intercede for us, to reign over our conscience, to guide, defend, and lead us to victory. His qualification for these offices, being "the Son of God, the only begotten of the Father," renders him infinitely worthy of our confidence, and constrains us to trust in him with all our hearts. To his word, as our prophet, we look for instruction; to his sacrifice and intercession we look for pardon and acceptance; and to him, as King on the throne of the universe, we yield implicit obedience, and are assured, if we put ourselves under his guidance, he will lead us to complete and triumphant victory. As we have used, and may often use the phrase "Jesus is the Christ," we thought it expedient to give this brief statement of the ideas attached to that phrase. EDITOR.

The foundation of Hope and of Christian Union.

MESSIAH is born in the city of David, in the awful crisis alluded to in the first essay in this number. Science had proved itself systematic folly; philosophy, falsely called moral, had exhibited its utter incompetency to illumiaate the understanding, to purify the heart, to control the passions, to curb the appetites, or to restrain the vices of the world. A scepticism that left nothing certain, a voluptuousness that knew no restraint, a lasciviousness that recognized no law, a selfishness that proscribed every relation, an idolatry that deified every reptile, and a barbarity that brutalized every feeling, had very generally overwhelmed the world, and had grouped those assimilated in vice, under every particular name, characteristic of every species of crime. Amidst the uncertainty, darkness, and vice that overspread the earth, the Messiah appears, and lays a foundation of hope, of true religion, and of religious union, unknown, unheard of, unexpected among men. The Jews were united by consanguinity, and by an agreement in a ponderous ritual. The Gentiles rallied under every opinion, and were grouped, like filings of steel around a magnet, under every possible shade of difference of thought, concerning their mythology. So long as unity of opinion was regarded as a proper basis of religious union, so long have mankind been distracted by the multiplicity and variety of opinions. To establish what is called a system of orthodox opinions as the bond of union, was, in fact, offering a premium for new diversities in opinion, and for increasing, *ad infinitum*, opinions, sects, and divisions. And what is worse than all, it was establishing self-love and pride as religious principles, as fundamental to salvation; for a love regulated by similarity of opinion, is only a love of one's own opinion; and all the zeal exhibited in the defence of it, is but the pride of opinion.

When the Messiah appeared as the founder of a new religion, systems of religion consisting of opinions and speculations upon matter and mind, upon God and nature, upon virtue and vice, had been adopted, improved, reformed, and exploded time after time. That there was always something superfluous, something defective, something wrong, something that could be improved, in every system of religion and morality, was generally felt, and at last universally acknowledged. But the grandeur, sublimity, and beauty of the foundation of hope, and of ecclesiastical or social union, established by the author and founder of christianity, consisted in this, that the belief of one fact, and that upon the best evidence in the world, is all that is requisite, as far as faith goes, to salvation. The belief of this one fact, and submission to one institution expressive of it, is all that is required by Heaven to admission into the church. A christian, as defined, not by Doctor Johnson, nor any creed-maker, but by one taught by Heaven, and in

Heaven, is one that believes this one fact, and has submitted to one institution, and whose deportment accords with the morality and virtue taught by the great Prophet. The one fact is, that Jesus the Nazarene is the Messiah. The evidence upon which it is to be believed is the testimony of twelve men, confirmed by prophecy, miracles, and spiritual gifts. The one institution is baptism into the name of the Father, and of the Son, and of the Holy Spirit. Every such person is a christian in the fullest sense of the word, the moment he has believed this one fact, upon the above evidence, and has submitted to the above mentioned institution; and whether he believes the five points condemned or the five points approved by the synod of Dort, is not so much as to be asked of him; whether he holds any of the views of the Calvinists or Arminians, Presbyterians, Episcopalians, Methodists, Baptists, or Quakers, is never once to be asked of such a person, in order to admission into the christian community, called the church. The only doubt that can reasonably arise upon these points, is, whether this one fact, in its nature and necessary results, can suffice to the salvation of the soul, and whether the open avowal of it, in the overt act of baptism, can be a sufficient recommendation of the person, so professing, to the confidence and love of the brotherhood. As to the first of these, it is again and again asserted, in the clearest language, by the Lord himself, the apostles Peter, Paul, and John, that he that believes the fact that Jesus is the Christ, is begotten by God, overcomes the world, has eternal life, and shall, on the veracity of God, be saved. This should settle the first point; and as to the second, it is disposed of in a similar manner; for the witnesses agree that whosoever confesses that Jesus is the Christ, and is baptized, should be received into the church; and not an instance can be produced of any person being asked for any other faith, in order to admission, in the whole New Testament. The Saviour expressly declared to Peter, that upon this fact that he was the Messiah, the Son of God, he would build his church; and Paul has expressly declared, that "other foundation can no man lay (for ecclesiastical union) than that Jesus is the Christ." The point is proved that we have assumed, and this proved, every thing is established requisite to the union of all christians upon a proper basis. Every sectarian scheme falls before it, and on this principle alone can the whole church of Christ be built. We are aware of many objections to this grand scheme, revealed by God, to establish righteousness, peace, and harmony among men; but we know of none that weighs a grain of sand against it. We shall meet them all (*Deo volente*) in due time and place. Some of them have been anticipated in one or two articles preceding. But of these more fully hereafter.

It must strike every man of reflection, that a religion requiring much mental abstraction or exquisite refinement of thought, or that calls for the comprehension or even apprehension of refined distinctions and of nice subtleties, is a religion not suited to mankind in their present circumstances. To present such a creed as the Westminster, as adopted either by Baptists or Paido-Baptists; such a creed as the Episcopalian, or, in fact, any sectarian creed, composed, as they all are, of propositions deduced by logical inferences, and couched in philosophical language, to all those who are fit subjects of the salvation of Heaven—I say, to present such a creed to such for their examination or adoption, shocks all common sense. This pernicious course is what has paganized christianity. Our sects and parties, our disputes and speculations, our orders and casts, so much resemble any thing but christianity, that when we enter a modern synagogue, or an ecclesiastical council, we rather seem to have entered a Jewish sanhedrim, a Mahometan mosque, a Pagan temple, or an Egyptian cloister, than a Christian congregation. Sometimes, indeed, our religious meetings so resemble the Areopagus, the Forum, or the Senate, that we almost suppose ourselves to have been translated to Athens or Rome. Even christian orators emulate Demosthenes and Cicero; christian doctrines are made to assume the garb of Egyptian mysteries, and christian observances put on the pomp and pageantry of pagan ceremonies. Unity of opinion, expressed in subscription to voluminous dogmas imported from Geneva, Westminster, Edinburgh, or Rome, is made the bond of union, and a difference in the tenth, or ten thousandth shade of opinion, frequently becomes the actual cause of dismemberment or expulsion. The New Testament was not designed to occupy the same place in theological seminaries that the carcases of malefactors are condemned to occupy in medical halls—first doomed to the gibbet, and then to the dissecting knife of the spiritual anatomist. Christianity consists infinitely more in good works than in sound opinions; and while it is a joyful truth that he that believes and is baptized shall be saved, it is equally true that he that says, "I know him, and keeps not his commandments, is a liar, and the truth is not in him."   EDITOR.

From a Baptist in Ohio to the Editor.

SIR—I would ask you, in the name of my calling, are you trying to raise the dead? Why do you make so much ado about primitive christianity, which I had thought had been buried together with the scriptures for sixteen hundred years? It is true, Luther, Calvin, and some others took some pains to raise some part of it, while the remainder was out of reach of their popular views, and would not be suitable to the taste that then prevailed. Now, sir, let me ask you if you are not afraid that your efforts will terminate to your injury? Were not these men as capable of judging for themselves as you are? and did they not know that modern things were better suited to modern people, than old fashions? Besides, sir, christianity has been so long buried, that it may be said of it as was said of Lazarus—it gives an offensive smell—it is disgusting to our taste. Hence, when you recommend any primitive practice, the moderns cannot endure it, but cry out, " away with it! away with it!" Do you think that it would avail any thing to tell the ladies of fashion that the old fashions were better than the modern? Would they not reply that it makes no matter—the modern are now in vogue, and the ancient are out of vogue. Just so the people in religious matters. When I say that the bible is buried, do not mistake me—it is only the simple and plain meaning of it, that has been long since discarded.

As for the clergy, why do you assail them? Do not you know that it is as easy to remove mountains as to convince a man that the very object of his dependance, the very thing that procures him an easy, if not a luxurious living, is all a foolish device—an imposition on the credulity of mankind? What could be more suitable to an indolent man than to have to work only one day in seven to maintain himself and family, and to be esteemed too as a gentleman of the first rank; to march at the head of grand processions; to be placed in the uppermost seats in public assemblies; nay, to be placed, as you once told us, on a wooden throne in the midst of a popular assembly. I think, sir, you would betray no ordinary ignorance of human nature, if you would persevere to convince a man so circumstanced that it was the belief of a falsehood put him in such snug and happy circumstances.

I fear, sir, you read the bible in the old-fashioned way—such as, "Feed the flock of God which is among you, taking the oversight thereof, not by constraint, but willingly; not for filthy lucre, but of a ready mind. Neither as being lords over God's heritage, but being ensamples to the flock; and when the Chief Shepherd shall appear, you shall receive a crown of glory that fades not away." Whereas the clergy read it thus to one another, in its modern sense: "Feed yourselves on the flock of God which is among you, by constraining them to feed you if they do it not of a ready mind; taking the oversight of the flock for filthy lucre's sake, and not from a willingness to give, but from a willingness to receive. Being as lords over God's heritage, and by no means ensamples to the flock; and when we ministers sit in council you shall have double honor." I will only refer you to another instance of the modern reading, that you may be admonished to abandon the project of getting the people to read in the old style. The clergy read *Acts* viii. 36—39. thus: " And the parents took their child to a certain meeting-house, and said, See here is water in the basin, what does hinder us to have our infant christened? The minister answered and said, If either of you believe, it may be done. The father then answered, saying, I believe in the Westminster Confession of Faith, and Catechisms Larger and Shorter. Then the priest, the parents, and the child drew near to the basin, and after consecrating the element, the priest besprinkled the infant's face. Then the spirit of Antichrist caught away the parson and he was found in the sacred desk, and the parents went on their way with the child crying, until its tears mingled with, and washed off, the sacred dew." Unless you can get the people to read the bible in the old-fashioned way, your efforts, sir, will be unavailing. Yours truly,
                          STEADY SEEKTRUTH.

No. 10.]   MAY 3, 1824.
Essays on Ecclesiastical Characters, Councils, Creeds, and Sects.—No. II.

HAVING in the preceding number introduced the opinions and speculations of the philosophical religionists, before and at the christian era, we will now give our readers an account of the corruption of the christian religion by those opinions and philosophical religious teachers. This we shall do in the words of one who cannot be much suspected for an extraordinary attachment to primitive christianity. Mosheim, from the mass of evidence upon this subject to which he had access, satisfactorily shows that the first "theological seminary," established at Alexandria in Egypt, in the second century, was the grave of primitive christianity. Yes, it appears that the first school instituted for preparing christian doctors was the fountain, the streams whereof polluted the great mass of christian professors, and completed the establishment of a paganized christianity in the room of the religion of the New Testament. But let us hear a popular doctor tell the awful tale in his own words:—

"Towards the conclusion of this century, a new sect of philosophers arose of a sudden, spread with amazing rapidity throughout the greatest part of the Roman empire, swallowed up almost all the other sects, and was extremely detrimental to the cause of christianity. Alexandria in Egypt, which had been for a long time the seat of learning, and, as it were, the centre of all the liberal arts and sciences, gave birth to this new philosophy. Its votaries chose to be called Platonics, though far from adhering to all the tenets of Plato. They collected from the different sects such doctrines as they thought conformable to truth, and formed thereof one general system.

"This new species of Platonism was embraced by such of the Alexandrian christians as were desirous to retain, with the profession of the gospel, the title, the dignity, and the habit of philosophers. It is also said to have had the particular approbation of Athenagoras, Pantænus, Clemens the Alexandrian, and all those who, in this century, were charged with the care of the public school* which the christians had at Alexandria. These sages were of opinion that true philosophy, the greatest and most salutary gift of God to mortals, was scattered in various portions through all the different sects; and it was, consequently, the duty of every wise man, and more especially of every christian doctor, to gather it from the several corners where it lay dispersed, and to employ it, thus reunited, in the defence of religion, and in destroying the dominion of impiety and vice.† The christian eclectics had this also in common with the others, that they preferred Plato to the other philosophers, and looked upon his opinions concerning God, the human soul, and things invisible, as conformable to the spirit and genius of the christian doctrine.

"This philosophical system underwent some changes, when Ammonius Saccas, who taught with the highest applause in the Alexandrian school about the conclusion of this century, laid the foundation of that sect which was distinguished by the name of the New Platonics. This learned man was born of christian parents, and never perhaps gave up entirely the outward profession of that divine religion in which he had been educated. As his genius was vast and comprehensive, so were his projects bold and singular; for he attempted a general reconciliation or coalition of all sects, whether philosophical or religious, and taught a doctrine which he looked upon as proper to unite them all, the christians not excepted, in the most perfect harmony.‡ And herein lies the difference between this new sect and the Eclectics, who had, before this time, flourished in Egypt. The Eclectics held that in every sect there was a mixture of good and bad, of truth and falsehood; and accordingly they chose and adopted out of each of them such tenets as seemed to them

conformable to reason and truth, and rejected such as they thought repugnant to both. Ammonius, on the contrary, maintained that the great principles of all philosophical and religious truth were to be found equally in all sects; that they differed from each other only in their method of expressing them, and in some opinions of little or no importance; and that, by a proper interpretation of their respective sentiments, they might easily be united into one body. It is further to be observed, that the propensity of Ammonius to singularity and paradox, led him to maintain that all the gentile religions, and even the christian, were to be illustrated and explained by the principles of this universal philosophy; but that, in order to this, the fables of the priests were to be removed from paganism, and the comments and interpretations of the disciples of Jesus from Christianity.

"This arduous design, which Ammonius had formed of bringing about a coalition of all the various philosophical sects, and all the different systems of religion that prevailed in the world, required many difficult and disagreeable things in order to its execution. Every particular sect and religion must have several of its doctrines curtailed or distorted before it could enter into the general mass. The tenets of the philosophers, the superstitions of the heathen priests, the solemn doctrines of christianity, were all to suffer in this cause, and forced allegories were to be subtilely employed in removing the difficulties with which it was attended. How this vast project was effected by Ammonius, the writings of his disciples and followers that yet remain, abundantly testify. In order to the accomplishing his purpose, he supposed that true philosophy derived its origin and its consistence from the eastern nations; that it was taught to the Egyptians by Hermes; that it was brought from them to the Greeks, by whose vain subtleties and litigious disputes it was rendered somewhat obscure and deformed; but was, however, preserved in its own original purity by Plato, who was the best interpreter of Hermes and of the other oriental sages. He maintained that all the different religions that prevailed in the world, were, in their original integrity, conformable to the genius of this ancient philosophy; but that it unfortunately happened that the symbols and fictions under which, according to the eastern manner, the ancients delivered their precepts and their doctrines, were, in process of time, erroneously understood, both by priests and people, in a literal sense; that, in consequence of this, the invisible beings and demons whom the Supreme Deity had placed in the different parts of the universe as the ministers of his providence, were, by the suggestions of superstition, converted into gods, and worshipped with a multiplicity of vain ceremonies. He therefore insisted that all the religions of all nations should be restored to their original purity, and reduced to their primitive standard, viz. "the ancient philosophy of the east;"* and he affirmed that this his project was agreeable to the intentions of Jesus Christ, whose sole view in descending upon earth was to set bounds to the reigning superstition, to remove the errors that had crept into the religions of all nations, but not to abolish the ancient theology from whence they were derived.

"To this monstrous coalition of heterogeneous doctrines, its fanatical author added a rule of

---

* These were similar to our Rev. D. D.s, presidents of theological schools—the great luminaries of those days, as famous as our Andover and Princeton professors and schools.

† This is the argument now used in defence of the study of "moral philosophy" by those who advocate a learned priesthood.

‡ This was similar to Dr. Mason's "Plea for Catholic Communion," predicated upon grounds different from the one foundation already laid by divine authority.

* This is analogous to making the "Westminster Creed" the grand standard of christian truth and the bond of union.

life and manners which carried an aspect of high sanctity and uncommon austerity. He, indeed, permitted the people to live according to the laws of their country and the dictates of nature; but a more sublime rule was laid down for the wise. They were to raise above all terrestrial things by the towering efforts of holy contemplation, those souls whose origin was celestial and divine. They were ordered to extenuate, by hunger, thirst, and other mortifications, the sluggish body, which confines the activity and restrains the liberty of the immortal spirit; that thus, in this life, they might enjoy communion with the Supreme Being, and ascend after death, active and unencumbered, to the Universal Parent, to live in his presence forever.* As Ammonius was born and educated among the christians, he set off, and even gave an air of authority to these injunctions, by expressing them partly in terms borrowed from the sacred scriptures, of which we find a vast number of citations also in the writings of his disciples. To this austere discipline, he added the pretended art of so purging and refining that faculty of the mind which receives the images of things, as to render it capable of perceiving the demons, and of performing many marvellous things by their assistance. This art, which the disciples of Ammonius called *theurgy*, was not, however, communicated to all the schools of this fanatical philosopher, but only to those of the first rank.

" This new species of philosophy, imprudently adopted by Origen and many other christians, was extremely prejudicial to the cause of the gospel, and to the beautiful simplicity of its celestial doctrines.† For hence it was that the christian doctors began to introduce their subtle and obscure erudition into the religion of Jesus, to involve in the darkness of a vain philosophy, some of the principal truths of christianity that had been revealed with the utmost plainness, and were indeed obvious to the meanest capacity, and to add to the divine precepts of our Lord many of their own, which had no sort of foundation in any part of the sacred writings.‡ From the same source arose that melancholy set of men, who have been distinguished by the name of Mystics, whose system, when separated from the platonic doctrine concerning the nature and origin of the soul, is but a lifeless mass, without any vigor, form, or consistence. Nor did the evils which sprung from this Ammonian philosophy, end here. For, under the specious pretext of the necessity of contemplation, it gave occasion to that slothful and indolent course of life, which continues to be led by myriads of monks retired in cells, and sequestered from society, to which they are neither useful by their instructions nor by their examples. To this philosophy, we may trace, as to their source, a multitude of vain and foolish ceremonies, proper only to cast a veil over truth, and to nourish superstition; and which are, for the most part, religiously observed by many, even in the times in which we live.§ It would be endless to enumerate all the pernicious consequences that may be justly attributed to this new philosophy, or rather to this monstrous attempt to reconcile falsehood with truth and light with darkness. Some of its most fatal effects were, its alienating the minds of many in the following ages, from the christian religion; and its substituting, in the place of the pure and sublime simplicity of the gospel, an unseemly mixture of platonism and christianity.

" The number of learned men among the christians, which was very small in the preceding century, grew considerably in this. Among these there were few rhetoricians, sophists, or orators. The most part were philosophers attached to the eclectic system, though they were not all of the same sentiments concerning the utility of letters and philosophy. Those who were themselves initiated into the depths of philosophy, were desirous that others, particularly such as aspired to the offices of bishops or doctors, should apply themselves to the study of human wisdom, in order to their being the better qualified for defending the truth with vigor, and instructing the ignorant with success.* Others were of a quite different way of thinking upon this subject, and were for banishing all argumentation and philosophy from the limits of the church, from a notion that erudition might prove detrimental to the true spirit of religion. Hence the early beginnings of that unhappy contest between faith and reason, religion and philosophy, piety and genius, which increased in the succeeding ages, and is prolonged even to our times, with a violence that renders it extremely difficult to be brought to a conclusion. Those who maintained that learning and philosophy were rather advantageous than detrimental to the cause of religion, gained, by degrees, the ascendant, and, in consequence thereof, laws were enacted, which excluded the ignorant and illiterate from the office of public teachers.† The opposite side of the question was not, however, without defenders; and the defects and vices of learned men and philosophers contributed much to increase their number, as will appear in the progress of this history."‡

Mosheim's Ecc. Hist. p. 163—173.

Let the reader bear in mind that a high churchman unequivocally represents primitive christianity as having been buried in the rubbish of Egyptian philosophy by the first doctors of divinity in the first theological seminary that ever existed in the christian church; and that many of those vanities, ceremonies, mysteries, and Ammonian institutes are come down to our times, and inserted in our creeds. Christians, read your bibles, and be admonished to explode from your religious faith and practice what you cannot find in the scriptures. The New Testament is the creed, discipline, and formula of christianity. Most of the popular schemes, and dogmas, and institutes are Egyptian, Babylonish, or Roman.

Our Essay on Experimental Religion

HAS been received with considerable diversity of feeling. Some are pleased with it, others displeased, and not a few know not whether to

---

* Modern religious fasts and austerities are just the same as those of Ammonius and the Egyptians.

† This Origen was the greatest doctor of divinity that ever lived, and disseminated more error and absurdity than any other writer of ancient or modern times. He got it from Egypt.

‡ Many of these remain unto this present time, and are adopted by Catholics and Protestants.

§ Reader, mark this well. Read it again, and see if you can find out any of those "vain and foolish ceremonies which cast a veil over truth."

* This is just in modern style; but remember this notion came from Egypt.

† This is similar to the laws of many sects yet existing, which decree that so many years must be spent at colleges and theological schools to qualify a man "for defending the truth," and, most frequently, error, " with vigor."

‡ We must thank Heaven that all did not worship this beast, that a few names in Sardis escaped this awful calamity.

approve or disapprove. We are sorry to find that almost all the objections we have heard against it have arisen from a misunderstanding of our design and meaning. It is said that we have taught that there is no necessity of being born again by the Spirit of God; that we have denied that Christians are new creatures, and that we have confined all divine grace to the apostolic age. Now we must confess that we did not intend to communicate such ideas; nor do we think that such can be fairly gathered from our words. But so consecrated is the phrase "experimental religion," that if you make the least freedom with it every feeling is excited, and it is like calling in question a man's title to his estate.

But in exposing the vain conceits of many about the nature and manner of this renovation, we were led, as we hinted, into a species of the same kind of metaphysical reasoning, which we feared would lead to mistakes. It is universally acknowledged by those who have attended to the operation of their own minds, that it is extremely difficult, if not impossible, to form any tolerable idea of the nature or manner of those operations. But it is agreed that the mind operates in its own way, whether we adopt a right or a wrong theory about its method of operating. Just so with respect to divine operations, or the operation of supernatural intelligences. We know such operations exist, but the *modus* or manner of these operations is inscrutable; and let our theory be right or wrong, these operations proceed in their own way—neither guided, controled, nor prevented by our theories. But wrong views of this subject may greatly injure both the peace and happiness of those that entertain them. And whenever any theory leads us to disregard the written word of God, or to neglect the constant reading and examination of it, and the practice of its plain injunctions, that theory is erroneous and dangerous.

As to the effects attendant upon the truth believed, we are clearly taught that these are such as to fitly characterize the believer as a *new man*. He is possessed of three principles of action, the most powerful and triumphant: these are faith, hope, and love. All revealed truth is the matter, or, as some call it, the object of faith. Future good things promised by God are the object or matter of hope, and the Lovely One, and every one that is like him, are the object of the christian's love. These principles purge, purify, elevate, and ennoble the mind that possesses them. "The gospel," as one in a certain place beautifully observed, "presents a faithful testimony to be believed, good things to be hoped for, and the most amiable one to be loved." The purification of our hearts, the refinement of our feelings, the elevation of our character, the reformation of our lives, are the inseparable fruits of the belief of the one fact, upon the evidence contained in the faithful record.

We have been censured for our manner of treating the enthusiastic and sectarian religion of our times. Perhaps, in this instance, we were too much in the spirit of Elijah, who thus addressed the false teachers of his time, and in relation to their god, said to them, "Cry aloud, for he is a god; either he is talking, or he is pursuing, or he is on a journey, or peradventure he sleeps and must be awaked." 1 Kings, xvii. 29. Yet this Elijah was one that feared, and loved, and served the God of Israel, though a little profane," as some would say, on this occasion. Paul, in the same spirit, said, "Ye suffer fools gladly, seeing you yourselves are wise;" and also besought the Corinthians to "forgive him the wrong" he had done them, in not being burdensome to them. On sundry occasions he speaks thus "profanely," especially when he said, "The things which the gentiles sacrifice, they sacrifice to demons and not to God." It was also "very impudent" in him to say, "The Cretans are always liars, evil beasts, slow bellies."

We have discovered that something under the name of "experimental religion," is the very soul of the popular system, and that this subject is worthy of a very serious and profound discussion; we will therefore promise our readers a series of essays on the office assigned to the Holy Spirit in the salvation of men, as this is developed to our view in the holy scriptures. Every thing called grace in the heart, christian experience, experimental religion, regeneration, &c. will come under this head. Patience, however, will be necessary on the part of our readers; and let those who are disposed to know what is truth upon this subject, as well as every other, in the mean time devoutly examine the scriptures for themselves.

We have just got out of our hands a heavy job of writing, which has engrossed much of our time and attention during the winter and spring. We hope to be able to bestow more time and labor on this work than we have hitherto been able to bestow on it.   EDITOR.

Awful Calculation.

AN ingenious, authentic, and valuable statistical work, published a few years since, calculates that the number of inhabitants who have lived on the earth amount to about 36,627,-843,275,075,846. This sum, the writer says, when divided by 3,096,000, the number of square leagues on the surface of the globe, leaves 11,-830,698,732 persons to each square league.—There are 27,864,000 square miles of land, which being divided as above, give about 1,314,522,076 persons to each square mile. Let the miles be reduced to square rods, and the number, he says, will be 2,853,273,600,000, which being divided as above, gives 1283 inhabitants to each square rod, which rod being reduced to feet and dividing as above, it will give about 5 persons to each square foot of terra firma on the globe. Let the earth be supposed to be one vast burying ground, and, according to the above statement, there will be 1283 persons to be buried on each square rod; and a rod being capable of being divided into 12 graves, it appears that each grave must have contained a hundred persons, and the whole earth have been one hundred times dug over to bury its inhabitants, supposing they had been equally distributed! What a lesson to human pride, vanity, and ambition!—*N. A. Eagle.*

No. 11.]   JUNE 7, 1824.

WE omit in the present number, our third Essay on Ecclesiastical Characters, &c. to give room for the following article written by one of our correspondents. It is not intended that it should be considered as occupying the place of any one of those essays we have proposed on the office of the Holy Spirit, as promised in our last. These essays we shall defer commencing in the present volume, but we shall attend to them in our second. The following letter is worthy of the examination of our readers:

To the Editor of the Christian Baptist.

SIR: When your eighth number of the Christian Baptist came to hand, upon reading your animadversions on experimental religion, I was persuaded that it would likely give offence to many of your pious readers; and that, instead of obviating the charge brought against you and your associates, of "denying experimental religion," it would rather increase it. This I have since understood to be actually the case. I, therefore, for my part, could have wished, that you had treated that very delicate, and, at the same time, very important subject, in a different manner. I am not to be understood as objecting to the detection and exposure of a false and unscriptural experience, which, from your words, appears to be the thing intended; for, in your foot note, page 141, you assert, that we are taught, that "since those gifts have ceased, the Holy Spirit now operates upon the minds of men only by the word;" and at the close of said note, you further assert, that "we are positive of one point," namely, "that the scriptures teach us not the doctrine of physical operations of the Divine Spirit in order to faith." With these declarations as I understand them, I am quite satisfied; for, since the sacred canon has been completed, it seems to be the general opinion, at least of all the most eminent Protestant writers that have adverted to this subject, that we are not to look for any new revelations of the Spirit; and that, of course, his saving operations in the production of faith and repentance, and of every other gracious effect by which we are made partakers of a divine nature, (*2 Peter* i. 4.) is by the word of truth being put into the mind and written upon the heart, (*Heb.* viii. 10.) for this certainly is one of the exceeding great and precious promises above referred to, (*2 Peter* i. 4.) by which the Lord has graciously engaged to save his people, (*Heb.* viii. 10.) As to regeneration itself, or, as it is commonly termed, the new birth, we are divinely assured, that it is effected by the word of truth. (*James* i. 18.) Of his own will begat he us by the word of truth; and (*1 Peter* i. 23—25.) Being born again not of corruptible seed, but of incorruptible, by the word of God, which lives and abides forever. And this is the word which by the gospel is preached to you.

Again—both the beginning and progress of Messiah's kingdom are ascribed to the word. Compare *Matthew* xiii. with *Mark* iv. and *Luke* viii. "Behold a sower went forth to sow," namely, the word of the kingdom; for the sower sows the word. "And he that received seed into the good ground, is he that hears the word and understands it; who, in an honest and good heart, having heard the word, keeps it, and brings forth fruit with patience." Again, (*Mat.* xvi. 16, 18,) Simon said to Jesus, You are the Christ, the son of the living God. Jesus answered and said to him, Upon this rock will I build my church and the gates of hell shall not prevail against it. Accordingly John, in his first Epistle, chap. v. verse 1, asserts, that whosoever believes that Jesus is the Christ is born of God. And Peter, in his first Epistle, chap. ii. verse 2. exhorts all such, that "as new born babes, they would desire the sincere milk of the word, that they might grow thereby." Again, Christ's farewell prayer for his disciples, is, "Holy Father, sanctify them through your truth; your word is truth. Neither pray I for these alone, but for them also who shall believe in me through their word." *John* xvii. 17—20, and *Paul to the Ephesians*, v. 25, asserts that "Christ loved the church

I

and gave himself for it that he might sanctify and cleanse it with the washing of water by the word." Also, Peter in his first epistle, chap. 1, verse 22, addresses the brethren to this effect: "Seeing you have purified your souls in obeying the truth through the Spirit, to unfeigned love of the brethren, love one another with a pure heart fervently." Lastly, to close this chain of quotations, it is worthy of remark, that the whole body of the persecuted disciples of Jesus is represented as overcoming the grand adversary by the blood of the Lamb, and by the word of their testimony. *Rev.* xii. 11. Now "who is he that overcomes the world, but he that believes that Jesus is the Son of God? And this is the victory that overcomes the world, even our faith." *1 John* iv. 5. Upon the whole of the evidence before us respecting the instrumentality of the word in the salvation of men, we find that it is the beginning, middle and end; that every thing is done by it, and that there is nothing done without it. That where the word of the truth of the gospel is not published, the Spirit of Christ has nothing to do, is farther evident from *John* xvi. 3—14, where his reproving or convincing the world of sin, of righteousness, and of judgment, is confined to his testifying the things concerning Jesus. In short, his very character as the spirit of Christ, as the spirit of wisdom and revelation, for enlightening, convincing, comforting and establishing, in the knowledge and belief of the truth, is ascribed to him exclusively as revealing and testifying the things concerning Jesus. Compare *John* xiv. 26, and xvi. 14, 15, with 1 *Cor.* xii. 3—13, with *Eph.* i. 13—18, and 1 *Pet.* i. 10—12, and ii. 18, 19, with Jude 14, 15.

For the more full illustration of the truth and certainty of this conclusion let us again review and examine the evidence, that we may clearly perceive the connexion of the word with the kingdom of Christ in its rise, progress and consummation, or ultimate triumph and perfection in this world.

1. And first we shall find that the word of the gospel is the seed of the kingdom; that every subject of it is begotten by, and born of that seed. See *John* i. 13, *James* i. 18, 1 *Peter* i. 23, 25, 1 *John* iii. 9. Upon this point of the testimony three things are expressly evident.

First, that every subject of Messiah's kingdom is born of God.

Second, that his birth is by the means, or through the instrumentality, of the word of truth.

Third, that this seed in each is the very and imperishable substance of his new being. Consequently, till this seed is sown and takes effect, there cannot be an existing subject of the Redeemer's kingdom upon earth.

II. Again, it appears from the evidence before us, that the radical formative truth, the inwrought perception, and real persuasion of which gives birth and being to the new creature, is that expressed by our Lord in his declaration to Peter, *Matt.* xvi. 16—18, with 1 *John* v. 1. It farther appears, that it was for the demonstration of this truth, that both the predictions, types and promises of the Old Testament were exhibited and recorded, and also the things that are written concerning Jesus by the four Evangelists. See *Luke* xxiv. 25, 27, 44, 45.: *John* xxiii. 30, 31. Consequently there cannot be one born of God, but by means of the scriptural persuasion and hearty reception of this truth, in the light of its proper evidence, and true scriptural import; for if Jesus be truly received as the Messiah, the Christ, he must be received in character; that is, in the true scriptural import of his personal, relative and official appellations. But who sees not that all this is virtually and truly implied in the belief of the great fundamental truth under consideration, viz. "That Jesus is the Christ, the Son of the living God." For whosoever is persuaded of the truth of this grand fundamental article, upon the evidence which God has afforded, the same is heartily disposed to receive whatever this glorious personage has affirmed, or caused to be taught concerning himself, and his Father, and the salvation, which he has accomplished.

III. Hence, thirdly, according to the evidence before us, we are justified, sanctified, nourished, and obtain a final victory and triumph over all the power of the enemy, by the belief of the truth; that is, by the word of the truth of the gospel, believed and acted upon.

First. We are actually justified in believing the apostles' testimony concerning Jesus, that is, the gospel. Compare *Mark* xvi. 15. 16, *Rom.* v. 1, with *Acts* xiii. 38, 39, and 1 *Cor.* ii. 1, 2, and xv. 1—6.

Second. We are also sanctified by the same word believed. See as above. *John* xvii. 17, *Eph.* v. 26, 1 *Peter* i. 22.

Third. By the same word the believer is nourished, comforted, and made to grow in grace. 1 *Peter* ii. 2, *Jer.* xv. 16, 1 *Thess.* iv. 18, 1 *Tim.* iii. 6.

Lastly. By faith, which is a belief of the divine testimony concerning Jesus, believers are made victorious over sin, Satan, the world and death. See *Rom.* vi. 14, 17, 18, 1 *Peter* v. 3, 9, *James* iv. 7, *Rev.* xii. 11, 1 *John* v. 4, 5, *Heb.* ii. 15. Therefore may all believers say, "Now thanks be to God, who gives us the victory through our Lord Jesus Christ." 1 *Cor.* xv. 57. Upon the whole, it is evident that all the salvation that is known or experienced in this world, is in consequence, and by virtue of, the knowledge and belief of the truth, which works effectually in them that believe. 1 *Thess.* ii. 13. Neither is there any other means appointed or acknowledged by God, for the salvation of men, but the scripture revelation of Jesus Christ. Compare *Mark* xvi. 15, 16, with *Luke* xxiv. 46, 47, and *Acts* iv. 12. That where this scripture revelation is not heard, not known, there neither is, nor ever was, nor indeed can be, any faith in Christ Jesus, (see *Rom.* x. 9, 14,) nor of course any regenerate, any purified in heart, (see *Acts* xv. 7, 9,) nor any endued with the spirit of adoption, crying Abba, Father. *Rom.* viii. 14, 16, with *Gal.* iv. 6, 8. But, instead of such characters, the debased and stupid practisers of horrid cruelties and abominable idolatries, "do service to them who by nature are no gods." This, all may know to be the present as it most certainly was the ancient state of the heathen world, in the days of the apostles and long before. Nor can it be shown, that since the gospel was first preached to the nations, from the day of Pentecost, (*Acts* ii. 1,) until this day, that any portion of the human family were ever reformed from their idolatries and disgraceful immoralities by any supposed physical operations of the Holy Spirit without the word. To talk, therefore, of christian experience by any supposed operations of the Holy Spirit without the word, or previous to, and independent of, the knowledge and belief of the truth, is not only contrary to most express declarations of holy scripture and universally established fact, but to reason also. It supposes a fact without a proper and adequate cause. It supposes a conversion from error and wickedness, without the proposal of truth and goodness

to the understanding and heart of the creature. It supposes faith without the exhibition of a testimony to be believed, a thing absolutely impossible. It also supposes love to God in his true and lovely character, of just and holy, merciful and gracious, which the gospel alone manifests, which, without the knowledge and belief of that gospel, is a thing equally impossible with the former. Love and devotion to an unknown God!! Again, to speak of experimental religion by way of contradistinction to a false religion, appears equally absurd. Whoever heard of a religion, Jewish or Christian, Pagan or Mahomedan, Popish or Protestant, that is not productive of some kind of experience —that produces no sensible effect upon the mind of the sincere professor of it? Can such a religion be found upon earth? Let us have done, then, with this unscriptural, indefinite, unmeaning phrase, which, at best, is only calculated to perplex, mislead, and deceive. When we speak of our holy religion, let us speak of it, and distinguish it by proper epithets, such as the scriptures afford, instead of those vain delusive epithets, which the wisdom, or rather the folly, of men has invented.

Yours respectfully, T. W.

Extracts from my Sentimental Journal.
No. II.
Social Prayers.

BEING shipwrecked on the island of Ila, on Friday, the 7th of October, 1808, on the first day of the following week I went to the parish church, and was entertained with a specimen of good old Scotch divinity, pronounced with all the gravity of aspect and solemnity of tone, for which the Scotch divines of the Presbyterian establishment, in the pulpits purified by the fire of the Scottish apostle John Knox, are eminently distinguished. The nobleman, who was Laird of the island, a distinguished member of the duke of Argyle's family, was present with his family; and as his patronage extended over the pulpits as well as the lands of the island, they occupied a very ostensible pew in the kirk, and a very conspicuous place in the prayers of the good parson. His temporal and spiritual welfare, and that of every branch of his illustrious family, next to that of King George III. and all the princes and princesses of the royal blood, were the burthen of his concluding prayer. Pleased with the aspect, pronunciation, and gravity of this venerable parson, I visited the same kirk, the next first day, called in Scotland, "the Sabbath." Archibald Campbell, esq., for that was the name of the Laird of the island, was absent, being about to take his seat in the British parliament. His pew being empty, the good old parson forgot to give him any place in his prayers, and the king's place in his petitions was considerably contracted since the preceding "Sabbath." Being detained by adverse winds and the inclemencies of the season until a third "Sabbath," I revisited the synagogue again. The doctrine was precisely orthodox, according to the standards of that kirk; but as the nobleman's pew was still empty, he had no portion in the prayers of the day. I bade adieu to the island and its hospitable inhabitants, the recollection of whose kindness yet awakens many grateful feelings, and sincere desires for their happiness.

How a man so devout as the parish parson, could forget to pray for his patron when absent, and be so mindful of him in his addresses to heaven when he was present, remained deeply impressed upon my mind, and was frequently a subject of curious reflection. I had not, however, travelled very far, nor continued many weeks amongst the pious Highlanders, till I found that it was a general practice in all parish churches, when the patron was present, to give him a large portion of the evening prayer, but always when absent he was forgotten. Being but just arrived at the period of reflection, and determined to study men as well as things, I became very attentive to the prayers of not only the parish clergy, but of all others. I observed it to be a general rule, that when two or three ministers of the same party happened to be present in the same pulpit, which ever one prayed, he made particular supplications for his ministering brethren. Thus the parson A prayed very ardently for his brothers parson B and C, when they were present; but when B and C were absent, A asked for no blessings for them. I do not recollect that I ever saw it otherwise in any sect or in any country. I noted this fact in my pocket book of memorandums, and placed it under the same head with those of the prayers of the parish ministers for their patrons. I think I headed this chapter, in my juvenile fancy, with the words, "*Complimentary prayers,* or prayers addressed to human beings not yet deified." In process of time, I happened to make a tour with a very devout divine; and, as he always spent the night in the house of some of his "lay brethren," in offering up his evening sacrifice, or what is more frequently called "leading in family worship," he never forgot to pray in an especial manner for his host, earnestly desiring that the family among whom he spent the night might be peculiarly blessed. During fourteen days and nights which I spent in his company, he never once forgot to pray for the proprietor of the house that gave him his supper and bed. In justice to his devotion I should remark, that one evening was spent in an inn, where he asked the liberty of attending upon family worship; and there he also prayed as fervently for his landlord and landlady as if in a private family. In justice to the landlord too, I should observe, that he remitted to him his bill in the morning, with an invitation to give him a call when convenient. Now custom had so familiarized the practice, that it was as natural for me to expect to hear the householder and his handmaid prayed for, as it was for me to kneel down when the prayer commenced. But even yet I was struck with the curious nature of that devotion which led his reverence to pray for X and his family, and for Y and his family, when he was in their house, and that although so very fervent this night in praying for X and his family, the next evening he forgot X and prayed for Y only, and so on without variation. This I also noted down under the head of "Complimentary prayers."

I would not be understood as censuring the practice of one christian praying for another, when it is by request, or when from any consideration it becomes necessary; or of a whole church praying for another church, or for one member, or for those that are not members, either in their presence or absence. But this is quite a different thing from those prayers which we call complimentary, which, if not intended as a mere compliment, most certainly appear so, in the above instances at least, and in many others which might be adduced.

But there is something very incongruous in these complimentary prayers. A enters the house of B and his wife C, and joins with them in prayer; he speaks in the first person plural, "we ask," "we pray," "we beseech," &c. By and by he begins to supplicate blessings on the persons of B and C. He still uses the same style, "we." Now B and C either join with him or they do not. On either hypothesis the prayer is no longer social. It is A praying for B and C, and B and C praying for themselves. A does not merely pray for them—they pray for themselves, and he is only included in such petitions as are of a general nature. He acts the part of an intercessor in one part of his petitions, and they, in another part, pray for him equally as themselves. Custom familiarizes, recommends and sanctions every thing. But there is neither reason nor scripture for such a practice. If two or three persons unite in prayer they should have some definite object which mutually interests them all alike.

It is usually allowed that it is one of the greatest and best of blessings that we should be admitted to lift up our voices to the throne of the universe. But if ever there be a moment in a christian's life when humility and sincerity become him well, this is the moment, when he is speaking to that glorious and Mighty One, before whose throne seraphs veil their faces and "angels prostrate fall." Our words assuredly should be few and well ordered; no pomp of language, no vain parade of words, no compliment to men, when we claim the audience of our Almighty Maker.

In visiting the family of an old friend ten years ago, I heard him confess the sins of his childhood, youth, and manhood, and pray for their forgiveness. I continued with him for one week. As often as he prayed in his family he made a repetition of the same confession of his and his family's sins, and a similar petition for their remission. In the course of a few years I visited him again, and heard the same confessions and petitions. Not long since I spent an evening with the same old gentleman, and heard the same without any sensible variation.

Methinks this aged professor has yet to learn the import of the "glad tidings of great joy to all people," one item of which most certainly assures the believer of the remission of all his sins committed previously to the hour he trusted in the Saviour. Hence the primitive christians never once prayed for the remission of the sins of their childhood, youth, manhood, or old age, committed previously to their reception of the good news. Not one instance can be produced of any saint, from the full revelation of the gospel of Christ on the day of Pentecost, praying for such a remission; but we find them thanking God that he had already, for Christ's sake, forgiven them all trespasses. They were commanded by the apostles to forgive one another, even as God, for Christ's sake, had forgiven them.

In short, to have prayed for the remission of the sins of childhood, youth, &c. committed while they were ignorant of the salvation of the gospel, would have evinced a total want of faith; for the asking for any favor plainly implies that the person who asks is not in possession of it. Suppose, for illustration, that I should go to my creditor and say, "I confess, sir, that I owe you a thousand talents, and as I am unable to pay you, I beseech you to forgive me." He replies, "Whatsoever you ask of me, of this nature, believe that you shall receive it, and you shall have it. Do you believe that my benevolence and ability are adequate to remit you this debt?" I answer, "Yes." Now suppose I should, every evening and morning, go to this rich and benevolent friend, and say to him, "I owe you a thousand talents—I am unable to pay you—I beseech you to forgive me that debt"—might he not, with propriety, say to me every time I went to renew my request, "Sir, you insult me. You profess to believe my word, and, in fact, you declare every day that you do not believe that I have been as good as my word. You either distrust my ability, my disposition, or my veracity. You dishonor me. Begone from my presence! but know assuredly, that whenever you trust in my ability, benevolence, and veracity, you are remitted." I must hang my head and remain speechless. Alas! the gospel of the blessed God is sadly mistaken by thousands who profess to believe it; who, not only in their ordinary deportment, but even in their religious observances, declare they believe it not. Alas! how many teachers of the gospel are in the habit of confessing and praying in the public assembly, as my old friend; and thus proving to the intelligent that, believe the gospel who may, they do not. Under the law, in their great sacrifices, there was a remembrance of sins made once a year, which the apostle adduces as an evidence of the imperfection of that state; but if there is to be a remembrance of sins once a week or once a day by the priests and the people now, we are in worse circumstances than the Jews. It is, indeed, evident, that few of the popular worshippers have received that one purification which leaves no consciousness of sins.   EDITOR.

Address to Christian Mothers.

Daughters of Zion:

THE christian religion has elevated your sex to a very high degree. To it you are indebted for that amelioration of your circumstances, that mitigation of your present grievances, incurred by your having been first in the transgression, that important place you occupy in the christian affection and esteem of him to whom you were put in subjection. Although some of your sex, in the history of the Old Testament, shine with distinguished lustre; yet it is in the New Testament alone where you appear to the highest advantage. Never, we presume, was Gabriel despatched upon a more honorable or a more acceptable errand, than when he visited the cottage of her that was espoused to the son of Jacob; than when he addressed the humble and virtuous virgin in these transporting words, "Hail! favorite of Heaven! The Lord is with you! Blessed are you among women!" From that moment your sex, as the sun after a long gloom, bursts forth with more attractive splendor. All the queens of eastern palaces, in all the pomp of eastern grandeur, never tasted the sweets of such an interview as that between Elizabeth, the mother of the harbinger, and the mother of Israel's King. All the expressions of imperial courtesy, how meagre in comparison of the welcome with which Elizabeth received that visit of her cousin, the salutation with which she embraced her! "How have I this honor, that the mother of my Lord should come to me!" The pious and virtuous Mary, and the humble swain that was made her husband guardian, exhibit a new scene of matrimonial bliss of which mortals never before tasted. He derives all his honor and his bliss from her entrusted to his care. A woman now elevates not only her own sex by the favor of Heaven, but also renders conspicuous in the annals of the world a descendant of that royal family that once reigned over Israel.

But we do not dwell at present on these illustrious incidents in your history, as if they were the only occurrences that gave importance and elevation to your sex. Let us just glance at a few others. The first miracle of this incomparable child, born, this only-begotten Son given, was wrought in honor of the mother that nursed him, and in honor of the first commandment with promise. His mother, at the famous marriage of Cana of Galilee, with all the deep solicitude of one concerned in every circumstance that concerned the reputation of the family with which she was in the intimacies of friendship, prompted her to appeal to her son, saying, "they have no wine." He shows it to be an occurrence which was of no concern to him, abstractly considered; but in honor of his mother, who commanded obedience to his will, the water when presented—yes,

"The modest water, aw'd with power divine,
Beheld its God, and reddened into wine."

This was the beginning of his fame, the first exhibition of his glorious power. And the last expression of solicitude for the temporal welfare of one of our race, which dropped from his lips amidst the agonies of the cross, was prompted by the keenest sensibilities of humanity, by that grateful recollection of the care of a mother, which is never to be forgotten; by that profound respect which every wise man exhibits to the woman that watched and wept over his childhood; yes, his last concern was for the future welfare of his mother. He says to John, his favorite disciple, casting his eye towards his mother, "Son, behold your mother;" and to his mother, "Behold your son." Thus he bequeathed his mother, as his richest legacy on earth, to that disciple whom he loved most of all.

Christian women, your praise and your fame, your zeal, your affection, and even your courage, shine with so much resplendence in the New Testament history, as to throw the most distinguished of our sex much, very much, into the shade. The fame of that Mary who sat at the feet of the Messiah, who anointed the Lord with ointment, and wiped his feet with her hair, transcends the fame of all the statesmen, warriors, monarchs, philosophers, and poets, that ever lived. Yes, while the fame of the statesman is bounded by our tenure of the soil on which we live; while the laurels that deck the brow of the warrior are stained with the blood he shed, and wither near the cypress that covers the tomb moistened by the tears of the widow and the orphans which he made; while the gems that sparkle in the crown of the monarch are dimmed and obscured by the cankering hand of time; while the renown of the philosopher fades in the presence of every insect, and of every plant, which says to his wisdom, "How limited you are!" and while the praises of the poet and the charms of harmony live only in the fastidious taste of men, O Mary, your memorial, the sweet perfume of your fame, extends to all generations! and that which you have done shall be told with extacy unalloyed, when time itself shall be no more!

And let the christian heroes remember, that when the highest and noblest names on their list of eighteen centuries fled like cowards from the scene of danger, and in the hour of darkness and terror deserted their suffering chief, christian women kept their place, and stood spectators near the cross. Yes, to the eternal praise of female piety, let it be published in all lands that women were the last at the cross, and the first at the tomb of their great and mighty Saviour. And as a token of his remembrance and acknowledgment of their devotion, pious courage, and unabated affection, to them he first showed himself alive after his death, and alleviated their sorrows.

But as it is not our intention to make these illustrious incidents in your history a theme form which to deduce all the reflections which they naturally suggest, we proceed to our design.

Your usefulness to the church is not curtailed by the apostolic injunction which allots to you that silence and submission which comport with that modesty and diffidence which are now and ever have been the highest ornaments of female character. You are to nurse and nourish every one that comes into the world; and the God of your offspring has given to you an authority over the mind in its most pliant state, paramount to every other. The babe that smiles in your arms, and finds its support and its refuge in your bosom, receives its first impressions from you. It recognizes a relation existing between you and it before it forms an idea of a father.— It views you as its best friend, and most willingly submits to your control. Your countenance is the first volume it reads; and it is a volume which conveys to its apprehension more ideas than perhaps any of us imagine. Its articulations are formed from yours, and your language is the first it can understand. You can converse with it, and communicate to its tender mind ideas which the greatest linguists and philosophers that ever lived could not.— You, then, occupy a place which cannot be rivalled, and which, if discreetly managed, may, under the blessing of Heaven, be of eternal importance to it. Do not be startled when I tell you that you are, by the law of nature, which is the law of God, as well as by his written word, ordained to be the only preachers of the gospel, properly so called, to your own offspring. You can tell them in language more intelligible to their apprehension, the wonders of creation; you can, from the lively oracles, teach them the history of our race; you can preach the gospel to them better than any Doctor of Divinity that ever lived. You can narrate to them the nativity and life, the words and deeds of Messiah; you can open to their minds how he died for our sins, and how he rose for our justification. You can tell them of his ascension to the skies, of his coronation in heaven, and that he will come to judge the world. When you have done all this, in a style which you can adopt, more easy of apprehension than any other—if Paul the apostle was again to visit the world and call at your house, he could not preach to them with greater effect. Nay, you have anticipated all that he could say, and done all that he could do, to give the word effect. If he were to attempt to make known the glad tidings of great joy, to announce the good news to your children—when he had done they might say, "Kind and benevolent friend, this is no news to us; we rejoice to have heard it all from a preacher before; a preacher too, whose love and benevolence were equal to yours, and whom we understood as clearly as we understand you." If he were to ask who the preacher was, and by what authority he spoke, the children might reply, It was from a preacher which you, beloved friend, yourself licensed; it was our mother whom you commanded "to

bring us up in the nurture and admonition of the Lord." O yes, replies the apostle, I did authorize an order of preachers which were to take my place after my decease, amongst whom your mother was one. My place and my office was to make known to all my contemporaries those glad tidings in the first place; for I was ordained a preacher as well as a teacher, and your parents can best occupy my place, as they can first make known to their offspring the same good news.

These hints, my dear friends, go to show you what is expected from you, and what you ought to do. And surely you will agree with me that the word of God, thus communicated by the fireside, from your own lips, under the blessing of Heaven, is just as efficacious as if pronounced from a pulpit of mahogany, covered with scarlet, and decked with tapestry, from a pontiff, or a rabbi covered with silk and a wig as white as Alpine snow. Remember Lois, Eunice, and Timothy, and Paul's commands to you. The giving of such an injunction to fathers and mothers implied that they were competent to perform them to the best advantage. The efforts of the clergy to take from you the office of preachers, under a pretence that either their authority or their ability is superior to yours, believe your friend, or rather believe the apostles, is an unjust encroachment upon your rights and privileges. Your example and your prayers, your authority, and your well proved affection and sincerity in all that you say, are worth more than all the logic, mathematics, algebra, and rhetoric, which ever were collected in all the seminaries upon earth, to give efficacy to your sermons. How blissful the privilege, and how high the honor conferred on you! Do then, christian matrons, from your love to your own offspring, and from your love to him that raised your sex to honors so illustrious, and from your hopes of immortality and eternal life in that world where they neither marry nor are given in marriage, but are as the angels, being the children of God and of the resurrection, bring up your children in the nurture and admonition of the Lord.					EDITOR.

WE design to give our readers every opportunity of judging for themselves, suppressing nothing written by friend or foe that respects our views. We have so far given them a specimen of what our opponents have said concerning this paper. The following letter, received a few days since, is from the pen of a very intelligent writer, who is the bishop of a respectable church, and with whom we are very sorry to differ in any opinion connected with the christian religion. We have the highest opinion of the integrity, uprightness, and christian deportment of this correspondent. I trust he will have the goodness to forgive me for publishing what was merely intended for my own consideration, when I assure him that it is purely for the benefit of my readers, as I have no doubt but it will be profitable to many.					EDITOR.

—

APRIL 22, 1824.
Dear Sir—I HAVE deferred writing to you longer than I designed when you left us.

I have received regularly your numbers of the Christian Baptist, and have read them with some care that I might understand with certainty the leading opinions which you design to defend, and those which you purposely oppose. I find much to condemn, and many things to approve.

Your opposition to the principle of missions is based upon an opinion which is altogether a new one, and which, I think, you have adopted without consideration, and is palpably erroneous. It is this: that the church is now in the place of the miraculous gifts, and is, "*in propria forma*, the only institution of God left on earth to illuminate and reform the world," as contra-distinguished from preaching the gospel, the commission to preach having ceased with the cessation of miraculous gifts. *No. 2. p. 16.*

I understand that the record is in the place of the miracles wrought by Christ and the apostles, and the words they used explanatory of them in proof that Christ is the Son of God; and that this record is the mean, preached and read for building up the church, so far from the church being in the place of the miraculous gifts. The conversion of individuals, by whose association the christian church is, and ever has been formed, is effected by the gospel record, comprehending the miracles. Yes, the record is in the place of the miraculous gifts, and not the church, which is in fact the effect of the record believed and acted on. The miracles are written and they are preached for the same purpose they were originally wrought, viz. that men might believe that Jesus Christ is the Son of God, which is the great principle of christian church union. They are as competent for that purpose now as they were when they were actually and sensibly exhibited. The church is of no use in illuminating and reforming the world, except so far as the saints who compose it are engaged in the work of the ministry, not only in preaching the gospel, but in illustrating its truths by a righteous and godly life. These two requisites ought never to be separated. A word to the wise is sufficient.

I regret exceedingly the opposition you have made to the missionary and bible society cause. It has greatly injured your usefulness, and put into the hands of your Paido-Baptist opposers a weapon to break the heads of the Baptists. They associate all that are peculiar to Baptists with your peculiar and strange notions on the subject of the bible and a preached gospel, that they may the more effectually destroy the effect of your debate with Mr. Maccalla.

My dear sir, you have begun wrong, if your object is reformation. Never attack the principle which multiplies the number of bibles, or which promotes the preaching of the gospel or the support of it, if you desire christianity to prevail. As I informed you when here, I repeat it again, your opposition to a preached gospel, to the preachers and bible societies, secures to you the concurrence of the covetous, the ignorant, the prayerless and Christless christians. Should they have had any religion, they cease to enjoy it as soon as they embrace your views; at the same time you wound the hearts of the zealous and devout christians. These are not the expressions of one who has an interest in defending the kingdom of the clergy, or the hireling system, but of one who, like yourself, has been providentially thrown into the possession of a competency of the good things of this world. I am as anxious as you can be for the correction of all errors, but in making the correction, or in aiming at it—spare, I beseech you the grand mean that God has employed and is still using for extending Christ's kingdom—I mean a preached gospel. I agree with you in the use and operation of every other mean in its proper place; but I must insist on it, that the preaching of the gospel is a most powerful one.

Would to God that all the saints were engaged in the work of the ministry for building up the body or church of Christ, and that they were all New Testament saints.

I am yours, &c.   —— ——

—

Very Dear Sir—I am much obliged to you for the above letter, knowing the sentiments which dictated it; and I trust you will consider that it is purely from a sense of its importance that I have published it without first soliciting your consent.

Your remarks upon what you call "a new opinion," on which is based my opposition to the principle of missions, and which you think is "palpably erroneous," I perfectly approve. But it never was an opinion of mine that the church, without the record, was left on earth to illuminate and reform the world. As you considered this to be my meaning, and as I now assure you that I never entertained such an opinion, you will perceive that we both agree in calling such an opinion erroneous. I am pretty certain that you and I view the church of our Immortal King in one and the same light. I am taught from the record itself to describe a church of Christ in the following words:—It is a society of disciples professing to believe the one grand fact, voluntary submitting to his authority and guidance, having all of them in their baptism expressed their faith in him and allegiance to him, and statedly meeting together in one place, to walk in all his commandments and ordinances. This society with its bishop or bishops, and deacon or deacons, as the case may require, is perfectly independent of any tribunal on earth called ecclesiastical. It knows nothing of superior or inferior church judicatories, and acknowledges no laws, no canons, nor government other than that of the Monarch of the Universe and his laws. This church, having now committed to it the oracles of God, is adequate to all the purposes of illumination and reformation which entered into the design of its founder. If I thought there was any difference in our views on this topic, I would be more definite and explicit. But to be more explicit in expressing my views of the means which the church is to use for the salvation of the world, I would remark, that having the record, or testimony of God in it, and every member professing it, it becomes the duty and high privilege of every member of it to be a preacher of the gospel, in the only sense in which any person can now be called a preacher.

I need not tell you that I do not mean to say that every man and woman that believes the gospel is to commence travelling about as the popular preachers do, or to leave their homes and neighborhoods, or employment, to act as public preachers. But the young women are to declare to their coevals and acquaintance—the elder women to theirs—the young men and elder men to theirs, the glad tidings, and to shew them the evidence on which their faith rests. This, followed up by a virtuous and godly life, is the most powerful mean left on earth to illuminate and reform the world. In the meantime the bishop of the church in their weekly meetings, teaches the religion in its sublime and glorious doctrine and bearings, and thus the members are still educating or building up in the most holy faith, and thus the church, in all its members, "speaking the truth in love, grows up into Him in all things, who is the Head, even Christ; from whom the whole body, fitly joined together, and compacted by that which every joint supplies, according to the effectual working in the measure of every part, makes increase of the body, to the edifying of itself in love." When the bishop rests from his labors, the church, of which he had the oversight, by his labors, and by the opportunity afforded all the members of exercising their faculties of communication and inquiry in the public assembly, finds within itself others educated and qualified to be appointed to the same good work. The church of the living God is thus independent of theological schools and colleges for its existence, enlargement, comfort, and perfection; for it is itself put in possession of all the means of education and accomplishments, if these means be wisely used.

The spread of the gospel, the multiplication of the number of the faithful in the apostolic age, is, in a great measure, attributable to the great company of them that declared the faith. The whole church of Jerusalem became preachers in a very short time. We are told (*Acts* viii.) that there was a great persecution against the congregation that was at Jerusalem; and all, except the apostles, were scattered through the regions of Judea and Samaria—"They, however, who were dispersed, (all but the apostles,) went about proclaiming the glad tidings of the word." No wonder, then, that so many myriads of the Jews were converted. No wonder, then, that so many congregations of christians were formed throughout Judea and Samaria, when one church sent out such a swarm of publishers of the glad tidings.

Dear sir, my very soul is stirred up within me, when I think of what a world of mischief the popular clergy have done. They have shut up every body's mouth but their own; and theirs they will not open unless they are paid for it. This is the plain blunt fact. And if I cannot bring facts, and documents, and arguments to shew that the paganism of the world is, in a great measure, attributable to them; that the ignorance and prejudice of our times, and that the incapacity of the believers to publish the glad tidings is altogether owing to them; that they, as a body collective, are antichrist—then I will say that I cannot prove any proposition whatever.

But to return. Moses we are told was preached, being read in the synagogues. Paul tells us that he was ordained a preacher and a teacher of the truth among the gentiles. We are told that, daily in the temple, and from house to house, they ceased not to teach and to preach that Jesus was the Messiah. I need not say to you, that to preach is merely to publish news; but as this will be read by many, for their sakes I say that myriads may be qualified to preach, either as Moses was preached, or *viva voce* to publish what Paul published to the nations, that are not qualified to teach the christian doctrine. And no man believes any fact but he can tell the reason why, and produce the evidence on which he believes it. This is all the New Testament means, and all I mean by preaching. A bishop must be "apt to teach," but nothing is said about being apt to preach, and you and I agree that preaching and teaching are two things essentially different. To have said that a bishop must be apt to preach, in that age, would have been absurd—when even women as well as men could preach. Paul mentions women of note who were his fellow-laborers: and all know how Priscilla explained to the eloquent Apollos the way of God more accurately. Euodia and Syntyche are mentioned as women who labored with the apostle Paul in the publication of the gospel. Yet in the church they were not allowed to teach, nor even to speak in the way of asking questions.

These hints are not submitted as proof of my grand proposition, "that the association called the church of Jesus Christ is, in *propria forma,* the only institution of God left on earth to illuminate and reform the world," only as illustrative of the means by which the church is to illuminate the world. I know many will attribute it to my vanity, nevertheless I will hazard the expression that I can fill a volume of at least four hundred pages in illustration and proof, with facts, and documents, and arguments, in confirmation of the truth of the above proposition. My reason for so saying, is not to convince any person of its truth, but to form an apology for the disadvantage under which such a proposition must appear, detached from the demonstration and proof on which it rests in my mind. This work is entirely too small to do justice to the numerous topics that call for notice and exposition. Our first volume is but an outline, and a very imperfect outline, of the course we design to pursue; and with all our exertions we will not be able, this year, to even introduce all the topics in our prospectus.

But to come more particularly to those items to which you object, I observe, that with respect to the preaching of the gospel, you see that, instead of being opposed to it, I advocate it on a principle and scale that leaves far in the rear all the popular expedients; and I can assure you that I know some churches in the United States that are already so far advanced in their knowledge of, and conformity to the primitive model, that all their members are now either almost, or altogether, accomplished preachers. I know personally, and by credible report, several Phebes, and Euodias, and Syntyches, and Eunices, and Eclectes, and Priscillas, as well as several Philips and Aquilas, &c. &c.

I am aware that there is no proposition nor course of conduct to which objections may not be made; but I must say, that I know of none that weighs a feather against this divine plan of preaching the word; and it affords me some pleasure to know that the Baptist society in former times acted in a good measure upon this principle; but I am sorry to witness their rapid strides in imitation of the corrupt systems around them in this day. I am determined, if the Lord will, in some future number to demonstrate that if a few doctors of divinity in the United States succeed in their plans, the Baptist society will inevitably be so like Babylon the Great, that no man will be able to distinguish between it and its idolatrous neighbors. I need not to inform you that some of them have actually recommended, in base imitation of the Paido-Baptists, the dedication of infants in the church by the parson, or shall I call him the bishop. Yes, they are determined to have the young St. Giles in lieu of the old St. Giles.

As to the missionary plans, I am constrained to differ from many whom I love and esteem, and will ever esteem if we should never agree upon this point, as well as from many whom I cannot love for the truth's sake. At the same time I am very sorry to think that any man should suppose that I am either regardless of the deplorable condition of the heathen world, or opposed to any means authorized by the New Testament for either the civilization or salvation of those infatuated pagans. But, my dear sir, how can I, with the New Testament before my face, approve the Catholic, the Episcopalian, the Presbyterian, &c. missionary schemes. Are they not evidently mere sectarian speculations, for enlarging their sects, and finding appointments for their supernumerary clergy. Look again at the sums of money squandered at home and abroad under the pretext of converting the world; and again, wherein is the heathen world benefited by such conversions? Is the hand of the Lord in this business? Does he work in it as in the days of yore? Look at our own country—our Indian neighbors and our African bondmen. Are not these, equally as the Japanese or Birmans, objects worthy of our sympathy and regard? I do not oppose, intentionally at least, the scriptural plan of converting the world. My opponents, amongst whom I am very far from ranking you, (for I know your personal regard and your attachment to the cause of our King) do represent me as opposing the means of converting the world, not wishing to discriminate, in my case at least, between a person's opposing the abuses of a good cause, and the cause itself. I did contribute my mite and my efforts to the popular missionary cause, until my conscience forbade me from an acquaintance with the abuses of the principle.

In the multiplication of the copies of the scriptures I do rejoice, although I conceive even this best of all good works is managed in a way not at all comporting with the precepts of the volume itself. And shall we not oppose the abuses of any principle because of the excellency of the principle itself? It might as reasonably be alleged, that while I oppose the abuses of the divine word, or of the ordinances of Christ, that I oppose both it and them.

As to the Christian Baptist securing "the concurrence of the covetous, the ignorant, the prayerless," &c. I cannot help it. I hope it may do them good—they have the most need of instruction. But I cannot conceive that this should be an argument against it; for you will say it is no argument against the Baptist system, that men of the world, deists, statesmen, &c. prefer it, as more rational and more conducive to civil liberty than any other. But I have no doubt it will give you pleasure to be informed that, as far as my acquaintance with the subscribers extends, a very considerable proportion of them are such christians as you yourself would cheerfully embrace in christian communion. And I will farther add, that a majority of them are amongst the most intelligent, the most respectable, and the most devout members of the community. I will also add, that its greatest opposers are, for the most part, the interested priests, the young beneficiaries, ruling elders, those aspiring to posts of honor and profit in the kingdom of the clergy, and their friends and relatives. I confess there is nothing in that state of things which the New Testament authorizes, that flatters the prospects and aims of most of the popular leaders.

My circumstances, I thank God, are such, as with a moderate attention to the things of this world, will afford me the necessaries of life; but they are such as would authorize me to receive a few hundreds a year without any material injury to myself or family. I know some of the neighboring clergy who are in better circumstances than I am, that complain of great difficulties in " getting along," who receive as good as $500 or $1000 a year. I do not mention it with any other reference to your remarks, than because they afford me an opportunity of dropping a hint to some who have ascribed my

course of what is called " preaching" for ten or twelve years without any compensation whatever, to my not having *need* of support; that when I arrived a stranger in this western country, without any other property than my education, I did, from a confirmed disgust at the popular schemes, which I confess I principally imbibed when a student in the university of Glasgow, determine that I should, under the protection and patronage of the Almighty, render all the services I could to my fellow creatures, by means of the bible, without any earthly compensation whatever. On these principles I began, and having no other prospects than to turn my attention to some honest calling for a livelihood, I prosecuted this design without looking back. At the same time I did not censure, nor do I censure, any christian bishop who receives such earthly things as he needs, from those to whose edification and comfort he contributes by his labors. And I do know many professed teachers, who ought rather to impart a considerable per annum to their poor brethren, than to receive from them one cent. I know there are extremes on every side—I wish to avoid them. And I do know that the popular clergy are not entitled to receive one cent from the people, because they have put themselves into an office which Heaven never gave them, trample upon the rights of the people, keep them in ignorance, and practically deny that heavenly aphorism of our Lord, which says, " It is more blessed to give than to receive." They practically say, " It is more blessed to receive than to give."

I trust, from this lengthy reply to your friendly letter, you will see that there is much less difference between our views than you anticipated. There is but one saying in your letter that I cannot reconcile to your own views, nor to the fact as it occurs to my observation; which is, "that my readers cease to enjoy their religion when they embrace my views." If they do, I think their religion is of such a kind that the sooner they get rid of it the better.

As to the Paido-Baptists endeavoring to destroy the effects of my debate with Mr. Maccalla, by alleging my "peculiar views," it matters nothing. If they had not these means they would find some others. Remember how Mr. Pond attacked Mr. Judson, how Mr. J. P. Campbell attacked Mr. Merril, and how all the Paido Baptists attacked Mr. Robinson. I am told that a certain beneficiary from Kentucky, on his way to Princeton, stopped at Washington, Pa., to inquire into my reputation, and wrote home to Kentucky that I was a very bad character, and an exile from religious society. This right that maintains the clergy must be maintained at any rate.

Desirous of hearing from you as soon as convenient, and assuring you that no difference of opinion upon these two points which you have mentioned shall ever alienate my affection and esteem for you, I remain your fellow servant.
                                                    EDITOR.

May 25.

———

No. 12.]   MONDAY, JULY 5, 1824.

Essays on Ecclesiastical Characters, Councils, Creeds, and Sects.—No. III.

IN the two preceding essays under this head, we partially adverted to the causes that concurred in ushering into existence that " *monstrum horrendum informe ingens cui lumen ademptum;*" that " monster horrific, shapeless, huge, whose light is extinct," called an ecclesiastical court.

By an ecclesiastical court, we mean those meetings of clergy, either stated or occasional, for the purpose of either enacting new ecclesiastical canons or of executing old ones. Whether they admit into their confederacy a lay representation, or whether they appropriate every function to themselves, to the exclusion of the laity, is, with us, no conscientious scruple.— Whether the assembly is composed of none but priests and levites, or of one half, one third, or one tenth laymen, it is alike antiscriptural, antichristian, and dangerous to the community, civil and religious. Nor does it materially affect either the character or nature of such a combination whether it be called presbyterian, episcopalian, or congregational. Whether such an alliance of the priests and the nobles of the kirk be called a session, a presbytery, a synod, a general assembly, a convention, a conference, an association, or annual meeting, its tendency and result are the same. Whenever and wherever such a meeting either legislates, decrees, rules, directs, or controls, or assumes the character of a representative body in religious concerns, it essentially becomes "the man of sin and the son of perdition."

An individual church or congregation of Christ's disciples is the only ecclesiastical body recognized in the New Testament. Such a society is "the highest court of Christ" on earth. Furious controversies have been carried on, and bloody wars have been waged on the subject of church government. These in their origin, progress, and termination, have resembled the vigorous efforts made to obtain the Saviour's tomb, or like the fruitless endeavors of the Jews to find the body of Moses.

As we intend to pay considerable attention to this topic, and to give details of the proceedings of ecclesiastical courts, &c, we think it necessary, in the first place, to attend to the import of the phrase "church of Jesus Christ," and also to the nature of the bishop's work. In the present essay, I will introduce a few remarks from the "Reasons of Alexander Carson, A.M. for separating from the General Synod of Ulster." These will cast some light on the import of the phrase "church of Jesus Christ."*

Matt. xviii. 15—18. "Moreover, if your brother shall trespass against you, go and tell him his fault, between you and him alone. If he shall hear you, you have gained your brother. But if he will not hear you, then take with you one or two more, that, in the mouth of one or two witnesses, every word may be established. And if he shall neglect to hear them, tell it to the church: but if he shall neglect to hear the church, let him be to you as a heathen man and a publican." Here the last appeal is to the church. He does not say, If he does not hear the church, take him to the presbytery; and if he does not hear the presbytery, take him to the synod, &c. but if he hear not the church, "let him be to you as a heathen man and a publican." I know, indeed, that various subterfuges have been invented to evade the force of this plain scripture. Every sect has attempted to find its own discipline in this passage; whilst individuals, to apologize for what they cannot justify, have attempted to darken its meaning

so as to make it of no practical use. The multiplicity of interpretations, in the opinion of Dr. Stillingfleet, is an argument to prove that it is totally inexplicable; in my opinion it proves only what is proved by the variety of sentiments on every other point in scripture, the perversity, the selfishness, or the prejudice of professing christians. What! has the Lord Jesus given a precept, in a case of such importance, and of such frequent occurrence, which cannot be understood? Did he wish to be, or could he not avoid being unintelligible? Must the Holy One of Israel speak with the darkness and evasion of a heathen oracle? If he did not mean to be understood, why did he speak? If he meant to be understood, why did he not speak in intelligible language? If we cannot find out who are the divinely appointed arbitrators of our differences, he might as well have said nothing on the subject. What an insult upon the Holy Ghost to represent his language to be so vague and indeterminate that it cannot be understood! Christ has said, "tell it to the church." Is there no way of coming at his meaning? Has the word *church* no determinate meaning in the New Testament? But Dr. Stillingfleet is of opinion, that if the discipline Christ has appointed be executed, it is not material by whom. Is it then the same thing whether a law be enacted by the lawfully appointed legislators, or by any other body of self constituted men? or that a criminal be tried by a lawful judge and jury, or by men who assume the right of judgment, without the countenance of lawful authority? If Christ has appointed any particular referees, it is as really a breach of his injunction to appoint any other, as it would be totally to neglect that instance of discipline. But is there any native, necessary obscurity in the precept arising from the promiscuous use of the word church in the New Testament? If it is now in any measure obscure, it has been rendered so not from the ambiguity of the scripture use of the word, but from its prostituted application in modern acceptation, and the sophistry and subtleties of interested, prejudiced, or bigoted men: we find no difficulty in the passage until we hear the forced explanations of it given by controvertists, and our mind begins to be distracted, and the subject obscured by the smoke of their unhallowed fires."

"I lay it down, then, as an axiom, that Christ meant some determinate thing by the word church, and that there must be sufficient evidence in the New Testament to lead the humble, teachable inquirer into that meaning.— Christ must have spoken intelligible language. Now, to investigate the scripture use of the word church."*

"*Ekklesia* literally signifies an assembly *called out* from others, and is used among the Greeks, particularly the Athenians, for their popular assemblies summoned by their chief magistrate, and in which none but citizens had a right to sit. By inherent power it may be applied to any body of men called out and assembled in one place. If ever it loses the ideas of calling out and assembling, it loses its principal features and its primitive use.

"Such being the origin and use of this word among the Greeks, to what is it be legitimately applied when used in sacred things? It may signify any assembly called out from the world, and united in Christ. Agreeably to this, whenever it is used in scripture in a sacred

---

* Mr. Carson, as to talent, erudition, and high standing among the Presbyterians in Ireland, was not surpassed by any minister of that denomination. We shall give his preface to these reasons in the present number. He is now the bishop of a christian church at Tubermore, Ireland.

K

* Of his remarks on this topic, we select only a few.

sense, that is, as applicable to believers, we find that it is invariably appropriated to an individual assembly of christians, meeting to enjoy the ordinances of Christ, or the christian community in general."

" But with equal propriety may this word be applied either to all the christians on earth, or all both in heaven and earth, as assembled in Jesus. Nor does this application stretch it a whit beyond its natural and intrinsic meaning. It is as literally and as truly applied to the one as to the other. All the saints on earth, all the saints in heaven, are assembled in him, as really as the branches of a vine are united in the trunk, the stones of a building upon the foundation, or the members of the body with the head. With the strictest truth all christians may be said to be already " in heavenly places in Christ." This double application of the word is neither foreign nor forced, incorrect nor indistinct. When it is used indefinitely, it is applied to the community of believers assembled in Christ: when it is used with respect to an individual church, which is its most general application, the context or the nature of the circumstances gives sufficient intimation. Let any one take the trouble to run over all the places where it is found in the New Testament, and I will be bold to say, he will not find a single text which will not fairly explain on this hypothesis. The cases where it may occur in the civil or unappropriated sense, are not accompanied with the smallest difficulty; the context, or a note of appropriation, as " church of Christ," &c. sufficiently marking the difference.

" Having stated the literal meaning, the profane and sacred application of the word *ekklesia*, let us next examine the claims of its modern* acceptations. It is quite a chamelion. It is as various in its meaning as the necessities of each party require. Sometimes it is a church session, sometimes an individual church; sometimes a classical presbytery; sometimes a synod; sometimes a general assembly; sometimes church rulers; sometimes all the churches of a province or kingdom. Truly, if the scripture gives ground for all these, it is more dark and perplexing than was ever an answer of the Sybil. Is not the bare statement a refutation of the fact, and the supposition a calumny on the oracles of God? But the practice of presbyterians themselves, is a complete refutation of this hypothesis. They do not speak promiscuously of all their assemblies by the name church, but have a distinct name for each, as the congregation, the session, the presbytery, the synod, &c. Now, if each order of these courts be a church, as well as each congregation, and the collective congregations, why do they not speak of them by the scripture name? Why have they imposed upon them names of their own invention? Evidently because they would otherwise be unintelligible. If one of their writers on church discipline was to speak of all their assemblies by the name church, without additional marks of distinction, his readers would not understand him; yet this is the very inaccuracy they charge upon the writers of the New Testament. They suppose them to speak promiscuously of the greatest variety of subordinate courts, as well as assemblies of a different nature, by the same name, without any mark of distinction to guide the reader. Now, I think this is a very fair criterion; scripture ordinances should be sufficiently intelligible by scripture names, without the use of any

* I call them modern, because they are later than the New Testament.

other. I believe it will be found a very just conclusion, that the institutions which have not a name in scripture, have not an existence in scripture. Let presbyterians, then, use nothing but the scripture names, and the doctrine of their subordinate courts will be jargon. By their unnatural extension of this word, they have taken it in modern use from that which alone deserves it—the individual assemblies of the saints. Let us suppose, then, that *ekklesia* might have been legitimately appropriated to denote any one of these assemblies, this appropriation will take it from all the rest. If a session is a church, then a congregation cannot be a church; if either of these be a church, then a presbytery cannot, without confusion, be usually so denominated; and if a presbytery is a church, then it will take that name from all inferior and superior courts. Now, if these courts be scriptural, let their advocates produce their distinct scriptural names. No word can have two appropriate meanings upon the same subject; *ekklesia* may be a civil assembly and appropriated also to a religious assembly; but in neither civil nor religious matters can it be appropriated as the distinctive name of two different assemblies, the one subordinate to the other. It may denote a particular assembly of saints, and the community of christians assembled in Jesus; but without confusion, it cannot be used as the appropriated name of a particular and general assembly of the same sort. This is clear from the names of civil courts. Though some of these be such as to be literally applicable to all, yet they are not so appropriated. Thus sessions, assizes, &c. Thus also in the church of England, though each of the orders are called clergymen, yet for this very reason it could not be the appropriated distinctive name of any one of them. There is curate, rector, bishop, &c. For the same reason, though bishop was the common name of all presbyters originally, yet when it was appropriated to one of the number, it was taken from all the rest. If, then, the word church be generally applicable to such a variety of assemblies, each assembly must have a distinctive name besides; to produce which out of scripture will be rather an arduous task. Besides, in speaking particularly of each of these assemblies, the common name could not be used, any more than the name clergyman would distinguish a bishop from a presbyter. When our Lord says, " then tell it to the church," if he intends presbyterian ecclesiastical courts, to which does he refer? If to the session, then all higher appeals are cut off; for if the offending brother will not " hear the church, let him be a heathen man and a publican:" if it means a general synod or assembly, then all inferior courts are cut off. But if church be also the scripture name of an individual assembly of saints, consisting of pastors and church members, is not the obscurity still increased? Whether must the congregation or the session be appealed to?"

" There is not the least intimation in any part of the New Testament of a representative government. Nothing is said about a number of church rulers being selected as an ecclesiastical council over a number of individual churches; nor any such use of the word church, as including a number of individual churches. When the inspired writers speak of a single assembly of saints, they invariably call it a church; when they speak of a number of churches, or the churches of a province or district, they do not call them a church but churches. Thus when Paul writes to the Corinthians, he addresses the

" church of God which is at Corinth;" but when he writes to the Galatians, he addresses the churches of Galatia. Thus also when the church of Jerusalem is spoken of, it is called a church; but when the aggregate of the individual churches of Judea and Samaria is spoken of, they are not called the church of Judea, or the church of Samaria, but the churches of Judea, and the churches of Samaria. Thus also the church of Cenchrea, (*Rom.* xvi. 1.) and the churches of Achaia; the church of Ephesus, the church of Smyrna, &c. But when they are spoken of in the aggregate, it is the seven churches of Asia, not the church of Asia, (*Rev.* i. 4. and ii. 1. &c.) I know indeed with respect to Jerusalem and Corinth, it is alleged that the saints in those cities must have been too numerous to have assembled in one place. But I need not take up my time in showing how or where they might assemble, or in ascertaining their numbers.— They are not more numerous than I wish them to have been; and the scripture itself refutes the objection in both instances. *Acts* ii. 44. 1 *Cor.* v. 4. and xi. 18. In these passages they are expressly shown to have met in the same place."

PREFACE
To " Reasons for separating from the General Synod of Ulster."
BY A. CARSON, A. M.

EVERY christian is a member of two kingdoms perfectly distinct, but perfectly compatible in their interests. In each of these, he has peculiar duties, in the discharge of which he is to pursue a very different conduct. As a subject of civil government, he is called to unreserved, unequivocal obedience, without waiting to inquire into its nature and quality, or even the legitimacy of the title of those in power. If he understands his bible, he knows that "the powers that be are ordained of God," and that he must " submit to every ordinance of man, not merely for wrath, but also for conscience' sake." In Britain he will submit to monarchy; in America, to a republic; and in France he will obey, without puzzling himself in determining whether Bonaparte is a legal governor or a usurper.* But it is not so in the kingdom of Christ. Here it is his duty in every thing to judge for himself, and in no instance to be the disciple of man. He is commanded to examine, not blindly adopt the dogmas of his spiritual guides. He is no where required to conform and submit to that form of church government under which he has been educated, or to which he may at any time have thought it his duty to attach himself. He is enjoined to " prove all things and to hold fast *only* that which is true." He is Christ's freed man, and should not suffer himself to become the servant of man, nor to be fettered by human systems.

Convinced that this is both the duty and privilege of every christian, I have largely and leisurely examined the original nature and present state of that church† in which I was educated, and in which I have for some years acted as a minister. I have examined, and am convinced,

---

* We Americans think that it is not incompatible with christianity to make our own rulers by all constitutional means; and that the members of every state, not governed according to the maxims of reason and justice, have a right inalienable to effect a revolution by all lawful means, or to emigrate. Mr. Carson here speaks of submission to the constituted authorities, and in this he doubtless speaks as a christian.—EDITOR.

† I am obliged sometimes in this pamphlet to use the word church in this common acceptation, though not so used in any part of the New Testament.

that both in plan and administration, it is contrary to the word of God. It must appear to every man of candor that I could have no interest in deciding as I have done. Every interest of a worldly nature was surely on the other side. The day I gave up my connexion with the general synod, I gave up all that the world esteems. I sacrifice not only my prospects in life, and my respectability in the world, but every settled way of support. It is usual for men to desert a church under persecution; I have deserted one in the tide of her prosperity, or, as some of her friends speak, in her " meridian glory." If people never begin to think any thing amiss in their religion till they are persecuted for it, or till superior honors and advantages are held out to view, they have reason to suspect their judgments. But when wealth and respectability in society are in the gift of the church, when one of her members sits in judgment upon her, she is likely to get a fair trial. A man is not apt, upon slight grounds, to reason himself out of his living, his friends, and his reputation. It will not be out of whim he will exchange ease for labor, respect for calumny, present competency for the naked promise of God. Notwithstanding this, I am perfectly aware that the worst motives and designs will be attributed to me. I would indeed know little of human nature, and less of the bible, if I did not expect the reproaches of the world. If they have called the master of the house Beelzebub, much more those of his household. He himself experienced such treatment from the world, and he knows how to succor his children in like circumstances.

The divine right of the Presbyterian form of church government, it may be expected, will now become the *present truth* among all sects of Presbyterians in this country. Their inveterate rage against each other will for a time be suspended that they may unite against the common enemy. Every pulpit will resound with the cry of innovation; many an affecting representation will be given of the sufferings of our worthy forefathers, in erecting the venerable fabric. I would caution christians not to suffer themselves to be imposed on by such senseless declamations. The appeal on both sides must be to the scriptures; not a stone of the fabric can be lawfully rested on any other ground. If classical presbytery is in the New Testament, let its advocates come forward and fairly refute my arguments. I have no object but truth, and whatever may be published against my pamphlet, in a christian and candid manner, shall receive every attention. But let them not lose their temper, nor substitute railing for argument. Neither let them nibble round the surface of the subject, but let them enter into the essence of the debate. If any are convinced, let them beware of stifling convictions. Let them not suffer interest, prejudice, or the fear of reproach, to deter them from obeying the least of the commandments of Christ. " Whoever shall be ashamed of me and my word in this sinful and adulterous generation, of him also shall the Son of Man be ashamed when he comes in the glory of his Father with the holy angels." *Mark* viii. 38. " He that loves father or mother more than me, is not worthy of me; and he that loves son or daughter more than me, is not worthy of me. And he that takes not his cross, and follows after me, is not worthy of me. He that finds his life shall lose it, and he that loses his life for my sake, shall find it." *Mat.* x. 37—39.

Though I am decidedly convinced of the complete independency of the apostolical churches, and of the duty of following them, I would not be understood as placing undue importance upon this point. Christians of every denomination I love; and I will never, I hope, withhold my hand, or my countenance from any who, after impartial investigation, conscientious y differ from me. I can from my heart say, " ɜrace be with all those who love our Lord Jesus Christ in sincerity and truth." Pity, indeed, while there are so few friends of Jesus, that those should harbor hard thoughts of each other for conscientious differences. But it is not to be expected from this, that I shall "know any man according to the flesh," or avoid freely censuring whatever I judge unfounded in scripture, out of compliment to any friend who may countenance it. This would be "to walk as men."

In endeavoring to overthrow the system of Presbyterianism, I have only assaulted the main pillars of the edifice; if I have succeeded, the roof and all the rubbish will fall of course.— The voluminous defences of presbytery, of former days, I consider too stale to be particularly noticed. I wait till their advocates recognize them. But though every pin of that system could be proved to be divine, it would not affect my opinion of the duty of separating from the synod. I would stand upon ground still tenable. I do not shrink from discussion. Truth will finally prevail.

A familiar Dialogue between the Editor and a Clergyman.

PART I.

Clergyman. WHY do you preach, seeing you decry all preaching?

Editor. I do not decry all preaching. I have said that it is the duty of every disciple to preach.

C. But how can they preach except they be *sent?*

E. I presume there are no preachers upon earth who are *sent* in the sense of those words quoted from the apostle.

C. Yes; I believe I am as much *sent* as any preacher ever was; and if I did not believe that I was *sent* I would not preach a word.

E. Well, sir, I find myself happy in meeting with a preacher sent from God. I will sit down at your feet and believe every thing you say, only remove some few doubts I have respecting your mission.

C. I do not want you to receive all that I say. Judge for yourself.

E. You do not, then, believe you are sent by God; for, assuredly, if you were sent by God, I should be a great sinner not to believe every word you say. For God would not send you to declare falsehoods, nor to deceive mankind.— If you will then prove that you are *sent,* I will examine no more for myself. I will believe what you say. Who ever was sent by God with a message to men, that it was not lawful and necessary implicitly to receive upon his word? or, in other words, was it not highly criminal in every instance, and at the peril of the hearer, to refuse implicit faith in the word of every heavenly messenger?

C. I do not pretend to plenary inspiration; but I contend that I am sent, or *called* by God, to preach.

E. To preach what?

C. The gospel.

E. What do you mean by preaching the gospel?

C. I mean to make it known.

E. You are not, then, sent to us in this region, for the gospel has been made known to us already by such preachers as leave us without excuse; whom, if we believe not, we would not be persuaded though one rose from the dead. I mean Matthew, Mark, Luke, John, and Paul and Peter, if you please. Have you any thing new to add?

C. I do not mean to make it known as if it had never been read or heard before; but to make known what they have said about it.

E. You mean to explain it, I suppose.

C. Yes, and to enforce it upon the attention of mankind.

E. To make a fact known is to preach, and to explain the meaning of that fact is to teach. But on your own views I would humbly ask, Did ever the Father of our spirits send one class of preachers to make known his will, and afterwards send another class to explain their message and to enforce it?

C. Yes, he sent the apostles to explain the prophets.

E. And he sent you to explain the apostles; and, by and by, he will send other preachers to explain you; and so explanations will never cease, and new missions will succeed each other till time be no more. Your saying that he sent the apostles to explain the prophets, is not more ingenious than Tobiah's saying, "He sends the event to explain the accomplishment of prophecy."

C. And are there not many things in Paul's writings "hard to be understood, which the unlearned and ignorant wrest to their destruction?"

E. I hope you do not suppose the explanation of these things is preaching. But as you and many of your brethren often cite these words, will you hear a remark or two upon them. It is not the *epistles* that is the antecedent to " *hois*," but "the things" mentioned by Peter. I need not tell you that *epistolais* is feminine and *hois* neuter; consequently, it is not the language or style of Paul that is referred to in this passage, but the things themselves of which he spoke.— However, I lay no stress on this distinction, as we admit the scriptures are often wrested—but by whom? Peter says the unteachable, (*amatheis,*) not the unlearned, but, as Macknight says, "the unteachable" and the double-minded; and these are always the learned or those who think themselves wise. You know that the Romanists infer from these words the necessity of an infallible interpreter. Their words are, "The scriptures are not sufficient for deciding controversies concerning the articles of faith; and the decision of these matters is to be sought from the Catholic church." But the misfortune is, that the Catholics do not tell us " whether it is the Pope alone, or the Pope in conjunction with his own clergy, or a general council of his bishops, or any particular council, or any other body of men in their church distinguished by a particular denomination." This is good policy; for all those to whom they have attributed infallibility have erred, as they are constrained to admit. And I think you will admit that none now differ more about the meaning of scripture than the learned.

C. But do not you say it is the duty of all disciples to preach, and what are they to preach, and to whom?

E. The disciples can preach only in the same way that Moses was preached, being read in the synagogues. This they may and can do, either by declaring the same things *viva voce,* or by reading the gospel and exhibiting its evidences to them who either cannot or will not read the Evangelists and Apostles.

C. But have they not all heard already? and can you, on your own principles, make known to them what they have already heard?

E. They have not all heard; for there are all the children born to the disciples, which it becomes their duty to disciple to Christ, and therefore christian parents stand in the relation of preachers to their own children. There are also some parents that are not disciples, and consequently their children are brought up in darkness. Now, as every disciple has access to these, it becomes his duty to instil into their minds, as far as human agency can extend, the words of eternal life.

C. Yes, and miserable preachers the mass of disciples will make—can't put three sentences together—not one in ten of them can explain one verse intelligibly. And you will set the women's tongues loose too, and they have always been too troublesome even when under every possible restraint; but you have removed all barriers and turned them loose upon us.—Believe me, sir, your principles are of a disorganizing character.

E. And to what is the incapacity of the disciples to preach and speak intelligibly owing? Doubtless to their religious education—to their teachers. Every person who has ideas upon any subject can communicate them. If his ideas are indistinct, his communications will be so too; but if his perceptions are accurate and clear, his addresses will be plain and intelligible. But you who occupy the pulpit, are the very persons who are to blame for this incapacity. This useless and senseless way of talking, which you call preaching, into which the old pagans led you, is the very way to make the people ignorant, to confound, perplex, and stupify them. This everlasting sermonizing! what good is in it? It resembles nothing that is rational in all the compass of thought. A B professes to teach arithmetic; he gets a class of forty boys from twelve to fifteen years old, we shall say. He tells them to meet once a week and he will give them a lecture or a sermon on some important point in this useful science.—The first day he lectures on the cube root for an hour. They sit bookless and thoughtless, heedless, and, perhaps, often drowsy, while he harangues them. He blesses them and sends them home, to return a week hence. They meet. His text is arithmetical progression.—He preaches an hour; dismisses as usual. The third day of the meeting up comes vulgar fractions; the fourth, rule of three; the fifth, addition; the sixth, notation; the seventh, cube root again, &c. &c. Now in this way, I hesitate not to say, he might proceed seven years and not finish one accountant. Who ever thought that a science or an art could be taught this way? And yet this is the only way, I may say, universally adopted of teaching the christian religion. And so it is that many men have sat under the sound of the gospel (as they call it) for forty years, that cannot expound one chapter in the whole New Testament. And yet these same christians would think it just to prosecute by civil law that teacher who would keep their sons four or five years at English grammar or arithmetic, and receive their money, and yet not one of their sons able to expound one rule in syntax or arithmetic. They pay the parson—they are of maturer minds than their children, and they have been longer under his tuition,

and yet they will excuse both the parson and themselves for knowing just as little, if not less, of the New Testament, than their striplings know of grammar or arithmetic.

C. Then you will reduce the christian doctrine to a level with common arithmetic, and you suppose that christianity can be taught just as easily as arithmetic.

E. You profess to be a Calvinist, if I mistake not; and do you not suppose that a disciple is as capable of being taught christianity as arithmetic, provided he is "a subject of divine grace," and you know that otherwise he would not be a disciple on the Calvinistic hypothesis. But upon either the Calvinistic or Arminian hypothesis, a disciple of Christ can be taught the christian religion in a proper course of education as soon as he can be taught any human science.

C. And so you suppose there is nothing more grand, sublime, deep, or unsearchable in the christian religion, than in a human science, such as arithmetic?

E. That does not follow from my assertion. There are many things incomprehensible and sublime in various sciences; but a person is said to understand and to be able to teach them, who is not able to comprehend and to explain every topic connected therewith. Many persons can teach arithmetic very well who do not understand one proposition of Euclid's ratios.

C. But it is only when the Spirit of God accompanies the preacher's words that the people learn; and that Spirit is not at the command of the preachers.

E. I know of no passage in the New or Old Testament that says that the Spirit of God accompanies any of our preachers' words. Besides, the disciples are the sons of God, and have the Spirit of Christ, and are therefore every way qualified to learn, under a proper teacher, according to your own hypothesis But, sir, they can never be taught the christian religion in the way of sermonizing. Public speeches may be very useful on many occasions; but to teach a church the doctrine of Christ, and to cause them to understand the Holy Scriptures, and to enjoy them, requires a course essentially different from either hearing sermons or learning the catechism.

C. I wish to resume sundry topics in the commencement of our interview, but will have to postpone it for the present. Adieu.

A Circular Letter

APPEARED in the "Columbian Star" of June 19th, addressed to every Baptist church in Massachusetts, and signed by Thomas Baldwin, Lucius Boles, N. W. Williams, Jonathan Going, F. Wayland, jun., recommending as "a good work" the formation of a state convention, to be entitled, "The Baptist Convention of the State of Massachusetts." As an inducement to the churches in Massachusetts to form such a convention, they are told that similar conventions "are formed and forming" in Connecticut, Vermont, Maine, New Hampshire, and New York, besides in several of the southern states.

Provided three associations concur in the constitution recommended and in the measure as a whole, the first meeting is to take place in Boston the last Wednesday in October next. It is also proposed under the tenth article of this constitution, that "whenever a general convention formed from state conventions throughout the United States shall be formed or designed, it shall be in the power of this convention to send delegates to such conventions and to instruct them to enter into any arrangements to promote the interests of religion," &c.

The Baptist churches send three or four delegates or representatives to the associations. The associations are, according to this constitution, to send one delegate for every five churches to the state convention, and the state convention is to send delegates on some ratio to the general assembly or convention.

And so we Baptists are to march forth in solid phalanx, "terrible as an army with banners." I would propose an amendment to this plan. I dislike tautology and monotony, and would, instead of so many kinds of conventions, move that the names of those highly useful meetings be changed as follows:—

Those councils that are sometimes called churches, let them be called church sessions. Let the associations be called presbyteries; the state conventions, synods; the general convention, let it be called the general assembly of the Baptist church of the United States. Let there be a fund attached to this establishment called the delegates' fund; and let it be enjoined at the first meeting of the general convention or general assembly, that every minister shall dedicate to the Lord every male and female child, born of baptized parents, at any convenient time within forty days after its birth; and let this rite be called spiritual baptism adapted to infants; provided always, that the parents are willing to bring their infants to the church to the parson to bless them; and that the parson's hand which shall be laid upon their head shall be duly dry at the time of imposition.*

Under this arrangement and modification, I think we shall be the most popular and powerful party in the union; and as for being orthodox,

* The original and scriptural simplicity of the Baptists is fast departing in the introduction of these associations, instrumental music in their worship, &c. &c.

PUBLISHER.

there can be no doubt upon that subject, seeing we shall have the concurrence of the Presbyterian and Congregational brethren, who will assuredly send us annually a few delegates, indicative of their great good will and high approbation of our charity, liberality, and soundness in the faith. I hope we Baptists in the western states will have no conscientious scruples on the propriety of this "motion," nor even call into question the "scripturality" of such a scheme, seeing the New England states and those in the south have said, "Go forward!" "Keep not back!" And especially as Jethro in the wilderness advised Moses to appoint captains over tens, captains over fifties, captains over hundreds, and captains over thousands. All of which is respectfully submitted to our brethren in the east and west—by   THE EDITOR.

———

I HAVE acted very imprudently, say many, in the exhibition of the matter contained in this volume. If I had not been so plain and so full in opposing many popular plans, just in the commencement, I might have, say they, obtained a more extensive circulation for this paper. I confess I used none of this sort of policy. My great object was to please myself. And as to policy, I acted under the impression of the truth of that adage which says, "Honesty is the best policy." Whenever I cannot obtain a circulation for what I believe to be the truth, I will cease to be an editor; and while this paper will quit cost, I shall bestow all my labor rather than be a silent spectator of the proceedings and events of the times. Its circulation, however, has far surpassed my anticipations. I think I may promise that the second volume will be more interesting than the first, as my time during the past year has been chiefly devoted to objects that did not enter into my views when the prospectus was issued. We flatter ourselves that our labors have not been altogether in vain.

EDITOR.

END OF VOLUME I.

CHRISTIAN BAPTIST.

NO. I.—VOL. II. BUFFALOE, (BETHANY) BROOKE CO. VA, AUGUST 2, 1824.

Style no man on earth your Father: for he alone is your Father who is in heaven: and all ye are brethren. Assume not the title of Rabbi; for ye have only One Teacher; neither assume the title of Leader; for ye have only One Leader— the Messiah.   *Messiah.*

PREFATORY REMARKS.

THE priesthood of the East and West, or those who claim a divine right of teaching authoritatively the christian religion, have been, and now are, sedulously at work, some in their weekly harangues, and others in their parochial visitations, shewing to their good and loyal subjects the awful danger of reading the "*Christian Baptist.*" They express a great concern about the souls of their hearers, and the dangerous tendency of our feeble efforts to persuade the people to read, examine, and judge for themselves. But whence this alarm—this Demetrian cry of the church in danger! Do these divines sincerely believe that it will be injurious to the souls of their worshipers to read this work! If so, then they only prove how useless they have been to their hearers. Why have they not instructed their hearers better, and thus have rendered them superior to imposition! What would we think of a teacher of grammar or arithmetic, who, after spending seven, seventeen, or twenty-seven years in teaching his pupils those sciences, should afterwards express a great fear of their reading any treatise on those same sciences, which had for its object either the approbation or reprobation of his instructions? Would he not, *ipse facto*, betray himself?

But, however uncharitable it may appear, we sincerely believe that they are unwilling to have their authority called in question, and fear the experiment of an effort to maintain it. The learned and the unlearned clergy have always exhibited an eager desire to pass themselves off for ambassadors for Christ, or a sort of plenipotentiaries, whose preachings, prayers, and exhortations, have a peculiar efficacy in heaven and earth, of which the prayers and exhortations of a christian cobbler or a christian maid-servant are divested. Now I am just such a simpleton as to believe that the preachings, exhortations, and prayers of sister Phebe, the maid-servant of his Grace the Lord Archbishop of Canterbury, are possessed of as much authority and efficacy as those of her master. By authority, here, I mean just every thing that the clergy claim to have peculiarly conferred on them from heaven. Such pretensions to authority, or a divine right to officiate as they do, are, no doubt, as useful to make the people fear them and pay them, as a mitre, a surplice, a cloven cap, or a sable gown is to a Popish priest, for all the wise and noble ends of his calling. But either the clergy possess an authority or a divine right to preach, pray, and exhort in public assemblies, on "the sabbath day," which every other member of the religious community does not possess, or they do not. Now if they do, it can be proved that they do; and if they do not, it can be proved

that they do not. I have already pledged myself to the public to prove that they do not, whenever any of them attempts to prove that they do. And I will add, that if I cannot prove, and satisfactorily too, to every umpire, that their pretensions, right, and authority to act as they do, is given them, not from heaven, but from men; then I will say that I can prove no point whatever. But how to reconcile their conduct to any correct principles, religious or moral, I find not. If I had a piece of genuine gold, or a coin that I thought genuine, soon as its genuineness was called in question, I, being conscious that the more it was tested the brighter it would shine, would not fear to have it subjected to the severest scrutiny. But were I possessed of a base coin, or of a counterfeit bank bill, which I wished to be reputed genuine, I would endeavor (being a rogue) to pass it off amongst the ignorant and unsuspicious, and fearfully avoid examination. The Protestant clergy have, when it suited their interest, laughed at the arrogant pretensions of the Papist clergy to infallibility. We view their pretensions to authority just in the same light.

The great body of the laity are so completely preached out of their common sense, that they cannot guess or conjecture how the christian religion could exist without priests. And I believe it to be as difficult to persuade many of them that they could do much better without them, as it once was, or as it is now, to persuade the loyal subjects of an eastern monarch, that a nation could exist without a king and nobles at its head. The United States, however, has proved the fallacy of such doctrine; and the primitive church, as well as many congregations of saints in modern times, have proved to those acquainted with their history, that either a learned or an unlearned clergy are now, and ever have been the cause of all division, superstition, enthusiasm, and ignorance of the people.

These sentiments are, we know, obnoxious to the wrath and vengeance of this order; and woe awaits him that rises up against the Lord's anointed. Our remarks, puny and insignificant as the clergy view them, are honest, well meant, and above board. Their efforts to defend themselves, strong, powerful, and valiant as they are, are in secret, by the fireside, or in the wooden box, where they think themselves protected from exposure and defeat. Two honest men, it is true, my friend, Thomas G. Jones, and the reverend editor of the Pittsburgh Recorder, have once, but not twice, manfully lifted up their pen like a two-edged sword; but alas! for the honor of the cloth, it soon sought its scabbard. They cannot, either in honor to their own well meant efforts, nor to the sacredness of their calling, say I am so worthless and vile as to be unworthy of their notice. For why, then, have they noticed me at all? And were they as sacred as the Saviour of the world, and I as vile as the woman of Samaria, they would do well to remember that the former deigned to converse and reason with the latter. Or if they are ambassadors of Heaven's Almighty King, and I as common as an Epicurean, a Stoic, or an idolatrous Lycaonian, they should remember that Paul, as great and as well attested an ambassador as they, disputed with Epicureans, Stoics, and Lycaonians. Or if they view me as an erring brother, as Paul did some in his time, they should be as open and as explicit as Paul, who, before them all, rebuked Peter to his face. It is true, indeed, that some of them have made me worse than any of these; for the president of a western college who took it into his head that he was the eloquent orator noticed in a former number, to a friend who asked him his opinion of it and me, very laconically replied, "He is the Devil." Supposing this were the case, and that Satan had actually appeared in human form, his serene highness, though marked D. D. should remember that the Saviour of the world rebutted the Devil with "It is written," and not with saying "You are the Devil."

I honestly confess that the popular clergy and their schemes appear to me fraught with mischief to the temporal and eternal interests of men, and would anxiously wish to see them converted into useful members, or bishops, or deacons of the christian church. How has their influence spoiled the best gifts of heaven to men! Civil liberty has always fallen beneath their sway—the inalienable rights of men have been wrested from their hands—and even the very margin of the bible polluted with their inventions, their rabbinical dreams and whimsical nonsense. The bible cannot be disseminated without their appendages, and if children are taught to read in a Sunday school, their pockets must be filled with religious tracts, the object of which is either directly or indirectly to bring them under the domination of some creed or sect. Even the distribution of the bible to the poor, must be followed up with those tracts, as if the bible dare not be trusted in the hands of a layman, without a priest or his representative at his elbow. It is on this account that I have, for some time, viewed both "bible societies," and "Sunday schools," as a sort of recruiting establishments, to fill up the ranks of those sects which take the lead in them. It is true that we rejoice to see the bible spread, and the poor taught to read by those means; but notwithstanding this, we ought not, as we conceive, to suffer the policy of many engaged therein to pass unnoticed, or to refrain from putting those on their guard who are likely to be caught by "the sleight of men and cunning craftiness."

As we have in the first volume devoted a number of articles to the exposition of modern devices, we shall still continue true and faithful to the principles on which we have set out; and in this volume, pay a little more attention to the primitive state of things, than we have in the former. For while we would endeavor to unmask the clergy and their kingdom, we would wish to call the attention of our readers, occasionally at least, to the contemplation of that glorious superstructure built by the founder and his skilful architects, described in the New Testament.

We have only to assure every one who may read this work, that any article written in proper style, by any person, clergyman or layman, in opposition to any sentiment we have expressed, shall be received with pleasure and correctly inserted. We will give every opportunity to our readers to judge for themselves; for we have never yet been afraid to publish the remarks of our warmest opposers; nor could we ever yet see the propriety of laying an embargo on the ears of those who hear us, lest they should be misled. We wish the exhortation of the apostle to have its fullest latitude—"Prove all things; hold fast that which is good." And as both the Old and New Testament wise men, teach us to answer different persons in a different style, for reasons there assigned, so we shall ever discriminate betwixt those "of whom we ought to make a difference," the interested and the disinterested errorist. We hope ever to manifest that good will is our motive, and truth our object.   EDITOR.

A Review of the General Assembly's last Report.

THIS ecclesiastical paper was published by order of the general assembly, and signed by the stated clerk. It is, therefore, an authentic document. It may also be fairly presumed that it is a fair specimen of the religious feelings and literary talents of this ambitious and aspiring party. It must be as interesting to the people of that religious community, as the president's message is to the good citizens of the commonwealth.

Every religious system, like every human body, has a spirit peculiar to itself. It is also true, that as there is a great similarity in human spirits, so there is a great similarity in the spirits of religious systems. This general similarity does not, however, annihilate or obscure the predominant peculiarities of each. This is as evident as that, although every perfect face exhibits eyes, nose, mouth and cheeks, yet there is such a variety in the adjustment of these, and other constituents of human countenance, as render the discrimination of face from face easy to all. The Presbyterian system exhibits a countenance specifically the same as other religious systems; yet the peculiarities in its aspect easily distinguish it from every other. One thing is certain, that the spirit of Presbyterianism is a lofty and aspiring one. Like a Roman chief, it cannot bear an equal or a superior. It aims for the chief place in the nation, and views every other system as an impudent intruder upon its rights and liberties. A full proof of this is afforded in all their plans and manœuvres, from the kirk session to the supreme court; and more especially in their synodical reports. Let us take a specimen from the title of the last report, the present subject of review:—

"A Narrative of the state of religion within the bounds of the general assembly of the Presbyterian church, and its corresponding churches, in the United States of America."

"The bounds of the general assembly;" that is, the whole United States, as would seem from the scope of the review. The Presbyterian church is, then, bounded on the North by the British provinces, on the East by the Atlantic ocean, on the South by the gulf of Mexico, &c., and on the West, for aught I know, by the Pacific ocean. A report of the state of religion within these bounds is a matter of no small moment. All the Arians, Socinians, Arminians, Deists, Quakers, Methodists, Episcopalians, Papists, Baptists, Shakers, New Jerusalemites,

&c. &c. &c., live within the bounds of the general assembly, and are consequently embraced in this report. An important document truly!! But as the report pays no very courtly attention to these residents within its bounds, it must be supposed that they do not consider these religionists at all, and observe, it is the state of religion, within these bounds, that is reported. This is, perhaps, the fact. This denomination, from the loftiness of its spirit, contemplates every other persuasion as irreligious and profane. Hence the editor of the Pittsburgh Recorder did positively declare, July 6, that he is the only religious editor in nine states and three territories; or to use his own words, "the Recorder is now the only religious paper published in all the western country, including nine states and three territories, with considerable parts of other states." And if even a Presbyterian paper tell of marriages, battles, tariffs, dry goods, silks and fancy goods, bank note exchange, tavern keepers, and candle manufacturers; it is all religious—for this only religious paper occupies more than half its columns in such religious intelligence. This is a plain proof that the altar sanctifies the gift; that the Pittsburgh Recorder, formerly of Chillicothe, is the only religious paper in nine states and three territories, and in considerable parts of other states. And so it is, that whatever a Presbyterian does is religious, and whatever any other man does is profane. But to the report again.

The report, perhaps, means better than it speaks—It means only a report of the state of religion amongst the communicants of the Presbyterian church—Let us try if this be its meaning. It reports that;

"Within our extensive bounds, there is a vast wilderness, filled with immortal souls who are destitute of religious instruction and hope. There are regions just beginning to enjoy the "day spring from on high," still dark in error and ignorance, and cold in indifference and sin. Where the gospel is preached, it is met with powerful opposition by error of every form, and it is assailed by enemies of every name. Amid many of our churches are to be found cold and worldly professors, and many who having a name to live are dead, and the enemies of Jesus are sometimes established in the house of his friends. We do not recollect to have heard more deep and afflicting representations from the presbyteries, of the want of zeal and the life giving energies of the Spirit. On every side there are complaints of prevailing error, of licentious practice, of gross intemperance, and disregard to the Lord's day. In many parts of our widely extended and extending church, the want of ministers is still most painfully felt, and even those who can support them cannot obtain them."

"From almost every direction we learn that the Lord's day is most shamefully profaned, and that even professors sanction this destructive and most offensive sin, by the looseness of their own example, or their open conformity to the world, in some of the most popular modes by which its sanctity is invaded. Even ministers, in some instances, have been known to travel in public conveyances on this "day of rest." The Assembly have learned the fact with pain; and while they deplore, they wholly disapprove it."

"In many parts of our country the odious and destructive sin of intemperance is, we fear, increased to an alarming degree; producing blasting and destruction to individuals, families, and churches. The Assembly, while they record the fact with shame and sorrow, and real alarm, will not cease to publish it, until those who profess to love the Lord Jesus shall awake to the dangers of our country and the church. We will warn our beloved people until they shall all arouse to duty and self-denial, to watchfulness and prayer."

What a picture of communicants of this church, and that from its own supreme court!!! If this learned and pious Assembly were to have reported the state of religion "within the bounds" of Arians, Socinians, and Papists, could its language have been more expressive of awful rottenness and corruption!!! Is this that church which is sanctified through the truth—"that chosen generation, that royal priesthood, that holy nation, that peculiar people," of whom the apostle spoke!!—We have never read a more lamentable account of any religious community than that under review. We have never seen any thing like it, if we except the report of a missionary, in the Recorder of July 13th, who gives an account of his tour through the New-Jersey Pines. He says—

"Had I not been an eye witness, I never could have believed such wretchedness, such total ignorance of divine things, could have been permitted in the sight of a theological seminary, containing upwards of one hundred students preparing for the ministry, and of the enlightened city of Philadelphia. What will the christian public say, if told that in the state of New-Jersey, a state abounding with men of science, talent and piety, there are whole neighborhoods which enjoy no preaching, no schools, no sabbaths, and no bibles; many precious immortals who never saw a bible—never heard of God their creator, nor of Jesus Christ who died to open a way for the salvation of our fallen race."

Mark it well—In sight of a theological school, in the vicinity of a hundred students of divinity, in the vicinity of the annual meeting of the supreme court of the church of the United States—a tract of country "seventy miles long and forty wide," the inhabitants are in a worse state than the Pagans in Asia!! *Query*—What has this theological school, and this general assembly been doing for years, when their highest neighbors have been so long without every thing they call christian?

But what is still worse, the very report itself partakes of the general deterioration. It is, in a literary point of view, one of the poorest of the poor; and in a moral point of view, (pardon the expression) the most defective. It is self-contradictory—Let us adduce the proof. The assembly says, in one part of it, that "we do not recollect to have heard more deep (mark the expression *more deep*) and afflicting representations from the presbyteries, of the want of zeal, and of the life-giving energies of the Spirit." Now, reader, mark what they say in another paragraph of the self-same report—"We believe that the cause of truth is advancing, that it is gaining victories over error, that knowledge is increasing, that the church is more engaged, steadfast, and prayerful, there is more zeal, more liberality, and more self-denial." Now put the two ends of the testimony together, and reconcile it, if you can. They say "we do not recollect to have heard more deep and afflicting representations from the presbyteries, of a want of zeal," and in a minute afterwards declare "there is more zeal" than formerly, and yet they never heard of less!!! But this is not all. They say they never heard "more deep and afflicting representations of the want of the life-giving energies of the Spirit;" and yet tell us of thirty-one revivals, of some of which they say, "One of the most extensive works of the Spirit, that has been known in our country, has occurred in Moreau, and has spread with astonishing power through the surrounding country." And stranger still, they say, "We learn from almost all our presbyteries that the word of God has been faithfully preached, and the people have attended with punctuality upon the stated worship of God, and in many instances have given earnest heed to the word spoken"—and yet "more deep and afflicting representations of the want of the life-giving energies of the Spirit, from the presbyteries, were not recollected ever to have been heard." Astonishing indeed!! Some of those ministers whom the Assembly deplored as sabbath-breakers, must certainly have penned this: but then, how could the others approve it!!— This is as astonishing as the reported revival in Jefferson College, which again appears in the report of the Assembly—But tell it not in India, nor publish it in the Isles of the Pacific, that the "Supreme court of the most learned (as they say) body of interpreters of scripture have, all, with one consent, ascribed to the words spoken by their divines the same character and epithets which belong to the oracles of God, and have styled themselves "the day spring from on high."

Once more, and we dismiss the report pro tem. The assembly says,

"The theological seminary at Princeton is every year becoming more and more important. Its present condition is flourishing. The number of its pupils is greater than at any former period; and it promises to be a favored and powerful instrument of disseminating the gospel through the earth."

Now, reader, remember that the only religious paper in nine states and three territories, did, on the 13th ult. declare, in the name of a sacred missionary, that there is a district of country, seventy miles long and forty broad, "in sight of this theological seminary, in darkness, great as any part of the Indies"—that there are "many precious immortals who never saw a bible, nor heard of God their creator, nor of Jesus Christ." How impudent is Satan thus to reign on the very borders of the camp of the Lord!!! How much are one hundred such students of divinity worth? One Benjamite with his sling and stone, would put a thousand such to flight.   EDITOR.

Essays on the Work of the Holy Spirit in the Salvation of men.—No. I.

To THE Spirit of God are we immediately indebted for all that is known, or knowable of God, of the invisible world, and of the ultimate destinies of man. All that ancient Pagans and modern Sceptics pretend to have known of these sublime topics, was either borrowed from the oracles of the Revealer of secrets, or was mere uncertain conceits or conjectures of their own. Were it our design, we could easily prove, upon the principles of all modern sceptics, upon their own philosophical notions, that unaided by the oracles of the Spirit, they never could have known that there is a God, that there was a creation or Creator, or that there is within them a spark of life superior to that of a brute. Indeed this has been unanswerably done already, in a work published a few years since, by James Fishback, D. D. This ingenious and profound reasoner has shown with demonstrative certainty, that, on the acknowl-

edged principles of Locke, "the christian phil osopher," and of Hume, the subtle sceptic, all the boasted intelligence of the deistical world is a plagiarism from the oracles of this Divine One. Indeed it all comes to this—if there be no innate ideas as these philosophers teach, then the bible is proved, from the principles of reason, and from the history of the world, to be what it purports, a volume indited by the Spirit of the invisible God. To pursue this argument is, however, foreign to our present purpose. We are not now, on set purpose, addressing infidels, but those who profess to believe that the christian religion is of divine authenticity. We may, perhaps, find it our duty to drop a few hints on this subject. In the mean time, we speak to those who profess faith in the sacred scriptures.

It being granted that the bible was dictated from heaven, it follows that it is revealed truth, that there is one God and father of all, one only begotten Son of God who is Lord of all, and one Spirit of God, who alone reveals to men the secrets of God. Leaving out of view all the metaphysical divinity of ancient councils or modern theological schools on the philosophical doctrine of the Trinity, we may safely assert, upon the plainest evidence, that these THREE must occupy the attention of every reader of the holy oracles. Scarcely have we time to exhaust one breath in reading the history of the creation, as written by Moses, until the Spirit of God is introduced to our view as operating in this marvelous demonstration of almighty power. And scarcely do we read a page in any one of the four Evangelists, until this Divine One appears to our view as a mighty agent in some work connected with the redemption of man. Even the New Testament closes with a gracious discovery of his benevolence, and the last welcome of heaven to the sons of misery and wretchedness is echoed by this self-same Spirit, who says, "COME and drink of the water of life FREELY."

Without presuming to roam in the regions of conjecture, or to indulge in the flights of imagination; or even to run at random through all that is recorded concerning this sacred name, into which we have been baptized, we shall confine our inquiries, and if possible, the attention of our readers, to that office which the Spirit of God evidently occupies in the salvation revealed in the New Testament.

That the christian religion was to be established and consummated by the ministration of this Spirit, is one of the plainest truths in revelation. It was a subject of ancient prophecy, and the facts recorded in the New Testament concerning the gifts and operations of this Spirit, are but the accomplishment of what was long foretold and anxiously expected.

The christian religion was established by the personal labors of its founder, who appeared to be no more than a Jewish peasant, and the labors of a few illiterate fishermen. It is the most singular fact on the page of history, sacred or profane, the best established, and most universally admitted, by friends and foes, that a Jewish peasant (as his enemies called him) and a dozen of individuals, without learning, without money, without family, without name, without any kind of human influence, revolutionized, in a few years, the whole world, as the Roman empire was then called; and that, too, at a crisis the most forbidding in its aspect, the most unfavorable that ever existed. Paganism was long established and strongly guarded by the sword of the civil magistrate, and myriads of hungry, cunning, and avaricious priests. Judaism, still better confirmed, as it had truth well attested on its side, and the imposing influence of the most venerable antiquity. On the one side, prejudices, creeds, rubrics, temples, gods in the Gentile world innumerable and indescribable—established and confirmed by many succeeding generations. On the other, the most inveterate antipathies, the most unrelenting malevolence, aggravated and embittered by a superstition that once had much to recommend it. Before their face, poverty, shame, sufferings through life, and martyrdom at last, were presented, not as matters of conjecture, but as awful certainties, to forbid their efforts and to daunt their souls. But by the energies of this Holy Spirit, its gifts and its endowments, they triumphed. Temples were vacated, altars pulled down, and idols abolished in every land, and a new religion established in Asia, Africa, and Europe. Such is the fact, the marvelous fact, recorded, recommended, and proved by a combination of evidence, the splendor of which throws into the shade all the evidence adduced in support of any other historical fact in the annals of the world.

In the contemplation of this wonderful revolution, the Holy Spirit is the most striking object presented to our view, and to it are to be ascribed all these marvelous results. And here we open the New Testament and commence our inquiries into the character of its operations.

That faith is necessary to salvation, is a proposition the truth of which we need not now attempt to prove, as all professors of christianity admit it; and that testimony is necessary to faith, is a proposition equally true, evident, and universally admitted. He that believes, believes something, and that which he believes is testified to him by others. A man, every body who thinks, knows cannot see without light, hear without sound, nor believe without testimony. Some people, we know, say they believe what they see; but this is an abuse of language. I know what I see, and I believe what I hear—upon the evidence adduced in the first case to my eye, and in the second to my ear. It is as natural for a child to believe as it is to hear, when its capacity expands: and were it not for lying and deceit, it would continue to believe every thing testified to its understanding. Children become incredulous merely from experience. Being deceived by lies and deceit, they become incredulous. Having experienced that some things reported to their ears are false, they afterwards refuse to believe every thing which they hear. The more frequently they have been deceived, the more incredulous they become. Hence the examination of testimony becomes as natural, in a little time, as it is necessary. The first lie that was told on earth was believed to be a truth. Fatal experience has rendered the examination of testimony necessary. These observations are altogether gratuitous, as all we demand is cheerfully granted by all professors of christianity, viz. that faith is necessary to salvation, that testimony is necessary to faith; and that owing to the existence of falsehoods and deceits, the examination of testimony is necessary to full conviction. These positions being adopted as indisputable truth, we proceed to observe that Matthew, Mark, Luke, and John testify that there was a woman named Mary who brought forth a son supernaturally, who was called Jesus; that the child was announced by John the Baptist as the Redeemer, or Lamb of God, that was to take away the sin of the world, who had been

foretold and expected for many generations; that he was distinguished above all that were born of woman, in the circumstances of his nativity, childhood, baptism, and in every personal accomplishment; that he spoke and taught truths, and performed actions peculiar to himself; that he was maliciously put to death in Judea in the reign of Tiberius Cæsar, under the procuratorship of Pontius Pilate, by the Jewish sanhedrim; that he rose from the dead the third day, and after appearing alive for forty days on the earth, he afterwards ascended into heaven, and was placed upon the throne of the universe, and appointed Judge of the living and the dead; and that until his second coming to Judge the world, he is exalted to bestow repentance and remission of sins to all that call upon him. These things and many others of the same character the Evangelists and Apostles, *una voce*, declare. Now their testimony is either true or false. If false, then all christians are deceived, and all the religion in christendom and in the world is delusion; for if christianity is not true, it will be readily admitted by my readers that neither is Mahometanism, Judaism, nor Paganism. If true, then all the christian religion depends upon their testimony. Their testimony, on either hypothesis, is worthy of the most impartial and patient investigation. But such a testimony required supernatural attestations. For although there is nothing in this astonishing narrative impossible in the nature of things, nor indeed improbable on the acknowledged principles of human reason itself; yet the marvelous character of the facts testified, the frequent impositions practised, and, above all, the momentous stress laid upon them, required that they should be authenticated from heaven. In the attestation of this testimony, and in the proof of these facts, the office of the Holy Spirit first presents itself to our notice.

It was not enough that the Apostles were qualified by the Spirit to deliver a correct, intelligible, and consistent testimony, but for the reasons above specified, that this testimony be attested by such accompaniments as would render the rejector of it damnably criminal, as well as afford the fullest ground of certainty and joy to all that received their testimony. Nor are we in this inquiry so much called to consider the import of their testimony or their qualifications to deliver it, as we are to exhibit the attestations afforded by the Holy Spirit.

Miracles were wrought by the influence of the Holy Spirit in confirmation of their testimony—that is, signs or proofs of a supernatural character followed their testimony. The very circumstance of miracles being added, proved their necessity; for all declare that God does nothing in vain. If miracles were wrought by the Saviour and his apostles, those miracles were necessary appendages to their testimony. For if faith, which we have agreed, is necessary to salvation, and if testimony is necessary to faith, as also admitted, then, in the case before us, miracles were necessary in order to the confirmation of this testimony, or to its credibility; for this is apparent from the fact that they were exhibited, and from the acknowledged principle that God does nothing in vain. But our remarks upon miracles must be postponed to the next number.

Two conclusions are fairly deducible from the preceding observations. The first is that the truth to be believed could never have been known but by the revelation of the Spirit; and secondly, that though it had been pronounced in the most explicit language, yet it could not have been believed with certainty, but by the miracles which were offered in attestation of it. It may then be safely affirmed that no man could believe the gospel facts without this work of the Holy Spirit in attestation thereof; for the Spirit of God would not have empowered those witnesses to have wrought those miracles if their mere testimony without them was sufficient to produce faith. For let it be remembered, that it is universally granted that God's works are all perfect, and that he does nothing superfluous or in vain.   EDITOR.

A Familiar Dialogue between the Editor and a Clergyman.—Part II.

Clergyman. I TOLD you at our last interview that I wished to resume the passage in the Romans which says, "how shall they preach except they be sent?" This I suppose to be applicable to all preachers authorized according to the law of God.

Editor. I presume it is. But I think it is by no means applicable to those licensed by a presbytery, except you can prove that a presbytery is authorized by God to send, in his name, whom it pleases. And for my part, I have long thought that those sent to preach by a presbytery are not sent by God; and amongst many other reasons I have for so thinking, this is one, that the presbytery has authorized itself so to act, and consequently its authority being self-bestowed, its acts and deeds are altogether human. Those whom it commissions are sent by men, as much so as a physician, who is authorized by the medical board under the recent law in Ohio, is sent by men to practice.

C. But is not a physician licensed by the board, authorized by the state, seeing the state constituted the medical board? Every licensed physician in Ohio is really sent or commissioned by the governor or the highest authority in the state, to act as a physician; and consequently the board is but a mean appointed to convey the authority of the state to the individual. Just in this sense I argue that a person licensed to preach by a presbytery is licensed by God, inasmuch as the presbytery is a means appointed by God to convey his authority to the individual. Now that a presbytery is a divine institution, and that it did in the age of the apostles convey such a right as I contend for, I will explicitly prove. Read with me if you please, 1st. *Tim.* iv. 14. Paul says to Timothy, "Neglect not the gift that is in you, which was given you by prophecy with the laying on of the hands of the presbytery."

E. I confess you have found the word presbytery once in the New Testament, and in the connexion with the imposition of hands too; but really I had thought that none but those sometimes called the ignorant laity, who are wont to be carried more by sound than sense, would appeal to this passage in proof that a presbytery, in modern style, is a means appointed by God to license, commission, or send forth preachers in the name and by the authority of God. Before you can bring this passage into your service, three things must be done—First, show that the word presbytery meant in that age, what you mean by it in your church style. In the second place, prove that the gift here said to be conferred on Timothy, was a license to preach, or to exercise his ministry in one congregation. In the third place that the laying on of the hands of the presbytery conferred this gift. I should be glad to hear you attempt these things because

I think that there lives not the man who can do any one of the three, and because I think that these three things must be explicitly proved before you can at all quote the passage in your favor. You yourself, in arguing with a Romanist, would adopt this same method. Suppose your controversy was about the church, or the church of Rome, and he should say that the "church of Rome" was actually once mentioned in the New Testament, therefore of divine authority; but as the church of Scotland was never mentioned, therefore it is an imposition. You would immediately say that he was now using the words church, or church of Rome, in a sense of his own, and not in the New Testament sense. So I say of your presbytery. You may call your son Paul or Peter, if you please, but your son and the Paul and Peter of the New Testament are very different characters. Six men may meet in an inn and form a constitution for themselves, and call themselves a presbytery, but you would dispute their right to the name. Now every argument you would bring against their assumptions I would turn against your canonized presbytery. It is to me all one and the same, whether your system of presbytery be five or five hundred years old. I pay it no more deference than I do the modern discoveries and improvements of the most modern errorists.

Your laying hold of the word "presbytery" in Paul's Epistle to Timothy, reminds me of an anecdote I read somewhere a few years ago, perhaps in Hunter's Sacred Biography. Some Jew I think it was, in his researches in Asia, found in some mound or other singular place, a tomb at some distance from the surface of the ground. On examination of the inscription it was found that, in ancient style, there was written upon it these words, "Here lies the body of Moses, the servant of God." Great speculations were afloat, and in a little time it was agreed that this was actually the tomb of that Moses who brought Israel out of Egypt. The discoverer was just upon the eve of making his fortune by his discovery, when it unfortunately was found out that this was the tomb of a Moses who had died a century or two before, who was reputed a servant of God. So ensnaring and dangerous is it to appropriate names of great antiquity, or of sacred import, to things which are every way incongruous. Believe me, sir, that they who thought they had got the body of Moses, the servant of God, were not more cheated than they who think they have found the presbytery of Lystra or of Ephesus in one of your church courts.

C. And do tell me what ideas you attach to the word presbytery? You admit it is a bible term. Now it must have a bible signification.

E. This I have no objections to do, provided you first give me a definition of what you call a presbytery.

C. I will. "A presbytery consists of the ministers and representative lay elders of the congregations of a certain district."

E. Now let me ask, Did you ever read in the scriptures of "representative lay elders" or ministers of a certain district meeting for any purpose? or rather, Was there ever such a being as a lay elder in the primitive church?

C. You promised me a definition of the word presbytery in its bible import. I am waiting to hear it. Those questions you ask will lead us off from the subject altogether. Let them be reserved till another time.

E. In doing this, then, I will read you a Presbyterian Doctor's translation of this verse.

6

Your brother Macknight thus translated it: "Neglect not the spiritual gift which is in you, which was given you according to prophecy, together with the imposition of the hands of the eldership."

C. But what was this eldership?

E. I will let Macknight explain it. His comment on the verse reads thus; " That you may understand the scriptures, neglect not to exercise the spiritual gift which is in you, which was given you by the imposition of my hands, according to a prophetic impulse, together with the imposition of the hands of the eldership, at Lystra, who thereby testified their approbation of your ordination as an evangelist." It seems, then, that the Greek word presbytery, according to the most learned of your own fraternity, implied no more than the eldership of one congregation. And so we read that the apostles ordained them elders in every city or church. As for your "lay elders," they were not yet got into fashion. If you cannot bring some other scripture to countenance your presbytery, it must appear altogether destitute of scripture warrant. Again, Paul, in the next epistle to Timothy, declares that this gift was given by the imposition of his own hands; and in no instance on record, does it appear that spiritual gifts of any kind, were bestowed by the imposition of any hands save those of the apostles. But, as you have already said, this may lead us into another discussion. I would then in the mean time propose that we would confine our attention to the passage in Romans, until its meaning is ascertained; as you see nothing can be obtained in support of your views, from 1st. *Tim.* iv. 14.

C. And what do you say of the passage in the Romans?

E. I appeal to the context for its meaning—to the design of the apostle in the passage. If this does not determine the meaning, it must be indeterminate, as you will readily admit.

C. And was not the apostle speaking of the ordinary preachers of the gospel—of those we now call ministers of the gospel?

E. Those you call the ordinary ministers of the gospel, are very ill defined in the popular creeds, and not at all defined in the New Testament. But I will say without hesitation, that the passage in dispute exclusively appertains to those who received a commission from Jesus Christ to announce or to publish the gospel to all nations, and that the prophetic allusion in the prophecy of Isaiah, which, in the style of the Easterns, and indeed in the style of Sophocles, the Grecian poet, is descriptive of the feet of those who publish good news, is wholly applicable to the apostles and their associates and to none else.

C. And have the apostles no successors in this commission; or are there none now divinely commissioned to do the things enjoined in that commission?

E. I know of none. If you and your brethren in office, conceive yourselves acting under this commission, your conduct is altogether unjustifiable. You should be always employed in announcing the gospel to all nations, and not stationed in a parish.

C. Strange and singular as your views are on many topics, I did not think that you were so extravagantly wild as to say or to think that the commission given in *Matt.* xxviii. 18, 19, had ceased to be a commission authorizing a regular ministry, seeing it expressly says, "I will be with you always to the end of the world." Did the apostles live to the end of the world, or are they yet alive?

E. Novel and extravagant as you view the sentiment offered, and ancient and sacred as you view that opposed to it, I confidently assert that yours is unfounded and novel, and that mine is capable of the clearest proof, and that the very words you quote to prove its perpetuity, prove that it was but temporary.

C. What! the promise, "I will be with you always to the end of the world," you say will prove that it was only of limited duration!!!

E. Yes, and with confidence of making it evident too. Let me read the commission, and as I read, propose a few queries: "And he said to the eleven, [what eleven?] Go you, [who] therefore, and teach or disciple all nations, baptizing them, &c., teaching them to observe all things whatever I have commanded you, [who?] and lo! I am with you [who] always—even to the end of the world!" What is meant by "the end of the world?" There is one question yet of great consequence which I have intentionally omitted to the last, merely to give it a marked emphasis. It is this: What does he mean by the promise, "I AM WITH YOU?" Now I conceive the very promise, "I am with you," determines the whole matter.

C. I will hear your exposition of it before I offer any remark.

E. You shall have an infallible exposition of it from the pen of an infallible writer. John Mark gives the promise "I am with you," in the following words. See his statement of the commission, xvi. 15—17. Campbell's translation. It reads thus: "And these miraculous powers shall attend the believers—(I am with you.) In my name they shall expel demons—they shall speak languages unknown to them before—they shall handle serpents with safety, and if they drink poison it shall not hurt them. They shall cure the sick by laying hands upon them." Thus the Lord was with them. Hear John Mark once more, and more explicit still, 20th verse: "They went out and proclaimed the tidings every where, the Lord co-operating WITH THEM, and confirming their doctrine by the miracles wherewith it was accompanied."

The promise, "I am with you," then, is infallibly explained to denote that Christ would, upon the invocation of his name, be present with all his power, to confirm their testimony by open and visible miracles, performed not only by the apostles themselves, but also by their immediate converts. So says Paul in his exposition of it, (*Heb.*) "God also bearing them witness, with signs and wonders, with diverse gifts and miracles." If such be the meaning of the promise, "I am with you," as it doubtless is, then where are the pretensions of those who suppose themselves authorized by this commission? Let any one of them prove that Christ is with him in the common sense of the words, and I will sit down at his feet and open my mouth only to echo his oracles. And in fact there is no other way it can be understood that will help your views. For if Christ be not with the clergy in some peculiar sense in which he is not with other men, then all their pretensions are vain. That this is the very sense in which it was necessary for him to be with the commissioned preachers, the very sense in which he was with them, and the only sense in which he was understood by them, I presume no man of common (I mean ordinary) sense can or will controvert. If so, then the commission is not to be extended to any in our time, nor is it given to any in our time.

C. Until I hear you define the last clause, "always, to the end of the world," I will make no remarks.

E. Your Presbyterian brother, Dr. George Campbell, offers a very handsome criticism, and a very correct one too, on this passage, and shews that it ought to have been translated "to the conclusion of this state." I have some remarks to offer upon the Greek phrase, "*sunteleia tou aionos*," which the present moment will not permit.

C. I will make only one objection, which I think is enough to destroy your whole theory, viz. On your speculations on the commission Paul was not included, for he was not one of the eleven, and so you have reasoned away Paul's apostolic character—so dangerous it is to follow seemingly ingenious speculations without adverting to facts.

E. My dear sir, I am often confirmed in the truth by the puny efforts of those who attempt to overthrow it. Some, however, thought with you in ancient times on this subject; for they would make Paul some kind of a little apostle, or a second-hand one, because he was called after the others were commissioned; and, indeed, both your objection and theirs to Paul would have been well founded, had it not been that he received a peculiar commission of his own, which I need not tell you is often referred to in the New Testament. But you may consult *Acts* xxvi. 16—18. where the items of his commission are specified; so true it is that Paul's commission differed from the others, that he was not sent to baptize, but to evangelize the heathen.

But as the evening is far advanced, I will leave you with these views of the commission till our next interview, hoping then to find you reconciled to them, or to hear a more vigorous defence of your own. I understand the commission as follows: 'Go you, Peter and Andrew, James and John Zebedee, Philip and Bartholemew, Thomas and Matthew Levi, James Alpheus and Lebbeus Thadeus, with Simon the Canaanite, and disciple all nations, immersing the believers of all nations into the faith of the Father, and of the Son, and of the Holy Spirit, teaching the baptized disciples to observe all things whatsoever I have commanded you, either before or since my resurrection from the dead—and take notice that I shall be ever present, with signs and wonders, to confirm your testimony, to the end of this state; for before this generation shall have passed away, the gospel shall be preached to all nations for a testimony to them.'

C. If such be the meaning of the commission, I have yet to learn the meaning of all the New Testament.

E. And if this be not the meaning of the commission, pray inform me what it is!

C. Adieu for the present.

Lay Preaching.

Mr. CHURCH, of Pittsburgh, at his baptism on the 11th ult. delivered a discourse of three hours and one quarter in length, in the presence of a very numerous congregation, assembled on the banks of the Allegany. Having myself been one of his hearers, I can give my readers a brief outline of his object and method. Mr. Church had been a member of different religious communities, and once a ruling elder of a congregation of Covenanters. He is well versed in all the systems of presbyterianism, and has, for a number of years, been a diligent searcher after truth. He brought with him to the water the creeds, testimonies, and formulas of those churches, as well as the holy scriptures. After having vindicated himself from the foul aspersions of some of his quondam brethren. and friends, which are the usual lot of those who

presume to judge and act for themselves in religious matters, he informed his audience that he would,

1st. Prove from the holy scriptures and the standards of the different churches his right to search, judge, and act for himself, and especially that he had an inalienable right, as well as the most justifiable reasons, to separate from every branch of the presbyterian church.

2d. Demonstrate from the scriptures the true nature and character of the church of Jesus Christ, her members, ministers, modes of worship, discipline; and contrast these with the genius of those societies that had assumed the title of christian churches, their members, ministers, modes of worship, and government.

3d. Exhibit the sacred import of christian baptism, its various corruptions and abuses in the Presbyterian churches, and others, as well as the character of those who were admitted to this ordinance in primitive times.

It would be altogether out of our power, in the size of this number, even to give any thing like a fair miniature of this discourse. Suffice it to say, that Mr. Church redeemed the pledge he had given in his method; and did, at least to my satisfaction, as well as, no doubt, to that of many of his auditors, fully prove his right of search from all the documents mentioned, and exhibit the corruptions of the systems proposed. He stripped the clergy of all their exorbitant claims and pretensions, and fully expatiated on the vices and deformities of the clerical system. He read many extracts from the popular creeds and testimonies, the national covenant and solemn league, on which he presented many appropriate remarks. And such was the efficacy of his remarks, that they produced, in some instances, the same effect on some of the sons of the national convention and solemn league which the discourse of Stephen produced on the Jews, such as a literal gnashing of the teeth, and an equivalent to stopping of the ears. He was, however, patiently heard by a respectable congregation to the close, although it rained for more than an hour of the time, and the people were by no means comfortably circumstanced. The discourse has, we have since understood, caused a great "shaking among the dry bones." Indeed, he sometimes appeared to me like Sampson amongst the Philistines, at least likely to kill more by his emblematical death, and in his emblematical burial, than during his former life. Very few of the regular clergy could have made so lengthy and so appropriate a discourse, and have assembled such a congregation, as this erudite layman.   EDITOR.

THE following QUERIES came from the pen of a diligent student of the Bible. We wish our readers to attempt, each, to answer them for himself.

1st. The order of the first churches when supernatural gifts were abundant, being discovered; what, if any example, will it form to us who live in these last days when supernatural gifts have ceased?

2d. What duty or duties are peculiar to the Bishop and not common to the brethren?

3d. Was it the Bishops who chiefly spoke in the first churches where they presided, or did they commonly sit as judges (1 *Cor.* xiv. 29.) to correct, &c. while the brethren edified the body in love? *Eph.* iv. 16.

4th. What are the peculiar duties of a Deacon?

5th. Was it to the deaconship that those seven mentioned in *Acts*, 6th chap. were appointed, or what were they?

No. 2.]   September 6, 1824.
Primitive and Modern Christianity.

A Series of almost 2000 years has now fled away since the gospel announced light and religious liberty to the enslaved world; since Messiah, emerging from the rocky sepulchre, destroyed Death, and delivered those who, through fear of his merciless domination, were all their lifetime subject to bondage. Strong and implacable were the enemies of Jesus; many were the foes with which the Captain of our salvation had to contend, and for a moment they seemed to prevail. They crucified him, and thought themselves secure; they entombed his murdered body, and vainly imagined the conquest was complete. Unhappy men! how blind to the future! Scarce was the palm of victory lifted to their brows, when it withered; scarce did the dawn of conquest rise upon their marshalled efforts, when it set in the midnight of everlasting dismay. They succeeded in depriving the Champion of Israel of the light of life; but in the awful moment he only groped for those pillars on which the whole temple of Jewish and heathen superstition stood. Then, indeed, he bowed himself. The grave could not retain him who made the world. The Shepherd of Israel descended into the pit, but it was only to destroy the enemy of the flock, and having seized him he slew him. When the son of God rose from the dead, and thereby brought life (eternal life) and immortality to light, ignorance, the cause of all Jewish, heathen, and antichristian superstition fled before him; and seeing that the world were in great bondage through fear of death, and especially through their ignorance of that life which lay beyond death, it was necessary that he who gave his life for the world should deliver his children from the bondage of this fear. Having risen from the dead, and removed the cause of all uncertainty respecting a resurrection and eternal life, nothing remained but to let the children know it. To effect this, to remove all fear, to inform the body of the resurrection of its head, to let all flesh see the salvation of our God—the Lord Jesus called the twelve, and, *viva voce*, commissioned them to go into all the world and to preach the gospel (*i. e.* his death and resurrection) to every creature: "He that believes shall be saved—he that believes not shall be damned." This, by the way, is the only constitution of a christian assembly, in opposition to all written instruments. Having received this gospel in charge, the apostles went forth every where preaching it, God bearing them also witness in signs and wonders, and diverse miracles, and gifts of the Holy Spirit, according to his will. Having made disciples in Jerusalem and every where among the gentiles, it became necessary to assemble the brethren on that fact which they had believed, in order that they might edify one another, grow in grace and knowledge, increase in every good word and work, and finally show forth the death of Jesus in the eating of the supper.

To manage the business of the church in all ages, it pleased the Head of the church to appoint bishops and deacons. The apostles were chiefly employed in ordaining elders "in every church" on their return from their first tour through the Lesser Asia. Titus was left in Crete for the express purpose to "ordain elders in every church," and Timothy had this business in charge in the church at Ephesus. And in all those appointments the bishops and deacons were chosen from among those who believed; and they had previously assembled themselves, like others, to eat the supper. Besides this, they were numerous in every church.

Of the elders or bishops at Ephesus, it is said that they "all fell upon Paul's neck," &c. but the word "all" is never used of one or two, but of a considerable number of persons. The epistle to the Philippians is addressed to the church there with the bishops and deacons. Two things, then, are remarkable in the choice of the primitive bishops: 1st. They were selected from among the brethren—2dly. they were numerous in every church. Two things are remarkable of modern teachers also: 1st. That they are not chosen from among the brethren—2dly. that there is uniformly but one in every church. The order established by the apostles, was the same in every church, and was very simple; but the world, which perverts all things, soon began to make inroads into the beautiful and simple institution of the Lord Jesus, and from the most instructive and pure society, it has become the nest of every unclean bird. Evil men did not wait until the apostles were dead, but even while they were alive commenced their antichristian labors, which caused the apostle to say that even now, i. e. while the all-authoritative apostles and chief servants of the Lord Jesus were present, the mystery of iniquity was a working; yes, even then there were evil men and seducers, who were to wax worse and worse; and those men were not without, but within the church, like Diotrephes, who loved to have the pre-eminence, who received not even the apostles, but prated against them with malicious words. So says John. Peter tells us that these false teachers were to be remarkable for false doctrine, for covetousness, for their contempt of the magistrates, for their corruption, for loving the wages of unrighteousness, for speaking great swelling words, &c. &c. They even dared, under the name of christians, to call in question the authority of the apostle, which occasioned him to speak as follows to the Corinthians; "Am I not an apostle?" and to say of those pretended servants of Christ, that seeing Satan himself was transformed into an angel of light, it was no wonder therefore if his ministers were transformed into the ministers of righteousness. This is a singular incident, that the sons of God, the disciples of our Lord Jesus, should really be subject to the impositions of the servants of the Devil, transformed in appearance into servants of Christ. What is the christian to do after being told so by the Spirit of his Father? Where is he to look for these transformed ministers? How is he to detect the cloven foot?

This difficulty is greatly increased in the present age. Teachers are so numerous and so contradictory, so learned and yet so ignorant of the scripture, so covetous and yet so lofty in their requirements, that even the well meaning are at a loss sometimes how to act in regard to their claims. Is the disciple to look for these transformed ministers among those who have thrown off not only the power, but the form, of religion? Surely not! The apostle says they assume the color of servants of Christ, and therefore must be looked for among christians. When any truth in the New Testament is contended for by any number of combatants, it is possible for all to be wrong, but they never all can be right. If one man call himself a servant of Christ because he holds a license of the Pope; another, because he holds it of an Episcopalian bishop; a third, of a classical presbytery; a fourth, of an association; and a fifth, of any body that has plenty of influence with the public—surely they cannot all be right when they come to contend with each other about the *jus divinum* of their respective ordinations. The first of these tells the world he can make his God! and the disciples eat him! The second half denies this, and the rest deny it altogether. This, one would suppose, is a very delicate point to be divided upon—yet so it is; and the Lord pity the poor disciple who has to confide in any of them, for they are very wolves! O! reader! is it not a desideratum then to have a rule by which the disciple may distinguish the ministers of Christ from the ministers of Satan transformed? Surely it is; and the Bible is that rule—the bible, declared to be profitable for doctrine, reproof, correction, and instruction in righteousness, and is given by inspiration, that the man of God may be perfect, fully furnished, says the apostle. I shall suppose myself a christian greatly embarrassed by the above saying of the apostle, viz. that the ministers of Satan are transformed into the ministers of righteousness, and feel anxiously desirous to be able to distinguish them from those who are the true shepherds or bishops of Christ's flock.

I have no guide under heaven but the Bible. This is either allowed, or ought to be, by all. There is no legitimate authority in religion that is not derived immediately from the scriptures; they are God's umpire in all christian questions; and to them, and them alone, in the dernier resort, must we appeal; so that the only question remaining is, Whether the Bible contains descriptions of the real and transformed ministers, particular enough to enable me to distinguish them from each other. I can know this only by opening the Bible and reading it. I proceed, with respect to both, by induction of particulars, thus:—First, all the bishops and deacons in the churches of Jerusalem, Judea, Samaria, Ephesus, Greece, Crete, &c. &c. were uniformly, without a single exception, selected from among the brethren of the particular churches in which they were to officiate; and this particular I hold to be a *sine qua non* in electing or ordaining a bishop of Christ. He must be chosen from among the flock. Step aside from this, and the hireling system at once enters with all its train of religious spouting, preaching, &c. If the brethren, therefore, require or desire to have bishops and deacons, it is indispensable that they look out from among themselves holy men, answering to the description of such persons, in Timothy, Titus, and elsewhere. Now in selecting bishops and deacons, a church, or a number of people calling themselves a church, may choose to depart from this uniform practice of the apostolic churches, *i. e.* they may hire a school or college man, who, allowing the assembly so hiring him, to be what they profess to be, a church of Christ, can never, in any sense, be said to be selected from among the brethren of said church; and for their practice in so doing it is certain that they can plead neither scripture, precedent nor precept. In such a case, then, we have great and manifold reasons to suspect the character of the church, as well as that of the minister. The first may be, and I only say *may be* a synagogue of Satan, and the preacher his minister transformed into a minister of righteousness. However, it would be premature in me to say that every minister so appointed is a minister of Satan, because this would, even in my own opinion, be deducing the general conclusion for which I am searching, from too limited a number of experiments. I only say then that such a person and such a church are wrong, *i. e.* astray from scripture authority in the very first step, and therefore I must proceed with the induction. But here I shall turn a leaf, and look through the medium of the scriptures at the hireling or transformed minister. We have seen how any

number of individuals in the apostolic churches arrived at the episcopal office, i. e. through a choice from among the members of the church where said bishops were to officiate. We are sure, then, that one so appointed " comes in by the door," i. e. in the only manner authorized by scripture precept and example. But for the hireling—how comes he in? " Verily, verily, I say to you, he that enters not by the door into the sheepfold, but climbs up some other way, is a thief and a robber." It would appear from this declaration, then, that the step which a man makes at the threshold, may finally determine his character as a minister. The reader may, perhaps, be afraid to look at things in this frightful point of view, seeing he may never have heard or seen of ministers being got by selecting them from the christians in the church where they are to officiate. We grant that this manner of viewing things bears wonderfully on the preachers of the present day, notwithstanding all their pretensions. But to go on: It may be objected that the Saviour used the above language (*John* x.) in reference to the Pharisees with whom he was speaking. It will be granted; but let us try to discover the meaning of the Saviour's account of the hireling in *John* x. First, then, he spoke this address to the Pharisees, as appears from the latter end of the preceding chapter; and when he had done so, the Apostle John makes this observation on the matter, (verse 6.) " This parable Jesus spake to them, but they understood not what things they were which he spake to them." A second matter worthy of observation then is, that those same Pharisees, whom he plainly indicated to be thieves and robbers, did not understand what he meant in this speech. In short, it would appear that those ministers were not aware of their own origin—were not aware that they had no right to labour among the flock of God, and had no authority from him. Let us see, then, how these men climbed up to the office of teachers in Israel!—how they came by the name Reverend or Rabbi.

All the world knows that there was no foundation in the law of God for the sectarian distinction of Pharisee and Sadducee. These sectaries, therefore, owe their origin to some heresiarch, who lived either at or before the return from Babylon. Well, therefore, might the Saviour style them an offspring of vipers, *i. e.* the followers of unauthorized, heretical assemblies, who, instead of adhering to the law of God, and that alone, would wickedly frame their own religious course, and even set aside the law of God by their traditions. But if they had no liberty from the law to assume these names, they had far less for assuming to themselves the office of teachers. It was declared by God in Deuteronomy, that the house of Levi should teach Jacob his judgments, and Israel his law; that they should put incense before him and whole-burnt sacrifice upon his altar. And on this account the lands of the house of Levi, which amounted to the one-twelfth of all Canaan, were divided among the other tribes, who returned one-tenth of their annual increase for the service appointed them by God, viz. for teaching his judgments and law, and for waiting on the service of the tabernacle. And here it must be remarked, to the confusion of those who plead for the tenth, that the lands of the tribe of Levi being taken into account, the priests received only one-tenth of the produce for one-twelfth of the soil, which is about one-sixtieth of the whole, besides what in reality was their own; so that Israel paid to the priests, in fact, a very poor stipend, considering the business and important service appointed them by God. The house of

Levi, then, were the true teachers in the church of Moses. And now conceive for a moment the fatal effects which the violation of the law would have upon the condition of the Levites; conceive how easily this paltry return might be diminished, and how quickly the ministers of God might be deprived of their due and necessary means of subsistence. If a host of individuals from the other tribes should arrogate to themselves the office of teachers and expounders of the law, the Pharisees, then, who were chief teachers, and compounded of individuals from every tribe, are therefore, by our blessed Saviour, declared to be a plantation which his heavenly Father had not planted, and were to be rooted out. Josephus, as quoted by Whitby, says that many of the priests were starved to death in consequence of the people not bringing in their tithes. It appears to me that the Pharisees had got up an order of things very much resembling our theological institutions, where all comers indiscriminately were instructed in the divinity of the day, without the least respect to the law of God on this point, without the least regard to the rights and dues of the Levitical ministers; and who does not see that the young Pharisee, Paul, who was no Levite, but of the tribe of Benjamin, was one of the young divines at the moment of his conversion? What right had Paul to teach the judgments and law of God to the Jews? He was a Benjamite, concerning which tribe God said nothing about teaching. Yet was this young gentleman sent to college—schooled in the traditions of his sect—distinguished for his zeal, and for his progress in the study of self-deception, as well as for being the student of the famous Gamaliel. Now, then, we can easily perceive, I hope, what the Saviour meant by the Pharisees' climbing up into the sheepfold another way, and being thieves and robbers. First, they had no authority for teaching from God. Secondly, they robbed both the priests and the people; as the Lord Jesus said, "You rob widows' houses, and for a pretence make long prayers." The priest's lips were to keep knowledge, and the people should seek the law at his mouth: for, says Jehovah, "He is the messenger of the Lord of hosts." The Pharisees and others then had come in between the people and the teachers whom God had appointed, and thus threw the nation into sects, as the schoolmen have done in the christian church; for, whereas our blessed Saviour has ordered us to look out for officers from among ourselves, and has given us examples of it in all primitive churches of his apostles' planting, these learned divines have come in between the holy brethren and the law of Christ, and have not only done away the ancient custom of selecting bishops from among the brethren, but even succeeded almost generally in foisting their own young men on the sons of God for teachers. When I look, therefore, through the medium of scripture at the christian bishops, I see that they are distinguished for being selected from among the disciples; and this I call the door into the sheepfold, because it is the way authorized by Christ. When I look through the scriptures at the transformed minister of Satan, I behold him coming into the fold by another way. *i. e.* in a way not authorized by Christ, not chosen from among the brethren, but foisted over the heads of the most aged and experienced into an office which is due only to one of themselves. "He that enters not by the door into the sheepfold, but climbs up some other way, the same is a thief and a robber." Now, then, in searching the scriptures, I have discovered one difference between the bishop and transformed minister—they do not

M

come in alike—the manner of their induction is absolutely diverse—the one by the door, the other by the wall—the one by an authorized method, the other by an unauthorized method. But this induction may be pursued to greater length in some future paper. PHILIP, *alias Walter Scott.*

Essays on the Work of the Holy Spirit in the Salvation of Men.—No. II.

IN our last essay it was, we hope, fully proved, that with regard to the truth to be believed and the evidences of it, we owe every thing to the gracious ministrations of the Holy Spirit. The matter of faith preached is, that "Christ died for our sins, was buried, and is risen from the dead;" but even this fact is attributed to the immediate agency of this Glorious One. He, therefore, may be said to have made the truth, as well as by the most illustrious displays of his power in its behalf, to render it credible to men. His testimony in its behalf consists of miracles and prophecy, but it is with the first of these only we have to do in our present essay. The term miracle is general, and comprehends not only those displays of power whose legitimate and single purpose was to establish the fact that Jesus was risen from the dead, but the gifts also which were vouchsafed to those who believed, and whose primary intent was to fill with light and wisdom the new converts to our holy religion.

It has often been asked, what necessary connexion is there between a miracle and a revelation from Heaven? If the term miracle is properly defined to be "the suspension of some known law of nature," the connexion will be as follows:—The suspension intimates the certain presence of a power superior to the law, and this is all it proves. The miracle, I say, only proves that a power superior to the law operates in its suspension, but the moral character of the agent is to be deduced from the nature of the miracle combined with the end for which it is said to be performed.

The miracles of our Saviour are chiefly of a beneficent kind, and the declared end of them is to establish a mission the most salutary. From a consideration of the character of his miracles and the salutary end for which they were wrought, we are constrained by the rules of right reason to believe that they were effected by the Spirit of God, and not by Beelzebub, as the infidel Jews evilly suggested. The moral character of the power is to be known by its effects; and so the Saviour, as a key to guide us in this difficult step, tells us that we are in this case to judge as in the case of trees bearing fruit. If the fruit is good, the tree is good—if bad, the tree is bad. If the miracle is of a beneficent character and its declared end good, the agent by whom it is effected is good. It was not our Saviour's finger that performed the miracles—his touching the cured was only to connect the miracle with the end for which it was wrought, viz. to show that he was the Messenger of the Most High, that this display of power was in behalf of his pretensions, and not of others who might be present. The work of the Holy Spirit in this respect, then, is most glorious, and becoming Heaven in the highest degree.

The Jewish religion and the Christian are the only two religions that ever were received by men, purporting to be confirmed by miracles. Neither the Mahometan religion nor any system of pagan superstition at its first publication claimed the evidence of miracles. On this topic we shall present an extract from Dr. Campbell's "Essay on Miracles," in reply to Mr. Hume. He says:

"Can the pagan religion—can, I should rather say, any of the numberless religions (for they are totally distinct) known by the common name of pagan, produce any claim of this kind that will merit our attention? If the author knows of any, I wish he had mentioned it; for in all antiquity, as far as my acquaintance with it reaches, I can recollect no such claim. However, that I may not, on the one hand, appear to pass the matter too slightly; or on the other, lose myself, as Mr. Hume expresses it, in too wide a field, I shall briefly consider whether the ancient religions of Greece or Rome (which of all the species of heathenish superstition are on many accounts the most remarkable) can present a claim of this nature. Will it be said, that the monstrous heap of fables we find in ancient bards, relating to the genealogy, productions, amours, and achievements of the gods, are the miracles on which Greek and Roman paganism claims to be founded?

If one should talk in this manner, I must remind him first that these are by no means exhibited as evidences, but as the theology itself; the poets always using the same affirmative style concerning what passed in heaven, in hell, and in the ocean, where men could not be spectators, as concerning what passed upon the earth. Secondly, that all those mythological tales are confessedly recorded many centuries after they are supposed to have happened; no voucher, no testimony, nothing that can deserve the name of evidence having been produced, or even alleged in proof of them. Thirdly, that the intention of the writers seems to be solely the amusement, not the conviction of their readers; that accordingly no writer scruples to model the mythology to his particular taste, or rather caprice; but considering this as a province subject to the laws of Parnassus, all agree in arrogating here the immemorial privilege of poets to say and feign, unquestioned, what they please. And fourthly, that at least several of their narrations are allegorical, and as plainly intended to convey some physical or moral instruction, as any of the apologues of Æsop. But to have said even thus much in refutation of so absurd a plea, will perhaps to many readers appear superfluous.

Leaving, therefore, the endless absurdities and incoherent fictions of idolaters, I shall inquire in the next place, whether the Mahometan worship (which in its speculative principles appears more rational) pretends to have been built on the evidence of miracles.

Mahomet, the founder of this profession, openly and frequently, as all the world knows, disclaimed such evidence. He frankly owned that he had no commission nor power to work miracles, being sent by God to the people only as a preacher. Not, indeed, but that there are things mentioned in the revelation he pretended to give them, which, if true, would have been miraculous; such are the nocturnal visits of the angel Gabriel, (not unlike those secret interviews, which Numa, the institutor of the Roman rites, affirmed that he had with the goddess Egeria) his getting from time to time parcels of the uncreated book transmitted to him from heaven, and his most amazing night journey. But these miracles could be no evidences of his mission. Why? Because no person was witness to them. On the contrary, it was because his adherents had previously and implicitly believed his apostleship, that they admitted things so incredible, on his bare declaration. There is indeed one miracle, and but one, which he urges

against the infidels, as the main support of his cause; a miracle for which even we in this distant region and period, have not only the evidence of testimony, but, if we please to use it, all the evidence which the contemporaries and countrymen of this military apostle ever enjoyed. The miracle I mean is the manifest divinity, or supernatural excellence, of the scriptures which he gave them; a miracle, concerning which I shall only say, that as it falls not under the cognizance of the senses, but of a much more fallible tribunal, taste in composition, and critical discernment, so a principle of less efficacy than enthusiasm, even the slightest partiality, may make a man, in this particular, imagine he perceives what has no reality. Certain it is, that notwithstanding the many defiances which the prophet gave his enemies, sometimes to produce ten chapters, sometimes one, that could bear to be compared with an equal portion of the perspicuous book, they seem not in the least to have been convinced, that there was any thing miraculous in the matter. Nay, this sublime performance, so highly venerated by every Mussulman, they were not afraid to blaspheme as contemptible, calling it "a confused heap of dreams," and "the silly fables of ancient times."

While modern sceptics would tell us of miracles wrought in support of paganism, and of the Roman priesthood, they have not as yet attempted to say that either the "lying wonders" of the "mother kirk," or the false miracles of the Pagan temples, were exhibited in the first exhibition of a religion or for the establishment of it. Mr. Hume, indeed, would compare the miracles of Christ and his apostles to some things he calls Pagan and Popish miracles;—but there is not, in fact, one point of coincidence or resemblance between them. What were the tales of Alexander of Pontus, the celebrated Pagan fortune-teller, or of Vespasian the Roman emperor, in common with the miracles of Christ and his apostles? What has the miracle reported in the memoirs of the cardinal De Retz, or those said to have been performed in the church yard of Saint Medard, at the tomb of abbe Paris, to do with the christian miracles? Is there one point of coincidence in the alleged design of these miracles, or in their character and use? Not one. Mr. Hume himself was constrained to yield the point. And those miracles mentioned by Mr. Hume were the best suited to his design of any "lying wonders" in the annals of the world. Those Pagan and Popish miracles, as far as the sceptic has introduced them, were not wrought in confirmation of any new religion as proofs of its divine origin. The cures said to have been performed, were, even by their own testimony, few in comparison to the number of applicants who received no cures, and few in comparison to the number who were thrown into diseases in seeking remedies. In these false miracles impostures were often detected and proved, and as Dr. C. has shown that all the cures said to have been effected were such as could have been effected by natural means. Again, none of those cures were instantaneous; many of them were the effects of medicine before used, and in many instances the maladies had evidently abated before application for remedies was made. Many of those miraculous cures were incomplete, and the relief afforded was in many instances temporary. Now if all the false miracles which one of the most ingenious and most learned of unbelievers was able to assemble from history and from fable, were liable to all the above imputations; and if the gentleman himself who advanced them was put to silence on these grounds, how transcendent this species of evidence afforded our holy religion. The miracles wrought by the Holy Spirit in attestation of the preaching of the apostles, were numerous, public, beneficent; no imposture was ever detected, the adversaries of the christian faith themselves being judges; the cures were always instantaneous, always complete and always permanent. To this Holy and Eternal Spirit, then, is every christian indebted for that most splendid and powerful of all evidence, which puts out of countenance all opposition, which covers with shame and confusion the subtle and presumptuous infidel, and which, in fact, presents the whole phalanx of opposers to the christian faith in the same ridiculous and absurd attitude as the dogs in the fable, which conspired to bark down the moon walking in brightness.

We must reserve our remarks on spiritual gifts to the next essay, which in the department of miraculous evidence, are the most triumphant and glorious of all.   EDITOR.

Address to the Public.

IT is no doubt known to some of you that a pamphlet, titled, "*Letters to Alexander Campbell, by a Regular Baptist*," has been published at Pittsburgh a few days ago. It will, doubtless, be expected that I would pay some attention to this work. The spirit and style of this "Regular Baptist" forbids my addressing one word to him. I will, therefore, without prepossessing my readers by expressing any opinion of the motives and object of this letter-writer, proceed to review his performance.

This "Regular Baptist" informs me that my character is of two kinds—*extrinsic* and *intrinsic*. My "intrinsic character" is that which he investigates, and on which he pronounces judgment. In coming at my intrinsic character, or the character of my heart, he has, he says, adopted "as a standard of judgment," principles admitted by "the christian and the philosopher." These principles, he adds, "direct to a general investigation of life, the whole area of action." But he regrets that the whole area of my action is unknown to him, every thing previous to my arrival in these United States being with him "something of conjecture." But although my "intrinsic character" is the object of investigation, and the principles of the christian and the philosopher require that the "whole area of action" should be examined, yet the ingenious author views "the area of my action" only since I joined the Baptists—and, in fact, while he professes to do this much, he only fixes his eyes upon me since 1820. And of all the area of my action from which my intrinsic character is to be ascertained, only four years come in review—and of these four years but my "two debates and the Christian Baptist" are particularly noticed. To what a span is the whole area of my action reduced! And from how few documents does he undertake to prove that I am unregenerated. Let not the reader be startled at the word *unregenerated*; for this is the point of investigation, and the whole area of this Regular Baptist's letters is filled with mighty and convincing proofs, as he alleges, that I am an unregenerated man. But the strangest point of all remains to be noticed, and that is, that of all the actions of my life, and of all the words I have spoken or written, not one is adduced as proof of his favorite position, but only his conjectures, with a reference to the Debates on Baptism, and the Christian Baptist. Of all that I have written not one word is cited. These letters then are, if any thing can be so named, "a new

thing under the sun." For I am tried and condemned upon mere conjecture, and worse than all, these conjectures are predicated either upon the most evident falsehoods, or upon a false view of facts. So much by way of introduction to my review.

A few remarks upon the writer of these letters are also necessary to their easy comprehension. They are anonymous, and necessarily to be ranked under the very common and general head of anonymous abuse. As such, I was not bound to notice them; for who knows not that the ebullitions of anonymous foes carry their own condemnation in their preface. But believing that medicine may be deduced even from the carcass of a serpent that has poisoned itself, I am induced to notice them under the conviction that good may result therefrom. The writer of these letters is the Reverend Mr. GREATRAKE, from the city of Baltimore, or somewhere thereabouts. He is now located in the city of Pittsburgh, and calls himself a "Regular Baptist." It is true that he either promised or prophesied in the conclusion of his address to the Baptist churches in the West, that while on earth he would "be known to them only by the name of a Regular Baptist." In his last letter to me he was kind enough to appear willing to give me his real name, on presenting to the publisher a "fair reason" for demanding it. But when I called on the publisher he presented me with written conditions which the "Regular Baptist" had given him, which precluded him from giving up his name except upon such conditions as the civil law would oblige him to give it up or suffer prosecution. This gentleman is at present hired by a party, who were excluded from a regular Baptist church, at least by a church which at the time of their exclusion, was recognized as such. He seems to glory in the name of "a Regular Baptist," yet with what propriety I cannot see, as he is ordained over a party that cannot be called regular Baptists. It is a truth that the last Redstone association recommended the calling of a committee to endeavor to promote a re-union of those excommunicated ones; or as they express it, "to compromise the difficulties;" and that a committee was called by the excluded party, which leaving undone what was the only thing recommended by the association to be done; they proceeded to do that which they were not commanded to do, and did, without any authority from the association, call or denominate the excommunicated ones a church; and thus, as far as in them lay, prevented their re-union on such grounds as could, on regular Baptist principles, constitute them a regular Baptist church. Although, then, Mr. Greatrake glories in the name of a Regular Baptist, as though the very name should "cover a multitude of sins," he is not at present acting as such, in the instances specified. This with me is, however, a very small matter, as I lay no stress on such names, whether assumed or bestowed. There is a church in Pittsburgh that would rejoice much more in being a regular church of Christ, than a regular Baptist church; which church has two bishops, who while they watch over and labor among the saints, labor working with their own hands according to the apostolic command; and not only minister to their own wants, but are ensamples to the flock in beneficence and hospitality. This church, by walking in the fear of God and in the comfort of the Holy Spirit, is edified and enlarged by regular accessions—and their example in that city is a dangerous one to those who would maintain themselves by maintaining such opinions as will maintain them. The object of the letter-writer evidently being to defame this church as well as myself, it was necessary to present the reader with this brief notice of things in relation to the Rev. Mr. Greatrake. Now to the letters.

There are four conjectures, in some respects different, and in some respects not very distinct, by which Mr. Greatrake demonstrates that I am unregenerated. The first is, that I "must have received some personal pique or experienced some severe disappointment, if not both, from the denomination or church to which I formerly belonged." The second is that I must be stimulated by an " insatiate vanity." The third, that I am actuated by avarice, or, as he expresses it, by my "pecuniary interest." The fourth is, that I am aiming at being the head of a party. Into one or more or all of these evil motives, he resolves my two Debates on Baptism and the "*Christian Baptist*," and thence concludes that I am a very bad man—although my extrinsic character he acknowledges is good.

I could have wished that my biographer had taken a little more time, and a little more of the advice of his friends, in waiting to get acquainted with my history and myself, and have left it to some more skilful, though less benevolent hand, to write memoirs of my life. I have only to make a statement of a few facts and occurrences of general notoriety, and I think his efforts will require no comment nor praise.

I sailed from the city of Londonderry on the 3d day of October, 1808, destined for the city of Philadelphia; but being shipwrecked on the coast of the island of Ila on the night of the 9th of the same month, I was detained until the 3d day of August, 1809, on which day I sailed from the city of Greenock for New York. On the 27th of which month I and the whole ship's company had almost perished in the Atlantic; but through the watchful care and tender mercy of our Heavenly Father, we were brought to the harbor which we desired to see, and safely landed in New York on the 29th of September, 1809. On the 28th of the next month I arrived in Washington, Pennsylvania, to which place I have been known ever since. I arrived in this country with credentials in my pocket from that sect of Presbyterians known by the name of Seceders. These credentials certified that I had been both in Ireland in the presbytery of Market Hill, and in Scotland in the presbytery of Glasgow a member of the Secession church, in good standing. My faith in creeds and confessions of human device was considerably shaken while in Scotland, and I commenced my career in this country under the conviction that nothing that was not as old as the New Testament should be made an article of faith, a rule of practice, or a term of communion amongst christians. In a word, that the whole of the christian religion exhibited in prophecy and type in the Old Testament, was presented in the fullest, clearest, and most perfect manner in the New Testament, by the Spirit of wisdom and revelation.

This has been the pole-star of my course ever since, and I thank God that he has enabled me so far to prosecute it, and to make all my prejudices and ambition bow to this emancipating principle. I continued in the examination of the scriptures, ecclesiastical history, and systems of divinity, ancient and modern, until July 15th, 1810, on which day I publicly avowed my convictions of the independency of the church of Christ and the excellency and authority of the scriptures, in a discourse from the last section of what is commonly called "Christ's Sermon on the Mount." During this year I pronounced one hundred and six orations on sixty-one primary topics of the christian religion in the western part of Pennsylvania, Vir-

ginia, and the neighboring part of Ohio. On the 12th day of March, 1811, I took to myself a wife of the Presbyterian connexion, and on the 25th of the same month became a resident in Virginia. I became a citizen of Virginia as soon as the laws of the state permitted, and have continued such until this day. In conformity to the grand principle which I have called the pole-star of my course of religious inquiry, I was led to question the claims of infant sprinkling to divine authority, and was, after a long, serious, and prayerful examination of all means of information, led to solicit immersion on a profession of my faith; when as yet I scarce knew a Baptist from Washington to the Ohio, in the immediate region of my labors, and when I did not know that any friend or relation on earth would concur with me. I was accordingly baptized by Elder Matthias Luse, who was accompanied by Elder Henry Spears, on the 12th day of June, 1812. In the mean time I pursued the avocations of a husbandman as the means of my subsistence; and while I discharged, as far as in me lay, the duties of a bishop (having been regularly ordained one of the Elders of the church of Christ at Brush Run) and itinerated frequently through the circumjacent country, I did it without any earthly renumeration. I did not at first contemplate forming any connexion with the Regular Baptist Association called "the Redstone," as the perfect independency of the church and the pernicious tendency of human creeds and terms of communion were subjects to me of great concern. As a mere spectator, I did, however, visit the Redstone Association in the fall of 1812. After a more particular acquaintance with some of the members and ministers of that connexion, the church of Brush Run did finally agree to unite with that Association on the ground that no terms of union or communion other than the Holy Scriptures should be required. On this ground, after presenting a written declaration of our belief (always distinguishing betwixt making a declaration of our faith for the satisfaction of others, and binding that declaration on others as a term of communion) we united with the Redstone Association in the fall of 1813; in which connexion the church of Brush Run yet continues. In the close of 1814 and beginning of 1815 I made an extensive tour through a part of the eastern region, visiting the cities of New York, Philadelphia, Baltimore, and Washington, and did to my present shame, by milking both the sheep and the goats, obtain about 1000 dollars for the building of a meeting-house in Wellsburgh, a place then destitute of any house for religious meetings. In 1816 I delivered a discourse on the law before the Redstone Association, which being published by request, gave rise to some discussion, which resulted, we believe, in some benefit to the searchers after truth. January, 1818, I undertook the care of a classical and mercantile academy, known by the name of the "Buffaloe Seminary." I continued the principal of this seminary for five and a half years. In 1820, after being thrice solicited by the Baptists, I did consent to debate with Mr. Walker on the subject of baptism. Of this debate two editions have been published—one by myself, of one thousand copies, and one by Messrs. Eichbaum and Johnson, of three thousand. In 1823 I commenced editing the Christian Baptist, and in the fall of 1823 held a public debate with Mr. MacCalla, which grew out of the former with Mr. Walker. These outlines bring me up till the present year, and render a further detail unnecessary. I should have observed that a church was organized in the town of Wellsburgh in 1823, which was composed for the most part of members dismissed from the church at Brush Run, of which church I was appointed a bishop.

The reader will agree with me in the result that it was expedient for me to give the above abstract with circumstantial accuracy, and we can, not only solemnly testify the above statement to be correct and strictly true, but we are able to prove every item of it of any importance before any tribunal, civil or ecclesiastical. With this document before us, let us now attend to the first conjecture. It is founded on a falsehood. I never received any personal pique or experienced any disappointment from any Presbyterian sect, Seceder or other. I never asked one favor from any Paido-Baptist sect, and therefore never received any disappointment. Nay, so far from this, favors were offered and not accepted. Immediately after my arrival in this country the academy at Pittsburgh was offered me, and invitations to union with the Paido-Baptist sects presented to me. Every thing is just the reverse of Mr. Greatrake's conjecture. Time after time favors, ecclesiastical favors, were offered me, and no consideration under heaven, but conscience, forbade their acceptance. Indeed I am bound gratefully to remember the kind offers and offices of many Paido-Baptists; and a better return I cannot (as I think) make, than to admonish them of their errors.* But this gentleman, to destroy my influence and my power to do them good, would persuade them that I am an enemy because I tell them the truth, and would conjecture that I was avenging an affront or an injury which I never received. Insults and injuries I have received from some Baptists, but until my appearance on the stage in defence of the truths I had espoused in common with them, no insults or injuries are recollected ever to have been received from any body of Paido-Baptists. †   Editor.

Remarks on Confessions of Faith.

Mr. Greatrake in his letters, says—"Again, we know that you propagate the doctrine of the church's independency, so far as to exclude all reference to articles of faith, and principles of order upon which they have been founded, (I am now speaking of the Baptist church) this your writings are uniformly understood to aim at. And really, sir, your attempt to disseminate this sort of sentiment, in the Baptist church in particular, demonstrates your very great attainment in impudence, or that you are extremely ignorant of the constituents of social unity and order, as I shall hereafter endeavor to exhibit. Can you suppose that any reflecting, intelligent member of the Baptist church, will ever conceive favorably of that man, or have confidence in the purity of his motives, who attempts to destroy the very foundation upon which the denomination has risen to such imposing magnitude, in such fair proportions, and with such solidity? Indeed, sir, the attempt on your part, or that of any other person, bears testimony of a radical defect in understanding, and can only leave you, in the exercise of all possible charity, the character of the knight of La Mancha, or the phrenzied Swede."‡

* The first night that I spent in Washington county, Pa., I enjoyed the hospitalities of Doctor Samuel Ralston.

† The remainder of this address, relating to the unfounded charge of avarice, is useless to this work, as it would, were it inserted, prove uninteresting to the reader. All personalities as far as possible, are excluded from this edition.   Publisher.

‡ We never descend to reply to such composition. We think the mere citation of it a sufficient act of humiliation, and a sufficient refutation of it, in the estimation of all sober christians.

I had thought that the Baptist denomination gloried not in the Westminster creed, but in the New Testament. I think Mr. Benedict in his history of the Baptists, more than once represents this as a fact, that the bible without comment, is the creed and confession of the Baptists. I know that he declares of the first Baptists in the United States, (vol. 1. p. 487.) in giving the history of the oldest church in the union, that, "from first to last, the bible without comment has been their confession of faith." And I am very sure that it is only in so far as they have adopted and acted on this principle that their progress is estimated in heaven. If they should, on any other principle, proselyte the whole world, they might become famous and respectable on earth, but all in heaven would frown upon them. And there is one fact which all my Baptist friends in this country know, that when the church to which I belonged associated with them, we protested against all creeds of human composition as terms of communion; at the same time declaring what we believed to be christian truth, in opposition to reigning errors. And although some seem to think there is no difference between a verbal or written declaration of faith and recognizing a human creed as a term of communion, we see a very great difference, so much at least as to forbid an effort on our part to make our own declaration of faith a term of communion to others. The New Testament, as respects christian faith and practice, is our only creed, form of discipline, and the avowal of the One Foundation, our only bond of union. I object to all human creeds as terms of communion from the following considerations:—

1. They are predicated upon a gross insult to the wisdom and benevolence of the Founder of christianity. They, in effect, say, that "the form of sound words," which he has communicated in writing, is not so well adapted to the exigencies of christians as some other form into which human wisdom and benevolence can place them. For if the New Testament is not so sufficient and suitable as a creed of human contrivance or arrangement, this creed exhibits greater wisdom and benevolence than the New Testament.

2. All creeds as terms of communion, being designed to exclude the evil and receive the good, are the most foolish of all expedients which human folly has adopted. For who that will see, does not see, that good men, that is men of christian integrity, will never subscribe or swear to believe that which they do not believe, for the sake of a name, a place, or an office in any church; whereas evil men who want a name, or a place, or an office in any church, will subscribe whether they believe or not.

3. They are the sources of division. They make an assent to philosophical views of revelation a bond of union, and consequently every new discovery, or dissent from an ancient one, occasions a new heresy and a new sect. Exclude him; for "how can two walk together unless they are agreed?" says the orthodox.

4. They are, in one word, every way wicked—inasmuch as they have always led to persecution, and have produced enmity, variance, and strife as their legitimate results. For these and a hundred other reasons, which time may specify and illustrate, I will never subscribe, nor swear to any other confession of my christian faith, than the New Testament.   Editor.

No. 3.]   October 4, 1824.

Address to the Public.

" There is one spirit in all the clergy, whether they be Romanist or Protestant, Baptist or Paido Baptist, learned or unlearned, their own workmanship, or the workmanship of others."

Sentimental Journal.

Amongst the Baptists it is to be hoped there are but few clergy; and would to God there were none! The grand and distinguishing views of the Baptists must be grossly perverted before they could tolerate one such creature. The Baptist views of a congregation of saints, if I understand them correctly, are such as the following:—

1. A congregation or church of Jesus Christ is an assembly of intelligent individuals, who, "by the washing of regeneration, and renewal of the Holy Spirit," voluntarily associate to walk in all the commandments and ordinances of the Lord Jesus Christ, declaring allegiance to the King Eternal, Immortal, and Invisible; and renouncing every other authority in heaven, on the earth, or under the earth.

2. Such a society having pledged themselves to one another, by the profession of the faith, and by the baptism ordained by Jesus Christ, have all power, liberty, and right to administer all the ordinances of Christ; and to do every act and thing that appertains to the order, discipline, and worship of the christian church; to choose out from among themselves bishops and deacons, that is, overseers and servants, to ordain or appoint such; and then to submit themselves, as to them that watch for their souls, and must give account, and all this without the interference of any ecclesiastical authority on earth.

A pretty good illustration of this principle, we find in the first Baptist church in the United States, A. D. 1636, a little over a hundred years after the reformation. Twelve persons, among whom was the famous Roger Williams, the first settler and founder of Rhode Island, desirous of forming a church, and first of being immersed in the primitive style—did meet together to deliberate on these topics. How to obtain a suitable administrator, was a point of some difficulty. " At length," as Benedict said, when they understood the scriptures, the " candidates for communion nominated and appointed Mr. Ezekiel Holliman, a man of gifts and piety, to baptize Mr. Williams; and who, in return, baptized Mr. Holliman and the other ten." Although the circumstances of the case compelled this measure, yet if it were not essentially right, that is, scriptural, it never could be justified; and I think that man is very inadequate to teach the Christian religion, who is not able to justify this procedure upon the grand principles of revelation and of reason. This first church in the union also appointed its own bishops and deacons according to the primitive style.*

Every person possessed in a good degree of the qualifications laid down by the apostle Paul as essential to the christian bishop, and who, after having been first well proved by a congregation of disciples, is ordained or appointed by the congregation to the overseer's office, in which he is to exercise the functions of a bishop, every such person, I say, is to be esteemed and valued as a bishop, and by no means to be ranked among the clergy. But some few Baptists, tickled by the love of novelty, and lured by the false majesty of Presbyterianism, exhibited in a classical priesthood, of ordinaries, co-ordinates,

* See Benedict's History, vol. 1, p. 475.

subordinates, priests and Levites; ruling elders, licentiates, reverends and doctors of divinity, have compromised the distinguishing features of their own grand peculiarities, and palmed upon themselves a species of demagogues, who, while they have all the airs, hauteur, and arrogance of some Paido-Baptist priests, have neither their erudition, nor their talents, nor their policy. They can neither wear the gown decently, nor conceal the cloven foot.

To do this in such a way as not to give umbrage to the pious members of this community, it is necessary to mock the ancient principles of this once humble and unassuming people. And so it comes to pass that a number of pious young men, of poor circumstances, but of virtuous habits, are taken out of the churches, to be made bishops of other churches, and after taught to conjugate *amo* and *tupto*, are sent to a theological school, now called a school of the prophets, and being drilled in the art and mystery of making a sermon, set out to find a church which wants a young foppish gentleman, who says to the old bishops, "Stand by—I have seen, and sure I ought to know." But how will he get into the church so as to be chosen from among the brethren is the point! The teachers of the schools of the prophets have settled this point. He gives in his letter, becomes a member a week or two, and is then chosen from among themselves: and so the Baptist principles are compromised. Thus a young gentleman filled with vast ideas of his own little though noble self, mounts the rostrum, and is called elder, though the word is a lie when applied to him, and obliges all the old and experienced saints to be silent, who are a thousand times better qualified than he to be overseer. Thus I have known a young Baptist priest made and finished in Philadelphia, go to the state of New York, preach a few times to a rich congregation, give in his letter, and in two or three weeks be called out from among the brethren to become their bishop; and that too, before he has got a wife, or a house, or a family to rule well. Such teachers I must rank among the clergy, and, indeed, they soon prove themselves to have a full portion, and sometimes a double portion, of the spirit of the priesthood. I hope, however, the number of such amongst the Baptists is small. Perhaps the whole aggregate number is not greater than the aggregate of good well meaning men among the Paido-Baptist clergy. They are not all Israel, which are of Israel, is proverbially true, of Baptists, and Paido-Baptists; though in different acceptations of the word Israel.

There is one vast difference, one essential and all-important difference betwixt the Baptists and Paido-Baptist views and societies. The Baptist views of the church of Jesus Christ are constitutionally correct; the Paido-Baptist views are unconstitutional. To make myself more intelligible—there are to be found in the Baptist system such views of the christian church, as, if carried out to their legitimate issue, will place them on apostolic grounds; but the Paido-Baptists would, if carried out, place them in the bosom of the Roman pontiff. Yes, the one system would place the church upon the foundation of the apostles and prophets, Jesus Christ himself the chief corner-stone. The other system would place it upon St. Peter as the rock. The Baptist system is capable of being reformed or brought back again to the constitution of the kingdom of heaven; the Paido-Baptist cannot. It must be destroyed. The one system carries in its bosom the means of its purification, the other, the fire

16

that must consume it. The foundation of the former needs but to have the rubbish cleared away; the foundation of the latter must be totally razed. The constitution of the one is essentially of Divine construction; the constitution of the other is altogether human. The good confession of the King of Martyrs before Pontius Pilate, is received by the Baptist and rejected by the Paido-Baptist system.

Essays on the Work of the Holy Spirit, in the Salvation of Men.
No. III.
Spiritual Gifts.

DAVID the king and prophet foretold that when Messiah the Lord would ascend to his throne, he would bestow gifts upon men. This passage of *Psalms*, lviii. 18. Paul (*Eph.* iv. 8.) applies to our Lord. When he ascended he says, "he gave," and by spiritual gifts qualified "some apostles, and some prophets, and some evangelists, and some pastors and teachers." Peter also, on the day of Pentecost, ascribed all the stupendous gifts vouchsafed on that day to the Lord Jesus. "Therefore," says he, (*Acts* ii. 33.) "being exalted by the right hand of God, and having received the promise of the Holy Spirit from the Father, He hath poured out that which you now see and hear." These "distributions of the Holy Spirit," as Macknight renders *Heb.* ii. 4. issued in the perfect qualification of apostles with "the word of wisdom;" prophets with the "word of knowledge;" evangelists with "tongues and miracles;" pastors with an immediate possession of all the requisites to feeding the flock, and teachers with the means necessary to instructing the novices in all the christian doctrine. It may be necessary to remark, that the pastors and teachers mentioned in this passage are to be distinguished from the ordinary bishops or elders of a christian church, inasmuch as the elders or bishops are to be qualified by ordinary means and to be selected by their brethren for the possession of those ordinary attainments mentioned by Paul in his epistles; whereas those pastors and teachers given on the ascension of the Lord, were as instantaneously prepared for their offices as Paul was made an apostle; they were not only converted to the christian faith, but, in an instant, by the gifts of the Holy Spirit, qualified to teach the whole religion. That this is no conjecture, but matter of fact, will appear from *Eph.* iv. 8—13. Three things are distinctly stated in this context to which we refer the reader, and these three must be distinctly noticed to understand the passage. The first is, that these apostles, prophets, evangelists, pastors and teachers, were gifts bestowed by Jesus the Lord on his receiving the throne of the universe. The second is, that they were given for an immediate exigency, or for a purpose which the infant state of the church required, that is, says the apostle Paul, (v. 12.) "for the sake of fitting the saints for the work of the ministry, in order to the building of the body of Christ"—(Macknight)—for fitting the converted Jews and gentiles for the ordinary work of the ministry or service requisite to the building of the church. The third is, that these supernaturally endowed apostles, prophets, evangelists, pastors and teachers, were to continue only for a limited time, marked by an adverb in Greek and English, which always denotes the time how long—*mechri*, "*until* we all come to the unity of the faith and of the knowledge of the Son of God, to a perfect man, even to the measure of the stature of the fulness of Christ, that we, the church, be not always composed of *nepioi*, babes."—Dr. Macknight in the following words: "These supernaturally endowed teachers are to continue in the church until, being fully instructed by their discourses and writings, we all who compose the church, come through one faith and knowledge of the son of God, to perfect manhood as a church, even to the measure of the stature which when full grown it ought to have: so that the church thus instructed and enlarged, is able to direct and defend itself without supernatural aid."

These three things being noticed, it is evident that these apostles, prophets, evangelists, pastors and teachers, were all supernatural characters, for a precise object, and for a limited time; that this object was answered by their discourses and writings, and, that this limited time has expired. For the benefit of those of weak understanding it may be observed, that although apostles were appointed before Pentecost, even from the commencement of the Lord's ministry, yet they were not qualified fully for this peculiar work, until endowed with those supernatural gifts bestowed on Messiah's sitting down on the throne of his Father, after his ascension into heaven; and consequently, it might be said, most justly, that on his ascension, "he gave apostles," as well as "prophets, evangelists, pastors and teachers." It may also be noticed for the benefit of the same class of readers, that while the word of wisdom was given to one—the word of knowledge to another—faith to work miracles to a third; to another the gifts of healing; to another the inworkings of powers, that is ability to produce or work in others the ability of working miracles; to another prophecy; to another discerning of spirits; to another diverse kinds of foreign tongues; to another the interpretation of foreign tongues by one and the same spirit; yet some individuals possessed more than one of those gifts, and the apostles many, if not all of them; and one in particular, which distinguished them from, and elevated them above all others, viz. the ability of conferring some particular gift by the imposition of their hands.

These gifts differed both in their nature and dignity, and some envied those possessed of the more splendid gifts, which gave rise to the apostle Paul's illustration of these gifts, in the 12th, 13th, and 14th chapters of his first epistle to the Corinthians, where he shows that although there was a great diversity of gifts, yet the matter of those gifts, if I may so speak, was the same; for they were all distributions of the same Spirit; their object was the same, for they were ministries of the same Lord; and their origin or authority was the same, for the same God inworked them in all the spiritual men. And while some were eminent for the word of wisdom, which appears to have been the doctrine of the gospel communicated by inspiration; others for the word of knowledge, or an inspired knowledge of the types and prophecies in the ancient revelations; others for faith which, as a spiritual gift, "led the spiritual men, without hesitation, to attempt the working of miracles;"* others for the gifts of healing, &c. &c.

* This faith, which the apostle calls a spiritual gift, he contradistinguishes from the common faith of christians in this discourse. " A faith that removes mountains" he shews to be different from the faith of christians, in this grand respect, that the spiritual gift called faith was to pass away—was but for a time; but the faith that saves the soul was to abide always. The scope and spirit of his argument in the 13th chapter of this epistle, taken into view with the context, is, " You Corinthians are coveting the best gifts, but come, now, and I will show you a bet

it was to be remembered that these distributions or these manifestations of the Spirit were given to every member of the church of Corinth; or a manifestation of the Spirit was given to every spiritual man to profit withal, not for his own honor or benefit, but for the good of the brotherhood; which the apostle in the subsequent context compares to a human body composed of many members—no member created for itself, or for its own benefit, but for the service of the whole.

To shew more fully the nature and use of those gifts, it may be necessary to take a view of the church of Corinth, of which church the apostle says, "It came behind in no gift." "You," says he, speaking to the Corinthians, "are enriched with every gift by him, even with all speech and knowledge." "When the testimony of Christ was confirmed among you by the miracles which I wrought and the spiritual gifts I conferred on you, so that you come behind in no gift." In the history of this church, then, we may expect to learn the nature and use of those gifts, to as much advantage as from the history of any other.

Corinth at this time was the metropolis of the province of Achaia, and was as famous as Athens itself for the Grecian arts and sciences. Cicero calls it "*totius Græciæ lumen*," the light of all Greece; and Florus calls it "*Græciæ decus*," the ornament of Greece. Refined and intelligent as Corinth was by Grecian sciences and arts, it was, through its luxuries and wealth, the most dissolute, lascivious, and debauched city in its day. Here Paul preached and taught for eighteen months the doctrine of Christ, and converted a very numerous church, composed of some distinguished Jews, but chiefly of the idolatrous and profligate Pagans. Luke tells us, "Many of the Corinthians, hearing, believed and were baptized." From the history of this church, gathered from the Acts of the Apostles and these epistles, it appears that there was a schism in it, envying, strife, and many irregularities; so that the presence of those gifts did not place the church out of the reach of those human corruptions, but were necessary to the illumination and confirmation of the disciples

in the faith which purified the heart by its intrinsic influences. Indeed, we find that even the spiritual men themselves needed the word of exhortation and admonition for their imprudence in the management of those gifts; which at once teaches us that those gifts had no general influence, and were not necessarily productive of the appropriate effects of the saving and sanctifying truth in the minds of the subjects of them. No wonder, then, that the apostle Paul commended the cultivation of brotherly love as a "more excellent way" than the coveting of the most splendid gifts. It is evident from the face of the first epistle, that even among the spiritual men there were blemishes and imprudences that required the castigation of the apostle. The apostle, indeed, settles the contest about the precedency of those gifts, and places them in due subordination to one another. A free and full translation of the 28th verse represents the matter thus: "The chief members of the church are thus to be ranked as God has distinguished them by gifts. First, apostles, who being endowed with the word of wisdom, from them all must receive the knowledge of the gospel. Secondly, the superior prophets, who, possessing the word of knowledge, are qualified to interpret the ancient revelations. Thirdly, teachers, embracing all who boldly declare the doctrine of Christ, illustrate it, and confirm it by miracles. Next, those who communicate to others the spiritual powers. Then, those who possess the gifts of healing diseases. Helpers, who, speaking by inspiration to the edification of the church, are fitted to assist the superior teachers, and to help the faith and joy of others. Directors, who, by the gift of discerning spirits, are fitted to direct the church. Lastly, persons who, having the gift of speaking different kinds of foreign languages, can preach to every nation in its own language." But yet the church can never be composed of all such, no more than the body can be all eye or all ear; for, says the apostle, "Are all apostles? Are all prophets?" No, indeed. The nature of those gifts, however splendid, was evidently only adapted, and their use merely designed, to illustrate and confirm that doctrine, which in its primary and essential results, when received and understood, purges, purifies, elevates, and ennobles the mind of the recipient. Hence the Holy One prayed, "Sanctify them through your truth."

Again, when the Lord spake of the Holy Spirit, (which was to proceed from his Father and himself, when he should be glorified,) he assured his disciples that this Monitor would testify of him, and would not only conduct them into all truth, but when he is come, "he will convince the world concerning sin, and concerning righteousness, and concerning judgment: concerning sin, because they believe not on me; concerning righteousness, because I go to the Father, and you see me no longer; concerning judgment, because the Prince of this World is judged. He will glorify me."* The signs and wonders, and distributions of this Holy Spirit, the apostle Paul declared were the confirmations by which Jesus was glorified in the world, and the testimony of the witnesses rendered credible and omnipotent. So, on Pentecost, the unbelieving Jews were convinced of their sin in not believing that Jesus was Lord Messiah, by the Holy Spirit confirming their word by signs following or accompanying. They were con-

---

ter way;" for, says he, all these gifts shall cease, tongues, &c. shall vanish away. And when all these gifts shall have ceased, faith, hope, and love, these three abide co-existent with the present world; but the greatest of these three graces is love, which will continue forever, not only co-existent with the present state, but when this state shall be consummated. Now the better way is to cultivate love, than to be coveting spiritual gifts, though of the most splendid rank. To see that this faith, hope, and love, and even love which is the greatest and best of all, is emphatically contradistinguished from spiritual gifts, we have only to read the close of the 13th and the commencement of the 14th chapter. It reads thus: And now abides faith, hope, love, these three, but the greatest of these is love. Follow after love, therefore, and desire spiritual gifts, but of these the chief is prophecy. The faith that was always to abide is not once classed amongst spiritual gifts. The only passage in our translation that might, by common readers, be so understood, is *Eph.* ii. 8. "For by grace are you saved through faith; and that not of yourselves: it is the gift of God." Leaving system out of view and following the scriptures, we find the sentiment to be as Macknight has rendered it. "For by grace you are saved through faith, and this affair is not of yourselves; it is the gift of God"—not *charisma*, a spiritual gift, but *doron*, a favor or common bounty. Indeed, the antecedent to that, every linguist knows is not faith; for *pistis*, faith, is feminine, and *touto*, that, is neuter. Let not, however, any systematic conscience be alarmed at this translation of the celebrated Calvinist. It is unanswerably correct. Nor does it at all interfere with the idea of salvation being of grace, of free grace; for if salvation, as a whole, is through the grace of God, faith, a part of that salvation, is of grace also; but here we are speaking of spiritual gifts, amongst which this faith is not one.

* Campbell's translation of *John* xvi 8—14.

18

vinced of his righteousness, or of his being the righteous Messenger of Jehovah, by the proofs the Spirit gave of his having been well received in heaven by his Father; and they were convinced of judgment, because it was evident from the testimony of the apostles, confirmed by those splendid signs of the Holy Spirit, that, by his cross, Jesus had triumphed over principalities and powers, and had vanquished him that had the power of death. Thus the Saviour promised and thus it was performed, and thus the world, infidel Jews and infidel Gentiles, were convinced of sin, of righteousness, and of judgment. The apostle Paul also declares in that same epistle, chapter xiv. that "foreign languages are for a sign, not to believers, but to unbelievers." Now the sign by which the Holy Spirit glorified Jesus on the day of Pentecost, was that of foreign tongues; diverse, or separated tongues of fire, appeared on the heads of the witnesses, and they spake in foreign tongues as the Spirit gave them utterance. This, then, was such a sign to the unbelieving Jews as to convince three thousand of them of sin, of righteousness, and of judgment; and hence they gladly received the word that announced to them the remission of their sins and the promise of the Holy Spirit. Thus the word came in "demonstration of the Spirit and with power," and their faith rested not on the wisdom of human reason, but on the power of God, thus exhibited with the word.

In our next essay this same topic will be further illustrated. As we promised to investigate this important subject with some degree of attention, we must request the patience of our readers to be put into requisition; and we must also remind them, that our object is to present just, what the scriptures teach on this subject, not attempting to support any system of divinity, however canonized or extolled. But in these things every disciple of Christ will suffer no man to judge for him while he is able to read the revelation of God in his own tongue—at least such ought to be his determination.

EDITOR.

To the Editor of the Christian Baptist.

DEAR SIR—As you are decidedly opposed to all intrigue, corruption, and tyranny of those courts called ecclesiastical, in whatever denomination they exist, I have concluded to make a statement to you for the benefit of the whole religious community at large, and of the Baptist community in particular, of some recent occurrences in an association with which you are well acquainted. You not being present at that association, but as I understood the church of Wellsburgh being now a member of the Mahoning Association, Ohio, it was supposed you had been there; and therefore I suppose that you will be yourself, as much as others, much interested in hearing of this matter.

You need not be informed that there have been, for seven years, two or three choice spirits of the old hierarchal system in that association, who have been, for some time, in the spirit of Diotrephes, seeking for the pre-eminence. Baffled in every attempt for a long time, their zeal, like a concealed fire, only waited for a fair opportunity of bursting forth with destructive fury. By a concurrence of fortuitous incidents, as we sometimes say, they conceived a favorable opportunity had occurred, which gave them some hopes of realizing their darling project. There were a few churches, and one in particular, whose messengers some way or other stood

in the way of their gaining the ascendant. How to get these out of the way was the difficult point. And how these gentlemen could acquire the eminence which they courted, without getting them out of the way, was a point still more difficult. There was one scheme, which, of all others, seemed to favor their project. It was known that some of the churches, in their annual letters, simply appealed to the scriptures, and gave from them a statement of their faith; and that some clause or article in the archives of the constitution of this association required an acknowledgment of the Philadelphia Confession of Faith. The junto, before the meeting of the association, began to intrigue in this way: they, as far as possible, obtained an appointment of such messengers as would favor their project, and I can assure you that I know of one church whose appointment of messengers was set aside by the parson, a member of the junto, and two of them removed because they were supposed to be men of an independent mind.

As soon as the association met, all the letters that did not appeal to the aforesaid Confession, were ordered by the head of the party, to be "marked for further investigation." When the letters were all read, it appeared that but nine had appealed, and thirteen had not. After the reading of the letters a committee was appointed to arrange the business, and chiefly of the leading members of the junto. They agreed that the nine churches only should be the association, and therefore made out a list of the messengers of the nine churches—and at once proscribed the thirteen. But, on a number of the messengers from the proscribed churches declaring that they would leave the house instantly if not permitted to take their seat, it was agreed to give them a seat while they investigated their claims. Then came on the investigation of their claims.

Various reasons were assigned for not appealing to the Confession by the messengers, as severally interrogated by the court. Some of the churches had not seen the little book called the "Confession of Faith," and knew nothing about it but from report. This was a fact true of the most of them, and not all the members of any one church in the association had ever read it. Some of those who had seen the little book, did not understand it, but said that as far as they understood it, they made no objections to it. Some alleged that there was so great a diversity of opinion about the lawfulness, propriety, and utility of such confessions, that they could not decide the point. Others affirmed that the scriptures were sufficient, and that stating their faith in them in direct terms, which they understood, appeared more consistent and satisfactory, than a mere appeal to any creed made ready to their hand. Two only of the churches, in their letters, utterly refused to adopt it as an expression of their faith; not, however, as opposing its doctrines, but on principles of pure scriptural independency. These things were all known to the junto, as well before as after the investigation; and therefore the long investigation of these letters was but a mere covering for their plot. One of the two churches was the one for which the whole plot was laid, and nothing now remained but to reject the one and to retain the other by an arbitrary usurpation of power. Several things were alleged in order to make a difference to cover the design, but nothing could be proved, or even investigated. The measure was carried amidst the frowns and marked contempt of every umpire in the assembly. Thus churches have been distracted into schisms, and an association, in fact, rent in twain by the unhallowed ambition and manifest envy of three or four leaders, at the expense of their own disgrace and public reprobation. Other acts of injustice and wanton tyranny were perpetrated by these individuals, under the pretence of being an ecclesiastical court, which I will not at present trouble you with. I am resolved, however, with your permission, to exhibit, if the case may require, some of the most flagrant violations of right which the ecclesiastical history of this century affords. In the meantime, I cannot conclude this communication without declaring the striking resemblance which appeared to me between this would-be ecclesiastical court and an ecclesiastical court of courtiers, that procured the signature of a Median prince to their decrees. This council sat two thousand three hundred and sixty-one years ago. Daniel, a prophet of the God of heaven, had been elevated to very high honors by the king, and was extolled above all the nobles of the land. "Then the presidents and princes sought to find occasion against Daniel concerning the kingdom or church; but they could find no occasion nor fault, forasmuch as he was faithful; neither was there any error or fault found in him." So far the cases are exactly similar. "Then said these men, We shall not find any occasion against this Daniel, except we find it against him concerning the law of his God." So far the coincidence is striking. "Then these presidents and princes assembled together," that is, the ministers and messengers associated; "and they said, O king! live forever!" So said these—O constitution! live forever! Again, "all the presidents of the kingdom and counsellors have consulted together to establish and make a firm decree, that whosoever shall ask a petition of any God or man, for thirty days, save of you, O king, he shall be cast into the den of lions." The resemblance is still apparent by substituting the words "whosoever shall acknowledge the bible as the confession of their faith, or any other confession of faith, save the Philadelphia one, shall be cast into purgatory." These pious divines well knew they had got Daniel now, provided they could establish the decree. Daniel, as soon as the decree was established, invoked the God of heaven as before. The consequence was, might gave right, and into the den of lions he was cast. The only essential difference between these two courts is, that the former was the most impartial and consistent of the two, because it cast all who departed from the decree into the den of lions; but in the latter, of thirteen which did not comply with the decree, but one suffered the vengeance of the law.

These late events have contributed more to demonstrate the correctness of the principles delineated in your paper, than any thing I have witnessed; for, to use an ancient proverb, "If these things be done in a green tree, what shall be done in a dry?" If, amongst a people who advocate the independency of the church of Christ, and who, in their meetings, say they are no more than an advisory council, such flagrant assumptions of power and violations of right can take place, what may not be expected from those who declare that all the congregations in the land are under the control of inferior and superior church judicatures? I know that such occurrences are extremely rare in our connexion; but although I am a Baptist, and the son of a Baptist, I would not conceal these flagrant abuses of principle amongst Baptists more than had

they happened amongst Paido-Baptists. I send you a number of new subscribers which grew out of the late scenes of ecclesiastical despotism. I have only to add, that I was an impartial contemplater of these occurrences, and neither a minister nor a messenger at this meeting, and that I can vouch for the truth of all that I have stated. Your friend,   Titus.

To the Editor of the Christian Baptist.

Sir—In the numbers of this work already published, we meet with several essays upon the christian religion, all justly tending to enhance its value by pointing out its consummate excellence, and peculiar adaptation to ameliorate, as far as possible in this life, the wretched condition of a guilty, ruined, perishing world; not only, by bringing into view the consoling prospect of a blissful and glorious issue to all our toils and sorrows, by a revelation of good things to come; but, more immediately, by inspiring us with principles, and leading to practices which have a direct tendency to strengthen our minds against the pressure of worldly calamities and guilty fears; filling our hearts with joy and gladness in the apprehended favor and fellowship of God through the Spirit, by the mediation of Jesus Christ. See *Hebs.* xii. 22—24. I could wish, however, to see those things more distinctly developed, not only by pointing out, as above, the high and distinguishing peculiarities of the christian religion; and by an upright endeavor, to extricate and defend it from the innumerable perversions and abuses, with which it is, and has been corrupted and subverted; as you evidently have been in the habit of doing from the commencement of this work; and which, indeed, appears to be the very design of it; but also by pointing out, and defending as clearly as possible, the religion of christianity, (pardon the expression;) for in this, if I mistake not, the christian religion has suffered most. For what does the Spirit predict, as the combined issue of the evil and perilous times that should come in those last days of the Gospel Dispensation, when the great body of professors should be such as are described in 2d *Tim.*, 3d and 4th chapters—"lovers of pleasure, more than lovers of God,—after their own lusts heaping up to themselves teachers, having itching ears,—turning away their ears from the truth, and being turned to fables,—not" so much as "enduring sound doctrine,—having a form of godliness, but denying the power thereof." Mark this—these professors of the christian religion would have a mere form of godliness, instead of the religion —the pure, blissful, and substantial religion of christianity. If you think, sir, the following essay any way conducive to answer the above purposes, and you approve of the sentiments it contains, as I believe you do, please give it an insertion in your useful paper.

I remain, sir, yours, very respectfully,
T. W.

Essay on the Religion of Christianity.

While many writers and teachers, some of them too of high repute in the christian world, so called, compliment christianity, I mean the New Testament exhibition of it, upon the super-excellency of its moral dictates, who, at the same time are ignorant of, and even averse to, the religion it inculcates; and whilst others profess to embrace it as a system of religion, without imbibing the spirit, realizing the truth, and experiencing the power of its religious institutions; but merely superstruct to themselves, rest in, and are satisfied with, a form of godliness; and that, very often, a deficient, imperfect form, or such as their own imagination has devised; let us, with an open bible before us, distinguish and contemplate that religion which it enjoins and exhibits—I mean the religion of christianity, for it also exhibits the religion of Judaism; but with this, in the mean time, we christians have nothing directly to do—we derive our religion immediately from the New Testament.

The author and ultimate object of our holy religion, is the God and Father of our Lord Jesus Christ, by his Spirit, speaking in Christ and his holy apostles. The principle of this holy religion within us, is faith, a correspondent faith; that is, a belief, or inwrought persuasion by, and according to, the word of truth, in all points corresponding to the revelation which God has made of himself through Jesus Christ by the Spirit. Hence, being rooted and grounded in the truth of this revelation, by faith in the divine testimony, we contemplate and worship God inwardly; that is, adore and reverence him in our souls, according to the characters and attributes under which he has revealed himself to us. Thus we worship the Father, through the Son, by the Spirit, relying upon his teachings in and by the word, to lead us into all the truth which he has testified for our edification and salvation; and also upon his internal influence to excite, instruct, and comfort us, by the truth; to help our infirmities, and to enable us to think and pray as we ought, both as to the matter and manner of our prayers. See *Rom.* viii. 26, and *Jude* 22, 21, with a multitude of other scriptures. Thus we have the internal religion, the habitual worship of the real believer, the sincere bible-taught christian with its principle; which is the faith above described. See *Rom.* x. 12—15.

Now this internal religion, externally manifested by certain acts and exercises of divine appointment, is what is commonly called worship, and rightly too. See the whole bible upon this word. The first instituted act of christian worship is baptism into the name of the Father, and of the Son, and of the Holy Spirit. Why is it translated "*in* the name," &c. contrary to the literal and almost universal translation of the particle *eis?* In the name of any dignified character, universally imports, by the authority of such a person. Whereas this is not the proper and obvious meaning of the baptismal institution. For although it is done by virtue of the divine authority enjoining it, that is, by the authority of Christ; yet its proper and primary import is not a mere exhibition of authority on the part of the institutor, and of submission on the part of the baptized, though this is certainly implied in every act of worship; but it is of a much more consolatory and blissful import, being an expression of faith and obedience on the part of the baptized; nay, the very first instituted act of the obedience of faith, in and by which the believing worshipper is openly declared to be of the household of faith and of the family of God, being baptized into "the name of the Father," of whom the whole redeemed family in heaven and earth is named; and into the name of the Redeemer, the Son, and heir of all things, who makes his people free; and into the name of the Holy Spirit, the sanctifier, the comforter, and perfecter of the saints; that by virtue of his indwelling and sanctifying presence, he, the baptized believer, may be separated to God, with all the redeemed, for a habitation of God, through the Spirit. Thus a new and

blissful relation to the Father, and to the Son, and to the Holy Spirit, is publicly recognized towards the believer, by an ordinance divinely and graciously instituted for this purpose. Being thus openly and explicitly declared to be of the family of God, through Jesus Christ, by the Spirit, he is declared free—justified from the guilt, and washed from the pollution of sin, by this washing of regeneration and renewing of the Holy Ghost, which is the privilege of all those that believe and thus obey the gospel, by a worshipful and obediential compliance with this divine appointment. His faith corresponding with every item of the divine testimony, thus exhibited, he joyfully recognizes his new, justified, sanctified, and filial relation to God; and realizing this, is filled with peace and joy in believing; and so goes on his way rejoicing, as well he may. See *Acts* viii. 39. So much for the first divinely instituted act of the worshipful obedience of faith.

The next in the immediate order of connexion is prayer. See *Acts* xxii. 16, with *Luke* iii. 21. With what a beautiful and holy consistency is the religion of christianity ordained and exhibited! First, "Be baptized and wash away your sins," then "Call upon the name of the Lord." The heart first sprinkled from an evil conscience by faith in the blood of atonement; and next, the body washed with pure water, declarative of the universal sanctification of the whole man, body, soul and spirit. Then, and not till then, can the believing subject draw near with a true heart, in full assurance of faith, and worship the Lord in the beauty of holiness, first having believed and obeyed the gospel. For "it is not by works of righteousness that we have done, but according to his mercy he saved us, by the washing of regeneration, and renewing of the Holy Ghost, which he shed on us abundantly through Jesus Christ our Saviour; that, being justified by his grace, we should be made heirs according to the hope of eternal life." *Tit.* iii. 5—7. Now, and not till now, can the believing sinner, first sprinkled at the altar, and then washed in the laver, enter into the holy place without fear, as a qualified and acceptable worshipper. For as it was in the typical, so it behoved to be in the antitypical worship; the laver still keeps its appointed place; still stands between the altar and the tabernacle. Having therefore, brethren, boldness to enter into the holiest of all, by the blood of Jesus, by a new and living way, which he has consecrated for us through the vail, that is to say, his flesh; and a high priest over the house of God; having our hearts sprinkled from an evil conscience, and our bodies washed with pure water, let us draw near with a true heart, in full assurance of faith. Compare *Exod.* xl. 30, with the above quotation from *Heb.* x. 19—22. The christian's faith, duly realizing those things, and observing the appointed way, he can draw near with confidence to his Heavenly Father, under the gracious and powerful protection of his Great High Priest, who ever lives to make intercession for him. Let him now pray with all manner of prayer and supplication, and intercessions for all saints, and for all ranks and degrees of men; let him also abound in praise and thanksgivings; offering up the sacrifice of praise to God by Jesus Christ continually; for this is he graciously instructed and authorized to do in his religious directory, with the goodly assurance that he is heard and accepted in all his addresses, according to the word of God; and that even when through ignorance he asks amiss, the Lord will graciously pardon. Hence praise and prayer become the christian's delightful exercise, because he realizes the greatness of the privilege; not only of being thus permitted to address the glorious fountain of being and blessedness without servile fear, in confidence of being always graciously heard and accepted; but more especially because it gives vent to the grateful and dutiful feelings of his heart, both toward God and man, and always increases them; and thus constantly furnishes him with the happy opportunity of growing in every grace, of subduing every vice, and of promoting and strengthening every virtue; also, of alleviating every woe, of mitigating every affliction. In a word, of bringing down upon himself all the blessings of Heaven that can be enjoyed upon earth—as well as of doing much good, both spiritual and temporal to others. Where is the genuine bible-taught christian, then, that does not delight to abound in the exercise of praise and prayer—to embrace and improve every favorable opportunity for those goodly purposes.

But that this may be the case, the next immediate ordinance of the christian religion, namely, the reading, I mean the musing upon, or studying the Holy Scriptures; taking them up in their connexion, and meditating upon the subjects they propose to our consideration, with a fixed contemplation of the various and important objects which they present. This dutiful and religious use of the bible, (that most precious, sacred record of the wonderful works of God, the only authentic source of all religious information,) is inseparably connected with, and indispensably necessary to, the blissful and all-important exercises of prayer and praise. Without this, those exercises must dwindle away to a trite form—must degenerate into a lifeless formality. It is from this dutiful and religious use of the divine word, that we derive the proper materials for those holy exercises. Hence says the Apostle, " let the word of Christ dwell in you richly; in all wisdom teaching and admonishing one another in psalms, and hymns, and spiritual songs, singing with grace in your hearts to the Lord. And whatsoever you do (of a religious nature) in word or deed, do all in the name of the Lord Jesus, giving thanks to God and the Father by him." *Col.* iii. 16, 17. And again, " Be you filled with the Spirit; speaking to yourselves, in psalms, and hymns, and spiritual songs, singing and making melody in your heart to the Lord; giving thanks always to God and the Father, in the name of our Lord Jesus Christ." *Eph.* v. 18—20. Hence it is evident, that if we would be spiritually minded, spiritually exercised in this delightful and heavenly employment, we must be filled with the Spirit; and if we would be filled with the Spirit, we must be filled with the word; the word of Christ must dwell in us richly; for we have no access to the Spirit but in and by the word. Therefore, "he that has ears to hear, let him hear what the Spirit says to the churches." To take up the Word, then, in this manner, that we may thus come to God by it, learn his glorious character, be taught by him, enjoy the blissful communications of his Spirit, be made wise to salvation, thoroughly furnished to all good works, is to make the proper and religious use of it; is to worship God by it; and to enrich our souls with all spiritual and heavenly blessings that can be enjoyed in this life. Thus says the Lord, " Hearken diligently to me, and eat you that which is good, and let your soul delight itself in fatness. Incline your ear and come to me; hear, and your soul shall live." *Isaiah* lv. 2, 3. Again, " Blessed is he that reads, and they that hear the words of this prophecy, and keep those things which are written therein." *Rev.* i. 3. " Moreover, we have more sure the prophetic word, to which you do well to take heed, as to a light that shines in a dark place, until the day dawn, and the day star arise in your hearts; for the holy men of God, spake as they were moved by the Holy Ghost." 2d *Pet.* i. 19—21. "This second epistle, beloved, I now write to you, that you may be mindful of the words which were spoken before by the holy prophets, and of the commandments of us, the apostles of the Lord and Saviour." 2d *Pet.* iii. 1, 2. "For whatsoever things were written aforetime, were written for our learning, that we, through patience and comfort of the scriptures, might have hope." *Rom.* xv. 4.

So much for the three primary, comprehensive and all-important ordinances of the christian religion; the particular and individual observance of which, constitute the religion of every real christian. Here let us pause a little, reflect, and compare these ordinances, in their proper and primitive import, order and connexion, as above deduced from the holy scriptures, and contrast them with the present views and practice—with the dull, listless, formal, ceremonious—nay, even superstitious and absurd formalities, which have almost every where, taken place of these.

What is the sprinkling of a few drops of water upon the face of a thoughtless, unconscious infant, when contrasted with the all-important significancy, and blissful effects of that first great ordinance of christian worship—that first constitutional act of the obedience of faith. Courteous reader, do but reflect, compare, and consider.

Laying aside all popular prejudice, say which you would choose—the joyous, blissful baptism of the Ethiopian eunuch, or the unauthorized sprinkling of a poor unconscious babe; never to be so much as remembered; and, in consequence of which, it is never after allowed to enjoy this blissful privilege; for which, through the grace of God, it might be duly qualified in due time. Again, consider the principle upon which this baptism is to be enjoyed; the inward preparation essential to its profitable reception, and then say what a sorry substitute is even the scriptural administration of this ordinance, (I mean as to the external form of it,) for the most part, in our day, when, instead of the demand of a good conscience towards God, by the resurrection of Jesus Christ, in consequence of correct views of the gospel, rightly taught, understood, and believed; the demand is concerning inward impressions, exercises, and feelings; predicated upon some peculiar inward work of the Spirit, in order to ascertain the regeneration of the subject; which, if approved, the person is then admitted to baptism; not, indeed, as the first instituted act of christian worship; as a divine appointment, declarative of the justification, adoption, and entire sanctification of the believing worshipper; but merely as an act of obedience to a positive command, and in imitation of Jesus Christ; having, thus, no farther tendency to produce a good conscience, than merely the pleasing sense of having performed a duty—of having obeyed a divine command. Thus this great gospel ordinance is sunk to the dead level of a mere moral duty; an ordinance great indeed in its import, and corresponding privilege, to the intelligent, believing worshipper; who, in the faith of its declarative and real import, receives it; and therein, and thereby, yields and presents himself, soul and body, a living sacrifice, holy and acceptable to God by Jesus Christ. See Romans, 6th chapter, upon the doctrine of baptism, with the consequent exhortations tendered thereon, chapter xii. 1—&c.

But herein is that old saying verified, "*There shall be like people, like priest.*" "For the leaders of this people cause them to err, and destroy the way of their paths." Therefore "have they turned away their ears from the truth, and are turned unto fables;" for "they have heaped to themselves teachers, having itching ears." Again, to what a lifeless formality—nay, even disgusting drudgery, is that next immediate and delightful ordinance, prayer, reduced under the present corruptions of christianity! Formerly it was from the altar to the laver, from the laver into the holy place. *Ex.* xl. 30. Jesus being baptized, and praying, the heavens were opened to him; and the Holy Ghost descended in a bodily shape, like a dove, upon him. Compare Matthew iii. 16. with Luke iii. 21. &c. Paul, also, having washed away his sins, calls upon the name of the Lord, (Acts xxii. 16.) and so of all the rest. The uniform doctrine was, First, believe the gospel—next be baptized—and then pray. Look back, courteous reader, to the doctrinal exhibition of this article, and you will not only see the propriety, but also the indispensable necessity of this order of proceeding, God having so ordered his worship; and, in this order and connexion, made ample provision for the comfortable and profitable access of his people. But how is it now? Some are taught forms of prayer from their infancy; others are taught to pray by set forms all their days. Prayer, or rather saying of prayers, is taught and considered by many merely as a duty, the neglect of which brings guilt upon their conscience; and the performance, no other comfort but merely a sense of having done their duty. Men are indiscriminately urged to pray, as a means of salvation, that they may escape hell, without any immediate respect either to the altar or the laver. Hence the great majority pray in their sins all their days, and, for aught that appears, die so. Do you not hear those men-taught, formal people, confessing always, from day to day, the same sins; the sins of their nature and practice; of omission and commission; of thought, word and deed; of childhood and youth, &c. or under whatever terms they are accustomed to make their confessions; withal, praying continually for pardon of the same sins: thus daily confessing their unbelief, their unpardoned, guilty condition. Not so the apostolic christians. These primitive worshippers, once purged, had no more conscience of sins. *Heb.* x. 3. For Jesus, that he might sanctify the people with his own blood, suffered without the gate, (xiii. 12.) and by one offering perfected forever them that are sanctified. (x. 14.) Whereas the ancient sacrifices could not make him that did the service perfect, as pertaining to the conscience, (ix. 9.) for in those sacrifices there was a remembrance again made of sins every year, (x. 3.) Hence those poor, men-taught, formal people, are in a much worse state than the ancient Jews, whose sacrifices, &c. being a shadow of good things to come, though they could not perfect them as pertaining to the conscience, yet afforded them some relief against despondency, in hope of the good things that were to come: but now the good things prefigured being come, and, after all, those formal worshippers not being perfected, not being purged from the guilt of dead works, to serve the living God with a true heart, in full assurance of the faith of the remission of their sins, through the offering up of the body of Jesus Christ once—

there remains for them no farther hope, no other sacrifice to be hereafter offered for sins: so they must either receive and enjoy pardon through faith in his blood, or live and die with a guilty conscience. Alas! for the present corruptions of christianity! Alas! alas! for its corruptors! Thus says the Lord of Hosts, Hearken not to the words of the prophets that prophesy to you: they make you vain. They speak a vision of their own heart, not out of the mouth of the Lord. They say still to them that despise me, The Lord has said you shall have peace: and they say to every one that walks after the imagination of his own heart, No evil shall come to you. For who has stood in the counsel of the Lord, and has perceived and heard his word? Who has marked his word and heard it?—I have not sent these prophets, yet they ran: I have not spoken to them, yet they prophesied. But if they had stood in my counsel, and caused my people to hear my words, then they should have turned them from their evil way, and from the evil of their doings. Therefore, behold I am against the prophets, says the Lord, that steal my words every one from his neighbor. Behold I am against the prophets, says the Lord, that use their tongues, and say, He says. Behold I am against them that prophesy false dreams, says the Lord, and do tell them, and cause my people to err by their lies, and by their lightness. The prophet that has a dream, let him tell a dream; and he that has my word, let him speak my word faithfully; what is the chaff to the wheat? says the Lord. Is not my word like as a fire, says the Lord, and like a hammer that breaks the rock in pieces? *Jer.* xxiii. 16—32. In consequence of such teaching as this, how is the third great and fundamental ordinance of our holy religion, the religious use of the Divine Word, obscured and perverted. With what uninteresting formality, and coldrife indifference, do many read it; even of those who place some part of their religious worship in daily reading a portion of Holy Scripture, as if the mere reading of it were to save them. Under what a cloud of errors and prejudices are the generality introduced to this sacred book! Some calling it a sealed book; others, a book hard to be understood, nay, almost unintelligible, except to the learned or inspired; and others again, a dead letter. The great majority of our modern teachers, like the false prophets of old, countenance and promote these errors and prejudices by their pretendedly learned or whimsical interpretations, spinning out lengthy discourses from a single sentence or clause of a sentence, thus teaching the hearers to believe that nobody can understand it but themselves. In this manner they steal the word from the people, feeding them with their own dreams and notions, instead of causing them to hear, and attend to the word of the Lord.

From this brief scriptural view of the private and personal religion of every intelligent bible-taught christian, both internally and externally considered; and this briefly contrasted with the popular religion of our day, we may clearly perceive an essential difference, and be hereby enabled both to examine ourselves, and admonish others.   T. W.

No. 4.]   NOVEMBER 1, 1824.

Essays on the work of the Holy Spirit in the salvation of men.—No. IV.

How transcendently kind and excellent is the work of the Holy Spirit in glorifying Christ, in advocating his cause, and in affording to men

23

such a gracious confirmation of that testimony, which, when believed, puts them in possession of the most certain, cheering and animating hope—the hope of immortality and eternal life! How diverse its gifts and operations! This persecuting Jew, in a moment, is converted, not only to the christian faith, but becomes himself the subject of its powers, the temple of its residence. The converted Jew, by its influence, is filled with the word of wisdom, and, while his tongue pronounces divine oracles, his finger communicates health to the incurable, and life to the dead. Another, who, yesterday, could not read an ancient prophecy or explain a Jewish emblem, to-day, filled with the word of knowledge, infallibly expounds all the secrets concealed in dark oracles, in obscure allegories, and in mysterious types of the oldest times. Another, who a moment before had no confidence in the crucified Nazarene, has that peculiar faith which impels and emboldens him to bid a demon depart, or a leprosy withdraw, in the assurance of seeing his command obeyed. Another, who, just now, ignorant of the past, and even of the present times, can, by the gift of prophecy, foretell infallibly what will happen next week, next year, or a century to come. Another, who, till now, knew not what manner of spirit was in himself, can, by the gift of discerning spirits, detect the inmost thoughts of a stranger who has put on the christian name. Another who never knew a letter, an obscure and idolatrous pagan, who never learned the grammar of his vernacular tongue, can speak foreign tongues with all the precision and fluency of an orator. And another, in the twinkling of an eye becomes an able and accurate expositor and interpreter of languages, a letter of which he never learned. Yes, all these gifts, and many more, did one and the self-same Spirit distribute to every individual, respectively, as he pleased. These glorious, inimitable, and triumphant attestations to the truth concerning Messiah, did the Spirit of God vouchsafe, as well as reveal the truth itself. And, although these gifts were not bestowed on every first convert; yet in some instances, whole congregations, without an exception, became the temple of these gifts; and, for the encouragement of the gentiles, who, for ages, seemed to be proscribed from the favors of Heaven, the first gentile congregation to which the glad tidings were announced, was filled with these gifts, and they all, in a moment, spake foreign tongues, as the Spirit gave them utterance.

Let it, then, be distinctly noticed, from all these premises, that these gifts had for their object, first, the revelation of the whole christian doctrine; and secondly, the confirmation of it; and without them, no man could either have known the truth or believed it. To this effect does the apostle reason, 1 *Cor.* ii. 9—16. He shews that none of the princes, the legislators, or wise men of Judea, Greece or Rome, ever could, by all their faculties, have discovered the hidden wisdom, "which God had determined before the Mosaic dispensation began, should be spoken to the honor of those apostles, gifted by the Holy Spirit." For so it was written, "Eye has not seen, and ear has not heard, and into the heart of man (before us apostles) those things have not entered, which God has prepared for them who love him. But God has revealed them (those unseen, unheard, and unknown things) to us (the apostles) by his Spirit" —"Which things (before unknown, unheard, and unseen,) also we (apostles) speak (to you

Gentiles and Jews, that you may know them) not in words taught by human wisdom, (in Judea, Greece or Rome,) but in words taught by the Holy Spirit, explaining spiritual things in spiritual words." "Now, an animal man, (whether a prince, a philosopher, a legislator, or a rhetorician, in Judea, Greece or Rome, by the means of all arts and sciences) receives not the things of the Spirit of God, for they are foolishness to him; neither can he know them, (by all his faculties and attainments,) because they are spiritually examined" (by the light which revelation and not reason affords.) "But the spiritual man (the man possessed of a supernatural gift) examines, indeed, all things; yet he cannot be examined by any animal man (because such cannot judge of the principles suggested to him by the Spirit;) for what man (who is merely animal) has known the mind of the Lord, (his deep designs respecting Jews and Gentiles, now made known to us apostles,) who will (or can) instruct him (the spiritual man.) But we (apostles) have the mind of Christ," and are able to instruct your spiritual men, with all their gifts. O! you Corinthians! How has this beautiful passage been perverted by system into a meaning the most remote from the mind of the Spirit! The translation above given is most consistent with the original, and, indeed, is the translation of Dr. McKnight, who seems to have rendered all those passages that speak of spiritual gifts, in all the epistles, much more accurately and intelligibly than any other translator we have seen. The animal man, or what our translators call a natural man, spoken of by the apostle, is quite another sort of a man than the Calvinistic or Arminian natural man. The apostle's natural man, or his animal man, was a man who judged of things by his animal senses or reason, without any revelation of the spirit; but the natural man of modern systems, is a man who possesses the revelation of the Spirit, and is in the "state of nature" as it is called. The apostle's natural man's eye had never seen, his ear had never heard, his heart never conceived any of those things written in the New Testament—our natural man's ear has heard, and it has entered into his mind to conceive, in some way or other, the things which were revealed by the Holy Spirit to the apostles. To argue from what is said of the one by the apostle, to the other, is a gross sophism, though a very common one; and by many such sophisms is the word of God wrested to the destruction of thousands.

While we are upon this subject, we conceive we cannot render a more essential service to our readers than to detect and expose a few such sophisms connected with the work of the Holy Spirit; in doing which we will still farther illustrate the topic under investigation.

Before coming to specifications, we shall make but one preliminary observation, viz. that in the fixed style of the New Testament, there are certain terms and phrases which have but one meaning attached to them; and when we use those phrases or terms in any other meaning than that attached to them in the sacred style, we as infallibly err, as if in using the term Jupiter, I should always attach to it the idea of a planet, whereas the author, whose work I read, always attaches the idea of a god to it. In such a case, I must, in every instance, misunderstand him and pervert his meaning.

The first specimen (and we can only give a few specimens) we shall give is from 1 *Cor.* xii. "But the manifestation of the Spirit is given to every man to profit withal." A thousand times is this sentence quoted to prove, and many a sermon is preached from it to show, that there is some kind of communication, afflation, or gift of the Holy Spirit given to every man to improve, or profit withal, to his own salvation. Three notable mistakes are obvious in such a perversion of the text: First, the manifestation of the Spirit denotes in this context, some spiritual gift by which the Spirit is visible, or, at least, evidently manifested to be in or with the person. Secondly, the *every man* denotes the spiritual men only, or every one that possessed a spiritual gift; for of these only the apostle here speaks. Thirdly, to *profit withal* denotes that the spiritual man did not receive this gift for his own benefit especially, but for the profit of the other members of the body; as the ear or eye does not receive impressions for its own benefit merely or primarily, but for the benefit of the whole body. This is just the design of the apostle in the whole passage.

We shall find another specimen or example of this same sophism in the 2d chapter, 4th verse: "And my speech (or discourse) and my preaching was not with persuasive words of man's wisdom, but with the demonstration of the Spirit and of power." How often do we hear the modern sermonizers praying that their preaching may come with the demonstration of the Spirit and of power, meaning thereby some internal operation of the Spirit;* whereas, the apostle uses these words to remind the Corinthians that his preaching was not successful among them by means of his eloquence, but because of the demonstration of the Holy Spirit; or that his mission was established by the gifts of the Spirit imparted to them, and by miracles wrought in their presence. The next verse makes this evident; for the design of this was, he adds, "that your faith might not stand in the wisdom of men, but in the power of God," in the miracles which God empowered me to perform; for such is the fixed meaning of the term power in this connexion. "God anointed Jesus of Nazareth with the Holy Spirit and with power." "You shall be endued with a power from on high." Those who were converted by seeing, and those who are converted by hearing of the miracles which God vouchsafed to the witnesses, their faith rests or stands upon the power of God. I know that some, to countenance the above-mentioned perversion, are wont to cite the 19th verse of the 1st chapter of the Ephesians, which reads thus: "And what is the exceeding greatness of his power to us-ward, who believe according to the working of his mighty power, which he wrought in Christ when he raised him from the dead." Here, say the populars, is a plain proof "that the power that produces faith in us is equal to the power that raised Jesus from the dead." This will

* We are not calling in question, nor purposely disproving any of the popular theories of the operations of the Spirit, in these examples of sophisms which we now adduce. We are merely exhibiting the way in which scriptural phrases are perverted, or wrested from their fixed meaning in the New Testament. And here it may be observed, that not unfrequently the scriptures are wrested to prove what is scriptural truth. For instance, it is a scriptural truth that there is but one God; yet, admitting 1 *John*, v. 7, to be a genuine reading, it is perverted when it is quoted to prove that there is but one God; for John's argument is not, that the Father, the Word, and the Holy Spirit, are one God; but that the witness, or record given from Heaven, is one and the same. "There are three that bear witness in Heaven: the Father, the Word, and the Holy Spirit, and these three are one" in respect of the unity of their testimony. I am happy in having the concurrence of Calvin, Beza, and Macknight, in this instance, for so they declare.

serve as a third example of this species of sophistry. Without either denying or affirming the truth of the popular sentiment, as an abstract speculation, let us see whether this was the meaning of the apostle. The apostle, from the 17th verse, is declaring his prayer to God for the Ephesians; and, in the 18th verse, mentions one item of his request, viz. "that the eyes of their understanding being enlightened, they might know what is the hope of their calling, and what the riches of the glory of his inheritance prepared for the saints: and that they might know what the exceeding greatness of his power will be (in the resurrection and glorification of their bodies) with relation to us who believe (which will be similar in glorifying the bodies of the saints to what it was in raising and glorifying Christ's body) according to the working of his mighty power, which he wrought in Christ, when he raised him from the dead, and exalted him," &c. So that the power here spoken of is a power to be exhibited in raising the bodies of the saints, and not a power to be exhibited in producing faith; for the Ephesians had already believed.

Another example of the same sophism we often observe in the citation of Acts vii. 51. "O! stiff-necked and uncircumcised in heart and ears! You do always resist the Holy Spirit: as your fathers did, so do you." Hence it is argued that there is some kind of operations of the Holy Spirit which are called common, and which are equally enjoyed by all men, the saved and the damned; and on this, and another saying or two, is the whole doctrine of common operations predicated. But that Stephen, who was full of the Holy Spirit and of wisdom, had no reference to any internal or external operations upon the unbelieving Jews, is most evident from the context. He shewed that his audience, as did their fathers, persecuted the prophets who spoke by the Spirit, and in resisting his word delivered by the prophets, they resisted the Spirit of God: for to resist a person's word and to resist himself, is, in all idioms of speech, the same thing. The unbelieving Jews, in resisting the testimony of Stephen and of the apostles, resisted the Holy Spirit; and many in our time, who resist the testimony of the apostles, dictated and confirmed by the Holy Spirit, do, in fact, resist the Holy Spirit. And, as in the days of Noah, the Spirit of God, by the preaching of Noah, strove with the antediluvians; so the Spirit of God, by the preaching of the apostles, committed to writing, does strive with all those to whom the word of this salvation is sent; and yet many still resist the cogency and power of the truth, and the arguments that confirm it. They did not all believe who saw the miracles, and such of the spiritual gifts as were visible; neither do all, who read or hear the apostolic testimony and its confirmation, believe it. It has, however, been shown in the first volume of this work, that the miracles and signs were written for the same purpose that they were wrought. This, indeed, needs no other proof than the testimony of John the apostle. He says, *chap.* xx. 30, 31. "Many other miracles Jesus likewise performed in the presence of his disciples, which are not recorded in this book. But these are recorded that you may believe that Jesus is the Messiah, the Son of God; and that believing (this) you may have life through his name."

Curiosity inquires, How long did this age of miracles and spiritual gifts continue? It would be no matter of great consequence to settle this point, and, therefore, it cannot be precisely determined. A few hints, however, on this subject, may be useful, in connexion with the design of these essays. It must be remarked, that when Peter first opened the reign of heaven to the Jews, these gifts were showered down in a more copious manner, than at any one period afterwards among the Jews. The proof of this fact will presently appear. When the same apostle Peter, who was exclusively honored with the keys, opened the reign of Messiah the King to the Gentiles, in the house of Cornelius, the Holy Spirit fell on all the congregation, as it did on the Jews "at the beginning." This phrase, "at the begining," denotes that the Spirit of God had not fallen on the Jewish congregation, as it did on Pentecost; and from Pentecost, till the conversion of the Gentiles, such a scene was never witnessed, even by the apostle; for he could find no parallel case, to which he could refer in giving a description of it, save that which happened in Jerusalem on Pentecost. The Samaritans did not receive it in the same manner as the Jews and Gentiles received it. Until Peter and John went down from Jerusalem, after many of the Samaritans had believed and were baptized, the Holy Spirit had fallen on none of them; but Peter and John imparted it to them by laying on their hands.* In almost every other instance, if not in all other instances, the Holy Spirit was communicated by the apostles' hands; consequently, when the apostles all died, these gifts were no longer conferred; and gradually all the converts who had those gifts died also; and, therefore, these gifts did not long survive the apostles. A reason for their ceasing to be conferred will appear in our next essay, which will be devoted chiefly to the third species of evidence, which the Holy Spirit vouchsafed to the testimony concerning Christ. Correct views of the office of the Holy Spirit in the salvation of men, are essential to our knowledge of the christian religion, as also to our enjoyment of it. On mistaken views of it are engrafted most of the extravagant systems of our times.   EDITOR.

King James' Instructions to the Translators of the Bible—with extracts and remarks.

[The following copy of instructions, with the extracts, are taken from Lewis' History of the English Translations of the Bible. They are here inserted, not to introduce the controversy about baptism, but to shew (what is little known) that King James actually forbade the translators of our Bible to translate the words *baptism* and *baptize*, and that these words accordingly are not translated by them. If any of our readers should doubt of the correctness of the extracts made, we refer them to the above work, that they may read for themselves.]
                                        ED.

" For the better ordering of the proceedings of the translators, his Majesty recommended the following rules to them, to be very carefully observed :—

1. The ordinary bible, read in the church, commonly called the Bishop's Bible, to be followed, and as little altered as the original will permit.

2. The names of the prophets and the holy writers, with the other names in the text, to be retained, as near as may be, according as they are vulgarly used.

3 The old ecclesiastical words to be kept; as the word church, not to be translated congregation, &c.

4. When any word has divers significations, that to be kept which has been most commonly used by the most eminent fathers, being agreeable to the propriety of the place, and the analogy of faith.

5. The division of the chapters to be altered, either not at all, or as little as may be, if necessity so require.

6. No marginal notes at all to be affixed, but only for the explanation of the Hebrew or Greek words, which cannot, without some circumlocution, so briefly and fitly be expressed in the text.

7. Such quotations of places to be marginally set down, as shall serve for the fit references of one scripture to another.

8. Every particular man of each company to take the same chapter or chapters; and having translated or amended them severally by himself where he thinks good, all to meet together, to confer what they have done, and agree for their part what shall stand.

9. As any one company has despatched any one book in this manner, they shall send it to the rest to be considered of seriously and judiciously: for his majesty is very careful in this point.

10. If any company, upon the review of the book so sent, shall doubt or differ upon any places, to send them word thereof to note the places, and therewithal to send their reasons, to which if they consent not, the difference to be compounded at the general meeting, which is to be of the chief persons of each company, at the end of the work.

11. When any place of special obscurity is doubted of, letters to be directed by authority to send to any learned in the land for his judgment in such a place.

12. Letters to be sent from every bishop to the rest of the clergy, admonishing them of this translation in hand, and to move and charge as many as being skilful in the tongues, have taken pains in that kind, to send their particular observations to the company, either at Westminster, Cambridge, or Oxford, according as it was directed before in the king's letter to the archbishop.

13. The directors in each company to be the deans of Westminster and Chester, and the king's professors in Hebrew and Greek in the two universities.

14. These translations to be used when they agree better with the text than the Bishop's Bible, viz. Tyndal's, Coverdale's, Matthews',* Wilchurch's, Geneva.''

"A copy of these orders or instructions being sent to Mr. Lively at Cambridge, and other copies to Dr. Harding, the king's reader of Hebrew at Oxford, and Dr. Andrews, dean of Westminster; it seems as if some other doubts arising concerning them, application was made by the vice-chancellor to the bishop of London for the resolution of them. To which his lordship replied, that "To be sure, if he had not signified so much to them already, it was his majesty's pleasure, that, besides the learned persons employed with them for the Hebrew and Greek, there should be three or four of the most eminent and grave divines of their university assigned by the vice-chancellor, upon conference with the rest of the heads, to be the overseers of the translations, as well Hebrew as Greek, for the better observation of the rules appointed by his highness, and especially concerning the third and fourth rule; and that when they had agreed

---

* Some sophistically talk of outpourings of the Holy Spirit now-a-days; yet, in the apostolic age, when the phrases poured out and shed forth were fixed in their meaning, there were but two outpourings of any note of which we read; in other cases it was given in another manner.

* This seems to intend the great bible printed 1539–40, by Edward Wilchurch, one of king Henry VIII's printers, and Grafton.

upon the persons for this purpose, he prayed them to send him word thereof."

The author from which the above is extracted, observes, that the translators, in their preface to the reader, affixed to their translation, declare as follows: "They had," they said, " on the one side avoided the scrupulosity of the Puritans, who left the old ecclesiastical words and betook them to others, as when they put washing for baptism, and congregation for church: and on the other hand, had shunned the obscurity of the Papists, in their azymes, tunike, rational, holocausts, prepuce, pasche, and a number of such like, whereof their late translation (at Doway and Rheims) was full, and that of purpose to darken the sense; that since they must needs translate the bible, yet, by the language thereof, it might be kept from being understood." The same author says, " Of this translation the learned Mr. Matthew Poole has given the following character. In this royal version, says he, occur a good many specimens of great learning and skill in the original tongues, and of an acumen and judgment more than common. By others it has been censured as too literal, or following the original Hebrew and Greek too closely and exactly, and leaving too many of the words in the original untranslated, which makes it not so intelligible to a mere English reader. This last was perhaps in some measure owing to the king's instructions, the third of which was, that the old ecclesiastical words should be kept. However it be, we see many of the words in the original retained, as, hosanna, hallelujah, amen, raka, mammon, manna, maranatha, phylactery, &c. for which no reason can be given but that they are left untranslated in the vulgar Latin." This author further declares, that Nary, in his preface to the bible, (printed in 1719,) remarks, there were certain words in the scripture, which use and custom had in a manner consecrated, as, sabbath, rabbi, baptize, scandalize, synagogue, &c. which, he said, he had every where retained, though they were neither Latin nor English, but Hebrew and Greek, because they are as well understood, even by men of the meanest capacity, as if they had been English." Speaking of Wickliffe's translation, he adds, " In Dr. Wickliffe's translation of the bible, we may observe that those words of the original which have since been termed sacred words, were not always thus superstitiously regarded: thus, for instance, *Matt.* iii. 6. is rendered *weren waschen*, instead of were baptized, though, for the most part, they are here left untranslated, or are not rendered into English so frequently as they are in the Anglo-Saxonic translation."

From the above instructions given by king James to the translators, and the subjoined extracts, the following observations are obvious, and are submitted to the consideration of the disciples of Jesus Christ.

1. It is evident from rule third of the king's instructions to the translators, that he forbade them to translate the old ecclesiastical words; and in rule fourth he commands, that when any word has divers significations, they should retain that in their translation which has been most commonly used by the most eminent fathers, being agreeable to the propriety of the place and the analogy of faith.

From the first extract subjoined to the above instructions of the king, it appears that his majesty was careful that his instructions should be observed by the translators, and especially the third and fourth rules. "It was his majesty's pleasure, that besides the learned persons employed with them for the Hebrew and Greek, there should be three or four of the most eminent and grave divines of their university assigned by the vice-chancellor, upon conference with the rest of the heads, to be overseers of the translations, as well Hebrew as Greek, for the better observation of the rules appointed by his highness, and especially concerning the third and fourth rules." In the second extract, the translators, in their preface to the reader, declare that they had observed at least his majesty's third rule respecting the old ecclesiastical words. They say, they had " on the one side avoided the scrupulosity of the Puritans, who left the old ecclesiastical words and betook them to others, as when they put washing for baptism," &c. In the third extract, though highly commended (and we believe justly) by Mr. Poole, their translation was censured by some others. The grounds of this censure are, that their translation is "too literal, or following the original Hebrew and Greek too closely and exactly, and leaving too many of the words in the original untranslated, which makes it not so intelligible to a mere English reader." It is said by the author from whom the instructions and extracts were taken, that "this was perhaps in some measure owing to the king's instructions, the third of which was, that the old ecclesiastical words should be kept." He adds, that "however it be, we see many of the words in the original retained, as, hosanna, &c. for which no reason can be given but that they are left untranslated in the vulgar Latin." This author also informs us that Nary, in his preface to the bible, printed 1719, says, that " he had every where retained these consecrated words, though they were neither Latin nor English, but Hebrew and Greek." And he adds in the last extract, that Dr. Wickliffe, in his translation, though he has in *Matt.* iii. 6. rendered the word baptized by washed, yet these words termed sacred words, are, for the most part, left untranslated by him, or are not so frequently translated into English as in the Anglo-Saxonic translation.

2. Let it be particularly noticed, that among those words called consecrated ecclesiastical words, and which were forbidden by the king to be translated into English, are the words baptism and baptize. This must be obvious to any person who will compare the king's instructions with the extracts made above. The king, in his instructions to the translators, rule third, commands " the old ecclesiastical words to be kept," and gives the word church not to be translated congregation, with an *et cetera*, as a specimen of these words. The translators, in their preface quoted above, declare that they, in order to avoid being puritanical in their translation, had put baptism where the Puritans had put washing. They also say that the puritans, by so doing, " left the old ecclesiastical words," which chiefly demonstrate that the word baptism was one of those words reckoned both by the king and the translators to be an old, a consecrated, and an ecclesiastical word. This, the translators add, was one of the puritan scrupulosities, and that they had, in their translation, avoided it. This is also proved from what was said by Nary in his preface to the bible, printed 1719. He declares, in the extract made above, that baptize was one of the consecrated words which he had every where retained in his translation, and which he allows are neither Latin nor English, but Greek. If more evidence of this fact was necessary, we might add that the author of the

work from which the extracts above are made, declares that these words called sacred words (of which baptism and baptize are two) were not always thus superstitiously regarded. As evidence of this, he remarks that Dr. Wickliffe, in his translation of Matt. iii. 6. rendered the phrase were baptized by *weren waschen*, though in his translation the old ecclesiastical words are, for the most part, left untranslated, or are not rendered into English so frequently as they are in the Anglo-Saxonic translation.

3. From the above instructions and extracts, it is very evident that whatever the words baptism and baptize may signify in the Greek language, they are words which are not translated in our version of the bible. The king virtually prohibited their being translated, the translators declare they left them untranslated, and others allow that they are neither "Latin nor English," but Greek. This surely should rouse the attention of every one who has any regard to the authority of the Divine Saviour, to inquire what do these words mean when correctly translated into English. If they signify sprinkling or pouring, let them be so translated. Had the king and the translators been baptists, and believed that these words signified immersion or dipping, would it not have been singular that they should agree to conceal their meaning by giving us only the Greek words anglicised? If they did mean sprinkling, as is generally asserted, there surely could have been no harm in translating them accordingly, when it was both the duty and interest of those who superintended the translation to do it. Why, then, all this concealment of their signification? It is said that they were old, ecclesiastical and consecrated words. It is believed that consecrated and ecclesiastical as the king and translators esteemed them, had they meant any thing but immersion, these qualities would not have saved them from being rendered into English. But who said those words were consecrated and ecclesiastical words, which should not be translated? The king and ecclesiastics, whose practice required this pious fraud to justify their kind of baptism, or at least to conceal that their practice was unscriptural. In no place of the bible, that I remember, does God say that there are certain old, consecrated, and ecclesiastical words, which must not be translated into the English language. The translators themselves only thought that these words were consecrated and ecclesiastical, when they occurred in certain places, and when used to express the mode of christian baptism. Thus, in the following passages, where the same Greek words occur, they disregard their age, their consecration, and their ecclesiastical nature. "He it is to whom I shall give a sop when I have dipped it. And when he had dipped the sop, he gave it to Judas Iscariot, the son of Simon." "And he was clothed with a vesture dipped in blood, and his name was called the Word of God." *John* xiii. 26. *Rev.* xix. 13. See also *Matt.* xxvi. 23. in the Greek. The translators in these, and in other instances, have inadvertently, or rather unavoidably, to make sense of these passages, shown us that they believed the Greek word *baptisma* means dipping. It may be presumed that there were particular reasons for leaving these words untranslated where christian baptism is spoken of, unless we can make ourselves believe that in those days king James and the translators in this acted without any reasons at all. But it is not easily believed that they acted without these reasons, when it is remembered that they had every inducement to

translate the words if they meant nothing contrary to their practice. It was with these old ecclesiastical words that the clergy succeeded in preserving the fascination of priestcraft. When Tyndale issued his translation of the bible, because he had in it disregarded the words which the clergy esteemed sacred, they condemned it. He had, for instance, changed charity into love; church into congregation; priest into senior; grace into favor; confession into knowledge; penance into repentance; and a contrite heart into a troubled heart. Sir Thomas Moore, who warmly espoused the cause of the clergy against Tyndal's translation, wrote a dialogue, with a view to bring it into contempt among the people. Tyndal, in answer to it, (as quoted by the author from whom we have taken our extracts) thus speaks: "What made them whose cause Sir Thomas espoused, so uneasy and impatient, was, they had lost their juggling terms wherewith they imposed on and misled the people. For instance, the word church, he said, was, by the popish clergy, appropriated to themselves; whereas, of right, it was common to all the whole congregation of them that believe in Christ. So, he said, the school-doctors and preachers were wont to make many divisions, distinctions, and sorts of grace; with confession, they juggled and made the people, as oft as they spake of it, to understand it by shrift in the ear. So by the word penance, they made the people understand holy deeds of their enjoining, with which they must make satisfaction for their sins to God-ward." The bible is not yet free from these juggling terms, when words are left untranslated and another meaning is affixed to them than what they originally signify, and that meaning sanctioned by very extensive practice. Whether this has originated in kingcraft or priestcraft, or in both, justice demands that it should be detected. A sacred regard to the authority of God ought to lead us to reject an error, however old, sanctioned by whatever authority, or however generally practised.

Extracts from Letters addressed to Elder Henry Toller, by James Fishback, pastor of the First Baptist church of Lexington, Ky.

In order to show that faith is more than a belief, a number of absurd distinctions have been made use of upon this subject. Many distinguish the belief of the head from the belief of the heart, as if a man could perceive a thing to be true with his head, whilst in his heart he perceived it to be false. If they mean by this, to distinguish faith from love, the terms are proper; for love is not belief, but an affection of the heart. They both unite in saving faith. The Spirit of God harmonizes the head and the heart, by imparting right apprehensions to them, and suitable impressions upon them, through and by the gospel of God's grace. It is common to distinguish true faith from a historical faith, as if there could be any true faith, without believing the gospel history! The gospels written by the four evangelists, contain the history of Christ's incarnation, life, doctrine, miracles, death, resurrection, ascension, and intercession, and one of the evangelists tells us the design of this history:—"These are written, that you might believe that Jesus is the Christ, the Son of God, and that believing, you might have life through his name." *John* xx. 31. Surely that belief, which has life eternal connected with it, must be true faith. A distinction is also made between believing the doctrine of the gospel, and receiving the person of Christ; as if Christ's person was not the object of the gospel doctrine, or as if we could receive Christ in any other way, than by believing that doctrine! John says " as many as received him, to them gave he power to become the sons of God," which receiving, he explains in the following words, " even to them that believe on his name." *John* i. 12. For another apostle says, "you are the children of God by faith in Christ Jesus." *Gal.* iii. 26. And it is plain, to receive him, or believe on his name, is to believe the doctrine of the gospel concerning him; for "he that abides in the doctrine of Christ, he has both the Father and the Son." 2 *John*, ver. 9.

Some describe faith to be an inward principle of grace, implanted in the heart by the operation of the Spirit, separate from, and previous to the knowledge of the word of God. But it is impossible to conceive what is meant by such a principle of grace as this. It cannot be any sentiment respecting Christ or his salvation, since it is supposed to be previous to the knowledge of the word of God, wherein alone he is revealed. Nor can it be any disposition or affection of mind towards Christ; for the mind cannot be affected with any object of which it has no knowledge; and our confession of faith makes the principal acts of saving faith to have immediate relation to Christ, trusting on him alone for justification, &c. But the Holy Ghost is the Spirit of truth, and operates upon the mind not abstracted from the word, which is truth, or without it, but by means of it, enlightening the understanding in its doctrines, and influencing the will by its motives: so that the word itself, is the very principle established in the heart by the Spirit. Men are born of the spirit; but it is by the incorruptible seed of the word, 1 *Pet.* i. 23. It is of his own will that God begets men to the faith; but it is with the word of truth, *James* i. 18. for faith comes by hearing, and hearing by the word of God, *Rom.* x. 17. To suppose, therefore, that the Spirit implants faith, as a principle of grace in the heart, without the word, or previous to any knowledge of it, is unintelligible, and unscriptural, and contrary to the word of God, and the confession of Faith:—it makes the word of God of little consequence—supercedes the necessity of preaching it to sinners, or of its being read by them in order to faith; and the Spirit does not glorify the Lord Jesus Christ in his operations, as he was promised to do, in imparting it. It opens a flood-gate of wild enthusiasm, and sets aside the scripture rule for distinguishing the Spirit of truth from the spirit of error. *Isai.* viii. 20. 1 *John* v. 1—6.

When men conceive faith to be a principle wrought in the heart by the Spirit, abstract from the word, it will lead them to look within themselves, for the operation of some spirit, very different from the spirit of truth, who speaks in the scriptures, whose work is to guide into all truth, to testify of Christ, and take of his, and show it to us. *John* xvi. 13, 14. It will make them seek after this inward principle, in the first instance, as the main hinge of their hope, and prevent them taking any comfort from the word till they find, or rather they fancy they find, this mysterious principle wrought in them: which, after all, seems to be only a principle of blind enthusiasm or self-conceit.

On the other hand, when faith is confounded with its effects, and made to consist of a number of good dispositions and vigorous exertions of the mind, it limits the extent, and clouds the immediate freeness, of divine grace to the chief of sinners, by confirming it to such as are supposed to be better qualified than others. It sets the gospel ground of hope at a distance from the self-condemned, who cannot find such good dispositions in themselves, and puts them upon striving to attain them, or to exert some act in order to be justified. The consequence is, that they either, discouraged, sink into despondency, or fall into despair after much fruitless labor, or, if they obtain some fluctuating peace in this way, it is not founded on what they believe concerning Christ, but upon a better opinion of themselves, or of the dispositions and actings of their minds towards him; and in this case it signifies little, whether they call these things acts of faith, or works of the law; or whether they thank God or themselves that they are not as other men are. This is surely a wide difference between believing "that God will justify only such as are well disposed and properly qualified," and believing "that he justifies the ungodly freely by his grace, through the redemption that is in Christ Jesus." *Rom.* iii. 24, ch. v. 5. and the effects of these two faiths are equally different. The former leads a man to seek relief to his guilty conscience, and peace with God from something to be wrought in him or done by him. The latter leads a man directly to the character and work of Christ, as the sole foundation of his justification, and of his hope and peace with God.

Saving faith is distinguished from every other, by its object and effects. Faith cannot so much as exist without an object; for, when nothing is believed, there can be no belief. It saves in no other way than that it has a saving object; and all its influence upon the heart and life, is, properly speaking, the influence of truth believed.

Though there can be no true faith without knowledge, yet there may be a kind of speculative knowledge without true faith. There is a wide difference between understanding the terms of a proposition, and believing the truth of it.

Whatever men may think of their knowledge and belief of the gospel, yet if they do not in some measure perceive its excellence, suitableness, and importance to their lost condition as sinners, they do not in reality know, and believe it—it is the operation of God's Spirit that produces this.

Christ told his disciples that the Spirit of truth, the Holy Ghost, when he came, would not speak of himself—but would glorify him. Accordingly, his operations, during the age of miracles, were all performed in glorifying Jesus Christ, and in his name. The gospel of Christ, since the days of the apostles, has been the theme he has blessed, in convincing the world of sin, of righteousness, and of judgment, and through which he has imparted saving faith in the Lord Jesus Christ. It was in the name of Jesus, all the miracles were wrought; and by the preaching of Christ, and him crucified, as he is exhibited in the record God has given of his Son, the same Spirit has exerted his power, through this preaching, in regenerating the hearts of men. Hence, it is by preaching Christ to sinners, and not the Spirit, that the Spirit operates in glorifying Jesus in their conversion. If I preach to sinners less about the Spirit, it is that they may experience the operations of the Spirit more, by preaching Christ and him crucified, which is the sum and substance of the gospel. On believers I urge the necessity of praying the Father, through the Son, for the Spirit, that he may enlighten and sanctify them, &c.

Communicated from Providence, Rhode Island.

That Christianity is at present most grossly corrupted, many sincere and spiritual christians see and deplore. In this town we have our share in this soul-sickening state of things. One church (one of the orthodox ones too) has in its bosom men who are notorious for profanity! This is one of that vast combination of churches which is now so active in the promotion of the modern plans of christianizing the world. If they would christianize themselves, and get rid of their abominable pride of life, and pompous religious parade, they would remove a great cause of grief from the minds of all meek and lowly christians acquainted with them; and the more especially, seeing they pass in the christian world for orthodox and evangelical.

It was formerly a saying among the Baptists, "Reading, no preaching;" but they have got so now, in this place, that they can read their prayers! Yes, the *Baptists* in Providence, R. I. do not scruple to read their prayers! At the celebration of Independence, this novel spectacle was exhibited, for the first time here, by a Baptist minister of this town, who was selected to pray on the occasion by the *Military* Committee of Arrangements! This same Baptist minister wears a gown in his pulpit, and, for preaching, *pronounces* a very flowery oration, written at full length. He is, therefore, a tolerable Episcopalian. But if he should take a little trip among country brethren, he would find disapproving countenances there. But who would have imagined, a few years ago, that the Baptists would ever have come to this? Where is the raiment of camel's hair, and leathern girdle of John the Baptist? *Ichabod* may with propriety be written upon the walls of their temple.

In one of our heterodox societies, people are taught a new birth of this nature; when the drunkard leaves off drinking, he is, in that, regenerated—and so of every thing else. Now every one that has been born of the Spirit, knows that this is not what is meant by being born again; and yet this doctrine is publicly held forth, and many embrace it. O! in what a lamentable case are blind people, when led by such blind guides!

Our singing here, as in other places, is performed by professors and non-professors all together, headlong; and thus people are made to utter solemn lies, singing of their heavenly birth when they never experienced any; and of their love to God when they are at enmity with him. This public sham is a public shame; and why it is suffered to go on in quiet as it does, is inconceivable. It is not my place to judge; but I should dread to be in the place of that minister who should promote or consent to this abominable outrage upon common sense and the worship of God. And yet this is the universal custom among us—orthodox and heterodox; and it is enough to make the heart of a servant of God ache.

The abomination of having men of the world meddle with the religious affairs of meetings, is here common. O christianity! O abused gospel! you need not the hateful, polluted embraces of your enemies. If they withhold their hearts from you, their money is your affliction when proffered to you.

As to the numerous societies of the day, things are here as in other places. Characters of the worst sort and church members mingle together, and talk of restoring the Jews, and of bringing about the Millennium, &c.—and the reverends, and honorables, and rabbies, and lawyers, and scribes, (I go no further,) trumpet their wonderful doings in the papers, and get their names upon these rolls of immortality. I see not how these people can teach the world christianity, seeing they do not appear to understand it themselves. And I should suppose that the members of those societies who are not christians, would be more consistently employed in healing themselves before undertaking to heal others. It is truly ridiculous that men, who know nothing about religion, should be zealously engaged in missionary matters. It seems to me this is the most foolish age that has ever yet been.

So much for the fountain. The streams which flow from it may be expected to be like it.—Worldly policy, ambition, and vanity, seem to be the governing principles throughout. Young men are sent to college to get qualified to preach! One way to learn to preach with a witness!—How edifying must it be to the mind of the young *theologian* to read the obscene and idolatrous Pagan tales of antiquity! How favorable an influence must the wanton legends of yore have upon him! And to see the vanity, lightness, self-importance, and apparent want of devotion of great numbers of those designed for the ministry, is enough to sicken and sadden the heart of every serious, humble christian.

The foregoing is but a glance at a few things —but it is enough to show us that the christian world is in a wretched, wretched state. O for the Spirit to come and make searching work among christians! Instead of being in a prosperous condition, the christian world is daily getting worse; and there is, at present, scarcely any pure christianity on the earth; and yet, our *college divines* will come in with their sophistry, and try to make us believe that things are going on finely! Out upon such nonsense, I say. I do not believe that a brown loaf is a leg of mutton.

ORION.

No. 5.]   December 6, 1824.

Essays on the work of the Holy Spirit in the Salvation of Men.—No. V.

All the evidences of the marvellous love of Jehovah, exhibited in the salvation of men, are like itself, superlatively grand and sublime. The evidences which command belief, are all miracles; the evidences which corroborate and strengthen that belief, sometimes called "the internal evidences of the record," are admirably moral and rational. The evidences on which the faith of the intelligent rests, are, in the first instance, all miracle. But when we discourse intelligibly on this miraculous evidence, we distinguish miracles, spiritual gifts, and prophecy. We have briefly suggested a few thoughts on miracles, properly so called, and on spiritual gifts, and are now to attend to prophecy. We have already found prophecy amongst the spiritual gifts, as also, indeed, the power of working in others the power of working miracles. But we are now to consider prophecy in a higher and more exalted sense.

Many of the primitive christians were possessed of the gift of foretelling future events. Paul declared that the Holy Spirit testified to him in every city, that "bonds and afflictions awaited him." In what manner the Holy Spirit testified this in every city we are informed. Let us take a few instances which settle this point. Acts xxi. 3. Paul found some disciples "who said to him, through the spirit, that he should not go up to Jerusalem," because of those afflictions that awaited him. Philip, the deacon, had "four

30

daughters which did prophesy," and while Paul was there a certain prophet named Agabus, came down from Judea, and when he came into the presence of Paul, he took his girdle and bound his own hands and feet, saying, "Thus says the Holy Spirit, so shall the Jews at Jerusalem bind the man that owns this girdle, and shall deliver him into the hands of the Gentiles." Thus the Holy Spirit testified to Paul by the words of the prophets. This Agabus was a prophet of some note, as appears from Acts xi. 28. "There stood up Agabus, and signified, by the spirit, that there should be a great dearth through all the world: which came to pass in the days of Claudius Cesar." This gift of prophecy differs from another gift of the same name. To prophesy, in the church of Corinth, imported no more than to speak, by inspiration, in a known tongue, to the edification of men; but to foretell future events, by the spirit of inspiration, is, what we are now contemplating. Nor is it our design to attend to those prophecies, which many individuals, in the age of spiritual gifts, uttered for the immediate exigencies of that period, for either the conviction or confirmation of their cotemporaries; but we are now to view the recorded prophecies, which were designed as a standing evidence of the truth testified concerning Christ. We all see the advantages which resulted to both Jews and Gentiles from the recorded prophecies of the ancient revelations, in the times of the Saviour and his apostles. Indeed, the prophecies, written and read, were the last appeal, and the all-convincing or silencing one, against which there was no rising up. But it is not prophecy, in that enlarged sense, which includes the evidence given to the Messiah, before his appearance in Judea, by the Jewish prophets; but it is the prophecies of the New Testament, afforded by the Holy Spirit, in honor of the Messiah and his cause, since his appearance in the flesh, which I am now to consider under this head.

The greatest wisdom is apparent in this department of evidence. The Spirit, given immeasurably to Jesus, afforded him all means of confirming his mission. His wisdom in exercising the gift of prophecy was admirably adapted to the exigencies of the time. He did not, in the first exercises of this gift, utter predictions that respected events long future: no, this would have been altogether useless in the first place; and, therefore, his first predictions respected events soon to happen with respect to himself and his apostles. If I possessed the gift of prophecy, and wished it to contribute to my honor, I would, doubtless, foretell some events which would soon happen, in order to obtain credit to predictions of greater futurity. So did the Saviour. His first predictions respected events just on the eve of being born. He foretold to Peter, that, on going to the sea, and in casting in his line, he would take a fish with a *stater* in his mouth. This was a small matter, but as difficult to tell as an event two thousand years distant. He prophesied that he would be killed by the chief priests, and that he would rise from the dead the third day, a few months before it happened. When they were on their way to Jerusalem, he sent two of his disciples to a village, predicting to them that they would there find an ass tied, and her colt with her, and ordered them to bring them to him; at the same time assuring them that, on telling the proprietor that the Master wanted them, he would send them. These little matters all tended to confirm the disciples in their faith concerning him. And, indeed, there was much need that their faith should be well confirmed, as it was soon to be put to a most severe trial. He, therefore, gives as a reason for his numerous predictions, the following: "This I tell you now, before it happen, that when it happens, you may believe." But, to pass over the numerous predictions that respected minor matters and approaching events, we shall proceed to notice a prophecy of great utility, which respected an event about forty years distant. This prediction was designed for public conviction, and was perfectly adapted to this end. It was of that character of events which must necessarily be notorious and eminently conspicuous. Let us attend to it. When all was tranquil in Jerusalem, the city and the temple standing guarded by the enthusiasm and patriotism of a powerful people, under a Roman procurator; when religion and business were going on in their regular course as for ages, he foretold, that, before the people then living, died; before the existing generation passed off the stage, the city and the temple should be razed, and not one stone left on another that should not be thrown down. "On the Mount of Olives his disciples accosted him privately, saying Tell us, when shall this happen? What shall be the sign of your coming, (to do this,) and of the conclusion of this state?" These questions he minutely answered. He declared the preceding events—the means by which the city and temple would be destroyed—gave directions to his disciples how they might escape this impending calamity, frequently called "the wrath to come," or "impending vengeance." And, as to the precise day, he informed them that he was not authorized to communicate it, for the Father had reserved this in his own bosom, and willed not men or angels to know it; but at the same time, he would so far satisfy them as to assure them that the people then living would not all die till it actually came to pass. This was as definite as a prophecy, so public and comprehensive, ought to be.

Let the reader remember that this circumstantial prediction concerning an event to be notorious through all the earth, was committed to record, and published through Judea, Greece, and Rome; in a word, through Asia, Africa, and Europe, many years before it came to pass.—And also let it be noted that the apostles, while they published it, gave exhortations in their epistles to the christians concerning it. Matthew's gospel was published in Judea thirty-two years before the destruction of the city and temple; Luke's memoirs of Christ were published in Greece seven years before Titus, the Roman general, razed Jerusalem and made the plough pass over it. Mark's memoirs of Christ were published in Rome five years before this era of vengeance. But, besides these written records, there were all the publishers of Messiah's words and deeds going to and fro through all the world. These are facts, which christians acquainted with the New Testament and the history of the world, believe; and which learned infidels are constrained to admit. That the apostles declared this prophecy to the churches, and that it was uniformly believed, and its accomplishment anxiously looked for, can be easily shewn from their writings. I say, *anxiously* looked for, because the persecuting power of the Jews was to fall with their city and temple; and the apostles solaced the disciples with the hope of its speedy fall. Paul assured the suffering Hebrews that their sufferings by the Jews would soon cease;

"For," said he, "yet a little while, and he who is coming will come, and will not tarry;" he will destroy the Jewish state, and then your infidel countrymen will have to cease persecuting you. This the context declares.   He tells the Thessalonians, that the Jews killed their own prophets and the Lord Jesus; that "they were hindering us (apostles) to preach to the Gentiles that they might be saved; so that they fill up their iniquities always.   But the wrath of God *is coming upon them at length.*" (Macknight's Translation.) Paul also assures the Romans, that the God of Peace would soon put under their feet the infidel Jews and the Judaizers.   The Jews he calls Satan, or the enemy, and adversary.   He comforts them with the assurance that God "would bruise Satan under their feet *soon.*"   It seems from what Peter says in his epistles, (the latter of which was written three years before the Lord came to avenge his quarrel with the Jews,) that the infidel Jews scoffed the idea of Christ's ever coming, as if the apostles had been long talking about it, and yet he had not come.   He consoles the dispersed brethren with these words, "Know that there shall come scoffers in the last days, walking after their own lusts, and saying, Where is the promise of his coming?"   And James, in the clearest style, after speaking of the wickedness of the Jews, in a tremendous gradation, which ends in these awful words, "You have condemned and killed the Just One, who did not resist you," exhorts and comforts the christians in these words, "Be patient, brethren, unto the coming of the Lord; strengthen your hearts, for the coming of the Lord draws nigh."   From these, and many more expressions and references in the epistles to the predicted fall of Jerusalem, and the power of the Jews, we are authorized to say that this catastrophe was, by all the christians, universally expected for years before its arrival, and therefore they required exhortations to patience under their persecutions, and were consoled by the certainty of the accomplishment of their Lord's prophecy.   In the year 70 Jerusalem and its temple were levelled to the dust, after being immersed in all the calamities the Saviour foretold.   This event, then, gave a terrible blow to the Jewish adversaries of the christian cause, and stimulated the christians with fresh courage.   Their patience having been tried for many years, the deliverance would be the more appreciated, and their faith would be greatly confirmed.   The more extensive the hatred, opposition, and persecution of the Jews had been, the greater publicity was given to the prophecy, and the more convincing the accomplishment. Had I lived in those days, and been so happy as to have been one of those persecuted christians who had witnessed the catastrophe, I would have argued thus with all opposers of the christian faith—"That Jesus the Nazarene was the promised Messiah, the Son of God, and now the Governor of the Universe, is abundantly proved, not only from the ancient prophecies, from his resurrection from the dead, from the gifts he has bestowed on many of his disciples, from the private prophecies he gave, which have been all accomplished, from his continued presence with his apostles, from the success attendant on their labors; but *now*, from the accomplishment of one of the most public and particular predictions in the annals of the world.   It cannot be denied that this prediction has been *read* by thousands in the writings of his apostles, has been *heard* proclaimed a thousand times by his followers; yea, that some are still living who heard him pronounce it; and that it is literally fulfilled, all

the world is now witness.   I pass over every thing of a mere private character—I fix my eyes exclusively on this astonishing circumstance.   I see every thing so exactly fulfilled in it; not one of his disciples perished in the siege; they all obeyed his commands; when they saw Jerusalem invested with armies, they fled; the people that were considered an abomination, that makes desolate, have come; the walls of Jerusalem are levelled to the ground; the temple laid in smoking ruins; the nation dispersed.   The blood of the righteous prophets has been avenged; and the curse the rulers invoked upon themselves and their children, has come upon them.   'This is the Lord's doing and marvellous in our eyes.' Kiss the Son, lest he be angry.   If his wrath be roused for a little, blessed are all they that put their trust in him."

Such an argument would, we think, be omnipotent with all who would hear and consider it. Besides, this prediction gave a vast weight, and a new impetus to the other prophecies delivered by the apostles in their writings.   For when this one, which figured so prominently in all their writings and speeches, was so exactly fulfilled, who would hesitate in looking for the accomplishment of the others in their proper seasons.

The prophecies delivered by Paul and John concerning the fate of christianity in the world occupy the next place in the written prophecies, and immediately succeed in train to that one now noticed.   The size of this paper forbids a minute attention to them.   The intelligent will readily perceive, what an essential service they render to the testimony of the apostles.   I will only set down the items of Paul's prophecy concerning the great apostacy, which we have lived to witness.   "That day (speaking of the last day) shall not come unless there come the apostacy first, and there be revealed that man of sin, that son of perdition, who opposes and exalts himself above every one who is called a god, or an object of worship; so that he, in the temple of God, as a god sits, openly shewing himself that he is a god.   Do you not remember that when I was still with you, I told you these things?   And you know, what now restrains him, in order to his being revealed in his own season.   For the mystery of iniquity already inwardly works, only till he who now restrains, be taken out of the way.   And then shall be revealed that lawless one.   Him the Lord will consume by the breath of his mouth, and will render ineffectual by the bright shining of his coming.   Of whom the coming is after (or similar to) the strong working of Satan, with all power, and signs, and miracles of falsehood." [2 *Thess.* ii. 3—9. Macknight's Translation.] This is as minutely descriptive of the apostacy, called anti-Christ, as the Messiah's description of the destruction of Jerusalem.

John informs us that he was in the Spirit, in Patmos, on the Lord's day, when the Messiah vouchsafed him a prophetic view of the church's history till the end of time.   In this prophecy, declared to be the fruit of the Spirit, we have a most signal evidence of the truth of the apostle's testimony.   The prediction of the destruction of Jerusalem, forty years before it came to pass; the prediction of the dispersion of the Jews, which yet exists; the prediction of the rise of the apostacy, and the removal of the Pagan power of imperial Rome, hundreds of years prior to the event; and the prediction of the downfall of the anti-christian kingdom, with the means eventuating therein; (a part of which we have lived to see,) constitute a sort of standing miracle, in attestation of the truth of the divine authenticity of the christian religion, which we owe to that Holy Spirit, which searches and reveals the deep designs and counsels of God.

These brief notices of the work of the Holy Spirit in revealing the saving truth, and in confirming it by miracles, spiritual gifts, and prophecy, merely suggest to the intelligent reader a train of reflections, which, if followed out, may lead to a further acquaintance with this most interesting subject, than could be communicated in volumes of essays of this diffuse and general character.

It must be remembered in all our inquiries into this, and every other question pertaining to the revelation of God, that it was all given since men fell into a state of sin and misery; and that, like every other work of God, it is perfectly adapted to the end for which it was given; that is, to make wise to salvation those that are ignorant and out of the way, and to guide those that are reclaimed by it in the paths of righteousness and life.

Hitherto we have been considering the Holy Spirit as the Spirit of Wisdom, and the Spirit of Power. We have not yet introduced him as the Spirit of Holiness or of Goodness. This will be more particularly attended to by and by.— For it is not only revealed as the spirit of wisdom and of power, but also as the spirit of all goodness in man. As the Spirit of Wisdom and of Power, it was the author of all the miracles, spiritual gifts, and prophecy; but as the Spirit of Goodness, it is the author of that principle in christians, which inclines and enables them to cry Abba, Father.　　　Editor.

To the Editor of the Christian Baptist:

Sir—Upon receiving the proposal for your intended monthly paper, I immediately became a warm and interested advocate for the encouragement of the work, and have ever since continued to read it with pleasure, and, I hope, with profit. The first and leading sentence in your proposal was that which chiefly and forcibly engaged my attention; namely, that "the Christian Baptist shall espouse the cause of no religious sect, excepting that ancient sect, called christians first at Antioch." I was naturally led to expect, according to my conception of things, that you would have commenced with, at least, a brief, comprehensive, and authenticated view, or scriptural demonstration, of the religious principles and practice of that ancient and venerable sect: a sect which I long wished to see drawn forth out of the obscurity of antiquity, and justly exhibited to public view—not, indeed, in the glowing colors of the poet or orator, but in the incontrovertible items of scriptural facts, which no intelligent professor of the divine authenticity of the sacred record, could, with any show of reason, controvert. Such an exhibition, distinctly and fairly delineated, would, in my opinion, have happily served as an expressive life-picture or a frontispiece to the work; and furnished the reader with a proper and authentic contrast to the present corrupt exhibitions of christianity. Though you have not attempted this, in the manner I supposed, and fondly expected; yet I must acknowledge, as I most cheerfully do with heartfelt approbation, that you have contributed much towards it in a variety of interesting particulars; which it is not my intention at present to collect, and present together in a combined point of view; but rather, with your permission, to submit to the consideration of your readers what appears to me, on incontrovertible documents, to have been the peculiar and distinguishing principles and practice of that ancient and venerable sect, whose cause you so decidedly and zealously appear to advocate, in the face of almost universal opposition. If what I shall offer, shall appear, what I most sincerely desire and intend, a genuine exhibition, or life picture, of the ancient Antiochian sect under consideration, it is well: if otherwise, I shall thank you, sir, or any of your readers, to favor me, and the public, with such corrections as will do justice to the original, and cause those prime heritors of the christian name to live once more within the sphere of human contemplation, should it be only on paper.— Your compliance, &c. will much oblige, sir, yours and the public's humble servant,

　　　　　　　Theophilus.

The disciples were called Christians first in Antioch.—Acts xi. 26.

The distinguished subjects of this essay were, by their historian Luke, denominated " the disciples" and " the saints," and both with a manifest reference to the Lord Jesus. The same author also informs us that they were accustomed to consider and address each other as brethren; wherefore he likewise uses this epithet in speaking of the characters under consideration. He also styles the aggregate or assemblage of those collected and dwelling together in any place, " the church in," or " at," such a place; or simply " the church;" and in the plural, " the churches." For the authenticity of these remarks, as well as for a variety of other important items respecting the subjects of our present inquiry, the reader is humbly and earnestly requested to peruse with attention the first twelve chapters of the history of these people, with the first three verses of the thirteenth; viz. of the Acts of the Apostles.

Now, as descriptive epithets are always intended to convey to us some knowledge of the thing described, let us advert a little to the import of the above epithets which were given to those people individually and collectively considered; and also how they came by those epithets, or on what account they received them. As to the first, namely, " disciple," we know it signifies scholar or learner; that is, one who subjects himself to, or under the teaching of, a certain master, that he may learn and practise his instructions for the very purpose for which they were given. Now, when any person puts himself thus under the guidance and direction of another, he actually becomes his disciple. It has been already observed, that the members of this ancient sect received the appellations both of disciples and saints in relation to the Lord Jesus: it therefore necessarily follows, that they acknowledged him their only Master; for this was one of his primary injunctions, that his disciples should acknowledge no master but himself. *Matt.* xxiii. 8—10. Again, addressing his disciples, he says, " You call me Master and Lord, and you say well, for so I am." *John* xiii. 13. These, then, were his exclusive claims on his disciples, that they should acknowledge him exclusively their immediate and only Lord and Master, or Teacher, under God the Father, who had delivered all things into his hand. And here let it be noted that it was in direct opposition to him in these his righteous claims, that the Jews cleave to Moses, as their only Teacher under God; saying to one of his followers, " You

33

are his disciple; but we are Moses' disciples." *John* ix. 28.

We have found, then, the first grand distinguishing peculiarity of that ancient sect of religionists, viz. that in all matters of a religious nature; that is, all matters of faith and obedience, or whatsoever respected the conscience; they acknowledged but one Lord and Master, one divine authoritative teacher, even Christ. Wherefore, in compliance with this leading principle, we find the apostles, those prime ministers of the gospel, always addressing their disciples in the name of the Lord Jesus Christ, whether they command or exhort. Moreover, in order to substantiate their claim to the discipleship, it was indispensably necessary that they should not only profess to receive Christ as their only Master and Lord, but they must also abide in him by abiding in his word, and his word abiding in them. *John* xv. 7—10. If you continue in my word, said he to those Jews that believed in him, you are my disciples indeed; and you shall know the truth; and the truth shall make you free. *John* viii. 31. 32. Under this particular we shall notice at present but one item—one primary clause; to which all that would become his disciples must heartily submit. See *Luke* ix. 23. And he said to all, if any one will come after me; (that is, if any one will become my follower—will put himself under my guidance and direction,) let him deny himself, and take up his cross daily, and follow me: that is, and *then* follow me; for no one, as if he had said, can become my follower upon any other terms. For this see also *Luke* xiv. 26—33. Thus, we may rest assured (as appears from their history) did those who were afterwards called christians at Antioch, come to enjoy the distinguishing and blissful privilege of discipleship.

But before they were called christians, we find they had been also called saints; that is, according to the real import of the term, persons separated to God—holy persons; for all persons or things that are in some peculiar or special manner—for some peculiar or special purpose—separated to the service of God, are, in the fixed style of the Holy Scriptures, termed sanctified or holy. Now we may clearly perceive in the foregoing items respecting the persons under consideration, that they were justly entitled to this epithet; and also upon what account they were so. They had professedly received Christ in his proper character; had manifestly complied with the terms of discipleship as above, "had purified their souls in obeying the truth through the Spirit," and thus had become sanctified through the truth, according to *John* xvii. 17. and were actually manifesting the truth of their discipleship by walking in love, according to *John* xiii. 35. "By this shall all know that you are my disciples, if you have love one to another." Now being thus affected with the truth, they had manifestly become "a chosen generation, a royal priesthood, a holy nation, a peculiar people; to shew forth the praises of God, who had called them out of darkness into his marvellous light." They were, therefore, upon the highest considerations known amongst men, properly called saints. What a beautiful gradation in the process of the divine economy towards this ancient and highly distinguished people! First called disciples, being really made such by divine teaching; that is, by the word of the truth of the gospel; next called saints, being sanctified through the truth, believed; then, brethren, being united in and by

the truth under one head, namely Christ; the head of the redeemed family of mankind, under his Father; for "the head of Christ is God;" "of whom (as the Great Father of All) the whole family in heaven and earth is named." Put these items together, and we shall find those favored people at length rightly called Christians, who were first by an orderly succession and concatenation of effects, the disciples, the saints, and the brethren of Christ. The propriety of this crowning epithet will appear conspicuously evident if we consider its import. "Christian" is a derivative from Christ. Now the term "Christ" signifies anointed, or the Anointed One; of course the term "Christian" naturally and necessarily signifies a partaker of the same anointing by derivation and communication, but in a lower and subordinate degree; as derivatives are also frequently diminutives, both in the ancient and modern languages. Upon this interpretation of the import and relation of the terms, let us advert to divine declarations upon this subject. *John* i. "We beheld his glory, the glory as of an only begotten of the Father, full of grace and truth; and of his fulness have we all received, even grace for grace." "For it pleased the Father that in him should all fulness dwell." *Col.* ii. 19. "You have an unction from the Holy One, and know all things. The anointing which you have received of him abides in you. The same anointing teaches you all things, and is truth," &c. *John* ii. 20—25. Hence we see the above interpretation fully established. In this epithet we may perceive the accomplishment of ancient prophecies.—"For thus says the Lord God, (speaking of Messiah's people in the aggregate, under the ancient terms of Zion and Jerusalem,) "The Gentiles shall see your righteousness, and all kings your glory; and you shall be called by a new name which the mouth of the Lord shall name." Again, in relation to this new name, speaking of the same people, in contradistinction to the unbelieving, stiff-necked, and rebellious Jews, (those obstinate adherents to Moses to the rejection of Jesus,) he says: "Behold, my servants shall eat, but you shall be hungry; behold, my servants shall drink, but you shall be thirsty; behold, my servants shall rejoice, but you shall be ashamed; behold, my servants shall sing for joy of heart, but you shall cry for sorrow of heart, and shall howl for vexation of spirit. And you shall leave your name for a curse to my chosen; for the Lord God shall slay you, and call his servants by another name. For behold, I create new heavens and a new earth; and the former shall not be remembered, nor come into mind." And, "as the new heavens and the new earth which I will make, shall remain before me, says the Lord, so shall your seed and your name remain." *Isaiah* lxii. 2. lxii. 13—15. 17. lxvi. 22.

How completely verified these ancient predictions, both in Messiah's people, and in the Jews that rejected him, no one, who has attentively read the New Testament as an authentic record, can be at a loss to determine. Those especially who have read Josephus' account of the final destruction of Judea and Jerusalem by the Romans, can be at no loss to perceive the awful verification of the above predictions in relation to the latter. It farther appears from the above citations, that the new name of Christian, first given to the primitive disciples at Antioch, was of divine original, and not merely by accident, or of man's devising. See *Isaiah* lxii. 2. as also the common use of the word "*chrematisai*," (called) seems to signify. This will also appear reasonable, both from the character of the subjects so called, its perpetuity and extent, and the important ends to be answered by it. Indeed all these things are recognized in the documents before us. It was to be the name, the only distinguishing name of the Messiah's people; therefore, it was meet that it should be imposed by himself—that "the mouth of the Lord" should name it. Again, its perpetuity was to be equal to its extent; for as this important name was to cover or include the whole of Christ's people co-existing upon earth at any one time, so it was to continue to the end of time—"so shall your seed and your name remain." Again, it was to answer the most important ends to the subjects; it was to absorb and obliterate for ever all names of partial distinction in the grand republic of religion and morals; and thus to unite in one grand religious community, without distinction, the whole human family under Christ—we mean as many of all nations as should believe in his name. Accordingly we find this name first given to the disciples at Antioch, in Syria, shortly after the gospel had been first preached to mere Gentiles, in Cesaria, in the house of Cornelius; the immediate consequence of which, as appears, was the exhibition of the gospel to the citizens of Antioch, without distinction of Jew or Gentile; and that with great success amongst the latter. See *Acts* xi. 19—24. Now for the first time, a great and mixed multitude, but chiefly Gentiles, were converted in the same city, and became together disciples of the same Lord. Now was the time, the precise time, when a new and appropriate name became necessary in order to unite these hitherto dissociated and jarring characters into one associate body: a name, too, of such powerful import, as might supersede and bury forever all offensive recollection of former hateful distinctions. Now we see that it was at this critical juncture, this precise point of time, and not before, that the new name was given. Indeed, it had never been necessary before, while discipleship was confined to the Jews, and their religious proselytes only; for these were already united in the religion of Moses. See, reader, the wise and gracious management of the divine economy! and that the Lord does nothing in vain! Well might the apostle say, that, "in the exceeding riches of his grace, he has abounded towards us in all wisdom and prudence." We come now to the last of those descriptive epithets by which the sacred historian denominates the aggregate of the christians dwelling together in the same vicinity, and statedly assembling together in the same place for religious purposes, viz. the church in or at such a place; and speaking of a number of such assemblies in any country, province, or district, he calls them the churches within such limits. See *Acts* ix. 31. &c.

If we advert to the literal and intrinsic force or meaning of the original term which we translate church, we will find it equivalent to called or chosen out of. Now the propriety of this epithet to a society or association of such characters as we have been considering, is sufficiently manifest from the whole of the premises before us taken together. Considered as disciples, they were separated from the authoritative teaching of all others in religious matters, to the One Master; in consequence of receiving him and his doctrine, they became saints, i. e. separated to God. Thus united under one head, they became brethren; and, as such, associated

for religious purposes, they became manifestly the called or chosen out of the rest of mankind, to the worshipping of God according to Christ Jesus.

Having thus briefly, and, we hope, strictly, according to the true import of the record, investigated the distinguishing peculiarities of that ancient sect, called "Christians first at Antioch," through the medium of the descriptive epithets by which they were originally denominated, let us now proceed to inquire more particularly into their religious tenets and practice, through the medium of other authentic documents concerning them, which we also find upon the sacred page.

We have already observed that their prime original epithet was simply that of "disciples" in relation to Christ, whom they considered as the only authoritative teacher under God, to whom only they were to hearken in matters of religion, according to the voice that proceeded from the Excellent Glory at his baptism and transfiguration—"This is my beloved Son, in whom I am well pleased—hear you him." But, upon this, it will naturally occur, that it was the privilege of a few only of those who were afterwards called "disciples" to have been personally acquainted with Christ, and, of course, to have been under his immediate teaching, and probably none of those at Antioch who first received the christian name. How, then, did they become his disciples, in the strict and proper sense of the term, as we have scripturally understood and considered? The answer is obvious. It was in consequence of the commission given to his apostles after his resurrection, and shortly before his ascension, to "go into all the world, and preach the gospel to every creature; to disciple, or make disciples of all nations," &c. We say, then, that the principle which originated their discipleship, and that of all others, from the day of Pentecost and afterwards, to the end of the world, was laid in the above commission—can be found no where else, and must be traced up to that source.

In the first commission Christ gave to the twelve, with particular instructions to go only to the lost sheep of the house of Israel, (*Matt.* x. 40.) he sent them forth with this declaration, "He that receives you receives me; and he that receives me, receives him that sent me." Again, in his instructions preparatory to this last and great commission, addressing his heavenly Father in their behalf, he says, "As you have sent me into the world, even so have I also sent them into the world." *John* xvii. 18. And addressing them, he says, "As the Father has sent me, even so send I you. And when he had said this, he breathed on them, and says to them, Receive you the Holy Ghost. Whosesoever sins you remit, they are remitted to them; and whosesoever sins you retain, they are retained." *John* xx. 21—23. Thus instructed, qualified, and commissioned, they were sent forth into all the world, as the ambassadors and representatives of Jesus Christ to the nations, to disciple them in his name, with the assurance of his continual and manifest presence with them. "And they went forth, and preached every where, the Lord working with them, and confirming the word with signs following." *Mark* xvi. 20. Thus it appears that they were, in the most strict and proper sense of the terms, the representatives of Jesus Christ to the world—even as he was of the Father. He identifies them with himself, even as he identifies himself with the Father. And as he, the Great Apostle of the Father, received from him the Holy Spirit, with power also to acquit, or hold guilty, according to the tenor of his commission to a guilty and rebellious world; so he likewise imparts the same powers and privileges to his apostles. See the above citations. With the strictest propriety, may all who received them in character, and, through faith in their testimony concerning Jesus, became obedient to their doctrine, be called the disciples of Christ: for they preached not themselves, but Christ Jesus the Lord; and whatsoever they did, taught, or commanded in the accomplishment of their commission, it was all in the name of the Lord Jesus.

But it farther appears, from the history of this ancient sect, that the disciples at Antioch, who first received the christian name, did not receive the gospel immediately from the apostles. See *Acts* xi. 19—24. Nevertheless, they received it, as all did, who, from the commencement of the gospel dispensation, that is, from the day of Pentecost, believed in Jesus, and were baptized into his name. We mean, they received the gospel in consequence of the apostolic commission; upon the execution of which the apostles were fully instructed and authorized to enter on the day of Pentecost, but not before. Compare *Luke* xxiv. 46—49. with *Acts* i. 4—8. and the second chapter throughout. We say, then, that all who received the gospel from that day to this, received it by means of the execution of this commission, which actually commenced on the day of Pentecost, by the preaching of repentance and remission of sins, in the name of Jesus, to all nations; a sample of which was, that very day, providentially assembled at Jerusalem. Some of all these, it appears, gladly received the word, were baptized, and afterwards, upon the persecution that arose about Stephen, being scattered abroad, went every where preaching the word. And some of them were men of Cyprus and Cyrene, who, when they were come to Antioch, spake to the Grecians, preaching the Lord Jesus. And the hand of the Lord was with them: and a great number believed and turned to the Lord. *Acts* viii. 1. 4. with xi. 19—21. Thus the Antiochians received the gospel, not immediately from the twelve, but from persons whom they had discipled. But these also had the promised presence, for "the hand of the Lord was with them;" which plainly shews that the commission was so limited as to confine the whole work of evangelizing, or discipling the nations, to the twelve or thirteen primary apostles, (adding Paul to the number;) but was intended to include all who, receiving those in character and believing their testimony, were thus qualified and disposed, by the grace of Christ, to co-operate for accomplishing the grand object of the commission; and these also it appears were made partakers of miraculous powers, (see *Mark* xvi. 17. 18. with *Acts* viii. 5. 6.) some of one kind, and some of another; but none of them were equal to the apostles; for they, as the complete and immediate representatives and plenipotentiaries of Jesus Christ, possessed, in the most eminent degree, all the powers he had received of the Father, as the great Preacher and Apostle of God. He had power on earth to forgive sins—so had they. He had power to communicate the Spirit to empower others to work miracles—so had they. He had power to work all kinds of miracles himself—so had they, &c. &c. &c. And all who, after them, received the Spirit, received it through their ministry, either mediately or immediately. Hence they are enthroned heads,

judges, and lawgivers in the christian church; and, in this sense, the founders or foundation of it, next to Christ himself; for they also labored, suffered, and died for its sake: but in all things he must have the pre-eminence, who purchased the church with his own blood. In short, Christ had so completely identified the apostles with himself, that whosoever received them, received him; that whosoever persecuted them, persecuted him; and that whosoever kept their sayings, kept his also; for the words they spake were not theirs, but the words of him that sent them. Hence, even in the most difficult circumstances, they were not to premeditate what to say; for, upon every emergency, it should be given them immediately what they ought to say. These things being so, it necessarily follows that whosoever received the word which they preached, upon the confirmatory evidence which the Lord by them exhibited, received Christ and his word; submitted to him, and were taught by him, and so became, to all intents and purposes, his real and genuine disciples, (whoever the immediate preachers might be,) and were therefore justly entitled to the new name of Christian. And here let it be strictly noted, that all who were divinely called to co-operate with the apostles, in the first instance, under their commission for evangelizing and discipling the nations, were also indued with a portion of their spirit, enabling them to speak the necessary languages, and to work miracles for the confirmation of the word. See the above quotations, with 1. *Cor.* 12th and 14th chapters.

Having thus briefly substantiated the claims of the Antiochian converts to the discipleship of Jesus, and of all others who received the word as they did, not immediately from the lips of the apostles, but from some of those whom they had discipled, or that had heard and believed their word—we come now, in the last place, to investigate more particularly the religious principles and practice of those primitive disciples; and this we shall attempt through the medium of the commission itself, and of those authentic documents which we have on record respecting its execution. For this purpose we shall advert to the items of the commission in their natural and proper order. To proceed, then, we find it prefaced thus: "And Jesus came and spake to them, (the eleven,) saying, All power (that is, all authority,) is given to me in heaven and in earth; go you, therefore," &c. Here we perceive that the commission is predicated upon the unlimited authority of Jesus. "Go you into all the world, preach the gospel to every creature," or disciple all nations, "baptizing them into the name of the Father, and of the Son, and of the Holy Spirit; teaching them (the discipled) to observe all things whatsoever I have commanded you. He that believes and is baptized shall be saved; but he that believes not shall be damned. And, lo! I am with you always, to the end of the world." *Matt.* xxviii. 18—20. with *Mark* xvi. 15. 16.

Here, then, in the first place, it is evident that whosoever believed what the apostles were commissioned and commanded to preach throughout all the world, to every creature, (that is "the gospel,") and were baptized as above, the same were discipled, that is, were made disciples of Jesus, and became thereby entitled to the promised salvation.

In the second place, it is equally evident that the discipled were to be farther instructed; namely, to observe, that is, to keep in mind and reduce to practice the "all things" that Christ had commanded, or should command his apostles to teach the disciples. Farther (with respect to the duties either of apostles or disciples) the commission saith not. Consequently the religious principles of the disciples were principles of faith and obedience; to believe the gospel which the apostles preached, and to reduce to practice what they enjoined in the name of Jesus, completed the character of a disciple. So much we evidently learn from the commission itself: for farther particulars we must have recourse to the execution of it; that is, to its actual accomplishment in the preaching and teaching of the apostles. In this part of the investigation two important points respecting christianity, necessarily come to be determined, viz. What is the gospel, and what the law of Christ? The belief of the former, constituting the faith; and the obedience of the latter, the duty of the christian. " For the christian is not without law to God, but is under law to Christ." It has been already observed that the preaching of the apostles under this last and great commission, the object of which was the evangelizing of the world, commenced on the day of Pentecost. On that memorable day repentance and remission of sins began to be published in the name of Jesus, to all nations, at Jerusalem, viz. that whosoever believed in him and was baptized into his name, should receive the remission of his sins, and the gift of the Holy Spirit." See *Acts* ii. 22—39. In the course of this sermon Jesus of Nazareth is proclaimed as " a man approved by God—by miracles, and wonders, and signs, which God did by him:" that, " being delivered by the determinate counsel and foreknowledge of God—he was taken and by wicked hands crucified and slain"— that God raised him from the dead—that he exalted him to his right hand—that " having received of the Father the promise of the Holy Spirit," he had poured forth upon his apostles and the other disciples assembled with them, the wonderful things which were then apparent: in a word, that he had made that same Jesus, which they had crucified, both Lord and Christ. As many as appeared convinced of the truth of this testimony, were exhorted to repent; that is, to be of another mind; to cease from their opposition; and be baptized into his name, in order to the remission of their sins. The result was, as many as believed the things thus testified concerning Jesus, gladly embraced the invitation, and were baptized, and so became his disciples, and were added to the hundred and twenty; and the Lord continued to add to their number daily such as should be saved. The effect of the next sermon (recorded Acts iii.) is the addition of five thousand. In the eighth we are informed that the number of the disciples multiplied in Jerusalem greatly, and that a great company of the priests were obedient to the faith; that is, became baptized professors of the truth which the apostles testified concerning Jesus; for all the obedience the gospel calls for, in order to salvation, is, that men believe it, upon the evidence which God has afforded, and so be baptized. " He that believes and is baptized, shall be saved." We have only yet advanced in our inquiry from the beginning of the 2d to the 8th verse of the sixth of the Acts, and we find ourselves introduced to a great multitude of disciples, the great majority of whom afford the most striking evidence of entire devotedness to the truth, and of its most blissful effects: they afford, we say, the most convincing marks of genuine discipleship. Are these not christians? Are they not justly

entitled to this new and distinguishing name? Are we not justifiable in considering them as a sufficient sample or specimen of christian character? We certainly think we are. If not, we despair of finding their superiors upon record. If ever the gospel was purely preached, they did it. If any thing believed amongst men could produce supernatural and heavenly effects, sure they were in possession of it. We speak of the mother church, the church of Jerusalem, which at this time was exceedingly numerous—full of benevolence, of hospitality, of brotherly kindness, and charity. Let us then pause here a little, and review with all possible attention the history of those wonderful people that we may distinctly apprehend what was preached and believed amongst them that produced such wonderful effects.

It was preached that Jesus of Nazareth, with the fame of whose character they were well acquainted, as " a man approved by God by the miracles, and wonders, and signs which God did by him," was the great prophet predicted by Moses. That he was the Messiah, the Son of God, whom they had wickedly crucified; that God had raised him from the dead; that he had exalted and glorified him at his right hand, a Prince, and a Saviour, to give repentance to Israel and forgiveness of sins; that the Father had constituted him Lord of all; had conferred upon him the promise of the Holy Spirit, that he might send him down upon his disciples; that he must reign until all his enemies be made his footstool; that heaven must be his residence till the times of the restitution of all things; they also preached through Jesus the resurrection, and, of course, the final judgment; and that there is no other name under heaven, given among men, whereby we must be saved; that whosoever believed in him and was baptized, should receive remission of sins and the gift of the Holy Spirit. These various items, taken in connexion with the proper arguments, will be found to be the amount of the apostles' preaching concerning Jesus, in the portion under consideration, down to the 8th verse of the 6th chapter. And, indeed, the whole of their preaching, in as far as we have any specimens upon record, is concerning Jesus. And if we should add all that is found in the Acts of the Apostles to the above items, it would scarcely add a new idea. Thus we find the apostles preached, and thus the primitive disciples believed. How simple! how comprehensive their faith!

As to their practice, they continued stedfastly in the apostles' doctrine, and in the fellowship, and in the breaking of bread, and in the prayers. Thus they manifested the stedfastness and reality of their faith, by their cheerful and persevering obedience. But were we, in the mean time, to condescend to all the particulars relative to their practice, according to the injunction in the second item of the commission, it would lead us to transcribe the greater part of the epistles afterwards addressed to the churches. This, however, we shall not attempt. But, taking for granted, what all must grant, namely, that they were obedient in all things, to the commands and exhortations of the apostles, with the exception of some incidental irregularities, which, upon being reproved, were speedily corrected, we may justly view their character through the medium of those epistles, placing to their account all the commendations, with the obedience of all the commands and exhortations contained in them. This being granted, we have before us on the sacred page the most precise

37

view of the religious principles and practice, or of the faith and obedience of the primitive christians. For whatsoever the apostles preached concerning Jesus and the blessings to be enjoyed through him, or concerning the punishment by him to be inflicted upon the unbelieving and disobedient, constituted their faith, in contradistinction to all others, whether Jews or Gentiles. In like manner, whatsoever the apostles taught them, in the name of Jesus, to observe and do, constituted their obedience. And here let it be carefully noted once for all, that faith and obedience comprehend the whole of christianity; and that, upon the premises before us, we have a distinct and complete view of the gospel and law of Christ, the belief and obedience of which constituted the religion of the primitive christians. These things being so, we can be at no loss, with the New Testament in our hands, to attain to the pure, original, uncorrupted religion of Jesus; if we only attend to it, and place all our religion in the belief of what the apostles have declared concerning him; and, in the obedience of what they have enjoined in his name, as therein recorded. We think it, therefore, needless to be more particular, as it is by no means our intention to transcribe the New Testament; but only to exhibit the leading and comprehensive outlines of the religious character of that ancient and famous sect, called "Christians first at Antioch." We shall therefore conclude with a review of the characteristic outlines of the picture which we have drawn.

In the first place, then, considering this ancient sect in the light of the descriptive epithets by which they were originally distinguished before they received the appellation of "christians," we found they were at first called "the disciples" in relation to Jesus of Nazareth, on account of their exclusive adherence to him as their only master or teacher in all matters of religion and morality: next, that they were also called "the saints," and "your saints" in relation to Jesus as separated to him, and sanctified by the belief of his word: afterwards, that they were called "brethren," as united by those bonds under one head into one family; the aggregate, or assemblage of which, in one place, was called "the church," that is, the assembly of the called or chosen out of the common mass of mankind, in that place. And lastly, upon the union of Jews and Gentiles into one associate body, which appears to have taken place first in Antioch, they received the new, appropriate, and distinguishing name of "christians," as partakers with Christ in that divine unction wherewith he was anointed; the great Prophet, High Priest, and King of his church: by a participation of which they also became a royal priesthood, being thereby made kings and priests to God. This, then, was that new and royal name by which the Lord was graciously pleased to designate and distinguish his people.

In order to a more full developement of the religious principles and practice of this distinguished people, we had recourse to the apostolic commission, the execution of which gave birth and being to christianity, being persuaded that whatever these were, they were such in consequence of the accomplishment of this commission. In this part of our investigation we found the apostles authorized and instructed to preach the gospel throughout the world, to every creature; to baptize the believers of it; and afterwards to teach them to observe all the commandments of the Lord Jesus, with the gracious promise of his presence to be with them continually

in so doing; that, therefore, to believe the gospel which the apostles preached, and to reduce to practice what they commanded in the name of Jesus, completed the character of a disciple; faith and obedience being all that was contemplated and required in the commission: consequently, that the religious principles of the disciples were principles of faith and obedience.

In order to determine more particularly the subject matter of their faith and obedience, or what they believed and practised, we had recourse to the authentic record of the apostles' preaching and teaching from the beginning of the second to the eighth verse of the sixth chapter of the Acts of the Apostles. Upon the whole, without resuming particulars here, we found that the entire subject of their preaching was Jesus Christ, and him crucified; and that the whole of their teaching was brotherly kindness and charity, with a stedfast and persevering attention to the ordinances; viz. to the fellowship, to the breaking of the bread or of the loaf, and to the prayers. See the original, Acts ii. 42. For the continual observance of all which, it appears they were pre-eminent. Hence we clearly perceive what they believed and practised; namely, that the subject matter of their faith was the gospel, or every thing the apostles preached concerning Jesus—and of their practice, every thing the apostles commanded them to do in obedience to his authority. Neither more nor less than this was required in the commission, nor exhibited in the execution of it, as to faith and obedience. As to farther particulars respecting the moral and religious practice and conduct of those primitive saints, we think we have justly placed to their account the observance of all the practical injunctions contained in the epistles to the churches. Reader, if you would contemplate them in the beauty of a full drawn character, extract from the Holy Scriptures whatever is clearly asserted concerning Jesus, and place the sum total to the account of their faith:—next proceed in the same manner, from the commencement of the gospel dispensation, (Acts ii.) to the end of the book, and place to the account of their obedience every injunction moral and religious, you can collect; and you will have a complete picture of a genuine and approved disciple. "If you continue in my word," said Jesus to those Jews that believed on him, "then are you my disciples indeed." John viii. 31. And when you have done this, see that you realize the same faith, upon the same evidence, and that you reduce to practice the same injunctions, in obedience to the same authority: so shall you also be a disciple indeed; suppose you had never seen a religious book but the Old and New Testament; and, in so doing, you will not lose your labor.

Lastly, for the detection of error, please to contrast this full drawn picture of pure primitive christianity with its present exhibition in the world; and you will see how vast the difference, both in principle and practice. In the former, the gospel preached by the apostles, and believed, was the faith: their commands, directions, and exhortations, delivered in the name of the Lord Jesus, was the law. The belief of the former, confessed in and by baptism, constituted a disciple, and entitled the person to the enjoyment of the remission of his sins and the gift of the Holy Spirit; the grand, comprehensive, and essential principles of salvation. The obedience of the latter evinced the reality of his discipleship, recommended him to the esteem of his brethren, kept him in the love of God, and in the enjoyment of that peace which passes all understand-

38

ing but of him that has it; nourished up and ripened his soul for a blissful and glorious immortality. Here all was evident, certain, and satisfactory; founded upon a divine testimony, divinely attested; God himself, by signs and wonders, and divers miracles and gifts of the Holy Spirit, bearing witness to the truth and certainty of every item of the faith and obedience inculcated. Here was nothing of human authority—nothing of the opinions or inventions of men. No contested propositions to be first proved by human reasonings, and then to be believed or practised by the disciples who acknowledged apostolic authority. But how is it now! Surely the very reverse. Alas! when will it be so again? Never, surely, until the professors of christianity return to the original standard of christianity—the New Testament; and until they be persuaded, with the primitive disciples, to place the whole of christianity in believing what the apostles preached and taught concerning Jesus, and in obeying what they enjoined upon disciples individually and collectively—that is, upon individuals and churches.   THEOPHILUS.

No. 6.]   JANUARY 3, 1825.
Essays on the Work of the Holy Spirit in the Salvation of Men.—No. VI.

BEFORE dismissing the subject of miracles, spiritual gifts, and prophecy, we may inquire into the necessity and use of this work of the Holy Spirit. That it was necessary to render the testimony credible, and that this is its use, will appear from the fact that it was vouchsafed, and from a brief reference to a few passages of scripture. The effect of miracles is thus declared, *John* ii. 23. "Many believed in his name when they saw the miracles which he did." *John* iii. 2. "Nicodemus came to Jesus and said, Rabbi, we know that thou art a teacher sent from God; for no man can do these miracles which you do, except God be with him." *John* vi. 14. "Those men, when they had seen the miracles that Jesus did, said, This is of a truth that prophet that should come into the world." Chapter vii. 31. "And many of the people believed on him, and said, When the Messiah comes will he do more miracles than these which this man has done." *John* viii. 30. When speaking in relation to his claims, and when prophesying of what was to be done to him, to those who had seen his miracles, we are told, "as he spake these words many believed in him." At another time, (*John* xii. 42.) when explaining and applying the ancient prophecies to himself, we are told that, "among the chief rulers many believed on him."

But in his own preaching he shows the use he would make of this work of the Holy Spirit; *John* v. 31—39. He appeals, when speaking to the people that discredited his pretensions, to the evidences on which he claimed their attention and their reception of him. He classifies the evidences on which he rested his claims under four items:—1st. He appeals to the miraculous, and every way credible testimony of John the Dipper. 2d. He appeals to his own marvellous works. 3d. He appeals to the testimony the Father had given, *viva voce*, at his baptism, and the Holy Spirit by its visible descent. And, 4thly, he appeals to the ancient prophecies which the Jews had received as of divine authority.

The works which Jesus did he often said were works given him to do by his Father; that his Father worked with him; and so necessary were those works to the credibility of his mission and pretensions, that he declared that "no man can

come to me except the Father which sent me draw him;" as if he had said, 'Neither my personal attractions as a man, nor my saying that I am the Son of God, would be sufficient to lead any person to receive me as God's Messiah; and therefore no man can, consistently with reason or the common principles of human action, come to me, except the attestations the Father has afforded, in these works which I do by his authority, draw him or persuade him to receive me as such.' So that in fact, faith in him or a reception of him, he declares impossible, but by the evidence of miracles.

Many, it is true, of those that received him, and especially before the Holy Spirit was given to his disciples, fell away; and, from the love of the praise of men, or the fear of persecution, apostatized. He, however, encouraged those that believed on him, on the evidence of miracles, (which was not perfected during his lifetime,) to persevere, with this assurance, that whosoever believed in him, "out of his belly shall flow rivers of living water." This figure the Evangelist thus explains, (*John* vii. 39.) "This he spake of the Spirit which they that believe on him would receive; for the Holy Spirit was not yet given, because that Jesus was not yet glorified."

Here, by the way, we must pause on this remarkable explanation which John the apostle gives of this promise. The Holy Spirit was not yet given, because Jesus was not yet glorified. The Spirit, then, it is evident, could not be given till Christ was glorified. Now we know that he did not expect to be glorified until his ascension to his Father's throne. He prays just before his death for this glorification. No man could enter into the kingdom of God until it was revealed, or come under the reign of God until this reign commenced. And it has been already proved that this reign did not commence till the Messiah was crowned Lord of all. Hence the Holy Spirit was not given till Christ was glorified, and until his reign commenced. The commencement of this reign is called the regeneration, or renovation, and therefore the apostles were not themselves regenerated in the sense of the Lord's discourse with Nicodemus; until the period called the regeneration came. The Saviour declared to Nicodemus that except a man were born again he could not see the reign of God. A man that was regenerated would, then, see or understand this reign. But none of Christ's disciples saw or understood this reign till Christ was glorified; for, before his ascension, they asked a question concerning his reign, which showed that they did not understand it; consequently, had not yet been born in the sense of John iii. 3. But it was promised to every one that believed on him, on the evidence of miracles, that he would be regenerated; for "he that believes on me," as the scripture says, "shall prove a cistern, whence rivers of living water shall flow." "This he spake of the Spirit, which they who believed on him were to receive; for the Spirit was not yet (given) because Jesus was not yet glorified." [Campbell's Translation.]

There is one great and distinguishing difference between the disciples of Christ before, and since he was glorified. Those who believed and became his disciples, seeing the miracles which he wrought, on the evidence afforded them, had to wait for the promise of the Spirit, through faith, a good while, and some a long time, till Christ was glorified. But now they who became his disciples after he was glorified, soon received the Holy Spirit. For in one day after Christ was glorified thousands were born of the Spirit and of water, and entered into the kingdom, and immediately were filled with love, peace, joy, long suffering, goodness, fidelity, meekness, and temperance—the blissful cluster of heavenly fruits of which the sons of God are all partakers.

But to resume the subject of the necessity and use of the work of the Spirit, I would request my readers not only to examine the use and necessity of this marvellous evidence before the Saviour was glorified, but let us see its necessity and use since.

Beginning with the first preaching of the gospel after the Holy Spirit was given, (Acts ii.) we see that the miracles and spiritual gifts, or the miraculous evidence, was indispensable to the production of faith. The sudden tumult of apparent rushing tempests in the air, drew together a great concourse of Jews. When they entered the house where the one hundred and twenty disciples were assembled, they saw and heard. They had heard a sound which brought them there. They now saw tongues resembling fire distinctly separated from each other, on the heads of the apostles. They heard them explain the meaning of all this. For miracles will not produce faith without their meaning be apprehended—the end or design understood. They were convinced by what they saw and heard. What they heard assured them that what they saw was the fulfilment of prophecy, and that the crucified Jesus was now on the throne of his Father. What they saw convinced them that what they heard was true, for God would not confirm a falsehood by his signature. They had not yet heard that there was pardon; and, therefore, knew not but God was about to take vengeance on them for their iniquities—Peter had not yet opened to them the door of faith and hope. They cried out in distress, "What shall we do?" Peter promised them pardon and the gift of the Spirit, on repentance and baptism. They heard him gladly, and were baptized, and then received *ten dorean*, the favor or gift of the Holy Spirit. Here we see the necessity and use of the miraculous evidence.

In the third chapter of the Acts we read of another splendid conversion. Thousands believe. But there was a signal miracle wrought in the name of Jesus the Nazarene. Peter, taking by the hand a notable cripple, commanded him to rise up and walk. He obeyed. Multitudes assembled: they saw and heard. Peter explained the meaning of the miracle, and it was understood as a witness from heaven that he spake the truth. They believed. See again the necessity and use of miraculous evidence.

Acts 4th, we read of the terror these miracles gave the enemies of Messiah's cause. They threatened the apostles. The apostles prayed, that with all boldness they might speak the word, and that God would stretch forth his hand to heal, and that signs and wonders might be wrought by the name of Jesus. The prayer was heard. The house shook. And so we soon read, that "by the hands of the apostles were many signs and wonders wrought among the people, by which believers were the more added to the Lord, multitudes both of men and women."

Saul of Tarsus was not only converted, but he was made a minister at the same time. Hence, said the Saviour, I have appeared to you to make you a minister. Those who suppose that all that happened to Saul, on his way to Damascus, happened to him for his conversion, pay no respect to this declaration. It is, however, true, that what he saw and heard, caused him to believe that Jesus whom he persecuted was the

Son and Saviour. He received the Holy Spirit by a special messenger whom the Lord appointed. Ananias came to him—laid his hands upon him—he received his sight, and was filled with the Holy Spirit. Paul said that, by the help of God, (in signs and wonders,) he continued always testifying the truth that Jesus was the Messiah. And a better summary of his labors and success we cannot give than in these words—"Christ has wrought by me to make the gentiles obedient in word and deed, through mighty signs and wonders, by the power of the Spirit of God; so that from Jerusalem, and round about into Illyricum, I have fully preached the gospel of Christ."

I need not, as if proving a point that required a specification of every item on record, be further tedious in showing the necessity and use of this miraculous evidence. It is, however, necessary to state, that the reading or hearing of these things now recorded, stands precisely in the same relation to faith, as the seeing of the apostles work the miracles, or the hearing them declare the truth. The words they spake are as much the words of the Holy Ghost when in written characters as they were when existing in the form of sound. And we have often shown that the miracles are recorded for the same reason they were wrought. And that the word written is as capable of producing faith as the word preached, is easily shown from the same record—*Acts* xvii. 11. 12. These noble-minded Thessalonians "received the word with all readiness of mind, and searched the scriptures daily whether these things were so;" therefore many of them believed. The truth to be believed is supernatural, and the evidence on which it is to be believed is of the same character. So says the apostle, "Faith, (while it is the offspring of the Spirit,) comes by hearing, and hearing comes by the word of God." And to the same effect says Peter, "Love one another with a pure heart fervently, having been regenerated not of corruptible seed, but incorruptible, through the word of the living God, which remains forever. But the word of the Lord (not *logos* but *rema*) remains forever. Now this is that *rema*, or word, which by the gospel is preached to you." [Macknight's Translation.]

Having occupied so much of this essay in exhibiting the necessity and use of the miraculous evidence, in order to rendering credible a miraculous testimony or narrative, I shall not introduce the topic primarily designed for this number, reserving it for our next.

I would only add, as a concluding observation, and I place it by itself that it may be distinctly noted, viz. That no person ever has believed the gospel to the salvation of his soul, but in the same manner and upon the same evidence, that all who now believe, or who will hereafter believe to their salvation, do believe or will believe on the same evidence and in the same manner as they who believed after the Holy Spirit was given. The difference, in the most rigid criticism, betwixt seeing and hearing, never, in my judgment, affecting the truth of the proposition. The blind men who applied to Christ for cures, believed that he was able to cure them as strongly, on the same evidence and in the same manner as they who had the use of their eyes.

EDITOR.

Proper use of the Sacred Writings.

THE following essay towards the proper use of the Holy Scriptures, is respectfully submitted to the readers of the Christian Baptist, by their humble servant in the truth,   THEOPHILUS.

"All Scripture is given by inspiration of God, and is profitable for doctrine, for reproof, for correction, for instruction in righteousness; that the man of God may be perfect, thoroughly furnished to all good works." 2 Tim. iii. 16, 17.

THIS is one of the many encomiums passed upon the sacred writings, which we meet with in the perusal of them; and a comprehensive one it is. It embraces the whole of the sacred canon, though it appears principally intended of the Old Testament Scriptures. [See the preceding context.] Nevertheless, as all that we call Holy Scripture is equally "given by inspiration of God," the above commendation will hold equally good of it all. It also appears to have been given for the same blissful end, viz. "to perfect the man of God." We find the appellation "Man of God" first given to Moses, afterwards to Samuel and David, and to many of the Old Testament prophets. It is also once given to Timothy, (1 *Epis.* vi. 11,) who is the only person to whom it is applied in the New Testament; in which it occurs but twice. In the place before us it is not restricted to Timothy, or any other, either personally or officially considered, but appears to designate the object of divine teaching—the student of the Holy Scriptures, that is, "the man taught by God" by the perusal and study of his word. In this sense we here take it. This we are sure is the end of the divine goodness in relation to all to whom it is sent. It is thus the Holy Scriptures stand recommended as "able to make us wise to salvation, through faith which is in Christ Jesus."

The grand subject of inquiry is, Are the scriptures, in and of themselves, independent of all external helps, able to do this? The answer to this important question, together with their proper use, is the precise object of this essay; and we hope to make it evident to all concerned, to know the truth, that the Holy Scriptures do, in and of themselves, independent of all external helps, possess a real intrinsic sufficiency to make the diligent student of them "wise to salvation," "thoroughly furnished to all good works."

To prevent mistakes, let it be clearly understood, that, by the independent and intrinsic sufficiency of the Holy Scriptures, we do not mean such a sufficiency as would, in the first instance, obviate the necessity of proper teaching. Teaching, in general, is indispensably necessary to mankind for every valuable purpose. We came into this world entirely and equally ignorant of every thing; therefore, we can know nothing without teaching, of some kind or other. The child is first taught by experience that fire will burn; that a knife will cut, &c. and every particular art and science, how plain and rational soever, must be learned before we can know or practise it. Of course, language, which is the vocal and written medium of communication, or something equivalent to it, must be learned before we can communicate our ideas to each other. Again, the language of a particular science, with its proper object, must be acquired before we can become proficients in it. It is just so with the Holy Scriptures. It is not only necessary that we understand to speak and read our native language in general, through the medium of common teaching, for the common purposes of life; but if we would understand the Scriptures, we must be taught the Scriptures; not merely to read them as a common book, but as a book of divine revelation, given for a certain purpose—having terms and phrases peculiar

to itself. Being thus properly introduced to the knowledge of the book, our attention called to its authority, its authenticity, its distinct and diversified subjects with their proper objects, its ultimate end, or the grand intention of the whole work, we are qualified to make the proper use of it, as a book written for our learning, in as far as teaching is concerned; we mean the teaching of the schools, or that preparatory teaching, to which every youth bred in a christian country is in justice entitled. This it appears was Timothy's privilege, as being descended of Jewish parents, so that "from a child he had known the Holy Scriptures," (of the Old Testament at least.) This he had of his grandmother Lois, and of his mother Eunice, according to the injunction, *Deut.* vi. 6—9. To the Jews the Old Testament presented itself immediately as the authentic record of the origin of their nation, and of all things; of their religion and laws, &c. of the singular interpositions of God in their favor. It was, therefore, to them a most interesting book, plain and intelligible: it needed no comment nor explanation. Written originally in their own language, it appears to have been, at least for a long time, their only book. To them, therefore, it always presented itself in the proper point of view in which it was to be considered. The series of events in the order of the narrative, from the beginning of Genesis to the end of Deuteronomy, was the natural and proper order in which the serious and attentive mind was to consider and contemplate the various things thus presented in succession. This book was also to be publicly read, at the appointed seasons, in the great solemnities of the nation. But we hear of no explanations, either allowed or attempted, for upwards of a thousand years, even to the days of Nehemiah, when explanation, in some measure, became necessary, the people having lost the purity of their native language during the seventy years captivity of the nation. There was, then, neither explanation nor comment upon the Jewish Scriptures for upwards of a thousand years; and what was done by Ezra and his companions at the time referred to, was merely accidental, owing to the reason already assigned. But are the Scriptures presented to us in the same natural, easy, and obvious light? Are we taught to consider them, as a plain and simple narrative of facts, divinely authenticated, namely, as a genuine and faithful record of what God did, and taught, and caused to be recorded by Moses and the prophets, by Christ and his apostles, for the instruction and salvation of mankind? And as such are we taught to consider the book, as it now presents itself to us, consisting of two grand and distinctive divisions, called the Old and New Testaments; the former as having for its immediate object the instruction of the Israelitish nation, or (according to modern style) of the Jews, containing the doctrine, laws and institutes of their religion and government; the latter as having for its immediate object the instruction and salvation of mankind, by the knowledge, belief and obedience of the Son of God—containing the doctrines, laws, and institutes of the christian religion? Are the successive generations of those called christians, we say, thus introduced to an acquaintance with the Holy Scriptures as they now appear amongst us in their complete and finished form? Are we thus successively taught to consider and understand them? Far otherwise. But ought we not? Who will say that we ought not? We fear there are very many; yea, a great majority among those that are called christians. Do not many forbid the common popular use of the Scriptures? They say it is a dangerous book in the hands of the common people—only fit for the learned—for the clergy. Do not others again, who differ from these, materially concur with them in the depreciation of the Holy Scriptures, considering them as a dead letter, as a sealed book, as scarcely intelligible; in short, as of no use except to the clergy, or, at least, to the regenerate; whereas the most precious, important, and mysterious portions of those Holy Writings were, by a divine command, published to an ignorant and ungodly world. See *Matt.* xxviii. 19, 20. *Mark* xvi. 15, 16, with 1 *Tim.* iii. 16. &c. &c. These poor, ignorant, deluded people, certainly do not know that God has prepared and ordained his word to be the only means of salvation amongst men, and, of course, the exclusive means of regeneration. Compare *James* i. 18, 1 *Peter* i. 23 —25, with the above citations. But do not the clergy of all denominations concur with the opinions under immediate consideration, else why attempt to expound or explain every portion without exception? Why pretend to the necessity of a classical education to understand the Scriptures; or, in lieu thereof, to a kind of secondary inspiration?

But after all these pretensions, to the manifest defamation of the Holy Scriptures, may we not inquire what hurt can result from the sayings and doings of God, or of man, recorded in the Holy Scriptures? Are the teachings and example of Jesus Christ and his apostles calculated to do injury? Again, is it not evident that the Scriptures, both of the Old and New Testaments, were, in the first instance, delivered to mixed multitudes of all descriptions; or, when Moses and the prophets, Christ and his apostles, addressed Jews and Gentiles in the words that are recorded, did they carry about with them learned interpreters to explain their sayings to the people? or did they ever suggest the need of such helps? How, then, has it come to pass, as at this day, that there is such an innumerable host of scripture interpreters, and such a universal acknowledgment of the almost indispensable necessity of such. The answer is obvious—the people are bewitched as formerly; (*Gal.* iii. 1. &c.) for from the beginning it was not so, as we have already seen. That a kind of teaching, peculiarly adapted to the subject, is necessary, at least to beginners, in order to a right understanding of the scriptures, has been granted. We might add that such a kind of teaching has become necessary, not only to beginners, but almost to every body in this dark and deluded age. The kind of teaching which we mean, however, is not the clerical teaching of our day. It aims at no more than a just analysis of the subject in order to the end proposed; namely, that the diligent student may be made "wise to salvation, thoroughly furnished to all good works;" for this intrinsic sufficiency the apostle asserts is in the Holy Scriptures, connecting the Old Testament with the New, as he manifestly does in the place alluded to, by adding, "through faith which is in Christ Jesus."

First, then, as to the analysis, let the student be duly informed concerning the character and design of this singular book; that it is a book of a sacred character, claiming God for its author, and having for its professed object or design the present and everlasting happiness of mankind; that it rests its claims upon the singularity of its contents, which are of such a nature, and so authenticated, that none but the God which it re-

veals could be the author of them. That it is the proper business of the student to advert both to its import and evidence, that he may clearly perceive both its meaning and authority; that the instructions it is designed to convey, in order to its professed object, resolve themselves into the following comprehensive and important particulars, viz. the knowledge of the divine character; of the original and present character and condition of mankind in the sight of God; of the divine procedure towards mankind in their present guilty and wretched condition, for their effectual relief and deliverance; of their present duties and privileges; and of the future and everlasting destinies of the whole human race. That, for the attainment of those necessary and important points of information, the scriptures furnish us with historical records of the doings and sayings both of God and men; by a due attention to which, we may learn the characters of both.— And here it should be observed, that there is no other way known to us, by which we may acquire the knowledge of any character, human or divine, but by words and deeds. Hence the necessity of a strict and studious attention to every item of the sacred records, in order to a particular and enlarged acquaintance with the character both of God and man—both of saint and sinner. Hence also the necessity of such faithful and authentic records. Moreover, the scriptures furnish us with prophetic declarations of things not seen as yet, by which we may learn the future destinies of mankind:—by others, that have been fulfilled, we have a certain proof of their divine original. They also furnish us with commands and examples, promises and threatenings, exhortations and dissuasives, religious ordinances and exercises, for our moral and religious instruction; that we may be happy in ourselves, enjoy social happiness one with another, and be ultimately happy in the complete and everlasting enjoyment of the favor and fellowship of God. Lastly, they present themselves to us under two grand divisions, called the Old and New Testaments; the former of which had for its proper and immediate object the instruction of the Israelitish nation; and contains the institutes of their religion and government; the latter has for its proper and immediate object the discipling of all nations, and the instructing of the discipled how they ought to walk, so as to please God, both in respect of religion and morals.— Hence the Old Testament contains a complete exhibition of the Jewish religion—and the New Testament, that of the Christian.

With these, or similar instructions, let a *correct* translation of the Holy Scriptures be put into the hands of the rising generation successively, from age to age; and those who are able to read and understand correctly their native language, will be at no material loss for farther explanation. As for those that are so deficient that they cannot read and understand their native language, let the public and private reading of the scriptures, with frequent recurrence to the above analysis, supply the deficiency. If such a use of the Holy Scriptures, in connexion with the other appointed exercises of religion, public and private, does not answer the purpose of religious edification, we have reason to fear that nothing human wisdom can devise will have the desired effect.

It may here be objected, "If the scriptures be so completely adapted to answer the gracious and blissful end for which they were given, independent of all explanation or comment, they must, of course, be exceedingly plain; and if so,

42

what need of any preparatory instructions—of any peculiar teaching, or introductory analysis to direct our studies, or to prevent mistakes?—Would it not be sufficient to put the book itself into our hands, at a proper period, in the ordinary course of our reading, without any kind of preface or introduction?"

To this we may justly reply, that, to convey the book in this manner, from hand to hand, from age to age, from one generation to another, would be next to impossible. Men are not accustomed to act so tacitly, and with such apparent indifference in things of high esteem—of great and acknowledged importance. Something, therefore, must and will be said; yea, in justice ought to be said, in relation to so invaluable a privilege. You will say, then, " Let it be called the Book of God—the Book of Life—the Holy Scriptures, or Sacred Records of the Old and New Covenants, Constitutions, or Dispensations; or by any other suitable and appropriate name: and, as such, be exhibited, read, and considered, without more ado." Granted; and what then? Will nothing more be said about it? Impossible. It must be read over, talked over, believed, obeyed, sung and prayed over; it must, therefore, necessarily be analysed. The mind will necessarily make distinctions in it; and, of course, make distinct uses of it, according to the variety of matter it presents to our consideration. The grand desideratum is, that the distinctions be just and natural; and that the proper, immediate, and ultimate design of every portion of it, be duly understood and realized. A just and correct analysis, such as has been attempted above, would, we presume, be of considerable advantage to the young student, especially for those important purposes. That the attentive and discerning mind, however, if unbiassed with erroneous system, would ultimately come to a right understanding of the Holy Scriptures, independent of all preparatory instructions, is cheerfully granted; but it might not be until after a long time and many mistakes. As, therefore, much good and no hurt is likely to ensue from the plan proposed; as it casts no manner of reflection upon the Holy Scriptures, on account of obscurity; or in any wise prejudges the free and independent use of the student's intellect; and, at the same time, gives proper scope for the performance of a grateful and important duty: we think there can be no just objection brought against it. At all events, it appears the only kind of human teaching that is necessary to render the word plain and profitable to every one that feels disposed to profit by it; while, at the same time, it does not pretend to explain it, but merely to direct the attention of the reader to the various subjects and objects it presents to his consideration, that he may be led to distinguish and make the proper use of them.

It may be farther objected, that, to introduce the reading of the Holy Scriptures through the medium of such analysis, might be made subservient to sectarian views, and, of course, have a tendency to bias the mind of the student in favor of a particular sect. To this we may justly reply, that simple analysis, which is all we plead for, can have no tendency whatever to bias the mind of the student, in any department of science. What biassing tendency can be produced by acquainting him with the name and intention of his author, and by furnishing him with an index of the contents or arguments which the author exhibits in order to accomplish his object? To do merely so much as this, to excite

the attention of the learner, and prepare his mind for forming a discreet and satisfactory judgment of the true import, relevancy, and tendency of the several items or arguments towards establishing a certain conclusion; so far from biassing his judgment in any respect, rather serves to put him upon his guard against mistake and deception. It can have no tendency, even in the first instance, to prejudice him in favor of the work. In short, it is doing him all the justice imaginable, in every respect. In putting a valuable work into his hand, it is calling him to the proper use of his talents, and at the same time rendering him all the just and necessary assistance that can be, in order to his reading it with profit, without so much as prejudicing him in its favor; that, by adverting to the import and evidence of every part, he may come to a just conclusion upon the whole. Had mankind been thus introduced to the bible at a proper age, without any farther comment, ever since christianity was established, and the sacred canon completed by the ministry of the apostles, we may fairly presume that things would have presented a very different aspect in the christian world. We should not have had so much mere educational faith, so many human traditions, such variety of sects, and so many shameful apostacies.

It will, perhaps, still be objected, that upon this plan of proceeding, the children of christians would have continued mere nondescripts, till after they had become of age—were well educated—had studied the scriptures—and formed a discreet and rational judgment upon the whole subject. In a word, till they became rational believers. To this we reply, with all firmness, without a moment's hesitation, it would then be soon enough; soon enough to assume a religious character, when rationally convinced of the truth and authenticity of the holy scriptures; of the true character of God; of the real character and condition of man; of the gracious procedure of God towards fallen man, for his effectual relief and deliverance; of his present duties and privileges, and future hopes. The profession of religion without a scriptural knowledge and certainty, we mean, a divine certainty of these things, is indeed but little worth. It is a mere forced production; a premature assumption. It brings to mind the common adage about mamma's pet; "a man at twelve, and a child all his days." This is too often the case with those premature professors. But at what age might such a proficiency in scriptural knowledge be rationally attained? We presume, that, under the proper means, it might be as early, as professions are commonly made; say, from the age of twelve to fifteen. It is no very uncommon thing, to find youths of this age good arithmeticians; yea, many tolerably good linguists. So far, then, as a competent proficiency in divine knowledge, depends on age, there appears no forbidding consideration, if the proper means be used. Timothy, "from a child, had known the holy scriptures." There is a proper course of divine or scriptural teaching adapted to every age, from the first dawnings of rationality. It is the province of every christian parent to judge of the capacity of his child, and to adapt his instructions accordingly. But there is a time, it may be about the age of ten, or shortly after, when the dutiful and intelligent christian parent may and ought to address his child to this effect: " My child, you have always seen me worship God both in my family and in the church. You have had the advantage of a reli-

Q

gious education so far under my example and direction. The time is now come when you must begin to understand, to think, and act for yourself. I, and the church in which you have always seen me worship, have concurred in teaching you to read and understand the language of the holy scriptures. These are the sources of our religious belief and practice. These you must now begin to read and study for yourself. We believe them to be the word of God—we call them by that name. But this is not a sufficient reason that you should consider them to be so, unless you are convinced by the proper authority; that is, the authority of God himself, who affords the proper evidence to those that seek it. This evidence is the word itself. Search the scriptures, and you will find it there. If not there, it is no where to be found. Therefore, if you would find it, you must search the scriptures; you must read and study them with the greatest attention. They claim to be the word of God, and we consider them as such, because they make him known. God is known by his word and by his works, or by his sayings and doings: now the scriptures are professedly a record of both. By the names and attributes, the sayings and doings, they ascribe to him, we become acquainted with him; that is, we learn his character. And the very existence of such a record, is to us itself, a demonstrable evidence of the truth of it. But you must gradually and progressively acquaint yourself with those things, and thus form your own judgment. You will perceive, the bible divides itself into two grand divisions; the former called the Old Testament, immediately addressed to the Jews, containing the institutes of their religion and government: the latter, called the New Testament, addressed to all nations, containing the history and gospel of Jesus Christ, and the institutes of the christian religion. It is with the latter that we, as christians, have immediately to do. Its declarations concerning Christ, and the salvation that is by him, constitute our faith; and the injunctions inculcated by his apostles upon individual believers, and upon the churches composed of such, constitute the rule of our duty. So we understand the scriptures, and sowe have received them: but for the divine authenticity of the whole, and the propriety of our so understanding them, you must judge for yourself by a careful and studious perusal, that you may come to know the truth upon its proper evidence; having this gracious promise upon record from the glorious and benevolent Author, that "they that seek him early shall find him." With such an address, and under the influence of such preparatory instructions, were the rising generation amongst professors of christianity seasonably introduced to the study of the holy scriptures, what happy consequences might be expected. How much more rational and scriptural such a procedure, than training them up in the dogmas of any party. Having first qualified them to read and understand the language of the scriptures, thus to commit and recommend to them the Word of God, as the means of their farther instruction, could certainly be productive of no bad consequences. Whereas, the neglect of this, or the contrary course, which is almost universally pursued, has a tendency to make sectarians, bigots, or enthusiasts, instead of rational, intelligent christians. For want of such a just and rational introduction to the scriptures, when a youth, what a loss of precious time and privilege has the writer of this essay experienced; though

early introduced both to the reading and memorising of the sacred records! He remembers, with regret, the many years of his life spent in the possession of the bible, without knowing the proper use and inestimable value of it. He was early taught, indeed, to consider it as the Word of God—as the alone head and source of all religious knowledge; but without any distinct view of that religious knowledge it was designed to communicate,—wherein it consisted,—or how it was to be ascertained: whether directly and immediately from the declarations of the book itself, or from the expositions and comments of men upon it:—what was the particular use and design of its distinct parts, and the ultimate object of the whole, in relation to religious attainment. In a word, whether he was to learn his religion directly and immediately from Moses and the prophets, or from Christ and his apostles:—whether he was to worship in the style and spirit of the ancient Jews, or of the believing Gentiles; or whether he was to join issue with both, and combine—the two religions into one, with some external and ritual distinctions: and how far such distinctions ought to be carried he was at a loss to conjecture, having no certain instructions how to determine. Like an unskilful traveller, who, accidentally introduced into a strange and highly improved country, though every where presented with beautiful and interesting objects, yet, for want of an intelligent guide to direct his attention, knows not how to avail himself of them; so was the writer of this, and, as far as he knew, so were all his acquaintances, in relation to the various, beautiful, and highly interesting objects presented to view on the sacred page. He knew not, for the most part, what to make of them;—could form no consistent apprehension of their scope and import;—or what that religion was they were designed to inculcate. He recollects that himself, for a time, with others of his acquaintance, took the bare reading of the scriptures to be religion;—at other times, the performance of what are called religious duties,—such as fasting and prayer, and attending to social worship, &c. again, the holding of a certain system of religious opinions, supposed to be drawn from, and proved by, the scriptures. This last mistake, (for such the writer conceives it to be,) led into a vast field of controversy, of contention, and vain jangling; for great is the diversity of human opinions in religious matters; and high and positive are the claims and pretensions of the respective sectaries, whether ancient or modern. It was not, however, till after the better part of his life was spent in those mistakes, that he came to discern the peculiar character, scope, and import of the holy scriptures, and wherein that real religion consists, which they are designed to communicate; namely, that it consists in that knowledge of God and man; or of the divine and human character, which the holy scriptures throughout, taken from beginning to end, as a complete whole, distinctly and luminously inculcate; and which terminates practically in the faith and obedience of the gospel, blessing the mind with peace and comfort in God, through the mediation of Jesus Christ, and replenishing it with holy and virtuous dispositions both towards God and man. This religion manifests itself in a confessed and stedfast belief of all divine declarations, and in a manifest and persevering obedience to all divine ordinances and injunctions, according to the just and obvious import of the words and phrases in which they are delivered; which belief and obedience rests simply and solely upon the authority of God. Thus receiving and understanding the holy scriptures as a perfect and intelligible rule of faith and obedience, independent of all human interposition, the writer has, at length, found himself quite at home, under the immediate teaching of the Great Teacher himself, and of his holy apostles and prophets. Thus brought home, and reconciled both to God and man, upon gospel principles, through the knowledge of the scriptures, after many wanderings, and the loss of much precious time and privilege, merely, as appears, for want of a proper and suitable introduction at first to the consideration of that sacred book, (for the writer, was, to the best of his recollection, as religiously disposed forty years ago as he is at present,) he would, if possible, and as far as possible, prevent the same pernicious and unhappy consequences from accruing to others. This he begs leave to assure his readers is his sole motive for calling their attention to this important subject.   THEOPHILUS.

"Worthy of Imitation."

UNDER this head, we are told by our missionary prints, that "the children of Catskill have contributed one hundred and fifty dollars to make Lafayette a Director for life of the American Bible Society." From the same source we learn that a "company of young ladies," at Richmond, Virginia, presented to him a certificate, announcing the fact that he was a member for life of the Bible Society of Virginia. The very next day, at the same place, we hear of his attending the races, and going to a ball in the evening. It is thus announced in the New York Gazette of November 4:—

"General La Fayette attended the Jockey Club Races at Richmond last Thursday. After the match race was decided, he sat down to a sumptuous repast, prepared by the members of the Jockey Club, on which occasion a number of toasts were drank. In the evening he attended a ball at the Eagle Tavern, where there was a most brilliant assemblage of beauty. The company consisted of about fifteen hundred ladies and gentlemen. The room was tastefully adorned."

We cannot perceive what possible good can result to the cause of religion, by dragging the General and other popular and distinguished characters, "by the hair of the head," into these clerical associations. Our missionary prints tell us "this is one of the happiest methods, which has yet been adopted, of testifying respect for the General's character." On this subject the Berean remarks—

"The character of La Fayette is founded on his political and military career. As a religious man, or a "Bible christian," we have never heard him spoken of. In one of his communications, written some time ago, and lately published in the newspapers, he speaks of Hume and Voltaire as his closest companions. We do not perceive in this any thing to entitle him to a directorship in a Bible Society; and so far from being the "happiest method" of testifying "respect for the General's character," we should not be surprised if he were to take it as a burlesque! But this detestable species of priestcraft has in it the triple purpose of increasing the funds of the clergy, giving an eclat to their proceedings, and extending their influence. Beyond this, the General's character has no affinity nor connexion with the concern."

The disposition of General La Fayette appears to be mild and condescending, and hence he would not willingly give offence to any class of citizens. In the following letter, copied from the London Examiner, we have exhibited an opposite character—one whose mind must be of a more bold and independent cast, and who is less concerned about giving offence. The letter is said to have been written by Lord Orford to the Secretary of the Norwich Tract Society, in answer to an application made to him to become its President:—

"Sir—I am both surprised and annoyed by the contents of your letter—surprised, because my well known character should have exempted me from such an application; and annoyed, because it obliges me to have even this communication with you. I have long been addicted to the gaming table—I have lately taken to the turf—I fear I frequently blaspheme—but I have never distributed religious tracts. All this was well known to you and your Society; notwithstanding which, you think me a fit person for your President! God forgive your hypocrisy! I would rather live in the land of sinners than with such saints. I am, &c."—The Reformer.

Editor's Tour.

I HAVE just returned home from a tour of more than three months, and have only time, before the close of the present number, to inform the readers of this paper, that, like those who say they have travelled in quest of knowledge, I have come home richly laden with intelligence derived from observation, conversation with many of the most intelligent and pious teachers of the christian religion, and from reflection on religious men and things of our own times. There is a great difference between sitting by the fire and reading the geography of a country, and travelling over its surface. We can read of mountains and hills, without the toil of climbing them; of rivers and morasses, without the perils of crossing them; of plains, fields, and meadows, without the pleasure of tasting their fragrance or feasting on the beauties of nature which they present to the eye of admiration. But in travelling it is all reality. The steep ascent must be with toil subdued. The desert must be traversed with patience and perseverance. The objects that salute the senses are not so fugitive as the characters on paper, which are soon left behind by the eye and mind of the reader. There is, moreover, a difference between words and things, which is easily apprehended by the most superficial observer. We can read of some tremendous battle, in which thousands have been slain, with less than half the emotion which we feel in seeing one man shot or gibbeted. This is a happy circumstance in the constitution of man, as respects temporal objects.

Owing to the character this work has assumed, I was necessarily called upon for explanations, presented with many interrogations, and drawn into many discussions. For more than two months my public speeches and private discussions and conversation on religious topics, averaged at least five hours per diem. That in so much speaking, and with so great a variety of character, talent, and information, I should not have profited much, would be rather strange. Of whatever advantage my tour has been to others, in these respects, it has doubtless been of much to me. The kingdom and dominion of the clergy, the necessity of a restoration of the ancient order of things, and the proper method of accomplishing it, have opened with greater clearness to my view.

I trust I shall be able to render this work
45

much more interesting to the community than it has hitherto been. A greater variety will be given to its pages, as the necessity for long essays on subjects purely sentimental, will not, we anticipate, much longer exist.

———

In many towns and neighborhoods in this western world, it becomes necessary, in order to success in any business or profession, that a person profess some sectarian creed. In some places, it is true, that there is a majority of non-professors; amongst these a man without any creed may succeed. These situations are, however, comparatively few, and still becoming fewer. The only chance of success in most places for a non-professor of a sectarian creed, (and there are many who seem to understand it,) is, to pay a tribute of respect, or a tribute of money, to the more powerful or more popular creed in his vicinity. Next to this, it behoves him to speak "charitably" of all. But wo awaits him who has so little policy as to profess no creed, and at the same time to speak disrespectfully of any or of all. William Pedibus, the shoemaker, lost the custom of all the Presbyterians in town, because he said that Parson Trim denied free agency. And Thomas Vulcanus, the blacksmith, never shod a Methodist's horse since the time he censured Elder Vox's sermon on the possibility of falling from grace. John Paidogogus, the free thinker, though an excellent teacher, lost the school of the village Romance, because his competitor, though of limited acquisitions and less talents, could say "*shibboleth.*" The editor of the "Times" failed to continue his paper, more than six months, in the county of Knox, because of his editorial remarks on the avarice of a clergyman in his neighborhood, who sued at law, through the trustees of his congregation, three widows and four paupers, for seven and sixpence a piece. Having failed, and made his hegira to the county of Hopkins, he commenced with some encomiums on a sermon of the Rev. Bene Placit—his subscription list was speedily and greatly enlarged, and by frequenting three meeting houses in town in due succession, and by giving a little stipend to the three parsons in town, he has got rich by his editorial labors. The motto to his paper is very *apropos:* it reads, "*Experientia docet.*" His former motto was, "*Principia non homines.*" Joannes Baptistus lost an election to congress, because his rival, John Melancthon, was taken up by two Congregational ministers. And the time was, in Western Pennsylvania, when the candidate taken up by the Presbyterian congregations, was carried over all opposition from superior talents, erudition, and fidelity. But since the father of the western Presbyterians failed to elect a governor for Pennsylvania by a single letter of recommendation, so marvellous as to exceed the power of faith, the congregational ticket scheme has been completely dropped.

In the agonizing struggle for the next President, it has been alleged by some that the wife of General Jackson is a pious Presbyterian, and some have been so bold as to say that the General himself either was, or was about to be a ruling elder. Mr. Adams, too, is a Congregational saint, as his friends say; but Messrs. Crawford and Clay are neither sanctified themselves, nor by their wives; and, see, how far they are behind. In fine, the sectarian creeds, according to their popularity, less or more, fill the chairs in the legislative halls of the states,

and even threaten the seat of the chief magistrate of the United States. Synods, too, like the first Popes, have actually passed resolutions approbatory of the measures of government; thereby shewing the right, and reserving the power, to pass resolutions disapprobatory of the proceedings of government, when either their temper or the times require it. Indeed, sectarian pride, ambition, and avarice threaten, evidently threaten the continuance of our present free and beneficent institutions.

But this is not all. Modern sectaries are so consolidating their energies and their influence, that in many of our towns and neighborhoods, when a young man gets himself a wife, he must either join some sect, or, at least, support one, if he intends to have bread and butter. Thus inducements are presented to hypocrisy, and men are forced into a profession which neither their judgment nor their inclination prompts them to, but which becomes necessary to success in their calling.

The clergy have ever been the greatest tyrants in every state, and at present they are, in every country in Europe, on the side of the oppressors of the people who trample on the rights of men. Nor are we to suppose that this is an accidental, but an essential characteristic of their assumptions. It is neither the air which they inhale, nor the soil on which they are supported, nor the government under which they live; but the spirit of their pretensions, which generates the hauteur, the ambition, and the love of sway, so generally conspicuous in their character. We know that there are some exceptions; but these only occur where the spirit of the man preponderates over the spirit of the system. It is by no means a marvellous thing to find individuals amongst the clergy exhibiting traits of character very opposite to the distinguishing features of the priesthood. While we cheerfully discriminate, let us cautiously, and with a jealous eye, observe their manœuvres as a fraternity ever to be feared, but never to be trusted, especially as respects the affairs of this present world.

EDITOR.

———

No. 7.]   FEBRUARY 7, 1825.

Essays on the work of the Holy Spirit in the salvation of men.—No. VII.

In the preceding essays on this subject, we have, as far as the limits of this work admitted, glanced at the outlines of those grand and benevolent displays of the Spirit of God, afforded in the revelation and confirmation of the christian religion. His multiform and splendid distributions as the Spirit of Wisdom and the Spirit of Power to the holy apostles, and to many of the first converts to the christian faith, in the introduction of the christian age, have just been noticed.

As the Spirit of Wisdom, he bestowed those gifts of wisdom, of the word of knowledge, of prophecy, and of tongues, to the ambassadors of Messiah, to qualify them to reveal, in words adapted to every ear, the character and achievements of God's only Son, and the benevolent purposes of the Father, through him, towards the human race. As the Spirit of Power, he clothed them with all those magnificent gifts of power over the bodies of men, by which they were always able to prove their mission and demonstrate their authority as the plenipotentiaries of the Son of God. What remains is to notice, with the same brevity, what the scriptures teach us of him as the Spirit of all Goodness. The apostle says: "The fruit of the Spirit is in all goodness, and righteousness, and truth." This fruit, on another occasion, he particularizes thus: "The fruit of the Spirit is love, joy, peace, long suffering, gentleness, goodness, *fidelity, meekness, temperance."

While his distributions, as the Spirit of Wisdom and of Power, were confined to the apostolic age, and to only a portion of the saints that lived in that age, his influences, as the Spirit of all Goodness, were felt and realized by all the primitive saints, and are now felt by all the subjects of the new reign, or by all the citizens of that new kingdom which the God of Heaven set up in the reign of the Cesars. The citizens of this kingdom, which commenced on the literal Mount Zion, and which will extend to all nations, tribes, and tongues, have ever experienced, and will, to the end of time experience, the influences of this Spirit, as the Spirit of all goodness, righteousness, and truth. The full development of these influences requires us to take a brief view of the Old Covenant and the New, or of the Letter and the Spirit.

Whatever illuminations were enjoyed by, and whatever prospective views were communicated to, the ancient saints and Jewish prophets, respecting the christian age, one thing is certain, that the Old, or Sinaitic Covenant, was a covenant of letter, and not a covenant of spirit. It is equally certain and obvious that the Jewish church, with all its privileges, had but the shadows of good things to come; that their condition was as different from ours as flesh and spirit; and their rank as unlike ours, as that of servants and sons. We are authorized in speaking thus by no less a personage than that distinguished Jew and great apostle to the Gentiles—Paul. He represents the Jews as being in the flesh while under the law, or covenant of letter, and the christians as being in the spirit, as under the gospel, or covenant of spirit. He speaks of the service of the Jews as a service in "the oldness of the letter," and of the christians, as a service "in newness of spirit." He speaks of the Jews while under the covenant of letter, as in the bondage of slaves and possessed of the spirit of servants; but when in the covenant of spirit, as being the sons of God and possessed of the spirit of adoption—"not having a second time received the spirit of bondage, but as having received the spirit of adoption, crying, as new-born babes, Abba, Father." Wherefore, he argues, the believing Jews are no longer servants, but raised to the rank of sons.

There are three passages in the writings of Paul to which we will at present refer in illustration of these two covenants. The first in his epistle to the Romans, chap. vii. "For when we were in the flesh, the sinful passions which we had under the law wrought effectually in our members to bring forth to death. But now we are loosed from the law, having died in that by which we were tied; so that we ought to serve in newness of the Spirit, and not in oldness of the letter." So the apostle represents the state of the Jews—first under the covenant of letter, and again under the covenant of spirit. The bondage and fear of the first covenant forms a perfect contrast to the liberty and confidence of the worshippers under the second. As we have given this passage in Macknight's translation, we shall also give it in Thompson's for the comparison of our readers: "For when we were in the flesh the sinful passions which subsisted under the law exerted their energy in our members

* Macknight's Translation.

to bring forth fruit to death; but we are now set free from the law by the death of that by which we were holden, so that we may serve with a new spirit and not by the old letter."

The second passage to which we shall refer, is 2d *Cor.* iii. In this chapter the apostle contrasts the two covenants, the manner of introduction or establishment of each, and the tendency and result of each. The covenants he contrasts by calling the law or old covenant the covenant of letter, and the new, or second covenant, the covenant of spirit. The literal and correct translation of the sixth verse makes this manifest. The apostle says of himself and his associate apostles, "Our sufficiency is of God, who has qualified us [apostles] to be ministers of a new covenant, not of letter, but of spirit. Not a new covenant of letter, but a new covenant of spirit, then, was ministered, or introduced and established by the apostles. The reason of the introduction and establishment of a new covenant of spirit the apostle gives by contrasting the tendency of each; for, adds he, the letter kills, but the spirit gives life. The tendency of the first, or Sinaitic covenant, was to condemnation and death. The tendency of the New Covenant or Testament* is to justification and life. The apostle next and chiefly contrasts the manner of the introduction of each, called the ministration. In strict propriety of speech he does not call the one the ministration of death, nor the other the ministration of spirit; but he speaks designedly and particularly of the manner in which they were ministered or introduced; that is, the manner in which the letter and the spirit, the law and the gospel were introduced. These things premised, and the passage is plain and instructive in the highest degree. Now, says he, if the manner of introducing the letter which ends in death, that letter "of death, engraven in stones," was attended with glory, shall not the manner of introducing [by us apostles] the Spirit be much more attended with glory. Nothing could be more natural, when the apostle had called himself a minister, and while he was defending his mission, than to call the service which he was called to perform, a ministry, or ministration. After being so diffuse in these remarks, we shall now briefly give the sense of the whole passage, varying the terms for the sake of clearness. He has qualified us apostles with suitable and splendid miraculous powers to introduce a new covenant—not of letter, but of spirit. For the covenant of letter issued in death, but the covenant of spirit issues in life. Now if a covenant of pure letter, written and engraven on stones, and which issued in death, was introduced by Moses from God with considerable glory, so that it shone in the face of Moses who introduced it, shall not the introduction of a covenant of spirit from God, by us apostles, which issues in life, be attended with greater glory, inasmuch as spirit is superior to letter, and life more desirable than death. I say—if the introduction of that letter which immediately began to work condemnation, was attended with glory, much more does, in the present time, the introduction of that spirit which puts men in the enjoyment of righteousness, abound in glory. For, again, if that which was only of temporary duration was introduced with glorious accompaniments, much more shall the introduction of this, which is to

* The terms covenant and testament are both the rendering of one and the same term in the original. Where we have testament and covenant the Greeks had one word, viz. *diatheke.*

be permanent, be attended with miraculous accompaniments, incomparably more glorious. Let it be noted that in varying the terms we are not translating; but giving the ideas in other terms for the sake of perspicuity; and let it be remembered that the terms letter and spirit denote the law and gospel, of which the apostle speaks, and above all, that the design of the apostle in this chapter was to vindicate his official character, as one called and qualified to introduce the spirit or new covenant.

We hasten to the third reference, which is designed to illustrate the two former. It is *Heb.* viii. The apostles were the ministers of the new covenant or the persons to whom the service of introducing it was committed, but Jesus is the mediator of it—for the grace came by Jesus Christ. Now then, says the apostle, he has more noble services allotted to him, inasmuch as he is the mediator of a better covenant, [not a mediator of the old one] which is established on better promises, [than the old one.] For if the first covenant had been faultless [but it was not, because it was letter engraven on stones,] there would have been no occasion for a second; for finding fault with them, [who had the letter, which made them faulty by condemning them] he says—by Jeremiah a Jewish prophet,—"Behold, days are coming, says the Lord, when I will make a new covenant [not of letter but of spirit] with the house of Israel and the house of Judah—not such a covenant [of letter] as I made with their fathers on the day when I took them by the hand to lead them out of Egypt (when at Sinai) because they did not abide by that covenant (of letter) of mine; therefore I took no care of them, says the Lord, (but gave them up to their enemies.) This is the covenant I will make with the house of Israel, after these days, (for the letter was to be temporary) says the Lord, I will put my laws into their mind (without letters on stone) and write them upon their hearts, (not by letter but by spirit,) and I will be to them a God and they shall be to me a people. And they shall not (as the people under the letter) teach every man his neighbor, and every man his brother, saying (according to the letter,) Know the Lord, for all shall know me (under this covenant of spirit,) from the least of them to the greatest of them. For I will be merciful to their unrighteousness, and their sins and iniquities I will remember no more." By saying a new covenant, God has made the former old. "Now that (old covenant of letter) which decays and waxes old, is ready to vanish."—*Macknight and Thompson.*

We here see the new covenant is called *spirit,* and the old one *letter.* In the former a letter was presented to the eye, but in the latter it is written on the heart. The tables of the old covenant were marble—the tables of the new covenant are the spirit or mind of man. The letter when engraved upon the marble was as cold and as dead as the marble itself—the gospel, when believed or engraven on the heart, inspires a spirit as active and powerful as the spirit on which it is written. The old covenant left its subjects *in the flesh* where it found them. The *letter* addressed them as men in the flesh, and the covenant when first promulged was marked in the flesh of the subjects by a bloody excision. Neither righteousness nor eternal life was enjoyed by it. The saints under it were saved by the provision of a better covenant. The apostle said if any man might have confidence under that covenant, or *in the flesh,* he might have had

more; and then tells that he was "circumcised the eighth day," &c.—and that "touching the righteousness that was in the law he was blameless;" yet he counted all the privileges he had *in the letter* as nothing, in comparison of the knowledge of Christ. Christians are told by the same instructor, that they "are not in the flesh, but in the spirit; not under the law, but under grace." All the religious institutions under the *letter* terminated in the flesh. They sanctified and purified only as respected the flesh, and could never make them that came to them perfect as pertains to the conscience.

The new covenant is, then, fitly called *a covenant of spirit,* because it respected not the flesh, but the mind of man, and because it is consummated by the spirit of God. There are, it is true, *written words* in the book of the New Testament, as there are *written words* in the book of the law. *But there is a* MORAL *fitness in the words of the* NEW *to be the medium of the inspiration of the Holy Spirit, as the Spirit of all goodness, righteousness, and truth, as there was a* MORAL *fitness in the engraven words of the former, to be the medium of the inspiration of a spirit of bondage, fear and dread.* There is a *natural* fitness in the pen in my hand to form letters on paper, but there is no natural fitness in it to cut down trees. Again, there is a natural fitness in an axe to cut down trees, but no natural fitness in it to answer the purposes of a pen. The exhibition of those attributes of the Deity, which the letter or law presented to them in the flesh, was, in like manner, *morally* fitted to produce guilt, and fear, and bondage. Just so, the exhibition of the inexpressible love, mercy, and condescension of God in the gospel, concerning his Son, is morally fitted to produce peace, love and joy in the minds of those who apprehend it.

In a word, the covenant of letter could not inspire men with the spirit of sons. It demanded what it did not impart strength to yield. It presented a perfect rule, but left the heart unable to conform to its requisitions. The more clearly a Jew understood it, the less comfort he derived from it. It filled his heart with the spirit of bondage, and issued in condemnation and death. Moreover, the law entered that the offence might abound; and it was added to the promise of the inheritance, because of transgression, till the Seed should come. But the new covenant developes that love which is morally adapted to inspire the spirit of adoption.— It makes sons. And because you are sons, God has sent forth the Spirit of his Son into your hearts, crying *Abba,* Father.

Thus far we have viewed the old covenant and the new, with a reference to the developement of the influences of the Holy Spirit, as the spirit of goodness, righteousness, and truth in the hearts of the faithful. We have merely noticed the means which God has employed, that his spirit might dwell in his church as in a temple. Submitting these remarks to the consideration of our readers, we shall postpone further remarks on this subject till our next.   EDITOR.

A Restoration of the Ancient Order of Things.
No. I.
Extract from the Minutes of the Baptist Missionary Association of Kentucky, began and held at the Town-Fork Meeting House, in Fayette county, on Saturday, the 11th September, 1824.

" THE next meeting of this association will be in the first Baptist meeting house in Lexington,

* This will be further developed in our next essay on this subject.

on the 30th of July next, which will be on the fifth Saturday of that month, at eleven o'clock, A. M.

" It is proposed also to have a meeting of all the Baptist preachers who can attend, on Friday, the day preceding the meeting of the association, at eleven o'clock, A. M. at the same place, for the purpose of *a general conference* on the state of religion, and on the subject of reform. All the ministers of the gospel in the Baptist denomination favorable to these objects, are invited to attend, and, in the spirit of christian love, by mutual counsel, influence, and exertion, according to the gospel, to aid in advancing the cause of piety in our state.

" *It is obvious to the most superficial observer, who is at all acquainted with the state of christianity and of the church of the New Testament, that much, very much is wanting, to bring the christianity and the church of the present day up to that standard—In what this deficiency consists, and how it is to be remedied, or whether it can be remedied at all, are the points to be discovered and determined.* In the deliberations intended, it is designed to take these subjects into serious consideration, and to report the result by way of suggestion and advisement to the Baptist christian community, and to the churches to which the members of the meeting may particularly belong.— We know very well that nothing can be done *right* which is not done according to the gospel, or done *effectually* which is not done by the authority, and accompanied by the blessing of God. While God must do the work, we desire to know, and to acquiesce in his manner of doing it, and submissively to concur and obediently to go along with it."

The sentences we have *italicised* in the preceding extract, are sentences of no ordinary import. The first of them declares a truth as evident as a sunbeam in a cell, to all who have eyes to see. The second presents a subject of inquiry of paramount importance to all who expect to stand before the Son of God in judgment. It affords us no common pleasure to see christians awaking from their lethargic repose to the consideration of such subjects. That the fact should be acknowledged and lamented, that VERY MUCH IS WANTING TO BRING THE CHRISTIANITY AND THE CHURCH OF THE PRESENT DAY UP TO THE NEW TESTAMENT STANDARD amongst a people so intelligent, so respectable in numbers, and so influential, as the Baptist society in Kentucky; and that leaders of that community, so erudite, so pious, and so influential, should call upon their brethren to lay these things to heart, and to prepare themselves to make an effort towards reform, we hail as a most auspicious event.

As I feel deeply interested in every effort that is made, either among the Baptist or Paido Baptist societies, for the avowed object of reform, and as this subject has become familiar to my mind, from much reflection and a good deal of reading, I trust I shall not be considered as obtrusive in presenting a few remarks on the above extract, or rather in presenting certain thoughts, a favorable opportunity for which it presents.

Since the great *apostacy*, foretold and depicted by the holy apostles, attained to manhood's prime, or rather reached the awful climacteric, many *reformations* in religion have been attempted; some on a large and others on a more restricted scale. The page of history and the experience of the present generation concur in evincing that, *if any of those reformations began in the spirit, they have ended in the flesh.*—

This, indeed, may be as true of the reformers themselves as of their reformations. I believe, at the same time, that the reformers have themselves been benefactors, and their reformations benefits to mankind. I do cheerfully acknowledge, that all they who have been reputed reformers, have been our benefactors, and that we are all indebted to them in our political and religious capacities for their labors. Because they have not done every thing which they might have done, or which they ought to have done, we should not withhold the meed of thanks for what they have done. Although two systems of religion, both end in the flesh, one may be greatly preferable to the other. This will appear evident when it is considered that, amongst religious persecutors, some are more exorable and lenient than others. Now, if there should be two systems of religion that both lead to persecution and issue in it, that one which carries its rage no farther than to the prison and the whipping-post, is greatly to be preferred to that which leads to the torturing wheel and to the faggot. The reason of this is very obvious, for most men would rather be whipped than burned for their religion. In other respects there are differences, which are illustrated by the preceding.

Those reformers are not most deserving of our thanks who stand highest and most celebrated in the annals of reformations. We owe more to John Wickliffe than to Martin Luther, and more, perhaps, to Peter Bruys than to John Calvin. The world is more indebted to Christopher Columbus than to Americus Vespusius, yet the latter supplanted the former in his well earned fame. So it has been amongst religious reformers. The success of every enterprize gives eclat to it. As great and as good men as George Washington have been hung or beheaded for treason.

The reformations most celebrated in the world are those which have departed the least from the systems they professed to reform.— Hence, we have been often told that there is but a paper wall between England and Rome. The church of England, with king Henry or George IV. as her head, though a celebrated reformation, has made but a few and very short strides from her mother, the church of Rome, with the pope at her head. So sensible of this are the good members of the reformed church of England, that they yet give to their king the title of " Defender of the Faith," although the title was first given him by the pope for defending his faith. The reformation of the church of England, effected by Mr. Wesley, which issued in Episcopal Methodism, has entailed the same clerical dominion over that zealous people, which their forefathers complained of in the hierarchies of England and Rome. And not in England only does this dominion exist, but even in these United States, of all regions of the earth the most unfriendly to a religious monarchy, or even a religious oligarchy. The question remains yet to be decided, whether a conference of Methodistic clergy, with its bishop in its chair, and laity at home, is any reformation at all from a conclave of English prelates, headed by a metropolitan or an archbishop. It is even uncertain whether the Methodistic discipline has led more people to heaven, or made them happier on earth, than the rubric or liturgy of England.

All the famous reformations in history have rather been reformations of creeds and of clergy, than of religion. Since the New Testament was finished, it is fairly to be presumed that there cannot be any reformation of religion, properly so called. Though called reformations of religion, they have always left religion where it was. I do not think that King Harry was a whit more religious when he proclaimed himself head of the church of England, than when writing against Luther on the seven sacraments, as a true son of the church of Rome. It is even questionable whether Luther himself, the elector of Saxony, the Marquis of Brandenburg, the Duke of Lunenburg, the Landgrave of Hesse, and the Prince of Anhalt, were more religious men when they signed the Augsburg Confession of Faith than when they formerly repeated their Ave Maria.

Human creeds may be reformed and re-reformed, and be erroneous still, like their authors; but the inspired creed needs no reformation, being, like its author, infallible. The clergy, too, may be reformed from papistical opinions, grimaces, tricks, and dresses, to protestant opinions and ceremonies; protestant clergy may be reformed from protestant to presbyterial metaphysics and forms; and presbyterian clergy may be reformed to independency, and yet the Pope remain in their heart. They are clergy still—and still in need of reformation. Archbishop Laud and Lawrence Greatrake are both clergymen, though of different dimensions. The spirit of the latter is as lordly and pontifical as that of the former, though his arm and his gown are shorter. The moschetto is an animal of the same genus with the hornet, though the bite of the former is not so powerful as the sting of the latter. A creed, too, that is formed in Geneva or in London, is as human as one formed in Constantinople. They have all given employment to tax gatherers, jail-keepers, and grave diggers.

All reformations in religious opinions and speculations have been fated like the fashions in apparel. They have lived, and died, and revived, and died again. As apparel has been the badge of rank, so have opinions been the badge of parties, and the cause of their rise and continuance. The green and orange ribbon, as well as the blue stocking, have been as useful and as honorable to those that have worn them, as those opinions were to their possessors, which have been the shibboleths of religious parties.

Human systems, whether of philosophy or of religion, are proper subjects of reformation; but christianity cannot be reformed. Every attempt to reform christianity is like an attempt to create a new sun, or to change the revolutions of the heavenly bodies—unprofitable and vain. In a word we have had reformations enough. The very name has become as offensive, as the term "Revolution" in France.

A restoration of the ancient order of things is all that is necessary to the happiness and usefulness of christians. No attempt " to reform the doctrine, discipline and government of the church," (a phrase too long in use,) can promise a better result than those which have been attempted and languished to death. We are glad to see, in the above extract, that the thing proposed, is to bring the christianity and the church of the present day up to the standard of the New Testament. This is in substance, though in other terms, what we contend for. To bring the societies of christians up to the New Testament, is just to bring the disciples individually and collectively, to walk in the faith, and in the commandments of the Lord and Saviour, as presented in that blessed volume; and this is to restore the ancient order of things. Celebrated as the era of reformation is, we doubt not but that the era of restoration will as far transcend it in impor-

tance and fame, through the long and blissful Millennium, as the New Testament transcends in simplicity, beauty, excellency, and majesty, the dogmas and notions of the creed of Westminster and the canons of the Assembly's Digest. Just in so far as the ancient order of things, or the religion of the New Testament, is restored, just so far has the Millennium commenced, and so far have its blessings been enjoyed. For to the end of time, we shall have no other revelation of the Spirit, no other New Testament, no other Saviour, and no other religion than we now have, when we understand, believe and practise the doctrine of Christ delivered to us by his apostles.   Editor

---

A Presbyterian University at Danville, Ky.

A Bill has been before the legislature of Kentucky for the incorporation of a University at Danville, 32 miles from Lexington, the seat of the Transylvania University; and for vesting the whole institution, its government and control, in the Presbyterian synod of Kentucky, not only till the millennium commence, but for ever. We have not yet understood the fate of this bill. We saw an unusual assemblage of the clergy of this synod at Frankfort, in November last; at which time, the reverend members of the synod were sweetly and gently opening the way for the introduction of the above bill. I not only hope, but I believe, the legislature of Kentucky understands the principles of republican government, of civil and religious liberty, better than to create or incorporate universities, and then to give them into the hands of any number of clergy, how intelligent and virtuous soever, for the purpose of subordinating them to a religious aristocracy. If the Synod of Kentucky stand in need of a college *de propaganda fide* for the propagation of their religion, let them build and endow themselves. To solicit the legislature to incorporate and to endow a University, and to give the control of it to a body of divines, is a very plain way of telling the public, that they intend to manage it for their own purposes, and not for state purposes. If the legislature, in their wisdom, think that it is necessary to incorporate and endow another University in the state, it must be either for the religious or literary interest of the state. If the literary interests of the state require it, why vest the control of it in an aspiring ecclesiastical body? Why endow, or even invest with corporate powers, a seminary for the advancement of classical and scientific knowledge in the state, and then give it to one religious establishment to convert it into an engine for their own sinister purposes—I say sinister, for their purposes are not the same as the purposes of the state in erecting an institution merely for literary objects.

But if on the other hypothesis, the legislature deem it expedient to erect, incorporate, or endow a literary institution for the religious interests of the state; why then give the preference to any one religious party, as there is no state religion in Kentucky? If the legislature incorporate a University for creating priests, let all the religious sects in Kentucky, who desire to have priests manufactured in modern style, have a fair, that is, an equal chance of participating in its advantages. I think that all the priests should have an equal chance. But, perhaps, it may be thought expedient to have a few high priests in the state; if so, then, do not give the control of the University to the Presbyterian synod, for they stand in the least need of it, inasmuch as they are pretty generally
50

high priests already. I do not know that the Presbyterian synod have any stronger claims upon the people's money, or the time and powers of the legislature, than any other good citizen of the state. Why, then, take them by the hand and aid and abet them in any sectarian project?

But, as I said before, if the literary interests of the state require the incorporation and the consequent endowment (for to give birth to an institution of this kind, and not to feed, and cherish, and nurse it, would be cruel!!) of another university, let the state retain, in its control, the management of it, and entrust it not in the hands of a would-be religious nobility. Knowing, however, that the legislature will act (or perhaps have already acted) as in their wisdom they think most conducive to the public weal, we shall only take a peep into the spirit of the synod in urging this matter.

What sort of a spirit do they exhibit in this effort? What moved them to solicit such a favor for themselves, to the exclusion of all other christian sects? I see in them the spirit of the two sons of Zebedee. They beg for the highest places in the kingdom. They obsequiously approach the legislature of Kentucky, and pray them to grant that their sons may sit at their right hand in their dominion and rule. I trust the legislature will feel the same indignation at their request, as the other disciples felt at the request of the two brethren, headed by their old mother. How like the spirit of circumcision, and of the commonwealth of Israel, is the spirit of the synod! They will yet be the circumcision, to whom pertain the oracles, the covenants, and the colleges! How modest their requests, and how benevolent and humble too! Let us have the high places in the land, for we deserve them better than other sects; we can make a better use of them; we are up—we wish to be higher, and to see our brethren among the vulgus. We want the throne—we know how to wield the sceptre; for we were born to rule, and other religious sectaries to obey. We are no friends to equal rights and immunities—we would rather have peculiar rights and privileges ourselves.

Yes, says the spirit of the synod, I have always been the pampered child in my mother's house; I cannot live like the other children of the family. I was never used to make my living by the bible and common sense; no, I have been fed, and nursed, and strengthened by good Latin and Greek and science. My brothers and sisters are hardy fellows; they can maintain themselves, or endure hardships. I have never been accustomed to such homely fare. Let them stand aloof, for I am holier than they. I am Jacob—they are Esau. Let them go and dwell in Mount Seir—I shall dwell in the goodly land, and must have the excellency. Yea, I am Joseph whom his father loved. I have always worn the variegated coat; and in former times ruled Egypt. Yes, I am that Joseph to whom his brethren bowed; that Joseph who taxed the Egyptians and mortgaged their lands to Pharaoh. Why, then, refuse me the throne, seeing I have so long sat thereon, and so long sworn by the life of Pharaoh? You princes of Egypt, you rulers and senators of the land, withhold not from me my rights and my honors. Bless me with your smiles and your money, and I will bless you with my prayers. Yes, I will pray for your long life, and in the days of famine you shall not starve; for I will give you goodly portions; indeed you shall be as Benjamin mine own brother; and a portion like that of Benjamin's shall be

yours. But if you will not exalt me now in my humiliation, the Philistine shall come upon you; yea, the Philistines from Philistina—and your wives and your little ones shall be for a prey to them that hate you.

Such is the language of the spirit of this synod which would rather reign in Danville than serve in Transylvania. I hope the legislature have admonished them to go home and study their religion a little better, and to endeavor to exhibit that humility and benevolence to all, which ought at least, to have some appearance in their character, and at the same time, have told them, it is not theirs to grant the sovereignty to them, rather than to others equally worthy, though not quite so clamorous as they.   EDITOR.

Oath of Allegiance to the Seceder Clergy; or to the principles of the associate synod of North America.

WITHIN a few months past, some of the congregations of Seceders, or, as they call themselves, the Associate Presbytery of Pennsylvania, have been swearing loyalty to their opinions and their clergy. This is the consummation of priestcraft, and an awful lesson to their cotemporaries, of the tremendous length to which an infatuated people may be led by the nose by a cunningly zealous and aspiring priesthood. Some of them no doubt, are conscientious too; for those that count their beads, and say prayers to St. Andrew, and the Holy Virgin, and kill heretics, are conscientious too. I have heard men swear most profanely, and in the same breath pray to God to forgive them. But really that, in the United States of North America, in the autumn of 1824, a congregation should be found so priest-ridden, as it appears most of these congregations are, is, to me, a phenomenon. From eighty to one hundred members of one of these congregations, in this vicinity, a few weeks ago swore as follows:

"We do, with our hands lifted up to the Most High God, hereby profess, and, before God, angels, and men, solemnly declare, that we desire to give glory to the Lord, by believing with the heart, confessing with the mouth, and subscribing with the hand, that in him we have righteousness and strength. We avouch the Lord to be our God; and in the strength of his promised grace, we promise and swear, by the great and holy name of the Lord our God, that we shall unfeignedly endeavor to walk in his ways, to keep his commandments, and to hearken to his voice, in love to him who has delivered us out of the hand of our enemies; and to serve him without fear, in holiness and righteousness before him all the days of our life.

"And seeing many at this time in a state of progressive apostacy from the cause and testimony of Jesus Christ, and many snares are laid to draw us after them; though sensible that we are in ourselves as liable to go astray as any, yet, entreating the Lord to hold up our goings in his paths, that our footsteps slip not, and trusting that through his mercy we shall not be moved forever, we do solemnly engage before him that lives forever and ever, that in every place where we may in providence be called to reside, and during all the days of our life, we shall continue steadfast in the faith, profession, and obedience of the true reformed religion, in doctrine, worship, Presbyterial church government and discipline. as the same is held forth in the word of God, and received in this church, and testified for by it, against the manifold errors and latitudinarian schemes prevailing in the United States of North America."

Now let it be noted that all this parade of words of solemn sound and awful moment, interspersed through this long oath, an extract of which has been given, and all the other clauses of this solemn oath are merely subservient to this one point, viz. " We solemnly engage [their hands at the same time lifted up to heaven] before Him that lives forever and ever, that in every place where we may be called to reside, and during all the days of our lives, we shall continue steadfast in the faith, profession, and obedience of the true reformed religion, [i. e. we shall continue Seceders] in doctrine, worship, Presbyterial church government and discipline, as the same is held forth to us in the word of God, [a mere manœuvre, as the next words show,] and received in this church and testified for by it." In plain English, I swear by him that lives forever and ever, that I will continue in the belief of the doctrine, worship, Presbyterial church government, and discipline, as received by the Secession church, go wheresoever I may, and as long as I live. Yes, " as testified to by it." Now any man of common sense, who reads the "Declaration and Testimony of this church," may at once see the import of the oath. In the Declaration and Testimony, page 118, they testify against all christians, who will not subscribe to, and contend for, written confessions of faith drawn up by fallible men. In page 121, they testify against all who oppose the duty of covenanting, or who assert that it is not a duty in New Testament times. They also testify against singing any other psalms or hymns than king David's, and against occasional communion with other churches, and constructively against occasionally hearing any other preacher than a Seceder. They might have shortened the oath, and have rendered it more plain, and more easy to be remembered. Thus—I swear I am a Seceder now; and I will be a Seceder while I live; and I swear that I will avoid every thing that might endanger perjury, by staying at home when I cannot hear a Seceder minister; that I will not in conversation either argue in support of my own sentiments, nor against those that oppose them.*

King Henry called a parliament, and obtained an act requiring all his subjects, under the pain of treason, to swear that he himself was supreme head of the church of England. Yes, and three friars, four monks, with John Fisher, bishop of Rochester, and Sir Thomas Moore, lord chancellor of England, were put to death for refusing to swear that king Henry was head of the church under Christ.†

Now it might be a question amongst moral philosophers and theological casuists, whether he that swears, that during all the days of his life, even to the last breath, he will continue a Presbyterian of the associate order, and he that swears that king Henry or king George is the head of the church, do not exhibit the same ignorance of human nature, and of christian religion; and whether the creatures of the king, or the creatures of the priest, are the more pliant and servile. I think it requires no great skill in mental philosophy to decide that the policy which led the king to require this oath of supremacy in favour of himself, and that which moved the worthy associate divines to require their subjects to swear allegiance to them, under the mask of supporting the true religion, is one and the same policy.

* I have understood that their clergy have given this counsel lest they should perjure themselves.

† Neal's History, vol. 1, page 71.

According to the rules of interpretation of former oaths and covenants, adopted by this religious community, the obligations of this oath are hereditary; their children now existing, and those yet unborn, are under its sanction, and are bound to be of the same true religion of their fathers. I am informed by those who witnessed this strange and awful scene of priestly domination and lavish servility, that it was performed with all the awkwardness of a militia muster. The priest obliged to keep his eye upon the book in reading the oath, and upon the behaviour of those before his altar, who at a signal given, were to lift their hands, and continue in a certain posture until informed to change their attitude. O! that some intelligent and benevolent tongue could have addressed the poor people, and have told them the nature and design of what they were about to do, before they lifted up their hands to heaven to swear that they would be Seceders all the days of their lives!*

EDITOR.

History of the English Bible.—No. I.

FOR the information of those of limited reading, we design to give a few historical facts respecting the progress of the English bible. The importance and utility of these historical notices will be apparent as we proceed.

It is a remarkable coincidence in the history of all the noted reformers from Popery, that they all gave a translation of the scriptures in the vernacular tongue of the people whom they labored to reform. There are other striking coincidences in the history of these men which may hereafter be noticed. John Wickliffe, who was born 1324, and died 1384, was the first reformer that disturbed the peace and unity of the church of Rome, and he was the first man that translated the New Testament into the English language. One of the errors which the popular clergy of that day laid to his charge, was, that he taught—that the New Testament is a perfect rule of life and manners, and ought to be read by the people. He also taught that there were but two officers in the christian church, viz. the bishops and the deacons. "That christians must practise and teach only the laws of Christ." His disciples were called Lollards. Wickliffe's Testament was in manuscript circulated amongst the laity and read with great avidity. But the reading of this blessed volume was attended with great danger, for in the beginning of Henry Fifth's reign a law was passed, which enacted— " That whosoever they were, that should read the scriptures in the mother tongue, (which was

* The philosophy of this mysterious thing is hid from the vulgar. I will explain it—The Presbyterians of the General Assembly and Dr. John Mason's Presbyterians are generally more popular than the Seceders. They are not quite so contracted as the members of the Secession. Their preachers not quite such old fashioned, moonshine, clear, cold, and pious orators as the Secession ministry but somewhat modernized. There was some danger of the people of the associate Presbytery falling in with and uniting with their other Presbyterian neighbors, especially since Dr. Mason's Plea for Catholic Communion appeared —and consequently the most popular preachers and parties would, by and by, engross the most of the Seceders. The Seceder ministry foreseeing this, knowing their own talents too, and fearing to risque their future destinies on such an experiment, determined to revive the remembrance of the former misdeeds of their Presbyterian forefathers in Scotland, and to widen the breach between themselves and their more popular neighboring preachers. They insisted on receiving the old covenants, adapted to existing circumstances, and after long drilling, have got many of their people secured from apostacy, by the impregnable bulwark of an oath, binding forever on themselves and their posterity. Knowing the policy of the measure, I hesitate not to call it " a consummation of priestcraft."

then called reproachfully Wicleu's Learning,) they should forfeite lande, catel, lif, and godes, from theyre heyres forever, and so be condempned for heretykes to God, enemies to the crowne, and moste errant traitors to the lande." So great was the rage of the clergy against reading the New Testament in English, when it first made its appearance. Every one who read it was suspected of heresy, and many were suspected of having read it, against whom it could not be proved, because they were a little more intelligent than their neighbors. For the reading of this volume will soon make a layman more intelligent than a priest who only uses it as a text book. John Keyser became so intelligent as to say, that although the Archbishop of Canterbury had excommunicated him, " he was not excommunicated before God, for his corn yielded as well as his neighbors." This much light was however dangerous to this man, for he was committed to jail for knowing and saying this much. This happened in the reign of Edward VI.

John Wickliffe made his translation, A. D. 1367, not from the Greek but from the vulgate New Testament as read in the Catholic church. This vulgate, which was read for many centuries, was a correction of the old Italic version, conjectured to have been made in the middle of the second century, not long after the first Syriac version was made. The old Italic was made from the Greek and Old Testament from the Septuagint. Jerome, A. D. 382, translated the Old Testament into Latin from the Septuagint, or rather corrected from the old Italic version. The Italic version, mended by Jerome, has been long in great repute amongst the Romanists, and is what is commonly called the Vulgate, from which Wickliffe gave the first English New Testament.					EDITOR.

No. 8.]					March 7, 1825.

Essays on the work of the Holy Spirit in the salvation of men.—No. VIII.

Ever since the creation of the heavens and the earth, God has always employed means, fitted to the ends he designed to accomplish. Indeed, the creation of this mundane state, is a creation of means suited to certain results. The means, as well as the end, are the creatures of God. His wisdom is most strikingly conspicuous, through all his works, in adapting his means to his ends. When he designs to bless the inhabitants of this globe with abundance of food, he sends the early and the latter rain. But does he intend to scourge them with famine? then the heavens become as brass, and the earth as iron. Or, perhaps, to vex them more grievously, he sends forth his armies of insects, apparently imbecile, but terribly victorious and puissant by their numbers. Or does he waste the race of men by diseases incurable? then the pestilence is inhaled in every breath, and a burning impetus given to every pulse, the means of which elude the philosopher's eye, and triumph over the physician's hand. When ships are to be engulphed in the fathomless ocean, and their crews buried beneath the foundations of the mountains; when forests, and villages, and cities, are to be prostrated to the earth in his vengeance, the whirlwind marches forth in awful grandeur, and knows no restraint but the will of him who rides upon its wings; or the earth rent with internal fires, trembles to its centre, and, while in convulsive throes, it spues up new islands in the ocean, it swallows myriads of men and their devices in a single respiration. Or, perhaps in the multitude of his resources, he sends the flaming thunderbolts, which fall with resistless power on those doomed to a more instantaneous destruction.

The means are always suited to the end. In the accomplishment of a moral renovation, or regeneration of the human mind, the same fitness in the means employed is exhibited in every respect. No new faculties are created in the human mind, nor are any of the old ones annihilated—no new passions, nor affections are communicated. He that possessed a quick perception, a steady and retentive memory, a strong discriminating judgment, a vigorous and vivid imagination before he was regenerated, possesses the same without any change after he has been renewed in the spirit of his mind. Indeed, the whole temperament of the human mind remains the same after as before. He that was before of a volatile, irascible, bold and resolute temperament, or the contrary, is the same when regenerate. The biography of Saul of Tarsus, and of Paul, the apostle; of Simon, son of Jonas, and of the apostle Peter; of John, the son of Zebedee, and of John, the apostle, fully and unanswerably demonstrate and confirm these remarks. Indeed, who does not admit that men perceive, remember, reason, love and hate, fear and hope, rejoice and tremble, after they have been regenerated, as before. The experience of every man concurs in this fact. The renovation of the human mind, or the purification of the human heart, is not then affected by a new creation of faculties or affections, which would be the same as creating a new soul. The soul or spirit of Saul of Tarsus was the soul or spirit of Paul the apostle. The spirit of Saul was not destroyed and a new spirit infused into Paul; for then the spirit of Saul was annihilated, and not saved. It appears, then, that the faculties of the human spirit and the affections of the human mind are affected no more by regeneration than the height of the human stature, the corpulency of the human body, or the color of the human skin are affected by it. The memoirs of every saint recorded in the bible are appealed to as proof of this.

If, then, as is proved, no new faculties are created, no new passions nor affections bestowed in regeneration, it may be asked, What does the *renewal of the Holy Spirit* mean? The scriptures authorize us in declaring that it consists in presenting new objects to the faculties, volitions, and affections of men; which *new objects* apprehended, engage the faculties or powers of the human understanding, captivate the affections and passions of the human soul, and, consequently, direct or draw the whole man into new aims, pursuits, and endeavors.

A partial illustration of this may be taken from the history of Joseph, governor of Egypt, and David, king of Israel. Joseph and David, in their childhood and youth, were employed in the cares, enjoyments, and pursuits of the shepherd's life. All their faculties of understanding, all their passions and affections as boys, were engrossed in the rural objects attendant on the shepherd's life. When elevated to the throne, their powers of understanding, affections, and passions were engrossed in the affairs of state, in the concerns of human government and royalty. A great change in their views, feelings, and pursuits, was necessarily effected by an entire change of objects. Or suppose an African child were transplanted from a Virginian hut to an African palace, at the age of ten or twelve; new scenes, new objects of contemplation, a new education, new companions, and new objects of pursuit, would revolutionize its whole mind, affections, and passions. But all these instances, although it might with truth be said, "Old things are passed away and all things are become new;" yet their mental faculties, powers of volition, and affections, are the same as when boys. This is, as was said, but a partial illustration; for in that renewed state of which we are speaking, heavenly objects of contemplation and pursuit are presented to all that is within man, and the change produced rises to a level with the magnitude, purity, and glory of the objects proposed. But lest we should get into metaphysical speculations, and fall into the errors we labor to correct, let it suffice to say, that before we can understand or admire the wisdom of God, in the adaptation of the means of regeneration, we must first know what the renewal of the Holy Spirit is. If regeneration, or the renovation of the human mind, were the result of the mere creative energy of the Divine Spirit, then, indeed, it were vain for us to talk of any means of renovation; then, indeed, a revelation in words, spoken or written—preaching or reading, are idle and unmeaning. This matter is at once determined with the utmost certainty, not by human speculations, nor reasonings, but by a sure and infallible testimony; and on this alone would we rest our views. Paul declares that Jesus Christ told him that he would send him to the gentiles to accomplish the following results: "To open their eyes, to turn them from darkness to light, and from the power of Satan to God; that they might receive forgiveness of sins and inheritance among them which are sanctified by faith that is in me." *Acts,* xxvi. 18. Or, as it is more correctly translated by Thomson, "To open their eyes that they may turn from darkness to light, and from the power of Satan to God; that they may receive a remission of sins and an inheritance among them who are sanctified *by the belief in me.*" Such was the object of the Messiah in sending Paul to the gentiles. Now who will not say, that when all this was done, those gentiles were regenerated or renewed in the spirit of their minds, and that the presentation of new objects to the mind was the means employed for the accomplishment of this end? Their turning from darkness to light, and from the power of Satan to God, are made dependant on, and consequent to, the opening of their eyes; and we all know that Paul, when sent to open their eyes, always presented to their minds new objects, or *the light of the world.* And, indeed, this was all he was commissioned to do, because it was all that Jesus Christ deemed necessary to be done, and all that Paul was empowered or capacitated to do. There was, then, the same fitness in the means Jesus Christ employed to the end proposed, as appears in the whole kingdom of means and ends. Paul declares that the ministry of reconciliation was committed to him as to the other apostles, and that the *word of reconciliation* was summarily comprehended in this one sentence: "God was in Christ reconciling a world to himself, not reckoning to them their transgressions; for he has made him who knew no sin a sin offering for us, that by him we may be made the righteousness of God." The means employed to reconcile enemies must ever fail of effecting a reconciliation, unless the means are adapted to their state and character. Now herein consists the great and the apparent difference between the majority of the popular preaching and the apostle's preaching. The former pays no attention to the suitableness of

means, but the latter always did. This we shall be at some pains to illustrate. Let a popular preacher of one school preach his gospel to a congregation he desires to see converted, and somewhere in his sermon a few dogmas of his school are presented to neutralize the other parts, or to orthodoxize the whole of it. He will say, it is true, that "natural men are spiritually dead, and as unable to believe in the Messiah as they are to scale heaven by a rope of sand, or to create something out of nothing;" or he tells the people that "God has foreordained a part of the world to everlasting life, and left the rest in their imbecile and bankrupt circumstances to sink down into everlasting death; that for these Christ died, and for a great portion of the human race no sacrifice was offered: no man can believe unless he to whom it is given;" and it must remain a matter of awful uncertainty whether any of the congregation he addresses are among those for whom Christ died, or to whom it shall be given to believe. Another preacher, of another school, tells his unconverted hearers that "their *wills* are as free to good as to evil, and that they are as able to believe in the Messiah as they are to eat and drink; that Christ died for all mankind, savage and civilized; and that it is still uncertain whether any of his congregation will be saved or not, or whether those who now believe will be saved or damned; but God did not foreordain the salvation or damnation of any man." These dogmas of the two great schools are continually heard from a vast majority of all the pulpits in the land. For, in fact, although there are perhaps ten thousand preachers in the land speaking every Sabbath day in all the synagogues, yet but two men speak in them all—and these two are John Calvin and James Arminius. Now it must be confessed that such preachers were not the apostles. Such means as these the Spirit of God never did employ in the conversion of Jews and Gentiles, in the age of primitive simplicity. And the reason is obvious, for there is no moral fitness or suitableness in those means to the end proposed. For what fitness is there to produce faith in telling a man that he cannot believe? or what fitness is there in telling a man that until he is quickened or regenerated by the Spirit of God, he cannot become a disciple of Christ in truth? Can such dogmas, however solemnly declared, or however often repeated, cause the Spirit to descend or to regenerate the man? But he must say these things in order to be, or to appear to be, orthodox! Again, what fitness is there to produce faith in telling a man that he is able to believe? Did ever a discourse upon what is called "the freedom of the human will," or men's natural powers, incline a man to choose what is good, or cause him to exert his displayed powers to believe? As rationally might one man attempt to persuade another to go to Spain or the Cape of Good Hope, by telling him his will was free to choose or to refuse, and that his natural abilities were sufficient. All such preaching is as absurd as it is unprecedented in the New Testament.

I enter not into the merits or abstract truth of the above systems. This would be to run the same old metaphysical race again. Some of those dogmas may be metaphysically true, but they are distilled truths. They have come from the Calvinistic or Arminian distillery. That is, in other words, certain parts of the bible, mingled with philosophy, and put through a Calvinistic or Arminian process of distillation, issue in these abstract notions. The men who deal in those distilled truths, and those who drink those distilled doctrines, are generally intoxicated. For even here there is a certain analogy between the revelation of God, and the corn and wheat of God. When the whole wheat or corn of God are used for food in their undistilled state, or when eaten in all their component parts, those who eat them are healthy and enjoy life; but when the component parts of those grains are separated by a chemical process, and the distilled spirit presented to human lips, men cannot live upon these spirits, but become intoxicated, and in process of time, sicken and die. This analogy is complete. They who believe and obey the New Testament, as God has presented it, live upon it, and enjoy life and spiritual health; but they who attempt to live upon those theories sicken and die. Those who feed themselves upon their free will and sufficient strength, often take care not to will to obey the apostle's doctrine; and those who complain that the will is not free, often appear " freely willing" to neglect the great salvation.

But some of the orthodox contend that it is not safe to permit a man to preach, or to speak to men on religion, who will not expressly and publicly declare that his theory is that men cannot believe unless they are first regenerated by the Spirit of God. This is the consummation of absurdity on their own principles. For surely they do not think that the Spirit of God will suspend or change the order of its operations according to the opinion of the speaker. On their theory, the Spirit of God will operate in its own way, whatever be the private theory of the speaker; and whether a man think or do not think that men can believe only as the Spirit of God works faith in them, the result on their own principles must be the same. But we have gone farther into this subject than was intended. I had intended, in this essay, merely to illustrate that there is a moral fitness in the word of reconciliation to become the means of the impartation of that Spirit of Goodness which we stated in our last as the peculiar characteristic of the covenant of Spirit, under which all christians live. And how much happier would the majority of Christians be, if, instead of eagerly contending about the fashionable theories of religion, they would remember that every good and perfect gift comes down from the Father of Lights —that he has promised his Holy Spirit to them that ask him, and that every necessary blessing is bestowed upon all them who, believing that God is a rewarder of them that diligently seek him, ask for those favors comprised in the love of God, the grace of the Lord Jesus Christ, and the fellowship of the Holy Spirit.　　　EDITOR

A Restoration of the Ancient Order of Things.
No. II.

HAD the founder of the christian faith been defective in wisdom or benevolence, then his authority, his testimony, and his commandments, might be canvassed with as little ceremony as the discoveries and maxims of our compeers and cotemporaries; then his religion might be improved, or reformed, or better adapted to existing circumstances. But as all christians admit that he foresaw and anticipated all the events and revolutions in human history, and that the present state of things was as present to his mind as the circumstances that encompassed him in Judea, or in the judgment hall of Caiaphas; that he had wisdom and understanding perfectly adequate to institute, arrange, and

adapt a system of things, suitable to all exigencies and emergencies of men and things, and that his philanthropy was not only unparalleled in the annals of the world, but absolutely perfect, and necessarily leading to, and resulting in, that institution of religion which was most beneficial to man in the present and future world. I say all these things being generally, if not universally agreed upon by all christians, then it follows, by the plainest and most certain consequence, that the institution of which he is the author and founder, can never be improved or reformed. The lives or conduct of his disciples may be reformed, but his religion cannot. The religion of Rome, or of England, or of Scotland may be reformed, but the religion of Jesus Christ never can. When we have found ourselves out of the way we may seek for the ancient paths, but we are not at liberty to invent paths for our own feet. We should return to the Lord.

But a restoration of the ancient order of things, it appears, is all that is contemplated by the wise disciples of the Lord; as it is agreed that this is all that is wanting to the perfection, happiness, and glory of the christian community. To contribute to this is our most ardent desire—our daily and diligent inquiry and pursuit. Now, in attempting to accomplish this, it must be observed, that it belongs to every individual and to every congregation of individuals to discard from their faith and their practice every thing that is not found written in the New Testament of the Lord and Saviour, and to believe and practise whatever is there enjoined. This done, and every thing is done which ought to be done.

But to come to the things to be discarded, we observe that, in the ancient order of things, there were no creeds or compilations of doctrine in abstract terms, nor in other terms other than the terms adopted by the Holy Spirit in the New Testament. Therefore all such are to be discarded. It is enough to prove that they ought to be discarded, from the fact that none of those now in use, nor ever at any time in use, existed in the apostolic age. But as many considerations are urged why they should be used, we shall briefly advert to these, and attempt to show that they are perfectly irrational, and consequently foolish and vain.

I. It is argued that confessions of faith are or may be much plainer and of much more easy apprehension and comprehension than the oracles of God. Men, then, are either wiser or more benevolent than God. If the truths in the Bible can be expressed more plainly by modern divines than they are by the Holy Spirit, then it follows that either God would not or could not express them in words so plainly as man. If he could, and would not, express them in words so suitable as men employ, then he is less benevolent than they. Again, if he would, but could not express them in words so suitable as men employ, then he is not so wise as they. These conclusions, we think, are plain and unavoidable. We shall thank any advocate of human creeds to attempt to show any way of escaping this dilemma.

But the abstract and metaphysical dogmas of the best creeds now extant, are the most difficult of apprehension and comprehension. They are farther from the comprehension of nine-tenths of mankind than the words employed by the Holy Spirit. We shall give a few samples from the Westminster creed, one of the best in the world:—

Sample 1. "The Father is of none, neither begotten nor proceeding; the Son is eternally begotten of the Father; the Holy Ghost eternally proceeding from the Father and the Son."

Sample 2. "God, from all eternity, did, by the most wise and holy counsel of his own will, freely and unchangeably ordain whatsoever comes to pass; yet so as neither is God the author of sin, nor is violence offered to the will of the creatures, nor is the liberty or contingency of second causes taken away, but rather established."

Sample 3. "Although God knows whatsoever may or can come to pass, upon all supposed conditions; yet has he not decreed any thing because he foresaw it as future, or as that which would come to pass upon such conditions."

Sample 4. "These angels and men, thus predestined and foreordained, are particularly and unchangeably designed, and their number is so certain and definite, that it cannot be either increased or diminished."

Sample 5. "Although in relation to the knowledge and decree of God, the first cause, all things come to pass immutably and infallibly; yet, by the same providence, he orders them to fall out according to the nature of second causes, either necessarily, freely, or contingently."

These samples are taken out of the 2d, 3d, and 5th chapters, and may serve as a fair specimen of the whole. Now the question is, whether are these words more plainly, definitely, and intelligibly expressive of divine truths than the terms used by the Holy Spirit in the scriptures? We do not ask the question, whether these things are taught in the Bible? but merely whether these terms are more plain, definite, and intelligible than the terms used in the Bible? This we refer to the reader's own decision.

II. But, in the second place, it is argued that human confessions of faith are necessary to the unity of the church. If they are necessary to the unity of the church, then the church cannot be united and one without them. But the church of Christ was united and one in all Judea, in the first age, without them; therefore, they are not necessary to the unity of the church. But again, if they are necessary to the unity of the church, then the New Testament is defective; for if the New Testament was sufficient to the unity of the church, then human creeds would not be necessary. If any man, therefore, contend that human creeds are necessary to the unity of the church, he at the same time and by all the same arguments, contends that the scriptures of the Holy Spirit are insufficient—that is, imperfect or defective. Every human creed is based upon the inadequacy, that is, the imperfection of the Holy Scriptures.

But the records of all religious sects, and the experience of all men of observation, concur in attesting the fact that human creeds have contributed always, since their first introduction, to divide and disunite the professors of the christian religion.*

Every attempt to found the unity of the church upon the adoption of any creed of human device, is not only incompatible with the nature and circumstances of mankind, but is an effort to frustrate or to defeat the prayer of the Lord Mes-

* The confirmation of this we shall reserve to another time, when it will be convenient to introduce a detail of historical facts. In our next number we intend to give a brief and faithful compend of the history of the formation of the Westminster Creed, from a source that cannot be questioned.

siah, and to subvert his throne and government. This sentence demands some attention. We shall illustrate and establish the truth which it asserts.

Human creeds are composed of the inferences of the human understanding speculating upon the revelation of God. Such are all those now extant. The inferences drawn by the human understanding partake of all the defects of that understanding. Thus we often observe two men sincerely exercising their mental powers, upon the same words of inspiration, drawing inferences or conclusions, not only diverse but flatly contradictory. This is the result of a variety of circumstances. The prejudices of education, habits of thinking, modes of reasoning, different degrees of information, the influence of a variety of passions and interests, and, above all, the different degrees of strength of human intellect, all concur in producing this result. The persons themselves are very often unconscious of the operation of all these circumstances, and are, therefore, honestly and sincerely zealous in believing and in maintaining the truth of their respective conclusions. These conclusions, then, are always private property, and can never be placed upon a level with the inspired word. Subscription to them, or an acknowledgment of them, can never be rationally required as a bond of union. If, indeed, all christians were alike in all those circumstantial differences already mentioned, then an accordance in all the conclusions which one or more of them might draw from the divine volume, might rationally be expected from them all. But as christians have never yet all possessed the same prejudices, degrees of information, passions, interests, modes of thinking and reasoning, and the same strength of understanding, an attempt to associate them under the banners of a human creed composed of human inferences, and requiring unanimity in the adoption of it, is every way as irrational as to make a uniformity of features, of color, of height and weight, a bond of union. A society of this kind never yet existed, and we may, I think, safely affirm never will. Those societies which unite upon the thirty-nine articles of the Church of England, and the thirty-three chapters of the Kirk of Scotland, do not heartily concur in those creeds. Most of them never read them, and still fewer heartily concur in yielding the same credence, or in reposing the same confidence in them.

Their being held as a nominal bond of union, gives rise to hypocrisy, prevarication, lying, and, in many instances, to the basest injustice. Many men are retained in those communities who are known not to approbate them fully, to have exceptions and objections; but their wealth or some extrinsic circumstance palliates their non-conformities in opinion; whereas others are reproached, persecuted and expelled, who differ no more than they, but there is some interest to consult, some pique, or resentment, or envy to gratify in their excommunication. This is base injustice. Many, like the late Rev. Dr. Scott, subscribe them for preferment. He declared that he was moved by the Holy Spirit to enter into the ministry, and yet he afterwards avowed that then he did not believe that there was any Holy Spirit. This is lying and hypocrisy. These are, however, incidental occurrences. But the number of such cases, and the frequency of their occurrence, are alarming to those who believe that God reigns. Again, the number of items which enter into those creeds is not amongst the least of their absurdities. In the Presbyterian Confession there are thirty-three chapters, and in these one hundred and seventy-one dogmas. In receiving "ministers," or in "licensing preachers," it is ordained that the candidate be asked, "Do you sincerely receive and adopt the Confession of Faith of this church, as containing the system of doctrine taught in the Holy Scriptures." Observe the words, "*the system.*" Yes, the identical system taught in the Scriptures—that is the one hundred and seventy-one dogmas of the Confession is the system of truth taught in the Holy Scriptures. Neither more nor less! But I am digressing. I only proposed in this place to show that the imposition of any creed of human device is incompatible with the nature and circumstances of man. This, I conceive, is rendered sufficiently plain from an inspection of the circumstances and character of the human mind already noticed.

But it was affirmed, that every attempt to found the unity of the church upon the adoption of any creed of human contrivances;—upon any creed, other than the apostle's testimony, is not only incompatible with the nature and circumstances of mankind, but is also an effort to frustrate and defeat the prayer and plan of the Lord Messiah, and to subvert his throne and government.

It will be confessed, without argument to prove, that the conversion of men, or of the world, and the unity, purity, and happiness of the disciples of the Messiah, were the sublime subjects of his humiliation to death. For this he prayed in language never heard on earth before, in words which not only expressed the ardency of his desires, but at the same time unfolded the plan in which his benevolence and philanthropy were to be triumphant.

The words to which we refer express one petition of that prayer recorded by the apostle John, commonly styled his intercessory prayer. With his eyes raised to heaven, he says;—"Holy Father—now, I do not pray for these only (for the unity and success of the apostles) but for those also who shall believe on me through, or by means of their word—that they all may be one,—that the world may believe that you have sent me." Who does not see in this petition, that the words or testimony of the apostles, the unity of the disciples, and the conviction of the world are bound together by the wisdom and the love of the Father, by the devotion and philanthropy of the Son. The order of heaven, the plan of the Great King, his throne and government, are here unfolded in full splendor to our view. The words of the apostles are laid as the basis, the unity of the disciples the glorious result, and the only successful means of converting the world to the acknowledgment, that Jesus of Nazareth is the Messiah or the Son of the Blessed, the only Saviour of men.

Let us attend to the argument of the prayer. The will of Jesus was the same as the will of him who sent him. The will of heaven, that is, the will of the Father, and of the Son, and of the Holy Spirit, is, that all who believe on the Messiah through the testimony of the apostles may be one; consequently, they do not will that those who believe on him through the Westminster divines shall be one. The words of the prayer alone demonstrate this. And who does not see, and who will not confess, that the fact proves, the fact now existing, that those who believe in him through the words of the Westminster divines are not one? They are cut up or divided into seven sects at this moment. While the Saviour prays that those who believe on him through the apostles may be one, he in fact, and in the plain meaning of terms, prays that they who believe on him through any other media or means may be divided, and not be one.

To attempt to unite the professing disciples by any other means than the word of the apostles, by the Westminster, or any other creed, is, then, an attempt to overrule the will of heaven, to subvert the throne of the Great King, to frustrate the prayers of the Son of the Blessed. As the heavens are higher than the earth, so are God's thoughts and ways higher than ours. He knows, for he has willed, and planned, and determined, that neither the Popish, the Protestant, the Presbyterian, the Methodistic, nor the Baptist creed shall be honored more than the apostle's testimony, shall be honored as much as the apostle's testimony, shall be honored at all. These creeds the Saviour proscribed forever; they are rebellion against his plan and throne, and they are aimed at the dethronement of the Holy Twelve—He put them on thrones, he gave them this honor. All creed makers have disputed their right to the throne, have attempted, *ipso facto*, their degradation, and have usurped their government. But he that sits in heaven has laughed at them, he has vexed them in his sore displeasure, he has dispersed them in his anger, and confounded their language as he did their predecessors, who sought to subvert his throne and dominion by the erection of a tower and citadel reaching to the skies. The votaries of those creed makers have also concurred with their masters, and have attempted to raise them upon their shoulders to the apostolic thrones; but he has broken their necks, and they go bowed down always. He has made them lick the dust, and caused children to reign over them.

But the conversion of the world is planned and ordered by the will of heaven to be dependant on the unity of the disciples, as well as this unity dependant upon the apostle's testimony. An attempt to convert Pagans and Mahometans to believe that Jesus is the Son of God, and the sent of the Father, until christians are united, is also an attempt to frustrate the prayer of the Messiah, to subvert his throne and government. There are unalterable laws in the moral world, as in the natural. There are also unalterable laws in the government of the moral and religious world, as in the government of the natural. Those laws cannot, by human interference, be set aside or frustrated—we might as reasonably expect that Indian corn will grow in the open fields in the midst of the frost and snows of winter, as that Pagan nations can be converted to Jesus Christ, till christians are united through the belief of the apostle's testimony. We may force corn to grow by artificial means in the depth of winter, but it is not like the corn of August. So may a few disciples be made in Pagan lands by such means in the moral empire; as those by which corn is made to grow in winter in the natural empire, but they are not like the disciples of primitive times, before sectarian creeds came into being. It is enough to say, on this topic, that the Saviour made the unity of the disciples essential to the conviction of the world; and he that attempts it independent of this essential, sets himself against the wisdom and plans of heaven, and aims at overruling the dominion and government of the Great King. On this subject we have many things to say, and hard to be uttered, because the people are dull of hearing. But we shall leave this prayer for the present, having just introduced it, and noticed the argument of it, by reminding the reader that instead of human creeds, promoting the unity of the disciples, they have always operated just the reverse; and are in diametrical opposition to the wisdom and benevolence of the Heavens. Should the christian community be united upon the Westminster, or Methodistic, or Baptist, or any human creed, then the plan of heaven is defeated, the apostles disgraced, the Saviour's prayer unanswered, and the whole order of heaven frustrated, and the throne of the universe subverted. He that advocates the necessity of creeds of human contrivance to the unity of the church unconsciously impeaches the wisdom of God, arraigns the benevolence of the Saviour, and censures the revelation of the Spirit. He, perhaps, without reflection attempts to new modify the empire of reason, of morality and religion; to rise above, not only the apostles, but the Saviour himself, and arrogates to himself a wisdom and philanthropy that far surpasses, and in fact covers with disgrace, all those attributes that rise to our view, and shine with incomparable effulgence in the redemption of man.

EDITOR.

History of the English Bible.—No. II.

ANNO DOMINI 1526, the New Testament was translated into English by Tyndal. This translation was printed at Antwerp. It had an astonishing circulation amongst the people. The bishops of the English hierarchy condemned it. They not only condemned it as a dangerous book for the laity, but complained of it to the king, and proceeded against those that read it with great severity. His majesty, Henry VIII. called it in by way of proclamation, June, 1520, and promised a more correct translation. But says Neal, " It was impossible to stop the curiosity of the people so long; for though the bishops bought up and burnt all they could meet with, the Testament was reprinted abroad and sent over to merchants in London, who dispersed the copies privately among their acquaintance and friends." " At length it was moved in convocation that the whole bible should be translated into English and set up in churches; but most of the old clergy were against it. They said this would lay the foundation for innumerable heresies, as it had done in Germany, and that the people were not proper judges of the sense of scriptures. To which it was replied that the scriptures were written at first in the vulgar tongue; that our Saviour commanded his hearers to search the scriptures, that it was necessary the people should do so now. These arguments prevailed with the majority to consent that the petition should be presented to the king, that his majesty would please to give order about it. But the old bishops were too much disinclined to move in it. The Reformers, therefore, were forced to have recourse to Tyndal's translation."*

Two remarkable facts in the history of the first translations of the scriptures are worthy of particular notice. The first is, that all who attained to the honor of first reformers attempted to give a translation of the scriptures in the vulgar tongue of the people they labored to reform. Peter Waldus, A. D. 1160, attempted a translation of the four Gospels into the French language. John Wickliffe, A. D. 1367, translated the New Testament into English. Martin Luther gave a translation of the bible in the German. Olivetan translated into the French, and Beza, the friend and companion of Calvin, rendered the New Testament into Latin. The

* Neal, vol. 1. p. 68.

second fact is, that the reigning clergy uniformly opposed these translations under the pretext of their inaccuracy, and their dangerous tendency amongst the laity.

But to return to the English bible, it is a fact worthy of some attention, that Wickliffe, who gave the first translation, was condemned as a heretic, and after his death, the orthodox dug up his bones and burned them. William Tyndal, too, who gave the second English translation, was condemned to death and executed as a heretic.

William Tyndal's New Testament was printed in one octavo volume, without a name, without any marginal references, or table at the end. In the year 1536 it had passed through five editions in Holland. Tyndal also made a good progress in translating the Old Testament. The five books of Moses, the books of Joshua, Judges, Ruth, the two books of Samuel, the Kings, and Chronicles, with Nehemiah and Jonah, were translated by him. Miles Coverdale and John Rogers finished it. Some marginal notes were added which gave offence to the clergy, and the whole work was prohibited by authority. Tyndal translated, as Wickliffe before him, from the Vulgate Latin, and not from the Greek. Archbishop Cranmer reviewed and corrected it, leaving out the notes and prologue, cancelled the name of Tyndal, and gave it the fictitious name of Thomas Matthews' bible. It was sometimes called Cranmer's bible, though in fact it was still Tyndal's translation corrected. The Archbishop's name and influence obtained the royal authority, and it was read by all sorts of people.

EDITOR.

The Apocalypse Explained.

THROUGH the kindness of a friend from Kentucky, at the city of Washington, we obtained direct from the press, Alexander Smyth's Explanation of the Apocalypse, or Revelation of John. Much was promised by Mr. Smyth, and he was a good deal snarled at by sundry editors for his impertinence in invading the dominions of the clergy. Some, indeed, were so candid as to allow that as a monk had invented or discovered the art of making gunpowder, it was not unreasonable to suppose, that a military general might discover the meaning of the Apocalypse. Now, although we had no prejudices against the general, we had not much faith in his pledge staked on the discovery; and, indeed, we are sorry that he has fallen so far short of the monk alluded to. He has made a great noise, but that appears to be the whole he has done. His pamphlet is, indeed, likely to sell well at fifty cents, though it does not contain as much matter as the present number of this work. But the size of it is the best property it possesses. The omnipotent key which he promised to this revelation has been long in the possession of the infidel world. It is this: " it now appears that, although the christian church has received the revelation of John the divine as genuine, for more than sixteen centuries, it is a pious forgery." This omnipotent key would unlock all the mysteries of the bible with the same ease it unlocks the revelation of John. But how will the general maintain the character of an honest man in professing to have discovered an infallible key to unlock this revelation, which the deists have worn out, and got welded a hundred times, and which is yet unable to open the lock! But this is not all: it illy comports with the declaration that he had found out such a key of interpretation, which leaves him in the rank of may-bes and perhapses. He has to say occasionally, This may mean and that perhaps may signify. This is a slippery key— a key that often misses the bolt. He supposes that Ireneus, who died A. D. 202, was the pious forger of this revelation, and that it was written as an enigmatical representation of events prior to that time; and yet some of the events which he brings forward as a part of this enigmatical history, happened after the death, or just at the close of the life of Ireneus. He has not attempted to explain many of the most important items in this book, otherwise than by telling us it is "a pious forgery." When the fact that the revelation of John existed and was quoted and referred to by writers from A. D. 100 till 200, presented itself, he discredits the testimony of historians, but afterwards quotes them as of authority in other instances. At one time Eusebius is a writer of no credit when his testimony opposes the general; at another time he is quoted without a demur. The same infallible key some of the infidels of the first centuries found out for unlocking the prophecies of Isaiah. They declared that what Isaiah said of the sufferings of the Messiah was written after the events had occurred, and that his prophecies were a pious forgery, although the Jews had held them sacred for many centuries before the christian era. Indeed the general's Explanation affords another instance that sceptics are the most credulous of mankind, while they object to the credulity of others. We have not time at present to give this work any more attention, nor, indeed, do we suppose it deserves any more. Perhaps the general intended to write a burlesque on the commentaries of the age.   EDITOR.

Episcopalian Diocess in Ohio.

It appears from the journal of the proceedings of the seventh annual convention of the Protestant Episcopal church, in the state of Ohio, that the Right Reverend Bishop Chase received on his tour through England, in solicitations of donations, property to the amount of twenty thousand dollars, for the establishment of a theological institution for the qualifying of clergymen for the church of England in this diocess. In his episcopal address to his convention he tells his clergy and laity that he generously presented a sum of money bequeathed to himself, by John Bowdler, esq. of England, having converted this money into a "well-wrought set of communion plate for the chapel of the intended seminary." To perpetuate this disinterested act of benevolence to the clerical praise of the first and second donor, on the chief piece of the plate is engraved as follows:—

"A flagon, two chalices, two patens, and collecting plate. This communion plate was purchased with a sum of money which the late John Bowdler, Esq. of Eltham in Kent, England, appropriated to the use of the Right Reverend Philander Chase, D. D. bishop of Ohio, and was, by the bishop's desire, dedicated forever to the service of this chapel. A. D. 1824."

Well may it be said that the righteous shall be held in everlasting remembrance, when their names are thus engraved on silver, and their piety commemorated by their own hands in letters as durable as the precious metal. This disinterested act of munificent benevolence of the Right Reverend bishop of Ohio, will, no doubt, in the eyes of the pious protestants, cover the policy of the subordinating these twenty thousand dollars to the interest and personal benefit of the bishop for life or good behaviour. For in the aforesaid journal, we are told that all the donations made to the bishop in England, were made upon the basis that the bishop is to reside at the seminary wherever located, and to have the charge and direction of it as one of the principal professors, and president; and, as such, to receive a proper compensation out of the funds contributed. The interest of twenty thousand dollars, at six *per cent.* is twelve hundred dollars *per annum.* Now, should the bishop only receive as "a proper compensation," the interest of this sum per annum, it will be obvious that, by his late tour, he has not only essentially subserved the interest of the church of England, but secured for life a handsome support in Ohio—a sum exceeding that paid to the governor of the state. But we are informed that, "according to the bishop's deed, upon which all donations are predicated, the real estate proposed to be given, and the appendages to it, will revert to the present bishop, the proprietor, in the event of establishing the seminary at any other place, (than the estate conveyed by the bishop;) but notwithstanding such reversion, it will become the duty of the bishop to reside personally at the seminary." Thus the welfare of the bishop is secured by every means, as well as the protestant church. And who would not go on a similar tour, having any prospect of thus consolidating the property of the church and his own upon the same basis. Such is the policy of this measure, and such are the prospects of building up this Zion in the wilderness. But where is the spirit and the resemblance of the new testament church and its bishops, in all this management? But we ought not, perhaps, to think of comparing this Right Reverend Bishop and his diocess to any congregation of saints and its bishops, mentioned in the age of uncorrupted simplicity. One thing is incontrovertible, that neither the founder of the christian institution, nor any of his immediate followers, ever saw such a flagon, two chalices, two patens, and collecting plate, as suited the taste of the Right Reverend Bishop Chase, D. D.
                                        EDITOR.

No. 9.]   APRIL 4, 1825.
Essays on the work of the Holy Spirit in the Salvation of Men.—No. IX.

THE gospel, or glad tidings of the benignity of God to mankind, is emphatically called *the grace of God.* Grace is a term of frequent occurrence in the New Testament, and always signifies the *favor* of God towards sinners.— This is no where so fully exhibited as in the gift of his Son. Hence the full, free favor of God came by Jesus Christ; and this is termed the grace, or the grace of God. The Spirit of God, by whose agency this grace is exhibited, is therefore called *the Spirit of Grace.* Those who have apostatized from the faith of the gospel, are said to have done despite, or to have offered an indignity to the Spirit of Grace, because they have treated with contempt that record which he inspired, and have contemned those splendid attestations which he vouchsafed in proof of its authenticity.

A great many enthusiastic and extravagant things are said about the grace of God—by those, too, who profess to teach the christian religion. Hence we often hear grace spoken of as a sort of fluid, resembling the electric, which bursts from the clouds that pass over our fields. Free grace, sovereign grace, and grace in the heart, are terms long consecrated and hackneyed in sermon books, until many suppose that they are bible terms and phrases. Hence the grace of some religious sectaries is free, and of others not free—is sovereign, and not sovereign—is in the heart, or not in it. There is a grace, too, which is called special, and a grace that is irresistible and efficacious. With some the day of grace is sinned away; with others it never comes, or never passes away. From all this confusion in the modern Babel, let us turn to the style of the New Testament. There we find that every bounty expressive of the favor of God towards man, is called a grace; that the bounty which one christian exhibits to another, is called a grace; that the written or spoken gospel is called the grace of God; and when this gospel is announced, the grace of God is said to appear, or to shine forth. Those who hold or stand in the gospel, as delivered by the apostles, are said to stand in the true grace of God, contradistinguished from those who blended the law and the gospel. Those who did not correspond in temper and deportment to the gospel, "received the grace of God in vain;" and those who did so correspond are exhorted "to continue in the grace of God." Those, then, who believe the gospel, receive the grace of God; for, in receiving the gospel, they, in other words, receive the grace of God. When the gospel is exhibited to any people, "the grace of God has appeared," or "shone forth" to them. When they believe it in their hearts, or receive it sincerely, then, and not till then, they have the grace of God in their hearts. This is all the countenance the scriptures give to the popular phrase, "the grace of God in the heart." When men have believed the gospel, they are under the reign of grace—they are under the favor of Jesus Christ, and all the benefits they enjoy are so many multiplications of his favor. So that when the apostle prayed that grace might be multiplied to, or that the grace of the Lord Jesus Christ might be with the saints, he, in other words, desires that the favor or benefits of his reign might be with them. While christians keep the commandments of the Saviour, they grow in his favor, or grow in grace, which is exhibited in the increase of all those dispositions and tempers of mind which are compatible with their state, as standing in the true grace of God.

This grace of God works in the hearts of the recipients. By it the peace of God rules, and the love of God is diffused in the hearts of men. A heart ruled by the peace of God, and warmed by his love, is as conscious or as sensible of it, as of any of its own emotions. Every person knows or is conscious that he loves, or fears, or dislikes any person, or thing. When two individuals are at enmity against each other, they are conscious of it, and of the cause. When they are sincerely reconciled to each other they are just as conscious of it, and of the means or cause of their reconciliation. And shall it be, when men are reconciled to God through his Son Jesus Christ, that they are, in this instance only, inconscious of it! Were this the case, with what propriety or truth could the apostle say to the christians of his time concerning the Saviour, " Whom, having not seen, you love; on whom, not now looking, but believing, you greatly rejoice in him with joy unspeakable and full of glory!" That a person could believe on, or trust in another, that he could love him, and rejoice in him, without being conscious of it, is altogether inadmissible. A persuasion that God is so benign, that he is so philanthropic, as to account faith for righteousness to him that believes the record given of his Son, as necessarily produces peace with God, as the appearance of the sun dissipates darkness. " Being justified

by faith we have peace with God through our Lord Jesus Christ, through whom, by this belief, we have obtained access to his favor in which we stand, and rejoice in a hope of the glory of God."

Indeed a transition from darkness to light, from enmity to friendship, from hatred to love, from distrust to confidence, from despondency to hope, from sorrow to joy in those of adult age, is marked with so many sensible attributes, as to render the inconsciousness of it morally impossible. Those, however, who are from infancy brought up in the education and discipline of the Lord; on whose infant minds the sun of righteousness has shone, are not capable of contrasting their present views and feelings with their former. From the earliest recollection they have believed in Jesus, and have, in some measure, enjoyed the benefits of a hope of acceptance with God. As their capacities of understanding have expanded, as their faith and confidence have increased, their enjoyments of the grace of God have also enlarged—But, perhaps, in no case amongst those born in a land where christian revelation is so generally diffused, can the contrast be so sensible and so obvious as in the first age of christianity. For thousands of men and women who yesterday were perfect Pagans, to-day rejoice in the hope of eternal life. Once they were darkness, but now they are light. Their renovation was as sensible, as obvious, and as striking to themselves, as the emancipation of an adult slave, as the liberation of a captive, or as the opening of the eyes of a blind man is to himself. Not adverting to the extreme disparity in our circumstances in these instances, from those of the first converts, has given rise to a perplexity, and sometimes, to a perturbation of mind, extremely prejudicial to the happiness of many disciples. To this the popular harangues have contributed in no small degree.

It is, perhaps, chiefly owing to the religious theories imbibed in early life from creeds, catechisms, and priests, that so few comparatively enjoy the grace of God which brings salvation. The grace of God, exhibited in the record concerning Jesus of Nazareth, affords no consolation. The hopes and joys of many spring from a good conceit of themselves. If this good conceit vanishes, which sometimes happens, despondency and distress are the consequences.— While they can, as they conceit, thank God that they are not like other men, they are very happy; but when this fancied excellency disappears, the glad tidings afford no consolation: anguish and distress have come upon them. This, with some of the spiritual doctors, is a good symptom too: for, say they, " if you do not doubt we will doubt for you." When they have worked them into despondency, they minister a few opiates, and assure them that they are now in a safe and happy state. Now they are to rejoice, because they are sorrowful; now they are to feel very good, because they feel so very bad. This is the orthodox "christian experience." This is the genuine work of the Holy Spirit!

Now in the primitive church the disciples derived all their strength, confidence, peace, hope, and joy, from the grace of God appearing in Jesus Christ. In this grace they saw their sins forgiven, themselves accepted, and, on the promise and oath of him that cannot lie, they looked for eternal life. They continued in this joy while they continued keeping the commandments of their Lord, and thereby continued in his love. By this grace of God appearing in Jesus Christ, the Spirit of God comforted their hearts; through it the spirit of adoption was received, and by it they cried Abba, Father. Their life and their joys sprang from him in whom they confided, and not from a high opinion of themselves. The foundation of their hope made them humble; the foundation of the hope of many moderns makes them proud. The fruits of the Spirit which they received were love to him that loved them, and to the saints for his name's sake; joy, springing from their acceptance with God and hope of eternal life; peace with God through the sacrifice of his son; forbearance towards all, springing from the Divine forbearance which they were every day conscious of; goodness exhibited to friends and enemies, in overt acts of kindness; faithfulness to God and man; meekness in their temper; and temperance in restraining all their appetites, springing from the example of their glorious Chief. The fruits of the Spirit of the fashionable christians, are love to themselves, and to those who unite with them in subscribing the same creed, and in paying the same priest; joy, springing from a high conceit of their moral worth; peace with God, through their having made a covenant of peace on conditions of their own stipulating; forbearance towards the rich or honorable transgressors of their laws, or those of God; goodness to them that love them; faithfulness to men, so long as their interests are consulted thereby; meekness in their temper to those who flatter them that they are every way excellent; and temperance wherein appetite makes no farther demands. In others the fruits of the spirit of orthodoxy are various:—doubts, which spring from their want of certain good symptoms; fears, which arise from a conscience not purged from dead works; and alternate joys and sorrows arising from a good or bad opinion of themselves —censoriousness towards them who cannot say *shibboleth* as articulately as themselves, and pride originating from a notion that they are exclusively the elect of God. We hope that amongst the popular establishments there are many whom the picture will not suit; but it is with sincere regret that we declare, it is drawn to the life and deportment of very many who stand very high in the religious world, who are pillars, too, in the temples in our favored land.

But to conclude, we commenced this essay with the intention of exhibiting the import of the grace of God, in the fixed style of the New Testament, regardless of the spurious dialect, or new nomenclature of modern divinity. The prominent ideas intended to be exhibited are, that the gospel of Jesus Christ is emphatically the grace of God; that this gospel received is the grace of God received; that this grace of God when received, works in the hearts of them that believe, that the Spirit of grace therein dwells in the hearts of men, and teaches them to deny ungodliness and worldly lusts; to live soberly, righteously, and godly in this present evil world; that they have "received the grace of God in vain" who do not exhibit its fruit; that "christians continue in the grace of God" while they abound in these fruits; and that while men hold fast the gospel as delivered by the apostles, they "stand in the true grace of God."

Thus we see that the whole work of the Spirit of God in the salvation of men, as the spirit of wisdom, the spirit of power, and the spirit of grace or goodness, is inseparably connected with, and altogether subservient to the gospel or glad tidings of great joy to all people, of the love of God exhibited in the humiliation to death of his only begotten Son. De-

tached from this we know nothing of it, because nothing more is revealed. And to indulge in metaphysical speculations, or to form abstract theories of our own, is not only the climax of religious folly; but has ever proved the bane of Christianity. If, at any time, in these essays, we approached the precincts of those regions, it was in following the gloomy doctors who begin and end there.   EDITOR.

A Restoration of the Ancient Order of Things. No. III.

"HOLY FATHER—now I do not pray for these only, but for those also who shall believe on me through their word, that they all may be one— that the world may believe that you have sent me." The testimony of the apostles, the Saviour makes the grand means of the enlargement and consolidation of his empire. He prays that they who believe on him through their testimony may be united. And their union he desires, that the world may believe that he was sent by God, and acted under the authority, and according to the will of the God and Father of all. The word of the Apostles, the unity of those who believe it, and the conviction of the world are here inseparably associated. All terminate in the conviction of the world. As the Father so loved the world that he gave his only begotten Son; as the Son so loved the world as to become a propitiation for its sins, and as the Spirit came to convince the world of sin, of righteousness and of judgment, the conviction of the world is an object of the dearest magnitude in the estimation of the Heavens. All the attributes of Deity require that this grand object be achieved in a certain way, or not at all. That way or plan the Saviour has unfolded in his address from earth to heaven. We all must confess, however reluctant at first, that, in the government of the world, there are certain ways to certain ends, and if not accomplished in this way they are not accomplished at all. The fact is apparent, and most obvious, whether we understand, or can understand the reason of it. As well might Israel have dispossessed the Canaanites in any other way he might have devised, as we attempt to carry any point against the established order of heaven. Israel failed in his own way; in God's way he was successful. We have failed in our own way to convince the world, but in God's way we would be victorious. Wisdom and benevolence combined constitute his plan, and although his ways may appear weak or incomprehensible, they are, in their moral grandeur of wisdom and benevolence, as much higher than ours, as the heavens are higher than the earth.

For any thing we know, it was in the bounds of possibilities for the Saviour to have founded his kingdom without apostles or their word; but we are assured, from the fact of their having been employed, that his wisdom and benevolence required, in reference to things on earth, and things in heaven, that they should be employed. If, then, as is evident, there is a certain way in which christianity can pervade the world, and if the unity of the disciples is an essential constituent of this way, how grievous the schisms, how mischievous the divisions among them!! While they are contending about their orthodox and their heterodox*isms*, they are hardening the hearts of the unbelievers at home, and shutting the door of faith against the nations abroad. While the Saviour, in the prospect of all the sorrows that were about to environ him, in the greatness of his philanthropy, forgetful and regardless of them all, was pouring out his fervent desires for the oneness of his followers, many who call themselves his disciples are fomenting new divisions, or strenuously engaged in keeping up the old ones. They in fact prefer their paltry notions, their abstract devices, their petty *shibboleths* to the conversion of the world. Yes, as one of the regenerate divines said, some time since, he would as soon have communion with thieves and robbers, as with those who disputed his notions about eternal generation, or eternal procession, or some such metaphysical nonsense; so, many in appearance, would rather that the world should continue in pagan darkness for a thousand years, than that they should give up with a dogmatic confession, without a life giving truth in it.* From the Roman pontiff down to a licensed beneficiary, each high priest and Levite labors to build up the shibboleths of a party. With every one of them, his cause, that brings him a morsel of bread, is the cause of God. Colleges are founded, acts of incorporation prayed for as sincerely as the Saviour prayed for the union of christians in order to the conversion of the world, theological schools erected, and a thousand contributions levied for keeping up parties and rewarding their leaders.

I have no idea of seeing, nor one wish to see, the sects unite in one grand army. This would be dangerous to our liberties and laws. For this the Saviour did not pray. It is only the disciples of Christ dispersed among them, that reason and benevolence would call out of them. Let them unite who love the Lord, and then we shall soon see the hireling priesthood and their worldly establishments prostrate in the dust.

But creeds of human contrivance keep up these establishments; nay, they are declared by some sects to be their very constitution.— These create, and foster, and mature that state of things which operates against the letter and spirit of the Saviour's prayer. The disciples cannot be united while these are recognized; and while these are not one, the world cannot be converted. So far from being the bond of union, or the means of uniting the saints, they are the bones of controversy, the seeds of discord, the cause as well as the effect of division. As reasonably might we expect the articles of confederation that league the "Holy Alliance" to be the constitution of a republic, as that the Westminster or any other creed should become a means of uniting christians. It may for a time hold together a worldly establishment, and be of the same service as an act of incorporation to a Presbyterian congregation, which enables it to make the unwilling *willing* to pay their stipends, but by and by it becomes a scorpion even among themselves.

But the constitution of the kingdom of the Saviour is the New Testament, and this alone is adapted to the existence of his kingdom in the world. *To restore the ancient order of things* this must be recognized as the only constitution of this kingdom. And in receiving citizens they must be received into the kingdom, just as they were received by the apostles into it, when they were in the employment of setting it up. And here let us ask, How did they receive them? Did they propose any articles of religious opinions? Did they impose any inferential principles, or require the acknowledgment of any dogmas whatever? Not one. The acknowledgment of the king's supremacy in one proposition

* The history of the world has not informed me of one sinner brought to repentance or converted to Jesus Christ by any confession of faith in existence.

expressive of a fact, and not an opinion, and a promise of allegiance expressed in the act of naturalization, were every item requisite to all the privileges of citizenship. As this is a fundamental point, we shall be more particular in detail.

When any person desired admission into the kingdom, he was only asked what he thought of the king. "Do you believe in your heart that Jesus of Nazareth is the Messiah, the Lord of all," was the whole amount of the apostolic requirement. If the candidate for admission replied in the affirmative—if he declared his hearty conviction of this fact—no other interrogation was proposed. They took him on his solemn declaration of this belief, whether Jew or Gentile, without a single demur. He was forthwith naturalized, and formally declared to be a citizen of the kingdom of Messiah. In the act of naturalization which was then performed by means of water, he abjured or renounced spiritual allegiance to any other prince, potentate, pontiff, or prophet, than Jesus the Lord.— He was then treated by the citizens as a fellow citizen of the saints, and invited to the religious festivals of the brotherhood. And whether he went to Rome, Antioch, or Ephesus, he was received and treated by all the subjects of the Great King as a brother and fellow citizen. If he ever exhibited any instances of disloyalty, he was affectionately reprimanded; but if he was guilty of treason against the king, he was simply excluded from the kingdom. But we are now speaking of the constitutional admission of citizens into the kingdom of Jesus Christ, and not of any thing subsequent thereto. The declaration of the belief of one fact, expressed in one plain proposition, and the one act of naturalization, constituted a free citizen of this kingdom. Such was the ancient order of things, as all must confess. Why, then, should we adopt a new plan, of our own devising, which, too, is as irrational as unconstitutional.

Let me here ask the only people in our land who seem to understand the constitution of our kingdom and the laws of our King in these respects, Why do you, my Baptist brethren, in receiving applicants into the kingdom, ask them so many questions about matters and things which the apostles never dreamed of, before you will permit them to be naturalized? Although you do not, like some others, present a book for their acknowledgment, you do that which is quite as unauthorized and as unconstitutional.

Your applicant is importuned in the presence of a congregation who sit as jurors upon his case, to tell how, and why, and wherefore, he is moved to seek for admission into the kingdom. He is now to tell "what the Lord has done for his soul, what he felt, and how he was awakened, and how he now feels," &c. &c. After he has told his "experience," some of the jurors interrogate him for their own satisfaction; and, among other abstract metaphysics, he is asked such questions as the following: "Did you not feel as though you deserved to be sent to hell for your sins? Did you not see that God would be just in excluding you from his presence for ever? Did you not view sin as an infinite evil? Do you not now take delight in the things which were once irksome to you?" &c. &c. If his responses coincide with the experience and views of his examiners, his experience is pronounced genuine. He not unfrequently tells of something like Paul's visions and revelations, which give a sort of variety to his accounts, which, with some, greatly prove the genuineness of his conversion.* Now what is all this worth? His profession is not that which the apostles required; and the only question is, whether the apostolic order or this is the wiser, happier, and safer. When the eunuch said, "Here is water, what does hinder me to be baptized?" Philip said, "If you believe with all your heart, you may." He replied, "I believe that Jesus Christ is the Son of God." Philip then accompanied him into the water, and immersed him. None of your questions were propounded—no congregation was assembled to judge of his experience. Philip, as all his contemporaries did, took him on his word. Now I think, brethren, that you cannot say I assume too much when I declare my conviction that the apostolic method was better than yours. You object that a person's *saying* he believes what the eunuch believed does not afford you sufficient evidence to disciple him. Well, we shall hear you. But let me ask, If he heartily believe what the eunuch believed, is he not worthy of baptism? "Yes," I hear you respond. Now for his *saying* he believes. What have you but his *saying* that he feels or felt what he described as his experience? You take his word in that case when accompanied with manifest sincerity, why not, then, take his word in this case when accompanied with manifest sincerity? Yes, but say you, any person can learn to say that he believes what the eunuch believed. Admitted. What then? Cannot any person who has heard others catechised or examined for his experience, *learn too* to describe what he never felt? So far the cases are perfectly equal. The same assurance is given in both cases. You take the applicant on his own testimony—so did they. We both depend upon his word, and we grant he may deceive us, and you know he has often deceived you. But we could easily shew, were it our intention, that you are more liable to be deceived than we. But we leave this, and ask for no more than what is abundantly evident, that the apostolic plan affords the same assurance as yours. We have the word of the applicant, and you have no more. These considerations shew that the apostolic plan is the wiser and the safer. It is more honorable to the truth too. It fixes the attention of all upon the magnitude of the gospel faith—upon the magnitude of the fact confessed.

* The reader may, perhaps, think that we speak too irreverently of the practice and of the experience of many christians. We have no such intention. But there are many things when told or represented just as they are, which appear so strange, and, indeed, fanciful, that the mere recitation of them assumes an air of irony. I confess, upon the whole, that this order of things appears to me as unreasonable and as novel as the following case:—James Sanitas once had a consumption. By a few simples, a change of air, and exercise, he recovered his former good health. He was importuned by Thomas Medicus, a physician, to converse about his former disease and recovery. The Doctor doubted whether he was really restored to health. He asked what medicines he used.—James Sanitas replied. The Doctor asked him whether he felt an acute pain in his breast or side for so long a time. He next inquired if certain simples were used, and how they operated. Last of all he inquired what his present feelings were. The answers of James did not correspond with Dr. Medicus' theory, and was told that he had still the same malady, and was in circumstances as dangerous as before. James assured him he felt perfectly sound and vigorous, and appealed to the manifest change in his appearance, corpulency, color, strength, &c. The Doctor settled the controversy by telling him that unless he felt certain pains so long. and a peculiar class of sensations while using the simples prescribed, he is deceived, he cannot be cured, he is yet consumptive, and must die.

It exalts it in the apprehension of all as the most grand, sublime, and all-powerful fact. It makes it to the disciple, in his views, what the Saviour is in all the counsels of God—the *Alpha* and the *Omega*. It shews its comprehensive and fundamental import, which in fact transcends every other consideration. Moreover, the disciple thus baptized is baptized into the faith, but in the modern plan he is baptized into his own experience. It is then most honorable to the saving truth.

When your applicant appears before your assembly, say of one hundred disciples, and has satisfied them all, they lift up their hands or otherwise express their approbation of his experience, and their consent to his naturalization. Now admit that his profession were sincere, that he felt all that he described, still he may not be a disciple in truth. He may, indeed, have been in doubts himself whether his experience were genuine. But in your judgment he has some confidence, or he would not sincerely appear before you. He has then, in your decision, the concurrence of one hundred persons approving his experience as genuine. This emboldens him. He now feels himself somewhat assured that he is a true convert, for a hundred converts have approbated his experience, and stamped it as genuine as their own. He may be deceived. And you must admit it, or else contend that all such approbated ones, who speak what they have felt, are genuine disciples. I argue that there is, on your plan, a possibility of deceiving or of confirming an applicant in self-deception. On the apostolic plan no such possibility exists. For admitting in this case, as in the former, that he sincerely believes what he professes, then he is a true disciple. And they who receive him on this ground, only express their approbation of the faith he has professed. They assure him, by their concurrence, that believing what he professes, he is a disciple.— This, then, fixes his attention upon the truth professed. In the one case the faith he has professed is only attested by the brethren as of paramount importance, which is so in fact; and in attesting which, there is no possibility of deceiving, whether his profession be feigned or sincere. In the other case his experience is attested by the brethren, as of paramount importance, which it may not be in fact; and in attesting which, there is a possibility of deceiving, whether his profession be sincere or feigned.

But, says one, you may soon get many applicants in this way. Stop, my friend, I fear not so many. You will, if you interrogate the people, find many to say they believe what the eunuch believed, but you cannot persuade them to do as the eunuch did. They will confess with their mouth this truth, but they do not wish to be naturalized or to put themselves under the constitution of the Great King. Their not moving in obedience proves the truth does not move them. But when any person asks what the eunuch asked, he, *ipso facto*, shews that his faith has moved him, and this authorized Philip to comply with his desires, and should induce us to go and do likewise. When the ancient order of things is restored, neither more nor less will be demanded of any applicant for admission into the kingdom, than was asked by Philip. And every man who solicits admission in this way— who solemnly declares that, upon the testimony and authority of the holy apostles and prophets, he believes that Jesus is the Messiah, the Son of the living God, should forthwith be baptized without respect to any questions or dogmas derived either from written creeds or church covenants. But I have wandered far from my investigation of the merits of the arguments in favor of creeds—so far that I cannot approach them until my next.   Editor.

The following epistle will serve as a specimen of the many received relating to the contents of this work, and will, perhaps, be of some use to its numerous and diversified readers. Prejudices which existed against this paper, and the panic which its first numbers produced, have greatly subsided, and its circulation has increased with unusual rapidity. It is high time that the religious community should awake to a just sense of the circumstances, and to the signs of the times, and we are peculiarly happy to witness the spirit of inquiry and investigation which at present threatens the downfall of those establishments projected in ignorance and enthusiasm and consummated by superstition.

To the Editor of the Christian Baptist.

Dear Sir,—I have been a constant reader of your periodical work from its commencement, and have been entertained and I think much edified; but I find some difficulties in comparing your views with the New Testament.

In your Sentimental Journal, page 58, you say, "evidence alone produces faith, or testimony is all that is necessary to faith," and, section sixth, same page, you say, "no person can help believing when the evidence of truth arrests his attention." Here I wish an explanation. Were there not many attended on Pentecost besides the three thousand who believed on that occasion? I ask, Why did they not all believe, for I presume they all heard and saw all that the three thousand saw and heard. The same may be said of the event that took place in the temple when Peter and John performed the miracle of healing the crippled man. There were many others who saw and heard. But five thousand believed—others persecuted. I wish here to refer you to a few passages of scripture that seem to me a difficulty to reconcile to your view of faith. *John* x. 24—28. *John* vi. 37 and 39. and *John* viii. 30. to the end of the chapter. Did not those persons hear the word of truth and see the miracles wrought in attestation of the truth? Did it not arrest their attention, and what sort of faith was theirs? Did not Judas Iscariot see the miracles and hear the words of Jesus for a length of time, and on various occasions, and what sort of faith was his?

There is another difficulty that occurs to me in comparing some of your views (as I understand them) with the scriptures. If I understand you, your views are that no divine influence is necessary in order to faith, nor is any afforded to any, more than is contained in the divine record. I would then ask why one person embraces the gospel gladly and another rejects it, and what we are to understand when we are told that the Lord opened the heart of Lydia that she attended to the things spoken by Paul; and what made the good ground or who gave the good and honest heart named in the parable of the sower. I think there is a text somewhere that says, "the preparation of the heart in man and the answer of the tongue is from the Lord;" and we know that we farmers do not prepare our ground by sowing our seed on it; neither can we understand that the Saviour meant that the sowing of the seed prepared the ground, or made the good and honest heart,

or it would have had the same effect on the stony places, or amongst the thorns.

Permit me to make one more request: Do give me a short explanation of a part of the epistle to the Romans, beginning at the 28th verse of the 8th chapter and ending at the 11th chapter. If this will be too much, confine yourself to two words that occur so often in the New Testament. They are these, "called," or the called, and "elect," or elected, or election. In complying with these requests you will confer a particular favor on an inquirer after truth.

P. H.

Kentucky, January 25, 1825.

Reply.

My Dear Sir,—Could I satisfactorily remove all the philosophical difficulties presented in your friendly epistle, and answer to your conviction every inquiry, I dare not do it for one sub stantial reason, viz. the next mail would bring me perhaps five hundred questions as difficult as they, and thus we should have in a little time a catechism as long and as metaphysical as the Westminster. I need not tell you of my unfeigned respect for you, nor of my sincere desires to render you all possible satisfaction, as I think you have already assurances as unambiguous as any which I could afford. Besides, in the prosecution of this work it will appear that not the bible but the schoolmen have raised those difficulties; and if it has not already appeared, I trust it will yet be manifest that those difficulties neither stand in the way of the salvation of the soul nor of the body.

Difficulties that arise from my remarks on faith in the passages quoted, may be easily solved by attending to the fact, that, in those remarks, we were speaking simply of faith itself, as existing in the human mind, independent of the theory of remote causes. A tree, a bird, and a fish, are easily distinguishable from one another by essential attributes or properties evident to all. There are many questions, however, about the remote causes of their existence, their attributes, and properties, which might be proposed, the solution of which would be as puzzling and curious as unprofitable. The unlettered swain who is possessed of an apple, a bird, and a fish, can easily distinguish them; and when eaten they are as conducive to his health and vigor as though he could comprehend and explain every principle and item that enters into their constitution. Faith, hope, and love, are just as distinct and distinguishable; with this difference, perhaps, that mental things not being subjected to the scrutiny of the external senses, require more reflection than those things submitted merely to the eye or hand. Now faith is neither more nor less than the belief of some testimony. This is what, in all ages, and amongst all people, is called faith. Faith without testimony is impossible; and nothing more nor less than testimony believed constitutes faith. I might be asked why such testimony was exhibited—who gave it—who caused it to be given—why I heard it—why I did not hear it sooner—or why I did not attend to it when heard,—and a thousand things besides; but still faith remains the same thing let these questions be answered as they may. And whether one man think that a man can, by the mere testimony of the witnesses, believe, or that God works faith in the heart by his Holy Spirit, still faith, however it comes into existence, is the belief of testimony. And such is the constitution of the human mind, that a man is as passive in believing as he was in receiving his name, or as the eye is in receiving the rays of light that fall upon it from the sun; consequently no man can help believing any testimony when the evidence of its truth arrests his attention.

But here we are asked, Why does not the same evidence arrest the attention of all? Why do not all believe the same testimony? The fact exists that all do not believe the same testimony, either human or divine. The evidence, then, does not arrest the attention? Why does it not? Prejudices, indisposition, antipathies, predilections, &c., shut the eyes and harden the heart. But here curiosity is not yet satisfied. It inquires again, Why is one more prejudiced than another, or why is one more indisposed than another? It is answered that the constitution of mind and body, habits, and the growth of certain passions, make the difference. This will not suffice. Another and another why is proposed. Why were these things so? It is answered, It was so decreed. Then comes why was it so decreed? It is answered, Because God so pleased. This is not yet satisfactory. It is asked, Why did it so please him? Because it was most conducive to his glory. Why was it most conducive to his glory? Because it was. And why, and why, and why? and so it ends with a why, just where we began.

But the parable of the sower presents a difficulty of the same kind. Why four kinds of ground? It is a fact that there exist four kinds, and that the seed did not alter the ground—did not change its nature. The ground was the same before and after the seed was cast. What then made the difference in the ground?—was it naturally or supernaturally so? If naturally, why four and not two kinds? If supernaturally one was good, why were three not so? If supernaturally three were bad, why was but one good? Many such questions the scholastic divines have given birth to. But when solved they contribute nothing to our happiness.

The parable of the sower and the other scriptures referred to in your letter, were not pronounced with a reference to settling such questions. In the parable of the sower the Saviour acquainted his apostles with the reception his word would meet with from the Jews when promulged to them. Some of them who believed the ancient revelations, like Lydia, and whose hearts were thereby opened or honestly disposed towards the hope of Israel, received the glad tidings of his advent without prejudice, and brought forth fruit in different degrees, according to a variety of circumstances. Others received the word, but the anxieties and the lusts of other things rendered it unfruitful. Others soon apostatized, and went back to the Jews because of tribulation; and on others it took no effect. Thus they were apprized before they set out of the result of their mission, and the fact proved the Saviour's prophecy to be correct. Both amongst the Jews, religious proselytes, and the Gentiles, it so came to pass. He did not intend in this parable to teach that some men's hearts were either naturally or supernaturally disposed to believe, and that others were not. He did not make excuses for men's infidelity by teaching them that the reason why they could not believe was because they were not the elect; nor did he flatter the pride of any who considered their natural powers and good dispositions were the cause of becoming his disciples. No such questions were before him; and to apply this parable to other purposes than those in reference to which it was pronounced, is wresting the scriptures.

Solomon's maxim that "the preparations (or Hebrew, disposings) of the heart and the answer of the tongue are both from the Lord," has been quoted by many divines to prove what Solomon never intended. Solomon was not speaking of the salvation of Jesus Christ in these words, but of the general management of the hearts and tongues of men. The answer of the tongue, as much as the disposing of the hearts, in some men, is from God,

While we thus contend, my dear friend, that "the sense of scripture is not manifold, but one;" that every period must be interpreted subordinately to the scope or design of the writer, thus endeavor to understand the revelation without any human system before our eyes, I am not to be understood as asserting that there is no divine influence exercised over the minds and bodies of men. This would be to assert in contradiction to a thousand facts and declarations in the volume of revelation—this would be to destroy the idea of any divine revelation—this would be to destroy the idea of any divine government exercised over the human race—this would be to make prayer a useless and irrational exercise—this would be to deprive christians of all the consolations derived from a sense of the superintending care, guidance, and protection of the Most High. But to resolve every thing into a "divine influence," is the other extreme. This divests man of every attribute that renders him accountable to his Maker, and assimilates all his actions to the bending of the trees or the tumults of the ocean occasioned by the tempests.

There are many things which are evident, yet altogether inexplicable. Some animals, even of those domesticated, are naturally, we say, kind and obliging, good natured and affectionate; while others of the same species are just the contrary. These sometimes, too, are moved by a divine influence. The dove returning with the olive branch, the raven with the food for the prophet, the fish with a stater in its mouth for tribute, another bringing Jonah to shore, and an ass preaching to a wicked prophet, were moved by "a divine influence." Until we know more of God than can be revealed or known in this mortal state, we must be content to say of a thousand things a thousand times, we cannot understand how, or why, or wherefore they are so.

But he would be a foolish husbandman who, going forth with precious seed to cast upon his field, would cease to scatter it because a philosopher had asked him some questions about its germination and the influences requisite to its vegetation, which he could not explain. As foolish would a hungry man be who would refuse to eat bread because he could not explain the process of digestion, nor tell how it conduces to the preservation of life. And just as foolish he who refuses to meditate upon the revelation of God and to practise its injunctions, because there are some why's or wherefore's for which he cannot give a reason.

My limits forbid me at present to be more particular. The scriptural import of some terms and phrases in your letter will be attended to hereafter. I wish to avoid all philosophical questions which have been introduced into the christian system, because they are utterly unprofitable, vain, and endless. For instance, were I to discuss philosophically the dogma founded on *John* vi. 37, "All that the Father gives me shall come to me," I should soon be

65

asked to solve a difficulty founded on *John* xvii. 13. " I have lost none of them you gave me, except one, the son of perdition." When I should have solved a difficulty on *John* x. 24, " You believe not because you are not of my sheep," I should have another upon these words, " You believe not because you seek honor from men," &c. I am not to be understood that there are difficulties really existing upon these passages, for they are plain in their context; but systems have made them difficulties as respects other systems. But those "texts" when torn out of their scope, are like the human eye when torn from the head and placed in the palm of the hand—it is useless, except as a subject of dissection and amusing speculation.

Hoping that your faith, and love, and hope, grow exceedingly, I remain your affectionate brother in the hope of immortality.   EDITOR.

Mason county, Kentucky, February 16, 1825.

Brother Campbell,

YOUR last number of the " Christian Baptist" has just arrived; and I must say, in justice to my own conscience, and in accordance with the sentiments of all those who have expressed themselves, that it is unusually interesting. Your readers are well pleased with your piece on the Spirit; but they are better pleased with your piece on the subject of the incorporation of the Danville University. I would say, for your information, as you seem, from your remarks in the last number, not to know, that the legislature had passed the act of incorporation, which you intimated or insinuated would be anti-republican, and which seems to be the universal opinion of all disinterested persons. How this is reconcilable with the equal and unalienable rights of mankind, and with the genius of our government, (when, as I have been informed, Congress has refused to incorporate religious institutions in the manner in which our legislature has done;) remains for them to explain to us. Although I do not cordially approve of every sentiment advanced in your publication; yet I am constrained to say, that it is better calculated " to restore the ancient order of things," to elicit an earnest, diligent, accurate, and thorough investigation of facts generally, and scripture particularly, to expose and dismember those illegal, dangerous, and antiscriptural confederacies, hierarchies, and aristocracies, which are so often, and so cunningly formed, and which are so sedulously sought, and so assiduously maintained, at the expense of us laity, truth and righteousness; and for the aggrandizement, the sole aggrandizement, of domineering, ambitious, not to say, designing and licentious clergy, than any publication I ever saw: and I do not hesitate to allow, that I do most conscientiously believe that it is doing more good than any publication in the western country. Moreover I do most earnestly wish it could have a more extensive circulation, even throughout the whole United States; and particularly in the middle and southern states, where the abominable abuses, irregularities, and usurpations, are the most prevalent and powerful. Your paper has well nigh stopped missionary operations in this state. I hope it will destroy associations, state conventions, presbyteries, synods, and general assemblies; all of which are as assumed and as antiscriptural as the infallibility and pontificate of the pope of Rome. I have long been a member of associations; and to the best of my knowledge, all the rivalships, divisions, schisms, jealousies, and antipathies, which have existed in our state for the last fifteen or twenty years, have been generated, nourished, and measurably matured, in associations. By adopting the same rule by which associations and conventions are formed, we might have a national convention of all the kindreds, tongues, people, tribes and nations under heaven, to meet once in every ten or twenty years, in London, Constantinople, Pekin, or Philadelphia. Let each nation send one ambassador, plenipotentiary, messenger, priest, high priest, pontiff, or king, just as the urgency of the case may require. I have thought that Satan would have to go to work afresh, before long, in order to forge names suitable to modern manœuvres. I am no priest, but if you will allow a suggestion from a plain man, I would say that the time of which Paul speaks in 2d *Thess.* ii. 3—5, has arrived, when there shall be a falling away from the ancient order of things, and that man of sin be revealed, the son of perdition, who opposes and exalts himself above all that is called God, or that is worshipped. So that he as God, sitting in the temple of God, shows himself that he is God. Hoping that you will persevere in pulling down this man of sin, and wishing you all success,

I remain yours respectfully,
A READER OF THE C. B.

History of the English Bible.—No. III.

" IN the reign of queen Mary [1555] the exiles at Geneva undertook a new translation, commonly called the Geneva Bible; the names of the translators were, Coverdale, Goodman, Gilby, Whittingham, Sampson, Cole, Knox, Bodleigh, and Pullain, who published the New Testament first in small twelves, 1557, by Conrad Badius. This is the first that was printed with numerical verses. The whole bible was published afterwards with marginal notes, 1559, dedicated to queen Elizabeth. The translators say, " They had been employed in this work night and day, with fear and trembling—and they protest from their consciences, that, in every point and word, they had faithfully rendered the text to the best of their knowledge." But the marginal notes having given offence, it was not suffered to be published in England till the death of archbishop Parker, when it was printed [1576] by Christopher Barker, in quarto, *cum privilegio*, and met with such acceptance, that it passed through twenty or thirty editions in this reign.

" Cranmer's edition of the bible had been reprinted in the years 1562 and 1566, for the use of the churches. But complaint being made of the incorrectness of it, archbishop Parker projected a new translation, and assigned the several books of the Old and New Testament to about fourteen dignitaries in the church, most of whom being bishops, it was from that time called the Bishop's Bible, and was printed in an elegant and pompous folio, in the year 1568, with maps and cuts. In the year 1572, it was reprinted with some alterations and additions, and several times afterwards without any amendments.

" In the year 1582, the Roman Catholic exiles translated the New Testament for the use of their people, and published it in quarto, with this title, " The New Testament of Jesus Christ, translated faithfully into English, out of the authentic Latin, according to the best corrected copies of the same, diligently conferred with the Greek and other editions in divers languages; with arguments of books and chapters, annotations, and other necessary helps for the better understanding of the text; and especially for the discovery of the corruptions of divers late translations, and for clearing controversies in religion of these days. In the English college of Rhemes. Printed by John Fogny." The Old Testament of this translation was first published at Doway in two quarto volumes, the first in the year 1609, the other 1610, by Lawrence Kellam, at the sign of the Holy Lamb, with a preface and tables; the authors are said to be cardinal Allen, sometime principal of St. Mary Hall, Oxford, Richard Bristow, fellow of Exeter College, and Gregory Martyn, of St. John's college. The annotations were made by Thomas Worthington, B. A. of Oxford; all of them exiles for their religion, and settled in Popish seminaries beyond sea. The mistakes of this translation, and the false glosses put upon the text, were exposed by the learned Dr. Fulke and Mr. Cartwright.

At the request of the Puritans in Hampton court conference, king James appointed a new translation to be executed by the most learned men of both universities, under the following regulations.

1. That they keep as close as possible to the Bishop's Bible.

2. That the names of the holy writers be retained according to vulgar use.

3. That the old ecclesiastical words be kept, as church not to be translated congregation, &c.

4. That when a word has divers significations, that be kept which has been most commonly used by the fathers.

5. That the division of chapters be not altered.

6. No marginal notes but for the explanation of a Hebrew or Greek word.

7. Marginal references may be set down.

The other regulations relate to the translators comparing notes, and agreeing among themselves; they were to consult the modern translations of the French, Dutch, German, &c. but to vary as little as possible from the Bishop's Bible.

The king's commission bears date 1604, but the work was not begun till 1606, and finished 1611. Fifty-four of the chief divines of both universities were originally nominated; some of whom dying soon after, the work was undertaken by forty seven, who were divided into six companies; the first translated from Genesis to the first book of Chronicles; the second to the prophecy of Isaiah; the third translated the four greater prophets, with the Lamentations and twelve smaller prophets; the fourth had the Apocrypha; the fifth had the four Gospels, the Acts, and the Revelations; and the sixth had the canonical epistles. The whole being finished and revised by learned men from both universities, the publishing it was committed to the care of bishop Bilson and Dr. Miles Smith, which last wrote the preface that is now prefixed. It was printed in the year 1611, with a dedication to king James, and is the same that is still read in all the churches."   NEAL.

No. 10.]   MAY 2, 1825.

Texts and Textuary Divines.

I DO not know whether we ought to agree with those lexicographers who make the Roman *textus* a term equivalent to the Grecian *ploke*, a weaving. Some may justify this etymological interpretation, because, they may suppose, that there is an analogy between the making of a web from thread, and the weaving of a sermon from a few detached words, called a text. I would rather derive the term text directly from the Greek verb *tixto*, to beget or bring forth, from which *texos* or *textus* might be ingeniously formed, and

this might be translated an egg, or something pregnant with life, which by the laws of nature might become a living animal, as a text by the laws of sermonizing easily becomes a full grown sermon. But waiving this as a question for the literati, we shall proceed to our subject.

An ingenious or an enthusiastic preacher may bring forth or create any dogma or doctrine he pleases from a text or sentence, detached from the scope or design of the writer; even from the same text sermons may be woven of the most discordant texture, as all the pulpits in the land attest. A whole system of theology has been deduced from one text, and a score of sermons have been woven from one thread. Particular election, particular redemption, effectual calling, progressive sanctification, and final perseverance, have all been deduced from, and proved by Isaiah lxii. 12. "And they shall call them the holy people, the redeemed of the Lord; and you shall be called, sought out, a city not forsaken."

I find amongst my father's old manuscripts of twenty years' standing, the outlines of twelve or thirteen sermons upon these words, "Bind up the testimony, and seal the law amongst my disciples." On these words was raised a doctrine so comprehensive, as to include almost the whole New Testament, and it appears from the manuscript as though this text had furnished matter for a quarter of a year's discussion. Such was the good old way of our worthy ancestors. He was, half a century ago, the greatest divine, who could bring the most doctrine, and pronounce the most sermons from a clause of a verse.

A fine orator in Belfast, a few years since, astonished a brilliant audience with an enchanting discourse upon these words—*Rev.* xii. "And there appeared a great wonder in heaven, a woman." He omitted the description, and raised his doctrine on those insulated words. He amused his hearers with a rare exhibition of pulpit eloquence; though some of the ladies were not so well pleased with "the doctrinal part."

I remember to have read, when about fourteen years old, a sermon delivered by a Scotch divine to a congregation of beer drinkers, from the word Malt. In the dignified pulpit style, after a pertinent exordium, he stated his method to be the following, as well as my recollection serves, (for I have not seen it since.)

1. In the first place, my beloved auditors, I will explain the different figures of speech in my text.

2. In the second place I shall attempt to exhibit the fourfold effects of malt in this life.

3. In the next place I will detail its fourfold effects in the world to come.

4. And in the last place, my dear hearers, I will deduce a few practical instructions and exhortations for your benefit.

In discussing the first head his topics were also four, corresponding with the four letters of his text—M, A, L, T. He very elegantly demonstrated; 1st, that M was metaphorical; 2d, that A was allegorical; 3d, that L was literal; and 4th, that T was theological.

The particulars under head second were also four, corresponding with the same four letters— Its effects in this life, were, 1st, M, murder; 2d, A, adultery; 3d, L, lasciviousness; and 4th, T, treason. On these he expatiated at great length.

Under head third the items were also four. The effects of an undue attachment to Malt in the next world, were, 1st, M, misery; 2d, A, anguish; 3d, L, lamentation; and 4th, T, torment.

His fourth head was as methodical in its dis-

T

tribution as any of the others, and closed with four exhortations on the same four letters, 1st, M, my dear hearers; 2d, A, all of you; 3d, L, look diligently; 4th, T, both *to* my text, and *to* yourselves, and above all *to* abstain from a free use of M-a-l-t liquors. We were told it had the happy effect of reclaiming and converting all his congregation from their intemperate habits.

Whatever may have been the intention of the publisher of this sermon, it was no doubt not only orthodox, but strictly methodical, and a just satire upon the textuaries. And I doubt not that it was a better sermon, and more edifying, than nine out of every ten of the fashionable harangues. I am very certain, also, that it had as much authority from the Bible as any of them. Nothing but the grossest ignorance, the native offspring of the dark ages, could have originated this text or scrap preaching; and nothing but the indescribable influence of custom, could have reconciled a thinking and rational being to its continuance amongst us.

But it is not only in the public assembly that the textuaries pervert the record of heaven, and impose upon the revelation of God as many meanings as there are letters in their text; but all their creeds, and treatises on theological subjects, are formed on the same principles. Now we are always prepared to show that to cite a sentence from the body of a discourse, to extract a sentiment from the scope of a speaker or writer, to confirm a position which he had not before his mind when those words were pronounced or written, is always hazarding an error, mostly wresting the author, and frequently just the same as interpolating or forging a revelation, and imposing it upon the credulous and unwary.

The Westminster Confession, now lying before me, affords hundreds of instances of this sort. I will open it almost at random, and find in every page the best means of illustrating the views just now offered.

The book, at my first opening, presented to my view pages 378 and 379. We shall give the whole article, commencing on page 378, (Philadelphia edition, 1797,) to our readers, and then our exposition.

"The pastoral office is the first in the church, both for dignity and usefulness.(*a*) The person who fills this office, has, in the scripture, obtained different names expressive of his various duties. As he has the oversight of the flock of Christ, he is termed bishop. (*b*)* As he feeds them with spiritual food, he is termed pastor. (*c*) As he serves Christ in his church, he is termed minister. (*d*) As it is his duty to be grave and prudent, and an example to the flock, and to govern well in the house and kingdom of Christ, he is termed presbyter or elder. (*e*) As he is the

(*a*) Romans ii. 13.
(*b*) Acts xx. 28. Take heed therefore unto yourselves, and to all the flocks over which the Holy Ghost hath made you overseers, (bishops) to feed the church of God, which he hath purchased with his own blood.
(*c*) Jer. iii. 15. And I will give you pastors according to mine heart, which shall feed you with knowledge and understanding. 1 Pet. v. 2, 3, 4.
(*d*) 1 Cor. iv. 1. Let a man so account of us, as of the ministers of Christ, and stewards of the mysteries of God. 2 Cor. iii. 6. Who also hath made us able ministers of the New Testament.
(*e*) 1 Pet. v. 1. The elders which are among you, I exhort, who am also an elder, and a witness of the sufferings of Christ, and also a partaker of the glory that shall be revealed. See also Tit. i. 5. 1 Tim. v. 1, 17, 19.

* "As the office and character of the gospel minister is particularly and fully described in the holy scriptures, under the title of bishop; and as this term is peculiarly expressive of his duty as an overseer of the flock, it ought not to be rejected."

messenger of God, he is termed the angel of the church.(*f*) As he is sent to declare the will of God to sinners, and to beseech them to be reconciled to God through Christ, he is termed ambassador.(*g*) And, as he dispenses the manifold grace of God, and the ordinances instituted by Christ, he is termed steward of the mysteries of God." (*h*)

In this chapter there are nine positions or propositions distinct from each other, requiring, as the authors thought, distinct proof. Ten texts are adduced, and six referred to, in proof of those positions.

Five of these nine positions I will prove to be erroneous, untenable, and the proofs, in every instance, wrested or perverted. Three of the remaining four, are, on scripture premises, objectionable: one of them, excepting the awkwardness of the expression, is perfectly correct and fairly confirmed or proved. This is the third one. But my limits forbid that I should dwell on any of them, save those that are erroneous and untenable.

Of the five thus classified the first is,—"As he (the bishop) serves Christ in his church, he is termed minister." 1 *Cor.* iv. 1. is adduced as proof. Now that this text is wrested will appear when the question is asked:—Did the apostle Paul in this sentence, or even in this chapter, speak at all of a bishop? This is the first question which a grammarian, or a logician, or a man of plain common sense will ask, who is intent on understanding such a question. Were these words spoken of a bishop, or bishops, in general, or particular? I fearlessly answer no. Suppose the pope of Rome, or the patriarch of Constantinople appropriated to himself the title of minister of Jesus Christ, and adduced this proof, which is the only one the Westminster divines adduced in support of their claims; what would a presbyterian doctor tell him? Would he not rationally and consistently say—Sir, Paul did not here speak of such ecclesiastical characters as you. He did not say—"Let a man so account of us popes, or patriarchs, as the ministers of Jesus Christ." This would be sound logic, or good sense. Well let us read the supplement to suit the Westminster appropriation. It reads thus—"Let a man so account of us bishops, as the ministers of Jesus Christ." This is as glaring as the preceding. But now read the verse with the supplement which the scope or context imperiously demands, and both the papistical and presbyterial appropriations are perfectly exploded—"Let a man so account of us apostles as of the ministers of Christ, and stewards of the mysteries of God." Now either the creed makers supposed that apostles and bishops were the self-same order, or they either ignorantly or wilfully appropriated the passage to themselves. On any hypothesis the perversion here is equal to the forging of a scripture authority. And did those men really believe that what was said of the apostles, applied to every bishop in the christian church! Or were they so dull of apprehension as to suppose that Paul here spake of bishops! So far will suffice as an exposition of the perversion of scripture in general, and of this passage in particular.

(*f*) Mal. ii. 7. Rev. ii. 1. Unto the angel of the church of Ephesus, write. Rev. i. 20. The seven stars are the angels of the seven churches. See also Rev. iii. 1, 7.
(*g*) 2 Cor. v. 20. Now then we are ambassadors for Christ, as though God did beseech you by us; we pray you in Christ's stead, be ye reconciled to God. Eph. vi. 20.
(*h*) Luke xii. 42. Who then is that faithful and wise steward, whom his lord shall make ruler over his household, to give them their portion of meat in due season? 1 Cor. iv. 1, 2. Moreover it is required of stewards, that a man be found faithful.

But, say some, it is a trifling mistake, a matter of no consequence. But it is undeniable that this method of quoting scripture, regardless of the scope of the writer, may issue, in other instances, in dogmas of the most dangerous import. We assert, however, that the above perversion is no little mistake, it is no trifling matter. It is a haughty and arrogant assumption of the clergy to give themselves the title of "the ministers of Christ," and thereby to claim the honors and regards due to those properly so called. Names have an imposing influence and lead thousands captive. But there is something in this clerical appropriation of this title as unjust as for one of seven heirs to an estate to pass himself off amongst strangers as the heir of such an estate, or as it would have been, during the negociation of Ghent, for one of the plenipotentiaries to have called himself the minister of the United States. And there is something in it as arrogant too, as it would have been for a few American consuls, in other European countries, to have called themselves the ministers of the United States.

But in this appropriation of the title, the ministers of Christ, there is a variety of error, and of arrogance. The term *diakonos*, in Greek; *minister* in Latin, and servant in English, are expressive of the same character or standing, are titles of the same import. The term minister, a general or unappropriated title, designates any servant, and belongs to every obedient disciple of Jesus Christ. In the general sense of the term it belongs to sister Phœbe, as well as to any apostle or bishop. And, indeed, the widow who cast in her two mites, was a much greater minister or servant of God, than any of the Westminster clergy, who were servants of God and the long parliament. To call the clergy the ministers of Christ, is, therefore, a pious robbery of the obedient disciples of Christ, who are ministers of God as well as they, to speak in the most humble terms.

But in the text taken from 1 Cor. 4. it is not *diakonos*, but *huperetes* that Paul appropriated to himself and his associates, the apostles. This term is defined, "official servants of those in authority," the office of a judicatory. It occurs, Matt. v. 25. translated officer; xxvi. 28. translated servant, but properly officers, as Dr. Campbell insists. It is applied to the servants or attendants of persons in authority, Luke xvi. 20. John xviii. 36. Acts xiii. 5. And Jesus said to Paul, Acts xxvi. 16. I have appeared to you to make you a *hupereten*, a servant or minister of myself—It is no where applied to a bishop, except in the writings of John Calvin, and the Westminster divines and their followers.

Position 2. "As it is his duty to be grave and prudent, and an example of the flock, and to govern well in the house and kingdom of Christ, he is termed presbyter or elder. 1 *Pet.* v. 1." The passage quoted does not prove this position. Nor is there any passage that says they were called elders for such reasons assigned. But the passage quoted proves that the term elder was sometimes applied to the first converts, to distinguish them from the novices. So Peter applies it to himself in the words quoted—I am also an elder, one of the first converts, (*kai*) even so old a disciple, so early a convert, as that I witnessed the sufferings of Christ—Hence Paul exhorts that a bishop should not be selected from the novices, or recent converts, but that he should be one of the elders, or first converts, lest not having experience, he might be puffed up with pride and fall into the condemnation of the devil. Hence they were fitly styled elders because of their age and experience in the school of Christ, and overseers from the nature of their office.

Position 3. "As he is the messenger of God, he is termed the angel of the church. *Rev.* ii. 1." The bishop is no where called an angel of the church. Many critics have spent all their genius and talents in endeavoring to find out who the seven angels of the seven churches mentioned in the second and third chapters of the Apocalypse were, and most certainly none of them has satisfactorily found them out. Not one of them can afford any thing but a vague conjecture to support his theory. I do not so much wonder that the Westminster divines mistook here; as many of the most learned since that time have been evidently mistaken in their conjectures on the angels. My correspondent Philip was the first person and the only person, who suggested to me the true import of the term in those passages. Its simplicity and plainness constitute the chief reason, in my judgment, why the learned critics, who are always looking for mysteries where there are none, could not find it out.

The term *angel*, every smatterer in Greek knows, signifies *messenger*. Now John, the writer of these seven epistles, we all know, was an exile in Patmos, when he wrote; and had not the liberty of travelling to visit those seven churches. He had no way of either receiving or communicating intelligence as respected them, but by messengers. When the Lord appeared to him in Patmos he commanded him to write for seven messengers, seven epistles, to be carried to seven churches—For the messenger to Ephesus, says he, write as follows. For the messenger to Smyrna, write as follows. For the messenger to Philadelphia, write as follows, &c. A natural and correct translation of the original, according to the common signification of the terms, solves the whole difficulty, and puts to shame the guesses of those who were too learned to regard common sense. The last words of the first chapter furnish the key to this difficulty; "The seven stars, are messengers to the seven churches." Not *the* messengers. *To* and *for* are equally signs of the dative case in the Greek language. To write a letter for a messenger to carry, is precisely accordant to the original, and to the fact. For how, in the name of common sense, could an exile in Patmos send letters to several churches in Asia but by messengers! And what more natural than that each of these churches, not more than one hundred and fifty miles apart, would send a messenger to the distinguished exile at Patmos! If they had a spark of christian love or veneration for the aged and only surviving apostle now a prisoner of Jesus Christ, could they refrain from visiting him by a messenger!—"I was in prison and you came to me," would suggest their duty. To those, or for those messengers of these churches was John to write according to the commandment. So that the plain and most obvious translation of this passage solves all difficulties which the writers on church government for ages have been unable, in all their researches, to solve. Indeed there was no difficulty here, but what their systems made. They wished to find a bishop converted into an angel, at the close of the first century; and having before John died, made him an angel, it would be easy in a century or two to make one a "god on earth, and disposer of all earthly crowns." So the Westminster position is false, and the text again wrested to prove what is untenable.

Position 4. "As he is sent to declare the will of God to sinners, and to beseech them to be reconciled to God through Christ, he is termed ambassador." The bishop of a church is called an ambassador no where in the inspired writings, nor is the term applicable to him in any sense whatever. It would be an offence of a very high degree against truth and reason to call a modern missionary an ambassador of Christ: but still a much grosser outrage to call an overseer of one congregation of professed disciples an ambassador of Christ. It is, however, sufficient for our purpose to show that the term is, by the apostles, exclusively appropriated to themselves. The text adduced by the Westminster divines is 2 *Cor.* v. 20. "Now then we are ambassadors for Christ," &c. Let common sense inquire, To whom does the pronoun *we* belong? or of whom does the apostle speak? Surely no man with any regard to the reputation of his understanding, will say that the apostle here spake of bishops or deacons. Jesus Christ is represented as God's chief ambassador, and the apostles sent by him as his ambassadors, to whom he committed the word of reconciliation, were his substitutes. Hence, says the apostle, We, the ambassadors of Christ, in his stead, as the ambassadors of God, beseech men to be reconciled to God. Since John Calvin's time, the clergy of that school have boldly assumed the title of ambassadors of Christ. This honor they disputed with the Romanists, who contended that their priesthood were the plenipotentiaries of heaven, and were incorporated a court by a decree of heaven, with full powers to negotiate with the Deity on the behalf of men, to remit sins and do all other acts and deeds belonging to the Sovereign of the Universe, by their delegated powers. It appears altogether unnecessary to expose the absurdity of this arrogance any further; but as the clergy contend for the title with so much warmth, and as the people are argued out of their common sense in many instances—it may be expedient to observe that the title ambassador amongst men, from whose usage of the term the apostles borrow it, exclusively belongs to those commissioned by the chief magistrate, and invested with full powers to exhibit terms of reconciliation to those at variance with the government, whose plenipotentiaries they are. Before they can be accredited as such, it is necessary that they produce their commission in the handwriting of the highest authority in the government, and the great seal of the state annexed. Our ambassadors at Ghent are referred to in illustration of this peculiarity. When the embassy is announced, the powers exhibited, and all the propositions declared, the embassy ceases. Those who afterwards descant upon, or interpret the articles of the embassy, are never called ambassadors or ministers plenipotentiary. Were the first orator in the land to travel through the world delivering lectures on the treaty at Ghent, exhorting the interested parties to a strict observance of all the items, and praying for their prosperity in so doing, he could not be called an ambassador. No man in the world can be called our ambassadors to Ghent, or to the court of St. James, but those who held that commission; nor could those commissioners themselves deliver the same authority to others. In case of indisposition or death, they cannot constitute or appoint others. The power that ordained them is the only power that can ordain others. These are common place remarks. And for the same reasons, on the same grounds, and by all the same rules, no man breathing the breath of life is an ambassador of Jesus Christ. The ambassadors are all dead, and returned to the high court that commissioned them. The articles of their embassy are all in writing delivered to the nations, the finger of God and the seal of heaven attached thereto; and no man, nor combination of men on earth have any power to subtract from, or add one item to, the whole embassy exhibited in the New Testament.

Should different political parties arise in the state, on different interpretations of the treaty alluded to, and different orators expound and discuss the treaty, it would be no more ridiculous nor arrogant in them, to call themselves ambassadors of the government of the United States, than for those creatures of theological schools, those rabbies of modern divinity, those self-made bishops, to call themselves the ambassadors of Jesus Christ.

So stands the fourth position we promised to expose; and such is the authority adduced to prove it. Indeed, as if ashamed to cite the passage, they refer to *Eph.* vi. 20, as a second proof where Paul says, "for which I am an ambassador in chains." Here I must call to my aid all the logicians, grammarians, and critics in the land, to explain by what rule, by what principle, by what authority, it may be said, that, because Paul was at one time an ambassador in chains, therefore every bishop in christendom is an ambassador of Christ in chains!!! Yet this is the logic of the Westminster divines!

The last position we shall notice, is,—"As he dispenses the manifold grace of God, and the ordinances instituted by Christ, he is termed steward of the mysteries of God." This is perfect popery. This assumption of the clergy is haughty beyond expression. A steward is one entrusted with the property of another, the dispensation or management of which, is under his control, for the time being, as though he were the proprietor; nor is he accountable to any, but to him who appointed him to his stewardship.— Such were the apostles. They were entrusted with the dispensation of the gospel, with the mysteries of God, and were to him alone accountable for their stewardship—The ministry of reconciliation was committed to them, and to none else. The dispensation of the gospel was theirs, and a wo from heaven awaited them, if they were not faithful in his work: for had they kept it back, or kept it a secret, and not fully made it known, the salvation of men by Jesus Christ would have been frustrated. When he repaired to heaven and left them on earth, inspired by his Spirit, all depended upon their fidelity. They, however, were faithful; dispensed the gospel; showed the mysteries fully; published them with their tongues and pens, and committed them to the church, the repository of the truth. They made their knowledge of these mysteries public property, revealed them plainly and announced them to all men. They did not lock them up in the bodies of the clergy, they did not secretly communicate them to theological schools, they did not delegate their authority to others, or sell the gift of God for money.

But in what light do the Presbyterian clergy present themselves to our view, in the above appropriation of the title, "stewards of the mysteries of God," and "dispensers of the manifold grace of God?" They expressly declare that they have the care and management of the manifold grace of God, and his ordinances entrusted to them, as the steward of an English lord has his estate put under his management during the absence of his master!! Amenable to their masters alone, they can communicate or not, dispense or retain the manifold grace of God by official right!! And worse than all, they will not do it without money! So that in fact these stewards, while paid by their master, make their official duties a source of revenue to themselves, But these donations are the perquisites of office! These stewards have, in too many instances, afforded the people sufficient evidence that they have no manifold grace to themselves, much less a stock to communicate or dispense to others. And, instead of having one new mystery of God to exhibit, they are daily striving to make mysteries of their own, and do not understand the mysteries of God, unfolded by the apostles. I am as much the steward of the emperor of Russia, as any one of them is a steward of the mysteries of God. The texts they have cited are just like those already reviewed. Luke xii. 42, was a parable addressed to the apostles by their master, who was preparing them for the stewardship. Their quotation of 1 Cor. iv. 1, has already been considered; and their adding this general maxim, "Moreover it is required in stewards that a man be found faithful," will apply to the keeper of lord North's park more pertinently than any Presbyterian pastor in the commonwealth.

These strictures will show what reliance should be placed in the textuaries, whether employed in making creeds or sermons. They will also furnish matter worthy of consideration to those who wish to look through a black coat and the titles of office to the spirit of the priesthood. We shall find many pages in the Westminster Confession more exceptionable than that noticed.—It is one of the best creeds, too, in the land. But they are all "like to a bow that shoots deceitfully."   EDITOR.

A Narrative of the Origin and Formation of the Westminster or Presbyterian Confession of Faith. No. I.

IT will be necessary, before any notice is taken of the Westminster Assembly of Divines, to state a few historical facts relative to those times.

Charles I. had dispensed with the call of parliaments, and had acted the tyrant in church and state for twelve years previous to the sitting of the long parliament. During these twelve years the puritans, or non-conformists to the English hierarchy, had suffered much from the Court of High Commission, the Star Chamber, and especially from the arbitrary, cruel, and tyrannical proceedings of Archbishop Laud, who was at the head of the English church. The insolence of the archbishop, supported and patronized by the king and court, terminating in the famous *et cetera* oath decreed in his convocation for preventing innovations in doctrine and church government, had arrived to a degree beyond the endurance of a great proportion of the king's subjects in England and Scotland. Tumults and insurrections in Scotland, together with the embarrassed state of the king's finances, obliged the king to call a parliament once more.

This parliament which assembled A. D. 1640, kept their seats for about eighteen years. It was as anxiously looked up to by the church for a redress of grievances as it was by the state for a redress of hers. As we are more concerned at present with the religious views and proceedings of this parliament, than with its political, we shall advert to these.

The king, if he had any conscience at all, was hampered, says Neal, with conscientious attachments to the divine right of diocesan epis-

copacy; but the parliament, almost to a man, excepting the bishops, were Erastians. "Erastus maintained that Christ and his apostles had prescribed no particular form of discipline for his church in after ages, but had left the keys in the hands of the civil magistrate, who had the sole power of punishing transgressors, and of appointing such particular forms of church government from time to time as were most subservient to the peace and welfare of the commonwealth." Indeed these were the sentiments of our church reformers, from Archbishop Cranmer down to Bancroft. And though the Puritans in the reign of Queen Elizabeth wrote with great eagerness for the divine right of their book of discipline, their posterity in the next reign were more cool upon this head, declaring their satisfaction if the present episcopacy might be reduced to a more primitive standard. This was the substance of the minister's petition to the parliament, in the year 1641, signed by several hundred hands. And even those who petitioned for pulling down the hierarchy, root and branch, were willing to submit to a parliamentary reformation till the Scots revived the notion of divine right of presbytery in the assembly of divines."

A few historical facts, characteristic of the views and spirit of the parliament and of the times, will be of importance in this narrative.

All the members of parliament took the sacrament from the hands of Bishop Williams, in the episcopalian order, shortly after their meeting.

They appointed committees to receive petitions on grievances in religion.

They resolved that, without act of parliament, a convocation of clergy could make no canons binding on the clergy and laity of the land.

As the parliament increased in popularity and power, the Puritans stiffened in their demands, and accommodation between them and the episcopal bishops became more and more impracticable.

Two petitions of great note were sent up to the parliament; the one called the Root and Branch Petition, signed by fifteen thousand citizens and residents of London, praying that the whole hierarchy might be destroyed. The ministers' petition, signed by seven hundred beneficed clergy and an incredible number of citizens from different counties in England, prayed that the hierarchy might be reformed. Nineteen petitions, signed by one hundred thousand hands, of which there were six thousand nobility, gentry, and beneficed clergy, prayed that the hierarchy might be continued as it was. In these nineteen petitions it was stated, "that there can be no church without bishops; that no ordination was ever performed without bishops; that without bishops there can be no presbyters, and consequently no consecration of the Lord's Supper; that a bishop has a character that cannot be communicated but by a bishop; and that the church had been governed by bishops for fifteen hundred years." The tacking of one hundred thousand names of freeholders to such petitions only prove that the honest countrymen acted too much with an implicit faith in their clergy.

Loud complaints were made to parliament of unfair means of obtaining names to petitions. The Puritans are said to have drafted a petition for remedying some palpable grievances, which obtained thousands of names to it, and afterwards cut off the names and prefixed another petition to them praying for a destruction of the hierarchy. This is affirmed by Lord Clarendon, vol. 1. p. 204. But, be this as it may, when the House of Commons appointed a committee to examine into these matters, so many faults of this kind appeared on both sides, that the affair was dropped.

The parliament resolved "that whosoever would not swear to support their liberties and the Protestant religion, was unfit to bear office in the church or commonwealth."

That the Puritans, afterwards called the Presbyterians, did not at first think of contending for presbyteries, or indeed for presbyterial church government, is evident from the plan of church government which they proposed to this parliament for their ratification, at an early period of its session. This plan was pretty similar to Archbishop Usher's. The outlines of this plan were as follows:—

1st. "That every shire (or county) should be a distinct diocese or church."

2d. "That in every shire or church twelve or more able divines should be appointed in the nature of an old primitive constant presbytery."

3d. "That over every presbytery there should be a president, let him be called bishop, or overseer, or moderator, or superintendant, or by any other name, provided there be one in every county for the government and direction of the presbytery, in the nature of the speaker of the House of Commons, or chairman of a committee."

Accordingly it was resolved, July 10, 1640, "that ecclesiastical power for the government of the church be exercised by commissioners." July 31, "Resolved, that the members of every county bring in the names of nine persons to be ecclesiastical commissioners, on whom the power of church government shall be devolved, but that no clergyman be of the commission." This shews that the Puritans of those times did not intend the presbyterian government, but only a reduction of episcopacy to a more moderate standard.

The parliament willing to reform faster and farther than the king, and to limit and circumscribe the prerogative beyond the desires of the king and bishops, became obnoxious to the king's displeasure, and finally the king left his palace and retired to York; and his queen, a bold and resolute Catholic, having absolute dominion over him, together with some of the English bishops and members of the court, drove the king into a war against his own parliament; so that the nation was divided—one part for the king and the other for the parliament. It were tedious to go farther into a detail of the causes of this civil war, which brought so many calamities on the nation and the king to the scaffold, and it is unnecessary to our present object.

The king, in the prosecution of this war, was reduced to the necessity of accepting the service and affection of the Papists; and on the other hand the parliament took all possible care to cultivate friendship with the Scots, and to secure that nation to their interests. The king rejected a mediation, offered by the Scots, to effect a reconciliation between him and the parliament, because the Scots insisted upon the abolishing of episcopacy, and a uniformity of presbyterian government in the two nations. The members of parliament, being Erastians, as before observed, were under no conscientious scruples about a change of discipline, believing that the civil magistrate had the keys, and might establish whatever form might be conducive to the public good, readily complied with any propositions made by the Scots, readily accepted the mediation, and wrote to the Scots assembly, which was soon to meet, desiring their advice and assistance in bringing about such a reformation as was desired.

August 3, 1642, the Scots parliament wrote to the English parliament expressing their desires "for unity of religion, that there might be one confession of faith, one directory of worship, one public catechism, and one form of church government." The Scots parliament say, "that they were encouraged to enter upon these labors by the zeal of former times, when their predecessors sent a letter into England against the surplice, the tippet, and corner cap, (worn by the clergy) in the year 1566, and again 1583, and 1589. They therefore advise to begin with a uniformity of church government; for what hope can there be of one confession of faith, one form of worship and catechism, till prelacy be plucked up root and branch, as a plant which God has not planted? "Indeed," add they, "the reformed kirks hold their form of government by presbyteries to be *jure divino* and perpetual, but prelacy stands by *jure humano*."

The English parliament bowed to all these overtures, as they well knew they needed the Scots' assistance in carrying on the war, and as they wished to engage them on their side against the king. Lord Clarendon observes very justly, says Mr. Neal, vol. 2. page 571, that the parliament were sensible they could not carry on the war but by the help of the Scots, which they were not to expect without an alteration of the government of the church, to which that nation was violently inclined. But then to induce them, says Mr. Neal, to consent to such an alteration, it was said the Scots would not take up arms without it; so that they must lose all, and let the king return as conqueror or submit to the change. From this source sprang the Westminster Creed. The policy of war, the fears of conquest, and the hopes of victory, gave birth to the meeting of the divines. In fact the meeting of the divines at Westminster, and their proceedings, at the instance of the English and Scots parliaments, was as perfect a political measure as was the queen's pledging the crown jewels on the continent in order to raise gunpowder and firearms for her husband to fight his subjects into a belief that the hierarchy of England was of divine origin, and that the king reigned absolutely by *jure divino*, or by a divine right.

The necessity of receiving assistance from Scotland in carrying on the war, and the condition on which the Scots parliament agreed to lend that assistance, obliged the English parliament to pass an ordinance for the assembling of divines to determine on a uniformity of doctrine and discipline for the two nations, or to establish a system of doctrine and discipline for the church of England that might assimilate it to the views of the kirk of Scotland.

The ordinance bears date June 12, 1643, and is thus entitled, "An ordinance of the Lords and Commons in Parliament, for the calling of an assembly of learned and godly divines and others, to be consulted with by the parliament, for settling the government and liturgy of the church of England, and for vindicating and clearing the doctrine of the said church from false aspersions and interpretations."*

The ordinance ordered one hundred and twenty reverend gentlemen, ten peers, and twenty commoners of illustrious birth, whose names are all mentioned in the ordinance, and now lying before me, to assemble at Westminster, in the chapel called king Henry VII's chapel, on the 1st of July, 1643. Forty of those persons were to be sufficient for doing business, or to compose a competent quorum for the purposes

* Rushworth, vol. v. page 337.

72

of parliament. They were prohibited from introducing any topic of discussion from among themselves, and were to be confined "to such matters and things concerning the liturgy, doctrine, and discipline of the church of England, as shall be proposed by either or both houses of parliament, and no other." They were "not to divulge their opinions or advices touching the matters aforesaid, either by printing, writing, or otherwise, without consent of parliament. If any difference of opinion arose, they were to represent it to parliament, with their reasons, that the houses might give further directions. Four shillings per day were allowed for each one during his attendance. Dr. William Twisse of Newbury was appointed prolocutor; and, in case of sickness or death, the parliament reserved to themselves the choice of another." The ordinance concludes with the following proviso: "Provided always, That this ordinance shall not give them, nor shall they in this assembly assume or exercise any jurisdiction, power, or authority ecclesiastical whatsoever, or any other power than is herein particularly expressed." The divines were chosen out of such lists as the knights and burgesses brought in out of their several counties, from each of which the parliament chose one, or at most two.

"Before the assembly sat, the king, by his royal proclamation of June 22, forbade their meeting, for the purpose therein mentioned, and declared that no acts done by them ought to be received by his subjects. He also threatened to proceed against them with the utmost severity of the law. Nevertheless, sixty nine assembled in king Henry VII's chapel the first day, according to summons, not in their canonical habits, but chiefly in black coats, and bands in imitation of the foreign protestants. Few of the episcopal divines assembled; and those who did, after some time withdrew for these reasons: First, "Because the assembly was prohibited by the royal proclamation." Second, "Because the members of the assembly were not chosen by the clergy, and therefore could not appear as their representatives." Third, "Because there was a mixture of laity with the clergy, because the divines assembled were for the most part of a puritanical stamp, and their business, as they apprehended, was to pull down that which they would uphold."

Very different characters are given to these divines by ecclesiastical writers. Perhaps they are all exaggerated. We shall, however, give the statement of one on each side. Lord Clarendon says, "About twenty of them were reverend and worthy persons, and episcopal in their judgments; but as to the remainder, they were but pretenders to divinity. Some were infamous in their lives and conversations, and most of them of very mean parts and learning, not of scandalous ignorance, and of no other reputation than of malice to the church of England." Mr. Baxter, on the other hand, affirms, that "they were men of eminent learning, godliness, ministerial abilities and fidelity." As politicians, we may say, from their works, that they did not understand the principles of civil liberty, for "they would allow no toleration to those whom they called sectaries;" and had they understood the christian religion they would never have assembled in king Henry VII's chapel to help the parliament to make a creed that would be the means of attaching the Scotch parliament to the English in carrying on a war against their king; nor, indeed, would they ever have been induced to meet for the purpose of establishing any creed or

form of discipline for any community holding the apostolic writings as of divine origin. We shall resume this narrative in our next. Every thing we have stated or may state on this subject is derived from the most authentic source. We pledge ourselves for the accuracy of every fact stated on historical ground, the vouchers being of the highest reputation as historians.

EDITOR.

To the Editor of the Christian Baptist.

DEAR SIR—Our friend Dr. Fishback, of Lexington, has proposed a plan of reformation in Transylvania University which is exciting a considerable interest in our state. As you have had an opportunity of much experience and observation in reference to universities and seminaries of learning in Europe and America, will you be so good as to give us your opinion on the subject?

The plan of reformation proposed seems to be to exclude all sectarianism in reference to religion from the institution, and to make the scriptures the only school book on that subject; to be read and learned by the students until they become acquainted with the principles, evidence, design, and character of the christian religion, as deduced from the bible. This is the religion of the country, in which all sects and denominations agree.

It is also proposed that the different christian denominations be admitted to an equal participation of the management and superintendency of the concern, in the board of trustees, and in the academical faculty, as far as practicable; and thereby to effect and cherish a unity of spirit in the bonds of peace, with an undivided confidence in all, in behalf of the institution. At the same time, to adopt a wise system of economy in the dress and expenditures of the students, so as to give to every man who is not rich an opportunity to educate his sons.

Would it be proper to exclude scholastic theology and natural religion, as they are called among the learned, from the course of instruction, which you know are taught in colleges? or are they true?

In Transylvania are taught, I observe from a catalogue, in the senior year, philosophy of mind, including the first principles of theology, by the President—I suppose without the bible.

Would or would not the above system, if adopted, in a great measure supersede the necessity of theological schools, except when established for sectarian purposes, and secure to parents and guardians, and to the country at large, instruction to the educated young men in the most important of all sciences—the science of spiritual things, which has been heretofore in a great degree neglected? My observation proves to me, that, if young men who are determined to fill situations in life which make education a prerequisite, do not bestow a particular, a critical attention upon the principles, nature, and evidence of the christian religion, in their course of previous education and academical study, they live for the most part their life time altogether ignorant of that religion; for as soon as they end their studies in college, they become immediately engrossed by others which exclude it from their minds, perhaps already barred by ignorance, pride, and prejudice, against any degree of attention to "the wisdom that comes from above," which is necessary for understanding it. This is the reason why we have so much infidelity and ignorance in the christian religion, dissolute morals, too, among the learned

73

professional men in christendom. This is the reason, too, why christianity is regarded by so many of that description of men as a system of inconsistencies and contradictions. Am I right, or am I wrong?

Ought Baptists to support and advocate the plan of reformation as suggested in the above sketch? I wish for information, because, from what I can learn, petitions will probably be circulated for subscription to the next legislature on the subject.   A Constant Reader.
——, Ky. March 10, 1825.

Reply to the above.

April 7, 1825.

Dear Sir—Your favor of the 10th ult. came to hand at too late an hour to be attended to in the April number. The subjects on which it treats are of great importance, both in a political and religious point of view. Seminaries of learning, for ages immemorial, have had a very great influence upon the political, moral, and religious character of society. And so long as the men who govern society owe their distinction to their education, and are elevated to these places that give them a formative influence on the views and habits of their contemporaries by means of their literary acquirements, literary institutions must be viewed with peculiar solicitude by the political, moral, and christian philanthropist. Whether christianity ever was at all indebted to colleges and universities, either directly or indirectly; or if indebted, whether it is more indebted to the popish or protestant literary establishments are not the questions now to be discussed. That they have done much evil to mankind admits of no disputation, but that they may do good, and that the evil done is accidental and not essential to them, is equally as indisputable.

That a course of instruction might be adopted and faithfully pursued, or that the present system might be reformed in the very best institutions, in such a way as to make them incomparably more advantage to society, is, I presume, to all who are conversant in such matters, a very plain and evident proposition. Indeed, the attempts of the present century to new-modify literary institutions, and the progress made in reformation in several seminaries, is proof positive that they are yet, in the judgment of the best informed, in an imperfect state, and that great advances towards perfection may yet be made. That Transylvania University, for whose prosperity you seem to be much concerned, may be elevated not only to still higher reputation at home and abroad, but that she may be rendered of incomparably more benefit to Lexington, Kentucky, and the whole Union, is, with me, a matter demonstrably evident.

The plan proposed by Dr. Fishback, while it merely alludes to some of the more glaring defects in almost all the seminaries of the union, recommends to the consideration of the community a system of reformation, which if adopted in substance or in the principle, if not in the whole form, would not only place the institutions adopting it on a basis superior to all the colleges in the union on the present establishments, but would also divest those institutions of some, if not of all those blemishes which present themselves so forcibly to the eye of the sagacious and benevolent members of the community.

One of the greatest blemishes in the character, and one of the greatest defects in the system of most of our literary institutions, is that they are religiously sectarian, and politically aristocratic in their constitution and administration. They are even in many instances much more so, strange as it may appear, in the American republic than they are in the British empire. This is perhaps more owing to the boards of trustees entrusted with the management of those institutions, and to the mighty spirit of emulation which seems to actuate religious sectaries in the contest who shall be greatest. The constitution and laws of the United States, founded upon the grand principles of civil and religious liberty, having placed all denominations on the same race-course, and having given to every one a fair start, presents the goal equally accessible to all, and the palm of distinction to that which runs fastest by its own strength—has indirectly contributed to that emulation which makes each one of the coursers willing to take hold of all the literary institutions he can grasp, in order to outrun, in this struggle for popularity, his competitors. It is perhaps owing to this that almost all our colleges are converted into sectarian schools, and are really more sectarian than under the English monarchy. For a similar reason they are more aristocratic too. In this country we have no noble nor ignoble blood—it has all come down from Adam and Eve; but in Britain and throughout Europe there is noble and ignoble blood—how it originated is unknown to us, but the fact is that it is one of the most dangerous realities in the world. Noble blood makes noble men, and royal blood makes kings; but Latin and Greek make lords in America—and Hebrew and Chaldee, with natural religion, make kings. Hence, when the nobility of Europe condescend to visit our ignoble blooded Americans, they can hold cast amongst us only by repairing to our colleges and universities where they find our noblemen. I have said that our literary institutions are more sectarian and aristocratic in this country than in Britain, and the natural causes or philosophical reasons for this fact are to be found in these hints.

In the University of Edinburgh, at the date of my last advices, there were two thousand two hundred and fifty students; and in Glasgow university, forty miles distant, there were two thousand two hundred, of all religious persuasions. Every parent and guardian commits the object of his greatest solicitude to those seminaries without the least apprehension or fear of any stratagem, or scheme, or undue influence to bias his understanding or to proselyte him. The work of making sectaries and of confirming them belongs to the divinity chairs, which every student is free to choose for himself after he has finished his academical course. The students are not even obliged to attend the sermons delivered in the chapels of these universities. On presenting a certificate that he attends any religious assembly in the city or suburbs, he is just in the same standing as those who frequent the chapel worship.

The rapid advances made by the Belfast Seminary upon Trinity College, Dublin, and upon Manooth College, furnish ample proof of the correctness of the principles contended for by Dr. Fishback. Trinity College, in the metropolis of the kingdom, existing for centuries, and devoted to the Church of England; Manooth too, of respectable antiquity, in the midst of a dense Roman Catholic community, and devoted to that religion, are outrivalled by an institution of twenty years standing, and comparatively fundless with regard to the others. Belfast, not sectarian in its character, has, in twenty years, equalled, and if I mistake not, excelled them both in the number of its students. Yet all these seminaries need reformation; but in proportion as they are not sectarian, in other respects, *ceteris paribus*, they are more popular and respectable.

Dr. Fishback's plan of giving to the board of trustees all the variety of sectarian feeling, by affording to every religious sect in the state a representation equal to its numbers, and by giving, as far as practicable, to its academical faculty the same variety of feeling and character, most obviously divests the institution of a sectarian character, makes it so far republican, and would no doubt, if adopted, elevate Transylvania as far above herself as above all the institutions in the western states. That one or two sects composed of a few congregations in the state, should have a majority of members in the board, and have thereby the direction of a state seminary, will not suit the genius of our country, and much less the enlightened republican spirit of Kentucky. Reason, common sense, and republicanism, without a jarring voice, declares that, in a state institution, the members of that state, whether natural religionists or sectaries under the profession of christianity, should, in so far as that institution is likely to affect their consciences, have a control in its management proportioned to their numbers.

Our colleges in the middle states are generally mere sectarian schools—most of them mere Presbyterian cradles, called by the clergy "the streams that make glad the city of *their* God." Hence they are fed by reviving showers, and, like rickety children, grow and languish at the same time, but always thrive disproportionally. But by these means the Presbyterian courser runs faster than his competitors. The Methodists and Baptists have "tried their luck" too by getting hold of colleges, but their systems do not so well correspond with those institutions. Instead of riding faster, they are only in danger of breaking their bones. Their skill in managing their steeds being inferior to their better disciplined brethren, they are likely in most instances to get thrown off into the mud.

You know that I discard the idea of qualifying a man to teach the christian religion by studying heathen mythology, dead languages, and natural religion, and, therefore, when I speak of advantages resulting to society from literary institutions, it is not in this way that I expect any, but in the general benefits of education communicated to society, and afterwards to be appropriated, like every other blessing of heaven, by the directions of the Holy Spirit speaking in the bible. When any community becomes intelligent, and when the advantages of education are generally diffused, the christian church will have her share of the benefits. To train any young man, purposely to make him a teacher of christianity, I am always ready to show, to be ridiculous and absurd; contrary to reason and revelation.

When I speak of divesting literary institutions of a sectarian character, it is with a reference solely to the public good; and as a measure of policy, I know of none that would contribute more to the reputation of any university, and consequently to increase its usefulness, by enlarging the number of its students, than to adopt such a course. Besides, as those political states will profit most from the South American independence, who were the first to acknowledge their independence; so those colleges will profit most from this policy who first adopt it.

U

But while I contend that no sectarian creed should be directly or indirectly taught in colleges, with all the same arguments, and for the same reasons, with, perhaps, a few more, I would contend that this phantom of the schools, called *natural religion, alias,* deism, should be discarded equally as any other sectarian project.—While I would not have presbyterianism or any other anti-christian *ism* taught, I would not have deism inculcated. The exclusion of this chimera from all our schools would be a reformation as great as was the expulsion of the Aristotelian predicaments and jargon from the colleges; and would be as benignant to christianity, as the expulsion of the Aristotelian logic was to science in general. And here you see I would as cordially agree with the second grand item of reformation suggested in the Doctor's plan, as with the first. A seminary of learning ought neither to be sectarian nor deistical. We know, too, there are sects and sectarians among Deists as among christians. And it is a fact, the reasons of which, too, can be as easily explained, that the natural religion of John Calvin is as deistical in its tendency as the natural religion of lord Herbert. A more elegant display and vindication of natural religion on John Calvin's principles, we do not recollect to have heard in any seminary, than that which I had the pleasure of hearing, last November, from the lips of Dr. Caldwell in the Transylvania University, in his introductory lecture to the medical class. I regret the loss of the notes which I had taken of this learned and elegant lecture. Yet I am able to show, as I conceive, that if the principles adopted in that lecture are tenable, the sooner we get rid of the bible the better. I know that the learned lecturer spoke, too, in commendation of the bible, but in this he was inconsistent with himself. Though I presume he borrowed nothing from John Calvin; yet, the old Reformer stood at his back with both his shoulders. On those principles, the bible might be of some little use to the stupid herd of mankind who cannot reason well; but to the philosopher who can look up "through nature's works to nature's God," it is as superfluous as a third wing to an eagle. It is, I have said, inconsistent for a natural religionist to commend the bible, seeing it flatly contradicts his whole system. It declares, "The world by wisdom, or philosophy, knew not God." It declares that it is by faith and not by reason that men can know the world was created. It declares, that we must *believe* that God exists—and that we cannot *reason* ourselves into a knowledge that God exists. Though I have not leisure nor room at present for this investigation, it is, I conceive, demonstrably evident, on the principles of reason, too, that without a revelation from God, no man can know that he exists. We are aware of many objections to this proposition, but we are prepared to show that they are as light as a feather, and that it is as true as the bible itself.

It is, to every rational and sober mind, a matter of the deepest regret, that almost all our young men return from college, graduates in extravagant and vicious habits. They are most generally sceptics, except those who are destined for the priest's office before they enter; these are generally firm believers in the religion which they intend to teach. Now that the course of instruction tends this way, needs no other proof than the fact just stated. And, indeed, I never could see how it was possible for it to issue otherwise on natural principles.

On religious, moral, and political principles, it

is necessary that the evidences of the christian religion should be fairly, fully, and forcibly taught in every seminary in our country. This no sectary can object to.—In the next place this proposition should be as fully, fairly, and forcibly taught as the preceding, viz. That Jesus of Nazareth is the Messiah, the Son of the living God, and the only Saviour of men. This is what distinguishes the Christian from the Jewish religion as now professed in the world, but is not peculiar to any religious sect, but common to all among us. This is all the teaching of religion that appears consistent with the plan and design of literary institutions. Indeed, "Paley's Evidences" contain, perhaps, the best outlines of a course of instruction of this kind to be met with. This far is necessary to save our young men from the sceptical tendency of the other parts of an academic course; and I know of no people in our state, or in any other, who could object to such a course, whether deist or christian.

So far I have just simply adverted to the queries in your letter, without doing more than to express a naked opinion or two. It may become necessary to be more full on some topics in your communication, but this is impossible at present. The plan of reform in those grand outlines already noticed, I conceive to be so evidently beneficial, and, indeed, liable to no serious objection from any sectary in religion or politics, as not only to deserve, but to command the co-operation of not only baptists, but paido-baptists in carrying it into effect. I know of but one objection that can be made to it, viz. Those who have the control already, in this, or any other establishment, and those who wish to make it subservient to their own particular interest, and are intent thereon, will say, it is better that we and our friends should have its control as we think we can manage it better to our own interest, than if all the community were to have a part in its management; in that case we could not expect to be either the sole, or the chief gainers. Believe me, my dear sir, in this is a very strong argument, and one that is always difficult to refute.

I remain respectfully yours,
EDITOR.

No. 11.]   JUNE 6, 1825.
A Narrative of the Origin and formation of the Westminster or Presbyterian Confession of Faith. No. II.

As THE Regular Baptist Confession of Faith is, in its doctrinal parts, but a mere transcript of the Westminster creed; and as the whole of it is founded upon the same principles of creed making—a narrative of the origin and formation of the Westminster, its grand model and parent, cannot but be highly interesting to the admirers of this creed amongst the baptist community. It is true, however, that the drafters or copyists of the Westminster creed amongst the baptists did not intend to bind it either upon churches or individuals, as the presbyterians or puritans do theirs; but only designed to show the puritans, who reviled them as damnable heretics, that their faith was substantially the same with their own. Yet many of the baptists, ignorant of the design of their own little confession, wish to have it riveted upon the congregations of their fraternity on pain of excommunication, as the system of truth taught in the holy scriptures. This occurrence in the history of the baptists serves to show how dangerous it is to traffic in the merchandize of Babylon. "Can a man take fire in his bosom and his clothes not be burnt?" But to resume the narrative.

It has already appeared that the Westminster confession owes its origin to a political contest; that the convulsions of England forced it into being; that it is a small morsel of the religious lava that belched forth from the crater of that political volcano which made Britain tremble from north to south, from the Orkney Isles to the Straits of Dover. It is also evident that the civilians and politicians that projected its formation, although abetted by the clergy, designed to help themselves to soldiers and munitions of war by the project; that they, being Erastians, had no objections to any form of ecclesiastical policy which might be adopted; that, indeed, that form was most eligible which would best suit the exigencies of the times; and, as every thing in the civil war, then levied, depended on Scotland, that creed and form of discipline was conscientiously to be preferred which would insure the co-operation of the Scots. Besides, two monstrous errors, arising, no doubt, from the mist of the dark ages, not yet dissipated, characterize the whole proceedings of the church and state in this assembly. The first is now so palpable that all men in these United States reprobate it. It is the notion that the doctrine and worship of what is called the church, is to be regulated by acts of parliament; that the civil authority necessarily must take cognizance of the doctrine, discipline, and worship of professed congregations of christians; that the civil sword must purify the hearts of the worshippers, and regulate their devotions. The other mistake, no less absurd, though perhaps not so manifest to all, was conspicuous in the clergy and laity, who indeed fostered and matured the assumptions of the civil rulers by appealing to them, and in constituting them arbiters and judges of what was sound doctrine and true piety. They appealed to them with all the confidence and earnestness that a christian appeals to the apostles, or as the Phillippian jailor appealed to Paul and Silas. The civil rulers erred most palpably in assuming such a jurisdiction over men's consciences; and the clergy and their supporters erred as absurdly in looking up to them to exercise authority in their behalf; and thus flattered them into the belief of a lie, that in decreeing what was sound doctrine and true piety they were serving God and his church.

We had in our last number left the divines in king Henry VII's chapel, regularly summoned, systematically hired, and patronized by the long parliament, waiting for their orders. Saturday, July 1, 1643, the assembly was opened with a sermon by Dr. Twisse, both houses of parliament being present. The ordinance for their convention was then read; and the members called by name, after which they adjourned to Monday.

Among the rules by which they were to be governed, the following oath or protestation was to be taken by every member, and, to refresh their memories, it was to be read every Monday morning:

"I, A. B., do seriously and solemnly, in the presence of Almighty God, declare that, in the assembly whereof I am a member, I will not maintain any thing in matter of doctrine, but what I believe in my conscience to be most agreeable to the word of God; or in point of discipline, but what I shall conceive to conduce most to the glory of God and the good and peace of the church."

The parliament would not trust them without an oath, and they succumbed to the above form. But let the reader remember the distinction between doctrine and discipline marked in this vow. In doctrine they vowed to maintain what in their consciences they believed most agreeable to the divine oracles; but in discipline they were not under the same obligation—they were to maintain what they conceived most to conduce to the glory of God and the peace of the churches. They were in fact sworn to act, if not to believe, as Erastians. The form of oath is predicated upon Erastian principles; that is, that there is no fixed form of discipline in the Scriptures, but that it was left to the civil magistrate who has the keys. Yes, they vowed to make the Bible the *standard* of doctrine, and their own conceptions of God's glory and the peace of the church the standard in matters of discipline. Under this vow or oath they entered upon their work.

The parliament, on Thursday, 6th July, sent them farther regulations, amongst which it was appointed that two assessors be joined with the prolocutor to supply his place in case of absence or sickness. Those first appointed were Dr. Cornelius Burges and John White. It was also ordered by the parliament, "that all things agreed upon and prepared for the parliament, shall be openly read and allowed in the assembly, and then offered to the parliament to act upon (as the higher house) if the majority assent; provided that the opinions of the persons dissenting, with their reasons, be annexed, if they desire it, and the solution of those reasons by the assembly."

The rules being prescribed, and the manner of proceeding being settled, the parliament sent the assembly an order to review the thirty-nine articles of the Church of England. Before the assembly began, they petitioned parliament to appoint a fast. Of this petition Bishop Kennett said, "Impartially speaking, it is stuffed with schism, sedition and cruelty." Our limits forbid us to publish this petition. The prominent features of which are: They petition the parliament in the name of Jesus Christ, "your Lord and ours," that "they would set up Christ more gloriously in all his ordinances, and reform all things amiss throughout the land." Besides praying for the fast, they pray the parliament to "suppress all the bold venting of corrupt doctrines; to charge all ministers to catechise the children and the ignorant adults; to have a care to punish all profanation of the Sabbath and of fast days, by unlawful labor or sports; to put down by a "thorough proceeding" all blind guides and scandalous ministers; to quicken the laws against swearing and drunkenness: to take a severe course against fornication, adultery, and incest; to abolish popery," &c. &c.

Friday, July 21, was appointed a fast, and three of the divines preached before parliament, and the fast was observed with great solemnity. Next day a committee was appointed to examine what amendments were proper to be made in the thirty-nine articles, and to report to the assembly. They spent ten weeks in debating upon the first fifteen, before the arrival of the Scots commissioners. Their design was to render their sense more express against the Arminians, whom they cordially hated, and to make them more determinate in favor of Calvinism. They appeared as solicitous to condemn antinomianism as to strengthen the churches against arminianism, and appointed a committee to peruse the writings of Dr. Crisp, Eaton, and Saltmarsh, who drew out some of the most dangerous positions. The assembly then condemned them, and endeavored to confute them in their public preachments.

The Scots in the mean time got up a general assembly to consider of the state of religion, as well as a political assembly, as conservators of the peace. The king gave them orders to confine their attention to their own country, and to let England alone. The parliament of England sent five dignified laymen and two distinguished divines from Westminster, with letters to each of the Scotch assemblies, desiring their assistance in the war, and some of their divines to assist those assembled at Westminster "to settle a uniformity of religion and church government between the two nations." These seven commissioners arrived at Edinburg on the ninth of August, and were well received by the Scotch Assembly, which (in profound policy) proposed as a preliminary, "that the two nations should enter into a perpetual covenant for themselves and their posterity, that all things might be done in God's house according to his will." The Scots appointed some of their number to confer with the English commissioners on the form of this covenant. This being done, they chose delegates for the Westminster assembly, and unanimously advised the convention of states to assist the English parliament in the war, for seven reasons, viz. "1. Because they apprehended the war was for religion. 2. Because the Protestant faith was in danger. 3. Gratitude to the English for former assistances to the Scots required a suitable return. 4. Because the churches of England and of Scotland being embarked in one bottom, if one be ruined the other cannot subsist. 5. The prospect of uniformity between the two kingdoms in discipline and worship will strengthen the Protestant faith at home and abroad. 6. The present English parliament had been friendly to the Scots and might be so again. 7. Though the king had lately established their religion, yet they could not confide in his royal declarations, having so often found *facta verbis contraria*, i. e. his deeds contrary to his words."

The instructions of the commissioners sent to the assembly at Westminster were to promote the extirpation of popery, prelacy, heresy, schism, scepticism, and idolatry, and to endeavor a union between the two kingdoms in one confession of faith, one form of church government, and one directory of worship. The committee for drawing up the solemn league and covenant delivered it into the Assembly, August 17, where it was read and highly applauded by the ministers and lay elders, none opposing it except the king's commissioners, so that it passed the assembly and convention in one day!! It was despatched the next morning to London, to the Westminster divines and Parliament, with a letter to the two houses, wishing that it might be confirmed, and solemnly sworn, and subscribed in both houses, as the surest obligation to make them stand and fall together in the cause of religion and liberty. The two divines, Marshall and Nye, who were sent into Scotland as commissioners with the five noble laymen, wrote, August 18, to the Westminster Assembly, "to assure their brethren that the Scotch clergy were entirely on the side of the parliament in this war against the popish and episcopalian faction; so that if the English parliament (say they) comply with the form of this covenant, they were persuaded that the whole body of the Scotch kingdom will live and die with them, and speedily come to their assistance."

When the commissioners arrived in London they presented the covenant to the two houses, who referred it to the Assembly of divines.— Some of the divines opposed some articles of the covenant. Dr. Featly declared he dare not abjure prelacy absolutely, because he had sworn to obey his bishop in all things lawful and honest. Dr. Burges objected to several items, and it was with difficulty he was persuaded to subscribe after he had been suspended. The prolocutor and many others declared for primitive episcopacy. They refused to subscribe until a parenthesis was inserted declaring what sort of prelacy was to be abjured, viz. (church government by archbishops, bishops, deans, and chapters, archdeacons, and all other ecclesiastical officers depending upon them.)

Bishop Burnet says the English commissioners pressed the Scots for a civil league, but the Scots would have a religious one. Sir Henry Vane put the word league into the letter, as thinking that might be broke sooner than a covenant; and in the first article inserted these words after the term reform, "according to the word of God;" but the Scots relied upon the next words, "and according to the practice of the best reformed churches." When Mr. Coleman read the covenant before the house of Lords, in order to their subscribing it, he declared that by prelacy all sorts of episcopacy were not intended, but only the form therein described. Thus, says Mr. Neal, the wise men on both sides endeavored to outwit each other in wording the articles; and, with these slight amendments, the covenant passed the assembly and both houses of Parliament, and by an order dated September 21, was printed and published. Thus originated and progressed the solemn league and covenant, which is appended to the Old Confession of Faith, which must be identified with it because of the same character and emanating from the same source, and designed for the same end. The first two articles of which, as a specimen, we shall here insert:—

"We, noblemen, barons, knights, gentlemen, citizens, burgesses, ministers of the gospel, and commons of all sorts, in the kingdoms of England, Scotland, and Ireland, by the providence of God living under one king, and being of one reformed religion; determined to enter into a mutual and solemn league and covenant, wherein we all subscribe, and each one of us for himself, with our hands lifted up to the Most High God, do swear—

"1st. That we shall sincerely, really, and constantly, through the grace of God, endeavor, in our several places and callings, the preservation of the reformed religion in the church of Scotland, in doctrine, worship, in discipline, and government, against our common enemies; the reformation of religion in the kingdoms of England and Ireland, in doctrine, worship, discipline, and government, according to the word of God and the example of the best reformed churches; we shall endeavor to bring the church of God in the three kingdoms to the nearest conjunction, and uniformity in religion, confession of faith, form of church government, directory for worship, catechism; that we, and our posterity after us, may, as brethren, live in faith and love, and the Lord may delight to dwell in the midst of us.

"2d. That we shall, in like manner, without respect of persons, endeavor the extirpation of popery, prelacy, (that is, church government by archbishops, bishops, their chancellors and commissaries, deans and chapters, archdeacons, and all other ecclesiastical officers depending on that hierarchy,) superstition, heresy, schism, profaneness, and whatsoever shall be found to be contrary to sound doctrine and the power of godliness, lest we partake in other men's sins, and thereby be in danger to receive of their plagues; and that

the Lord may be one, and his name one, in the three kingdoms."

"Monday, September 25, 1643, was appointed for subscribing this covenant, when both houses, with the Scots' commissioners and assembly of divines, being met in the church of St. Margaret's, Westminster, the Rev. Mr. White, of Dorchester, opened the solemnity with prayer; after him Mr. Henderson and Mr. Nye spoke in justification of taking the covenant from scripture precedents, and displayed the advantage the church had received from such sacred combinations. Mr. Henderson spoke next, and declared that the states of Scotland had resolved to assist the parliament of England in carrying on the designs of this covenant; then Mr. Nye read it from the pulpit with an audible voice, article by article, each person standing uncovered, with his right hand lifted up bare to heaven, worshipping the great name of God, and swearing to the performance of it. Dr. Gouge concluded the solemnity with prayer, after which the House of Commons went up into the chancel, and subscribed their names in one roll of parchment, and the assembly in another, in both of which the covenant was fairly transcribed. Lord's day following it was tendered to all persons within the bills of mortality, being read in several churches to their congregations as above. October 15, it was taken by the House of Lords, after a sermon preached by Dr. Temple, from Nehemiah x. 29. and an exhortation by Mr. Coleman. October 29, it was ordered by the committee of states in Scotland to be sworn to and subscribed all over that kingdom, on penalty of the confiscation of goods and rents, and such other punishment as his majesty and the parliament should inflict on the refusers. All the lords of the council were summoned to sign the covenant, November 2, and those who did not, to appear again the 14th of the same month, under the severest penalties; when some of the king's party not attending, were declared enemies to their religion and to their king and country. November 17, their goods were ordered to be seized, and their persons apprehended; upon which they fled into England. Such was the unbounded zeal of that nation. February 2, following, the covenant was ordered to be taken throughout the kingdom of England, by all persons above the age of eighteen years; and the assembly were commanded to draw up an exhortation to dispose the people to it, which being approved by both houses, was published."

Here we shall leave the Westminster assembly for the present, engaged in forming exhortations to induce all persons from eighteen years and upwards to swear to extirpate popery and prelacy, and to maintain presbytery themselves and their children forever.   EDITOR.

A Review of Dr. Miller's Lecture on the Utility and Importance of Creeds and Confessions.

THIS lecture was delivered at the opening of the summer session of the Theological Seminary of the Presbyterian church, Princeton, July 2d, 1824, by Samuel Miller, D. D. Professor of Ecclesiastical History and Church Government in the aforesaid Theological School. It is therefore a precious document, as it affords a fair specimen of the theological views of this great school of the Presbyterian prophets, and as it brings to a focus all the lights of this learned body of divines on this much disputed subject. It has been in circulation for a few months and has received the approbation of all the admirers of the

Westminster Creed in this country, as far as we have learned. The editors of the West, as well as those of the East, extol it as a prodigy of genius, learning, and sound doctrine. As it brings down to July 2, 1824, all the discoveries and improvements of fifteen centuries in defence of human creeds, by a Master in this Israel and a Professor of Ecclesiastical History, we may naturally expect much light from it on the topic on which it treats; and that as it is the *last*, so it is the most *able* defence of human creeds.— As such we are bound to consider it, and as such we shall offer a few remarks upon it.

In our series of essays upon the restoration of the ancient order of things, we had begun and resolved to prosecute an investigation of the merits of the arguments in favor of those creeds; but as we have got them all offered to us at once, and by so able a hand, from such a dignified chair, we are exonerated from the labor of gathering them from many sources, and shall therefore consider ourselves in possession of the most important in possessing the defence of Dr. Miller. We shall therefore detach from those Essays on the Restoration the subject of human creeds, and in detail examine their merits *per se*, as the Doctor presents them.

After a fashionable exordium, such as Horace would approve, in which Dr. Miller teaches the young prophets to consider themselves like Jesus of Nazareth, as "set for the fall and rising again of many in Israel," he proceeds to his subject, which he states to be "the importance of creeds and confessions for maintaining the unity and purity of the visible church." He next gives his reasons for calling his candidates for the holy office of the Presbyterian ministry to this subject; amongst these the chief is, "that latitudinarians and heretics" are animadverting too severely on this subject—for, with the Doctor, they who oppose human creeds are almost exclusively either latitudinarians or heretics.— No doubt in this he is correct; for Paul himself, when he ceased to argue in defence of the traditions and dogmas of the theological seminary in Jerusalem, became an incorrigible heretic, and a wild latitudinarian; and no wonder if his followers should still be considered and called heretics by all Gamaliels.

But that the reader may be able at one view to see the whole phalanx of arguments which have been gathered and condensed for one thousand two hundred and threescore years, in support of the utility and importance of these standards, we shall present in one view the sevenfold reasons of the Doctor:—

"Now I affirm that the adoption of such a creed is not only lawful and expedient, but also indispensably necessary to the harmony and purity of the visible church. For the establishment of this position, let me request your attention to the following considerations:

"1. Without a creed explicitly adopted, it is not easy to see how the ministers and members of any particular church, and more especially a large denomination of christians, can maintain unity among themselves.

"2. The necessity and importance of creeds and confessions appear from the consideration, that one great design of establishing a church in our world was, that she might be, in all ages, a depository, a guardian, and a witness of the truth.

"3. The adoption and publication of a creed, is a tribute to truth and candor, which every christian church owes to the other churches and the world around her.

"4. Another argument in favor of creeds, publicly adopted and maintained, is, that they are friendly to the study of christian doctrine, and of course to the prevalence of christian knowledge.

"5. It is an argument of no small weight in favor of creeds, that the experience of all ages has found them indispensably necessary.

"6. A further argument in favor of creeds and confessions may be drawn from the remarkable fact, that their most zealous opposers have generally been latitudinarians and heretics.

"7. The only further argument in support of creeds on which I shall dwell, is, that their most zealous opposers do themselves virtually employ them in all their ecclesiastical proceedings."

After the amplification and elucidation of these seven strong "arguments" or affirmations of the Doctor, he meets and refutes five objections, viz:—

"1. And the first which I shall mention is, that forming a creed, and requiring subscription to it as a religious test, is superseding the bible, and making a human composition instead of it a standard of faith.

"2. Another objection frequently made to church creeds is, that they interfere with the rights of conscience, and naturally lead to oppression.

"3. A third objection often urged against subscription to creeds and confessions is, that it is unfriendly to free inquiry.

"4. A fourth objection frequently brought against creeds is, that they have altogether failed of answering the purpose professed to be intended by them.

"5. The last objection which I shall consider is, that subscription to creeds has not only failed entirely of producing the benefits contemplated by their friends, but has rather been found to produce the opposite evils—to generate discord and strife."

He then concludes with sundry warm exhortations to the young candidates for the sacred office to contend earnestly for the faith once delivered by a synod and parliament to the militant kingdoms of England and Scotland, as necessary to the unity and purity of a visible church militant.

After thus surveying the bounds and limits of this defence, we may take it up in piecemeal, and examine each fold of this sevenfold shield. But that the reader may be able to take as general a view of the ground we occupy as of that occupied by the Doctor, we shall, by way of preparation, suggest what we must call the two grand sophisms on which his defence rests.

1st. The Doctor, by some fatal accident to his scheme, identifies the church or congregation of Jesus Christ with the visible Presbyterian congregation or church. Now we will readily agree with the Doctor that some of his arguments are conclusive, admitting this sophism to be a truth. For his first argument shows that "it is not easy to see how the ministers and members of any particular church, and more especially a large *denomination* of christians, (that is, a Presbyterian or Episcopalian denomination,) can maintain unity among themselves without a human creed." I agree with the Doctor here, that a human creed is essential to the unity of a political or worldly establishment, such as the Presbyterian or Episcopalian *denomination*. And I think it would require better eyes than the Doctor's or mine "to see" how the ministers and members of the large denomination of Presbyterians could maintain unity without a human creed. Any human establishment requires human contrivances to keep it together. I do not believe that Free-Masons could maintain their unity and harmony without a creed, and formula, and catechism. I will agree with the Doctor that it is not easy to see how either the large and respectable denomination of Free-Mason christians, or the large and respectable denomination of Presbyterian christians could maintain their unity of spirit without a written creed deduced from the bible. And I will add that I am assured, were it not for the Presbyterian Confession of Faith, the Presbyterian church would soon become extinct, as others before it have done, built upon human creeds. A human creed is the very rock on which a sect or denomination is built. " If the foundation be destroyed what can the builders do?" Indeed the creed of Westminster is called "The Constitution of the Presbyterian church in the United States." Now who does not know, that if the constitution be destroyed, the social existence of those confederated by it, is destroyed!—The misfortune, then, is that the Doctor's able defence only proves that human creeds and confessions are necessary to preserve sectarians, or to unite one denomination in a league defensive and offensive against all others. For this he reasons, and demonstrates, and proves, as a Doctor ought, when employed in drilling young recruits for the ranks and wars of their sect. They will march forth in this panoply, invincible in fight. That human creeds are necessary to the existence of sects of human contrivance, the Doctor has well proved; but the sophism is here, that he argues that human creeds are therefore necessary to the unity of the church of Christ. This is the deception, this the sophistry of six of the seven arguments. A greater blunder we do not remember to have seen committed by any Doctor since the days that the Jesuits wrote in favor of themselves, as a brotherhood confederated by divine authority, than that which Dr. Miller has unhappily committed in arguing that, because a human creed is necessary to the unity of one sect, or for the maintenance of one division in what he calls the church of Christ, therefore a human creed is necessary to the unity of that church. In plain English, that which makes and keeps up one division, is necessary to the unity of the whole.— This is Princeton logic, and Presbyterian divinity! But after all, the Doctor may have meant, by the unity of the church, the unity of the Presbyterians. And, indeed, this appears to be the design of his whole defence, for in his exhortation he rather censures the Presbyterian ministry for not being sectarian enough. His words are—

"We are so ready to fraternize with all evangelical denominations that we almost forget that we have a denomination of our own, to which we are peculiarly attached. Now this general spirit is undoubtedly excellent; worthy of constant culture, and the highest praise. But may it not be carried to an extreme? Universal active benevolence, is a christian's duty; but when the head of a family, in the ardor of his exercise, feels no more concern or responsibility respecting his own household, than he does about the households of others, he acts an unreasonable part, and, what is worse, disobeys the command of God. Something analogous to this, I apprehend, is the mistake of that christian, or that minister, who, in the fervor of his catholicism, loses sight of the fact, that God, in his providence, has connected him with a particular branch of the visible church, the welfare and edification of which he is peculiarly bound to

seek. If his own branch of the church has any thing of peculiar excellence in his estimation, on account of which he prefers it,—which is always to be supposed,—can it be wrong for him to desire that others should view it in the same light? And if he be justifiable in recommending these peculiarities from the pulpit—as all allow —is he not equally justifiable in recommending them from the press, especially by means of accredited publications?"

Now this is in brief—it is good to be charitable to all, but see that you keep up your own sect. Keep up the presbyterian denomination, as every good father keeps up his own house. Be good neighbors, but remember the interests of your own house.

Such is the sophism that constitutes the basis of six of his seven arguments. And they are plausible if we admit that the presbyterian denomination is exclusively the church, but on any other principle they are ridiculous and absurd. And let it be remembered that there is no controversy between us and the doctor upon the necessity and utility of his confession of faith to the existence of his own sect. But this we shall, until we obtain new faculties, consider a subject as distinct from the unity of the disciples of Christ, as the union of the Turks against the Greeks is distinct from the American union on the grand principles of civil and religious liberty.

The second sophism which constitutes the second pillar of the Doctor's superstructure is, that those who discard human creeds as important and useful to the church of Christ, reject all creeds. His seventh argument is predicated entirely upon this, and some of his remarks upon the others partially. Now this is making a man of wax and blaming him for not speaking. While we contend that human creeds are every way unscriptural and destructive to the unity and purity of the church of Christ, we contend that his church has, and must have a creed, and that he has himself drawn it out and committed it to writing by his apostles. If he had thought, as he knew all that would come to pass in the dark ages, that any other creed or formula was necessary for present exigencies, he would have given directions and authority to some persons to have formed it; but as he has not done this we are sure it is unnecessary, just because he thought so. Having taken this general view of Dr. Miller's lecture, and of the sophisms on which it is based, we dismiss it for the time being, reserving particulars until another opportunity.   EDITOR.

A Restoration of the Ancient Order of Things.
No. IV.

THAT the word of the apostles shall be the only creed, formula, and directory of faith, worship, and christian practice, when the ancient order of things is restored, we have offered some evidence to show. The constitution and law of the primitive church shall be the constitution and law of the restored church. As the constitution and law then admitted all the faithful disciples of the Lord to an equal participation of all privileges; so when the same is again adopted, the same privileges will be extended to every orderly citizen of the kingdom. Without any of our modern creeds in substance or in form the church was once united, complete, and happy, and will be so again. For the same cause will always produce the same effect. When the disciples shall return to the Lord he will return to them.

In receiving members or citizens into the kingdom, or in naturalizing foreigners, it appeared, in our last essay, that nothing was required of them but an acknowledgment of the word or testimony of the witnesses concerning the King, Jesus of Nazareth. A hearty declaration, or confession with their lips, that they believed in their hearts, that Jesus of Nazareth was the Messiah, the Son of the living God, the King and Lord of all, qualified them as applicants for naturalization. In the act of immersion into this name, they renounced every other Messiah, Lord, King, or Saviour; they put off their former religion, and renounced every other religious obligation to any other system or authority, and put on Jesus, as their Lord and King. From a consideration of the ancient order it appeared, that the apostles did not command men to be baptized into their own experience, but into the faith then delivered to the saints. It was affirmed that the ancient order was wiser, safer, and more honorable to the saving truth, than the modern way of receiving members into a baptist society, and some proof was presented.

In the present essay we shall make a few remarks upon another important preliminary to the restoration of the ancient order of things. There must be, and there shall be, an abandonment of the new and corrupt nomenclature, and a restoration of the inspired one. In other words, there must be an abandonment of the Babylonish or corrupt phraseology of the dark ages and of modern discoveries, in the fixed style of the christian vocabulary. This is a matter of greater importance than may, at first sight, appear to all. Words and names long consecrated, and sanctified by long prescription, have a very imposing influence upon the human understanding. We think as well as speak by means of words. It is just as impossible for an adult to think as to speak without words. Let him that doubts make the experiment. Now as all correct ideas of God and things invisible are supernatural ideas, no other terms can so suitably express them as the terms adopted by the the Holy Spirit, in adapting those supernatural truths to our apprehension. He that taught man to speak, would, doubtless, adopt the most suitable terms in his language to reveal himself to his understanding. To disparage those terms, by adopting others in preference, is presumptuous and insolent on the part of man. Besides, when men adopt terms to express supernatural truths, it is not the truths themselves, but their ideas of them they communicate. They select such terms as suit their apprehensions of revealed truth, and hence the terms they use are expressive only of their conceptions of divine things, and must just be as imperfect as their conceptions are. It is impossible for any man, unless by accident, to express accurately that which he apprehends imperfectly. From this source spring most of our doctrinal controversies. Men's opinions, expressed in their own terms, are often called bible truths. In order, then, to a full restoration of the ancient order of things, there must be "a pure speech" restored. And I think the Lord once said, in order to a restoration, that he would restore to the people "a pure speech." We know that the ancient order of things, amongst the Jews, could not be restored, after their captivity in Babylon, until the law of the Lord, containing the primitive institutions of the Jews' religion, was read and understood by the people, and the dialect of Babylon abandoned, as far as it corrupted the primitive simplicity of that religion. Hence the scribes read them the law from morning to evening, gave them the sense and made them understand the reading. This became necessary because of the corrupt dialect they had learned in Babylon, on account of which their revelation was unintelligible to them, until the language of Canaan was purged from the phraseology of Ashdod. It will, we apprehend, be found precisely similar in the antitype, or in the return of the people of God from the captivity of Babylon the great, the mother of abominations.

But we shall go on to specify a sample of those Babylonish terms and phrases which must be purified from the christian vocabulary, before the saints can understand the religion they profess, or one another as fellow disciples. I select these from the approved standards of the most popular establishments; for from these they have become current and sacred style. Such are the following: "Trinity. First, second, and third person in the adorable Trinity: God the Son; and God the Holy Ghost. Eternal Son. The Son is eternally begotten by the Father; the Holy Ghost eternally proceeding from the Father and the Son. The divinity of Jesus Christ; the humanity of Jesus Christ; the incarnation of Jesus Christ. This he said as man; and that as God. The common operations, and the special operations of the Spirit of God. Original sin, and original righteousness. Spiritual death; spiritual life. Covenant of works, covenant of grace, and covenant of redemption; a dispensation of the covenant of grace, and administration of the covenant. Effectual calling. Free will. Free grace. Total depravity. Eternal justification. Eternal sleep. Elect world. Elect infants. Light of nature. Natural religion. General and particular atonement. Legal and evangelical repentance. Moral, ceremonial, and judicial law. Under the law as a covenant of works, and as a rule of life. Christian sabbath. Holy sacrament. Administration of the sacrament. Different kinds of faith and grace. Divine service; the public worship of God," &c. &c.

These are but a mere sample, and all of one species. It will be said that men cannot speak of Bible truths without adopting other terms than those found in the written word. This will be granted, and yet there will be found no excuse for the above species of unauthorized and Babylonish phraseology. It is one thing to speak of divine truths in our own language, and another to adopt a fixed style of expressing revealed truths to the exclusion of, or in preference to, that fixed by the Spirit, and sometimes, too, at variance with it. For instance, the terms Trinity, first and second person of—Eternal Son, and the eternal procession of the Spirit, are now the fixed style in speaking of God, his Son Jesus Christ, and of the Spirit, in reference to their "personal character." Now this is not the style of the oracles of God. It is all human, and may be as freely criticised as one of the numbers of the Spectator. Yet because of the sanctified character of these terms, having been baptized, or authorized by the orthodox and pious for centuries, it is at the risque of my reputation for orthodoxy, and at the expense of being charged with heresy, that I simply affirm that they are terms that the wisdom of this world teaches, and not the Spirit of God. I would not be startled to hear that I have denied the faith and rejected the revealed character of the Father, Son, and Holy Spirit, because I have said that the fixed style in speaking of them in the popular establishments is of human origin and of the language of Ashdod, and not of the language of Canaan. This, however, only proves that the terms of human philosophy are held more sacred, than the words of the Holy Spirit.

81

These terms originate new doctrines. Thus the term "trinity" gives rise to the doctrine of the trinity. And what fierce controversies have originated out of this doctrine! How many creeds and martyrs has it made! Courteous and pious reader, would it not be as wise, as humble, and as modest, too, for us, on such topics, to prefer the words of the Holy Spirit, and to speak of God, his Son, and Spirit, as the apostles did. Moreover, these terms do not help our conceptions of God at all. They rather impede than facilitate our understanding the divine oracles. It is more difficult to conceive of an eternal Son eternally begotten, and of a Spirit eternally proceeding, than to understand any thing God has ever spoken to men. And see on what a slender thread those distinctions hang! Because Jesus Christ told his disciples that he would send them the Spirit, which Spirit would or was to proceed from his Father, or to be sent forth by his Father as well as by himself; therefore the schoolmen affirm that the Spirit eternally proceeded, or was eternally coming from the Father!! This is the whole thread on which this "doctrine" hangs. I only instance this, and cannot now pause on the others.

But besides this species of sophistry there is another more dangerous, because more specious. This is really as foreign and as barbarous a dialect as that we have noticed, though in Bible terms. It consists in selecting Bible terms and sentences and in applying to them ideas totally different from those attached to them by the Holy Spirit. Of this sort are the following: "The natural man, spiritual man; in the flesh, in the spirit; regeneration, washing of regeneration; ministration of the Spirit, demonstration of the Spirit; power of God, faith of the operation of God, the grace of God; the letter, the spirit; the old and new covenant; word of God; the ministry of the word; truth of the gospel; mystery, election, charity, heretic, heresy, blasphemy, church communion, baptism, faith," &c. &c. &c. The former dialect rejects the words of the Holy Spirit, and adopts others as more intelligible, less ambiguous, and better adapted to preserve a pure church. The latter dialect takes the terms and sentences of the Spirit, and makes them convey ideas diverse from those communicated by the Spirit. We shall in this, as in the former dialect, specify one instance. Take for this purpose the sentence, "Through faith of the operation of God." This the populars use to designate a faith wrought in the human heart by the operation of the great power of God. But the Spirit of God intended by this phrase to shew that christians in baptism had represented to them their resurrection with Christ to a new life, through a belief of the great power of God, exhibited in raising Christ from the dead. So the wisest teachers, and so all the learned translators of the last century understood it, amongst whom are, Pierce, Tompson, Macknight, and others. Macknight reads it thus: "Being buried with him in baptism, in which also ye have been raised with him through the belief of the strong working of God who raised him from the dead." Now in relation to these two dialects there is one easy and safe course. The first is to be totally abandoned as transubstantiation and purgatory are by Protestants, and the other is to be tried by the context or design of the writer.

We cannot at present be more particular; but of these terms and sentences we shall not be forgetful hereafter. It is enough at one time to suggest them to the consideration and examination of our readers.

The adoption and constant use of this barbarous dialect, was the cause of making divisions, and is still one existing cause of their continuance. This style furnishes much matter, and many a topic to the gloomy Doctors who delight in metaphysical subtleties, and gains them much credit for their skill in mysteries, which they exhibit in their weekly attempts to unravel the webs which themselves and their worthy predecessors have woven. Let it be remembered that, as these terms were not to be heard in the primitive church, in restoring the ancient order of things they must be sent home to the regions of darkness whence they arose.

Editor.

History of the English Bible.—No. IV.

Many objections have been made against king James' translation. The Greek New Testament which the king's translators used was that of Robert Stephen's. It was the third and fourth editions of R. Stephen's Greek New Testament, published 1550 and 1551. In the fourth edition of R. Stephen's Greek New Testament the text was, for the first time, divided into verses. The translators followed Stephen in his chapters and verses, and thus the first edition of the English Bible was as mangled and as unintelligible as the present. Dr. Macknight, in the general preface to his translation of the Apostolical Epistles, presents the common objections to the present version in one section, which reads as follows:—

"To this edition of the bible it has been objected, 1st. That it often differs from the Hebrew to follow the seventy, if not the German translation, particularly in proper names. 2d. That the translators followed the Vulgate Latin, have adopted many of the original words without translating them, such as *hallelujah, hosannah, mammon, anathema,* &c. by which they have rendered their version unintelligible to a mere English reader. But they may have done this in compliance with the king's injunction concerning the old ecclesiastical words, and because, by long use, many of them were as well understood by the people as if they were English. 3d. That by keeping too close to the Hebrew and Greek idioms, they have rendered their version obscure. 4th. That they were a little too complaisant to the king in favoring his notions of predestination, election, witchcraft, familiar spirits, &c. But these, it is probable, were their opinions as well as the king's. 5th. That their translation is partial, speaking the language of, and giving authority to one sect. But this, perhaps, was owing to the restraint they were laid under by those who employed them. 6th. That where the original words and phrases admitted of different translations, the worse translation, by a plurality of voices, was put into the text, and the better was often thrown into the margin. 7th. That notwithstanding all the pains taken in correcting this and the former editions of the English bible, there still remain many passages mistranslated, either through negligence or want of knowledge: and that to other passages improper additions are made, which pervert the sense, as *Matt.* xx. 23. where, by adding the words, "it shall be given," it is insinuated that some other person than the Son will distribute rewards at the day of judgment.

"Such are the objections which have been made to the king's translation by the Protestants. They are mentioned here as historical facts. How far they are just, lies with the reader to consider. The objections made by the

Papists were the same with those which were made to the former translations, and particularly that several texts are mistranslated, from the translators' aversion to the doctrine and usages of the church of Rome."

Such are the most common objections to the translation made by king James' authority, as Dr. Macknight has briefly stated in his prolegomena to his translation of the Apostolic Epistles. Besides this, the divisions of the scriptures of the New Testament into chapters and verses by Romanists of small learning, and less intelligence in the meaning of the inspired writings, in imitation of the Jewish Rabbins' division of the Old Testament, has been long complained of by all the judicious and intelligent scripturians of the last century. It was indeed impossible for Robert Stephens, a monk, while making a tour through some of the richest provinces of the Roman church, to make a judicious division of the New Testament into verses, and yet this is the division still used by all Protestants.

To remedy those evils, so long and so justly complained of, we have issued proposals for publishing a new translation of the New Testament, made by Doctors Campbell, Macknight, and Doddridge, decidedly the best that has appeared in our language. As the plan and character of this most valuable work is already before the public in the form of a prospectus and proposal, we deem it unnecessary to say much about it on the present occasion.

EDITOR.

Precious Confession.

THE following is an extract from the sentiments delivered by the Rev. Dr. Burton, at an association of the congregational clergy, at Thetfort, in the state of Vermont, and published by the Rev. Ignatius Thompson, who was present at the association. It may be depended upon as authentic :—

"The Calvinistic sentiments never will prevail till the colleges are under our influence. Young men, when they go to college, generally have not formed their religious sentiments. We ought to have a president and instructors who have the address to instil the Calvinistic sentiments without the students being sensible of it—then, nine out of ten, when they leave the college, will support the Calvinistic doctrine—they will go out into the world, and will have their influence in society. In this way we can get a better support, without law, than we ever had with it. And besides, when once all our colleges are under our influence, we can manage the civil government as we please."

[*Western Herald.*

No. 12.]　　　　JULY 4, 1825.

A Narrative of the Origin and Formation of the Westminster or Presbyterian Confession of Faith.
No. III.

IN taking a correct view of the Westminster Confession it is necessary to take a correct view of the divines that formed it; and in doing this it will be necessary to pay a due attention to their proceedings. In our last number we left them preparing an exhortation to engage all persons above eighteen years of age in England to swear to and subscribe the solemn league and covenant. Many schemes were adopted, and many equivocations and intrigues exhibited by the clergy, then called the loyalists, to avoid the

oath. The Puritans now had the power on their side, and that has always given right to the clergy to do what was conducive to their dominion. Confiscations, ejectments, proscriptions, and penalties, were now the order of the day. But this was only establishing a precedent, which, in the reign of the next king, occasioned many to repent of their cruelty and intolerance; for men generally hate persecution when themselves are the objects of it. The king forbade his subjects to swear to the covenant, but some of them tauntingly exhorted him to take the covenant himself.

In pursuance of an order from the parliament the divines wrote to the Belgic, French, Helvetian, and other reformed churches. They sent them a copy of the covenant to shew how pious they were, and besought them to own them in any way they pleased, "as contemptible builders, called to repair the Lord's house in a troublesome time," and to pray for them that "they might see the pattern of this house; and that they might commend such a platform to our Zerubbabels (i. e. the members of parliament) as may be most agreeable to his word, nearest in conformity to the best reformed churches, and to establish uniformity among ourselves."

All the Episcopalian divines left the assembly before the bringing in of the covenant, except Dr. Featly, who was expelled for corresponding with archbishop Usher, and for revealing the proceedings of the assembly contrary to their rules. From the time of taking the covenant Mr. Neal dates the entire dissolution of the hierarchy, though not formally abolished by act of parliament.

January 19, 1644, the Scots army, consisting of twenty-one thousand soldiers, commanded by Gen. Leven, crossed the Tweed and entered into England. This event changed the proceedings of parliament and the assembly. The controversy about church discipline was now changed. Before the arrival of the army, a reformation of the hierarchy was only insisted upon; but now the total extirpation of it was attempted. The first step to do this effectually was to purify the universities, which were the head quarters of the hierarchical divines, and to make them puritanical fountains. The colleges were then all for the king and the hierarchy. But the Calvinists were determined to purify them. They began with Cambridge. The Puritans represented the teachers in that university, or the clergy controlling it, as "idle, ill-affected, and scandalous." The parliament, by an ordinance of January 22, gave the work of purifying this university to the Earl of Manchester, with full power to "eject" from office whom he pleased; "to sequester their estates, means, and revenues; to dispose of them as he thought fit, and to place others in their room, being first approved by the assembly of divines sitting at Westminster." He was to use the covenant as a test. On March 18, 1644, the covenant was offered to such graduates only as were supposed to be disaffected towards the parliament and divines; after which about two hundred were expelled. Mr. Neal gives the names of eleven doctors of great attainments who were displaced, and thinks that, because of their love of monarchy and hierarchy, the times required their expulsion. As the Westminster divines had the filling up of the vacancies they took special care to fill the empty chairs with good orthodox teachers and divines, and therefore filled more than half the vacancies, occasioned by the expulsion of the Doctors, out of their own assembly. During the year 1644, fifty-five persons were examined and appointed to the vacant fellowships in this university by the makers of the confession.

"Before we notice the debates of the assembly of divines, it will be proper, says Mr. Neal, to distinguish the several parties of which it was constituted. The Episcopalians had entirely deserted it before the bringing in of the covenant, so that the establishment was left without a single advocate. All who remained were for taking down the main pillars of hierarchy before they had agreed what sort of building to erect in its room. The members of the assembly which now remained were divided as respected discipline and church government, into three parties—Presbyterians, Erastians, and Independents. The name Puritan is from this time to be discarded. It once covered them all; but now they are distinguished by their views of church discipline. The majority of the assembly at first intended only the reducing episcopacy to the standard of the first and second age. But for the sake of the Scots' alliance, they were prevailed with to lay aside the name and function of bishops, and attempt a presbyterial form; which at length they advanced into *jus divinum,* or a divine institution. The Erastians were for giving the keys to the civil magistrate, and denied that there was a *jus divinum* for any form of church government. The independents or congregational brethren, composed a third party, and made a bold stand against the high proceedings of the presbyterians, and plead the *jus divinum,* or the divine institution of the congregational plan. There was not an anabaptist in the assembly; but out of doors they joined with the independents on the subject of church government. They made a considerable figure at this time, and joined with the independents in contending for a toleration of all nonconformists. Lord Clarendon represents the independents as abhorring monarchy, and approving of none but a republican government; and that as to religion, their principles were contrary to all the rest of the world; that they would not endure ordinary ministers in the church; but every one among them prayed, preached, admonished and interpreted scripture without any other call than what himself drew from his supposed gifts and the approbation of his hearers. Yet, with all their ignorance, they were an overmatch for the presbyterians and Erastians in the assembly, who out voted them, but dare not debate with them, as we shall see in their debates on church discipline.

October 12, 1644, the parliament ordered the assembly "to confer and treat among themselves of such a government and discipline as may be most agreeable to God's holy word, and most apt to procure and preserve the peace of the church at home, and a near agreement with the church of Scotland, to be settled in this church, instead of the present church government, by archbishops, bishops, &c. which it is resolved to take away, and to deliver their advices touching the same to both houses of parliament with all convenient speed." The ancient order of worship and discipline in the church of England was set aside twelve months before any other form of government was appointed.

Upon the petition of the divines, the parliament passed an ordinance for the ordination of ministers, and appointed ten members of the assembly to constitute an ordaining committee; to appoint or ordain by imposition of hands all those whom they deemed qualified to be put into "the sacred ministry." This was an ordinance *pro tempore.* They appointed other ordaining committees in different parts of the kingdom. To these ordinances and measures the independents entered their dissent, unless the ordination was attended with the previous election of some church.

They were next engaged in making out "a directory for public worship" instead of the old liturgy. This directory passed the assembly with great unanimity, none but the independents demurring much about it. It was, however, with much difficulty introduced into the congregations throughout the kingdom, and the parliament were obliged the next summer to pass another ordinance obliging the "common prayer" to be cast out of all the churches, and the new directory to be the law of worship. Great tyranny was exercised in getting the people to worship according to the new directory. A fine of five pounds for the first offence, ten for the second, and a year's imprisonment for the third, was the penalty for only reading the common prayer in private families. "All ministers who do not observe the directory in all cases of public worship, shall forfeit forty shillings." This ordinance was issued August 23, 1645. "These," says Mr. Neal, "were the first fruits of presbyterian uniformity." The baptists, too, at this time, were written against, preached against, and some of them shut up, in prison; and even one Mr. Otes, in Essex, was tried for his life for the murder of Anne Martin, because she had died a few days after she was baptized. "On the next day after the establishment of the directory, Dr. William Laud, archbishop of Canterbury, received sentence of death. He had been a prisoner in the Tower almost three years, upon sundry impeachments. His trial excited great interest and occupied much time. He had been a tyrant in church and state, and a cruel persecutor. But the Presbyterians measured to him as he had measured to others. Mrs. Macauly in her History of England, vol. iv. page 143, very correctly observes that "the parliament ought to have left this aged prelate an example of their mercy, rather than to have made him the monument of their justice." "It is plain, adds she, that he fell a sacrifice to the intolerant principles of the Presbyterians, a sect who breathed as fiery a spirit of persecution as himself." The archbishop died by the executioner in the seventy second year of his age, and the twelfth of his archepiscopacy. Such were the religious spirit and zeal of the times, and such the proceedings at Westminster while the creed of myriads was on the stocks, and the faith of the orthodox was delivering to the saints. Their debates on ordination and presbyterian government shall be noticed in our next.   EDITOR.

Christian Union.—No I.

READER, attend to what I am about to write. I address all denominations of christians, not with a design to oppose or to defend one sect more than another, or to pull down one system and build up another; but to show the error of all and to point out an infallible remedy.

It is high time that the christians in these United States consider the occasion of their divisions and strife, and bestir themselves to their correction and removal. Disunion among christians is their disgrace and a perpetual reproach and dishonor to the Lord Jesus Christ. To attempt union among jarring sects which are established upon different foundations, without the explosion of their foundations, is altogether fruitless. They may cozen one another a little by attempts at open communion, but it will amount to nothing valuable. They must all be built upon the same foundation before there can be a sameness of feeling and a unity of faith in the bonds of peace.

Christian union can result from nothing short of the destruction of creeds and confessions of faith, as human creeds and confessions have destroyed christian union. When ever the setting aside of creeds and confessions shall be attempted, christians will give to the world, and to angels and to themselves, proof that they do believe in the word of God.

The adjustment of a single word in the bible, according to the scriptural import and use of it, in principle and practice, will cure all errors in religion, and supply all that is wanting in uniting and making christians happy, and in giving a death-blow to scepticism and infidelity, and in converting the world. That word is *faith*—a word which has been perverted from its proper meaning and use in religion for more than sixteen hundred years by false philosophy and by the impious assumptions of civil authority in the establishment and regulation of religion. By these means King Messiah has been excluded from his own dominion, and human wisdom or ignorance has supplanted the wisdom that comes from above, and the church has been shorn of her glory.

What is the scripture meaning of the term "*faith?*" I answer that faith comprehends a system of truths, of which God is the great author, and a system of affections and conduct, of which he is the supreme object, all of which are revealed or made known by his word. Faith is the substance of things hoped for, the evidence of things not seen, which comes by hearing the word of God. The objects of faith are not objects of sense or of sight, any more than visible objects are objects of sight to a blind man. God is an object of faith, and has revealed himself by name, for no man has seen him at any time; and all that system of truths, of which he is the great subject and object, which are comprehended in the term "*religion*," are made known by his word. By this word the things that are seen are associated in the mind with God who is unseen, as their creator.*

The church of Christ is an assembly of believers, or of saints called out of the world and constituted by his authority. In this church the gospel is the mean and rule of faith and practice. Without faith the church cannot be formed—as without it, it is impossible to please God; and without his word there can be no faith or religion. The heathen, in their religion, have some broken traditional fragments of an original revelation.

We are dependant on the doctrinal statements and facts in the gospel for true views and correct impressions of the divine character.

The names, doctrinal statements, and facts, in the gospel, must be preserved in their order and connexion, and perceived, if we would know the truth.

In religion we cannot think any thing of ourselves, as of ourselves, but all our sufficiency is of God. The word of God is the instrumental cause of thought. We cannot think of God without an idea of him, and we cannot have an idea of him without his word. We are taught by, and we think and speak in, the words which the Holy

Spirit has taught, when we learn, or when we think or speak the truth in religion. 1 *Cor.* ii. 13.

If we cannot think any thing true or right without the word of God in religion, when we leave that word, or change or alter the connexion in the statements, or alter the terms with their associations in it, our thoughts in religion are wrong. God's word is truth. It teaches us the actual state of things as they are in his own existence, character, and will, and the relations we and the universe sustain to him, as far as we are capable of knowing them.

Alter this word of truth by adding to or taking from it, or by changing the order of its doctrinal statements, and facts, and names, and their qualifications, and you change in the same degree, in the views, and in the feelings of the mind, the actual state of things as they exist in Jehovah and in his character, and as they exist in the relations which men and the universe sustain to him. By this alteration you convert truth into error, and you obscure, mar, or mutilate the glorious image of God as it shines in the face of Jesus, which is designed, and is the only ordained mean too, as it shines there, to renew the heart of man, and the world of men, into the image of him who created him by the knowledge of him. You moreover form the very elements of sectarianism and sectarian hatred. God's nature is love, and his perfections form a unity. The knowledge of them produces love and unity in all those who receive a full renovating impression of them in the gospel.

What is a creed? I answer that it is a short, or a summary account of the chief articles of the christian faith compiled by men.

What is a confession of faith? I answer that it denotes a list or enumeration and declaration of the several articles of belief in a church. Such are professedly taken from the scriptures,—they are, however, *not* the scriptures. They have different names, and are the covenants or the constitutions of different churches, which are not found in the scriptures. Where do you find the Philadelphia Confession of Faith, or the Westminster, or the Methodist Book of Doctrine and Discipline, or a Baptist church, or a Presbyterian church, or a Methodist church, or any other church than the church of Christ, in the New Testament?

But it is asked, Are we not free to do as we please in these matters, and have we not a right to form creeds and sects? I answer in the name of the Lord Jesus Christ, *No!* they have not a right to act thus! The assumption that they have the right, is the foundation of popery, both in the exercise of human legislation and of human authority in religion. What! shall we who cannot think, or know, or feel, or act righteously and truly in any thing relative to religion, without the names, and doctrinal statements, and facts in the gospel, change or alter them, and substitute others in their place? In this case they cannot fail adding to, or taking from the word of God. There is one lawgiver who can save the obedient and destroy the disobedient, who has forbidden, under a most awful penalty, any alteration in the words of his book. *Rev.* xxii. 19.

The gospel is the charter of the mutual rights of all christians. No man or set of men has a right to alter that charter. He that does so, forfeits his rights and privileges under it. He invades the prerogative and sovereignty of King Messiah, and impairs or destroys the rights of his subjects. The glory of Immanuel is essentially concerned in the unity and happiness of the members of his body. The gospel, in its

* I presume the writer of this excellent essay uses the term faith here as it is sometimes used in scripture, not to express the belief of the truth, but the truth to be believed.   [ED. C. B.

integrity, is designed to produce them and to advance his kingdom, and it must and will produce these effects when unaltered.

What! establish new names and sects in the christian religion, to the exclusion of Christ and the name Christian? Is this true? Look into the New Testament. There the church is the church of Christ, and his disciples are christians. Look out of the New Testament, and look into creeds and confessions. Here we see a Baptist church, a Methodist church, and a Presbyterian church, &c. and answerable to these, here, we see, Baptists, Methodists, Presbyterians, &c.

The New Testament names, which all must approve of, are thrown aside to give place to sectarian names, which all are offended at, in some degree, and think invidious, except those who belong to them, and they ought to be tired of them. With these sectarian names are united sectarian feelings and affections, and sectarian sympathies and antipathies, which have taken the place of true christian feelings and affections.

But it is said, these are only *names*. We have seen that, in religion, names, and words, and sentences, are every thing in order to right ideas. If we alter them by adding to them or taking from them, in the original order of the revelation, we change the truth and the effects of it into error; and when this is done there is nothing to correct it by. In nature, if we give a wrong description of an object, that description can be corrected by examining the object. In religion, the objects, the facts, and the doctrines are only known through the description—alter that, and the error is without remedy.

When we give a name and a creed to a church, other than the name of Christ, or Christian, and the New Testament, or the Gospel, that church acquires immediately in our *imaginations* and *feelings*, and in fact, a character altogether different from what the church of Christ really possesses in the light of the New Testament. The character of Christ in authority and dominion, as the one lawgiver; and the character of christians in faith, and hope, and love, are merged in the sectarian names given to the church and to the members.

In this case we see that a difference of names is more than a verbal difference. Different names and different creeds have occasioned a more persevering combat in the christian world, among christians in their ecclesiastical councils, bitter controversies, and bloody persecutions and wars, to settle what they have called the christian faith, and the order of the church, according to their names and creeds, than all the conquerors of the world have employed to make themselves masters of it. All this has arisen from entire ignorance of the use and the design of the gospel.

But it is asked, Are all christians to agree in this union? I answer, that in all the fundamental truths they must and do agree. The union requires of them that they throw away nothing that they possess but error and falsehood. They must agree, and they do agree, in the character of King Jesus, and in the authority of his statute book, agreeably to the scripture statements of both. Without these men cannot be christians, and ought to have no place in a church. Receive members into the church and discipline them according to the gospel, and all things will be done in good order.

Every christian has a divine right to admission into the church of Christ, and to enjoy all the rights and privileges therein, wherever he may be, if he presents himself according to the gospel, unencumbered by sectarian names and creeds; and no church has a divine right to refuse him admission, or to require of him sectarian conditions in order to his admission. Two *opposing divine rights* is a contradiction. The love and fellowship of christians is the inheritance and happiness of every individual saint. They are his spiritual property, and in the possession and enjoyment of them the Saviour has given it to him in charge to "stand fast in the liberty wherewith Christ has made him free." He has a right, a divine right, to require of every church to relinquish its sectarian name and creed in order to his entering it. If the church refuse this, he has a right to complain to his Lord against the injury done to him, and that complaint will be sustained.

The great error among christians is in their forming their consciences in religion on the opinions of men. By reason of this, that love and zeal which ought to be felt for God and man, are transferred to a party, and are engrossed by sectarian views and principles. Hence the conscience is performing different sentences in different churches and sects at the same time, and in direct opposition to each other. There is a Baptist, Methodist, Presbyterian, Episcopalian, and Roman Catholic conscience, and a Christ to answer each, and thus Christ is divided. In Kentucky there is a *Licking Association conscience* among the Baptists, or a *Particular Baptist conscience*, founded by cutting up the scriptures, and taking out and stringing together a few scraps or verses torn from their connexions.

Conscience should refuse her homage to any other than God in his word. The man who submits his conscience to the unauthorized decisions of men in religion, does not in his conduct rise to the dignity of religious worship. Such a subjection is a criminal surrender of christian liberty, and a violation of the apostolic precept, "Stand fast in the liberty wherewith Christ has made you free." Nor can they who make it feel the true spirit on which the whole law and prophets, the gospel, Christ, and the apostles, hang; viz. "love to God and love to man."

I repeat what I formerly observed: Adjust the term faith according to the scriptural meaning of it, which is agreeable to the true philosophy of the human mind in spiritual knowledge, and you rectify all error. You extinguish the deist's and the divine's natural religion or deism, and all human inventions in religion, or forgeries and corruptions—you establish the Bible as the only instructor in religion in our schools and out of them, and you wipe out all sectarian names and creeds, and unite the whole church in one name, and establish it upon Jesus Christ as the Son of God, and the gospel, or the New Testament, as the statute book of his kingdom. This will be the commencement of millennial glory. The happiness of christians will approach to the heavenly state. Jesus will be all and in all.

In the present divided and distracted state of opinion and practice, I would say to every one, throw aside your sectarian names and human creeds as soon as practicable, and assume the name given to the disciples at Antioch—christians—and admit the name of Christ to grace your association and to be the crown of your rejoicing. Open your hearts and consciences to the light and influence of the word of God in the gospel, and be always exercised to have a conscience void of offence towards all in what you do. If that word tells you to sprinkle infants, do it; or if it tells believers to be immersed, obey. Do all in the name and by the express authority of Jesus Christ. I would not have dominion over your faith, but be a helper of your joy. Continue in the word of Christ, then shall you be his disciples indeed, and you shall know the truth, and the truth shall make you free. In that case we will lose nothing but error, and ignorance, and sectarian bigotry, and we shall gain the knowledge of the truth and the true christian character, and our hearts will be filled with love to God and love to man; and we will necessarily be one as certain as that Jesus lives; and the world will believe in him. *John* xvii. 20, 21.

I have much more to write.

CHRISTIAN UNION.

A Restoration of the Ancient Order of Things.
No. V.
Order of Worship.

WE shall now inquire what was the ancient order of worship in the christian church. Preparatory to this it may be expedient to consider whether there be any divinely authorized worship in the assembly of saints. As this is a theme of great importance, and of much difficulty with some, we shall bestow some attention to it. And in the first instance we shall attempt to demonstrate from rational principles, that there is a divinely instituted worship for the assemblies of the disciples. In order to do this as convincingly as possible, and to circumscribe the arena of conjecture, we shall take but two positions, which we hope to hold as impregnable fortresses against all assault. These we shall exhibit in the form of dilemmas. The first is, either there is a divinely authorized order of christian worship in christian assemblies, or there is not. This every man must admit, or cease to be a man. Now to remove all ambiguity from the terms of this dilemma, we shall explicitly state that, by a christian assembly, we mean a congregation or assembly of disciples meeting in one place for social worship. The day agreed upon by christians for this meeting is the first day of every week. The authority that ordains this day we have already noticed in this work, and it is not now a subject of inquiry. It is also unnecessary to our present purpose, inasmuch as this day is agreed upon by all christians, with the exception of some Sabbatarians, for whose consideration we have something to say at another time. By the phrase, "order of christian worship," we do not mean the position of the bodies of the worshippers, nor the hour of the day in which certain things are to be done, nor whether one action shall be always performed first, another always second, and another always third, &c. &c. though in these there is an order which is comely, apposite, or congruous with the genius of the religion, and concerning which some things are said by the apostles; and, perhaps, even in some respects, these things may be determined with certainty as respects the practice of the first congregations of disciples; but that there are certain social acts of christian worship, all of which are to be attended to in the christian assembly, and each of which is essential to the perfection of the whole as every member of the human body is essential to the perfect man—is that which we wish to convey by the phrase, "order of christian worship." These remarks may suffice in the mean time to prevent misapprehensions; but in the prosecution of our inquiries every ambiguity will be completely removed. We shall now repeat the first position we have taken—either there is a divinely au-

thorized order of christian worship in christian assemblies, or there is not.

On the supposition that there is not, then the following absurdities are inevitable: There can be no disorder in the christian assembly; there can be no error in the acts of social worship; there can be no innovation in the department of observances; there can be no transgression of the laws of the King. For these reasons, viz. where there is no order established there can be no disorder, for disorder is acting contrary to established order; where there is no standard there can be no error, for error is a departure or a wandering from a standard; where there is nothing fixed there can be no innovation, for to innovate is to introduce new things amongst those already fixed and established; and where there is no law there can be no transgression, for a transgression is a leaping over or a violating of legal restraints. Those, then, who contend that there is no divinely authorized order of christian worship in christian assemblies, do at the same time, and must inevitably maintain, that there is no disorder, no error, no innovation, no transgression in the worship of the christian church—no, nor ever can be. This is reducing one side of the dilemma to what may be called a perfect absurdity.

But, to make this matter evident to children as well as men, we will carry it a little farther. One society of disciples meets on the first day morning and they all dance till evening, under the pretext that this is the happiest way of expressing their joy, and when they have danced themselves down they go home. Now in this there is no disorder, error, innovation, or transgression, for there is no divinely authorized order of christian worship. The reader will observe that we do not suppose human laws or regulations of any consequence in this matter. Men may regulate the worship they require for themselves and for one another; and in relation to those regulations there may be disorder, error, innovation, and transgression. But as none but the Lord can prescribe or regulate the worship due to himself and profitable to us; so, if he have done it, human regulations are as vain and useless as attempts to prevent the ebbing of the sea or the waxing and waning of the moon. But to proceed: Another society meets for worship, and they sing all day; another shouts all day; another runs as in a race all day; another lies prostrate on the ground all day; another reads all day; another hears one man speak all day; another sits silent all day; another waves palm branches all day; another cries in the forenoon and listens to the organ in the afternoon; and it is all equally right, lawful, orderly, and acceptable; for there is no divinely authorized order of christian worship. We are then, on the principles of reason, constrained to abandon this side of the dilemma, and give up the hypothesis that there is no divinely authorized order of christian worship. Now as one of the only two supposable cases must be abandoned, it follows by undeniable consequence, that there is a divinely authorized order of christian worship in christian assemblies.

Our second position we hope to make appear equally strong and unassailable. Having now proved that there is a divinely authorized order of christian worship in christian assemblies, our second dilemma is, Either this christian worship in christian assemblies is uniformly the same, or it is not. To clear this position of ambiguity, it will be observed that we speak of the assembling of the disciples on the day agreed upon for the purpose of social worship, and that the same acts of religious worship are to be performed on every first day in every assembly of disciples, or they are not. If the same acts of worship, or religious ordinances, or observances, be attended to in every assembling of the saints, then their worship is uniformly the same; but if not, then it is not uniformly the same. The position we again repeat, this exposition being given, Either the christian worship in christian assemblies is uniformly the same, or it is not.

We shall follow the same method of demonstration as in the preceding dilemma. We shall take the last of the only two supposable cases and try its merits. It is not uniformly the same. Then it is different. These differences are either limited or unlimited. If they are unlimited, then it is uniformly different; and what is uniformly different has no order, standard, or rule, and thus we are led to the same absurdities which followed from supposing there was no divinely authorized order of christian worship; for a worship uniformly different is a worship without order. But supposing that those differences are limited, those limitations must be defined or pointed out somewhere. But they are not. Now differences that are no where limited or pointed out are unlimited, and consequently may be carried *ad infinitum*, which is to say there is no order appointed, and thus we are again encompassed with the same absurdities.

To level this to every apprehension, it may be remarked that the worship of the Jews, though divinely authorized, was not uniformly the same. The worship at the feast of Tabernacles, at Pentecost, at the Passover, and in different seasons of the year, and even of the Moon, varied from what was attended to on ordinary occasions. These varieties and differences were pointed out in their standard of worship. But no such varieties are pointed out, no such differences are ordained in any part of the standard of christian worship. Yet we find amongst the professed christians as great variety existing as amongst the Jews—though with this difference, that divine authority ordained the one, and human authority the other. The worship of a class meeting, of a camp-meeting, of a monthly concert, of an association, of a sacramental occasion, of a preparation, and of an " ordinary Sabbath," differ as much as the Jewish Passover, Pentecost, annual atonement, or daily sacrifice. Now there were in the Jewish state solid and substantial reasons for all these varieties, but in the christian state there is no reason for any variety. The changing types of the Jews religion have received their consummation, and now there exists at all times the same reasons for the same observances. There is no reason why a society of disciples should commemorate the death or resurrection of Jesus on one first day more than another. All the logic and philosophy of the age, as well as the New Testament, fails in producing one reason. He that invents or discovers it, has discovered a new principle. But we are only establishing or demonstrating on rational principles that the worship of a christian assembly is uniformly the same, and the method we have chosen is that of supposing the contrary and reducing the hypothesis to an absurdity, or a series of absurdities. In brief, the sum of our remarks on this position is, that if the worship of the christian church is not uniformly the same, then it is either occasionally or uniformly different. If uniformly different, then there is no established order, as proved in the first dilemma; and if occasionally different,

there must be some reason for these varieties; but no reason exists, therefore a difference without reason is irrational and absurd. It follows then that there is a divinely authorized order of christian worship in christian assemblies, and that this worship is uniformly the same, which was to be demonstrated on principles of reason.

These positions are capable of rational demonstration on other grounds than those adopted; but this plan was preferred because it was the shortest, and, as we supposed, the most convincing.

This is only preparative or introductory to the essays which are to follow upon the ancient worship of the christian church. We are hastening through the outlines and shall fill up the interior after we have given an essay on each of the following topics. They continued stedfastly in the apostles' doctrine—in breaking of bread—in fellowship—in prayers—praising God. As we have paid more attention in the general to the apostles' doctrine than to the other items, our next essays will be on the breaking of bread, the fellowship, and prayers of the primitive church.

Hoping that the christian reader will bring all things to the test, and hold fast that which is good, we bid him adieu for the present.

EDITOR.

The Third Epistle of Peter, to the Preachers and Rulers of Congregations.—A Looking Glass for the Clergy.

ONE of the best proofs that a prophecy is what it purports to be, is its exact fulfilment. If this rule be adopted in relation to the " Third Epistle of Peter," there can be no doubt that it was written in the true spirit of prophecy. We thought it worthy of being preserved, and have therefore given it a place in this work.

ED. C. B.

Preface.

How the following epistle came to be overlooked by the early saints of christendom and by all the fathers, or whether it was purposely suppressed by the Council of Nice, and why it was at last destined to be found with other old manuscripts among the ruins of an ancient city by a miserable wandering Monk, are all circumstances which my limited knowledge of these subjects does not enable me to explain. I am answerable only for the accuracy of the translation from a French copy presented by the Monk himself. Neither can I prove the authenticity of the original, unless it be on the strict correspondence of the actual state of the church with the injunctions contained in the epistle, a correspondence which seems to hold with as much veracity as that which is found in the fulfilment of any prophecy with the prediction itself.

TRANSLATOR.

CHAPTER I.
The Style and Manner of Living.

Now you who are called and chosen to go forth to all nations and among all people, in time present and time to come, to preach the word, see you take to yourselves marks, nay, many outward marks, whereby you shall be known by men.

Be you not called as men are called; but be you called Pope, Archbishop, Archdeacon, or Divine, or Reverend, and Right Reverend, or some like holy name; so may you show forth your honor and your calling.

And let your dwelling places be houses of splendor and edifices of cost; and let your doors be decked with plates of brass, and let your names, even your reverend titles be graven thereon; so shall it be as a sign.

Let your garments in which you minister be garments not as the garments of men, neither let them be "seamless garments woven throughout;" but let them be robes of richest silk and robes of fine linen, of curious device and of costly workmanship; and have you robes of black and robes of white, that you may change the one for the other; so shall you show forth your wisdom and humility.

Let your fare be sumptuous, not plain and frugal as the fare of the husbandman who tills the ground; but live you on the fat of the land, taking "good heed for the morrow and wherewithal you shall be fed."

And drink you of the vines of the vintage brought from afar, and wines of great price; then shall the *light* of your *spirits* be the light of your *countenances*, and your faces shall be bright, even as the morning sun shall your faces glow in brightness; thus shall you show forth your moderation and your temperance in all things.

Let the houses in which you preach be called churches, and let them be built in manner of great ornament without, and adorned with much cost within; with rich pillars and paints, and with fine altars and pedestals, and urns of precious stones, and cloths and velvet of scarlet, and vessels of silver.

And let there be rooms for the changing of robes, and places for the precious metals and mitres.

And let the houses be divided into seats for the congregation, and let every man know his own seat; and let the first seats in front of the altar be for the rich that pay by thousands; and the next for the poorer that pay by hundreds; and the last for those that pay by tens. And let the poor man sit behind the door.

And let the seats be garnished with cushions and crimson cloth, and with fine velvet; for if the houses of players and vain people who deal in idle sayings and shows of mockery, be rich and gorgeous, how much more so should be the houses that are dedicated to him "that is meek and lowly of spirit."

CHAPTER II.
The Choosing of Ministers.

WHEN you go out to choose holy ones to be of your brethren, and to minister at the altar, choose you from among the youth, even those whose judgments are not yet ripe, and whose hearts know not yet whether they incline to God or Mammon.

But you are wise, and you shall know the inclining of their future spirits, and you shall make them incline to the good things which the church has in store for them that are called, even those that shall be called by you.

Then shall you have them taught exceeding many things. They shall not be as "ignorant fishermen," or husbandmen, or men speaking one tongue, and serving God only by the knowledge of his law.

Nay, you shall make them wise in the things of your wisdom; yea, exceedingly cunning in many *mysteries*, even the *mysteries* which *you* teach.

Then shall they be fitted for the "laying on of hands," and when the bishop has done his office then shall they be reverend divines.

But if any man believe that he is called by God to speak to his brethren "without money

and without price," though his soul be bowed to the will of the Father, and though he work all righteousness, and "speak as with the tongue of an angel"—if he be not made a divine by your rulers and by the hands of a bishop, then is he not a divine, nor shall he preach.

He that is chosen by *you* shall give *you* honor, and shall be honored by men, and honored by *women;* and verily he *expects* his reward.

CHAPTER III.
The Performance of Preaching.

WHEN you go to the church to preach, go not by the retired way where go those that would shun the crowd, but go in the highway where go the multitude, and see that you have on the robes of black, and take heed that your pace be measured well, and that your march be stately.

Then shall your "hearts be lifted up," even as the hearts of mighty men shall they be lifted up. And you shall be gazed upon by the multitude, and they shall honor you; and the men shall praise you, and the *women* shall glorify you, even by the women shall you be glorified.

And when you go in, go not as the ordained, prepared *only* with a soul to God and with a heart to men, and a spirit filled with the Holy Ghost; but go you with your pockets full of papers and full of divine words; even in your pockets shall your divinity be.

And let your sermon be full of "the enticing words of man's wisdom," and let it be beautified with just divisions, with tropes and with metaphors, and with hyperbole, and apostrophe, and with interrogation, and with acclamation, and with syllogisms, and with sophisms, and throughout let declamation be.

And take good heed to your attitudes and your gestures, knowing when to bend and when to erect, when to lift your right hand and when your left, and let your motions be graceful, even in your attitudes and in your gestures let your *grace* be. Thus shall you be pleasing in the eyes of the people and *graceful* in their sight.

Let your voice at times be smooth as the stream of the valley, and soft as the breeze that waves not the bough on its bank; and at times let it swell like the wave of the ocean, or like the whirlwind on the mountain top.

Then shall you charm the ears of your hearers and their hearts shall be softened, and their minds shall be astounded, and their souls shall incline to you; and the men shall incline to you, and likewise the women; yea, to your sayings and to your persons shall they be inclined.

And be you mindful not to offend the people; rebuke you not their sins; but when you rebuke sin, rebuke it at a *distance;* and let no man apply your sayings to his own case; so shall he not be offended.

If a brother shall raise up the banner of war against brother, and christians against christians, rebuke them not; but be some of you on the one side and some on the other; and tell the one host that God is on their side, and the other host that he is on their side; so make them bold to kill. And even among swords and lancets let your black robes be seen.

Preach you not "Peace on earth and good will to men," but preach you glory to the victor, and victory to the brave.

If any man go into a foreign land and seize upon his fellow man, and put irons on his feet and irons on his hands, and bring him across the great deep into bondage; nay, if he tear asunder the dearest ties of nature, the tenderest leagues of the human heart; if he tear the wife from the husband, and force the struggling infant from its mother's bleeding breast, rebuke him not!

And although he sell them in foreign slavery to toil beneath the lash all their days, tell him not that his doings are of Antichrist; for lo! he is rich and gives to the church, and is esteemed pious, so shall you not offend him, lest peradventure he withdraw himself from your flock.

Teach them to believe that you have the care of their souls, and that the saving mysteries are for your explaining; and when you explain your *mysteries*, encompass them round about with words as with a bright veil, so bright that through it no man can see.

And lo! you shall bind the judgments of men, (and more especially of women,) as with a band of iron: and you shall make them blind in the midst of light, even as the owl is blind in the noon day sun; and behold you shall lead them captive to your reverend wills.

Chapter IV.
The Clergy's Reward.

"In all your gettings" get money! Now, therefore, when you go forth on your ministerial journey, go where there are silver and gold, and where each man will pay according to his measure. For verily I say you must get your reward.

Go you not forth as those that have been sent, "without two coats, without gold or silver, or brass in their purses; without scrip for their journey, or shoes, or staves;" but go you forth in the good things of this world.

And when you shall hear of a church that is vacant and has no one to preach therein, then be that a *call* to you, and be you mindful of the call, and take you charge of the flock thereof and of the fleece thereof, even of the *golden* fleece.

And when you shall have fleeced your flock, and shall know of another *call*, and if the flock be greater, or rather if the fleece be greater, then greater be also to you the call. Then shall you leave your old flock, and of the new flock shall you take the charge.

Those who have "freely received" let them "freely give," and let not men have your words "without money nor without price," but bargain you for hundreds and bargain for thousands, even for thousands of silver and gold shall you bargain.

And over and above the price for which you have sold your service, take you also gifts, and be you mindful to refuse none, saying, "Lo! I have enough!" but receive gifts from them that go in chariots, and from them that feed flocks, and from them that earn their morsel by the sweat of their brow.

Yea, take you gifts of all, and take them in gold and in silver, and in bread; in wine and in oil; in raiment and in fine linen.

And the more that the people give you the more will they honor you; for they shall believe that "in giving to you they are giving to the Lord;" for behold their sight shall be taken from them, and they shall be blind as bats, and "shall know not what they do."

And you shall wax richer and richer, and grow greater and greater, and you shall be lifted up in your own sight, and exalted in the eyes of the multitude; and lucre shall be no longer filthy in your sight. And verily you have your reward.

In doing these things you shall never fail. And may abundance of gold and silver and bank notes, and corn, and wool, and flax, and spirits and wine, and land be multiplied to you, both now and hereafter. Amen.

Extracts from my Sentimental Journal.—No. III.
Popular Worship.

Shortly after my arrival at N—— I went to the Presbyterian meeting-house. It was a tasty and magnificent edifice, and well filled with fashion and beauty. The wooden throne was superb, and in the first boxes sat and reclined the wealthy and proud on seats as soft as sofas. After a silent contemplation of the polite crowds entering and walking to their respective pews, in all the majesty of the theatre, which feasted the eyes of those already seated, and furnished texts for the first half of the week, the grave young parson commenced the public worship of God, who delights in a fine exterior, and in a proud and aspiring heart; who despises the poor cottage and the cottager, the rough meeting-house, and the rude and rough frequenters of it. He sang and prayed one hour and six minutes; or rather he offered songs for the sweet singers, who expressed their piety in all the gracious flexions of symphonious voices, while the devout audience worshipped in admiring the harmony of music, and praised their God for having given such fine voices and charming music to men and women. His prayer was well pronounced, in periods such as Dr. Blair commends; and, in the true philosophy of rhetoric, he worshipped, if not in spirit and in truth, certainly in taste and elegance. His sermon was forty-five minutes long, and was all built on this clause, "Why will you die, O house of Israel!" He finished with one song and prayer twenty-seven minutes long, and then blessed the people and sent them home for one week. Next day I inquired after his stipend and found it was annually two thousand dollars, besides marriage fees and funeral sermons extra, amounting to perhaps one thousand more. Six months in the year he gave them two orations *per diem*, and six months one, averaging forty-five minutes each, making in all fifty-eight hours and one-half in a year, valued at thirty-four dollars per hour, or twenty-six dollars per sermon. His sermon on "why will you die, O house of Israel!" cost the congregation twenty-six dollars, except we should count something on the prayers; but as he was hired to preach, and not to pray, it is just to fix this value upon his sermons. Now if one clause of a verse cost that people twenty-six dollars, the question with me was, How much would it cost them to have the whole bible thus explained? I soon found, by the rule of three, it would require rather more than a thousand years to get once through, and cost the congregation one million three hundred thousand dollars to have it thus explained. But the misfortune was, that they must all die before they would hear it all explained, and pay all their lives for that which would never be accomplished. But they were amused once in a week for their money, and their life was only a frolic throughout, and the parson might as well have some of their money as the play-actor or the confectioner. During the evening I was entertained by contrasting the present state of the "christian congregations" with that of the first disciples, and their teachers with those who were first employed in this work. Blessed revolution! when the same sort of men, and actuated by the same motives too, now pay dollars instead of stripes for hearing preachers; when the children of those who whipped and scourged the first teachers now contribute by tens and twenties to those who call themselves the successors of those who freely received and freely gave. Editor.

Five Queries Answered.

The following questions are from a teacher of the christian religion in Ohio:

" 1st.   Was Jesus a priest while on earth?

" 2d.   Did he make an atonement when he died on the Roman cross?

" 3d.   Did he appease the wrath of himself according to the common preaching of the clergy?

" 4th.   Did humanity die and divinity leave the Son of God?

" 5th.   What kind of a body will the ungodly rise with in the resurrection?

" My design is to understand the scriptures and act accordingly, not fearing the frowns of the clergy nor the power of the Sectarians.

" *April* 18, 1824."

To the first question the scriptures answer, No. The life of the victim was taken without the tabernacle, according to the types of Israel, and the priest officiated in the holy place in offering or presenting the sacrifice and in interceding. The Messiah's life was taken on earth; and in heaven, the true holy place, he officiates as priest. He could not be a priest on earth according to the law; but having suffered without the gate, he entered into heaven itself, and there officiates as our great High Priest, consecrated by an oath, a Priest upon his throne after the order of Melchisedec.

To the second question the scriptures respond, and inform us that he died for our sins, or was delivered up for our offences, and has by his death atoned or reconciled us to God. The phrase " atonement of Christ" is unscriptural. We have, by him, received the reconciliation. It is rather our atonement by means of his death. God has reconciled or atoned us to himself by the death of his Son. His death upon the cross is, then, the means or cause of our atonement.

To the third question the record gives no answer. It is an absurdity growing out of the dogmas of the schools. It was the love of God and his lovely character that required the death of his Son. The death of Jesus is the highest proof in the universe of God's philanthropy.

To the fourth question the scriptures do not respond. It has arisen from the dissecting knife of theological anatomists. It is the northern extreme of frigid Calvinism. The immense ice mountains of those regions have prevented their most expert captains from finding a passage to those latitudes which would confirm their theory of sphere within sphere. They are as skilful to separate and treat of humanity and divinity in the Son of God, as is Colonel Symmes in forming this globe into so many hollow spheres, each having its own properties and inhabitants.

To your fifth question the new testament deigns no reply. It is kind enough to inform us of the bodies of the saints at the resurrection, and thus sets before us an object of hope the most engaging, purifying and ennobling, that is conceivable, and leaves the bodies of the wicked in impenetrable darkness and awful gloom; and it might be as impious and as absurd for us to attempt to draw an image of that which has no model and which is designedly as far from human view as those chains of darkness which bind fallen angels unto the judgment of the great day.

Things not revealed belong to the Lord, and those revealed belong to us and our race in all ages. And happy are they who believe and obey what God has revealed, and who labor to stand approved before him at his coming.

                                        Editor.

Several baptist congregations in the western part of Pennsylvania, and in the state of Ohio, have voted the Philadelphia Confession of Faith out of doors, as not worthy of a place among them. They are determined on being free to be guided by that old fashioned book that exhibits the faith once delivered to the saints, in the order and connexion best adapted to mankind, as appeared to the founder of the religion.

                                        Editor.

At a meeting of sundry teachers of the christian religion and brethren from different sections of the country, held in Warren, Trumbull county, Ohio, on the last day of May and first of June, at which the editor was present, the greater part of two days was occupied in discussing the ancient order of things. A great desire was expressed by most of those present to see the ancient order of things restored; and the discussion was free, candid, and general. Many topics were introduced subservient to the grand topic of investigation; and from the zeal and harmony that was apparent in this investigation, it is to be hoped that those congregations of disciples who have begun in the spirit will not end in the flesh, but that the ancient order of things will soon be exhibited in the practice of the disciples meeting on the first day of the week.

                                        Editor.

END OF VOLUME II.

W

CHRISTIAN BAPTIST.

NO. I.—VOL. III. BUFFALOE, (BETHANY) BROOKE CO. VA., AUGUST 1, 1825.

Style no man on earth your Father: for he alone is your Father who is in heaven: and all ye are brethren. Assume not the title of Rabbi; for ye have only One Teacher; neither assume the title of Leader; for ye have only One Leader— the Messiah. *Messiah.*

PREFATORY REMARKS.

Notwithstanding the flood of opposition which was intended to have overwhelmed this work, and aimed at its destruction by an ambitious priesthood and their deluded admirers, it has acquired an extensive growth in its circulation, and a vigor which opposition alone could give it. A spirit of investigation and of unbiased inquiry, which we had scarcely anticipated, appears to have aroused into activity the dormant energies of a priest-ridden community. We have every reason to hope that this spirit will not give sleep to its eyes, nor slumber to its eye-lids, until many shall clearly see and comprehensively understand, the mighty difference existing between the kingdom of the Clergy, and that of the Saviour of the world. We have little to promise but *perseverance* in the arduous conflict, so long as the same necessities exist, and until we shall see the ancient order of things restored in some good degree. Our constant readers have, perhaps, been expecting a series of essays upon some topics in our prospectus, scarcely yet touched. We have only to request a due exercise of patience on their part, and to offer as an apology the great press of many matters more immediately bearing upon existing circumstances. We intend to leave nothing undone, and to accomplish all that has been promised, as we have opportunity; but prudence is necessary to direct. We have also the proffered assistance of some of the most able and distinguished Nicodemuses of the times, and shall thankfully receive and promptly attend to their communications upon general and important matters. For there are a goodly number of those even amongst the priesthood that bid us God speed, although for the present distress they think it expedient to remain in the conclaves of the powerful. We must sympathize with them a little, for as Paul said, "all men have not faith," so we see all men have not courage.

While the press is pouring forth every day fresh oil into the lamp, which guides the devotion of the thoughtless, and makes them think that they see the sun in a smoky wick, not an editor in the East nor in the West of all the Luminaries and religious Heralds, has ventured to dispute one inch of the ground that we claim. And yet their snarling shows they would bite if they could. They seem to know that the less they say the better for them and their cause; and perhaps they are right. The editors of the Western Luminary did positively promise in December last, to enter the field of investigation, and to oppose us manfully; but not a syllable has appeared on the subject in any of their numbers that we have seen. They have either quit publishing, or ceased to send us their paper, for we have not seen one for a month. Perhaps they are of the same spirit with our neighbor the *Pittsburgh Recorder*, who, after he had agreed and promised to exchange papers with us, soon as we began to inquire what he was doing he forgot his agreement and ceased to send us his paper. These gentry seem to know, or at least to think, that their cause will not bear the light of open discussion, and that a *silent* course is the best policy. They have given sufficient evidence by their occasional notices, that if they could do any thing in the way of public discussion, they would soon be at it. We do not say these things to provoke them into a controversy, for we have no expectation that there is any excitability in them, but merely to show the manner of spirit they are of. We must confess that we cannot view with other feelings than those due to a thief and a robber, who covers himself with the curtains of night, that he may execute his designs, those who attempt to extend their empire over the human mind and conscience, by suppressing the truth or withholding the light from the eyes of those who look up to them as their guides. This they do by prejudicing the minds of many against the truth. We hope the day is not far distant, in which it will be admitted, that true charity, benevolence and philanthropy consist not in flattering the wicked, nor in speaking peace to every body, but in withstanding to the face, as Paul did Peter, all those errorists, whether acting the part of the deceiver or the deceived.

EDITOR.

Christian Union.—No II.

I am aware of the prejudices which each christian sect feels for their own name and creed, and of the great difficulty there will be in getting them to drop them, or to exchange them for the name of Christian and the word of God. I fear that there are many professing christians among what are called *Protestant* sects, who, rather than make this exchange, would unite with the Roman Catholics in defence of human authority, in legislating for, and dictating to the consciences of men in religion. In this they would act consistently, if they really entertain the sentiment expressed by Dr. Miller, "that the adoption of a creed," (or confession of faith such as the Westminster,) "is not only *lawful* and *expedient*, but also *indispensably* necessary." They ought, however, in that case to be consistent throughout, and to join themselves to the church of Rome. For if any church or people have authority from God to form creeds and confessions in religion, (and without divine authority there is no right,)

1

the church of Rome had it before, and, as the elder and mother church ought to have been obeyed; and consequently the Reformation, as it has been called, was a rebellion against superiors, a disobedience of the divine authority vested in that church, and ought as such to be renounced by returning to it. If indeed it be lawful for men to substitute their speculations and notions derived from nature, and their views of scripture for scripture itself, and to impose them upon men's consciences, it will be very difficult to show upon what principle the church of Rome can be condemned for having thus acted. It will not do to say that they went too far, for they had as good a right to judge how far they might go as those have who condemn them. Dr. Miller's whole defence of creeds is based upon the deism or natural religion of John Calvin. This deism is at the foundation of, and pervades every system of sectarian religion in christendom; it had its origin in Pagan philosophy, relative to innate ideas of God which was at an early period incorporated with the christian religion. The following sentiments are extracted from Calvin's *Institutes*, vol. I. *chap.* iii. "*The human mind naturally endowed with the knowledge of God.*"

"We lay it down as a position not to be controverted, that the human mind, even by rational instinct, possesses some sense of a Deity—for God has given to all some apprehension of his existence; some sense of divinity is inscribed on every heart. All men have by nature an innate persuasion of the divine existence, a persuasion inseparable from their very constitution. The sense of a Deity is a doctrine not first to be learned in the schools, but every man from his birth is self-taught. Men need not go out of themselves for a clear discovery of God—the seeds of divinity are sown in the nature of man." In opposition to all this, the word of God says that "the world by wisdom knew not God;" and so say the history of the world and the experience and consciousness of every individual. Locke exploded the doctrine of innate ideas. All the present systems, however, retain the consequences of that doctrine, which are seen in natural religion or deism, which is a religion without revelation, and in scholastic theology, and mystic divinity. These are taught in all theological schools, colleges, and universities in christendom. True philosophy and the bible make revelation essential to religion. Men are born with innate capacities or susceptibility for acquiring the idea or knowledge of Deity; but revelation, supernatural revelation, is necessary for enlightening or improving that capacity, for giving the idea or knowledge of God.

The point must be sooner or later conceded, that Christ is the light of the world in religion and spiritual things, and that in his church he is himself the only sovereign and head; that he only has power to decree articles of faith and the authority thereof, and that he alone has a right to ordain rites and ceremonies, and to fix the terms of communion and of church membership; and consequently that no ecclesiastics or earthly princes have power to make laws in his kingdom which shall bind the consciences of his subjects, *Matt.* xx. 25—27. chap. xxiii. 8, 9. chap. xxviii. 18—20, 1st *Cor.* viii. 6. *Eph.* i. 22. *Jas.* iv. 12. According to Christ's system of laws, and the principles of his kingdom, the members of that kingdom may differ in opinion and in conscience too, in some matters of religion, without disunion, and without forming creeds, and confessions, and sectarian churches, in opposition to each other. It is made even a part of christian duty for members of his church to tolerate a difference of opinion and

sentiment, not in respect to human creeds, for their very existence is an abomination: they produce divisions, and are to be opposed every where.

Read the fourteenth chapter of Paul's Epistle to the Romans. The principles contained in that chapter should be regarded as the great charter of christian liberty. They are the strongest barriers against all usurpations on the rights of conscience, whether by ecclesiastical or civil powers. The kingdom of God is in righteousness, and peace, and joy in the Holy Ghost: we are therefore commanded to follow after the things which make for peace, and things wherewith one may edify another.

Do, Mr. Editor, print for us in the Christian Baptist the substance of Macknight's "view and illustration of the matter contained in the 14th chapter of the Epistle to the Romans." And do you, reader, read that chapter in connexion with 1st Cor. viii. chapter, with care. The principles of moral conduct for christians towards each other united in Christ, in these chapters are less understood, seldomer thought of, and less practised than many of us are aware of.

With respect to the christian religion, nothing appears to me to be more absurd and contradictory than for men to talk or think of speaking divine or supernatural things in human language. This is very common, however, in theological schools, and in lectures on divinity: this is according to the Calvinistic vocabulary, with which Thomas Paine and all the Deists agree. Then in comes the mystic agencies, by which human and natural language is made to produce divine or supernatural effects!!

Human language, that is words and sentences invented by men, cannot rise higher than the objects of human thought, and the ideas of nature; nor can it exist antecedent to them. The ideas of supernatural or divine things are obtained by or through supernatural or divine language; that is, by language which originated with God. But according to the system of natural religion, the mind possesses these ideas naturally, or obtains them by reasoning, and invents the language which communicates them without revelation. If we would ourselves speak divine truths, or teach others, we must use the terms in which it was revealed. It is one thing to speak of divine things, and another to speak divine things. We may use our own language, the language arising from sensation, and reflection in speaking of or concerning them, after the divine objects are known: the knowledge, however, and belief of them must be first obtained by the scriptural terms and statements in which they were revealed; and if we would retain them, and communicate them to others, they must be retained and communicated, in the terms and statements in which we learnt them.

There is a state of mind, of feelings, of affection or emotion arising from the operation of the Divine Spirit, through, or with, or by, his gospel truth upon the human heart, which is termed an experience of grace, or religious experience, which accords with the word of God. In detailing of this experience the language used derives its qualifications from the states of feelings and sensation which it describes. No person who has not experienced these states can speak of them from the heart. To obtain this we must use gospel truth as the Spirit operates by and through it.

It is thought by some that the opposition to human creeds and confessions may be applied with equal force against the public preaching and teaching of religion. I think not. Public addresses are made on the subject of religion to bring to people's minds scriptural views of divine things which have been learnt by the speaker, and to assist the hearers by a language addressed to their understandings and feelings, and which associates their best interests and chief happiness with the objects of faith as revealed in the gospel, to understand the scriptures and to believe them; but these addresses are never designed to be creeds and confessions for the hearers. Nothing that teachers say in their public discourses is intended to be paramount to the word of God; in many cases creeds are, insomuch, that men are liable to be treated as heathen men and publicans under their operations, who in all respects, according to the gospel, are entitled to the rights and privileges of Christ's church. Yes, they may be accepted by God, and yet refused admittance into this sectarian kingdom; or if already members of a church constituted upon a human creed, are liable to be cast out by the operation of that creed, in the name of the Father, Son, and Holy Ghost, and given to the Devil, and for no other reason than an uncompromitting adherence to the word of God, and authority of Christ according to the gospel, in preference to the authority of the Westminster assembly, or of John Wesley and his hierarchy, or of the Philadelphia association, or the authority of Henry VIII. and his bishops and successors in the Episcopalian church! This is no extraordinary operation of creeds and confessions, for it arises necessarily from sectarian constitutions, and every christian who is faithful to the Lord Jesus Christ, and is determined to "stand fast in the liberty wherewith he has made him free," ought to be turned out, must and will be turned out, of the churches built upon human creeds, if they exercise consistent discipline! Paul himself would be! Reader, weigh this well and you must see and feel the contrariety of opposition which exists between sectarian churches and the church of Christ. This is the reason why Christianity, as it is improperly called by the different sects, produces so little good in the world.

The christian religion was designed by its Divine Author to remedy all the evils which are incident to man's state of sin and misery in the world, and to make men happy and united in peace and love. This design has not been, and is not accomplished but in a very partial and imperfect degree, among even the professors of religion. And why is this the case? I answer, That by reason of Christ having been divided, christianity has been converted into a system of war, of persecution, and oppression, not against the common enemy, the destroyer of men's souls and of their happiness, so much as against each sect, and by each to the destruction of the spirit, and character and felicities of that religion as revealed in the gospel.

Who has not seen and felt the operation of sectarian indignation in our country, in arraying citizens, relations, and friends, against each other, who were at peace before they assumed the sectarian badge? Yes reader, you have seen the peace and happiness of families wounded and destroyed by this fiend-like influence; and have you not felt some of it too? Can that system of things which produces these effects be the religion of Jesus Christ as it appears in the gospel, the religion of him who is the Prince of Peace, and the author of good will, and kindness, and love among men? Oh no! an enemy has done this; it was done by "false Apostles, deceitful workers, transforming themselves into the Apostles of Christ; and no wonder, for Satan himself transforms himself into an angel of light." 2d Cor. xi. 13, 14

This old enemy has imposed upon the people of God, as he did upon Eve and Adam in Paradise, by adding a new chapter to the Bible under the alluring and apparently innocent title of "Non-Essentials," with a view of dividing Christ, and of securing his influence, and retaining human creeds, and sects, and authority, in religion.

Is it a non-essential that the new name, the name of Christ, and of Christian be made to give place to the name of Presbyterian, or of Baptist, or of Methodist, or of Episcopalian? Is it a non-essential that men should believe in, and serve the Lord Jesus, by the lessons, and instructions, and authority, of human wisdom, taught in creeds, confessions, books of discipline, and liturgies, rather than through the word of the Apostles and the authority of Christ? Is it a non-essential that christians be divided by reason of this into different factions, and be involved in conduct towards each other which occasions the christian religion often to be derided by the world as a curse to the peace of society, and the name of Jesus Christ to be blasphemed among the Gentiles? Is it a non-essential that the world of mankind should remain in unbelief and be damned? Reader, answer these questions in reference to the part you have acted, and are now acting in this sectarian business, with the awful truth impressed upon your mind, that "we shall all stand before Christ's judgment seat, and every one of us shall give an account of himself to God." Hear the Saviour's prayer for unity through the word of the Apostles, amongst his disciples, and in his church, that the world might believe on him. This prayer he put up before he entered upon his sufferings; and to accomplish the objects of which he endured the agonies in the garden and on the cross, descended into the tomb, rose from the dead, and now fills his Father's throne with all power in heaven and in earth. "Neither pray I for these (the Apostles) alone, but for them also which shall believe on me through their word, that they may be one; as you, Father, are in me and I in you, that they also may be one in us, that the world may believe that you have sent me." *John* xvii. 20, 21.

This is God's plan for union and for the conversion of the world, Satan's chapter of Non-Essentials notwithstanding. We are constantly praying and laboring for the conversion of sinners among us, and for the conversion of the heathen; but as long as we retain our sectarian divisions, God is bound to his Son, as far as these divisions are concerned, not to hear our prayers nor bless our exertions. The prayer and intercession of Jesus Christ are, that all christians may be one through the word of the apostles, that the world may believe in him: his honor, and glory, and faithfulness are bound up in this order. Should our prayers and exertions be heard, and blessed, in the present state of division and disunion, as far as they are concerned, the Lord Jesus Christ would be dishonored, his truth would fail, and the covenant of the Father to the Son, that he will give the Jews and the Heathen to him for his inheritance, according to the principles of the new covenant in the gospel, would be broken. None are converted to Christ on sectarian principles. Then why retain them? The different sects have not sufficiently realized that God in the conversion of sinners does nothing more than to make them christians, and place them immediately in the love, and under the direction, instruction and government of Jesus Christ. The inquiry of the new convert is, "Lord what will you have me to do?" The Lord directs him to search the scriptures, and in them he gives precisely the same directions to all, and which,

3

when humbly received and practiced, produces the unity and happiness of the saints, and the employment of the means for the conversion of the world. Sectarianism, with the chapter of non-essentials in its hand, and with the pestilential breath that blasted men's happiness in Eden, interposes, and as far as possible, robs the saint of the name of his Saviour; and of his authority too, by giving him the name of a sect and its book of laws: by its subtilty it kidnaps him, and takes from him his christian liberty, and makes a galley slave of him to tug the balance of his days at a sectarian oar; or plundered of his divine inheritance as far as the universal love and fellowship of the saints, and the sweet smiles of the Saviour are concerned; and as far as active usefulness in promoting the common salvation, and human happiness, from parts of it in the present life, he appears an exile from his father's home in a far country, engaged in feeding swine and in eating husks. The language of the Saviour to such is, " return you backsliding children, and I will heal your backsliding; wherefore do you spend money for that which is not bread, and your labor for that which satisfies not?" The answer of every christian ought to be, " behold we come quickly to you, for you are the Lord our God."

I know it is said that all these things will be brought right when the millennium shall come. I reply that it will be by the correction of these errors that the millennial day will be ushered in. It is moreover alledged that the different sects of christians must be greatly changed from what they are at present in their religion, before they will agree to unite upon the gospel and throw away their creeds. I think otherwise. Every real christian will obey God, rather than men. " My sheep" said the Saviour, " hear my voice and they follow me—a stranger they will not follow." All that is needed for the restoration of the church to the apostolic order, is, that christians be christians, and act as the disciples of Jesus Christ. Let them throw aside their sectarian distinctions, and the commandments of men, and take the name of their Lord, and the word of God, and cultivate mutual forbearance towards each other, and tenderness for each other's conscientious differences in opinions, according to *Romans* xiv. and they will quickly feel the truth and meaning of what the Saviour said, " If any man will do his will, he shall know of the doctrine whether it be of God." And again, " If you continue in my word, then are you my disciples indeed: and you shall know the truth, and the truth shall make you free." And " If the Son shall make you free you shall be free indeed:"—free from error, and ignorance, and sectarian bigotry, and free to love Christ and his people and cause universally, and free to be engaged in all christian duties for promoting the conversion of the world, and for making mankind happy and glorious.

But I am asked whether I design to drop the ordinance of baptism by throwing away the name of Baptist? Without saying a word about sprinkling, pouring, washing, or dipping of adults or infants, I answer that my design is that every doctrine and ordinance be preserved in their proper place according to gospel order, and that every thing be called by its proper name, in the fixed style of the Holy Ghost. The Baptist said, (we have no account in scripture of but one Baptist,) " Christ must increase, but I must decrease." It is high time that this be the case. Paul was greater than John the Baptist, (*Matt.* xi. 11.) yet he would not permit any of Christ's

disciples to call themselves by his name, or by the name of Apollos, or of Peter. All sects may have something good among them; but that good is common property, and ought not to be limited by sectarian barriers or conditions. God makes it the duty of every christian to oppose every sectarian name and creed, and they have a divine right to do so; but none have a right to oppose the name of Christ or his oracles. He makes it the duty of all who are built upon the Lord Jesus Christ by faith in him, for his name's sake to exercise tenderness and forbearance towards each other in points of conscientious differences, but never to divide or form new sects or creeds. I shall say something about the origin, and growth, and effects of creeds hereafter, in promoting orthodoxy, &c., beginning with what has been falsely called " the Apostles' Creed." I will then address the clergy particularly on their duty in these United States.

                    CHRISTIAN UNION.

A Restoration of the Ancient Order of Things.
No. VI.

On the Breaking of Bread.—No. I.

IN our last number we demonstrated from rational principles, that there necessarily must be, and most certainly is, a divinely instituted worship for christian assemblies; and that this worship is uniformly the same in all meetings of the disciples on the first day of the week. That the breaking of bread in commemoration of the sacrifice of Christ, is a part, or an act of christian worship, is generally admitted by professors of christianity. Romanists and Protestants of almost every name agree in this. The society of Friends form the chief, if not the only exception in christendom, to this general acknowledgment. Their religion is all *spiritual*, and may be suitable to beings of some higher order than the natural descendants of Adam and Eve; but it is too contemplative, too metaphysical, too sublime, for flesh and blood. We have tongues and lips wherewith men have been impiously cursed, but with which God should be blessed. We have bodies too which have become the instruments of unrighteousness, but which should be employed as instruments of righteousness. And so long as the five senses are the five avenues to the human understanding, and the medium of all divine communication to the spirit of man, so long will it be necessary to use them in the cultivation and exhibition of piety and humanity. But we have a few words for them in due time, for we esteem them highly on many accounts. But in the mean time, we speak to those who acknowledge the breaking of bread to be a divine institution, and a part of christian worship in christian assemblies, to be continued not only till the Lord came and destroyed Jerusalem and the temple, but to be continued until he shall come to judge the world.

That the primitive disciples did, in all their meetings on the first day of the week, attend on the breaking of bread as an essential part of the worship due their Lord, we are fully persuaded, and hope to make satisfactorily evident to every candid christian. Indeed this is already proved from what has been said in the fifth number under this head. For, if there be a divinely instituted worship for christians in their meetings on the first day of the week, as has been proved; if this order, or these acts of worship are uniformly the same, as has been shown; and if the breaking of bread be an act of christian worship, as is admitted by those we address—then it is

                                                    4

fairly manifest that the disciples are to break bread in all their meetings for worship. This we submit as the first, but not the strongest argument in support of our position. We confess, however, that we cannot see any way of eluding its logical and legitimate force, though we are aware it is not so well adapted to every understanding as those which are to follow. Our second argument will be drawn from the nature, import and design of the breaking of bread. This we shall first illustrate a little.

While Romanists, Episcopalians, Presbyterians of every grade, Independents, Methodists, Baptists &c., acknowledge the breaking of bread to be a divine institution, an act of religious worship in christian assemblies, they all differ in their views of the import of the institution, the manner and times in which it is to be observed, and in the appendages thereto belonging. In one idea they all agree, that it is an *extraordinary* and not an ordinary act of christian worship; and consequently, does not belong to the ordinary worship of the christian church. For this opinion they have custom and tradition to show, but not one argument worthy of a moment's reflection, not even one text to adduce as a confirmation of their practice. Who ever heard a text adduced to prove a monthly, a quarterly, a semi-annual, or an annual breaking of bread. This course in regard to this institution, I conjecture, drove the founders of the Quaker system into the practice of *never* breaking bread—just as the views of the clergy make and confirm Deists.

Much darkness and superstition are found in the minds and exhibited in the practice of the devout annual, semi-annual and quarterly observers of the breaking of bread. They generally make a Jewish passover of it. Some of them indeed, make a Mount Sinai convocation of it. With all the bitterness of sorrow, and gloominess of superstition, they convert it into a religious penance, accompanied with a morose piety and an awful affliction of soul and body, expressed in fastings, long prayers, and sad countenances on sundry days of humiliation, fasting and preparation. And the only joy exhibited on the occasion, is, that all is over; for which some of them appoint a day of thanksgiving. They rejoice that they have approached the very base of Mount Sinai unhurt by stone or dart. In the opposite degrees of their ascent to, and descent from this preternatural solemnity, their piety is equal. In other words, they are as pious one week or ten weeks after, as they were one week or ten weeks before. If there be any thing fitly called superstition in this day and country, this pre-eminently deserves the name. A volume would be by far too small to exhibit all the abuses of this sacred institution in the present age.

The intelligent christian views it quite in another light. It is to him as sacred and solemn as prayer to God, and as joyful as the hope of immortality and eternal life. His hope before God, springing from the death of his Son, is gratefully exhibited and expressed by him in the observance of this institution. While he participates of the symbolic loaf, he shews his faith in, and his life upon, the Bread of life. While he tastes the emblematic cup, he remembers the new covenant confirmed by the blood of the Lord. With sacred joy and blissful hope he hears the Saviour say, "This is my body broken—this my blood shed for you." When he reaches forth those lively emblems of his Saviour's love to his christian brethren, the philanthropy of God fills his heart, and excites correspondent feelings to those sharing with him the salvation of the Lord. Here he

knows no man after the flesh. Ties that spring from eternal love, revealed in blood and addressed to his senses in symbols adapted to the whole man, draw forth all that is within him of complacent affection and feeling to those joint heirs with him of the grace of eternal life. While it represents to him all the salvation of the Lord, it is the strength of his faith, the joy of his hope, and the life of his love. It cherishes the peace of God, and inscribes the image of God upon his heart, and leaves not out of view the revival of his body from the dust of death, and its glorious transformation to the likeness of the Son of God.

It is an institution full of wisdom and goodness, every way adapted to the christian mind. As bread and wine to the body, so it strengthens his faith and cheers his heart with the love of God. It is a religious feast; a feast of joy and gladness; the happiest occasion, and the sweetest antepast on earth of the society and entertainment of heaven, that mortals meet with on their way to the true Canaan. If such be its nature and import, and such its design, say, ye saints, whether this act of christian worship would be a privilege, or a pain, in all your meetings for edification and worship. If it be any proof of the kindness of the Saviour to institute it at all, would it not be a greater proof to allow the saints in all their meetings to have this token of his love set before them, and they called to partake? If it were goodness and grace on his part to allow you twice a-year in your meetings the privilege, would it not be inexpressibly greater goodness and grace to allow you the feast in all your meetings. But reverse the case, and convert it into an awful and grievous penance, and then grace is exhibited in not enforcing it but seldom. On this view of it, if it be an act of favor to command it only twice a-year, it would be a greater good to command it but twice or once during life. Just, then, as we understand its nature and design, will its frequency appear a favor or a frown.

It is acknowledged to be a blissful privilege, and this acknowledgment, whether sincere or feigned, accords with fact. It was the design of the Saviour that his disciples should not be deprived of this joyful festival when they meet in one place to worship God. It will appear (if it does not already) to the candid reader of these numbers, that the New Testament teaches that every time they met in honor of the resurrection of the Prince of Life, or, when they assembled in one place, it was a principal part of their entertainment, in his liberal house, to eat and drink with him. He keeps no dry lodgings for the saints—no empty house for his friends. He never bade his house assemble but to eat and drink with him. His generous and philanthropic heart never sent his disciples hungry away. He did not assemble them to weep, and wail, and starve with him. No, he commands them to rejoice always, and bids them eat and drink abundantly.

Man is a social animal. As the thirsty hind pants for the brooks of water, so man pants for society congenial to his mind. He feels a relish for the social hearth and the social table; because the feast of sentimental and congenial minds is the feast of reason. Man, alone and solitary, is but half blessed in any circumstances. Alone and solitary, he is like the owl in the desert, and pelican in the wilderness. The social feast is the native offspring of social minds. Savage or civilized, man has his social fire, and his social board. And shall the christian house and family be always the poorest and the emptiest under heaven? Is the Lord of christians a churl? Is he sordidly selfish? Is he parsimoniously poor and niggardly?

5

Tell it not amongst the admirers of anniversaries! publish it not amongst the frequenters of any human association! lest the votaries of Ceres rejoice! lest the sons of Bacchus triumph!

The christian is a *man*. He has the feelings of a man. He has a taste for society; but it is the society of kindred minds. The religion of Jesus Christ is a religion for *men*; for rational, for social, for grateful beings. It has its feasts, and its joys, and its extacies too. The Lord's house is his banqueting place, and the Lord's day is his weekly festival.

But a sacrament, an annual sacrament, or a quarterly sacrament, is like the oath of a Roman soldier, from which it derives its name, often taken with reluctance, and kept with bad faith. It is as sad as a funeral parade. The knell of the parish bell that summonses the mourners to the house of sorrow, and the tocsin that awakes the recollection of a sacramental morn, are heard with equal dismay and aversion. The seldomer they occur, the better. We speak of them as they appear to be; and if they are not what they appear to be, they are mere exhibitions of hypocrisy and deceit, and serve no other purpose than as they create a market for silks and calicoes, and an occasion for the display of beauty and fashion.

Amongst the crowds of the thoughtless and superstitious that frequent them, it is reasonable to expect to find a few sincere and devout; but this will not justify their character, else the worshippers of saints and angels might be excused; for many of the sincere and devout say, Amen!

From the nature and design of the breaking of bread, we would argue its necessity and importance as a part of the entertainment of saints in the social worship of the Lord in their assemblies for his praise and their comfort. We cannot prosecute the subject farther at present. We have been preparing the way for opening the New Testament in our next number, to produce evidence and authority of a higher order. In the mean time, let the christian who apprehends the nature, meaning and design of this institution, say whether it be *probable* that it is, or could be an *extraordinary* observance, and not an ordinary part of christian worship in the meeting of saints.

EDITOR.

Notification.

WHEREAS the Rev. Mr. *Blackburn*, D. D. a Presbyterian of the town of Louisville, Kentucky, has declared that he did, in a sermon pronounced in Frankfort, "sweep from the arena" the sentiments and views expressed by me in an address delivered in the chamber of the Representatives of the state of Kentucky in November last, and that in my presence too; (in this point, however, he is mistaken, as I was in Lexington the time he spoke on that subject,) this is to inform the said Rev. Mr. Blackburn, D. D. that I am prepared to defend, illustrate and establish those sentiments and views before his face, and where he shall have an equal liberty of opposing all he has to say in defence of his views and sentiments, on the same subject. It will be remembered by many present at that time in Frankfort, that the most offensive item in my address and the most obnoxious to the displeasure of the priesthood, was, "that it was no part of the revealed design of the Saviour to employ clergymen, or an order of men resembling the priesthood, in the diffusion, spread, or progress of his religion in the world. In brief, that the whole Paido-Baptist priesthood is an order of men unauthorized by Heaven. They are neither constituted, commissioned, nor authorized by the Head of the Church to officiate in any one of their assumptions."

I would most respectfully inform the Rev. Mr. Blackburn, D. D. that I feel ready, as far as in me is, to contend for the truth of every sentiment advanced on that subject; and am disposed, all things concurring, to meet him any where within one hundred miles of Louisville, in the month of May or June next, for the discussion of that proposition. I engage upon his taking the affirmative, to show that the whole fraternity of Paido-Baptist clergymen, divines, or ministers, is a human institution, neither commanded, appointed, or decreed by God, to officiate in the office which they have assumed; that all their right so to officiate is self-constituted and bestowed; and is supported merely by a laity whose consciences are, in this respect, created and made by those priests that made and created themselves, and who preached the people into a deep sense of the reverence due to them as the Lord's anointed ones.

I would wish to have it distinctly understood that the whole grounds of debate on this subject are expressed in the following proposition, viz.—

That the Presbyterian clergy, or any other fraternity of Paido-Baptist clergy, is an order of men divinely constituted and authorized.

The Doctor and his brethren say that this proposition is *true* as far as respects their denomination. I am constrained to think, and therefore say, that it is *false*.

Now as public discussion, conducted with moderation and good temper, is of all means the best adapted to elicit inquiry and exhibit truth, I am constrained, from a sense of the high importance of this question, to propose (should the Doctor decline) to meet in conference any minister of the synod of Kentucky, on this proposition; and should they all decline calling this matter into question, I will agree, as far as in my power, to meet any minister of learning and good standing, of any denomination, who will agree to support the above proposition or any one equivalent thereto, and endeavor to show that it is as false as the assumptions of the Roman Pontiff.

As the Doctor has boasted that he has already "swept from the arena" my sentiments and views on this subject, it gives a peculiar direction to this invitation to him. My duty requires me to give him a welcome invitation to do it again in my presence, and before all who may please to hear him do it. He shall have every respect due to his standing and reputation; and I hereby pledge myself to submit to any rules of decorum any three respectable citizens shall appoint, one of them being chosen by him, another by me, and a third by these two.

I do not suppose that any intelligent man, or any friend to free inquiry, will snarl at this proposal. If it be lawful to advance a proposition, it is lawful to defend it; and if it be lawful to defend, it is lawful to defend it in the presence of them who say they can assail it. And if it be lawful, generous and christian-like, to attack the sentiments of those whose views differ from our own, in their absence, it is surely as christian-like, as generous and as lawful, to do so in their presence. And if the Doctor has done all he says he has done once, he can more easily do it a second time—and to much greater advantage. Few comparatively had the benefit of his address on that occasion: many would have the benefit of his views in such a full discussion. Public feeling, the circumstances of the times, zeal for truth, and a respect to all that is manly, good and fair, render this call upon this Divine truly imperative.

July 16, 1825.   A. Campbell.

To the Editor of the Christian Baptist.

Dear Sir—I have read a series of numbers of the "*Christian Baptist*" with interest, and am much pleased with your professing to discard from your creed every thing that has not the express sanction of the Holy Scriptures. These, if I rightly understand you, you consider the christian's *only rule* of faith and practice. Thus far I cordially agree with you. I am likewise much pleased with your generous offer to publish in the *Christian Baptist* any well written piece in opposition to any sentiment you have therein advanced. From the above I have taken the liberty to present the following queries for your inspection, presuming you will feel no reluctance to give a reason for any thing you believe or practice:—

Where have the scriptures declared that the New Testament is exclusively the christian's guide?

Where do you find authority for calling the first day of the week "Lord's Day?"

Where are you commanded to celebrate the resurrection of Christ every week?

In all my biblical researches I have never been able to find a warrant for either.

That the ceremonial law is abolished, and that the political law of the Jews never was obligatory on any other nation, I cheerfully admit; but that the moral law was confined to the Jews, or that it has ever been abrogated, I have yet to learn. If I do not misapprehend the New Testament writers, they have every where (when speaking of the moral law) spoke of it with respect. "Think not," says the Saviour, "that I am come to destroy the law or the prophets. I am not come to destroy, but to fulfil," &c. *Matt.* v. 17—19. To argue that he came to fulfil, and thereby destroy it, would be directly charging him with self contradiction. If he destroyed by fulfilling it, then he accomplished what he never came to do. Besides, I cannot conceive how a man could justly be censured for breaking one of these commandments, or for teaching others so to do, if Christ had destroyed the whole. Many other places might be quoted where the New Testament writers "establish the law."

If the Scriptures do not call the first day Lord's Day, and we take the liberty to apply that title to it; or if God has not commanded us to celebrate the resurrection of Christ weekly, and yet we attend to it—in either case we are found on Paido-Baptist ground; and if we can walk with them thus far without an express warrant, I conceive we cannot censure them for sprinkling infants, without manifesting the most glaring inconsistency.

As in the second volume of the Christian Baptist you refer to the first, I have taken the liberty to send you the numbers of our Magazine complete, and request you in turn to send us the first volume of the Christian Baptist. We have suspended the publication of our magazine for a short period, but expect to resume it soon. We invite you to a cordial perusal of its contents, in which you will find several typographical errors, especially in the Greek, which you will have the goodness to correct in reading.

We cheerfully reciprocate your offer to publish in our future numbers any friendly remarks in opposition to any thing published in our magazine. We conceive that free inquiry is the open road to truth; and if we are wrong, we will thank our friends to set us right. I flatter myself that you will give an answer to my queries, either in the Christian Baptist or by letter.

Yours respectfully,   Eli S. Bailey.

To Mr. Eli S. Bailey.
One of the Editors of the Seventh Day Baptist Magazine.

Dear Sir—I am ready to give you a reason for my belief and practice touching those things whereof you inquire of me. In relation to your first query, I have to object to the terms in which it is proposed. The example of Abraham and of the Jewish worthies, together with many of the admonitions and precepts found in the Jewish Scriptures, may be, and doubtless are, of importance to guide and encourage christians in the right way. The things, too, that happened to the Jews, happened to them for ensamples, and they are written for our admonition upon whom the ends of the world are come; consequently, of use to guide us. But if you ask, Where do the Scriptures of the prophets or apostles declare that the apostolic writings are to be our exclusive guide in the christian religion, I am prepared to say that we are expressly and repeatedly taught, in all matters of religious observance or of christian obedience, to be guided by Jesus the Messiah, and not by Moses—by the apostles, and not by the Jewish prophets. "The law was given by Moses, but grace and truth came by Jesus Christ." Now Moses commanded the people to obey that prophet whom the Lord should raise up to them like to him. Moses and Elias, when they descended from heaven and laid their commission at his feet, recognized his character as the one, or only Christian Lawgiver; and a voice from the excellent glory commanded the disciples to hear the beloved Son when Moses and Elias were taken to heaven. The law and the prophets also were to continue only until the seed came; for the law and the prophets were until John, but since that time a new religion and a new kingdom were set up. Christians are declared not to be under the law, but under the gospel, or the grace. Even the Jews, who believed in Jesus as the prophet and king whom God sent to Israel, were said to be like a woman whose former husband was dead; no longer bound to obey him, but at liberty to be married to, and to become subject to another lord or husband. Indeed a considerable part of the Epistles to the Romans, Galatians, and almost all the Epistle to the Hebrews, are written to prove that believers in Christ are not under Moses as a guide in the christian religion, but under Christ, who is a Son over his own house, and not a servant in another's house, like Moses. Moses, as a servant, faithfully delivered laws to the people over whom he reigned; but Jesus Christ, as a Son, gives laws to those over whom he reigns as our prophet and king. For further reasons why we believe that we are now to continue in the apostles' doctrine, and to submit to them exclusively in Christ's house, see Christian Baptist, vol. I. p. 38—40. To this add, that when Jesus promised thrones to the Apostles in his church, he left none for Moses nor Elias—not Moses, but the twelve apostles of the Lamb, were to judge or give statutes to Israel. And when the Great King commissioned them, he commanded them to teach only what he commanded them. "Teach the disciples," said he, "to observe all things whatsoever I have commanded you." The *I* is inclusive of all Christ commanded, and exclusive of every thing else. Hence, so long as we believe the apostles to be faithful men, their example, or the examples of the churches whom they commended, are exactly of the same force as a broad precept. If you had seen the first volume of this work and the address alluded to (a copy of each I have now sent you) I think those questions would have appeared to you unnecessary, at least the first one.

Under the new constitution all disciples live if they knew it; and if you go back to Moses for a Sabbath, you may go back to him for a new moon, a holy day or what you please. And indeed we are, and must be confessed to be, either under the old constitution or the new. We cannot be under both. We cannot live under the English and American constitution at the same time. If I were to go to Moses for a "*Seventh Day Sabbath*," I should not blush to take from him an eighth day circumcision or an annual passover. I have paid a good deal of attention to your Magazine, particularly on this topic of your peculiarity, and must think that you are inconsistent in telling me any thing about Paido-Baptist ground. But I should be glad to see the seventh day kept by those who have a conscience in this matter, as the law requires; and perhaps in keeping it this way, at least *once* in a life-time, they might become enlightened in its meaning. Please see vol. I. p. 43—46.

Your second question I will briefly answer. For the same reason that Paul calls the table on which the emblems of Christ's death are exhibited "the Lord's table," we call the day on which he rose from the dead and brought life and immortality to light, the Lord's day. It is true that every day in the week, as some say, is the Lord's; and so is every table in the world, for "the earth is the Lord's and the fulness thereof;" yet an apostle *once* calls this table the Lord's table. But if this reason will not be satisfactory to all, we have another. We have as much reason to believe that the first day of the week is once called by an apostle *the Lord's day*, as we have to believe that the table alluded to is once called the Lord's—"I was in the Spirit on the Lord's day." Now after hearing all that I could hear, and reading all that I could read, from the Sabbatarians and others, on these words, I must contend that no meaning can be affixed to them, from any thing in the whole record, but that the writer intended the day of the Lord's resurrection. For if he meant the gospel day, as some would have it, then the apostle degrades himself to a puerility, incompatible with his standing as a man—much more as an apostle. For as he intended to acquaint the reader addressed with that day in his exile on which he received the revelation, to have taken a name that was as indefinite as the whole gospel age, or to have taken a name not generally understood at that time as expressive of any particular day, would have been childish in the extreme.

But again, the first day of the week is emphatically the Lord's, for this reason, that on this day he was *begotten*—at least Paul says so. See his application of a part of the second psalm, *Acts* xiii. 34. "This day have I begotten you, my Son." Now these are my reasons (at least a number of them) for sometimes calling this day the Lord's day. I say *sometimes*, for I am not tenacious about its name. If you conscientiously prefer calling it the *first day* of the week, and regard it to the Lord as the first christians did, I am not conscientiously weak about the name, and should never force what may be a conclusion of my mind upon the religious practice of others. For I will admit that these reasons may not carry the same weight to every mind. But as you demanded my reasons for so denominating it in this way, (which is far from being a general practice)

I have given you them freely. They are at your service.

An answer to your third query you will find in the 6th and 7th numbers on the "*Restoration of the Ancient Order of Things.*" This is of more importance than the *name* we give the day.

I feel gratified with the spirit and temper of your letter, and am only sorry that my limits forbid me giving it a more lengthy notice. The numbers which I have sent you, and which you had not seen before writing your communication of the 30th ultimo, are, I think, a full answer to the subject matter of your queries, and much more minute than I could now find room for. I would request you to examine very closely the two articles referred to in the first volume, and to consider them as an answer to your difficulties upon the Sabbath day of the Jews, and the Lord's day.

The distinctions of moral, political and ceremonial law, which run through your Magazine and letter, are of the same family with infant baptism. Some might make them twin-sisters; but I would rather view them as the elder and younger branches of the same root.

Your quotation of *Matthew* v. 17, is entirely irrelevant, as it equally applies to your ceremonial as to your moral law, and he was as exact in the ritual of Moses as any other minister of the circumcision. It applies to the prophets too, as well as to the law; yet it is said of him that he delivered his brethren the Jews from the law, and that when the object of faith was come, they were no longer under a schoolmaster. In contending for the due observance of the Lord's day we establish the law—as Paul did by faith. But in making Sabbath days for Gentiles in this northern latitude, we put a yoke on the necks of the disciples, which makes Christ of as little effect to them as he was to those who circumcised in order to be saved.

Yours respectfully,   A. Campbell.

An Epitaph.

Bold infidelity, turn pale!
Beneath this stone four infants' ashes lie:
   Say, are they lost or sav'd?
If death's by sin, they sinn'd, because they're here:
If heaven's by works, in heaven they can't appear.
   Reason, ah! how deprav'd!
Revere the bible's sacred page, the knot's untied:
They died, for Adam sinn'd;—they live, for Jesus died.
          The Witness.

No. 2.]   September 5, 1825.
A Narrative of the Origin and Formation of the Westminster or Presbyterian Confession of Faith.—No. IV.

The parliament ordained, April 26, 1615, that "no person shall be permitted to preach who is not ordained a minister in this or some other reformed church, except such as intend the ministry, who shall be allowed for the trial of their gifts, by those that shall be appointed thereto by both houses of parliament; and it is earnestly desired that Sir *Thomas Fairfax* (a military chieftain) take care that this ordinance be put into execution in the army. It is further ordered to be sent to the lord mayor and committee of the militia in London, to the governors and commanders of all forts, garrisons, forces, cities and towns, with the like injunctions; and the mayor, sheriffs and justices of the peace, are to commit all offenders to safe custody, and give notice to the parliament, who will take a speedy course for their punishment."* This is the way to make

* Neal's History, vol. 3, p. 281.

and establish orthodoxy, and to show the divine institution of the clergy and presbytery, without the trouble of interrogating the twelve apostles. Thus the clergy had their lips opened, and the laity had theirs shut by the laws of the land; and the military and other rulers were to guard the consciences of the people with a drawn sword.

"At the same time the lords sent to the assembly of divines to prepare a new directory for the ordination of ministers of the church in England, without the presence of a diocesan bishop. This took up a great deal of time by reason of the opposition it met with from the Erastians and Independents; but was at last accomplished, and passed into an ordinance November 8, 1645, and was to continue in force by way of trial for twelve months. On the 28th of August following it was prolonged for three years, at the expiration of which time it was made perpetual."*

The two fundamental rules of this *new* directory, which is now thought by many to be as *old* as Paul's time, ran thus:—*First*. "The person to be ordained must apply to the presbytery, with a testimonial of his taking the covenant, of his proficiency in his studies," &c., whether he can conjugate *tupto*, and decline *hic, hæc, hoc*, &c. &c. *Second*. "He is then to pass under an examination as to his religion and learning and call to the ministry." If he be called by God as Aaron was, to be a high priest, and can tell how religious he is, he is then to be anointed by the presbytery; if not he must return to the plough or loom, and forever after hold his peace. *Lastly*. "It is resolved, That all persons ordained according to this directory, shall be *forever* reputed and taken, to all intents and purposes, for lawfully and sufficiently authorized ministers of the church of England, and as capable of any ministerial employment in the church, as any other presbyter already ordained or hereafter to be ordained." So this point is made orthodox and of divine authority.

The Independents maintained the right of every particular congregation to ordain its own officers. This was debated ten days. The arguments on both sides were afterwards published in a book titled "*The Grand Debate between Presbytery and Independency*." At length the question was put, "that it is requisite no single congregation that can conveniently associate with others, should assume to itself the sole right of ordination." It was voted in the affirmative. The following distinguished ministers entered their dissent:—Thomas Goodwine, Philip Nye, Jeremiah Burrows, S. Simpson, W. Bridge, W. Greenhill and W. Carter. The majority, however, ruled, and in such cases always regulates the conscience and decides what is divine. For the voice of the majority is the voice of God.

"It was next debated whether ordination might precede election to a particular cure or charge." That is, whether a man might be married without a wife, and afterwards take whom he could get by virtue of his marriage, or whether a man might be appointed to a charge without having any. This could not be fairly carried, and was compromised with the Independents, who agreed to the imposition of hands in the ceremony of ordination, "provided that it was attended with an open declaration that it was not intended as a conveyance of office power."

A debate of thirty days was held in the assembly on this proposition, "that the scripture holds forth that many particular congregations may, and BY DIVINE AUTHORITY OUGHT to be under one pres-

* Neal's History vol. 3, p. 181.

byterial government." The Erastians would not except against the presbyterial government as a political institution, but opposed the claim of divine right. But the Independents opposed the whole proposition and advanced a counter divine right of independency. Fifteen days they took the part of opponents, and fifteen days they were upon the defensive.

The chief inquiries were concerning the constitution and form of the first church of Jerusalem, the subordination of synods and of lay elders. The Independents maintained that the church of Jerusalem was *one* congregation; the Presbyterians affirmed that there were many congregations in this city under one presbytery. The ablest critics in the assembly, such as Dr. Temple, Selden, Lightfoot, Coleman, Vines, &c., were divided upon this head, but it was carried for the Presbyterians. The Jewish Sanhedrim was proposed in the assembly as a model for their Christian presbytery, and great skill in the Jewish antiquities was exhibited in this part of the debate in settling what were the respective powers of the ecclesiastical and civil courts under the law.

As the reader, not acquainted with the origin of the present religious institutions, will be curious to know how the lay elders or ruling elders, got into existence, we shall, while noticing these proceedings of the assembly, just remark, that while they were inquiring into the constitution of the Jewish Sanhedrim and defining its ecclesiastical and civil powers, it was remarked that "Moses appointed that he that should not hearken to the priest or the judge should die." Deut. xvii. 12. It was inferred in favor of church power that the priest held one court and the civil magistrate another. But Mr. Selden observed that the Vulgate Latin, until within these 40 years, read thus, *Qui non obediverit sacerdoti ex decreto judicis morietur*. "He that will not obey the priest shall die by the sentence of the judge." Mr. Lightfoot added, that when the judges of inferior courts went up to Jerusalem by way of appeal, it was only for advice and consultation. But when the question was put for a subordination of synods and lay elders, as so many courts of judicature, with power to dispense church censures, it was carried in the affirmative, and asserted in their humble advice to parliament, with this addition, "So Christ has furnished some in his churches besides ministers of the word, with gifts for government, and with commission to execute the same when called thereto, who are to join with the minister in the government of the church, which officers the reformed churches generally call elders." Hence their name, authority, and office.

When this point was carried by a large majority, the Independents entered their dissent in writing, and complained to the world of "the unkind usage they met with in the assembly; that the papers they offered were not read, and that they were not allowed to state their own questions, being told they set themselves industriously to puzzle the cause and render the clearest propositions obscure, rather than argue the truth or falseness of them; that it was not worth the assembly's while to spend so much time in debating with so inconsiderable a number of men." They also declared that "the assembly refused to debate their main proposition, viz. Whether a divine right of church government did not remain with every particular congregation." To all which, says Mr. Neal, it was replied that the assembly were not conscious they had done them any injustice; and as for the rest, they were the proper judges of their own methods of proceeding. So these matters were carried in the Westminster Assembly. But the Erastians reserved themselves for the House of Commons, where they were sure to be joined in opposing these decisions of the assembly by all the patrons of the Independents. For it mattered not what was decided by the assembly—it was neither divine nor orthodox untill sanctioned by the parliament. The English and Scots commissioners were very solicitous about the fate of this dogma of the divines in the House of Commons, and were determined to carry the point by stratagem. The scheme was, to carry the question before the house should be full. "They gave their friends notice to be early in their places; but Mr. Glyn, perceiving their intentions, spoke an hour to the point of *jus divinum*; and after him Mr. Whitelocke stood up and enlarged upon the same argument till the house was full; when the question being put, it was carried in the negative, and that the proposition of the assembly should stand thus, *that it is lawful and agreeable to the word of God*, that the church be governed by congregational, classical, and synodical assemblies."*

Because the House of Commons would not go the whole length with the Assembly in establishing the *jus divinum* of presbytery, the Scots commissioners and the high Presbyterians in England alarmed the citizens with the danger of the church, and prevailed with the common council to petition the parliament (November 15) "that the Presbyterian discipline shall be established as the discipline of Jesus Christ." But the commons answered with a frown. Not yet discouraged, they prevailed with the city ministers to petition, who, when they came to the house, were told by the Speaker they "need not wait for an answer, but go home and look to the charge of their congregation."

"The Presbyterian ministers, despairing of success with the Commons, instead of yielding to the times, resolved to apply to the House of Lords, who received them civilly and promised to take their request into consideration; but no advances were made for two months, and they became impatient, and determined to renew their application; and to give it the greater weight prevailed with the lord mayor and court of aldermen to join them in presenting an address, which they did June 16—"for a speedy settlement of church government according to the covenant, and that no toleration might be given to popery, prelacy, superstition, heresy, profaneness, or any thing contrary to sound doctrine, and that all private assembles might be restrained." But it was all in vain. The House of Lords and the House of Commons would not be moved by their disagreeable importunity. "However, adds Mr. Neal, this laid the foundation of those jealousies and misunderstandings between the city and parliament, which in the end proved the ruin of the Presbyterian cause."

The next and fiercest controversy between the parliament and the assembly was upon the power of the keys. But upon this we cannot now speak particularly.

From the preceding details of facts we may easily discover the spirit of the founders of Presbyterianism, and what sort of times we would have had could they have obtained their wishes. But there was more moderation and benevolence in the army and the parliament than in all the high-toned clergy of that day. And yet the parliament was priest-ridden down to no ordinary degree of servility to the superstition of those times. EDITOR.

* Neal's History, vol. 3, p. 290.

A Restoration of the Ancient order of Things.
No. VII.
On the Breaking of Bread—No. II.

THE apostles were commissioned by the Lord to teach the disciples to observe all things he had commanded them. Now we believe them to have been faithful to their master, and consequently he gave them to know his will. Whatever the disciples practised in their meetings with the approbation of the apostles, is equivalent to an apostolic command to us to do the same. To suppose the contrary, is to make the half of the New Testament of non-effect. For it does not altogether consist of commands, but of approved precedents. Apostolic example is justly esteemed of equal authority with an apostolic precept. Hence, say the Baptists, shew us where Paul or any apostle sprinkled an infant, and we will not ask you for a command to go and do likewise. It is no derogation from the authority for observing the first day of the week, to admit that christians are no where in this volume commanded to observe it. We are told that the disciples, with the countenance and presence of the apostles, met for worship on this day. And so long as we believe they were honest men, and taught all that was commanded them, so long we must admit that the Lord commanded it to be so done. For if they allowed, and by their presence authorized, the disciples to meet religiously on the first day, without any authority from their King, there is no confidence to be placed in them in other matters. Then it follows that they instituted a system of will-worship, and made themselves lords instead of servants. But the thought is inadmissible, consequently the order of worship they gave the churches was given them by their Lord, and their example is of the same force with a broad precept.

But we come directly to the ordinance of breaking bread, and to open the New Testament on this subject, we see (Matt. xxvi. 26.) that the Lord instituted bread and wine on a certain occasion, as emblematic of his body and of his blood, and as such, commanded his disciples to eat and drink them. This was done without any injunction as to the time when, or the place where, this was to be afterwards observed. Thus the four gospels, or the writings of Matthew, Mark, and John leave it. At this time the apostles were not fully instructed in the laws of his kingdom; and so they continued till he ascended up to his Father and sent them the Holy Spirit. After Pentecost, and the accession gained that day, the apostles proceeded to organize a congregation of disciples, and to set them in the order which the Lord had commanded and taught them by his Spirit. The historian tells us minutely that after they had baptized and received into their society three thousand souls, they continued steadfastly in a certain order of worship and edification. Now this congregation was intended to be a model, and did actually become such to Judea, Samaria, and to the uttermost parts of the earth. The question then is, What order of worship and of edification did the apostle give to the first congregation they organized? This must be learned from the narrative of the historian who records what they did. We shall now hear his testimony, (Acts ii. 41.) "Then they who had gladly received his word were baptized, and about three thousand were that day added to them : and they continued steadfastly in the apostles' doctrine, and in the fellowship, and in breaking of bread, and in prayers." Other things are recorded of this congregation distinct from those cited, such as their having a community of goods, and for this purpose selling their possessions of houses and lands. But these are as peculiar to them and as distinct from the instituted order of worship, as was the case of Ananias and his wife Sapphira. Their being constantly in the Temple is also added as a peculiarity in their history. But it may be correctly inquired, How are we to distinguish between those things which are as peculiar to them as their vicinity to the Temple, and those things which were common to them with other christian congregations? This must be determined by a comparison of the practice of other congregations as recorded by the same historian, or as found in the letters to the churches written by the apostles. From these we see that no other christian congregation held a community of goods; no other sold their possessions as a necessary part of christian religion; no others met constantly in the Temple. Indeed, Luke, from his manner of relating the order of worship and means of edification practised by this congregation, evidently distinguishes what was essential from what was circumstantial. For after informing us, verses 41 and 42, of the distinct parts or acts of their social worship, he adds in a separate and detached paragraph the history of their peculiarities. "Now," adds he, "all they who believed were together and had all things in common, and they sold their possessions and goods," &c. This, too, is separated from the account of their social acts of worship by a statement of other circumstances, such as the fear that fell upon every soul, and the many wonders and signs which were done by the apostles. From a minute attention to the method of the historian, and from an examination of the historical notices of other congregations, it is easy to distinguish between what was their order of worship and manner of edification from what was circumstantial. And, indeed, their whole example is binding on all christians placed in circumstances similar to those in which they lived at that time. For though the selling of their possessions is mentioned as a part of the benevolent influences of the christian religion clearly understood and cordially embraced, as a voluntary act suggested by the circumstances of the times and of their brethren; yet were a society of christians absolutely so poor that they could live in no other way than by the selling of the possessions of some of the brethren, it would be an indispensable duty to do so, in imitation of him who, though he was rich, made himself poor, that the poor, though his impoverishing himself, might be made rich. But still it must be remarked that even in Jerusalem at this time the selling of houses and lands was a voluntary act of such disciples as were possessors of them, without any command from the apostles to do so. This is most apparent from the speech of Peter addressed to Ananias and his wife; who seem to have been actuated by a false ambition, or love of praise, in pretending to as high an exhibition of self denial and brotherly love as some others. Their sin was not in not selling their property, nor was it in only contributing a part; but it was in lying, and pretending to give the whole, when only a part was communicated. That they were under no obligation from any law or command to sell their property, Peter avows in addressing them, and for the purpose too of inculpating them more and more: "While it remained," says he, "was it not yours? It was still at your own disposal." You might give or withhold without sin. But the lie proved their ruin. Thus it is easy to discover what was essential to their worship and edification from what was circumstantial.

Their being baptized when they gladly received the word, was not a circumstance, neither was their continuing steadfastly in the apostles' doctrine, in fellowship, in breaking of bread, and in prayers. This the order of all the congregations gathered and organized by the apostles, shows. With regard to our present purpose, enough is said on this testimony, when it is distinctly remarked and remembered that the first congregation organized after Pentecost by the apostles, now gifted with the Holy Spirit, CONTINUED AS STEADFASTLY IN BREAKING OF BREAD as in the apostles' doctrine, fellowship, or prayers. This is indisputably plain from the narrative, and it is all we want to adduce from it at present. It is bad logic to draw more from the premises than what is contained in them; and we can most scripturally and logically conclude from these premises, that the congregation of disciples in Jerusalem did as steadfastly, and as uniformly in their meetings, attend on the breaking of bread, as upon any other mean of edification or act of worship. It cannot, however, be shown from this passage how often that was, nor is it necessary for us to do so in this place. We shall find other evidences that will be express to this point. We dismiss this passage in the mean time, by repeating that the first congregation organized by the apostles after the ascension of the King, did as steadfastly attend on the breaking of bread in their religious meetings, as upon any act of worship or means of edification.

We shall again hear Luke narrating the practice of the disciples at Troas, (*Acts* xx. 7.) "And on the first day of the week, when the disciples assembled to break bread, Paul, being about to depart on the morrow, discoursed with them, and lengthened out his discourse till midnight." From the manner in which this meeting of the disciples at Troas is mentioned by the historian, two things are very obvious: 1st. That it was an established custom or rule for the disciples to meet on the first day of the week. 2d. That the primary object of their meeting was to break bread. They who object to breaking bread on *every* first day of the week when the disciples are assembled, usually preface their objections by telling us that Luke does not say they broke bread *every* first day; and yet they contend against the Sabbatarians that they ought to observe *every* first day to the Lord in commemoration of his resurrection. The Sabbatarians raise the same objection to this passage when adduced by all professors of christianity to authorize the weekly observance of the first day. They say that Luke does not tell us that they met for any religious purpose on *every* first day. How inconsistent, then, are they who make this sentence an express precedent for observing *every* first day, when arguing against the Sabbatarians, and then turn round and tell us that it will not prove that they broke bread *every* first day! If it does not prove the one, it is most obvious it will not prove the other; for the weekly observance of this day, as a day of the meeting of the disciples, and the weekly breaking of bread in those meetings, stand or fall together. Hear it again: "And on the first day of the week, when the disciples assembled to break bread." Now all must confess, who regard the meaning of words, that the meeting of the disciples and the breaking of bread, as far as these words are concerned, are expressed in the same terms as respects the frequency. If the one were *fifty-two* times in a year, or only *once*, so was the other. If they met every first day, they brake bread every first day; and if they did not break bread every first day, they did not meet every first

11

day. But we argue from the style of Luke, or from his manner of narrating the fact, that they did both. If he had said that on *a* first day the disciples assembled to break bread, then I would admit that both the Sabbatarians and the semi-annual or septennial communicants might find some way of explaining this evidence away.

The definite article is, in the Greek and in the English tongue, prefixed to stated and fixed times, and its appearance here is not merely definitive of one day, but expressive of a stated or fixed day. This is so in all languages which have a definite article. Let us illustrate this by a very parallel and plain case. Suppose some five hundred or a thousand years hence, the annual observance of the 4th of July should have ceased for several centuries, and that some person or persons devoted to the primitive institutions of this mighty republic, were desirous of seeing every fourth of July observed as did the fathers and founders of the republic, during the hale and undegenerate days of primitive republican simplicity. Suppose that none of the records of the first century of this republic had expressly stated that it was a regular and fixed custom for a certain class of citizens to pay a particular regard to *every* fourth day of July—but that a few incidental expressions in the biography of the leading men in the republic spake of it as Luke has done of the meeting at Troas. How would it be managed? For instance, in the life of John Q. Adams, it is written, A. D. 1823, " And on the fourth day of July, when the republicans at the city of Washington met to dine, John Q. Adams delivered an oration to them." Would not an American a thousand years hence, in circumstances such as have been stated, find in these words *one* evidence that it was an established usage during the first century of this republic to regard the fourth day of July as aforesaid. He would tell his opponents to mark that it was not said that on *a* fourth of July, as if it were a particular occurrence, but it was in the fixed meaning of the English language expressive of a fixed and stated day of peculiar observance. At all events he could not fail in convincing the most stupid that the primary intention of that meeting was *to dine.* Whatever might be the frequency or the intention of that dinner, it must be confessed, from the words above cited, that they *met to dine.*

Another circumstance that must somewhat confound the Sabbatarians and the lawless observers of breaking of bread, may be easily gathered from Luke's narrative. Paul and his company arrived at Troas either on the evening of the first day, or on Monday morning at an early hour; for he departed on Monday morning, as we term it, at an early hour; and we are positively told that he tarried just seven days at Troas. Now had the disciples been Sabbatarians or observed the seventh day as a Sabbath, and broke bread on it as the Sabbatarians do, they would not have deferred their meeting till the first day, and kept Paul and his company waiting, as he was evidently in a great haste at this time. But his tarrying seven days, and his early departure on Monday morning, corroborates the evidence adduced in proof that the first day of the week was the fixed and stated day for the disciples to meet for this purpose.

From the 2d of the Acts, then, we learn that the breaking of bread was a stated part of the worship of the disciples in their meetings; and from the 20th we learn that the first day of the week was the stated time for those meetings; and, above all, we ought to notice that the most prominent object of their meeting was to break bread.

But this, we hope, will be made still more evident in our next.　　Editor.

Public Notice.

I, ezra stiles eli, stated Clerk of the General Assembly of the Presbyterian Church in the United States of America, do hereby certify to all whom it may concern, that said Assembly having resolved to establish a *Western Theological Seminary,* did on the 30th day of may last, appoint

Major Gen. Andrew Jackson, of Tennessee;
Hon. Benjamin Mills, of Paris, Kentucky;
Hon. John Thompson, of Chilicothe, Ohio;
Rev. Obadiah Jennings, of Washington, Pa.
Rev. Andrew Wylie, of Washington College, in Pa.

to be commissioners of the assembly to examine carefully the several sites which may be proposed for the contemplated seminary, as to the healthiness of the place and regions where these sites may be found, as to the amount of pecuniary aid and other property which may be obtained from the inhabitants of these sites and their vicinity severally, in establishing the contemplated seminary, and as to all other circumstances and considerations which ought to have influence in deciding on the location of the seminary. These commissioners are to report to the board of directors of the Western Theological Seminary, the proposals that have been made to them, and their opinion of the whole subject of the seminary, that the said board after considering the report of the commissioners, may recommend to the next general assembly the most suitable place, in their judgment, for the establishment of the Western Theological Seminary.

Of these commissioners Gen. Andrew Jackson is chairman; and they, as well as the directors, are appointed first to meet at Chilicothe, Ohio, on the third Friday of July, at 2 o'clock P. M. and subsequently on their own adjournments.

The agents appointed by the assembly to solicit and receive donations for the Western Theological Seminary, are the Rev. James Hogue, Rev. David Monfort, of Millville, Hamilton county, Ohio; Rev. James Culbertson, Rev. Thomas Barr, of Wooster, Ohio; Rev. William Wylie, Rev. Elisha P. Swift, and Rev. Obadiah Jennings.

This publication is made that due notice of their appointment may reach the commissioners, directors, and agents, even should they fail of receiving the written circular of the subscriber; and that literary corporations and enterprizing individuals in the flourishing western towns, may have an early opportunity of making proposals to some one of the commissioners above named concerning the location of the seminary.

Those printers in the South and West who will give this notice a gratuitous insertion in their papers, will confer a favor on the Presbyterian church.

By order of the General Assembly.

EZRA S. ELI.

When the following Public Notice is read, it will appear that the General Assembly of 1825 yet possesses in an eminent degree the primitive evangelical, and apostolic spirit of the first laborers in planting christianity in the Roman empire. How this precious relique escaped the ravages of Vandalism and the reign of Night, in the ages of undisturbed superstition, is left to the conjectures of the reader.

Public Notice.

I, Simon Peter, an apostle and stated clerk of the General Assembly of the Presbyterian church of the Western Roman Empire, do hereby certify to all whom it may concern, That said assembly having resolved to establish a Western Theological Seminary, did, on the ides of May last, appoint

Major General CLAUDIUS CAESAR, commander in chief of the army of invasion into Britain;

Hon. JULIUS AGRICOLA, of South Britain;

Hon. QUINTUS CURTIUS, of Rome;

Rev. SENECA, of Spain, the true moralist;

Rev. MAECENAS, son of the patron of Horace—to be commissioners of the assembly to examine carefully the several sites which may be proposed for the contemplated seminary, as to the healthiness of those sites, as to the amount of the mammon of unrighteousness and other means which may be obtained from the inhabitants of those sites, in establishing said fountain of grace in their vicinity. These commissioners are to report to the Rev. Matthew Levi, Joannes Markus, Saulus Paulus, D. D. and the other directors of the Western Theological Seminary, the proposals that shall have been made to them, and their opinions on the same.

Of these commissioners, Gen. Claudius Cesar, because he has been a celebrated duellist and warrior, and has no children, is chairman, and particularly qualified to take the command in a cabinet of clergy, as in a council of war; and they, as well as the directors, are to meet at Damascus on the first of the ides of July, at the 8th hour of the day, and subsequently on their own adjournments.

The agents to solicit and receive donations for the Western Roman Theological Gentile Seminary, are, the Rev. Mr. Simon Magus, Rev. Mr. Tertullus, Rev. J. Sergius, Rev. T. Timothy, Rev. T. Titus, Rev. O. Agabus.

It is hoped that the friends of religion in the flourishing towns of the Western Roman Empire will contribute spiritedly on this occasion to a western source of life, as they have done in the neighborhood of Jerusalem, to the Eastern.

Those scribes and heralds in the South and West, who will publish this notice without any mammon in return for it, as we are very scarce of the images of Augustus, will confer a favor on the Presbyterian church, for which its head will reward them in Paradise.

By order of the General Assembly,

SIMON PETER, Stated Clerk.

"The Presbytery of Onondaga.

"DEEPLY affected with the deplorable situation to which the children of the professed people of God have been reduced by a neglect of religious instruction, and the ignorance in which they have been kept of the privileges of their birthright, secured to them by divine constitution—do most earnestly and solemnly recommend to the churches a careful and prayerful observance of the following RULES:—

1. That every professing parent, guardian, or master of a family, observe the duty of instructing his household in the great doctrines of our holy religion, of inculcating on their minds the obligations they are under to God, and the covenant relation they stand in to him: taking for a general text-book of instruction, the Catechism of the Westminster Assembly of Divines.

2. That such parents, guardians, or masters, commit their household to the instructions of the church, and bring them, or cause them to be brought, to such place or places of instruction as the regular authority of the church may from time to time appoint.

3. That each church within the bounds of this presbytery appoint certain judicious and pious male members of the church as catechists, to go from house to house, and confer with professing christians and their households on the importance of instructing children in the principles of religion, and to appoint certain places where the children of a particular neighborhood or section of the congregation, may, at stated times, meet for the purpose of receiving instruction from such Catechists.

4. That the ministers and elders, or other authority of the churches, call a general meeting of all the children of the church, quarter-yearly, for the purpose of furnishing them such religious and moral instruction, as their several circumstances, on an examination of their views and feelings, shall appear to require.

5. That every church hold all the children of the church, under twelve years old, responsible to the church for their future conduct; that the church never afterwards relinquish their inspection and discipline; that such children hereafter stand on the same ground, submit to the same salutary correction for their reformation and repentance, or the same sentence of exclusion to which the other members are subject, and that the names of all such children be added to the catalogue of members now enrolled as constituting the church. It being understood, at the same time, that they shall profess their faith, in order to a participation of the Lord's Supper.

6. That each church collect all other baptized persons, who have hitherto been non-communicants, and who will assemble at the call of the church, and ascertain who among them are now willing to be responsible to the church, to stand in their lot in the kingdom of Christ, and publicly profess their attachment to him and the doctrines contained in the Assembly's catechism; and, in fine, to view themselves, and be treated by the church, as ever afterwards members. And that all such persons be also added to the catalogue of members composing the church.

7. That all minors who shall hereafter be baptized, be immediately enrolled with the church, considered as members, and treated accordingly.

8. That when parents from abroad come and are received into our churches, their children, under twelve years of age, be received and enrolled as members with them.

Done in Presbytery, at Homer, Dec. 31, 1812.

DIRCK C. LANSING, Moderator.

JABEZ CHADWICK,　Clerk."

AN excellent plan, truly, to make and confirm Presbyterians, but not *Christians.* These rules expressly avow principles of these sectaries which but few of their leaders at this time are willing openly and explicitly to declare—such as,

1st. Not the Holy Scriptures, but the Westminster catechism, is the "text-book" for the religious instruction of the offspring and households of Presbyterians. Thus the understanding, and consequently the conscience of those youths are biassed and moulded into the Presbyterian form.

2d. That all the children, under 12 years old, born of the flesh, are to be enrolled as members of the church, and to be held responsible to the church, faith or no faith.

3d. That those children of the flesh are to be accounted as the seed, and to be the subjects of church discipline, of correction and exclusion, as other members; yet precluded from the privileges of the senior members.

4th. But it is avowed that of these under twelve-year-old members, only a part shall be communicants; and the other part, though equally members, are not to be communicants.

5th. That all other baptized persons, whether under or over twelve years old, who are non-communicants, be collected and interrogated whether they will stand in their lot in the kingdom of Christ, avows that those non-communicants have a place or lot in this kingdom, whether christian or infidel. A worldly and carnal kingdom, truly!

6th. That all baptized minors are considered as members, and forthwith to be treated as such.

QUERIES.

1. Why not enrol them as members at the age of ten days or ten years?

2. What course of discipline is to be practised on three-month or on three-year-old members; for these are members under twelve, and to be disciplined by these canons?

3. Whether is it their birth or baptism that makes these babes and minors members of the Presbyterian church?

4. If their birth make them members, why baptize them, seeing members of the church are not to be baptized? Or if baptism make them members, why compare it to circumcision, for circumcision did not make members of Abraham's family?

5. Can one code of laws suit a church of three sorts of members—speechless babes, unregenerated minors, and regenerated adults?

In what a miserable condition is that church which is under such lawgivers as the Onondaga Presbytery!!

6. Who placed them on thrones to give laws to any society calling itself the kingdom of Christ?

7. Does not the passing of such laws declare that the New Testament is silent on such things?

8. Ought they not to read Revelation xxii. 18. and tremble?

ED. C. B.

To the Editor of the Christian Baptist.

DEAR BROTHER,—WHILST your worthy friend and correspondent, "P. H." is puzzling his brain with some of those many difficulties originating in scholastic theology and science, falsely so called; I am equally concerned in trying to ascertain what method to pursue in order to introduce "the ancient order of things" amongst churches called churches of Christ. And as you are undoubtedly an advocate for this reform, and possessing more information than myself, I take the liberty of asking for some instructions. But before I proceed to any specifications, I wish to make known to you that my case is somewhat singular; and, as such, shall give you a short sketch, which, perhaps, may answer some good purpose, especially should this ever meet the public eye.

I have been for a considerable number of years what we call a preacher of the Gospel, and have been solemnly ordained to that office by men of the highest respectability in my order. I have itinerated much through the country, and have honestly endeavored to recommend the religion of Jesus Christ to my ignorant and perishing countrymen, and in doing of which (if I am a proper judge) I have gained considerable applause, and have been looked upon as a promising young man. During this state of things my vanity has often been flattered; and had it not been for one serious difficulty with which I had to grapple, it is uncertain to what a degree of self-importance I might have arrived—and that was, whether I was really called by God to the work of the ministry; for my teachers had caused me to believe that there was a special call for the ministry, differing from that call which was

necessary in order to make men christians. After laboring under this difficulty for many years, and still unable to ascertain whether I was really called or not, I made an exertion of mind and discovered that it could not be wrong in any man to recommend that religion which was ordered to be published, call or no call; and so I acted, and felt considerably relieved from my most serious difficulty. This was my situation when I first saw your views on that subject in the *Christian Baptist*; and no sooner had I read them and compared them with the word of God, than I abandoned entirely, what I had before partially, and am made now to wonder why the christian world could have been kept in ignorance so long, an ignorance too which is fraught with so much distress to an honest-minded christian. Having given up my former views relative to the call, I now only esteem myself a christian, as one who has obtained like precious faith with all saints; and in consequence of this hope of eternal life, I now, from a principle of gratitude to God for his goodness to me, wish still to recommend that religion to all men, which is the source of all my substantial joys—

"Nor can I willing be his bounty to conceal
"From others, who, like me, their wants and hunger feel.
"I'll tell them of his bounteous store,
"And try to send a thousand more."

Although I am satisfied on the subject above touched, still I have cause of great and increasing distress in consequence of viewing the state of the churches, as being yet in the wilderness, and bearing so little likeness to their ancient simplicity and glory. For this restoration I ardently pray; but I am greatly at a loss to know how to make a move, seeing the prejudices with which we will have to contend. It is an easy matter for you, my brother, to theorize on this subject, but how to reduce it to practice, I have not yet found; and this is the subject on which I ask advice. For sure if we do not go to work right, we shall not prosper—we shall only be making bad worse. My inquiry more particularly respects the churches that are already in existence, and whether they can be reformed without creating additional difficulties and distresses. Your answer to the above inquiry (should you give one) will be read with avidity.

Hoping you may prosper in your inquiry after truth, I subscribe myself

Your brother in Christ,
FAITHFUL.

Reply to Faithful.

Dear Brother,

THE difficulties which you mention in your epistle of July last are apparently great, and in some respects, no doubt, really so. The things that happened to the Jews, once the people of God, happened to them for types or examples, and they are written for our admonition, to whom the grace of God has appeared, and upon whom the ends of the world have come. They apostatized from the divine institution given by Moses; they lost the primitive simplicity and excellency of the Jews' religion, and departed far from both the letter and spirit of the covenant under which God placed them. They were carried captive into Babylon for their iniquities, and while in Babylon they lost the primitive meaning of the sacred language, the medium of the revelation made them; and thus both the law and the worship under it were not exhibited among them. While in Babylon their condition became worse and worse. It pleased the God of Abraham to turn the captivity of Jacob. But the dangers and difficulties that attended their return were great and appalling. To restore the ancient order of things then was a work of no small difficulty. They had lost a living model of the Lord's house; they were ignorant of the manner in which the religious festivals and institutions were to be observed; they had formed many alliances that were difficult to be broken; and, worse than all, they had lost the true meaning of their apostles and prophets. Now, so similar has been the apostacy from the new covenant, that almost all the same misfortunes attend it, and the same names are, in the new covenant prophecies, attached to it. To complete the analogy, and to make it a type of that which it doubtless circumstantially represented, we may expect to find the same difficulties attendant on a return to Jerusalem, and a restoration of the divinely authorized institutions of the new covenant. Some of the professing people of God will now, as formerly, oppose a return; many will despair of its practicability; a living model of the house of God is wanting; and the sacred dialect has been so much perverted, and is so generally misunderstood, that but few of even those who feel the thraldom of the captivity of Babylon the Great, know whence they are fallen, and of what things they should repent.

To make a move in the business of restoration, and in returning to the covenant, is, I confess, quite a different thing from speculating or talking about it; and yet it only requires an intelligent mind and a willing heart. These will direct and embolden every effort. The people must abandon the language, customs, and manners of Ashdod. For this purpose they will meet, and read, and examine the New Covenant writings. They will also look to Heaven for wisdom and courage, and as soon as any item of the will of Heaven is distinctly apprehended, it will be brought into their practice. But, my dear sir, personal reformation, or individual conformity to the spirit, and temper, and morals of christians, must be the basis of every attempt at a social or united representation and enjoyment of the christian religion. This personal reformation will, however, grow with, and be accelerated by, a social and united effort to understand and practise the apostolic instructions. These cannot be separated. It is admitted the form of godliness in individuals and in societies may exist without the power; and a congregation may, like a well-disciplined army, be clothed with all the regimentals, and perform all the involutions and evolutions to an *iota*, and yet not a soldier among them—not a christian in spirit and temper—in life and deportment.

But this is more likely to be the case any where than amongst those who are daily and ardently cultivating a knowledge of the Holy Scriptures, and aiming at standing perfect and complete in the will of God. This course is a sovereign antidote against that state.

But to come to the pinching question in your communication, it must be observed that, amongst the congregations with which you are connected, there is found this happy circumstance—they have taken the scriptures of the New Testament for their constitution. Perhaps some of them have made their obeisance to something called the Constitution of the Elkhorn or Licking Association, or to something surnamed after the fish ponds or mill seats of your country; but these are such modern playthings they can very easily be drowned in the waters that christened them. But in all those congregations

Y

which have recognized that Christ's kingdom is not of this world, and not composed of all born into the world by natural generation, methinks it were easy, if the hearts of the people are regenerate, to have the ancient order of things restored.

As I have no dictatorial authority in these matters, and would by no means covet such; and, indeed, as nothing can be done but by the people themselves, examining, judging, and acting for themselves, I can only say, that all those desirous of knowing, enjoying, and exhibiting the christian religion in its original purity and excellency, must individually, and in their public meetings, search and examine the apostles' doctrine, and pay no manner of respect to any opinions or practices which they have formerly regarded, except so far as they see, and learn, and know them to be the teachings of the Holy Spirit. If they cannot get into this way of reading and examining the Holy Scriptures to their profit, let them begin and inquire into the reasons of their present conduct. It is easy to put them on the search, by proposing them a few questions to solve—such as, By what authority and for what reason do we meet once in a month or once in two weeks to hear a sermon? By what authority and for what reason do we agree with a man, called "a preacher," for the one fourth, or the one half, or the one third of his time to preach to us? By what authority and for what reason do we all forsake the assembling of ourselves together except when our preacher draws us out? By what authority and for what reason do we at one time attend on certain acts of worship in our assemblies, and not at another? or why have we ordinary and extraordinary acts of worship? Why should we not devote a part of the time employed in our meetings in inquiring into the grounds and reasons of our own acts and deeds, and in comparing our views, enjoyments, and practices, as christians, with those of them who first trusted in Christ? And why should we not, as soon as we discover any incongruity, deficiency, or aberration in our views or practices, immediately abandon them, and become followers of them who among the Jews and Gentiles, first turned to the Lord?

My dear sir, I think by the time these matters are ascertained, the views and dispositions of all who fear God will be considerably improved; and, as the best solution of these difficulties, we intend to give the history of the progress and proficiency of some congregations who have taken this course, and are now enjoying a participation of the fulness of the blessings of the gospel of Christ. It will not be surprising to find some members of your best regulated churches who will rather walk as other professors walk, than in the paths consecrated by the authority of the Lord and the examples of his first followers. Thus the chaff will be purged from among the wheat; and the disciple in deed will be distinguished from him who has merely the name.

With prayers for your success in the noblest of all attempts, I am your brother in the hope of immortality.				EDITOR.

No. 3.]			OCT. 3, 1825.

A Narrative of the Origin and Formation of the Westminster or Presbyterian Confession of Faith.
No. V.

It would be tedious, though, perhaps, very profitable to go into the detail of the acts and deeds of the Westminster Assembly, and those proceedings of the long parliament connected

15

with the call and session of those creed makers. An assembly which sat five years six months and twenty two days, in which they had one thousand one hundred and sixty three sessions, must have done a great deal of ecclesiastical business, right or wrong. Their deeds will appear to posterity either good or evil, according to the medium through which they are viewed. If viewed through the medium of the popular and fashionable systems of this age, a majority of their acts will appear good and commendable to those who are their children; but if viewed through the medium of the twelve apostles, by those who venerate their character and authority, their deeds will appear every way out of character, and worthy of the severest reprobation. It is a very slim commendation of them to allow that they declared many truths in their confession; for so did the council of Trent and the council of Nice.

After they had spent the above term of five years six months and twenty two days, in creed and discipline manufacturing, those who yet kept their seats were converted into examining committees. After making the laws of conscience and conduct, they became examinators of such ministers as presented themselves for ordination or induction into livings. In the form of examining committees they might have sat till their last breath, had not Oliver Cromwell, on the morning of March 25, 1652, turned the long parliament out of doors, and thus being deprived of their patron, preserver, proprietor, benefactor, and guide, they broke up without any formal dissolution. *Sic transit gloria mundi* —and so may all the enemies of civil and religious liberty, all usurpers of the thrones and authority of the Lord and the apostles, whether intentionally or unintentionally such—so let them be dispersed! Let their language be confounded, and " confusion on their banners wait!"

They did not like their own establishment when they had it built. There was not enough of the dungeon and the sword in it. This will appear in the sequel.

That our remarks may appear just, if they do not already from the facts exhibited, we shall, in this number, give an extract or two from the history of their contest about the keys. Those who would wish to have a full statement of their proceedings would do well to consult Rushworth's, and Whitlocke's Memoirs, or Neal's History of the Puritans, vol. 3. The following hints will be found in Neal's History, vol. 3. page 392—5.

"But the fiercest contention between the assembly and parliament arose upon the power of the keys, which the former had voted to be in the eldership or presbytery, in these words: "The keys of the kingdom of heaven were committed to the officers of the church, by virtue whereof they have power respectively to retain and remit sins, to shut the kingdom of heaven against the impenitent both by the word and censures, and to open it to the penitent by absolution; and to prevent the profanation of the holy sacrament by notorious and obstinate offenders, the said officers are to proceed by admonition, suspension from the sacrament of the Lord's supper for a season, and by excommunication from the church, according to the nature of the crime and demerit of the person;" all which power they claimed, not by the laws of the land, but *jure divino*, or by divine appointment.

The Independents claimed the like power for the brotherhood of every particular congregation, but without any civil sanctions or penalties annexed; the Erastians were for laying the communion open, and referring all crimes to the civil magistrate. When the question therefore came under consideration, in the house of commons, the learned Mr. Selden delivered his opinion against all suspensions and excommunications, to this effect, " that for four thousand years there was no law to suspend persons from the religious exercises. Strangers, indeed, were kept from the passover, but they were pagans, and not of the Jewish religion. The question is not now for keeping away Pagans in times of christianity, but Protestants from Protestant worship. No divine can show, that there is any such command as this to suspend from the sacrament. No man is kept from the sacrament, *eo nomine*, because he is guilty of any sin, by the constitution of the reformed churches, or because he has not made satisfaction. Every man is a sinner, the difference is only that one is in private, and the other in public. *Dic ecclesiæ* in St. Matthew were the courts of law which then sat at Jerusalem. No man can show any excommunication till the popes Victor and Zephorinus (two hundred years after Christ) first began to use them upon private quarrels, whereby it appears that excommunication is a human invention, taken from the heathens."

Mr. Whitlocke spake on the same side of the question, and said, " The assembly of divines have petitioned and advised this house, that in every presbytery, or Presbyterian congregation, the pastors and ruling elders may have the power of excommunication, and of suspending such as they shall judge ignorant or scandalous. By pastors, I suppose they mean themselves, and others who are or may be preachers, and would be bishops or overseers of their congregations. By ruling elders they mean a select number of such in every congregation as shall be chosen for the execution of government and discipline therein. A pastor is one who is to feed his sheep; and if so, how improper must it be for such to desire to excommunicate any, or keep them from food; to forbid any to eat, or whomsoever they shall judge unworthy, when Christ has said, Take, eat and drink, you all of it, though Judas was one of them. But some have said, it is the duty of a shepherd, when he sees a sheep feeding upon that which will do him hurt, to chase him away from that pasture; and they apply this to suspending of those from the sacrament who they fear, by eating and drinking unworthily, may eat and drink their own damnation. But it ought to be observed, that it is not receiving the sacrament, but the unworthiness of the receiver, that brings destruction; and this cannot be within the reach of any but the person himself who alone can examine his own heart; nor can any one produce a commission for to be judge thereof. But it is said, that ruling elders are to be joined with the pastors; now in some country villages and congregations, perhaps they may not be very learned, and yet the authority given them is very great; the word *elders*, amongst the Hebrews, signified men of the greatest power and dignity; so it was amongst the Romans, whose senate was so called, from *senes*, elders. The highest title amongst the French, Spaniards, and Italians, *seigneur* and *seigniori*, is but a corruption of the latin word *senior*, elder. The same may be observed in our English corporations, where the best and most substantial persons are called aldermen or eldermen. Thus the title of elders may be given to the chief men of every presbytery; but if the power of excommunication be given them, they may challenge the title of elders in the highest signification.

"Power is desired to be given to suspend from the sacrament two sorts of persons, the ignorant and scandalous; now it is possible, that they who are judged to be competent in one place may be deemed ignorant in another; however, to keep them from the ordinances is no way to improve their knowledge. Scandalous persons are likewise to be suspended, and this is to be left to the discretion of the pastors and ruling elders; but where have they such a commission? Scandalous sinners should be admonished to forsake their evil ways, and amend their lives; and how can this be done better, than by allowing them to hear good sermons, and partake of the holy ordinances? A man may be a good physician, though he never cuts off a member from his patient; and a church may be a good church, though no member of it has ever been cut off. I have heard many complaints of the jurisdiction of the prelates, who were but few; now in this ordinance there will be a great multiplication of spiritual men in the government, but I am of opinion, that where the temporal sword is sufficient for punishing of offences, there will be no need of this new discipline."

Though the parliament did not deem it prudent wholly to reject the ordinance for excommunication, because it had been the popular complaint in the late times, that pastors of churches had not power to keep unworthy communicants from the Lord's table; yet the speeches of these learned gentlemen made such an impression, that they resolved to render it ineffectual to all the purposes of church tyranny; accordingly they sent to the assembly to specify, in writing, what degree of knowledge in the christian religion were necessary to qualify a person for the communion? and what sort of scandal deserved suspension or excommunication? Which, after much controversy, they presented to the houses, who inserted them in the body of their ordinance for suspension from the Lord's supper, dated October 20, 1645, together with certain provisos of their own, which stripped the presbyteries of that power of the keys which they were reaching at:—

"Provided always, that if any person find himself aggrieved with the proceedings of the presbytery to which he belongs, he may appeal to the ecclesiastical eldership; from them to the provincial assembly; from them to the national; and from them to the parliament."

"It is further provided, that the cognizance and examination of all capital offences shall be reserved entire to the magistrate appointed by the laws of the kingdom, who, upon his committing the party to prison, shall make a certificate to the eldership of the congregation to which they belonged, who may thereupon suspend them from the sacrament."

By these provisos it is evident the parliament were determined not to part with the spiritual sword, or subject their civil properties to the power of the church, which gave great offence to the Scots commissioners, and to most of the English Presbyterians, who declaimed against the ordinance, as built upon Erastian principles, and depriving the church of that which it claimed by a divine institution. The parliament observing their ambition of making the church independent of the state, girt the laws closer about them, and subjected their determinations more immediately to the civil magistrate, by an ordinance dated March 14th, 1645—6.

This ordinance of suspension from the sacra-

ment was extorted from the two houses before the time, by the importunate solicitations of the city clergy; for as yet there were no classes or Presbyteries in any part of England, which ought to have been erected before they had determined their powers. The houses had voted that there should be a choice of lay elders throughout England and Wales, and had laid down some rules for this purpose, August 19, 1645; but it was the 14th of March following before it passed into a law.

It was then ordained, "1. That there be forthwith a choice of [ruling] elders throughout the kingdom of England, and dominion of Wales.

"2. That public notice be given of such election in every parish, by the minister of the parish, a fortnight before; and that on the Lord's day on which the choice is to be made, a sermon be preached suitable to the occasion.

"3. Elections shall be made by the congregation, or the major part of them then assembled, being heads of families, and such as have taken the covenant."

The parliament apprehended they had now established the plan of the Presbyterian discipline, though it proved not to the satisfaction of any one party of christians; so hard is it to make a good settlement when men dig up all at once old foundations. The Presbyterian hierarchy was as narrow as the prelatical; and as it did not allow a liberty of conscience, claiming a civil as well as ecclesiastical authority over men's persons and properties, it was equally, if not more insufferable. Bishop Kennet observes that the settling presbytery was supported by the fear and love of the Scots army, and that when they were gone home it was better managed by the English army, who were for independency and a principle of toleration; but as things stood nobody was pleased; the Episcopalians and Independents were excluded; and because the parliament would not give the several presbyteries an absolute power over their communicants, but reserved the last appeal to themselves, neither the Scots nor English Presbyterians would accept it.

The English Presbyterians, having resolved to stand and fall with the Scots, refused peremptorily to comply with the ordinance, relying upon the assistance and support of that nation.

It was a sanguine and daring attempt of these divines, who were called together only for their advice, to examine and censure the ordinances of parliament, and dispute in this manner with their superiors; the commons, alarmed at this petition, appointed a committee to take into consideration the matter and manner of it; who, after some time, reported it as their opinion, that the assembly of divines, in their petition, had broken the privileges of parliament, and were guilty of a *præmunire;* and whereas they insisted so peremptorily on the *jus divinum* of the Presbyterian government, the committee had drawn up certain queries, which they desired the assembly might resolve for their satisfaction. The house agreed to the report of the committee and on the 30th of April, sent Sir John Evelin, Mr. Nathaniel Fiennes, and Mr. Browne, to the assembly, to acquaint them with their resolutions. These gentlemen set before them their rash and imprudent conduct, and in several speeches, showed wherein they had exceeded their province, which was to advise the houses in such points as they should lay before them, but not to dictate to those to whom they owed their being an assembly.　　　　　EDITOR.

17

A Restoration of the Ancient Order of Things.
No. VIII.

On the Breaking of Bread.—No. III.

WE have proposed to make still farther apparent that the primary intention of the meeting of the disciples on the first day of the week, was to break bread. We concluded our last essay on this topic with a notice of Acts xx. 7. "And on the first day of the week when the disciples assembled to break bread." The design of this meeting, it is evident, was to break bread. But that this was the design of all their meetings for worship and edification, or that it was the primary object of the meetings of the disciples, is rendered very certain from Paul's first letter to the Corinthians, chapter xi. The apostle applauds and censures the church at Corinth with respect to their observance of the order he instituted among them. In the second verse he praises them for retaining the ordinances he delivered them, and in the conclusion of this chapter he censures them in strong terms for not keeping the ordinance of breaking bread as he delivered it to them. They retained in their meetings the ordinance, but did abuse it. He specifies their abuses of it, and denounces their practice as worthy of chastisement. But in doing this, he incidentally informs us that it was for the purpose of breaking bread they assembled in one place. And the manner in which he does this is equivalent to an express command to assemble for the purpose. Indeed there is no form of speech more determinate in its meaning or more energetic in its force than that which he uses, verse 20. It is precisely the same as the two following examples. A man assembles laborers in his vineyard to cultivate it. He goes out and finds them either idle or destroying his vines. He reproves and commands them to business by addressing them thus—"Men, ye did *not* assemble to cultivate my vineyard." By the use of this negative he makes his command more imperative and their guilt more apparent. A teacher assembles his pupils to learn—he comes in and finds them idle or quarrelling. He addresses them thus—"Boys, ye did *not* assemble to learn." In this forcible style, he declares the object of their meeting was to learn, and thus commands and reproves them in the same words. So Paul addresses the disciples in Corinth—"When ye assemble, it is *not* to eat the Lord's supper;" or (*Macknight*,) "But your coming together into one place, is *not* to eat the Lord's supper," plainly and forcibly intimating that this was the design of their meeting or assembling in one place, commanding them to order, and reproving them for disorder. Now it must be admitted that Paul's style in this passage is exactly similar to the two examples given, and that the examples given mean what we have said of their import; consequently, by the same rule, Paul's reminds the Corinthians, and informs all who ever read the epistle, that when the disciples assembled, or came together into one place, it was primarily for the purpose of breaking bread, and in effect most positively commands the practice. To this it has been objected that the 26th verse allows the liberty of dispensing with this ordinance as often as we please. In the improved translation of Macknight it reads thus: "Wherefore, as often as you eat this bread and drink this cup, you openly publish the death of the Lord till the time he come." Either these words, or those in the preceding verse, ("This *do*, as often as you drink it, in remembrance of me,") are said to give us the liberty of determining when we may break bread. If so, then the Lord's supper is an anomaly in revelation. It is an ordinance which may be kept once in seven months, or seven years, just as we please, for, reader, remember, "where there is no law there is no transgression." But this application of the words is absurd, and perfectly similar to the papists' inference from these words; for they infer hence that "the cup may sometimes be omitted, and under this pretence have refused it altogether to the laity." And certainly if the phrase, "as often as you drink it," means that it may be omitted when any one pleases, it is good logic for the papists to argue that it may be omitted altogether by the laity, provided the priests *please* to drink it.

But neither the design of the apostle nor his words in this passage have respect to the frequency, but to the manner of observing the institution. If this is evident, that interpretation falls to the ground; and that it is evident, requires only to ask the question, What was the apostle's design in these words? Most certainly it was to reprove the Corinthians, not for the frequency nor unfrequency of their attending to it, but for the manner in which they did it. Now as this was the design, and as every writer's or speaker's words are to be interpreted according to his design, we are constrained to admit that the apostle meant no more than that christians should always, in observing this institution, observe it in the manner and for the reasons he assigns.

And last of all, on this passage, let it be remembered, that if the phrase, "as oft as," gives us liberty to observe it seldom, it also gives us liberty to observe it every day if we please.— And if it be a privilege, we are not straitened in the Lord, but in ourselves.

But, say some, "it will become too common and lose its solemnity." Well, then, the seldomer the better. If we observe it only once in twenty years, it will be the more uncommon and solemn. And, on the same principle, the seldomer we pray the better. We shall pray with more solemnity if we pray once in twenty years!

But "it is too expensive." How? Wherein? Is not the "earth the Lord's and the fulness thereof?" It costs us nothing. It is the Lord's property. He gives us his goods that we may enjoy ourselves. We never saw or read of a church so poor that could not, without a sacrifice, furnish the Lord's table. To make one "sacrament," requires more than to furnish the Lord's table three months. I hate this objection most cordially.—It is antichristian—it is mean—it is base.

"It is unfashionable." So it is to speak truth, and fulfil contracts. So it is to obey God rather than man. And if you love the fashion, be consistent—dont associate with the Nazarenes—hold up the skirts of the high priest, and go to the temple. But all objections are as light as straws and as volatile as a feather.

To recapitulate the items adduced in favor of the ancient order of breaking bread, it was shewn, as we apprehend—

1. That there is a divinely instituted order of christian worship, in christian assemblies.

2. That this order of worship is uniformly the same.

3. That the nature and design of the breaking of bread are such as to make it an essential part of christian worship in christian assemblies.

4. That the first church set in order in Jerusalem, continued as stedfastly in breaking of bread, as in any other act of social worship or edification.

5. That the disciples stately met on the first

day of the week, primarily and emphatically for this purpose.

6. That the apostle declared it was the design or the primary object of the church to assemble in one place for this purpose, and so commanded it to the churches he had set in order.

7. That there is no law, rule, reason, or authority for the present manner of observing this institute quarterly, semi-annually, or at any other time than weekly.

8. We have considered some of the more prominent objections against the ancient practice, and are ready to hear any new ones that can be offered. Upon the whole, it may be said that we have express precedent and an express command to assemble in one place on the first day of the week to break bread. We shall reserve other evidences and considerations until some objections are offered by any correspondent who complies with our conditions.   EDITOR.

Christian Union.—No. III.

NOTHING can reconcile the different sects in religion to relinquish their sectarian names and creeds for the name of christian and the word of God, but a clear proof that their names and creeds are not only unscriptural, but are subversive of the christian character, and in their consequences prevent the world believing in Jesus Christ. In my two former numbers I have shown, in some degree, the truth of these things, and feel sure that every tender-hearted christian cannot fail to feel much affected by the considerations there exhibited.

I promised, in my last number, to give a short account of the origin of creeds as distinguished from the word of God in the gospel. This I do, the more effectually, to evince the deception that is practised upon the world and the delusion under which it labors on this subject.

The first creed of which we are informed, as distinguished from "the faith which was once delivered to the saints," is presented to us under the imposing but false title of "The Apostle's Creed," which is so often repeated by the Roman Catholics and the Episcopalians as of divine origin. Dupin, in his Ecclesiastical History of the first century, than whom a more correct and impartial historian has not lived, though of Catholic profession, makes it abundantly evident that this creed was not composed by the apostles. Saint Jerome says that the faith of the creed was an apostolic tradition, and was not written on paper by the apostles. "The fathers of the three first ages," Dupin observes, "disputing with heretics, do not pretend to say that the creed was composed by the apostles, but that the doctrine comprised in the creed is that of the apostles." "We find," he farther remarks, "in the second and third ages of the church as many creeds as authors, and the same author sets the creed down after a different manner in several places of his works, which plainly shows that there was not then any creed that was reputed to be the apostles, nor even any reputed or established form of faith except that which was written in the word of God. St. Jerome exhibits two different creeds, and Tertullian made use of three different creeds in three several places; all of which creeds are different from the Vulgate." So much for the origin of the first creed, which is rung upon all the changes so often every Sabbath by Catholics and Episcopalians as apostolic.

The next one which we shall notice, and which is the most distinguished instance of creed making in history, is the Nicene Creed, which was made by and under the authority of Constantine the Great, in the year 325, and was established as the constitution and test of the true Catholic church, and the divine measure of all orthodoxy.

The history of this creed is the following. There were in the church of Alexandria, in Egypt, two pastors, one named Alexander, and the other Arius. Alexander, on a certain occasion, affirmed in reference to the Trinity, that there was "an unity in Trinity, and particularly that the Son was co-eternal, and co-substantial, and of the same dignity with the Father." Arius objected to the language, and urged that "If the Father begat the Son, he who was begotten must have a beginning of his existence as Son; and from hence, said he, it is manifest that there was a time when the Son was not," &c. This difference in speculation between these two men, neither of whom seems to have attended to the scriptural statements on the subject, involved all christendom in a flame and set bishops against bishops, who set the people together by the ears, and gave occasion, as Louates observes in his church history, to the heathen to ridicule the christian religion upon their public theatres. Julian, the nephew of Constantine, who, by reason of these disputes, renounced christianity and returned to Paganism, used to call into his presence the boxers on each side of the controversy, to abuse each other for his amusement.

The dispute between Alexander and Arius occasioned Constantine to call his Œcumenical Council—the council of the whole world, as it was called, to settle the orthodoxy on the subject, who decreed as follows:—"We believe in one God, the Father Almighty, maker of all things, visible and invisible; and in one Lord, Jesus Christ, the Son of God, the only begotten, begotten of the Father, that is, of the substance of the Father, God of God, Light of Light, true God of true God, begotten, not made, consubstantial with the Father," &c. This was the established creed, or the iron bedstead by which every man was to be measured, and to be lopped or stretched as he might be too long or too short, according to its dimensions. With its erection was forged "the infernal instruments of torture and death for effecting uniformity in religion," which were put into the hands of the clergy by civil authority. This occurred in A. D. 325, and was the first regular establishment of christianity by civil authority, and has been perpetuated down to the present time in the old world. At that time Constantine, though unbaptized, assumed the title of Universal Bishop. With this creed, and the power of punishing heretics, was exhibited the full revelation of the Man of Sin, and with it was established the kingdom of the clergy. See Jones' History of the Church, vol. 1. It was at this time, as Dupin remarks, that "bishops met together with liberty, being supported by the authority of princes, and made abundance of rules concerning the ordinances of the church. Previous to this the discipline was plain and simple, and the church had no other splendor to recommend it but what the holiness of the manners of the lives of the christians gave it."

Had the poor worms of the dust, Alexander and Arius and Athanasius, been let alone to enjoy their speculations, with a moderate attention to the word of God, their differences of opinion would either have done no harm, would have been healed, or would have died with them.

Jones, in his history, remarks, that "the effects of this general council were to lay the foundation of a system of persecution of a complexion altogether new, professing christians tyrannizing over the consciences of each other, and inflicting tortures and cruelties far greater than they had sustained from their heathen persecutors." Each side of the Arian controversy, when in power, persecuted the other with the most ruthless sanguinary violence. True christianity had nothing to do in this dark business. This was the revelation of the Man of Sin which had been previously let or hindered by pagan emperors.

The difference between Alexander and Arius arose from the neglect or disregard of the doctrinal statements and facts as revealed in the word of God on the subject of the nature and character of Christ, and by indulging in metaphysical speculations, aided by Clement's natural religion, without regard to the word.

It is impossible for those who entertain a reverential regard for the great God not to be struck with the presumption of sinful, ignorant, erring mortals, who would dare to investigate a subject of such awful import as the *modus* of the divine existence, or who would presume to go further in the discovery of God than he has revealed himself.

It would now seem, that, according to the most enlightened scripture views of the subject, both sides of the Arian controversy in the fourth century were wrong, and yet both in some degree were right:—for, as has been observed by a distinguished orthodox writer of Europe of the present day, and which agrees pretty much with the principles of the Andover school in Massachusetts, "Divine revelation never leads us to conceive of the Son of God abstractly from the incarnation of the Word. The Word that was God was made flesh. The Holy Ghost overshadowed the Virgin Mary;—this was the reason, not only of her conceiving that holy thing, but also of its being called the Son of God. Although the sonship of Christ always supposes and includes his godhead, in which the eternal original and essential dignity of his person consists; yet it does not appear from scripture that he is called the Son of God, merely as God, or to teach us the origin and manner of his existence in the godhead; it seems applicable to him as Emanuel, God with us." Human knowledge of Jehovah can go no further than the terms in which the divine nature as Father, Son, and Holy Ghost are revealed. The cherubim veil the rest with their wings.

In the western states a very unprofitable controversy has existed on this subject. If men could be content with the scripture statements of the nature and character of Christ, and could realize the fact that he was worshipped as God by inspired apostles and christians, for which they suffered death, and which was indeed the first cause of their persecution, it would end all controversy, and we would soon see a union of sentiment. Without the agreement that Christ is really an object of worship, and is of course Divine, there can never be christian union between them.

These disputes have originated a technical phraseology on both sides, which has greatly narrowed the vocabulary in religion, and has rendered some modes of expression almost obsolete, which were indulged in without scruple by the sacred writers. They have occasioned, on the Arian side of the question, in many instances, the relinquishment of the latitude with which the scriptures express themselves on the nature and glory of Christ, and have produced a scrupulous and systematic cast of diction which is altogether inconsistent with the noble freedom displayed by the inspired penmen. Many expressions are employed, without hesitation, in scripture, which are rarely found even in the direct form of quotation in their writings, and are never heard in their public addresses but with a view of subjecting them to explanations and speculations, which so mutilate and mar the character of Christ as to render him altogether an object unfit for the worship of christians; and who, if thus seen, had never been worshipped by Stephen and Paul and the apostolic christians. Paul wrote his first epistle to "the church of God which is at Corinth," and "to all that in every place call upon, or invoke, the name of, or worship, Jesus Christ our Lord, both their and our Lord."

The next instance of creed-making was in the reign of Henry VIII. and his immediate successors. This is said to have formed the dawn of the Reformation, which has eventuated in the formation of the Episcopal church in England and in these United States, with which also the Methodist Episcopal church is identified.

After having been married to Catharine of Arragon for a number of years, Henry VIII. became attached to Anne Boleyn, and petitioned the Pope to divorce him from Catharine that he might marry Anne, which the Pope refused or delayed. He then obtained a sentence annulling his marriage from Bishop Cranmer. The Pope rescinded Cranmer's sentence and excommunicated the king. This induced Henry and his parliament to pass an act abolishing the Pope's power in England, and v another act they declared the king supreme head of the church, and all the authority of which the Pope was deprived in England was vested in, and assumed by, Henry.

Henry was a devoted Roman Catholic in heart, and becoming jealous of Ann Boleyn's attachment to the Protestants, had her beheaded, and the next day married Jane Seymer, who dying, he married Anne of Cleves, and in a short time put her away and married Catharine Par.

Edward VI. the son of Jane Seymer, succeeded his father, Henry VIII. to the throne, when nine years old. He was a good little boy, and friendly to the Protestants. He and his bishops did something towards forming and improving the church of England. Mary, daughter of Catharine of Arragon, succeeded him, restored the supremacy of the Pope of Rome, and beheaded Cranmer and others. After Mary, came to the throne Elizabeth, daughter of Anne Boleyn, who restored the ecclesiastical order appointed by her father, and was the first female Pope of England; for she "arrogated to herself that ecclesiastical supremacy over the faith and worship of her subjects which before was supposed exclusively to belong to the court of Rome." The bishops and clergy were so far from having any hand in forming the present established church of England or in ordaining its rites and articles of faith, that it was done not only without them, but in actual opposition to them. The parliament and the queen alone established her supremacy and the common prayer-book, in spite of all opposition from the bishops in the House of Lords; and the convocation then sitting was so far from having any thing to do, in those church articles for reformation, that it presented to Parliament several propositions in behalf of the tenets of popery, directly contrary to the proceedings of parliament.

Such is the pure spiritual origin, if I may speak ironically, of the Episcopal church of England and of these United States. Are there not many of the marks of the Beast upon it? In the church of Christ he is the sole head, founder and lawgiver; all authority and jurisdiction are in him and flow from him; but in the church of England the king or queen is "supreme head, possessing all power to exercise all manner of ecclesiastical jurisdiction, and archbishops, bishops, and archdeacons, and other ecclesiastical persons have no manner of jurisdiction ecclesiastical, but by and under the king's majesty, who has full power and authority to hear all manner of causes ecclesiastical, and to reform and correct all vice, sin, errors, heresies and abuses whatever." 29th Henry viii. ch. 1, 37th Henry viii. ch. 17, 1st Eliz. ch. 1. The bishops for these United States, after the Revolution, could not be ordained in England without the consent of his ecclesiastical supremacy, George III. and it was with difficulty that the succession could be obtained on that account.

In consequence of this supremacy, the king or queen has power to excommunicate from, or re-admit into the church, independent of, yea, in direct opposition to, all its bishops and clergy. They revoke, if they please, any spiritual censure; suspend or excommunicate any bishop or other clergy; and by proclamation, without repentance, can restore the vilest offenders to the bosom of the church. They have power to forbid all preaching for a time, as did Henry VIII. Edward VI. queens Mary and Elizabeth; to limit, instruct, and prescribe to the clergy what they shall and what they shall not preach, as did Elizabeth, James I. Charles, and king William. Such is the channel of legitimacy through which Episcopalians allege that the apostolic succession has been handed down to them, who, with the Roman Catholics, assume the exclusive right to preach the word of God and to administer the ordinances of the New Testament by virtue of this pure spiritual legitimacy, and this, too, in these United States! Can that be the church of Christ, with such a head to it, which exalts itself above all that is called God!

He who reads Jones' History of the Church of Christ, the history of that society of christians which we see described in the Acts of the Apostles and in the Apostolic Epistles, which has been persecuted since Constantine by such secular ecclesiastical establishments as that of the English episcopacy, will readily perceive that the church of Christ is quite a different thing from such hierarchies, and that their creeds and confessions have no claim to divine authority, but are reprobated by it. It will be seen that that which has been described by Mosheim and Milner as the church of Christ has been the beastly persecutor of his church.

The Methodist Society and system was first formed in 1729 by the association of John and Charles Wesley and some other persons, for religious exercises and their own improvement in reading the scriptures. Their regularity and seriousness procured for them the name of *Methodists.* Mr. Wesley gives us the following account of Methodism:—"The first rise of Methodism (so called) was in November, 1729, when four of us met together at Oxford; the second was at Savannah, in April, 1736, twenty or thirty persons met at my house; the last was at London on this day, (viz. May 1, 1738,) when forty or fifty of us agreed to meet together every Wednesday evening, in order to a free conversation, begun and ended with prayer." From 1760 to 1790, several persons of Mr. Wesley's society emigrated from England and Ireland and settled in various parts of America. During the war between England and America all communication between the two societies was cut off. This was very much felt by the American Methodists. Mr. Asbury, the senior minister, was importuned to take proper measures that the societies might enjoy the privileges of other churches, by the ordination of ministers. This he refused because of his attachment to the church of England. On this, a majority of the preachers separated from him and chose out of themselves three senior brethren, who ordained others by the imposition of hands. Mr. Asbury prevailed on them to return, and by a vote at one of their conferences, the ordination was declared void. After the war Mr. Wesley drew up a plan of church government, &c. for the American Methodists, and ordained Dr. Coke a *joint superintendent* with Mr. Asbury over the Methodist connexion in North America. The reason Mr. Wesley assigned for this measure was the following, which he gave in answer to a question put to him by William Jones, a chaplain of lord bishop Horn, in the following words: "Whether it was true that he (Wesley) had invested two gentlemen with the *episcopal* character, and had sent them in that character to America?" "As soon," said Mr. Wesley in answer, "as we had made peace with America, and allowed them their independence, all religious connexion between this country and the independent colonies was at an end; in consequence of which the sectaries fell to work to increase their several parties—and the Anabaptists, in particular, were carrying all before them.—Something was therefore to be done, without loss of time, for this *poor people* (as he called them) in America; and he had therefore taken the step in question with a hope of preventing further disorders." Thus Mr. Wesley, who was only a presbyter, consecrated two bishops, which was complained of by bishop Horn in his charge to the clergy of Norwich. See Jones' Life of Horn in Horn's works, vol. i. p. 161. and vol. iv. p. 52.

I frankly confess that Mr. Wesley had as much of a divine right to ordain bishops, to form a creed, to make a book of discipline, and to ordain and establish rites and ceremonies in the church, as the pope of Rome and all his cardinals had; or as had Henry VIII. and pope Elizabeth with their parliaments and bishops; or as had parliament with the Westminister Assembly, who made the Presbyterian Confession of Faith; or as had the seven Baptist churches of London, or the one hundred churches who composed the Philadelphia Confession of Faith. In behalf of the Lord Jesus Christ, who is the one lawgiver, and head of the church, however, I aver that all these powers have been exercised without right, and in opposition to his authority; and any man who submits to them as authoritative in religion, worships the image of the Beast and bears his name.

The Westminster Confession of Faith was formed by the Westminster Assembly, which was convened as an ecclesiastical council of parliament in 1643. The ordinance which convened them stated that they were "to be consulted with by parliament for settling the government and liturgy of the Church of England." Its professed design was to reform Episcopacy to the standard of former times. But the interests of parliament, in opposition to king Charles I. became so reduced that they were obliged to call in the aid of the Scots. Their aid was offered on condition that the Parliament and the Westminster Assembly would abandon Episcopacy, and attempt the establishment of

Presbyterianism, which at length they advanced into *jus divinum*, or a divine institution, derived expressly from Christ and the apostles. On the 17th of August, 1643, the Solemn League and Covenant, embracing these objects, was delivered into the assembly by Dr. Henderson. It was adopted by parliament and sent over the three kingdoms to be sworn to and signed. The objects stated in the covenant were to promote the extirpation of popery, prelacy, heresy, schism, scepticism, and idolatry, and endeavor a union between the kingdoms in one confession of faith, one form of church government, and one directory of worship. They took an oath to be orthodox in doctrine agreeably to the word of God; and in discipline to do what they should conceive would be most to the glory of God and the good and peace of the church." The Westminster Confession of Faith was the result of this holy alliance. The General Assembly of the Presbyterian church in these United States say, in their minutes of 1824, in reference to the Westminster Assembly, that "its members were full of the Holy Ghost" when they produced that Confession.

The Baptist Confession of Faith was published in London in 1643, not under the name of a baptist confession, but "of seven congregations in London." "The name of baptist," as is observed by Adams in his History of the Religious World, "is only of modern date and of local application." Anabaptists and anti-paido-baptists had been the usual epithets by which christians who believed that the immersion of believers was baptism, had been called by their opposers. They professedly published the confession of faith for the information and satisfaction of those that did not understand what their principles were or had entertained prejudices against them, and persecuted them, on account of sentiments which they did not entertain.

In their confession they say, "We confess that we know but in part; to show us from the word of God, that which we see not, we shall have cause to be thankful to God and to them. But if any man shall impose upon us any thing that we see not to be commanded by our Lord Jesus Christ, we should, in his strength, rather embrace all reproaches and tortures of men, and if it were possible, to die a thousand deaths, rather than do any thing against the truth of God, or against the light of our own consciences." They did not assume or bear the name of baptists, but professed themselves to be baptized congregations.

Thus I have given a short but just sketch of the origin of the sects and creeds of our country. In my next number I design to address the preachers of all denominations on the subject of CHRISTIAN UNION.

General Smyth and C. Schultze.

A Mr. SCHULTZE, of Virginia, has given a bold challenge to all the clergy in general, and to Bishop Hobart, of New York, in particular, to stand to their arms; for if not, he will publish to the world a treatise " on the doubtful origin of all our miracles, and also all religions, except ancient Theism." This ancient Theism of his is supposed to be the invention of somebody before Moses, whom he represents as a most wicked knave and impostor. We cannot but admire the intrepidity of this strong-minded layman, as he represents himself, who, after forty years' study and twenty years' praying, discovered how Aaron's rod budded and blossomed, and that was by soaking it in warm water or oxyge-

nated muriatic acid, mingled with water, &c. We have no room at present to publish any strictures on a piece of his composition which has appeared in a late Philadelphia paper. But as Mr. Schultze appears a very conscientious Deist, and really a very devout one too, and as he declares his belief to be established in the unity of God, the immortality of the soul, and a future state of rewards and punishments, and has very respectfully challenged the clergy—we, though not included in his general challenge, would promise, if the clergy fail to convince him that he is mistaken, to show that his creed is stolen from the bible; for, according to right reason and common sense, the unity of God, the immortality of the soul, and a future state of rewards and punishments, are not knowable by our five senses, the sole avenues to the human understanding. And we will engage to show, if Mr. Schultze pleases to favor us with his manuscript, (without a penal bond for five thousand dollars for its return, though we will pledge our word to return it if possible,) that he must, on his own principles, renounce his own creed too, and become a downright Atheist, instead of a Theist. And, indeed, there is no man who can stop on this side of pure Atheism who rejects the Christian religion. And this is equivalent to saying that no man can reasonably be a disbeliever of the Christian religion. EDITOR.

No. 4.]   NOVEMBER 7, 1825.
A Narrative of the Origin and Formation of the Westminster or Presbyterian Confession of Faith. No. VI.

THE Parliament, desiring to comprehend the Independents within the new establishment recommended by the Assembly at Westminster, or to give them a full toleration, did, on the 13th of September, 1644, order a grand committee of accommodation to consider the points of difference. The Independents would have stated the points of difference and would have endeavored a compromise while the discipline of the church was pending in the Assembly; but, at that time, the Presbyterians insisted that the new form of government should first pass into a law as a standard, before the exceptions of the Independents should be considered. Upon which they were adjourned by the House of Commons till the affair should be determined in the Assembly; who agreed, April 4, 1645, "that the brethren who had entered their dissent against the Presbyterian government should be a committee to bring in the whole frame of their government in a body, with their grounds and reasons." The Independents desired liberty to bring in their objections by parts as the Presbyterians had done their advices; but this not being admitted, they desired time to perfect their plan before any other scheme passed into a law, but the Presbyterians, without any regard to the compromise, by the assistance of their Scotch friends, pushed the affair to a conclusion in Parliament; upon which the Independents laid aside their own model, and published a remonstrance complaining of the artful conduct of the Assembly; and that the discipline of the church being fixed, it was too late to think of a comprehension.* Thus the Presbyterians jockeyed the Independents, and intrigued their *jus divinum*.

The Parliament saw the mistake, and by their own hands resumed the affair, and revived the committee of accommodation, Nov. 6, 1645.

A committee of the most distinguished Independents, and also of the leading Presbyterians,

---

* Neal, volume 3. page 307.

met several times on the subject of accommodation and toleration. At their last meeting, March 9, the Presbyterian paper in answer to the overtures of the Independents, concluded with these remarkable words—" That whereas their (Independent) brethren say that uniformity ought to be urged no farther than is agreeable to all men's consciences, and to their edification, it seems to them as if their brethren (the Independents) not only desired liberty of conscience for themselves, but for all men, and would have us think that we are bound by our covenant to bring the churches in the three kingdoms to no nearer a conjunction and uniformity than is consistent with the liberty of all men's consciences; which, whether it be the sense of the covenant, we leave with the honorable committee." Hereupon " Jeremiah Burroughs, a divine of great candor and moderation, declared in the name of the Independents, that if their congregations might not be exempted from that coercive power of the classes—if they might not have liberty to govern themselves in their own way, as long as they behave peaceably to the civil magistrate, they were resolved to suffer or go to some other place of the world where they might enjoy their liberty. But while men think there is no way of peace but by forcing all to be of the same mind—while they think the civil sword is an ordinance of God to determine all controversies of divinity, and that it must needs be attended with fines and imprisonments to the disobedient; while they apprehend there is no medium between a strict uniformity and a general confusion of all things; while these sentiments prevail, there must be a base subjection of men's consciences to slavery, a suppression of much truth, and great disturbances in the christian world."

Thus ended the last committee of Lords and Commons and Assembly of Divines for accommodation. Nothing was more detested and abhorred by the majority of the Presbyterians than toleration. The London divines, who often at this time held their meetings at Zion College, and had a synod every Monday to consult in order to aid the Westminster Assembly in carrying their points favorable to their own establishment, and in opposition to any toleration of other sectaries—besought, in a letter of January 15, 1645, the Assembly "to oppose with all their might the great Diana (toleration) of the Independents." In this letter these words are to be found—" Not, say they, that we can harbor the least jealousy of your zeal, fidelity, or industry in the opposing and extirpating of such a root of gall and bitterness as toleration is, and will be both to the present and future ages." The city ministers, in a provincial assembly, Nov. 2, 1749, in a vindication of their beloved presbytery, "represent universal toleration as contrary to godliness, opening a door to libertinism and profaneness, and a tenet to be rejected as soul poison." *

Such was the spirit of the Presbyterians both in and out of the creed-making assembly; and, as Mr. Neal justly observes, this *no toleration* was turned upon themselves by the prelatists in twenty years; so that they who would, and who did shut the gates of toleration and of mercy upon others, had these very gates shut in their own face. Mr. Baxter, tyrannical as he was, lived to deplore the blindness and obstinacy of this assembly upon this subject. His words are, "The Presbyterian ministers were so little sensible of their own infirmities, that they would

* Neal, page 313.
Z

not agree to tolerate those who were not only tolerable, but worthy instruments and members in the churches, prudent men, who were for union in things necessary, for liberty in things unnecessary, and for charity in all; but they could not be heard."

We shall notice but one other act of this assembly, and dismiss them from our view for a while. The Parliament requested them to recommend some other version of the Psalms of David than Sternhold's and Hopkins'. They read over Rouse's version, and, after several amendments, sent it up to the House, Nov. 14, 1645, with the following recommendation: " Whereas the honorable House of Commons, by an order bearing date Nov. 20, 1643, have recommended the Psalms published by Mr. Rouse to the consideration of the Assembly of Divines, the Assembly has caused them to be carefully perused; and as they are now altered and amended, do approve them; and humbly conceive they may be useful and profitable to the church if they be permitted to be publicly sung. Accordingly they were authorized by the two Houses."

Thus we have seen how the Presbyterian Confession of Faith, Solemn League and Covenant, Directory for Public Worship, Form of Discipline, Presbyterian Church Government, and Rouse's version of the Psalms of David, got to be canonical and of divine authotity. And with deep sorrow, too, we have seen that no toleration was the first sprout from this sweet or bitter root. The following items give the whole in miniature :—

1. When king Charles I. sought the assistance of his Catholic subjects in carrying on a war for his own prerogative, the Parliament which opposed him sought the assistance of the Scots nation in resisting his claims.

2. The Scots, prejudiced in favor of Calvinism, through the preaching of Knox and others of the Geneva school, agreed to assist their English neighbors upon condition that they would assist them or unite with them in establishing one creed, one discipline, one ecclesiastical government in both nations.

3. In order to this, it was stipulated that an assembly of divines be called as an ecclesiastical council, to aid the Parliament in settling a religious establishment that would meet the views of the Scots.

4. That the assembly at Westminster was summoned, convened, sworn, instructed, paid, and controlled by this parliament.

5. That the solemn league and covenant was introduced, fashioned, matured, and established by the same divines and parliament.

6. That Rouse's psalms were canonized and legitimized by the same authority.

7. And that the whole ended in religious despotism, tyranny, and *no* toleration. That swords and constables, exiles, confiscation, and death, were the attendants and sanctions of this system.

It is to be hoped that many of the modern Presbyterians have seen the folly of their creed makers, and do lament that such should have been the circumstances which gave birth to their system.   EDITOR.

——————

In presenting our readers with the following extract, we are afraid of being charged with the crime of plagiarism; because it will be remembered that, if we have not used the very words and phrases in some of our public addresses, we have certainly on various occasions, *viva voce*,

194 THE CHRISTIAN BAPTIST. [Vol. III.

and, perhaps, with the pen, too, expressed every idea in the extract, and yet never acknowledged Mr. Locke as our tutor in any instance. Yet, strange as it may appear, we are perfectly innocent of the crime. For, until a few days ago, we had never seen or read one sentence in this work. In preparing for the edition of the New Testament, among other words lately received, this of the justly celebrated Locke came into our hands. It is the 3d edition, published in London, 1733, nearly a century ago. This great layman, commentator, and philosopher, to whom all the British empire and all America are indebted for his essays on Toleration, on the Human Understanding, and on other accounts, did, in our judgment, and in that of the great Dr. Pierce, and many others, make the best effort towards understanding the apostolic epistles ever made since the great apostacy took place. But he was a layman, else he should have been better known and more universally read as a commentator. His praise as a philosopher is commensurate with the English tongue—and, indeed, with modern Europe; but his character as a biblical critic is not so well known, because he had never been consecrated. We publish this extract on account of its intrinsic importance, and to show that some of those views which are said to be peculiarly our own, were entertained a hundred years ago, and concur in showing the necessity of the translation of the New Testament which we are about to publish.
Ed. C. B.

Extract from the Preface to Locke's Paraphrase and Notes on Four of Paul's Epistles.

"To these we may subjoin two external causes that have made no small increase of the native and original difficulties that keep us from an easy and assured discovery of St. Paul's sense, in many parts of his epistles, and those are—

"First. The dividing of them into chapters and verses, as we have done; whereby they are so chopped and minced, and, as they are printed, stand so broken and divided, that not only the common people take the verses usually for distinct aphorisms, but even men of more advanced knowledge, in reading them, lose very much of the strength and force of the coherence, and the light that depends on it. Our minds are so weak and narrow, that they have need of all the helps and assistances that can be procured, to lay before them undisturbedly the thread and coherence of any discourse; by which alone they are truly improved, and led into the genuine sense of the author. When the eye is constantly disturbed with loose sentences, that, by their standing and separation, appear as so many distinct fragments, the mind will have much ado to take in, and carry on in its memory, a uniform discourse of dependent reasonings; especially having from the cradle been used to wrong impressions concerning them, and constantly accustomed to hear them quoted as distinct sentences, without any limitation or explication of their precise meaning from the place they stand in, and the relation they bear to what goes before or follows. These divisions also have given occasion to the reading these epistles by parcels and in scraps, which has farther confirmed the evil arising from such partitions. And I doubt not but every one will confess it to be a very unlikely way to come to the understanding of any other letters, to read them piecemeal, a bit today, and another scrap tomorrow, and so on by broken intervals; especially if the pause and cessation should be made as the chapters the apostle's epistles are divided

into, to end sometimes in the middle of a sentence. It cannot therefore be wondered at, that that should be permitted to be done to Holy Writ, which would visibly disturb the sense and hinder the understanding of any other book whatever. . If Tully's epistles were so printed, and so used, I ask whether they would not be much harder to be understood, less easy and less pleasant to be read by much than now they are?

"How plain soever this abuse is, and what prejudice soever it does to the understanding of the sacred scripture, yet if a bible was printed as it should be, and as the several parts of it were writ, in continued discourses where the argument is continued, I doubt not but the several parties would complain of it as an innovation and a dangerous change in the publishing those holy books. And, indeed, those who are for maintaining their opinions, and the systems of parties by sound of words, with a neglect of the true sense of scripture, would have reason to make and foment the outcry. They would most of them be immediately disarmed of their great magazine of artillery wherewith they defend themselves, and fall upon others. If the Holy Scripture were but laid before the eyes of christians in its due connexion and consistency, it would not then be so easy to snatch out a few words, as if they were separate from the rest, to serve a purpose to which they do not at all belong, and with which they have nothing to do. But as the matter now stands, he that has a mind to it may, at a cheap rate, be a notable champion for the truth; that is, for the doctrines of the sect that chance or interest has cast him into. He need but be furnished with verses of sacred scripture, containing words and expressions that are but flexible (as all general, obscure, and doubtful ones are) and his system that has appropriated them to the orthodoxy of his church, makes them immediately strong and irrefragable arguments for his opinion. This is the benefit of loose sentences and scripture crumbled into verses, which quickly turn into independent aphorisms. But if the quotation in the verse produced were considered as a part of a continued, coherent discourse, and so its sense were limited by the tenor of the context, most of these forward and warm disputants would be quite stripped of those which they doubt not now to call spiritual weapons; and they would have often nothing to say that would not shew their weakness and manifestly fly in their faces. I crave leave to set down a saying of the learned and judicious Mr. Selden:—'In interpreting the scripture,' says he, 'many do as if a man should see one have ten pounds, which he reckoned by 1, 2, 3, 4, 5, 6, 7, 8, 9, 10, meaning 4 was but four units, and 5 five units, &c. and that he had in all but ten pounds. The other that sees him, takes not the figures together, as he does, but picks here and there; and thereupon reports that he had five pounds in one bag, and six pounds in another bag, and nine pounds in another bag, &c. when as, in truth, he has but ten pounds in all. So we pick out a text here and there to make it serve our turn; whereas, if we take it all together, and consider what went before and what followed, we find it meant no such thing.'"

A Restoration of the Ancient Order of Things.
No. IX.
On the Breaking of Bread.—No. IV.

I do not aim at prolixity, but at brevity, in discussing the various topics which are necessary to be introduced into this work. We are not desirous to shew how much may be said on this or

24

any other subject, but to shew how little is necessary to establish the truth, and to say much in a few words. We shall not, then, dwell any longer on the scriptural authority for the weekly breaking of bread; but for the sake of those who are startled at what they call innovation, we shall adduce a few historical facts and incidents. We lay no stress upon what is no better than the traditions of the church, or upon the testimony of those called the *primitive* fathers, in settling any part of christian worship or christian obedience. Yet, when the scriptures are explicit upon any topic which is lost sight of in modern times, it is both gratifying and useful to know how the practice has been laid aside and other customs been substituted in its room.— There is, too, a corroborating influence in authentic history, which, while it does not authorize any thing as of divine authority, it confirms the conviction of our duty in things divinely established, by observing how they were observed and how they were laid aside.

All antiquity concurs in evincing that for the three first centuries all the churches broke bread once a weak. Pliny, in his Epistles, book 10th; Justin Martyr, in his Second Apology for the Christians; and Tertullian, De Ora. p. 135, testify that it was the universal practice in all the weekly assemblies of the brethren, after they had prayed and sang praises—"then bread and wine being brought to the chief brother, he takes it and offers praise and thanksgiving to the Father, in the name of the Son and the Holy Spirit. After prayer and thanksgiving the whole assembly says, Amen. When thanksgiving is ended by the chief guide, and the consent of the whole people, the deacons (as we call them) give to every one present part of the bread and wine, over which thanks are given."

The weekly communion was preserved in the Greek church till the seventh century; and, by one of their canons, "such as neglected three weeks together were excommunicated."—*Erskine's Dissertations*, p. 271.

In the fourth century, when all things began to be changed by baptized Pagans, the practice began to decline. Some of the councils in the western part of the Roman empire, by their canons, strove to keep it up. The council held at Illiberis in Spain, A. D. 324, decreed that "no offerings should be received from such as did not receive the Lord's Supper."—*Council Illi. canon* 28.

The council at Antioch, A. D. 341, decreed that "all who came to church, and heard the scriptures read, but afterwards joined not in prayer, and receiving the sacrament, should be cast out of the church till such time as they gave public proof of their repentance."—*Council Ant. canon* 2.

All these canons were unable to keep a carnal crowd of professors in a practice for which they had no spiritual taste; and, indeed, it was likely to get out of use altogether. To prevent this, the council of Agatha, in Languedoc, A. D. 506, decreed "that none should be esteemed good christians who did not *communicate* at least three times a year—at Christmas, Easter, and Whitsunday." *Coun. Agatha, canon* 18. This soon became the standard of a good christian, and it was judged presumptuous to commune oftener.

Things went on in this way for more than six hundred years, until they got tired of even *three* communications in one year; and the infamous council of Lateran, which decreed auricular confession and transubstantiation, decreed that

"an annual communion at Easter was sufficient." This association of the "sacrament" with Easter, and the mechanical devotion of the ignorant at this season, greatly contributed to the worship of the Host. *Bingham's Ori. B.* 15. c. 9. Thus the breaking of bread in simplicity and godly sincerity once a week, degenerated into a pompous sacrament once a year at Easter.

At the Reformation this subject was but slightly investigated by the reformers. Some of them, however, paid some attention to it. Even Calvin, in his *Ins. lib.* 4. chap. 17. 46. says:— "And truly this custom, which enjoins communicating once a year, is a most evident contrivance of the Devil, by whose instrumentality soever it may have been determined."

And again, (*Ins. lib.* 6. chap. xviii. sec 46.) he says:—"It ought to have been far otherwise. Every week, at least, the table of the Lord should have been spread for christian assemblies, and the promises declared, by which, in partaking of it, we might be spiritually fed."

Martin Chemnitz, Witsius, Calderwood, and others of the reformers and controversialists, concur with Calvin; and, indeed, almost every commentator on the New Testament, concurs with the Presbyterian Henry in these remarks on Acts xx. 7. "In the primitive times it was the custom of many churches to receive the Lord's Supper every Lord's day."

The Belgic reformed church, in 1581, appointed the supper to be received every other month. The reformed churches of France, after saying that they had been too remiss in observing the supper but four times a year, advise a greater frequency. The church of Scotland began with four sacraments in a year; but some of her ministers got up to twelve times. Thus things stood till the close of the last century.

Since the commencement of the present century, many congregations in England, Scotland, Ireland, and some in the United States and Canada, both Independents and Baptists, have attended upon the supper every Lord's day, and the practice is every day gaining ground.

These historical notices may be of some use to those who are ever and anon crying out *Innovation! Innovation!* But we advocate the principle and the practice on apostolic grounds alone. Blessed is that servant who, knowing his master's will, does it with expedition and delight.

Those who would wish to see an able refutation of the Presbyterian mode of observing the sacrament, and a defence of weekly communion, would do well to read Dr. John Mason's Letters on frequent Communion, who is himself a high-toned Presbyterian, and, consequently, his remarks will be more regarded by his brethren than mine.   EDITOR.

———

Paraphrase on Rom. VIII. 7—25.—By Request.

The proposition which the apostle has in design to enforce, is that contained in the last clause of verse 17. viz. "If we believing Jews and Gentiles suffer, without apostacy, the bodily afflictions incident to our obeying the Lord, as he suffered the afflictions attendant on his humiliation, we shall be glorified with him at the resurrection of the just, at which time we shall be fully revealed as the adopted sons of God."

For my part, says Paul, I do not esteem the afflictions of our bodies in the present life as worthy to be compared with the glory that shall be exhibited in us at the resurrection of our bodies from the grave. For such is the transcendant glory to be revealed in us, that the earnest desire of the believing Jew and Gentile looks in hope for the manifestations of the sons of God in their glorified bodies, in which they will appear in character as the adopted sons of God. For the believing Jew and Gentile, as respects the body, were, in consequence of one man's sin, subjected to corruption in the grave; not, indeed, with their own consent; but they now cheerfully submit their bodies to the dust of death because God has subjected them to it, in hope that these mortal bodies shall be liberated from the bondage of corruption in the grave, and introduced into the freedom of the glorious immortality of the children of God. Besides, we know that bodily suffering is not exclusively the lot of christians, for the whole human race groan together and travail in pain even yet with all their efforts to escape these evils. And not only the unbelieving Jew and Gentile, but ourselves, who, by faith in Jesus, are become the sons of God, who have the chief and most exalted gifts of the Holy Spirit, even we ourselves groan within ourselves, anxiously waiting for the full adoption of the sons of God; namely, the redemption of our bodies from the grave at the resurrection of the just. For we are sustained in these bodily sufferings in hope of this glorious resurrection. Now you know, O Romans! that hope which has obtained its object is not hope; for what a man sees, how can he hope for it? But if we hope for that which we do not see, then we patiently wait for it, as is the case with respect to the resurrection and glorification of our bodies.

To the Editor of the Christian Baptist.

Mr. Campbell—As different persons understand the same expressions very differently, so it happens in my neighborhood with the readers of the *Christian Baptist*, until it is at length agreed to refer to you for your real meaning on one point, with regard to which many are very tenacious.

The fact is just this, that while I cannot, for certainty, see any thing to fault in what you have advanced (so far as I have happened to see and read) but much to admire and approve, being long since convinced that all those hireling preachers and high-flying professors with them, who are so hand-and-glove with the world that they bear none of that persecution, hatred, and odium, which Christ promised as the sure and inevitable lot and portion of all his true followers—I say, while I am fully convinced that these are not the true and real followers of Christ, in that strait and narrow way pointed out by him, many think otherwise for want of knowing and duly considering those well pointed truths in proof of it, which you are gradually furnishing, and which, I trust in God, will in the end be attended with great moral good.

A religious Archimedes has long been wanted to raise the moral world from its chaotic darkness as to true and abstract religion.

But, sir, many think that you go too far, and condemn all, because (like or as a man of true and accurate science and extensive erudition) you do not, as such ones cannot, agree fully and exactly with any one of the sects—because, say they, you seem to condemn all the sects, except perhaps the society of the Friends, called Quakers; and that you seem rather to bear on them, by suggesting that revelation is full (by which I understand you to confine your ideas essentially to scripture revelation, or the like,) whereas they avow a belief that they are, by times, under the monitions of the Spirit, which I am inclined to believe of some of them, except when they, like others, run into the heathenish and unscriptural practice of making long public prayers, which my bible wholly condemns—neither can I believe that the Spirit of God ever taught any thing so totally unreasonable and absurd. However, to do them justice, I think that they do not make so long prayers, full of "vain repetitions," and pompous dictatorial matter.

But, sir, if you should utterly deny all the monitions of the Spirit and every kind of revelation in our times, then we should certainly be at issue on that point. For I fully believe that, in this respect, God is the same, to his true and faithful followers, at least, as he was in the days of Abraham, Isaac and Jacob, Joseph and others, and that he still, by times, reveals certain things to some men and women, and points out to their understandings certain things which are, and things which shall come to pass—I say, I believe this, because my experience has proved it; because I have, several times in my life, been advised of things to come, in such a way and manner, and upon such a particular crisis, that it seemed impossible for me to mistake what was intended.

And though these monitory impressions of something to come, were several times limited to things most improbable and unlikely to take place, still they never once failed. Also, being generally accompanied with an impression that I must heed, mind, or remember them, as things which would certainly take place in due time, I was therefore generally quite unable to doubt of them for a moment of time.

I have judged these monitions as coming directly from Deity, because I think that no one else knows all things to come, and is also friendly enough to advise us of them beforehand.

To conclude, sir, let me plead for the rights of conscience and opinion, especially for the society of Friends; for, if our Saviour's words are verified at all, by any people, it must be allowed to be by them—I mean in what he said to his followers, when arraigned for their opinions and preaching; and whereon he commanded them not to meditate what they should answer, or what they should say, adding that he would give them words and arguments which none of their adversaries should be able to gainsay or resist. If this promise can be consistently extended to any of his followers of latter times, it would seem to me to be most applicable to them, because their opponents cannot refute their arguments—they cannot hold way with them in dispute upon scripture ground (see their evasive excuses upon Berkely and other of their writers,) and therefore have had recourse to civil power to crush and silence them, just as your opposers would now silence you, if they could, by the same means, and for the very self-same reasons; namely, because they cannot hold out a fair argument with you, either upon scriptural or philosophic ground, right reason or common sense.

It is for this reason, sir, that priestcraft is at its very wit's end, and in the very raving paroxysms of desperation, for fear of the loss of its empire over the understandings of the multitude. It fears that people will begin to use their brains properly, and to think and reflect on the nonsense of their arrogant pretensions, as though God had given them a power which mortal never had, namely, to be the real and efficient cause of the salvation of others, which would leave this plain and horrid inference as an inevitable result, namely, that if by their presence and exertions many souls would actually be saved, that it is hence most clearly and fairly deducible, that, by their absence or remissness, many souls would be lost. This, although not perceived by many truly honest and religious minded persons (who are therefore zealous to send missionaries out to all the world) is a most horrid and abominable doctrine. For as such circumstances depend on the providence of God, which has not left it to any one to choose in what age and place he should be born, so as to have a religious education and an able and faithful teacher, therefore it refers back the whole blame on Deity and his providence for all that are supposed to be lost in that way; and which, therefore, as a Mr. Witherell justly remarks, in a like case, makes God more cruel than the Devil can possibly be, because the Devil has not power thus to plan and execute the loss and destruction of nearly all, thus unconditionally, as to any thing in their power to fix, control, or alter in the least degree.

Christ said, "Follow me, and I will make you fishers of men;" but he has no where told us, as I understand, that these same men would otherwise be lost; for this would reflect great injustice upon God and his providence, which is said to notice even the little sparrow.

Again we read, that "they who turn many to righteousness shall shine as the stars for evermore;" by which I understand that they who are the willing and faithful instruments of God's providence, in this way, shall, in due time, reap the just reward of all their labors and exertions.

But I must not enlarge much, because it is quite an incorrigible task to undertake to make the multitude see that every genuine religious tenet must have fair reason as well as scripture for its support.

And again, because I think that right reason and scripture, and the obvious character of Deity, fully warrants the idea that he would be disposed to reveal certain things, in some peculiar cases, directly to mortals like us; and that he accordingly does reveal them, while on my part I may not be able to make people see it to be so, any better than I can make them see and believe that, according to scripture and reason, God is far too just to ever let or suffer one single soul to be ultimately lost, because, in his providence, no christian professor was ever sent to teach and instruct it. Or, again, any better than I can make them see and understand that, although the things taught by the preacher may be, as the scripture says of good works, "good and profitable to men," yet that they never can be the entire and efficient cause of their salvation.

AN OCCASIONAL READER.

—

To " An Occasional Reader."

DEAR SIR,—ALL that I know of God, and I believe all that can be known of him, is from the revelation he has given us. If, without a revelation from himself, men could have known his existence or his character, a written record or a verbal representation of himself was superfluous. And if, without the revelation, he can be known, they who have it not are just in as good circumstances as we, if not in better. I cordially embrace and cheerfully subscribe the aphorism of Paul, which affirms that the world by its philosophy knows not God. This is not only an article of my faith, but an item of my experience. Is any child born with innate ideas of God? Do we not see that they must all be taught his being and perfections? Where is the nation which knows him without a written revelation or some remnants of tradition originally derived from the bible? These questions I do not propose to you as if you were of a contrary opinion; but to enforce the truth that all that is known or knowable of God is derived either directly or indirectly from his verbal communications to men—and aided by these, the heavens declare his glory, and the earth proclaims his goodness, and every thing in the universe pays its tribute to the bible. So long, then, as I believe the bible to be from God, so long I must believe it to be a perfect revelation—not perfect in the absolute sense of the word, for this would not suit us any more than Paul's communicating revelations which he had in the third heavens; but it is perfect as adapted to man in his present circumstances. Many things are only hinted, not fully revealed; and while here we must see as through a glass darkly, but in another state we shall have a revelation of his glory which will be perfectly adapted to us in those circumstances; but even then that revelation will not be absolutely perfect, for a revelation absolutely perfect would make God as well known to his creatures as he is to himself, which I would humbly say appears to me impossible.

As to those monitions and impressions of which you speak, I know some things certainly, and I conjecture others. The bible tells me that communications, monitions, and impressions have been made upon the minds of men in dreams, visions, trances, &c. yet the knowledge of salvation was not communicated in this way. It would have been as easy, by a dream or a monition of the Spirit, as you speak, to have made Cornelius and his friends acquainted with the salvation of Jesus Christ, as to have vouchsafed the vision to Cornelius and to Peter. Yet this was not done, because not agreeable to the divine mind, who sees not as man sees. When there appeared to have been a necessity for communications of this kind they were not made. And now that the revelation is completed and given to us with awful sanctions, and the most tremendous threats against innovators, and against those who either add to it or diminish from it; it is as absurd to expect such monitions as it is to trust in dreams and visions. This far may be known with certainty. With regard to impressions and monitions now made on the human mind respecting passing events, either when the body is asleep or awake, we have heard much, experienced something, and know nothing. I once ventured to predict a future event from a dream which I then believed would come to pass, and which did actually come to pass contrary to any expectation derived from things known. But what of this? How many such things would be necessary to form a systematic theory? It might be conjectured that, as angels are ministering spirits, employed by him that rules over all and knows all things, in performing their respective missions, they do impress the mind of those to whom they minister, and sometimes preadmonish them of future events. But again, others are punished, as was Pilate's wife, by such impressions; and many, if not most of these monitions, are useless, as the persons premonished cannot make any use of them; for this would destroy their character as predictions, which necessarily are unconditional. So that after all, our wisest and happiest course is to attend on the written monitions of the Spirit; for however we may amuse ourselves with speculating upon the subject, we must be ignorant of them until we know what sort of an intercourse exists between embodied and disembodied spirits, which we can never attain to in this state. All the light we have or can have is as useless as the feeble ray that finds its way through a small aperture into a cell—it neither enlightens, warms, or cheers the solitary prisoner. Let us then attend to the certain prophetic word, as to a light that shines in a dark place, until the full splendor of heavenly light bursts upon our spirits when disencumbered with these clay tenements. Of these remarks it may be said, they are more amusing than instructive.   EDITOR.

Anecdote.

DURING a late revival at Camillus, New-York, a man who had been sprinkled in his infancy wished to be baptized and join the Presbyterian church. The Presbyterian divines would not baptize him, because he had been sprinkled. The Baptists would not immerse him, because he wanted to join the Presbyterians. At length a new sort of christians, called "Smithites," immersed him. He then joined the Presbyterians. The church was satisfied with his sprinkling, and he with his immersion.

No. 5.]   DECEMBER 5, 1825.
Notes on a Tour.

WE have been in the practice of making pretty extensive tours for the last three years, with a special reference to gaining correct information on the actual condition of the religious communities in this extensive and prosperous country. We have both read and travelled in quest of information, and have found additional proofs that there is a great difference between reading geography and travelling over the surface of a country; between hearing of, and seeing the religious world; between viewing men and things with our own eyes, and looking at them through the media of books and newspapers; between contemplating society in the closet, and mingling with it in actual operation. We have been long convinced that to live to purpose in any society, it is necessary to be well acquainted with the state of that society; it is necessary, in a certain sense, "to catch the living manners as they rise." Man is a creature incessantly developing himself—perpetually exhibiting new and strange appearances. And while it is true that, "as in water face answers to face, so does the heart of man to man," it is equally certain that the varied year and the ever-shifting scenery of the heavens and the earth are but emblems of the changes continually exhibiting in human society.

Society is continually in a progressive state. It is either advancing in intelligence and virtue, or marching downwards in ignorance and vice. Regardless of the spirit and character of this age and of this great community, many are for holding the people down to the standards of the 16th and 17th centuries. Hence we find the creeds and forms that suited the age and circumstances of our ancestors, cotemporary with Charles I. bound with new rivets on the necks of our countrymen. This is not more absurd than to oblige men to wear the apparel which suited them when boys, and to compel men when they have no taste for the pranks and amusements of children, to go through all the forms.

We are happy to find that, in spite of the reigning doctors of traditions, the people are gradually awaking to a sense of their religious rights and privileges. We find a large majority of most religious communities are quite unsettled in their views of religious principles and practices. They have lost the greater part of that confidence of being the most reformed christians, and the wisest in the world, which was the characteristic of every sect some quarter of a century ago. Many who thought their church almost infallible, now readily admit that she not only may, but that she actually does, frequently err. And there is a spirit of inquiry marching forth, before which, most assuredly, the rotten systems of tradition and error must and will fall.

We learn, however, from experience, as well as from books, that the human mind is prone to extremes in all circumstances. We see when men have been long enslaved in church or state, they become anarchists in both. Tyranny and anarchy, if not themselves opposites, are, in this respect, the extremes of certain principles and practices. When a tyrant is dethroned, and his vassals liberated, he finds his quietus in a guillotine, and they convert his palaces into towers and strong holds for each other in rotation. So in the church. They who call the Pope Antichrist, and renounce any successor of St. Peter, set themselves up as Popes, and thus a whole congregation of protesters become a college of cardinals, and they will have no Pope because each one wishes to be Pope himself. Democrats in politics, and Independents in religion, are not unfrequently the greatest tyrants in the world. I am a democrat because I love kingly power, and dont like to part with it to other hands. And you are an Independent because you like papal supremacy, and wish to have your share in full. I only mean to say (for I am called a democrat and an Independent) that such is the issue of both, if not closely watched and constantly guarded.

There is anarchy in the church as surely as there is anarchy in the state, and mutinies and insurrections are not confined to sailors and soldiers. My friend Thomas Biblicus, in every sect of which he was a member, and he had been a member of at least four, always opposed every appearance of tyranny in the priests and rulers of the congregations of which he was a member, and was ever and anon talking against his ecclesiastic ruler and priest, and declaiming loud and long on the liberties of the children of God. Finally he became an Independent, and was called to become the president of the meeting, and soon became a full grown despot that could bear no contradiction, and aimed at absolute power in the church.

James Libertas, too, an old acquaintance, eternally declaimed against creeds as impositions on men's consciences, and yet he was always employed in imposing his own opinions upon his brethren, and frittered the society of which he was a member to nothing, by multiplying non-conformists at every meeting. Indeed, many are praising the life they will never lead, and condemning others for their own sins. My cousin, William Puritan, was always lamenting that he never heard "a sermon preached" against evil speaking, and was always telling what evil things his brethren were saying of one another, and yet he always concluded his remarks by observing, that while so many indulged in evil speaking, he must call them all hypocrites and railers.

In my late tour of a thousand miles I was reminded of what I had before discovered, that religious sects and forms cover the earth as the different sorts of timber the soil. In one place it is all oak; in another, all pine; in no place all hickory; in some places every sort of timber. Here it is all Presbyterian, and Methodist underwood; there it is all Methodist, and Presbyterian underwood. Here it is all Baptist, and there it is.all sorts. Here some bend before they break, and there some break before they bend. I often asked myself, Is this all nature and that all grace? Or is it nature that covers this soil with Baptists, and grace that covers that with Presbyterians? Here Calvinism reigns predominant, and there Arminianism. On one side of the hill they pray to be kept from Arminian errors; on the other side, from Calvinistic errors. To tell a man in one county that he is an Arminian, is to traduce him; to tell him in another that he is a Calvinist, is no honor to him. Again I asked myself, Is this nature or grace? Upon the whole, I discover that many are Calvinists in the things pertaining to the next world, but Arminians in the things pertaining to this. They believe that all things in the next world will be as decreed; but in this they believe that men are rich or poor, honorable or base, according to their works.

Among the strangest occurrences which I witnessed, I note the fact that I visited three associations this fall, having no written creed other than the scriptures of the apostles, and disclaiming any jurisdiction over the churches; they met, had a social interview, and parted without a quarrel. This, indeed, was to me a strange occurrence; for it is almost impossible to assemble half a dozen of teachers of any sect, and to keep good friends for one day.

But one of the most prominent signs of the times, and one of the most significant, I cannot close these desultory remarks without noticing. It is this: The people every where have an insatiable appetite for sound doctrine. They eat whole sermons after sermons, and run after this and that preacher for sound doctrine, and are as hungry as before. Is he sound—is he sound in the faith? This is the all important question, on the solution of which depends the character of the preacher for orthodoxy or heterodoxy—and his reputation is all in all to him. The preachers too generally labor all their lives to die with the reputation of having been great and orthodox preachers; and the people follow them up to hear sound doctrine, to sit as jurors upon their views and abilities, and to bring in a verdict, which, if true, makes them good christians, and the preacher either great or little, sound or unsound in the faith. "But, worse than all, and most to be deplored," sound doctrine is made, like charity, to cover a multitude of sins. One man gets drunk: he is arraigned before the bar of the church: he confesses his fault, and apologizes for it by a dogma of sound doctrine, viz. he is not his own keeper. He is pardoned. This is a sample of the use and importance of sound doctrine. Errors of opinion become in many places the cause of ecclesiastical degradation and of exclusion from the church, while immoralities are overlooked and ascribed to the "remaining corruptions" of human nature. Errors in opinion are treated as felons, while immoralities are indulged as a wayward child, the darling of his mother. This is not so much a sectarian peculiarity, as it is the characteristic of the times. It would be of infinite importance to the religious community and to the rising generation, if, from the teacher's chair, in the church, and in every christian family, less was said about this sound doctrine, and the time occupied therein devoted to recommending, enforcing, and practising that "holiness without which no man shall see the Lord."

                                             EDITOR.

_____

Conscience.—No. I.

THERE is a proposition in proof of which a thousand arguments and facts can be adduced. It is the following: _Throughout christendom every man's religious experience corresponds with his religious education._ If any ambiguity rests upon this proposition, it arises not from the terms in which it is laid down, but from the religious systems we have received. This will be removed by a minute attention to what has passed and is now passing in our own minds, and under our own observation amongst men.

One fact will throw much light on this subject. It is this: All those feelings, sensibilities, experience, called religious, begin with the conscience. Conscience is, by the popular philosophers in morals and religion, called the moral sense. Admitting the name as a correct one, it follows that, without conscience, or this moral sense, a man can have no more religious apprehension, feeling, or sensibility, than a blind man can have of colors, or a deaf man of sounds.

But to adapt the above proposition to every apprehension, let it be noted that all systems lay down a consciousness or a conviction of sin or guilt, as previous to repentance and conversion—as the commencement of all true experience. Now in this, conscience is concerned, as all must admit; and this is all that is necessary to prove that all religious feeling, experience, sensibility, or whatever men may please to call it, begins with the conscience. Now if it can be proved that the consciences of men vary according to their education, our proposition is easily proved—that every man's religious experience corresponds with his religious education.

A B feels guilty, or his conscience accuses him of sin, if he eat pork on Friday, or beef during lent. Whereas C D can eat fish, flesh, or fowl, whenever he is hungry and can be so fortunate as to get it, without the least sensibility of guilt, or conviction of sin. It must be admitted in this case and in ten thousand parallel ones, that there is a deep sense of guilt in the breast of A B, and none in the heart of C D, and that a difference of religious education is the cause or reason of this variety of conscience and diversity of religious experience.

E F is convicted of guilt because his children have not been baptized—because he has not dedicated them to the Lord in baptism; and G H could not and dare not have his baptized for the same reason that E F feels guilty in not doing it—because he thinks it a sin.

J K will not be baptized himself in water—his conscience will not permit him; because water baptism is done away as a work of the flesh. L M would feel guilty to commune with N O, the Baptist, and N O would feel guilty to commune with L M, the Presbyterian. In fine, we might go on to show that there are as many consciences as sects, but it is superfluous; enough is said to show that every man's conscience is formed and varies from another according to his education.

Many I know very improperly call convictions of sin, sensibility of guilt, and all the commotions of mind, perturbation and confusion through which they pass, and of which they are conscious—I say, they call it all christian experience. But in so doing, they make Turks, Jews, and Pagans Christians; for all have these religious sensibilities and experiences of which we speak. Infidels themselves have consciences; they fear and tremble though they do not believe, as demons. The conflicts, agonies, remorse, doubts, fears, horrors, reformations, penances, often

                                                       29

christened and confirmed as christian experience, have no christianity about them. Men that are not christians experience such things. Love, joy, peace, long suffering, gentleness, goodness, fidelity, meekness, temperance, are the fruits of God's Spirit in the hearts of christians.

A man may put out his own eyes, and stop his own ears, and he may sear his own conscience; but all men have some religious sensibility about them at one period or other—they have a conscience which accuses or excuses, according to their education; and doubts, fears, agonies—hopes and joys too, originate, proceed, and terminate according to their moral sense.

There are some monstrous or unnatural consciences which we can reduce to no system. If we were to attempt it, however, we should fail altogether, unless we could bring them to quadrate with a monstrous or unnatural education. Of this kind is the conscience of X Y W. X could not admit a Methodist preacher into his meeting-house and pulpit, but he could conscientiously admit a theatrical exhibition of folly, vanity, and vice into it, and sit, look on, and laugh at it. Y could not conscientiously, on the Sabbath, go to hear a moral and conscientious teacher of what is called free grace, because of his views of the atonement; and yet he could sit in his house all the Sabbath day and revile his religious neighbors; and on Monday lie and cheat if his interest required it. W debarred all from his communion table who would frequent plays and theatrical exhibitions, and yet he wrote several farces himself, and taught his students to act them in *propria forma.* He debarred all those who were guilty of occasionally hearing any other preacher than himself and his brother field marshals, and yet he could allow his people to hear and read plays and romances without ecclesiastic censure. In short, I see so much of this sort of conscience, as to induce some doubts whether those people have not seared their consciences altogether, and to have arrived at that state which is called by an apostle "past feeling." If they have any qualms of conscience, they are like the pulsations of a dying man or the last throes of a slaughtered ox.

But I find myself digressing from my subject, and shall have to postpone the further illustration of the proposition with which I set out till my next. EDITOR.

Review of " Remarks on the Rise, Use, and Unlawfulness of Creeds and Confessions of Faith in the Church of God—By John M. Duncan, Pastor of the Presbyterian Church, Tammany Street, Baltimore."—Part First.

I SINCERELY lament the one sided zeal and squint eyed piety of our religious polemics on the subject of Mr. Duncan's book. Dr. Miller, of Princeton notoriety, published a short pamphlet in support of creeds, traditions, and clerical domination, which had for its passport into the hands of the laity, the combined influence of the whole theological school at Princeton, the heads of all the Presbyterian departments, and the priestly presses of the religious editors of that denomination. It was extolled by the ambitious clergy, recommended by the itinerants, extracted and eulogized by the Presbyterian editors, sold by book sellers, presidents of colleges, and ruling elders, lent by all the superstitious, and bestowed by the zealots of all the Presbyterian ranks. But Mr. Duncan's book, abounding with good sense; dressed in an elegant style; replete with sound logic; clear, forcible, and all persuasive in argu-

ment, exhibiting a happy alliance of reason, history, and revelation in establishing his views; and breathing a spirit, humble, affectionate, and pious—finds its way without any of Dr. Miller's auxiliaries. Not an editor, not a priest, high or low, to recommend it, and in the western country scarcely a bookseller to attempt to sell it. This is, however, just what I would have expected. The same spirit that prompted my neighbor, the president of Canonsburgh, to cram one of Dr. Miller's pamphlets into the pocket of every student that had room for it on any condition, prompts him, and all the lovers of the reigning ecclesiastics, to be as silent as the grave on Mr. Duncan's *unanswerable* performance. I say unanswerable; for I hesitate not to affirm that amongst all the advocates of creeds on this continent, not one can fairly meet and even plausibly answer the arguments in this book—It is consoling to observe, that notwithstanding the well concerted opposition of the lordly keepers of the keys of intelligence and consciences of the laity, this book is, by its own merit, and the majesty of its strength, commanding the attention, and enlightening the minds of many. I have only to subtract one single item from an unrestricted recommendation of this book, to all in the pulpit and out of it, as a book every way adapted to conciliate the attention, and to illuminate the mind of every reader; and that item is one in which few, if any, of the populars, will agree with me—It is this;—a number of scriptures are quoted in it, and applied in the popular sense. This, however, gives it more force with the populars, and will be regretted only by those who are laboring to affix the same ideas to the words and sentences in the New Testament, which the penmen attached to them. Perhaps Mr. Duncan, in thus quoting them, intended an " *argumentum ad hominem.*"

Although the subject of this book is to me now a trite one, and one which has become stale, the writer of it now standing in the same predicament, and with the same views, in which I found myself about a dozen years ago, I read it with both profit and delight. It caused me to do what Paul did when he met with his brethren at Appii Forum and the Three Taverns; " He thanked God and took courage."

I am happy to find that Mr. Duncan is not the only Presbyterian who has the same views on the subject of his book. He is not the only one who teaches his hearers and his readers that creeds, confessions of faith, and ecclesiastical courts are all human institutions, and unlawful. That the Bible is perfectly adapted to all the ends and intentions of its author. He is not alone. There are several other members of the general assembly, who accord with his sentiments, and will unite with him in his efforts to liberate the people from the influence and thraldom of human creeds and church courts. Before giving a few extracts from this book I have only to express my desires and my hopes that Mr. Duncan, and all of the same views, may carry out their sentiments and arguments to their legitimate issue; and exhibit as ably in their lives, as he has in his views, that consistency which has in times past, and will in all time to come, be the greatest ornament of character, and the most convincing evidence that the disciples of Christ are all taught by God.

We simply give a few of the sentiments of the writer without entering into his proof, to give our readers an idea of the work.

In page 4 he expresses a just view of this age. —"All the world is in commotion; or, if not

30

roused, is waiting in awful suspense for what tomorrow may bring forth. The human mind is in search of something which it has not yet learned to define:—It is the simplicity of the gospel of Christ."

To the same purpose he says, page 23.—"That a change, and a very great change too, is coming, Dr. G. himself believes; and so does every christian who has read his bible. God forbid that we should be disappointed; for, really, ecclesiastical matters are, at present, most terribly distracted."

The author characterizes the times very correctly and beautifully, by telling what he has been made to feel. Page 36.—"We feel, that we cannot disown the supreme authority of our fathers, and determine to think for ourselves, without provoking the displeasure of professing christians. We feel, that we cannot furnish illustrations of evangelical truth, framed according to our own best conceptions; and modified to meet the peculiarities of the day in which we live, as far as we apprehend those peculiarities; without incurring the heaviest censure, under a gratuitous assumption that we are not " walking in the footsteps of the flock." We feel, that we cannot whisper a doubt as to the theological views of divines of " the olden time," or review the crude notions of our youth by the severer thoughts of maturer years, without finding our change to be our reproach, in the estimation of thousands whose good opinion we value. We feel, that to abandon that mode of scriptural exposition, which makes every text to utter some Calvinistic or Arminian dogma; and to exchange it for that which brings up every conscience to the bar of divine revelation, to answer for itself; or which pours the full radiance of the bible over the individual and social habits of men; is to subject ourselves to be reviled for a breach of ordination vows. These things we have been made to feel: and we cannot resist the testimony of our senses. The doctrines of our forefathers have been constituted, in practical life, the rules of our faith. We must have their ideas, their terms, their intellectual associations; every thing must be consecrated by antiquity, or we are not orthodox. Once more we ask, Who would not labor to redeem society from such mental servitude? Who can suppose that he has too much to sacrifice, to bring men back to God, and to induce them to think for themselves, as if they had a mind and conscience of their own.

In page 12 he acquaints us with his design of writing.—"I write for truth, not for victory; and to demonstrate to the public, that some good reasons exist for my scruples on the subject of creeds and confessions. No man, who has a good cause to manage, has any need to grow vulgar, and descend to personalities; or if he does, he is a feeble advocate, and his cause would succeed much better without him. At the same time, it would be carrying the rules of politeness too far, to require a writer to enfeeble his argument, or not to give it all the force which the circumstances of his subject demanded. On these terms the principles of Dr. M's lecture shall be fairly controverted in the following pages; for I verily believe that he is erroneous, and very erroneous too, in what he has advanced, and that the sentence of heresy is not due to those to whom he awards it."

In page 25 he admits the views ascribed to him in the following words:—"I do not deny the views which are ascribed to me: that is to say, I am an undisguised advocate of the follow-

ing truths:—That God *alone* is Lord of conscience, and that his bible is the *only* rule of faith and practice: Or, if the reader pleases, that church courts and human creeds or confessions are not entitled, in any shape whatever, to control the human conscience."

In page 91 he places himself under the banners of the motto which designates this paper. "We are to call no man or body of men, Master on earth. One is our Master, even Christ. His word is the sole standard by which, as christians, or as churches, we must stand or fall. Happy will it be for us, if we can appeal to the Great Searcher of hearts, that we have not followed the traditions and inventions of men, but the sure word of prophecy, which is given to us to be a light to our feet, and a lamp to our path, to guide us in the way of peace."

In page 101 we have the true philosophy of the difference between primitive and modern christianity.—"We believe, that thus the primitive church did actually live in purity and peace, and that her purity was never corrupted, nor her peace destroyed, until the idea of ecclesiastical power had maddened and degraded her sons and daughters; and led them to substitute human for divine law. We believe, that the whole world is, at this present moment, aiming at a return to the principles and habits of original simplicity, in political, as well as ecclesiastical matters; and that all the political and ecclesiastical powers on earth, cannot prevent the changes which have commenced their reforming and revolutionizing process."—This is not more bold than true.

From page 109 to page 112 he adduces five facts that explode Doctor Miller's theory of ancient human creeds. Of these I can adduce but one as a specimen, page 108.—"The *second* fact is, that synods and councils, whose province it is to form these authoritative rules, did not appear in the christian church until the middle of the second century; were a pure human contrivance, when they did appear; and did nothing but mischief, by interfering with the immensely important, and greatly chequered, interests of christendom, which they were not qualified to manage."

In opening the pages of Mosheim, which he does to great effect against Dr. Miller's views, he pays the following pretty compliment, *en passant*, to such creeds as the Westminster, page 119.—" It is altogether a mistake to suppose, that these ecclesiastical documents, are unsuspected, and untreacherous guardians of truth. They never protected truth nor promoted unity; they never gave health to the church's soul, nor grace and beauty to the church's form; they never hushed contention, nor reconciled conflicting opinions, since they were first introduced. They do none of these things now; but, as of old, they do at this day tarnish the beauty, distract the peace, and cripple the efforts of the church of God. They did then, and they do now, set brothers at variance, and teach them to divide their inheritance on unfair principles, and in the midst of strife and discord. And these things they will always do, while they are permitted to regulate ecclesiastical matters, and divide the church into voluntary associations."

In page 174 we have the following apostrophe to the advocates of creeds—with which we shall close our random extracts at present, promising a few more hereafter on the superlative character of the bible.

"O inhabitants of Jerusalem, and men of Judah, judge, I pray you, betwixt me and my vineyard. What more could have been done to my vineyard, that I have not done in it?" says the Lord. Come, you ministers of Christ, accept the challenge and reason with your master. Tell him of the insufficiency of his bible, and of your happier legislation in forming creeds! Make it appear in his presence, that there is a necessity for other tests of christian character, than the one he has furnished. Tell him that it is impossible for him to get along in peace and love, unless the form in which he revealed truth be altered, and a concise summary of moral doctrines be framed, as a companion for the bible. Take your stand on the threshold of his holy temple, and proclaim aloud, that men who will not listen to Moses and the prophets, to Christ and his apostles, will be persuaded by your creeds; and that unless this demand is gratified, the church must crumble to pieces. The whole angel host would frown at such presumption."

                                                    EDITOR.

Universalism.

THERE is a great deal said in this age upon the universal restoration of all demons and wicked men to the eternal happiness of saints and angels. It is true that the demons are yet in purgatory, and that those that die in their sins are to go through a purgatorial punishment proportioned to the number and magnitude of their sins at the allowance of ———— years for each transgression according to some systems; and according to others on the ratio of ———— hundreds of years. Satan and his colleagues have been out of the presence of God now for six thousand years, and how far they have got through this purgatorial punishment is not yet settled. We have had, for the last year, so many questions proposed to us from correspondents on this system, that a little volume would be requisite to give them suitable answers. We are not at leisure, nor have we so much energy of mind, or body, as would be sufficient to give them even a respectful answer. We can only, in a summary way, acknowledge the receipt of them. Some, indeed, speak with as much certainty upon this subject as if they had just finished and gone through this purgatorial chastisement, and visited our world fraught with intelligence from Hades. They have discovered that all the caveats and threats in the New Testament are like the bugbears, and stories of ghosts and witches, which nurses tell to their peevish children when they would scare them to sleep. They tell lies; but it is with a good intention. They know there are no ghosts nor witches to disturb the children; but it would not be safe to tell them so. It is necessary to lie. Just so, when the apostles and the Saviour spoke of *aionion* or everlasting punishment, and of *aionion* or everlasting destruction, they knew there was no such thing; but they found that men could not be governed or managed without those bugbears, and were under the necessity of doing as the nurses aforesaid. They were under the necessity of telling lies from a good intention. They used such words and phrases in representing the duration of the punishment of the wicked, as they used in representing the continuance of the happiness of the righteous; yet they knew that the one was to terminate some fifty thousand years hence, while the other would never end. I have sometimes thought that it was exceedingly ungrateful in those knowing ones to disclose the secret. For if God was so kind to them as to afford them a special revelation for their own comfort, while he evidently holds out tremendous prospects to the wicked *in terrorem*, it is unkind on their part, to blab out

the secret, and thus divest the governor of the world, of the most puissant means of keeping it safe for the righteous to live in it. They seem to act the part of an intruder into the family of a matron who was succeeding pretty well in managing her restive children, by the terrors of ghosts and wizards, but the intruder tells them their mother is deceiving them; and thus the little pests scream out afresh, and bid defiance to all the ghosts and demons in the nation.—I say there is such a similarity in the cases, that we cannot avoid associating them in our mind, and we think it not unreasonable to inscribe them on paper.

I know the mighty war of words that can be paraded on any subject. Since Peter De Alvo wrote forty volumes on the nativity of the Messiah, I am afraid to enter the list with those worthy champions, if it were only on one of Horn Tooke's *ifs*. The Universalists have a pretty theme too—the benevolence of God, and the ultimate felicity of every creature, and thousands will hear them gladly.* When a few weeks ago I visited the Baltimore penitentiary, and saw more than three hundred and fifty convicts suffering for their evil deeds, it struck me what a fine popular topic it would have been there to have announced to the suffering miscreants, that while the lawyers, judges, and their keepers, made them believe that the governor and the laws of the state required their continuance there for life, it was all craft and policy; that neither the moral character of the governor, nor the just exposition of the laws, would authorize any such long and cruel treatment. No, no. His character and his promulgations require that if you only feel sorry for what you have done and promise to do better, you will be set at liberty in a few days or hours. I say, something like this would have been a popular topic in such a place, and I am sure if I could have harangued them thus, under specious circumstances, I would have had many to hear me gladly, and to wish that it were true.

I do not, however, think that the Universalists are sinners above all others, in that they have run to one extreme, because some sectaries have run into the opposite. When I hear one man talk about his elect and reprobate infants, and little ones in hell not a span long; and hear another describing the flight of the demons from Stygian darkness, and representing the Devil and his messengers ascending to that heaven whence they were once excluded; I view them both alike—each mounted on his winged horse, and attempting to soar beyond the regions of re-

* And yet the benevolence of God, on which Universalists so often talk, is a lame benevolence on their own principles.—They are much concerned for the character of the Divine benevolence, and the standard by which they adjust it condemns their own system. They must, and they ought, to banish from this world and from the next, any such idea of God, as that of vengeance, and teach that neither vengeance nor punishment belong to the Lord.— For so long as they teach a purgatorial punishment of ten or fifty thousand years continuance after death, so long they destroy their own arguments drawn from the Divine benevolence. For if God can, on their own theory, be so benevolent in making men unhappy so long, it will be difficult to show why he cannot be benevolent in lengthening it out for another age, or for ages of ages, *ad infinitum*. In short, while they talk so much about the cruelty of other systems, they ought to divest their own system of so much of it, and deny future punishment altogether; and even then their system will be imperfect: for, to be consistent, they must show that all the pains, afflictions, and miseries of this world, constitute perfect happiness: and that will be a hard task—for the testimony of our senses will come in their way. But until they reconcile present evils to their system of Divine benevolence, it is in vain to object against them who say that God will punish the wicked, and bless the righteous, hereafter.

velation. Because A disapproves the theory of B on any subject, I am not convinced that A's theory is correct. It is a bad way to correct one extreme by running into another. One may as well be wrecked on Scylla as on Charybdis.

But, to change my voice, I would earnestly request those preachers of universal deliverance from hell, to stop and think how far the drift and scope of their efforts correspond with the obvious drift and scope of the preachings found in the New Testament. As Mr. Kneeland will have it, *aionion* life, and *aionion* death, or *aionion destruction*, are the mighty and majestic sanctions of the gospel of Jesus the Messiah. Now without saying a word upon his translation, if such it may be called, (and I have it now on the table before me, and Griesbach lying under it) it must be admitted that the bible always holds out something terrible to the wicked, to them who disbelieve and disobey Jesus the King, at his coming to judge the world. This, I say, must be, and, I believe, is, admitted, by all Universalists. Now, if it be admitted, as it must be, and as it most generally is, that the wicked shall be cast off from the presence of God and his holy messengers, into inconceivable and inexpressible anguish and misery, in the judgment; it is all idle to talk and contend about the termination of it. There is neither days, weeks, nor months, in that state. There is no standard conceivable, nor revealed, by which the length or continuance can be measured. If they are damned or condemned at all, it is in vain, on rational principles, to attempt to date it in a world where there is no calender; and we are very sure that all the Universalists on earth cannot produce one sentence in all the revelation of God that says any thing about the termination of the punishment of the wicked. The bible often tells us of its commencement; but not once of its end. It is wise for us not to live upon conjectures, nor to build systems upon dreams and visions, which may cover us and our children in the ruins, and one day cause us to exclaim—It would have been better for us that we had never been born.—I am content to be assured that whosoever hears the gospel and believes and obeys it, *shall be saved*, and that whosoever hears it and disbelieves it, *shall be damned.*—I know no gospel in proclaiming *to sinners on earth* that after they are damned in judgment, they may, by a long series of awful punishment, be brought to repentance, and be delivered from hell. This I am sure is no gospel in this world, and what it might be if announced in Hades or Gehenna, or by whom it could be preached there, I will not, I dare not, conjecture.—But of one thing we are assured, that it is a fearful thing to fall into the hands of the living God; and an awful experiment to attempt to relax or weaken the glorious and tremendous sanctions of the gospel of his grace.

EDITOR.

The Textuaries.

THE scrap doctors or text expositors have not only very generally obscured the words they proposed to illustrate, but they have made their office accessible to every novice, and introduced a band of "public preachers" that are a disgrace to the age in which we live. Any body with, or without common sense, can become a scrap doctor. A man that can neither read nor spell can "preach a sermon *on* a text, or preach *from* a text." I am authorized to state, as a well attested fact, that, not long since, in the District of Columbia, hard by the capital of the United

States, where all the heads of department live, and all foreigners resort, a certain textuary did take for his text the words of a wicked man, found in Matthew 25: the false accusation of the wicked servant who told his lord—"You are an austere man." This was the text. The preacher could not spell well, and he made it, "You are an *oyster* man." But the misfortune was, "he raised his whole doctrine" on the word *oyster*. In his exordium, for he too was an orator, he told his audience that his object was to show how fitly the Saviour was compared to an oyster-man, or oyster-catcher. Accordingly his method was—1st. To show the coincidence or resemblance between his Saviour and an oyster-man. 2d. To point out how suitably oysters represented sinners. 3d. To demonstrate how beautifully the *tongs* which the oyster-man uses to take up oysters, represented "ministers of the gospel." 4th. To prove that the oyster-man's boat was a fit emblem of the gospel and of a "gospel church," into which the oysters or sinners are put when caught or converted. His fifth head I have forgotten; but perhaps it was to show how the cooking and eating of oysters represented the management and discipline of those sinners caught by those ministers of the gospel. He concluded with a few practical hints according to custom.

What a happy mistake was this and how fortunate for the audience! And yet he was called and sent by God to preach his gospel!!!!

I once heard, with my own ears, a pious textuary deliver an introductory sermon to an assembly of divines from the words of the devil, or from what was equivalent—the words of a damsel speaking from the impulse of a spirit of divination. The soothsayer said of the apostles—"These are the servants of the most high God which show to us the way of salvation." He did not "stick so well to his text" as the aforesaid textuary; for while the divining damsel applied her words to the apostles, the divine preacher appropriated them to himself and such folks as the oyster expositor.

A pious divine, who may, for aught I know, be yet dubbed D. D. whose spirit within him was vehemently moved at the knots of ribbon on the ladies' bonnets, ransacked from Genesis to Jude for a text to afford a pretext for giving scope to the fervor of his soul against those obnoxious knots, found the following words—"Let him that is on the house *top not come down.*" Not being a perfect speller, though a good preacher; and wishing to have a text just to the point, he selected these four words—"Top not come down." *Pro causa euphoniæ* he prefixed a *k* to the negative particle and converted it into a noun theological. His method was natural and easy—1st. He proposed, to explain the top knots. 2d. To give a divine command for their demolition. 3d. To expatiate on the reasonableness of the injunction, *come down.* 4th. To denounce the eternal perdition of the disobedient. He, too, was a preacher who appropriated the words of Isaiah: "How beautiful are the feet of them that publish the gospel of peace, that bring glad tidings of good things." He was sent by God—if we could believe him.

Now, courteous reader, will you allow me to say what I am sure is a fact; that I have heard hundreds of sermons, and read volumes of them, on texts, and from the learned too, which, though not so evidently ridiculous to every body, were really as absurd as the above.

EDITOR.

To the Society of Friends, commonly called Quakers.

RESPECTED AND RESPECTABLE FRIENDS: You have, as a society, long contended against water baptism, on the supposition that it once was, but is now done away. The Spirit that moves you, has moved me to address you, not, indeed, to provoke you to a controversy with me, nor to speak to you as some sectaries speak to you. I am not about to use the same arguments against your views, which you have often heard, and as often considered. But for some time past, that Spirit which has suggested so many good things to you, has suggested one consideration to me, which I am constrained, by it, to make known to you, believing it to be enough to settle all doubts on the subject of baptism. This consideration will appear the more weighty to you, inasmuch, as it is founded upon your own acknowledgments. I have never seen it presented to you by any of those who would slander you into a compliance with their clerical schemes. I intreat you to pay it due attention. It is this: You believe that there is one Lord, one faith, and one baptism. But the fooleries of your opponents drove you to say that this one baptism, is the baptism of the Spirit. Now if I can show that this one baptism cannot mean the baptism of the Spirit, you will, no doubt, admit that while there is but one baptism, you ought to submit to it. In the first place, then, I offer you this proposition: That no gift, operation, or influence, of the Spirit, was ever, by any inspired writer, called the baptism of the Holy Spirit, save what happened on Pentecost, and in the first calling of the Gentiles in the house of Cornelius. If this be true, then this one baptism, of which Paul speaks, is an immersion in water.

Now, that this position may evidently appear to be true, it will be necessary to notice two points: First, That no man who was the subject of any gift, impression, influence, or operation of the Spirit of God, other than the Pentecostian, is said to have been baptized in the Holy Spirit. And, in the second place, that the promise of being baptized in the Holy Spirit, and its accomplishment, are, by the New Testament writers, exclusively applied to the times and places above specified. In illustration of the first point, it is only necessary to observe, that it is confessed that many of the Old Testament saints were the subjects of influences, gifts, and operations of the Spirit. By it the prophets spake, and by it the oracles were composed. Yet not one of these are said to have been baptized by the Holy Spirit. Again, during the ministry of John and labors of the Lord on earth, many persons, and especially the apostles, were the subjects of gifts, impressions, operations, and influences of the Spirit, yet those persons were not said to be, and, in fact, were not baptized, in the Spirit. For this plain reason, with all their gifts, they were the subjects of the promise, "He shall baptize you in the Holy Spirit and in fire." To them was the spiritual baptism promised by the Saviour. The demonstration of the second point will confirm and establish the first.

Acts i. 5. The Saviour, after he rose from the dead, and just before his ascension into heaven, promised his disciples that they would soon be baptized in the Holy Spirit. His words are—"You shall be baptized in the Holy Spirit not many days hence." Now, my dear friends, observe this baptism was then future, consequently all the spiritual influences they had hitherto experienced did not constitute this baptism, for why then should it be a matter of promise?

Please observe again, the time for its accomplishment is fixed and defined—"Not many days hence"—Pentecost was not many days hence. Not many days after the Lord's ascension they were baptized in the Holy Spirit, and in fire, *Acts* 2. Peter there and then demonstrated that this outpouring of the Spirit which put all the apostles and others fully under its influence, called on this account a baptism or immersion, was the accomplishment of former promises. This baptism was never repeated till God called the Gentiles. And in order to show his impartiality he made no difference between them and the Jews. Peter shows that there was no other outpouring of the Spirit from Pentecost till the calling of the Gentiles. "God, says he, gave the Gentiles the same gift that he did to us Jews at the beginning" of the reign of his Son, or of the christian age. There had been no outpouring from Pentecost till that time. Pentecost was the only day, and Jerusalem the only place, analogous to this. From all which it is apparent that no other gifts, operations, or influences of the Spirit from the beginning of the world till Pentecost are called the baptism of the Holy Spirit; and that no similar outpouring had intervened from the first calling of the Jews till the first calling of the Gentiles, and that the various graces, called the fruits of the Spirit, neither are nor can be called the baptism of the Spirit.

Once more observe that the baptism of the Holy Spirit, was to be a visible baptism. This the promise implied. We all know that the two occasions called the baptism of the Spirit were visible and brilliant—but, my friends, is your baptism of the Spirit visible or invisible? They were enveloped in fire and covered with tongues —And it is worthy of note that all the subjects of this baptism could instantaneously speak foreign languages which they never learned—Can the subjects of your spiritual baptism do this also?

Now the one baptism of which Paul speaks in the present time, when writing to the Ephesians, was not that past on Pentecost, nor can it, by any arguments deduced from scripture, be applied to any influences in our day, whether "ordinary or extraordinary." While then you admit that there is one baptism, and as you see it is not the baptism of the Holy Spirit, for which there is now no use nor promise; and which we have never seen as exhibited on those occasions; this one baptism is that in water; and you will, no doubt, remember that when Cornelius and his friends had received the baptism of the Holy Spirit, the great apostle Peter commanded them to be immersed in the name of the Lord. And I know you would rather say that it is more probable that George Fox might have erred than the apostle Peter.

Accept these hints from your friend,
THE EDITOR.

MANY letters, like the following, are on file, and remain to be answered. This is one of the oldest date, and priority, in this respect, ought to be regarded.

V——s, August 29, 1825.

DEAR BROTHER,—For the last year past, I have been both a subscriber and a reader of your Christian Baptist. I think I have, upon many subjects, been much interested and benefited; and am of opinion that the principles which you advocate, will prove more and more interesting to the christian who inquires after the truth. You have, in some one of your numbers, suggested a plan for reading and understanding, more easily, the word of God. I have thought it a good one, and immediately determined to pursue it. I have progressed as far as the Acts of the Apostles. And find some scriptures in the meaning of which I cannot satisfy myself; and from your disposition to make known the truth, I take the liberty of asking from you your views upon some verses which I shall put to you for explanation, believing that you will communicate your views of them to the public through your useful paper: *Matt.* v. 22. 39. ch. vi. 25. ch. xix. 12. The only way to serve God acceptably, according to my views of his character, is to do his will, and in order to do that will, we should understand what he requires of us in his written word.—Respectfully, &c.

Dear Brother,

A PARTIAL answer to your request is all I can give you at this time. A correct translation of Matthew v. 22, renders it more intelligible:— "Whosoever is vainly incensed against his brother shall be obnoxious to the judges; whosoever shall call him fool shall be obnoxious to the sanhedrim; but whosoever shall call him miscreant (or apostate wretch) shall be obnoxious to a Gehenna of fire," (or to burning alive in the vale of Hinnom.) The Saviour informs his disciples that while the Jews then only brought those guilty of actual murder before the judges; under his reign, the least degree of anger would subject a person to a punishment analogous to that which was usually inflicted by the inferior courts; that the expression of anger in the way of contempt of a brother should render the persons obnoxious to the punishment analogous to that inflicted by the sanhedrim, which was stoning to death; and that the highest expression of anger with the tongue should expose the transgressor to a punishment analogous to being burned alive in the vale of Hinnom. He, in this instance, as his method was, communicates the doctrine of his reign through the medium of existing customs, institutions, and avocations of men. He, through these allusions, teaches his disciples that every aberration from brotherly love would be taken cognizance of by him.— Anger in the heart, anger expressed in the way of contempt, and anger expressed with marked hatred. All laws, human and divine, award punishment proportioned to the crime or offence. His *design* in the context renders his meaning apparent, and teaches all the disciples that while he mercifully forgives the offences of those who confess their faults and forsake them, he severely scrutinizes their thoughts and words, with even more severity than men are wont to exhibit to the overt acts of iniquity.

Matthew vi. 25, becomes perfectly plain when fairly translated. Thus—"You cannot serve God and Riches. Therefore I charge you, be not anxious about your life, what you shall eat, or what you shall drink, nor about your body what you shall wear."

The context gives the following as the spirit and design of Matthew xix. 12. The question was—Whether it were not better in some conditions to live unmarried. The Saviour answered, "They alone are capable of living thus on whom the power is conferred. For there are some persons who never had any desire to enter into the nuptial bonds. Others have been prevented by violence, and others from their zeal to publish the reign of heaven, have divested themselves of any such desire. Let him act this part who can act it." This is the spirit of the reply and the reasons for his answer. My limits will not permit me to be more particular at this time

Wishing you God speed in your inquiries, I am your brother in the search of truth.   EDITOR.

THE following Ode we understand was written by an emigrant to this country, who, in the midst of misfortunes in a foreign land, was brought to remember the blessings he enjoyed when under the pious tutelage of his christian parents. To what extent the tuition and example of the parents was a blessing to the son, we have not yet learned; but one thing is certain, that it is seldom in vain.—ED.

To the Family Bible.

How painfully pleasing the fond recollection
    Of youthful connexion and innocent joy,
While bless'd with parental advice and affection,
    Surrounded with mercies and peace from on high.
I still view the chairs of my father and mother,
    The seats of their offspring as ranged on each hand,
And the richest of books. that excels every other—
    The Family Bible that lay on the stand—
        The old-fashion'd Bible, the dear blessed Bible,
        The Family Bible that lay on the stand.

The Bible, the volume of God's inspiration,
    At morning and evening could yield us delight;
And the prayer of our sire was a sweet invocation
    For mercies by day and protection by night.
Our hymn of thanksgiving with harmony swelling
    All warm from the hearts of a family band,
Hath raised us from earth to the rapturous dwelling
    Described in the Bible that lay on the stand—
        The old-fashion'd Bible, the dear blessed Bible,
        The Family Bible that lay on the stand.

Ye scenes of tranquility, long have we parted,
    My hopes almost gone, and my parents no more;
In sorrow and sighing I live broken hearted,
    And wander unknown on a far distant shore.
But how can I doubt a bless'd Saviour's protection,
    Forgetful of gifts from his bountiful hand;
Then let me with patience receive the correction,
    And think on the Bible that lay on the stand—
        The old-fashion'd Bible, the dear blessed Bible,
        The Family Bible that lay on the stand.

No. 6.]   JANUARY 2, 1826.

Review of " Remarks on the Rise, Use and Unlawfulness of Creeds and Confessions of Faith in the church of God—By JOHN M. DUNCAN, *Pastor of the Presbyterian Church, Tammany street, Baltimore."—Part Second.*

THE more deeply we drink into the spirit of the New Testament, the less we relish the dry and lifeless dogmas of human creeds. As we ascend in clear and comprehensive views of the Holy Oracles, human formularies descend in our estimation. Hence we invariably find an ardent zeal for human systems, accompanied with glaring ignorance of the revelation of God, and true veneration for the records of God's grace, is always attended with intelligence and liberality. The following extracts from Mr. Duncan's work, so fully confirm these sentiments; so exactly correspond with many pieces published in this work, that we cannot deny ourselves the pleasure of presenting them to our readers.— Their value will apologize for their length; and, indeed, we have done violence to the author in garbling his pages, and have rather detracted from the force and beauty of his remarks, by selecting only a few sentences of many which ought to appear together in the order he has given them. We wish our readers to have some tolerable idea of the work, and hope that many of them may be induced to add this book of Mr. Duncan's to their library. These selections are made from page 184 to page 208.   ED. C. B.

"Our second principle is, that the bible being the word of God, it must necessarily be precisely suited to human beings as sinful and fallen; and therefore it embraces in its provisions all that is peculiar, either in their character or condition."

"And what is the Bible, for which we plead so ardently? It is not merely a high wrought eulogy upon the character of Jehovah; but it is his condescension to men upon earth. It is not a stern display of abstract righteousness; but it is the mingling together of justice and peace, of mercy and truth. It is not the impracticable requisition of absolute purity, made with an unpitying eye and an oppressive hand; but it is the proclamation of "the righteousness of faith," that glorious principle of which angels and the redeemed shall talk together throughout eternity. It is not the statute of an indescribable sovereignty, which no prayer can relax and which no tears can soften; but it is the opening of the prison doors, it is a universal call, it is an indiscriminate overture;—whosoever will, may come; and whosoever comes, shall in no wise be cast out; and all its agents act upon its own liberal commission. "The Spirit and the bride say, Come. And let him that hears, say Come. And let him that is athirst, Come. And whosoever will, let him take of the water of life freely." None of our Calvinistic brethren, as they may be pleased to denominate themselves, will halt at the foregoing statement. If they do, let them pause and reflect whether, under the guise of Calvinism, they have not sunk into a system of the most haughty, joyless, and chilling fatalism?

"Again, the Bible is intended to be a system of practical morals. It reveals not doctrines for the sake of doctrine, but as they may serve to fulfil practical purposes; or it never was designed to establish theory independent of practice.—God did not send his only begotten Son into our world merely to display the brightness of his glory; he veiled all that glory that men might look at it, and sent his Son "in the likeness of sinful flesh," that men whose moral perceptions were very low by reason of the "weakness of the flesh," might have an "express image of his person," which they could adore with a degree of intelligence consistent with their infirmities. The Holy Spirit has not come down merely to astonish by his own mysterious movements; his official work is to build up a temple on earth for the habitation of God—a spiritual house, resting on Jesus as a living stone, and into which he inserts, as living stones, all whom he sanctifies. The gospel, even when angels have tuned their harps to its lofty strains, is not simply, Glory to God in the highest; but it is, Peace on earth and good will toward men."

The simplicity of the Bible, or its happy adaptation to the circumstances of mankind, is one of the most striking proofs of its divine original. That the blind should receive their sight and the lame walk, that the lepers should be cleansed and the deaf hear, and that the dead should be raised up, form an irresistible demonstration in favor of any thing they can be brought to prove; but when the Redeemer stated all these things in testimony of his own pretensions, he did not think the train of evidence complete, and added, "the poor have the gospel preached to them." The heavenly visions which he had seen with his Father, and the particulars of which he came down from heaven to reveal on earth, are made plain and distinct to the human mind; level to the comprehension, not only of the divine, the philosopher and the scholar, but to the poor. They are like Habakkuk's message, made plain upon tables, so that he who runs may read. It is this very thing which reveals the author of the bible with peculiar glory; for infinite wisdom is ever displayed by the perfect adaptation of means to an end. Instead, then, of needing any of those perplexing summaries, which different religious denominations have given us as the product of their own wisdom, the bible, by its own plainness, evinces its own perfection, and recommends itself to the most uninformed, as a sure guide to everlasting life. If in it "there are depths where an elephant might swim," there are in it also "shoals where a lamb may wade." If it administers strong meat to those who are of full age, it serves the babe with milk. If it prescribes perfection to its reader, it begins by communicating first principles; and he who has learned rightly to divide it, has learned how to give to each his portion of meat in due season."

"And what, we ask, would become of the mass of mankind—what of the majority of professing christians—what of our children, whose very praise in the presence of the Redeemer may be that from childhood they knew the Holy Scriptures which are capable to make even them wise to salvation, if the bible was not thus modified to meet the imbecility of human powers?"

"It is manifest that the scriptures must be plain to the human mind, or they can be of no use to the *poor;* and the mass of mankind could have no divine book which they can profitably read. It must be a volume suited to the illiterate and the busy, the bond and the free; fitted to the tottering old man, bowed down with years, who has no time to waste on our speculations, and to the young child that cannot comprehend them. It must be a book which the mother can explain to her little ones, and from which the father can read to them, under the sanctions of divine authority, a morning and evening lesson. Say it is otherwise, and then the fact that to the poor the gospel is preached, is no longer a proof of the divine authenticity of the scriptures, seeing they cannot be put to that use as a system of moral truths. To them its page is unintelligible; its very doctrines mysterious, its propositions unformed; its promises irrelevant; and, by a reference to a human creed, imposed upon them as the meaning of the scriptures, *their faith must stand in the wisdom of men.*"

"If, then, we are right in saying that God has in the bible given us moral truth in the best form it could wear, considering the character of the being for whom it has been prepared—and who can say we are not right? Then, under what principle have synods and councils undertaken to alter that form? For our creeds and confessions of faith do take the truth which God has revealed out of its scriptural connexions; and they do modify it according to the conceptions of the men who make them, or the prejudices and feelings of the age which creates and enforces them. And why do they this? It certainly becomes them to give the best of all reasons for so eccentric an adventure. Can they make truth more tangible? Have they the promise of the Spirit to superintend their deliberations, when they undertake to revise and correct God's institutions? Have they any divine promise to guarantee a good result? Or do they suppose they have a sufficient warrant to take such a step, from the fact that they have a sectarian object to accomplish, or that the interest of a voluntary association may require it? Then they must remember that they have the very same argument to meet in application to these voluntary associations; and to justify themselves for so dividing the church of the living God, and altering her external form. And we really do not wonder that these two things are put together; for as Paul argues with the Hebrews, "The priesthood being changed there is of necessity a change also of the law."

"But perhaps it may be denied that our creeds do alter the form in which truth is brought to bear upon the conscience. We must then make our assertion good. Are not our creeds professed summaries? And what is a summary? Is it the same thing with that which it abridges, or is it a different thing? If the original and the abstract be drawn out by different hands, will they present the same intellectual image? Is this summary needed? Did the Master give us one, or empower us to make one, because his bible was a deficient instrument of operation upon the human spirit? Every man at a glance may perceive that he has not framed the scriptures upon the same principle on which our theological systems are constructed. The bible is not a collection of abstract propositions, systematized into regular order, nor is it a schedule of difficult metaphysical subjects, arranged under general titles, such as the attributes of God, the divine decrees, the perseverance of the saints, &c. On the contrary, it is a transcript of social transactions; it is an exhibition of human life; it is that species of composition which all the world knows is most interesting to the mass of mankind. It is true some lofty speculators, some profound thinkers, who are capable to reason both matter and spirit out of God's creation, might prefer a volume of mental abstractions; but then the reader must remember that the bible was written for the *poor;* that it was intended to throw a beam of the life that shall never end upon the infant mind; to cheer the humble, the lowly, and the contrite spirit; and, while the dews of its blessing are falling upon the dying old man, to stretch the bow of the covenant of grace across the firmament of truth, that his closing eyes may be opened upon the cloudless light of an eternal day. Had such an epitome or compend of moral truths, as our creeds profess to be, been the best form of revelation by which the human mind could be spiritually enlightened, doubtless God himself would have adopted that form; for he declares that he has done for man all that he could do for him; and indeed, he has too much pity and compassion for this fallen child of his love to leave any thing undone which could have been done. If he had intended to write a book for a race of philosophers, instead of rejecting such for being wise in their own conceits; and if philosophers really know how to make systems, or are themselves best instructed in that way, doubtless he would have given them his revelation in a more logical form. Most certainly, however, he has not done it; and the inference fairly is, that our systems are constructed on false views of human nature, or that our creeds are not at all fitted for man in his present state. There is a better way of teaching mankind the science of morals: for Jehovah himself, who needs not that any should tell him what is in man, has adopted another way. Surely we may safely follow where God leads, and to imitate his example never can jeopard the prosperity or peace of his church."

"The practical result of our creeds confirms our argument. Can children understand the abstract propositions contained in the Shorter Catechism? Have not scientific men long since learned that every thing must be simplified, and, if possible, illustrated by example, in order to interest, impress, and benefit the infantile mind? Are they not descending from their own lofty eminence, and, taking these little immortals by the hand, leading them up step by step? And shall we leave their moral nature uncultivated, or fatigue their tender spirits by the incessant repetition of things which they do not understand? Are our grown up christians better treated by this system of perplexed legislation? Do not these creeds drag away the christian mind from scriptural exposition to dwell upon polemic propositions? Do they not make it necessary for us to contend with those whom we ought to love; and even to divide families, as if the husband and the wife, the parent and the child, worshipped different Gods? Do they not present truth in philosophical forms, about which men are every where at liberty to reason according to their own apprehensions? Do they not teach men to feel comparatively irresponsible about religious things, because they consider themselves to be reasoning with man about his notions, and not with God against his institutions? Let the reader judge for himself whether we do not recite facts. As Calvinists, we almost intuitively shrink away from being thought Arminians; and as Arminians we are equally frightened by a charge of Calvinism.— The past age has made a controversy between these two sets of opinions exceedingly popular, and our creeds have served to perpetuate strife! He is thought to be a clergyman of secondary consideration, and to possess talents of a very inferior order, who cannot perspicuously arrange and skilfully discuss the *five points;* while on the other hand, Whitby and the Lime-street Lectures have obtained immortal honor. Neither party seems to know that if they would cease to contend, and declare what they are honestly convinced is in the bible, they would blend in most perfect harmony, as soon as long established habits, running throughout society, could admit so happy a revolution. But they have formed their opinions; they have chosen their theological system; they have entered into their ecclesiastical connexions; and of all things that are inimical to harmony, these voluntary associations are the worst—because by them all society is thrown into commotion. It is really admirable to hear how controversialists, belonging to different voluntary associations, will treat a scripture text which they have abstracted from its own relations, and how clearly they will demonstrate it to utter their own opinions. Who does not feel some concern when he hears a minister of the gospel endeavoring to establish a doctrine which every one knows is employed to evolve a sectarian, rather than a scriptural principle? And who, that has even thought dispassionately upon the subject, would not prefer to have the bible explained to him as other things are explained, than hear the most eloquent discussion on a sectarian tenet? Surely the study of the scriptures, and an effort to make men feel truth as spoken by divine wisdom, and enforced by divine authority, would entirely change the complexion of such ministrations, and impel the human mind into trains of thinking and habits of application much more spiritual and edifying. We say again, let the reader judge for himself; the whole subject is presented to him in real life; it is pressed out to its very extreme; and he may even hear, as an argument in favor of theological strife, that division is necessary to unity. A lovely paradox! An unexpected, but happy union of contraries! Its framers are fairly entitled to all the credit of its ingenuity. We dare not envy them their happy talent for invention."

THE Synod of Baltimore have again proved that they make and hold the confession and formulary as authoritative rules of faith and practice, and as terms of communion between Christ and his disciples. The following is positive proof thereof.

" The Rev. John M. Duncan, of Baltimore, and the Rev. Charles M'Lean, of Gettysburgh, in this state, have both declined the jurisdiction of the Presbyterian church in the United States, on the ground that they object to creeds and confessions as terms of christian or ministerial fellowship; and the Synod of Baltimore have accordingly declared their congregations vacant, and have put them under the care of the respective presbyteries of Baltimore and Carlisle."—*Pittsburgh Mercury, Nov. 30.*

So Messrs. Duncan and M'Lean are to be viewed and treated as heathen men and publicans, because they aver that there is but one authoritative rule of christian faith and practice, and that this is the Bible. But behold they have declared their congregation vacant! This is another acceptation of the word "vacant." They have vacant territories in their church, with only two hundred thousand inhabitants on them; vacant churches, because the pulpit is sometimes empty; and vacant congregations when their pulpit is every day filled with a good man who happens not to be orthodox in this article of the fallible rule of faith and practice.

"They can create and they destroy."

They have annihilated Messrs. Duncan and M'Lean, as well as paganized them. Great are their tender mercies for those transgressors, and inexpressible their sympathies for their dear and precious congregations. We have it from good authority in Baltimore, that Mr. Duncan's congregation was as unanimously determined to adhere to the sentiments in his book as any congregation of orthodox christians in the country is determined to hold fast its form of sound words imported from Scotland on board the ship Enterprize, and guarded by two frigates laden with soldiers and munitions of war.   ED. C. B.

On the Rights of Laymen.—No. 1.

FOR more than half a century past, no theme has been more popular, no topic has been more fully discussed, than the rights of men. The result has been, that very generally, in the New World at least, it is conceded that all men are born to equal rights. But our theme is not the rights of men, but the rights of laymen.

Some, no doubt, will inquire, What is a layman? We answer, a man is the creature of God, but a lay-man is the creature of priests. God made men, but priests made laymen. In the religious world we often hear of clergy and laity. These are terms of Grecian extraction. The term clergy denotes the Lord's lot, or people; the term laity denotes the common herd of mankind, or the clergy's lot or people. We shall attend first to the inalienable rights of the laity, and secondly to the inalienable rights of the brethren in Christ.

In the first place, a layman has a right to consider himself as possessed of five senses, viz. seeing, hearing, tasting, smelling, and feeling. If misfortune or vice has not deprived him of the use of any of them, he is always to bear in mind that his Creator gave him eyes, ears, a mouth, nose, and hands, and that he designed he should use them all. These five senses completely adapt man to this present world. As an animal, he has no use for a sixth sense. His eye feasts upon light, his ear upon sound, his mouth, tongue, and palate, upon tastes, his nose upon odors, and his hands inform him of the heat and cold, roughness and smoothness, hardness, and softness, and all such properties of the bodies around him. These all serve him as guards and defences, as well as minister to his enjoyments. As in a world of matter his whole body is liable to many inconveniences, his Creator has transfused through his whole system the sense of feeling, which exists most exquisitely in his hands. In one sentence, there is not a single property in any material thing of any use to man, that is not distinguishable by some one or all of these senses. Now a layman is endowed with all these senses as well as a priest. Therefore he is to use them, and believe their testimony in preference to any thing a priest tells him. For example: If a priest tell him that he can turn wine into blood, and bread into flesh, the layman must taste them, and if this blood have still the taste of wine, and this flesh of bread, he must believe his senses in preference to the priest's tongue. For God gave him those senses, and they are to be relied on more firmly than the words of any man. Again, when a priest tells him that he immerses or washes a person in water, when he only besprinkles his face or his hands, he must believe the testimony of his eyes, and not the lips of the priest, for his eyes are more to be trusted than the lips of a thousand priests. Now it is the inalienable right of every layman to exercise his five senses, and never to be argued out of them or to believe any thing contrary to them.

But let it be remembered that those five senses give a man no other intelligence than what concerns the material world around him. They cannot introduce him to an acquaintance with a world of spirits, or a future state. But in order to fit him for this, God has given him another class of faculties which exist in his spirit, as those senses exist in his body. These faculties are all comprized in one sentence, which affirms man to be a reasonable being. But each of the faculties which constitute a reasonable being, are as distinct from one another as are his five senses. The eye and the ear are not more distinct than perception and reflection, than memory and judgment. These being within the man, are not so easily apprehended as his senses which are without. The spirit of a man dwells within him, and as through windows, views, through the five senses, the objects around him. What it cannot perceive through one of those windows, it can discern through another. Besides this, it can look upon itself and become conscious of its own actions. But these are not so obvious to all mankind. The mass of men attend much more to what is passing without than to what is passing within them, and therefore know more of the former than of the latter.

But of all the faculties with which the spirit of man is endowed, none exalt him so high, none put him in possession of intelligence so important as the *faculty of believing.* Whether this faculty be a combination of other faculties, or one distinct from all others, is not worthy of a moment's investigation, as every man knows that he *can* believe, and *does* believe human testimony when it possesses certain attributes. Indeed, all that we do know, and all that we are assured of beyond the narrow sphere of our own experience and observation, all that we know of the past, the present, and the future, beyond the limits of our horizon, we have acquired by this faculty of believing.

As men spoke before they wrote, and as intelligence respecting facts is reported before it can be written, the ear is the first medium through which testimony reaches the spirit of man. Consequently our conviction, or assurance of things reported, commonly called *faith*, "comes by hearing," or by the ear. Through this window of the ear the spirit of man sees incomparably more objects and acquires incalculably more information than by the other four windows or avenues of information.

Reading what is written is a sort of hearing by the eye. If the assurance of things unseen be acquired from reading, it derogates nothing from the rational and biblical truth, that "faith comes by hearing;" for writing is a substitute for speaking, and reading is but a substitute for hearing. I would not spend time in illustrating a matter so plain, were it not, that some of the priests, in order to enhance their services, have boasted that faith comes by hearing, and not by reading. By hearing *them* too, rather than by reading Paul!*

But as the eye of man would be of no use to him if there was no sun or no light, so the faculty or power of believing testimony would be of no consequence if there was no testimony to be believed. And although he may have testimony concerning things present and visible, which is of much importance in the present life; yet, if the exercise and use of this faculty is to be confined to human testimony respecting present objects, still he is completely in the dark as respects the unseen and future world, and but little elevated above a bee, a beaver, or an elephant. Now of the unseen and future world he can have no human testimony, properly so called; for no man has returned from the unseen world and testified any thing about it; and if we have no testimony from God concerning the unseen and future state, the faculty of believing is of no more consequence than the sense of seeing, as regards the world of spirits.

And if, upon the hypothesis of the truth of "natural theology," a man could arrive at the knowledge of the being, and of some of the perfections of God, yet still every thing concerning his will, and the future destinies of man, is unknown and unknowable. But the Bible is to man the sun and light of the world of spirits, or of the unseen and future state. The testimony of God is addressed to, and fitted for, this faculty of believing, with which he has endowed man, and of which he cannot be divested so long as he is rational, except by his own depravity—as by an abandoned course a man may destroy, or sear his own conscience until it is past feeling, so he may abuse his faculty of believing, so far as to believe a lie and reject the truth.

But in making a Bible, the author of it has indirectly given us some of the best lessons in the world upon this faculty of believing. By attaching to it, and stamping upon it, and working into it certain evidences of its origin, he has taught us what a being like man requires, in order to giving full credence to testimony, human or divine. In adapting this book to fallen men, he has shown us what this faculty of believing now is, and not what it once was. And he has given so much of this sort of evidence as to render every man inexcusable who continues in unbelief.

To conclude this item, we would add, that by our reasoning faculties we are to try and deter-

mine whether the book called the Bible came from heaven or from men; and having determined that God is its author, we are then to receive its instructions and implicitly to follow them. It is, then, in the second place, the inalienable right of all laymen to examine the sacred writings for themselves, and to exercise this faculty with which God has endowed them, and not to believe what the church believes, nor how the church believes, because the church believes it; but to judge and act for, and from themselves.   A BEREAN.

A Restoration of the Ancient Order of Things.
No. X.
The Fellowship.

H ΚΟΙΝΩΝΙΑ, *koinonia*, translated fellowship, communion, communication, contribution, and distribution, occurs frequently in the apostolic writings. King James' translators have rendered this word by all those terms. A few specimens shall be given. It is translated by them fellowship, *Acts* ii. 42. "They continued steadfastly in the fellowship." 1 *Cor.* i. 9. "The fellowship of his Son, Jesus Christ." 2 *Cor.* vi. 14. "What fellowship has light with darkness." *Gal.* ii. 9. "The right hand of fellowship." *Philip.* iii. 10. "The fellowship of his sufferings." 1 *John* i. 3. "Fellowship with the Father." 2 *Cor.* viii. 4. "The fellowship of the ministering to the saints."

They have sometimes translated it by the word communion, 1 *Cor.* x. 16. "The communion of his blood.—"The communion of his body." 2 *Cor.* xiii. 14. "The communion of the Holy Spirit."

They have also used the term communicate or communication, *Heb.* xiii. 16. "To communicate," or "Of the communication be not forgetful, for with such sacrifices God is well pleased."

Where it evidently means alms giving in other places, they have chosen the term distribution, 2 *Cor.* ix. 13. "For your liberal distribution to them, and to all."

They have also selected the term contribution as an appropriate translation, *Rom.* xv. 26. "For it has pleased them of Macedonia and Achaia to make a certain contribution for the poor saints at Jerusalem."

It is most evident, from the above specimens, that the term ΚΟΙΝΩΝΙΑ imports a joint participation in giving or receiving; and that a great deal depends on the selection of an English term, in any particular passage, to give a particular turn to the meaning of that passage. For instance, "The right hand of contribution" would be a very uncouth and unintelligible phrase. "The contribution of the Holy Spirit," would not be "much better." Again, had they used the word contribution when the sense required it, it would have greatly aided the English reader. For example—*Acts* ii. 42. "They continued steadfastly in the apostles' doctrine, in the breaking of bread, in the contribution, and in prayers," is quite as appropriate and intelligible, and there is no reason which would justify their rendering *Rom.* xv. 26 as they have done, that would not equally justify their having rendered *Acts* ii. 42. as we have done. In *Rom.* xv. the context obliged them to select the word contribution, and this is the reason why they should have chosen the same term in *Acts* ii. 42. The term fellowship is too vague in this passage, and, indeed, altogether improper: for the Jerusalem congregation had fellowship in breaking bread, and in prayers, as well as in contributing; and as the historian contradistinguishes the *koinonia* (or

----

"fellowship," as they have it) from prayer and breaking bread, it is evident he did not simply mean either communion or fellowship as a distinct part of the christian practice or of their social worship.

Thompson has chosen the word community. This, though better than the term fellowship, is too vague, and does not coincide with the context, for the community of goods which existed in this congregation is afterwards mentioned by the historian apart from what he has told us in the 42d verse—There can be no objection made to the term contribution, either as an appropriate meaning of the term ΚΟΙΝΩΝΙΑ, or as being suitable in this passage, which would require an elaborate refutation, and we shall, therefore, unhesitatingly adopt it as though king James' translators had given it here as they have elsewhere.

As christians, in their individual and social capacity, are frequently exhorted by the apostles to contribute to the wants of the poor, to distribute to the necessities of the saints: as the congregation at Jerusalem continued steadfastly in this institution; and as other congregations elsewhere were commended for these acceptable sacrifices, it is easy to see and feel that it is incumbent on all christians as they have ability, and as circumstances require, to follow their example in this benevolent institution of him who became poor that the poor might be made rich by him.

That every christian congregation should follow the examples of those which were set in order by the apostles, is, I trust, a proposition which few of those who love the founder of the christian institution, will question. And that the apostles did give orders to the congregations in Galatia and to the Corinthians to make a weekly contribution for the poor saints, is a matter that cannot be disputed, see 1 Cor. xvi. 1. That the christian congregations did then keep a treasury for those contributions, is, I conceive, evident from the original of 1 Cor. xvi. 1, which Macknight correctly renders in the following words: —"On the first day of every week let each of you lay somewhat by itself, according as he may have prospered, putting it into the treasury, that when I come there may be then no collections."

Some who profess to follow the institutions of Jesus Christ, as found in the New Testament, do not feel it incumbent on them to make a weekly contribution for the poor, and urge in their justification, among other excuses, the two following: 1st. "In these United States we have no poor;" and, in the second place, "It was only to some churches, and with reference to some exigencies, that those injunctions were published." The Saviour said, "The poor you have always with you;" but it seems we have lived to see the day when this is not true, in the bounds of the New World. "But," says another, "the poor clergy exact from us all we can contribute, and all the cents which our mourning bags every week collect, are lost in this vast abyss!!"— "Two wrongs will not make one right!"

That some churches, on some particular occasions, were peculiarly called upon to contribute every week for one definite object, is no doubt true, and that similar contingencies may require similar exertions now as formerly, is equally true. But still this does not say that it is only on such occasions that the charities of christians must be kept awake, and that they may slumber at all other times. Nor does it prove that it is no part of the christian religion to make constant provision for the poor. This would be to contradict the letter and spirit of almost all the New Testament. For, in truth, God never did institute a religion on earth that did not look with the kindest aspect towards the poor—which did not embrace, as its best good works, acts of humanity and compassion: In the day of judgment, the works particularized as of highest eminence, and most conspicuous virtue, are not, You have built meeting-houses—you have founded colleges, and endowed professorships—you have educated poor pious youths, and made them priests—you gave your parsons good livings; but, You visited the sick, you waited on the prisoner, you fed the hungry, you clothed the naked christian.

But some excuse themselves by shewing their zeal for sound doctrine. "We," say they, "do not build colleges nor give fat livings to priests." No, indeed, you neither contribute to rich nor poor; you do not give to things sacred, or profane; you communicate not to the things of God, nor the things of men. You keep all to yourselves. Your dear wives and children engross all your charities. Yes, indeed, you are sound in faith, and orthodox in opinion. But your good works are not registered in the book of God's remembrance, and there will be none of them read in the day of rewards.

But this is not my design. *The contribution*, the weekly contribution—the distribution to the poor saints, we contend is a part of the religion of Jesus Christ. Do not be startled at this use of the term *religion*. We have the authority of an apostle for it. James says, "Pure and undefiled religion in the presence of God, even the Father, is this—viz. to visit (and relieve) the orphans and widows in their afflictions, and to keep unspotted by the vices of the world."— There is a *sacrifice* with which God is well pleased, even now, when victims bleed no more.— James has told it here, and Paul reminded the Hebrew christians of it. And when any one undertakes to show that our present circumstances forbid our attending to a weekly contribution for the poor, whether in the congregation or out of it, we shall undertake to show that either we ourselves are proper objects of christian charity, or we are placed in circumstances which deprive us of that reward mentioned in Matthew xxv. And if there is need for private and individual acts of charity, there is more need for a systematic and social preparation for, and exhibition of, congregational contributions. But let it be remembered, that it is always "accepted according to what a man has, and not according to what he has not."

I shall close these remarks with an extract from one of the best fragments of antiquity yet extant, which was first published when christians were under the persecutions of Pagan Rome. It is from an apology of one of the first bishops, which being addressed to a Roman emperor, shows the order of the christian church before it was greatly corrupted. It is equally interesting as respects the weekly breaking of bread and the weekly contribution. Justin Martyr's Second Apology, page 96—"On Sunday all christians in the city or country meet together, because this is the day of our Lord's resurrection, and then we read the writings of the prophets and apostles. This being done, the president makes an oration to the assembly, to exhort them to imitate, and do the things they heard. Then we all join in prayer, and after that we celebrate the Supper. Then they that are able and willing give what they think fit; and what is thus collected is laid up in the hands of the president, who distributes it to orphans and widows, and other christians as their wants require."

Would to Heaven that all the congregations in these United States approximated as nearly to the ancient order of things, as did those in behalf of whom Justin Martyr addressed the Roman emperor, not more than fifty years after the death of John the apostle!   Editor.

Communication.

Bishop A. Campbell—

Dear Sir,—In reading your "Christian Baptist" of October last, on "Christian Union, No. 3," my attention was particularly arrested and drawn to a few statements on the doctrine of the "Son of God." The author, after having given us the history of the dispute between Alexander and Arius, and the unhappy result of that dispute, proceeds to state one of the most uncharitable sentiments I ever saw or heard. This appears to me the more strange, as proceeding from the pen of one professing such liberal principles, and so ably advocating the doctrine of christian union. I am heartily sorry that this, and a few other remarks of the writer, ever found a place in your pages. The sentiments to which I allude are as follows:—

"It is impossible for those who entertain a reverential regard for the Great God, not to be struck with the presumption of sinful, ignorant, erring mortals, who would dare to investigate a subject of such awful import as the *modus* of the divine existence, and who would presume to go farther in the discovery of God, than he has revealed himself." Have not the presbyterians —have not the regular baptists—have not most of the different sects—have they not "dared to investigate the *modus* of the divine existence?" Have they not "presumed to go further into the discovery of God than he has revealed himself?" Most certainly it is acknowledged. For they assert in their creeds, that "God exists in three persons, the Father, Son, and Holy Ghost; that the Father is of none, neither begotten nor proceeding; the Son is eternally begotten of the Father, and the Holy Ghost eternally proceeding from the Father and the Son." This is not merely an attempt to investigate, but to explain the *modus* of divine existence. This is certainly going further into "the discovery of God, than he has revealed himself." But for this must they all be considered as having no reverential regard for God? If they had, they would not dare—they would not presume to do it! Nay, more; they would be struck to see another dare or presume to do it. The attempt to investigate the *modus* of divine existence, and to go beyond revelation, I cordially disapprobate; but feel unwilling to proscribe all who have dared it. Your writer tells us, that "in the western states a very unprofitable controversy has existed on this subject. If men could be content with the scripture statements of the nature and character of Christ, and could realize the fact that he was worshipped as God by inspired apostles and christians, for which they suffered death, and which was, indeed, the first cause of their persecution, it would end all controversy, and we should soon see a union of sentiment. Without the agreement that Christ is really an object of worship, and is of course divine, there can never be christian union between them."

And is this, sir, the end of all your labors to destroy authoritative creeds and confessions, and unite christians on the broad, unerring base of the bible? Must we adopt this writer's creed, an authoritative creed too? for, without it, "there can never be christian union?" Permit me, sir, to take a view of this creed, and make a few strictures on it."

1. Men must be content with the scripture statements of the nature and character of Christ.

2. They must realize the fact that he was worshipped as God by inspired apostles and christians.

3. That the apostles and christians for worshipping Christ as God, suffered death.

4. That their worshipping him as God was the first cause of their persecution.

5. That believing these things would end all controversy, and produce union of sentiment.

6. That, without the agreement that Christ is really an object of worship, and is of course divine, there can never be christian union.

Article 1. Men must be content with the scriptural statements of the nature and character of Christ.

With this I agree; but your writer has, in the following articles, fixed the doctrine of his nature and character, as being God and divine; and this in the supreme sense; for, on the same page, he says, "the worship of Christ always supposes and includes his godhead, in which the eternal, original, and essential dignity of his person consists." He also informs us on the same page, that this divine person, this person of eternal, original, and essential dignity, called the *Logos*, was made flesh, or conceived in the Virgin Mary, and therefore called the Son of God, by which name he was never called, till born of Mary. Now, sir, who can subscribe this article? Unitarians of every class reject it. Trinitarians will never receive it, for they never will admit the soul revolting, the heart chilling idea of the God supreme being conceived and born of a woman. Can men, thinking men, with the bible in their hands, be content with your writer's statement of "the nature and character of Christ?" Impossible! "It is presuming to go further in the discovery of God than he has revealed himself."

Art. 2. They must realize the fact that he (Christ) was worshipped as God by inspired apostles and christians.

This, though stated as a fact, we think, needs proof; and until this can be brought from the bible, we humbly deny it as a fact. We admit that he was worshipped by inspired apostles and christians, not as the only true God, but as the Son of the only true and living God.—Him, who was obedient to the death of the cross, has God highly exalted, and given a name above every name, that every knee should bow, of things in heaven, in earth, and under the earth, and every tongue confess him Lord, to the glory of God the Father. *Phil.* ii. 6. Here is an object of worship, and one, too, worshipped not only by inspired apostles and christians, but also by all in heaven. Can any one believe that this was the only true and living God? I think not. Again, in *Rev.* i. 5. 6. To him that loved us, and washed us from our sins in his own blood, and has made us kings and priests to God, and his Father, to him be glory and dominion forever and ever. Amen. Here Christ is evidently an object of worship; and it is equally evident that this object is not the only true God. Again, Rev. v. 9. And they sang a new song, saying, You are worthy to take the book and loose the seals thereof, for you were slain and have redeemed us to God by your blood, out of every kindred, and tongue, and nation; and have made us to our God kings and priests. v. 12. Worthy is the Lamb that was slain, to receive power, and riches, and wisdom, and strength, and honor, and glory, and blessing. v. 12. Blessing, glory, honor, and power, be to him that sits on the throne and to the Lamb, forever and ever. This worship is given by all in heaven, earth, and sea. None can doubt that the Son of God is the object as well as his Father. Were it necessary, I could produce abundantly more evidence to the same effect; but these are conclusive that Christ was worshipped, not as the only true God, but as his Son. We cannot subscribe this article.

Art. 3. That the apostles and christians, for worshipping Christ as God, suffered death. This article is positively denied, and we believe the writer cannot produce any evidence to establish the affirmation.

Art. 4. That their worshipping him as God, was the first cause of their persecutions.

This we as positively deny. Proof is again called for. We believe it is called for in vain, for it can never be produced.

Art. 5. That believing these things would end all controversy, and produce union of sentiment.

This we presume not fully to deny; for if all men could believe these things, there would be thus far a union of sentiment, and on these points controversy would cease of course. But are not Calvinists and Arminians generally agreed on the main points in the articles above? and is there an end of controversy between them? Is there a union of sentiment?

Art. 6. That without the agreement that Christ is really an object of worship, and is of course divine, there can never be christian union between them.

That Christ is really an object of worship, and that he is divine, none of us deny. We could readily subscribe this article; but as the writer has defined them, we dare not do it. Uniformity of sentiment is yet contended for, and without it, no christian union.

If these be your sentiments, you will need a new confession of faith, by which to receive members into your societies and communion. If this be your object, to exclude all other creeds to make way for one of your own make, I have been deceived in you. But I think you do not agree with the sentiments of your writer. I had thought, and yet think, that your object was to admit the bible only as authoritative—the only rule of faith and practice—and that the only terms of admission into the church was to believe with all the heart that Jesus Christ was the Son of God, and a holy, obedient conformity to his word through life.

It is the desire of a number of your patrons that you publish this short tract in your next number. Respectfully, your friend,
AQUILA.

—

THERE appears, at first sight, a much greater discrepancy between "Christian Union" and "Aquila" than there really is. In the first instance, they both disapprobate any attempt "to investigate the *modus* of the divine existence, or that would go farther in the discovery of God than he has revealed himself." And both agree that Presbyterians, Baptists, Calvinists, and Arians have made such attempts. And, indeed, every one of those metaphysical doctors, who have written most largely on this controversy, was wont to accuse his opponent with "too much presumption," and the want of "a reverential regard for the Great God." I think, too, that both "Aquila" and "Christian Union" are unwilling to proscribe all who have dared it.

There is too, in the quotation which "Aquila" has made from page 120, a much greater agree-ment than his strictures upon it would seem to import. But one unscriptural phrase is the cause of all this controversy. Had "Christian Union" not introduced the Andover school divinity into his essay, nor this phraseology into his style—had he contented himself with the words which the Holy Spirit teaches in speaking of the Lord whom all christians worship and adore as God's only begotten Son—I say, had he been as fortunate in avoiding the language of Ashdod in this instance as he has been on other occasions, he would not have been so obnoxious to the criticisms of "Aquila." And while these two christians contend that men should be content with the scriptural statements of the nature and character of Christ, they should themselves watch their pens, lest they should offend against their own principles; for we all know that it is much easier to lay down good rules than it is to walk up to them; and I think I can find in both their essays, what I dare say they may both find in my remarks, departures from the style which we all commend. I do not enter into the merits of either of those pieces; they are both before the public; and from my knowledge of both the writers, I am pretty confident their views are very similar on the topics of this letter. But appearing in the regimentals and with the dialect of foreigners, they are likely to mistake one another. That the first christians were persecuted for worshipping Jesus Christ, the Son of God, as Lord of all, and that none can be called or esteemed christians, or unite in christian worship, who do not so believe in him, and so worship him, is what I am convinced both these writers believe. I heard of a man who undesignedly killed his own brother in an engagement with the enemies of his country, in consequence of his brother having put on a red coat.
EDITOR.

—

Messrs. Duncan and M'Lean.

AFTER almost all the political papers in the western country had noticed the withdrawal of these gentlemen from the Presbyterian sect, the editor of the Pittsburg Recorder, the "only religious paper in nine states and three territories," announced the fact; and, by way of comment, added the following very sensible anathema:—"It is said these ministers disown and oppose the Confession of Faith and Form of Government of the Presbyterian Church in the United States, and are acting on a disorganizing plan, tending to anarchy, and to open a way for the corruption of the church by the ingress of the most pernicious errors."

Faithful centinel! True to yourself and to your cause! But tell me how comes it to pass, that when any one affirms that there is but one infallible rule of faith and practice, and that there is no use in adding to it a fallible one, that, in so doing, he becomes a heretic, a disorganizer, an anarchist, a demon? And how is it, tell me, sage, divine, and sagacious watchman! that when any one affirms that we ought to have a fallible and imperfect rule of faith and practice, he then becomes orthodox—sound—a friend of order and good rule—a saint? Does every one who says the scriptures are of divine authority, a revelation of God, and, like their author, perfect and complete—does every such one open the way for the corruption of the church, and introduction of "the most pernicious errors?" But if your fallible rules are your wall of fire, your bulwark, and strong tower, why did they not keep such monsters as Messrs. Duncan and M'Lean from invading your dominions and

42

drawing away so many disciples after them; men who are so wicked as to say that the bible is from Heaven, and your confession from—Edinburgh; men who are so impious as to affirm, even within your sacred walls, and before your awful tribunal, that it is worse than farcical trifling to add to a perfect and infallible rule, an imperfect and fallible one; men who are so obdurate as to say that your creeds began in error, were consummated by ignorance and superstition, and terminated in discord, division, hypocrisy, and persecution. Tell me these things, or rather tell the world, that they may see how wise, and good, and just you are, in consigning to infamy and perdition those unfortunate malefactors who had resolution to think correctly, and honesty and firmness to avow their convictions. When you have done these things, be assured we will join you in holding up to public scorn and contumely the above named gentlemen and all who espouse their sentiments. Till then you will have to pardon us for viewing your efforts as exactly in the spirit, and up to the model, of the Romanists against the Protestants, or of the Jewish Sanhedrim against the first promulgers of the christian faith.   EDITOR.

No. 7.]   FEBRUARY 6, 1826.
Bigotry and Partiality.

THIS is a time of religious and political earthquakes. The religious communities of the new world, and the political states of the old world are in circumstances essentially the same. A great political earthquake threatens to bury in its ruins tyrants and their systems of oppression. The ecclesiastical systems of the clergy appear destined to a similar fate. It is to be hoped that, as the New World took the lead in, and first experienced the blessings of, a political regeneration; so they will be foremost in the work, and first in participating the fruits of an ecclesiastical renovation.

All sects, new and old, seem like a reed shaken by the wind. Even the authority and infallibility of his Roman Holiness has been questioned by his own children in the New World. And who that has eyes to see, does not know that nothing but the sovereign charms of a monarch's smiles, and the strong chains forged from eight hundred millions of dollars in real estate,* keep up the forms of Pope Eliza in the church of Saint Harry. The Solemn League and Covenant too, with the awful dogmas of the long parliament divinity; the test-oaths, and the sacred subscriptions to the saving canons of the kings of Saint Andrew, have failed to preserve, hale and uncorrupted, the pale of Presbyterian communion. The veteran chiefs, and the sanctified magi of the cause of uniformity, fear a volcanic eruption, alike ominous to themselves and their systems. Their "Religious Almanacs" portend comets, falling stars, and strange signs in the heavens, accompanied with eclipses of the greater and lesser lights that rule the night. Their constitution is motheaten, and the tinsel upon their frame of discipline has become dim.

And not less strange, the Reformation of John Wesley is already in need of reform. His people had scarce tested his system of government by the light, not of the bible, but of our political

* "*Wealth of the Church of England.*—It is stated in a late paper, that the fee simple of the established Church of England, is in value equal to £200,000,000, or $888,-888,888; which, allowing sixteen dollars to a pound, would make 24,801 tons of silver. With the income of such a fund, no wonder the church is powerful and has its votaries, and can keep up its existence without possessing any true religion."—*Reformer.*

institutions, until they found it would eventuate in diocesan episcopacy, as tyrannical and as cruel as that which exiled Whitefield and the two Wesleys from the cloisters of "Christ's College" for reading the scriptures and praying.

The motto of the spirit of this age seems to be taken from the gigantic Young—
    "Flaws in the best—full many flaws all o'er."

The Methodists, in the greatness of their strength, are rising to break the chains which threaten to bind them in the house of the Philistines. A host of reformers are about to reform this reformed system. We have seen their efforts, and rejoice. Though we are assured that when they shall have completed their projected reformation, they will then need a reform more thorough than yet they have attempted. We do not despise "their day of small things."

The following sensible remarks do honor to a work entitled "The Mutual Rights of Ministers and People," published in Baltimore by a reforming Methodist committee. We have only to add, that we have lamented that none seem to regret the evils of bigotry, partiality, and persecution, until they feel their dire effects; and that sometimes those who have once plead against persecution when themselves were the objects, plead for it when they had the sword by their side. But we give place to the following pertinent remarks. They are extracted from No. xiv. p. 28—31.   ED. C. B.

"SERIOUS reflection may convince us all, that reformation is highly necessary, not only in matters of church government, but even in our general views of experimental and practical religion. Let us instance one or two particulars.

"While the ministers of religion have been crying aloud, and very justly, against pride, and covetousness, and sensuality, and many other evils: how is it that the great evil of bigotry has been nourished in the heart of the christian church, as though it were an innocent or an indifferent thing? By bigotry, is meant, A man's obstinate attachment to an opinion, or set of opinions, which indisposes him to give a candid hearing to any thing else, and makes him unwilling that his brother should have the same liberty of judgment which he claims for himself. This is one of the deepest and most violent roots of moral evil. It is a great, and seemingly insurmountable obstruction to the progress of truth and righteousness over the whole earth. It affords nourishment and defence for Infidelity, Mahometanism, Judaism, and for every other erroneous system under the sun. Its practical fruits also are abundant. It may be doubted whether covetousness, or sensuality, or the love of power, or the love of praise, have produced a more plentiful harvest of internal and external ungodliness, than this bitter enemy of all righteousness, which Zion's watchmen appear almost to have overlooked. For let it be considered that this same bigotry is the parent of almost all the evil surmisings, heart-burnings, rash judgments, hard speeches, oppressions, and persecutions, that can be found in the christian world. It not only makes null and void the arguments of an opponent; but, alas! it boldly impeaches his motives, and assails his moral character. Not only are his talents to go for nothing—not only are his labors to be despised; but his virtue and piety—his zeal and heavenly-mindedness, though supported by an unblamable life—all, all must be disposed of with indifference or contempt, by the high, and bitter, and sovereign dictates of bigotry! And yet this dark and dread-

43

ful evil is not only winked at, but nourished in the hearts of all the churches in christendom! Would to Heaven this were a mistake! but, alas! the evidence is too manifest, that every church upon earth greatly needs a reformation in this particular. Infidels, and Mahometans, and Heathens, and sinners of every description, may look on with astonishment, and see christians of every name, through the influence of this evil principle, animated with a more constant and flaming zeal against each other, than against the spirit of hell and all the works of darkness! And yet many seem not to be aware that it is to be regarded as a moral evil. Some, perhaps, may be found making high professions of justification and sanctification, and at the same time habitually nourishing this root of bitterness in their hearts. This is a mystery of mysteries, and can only be accounted for by supposing that a thick cloud of intellectual darkness has been overspreading the christian world, especially upon this subject. For a candid and faithful examination of the matter must surely convince every intelligent mind that it is as perfectly vain for a confirmed bigot to make professions of holiness, as for a confirmed thief to make a profession of honesty.

"Whether partiality must be regarded as the daughter, or as the sister of bigotry, may perhaps bear a dispute; but as they have the striking and identical likeness of twins, we may safely call them sisters. The just definition of partiality, is, the confined affection and confidence which a man has for his own party, and which produces a corresponding disaffection and distrust towards all others. How lovely, in the estimation of such a man, are all the peculiarities comprehended under the particular *ism*, by which he and his party are distinguished! and how dark and doubtful is all beside! While his mind is amusing itself in surveying the vast beauties of his party, and inimitable excellencies of its plan, the cloud which obscures the horizon of every other, appears to grow darker every hour! His feelings are sublime and inexpressible, and perhaps advance almost to that state of devotion which is due alone to the Deity, whose only plan is unexceptionable, and who has no party under the sun. Now as God has no party, and as his ministers are to do nothing by partiality, and as the wisdom which is from above is without partiality, as well as without hypocrisy, we might as well doubt whether hypocrisy be a moral evil, as to doubt whether partiality be such. And yet, alas! how has this great evil been spared in the christian world! And not only spared, but the presumption is, that both it and bigotry have been protected and encouraged as the great champions and defenders of each sectarian cause. They make a man zealous and decided —they make him resolute and courageous! Yes, and let it be added, they make him uncandid, fierce, dogmatical, and blind. They are as fine and acceptable allies for a Jew or a Turk— for a Pagan or an Atheist—as they are for a sectarian christian.

"Let us survey, a little further, these evil dispositions in human nature, that we may judge of them by their fruits.

"First, consider their effects within any religious denomination. They say to the soul of every member, So far shall you go in your meditations, and no farther: your business is not to inquire what is true, but merely to inquire what are the sentiments of our church, that you may defend them to the end of the world. You are not only to avoid contradicting them, but you are

to make no addition to them; because our lovely plan is not only free from errors, but also contains the whole body of truth completely. You must silence every heretical thought of improvement, and merely walk in the good old way, as we have pointed it out to you. Thus, whatever error may be in the church, it seems it must be held fast to eternity. The intellectual faculties of the members must be hampered, and their hearts corrupted, by doing violence to honest conviction, and by warping both reason and revelation into the pale of their sectarian boundaries. And even the truth itself is hindered by these evils from producing its native and salutary effects: for truth, when believed merely with the faith of bigotry, is little better than error. Its evidence is not examined, and its value, as truth, is not apprehended; but merely its subserviency to the support of our beloved cause. For if we made our cause subservient to the truth, instead of making the truth subservient to it, we should be willing for our churches to follow the truth wheresoever it might lead the way.

"Secondly, consider their effects upon the different denominations, in their relation to each other. We stand with surprize and wonder, to behold the errors and absurdities of other denominations: they stand with equal surprize and wonder, to behold the errors and absurdities of ours: while the true cause of wonder is, that each party cannot see that they are all holding fast the same identical error, namely, the infallibility of our own party. One party enjoins on all its members to defend every thing here, and to oppose every thing there: the other party does the same. Thus the inquiry, What is truth? is neglected and laid aside. One says, There is no religion with you; and another, There is no religion with you. One says, That is a damnable heresy; and the other says, That is a damnable heresy. One wonders at the blindness and obstinacy of this people; the other wonders at the blindness and obstinacy of that people; while all Heaven pities the selfish vanity of man, and all Hell is pleased with our destructive and ridiculous conduct."

Bigotry.

AMONGST the indiscriminate usage and application of the term *bigotry*, it is not uncommon to find it very unwarrantably applied. It is used to excite public odium, where the thing which it is used to represent is no way disgusting. Hence some are called bigots, and accused of bigotry, for rejecting all written creeds except the bible; for being strict in worshipping God according to his commandments; for requiring the members of a christian community to obey God rather than men. And I have known infidels accuse a christian church of bigotry, because they would not retain in their fellowship immoral persons, or persons who denied the Lord that bought them; and those who, in the apostle's estimation, denied the faith and were worse than an infidel. Those who dislike the institutions of the Messiah are often found reproaching those with bigotry who love and obey them. Indeed, there is no term, whether received in a good or a bad sense, that may not be most egregiously misapplied.   EDITOR.

The Casting Vote, or the Creed triumphant over the Bible.

IN the Long Run Association, Kentucky, reporting three thousand and sixty four members, at the last annual meeting, the first Friday in September last, in Bullit county, a circular letter, written by P. S. Fall, Bishop of the church in Louisville, in said state, advocating the scriptures as the one only sufficient, perfect, and infallible rule of christian faith and manners, and was rejected by the casting vote of Elder George Waller, Moderator of said meeting. It is not a little remarkable that the moderator, a descendant of the Wallers of Virginia, once persecuted by the friends of an orthodox creed, should have saved this little relic of Papal Rome from the sepulchre of human traditions, just in the same manner as his prototype, Dr. Lightfoot saved infant sprinkling in the Westminster Assembly. The house was equally divided on both occasions, and the moderators in the same manner, and for the same reasons, saved their favorite relics. A handsome way, indeed, of establishing orthodoxy! Might not only makes wrong *right*, but changes error into *truth*. The minority had the proscribed letter published; and we are happy in being able to lay before our readers a few sketches of it. We are sorry that our limits forbid more lengthy extracts.

"It is not unfrequently said, by word of mouth, as well as in creeds, *that* "the word of God is the only, and the sufficient and perfect rule of faith and practice." While this is admitted in word by all religious denominations, it is to be feared that but few feel the force, or understand the import of their own declaration. Let them but critically examine every part of this sentence, and while it appears in direct accordance with the word itself, it is in complete violation of the practice of almost all; for if the declaration be true, that the "word of God" is the only, sufficient, and perfect rule in ALL things pertaining to belief or conduct, why are creeds, confessions and human formulas of doctrine, practice, government and experience, established as the exclusive tests of all, to the manifest deterioration of the bible, while churches rest contented with the bare declaration of its sufficiency?"

"In illustration of the importance of the Holy Bible, permit us to examine the position that the word of God is the only sufficient and perfect rule of our faith and practice."

"We observe, first: It is "the rule of faith." When we speak of "faith," we do not allude to a system of doctrine, in the common acceptation of the term, but to the very facts and truths which must be believed in order to salvation. It is supposed to be of very little importance whether a man be a Calvinist or Arminian; whether he adopt the Gillite, Fullerite, Hopkinsian, or Triangular system of Calvinism; or whether he reject all, (these systems themselves being judges,) so that he believe "the record God has given of his Son," and move in obedience to the truth; so that his "experience" coincides with the bible; all is then supposed to be right, whatever system he adopts. Now there is a manifest inconsistency between the two parts of this hypothesis; for all these systems propose themselves to us as true, yet they are all contrary, the one to the other; and if really thus at variance, and persons of equal intelligence and supposed piety be found among their advocates, how can all believe the record God has given of his Son, when all believe things so different? How can all move in obedience to the truth, when all move different ways? How can all have experiences coincident with the bible, when all have experiences coincident with the systems they maintain, thus at variance with each other? In fact, it is absurd to distinguish between a man's faith and what he believes, between a man's experience and what he

knows; for faith is belief—experience is knowledge."

"Thirdly. They are the only rule of both. As our faith and conduct are so intimately connected, that if the former be defective, the latter must be so of consequence—it is of vast importance to us that there be some definite standard by which to measure both, and ascertain their character. If there were more rules than one, and all agreed, all but one would be unnecessary; and if they disagreed, no one could ascertain which had the highest claim on our attention. We therefore should be left without any. There can, therefore, be but one only infallible standard of faith and practice; and this must be supported by evidence, internal and external, sufficient to prove its truth. It is not for us now to enter upon the consideration of the evidences of the inspiration of the Holy Bible; but there is one which demonstrates it to be that one only and infallible rule. It is the plainest book in the world. It is better adapted to all capacities than any other; and, as the Confession of Faith says, "any one with ordinary sense can understand it." When we read the Bible, we are often apt to look for some dark hidden meaning, which none but the preachers are supposed capable of understanding; (and hence the necessity of a special call and the communication of peculiar powers from on high;) but it is abundantly clear, that the meaning of every part of the New Testament is to be ascertained by an attentive study, not only of what is written, but why it was written, and that the literal and obvious meaning of words and phrases is the true meaning of those employed in the communication of divine truths."

"We observe, fourthly, that the word of God is the only sufficient rule of faith and practice."

"If we were to suppose that it were insufficient, should we not arraign the wisdom and benevolence of Heaven? If Jehovah could have given a sufficient rule of faith and practice, and would not do it, what ideas could we form of his benevolence? If his benevolence would have prompted him to give a sufficient rule, and he could not do it, he is of necessity deficient in wisdom; but he has given us the Holy Volume and has declared it to be sufficient—"able to make us wise to salvation," to give us "an inheritance among all them which are sanctified," and "to save our souls." *Jas.* i. 21. Now every attempt to attach importance to any other rule than this, is evidently a blow aimed both at the wisdom and benevolence of God; since these have furnished us with the Holy Bible, and we lay it aside to examine ourselves, our brethren, and christian churches, by the works of men's hands—creeds and confessions of faith, and by these determine who is orthodox or the contrary. These things may not be palatable, brethren, but they are lamentably true, and require our most serious consideration."

"Lastly, the word of God is the only, sufficient, and perfect rule of faith and obedience."

"To suppose that God would communicate to his creatures any revelation that is imperfect, would shock all common sense. The denunciations against those who add to, or take from the Holy Volume, demonstrate that it needs neither increase nor diminution. All that God intends to reveal to the children of men, is to be found in the Bible. No new revelation need be expected, nor is one requisite, since all things necessary to know, to believe, and to do, in order to salvation, are given us already."

WE are happy to discover in the Minutes of said Association, the progress of principles which augur a growing regard for, and investigation of, the infallible rule of faith and practice, as the following items show:—

"*Query from Elk Creek.*—Is it for the honor of the cause of Christ, that all ordained Baptist preachers be called Bishops? If not, who are to be so named?

"In reply to this query we state, that it was evidently the practice in the first churches to denominate the Pastor of one congregation a Bishop. It is also clear that the terms Elder, Shepherd, Teacher, and Overseer, all refer to the same persons. It is, therefore, according to the word of God, and for the honor of the cause of Christ, that the teacher of one congregation be called a Bishop.

"The following queries from the church at Louisville, were referred to the churches for their investigation, with the request that they will express their sentiments upon them in their next letters:—

"1. Is there any authority in the New Testament for religious bodies to make human creeds and confessions of faith the constitutions or directories of such bodies in matters of faith or practice?

"2. Is there any authority in the New Testament for Associations? If so, what is it? If not, why are they held?

"The following query from the church at Shelbyville, is also referred as above, viz.

"Are our Associations, as annually attended, of general utility?"

Confessions of Faith—Confessions of Opinion.

AFTER all that has been said on this subject, there is not a sect in this country, of which we have heard, that has a confession of faith, properly so called. They have books and pamphlets, which they call by this name, and by which they impose upon themselves and upon one another. If it be not too late, we would give them a true and proper name, a name which we are assured every man of good sense and of common education must approve, as well as agree to discard the common name as a misnomer, as incorrect, and as absurd. The proper name of those instruments is, doubtless, according to the English language, A Confession of Opinions, or, Confessions of Opinions. If there be any difference between faith and opinion, (and that there is, all languages and dictionaries declare,) then the name we have given them is perfectly *apropos*, and their common name perfectly incongruous.

All writers on faith, properly so called, define it to be, "the belief of testimony, either human or divine." And opinion is, "the notions, judgment, or view which the mind forms of any thing." For example, I believe the testimony which God has given to Jesus of Nazareth, or I believe that Jesus of Nazareth is the Messiah, the Son of the living God. This is a well attested fact, in proof of which the Father, the Word, and the Holy Spirit have given, or agree in one testimony. Concerning this person, his mission, and character, various opinions may be formed. All things testified of him are articles or items of belief; and all views, judgments, or notions formed of the things testified, are matters of opinion. Now all the abstract views of God and man, of things present and future, with which these confessions are replete, are matters of opinion; and as the general character of these books should fix upon them their name, they should be styled Confessions of Opinions. To

speak philosophically, I believe what is testified, I know what I have observed or experienced, and I am of opinion in all things speculative. It is true, in one sense, I may be said to know what I have believed, when my faith has been proved by observation and experience. But the terms faith, knowledge, and opinion, should never be confounded. I believe that Jesus Christ died for our sins, I know that the sun gives us light, and I am of opinion that all infants dying shall be saved.

A person's faith is always bounded by testimony; his knowledge by observation and experience, and his opinions commence where both these terminate, and may be boundless as God's creation or as human invention. Perfect freedom and liberty should be granted to all opinions. The faith of christians should be guarded and circumscribed by the revelation of God, and every man's knowledge admitted to be co-extensive with his observation and experience. In matters of this world those distinctions are realized and acted upon every day. A killed B. C believes it, D knows it, and E is of opinion that A killed B. C believes it to be true, because three credible persons have sworn that they saw him do it. D, one of the three witnesses, knows it to be true because he saw it done. And E, who neither heard the testimony nor saw the deed, but from some circumstances detailed to him, is of opinion that it is true. These distinctions are, we presume, evidently correct. A superficial reader may object that Thomas is said to have believed what he saw. But those who attend to all the circumstances will see that he believed the testimony which he had before heard, when certain evidences were presented to his eyes. In this sense the term may, by even correct speakers, be often used. But enough is said to suggest a train of reflections which must issue in the conviction that our confessions of faith are confessions of opinions, and as such ought to have nothing to do with the union, communion, and harmony of christians. "There is one faith," says the apostle; but no where in the volume is it said, There is one opinion. Every new religious establishment, founded upon one opinion, will come to ruin, as all the past have done, and as all the present are doing. But the gates of Hades shall not prevail against those who build on the one faith, which is beautifully and properly called "the Rock."   EDITOR.

Boone county, Missouri, Nov. 23, 1825.
To the Editor of the Christian Baptist.

DEAR SIR—I TAKE my pen in hand to inform you that your influence is much injured in this country among the United Baptists, through a report that you belong to the Unitarians, and that you yourself are one. This report has been circulated by the Unitarians in this country.— Feeling tolerably well satisfied that you are not, I have labored considerably to prevent a belief of this kind. But not having seen any thing in your writings decisive on that topic, have not been able to keep the people from harboring a suspicion that you may be an Arian or Unitarian.

You will please do yourself the justice, and me the pleasure, of informing me of your standing; that is, what society you are in, and your belief of our glorious Redeemer.

I remain yours in gospel bonds,
          T. T.

Reply to "T. T."

DEAR BROTHER—YOUR favor of the 23d November was duly received; but my numerous and multiform engagements hitherto prevented my replying to it; and I now do it through a medium that may prevent the necessity of my having frequently to furnish such replies. Many heresies and errors are ascribed to me by those who are interested in keeping the people in ignorance and bondage. The only favor that I ask of the public, is, to accept my own statements and avowals of my sentiments, instead of the railings of my opponents, who, because of their own imbecility, or that of their cause, find it more easy to defame than to refute. And, of all calumniators, they do it with the most effect, and are consequently most obnoxious to reproof, who commend that they may defame; who say such a sentiment is true, and in this he is undoubtedly right; "*but*" (O! the tremendous BUT) "he is a Socinian or an Arian."

None of these pulpit defamers or fireside traducers dare, through the same medium through which I publish my sentiments, publish their slanders and defamations. But by their more private inuendoes and reproaches, and by whole phalanxes of omnipotent *buts*, like moles, work under ground, and bury themselves and their followers in the heaps they raise.

In different regions in this vast country they use different slanders. Their general rule appears to be this: Whatever seems to be the most odious heresy in the neighborhood is placed to my credit. Thus, in one place, I am a Socinian; in another, an Arian; in a third, a Trinitarian; in some places I am all at once an Arminian; in others, a Calvinist; here a Pelagian, and there an Antinomian; yonder I am a Universalist, and elsewhere a Sabellian. If these calumnies were drawn from what I have spoken or written, I would at once compliment myself as a very close follower of Paul. For as each of these sectaries contends that Paul favors his heresy, if any one teaches *all* Paul taught, he will be as likely to be represented as favoring these heresies as Paul himself is. Thus with the Methodist, Paul is a Methodist; with the Calvinist, he is a Calvinist; with the Universalist, he is a Universalist; and with the Socinian, Paul is said to have been a Socinian, &c. &c. But if none but Calvinists approved my course, or if none but Arminians censured me, I would conclude that I had disowned Paul. For to me it is certain, if any man teach *all* that Paul taught he will sometimes be approved by all, and sometimes blamed by all. There is no sect that does not contend for some things Paul taught. It is, therefore, most apparent, that he who is approved by one sect only, is, *ipso facto*, proved to be a setter forth of some new doctrine, or a retailer of some antiquated error.

But the misfortune is, that I cannot enjoy the above compliment in full, because I know that the rule of slander most generally approved, is, to accuse me of holding that error or heresy which is most damnable in the estimation of those amongst whom it is circulated. And when this will not serve the purpose, even my moral character is assailed. In Kentucky, some time after my debate with Mr. M'Calla, it was reported that I had stolen a horse; and not long since, in Illinois, it was said that I was excommunicated for drunkenness. Not far from Lake Erie I was said to have turned Deist, and by those too who bought their sermons in Boston, and read them in Ohio; and in many places, that I was known to be an "*extremely immoral man*" in my own vicinity. In fact, as a Doctor of Divinity told his people near Lexington, I am "*a very bad man*" in the estimation of many,

and it would afford them a satisfaction, which I trust they will never enjoy, (and yet it is *cruel* on my part to deprive them of it) to be able to publish my fall and ruin to the utmost bounds of this union. I am sure of it. They would rejoice to be able, with some degree of plausibility, to accuse me of some high misdemeanor. For their own deeds and lispings avow it.

That I am not a Socinian, you may see by turning over to No. 8, 1st vol. C. B.—and as you know I have no faith in the *divine right* of Associations, yet, to shield me from such *far-off* and *underhand* attacks, as well as for other important purposes, that I may be under the inspection and subject to merited reprehension, I and the church with which I am connected are in "full communion" with the Mahoning Baptist Association, Ohio; and, through them, with the whole Baptist society in the United States; and I do intend to continue in connexion with this people so long as they will permit me to say what I believe, to teach what I am assured of, and to censure what is amiss in their views or practices. I have no idea of adding to the catalogue of new sects. This game has been played too long. I labor to see sectarianism abolished, and all christians of every name united upon the one foundation on which the apostolic church was founded. To bring Baptists and Paido-Baptists to this is my supreme end. But to connect myself with any people who would require me to sacrifice one item of revealed truth, to subscribe any creed of human device, or to restrain me from publishing my sentiments as discretion and conscience direct, is now, and I hope ever shall be, the farthest from my desires, and the most incompatible with my views. And I hope I will not be accused of sectarian partiality when I avow my conviction that the Baptist society have as much liberality in their views, as much of the ancient simplicity of the christian religion, as much of the spirit of christianity amongst them, as are to be found amongst any other people. To say nothing of the things in which they excel, this may be said of them without prejudice to any. And that they have always been as eminent friends of civil and religious liberty as any sect in christendom, will not, I presume, be denied by any. But that there are amongst them some mighty Regulars, who are as intolerant as the great Pontiff of regularity and good order, no person will deny. And that there is in the views and practices of this large and widely-extended community, a great need of reformation, and of a restoration of the ancient order of things, few will contradict. In one thing, perhaps, they may appear in time to come, proudly singular, and pre-eminently distinguished. Mark it well. Their historian, in the year 1900, may say, "We are the only people who would tolerate, or who ever did tolerate, any person to continue as a Reformer or a Restorer amongst us. While other sects excluded all who would have enlarged their views and exalted their virtues; while every Jerusalem in christendom stoned its own prophets, and exiled its own best friends, and compelled them to set up for themselves, we constitute the only exception of this kind in the annals of christianity—nay, in the annals of the world." I think it is not a very precarious *perhaps*, that this may yet be said of this ancient and singular people.—But should it come to pass that neither they nor any other people can say this of themselves, then, most assuredly, if ever there be a united and a happy state of the church upon this earth; if ever there be a millennium; the Baptist society, as well as every other, will have to be immersed in that general catastrophe which awaits every sect who holds a principle incompatible with this millennial state of the church.

Your brother, in the hope of the resurrection of the dead.   Editor.

January 17, 1826.

P. S. There was a *John* Campbell in Pittsburgh, who was said to have been a Socinian. He is no longer one. He has gone to *Hades*, where there is not a Socinian, an Arian, nor a Trinitarian. Perhaps I may, in Missouri, have been identified with, or mistaken for this person. I need not cause you to pay the postage for the minutes of our Association, or any other documents, as I presume the above will be satisfactory.

Conscience.—No. II.

In a former number we set out with this position, viz.—" Throughout christendom every man's religious experience corresponds with his religious education." This was partially illustrated in that number. We will make some additions in the present.

As there are some things similar and some things different in the education of most persons; so there are some things alike and some things unlike in their religious experience. In our last number on this subject we took notice of the influence which conscience has upon the religious experience of all; and that conscience was framed by those who first had access to the infant mind. This was proved by observing the varieties which appear in the consciences of different individuals.

What is called "the work of conversion," is, in many instances, but the revival of early impressions. And what a poor progress the teachers of religion, as they are called, would make in converting persons, were it not for the early impressions made by parents and guardians, may be easily ascertained by comparing their success amongst Pagans and amongst the descendants of christian parents. And even amongst the latter, their success is proportioned to the degrees of care bestowed upon some, in comparison of others.

Amongst the numerous accounts of "christian experience" which we have heard from the lips of the converted, and the histories of their conversion, we do not remember to have heard one which was not to be traced to, or resolved into, parental influence, or its equivalent. This appears to be the *preaching* which is most commonly instrumental in bringing sinners into the fold of God. I have sometimes thought that not one preacher in these United States has had the honor of being the entire and exclusive means of converting one of the descendants of those who made any pretensions to christianity, except in the case of his own family. Their hearers and attendants, in public assemblies, have heard that there is a God, a heaven, a hell, a Saviour, before they hear it from their lips. They predicate their pleas, arguments, exhortations, and addresses to their hearers, upon the hypothesis that they are in possession of these first principles. When any one is moved to *fear* or *hope* from their addresses, it is from comparing what he has heard, or from associating it with his former conduct and convictions.

This person was awakened on hearing a preacher read for his text these words, "How shall we escape if we neglect so great salvation."— On hearing these words he was struck with fear; his whole soul was harrowed up; he was almost driven to despair: but in the conclusion he was made to hope in God and to trust in his salvation. Ask him what he feared and why he feared, and he will tell you that he feared the wrath of Heaven for having neglected this salvation. But had he not previously believed that there was a future punishment awaiting the disobedient, how could his fears have been excited? "But," adds he, " I was not only afraid of the wrath of Heaven on account of my neglect, but I would rather than all the world that I could have believed in the Saviour and shared in his salvation." Well, why did you desire to believe in the Saviour if you had not previously believed there was a Saviour? Why did you wish to share in his salvation, if you had not before believed that you were a sinner, and that there was salvation? Your doubts and fears, then, were all founded upon your former convictions. And had it not been for these, neither the reading of these words, nor the preacher's remarks, would have produced one emotion. Nay, his strongest appeals to your conscience were based upon the supposition that you were in possession of these convictions. If he have been instrumental in any respect, it was in causing you to hope that notwithstanding you had long sinned against the light you had since an infant, there was room in the divine mercy for your pardon and acceptance, in believing and obeying the truths you had once received and acknowledged, and had been taught, whether your father was Protestant or Papist, High Churchman or Dissenter. He may have revived those impressions, and been instrumental in leading you to repentance for having lived in opposition to your own acknowledgments; but the seeds were sown before.

In the same manner the influences of Heaven take hold of these truths, however first communicated to the mind; and persons are not unfrequently, without a preacher, influenced to act according to the light formerly received, and *then* illustrated and revived—'tis true, not without a preacher, in the scripture sense, but in the popular sense. For parents, guardians, or whosoever pronounces the words of the preachers specially called and sent by God, only gives extension or sound to words long since announced.

But the seeds are sown in "a land of bibles," always in infancy or childhood, which, under the divine blessing, in riper years, bring forth fruit to everlasting life. Conscience is then formed, and without this, a man might as rationally expect to be instrumental in converting fish as men. But it most commonly happens that *tares* are sown with the *wheat* in the mind, though not in the sense of the parable; or, in other words, improper views are communicated with the truth of God, which, in after life, give rise to that mental perturbation and those varied feelings of which many are conscious. The catechisms and little manuals, put into the hands of children, together with the old wives' fables which they are wont to hear, lay the foundation for many a doubt and reverie, of which, otherwise, they never would have known any thing.

Every person who will reflect, and who can reflect upon the workings of his own mind, will readily perceive how much trouble he has experienced from mistakes. Nay, much of his present comfort is derived from the correction of former mistakes and misapprehensions.— Who that has read John Bunyan's conversion, John Newton's, or Halyburton's, or any of those celebrated standards of *true* conversion, has not observed that glaring mistakes and erroneous views were amongst the chief causes of their long and gloomy trials; and that their after peace, and joy, and hope, arose from the correction of mistakes which the errors of education had thrown in their way.

For example: The numerous speculations on the different kinds of faith has pierced with many sorrows innumerable hearts. In all the varied exhibitions of christianity, much stress is laid on faith. And as soon as it is affirmed that he that believes shall be saved, and that care should be taken that faith be of "the right kind," the attention of the thoughtful is turned from the truth to be believed to "the nature of faith." The fears and agonies which are experienced are not unfrequently about "believing right." The great concern is about true faith. This person is looking in himself for what he has been taught are the true signs of regeneration, or of the faith of regeneration. He is distressed to know whether his faith is the fruit of regeneration, or whether it is mere "historic faith." Unable to find such evidences as he is in quest of, he is distracted, he despairs, he agonizes. He tells his case. He is comforted by being told that these are "the pangs of the new birth." He draws some comfort from this consideration, which increases or decreases as these pangs are supposed to be genuine or the reverse. Thus he is tossed to and fro in awful uncertainties, which are more or less acute according to his moral sensibilities. By and by he hopes he is regenerate, and a calm ensues, and he is joyous because he fancies he has been regenerated. Thus his comforts spring not from the gospel, but from his own opinion of himself.

Another, under the same system, receives no comfort because he has not found the infallible signs in himself of being a true believer. He despairs—he is tormented. He concludes that he is one of the reprobates. He is about to kill himself. What about? Not because there is no Saviour, no forgiveness, no mercy. Not because the gospel is not true; but because it is true, and because he cannot find in himself the true signs of genuine conversion. Thousands have been ruined—have been shipwrecked here. This the bible never taught. This case never occurred under the apostles' teaching. It is the genuine offspring of the theological schools. It is the experience of a bad education. A few drops of acid sour a puncheon of the sweetest wine. And thus a few wrong notions convert the love of the Saviour into divine wrath—make the gospel of non-effect—embitter life—and make it better not to have been born.

I well remember what pains and conflicts I endured under a fearful apprehension that my convictions and my sorrows for sin were not deep enough. I even envied Newton of his long agony. I envied Bunyan of his despair. I could have wished, and did wish, that the Spirit of God would bring me down to the very verge of suffering the pains of the damned, that I might be raised to share the joys of the genuine converts. I feared that I had not sufficiently found the depravity of my heart, and had not yet proved that I was utterly without strength. Sometimes I thought that I felt as sensibly, as the ground under my feet, that I had gone just as far as human nature could go without supernatural aid, and that one step more would place me safe among the regenerated of the Lord; and yet Heaven refused its aid. This, too, I concealed from all the living. I found no comfort in all the declarations of the gospel, because I wanted one thing to enable me to appropriate them to myself. Lacking this, I could only envy the happy

favorites of heaven who enjoyed it, and all my refuge was in a faint hope that I one day might receive that aid which would place my feet upon the rock.

Here this system ends, and enthusiasm begins. The first christians derived their joys from an assurance that the gospel was true. Metaphysical christians derive theirs not from the truth of the gospel, but because they have been regenerated, or discover something in themselves that entitles them to thank God that they are not as the publican. The ancients cheered themselves and one another by conversing on the certainty of the good things reported by the apostles—the moderns, by telling one another what "the Lord has done for their souls in particular." Their agonies were the opposition made by the world, the flesh, and the devil, to their obeying the truth. Our agonies are a deep and solemn concern for our own conversion. Their doubts were first, whether the gospel were true, and, after they were assured of this, whether they might persevere through all trials in obeying the truth. Ours, whether our conversion is genuine. More evidence of the truth removed their first doubts, and the promises of the gospel, with the examples around them, overcame the last. A better opinion of ourselves removes ours. In a word, the philanthropy of God was the fountain of all their joys—an assurance that we are safe is the source of ours.

The experience of the Moravians differs fom the experience of almost every other sect. They teach their children that God is love, and through his son loves all that obey him. This principle is instilled from the cradle. Their history does not furnish an instance of a work of conversion similar to those which fill the memoirs and magazines of all the different bodies of Calvinists. Perhaps enough has been said to prove our position, that "throughout christendom every man's religious experience corresponds with his religious education." If not, a volume of evidence can be adduced. EDITOR.

Honorable Title of "D. D." Refused.

IN some eastern papers "the Rev. Spencer H. Cone, a Baptist clergyman," was reported as recently dubbed D. D. But this was a mistake. It was the Rev. Samuel H. Cox who was dubbed and refused the honor. We are sorry to observe a hankering after titles amongst some baptists, every way incompatible with their profession; and to see the remarks lately made in the "Columbian Star," censuring Mr. Cox for declining the honor. Those who deserve honorary titles are the least covetous of them. We have not met with any baptist bishop who is more worthy of a title of honor, if such these double D's be esteemed, than Robert B. Semple of Virginia; and when the degree was conferred on him, he, like a christian, declined it.

The following remarks are worthy of a place in this work:—

"In the New York Observer of the 26th ult. we find an article occupying nearly two closely printed columns, with the signature of Samuel H. Cox, Pastor of the Lightstreet Presbyterian Church, N. Y. in which the writer, after stating that he had seen a newspaper paragraph from which he learned that the trustees of Williams College, Mass. had taken with his name the very customary liberty of attaching D. D. to it, says, "I ask the privilege of announcing that I will not accept of that appendage." And after some other observations, he adds, "It is high time— the spirit of the age demands it—that this mania of graduating should itself be graduated, and that without favor in the enlightened estimation of the public. *Itaque illud Cassianum. Cui bono fuerit, in his personis valeat.* The *cui bono* question in reference to those academico-theological degrees, and for the best possible reason, has never been answered. It is an affair that belongs to another category. It has nothing to do with *good*, but only with—*honor!*"

Having disavowed any disrespect to Williams College, or to his clerical brethren, especially the order from which he repudiates himself, he makes the following remarks:

"The purely academic and literary or professional degrees, such as A. B. or A. M. or M. D. or L. L. D. and such as merely indicate office or station, and which colleges do not confer, as V. D. M. or S. T. P. are out of the argument, and "against such there is no law." If doctorates in divinity meant any thing, they would sometimes be libellous. There are those, it is too notorious, who need a great deal more than collegiate or colloquial doctoration to impart to them intellectual, or literary, or theological, or (I blush to write it) even moral respectability; and whose doctoration, while it is the acrimonious laugh of the million, becomes a solid reason, were there none better, to those who prize good company, for abdicating the eminence of being classed with them in the associations of the community. "To their assembly, mine honor, be not thou united."

In assigning reasons for refusing the honorary title of D. D., Mr. Cox makes the following remarks:

"I believe that the principle of ministerial party is both evangelical and important, and that the system in question is very inimical to it; that there is no higher earthly honor in the relations of life than that of a minister of Jesus Christ, who loves his master and understands the truth and magnifies his office; and consequently I dislike a system that so evidently and popularly implies something unintelligibly more, and arrays one ministerial brother in an adventitious superiority over his peers; and that it is anomalous for a secular and literary institution, without any faculty of theology, to come into the church universal of Jesus Christ, and diversify his officers, and confer permanent degrees of official honor, which neither deposition nor excommunication, should they succeed, has power to annul; and all this where he has said, "Be not you called Rabbi; for one is your master, even Christ; and all you are brethren." It is also a grand reason that I think it a "scarlet" relic of papacy, and that demands retrenchment; but the greatest reason is, that it is earthly, and at variance with the spirit, if not with the very letter of the gospel. The passage in Matt. xxiii. 5—12. appears incapable of a fair solution in coincidence with the innocency of doctorial honors in the church. Many other scriptural references might be made. Take a few more: *Matt.* xviii. 1—6. v. 19. *Luke* xxii. 24—27. xx. 45—47. *John* xvii. 18. xii. 25. 43. v. 41. 1 *Cor.* 1—5. *Rev.* iii. 21. xii. 4. xvi. 15. xvii. 12. The Old Testament contains much to the same purport.

To conclude, I believe that the usefulness, the moral worth, the genuine respectability of the sacred profession, and, of course, the honor of our common Master, require the abjuration of Doctorates."

Unity of Opinion.

Unity of opinion, abstractedly considered, is neither desirable nor a good; although considered not in itself, but with reference to something else, it may be both. For men may be all agreed in error; and, in that case, unanimity is an evil. Truth lies within the Holy of Holies, in the temple of knowledge; but doubt in the vestibule that leads to it. Luther began by having his doubts as to the assumed infallibility of the Pope; and he finished by making himself the corner stone of the Reformation. Copernicus and Newton doubted the truth of the false systems of others before they established a true one of their own. Columbus differed in opinion with all the old world before he discovered a new one; and Galileo's terrestrial body was confined in a dungeon for having asserted the motion of those bodies that were celestial. In fact, we owe almost all our knowledge, not to those who have agreed, but to those who have differed, and those who have finished by making all others think with them, have usually been those who began by daring to think for themselves; as he that leads a crowd, must begin by separating himself some little distance from it. If the great Hervey, who discovered the circulation of the blood, had not differed from all the physicians of his own day, all the physicians of the present day would not have agreed with him. These reflections ought to teach us that every kind of persecution for opinion, is incompatible with sound philosophy. It is lamentable, indeed, to think how much misery has been incurred from the intemperate zeal and bigoted officiousness of those who would rather that mankind should not think at all, than not think as they do. Charles V. when he abdicated a throne, and retired to the monastery of St. Juste, amused himself with the mechanical arts, and particularly with that of a watch-maker; he one day exclaimed, "What an egregious fool must I have been, to have squandered so much blood and treasure in an absurd attempt to make all men think alike, when I cannot even make a few watches keep time together." We should remember also that assent or dissent is not an act of the will, but of the understanding. No man can will to believe that two and two make five, nor can I force upon myself the conviction that this ink is white, or this paper black.—[*National Gazette.*

[This is all very good; but in the christian religion there are no new discoveries, no new improvements to be made. It is already revealed and long since developed in the apostolic writings. We may discover that there are many new errors and old traditions, which are alike condemned in those sacred writings. But truth is at least one day older than error; and what many now call "the good old way," was two or three hundred years ago denominated a wicked innovation or a chimerical new project. Old things become new when long lost sight of, and new things become old in one generation. But truth is eternal and unchangeable.]

Ed. C. B.

No. 3.]   March 6, 1826.
Review of a Sermon on the Duty of the Church to prepare Pious Youth in her bosom for the Gospel Ministry.—By the Rev. Gideon Blackburn, D. D. Pastor of the Church in Louisville, Ky.—Text, Eph. iv. 11, 12.

" And he gave some apostles ; and some, prophets ; and some evangelists ; and some, pastors and teachers, for the perfecting of the saints, for the work of the ministry, for the edifying of the body of Christ."

This is that Rev. Gideon Blackburn, D. D who boasted that he had " swept from the arena"
50

a discourse of mine before the legislature of Kentucky, in 1824, on the subject of what he calls "the gospel ministry;" and whom I had invited to do in my presence what he had so easily done in my absence. This he has since declined and begs to be excused. But as a substitute he has offered this sermon on that subject, fraught with all the logic and rhetoric for which he has been honored with the title of D. D. We may then expect to find in it all those arguments which "swept from the arena" my cobwebs; which dissipated to the four winds of heaven the dust of my reasonings, arguments, and proofs. As a fair and full specimen of what the Doctor can advance in support of his views, we are bound to consider it. This is his cool, deliberate, studied, and, no doubt, best effort, against what some "wiseacres" have said against modern clergymen as the successors of the apostles, as the ambassadors of Christ, as the called and sent of the Holy Spirit. We shall therefore bestow a little attention upon it. For as the author of it is at the head of the priesthood of his state, and as he is one of the honored called ones, whom the Holy Spirit has sent to Kentucky; and, in attestation of which, and to show how far the men of this world have approved of the Holy Spirit's choice and work, they have honored him with two capitals of mighty power and awful import; and as he is a father in Israel, his sayings and reasonings are entitled to great respect. It is but seldom the patrons of the science of this world approve of the appointments of the Holy Spirit. For of the thousands whom he calls and sends, not more than one in ten is recognized by colleges and their trustees as worthy of an honorary title. When, therefore, the Holy Spirit, the presbytery, and the patrons of science, infidels and all, concur in attesting an ambassador of Christ, most assuredly we ought, with due submission, to sit at his feet. But this rebellious heart of mine wants something more than all the presbytery and the board of trustees can confer, in proof that Gideon Blackburn, D. D. Pastor of the church in Louisville, is sent by the Holy Spirit, and a true ambassador of Jesus Christ. It is true that this sermon exhibits him very much in the true character of an ambassador, for as soon as an ambassador has proved his mission, his mere assertions and *say so's* are equal to all the logic and rhetoric of Demosthenes and Cicero united in one head. Consequently the Doctor, laying infinite stress upon his own infallibility, has not adduced one single scrap from Moses to John, to prove the subject of his discourse. This is, indeed, ambassador-like. The Holy Spirit, the college, and the presbytery, having chosen, and called, and sent, and honored him, it would have been beneath the dignity of them all that he should have to prove what he says. This would be placing him upon a level with a Methodist or Baptist elder. This would destroy all his high pretensions. It is necessary for a Methodist or Baptist teacher to prove all that he advances, but entirely unnecessary for Gideon Blackburn, D. D. Right well he knows this! and consequently, in the true style of an ambassador, he deigns no proof!

His sermon is intended to proclaim that it is the duty of the church to prepare in her bosom pious youth for the gospel ministry. Now this is really a new message from the skies, for there is not one word, from Genesis to John, which says that it is the duty of the church to prepare pious youth for the gospel ministry. This point could not be proved from the words of any pre-

vious ambassador, and it is unnecessary for an ambassador to prove his own communications to be true. But now this reverend ambassador informs the world that it is the duty of the church to train young men for the gospel ministry, and of these young men to make presbyters or elders.

His text, to have been pertinent to his purpose, ought to have read, "When Jesus ascended to his throne, he gave apostles, prophets, evangelists, pastors, and teachers, supernaturally qualified for the work, and in a moment prepared to discharge the duties of their calling—and then gave orders to the churches to train up young men, artificially and mechanically, to be their successors in the manner hereinafter specified." This text would have suited his subject. But I am wrong. An ambassador, prophet, or evangelist, &c. ought to take no text at all, but make a text for himself. The taking of a text implies inferiority and dependance, every way unbecoming "the legate of the skies." And the Rev. Doctor is aware of this; for although he conforms to the custom of his modern peers in writing a text at the head of the page, he simply adduces it as a motto, and troubles his head no more about it, but proceeds to something more sublime and glowing from the skies—no old revelation, but one new and brilliant, occupies his tongue and pen.

This sermon occupies twenty octavo pages, and has not one argument in it to show that the text has any more bearing upon the present day, nor upon his subject, than "Abraham begat Isaac, and Isaac begat Jacob." Indeed there is not a single sentence of scripture adduced in the way of argumentative proof, in the whole discourse. Some two or three scraps round off as many periods, and the bible is upon a par with the Koran through the remainder of the sermon. But this was wisely done, for the bible has nothing to do with his object or design. His mock explanation of apostles, prophets, pastors, &c. is a burlesque on modern commentators. The "teachers" mentioned in the text are represented as professors of divinity and presidents of theological schools. "Some teachers," says he, "whose business it is particularly to explain the doctrines and regulations (canons) of the church, and carefully instruct young men in the course of theology taught in the bible."

His method of sweeping from the arena all argument and proof, is fairly exhibited in the following words:—"The general idea implied in the office of minister or ambassador for Christ, was designed to continue in the church to the end of time; but the special idea attached to the ministry, under the word apostles and prophets, ended with the completion of the canon of scripture." This single assertion of one D. D. "sweeps from the arena" all that ten thousand such as I am might say in a century. So the Doctor thinks, for he adduces no more. This is just the topic, too, in substance, on which all turns, and every thing is decided, that came upon that "arena" which the Doctor swept so clean. This is a besom of destruction, indeed! this mighty, this omnipotent assertion. 'Tis well for you that you are an old man, and of a privileged order; for had a pious young man asserted so roundly, we would have demanded the proof. But there is no need of proof—an ambassador from the skies says so!

But after all, the assertion is a little wanting in common sense, and borders upon what, amongst young men, is called nonsense.—A "general idea" continues in the church till the end of time, and a " special idea" died with the completion of the inspired canon. This reminds me of a waggish epitaph written on the tomb of the materialist and sceptic historian, David Hume. A student in Edinburgh is said to have written it.

" Beneath this circular idea,
Vulgarly called tomb,
Impressions and ideas rest,
Which constituted Hume.'

So the general idea implied in ambassador and minister is immortal, and the special one is in the tomb of the apostles! I yet remember the rhetorical flourishes of this textuary when I last heard him, and this is a pretty good sample of them, excepting what pertains to his hands.

In describing this general idea which is found in the persons of modern ambassadors, he says, "He," to wit, the idea, "must have a correct knowledge of theology in its radical principles," [the branches, no matter about them,] "its systematic arrangement," [at Westminster,] "and the dependance of its parts," [the five points,] "upon each other, together with a good knowledge of the classes of texts on which each leading idea is bottomed." He has only to study the classes of texts on which the leading ideas of his system is bottomed. Thus the Doctor aims at making a good textuary.

But in farther describing this textuary, who on a sudden becomes a general idea, and assumes to be an ambassador with his good knowledge of general ideas, bottomed on classes of texts, he says, he " is employed by Christ to be his agent on earth in negotiating with the souls of men." What a general idea is this! A pious youth becomes a beneficiary, then a textuary, next a minister or ambassador—Christ's agent, negotiating with the souls of men!!! A fine picture! an important office! a high calling!

In finding a model for this plan of procedure, the Doctor ransacks the bible in vain; but he finds in some old copy, or, may be, in the apocrypha, a piece of church history I never saw before. Perhaps it is a new revelation. As it is of great consequence to the community, I shall therefore quote it. It is designed to tell us how the primitive church got a supply of the general ideas, called ambassadors:—"Some one who appeared to be best qualified to lead the devotions, was appointed to that office. He devoted himself to reading and study, that he might acquit himself properly in that station. After he had acquired sufficient theological knowledge and a good degree of boldness in the faith, he was set apart to the work of the ministry by the laying on of the hands of the presbytery." This is a precious piece of ancient history, and we shall ever after quote it as of undoubted authority, because an agent of the Saviour's in negociating with the souls of men in Kentucky, has favored us with it.

In dividing these agents into proper classes, and in assigning them their portion of labor, he wills some to be editors of religious newspapers, and authors, who are to be qualified "to defend the minute parts of the christian system." Some to be able " logically and mathematically to explore the whole field of theory, and to clear off the heterogeneous matter cast on the truth by the sophistry and wickedness of men of perverse minds." Some "for parochial duties." Some " for pioneers in the wilderness," and a host of " minute men on all the essential doctrines of the gospel." These are to be ready at a minute's warning to put on their armor of texts, and to march into the field panoplied with general ideas.

But the doctor aims at a new plan of augmenting the number of the presbyterian clergy, from 1080, the present number, to twenty thousand, in the lapse of twenty years. Theological schools will not answer the purpose—too slow in their operation. He laments that pious youths of respectable parents are deterred from becoming ambassadors. " Many parents even discourage their pious sons from preparing for an office so destitute of pecuniary returns." The poor, then, by means of gratuitous contributions, are to be converted into agents of Heaven; and he will have every fifty members to make one priest in five years. It will not do, he says, " to leave to parents to select and educate" their sons for ambassadors. This will produce no favorable results. " There are two thousand congregations of Presbyterians in the union. Let each of these educate one beneficiary in five years;" or "every fifty members by paying 25 cents per month, could furnish one agent to negotiate for Heaven, every five years." Thus, for the small sum of seven hundred and fifty dollars, one ambassador could be furnished with sufficient "general ideas," bottomed on "classes of texts," and might become a " minute man" in all the " essential doctrines of the gospel; and thus a supply of one for every five hundred souls could be easily obtained, if avarice were subdued." But he will have those young men put under some member of presbytery to study divinity, and thus recommends a departure from that fragment of ecclesiastical history which he made known to the world.

Unless efforts similar to these are made, " the period is not far remote when missionary efforts must be paralyzed—the very foundation of the church" [viz. Jesus Christ and the apostles,] " must give." As an argument to enforce the burden of his message, he reminds the people that he was the originator " of the plan of instruction now adopted amongst the American savages; the plan which was at the bottom of the present missions, and which now gives them support;" and hints, modestly enough, that some have not honored him for it, but " have attempted to conceal" this fact. If one plan of operation which he has introduced, and of which he is the inventor, has been so successful, it is a a fair and necessary conclusion that this plan of augmenting the number of priests must be alike wise and practicable, and that similar results will follow its adoption. With such weapons as these, the Rev. Gideon Blackburn, D. D. " sweeps the arena" of all false doctrine, and carries conviction to the hearts of his hearers. Editor.

A Restoration of the Ancient Order of Things.
No. XI.
To the Editor of the Christian Baptist.
W——Co. Ind. Dec. 12, 1825.
Dear Sir:—A sincere desire to know the truth as it is in Christ, is the sole cause of these lines. I need not tell you that I am not a scholar—that these lines will manifest. Neither do I approve of the popular doctrines of the clergy, or even of such an order of men; but think it my duty to let you know that I belong to a church called " German Baptists," sometimes " Dunkards," whose government is the New Testament only. They are not the same in principle or faith with those of the old connexion in Pennsylvania, Virginia, Maryland, and Ohio; but an order that took rise from them in Kentucky, by one Teacher, in Shelby county, about six years ago, amounting now to about two thousand, having

about twenty-four teachers, and increasing fast. Our views of christianity you have expressed in the Christian Baptist, vol. 2d, and on the grace of God, volume second, Nos. 8 and 9; and in the whole second volume I do not see any thing to divide us in sentiment, though I do not approve of some things in your first and third volumes. The Calvinists here generally anathematize the Christian Baptist because it condemns their metaphysical speculations. I read your debate with McCalla, and also the first and second part of the 3d vol. of the Christian Baptist, and find myself edified, my views enlarged, and my faith strengthened; yet I was astonished, finding you so great an advocate for primitive christianity, to hear you say that whatsoever the apostles commanded constituted the practice of the first christians, and yet not notice the plain commandment of washing feet, and that of the kiss of charity; and to hear you say that the practice of the apostles constituted a law for us, and upon this ground contended for weekly communion, and yet not stating that the night was the time, yea, the only time, according to Christ's institution and the practice of the apostles to observe this ordinance. Though I am not convinced of the necessity of weekly communion, not seeing how it could be kept so often in our back country, owing to our scattered state of living from ten to fifteen miles apart; yet I think that whenever it is observed, it should be done according to the primitive model. This much I have written for your own meditation, and now request you to write to me personally, and give me your views on *trine* immersion. You have plainly proved in your Debate that immersion was the only baptism the New Testament authorizes; but you have not stated whether trine or single immersion is the proper action of baptism. In your Debate you state that trine immersion was practised within two years of the lives of the apostles, and we know, according to Robinson's History, that it was the practice of the christians, in the time of Constantine, and yet is among the Greeks. From the commission to baptize, Matt. xxviii. 19. I yet think it is the proper action of baptism, and think that it should not be performed transversely, but forwards, in the most humble manner of obedience, Romans vi. 5. I have written this to let you know my views; and now beg you, in the name of Christ, to inform a poor, illiterate man, who never has had the opportunity of receiving education, though he has always desired it, the whole truth with respect to this matter. I wish you to be concise and very particular, as I shall depend on what you write to me; and every earthly advantage and popularity would I freely forego to follow the truth. I am sincerely your friend, &c.   J. H.

Reply to the Above.

DEAR BROTHER—For such I recognize you, notwithstanding the varieties of opinion which you express on some topics, on which we might never agree. But if we should not, as not unity of opinion, but unity of faith, is the only true bond of christian union, I will esteem and love you, as I do every man, of whatever name, who believes sincerely that Jesus is the Messiah, and hopes in his salvation. And as to the evidence of this belief and hope, I know of none more decisive than an unfeigned obedience, and willingness to submit to the authority of the Great King.

Your objection to the weekly breaking of bread, if I can call it an objection, equally bears against the meeting of disciples at all, for any purpose, on the first day. For if you will allow that if they meet at all, there is no difficulty insurmountable, in the way of attending to this, more than to any other institution of Jesus. As often as they can assemble for worship on that day, let them attend to all the worship, and means of edification, and comfort, which their gracious sovereign has appointed.

As to the time of the day or night when it should be observed, we have no commandment. But we have authority to attend upon this institution at whatever time of the day or night we meet. The Lord's having instituted it at night, will not oblige us to observe it at night, more than his having first eaten the passover should oblige us first to eat a paschal lamb, or to observe it in all the same circumstances. We are always to distinguish what is merely circumstantial in any institution, from the institution itself. The disciples at Troas came together upon the first day of the week to break bread; and the apostle Paul commanded the disciples at Corinth "to tarry one for another, to wait till all the expected guests had arrived," which shews that it occupied an early as well as an essential part of their worship. Any objection made to the hour of the day or night in which any christian institution should be observed is founded upon the doctrine of holy times, or sacred hours, which are Jewish and not christian. Besides, it is bad logic to draw a general conclusion from any particular occurrence. We might as well argue that, because Paul immersed the jailor at the dead hour of night, every person should be immersed at the same hour, as that because the Lord instituted the supper the night in which he was betrayed, it should be always observed at night. Nay, the same sort of logic would oblige us to observe it only the last night in our lives, if we could ascertain it, and to have no more than a dozen fellow participants. We should, on the same principle, be constrained, like the Sabbatarians, to reform our almanacs, and to decide whether it was instituted at nine or twelve oclock at night, &c. But apostolic precedent decides this point, and not inferential reasoning.

As to the washing of the saints' feet, there is no evidence that it was a religious ordinance, or an act of social worship. Yea, there is positive evidence that it was not. Paul, in his directions to Timothy, at Ephesus, tells him that certain widows were to be supported in certain circumstances by the church. These widows were members of the church; and, as such, must have been regular attendants on, and partakers of, all its institutions.

Now, in describing the character of those widows which were to be supported by the congregation, Paul says, "If she have brought up children, if she have lodged strangers, if she have washed the saints' feet, if she have diligently followed every good work." Had the washing of the saints' feet been a religious, or what is called a church or social ordinance, it would have been impossible for her to have been in the congregation, and not to have joined in it. He might as well have said, If she have been baptized, if she have eaten the supper, as to have said, "If she have washed the saints' feet" had it been a religious institution. But he ranks it not amongst social acts of worship, not amongst religious institutions, but amongst good works. When, then, it is a good work, it ought to be performed, but never placed on a level with acts of religious worship. It is a good work when necessity calls for it; and, though a menial service, the Saviour gave an example that no christian should forget, of that condescending humility which, as christians, we are bound, both from precept and example, to exhibit towards our brethren in all cases when called upon. Besides the design of it at the time he practised it, is ascertained from a regard to the mistaken and aspiring views of the disciples respecting the nature of places of honor in his kingdom.

It was a good work, and still is a good work, more frequently in Asia than America. The soil, climate, and dress of the Asiatics more frequently called for it, than our circumstances require it. But we argue not from these circumstances—we use them as illustrations of the fact, that Paul the Apostle has positively decided that it is not a religious institution, an act of religious worship, or an ordinance in the church, but simply a good work, and I have experienced it to be a good work, in my own person, more than once, even in these United States.

Much the same sort of evidence exists in proof that the kiss of charity is not a social or church ordinance. A great deal more, however, can be said in behalf of it, than of either of the preceding items. It is argued that it is five times positively commanded in the epistles written to the congregations, set in order by the apostles. From this I would conclude that it had not been established by the apostles as an act of religious or social worship in those societies, as a part of their usual and stated worship; for if it had, there could not have existed a reason for enjoining it so repeatedly as we find it enjoined. Hence we do not find one commandment in all the epistles to the churches, respecting baptism, the Lord's supper, or the Lord's day: certain things are said of them, and in relation to them, as already established in the church, but no command to observe them. From the fact of the kiss of charity being so often mentioned, and from the circumstances of the congregations to which it is mentioned, I argue quite differently from many zealous and exemplary christians.

Another argument in favor of it is deduced from the fact that these letters were written to the churches, and that consequently the things enjoined in them, were enjoined upon the disciples in their collective capacity. True in part only. For it is not a fact that the injunctions in those epistles all respected the brethren in their meetings only, but also their conduct in the world, in their families, and in all the various relations of life.

It is admitted that the usual method of salutation in the East was, and still is, by kissing the cheek or neck of a relative or friend. In some countries, in Europe, too, this custom is quite common; but the farther west or north we travel from Constantinople or Rome, the custom is less frequent. Shaking hands is one of the most usual methods of expressing friendship and love in Europe and America.

Christians are to love one another as brethren. This is the grand standard of their affection. Whatever way, then, I express love to my natural brother, I should express it to my christian brother. If the custom of the country and those habits of expressing affection which it familiarizes to our minds, require me to salute my natural brother when I meet him, by a kiss on the lips, neck, or cheek, so let me salute my christian brother. But if the right hand of friendship and love be the highest expression of love and affection for a natural brother, to salute a christian brother otherwise is unnatural. For example—suppose that after an absence of seven years, I were introduced into a room where one of my natural brothers and one of my christian brethren were assembled, and that I should kiss the latter and shake hands with the former; would not this diversity be unnatural and contrary to the generic precept, "Love as brethren." I contend, then, that neither the customs in dress, wearing the beard, or mode of salutation, is the meaning of the requirements, of the precepts, or examples of the apostles; but that the genius and spirit of their injunctions and examples, are, in these things, expressed by the customs and habits which our country and kindred adopt, and by means of which we express the spirit and temper which they inculcated and exhibited.

But to make this a regular and standing ordinance of christian assemblies, appears to be entirely unauthorized by any hint, allusion, or command, in the apostolic writings. I speak neither from prejudice nor aversion to this custom. For my own part, I can cordially comply with either custom, having been born in a country where this mode of salutation was more common than in this; but to advocate or enjoin it as of apostolic authority, I cannot. When misunderstandings and alienations take place amongst brethren, and a reconciliation has been effected; when long absence has been succeeded by a joyful interview; or when about to separate for a long time, the highest expressions of love and most affectionate salutations are naturally called for, which the customs of the country have made natural. And these become holy amongst christian brethren on account of the high considerations which elicit them.

In a word, whatever promotes love amongst christian brethren, whatever may increase their affection, or whatever expressions of it can best exhibit it to others, according to the customs and feelings of the people amongst whom we live, is certainly inculcated by the apostles. And if christian societies should exactly and literally imitate and obey this injunction, no man, as far as I can learn, has a right to condemn or censure them. Nor have they who practise according to the letter, a right to insist upon others to think or practise in a similar way, so long as they exhibit that they love one another as brethren.

With regard to trine immersion, and the manner in which the action should be performed, we have neither precept nor precedent. In the debate alluded to, instead of two, it is, I think, in the errata, two hundred years after the apostolic age, when we first read of trine immersion. That immersion is always spoken of as one act, is most evident from all that is said about christian immersion. It is true that the scribes and elders, as indeed the Jews generally, had a plurality of immersions; but the christian action is a unit. There is no command that a person should be immersed three times in order to constitute one baptism or immersion. Nor is there an example of the kind on record, not even a hint or allusion to such a custom. Therefore, we cannot teach it as of divine, but as of human authority. And in what position the body should be disposed of in the act, is as immaterial as in what fashion a coat or mantle should be made. To bring the christian religion to inculcate matters of this sort, would be to convert the New Testament into a ritual like the book of Leviticus, and to make christian obedience as low and servile as that of the weak and beggarly elements.

Thus, my dear sir, I have hinted at the topics you proposed. I should have written to you "personally" long since; but in such cases, here the matter is of general interest, I prefer, as opportunity serves, to lay it before the public. And as to the long delay, I have to urge by way of apology, that I am this winter, more than ever before, absorbed in business of the highest, most solemn and responsible nature. I have under my care the publication of a new Translation of the New Testament. Though the translation was made ready to my hand, yet the necessary examination of every word, and comparison of it with the other translations of note, for the purpose of assisting the English reader with the best means of understanding this blessed book, has given me incomparably more labor than I had any idea of. It is indeed, to me a delightful and profitable employment, having assembled all translations of note, and even those of no great reputation, I am under the happy necessity of reading, examining, and comparing all, and in notes critical and explanatory, elucidating the text when it can be improved. But a small portion of my labor can be seen, or will meet the public eye, because, in many instances, after the most diligent examination and comparison, the translation given is adopted in preference to all others; and my labor simply results in the conviction that the translation of the standard works is the best. It is a work that I dare not delay, or yield to any other demands upon me, however imperious. I have more than sixty letters at this time on file unanswered, and many of my correspondents are got out of patience with me; but I have a good, or many good apologies to make. If they will only bear with me this once, I hope to make them returns in full.

Wishing you favor, mercy and peace, from our Lord and Saviour, and glad to hear from you at any time, I subscribe myself your brother in the hope of immortality.   A. C.

February 25, 1826.

The Bible.

THERE is, perhaps, no book read more than the bible, and it appears as though no book generally read was less understood. This, no doubt, has arisen from a combination of causes which exists in relation to no other book in the world. If any other book in the English language had as many commentaries written upon it, had as many systems based upon it, or upon particular constructions of it; if any other book were exhibited in the same dislocated and distracted light, had as many debates about its meaning, and as many different senses attributed to its words; if any other book were read as the scriptures are commonly read, in the same broken, disconnected and careless manner; with the same stock of prejudices and preconceived opinions, there is every reason to believe that it would be as unintelligible and as little understood as the bible appears to be. We often wonder at the stupidity of the Jews in our Saviour's time in relation to his pretensions and claims, and no doubt posterity will wonder at our stupidity and ignorance of a book which we read so often and profess to venerate so highly. There is a greater similarity in the causes and reasons of their and our indocility than we are aware. The evil one has the same interest in obscuring this volume which he had in obscuring the evidences of his mission; and the vitiosity of man, both natural and acquired, exhibits itself in the same aspect towards the

bible as it did in reference to the person concerning whom it was all written.

But among the myriads who religiously read the bible, why is it that so little of the spirit of it, seems to be caught, possessed, and exhibited? I will give one reason, and those more wise may add to it others. Many read the bible to have a general idea of what it contains, as a necessary part of a polite education; many read it to attain the means of proving the dogmas which they already profess; many read it with the design of being extremely wise in its contents; many read it that they may be able to explain it to others; and alas! but few appear to read it supremely and exclusively that they may practise it; that they may be conformed to it, not only in their outward deportment, but in the spirit and temper of their minds. This is the only reading of it which is really profitable to men, which rewards us for our pains, which consoles us now, and which will be remembered for ages to come, with inexpressible delight. In this way, and in this way only, the spirit of it is caught, retained and exhibited. Some such readers seem to be enrapt or inspired with its contents. Every sentiment and feeling which it imparts seem to be the sentiments and feeling of their hearts; and the bible is to their religion what their spirit is to their body—the life and activity thereof. The bible to such a person is the medium of conversation with the Lord of Life. He speaks to Heaven in the language of Heaven, when he prays in the belief of its truth, and the Great God speaks to him in the same language; and thus the true and intelligent christian walks with God and converses with him every day. One hour of such company is more to be desired than a thousand years spent in intimate converse with the wisest philosophers and most august potentates that earth ever saw.   EDITOR.

The Many against the Few.

THE few have had a conflict with the many in every attempt towards reformation since error got the better of truth. This for a long time must uniformly be the case. Therefore, none ought to be discouraged because of the number or influence of those leagued in support of any error. The history of the world is replete with information and encouragement on this subject. Truth fairly presented, and enforced by the good examples of its advocates, has ever triumphed, and will continue to triumph till the victory is complete.   EDITOR.

No. 9.]   APRIL 3, 1826.
Christian Morality.—No. I.

THE history of the world down from its first page till the present time represents man to be precisely such a being, in respect to moral character, as the bible describes him. In his natural, or rather preternatural character, he exhibits himself to be ignorant of God, alienated from him, filled with enmity, hatred, selfishness, ingratitude, and a false ambition. However the reflex light of christianity in civilized nations, and what is called the science of morals approbated and enforced in the social compact and forms of government of Pagan nations, have imposed restraints upon these evil principles, have offered rewards to virtue, and assigned punishments to vice, still the radical principles of human depravity exhibit themselves in the children of nature, under the best human culture; and thereby prove, that, however they may be restrained, they still exist in all the bitterness of moral corruption. Hence all the crime, misery, and wretchedness, which appear in the human family.

A mind alienated from God is alienated from man. This is a truism of greater momentum in morals, than any axiom of Newton's is in physics. Hence every scheme which has been adopted for moralizing and improving the social character of man, which has not been based upon the above truism, has failed of its object. Like the universal *specifics* of empyrics, or the nostrums of quacks, they have proved the disgrace of their authors, and the injury, if not the ruin, of the too credulous recipients. The christian scheme of moralizing and improving the world recommends itself to the philosopher upon his own principles; while false philosophy ascribes effects to inadequate causes, and would produce results regardless of the fitness of means, true philosophy requires adequate causes, and means suitably adapted to the ends in view.— Thus the christian scheme of moralizing and felicitating the world is based upon the actual condition of the human family, and regards every symptom and exhibition of the complex case of human vileness. But it begins at the root of the disorder. Perfect moral health can be enjoyed only in the temperature of perfect love to God, and on the food of perfect obedience to his will. A comfortable degree of this health can be enjoyed in this life only by a reconciliation of the mind to God, which necessarily produces benevolence in its manifold exhibitions towards man. The christian scheme of ameliorating society in this world, and fitting man for heaven, is based upon these leading principles:—

1. That man is alienated from God through ignorance of him, and by his wicked works.

2. That this ignorance, alienation, and these wicked works, must necessarily eventuate in his ruin, unless he be delivered from them.

3. That wicked works proceeding from alienation of mind, and alienation of mind proceeding from ignorance of the moral character of God, the true and rational course of procedure in the deliverance of man from this state, commences with imparting to his mind just views of the character of God, which, when apprehended, reconcile the mind to God and necessarily produce philanthropy or benevolence to man. On these principles, which the wise men of this world on other subjects call philosophical, does the christian religion proceed.

The rudiments of christianity, or the first lessons which it imparts, are comprehended in one sentence, viz. "God is love." This does not, in its scriptural connexions, represent him as having no other perfections, natural or moral, but that of love; but it represents him in his procedure to men, in the whole origin and process of the work of reconciliation, in the amelioration of the character and condition of men, as supereminently displaying benevolence or philanthropy.

It is the love of men, and not of individuals, which is called "philanthropy" in the New Testament. Those systems of religion which begin and terminate in one principle, viz. that God loves only one nation or a few individuals of all nations as men, divest the christian religion of God's means of reconciling human beings to himself. On this principle it becomes equally unavailing to the few who are loved as sinners, as it does to the many who are not loved as sinners. For no means are adapted to reconcile the mind of man to God but such as exhibit his benevolence to men indiscriminately. So long as the divine benevolence is represented as without any known object, as being a secret to every human being, neither those who are embraced in it, nor those who are left out of it, can derive one ray of hope from all the preacher can say about it, until they discover something in themselves which warrants an opinion that they may be amongst the special objects of it. Hence their piety originates from a religious selfishness which enters into all their thoughts and expressions on the subject of the favor of God!

All the terrors of the Lord cannot produce love in any creature alienated from him, else those evil spirits which kept not their first estate would long since have been reconciled to him. Nothing but the exhibition of love can destroy enmity. Hence, in the word of reconciliation, which the apostles announced, the most emphatic sentence is, "God so loved the world that he gave his only begotten Son, that whosoever believes on him may not perish, but enjoy eternal life." They never told any congregation that God loved a world which nobody knew any thing about; that he loved a few here and there; and who was or was not one of these, nobody could tell. Such a representation of God's election, or purpose, is not worthy of the name of gospel or "good news to all people," or indeed to any people. But of this again.

To bring man to love God and one another, is the high end of the christian religion. This is happiness. The happiness of heaven is the happiness of perfect love. The intelligent christian expects to be introduced into a society of the most refined and exalted intelligences, whose love to each other will be incapable of augmentation. Hence the standard of christian perfection is graduated by love to the brethren—and just in so far as we have progressed in the cultivation of complacent affection and benevolence, so far have we obtained a taste for the society of the saved.

One leading design of the institution called the church, was to give its members a taste for the society of heaven; for the fact is, but very few have any taste for such a society, and for such entertainments as the intelligent and perfect christian pants after, in the upper world. Many christians talk a good deal about heaven; but from their taste, as it exhibits itself, they would like, it is true, to be in the palace of the Great King, but they would rather be in the kitchen amongst the servants, than amidst his attendants that wait upon his royal person. They think more upon being safe than upon the high enjoyments, and talk more on escaping the burning lake than on all the rational delights of pure and exalted spirits before the throne of the Almighty.

Men have made many attempts to promote good will amongst a few—whom nature, interest, solemn pledges, climate or country had united. But these are poor substitutes for the grand scheme of consociation devised and published by the Almighty. Every tie has been broken or worn out, which men have devised as a substitute for the ties of enlightened christian affection. But what consideration can unite men in the purest affection, as the manifold cords of the christian religion?

To the ties of nature, to all the bonds that draw the heart of man to man, christianity adds considerations infinitely more endearing. The one faith, the one hope, the one Spirit, the one Lord, open a new world of relationships. Christians are united by the highest, strongest, noblest ties that human reason knows; each of which is stronger than death, more triumphant than the grave. That we are redeemed by the same blood, bought by the same Lord, purified by the same Spirit, embraced in the same love of the Father; that we are to be joint participants of the same glorious resurrection, co-heirs of the same immortality, and joint inheriters of the same triumphant kingdom: that we are to be fellow guests at the marriage supper of the Lamb, to attend the funeral of nature, and to be fellow citizens with all the pure and exalted intelligences in the universe in one enraptured throng forever, are considerations, if realized, which ought, one would think, to produce but one feeling towards all the household of faith, banish all discord, cover all defects, excite all sympathies, and elicit all brotherly love.

This is that fountain, the streams of which are pure morality. That formal, stiff, forced, mechanical, and legal morality which appears detached from these principles, which grows from another root, is like the wild olive or forest grape, which, while exhibiting some of the appearances, possess not those valuable properties, on account of which, we appreciate those cultivated by man.

We are sorry to have to remark, that there appears to be a great falling off from the morality of the christian religion, as well as from the ancient order of things in the christian communities. This is in a measure to be traced to the new bonds of union which have been adopted in different religious communities, and to attaching an undue importance to the little party shibboleths, which, in some societies, become at once the standard of both religion and morality. These are desultory remarks, and intended as prefatory to a series of essays on christian morality. In the course of which we are apprehensive that we shall find even amongst christians of the present day, that the standard of christian morality is many degrees lower than the apostolic.   EDITOR.

———

THE following letter is from the pen of one of the most intelligent, pious, and worthy bishops in Virginia; whose standing in the learned world obtained for him the honorary degree of D. D. and whose piety and intelligence refused the title as a badge of popery. Believing this letter to be of importance to myself, and to the religious community at large, I here lay it before the public with my remarks in reply to the same.
                                        ED. C. B.

King & Queen Co. Va. Dec. 6, 1825.
Brother Campbell,

DEAR SIR—ACCORDING to my promise to you (and I may say to God also) I commence a letter of correspondence with you.—Your preaching among us reminded me of Apollos who displayed, as we moderns say, great talents, or, as the scripture says, "was an eloquent man, and mighty in the scriptures." Apollos, however, with all his eloquence and might in the scriptures, submitted to be taught the way of God more perfectly, and that too, by a mechanic and his wife. After this he helped those much who had believed through grace. May I, though inferior to Aquila, &c. attempt a reformation in principle of one, not only eloquent and mighty in the scriptures, but deeply learned in all the wisdom of the Greeks and Romans. So far as I can judge by your writings and preaching, you are substantially a Sandemanian or Haldanian. I know you differ from them in some points, but in substance you occupy their ground. Now I am not about to fall out with them as heretics of the black sort. I think they have many excellent things among them, things I

would gladly see more prevalent among us. But in some respects they are far from pure christianity. Forbearance is certainly a christian grace, strongly recommended both by precept and example, in the word of God. It is an important branch of charity, without which knowledge is nothing, and the eloquence of angels nothing more than a tinkling cymbal. Without christian forbearance, no church fellowship can be maintained; at least, so I think. The Haldanians, I am persuaded, are greatly deficient on this head. I do not say they are wholly without forbearance, but they limit its exercise to too narrow bounds. In all church decisions, say they, there must be an unanimity, all must think alike. However desirable this may be, it is impossible—men will differ in opinions honestly; hence, unless allowance be made for ignorance, for humors, and even for obstinacy, there will be little peace; or, however, peace cannot subsist long. The strong must bear the burdens of the weak, and not please themselves. I name this one case out of many in which they use too little forbearance. You will ask, are there no limits? Doubtless the same apostle who in one place says, "I please all men in all things," in another says, "do I seek to please men?" The essence of the gospel must be maintained at the expense of even life itself, and to do this more effectually, we must use forbearance in minor things. Gentleness of spirit becomes a servant of the Lord, and especially towards those who oppose truth as being the most likely to bring them to repentance. But among the Haldanians (judging from writings) a gentle spirit is rarely to be found. Harsh and bitter sarcasms are the weapons with which they fight their opponents. This too I am the more disposed to think applies to them as a sect, because I have known some of their party who have appeared, in private conversation, to be mild and gentle indeed, and every way pleasant; but when brought out in writing or public speaking, seemed to have another kind of temper. If you will bear with me, I will suggest that this seems to be the case with the editor of the Christian Baptist. As a man, in private circles, mild, pleasant, and affectionate; as a writer, rigid and satirical, beyond all the bounds of scripture allowance. I have taken the Christian Baptist now from its beginning, i. e. I have read them from their first publication, and my opinion has been uniformly the same.—That, although sensible and edited with ability, it has been deficient in a very important point, *a New Testament spirit.* It will not do to say there are hard sayings to be found in the scriptures. True; but that is far from being the general tenor of them. These hard expressions are to be found only at the end of long forbearance, and then they are not contrary to the spirit of christianity. This, may I say, is the most serious objection to the Debate on Baptism. The book exhibits baptism in a most lucid point, sufficient, I should think, to convince every Paido baptist that may ever read it. But the bitterness of the expression universally blinds their minds with resentment so as to stop up the entrance to truth. You will say it was but a retort to more bitter things from the other side. I answer, truth requires no such defence. Hence the persecutions of every age have been on the side of error. But truth, holy truth, with God on its side, requires no such support. 'Tis a tender plant that dwindles under such rough culture. So much for forbearance, gentleness, &c. Your opinions on some other points are, I think, dangerous, unless you are misunderstood, such as casting off the Old Testament, exploding experimental religion in its common acceptation, denying the existence of gifts in the present day, commonly believed to exist among all spiritual christians, such as preaching, &c. Some other of your opinions, though true, are pushed to extremes, such as those upon the use of creeds, confessions, &c. &c. Your views of ministerial support, directed against abuses on that head, would be useful; but levelled against all support to ministers (unless by way of alms) is so palpably contrary to scripture and common justice, that I persuade myself that there must be some misunderstanding. In short, your views are generally so contrary to those of the Baptists in general, that if a party was to go fully into the practice of your principles, I should say a new sect had sprung up, radically different from the baptists as they now are. But I have almost gotten through my paper with finding fault, an article too, that I have not heretofore dealt much in. Shall I close by telling you that we all feel much interest in your welfare personally, that your mild and sociable manners, &c. procured among us not respect only, but brotherly love and christian affection, and that much of your preaching was admired for its eloquence and excellency, and that if you would dwell upon these great points chiefly, such as faith, hope, charity, &c. you would be viewed by us as having a special command from Him whom we hope you love, to feed his lambs and his sheep. By way of apology for you, and a small compliment to our folks, I was really struck while you were among us, that the acrimonious treatment that you had received from others had pushed you to certain severities and singularities, which, if you dwelt among us, you would relinquish. This letter is designed as a private correspondence, but if any good should arise from its publication, I should have no objection, provided it came out wholly.

Yours affectionately,   R. B. S.

P. S.—I was writing this, from first to last, two or three weeks. I yesterday got your December C. B. with which I am much pleased.

Reply.

Very Dear Sir:—Being very sensible that sundry items in your letter are matters of general importance, and of general interest, after due deliberation on its contents, I considered it my duty to lay it before the public. And had it not been that you wished, in case of its publication, that it should wholly appear, I would have suppressed certain complimentary expressions, which, however kind the motives which dictated them, are more flattering on your part, than deserving on mine. The benevolent christian spirit which appears in every sentence, while it explains and seasons your commendations, gives weight and emphasis to your censures. The latter, however, are those in which I am most concerned, and in which most will agree in opinion with you. To myself, indeed, they are the more acceptable; having long since learned that the rebukes of a friend are faithful, while the kisses of an enemy are deceitful.

I have no design to plead not guilty to the whole of your corrections, nor to say that I do not need some of your reproofs and admonitions; but I have some explanations to offer, and misunderstandings to correct, which, I believe, will be as acceptable to you, as they are necessary for the sake of others.

To pay due regard to the sundry items in your letter, I shall follow the order in which they appear; and, in the first place, you say, "So far as I can judge by your writings and preaching, you are substantially a Sandemanian, or Haldanian." This is substantially affirmed of me by many who have never seen nor read one volume of the writings of Sandeman or Haldane: and with the majority it has great weight, who attach to these names something as heretical and damnable as the tenets of Cerinthus and the Nicolaitans. I have not myself ever read all the works of those men, but I have read more of them than I approve, and more of them than they who impute to me their opinions, as heresy. I was some fourteen years ago a great admirer of the works of John Newton, I read them with great delight, and I still love the author and admire many of his sentiments. He was not a staunch Episcopalian, though he died in that connexion. In an apology to a friend for his departure from the tenets of that sect in some instances, he said, "Whenever he found a pretty feather in any bird, he endeavored to attach it to his own plumage, and although he had become a very speckled bird, so much so that no one of any one species would altogether own him as belonging to them, he flattered himself that he was the prettiest bird among them." From that day to the present I have been looking for pretty feathers, and I have become more speckled than Newton of Olney; but whether I have as good a taste in the selection, must be decided by connoisseurs in ornithology.

Concerning Sandeman and Haldane, how they can be associated under one species, is to me a matter of surprise. The former a Paido-Baptist, the latter a Baptist; the former as keen, as sharp, as censorious, as acrimonious as Juvenal; the latter as mild, as charitable, as condescending as any man this age has produced. As authors I know them well. The one is like the mountain-storm that roars among the cliffs; the other like the balmy zephyrs that breathe upon banks of violets. That their views were the same on some points, is as true as that Luther, Calvin, and Wesley agreed in many points.

I was once much puzzled on the subject of Harvey's Dialogues, I mean his Theron and Aspasio. I appropriated one winter season for examining this subject. I assembled all the leading writers of that day on these subjects. I laid before me Robert Sandeman, Harvey, Marshall, Bellamy, Glass, Cudworth, and others of minor fame in this controversy. I not only read, but studied and wrote off in miniature their respective views. I had Paul and Peter, James and John, on the same table: I took nothing upon trust. I did not care for the authority, reputation, or standing of one of the systems a grain of sand. I never weighed the consequences of embracing any one of the systems as affecting my standing or reputation in the world. Truth (not who says so) was my sole object. I found much entertainment in the investigation. And I will not blush, nor do I fear to say, that, in this controversy, Sandeman was like a giant among dwarfs. He was like Sampson with the gates and posts of Gaza on his shoulders. I was the most prejudiced against him, and the most in favor of Harvey, when I commenced this course of reading. Yet I now believe that not one of them was exactly on the track of the apostles. I have also read Fuller's Strictures on Sandemanianism, which I suppose to be the medium of most of the information possessed on that subject in this country. This is the poorest performance Andrew Fuller ever gave to the world.

58

I have not read it for a long time: it is on the shelves of my library, but I will not at this time brush the dust off it. If I remember right, he concedes every thing in the first two or three pages, which he censures in the rest of his work, except it be the spirit of the system. And the fact is (which, indeed, he indirectly acknowledges) that Andrew Fuller was indebted more to John Glass and Robert Sandeman, than to any two men in Britain, for the best part of his views —I will not here pause to inquire whether he wrote those strictures to save himself from the obloquy of being called a Sandemanian, as some conjecture, or whether he wrote them to give a blow to Archibald M'Lean, of Edinburgh, who had driven him from the arena some years before: but I will say it is a very poor production, and proves nothing that either Robert Sandeman or Archibald M'Lean felt any concern in opposing.

But, my dear sir, while I am pretty well acquainted with all this controversy, since John Glass was excommunicated by the high church of Scotland, for preaching that Christ's kingdom is not of this world, which is now more than a century ago; and while I acknowledge myself a debtor to Glass, Sandeman, Harvey, Cudworth, Fuller, and M'Lean; as much as to Luther, Calvin, and John Wesley; I candidly and unequivocally avow, that I do not believe that any one of them had clear and consistent views of the Christian religion as a whole. Some of them, no doubt, had clear and correct views of some of its truths, nay, of many of them, but they were impeded in their inquiries by a false philosophy and metaphysics, which fettered their own understanding in some of the plainest things. For instance, with the exception of Fuller and M'Lean, they all contended for the popish rite of baby baptism or sprinkling. As to James Haldane, I am less indebted to him than to most of the others. I was much prejudiced against his views and proceedings when in Scotland, owing to my connexion with those who were engaged in a controversy with his brother Robert, and against the system in general. I have, since my arrival in this country, read some two or three pieces from his pen:—one in favor of infant baptism, and one against it, and some others I do not recollect. I have heard a great deal of him and his brother Robert, from members of their connexion, who have emigrated to this country; and while I do not believe that there lives upon the earth a more godly, pious, primitive, christian, than James Haldane of Edinburgh; and few, if any, more generally intelligent in the christian scripture, you express my views of that system generally. Being possessed of a very large estate, and connected by marriage with some of the most illustrious families of North Britain; these two brothers, especially the elder, had much in their power. From the best information I have gathered, Robert Haldane has expended something like four hundred thousand dollars, in what he deemed to be the cause of the Redeemer; and, no doubt, will have his reward. He now sees, and acknowledges, that much of this money, though benevolently appropriated, was misapplied—He had, at one time, a great notion for training poor and pious young men for " the gospel ministry," and I think, in a few years he had some fifty or sixty educated, boarded, and equipped for the field, at his own expense. Many of those, without the spirit of their master, became just such spirited men as you describe. Some of them, too, excellent men, caught the spirit of Robert

Sandeman, and became fierce as lions in the garb of lambs, Hyper-Calvinists, Separatists, with whom "tenth or ten thousandth broke the chain alike." No matter if an agreement existed in nine hundred and ninety-nine opinions, if in the thousandth there was a difference, the chain was severed, and they were to one another as heathen men and publicans.

While I thus acknowledge myself a debtor to those persons, I must say, that the debt, in most instances, is a very small one. I am indebted, upon the whole, as much to their errors as to their virtues, for these have been to me as beacons to the mariner, who might otherwise have run upon the rocks and shoals. And, although it is a catachresis to say, that a sailor is indebted to those who have fallen upon rocks, on which he might have been wrecked, had not others before him been unfortunate in this way; yet, I must acknowledge, that the largest amount of my debts is of this kind, though, in some instances, I have been edified and instructed by their labors.

For the last ten years I have not looked into the works of any of these men; and have lost the taste which I once had for controversial reading of this sort. And during this period my inquiries into the christian religion have been almost exclusively confined to the holy scriptures. And I can assure you that the scriptures, when made their own interpreter, and accompanied with earnest desires to the author of these writings, have become, to me, a book entirely new, and unlike what they were when read and consulted as a book of reference—I call no man master upon the earth; and although my own father has been a diligent student, and teacher of the christian religion since his youth; and, in my opinion, understands this book as well as any person with whom I am acquainted, yet there is no man with whom I have debated more, and reasoned more, on all subjects of this kind, than he—I have been so long disciplined in the school of free inquiry, that, if I know my own mind, there is not a man upon the earth whose authority can influence me, any farther than he comes with the authority of evidence, reason, and truth. To arrive at this state of mind is the result of many experiments and efforts; and to me has been arduous beyond expression. I have endeavored to read the scriptures as though no one had read them before me; and I am as much on my guard against reading them to-day, through the medium of my own views yesterday, or a week ago, as I am against being influenced by any foreign name, authority, or system, whatever.

You say that "those people have many excellent things among them—things you would gladly see among us." So say I. You think "they are very defective in forbearance." This may be still true for any thing I know; but one thing I do know, that several congregations in this connexion are far more "forbearing" than the Baptists in Virginia; for several of them receive unbaptized persons to the Lord's table, on the ground of forbearance. The congregation in Edinburgh in connexion with James Haldane, and that in Tubermore in connexion with Alexander Carson, two of the most prominent congregations in the connexion, do actually dispense with baptism on the ground of "forbearance." I believe there are some others who carry "forbearance" thus far. These people have been much slandered at home and abroad by an interested priesthood, and I do know that many things reported of them in this country are false.

They say that when a Paido-Baptist gives evidence that he is a christian, and cannot be convinced that infant baptism is a human tradition, he ought to be received into a christian congregation as a brother, if he desires it, irrespective of this weakness. They were once more tenacious of their peculiar views than at present.

But on the subject of forbearance I have to remark that there is no greater misapplication of a word in our language that I know of, than of this one. In strict propriety it does not apply at all to the subject in relation to which it is commonly used. No man can be said to forbear with another, except in such cases as he has done him an injury. Now when christians differ in opinion upon any subject, unless it can be made appear that the opinion of A. is injurious to B. the latter cannot forbear with the former. There is no room nor occasion for forbearance; for B. is not injured by the opinion of A. To say that christians must exercise forbearance with one another because of difference of opinion, is admitting that they have a right to consider themselves injured, or that one christian has a right to consider himself injured because another differs in opinion from him. It is precisely the same mistake which is committed by those who ask the civil authorities to tolerate all or any religious opinions. The mere asking for toleration recognizes a right which no civil government possesses, and establishes a principle of calamitous consequences, viz. that opinions contrary to the majority, or the national creed, are a public injury, which it is in the power of government to punish or tolerate, according to their intelligence and forbearance. Civil rulers have no right to tolerate or punish men on account of their opinions in matters of religion. Neither have christians a right to condemn their brethren for differences of opinion, nor even to talk of forbearing with one another in matters of opinion. The scriptures speak of the forbearance of God, and teach that christians in certain cases should forbear with one another in cases of injury sustained; but never, that I can see, on account of matters of opinion. A person might as well be said to forbear with his natural brother because he was only ten years old, or five feet high, or because he had grey eyes; as to forbear with his christian brother because he differed from him in some opinions. I know that we all use the term forbearance in a very unwarrantable sense, and that it is difficult to find a term every way appropriate to communicate correct ideas on this subject. To bear with, or allow a brother to exercise his own judgment, is no doubt all that you intend by the term, and this is certainly inculcated in the apostolic writings. And I am willing to carry this principle to its greatest possible extent; though, as you say, there is and must be a stopping place. So long as any man, woman, or child, declares his confidence in Jesus of Nazareth as God's own Son, that he was delivered for our offences, and raised again for our justification; or, in other words, that Jesus is the Messiah, the Saviour of men; and so long as he exhibits a willingness to obey him in all things according to his knowledge, so long will I receive him as a christian brother and treat him as such.

What you say of the "*Christian Baptist*," as being deficient in one important point, "a New Testament spirit," next merits my attention.—This may be true; and I am thankful to you for your kind remarks upon this topic. One thing, however, I can say, that I am conscious of the most benevolent intentions and kind feelings towards the persons of those very men on whose conduct and measures I have animadverted with the most apparent severity. But I will not say that what I have written exhibits this spirit to the best advantage. I can, I acknowledge, with the utmost good nature and benevolence, say and write many things that may appear, and that to strangers do appear, to be dictated by a very different spirit. I know that what you say of the general spirit of the New Testament is true; but there is one thing on which I have thought a good deal, which I think escapes the observation of many, viz. that if the apostles were on earth now, and were to write upon the present state of things in christendom, their writings would appear to be very different in spirit from those which they wrote when first declaring God's philanthropy in the gift of his Son. They then spoke and wrote in the full spirit of this benevolence. But when a defection began to appear, and apostacy began to shew its face, the apostle began to "change his voice," and to exhort others to carry on *a good warfare* against those seducing spirits, and to reprove, rebuke, and that with sharpness too. Judging from what they said when false teachers began to appear, both of them and to others concerning them, I am of the opinion that the same spirit of benevolence which appears in their public annunciation of the gospel, would lead them now to speak in a style similar to that in which the epistle of Jude and the second epistle of Peter was written.—These things I do not advance as an excuse for myself in all respects, for I know that few will apprehend that the "Christian Baptist" is written in the spirit in which I am conscious it is. But I think that the New Testament spirit is a spirit of meekness, of mildness, of benevolence, and of decided hostility to all and every corruption of the gospel. The physician is not less benevolent when, as a surgeon, he amputates a limb, than when he administers an anodyne.—Yet there would be a manifest difference in his spirit and temper in the judgment of a spectator who did not enter into his views and motives in these two actions. There is one fact which will not be out of place to state here. It is this:—There are many topics which would lead to the exhibition of what would appear in the fullest sense, and in your own sense of the words, "a New Testament Spirit," which I would have gladly introduced into this work; but owing to its circumscribed dimensions and the force of opposition, I have had to withhold or to cause them to yield to those topics which are the least conducive to what, in the estimation of the majority, is the spirit you would wish to see more strikingly exhibited. Hence so much of one species of composition gives a general character, both to the matter and manner of the work. So much for a "New Testament spirit." I will conclude this item by observing that I hope to profit from your remarks on this subject.

On my "casting off the Old Testament, and exploding experimental religion, in its common acceptation; denying the existence of gifts in the present day, commonly believed to exist among all spiritual christians, such as preaching," which you think "are dangerous," unless I am misunderstood, I have not room to say much at present. On the subject of "experimental religion" some remarks will appear in the next number under another head; and with reference to "casting off the Old Testament," I will just observe that I know not of one sentence in the Christian Baptist that holds out such an idea. As to divine authority, I have at all times viewed it and represented it as equal to the New. But that christians are not under it, but under the New, I have contended, and must still contend. And as to the present existence of " spiritual gifts" in the church, in the New Testament sense of these words, I do not believe that any such exist. But if you mean to call preaching, teaching, praying, praising, exhorting, and ruling, *spiritual gifts*, I do believe that such gifts do exist, and that there is sufficient room for a very liberal exhibition of them in the present day. I have thought that my essays on the work and office of the Holy Spirit had sufficiently exhibited my views on this subject, so as to preclude misapprehension. Any objections, candid or uncandid, against the views exhibited in these essays, I will minutely consider whenever presented to me in an intelligible form.

But I hasten to your remark on ministerial support. You say—" Your views of ministerial support, directed against abuses on that head, would be useful; but levelled against all support to ministers, (unless by way of alms,) is so palpably contrary to scripture and common justice, that I persuade myself that there must be some misunderstanding." Now, my dear sir, the words " ministerial support" are so vague and so latitudinarian, that I do not believe that I could be understood by any person who uses them in the common acceptation, if I speak in the style of the New Testament. On this subject I have said but little, except by way of allusion to existing customs, and have generally condemned, and must condemn the popular course. I have said something on the word *minister*, which I believe to be of importance in this question. But I have not arrived in my course of essays on " the Restoration" to that place which would lead me to exhibit what I deem the views of the New Testament on the bishop's office, call, ordination, and support. That any man is to be paid at all for preaching, *i. e.* making sermons and pronouncing them; or that any man is to be hired for a stipulated sum to preach and pray, and expound scripture, by the day, month, or year, I believe to be a relic of popery.

The difference between a hireling " minister" and a bishop, I will endeavor to illustrate in my next essay on the "*Ancient order of Things*," to which I would refer you for the present. I do know, for I inquired when in your vicinity, that you have never esteemed gain to be godliness, and that although you have labored much as a bishop and as a preacher, you have never made it, sought it, or found it to be a lucrative calling. And I am sure that you do not object to any thing you have seen in the Christian Baptist on this subject, because it either has operated, or was feared to operate, against you. In the words of the apostle, " You have not thus spoken that it should be so done to you." I say I am convinced of this, and that you speak in behalf of others, and for the sake of consistent views of the Christian religion.

Your last observations in your table of corrections I come now to notice. It is this: " In short, your views are generally so contrary to those of the Baptists in general, that if a party was to go fully into the practice of your principles, I should say a new sect had sprung up," &c. This is neither a commendation nor a reprobation of the " Christian Baptist," until one or two questions are answered.

In the first place, Are the Baptists generally now following in the steps of the primitive church? Are they up to the model of the New Testament? Upon the answer given to this query your last remark conveys praise or blame. If they are in the millennial state, or in the primitive state of the church, then every thing that would change their order and practice is to be reprobated and discountenanced by every christian. But if not, every well meant effort to bring them up to that state, as far as scripture and reason approbate, ought to be countenanced, aided, and abetted by every one that loves the Lord Jesus Christ in sincerity.

Again it may be asked for the sake of variety, Would not a congregation of saints, built exactly upon the foundation of the apostles and prophets, and walking in all the commandments and ordinances of the Lord blamelessly, appear like a new sect arising amongst the Baptists, or any other sect in this country?

And, in the third place, Ought not every christian who prays for the millennial state, or a restoration of the ancient order of things, to labor to promote so desirable an event by all the means in his power?

On the view taken of these questions, and the answer given to them, depends the import and weight of your last remark. In the mean time I must come to a close, referring you on this last topic to my reply to " An Independent Baptist" in the next number, for a more luminous expose of the principle embraced in it; assuring you at the same time that I will maturely weigh and candidly attend to any remarks you may please to favor me with on any topic embraced in this reply, or on any other embraced in this work. I hope always to possess, and to be able to exhibit, the spirit and temper of a disciple of him who taught his followers to love and obey the truth, and who gave us an example in his own person, that the most exalted, glorious and happy course of life, is to do the will of our Heavenly Father.

With sentiments of the highest respect and affection, I remain your fellow servant in the hope of immortality.   EDITOR.

A Restoration of the Ancient Order of Things.
No. XII.

The Bishop's Office.—No. 1.

A BISHOP without a charge or cure, is like a husband without a wife, a contradiction in sense, if not in terms. There must be sheep before there can be a shepherd, and there must be a congregation before there can be an overseer. There must be work to be done before there is occasion for a workman. From all which it is plain there must exist a congregation of disciples before there is any office, officer, call, ordination, or charge concerning them. A bishop without a congregation, a president without a people, a teacher without pupils, is like an eye without a head, a tongue without a mouth, a hand without a body. From these incontestible dictates of common sense, if there were not a hint in the Oracles of Heaven upon the subject, it would appear that the existence of bishops or overseers was, in the order of nature, in the order of reason, in the order of God, posterior to the existence of churches or congregations. But the apostolic writings are as plain as the dictates of common sense upon this subject. They teach us that the office of bishops was the last thing instituted, or, in other words, that the apostles and evangelists, had fulfilled their commission, i. e. had proclaimed the gospel, made disciples, baptized them, convened them, and taught them.

61

the christian doctrine, before they suggested to them the necessity, utility, and importance of the office of a bishop. Thus we find the apostles in their subsequent or last visits to the congregations which they had planted, instituting, appointing, and giving directions concerning the bishop's office.

From these premises it must follow that, as the enlisting of soldiers is previous to their training; the making of disciples, to teaching them; the gathering of congregations, to setting them in order; necessarily the bishop's work is different from that of a missionary, a preacher, an evangelist, in the New Testament import of these terms. That the work of a bishop is different from every other work requisite to forming a congregation is self-evident from one fact, viz: *That this work or office did not originate until congregations existed.*

How congregations first came into existence, is one question; how they are to be brought into existence now, is another question; and what is a christian bishop, or his work, is a question essentially distinct from both. To arrive at clear and distinct views on any subject, we must simplify, not confound; we must take one topic at a time; we must view it in all its bearings, and still keep it separate and distinct from every other.

We are now on the bishop's office, as presented to us in the primitive congregations, and not the question how these congregations were gathered then, nor how congregations are to be gathered now. On these questions we have dropped some hints already, and may hereafter be more diffuse. We begin with a congregation such as that in Antioch, or that in Ephesus. The apostles and evangelists had converted, baptized, and convened the disciples in those places, had opened to their minds the christian doctrine. In process of time they had so far progressed in this doctrine, as to be able to edify one another; some, as in all societies, progressed faster and farther than others. Some were better qualified to preside, to rule, and to teach, than others; and the constitution of man as an individual, and of men in society, is such as to require, for the sake of intelligence, order, peace, harmony, and general good, that there be persons set apart or appointed to certain functions, which are necessary to the good of the whole associate body. The exigencies of the congregations required this, both with regard to themselves and to others. Thus originated the bishop's office.

The nature of the bishop's office may be learnt either from the exigencies of the congregations, or from the qualifications by which the apostles have designated bishops. The qualifications which the bishop must possess show what was expected from him. These qualifications are of two sorts, such as respect the work to be done by the bishop; and, secondly, such as respect the dignity of character which his prominence in the christian congregation behoves him to possess. The former are those which some call gifts, or talents, of the intellectual order; the latter are endowments purely moral or religious. Those with which we are at present concerned are of the intellectual order. These are comprized under two general heads, viz. teaching and presiding. He must be qualified to teach, and be able by sound teaching both to convince and exhort those who oppose the truth. He must feed the flock of God with all those provisions which their exigencies require, or with which God has furnished them in the christian institution. He must preside well. He is from office

the standing president of the congregation; and it being requisite that he should be one that presides well in his own household, plainly imports what is expected from him in the christian congregation.

In our ordinary meetings, according to the prevailing order in our congregations, we have no need of a president—we only desire and need an orator. Hence we have often been asked, what are we to understand by a bishop's ruling or presiding well? I have generally replied, (perhaps rather satirically,) that the ancient congregations were not so well bred as the modern; that they were apt to ask questions and propose difficulties; and some arose to address their brethren in the way of admonition and exhortation; but that we Americans were a well bred people, had studied the etiquette of gentility in our meetings; and that our bishops needed not the qualifications of a president of a family, tribe, or community, no more than the president of the United States wanted a lifeguard in these peaceful times, or a shepherd a staff to guard his sheep when wolves and dogs were extinct.

In what are called "meetings of business," once a month, or once a quarter, there is some apprehension that a president or "moderator" may be necessary, and the first thing done is to elect or appoint one; never considering or viewing the bishop as any more president from office than any other member, a positive and explicit proof that even the idea of presiding well is not so much as attached to the bishop's office in these times, amongst the Baptists too.

A congregation of disciples, which is modeled upon the New Testament, will find that presiding well, is just as indispensable as teaching well, and that the prohibition of novitiates, or young inexperienced disciples, from the bishop's office, is as wise a provision as any other in the christian institution.

The bishop of a christian congregation will find much to do that never enters into the idea of a modern preacher or "minister." The duties he is to discharge to Christ's flock in the capacity of teacher and president, will engross much of his time and attention. Therefore the idea of remuneration for his services was attached to the office from its first institution. This is indisputably plain, not only from the positive commands delivered to the congregations, but from the hints uttered with a reference to the office itself. Why should it be so much as hinted that the bishops were not to take the oversight of the flock "for the sake of sordid gain," if no emolument or remuneration was attached to the office? The abuses of the principle have led many to oppose even the principle itself. We have said much against the hireling system, and see no ground as yet to refrain; so long as the salvation of the gospel, the conversion of the world, and heaven itself, are articles of traffic, and in the market, like other commodities, accessible to the highest bidder. The motto over the spiritual warehouses is, "The highest bidder shall be the purchaser." And we are persuaded by a hundred venal prints, that if the church had the bank of the United States, that of London, and Paris, it could, in twenty years, convert the whole world, with the exception of a few millions of reprobates. I say while such is the spirit breathed from the pulpit and from the press, there exist ten thousand good reasons for lifting up our voices like a trumpet, crying aloud, and sparing not.

But to discriminate on this subject, and to exhibit where, and when, the hireling system begins; to graphically define, bound, and limit, beyond the power of cavil, on the one hand, and abuse on the other, has appeared to be a desideratum. While on the subject we shall make one effort here, subject to future and farther amendments, as circumstances may require.

A hireling is one who prepares himself for the office of a "preacher" or "minister," as a mechanic learns a trade, and who obtains a license from a congregation, convention, presbytery, pope, or diocesan bishop, as a preacher or minister, and agrees by the day or sermon, month or year, for a stipulated reward. This definition requires explanation. That such, however, is a hireling, requires little demonstration. He learns the art and mystery of making a sermon, or a prayer, as a man learns the art of making a boot or a shoe. He intends to make his living in whole, or in part, by making sermons and prayers, and he sets himself up to the highest bidder. He agrees for so much a sermon, or for fifty-two in the wholesale way, and for a certain sum he undertakes to furnish so many; but if a better offer is made him when his first contract is out, (and sometimes before it expires,) he will agree to accept a better price. Such a preacher or minister, by all the rules of grammar, logic, and arithmetic, is a hireling in the full sense of the word.

But there are other hirelings not so barefaced as these, who pretend to be inwardly moved by the Holy Spirit to become ministers, and who spurn at any other qualification than the impressions and suggestions of the Holy Spirit, who are under an awful wo if they do not preach; and yet agree merely in the capacity of supplies, or preachers, to act the preacher for some small consideration. Upon the whole, I do not think we will err very much in making it a general rule, that every man who receives money for preaching the gospel, or for sermons, by the day, month, or year, is a hireling in the language of truth and soberness—whether he preaches out of his saddlebags, or from the immediate suggestions of the Holy Spirit.

The christian bishop pleads no inward call to the work, and never sets himself to learn it. The hireling does both. The christian bishop is called by the brethren, because he has the qualifications already. The minister says he is inwardly called, and prepares himself to be called and induces others to call him. The former accepts of the office for the congregation of which he is a member, and takes the oversight of them, and receives from them such remuneration as his circumstances require; and as they are bound in duty to contribute to him, not for preaching the gospel at all, for this they have already believed, enjoyed, and professed; but for laboring among them in teaching and watching over them, in admonishing them, in presiding over them, in visiting them in all their afflictions, and in guarding them against seduction, apostacy, and every thing that militates against their growth in knowledge, faith, hope, and love, and retaining their begun confidence unshaken to the end. The latter goes about looking for a flock, and when he finds one that suits his expectations he takes the charge of it for a year or two, until he can suit himself better. The former considers himself the overseer or president of the one congregation only who called him to the office, and that when he leaves them he resigns the office and is no longer president. The latter views himself as a bishop all his life. He was one before he got his present charge, and when he abandons it he is one still. He has

been called by God as Aaron was, and remains a priest for ever. The christian bishop was chosen and ordained from his outward and visible qualifications which the apostles described and required. The "minister" is licensed because of some inward impressions and call which he announces; or because he has been taught Latin, and Greek, and divinity, and because he can make a sermon, speech, or discourse, pleasing to the ears of a congregation or presbytery. Thus they differ in their origin, call, ordination, and work. Money is either the alpha or the omega, or both, in the one system. The grace of God and the edification of the body of Christ, are the alpha and omega of the other. Money makes, induces, and constitutes the one, unites him and his charge, dissolves him and his charge, and reunites him with another; again dissolves the union, and again and again originates a new union. Hence in the hireling system there is a continual tinkling of money, writing of new contracts, giving new obligations, making new subscriptions, reading of new calls, installing of old bishops, and a system of endless dunning. In the other, the love of God, the grace of Jesus Christ, who gave himself for the church, the eternal ties of christian affection, the superior blessedness of giving to receiving, of supplying our own wants, of laboring with our own hands when it would be oppressive to others, either to relieve us or others, the example of Jesus who made himself poor, are the darling topics and the constant themes. That the bishop who thus labors in the word and teaching is worthy of double honor, and justly entitled to the supply of his wants, whether of food, raiment, or money, or all. Paul himself declares, and reason itself teaches; and those christians deserve not the name, who would suffer such a bishop to be in need of any necessary good thing which they had in their power to bestow. If he wave his right to receive it, he is the more worthy; but the right exists whether he uses or waves it; whether it is or is not recognized by others. So says the christian institution, so says reason, and so say I. But of the bishop's office again.

EDITOR.

No. 10.]   MAY 1, 1826.

I DO not wish to occupy many pages of this work with a controversy on a subject which has most generally terminated in metaphysical jargon, and which usually becomes a mere logomachy, or war of words. If the scripture statements, in scripture connexions, and in scripture words, will not prove satisfactory on this subject; and if union, confidence and harmony, cannot be established and retained on such a basis—in vain will recourse be had to speculation, scholastic terms, and philosophical distinctions.

[ED. C. B.

For the Christian Baptist.

THE communication of Aquila, published in the Christian Baptist of January last, in reference to some things said in the third number of *Christian Union*, demands some attention.

The union of christians it is believed is essential to the glory of God, the happiness of the saints, and the conversion of the world. Jesus Christ is the foundation and the head of this union; and faith in him, according to the scriptural account of his nature and character, is the bond of it. Aquila, I suppose, will agree to these things; and whether he, or the writer of Christian Union, be correct or not in their views, it is impossible that they and those who think with them

2 E

can realize christian union as long as their ideas of the foundation and head of this union are materially different.

There is in the scriptures one doctrine, in which all the lines of divine revelation meet as in a common centre, and which is therefore, by way of eminence, denominated the truth. That doctrine may be thus briefly stated that Jesus of Nazareth is the true Messiah, the Son of God, and Saviour of sinners: that he was delivered for the offences of the guilty, and was raised for their justification, and that in him the Father is well pleased. This is the truth which came by Jesus Christ, (*John* i. 17) to which he himself bare witness, (*John* xiv. 6) which was attested by the voice at his baptism, (*Matt.* iii. 17,) and at his transfiguration, (*Luke* ix. 35.) To this truth all the apostles bare witness in their doctrine.— "Many other signs truly did Jesus in the presence of his disciples which are not written in this book; but these are written that you might believe that Jesus is the Christ, the Son of God; and that believing, you might have life through his name." *John* xx. 30, 31. "Let all the house of Israel know assuredly that God has made that same Jesus whom you have crucified both Lord and Christ." *Acts* ii. 36. Thus far I suppose there is no difference between Aquila and Christian Union.

Aquila agrees that men must be content with the Scripture statements of the nature and character of Christ; that Christ is really an object of worship, and that he is Divine. But he denies that Christ was worshipped as God, and only as the Son of the only true and living God. He denies also that the apostles and christians for worshipping Christ as God suffered death, or that it was the first cause of their persecution. The only point that is of any importance here is included in the question, What were the views of inspired apostles of the nature and character of Christ as an object of worship? Did they worship him as a man, or as an angel, or as a superangelic creature, or as a demi-god or as the only true and living God? Aquila will answer, that they viewed him as the Son of the only true and living God. I ask, What were their views of his nature and character as the Son of God? Did they view him as a man, or as God, or as neither, as do the Arians? Or did they view him as God and man? Whatever were the views of the apostles on this subject, it will be readily conceded they are essential to true christianity, and to the union of christians in truth and love. And it will be also agreed that the apostles in worshipping Christ had the same views of him which they have written in the New Testament. These things being premised, I observe, that the apostles did denominate Christ *God*, and ascribed to him the attributes of Jehovah. Paul tells us that as concerning the flesh, Christ came from the fathers, who is over all God blessed forever. *Rom.* ix. 5. This is a scripture statement, agreeably to which Paul, an inspired apostle, must have worshipped Christ; he worshipped him as God blessed forever, and so ought we.

But he is not only called or denominated God, but the perfections of God, such as creative power, omnipotence, omniscience, divine worship, divine honors, and eternal existence are ascribed to him in scripture statements. He is also described as a real man and is so denominated, yet without sin; he by the power of the Holy Ghost was conceived by the Virgin Mary, was born, increased in wisdom, grew in stature and in favor with God and man; he ate, drank, slept, labored; was fatigued, hungered, thirsted; rejoiced and sympathized with his brethren; wept and was in an agony; prayed, bled, died, and was buried, and rose again.

The ascriptions of divinity to him are sustained by divine words, as the ascriptions of human nature to him are sustained by human actions and sufferings.

Those who object to Christ being God as well as man, do it because they cannot understand the *modus* of the connexion between Deity and humanity—how a union of the divine and human natures could take place; and yet they believe, at least some of them do, that a human body was united to a soul not human They have never yet told us to what order or class of beings this new compound belongs. According to their views he is not divine, only in the same way, but in a higher degree than the apostles were; he is not human, for a human soul is essential to human nature; nor is he angelic, for angels have no corporeal powers.

If Christ possesses not only the nature according to the flesh, that is human nature, which he derived from the fathers, but is also God blessed forever, Aquila will surely agree that " the worship of him always supposes and includes his godhead, in which the eternal, original, and essential dignity of his person consists." Again —the inspired evangelist John has told us that the Word was God and was made flesh, who is the same that Paul spoke of as above. Aquila, by reason of his not being able to comprehend, or even to understand the manner of the conception, or the mode of the union between the Deity and humanity of Christ, ought not to regard it as "a soul-revolting and a heart-chilling idea," for great is the mystery, God was manifested in the flesh. Instead of this being a heart-chilling and a soul-revolting idea, it is the delight and joy of the saints. It is also essential to christian union and to true christianity, according to apostolic views of it.

Every thing said of Christ in respect to his human nature, must necessarily be spoken of him in a capacity in which he is inferior to the Father. But it may be asked, How are we to distinguish between Christ's human and his divine nature? I answer, Just as when we speak of a man we distinguish whether what is said is said of his body or of his soul. When we say that Abraham is dead, we mean his mortal part. When we say that Abraham is alive, we mean his immortal part. When the Evangelist says that Jesus increased in stature and wisdom, and in favor with God and man; that he ate, drank, slept, wept, &c. he obviously means that his human nature did this, comprehending his body and soul. When he affirms that the Word was God, and made the universe; and when the apostle Paul says that Christ is supreme, God blessed forever, these are predicated of his divinity which can neither increase in stature or in wisdom.

Christian union is vitally concerned in unity of view and sentiment in relation to the nature and character of Christ. There can be no union in worship without this, as there cannot be in faith and love, for he is the Alpha and the Omega of both. Arians, who deny the Deity of Jesus Christ, do actually charge those who believe in it and worship him as such, with idolatry. How would those who entertain such discordant views commune with each other—realize a joint participation of the same blessings? those things which are soul-revolting and heart-chilling to one, are soul-attracting and heart-cheering to another.

I have written with much frankness, and perhaps the things I have written may be considered as savoring too much of the language of Ashdod. Be it so. I cannot understand the use of facts, natural and supernatural, and of correspondent words and sentences as means of information, if they be not intended for, and used to impart ideas and knowledge of existences, natures, qualities, and characters, in relation to the objects and subjects to which they belong and apply.

In nature natural phenomena or appearances indicate and prove natural existences and properties, and form the bounding circle of all that can be known of nature. Supernatural phenomena, miracles, or divine works as distinguished from the operations of nature, properly so called, indicate and prove supernatural or divine existences, when associated with verbal explanation and used by the agents for that purpose. These, comprehending the phenomena and language, form the bounding circle of all that can be known of spiritual existences exclusive of the knowledge of the human mind, if indeed that can be termed spiritual knowledge, which may be known of the mind without revelation.

It may be objected that the number of places in the New Testament in which Christ is called God, are so few that they ought not to be relied on in fixing so important an article of faith as his Deity. To which I reply, that it is no more necessary that the fact should be stated in every chapter in the New Testament that Jesus Christ is God, in order that it should be known and believed as an essential article of christian faith and of christian union, than it is necessary that we be informed in every chapter of the bible that in the beginning God created the heavens and the earth, that it should be known and believed; or that a law of the state shall be re-enacted every day by the legislature, to make it obligatory on the people of the state.

In casting my eyes over Aquila's publication, I was sensibly impressed with the truth of some of the remarks made in the third number of Christian Union, and which apply in a considerable degree, although not in the same way or in relation to the same subject, to all sectary christian associations, so far as their peculiarities are concerned. With the quotation of it I will conclude this paper.

"These disputes have originated a technical phraseology on both sides, (the Arian and Athanasian,) which has greatly narrowed the vocabulary of religion, and has rendered some modes of expression almost obsolete, which were indulged in without scruple by the sacred writers. They have occasioned, on the Arian side of the question, in many instances, the relinquishment of the latitude with which the scriptures express themselves on the nature and glory of Christ, and have produced a scrupulous and systematic cast of diction, which is altogether inconsistent with the freedom displayed by the inspired penmen. Many expressions are employed without hesitation in scripture, which are rarely found even in the direct form of quotation in their writings, and are never heard in their public addresses, but with a view of subjecting them to explanations and criticisms, which so mar and mutilate the nature and character of Christ as to render him altogether an unfit object for the worship of christians; and who, if he had been thus seen by Stephen, and Paul, and apostolic christians, had not been worshipped by them."

PHILO-CHRISTIAN UNION.

WE have always designed and endeavored that this work should not present a one-sided representation of things, of sentiments, and practices of the time in which we live. We have nothing to lose in the pursuit of truth; and we never desired that our own views should ever obtain any other authority over the minds of our brethren, than as they are authorized and supported by the apostles and prophets. We have therefore given publicity to all the objections, candid or uncandid, which have been respectfully submitted by our brethren or opponents. We wish to give our readers every opportunity of judging correctly of every thing we advocate, and have therefore given much more of the objections offered by our correspondents, than of the commendations and encomiums which have been received. The FOLLOWING LETTER speaks for itself, and demonstrates that its author possesses talents of the first order. I publish this letter *literatim et punctuatim;* but had I taken any liberty with it, there are two or three words and phrases which I would, for his sake, have erased. I need not add that my giving publicity to this document affords some evidence that I am willing to meet any objections which can be made to my views or to my course.   EDITOR.

Saturday Morning, February 11th, 1826.

MR. EDITOR,—MY own consciousness approbates the goodness of the injunction, "Judge not," and intimates the folly of expecting "perfection" in any man living: but we expect "consistency," especially in a *reformer,* and *a restorer of the primitive order* of things in the church of Christ. Suffer me to call your attention to a few things which demand, on your part, a public elucidation. In your reply to T. T. of Boone county, Missouri, you say "I and the church with which I am connected, are in full communion with the Mahoning Baptist Association, Ohio; and through them, with the whole Baptist society in the United States; and I do intend to continue in connexion with this people," &c. Now, sir, I have no doubt but you feel honestly about this "full communion" with the whole Baptist society, but in fact and in effect, it is but a *white lie;* an equivoque, a time-serving expedient and tends to shake the confidence of those who love you, as to the downright sincerity of the Christian Baptist. It has, at least, disturbed me not a little. Pray sir, what is "full communion?" Is it not "full union in the common worship, doctrine and institutions of any church or denomination." Yes, this is the understanding where the language comes from the lip, or pen of integrity. Your profession implies, according to your own principles, a sincere conviction that the whole Baptist society (regular associated Baptists) is the church of Christ, of which Jesus is the head, and that they are conformed to the New Testament law as respects doctrine, worship, and order. You, by this, publicly avow that in your judgment, the regular associated Baptists exhibit the model of Christ's house, are the election of grace, and may be pointed out as the living epistle of the Holy Ghost to be seen and read of all men. This is not what the Christian Baptist says, but it is what your visible standing and professing conduct says. If so, in what sense are you a restorer of primitive christianity? If they, as a society, are the church of Christ, what right have you to interfere with their existing order and state? But if, at heart, you do not confess them as holding that order, which would rejoice the soul of an apostle, what do you mean by professing "full communion" with them?

Pray sir, who or what are the associated Baptists in the United States? Are they not a large denomination of religionists, differing from the other religious sects in no respect, affecting this question? After you have approved their *dipping*, and reprobated the *sprinkling* of the others, in what other particular are the associated Baptists a peculiar people, unless it be that after having made one right movement, their conformity to the "course of the (christian) world" is more sinful as it is more inconsistent and glaring? This may be contradicted, but cannot be disproved from God's word; and he who has "full communion" with the whole Baptist society, as the New Testament church, and yet refuses to extend the right hand of fellowship to the rest of the evangelical sects, is a purblind pharisee, straining out a gnat and swallowing a camel.

Dialogue between "Regular Baptist" and the "Editor," who are professedly of *one* faith, of *one* mind, of *one* church, speaking the *same* things, and of *one* heart to serve the King of Zion, as he has commanded, &c.

Reg. B. Our churches are founded on the Philadelphia Confession, as the bond of union, and the statute of discipline; is not that proper and scriptural?

Ed. By no means; it is antichristian and must be considered rebellion against the Great King and Head of the Church!

Reg. B. It prevents varieties in doctrine, which could not be tolerated among us as particular Baptists, and sound Calvinists. Is not Calvinism according to the scriptures? I mean the limited supra-sub-lapsarian plan?

Ed. I think not. Calvinism is a corruption of christianity, and of course a curse to the world, by perverting men from the simplicity of the faith!

Reg. B. Indeed! but Mr. Editor, what think you; ought the Lord's Supper to be attended oftener than once a month, or is it a matter left to the churches to fix, as suits their views? You know the scriptures say "as oft," without telling how oft, and the Associated Baptists throughout the union consider it a matter of indifference until determined by a vote of the church. They generally commune once a month, or at least once in three months, in the country churches. Is not our order scriptural?

Ed. Unquestionably it is not. The church of Christ must break bread every first day; nay, it is the main design of their coming together. Monthly communion is a vile deviation from gospel order!

Reg. B. At any rate the Associated Baptists are right in casting out of the Associations any church that has more than one Bishop or Elder. It has been lately done; was that not strictly scriptural?

Ed. No! The primitive churches had each a plurality of elders or bishops, and without at least two bishops was not fully organized. They grew up in the church and were never imported. Know sir, that in each church there was a presbytery! Examine and you will be satisfied of this too.

Reg. B. Well, well, Mr. Editor, though we don't agree in most things, yet we are one as respects the glorious duty of going down into the water and coming up out of the water. We both despise babyrantism, do we not?

Ed. Even here, you are blind and uninstructed. You are dipped for no better reason than

binds you to any other duty, such as speaking the truth, or paying a debt. Learn sir, that the baptismal water washes away sin, and is the only divinely appointed pledge that the blood of Christ has cleansed the conscience of the obedient disciple. Why do you stare so? Go home and read your bible and you will see that your regular, particular, Calvinistic, Associated Churches are of the world, and their services an abomination, for it is written "In vain do you worship me, teaching for doctrines the commandments of men!"

Reg. B. O dear sir! I was mistaken in you— Pray Mr. Editor are you a Regular Baptist?

Ed. Why yes I am and I intend to be in "full communion" with the whole Baptist society in the United States. Though I agree with you in almost nothing, yet by keeping up this nominal fellowship, I can be more extensively useful! I confess that this plea is preferred by almost all the Evangelical in their respective communions, as a reason for infant sprinkling, episcopacy, but what then?

Reg. B. O nothing! As our brother Doctor says, utility is the standard of virtue, and conscience is the creature of circumstances. Besides you will, Mr. Editor, be better protected by the Association at your back, than if you only relied on Christ's promises. It is at least a good thing to "lay heavy burthens on the shoulders of other men, though we do not touch them ourselves with one of our fingers."

Ed. Well, let us say no more on this head. Good by my brother!

Dear sir, I have used plainness of speech— print this, and speak in your own behalf—If Associations are scriptural, why then, say so— If not, then "Come out from among them"—If you are acting a part from pride, love of popularity or singularity, be assured that in their train comes contempt. These things have I written, hoping you are desirous of consistency— a man of integrity and uprightness, and from a desire to make you more and more amiable, that I may love you more for the truth's sake.

AN INDEPENDENT BAPTIST.

To an Independent Baptist.

DEAR SIR,—AFTER thanking you for your fidelity, and great plainness of speech, and for the favorable opportunity you have afforded me for vindicating my course from imputations, which many may make, when, and where, I should never hear them; and also for the occasion which you have given for illustrating more fully a principle which I think is not yet well understood by many intelligent christians, I proceed to observe that your very ingenious dialogue, and, indeed, your objections altogether, proceed upon the hypothesis, and terminate in one point, viz. that my course, or rather my declaration that "I and the church with which I am connected are in full communion with the Mahoning Baptist Association, and through them with the whole Baptist society," &c. is inconsistent with the sentiments and views exhibited in the "Christian Baptist." If so, your dialogue and letter are unanswerable; I must lay my hand upon my mouth: if not, your shafts have missed the mark, and carry no conviction to my mind; and cannot to any intelligent reader.

I agree with you that consistency, though a very rare commodity, is essential to a good character, and especially in any person who would call the attention of men to the bible. It is a misfortune, however, to see men always consistently doing wrong. Consistency is a virtue only when the professed principles of action are good. In every other case it is very far from being commendable. Perhaps Satan is a very consistent character since the seduction of Eve. Neither sincerity nor consistency are virtues abstract from the qualities which constitute a good man. But without them no man can claim any regard from his fellow-men, nor can his conduct or example be worthy of imitation, whatever other good qualities he may possess. I consider, therefore, that the charge of inconsistency, when the professed principles of action are good and sacred, is no trivial imputation.

But what constitutes consistency? In acting conformably to our own professed sentiments and principles, or in acting conformably to the professed sentiments and principles of others. In answering this question, your letter is answered. I have no doubt of being able to make it quite obvious that this obnoxious sentence is perfectly consistent with the views and principles exhibited and advocated in this work. But if consistency requires a person to act conformably to the views of "An Independent Baptist," (a proud and imposing name) or to the views of any other person differing from his own, in that case you are unanswerable; but if not, a pigmy is an overmatch for a giant panoplied with dialogues.

To come to the point at once, what are the principles of union and communion advocated in this work? Has not the one foundation which the apostle affirmed was already laid, and besides which no other can be laid, which will stand the test of time and of critics, which is the only one on which all christians can unite, and have "full communion," and against which the gates of Hades shall not prevail; I say has not this been the only bond of union which the "Christian Baptist" ever advocated? And what is it, but a sincere and hearty conviction, expressed or confessed by the lips, that Jesus is the Christ: and this belief, exhibited by an overt act of obedience which implies that the subject has put on Christ, prepares him, or qualifies him, if you please, to be saluted as a brother. So long as he confesses with his lips that he believes in his heart this truth, and lives conformably to it and supports an unblemished moral character, so long he is a worthy brother.

Your dialogue artfully keeps out of view every thing about the one Lord, the one faith, the one hope, and hardly will admit the one baptism, and every other point of general agreement in the Baptist society, and to the best advantage exhibits the points of difference. Now a person equally ingenious with yourself could frame a dialogue on the other side, showing how inconsistent I would be, with the principles asserted in this work, if I had refused communion with the whole Baptist society. Did I say as ingenious as yourself? Nay, with the ingenuity of a stripling, he might confound me. On the hypothesis that I refused or declined union or communion with the Baptist society, he would introduce an artificial, regular, or associate Baptist, who would ask me, Do not the associate and unassociate Baptists believe that Jesus is the Christ? Nay, do they not believe that he died for our sins, that he was buried, that he rose the third day, that he ascended into heaven, that he sent down the Holy Spirit to advocate his cause, to convince the world of sin, of righteousness, and of judgment; that he will come again to raise the dead, and to judge the world. Nay, do they not declare their belief that his kingdom is

not of this world. That the subjects of it are born again, new creatures, and must maintain good works, and cultivate holiness; without which no man shall see the Lord? To all such queries I would be constrained to answer yes.

He would next say, Do you not contend that unity of opinion is not essential to christian union; that the one Lord, the one faith, the one hope, and the one baptism, comprehend all that can legitimately be required? To this I must consistently answer yes. Well, then, says he, you are a hypocrite, a pharisee, insincere, and most inconsistent, and a transgressor, building the things which you have demolished. To which I must consistently plead guilty.

You see, then, how little ingenuity would be requisite to confound and silence me, should I act the part of an "Independent Baptist" while contending for the principles exhibited in this work. The inconsistency of which you complain is therefore not in me, but it is in your own views.

I am yet but entering upon the subject. I shall now give my own explanation of this offensive "full communion" with the Baptist society. Your full communion and my full communion are very different things. You define your full communion to be "full union in the common worship, doctrine, and institutions of any church or denomination." Again you say, "Your profession implies, according to your own principles, a sincere conviction that the whole Baptist society (regular associated Baptists) is the church of Christ, of which Jesus is the head, and that they are conformed to the new testament law, as respects doctrine, worship, and order, exhibiting the model of Christ's house," &c. I question very much whether you yourself have this sort of full communion with the one congregation with which you associate. But this will not excuse me. Again, I question very much whether Paul the apostle could have broken bread with the congregation in Rome, in Corinth, in Thessalonica, or with the congregations in Galatia, and others, at the time he wrote his letters to them. Nay, I do not think that the Saviour himself could have instituted the supper amongst the twelve, or that they could have had full communion on your principles in that one institution the night in which he was betrayed. For none of these congregations at the times alluded to were exhibiting the model of Christ's house, "were conformed to the new testament, as respects doctrine, worship, and order," or had this sincere conviction that all was perfect—just up to the standard of full perfection in all these particulars.

In the full import of the words full communion, when carried to their utmost extent, I do not know that such a communion ever was, or ever will be exhibited upon earth. The word full, I admit, may be so explained as to confine this sort of communion to the heavenly state. But in ordinary acceptation, or in its loose acceptation, it means no more than joint participation in a certain act or acts. When I unite in prayer with a society of disciples, I have full communion with them in certain petitions, confessions, and thanksgivings; but requests may be presented, confessions made, and thanksgivings offered, in which I have not full communion. The same may be said of any other social act of worship. All that I intend by the phrase is,* that I will unite with any Baptist society in the Uni-

* The words full communion are marked with inverted commas, in my letter to T. T. Missouri, thereby implying that I use them in accommodation to their current use.

ted States, in any act of social worship; such as prayer, praise, or breaking bread in commemoration of the Lord's death, if they confess the one Lord, the one faith, the one hope, and the one baptism: provided always, that, as far as I can judge, they piously and morally conform to their profession. But that congregations may be found, under the banners of this profession, with whom I would not unite in one single act of social worship, as well as individuals, I will cheerfully declare. And with not one would I unite in prayer or praise, or breaking bread, if that act is to be interpreted into a full, perfect, and entire approbation of all their views, doctrine, and practice, as a society or individuals. Here then is the fundamental difference between your full communion and mine. Every act of the one, you understand, as unequivocally expressing full and entire approbation of every thing among them. I consider every act as only expressing approbation of the thing represented, and of them in so far as they conform to it. Therefore, I frankly and boldly declare to them, as Paul did to the Corinthians, the things in which I praise them, and the things in which I praise them not. And I know of no way, of no course, that any christian can pursue consistently with the whole new testament, consistently with his serving God and his own generation, but this one. Therefore I advocate it and practise it.

I have tried the pharisaic plan, and the monastic. I was once so straight, that, like the Indian's tree, I leaned a little the other way. And however much I may be slandered now as seeking "popularity" or a popular course, I have to rejoice that to my own satisfaction, as well as to others, I proved that truth, and not popularity, was my object; for I was once so strict a Separatist that I would neither pray nor sing praises with any one who was not as perfect as I supposed myself. In this most unpopular course I persisted until I discovered the mistake, and saw that on the principle embraced in my conduct, there never could be a congregation or church upon the earth.

As to "the purblind Pharisee who strains out a gnat and swallows a camel," because he will not have full communion with all the evangelical sects in the mass, I have to remark, that it is not optional with me or you whether we would have christian communion with them. They have something to say upon that subject; and here, once for all, it must be noted, that my having communion with any society, Baptist or Paido-Baptist, depends just as much upon them as upon myself. Some Baptist congregations would not receive me into their communion, and if any Paido-Baptist society would, it is time enough to show that I am inconsistent with my own principles when any "evangelical sect or congregation" shall have welcomed me to their communion, and I have refused it. At the same time, I frankly own, that my full conviction is, that there are many Paido-Baptist congregations, of whose christianity, or of whose profession of christianity, I think as highly, as of most Baptist congregations, and with whom I could wish to be on the very same terms of christian communion on which I stand with the whole Baptist society.

There is, I confess, a great inconsistency somewhere; yes, every where, on the subject of communion. Baptists, and Paido-Baptists generally confine communion to the Lord's table, and, indeed, call it, by way of distinction, *the communion.* Hence full communion, with the majority, means no more than the *breaking of*

bread together, or sitting down at the same "communion table." Here originates all error on the subject of your dialogue, and on the whole subject of intercommunity with the christian world. Another proof, too, that conscience is a creature of circumstances.

There is a certain place called "The Family Altar." Baptists and Paido-Baptists, of different name, often meet at this "family altar," and there unite all in one communion. In their monthly concerts for prayer, &c. there is another "altar," at which all sects sometimes meet; and all have full communion in prayer and praise. But if on the next day the Lord's table was furnished, they would rather be caught in company with publicans and sinners, than sit at the side of those with whom they had full communion in prayer and praise a few hours before. Their consciences would shudder at the idea of breaking bread in full communion with those, with whom, yesterday, or last night, they had full communion in adoring, venerating, invoking, and praising the same God and Redeemer. There is something like inconsistency here. It must be confessed, too, that the New Testament presents baptism as prior to social prayer and praise, as indispensably preceding these, as the Lord's supper. I have thought, and thought, and vascillated very much, on the question, Whether Baptists and Paido-Baptists ought, could, would, or should, irrespective of their peculiarities, sit down at the same Lord's table. And one thing I do know, that either they should cease to have communion in prayer, praise, and other religious observances, or they should go the whole length. Of this point I am certain. And I do know that as much can be said, and with as much reason and scripture on its side, to prove that immersion is as necessarily prior to social prayer, praise, &c. as it is to eating the Lord's supper.

Dear sir, this plan of making our own nest, and fluttering over our own brood; of building our own tent, and of confining all goodness and grace to our noble selves and the "elect few" who are like us, is the quintessence of sublimated pharisaism. The old Pharisees were but babes in comparison to the modern: and the longer I live, and the more I reflect upon God and man—heaven and earth—the bible and the world—the Redeemer and his church—the more I am assured that all sectarianism is the offspring of hell; and that all differences about words, and names, and opinions, hatched in Egypt, or Rome, or Edinburgh, are like the frolics of drunken men; and that where there is a *new creature,* or a society of them, with all their imperfections, and frailties, and errors in sentiment, in views, and opinions, they ought to receive one another, and the strong to support the infirmities of the weak, and not to please themselves. To lock ourselves up in the bandbox of our own little circle; to associate with a few units, tens, or hundreds, as the pure church, as the elect, is real Protestant monkery, it is evangelical pharisaism.

If we would heal the sick, we must visit them; if we would restore the lame, we must take them by the hand; if we would correct, inform, or reform erring christians, we must do as the Saviour did;—bear with their weaknesses. We must seek every opportunity of converting the sinner from the error of his way, of instructing the weak and feeble-minded. It is lame charity which requires all its objects to be as rich, as wise, and as strong as ourselves. And the history of the world does not afford one instance

of any man, or set of men, reforming, or restoring, or enlightening, or comforting the society
from which they separated. And the systems
and sects which they built, in the lapse of a few
years, were as much in need of reformation, as
those from which their founders separated.

The Baptist society exhibits a greater variety
than any other society in christendom. They
are a people made up of all religious persuasions,
and, generally speaking, their platform is more
consonant to the freedom of inquiry, to freedom
from ecclesiastical tyranny, and to the independence of congregations, than any other. With
the exception of some rigid "regulars," confes-
fessions of faith and the authority of associations, are held in no great esteem. The congregations in most places are extremely jealous of
their rights, and delegate nothing to any superior
judicatory. I know some associations whose
meetings are as innocent as a tea party, or any
social or friendly interview. Some, I know, do
imitate the *beast*, only they want horns. They
resemble a hornless ox; they push with their
heads, but cannot gore. But so long as they
will bear reproof, suffer exhortation, and allow
us to declare our sentiments without restraint;
so long as they manifest a willingness to know
the whole truth, and any disposition to obey it;
so long as they will hear us and cordially have
fellowship with us, we will have fellowship with
them, we will thus labor for their good, and
endeavor to correct what appears to be amiss—
commending when praise is due, and censuring
when it becomes necessary. I do hope in this
way always to have the approbation of Him
whose commendation is more to be desired than
the admiration and praise of ten thousand worlds.
This, I think, you must see, I do in perfect consistency with the sentiments advocated in this
work. But if you still think otherwise, I am
willing to hear from you again, and pay due
regard to what you have to advance.

With best wishes, I remain, &c.
EDITOR.

The Baptist Recorder.

WE have duly received seven numbers of The
Baptist Recorder, edited by Messrs. George Waller and Spencer Clack, Ky. Sundry articles in
these numbers exhibit a belligerent aspect towards this paper. The anonymous pieces over
the signatures S. M.—S. W.—and P. D. we pass
without a single criticism, for two reasons. First,
because when a writer opposes a person who is
known, and disliking to be known himself, conceals himself behind two letters as a mask, there
is something so suspicious in his character,
so undeserving of notice, except from a person
like himself under a mask, that we cannot deign
him a reply. We appear unmasked. Those
who expect from us any attention must come
forward in their full name. And in the second
place there is no reason, argument, or good sense
in those pieces, that should induce us either to
desire to know their authors, or, if known, to
require a moment's reflection. If the authors
make themselves known, I will publish some
of their pieces in this work without a single
remark, believing that their very appearance in
this work would be a sufficient exposure of their
imbecility, or of that of their cause, if they have
any.

I feel myself in duty bound to pay some attention to the editorial department of this work, or
to what the editors themselves have to say on
the great things of the kingdom of Jesus in the
present and future state. I am, indeed, much

pleased to see them come forward to oppose
what they do not like, and to correct what they
think wrong. I do assure them that it will give
me great pleasure to be corrected by them in
any respect whatever. I trust I have not yet
to learn the value of truth. Like gold, every
particle of it is precious. I do earnestly desire to
be in the full possession of as much of it as I
can by any means acquire, and I am always
thankful to every man, woman, or child who
imparts to me the knowledge of what I knew
not before. Besides, I am much pleased with
their efforts on another account. The Christian
Baptist is extensively read in Kentucky, and if it
is doing any injury it will be corrected and repressed in its career; and if it is doing any good
it will receive a new impulse and be accelerated
in its course. I care not for its circulation on
any other account, than as it does good. If it
does evil, the sooner it dies I will rejoice. But
I must be convinced before I can be converted
to any thing. And such is the constitution of my
mind, that nothing will operate upon it but truth,
reason, argument and evidence.

There are, in the numbers which have been
issued, but two topics that demand our attention.
The one is the editorial remarks upon "experimental religion;" the other is some remarks of
Mr. George Waller upon his "casting vote in the
Long Run Association." Had Mr. Waller confined his remarks to the subject on which he
professedly wrote, we should have endeavored
to have found room for his whole piece; but he
has indulged in too much acrimony, and gone
off in a tangent from his subject to insinuations
which are neither creditable to himself nor his
cause. We shall, however, present the reader
with what pertains to his casting vote:—

"Finding in the last number of the work
alluded to, [Christian Baptist,] page 215, under
the head of "the Casting Vote, or the Creed
triumphant over the Bible," a few remarks, in
which I (with the Long Run Association) am
implicated as acting an unworthy part, and considering myself in that connexion singled out as
an object of slander, it seems altogether important that I pay some attention to that subject.
It is true, as stated in said number, that the Long
Run Association, at her session of September,
1825, reported three thousand and sixty-four
members; that I did preside in said meeting as
Moderator; that a circular letter, written by
P. S. Fall, pastor of the Baptist church in Louisville, Ky. was presented for inspection, the subject of which was as stated in said number. It
is also true that I am a descendant of the Wallers of Virginia; once persecuted by those who,
having the form of godliness, but denying the
power of it: and so great is my attachment to
my predecessors, and that gospel which they so
warmly espoused, that I am content (if the will
of God be so) to suffer persecution from a similar
source. It is not true, as expressed at the head
of said remarks, that in the rejection of said
letter, the creed was triumphant over the Bible.
Nor is it true that in giving the casting vote in
that case, I copied the example of Doctor Lightfoot by acting from the same reasons. I must
acknowledge myself at some loss to understand
the allusion in the expression, "for the same
reasons:" if reference is had in this expression
to the reason given by the publishers of said
circular letter, for the decision of the moderator.
Although I have no disposition to impeach the
motives or veracity of the publishers, yet, to say
the least of it, manifest injustice is done to the
moderator on the subject of his vote. It is ad-
69

mitted that something to that effect may have occurred in the course of examination on that subject, but not in the shape of a reason for the casting vote. It is not true, as insinuated by the Christian Baptist, that the creed and the Bible were in question before the Association; and I cannot persuade myself that Mr. Campbell believes they were; for he knows too well the views of the Baptists in the adoption of the creed, to be innocent when he thus represents them; for support of these remarks, see Confession, ch. i. of which Mr. C. cannot be supposed to be ignorant, especially as he has so much to say against them. It will be recollected by those who were attentive to the proceedings of the Long Run Association, that after the circular written by P. S. Fall, had passed the examination of the committee, and it was presented to the Association for adoption, there were two additional notes, one of which declaring that it was not the intention of the writer to call in question the propriety of creeds: this was done at the suggestion of the moderator, in committee, and with a design to waive any objection to the letter, before the Association, which might arise from the supposition that the letter was designed to oppose and put down the creed. Not having the manuscript (as it appeared after amendments) before me, I do not pretend to detail the facts precisely as they occurred; but the substance is given, to the best of my recollection. These things in view, and it is impossible that any person can believe, either that the creed or Bible were in question before the Association, or that the casting vote of the moderator rendered the creed triumphant over the Bible."

Now let the reader observe that every thing stated in the article alluded to in the seventh number is admitted by Mr. Waller, excepting the head or title prefixed to the article. That the creed was triumphant over the bible was the natural consequence in my mind, for this reason: First, because the letter advocated neither more nor less than that the bible is "the one only sufficient, perfect, and infallible rule of christian faith and manners." And Mr. Waller admits that the extracts given in the seventh number do, in truth, express the substance of the whole letter. Has Mr. Waller assigned any other reason for giving his casting vote, other than stated by the publishers of said letter? Does he now give his reasons for said vote? And what damnable or condemnable doctrine was in said letter, except that it contended that the bible alone was the only sufficient, perfect, and infallible rule of christian faith and manners? Was not the substance of the letter the reason why he rejected it by the casting vote? If not, pray what was it? And if it was the substance, I must again declare, notwithstanding the question was not put in the very words whether the creed or the bible shall be the only perfect and infallible rule, &c. that still it was in fact and in effect, "the creed triumphant over the bible;" and to quibble now about the form in which the question was put, or to make that an excuse for the vote, is only weak and childish. Will the reader please turn over to the seventh number of this volume and read the extracts of said letter there given, and remember that Mr. Waller has affirmed them to be correctly stated, and then ask himself whether the title given to the casting vote is just or unjust, and I will abide by his decision.

As to what he says about copying the example of Dr. Lightfoot, I did not say he "copied" it. And his saying that he was not actuated by Dr. Lightfoot's reasons, and then declaring that he did not know what they were, I must charitably say, deserves no notice. I am glad to observe that he is now ashamed of his vote, and that he considers it "slander" to be reminded of it, or to have it published without a disrespectful word. I have only to add my earnest desires that all who vote as he did against such a document as said letter, may consider it "slander" to be told of it again.

I will give another extract immediately following the preceding, which I am sorry to say is but a poor defence of himself, and unworthy of a good cause. This I consider undeserved slander, and of the lowest kind:—

"I take this to be the whole secret: Mr. C. has set out to cut a figure in the learned world, and no plan so likely to succeed as to set himself to oppose the whole religious world. If this course can be freed from the charge of bigotry, (against which he inveighs so vehemently,) I can only say that I am mistaken: this, however, is no new thing under the sun, for in every instance where new sects start up, their leaders must (in order to success) show that every body else is wrong as to religious matters, and themselves right: it is true, the baptists are complimented, not only with assertions that they are right on the subject of baptism, but to their support on that subject one public controversy after another has been bestowed upon them. This, however, is not surprising, when it seems a reasonable calculation, that by means of a press at hand, publications of those controversies might be productive of a considerable income to the donor. The exertions of Mr. C. in opposition to associations and confessions of faith, or opinions, cannot be accounted for upon principles satisfactory to me, in any other way than by admitting the following as the cause. That in order to enlarge the sphere of his operations every thing like dependence of the churches, one upon another, must be destroyed by the destruction of associations, and that of the members of churches by the destruction of confessions of faith. And why must associations and creeds be destroyed? Because they are human productions. No person pretends that there is express precept or example in the word of God, yet I esteem it impious that the scripturality of associations or creeds should be denied."

Here my motives of action are represented as vile, and what I have said must be false, because my motives are judged, condemned, and execrated. I had thought that "God alone searched the hearts and tried the thoughts of the children of men." On this I will make no comment. I do not impute any thing to the motives of Mr. Waller; I trust they are pure and upright, and I assure him I will be the last to impeach them. It is with what he says and does I have to do. I leave the rest to him "that sees not as man sees."

I have not room to be more particular in my remarks, nor more full in my extracts on this subject. There are some sentiments expressed on the subject of creeds and associations which I cannot believe are the real sentiments of the author. He says, "I esteem it impious that the scripturality of associations or creeds should be denied." I will not comment upon this saying until the writer avows it to be his real sentiment on this subject, believing it to have been written at an unfavorable moment when under the influence of some mental perturbation. For assuredly no Baptist can think that it is a sin against God, or the want of reverence for him, to deny that human creeds and associations are commanded in scripture.

Again he says, "To say that creeds and associations were introduced among us, with any other than religious feelings, desires, and motives, is unpardonable impiety." Now I would rather think and say that Mr. Waller did not understand or weigh the import of his own words, than to think he really means that the mere saying that creeds and associations were introduced not as he represents, is a sin against God that has no forgiveness, neither in this world nor the next. There are so many things of this kind in brother Waller's piece, that I would rather impute them to any cause than to suppose them the genuine views and feelings of his mind. His remarks upon the new version of the New Testament, which he never saw, are of the same kind, and indicate some mental perturbation, which forbid my commenting upon them until I am assured that they are his cool and deliberate sentiments.

On the subject of "experimental religion" the editors have been hinting, hoping, and doubting something about my orthodoxy. I am glad they have begun here, and that they have published my first essay on this subject. Had they also been so obliging as to have published my last one, or even an intermediate one on the same topic, I should have appreciated their candor and liberality still more. I think my remarks on Conscience, vol. 3, No. 7, being the last thing said on that subject, ought to appear in connexion with No. 8, vol. 1. I shall feel obliged to acknowledge a favor done to myself individually, and to the cause which I espouse, should the editors publish the article on "Conscience," No. 7, vol. 3.

While on this topic, I must just remark, that as the editors have not as yet attempted to elucidate this subject, or to give their views, or any views, other than a few vague expressions, it would no doubt be of importance to the community that they should fully discuss the subject. And still I put the question, What is "experimental religion?" The words import neither more nor less in any acceptation of them, according to the English language than a religion founded upon experiment, or proved by experiment. It is optional with those who contend for the thing signified by the phrase, to say which of the two. If it mean a religion founded upon experiment, let them illustrate the nature and properties of those experiments: if proved by experiment, let the experiments be explained. I will not do it for them, because I cannot. Let them who so warmly contend for the name and for something under the name, explain it, and I will examine and declare unequivocally my views upon their exposition. As to "christian experience," the language is intelligible, and I understand the words precisely. They mean the experience of a christian. And I am persuaded that every christian in the world has experience. Yet a great portion of what is commonly called "christian experience" is as much the experience of deists and apostates, as it is of christians. Neither convictions of guilt, nor fears of punishment, nor hopes of exemption, nor desires for reformation, are peculiar to christians. Simon Magus, and Judas Iscariot, and ten thousand others have experienced these, whom few of the populars would put on their lists of christians. If the phrase "christian experience" must be retained, let it be defined; let those who consecrate it give us a definition of it that comports with the import of the words or with their views. My remarks in the 8th No. vol. 1, on this subject, may be ridiculed and laughed at by those who

do not understand them, or by those who have been misled and are misleading others in this wild course; but they have not yet been able to show that they are either logically or scriptually erroneous. I have too many documents to prove that thousands are depending upon their experiences and experimental religion as the bases of their hope towards God, whose experience and experimental religion are not worth a straw.

I am assured that every one that is born of God feels as well as believes, hopes and fears, loves and abhors, rejoices and trembles, and that they are conscious of all these; that they are purified in their hearts, reformed in their lives, and zealous of good works; that they are fervent in spirit, constant in prayer, and intent on showing forth the praises of him who has called them out of darkness into his marvellous light. And I contend that, without these, a man is blind and cannot see far, and dead while he lives.

As to the modus operandi, as described by the populars, it is all foolish philosophy; vain and deceitful jargon, and a ship load of such theories is not worth one inspired word. If I cannot prove them such by unanswerable arguments, I will become a spiritual metaphysician, a theoretic doctor, a retailer of theological receipts, as orthodox as Beza or Calvin.

I have now to propose to the editors of the Baptist Recorder:—You, gentlemen, have selected what you call my views of experimental religion, out of the numerous topics in the Christian Baptist. This appears from your beginning with this topic. If, of the numerous essays on this subject, you think the first one on this topic answers your purpose better than any other, I have no objections to your availing yourselves of it, irrespective of any thing afterwards published on the same topic; or if you please to select any other one down to the article headed "Conscience," No. 6, vol. 3. or if you prefer to publish your own sentiments on the subject, I will promise to publish any thing you write on the subject, to the amount of four or five pages in one number, and will take no more to myself in replying to it—on the following conditions: 1st. That you publish my replies in full in your paper; and 2dly. That you confine yourselves to one topic at a time, and abstain from every expression of passion, from every insinuation about my motives, which you know nothing about; in a word, that you confine yourselves to argument and scripture. I do not stipulate these conditions as though I feared a non-compliance, or any thing like injustice on your part; but the insinuations over the name of Geo. Waller have given some apprehension that the latter may not be an untimely hint. My willingness to be instructed or put to rights, and to give every opportunity to my readers to judge for themselves, have dictated the first condition. I court investigation, and only ask for what is commonly called "fair play," and good order in the plan of conducting it.

One topic at a time, and a firm adherence to the oracles of truth and to argument, are conditions which common sense and common justice dictate, and against which we know of no objection which honesty, integrity, and the consciousness of a good cause can offer. All of which is respectfully submitted, by your humble servant for the truth's sake,   THE EDITOR.

———

MANY of the great men of all departments of science, in their lucid intervals, have expressed the same views of the bible and of systematic theology:

Milton's Treatise on Christian Doctrine.

"If, then, the scriptures be in themselves so perspicuous, and sufficient of themselves to make men wise unto salvation through faith, and that the man of God may be perfect, thoroughly furnished unto all good works, through what infatuation is it that even Protestant divines persist in darkening the most momentous truths of religion by intricate comments, on the plea that such an explanation is necessary; stringing together all the useless technicalities and empty distinctions of scholastic barbarism, for the purpose of elucidating those scriptures which they are continually extolling as models of plainness? as if scripture, which possesses in itself the clearest light, and is sufficient for its own explanation, especially in matters of faith and holiness, required to have the simplicity of its divine truths more fully developed, and placed in a more distinct view, by illustrations drawn from the abstract of human science, falsely so called."

Dr. George Campbell's views of Commentators and Commentaries, extracted from his Lectures on Systematic Theology.

"The dogmatist knows nothing of degrees, either in evidence or in faith. He has properly no opinions or doubts. Every thing with him is either certainly true, or certainly false. Of this turn of mind I shall only say, that so far from being an indication of vigor, it is a sure indication of debility in the intellectual powers."

"Of most of our commentaries we may almost say, they speak an infinite deal of nothing.— Their reasons are as two grains of wheat hid in two bushels of chaff; you shall seek all day ere you find them, and when you have them they are not worth the search."

"Almost every commentator hath his favorite system, which occupies his imagination, biasses his understanding, and more or less tinges all his comments."

"How unsafe, then, must it be to trust in men. When we thus implicitly follow a guide before inquiry, if we should even happen to be in the right, it is, with regard to us, a matter purely accidental."

"Whilst, therefore, it is by far the too general cry, 'Read, read commentators, systematists, paraphrasts, controvertists, demonstrations, confutations, apologies, answers, defences, replies, and ten thousand other such like;' I should think the most important advice to be, devoutly study the scriptures themselves, if you would understand their doctrine in singleness of heart."

"Rica having been to visit the library of a French convent, writes thus to his friend in Persia concerning what had passed: Father, said I to the librarian, what are these huge volumes which fill the whole side of the library? These, said he, are the interpreters of the scriptures.— There is a prodigious number of them, replied I; the scriptures must have been very dark formerly, and very clear at present. Do there remain still any doubts? Are there now any points contested? Are there? (answered he with surprise,) Are there? There are almost as many as there are lines. You astonish me, said I; what then have all these authors been doing? These authors, returned he, never searched the scriptures for what ought to be believed, but for what they did believe themselves. They did not consider them as a book wherein were contained the doctrines which they ought to receive, but as a work which might be made to authorize their own ideas."

No. 11.]   June 5, 1826.

A Restoration of the Ancient Order of Things. No. XIII.

The Bishop's Office.—No. II.

Some of the populars sneer at the term *bishop*, as if the Spirit of God had not chosen it to designate the only legitimate "officer" in a christian congregation, who is, from office, to teach and rule. They love *Rabbi, Rabbi*, or *Reverend and Right Reverend*, too well to lay them aside, or to exchange these haughty titles for the apostolic and humble name of overseer or bishop. And I see that some of the Baptists too, who love the present order of things, and who contend for the traditions of the fathers in the mass, in their editorial labors either capitalize, or italicize, or by some outlandish mark, erect a monument of admiration at every inscribing of the name Bishop. Yet their dear "Confession of Faith" says, p. 43:

"8. A particular church gathered and completely organized according to the mind of Christ, consists of officers and members; and the officers appointed by Christ to be chosen and set apart by the church, so called and gathered, for the peculiar administration of ordinances, and execution of power, or duty, which he intrusts them with, or calls them to, to be continued to the end of the world, are bishops, or elders, and deacons."

Some again, because of the impieties of England and Rome in appropriating this term to a man who wore a wig, and a gown, and trappings, have considered it very profane indeed, to call any man a bishop who does not wear a wig and kiss the pope's toe. But to those who have got an apostolic taste, the title or name of office which Paul and Peter adopted and designated is incomparably preferable to the prescriptions of Geneva or Westminster. I have lately heard that some Baptist teachers who at first recognized the "divine right," at least of the name, and were desirous of coming up to the ancient model in all things, are now startled, if not considerably shocked, when saluted "Bishop;" but the term *reverend* can be heard without any nervous spasm. Perhaps this may be accounted for on good principles; and, indeed, if so, it is the best argument we can find for giving an exclusive preference to the terms adopted and fixed by the Spirit of Revelation. The reason why they are startled at the title on this hypothesis, they see some incongruity in its application to them. There is no incongruity arising from their want of an academical education, from their being merely acquainted with their mother tongue, from their not having a doctorate or an honorary degree. It is not on this account they are startled or affrighted at being called Bishop. But they never read in the New Testament of a bishop of two, three or four congregations; of a bishop having the "pastoral care" of a church in Rome, and Corinth, and Ephesus—in Philadelphia, Pergamos, and Thyatira, at the same time. They might have read of a plurality of bishops in one congregation, but never of a plurality of congregations under one bishop. This they may have read in the history of diocesan episcopacy, but not in the history of primitive episcopacy. But some of them are startled perhaps, on another consideration. They were not made bishops according to law. Their declaration of a special call to some work entirely distinct from the bishop's work, was the ladder which reached from the floor to the pulpit. And they do not read that any were made bishops in the hale and undegenerate days of the christian kingdom, because of their having declared that they were inwardly moved by the Holy Spirit to take upon them the office of a bishop. In fine, there is no occasion for being particular or minute in finding out incongruities, which may appear to some a good and lawful reason why *they* should not be so designated. But they can discover no incongruity in being called minister, preacher or divine; for every one that makes public speeches or harangues on religion, is so called by their cotemporaries. The term *reverend*, too, is become such common property, that the preacher of the dreams of Swedenborg, or the leader of the dance of a Shaker meeting is fully entitled to all its honors and emoluments—equally heirs to its privileges in this world and that which is to come. That some half dozen of Baptist preachers have become shy of the name bishop, for the reasons above specified, is, indeed, a good symptom in their case. It proves that their acquaintance with the ancient order of things is increasing, that they see a discrepancy between the ancient order and the present—between themselves and the bishops instituted and appointed by the apostles.

As to our Presbyterian brethren, they make little or no pretensions to the name. They are wise enough to know that it is unsuitable to their character; but they would have some to think, that their minister and Paul's bishop are one and the same character.

Our methodist friends have not quite forgotten the glory and majesty of the Lord Archbishop of York:—for even until this hour archepiscopacy has some charms in their eyes. In other words, a few of this brotherhood still like the remains of diocesan episcopacy. They seem to admire it, even in its ruins. I believe, however, such is the progress of light amongst this zealous people, that few, if any of their leaders, consider there is a divine right for either their bishops or form of church government, other than " *vox populi, vox Dei.*" Yet still their " church government" has too many heads, even when the horns are broken off.

The good old *high* church bishops are not within the sphere of comparison. There is no point of contact; no one side of the system that can be measured by any side of primitive episcopacy.

Our baptist brethren began in the spirit, but ended in the flesh, on their adopting a species of presbyterial independency—licensing of preachers, and then converting these preachers into elders, with the exclusive right of administering " sealing ordinances," and creating or finishing an order of its own kind.

But the fact is, very generally, that few of the leaders of religious assemblies seem to know, or are able to decide, whether they should be called evangelists, preachers, elders, bishops, or ambassadors; but the term minister or divine seems to embrace them all.

To many it seems but of little consequence to be tenacious of the name. Why not then call the leaders priests? Why not then call them astrologers, soothsayers, or oneirocritics, if the name be indifferent? Because, says one, those names are used to denote quite different characters. For the same reason, therefore, let the names which the apostles adopted be used in their own acceptation, and let those things, persons and offices which the apostles said nothing about, be named or styled as the inventors please, but call not bitter sweet, nor sweet bitter. Let us not call the messenger of a congregation, an elder. Let us not call a preacher, a bishop. Let us not call a bishop, a divine; nor a deacon, a ruling elder. In a word, let us give to divine institutions divine names, and to human institutions human names.

Were christian societies to constitute christian bishops, and to designate them by their proper title or name of office, many important results would exhibit themselves, amongst which, none of the least would be the levelling the haughty and supercilious pretensions of those who claim another office under this name, and designate themselves as the only persons to be so viewed and denominated.

Another happy circumstance resulting from this course, would be the discountenancing and suppressing the pretensions and enthusiastic conceits of those who are imposing themselves upon society, under the pretence that they are specially called and sent by the Holy Spirit of God to preach. If they are sent to preach, let them go to preach—but they can plead no right to officiate as bishops under the call to preach. If they are *called* to go and preach the gospel to every creature, they dare not, of course, refuse to go; nor dare they assume a work in relation to which they are not called, and to which no man was ever otherwise called, than as the brethren, under the direction of the Holy Spirit, called him. For amongst all the qualifications by which Paul would have a bishop chosen—the modern special call is not to be found—I again repeat, that the adoption of the course divinely recommended, would, in due time, suppress the impositions practised upon the unsuspicious, by a class of raving, ranting mountebanks, who are playing themselves off as a kind of little half inspired ones, who just give to the people what they pretend they have got from heaven; and say that so clear is their divine mission and call, that eternal woe awaits them if they preach not the gospel.

The bishops of apostolic creation are sometimes called elders—because they were generally aged persons, and always amongst the oldest converts in the community in which they officiated. But the office is no where called the elder's office. There is nothing in the term elder, which can designate the nature of any office. But the term bishop implies a good and arduous work.

While on the term elder, it may be remarked, that there is no greater incongruity than to see a stripling or a young man from twenty to thirty, styled elder; and if the name does not suit his years, it is a very strong reason in favor of the conclusion that the office of a bishop does not.

Here I had intended to have called the reader's attention to the call and appointment of a bishop—but circumstances beyond my control, forbid an effort of this kind for the present.

EDITOR.

To the Editor of the Christian Baptist.

B—— Co. (Md.) April 1, 1826.

DEAR BROTHER,—ALTHOUGH a stranger to your correspondents Faithful, see page, 184 and J——H——, see page 222, I feel an affection that proceeds for the truth's sake, that I cannot withhold from their view a statement of a church of Jesus Christ attending to the ordinances in their simplicity. Although I am in practice for years with the order described below, yet to copy this account is far better than I could do it otherwise—and your time being so much occupied with printing the New Testament, you have not been able to comply with what you say at the close of yours to Faithful, that is—" We intend

to give the history of the progress and proficiency of some congregations who have taken this course, and are now enjoying a participation of the fulness of the blessings of the gospel of Christ." You will please publish this account in the present volume, and my anxiety for the dear brethren, Faithful and J— H—, will be relieved.   Yours in love,
                                W——— C———.

The following is copied from the first volume of the Christian Magazine, printed in Edinburgh, in 1819.

An Account of a Remarkable Occurrence in a Late Journey.—An Apostolic Church.

HAVING occasion, some time ago, to travel in the county of ——, I arrived, on Saturday evening, in the town of ——. Being a stranger, I made inquiry of my host respecting the places of worship in the town. He told me there were two established churches, a Burgher and an anti-Burgher meeting, an Episcopal chapel, and of late, said he, another meeting has been set up, whose mode of worship is different from all the others. I was curious to learn wherein it differed; but he could give me no distinct answer, only, he said, that many of the town's people did not approve of it, though, he had heard, some of the graver cast liked it very much. Next morning I inquired where I should find the new place of worship he had mentioned, and being directed, I repaired to it.—Two persons, whom I supposed to be the elders of the church, soon entered.— One of them, after a short prayer, imploring the divine presence, gave out a hymn, celebrating the resurrection of the Lord Jesus. He then read a portion of scripture from the Old Testament and another from the New. That from the New Testament was judiciously chosen, as illustrating some part of what had been read from the Old. Having mentioned several of the members by name, who were variously afflicted, he called on one of the brethren to pray. He was an aged disciple of grave appearance; his prayer seemed to be the effusion of a heart alive to God—plain, artless, and appropriate. I was particularly struck by the affectionate manner in which he prayed for these distressed brethren. It reminded me of the apostle's description of the body of Christ, "Whether one member suffer, all the members suffer with it." After again uniting in praise, the other elder addressed the church, in terms which made such an impression on my mind, that, I believe, I repeat his words almost *verbatim*—" I have now," said he, " brethren, to lay before you a matter peculiarly painful, it is the case of our brother ———. His crime is described in the fifth chapter of the Galatians, the 19th verse. The fall of our brother, I lament to say, is well known to the world, and has caused the enemies of the Lord to blaspheme. By the offence of this person (for he did not again name him) the church is called to deep humiliation before God. In this mournful case, we have a striking instance of the fatal effects of unnecessarily mingling with the world. This was the first step of his defection, and it paved the way for all that has followed. When first spoken to on the subject he positively denied it; but has now confessed it to me and two of the brethren." [Here these two brethren simply attested the truth of the statement.]— After a short pause he proceeded—" With the law of our Lord and Master in our hands, we can be at no loss as to our duty in this case. That law is explicitly stated in the fifth chapter of the 1st epistle to the Corinthians, from the fourth

verse to the end, [which he read.] Here then, you perceive, brethren, there is no alternative; the Lord Jesus commands us, both for this person's good, and that of the body, to separate him from our fellowship." The church, (who I now perceived were sitting together in one place) having signified their conviction that this was their duty, the elder, with much solemnity said, "We then, as a church of Jesus Christ, and acting by his authority, do, in obedience to his commandment, separate ——— ——— from our fellowship." He then prayed, in a very appropriate and impressive manner, for the unhappy subject of discipline, that the ordinance of God which had now been attended to, might be blessed to his soul, in bringing him to repentance—and to the church, in leading them to watchfulness, self abasement, and continual dependance on the grace of Jesus. After prayer, the 101st psalm was sung, which formed an extremely suitable conclusion to the solemn service. I never witnessed a scene more deeply affecting. The countenance of every person present bespoke his feelings. How is it, said I to myself, that I have lived so long among christians, and have never, till now, seen this plain and positive law of Jesus carried into effect? How beneficial are the laws of his kingdom! how much are they calculated to promote the spiritual life of his people, and to awaken the thoughtless and inconsiderate! The church now proceeded to— what I afterwards understood was a stated part of their service every Lord's day—the observance of the Lord's supper. The simplicity with which this divine ordinance was attended to, was, in itself, edifying. I beheld a representation of the unity of the body of Christ, which I never before witnessed. The words of the institution were read by one of the elders, a few remarks were then made on the nature of the Lord's supper, and on the spirit in which it ought to be observed. He then gave thanks; and then breaking the bread gave it to the disciples, who divided it among themselves. Having again united in thanksgiving, he gave also the cup, and when all had drank of it, concluded with a short exhortation, and singing an appropriate hymn. This part of the service being closed, the elder said, " Let us now, brethren, attend to the ordinance of mutual exhortation:" when some of the members spoke, for a few minutes alternately, with much simplicity, earnestness, and evident humbleness of mind. The addresses of the brethren were, properly speaking, exhortations— calculated to excite to the performance of duty, and to bear, with patience, the various sufferings of the present life: each of them had some relation to the others, and their combined influence was highly salutary. Is not this, said I to myself, an exhibition of what the apostle means, when he speaks of " the body of Christ edifying itself in love?" The exhortations of the brethren were followed by an address from one of the elders, in which he briefly recapitulated the topics brought forward by the members, and enforced the duties to which their attention had been called. One of the brethren was again called on to pray. After again uniting in praise, the elder, in a short prayer, implored the divine benediction on all their services, and entreated the blessing of God, while they attended to the fellowship of the saints. The church then sat down, when a collection was made, and the worship closed. The two hours which I thus spent with these dear people, were among the happiest and most profitable I ever enjoyed on earth. I bless God, that unexpectedly I had an opportunity of witnessing the order of a church, which commended itself to my mind, as combining all the ends of christian association, and of which I had previously formed some idea from reading the New Testament. After an interval the service proceeded, and the time was occupied by prayer and praise, the teaching of the elders, and the reading of the word of God; which last, I observed, throughout the day formed a conspicuous part of their worship.

"Being under the necessity of leaving this town early next morning, I was very desirous of learning their history. Accordingly, when worship was over in the evening, I accosted a person whom I had noticed among the members: 'Sir,' said I, ' I am a stranger in this place, and was happily led to your place of worship to-day. Although unknown to any of you in the face, I trust I am one with you in the faith and hope of the gospel. I was very much edified with your order, and would esteem it a great favor if you would give me some particulars of your history.' He very kindly invited me to his house, and gave me the following interesting detail:—'I have no doubt,' said he, ' that the motives of your inquiry are good; I shall, therefore, without reserve, give you the information you request. We have met together as a church for these six years past. The original members were intimately acquainted with one another. Each of us had, for a considerable time, been groaning under the defects of the societies with which we were then connected. We clearly perceived that they bore none of the features of the churches set in order by the apostles; but we sinfully contented ourselves with our condition. Our chief comfort, as to christian society, arose from assembling together once a-week in what is called a fellowship meeting. On one of these occasions a member spoke with some freedom on the distress he felt, arising from the cause above mentioned. This led the way to a free conversation; and we soon found that our distress was not that of an individual, but common to us all. We therefore resolved to walk together as a church in all the ordinances and commandments of the Lord Jesus, diligently searching the scriptures to know his will, and fervently praying to be guided by him. From that period we have assembled regularly on the first day of the week. The Lord has been pleased graciously to countenance us. Our beginning was indeed small; we were few and despised; but walking, as I trust, in the fear of the Lord and in the comfort of the Holy Spirit, we have been greatly multiplied. We had soon the satisfaction of choosing two of our brethren, with whose qualifications we were entirely satisfied, as our elders. Their labors of love have been much blessed, and one and another has from time to time been added to our number. Our communion commenced," he continued, " in the full conviction that we were yielding obedience to the Lord Jesus. And now we have increasing experience of the truth of our Saviour's declaration, that if any man do his will he shall know of the doctrine whether it be of God. We have no standard but the will of our Master; and this we find so clearly stated in the scriptures, that, with the teachable spirit of disciples, we are in no danger of misunderstanding it." "The brethren," said I, "appear to have much love to each other." "Yes," he replied, " we know the benefits of christian fellowshp, by coming together into one place on the first day of the week, and regularly observing the ordinances of Christ, we not only get better

acquainted, but our interest in each other is greatly promo ed. If a brother or a sister be absent they are immediately missed, and inquiry is made for them. Our elders know well the situation of every individual; and in case of distress, the church is particularly informed. Thus our sick, or otherwise distressed brethren, are not neglected. Christian sympathy is excited, and we are stirred up to the duty of weeping with those that weep. In short," continued he, " we have convincing proof of the wisdom of all the appointments of Christ, and how eminently the observance of them is calculated to cherish and mature every christian grace, the people of God are not aware of the loss they sustain by neglecting any one of them." " I was much gratified," said I, "by the short exhortations of the brethren to-day; is every brother called on to exhort in the church?" " Yes," he answered, " we think the commandment to exhort one another, can be limited no otherwise, than by a brother possessing no talent for it. It is the duty of our elders to take care that the edification of the church be not marred; and if a church be composed of real disciples abuses will rarely occur. We have no right to make laws to ourselves; it is our province to follow implicitly the injunctions of our master. A few Sabbaths ago, one of our brethren spoke on the consolations which the gospel affords to believers under the heaviest trials, and with much feeling urged the duty of cordial submission to the will of God. The advice came with peculiar impression, from one whose deep affliction was well known to his brethren. Indeed, who that knows the Lord is not fitted to suggest a word in season, and how gracious is the Saviour's appointment, that his disciples should comfort one another with the words of truth. Individual experience thus becomes a general benefit. The Lord Jesus, my friend, bestows gifts on his people, and every one knows that gifts are improved by exercising them." " But does not the singularity of your observances, draw upon you the censure of others?" "I believe it does; but," added he, with a look of peculiar satisfaction, "a full conviction that we are obeying the commandments of the Lord Jesus, raises us superior to these little obstacles. While we follow our own convictions of duty, and are thankful, that, in this highly favored country, every man enjoys liberty to worship God according to his own conscience, we, at the same time, cherish a loving spirit towards all who truly fear God; we earnestly desire the universal spread of the gospel; and use every means in our power for the salvation of perishing sinners around us." I thanked this worthy man for the free and open manner in which he had talked with me, and, with much regret, bade him adieu!

Next morning I pursued my journey, but not without casting a wishful eye on the spot where these disciples sojourn. The occurrences of this day I shall not soon forget. Never do I read of the churches of the New Testament but I realize the christians at ———. Send forth, O God! thy light and thy truth, unite thy people. Thou hast indeed given them a good law; thy commandments concerning all things are right. "Thus says the Lord, I am the Lord your God, who teaches you to profit, who leads you by the way that you should go. Oh! that you had hearkened to my commandments, then had your peace been as a river, and your righteousness as the waves of the sea!" *

* Would the churches at Jerusalem, Philippi, &c., the models of the above, be esteemed orthodox now?—PUB.

Christian Morality.—No. II.

THERE is as much wisdom exhibited in concealing some things as there is in revealing others. Parents, in relation to their own children, have incontestible proofs of this, if they are parents of discernment. Our Heavenly Father, in revealing himself and his designs to the children of men, has purposely concealed many things which it would have been unwise, in relation to all ends and results, to have discovered. There was evidently some principle, some statute in the counsels of the Omniscient, which allowed the discovery of certain things, and forbade the disclosure of others. When this principle or rule of revelation is apprehended many important results are acquired, many reflections present themselves which are of much value to the student of the Bible.

We have no doubt but it is quite practicable to ascertain the rule or principle which authorizes the revelation of some things, and which withholds from mortal man the knowledge of others.

When we take into view the object proposed, in giving to the world the bible, we have got into the possession of more than half the secret. And what was this? It will be said, The illumination of the world. But in reference to some end? Assuredly in reference to some end; for, without this end in view, there could be no selection of items or topics on which to address men. God has not disclosed the principles of astronomy or navigation in any part of his revelation; yet if the object of his revelation had been the mere illumination of the mind on subjects hitherto unknown, the systems and laws of astronomy or chemistry, would have been in times past a proper subject of revelation. But it is not the mere illumination of the mind which constituted a primary object in any communication from God to man.

To come directly to the point before us, it must be observed that the volume of revelation was not given to angels, nor written for them; nor was it given to man in his primitive state, nor adapted to a perfect innocent being; but it was designed for, addressed to and conferred upon fallen and polluted human beings, composed of soul, body and spirit, in such circumstances as those in which we first find ourselves when introduced to life. From all which the inference is unavoidable, viz. That the bible is designed for, and adapted to, the children of men in their present circumstances, to improve their condition here, and to fit them to become members of a pure, refined and exalted society hereafter.

It has long been discovered, and almost universally admitted, that three words constitute the sum total of human misfortune in this life.— These are, ignorance, guilt and bondage. From the brutal ignorance of the Hottentot, up to the refined ignorance of a sceptic philosopher, there are many intermediate degrees; but as respects the true knowledge which the bible communicates, there is a total blank in the extremes and in all the intermediate degrees.

To fit man for heaven, in one sentence, is the design of the whole volume. This being admitted, then it follows that nothing is revealed which is not directly or indirectly conducive to this end. The grand rule or principle on which all revelation has ever proceeded, is this—whatever may or can purify man, is lawful and benevolent to communicate; whatever cannot accomplish this, Wisdom says, Disclose it not.

Curiosity has prompted a thousand queries, to which the bible deigns no reply. And why?

Because, if answered, they would contribute nothing to the purification of the heart, or to the reformation of the life. God's sublime and glorious scheme of ameliorating and reforming the world is founded upon the actual condition of man. And as intelligence, purity of heart, and rectitude of life, are as inseparably connected with present and future happiness, as ignorance and guilt are with bondage and wretchedness, both here and hereafter, the bible is prepared, was bestowed, and is adapted, to the promotion of intelligence and purity, as prerequisites, as indispensables, as a *sine qua non* to happiness. "The whole scripture is divinely inspired, and is profitable for teaching, for confutation, for instruction in righteousness, that the man of God may be perfect, and thoroughly fitted for every good work." Intelligence, purity of heart, and uprightness of life, are the sole objects for which the bible was bestowed on the world. As ignorance, guilt and bondage, constitute the sum total of human misery, so intelligence, purity and the freedom of the truth, comprehend the whole object, design and end of divine revelation.

Christians, then, egregiously mistake, who value themselves on the account of their superior intelligence, or who pursue information in the things revealed, merely for its own sake. Unless this knowledge is conducive and allied to the art of living well, it merely puffs up and avails nothing. I have seen some christians who seem to think that the clearness of their views and the comprehension of their understanding would invade the kingdom of heaven and take the citadel of God, whose piety and purity were far below the standard of a Syrophenician woman, were far below the scale on which Zaccheus the publican was measured. In fact, a man who glories in his intellectual attainments in the bible, (and of this class there are not a few) and pursues the knowledge of the volume for its own sake, resembles a foolish husbandman who boasts of his thousand measures of wheat and his thousand measures of corn, who, as yet, has but ploughed his fields, and intends nothing more until harvest. Yet intelligence is one of the noblest of all things; for without it there is no purity. It is only, however, when it is pursued and acquired for the express purpose of living piously and virtuously, that it is a blessing to the possessor. We sometimes meet with more piety, purity and virtue, amongst those of inferior intellectual endowments, than amongst those of superior attainments. "For knowledge puffs up." As, therefore, the bible was written to impart intelligence to men, as this intelligence was designed to promote purity, and as purity is essential to happiness, we may see what ought to be our constant aim in all our studies, in all our inquiries into the meaning of the bible. And that, as Solomon says, "the fear of the Lord is the beginning of wisdom," so the conclusion of the whole matter is, "Fear God and keep his commandments," for this is the whole happiness of man.   EDITOR.

Theoretic, Scholastic, Metaphysical, Speculative Theology.

THE editors of the *Baptist Recorder* appear to be very strongly attached to dogmatic theology. With many, indeed, of the admirers of Aristotelian logic and the Geneva theology, *soundness in the faith* means no more than pronouncing with an unfaltering tongue a few dogmas in the quaint style of puritanical divinity. Greater fears are entertained, and stronger doubts of my orthodoxy are expressed by those zealous and *sound* divines, because I will not subscribe a few unprofitable and foolish dogmas, than if I had denied the resurrection of the dead and the final judgment—at least so it appears to me. Great efforts are made to enlist the feelings and prejudices of those with whom *sound* is infinitely more important than *sense*, against my endeavors to call the attention of christians off from the vanities of spiritual quacks, to the pure milk of the divine word. I am represented, if not in so many words, yet in effect, as " in the gall of bitterness and bond of iniquity," because of my essay on experimental religion. In a late Recorder an extract is given from some Christian Secretary, pronouncing encomiums upon Messrs. Waller and Clack for their *able* efforts to expose my heresy, in which there is about a round half dozen of plump falsehoods, gravely told, and no doubt undesignedly from the overflowings of an honest zeal in defence of orthodoxy, which led the author to speak on a subject with which he was entirely unacquainted, and concerning a person of whom he scarcely knows the name. Yet this will pass very well with those whose "inward consciousness" is made a test of divine revelation, and whose "experience" constitutes a tribunal from which there is no appeal. May the Lord have mercy upon those who oppose the restoration of the ancient order of things, and teach them the lesson which Gamaliel taught his compeers in the Sanhedrim! Poor men! I can enter into their views and feelings, for I know their system; I know my own motives too: and were they a little wiser they would be the first to aid, and the last to oppose, what all who are born of God are praying for every day—the union, peace, harmony, and love of christians on the foundation which the Great Architect himself laid for his spiritual temple. Should they succeed in securing the attachment of the misguided to their moth-eaten systems, what reward can they expect, and what do they anticipate from the Judge of All? Will he praise them for preferring the dogmas of the schools to the testimony of the apostles? Will he commend them for flattering the people that they are just up to the model of the New Testament; that they are perfect in their views and practices, wanting nothing? Will he thank them for their zeal in maintaining the traditions of synods and councils in contravention of his own apostles? O! that they who have influence among the people, would use that influence to enlighten and purify their minds, and not to confirming them in cold, and sterile, and lifeless theories.

The following dogmas are expressive of the views of the editors on one topic, in relation to which they have something in almost every paper.

" 1. The regeneration of the heart is the work of God, by his Spirit exerted immediately and directly upon the hearts and understandings of men."

" 2. The regeneration of the heart is not the work of God, by his Spirit exerted immediately and directly upon the hearts and understandings of men; but it is the effect of the word believed. The word itself is *spirit* and *life*. All that is necessary to produce what is called the *new man*, is an honest reception and firm belief of the truths of the gospel; for the operation of faith is always in perfect accordance with the nature of the truth believed."

The first of these positions the editors declare to be a true one, and that the Baptists have long since "adopted" it. It is an alien, and they have adopted it. Who "adopted" the second position, the editors do not say, and for my part I do not know. For I have never met with a creed which says, "the regeneration of the heart is not the work of God, by his Spirit," &c. &c. I hope the editors are so far regenerated themselves as not to invent dogmas for others that they may injure the reputation of others, and gain credit to themselves for their orthodoxy. But they avow the first dogma to be their own creed, and bolster it up by the "internal evidence of consciousness'" and the right it has to be true because the Baptists have long since adopted it. This last bulwark of the dogma J hesitate to admit. For neither the Baptist Confession of Faith says so, nor do I believe that the Baptists generally teach this dogma. However, whether they do or do not teach it, is, with me, a matter of no moment; for I am assured that neither John the Baptist, nor any Baptist congregation in the apostolic age, either taught, or entertained, or expressed such a dogma. But it is either expressed with ingenuity, or mental reservation; and where two opinions may be formed of an action or expression, charity says, always prefer the more favorable one. We shall do so. Now the proposition says, " the regeneration of the heart is the work of God, by his Spirit exerted immediately." Mark this word *immediately, i. e.* without the intervention of any other cause—independent of the word. So, then, Messrs. Waller and Clack declare in favor of this dogma, that the regeneration of the heart is the work of God, by his Spirit exerted independent of the word or revelation of God, directly upon the hearts and understandings of men.— This they positively declare to be, with them, the standard of orthodoxy. Now the question is, What advantage will result to any person from implicitly or explicitly believing, avowing, or teaching this dogma? It can effect no change in the heart or affections of any human being. " For men are regenerated by the Spirit of God, independent of the word," and, most assuredly, independently of this dogma. The believing of it can regenerate no body, if it be a true dogma. If this dogma be true, the Bible and the Alcoran are alike concerned in the regeneration of the human heart. This is no enthusiasm. It is the deliberate, premeditated, and written position of brethren Waller and Clack. The Spirit of God immediately and directly regenerates the heart! I have given Walker's definition of the term *immediately,* lest I should be supposed to give too high a coloring to the terms in which this position is expressed. There is one thing which they say of this position which I think passing strange. It is this: "On its truth are founded all their (the Baptists') exertions for the salvation of sinners." That is, because the regeneration of the heart is the work of God, by his Spirit exerted independent of the Old and New Testament, the Baptists are themselves to be the means of regenerating men by the Old and New Testament, printed, published, read, and preached, as the medium or means of regeneration; and all the while adopt, maintain, and proclaim the position that men are regenerated immediately by the Spirit of God. If notes of admiration were not too common things, we should here call for battalions of them. No wonder, then, that an improved version of the New Testament is considered by brother George Waller as a superfluous and useless thing. In fact, the reading of it in Greek or Syrochaldaic to an English scholar is just as useful, on the adopted position, as profitable as any thing else. No wonder that these divines contend for a special call to convert men. Did I say no wonder? Yes, it is a great wonder; for what use is their call and preaching, if the Spirit of God regenerates the human heart independent of all second causes. I will not further expose the ruinous influence of such a dogma if it be true. I will just leave with these brethren one dilemma—either their dogma is true or not true. If true, then it matters not what doctrine is taught by me on the subject of regeneration; for the Spirit of God regenerates the human heart independently of all doctrine, true or false, even of the bible itself. But if untrue, then, indeed, to act under its influence is most injurious, as it will necessarily make the scriptures a dead letter, and all preaching vain.

I have no disposition to enter into the field of speculation on such dogmas. But were I disposed to make the most of such a position, did I wish to gain an advantage over an enemy, I could not wish for a more favorable dogma; for I do not think that any other theorem of the Jansenites, not even their invocations for the dead, is more vulnerable than this dogma. I do fondly hope that these brethren speak and act otherwise than this dogma will authorize, in addressing men on the subject of religion. Perhaps there is some error in the composition of the sentence which they have overlooked, for I would rather account for it in any other way than to suppose this sentiment to be a principle of action with them. Indeed I almost know it is not a principle of action with them: however pretty it may look on the lid of a snuff-box, or on vellum, I think it is not written on their hearts.

But all such preaching and teaching, all such theory is worse than mere trifling. A theory about the formation of Adam out of the dust, whether his creation began with his head or his feet, or whether he was instantaneously or immediately complete, and all his members simultaneously formed, is just as useful, as profitable to men, as any theory of regeneration which I have seen; and I am always ready to shew that he who preaches any theory, orthodox or heterodox, preaches not the gospel of Jesus Christ. To this sentence I invite attention, and challenge investigation.

I have not heard from the editors of the Recorder on my last. I have seen their ninth but not their eighth number, and seeing so much insinuation and indirect opposition to, I am persuaded, they know not what, I thought it expedient just to give them a hint how vulnerable they are, to assure them that their either propping an old theory, or attempting a new one, is out of the question altogether.   EDITOR.

Church Government.

THE ancient independent writers have poured forth abundance of nonsense about meetings for counsel and advice. Some of them have supposed that though *Acts* xv. does not afford a model for meetings of ministers to make authoritative decrees for the churches, yet that it sanctions such meetings for the purpose of giving counsel and advice to the churches. But it is not possible to explain this passage in such a manner as to establish the divine right of assemblies for advice. This meeting gave not advice, but decrees; did not submit opinions to be canvassed, but doctrines to be believed, and precepts to be observed. If it is at all a model for any foreign interference, it establishes absolute

authority on the one hand, and passive and unlimited obedience on the other. I cannot see any thing that could tempt inquiring christians to adopt this theory, except that they have not been thoroughly purged from Presbyterian prejudices, or a desire not to appear all at once to go so great a distance from the churches of this world. Perhaps a mixture of these motives have operated with them. They are a little shocked themselves, and perhaps are afraid that others will be more so, with the idea of being so unlike to other societies called churches, in every distinguished feature. On the contrary, I am of opinion that we ought not to wish to hide from the churches of the world how much we differ from them. We ought to be solicitous rather to show them that, in every distinguishing feature, the kingdom of Christ differs from the kingdom of this world. We ought not to keep the worshippers of the Beast in countenance by making an image of the Beast. There is no reason to fear alarming the prejudices of the world, or of christians. If the cause is the Lord's, we may safely rest it upon his shoulders. If men will receive instruction from the word of God as to the nature of Christ's kingdom, it is well; but if any man will be obstinately and perversely ignorant, let him be ignorant. It is our duty to hold forth the word of life in every part of it; it is in the Lord's hand who shall receive it. He has no need of our wisdom to help forward his plans.

But if such meetings are not instituted from this passage, *jure divino*, they cannot plead it to sanction their innocency. If they are not the offspring of the wisdom of God, they must be the offspring of the wisdom of man; and the Lord will no more countenance one human religious institution than he will another. To say that such assemblies are useful, yet not instituted, is to arraign the wisdom of Jesus as a legislator, and to deny the competency of his institutions. If they are not divinely appointed they cannot be useful, they cannot be innocent. I am bold to predict that wherever they are tried, either an increasing acquaintance with the word of God, or a deeper knowledge of the nature of Christ's kingdom, will lay them aside, or they will degenerate into an engine of Satan. In the very first instance they must tend to damp inquiry in the churches, and gradually habituate them to allow others to have the trouble of thinking for them.—*Carson's Reply to Brown on Discipline.*

Two Anecdotes.

"WE know," says Campbell in his Lectures on Ecclesiastical History, "who they were in ancient times that sought honor one of another, who affected the principal seats in the synagogues and the uppermost rooms at feasts, who loved greetings in the markets, and to be called by men, Rabbi, Rabbi. We know also who it was that expressly prohibited, amongst his disciples, such unbecoming emulation and worldly vanity, who enjoined them not to seek honor of men, or to contend who, in the judgment of men, should be greatest; but to seek that honor only which comes from God. We know also who it was that made usefulness the standard of greatness, and pronounced him to be possessed of the highest dignity who is most humble and serviceable; who, instead of courting, is solicitous to avoid such enviable distinctions. On which of these models the convention at Trent and other preceding councils were formed, I shall leave to the candid and impartial to determine. I shall conclude this lecture with a story, homely indeed, but apposite:—An English country parson was bragging in a large company of the success he had had in reforming his parishioners, on which his labors, he said, had produced a wonderful change for the better. Being asked in what respect, he replied, that when he came first among them they were a set of unmannerly clowns, who paid him no more deference than they did to one another; did not so much as pull off their hat when they spoke to him, but bawled out as roughly and familiarly as though he were their equal; whereas now they never presumed to address him but cap in hand, and in a submissive voice, made him their best bow when they were at ten yards distance, and styled him *Your Reverence* at every word. A Quaker who had heard the whole patiently, made answer—"And so, friend, the upshot of this reformation, of which thee hast so much carnal glorying, is, that thee hast taught thy people to worship thyself."

"IMPLICIT FAITH has been sometimes ludicrously styled *fides carbonaria*, from the noted story of one who, examining an ignorant collier on his religious principles, asked him what it was he believed. He answered, "I believe what the church believes." The other rejoined, "What, then, does the church believe?" He replied readily, "The church believes what I believe." The other, desirous if possible to bring him to particulars, once more resumes his inquiry: "Tell me, then, I pray you, what it is that you and the church both believe?" The only answer the collier could give was, "Why truly, sir, the church and I both—believe the same thing." This is implicit faith in perfection, and, in the estimation of some celebrated Doctors, the sum of necessary and saving knowledge in a christian."—*Campbell's Lectures.*

No. 12.]   JULY 6, 1826.
For the Christian Baptist.

WHEN deep sleep comes upon man, and mortals, tossed and harrowed in their minds, enjoy, for a moment, the sweets of forgetfulness, which, upon the whole, has been conducive to my happiness; having been for months past disturbed, not only by day, but sometimes by night, on the great difficulty of deciding who, of all the guides of the people, are under the guidance of the Holy Spirit. If, Mr. Editor, the vision will, in your view, be of any use to any, please lay it before the public.   MIRZAH.

IN visions of the night I saw most distinctly through the whole area of a field, which I supposed to be many thousand miles square, the most extensive groupes of human beings, which fancy when awake could well conceive of. The field itself exhibited no little variety. On all sides there were hills and vallies, woods and rivers, of singular aspect, yet presenting no obstruction to my sight, for every elevation and protuberance appeared to be transparent as glass. The field, as already described, was square, though at intervals it appeared to be octagonal, and sometimes to have a hundred equal sides. Of the numberless curious and attractive scenes which crowded upon my sight, few of which can either be distinctly recalled or related, I shall attempt, at present, the recital of but a few. Never on earth before did I see a field of any dimensions so diversified with roads and paths. Indeed, it sometimes appeared as though the whole area had been once trodden with human feet in the way of large and small roads, straight and crooked paths. Even at the present time,

during my vision, it appeared as if the whole premises were allotted to engineers and supervisors for the purpose of making experiments in the construction of roads and paths. No conceivable design could have located several hundred paths, side by side, sometimes paralel to each other, and sometimes as serpentine as the milky way, other than the mere project of experiment. For notwithstanding the myriads of paths in every direction in this vast field, there were but two gates and principal roads, which all seemed at one time or another to frequent.

The whole scenery was illuminated with a very strange and fluctuating sort of light, which seemed to emanate from no fixed fountain or source, but differing in degrees at different intervals, and sometimes so very faint that objects quite contiguous could not be discriminated from one another. The countless myriads which were always in motion in this vast area, kept up such a continual noise, that for a long time, though extremely anxious to learn something about them, I could not distinguish one articulate sound. They often appeared in great agitation, and in large and small groupes appeared to oppose each other, and the stronger often compelled the weaker to desert one path and flee to another. Either a gleam of light, or something under that appearance, often seemed to arrest the attention of those in its vicinity, and all seemed attracted by it, and, for a while, appeared tranquil in contemplating it; but in a shorter or longer period it vanished, and they all became as restless as ever.

After many fruitless efforts to acquire some information on all that pressed upon my attention, I resolved to mingle with some crowd or to set out a solitary traveller in quest of information. While thus pondering in my mind, a venerable figure approached me, and looking very earnestly in my face, said, "Whence camest thou hither?" I could make no reply. He, without giving me time to propose a question, said "It is all as uncertain as before." What? said I. "Paradise," he replied, and instantly leaving the path in which he stood, began his march in another, and vouchsafed me no farther information.

At this moment, turning to the East, I saw an immense crowd assembled before a chair of huge magnitude, in which many hundred persons could be comfortably seated, yet but one august personage sat in it, beneath whose feet, on platforms of different elevations, stood myriads of mitred dignitaries, having inscribed upon their foreheads "The Called and Sent." At the right hand of the chair stood a huge cross, on which, as well as on the chair, was inscribed J. C. V.* While I was gazing with astonishment on these strange scenes which I could not understand, I observed many individuals, and sometimes considerable groupes, abandoning the countless millions which stood in solemn gaze upon the chair, its occupant, and the dignitaries beneath, and saw them pass through a grotesque and antique gate, on the side of which, fronting the chair was inscribed *Heresy* and on the other side *Reformation.* Through this gate of enormous dimensions, which permitted not only whole groupes to pass together without inconvenience, but also to carry with them immense loads, resembling bales, each inscribed with M. E. T.† I directed my course, and saw *two* chairs, something smaller than the former, and not quite so venerable, dig-

* I suppose the letters, J. C. V. denote the Vicar of Jesus Christ.

† It is presumed these letters are the Latin initials of Traditions of the Mother Church.—ED.

nified with two patriarchal rabbis resembling the archbishops of York and Canterbury; a crown of gold, engraved and lettered, " *Defender of the Faith*," hung at equal distance from them both.   Around them stood twenty-four fathers, with beautiful vestments covered with sentences of Hebrew, Greek, and Latin, all importing " *The Called and Sent.*"   Many thousands kneeled before them with four cornered tiaras, having the same inscription, " The Called and Sent."

A gate fronting these chairs, less than the former, but having the same inscriptions on both sides, was equally thronged with dissenters, who, after gazing a while at those exalted pontificals, withdrew through it and disappeared.   I pursued them in great haste, determined to obtain some certain information. But, to my astonishment, on passing through it, more than a hundred paths diverged from its threshold in all directions, each one leading to a small eminence covered with chairs, and all filled with incumbents, bearing upon their little tiaras, in small capitals, the same inscription, "The Called and Sent."   Larger or smaller crowds stood before them all; but so fluctuating that no one could tell which was likely to become the greatest or the least.

The unceasing din and commotion between the outposts of each crowd reminded me of nothing so much as the swarms and commotions of a large assemblage of bees when the sun approaches Cancer.   I could distinguish not one sentence, though every chair was filled with an orator, and in every crowd a multitude appeared repeating the same sentences.   In despair I retired to a long skirt of woods which covered the margin of a tranquil stream, and there expected to find a requiem for meditation.   But soon as I descended towards its borders, I observed a great many stragglers who had deserted all the crowds and hastened to the river.   These seemed at first to be following me, but passed me by without uttering a word, until they reached the stream, into which they plunged themselves as though they were weary of life and sought a termination of its toils and uncertainties.   I looked to see them emerge no more, but with no little surprise I saw them every one ascend the opposite bank, and were met there by twelve long bearded men, wearing leathern girdles and camblet gowns.   Each of these seemed eager to seize by the hand every one who emerged from the river, and to lead them into beautiful arbors and booths pitched at a respectful distance from each other along the stream.   Each of these twelve primates had a different head dress, but all inscribed with "The called and sent."   At this moment I found my feet wet with the water of the stream, the edge of which I had unconsciously approached.   At this instant I was hailed and invited to cross by a very humble and venerable figure on the opposite shore.   But while in suspense I was caught by the skirts by a number of " The called and sent"* of the crowd nearest the river, having " liberty and independence" added to all their other inscriptions.   These pulled me back, while I was zealously invited by those on the opposite side to enter their arbute arbors.   One exclaimed, " If you fear the stream I will send you a canoe;" another said, " Nay, here is a balloon;" a third pointed to a rainbow over a bridge, and a fourth said, "Swim the stream, or be lost forever."   In the mean time a crowd like harpies had a hold of every protuberance on my raiment; not a button

* I conjecture the sect called Independents is here alluded to.—ED.

was left on my garments, and I was likely to be rent from head to foot.   In the mean time, frantic with despair, I struggled for life, and by a fortunate effort disentangled myself and plunged into the stream.   Soon as I had crossed I was seized by at least half a dozen of the sages I had seen, and was as likely to be torn to pieces as before.   I begged for time to change my apparel, which being granted, I made my escape to a cavern I descried in an unfrequented spot at some distance, where I sat musing on all that had passed.   After some time a refugee, like myself, entered the same cavern, and, after discerning me, said, "Friend, how camest thou hither?"   I told him my story, and he told me his.   He informed me that he had been for many years on his feet, running in the different paths, and now, for the first time, had sat down.   He told me he had found a map in a cave which he had long wished to peruse, but never till now had found an opportunity.

All the information he had gathered during many years traveling amounted to no more than this: That it had been once announced in these regions that a happier country, called Paradise, had been once prepared for all who desired it; that the way to this country had been graphically laid down, but that a predecessor of that godlike man who sat upon the first huge chair which I noticed, had secreted the map of the country and the high road that led to it, and that his successors said they could describe it better by words than by maps, and that all the different roads and paths which I had noticed had been laid down by different great and wise men of former times; that all those different orders of chaired pontificals claimed the honor of being "The called and sent" of the author of the original map to put the inhabitants of these regions in the sure and certain road to that celestial country.   He also informed me that many had traveled for years in different paths, and had followed different guides, all called and sent; but that they, depending upon those guides, had never found that country; and that so great was the increase of new and improved guides, that all the dominions which they enjoyed were likely to be cut up with new roads and paths, without promising a happier result than before. "But," says he, "come let us open this map." We opened it, and to our surprise, found that not one of those guides who claimed the patronage of the author of the map, had been authorized by him, but that he had once authorized a sufficient company of surveyors and engineers, who had exactly defined the country and the way thither.   We followed the map, and soon found a road which, although almost covered with grass, shrubs, and trees, led us safely into the confines of Paradise, where in transport I awoke, and found it but a vision.   MIRZAH.

On the Millennium.—No. I.

MANKIND are certainly moving in the horizon of some great and eventful change, into the centre of which all society must inevitably and speedily be carried.   The world is in strange commotion; expectation is all aroused—anticipation of something good, splendid, and unknown, is become undoubting and impatient, even to painfulness; and the time is at hand when a plenteous harvest of toil and talent must be reaped from all orders of society, that many run to and fro, and knowledge be increased.

The time is certainly arrived, when the great political establishments, the powers and principalities of the world, which have created and fostered those warlike feelings, and mercantile and rival interests, so hostile to the spirit of the gospel, and which have led men so far away from nature, must speedily be dissolved; and when the economy of God, which shall be more in unison with the religion of his Son and with nature, shall suddenly make its appearance.

The object of this paper is to show that God has designs of high favor towards man, and will vouchsafe him an age of happiness, in which the entire sum of physical, moral and intellectual good, which can be enjoyed on earth, will be granted.

The subject is one of immense depth and extent. It involves the whole series of scripture history, and prophecy, and is as protracted as the duration of the world itself. Accordingly the reader will not expect the author of this paper to go into a detail of the subordinate parts of a subject of such plenitude and sublimity; but if the two extremes of the providential chain, with a few of the more illustrious links by which they are connected, shall be clearly pointed out, so as to furnish christians with an elementary clue to this grand topic, it is presumed the reader will be sufficiently remunerated for his trouble in reading this essay.

All men exist under a threefold order of relations; first to the natural world; secondly, to one another; and thirdly, to God; and the history of the world demonstrates, that, to mankind in the aggregate, as to each individual, the knowledge of these relations is slow and progressive; that it is not incident to the infant child alone, but also to the infant family of mankind, to stop at these immediate and more obvious relations which subsist between us and matter; that mankind in the aggregate, as well as each individual, have their physical pursuits; and that, therefore, the antediluvian period, characterized by the absence of all governmental arrangements, may, with propriety, be called the physical age of the species.

Secondly, the middle period of the world's history is pre-eminently distinguished for a high regard to that more remote order of relations, which subsists in great and populous empires, as the Babylonian, Persian, Grecian and Roman; during which long epocha personal liberty and personal security have been better established; and happiness, which is the end of our existence, less fluctuating and uncertain than it was during the merely physical age, which passed before the flood. This may be styled the *secular* age of our species, concerning which the prophet says, "I beheld until the thrones" i. e. of those empires "were cast down." But,

Thirdly, Mankind having nearly exhausted the limits allotted to them for pursuits purely physical and political, and having, by dint of long experience, learnt the inefficiency of commerce and war to secure happiness, are now deeply inspired with a premonition of some great and incomprehensible change, the present nature of which time alone can fully clear up. This is the *millennial* or *evangelical* age of the world; during which the human race will enjoy great happiness, and that third order of relations which have been revealed as subsisting between men and their Creator and Redeemer, shall be fully investigated, developed, and enjoyed.

Let it not be supposed, however, that these observations are made merely to arrive at the trite conclusion that man is a physical, moral, and intellectual being; but for the important purposes of showing the chain of high and holy providences, by which the God of all mer-

cy and grace, has long been conducting the human family to an age of virtue and happiness; also that he has done it by a course of physical and politico-moral experience, perfectly adapted to human nature, without which mankind would never, for any length of time, have remained either virtuous or happy; and this division of the world into physical, secular, and evangelical ages, is neither arbitrary nor fanciful, but is founded in matter of fact, and abundantly supported by divine declaration. The first age being marked out by a judgment not less notable than the flood; the second issuing in the judgment and total overthrow of the anti-christian governments; and the evangelical age terminating in the final judgment itself. And let no one say that in order to induct the human family into the evangelical age, God has too much protracted the physical and secular ages. Such language would be improper, even if we had made all of past experience which we ought to have made of it. But what improvements have we made of past experience? Do not facts the most numerous, obvious and striking, demonstrate that we have not advanced one step in the art of applying the liberty and security so richly enjoyed in America to the promotion of our happiness, which is the grand and glorious end of all the present, past, and future dispensations of providence in regard to us. For of what value is personal liberty, and personal security, so long as they are prostrated to ambition, speculation, and war; for granting, that the intervention of science, and the milder influence of the gospel has quenched the spirit of war in these states, yet mark the rival interests and intense passions excited by the commercial spirit that is abroad. If the spirit of war is hushed, the fact resembles the case where one unclean spirit makes room for seven others still more abominable than himself; for, at this moment, the United States, the noblest nation in the world, is on the verge of becoming a race of speculators; while their boundless territories, the nation's real estate, lies comparatively unappropriated to their real happiness.

Meanwhile, let the reader bear in mind that history, and especially the holy scriptures, show us that the march of man towards virtue and happiness has been slow and progressive; they show us also that God is exceedingly opposed to, and displeased with, aristocratic and oppressive governments; while, at the same time, the fatal destruction of the antediluvians, clearly evinces the impracticability of existing in any way but under some general government, to secure us at once against foreign force and domestic broils. That, in the approaching age, political authority will be confined to the regulation of its proper concerns, and while all enjoy the sum of physical, moral, and intellectual good—the word of the Lord will have free course and be glorified in the salvation of thousands. So much, at present, for the physical, secular, and evangelical ages, by which the scripture, history, and age of prophecy, are seen to harmonize so admirably with the course of human improvement.   PHILIP.

To the Editor of the Christian Baptist.
On Faith.
Connecticut, April 25, 1826.

I FULLY believe with you that much has been said and written on this subject inconsistent with the simplicity of the Word, and tending much to perplex the minds of the disciples of Christ. I accord with you, that faith is the belief of testimony; that the faith with which salvation or eternal life is connected, is the belief of the testimony of the Son of God in the scriptures of truth. But the distinction you appear to make between faith and repentance, in respect to divine influence producing these, appears to me to be unscriptural. You admit the scriptural truth that Christ "is exalted to *bestow* repentance," (No. 1. vol. ii. p. 85) but you say, (Sentimental Journal, p. 58,) "evidence *alone* produces faith, or testimony is *all* that is necessary to faith." I wish you to try this principle, and place before your calumniators "evidence" that you are an honest man, and see whether it "produces faith." What means this scripture?— "How can you believe that receive honor one of another, and seek not the honor that comes from God only," or the alone God? Does not Jesus Christ here plainly teach that the evil disposition of the heart biasses the man and causes it to resist, or prevents it from perceiving the evidence which is placed before it? Did he not teach that the cause why the Jews would not come to him, or believe him, was, that they loved darkness rather than light? Do you not think that the cause of some persons defaming you is the prejudice of their own minds, and not any deficiency in the evidence of your good character, which you have given them? Jesus told the Jews, "Because I tell you the truth, you believe me not." They could believe the lies of false prophets. If some other came in his own name, him they could receive; but because the Son of God came in his Father's name, or to exhibit and establish the goodness of that law which they had broken, they would not receive him. They *repented* not that they might believe. Matt. xxi. 32. When Paul was at Corinth preaching "the things concerning the kingdom of God," the cause of many believing not was not a want of evidence of the truth of the divine testimony, but that they "were hardened." *Acts* xix. 9. Passages of similar import might be added to prove that the cause of unbelief and impenitence is the same, and consequently divine influence is as necessary to remove one as the other. The cause is loving darkness or sin rather than light or holiness. You will please to observe also that Jesus Christ condemned the Jews, which is additional proof that unbelief arises from an evil heart or disposition, and not for want of evidence. Again, "Whosoever believes that Jesus is the Christ, is born of God." There is, in my view, abundant evidence in the scriptures of truth that the faith which is connected with justification is as much "the gift of God" as repentance or any other fruit of the Spirit. Faith and repentance, &c. are indeed acts of our own minds, but they are all effects of the renewal of our minds by the Holy Spirit. It is no more congenial to the mind of a sinner to believe to the saving of the soul, than it is to repent of sin or to love God. I have no desire to go beyond the word on this or any other divine subject; neither will I reject the plain testimony of that word, because the judgments of God are unsearchable, and his ways past finding out. I apprehend that "the matter" of saving faith is something more than "that Christ died for our sins, and was buried and is risen from the dead," unless we suppose that the belief that Christ died for our sins, implies a belief of his holy doctrine respecting the law of God, the evil of sin, and our just condemnation. I am very confident that I believed the facts that Christ died on the cross, was buried and rose from the dead, long before I had any faith that "overcomes the world." These facts may be

believed, while the holy truth connected with these, is denied and rejected. Mr. Fishback, in the extracts you have published, well observes, when considering the truth to be believed, that "the gospels written by the four evangelists, contains the history of Christ's incarnation, life, doctrine, miracles, death, resurrection, ascension, and intercession; and one of the evangelists tells us the design of his history:— "These are written, that you might believe that Jesus is the Christ, and that, believing, you might have eternal life through his name." He remarks, "It is of his own will that God begets men to the faith, with the word of truth." He also declares that belief and love "unite in saving faith." If so, divine influence must be as necessary to produce saving faith as love. Mr. Fishback likewise remarks, "He (the Spirit) has imparted saving faith in the Lord Jesus." I notice these remarks of Mr. Fishback's, because you remark that his "observations concerning faith" are "expressive of (your) sentiments." I have no idea of faith as a principle in the heart separated from the word of truth; but I understand that it is by the operation of the Spirit that the truth is believed to the salvation of the soul. In your reply to P. H. [No. 9 vol. ii.] you observe, "Some of them who believed the ancient revelations, like Lydia, and whose hearts were thereby opened, honestly disposed," &c. I beseech you, dear sir, to compare this representation of the subject, with that of the Holy Spirit. The inspired historian, writing of Lydia, remarks, "Whose heart the Lord opened, that she attended to the things that were spoken by Paul." You represent the opening of the heart, as the effect of attending to, or believing the truth. The Spirit of Truth represents it as the cause. You observe, "We are asked—why do not all believe the same testimony?" and "another, and another why is proposed. And so it ends with a *why* just where we began." I would rather say it ends just where the Spirit of Truth ends it. We may propose questions which are answered by the revealed truth. Thus far we may go; but here curiosity and pride must be stayed. If we ask, Why do not all who have the gospel believe it? The answer is, Because they love darkness rather than light. "You *will not* come," &c. said the faithful witness. If the question is, Why do some believe rather than others? the answer is, "As many as were ordained to eternal life, believed." "You has he quickened who were dead in trespasses and in sins," &c. "But God who is rich in mercy, for his great love wherewith he loved us, even when we were dead in sins, has quickened us together with Christ." "By grace you are saved," &c. "For we are his workmanship, created in Christ Jesus to good works," &c.

If the question is, why does God thus quicken some rather than others? the answer is, "He has mercy on whom he will have mercy." "For your pleasure all things are," &c. Here the divine testimony ends the subject, and here we ought to end. But if any are disposed to murmur against this truth, there are a few questions for them to answer. "He that reproves God, let him answer it." "Is your eye evil because I am good?" "Shall I not do what I will with my own?" "Who are you, O man! that reply against God," &c. "Surely the Judge of all the earth will do right." Amicus.

———

To Amicus.

If, as you say, "faith is the belief of testimony," there can be no faith without testimony;

and if faith be no more than the belief of testimony, nothing more than testimony enters into the nature of faith. This is admitted by all persons of reflection on the subject of faith properly called human. But many will have that faith which is so often spoken of in the christian scriptures, to be something more than the belief of truth, or the belief of the testimony of God; and even of those who contend that faith is simply the belief of the gospel, or testimony concerning Jesus the Lord, some will have this faith distinguished in some way, either as the effect of regeneration, as a holy or spiritual act, as inwrought by some physical agency in the heart, or some way differing from the usual and commonly received import of the term. Hence so much mystery, and mysterious reasoning on the subject of "saving faith." As nothing of this kind of reasoning or definition appears in the inspired writings, we are naturally led to look for its origin and progress somewhere else. We can soon trace it to "Mystery, Babylon the Great," but no farther. And here I am willing to leave it. But many wish to leave only a part of it there, and seek to introduce an improved system of definitions into the christian vocabulary.

If we receive the testimony of men, the testimony of God is more worthy of reception, and produces greater certainty; and this is all the difference the New Testament presents to me betwixt faith in the testimony of man, and faith in the testimony of God. But this will not satisfy those of a metaphysical taste, who are philosophically inquisitive into the doctrine of causation. They must, step by step, ascend to the ultimate cause, or to the most remote cause of every thing; and while each one pursues the course which education or chance opens to his feet, and terminates his inquiries only because he can travel no farther, the christian taught by God is meditating the things revealed, which seraphs admire, and seeking to enjoy a fulness of the blessing of the gospel of Christ. But this is not the worst of it. One believer not unfrequently contemns another because he cannot soar so high in the doctrine of causation as himself. He dislikes him, too, not because he is not as good a christian, but because he is not so wise a philosopher as himself. Hence one christian philosopher terminates his inquiries here—"As many as were ordained to eternal life believed;" or, "You believe not because you are not my sheep." Another, who is not so strong, or perhaps stronger, terminates his inquiries here—"They searched the scriptures with all readiness of mind; many of them, therefore, believed." Each one loves his own theory, and is zealous for it as though it were the gospel of Christ. Indeed, some often call their doctrine of grace "The Gospel." Many texts are brought into the field, and strung together, whose connexion is dissevered; and not one of which was, perhaps, designed to prove any such theory. Some texts are of doubtful import as respects either theory. These are declared to be lawful plunder, and each belligerent, according to his martial skill, captivates them to his service. Thus the war is protracted and the strife maintained, which it is the desire of every christian to see terminated. To come to the drift and scope of your communication, I would observe, First. That you seem to gather from the Christian Baptist (how lawfully I will not inquire) that I make a distinction between faith and repentance as respects divine influence in their production. This I never intended; nor do I see that affirming that "evidence alone produces faith," and

that "repentance is bestowed," implies that there is any difference in the origin of either as respects divine influence. In one instance we spoke not of the origin of faith, but of its nature. In the other, of the origin of repentance, and not of its nature. But we are so much accustomed to a quaint orthodox style, that if a person speaks of faith or repentance, and does not always preface his remarks by observing that both are "the gift of God," he is at once supposed not to be sound in the faith.

It has often surprised me to find with what tenacity the sound of some texts is held, regardless of the meaning, because the sound, more than the sense, suits some favorite position. Of this very species is the text now before us. I am quite certain that it is generally quoted to support a position which was not before the mind of the writer. In the new translation, which we have just published, of Campbell, Macknight, and Doddridge, it reads thus: "And when they had heard these things, they acquiesced, and glorified God, saying, God has then given to the Gentiles also reformation to life." Taken in all the attendant circumstances, it just means—God has then no longer confined his benignity to the Jews, but has, to the Gentiles, as to them, given the same reformation to life. But this is not the text to which the allusion is. It is, "Him has God exalted at his right hand to be a Prince and a Saviour, to give reformation to Israel and remission of sins." This as evidently refers to the Jews as a people, as the former does to the Gentiles as a people. And both, I apprehend, mean no more than that Jesus, as a Saviour, has conferred upon both Jews and Gentiles the blessings of life through a reformation proceeding from a belief of the favor of God through himself. And the term "also," in reference to the Gentiles, shows that it had already, prior to their calling, been granted to the Jews. But this is *toto cœlo* different from the popular notion of what is called "evangelical repentance" wrought in the heart of any individual, Jew or Gentile.

In the second place, I observe that I perfectly accord with what you say, that "it is not the want of evidence, but the want of disposition;" so not the want of ability, but the power of prejudice, and vicious inclinations, or a wicked heart, which prevents many from hearkening to, believing, and obeying the gospel. Hence unbelief is a sin. But were it so that a want of evidence, or of ability to believe, was the cause of so many infidels, then infidelity could not be a sin, or a worthy cause of condemnation. But God has given sufficient evidence, and consequently sufficient ability to every man to believe the testimony of his Son; and, therefore, the unbelief of every man is chargeable to his own wickedness. Nor is there, in my view, the least discrepancy between these positions and that "that evidence alone produces faith, or is all that is necessary to faith," when speaking of the nature of faith.— For faith, however it comes into existence, is no more than the belief of truth; and it is evidence alone that ascertains and demonstrates what is truth. That the evidence of truth does not arrest the attention of all, is equally true of things human and divine. And it has been often and long remarked how easily men assent to a proposition which they wish to be true, and with what difficulty they assent to one averse from their inclinations. This only proves the influence which the will has upon the understanding. In other cases, where there is no previous bias for or against any proposition, the assent is just proportioned to the evidence. These remarks are as true in reference to the dogmas of sectaries, as they are with regard to matters of simple belief.

I observe in the third place, that what you call "the matter of faith," or the truth to be believed, as more than that "Jesus died for our sins, was buried, and rose again," does not exactly accord with the emphasis which the holy apostles lay upon these superlative truths. It has often been admitted that thousands acknowledge these as facts from common education, as the Turks do that Mahomet was heaven's last prophet, who do not understand their import, nor recognize the evidence on which they rest. On this we lay no stress. No man can truly believe them and not overcome the world. We have never said or supposed that a man's *saying* he believed them, while they did not work effectually in his heart and life, was any evidence that he believed them; nor do we think that they can operate to the saving of the soul, unless when received in their scriptural import. On this topic we have repeatedly written very plainly.

I remark in the fourth place, that the greatest objection I have to the scope and drift of your communication, is, that it goes to the trite, inoperative, ineffectual, and cheerless conclusions of the Geneva metaphysics. I know right well how many texts can be paraded in support of these conclusions, and you know very well how many texts can be paraded on the other side. I advocate neither side of this controversy, because neither, in my judgment, was the design of the apostolic writings. And I am very sure that to *sinners* there is no gospel in the Calvinistic system, as it stands in the creeds of those sects who embrace it. It is no gospel to proclaim, that "God from all eternity elected a few individuals to everlasting life; that these few of Adam's progeny are all that he loved; the rest he doomed permissively to everlasting death; for these few elect ones, and for these only, his Son was born, lived and died. These only he effectually calls, these he quickens by his Holy Spirit, and these shall, in spite of all opposition, persevere to the end and be saved." I say this *honest front* of Calvinism, how true soever in metaphysics, is not the gospel of Jesus Christ our Lord, and all those texts which are brought to prove it are either wrested, perverted, or misapplied.

Though born, educated, brought up, and I might say, confirmed in this system, by all the reading, and study of my life; I am, from the apostolic writings alone, convinced, that to teach, preach, or proclaim such a system, is not to teach, preach, or proclaim the gospel I find in the New Testament. And I can see no reason nor propriety in opposing such a system to deny that God rules over all, that his counsel stands, that he does all his pleasure, that he influences the heart of every one that believes, as he did that of Lydia. If you please, that he gives his Holy Spirit to all that ask him or to all them who believe—that our whole salvation is of favor, free as the light of the sun, and that God is its sole author: for all things in it and connected with it are of God. I say, I see no reason to deny or oppose these positions, to maintain the conclusion—that every man who hears the glad tidings may believe them and be saved if he pleases, or if he truly desires it.

This conclusion, strange as it may appear, I find no intelligent Calvinist able or disposed to controvert, however tenacious about his original sin, his total depravity, and his effectual calling. I thank God that he has given the fullest proofs

of philanthropy, and not of personal regards; that he has in sincerity called men to look to his Son and be saved, and given the fullest assurance that whosoever will, may, can, and ought to come to him, and be saved; and that all that disobey this call have no excuse for their sin. This may be called any *ism* men please, but that it is in accordance with the whole scope, design, and letter of the inspired volume, I doubt not.

That multitudes love darkness rather than the light, and the gratification of their brutal and animal appetites rather than obeying the gospel, I have to lament; but one thing I know, they can not implicate the benevolence of God, nor charge him either with partiality or injustice in condemning them for this course.

That the Lord opened the heart of Lydia, and delivered Paul out of all his tribulations, is equally true; and that Lydia, before that day, was a pious worshipper of God, and that Paul escaped by his own feet, and once by a basket, is just as true. It is also true that the corn which I eat is the gift of God, and so is the faith and reformation which I enjoy. I say this merely as a hint to show how easily all those texts can be rationally and scripturally understood, which are so often presented to prove dogmas which prophets and apostles never thought of, nor entered into their hearts to conceive. You will see, then, that there is no necessity for stopping to inquire into the truth or falsehood of those dogmas, so long as the scope and drift of these conclusions are at variance with the whole current of revelation, nor of examining particular proofs, so long as the conclusions themselves make both law and gospel a dead letter, and represent men as dead as the stones of the field in a sense called "spiritual."

Many have labored with great toil to take the texts one by one from their opponents; but the whole contest is mere logomachy. Of this species is the text you have quoted from Luke's history: "As many as were ordained to eternal life believed." A correct translation, in most instances, is all that is necessary to settle many of these controversies. Doddridge, a Calvinist too, renders it "As many as were determined for eternal life believed." This is as ambiguous as the original, which Dr. Campbell has proved to be the true method to be pursued in giving a fair translation. For the determination may either be that of the Creator or the creature, which of the two must be ascertained from other considerations than the mere import of the term. Whitby has it, "As many as were disposed for eternal life believed," and argues that the original term is used but once in the same form by Luke in this treatise, and there it must signify one's own disposition—"Paul was disposed to go on foot." I mention this to show much may be subtracted from the imposing authority of a few texts whose sound seems to sanction dogmas at variance with the whole scope of the gospel of Jesus.

You will not, my dear sir, suppose that I consider you as wishing to support the dogmas of Calvin or any other man: I have a far higher opinion of your intelligence and virtue than to suppose this. I know you aim at the mere understanding of the scriptures, and acknowledge no man as a master in these things. But I think your communication, however well intended, and of this I entertain no doubt, is modelled upon that system, and terminates in sheer fatalism. And I know from experience how easy it is to be under the influence of impressions and biasses directing our views into particular channels when it is not our intention to go farther than the bible seems to authorize us. There is one thing, I think, must be obvious, that it can be of no use to any sinner or unregenerate person, either to believe, or to have preached to him, that only the elected sinners can believe the gospel. I would wish to attend to all the items in your communication; but time and space forbid. I have been on generals—for particulars again.   EDITOR.

Independent Baptist to the Christian Baptist.

MR. EDITOR—IF, in my last epistle, I have sinned against the law requiring us to love as brethren, my defence must be that it was not intended. As "perfection" was not pretended to, you will forgive the exceptionable words and phrases, arising from a strong feeling on the subject of discussion. It is a difficult attainment to be able to admonish in the simple and mild language which soothes while it sanctifies. The defence you make in reply to me has been carefully read. I am *not* satisfied; and, to speak candidly, it is, in my opinion, the first instance where the editor of the "Christian Baptist" seemed to be at a loss. *Aliquando Homerus dormitat.* The real question is not touched, and instead of a manly and triumphant appeal to apostolic principle and example, you have produced a *thing* made up of verbose declamation and sophisticated special pleading. With the remark that what you say of "consistency" may be generally true, but not called for, I hasten to the point.

With the hope of escaping from the clutches of the Dialogue, you assert that the "only bond of union among christians, advocated by the Christian Baptist, is a sincere and hearty conviction expressed or confessed by the lips, that Jesus is the Christ," &c. Taking advantage of the simplicity of this proposition, you go on to say that when this belief exhibits itself by an overt act, the individual so confessing and acting must be recognized as a brother. Now this is all true in terms, and yet in fact it is sheer trifling. Let me follow your example by way of illustration. Suppose I affected to prove the whole christian world to be one society of enlightened, sanctified and regenerated individuals, in a state of gracious acceptance and reconciliation with the true God. Having you for a model, I would declare in favor of charity in loose and general terms, and close with "It is written," "Every spirit that confesses that Jesus Christ is come in the flesh is of God." Who does not perceive, that excepting a few obstinate Jews, I have (according to your mode of argument) demonstrated the new creatureship of the Quaker, the Pope, and the "Christian Baptist," with all the christian world, man, woman and child. Nay, it might secure the salvation of the Turk and the "restitution" of devils. My antagonist, if I had one, would no doubt reply, "It is so written, but the use you make of the text is sophistical; you have no right to dislocate and insulate these words, thereby giving them an application not intended by the Holy Spirit. Does such a confession (he would ask) imply the expression of so many words, or the belief of a character, the ingredients, features, and qualities of which are to be learned in the rest of the divine testimony?" The only answer which this question admits of, would contain the refutation of my theory, and *mutatis mutandis*, it is your refutation also.

Waving the advantage I might claim, by a general view of the Messiah's character, I will confine myself to a single trait. When Peter said, "God has made that same Jesus whom you have crucified both Lord and Christ," and it was believed by a Jew, was not his confession that Jesus is the Christ at least tantamount to the following, viz. "I confess Jesus of Nazareth to be the promised Messiah—the Prophet like to, nay, greater than Moses; that he is King of Zion; and that (if possible) I am bound to "hear" Jesus with greater submission and obedience more exact than ever Jew heard Moses the servant of God?" If so, the one foundation implies a hearty conviction of Christ's royal supremacy as sole lawgiver in Zion, and instead of an "overt act," (as you loosely express it) as the exhibition of this conviction, it will, nay, must be followed by obedience to the peculiar institutes of his house or kingdom. Your very charitable recognition of Paido-Baptists, &c. as brethren, serves to neutralize the distinction between truth and error —between allegiance and rebellion. As for the societies of sprinkled "new creatures," with whom you could wish (if they would let you) to have "full communion," equal to what you have with the whole Baptist society, they resemble what a synagogue of Jews would be, who rejected circumcision, sacrificed swine, and new-modelled and modified the law to suit convenience and expediency. They might think themselves Jews—some time-serving Rabbi might call them brethren Jews; but if they claimed Moses as their lawgiver, I would justly charge them with gross inconsistency; a charge which, upon analogous ground, is now proved against the "Christian Baptist."

Your reply suggested the query, "Where now are all the scripture proofs to which Mr. Editor, in a good cause, can make so powerful appeal?" The feeling was natural; for, in christian sincerity, I consider your bible knowledge to be immense. True, in one instance you call upon Paul to help you, by raising a question as to the probable pliability of the apostle's conscience in certain cases. But I am verily persuaded that Paul rejects this unholy alliance. His Master commissioned him to teach the baptized disciples to observe all things whatsoever had been commanded. This tested and increased their love. When churches were built on the one foundation, the divine pattern was carefully copied. If irregularities crept in, he reproved and admonished; if they repented and confessed him the ambassador of the Great King, he rejoiced and approved them as brethren; if they repented not, he denounced them as fallen; and trampling on the accommodating conscientiousness of degenerate men, in the majestic moral attitude of a man acting "in Christ's stead," he decreed, "We have no such custom, neither the churches of God." This is a church question, and not a judging any man's personal piety and conversion. If a man says, "I believe," &c. well, I judge him not as concerns his final salvation. But if he hint at "full communion" with the church of Christ, I must reply, "Arise and be baptized," &c. "O, says he, I have been solemnly sprinkled by a Levite already." Here I pause till he obey. But what would you do? You would call him brother Paido, and eat and drink with him in "full communion," expressing approbation of the thing represented and of him in so far as he conforms to it. If this new creature should ask me why I refused him, holding, as he said he did, to one Lord, one faith, one hope, &c. I would tell him that faith without works is dead; that he could not break bread; that Christ must be obeyed; and that no instance, divinely authenticated, had ever appeared of any man having believed the gospel, in whom it failed to produce a desire, and willingness to be baptized, and to continue "stedfastly in the apostle's doctrine," &c. Here your practice and mine would be directly opposite, and yet I appeal to the readers of the "Christian Baptist," whether I do not exactly conclude with your printed sentiments. If so, the charge of inconsistency remains, and the panoply of the Dialogue is impenetrable. But what need of argument; it is a palpable evasion of the question, to talk of recognising a society of "new creatures" as a New Testament church, who, whatever may be their piety and solemnity, are not ashamed to confess that their church is organized and upheld according to the suggestion of human policy. *Horresco inferens!*

You attempt to fix the charge of inconsistency on me by a counter-dialogue, going to show that your Christian Baptist agrees in many respects with the Regulars, and that, therefore, you would be inconsistent if you did not maintain "full communion" with them—"the legs of the lame are not equal." That another objector could prove you inconsistent, by a different road, is surely not my fault, neither does it invalidate the force and truth of my position. "See you to that." Besides, your argument is inconclusive. It is as if I had engaged to show that gold and tin are both metals, but essentially different, and in order to do so I have pointed out the differential quality. You have endeavored to prove them to be one and the same metal, by enumeration of the qualities common to both—and with the same truth and fairness with which you attempt to roll over the reproach upon me, you might affect to assure the world that you had proved the identity of gold and tin. To make the best of your argument, the "full communion" which you enjoy and advocate, if carried out to its legitimate extent, instead of producing in the church the visible image of Christ, would create a resemblance to a certain "great image, his legs of iron, his feet part of iron and part of clay!" This is the dream; cannot you, Mr. Editor, tell the interpretation thereof?

The declamation you have indulged in, with the view of decrying strictness, separation, &c. is what is termed in these days, liberal, charitable and kind; but most astonishing as coming from you. It breathes the spirit which has lowered the tone of scriptural feeling, and gone far already in the production of a homogeneous nondescript, in which the church and the world are blended and the eternal distinction lost. Suffer the word of respectful and affectionate admonition—Ponder well the paths of your feet—Be warned—You have been at the monastic tropic, and are now it seems leaving the line—Watch and pray, or by and by you will be at the latitudinarian tropic—and instead of shining (as my prayer has been and now is) in the firmament of the kingdom of heaven, a fixed star—you may yet resemble (which may God's mighty power prevent) the moon, at best but a satellite of the earth, having this motto, "Little light, less heat, and many changes."

May God keep you in his way—and long preserve you an instrument of good in his church—"Now therefore, O God, strengthen his hands"—Instead of leaning upon "Associations" as a prop, when the regular or irregular Sanballats are wishing to prevent you from repairing the wall, craftily saying "Let us meet together in the house of God within the temple," &c. then is your time to stretch forth your hand like good

Nehemiah and say, "should such a man as I flee? and who is there that being as I am, would go into the temple to save his life? I will not go in." May your leaf never wither and your end be PEACE! I remain yours, &c.

AN INDEPENDENT BAPTIST.
Saturday morning, May 20th, 1826.

To an Independent Baptist.

DEAR SIR,—It appears from your favor before me that the grounds on which your first charge of inconsistency was based are sandy. You labor, indeed, to fasten upon me the same charge, but rather on new grounds than on the old. For your remarks upon what I have called the bond of union and peace, are directed more to affect the principle of union itself, than my declaration on which your first letter was founded. So that in fact, and in effect, you now contend with the principle itself, and not with my practice. You do not now admit, that the only bond of peace, and consequently of christian union, is "a sincere and hearty conviction expressed or confessed by the lips that Jesus is the Christ," &c. You ought then to have manfully and explicitly attacked the principle when first advanced, in the first volume of this work; and not now have demurred at the carrying of this principle into practice. For with all your ingenuity, this, to the judicious, must appear to be the sticking point with you; the very thing itself against which you object.

It was not "with the hope of escaping the clutches of the dialogue" that I now assert this principle. Nay, verily, it has been asserted and contended for more than once or twice in the first volume of this work. I take no "advantage of the simplicity of this proposition" when I observe "that when this belief exhibits itself by an overt act the individual so confessing and acting must be considered as a brother." This you say, even in your last, "is true in terms"—and strange to tell, "yet in fact it is sheer trifling." This last assertion is yet to be proved. And here you fly off in a tangent. Why, dear sir, do you labor to show me that the simple pronunciation of the terms of any position, such as "that Jesus is the Christ;" or "that every spirit that confesses that Christ has come in the flesh is of God," regardless of the import of these terms in the scripture sense of them, is not sufficient to produce confidence in the person, so pronouncing these terms, as a christian? Is there such a position or declaration in this work? I say there is not. You are really fighting with a creature of your own formation, and not with me. And here, give me leave to observe, you afford me fresh evidence of the unassailable character of the ground on which I stand; for with all your ingenuity and dexterity, and these I admit are conspicuous, you cannot touch the principle otherwise than by caricaturing an abuse of it. And with your remarks of making the pronunciation of any terms, found in the bible, regardless of the biblical import, the criteria of a disciple, or a bond of union, I most cordially agree. You must perceive then that you are at war with some creature of your own formation, and not with me, for I will join you and aid in annihilating this spectre of your own imagination. Strike it once, and I will strike it twice. We can annihilate it, for it has nothing immortal nor indissoluble about it. But here let me put you on your guard. Take heed that when fighting against a monstrous production, you do not imperceptibly direct your artillery against the offspring of heaven, and be found in the ranks of creed makers and dogmatists who defame the one foundation, and, Babel like, project the basis of a city and tower which is to reach from the plains of Shinar to the heavens.

When this half of your letter is disposed of, it is all disposed of as respects the topic on which you commenced your correspondence. The charge of inconsistency is disposed of; and whether you or I will have to patronize it, is not for you or me to say. Neither of us would, in civil courts, be admitted as evidence on a question of this kind—This is the province of the jurors. And with their verdict I am satisfied. Are you?

The new ground of inconsistency which you have now taken, arises not from my remarks to a correspondent in Missouri; but from my remarks to an "Independent Baptist." And here permit me to remark, that you have taken for granted what has not been asserted yet; that Baptists and Paido-Baptists should, irrespective of their difference on the subject of baptism, break bread together. Whether they ought or ought not, has not been asserted by me. This question is yet, with me, *sub judice.* It is true that I expressed a wish to be on the same terms of communion with the pious of all denominations as with the Baptist. This is a desire I am very far from hoping is peculiar to myself. But if I had asserted it as my conviction, and upon that conviction had acted so far, as to break bread with Paido-Baptists on the same principles as those on which I would unite with a Baptist community, your remarks would rather confirm me in the practice than have caused me to doubt of its propriety. For I reckon that when any person attacks any principle or practice, and either fights with something else under that name, or is compelled to adopt principles of argument which would condemn other principles and practices of the propriety of which there is no doubt, at least with himself, this procedure rather proves than disproves the position against which he argues. This appears, if you will indulge me once more, to be a little the case with the Independent Baptist. Your arguments will equally condemn any intercommunity of worship with them. You cannot, on your principles, pray with them, sing praise with them, or unite with them in one individual act of social worship—I pray you consider this.

With what propriety you compare a "society of sprinkled new creatures," to a "synagogue of Jews who reject circumcision and sacrifice swine," I confess I do not see. There is no analogy between the two cases. Erroneous and weak as the sprinkled new creatures are, they do not reject circumcision in some sense, nor baptism in some sense; nay, they are too much attached to circumcision. They dislike the knife and prefer water. But there is no "rejection" of the ordinance of baptism by sprinkled new creatures; but a mistake of what it is. I think we can find an exact comparison which expresses the full amount of the pravity of the error and practice of the honest baby-sprinklers. It is this:

Paternus says to Filius bring me a book; Filius, eager to obey his father, goes and brings him a *leaf* of paper. Paternus, Why did you not obey me? Father, says Filius, I did; I went at your command, and lo, here it is, pointing to the leaf. That is not a book, says Paternus. I thought it was, replied Filius. Paternus says, well my son, I accept your obedience, and pardon your mistake, because it was not a wilful one. Paternus calls another son. Go Junius, says he,

and bring me a book. Junius goes to play at tennis. His father indignant calls for him. He appears. Where is the book, says he, for which I sent you? O father, replied Junius, I preferred a game at tennis to bringing you the book; I thought you might go for it yourself, send somebody else, or do without it. "You are a rebel, sir, and you shall be beaten with many stripes." This, Mr. I. B. is your Jew, and that is my Paido-Baptist christian brother. Now make you the comment, there is the text.

You are equally unfortunate in your comparison of "gold and tin." You make water the differential quality. It is a pretty comparison; but ill adapted. I did not make myself gold, and the Baptists, in general, tin, nor *vice versa:* consequently I was not engaged in proving gold and tin to be one metal; and if I had, you would not have proved them to be different by making water the essential differential quality. You will consider this.

Your "dream" and Nebuchadnezzar's are nothing akin. His image was partly gold, silver, brass, iron, and clay. Mine is the representation of a family of babes, striplings, young men, and fathers all of one faith. Now to compare this image to Nebuchadnezzar's is worse than to make water the essential difference between gold and tin.

It was not the paucity of scripture documents which I have to urge in defence of the grounds assumed in my former letter that caused me to content myself with a reference to the alleged practice of Paul in breaking bread with the congregations to which he wrote letters of commendation, reproof and admonition. It was because I thought a hint of this sort was enough. For, indeed, I find no point more fully developed, in all the epistles, than the one foundation, and the duty of all christians to maintain the unity of the spirit in the bond of peace. Were I to enter upon this topic, I would find line upon line, and precept upon precept, enforcing this maxim, "wherefore receive you one another without regard to difference of opinion," on which the apostle writes the largest section in the epistle to the Romans. (Chapters xiv. and xv.) I would call to my aid, his letters to the Corinthians, and his demonstrations, to other congregations, of this principle, that "In Christ Jesus neither circumcision nor uncircumcision avails any thing, but a new creature, but faith which works by love." But of this again. If there is any position laid down with unusual plainness, and supported with more than ordinary demonstration, in the epistolary part of the New Testament, it is this: That christians should receive one another as Christ has received them, *with all their intellectual weaknesses.* This you may call Latitudinarianism; and such a Latitudinarian, I pray you may become.

If you have any thing to add upon the principle or practice resulting from the bond of peace which I have long since advocated, I will hear you cheerfully again. You have one advantage over me. No person knows who the Independent Baptist is; but alas! I am as a target on a naked hill. Perhaps if you would authorize me to unbutton your coat it might contribute to explain some items in your correspondence; but without your consent not one button shall be unplaced.

In the mean time, however, I cannot close without most sincerely reciprocating your kind wishes and unfeigned desires for myself and the cause in which I am engaged.

Yours sincerely,　　　EDITOR.

CHRISTIAN BAPTIST.

NO. I.—VOL. IV. BUFFALOE, (BETHANY) BROOKE CO. VA., AUGUST 7, 1826.

Style no man on earth your Father: for he alone is your Father who is in heaven: and all ye are brethren. Assume not the title of Rabbi; for ye have only One Teacher; neither assume the title of Leader, for ye have only One Leader— the Messiah. *Messiah.*

PREFATORY REMARKS.

ON the subject of religion I am fully persuaded that nothing but the inspired scriptures ought ever to have been published. On all sciences and arts merely human, and pertaining to the things of this life, author may succeed author, and volume be added to volume, keeping pace with the expansion of human intellect and the accumulations of human experience—But what is the reason? The answer is ready. No author is perfect; and no volume absolutely complete; no science has arrived to absolute perfection; and no art has been carried to a consummation beyond which ingenuity cannot reach. Hence we conclude that authors and their works on all subjects merely human may with propriety and advantage be multiplied manifold. And because God is the author of the sacred volume, a perfect teacher of one science and of one art; that science and that art, incapable of any improvement from human intellect, requires not another author than himself, nor another volume than the bible. The great God has condescended to teach but *one science* and that is the science of religion, or the knowledge of himself, and of man in all his relations, as his creature. He has taught but *one art*, and that is the art of living well in relation to all the high ends and destinies of man. Now the bible contains this *science* and teaches this *art* in the same perfection which its author exhibits in all his works. From this I infer that no treatise on religion, that no rules of practice can be introduced, but at the expense of impeaching the character of the author of this volume. Such efforts say—in language loud and daring;—indeed their proper title is, " A new improvement on the science of religion, and the art of living well, in which this science and art are exhibited, in relation to some, if not to all the divine ends, to much better advantage than they are by God in his writings; by the public's most wise and benevolent friend—*A Fellow Erring Mortal.*" I say this is the language, meaning, and the proper title of every such volume and its author.

No tongue could express, no heart conceive, no power of numbers calculate the advantages which the world would this day have enjoyed had not one volume, on the science and art before mentioned, been announced to the world save the oracles of God. For such a globe as that which we inhabit there is no occasion for *two suns* even of divine architecture; and much less for one of human formation. As little need is there for another treatise on this subject than God's own volume.

" Why then do you, Mr. Editor, propose and commence another volume?" I was anticipating this from the first sentence, and am prepared to answer your question. So many systems other than God's own system, and so many rules besides his, have appeared, confounding, dividing and distracting the human family, that to call men off from these appears just as necessary as when men have perverted and abused any gift of heaven, it becomes the duty of every philanthropist and faithful subject of the great King to apprize men of the consequences, and to call them off from what may prove their utter ruin. There was no occasion to denounce drunkenness before men had discovered the art of making, and a taste for using to excess, fermented liquors. But now that drunkenness has become the common or a common sin of the community, there is need for dehortations against this horrid abuse of God's bounty.

"God made man upright; but he has sought out many inventions." To restore man to uprightness and happiness is the grand end of the whole remedial government of God. To be instrumental in introducing that state of things which God instituted, and which was once exhibited; of leading the disciples to see that they need but one bond of union, one prophet, priest and king, one bible, one book on the science of religion, and one treatise on the art of living well, is the supreme object of all our efforts.

That such has been our design I hope has been already gathered from the preceding volumes, and we are thankful that we are not without witness that our labor has not been in vain. The sphere of usefulness allotted to this work has increased and been enlarged with every volume. The present volume is commenced with incomparably more sanguine anticipations than those which animated our first efforts. We are assured that the religious mind is marching forward with strides geometrically proportioned to its progress not many years back.

The opposition made to our course has only stimulated our speed, and affords fresh evidence of the goodness of the cause to which we are indissolubly wedded. The pusilanimity of our opponents, the imbecility of their attacks—and the manifest management of their resources, while they exhibit the true foundation of their standing in public estimation, have confirmed our hopes, and given the assurance that not only the decline, but the overthrow of human religious establishments, and of a religion founded upon human tradition and upheld by prejudice is at hand.

Had they never been employed in an effort to defeat our attempts, we could have known nothing of their disposition and could have argued nothing from their silence; but their exertions have

1

shown, that to will is ready with them; but how to perform they find not.

We boast not of ourselves; but of the excellency of those principles which we have been led to espouse: and our unfeigned desire is that our opponents would either manfully, argumentatively and affectionately produce their strongest reasons; or come over and help us.

While the press is laboring every day and pours forth upon the public eye volumes of declamation, of commendation, of eulogy upon the toys of childhood, and the trifles of old age; upon the glorious fruits of *tracts*, the exploits of the heroes of modern invention; while holy romances, fictitious travels and religious novels are gravely recommended by the pulpit and the press, methinks there is room and need for a few faithful advocates to plead the cause of the bible, and to argue its superiority over all human expedients to convert the world.

The great majority of papers called religious, are as much political, commercial and facetious as they are religious. The Luminaries, Stars, Suns, Registers, Recorders, Secretaries, &c. &c. in one column tell us the way to heaven, and in the next how to engraft trees, make canals, raise revenue: and some advertise strayed or stolen horses, hogs and negroes. In the same column I lately saw the way to escape the wrath to come, and to clean black silk, separated by a single line. In another, a direction to devotion followed by a direction to find the residence of the barber. A famous conversion is, in another, followed by a broker's list of the rates of exchange. The necessity of humility and temperance is argued in one paragraph—fancy goods, gewgaws and sweetmeats announced in the next. In a word they are a heterogeneous mass of the

—————————" *Congestaque eodem*,"
" *Non bene-junctarum discordia semina rerum.*"

" Any thing to please every body and any body for the sake of two dollars a year," is their motto. If not the letter or design, it appears to be the only appropriate motto. We might as well call Thomas Paine a christian apostle, as call any one of them the only religious paper in seven states and three territories. Now and then, in splendid capitals, is hung up the glorious fruit of a "Tract of four pages;" of the conversion of a whole neighborhood by one single prayer of a pious beneficiary fresh from some theological school; of the brilliant success of a religious beggar; and of a new batch of presidents, secretaries, managers and trustees—of what——? I say of what?——The dictionary affords not words to designate of what.

In this state of things I sincerely think that there is need for somebody to attempt to serve *one master*—to plead one cause—to contend for one system which can boast of a divine and infallible origin. And such may we be found, is the prayer of the   Editor.

—————

A Restoration of the Ancient Order of Things.
No. XIV.

The Bishop's Office.—No. III.

It is admitted by the Apostle Paul that a person not invested with the office of a bishop may desire the office. "If a man earnestly seeks the office of a bishop, he desires an excellent work," He then proceeds to lay down the indespensable moral and intellectual qualifications which he must possess. In doing which he plainly supposes that one may earnestly desire this work who is not eligible to it. Experience, also, a good teacher, teaches the same thing.

But having already glanced at the moral and intellectual endowments of a bishop in a previous number, we proceed to his call and appointment to office.

In the first place, then, the call is based upon the qualifications; without these he is not eligible; with them he is eligible. Consequently a due estimate of his endowments must be formed by somebody; and most certainly not by himself, nor by those who belong not to the flock to be instructed and presided over. By whom then? Assuredly by those amongst whom he is to labor, and over whom he is to preside. His qualifications in the intellectual department must then be viewed in relation to the capacity and attainments of the flock: for a man may be fit to teach, and to preside over one flock, who would not be qualified to teach or preside over another. The flock then in calling or electing a person to this office will turn their attention to themselves as well as to the candidate. They will consider his intellectual attainments with a reference to their own, and will conclude whether his aptitude to teach and his capacity to preside is of such a degree as will correspond to their circumstances. If so, he is apt to teach them, and eligible to preside over them. His election or call is from them and must be audibly, distinctly, and emphatically expressed. They are constituted the judges in this case. For no matter how eagerly he may desire or seek the office, he can make no pretension to it from such considerations. He cannot make himself an overseer. This the flock must do.

On the mode or manner of expressing this call or election we have only to remark that the inspired writers use the term which the Greeks were wont to use in their elections of officers. The inference is, that in using or adopting the same term, they attached to it the current ideas; which were, that the person to be appointed should be publicly announced and that by the voice or stretched out hand of the members entitled to choose, he was to be elected. The consent of the people or their wish unequivocally expressed, was all that ever was, amongst the Jews or Greeks, deemed essential to the election or appointment of any officer. Whether the hand should be stretched forward, or elevated; whether the electors sat or stood, or whether they spoke aloud, each one separately or with one consent arose and simply answered in the affirmative, the election was always good and valid;—provided always the desire of the people was clearly and fully expressed.

As to the act called ordination or inauguration, if ever there was such an act peculiarly so called, it consisted in the imposition of the hands of the seniors or elders of the congregation. The Apostles did express their concurrence with the people's choice by an act of this sort, and when congregations were fully set in order there was always a plurality of elders or a presbytery instituted in each congregation, who always did express their concurrence with the brethren's call by inducting the elected into office by the joint imposition of their hands. But this eldership was not a collection of elders from different congregations assembled; but those of one congregation.—The history of this institution stands thus, and would have continued thus but for the man of sin;—Every thing essential to appointment, call, or ordination was vested in the minds of the brethren. Their desires, however expressed, gave the office to the candidate, however he was announced. The apostles so taught them. They, in the first instance, took a part, not in the call or appointment; but in the introduction and inauguration of the

Q

bishops elect. This was done in conformity to the Jewish custom of imposing their hands upon the head of the person or animal devoted. This being done, a plurality of bishops being thus introduced into any particular congregation, when, either the death of one of the eldership, or the increased demands of the congregation required another, the brethren called or elected and the eldership expressed their concurrence, and the brethren's desire, by a formal sign expressive of the devotion of the person to the work. I say this is all that can be legitimately gathered from the volume, as to the forms of investiture; but as to the right of the brethren so to choose, and of the bishop, on this choice to officiate, there is the most ample evidence.

Here I would take the liberty to remark that in process of time, as corruption and defection progressed, it came to pass that what was, with the apostles, but the mere sign or mark, expressive of their concurrence with the brethren's election and appointment, came by degrees to be considered as the ordination itself, independent of the brethren's voice—Now no instance can be found in the inspired writings, where the circumstances are detailed, of the call and appointment of any brother to any office, where the call and appointment is not distinctly represented as the act of the brethren, and in no case is an ordination or appointment made without them. But their call is what, in all cases, gives the right to officiate. This is the essential thing, and the other accompaniments are the accidental properties of this thing.

The analogy between such an appointment and that of a presiding officer in a free community is as exact as any other analogy. For example, what gives any man a right to officiate as a governor or a president in a free community—Is it not the call and appointment of the people composing the community? Whether is it the voice of the people, or the form of inauguration after the people have made the appointment, which constitutes the essential consideration in creating such officers? The application is easy.

The Grecian and Roman republics, the commonwealth of Israel in its primitive integrity, the republics of America, and the congregations of christians in this one instance are essentially the same. In their first origin the people did every thing, both elect and ordain. No republic ever sent to another republic for their officers to come and make ordinations for them. No kingdom or monarchical empire ever sent for a foreign king or potentate to come and make a king for them. No christian congregation, in the age of primitive propriety, ever sent to another for their officers to come and ordain officers for them. The imposition of hands, when first instituted among the Jews, was practised by the laity.

In process of time persons were set apart in every community under every form of government for the purpose of inaugurating those constitutionally made officers. It was so in the Jewish, it was so in the Grecian, the Roman and the American republics. It was so in the christian, and it will be so again.

With the history of the world, with the pages of Jewish and christian history before me, I would contend that any congregation has a right to call, appoint, or ordain any person to any office laid down in the volume, and to do all the acts and deeds thereto appertaining, without calling to their aid the assistance of any foreign deacon, bishop or officer.

EDITOR.

In looking over the Baptist confession of faith in order to find out the nature, design and authority of the annual associations of messengers, I find the following paragraph, which contains the whole law and testimony on this subject. It is not a part of the good old confession of the English churches of 1689, but it is a part of the "Treatise of Church Discipline" drawn up by Benjamin Griffith at the request of the association which met in Philadelphia, September 25, 1742, and added it is presumed, by the authority of said association, to the confession, and made an essential part of the canons of the associated churches.

As this document contains the nature, design, and the authority of such meetings, we shall lay it before the public in full, accompanied with a few

Remarks on the Communion of Churches.
[Last Section.]

"And forasmuch as it falls out many times that particular churches have to do with doubtful and difficult matters, or differences in point of doctrine or administration, like the church of Antioch of old, wherein either of the churches in general are concerned, or any one church, in their peace, union, or edification; or any member or members of a church are injured, in or by proceeding in censures not agreeable to gospel rule and order; it is according to the mind of Christ, that many churches holding communion together should meet by their messengers and delegates, to consider of, and to give advice in and about such matters in difference; and their sentiments to be reported to all the churches concerned: and such messengers and delegates, convened in the name of Christ, by the voluntary consent of the several churches in such mutual communion, may declare and determine by the mind of the Holy Ghost, revealed in the scripture, concerning things in difference; and may decree the observation of things that are true and necessary, because revealed and appointed in the scripture. And the churches will do well to receive, own and observe such determinations, on the evidence and authority of the mind of the Holy Ghost in them, as in *Acts* xv. 29. Yet such delegates thus assembled are not intrusted or armed with any coercive power, or any superior jurisdiction over the churches concerned so as to impose their determinations on them or their officers, under the penalty of excommunication or the like. See the Confession, chap. xxvii. sect. 14, 15. See also Dr. Owen, On the Nature of the Gospel Church, chap. xi. and Dr. Goodwin, vol. iv. book v. chap. viii. ix. x. &c., Of the Government of the Churches of Christ."

As reference is had in this paragraph to the English part of the confession, that both the American and English views may appear in full, we shall here insert the two sections of chap. xxvii. above referred to:—

14. "As each church and all the members of it, are bound to pray continually for the good and prosperity of all the churches of Christ, in all places, and upon all occasions to further it, every one within the bounds of their places and callings, in the exercise of their gifts and graces, so the churches, when planted by the providence of God, so as they may enjoy opportunity and advantage for it, ought to hold communion among themselves, for their peace, increase of love, and mutual edification."

15. "Cases of difficulty or differences, either in point of doctrine or administration, wherein either the churches in general are concerned, or any one church, in their peace, union and edifi-

3

cation; or any member or members of any church are injured in or by any proceedings in censures not agreeable to truth and order; it is according to the mind of Christ, that many churches holding communion together, do by their messengers meet to consider and give their advice in or about the matter in difference, to be reported to all the churches concerned; howbeit these messengers assembled, are not intrusted with any church power properly so called; or with any jurisdiction over the churches themselves, to exercise any censures either over any churches or persons, or to impose their determination on the churches or officers."

The grand points embraced in the sections here exhibited, are,

1st. That cases of difficulty and difference either in point of doctrine or administration, affecting one particular congregation or others with them, may occur.

2d. That in cases of either sort, particularly of mal-administration, individual members may be injured by the censures or proceedings of the particular congregation to which they belong.

3d. That because of such things, it is the mind of Christ that the particular congregations should, by messengers or delegates, meet to consider of such cases, and to give advice to the congregations.

4th. These delegates in association assembled may "decree the observation of things that are necessary, because revealed and appointed in the scripture. And the churches will do well to receive, own and observe such determinations, on the evidence and authority of the mind of the Holy Spirit in them."

5th. That these messengers when assembled have no power to oblige the congregations or individuals to take their advice, by inflicting any penalty whatever. They are neither to "impose their determinations on the congregations nor their officers under the penalty of excommunication or the like."

Such are the prominent items in the preceding extracts, and they contain the whole law and testimony on this subject.

Now there are some things here on which I want more light; and first on the subject of these delegates. Are they the representatives of the churches? If so, what do they represent? Do they represent the wish, desire, conscience and interest of those at home? I can see how a person may be my representative in the national councils, in matters and things pertaining to this life; but I cannot see how any person can be my representative in any thing belonging to my conscience, in the things pertaining to the kingdom of Jesus Christ. If viewed simply as delegates, what is delegated to them? Is any thing pertaining to the doctrine, worship, or discipline of the congregation which sends them? If so, what is it, or what may it be? If not the doctrine, worship, or discipline of the church, what is delegated to them? As messengers going to a general meeting to carry intelligence to that meeting, and to bear home intelligence from it, I can understand the nature and utility of their mission; but I do not understand them when viewed in the light of delegates or representatives. I will thank any person to afford me some information on this subject.

In the next place I am at a loss to understand how it comes to pass that these delegates may decree things that are necessary, and yet the congregations be absolved from regarding these decrees any more than the advice of an infant which may be taken or rejected with perfect impunity. And how it may be *well* for the con-

gregation to take the advice of the council, and yet they cannot and must not be censured for not taking it! On this subject I earnestly solicit information.

Again, I cannot see how these associations can have the authority of Christ so to decree or advise, and that congregation be guiltless who refuses or rejects their decrees. For I can find no parallel case where the Great King authorizes any agents to act for him, and yet holds those guiltless who disobey his own institution.

There is another difficulty here. The English and American Baptists in times past have quoted *Acts* xv. in support of their meetings and of their authority so to decree. Yet they will not allow that their decisions are to be received as the decisions of the "association that met in Jerusalem." They do not consider their decision as the decisions of the Holy Spirit, and cannot even say that they are *infallibly* according to the decisions of that Spirit, and therefore they very prudently say their people may receive or reject their decisions, as they deem them agreeable or otherwise to the Divine Word, of which they are supposed to judge with the same authority at home, as their delegates do abroad or in council assembled.

But that difficulty which is to me the greatest and most incomprehensible is this. Seeing that the associated Baptists do view associations in the light before given, and withhold all authority from the decisions of their delegates; seeing they deny that associations have any right "to impose their determinations on the congregations or other officers under the penalty of excommunication or THE LIKE;" how in the name of all consistency, do they sometimes excommunicate congregations, or churches, and cast them out of the association, as the penalty for refusing to take their advice or receive their decrees. This is the most inexplicable thing of the whole, and I do earnestly solicit light on this subject, if it should be refused on every other.

As the time of associations for the year 1826 is fast approaching, it seemed good to me to propose those embarrassments to such brethren as have paid more attention to such things than I have. For on reading the Confession of Faith and the Treatise on Discipline thereto affixed by Benjamin Griffith at the request of the Philadelphia association, I thought that all jurisdiction and authority over churches was disclaimed, and that no penalty was attached to any refusal on the part of any congregation to conform to the decisions of their delegates in council assembled.

The power of an association is declared in fact to be inferior to the power of a single congregation. The association is not even co-ordinate with, but subordinate to, a single congregation. Except as a meeting for mutual intelligence, exhortation, and comfort, they have nothing to do which cannot be undone by a single congregation. If then they attempt to imitate the ecclesiastic courts of other denominations, they become more awkward than the ass covered with the skin of the lion. They appear like a lion, but bray like an ass. At least such is the construction, and the only construction I can put upon the words quoted until better informed, till which time I must think and speak as I do.   EDITOR.

—

AN association once on a time advised a church to put away its teacher. The congregation at home examined the advice of the association, and on comparing it with the decisions of the Holy Spirit, as they understood them, refused to take the advice of the delegates assembled; for which cause they were excommunicated from the communion of the association for their contumacy. Now the question is, Did this association act according to the law and testimony contained in the little book? and if they did, where then is the difference between the decrees of an association and those of a college of cardinals, or a bench of English prelates? This query is respectfully submitted.   EDITOR.

Acts of Incorporation.

MR. EDITOR—ARE we to consider congregations of christians acting comformably to either the letter or spirit of the religion which they profess, when they solicit acts of incorporation from the civil authority; and having obtained them, proceed to exercise the new powers with which they are invested? As you say so much, and propose to say more on the subject of christian morality, would you oblige a few of your Virginia friends with a few remarks in reply to the above query?   OLD VIRGINIA.

LET me answer one query by proposing another. Why do christian congregations solicit such acts of incorporation? The chief and substantial reason is, that they may be able to compel, by the arm of flesh, those who do not willingly contribute to the "Lord's treasury." The naked truth is this; an unincorporated congregation is no party in law: consequently the trustees thereof are like their creators, not recognized in law. They cannot raise or collect funds from those who promise, and afterwards repent, by any legal process. But when incorporated or invested with such privileges as make them a party, they can levy, distrain; in a word, they can compel every man to pay whatever he once promised; they can receive legacies: they can raise, and husband, and appropriate funds, as any other company, for building roads, canals, or bridges.

Acts of incorporation are therefore solicited and obtained for the self-same reasons which induce canal, road, and bridge builders to solicit them. They are of the same use and advantage to both. When, then, a christian congregation solicits from the state legislature an act of incorporation, in plain English it says, "Give us the right to compel by all the civil pains and penalties which are allowed to all corporate bodies of this world, such as fail in making good their promises. We say, give us the power to compel them, against their own inclination, to contribute the sums which they once promised. For we have found all other means, all arguments and inducements drawn from the christian religion, unavailing. We do not like such christians, it is true; but we want their money. They once subscribed, and they ought to pay; but they will not be induced by any other argument than those eloquent appeals, which the constable or sheriff can make to their feelings. Grant us then, O ye powers that be! the right of compulsion—that glorious right, by which we can move the widow's soul and the orphan's guardian to do what is right in its own nature and profitable for us to enjoy; and we will, as in duty bound, ever pray that you may share liberally in our tender mercies. If any one has a bequest to make us, we cannot receive it. Many a well disposed old maid, and childless old bachelor would, in their last moments, will and bequeath to us the remnants of their fortune; but we have no power to receive it or to retain it against the legal heirs. Grant us then, we humbly beseech you, the right of receiving and retaining such legacies, if the natural or legitimate heirs should mourn all their days in sorrow for it. Make our plea stronger than their

plea, and we shall doubly pray." I say, this is in plain English the spirit, and meaning, and language of all such solicitations. Whether, then, such requests are compatible with the Christian spirit, I leave you to judge. I make no comment, as the text is plain enough already.

This is the best substitute for a religious establishment in this country, and in a certain degree has answered all the purposes. I do not here inquire into the policy of granting such petitions; I do not inquire into the constitutional right which any assembly has to grant such favors. But I am willing to shew by many arguments, (if this is not satisfactory,) that in asking for such immunities, every grand principle of christianity is lost sight of, all dependence upon Jesus Christ is renounced, all faith in his promises and all regard to christian character is abandoned.

Many preachers and ministers of such congregations contend that they have a right to live on the gospel. For the sake of argument let it be admitted. Let us then suppose a case which has within our own knowledge actually occurred. A clergyman preaches the gospel; he has an incorporated congregation. Forty-five dollars of one year's subscription were collected by the arm of flesh. The money was brought by the trustees to the priest. His bread and his meat for a certain time were purchased with it. He and his family eat it. Now the question is, When he eats this bread and meat, whether does he live on the law or on the gospel? Whether does he eat the free-will offering of devotion, or the exacted tribute of sordid poverty, or the constrained oblation of covenant breakers? Can he return thanks to Heaven for his food, as the bounty of God, or must he thank the "the powers that be" for it? An infant becomes an Aristotle here. The case is a plain one. And many such there are, who "preach the gospel" and live upon the law.

Every attempt to hold in subjection either the conscience or the purse of any people by legal restraints on religious grounds ultimates in an inquisition: and if it stop short of fire and sword it is owing to the mildness of the people, and not to the spirit of the system.

We have no doubt but many unsuspicious souls, without evil motives or designs enter into such measures; but still the thing itself is a great evil and has already in some instances, and may yet in many more, become a source of sorrow and of suffering to those who have been caught unawares in an evil net.

That we are not singular in this view of the tendency of those measures, the following extracts from a correspondent in Amelia county, Va. will shew:—

"At a meeting of the Presbyterians some time since, not far from this place, among other things it was proposed to petition the next session of the Virginia legislature for a charter of incorporation; but the motion was opposed by some upon the ground that it would not go down well with the people yet. It was consequently postponed to a more convenient season, while they in the mean time intend to use their best endeavors to prepare the minds of the people for this measure. This, dear sir, is regarded by us as a bold stride towards an establishment. We would like to hear you upon this important point."—

"By demonstrating to an enlightened public that religious incorporation is the foster mother of establishments; that death-like inquisition is her legitimate offspring; imprisonment her only process; the stake her only tribunal; and death

5

the only anodyne of her opponents; the evil day may be delayed in its coming; nay, the impending danger may be entirely averted. If so, happy for us who oppose the measure! thrice happy for those who urge its rejection! happy for all our fellow-citizens!"

Christian Morality.—No. III.

MY text will be found in the Baptist Recorder, vol. 1. No. 13. It reads thus: "In our next number we shall give his criticism in full (that is on the two positions which appeared in the 10th No. of the Recorder. See C. B. Volume third) that our readers, whom brother C. represents as persons with whom sound is infinitely more important than sense, may judge for themselves." Now, courteous reader, you see the Recorder represents me as having stigmatized its readers as persons "with whom sound is infinitely more important than sense." Let us turn over to Volume third. Here we find these words: "Great efforts are made to enlist the feelings and prejudices of those with whom sound is infinitely more important than sense, against my endeavors," &c. These words the genius of controversy converts into a direct and formal imputation of one particular class of readers. Let us now for example take a parallel case. Suppose that the National Intelligencer, had said of the efforts of the United States Gazette that great efforts were made to enlist the feelings and prejudices of those who are tories against the present administration; would it be a truth or a falsehood to say that the National Intelligencer had represented the readers of the United States Gazette as tories? To what should we attribute such a misrepresentation? Should we call it an error of the head, or of the heart? If of the head, should we attempt to reason with a person of such intellectual powers? If of the heart, could we suppose it to be under the influence of the Holy Spirit? From an intellectual or moral defect such perversions and misrepresentations must proceed. The above is the only notice which the editors of the Recorder have yet taken of my remarks on experimental religion. The 11th and 12th Nos. which have been issued since our first notice of them was written, have not been received; but it appears from the 13th that they have not in these Nos. published any thing upon the subject. I do hope these gentlemen will make reparation for the injury they have done me in the apprehension of their readers. It was for their benefit I wished my remarks inserted in the Recorder, consequently could not suppose them persons of this stamp; but if my remarks are to be thus perverted, and if I must be brought before them in such disadvantageous circumstances, I could not wish to appear before them. They might as truly tell their readers that I had represented them as men-stealers or homicides, for if my saying that some persons are of such character, implies that I represent all the world of this character, they might with a good grace tell their readers, in particular, that I had thus represented them. But from this unpleasant topic I turn to one of the exalted items of christian morality.

With most men of refined moral sensibility reputation is next to life—with some it is dearer than life. The christian religion cherishes this feeling, and while it guides and stimulates our pursuits after good fame, it teaches us by the broadest precepts, and the most powerful examples to take care of the reputation of others. "A good name is better than great riches," was an axiom of the wisest man. Philosophers and poets have dwelt upon this theme with more than usual pathos. How often do the apostles exhort the christians to seek the reputation of those who in former times had obtained an illustrious fame? With how many arguments and exhortations do they induce them to shine amongst the excellent.

It is no inconsiderable evidence of the Divine excellency of this religion, that it teaches its disciples to pay a due regard to that in others which they appreciate most in themselves. Hence what is dearest in the christian's estimation is to be guarded in another in exact proportion to the importance which he himself attaches to it. Thus a man to whom the reputation of virtue and wisdom is dearer than any earthly acquisition, is taught from the golden rule itself, to pay the highest regard to the reputed virtue and wisdom of others. But there is this peculiarity in the christian system, it does not allow any of its disciples to derive any satisfaction from a comparison of themselves with others. All human systems are founded upon false principles as respects the satisfaction to be derived from reputation. They allow their admirers to be pleased in excelling others; not seeing that if it afford pleasure to excel others, it must inevitably afford pleasure not to see others as commendable as one's self. But the christian system, as the heavens are higher than the earth, excels that which is based upon such principles. It teaches us while eagerly bent upon the reputation of christian wisdom and virtue, to derive pleasure from the superior displays in others of that which we would admire in ourselves, and inciting us rather to look with pity and regret on those in our rear. There is a delicate distinction here which we regret to see so seldom noticed.

Slander, revilings, backbitings, whisperings, evil speaking, and every species of detraction is reprobated in the most forcible terms which human language affords, by all the inspired writers who touch upon this topic. And amongst the essential characteristics of the man who shall inhabit the heavenly mansions, this has a chief place—"He does not take up an evil report against his neighbor." "He despises a vile person, also, and honors them that honor the Lord."

What a massacre of character do the public prints, the public places of resort, and even the social hearth in this day exhibit. When commendation is volunteered or extorted, how often is it circumscribed, and what immense subtractions are made, by one or two of those terrific *buts*!! The very thing of which all are so covetous, viz. a good name, they bestow with the greatest frugality upon others; and too many, like the shamble fly, seem to feast upon the putrid spots in human character.

The sycophant too and the detracter are nearer akin than a cousin-german. But we are digressing. Paul exhorts, "Render to all their dues: honor to whom honor is due, and respect to whom respect is due." No toleration is granted, no allowance is made in the treatment of any person, whether viewed in the light of a friend or a foe.

It has been a thousand times lamented, that religious controvertists pay the least regard to the reputation of those from whom they differ in opinion. As charity hides a multitude of sins, so a difference in opinion covers a multitude of virtues. Reformation in this respect should be every where preached and practised.

EDITOR.

Scripture Quotations.

WE have often had occasion to notice the pernicious influence of the text system of expounding scripture—No practice has done more to obscure the meaning of scripture, and to originate the most romantic and enthusiastic tenets. The thoughtless manner in which the multitude of textuaries follow each other, not merely in their sermons, but in their quotations of scripture, only affords another instance that not one in a thousand dares to think for himself, and to exercise his own faculties on the scriptures. I have found myself, in countless instances, quoting scriptures in a sense which I had heedlessly attached to them because I always heard them quoted in this manner. Nothing but my own experience and observation has taught me that the great mass of mankind are but mere imitators, and the disciples of men. I have found too, that many sentences are, I may say, universally quoted in a sense which not one sentence of scripture will justify, and that too, on some of the most common topics. I will exhibit a few specimens:—

Psalms cxlv. 9—"The Lord is good to all, and his tender mercies are over all his other works." The last clause I never once heard quoted right, or in its true sense. If I have not been greatly deceived, I have, in every instance, heard it quoted thus: "His tender mercies are superior to all his other perfections, over them all in greatness and glory, transcending every other attribute of his nature." This is the sense universally attached to the words in their frequent application. Now let the whole context be considered and this application of them must be discarded—The sense in which the Psalmist evidently uses these words is—"The Lord is good to all men, and his tender mercies are over all his other creatures upon the earth. He feeds the raven, the young lion, and the eyes of all things wait upon him, and he upholds and feeds them." God's perfections are never in scripture called his works, and David often exhibits his goodness and mercy manifested to the meanest of his creatures.

David is often called "the man after God's own heart," from the sound of a passage frequently quoted—He is said to have been a man such as God's heart or mind exactly approved. Thus the populars always apply these words: And of all the men that ever lived David is represented by them as "THE man after God's own heart." Now let 1st. *Samuel* xiii. 14, be examined and this sense will totally vanish. Here it is—"Saul has not answered my purpose, mind, or will in governing my people; but I have found a man that will just suit my purpose, viz. David the son of Jesse." That this is the true sense of the words in sacred scripture, methinks is evident when declared without further exposure.

At a certain crisis in the vision of John, long before the end of the world comes in his view, a heavenly messenger is introduced who solemnly declares "time shall be no more." Hence in the numerous allusions to the period here spoken of, all speak of a period when time ceases to exist. Sermons are spoken and even published on the text "time shall be no more;" whereas the sense, and indeed, the true translation, says, "there shall be no longer delay, the judgment spoken of shall be immediately executed"—that other things which require the continuance of time may regularly be introduced.

In these examples I prefer those on which no sectarian tenet depends, to illustrate what egregious blunders, and how universally followed, are passing current, as the sense of the sacred writings, under the popular system of text preaching and text quoting.   EDITOR.

No. 2.]   SEPTEMBER 7, 1826.

On the Millennium.—No. II.

THE division of the history of our world into the physical, secular and millennial ages, besides spreading before the mind the beginning and end of things, has also this great and desirable advantage, that the inquirer after truth, having once ascertained the distinguishing characteristics of each age, it enables him to distribute the prophecies accordingly, and to acquire a correct general knowledge, not only of his own age, but also of that which has preceded or may follow it.

To understand the course of human events as glanced at in the rapid sketches of the prophets, and to know the relation which our own times and labors bear to what has actually gone before or may be reasonably and scripturally hoped to follow after, is, of all things, the best calculated to inspire the christian with resignation, and to endow him with those qualities of reasonableness and sobriety which his high profession so imperiously demands.

To hear the servant in the house of Christ confounding all times and events, and ignorantly setting forth the secular church and authorities, in the terms of the splendid but unaccomplished prophecies which relate to the millennial church and authorities, is very unbecoming, and it may be highly criminal and dangerous—criminal, because it flatters secular and opposing institutions, which God has largely condemned; and dangerous, because it tends to mislead the public mind, and consequently to retard general improvement.

It is a crime, however, of which the ecclesiastical dignitaries are exceedingly guilty. Where a complimentary sermon is to be delivered, I speak of the European world, the preacher seldom fails to select a text which affords him a fair opportunity of flattering the prince; the scriptures which relate to the millennium are generally resorted to, and the prince whom God has set forth in the scriptures as a wild beast, or the horn, which is the very instrument of terror or rage in a wild beast, is thus painted by the preacher as an inimitable diadem in the hand of Jehovah and a nursing father in the church. The prince is flattered. The priest is rewarded—and so the way of thus confounding things proves a chief art by which the abettors of bad government and false religion mutually encourage and deceive one another.

We ourselves are not behind in the practice of this art, and were we not kept humble by the manifest prevalence of the secular plagues, debates, envyings, wraths, strifes, backbitings, whisperings, swellings, tumults, we should seldom fail to flatter ourselves that among us, and among us alone, Christ was enthroned in his Millennial glory. But alas! the thrones are not yet cast down, the secular age has not yet expired, war, commerce and ambition, with the rival passions created by them, pride, envy and emulation every where prevail.

It has been observed, in a former paper, that the physical, secular and millennial ages are marked out on the face of scripture by three attendant judgments—the *Flood*, the *extinction of immoral government*, and the *resurrection of the dead*. The remainder of this paper I devote to remarks rather on these judgments than the ages to which they severally belong.

The flood, an amazing catastrophe drawn from the resources of the material world, constituted the judgment of the first age. The gratification of the sexual and other appetites formed the chief guilt with which the age was chargeable, "until Noah entered the ark," says the Redeemer, "they were eating and drinking, marrying and giving in marriage," &c. it was with great propriety, therefore, that God swept away the animal crimes of a race so sensual by the judgment of the flood.

The corruption of the secular or middle age being of a higher and more refined nature i. e. of those political and social relations which subsist in large communities, the judgment which shall wipe it away, the scriptures describe to us as being of a more artificial and complex nature. It consists in the extinction of immoral government and false religion, by means of war, conducted under the united aid, and upheld by the united lights of revelation and general science.

Still more extraordinary, however, will be the final judgment, the resurrection of the dead, sudden, general, and conclusive, it will be effected by an immediate effort of the strong hand of Jehovah—when all the men of all the ages physical, secular, and millennial, shall stand before the judgment seat of Jesus Christ and give to him an account of the deeds done in this body, whether they be good or evil.

The first judgment then was effected by natural means—the second will be by artificial means—and the third and last by super-natural means, when the human family, which has so apostatized from God, shall be judged and the material world shall be dissolved.   PHILIP.

———

THERE is a great advantage resulting to the community from the art of letter writing of which all are sensible. The letters I receive, and frequently lay before the public in this work, I consider of great interest and advantage to myself, and to my readers. These communications bring before the reader the sentiments and views of many persons of great intelligence and unfeigned piety on the grand subjects on which we treat. I have read some works a century or two old, in reference to which I should have been much edified and delighted, had the authors of those works possessed and given to their readers the sentiments of the distinguished men of their own times. What I have often regretted in works of considerable merit, as a defect, I have always wished to supply in this. I am peculiarly happy in having a number of correspondents of the first order in the literary and religious world, and on the present occasion have more than ordinary satisfaction in introducing, to the acquaintance of my readers, the sentiments of a new correspondent, whose intelligence, piety, and high standing among the churches of Virginia, require no eulogy nor notification from me. The letter itself is sufficient recommendation. I have only to solicit, on my behalf and that of my readers, a continuance or repetition of such favors, both from himself and some others, particularly from a correspondent in King and Queen county, from whom we have not heard for some time. I would delight in a private correspondence with many of my brethren in the east and in the west on all the topics which appear in this work; but the immense labor of my fingers and mind for some time past has prevented me of that pleasure, and therefore, I have, in some instances, where matters of great moment present themselves, preferred, even when the writer did not intend it, to publish his letters and my answers, for the public good. I have no idea of suppressing any thing of consequence because the writer and I may differ in some points. And while

I edit this work it shall be open to every decent passenger of whatever creed, who holds the Head.

———

Paulinus to the Editor of the "Christian Baptist," wishes grace, mercy, and peace.—1st Epistle.

DEAR SIR.—FINDING the Christian Baptist to be a vehicle, free for all passengers who behave with tolerable decency, and considering myself to be one of that description, I have a mind, if there should be room, to take a seat and try a little trip. By the way, I doubt you will find it necessary to enlarge your vehicle, or submit too often to see yourself and some of your passengers crowded out. But let me drop the figure: I am fond of figures, and therefore would not wish to chase them out of breath. I feel a desire to offer you some thoughts, which, however you may estimate them, will be received, I am confident, in that spirit of friendship and good will, in which they are communicated. This confidence I am disposed to cherish, not only from the impression produced by a slight personal acquaintance with you, but from the candid manner in which, (as far as I have observed,) you have replied to your correspondents—those who have censured, as well as those who have approved.

With regard to the Christian Baptist, (the object in view in this communication,) or rather, with regard to the principles and sentiments you maintain in that publication, my letter, as you will see, will wear a sort of mixed aspect. I have not yet had the opportunity of perusing all the numbers, from the commencement of this work; but as far as I have seen, I find much to approve, something to doubt, and something too from which I must dissent. Possibly, however, my dissention may be owing, (in part at least,) to the want of a full and correct understanding of your sentiments.

I said, "much to approve;"—I might use a stronger term and say, much to admire. With several of your essays, I have been not only pleased but delighted. Many of your remarks too, in opposition to the errors and follies, too prevalent in the religious world, meet my own views and receive my warm and hearty commendation. In a word, I am greatly pleased with what appears to be your drift and aim, viz. to clear the religion of Jesus of all the adventitious lumber with which it has been encumbered, and bring back the christian church to its primitive simplicity and beauty.

After these general remarks, it will of course be expected, that I should notice some particulars.

In the first place then, your views of the christian religion, considered as a dispensation, appear to me to accord, in general, with the spirit of the New Testament. I recollect, particularly, an essay on Christianity, which I had the opportunity of reading in the first Vol. which, in the main, I thought superlatively excellent; as well as that also on the Jewish Sabbath and the Christian Lord's day. In the same volume I think too, was an essay, the subject of which was, the cessation of Old Testament obligations under the Gospel dispensation. Some things, according to my present impression, were there advanced, to which I am not prepared to assent, without a re-perusal of the piece; but the leading sentiment appeared to me to be perfectly defensible on scriptural grounds.

That we are not under the old dispensation, but under the new, is admitted by all christians: and that the obligations imposed upon us, by the revelation of God's will, do not arise from the

Old Testament, but from the New, seems not only to follow as a consequence, but to be abundantly manifested in the christian scriptures. If this therefore, is all you mean by denying the perpetual obligation of the Old Testament, then, as far as I can see, you are right in this point. That the old testament is of divine authority;—that it is a fund of sacred instruction—calculated, by divine wisdom, as a proper rule for the patriarchal and Mosaic dispensations, and an aid to christians in the present day, are facts not to be called in question. A great proportion too of the prohibitions, injunctions, and precepts, found there, (all those indeed of the nature called moral,) are, doubtless, of perpetual obligation: but then they are such as are substantially introduced into the New Testament, and incorporated with its glorious truths. Or else, how, (I would ask,) are we to distinguish these moral matters, from those of a different character? from ceremonial and judicial ordinances? Is the light of nature to sit in judgment, in this case, in order to discriminate and decide? I should think not;—at any rate, while we have the light of the New Testament to guide us.

Thus then it would seem that we may correctly and safely take this position:—That the old dispensation has passed away, and with it, all institutions, ordinances, and obligations, not re-sanctioned by the New Testament. This is a position which presented itself to my notice several years ago, and appeared then, as it does now, not as a mere speculation, but as an instrument the most effectual for sweeping off all that rubbish which has been gathered from the old ruins of former establishments, to build withal on christian grounds. But to take the position, that all Old Testament requisitions and laws, not specially repealed in the New, are now binding on christians, appears to be placing us among the tents of the patriarchs and the tabernacles of the Israelites, in the midst of bewildering researches that can have no end.

It is, as you will observe, with your views of the christian religion, considered as a dispensation, that I have thus the pleasure of expressing my concurrence; and I do hope that upon a more explicit declaration of your sentiments, I may find no cause to disagree with you, as to what more nearly concerns the nature of that religion;—the agency, I will say, which produces it in us. I do not wish you to consider me, at this time, as really differing from you on this point: I only desire to be better satisfied. Let me explain myself.

There are some among us possessed of strong apprehensions, that you are disposed to deny the existence of the regenerating and sanctifying operations of the Holy Spirit on the spirit or the heart of man; and that you would ascribe all the religious effects produced in us, solely to the influence of the written word, or the external revelation of God. And these apprehensions, permit me to add, are not, in all cases, the effect of any prejudice against you.

For myself, I have said to others, as I now say to you, that I cannot think this of you. I have seen indeed many things in your writings which appear inconsistent with such a sentiment;—a sentiment which obviously goes to the annihilation of all hope for gracious aid in the christian warfare, and of course, to the annihilation of prayer for any such aid. A sentiment which would thus cut off communion with God, and let out, (as I may say,) the very life's blood of religion, I cannot think you would maintain. Still, however, I would fain see you more explicit on this point: it appears to be due to yourself, as well as to others; and to a compliance with this wish, I should suppose you can have no objection.

That the word of God is the instrument of our regeneration and sanctification, I have no doubt; nor would I think of saying it is his usual method, (whatever he may in some cases choose to do,) to operate on the soul, independent of the word. But that there is a living, divine agent, giving life and energy to the word, and actually operating on the soul, is, in my view, a truth which forms one of the glorious peculiarities of the religion of Jesus: and thus I would say, in the language of the apostle, we are " born again, not of corruptible seed, but of incorruptible, by the word of God which lives and abides forever." You will not place this matter, I am persuaded, among those unprofitable disquisitions about causation, of which you complain in your answer to Amicus, in the last number of the C. B.

In commencing my letter I had several other matters in view; but the room I have already occupied forbids any thing more than a passing notice of them, in the present communication.

It was my wish, not only to express my hearty approbation of your avowed hostility to certain abuses and follies, prevalent in the religious world; but to lend any little aid in my power, towards a correction of these evils. Among the objects here alluded to, let me just mention—the adoption of Creeds and Confessions of Faith;— those fruitful sources of dissention, and stubborn barriers against the admission of divine light from the word of God, and the high pretensions of many amongst the clergy, (so called) together with their pompous human titles;—the food of spiritual pride, and the fetters of free enquiry and decision amongst christians. Here, however, it was my intention to state to you, how I considered you as having suffered yourself to be carried to an extreme, in discarding the office of preacher, and the practice of public preaching, and confining your views of public ministration wholly to teaching and admonitoin in the church. On this point I can at present only express my wish that you would re-consider the matter, and see whether there be not room for qualifying your sentiments; —whether the work of an evangelist (or gospel preacher) be not proper and requisite, as well as the office of a bishop;—requisite, I will say, not to the order of a gospel church, but to the present state of the new dispensation.

Another matter (perhaps the most interesting) yet remains to be mentioned: I mean such a reformation in the church as shall restore what you term "the ancient order of things." That some reformation is requisite, I think there can be no doubt: to what extent I do not yet feel myself prepared to say. Some of the things which you insist on are with me (like a certain point with you) matters as yet *sub judice*. May the great Head of the church direct his people, by whatever means he may see proper.

Before I conclude, permit me to suggest a query, whether, in opposing what you deem the errors of the day, you ought not to be cautious to preserve a due degree of moderation in your language. In this opposition I do not wish to see you abate "one jot or tittle" of the firmness with which you take your stand, or the keenness with which you make the attack. I am only apprehensive, that the occasional asperity of your language may afford a pretext to your adversaries, to represent you as one of those censorious spirits who take pleasure in dealing out invectives; and thus your arguments and remarks, though well

9

directed, may in some degree fail of their effect. In some cases, you know, the opposers of truth find a convenient asylum from its shafts, in an affec'ed contempt for their assailant: and when they dare not treat his talents in this way, they will sometimes affect to despise the spirit by which he is actuated: and thus, dreading his weapons, and the skill with which he wields them, they cover themselves with this pretext in order to avoid the battle. Indeed I cannot help suspecting, that there are Editors of religious journals, who, in regard to the Christian Baptist, have betaken themselves to this convenient refuge. But though I would wish to see you "cut off occasion from those who desire occasion," pray observe, I would not wish you to cut off the points of your arrows, whenever they are directed at error or folly.

That you may steer a straight-forward course, —alike unawed by custom—unprovoked by opposition—unseduced by novelty, is the prayer of,

Yours in the gospel,

PAULINUS.

Virginia, July 25th, 1826.

To Paulinus.

DEAR SIR,—SINCE the commencement of this work I have not received a letter from any correspondent with more pleasure than that produced by the reception of yours. And there has not, in my judgment, appeared in this work, a letter from any correspondent more evangelical in its scope, more clear and luminous in its object, more unexceptionable in its style, more perfect in its soul, body, and spirit. I am not conscious that there is one point of controversy between us in all the items of practical truth embraced in your letter. Whatever diversity of opinion might possibly exist between us in carrying out some principles to their legitimate issue, I am conscious of none in the premises. We know, owing to causes quite familiar to us both, that it is possible for persons of unquestionable honesty to agree in the premises and differ in the conclusions. I do not, however, make this observation, from a surmise that this would be the fact, or that it is the fact in our case, respecting the premises in your epistle.— Permit me then to glance at the items which it presents to my reflection.

And first of the Old and New Dispensation.— The position which you say may be "safely taken" embraces every thing for which I contend, viz:—"That the Old Dispensation has passed away, and with it all institutions, ordinances, and obligations, not re-sanctioned by the New Testament," or in the New Dispensation. You will see this position contended for at considerable length in a discourse which I pronounced ten years ago, (a copy of which I herewith transmit you) before an association in the western part of this state. For the heresy of which, I have been persecuted ever since by a small banditti of the orthodox. You will see that I was but a stripling at the time this discourse was delivered; and that I was quite metaphysical upon the atonement. The mists of the river Nile had not then ascended to the tops of the mountains; but were thinly spread and gently reclining upon the sides of the hills. In a series of essays on the Patriarchal, Jewish, and Christian states or ages, now in contemplation, the Divine authority, incalculable importance, and practical use of the Old Testament, will, I hope, be fully developed to all inquisitive minds.

But to proceed to the next and more interesting item, "the nature" of the christian religion, or what you call the "agency" which produces it in us. Were it not for the pernicious influence of the theories afloat on this subject, I would assert my concurrence in opinion with you. This may appear a strange saying; but it is in accordance with the genius of this work. I have taken a stand which I am determined, by the grace of God, not to abandon. I will lay down no new theories in religion, contend for no old theories, nor aid any theory now in existence. For why? Because no theory is the gospel of Jesus the Messiah. Nor can the preaching or teaching of any theory, be the preaching or teaching of the gospel. And, please mark it well, *no man can be saved by the belief of any theory, true or false: no man will be damned for the disbelief of any theory.* This position I hold worthy to be printed in majestic capitals. No consumptive body, no chronic disease, not even the dyspepsia, can be cured by adopting any theory of disease or of the *modus medendi;* else I should have been cured of the latter malady long since.

Those who ascend in balloons have proved that the nigher they approach the thin blue ether, the air becomes clearer, and as it becomes clearer it becomes cooler. They have found that there is a region a good way on this side too, of the azure fields, where mercury itself would freeze on midsummer day at noon. Man could not live in those pure, clear, and lofty regions. He requires an atmosphere highly impregnated with terrene qualities; and it has been long known that the sun's rays give no heat to the etherial regions through which they pass. They must come in contact with the matter or the effluvia of this globe before they possess any vitality, or power to support life. There is a good analogy here. Man has so much of the animal in him and about him that he cannot now mentally, any more than corporally live upon abstract views. Hence, as you have, my dear sir, no doubt frequently observed, the Bible teaches every thing in the *concrete,* and nothing in the *abstract.* This is the radical, distinguishing, or most essential differential quality of this book in comparison of all others in the world, and especially of all systems of religion.

On this point I would wish to be well understood: for if well understood on this point, I cannot be easily misunderstood on many others. I will, therefore, impose on your patience a little longer. And as I sometimes prefer to present a whole broadside of assertions to arrest attention, I now assert that there is not one abstract truth propounded in all the Bible. Where is the position lain down, that the spirit of God, independent of the word, regenerates an unbeliever? And which of the prophets or apostles inculcates that the word of God, independent of the spirit, regenerates an unbeliever? Again, where is the position found in the sacred volume, that the spirit, accompanying the word, regenerates a man? Once more, where does it assert, that men can, without the Holy Spirit, believe, or that they cannot? Some, no doubt, view some of these positions as Bible truths, and fancy that they are abstractly taught in the sacred volume I ask them, *where?* For I have never found them there. They are all abstract views, or mere speculative conclusions drawn from the scriptures by each speculator according to his logical implements and prowess.

There can be no doubt, either, but that there are abstract or speculative views which can be drawn from, or pressed out of the bible. If alcohol was not in corn, no process of distillation could bring it out. If croton oil was not in the croton bean, no press could abstract it from it. But who can live on alcohol!—And who can be saved by abstract views!

Believe me, my dear sir, that the art of making sermons after the fashion, is the art of making fermented liquors out of the streams of the waters of eternal life. Our great theological writers are gigantic elaborators, their works are immense distilleries, and the systems which they rectify, especially when mellowed with age, like good old cogniac, are sought after and swallowed down with a zest peculiar to tiplers. I know some theological tiplers that in all probability have not gone to bed duly sober once in forty years. There is among them, too, some rare instances of longevity. They are, however, generally bloated in youth, and shrivelled in old age. There are, too, some awfully alarming apoplectic explosions; but still *ardent spirits* are in demand, and the religious retailers are enriched.—Oh, when shall men relish the aliment of nature, and learn to live upon the simple bread of God, and the pure water of life!

But who can live on essential oils? Or will the act of speculating or inferring; or will the inferences when drawn—that the spirit without the word, or the word without the spirit, or the spirit and word in conjunction regenerates the human soul; I ask, will the act of drawing these inferences, or these inferences when drawn, save the soul? If they will not, why make them essential to christianity, beneficial to be taught. And why, oh why, condemn him as a heretic whose head is too weak to draw or drink them!

Some boisterous spirits, who have more sail than ballast, who have become confirmed theological tiplers, are ever and anon teaching and preaching up their theory of regeneration. Without it they could not make a sermon any more than a cordwainer could make a shoe without a last. Some of this class say of me—"He is not sound in the faith; see how ambiguously he talks about regeneration; if his views are consistent with ours why does he not come out flat footed; why all this reserve; why does he not roundly assert in so many words, what his theory is."—Yes, says the drunkard; you must drink, "tell me whether you will have cider, strong-beer, wine or brandy; you must drink something, or you are no company for me." But to lay aside an excellent metaphor lest I should allegorize, I will say in plain English, if I were to act politically and dishonestly, I would adopt one theory, and impugn every other. But what then? I would have to be swept off with all my predecessors in Babylon, before the millennium appears, before the temple of the Lord appears in its glory. It is, therefore, that I am at war with all theories both true and false. Because, in addition to what has been said of their inutility, the world is intoxicated with them; men are loving and hating one another on theoretic grounds, they are fighting about their theories, either making them the bond of union or the signal of war. Yes, men hate one another for God's sake, if we may believe them in earnest, or acting consistent with their feelings.

I have in the second volume of this work, written a series of essays on the work of the Holy Spirit in the salvation of men, without laying down any theory or terminating in any speculative conclusions. At least, I studiously avoided such a speculative result. My aim was to understand and exhibit what the scripture says on this subject, regardless of those theories. But because I would not exclaim *Shibboleth*, I have been reprimanded as heterodox.

To most of us it is impossible to think upon religion, or to talk upon it without running out into mere speculation. For this reason:—Ninety-nine books, and ninety-nine preachers in every hundred are wont to treat religion as a speculative science, in which every thing depends upon having right theories. Whereas the bible always represents faith in Jesus, as the Lord Messiah, and obedience thence resulting, as the all in all—"As the twig is bent the tree's inclined."—Hence we have churches of religious speculators. Our congregations are large juries empanneled to sit in judgment on the preacher's orthodoxy: and if theoretically right, he is a brother, a saint, and sound in the faith. Hence, say the people, we go to *hear* the Rev. Mr. Such-a-one, not to *worship* God. They are assemblies of critics, from whose tribunal there is no appeal—no Cesar; no Areopagus.

The preceding remarks will, I hope, my dear brother, afford some satisfaction as far as respects the reason why I do not contend for any one theory of regeneration. But if any man accustomed to speculate on religion as a mere science, should infer from any thing that I have said on these theories, that I contend for a religion in which the Holy Spirit has nothing to do; in which there is no need of prayer for the Holy Spirit; in which there is no communion of the Holy Spirit; in which there is no peace and joy in the Holy Spirit, he does me the greatest injustice; he is ignorant, doting about questions, and strifes of words, from which proceed envy and contention.

All whom I baptize, I baptize into the name of the Father, and of the Son, and of the Holy Spirit. I pray for the love of the Father, the grace of the Son, and the communion of the Holy Spirit, to remain with all the saints. A religion of which the Holy Spirit is not the author, the subject matter, and the perfecter, is sheer Deism. To a man who teaches otherwise, I would say, "are you a teacher of Israel, and know not these things?" And to the speculators I rejoin, "the wind blows where it lists, and you hear the sound thereof; but can not tell whence it comes, nor whither it goes." If he will yet contend, I add, tell me how the human spirit is first formed in the infant man, or how the bones of the human body are first fashioned, and I will tell him how his theory is wrong. One thing we know, that except a child be born it cannot come into this world, and unless a man be born of spirit and water he cannot enter the kingdom of Jesus. When an infant is born into the world it feeds upon no theory, nor does it come into the world by the efficacy of theory. And were we to philosophize till the last trumpet is heard, children will be born into the world in the same old-fashioned way, and so will they enter the kingdom of Jesus in the way ordained and framed by God, the Father of our spirits. The incontrovertible fact is, men must be born from *above;* and for this purpose the glad tidings are announced. Let us simply promulgate them in all their simplicity and force, unmixed with theory, uncorrupted with philosophy, unsophisticated with speculation, and unfettered by system, and mark the issue. Hitherto shall you come and no farther; and here let all the waves and billows of human passion and human feeling be stayed!

Whatever the scriptures say, I say, The only question with me is to understand each sentence in the light of its own context. And I will not refrain from any inquirer my views of any passage, without either theorizing or dogmatizing. To make *new* theories is the way to make *new divisions.* To contend for the *old* is to keep up the *old divisions;* either of which would be in direct opposition to all my efforts, and, what is still worse, in direct opposition to the decisions of the Holy Spirit.

"That the work of an evangelist or a preacher is requisite, not to the order of a christian church; but to the present state of the new dispensation," is a position which I will not contend with you. The Holy Spirit says, "let him that hears *say come;*" and why should I say to him that hears, do not *say come;* hold your tongue. No; forbid it heaven! "Let him that hears say come," is a license which the Holy One gave when he was closing the canon, sealing up the law and the testimony. And thanks be to his name, he left no tribunal on earth to controvene this decision. While then there are any who have not come to the fountain of life, and when any one who has heard and come, and tasted, finds such an opportunity to say come, let him say it in word and deed.

I thank you most cordially for your hints on moderation. I will attend to them. 'Tis hard, indeed, for any one to have a quiver full of sharp arrows, well pointed, and well bearded, and not to draw blood. And there is still so much sympathy in human nature, that it will sometimes drop a tear on witnessing the last throes of an expiring foe. Hence when the enemies of truth are sorely wounded, its friends exclaim, refrain a little.

I appreciate very much, indeed, your christian exhortation; and will always be glad to hear from you. Pray lend a helping hand. It is neither *my* cause nor *yours,* but *our* cause. I have only room to express my unfeigned prayer that your kind wishes for me may be returned manifold into your own bosom.

Your brother in the hope of immortality,
EDITOR.

OHIO, JULY 26, 1826.
To the Editor of the Christian Baptist.

DEAR SIR,—You will, no doubt, be surprised at receiving a letter from a boy; and one who is entirely unknown to you;—nothing but considerations of the deepest interest to myself, could have induced me to address you in this manner: I do it to obtain information from you on the subject of *christianity;* and I anxiously hope, if time will permit you, that you will have the kindness to comply with my request. That you may understand my case rightly, I will state it as fully and clearly as I can.

Impelled by the death-bed injunctions of a beloved mother, and the necessity I saw for living a religious life, I seriously determined on leaving my evil habits, while young, and endeavoring to have religion firmly seated in my heart; fearful that if I deferred it until a later period of life, vice might attract my affections, and I would end my life in sorrow; I therefore strove against any improper desires; avoided bad company and bad books; read my bible and such books as I thought beneficial; attended public worship; and sought for divine aid in private devotion. I had been irresistibly led on, by the importance of religion, in my endeavors to attain it, although I had never experienced one feeling of repentance. This made me unhappy. I saw some rejoicing in religion, who had once trembled in despair; I envied their feelings, but could not enjoy them; a coldness and apathy made me insensible to both the threatenings and promises of the gospel; all my endeavors to shake off this lethargy from my mind, were either unavailing, or if successful, it was but for a moment—despair, or any thing to have excited my feelings, would have been a relief from this unhappy situation of mind. I at last concluded to avail myself of the advice and encouragement of the pious. I had examined the principles of several sects, and settled in a preference of the Methodist church, of which I became a member. I had continued in that for nearly a year, seeking the Divine favor and anxiously desiring that my stubborn heart might be changed; but still I remained unrelieved. I was not alarmed for my safety—nor was I panting for the river of life; but yet, was most anxious that I should be. I now began to conclude there was some radical defect in the grounds of my faith, and determined to look again at the evidences by which the bible was supported as a revelation from heaven. While reflecting one day on the subject of the truth of revealed religion, a thought occurred to me with peculiar force, it was, Whether the Deity would have created any being and placed him in such a situation in which it was possible for him to make himself deserving of eternal torment. My view of the character of Deity induced me to believe he would not; and from this I was led strongly to doubt the divinity of the bible. From further reflections on the prescience of Deity, many considerations of like nature were urged upon my mind. I thought that as the greatest degree of happiness was the only object of creation, the design of the Almighty would have failed, if, as the scriptures authorize us to believe, a majority of mankind will be forever damned; that his goodness would not have rested the decision of such an inconceivably important question, with so weak and corrupt a being as man, and who was, moreover, placed in circumstances which so strangely nourished a distaste for the duties which the bible enjoins. I thought that as the Deity was the *first cause* of all things, he was responsible for all things, especially for *evil,* as he possessed a greater power to prevent it than the immediate cause, and if so, he could not punish any of his creatures with eternal misery; that if man was accountable for his actions to the awful extent mentioned in the bible, free will would be a curse instead of a blessing; that if our Maker was ALMIGHTY he could have created universal happiness, and to this end I conceived every thing in nature had a direct tendency—I could reconcile the evils we felt here, as necessary to our peculiar state of existence; but could not satisfy myself of the necessity or justice of *God's* punishing a being, eternally, for the effects of a weakness in which he was born. Punishment, I thought, should be proportioned to criminality: but in inflicting eternal punishment for temporal crimes, this principle of justice is violated. Could the God of compassion have sat on his throne of untroubled felicity, whilst a being whom he had called into existence, who would never have been *liable* to pain but for him, was enduring the pains of hell fire! And besides these it appeared to me inconsistent with the Deity to require from us, *on pain of damnation* if we failed, implicit belief in an account of transactions which occurred several thousand years ago, (and considering the imperfect medium through which information was communicated from one age to another,) and of which it required the utmost stretch of intelligence to comprehend even the probability. I have thought that if there is a place of reward and punishment, my destiny is foreseen by the Omniscient eye, and nothing which I can do, will alter it.

If these thoughts are correct, I will be obliged to abandon the book I was taught to love, and the profession I felt bound to make; I must draw down upon my head both the pity and the censure of society, and the tears of afflicted friends. If they are erroneous, I beg you to explain them, for my satisfaction, as soon as it is convenient for you to attend to it. If convinced of the truth of the Bible, I feel desirous to take up the cross and bear the burden and heat of the day. More than myself may be benefited by an answer to this.—And I shall ever remain

Your grateful friend,   D.

Replication.—No. 1.

DEAR SIR,—ALTHOUGH I saw the word "private" at the head of your communication, I have made it public in one sense. I shall however, keep it private as far as respects the author until the injunction is removed. The reason why I give publicity to a private letter is, because it may be of much use to others, and can be of no injury to the author, while the injunction is virtually regarded by me. I conceive the difficulties, however you may have been entrammelled with them, as not peculiarly your own, and whether I may succeed in removing them, I doubt not but the very effort may be of general use. I can easily conceive of your difficulties before you joined, and while you were in connexion with the Methodistic society. You were too rational to become a downright enthusiast, and not rational enough to begin at the right place in examining the evidences of the christian religion. You are not to imagine that I suppose that all Methodists are enthusiasts, very far from it. I would be glad, however, that there were no Calvinistic enthusiasts. But I know there are many "seeking for religion" who find a sort of religion that does not wear well; a whole suit of it will become thread-bare in a few months. I have seen the elbows looking out of some new suits in less than the regular wear of seven days. I know also that there is a possibility of keeping a suit of this sort decent for a good while; but then it must be worn only on Sundays, and only while at meeting. It must be hung up in the wardrobe all week and brushed on Sunday morning in time for meeting.

But I have said that you were too rational to become an enthusiast. Weak minds, like gun powder, are easily blown up. And like phosphorus some of them take fire without a single spark. Animal heat alone has set a housefull all in a blaze: but it was an innocent sort of a flame, it did not singe a single hair—The smell of fire was not left on them.

The method of teaching those "who seek for religion" among the Methodists is no better than that practised by other religious sectaries. The New Testament is not, neither can it be developed on any such a system. The Divine attestations to the truth of christianity, the miracles and the prophecies, with all the thousands of internal evidences are not opened to the minds of the hearers. Hence there is more religion in the blood than in the heart or head of those who begin in the flesh and think to end in the spirit.

But I cannot see how your difficulties could make you a Deist. This would be a most irrational conclusion. I can easily see how you might become an Universalist; but there is no connexion between your difficulties and Deism. Do you ask me, why? I will tell you: your difficulties never could have existed but for the belief of the truths revealed in the bible—Do you say, *what truths?* I answer, you believe,

1st. That there is one self existent independent eternal God.

2d. That the world was created by Him.

3d. That you have within you an immortal spirit.

4th. That there will be an end or termination of this present state of things.

5th. That there will be a future state of rewards, if not of punishments.

You admit all these to be unquestionable truths. I ask; upon what evidence? Not by the testimony of your five senses—for they give no revelation of this kind; all they can tell you is that all nature concurs in attesting these truths. But, remember well, they do not originate in your mind these truths—else all nations, all tribes and tongues would be in possession of them, which you know, if you know any thing of history, is not at all the fact. All the ideas you have by the five senses are the mere images of sensible objects, or objects of sense; but on subjects that are not objects of sense they give you no information. Hence the deaf know nothing of sounds—Hence the blind know nothing of colors. The reason is, the other senses give no information of any kind but what belongs to them, consequently all the senses are limited by things material and mundane; consequently can give no information on things spiritual, such as God, human spirits, heaven, &c. These truths then, however Deists may boast, are all borrowed from the bible. Hence there is not a rational Deist in the universe. Of this subject I am master; if of no other. I have, therefore, found them skulking off into Egypt or Hindostan and calling upon the mountains and hills to cover them, when they have been sensibly attacked upon the principles of reason which they so unmeritoriously glory in. They are the poorest drivelling philosophers that ever assumed the name. And, like lord Herbert, while they declaim against enthusiasm, they are the veriest enthusiasts. For they pretend to hold principles which have no foundation at all, which is sublimated enthusiasm. They boast in the belief of one God, of the immortality of the soul, and a future state—but ask them, how they came by it, they will tell you, *by the use of their reason!* Reasoning on what? the things that are made—but who made them? Thus it goes in a circle; they prove that there is a creator, from the things created; and they prove that things are created, because there is a creator. Sagacious doctors! But pray, good doctors, where is the archetype or original of a human spirit from which you were put in possession of the idea, where did you see any thing created by a mere exertion of Almighty power? Tell me, why cannot the dumb speak, who have tongues? because they have no archetype of sounds! Are not all our simple ideas the result of sensation and reflection! And how is it that you can see things which are invisible, and hear sounds which are made beyond the regions of air!

But I have not to do with a sceptic in the truth of revelation: for you, my friend, do admit of many revealed truths—Truths too which are supernatural, which are spiritual; truths which no man without a revelation, either oral or written, ever knew. Either Atheism, unqualified Atheism, or faith in Jesus as the Son of God are the legitimate stopping places on the principles of sound reason and good logic. All that halt between these extremes, are besotted with a brutish stupidity. The ox and the ass are their reprovers.

Nor can you rationally, from your statement of difficulties become an Universalist. If one point were conceded to you perhaps you might. But then this is a point which no man can ever concede as a man. I can sympathize with you here, because I was once embarrassed between this Scylla and Charybdis. I shall first state your capital difficulty, and then this point. Your capital difficulty is, "Whether the Deity would have created any being, and placed him in such a situation, in which it was possible for him to make himself deserving of eternal torment." This difficulty arose in your mind, as you state, from your views of the character of Deity. Now the question is, whether a being perfectly righteous himself; suppose for example, a seraph of greater capacity than you, and of uncontaminated purity, might not, from his view of the Divine character, find a greater difficulty to reconcile than yours, upon the hypothesis that God rewarded the wicked with endless felicity: or in other words, that he should originate a system in which it was possible for any rational creature to become corrupt, and yet this corruption be no barrier in the way of his rising to eternal glory and felicity. You will readily perceive that this *supposed* difficulty of a seraph, and your *real* difficulty, have to encounter one and the same fact, viz. that God has created rational beings which some way or another have become corrupt. This you must admit or identify virtue and vice, truth and falsehood, benevolence and malevolence, in one word, moral good and moral evil—We all know that, to a criminal, mercy is the most darling attribute in his judge: but to a sinless being, justice, inflexible justice, is the most delightful perfection. And here another question arises, whether the government of God (for God is a governor as well as a creator) should be conducted on such principles as to meet the difficulties of those creatures lowest in intellect and immersed in crime; or the difficulties of those most exalted in capacity and of unsullied purity.

But this question is out of my way, for this is not the point to which I had reference. We all know from experience that a system of government which is based upon rewards and punishments is the most beneficial to the present state of society. Now it must be decided, before we proceed to your difficulty as a real one; whether future rewards and punishments may not be most beneficial to the future state of society. But if this question is to be decided without our observation and experience it must be decided upon mere theory, and such a decision, we know from experience, is, until tested by experience, unsafe. But your difficulty rests upon what is not proved to be a fact, and which cannot by any mortal man be proved to be a fact, viz. that punishment will not be beneficial to society in a future state. Your difficulty then is a purely theoretic one, and not one predicated upon any known fact. Consequently can be of no real importance in deciding either upon the evidences of revelation nor upon its meaning.

But still I am not come to the point which I had proposed. I will now state it. For the sake of argument, then, I will admit that before any creature was made, the result, or final termination of all things, on the present plan of things, was as perfectly well known to the Creator as it will be in any future period, and also that any other possible result on any other plan, was just as well known. The question then was with the Creator, if we dare suppose him either in deliberation, or in suspense on the question, which plan was best to adopt; which plan of creation shall I adopt. If any, the plan which was actually adopted, as the fact proves. But it might have been proposed as a difficulty, if the plan adopted, with perfect prescience, was the best which possibly could be adopted, then a final question

might occur, whether it was better to create or not to create, admitting the result to have been clearly foreseen? The fact proves that to the Omniscient One it appeared most advisable to create. Now you will observe upon the premises before us that it is conceded that the actual state of things now existing was the best possible state in which they could exist with a reference to all final results. It may, then, in the spirit of true devotion, and genuine humility be affirmed that God *could not*, with a reference to all final results, give birth to a more perfect system of things than the present. In other words, God could not make an infallible fallible creature. Now before your difficulty becomes too heavy for the strength of an ordinary mind, it must be proved that God could have given birth to a system in which moral evil could find no place, and in which there would be no need of a governor, and that he did not. But no living man can show that this is the fact, consequently your difficulty is one in which imagination is solely or chiefly concerned, and not reason nor fact. It must then be conceded that God could, in reference to all results, have given birth to a better system, or to one in which moral evil could have no place, and that he did not, before you have any grounds on which to constitute a plea. Again, such a system would have forever precluded the possibility of any creature being happy: because the knowledge of God is essential to the happiness of a rational creature, and if God had given birth to a system which in its very nature excluded the possibility of evil, it would have also excluded the possibility of his being a governor. A creator he might have been, but a governor he could not have been; and unless exhibited as a governor, no rational creature ever could have known him in that way essential to happiness. These principles being apprehended: it follows, that if God had not given birth to a system in which it was possible for some to be miserable hereafter, it would have been impossible to have given birth to a system in which any could have been eternally and perfectly happy.

I am decidedly of the opinion that there is not one rational objection can be adduced against any thing in the Bible. All those objections which have a show of reason are but evidences of the weakness of the objector, and of the influence of prejudice and evil habits. It is very hard to convince a person against his will, and it requires no great ingenuity to propose such difficulties upon any subject as no wise man could answer. Yet this will not prove that the difficulties or objections are reasonable. It only shows that no man knows every thing—It may be necessary for me to state that I do not conceive that you are actuated by any other than the most sincere intentions in your communication, and that I feel a sanguine hope of being able to remove your objections; for I feel as able to prove that the Bible is from God, as that the sun is the workmanship of his hands. A sceptic might as successfully attempt to convince me that men made the sun, as that they invented the Bible.

I will hear any other difficulties you have to propose, when I shall have finished my reply to your communication before me, which I intend to prosecute farther in my next.

Your obedient servant,   Editor.

In a straggling number of the Baptist Recorder, which is dated May 27; but came to hands only a few days ago—I perceive the editors of that Journal have virtually declined the discussion proposed on the subject of "experimental religion." It appears their papers are either mis-sent to me, directed to Buffaloe, Mason Co. Va. instead of Brooke Co. or else not regularly mail-ed at the time of publication. The following re-marks, in the aforesaid number, show how the subject is evaded.

"As to the proposed plan for a discussion of this subject we would say to the Editor—Dear Sir, what need is there for the discussion of this subject? Is it not as yet understood? Has not God taught every christian by his Spirit to know the import of the thing signified by the term? But if the discussion be deemed necessary, will it not be best in the first place, to ascertain wherein we differ, and in what we agree? In order to this we will propose a few questions—we do it in the spirit of christian love, not with the intention to produce debate and altercation.

1. "Will you be so kind as to tell us your own experience? You have read Bunyan—you have heard experiences related in the church, by candidates for admission—you know our mean-ing.

2. "Do you, or do you not hear the experiences of persons before you baptise them.

3. "And since you know what the Baptists mean when they speak of experimental religion, will you be so kind as to tell us, whether accor-ding to the known and common acceptation of the term, you agree with them or not? If you do not agree with them, please to inform us in what respects you differ and the reasons why.

"A candid, honest answer to these interroga-tions is very desirable; it may at once remove the necessity of a further discussion. We design to give you "fair play"—if in any thing your ideas have been misrepresented by us, we hold ourselves responsible for the correction, when informed of it. We present your views entire—by copying the above into your paper you will reciprocate the favor.

"Wishing you health of body and experi-mental religion in the heart,
            We subscribe ourselves yours, &c.
                                THE EDITORS."

—

So I must tell Messrs. Waller and Clack my "experience," which the three past volumes of the C. B. would not hold, before they will enter on the discussion. In the next place I must in-form them in what manner I baptize, as prepar-atory. And, in the third place, I must argue their side for them, and my own side too.—Their method of getting off from the discussion reminds me of a priest and a layman who once agreed to arbitrate a question on which they differed. The layman, confident that he would have a decision in his favor, agreed that any three men might be chosen by the priest. Whereupon the priest chose Abraham, Isaac and Jacob, and referred the case to their decision. In this way the matter was postponed *sine die*.

The objection which these gentlemen offer against the discussion should, (were they to act consistently) lead them to be silent on every top-ic of the christian religion, viz.—"Has not God taught every christian by his Spirit the import of the thing signified by the term?" Why then, Messrs. Editors, do you presume to teach them any thing, since the spirit teaches them every thing? Again, if I must yet tell these brethren wherein we differ, why did they pretend to tell others how heterodox I am. This would be a **work** of supererogation.

                                EDITOR.

———

No. 3.]   OCTOBER 2, 1826.

To Mr. D.—A Sceptic.—Replication.—No. II.

DEAR SIR:—I HAVE, as you see, affixed the ep-ithet *sceptic* to your address. I mean no censure or reproach in so using this term. You are, in one sense of the term, a sceptic; you are incred-ulous and distrustful in the christian religion; but you tell us your difficulties. You say, like Thomas, unless I see so and so, I will not believe. Thomas, however, wanted evidence to establish a certain fact, without distrusting any sentence or sentiment in the ancient revelations. Your scepticism is founded upon imaginary difficul-ties; or rather by some ill directed genius you would make a lever and a fulcrum of imaginary difficulties, by which you would hurl either the bible or hell out of the universe. You would like a bible that had no hell in it; a bible that made men deserving of eternal happiness, because they were incapable of being made deserving of eternal misery. But to proceed—

In my last I paid some attention to your first great difficulty. Such remarks were made upon it as, I conceive, prove it to be an unreasonable difficulty. One in which imagination, wild and uncontrolled, was wholly concerned, and in which reason has nothing to do. I now pro-ceed to consider the next sentence in your let-ter. It is this:—"my view of the character of Deity induced me to believe he would not (have created any being, and placed him in such a situation in which it was possible for him to make himself deserving of eternal torment,) and from this I was led strongly to doubt the Divin-ity of the bible." In this sentence you proceed upon a principle which is inadmissible. You represent yourself as having certain views of the character of Deity so independent of the bible, as that you are constrained rather to reject the bible than your "views of the character of De-ity!" Your views of the character of Deity are not then derived from the bible; for it would be absurd, as you will admit, for a per-son who derived all the light he ever enjoyed from the sun, to say, that his views of light were such as to induce him to believe that the sun could not be the fountain of it, be-cause it was not clearer, without intermission, or omnipresent, &c. &c. Your views then of the character of Deity are so correct, that rather than abandon them you would abandon the bible. You doubt the divinity of the bible because, as you understand it, it opposes or clashes with your views of the Divine character. Very well, indeed! In my last I demonstrated in part that you could not know that there is but one self-existent, independent and eternal God, but from the bible. But here you advance one step far-ther than even lord Herbert, who, by seeing one miracle, was enabled to disbelieve all miracles! You have got a character of Deity some where that annihilates the divinity of the bible. Tell me, my friend, where did you obtain this char-acter? From the exercise of your five senses, which some call the exercise of your reason. Your five senses must be many millions of times more acute and penetrating than mine. One glance of your eye scales not only the summit of Chim-borazo, but the loftiest gem that sparkles on the summit of Mount Zion. Nay, it surveys the com-et's flight, and pierces down to the chambers of Leviathan in the depths of ocean, and thence draw a character of Deity. Your ear discriminates the winds that whistle on the peaks of the planet Jupiter, from those that roar on the cliffs of the Georgium Sidus. And so with all your senses.

But tell me gravely, if your senses are not better than mine, how you came by this divine character. Just from what has presented itself to you in the township in which you were born, and in which you live, in the state of Ohio.—A sublime character for the Deity it must be, which you could manufacture from the township of ———, in the state of ———, by working your five senses under the guidance of reason for twenty years. Yet it is so finished that you would prefer it to all the bible reveals. Nay, you would rather deny the divinity of the bible than abandon *your views* of the character of Deity!

I shall try what sort of a character I could form of Deity from my five senses controlled by reason, after I was told that there is but one God. I suppose myself in the possession of the truth that there is but one God, without ever hearing a word of a single attribute he possessed, and then I set about to form a character for him; or, which is the same thing, to endeavor by the exercise of my five senses on the things around me, guided my reason, to attain correct views of his character.

I began my enquiries on the first of April, 1800, when I was five years old. That morning I was told for the first time there was a God who made all things. What sort of a being he was nobody would tell me. I went to work to find him out. I was told he had made all things; but not knowing how long since, I could not tell any thing about him from the things made, because I could not tell how much they might have been changed since he made them. I stumbled at the threshold and fell into despair just at the beginning of my enquiries. I went back to my guide and told him he must tell me one item more before I could learn any thing about this one God.—But before I thought, I had proposed a dozen of questions. Where did he live? Did he concern himself any more with the world after he made it? Has he committed it to other agents? Who are they? Is the sun one, the moon another, the winds a third, the clouds a fourth? Has he done creating yet? Does he not make more water, more wind, more earth, more animals, &c. &c. &c. Thus I had thronged upon the ear of my preceptor a score of questions. He replied, I told you there is one God who made all things, and that is enough to introduce him to your acquaintance, if you reason right; but as you are a little stupid, I will tell you that he made all things six thousand years ago, and still governs them; but I will tell you no more until you have found out his character yourself. I made a second effort. By the end of April, I had seen the peach-trees and the apple-trees all in blossom, and the young fruit, of which I was very fond, began to exhibit itself as the blossoms fell off. But up came the north wind one night and something called frost came behind it, and in one night all the fruit was destroyed. I looked with great fury in my eyes at this monstrous hard-hearted north wind which prostrated all my hopes. I blessed the south wind and cursed the north. But on reflection, said I, there is but one God, who made all things and governs all. Now he must have sent the south wind for these two weeks past, and cherished all these millions of blossoms, and then he must have sent up Mr. Boreas with his cold blasts and swept them all to ruin. Thought I, he is a very changeable and whimsical being this who puts himself to so much trouble to make young apples and peaches, and then, in a moment, or fit of passion, because I *lied* the other day, turn right round and destroy them every one; and how unjust he is to make all my brothers and sisters, my uncles and aunts to want apples and peaches a whole year because *I told a lie.* Enraged by my own reasonings, I ran to my cages, and nests of young birds, and found them all frozen to death. Thinks I, what a cruel God this is who has killed all these dear little innocent birds just because he got angry at me. I thought, the other day, he was very good, when every thing was blooming and smiling around me; but now he appears most whimsical, notionate, cruel, and unjust. I was going back to my informant with a score of new questions, but he frowned me from his presence, and said he would not tell me one word more: if I could not make out, for myself, a character for the Deity, said he, you must wait till you grow older and can reason better. So my enquiries stopped, and I settled down in the opinion that God was either not almighty; that winds and rains were stronger than he, or that he was the most notionate, irrational, and whimsical being in the universe: sometimes kind and sometimes cruel, as he pleased.

Early impressions and first views have a great influence upon the reasoning powers in subsequent life; and these first impressions of the character of Deity, drawn from the destruction of the apples and peaches, and the destruction of my young birds and chickens, remained for many years. If others could have reasoned better or had other data to reason upon, they might have come to different conclusions; but these were the best I could command. I began to read geography at the age of thirteen, and astronomy came in my way. When I read of different climates and their effects upon the human family, I thought that God was either not the wisest being, the most powerful, nor the most impartial. I thought if he made the whole earth he might have made it alike fertile, salubrious, and comfortable, if he had been omniscient and omnipotent. If he could and did not, I thought he was very partial and unjust, arbitrary and unreasonable.

"The frozen Icelander and the sunburn'd Moor," both told a strange story, and reflected much upon their Maker. I saw a good deal of order in the revolutions of the heavenly bodies: but I saw, or thought I saw, a good deal of disorder, of doing and undoing. Astronomers had told me that some stars had disappeared from the heavens, having been struck and consumed by blazing comets, and I began to fear that one of those comets might, in a fit of anger, strike our wooden country and burn it up. That if other stars had shone for thousands of years and were consumed, I could find no reason why our planet might not be subject to a similar fate, from some freak of a mad comet. And as the Deity allowed a system of destruction to follow up a system of providence and preservation, I could not tell but this was his darling pleasure to be always creating and always destroying. I read something in geography of different nations having different gods; gods of the hills and of the vallies, of the mountains and of the plains, of the seas and of the rivers, of the winds and of the other elements; and thought this explained many difficulties—I was just reconciling my difficulties growing out of the destruction of my apples and peaches and chickens, upon the hypothesis that there was a plurality of gods; that they had been quarrelling amongst themselves; that the god of the north wind had, in a rencontre, gained a triumph over the god of the south wind, &c. But while I was thus meditating, I opened a page in the travels of Curosus, who was describing an Asiatic islander carving a branch of the bread-tree into a little pocket God; which he was to invoke when he became hungry. This occurrence drove me into scepticism upon the doctrine of a plurality of gods: and so I resumed my early prepossessions in favor of but one God.

In the midst of my excursions in quest of the Divine character, I was struck dumb with an occurrence in my own neighborhood. I had been just concluding that God was *perhaps* a benevolent being, when I was told of the death of an idiot who had lived twenty years in idiotism and worn to a skeleton by epilepsy, while his brothers and sisters were all *compos mentis*, intelligent, healthy, and affluent. Thought I, this is a proof that God is partial and unreasonably cruel, for it had been a maxim with me that he that is unjust in a little is unjust, as well as he that is unjust in much: and if God could for twenty years thus punish one of a family and bless all the rest, I could neither tell what he was in himself or what he might or could do.

If I have reasoned wrong, it was the best I could reason on the data before me; and while I found others reasoning differently on the same data, and on different data, I was led to question whether there was any such thing as a reasonable being, and thus in attempting to find out by reason, a character for God, I was likely to find no character for man: but that he was a central point of contradictions.——So Inquisitas tells his story.

Now, my friend, your views of the divine character independent of the divinity of the bible, are not worth one grain of sand. And every system of scepticism founded upon the divine attributes, and of religion at variance with the bible facts, is a mere spider's web woven out of its own bowels, and designed only to catch flies.

I know our colleges are schools of scepticism, and that pure deism is taught in one department in every college in Europe and America, wherever natural religion is taught. But so much for your view of the divine character at present, on account of which you are compelled to reject the divinity of the bible. In this you resemble a child who says it would rather have the light of a glow-worm than that of the sun.

Your friend,   The Editor.

Ecclesiastical Tyranny.

I have had the pleasure and the pain of visiting three associations since writing our last number. To the first, viz. the Stillwater, Ohio, I went as a spectator. To the second, viz. the Mahoning, Ohio, I went as a messenger; and to the Redstone, Pennsylvania, I went as a corresponding messenger from the Mahoning. My visit to the Stillwater and Mahoning associations was altogether agreeable. There was no vain jangling about creeds and forms; no controversy about who should be pope and cardinals. There was no interference with the inalienable rights, nor encroachment upon the liberties of the brethren, considered as individuals or as congregations. All was harmony and peace. I never witnessed greater harmony or more brotherly love at any public meeting than at these two meetings, especially the latter. I returned home edified and refreshed. After the respite of a day, I set out for the Redstone. As I approached its horizon, the sky began to gather blackness, the reverberation of distant thunders and the reflected glare of forked lightnings from

the regions of the Laurel Hill portended a tremendous war of elements, if not a crash of worlds. Three clouds of ominous aspect surcharged with wind, one from the east, one from the north and one from the south, seemed to concentrate not far from the Old Fortification. As they approximated towards each other, they rolled out great volumes of hydrogen gas, which ignited by some electric sparks, exhibited a frightful aspect, and seemed to threaten a fiery desolation, and to hurl ruin far and wide. But to our great and agreeable disappointment it eventuated in a mere explosion of wind, which injured no green nor living thing. It purified the air, and was succeeded by a grateful and cheering calm. After having stated these meteorological observations, I proceed to give a faithful description of the meeting itself. And that our readers may have the premises before them, I will state a few historic facts.

One man whom I will not name, in the true spirit of Diotrephes, has for at least fifteen years past, lorded over the faith of the whole association, or sought to do it. He was converted under the ministry of a Methodist, and became all at once a Methodistic preacher; and having burned out somewhere near the tropic of capricorn, the cinder was carried to the arctic circle, and became a Calvinistic Baptist, of the supralapsarian order. As is usually the case with men of little information and strong passions, when converted from one extreme they run into the opposite; so with this zealous divine. And as he was extremely lax in his faith in former times, he has bound himself with a seven fold cord never to have any communion with those who will not *say* they believe in the whole "*Philadelphia Confession of Faith.*" He forms a league with two others, offensive and defensive. One of them of no standing in church or state, and the other I know nothing about, save that he has a remarkable red face, and cannot speak only at times. I mean no insinuation against his moral character; for of this I know nothing. I choose to represent each of the triumvirate by their most remarkable traits; for I do not know that I shall ever write their names in this work. These three brothers combined their efforts for the last two years to carry one point: in plain English, that one of them should be Pope, and the other two his Cardinals, the one Cardinal of the Right, and the other Cardinal of the Left. The reason of this combination was, that for a few years past the two first had fallen into their proper ranks, and could not rise to any notice but in the cause of orthodoxy. Who that has his eyes open has not seen that men of the lowest intellect and of the lowest moral endowments are the most zealous in the cause of orthodoxy? and that the reason is, they are conscious that unless they can raise a clamor about orthodoxy they are likely to pass off the stage as they ought? I have always found those of the most orthodox scent the slowest in the race, and the loudest in the sound. The foremost hound makes the least noise about the course, but those hindmost are always sounding lo here! or lo there! Having given this faithful and honest introduction to these triumvirate which is as much too circumstantial, as it is too long, I proceed to the history of the manœuvre and intrigue by which they made themselves Pope and Cardinals.

The physical forces which they could bring into the "advisory council" they knew were inadequate to their object. For of twenty-three or twenty-four churches composing the association they were conscious that a majority would be against them. According to the constitution of the association each church could legally send three messengers which could have a seat and a vote in their resolves. After exploring the ground and doing every thing which could be done to increase their physical forces, it was found to amount to ten congregations; that is, they could not find *ten* whole congregations in the association to come into their views, but they could find a majority in their favor in the whole fractional parts of these ten churches. So that they were entitled to a representation of thirty voters. These thirty voters out of seventy-two which would have been a full representation of the whole association, have now to constitute themselves into the whole association. Orthodoxy must now lend its aid, and the good old constitution must be revived, though it has always been a dead letter; for not one association that ever met was regulated by it for two hours at a time. But in the constitution it is written that the churches in writing their letters shall refer to the *Philadelphia Confession of Faith*. They must make a bow to it *in limine*. This matter has been for years discussed in this association; and the more it has been examined the less it has been relished. The children in many places now see the absurdity of their fathers and mothers declaring their faith to be expressed in the Philadelphia Confession of Faith, which not one in ten of them ever saw; and not one in a hundred of them could understand if they did see it; and which not one church in America believes to be the system of truth taught in the holy scriptures; for some one chapter in it is rejected by every church in America. However, it will answer a good purpose to carry this point. So it was resolved by the triumvirate to cut off from thirty-six to forty-two voters, that the thirty above referred to might be the association. And so it came to pass; for soon as the letters were read, every one that did not mention the *Philadelphia Confession of Faith* was handed back to the messenger, and all the voters included in the letter were rejected from the list. So that thus, in direct violation of this *dead-and-alive constitution*, which says, "the letters when read shall be delivered to the moderator or clerk," the representatives of thirteen or fourteen churches were denied a seat and a vote in the association; and thus the friends of the would-be Pope and Cardinals have the association to themselves. Then the thirty voters appoint their own officers. One becomes a captain of twenty-nine individuals, and there is room for two under officers to preside over thirteen each. After having elected their own officers and invited only such of the strangers to a seat as would answer their views, they proceed to the greater excommunication, having by the lesser excommunication already despatched about the *three-fifths* of the whole body. And here I am constrained to say, that in all my own experience and reading I have found no parallel to the procedure of these thirty voters. No inquisitorial process was ever so *informal*, and none more shameless and remorseless. The only thing to which I could compare it was the tyranny of Robespierre during the reign of terror in the French revolution.

An instance or two must suffice:—The first church on the list to be given over to Satan was that in Washington. The guillotine was now erected and the instruments were all prepared for execution. The Pope and his two Cardinals in succession belabored this church for about one hour, calling them Arian, Socinian, Arminian, Antinomian, and every thing that is bad, because

they had in their letter refused to call any man Pope or Master on earth. Not one word were they allowed to say for themselves. They did not even ask the messengers of this church if they had any thing to say why the sentence of the law should not be executed upon them. By a species of what is sometimes called legerdemain, or, in the Welsh dialect, *hocus pocus*, one messenger, or perhaps two, had been introduced to a seat out of the forty-two excluded voters, before this case of the Washington church came to judgment. One of these messengers attempted to call a halt to their procedure, but it was all in vain. The church was doomed to destruction, and a majority of thirty hands lifted up to heaven gave their head to the guillotine and their mortal remains to Satan. Next was brought up to trial Maple Creek Church, with its good old Bishop, Henry Spears. The good old man mounts the scaffold with a serene countenance, and after the triumvirate had shed a few crocodile tears over the old man and his church, whom they said they loved as their own souls, and against whose faith they had not one objection, save they had omitted to mention these words, "*Philadelphia Confession of Faith*." I say, out of a flow of unusual clemency they asked the good old man if he had any thing to say why he should not be beheaded and his carcase given over to Satan. He mildly having answered in the negative, the signal was given and he was despatched without a groan. Next came the venerable old Matthias Luse and his church on Pigeon Creek. In addition to the crime of not having mentioned the "Philadelphia Confession of Faith," it was alleged by the Cardinal of the Left Wing that they had been guilty of contumacy and unofficer-like conduct. This gave rise to a long debate whether they should be executed for a sin of omission or commission, which was finally decided in favor of the former. Old Matthias made no confession at the stake, but died like a sheep. At this time I stood in need of some fresh air and made my way out of the crowd. I next attended the funeral of the martyrs, and appeared no more in the presence of the sanhedrim. While I was engaged in carrying off the slain, having occasion to come nigh the guillotine, I heard the last groans of the Somerset church.

In the meantime, I found it convenient to retire from the premises, not knowing but by some arbitrary stretch of power I might be put to death; and so I mounted my horse, and escaped out of their hands. What was done during the night I cannot tell; but so far as I have narrated I pledge myself for the truth substantially of all that I have stated upon the evidence of my own senses.

While I confess myself very doubtful of all those meetings called associations, conventions, conferences, &c. which view themselves either as a church representative, or as representatives of churches, I willingly own that the misdemeanors of these thirty voters are not to be charged to the account of, or preferred as objections against associations: for one reason; viz. they possessed not one attribute, but divested themselves of every feature, of a Baptist association. For example: suppose thirty members of congress should arrive at Washington city a few days before the others, and after several *night* meetings agree, that, as each newly elected member must produce, from the proper authority in his district, a letter, attesting him to be duly elected, they would reject, from a seat in that body, every member whose letter was not worded in the same set phrase, which they themselves had fixed upon as constitutional: I say, suppose that these thirty congress-men, after dismissing all the others, should proceed to call themselves *the Congress of the United States,* and to claim the rights, and profess to perform the duties, of that body; would any man in his senses call them such, or would he object to all or any meetings of congress, because thirty individuals had taken it into their heads to tyrannize over the nation? Not the system, but the men, in this case would become the proper subjects of reprehension. It is as nearly analogous to the case in hand, as any we can well imagine. I would not, then, attack all general or public meetings of messengers from christian communities, thro' the medium of such monstrous occurrences; nor lay to their charge the conduct of these modern religious knight errants. But as there are the leaders and the led in this, as in all similar occurrences; and as the led are perhaps conscientious in their votes, while the leaders cannot reasonably be thought to have any conscience about it, it may be necessary to ask a few questions designed to awaken them to reflection.

When your moderator prayed in the morning of this day of slaughter that you might "act in all your proceedings from unfeigned love to the Saviour, and the brethren, and with a single eye to the glory of God," did you say, Amen? If you did, were you in earnest? When he prayed that you "might be directed in all the proceedings of the day by the Holy Spirit," did you not remember that you had, the night before, determined on the course you would pursue? Did you ever think of the similarity of your proceedings in council to those of that Sanhedrim which condemned the Just One to the cursed tree? Did you act as a church representative, or as representatives of the consciences of your friends at home? By what law or rule in the testament, or in the Confession of Faith, did you pretend to excommunicate churches? From what did you excommunicate them? Do you think that their not *naming* "the Philadelphia Confession" will preclude their admission into heaven? And if your excommunication cannot affect their standing in the estimation of the Great King and the holy angels, how much is your excommunication worth? Will it degrade them in the estimation of men, or does it not degrade you? Do you not rank a refusal to acknowledge the Confession of Faith, with murder, adultery, and theft: inasmuch, as you affix as grievous a censure, and as heavy a punishment, to the one as the other? Do you not make a denial of the Bible and of your human creed equally criminal, and equally worthy of the greater excommunication? What assurance does it give either of the faith of a church or of an individual to say:—"We believe in the scriptures of the Old and New Testament, as they are explained and held forth in the Philadelphia Confession of Faith?" Does this Redstone patented form of a church letter, give any assurance at all, that the church is a christian church? Would not their saying or writing any thing else be just as good proof? What sort of a foundation for christian love is this: "We believe in the Bible as explained in the Confession of Faith?" To love for this sake, is it to love for Christ's sake? Do you think that the best way to save life is to cut off the head, to quench a flame by throwing oil upon it; or to reconcile the injured by adding to their grievances? Do you think that the Lord will thank you now, or smile upon you hereafter, for having declared that you will have no christian fellowship with those who own the same Lord, claim the same Spirit, worship the same God: hold the same faith, hope, and baptism with you, because they would neither bow the head, nor bend the knee, to your little Philadelphia Confession of Opinions? Do you think your consciences will approve it when you come to die, and that you will glory in having done so in the day of Judgment? Lastly, would you not, and ought you not, was it in your power, according to your proceedings, to bolt the gates of heaven against those churches, and banish out of that kingdom all who will not subscribe your book of dogmas?

I do not think you either will or can answer these queries; but my desire is that you may from your inability to answer them, be brought to repentance before it be measured to you, as you have measured to others.　　EDITOR.

A New Association.

As I have been informed, the messengers of the non-conforming congregations agreed to go home, and report progress to the churches which sent them, and to propose to them to send messengers to Washington, Penn. on the Saturday preceding the second Lord's Day in November next; which churches, it is expected, will send persons duly empowered to act in the forming of a new association. As a majority of the non-conforming churches are in Washington county, the probability is, this new association will be called the Washington Association. It is also probable it will be constituted on more liberal principles than that which has imposed upon them the necessity of setting up for themselves. And here it may not be amiss to speak in *parables* to the wise; for to them similitudes are plain.

Parable of the Iron Bedstead.

In the days of Abecedarian Popes it was decreed that a good christian just measured three feet, and for the peace and happiness of the church it was ordained that an iron bedstead, with a wheel at one end and a knife at the other, should be placed at the threshold of the church, on which the christians should all be laid. This bedstead was just three feet in the casement on the exactest French scales. Every christian, in those days, was laid on this bedstead; if less than the standard, the wheel and a rope was applied to him to stretch him to it; if he was too tall, the knife was applied to his extremities. In this way they kept the good christians, for nearly a thousand years, all of one stature. Those to whom the knife or the wheel were applied either died in the preparation, or were brought to the saving standard.

One sturdy fellow, called Martin Luther, was born in those days, who grew to the enormous height of four feet: he of course feared the bedstead and the knife, and kept off at a considerable distance deliberating how he might escape. At length he proclaimed that there was a great mistake committed by his ancestors in fixing upon *three feet* as the proper standard of the stature of a good christian. He made proselytes to his opinions; for many who had been tried on the three-foot bedstead, who were actually *four feet*, had found a way of contracting themselves to the popular standard. These began to stretch themselves to their natural stature, and Luther had, in a few years, an iron bedstead *four feet* long, fashioned and fixed in his churches, with the usual appendages. The wheel and the knife soon found something to do in Luther's church; and it became as irksome to flesh and blood to

19

be stretched by a wheel and rope to four feet, or to be cut down to that stature, as it was to be forced either up or down to the good and sacred *three-foot* stature. Moreover, men grew much larger after Luther's time than before, and a considerable proportion of them advanced above his perfect man; insomuch that John Calvin found it expedient to order his iron bedstead to be made six inches longer, with the usual regulating appendages. The next generation found even Calvin's measure as unaccommodating as Luther's; and the Independents, in their greater wisdom and humanity, fixed their perfect christian at the enormous stature of *five feet*. The Baptists at this time began to think of constructing an iron bedstead to be in fashion with their neighbors, but kindly made it six inches longer than the Congregationalists, and dispensed with the knife, thinking that there was likely to be more need for two wheels than one knife, which they accordingly affixed to their apparatus. It was always found, that in the same proportion as the standard was lengthened, christians grew; and now the bedstead is actually proved to be at least six inches too short. It is now expected that six inches will be humanely added; but this will only be following up an evil precedent; for experience has proved, that as soon as the iron bedstead is lengthened, the people will grow apace, and it will be found too short even when extended to *six feet*. Why not, then, dispense with this piece of popish furniture in the church, and allow christians of every stature to meet at the same fireside and eat at the same table?—The parable is just, and the interpretation thereof easy and sure.

Every attempt at reformation since the rude but masculine efforts of Luther, has been based upon the same principles. He did not like the popish superstructure, notwithstanding he built upon the same foundation. So did all his successors. They all divided the New Testament into two chapters. The title of the one was, *the essentials*—and the title of the other was *the nonessentials*. In one party the one chapter, and in another party, the other, is much the larger. Still the volume comprizes but two chapters, however disproportioned they may be. Many efforts have been made to reduce the chapter of Essentials into narrower limits; but as it is reduced the other is enlarged, and the old division is kept up. The book called The Creed contains all the essentials; and as they are there correctly arranged and soundly digested, this book is more the subject of controversy than the Testament, which has the essentials and the non-essentials all jumbled together.

Suppose, then, that a number of churches should agree to throw aside the iron bedstead, and take the book in one chapter, and call it their Creed and Book of Discipline. What then? Oh! says Puritanus, Methodists, Presbyterians, Episcopalians, &c. &c. do this. Stop, my friend, not one of them dare trust themselves upon this bottom; they all have their creeds and disciplines to keep them from sinking. What then if an experiment should be made, and a fair trial of the adequacy of the Divine Book should be given; and whenever it fails of the promised end, let any other device be tried. But among all the experiments of this age and country, it is nowhere recorded that such a trial has been made and failed. I am aware of all that can be said on the other side, and still I assert that no such an experiment and result are on record. And moreover, I do not think it is likely that it shall ever be proved by actual experiment that the New Testa-

ment, without a creed, is insufficient to preserve the unity, peace, and purity of any one congregation, or of those of any given district. But above all, let us have no more iron bedsteads, with or without wheels or knives. EDITOR.

Review of Miller and Duncan.

DR. MILLER has resumed his pen against Mr. Duncan. His pamphlet is titled "A letter to a gentleman of Baltimore in reference to the Rev. Mr. Duncan, by Samuel Miller, D. D. Professor of Ecclesiastical history and church government in the Theological Seminary, at Princeton, N. J."

The following summary embraces the outlines of the whole pamphlet of 90 pages—

I. Reasons why D. Miller should not reply to Mr. Duncan's book. These are: 1st. An aversion to controversy—2d. The professional avocations of the Dr. were of too pressing a nature. 3d. That formerly he had resolved to have no controversy with Mr. Duncan. 4th. Because he saw no good end to be gained by the controversy. 5th. Because Mr. D's book required no answer. Yet, notwithstanding all these strong objections, the fact is the Doctor has taken up his pen, and is pledged by all that's manly, good, and fair, not to lay it down until convinced, confuted, or triumphant.

II. The second item in the Dr's book is six charges against Mr. D's book. These are: 1st. Mr. Duncan is contending without an adversary in all he says about the Bible as the one, only, sufficient, and infallible rule of christian faith and practice; and in all he says of the secular, ambitious, encroaching and tyrannical spirit of the clergy from A. D. 100, till A. D. 400, or to the council of Nice, also in his remarks on the corruptions and errors of the early ecclesiastical councils and creed makers—2d. That while Mr. D's premises are acknowledged by Dr. Miller, he dissents from him in the logical propriety of his conclusions. That is, the Dr. and Mr. Duncan agree in the premises, that there is but one infallible rule of faith and practice; but the Dr. thence infers we ought to have a fallible one, and Mr. Duncan very illogically concludes that we ought not—Concerning the primitive fathers and their councils Mr. Duncan and the Dr. agree; but Mr. D. infers their decisions and their creeds were like their makers; and Dr. Miller infers that a clean thing may and can come out of an unclean.—3d. His third charge against Mr. D's book is, that it proves too much for Mr. Duncan himself; that is, because Mr D. will have no human creed he ought to have no preachers nor commentators, &c. and the Dr. alleges that the arguments which prove no human creed, also prove no preachments nor expositions of scripture. This is equivalent to saying, If a person contend that men should be free, they ought, for the same reasons, to contend that men should be ignorant. 4th. A fourth charge against Mr. D's book is, that it no where tells how the important ends may be attained without creeds, which the Dr. contends are attained by them, such as uniformity in opinion, &c. 5th. His fifth charge is, that while Mr. D. contends against the unlawfulness of creeds, he allows the indispensable necessity of having a confession of faith himself—i. e. while he contends that men's consciences should not be enslaved by human creeds, he requires men to confess that they believe the gospel, &c. 6th. The Dr's sixth and last charge against this book is, that it is wholly irreconcilable with the constitution of any Presbyterian church.

After making out these six crimes against this guilty book, the Dr. proceeds to defend himself from the attacks of Mr. D. and to show that the concessions which Mr. Duncan found in the Dr's other works which subvert his own argument in favor of creeds, are not to be used in any other controversy than with an Episcopalian. That what the Doctor says when addressing Episcopalians is not to be remembered when he writes in defence of his own system—He next gives us his *opinion* of the judicial proceedings of the synod of Philadelphia in the case of Messrs. Duncan and M'Lean; which, indeed, is very flattering to the synod. Then he comes to discuss the question; whether creeds, if adopted, ought to contain any other than a few fundamental truths? He thinks they ought. To this item follows a vindication of Presbyterianism from the imputations of an ambitious, encroaching, tyrannical, and anti-American spirit. A question is then started whether Dr Miller's views of creeds are favorable to the circulation of the bible without note or comment, by the bible societies? That his views are favorable to such a circulation of the bible he would wish us to entertain; but in fact, as he afterwards states, the question is, "Whether the bible shall be circulated *without note or comment*: or not at all?" His answer is, that it would be better to have it "accompanied with an enlightened, perfectly orthodox and judicious commentary:" but if the bible cannot be accompanied with such a comment (which he thinks it could not yet awhile) he would prefer to see it circulated without note or comment *rather than not at all.* He concludes by an attempt to mitigate the evil of subscription to creeds, by showing that it is only the teachers of religion who must unequivocally subscribe to creeds as THE *system* of truth taught in the bible. It would be desirable that the laity were *orthodox* as well as pious; but for the present distress it will suffice if the clergy subscribe; for in that case there is a probability the laity may be kept orthodox.—Such are the outlines of Dr. Miller's defence. From all which it appears that in the Dr's opinion religious sects are still necessary, and creeds are necessary to keep them up; that Presbyterianism is just the identical religion of the New Testament, and that when the millennium commences all the christian world will become Presbyterians; that the tenets of this party will triumph over all other tenets, and be universally believed and obeyed—that the bible will be circulated yet for a little while without note or comment; but after a little it will be accompanied with the Westminster Creed, and Catechism, and Matthew Henry's notes, or some such orthodox and pious commentaries: and that then it will come to pass in religion, as it was before the project of the Free-Masons in the plains of Shinar of building a tower to reach to heaven, the earth will be all of one language and of one speech.   EDITOR.

To this "Letter to a Gentleman in Baltimore," Mr. Duncan has written a reply of 143 pages, duodecimo. This reply is divided into six sections, with prefatory remarks and a general conclusion. In the first section Mr. D. gives his reasons for not following step by step the arrangement Dr. M. was pleased to make in his lecture; and very mildly calls the Doctor to an account for a number of unwarrantable assertions which he was pleased to make in his "Letter to a gentleman in Baltimore." The victory gained over Dr. Miller in this first section is chiefly embraced in the following items:—1. Dr. M. had, in his lecture on the utility of creeds, asserted that

"the experience of *all ages* has found creeds indispensably necessary." This position he asserts in his letter was unassailed by Mr. D. or, at least, was left in all its force. By an induction of historical evidence which is irrefragable, Mr. D. had shewn before, and again shews, that no such experience exists; and that the age or *ages* anterior to the Council of Nice had no such instruments; that "human creeds" and "scholastic theology" are the creatures of ecclesiastical power, and the offspring of a degenerate age. Dr. M. is manifestly foiled in this point; for having asserted that the experience of *all* ages had found creeds indispensably necessary, it behoved him to shew that they were in use in the primitive age and in the ages anterior to the Council of Nice. His failure in this instance makes his assertion not worth a goosequill. And their being of indispensable utility in keeping up popery, prelacy, or presbyterianism, or any sect, so far from being an argument in their favor, is, in my humble opinion, just the reverse. Dr. M. fails as much in the hands of Mr. Duncan in making out the following position, as in the instance just mentioned, viz. "Human creeds are friendly to the study of christian doctrine, and, of course, to the prevalence of christian knowledge." This position is fairly demolished both by reason and fact.

Mr. D. remarks, page 13, "Creeds are considered as unfriendly to the acquisition of christian knowledge, because they take divine truth out of its biblical connexions; throw it into scholastic forms; substitute abstract propositions, as disputable as they are philosophical, for plain practical law, and interfere with the varied operations of different minds, by forcing a unity of sentiment at the expense of free inquiry. This view of creeds, which every man may see exemplified in the controversies of the present day, was traced up to the same degenerate ages, when scholastic theology, as correlative with ecclesiastical power, was introduced as another active cause, creating the *indispensable necessity* for these instruments. Thus history, instead of passing any eulogy upon their power to extend spiritual erudition, proclaims them from the first to have been mere tests of philosophy, and therefore the ministers of strife and controversy. Such they have always been, and such they are now."

Mr. D. is never more successful than when he fights Dr. M. with his own weapons. Most unfortunately for the Dr. he had once a controversy with the Episcopalians in a series of "Letters;" and as the prelatists argued in favor of their establishment from the primitive fathers, ancient councils, canons and creeds, the Doctor was obliged to storm their citadel, and in doing this he came out in favor of the *bible alone.* Here I must give Dr. Miller's own words, as quoted by Mr. Duncan. Mr. D. in addition to the quotations in his former "Book on the Unlawfulness of Creeds," adds as follows, page 16.

"In the "Letters" he (Dr. M.) speaks of the bible *alone*—of the word of God as being the *sole standard*—of the traditions and inventions of men as *not* to be *followed*—of our having but *one master*, even Christ; of our obligation to call no man or body of men masters, on earth, &c. *i. e.* I supposed him to be maintaining, in all its integrity, his argument against the Episcopalians—that it was death to any cause which could not be sustained by the bible *alone.* To quote some new extracts: Thus he smiles at a prelatical concession: "In other words, they confess that the scriptures taken *absolutely alone*, will not bear them out in their claims. But they suppose, and insist, that the

21

facts which are mentioned in the sacred history, *taken in connexion* with the writings of the *early fathers,* decidedly support this claim. That is, the New Testament, in its own divine simplicity, is insufficient for their purpose; but *explained,* and *aided,* by the writings of fallible men, it declares positively in their favor. Is it so?—What is this but saying, that the bible is not a rule either perfect or sufficient for the church? What is this but embracing a principle which makes human testimony co-ordinate with that of God; and which must involve us in all the mazes and uncertainty of tradition." Thus also he quotes the declaration of the celebrated *Chillingworth* with great commendation:—" I, for my part, after a long, and I verily hope and believe, impartial search of the true way to eternal happiness, do profess plainly, that I cannot find any rest for the sole of my feet, but upon this rock only, viz. the *Scriptures.* I see plainly, and with my own eyes, councils against councils; some fathers against other fathers; the same fathers against themselves; a consent of fathers of one age against the consent of fathers of another age; and the church of one age against the church of another age." " But it is needless," continues Dr. M. "to multiply reasonings, or authorities on this subject. The sufficiency and infallibility of the scriptures *alone,* as a rule of faith and practice, was assumed as the grand principle of the reformation from popery, and is acknowledged to be the foundation of the protestant cause."

These principles and observations of Dr. M. in his argument with the Episcopalians, are just as forcible against himself when they come from the pen of Mr. D. So that if Dr. M. in this way triumphed over the prelates, Mr. D. triumphs over him by his own words. In the first section of Mr. D's reply these points are obviously gained, together with others of minor importance; so that in the first rencounter he has actually got within the intrenchments of his antagonist.

In the second section he advances towards the pavillion of the general himself. I would gladly be more copious in my extracts here, but my limits confine me to the following:—

Page 21. " In continuing his objections, Dr. M. says—" A still more remarkable charge to which Mr. D's book is liable, is, that while he maintains, with so much zeal and vehemence, the unlawfulness of all creeds and confessions, he distinctly allows the indispensable necessity of having a confession of faith, and confesses that he has, and employs one himself." I beg leave very respectfully, to say, that the charge is most remarkable; so much so, that it is far from being *correct.* One of the necessary qualities of a good controvertist is, that he should carefully endeavor to understand his opponent; and most scrupulously avoid misrepresenting words, or phrases, or sentences, which it would require some ingenuity to misunderstand. I did not condemn *all* creeds, taking the term *creed* in its literal sense; but I did condemn all creeds, taking the term *creed* in its ecclesiastical sense, *i. e.* as expressing a rule of faith and manners, composed, authorized and *enforced* by a voluntary association: I did not confess that I employed a creed, in the ecclesiastical sense of that term; but did confess that I had one, in the literal sense of the term; and admitted that every man must have one, as far as he has investigated, to his own satisfaction, any set of subjects which may be proposed to his belief. It is difficult to perceive how my meaning could have been mistaken, or not be grieved by the use of such unfair artifice in argument."

The burthen of this section is the explanation of the position "that every real christian has a creed," and to contradistinguish this from the documents in question, from ecclesiastic creeds, and authoritative terms of communion. The pernicious influence of these human creeds is clearly developed in this section, and towards the conclusion of it the case is forcibly stated in the following words, with which we shall conclude at present.

Page 33. " Now, if the church cannot live simply with her Bible, but flourish with her creed —if the Bible affords no effectual guard against the inroads of heresy, while a creed does—if the privileges of the ministry are to be determined, not by the Bible, but by a creed—then is not the one practically put in the place of the other? Is not one practically better than the other, insomuch as it does what the other cannot do? In short, is it not the supposed practical usefulness of creeds, which has obtained for them all the labored eulogy they have received?"

Star of the South.

A PAPER under the above title has recently appeared in Milledgeville, Georgia. This is one of the luminaries of the day, just adapted for the relaxing influence of a southern climate; for the editor is busily employed in relaxing the sanctions of the gospel. He has reasoned himself into the belief that all men will be saved, and is now employed in teaching the readers of his paper that no man will be punished in hell. So that the murderer and the saint shall ultimately enjoy the same eternal felicity. So that all the threatenings of the Living God are empty sounds, and they that reform, and they that reform not, shall be equal in the enjoyment of the same felicity. By a telescope of prodigious power this rational editor has descried Paul and Nero, Elijah and Jezebel, Caiaphas and John—Herod and the Baptist, all standing in a glorious group before the throne of God. He sees Death and Hades cast into the lake of fire, and passing thence to Heaven—with many other rare sights.

He has also discovered that " it is a violation of the directions of the Saviour for any one to pray in *public;* to pray to any being but the Father; to pray for any thing except *bread,* for the forgiveness of sins, and deliverance from evil."!! So that all the apostles have seduced mankind both by precept and example, by teaching them to pray for every thing which they wanted; and especially in teaching them to pray for one another. When Paul prayed repeatedly for the saints, and for so many favors for them, "he violated the directions of the Saviour."— What strange light does this Southern Star afford! Should it mingle its rays with the Middle and Northern Stars, what a blaze of light will shine upon these states!!!   EDITOR.

The New Testament.

SOME of the priests in Ohio, who pretend to great erudition, have raised an evil report against Campbell's translation of the four gospels, giving out that Dr. Campbell was a Socinian, and the head of a faction of this stamp in the Kirk of Scotland. This is a gratuitous slander. Such a charge was never before exhibited against Dr. George Campbell. Another person named Campbell did, half a century before Dr. Campbell's translation was published, raise some noise in the Kirk of Scotland about Socinianism. If the above slander was not invented by its author in

Ohio, he should have known better than to have confounded two persons so essentially dissimilar in views—especially in a matter so important. I am not sure but that the same gentleman will be sorry to find that he was mistaken; for generally they who propagate an evil report wish it to be true.   EDITOR.

No. 4.]   NOVEMBER 6, 1826.

To Mr. D.—A Sceptic.—Replication.—No. III.

DEAR SIR:—IN again reading your letter, I have already, I perceive, got my lever under the heavier end of your difficulties. What you next say is rather a farther developement of those noticed, than a detail of new ones. I will, however, still prosecute the subject farther, and pay a due regard to those sentences which exhibit your difficulties in a new, or in a stronger light.

There is in all the productions of sceptical writers which I have seen, a singular confounding of things revealed, with their own reasonings. More than half the time their premises are in the Bible, while they are cavilling against it. *You* seem to have fallen into the same predicament. The sentence in your letter, next to those I have examined, is of this character. It reads thus:—" I thought that as the greatest degree of happiness was the only object of creation, the design of the Almighty would have failed, if as the scriptures authorize us to believe, a majority of mankind will be forever damned."

Let me now ask you, How did you come to think that the greatest degree of happiness was the only object of creation? If not from the Bible—from what source? It will serve no purpose to say, " *By reasoning;*" for this is but a mere excuse for plagiary. For a man might as rationally propose to create something out of nothing, as to propose to reason without something to reason upon. And now I ask you (for your own conviction,) *Upon what* were you reasoning when you came to the conclusion that " the greatest degree of happiness was the only object of creation?" Upon something in the Bible, I conjecture; for there is nothing out of it from which this can be legitimately inferred on principles of reason.

The grave terminates all reasonings about happiness. No person can look beyond it without the telescope of faith—without the Bible. Now no man can rationally conclude from all that passes from the cradle to the grave, that " the greatest degree of happiness was the only object of creation." If there be a truth in the Bible which human experience approbates, it is this, " the whole creation groans and travails in pain." I positively deny that there is any such data afforded in the material world, from which any man can legitimately conclude that " the greatest degree of happiness was the only object of creation." In fact, all human experience is to the contrary of such a conclusion; for no one in this life ever tasted one drop of the greatest degree of happiness; and how, in the name of the whole five senses, could he conclude, either from his observation or experience, that the greatest degree of happiness was the only object of creation!!! From this, methinks, you may see that you are indebted to the Bible, either understood, or misunderstood for your premises; and that there is no logical connexion between your premises and your conclusions.

But, again—You *add* to the Bible with as little ceremony as you borrow from it without acknowledging the debt. Pray where does " the Bible authorize you to believe that a majority of mankind will be forever damned?" This may be a fact; and it may be admitted without in the least invalidating the truth of the Bible. For no man can argue from the fact that there are ten times more blossoms in spring than apples in autumn, that the world is not under the government of God. But without questioning the truth of such a termination of things, I ask Where does the Bible authorize such a belief? That in past ages, or in the present, a majority of mankind have walked in the broad way, and but few comparatively in the narrow way, may be admitted as a Bible truth; and yet it will by no means follow that a majority of mankind will be forever damned. For one or two substantial reasons: For any thing you or I know, all the human beings that have yet lived may be as a drop out of a bucket in comparison of the whole human family. Again—Of the millions of human beings that have been born, one-third, at least, have died in infancy, concerning the eternal destiny of which the Bible says just not one word. But that a period of many generations is yet to come, in which the knowledge of God shall cover the earth as the waters cover the sea, the Bible explicitly declares; and concerning what numerical proportion of the whole human family shall be saved, the Bible says not one word. Of the saved it says, " they shall be an exceeding great number, which no man can number," and this is more than it says of the number which shall be cast off into hell. You will see that I determine nothing about the comparative number, but only say that you have no scriptural authority for believing that a majority of the whole human family will be eternally damned. I would add, that in reasoning against, or in calling in question, the divine authority of a book to which yourself and all intelligent persons are obviously indebted for every correct view of the invisible and future world, it behoves you not to reason from conjectures, or ill formed views, which are based upon mere imagination. But as I before said, nothing can be inferred from the numbers saved or lost against the divinity of the book, from mere principles of reason.

The subsequent part of this period is engrossed in my *Replication No. 1.* You add, " I thought that as the Deity was the first cause of all things, he was responsible for all things, especially for evil, as he possessed a greater power to prevent it than the *immediate cause;* and, if so, he could not punish any of his creatures with eternal misery." This much will suffice for the present epistle.

When you talk of the Deity being *responsible,* you lose sight of the essential attribute of Deity. A Supreme can neither be responsible nor accountable; for responsibility and accountability imply dependance. To whom can a Supreme be responsible? An independent dependant being is no greater contradiction than a responsible Supreme. To whom could the Creator be responsible for creating so much sea, so much cold, so much darkness, so many reptiles, so many monsters in the ocean, so many conflicting and jarring elements in this material system? If to his creatures, then he is like them; if not to them, to none.

Some talk of his preventing moral evil by an exertion of Almighty power; of his having " greater power to prevent it than the immediate cause;" of his being stronger than Satan. But all such notions, if they have any foundation at all, are built upon the most palpable inattention to rational nature. And here I would affirm that it is impossible to conceive of a ration-

2 L

al creature of an *infallible* nature. But in affirming this I am brought to the shore of an immense ocean where weak heads are sure to be drowned. Let us try whether we can swim a short distance in sight of land.

Let us then try an hypothesis of this sort, viz. Suppose that all those beings called angels, of which you have doubtless heard, had been created infallible creatures. What then? None of them *could* have become Satan. But what next? None of them could have been capable of moral good. For it is essential to moral good that the agent act freely according to the last dictate, or the best dictate of his understanding. Moisture is not more essential to vegetation than this liberty of acting according to the views or feelings of the agent is to moral good. Please consider, that if a rational being was created *incapable* of disobeying, he must, *on that very account*, be incapable of obeying. He then acts like a mill wheel, in the motions of which there is no choice; no virtue, no vice, no moral good, no moral evil. A little reflection is all that is wanting to see that a race of beings created incapable of disobeying, (i. e. *infallible*,) are as incapable of moral good or moral evil; of virtue or vice; of rewards or punishments; of happiness or misery, as the stones of the field. There are some things impossible to Omnipotence. Hills cannot be made without vallies; shadows, without substances; nor rational beings, without free agency. "It is impossible for God to lie." It is impossible to create a being that shall be capable of obeying, and at the same time incapable of disobeying. If, then, an order of beings had been created among which it was impossible for any one to become Satan, it would have been as impossible for any one of them to be either morally good, virtuous, or happy. So ends the first hypothesis. And who can bring it to any other issue?

Let us try another. Suppose that when one or more of those beings called angels had disobeyed and fallen, that he had been annihilated by an exertion of almighty power. What then? Physical power triumphs over an evil agent. What next? Moral evil is not subdued by moral means. Therefore the possibility of its recurrence in the same order of beings is not prevented. To prevent its recurrence in the same order of beings a mere display of physical energy is insufficient; wisdom must be displayed as well as power; goodness and justice must be exhibited as well as omnipotence. To have crushed the first rebel by an immediate display of simple omnipotence would not have prevented the rebellion of others; it would not have been godlike, but it would have been in the style of mortals, who, when foiled in one department of energies, seek redress in another.

To launch out into the developement of views purely metaphysical, in order to correct metaphysical errors, is at best only calculated to create a distrust in those visionary problems on which some build as firmly as if on the Rock of Ages. I never wish to establish any one point in this way; but I desire to throw a caveat in the way of those who are willing to risk eternity itself upon a visionary problem.

How "God's possessing a greater power to prevent moral evil than its immediate cause, prevents his punishing any creature for his evil actions," is to me altogether unintelligible. No father would reason thus with respect to a disobedient child. God has power to prevent A from killing B; ought he not therefore to ordain the death of A, or inflict any punishment on A for killing B? We sometimes reason on such principles against the ways of God as would condemn every human being.

But leaving this ocean of speculation, (for my head aches,) let us approach the shore. Moral evil exists as sure as we exist. From all that we can reason on its origin, nothing can be concluded against the divinity of the Bible. The Bible is the only book in the world which pretends to give us a history of its origin, progress, and cure. We do know that it exists; for of this we have indubitable testimony, and there is nothing repugnant to reason in the sacred history of its origin, which is simply this. God made rational beings of different orders, that is, beings capable of obeying and disobeying his will, without which capacity we have seen they could be neither virtuous nor vicious, happy nor miserable. Those beings were necessarily created under a law. One or more of them disobeyed that rule of action. This first act of disobedience was the first moral evil in the universe.— God did not immediately destroy it, as we have seen and the Bible testifies. It is in the nature of moral evil to multiply its exhibitions. This it has done. And God has adopted a course of government adapted to its nature, which the Bible unfolds, and at which some men cavil. This is an additional proof of its nature and existence. He has devised and revealed a remedy for those laboring under its consequences. Those who receive the remedy are cured. Those who do not, remain under its influence.

Now what other or more rational history of moral evil can be given? Nay, is there any history of it besides the Bible history in the world. What can—what does Deism present? Is there a slippery *perhaps* on the subject in all their systems? Does not Deism make God as directly and immediately the author of moral evil as of moral good? Is not men's aptitude to it called by them *nature*. Yes, the course of human nature. And whether they represent man as springing from the ground as a mushroom, or as the fortuitous concourse of atoms, do they not view him as just the same being now that he was when he first opened his eyes, or from a vegetable began to have the power of locomotion?

To those who are modest enough to question their own capacity to decide on all things supernatural, invisible, in heaven, earth, and Hades, with infallible certainty, I doubt not but the Bible account will appear at least *rational*; and I am now, and I hope always will be, able to prove that any other account, theory, or conjecture different therefrom, is just as futile and as childish as the schoolboy's theory of the earth, which made the globe rest on the back of a large turtle, but could find nothing for the turtle to stand upon.

You shall, God willing, hear still farther from your friend,   THE EDITOR.

A Restoration of the Ancient Order of things.
No. XV.
Love Feasts.

THAT the bible is precisely adapted to man as he is, and not as he was, or as he shall be in another state, is with me a favorite position; and one, as I conceive, of much consequence in any attempt to understand the Sacred book. Next to it in plainness and importance is this—that the religion of Jesus Christ is based upon the whole man, his soul, body, and spirit. There is not a power, capacity, or attribute, which man possesses, whether animal, intellectual, or moral, which it does not lay hold of; which it does not address, control, or direct, in the pursuit of the most dignified and exalted objects. From the loftiest faculties of the mind, down to the appetites and passions purely animal, it loses sight of nothing. Hence we may say of it as the Saviour said of the Sabbath, *"It was made for man."*

It is a religion essentially social, and the reason of this is found in the nature of man—for he is a social being. The religion of Jesus Christ refines the social feelings, and gives full scope to the exhibition of all that is social in man. No man can therefore either enjoy, or exhibit it to advantage, but in the midst of christian society. Hence "love to the brethren," and all that springs from it, forms so conspicuous a part of the christian religion.

A christian congregation established upon the New Testament exhibits the most perfect society of which human imagination can conceive. Every perfection and advantage that belongs to society is a constituent of it. When we have put every faculty into the most active requisition; when we have aroused all our powers to discover, or to exhibit the nature, properties, excellencies, and benefits of the most finished, polished, and sentimental society, we have only been seeking after or exhibiting that peculiar character of society which the New Testament gives birth to, and to constitute which is its highest object, as respects the present world. Neither reason, nor even fancy itself, can project a single ornament, can point out a single perfection or benefit that belongs to society, which does not belong to, and form a part of, that society of which we speak.

But I speak not of a degenerated state of a christian society, such as those dead and misshapen things which intriguing kings and sycophantic priests have given birth to; but I speak of a christian society in its pure and primitive state, such as that formed by the direction and under the guidance of the Holy Spirit. Many societies called "christian" are the habitation of envy, pride, ambition, selfishness; a rendezvous of moping melancholy and religious superciliousness; a conjunction of ignorance and superstition: a combination of gloom and invincible moroseness. A great majority of christian congregations assume an aspect more becoming an assembly of pharisees and monks than of christians. A severe austerity, a rigid sanctimoniousness, an awful penitential silence characterize their interviews. Their sunday apparel seems to sympathize with an agonizing piety within, and every movement indicates that there is something in their religion at variance with their lives and their comfort. These are but little things; yet they are symptoms of a diseased constitution, and like an unnatural pulse, assure the physician that the vital functions are laboring under a morbid influence. There can be no doubt to those who drink deep into the spirit of the New Testament, but that the aspect of a society of primitive worshippers was essentially different from ours. The hope, and joy, and love, and confidence in God, which their views of Jesus inspired, animated their countenances and their deportment, and shone forth in their whole demeanor; as the ignorance, the doubts, and fears, and awful uncertainty, of a company of cloistered friars and nuns, designate their faces and gestures. It is not going too far to say, that an intelligent mind makes an intelligent countenance, and exhibits itself even in the ordinary movements of the outward man. It is much more evident that the whole aspect and demeanor of a congregation of worshippers is an index to their peculiar views and sentiments. Who, that is acquainted with the views and sentiments of the individuals composing any congregation, does not see, or think he sees, in the outward man the character he has formed of the inward man. This I do not say as if it were my design to enjoin upon individuals or congregations to cultivate a system of appearances or movements, comporting with the sentiments, views, and feelings of others; but to lead them to reflect on the causes of these things, and to inquire after what that was, and what that is, which distinguishes us from the primitive disciples.

This leads me to remark that the primitive christians had, amongst other things which we have not, a particular kind of feasts, called in the New Testament, *"feasts of charity,"* or rather *"love feasts."* This was not a practice for which they had to work themselves up, but it was a natural and unforced expression of the spirit which dwelt in them. A marriage supper is not more natural than a christian *love feast.* There does not appear any precept enforcing or enjoining such feasts in any part of the apostolic writings. This would have been as inconsistent with the genius of the book, as for it to have given a commandment that christians should eat and drink together. It was as much the genuine result of their religion, as verdure is the result of the genial influences of spring. When God sends the rain and causes the balmy zephyrs to breathe, it is unnecessary to issue a command to the seeds of plants to germinate and grow. Thus it came to pass, that soon as the spirit of God was poured out on Pentecost, and disciples multiplied, they not only attended upon the ordinances of social worship enjoined upon them by the apostles; such as *"the breaking of bread,"* "the fellowship," "the prayers," "the praises," &c. but they were led to meet in each other's houses, and to "feast with gladness and singleness of heart." This going from house to house and eating their food with gladness and singleness of heart, or as it is more correctly and beautifully rendered, "and breaking bread from house to house, they partook of their refreshment with joy and simplicity of heart, praising God," is just what is fitly called a feast of love, or *the love feasts* of the New Testament; because christian love bade the guests, brought them together, and was president of the table.

Feasts, either public or private, are usually denominated from the cause that institutes them. Now when a number of christians are invited, purely on christian considerations to meet either in a particular family, or at a public place of rendezvous, for the purpose of social eating and drinking, or feasting; this repast, whether given by one individual brother, or made by the contributions of all, is a *christian love feast.* To these feasts was added the song; yes, the sacred song of joy and gladness was a prominent part of the the entertainment: for it is added, " they partook of their refreshment with joy and simplicity of heart, *praising God.*" What more natural than these christian feasts? Refined and elevated sociableness is the direct tendency of the christian religion. The table and the fireside; the scenes of festivity, of social converse, and of social song, consecrated by christian affection, become as joyful and cheering to christian hearts, as ever was the altar of Hymen to the bridegroom and the bride—as ever was the marriage supper to the nuptial guests.

When any intruded into these love feasts, or were bid to the entertainment undeserving of it, these were " spots and blemishes" in those feasts of love, and are so designated by the apostles. Hence it is inferred that none but those embraced in christian love were wont to be invited to those entertainments; and that no social eating and drinking of a mixed character, where our relatives and neighbors are invited, irrespective of christian considerations, can lawfully be called a *christian love feast* in the primitive sense of these words. It also follows that whenever a company is called together, all of which are disciples of Christ, to eat and drink, and to be cheerful, such a feast is a christian love feast, and forms no inconsiderable part of that system of means which is wisely adapted to enliven christian affection, and to prepare men for the entertainments of heaven.

When the ancient order of things is restored, these feasts of love will be found as useful for the promotion of humility, benevolence, joy, and peace, as they were in those hale and undegenerate days of primitive simplicity. They will be found as necessary for the perfection of enjoyment in this earthly state, as any of the acts of social worship are to the edification of the christian community in their weekly meetings. They are obviously distinguished from any of the acts of social worship ordained for the whole congregation on the day of life and immortality; but houses are not more necessary to shield us from the inclemencies of the weather, than those festive occasions are to the consummation of the entertainments, and finished exhibition of the sociability of the christian religion.   EDITOR.

THE following letters are from the students of theology in the Hamilton Seminary, New-York:

HAMILTON VILLAGE, *August* 24, 1826.

DEAR SIR—On a request made to you some time since, you very politely forwarded, to the Philomathesean Society, of the Literary and Theological Seminary, in this place, your paper styled "The Christian Baptist." You have not failed to remember us ever since, but have, without any remuneration, furnished us with it regularly. You have thus manifested for us a friendly feeling, a kindness in your attention for which we should be grateful, and for which we now, sir, tender you our unfeigned thanks.

But for reasons which we are willing frankly to avow, our society has recently come to the resolution to ask you to discontinue your publication.

It was hoped, respected sir, that your time, your influence, your talents, would all have been put in requisition to subserve the cause of God, and consequently the happiness of man. It was hoped, that thousands would rise up to call you blessed; and that the evening of your life would be calm and composed; cheered by an approving conscience, the approbation of your fellow creatures, and the smiles of indulgent Heaven. But upon a careful examination of your paper, among much that is good, we find much that we cannot approve; much that is repugnant to the best feelings of man, and subversive, as we apprehend, of vital piety. In this vale of tears, man needs all the comforts which can be derived from the light of divine revelation, all the consolation which God in infinite mercy has vouchsafed to man through a blessed Mediator; besides, he needs all the encouragements, all the persuasion, which can be afforded by the most devoted and godly men of the present age, to forsake the contracted views, and jealousy of feeling, which so strongly marked the conduct of our fathers. We admit that there may be much in the church at the present day that is

reprehensible. But what way is most likely to effect a change? Is it by a confirmed course of ridicule and sarcasm, or by a dignified, argumentative, and candid exposition of error, and a mild and persuasive invitation to amendment?

What consolation can we possibly receive, unless we can so live at all times, that when God calls us to his dread tribunal, we may be in readiness to appear? Oh! what will be the situation of that servant, who, when he is called, shall not have on the wedding garment? Shall we preach, shall we pray, shall we circulate our thoughts through the medium of the press, without the most scrutinizing search of our own hearts? and a petition at the throne of Divine Grace, that God may bless our every effort for the good of mankind? What are we, dear sir, but miserable worms of the dust? Shall we who hope to inherit, in a few days, the great and exalted privilege of the lowest place in Heaven, keep up a continual warfare with our fellow creatures, and expect to gain the approbation of a pure and infinitely Holy Being, by acts so deficient in charity? The cold hand of death may be upon you before this hasty and imperfect scroll shall reach you; and perhaps the hand which how sketches these lines will be no more active when this letter reaches the place of its destination. These may be considered trite remarks; but death, judgment, and eternity are solemn things—and they are at hand! Permit us to remind you of the great concern which some of the most able, devout, and pious writers have experienced, when publishing their works, apprehensive lest they might not be productive of good.

With a fervent prayer that your mind may be so directed by Divine Grace, and that you may be so governed by wisdom, that the best interests of your fellow creatures may be promoted, and God honored, we bid you farewell.

By order of the Society,
W—— D——, *Cor. Sec.*

YOUNG GENTLEMEN,—I CANNOT but feel indebted to your urbanity and admirable piety for the practical little sermon you have had the condescension to deliver to myself for my own exclusive benefit. Had it not been for your kind *mementos* I might have forgotten that I am a mortal being, and an accountable one. But you have been kind enough to assure me that I must die and be judged, and that at no distant period; for all these proofs of benevolence on your part, I should be extremely insensible were I not to feel grateful; and impolite, were I not to acknowledge my obligations to you. It is true, indeed, that it is not apparent from your letter to what religion you would have me proselyted—whether to the Jewish, Mahometan, or Christian; for as to any thing it contains of a distinguishing character, it might have been written by a Jew, a Mussulman, or a Christian. There is one thing sufficiently plain, however, that you would have me converted to a religion of more charity, and which would dispose me to sing with the charitable poet—

"Father of All! in every age,
"In every clime ador'd;
"By saint, by savage, and by sage—
"Jehovah, Jove, or Lord."

Or rather—

"For modes of faith let zealous bigots fight;
"His can't be wrong, whose charity is right."

Were it not apparently impertinent and somewhat invidious to deliver a lecture to one's superiors, especially to persons already so pious, I feel from the very bottom of my heart a strong,
26

a vehement desire to request you to read the New Testament of Jesus Christ once through, with all that pious concern which you so feelingly exhibit for me. For I feel as certain as I live, that you are not indebted to it for the piety which your communication breathes; else you could not have deliberately denounced the Saviour of the world and his holy apostles for their plain, and bold, and severe reprehension of the errorists of that age. This exhortation I would enforce, with many evidences of its necessity, with many proofs of its importance, with many directions for its adoption, were I addressing persons less pious than yourselves; and I would urge it with more concern upon you, as you are preparing yourselves to be guides of the blind, teachers of babes, and instructors of those ignorant and out of the way; but, as I before said, it would appear impertinent and invidious for me so to do.

You must not call this sarcasm nor raillery; for I assure you I doubt not but your pious souls have been sorely grieved with the impious spirit of "The Christian Baptist;" for it never has looked with a benign aspect either upon the professors of theological schools, nor their disciples. It has never flattered their pious efforts in making christian bishops for christian congregations by means of a system of speculation, and a few rules for collecting sermons, or manufacturing those of ancient times down to the present taste and fashion. But again I entreat you not to imagine that I do not conceive you pious students of divinity; nay, I doubt not but you are as pious as any of the students of Gamaliel, not even excepting Saul of Tarsus. But should you ever be born from above, I will expect to see your piety exhibit itself in a different way and to run in a different channel.

With unfeigned wishes for such an event, I subscribe myself your grateful friend,

THE EDITOR.

—

The following epistle from a minority of the students of said Seminary exhibits another kind of piety:

Brother Campbell,

DEAR SIR—PROBABLY the same mail which shall bring you this letter, will bring you another from the Philomathesean society of this place, requesting a discontinuance of your paper, which agreeably to their request, you have very liberally and regularly sent them. The truth is, sir, the society are, and ever have been, since your paper was sent for, divided on the subject. The propriety of keeping it has been frequently litigated with much warmth. Some have been very anxious to keep it, and others have been very bitter against it. But those opposed to it have at length prevailed; and, as members of this society, we must submit. Yet, as individuals, a few of those in favor of keeping your paper, have concluded unitedly to ask you, as a favor, to continue (to us) "The Christian Baptist." We ask it as a favor because we are here supported by the charity of the public, and are unable to defray the ordinary expense of it. Should it be your pleasure to gratify our request, we hope ever to remember it with gratitude. But whether you should comply with our request or not, may you ever share largely in that grace you so eminently need to succeed your endeavors to restore "the ancient order of things." May you have that wisdom which comes down from above which is pure, peaceable, gentle, and easy to be entreated. With undissembled piety, chris-

tian humility and apostolic devotion, may you by plain persuasive and christian-like argument, be enabled to expose the errors of the age, and establish that purity and simplicity which characterized the apostolic age. May the good will of him who dwelt in the bush rest upon you forever, and the fruits of genuine piety be your choicest blessing. May your age be clearer than the noon, and as a morning without clouds; and when you shall be called to pass the Jordan of death, may you have the peaceful satisfaction of reflecting upon a life spent in the service of God. May your sun set in tranquillity, and the beams of eternity salute your rising peace.

Yours, most sincerely, and most affectionately,

C—— S——

—

My Dear Friends,

WITH great pleasure I comply with your request and hope that you will be always ready, when you either adopt or reject any sentiment in this work, to produce good and scriptural reasons for so doing. I have never felt any disposition to censure those who differ from me in any of my views, provided always, they seemed to act reasonably and conscientiously, and had something like argument or evidence to support them. Indeed I cannot say I censure any differing from me on any account. It is not my province to censure. I may pity and lament their obstinacy, or their weakness; but if I view any thing more correctly, I have no ground of boasting in myself. I do love all them of every name under heaven that love my Lord and Master, and I would deny myself, to any extent the law of our King commands, to render any service to the humblest disciple in his kingdom. And while I write and labor as I do, he that knows the hearts of all flesh knows that I do it from the fullest conviction from his oracles that the christianity of our day is a corrupt christianity, and that the ancient order of things is lost sight of in almost all denominations of professing christians. I do consider that there are many, very many christians, in the present day, greatly out of the way, and that they are suffering famine and disease in their souls because of it. I am assured that good health cannot be restored but by the depleting and stimulating plan recommended by Paul in his letters to Timothy and Titus.

Should any of you, at any time, feel any objections which you deem insuperable against any thing in this work, it will give me great pleasure to have you state them to myself: or should any of your instructors dislike any thing in it, their objections shall be thankfully received, carefully considered, and most respectfully replied to. We must all give account of ourselves to the Lord, and whatever we think now, I am sure at that moment we would rather have his approbation than that of all the human race besides.

Praying that you may be prepared to give up your account with joy, and not with grief, I write myself

Your obt. servt. for the truth's sake,

THE EDITOR.

P. S. I make no apology to you, nor to the Philomathesean Society, for publishing your letters; believing that there is nothing which they contain that is of any private interpretation.

ED.

———

From the "Western Luminary" of September 27.

MR. EDITOR,—PERMIT me to call the attention of your readers to a work which is now circulating freely among our Baptist brethren in this state. I allude to the New Testament lately published by Mr. ALEXANDER CAMPBELL of Virginia; concerning which there is much false impression on the minds of many.

It was expected by people generally in this part of the country, that Mr. Campbell intended to furnish us with a translation executed many years since by Doctors Campbell and McKnight of Scotland, and Dr. Doddridge of England. If this expectation had been realized, the writer of this notice would have been satisfied, believing those translations to be generally faithful and correct; but finding on examination, that the deviations from those authors are exceedingly numerous, he asks leave to lay before the readers of your paper the following statement, in order that they may judge for themselves whether their impressions concerning this work have not been in many instances erroneous.

On the single subject of baptism, the alterations from the translations of the above authors are upwards of eighty. There are no less than seven of these in the third chapter of the "Testimony of Matthew." In all of the gospel by Matthew, there were found, at least, sixteen alterations on this subject—in Mark, twelve—in Luke, eight—in John, eleven—in Acts, nineteen—and a few in some of the other books, making at least the number mentioned above.

As it was found to be too tedious and troublesome to compare the whole work with the originals, in order to ascertain the deviations on all subjects, a selection was made of a single epistle for this purpose. This was the Epistle to the Hebrews translated by Macknight; and in this were found upwards of sixty alterations from that author.

Now, Mr. Editor, if this epistle be a fair specimen of the whole Testament, it will follow, that there are contained in it upwards of one thousand five hundred variations from the translations of the learned Doctors whose names are in the title page, although numbers of our wise men in Kentucky imagine that we have it almost verbatim from these translations.

Most of the variations in the Epistle to the Hebrews are of small importance, but they serve to shew us that Mr. Campbell was anxious to furnish the public with a gospel, shaped exactly to his own views.

In glancing my eye over other parts of his work, I perceived an alteration in the Acts of the Apostles, which, in my view, is of very considerable importance. I allude to *Acts* xx. 28. "Feed the church of God, which he has purchased with his own blood." It is translated "God" by Dr. Doddridge, and he gives a note stating that there is no good authority for the change which some propose to make, of "God" into "Lord." This has long been viewed, as a powerful text in opposition to those who deny the proper divinity of Christ; for it states positively, that he who purchased the church with his own blood, is God. This did not pass unnoticed by the Unitarians, and hence they have long endeavored to persuade people that the common version of the original is erroneous, and ought to be changed as above; and I am sorry to say that Mr. Campbell makes the change, although it is in opposition to the pious and learned Doddridge, from whom this part of his work is taken. I know indeed he passes over it silently, but it may not tend the less on that account, to unsettle the minds of common readers with regard to an important doctrine of God's word.

Mr. Campbell has been charged with leaning towards Unitarianism. I know not whether

there be a sufficient foundation for the charge or not; but if not, he ought to guard against giving a handle to the enemies of truth.

The above remarks are not intended as a discussion of the merits of this work, but simply to show to those who read it the necessity of guarding against the supposition that it is the identical translation furnished by Doctors Campbell, Doddridge and Macknight.

A FRIEND TO TRUTH.

A Refutation of the foregoing Misrepresentations.

THERE are many ways of making false impressions upon the public mind besides the telling of downright lies. But there is as much real falsehood in the sight of Heaven and all intelligent minds in giving such a representation of things, in whatever language it may be uttered, as gives a false impression to the hearer. And when it is done intentionally, it differs nothing from the grossest deception. The writer of the above article has, in my judgment, as really "borne false witness against" me, as if he had accused me of treason against the state; and what is far worse in the case, it is in a matter of incomparably and inexpressibly more momentum.

Reader, ask yourself what is the impression which the above statement makes upon your mind. 1st. Does it not lead you to think that I had cheated public expectation in the execution of a work contrary to my proposals and conditions of publication?

2d. Does it not lead you to think that I have secretly, and with an intention to deceive, foisted into the works of Doctors Campbell, Macknight, and Doddridge, "one thousand five hundred" and more alterations?

3d. Does it not lead you to think that I had some other "gospel" of my own, different from that of those Doctors, which I wished by a fraudulent artifice, to impose upon the public as theirs?

4th. Does it not lead you to suspect that I am an artful Socinian, changing and interpolating the sacred text to establish a favorite hypothesis?

5th. Does it not, lastly, lead you to believe that I am a very bad man, and a most impudent deceiver, deserving of no confidence as to honesty and integrity in my professions?

Such, I believe, are the impressions it is designed to make, and such I am certain are the impressions it is calculated to made upon the minds of all them who either know me not, or are prejudiced against me.

Now, courteous reader, I will ask you one question more. Do you not think, that if there be no foundation for any of these impressions—for any of these malignant insinuations—that the author of the above statement has as really violated the ninth commandment of the sacred ten written by the finger of God, as if he had accused me of murder, theft, or any other crime of which I am innocent?

Now for the proof. It is a fact which can be proved in any court of law or equity, that the work is as exactly executed according to my prospectus as it could be, with this one exception, viz. that I did not put upon the margin the different translations for reasons assigned in my General Preface, but placed them in an Appendix. See Preface, p. 10.

In the second place, it is a fact which can be proved in any court of law or equity, that I have faithfully given the translation proposed, and that the eighty alterations on the subject of baptism which the above statement mentions, are authorized by Dr. Campbell and proposed in my prospectus.

And here let it be noted, that this "Friend to Truth" tells eighty lies in telling one truth! for the eighty differences, if like the seven mentioned in the third of Matthew, (and this is the only specification he has made,) are only in one word, which it can be proved in any court of law and equity in England or America, is authorized by the said Dr. George Campbell, who this "Friend to Truth" says is "a faithful and correct" translator in general. Eighty times it is immerse or its derivatives, instead of the Greek word baptize and its derivatives, which we promised in our prospectus to attend to. Thus his eighty differences are in fact but apparently one, and in reality not one. For it can be proved as aforesaid, that Dr. George Campbell has said and published to the world that it ought to be done as I have done, and gives his reasons why he did not do it.

Again—I request the reader's attention to the following item in my prospectus:—

"There is also one improvement of considerable importance which ought to be made in this work, and to which we shall attend. Sundry terms are not translated into English, but adopted into those translations from long usage. Those terms are occasionally translated into English by Campbell and Macknight; but not always. We shall uniformly give them the meaning which they have affixed to them, wherever they occur, and thus make this a pure English New Testament, not mingled with Greek words, either adopted or anglicised. *But in doing this, we shall not depart in any instance from the meaning which they have declared those words to convey.*"

You see there is one promise of great importance in *italics* in this quotation. Now it can be proved in any court of law or equity where the English language is spoken, that I have not, in one instance, departed from this promise. I challenge all the colleges and divines on this continent to shew that I have not, in every instance, so done. Let this Doctor of Divinity, this "Friend to Truth!" make an attempt.

He finds "upwards of sixty alterations" in the Epistle to the Hebrews. How this sounds! True he admits them to be of little importance—but how numerous are they! Now, lovers of truth, he has not been half as ostentatious of his calculating prowess as he might be: for, in fact, there is more than one hundred and twenty "alterations" in the first six verses of the third chapter of this epistle!!! In other words, I have given six full verses of "alterations" from the translator of this epistle. But what are they? Why, when the matter is looked into, Dr. Campbell's translation of six verses is put into the text in preference to Dr. Macknight's. Thus I have departed one hundred and twenty times from Dr. Macknight in one half dozen of verses. And what has become of Dr. Macknight's translation of these six verses? Have I cheated the public, and made them believe that they were reading Macknight. No, indeed; Dr. Macknight is faithfully given in the Appendix, because there was not room for it in the margin, and about fifty times you will find Macknight in the Appendix in this one epistle. Now the fact is, this lover of truth to the contrary notwithstanding, these fifteen hundred "variations" are of this kind; and I am not sure but he might have made them twice fifteen hundred if he had been a little more at leisure.

This tremendous number of alterations will sound as terrific in the ears of the honest members of Dr. Blythe's or Dr. Breckenridge's congregation in Lexington, as did a sentence I met with in Michaelis' Introductory Lectures to the New Testament, when I was a "student of Divinity." Michaelis, a very learned and a very orthodox professor, informed me that in the Greek manuscripts of the New Testament, amongst the best of them too, there were more than forty thousand alterations or variations! But when I began to understand the nature of these alterations, there were not more than a hundred of them of much importance. Thirty-nine thousand of them were something like this Dr's eighty apparent differences in one word, but, in reality, no difference. But after all this alarm of the church in danger! the fact is, the public have all the translation of these three Doctors in the volume, and these fifteen hundred different translations into the bargain! So that if the matter be rightly understood, the direful, or rather ireful insinuations of this Friend to Truth are so many encomiums upon the work!

But this "Friend to Truth," this masked champion of orthodoxy, aims a deadly javelin at my heart. He would assassinate me in the dark! He would "rob me of my good name," and massacre my reputation, and destroy the influence of the best translation of the New Testament that ever appeared in our language; because, forsooth, he thinks it endangers his baby sprinkling. And in this *I* am not to blame. See Appendix No. 4. His own good and "faithful" Doctors are to blame. They were witnesses in secret, but now they have come out to the public gaze, and I must be called "a Socinian," and an "interpolater," that I may be burned by some good John Calvin, and that the witness of these three "faithful and correct" translators may be again imprisoned. And why am I a Socinian now? Because, on the authority of the acknowledged great, and learned, and mighty collator of versions and manuscripts, I have preferred the term *Lord* to *God*. And here again, have I cheated the public? Nay, verily, I have given both. Yes, both Doddridge and Griesbach. See Appendix No. 47. For although I am as firmly convinced of the proper divinity of the Saviour of the world, that he is as literally and as truly the Son of God as the Son of Man, as ever John Calvin was, I would not do as this "Friend to Truth" insinuates I ought to have done, made the text bend to suit my views. But in reality it is more in favor of the divinity of Jesus as it is in Griesbach than as it is in Doddridge. It is only against the awkward phraseology of those controvertists who make more Socinians than Calvinists by their efforts to convert the former. On this ground it was that Dr. Whitby preferred the reading of *God* instead of *Lord*, while he gives better authority for the latter than the former. But I was not thinking about favoring my views, nor any man's views, in preferring Griesbach to Doddridge. While I give the reader both, I leave him to judge for himself; but this "Friend to Truth" would have given but one, as he blames me for giving both. I said in the preface I gave the most conspicuous place to that reading or rendering which I thought deserved it—and so it happens here.

Now my reasons for preferring *Lord* in this place to the term *God*, are as follows:—Some ancient MSS. have it *God*; others, *Lord and God*; others, *God and Lord*: some, Lord God; others, Christ; others, Saviour; and some of the most ancient have it *Lord*. Griesbach gives all these readings, and decides in favor of the latter. Besides I added, in my own mind, to the authority of Griesbach, the following facts. Ireneus, one of the oldest writers who flourished A. D. 176, quoting this passage in L. 5. 14. quotes it as in the New Translation. Now I think this is of great weight, as he lived before any controversy arose about the passage, and before any of the MSS. now in existence were written.—Again—the Syriac translation, the oldest in the world, has it *Lord*. I do not know how much influence these facts might have had on the mind of Griesbach in deciding for himself on the manuscripts before him; but I mention them as adding in my mind to the weight of his decision.

But after all, I feel assured that this "Friend to Truth" examined the whole translation in order to find something to impeach my reputation, and that he fixed upon this as the only, and the most likely foundation on which he could rest his lever in order to hurl me down in the estimation of those whose conviction upon another subject he feared. And yet he has ten times more reason to impeach John Calvin and Theodore Beza on account of Socinianism than me, excepting that I have not given my voice in favor of burning any Servetus. For both these gentlemen argue that the famous passage which a hundred orthodox divines and critics have condemned as spurious, viz. 1 John, v. 7. does not prove the unity of three persons in one God, admitting it to be genuine.

Now I know that this "Friend to Truth" has a way to save himself from all these remarks. It is this: He has not pronounced any opinion upon "the merits" of the translation; he has not affirmed any of the things he has insinuated; and he only meant to correct the false impressions of others; and that he has not in so many words accused me of any unfaithfulness in the case—but we do not thank him for leaving this back-door open. He has done his best to blast my reputation and to destroy the influence of the work. I am glad to have it investigated with all scrutiny and severity, and to hear every objection to it from any quarter, because I am of opinion I can defend the work in every grand point against any opposition from any quarter whatever. Numerous attempts similar to that of this anonymous Divine, were made against the common version now in use, but the king's decree put them all to silence.

I have only to add, that my opinion is, that this slanderer was afraid to publish his name because he is of slender reputation already, and one of those Divines on whom I had to call when last in Lexington because of slanders which he propagated against me, and which he was obliged to retract or explain away.

If the editor of the "Luminary" has any regard to his character as a "Friend" of *Justice*, he will publish this statement, as I have published his, and thus "do to others as he would wish them to do to him."   Editor.

A Good "Christening."
"Go up, thou baldhead!"

Some *religious* editors in Kentucky call those who are desirous of seeing the ancient order of things restored, "the Restorationers," "the Campbellites," and the most reproachful epithets are showered upon them because they have some conscientious regard for the Divine Author and the divine authority of the New Testament.—This may go down very well with some; but all who fear God and keep his commandments will pity and deplore the weakness and folly of those who either think to convince or to persuade by such means.

The Points at Issue.

We contend that all christian sects are more or less apostatized from the institutions of the Saviour, and that by all the obligations of the christian religion they that fear and love the Lord are bound to return to the ancient order of things in spirit and in truth. Our opponents either contend that they are not apostatized, but are just what they ought to be; or if they admit of any defection, they contend that the time is not yet come—they must await the Millennium; and that it is better to keep up the present systems than to attempt any thing else. This is just the naked question, detached from all superfluity, and it would be well for both the friends and opponents of this work frequently to reflect upon it.   Editor.

No. 5.]   December 4, 1826.
To Mr. D.—A Sceptic.—Replication—No. IV.

Dear Sir—You say that "if our Maker was almighty, he could have created universal happiness." But his works prove him almighty, and experience shows that he has not created universal happiness; for even the temporary evils which millions feel are incompatible with the idea of universal happiness. You in this instance, therefore, argue against both observation and experience. But you add, "To this end, (*i. e.* universal happiness,) I conceived every thing in nature had a direct tendency." What "direct tendency" you can see between ideotism, decrepitude, penury, disease, and all the evils of the brutal creation towards universal happiness in this state, I cannot conjecture; and if you take into view a future state, you then admit the very truth at which your skepticism revolts. But what is no less strange, you say you are "able to reconcile the evils we feel here as necessary to our peculiar state of existence." This is like a person saying he is able to carry two hundred pounds upon his shoulders, but adds he is unable to carry fifty. You talk of a peculiar state of existence here; but when you reject the divinity of the Bible, where do you learn of any other than this peculiar state of existence here? Another state of existence hereafter is a Bible truth, but not one which can be derived from any other source.

I aim at no more in these remarks than to convince you that your whole style and sentiment is at variance with your doubts. The grand principles are already laid down which show your difficulties to be unreasonable, and emerging from an unchastened imagination. In the same style you affirm, "Punishment, I thought, should be proportioned to criminality: but in inflicting eternal punishment for temporal crimes the principle of justice is violated." What that principle of justice is I know not, which teaches us that a man should be punished no longer than the precise time he sins, or that if an offence is committed in one minute the punishment should be of no longer continuance. This is precisely the force of your objection. For the idea of punishment being longer than the time of sinning, is that which staggers you. It would, therefore, be a violation of this "principle of justice" to confine a man in a penitentiary for eighteen years for a crime which he perpetrated in half an hour. On this "principle of justice" it would be unreasonable to cut off a man's life for ever from the earth for an action which he committed in one minute. Men are in the habit of "punishing eternally" their fellow creatures for "temporal crimes." For when A kills B, he is by his peers and the laws of his country punished with an eternal separation from the whole human race existing upon the earth. But on this your "principle of justice," this is a gross violation of all right. But again, there is another sophism in the terms "temporal crimes." I know of none such; for as to the time in which any action, good or bad, is finishing, it is nothing. For instance; A kills B. Now B is in a moment cut off from all his relatives. His children lose him once for all. The effects of this murder are eternal; or, in other words, the children of B are ever deprived of their father, and B himself is forever deprived of his life by an action which was perpetrated perhaps in a minute. The consequences are eternal, and not temporal; and therefore it is out of all propriety to talk of "temporal crimes." It would require more logic than, I presume, is possessed by all the colleges in your state to show or prove on fair principles, that there is any crime temporal, in your sense of the words, or that there is any crime committed the consequences of which are not eternal.

You make some strong cases and propose some queer questions; but they only glance at one side of the difficulty, and are all capable of being turned to any point in the compass of human ingenuity and human weakness: such as, "Could the God of compassion have sat on his throne of untroubled felicity whilst a being whom he had called into existence, who would never have been liable to pain but for him, was enduring the pains of hell fire." You might have said, "Was enduring the pains of the gravel or rheumatism, or an infant enduring the pains of the cholic, or of a burned or scalded finger, or of a fever," &c. &c. for these cases are as much in point as yours when presented in connexion with "the God of compassion."

The consummation of your difficulties is, I presume, expressed in the following sentence: "And besides these, it appeared to me inconsistent with the Deity," (I suppose your ideas of the Deity) "to require from us, on pain of damnation if we failed, implicit belief in an account of transactions which occurred several thousand years ago, (and considering the imperfect medium through which information is communicated from one age to another,) and of which it required the utmost stretch of intelligence to comprehend even the probability." Your difficulties in this sentence are based upon false views of the gospel and of its evidence. It is not a fact that implicit faith in transactions at best probable, is required on pain of damnation. Every thing in this sentence is convulsed and distorted. Men are not, in strict propriety, even required to believe any thing on pain of damnation. For example; suppose you had swallowed the most deadly poison, and that some benevolent physician had voluntarily called upon you and told you that there was a medicine which would save your life, but if you did not take it you must most certainly die; would it be a truth for you to assert, when cavilling against the medicine, that you would not taste it because he had required you implicitly to receive it on pain of death. I say it would be a false representation of the whole matter, notwithstanding it is true that if you did not receive

the medicine you must die. Now I cannot conceive how it could be "inconsistent" with the most benevolent being to address a dying man as the physician in question had addressed you, and to assure him that eternal destruction must be his doom if he reject his medicine. Now the fact is, all men are sick of a disorder which must prove their eternal ruin if they are not cured of it. This is just as certain as death. I will not spend time in proving it. A remedy is provided. It is an infallible one. It is presented gratuitously, and directions for its use are appended to it. To excite interest, and to persuade men to receive it, they are told a solemn truth—that die they must—that perdition awaits them, if they do not receive it. Some say they are not sick, and they will live forever without it. Others say they are sick, but have no confidence in the medicine. Others have no objection to the medicine, but dislike its administration. Others receive the medicine gratefully, are thankful for it, and are cured by it, and would persuade others to come and be cured. Amongst those who object to the medicine, there is a great variety. Some will not take it because the physician tells them they cannot be healed without it. Some reject it because they think they ought not to have been sick, and are incensed against their Maker because he did not give them a constitution insusceptible of disease. They defy Omnipotence to arms, and console themselves that if they are lost, it will be their Maker's loss as well as theirs, and that it will pain him as well as them. They choose death to spite him. Others object to the medicine, because every body will not be cured, and all the world saved by it. They would believe its efficacy and partake freely if all were to be cured by it, but because they are told that all will not receive it and be healed, they will not taste it. So it goes. I have seen many men act the part of a spoiled child, which cried all morning about its breakfast, and though in need of food, it spurned the bread and butter, and threw it back upon the too kind and lenient hand of an affectionate parent, because its humor was not consulted in some peculiar way.

But it is not a fact that men are required to believe implicitly, on pain of damnation; nor is it a fact that the transactions to be believed occurred several thousand years ago; neither is it a fact that the medium of information is of such a character as you describe: nor is it a fact that it requires the utmost stretch of intelligence to comprehend the probability of those transactions which constitute the gospel. This is not the place, nor is the time so opportune, to enter largely into the nature of the gospel nor the evidence which supports it. But I will give you a brief statement of the gospel and a few remarks upon the evidence of its divine authenticity in my next. Your sincere friend, EDITOR.

Review of Miller and Duncan.—Continued.

IN the third section Mr. Duncan repels the third charge of his antagonist. It was confidently alleged by Dr. Miller that Mr. Duncan's arguments against creeds proved too much for Mr. D.; for if Mr. D. objected to creeds because they were human, he ought to object to expositions of scripture, or comments, verbal or written, because they are human; therefore, concludes the Doctor, Mr. Duncan's arguments prove too much for him. This is the way that men of talents impose upon the weak and unsuspicious. Mr. D. drives Dr. M. from this sophism by shewing that he wilfully changes the question, and misrepresents him: for Mr. D. does not object to creeds simply because they are human, nor indeed at all on this account; but he objects to men making human creeds authoritative, making them as binding on the conscience as if they were of divine authority: he would, he shews, object to human sermons and human commentaries too, if they were to be imposed upon the people as terms of communion, and he would not care that any church published a human creed every time they met, provided it was a mere declaration of their faith that day, and not intended to be binding upon them and their children after them while they met in that house. In p. 40 Mr. D. says—

"In relation to 'commentaries on the bible,' his argument is, if possible, still more defective. They may not be altogether harmless; and the church, upon the whole, might do as well, if not better, without than with them. For the most part they manifest very little intellectual independence, and are the depositories of the dogmas and notions of the day in which they were written. But still, no man is obliged to own or read them; no church court will try heresy or immorality by their interpretations; there is no difficulty in exchanging them, and no censure implied in rejecting them. But what of ecclesiastical creeds? Are they thus lightly esteemed? Do christians consider them as mere commentaries? Would Dr. M. listen for a moment to any overture, which would propose so to treat them?—Let men write as many creeds as they please, and publish them as often as they please. But let it be done on their own responsibility, and let ministers and christians read them or not, at their own option. On these terms our controversy would soon be over. Dr. M's third charge therefore is wholly unfounded."

In the fourth section of Mr. D's book he does more than defend himself, for he mortally wounds his opponent. With an air of triumph Dr. Miller had asked, "how the church can take effectual measures to exclude Pelagians, semi-Pelagians, Swedenborgians, Universalists, Arians, and Socinians from her ministry, without the use of creeds and confessions in some form?" This question Mr. D. treats in a most masterly manner. He shews in reply to the first, that "the man who cannot be condemned by the scriptures is not to be condemned at all." He shews that the very creeds which were made against those heresies and heretics did not keep them out. This he supports by historic facts well introduced, such as—

What did the Nicene creed (made against Arius himself) effect? "Was Arius converted, convinced, or silenced? Very far from it. Contentions abounded, angry debates were protracted, and Arius was banished. A little while after Arius was recalled, and *subscribed the creed*, remaining still unchanged in his heretical sentiments; so that this 'important end' of excluding Arius from the ministry, was not secured even by a *creed*.

"Nor did many years roll by, until a bishop of Rome was guilty of an equally disgraceful manœuvre. Pope Liberius, 'about the middle of the fourth century, when the Arian controversy was at its height, intimidated by the power of the reigning emperor Constantius, whom he knew to be a zealous disciple of Arius, declared publicly in favor of that party, and excommunicated Athanasius, whom all the orthodox regarded as the patron and defender of the catholic cause. This sentence he soon after revoked; and after revoking it, his legates, at the council of Arles, overawed by the emperor, concurred with the

rest in signing the condemnation of Athanasius, yielding, as they expressed it, to the troublesome times. Afterwards, indeed, Liberius was so far a confessor in the cause of orthodoxy, that he underwent a long and severe banishment, rather than lend his aid and countenance to the measures which the emperor pursued for establishing Arianism throughout the empire. But however firm and undaunted the pope appeared for a time, he had not the magnanimity to persevere; but was at length, in order to recover his freedom, his country, and his bishopric, induced to *retract his retraction,* to sign a second time the condemnation of Athanasius, and to embrace the Arian symbol (creed) of Sirmium. Not satisfied with this, he even wrote to the Arian bishops of the east, excusing his former defence of Athanasius; imputing it to an excessive regard for the sentiments of his predecessor Julius; and declaring, that now, since it had pleased God to *open his eyes*, and shew him how justly the heretic Athanasius had been condemned, he separated himself from his communion, and cordially joined their holinesses (so he styled the Arian bishops) in supporting the true faith. Before he returned from exile, meeting with the emperor, who was by this time turned semi-Arian, the pliant pontiff, impatient to be again in possession of his see, was induced to change anew, and subscribe the semi-Arian confession!' Will Dr. M. who has so earnestly asked me what I would have done with my doctrine as a member of the council of Nice, look at the contrast, and candidly answer to himself, who 'missed the point'—the ancient confessor or the creed-makers?"

But "admitting," says Mr. D. "that he may, by his creed, exclude Pelagians, semi-Pelagians, Swedenborgians, Universalists, Arians, and Socinians from the ministry, by what authority does he extend its operation, and exclude from the ministry, in his voluntary associations, men who are contaminated by none of these heresies? Men against whom he has not a word to say, but that they oppose the exercise of human authority in the church, and are scrupulous to preserve the rights of the human conscience, and the supremacy of the Lord Jesus, as King and Head of his church? Will he permit me respectfully to return his own words to him: "Why this almost entire silence concerning a part of the argument, which, first of all, and above all, demanded his whole strength? Not, I am persuaded, because he had not discernment enough to see the full front and force of the difficulty, but because he had nothing to say. Here his doctrine labors most deeply and fatally. Until he shall relieve it from this difficulty, he will have accomplished nothing. It is a millstone about the neck of his cause, which, unless detached, must sink it irrecoverably."

Here the Doctor receives an incurable wound. I am sorry that I cannot publish the whole of Mr. Ducan's answer to this question, because in giving a few slices of it I do injustice to the whole. In showing how the church may be preserved pure without these humanly authoritative human creeds, he is full and convincing. He asks, How did the primitive church, and down till the council of Nice, exclude heretics and heresies?—If creeds are necessary, Why did not the Master himself give us one? Why did not the apostles give us one, seeing the church must perish without it? Out of about forty pages of the most relevant mater in reply to this question, I can give but one quotation more:—

"If then the question is again pressed, how shall we exclude heresies and their advocates from the church, I reply, let christians quit their scholastic strife, and seek after nothing but biblical theology. Let young men, while training for the ministry, be turned to the study of the bible, and taught to learn for themselves what Jehovah has said. Systems of theology will always produce heretics; for they are always creating matters of "doubtful disputation," and ranging parties in hostile array. Few men examine every thing which belongs to any given system; and many men declare a vast deal more than they know. A principle is taken for granted, and then its legitimate consequence is boldly defended; whereas both should be discarded, if the first were candidly and fairly considered. Let young men be taught to investigate for themselves; to turn their attention to the scripture page, and declare no more than what they learn from prayerful and diligent inquiry. When this is done, the "millstone," which we are endeavoring to detach, shall roll to the bottom of the floods: and Dr. M. and myself, with our bibles in our hands, shall rise to the paradise of God, to differ no more forever. There we shall see as we are seen, and know as we are known; and charity, the greatest of all christian graces, now so loosely seated on our hearts, will adorn us with her mantle while eternity shall last."

Extract of a Letter from a friend in North Carolina, to the Editor, dated September 10, 1826.

—" I wish to encourage the more general circulation of them, as, in the general, I heartily approve of what they contain, especially the imposition of the priesthood; yet I must acknowledge there are a few things to which I have some objections. Objection 1st. The call to the ministry: you, if I mistake not, reject any thing like our having a knowledge of any special call of God to the work, as this call was confined to the days of the apostles, and accompanied with miracles as the evidence. This I acknowledge, and the calling may be said to be a miraculous calling, as well as many miracles attending their work, (the case of Paul;) but since the days of the apostles, I have to believe that the real ministers of the gospel of Jesus Christ are divinely and specially called to the work; not that I believe that every person who takes it upon himself to teach or to preach, is called by God to the work; no, far be it, for I believe that there are but few, compared to the number now engaged in this all-important work, know any thing like a work of grace upon their souls, and as little about a call to the ministry. I believe many are nothing better than wolves in sheep's clothing, and many, too many, are preaching for filthy lucre, feed and are kept fat on goat's milk; but yet I believe those that are owned by God are such as have passed from nature to grace, have experienced the new birth, and not all such called to preach: though I acknowledge that every lay member is to teach and preach both by example and precept, if they act up to their duty and privilege, as lay members and not pastors. Neither do I believe that every person whose mind may lead him out to public speaking, is to be considered as qualified for an elder or pastor; for in the church, God has placed diversities of gifts, by the same Spirit, some pastors, some teachers, some to exhortation, &c. and we are all called upon to the exercise of these public gifts; but I believe those that are called to labor in word and doctrine and to take charge of the flock of God, to feed them, &c. have some special exercise of mind not known

to others. I will tell you a little of the exercise of my mind. I entertained a hope about twenty-nine years ago, that God, for Christ's sake, had pardoned my sins; that I was justified in his sight through the all-atoning blood of the cross, &c. At this time I felt unspeakable love both to God and my fellow creatures, and it was my heart's desire that all might see and test the sweetness of this salvation, &c. but yet I can date no call to the work of the ministry. About six months after, I had a most transporting view of this glorious plan with its sweet and unbounded fulness—the beauty of holiness, the hateful nature of sin, the happy state of the saints, the deplorable state of the wicked, &c. that immediately my mind was impressed something like this; that as God had been so good as to reveal and make known these things to me, if I did not go forth and warn poor sinners of their danger and endeavor to point them to the Lamb of God that takes away the sin of the world, that God would require their blood at my hand, &c. I trembled, I tried to make my excuses, but yet it would awful sound in my ears and reach my very heart, Woe to me if I preach not the gospel! For seventeen years was this the case; but at length, with much fear and trembling, I had to venture upon the Lord. Since that, though doubts and fears often I have to labor under, I witness peace in venturing in the work. It would exceed the limits of a letter to detail minutely the exercise of my mind for seventeen years.

Objection 2d. You say, if I mistake not, that we only have to acknowledge that we believe that Jesus Christ is come in the flesh. Now I believe that there are thousands that are so well instructed in the scriptures, that they believe this in the head but not in the heart; and this belief may influence them so as to live moral lives with graceless hearts. I believe all such as have been and are delivered from the curse and bondage of the law, and have been put into the liberties of God's dear children, can render such an account of the exercises of their mind while under conviction, their deliverance, &c. &c. as is common with other christians, and in this way to get fellowship, which is desirable in the church of Christ. I only drop these few remarks, and must come to a close after noticing another objection—that of faith.

You hold out to view that the scriptures hold out but one faith. True, there is but one true and saving faith, which is that faith that works by love and purifies the heart from sin, &c. But the scripture speaks of a faith which we make shipwreck of, a faith of devils, &c. Probably I might have understood you better had you been a little more full on these subjects. I have been short in my objections and remarks, for it would require a letter of several pages to give you my views on the subject, which I may attempt another time.

Funeral sermons, so called, I believe to be anti-christian and traditional. I should be glad you would give us your views of this subject in one of your papers, as fully as possible.

Adieu, my dear brother, for the present. I hope ever to be your well-wisher and fellow-laborer in the common cause of our Divine Master, and that in much love.   J. C."

Reply.

Dear Brother,

WITH regard to the two objections stated in yours of the 10th September, I have a few things to remark. And with respect to the first it ought

33

to be considered that preaching, teaching and ruling embrace the whole duties belonging to the offices ordained by the Saviour relative to the conversion of sinners and the edification of disciples. These works were for a time to be performed by the same persons. And if we understood the precise idea attached to these terms by the apostles, there would be less difficulty in our minds as to the call and qualifications indispensable to these works. The term *call* itself is a scriptural term, and was used by the apostles in a certain and definite sense.

You have no doubt frequently observed that we contend that the scriptures never can be understood in any other way than by attaching to the terms found in the book the very ideas which the sacred writers and speakers affixed to them. To take their terms and attach other ideas to them, is the grossest imposition upon ourselves and others. To attempt to understand their terms or to investigate the meaning of them is not a mere controversy about words and names, as some would have it; for the whole of our salvation is found in words and communicated to us in terms; and unless these words and names are apprehended, we are just in the predicament of those who have no revelation. It is matter, therefore, of vast importance with me to understand the words found in these sacred writings in the very identical sense of the writers; and I am assured that when this is done all doubts on the subject of religion will vanish, and the New Testament will be perfectly understood. There is but one rule to be observed in order to gaining this end, and that is to take notice how the terms are either universally or specially used in all the places where they occur. This requires much reading and attention, which, however, always repays the diligent. The laborer is always rewarded with prompt payment. No man can labor one day in those mines but he must carry home with him the precious metal at night. God is not (like man) obliged to carry on any work upon mere credit. He always pays down at the moment the work is done. Nay, we can never bring him in debt; for he pays for every stroke while it is striking.

But to return. Let the term preaching and the term call be understood aright, and there can be no controversy between us upon the subject.— But you think " there is a call to the ministry." In this phrase the terms are all changed. I think there is a call to the office of a deacon, and I think there is a call to the office of a bishop; and I think, moreover, that no man can constitutionally assume, or take to himself, these offices, unless he is called according to the apostolic rule. But with regard to " the call to the ministry" the bible says nothing; and although I understand the ideas attached to these words in popular use, I reject them from my vocabulary altogether, because they mislead those who wish to understand the christian scriptures in their own simplicity and force. The bible knows nothing about " the ministry" of the Catholic, Episcopal, or Presbyterial church, nor any other ministry save that of Moses and Christ. There is no such office as that of a pope, cardinal, dean, chapter, archbishop, church warden, presiding elder, circuit preacher, class leader, lay presbyter, Presbyterian minister, Congregational or Baptist Divine, mentioned from Genesis to Jude. It is true, John, in the Revelation, mentions something about them, but it is when he is describing that curious animal that rose out of the sea, that spoke like a lamb, and which had horns and claws somewhere about it. Now as the bi-

ble knows nothing of these offices, it is unreasonable to expect to find a call to them mentioned in the volume. " A call" in some sects means so many hundred dollars a-year; in others it means a deep impression upon the mind; and in others it means no more than the voice of the congregation.

I know what you term " a call" is just what I felt a hundred times when a boy. And I still feel it. I feel that it is my indispensable duty to call upon sinners to reform, and to flee from the wrath to come. I also feel that it is my indispensable duty to write and publish this paper, and to make use of all righteous means to circulate it far and wide. I could not conscientiously abandon it. But shall I say that I am specially called by the Holy Spirit to edit the " Christian Baptist?" If there be any sense which can be put upon these words, which will justify their use in this connexion, I will add, that I am as much called by the Holy Spirit to publish the " Christian Baptist," as any man upon the earth is called to preach the gospel. What think you of this? A man that can read well, and who finds persons who cannot read the testimony of Matthew, Mark, Luke, and John, is also called by the Holy Spirit to read those testimonies; and in so reading, he is preaching the gospel. I think the whole amounts to this, and the whole controversy issues here; those who feel it their duty to preach the gospel, call this sense of duty " a call of the Holy Spirit;" and when they feel it their duty to visit the sick, and to feed the hungry, and clothe the naked, they consider this sense of duty a mere dictate of conscience, or a part of religion, and do not rank it so high as a special call of the Holy Spirit; whereas in fact it is the same in every respect. And did men feel that there is as much religion in feeding the hungry and visiting the sick, as they think there is in public speaking, I doubt not but that they would think they had as divine, and as authoritative a call, to the one as to the other. But many, from false views of things, after they have found peace and joy in the gospel, think that there is no way of serving God nor men but in preaching the gospel, and they can have no rest night nor day so long as they are not " serving God," *i. e.* in their view, preaching the gospel. Hence so many not only attempt to preach the gospel, but even to teach the christian religion, who have need themselves to be taught the very first principles of the doctrine of Christ. In this way they impose upon themselves, the church, and the world, with a good conscience, thinking they are serving God, and that they are either emphatically or exclusively the servants of God. Now I am led to think, from the apostles' doctrine, that the poor widow, or the waiting maid who labors industriously in her station, and who obeys Christ, is just as good a servant of God and " minister of Jesus Christ" as ever John Calvin was, or any other preacher or teacher is. On this topic I cannot be more diffuse at present.

As to your second objection, I will only observe that, although every christian can tell much of his own past and present feelings, there is no law, commandment, or rule, calling upon him to make them known for any purpose whatever. And there is no divine commandment, rule, or precedent, authorizing us to demand, in order to baptism, any such a recital; but a true, sincere, or hearty profession of the faith which the apostles required. Disciples are not to be baptized into their own experience, but into the faith; nor are we to love them because of their experience, but because they are partakers of the same precious faith. Nor is their telling their experience any more assurance that " their religion is seated in their heart" than their professing the faith. There is not one advantage to be gained by hearing or telling all the workings of unbelief, or all the conflicts of conscience, or all the agonies of despair, all the calms and storms of the experience of John Bunyan, or any other man; and it is absurd, in every sense of the word, to call such agitations and mental commotions as were prior to conversion—I say again, it is absurd to call such, " *christian* experience." Any thing it may be but *christian* experience; for a christian experiences no such things. And it is absurd on another account to require a candidate for baptism to tell us his *christian* experience, for it supposes that he must have lived a long time a christian without obeying the very commandment which points him out as a disciple of Christ. And for a Baptist to baptize any candidate on the recital of his christian experience while disobeying the gospel, is the climax of inconsistency. If I am to be entertained with such recitals, I would ask persons to tell me what they experienced while they disobeyed the gospel, and what have they experienced since they believed and were baptized. This would at least be consistent with Baptist proceedings; but the popular course is at war with the very elements of their own system. I have only to add one word more, that to call the experiences of men, before or after they believe, vital piety, is the greatest abuse of language and good sense that I know of.

On the subject of *funeral sermons*, the law of my King says nothing. Some may, perhaps, have read in their Testaments of the eloquent eulogy and pathetic funeral oration which the Rev. Simon Peter delivered on the death of Deacon Stephen; or of the feeling funeral sermon that the pious and Rev. Saulus Paul pronounced on the death of the Rt. Rev. and venerable James Zebedee. Those who have read the funeral sermons delivered by the apostles on the death of John the Baptist, and Mary the mother of Jesus, will no doubt admire the practice; but for us who have lost all these parts of the New Testament, we cannot be supposed to have much taste for this kind of orations. For my part, I would rather hear one resurrection sermon than ten burial sermons.

I have been sometimes asked how this practice got into fashion. The only history I can give of it is as follows:—In the days of popish uniformity it was usual to gather the friends of the deceased to contrive some way of expediting the progress of the departed in his journey through purgatory. For this purpose his relative gave oblations, and the priest was there ready to receive them. When the oblations amounted to something sufficient to make the gates of purgatory yield, the priest went down with the sum and gave his orders to the keeper of this prison to let the ransomed captive escape.

The followers of John Calvin and Martin Luther did not relish this custom; but in process of time some of their followers thought that the Romanists gained something from *the dead* for the benefit of the living; and they set about visiting the houses of mourning, and of making lamentation over the dead for the purpose of affecting the living. They professed not to benefit the dead, but the living. The rich had large funerals and many mourners, and consequently the priests were more attentive on these occasions, because it gave them a " greater opportunity of *doing good*." It then became a dishon-

orable thing not to have funeral sermons when relatives died, and so it passed off into a mere token of respect for the dead and living. It is now a mere complimentary thing; and you know when any thing is considered a *decent* thing, there are many excuses for it. And so it is said it is a good time to touch the feelings when the heart is melting with grief; and it is for the sake of the living and not for the dead that this custom is kept up. It has often astonished me how much more pains is taken, and how much more ingenuity is exhibited in finding authority or excuses for the support and continuance of human institutions, than for attending upon the Divine ordinances plainly declared in the New Testament. But how sensible christians can justify themselves to their own consciences for neglecting the ancient order of things, and in following up human traditions, is to me a matter of inexpressible surprize. I saw, not long since, a funeral sermon advertised on the occasion of the death of Jeremiah Beauchamp and his wife; and a funeral sermon has been delivered on the execution of malefactors in some of our cities. No doubt these were proper themes; but it is something like those " affairs of honor" amongst people of color, which are a good lesson to such men as the honorable John Randolph and the honorable Henry Clay.

Many, however, delivered funeral sermons from the best motives, and this is with them a sufficient excuse. Balls have recently been introduced in Paris by the prayers of a clergyman, and no doubt there was need for them. And " the grace" before a public dinner has been drunk down in a toast after dinner. Editors of newspapers pronounce encomiums upon the prayers of religious orators of the day. A cattle show and exhibition of horses and hogs must be carried to the church and consecrated by a priest; and nothing is wanting to sanctify a horse-race, and make it a sealing ordinance, but a small stretch of charity—about as much as will license a billiard table and a game of cards. What a religious people we are!! Wishing you and I may be content with, and live up to the piety ordained in the New Testament, I subscribe myself your affectionate brother and fellow-laborer in the doctrine which is according to godliness.   THE EDITOR.

Christian Morality.—No. IV.
On Speaking Truth.

" AND as he thinks in his heart, so does he truth express," is one of the distinguishing characteristics of a true disciple of Jesus Christ. Truth is the basis of all confidence amongst rational beings. Implicit confidence in every word spoken would have always been enjoyed had it not been for the introduction of lies. Unbelief and distrust are the natural results of a system of lying and deceit. God has thought proper to designate himself, since the introduction of falsehood into the universe, as " the God of truth." The Devil is always represented as a liar—as the father of liars—as the arch deceiver. Eve was seduced by a lie; and the belief of a lie became the cause of all distrust, and opened a fountain of deceit which has corrupted the whole race of Adam. By the belief of a lie death entered into the world; and God has thought proper, by the belief of the truth, to introduce men into the enjoyment of life. Every thing good is on the side of truth; and every thing evil is leagued with falsehood. The lying tongue and deceitful lips are an abomination in the sight of God; because from them have proceeded all that is the cause of misery and wretchedness in the world.

From these maxims, which are as universally admitted as the evidences of the christian religion, it is easily inferred that truth is a capital virtue, without which there is no goodness in man. Christians having experienced the evil consequences of the first lie that was spoken in human ears, and having been reclaimed and brought back to God by the belief of truth, are led not only to love the truth which brought them to reformation, but to love truth in general. To speak it and practice it are therefore indispensable duties of the christian.

All errors in religion are of two kinds; as we say, errors in doctrine and errors in practice. Errors in doctrine are simply lies; whilst errors in practice are transgressions of law. Doctrinal errors are doctrinal lies, or false views which the mind takes of things revealed. If, then, a man believe false doctrine, he simply holds that for truth which is, in plain English, a lie. Of those doctrinal lies some are inoperative speculations; others are operative falsehoods which issue in the transgression of law.

Some men, for example, teach for doctrine that reformation is not the immediate duty of all men yet unreclaimed. Some believe this to be a truth; consequently, do not reform: but are waiting for something as previous or preparatory to it. Now the holding of this error issues in the transgression of law, or in the transgression of a divine commandment, which expressly says, "God commands all men every where to reform." Again—some take up false views of this reformation, which issue in practical errors. Supposing it to mean no more than a change of views or a regret for the past, they are led to rest in a change of system or of sentiment, while their practices continue as they were. But did they view it as a truth, that in the proclamation of reformation, God commanded such a change of sentiment through the truth proclaimed, as commences forthwith a reformation of life, and that this reformation of life is the end or object of the commandment or proclamation, then nothing short of such a reformation could satisfy the person entertaining such a view of this proclamation. In this we see how errors in doctrine, or doctrinal lies, issue in transgression of law, either in the way of omission or commission.

The apostle John, both in his Epistles and in the Revelation, distinctly and boldly denominates the speakers or promulgers of false doctrine, liars. Those who profess to know God, but in works deny him, the same apostle calls liars. "If," says he, "a man says I know him, and keep not his commandments, he is a liar, and the truth is not in him." When the apostle John says, "all liars shall have their portion in the lake which burns with fire," there is every reason to believe, from a just regard to his style, that he especially means the propagators of false doctrine.

But we would call the attention of our readers to a great apostacy from truth, not only doctrinal or sentimental truth, but from speaking truth, and giving true representations to one another in the common intercourse of life. The time has been when a christian was understood to mean a person free from guile, deceit, and falsehood of every kind. He was understood to be a person purified in heart by the belief of divine truth; a person who made no false pretensions nor promises, and always gave a faithful representation of things. But there appears an awful declen-

sion in the general character of christians from this description, in the present day. "Christian nations" are as famous for lying and deceit, as they are for their refinements in the arts of war and an honest way of men stealing. The great multitude seems to have lost a regard for truth, and to have adopted a regular system of prevarication and deception. Even the most solemn promises and pledges are violated without any apparent contrition. A tells B, without any apparent compunction, that he cannot meet his engagements because the times are hard. He will not discommode himself, or make any sacrifice, and scarcely an effort to redeem his pledge, because it is fashionable to excuse oneself for failing to fulfil promises by laying all the guilt upon the depreciation consequent on our extravagancies. But this is not all. In speaking of one another, and to one another, exaggeration and hyperbole do not satisfy the propensity for the marvellous, do not give full vent to our passions, our loves or our hates; but downright fabrication and gross misrepresentation become necessary to carry favorite objects; insomuch that we scarcely know how much to subtract from all that we hear, in order to arrive at the truth. Those whose consciences will not brook downright fabrication and blunt lying, will nevertheless button themselves up to the chin in a garment of guile of as many plies as the seven-fold shield of Achilles; so that if you were to unbutton some of our giants in morality, they would be mere pigmies in stature. Equivocation, mental reservation, ambiguity, double meanings, high colorings, small subtractions, and little additions are the apparent order of the day. Now the genius and spirit of all the precepts and examples of christian morality on this point, are in direct opposition to the course of the world. Even hypocrisy and guile are denounced as most odious offences against the spirit of Christ; and yet hypocrisy and guile are the most decent of all the species of lying and deceit exhibited in the world. One of the ingredients in that famous recipe for long life which king David first promulged, and which the apostle Peter attests, is this: "If a man would live long and see good days, let him refrain his tongue from evil and his lips from guile." If christian societies do not reform in this respect, the character which Paul gave of the Cretans will soon accord with the great mass of the christian world—the Cretans are always liars."

Every pretence, profession, declaration, and promise that does not fully accord with simple fact, is to be ranked under the generic head of lying, and divests the character of that essential attribute of the inhabitants of heaven. "And as he thinks in his heart, so does he truth express."   Editor.

A Restoration of the Ancient Order of Things.
No. XVI.
The Spirit of Ancient Christians.

Amongst all that has been said in this work on the ancient order of things, we do not at present recollect of having received any objections from any quarter against any one position laid down in any essay under this head. We have received numerous communications presenting objections to some articles in this work, but none that we remember against any one item which we have said belonged to the ancient order of things. To what this is owing, I presume not to say. One thing is obvious from the face of this work, that our correspondents are not backward in exhibiting their objections, nor are we very scrupulous about laying them before the public. This silence, then, on this grand chapter of this work, is to be attributed either to a general conviction, or a patient investigation not yet finished, or to an entire apathy on the subject. We would rather ascribe it to either of the former two causes than to the latter.

Before we proceed to any new items under this general head, we shall offer a few remarks on that spirit and temper of mind which was exhibited while as yet the ancient order of things stood uncorrupted, and which it may be presumed must be possessed, and exhibited in order to the restoration of that order.

One of the most infallible signs of true conversion which I know any thing of—and one which the ancient converts generally exhibited—and one which Saul of Tarsus, at the moment of his conversion so eminently displayed, is couched in these words—"Lord, what will you have me to do?" This unfeigned and vehement desire to know the will of the Lord in order to do it, is, in my humble opinion, the surest and most general and comprehensive sign, proof, and pledge of regeneration. The spirit and temperament of the ancient christians inclined and drew them, as the laws of gravitation do all bodies to the centre of the system, to a most devout conformity to all the institutes of the Prince of Life. They loved his will supremely. Neither fire nor water, famine nor sword, good fame or bad fame prevented them in their obedience. They took joyfully the spoiling of their goods, and loved not their lives unto death rather than renounce their allegiance in any one point to him who died for them. His laws and institutions were all in all to them. No scribe, no rabbi, no sanhedrim, no human tribunal, no popularity amongst their own people or foreigners, no reproach, no privation could induce them to treat his will with either coolness, indifference, or neglect. They reasoned thus: If Jesus died for us, we owe our lives to him. We are his, and not our own. His will shall be ours. His statutes shall be our choice. Our only concern shall be, "Lord, what will you have us to do?"

Let the spirit, then, of the ancient christians be restored, and we shall soon see their order of things clearly and fully exhibited. "If the eye be sound the whole body shall be full of light;" and if the heart be right the practice will bear the test of examination. To have the ancient order of things restored in due form, without the spirit or power of that order, would be mere mimicry, which we would rather, and we are assured the primitive saints themselves would rather, never see. The spirit of the present order of things is too much akin to the spirit of this world. It looks with a countenance beaming too much complacency on the pride and vanity, on the tinsel and show, on the equipage and style, on the avarice and ambition, on the guile and hypocrisy of this world. Its supreme petition is not "Lord, what will you have me to do?" but "O you sons of religious fashion! you leaders of religious taste! you synods and councils! you creeds and systems! you mitred heads and patented divines! and you, O Mammon! tell us plainly, tell us fully, what you would have us to do to gain your admiration, and if possible too, to save our souls." This is not the spirit of all, of any creed or of any party; but this appears the leading and triumphant spirit of the present order of things.

The spirit of the ancient order always looked up to the throne of Jesus, while that of the modern looks around on the smiles of ecclesiastical rulers. The spirit of the ancient derived its joys from the complacency of the Founder of the Faith; the spirit of the modern, from the approbation of the leaders of devotion. The apostles' doctrine was the food and support of the former, while creeds and commentaries are the nourishment of the latter. The praise of God animated that—the praise of men enlivens this.

May I tell a little of my religious experience, as this is much the fashion now? I will once at least, comply with the will of the religious populars. Well, then, I once loved the praise of men, and thought it would be a great happiness could I so shape my course as to merit the praise of God and the approbation of men. I saw there was a kind of piety the people of fashion in the religious world admired, and I thought that a few small additions to it might make it pass current in both worlds. I set my heart to find it out. I saw but little difference in many sects as respected true piety, but a good deal as respected show and ceremony. I thought that which was most popular might upon the whole be the safest, as it would make sure of one point at all events, and might gain the other too. For there was a John Newton in the church of King Harry and a George Campbell in that of St. Charles. I vacillated here for a time. If I joined the most fashionable and profitable society, and adopted the most genteel order of things, I did not know but that if I were a pretty honest and faithful member, like some of those good Churchmen or Presbyterians, I might chance heaven as well as they, and at all events I would be sure of good entertainment on the road. As yet I felt not the attractions of the love of God; but soon as I was enabled to calculate the import of one question, viz. "What is a man profited if he should gain the whole world and lose his life?" and soon as I understood that it was "a faithful saying and worthy of all acceptation, that Jesus the Messiah came into the world to save sinners," even the chief of sinners, I reasoned on different premises and came to different conclusions. If bought at so dear a rate, and purchased at such an immense price, I found all my faculties, and powers, and means, and opportunities were claimed on principles at which no generous heart could demur. Had I a thousand tongues as eloquent as Gabriel's and faculties of the most exalted character, 'twere all too little to tell his praise and to exhibit his excellencies to men.

The only question then was, How shall I do this to the most advantage? In attempting to find an answer to this, I found that there was a way already laid down, which, if I adopted and pursued, must lead soonest and safest to this point. It was all comprised in two sentences—Publish in word what he has done, and as his own institutions will reflect the greatest possible honor upon him in this world, let them be fairly exhibited and the end is gained. This chain of thought just led me to the question, "Lord, what will you have me to do?" Now, in attempting to find an answer from his oracles to this petition, I took it for granted that there was no new communication of his will to be expected, but that it must be sought after in the volume. When any act of devotion or item of religious practice presented itself to my view, of which I could learn nothing from my Master's Last Will and Testament, I simply gave it up; and if I found any thing there, not exhibited by my fellow-christians, I went into the practice of it, if it was the practice of an individual; and if it was a social act, I attempted to invite others to unite with me in it. Thus I went on correcting my views, and returning to his institutes until I became so speckled a bird that scarce one of any species would cordially consociate with me: but I gained ample remuneration in the pursuit, and got a use of my wings which I never before experienced. Thus too I was led into a secret, which as I received freely, I communicate freely. It is this: There is an ancient and a modern order of things in the Lord's house. Now I am sure that if all my brethren had only the half of the religious experience I have had upon this subject, they would be doubly in the spirit of this ancient order, and their progress would be geometrically proportioned to what it now is. My friends will forgive me for so much egotism—and my enemies will find fault with me at any rate; so that it is little matter as respects them, what I say or do. In the mean time, however, I cannot conclude without again remarking, that if the spirit of the ancient christians and of their individual and social conduct was more inquired after, and more cultivated, we should find but little trouble in understanding and displaying the ancient order of things.   EDITOR.

Hilary, Bishop of Poictiers in Aquitanic,
Who flourished in the fourth century, speaks as follows of the spirit of creed-making in his time, which was but a few years after its rise:—

"It is a thing equally deplorable and dangerous, that there are as many creeds as there are opinions among men; as many doctrines as inclinations; and as many sources of blasphemy as there are faults among us; because we make creeds arbitrarily, and explain them as arbitrarily. And as there is but one faith, so there is but one only God, one Lord, and one baptism. We renounce this one faith, when we make so many different creeds; and that diversity is the reason why we have no true faith among us. We cannot be ignorant, that *since the council of Nice, we have done nothing but make creeds.* And while we fight against words, litigate about new questions, dispute about equivocal terms, complain of authors, that every one may make his own party triumph; while we cannot agree, while we anathematize one another, there is hardly one that adheres to Jesus Christ. What change was there not in the creed last year! The first council ordained a silence upon the *homoousion;* the second established it, and would have us speak; the third excuses the fathers of the council, and pretends they took the word *ousia* simply; the fourth condemns them, instead of excusing them. With respec to the likeness of the Son of God to the Father. which is the faith of our deplorable times, they dispute whether he is like in whole, or in part. These are rare folks to unravel the secrets of heaven. Nevertheless it is for these creeds, about invisible mysteries, that we calumniate one another, and for our belief in God. We make creeds every year; nay, every moon we repent of what we have done; we defend those that repent; we anathematize those that we defended. So we condemn either the doctrine of others in ourselves, or our own in that of others; and reciprocally tearing one another to pieces, we have been the cause of each other's ruin."

No. 6.]   JANUARY 1, 1827.
Note.—When I received the epistle from Mr. D, a skeptic, my father was on a visit at my house. I handed it to him and requested him to write a suitable answer; with an engagement that I would write an answer without seeing his, and that his should be written without seeing mine; that we should then read them and put it to vote which should be published. When writ-ten and read, we voted them "both best," and agreed that both should be published. Accordingly, without further ceremony, I lay his before the reader. It ought to be stated that he promised to confine himself to the mere difficulties.   EDITOR.

To Mr. D, a Sceptic.—Replication No. V.
Sir—In adverting to that part of your letter containing the difficulties which occurred to your mind in your re-examination of the evidences for the truth of divine revelation, with your request for a satisfactory solution; I perceive you assign me a task of no small magnitude, to the accomplishment of which two things appear indispensably necessary; viz. a competent ability on my part to propose a just and adequate solution, and on your part a capacity or state of mind competent to receive it; neither of which might be the case, and yet the difficulties not insolvable. In the mean time, however, before we attempt things so remote and apparently arduous, let us advert to things contiguous and which lie immediately before us; by this means we shall advance better prepared to encounter those huge and apparently insuperable difficulties, or they may vanish as we approach, and, like imaginary mountains upon the verge of a distant horizon, totally disappear. Two things which involve the whole are obvious and tangible; namely, the Bible and the World. The former of which corresponds as exactly to the latter as the reflection of the face in a glass answers to the face reflected. The Bible presents us with a certain description of human nature, that is, of the dispositions, conditions, conduct, and characters of mankind; and, at the same time, in connexion with this, with a correspondent display of the divine procedure towards mankind, either as approbatory or disapprobatory; on the one side proposing and conferring rewards or privileges; on the other, denouncing and executing punishments or privations. All this we find, both by our own and by universal experience, to be correct. The description exactly agrees with the thing described. The effects and consequences perfectly corresponding to the approbatory or disapprobatory annunciations, whether we trace them upon the ample and diversified page of universal history; or upon the more limited page of our actual experience and observation. We every where perceive a perfect coincidence between that which is and has been the character and condition of mankind, both individually and collectively, with the effects and consequences; and what the Bible presents us upon these topics; —the actual providence of God in the series of events perfectly corresponding to that which is written. Besides this display of facts, of which there can exist no doubt to him who will avail himself of the existing and obvious documents, the Bible further informs us of two things of which we must otherwise have remained entirely ignorant, as evidently appears from the existent state of all the nations that have not received it. Namely, how things came to be as they are; and what will be the future consequences after the termination of the present state of things. Of the truth and propriety of these two latter items of the divine testimony there are and have been great diversities of opinion, many difficulties and objections have originated to inquisitive minds, which, for aught I know, have never been, nor possibly can be resolved in this life: their truth and propriety, however, have never been attempted to be disproved by contrary testimony, and, I presume, never will. No credible witnesses ever have been, nor, I again presume, ever

38

can be produced to prove the contrary of what is recorded in the first three chapters of Genesis or in the last three of Revelations, whatever doubts may arise concerning the wisdom, the goodness or the equity of the proceedings and events therein recorded. Whereas much and satisfactory evidence has been and can be produced to evince the truth, that is, the divine authority and authenticity of these portions of the sacred record. But to come to the difficulties which you suggest, through the proper medium, let us first see how the quantum of evil, both physical and moral, which the bible and matter of fact, or, in other words, universal experience present to our consideration, may be shown to be consistent with the attributes of prescience, goodness, and power, which the bible, and the common consent of all that receive it as a divine revelation, ascribe to God. The bible and all that receive it in its proper character, indeed all that are tolerably well acquainted with the history of the world, with the past and present condition of mankind, do and must acknowledge that a vast and almost endless variety of evils, physical and moral, vex, torment, harass, and oppress the world; and that this has been the case from the earliest ages. The bible in the meantime informing us that the physical evils are the just and proper results and consequences of the moral; and that they are ordained by God as punishments, preventives, or correctives; and also that they shall not cease with the present state, but shall continue to afflict the wicked and impenitent during the whole course of their existence in a future state, for ever and ever. Now if penal evil be inseparably connected with moral in the constitution of things; if it be the just and settled order of the divine government, as the bible and universal experience testify, why should we suppose it to cease to afflict the wicked in a future state more than in the present: and that there will be a resurrection and future state of the wicked the bible most expressly testifies? And if it be not inconsistent with the prescience, goodness, and power of God to be the creator, preserver, and governor of such a world as this is, and has been now for near six thousand years; a very sink of moral evil, and constantly oppressed, racked, and torn to pieces with physical evil: why should we suppose it to be inconsistent with these divine perfections to continue the same for any indefinite duration? Upon what principle should we plead for its consistency with the above attributes to continue such a state of things for six thousand years, that might not as well apply, for aught that we know, to sixty thousand years? And if it be a just decision that the "wicked should travail in pain all his days," supposing him to live one thousand years; upon what principle should we show it to be an unjust decision supposing him to live one hundred thousand years? And if all the torture and torment that is and has been excruciating the human family for so many thousand years, has been compatible with the "untroubled felicity of the God of compassion;" may there not be similar or tantamount reasons that would render it compatible with his untroubled felicity, nay, with his infinite wisdom, goodness, and mercy to continue the punishment of the wicked to endless duration? Upon what principle should we suppose it? If he punish the wicked because they are wicked, from his essential and just abhorrence of their wickedness, because of its intrinsic malignity; shall we suppose he will ever change in this respect? And should we farther suppose that the sufferings inflicted and endured in this world on

account of sin are relatively useful to the purposes of the divine government; by what reason or upon what principle should we attempt to prove that the continued manifestation of the divine displeasure upon the wicked for their wickedness might not be equally useful to the purposes of the divine government in relation to a future state? In short, upon what premises soever we attempt to reconcile the present condition of the world to the revealed character of God, the same or similar premises will reconcile to the divine character the future state of rewards and punishments revealed in the bible.

Upon the whole, the investigation of this subject, if duly considered, has a powerful tendency to impress our minds with two important conclusions. The one is, as the bible happily expresses it, "Who by searching can find out God? Who can know the Almighty to perfection? It is high as heaven, what can you do? It is deeper than hell, what can you know? The measure thereof is wider than the earth; it is broader than the sea. How unsearchable are his judgments, and his ways past finding out!" The other is, How heinously malignant the nature, and how dreadful the consequences of sin! What a world of misery, what an infinity of evil has its introduction occasioned! To what a stretch of condescension and goodness has God vouchsafed to condescend, in sending his only begotten Son into the world, that we might be saved through him, from this deadly evil!

T. CAMPBELL.

THE following most excellent epistle is from the pen of one of the most experienced christian bishops in the city of Philadelphia. We have not one objection to a single sentiment it contains. The reader will see that I am still thought too severe in some of my strictures. I had thought that I had become extremely mild. In selecting terms and phrases, it is with me a matter of great self-denial to reject an appropriate one and to adopt one less appropriate, merely because the most appropriate is too true—that is, too severe. But as we grow older, I hope we will become wiser.　　　　EDITOR.

To the Editor of the Christian Baptist.

MY DEAR SIR,—Your answer to Paulinus in your September number is truly pleasing. I have rejoiced in Spirit, and praised the Father of Light for its contents. Your capitals deserve indeed to be written in capitals of gold—" NO MAN CAN BE SAVED BY THE BELIEF OF ANY THEORY, TRUE OR FALSE—NO MAN WILL BE DAMNED FOR THE DISBELIEF OF ANY THEORY."—Nor is your assertion less important—" the only question with me is to understand each sentence" [of the scriptures] "in its own context." Go on and prosper, till you have sapped and overturned the kingdom of the clergy, purged the churches from the old leaven and gathered multitudes to the Saviour. To understand what God says to us in his word, in the sense in which he speaks, is to hear that our souls may live. The moment we mistake his sense, we speculate and turn truth into falsehood in our corrupted minds; and then " if the light that is in us be darkness, how great is that darkness." Your close and pointed reasoning about theological tipplers is certainly excellent, but perhaps too highly figurative, and its language not understood by all your readers. Be sure that your ideas be understood by the babe in Christ, however illiterate, and you will rejoice the hearts of the simple, and put to flight the many speculatists in christianity. Besides, while I highly approve of the great leading ideas of your work, I can by no means approve of the harsh epithets and the much sarcasm that so easily flow from your pen. Why such expressions as "the populars," "banditti of the orthodox," or even "kingdom of the clergy," or any manner of expression that may make the truth a greater offence to the weak believer or the worldly professor than it really is. But it is likely that you account your pointed and even burnished arrows all blunt enough to rouse the dormant spirit of the age—and perhaps in this thought you are correct. I trust, however, you will remember that the weapons of our warfare are not carnal.

I am not at all surprized that the descriptions you give of faith, regeneration, christian experience, and the sanctifying influence of the truth, should occasion such opposition. No man will believe that faith is the belief of the gospel till he understand the gospel in the sense in which the apostles preached it. Express the gospel in every possible way, and exhibit in the most pointed manner that it is impossible to be saved in the very nature of things, in any way but by believing what God has said of his Son: Still the thing is not understood—the internal feeling and sentiment of every one, even the best instructed in speculations about the gospel, is, "What shall I do that I may work the works of God?" And if you are so plain and pointed that such persons cannot mistake you that you mean exactly what you say, that faith is no more than believing what God says of Jesus—then the carnal mind rises in wrath against God's only way of saving sinners. For in the ears of all such persons the words Jesus, faith, repentance, &c. mean no more to them than the same thing they have done, or are about to do to reconcile God to them, and thus avert his wrath. The work that God has wrought they will by no means believe. And it has appeared to me the more orthodox, as you would say, unbelievers are, the more they are opposed to salvation by faith. The fact is, that men are not disposed to be dependent on the Saviour for salvation, and therefore their heart rises in enmity against the doctrine of the gospel. And this is the real cause why their minds are blinded as to God's way of renovating the human soul and sanctifying all its powers. You have no doubt observed the striking beauty of the Saviour's words to Paul in reference to the effects of that gospel which he was to preach among the Gentiles, Acts xxvi. 18. "To open their eyes, to turn them from darkness to light, and from the power of Satan to God, that they may receive forgiveness of sins, and inheritance among them that are sanctified through faith that is in me."

Here the Saviour attributes the enlightening of the mind, the renovation of the heart, the forgiveness of sins, and the present and eternal inheritance of his people, to the faith that is in him. A mistake then with respect to this faith will be fatal, to the whole of personal salvation. Hence the great mistakes about what is called "christian experience." I do not, indeed, approve of the phraseology. The word "experience" is used, I think, only three times in our translation of the bible: first, in the book of *Genesis*, xxx. 27. where Laban says that he had learned by "experience" that the Lord had blessed him in worldly things on account of Jacob. Second, *Eccles.* i. 16. where Solomon boasts of his having great "experience" of wisdom and knowledge, evidently in worldly matters, above all that were before him in Jerusalem. And third, *Rom.* v. 4. where in Paul's beautiful climax he informs us that "patience works experience." The two first passages seem to regard altogether the things of this life; and Paul's "experience" seems plainly to refer to the proof we have of the interpositions of the Divine Providence in our behalf, when we patiently endure afflictions, especially for the sake of the gospel, or for righteousness' sake, as may be strikingly seen in the case of Joseph when imprisoned in Egypt. But this aside, I know what believers mean by "experience," viz. all the influence of the Spirit and gospel of God upon their minds and hearts. But others have a very different meaning. Their experience is their Saviour. That is, the many convictions of sin, and the law work they underwent before Christ, as they think, was made precious to them, and the sad struggle they have had since to persuade themselves that God loves them, and that they have an interest in Christ. That is, their religious feelings are their experience and their Saviour and their ground of hope, such as it is, before God. You would do well, then, to analyze and expose "experience" in this way. We may rest assured, that if we use the words "christian experience," or any other phraseology in a sense in which the Holy Spirit does not use them, some error lies at the bottom. When the Spirit of Truth describes the influence of divine truth upon the mind, he uses more emphatic and defined language—such as "light in the Lord," "righteousness," "knowledge," "the holiness of the truth," "the workmanship of God, created in Christ Jesus to good works;" or as Paul beautifully states it in few words, when enjoining on Timothy that he ought to charge the teachers of christianity that they teach no other doctrine than that which the apostles taught, he reminds him that the end of this charge which he gave him was "love out of a pure heart, and of a good conscience, and of faith unfeigned; from which some having swerved have turned aside to vain jangling." 1 *Tim.* i. 5. Now Paul's definition of vain jangling in christianity, let it be about what is called christian experience or any thing else, is that which is aside from love out of a pure heart and of a good conscience, and of faith unfeigned. I admire this definition of "christian experience," or, I would rather say, of the influence of the gospel upon all the powers of man. But what does Paul mean? His meaning is obvious and the more striking that he descends his climax. The last step of his ladder is "faith unfeigned." And this is that which saves the guilty, depraved, perishing sinner. "Faith feigned" is when a man professes with his lips what he does not believe in his heart, like Simon Magus,* who professed with his lips what he discovered by his works he did not believe in his heart. "Faith unfeigned" is the language of the lips expressing the belief of the heart. Instance the eunuch when put on examination of his faith, that is of what he believed; his answer seems to have been the express index of his heart, "I believe that Jesus Christ is the Son of God." *Acts* viii. 37. Or, as Paul himself expresses it, "If you shall confess with your mouth the Lord Jesus, and believe in your heart that God raised him from the dead, you shall be saved." But say many, you must believe with your heart and not with your head. Oh, fools, and slow of heart to believe, what even common sense dictates! Are there two ways of believing? If a man believes—he believes! I know of no other way of correcting the falla-

---

* "Simon himself believed also." *Acts* viii. 13. Pub.

cy. The question is, Does a man believe what God has said of his Son, or instead of this does he believe any religious conceit of his own imagination, or that of any of his fellow men? He may believe any thing in religion he pleases, but if he does not believe that Jesus of Nazareth is the only Saviour, he cannot be saved. Faith unfeigned, then, is to confess with the mouth, as an index of the heart, that Jesus of Nazareth is the Christ. Now the second step upward (of christian experience) or rather of the influence of divine truth upon all the powers of man, is "a good conscience." Conscience is that knowledge which men have of their connexion with the author of their existence, either from tradition or from the written word of God, whereby they understand that now and after death they must give an account of themselves to God. What an awful account this must be is beyond the power of utterance. Overpowered with the account men hear the gospel that the blood of Jesus, God's Son, cleanses from all iniquity, they believe it and escape to the blood, the sacrifice which the Saviour offered on Calvary, and see in this sacrifice that which satisfies the justice of God as to their crimes, and glorifies all the perfections of Deity in their justification, and obtain peace with God through the death of Christ; yea, the answer of a good conscience towards God through the resurrection of Jesus from the dead, because that resurrection evinces that the Deity was satisfied with the atonement made on Calvary, inasmuch as Jesus of Nazareth was raised from the dead, and placed at the right hand of the throne of the Almighty. Consequently, that which satisfies the justice of the eternal God, pacifies the conscience which is enlightened in the knowledge of the justice and holiness of God. Those who have their consciences satisfied with any thing less than that which satisfies the justice and holiness of the Deity, are building upon the sand. A good conscience is that which meets the justice and purity of the Divine Majesty, by the righteousness of God, the obedience to death, of Jesus the Son of God. We have the answer of a good conscience towards God, because we urge nothing in our justification before him but what magnifies his law and makes it honorable; namely, the death of his beloved Son. And we receive all our knowledge of right and wrong from this source. This, then, is a good conscience. The pure heart is defined by Peter—"Seeing you have purified your souls in obeying the truth through the Spirit to unfeigned love of the brethren," &c. 1 Pet. i. 22. The "truth" is the gospel of the Son of God, which exhibits every object in its true light, and stands opposed to all the lies of Satan and his children about any thing you please. Obeying this truth is believing it in the very sense, and in none other in which God speaks it, and this necessarily produces a pure heart, the purification of the whole soul—the mind is enlightened, the conscience is purified and at peace—the passions, the will, the affections, all the volitions are thrown into the gospel mould—the new creature is produced, the workmanship of God; or, as Paul beautifully describes the believing Romans, "God be thanked, that though you were the slaves of sin, you have obeyed from the heart that mould of doctrine into which you were cast." Rom. vi. 17. The gospel is the mould of teaching; obeying the gospel is submission to Messiah: by believing the gospel, the soul is cast into it, as metal in fusion is cast into a mould and receives all that divine impression; in every power of the soul which the

gospel believed is calculated to produce. Hence love to God who first loved us—love to all, whether persons or things, that bear his authority and his image. Hence especially the peculiar affection which is purely a christian affection—love to the brethren of Christ, because they are his brethren for the truth's sake, for the gospel's sake which is in them and shall be with them for ever, whether on earth or in heaven; and hence the benevolence to all men which the gospel breathes to the most inveterate of God's enemies. All this works that Spirit of the Truth which convinces men of sin, of righteousness, and of judgment by the gospel. Never was there any other work of the Holy Spirit to the personal salvation of men, to their being born from above, or being partakers of the divine nature. If any man have not this spirit of Christ with which he was anointed, he is none of his. This is the pure heart. And all this purity is from faith in the Son of God. No right sentiment, no peace of conscience, no holy feeling, no submission to the authority of God, no holy living but by the belief of the Son of God. Jesus must have all the glory. He has all the glory of the new creature, because he is the head of it; and his enemies who would have any religious experience from him, shall be eternally disappointed. I say, then, if I understand you, I wonder not that your little work meets with many enemies in what is called the religious world. But go on. I would say Macie, if it did not savor of the beast. Cut off every sentiment and every feeling that is not grafted on the cross of Christ, and care not who feels the severe incision. For every plant which the great husbandman has not planted shall be rooted up.

When I began this scribble I intended in the end of it to have given you specimens of speculation in christianity contrasted with the opposite truth, which have been among my papers for some time; but I have neither time nor room.

W. B.

Philadelphia, Oct. 12, 1826.

The World Ruled by Names.

I have met with the observation, though I do not at present recollect where, that the world is ruled by names. It matters not who said so; but experience shows us that there is more truth in the remark than any one at first hearing would be apt to imagine. When names are first assigned to offices, or even to orders of men, there is commonly an association of ideas, favorable or unfavorable in some respect or other, which is derived from the more ancient to the more recent application of the term. And even if the term should be coined for the occasion, the materials whence it is taken, that is, the known etymology, produces the same effect. It invariably gives rise to certain associations; these influence opinion, and opinion governs practice. We have seen the tendency which the distinction of mankind into clergy and laity had, to heighten in the minds of the populace, (that is, more than nine-tenths of the people) the reverence for the sacred order. The effect thus actually produced, in ignorant ages, through the arrogance of the one side, and the superstition of the other, is sufficiently manifest, and perfectly astonishing. I shall proceed to take notice of the consequences of some other innovations in the style adopted on these subjects.

A close resemblance, both in titles and functions, to the Jewish priesthood, came soon to be very much affected by the pastors of the church.

41

The very names of high-priest, priest, and Levite, which the inspired writers had never once applied to any class of ministers, ordinary or extraordinary, in the christian commonwealth, appeared to have a wonderful fascination in them, that rendered them incomparably superior to any appellations which Jesus Christ or his apostles had thought fit to bestow. Beside the fancied dignity, the sacerdotal titles had been always understood to convey the notion of certain rights which conduced both to the honor and to the emolument of those to whom these titles belonged. Now having availed themselves of the supposed analogy, they thought they had the best right in the world to extend their claims much further; arguing, that because the bishops, presbyters, and deacons, were the high-priests, priests, and Levites, of a superior, a more heavenly and spiritual dispensation, they ought to possess more of the unrighteous mammon, that is, more earthly treasure ·and greater temporal power. And, what is still more· extraordinary, by such wretched reasoning the bulk of mankind were convinced.

It is worth while to remark the great difference between the style adopted by the apostles, in relation to all sacred matters, and that which, in the course of a few ages, crept into the church and even became universal in it. Under the Mosaic economy, which exacted the rigid observance of a burdensome ritual, the only place devoted to the ceremonial and temporary service, consisting in sacrifices and oblations, ablutions, aspersions and perfumes, was the temple of Jerusalem, for no where else could the public ceremonies be lawfully performed. The places that were dedicated to what may be called comparatively the moral and unchangeable part of the service, consisting in prayers and thanksgivings, and instructive lessons from the law and the prophets, were the synagogues, which, as they were under no limitation in point of number, time, or place, might be built in any city or village where a suitable congregation of worshippers could be found; not only in Judea, but wherever the Jewish nation was dispersed, and that even though their temple and their polity should subsist no longer. The ceremonies of the law being represented in the gospel as but the shadows of the spiritual good things disclosed by the latter, and its corporal purifications, and other rites, as the weak and beggarly elements, intended to serve but for a time, and to be instrumental in ushering a more divine and rational dispensation, it was no wonder that they borrowed no names from the priesthood to denote the christian ministry, or from the parade of the temple service, much calculated to dazzle the senses, to express the simple but spiritual devotions and moral instructions, for which the disciples of Jesus assembled under the humble roof of one of their brethren. On the contrary, in the name they gave to the sacred offices, as well as to other things, regarding their religious observances, they showed more attention to the service of the synagogue, as in every respect more analogous to the reasonable service required by the gospel. The place where they met is once, James ii. 2. called a synagogue, but never a temple. "If there come into your assembly," *eis ten synagogen 'umon*. And it is well known that the names teacher, elder, overseer, attendant, or minister, and even angel, or messenger, of the congregation, were, in relation to the ministry of the Jewish synagogue, in current use.

When we consider this frequent recourse to terms of the one kind, and this uniform avoidance of those of the other; and when at the same time we consider how much the sacred writers were inured to all the names relating to the sacerdotal functions, and how obvious the application must have been, if it had been proper; it is impossible to conceive this conduct as arising from any accidental circumstance. We are compelled to say with Grotius, "*Non de nihilo est, quod ab eo loquendi genere, et Christus ipse, et apostoli semper abstinuerunt.*" It is indeed most natural to conclude, that it must have sprung from a sense of the unsuitableness of such a use to this divine economy, which, like its author, "is made not after the law of a carnal commandment, but after the power of an endless life." I may add, it must have sprung from a conviction that such an application might mislead the unwary into misapprehensions of the nature of the evangelical law.

In it Jesus Christ is represented as our only priest; and as he ever lives to make intercession for us, his priesthood is unchangeable, untransmissive, and eternal. A priest is a mediator between God and man. Now we are taught, in this divine economy, that as there is one God, so there is one mediator between God and men, the man Christ Jesus. The union of the mediatorship, and consequently of the priesthood, in the strictest sense of the word, is as really an article of our religion as the unity of the godhead. I do not deny, that in a looser sense every minister of religion may be called a mediator, or, if you please, a priest; inasmuch as he is the mouth of the congregation, in presenting their prayers to God, and is, as it were, also the mouth of God, on whose part he admonishes the people. The great reason against innovating by the introduction of these names is, not because the names are in no sense applicable, (that is not pretended,) but because, first, they are unnecessary; secondly, their former application mus unavoidably create misapprehensions concerning the nature of the evangelical ministry; and thirdly, because the inspired penmen of the New Testament, who best understood the nature of that ministry, never did apply to it those names.

But to return. The only proper sacrifice, under the new covenant, to which all the sacrifices of the old pointed, and in which they were consummated, is the death of Christ. This, as it cannot, like the legal sacrifices, be repeated, neither requires nor admits any supplement.— "For by one offering he has perfected for ever them that are sanctified." Sometimes, indeed, in regard to the Mosaic institution, an allegorical style is adopted, wherein all christians are represented as priests, being, as it were, in baptism, consecrated to the service of God, the community as a holy priesthood, to offer up spiritual sacrifices to him, the bodies of christians as temples destined for the habitation of God through the Spirit. The oblations are thanksgivings, prayer, and praise. The same name is also given to acts of beneficence and mercy. "To do good and to communicate forget not, for with such sacrifices God is well pleased."— This is also the manner of the earliest fathers. Justin Martyr, in his dialogue with Trypho the Jew, after mentioning Christ as our all-sufficient high priest, insists, that in consequence of our christian vocation, we, his disciples, not the pastors exclusively, are God's true sacerdotal family. *Emeis archieratikon, to alethinon genos esmen tou Theou.* In this allusive way, also, the terms circumcision, passover, unleavened bread, altar, sabbath, and the like, are sometimes allegorically applied by the sacred penmen. But no where are the terms high priest, priest, or Levite, applied particularly to the ministers of Christ.

Doctor Hickes, a zealous asserter of what he calls the christian priesthood, has a wonderful method of solving this difficulty. He supposes that Christ and his apostles acted the politicians in this particular. According to him, they were afraid, that with all the miracles and supernatural gifts they could boast, it was an undertaking too bold to be hazarded, to appear as rivals to the Jewish priests. Here he inadvertently ascribes a conduct to Jesus Christ, which, in my apprehension, reflects not a little on the sincerity of that spotless character. "As a Jew," says he, (let. I. chap. iii. sec. 1.) "he was to observe the law and the temple worship, and live in communion with the Jews; which, though he could do as a king and a prophet, yet he could not do it with congruity, had he declared himself to be their sovereign pontiff, that very high priest, of which Aaron himself was but a type and shadow." But allow me to ask, Why could he not? Was it because there was a real incongruity betwixt his conforming to the Jewish worship, and his character of high-priest? If there was, he acted incongruously, for he did conform; and all he attained by not declaring himself a priest, was not to avoid, but to dissemble, this incongruity. And if there was none in conforming, where was the incongruity in avowing a conduct which was in itself congruous and defensible? We are therefore forced to conclude, from this passage, either that our Lord acted incongruously, and was forced to recur to dissimulation to conceal it, or that Doctor Hickes argues very inconsequentially. The true christian can be at no loss to determine which side of the alternative he ought to adopt.

But to consider a little the hypothesis itself, the apostles might boldly, it seems, and without such offence as could endanger the cause, call their master the Messiah, the King, (a name with the Jews above every other human title.) They might, in this respect, say safely, that though their chief priests and rulers had killed the Lord of Life, God had raised him from the dead; nay, had done more, had exalted him to his own right hand to be a Prince and a Saviour, to give repentence to the people, and remission of sins. They might thus openly, if not put him in the place of the priest, put him in the place of the Almighty, to whom the priests are bound to minister, and from whom ultimately all the blessings must be obtained; nay, and represent his power as more extensive in procuring divine forgiveness and favor, (the great object of all their sacrifices,) than any that had ever been experienced through the observance of the Mosaic rites; inasmuch as " by him all that believe are justified from all things, from which they could not be justified by the law of Moses." Yet, says the Doctor, they durst not call him priest. Now we know that the usurping of this title was not, by the Jewish institute, either treason or blasphemy; whereas, the titles and attributes, which the apostles gave their master, were accounted both treasonable and blasphemous by the unbelieving Jews, and with too much appearance of truth, if Jesus had been the impostor they imagined him; for the disciples set him in their representations above every thing that is named, either in the heaven, or upon the earth. I might say further, Did the first preachers hesitate to maintain the cause of their master, notwithstanding that by implication it

charged the guilt of his blood on the chief priests and rulers, as those rulers themselves but too plainly perceived? But why do I say by implication? They often most explicitly charged them with this atrocious guilt. It was in the midst of the sanhedrim that Stephen boldly said, "Which of the prophets have not your fathers persecuted? and they have slain them who shewed before of the coming of the Just One, of whom you have been now the betrayers and murderers." Might they thus with safety to the cause, at least, though not with impunity to their persons, exhibit those priests as homicides, parricides, regicides, and, if I may be allowed a bold expression, even deicides; and yet durst not, without involving the whole in one general ruin, so much as insinuate that they also had their priests? *Credat Judæus Apella!*

In short, the whole pretext of this learned Doctor is precisely as if one should say, that if in a country like this, for instance, one were to raise a rebellion in favor of a pretender to the crown, the partisans might, with comparatively little danger or offence, style the sovereign in possession a tyrant and usurper, and proclaim the man they would set up, king of Great Britain, France, and Ireland, and even add, defender of the faith. But it would be imminently hazardous, and would probably ruin the cause, to insinuate that he had the patronage of any ecclesiastic benefices. They may with safety denominate him the head of the church, and of the law, the source of all honors and authority in the state, and even give him higher titles than ever monarch had enjoyed before; they may assume to themselves the names of all sorts of offices, civil or military, under him; but if they would avoid inevitable perdition, let them not style any of themselves his chaplains. In fact, the absurdity here is not equal to the former.

To Mr. D.—A Sceptic.—Replication.—No. VI.

In my last I promised you a brief statement of the gospel with a reference to your difficulties. In attempting this I must, owing to circumstances, be governed by the circumscribed limits of a sheet.

Through habit it frequently happens that the most sublime and interesting truths are heard with apathy and indifference. Because familiar with the terms, gospel, salvation, eternal life, love of God to sinners, &c. we often pronounce and hear them with as much indifference as the most common incidents of the day. But this is not all; ideas are often attached to the terms above mentioned, which contribute to the insensibility with which they are so often heard and expressed, and which divest the terms of that which most of all could interest the hearts of sinners. I will, therefore, present the gospel in the form of a proclamation, that the novelty of the *form* may awaken, if possible, attention, to *the thing.* It is not the definition of a name, but the exhibition of facts the most significant, at which I aim. I include in the proclamation that which makes it glad tidings of great joy to all people to whom it is promulged. It is in the name of him who has a right indisputable so to speak :—

Whereas all mankind have corrupted and debased themselves, have sinned against me and come short of my glory, in consequence of which they are estranged in heart from me, irreconciled to my government and will, and filled with enmity against my moral character: And where-

as there is no possibility of their restoration to
my favor, nor of their true enjoyment of themselves, in consequence of their ignorance, guilt,
indisposition, and subjection to their passions
and appetites by any means within their reach—
I DO HEREBY PROCLAIM TO ALL MANKIND INDISCRIM-
INATELY, That, moved by my own pity and compassion towards them as my own creatures,
though fallen and degraded, I have sent my only
begotten Son into the world to reveal to them my
true character; to acquaint them with their true
condition and circumstances; to expiate sin by
the sacrifice of himself, to honor and exalt my
name in all the earth, and to render it every way
compatible with my righteousness, to whomsoever I will. Be it known, therefore, to all mankind, irrespective of family, sectional or national
distinction, That it is my WILL to pardon, and
accept into my favor and friendship, every one
who believes and obeys him as my Son and the
only Saviour of men, and who is thereby reconciled to my character and will: And I do hereby
declare upon my own veracity, that I will raise
to life again all who die in the faith of my Son,
and glorify them at the consummation of this
state; that I will introduce them into my own
presence in heaven, and bestow upon them all
the happiness of life eternal in my kingdom of
glory for ever. But whosoever hears and rejects
this my proclamation, shall be condemned, and
shall share only in the resurrection of damnation.
In attestation whereof, I have sent my prophets
and apostles, accredited with all the powers and
gifts of my Holy Spirit, to promulge this my proclamation, and to demonstrate the truth and certainty thereof by all the signs and pledges which
rational beings can demand, and to commit the
same to writing, stamped with such evidences
as are requisite to gain it universal acceptance.
And I do give it in charge to every saved sinner
under heaven, to take all necessary pains, and
to use every possible means of giving publicity
to the same until I call him home; and I do most
solemnly declare, that eternal vengeance awaits
all them who do not obey this my proclamation,
and who shall corrupt, add to, or diminish aught
therefrom.

Such is the gospel in the form of a proclamation from the invisible God. Now the question
is, To what in this can any man reasonably object? I confess I know not. I admit, indeed,
that some objections are made to it, but they are
most unreasonable. For instance, it is objected
that faith or belief is made a condition or a *sine
qua non* to the enjoyment of this salvation, and
that this faith is an involuntary thing. This objection is perfectly unreasonable, and built upon
a mistaken view of faith. It is impossible that
any medicine can cure a diseased body, unless
it be received into that body. In the same
way, it is impossible that the gospel can save
any soul unless it be received into that soul.
And whatever answer you would give to him
who objects to a medicine simply because it will
not cure without being taken, I would give to
him who objects to the gospel because it will
not save without being believed. If the gospel

could save a man without being believed, I am
sure the benevolence which gave birth to it
would not have restricted its benefits to believers. But the benevolence and philanthropy of
God cannot affect our hearts unless it be known,
and it cannot be known unless it be believed,
because it is the subject of testimony. And
although faith may be said in some sense to be
involuntary, yet it so happens that unbelief,
where the gospel is promulged, is perfectly a
voluntary thing, and that is the reason they
who reject the testimony which God has given
of his Son, have no excuse for their sin. Also,
in rejecting this testimony, they prove their perversity by divesting themselves of all those
principles of reasoning which govern them
in the affairs of this life, and in admitting to be
true a thousand things which govern their conduct in this world, which are neither so important in themselves, nor supported by a thousandth part of the evidence which supports the
christian faith. In a word, in rejecting the gospel they reject their own reason, sin against
their own principles, degrade their own faculties,
and, what is still worse, they make God a liar, and
appropriate his attributes to their own conceits.

I am constrained to break off. If what I have
said in reply to yours is not satisfactory, I should
like to hear from you again. In the mean time
I should recommend you most humbly and pray-
erfully to take up the blessed volume, and (if
you can get a copy of the new translation I have
lately published, it will facilitate your inquiries
a hundred fold,) give it a regular and close investigation from beginning to end, about a dozen
of times, and then tell me what you think of it.
    Your Friend,   THE EDITOR.
Kentucky, Nov. 29th, 1826.

GOOD men of all sects have nearly the same
views of Creeds, Ecclesiastical Courts, of "Christian Experience," and of Pure Religion. The
following sentiments are extracted from one
volume of the works of JOHN NEWTON, of excellent memory.—ED.

"I dare not say what the Lord may or may
not do; but I have no present conception of love
without faith, or of faith without some communication of gospel truth and light to the mind."

"I am not very fond either of assemblies,
consistories, synods, councils, benches, or boards.
Ministers as individuals in their respective
places, are like flowers, which will preserve
their color and scent much longer, if kept singly,
than when packed together in a nosegay or
posey, for then they quickly fade and corrupt."

"It is possible to preach a very good sermon
from an English or Scotch proverb. Modes and
fashions alter in religious matters, as well as in
dress. Our first reformers usually preached from
common places; they did not take a text, but
discussed a subject—such as faith, repentance,
holiness, &c. yet surely they were preachers of
the gospel. The two volumes of Homilies, to
which our clergy are obliged by law to subscribe their assent, are a valuable collection
of sermons in this way."

"On our side of the river, many think as highly of Episcopal or Congregational order. Perhaps much of our differences of opinion on this
head, may be ascribed to the air we breathed,
and the milk which we drank in our infancy.
If I had lived in Scotland, and known the Lord,
my ministry, I suppose, would have been in the
Kirk, or the Relief, or the Secession: and if Doctor Erskine had been born and bred amongst us,
and regarded according to his merit, he might

44

perhaps have been archbishop of Canterbury long ago."

"May we not say with the apostle, Grace be with all that love the Lord Jesus Christ in sincerity? I think that is a latitudinarian prayer—I hope many agree in loving him, who sadly disagree about trifles. Such is the weakness and wickedness of the heart, even in good men. There is a great and old established house, which does much business, and causes no small disturbance in the world and in the church. The firm is Satan, Self, and Co. Till this powerful, extensive partnership be dissolved, we cannot expect perfect peace and union among all believers. It will be a joyful day, when its credit shall totally fail. Such a day we are warranted to hope for."

"I cannot speak as you do of remarkable discoveries, &c. I trust I do walk by faith—I certainly do not walk by sight. All my hope, light, and comfort is derived from a little book which I can carry in my pocket."

"If all lay preachers were like-minded with Messrs. H—— and A——, I would pray the Lord to increase their number a hundred fold. We have some such in England, but not a few would be better employed at the plough or the loom."

"A man who is more fond of novelty than of honest labor, or of being always called plain Tom or Dick, having a good stock of self-conceit, transforms himself into a preacher—he then expects to be styled Mr. Thomas, perhaps the reverend Mr. Thomas, to be excused from work, and to look almost like a gentleman. I fear such motives as these may stimulate some to be missionaries, both for at home and for abroad. When these are invited to the houses of the affluent, courted and caressed by people of the first characters, laden with gifts and presents, &c., considering what human nature is, I cannot wonder if this sudden transition from obscurity to honor and public notice, has a tendency to turn their heads, and make them think themselves persons of no small consequence."

"I pray the Lord to bless you and all who love his name in Scotland, whether Kirk, Circus, Relief, Burghers, Anti-Burghers, Independents, Methodists, or by whatever name they choose to be called. Yea, if you know a Papist who sincerely loves Jesus, and trusts in him for salvation, give my love to him."

"Study the text of the good word of God. Beware of great books. The first christians had none to read, yet they lived honorably and died triumphantly. Beware of leaning too hard upon human authority, even the best; you may get useful hints from sound divines, but call no man master. There are mixtures of human infirmity, and the prejudices of education or party, in the best writers. What is good in them they obtained from the fountain of truth, the scriptures; and you have as good a right to go to the fountain head yourself."

"There was a man and his wife who had no book but the Bible. In this they read daily, and received much comfort. One day their minister from the pulpit recommended some commentary. They attended to his recommendation, for they purchased the commentary and sat down to read it. After reading in it for some time, the man asked his wife how she felt now under the commentary. I will tell you how I feel. When I read the Bible itself, I felt as if I had drank a glass of wine; but this commentary tastes like a glass of wine in a pail of water. The wife acknowledged her feelings were the same; and by mutual consent they returned to the Bible."

So did write a good High Churchman.

Wealth of the Church of Spain.

The Pope having granted to the king of Spain the liberty of conferring pensions amounting to a third part of the bishops' revenues for one year, the Spanish government demanded of them (long before the revolution) an estimate of their amount. It may easily be supposed they would not rate them very high, and it is thought that, with the exception of the Archbishop of Toledo, they only valued them at half, or the third part of their real value. The following were the returns received and on file:—

Archbishop of		Archbishop of	
Toledo,	£110,000	Fortosa,	£6000
Zaragosa,	13,000	Coria,	5000
Santiago,	32,000	Astorga,	4000
Seville,	40,000	Almeria,	3100
Granada,	11,500	Santander,	3450
Valencia,	26,000	Palencia,	4300
Osma,	11,500	Gerona,	2500
Placentia,	8,000	Feruil,	3000

The total revenue of the Spanish Archbishops, and Bishops, according to their own estimates, amounted to £520,000 sterling; the revenues of the canons of the first and second class amounted to £469,845. Some of the canons whose incomes do not exceed £300 are enabled to keep coaches. Many of the bishops live in a style of magnificence surpassing even that of the grandees.

Income of the Spanish Clergy.

Tithes,	£10,900,000
Fees,	110,000
Alms,	1,950,000
Livings,	1,000,000
Produce of church yards,	600,000
	£13,660,000

At first sight it will appear incredible that a nation whose annual expenditure does not amount to £7,000,000, should ever have allowed the clergy to raise a revenue double that of the kingdom. But this phenomenon has been a consequence of their enormous power. Yet in spite of the inquisition, all the men of talent who have governed Spain, have endeavored to make the clergy contribute a portion of their immense wealth to the support of government. Long before the revolution they had more than once applied the ecclesiastical revenues to the public service, and when the Cortes did the same, they only followed the example given to them by many ministers of absolute kings, who reigned prior to Ferdinand.—*English Paper.*

No. 7.]   February 5, 1827.

Review.

There is just issued from the press, in this place, (Pittsburgh,) a work, titled, "*The Supreme and Exclusive Authority of the Lord Jesus Christ in Religious Matters, maintained; and the Rights, Liberties, and Privileges of the Children of God established from the Sacred Scriptures, in Opposition to the Assumed Powers of Ecclesiastics. In two Parts. By John Tassey, Pastor of the Congregational Church, Pittsburgh.*" This work contains 265 pages, duodecimo. The first part is based upon that ancient prophecy, *Deut.* chap. xviii. as quoted by Peter, *Acts* iii. 22. 23. " For Moses truly said to the fathers, A prophet shall the Lord your God raise up to you, of your brethren, like to me; him shall you hear in all things, whatsoever he shall say to you. And it shall come to pass, that every soul that will not hear that prophet, shall be destroyed from among the people."

In this part the author first illustrates the similarity between Moses the type, and Christ the antitype, in a variety of striking coincidences, both personal and official, in order to illustrate and establish the truth of the prophecy.

He next proceeds to develope and enforce the duty of unlimited obedience in all things. This he does with great apparent solemnity and elaborate pathos; and finds much to blame and lament, and justly too, on account of the manifest neglect of, and opposition to, the exclusive and universal authority of this great prophet amongst professors of every name and description.— "There is not," says he, "that entire subjection of mind to the instructions of Christ, discoverable among professing christians, that there ought to be. There is not that total and unqualified surrender of the soul to all the doctrines, and to all the duties which he inculcates. They not only listen to his word with a partial ear and straitened understanding, but with a prejudiced mind and a steeled heart. Determined at all hazards to maintain their ground, they cannot, they will not be persuaded to resign themselves to the entire control of the Lord Jesus. We complain not now of any particular description of professing christians. The evil is general and deep-rooted in them all, and demands immediate remedies. It is an eating gangrene that will soon corrode the vitals of religion, and eat out the very marrow of the gospel. And how can it be otherwise if the authority of Jesus is superseded by the authority of other principles? if pride, and party zeal, and selfishness, and love of systems, with all their close attendants in the train, march up, in rank and file, to dispossess the Son of God from his high seat as Lord of conscience?" Page 42.

Again, page 48—"Not that any professing christian will openly or avowedly deny the authority of Jesus. But whether his authority is set aside avowedly or otherwise, it matters not. It amounts to the same thing. 'You call me Master and Lord, and do not the things which I say. Many will say to me in that day, Lord! Lord! to whom I will say I know you not; depart from me, you workers of iniquity.' What we complain of, then, is that attachment to self-formed and conjectural principles, by which the authority of revelation is superseded;—that love of system which grinds down and newmodels every opposing passage of these holy records, until it is supposed to tally with our acknowledged creed; that blind and unconquerable love of party, which forces the Oracles of Heaven out of their natural and obvious meaning to support its unhallowed pretensions." Page 54. "Yet, singular to tell, that some of our most zealous advocates for *systems* talk of persons going to hell with an orthodox creed, as if religious truth had changed its nature, and become the soul's eternal enemy. Perhaps, however, there is some cause for thinking so; some real operative principle that works the effect; but surely in the word it is not, nor can it be. The doctrines which the Saviour taught tend not to lead men in the path to hell; but upward lead to glory and immortal joy. Whence is it, then, that such reflections rest on orthodoxy? We suspect the cause is near at hand, and quite within our reach. The general source from which men learn religious sentiments is not the word of God, but the formal systems of the day; or from the

party to which they respectively belong. In those systems the principles of religion stand invested with all the authority of ecclesiastical statutes, and enforced by ecclesiastical sanctions, but the authority of Christ attends them not. There they are exhibited in all the nakedness of systematic stiffness, stripped and leafless as the sturdy oak in winter, couched in the technical and logical phraseology of the schools; but they stand divested of those heavenly charms which engage our affections; of that sympathy and love which subdue the heart, and captivate the soul. There they are set forth contaminated with the foul breath of fallible and dying mortals, addressed only to the intellects of men; announced in words of human wisdom, and compounded of the most heterogeneous materials; and, consequently, cannot reach the conscience, nor carry conviction to the inquiring mind: they possess no attractions to catch the soul, no loveliness to engage the heart to the admiration of virtue. And every step we take in pursuit of truth, as exhibited in these formularies, is attended with uncertainty and doubt. We may talk, then, of the wisdom of our ancestors, and their claims upon our high regards; but their wisdom was certainly human wisdom, and the regard we owe them ought never to be placed in competition with that which we owe the Lord of life. How very differently do the scriptures teach us! They take every avenue to the human heart. They enlighten us with their instructions, and sanctify us by the purity of their truth, and the unction of the Good Spirit from on high; they command us into subjection by their authoritative voice; and deter us from the paths of folly by the thunders of heaven. They engage our sympathetic feelings by the sympathy and love of Jesus; and excite our imitative dispositions by the exhibition of all that is amiable and of good report in the conduct of those whom they set before us for our examples. Instead of an abstruse and metaphysical phraseology, we have the plain and obvious language, which his righteous servants spake, as they were moved by the Holy Spirit. Instead of the productions of fallible men, we have the pure and infallible testimony of the Lord Jesus. And in place of the dry systematic formularies of human wisdom, we have all the excellency, and beauty, and harmony, of the doctrines and duties of God's word, represented in their close connexion and dependency. And with all the charms with which virtue can adorn the human character, we see the Son of God invested, and in him morality and holiness assume a living form to attract and draw us from the fatal paths of folly, sin, and shame. *That* orthodoxy, therefore, which changes not the heart, but leads to ruin and despair, is the genuine offspring of human creeds: from the pure fountain of eternal truth it has not sprung. Surely the doctrine of Christ must be sadly compounded with false principles, or associated with most erroneous sentiments, when it ceases to produce those natural effects ascribed to it in the scriptures.— Were it received pure and unmixed from the fountain of truth now, as it was in apostolic days, it would still bring forth the peaceable fruits of righteousness, which are by Christ to the glory of God."

Page 59. "The doctrines and commandments of men, on whatever pretence introduced, ought to meet with that severity of rebuke, which they most justly deserve. They have ever been the source of discord and corruption in the church of God. If Christ is sole governor in his kingdom;

if he is given as leader and commander to his people; if he, as Moses was, is faithful in all his house; and if he possesses the exclusive right of dictating to the consciences of men, and of making laws for their regulation in religious matters; then every rule of expediency, every doctrine of human formation, every case of conscience determined in any shape, by persons possessing an assumed right to do so, is contrary to the rights and prerogatives of the Lord Jesus."

After insisting at length upon the exclusive and universal obligation of hearkening to the voice of our Great Prophet, and of the ruinous and dreadful consequences of rejecting or neglecting his authority, or in any wise interfering with it, he comes to the second part, p. 85, to treat more particularly of the supreme authority of the Lord Jesus in relation to his churches, and to vindicate the liberties and privileges of his people from the assumed authority of ecclesiastical courts of every description. He prefaces this part of the subject with a quotation from Acts xxii. 17—28, a part of Paul's farewell charge to the elders of the church of Ephesus.

Page 85. " Warped by the prejudices of education, or blinded by a superstitious attachment to a particular sect, some are of opinion that the bible lays down no specific rules for the management of Christ's kingdom, but leaves it to the prudential management of its friends to regulate its concerns."

In reply to this assumption, our author justly argues, that it goes " to arraign the wisdom of God,—to charge the oracles of Heaven with what would render them useless and nugatory." That " we can never conceive that an all wise God would leave his word imperfect; or that he would grant us a code of laws which would either be inapplicable or deficient; much less that he would leave his people altogether destitute of such *necessary* regulations." That, "of all the duties which devolve upon a governor, there is none more essentially necessary than the formation of wise and equitable laws for the management of his subjects. Without these it is impossible for him to maintain his authority, or prevent anarchy and confusion throughout his dominions." That " it is equally impossible for subjects to submit to law with which they are totally unacquainted." That " of course, it becomes the bounden duty of every wise ruler to govern by righteous and equitable laws, and to publish these for the benefit of all concerned. Also, that by the nature of the laws promulgated, we judge of the qualifications of the governor from whom they derive their authority and character." Therefore, that "if the Lord Jesus is King of kings, and Lord of Lords, it is but reasonable to expect that he will govern his subjects by regulations corresponding with his righteous character: that, as they are willing subjects, and must render a cheerful, and not a forced obedience, they must become acquainted with the laws of his kingdom, as promulgated by himself; and then their obedience will not be an act of submission to the authority of man, but to that of Jesus Christ: their faith will not stand in the wisdom of man, but in the power of God. But to suppose that the Lord Jesus governs his church without any fixed or determined laws; or that, if he does rule by such laws, he has not clearly or explicitly made them known to his people, ought to be regarded as too gross an insinuation to admit of the smallest consideration."

Thus he argues for the indispensable necessity of a distinct, intelligible, and competent ex-

hibition of law, both for the honor of the ruler, and the loyalty and comfort of the ruled. And certainly to good effect. For to acknowledge Christ as a ruler without a law; or by a law deficient and unintelligible, would, to say the least, be a foul imputation upon his character. What would we say of a civil governor, or of a government that would proceed in this manner? Would we not call that governor or government weak, foolish, or tyrannical?

After obviating an objection to the above statement, drawn from the informal and unsystematic exhibition of the laws by which the church of Christ is to be governed, our author proceeds [page 88] to an examination of the nature and constitution of those primitive societies called churches of Christ, in order " to ascertain the amount of the information furnished in the scriptures respecting their government, laws, and customs, as they existed in apostolic days;" and resolves his inquiry into the four following questions: "What is the church of God, which he has purchased with his own blood? What is its nature and constitution? What are the permanent officers and ordinances of a scripturally organized church? And what are the particular duties devolving upon those officers?"

In the prosecution of these inquiries, he confines himself wholly to the sacred records; except that, in one single instance, he refers to the well known Apologetic of Justin Martyr, in page 211, which shall be noticed in its proper place. He commences with exhibiting the certain and definite meaning of the term *church* in its appropriated application to the people of God, both in the Old and New Testaments. In the course of this investigation it is fully evinced that the term church, or congregation, (as some translate it) when applied to the people of God has always one of the two following significations; namely, either the whole body of the redeemed contemplated as co-existing either in heaven or earth; or else to one particular society met, or in the stated habits of meeting together in one place for religious purposes. That this latter and particular application of the term is sometimes attributed to the congregation as distinguished from their pastors and teachers, but never to the latter as distinguished from the former: as is also the term *clergy*, translated heritage, 1 *Pet.* v. 3. applied by the apostle to the people, contradistinguished from their bishops and pastors. It is also clearly evinced that the term church is never used to designate a confederation of churches; or a representative assembly composed of delegates from such confederation.

Page 102. " Moreover, we maintain that the word church, in the scriptures, can be understood neither literally nor figuratively, as applicable to an assembly of delegates from different churches or congregations. Not literally—for as we have shown before, it is already the appropriated name of those societies from which the delegates are supposed to be sent, and these various societies are never assembled in one place, so as to make but one society, and therefore can never be called a church; they are not literally a church, but churches; for they literally meet in a number of different places; and, surely, a number of distinct assemblies can never be called one assembly. But, you say, they are assembled figuratively in their representatives. Suppose they are, this does not alter the case; for the designation church cannot apply, in the singular number, to these representatives figuratively, no more than literally, for the best reason in the world—because the representatives assembled must, in this case, be designated by the very title by which their constituents are known. And as, in the present instance, their constituents are designated by the plural noun churches, for this very reason, if we wish to apply the appellation to a representative body figuratively, we must call them churches, not church; for all these different assemblies, according to scripture usage, are never known, nor described by the singular noun, church; but always by the plural, churches. Accordingly, it might be properly said, in a figurative sense, that the Presbyterian congregations enacted a certain law, thereby meaning that the general assembly did so. But we could never, with propriety, say the Presbyterian congregation did so; for all the congregations of Presbyterians are not known by the title congregation, in the singular number. Or suppose, for sake of illustration, that an assembly of delegates from Antioch, Syria, Silicia, &c., together with the apostles and elders resident in Jerusalem, met as a representative body there; this meeting could not, in a religious sense, be literally called a church, for this word was already pre-occupied, being the appropriated name of any particular assembly of the saints, who met for worship; consequently, could not become the designation of a meeting so differently constituted: nor could it be so called figuratively; for we could not say that the church in Jerusalem enacted certain decrees, for this would be false; the meeting of christians in Jerusalem, previously known by this designation, not being a delegated body at all, but a worshipping society; consequently it could not be the assembly called the church in Jerusalem, which enacted such decrees as the case supposes. And on the supposition that this representative body was the enacting authority, it could not be figuratively called the church in Jerusalem; for it was not the church in Jerusalem merely, that had delegates in the representative body; but, as is alleged, there were delegates from a great number of other churches throughout Syria, Silicia, &c. consequently, the decrees of these churches, made by their delegates assembled in Jerusalem, could never be figuratively called the decrees of the church in Jerusalem, but must, in consistency with the rules of rhetoric (he might have said, with the rules of common sense,) be called the decrees of the churches represented, inasmuch as these churches, by their representatives, enacted them."

Our author, after thus vindicating the term church from a gross misapplication, manifestly designed to give an appearance of scriptural authority to the representative system of church government, next proceeds to notice an unhappy sectarian abuse of the term:—

"By a strange and almost unaccountable revolution in the history of the appellation church, from being the designation of a christian society, it has come to be in connexion with some other descriptive word, the badge of distinction among the various sectaries. Hence we have the Lutheran Church, the Reformed Presbyterian Church, the Baptist Church, &c. all of which designations describe the boundaries of the respective sects to which they refer; or, as they are frequently used, represent the supreme judicatories belonging to these denominations. Hence the assemblies of God's people have been robbed of their proper scriptural name, and others substituted for it; and almost all that remains to the original proprietors of it, is, that they are permitted to grace the walls of their meeting-houses with this designation, and call them churches.

All the honors and privileges belonging to those who formerly were the rightful owners of the title, have been gradually assumed, and finally usurped, by what are now denominated church judicatories, together with the title itself. Yet for such an application of the word church to a representative body, the scriptures do not lay the smallest foundation. "The notion, therefore, of a church representative, how commonly soever it has been received, is a mere usurper of a later date, and it has fared here, as it sometimes does in cases of usurpation, the original proprietor comes, though gradually, to be at length totally dispossessed. Should any man now talk of the powers of the church, and of the rights of churchmen, would the hearers apprehend that he meant the powers of a christian congregation or the rights of all who are members of the christian community? It is, therefore, not without reason that I affirm, that the modern acceptation, though an intruder, has jostled out the rightful and primitive one, almost entirely."*

Our author modestly concludes this part of his investigation by submitting the result to the judgment of the candid and impartial; with the following protest:—

Page 141. "It only remains for us to declare, That we do most solemnly protest against all ecclesiastical courts of every description, as completely hostile to the supreme authority of our Lord Jesus Christ, and subversive of that pure and personal obedience which we ought to render to him, as king and head of his church. And still further, we do not hesitate to pronounce that system, which erects partition walls, or frames terms of communion, either congregational or ministerial, by which christians are prevented from joining together with their fellow christians in the service of God, or from engaging to perform their duty according to their talents or abilities, as destructive to the best interests of christianity, and as sanctioning the breach of that primary law of Christ's house—the law of love."   PHILALETHES.

December 6, 1826.

[TO BE CONTINUED.]

Paulinus to the Editor of the "Christian Baptist."

[Second Epistle.]

Virginia, November, 1826.

DEAR SIR—IT is time I had made my acknowledgments for the attention which you have paid to my first letter; not only in giving it a place in your interesting publication, but in replying so promptly and largely to the various points introduced to your notice. I am your debtor also, and in no small degree, for the copy of your discourse on the abrogation of the Old Dispensation, &c. It proved a mental treat, for which I beg you will accept my hearty thanks.

The metaphysical parts of this composition, however ingenious, (and ingenious they certainly are,) I let pass. You have yourself glanced at them, by way of disapprobation; and I have long been persuaded, that with metaphysical reasonings we have but little to do, in illustrating and enforcing the simple truths of the gospel. Nor do I mean to express unqualified approbation, as to the rest of the discourse. This could hardly be expected: and were you to revise and republish, I think it probable that the statements or remarks, even in regard to the governing object, might, in some two or three instances, wear a different aspect. The main point appears to me to be triumphantly carried; but

* Campbell's Lectures, p. 166.

48

there are expressions and sentiments which seem to be rather unguarded and defective, and to require some modification. The pamphlet is lent out; so that I cannot refer to it so definitely as I could wish; but as this matter is thought by some of the wise and good, to involve consequences of a dangerous tendency, I must ask your indulgence while I make a few remarks.

After proving that we are not now under the Legal Dispensation, or the Law, (so called,) and showing that we are to draw our views of actual duty from the New Testament, &c. when you come to the case of the unconverted sinner, you place him, I think, under the Law of Nature. True it is that you make the summary of the Law, ["You shall love the Lord your God," &c.] the basis of all Divine Law. This is, indeed, a thought as important as it is just and striking. Yes; this principle, no doubt, is carried round, through the vast range of the universe, as the foundation on which all particular obligations are built up: so that however the Law, as a Dispensation, may be branched out or modified, to suit different classes of rational beings, or different times and circumstances, it stands on the same eternal, unchanging basis. This sentiment commends itself at once to the mind of an intelligent reader of the bible: it taxes not our ingenuity for proof; and had some of our "divines" happily taken it up, in proof of the immutability of the "Moral Law," they need not to have set up their chymical apparatus; to convert one thing into another, by attempting to prove, that the law given to angels, the law given to Adam, and the ten commandments, are all the same.

I may seem to be digressing, but you will not consider me as having lost sight of the point. You place the unconverted sinner under the Law of Nature. And why not place him, my dear sir, under the whole of God's revealed will, according to the Dispensation under which he lives? This, I think, is perfectly consistent. Even the heathen are under the Law of Nature, (*Rom.* ch. i.) and wherever the New Dispensation comes, it lays hold of every human creature, with the grasp of divine authority, while it presents the exhibition of divine mercy. The basis of obligation is the same, in the benighted regions of paganism, and in the enlightened lands of christendom; but the dispensation, and the particular obligations, are certainly very different.

I might enlarge on this topic, but I consider it unnecessary; your own reflection no doubt will supply, or has supplied, whatever I might add by way of argument. A brief remark or two, however, I must beg leave to subjoin, in order to obviate misapprehensions; as to my own views of this matter of Old Testament and New Testament obligations. And first, it appears perfectly scriptural and proper, to consider us under the New Dispensation, as still under Divine Law, though not under "*The* Law," or the Legal Dispensation. The will of God, as exhibited under the New Covenant, so far as it consists of prohibitions and injunctions, is now his Law to us. Secondly, by this Law, or revealed will of God, (call it what we may,) unconverted sinners are certainly condemned; and by it, christians are to have their hearts and lives regulated. I only add, thirdly, that whatever is sanctioned, as of continued obligation, by the letter or spirit of the New Testament, is to be so received, wherever found;—whether in the Old Testament, or even as a dictate of nature.

Dismissing this point, I come now to notice

one of deep interest, on which, in your answer to my first communication, it is but justice to say, you appear to have bestowed much attention. I allude to the subject of Divine influence, or the operation of the Holy Spirit on the heart of man. I feel confident that you wish me to be free and candid in my communications; and I certainly feel as confident, that without full liberty of this sort, I should find no satisfaction in communicating my thoughts at all. This is all the apology I deem necessary. Freely and candidly then, I must say, that while many things in your answer—and many incidental remarks, in reference to this very point, met my admiring approbation, I felt some degree of disappointment at the manner in which you considered it proper to shape your reply, in this particular case. Your reasons are, no doubt satisfactory to yourself: perhaps they ought to be so to me and to all. I have heard much said about your answer to Paulinus; for it has excited amongst us a high degree of attention. Some of your readers are satisfied; some are not. And though, upon a candid, careful, re-perusal of your letter, I think it justly due to you to say, that you are an avowed friend to the Spirit's operations, in the production of genuine religion, I must own that I could still wish, you had found in your heart to dispense with what I consider an over degree of scrupulosity, and to answer in a more direct manner. I certainly do not think of dictating to you; nor do I wish, by any means, that you should do violence to your own conscientious views of propriety: but I must think you carry your scruples on the subject of theories and systems to some excess. Permit me to state, as briefly as I can, my own views. By the way, I did wish to introduce, in this letter, some new subjects; or at least to take up some that were just touched on in my former communication: but I must say out what I have to say on the matters in hand, before I can attend to any others; and there will then, I doubt, be but little room left, without occupying too many of your pages.

Now, my dear sir, be it known to you, and to all whom it may concern, that I am as little disposed to advocate or favor the "art and mystery" of manufacturing theories and systems in religion, as almost any other man—perhaps even, as brother Campbell himself. True it is, that I sometimes indulge my imagination in conjectures;—in attempting some little excursions in the unknown regions,—in the wide field of possibilities, &c. though I do not wander into so many fields as a certain D. D. whose sermon you reviewed; nor do I exhibit these conjectures as articles of faith. But these conjectures, I presume, are a different sort of thing from what you mean by theories in religion; and again I say, I am no advocate for the formation of mere theories; nor for the compiling of abstract truths: nor do I think that those laborious writers, who have attempted to manufacture a regular, connected system of divinity from materials such as they could collect, have thereby advanced the cause of unadulterated religion. I say, a regular, connected system: for though I believe such a system does really exist with God;—that the golden chain is complete; yet it appears to be exhibited only in some of its parts; the connecting links being hidden in impenetrable, adorable darkness. The skill of man is thus baffled; and wherever a fond system-maker exhibits what he would call the whole golden chain, we shall find, upon examination, that he has only some of the parts—(perhaps, indeed, only some of those which are actually revealed,) joined, here and there, by a hempen cord, or an iron link of his own making.

I have no disposition, I assure you, to carry the fruits I may be enabled to gather from the tree of life, (the bible,) to any *distillery*, Arminian or Calvinistic, to be run down into *alcohol*: I would rather take them in their own proper state. I do not consider myself obliged either to be laced up in the *stays* of John Calvin, or to wear the *surtout* of James Arminius: I like better "the robe of righteousness—the garments of salvation"—found in heaven's wardrobe, ready made, and to be procured "without money and without price."

This egotism, it is hoped, will be excused in the present case;—and so much with regard to theories and systems, shaped according to human skill. It is to be lamented, indeed, that systems seem to please some professors of religion, more than the good news of salvation by Christ; and that they manifest more solicitude for the preservation of their beloved plans, than for the maintenance of vital and practical godliness.— Touch every chord in the lyre of salvation;— they still remain listless, unmoved, till the darling notes be sounded to which their spirits are in unison. O for the time when divine truth— the *whole* of divine truth, shall be relished, as coming from God!—when the souls of professed christians, tuned by grace, shall respond to every declaration of the will of God;—now, with holy fear; now, with lively hope; now, with "joy unspeakable and full of glory;" and always, with obedient "faith that works by love." This will not be till the bible is taken, in good earnest, as the standard of faith and practice. O, sir, may God speed your efforts to call the people to this only standard! May He assist us to plant this standard, this milk-white banner, on the heights of Zion—no more to be insulted by the party-colored flags of Creeds and Confessions of Faith waving over it.

But after all that I have said, I am not so apprehensive—not so "tremblingly alive" to the danger of theory and system, as to avoid the direct expression of a sentiment on any proposed subject in religion, where indeed I have a sentiment made up on such subject. And why, my dear sir, should we be thus apprehensive? Is there any inconsistency, any impropriety, in so expressing our sentiments? Surely I should think not: or else, as far as I can see, we might narrow the limits of our liberty this way, to one solitary, general, proposition or declaration—*I believe what the Bible teaches.*

My letter grows long, and I must condense;— must throw out some two or three paragraphs, which I had scribbled off to be transcribed. As I can conceive nothing improper in the simple expression of religious sentiment, so, (to go a step farther,) I see no harm, no injurious tendency, in distinguishing and arranging any scriptural topics, for the sake of bringing the authorities of the bible to bear on them, and obtaining a more lucid view of the different subjects. But then, be it well observed, I would take all these matters simply as I find them in the scriptures;— not as mere abstract truths, but as having their adjuncts;—not as naked theories, but as practical lessons. I would not exhibit them as forming a system,—the connecting links of the different parts being here and there supplied from my own metaphysical reasonings; much less would I, for the sake of any system, sacrifice one part of divine truth to any favorite view of another part. Such are my thoughts in regard to theories and systems in religion. If now, while I think you rather in danger of fastidiousness on the one hand, you should consider me in any degree unguarded on the other, i should really wish to see the evil pointed out: for I again say, I am no friend to the "art and mystery" of system-making. And here I leave this matter: no doubt you will think it high time.

I have lately received my copy of the new translation of the New Testament,—a work which I think well calculated to aid the liberal-minded reader in his study of the sacred volume;—to relieve the mind on some passages which, in the common translation, appear difficult, if not unintelligible; to enlarge our comprehension of divine truth; and to confirm our belief, by bringing forward (as every good translation does) the same general representation of the sacred original. Of one or two of the *supplements* I stand in doubt; and, whether it be taste, or the effect of habit, or something better, I have now and then met with a new term which pleases me less than the old one. But as yet I have not given the whole book a perusal, and must be sparing of particular remarks. The four Gospels (or Testimonies) I had before read; —having in my possession Dr. Campbell's Translation, with his admirable Dissertations.

Before I leave this subject, and bid you adieu for the present, though I have occupied, I doubt, more than my share of room, I must take occasion just to say, how highly pleased I am with your "Prefaces," and "Hints to Readers," &c. and at the same time, how sorry I am to find one particular sentence, which to me appears to be seriously wrong. It is in the Preface to the Epistle to the Romans. "And here let it be noted, (you say,) that the justification by works, and that by faith, of which Paul speaks, and of which our systems speak, are quite different things. To quote his words and apply them to our questions about faith and works, is illogical, inconclusive, and absurd."

On this point I can now say but little. The sentiment you have expressed in the general preface to the epistles,—that we are to attend to the circumstances of the writer and the persons addressed, &c. is readily admitted to be correct and important; and that we are not to make every period a proverb, like one of Solomon's, &c. But then, dear sir, is it any thing uncommon in epistolary communications, (especially in those of a didactic nature,) occasionally to express a truth, a maxim, a position of general application? Certainly not, and to me it seems entirely clear, that the apostle has done so in the case above alluded to. While he assures the Jews that they could not be justified by the works of their law; while he reminds the Ephesians, that it is "not by works, so that no one can boast;"—and while he remarks to Titus, that we are saved, "not on account of works of righteousness which we have done, but according to his own mercy," &c.— am I not authorized to maintain the same truth, as of general application? Surely I should think so. If I have misunderstood you, excuse me; and be persuaded, my dear sir, that the interest I take in your labors, is one powerful motive with me to remonstrate, wherever I have done so. I need not remind you, that according to our motto, "The Bible our Standard," I must adopt no man's views, however right in many things, where he appears to me to be in an error.

Believe me, with best wishes,

Yours, in the gospel of our common Lord,

PAULINUS.

Experimental Religion.—No. 1.

THERE are a few topics in our religion to which the writers of the New Testament have paid very particular regard. They are, 1st. The Messiahship of Jesus. 2d. The history of the Apostles. 3d. The right ordering of the primitive churches; and 4th. The history of the church general, or whole body of christians.

In making a selection of the sacred books, it was, therefore, with great propriety that the first place was assigned to that order of them which particularly respected the founder of our religion—Jesus.

With equal propriety the second place has been given to those books which speak of the second order of religious character, viz. the immediate followers of Jesus, or the twelve apostles, a general history of whose labors has been delivered to us by Luke in the Acts or Actions of the Apostles.

The epistles addressed to particular churches occupy the third place, and discourse generally upon the various relations subsisting between them and the Messiah, whose mission they had recognized; their obedience to him; their worship, discipline, order, &c.

While the Revelations, which furnish us with a prophetic account of christianity in the aggregate, from the days of the apostles till the end of the world, occupy the fourth place.

That the mission of Jesus, the history of his twelve apostles, the constitution of the primitive churches, and finally the fortunes of christianity in the aggregate, are therefore subjects of great and popular importance, cannot, I think, be reasonably doubted.

But after all, what would it profit me to understand all that the Revelations have said of the church general, what happiness should I derive from the most perfect acquaintance with what is written of the primitive institutions, or of the twelve apostles, or even of Jesus himself, in all the scriptures generally, and in the four gospels in particular, unless at the same time I knew that I myself were individually and personally interested in the great salvation. This brings us precisely to what is vulgarly called "experimental religion;" a phrase which, by the way, means nothing more than those personal proofs and evidences of our individual adoption into the family of God, which are to be found in the character of every genuine christian. Other topics may be great and of general importance; but if I have rightly defined the expression experimental religion, then it stands for something of more vital importance to my present happiness than all other matters—it stands for the personal evidences of my own individual election to eternal life. Beings of a different order may possess great knowledge of Jesus, of the twelve apostles, the primitive churches, and also of the body of Christ in general; but they can have no experimental religion, no personal proofs that they are individually interested in this salvation; therefore they can derive no happiness from the belief and contemplation of those subjects. The devil possibly has a more extensive acquaintance with those topics than the most enlightened christian; yet his knowledge must inevitably result in trembling. He has no experimental religion.

Will any man assert, then, that it is of small importance to be convinced that I am individually interested in the salvation of God? I presume that no christian would willingly be guilty of such temerity; and I hesitate not to aver that it is of supreme importance to me to be well in-

formed on this grand point; therefore, it has pleased the Holy Spirit, besides those books written concerning Christ, his apostles, the particular churches, and the body general, to give us also another order of books written on this very topic. The epistles general, and especially the first of John's, are devoted to this subject, and detail to us the various evidences by which we may know that we are "in him that is true;" that we are "now the sons of God," and "have eternal life." In fact, I fear not to hazard the opinion that the New Testament had been incomplete without something on the topic indicated by the unsound phrase "experimental religion." Something on this point, indeed, was necessary to keep a man from being imposed upon in regard to his own character, while on the other hand, something seemed necessary to be said about the infidel or apostate to keep a man from being imposed on in regard to the character of others. This has actually been done by Peter and Jude, who, in their general epistles, have spoken both of unbelievers and apostates. This topic, I presume, we must, by way of analogy, style experimental infidelity!

Thus we have in the New Testament, books which inform us of Jesus Christ, the apostles, the first churches, the church general, the character of the unbeliever, and finally the character of the true believer, or of the personal proofs of a man's adoption into the family of the Most High.

Experimental religion, then, (for I scorn to fight about the sound when we have agreed upon the sense)—experimental religion, I say, is one of those subjects which the Holy Spirit has shown to be of importance, inasmuch as he has condescended to discourse upon the christian graces and gifts which constitute what we call by this rotten phrase, "experimental religion." In another paper, I may, perhaps, enumerate some of those particular evidences by which the christian may know that he is a son of God, though I may just add here, that the scriptures inform us that, 1st, Whosoever believeth that Jesus is the Christ, is begotten by God. 2d, Whosoever loves, has been begotten by God. 3d, That whosoever has the hope of the gospel in him, is an heir of God; and, finally, that all christians know that they have been begotten by God by the spirit which he has given them. Thus the faith, love, and hope of the gospel, with the gift of the Holy Spirit, are all proofs of our individual personal adoption.

PHILIP, *alias* W. SCOTT.

Extract of a Letter from the Editor.

I FIND the saints are yet in Babylon. Many, very many are conscious of it, and are desirous of coming out of her that they may not partake of her plagues. But they are beset with difficulties. They have lost not the copies of the law of their King, as did their types, the Jews, in the literal Babylon; but they have lost the sense, or rather have been preached out of the sense of the law, and many are even preached out of their common sense. They are sensible of this. But this is not all. There are too many Sanballats and Tobiahs, and too few Nehemiahs and Ezras. The captives, too, are so much attached to the chains that bind them, and so much wedded to the manners of the Babylonians, their captivators, that they are, in many instances, unwilling to hazard the dangers and to encounter the reproaches incident to an attempt to return to Jerusalem. I labor incessantly to convince and to persuade the people who fear God, both out of the law, prophets, psalms, and apostolic writings, that such are their character and circumstances, and to induce them to return. It happens in this case as it did when the gospel was first promulged—some believe the things that are spoken, and some believe them not. The number of believers is, indeed, very considerable. But when they think of repairing the breaches, and rebuilding the temple, some Sanballat says, "Will they revive the stones out of the heaps of the rubbish which are burned?" And, to scandalize them, some Tobiah adds his scoff, saying, "Even that which they build, if a fox go up, he shall even break down their stone wall!" However, many of the people "have a mind to work," and the wall will be reared. Out of Babylon they will—they must come; for the mouth of the Lord has spoken it. And should we never see the day, we will die in the full assurance of faith that the saints will separate themselves from the strangers, and renounce allegiance to their spoilers and captivators. Many of those friendly to a return, are attempting to persuade their communities to arise in the mass and to march in one phalanx, and flatter themselves that they may succeed. However much we do desire such an event, we cannot reasonably expect it; for such an event never happened. No community, either political or religious, ever was reformed in the mass. No people ever, all at once, returned from any apostacy. Even when God's typical people were brought back out of Babylon, of the whole nation, but forty two thousand three hundred and sixty at first returned.

I have been often interrogated on the subject of a model or a precedent for the restoration of the ancient order of things. Some seem to think that the New Testament ought to furnish an example of the sort, or some directions for the accomplishment of an object so important. It does, indeed, in some sense, though not in the way which some desire. It teaches us how Jews and Pagans were converted to the faith, and how both people were consociated into one community. It teaches us upon what principles they became one, and for what ends and uses they maintained the unity of the Spirit in the bonds of peace. It exhibits to us what they did in their congregations; but it does not, because it could not, afford a model of a people returning from a long and grievous apostacy. The christian communities had not then apostatized, and consequently no example of a return could be afforded. Until Rome was built there were no great roads leading thither, nor groups of people returning thence. For this reason the New Testament could not afford a model such as we want. But it foretells this apostacy; its rise, progress, and termination: it exhibits the thing in emblems, and in sacred symbols teaches us how to come out of THE MYSTERY, BABYLON THE GREAT. It imperiously commands a return to Jerusalem; and, in general principles, ordains the way. If, then, we only remember whence we are fallen, we may reform. We may return to the Lord. But it does more than all this. It not only minutely describes the apostacy, and characterizes the Man of Sin, and Son of Perdition; but it leads us, in the way of symbols, to understand where we are, and how to return. It tells us plainly that we may find, in the history of the Jews, our own history, and a remedy for all our grievances. To illustrate this point, I cannot do better than to present you the outlines of an oration delivered on this subject. It was the first time that I based a public speech

on the writings of Nehemiah; and I must (as they say, John Bunyan was wont to do) write down the discourse after it was pronounced, or give the items and outlines of an extemporaneous address:—

The outlines of an Oration, based upon the 4th and 6th chapters of Nehemiah, the 2d chapter of the Second Epistle to the Thessalonians, and the 17th and 18th chapters of the Revelation.

AFTER reading the above portions of the sacred writings, a few general remarks were made on the character of the inspired books, and particularly on the peculiar method which God had adopted in communicating instructions to men. The utility of the adoption of types or emblems, in communicating instruction, was next exhibited. The natural world, considered as a volume of natural types; and the sacred history of the Jewish people a volume of spiritual types. After these introductory observations, the Jewish scriptures were examined on the subject of types. From this examination it was found,

1st. That there were persons and things originally designed as types; and also that persons and things not originally designed as types, were in the New Testament, by the inspired commentators on the Old Testament, adopted as types, and used as such for the illustration of the christian doctrine. Of the former sort were the priests under the law, the altars, sacrifices, tabernacle, its vessels, the temple, &c. &c. Of the latter kind were Adam, the deluge, Sarai, Isaac, Hagar, Ishmael, &c. &c.

2d. By connecting the two Testaments, or the Jewish and Christian Scriptures, it was found that certain persons, in certain respects, were types of Jesus Christ; that his being called the second Adam, a priest after the order of Melchisedec, a Mediator such as Moses, &c. &c. were proofs and illustrations that he was considered the anti-type of many types. But this was not all. On the authority of the infallible commentator, Paul, it appeared that there were not only types of Christ in the Jewish scriptures, but that there were types of the christian people, their worship, and circumstances: and indeed that the history of the church was all found in type in the history of the Jews. In illustration and confirmation of this, the following particulars were noticed:

1. That all the same names which are in the christian scriptures appropriated to the christian assembly or church, were first appropriated to the Jewish people in the mass. Such were the terms called, elected, redeemed, bought, purchased, ransomed, chosen, a peculiar people, a holy nation, a kingdom of priests, my people, my beloved, my children, spouse, bride, saved, &c. &c.

2. That all the christian ordinances and worship were typified; such as the Lord's day, by the morrow after the Sabbath, when the first ripe sheaf was waved, christian immersion, by their being immersed once into Moses in the cloud and in the sea; their frequently eating the manna and drinking the water from the rock, an ensample or type of our participation of the emblems in the Lord's supper; their sprinkled altar, a type of our sprinkled consciences; their λουτρον, or laver or bath for cleansing the priests, a type of our bath of regeneration; their first tabernacle, or holy place, a type of the christian church; their common priests, a type of christians: and their high priest a type of Jesus; their thank offerings, of our praises; and their sin offerings, of the sacrifice of our great High Priest. Incidents in their history were also shown to be types of incidents in our history. Such as their being called out of Egypt;

their receiving of a law afterwards; their journey through the wilderness; their river Jordan; their promise of a rest in Canaan: their entrance into it; their city Jerusalem; their Mount Zion; their captivity in Babylon, and their deliverance thence. Other incidents were taken notice of; such as the rebellion of some of them; their failing in the wilderness; their chastisements; their reformations; the special government under which they lived; the rewards and punishments. The authority of the christian apostles was adduced in support of these facts; such as Paul's comments in the 10th of the 1st Epistle to the Corinthians; his letter to the Hebrews every where.

These remarks and illustrations were merely introductory to the portions of scripture read. We then proceeded to demonstrate the fact that the captivity of Israel was in all its prominent features a type of the present state of the christian world. This was proved,

1st. From the fact that Paul declares twice in his 1st Epistle to the Corinthians that these things (which happened to them) were τυποι, types to us. Chap. x. 6. "Now these things have become types or examples to us." And verse 11. "Now all these things happened to them as τυποι, types or examples, and are written for our admonition upon whom the ends of the ages are come."

2d. From the fact that John in the Revelation transfers the very name of the People, or city of captivity of the Jews—I say, he transfers that name to the city of our captivity and to the state in which we are, and calls our spoilers and captivators, Babylon the Great. There is a spiritual Sodom, Egypt, and Babylon. See Revelations, chapters xi. and xvii.

3d. From an analysis of the 2d chapter of the 2d Epistle to the Thessalonians. This led to an exposition of the more prominent features of the countenance of the Man of Sin, and Son of Perdition. That he was not a political, but a politico-ecclesiastical personage, was shown from his sitting not on a civil tribunal, but in the temple of God, and from the term MYSTERY in capitals upon his forehead. That his impious assumption of the character of God, consisted essentially in his claiming dominion over the faith or consciences of men, and a homage from men due to God alone.

In speaking of the Woman of Sin, viz. the Mother of Harlots, as well as of the Man of Sin, we did not confine neither him nor her to the walls of Papal Rome; but very briefly it was remarked, that although "the Mother of Harlots" might live in the great city, yet her daughters had married and left her; in plain English, that every council ecclesiastic which assumed the right of dominion over the faith and conscience, and claimed titles of homage, such as Reverend, &c. or any attribute of power or honor which belonged to God alone, was a legitimate descendant, daughter, or grand daughter of the woman on whose forehead was written "Mystery, Babylon, the Great, the Mother of Harlots, and Abominations of the Earth," cautiously avoiding offence, as some of her progeny were present. I went on to demonstrate from our own experience and observation, independent of the sacred testimonies, that we were now in Babylon. Waving all advantages which might have been derived from the time, and times, and the dividing of time; the three years and a half, the forty-two months, the 1260 days, the accordant emblems of 1260 years; their commencement and termination—waving a hundred minor evidences likewise of the fact, the attention of the audience was confined to three obvious proofs, viz.

1st. The confusion of religious speech now existing, analogous to the confusion of speech at Babel, and the confounding or mixing the language of Canaan with the language of Ashdod during the captivity; our creeds, systems, sermons, and scholastic terms, mingled with some biblical terms, terminating in an almost general ignorance of the sacred writings, and an impossibility of understanding the holy oracles, were just noticed illustrative of the exact analogy between us and the Jews while in Babylon.

2d. The almost total deprivation of the consolations of the christian religion, apparent in our private capacities and in our public meetings, in our individual experience, and in our social interviews; the melancholy and gloom; the prayers and feelings of the religious, expressed in the 137th psalm; in short, all the grand characteristics of our state, as respects the enjoyments of the religion we profess in its public institutions, and in its personal and family benefits, are exactly correspondent to the state of the Jews during their captivity. An appeal was here made to the experience and the prayers of the pious, based on the first six verses of the 137th psalm.

3d. The intercommunity with the world, the mingling of religion and politics, the alliance of church and state either in the European forms or by the more specious incorporations of these United States, the almost general conformity to the world in all its frivolities, in the gratification of all those appetites, passions, and propensities, purely animal, so common amongst christians; the great neglect, the very general neglect of the christian education of the youth, and the consequent irreligion and evil morals of many of the children of christian parents, are similar to the intermarriages between the Babylonians and the Israelites, and the almost universal assimilation of the children of those unauthorized marriages to the children of Chaldea. Thus, from the confusion of religious speech, the absence of the christian institutions, and the enjoyments dependent on their observance, and the deterioration of christian morals by an almost exact conformity to the course of this world, being the antitypes of the confusion of the Hebrew language in Chaldea, the absence of the temple and its worship, and the amalgamation of the Hebrews and Babylonians by marriage and familiarity, was argued the fact that we are yet in Babylon agreeable to the scripture declarations and evidences before mentioned.

Having found ourselves in Babylon; having seen the almost exact agreement of the types and the antitypes, we were led to inquire why the Jews were carried captive into Babylon, that we might in the analogy find a proof or evidence of the reasons assigned in the New Testament why christians are in spiritual Babylon. We found that the Jews had broken God's covenant with them as a nation, by which he had engaged to be their king and protector, and that in consequence he had permitted their temple to be burned, their city to be laid waste, their land to be turned into a desert, and themselves to be slaves to Pagan sovereigns. And so with the antitype. The christians departed from the new covenant. The threatenings declared by Jesus Christ to the seven congregations in Asia have been executed. The Lord Jesus has been disregarded as king, and his institutes forsaken. Other church covenants have been formed; other authorities have been acknowledged; other lawgivers have been obeyed, and other apostles than those sent by Jesus, have been enthroned in our hearts. Therefore are we in Babylon.

Their return is a type of ours, else the system of types is defective and fails of perfection.— Cyrus made a proclamation; liberty was granted by the state in which they were enslaved. The civil powers now are relenting, and our government has given us the liberty and acknowledged our right to be governed in our consciences by the Great King. The proclamation by Cyrus was not more friendly to the return of the Jews to their own land and laws than is the constitution and laws of these United States. The time has arrived that the return should be commenced.

But how is it to be effected was next proposed. Both the doctrine of the types of the New Testament agree—

1st. The Jews confessed their sins. See *Nehemiah* ix. 6. They said, "O Lord, many years did you forbear our fathers, and testified against them, by your Spirit in your prophets, (as he has to us by his Spirit in the apostles,) yet would they not give ear." "Neither have our kings, our princes, our priests, nor our fathers kept your law, nor hearkened to your commandments and your testimonies wherewith you did testify against them."

2d. But they did not only confess their sins. They personally reformed; they reformed their family discipline; they returned to the Lord with all their heart. 3d. They gave the people the law in its original import.

4th. And they solemnly engaged, as a society, to walk in God's law which was given by their lawgiver, and "to observe and do all the commandments of the Lord our God, and his judgments and his statutes." See *Nehemiah* x. 29. Let us go and do likewise, as respects our King, his laws, commandments and statutes.

We were then led to consider the parts of *Nehemiah* read, as typical of the difficulties, reproaches, and opposition which must be encountered by those who undertake to rebuild the city and the temple.

Such were the outlines of an oration designed to shew that the ancient order of things must be restored, and that the way is marked out, not only in the apostolic writings and prophecies, but also fully exhibited in the typical people.— These outlines you may consider and fill up at your leisure. But should you neglect this, remember the command of the Lord our King. "Come, out of her, my people, that you may not be partakers of her sins, and that you may not receive of her plagues."

P. S. There was something said on the reasons why the Mother of Harlots had *mystery* written on her forhead, which I have not room to give you at present.

Versailles, Ky., Dec. 26, 1826.

No. 8.]   MARCH 5, 1827.

A Restoration of the Ancient Order of Things. No. XVII.

Purity of Speech.

IF all christians "spoke the same things" they would doubtless be of the same mind. But, says the philosopher, if they were all of one mind they would all speak the same things. Grant, then, that speaking the same things is the effect of thinking the same things; and yet, perhaps, it might be true that speaking the same things might, in its turn, be the cause of thinking the same things. For example; William and Mary thought the same things concerning John Calvin —they spoke the same things concerning him to

their children; and their sons and daughters thought the same things of him. This is true in the general.

It is no uncommon thing in the natural world for an effect to be the cause of another effect, and the last effect to be similar to its cause. For example; there is a chain of seven links. A person with a hammer strikes the first link. The motion of the first link is the effect of the stroke of the hammer; but the motion of the first link becomes the cause of the motion of the second, because of the impulse it gives it; and the motion of the second becomes the cause of the motion of the third, and so on to the end of the chain. In each of these effects, so far as they become causes, there is something similar to the first cause. Now it is much more obvious that, in the world of mind or thought, this similarity exists to a much greater degree than in the world of matter. The reason is, men cannot think but by words or signs. Words are but embodied thought, the external images or representatives of ideas. And who is there that has paid any attention to what passes in his own mind, who has not perceived that he cannot think without something to think about, and that the something about which he thinks must either assume a name, or some sort of image in his mind, before his rational faculties can operate upon it; and moreover, that his powers of thinking while employed exercise themselves in every effort, either by terms, names, or symbols, expressive of their own acts and the results of their own acts? Now, as men think by means of symbols or terms, and cannot think without them, it must be obvious that speaking the same things, though it might be alleged as the effect of thinking the same things, is more likely to become the cause of thinking the same things than any natural or mechanical effect can become the cause of a similar effect. This much we say for the employment of the speculative reader; but for the practical mind it is enough to know that speaking the same things is both rationally and scripturally proposed as the most sure and certain means of thinking the same things. On this view of the matter, I would base something of great consequence to the religious world. Perhaps I might find something in it of more real importance to all christians of every name, than all the fabled powers of the philosopher's stone, had they been real. Perhaps in this one view might be found the only practicable and alone sufficient means of reconciling all the christian world, and of destroying all partyism and party feelings, with all their retinue and train of evils which have been more fatal to christian light and liberty than were all the evils which fell upon human bodies from the opening of Pandora's box, to the animal enjoyments of this world. But how shall we all speak the same things relating to the christian religion? Never, indeed, while we add to, or subtract from the words which the Holy Spirit teaches. Never, indeed, while we take those terms out of their scriptural connexions, and either transpose them in place, or confound them with terms not in the book. If I am not greatly mistaken, (and I beg to be corrected if I am) the adding to, subtracting from, the transposition of, and mingling the terms of the Holy Spirit with those of human contrivance, is the only cause why all who love the same Saviour are disunited.

Now every human creed in christendom, whether it be long or short, whether it be written or nuncupative, whether it be of "essentials or non-essentials," whether it be composed of five or of fifty articles—either adds to, subtracts from, or transposes the words of inspiration, or mingles things of divine and human contrivance together. No such volume, no such articles can be *the* form or a form of sound words. Every creed is a new mould of doctrine, and into whatever mould metal is cast, when moulded it must assume the size and impress thereof. Let silver be cast into a French, Spanish, English, or American mould of the same size, but differently constructed; and although it is all the same metal, and of equal size, each crown, whether French, English, or Spanish, assumes a different stamp. Now the apostle Paul uses this figure, *Rom.* vi. xvii. (see the new translation.) "You have obeyed from the heart that mould of doctrine into which you were delivered," or cast. Now does not reason and experience teach us that if ten thousand thousand pieces of coin were cast into the same mould they would bear the same impress. We have but one apostolic mould of doctrine in the world, and all the sons of men cannot construct a mould of doctrine like it. A human conscience cast into the mould of the Episcopalian, Presbyterial, Methodistic, or Baptist creed, and a human conscience cast into the apostolic mould, all bear a different stamp. The Episcopalian, Presbyterial, Methodistic, Baptist, and Apostolic coin, not only wear a different date, but a different image and superscription. Martin Luther's head, John Calvin's head, John Wesley's head, John Gill's, or Andrew Fuller's head is stamped upon each of them. Not only is the *Anno Domini* different, but the image or head is different on each. They may be all silver of equal purity for aught I know, till they are tried in the furnace; but they are not one, neither can they be in image, superscription, date, and other circumstances, and therefore cannot pass current in another country. Let them, however, be tried with fire, and melted down, and all cast into the apostolic mould, and they will come out with a new image and superscription, and pass current through all the empire of that head which is stamped upon them. The figure, I think, is the best in the world, and illustrates the whole matter. I am indebted for it to the Apostle Paul. He gave me the hint, and I am grateful for it.

Some of our Baptist friends here in Kentucky have tacked round, and thought of a new plan of making a mould to give no impress or stamp to the coin at all. They will have no image, superscription, or date upon it. They will have the coin to weigh so many grains or pennyweights, but without a stamp. A plan of this sort has been lately proposed by one of our good Doctors; but to the astonishment of all, the first coin that came out of this new mould was inscribed with the number "six hundred three score and six." Let him that has understanding explain how this could be. But of this hereafter.

Let, then, but one mould of doctrine be universally adopted, of standard weight, image, and superscription, and all christians will be one in every visible respect; and then, and not till then, will the kingdom be visibly one. There will be one king, *Dei gratia*, on every crown; and that crown, if of genuine metal, will pass current through all the king's dominions. It is admitted there may be some pewter, or brass pieces whitewashed; but the former will soon grow dim, and the latter, when rubbed a little, will show a baser metal.

I may be asked, How does this correspond
2 P

with speaking the same things? I will tell you, it is but a figure illustrative of the same thing. The same image and superscription engraved in the mould, answers to the same things spoken in the ear and conveyed to the mind. The same impression will as certainly, though not mechanically nor as instantaneously, be made upon the mind as upon the metal. And did we all speak the same things we would be as visibly one as all the pieces of coin which have been cast into the same mould. I again repeat, *that this unity never can be obtained while any other creed than the sacred writings is known or regarded.* And here I invoke all the advocates of human creeds in the world:—

Gentlemen, or christians, whoever or whatever you be, I will consider your attempt to disprove this position a favor done to me and the christian world. None of you have ever yet attempted to show how christians can be united on your principles. You have showed often how they may be divided, and how each party may hold its own; but while you pray for the visible unity of the disciples, and advocate their visible disunity, we cannot understand you.

But to come to the illustration of how speaking the same things must necessarily issue in thinking the same things, or in the visible and real unity of all disciples on all those topics in which they ought to be united, I will select but one of the topics of capital importance on which there exists a diversity of sentiment. For example: The relation existing between Jesus Christ and his Father. This is one of those topics on which men have philosophized most exuberantly, and on which they have multiplied words and divisions more than on any other subject of human contemplation. Hence have arisen the Trinitarian, Arian, Semiarian, Sabellian, Unitarian, and Socinian hypotheses. It is impossible that all these can be true, and yet it is possible that they all may be false theories. Now each of these theories has given rise to a diction, phraseology, and style of speaking peculiar to itself. They do not all speak the same things of the Father, Son, and Holy Spirit. But all who do speak the same things belong to one theory. Scripture words and sentences are quoted by each of the theorists, and to these words are added expositions and definitions which give a peculiar direction to the words of the Holy Spirit. Some portions are considered by each theorist as peculiarly favorable to his views, while others are not often quoted, and if quoted at all, are clogged with embarrassing explanations. Some of the words of the Holy Spirit are quoted with great pleasure and others with great reluctance. And why? Because the former are supposed more favorable to the theory than the latter. I have often seen with what pleasure the Arian dwells upon the words "first born of every creature;" "the beginning of the creation of God." And how seldom, and with what reluctance, he quotes "I am Alpha and Omega, the First and the Last;" "In the beginning was the word, and the word was with God, and the word was God." Again, the Socinian emphasizes with great force upon the words "the man Christ Jesus;" but never dwells with delight upon this sentence, "Who being in the form of God, did not think it robbery to be like God." The Trinitarian rejoices that "there are three that bear record in heaven, the Father, the Word, and the Spirit, and that these three are one;" that Jesus said, "I and my Father are one," &c. But seldom does he quote on this subject the texts on which the Arian and Socinian dwell with pleasure. Not one of them will quote with equal pleasure or readiness every thing said on this subject; and had they the liberty they would trim and improve the apostles' style to suit their respective theories. They would do, as I heard a preacher do this week, quote the scriptures thus: "If any come to you and bring not the doctrine of the absolute, unoriginated and infinite divinity, the doctrine of the eternal filiation and generation of Jesus Christ, receive him not into your house." They do not speak the same things of the Father, the Son, and the Holy Spirit. Now, suppose that all these would abandon every word and sentence not found in the bible on this subject, and without explanation, limitation, or enlargement, quote with equal pleasure and readiness, and apply on every suitable occasion every word and sentence found in the volume, to the Father, to the Son, and to the Holy Spirit; how long would divisions on this subject exist? It would be impossible to perpetuate them on this plan. I ask the world if it would not? But, says an objector, there would be as many opinions under any other phraseology as the present. This might be for the present generation, but they could not be perpetuated. And as to any injury a private opinion may do to the possessor, it could, on this principle, do none to society.

Again, could not men believe in, obey, love, fear, and rejoice in Jesus Christ as readily and to as great a degree by speaking and hearing all the words and sentences in the volume, as they now do in all the varieties of their new nomenclature. Let them be cast into the same mould; that is, speak and hear the same things, and there would not be a Trinitarian, Arian, Semiarian, Sabellian, Unitarian, Socinian, or any thing else but a christian on this subject, or an infidel in the world. It would be so on all other topics as on that instanced, if the same principle were to be adopted.

Men would, on this principle, learn to appreciate and love one another, and to estimate human character on the real standard of piety and moral rectitude. Unfeigned obedience to the Lord, guileless benevolence to all men, and pure christian affection to the household of faith, would be the principle of appreciation of human character. Not our wild reveries, our orthodox jargon, or our heterodox paradoxes would be of paramount importance. Never can this state be induced until a *pure speech* be restored—until the language of Canaan be spoken by all the seed of Abraham.

Our confessions of faith, our additions to, our subtractions from, our transpositions of, and our extractions out of the book of God, are all in open hostility to the restoration of a pure speech, and are all under the curse, and we are punished with famine and sterility on account of them.— I have seen a confession of faith all in bible terms, extracted and transposed, like putting the eyes and ears and tongue in the right hand. Now I object as much to a creed in bible terms transposed and extracted, as I do to worshipping the Virgin Mary instead of Jesus the Messiah. The transposition of the terms or the extraction of sentences from their connexions is just as pernicious as any human innovation. Samples of this sort will be afforded at another time.

No man is to be debarred the christian church who does not deny in word or in works the declarations of the Holy Spirit, and no man is to be received into the christian community because he expresses himself in a style or in terms not found in the christian books; which must be the case when a person is obliged to express himself in the corrupt speech or in the appropriated style of a sectarian creed in order to his admission.   Editor.

———

Review of Tassey's Vindication of "the supreme and exclusive authority of the Lord Jesus Christ in Religious Matters."—Continued from p. 303.

It appears a matter of such vast importance, especially in t' e present corrupt and divided state of christianity, to have the sole and exclusive authority of our Lord Jesus Christ in religious matters fully vindicated, and re-established in the hearts and minds of his professing people; that every publication which has this for its object appears peculiarly worthy of public notice. And as this appears to be the grand object of the "Christian Baptist," I have supposed a few extracts from the work under consideration would not be unacceptable to its readers. Mr. T's sole object in his vindication, is to establish the all-sufficiency and alone-sufficiency of the Holy Scriptures, as a plain and adequate expression of the divine will for the instruction and direction of the people of God in all matters of faith and duty; to enforce the most strict and conscientious observance of them in all things for this purpose, and to obviate the interference of all human authority between the word of God and the consciences of his professing people. In the prosecution of this object it necessarily occurs not only to vindicate the independent and intrinsic sufficiency of the Holy Scriptures as a complete rule of faith and obedience, by arguments drawn from the character and declarations of their divine author;—by an induction of leading particulars respecting the faith and order of the church, its officers and ordinances, and the qualifications and duties of its members; but also to attack and obviate the high pretensions of assuming ecclesiastics, by vindicating the sacred text from the false constructions forced upon it in support of their pretended claims. This he does by shewing, in the first place, that the fixed and appropriate meaning of the term church, in the New Testament, when used in relation to the subjects of the Redeemer's kingdom, is either universal or particular, as noticed in my last. In the prosecution of this part of his plan, (p. 94,) referring to apostolic times, he observes that, "in those days sectarianism had no existence, except as contemplated in prophetic vision."

The amalgamation of christian communities into one solid, compact, and united body, by representation in ecclesiastical councils, was not then heard of. Such worldly compacts of self-seeking and self-interested spiritual rulers, endeavoring to promote their ambitious designs, had not, at this time, as afterwards, subverted the liberties and privileges of the children of God. The wisdom of ecclesiastical councils had not, as yet, occupied the place of the wisdom of the Lord Jesus; nor had scholastic or systematic divinity destroyed the simplicity of the doctrine of Christ. Far otherwise do matters now appear. We must now have a system of government modelled upon the best establishments around us. We must have superior and inferior courts, legislative assemblies, and ecclesiastical judicatories. And what, at the best, makes but a bungling job of the whole of such systems, is that the same assembly is this moment legislative, and anon judicative; not only is it the maker, but the executor of its own laws; thus opening a door for the most tyrannical exercise of power. It is well that our liberties, civil and religious, are guaranteed by wise and liberal institutions. Were it not for this, we should soon be furnished with the necessary appendages of all such ecclesiastical establishments, to wit, inquisitorial racks and gibbets, the most convincing instruments ever used by ecclesiastical power. Matters, then, have mightily changed since apostolic times. The appellation *church*, from designating a few disciples associated together to sing praises to Jesus Christ," (and commemorate his death) "has come to signify a large and respectable body or sect of professing christians, once a year represented in general assembly, or in its convocation of bishops, usually convened to make laws to bind the consciences of their careless and submissive adherents. Accordingly, we have the Romish Church, the Episcopal Church, the Presbyterian Church, the Methodist Church, the Baptist Church; and their natural associates in power," (the Romish Conclave) "The Convocation of Bishops, the General Assembly, the Methodist Conference, the Baptist Convention; a kind of phraseology to which the New Testament is a total stranger. Little did the first christians think that the body of Christ should ever be split up into such fragments, and that its professed friends should become the rivals of earthly potentates in their thirst for splendor and power. Little did they suppose that the followers of Christ should so far lose sight of their Master's glory, as to become the mere dupes of a designing oligarchy, in promoting the prosperity of any particular sect or faction. Now that all this has come to pass, may be established from the most indubitable phraseology: what does such language as the Baptist *interest*, the Methodist *interest*, the Presbyterian *interest*, indicate? Who does not perceive that the secret spring of action which this betrays, is the aggrandizement of a party? This, and often this alone, is the grand moving cause of all that fury, zeal, and seeming earnestness with which our peaceful hours of rest have been broken in upon, and grievously misspent. And, to promote and gain this mighty end, have been the cause of collecting together synods and other ecclesiastical councils, since the commencement of those extended corruptions, by which the churches' beauty has been defaced. But who is there so blind as not to see, that, in proportion as the aggrandizement of a sect is promoted, so is the glory of Christ injured; and, the cause of truth and righteousness, of heavenly peace, of christian love and unity, more pleasing than the splendid offerings of mighty conquerors, is immolated at the shrine of this insatiable love of party?"

"Oh! then, let us return to the simplicity and purity of ancient times, when the disciples of Jesus, in their associated capacity, or as individuals, acknowledged no authority, either delegated or assumed, but that of Jesus Christ; and when, in their church assemblies, they could carry into execution the laws of Jesus, without the aid of self-constituted courts, either to new model or explain them; or any human authority to give them sanction!"

"Once more, we observe, that the language of the sacred writers, when they come to refer to the local situations of the various churches, decidedly proves that they had no conception of a consolidated earthly church, either extended" (as embracing the whole population of a district or country, as the church of Scotland, &c.) "or representative" (by delegates or otherwise.) "When they refer to any circumscribed or limited situation, as a town or city, they, in all such cases, use the singular number, as the church at Ephesus, at Corinth, at Cenchrea, which was about two miles from Corinth; evidently because there was no christian society in any of these places, but one, to which the designation *church* justly belonged.

But when they come to speak of a certain district of country, in which there was a number of such assemblies, they as invariably use the plural number; as, "the churches of Judea which are in Christ Jesus; the churches of the Gentiles; the churches of Macedonia; the churches of Galatia; the seven churches which are in Asia;" never the "church of Judea, of the Gentiles" (or the gentile church,) "of Macedonia, of Asia, or of Galatia." Now this phraseology proves that the word church, in the singular number, was so completely appropriated to a single congregation of Christ's disciples, and had become so universally the name by which such an assembly was distinguished, that nothing but local situation was necessary to subjoin to it, in order to make it explicitly refer to a particular society; and, that it would have been an absolute abuse of language to have used it as the appropriate name of any differently constituted meeting. The word congregation, which, through custom, has become the appropriated name of an assembly of people in the habit of meeting to attend to the worship of God, might as properly be applied to a session, a presbytery, a synod, and a general assembly, as to apply the appellation church to any of these. But, were we to adopt this course, confusion and obscurity would be the consequence, and language would cease to be (an intelligible) medium of communicating our ideas. Were the word congregation to be indiscriminately applied to the meetings above noticed, then it could be the appropriated name of none of them; and we would be obliged to use it with such expletives as would prevent mistakes. In like manner, if the word church became the appropriated appellation, by which a worshipping assembly of the saints was distinguished; it follows, that it could never have become the appropriated designation by which any differently framed assembly could be represented. Nor could it ever be used in reference to a representative assembly of any description, without the addition of such expletives; or, in such a connexion as would preclude misapprehension. But in none of the passages in which the appellative church occurs, where it is supposed to apply to a representative body, are there any expletives subjoined to intimate a change in the application of the word; nor is there any thing in the connexion which would indicate such a use of it, as shall afterwards more fully appear. If, then, this is the fact; and if the word church, after all, will be found to mean, at one time, a kirk session, or consistory; at another, a synod, or provincial conference; and again, a general assembly convened in judicature; or a general conference in conclave assembled; and yet no intimation of any of these different meanings in the connexion; nor any expletive annexed to intimate the change; must there not follow the utmost confusion and misapprehension? and would not every writer, who would commit such blunders, be justly chargeable with darkening counsel by words without knowledge? Should he not be reprehended severely for his ambiguous and unmeaning phraseology? And is it so, that it remains to be the province of the Holy Spirit alone, to write unintelligibly? To use words, yea, appropriated names, in a variety of different meanings, with-

57

out warning us of the change; or intimating the reason of such alteration from the fixed and determined meaning of such appellations! Far be it from any christian to think so improperly of the productions of inspiration;—to suppose that he ever meant to speak unintelligibly, or use language calculated rather to obscure, than to elucidate divine truth! Let us prefer charging the evil to its proper cause,—a disposition to make the scriptures quadrate with our respective systems. It is this that has affixed certain meanings to words, which the Spirit of God never intended them to convey. By this means men gratify their prejudices, and prop up those systems of religion to which they are attached, and give them the appearance of scriptural support; when the volume of inspiration directly discountenances and opposes every thing of the kind. So long, therefore, as we are to regard words as signs of our ideas, and the Divine Spirit sent to reveal to us every thing necessary for the proper management of his children, we ought to lay it down as a fixed principle, that when he speaks to us, he intends to be understood; and, consequently, that he uses words in their commonly acknowledged import."

Thus our author justly reasons against the perversion and abuse of the language of inspiration, and points out the true cause of it, while rescuing and defending the term *church* from the forced and incoherent meanings imposed upon it, in support of an assumed authority to dictate in matters of religion. And having done this, (as I think he most evidently and irrefutably has, in the course of his investigation,) all rule and authority in the church of Christ, (except that of a single congregation with its proper officers, over its own proper members, in the execution of the laws already made and provided in the holy scriptures for the government of the church,) are for ever abolished. Consequently, every distinct worshipping assembly, or particular church, remains in full possession of all that power of complete self-government, with which the apostles left the primitive churches fully invested, after they ha set in order amongst them the things that were wanting for this purpose.

In the course of his vindication, our author frequently refers to the modest assumption in behalf of synods and councils, recognized in the Westminster Confession of Faith, chapter xxxi. section 3. and adverts to the only two passages of scripture therein quoted in support of it without a formal reference to the Confession of a full quotation of the passage, which reads thus: "It belongs to synods and councils ministerially to determine controversies of faith and cases of conscience; to set down rules and directions for the better ordering of the public worship of God, and government of the church; to receive complaints in cases of mal-administration, and authoritatively to determine the same; which decrees and determinations, if consonant to the word of God, are to be received with reverence and submission; not only for their agreement with the word, but also for the power whereby they are made, as being an ordinance of God, appointed thereto in his word. *Acts* xv. 15—31. xvi. 4. *Matt.* xviii. 17—20. "These are the claims of the whole Presbyterian body on which they have continued to act, however otherwise divided in sentiment, from the year sixteen hundred forty-seven to the present day. Claims which justify the pretensions and acts of all synods and councils, from the council of Nice to the present day; for, according to them, and they are the judges, both the authority enacting, and the acts enacted, are

according to the word of God. It is true, but rather unhappily for them, it is conceded, sect. 4. that "all synods or councils since the apostles' times, whether general or particular, may err, and many have erred; therefore they are not to be made the rule of faith or practice, but to be used as a help in both." Eph. ii. 29. Acts xvii. 11. 1 Cor. ii. 5. 2 Cor. i. 24. "Therefore, before we can warrantably receive their help, we must first help ourselves; and ascertain by our own research of the holy scriptures whether those things, which they have determined, are so. A poor, uncertain, fallible help, indeed! And yet so invested with a divine authority, as to be an "ordinance of God!!" And which if we do resist, we are sure to receive present damnation!! For who ever resists the dogmas of such decreeing and enacting authority, without being cast out as heretics or schismatics, however unscriptural they might appear to the conscientious recusant? But this, it seems has only been the case "since the apostles' times." Happy, then, yea, thrice happy, the christians that lived in the apostles' times, whose helps were infallible. Helps that might be depended upon with the utmost confidence. Helps worthy of God to give, and of his people to receive. And would it not be better still to rest in the helps thus supplied, than to have recourse to such miserable supplements, —such super refinements of "rules and directions for the better ordering of the public worship of God, and government of his church?" Have we not reason to fear, yea, is it not evident, that the rules and directions superadded to what the apostles left behind them, under the pretence of the better ordering of things, have had the very contrary tendency? Did not the apostles, by means of the faith and order established by them in the churches, leave the christian communities in peace and love amongst themselves, and towards each other? But how is it now, after the better orderings, and additional improvements of, at least, fifteen hundred years? Let the reader judge.

But to proceed: Our author not only evinces by a copious induction of evidence from the holy scriptures against the allegations of Dr. McLeod and others, that the term church is never used in the singular to denote a plurality of assemblies in any place, united in a representative body, to regulate the concerns of its constituents; but also attacks and exposes the forced interpretations put upon Matthew xviii. 17, &c. and Acts xv. 15—in support of such representation. The reader will please to recollect, that it is upon these two passages, as upon an impregnable foundation, that the whole colossian superstructure of synods and councils, their divine constitution and mighty powers are predicated, in the above cited article, from the Westminster Confession of Faith. They ought certainly, therefore, to be proof of the most obvious and decisive character, in order to support such high pretensions, such vast assumption of power. But from what appears upon the face of the investigation before us, the former shrinks, nay, quite disappears at the first touch; and, considered as proof, goes rather to demolish than to support the superstructure founded upon it. For, as our author justly observes, the phrase "tell it to the church," in the above connexion, precludes forever the possibility of appeal, inasmuch as the sentence of the church is decisive, being ratified in heaven. If we understand the word church, then, in its appropriated scriptural import, for a single congregation of saints statedly meeting for religious purposes, a rejection of its decision admits of no appeal, and if we should understand it as Presbyterians do, to mean a kirk session, a presbytery or a synod, to whichsoever of these the complaint is made, by its decision the matter is determined, being ratified in heaven: consequently to the defendant, or rather to the recusant, there remains no room for appeal, though he should think himself aggrieved. "Tell it to the church," then, is the third and last step in the process; however we may understand the term. "In the reasoning which we have followed up, says Mr. T. in reference to this quotation, we have taken it for granted, that some one of the courts specified, might have been intended. But—whether you call it a consistory, a session, a committee, a bishop's court, a synod, or conference, what you please, there is not the most distant allusion to any one of such constituted judicatories, whatever in the passage. We would ask,—what hinders the word church from being here understood in its usual and determined acceptation?"—"By what rule of sound criticism," says Professor Campbell, "can we arbitrarily impose here on the word church, the signification of church representative, a signification which we do not find it bears in one other passage of scripture? To affirm, without proof, that this is the sense of it here, is taking for granted the very point in dispute."* Let it first be shewed that in the phraseology of the New Testament, the word church is applied to a representative body of any kind, and we will relinquish the point, &c. Our author next proceeds to investigate the claims in support of the representative system, founded on Acts xv. 15, &c. the other parts of the foundation assumed in the Westminster Confession, in support of the divine right of synods and councils: the whole of which claims appear, in the course of the investigation, to receive as little countenance from this latter passage, as they did from the former.

P. 124, "We shall now more particularly examine the 15th chapter of the Acts, which is supposed to present an example for courts of appeal, and to which all the different denominations refer with confidence in support of their respective systems. To conceive, however, that this chapter lays a foundation for papal usurpation, and diocesan episcopacy, and classical presbytery, is perfectly absurd: yet this is the grand proof to which they all appeal in support of these different hierarchies. That this chapter lays no foundation for any one of the above systems, and especially for those courts of appeal, or ecclesiastical councils, for which it is so triumphantly quoted, we propose now to demonstrate. Mr. M'Leod informs us, that "we have in this chapter an authoritative decree, enacted by a representative assembly, exercising ecclesiastical jurisdiction over churches and presbyteries." That it is an authoritative decree, we most readily admit; and who is there that denies it? But that this decree was enacted or ordained by a representative assembly, we refuse to acknowledge. The first argument by which he attempts to prove his position is this: "The apostles did not determine the question as inspired extraordinary teachers and rulers. When inspired they spake as they were moved by the Holy Ghost. This excludes disputation. But about the question there was much disputation!" On reading this paragraph we were struck with astonishment—What! the apostles did not determine the question as inspired, extraordinary teachers!! For what then are

* Campbell's Lectures, p. 164.

these uninspired decrees placed in the inspired volume? Not determine the question as inspired extraordinary teachers!! Why then does the language of the decrees declare the contrary? "It seemed good to the Holy Ghost and to us, to lay upon you no greater burden than these necessary things." What! this question not determined by inspiration, and yet "it seemed good to the Holy Ghost!!!" Oh! prejudice! oh! bigotry! what have you done? You cease not to pervert the right ways of the Lord. Need we, then, endeavor to argue out these decrees to be an inspired document, when they are expressly so called by the inspired writer himself, and also by the unanimous voice of the apostles and elders, with the whole church, who preface their letter with this declaration?—Who can deny it that believes the inspiration of the scriptures at all? This one fact, then, invalidates forever any argument that can be drawn from it in favor of ecclesiastical councils and enactments. But we are told, "About this question there was much disputation, and inspiration excludes disputation." Be it so. Among whom did this much disputation take place? Was it among the apostles? No such thing. Not a symptom of this kind is noticed as happening between those inspired characters. On the contrary, the three of them that spake are in perfect accordance in their views of the subject; as any person may see who will take the trouble of examining the narrative. Nor does the circumstance of the apostles' arguing the point from the Old Testament scriptures, or from the facts that had occurred under their own labors, alter the case respecting the inspiration of this document, more than the same course destroys the inspiration of the epistles, in which we find it pursued to great extent. This, therefore, was evidently an extraordinary meeting, because composed in part of inspired extraordinary men, who were competent to ordain inspired and extraordinary decrees, being authorized to do so by the Holy Ghost. Until then, you can find a synod partly composed of such characters as are competent to enact decrees under the infallible guidance of the Holy Spirit, as the above mentioned document was ordained, it is vain to plead this case as a precedent for ecclesiastical courts, or to talk of enacting authoritative rules of faith and manners for the disciples of Christ. The claims of the court of Rome, on this score, have some degree of consistency with them. It at once sets up for infallibility, and his Holiness tells you plainly, that he is the successor of Peter, and derives his authority immediately from Jesus Christ, whose vicar he is upon earth, but there are ecclesiastical courts claiming a right, authoritatively, to enact laws for the people of God; to determine articles of faith, and resolve cases of conscience, and that, at the very time they are disclaiming every thing like infallibility.—We would ask, then, What is the difference between a Presbyterian synod or assembly, claiming to be the successors of the apostles, exercising their assumed power in the name, and by the authority of Jesus Christ; and his Holiness the Pope, claiming to be the successor of Peter, and exercising his assumed power in the name and by the authority of Jesus Christ? For our part, we have a number, by whose combination they become the more dangerous.

Page 98. "But let us inquire more minutely into the materials of which this assembly was composed. Were they ministers and elders only? Yes," says our author, "the assembly was composed of presbyters." "No," says the inspired writer, "for it pleased the apostles and elders, with the whole church, to send chosen men of their own company to Antioch." And again, "the apostles, and elders, and brethren send, greeting." Here, then are two writers at issue upon this point; and the question simply is this, Shall we believe the assertion of Alexander M'Leod, because————? Or shall we believe the testimony of Luke, because he was inspired by the Holy Spirit?"

I shall close these extracts for the present with the following; see page 124:—"What, then, becomes of this *jure divino* system, or the divine warrant for ecclesiastical courts? Is there any warrant whatever contained in the inspired volume for such constituted courts? We reply unhesitatingly, that there is not, in any shape; neither directly nor impliedly. That there is nothing "agreeable to sound reasoning from established truths,—nor from approved example,—nor sanctioned by divine approbation,—nor established by divine acts,—nor recommended by directions from God," to be found in favor of such a system; and, consequently, that it cannot be of divine right, our author himself being judge."

PHILALETHES.

(TO BE CONTINUED.)

THE following Reply to a second communication of "*A Friend to Truth*," which appeared in the "Western Luminary," some time since, was intended first to have appeared in that paper.— The reason it was not published in the "Luminary," will probably be made known hereafter.

PRINTER.

Mr. Skillman,

DEAR SIR—It is said you are a christian. I will, therefore, address you as if in truth you were one. I profess to be a christian, and will speak to you as I think a christian ought to speak. Christians have a right to use a liberty with each other, not common to all mankind. They may exhort, admonish, reprove, and entreat one another in a way in which the children of this world dare not. They are all born again, and from above, and have kindred feelings, desires, aims, and pursuits. They are children of one family, are all taught by God, and under the government of one Divine King. They are mutually bound to be subject to the same laws, and to watch over one another. They sometimes err. Hence arise the obligations of reciprocal care for each other's good.

You published, about three months ago, a communication injurious to my moral and religious character. You saw my refutation thereof six or seven weeks ago. You promised, from a sense of justice no doubt, to publish my refutation a week after you saw it. But you did not meet your engagements, because it is presumed the author, or authors of the slander, had not their rejoinder ready. Dare you not let my reply appear as soon as you saw it, or as soon as you promised it? Were you afraid to let your readers see it, unpreceded by a second publication of the slander, and unsucceeded by a long rejoinder: lest they should be in danger of being convinced? There is either cowardice or injustice apparent in this thing; but which, I will not say; or whether either, until you vindicate yourself. If the sun ought not to go down upon a christian's anger, it ought not to rise and set for forty days on the columns of slander and evil report uncontradicted, when the refutation is in possession of the publisher. It is true you informed us you expected an addition of subscribers to your paper; and that you would ultimately have the pleasure

of publishing more generally my refutation.— But, sir, in gaining power you lost time; and one great act of kindness does not always compensate for two wrongs. Now I exhort you to do so no more. Be never ready to take up an evil report against your neighbor; and should it get into circulation, be ever ready to put it down.

But now to the rejoinder of your " Friend to Truth." He has tried to escape through the back door which I mentioned in my refutation he had left open for himself. He contends he said no harm of me, nor of the New Testament: nor did he intend to praise, or blame, or criticise the work, but merely to correct a false impression on the public mind, that prevailed among many.— This is, I grant, what he *professed* to do; but, in *reality*, he made a false impression upon the public mind, and most grievously slandered me.— He brings the foulest charge ever mortal man brought against me. Now for the proof. His own words are, "He (viz. myself) was anxious to furnish the public with a gospel shaped exactly to his own views." Now, Mr. Skillman, I ask you what more grievous charge could you conceive of, than to accuse a professed christian of wilfully, designedly, "*anxiously*" imposing upon the christian public a book, purporting to be a correct translation of the New Testament, "shaped exactly to his own views," and in which he makes the Spirit of God speak to suit himself, regardless of the true meaning thereof? It is a crime above all forgery, interpolation, and perversion, known in human affairs. If this be done without a shadow of proof, without a single specification, is it not slander of the highest character? I leave this question with you, sir, and the public. But the fact that I am so accused without a single specification in proof thereof, is manifest from the two pieces published in your paper over the signature "Friend to Truth."

I must not feel myself slandered nor injured by such an allegation; nor must I defend myself from it, unless I renounce all christian character! So this gentleman insinuates. It would be impolite and unchristian in me to plead not guilty. I have not so learned Christ. I have plead not guilty, and this pious and just lover of truth has written again. And what has he said?

1st. That he is not Dr. Blythe.
2d. That he "*brought no charge against me.*"
3d. He acknowledges that he made one false representation on Acts xx. 28.
4th. He attacks Griesbach.
5th. He proves me a Unitarian.
6th. He demands of me the proof, or to say that I am a Unitarian. And,
7th. He then charges me only with "fast winging my way towards the cold regions of Unitarianism." He then prays for me. The whole farce is then complete.

On these points I must of course say something. He says I "attribute his piece to Dr. Blythe." No where is this said in my reply. He then draws into view an interview I once had with Dr. Blythe, of which he gives a one-sided and incorrect representation. I feel not one unkind emotion towards Dr. Blythe. It is true he acted unkindly, and, I think, an unchristian part towards me. In the fall of 1824, when I was in the neighborhood of his congregation, as I was correctly informed, he commanded his people not to go to hear me, telling them I was "a very bad man and he could prove it." This was obviously an attack upon my moral and religious character. I called upon him for an explanation, and his reasons for so accusing me. I told him what I had heard. He did not deny having said so. I called on him for the proof. He said he knew nothing about or against my moral character, and that he did not mean my moral character; but that he considered me erroneous.— I said the people did not so understand his accusation, and that the term "*bad*" always related to moral character, and that if he had said an erroneous man I should never have inquired after it. I also added that a person acquainted with the meaning of words could not use the term *bad* as synonymous with *erroneous*. He again repeated as above, and thus retracted or explained away the import of his accusation. He then told me he pitied me. I replied, I also pitied him. He added, that I was laboring to pull down the kingdom of the clergy, and that he was determined to build it up. As to any challenge I gave him to " a debate before the sovereign people," I am not conscious; but Col. Drake will, no doubt, remember whether or not; and as he heard my conversation with the Doctor, I appeal to him whether the above is not correct. This is Mr. Friend to Truth's first proof that the New Testament is not faithfully published.

In the next place this good man reminds his readers that his sole object in his first piece, was, " to correct false impressions that prevailed among many with regard to the New Testament." But we have no evidence that any " false impressions" existed but the word of an anonymous scribe. And no man could have any such impression as he describes, who had read the work; as every thing is plainly stated both in the prefaces and appendix. So that his effort was altogether gratuitous, and uncalled for. And he admits he had never seen the prospectus; consequently, could say nothing about my fidelity in the matter. This is his second argument to prove the translation unfaithful.

On the subject of baptism, he had said that " the alterations were upwards of eighty," and complains of my saying that this was telling eighty lies in one truth. This, I own, as he understands it, was quite as impolite as it was for Paul to say that the "Cretans are always liars," or as it was for John to say, that " he is a liar who says he knows God, and does not keep his commandments." But he is too sanguine when he thinks that I admit he tells one truth in this matter. For, should a schoolboy say he had seen eighty pigeons when he only saw *one* eighty times, I would not allow that he had told one truth in his whole story. And the young student of which he speaks, and of whom he read in the spelling-book, who made three chickens out of two, reflects on himself, and not on me, if he had the sense to see it. It suited his conduct—not mine. He next passes by with a sneer the fact that Doctors Campbell and Macknight authorized every thing said on baptism in the whole work. Three facts are stated in my reply, showing that there is not in reality one alteration on the subject of baptism, in the whole eighty: and, Mr. Skillman, take notice, he does not attack one of the three. I demand of him a refutation, if he can of these three facts. All that he can say, these three unassailed, is only making instead of removing "false impressions." Thus we dispose of his " more than eighty alterations," or his third argument to remove false impressions.

He next tells us that Griesbach divided the collated manuscripts into three classes, and "if he mistakes not, changed the reading" of God into Lord (Acts xx. 28.) " on the authority of a

very few." As he appears afraid of committing himself here, we shall advise him to inform himself better before he next writes, and request him to give the names of the manuscripts upon the authority of which the reading is preferred, and then we shall see whether they are of more weight than the very many on the other side. But here he gives up the point about my making a false impression, and also passes by, without a single remark the testimony of Ireneus and the Syriac version. He also fails to charge Griesbach with Unitarianism, and Michaelis with Socinianism, which he ought to have done. He also studiously avoids telling us how the reading Lord instead of God, destroys the divinity of Jesus. Until this is done it is all a mere puff of noisy breath. I assert that Griesbach's Greek Testament is the most correct text in christendom—and this at least is a fair and full balance to all his assertions on Nolan. So goes his fourth argument.

His fifth argument is, that I am *almost* a Unitarian, and sorry is he that the evidence is not stronger. But this he is at great pains to prove. His first proof of this tremendous charge is, that " *Christian Union*," was Dr. Fishback, and " *Aquila*" was Barton W. Stone; and that I persuaded Dr. Fishback and B. W. Stone that there was no difference between them on the subject of worshipping Jesus. But unfortunately for his conclusion, the premises are false: for B. W. Stone never wrote one sentence in the Christian Baptist over any signature whatever. "*Sic transit gloria mundi*." His "good reason" to the contrary notwithstanding. His second reason why I am a Unitarian is, because I told a correspondent from Missouri that I was not a Socinian. Because I am not a Socinian, therefore, I must be a Unitarian. This is *sound* logic. He believes me sometimes. Well now, I will tell him, that I am neither an Arian, nor Unitarian, nor Sabellian. *Query*—Will he now believe that I am none of these, upon the same evidence on which he believes I am not a Socinian?

Third proof of my Unitarianism—I quote the Reformer. Now I never heard nor understood that the Reformer was a Unitarian, nor did I ever hear him so charged. But if he be, will my quoting him on historical matters, or any other, not on the doctrine of Jesus, prove me a Unitarian? If so, then every one is a Deist who quotes Hume or Gibbon; every one that quotes Dr. Blythe is a Presbyterian, and every one that quotes John Wesley is a Methodist. A fine critic on the New Testament truly!!!

His fourth proof is, that I sympathized with the rulers of Transylvania University when persecuted by the *righteous*. I pitied the *goats* when the *sheep* butted them prodigiously. Yes, I pitied the goats' *horns* when red with the blood of the sheep. And if a Protestant should knock out the brains of a Papist, and I should be so unfortunate as to pity the Papist, I must then turn Catholic, and worship the host. Admirable translator!! Profound interpreter!! Steel and lead might as soon elicit a spark of fire as your genius prove me a Unitarian. I never sympathized with the religious opinions of any ruler of the Transylvania University; for I never knew that they gave themselves nor the public much concern about supernatural religion of any sort; but I confess that I thought it unadvisable that the Presbyterians should control every fountain of literature in the West; and unreasonable that a state institution should become a *sectarian* school. After thus proving me to be a Unitarian, he asks me to say whether or not I am, by writing certain phrases which he has the goodness to prescribe, only attaching to them, without mental reservation, the orthodox sense. I see he thinks me conscientious! Well now, should I conscientiously avow that I am not a Unitarian, Socinian, Arian, Semiarian, or Sabellian, I wonder whether he would believe me. We shall try. If he does not, then my using his test words would be of no use: for, then, I spake feignedly. Strange case, indeed! I am accused of being or leaning to a Unitarian, and not one sentiment or sentence in all my writings or public speeches adduced in proof. I am accused of making a New Testament to suit my gospel; and yet my accuser does not say what my gospel is, nor does he say that I have perverted one single word to favor it—Yes, he has. Has he not censured the word Lord instead of God? But has he accused Griesbach, Ireneus, and the Syriac version, and many others, of having gospels of their own to foist upon the public?—No. Has he accused them of Socinianism or Unitarianism?—No. If, then, this "alteration," himself being judge, does not prove them interpolators and heretics, how can it criminate me!! But, sir, is it not passing strange, that of all the texts that speak of " the supreme deity of Jesus" in the whole New Testament, he has not found one against which to except in the new translation, save this one! and even this one he does not presume to shew to be Unitarian. Is it so that he has not another one in all the book to place along side of it. Surely, then, the new translation is most unexceptionable on this subject; for more than twenty have been excepted to in the common version on this account, by Calvinistic writers, as I can prove.

I do charge him with the crime of slander in this instance; and I call upon him to show that there is any gospel other than the apostolic supported in the new version. I have often given my reasons why I object to expressing myself in any creed language, upon any article of the christian religion. See also an essay on " purity of speech," in this No. on this very topic. I do believe that Jesus the Saviour is the *Word made flesh;* that this Word was "in the beginning with God, and that this word was God." I do believe and teach that he is "the Alpha and Omega—the First and the Last." I believe that " although he *was rich,* and thought it not a robbery to be like God, yet he made himself poor," and ten thousand persons are witnesses that I pray to him and teach others to pray to him, and to worship him with all their hearts, without reservation or equivocation. If this be a proof of Unitarianism or Arianism, I may be accused; but otherwise no man can accuse me without being guilty of slander. But I will speak of him in bible terms, and in the words which the Holy Spirit teaches, and not in the language of Ashdod. I do so on all other topics equally with this. But, like a true son of a sect, this anonymous slanderer first orders me to be scourged, and then asks me what I have done. He first accuses me of the basest crime, and then, unable to convict me of it, he *adjures* me to say, am I not guilty? He condemns me and then calls for the evidence. But I defy him to prove his charge, and to prove from the new version that I have not faithfully done every thing proposed to be done in the work. In his last piece he has, indeed, not even adverted to the essential parts of my former reply. He has not made a single objection to the 15th and 16th paragraphs of my reply, nor a single remark, that I can see, on them; and these unassailed, he has conceded every point of importance.

He thanks me, not for having given this translation to the public; but snarls at the idea of its being imprisoned, because two or three *clergymen* in the state have the whole work, and perhaps not more than *three* men in the whole state have *all the three works* which I have given in one volume. Many of them may have one of the three, some two, but very few indeed have the whole; and should not the "laity" have the work as well as the clergy? *I gave it to them*—and he will take it from them. I can prove, as soon as he gives his name, if I am not greatly mistaken, that he has actually took home to his own house the work from some of his lay brethren, first telling them its faults and then accepting of it as a present. His name, in full, will decide this point. But with all he says about the clergy having these works, I am told he had to ride to Winchester to a circulating library to get a peep into Doddridge on Acts xx. 28, that he might make out his case.

He requests me to publish his rejoinder. My rules require his name when a request of this sort is made. Let him publish his name, and I will publish them from Dan to Beersheba.

Mr. Skillman, as a christian, I can have no object but truth. I am not afraid to avow my sentiments on any subject. I am obliged to you for your last extract from the Christian Baptist; but cannot thank you for the head you made for it. But your head and my body will not make one man. I court investigation, special and strict investigation of the new version. I thank all for their criticisms, but none for their slanders. I feel able to defend the work against all opposition, and will think so until I am tried. You will publish this, I trust, as soon as you see it, especially as you have published the slanders of your friend twice, and tacked his rejoinder to the heels of my reply. You will excuse this hasty scroll, as your paper was received by me after night, on the 6th instant, at Louisville. I am now starting to Indiana, and cannot transcribe my Monday morning's lucubrations.

Your honest friend,   A. CAMPBELL.
Louisville, January 8, 1827.

Anecdote.

A SCOTCH blacksmith being asked the meaning of metaphysics, explained it as follows:— " When the party who listens dinna ken what the party who speaks means, and the party who speaks dinna ken what he means himself—that is metaphysics."

No. 9.]			APRIL 2, 1827.
Remarks on a Tour.

THROUGH the watchful care and supporting hand of the Father of Mercies, we have returned in safety from a tour in the states of Ohio, Kentucky, Indiana, and Tennessee, occupying a period of four months. On this tour I had the pleasure not only of visiting my old friends and acquaintances, but of adding many new ones to the number. To this pleasure, however, was annexed the pain of parting. For, to the uncertainty of meeting again in this pilgrimage, was added the uncertainty, in some instances at least, of meeting in the heavenly country. For, while we rejoice in the assurance of meeting many of our friends in that blessed state where there is no more separation, it must be acknowledged that there are some personally attached to us, and we to them, from various reasons, concerning whose eternal life we can entertain but a very slender hope. It is, perhaps, natural; but so it is, that while we exercise benevolence towards all mankind, we more ardently desire the salvation of some than of others. Hence it is, that on our list of friends there are some of whose salvation we are not always sanguine; yet, from their social and merely human virtues, we feel compelled, with more than ordinary zeal, to exclaim, "Would to God that they were not only almost, but altogether christians!" The Saviour once looked upon and loved a young man of extraordinary virtue, who, with a sad and sorrowful heart, bade him adieu. He was almost, but not altogether a disciple. There are, perhaps, few christians unacquainted with the feelings and views to which we allude. There is no doubt but that the Saviour of the world, his apostles, and the christians of the primitive age, had many friends who never became obedient to the faith. But this is a subject on which we can neither think nor write with pleasure. We shall therefore dismiss it with the expression of a wish that none may construe attachments or friendships, based on considerations merely human, into an affectionate regard for the Saviour and his disciples.

We added much to our knowledge of men and things religious, and returned home richly laden with materials for public edification. These materials have been quarried out of the actual condition of things in the religious world, and will require but little skill to adjust to advantage. We got into the cabinet of the popular systems, and into the *sanctum sanctorum* of the religious world. At these we had but peeped before, but now have looked full in the face the sacred effigies which fell down from Jupiter. We are often wont to conclude that from a few samples we know the whole, and that from a short acquaintance we know the man. Of the fallacy of such conclusions we have frequent proofs, but yet we are reluctant to suspect that we may be wrong. I would not raise expectation too high, nor give occasion to retort—

"Returning from his finish'd tour,
"Grown ten times perter than before;"

but I would say that I think I am better qualified to speak to the religious world on the subjects to which I have been calling its attention, than before. I have been questioned and cross-questioned a thousand times on a thousand topics; I have heard religious experiences, religious doubts; histories of conversions and relapses; of family religion, of family discipline, of christian congregations, of councils, conferences, and synods, of debates and strifes, of revivals and declensions, of persecutions and triumphs, of religious wars and commotions—so numerous and diversified, so ordinary and extraordinary, that I think little can be added to give variety to the religious scenery which I now have in retrospect.

If undissembled piety yet exists on earth, I have seen it; if christian friendship or brotherly love have yet their abode on earth, I have sojourned with them; if intelligent zeal and active philanthropy yet warm a human heart, or animate a human tongue, we have heard their eloquence and felt their power. And if there can be seen a dreary waste of frigid speculations; if there be on earth a barren desert of withered forms and parched ceremonies; if there be a valley of dry bones and lifeless sculls, strewed with the spoils of death, we have traversed it through. If there be superstition, delusion, enthusiasm, scepticism, infidelity, or atheism, yet alive, we have conversed with them.

Of the teachers of what is called religion, we have had a very full example. From the allegorizer, who preaches Christ and his church out of every verse of the Song of Solomon; from the mystic, who finds the whole plan of salvation in Paul's shipwreck and escape on Malta; from the inspired enthusiast, who tells of dreams and visions, of extacies and revelations all the day; from the drivelling paraphrast to the verbose and soporiferous commentator, we have had a perfect example. But on the other hand, we have also been conversant with the sapient doctors of biblical criticism, the shrewd and convincing reasoners upon the law and the testimony; the profound interpreters of scholastic theology; the eloquent declaimers against vice and immorality; the dispassionate and frigid metaphysician; the practical preacher, and the erudite bishop. But what is worthy of notice and still more of remembrance, we have heard some commend the life they will not lead, and approve the course they will not follow; who

"See the better way and approve it too,
"Detest the worse, and still the worse pursue."

Of the influence of these teachers there is every where illustrious demonstrations. Here is a congregation all on fire, and there another cold as Boreas. Here there is one intelligent and liberal; there another ignorant and bigoted. Here they are all intent on mysteries, and there on their interpretation. In one congregation it is all doctrine; in another, all practice. In a few the supreme question is, "Lord, what will you have us to do?" but in many it is in effect what is most fashionable?

Religious sects do not bound and limit these diversities, but they exist in all. We mingled with all, conversed with all, and found in all pretty much the same varieties. A few differences in opinion do not always, indeed very seldom, make a visible difference in the exterior or interior items of a profession. The Baptist and the Paido-Baptist, the New Light and the Old Light in the same latitudes vegetate alike. They wear different regimentals, rally round different standards, and fight under different captains; but neither the flag nor the cockade makes a difference in the soldiers. One is heroic and daring; another dastardly and timid under any insignia. As of nations it was once said, of sects it may now be said, "In every one he that fears God and works righteousness is accepted by him." And will not the sprinkled which by nature keep the precepts of our Lawgiver, judge you a transgressor, though immersed, who boast in your immersion, and keep not the commandments of your King?

The two greatest evils we have to deplore, because pregnant with the greatest evils to mankind in general, are the manifest want of congregational and family discipline. The easy terms on which many are admitted into christian communities, and the little attention paid to their after behavior; the great zeal manifested for the acknowledgment of the party *shibboleths*, and the little concern expressed for the good works of christians, have almost defaced the landmarks which bound the plantations of nature and of grace. The decent moralist without, and the precise professor within, the pale of christian society, are, in the main, one and the same character. And when the question is asked, What do you more than others? it is answered by comparing the best in the church with the worst out of it—a mode of reasoning the most sophistical in the world. It should have been by comparing the worst in the church with the most respectable deistical moralist, and not by demanding all the boot between the decent sceptic and the extravagant debauchee, or licentious rake, to make the odds between the christian and the unregenerate. But thus it is that many impose upon themselves and one another. They are content to say that they differ from others, inasmuch as they frequent not the ball-room, nor the theatre, nor the haunts of dissipation. To this add, that the reins of congregational discipline are held in such an enfeebled hand, that a group of the most motley character is held together whithersoever the impetus of passion, sense, or appetite guide the way. Though this is not universal, it is very general in all parties. The restraints of christian doctrine are relaxed by the artificial or rather mechanical restraints of wayward creeds, and an agreement in "essential" opinions, covers a multitude of actual aberrations from the morality of the Lord Jesus.

The most generally true and correct report of the Baptist churches which could be given is as follows:—Four congregations or churches are under the pastoral care of one shepherd. He visits them every fourth Saturday and Sunday. In their church capacity they meet once a month. They meet at twelve on Saturday, and after organizing themselves by prayer and the appointment of a moderator for the day, business is called up. If there be no "business" on the docket an effort is made to create some, lest they should be idle. The business generally consists in hearing the experiences of candidates for baptism, should any offer. Each member becomes a juror, and when the candidate tells his story, a verdict is agreed on according to the nature of the case. If a favorable opinion of the candidate is entertained, he is ordered to be baptized; and this matter disposed of, nothing remains but to hear a sermon, or to quote the eighteenth of Matthew over some case of discipline. The *first* day of the week, commonly called *Sunday*, is occupied in singing a few stanzas of something called hymns, which in general are the metrified articles of the creed of the church. Next comes a prayer, or the hymn turned into prose; that is, the opinions of the brethren, dressed up in the form of prayer; and then comes the sermon, in which one drop of wine is turned into a gallon of water. By this miracle the faith, that is the *opinions* of the brethren, is strengthened, and sometimes their heads become dizzy with the sound, or rather effervescence of the distillation, or decomposition of the concrete material. Speculations are sung and then prayed, and then preached and then sung, and then prayed and then blessed. And after being thus fed and feasted, the brethren go home for one month to ruminate and digest this hearty meal. Thus the lambs are fed, and the sheep feasted. As to the children at home, the little kids are playing about the shepherds' tents, or nipping the blossoms on the hills. It is altogether left to Heaven when and how to convert them. It is a work of sovereign grace which no education can accelerate or retard. So sovereign are the conversions and so supernatural, that there is as good a chance in the playhouse as in the chapel. A minute acquaintance with novels and romances is as well adapted to conversion as the historical books of the Old and New Testaments. The great concern about the children is, that they may be rich and honorable in this world; that they may be able to control a great many pounds of bread and beef, and to dispense it with a good grace. Thus their minds grow up a great moral waste, in which grow exuberantly the corrupt passions and appetites of nature.

This is not too highly colored for the present order of things on a general view; but we rejoice to know that there are many individual and some congregational exceptions. But when we describe things in the aggregate, we speak of them as becomes their more general features. A great majority of the families I visited do attend to family religion and to the religious instruction of their children, and some of them to the religious instruction of their servants. But on all hands I heard of, and in some instances I saw, "christian parents" in whose house the melody of praise and the voice of prayer is seldom heard except when a preacher calls. Neither is it uncommon to find a whole family reared and married, and not a professor among them!! Yet in the polite circle and amongst the honorable cits, none are more conspicuous than they. Were time eternity—this life eternal—this world heaven, and all things here immutable, reason and religion would unite in teaching us to devote our whole souls to the objects around us; but as we do not profess to think so, such christians are the greatest paradoxes in the universe. These remarks proceed from benevolence, and are designed not to flatter the wayward—not to allure the unsuspicious—not to conceal our shame—not to reproach the upright—not to palliate the froward—not to countenance the latitudinarians, nor to compliment the orthodox; but to warn, admonish, to reprove, confute and commend, when it is due. It is not he that commends himself who is approved, but him the Lord commends.   EDITOR.

A Restoration of the Ancient Order of Things.
No. XVIII.
Argument against it.

THE present general order of things is exhibited in miniature in the preceding remarks. There are many who advocate the present order of things—not, we hope, the effects of that order, but the system of things which legitimately issues in these results. They are, to say the least, false reasoners, or fallacious philosophers. They do not assign to effects their proper causes, or to causes their proper results. True philosophy consists in assigning effects to their true causes; false philosophy, in assigning effects to other causes than their own. We have often heard much of how the Lord has blessed the present order of things by the numerous converts and large accessions made to congregations under the reigning systems. This is most fallacious and dangerous logic. If it were true philosophy, it would equally prove that infant sprinkling, the invocation of saints, and the whole system of papistical and protestant managements were of divine origin and approbation. For how often do we hear the Papist and the Protestant appealing to the mighty achievements of their leaders in proof that the Lord is with them, and that he countenances all their movements? Each party numbers its Israel every year, and capitalizes its converts, in attestation that the Lord is there. Scarce a revival comes, but Presbyterians, Methodists, and Baptists come in for a share; though, in general, the two former out-count the latter. Now if the Baptist annual converts prove that the present order of things is of divine origin amongst them, it will as logically prove that the present order of things amongst Catholics, Presbyterians, and Protestants, is of divine approbation. All that my reasoning powers can conclude from these premises, is, first, That if the Lord's hand is not in these accessions, they are equally deceived; and though in different degrees, all distant from the equator of truth. One

64

is ten degrees south; another, ten degrees north; and though twenty degrees apart, they are equally distant from the equator of true religion. But, in the second place, if the Lord's hand is in these accessions, then it proves that he disdains equally their systems and their order, and bestows his favors indiscriminately on all. It cannot be argued that he approves all their systems; for this would terminate in the most absurd results. He would then approve of Papacy, Episcopacy, Presbytery, and Independency—of infant sprinkling and of believer's immersion, and of a hundred things flatly contradictory to each other. I say, then, it proves, on the best hypothesis, that he disdains all their systems and their order, and that he loudly proclaims it by the distributions of his favor upon the Baptist order, the Methodistic order, the Presbyterial order, and so forth. If the Lord approved of one of the present systems he would confer all his favors upon that people; or, in other words, he would assemble his elect under that standard, and signalize them as he once did the only nation he selected and made his own. They could exclaim, What people like us!! What people has the Lord blessed as he has blessed us!! I say, then, that to my reasoning faculties, the logic of the Baptist Recorder or that of the Presbyterian Luminary now confederated, proves not that the Lord approbates that for which they contend, viz. the present order of things in their respective circles, but that he equally disdains both their orders. I would like to see them try their logic here. He sends his gospel to them all, on the supposition that the work of these revivals is his, and thereby calls them to reformation. I have no idea of magnifying molehills into mountains, nor of consecrating the language of Ashdod into that of Canaan; I have no idea of amalgamating oil and water, of christening pagans, or of paganizing christians; I have no idea of raising up a holy seed from Egyptian or Babylonish wives, nor of proving that the Lord approves the present order of things, because the Methodists and Baptists annually count twenty thousand converts a-piece.

During the ancient order of things there was no church meetings for the purpose of receiving candidates for immersion. There were no monthly meetings to decide who should be baptized. There was no person who held his membership in one church and had the pastoral care of another in which he was not a member, and to which he was not amenable, as is now the case very generally. There was no church in those days of primitive integrity, composed of a hundred members, which, in a case of discipline, gave only eleven votes, six against and five for the delinquent, and they excommunicated him. There was no deacon appointed solely for the purpose of carrying about a plate four times a-year. There was no society whose whole code of discipline was the 18th of Matthew. There was no one who had any formulary, creed, or confession, other than the apostolic writings. Now let him that affirms to the contrary remember that the proof lies upon him. And we will assure him that his proof will be faithfully published by us, should he send it for that purpose. The subjects introduced here are intended for future developement.   EDITOR.

The Creed Question.

THIS question has been long and warmly contested in the United States. In Kentucky an anonymous writer, who it is believed has changed sides on this question more than once, who calls himself "*Aleph*," and very pertinently too, has thrown down the gauntlet in an extraordinary way indeed. Another, who goes a step higher, even to the second letter of the Hebrew alphabet, and calls himself "*Beth*," has severely castigated the temerity of his brother Doctor. It is passing strange that the only two Doctors of Divinity in the West, of the Baptist denomination, should thus become *Aleph* and *Beth*, and stand on the two sides of this question. The creed side has lost one hundred per cent. within a year or two past, if I mistake not. Its advocates have deserted the old ground, and Doctor Aleph in his recent challenge has got it fixed on no ground at all, but, like Mahomet's coffin, hung between heaven and earth. It would require a critic to understand his challenge. It is in the following words:—"If Mr. Duncan, Mr. Campbell or the Reviewer, should be inclined to meet the great question fairly in reference to the principle of having a creed, not in regard to the contents of any particular creed, nor in regard to church administration, for these are different subjects; if they will meet the single question above stated, their error shall be made apparent, even to the most ordinary capacity." So, then, Mr. "Aleph" will not contend for the contents of his creed, but for the principle of having one. Neither will he contend about the use to be made of his creed in church administration. But all he will engage to do is to contend for the principle or right of having a creed. This is with him the great question. But unfortunately or accidentally it happens that the Doctor has given his challenge so as to preclude the hope or fear of an opponent. The Doctor is a very amiable man, and I cannot think he designed to play the sophist here, though he has done it to extravagance. I ascribe it to his cause and not to his good sense. Suppose, for example, I had written against polygamy, or against the right or principle of having two wives. Suppose that some polygamist should have said, and defied the world on it, that "If Mr. Duncan or myself should be inclined to meet the great question fairly in reference to the principle of having a wife, not in regard to the number or character, nor their treatment; if they will meet the single question above stated, their error shall be made apparent to the most ordinary capacity"—what answer would it deserve? If it were not an insult to the good sense of the reader, I would say, Sir, you have changed the ground of controversy altogether. I contend not against the principle of having a wife, but, sir, you contend for the principle of having two; and before you will make my error apparent to the most ordinary capacity, you will first produce the divine authority or right reason of having two wives at one and the same time. I contend for one divine and infallible creed, and you argue for a human and fallible one along with it, or for the "principle" of having two creeds. "Now, sir, the proof lies upon the affirmer. Be so good, then, as to produce your divine authority or your good reasons for the principle of having two creeds, and then I pledge myself to make your error plain to the most ordinary capacity. Now, my kind friend Aleph, stick to your text, and, like an honest man, come out, not in the first letter of the Hebrew alphabet, but write your name in full.

I must not close till I have let Beth confute Aleph in his own words. The preceding challenge of Aleph is replied to by Beth in the following words:—

"I have never heard of any christian man who controverted the propriety and even the necessity of having a creed. The only question is, Whether or not Jesus Christ shall be the au thor of the creed, and of the constitution and laws of his church? or shall a voluntary association of men take this business out of his hands and form one to suit their own views and purposes, by either changing the doctrinal statements, facts, and connexions, as they appear in the word of God, or by adding to, or taking from his system of truth, or by epitomising it? It required the Father, Son, and Holy Ghost, to write the system of faith in the gospel, and shall a voluntary association of men presume to exercise the power of changing, modifying, or improving it? This would, in my judgment, savor very much of a conspiracy against the kingdom of Christ, and of a presumptuous sin. If one association of men have a right to form a creed, another and another have, and churches formed in accordance with them have equal claims to divine authority. The Presbyterians, Baptists, Methodists, Episcopalians, and Roman Catholics, all stand upon the same footing. Each one under this divine authority, claims the right to wage war upon the rest in defence of their faith; and thus we have five different organized armies, marshalled under different standards, commanded by different officers, and united by different creeds, in active conflict, *by divine authority too,* in direct violation of the express commands and authority of Jesus Christ in the gospel. All this is done under the pretext of keeping out Arians and other heretics. Every one assumes the right to be God's commentator and expositor, instead of the apostles; and all differ, and make their differences articles of faith." EDITOR.

ACTS xx. 28. "*Feed the church of God which he has purchased with his own blood.*"

Mr. Alexander Campbell, it seems, in his new translation, substitutes the term *Lord* for *God,* in the above passage. This, he tells us, he has done on the authority of Griesbach, Ireneus, who flourished A. D. 170, and the Syriac version. According to the alteration, it reads—"Feed the Church of the Lord," instead of "the church of God," as it is in our common version.

It does not appear to me, that any one should oppose the introduction of a various reading into the common text, when the change is evidently for the better, and is clearly supported by satisfactory evidence, as the genuine reading. But when this is not the case, it surely ought not to be attempted; because all attempts to alter the text in common use, tend to unsettle the public mind, in relation to, and destroy the confidence of the people in, the sacred scriptures.

As different opinions appear to be entertained relative to the above passage, permit me to inquire whether the phrase, *the church of the Lord,* is a New Testament phrase? *The church of God,* we know to be language quite common with Paul, as the following quotations will show:—

"Paul, called to be an apostle of Jesus Christ, through the will of God, and Sosthenes, our brother, to *the church of God,* which is at Corinth." 1 *Cor.* i. 2.

"Give none offence, neither to the Jews, nor the Gentiles, nor to *the church of God.*" 1 *Cor.* x. 32.

"But if any man seem to be contentious, we have no such custom, *neither the church of God.*" "What! have you not houses to eat and to drink in? or despise you *the church of God,* and shame them that have not?" 1 *Cor.* xi. 16. 22.

"For I am the least of the apostles, that am not meet to be called an apostle, because I persecuted *the church of God.*" 1 *Cor.* xv. 9.

"Paul, an apostle of Jesus Christ, by the will of God, and Timothy our brother, to the *church of God* which is at Corinth." 2 *Cor.* i. 1.

"For ye have heard of my conversation in time past in the Jews' religion, how that beyond measure I persecuted *the church of God.*" *Gal.* i. xiii.

"For ye brethren became followers of the *churches of God,* which in Judea are in Christ Jesus." 1 *Thess.* ii. 14.

"So that we ourselves glory in you in the *churches of God.*" 2 *Thess.* i. 4.

"For if a man know not how to rule his own house, how shall he take care of *the church of God?*"—"But if I tarry long, that you may know how you ought to behave yourself in the house of God, which is *the church of the living God.*" 1 *Tim.* iii. 5. 15.

If, now, it be inquired, "How often is the phrase, the church of the Lord, used in the New Testament?" I believe the answer must be, "Not once." If it be there, I have not been able to find it; and Horne, in his "Introduction to the Critical Study of the Sacred Scriptures," tells us it is no where in the New Testament. These facts render it evident that Paul was not accustomed to use such a phrase as the church of the Lord, but was in the habit of calling the church the church of God; and that, therefore, the strong presumption is, he did so in Acts xx. 28. in his address to the elders of the church at Ephesus. For it is to be remembered, that although Luke was the penman, yet the language is Paul's. And as it stands in our common version, it is just what we might expect from him. It "smacks" so much of Paul—is so much like him, that I can hardly help thinking we have the very language he used. But to change it into the church of the Lord, necessarily introduces to us a new speaker, and a new New Testament writer.

It is then evident, that the common reading in the passage under consideration is the authorized reading—authorized from parallel passages of scripture, which warrant the phraseology; while the change which Mr. C. has made, is in like manner unauthorized. With this strong and not easily refuted presumption in favor of the phrase as it stands in our bibles, it appears to me we ought to have powerful external evidence (as that which arises from a various reading in ancient MSS. and versions is called) in support of the change before it is introduced.

But when the external evidence is examined, there is no such weighty preponderance in favor of the alteration, that I know of. What if Griesbach does decide in favor of the change? At least one other critic,* of no ordinary talent and industry, and perhaps full as learned as Griesbach, and who has written since him, and profited by his labors; after having noticed all the various readings, and cited the evidence in favor of each, decides that the weight of evidence from ancient MS. versions, and the fathers, is in favor of the common reading.

The same author tells us that the old Syriac version is neither in favor of the common reading, nor of Mr. C's; but supports the phrase, *the church of Christ.* If so, there is a slight mistake in Mr. Campbell's piece, published in the Luminary of the 3d of January, which informs us that that version contains the reading which he prefers; and likewise a slight diminution of the evidence on which he makes his change.

From the same source we learn that Ignatius supports the common reading; a father, who

---

* I mean Thomas Hartwell Horne, in his "Introduction to the Critical Study of the Sacred Scriptures." Vol. 2 p. 350, 351, second London edition.

flourished considerably earlier than Ireneus, on whose testimony Mr. C. places so much reliance. "Ignatius, as it is testified by ancient writers, became bishop of Antioch, about 37 years after Christ's ascension; and therefore, from his time and place, and station, it is probable that he had known and conversed with many of the apostles." (vid. Paley's Evidences, p. 82, 83.) For the same reason, therefore, that the testimony of Ireneus is relied on for the change of the passage, that of Ignatius should be preferred to retain it as it is.

These considerations ought not to be unknown to a man who undertakes to alter the sacred text in common use. And when we reflect that Mr. C. is considered a man of talents and learning, it is difficult to shut out the suspicion that he has an *a priori* preference for the term Lord, or some other word, rather than the one which our version contains; which is well calculated to excite a fear, that he has a leaning to the Arian creed.
VINDEX.
Western Luminary, Feb. 7.

——

WERE it not for the fictitious name and the last period of the preceding critique, we would say that it has some appearance of reasonableness about it. The last period would, in cases of testimony, subtract much from the competency of the witness. There is not only a logical defect, but a manifest prejudice apparent in it. This will appear by substituting the name of Griesbach in lieu of mine. Then his last sentence will read, "And when we reflect that Griesbach is considered a man of talents and learning, it is difficult to shut out the suspicion that he has an *a priori* preference for the term Lord, or some other word, rather than the one our version contains, which is well calculated to excite a fear that he has a leaning to the Arian creed." Now, as this reading, in the opinion of "Vindex," excites no fears of the orthodoxy of Griesbach and others, it could not in relation to me, were the author as free from prejudice against me as against Griesbach. This, then, is a proof of prejudice, or of a defect in the logical power of this *avenger*. No man can reason fairly when under the tyranny of prejudice.

I will now, with the utmost frankness, examine his reasoning. It is obvious that his critique is based upon the singularity of the phrase, "church of the Lord." He has very satisfactorily shown that the phrase "church of God" is of frequent occurrence in Paul's style, and the phrase "church of the Lord" does not occur in any other passage. Now all this is well told and reasonable enough. From this he concludes very plausibly that the reading *church of God* ought to be preferred to the *church of the Lord.* This is much more specious than solid. To argue on this principle may, in his estimation, suit a case of this sort exactly; but I well know he would not abide by its application in many other passages. There are many phrases which occur but *once* in Paul's writings, which I know he would not like to see excluded on this account from the apostle's writings, though Paul uses others frequently which are nearly of the same effect; such as "the blood of Jesus," "one mediator," "the man Christ Jesus."

The strength of his objection is simply this, that the words "church of the Lord" occur no where else in his writings; but this equally applies to many other phrases; and consequently, as he would not exclude them on this account, to be consistent, he ought not here to object on this ground.

But I proceed to notice another and greater objection to his criticism. I will apply his own principles of reasoning to another clause or phrase in the common version of this disputed text. This is the phrase "blood of God," or "*his* blood," applied to God. Now I affirm, in my turn, that this phrase occurs no where else in the whole New Testament, but that other phrases as kindred as the phrases church of God and church of the Lord, are quite common on this subject. If then his logic be sound, it equally militates against the common version of this text as against the new: "Vindex" himself being judge. We have the phrases "blood of Jesus," "blood of Jesus Christ," "blood of Christ," "his blood," applied to the Lord, and "*thy* blood," "blood of the Lamb," and "blood of the Lord;" but no where have we the phrase "blood of God," or "*his* blood," applied to God. Some of these occur often, and all *once*, independent of the disputed text. Now if I have any reason about me, Mr. Vindex is confuted by his own argument. For his reasoning will exclude one part of the disputed text which he wishes to retain in the common version, for the same reasons precisely which he urges against the new. It is a good rule that works both ways. Indeed, the phrase blood of God, or his blood, applied to God, is just as great a solecism in the inspired style, as the phrase death of God, or his death, applied to God, would be. This, then, authorises me to conclude my criticism on Vindex' *critique*, in his own words: "To change it into the blood of God, or his blood, necessarily introduces to us a new speaker, and a new New Testament writer." Is not this another proof that "the legs of the lame are not equal?"

Now, admitting that the phrase church of the Lord occurs no where else in the New Testament, it militates no more against its genuineness than it does against the phrase blood of Jesus, which also occurs but once. But this is not all: there is no such incongruity between this phrase and the whole New Testament style, inasmuch as the phrase church of Christ is quite in the inspired style, as there is between the phrase blood of God, or his blood, and the apostolic phraseology. Here, then, we have the advantage in the new version over the old on the principle assumed by Vindex himself.

Vindex alleges, on the authority of Horne, that while Griesbach and Ireneus have it church of the Lord, the Syriac version has it the church of Christ. But in equipoise to Dr. Horne, I affirm that Dr. Whitby asserts that the Syriac version has it church of the Lord. This, however, on Vindex' own acknowledgement, affects not the merits of the question. I cannot at this time affirm, from my own inspection, that the Syriac version has it on the side of Dr. Horne or Dr. Whitby; but on either side, it is on the side of the new version rather than the old. Against this, prejudice itself cannot cavil. I cannot equal Horne to Griesbach with so little ceremony as Vindex seems to do. I subtract nothing from the merits of Horne, when I give it as my opinion that he does not rank at all with either Griesbach or Michaelis or any of the first collators. That was not his business, nor is it his merit.

I should like to see the words of Ignatius which favors the common version. I have not seen them; and if the allusions to them are similar to those in Paley, Dupin, Eusebius, and other ecclesiastic writers, they are not worth a grain of sand. It is not plead by Horne that Ignatius quotes those words of Paul directly, nor do I know of any reference to them in Ignatius' works which would establish any reading. Nothing short of a direct quotation will, or can be admitted in this case.

But in the last place on this subject, I have a greater reason to prefer Griesbach and other authorities to the common Greek, than any yet mentioned. And, strange as it may appear, it is for the very reason why many short-sighted critics prefer God to Lord. They conceive, like Matthew Henry, whom I esteem as a good man, but a very weak commentator, that the reading of God rather than Lord, exalts the dignity of the Saviour—exalts him more than reading Lord in preference to God. Now I conceive that there can be no higher dignity, personal nor official, than is contained in the phrase church of the Lord; especially when the same church is called the church of God by the same speaker. Here we have all that can be argued from the *name*, in favor of his dignity from the common reading.

I reason thus: There is more value in one human being than there is in one million of globes such as this we inhabit. If, then, the whole assembly, or church, or congregation of purified and glorified human beings belongs, *jure divino*, or by inheritance, or by redemption to the Lord Jesus; if it be his own, as it is his Father's, I can conceive of no glory superior to his personal glory and majesty. I can conceive that he is worthy, infinitely worthy, to receive all blessing, adoration, and thanksgiving from every rational and glorified being in the universe. I conceive that all the paltry criticisms and puerile notions about the phrase blood of God, fall infinitely short of those masculine and sublime contemplations, originating from the apprehension of that ineffable glory couched in the proprietorship of the whole assembly of immortal saints. For, when I scan, by all the lights of astronomy, the worlds and systems of worlds of matter which glimmer over the vast immensity of the spangled firmament; when I add to their real magnitude and grandeur all that the loftiest flights of imagination can bestow, and reflect that one immortal, one deathless spirit is of infinitely more value than they all; how inconceivable and inexpressible your dignity, glorious Lord, who claim them all as your own, by a right which no creature in all the orders of intelligence can ever, dare ever, or will ever dispute!

Thus I reason, and till better informed, must reason on the sublime view presented to my mind in Paul's farewell address to the elders of a congregation in Ephesus. But still I contend that no ideas I could entertain of the propriety of the phrase, nor of its accordance with the style of the speaker, and congruity with the sentiment of the whole volume, would authorize me or any one else in preferring the reading in the new translation, were it not supported by authority equal, or paramount to the other, which I think will appear to all who will or can weigh the authorities on both sides.

If I could expect any thing like candor or justice from Mr. Skillman, editor of the "Luminary," I would demand the insertion of this article in his paper; more especially as he gathers into his paper all the febrile, jejune, splenetic, and pusilanimous effusions of the masked tribe of dreamers which have honored the "Baptist Recorder" with their impalpable and nameless denunciations.

EDITOR.

The New Translation.

THE first edition of this work is, with the exception of a very few copies, disposed of. It has been well received and highly approved of by many competent judges, alike distinguished for their piety and erudition.* The objections made to this translation are not in the proportion of ten per cent. to those made to former translations; and I presume were it generally received, or rather circulated, the objections from all parts of the union would not proportionally amount to more than they now do. Many objections and petitions against the common version, it is said, were presented on its first appearance. The king's decree silenced them at first, or until use had rendered it familiar, and the youth accustomed to read it at school when they arrived to manhood thought well of it, and esteemed all the points and letters in it of divine authority. It is to be hoped that no such means will ever again be resorted to, to give currency to any translation. That only should obtain general reading whose merit deserves it. We have been often requested, (and it is probable at some future day it may be undertaken) to publish a pocket edition of this version. But before a second edition, either of a larger or smaller size, will be proposed or attempted, we wish to receive all the criticisms and emendations which can be proposed by the learned and pious of all denominations. We therefore humbly solicit from all concerned or interested, whatever light they have to throw upon the subject. We will be thankful for objections and criticisms, candid or uncandid, even as plausible as the article copied into this number from the "Luminary." Such investigations and criticisms, from whatever motive they proceed, are beneficial to the public, who are desirous of understanding the book.— The weak-minded only are afraid of new translations, or, at most, those who have not thought much upon the subject. I think the illiterate have stronger faith who read many translations, than the same class have who read but one.— The reason is obvious: Faith has to do with facts and events attested. Now as all translations, even the most imperfect, present all the same facts, and personages, and every thing historical to the mind of the reader, he, though unacquainted with the original tongue, becomes more assured of the certainty of the facts he believes, because he finds that all translators, which are to him as so many witnesses, give the same historical statements. Suppose, for example, an Englishman unacquainted with Greek, understands the French, Spanish, and German languages, and reads in them all the New Testament. He finds that all the persons, events, places, and occurrences—all the lives, labors, and successes of the apostles—in a word, every thing historical precisely the same—would not such a person have more rational ground of assurance of the correctness of any translation than he who has read but one version? Improved translations do not introduce any new articles of belief, because they attest no persons nor facts, no historical matters that were not attested before; but they have their value and importance from the plainness, force, beauty, and simplicity in which they present the testimony of God to the reader. In every thing that concerns faith, all translations are the same; but as re-

* It was *burnt*, however, in Jessamine county, Kentucky, after the incendiary, a preacher, who does not understand his mother tongue, had compared it with the *common version*, and prayed ten days! *Mirabile dictu!*
PUBLISHER.

spects a clear and comprehensive understanding of the book, there is as great difference as there is, or as there can be, in any number of witnesses giving testimony in any case. While nine of them declare all the same facts, it may happen that the tenth expresses himself with so much more perspicuity, that there is incomparably less difficulty in understanding him than the other nine. So much for the objection to new translations, as supposed detrimental to the faith of the reader. We solicit most earnestly all criticisms, objections, or emendations, which piety, biblical knowledge, or general information can present. We wish to live for the benefit of our contemporaries, and of the next generation. We are indebted to those that have gone before us, and that debt we can only discharge so far as we labor for the benefit of those who are to live after us.　　　　　　　　　EDITOR.

Mr. Robert Owen and the Social System.
No. 1.

MR. OWEN has attracted much attention in this country as well as in Britain from the singularity of his views, and the benevolent nature of his efforts for the amelioration of society. He has afforded evidence of "mental independence" never perhaps surpassed before. His talents, education, fortune, and extraordinary zeal in the prosecution of his favorite object, entitle him to a very liberal share of public respect. It is, I believe, very generally admitted that he is perfectly disinterested as far as respects pecuniary gain, in all that he has done, and is doing, for the establishment and developement of the social system. He has not been treated, however, with over much courtesy by many editors, both political and religious, who have animadverted on his principles and his plans. For my own part, I have felt some degree of sympathy for him, and of mortification too, at the nibblings of his opponents. I have waited for a better acquaintance with his principles and managements before I even ventured to form an opinion for myself, either of their wisdom or practicability; and am not yet able to form a satisfactory opinion of the social system as advocated by him. I have long endeavored neither to condemn nor approve any opinion either because it is old or new, popular or unpopular. Paul's maxim I esteem of equal importance in all things—"Bring all things to the test, and hold fast that which is good."

The benefits resulting from a co-operative system have been apprehended in theory and proved by experience, before we heard of Mr. Owen in this country. A social system of co-operation may be grafted on any system of religion, true or false; but that a social system of co-operation can at all exist without religious obligations has never yet been proved; but this appears to be the experiment now on hand at New Harmony, Indiana. In this Mr. Owen has afforded the most convincing proofs of "mental independence." The annals of the world fail to present one single league or confederation for any purpose that was not perfectly ephemeral, without religion of some kind or other. I have no notion of getting angry with Mr. Owen, or of belaboring him with harsh epithets for hazarding an experiment of this sort. It is true, indeed, that I regret that any person born in the eighteenth century, and educated in the kingdom of Scotland, should have profited so little by the circumstances around him, and should have learned so little from all that has gone before him, as to suppose that a being such as man is,

could be happy in any circumstances, without the hope of immortality beyond the grave.

I regret very much, indeed, that Mr. Owen has found it necessary to the completion of his plans to abolish every vestige of the religion of the bible—from the divine ordinance of matrimony down to the observance of the Lord's day. This I regret from my regard for the social system in particular, and also because of its pestiferous influence on certain classes of society, who need the benefits of something more than the social system to improve their morals and their circumstances.

It appears that the human mind may be so intensely applied to a favorite object of study or pursuit, as to lose its own equilibrium, so to speak; and that a man may become a downright enthusiast on any other subject as well as religion. There is a deistical, atheistical, political, economical, as well as a "christian" enthusiast. And Mr. Owen seems to have paid so much attention to the influence of circumstances upon human character, an influence very great indeed, as to have ascribed omnipotence to it, or rather to have deified it. This I presume to be the cause of his "mental independence." I know, indeed, it is not very easy to bound or limit the influence of surrounding circumstances, but still they have limits, even in forming human character. To make every thing in human character depend upon the power of circumstances, is to me as great an error as to make nothing depend on it. These are the two extremes. "*Media tutissima est.*" The true and safe way lies between. Education may do as much for the animal man as cultivation may do for plants, and I think it can do little, if any thing more. That moralist who conceives that he could, by an entire change of circumstances, effect an entire change of character, is not less deceived than the botanist who thinks he could make grapes grow on thorns, or figs on thistles, by a change of climate and of culture. No change of circumstances could make a goat produce wool, or convert a lion into a lamb. So no change of circumstances could make a Nero out of Mr. Owen, nor a Bonaparte out of Gen. Hull. There is more born into the world than flesh and blood, and yet a great deal depends upon corporeal organization. No change of circumstances could make a painter or a musician where the eye and the ear are not bestowed by nature, so no change of circumstances can make the naturally indolent, selfish, envious, ambitious, the contrary characters. I cannot, then, ascribe the attributes of Deity to the circumstances of birth or education, and therefore I cannot be so mentally independent as Mr. Owen. But Mr. Owen only dates the era of "Mental Independence" from the fiftieth year of political independence, consequently he does not owe his "mental independence" to the circumstances that surrounded him more than forty years ago.

Out of this "mental independence" has arisen the hostility to the Bible which so much characterizes the New Harmony Gazette. Free agency, responsibility, marriage, and every religious institute are exiled from the city of Mental Independence. These are not the circumstances which are to surround the infants born there. No, these are all inimical to "mental independence."

I am glad to see, upon the whole, that a series of essays against the Bible has commenced, and that an "*Enquirer*" has published his number one on the subject. I do not rejoice in the thing itself, but that we shall have a chance (as we are not free agents) of hearing all that mighty evidence in favor of no religion, and against the Bible which "the first year of mental independence" can bestow upon the world. If no abler hand will appear on the side of the Bible, I shall be compelled to volunteer in the service, for I am indebted more to the light which it contains than to all the circumstances else which surrounded me from infancy to man; and I am as certain that this new era of "mental independence" with all the circumstances to which it may give birth, will not be worth the testimony of John to the illuminated citizens of New Harmony, as I am that Mr. Owen did not create himself. But I will wait a few weeks until the work has progressed a little, and till I see the strength which is to come into the field.

I will only add that it is the deistical or rather atheistical part of Mr. Owen's system to which I am compelled at present to object, I should like to have his definition of the term "morality," for I think it is wanting to make his paper intelligible to most readers.   Editor.

To "Paulinus."—Letter II.

My Dear Sir,—My absence from home at the time of the publication of your favor of November last, will, I hope, be accepted as an apology for the delay of my reply. Your remarks upon the discourse on the abrogation of the Legal Dispensation perfectly meet my approbation. I do not object even to your placing the unregenerate descendants and neighbors of christians "under the whole of God's revealed will according to the dispensation under which they live." Nor, if I recollect right, does this militate with the doctrine of that discourse. In placing the unregenerate Gentiles under what is called the Law of Nature, as explained in that discourse, we had respect to them in the mass, without regard to specialities in their condition. But were I asked where I would place the unconverted Virginians, on the principles asserted there, I would answer under the New Testament. I would, in addressing them, demonstrate, that the principles, laws, or light in that volume, would prove their awful condemnation in the day of vengeance, if they obeyed it not. I would assure them that the first commandment obligatory on them, was, "Believe on the Lord Jesus Christ." That disobedience to this commandment would prove their condemnation. If asked for the second commandment, I would reply, "Be immersed, every one of you, in the name of the Lord Jesus, for the remission of your sins." Until these two commandments were obeyed, I would shew them that they are not in the kingdom of Jesus Christ, and that they were worthy of condemnation, if on no other account, on this, that light was come into the world, and they loved darkness rather than light, because their deeds were evil. These commandments not obeyed, I would endeavor to convince them that they could promise themselves nothing on any rational principle, but an eternal separation from the presence of the Lord, and the glory of his power in the day of righteous retribution. In addressing such a people, I would give such an exhibition of the matter, always emphasizing on the first commandment of the New Dispensation, without obedience to which no other commandment could be acceptably obeyed. Viewing the matter, then, in the light of law, I would proceed thus: To preach the law or decalogue of Moses to the citizens of Virginia, appears to me as irrational and unscriptural as it would be to command them, upon the authority of Moses, to emigrate to Canaan.

The metaphysics of that discourse I am glad to find you disapprove. It is for the same reason that I disapprove of the metaphysics on the influence of the Spirit in renewing the human heart. In my last to you on this subject, I went to the utmost line, as I conceive, marked in the Bible, and perhaps a little beyond it. I attribute a good deal of the general satisfaction which it has given, both in the West as well as in the East, to its having reached the threshold of the temple of metaphysics.

Still you think I ought to have answered "in a more direct manner" that part of your letter on the subject of divine influences, and you state that you "are not so tremblingly alive to the danger of theory and system as to avoid the direct expression of a sentiment on any proposed subject in religion." Neither am I, provided the subject in religion be a subject on which the bible treats. But at present there are two sorts of subjects in religion—one on which the bible says not one word, and one on which it says something. I was asked, on my late tour, very many questions on what are called religious subjects, to which I could give no answer from the bible, because the bible said nothing about them. It is true I gave direct answers to some of those queries, but they were answers derived from the same cistern whence the queries came. You are not ignorant, my dear sir, that in this catechetical age we have many queries of this sort.

A very zealous divine, who, before my arrival in his parish, had published a bitter, little, unmeaning piece, against my views of faith, as he called them, asked me at our first interview, "whether saving faith was an act of the intellect or of the heart"—whether it was an intellectual or approbatory act. This question was asked me, too, after he had published me as contending for a faith merely intellectual, and after he had declared himself pleased with all that I had said in the only discourse he had heard me deliver, being only "displeased with the things I had not said." Having previously published me as altogether intellectual, he had the kindness to call on me for the proof. It is true his letter was signed only with the initials of his name; but when I lately saw it in a very religious newspaper, I doubted not who the author was; for it was a *fac simile* of his views. Now, my dear sir, what answer from the bible could I give to such a query? I told him I could give him a metaphysical answer, but none from the book. Not waiting for this, he went on to talk about believing with the heart, as a scriptural phrase, and contrasted this with believing with the head. The former he called "approbatory faith"—the latter "intellectual faith." I found it very difficult to convince him that the contrast between the head and the heart was one of his own making; that Paul knew nothing, and said nothing about believing with the head. Paul, I added, contrasted the mouth and the heart, and not the head and the heart; or, in other words, that it required "the confession of the mouth" as well as the belief of the heart, to make a christian. "If you shall confess with your mouth the Lord Jesus, and shall believe in your heart that God raised him from the dead, you shall be saved. For with the heart man believes to righteousness, and with the mouth confession is made to salvation." I would not admit that there was such a thing at all as believing with the head. I hope I removed some of his prejudices, and might have removed them all, had he not first committed himself in the aforesaid publication. I give the above as a sample of such questions as cannot be answered out of the bible. If answered at all, the terms must be changed, and a new form assumed. You will not understand me as arranging your question on the Spirit's work under this head. I merely intend distinctly to mark the difference between those subjects in religion of which the bible says nothing and those on which it speaks.

In reply to those queries on subjects in religion of which the bible speaks, more is necessary than to say, "I believe what the bible teaches." That is not the question. The question is, What does the bible teach on such a subject? Such a question merits a direct reply. It sometimes happens that the subject is one on which the bible says so much that little more than the outlines can be given in the compass of an ordinary reply. This is the case on the subject of the operations of the Holy Spirit.

On this subject much has been said in the second volume of this work, because there is a great deal said by the apostles on this subject, and a great deal said in the present time not authorized by the apostles. The subject has not been exhausted; but there may be questions proposed on subjects of which the bible speaks, which the bible will not answer. For example; How does the Spirit influence the minds of men? is a question I cannot answer from the bible. But if I am asked, Does the Spirit regenerate the human heart? Does it influence the minds of men? I answer, The bible teaches it does. But I have a great scrupulosity of mind in going beyond what is written on this subject in particular. The reason is, some speculative theory of spiritual operations is the very essence, the very soul, of every system of religion in christendom. The deist, the lifeless formalist, the "rational christian," and the flaming enthusiast, have all their theories of spiritual operations. The "rational christian" you will perceive I rank among the others. I admit of no such a distinction. The bible knows nothing of rational or irrational christians—of good or bad christians. A christian designates all that the bible approves. A bitter sweet or a sweet bitter is not more incongruous; nor is a sweet sweet, nor a bitter bitter more redundant than these epithets attached to that name. When I hear a man contend that he is a rational christian, I know that he is in Babylon.

But to return. The popular theories about divine influence, or the operations of the Spirit, terminate either in one or the other of these two similitudes. A sea captain and his crew, intent on a voyage from New York to Palestine, had got all the tackling of the ship and all the necessary sea stores for the voyage aboard. Every thing was ready on the appointed day. But there was no wind. The captain and his crew amused themselves every day, sometimes in the city and sometimes in the ship. Thus day succeeded day, until the time arrived when the voyage should have been finished. The owner of the ship demanded of the captain why the voyage was not made. The captain replied, he and his crew were every day ready and every day at their post, but that there had not been a single breeze of wind. The ship, he added, was rotting and the provisions were daily consuming; but inasmuch as he could not create the wind, nor cause it to blow, he could neither blame himself nor his crew. The owner was chagrined but could not censure the captain or his crew.

Another captain bound from Egypt to Corinth, so soon as he had collected his crew and fixed upon the day of his departure, determined to make the voyage in a given time. Finding that there was no wind and that wind was necessary to his success, he invented a large pair of bellows, and set all his crew to work to blow upon the sails. They succeeded in getting the vessel, the tide being favorable, out of the harbor. But so soon as they had cleared the promontory, and fell into the current, their strength and their bellows inadequate to the current, they were carried off by it, and ultimately perished in the sea. The interpretation and application is easy to him that understands the secrets of the reigning systems.

Any theory on this subject which countenances the listless and inattentive, which disheartens the anxiously desirous, which emboldens the arrogant and presumptuous, is not of God, is not countenanced by the bible. I often think of a saying of old brother Asher's in Kentucky. He told me, in December last that he "believed in the doctrine of the final perseverance of the saints, and yet he believed that this doctrine would be a means of the damnation of thousands in Kentucky." In this laconic way I would speak of the operations of the Spirit.

If any man ask me how the influence and aid of the Spirit is obtained, I answer, By prayer and the word of God. Thus I will give direct answers, so far as, I think, the oracles authorize. But I am governed more in speaking upon this subject by the following, than by all other considerations. *The apostles preached Christ and not the Holy Spirit;* or rather, they preached the Holy Spirit when they preached Christ. So the Saviour instructed and commanded them. They preach the Spirit with most success who say nothing about his work in conversion. So did the apostles. In all the sermons pronounced by the apostles to unregenerated persons, of which we have so many samples in the Acts of the Apostles, they never once spoke of the works of the Spirit in conversion. Not one example in all the volume—not one model of the discourses we every day hear about the work of the Spirit. The apostles remembered that the Spirit was not to speak of himself, his own office and work, but of Christ. Their good news, therefore, was about Christ crucified. The gospel most admired in many places, is not the gospel of Christ, but the gospel of the Spirit, or the gospel of the preacher's experience. Because I do not in every sermon tell the people how bad I once was, and how good I am now, some of these new gospelizers declaim against me as unregenerate. And they pass themselves off as spiritual men and good teachers because they tell of the work of the Spirit upon their own hearts, instead of telling what Jesus has done for the world. Thus their hearers go home, looking into their own hearts for some consolation, instead of looking off to Jesus, the author of salvation. They rejoice in themselves and in their holy spirit, and not the Lord.

But I must break off in the midst of my reply, begging you, my dear sir, to have patience with me and I will pay you all. I cannot, however, close this part of my reply without assuring you of my perfect accordance with you on your remarks upon conjectures, theories and systems; and that the continuance of your correspondence affords me peculiar pleasure. I hope in my next to give you full satisfaction on the sentence to which you object in the preface to the Epistle to the Romans.

Wishing you health in soul, body and spirit, I remain your fellow-servant in the gospel,   Ed.

Fictitious Names.

In my late tour I found that some teachers who, in conversation and in their public discourses, sometimes approved of the sentiments published in this work, were wont to write against them under fictitious names. The assuming of a fictitious name, when writing against a person who appears in his own proper name, appears to me a cowardly and unjustifiable course: and I do think that every christian should be like Nathaniel, "an Israelite indeed, in whom there is no guile;" I therefore declare it my intention henceforth to make no replies to anonymous opponents, always considering them as unworthy of notice, because of the suspicion inseparably connected with the anonymous. Howbeit, this is not to be understood of my private correspondents, nor of those whom I have already noticed under the mask of an assumed name. This resolution will be carried into effect in relation to all those who may rationally be supposed to have seen it before they wrote. For in that case we will be authorized to conclude that they expected when writing to pass unnoticed, and feared to hazard an exposure.   Editor.

No. 10.]   May 7, 1827.
Deferred Articles.

The following letter is from one of the most intelligent churches in the western states with which we are acquainted. It was addressed to a very respectable Baptist Association in the state of Tennessee, and we are happy to learn that this Association had so much intelligence and liberality as to accept it as the platform and basis of a union with it and the church who wrote it. So long as associations are kept up, we think that were they to act up to the principles herein stated and recognized, much less injury could result to the christian community from their meetings than has hitherto been the result of them. This is a good step and a rapid advance towards the introduction of a better order of things.—Ed.

The Church of Jesus Christ at Nashville, to the Concord Association, sendeth Christian Salutation.

Dear Brethren,—After an interval of two years, we again address you by letter and messengers. Various circumstances induced us last year not to unite ourselves to any association, which circumstances it is not necessary to enumerate. We again present ourselves before you, and request to be admitted into your body.

Deeming it perfectly necessary that we distinctly understand each other, upon forming this union, we think proper to state our sentiments concerning associations, and the relation they bear to the churches composing them.

Your code of government, as published in 1825, declares that the association " shall have no power to lord it over God's heritage, neither shall it have any ecclesiastical power, or infringe upon any of the internal rights of the churches." To all this we cheerfully consent, and consider it an expression of our own feelings. We may not, however, understand it alike, and will therefore beg leave to exhibit our views of it.

We understand this sentence as saying, that the association has no power to determine what any church shall receive as her creed; or whether she shall have any creed or confession at all, other than the bible; and consequently that she has no power so to lord it over God's heritage, as to condemn any church for holding or teaching any scriptural truths, though they be at variance with the opinions of this body concerning such truths.

In this view of the subject, we presume it will not be required of us to subscribe to any human instrument of union, as the test of our doctrine or practice. For we cannot but believe, that the Holy Bible is as plain in expressing its own truth as it ought to have been; and consequently that no man can express more clearly than it does, what we are to believe and practise. If this be true, (and we presume it will not be denied,) it is useless for us, as a church, or for any other body, to hold up a twinkling taper to give light to the world, when the sun shines in his meridian splendor. If the fear of God and the love of the brethren will not hold the disciples in union, upon the one foundation, we may forever despair of any such instruments of union as creeds and confessions of faith obtaining so desirable an end.

Again—We understand the " constitution" of your body as saying, when it declares the association "shall have no ecclesiastical power," &c. that the association does not intend to interfere with any of the *internal rights* of the churches. That is to say: the association has no power to interfere with the *order, doctrine, government,* or *practice,* of any church, *governed in all,* by the great charter of our religious privileges—the *New* Testament of our blessed Lord and Saviour Jesus Christ. We consider all these to be the " internal rights of the churches"—rights given them by the Great Head of the church—rights expressly defined and limited by Him, " in whom are hid all the treasures of wisdom and knowledge;" and, therefore, rights which are inalienable, and over which no body of men on earth has any control. In short, we consider ourselves at liberty to appoint our own teacher or teachers, and all other officers, without molestation or assistance from any; and to judge for ourselves, when the sentiments delivered by our teachers, so appointed, are contained in the Holy Bible; without acknowledging the right of any others to interfere in the judicial investigation of such sentiments.

Indeed, brethren, we look upon your "constitution" as guaranteeing to every church connected with it, a full, free, and unmolested liberty of conscience—a liberty unshackled by any authority, except his who has set his people free; a liberty that is not, and will not be, used as a cloak for licentiousness by any one who fears God, and desires to walk by the light of the truth; and a liberty which none other than God who gave it has any right to destroy, and which this association, most certainly, will never assail.

It is our desire, beloved brethren, to live harmoniously with all our brethren; and while we acknowledge ourselves to be "of you," we think that these are the only principles on which unity can be maintained.

We do not consider ourselves the guardians of the public faith; nor as having any right to direct what any shall believe. Error requires not human efforts to overthrow it: the exhibition of the truth in its simplicity, has ever been found, in the hands of God, a weapon most mighty to the pulling down of strong holds.

We trust, brethren, that while we deny the authority of men in matters of religion, we feel bound to endeavor to ascertain the will of our glorious chief; and so far as we know it, to observe it. We are far from supposing that all is known, at the present day, of the Records of Heaven, that can be known; and are therefore willing to learn "what is truth," whoever be the instrument of pointing us to it. That there yet remains much to be known concerning divine things we must believe; for "if any man thinks he knows any thing, he knows nothing yet as he ought to know."

Review of Tassey's Vindication, &c.—Continued
from page 314.

Part 2, Section 3d, Page 143. "HAVING fairly, and, we trust, impartially investigated the import and application of the word *church*, as it occurs in the New Testament, and shewn that no part of the sacred scriptures gives any countenance or support to any description of ecclesiastical representation, or courts of appeal, by whatever name they may be called; we now proceed to inquire more particularly into the *nature* and constitution of a church of Christ; and to ascertain, from the test of all religious truth, what are its proper officers, ordinances, and particular duties. Long as this subject has occupied the attention of christians, it appears to be but partially understood; and among those who do know it, there are but few who have the resolution to stand forward in defence of what the scriptures represent as the path of duty." In the investigation of this important part of his subject, our author evinces that believers only are the proper and capable subjects of the duties and privileges of a christian church; and that the members of the primitive churches were all considered as such; that, therefore, the constituent members of a christian church are, and must be, professed and manifest believers. He farther adds, (page 149,) that, "In order to become a member of any of the primitive churches, faith in Jesus Christ was the only essential qualification looked for, or acted upon, in that age of christian simplicity." Both these positions Mr. T. fully establishes by quotations and arguments evidently just, pertinent, and conclusive; and proceeds to observe that "We are indebted to the refinement and subtle distinctions of modern times for that long catalogue of terms of communion which the various sects have drawn up, by which they oftener shut out the true child of God from partaking of the children's bread, than they do the dogs which have no right to it." How true this is, every intelligent and attentive observer of the present conduct and state of the churches must be satisfied. He also justly observes, (p. 147,) that "it is not subscription to the same creed, or confession of faith, scientifically framed, according to the philosophical or school divinity of the day, which is to attract the disciples of Christ to one another. The true gravitating principle here, is the love of Christ. They must gather together in his name. Where this is wanting, or any other principle substituted in its place, the assembly, however designated, is not, nor can it be, a church of Christ. They must gather together in his name. Not only must his authority induce them to assemble, but their attachment to him, and love to his name, must be the grand prevailing principle which draws them together, and binds in one compact, united, and indissoluble association, every individual of them, or else they cannot be recognised as being blessed with his presence, nor countenanced by the King and Head of his church. "If any man love not our Lord Jesus Christ, let him be anathema maranatha."

Having clearly evinced that faith alone, or a belief of the gospel, that is, the belief of what the apostles testified and taught concerning Jesus, is all that can be scripturally required in order to church membership; and that love to Christ, and to each other solely on his account, that is, on account of their common faith in Christ and attachment to him, is "the true gravitating principle, that is to attract the disciples of Christ one to another, and not the love of party nor of system," &c. &c. Our author next proceeds "to inquire into the particular and permanent officers requisite to a fully organized christian assembly." Of this description he finds but two, viz. the bishop and deacon; the former to rule and teach; the latter to receive and apply the contributions of the congregation to their proper objects. As for apostles, prophets, and evangelists, he shews that their offices were temporary, and could not by them be transmitted to others, because they could neither transmit their qualifications, nor yet the special commission under which they acted. That even Paul himself, though an apostle in the most strict and proper sense of the word, did not feel himself authorised to act under the primary commission given to the eleven, (Matt. xxviii.) nor did he assume it. "Christ," says he, "sent me not to baptize, but to preach the gospel." This he could not have truly said had he considered himself acting under the primary commission, or as included in it; for all such were expressly commanded to baptize as well as to preach the gospel. Our author further observes that all the churches planted and set in order by the apostles were furnished with a plurality of elders and bishops; and also, as far as appears, with a plurality of deacons: consequently, that each church, fully organized, had in itself an eldership or presbytery.

That the term Elder, Bishop, and Pastor, are indiscriminately applied to the same officer, and that the modern distinction of teaching and ruling elders is utterly devoid of scriptural authority—a mere human invention. P. 164. Adverting to 1 *Tim.* v. 17, upon which the above distinction is chiefly, if not solely founded, our author fairly shows that no such distinction can be intended; because all the elders there spoken of, however distinguished amongst themselves as to their respective talents or labors, are perfectly equalized as to office and maintenance; they all rule well, and are all accounted worthy of the same double honor; namely, respect and maintenance. "Again, we remark," says he, "that as the elders who labor in word and doctrine are evidently included in the general proposition, "the elders that rule or preside well," it naturally follows that all the elders spoken of were of one description; and although the passage plainly intimates that some may excel in one department of the pastoral office, while others may excel in another, yet they were all entitled to maintenance on account of their labor, and, therefore, were perfectly on a level—there was no disparity amongst them. But those who ruled well and devoted more of their time to teaching and preaching, were more particularly entitled to a double portion, because their expences would naturally be much greater." Now nothing could be more reasonable than this; for, as the apostle justly alleges, "the laborer is worthy of his reward." But, as our author observes, (page 157,) "It was the spirit of ambition and domination, which is not confined to secular rulers, but which has been felt with all its diabolical results, to pervade almost every department of trust in the religious community," that gave rise to this distinction, and, indeed, to all the other ambitious and anti-scriptural claims and pretensions of an aspiring clergy. And "that under whatever shape this aspiring spirit has thought proper to appear, the pretext for introducing it to the notice of mankind has uniformly been that of supporting and maintaining the unity of the church. Under cover of this pretended object an aspiring prelate has aggrandized his order, and by his intrigues and largesses, has gotten himself appointed to the head of his sect or party, under the name of pope, archbishop, &c. and in him the visible unity of the church is supposed to be displayed. The Pope is the visible head of the Catholic community, and styles himself universal bishop, as if none existed besides himself. The King is the head of the church of England, and all parts of that denomination are under his control. In him they are united. Episcopalians place at their head some particular leader; and call him archbishop, or primate, or metropolitan; and to him they voluntarily resign their liberties as christians, conceiving that thereby they are promoting the unity of the church. And under the pretence of exhibiting this unity, Presbyterians of every sect have adopted their representative system, that they might have a representative head to their respective denominations, inasmuch as they had become opposed to an individual earthly head. Hence all presbyteries, synods, and congregations, are placed in subjection to one national synod, or general assembly; which constitutes itself the bond of union, peace, correspondence, and mutual confidence among all the churches. (p. 242.) Now it must be manifest to every close observer, that there can be but little difference in reality, between all these contending parties. Their real object, the attainment of spiritual power, is the same; their pretext the same; and the means of accomplishing their ends are nearly similar. They all aspire after an earthly spiritual headship, which, wherever it is found, stands opposed to the (sole) headship and government of the Lord Jesus. They talk loudly of promoting the unity of the church, but it is not the church of Christ, but the unity of their particular party is meant. They are all zealous in the support of subordination and subjection, but it is that kind of it, which tends to aggrandize the head of their sect; but which, in proportion, derogates from the authority of Jesus, and from that submission which he most justly demands. The person, therefore, who most anxiously engages in promoting the unity of any one of these particular denominations, thereby proves himself to be the most zealous divider of the true church of God; and, consequently, deserves the name of schismatic or heretic, in the scriptural sense of those words. He is endeavoring to destroy the unity of the spirit, instead of keeping it in the bond of peace. For the more zealously any sect contends for its peculiarities, or those particular forms and ceremonies in which it differs from others, it thereby makes the breach wider betwixt those that adhere thereto, and other christians. It promotes and perpetuates that discord, which is the very bane of christianity, and which affords such cause of triumph to the abettors of infidelity." Our author next proceeds to animadvert upon the striking difference between the scriptural qualifications requisite for the pastoral office, and those prescribed and required by presbyteries, &c. in which, upon a fair investigation, there does not appear a single coincidence. Almost the same, it appears, may be truly said of the whole process of election and ordination. Mr. T's conclusions upon the whole are, that "the two, and the only essential things to be considered in relation to the appointment of officers in christian churches, are, First. That the candidate proposed be fully qualified for the office; that he possess every requisite demanded by the spirit of inspiration. Secondly. That he be unanimously elected or chosen by the church

to fill that office, for which he has been nominated. The mere ceremony of inauguration, if we may so call it, is of no consequence at all—it neither fits the candidate for the better discharge of his duty, nor does it communicate any power to him, of which he was not previously possessed. It only fixes the commencement of his official duties. The moment that an undue importance is placed upon this, or any other external ceremony pertaining to the religion of Jesus Christ, we ought to take the alarm, lest innovation and superstition come in like a flood and overwhelm us. P. 178—9. Animadverting upon the assumed prerogatives of presbytery in relation to the settlement and ordination of ministers, our author observes, (p. 189,) that "these modest dealers in spiritual ware can easily make a minister of Jesus Christ, and again unmake him: can induct him into the office, and at pleasure cast him out: can ordain him to the pastoral office, and therein bind him over to their party by oaths and promises; and, anon, if he prove restive and not sufficiently submissive to their will, can dissolve this contract without the consent of either party. Nay, if the church and congregation are determined to adhere to him under whose labor they have reaped so many advantages, and on no account will consent to such dissolution; yet the bull (or rather bill of divorce) runs thus, "Resolved, That the pastoral relation heretofore subsisting between the congregation of B. and the Rev. J. M. D. be, and the same is hereby declared to be dissolved." A bill of spiritual divorce! This, indeed, without the consent of either party! Strange!! "Such is one of the documents of religious oppression and tyranny which the nineteenth century exhibits, and in a land in which we boast of being freemen, and talk so loudly of the rights of conscience. Does not this very much resemble the thunders of the Vatican, and the haughty pretensions of the church of Rome? Did not the pretended successor of St. Peter take upon him to absolve subjects from their oath of allegiance, and to dissolve the most solemn contracts? And what less have some of our spiritual courts of late done? They have presumed to absolve congregations from their obligations to their pastors, and declared them vacant when they were not vacant; and this they have done without consulting any of the parties concerned, or having the consent either of the teacher or the taught. Now this is wonderful, and bespeaks a system well digested, and peculiarly adapted to the end proposed, the subjugation of the human conscience to these spiritual dominions." Here the right of ordination is wielded as the great instrument of power; the door by which this ascendency is introduced, and carefully shut over the intellects of men. P. 192. How improper, how superstitious is it, to make the validity of an office, of an ordinance, depend upon the dreams of ecclesiastics about regular ordination! How absurd, how iniquitous is it, to take advantage of the superstitious disposition of ignorant people, in order to erect upon such a visionary basis an ecclesiastical hierarchy, destructive of the union, peace, and liberties of the children of God! A system of ecclesiastical authority subversive of the authority of Christ, and calculated to rob every christian society of the privileges which he has granted them! How domineering, how tyrannical is it, to attempt to dissolve the pastoral relation between an elder and his flock, without the consent of either parties! How false and farcical to declare a congregation vacant, which has its own regularly chosen pastor to officiate!

In treating of the ordinances our author remarks, (page 211,) " that the Lord's supper was observed in apostolic times every Lord's day, may be established by the clearest evidence. The passage already referred to, Acts ii. 42, in Luke's account of the primitive christians, represents the breaking of bread as a permanent and continued practice in their assemblies. For their steadfastness in the apostles' doctrine, and fellowship, and breaking of bread, can be understood in no other sense consistently with the connection. Perhaps the best comment we can have on this passage is a statement given in the Apologetic of Justin Martyr, who wrote about forty-four years after the death of the Apostle John. He tells us, (page 98th,) that "on Sunday all christians in the city and country meet together, because it is the day of our Lord's resurrection, and then we hear read to us the writings of the prophets and apostles. This done, the president makes an oration to the assembly to exhort them to imitate and do the things they hear; and then we all join in prayer, and after that we celebrate the Lord's supper, and they that are able and willing give alms." Nothing can more expressly determine the uniform course pursued in the stated worship of God than this. And the statements both of the inspired writer, and of this ancient disciple, go to prove that the Lord's supper, formed as regular and permanent a part of the worship of God, as did the apostles' doctrine and prayer." Again, (p. 213,) "the same arguments that go to overthrow the weekly observance of the Lord's supper, will subvert the weekly observance of the Lord's day. For we affirm, that the evidences are of the same nature, drawn from the same sources, and consequently of the same force by which the weekly observance of the Lord's supper is proved, as those by which the first day of the week is established. What is the reason then that we attend to the one institution with an almost invariable unanimity, whilst we neglect attending to the other with that frequency which the authority of Christ requires? It cannot be supposed that this arises from any defect in the evidence. This is impossible; for it is completely and justly satisfactory in the parallel case alleged. It is prejudice, therefore, that prevents christians from following up their duty in this case as they do in the other." I am sorry that I cannot do more ample justice to the argumentative merits of Mr. T.'s performance, not only upon the above, but also upon other important topics which justly demand the attention of christians, and imperiously call for reformation. I could heartily wish that the work itself were not only in the hands of all the readers of the Christian Baptist, but of the religious public at large. Though not without its faults, a few of which, with the permission of the editor, I design to point out in a future number, it calls aloud for "the restoration of the ancient order of things." It is one of the many publications of the present day, that indicates the awakening of the human mind out of the letheal slumber of ages, and happily betokens the speedy approach of that radiant morning of universal light which will never henceforth give place to the darkness of superstition and error, but will shine more and more to the perfect day.　　　PHILALETHES.

The Trinitarian System.

DEAR SIR,—IN one of your fireside conversations, when interrogated on your views of " the Trinity," you gave an exposition of the first verse of the first chapter of John's Testimony, with which myself, and, I believe all present, were

much delighted. In conversing with those present on that occasion, I found that they, as well as myself, had forgotten some of the more prominent ideas. You will confer no ordinary favor on us all, and no doubt it will be pleasing to many of your readers, to give it in writing as nearly as possible to what you spoke on the subject. Do, then, oblige us so far as to give us the same in your next number of the Christian Baptist.

Yours, most affectionately,
　　　　　　　　　　　TIMOTHY.
Kentucky, March 1, 1827.

—

To Timothy.

DEAR SIR,—You will recollect that when I was interrogated on that subject, I gave sundry reasons why I felt reluctant to speculate on the incomprehensible Jehovah. It was also stated that there was no topic in common estimation so awfully sacred as that of the doctrine of " the Trinity," and if a man did not speak in a very fixed and set phrase on this subject, he endangered his whole christian reputation and his own usefulness. At the same time I remarked that I was very far from being afraid either to think upon this subject or to express my thoughts, although it was deemed so unpardonable to depart even in one monosyllable from the orthodox views. I moreover stated that I disliked any thing like speculation upon this topic in particular, because, if I differed in the least from the orthodox, I introduced something like a new theory, or something that would be treated as such, and either approved or rejected on theoretic grounds. If, however, you will neither make a new theory out of my expositions, nor contend for any speculations on the subject, nor carry the views farther than where I leave off, I will gratify you and other friends with my views of the first sentence in John's Preface to his Testimony—" In the beginning was the word, and the word was with God, and the word was God."

1. In the first place I object to the Calvinistic doctrine of the Trinity for the same reasons they object to the Arians and Socinians. They object to these, because their views derogate in their judgment from the eternal glory of the Founder of the christian religion. They will not allow the Saviour to have been a creature, however exalted, because they conceive this character is unbecoming him, and contrary to the scriptural statements concerning him. They wish to give him more glory than they think the Arians are willing to do. Now I object to their making him and calling him an "Eternal Son" because I think that if he were only the Son of God from all eternity, he is entitled to very little, if any more glory, than what the Arians give him. I wish to give him more glory than the Calvinists give him. They are as far below his real glory, in my judgment, as the Arians are in their judgment.

2. But in the second place, I have an insuperable objection to the Arian and Calvinistic phraseology—On the doctrine of the first relation existing between the Father and the Saviour of Men, because it confounds things human and divine, and gives new ideas to bible terms unthought of by the inspired writers. The names Jesus, Christ, or Messiah, Only Begotten Son, Son of God, belong to the Founder of the christian religion, and to none else. They express not a relation existing before the christian era, but relations which commenced at that time. To understand the relation betwixt the Saviour and his Father, which existed before time, and that relation which began in time, is impossible on

either of these theories. There was no Jesus, no Messiah, no Christ, no Son of God, no Only Begotten, before the reign of Augustus Cesar. The relation that was before the christian era, was not that of a son and a father, terms which always imply disparity; but it was that expressed by John in the sentence under consideration. The relation was that of God, and the "word of God." This phraseology unfolds a relation quite different from that of a father and a son—a relation perfectly intimate, equal, and glorious. This naturally leads me to the first sentence of John. And here I must state a few *postulata.*

1. No relation amongst human beings can perfectly exhibit the relation which the Saviour held to the God and Father of All anterior to his birth. The reason is, that relation is not homogenial, or of the same kind with relations originating from creation. All relations we know any thing of are created, such as that of father and son. Now I object as much to a created relation as I do to a creature in reference to the original relation of God and the word of God. This relation is an uncreated and unoriginated relation.

2. When in the fulness of time it became necessary in the wisdom of God to exhibit a Saviour, it became expedient to give some view of the original and eternal dignity of this wonderful visitant of the human race. And as this view must be given in human language, inadequate as it was, the whole vocabulary of human speech must be examined for suitable terms.

3. Of these terms expressive of relations, the most suitable must be, and most unquestionably was, selected. And as the relation was spiritual and not carnal, such terms only were eligible which had respect to mental or spiritual relations. Of this sort there is but one in all the archives of human knowledge, and that is the one selected.

4. The Holy Spirit selected the name Word, and therefore we may safely assert that this is the best, if not the only term, in the whole vocabulary of human speech at all adapted to express that relation which existed "in the beginning," or before time, between our Saviour and his God.

These *postulata* being stated, I proceed to inquire what sort of a relation does this term represent? And here every thing is plain and easy of comprehension. I shall state numerically a few things universally admitted by the reflecting part of mankind:—

1st. A word is a sign or representative of a thought or an idea, and is the idea in an audible or visible form. It is the exact image of that invisible thought which is a perfect secret to all the world until it is expressed.

2d. All men think or form ideas by means of words or images; so that no man can think without words or symbols of some sort.

3d. Hence it follows that the word and the idea which it represents, are co-etaneous, or of the same age or antiquity. It is true the word may not be uttered or born for years or ages after the idea exists, but still the word is just as old as the idea.

4th. The idea and the word are nevertheless distinct from each other, though the relation between them is the nearest known on earth. An idea cannot exist without a word, nor a word without an idea.

5th. He that is acquainted with the word, is acquainted with the idea, for the idea is wholly in the word.

Now let it be most attentively observed and remembered, that these remarks are solely intended to exhibit the relation which exists between a word and an idea, and that this relation is of a mental nature, and more akin to the spiritual system than any relation created, of which we know any thing. It is a relation of the most sublime order; and no doubt the reason why the name Word is adopted by the apostle in this sentence was because of its superior ability to represent to us the divine relation existing between God and the Saviour prior to his becoming the Son of God. By putting together the above remarks on the term word, we have a full view of what John intended to communicate. As a word is an exact image of an idea, so is "The Word" an exact image of the invisible God. As a word cannot exist without an idea, nor an idea without a word, so God never was without "The Word," nor "The Word" without God; or as a word is of equal age, or co-etaneous with its idea, so "The Word" and God are co-eternal. And as an idea does not create its word, nor a word its idea; so God did not create "The Word," nor the "Word" God.

Such a view does the language used by John suggest. And to this do all the scriptures agree. For "The Word" was made flesh, and in consequence of becoming incarnate, he is styled the Son of God, the only Begotten of the Father. As from eternity God was manifest in and by "The Word," so now God is manifest in the flesh. As God was always with "The Word," so when "The Word" becomes flesh, he is Emanuel, God with us. As God was never manifest but by "The Word," so the heavens and the earth, and all things were created by "The Word." And as "The Word" ever was the effulgence or representation of the invisible God, so he will ever be known and adored as "The Word of God." So much for the divine and eternal relation between the Saviour and God. You will easily perceive that I carry these views no farther than to explain the nature of that relation uncreated and unoriginated which the inspired language inculcates.

These views place us on a lofty eminence whence we look down upon the Calvinistic ideas of "eternal filiation," "eternal Generation," "eternal Son," as midway betwixt us and Arianism. From this sublime and lofty eminence we see the Socinian moving upon a hillock; the Arian upon a hill; and the Calvinist, upon a mountain; all of which lose their disproportion to each other because of the immense height above them to which this view elevates us. The first sentence of John I paraphrase thus: From eternity was the Word, and the Word was with God, and the Word was God. He was, I say, from eternity with God. By him all things were made, and he became flesh and dwelt among us. He became a child born and a son of man. As such he is called Emanuel, Jesus, Messiah, Son of God, Only Begotten of the Father.

I can give the above views upon no other authority than my own reasonings. I learned them from nobody—I found them in no book. It is true, indeed, I have held the idea for sixteen years that Jesus is called the Son of God, not because of an "eternal generation," (which I conceive to be nonsense,) but because he was born as the angel described to Mary. This is now pretty generally received by a great many christians. Nor would I dispute or contend for this as a theory or speculation with any body. I could, indeed, amplify considerably, and perhaps obviate some difficulties by following up farther the hints submitted; but such are my views of the import of the beginning of John's testimony. You will remember that I make no systems, and although there are some abstract reasonings upon terms (as indeed much of our reasonings about language are) in the preceding, it is only for the purpose of getting into the sacred import of a style from which we have been proscribed by a speculating philosophy. I have acceded to your request with more ease than I could have done, had it not been for a few prating bodies who are always striving to undo my influence by the cry of Unitarianism, or Socinianism, or some other obnoxious *ism*. From all *isms* may the Lord save us!   Yours truly,   EDITOR.

A Restoration of the Ancient Order of Things. No. XIX.
The Deacon's Office.

THE time once was that every christian congregation had a treasury. In those days they required a steward, a treasurer or a deacon, or more than one, as the exigencies demanded. For, although the terms steward, treasurer, almoner, and deacon, are not perfectly synonymous, they nevertheless express the office and duty of the scriptural deacon. The term deacon, as all know, is equivalent to the English word servant, but the word servant is a very general term, and in the state signifies every public officer, from the President down to the constable. They are all servants of the state. So the apostles, evangelists, prophets, and bishops were all servants of the Lord and of the church. But there was one set of servants in the apostolic churches who were emphatically the servants of the church in its temporal concerns. These were the deacons, or stewards, or treasurers of the church. For as the deacon's office had respect to the temporalities of the church, and as these are in general some way connected with pecuniary matters, the office of treasurer and almoner is identified with, or is the same as that of deacon; so much so that some translators have, out of regard more to the application than to the literal import of the term διακονος, uniformly translated it *almoner*.

The plain and simple state of the case is this: Christian congregations in primitive times, had need of money or earthly things as well as we. They had rich and poor members. Their poor were such as could not, either through bodily infirmities, or through the inadequate proceeds of their labor in times of embarrassment, furnish their own tables. Those who had to spare were then called upon to supply their wants. And in many instances they not only contributed to the wants of their own poor, but to the wants of those of remote christian communities, in times of general scarcity or pecuniary difficulties. Contributions, generally called the *fellowship*, were statedly attended to in all their meetings. So Paul gave directions to all the churches in Galatia and elsewhere to replenish the treasury every first day, as the Lord had prospered them in their temporal avocations. A deacon or deacons had the charge of this treasury, and were ex-officio treasurers; but this was not all. They were not only to take care of the contributions, but to dispense or appropriate them according to the directions of the brethren. Thus they were stewards. And as the poor were those in whose behalf this fund was created, and as the deacons dispensed to them, they became ex-officio almoners of the poor.

As they had not in those days of primitive simplicity so many different sorts of funds and officers as we have in this age of complexity;

the deacons attended to all pecuniary matters, and out of the same fund three set of tables were furnished. These were the Lord's table, the bishop's table, and the poor's table. A plurality of deacons was in most instances necessary because of the attention required from them and the trust reposed in them. It was not so much per annum to the bishop, nor so much per annum to the poor, nor so much per annum to the Lord's table; but according to the exigencies of each and the ability to contribute, was the extent of the treasury and the distributions of the stewards or deacons of the congregation. In this state of things the deacons had something to do. They were intimately acquainted with the families and wants of the brethren, and in paying a christian regard to these and the duties of their office they obtained an honorable rank and great boldness in the faith, or fluency in the doctrine of Christ. Conversant with the sick and the poor, intimate with the rich and more affluent brethren, familiar with all, and devoted to the Lord in all their services, they became eminent for their piety and charity, and of high reputation amongst their brethren. Once every week these contributions were made, and as often were the appropriations made in times and circumstances that required them. Out of the church's treasury, then, the poor and distressed widow above three score, or the sick and afflicted disciple was relieved. The Lord's table was continually furnished with bread and wine. The bishops' also, according to their labors and their need, were supplied. And thus every thing was promptly attended to in the Lord's institution which could afford spiritual and temporal comfort to all the subjects of his kingdom.

Amongst the Greeks who paid so much regard to differences of sex, female deacons, or deaconesses, were appointed to visit and wait upon the sisters. Of this sort was Phebe of Cenchrea, and other persons mentioned in the New Testament, who labored in the gospel. The seven persons mentioned and appointed to the service of tables, Acts vi. though not so denominated, were nevertheless invested with and fully possessed of this office. The treasury was entrusted to them—the widows' tables, and every table which required service was attended by them. The direction given to the Corinthians respecting the treasury, and the instructions to Timothy and Titus concerning the choice of deacons, also concerning the support of widows and bishops, all concur in furnishing the above views of this office and work.

But how has it degenerated in modern times into a frivolous and unmeaning carrying about a plate once a quarter, in all the meagre pomp of a vain world!—a mere pompous etiquette, without use or meaning. Often we find the office of treasurer and deacon contradistinguished, as that of moderator and bishop in the same congregation. It is a scriptural insult to appoint a moderator where there is a bishop, and the same to appoint a treasurer where there is a deacon. The deacon is, *ex officio*, treasurer, and the bishop, *ex officio* moderator or president. To appoint a president in any meeting where there is an appointed bishop, it is in effect saying that the bishop is not qualified to keep order; and to appoint a treasurer where there is a deacon, it is in effect saying he is not to be trusted, or not qualified for his office. The office itself suggests the propriety of those directions and qualifications laid down for both the deacons and deaconesses in Paul's letters before mentioned. What a wise, benevolent, and independent in-

77

stitution, a christian congregation is! Nothing is left out of view which can contribute to the temporal and spiritual weal of the brotherhood. They meet in full assembly once every week to remember, praise, and adore the Lord; to share in the participation of his favors. The temporal state of the brotherhood is not overlooked in these meetings. Contributions are made for the necessities of saints. The deacons are acquainted, and, through them, the whole fraternity, with the circumstances of all. Under its wise and wholesome discipline care is taken that every member capable of labor, work with his own hands, diligently at some honest calling. The contracting of heavy and oppressive debts is proscribed. No brother is allowed to enthral himself or others in any sort of worldly speculations which incur either anxiety on his part or inconvenience to others. The aged, feeble, and helpless are taken care of by the brethren. The indolent, slothful, and bad economists are censured, admonished, and reformed, or excluded. The Lord's table is constantly furnished. The bishops' wants and necessities always supplied, and no one deprived of any necessary good. There are persons fitted for every service; and those who attend continually on this good service, become eminent in the faith, and after refreshing others are again in turn refreshed themselves. In this view of the deacon's office, we cannot but concur with the sayings and views of the primitive fathers who considered the deacons as the treasurers of the congregation, and as appointed to the service of tables, viz. the Lord's table, the poor's table, and the bishop's table.　　　　　　　　　　　　EDITOR.

To "Paulinus."—Letter III.

MY DEAR SIR—THE sentence in the Preface to the Epistle to the Romans, which to you appears objectionable, is the following: "And here let it be noted that the justification by works, and that by faith, of which Paul speaks, and of which our systems speak, are quite different things. To quote his words and apply them to our questions about faith and works, is illogical, inconclusive, and absurd." When I penned this sentence, I anticipated objections to it, and knew that it would be out of place to obviate them in that preface. The question then was whether should I withhold or bestow it. The fact of its appearance shews my decision of that question. I am glad you have called upon me for an exposition of it. I trust I will be able to satisfy you and others who have objected to it. We shall now make the attempt.

The 4th chapter was that portion of the epistle to which I referred in that sentence. Now it must first be asked, What were the *works* of which the apostle there speaks? It will be admitted in the case of Abraham, from whose works and faith the apostle here argues, that the faith of Abraham was a belief that his seed would be as numerous as God had promised him: "*so shall thy seed be.*" This promise he believed, notwithstanding all in *nature* and *experience* was against it. He considered not his own body now *dead*, neither the *deadness* of Sarah's womb.—Against all hope founded on the nature of things, he believed in hope of being the father of nations by the aged Sarah. It was not his faith in a Messiah which was accounted to him for righteousness as our systems speak. It was not his faith in a Messiah that constituted him the father of all believers. Others believed in the Messiah as firmly as he. But relying on the faithfulness and power of God alone, he was confident that

his offspring by Sarah would be as innumerable as the stars, or sands on the sea shore—"*therefore it was counted to him for righteousness.*" By a reference to the 11th *Heb.* it will appear that the faith by which the ancients obtained a good report was as different as their names. In other words, the faith spoken of was the belief of particular promises or revelations made in their days. Their believing was the same, but the things believed were different. In every age of the world the faith of the approved consisted in the truths revealed to them and of the promise given them. So Paul, after speaking of Abraham's faith in God's promise to him, being accounted to him for righteousness, adds, "It was not written for his sake; but for us also, to whom faith shall be accounted for righteousness, if we believe the promise made to us, viz. that Jesus died for our sins, and was raised for our justification." Paul argues here that not his fleshly works of circumcising himself nor his children, nor his servants, justified him; but his faith in the promise, "*So shall thy seed be.*" Again, the law was not given to the seed of Abraham with a reference to Canaan. "The inheritance was not by law, but by promise." Canaan was unalterably promised four hundred and thirty years before the law; or the law was four hundred and thirty years after the promise—consequently no works of that law were spoken of in the case of Abraham. Neither the faith of Abraham nor the works of Abraham, here spoken of, are akin to our systematic faith and works. The affirmation in the above sentence is therefore true.—But what is gained by the affirmation? I answer, *Accuracy* in noticing the meaning, and *correctness* in applying the sentiments of scripture. A loose and indiscriminating citation of scripture words, without regard to their scriptural meaning, is the cause of nine-tenths, at least, of the errors of this age. And I would not prove a scriptural truth, by misquoting a scriptural passage, for the sake of the dearest sentiment I hold. Some quote the scriptures as if they thought it right to bring every word that can be cited from any similarity, in proof of a favorite point. Now a good cause is often more injured by one misapplied text, than it can be aided by a dozen of good arguments. On this subject I would be precise even to squeamishness. I would, in other words, object as much to a citation of scripture made at variance with the design of the passage in aid of my own most favorite topic, as I would to an erroneous argument advanced by an opponent.

But again, more is at issue than has yet been noticed. "Good works," "trusting to works," and "justification by works," are words and sentences of general currency. Many class under the head of *good works*—prayers—praises—baptism—the Lord's supper, and all acts of devotion; and seeking to be justified by these is often viewed as seeking justification by works; and i* is supposed that Paul had such works in view when he spake of works of law and justification by works.

Once more, "good works" are identified with "works of law" and works of human contrivance; and the consequence is, that what is said about good works in scripture is very generally misunderstood and confounded with works of law. All these mistakes can only be corrected by a minute attention to the scripture style.— And, as you know, I deal much in assertions sometimes, especially when I have neither time nor room for the proof, I will assert that all works called *good* in scripture have *men* for their object;

and that no act of devotion, or any work which has God only for its object, is called a good work. That may be an act of devotion, but a good work in the scripture style it cannot be. The kind offices performed to the Saviour when he was poor and needy, the kind offices performed by one disciple to another, and every work which has man's comfort or happiness in view, is, in the sacred style, a good work. The settlement of this small matter is with some mere trifling; yet such persons admit that ten mills make one cent, and one hundred cents make one dollar, and that one dollar and one-fourth will purchase one acre of land forever. Let the above view of good works be fairly established in the mind of a Catholic and he becomes a Protestant.

But what I fixed my attention chiefly upon in that passage was the meaning of the justification by faith and that by works which Paul and James taught. To understand which has been with many theologists a matter of such immense trouble. Faith and works must be apprehended in the apostolic sense before justification by either can be understood in that sense.

Sinners are justified by faith, and christians by works. But this is too laconic for the mass of mankind. It is one thing, however, to introduce a person into a state of acceptance, and another to live acceptably in that state. It is one thing to enter into the married state, and another to make a good wife. Now faith in God's promise through Jesus Christ, is argued by the apostles, as that which brings men into a state of intimacy, friendship, and familiarity, or, in other words, into a state of acceptance with God. Thus faith is accounted to a man for righteousness, by the mere favor of God. But the continued enjoyment of such a state is by the same favor made to depend on our behaviour. On this principle is founded all the apostolic exhortations. All that is addressed to the hopes and fears of christians is derived from this consideration. So that when Paul and James are understood, there will be no occasion for an effort to reconcile them, as Luther and Calvin laboriously attempted. Paul speaks of the justification of sinners, and James of the justification of christians. It is an astonishing act of favor to account faith in Jesus as righteousness to a sinner, and then to teach this justified person how to live as eternally to enjoy the favor of God. In the final judgment when men's actions and not their states will be examined, faith is not then accounted to any man for righteousness. But, I was hungry and ye fed me, naked and ye clothed me, &c. These shall go away into everlasting life, &c. This is an important point. Without holiness, then, no man can enter the heavenly kingdom—"If any man, therefore, draw back, my soul shall have no pleasure in him." Instead of attempting to show that these persons had not "true faith," let us endeavor to show that we have works. Was not Abraham justified as a sinner by faith in God's promise? And as a servant of God, was he not justified by works when he offered up Isaac his son upon the altar? But I must not attempt to write a treatise on faith and works. Nor need I attempt to satisfy all the lovers of systems. What rendered the faith of Abraham so remarkable was his belief of a promise which was beyond the power of nature to accomplish, and what rendered the work so famous, on account of which he obtained a good report, was that it was an act of self denying and unreserved obedience growing out of his former belief. I am not now speaking of how the just man lives by faith; but of the faith which justifies a sinner—

nor of the works by which sinners seek to be justified; but of the works which justify the faith of christians. Without faith it is impossible for a sinner to please God, and without works it is impossible for any to be justified in the day when every man shall be rewarded according to his works.

With regard to what you say of a writer in epistolary communications "expressing a truth, a maxim, a position of general application," I would observe, that there is no incongruity, no impropriety in so doing, and I admit that the apostles frequently did so. But you will please to observe, as indeed I doubt not but you have frequently observed, that these maxims, truths, and positions of a general nature, are no more general than the object he has in view, or the drift of his remarks; and that they are never abstracted from the subject on hand. But it may happen that they have a general bearing upon other subjects from analogy, and as such they are to be interpreted and applied by the most exact rules of analogy. To say, for example, that no man is justified by works is a general truth. But general as it is, it must, from its context, be restricted to unbelievers, for it is just as true and as general that every christian will be justified by his works. Nothing else comes in review on the day of judgment; if the Lord's account of the separation of the sheep and the goats is to be applied to that day. A great deal of wisdom and knowledge is requisite to the application of general truths. So sensible were the sacred writers of this that they most generally restrict those general truths either in their own exposition or application of them.

I see every day the ill effects of the two popular systems of faith and works. Some seem to be afraid of doing good works lest they should trust in them, and some have no use for faith nor a knowledge of the scriptures; but *talk* of doing justly, loving mercy, and walking humbly with their God. Again others call prayer, praise, baptism, and all religious observances, good works—and dehort men from trusting in them as they would the fleshy works of the Jew or of the law.

I will be asked, Are these *bad* works, and are not all works either good or evil? To the captious or weak disciple I would reply in your sense of the terms, All works are either good or bad; but this is not the distribution of them made in the scriptures—Good works are of the following classes: "A widow well reported for good works," of what species? "if she have brought up children, if she have lodged strangers, if she have washed the saints' feet, if she have relieved the afflicted, &c. *i. e.* if she have diligently followed every good work." From this style there is no deviation in the sacred writings. Acts of devotion towards God though we may call them good works are not so distinguished in the holy oracles. To most readers these remarks will appear hypercritical; but I know, my dear sir, that you will concur with me in saying that the time will come when a pure speech will be restored, and that as by a correct speaker the pronunciation of a monosyllable is a matter not to be overlooked, so to a correct devoted biblical student, every thing is of importance that throws light upon any sentence in the sacred books.

I am constrained to be much more succinct in this part of my reply than I had projected. To give the reasons is not now necessary. If, in any thing, these remarks are not satisfactory, I rejoice to know that your frankness and candor will prompt you to write me your criticisms and objections. I wish for, and anxiously solicit from you, dear sir, all the criticisms, objections, and inquiries which you may think expedient, either on the New Translation, or on the contents of this work.

In great haste, but with much affection, your brother in the hope of immortality,

EDITOR.

No. 11.]   JUNE 4, 1827.
Speculation in Religion.

BY speculation in religion we mean religious ideas that never enter into practice. Man is a religious creature, because, as an intelligent, immortal and accountable being, he is dependent on God, and the more dependent he feels himself, the more religious he is, while his speculations in religion bring him no nearer to God. Man, therefore, without the knowledge of Jesus Christ as the only mediator between God and man, has no godliness. By godliness we mean, the transformation of mind, passion, and conduct to the will of God as revealed in the gospel. Speculation in religion is that which does not affect, according to the will of God, either the sentiments, passions, or conduct of the religious being.

Speculation in philosophy has been wisely discarded from approved systems. Since the days of Bacon our scientific men have adopted the practical and truly scientific mode—That is, they have stopped where human intellect found a bound, over which it could not pass, and have been contented to go no further than material objects, analyzed, gave out their qualities, and left the manner of their existence, as beyond the bounds of created intellect. Since men have been so wise in handling and analyzing material objects, we have heard little or nothing about occult sciences: but the sciences and the arts have advanced with increased velocity to the great good of the human kind. We plead for the same principle in the contemplation of religious truth. The qualities of matter are to be found in the great elaboratory of the material world, by inducing matter by every process to give out its qualities, and to deduce nothing from hypothesis; so religious truth is to be deduced from the revelation which the deity has been pleased to give to man. And as in the elaboratory of the material world, every truth concerning the qualities of matter is to be deduced from the matter itself; so in divine revelation we are to deduce what is practical, avoiding all speculation.

Philosophers have become wise in their generation, and, therefore, we will not even mention the hypotheses of past ages with respect to the material world, which have been scouted by science; but come immediately to our point, namely, that the men of religion have been less wise than the men of science. A few examples shall suffice.

Specimens,

Of speculation in religion.	Of Truth.
God is too good to condemn and punish his creatures.	The Lord God is merciful and gracious,—slow to anger,—longsuffering,—forgiving iniquity, transgression and sin,—and by no means clearing the guilty.
Holiness is God's darling attribute.—Mercy is God's darling attribute.	The Lord is holy in all his works, and just in all his ways.
God's eternal Son.	That holy offspring which shall be born of you shall be called the Son of God. This is my beloved Son, in whom I am well pleased, hear you him.
The spirit proceeds from the Father and the Son by eternal procession.	If I go not away the comforter will not come, but if I go away I will send him to you—which proceeds from the Father, and he will take of mine and show it to you.
The Redeemer came to save the elect.	The Son of Man came to seek and save that which was lost.
The Redeemer will only save his elect people.	This is a true saying and worthy of all acceptation, that Jesus Christ came into the world to save sinners—the chief.
The elect infants that die in infancy shall be saved.	Suffer little children to come to me, and forbid them not, for of such is the kingdom of heaven.
Are there few that be saved?	Strive to enter in at the strait gate, for I say to you that many shall seek to enter in, and shall not be able.
The gospel is only good news to sensible sinners.	Good news to all people.
The gospel is not to be preached to sinners till they are sensible of their lost estate.	Go you into all the world, and preach the gospel to every creature, he that believes shall be saved, he that believes not shall be condemned.
Sinners in their natural state are dead in sin as the dead in the grave; they can do nothing—they cannot come to Christ, nor repent, nor believe, &c.	You do search the sacred scriptures, for in them you think you have eternal life, but you will not come to me that you might have life. The animal man discerns not the things of the Spirit of God, they are foolishness to him, for they are spiritually discerned. This is the condemnation, that light has come into the world, and men have loved darkness rather than light, because their deeds are evil. He that believes not the Son of God is condemned already, because he has not believed on the only begotten Son of God.
Faith is the gift of God, and, therefore, not the duty of sinners.	
Unbelievers cannot believe the gospel, and, therefore, they cannot be condemned for that which they are unable to do.	Jesus comes in flaming fire to take vengeance on all those who believe not God and obey not the gospel.
Faith includes in it truth, confidence, and many fruits of the Spirit, and, therefore, a man cannot possess faith without the Spirit of Christ.	Faith is the substance of things not seen, the confidence of things hoped for. He that believes on the Son of God has everlasting life.
If you have real faith.	There is one faith.
Many may believe all	The things verily be-

that the sacred scriptures say, and yet perish.

Regeneration is an inexplicable mystery.

In regeneration the soul is passive, and in conversion active.

Regeneration is the root of all goodness.

God often hides his face from his people in sovereignty.

Before that a man can ascertain that he is a child of God, he must love God for what he is in himself as the source of all perfection, without any relation to what he is to believing sinners.

Man shall not be justified till the last day.

Once in Christ always in Christ.

Christ has left no direct nor specific form of government for his church.

The souls of men sleep with their bodies till the resurrection.

With what body do they come?

It is vain talking.—We know that salvation is of God—and we know that if we strive ever so much we cannot be saved except we be elected.

lieved amongst us. He that believes on the name of God is not condemned.

Seeing you have purified yourselves in obeying the truth through the spirit.

They were pierced to their hearts, and cried out Men and brethren, what shall we do? Be converted every one of you.

Without faith it is impossible to please God—Purifying their hearts by faith.

Your iniquities have separated between you and your God, and your sins have hid his face from you.

We love him because he first loved us—God is love; he that dwells in love, dwells in God, and God in him.

Being justified by faith we have peace with God.

He that endures to the end, the same shall be saved—Kept by the power of God through faith to salvation.

Go you into all the world, disciple all nations, baptizing them—and teaching them to observe all things that I have commanded you; and lo! I am with you always, even to the end of the world.

To-day shall you be with me in Paradise. I have a desire to depart and be with Christ, which is better.

You fool! that which you sow is not quickened except it die. And God gives to every seed its own body.

Who are you, O! man, that reply against God? To-day if you will hear his voice, harden not your heart. Come let us reason together, says the Lord, though your sins be as scarlet, they shall be white as wool.—Let the wicked forsake his way, and the unrighteous man his thoughts: Let him turn to the Lord, who will have mercy upon him, and to our God, who will abundantly pardon.

It would, indeed, be an arduous undertaking to give specimens of all the ways in which men speculate in religion. The above specimens are given as an example of what is meant by speculation in religion. It is of great consequence to have spiritual discernment to distinguish between that which is speculation in religion and that which is truth. The more especially as such speculations put on the appearance of truth, or seem to have truth for their basis. Such was the first speculation in religion, by attention to which man fell from his original state. You shall be as God, knowing good and evil, is as true as any speculation that has been proposed since that time.

Speculations in religion may be known by this test: though they could be ascertained, they do no good; and agitated, and discussed, and acted upon, they have the most pernicious consequences. Such are the features of speculation as drawn by Paul—Foolish and untaught questions avoid, knowing that they do gender strife. Of this cast was the first speculation, "You shall be as God." Well be it so. What has been the consequence? Or take any of the above specimens of speculation. Say God is too good to condemn and punish his creatures. Well! agitate the question. Be emboldened in sin, and then find that he will by no means clear the guilty. Again, say that holiness is God's darling attribute, and then have all your powers hardened in despair. Proceed again to mercy as the favorite of the Most High, and speculate yourself into hardened insensibility. Speculate again, and say that the Saviour is God's eternal Son, and try if you can believe and act upon it, that the Son, as such, and the Father are equally eternal, as regards the Deity. Or if you try your powers upon what men call the eternal procession of the Spirit from the Father and the Son, endeavor to show what you have gained in knowledge of the influence of the Spirit in regeneration, and in that holiness without which no man shall see the Lord. Or say that the Redeemer came to save the elect only: discuss the question in all its bearings—Do you know who are the elect? or in what way are you to know your own election? Or if you contend that the gospel is only to be preached to sensible sinners, the truth leads to inquire who is the sinner that is truly sensible of his sins before he receives the gospel? Or are you such a sensible sinner as to value the gospel without believing it?

The pursuit of speculation leads further from truth and further from God. But the truth is one; always does good, and its practical tendency is happiness to the individual and benevolence to all.

The test of truth is the word of God in its plain sense, addressing itself to every man's conscience. The word of God is itself the truth, nor is there one speculation in all the word of God.

Speculations seem to be founded on the sacred scriptures. It is, however, only a false appearance. Say that speculation takes up the proposition that men in their natural estate are dead in sin, and do nothing pleasing to God, and cannot repent, nor believe the gospel without the Spirit of God. It is all true in a true sense, the bible says the same things, and much more strongly than men's words can express; but the bible does not say the same things by way of speculation. It speaks practically; that is, it represents man's entirely helpless state; that he may come to the Saviour, and that in not coming to the Saviour, he may condemn himself as a guilty and depraved enemy to God, and to the gospel, in his mind and by wicked works. Speculation always

leads from practice. Men, in their speculations, even about the guilty, depraved and totally helpless state of man by nature, become vain and proud of their accuracy of knowledge, and thereby are kept from the Saviour, while the reception of the truth of God upon the state of human nature leads to the Saviour, because it is derived from a knowledge of him that came to seek and save that which was lost.   W. B.
Philadelphia, Pa.

On Experimental Religion.—No. II.

In my last paper it was observed that a knowledge of general christianity, the primitive churches, the apostles, and even of Christ himself, as written of in the New Testament, was of too popular, too remote a nature to consummate personal happiness; and that while those high matters concerned mankind universally, our individual comfort terminated ultimately upon a knowledge of ourselves, viz. whether we were or were not personally possessed of those graces of faith in Christ, hope of eternal life, love of God and man; and the gift of a holy spirit, which, as was observed, go to define the unsound phrase "experimental religion." Of the four particular evidences of personal adoption, viz. faith, hope, love and a holy spirit, I shall select the last for the subject of this essay—the gift of a holy spirit.

Well, then, by way of premises, let it be observed that the visible universe, the law of Moses, and the gospel are to be regarded as so many oracles by Jesus Christ concerning the divine character, which it is his high office to reveal. These oracles set the divinity in the several attitudes of creating, commanding, redeeming; consequently in the universe we behold his physical grandeur—in the law we hear his moral authority—in the gospel we perceive him sympathizing. "Jesus wept." The universe, then, is God manifest in works—the law is God manifest in words—the gospel is God manifest in flesh; and thus Jesus Christ in these revelations causes the divine character to approach mankind gradually by three successive advances—from mere physical power to moral supremacy, and from that again to the intensest and most unparalleled sympathy and sensibility, sweating blood, and weeping tears and uttering shrieks at the painful idea of being shamefully hung on a cross, naked, in the presence of three millions of people. His feelings broke his heart—"Reproach has broken my heart." *Ps.* So much for the developement of the divine character in these three dispensations of nature, law and the gospel. But now in regard to the comparative advantages brought to the worshippers by the successive introduction of these economies, it will appear obvious from what has been stated that an increased degree of light respecting the divine existence and character, the origin of the universe, the creation and destiny of man, the causes of death and of immortality, and the federal relations by which we are made partakers of these, are the chief. But this is not all; it is but the one half, for as in each of these dispensations there is a primary revelation of God round which all others are made to play, so in each of them there is a fresh advantage bestowed upon the worshipper, round which his increased responsibility is made to turn. In nature, then, heathens see God's physical greatness; in the law Jews hear his moral authority; in the gospel christians experience his spiritual power.

In the first dispensation men sinned against the invisible power and godhead by changing his glory into an image made like to corruptible man, and to birds and four footed beasts, and creeping things.

In the law Jews sin against his moral authority, expressed on tables; but in the gospel, in which God has substituted spirit for literal sounds and natural symbols, the worshippers sin against the Holy Spirit, they grieve or quench the Holy Spirit, for the gospel is the ministration of Spirit. In the first dispensation, we see; in the second, we hear; in the last we enjoy God.—But how the uncreated Spirit dwells in a created spirit, filling it with joy, we know not; but certain it is that this fellowship is set forth in the following words: "Behold I stand at the door and knock: if any man hear my voice and open the door, I will come in to him, and will sup with him and he with me." Again—"If a man love me he will keep my commandments, and my Father will love him, and we will come in to him and make our abode with him!" Supping with Christ means joy in a holy spirit. In a word, some men are condemned because they believe not in the Son of God; and secondly, others are condemned because, believing in him, they "turn away," "love the present world," "mind earthly things," "deny the Lord who bought them," "trample under foot the blood of the Son of God, and do despite to the Spirit of Grace;" and to me it is evident that the present race of christians are to be censured not so much for their informality as their carnality and contempt of the Spirit of our God.

But now if any should ask why Jesus Christ made us to see the divine grandeur, and hear his moral authority, before he let us *taste* his spiritual power, my answer is this, That it was necessary that the law of God should be written on stone; first, in order that fallen nature might by experiment (and we are altogether creatures of experiment) discover its inadequacy to keep it; and second, that this same written law might be for a book of reference in the days of the Spirit; in the days or economy in which power to fulfil the law is fully and freely given by God to those who believe that whensoever men sin against the Spirit which they have of God, they may be reproved, corrected, instructed. The scriptures are therefore said to be profitable for all these ends.

Let us, then, christian reader, walk in the Spirit, and we shall not fulfil the lusts of the flesh; "for if any man have not the Spirit of Christ, he is none of his." If we live after the flesh, we shall die; but if we through the Spirit do mortify the deeds of the body, we shall live; and if the Spirit of God dwell in us, he that raised up Jesus Christ from the dead will quicken our mortal bodies also by his Spirit which dwells in us. Concerning the written law as a rule of life, I should think that "Book of Reference" were a better title for it, inasmuch as the Holy Spirit is both the christian's life and the rule of it; but by the present commercial, trading race of professors, our religion is transformed into a written law, a letter, a commandment; and by men so guilty of the spirit of gain, christianity, which is godliness, will never be experimentally understood to mean any thing else than a written instrument; nevertheless to some it is the "power of God."

But some will say, When is this gift of the Holy Spirit given—before or after belief? In reference to this good gift of God, I heard it observed a few nights ago that we had turned the gospel wrong end foremost—the modern gospel reading thus: "Unless you receive the Spirit you cannot believe!" the ancient gospel reading thus: Unless you believe you cannot receive the

Holy Spirit; or to give it in the terms of Peter, Believe and be baptized, and you shall receive the gift of the Holy Spirit, for the promise (*i. e.* of the Holy Spirit) is to you," &c. &c.   Indeed it must be confessed that if we say to sinners, When you receive the Holy Spirit you will believe; and the apostles say, When you believe you will receive the Holy Spirit, that there is manifestly an inversion of the apostolic annunciation concerning the heavenly gift, the question in the primitive age being, "Have you received the Holy Spirit since you believed?"   But without being *casuistical, i. e.* jesuitical in this matter, we shall drop it; and without striving about the time when the gift is bestowed, let us thank God that it is bestowed at all, and glorify him by walking in it, living in it, praying in it, and rejoicing in it; for "to be carnally minded is death, but to be spiritually minded is life and peace."

Again—Some will say, What does the expression *Holy Spirit* mean?   Well, in scripture it stands first for God the Holy Spirit, and secondly for the holy mind or spirit of a believer—for illustration, take Peter's words to Ananias, "Why has Satan tempted you to lie to the Holy Spirit; you have not lied to men, but to God," (the Holy Spirit.)   And the Saviour says, How much more will your heavenly Father give a holy spirit (as it should be translated) to those that ask him.   Again—Praying in a holy spirit. Again—Paul says he approved himself God's servant "by knowledge, by long sufferings, by kindness, by a holy spirit," i. e. by a mind innocent of the love of gain, or commerce, or sensuality.

Now then the expression stands for both God the Holy Spirit, and for a believer's spirit made holy by him.

I shall now answer, from scripture, the following questions.—When do we know that we are born of the Spirit?   I answer, when we know that our spirits are holy.   But it will be asked again, when do we know this?   I reply, when we behold our minds producing the fruits of a holy spirit.   But what are the fruits of a holy spirit?   Paul says they are joy, peace, long suffering, gentleness, goodness, fidelity, meekness, temperance, against such there is no (written) law.   Now how many unholy Baptists are there? how many unholy Presbyterians, how many unholy Methodists, Episcopalians, Independents, and schismatics of every name?   Well may the editor say we are still in Babylon!   Ah me! when shall we return, and discern between the righteous and the wicked: between him that serves God and him that serves him not?   Ah apostatizing christians, grievers and quenchers of the Spirit of our God, are we not ashamed?

Now, reader, let us return to God and holiness, for without it no one shall see his face—and believe me that a disputatious mind is not a holy mind—an intemperate, unmeek, or unfaithful spirit is not a holy spirit—neither is one that does not practise goodness, and gentleness, and long suffering, and peace—neither the mind that does not love, or does not rejoice in Jesus. Ye cavillers, ye conceited few, who boast of your scriptural knowledge; but whose spirits, nevertheless, cannot move even the elements of the heavenly oracles, let me whisper to you a secret, that the kingdom of heaven is not so much in an abundant knowledge, as in an abundant spirit of righteousness, peace and holy joy.   PHILIP.

To the Editor of the Christian Baptist.
O. S. Virginia, October 21st, 1826.

DEAR SIR,—ONE who wishes to see truth tri-umph over error in every thing, and who believes that the Christian Baptist is destined to be instrumental in bringing about this great desideratum in matters of religion, begs the favor of addressing the Editor a few lines upon a subject of great interest to one who believes himself out of the "ark of safety;" but whose supreme desire is to know the truth as it is in Jesus.

Regarding you as a teacher in Israel, I desire your aid in my researches after truth, and in the present instance I make the application with the strongest assurance of being satisfactorily answered, (if you see fit to answer me at all) as the subject upon which I solicit information once operated upon your mind precisely as it does on mine.

In your dissertation on Conscience, No. 7, vol. 3, you have *literally* told my experience.   This is the part to which I allude.   You say,

"I well remember what pains and conflicts I endured under a fearful apprehension that my convictions and my sorrows for sin were not deep enough.   I even envied Newton of his long agony; I envied Bunyan of his despair.   I could have wished, and *did wish* that the Spirit of God would bring me down to the very verge of suffering the pains of the damned, that I might be raised to share the joys of the genuine converts. I feared that I had not sufficiently found the depravity of my heart, and had not yet proved that I was utterly without strength.   Sometimes I thought that I felt as sensibly, as the ground under my feet, that I had gone just as far as human nature could go without *supernatural* aid, and that one step more would place me safe among the regenerated of the Lord; and yet heaven refused its aid.   This too I concealed from all the living.   I found no comfort in all the declarations of the gospel, because I wanted *one* thing to enable me to appropriate them to myself.   Lacking this, I could only envy the happy favorites of heaven who enjoyed it, and *all my refuge was in a faint hope* that I one day might receive that aid which would place my feet upon the rock."

Now, sir, you cannot conceive with what intense interest I followed you through every word of this paragraph; *every word* was in perfect coincidence with my own feelings.   I thought, as I read the piece, *at last* I have found a pilot who was once entangled in such quicksands and vortices as obstructed my passage, and who of course will be able to give me some important direction how to steer so as to reach the desired haven.— But alas! what was my disappointment when, instead of informing us how your feet were *ultimately* established, "upon the rock," you suddenly break off the thread of your narrative, and leave us in painful suspense as to your future destiny.   The sentence following the paragraph above quoted, began thus: "Here this system ends and enthusiasm begins."   I am at a loss what construction you would have us place upon these words.   I am sure you cannot mean that it would be enthusiasm to wish for *supernatural* aid in regeneration, for without such aid, as I understand the matter, no man can be a christian.   The following scriptures, I think, confirm my opinion—The natural man receives not the things of the spirit of God, for they are foolishness to him; neither can he know them, because they are *spiritually* discerned.   Now as the *natural* man has not and cannot have this discernment, the conclusion is inevitable that it must be a *supernatural* work.   Again, we are informed that faith is the gift of God, and of course I must say cannot be learned in the school of nature. But I am sure, as before said, that this cannot be your meaning—I would, therefore, fain see you resume the subject in a future paper. I want to hear again from you about the ONE thing which you *once* felt so much in need of, and which I have thought (with humility be it spoken) was the *one* thing I lack to become a christian—for my *judgment* has long since been convinced of the truth of christianity. The morality of the gospel, its rapid propagation under its first illiterate preachers in opposition to the prejudices of the world, the accomplishment of the Old and New Testament prophecies, the miracles wrought by the Saviour, &c. &c. constitute a chain of testimonies which infidels have in vain tried to break. I believe that Jesus Christ was the Son of God. But how did I become possessed of this kind of faith? So far as I know, by *my own efforts;* by reading and reflection, just as I learn and believe that Rome is situated on the Tiber, and that Oliver Cromwell usurped the liberties of his country. With grief, therefore, I am constrained to believe that *mine* cannot be *saving* faith. I know of no title by which I can be more fitly designated than the paradoxical one of

A Believing Unbeliever.

Reply to the above.

DEAR SIR—Your letter has been deferred beyond my intentions, having, with some others, laid off for immediate attention, been overlooked, in the accumulation of business. My experience broke off, you think, too abruptly. This may have been so for your case, but for my object at that time, which was to show *that every man's experience corresponded with his religious education,* it was conducted sufficiently far to demonstrate the point in hand. Persons educated by the apostles had no such experience as that which I related. The New Testament furnishes no such a case. The consummation of such a case is as unscriptural as is the commencement and progress through. It is not the result of apostolic but of systematic teaching. But few are able to trace their mental exercises and excitements to the proper cause. Hence divine and human causes are so completely blended together that few can discriminate the one from the other.

"Where this system ends enthusiasm begins." The system brings us down to a certain point of sadness, grief, or despair. To extricate us it is necessary that a door should be opened for conceits to arise. Hence we look for divine interpositions of a peculiar character at a certain crisis, and as the drowning man holds fast his straw, so we take hold of a dream, or a conceit, or an impression, or an impulse, or a voice, or a particular occurrence, and by a favorable interpretation imagine it a sign or token for good, and console ourselves that Heaven has now lent its long withheld aid. We begin to rejoice in our supposed personal safety, and, by a slight but quick transition, rejoice in God for his sovereign aid or grace bestowed on us. This gives a brighter color to every thing we see. An almost sensible difference is discovered on even natural objects around us. Now the landscape smiles and blooms which before hung in mourning.—The winds whisper peace. The waters roar no more.

"That very voice which thundered terrors to the guilty heart,
"With tongues of seraphs whispers peace."
"The swallow twittering from its straw-built shed," or the raven croaking on the leafless tree,

is heard with pleasure unknown before. A thousand springs of enjoyment are open now and overflowing which before were dry.

The strong minded are longest in the gloom. Where the rational faculties are vigorous the passions are weaker, and *vice versa.* Children are proof of this. The men of strong intellect and much reflection are not so easily satisfied when in doubts or fears. Hence the system leaves many in the mire whom no conceit or reverie can bring out. So much I add to my former statements in the essay referred to in your letter. To resume my experience where I left off. I rested for a while on the bare probability or possibility that divine aid would come to my relief. This I soon found to be but slender support to a troubled mind. It were long to tell, and worth little when told, how many efforts, how many hopes, and how many disappointments in succession agitated my mind. I was all the while looking for an aid which was never promised, and expecting an interposition without which I was taught I could derive no assurance of the favor of God. I was once, nay more than once, led to believe that I had received this aid in consequence of the vivid impression made on my mind on hearing a layman speak to me of a righteousness without law, a righteousness of God through a belief in facts attested by the law and the prophets. So soon as I imagined the aid was granted I felt a joy and peace unknown before. These feelings, I afterwards saw, arose not from a belief of the philanthropy of God; but in consequence of a special interposition on my behalf. Hope and fear alternated in my breast just as I thought upon the *help* which was afforded me. If I thought it was divine aid, I had hope; if I supposed it to be altogether human, I feared. I began at last to rest with more satisfaction on the proclamation "whosoever will." I reasoned thus, "I was most certainly willing, and God was most certainly a God of truth, and had most assuredly invited me to partake of his favor, and why should I not? But I could not boast like others, I had still something to fear which they had not; and this, like a worm unseen, made my leaf wither and my head droop. Nor was it until I clearly apprehended that it was quite compatible with the blessed gospel for a person to view himself as destitute of any peculiar or personal claim founded upon any supposed favor bestowed upon him, or assistance given him, or good quality in him, and at the same time to rejoice in hope of the favor of God abounding through the gift of Jesus that I could feel myself at all stedfast in the faith and hope of eternal life. I found ultimately that the gospel is the power of God to salvation to every one that believes it, and the divine aid was vouchsafed in a way which I had not expected. I had looked for it independent of all the grace revealed in the gospel, but found it inseparably connected therewith. My experience hitherto was the experience of a misguided education, and indeed the experience of unbelief. My present peace and joy and hope arise from a firm persuasion that in the Lord Jesus through the love of God, and the grace of the Holy Spirit, I have acceptance, and am adopted into the family of God. Of this I have assurance from the spirit of adoption which I have received, and from the love I have to all the saints. There is not a man, woman, or child upon the earth who sincerely loves the King, my Lord and Master, whom I do not unfeignedly love for his sake. And there is no commandment of the King, there is no expression of his will, to obey which, I feel the least reluctance Such is the head of the chapters of my christian experience.

I feel myself bound to give you this disclosure of my experience from the spirit and tenor of your epistle. But to say that it can be profitable to others for me or any other person to tell all their agitations and describe their journey to their present abode in the favor of God, is with me quite questionable. Myriads were brought to rejoice in the Lord in a few minutes or hours, and I blame my religious education for all the darkness, and gloom, and uncertainty, of which I have been conscious. I am now in the enjoyment of the blessings of the gospel of Christ; but this I might enjoy manifold more, and might have enjoyed much sooner, had it not been for the obstacles thrown in my way by an abstruse and speculative theology. Thousands by a different road have arrived at the same hope, and may much excel me, in their enjoyments and spiritual devotion, and therefore I cannot give this narrative as a standard by which any man's pretensions to the christian character may be tested.

As to the supernatural aid afforded in any case, I have to observe that it is all supernatural, the truth believed, the good things hoped for, and the amiable one loved are all supernatural. And if by your "own efforts" you could believe that Jesus is the Messiah the Son of God—by your "own efforts" you can believe in him to the salvation of your soul. That is "saving faith," (for there is but one faith,) which purifies the heart and works by love. If your faith does not work in obeisance to all the Lord's commandments, it is no faith, not even of your own efforts. We can have, and we do have, the blessing of God, or the aid of God, whenever we sincerely ask it. Your references to the "natural man," and to "faith being the gift of God," would have been unnecessary in this case had you read the essays on the work of the Holy Spirit, vol. 2, page 124, 131. To these I refer you. It is one of the monstrous abortions of a purblind theology for any human being to be wishing for supernatural aid to be born again. Transfer such an idea to the first birth and to what an absurdity are we reduced!!

Be assured, my dear sir, that other teaching than the apostles has confused you. You might, at this moment, have been a believing practitioner of the commandments of the Lord, instead of a believing rebel against the Lord, had you honestly read and examined the New Testament. For there the power of God is always exhibited, and supernatural aid displayed in behalf of every sinner who is disposed to receive it. If you have not, it is because you ask not; and if you ask and receive not, it is because you ask for an improper purpose. And no man living can now be excused for disobedience to the faith, or will hereafter be excused for his disobedience, because supernatural aid was withheld. It is just as sure as the genial influence of spring which now clothes the forests and the fields with verdant beauty; but to him whose fields are unprotected and uncultivated, the influences of spring are as though they were not. You might as well tell me that you can bake a loaf by your own efforts, without flour, water, and fire, as that you can believe that Jesus is the Son of God, by your own efforts. I refer you to the excellent essay in this number on speculation in religion, written by an elder in Israel, and to that on experimental religion, by Philip.

Yours, benevolently,   EDITOR.

————

The Social System and Deism.
No. II.

FROM the reception which my *Reply to Mr D,* a *Sceptic*, has received—from the requests of many of my readers—from a consideration of the prevalence of scepticism in this country—and from the bold and open attacks of Deists on the Scriptures of Truth, I feel it my duty to devote a few pages of this work to the Sceptics of the present day.

Of these there are two kinds—the inquisitive, speculating, and, in his own judgment, *sincere* Sceptic; and the ignorant, impudent infidel, who never seriously read the Christian Scriptures, and who glories in being an unbeliever, as if it was essential to his dignity to discard revelation, and to blaspheme the author of the christian religion. Their case is a hopeless one. They are too ignorant to be addressed by reason—too wise in their own conceits to learn any thing, and their conscience so perfectly seared as to have become insusceptible of conviction. There are moral disorders in the human race as incurable as any of those corporeal diseases which have been for ages, and still are, considered beyond the control of all remedies. Amongst these I would place the moral distemper of this latter class of infidels. Some of this class were given up by the Great Physician himself. Miracles could not be wrought in their presence; or, if wrought, could effect nothing. I do not say that it is impossible for God to raise the dead, or to cure such infidels; but it is incompatible with the principles of his moral government to display omnipotence this way. The Saviour could lament the catastrophe of Jerusalem; but could not, consistently with his government, heal them. But there are some of the former class who may be brought to their reason or right mind, and for their sakes I think some efforts ought to be made. The weak-minded christian, and the young convert too, may be strengthened, and the lame may be healed. When an apostle told christians to be always prepared to give a reason of the hope that was in them, he did not mean what the people of this time mean by these words. We in this day call our mental exercises the reason of the hope that is in us; but he meant the evidences of the gospel, and not our evidences of our interest therein. "Be always ready to afford to magistrates and rulers, when called before them, good reasons why you believe and hope in Jesus as the Messiah." I think, too, the New Harmony Gazette, which, in this country, is the focus of the lights of scepticism, to which, as Tacitus said of Rome, flows all the *cream*, shall I call it, of *enlightened* infidelity, merits a particular attention. The conductors of that journal are amongst the most assiduous, devoted, and persevering Sceptics of the 19th century. The bible, some how or other, stands in their way, and is supposed to be inimical to some favorite scheme, or darling hypothesis of the builders of the city of Mental Independence. At all events, we have not seen a number of that paper in which there is not either a popgun or a blunderbuss discharged at Revelation. For my part I rejoice to know that so much of the reflex light of christianity shines in our political institutions that no *bastile*, no *auto da fe* awaits the man who vends his sceptical reveries in books or papers, or publicly declaims against the bible and in favor of Deism. If our most pure, holy, and heavenly religion can be defended, supported, inculcated, and diffused by no other weapons than iron locks, swords, and faggots, I wish not to be in the rear or van of its advocates. No: on our banner is inscribed, *reason, argument, persuasion.*

I never censure a Deist for his eulogies on reason, but for his want of it. I have, indeed, regretted to see and hear men extol *common sense,* and immediately turn round and shew that they had not a particle of it. If there be in this country a reasonable Deist, I have not had the good fortune to become acquainted with him.— Some of them, I know, talk a great deal about reason; but, really, if I know the meaning of the word, they are the most unreasonable beings I have met with. But I would not get angry with them on this account, but rather I would pity and lend my aid to assist them.

I propose not in these essays to wear any suit of armor made ready to my hand, nor to panoply myself with the fashionable shields and breast-plates of the famous defenders of the bible. I know of few of them that have not in some way injured the cause they labored to defend. Nor will I direct an arrow at every pigmy who squeaks upon an oaten reed. Nor can I yield to the *liberales* at New Harmony the right of using every species of attack at one and the same time. But to drop the metaphorical and to come to the literal, I will premise a few things in this number—

1. The bible is commonly, by friends and foes, styled the Revelation of God, or a Divine Revelation; and under this title the Sceptics attack it with the most apparent effect and raise the loudest cry. I come not forward to be attacked through the media of other men's sophistical technicalities. I must tear them all off as David did Saul's armor. Any Sceptic that may deign me a reply, is to remember one thing above all others, that I am to be attacked only in my own style and acceptation of terms and phrases, and that I defend the bible, and not any man's system of religion, nor his arguments in favor of its divine original. Although not so rich in *mental independence* as the conductors of the social system, I have some little property of this sort of which I would be parsimonious.

I do not believe, then, that the book commonly called the Bible, is properly denominated a Divine Revelation, or communication from the Deity to the human race. At the same time, I am convinced that in this volume there are revelations or communications from the Deity to man. Revelation, properly so called, is an exhibit of supernatural things, a disclosure of things unknowable by any other means in the reach of mortals. Whatever can be known by reason, or the exercise of our five senses, is not a subject of revelation at all. But the things revealed are all reasonable when all the premises are understood. I grant that the simple statement of any thing not known before may in some sense be called a revelation. For example; the history of the French or American Revolution to a child who never read or heard any thing of it before, is a revelation, but not a divine revelation. To constitute a divine revelation, in our sense of the terms, it is not only necessary that God be the author of it, but that the things exhibited be supernatural, and beyond the reach of our five senses. For example; that God is a Spirit, is beyond the reach of our reasoning powers to discover, and could not be known by any human means. That a Spirit created matter, or that God made the earth, is a truth which no man could, from his five senses or his reasoning powers, discover. It is therefore a revealed truth. That man has a spirit in him capable of surviving his mortal frame, is also a supernatural truth.

That man will live again, and be either happy or miserable in a future state, is another supernatural truth. That God so loved the world as to send his only begotten Son to enlighten, purify, and happify men, is a supernatural truth. Now the Bible contains a thousand things that belong not to this class. For example; Moses writes five books in which he relates many thousand historic facts and incidents, none of which are supernatural, though there are many communications in his writings which are supernatural and rank under the head of Divine Revelations. The history of the bondage in Egypt, of their pilgrimage through the wilderness, of their possession of the land of Canaan, of their judges and kings, is no more than true and faithful history. From the perusal of which the divine character and human character is developed to the mind of the reader.

This is as true of the apostolic writings as of the ancient Jewish prophets. In the five historical books of the New Covenant or Testament, many thousand items are written which are no divine revelation; such as the reasonings, objections, and discourses of the Jewish priests, scribes, Pharisees, and Sadducees. Many historical facts, such as the decapitation of John, the calling of Peter, the enrolment of Augustus Cesar, the death of Herod, the martyrdom and burial of Stephen, the peregrinations of the Saviour and the apostles, &c. &c. These, and a thousand other items cannot be called, in our sense of the terms, a divine revelation. Many things in the prophetic books of the Jewish scriptures, and many things in the epistles of the christian scriptures are of the same kind. It would be as great a misnomer to call Paul's request about his cloak left behind him a divine revelation, as to call the Inquirer who writes against the Bible, a Christian. I mean that "Inquirer," in the New Harmony Gazette, who begins by pronouncing sentence, and afterwards calls for the proof. Now it must be remembered that generally both the Old and New Testament writers make a distinction such as I have made between those communications which were from God, and the other parts of their writings. The Jewish prophets were wont to call the divine communications a word from the Lord—the message or burthen of the Lord, &c. And the Saviour promised two things with a reference to this subject, of which we should be mindful. 1st. That the Spirit would qualify them to be faithful historians, by bringing all facts necessary to their narrative, to their remembrance; and, in the 2d place, he would guide them into all supernatural truth. This is quite a different work. It is one thing to recal to a person's remembrance that of which he was once conscious, and another to make him know things of which he, with all the world, knows nothing. The former qualified them to be faithful historians—the latter, to be ambassadors of God, or teachers of his will to men. Thus we believe Moses and all the historians in the Old and New Testament to be credible and faithful witnesses; but in reasoning upon the contents of these books, we must always discriminate between what is supernatural and what is not; we must distinguish what is a Divine Revelation from what is human. Not adverting to this, has been the means of much of that nonsense called argument against the Revelation of God. Now much superstition amongst christians owes its origin to the same cause. It is in the present time an enviable path which lies midway between scepticism and superstition. Thomas Paine never would have written his Age of Reason had it not been that he supposed the Bible was in the way of his politics. I will not say that he might save his life by avowing such principles as would be deemed orthodox by those who controlled the guillotine; but I will say that it was because he supposed, so long as the Bible was held sacred by the great mass of the community, that it would be impossible successfully to oppose the doctrine of the divine right of kings. Had he ever read, or at all understood the Old Testament, he would, from the same motives which led him to oppose it, have inculcated its authority upon the minds of the community. His devotion to a commonwealth, and his dislike of monarchy, which caused him to attack, would have induced him to defend the ancient oracles. For this good reason: the only form of government which God himself actually set on earth was that of a commonwealth. He permitted a monarchy for a punishment, but set up a commonwealth for a blessing to the nation which he took under his special care for special purposes.

Had the unreasonable author of the Age of Reason been better acquainted with the volume he oppugned, he would, even from his politics, have been obliged to plead its authority in his favor. I have some misgivings that none oppose the Bible who do not think it opposes them. And it might, perchance, be of some use to those who profess to inquire after truth, and yet oppose this book, to inquire amongst their other inquiries, why they at first found themselves sliding off to the opponents of Revelation. I have one great philosopher on my side in this hypothesis. He said men disliked the light that condemned them. To give it in his own words, "He that does evil hates the light, neither comes to the light lest his deeds should be detected."

But I must not omit to state another preliminary consideration, with me of much consequence. It is this: It is not the patriarchal, nor the Jewish, nor the Christian Revelation in piecemeal that I am about to defend against the querulous, captious Sceptic—it is the consummation of all the ancient revelations in the mission of the Son of God. In reference to this, I view the whole volume; for this is the Alpha and the Omega of the whole. The christian religion is the corn in the ear. It germinated in the patriarchal, it shot forth in the Jewish, and ripened at the christian era. It is not the bud, nor the stalk, nor the leaves, nor the blossoms, but the ripe ear which we are to eat. And it is this about which we are concerned. I know the Sceptics reason or talk as if the ripe ear should have come first; that it is unreasonable that there should be a root, a stem, leaves, and a husk. They are eccentric geniuses, when talking against the Bible.

To obviate the unfounded fears of some weak minds, arising from my remarks on Revelation, I will state distinctly, though it is fairly implied in my remarks, that, as historians, the sacred writers are infallible. Not only is their record of divine communications, but their narratives and episodes are infallibly correct. The account of the deluge, of the confusion of human speech, of the destruction of Sodom and Gomorrah, are as much to be relied on as the revelation of God's gracious purposes in the mission of his Son. But many, not discriminating between the history of human affairs, such as Jacob's obtaining the blessing, and Abraham's denying his wife, and the Israelites carrying off the goods borrowed from the Egyptians, &c. &c. and the revelations from God, impiously rail against divine revelation as if these were essential items thereof. It matters not whether these historians wrote

2 T

in part or in whole from tradition, from their own observation, or from immediate suggestions, their historical accounts are to us infallible, because sanctioned, approved, and quoted by those under the fullest influence of the Holy Spirit. These things premised, I purpose in my next to come in contact with the sceptics of the present day. And as I am determined to put them on the defensive, and to have half of the interrogations, and thus to meet them on fair grounds, I will propose them a few questions for consideration; and in order to obtain suitable answers, I will answer question for question, and divide to a scruple the *onus probandi*, or burthen of proving our respective positions.

Quest. 1. Is there a God who created all things? And if answered in the affirmative, upon what evidence is this known?

2d. Is there a spirit in man which will survive the body or live after the animal life is extinct, and upon what evidence is this known?

3d. Is there a future state of felicity or of torment, and if so, upon what evidence is this known?

I will not be further inquisitive at present. I will reciprocate the favors demanded on principles perfectly liberal. Definite answers and rational proof is expected from some of the enlightened Deists at New Harmony. I have no doubt that it will be conceded that questions and discussions, to the great mass of mankind, paramount to these cannot be conceived.

EDITOR.

Dear Sir,

ONE of our teachers in this county has refused to have the new translation read in a public meeting because it is not the word of God, alleging that the common version is received as the word of God, but that the new translation is not considered such. Pray whose word shall we call it? Answer this, if you please, for some of us are in doubt upon this subject.

Yours, truly,			CANDIDUS.

Reply to the Foregoing Letter.
Mr. Candidus:

DEAR SIR—YOUR teacher was certainly right, and you should all passively submit to his determination. For the common version is the word of God, but the new translation is not. The reason I will now tell you. The common version was made by forty-nine persons authorized by a king, paid for their trouble by the king, and when their work was published, the king ordered it to be read as the word of God in public assemblies and in families, to the exclusion of every other version. Now all the versions that were read before this king's reign, ceased to be the word of God when the king signed the decree; and from that moment the king's version became the word of God. You will see, then, that there are two things necessary to constitute any translation the word of God; first that it be authorized by a king and his court; and again, that it be finished by forty-nine persons. Every translation becomes the word of God, or is more or less the word of God, according to the number of persons that make it. Thus, if one hundred persons made a translation it would be doubly more the word of God than that made by the forty-nine, and four times more than that made by twenty-five, and thirty-three times and one third more than the new version, provided it was so decreed by a king. For you must remember that both are necessary, and that if a thousand men should agree to make a version, it would

87

not when made be the word of God, because it wanted the royal approbation. You will naturally conclude, from these plain facts, that if one man or three men should most exactly and perfectly translate the original Greek and correct very many errors and inaccuracies in the king's translation, it would nevertheless still be the word of man; for all the errors, inaccuracies and imperfections in the common version are the word of God, and the correction of them all or any number of them, by only one man or three men, would be no more than the word of man. This, sir, is not only sound, but most orthodox logic. It would, therefore be a profanation of the pulpit, and the holy place, to read within thirty yards of it, the new version. If it be read at all, it ought to be at least beyond the grave yard, or outside of all the consecrated ground. It may be read in families, just like Robinson Crusoe or any other romance; but never with the veneration of a sermon-book, and infinitely less of the word of God. For the sake of making this matter a little more plain, I will extract a few sentences and phrases out of the common version and out of the new, that you may see how the word of God differs from the word of man:

King's Version.	New Version.
The kingdom of heaven is at hand.	The reign of heaven approaches.
Baptism of repentance.	Immersion of reformation.
I bare record.	I testified.
The witness of God.	The testimony of God.
I could wish to be accursed from Christ.	I was wishing to be accursed from Christ.
The church of God.	The congregation of God.
God be thanked that you were the servants of sin; but you have obeyed from the heart that form of doctrine which has been delivered unto you.	But thanks to God, that though you were the slaves of sin, you have obeyed from the heart the mould of doctrine into which you were cast.
Generation of vipers.	Offspring of vipers.
Be angry and sin not.	Can you be angry and not sin?
Time shall be no more.	There shall be longer delay.

Now if forty-nine men, summoned and paid by a king, should, in obedience to the king not translate but anglicise such Greek words as baptism, bishop, angel, church, &c. &c. and should one or forty-eight persons, from their own better information and mental independence, translate those words into English, and give us immersion, overseer, messenger, congregation, &c. &c. this version ought not to be read in a public meeting because it is the word of Man; but the other being the work of forty-nine men, sanctioned by a king, should be read as the word of God. By such arguments as these, my dear sir, we prove the common version to be the word of God, and the new to be the word of man. If any man has any better arguments than these to offer, we shall cordially thank him for them. EDITOR.

No. 12.] BETHANY, JULY 2, 1827.

A POST-OFFICE having been established at my residence, it became necessary to change the name of this place because of a post-town in Mason county called Buffaloe.

To the Editor of the Christian Baptist.
HARTFORD, CONN., MAY 1, 1827.
DEAR BROTHER IN THE LORD,—We have for some time enjoyed the privilege of reading your pub-

lication, and have been edified by many of its communications. It has afforded joy to a few advocates for a strict adherence to the doctrine and ordinances of the New Testament in this place, to know that the ascended Saviour is raising up witnesses in different places to vindicate his truth, and bear testimony against those traditions which make void his holy commandments.

Deeply impressed with a sense of our duty, to keep the ordinances of him who has loved us, and given himself for us, as they are delivered to us in his word, we have found ourselves obliged to take the course you have so ably advocated, of renouncing all the diverse creeds of fallible men—all sectarian or denominational attachments, and of fellowshipping, what we understand to be the truth, and that only, wheresoever and in whomsoever we find it.

Assured of the truth and importance of our Saviour's testimony, "My kingdom is not of this world," and of the corresponding apostolical command, "Be you not unequally yoked together with unbelievers," we have separated from those worldly religious societies, whose origin is so manifestly found in that wisdom which is foolishness with God. We have assembled on the first day of the week to break bread, teaching and admonishing one another from the word of the Lord, in psalms and hymns, singing, &c. We have no desire, however, to separate from any who love our Lord Jesus in sincerity, any farther than we are obliged so to do in order to obey his commandments. We would not overlook, what we indeed conceive to be, a very important principle in our Master's kingdom, i. e. the law of christian forbearance; and while we desire in the spirit of meekness to come out from, and bear testimony against those things which tend to make void the laws of Zion's King, we wish to unite with all his true subjects in the observance of whatever we mutually understand to be his requirements.

With these views, you may well suppose we rejoice to co-operate in our humble measure, with those who are endeavoring to bring back the disciples of Christ to that simplicity of doctrine and practice from which they have been so awfully corrupted. We are happily agreed with the general views exhibited in the Christian Baptist; and if in any thing we are otherwise minded, we rejoice that your liberality has assured us of an opportunity for amicable discussion in your pages for the promotion of our union in the truth as it is in Jesus.

We wish now, we humbly hope for the truth's sake, to make a few remarks on the important and interesting subject of the character of our blessed Master. We have been perfectly satisfied with your remarks generally on this subject, as they have, like your remarks on other subjects, been obviously derived from the word of truth, and not from the systems of men. But we must frankly inform you that, in your last number, in defending yourself against the insinuations of your opponents, you have, in our opinion, adopted a phraseology, and expressed an opinion, opposed to the express testimony of our Saviour, and subversive of the great truth, that he is "the Son of the living God."

You reason thus: "There is more value in one human being than there is in one million of globes such as this we inhabit. If, then, the whole assembly, or church, or congregation of purified and glorified human beings belongs, *jure divino,* or by inheritance, or by redemption to the Lord Jesus; if it be his own, as it is his Father's, I can conceive of no glory superior to his personal glory and majesty."

Now we believe and rejoice in the truth, that the whole redeemed church belongs to the Lord Jesus; but, that it is "his own, as it is his Father's," we cannot believe without rejecting the following testimony of our Saviour, " I have manifested your name to the men whom you gave me out of the world: they were yours, and you gave them me."—"You have given him power over all flesh, that he should give eternal life to as many as you have given him." " I pray not for the world, but for them whom you have given me." *John* xvii. 2, 6, 9. Here the testimony is plain, repeated, decisive. The saints belong to the Son by gift. But do they belong to the Father by gift? Who has first given to him? They were originally, and by independent right, the Father's. " Yours they were, and you gave them me."

Moreover—to say, " I can conceive of no glory superior to (Christ's) glory and majesty," is, in our opinion, opposing the testimony of the Saviour in the following words, "My Father is greater than I." "My Father who gave them to me is greater than all."

We "reason thus:" " To us, there is but one God, the Father, of whom are all things;" who "works all things after the counsel of his own will." Therefore, the Father is exclusively the eternal underived, and independent source of all being, perfection, and glory, and is worthy, and demands to be loved and adored as such. To us there is " one Lord Jesus Christ, by whom are all things;" by whom the Father creates, governs, redeems, and judges his creatures, who is the "first begotten," the beginning of the creation of God—"the image of the invisible God"— "the first born of every creature"—the only "mediator between God and man," and is worthy to be loved and worshipped as such, "to the glory of God the Father." We worship and obey the Son as King in Zion, but we worship as the "one God, the Father" who set him there. *Ps.* ii. 6. We joyfully acknowledge him as "head over all things to the church," but we believe the divine testimony, that the Father "gave him" this authority. *Eph.* i. 22. The Father " has appointed (him) heir of all things;" *Heb.* i.—"has put all things under his feet;" 1 *Cor.* xv. 25.—and "has made subject to him angels, and authorities, and powers," 1 *Peter* iii. 22. We rejoice in the animating assurance that he must reign till he has " put all enemies under his feet:" but we know that " when all things shall be subdued to him; then shall the Son also himself be subject to him that put all things under him, that God may be all in all." 1 *Cor.* xv. 28.

Now then, dear brother, we "reason thus:" If we "conceive of no glory superior" to that of "begotten" or dependant existence—if we " can conceive of no glory," of power, or wisdom, superior to that which is derived from, and dependant on another, we must agree with you that we "can conceive of no glory superior to the personal glory and majesty" of the Lord Jesus. But if we can have any conception of a being who is self-existent, underived, (which reason itself teaches there must be) of infinite and independent knowledge, wisdom, goodness, and power; we must say that we can conceive of a glory superior to the personal glory and majesty of our Lord Jesus Christ. What conception, we ask, have you of the words of our Saviour, " My Father is greater than I?" To suppose that he meant (without giving the least intimation of such meaning) that the eternal Jehovah is greater than a man, is, to us, inadmissible. Moreover, it was not true that the Father was greater than he, if he was the eternal God and man. Had this been true, would he not have said, My father is greater than I am in my human nature?

Has not Jesus Christ plainly taught us that he is dependant on another, even the Father, for the highest glory he ever possessed, by praying (*John* xvii. 5,) for the glory he had before the world was? Did he not constantly declare his dependence on the Father, and not on the Word, or any second person in the godhead, for all things? And when the Jews charged him with " making himself equal with God," did he not repel the charge in the most unequivocal manner by the assurance, "Verily, verily I say to you, the Son can do nothing of himself?" Is it not manifest that the term God is applied to the Son figuratively, (as it is to beings of vastly inferior order) since it appears from *Ps.* xlv. and *Heb.* i. that as God, he has a God who " has anointed" him? These considerations, in connexion with many others, have long since convinced us that the common principle of referring every expression of dependence to his humanity only, is a violation both of scripture and reason.

To us there is no truth more plainly revealed from heaven, than that Jesus Christ is the SON of God. In this glorious character he was announced to a perishing world, as the object of faith and foundation of hope, by " the only true God," *Matt.* iii. 17.—by Christ himself, *Luke* xxii. 70.— and by his apostles, *Acts* ix. 20. 1 *John* iv. 15. But to say that the Son of God is God himself, (using the term in its highest import) is as manifest a contradiction as to say that the son of the president is the president himself. And as the affirmation concerning the son of the president, that he is president, would be an implicit denial that he is his son: so the affirmation concerning Jesus Christ, that he is the eternal God, is an implicit denial that he is his Son; and though we may "have found him of whom Moses in the law and the prophets did write, Jesus of Nazareth," we have yet to look elsewhere for the Son of God.

We submit these free remarks to your candid examination, in the confidence that you have the pure truth in view, and are determined to advocate it, so far as you understand it, however contrary it may be to preconceived opinion, or popular systems. We should have offered much more evidence on the subject, did we not fear intruding on your liberality, by occupying too much room in your pages. Commending you to God and to the word of his grace, which is able to build us up, and to give us an inheritance among all them that are sanctified, we subscribe ourselves your brethren in Christ.

HENRY GREW,
JAMES HANMER,
Members of a Church of Christ in Hartford.

THE writer of the preceding letter had not seen our essay on the Preface to John's Testimony when he wrote the above. To this we refer him as an answer to his communication. We have another communication from him on another subject, to which we will attend in its own time.   ED. C. B.

To the Editor of the Christian Baptist.
DEAR SIR,—STOP one moment and permit a stranger who feels much interest in the reformation that is now beginning to take place in the christian world, to take a short trip with you. I

will not be tedious, though I may be a little troublesome. I do not expect to please the fashionable and polite, for I am neither a clergyman nor a schoolman; but, sir, you know that it takes every body to make a world, and it may be there are some like myself. If so, I may be of some use to them.

I subscribed for the new translation and the Christian Baptist without knowing but very little of the character of either; and sorry was I for doing so, until they came to hand. I heard much said against you in relation to your christian character—you were called every thing almost but a christian. No wonder, then, living in Babylon as I did, being enveloped in darkness, and dreaming that all things were going on well, that I should be alarmed when the trumpet proclaimed, "Up! get you out of this place, for the Lord will destroy this city!" At length the Christian Baptist arrived. My fear increased to an alarming degree; for at the first broadside all my rigging went by the board, and I expected the next would send vessel, cargo, and all to the bottom. But after reading awhile, and finding the ship still afloat, my fear began to subside, and I at length became so calm in my mind that I concluded to examine the hull and the cargo. The rigging I did not look after. The hull I found had received no injury. I then examined the cargo. I found that fully three quarters of it was finally ruined. I got very anxious in the examination, and found that all that was damaged was *contraband*. I wish others would examine; for I do believe that there are thousands in the same situation with myself. Well for me that I examined before I got into port! If I had not, vessel, cargo, and all would have been exposed to condemnation. The christian world are dreaming in Babylon as I was.— They are infatuated. They are blind respecting the "highway" the prophet speaks of; and oh! what a poor stagger do they make in attempting to travel along that happy road. But ah! I see the cause of all their woes. They are intoxicated. They have been drinking of the wine of her fornication—the cup of her abominations which has caused all the world to wonder after the Beast. They have bought of her merchandize and have hid it among their stuff, and very few of them are willing to acknowledge their crime, or own their relation to the Mother of Harlots; and no wonder, for such is the nature of her bewitching cup, that every one says, " I am not drunk," a sure symptom that they have been tippling. I know that it is unpleasant to claim kin with so base a woman, but the relation we had better own until we have disposed of all her merchandize; for by that we have been detected, and we never shall, with all our priestcraft, be able any more to conceal the relation. I think there is a fire kindling among the plunder. The hay, the wood, and the stubble begin to smoke. And what makes me more sure of it is, the merchants are beginning to scold—(may God grant that soon they may have occasion to lament, saying, *Babylon is fallen! is fallen!*)—I mean the retailing merchants who live in the suburbs. The wholesale merchants live in the capitol. I am afraid they are out of the reach of your artillery. I hope, however, that you will mount your heaviest ordnance and level on the metropolis and if it should have no effect, I hope you will not be discouraged, but continue to remember her daughters and grand daughters until they remove out of her jurisdiction.

Many are very free in spending their opinion with regard to the Christian Baptist. I also will show mine opinion. My opinion is, that it is by far the most valuable human production that I ever saw. It not only discovers to us our errors, our maladies; but it points out to us the only antidote for all our diseases. It points us to the precious word of God. With us there are a number that have betaken themselves to the book of God as the only resort of safety, as the only standard by which they are to be governed. The church in this place have begun to tear away the rubbish, the commandments of men, and are trying to build according to the pattern left by the apostles of Christ. Some laugh, others mock and say that it will soon be at an end; but the work goes on, and we are in full belief that the church will ere long become the joy of the whole earth, though men and devils may oppose. Let all those that love God immediately lend a helping hand, and especially those that see their errors. Let no worldly interest prevent you from coming up to the help of the Lord against the mighty foe. It would be better not to have known the way, than after we have known to refuse to walk in it.

I will mention one circumstance that has taken place among us, which will be a satisfaction to you. It is concerning a man who was formerly a Deist. I presented him with your third number addressed to a Sceptic. After reading it all his arguments against the bible were blown away like chaff. He was left without hope; the distress of his mind was depicted in his countenance, and no relief could he obtain until he repaired to his long neglected bible. Here he found relief. He now believes the bible is from God. He now believes with all his heart that Jesus Christ is the Son of God. He has been immersed into the name of the Father, Son, and Holy Spirit. He is walking in fellowship with the saints, and looking for that blessed hope, the glorious appearing of our Lord and Saviour Jesus Christ. These, sir, are some of the effects of the above publication alluded to among us. I believe it is a very good criterion to judge of the nature of things by their effects. We cannot expect that the church will come out of Babylon without great commotions in the world. Heaven must be shaken as well as earth. The shaking has begun, and we hope that it will continue until every human invention is shaken out.

Numbers appear to find fault with your style. They think that you are too harsh, and that your strokes are too severe. One person, however, does not wish to have the points of your arrows cut off; yet he appears to be a little uneasy. I suspect that they wish to have some of the beards taken off. If this is what they wish for, I for one should be opposed to it; for there are some which I have heard of who have been wounded, who have got rid of the spear; the scar, however, I believe they will carry to their graves. I should think that a few more beards would be very beneficial for those people, and I cannot see what harm they would be to any person; but I leave you to manage that matter as you may think proper.

With regard to the new translation, I am highly pleased with it; and the more I read it the better I like it. It does not, however, escape the censures of the priests, and many others who follow their pernicious ways speak evil of it. It is my opinion that many of those that have got into Moses' seat would make the people believe, if they could, that the old version fell down from heaven just as it came out of the hands of the king's translators. They would feign have the

people believe that it is the blackest crime that a man can be guilty of, to attempt a new translation. They talk about men laying their hands on the very word of God; and yet after all their ado, I have not heard of one sentence being justly condemned. Oh what will not priestcraft do? I will answer the question; it never has, nor never will lead the people to their bible and to their Saviour. I have heard of one man that has burnt the new translation—I think that it was a brother to one of the editors in Kentucky. It appears that he has loved the old translation ever since he was a boy. I must think that he has a greater regard for the king of Great Britain than he has for Dr. Campbell. Why he should prefer the king I know not, unless it be for this reason, that he is styled "Defender of the Faith." If the gentleman should be called to part with either his creeds or the old version, I seriously fear that king James would share the same fate with the Doctors of Scotland. But after all, I think that his aim was to give you, sir, a deadly blow. Harmless, indeed, was his weapon, and so will every other one be that is aimed at truth. Their reaction, however, will be severe, for they will fall on their own pates. May Heaven shield you in the day of battle; and when your work on earth is done, may you enter into the joys of your Lord.   A Friend to the Restoration
Of the Ancient Order of Things.
Columbus, May, 1827.

Potent Reply to a weak Objection.

"Pulling down every thing, and building up nothing," is an objection often presented against the Christian Baptist. The following reply to it from an English paper, is a perfect expression of our sentiments on the subject. The same things have in substance appeared in this work before.
Ed. C. B.

"But the charge of pulling down and not building up any thing in its stead, is, unintentionally, the highest compliment that can be paid to us. It is to this building up something, instead of what was pulled down, that we owe the evils of all pretended reformations, and it has served more than any thing else to perpetuate error, as it is a lamentable fact, that from Luther down all parties have set up a system of their own; not always indeed so repugnant to reason as that which they have destroyed, but so encompassed with hedges, that whoever have dared to go farther than they have done, have been considered as enemies to religion.

"We have nothing to build up. The fair fabric of christianity stands still as firm and conspicuous in the New Testament as ever it did; all we have got to do is to remove the walls, the buttresses, and rubbish, which prevent inquiring men from beholding it in its native purity, splendor, and loveliness; and when this is done, the superstructure will present itself to view—an object deserving of universal admiration; then nothing more will be requisite than to invite men to examine it, as it is fairly and clearly depicted in the New Testament."

For the "Christian Baptist."

Mr. Editor,—I have read many of your numbers with much interest; and believe that you have done the church of Christ essential service through the medium of the Christian Baptist. I have been for some years a member of the Baptist church, and have believed it to be as near "the ancient order of things" as any other sect of the day, and indeed nearer. Nevertheless, some of her practices I cannot approve of, for I am not so prejudiced in favor of my own sect that I am insensible to its blemishes. Permit me to mention one which has been adverted to in one of your numbers, viz. the mode of receiving candidates for baptism, on what is denominated their experience before the church.

The bishop takes his seat in some conspicuous part of the house; the members of the church seat themselves adjacent to him in a semicircle, and sometimes in the presence of unbelievers. The humble candidate is called upon to advance and stand or sit in their midst, and relate over his "travels from nature to grace;" he begins, "A great while ago, I was struck in my mind," &c. But you know the old tale, and the whole process. This weak and trembling individual (perhaps a female) whose mind is in a state of dreadful perturbation, is obliged to give such a detail as agrees with the peculiar feelings of those present, or else she cannot be received as a candidate for baptism. Now, it is manifestly certain that such a course was not pursued by the primitive churches. Reason, the propriety of things, nor the word of God will not sanction it.

Reason will not sanction it. The candidate is so much overawed by the presence of the bishop, deacons, the church, *en masse,* and unbelievers, that it is impossible that she could have a perfect command over her mind. She is aware that every word she utters, every sentiment she discloses, every feeling she defines, must undergo the rigid scrutiny of all present. One false step and she is rejected. Awful crisis! Portentous moment! She stands as a criminal at the bar in the presence of her judges, who at the end of her confession will pass the verdict of *Guilty,* or *Not Guilty.* I have seen men of strong nerves, of good understanding, who could converse sensibly on the christian religion around the social hearth, and could even speak eloquently on other subjects in public, turn pale, shake like the aspen, and be perfectly unmanned in attempting to relate their experience before the church as candidate for admission. But how much more severe is the trial for the young, the poor, the ignorant, and those who have not acquired confidence by mingling in society—if ever they have known the truth, scarcely a vestige of it can be traced by them, in consequence of the ebullition that is going on within their minds. The propriety of things and the ancient order of things alike forbid this practice. C.

Brother Campbell,—I read, with a great deal of pleasure, your Christian Baptist. Your April No. was truly pleasing. On some topics, however, introduced into that work, I have doubted whether the editor has not, in opposing error, sometimes gone to an extreme. I will specify one case—that of receiving members into the church on the bare expression or declaration made by the eunuch to Philip, the evangelist. Now, that, amongst the Baptists, there are sometimes many unnecessary questions asked, and many, very many unnecessary and enthusiastic things told, is admitted and lamented. It is also admitted that in the New Testament there is no example of any being received into the church or churches by the relation of a christian experience. But, brother, you admit on some other cases, (and that of divine command too) that a change of circumstances and customs may justify a change of practice, where the manifest design and spirit of the practice or command of Christ and his apostles are not violated; as in the case of the "holy kiss," five times enjoined by the apostles,

being strictly obeyed by the christian shake-hands, and this is argued from the change of custom and circumstances. Now that there is a change in the circumstances of the people in christian countries, when compared with those of apostolic ages, is manifest. Then the great question was, Is Jesus of Nazareth *the Christ*, or is he not?—Did he really rise from the dead, or did he not? The apostles and disciples of Christ, on the one part, affirmed; the unbelieving Jews and Gentiles, on the other part, denied and contradicted—and so unpopular was the bare confession that Jesus was "the Christ," that it subjected the person to infamy and reproach, if not to death. Under these circumstances, a bare declaration that they did believe Jesus was the Christ, and a desire publicly to obey him, was a sufficient evidence to the apostles and brethren that there was a change of heart. Add to this, also, the notable case of Ananias and Sapphira, his wife, who, for deception, were struck dead, producing fear on all the people, "and of the rest durst none join themselves to them."—But now circumstances are very different, (at least in some of these things;) now no great disgrace to profess that *Jesus is the Christ;* no great dishonor to obey him; no great fear of scourgings, imprisonments, and torturing deaths; no signal judgments on hypocrites and impostors, to make others fear. If, therefore, the apostles required the strongest evidence that *then* could be given of sincerity of heart, is it not reasonable that we should require the strongest evidence that can *now* be given of a real change of heart in those whom we invite into our union and fellowship as members of the kingdom of our Lord Jesus Christ? You will not understand me as supposing that the strongest evidence of a change of heart consists in a *systematic experience,* or that in this matter we are to measure ourselves by ourselves, or compare ourselves among ourselves: but as you admit that men must be *born again,* and that this change is more or less known, or knowable to the subjects of it, in proportion to their age and circumstances, and that such change is always followed by correspondent fruits of *love* to Christ, to holiness, and to christians, with a manifest abhorrence of sin, whether discovered in themselves or in others; of *joy* in believing in Christ, and in doing his will; of *peace* with *God* the Spirit, in the heart, crying Abba, Father! with *men,* in seeking their good, &c. &c. Shall we not, I say, require such a confession with the mouth, as will give us a charitable conviction that they have "believed with the heart unto righteousness;" and that according to their age, or the circumstances under which they have been raised, or in which they have lived. These remarks I submit to you with the confidence of a brother in Christ, believing, when understood, there will be no material difference of sentiment on this subject. Indeed I think I already understand you, but wish you to be more explicit for general satisfaction. You can make what use you please of any part of this letter; and as my name affixed to any composition of mine will likely never bring me to great honor, I wish it always to appear. I remain your unfeigned brother in Christ Jesus our Lord.   B. ALLEN.
     April 23d, 1827.

Reply.

BROTHER ALLEN—I perfectly agree with you "that we should require the strongest evidence that can now be given of a real change of heart in those whom we baptize." The only question then is, what is that evidence? We must re-

member that we have no right, no law, nor precedent for putting off an applicant for one single day. The applicant may, and indeed ought, to solicit baptism the hour he believes. We cannot say to him, Go and shew us by your works for a week, a month, or a year, that you are a genuine convert. This would be a glaring infraction of every principle, law and precedent in the kingdom of Jesus. What then? Shall we require the testimony of others respecting the character of the candidate? This cannot be satisfactory. They may tell us he is moral, virtuous, and was always so; or they way tell us that he is reformed; but still this is not sufficient evidence. Nay, should they testify that he is known to be devout, still a question arises, Why was he not long since immersed if so good a man—if so devout? We are at length reduced to a necessity of taking his own word and acting upon that. Now the question is, In reference to what shall we take his word? Shall we require him to declare what he believes or what he feels, or both? For the first we have apostolic example, but for no other. Suppose, however, that we have found a safer way, (the apostles were deceived sometimes,) and that circumstances have changed so far as to render the ancient order obsolete or unsuitable; for there is now no shame in professing, no danger of all those evils and terrors which you very properly enumerate—how shall we prove our way to be safer than the good old way? They never told their experience in order to baptism; but it is supposed that this new way is not liable to the same objections as the old way. But will you please consider that all the shame and terror which you have very properly detached from saying, "I believe with all my heart that Jesus is the Son of God," is also detached from a narrative of our feelings, of our journey from nature to grace." Now if the shame and terror prevented hypocrisy then, they might, if they still existed, prevent it still. But they do not exist, either in relation to the confession of faith or the narrative of experience and consequently can have no effect in the one case more than in the other. If, from the love of honor and absence of human terrors, men will solemnly declare a lie in professing their faith, they will solemnly tell a lie in narrating an experience which they never felt, and which, if they did feel, is to us not so sure an evidence of a change of heart as a declaration of the precious faith. For we are assured that all who believe what they confess, are begotten by God; but we are not sure that all who have felt as that candidate feels, are begotten by God. I am, therefore, dear brother, fully convinced that the good old way affords us the strongest evidence that the nature of the case admits.

A change of circumstances cannot be plead against the ancient, nor in favor of the new way—for circumstances equally affect both. Nor would I carry the argument from a change of circumstances so far in relation to the topic which you mention against any instituted item of religious worship. A brother in Maryland wrote me a long letter in favor of the holy kiss, which was received after my departure from home last Fall. I had intended it for publication, but it has been jostled out. He lays great stress upon the five times commanded, and inveighs against my reasoning on a change of circumstances or customs. Had I published his letter, I should have illustrated one point not stated in my remarks upon "the holy kiss," and which would have shown that a change of circumstances and customs was not the reasoning which sets aside a holy kiss in our country. Advocates for this usage deceive themselves by inserting a definite article and by rejecting the indefinite which always precedes the terms holy kiss. It is not *the* holy kiss, but *a* holy kiss. All instituted acts of religion are characterized by the definite article, as, the Lord's table, the Lord's day, &c. It is one thing to command a holy kiss, and another to command the holy kiss. The former style is decisive evidence that it was no stated institution, while the latter would most certainly have shown it to be established—against which no change of circumstances could be plead; but as it is, a change of circumstances can be plead with good effect. This, in passing, is a caveat against a licentious principle of reasoning in opposition to plainly and solemnly ordained usages and sacred institutes.

I am willing, brother Allen, to give to your reasoning all due regard, and I have no doubt but what you have written is as much to the purpose as any man can adduce; but you will see that while we equally agree that the strongest evidence which can be adduced ought to be demanded, the only question of moment is, What is the strongest evidence?

I will admit that if there is any ground to suspect the sincerity of the applicant, or any intimation of any improper motive impelling him to solicit the ordinance, I would sift him to the bottom, and, on suspicious evidence, say to him, Go and bring forth fruits worthy of your profession. But where there is no ground of suspicion, and the person freely comes forward and solicits baptism upon a solemn declaration of what the eunuch professed, I would say nothing should hinder his baptism, and no experience be inquired after. A person can have little or no christian experience until he is born of water and of the Spirit; and it does appear to me preposterous to demand the experience of a christian from a person who has not yet put on Christ, not dead by sin, nor buried, nor risen with Christ. When a person has come out of the bath of regeneration, and has been born of the Spirit and the water, we look for the experience of a christian; but it will take more logic than all the colleges in your state possess, to persuade me that it is reasonable to demand a narrative of christian experience from a person who has never publicly confessed the Lord Jesus, nor assumed his name. Yours, most affectionately,

EDITOR.

Extracts from a variety of Letters,

The number and length of which preclude the insertion of them in any reasonable time.

Two Objections from a Correspondent in Richmond, February 8th, 1827.

OBJECTION 1st.

IT is objected to the adoption of the term *contribution* instead of the term *fellowship*, (*Acts* ii. 42.) "that the disciples at that time had all things common, and consequently there was no need for a *contribution*." We admit that where a perfect community exists, there is no need nor means for a contribution to create a fund. But even then there is need for a *distribution* from the common stock, and this distribution amongst the individuals is a *contribution* to their wants. But if a community of goods in the Jerusalem congregation did not divest the disciples of the means of their feasting in love from house to house, it could not supersede the necessity of statedly joining in *contributing* to the necessity of saints; either by a *distribution* from a common stock, or by a *contribution* continually augmenting both from new accessions and from the household portions of those who still superabounded. It is not necessary in order to a contribution that every individual must have something to give—there must be some to receive before there can be a fellowship in giving and receiving. The κοινωνια, or *fellowship*, (*Acts* ii. 42.) is something obviously distinct from every other part of the worship and order of the congregation in Jerusalem. They had what we call *fellowship* in every thing; but there was a certain joint participation in one work of religious obedience and brotherly love which emphatically was the fellowship, contribution, or distribution. The term *contribution* we yet think is the most appropriate, because it includes in the sacred usage the idea of distributing—of giving and receiving.

OBJECTION 2d.

"I allude to the note to Galatians iii. 20. "Now a mediator is not a mediator of one; but God is one." I cannot help thinking there must be an error in both translations, (or all given) and in your reasoning on the passage also; and that the error mainly consists in connecting the *mediator* with the *law*. I was, and still am, unable to see the propriety of this; and an examination of the text and context, particularly in the common translation, induced me to think that the error had arisen from a slight inversion of the words in the sentence. The term *law*, seems to carry with it nothing like the notion of an agreement of parties, either existing or proposed; but is the language of unconditional command, addressed by him who has full power and authority, to him who is bound to receive and obey. What place or propriety is there here for the office of a mediator? I can find none. The term *mediator*, however, while it necessarily supposes a variance, presents at once the idea of a proposed healing of that variance, and reconciliation of the parties—and to effect this is the great purpose of the mediatorial office. It appears to me then that the meaning of the passage will be given thus—"Wherefore then the law? Because of offences, it was added, to be in force till the seed should come, to whom was made the promise of the inheritance; which *promise* was ordained by angels in the hand of a *mediator;* or thus—which promise, being ordained through a mediator, was made known by the hand of messengers, (Moses and the other prophets.) Now a mediator necessarily implies two parties, and without the consent of both, a covenant between them cannot be annulled: but God, who gave the law, is only one party; therefore this covenant of promise cannot be impaired by the law." The *seed* and the *mediator*, I suppose, mean the same person; and though the promise be, in form, to him, it is, in *substance*, through him, to mankind, the offenders, and one of the parties at variance; and who, by reason of sin, were disqualified (as in worldly concerns are infants and *femes covert*) to covenant in person. The apostle has argued, *that faith in Christ delivers from the law:* and to remove the apparent objection to this position, presented by the question, To what end then was the law given? he recalls to their minds the fact, that the inheritance was promised through a *mediator;* a person whose name not only infers two parties at variance, but the proposed reconciliation of those parties; that this term *mediator,* then necessarily includes the idea of the concurring will of two parties uniting and centering in *the person of the mediator:* and affirms, that the *law* was added, to operate only until the mediator should appear and the reconciliation of these parties be effected by him; and that this *law,* which was the act of only one of these parties, could not possibly have the effect of diminishing the certainty and stability of the *promise,* which could only be annulled, altered, or impaired, by the will of both parties; and proves the necessity of the concurrence of both parties, to effect any such alteration, by the introduction of the *mediator,* the personal representative of both. Thus, I think, the apostle effectually removes the objection to his position, that faith in Christ delivers from the bondage of the law, supposed by the question, Wherefore then the law? by showing that there is nothing in the nature, or end, of the law, at variance with that position. I cannot regard Moses as possessing any of the great characteristics of *the mediator.* He was a faithful servant of God, as a messenger to the people; but had none of the distinguishing powers of the mediator, no power to negociate any permanent peace between the parties. Of this office, though faithful, he was not worthy. Nor do I believe that the term is applied to him in any instance; unless, indeed, in that we have been considering, which I consider a mistake. 2d *Timothy* ii. 5. Paul says, " There is one God, and *one mediator* between God and man, the man Christ Jesus." And as there is certainly but one God, I suppose Paul may be regarded as affirming that there is only *one mediator.*"

I have three insuperable objections to this interpretation of the passage:—

1st. It subverts the idea of the law being a covenant. This it most certainly was. It is repeatedly styled "*the covenant;*" the tables on which it was engraved are called "the two *tables* of the *covenant;*" and it is always kept in contrast with the *new* and *better* covenant, established on better *promises;* but this is not all—the whole circumstances of its promulgation make every precept a separate item of one grand national covenant. The preliminaries were distinctly stated and acceded to by the Jews before an item of it was pronounced; and when the whole was written on parchment, Moses, its mediator, by a divine command, sprinkled the book with blood, saying, " This is the blood of *the covenant* which God has enjoined upon you." They who violated these precepts were said to have " *broken* the covenant;" and so soon as the nation apostatized to idolatry, as a nation, they broke the covenant and were given over to their enemies.

2d. It destroys the character of Moses as a *mediator.* Moses most unquestionably was a mediator. He describes his office at the time of the giving of the law most minutely, (*Deut.* ii.) " The Lord our God made a covenant with us in Horeb. *I stood between* the Lord and you at that time to shew you tne word of the Lord." And Jesus is in contrast, as the antitype, styled " the mediator of a better covenant." *Heb.* viii. 6. The ministry of Moses as the mediator, is inferior to the ministry of Jesus as a mediator, and a correct idea of the latter can only be obtained through a scriptural view of the former. Independently of the passage under consideration, Moses is represented in the character and office of a mediator.

I beg leave to correct a popular mistake relative to mediation and the office of mediator. It never was necessary nor compatible with the relations between Heaven and Earth, that any person should be appointed both by Heaven and Earth to the office of mediator. The mediation and the mediator are gracious appointments of " one of the parties" only, if we may so use the term; nor is the mediation conducted on the same principles as if parties offended and of equal dignity were to be reconciled. The mediation of Moses and of his antitype are gracious appointments of the Father of Mercies, and are not to be exactly measured by our practices.

3d. It is at variance with the fixed principles of all languages I know any thing of, and most assuredly with the original, to substitute promise instead of law in the hand of angels. The word answering in grammatical construction with *diatageis,* "ordained," is not *epangelia,* "promise," but *nomos,* "law." To affirm that George IV. is queen of England, is not more at variance with our idiom, than to say that the promise was ordained by angels, or through a mediator. Law is masculine in Greek, and promise is feminine, and ordained is of the same gender with law and not with promise. I have sundry other objections to this interpretation, but these three I deem quite sufficient. I am still of opinion that the Note, No. 78, Appendix to the new translation, is the correct view of this passage. This opinion does not, however, stand the least in my way of hearing and examining any other that may be offered, nor of adopting a more satisfactory one when it comes documented with superior claims upon my reason. I have great respect for the writer of the letter from which the above extracts are made. He thinks closely on the great subject of christianity; but this passage has puzzled many commentators, and for many years I could see no meaning in it. I do not know that any commentator gives the views in the new translation.   EDITOR.

—

Queries.

The following four questions are from a correspondent in Essex county, Virginia:—

1. Has the gospel, as it now stands on record, influence or power in itself, without the agency of the Holy Spirit, to regenerate and make a man a new creature? And if it has or has not, please to tell us how that change is brought about.

2. Is not saving faith wrought in the heart by the influence of the Holy Spirit; and can a man have saving faith without that influence on his soul? I say saving faith, because it is evident that the New Testament speaks of two sorts of faith, let the Philadelphia bishop say what he may to the contrary.

3. What does the apostle mean when he says, " If by grace, then it is no more of works, otherwise grace is no more grace?"

4. And when he says, " Unto them which are called, both Jews and Greeks, Christ the power of God and the wisdom of God," what sort of a calling does he here allude to?

Answers.

1. To answer this question with a yea or a nay, might comport with a system already received or rejected by the querist; but either a yea or a nay would be incompatible with the genius and spirit of the inspired volume. To separate and distinguish the Spirit from its own word is the radix of unhallowed speculation. What the gospel, written or spoken, does in regenerating or purifying the heart, the Spirit of God does, and what the Spirit of God does, the gospel spoken or written does. Those who resist the gospel proclamation, resist the Spirit of God; and those who resist the Spirit of God, resist and reject the gospel

proclamation. Suppose I were asked, "Has the sun, the earth, the water, and the air, power or influence of themselves, independent of the influence of God, to make an ear of corn from one grain deposited in the earth," I could not answer it by a yea or a nay; but i could say that God creates the corn, and that the sun, the earth, the water and the air were media through which, and through which only, the divine influence was exhibited. So that they stand to the corn planted as the power of God. And if I were asked, Why does not the word written or spoken exhibit the same power in all who read and hear it, I would say it was owing to the same cause why every grain of wheat or corn which is deposited in the earth does not produce a ripe ear. The Saviour himself justifies this analogy between things natural and moral. See his parable of the sower and his seed.

2. From the answer above given to query first, I am authorized to say that "saving faith" is wrought in the heart by the Holy Spirit, and that no man can believe to the saving of his soul but by the Holy Spirit. I waive the question about two kinds of faith. Unfeigned faith or true faith is what is meant by "saving faith;" and feigned faith, "false" faith, or "dead" faith, are not saving.

3. Paul means that grace or favor, and desert are antipodes. Whatever is of the one cannot be of the other. Every thing in our salvation is of pure favor. A. by a mere act of favor, or a deed of gift, invests B. with a large farm amply sufficient for all the purposes of life. He afterwards writes him a letter, informing him that if he does not practise temperance, if he does not take exercise, if he does not mingle labor and rest, and avoid every excess, he cannot live nor be happy. Now he that argues that B. obtained the estate by his works, is in error; and every one who says that, without the works enjoined by A. in his epistle, B. can live and be happy, is in an error; and every one who says that B. got the farm as a reward of his works, says what is not true.

4. Christ is the power of God to all the called. The term called is used in a twofold sense in the New Testament: 1st. As descriptive of all who hear the word of life—and 2d. As descriptive of all those who receive it. The former is its general—the latter, its special acceptation. The "many called" are all who hear, the "few chosen" are all who obey. The former slight the call—the latter make it certain. The former treat their calling and election as idle and unmeaning compliments—the latter make them sure and enjoy the special benefits thereof. To the latter only, to those who accept the call, is Christ the power of God to salvation. The obedient are the "effectually" called, and the disobedient are the ineffectually called.

The writer of the above queries had not read the second volume of this work when he proposed them. Were it not for the extreme sensibility of some taught in human schools, either old or new, on these topics, we should exclude them from our pages, as the most fatal of all the speculations in religion which generated in the dark ages. That man has true faith or saving faith who obeys the Lord Jesus Christ, and he that disobeys him has either no faith at all, or a dead faith. He is regenerated who believes and obeys the Lord Jesus sincerely, and he is unregenerated who does not. The truth believed purifies the heart—and no heart can be purified without

it. And every question, which, when answered, does not lead to some good practice, is as idle as the theory of captain Symmes. His theory of the earth is of as much use to my corn field, as the grand things sought after in the above four queries are to the soul of the querist. The next generation will admit this; but few of the present can. Many seem to be more concerned about my regeneration than they are about their own; than they are about the many good things I am habitually calling their attention to. While I cannot but feel grateful to them for their solicitude, I should like to see them evince very clearly the purity of their hearts by a holy life; that is, by a life of obedience to the Son of God, in all the commandments and institutions of the King, whether of an individual or social character. Happy only are the pure in heart, for they shall see God.   EDITOR.

Queries.

1. WHAT is the work of an evangelist? It was the business of proclaiming the gospel to those who never heard it. It is the same thing still. Before the gospel was generally announced persons were devoted exclusively to this work. And now-a-days much of this work is done by christian parents to their children, and by the overseers of the churches. So that in christian countries there is not the same reasons existing for an order of persons exclusively devoted to this work as there was in the apostolic age. See the essays on the work of the Holy Spirit, volume second.

2. What should be the qualifications of those who administer the ordinances of the christian church? "The administration of ordinances" is a popish phrase, and ought to be cashiered from the christian vocabulary. Persons appointed by the church or christian congregation, having the qualifications which Paul lays down for overseers, and public servants, or deacons, when attending their respective duties, are "administering all the ordinances" of the christian church. The election or appointment of the church is that which gives them an official right to act in an official capacity. Any person appointed by a church to baptize, has a right to do it.

3. Did not Philip and other primitive preachers usually take "a text?" Philip's text was in *Isaiah* 53. when he converted the eunuch. And Paul preached in Athens from a text. This is more like a quiz upon the textuaries than any thing else. One might more easily make a pope out of Paul than a textuary. If there was any thing like a text in the case of Philip, it was the eunuch that selected it; and if answering a question upon any passage out of the Old Testament or New, or out of a Grecian poet, furnishes a model for text-taking and sermonizing—then the sprinkling of bells, and the wearing of official vestments, and the laying of corner stones, and the consecrating of grave yards, can easily be proved from scriptures. This query does not merit a serious reply. No prophet nor apostle nor divinely called preacher ever took a text or made a sermon in our sense of the words, from the days of Moses till the days of Origen, the inventor of a thousand errors. The quoting of any passage or the commencing with any sentence, no more makes that sentence a text in our usage, than the preaching of Balaam's ass made him a christian evangelist.   EDITOR.

CHRISTIAN BAPTIST.

NO. I.—VOL. V. BETHANY, BROOKE CO. VA., AUGUST 6, 1827.

Style no man on earth your Father: for he alone is your Father who is in heaven: and all ye are brethren. Assume not the title of Rabbi; for ye have only One Teacher; neither assume the title of Leader; for ye have only One Leader— the Messiah. *Messiah.*

PREFACE TO VOLUME V.

THOUGH opposed by a great variety of character, ways and means, and though opposing the defections and apostacies of this age, the Christian Baptist continues to extend its circulation, and to augment the number of its patrons. From the first number to the last published, it has progressively advanced in public regard and esteem, if a continued increase of friends and advocates may be considered a good omen. The fifth volume we are permitted to commence under circumstances still more propitious than those under which we commenced the last.

When I say that there is no periodical work of the same character amongst the scores of the day; none conducted on the same principles; none directed to objects perfectly similar; none exhibiting with equal fulness both sides of every subject discussed—I only say what hundreds have already said, and what all who read it, and other publications of the day do know. But when I say, I am interested and disinterested in the further progress and success of the work, I must offer an explanation. I am interested, because I am more and more confidently assured of the truth and importance of the general views which it exhibits, and because I cannot doubt but that a state of things, such as it contemplates, must supplant the carnal, worldly and superstitious establishments, so popular in this day; each of which owes its origin to an ecclesiastical council and its creed. With these views I cannot look around, even as a spectator, without feeling a high and intense interest in its success. I am also disinterested, inasmuch as I have committed it to the patronage of Heaven, and am satisfied to await the result. And I cannot but think it very unbecoming, when we commit any thing to the guidance, control, or blessing of the Lord of All, to feel solicitous about the issue. As to my worldly interest in the work, which the weakness and ill will of some have magnified into a *primum mobile,* I feel no concern. Sixteen years ago the devil whispered into my ear that I might get a good benefice in one of the honorable sects of the day; or if I would prefer a seat in the bar or in the temple of legal science, I might promise myself a good little fortune in wealth and fame. I will always thank God that, poor and inexperienced as I then was, I had strength to resist the temptation, and to vow allegiance to the bible. But if the contents of the volumes already published will not attest my independence of mind, singleness of object and aim, and disregard of human applause, except that of doing good, I should fear that reason and argument would be offered in vain.

The policy and the measures adopted both by my open, avowed and determined opponents, and by the masked, double minded, and double tongued, faltering and wavering adversaries, have inspired me with more confidence in my means and resources—with more assurance of the truth and triumphing pretensions of the cause I espouse—with more disdain for error itself, and the low cunning, pusilanimous intrigues and cowardly artifice by which it strives to creep into notice, or to keep fast its unauthorized hold upon the passions and prejudices of those who will not think, and therefore cannot act for, or from themselves.

Amongst all the combatants who have appeared in their proper name, or under a mask, in the "Baptist Recorder," the "Western Luminary," the "Pittsburgh Recorder," and the other "lights" of the day, who has made good a single position, a charge, accusation, or specification, either against the New Translation or any leading point in this work, by any thing like argument, reason or testimony? The history of my friend Skillman, with his friend Steel, alias "Friend of Truth," alias "Vindex," &c. &c. is the history of them all. The winking and hoodwinking, the insinuating and criminating, the masking and unmasking, the fearing and doubting, and I wish I had no reason to add, the equivocating and misrepresenting, of such opponents, only beget doubts in the bosoms of their friends, deepen the convictions, and confirm the confidence of those who cannot unite nor fraternize with them. Let my opponents name the man who has not retreated from the ground so soon as the troops were marshalled. Let them count how many have even stood till the battle was set in order. How powerful is truth, and how bold too!! How imbecile is error, and how dastardly too!!

I wish to state it again most distinctly, that not one of the essays on the "Restoration of the Ancient Order of Things," has been impugned or seriously objected to from any quarter whatever. The same, indeed, might be said of almost every leading position in the whole work. The truth is, light is increasing. Many of those who have opposed us in one way or another, have been convinced; and some of those yet opposing would much rather wear the mask than risk their persons. They have not confidence in themselves. Many, too, who have been for years teaching things which they now know they ought not to have taught, are extremely hard pressed between conscience and rabbinical pride. Conscience says, "Confess your error and reform." But the pride that comes from the sacred desk, says, "No; the people will honor me

1

no more." There is a volume here in one sentence. And since the days of John the Immerser until now, the kingdom of heaven is invaded, and invaders take possession by force. The laity have had to invade it, and to raise up captains, and colonels, and generals, from among themselves; for the disciplined, and by law established, captains and commanders would not march at their head.

I trust I will make this volume as interesting as any one which has preceded it. I have the means. I never was at any time in my life more open to conviction than I now am, and I never felt more confident of the cause of which I am the humble advocate—either of its superlative excellency or of its ultimate success. May the Lord grant his blessing, without which, Paul himself might plant, and Apollos, too, might water in vain. Editor.

Review of Dr. Noel's Circular.—No. I.

A circular letter written for the Franklin Association, Ky., 1826, by the reverend Silas M. Noel, D. D. on the creed question, was republished in the Baptist Recorder, and lately republished in Cincinnati. On my late tour I was often told that it was represented and held by the advocates of human creeds, as an unanswerable performance; as the best thing ever written on the subject; that it settled the controversy forever, &c. &c. Hearing it so highly extolled, and being so well acquainted with the versatile genius of its author, I read it with great attention, and whether it was owing to my expectation being too much elated, or to some other cause, I vouch not; but in truth, it appeared to me much below the ordinary talent of the writer, and extremely imbecile. It is, indeed, as strong in assertion and as weak in argument as any piece I have seen on the subject written in the current century. It is a condensed view of the Princeton pamphlet, in some of its strongest positions; but when apparelled in a new dress it is still more awkward and unsightly than in the full uniform of Doctor Miller.

The Doctor's starting point is this:—"Creeds formed or enforced by the civil authority, are usurpations leading to persecution and to despotism, while those formed by voluntary associations of christians, enforced by no higher penalty or sanction than exclusion from mere membership in the society, are not only lawful but necessary in the present state of the religious world." This is a mere assertion and a distinction without a difference. Creeds formed by "voluntary associations" whether convened by the state or the church are alike voluntary; alike in their tendency and results. And while the Doctor gravely makes the sanctions of those voluntary civil creeds greater than the sanctions of the voluntary ecclesiastical creeds, they are in fact, and in effect, the same. The sanction of such creeds as the Doctor advocates, he kindly and politely calls "*mere exclusion* from membership" in the kingdom of heaven, while the sanction of the creed he condemns is worse than mere exclusion from that kingdom; that is, civil pains, such as confiscation of goods, exile, imprisonment, or death. So that exclusion from temporal advantages is much greater in the Doctor's view than exclusion from the kingdom of heaven. The Doctor, I admit, does not speak out so explicitly as he would do in a better cause. He does not like to appear on this occasion, with Peter's girdle and the keys of the kingdom of heaven dangling on his loins. This he knew would illy comport with the leathern girdle of the Harbinger, and would not suit the spirit or taste of this age. But when we draw aside the Doctor's surplice we shall, under the leathern girdle, see the mighty keys, somewhat rusted it is true, but cast in the good old Roman mould, with the sublime initials of P. M. V. I. C. with the good old motto "*Procul profanes*"—Hence you profane.

The short metre of the Doctor's music is this: Our church is the church of Jesus Christ, called in the New Testament, "the kingdom of heaven," and all who are worthy members of it, shall be worthy members in the kingdom of glory; all who are justly excluded from it, are justly excluded from the kingdom of glory—because we act by the authority of the great King, and we all allow that the great King will not exclude, nor allow to be excluded, from his kingdom on earth, such as he will receive into his kingdom of glory.

I know how the Doctor would try to save himself here. He would tell us that he does not consider his church as the only church of Christ, and he will very courteously and kindly tell all his orthodox neighboring churches that they are all churches of Jesus Christ, equally with his own; and that by his sanctions to his creed, he means no more than to tell the excluded that he is not quite so good company as he could wish, but that he can be accommodated equally well with a place in some other good natured church of Christ; and that he hopes to meet him in the heavenly kingdom though he has some objections to fraternizing with him "in the present state of the religious world." Here Doctor Miller and Doctor Noel politely and graciously shake hands, and bid each other good bye—and in parting, say, You, dear Doctor, keep your church *pure* from me by your creed, and I will keep my church *pure* from you by my creed, but, God bless you, dear brother Doctor, for although "in the present state of the religious world" it is fitting that you should commune under your creed, and I under the banners of mine, I do believe we shall commune in heaven together, and be both welcomed there by the great King as good and faithful servants; *I* for *excluding you*, and *you* for *excluding me*. The Princeton Doctor says, O dear Doctor Noel! I will receive you into my pure communion, will you not receive me!! The Doctor of Oakley rejoins, farewell, Doctor Miller; I thank you for your assistance in the creed question; but while you rantize these little puklings I do not like to sit by your side—excuse me, dear Doctor, I love you and we will both feast at the same table above.

In this pithy, polite, and good natured way, our Baptist Doctor excuses himself for all the sanctions of his creed—which means neither proscription, nor persecution; tyranny, nor usurpation; but a little good natured chicanery.

But to quote Horace once more, as I know one Aleph in Kentucky, who has a dictionary of quotations,

"Sed tamen amoto queramas seria ludo;"

let us come to the starting point again. The Doctor begins this puissant circular with a *petitio principii*, and ends with an *argumentum ad verecundiam*. But for the present we shall canvass his Alpha or his Aleph, and leave Omega till another day. To tell the naked truth with that candor and simplicity which I desire always to be characteristic of my pen—it is all downright sophistry from first to last. And I did wish never to be called to notice this letter, because of my personal regard for its author. But when solemnly called to the task, we must know no man after the flesh. I will then, as far as in me lies, repress this pen of mine from all irony or satire, and with the utmost gravity examine the capital assumptions of the writer.

It is assumed that mere exclusion from membership in a society claiming the high title and character of a church of Jesus Christ, is a sanction to a human creed of no such great moment as the persecutions and proscriptions which sanction human creeds framed by civil power. This is obviously a fundamental error. The excluded are generally proscribed to the utmost extent of the excluders. If it be so that the excluded from any church in the government, are not injured in their political character and standing, we have reason to thank the liberality and independence of those who brought about such a state of civil society, and not the creed nor the priest which excludes. But I do most sincerely think that it is no small matter, no " mere" little thing to be solemnly proscribed the kingdom of heaven by those little idols which the sects worship, whether authorized by letters patent from the sceptre or from the mitre. And however we may choose to word it, when we desire to carry our point with guile, to exclude a man from " mere membership" in the church, is an act of the most awful import, and unless sanctioned by the great King and head of all authority and power, it is an usurpation and a tyranny, than which there is not any more heinous.

Again, the Doctor assumes that " creeds *formed* and *enforced*" by a voluntary association are *lawful*. But he has forgotten to lay before us the *law* and the testimony. To assert that such are lawful is not enough—we want to *see* the law. But this cannot be shown, and therefore we cannot see it. It may be lawful in the civil code of Kentucky or of Scotland; but we are not to be satisfied with civil statutes in matters of this sort. Let us have a divine law authorising a voluntary association to form and enforce any religious creed, and we will yield the point at issue. But until this is done we must view the assumption as perfectly gratuitous.

In the next place the Doctor assumes that churches are " voluntary associations." These terms ought not to pass current until tried. Human establishments of a sectarian character, may, perhaps, be called " voluntary associations," because begotten and born of the will of man. But I am far, very far, from granting that the church of Jesus Christ is a " voluntary association." Men and women, it is true, ought to become members of it with their own consent. But the constitution and laws and institutes of this society are not at our option nor rejection. No man can reject, or new modify, or refuse them obedience, and be guiltless. No man is allowed of his own will and free consent to make a church covenant, to decree church laws, or institute any religious observance. I wish for a definition of the terms *voluntary association* when applied to the church of Christ. I promise to show that if the Doctor attempts this he either refutes his own circular or directly assails the New Covenant or constitution of the kingdom of heaven.

I offer these remarks upon the Doctor's starting point alone. His letter wants method. He ought first to have given his definition of a creed, and then to have given the law and the testimony. But he begins as I have noticed and then gives his definition. His definition I will attend to in my next.

EDITOR.

Deism and the Social System.—No. III.

NONE of the gentlemen Free-Thinkers, none of the Deistical Philosophers of the city of " Mental Independence," nor any where else, as far as I have seen, have as yet, either deigned or ventured to meet me on the premises submitted in my last. Gentlemen, this will not do. This will neither comport with the artificial dignity of your profession, with the ground you have assumed, nor with the awful magnitude of the subject. You have erected a temple, in which you have constructed a throne, and on it you have crowned *Reason*, the arbiter of every question. I approach the altar you have dedicated— I have read the inscription thereon. I will dare to enter barefoot into your sacred edifice, and will make my appeal to your own goddess. Come then, and let us implead one another. In my last I stood at your threshold. I submitted my premises; I propounded the grand interrogatories, against which your sovereign arbitress said not one word. If you are silent here, it augurs badly for your reputation, it comports not with the loftiness of your pretensions, and with your former assurance.

If I may judge from all the samples I have ever seen of the whole of your resources, gentlemen, I must think your cause the most desperate of all causes ever plead at midnight or at noon. You have no premises, and how can you have any conclusion? If you have premises, let us see them explicitly and definitely laid down. Your friend, the "Inquirer," of whom I have made mention, in all the pieces I have seen from his pen, has given us not so much as an axiom, postulatum, or proposition. The sum of his first number is, that he was once a *true* believer in revelation, and that he is now a *true unbeliever;* and the reason he gives for being an unbeliever is, that he " could not help finding traces of ignorance in the scriptures." The only conclusion that I can draw from his first essay is, that he was once a true believer without evidence, and he is now a true unbeliever without reason. My conclusion I contend, is perfectly logical, for he gives no reason why he once believed, and I will show he gives no reason why he now disbelieves. A person who tells us that he was a true believer of a lie, means, I suppose, that he was a sincere believer of a lie, and intends that we should consider him at that time as a dupe of others. Indeed he publicly professes himself to have been once the dupe of others; for he sincerely believed what he now acknowledges to be a lie. This will not prove, either on Aristotle's or Lord Bacon's plan, that he is not now the dupe of others or of himself. For if he once sincerely believed a lie, it is neither absurd nor impossible to suppose that he *now* sincerely believes a lie. He would have saved himself of many a blunder, and us of a little trouble, if he had told us all the evidences on which he once believed the lie, and had contrasted them with all the evidences on which he now believes what he calls truth. The fact, however, is, that he has now no faith at all, either true or false; for faith without testimony cannot exist. And as he has no testimony that the Bible history is untrue, he cannot believe that it is not true. For a man to say that he believes the Bible is not true, is just as incongruous as for a man to say, I see without light. Now as there is no *opposing* testimony to that of the Jewish or Christian historians, no man can say that he believes the Bible history to be false. And here let me ask in passing this quagmire, Is there any cotemporary historian with Moses, Matthew,

Mark, Luke, or John, who contradicts their testimony? If so, produce it.

But I must not omit to show that this honest "Inquirer" is, in his own sense of the words, and in his own logic, as fully deceived now as he admits he once was. He was once a true believer without evidence. This he declares. Now I say that he is a "true" disbeliever without reason or evidence. And from his own pen I will bring the proof. In his first essay he says he 'could not help finding traces of ignorance in the writers of the Bible.' At this discovery his faith exploded. But what was the *ignorance* he could not help finding? This is the question. Would you laugh if I told you that it is this? He discovered that Moses was *ignorant* of the art of steam-boat building!! He does not say so, I admit; but, in effect, he says the same. His starting point is this, (No. 2.) "The ancients had no correct knowledge either of astronomy or natural history, and the writers of the scriptures if they *be not* inspired may be expected to exhibit such misconceptions on those subjects as we know to have characterized the age in which they lived. In this view of the subject let us examine the account of the creation according to Moses."——Ay, indeed, "in this view of the subject" he examines the account of the creation. Let us now state the counter part of his position in his own style. "The ancients had no correct knowledge either of astronomy or of natural history: and the writers of the scriptures, if they *be inspired*, must be expected to exhibit such conceptions on these subjects as we know not to have characterized the age in which they lived"—— And thus have rendered themselves incredible, I say. For should a man pretend to write the history of the first settlement of Virginia, and tell us about their navigating the James river in steamboats, two centuries ago, and pretend that he lived at that time, he would destroy the credibility of his own work. And so Mr. "Inquirer" would have had Moses to have exhibited, "*if inspired*," conceptions of astronomy and natural history as we know did not characterize the age in which he lived. This is the honest frontispiece of "all the ignorance he could not help finding in the Bible."

In the first step the "Inquirer" made, the following errors are adopted as axioms of undoubted truth:—

1. That men inspired to teach religion should be inspired with the knowledge of all natural science.

2. That to render a witness credible on one subject, it is necessary that he should speak our views on every conceivable topic.

3. That a writer who wrote three thousand years ago, should adopt a style of writing and exhibit views of things not known or entertained by any people on earth for a thousand years after he died, in order to make his narrative credible.

That I do no injustice to him will appear from the following question. After telling us the ancient and modern views of the earth's figure, and of the heavenly bodies, he asks "Does Moses, as an inspired writer, discover by preternatural (a blunder—it should have been *supernatural*) assistance the truth on these subjects; or does he, like an erring unenlightened man, give in to the popular errors of his times?" If not, I will not believe him to have been inspired in astronomy, [legitimate conclusion!]—no, not so reasonable—I will not believe him to have been inspired in any thing he wrote or taught!! No wonder this gentleman ceased to be a true believer in the Bible.

After all his feeble attempts to caricature the Mosaic account of the creation of this mundane system, he fails to shew that Moses committed one single blunder, Sir Isaac Newton himself being judge. His account of the gradual developement of things during the space of six evenings and mornings is neither contrary to, nor incompatible with, any established truth in the principles of Sir Isaac or of Galileo. But my intention was not to prosecute this subject farther in this essay than to expose the fallacy of the starting point of this true unbeliever. I wished to test the *rationale* of his system; and if I have not shewn it to his satisfaction, on hearing his complaint I will be more full and copious in the developement. It is the *rationale* of the system I first attack. I would not give a pin for an arithmetical defence of the size or of the contents of Noah's ark, nor for an astronomical explanation of the Mosaic account of the creation, to confute or refute the puerile cavils of any conceited sceptic; while I can, by a single impulse of my great toe, kick from under him the stool on which he sits, astride the mighty gulf, the fathomless abyss, whence he cannot rise by all the implements and tacklings in the great Magazine of sceptical resources.   EDITOR.

For the "Christian Baptist."

MR. EDITOR:—WILL you please present to the public generally, and to the person addressed particularly, through your columns the following remarks. I conceive them due to you and the public. A responsible person, has now presented himself before the public, in the shape of an opponent, and is bound by every tie that religion or good breeding can offer, either to bear himself out in his assertions, or to recall the remarks he has made. There are multitudes, both in Virginia and Kentucky, as well as elsewhere, deeply interested in the calm and able discussion of those points which now cause so much emotion.

I have not the pleasure of an acquaintance, personally with the excellent man I now address; but from my youth have heard his praises spoken. If any one be able to examine these matters in a christian-like and able manner, my information leads me to believe that he is the man. He will I doubt not, feel himself bound by the fear of God and the good of men, to avoid that light, ridiculous, and unmanly, as well as unchristian course, that his pupil "Aleph" has thought proper to adopt, for the purpose of bringing odium upon what he cannot confute, and which he has acknowledged to be "a state of things much to be desired."

I feel myself personally interested in this matter. If you are presenting the christian community with a number of "*chimeras*," I wish to reject them; and am certain that in thus saying I express the feelings, the sincere feelings of many pious and intelligent professors of the christian religion in Kentucky. But if this assertion is made without proof, the writer ought to consider himself responsible for circulating that which is without proof.

I hope, sir, that I shall not be considered in the light of an intruder in making this address, or as wishing by any means to provoke an unprofitable controversy: but that I shall be believed in saying that I desire, above all things, to see the christian communities united upon the one foundation.

I humbly conceive, sir, that our teachers do not go to the root of the matter in this examination. They (that is to say, the Baptists) seem to forget that there are any christians in the world but themselves, and that their own sect is the only religious community known. And this feeling is too common to all sects. Now, sir, there are other denominations in the world as numerous, as intelligent, and as pious as their own denomination, which they admit to be christians, but for which they will have no fellowship. Sectarianism is either right or wrong. If right, they are right in striving to keep up their own sect, and preventing the influence of any man, who wishes to induce a scepticism as to the divine authority for it. But if sectarianism be wrong, then all efforts of this kind are sinful. This, sir, is just the hinge, as I conceive, upon which your whole exertions turn. To destroy that which in word all condemn; but which in deed all religionists cherish, ought to be the effort of every man who fears God and loves the peace of society.

If, Mr. Editor, it should be necessary to present my name hereafter, you are at liberty to do so. I have hitherto been almost silent in the discussions which have for the last year, agitated this state; and am only now induced to present myself for the purpose of eliciting all the light of which the subject is susceptible. I have regarded with perfect indifference all the pusilanimous efforts of your opponents in the papers of the day; but confess that the extract furnished by the *Recorder,* from Dr. Semple's letter, has, in my estimation, more importance attached to it than the whole of them put together. I am aware of the imposing influence of great names, and know that much reliance will be placed upon the opinions of men celebrated for piety, learning and talents. I therefore wish to obtain, in full, the views of Dr. Semple on these "chimeras."

I am, Sir, Your brother
in the hope of eternal life,
QUERENS.

P. S.—Do you think it would be at all improper for you to publish in the *Christian Baptist* some of the letters which have been written you by my friend and brother Doctor Noel, alias "*Aleph,*" approbatory of your course and sentiments? *He* would not think it improper certainly.   Q.

To R. B. Semple, of Virginia.

DEAR SIR:—I OBSERVE in the last *Recorder* an extract from a letter, of which you are the writer. It is couched in the following words: "He (that is, *Paulinus*) wrote something last year, in which he certainly went too far., He is now convinced (I am persuaded) and is guarded against our friend Campbell's chimeras."

From the uniformly excellent character you have borne among those who either know you or have heard of you, I presume you are "a man fearing God and eschewing evil." Now if this be the case, you would not (since by our words we shall be justified and condemned) either write or speak any thing against another professing christian, for which you have not good reasons and sufficient authority. But you have pronounced the sentiments which "friend Campbell" and Paulinus have discussed, to be mere "*chimeras.*" Now you must have reasons for so saying, which, perhaps, many intelligent christians in this state have not. There are, too, in this western country, a number of persons who are perpetually abusing brother Campbell, and expressing their fears that "he is no christian." But it is to be remarked that among all the essays that have appeared, there is not one in which argument, or the scriptures, or any correct principles of reasoning have been resorted to for maintaining that he is an errorist I therefore call up-

on you, most affectionately, to make good your assertion by proving that the editor of the Christian Baptist is promulgating mere "*chimeras.*" You cannot, as a man of God, refuse this. The whole western community is concerned in it. The whole religious community is concerned in it, and your reputation for piety, learning and talents, lead us to consider you the very fittest person for attempting a refutation of these chimeras. If they are "*chimeras,*" they ought certainly to be exposed, and since you pronounce them such, you must of course be able so to prove.

Yours, &c.   QUERENS.

Letters Addressed to A. Campbell.—Letter I.

Bloomfield, Ky. May, 1827.

BROTHER CAMPBELL:—BEING desirous to see in our denomination unity of heart, of sentiment, and exertion, I have thought proper to address you in the loose style of epistolary writing, as one who is eminently qualified to do good. As I have but little leisure for either reading or writing, and withal labor under continual infirmities of body, you will please excuse my inaccuracies of style or expression, and regard me as a friend who approaches you unmasked, undisguised, open and free.

The church of Christ is compared to a human body. If one member suffer, they all suffer—if one be honored, all are honored. Of this body we all are members; we all have the same *rule,* the New Testament; the same master, Jesus Christ; the same hope and calling; and we all should be of *one* mind, and speak the same things. But this is not the case; every one has his "doctrine and his psalm;" schism exists, divisions are fomented, and party feeling aroused. I allude to the *effect* produced by your writings, orations and lectures. To this fact your Christian Baptist bears testimony. Some are for you, others against you; some believe, others reject; some approve, others censure and condemn. Such is the state of affairs; such the effect produced by your writings. But let me ask, What is the great good which such divisions will achieve? Will the disciples become better christians, love each other more fervently, be more humble and faithful? I fear not. A house divided against itself cannot stand; if we bite and devour each other, shall we be more prosperous, more happy, or exhibit a brighter example of christian forbearance, brotherly love, and charity? You will say no. What then is to be done? In what manner shall we fulfil the law of Christ? Have we no bowels of compassion, no sympathies for the church in the wilderness? I hope you have, that you would rejoice to see what I desire, and what constitutes the burden of my message at a throne of grace. Come then, my brother, come bow with me before our God, let us ask forgiveness for all the evils we have ever done; and pray for the future guidance of the Holy Spirit, that we may approve ourselves to God and to the conscience of every man.

You, if you have examined the editorial articles of the Recorder, are aware that I have used mildness in almost every thing which I have written either of you or your opinions. Except on the subject of experimental religion, I have neither censured, condemned, or approved any particular notion advanced by you or your correspondents; and even on that subject I spoke with caution; I was not certain that I understood your views, and therefore requested an explanation. This you did not think proper to give; and hence, our correspondence was closed. I now resume it under a different form, and on my own personal responsibility.

You object to creeds and confessions; and for the very same reason I could object to your "ancient order of things." You object to creeds because they are not the bible—are not *the only rule.*—Your ancient order is not the bible; is not the rule, and merits the same exceptions. Are creeds unnecessary? So is your ancient order, and your expositions. Do creeds influence the conduct of men? So does your ancient order. If creeds are unnecessary and injurious to the welfare of society; so is your Baptist; so your essays and expositions. But in this you differ from me in opinion. You think and believe that your Baptist is to produce great good in the world; that it will correct the errors of the times; will induce a pure speech—will bring the church out of Babylon—place her on Mount Zion—and rebuild the walls, the broken walls of Jerusalem. But I fear you are mistaken; it appears to me you have added to the confusion of tongues; you have introduced a new dialect—in some phrases somewhat different from the former. To be plain, you have, in part, formed a new creed; not a lifeless inefficient one—no, not so; but one which as effectually influences the conduct of your abettors as any confession of faith. Your creed, I mean your writings, is not the bible—is not the rule of conduct prescribed by Jesus Christ and his apostles: and yet it is manifest that those who embrace your views of divine truth and conduct, are governed by them. On this subject I shall enlarge in my next; in the mean time think on what I say. Though I may not possess your talents, leisure, or acquisitions, yet I hope to show you in the sequel that your brethren who reject your opinions, deserve your love and respect. Consider me not an enemy, but a friend, a brother.

Observe, between you and your Baptist brethren there is no difference of opinion as to the rule of faith and practice. On this subject we all speak the same language; we all acknowledge the same authority; all profess to be governed by it. What, then, is the difference between us? Simply this: We cannot agree as to what the bible teaches. The Baptists think the bible teaches the doctrine contained in their creeds; you think it teaches what you have written and published, and what you will hereafter write and publish. But more of this at another time.

As brother Waller has affixed his name to every article written by him and published in this paper, permit me to request you not to render him responsible for any errors committed by myself, and for what he has written he is personally responsible.

I subscribe myself yours, &c.
                    SPENCER CLACK.

☞ We have inserted several of your essays. As an act of justice this letter claims a place in the Baptist.

Reply to the above.—No. I.

BROTHER CLACK—I CANNOT but express my astonishment at the greatness of your charity in saluting me "*brother.*" Having been for more than one year the constant object of vituperation and detraction, of obloquy and misrepresentation in your paper; to be addressed by you as *brother*, sounded as wild in my ear as did *cousin* in the ears of the fox when seized by the dog. 'Tis true your editorial articles were extremely mild; but while you gave free and full scope to every anonymous reviler, while your columns were surcharged with the very lowest scurrility and

personal abuse, and by those too who dare not shew their face; your editorial moderation only served as a little seasoning to the dish; and your dexterity in selecting and extracting from every source such matter as would amalgamate on the doctrine of affinities with your original cavillers, only served to evince the sincerity of your intentions and the firmness of your efforts to put me down and the cause which I advocate in the estimation of your readers. You have certainly learned that I am extremely good-natured, or else you have sincerely repented of your way. If the latter be the fact, and you are determined to reform; and as you seem determined to pray for the forgiveness of the evils you have committed against the cause of God and truth, my religion teaches me to forgive; and therefore, so long as you evince sorrow for the past, and promise to do better for the future, I will call you Brother Clack.

Well, then, brother Clack, what is all the evil I have done in my "writings, orations, and lectures," for which you would have me join you in your prayers for remission? You tell me "divisions and schisms" exist: This is true; but whether my "writings, orations, and lectures," are to praise or blame, or neither, for these divisions and schisms, is a question not so easily decided. The gospel of the Lord Jesus, his preachings and teachings, or his orations and lectures, together with those of his apostles, caused much division, schism, and persecution. But whether they who proclaimed liberty to the captives, the opening of prisons to them in chains, the recovering of sight to the blind, and the year of acceptance with the Lord—were to blame for these evils; or whether the opposing party who contradicted and blasphemed, who slandered and persecuted the Lord and his apostles, is a question that would not, I think, puzzle you a long time to decide. And if any of the Pharisees or other praying people of that age had requested the apostles to join them in prayer for the forgiveness of the evils they had done, referring to schisms and divisions, it is a question whether any of them would have bowed the knee, which would not require me long to decide.

That my "writings, orations, and lectures," have produced some effect, is, on all hands, admitted; but whether these effects are to be more general, whether they are to be permanent, or whether good or evil, are questions on which every man will think for himself according to the bent of his feelings, prejudices, passions, interest, and conscience. One thing I do know, that if I were to put the question to vote with regard to the course I pursue in my "writings, orations, and lectures," in any convention of the clergy in the union, whether I ought to stop, say no more, and write no more, I would have their permission to spend the remnant of my days in inglorious ease. Or were I to submit the question to all the religious editors of religious newspapers, I would expect a similar decision. But were I to await the vote of all those who have diligently read the volumes now extant of this work, I do think I would have ten to one, saying, *proceed.* One thing I do know, that I have the concurrence, approbation, and prayers of many teachers in our Israel, and of very many of the most intelligent, experienced, and pious of our own denomination; and, indeed, of many in other denominations. And if I were to be moved, excited, or guided by commendations from men, I do sincerely think that I can produce as many written commendations, and high encomiums upon this work, from as many respectable

6

names and judges, as can be adduced in commendation of any religious paper of the same age on this continent. I am not to be guided, however, by such admonitions or commendations. I always approve the motives which urged me to undertake this work and to continue it, and I will persevere until the Lord says, stop. When I understand him thus signifying I will pause.

What good effects are to result to society from the many religious newspapers now in circulation, I know not. Most of them seem to be designed to sell so many reams of paper and kegs of ink per annum, and to furnish business for mechanics. The trash which they crowd upon the public ear and the public mind neither feeds body, soul, nor spirit.

As to what you say concerning the evils of division amongst christians, I have nothing to object. I sincerely deplore every division and every sectarian feeling which now exists; and if I thought there was any man on this continent who would go farther than I to heal all divisions and to unite all christians on constitutional grounds, I would travel on foot a hundred miles to see him and to confess my faults to him.

The intelligence, purity, and union of all who acknowledge the mission of Jesus our Lord, and the conversion of sinners to him, are, with me, the *magnum bonum*, the grand ultimatum of all my "writings, orations, lectures," and social prayers. On this ground I object to all your little human creed books, which yourself and your friend Dr. Noel advocate with so much warmth. I say Dr. Noel, as he is generally acknowledged to be the chief writer for the last year in your paper, under different masks, on this subject. I attribute the boyish, waggish, and theatrical style of those essays attributed to him, rather to the poverty of the subject than to any other cause. No man who fears God and reverences the Bible, can admire the frivolous, light, and fantastic style, which characterizes the incubations of your "Aleph." Wit and humor have their admirers—satire, and even declamation will not always disgust; but there is a style which is destitute of all these, and pleases none but the vitiated taste of those who never had, or have lost a true standard of appreciation. I reserve my remarks upon your, and the Doctor's definition of creeds, until my next on his circular; in which I will show that you both have abandoned the cause which you think and profess to advocate.

I have advanced many arguments in this work against creeds: which none of your writers have even noticed, and which I am sure none of them can set aside. And I have solid and substantial objections to them, which, I presume, no man living can remove. But it is creeds, in the legitimate and established sense of the word in ecclesiastical usage; and your not defending them, but changing the use and acceptation of the term, proves to the intelligent and discerning reader your embarrassment and impotency; but amongst those who cannot distinguish argument from declamation, whose passions and prejudices are strong, and whose judgment and powers of reflection are imbecile, any thing that pleases their taste passes for logic profound and unanswerable.

I do attribute to creeds, in the proper acceptation of the term, all the divisions and strifes, partyism, and sectarian feeling, of the present day; all the persecutions and proscription, all the havoc of human life, and all the horrors of the inquisition in the cause of religion, during many centuries before we were born. I attribute to them and the councils which gave birth to them, the greater part of the ignorance and superstition, enthusiasm and debates, and even the schisms and divisions of which you lament in the present day. I have yet to meet with the first church which holds a human creed with inflexible rigidity, and which is enlightened in the Holy Scriptures. The stronger the faith in human creeds the weaker the attachment to the Bible, and the greater the ignorance of its contents. This is, at least, in truth and fact, the result of my experience and observation.

But the peace, the harmony, the union, and love of Christians, the purity and joy of the household of faith, can only be promoted by a devout, spiritual, and unwearied attention to the lively oracles—no dry bones, no lifeless skeleton, no abstract miniature of doctrine, no cold formula of discipline, ever, brother Clack, promoted peace with God, conversion to God, harmony, union, and love amongst christians. Search the records of time and you will find ignorance, superstition, tyranny, division, and schism, on the one side. Humility and christian affection, spirituality and true charity amongst the leaders, expired in the Council of Nice, when the first creed received the imperial subscription.

You will find the Lord Jesus at the head of those who have opposed human creeds. Ever since the day that he lifted up his voice and inveighed against those who in vain worshipped God, teaching as doctrines the commandments of men—who set aside and rendered void the revelation of God, by their dogmatisms and traditions—who, by their glosses and dogmas, gave a different meaning to the commandments of God. From that day to this, creeds and creed-makers are anathematized from Heaven. Innocent and harmless as you suppose them, they are a root of bitterness, and justly condemned by all in Heaven. The prayers of the martyrs under the altar, the blood and tears of those who refused subscription to Pagan, Jewish, Papal, and Protestant creeds, cry aloud for vengeance on those who framed them, and on those who executed them. Many thought they did God service when they made them, and that they were necessary for the unity and purity of their church; yea, they thought they did God service when they killed them that opposed them, and stoned and gibbeted them who would not subscribe them. But you see *their* error, and cannot see your own, brother Clack. I would not be found in your ranks, neither as a commander nor a private, for all the fertile soil of your state—for all the honor which all your population could bestow. I would rather be in the ranks of the martyrs, at the head of which stands the illustrious chief who was crucified rather than subscribe. Yes, I desire to be with them living and dying. And when the hour of his indignation comes, when the awful day comes when he will answer the prayer from under the altar, may the thoughtless and inconsiderate advocates and abettors of a system essentially the same, find pardon and refuge in him.

I have only to request you to reciprocate the favor or the act of justice demanded in your first letter. In due time I shall attend to every item you have presented in your letters to me, and believe me to be most sincerely attached to every one who loves my Lord and Master, whether Baptist or Paido-Baptist, New Light or Old Light: and firmly determined to advocate the restoration of the ancient order of things to my last breath.

A. CAMPBELL.

2 V   7

A Restoration of the Ancient Order of Things.
No. XX.

THERE is no trait in the character of the Saviour more clearly marked, more forcibly exhibited in the memoirs of his life, than his unreserved devotion to the will of his Father and his God. How often do we hear him say, " I came not to do my own will, but the will of him that sent me." " It is my meat and my drink to do the will of him that sent me, and to accomplish his work." The motto of his life was sung by David in these words: " To do thy will, O God, I delight." An unfeigned and unreserved submission to, a perfect acquiescence in, and a fixed unalterable determination to do, the will of the Most High, is the standard of true devotion, and the rule and measure of true happiness.— Whence, let me ask, arose this devotion to the will of the Father in our Lord and Saviour? We answer, Because he knew the Father. He knew that God is, and was, and ever shall be love, and he received every expression of his will, whether pleasing or displeasing to flesh and blood, as an exhibition of God's love. He knew too, that there was no love like the love of God, either in nature or degree. The love of God is a love emanating from, incorporated with, and measured by, an infinite wisdom, and omniscience.— Human affection is often misplaced and misdirected, because of human ignorance and human weakness. The love of some men is much greater than that of others, because of the strength of their natural endowments. But as the wisdom and knowledge of God are unsearchable, so his love never can be misplaced, misdirected, never can be measured, nor circumscribed. It is perfect in nature, and in nature it is wisdom, power, and goodness combined. In degree, it cannot be conceived of by a finite mind, nor expressed in our imperfect vehicles of thought. It passes all created understanding. It has a height without top, and a depth without bottom. Every oracle of God, is a manifestation of it. As the electric fluid pervades the earth and all bodies upon it, but is invisible to the eye and imperceptible to the touch; but when drawn to a focus in a cloud by its law of attraction, and when it is discharged to another body which requires more of it than the point from which it emanated, it assumes a new form, and a new name, and becomes visible to the eye, and its voice is heard. Every expression of the will of God, every commandment of God, is only drawing to a certain point, and giving form and efficacy to his love. It then becomes visible—it is then audible—We see it—we hear it—we feel it.

The very term *devotion* has respect to the will of another. A devoted or devout man is a man who has respect to the will of God. When a person is given up to the will of any person, or to his own will, he is devoted to that person or to himself. But as the term devout is used in religion, we may say that every man is more or less devout, according to his regard to the will of God expressed in his holy oracles. The Saviour was perfectly so, and he is and ever shall be, the standard of perfect devotion. Not an item of the will of God found in the volume of the old book written concerning him, that he did not do, or submit to; not a single commandment did he receive in person from his Father which he did not perfectly acquiesce in, and obey. He was then perfectly devout.

Now, in proportion as men are regenerated, they are like him. Faith always purifies the heart. A pure, is an unmixed heart, that is, a heart singly fixed upon the will of God. The regenerated are therefore devout, or devoted to the will of God, and the unregenerate care nothing about it. Now every one that is devout, or devoted to the will of God, will continually be inquiring into the will of God. Hence his oracles will always be their meditation. Every regenerated man will therefore be devout, devoted to the revealed will of God, will seek to know, and understand, and practice it; therefore every regenerated man will be a friend and advocate of the ancient order of things, in the church of the Living God, because that order was according to the will of God, and every departure from it is according to the will of man. There is not a proposition in Euclid susceptible of a clearer or fuller demonstration than this: Every regenerated man must be devoted to the ancient order of things in the church of God—Provided it be granted as a postulatum, that the ancient order of things was consonant to the will of the Most High. A mind not devoted to the whole will of God, revealed in the New Book, is unregenerate. He that does not obey God in every thing, obeys him in nothing. Hearken to this similitude—

A householder who had one son and many servants, was about to depart on a long journey to a distant country; he called his son into his presence, and said to him, My son, I am about to be absent for a long time; you know I have a vineyard, and an olive-yard, and an orchard of various kinds of fruit. These I have cultivated with great care, and have kept my servants employed in fencing, and in cultivating each of them with equal labor and care. I now give them and my servants into your care and management until my return, and I now command you to have each of them fenced, and pruned, and cultivated as you have seen me do, and at my return I will reward you for your fidelity. He departed. His son calls all the servants together, and having a predilection to the grape above every other fruit, he assembles them all in the vineyard. He improves the fences, he erects his wine vat, and bestows great labor and attention on the pruning and cultivating the vines. They bring forth abundantly; but his attention and the labor of the servants is so much engrossed in the vineyard, that the oliveyard and orchard are forgotten and neglected. In process of time his father returns. He finds his vineyard well enclosed, highly cultivated, and richly laden with the choicest grapes. But on visiting his orchard and oliveyard, he finds the enclosures broken down, the trees undressed and browsed upon by all the beasts of the field. He calls his son. He hangs his head in his presence. His father asks, Why is it, my son, that my oliveyard and orchard are so neglected, and destroyed, while my vineyard flourishes, and is laden with fruit? Father, said he, I have always thought the grape was the most delicious of all fruit, the most salutary, as it cheered the heart of God and man, and therefore the most worthy of constant care and cultivation—I therefore bestowed all my attention upon it. His father rejoined, Unfaithful child, it was not my pleasure, my mind, nor my will, then which guided you; but your own inclination. Had you preferred any thing else to the vineyard, for the same reason that you neglected my orchard and my oliveyard, you would have neglected it. I thank you not for the cultivation of the vine, because, in doing this, you consulted not my pleasure, but your own. Undutiful son, depart from my presence—I will disinherit you, and give my possessions to a stranger.

So it is with every one who is zealous for keeping up one institution of the King of kings, while he is regardless of the others.

Some Baptists are extremely devoted to immersion. They have read all the baptisms on record in the New Testament, and beginning at the Jordan they end at the city of Philippi, in the bath in the Roman prison. The ancient mode and nothing else will please their taste. Away with your sprinkling and pouring, and babyism! The authority of the Great King is described in glowing colors. The importance of implicit obedience is extolled, and the great utility of keeping his commands is set forth in language which cannot be mistaken. But when the ancient mode of observing the Lord's day or of breaking bread is called up to their attention, they fall asleep. The authority of the Great King will scarcely make them raise their heads or open their eyes. Implicit obedience now has no charms, and the utility of keeping his commands has no attractions for them. Such Baptists are not regenerated, that is, they are not devout—not devoted to the will of God. They seek to please themselves. Let such compare themselves with the son of the householder in the preceding parable. They have got a *Baptist conscience*, and not the conscience of the regenerate. A Baptist conscience hears the voice of God and regards his authority only where there is much water. But a regenerated mind and a christian conscience, hears the voice of God and regards his authority as much on every Lord's day, or at the Lord's table, as on the monthly meeting, as at Enon or in the desert of Gaza. Many, we fear, think they are pleasing and serving God, while they are pleasing and serving themselves. They think they are devout, but they are devoted to their own will. So is every one who acknowledges any thing to be the will of God, and yet refuses to do it.

Ah! remember, my friends, that all flesh is as grass, and all the glory of man, rabbinical, clerical, regal, is as the flower of the grass: the grass withers, and the flower falls down, but he that *does* the will of God abides forever.— Ye Doctors of Divinity, who are doting about questions, and fighting about straws; ye Editors of religious journals, who are surfeiting the religious mind with your fulsome panegyrics upon those who second your views, and directing the public mind to objects lighter than vanity—remember that the will of Jehovah will stand forever, and that when " gems and monuments and crowns are mouldered down to dust," he that does the will of God shall flourish in immortal youth. Go to work, then, and use your influence to restore the ancient order of things. EDITOR.

Extract of a letter from a gentleman in Sparta, West Tennessee, to the editor of the Christian Baptist.

"UPON the supposition that 1 John v. 7. is genuine, I make the following remarks. Observe, John does not speak of this subject as being unknown previous to his writing this epistle; but rather offers it as a narration of things attendant on the life and baptism of the Saviour. That this epistle is a narration of past events, appears from the first chapter and first verse of this epistle. This, I presume, none will deny. " For there are three that bear record in heaven," &c. I cannot believe that this record or testimony had no object, neither that Jesus was the object, and at the same time a witness in the case himself. Believing him to be the object of said record or testimony, but not a witness in the case, I therefore conclude that he is not implicated by

the term " Word" in this passage, though he is in others; yet this is no direct proof that he is implicated in the above one. Observe again, John says, verse 6th, " This is he that came by water." When did Jesus come by water, if not at his baptism? Yes, at that very juncture said record or testimony was completed in heaven, while Jesus, the object, was on the earth—on the river side. Now if Jesus is the *Word*, then the passage should read thus: For there are *two* that bear record in heaven, and *one* on the earth, or river side. In the 9th verse, he says, " For this is the witness of God which he has testified of his Son." I would ask, With what degree of propriety do men speak, when they say, God has testified this witness of his Son, and add, at the same time, that the Son is a testifier in the case himself? I speak as to wise men. Judge you what I say. Was the business of the Saviour into the world to bear witness to himself, or to the truth? John xviii. 37. Hear his own words: " If I bear witness of myself, my witness is not true." John v. 31. And again, in the 10th verse he says, " Because he believes not the record that God gave of his Son."— Here the same record is said to be given by God himself. Now admitting that the Son bears a part of this record, can we speak the language of Canaan with reason, and say, This is the record God gave of his Son? From these and many other considerations of a similar nature, I am led to believe that the Son is not implicated by the term " Word" in this verse. Now you would ask me, What composed said record? To which I will answer in the following manner. Here let me observe, that this record is composed of three manners of attesting the same truth, viz. *that Christ is the Son of God:—*

First manner—The Father, by *Isaiah* xi. 2. " And the Spirit of the Lord shall rest *upon* him," &c. From this it is plain that the people were to see the Spirit rest *upon* him; and sure enough it was seen, (*Mark* i. 10.) Observe the term *upon. Isaiah* xlii. 1. " I have put my Spirit *upon* him, and he shall bring forth judgment to the gentiles." Here is another scripture that in my opinion, has reference to the descent of the Holy Spirit on Christ at his baptism. *John* i. 33. " And I knew him not, but he (the Father) that sent me to baptize with water, said to me, *Upon* whom you shall see the Spirit descending and remaining on him," &c. Through these scriptures, or in this manner, the Father bore *record* of his Son.

Second manner—The Holy Spirit descended *upon* Christ when he came up out of the water; or, in the language of verse first, " this is he that came by water." " And John saw and bare record that this is the Son of God." *John* i. 34.

Third manner—Matt. iii. 17. " And lo! a voice (the Word) from heaven saying, This is my beloved Son, in whom I am well pleased." Thus we see these three are one as to their origin and design, being given by one being, who by these three manners of attestation, designed to prove the heavenly, the heart-reviving and the soul-saving truth that Jesus Christ is his well beloved Son."

DEAR BROTHER:—I CAN neither admit the genuineness of the reading of 1st *John*, v. 7. nor your interpretation thereof, if genuine. The true reading, in my judgment, is the following, verse 6: " This is he who came (or was coming or was to come) by water and blood, Jesus the Christ; not by the water only, but by the water and the blood, and it is the Spirit which attested this, because the Spirit is the truth. Farther,

9

there are three that testify this—the Spirit, and the Water, and the Blood—and these three are one," or to one amount. Thus I literally translate the Greek text of Griesbach, which reading is moreover approved and confirmed by Michaelis, and other great critics and collators of ancient MSS.

That the common reading, if genuine, makes nothing in favor of the Trinitarians is admitted by both Calvin, Beza, Macknight, &c. &c. That it is not genuine was admitted at the era of the Reformation by Luther, Zuinglius, Bullinger and Erasmus, and by many eminent critics since that time. That it is wanting in all the ancient manuscripts, save one, and that of doubtful authority, is generally admitted; and that it is not found in any of the very ancient versions is indisputable, such as the old Syriac, the Coptic, Arabic, and Ethiopic. That it is not quoted by any of the primitive fathers, and scarcely referred to before the era of the Council of Nice, is also admitted. It was by Robert Stephens introduced into the common Greek text from *some* of the most ancient of the Vatican Greek Testaments, from which the Spanish theologians formed the Complutensian edition of the Greek Testament, and which Pope Leo X. gave them. Mill, in his note on the common reading, lays considerable stress upon its having been quoted by Tertullian and Cyprian before the middle of the third century; but the objections against these quotations render them of very doubtful authority; and it is most worthy of note that in the fierce controversies about the Trinity immediately subsequent to the Nicene Council and Creed, it is not once quoted by any writer, which shows it not to have been in the copies then generally read.

As in the judgment of Calvin, Beza, and the most learned Trinitarians, it makes nothing in favor of *three persons in one God:* and as neither the adoption of it as genuine, nor the rejection of it as spurious, favors the conceits of the Arians; neither sect should contend about it beyond the evidence which antiquity and the scope of the passage furnishes.

The translation I have above given of Griesbach is in the spirit and scope of the context; and as I understand the passage, it imports that Jesus was proved to be the Messiah or the Christ, supereminently at his baptism and death. He was, according to ancient type and prophecy, to come by water and blood—and according to these he did come fully attested at his baptism and death. Now there are *three* evidences of this truth that Jesus is the Christ, and that all who believe in him have eternal life. These three concur in one and the same thing. These are the spirit, not the Holy Spirit particularly, but the doctrine which Jesus taught. Thus John defines it in the passage itself: "The spirit is THE TRUTH." The article is overlooked in the common version. The *truth,* then, or the *spirit,* or the *doctrine* which Jesus taught, proves his mission and his claims. The water, or his baptism, and the baptism of the first christians, which was generally accompanied by some spiritual gift, is another proof of the same. His death inseparably connected with his resurrection, consummates the whole, and the ordinance that commemorates it is a standing monument of his mission. So that these three, the doctrine, the baptism, and the death of Jesus, all attested and accompanied by the most signal demonstrations of the Holy Spirit, constitute a summary view of the infallible evidence of the Messiahship of Jesus, and of the truth of God's promise of eternal life to all who believe in and obey him.

Farther than this your friend and brother cannot at present go. EDITOR

No. 2.] SEPTEMBER 3, 1827.

Deism and the Social System.—No. IV.

PERHAPS I should again apologize for the singular title of these essays. It would import that an inseparable alliance existed or was formed between scepticism and a system of social cooperation. There is no such necessary connexion. There was, and there is, scepticism without a co-operative system; and there is a co-operative system without deism.

I receive a German paper, edited by Henry Kurtz, a teacher of christianity, in Canton, Ohio, denominated the "Messenger of Concord," devoted to primitive christianity; in which some extracts from this work are translated into the German language. The writer is an admirer and advocate of the ancient order of things and of a social or co-operative system. An infant association of some pious and intelligent Germans already exists, whose constitution contemplates a community perfectly social, and devoted to the religion of the first congregation in Jerusalem. As far as I understand the genius and spirit of their system of co-operation and their views of christianity, I can cheerfully bid them God speed. But not so our friends at New Harmony. Their system of scepticism must inevitably render their co-operative system a system of disorder—a co-operation whose fate was long since portrayed in the plains of Shinar. Their system has been, now is, and ever shall be, the—"*Discordia semina rerum non bene junctarum congestaque eodem.*"—"The discordant seeds of things not fitly joined together and fitted together in the same place." Principles at war with reason, revelation, and a permanent co-operation, are strewed over the pages of their "Gazette," and the "mental independence" which is exhibited deifies both mind and matter, and annihilates both the idea of a creator, and of a moral governor of the world. But to return to our subject.

Since writing our last, the editor of the "New Harmony Gazette" has given in his paper of the 11th July, a few extracts from our No. 2. on this subject, with an invitation to some of his correspondents to come forward and maintain their cause. There is but one sentiment in the remarks of the editor which demands any notice from me. After commending my liberality, he adds—

"But though he would free us from punishment here, he would, we fear, be pleased to see us in another world suffering those pains and tortures which our scepticism justly merits from a merciful but just Creator. Such at least is the opinion [not the good pleasure then] of most christians. This is one of those erroneous ideas which are the great stumbling block in almost every system of religion. Merit and demerit is attached to a belief and disbelief in certain dogmas or doctrines, an idea which we know not how to reconcile, with the consciousness which we, in common with all other individuals of our species, possess, that our will has no power or control over our belief."

This "stumbling block" in the way of our sceptical friends, is one of their own creation, or one in which the bible is not concerned. How far metaphysical systems may have created it, I stop not to inquire. But I hesitate not to call this a palpable error, viz. that we have a consciousness that our will has no power nor control over our belief. This assertion, that our will has no control nor power over our belief, is found in substance or in form in almost every number of the "New Harmony Gazette," and is one of the most palpable errors in all that they say against christianity. The experience of every man who can think at all upon what passes in his own mind, is, and must be, directly to the contrary of this assertion. It is, indeed, almost a proverb, " that what men wish or will to believe, they do believe; and what they do not like or will to believe, they disbelieve." Stop, Mr. Editor, and examine yourself here. This assertion I know is a capital and an essential dogma of yours. I see it is a part of "the chain or filling" in every piece you weave against the bible. I know, too, the speciosity which it has; for there are many instances in which it would seem the will had no power over our belief; and I do know there are many cases where and when we cannot help believing and disbelieving when our will is on the other side. But still it is a truth capable of the fullest demonstration that your assertion is false; or, in other words, that the will has an immense control over our belief. You see, then, we are at issue here. And as this is your main fort and citadel, do examine its bulwarks and towers. They are most certainly built upon the sand. You assert that the will has *no power* over our belief. I assert that it has an *immense power* over it. My adage is, What men will to believe, they most generally, if not universally, believe. I assert that the understanding is not independent of the will, nor the will of the understanding. But I only call this subject up to your reflection at present. The design of my present paper is to offer some thoughts upon the nature of the evidence of christianity.

The evidence of christianity, or the proof that it is of divine origin and authority, are usually classified under two heads—the *Internal* and the *External.* The internal are those which appear in the volume itself, or the proofs which the religion itself, objectively considered, presents to the mind of a reasoner or student. The external are those attestations which accompanied the promulgation of the religion, and those arguments derived from, not the nature of the religion itself, but from the accompaniments of it; these are usually denominated the miracles and the prophecies. To those who were the cotemporaries of the promulgation of this religion, the external evidences first arrested their attention, and were, in a certain sense, to them the stronger evidences; but to us who have the whole on record, both the religion itself and the miracles and prophecies, the internal are the stronger, and first arrest our attention. It is, perhaps, improper to separate them, for the one is not without the other, either in the design or execution of this stupendous scheme, nor in the import of it. I am not about to adopt this trite method, nor to occupy the attention of my readers in the investigation of either distinctively; but in the mean time, would offer a few reflections upon the adjustment of the evidences to the condition of mankind in general.

I will, without hesitation, admit that the evidences of the truth of christianity might have been easily augmented if it had pleased the founder of it, or had it been compatible with the whole plan of things. From analogy I have reasoned thus. The sun might have been made to have produced a thousand times more light and heat. Animals necessary to our comfort might have been greatly multiplied, or those given us might have been endowed with a higher degree of instinctive knowledge. But again, if the sun had been made to afford greater light, the human eye would have been rendered useless, or have been made differently. If the heat which we attribute to the sun had been greatly augmented, our bodies could not have endured it. If domestic animals had been augmented, their support would have been more oppressive, or if those made for our convenience had been endued with more instinct or more extensive knowledge, they would not have served us at all, but have become our masters. And if the evidences of christianity had been augmented, it would not have been adapted to the condition of man. The adjustment of light to the eye and of the eye to light; of heat to animals and of animals to heat; of instinct to brutes, and of brutes to our service, is all graduated upon a divine scale; or, in other words, is perfectly adapted means to end, and end to means. Precisely so the evidences of the christian religion to the present condition of men, and of the religion itself to man. The christian religion is made for man, and absolutely and indispensably necessary to his comfort, as food is to the body. And the evidences of this religion taken together are as precisely adapted to the condition of man in this stage of his existence, as light is to the human eye, or sound to the human ear. Amongst the thousand ways in which the evidences of the christian religion might have been, and might now be augmented, I will mention but two or three. For instance, God might have spoken aloud to the Jews and Romans in their own language, in such a way as could not be misunderstood, and have attested the pretensions and claims of his Son. The Son himself might have, by the same power, given more general and conspicuous proofs of his mission. He might have gone to Rome, as to Jerusalem, and summoned all the heads of departments, magistrates, legislators, and priests, and given such proofs of his person and mission as would have revolutionized Rome and the world in a few days. At this time also, God might speak in all the languages of the world in the same instant of time, and inform all nations, *viva voce,* that the contents of the New Testament were worthy of universal acceptation. Or he might cause all the believers to escape all calamities in this first life, and live ten times as long as the infidels; he might cause them to pass off the stage in a deep sleep, as when Eve was made out of the side of Adam, and thus have exempted them from all pain. He might have made them prosperous and happy every way. But what imagination can conceive, what tongue express how many, and how signal proofs of the divine authority of the scriptures of truth, he might have given! So that I make it an argument of no little momentum in giving a reason of the hope that is in me, that God could have made the evidence omnipotent, but he has not done it, and for reasons the wisest that could be conceived of.

I write not now merely for the benefit of sceptics, but for Christians schooled in a false philosophy. Why, tell me, ye Christians, who are naturally and morally, or spiritually dead as a stone, why was there any adjustment of the evidences of christianity, or rather why had it any evidence at all but in the hearts of men? Why was not the evidence greater or less than it is? Your systems will not enable you to answer this question I am sure. Ask your Doctors, and they cannot tell you. Ask your systems, and they have forgotten it. Yet it is a fact that the evidences are adjusted upon a certain scale and amount to a certain maximum beyond which they do not go.*

Had they gone farther (I will blab out the secret,) all excellency in faith would have been destroyed. Had they fallen short one degree every mouth could not have been stopped. While a small proportion of the evidence is sufficient for some, it is all necessary for others; and those who do not believe upon the whole of it, and have one objection remaining when the whole is heard and examined, that which would remove this one objection would destroy every virtue and excellency properly belonging to faith. Faith built upon evidence greater than the whole amount divinely vouchsafed, would have nothing moral about it; it would be as unavoidable as the motions of a mill wheel under a powerful head of water, or as the waving of the tops of pines beneath a whirlwind.

I must break off in the midst of my illustration, and close my present essay, when I tell the New Harmony people that the faith which they talk of, over which " the will has no power," requires that species of evidence which is incompatible with all moral virtue and goodness, and which would make belief like the fall of one of those volcanic stones which a few months since shivered a tree a few miles from Nashville, Tennessee.

To such christians as are staggered at the above reasoning, I would just mention that the Saviour resolved the infidelity of his hearers on many occasions, entirely to the will—"You will not come to me," and "You would not."

Editor.

—

A Farmer once had a horse, which his son, a lad of ten years old, could ride with pleasure and safety. But no fence could keep this horse out of his master's corn field. The consequence was, he was confined to the stable and secluded from good pasture. The lad said to his father one day when riding out, 'Father, what a pity it is that this horse has not a little more wisdom—how much better he might live in the pasture than in the stable, if only he could learn from his first long confinement to avoid going into the cornfield. If he had only a little more sense how much better it would be for him and for us.' Stop, my son, replied his father—if he had a little more sense, just as much as you now wish him to have, he would not let you nor me ride him at all. Those who never think upon the adjustment of things to their respective ends and uses, will find an admonition here.   Editor.

―――

Remarks on Tassey's Vindication.
To the Editor of the Christian Baptist.

Sir—In the close of extracts from Mr. Tassey's vindication, &c. the last of which appeared in your No. of May 7th, I intimated an intention,

* If sinners be as spiritually dead as a stone, and if their conversion be the effect of omnipotent power, or of mere physical energy of God's spirit; then not only is any adjustment of evidence unnecessary, but all evidence of the truth of the scriptures is quite unnecessary. To afford evidence of any kind, or to augment it to any degree, would be as unmeaning or as superfluous as to create one, two, or three suns to enable those to see who are born blind. On the scheme that men are all born blind, and therefore cannot see any light, star light, moon light, or sun light, it would evince a want of wisdom in the Creator to have created any light at all, or to have tempered it to any degree whatever. What would we think of the skill of a physician who professed to restore the blind to sight, and who employed himself in making candles of different magnitudes, or of lighting lamps of certain capacities! Assuredly the rational would lose all confidence in his prescriptions.

with your permission, of adverting to a few faults which I was grieved to find in that otherwise excellent performance.

Though the author appears quite alive to a sense of the pernicious influence of the common prejudices of education, of system, of interest, &c. and speaks as loudly and as pointedly against them, as almost any I have met with, yet, strange to tell, he seems as completely under the influence of those pernicious evils, against which he declaims and admonishes with so just a vehemence, as are some of those, he so justly condemns. It is under this impression I feel induced to animadvert upon a performance which, in other respects, I so highly esteem—and that both for the sake of the author, and of the public into whose hands these animadversions may chance to come. But, before I proceed, permit me to correct a mistake which I made in relation to the author's not having formally cited the Westminster Confession of Faith, upon the powers of synods and councils, which he has precisely done, p. 233. This was an oversight.

Investigating the various striking coincidences between Moses the type, and Christ the antitype, from *Acts* iii. 22. 23. it is stated p. 21. that " Moses was the introducer of a new dispensation of religion; one which was different and distinct, in its leading features, from any that had preceded; and which was added, as an appendage, to the patriarchal dispensation, "because of transgression, until the seed should come to whom the promise was made." Moses was king in Jeshurun. "Our Lord, in this respect, most strikingly resembled his predecessor. He is the author and introducer of a new dispensation of religion, of which he is himself the sum and substance. He came to put an end to the carnal institutions, which consisted in meats, drinks, and divers washings; to these sacrifices, which could not make him that did the service perfect, as pertaining to the conscience; and to abrogate and forever abolish all the laws which pertained to the worldly sanctuary, and all the privileges that belonged to the Jews as a distinguished and separated people. He came, as the Sun of Righteousness, to enlighten a dark and benighted world, to teach and establish the worship of the true God, in its more spiritual and glorious form.—He came, also, to give laws and regulations to his people, adapted to the various circumstances in which they, as his followers, would feel themselves placed in this present world." So far the coincidence and contrast is clear, striking, and intelligible; and the natural and necessary consequences certain, easy, and obvious. We must then, as christians, look simply and solely to Jesus Christ for the whole of our religion; for he, as our king, has given laws and regulations to his people, adapted, &c. Christ is King in Zion.

Not so fast, for, says Mr. T. "We are not to consider the religion which the Saviour taught, as a distinct and different religion from that which was propagated by Moses. They are in substance and design the same, and are not in any measure to be considered as opposed to each other.

"Although, therefore, our Lord came to set aside that covenant or dispensation of religion, which had waxed old, and was ready to vanish away; yet it was not to abolish the religion itself; for a sinner was justified by faith and saved then, just as he is now: and though he introduced a new covenant or dispensation of religion, excelling, in glory, that which preceded it, yet the religion itself was essentially the same as that which had subsisted from the grant of the first promise to our progenitors before their expulsion from Paradise." Now, gentle reader, to reconcile Mr. T. with himself and with the truth; *hic labor, hoc opus est.* This appears, indeed, an insuperable difficulty. Moses, he says, was the introducer of a new dispensation of religion, one which was different and distinct in its leading features, from any that had preceded; and which was added, &c. In like manner, also, that our Lord, the great antitype, "is the author and introducer, of a new dispensation of religion; and that he came to abrogate and abolish forever all the laws which pertained to the worldly sanctuary, and all the privileges which belonged to the Jews as a distinguished people." Consequently, he did not leave one shred of the Mosaic dispensation, "which was added as an appendage to the patriarchal dispensation" in force: yet he says, "We are not to consider the religion which the Saviour taught, as a distinct and different religion from that which was propagated by Moses." And not only so, but after granting that both Moses and Christ, each introduced a new dispensation of religion, "distinct and different from any that had preceded;" yet that, "the religion itself," which our Lord introduced, "was essentially the same, as that which had subsisted from the grant of the first promise to our progenitors, before their expulsion from Paradise." Consequently that neither Moses nor Christ introduced any new dispensation, of religion; but that they are both the same as the patriarchal, and of consequence the same with each other. Do, reader, reconcile these things if you can. Moses introduced a new dispensation of religion distinct from the patriarchal; Christ introduced a new dispensation of religion distinct from both; and yet we are not to consider it as such; nay we are to consider these three distinct and different dispensations of religion, as one and the same religion essentially.

But perhaps the reconciling medium lies involved in the mysterious word, essentially; or in the pithete, dispensation, which our author, in his premises, always attaches to the word religion; or perhaps it may lie concealed in the term, religion, itself. Let us try then what assistance the common and established sense of these terms may afford us for reconciling our paradoxical and mysterious author with himself.

To begin with the last mentioned, namely, religion; that we may not mistake the meaning of this leading and important term, let us begin at the root:—it is derived from the Latin word, *religio,* and that from *religo,* to bind thoroughly, or strictly; that is, to all intents and purposes; hence the noun in the Latin language is frequently used to signify an oath; more commonly piety, the worship of God, or the rites and ceremonies of his worship. Hence a man of religion, of piety; or a pious and religious man, are phrases of equivalent import; expressive of the possession and exercise of an inward principle of love, adoration, and reverence towards God. In this sense, indeed, religion is the same in all true worshippers, both men and angels. In this sense, therefore, neither Christ nor Moses, officially considered, were the authors nor introducers of it. Our author therefore must needs understand it in the external exhibition of it, consisting in a devout and reverential observance of certain rites and ceremonies, or ordinances of divine worship, divinely appointed; for in no other sense can religion be properly the subject of a divine institution. Now our author has told us,

that, in all these respects, the patriarchal, Jewish, and Christian religions are distinct and different. How then can they all be the same; especially as he tells us that the last mentioned has abrogated and for ever abolished all the laws, ordinances, rites, and ceremonies which pertained to the worldly sanctuary; or which, in other words, constituted the Jewish religion. And it is as certain, that the religion of Moses abolished the preceding to which our author says it was appended; for under it, to have worshipped according to the preceding, would have subjected the worshipper to death.

The Jewish religion was, therefore, as destructive an appendage to the patriarchal, as the christian religion is declared to have been to the Jewish. It abrogated and forever abolished it to the Jews. But our author only says they were essentially the same. There may be something of mysterious importance in this, for the doctrine of essences is, confessedly, of difficult interpretation. The term *essence,* is generally understood to mean the being or substance of a thing, or the remote matter out of which it is made, or its prime constituent qualities, &c. And probably this is the meaning of our author; for he says, the Jewish and Christian religions, "are in substance and design the same;" "for a sinner was justified by faith, and saved then, just as he now is." If by the term *justified,* we are to understand a person's being sustained as righteous before God, as approved and accepted in his sight, we might argue in a similar way, that the religion of our first parents in the state of innocency, and of the faithful was essentially the same; yea of all true believers to the end of the world; for who knows not that the very essence, or prime constituent principles and essential qualities of acceptable worship, of all true religion, are faith and obedience; that by these Abraham, and true believers with him, are and have been justified, and ever shall be; and that by departing from these our first parents sinned, and fell into condemnation—even by their disbelief, and consequent transgression. But, after all, our author may perhaps be exculpated from the unpleasant charge of self-contradiction by the just import of the term *dispensation,* which he always annexes to the word *religion,* in the premises before us. He does not say that either Christ or Moses introduced a new religion; but only a new *dispensation* of religion. What may be the difference between a *new religion,* and a *new dispensation of religion,* seems difficult to define. The term dispensation strictly and properly implies a weighing or parcelling out of something, as a task or portion for present use or occupancy. Hence, in certain cases, there may be a new or repeated dispensation of the same things. Thus summer and winter, spring and autumn, day and night, are, and have been dispensed to the world, and shall continue so to be to the end of time. Yet no man considers any of these a new dispensation. The word covenant, which our author uses in this connexion, and which has the advantage of being a more scriptural epithet, goes to afford no assistance towards solving the difficulty; for a new covenant of religion, which signifies, a new constitution or establishment of religion, necessarily implies and designates the newness or novelty of the religion established; especially when the people for and amongst whom it is established, are already in possession of a religion or form of worship which the new religion goes to supercede, as our author acknowledges the christian did the Jewish, to all intents and purposes demolishing its whole fabric.

13

Upon the whole investigation of this subject of apparent self-contradiction, there appears no means in the compass of the common use of language, and of common sense, to exculpate our author; I mean of reconciling him with himself. This, however, would appear a matter of small moment, were it not for the importance of the subject, and the connexion in which it stands. But what a pity that so strenuous and able an advocate for reformation should have so committed himself, for the sake of maintaining an antiscriptural hypothesis, viz. that the christian church or kingdom of Christ is but a continuance and improvement of the old; and this not for the sake of priestly honors, and the tithing system, like the high pretensioned Episcopalians; but merely for the sake of infant sprinkling, founded upon the hypothesis of church membership, deduced from the rite of circumcision, the fleshy seal of the covenant of peculiarity, with the select seed of Abraham according to the flesh.   Philalethes.

[TO BE CONTINUED.]

Review of Dr. Noel's Circular.—No. II.

Rev. Silas M. Noel, D. D. thus defines his creed: "By a creed, we mean an epitome, or summary exhibition of what the scriptures teach." The Rev. Samuel W. Crawford, of Chambersburgh, Pa. who this year has printed a sermon on creeds, on the hypothesis that Dr. Miller and his predecessors had left something undone which he could achieve, has defined his creed thus, p. 6. "Creed is derived from the Latin word *credo*, I believe, and means simply that which any one believes, whether expressed by the living voice, or exhibited in written or printed language. It also signifies a system of evangelical truth, deduced from the scriptures by uninspired men, printed in a book, and made a term of ecclesiastical fellowship." The Rev. G. Waller defines a creed to be, every thing a man preaches or writes, and to this agrees the opinion of my friend and brother, Rev. Spencer Clack, who declares all that a man writes on religion to be his religious creed. I could fill a few pages very conveniently with definitions of creeds, but these will suffice at present. To begin with Dr. Noel, whose creed is "a summary exhibition of what the scriptures teach." As we have never seen the Doctor's creed in writing or in printed characters, nor heard him preach it all, for this he cannot do until he has preached his last sermon, we cannot form any opinion upon its perfection or imperfection, as coming up to his definition. He tells us it is not the scriptures themselves, but a summary exhibition of what they teach. This *summary exhibition*, then, is that which is to preserve the purity of the church. What the scriptures teach in their own proper arrangement, and in their own terms and phrases, is inadequate to this great end; but the summary exhibited in the Doctor's arrangement and terms will answer this glorious object. *Query.* How much more valuable is the *summary exhibition* than the whole inspired volume? *Query* again. What a pity that the Lord did not command his apostles to draw up a *summary exhibition*, knowing, as he must have known, that without this "summary exhibition," his church must have gone into dilapidation and ruin. Arians, Socinians, Universalists, Baptists and Presbyterians, must, without it, have formed one communion. And what a pity that the apostles had not, "out of their own head," given this "epitome or summary exhibition," before they died. But on Mr. Crawford's definition, this would not have answered the purpose, for his creed "must be deduced from scripture by *uninspired* men." And on Messrs. Waller and Clack's definition, it would have been impossible to have done it, for it required all "the sermons, orations, and lectures" of our Lord and his apostles to make their creed, and all that they wrote and spoke during their whole lives constituted their creed. For all that I have written, is, with them, so many articles of my creed—and how voluminous it may be before finished, neither I nor they can predict.

We want to see Dr. Noel's "*summary exhibition*" more than any other. For his creed is nuncupative. He has not yet committed it to writing. The little creed book made or adopted by the Philadelphia Association is not his creed. For he has declared he does not believe it all, and he sometimes "constitutes churches" on one creed and sometimes on another. I have heard of two or three which he constituted upon "no summary exhibition" whatever; but on the platform of the whole volume *in cumulo.* I do herein and hereby sincerely request him to publish to the world his "summary exhibition," and to show us what the scriptures teach. For as I do well know there is not in print on this continent one such summary exhibition as he approves, believes, or practices. For against the Philadelphia creed he has most serious and important objections. And it is not many years since he attempted to publish a creed, but for some reasons abandoned it. And although *Aleph* and *Beth* should "bury the tomahawk," and agree on other principles of operation, still it will be necessary to publish the summary, or cruelly to desert the church to wolves and tigers, stripped of its only guardian, an epitome of what the scriptures teach. I repeat, the Doctor ought, on his own principles, to print the summary; for he says, p. 5, "a nuncupative creed is not calculated to quiet disturbances, or to exclude corruption." "If," adds he, "we use a religious test at all, we should be honest and independent enough to avow it." Honesty and independence, then, as well as the fitness of things require the publication of an epitome. To pretend to hold to the Philadelphia Confession, when it is neither believed nor practised, is to make it, and treat it, no better than the bible. If the Doctor believes it to be the desired epitome, honor and honesty require him to avow it; if not, let us have a faithful one.

But on glancing over the Doctor's circular, I find an epitome stated in it, and lest I should be contradicted by it in inserting that there is no epitome or summary exhibition in print, such as the Doctor approves, I must lay this epitome before my readers. It is in the following words, p. 7. "The bible plainly teaches, as I read and believe, the deplorable and total depravity of human nature, the essential divinity of the Saviour, a trinity of persons in the godhead; justification by the imputed righteousness of Christ; and regeneration and sanctification by the Holy Spirit, as indispensable to prepare the soul for heaven." Is this the summary exhibition of all the bible teaches, or of what the bible teaches?—!! Are these "the only radical truths?" Oh! that we "could see ourselves as others see us!" What a pity that God should have employed so many prophets and apostles for so many centuries, who have written so many pages to teach us no more than may be summarily comprehended in the above epitome.

Not a word of the perseverence of the saints—not a word of the resurrection of the dead, of

14

eternal judgment, of eternal salvation or damnation in the above "summary exhibition of what the bible teaches." On this epitome Sadducees and Universalists might get into the bosom of the Doctor's church. Blessed be God that my faith is not to be measured out to me in spoonfuls by any such epitomizing Doctors! and that I can smile at the folly and deplore the weakness of such summary exhibits of what the bible teaches. I should not have been astonished at the above epitome, had not my friend, the Doctor, added, "These I believe to be the radical truths which God has revealed in his word," yes, "the fundamental principles." Mark it well—"THE radical truths"—THE fundamental principles!"

Now, reader, you know the definite article the is inclusive and exclusive—it includes and excludes every thing foreign to that to which it is applied. Doctors of Divinity are all Doctors of literary attainments. And Doctor Noel is distinguished as a belles-lettres scholar. The resurrection of the dead, and eternal life and death, are not among "the radical" nor "the fundamental truths;" and from all in the above epitome, I know not whether the Doctor would make them any truths at all taught in the Bible. Whether such an epitome, or a general declaration, "I believe what the Bible teaches," furnishes the more or the most satisfactory data on which to unite in church fellowship, I would not spend one sentence to prove. But as this matter is sufficiently exposed, I proceed to notice that there never has been, nor ever can be, "a summary exhibition, nor "an epitome of what the Bible teaches," written out by the hand of man. If all the Doctors on earth were to meet in one solemn conclave, and sit seventy years longer than the Council of Trent, they cannot write out such an epitome. And I do here promise, that if any man attempts to give such a summary exhibition, even Dr. Noel himself, I will shew that it is no epitome, no summary exhibition at all. So that if what I have now said be correct, and the Doctor's definition of a human creed be correct, then it follows no such a creed as he would make a religious test can be furnished from the pen of mortal man. Now remember we are at issue here, and that I stand pledged to shew, when any such epitome is written out, that it is not "a summary exhibition of what the Bible teaches;" and I think, my opponents themselves being judges, it will be awarded that I have now shewn that the Doctor's radical and fundamental truths are no epitome, compend or summary of what the Bible teaches. I do not care how the human creed advocates, transmografy or metamorphose themselves on the question—I do not care how they change the mode of defence or the definitions—I am just as conscious that I can ferret them out, and shew them and the world that it is all downright sophistry as I am that I can lift fifty pounds weight.

The Baptist Recorder editors have changed the question altogether. A creed, with them, is all that a man preaches or writes. "Your creed," says brother Clack in his first letter to me—"I mean your writings." Here is the proof, or a summary exhibition of it, that a man's writings are what they call his creed. But is not this most sophistical? Who contends that his writings should be made a term of communion—a test of christian character? If Messrs. Waller and Clack do so, I hereby declare I do not. If any man or set of men should attempt such a thing, I hereby protest against them. The indiscriminate use and application of the term "creed"

unsettles the question altogether. Now I candidly acknowledge there is much more honesty, independence, firmness, and candor, apparent in the writings of Dr. Miller and the Rev. Crawford, than in any of the Baptist advocates of creeds. The Paido Doctors boldly and unequivocally avow what they mean, and defend themselves as unambiguously as they can. But there is such shuffling and changing, such settling and unsettling, such defining and misdefining the terms or the chief term in this question, among the Baptist Doctors, that it exhibits either great misgivings within, or inability to reason on the subject. When a term is changed in its meaning by any controversialist, all logicians know and admit that the person who changes it either begs the question, abandons the cause, or misrepresents his opponent. To say that I make a creed of my writings, or that they come up to Dr. Noel's definition, is without all reason, argument, or proof. I have never once attempted to form a creed upon Dr. Noel's plan, Dr. Miller's, or any other plan. And if the question is now to be argued, Whether my writings constitute a creed, or in writing I am making a creed for others, let the former question be abandoned and I am at my post to defend myself at a moment's warning. But, gentlemen, no more of this sophistry. I have not yet done with Dr. Noel's definition, but I do not wish to weary him out, or my readers at one time on this trite question.

                                        EDITOR.

_____

Replication No. II. to Spencer Clack.

BROTHER CLACK,—WHEN you have read my No. 2. on Dr. Noel's circular, you will no doubt have observed that I represent you as having changed the subject of investigation on the creed question, and that you are considered as fighting with a phantom of your own creation. You have defined a creed to be all that a man writes on the subject of religion—a definition however true and correct you may consider it, is at war with all the creed systems in christendom. On your definition, the creed of the Presbyterian church is the writings of all the commentators, all the bodies of divinity, sermon books, and religious magazines, written by the orthodox clergy of that church, equally with the Westminster productions. On your definition, all writings of Dr. Gill, Andrew Fuller, and a hundred others, regular and orthodox Baptists, constitute the creed of the regular Baptist church. And so it comes to pass, that all the writings of every man is his creed, and all who adopt him as a brother or a member of their community, adopt his writings as their creed. I know you have not said so in so many words, but your definition of a creed most certainly represents the matter thus. For you call my whole writings my creed, and make them the creed of all who read them with approbation. This is not that question Dr. Noel, Dr. Miller, or I was discussing; and by introducing this view of the matter, you have changed the whole ground of controversy. For instance, when I commence a defence of myself from your imputations, I have only to show that I am making not a creed for myself or others, no test of religious character, no term of communion; and when I have done this the question at issue is never glanced at, which is proof positive that the question at issue is abandoned by you.

If you aim either at my conviction or that of others, you must not reason in this way; for to see you driven into this plan, establishes us in our views more and more: and weakens your cause, irreparably   I now beg your indulgence while I attempt to show you that you have mistaken the subject altogether. I say mistaken, for I would rather believe that you have mistaken, than that you have knowingly *misrepresented* it. You say in Letter 1. " You (meaning myself) "object to creeds and confessions, and for the very same reason I could object to your ancient order of things. You object to creeds because they are not the Bible." Now let me tell you that this is not fact. I never did object to creeds because they were not the Bible. And recollect I use the term creed in its ecclesiastical import; and I call upon you to show where I have objected to creeds for this reason. Nor can you object to my "ancient order of things" for the same reason why I object to creeds and confessions. I object to creeds and confessions because made authoritative " tests of religious character and terms of christian communion;" and never can you, " for the same reason," object to the essays I have written on the "ancient order of things," because I have never made them, hinted that they should be, or used them as a test of christian character or terms of christian communion.

You must, I think, now see that you are fighting with a phantom of your own creation. It is not the editor of the Christian Baptist that you assail, but an apparition or a ghost that has some moonless night appeared to you in the vicinity of Bloomfield. I have often said (and let me tell you that I am not like your friend *Aleph*, always veering about on this question or any other which I publicly avow, for I have declared in the first letter I ever presented to a Baptist Association many years ago) that I cared not how many creeds were published, or would not object to publishing a creed every year, provided that it was only to inform the world what I or those in union with me held : and not to be made a test of christian character nor a term of christian communion. It is just in this light only that I oppose them in this controversy. And so long as you defend them in any other light, or represent me as opposing them—so long you mistake the question—so long you are terrified by ghosts and witches—so long you abandon the cause which you seem, and would wish to appear, to defend. It is very true I might object to many creeds because of their contents; but that is not the question now. It is the right of making any human creed—any inferences drawn by fallible men and fallible reasoning from the scriptures—any epitome, or summary exhibition, made by short-sighted mortals, a test of religious character and a term of christian communion. Having then detected you in a gross mistake of the whole matter at issue, I hope I shall be excused for noticing any farther any thing you have said upon this subject, founded upon your misapprehension of the subject. You know when we have dug up the foundation, it is not always necessary to knock the wall to pieces.

Mr. Crawford of Chambersburgh gives the best definition of a creed of any of you human creed advocates: "It is a system of evangelical truth, deduced from the scriptures by uninspired men, printed in a book, and made a term of ecclesiastical fellowship." Although not a Doctor of Divinity, he has acquitted himself well here. Uninspired deductions of the understanding *from* the scriptures, made a term of ecclesiastical fellowship. This is the creed for which he contends, and such a one as he practically holds. Uninspired inferences is his bond of union. Faith, I

will contend, has respect to testimony alone, and facts attested are the only things that can be believed. The agreement of conclusions with premises, or the deducing of them, or the apprehending of them, is a work of reason, not of faith. A man might as properly say he believed that an equilateral triangle had three equal sides and three angles, as to say that any book of inferences, inspired, or uninspired, deduced from any premises, is a confession of faith.— Two men may agree in all the deductions or chapters in the confession of Mr. Crawford, but their agreement is in opinion, not in faith.—- And if he could apprehend this, his whole sermon on creeds is dissolved and vanished into thin air.

There is one other mistake in your first letter, which I beg leave to correct. You say, "Between you and your Baptist brethren there is no difference of opinion as to the rule of faith and practice." I wish this was true. I admit it is true so far as we profess to have one and the same bible; but I do not profess to walk by the rule of the Philadelphia Confession—and if you do, you have got one rule more than I have got. I have no idea of calling any thing a rule of life by which I do not walk, and no man can walk by two rules unless they are of the same length and breadth.

In illustrating this rule, you say the Baptists think the bible teaches the doctrine contained in their creeds. Now, brother Clack, you will pardon me in saying that I do not know a Baptist church on this continent that "thinks the bible teaches" the doctrine contained in the only regular Baptist creed I have seen. And not all the members of any one church which I have yet met with, have ever seen or read this creed. It is very questionable with me whether as many as five persons in every church in your state have read or seen this little book—and I think it is no great loss. Many Baptists have gone to heaven who never saw it; and I do not think a single soul would be lost in consequence of the destruction of every human book of dogmas, called creeds, in the United States.

What then are you, brother Clack, contending about? About an *ignis fatuus*—a dead carcase; a dead letter—uninspired deductions? the apprehension of the theoretic truth of which depends upon the strength of intellect, and not upon faith at all. The apprehension of which never saved a sinner, nor edified a saint. If you were to issue from your press this day one myriad of such creeds, you would only poison the minds, inflame the passions, and scatter the seeds of discord throughout your churches. I do most earnestly beseech you, brother Clack, to abandon this heart-hardening—this soul-alienating—this discord-making—this strife-breeding course. Lift up your voice, and wield your pen in behalf of the superlative excellency, heaven-born simplicity, divine sufficiency, majesty, and power of the sacred writings of the holy apostles and prophets of Jesus our Lord. Call sinners to behold the Lamb of God which takes away the sin of the world, as he has been presented to us by his holy messengers—and exhort the saints to keep his commandments—to abide in his love—and to love one another for his name's sake—and neither in the hour of death; nor in the day of judgment will it cause you to blush or tremble, because you have cast to the moles and to the bats the little book and all the sophistry which was attached to, and inseparably connected with, the keeping it in public esteem, as a form of sound words. A. CAMPBELL.

————, Miss. May 29, 1827.

Dear Sir,—On reading your essay in one of the late numbers of the Christian Baptist, on the "purity of speech," or being cast into the mould of the New Testament, or Covenant, my mind was involuntarily led to the following train of reflections, which I have concluded to pen down and transmit to you for publication, if you think them worthy of insertion.

The subject of my meditations was the first idolatry, or image worship, the worshipping of the molten calf as gods, a particular account of which may be read in Ex. xxxii. The Israelites said to Aaron while Moses was upon the Mount receiving the law, "Up, make us gods which shall go before us," &c. "And Aaron said to them, Break off the golden ear-rings which are in the ears of your wives, of your sons, and of your daughters, and bring them to me."— "And all the people broke off the golden ear-rings which were in their ears, and brought them to Aaron." Men wore these ornaments in the eastern countries as well as women, as we find in the story of the Israelitish and Midian soldiers. Judges viii. 24, 25, 26. And Pliny speaking of their ear-rings, says, "In the east it is esteemed an ornament for men to wear gold in that place." (See Beauchart's History, chapter 34,) "And they said, These be your gods, O Israel!" &c. "And Aaron built an altar before it, and made proclamation, To-morrow is a feast to the Lord." Now, what in this history struck me so forcibly, was, first they changed their glory into the similitude of an ox, a fat filthy ox that grazes on the green meadow, and then transferred to this beautiful ox with white and black spots intermingled, the fearful name, the character, the attributes, the perfections, the works and the worship of the *I am that I am*. For they rose up early on the morrow and brought burnt offerings and peace offerings. How easy the transition! This may appear a small matter to some who believe that whatever a man thinks to be right, is right to him; and to others who say that it is no matter what we call things, so that we mean the same thing; and by others it will doubtless be viewed in the light of a non-essential, as it was at most only a departure from one of the statutes. But let us trace this one act of the high priest through all its meanderings, as far as we have the facilities of doing so, and see if the ultimatum will support these persons in their indifference about celestial names and things.

It is generally supposed that they learned this idolatry or abomination from the Egyptians, among whom they had sojourned, and who were notorious for their love and use of hieroglyphics, and who accordingly worshipped Joseph, (who interpreted the dream of Pharaoh's seven fat and lean kine,) under the emblem of an ox with a bushel turned over his head. This is the foundation of all idolatry. This is the Apis, or Serapis, of the Egyptians; the Bel, or Belus, of the Canaanites, Chaldeans, or Babylonians; the Melianthus of the Phœnicians; the Molech, Moloch, Milcom, Melcam, Malcom, Rephan, Remphan, Chiun, of the Ammonites; the Baal, a male deity, of the Israelites; the Chemosh, Baalim, and Ashtaroth, feminine deities, of the Moabites; the Adonis of the Syrians; or the Rimmon of the Damascenes; the Thammuz of the Jews; the Dagon of the Philistines; the Saturn of the Carthagenians; the Light and Darkness of the Persians; the Jupiter, Apollo, Mars, Mercury, Bacchus, and, in short, the thirty thousand gods of the Greeks and Romans, made like to corruptible man, and to birds, and four-footed beasts,

and creeping things. They even deified the most abominable vices—

"Gods partial, changeful, passionate, unjust,
"Whose attributes were rage, revenge or lust;
"Such as the souls of cowards might conceive,
"And, formed like tyrants, tyrants would believe."

The properties of these idols transferred to St. Augustine, St. Ambrose, St. Cyprian, &c., forms the mysterious rites of the Holy Apostolic Catholic Church, and which lies deep at the foundation of the modern charitable and Babylonian churches, which claim the prerogative to change, alter, and abolish rites and ceremonies to suit times, places, and countries, (see the Prayer-Book, under head "Ceremonies,") and whose fall will be great. Thus we see that the whole system of ancient Pagan mythology is nothing more than the perversion of a plain historic fact of the Jewish law: a mixture of Judaism and Paganism, a misnomer. The modern systems of mythology are a mixture of Judaism, Paganism, and Christianity. Jewish and anti-christian names and ideas transferred to christians' names and things, a misnomer. After this survey, will any man say that it is immaterial what we call things, so that we mean the same things; that there are non-essentials in the word of God, connected with every word of which is, majesty, authority, power, wisdom and benevolence? The following reflections seem naturally to arise. How grateful should we be for "the Book" which gives us all the information we have, or can have, of the Almighty, and our own origin and destiny, in appropriate and intelligible terms! How careful should we be to preserve inviolate every phrase, word, syllable, and letter of this inestimable book! What robbery has God sustained by this one departure from the divine law! What innumerable millions of souls have perished in consequence of this one departure! How much evil have great men done at different periods of the world by lending their names and influence to sanction these departures! How difficult to return to the right way when once forsaken! How much trouble, vexation, opposition, persecution, tyranny, agony, horrors and bloodshed, and death, in a thousand forms, have the Christians experienced by this one departure! How has his glory been concealed and his significant and heavenly institutes perverted!   J. C.

———

Belmont, Ohio, July 28, 1827.

Mr. Campbell—From the perusal of your Christian Baptist, and known talents on theological subjects, I would come nearer to the truth of a question I would presume to propound. Before I lay down the question, I will state the history of the case which gave rise to it. I am a member of the Methodist Episcopal Church, and denominated a Reformer, being an adherent to that party. We, the reformers, of the said church, have got up a paper called the 'Mutual Rights, in which are discussed the principles of church government. We, the Reformers, wish the church to be modelled upon primitive usage, *i. e.* the people to be identified in the church with the ministers in the law-making department. Now it is contended for, in a pamphlet versus Reform, that, as the church originated from the preachers, that is, in the formation of the discipline to govern the Methodist Episcopal Church, as the people did not originate the discipline, they have not any right in the administration of the church. And again, that a man virtually surrendered his inherent rights in the church, or, in one word, that a member of the Methodist Episcopal Church has lost his liberty as Christ's freeman when a member of said church. You must recollect that the discipline of our church originated from Coke and Asbury, and that the present polity was surreptitiously introduced, being contrary to the desire of our founder, the episcopacy of the church. Now for the question: Can it be possible for any church to exclude its members from a participation in the law-making department of the church, merely and solely because the church government originated from the ministry? Was not the church for one hundred and fifty years governed according to the manner it is laid down in the New Testament, and as soon as the clergy debarred the people their legitimate rights, it sunk or merged to popery, with its concomitant evils? Now it is also contended in the pamphlet, that, as the Methodist polity is missionary, lay representation will bring it down to the congregationalist form, and naturally destroy the design of the missionary character. Now we have nothing to warrant that assumption from primitive times. I am certain that there were churches planted in different parts of Asia, Europe, Africa, and that under that economy, the spirit of the missionary character was glorious. Now how lay representation, in the councils of the clergy, can destroy the missionary effect, is an enigma to my mind, maugre the spareness of the number of the people and the extent of country the preachers have to travel, even if they have the world for a diocese.

Your attention to these, will command the grateful recollection of your sincere friend and well wisher. S. I. M.

—

"In the April, May, and June numbers of the "Mutual Rights," a periodical work, published by a committee of Methodists in Baltimore, there is an account of seven members being excluded by the preachers in North Carolina, for no other crime than peaceably attempting to obtain their rights as members of the church. Also, an account of a preacher being silenced for one year by the Baltimore Conference, for reading the "Mutual Rights," and recommending them to others—his moral character unimpeachable. These things have roused the members so in many parts, that they are determined no longer tacitly to submit to this Methodist Popery."

—

My Dear Sir—I am glad to see the efforts making by the more intelligent Methodists throughout the union, for divesting their system of those strong features of resemblance to the papal supremacy, which appear in this country so illy to comport with the spirit and genius of our government. A calf in rich pasture soon grows up into an ox; and when an ox, he can sometimes gore prodigiously. The calf which was raised by the hands of Messrs. Asbury and Coke, though not so well thriven as that on the banks of the Thames in Old England, has grown rapidly, and occasionally he terrifies the youngsters by the shaking of his horns.

I do hope that you will succeed in defacing one mark of the Beast from your system. But I do not understand so well what you mean by the laity participating in the law-making department. Neither the teachers nor the taught, as I understand the New Testament, have any law-making authority at all. Jesus Christ, the New Testament teaches me, is the one only lawgiver, and he is able to save them who obey his laws, and to destroy them that do not. You have no need of any other lawgiver, nor laws, as far as I can judge. I would ask those who wish to have a legislating power, to inform me how, and upon what subjects, they would exercise it.

I do not wonder at the logic used by the anti-reform good people. Men never like to part with power; and those in power will always find many tools by which to carry their projects into effect, by any means, sense or nonsense.

I answer your question with a capital NAY. But I am unwilling to put out one class of lawgivers and to put in another, when I know that every law they make for the church will be an attempt to usurp the throne and government of the Great King. You want less law-making and more law-keeping. If I were to set up a human religion, that is, a religion of human contrivance, I would ordain that all the law-making should be in the hands of the laity, and that the priesthood should have no part in it at all; but let them execute the law of the laity. Then you might expect something like your rights—your mutual rights—but if you let the clergy help you to make laws and execute them too, you will be duped at last. For were you to send two laymen for every priest, the priests would make the laws at last; and your reformation, like that of Luther, would need to be reformed again and again.

With the best wishes for your success in destroying idols and them that worship them, by the power of truth, I subscribe myself your friend and the friend of every man who loves truth and liberty. A. Campbell.

—

From the New Harmony Gazette of August 1.

In reply to the queries of the Christian Baptist, published in our Gazette of the 11th ultimo, we have received the following communication from our correspondent W. R.

To the Editor of the New Harmony Gazette.

Mr. Editor—Having in vain looked for a reply from some of your correspondents to the Queries of the Christian Baptist, published in your Gazette some weeks ago, I beg to offer the following remarks, without, however, claiming the appellation "enlightened Deist."

The questions proposed for our consideration are, Is there a God who created all things? Is there a spirit in man which will survive the body? Is there a future state of reward or torment? I answer, We can reply to these propositions neither in the affirmative nor in the negative, for we possess no positive knowledge on any of these subjects.

A God, the Soul, Heaven and Hell, if such existences and places do really exist, can never, from their nature, become cognizable by the senses of man. I therefore cannot conceive how we shall ever be able to acquire information regarding their nature or existence. W. R.

Can the editor of the Christian Baptist, or some of the "enlightened Deists" from whom he expected a reply, afford us any *positive* information on this subject? If so, we shall be pleased to hear from them, and shall insert their communications, reserving to ourselves our editorial privilege of closing the discussion, should it become too lengthy for our columns, or uninteresting to our readers.

—

I have only room for the present to remark, that, with all the improvements in philosophy for eighteen centuries, the world is no wiser with respect to God than it was when Paul lived. He then declared that neither Greece, nor Rome, nor Egypt, by all their philosophy, knew God. Even to this day, the God that was unknown in Athens, is unknown in New Harmony, and to all who have no other lights than what philosophy affords. And here is another and a striking proof: the people of the city of "Mental Independence" are said to have the best library on this continent, and with all the advantages of social converse in the best improved condition of human nature, having voluntarily extinguished the lights of supernatural revelation, have now candidly and honestly avowed that whether there is a God at all, a spirit in man that will survive his mortal body, a heaven or hell, is to them *unknown* and *unknowable*. This is the identical conclusion to which I knew most certainly, by all the knowledge of philosophy which I possess, they would be constrained to come. For, as I have frequently said, there is no stopping place between Deism and Atheism; and they are lame philosophers who, taking philosophy for their guide, profess to hold with Herbert, Hume, Gibbon, and Payne, that there is a God, an immortal soul, a heaven, or a hell. I give great praise to the New Harmony philosophers for their candor and their honesty in frankly avowing the conclusion which all the lights they have authorize them to maintain. I say they are good philosophers. They have reasoned well. I thank them for their polite and minute attention to the queries I proposed to them; and in the meantime, promise them a continuance of my essays on this most interesting subject.   Editor C. B..

———

No. 3.]   October 1, 1827.
Deism and the Social System.—No. V.
Randolph County, Ind. July 3, 1827.

Dear Sir,—In looking over some of your late numbers of the Christian Baptist, I found a series of essays addressed to Mr. D., whom you call a sceptic. Though I am not fond of useless "replication," yet when controversy is instructive, I have no objection to give ear to it, and learn what may be learnt from it. This being the case, I feel somewhat inclined to investigate some positions laid down (I will not say assumed) by you in the above essays; but at the same time, I will observe that I wield a young untutored pen—one in which it would be the height of presumption to undertake to vie with the masterly quill of the erudite A. Campbell.

In the first and second numbers of your Replication, you deny the possibility of the existence of a God being known without deriving that knowledge from the Bible. Strange, indeed, is it, that the all-wise Creator of the universe should make the most fallible kind of evidence, viz. testimony, the *only* possible vehicle through which he can be known to his creatures! It is strange that he should make the frail inventions of men, such as empty sounds, paper, &c. the archives of his name and character, in exclusion to the more durable work of his own hand—the Book of Nature.

I think that the evidence of the scriptures is of the most fallible class; because it is to us history, hearsay, or evidence resting on the testimony of others. There are but three kinds of evidence by which we assent to the truth of a proposition; and of these but one is infallible, and that is where the principles on which the evidence is founded are intuitive. Such is the evidence on which mathematical truths are founded. The next highest class of evidence is that which I call experience; and is that which is received immediately by the senses. It is on this kind of evidence that the truths of natural and experimental philosophy stand. This, though a very high kind of evidence, is still fallible: for we are liable to be deceived by our senses, since, to a man having the jaundice, every thing appears

yellow. The next and last class of evidence is testimony, wherein we give our assent or dissent to a proposition on the veracity of others. This kind of evidence is quite fallible: for the witness may either wilfully deceive by prevarication or lying; or though he wish to give correct testimony, his senses may have deceived him; and he being deceived, those who receive his testimony cannot but be deceived also.

The truths of the Bible are with us, founded on this kind of evidence. For though at the promulgation of the gospel, its truth was attested by miracles; yet *we* believe that it was attested in such a manner, on the evidence of testimony.—It is *possible* for the Bible to be all a fable or romance produced by priestcraft. And as it is possible for it to be so, you see that the vehicle which you would make us believe is the only one by which we can come at a knowledge of our Creator, may deceive us, and we may spend our whole lives in controversial bickering about fables.

Having said this much to show you that there is not so much credence necessarily attached to the scripture account of the Creator and his character as you would have us believe, I shall now undertake to show you that, notwithstanding you could not, by your senses, discover but that the Creator "was either not almighty; that the winds and rain were stronger than He, or that he was the most notionate, irrational, and whimsical being in the universe;" we can, by our senses, and reasoning faculties, be as imperatively convinced of the existence of a God, as we can by the scriptures. I would here observe that this is the main point in which I disagree with you in your "replication."

To show that we are capable of knowing that there is a God, and how it is we came by this knowledge, I think we need go no farther than ourselves. Man, beyond doubt, has a clear perception, and certain knowledge that he exists and is something. If any one is so sceptical as to deny this, he may enjoy his opinion, for me, till hunger or pain convince him of the contrary. For such are beyond the power of reason or demonstration to touch, if it were possible for such to be. But it is impossible for such rational creatures to exist; therefore, rational creatures that do exist, are certainly assured of their existence.

"In the next place, man knows, by an intuitive certainty, that bare nothing can no more produce real being, than it can be equal to two right angles. If a man knows not that non-entity, or the absence of all being, cannot be equal to two right angles, it is impossible that he should know any demonstration in Euclid. If, therefore, we know there is some real being, and that non-entity cannot produce any real being, it is an evident demonstration that, from eternity, there has been something; since what was not from eternity, had a beginning; and what had a beginning, must be produced by something else.

"Next, it is evident, that what had its being and beginning from another, must also have all that which is in, and belongs to its being from another too. All the powers it has must be owing to, and received from the same source. This eternal source, then, of all being, must also be the source and original of all power; and so *this eternal being must be also the most powerful.*

"Again, a man finds in himself perception and knowledge. We have, then, got one step farther; and we are certain now, that there is not only some being, but some knowing intelligent being in the world.

"There was a time, then, when there was no knowing being, and when knowledge began to be; or else there has been also a knowing being from eternity. If it be said there was a time when no being had any knowledge, when that eternal Being was void of all understanding—I reply, that then it was impossible there ever should have been any knowledge; it being as impossible that things wholly void of knowledge, and operating blindly, and without any perception, should produce a knowing being, as it is impossible that a triangle should make to itself three angles bigger than two right ones. For it is as repugnant to the idea of senseless matter that it should put into itself sense, perception, and knowledge, as it is repugnant to the idea of a triangle, that it should put into itself greater angles than two right ones.

"Thus, from the consideration of ourselves, and what we infallibly find in our own constitutions, our reason leads us to the knowledge of this certain and evident truth, that there is an eternal, most powerful, and most knowing being; which, whether any one will please to call God, it matters not. The thing is evident, and from this idea duly considered, will easily be deduced all those other attributes, which we ought to ascribe to this eternal Being. If, nevertheless, any one should be found so senselessly arrogant, as to suppose man alone knowing and wise, but yet the product of mere ignorance; and that all the rest of the universe acted only by that blind hap-hazard: I shall leave with him that very rational and emphatical rebuke of Tully, (C. 2. de leg.) to be considered at his leisure. What can be more sillily arrogant and misbecoming than for a man to think that he has a mind and understanding in him, but yet in all the universe beside there is no such thing? Or that those things which, with the utmost stretch of his reason he can scarce comprehend, should be moved and managed without any reason at all?

"From what has been said, it is plain to me, we have a more certain knowledge of the existence of a God, than of any thing our senses have not immediately discovered to us. Nay, I presume I may say, we more certainly know that there is a God than that there is any thing else without us. When I say we know, I mean there is such a knowledge within our reach, which we cannot miss, if we but apply our minds to that, as we do to several other inquiries."—Locke's Essay, B. 4. ch. 10.

Now, sir, do you think that you and "Inquisitas" made the best use of your reason, when you undertook to discover the existence and character of God? Your stories are as cogent reasoning in support of your hypothesis, as the story of the man who said he had lived 20 years at one place, and during the whole time he never found his head hanging down, would be to disprove the diurnal motion of the earth. Others might reason better; but you, Inquisitas, and the man, all reasoned alike, that is, "the best you could."

I do not wish you, from the above remarks, to think I am an enemy to the laudable work in which you are engaged. I do think it high time for a people who boast of their freedom, to have the fetters of superstition broken, and their minds liberated. But, conceiving that you reasoned wrongly on the above point, I have made free to give you some of my thoughts on the subject. Judging from your character as a disputant, I expect to be heard patiently and dealt with fairly.   A Lover of Just Reasoning.

Reply to the above.

Dear sir.—To the classification of evidence which you adopt, I offer no objection. But more has been said on the superiority of intuitive evidence than the subject deserves. Its superiority, in the estimation of philosophers, is greater than either in fact or utility. For the sake of argument, I am willing to admit that it produces infallible certainty; but this infallible certainty is of no greater importance in actual life than is the certainty, fallible or infallible, which results from the evidence of our senses or of testimony. I am intuitively certain that a whole is greater than a part. I am experimentally certain that fire will burn. I am, *by testimony*, certain that George Washington once lived. I doubt no more the truth or certainty of the last mentioned than of either of the former. You, in theory, place intuitive evidence above all other, as respects certainty; but, in fact, you place the evidence of your senses or experience above it. Take an instance in the close of your letter. You attempt to prove that there is a God from intuitive principles; and after reasoning for some time on these principles, you conclude your syllogisms by saying, "From what has been said, it is plain to me we have a more certain knowledge of the existence of a God, than of any thing our senses have not immediately discovered to us." But, what follows? Not so certain, or not more certain than we are of any thing which our senses discover to us. In this way the philosopher often forgets his theory when he comes in contact with fact. I attribute Locke's words to you, as you have adopted them.

But as men do not feel themselves certain upon, nor according to, the principles graduated by philosophers in their schools, it is a matter of no importance with me to spend many minutes in objecting to your remarks upon evidence in general. The Revelation of God was not first communicated by testimony: he did not choose to reveal himself in this way; but to us now it is all matter of history or testimony: but not merely so, as you represent it. The Revelation is addressed to the whole man, and it has within it its intuitive principles, which it presents to the honest student as Euclid does to his students. When the terms are understood, it is as intuitively evident that good men differ from bad men, as that 2 and 3 are not one and the same. There is no proposition in Euclid more capable of lucid and conclusive demonstration than this one. It is impossible that the bible could have been forged or introduced through priestcraft or kingcraft. To those acquainted with its contents, it is an axiom as evident in morals, as any respecting quantities in mathematics, that good men could not surreptitiously introduce this volume. Neither could bad men. But, without particularizing on a subject so plain, I proceed to remark that the evidence which supports the claims of this volume is not confined to any one species, but embraces the whole. Its truth becomes the subject of experience, properly so called. Jesus the Messiah puts it in the power of every person whom he addresses experimentally to prove the truth of his pretensions. He says, "Come to me, all you that labor and are heavy laden, and I will give you rest. If any man put himself under my guidance he shall know the truth, and the truth shall make him free." Thus we have the means of deciding experimentally on the reality of his pretensions. Whether he were an impostor, or the Messenger of the Great God, is submitted thus to be tested by our experience. Where is the man who has proved these promises false? Myriads have experienced their truth. Thus you see it is doing injustice to the wisdom of the author of this volume to say, that he has made it a matter of testimony only, properly so called. For its claims are supported by intuitive evidence, experience, and testimony.

But there is a shorter, and, to the bulk of mankind, a more cogent way of deciding the question, Whether the Book of Creation, or that called the Bible, is better adapted to communicate to the human mind the knowledge of God? This is by furnishing an answer to the following question: Whether do they who read the bible, or they who read nothing else but the Book of Nature, know most of God, or know him best? Which of them possess the more clear, consistent and rational views of Deity? The progress of the students is the better proof of the qualifications of the preceptor.

But the principal point is that which is yet to be noticed. You object in strong terms to my "denying the possibility of the existence of God being known, without deriving that knowledge from the Bible." Permit me distinctly to state the difference between my views and those of natural religionists, deists, and sceptics in general, on this subject.

1. I contend that no man, by all the senses, and powers of reason which he possesses, with all the data before him which the material universe affords, can originate or beget in his own mind the idea of a God, in the true sense of that word.

2. But I contend so soon as the idea of Deity is suggested to the mind, every thing within us and without us, attests, bears testimony to, and demonstrates the existence and attributes of such a being.

If the first position can be established, it will follow that there cannot be a rational deist on earth. If the second position be established, there cannot be an atheist amongst all the *compos mentis* of the human race. I think both of these positions can be triumphantly maintained against all objections whatsoever. The first one is that which you assail, and these essays are devoted to the establishment of it alone. I proposed three questions to the *illuminati* of New Harmony for this purpose, expecting that if they were deists, they would answer them in the affirmative, and then offer their proof. But not knowing whether they would affirm or deny, I could do no more than simply propose them.— They, very politically, and, I suppose, honestly, (for honesty is always the best policy) said they could neither affirm nor deny. But in their last number which reached me to-day, (September 10) they have exhibited more wit than logic on the subject of these queries. I will lay before you a second class of answers given to these three queries by another of these sage philosophers, and to which the editor says aloud, *Amen!*

"The editor of the Christian Baptist appears desirous to get rid of the *onus probandi*, the trouble of proving, by demanding from the sceptics of Harmony answers to three questions. This seems to me unphilosophical. As the writers in the Gazette are professed sceptics, the *onus probandi* can never, with propriety, be thrown upon them. When I say, *I doubt;* this wants certainly no other proof but my assertion. But I shall, nevertheless, answer his questions, and by doing so, show their philosophical impropriety."

1st "Is there a God who created all things?" I answer, from my heart, *I do not know. If you know*, pray *prove* it! This is the *norma dispu-*

tandi, as Miss Wright says, and I think with her, there is as much proof *pro* as *con.* If, by the word "creating," you mean producing out of nothing, I feel the irresistible weight of the axiom, *ex nihilo nil fit*, out of nothing nothing can come, which repels your assertion. If you call God the *first cause*, he is an effect *without a cause;* and this is again nonsense. Even as the proofs *pro* or *con*, temporarily preponderate in my mind, I call, at one time with Goethe, the world an "ever-devouring, ever-regurgitating monster," or at another I exclaim with Pope, "all discord's harmony not understood,"—"whatever is, is right!" When I observe benevolent design attained, I am for a God. But when I see design *not attained*, (as e. g. the nipples in males of men and quadrupeds, or muscles to move the external ear in man without a *nerve* to influence its motion, &c.)—or a bad design, attained or or not, (e. g. the claws of the tiger to tear the innocent lamb, or those of the hawk to pierce the heart of the harmless dove, &c.)—the idea of a God speedily vanishes. If the editor of the Christian Baptist can prove the existence of a God, he is heartily welcome: for my part, I cannot.

2d. "Is there a spirit in man?" &c. Here again I must impugn the irregularity of the opponent. He should first have given a definition of the word *spirit*. I should define it to be something not in the least like to any thing I know; and this would be a good definition of *nothing*.— Modern philosophy with the celebrated professor Kant, has quite set aside the unmeaning distinction between matter and spirit; for who can tell where matter ceases and spirit begins? The substances of electricity, galvanism, caloric, magnetism—are they *matter* or *spirit?* If he will let me substitute the word *substance*, *essence* for spirit, I will answer the question. The substance which thinks and wills in us, must last forever; for annihilation is nonsense to us, who have never witnessed it. But whether that substance, as an individual being, can think and act, when uncombined with other substances, as in man during life, is again a problem justly to be doubted. The editor of the Christian Baptist will here again have to prove, or wait with with me "*the great teacher, Death.*"

3d. "*Is there a future state of felicity or torment?*" Bitter and sweet are so equally mixed in the cup of life, that we can claim neither compensation in bliss, nor owe retribution in torments hereafter. If happiness be our lot after death, it is mere generosity that bestows it; and if misery, it would be sheer, wanton, unmerited tyranny.

"This is all I know about these matters; and if the editor of the Christian Baptist knows more about it, I implore him, in the name of all honest sceptics, to come forward and PROVE it!

"*Affirmanti incumbit probatio.*"

They are premature in alleging that I put, or was wishing to put, the *onus probandi*, or task of proving, upon them. I was waiting their affirmation or negation; and then if there was a necessity for proof, the "*norma disputandi*," or law of disputing, would decide who should have the *onus probandi*. I told them at first I was willing to divide the burden before I knew what it would be. You will at once perceive that you and they are at issue, or that they decide in my favor against you. So that I may very justly hand you over to them, or them over to you. You and they, not I and they, are at issue on the first position. They have renounced both christianity and deism. They call deism "*nonsense.*" Your argument and that of Locke, they boldly affirm to be "*nonsense.*" I have now, by the testimony or concessions of a plurality of the most enlightened sceptic philosophers in the world, gained the very point, to establish which, these essays were commenced. They are devoted to deists; and a competent jury of sceptics, the only umpires in this case, have given in their verdict that a "rational deist" is a contradiction in terms or equivalent thereto; and that all his philosophy is "*nonsense.*" My first position is established with them, and those who oppose it I hand over to them. You will please, then, if you have any doubts on my first position, after reading this essay, make them known to those philosophers. For my part, unless I were to edit a work devoted to scepticism in all its various forms, (and this I think would be very necessary in the present day) I can say but little more on the subject in this work, as its object is of a different kind. Should I find room for a series of essays on the 2d position, I would like to come in contact with the sceptics of the Gazette. But as atheism is rather a distemper of the moral powers, than a defect in the intellectual, and as it never has, and I think never can make headway in the human family, I do not feel myself imperiously called to demonstrate my second position. There is not one person in ten myriads who will dispute its truth; and therefore, so long as there are many other truths of great importance, against which many object, both good reason and benevolence suggest that these should first be attended to. If a hundred persons will furnish ten subscribers each to a monthly paper, the same size, execution and price of this work, per annum, to be devoted to scepticism in general, I will engage to do the duties of an editor as far as I am qualified. And indeed I have often thought that such a work is much needed in the present day. A word to the wise is sufficient for him, and ten will not move a simpleton.

But I must not conclude this paper without pointing out the grand error in your and the philosophers' reasoning upon intuitive principles to originate the idea of a Creator or first cause. You begin to work with the idea in your own mind, and fondly imagine you have acquired it by your reasoning. Your effort should have been to show how a person without such an idea is to originate in his own mind the whole idea of a God. You suppose him in possession of a part of the idea before he begins to reason at all.

All that the book of nature teaches is that every animal and vegetable is dependent on one of its own kind for its production. The whole volume does not afford a model or archetype for an idea of any animal or plant being dependant on any other of a different nature and kind for its production. You leap over the distance from earth to heaven in your reasoning, or rather, you fledge yourself with the wings of faith, and find in the bible the idea of all things being dependant on a Being unlike every other, who produces no being like himself, contrary to your analogy from the book of nature, and who produces all beings both unlike himself and one another. You flew so nimbly and so easily over this mighty gulf, that you were not conscious that you had got out of the region of earth-born ideas altogether, and were farther than all space from the volume of nature which you sat down to read. Ask Locke and Hume, and they will tell you that you cannot have a single idea—a simple uncompounded idea, the pattern of which or the thing of which it is the idea, is not first presented to some one of your senses. Ideas are images, and be-

fore the image is seen in the glass, or exists in the mind, an object must be presented. And when have you seen any thing creating or producing something out of nothing, or forming any thing essentially unlike itself? And if such an object is no where presented you, can you have the image of it!!!

A natural man might see, and have an idea, that every animal and vegetable is dependant upon one of the same kind for its existence; but by what steps he could arrive at an idea that an invisible being made one or all animals and vegetables, I think no man living can show. And that any man could logically infer that there is a first cause, which is the effect of no antecedent cause from any thing he ever saw or heard outside of the bible, no philosopher has yet shown, nor can it ever be shown until man gets six senses instead of five. Locke and other philosophers who have rejected the doctrine of innate ideas and who have traced all our simple ideas to sensation and reflection, have departed from their own reasonings when they attempted to show that, independent of supernatural revelation, a man could know that there is an eternal first cause uncaused. You have a lever, but like Archimedes, you must exclaim "*dos pou sto.*" You must beg a place on which to rest your fulcrum. And outside of the bible the universe does not afford you a speck of matter on which to place your fulcrum.

But I have a few facts which on your principles, are inexplicable—on mine they are easily understood:—

1. Not one of the terms peculiarly expressive of the idea of a God, such as spirit, eternity, immortality, &c. are to be found amongst any people antecedent to their being possessed of oral or written revelation.

2. No nation or individual, without oral or written revelation, can be found who has a single idea of any item in the deists' creed.

3. All the deaf and dumb that have been made to hear and speak, or who have been taught to communicate their ideas, have uniformly and universally declared that an idea of a God, or any thing under that name never entered their mind. This is decisive proof that the knowledge of God enters the human mind by the ear, or by communication, verbal or written.

4. Not one of the idolatrous nations pretend to have derived their religion from reason. These are facts which I can only state at present; but which, when developed, contain volumes of invincible argument on this subject.

My dear sir, all your philosophy ends in doubts. And you may see from the philosophers of Harmony, that so soon as the bible words and ideas are proscribed, man is left in total darkness, both as respects his origin and destiny, the two grandest and most sublime points ever imagined or expressed. While they boast of light, they make a man more ignorant than an ass which knows its master's crib. They divest him of all his majesty, and make him of no more consequence than a snail or a mushroom. *Sic transit gloria philosophiæ.*   EDITOR.

———

A Problem for the Editor of the Harmony Gazette and his Doubting Brethren.

You think that reason cannot originate the idea of an eternal first cause, or that no man could acquire such an idea by the employment of his senses and reason—and you think correctly. You think also, that the bible is not a supernatural revelation—not a revelation from a Deity in any sense. These things premised, gentlemen, I present my *problem* FOR ATHEISTS in the form of a query again.

The christian idea of an eternal first cause uncaused, or of a God, is now in the world, and has been for ages immemorial. You say it *could not* enter into the world by reason, and it *did not* enter by revelation. Now, as you are philosophers and historians, and have all the means of knowing, *how did it enter into the world?*　EDITOR.

Paulinus to the Editor of the "Christian Baptist."
[A NOTE. Aug. 11, 1827.]

DEAR SIR:—EXISTING circumstances seem to require from me a statement of facts, with a few explanatory remarks:—I hasten to offer them accordingly.

Some little time past, I received from my much esteemed friend, Bishop R. B. S. the Kentucky "Baptist Recorder" of June 2; with a letter containing a reference to an editorial article in that paper. In this article, (which is addressed to yourself by one of the editors,) notice is taken of a letter which it seems was written by my friend above mentioned, to a correspondent in Kentucky; and an extract is given, in which the writer, speaking of Paulinus, says, "He wrote something last year, in which he certainly went too far. He is now convinced, (I am persuaded,) and is guarded against our friend Campbell's chimeras." In the last number of the Christian Baptist, too, I find this extract introduced by one of your correspondents; a circumstance which tends to hasten me in this statement.

That the writer felt the *persuasion* here expressed, I am too well assured of his candor, for a moment to question; nor can I indulge any disposition to complain of his having mentioned this impression to his correspondent, in a letter, which, as he informs me, was not designed for publication. That he might feel such a persuasion—a persuasion that I had measurably receded from some of my positions, is easy to imagine; though I certainly never intended, by any thing I may have said, a retraction of what I had written in the Christian Baptist.

Among the several points introduced in the correspondence between you and myself, there were two especially, on which my friend above mentioned had thought that he and I differed considerably. These regarded the subject of the "Old Dispensation," and the questions concerning "Creeds and Confessions of Faith." In the course, however, of several conversations, friendly discussions, and mutual explanations, we conceived that the difference, if any, was immaterial. I understood him as maintaining the perpetual obligation of Old Testament injunctions, *only* in so far as they are of a *moral* nature; and all such are surely sanctioned in the New Testament; and on my part, while I maintained the impropriety and injurious tendency of creeds and confessions of faith, considered as *standards*, I conceded to him, that I could see nothing improper in a written declaration or explanation of our religious sentiments.

Now, it is very possible, that, in regard to these matters, my brother S. might consider me as yielding, in some measure, the points for which I had contended; while I might believe, (as I certainly do,) that in all this—taking my two epistles in the Christian Baptist together—there was nothing the least inconsistent with what I had there written.

This statement is not intended for the purpose of screening myself from the imputation of a change in sentiment. We know but in part; and I am far from thinking it dishonorable, when

conviction has taken place, to retract a former opinion or adopt a new one. In this case, however, I see no occasion to retract; being persuaded that what I have advanced will, if properly understood, abide the test of any examination.

But there is a point, (permit me now to say,)—a matter of deeper interest and greater importance than any I have here alluded to; on which brother S. and myself, with many others, are cordially agreed;—I mean, the necessity of a present divine influence from the Holy Spirit, for the renewal of the soul of man in the image of Christ; and on which I must say, you do not appear to us to come out with sufficient clearness. Since your answer to my second epistle, (for which I hereby offer you my sincere acknowledgments,) I have read your whole series of "essays on the work of the Holy Spirit in the salvation of men;"—"counting, (to use the words of Solomon,) one by one, to find out the account; which yet my soul seeks, but I find not." Amidst a display of masterly talent, and lucid argument, and excellent matter, I find not any explicit exhibition of the point above mentioned. But you seem to think that this would be going so far towards forming a mere *theory;* and you seem to think that this is a point of mere *speculation.* Well, my dear sir, I must say, I do most devoutly differ from you in this opinion. To me it appears that this would not be *theorizing* (if there is such a word) but expressing a *scriptural truth;* and that it is by no means a mere *speculation,* but a point of deep *practical importance.*

I forbear, at present, to enter into this subject; reserving it for an essay which (God willing) I intend to write when more at leisure; and for which I hereby give you notice, I shall solicit a place in the *Christian Baptist.*

With the other extract in the "Recorder," there is no occasion, I presume, for me to interfere; the particular object of this communication being an explanatory exhibition of what concerned my own case. My acknowledgments, however, are due to brother Clack, of the "Recorder," and I beg through this medium to make them—for his favorable opinion as to my *disposition.* I am, indeed, as he believes, "not disposed to rend the churches for the sake of establishing the constructions and interpretations" of any person: for though I think there is room for reformation even among the Baptists, I am persuaded that this desirable object should be attempted, and may be best effected, by other means than those which might be calculated to rend the churches: and I wish, that in treating on each others' errors, we might not forget to love each others' persons.

Asking an insertion of this (entire) in the *Christian Baptist,* and wishing you grace, mercy, and peace, I am, dear sir, yours for Christ's sake.

　　　　　　　　　　　　　　PAULINUS.

P. S. Although my note has already extended beyond the limits which I had designed, I cannot be content to send it on, without saying how well pleased I always am with your attacks on the follies and vanities, the avarice and ambition, too prevalent in the religious world, and among the clergy, (so styled,) as well as the laity. [Would that I could be as well satisfied in every thing!] While some species of errors should, I think, be met in the spirit of mildness, these evils deserve the keenest strokes. Whence comes the desire, among the christian ministry, to be honored by human titles, and elevated by a factitious dignity? Not from the spirit of Christ. And who gave to our colleges the authority to weave a spiritual chaplet for the brows of a preacher? Not he who said, "Be ye not called of men Rabbi." What a pity that Baptists, who profess to be followers of Christ in simplicity, should ever "cast one longing, lingering look" at such vain baubles: and be willing to follow, though at humble distance in the track of the grand hierarchy. Excuse the length of my *note*.

                                             PAULINUS.

To Paulinus.

VERY DEAR SIR,—IN the proposed communication, which I shall receive gladly, please be full on one point, viz. in showing that the decision of one question is "a point of deep practical importance." I mean that the teaching of the unregenerate the necessity of a divine influence to their renewal or conversion, is to them "a point of deep practical importance." I remain yours as ever.   EDITOR.

From the Christian Messenger To the Christian Baptist.

BROTHER CAMPBELL,—YOUR talents and learning we have highly respected: your course we have generally approved; your religious views, in many points, accord with our own; and to one point we have hoped we both were directing our efforts, which point is to unite the flock of Christ, scattered in the dark and cloudy day. We have seen you, with the arm of a Sampson, and the courage of a David, tearing away the long established foundations of partyism, human authoritative creeds and confessions; we have seen you successfully attacking many false notions and speculations in religion—and against every substitute for the Bible and its simplicity, we have seen you exerting all your mighty powers. Human edifices begin to totter, and their builders to tremble. Every means is tried to prevent their ruin, and to crush the man who dares attempt it. We confess our fears that in some of your well intended aims at error you have unintentionally wounded the truth. Not as unconcerned spectators have we looked on the mighty war between you and your opposers; a war in which many of us had been engaged for many years before you entered the field. You have made a diversion in our favor, and to you is turned the attention of creed makers and party spirits, and on you is hurled their ghostly thunder. We enjoy a temporary peace and respite from war where you are known.

From you we have learned more fully the evil of speculating on religion, and have made considerable proficiency in correcting ourselves. But, dear sir, how surprised and sorry were we to see in your 10th number, volume 4, a great aberration from your professed principles. You there have speculated and theorized on the most important point in theology, and in a manner more mysterious and metaphysical than your predecessors. We refer to your exposition of *John* i. 1. " In the beginning was the Word, and the Word was with God, and the word was God." Please, sir, attend to a few friendly remarks, designed to correct in time what may hereafter become of more serious injury, than any system before invented by the wisdom of man.

You have assumed very high grounds, from which you look down upon all the christian world, and see them at an immeasurable distance below you—the Calvinist midway between you and the Arian—the Calvinist on a mountain, the Arian on a hill, and the Socinian on a hillock. From this eminence you see a vast difference between the Calvinist and Arian; but on a page or two before, you could discover very lit-

tle, if any difference between their views of the Son of God. The ground you occupy is too high for common minds to tread. I should be afraid to venture, lest giddiness should be the consequence. I would advise my dear brother not to soar too high on fancy's wings, above the humble grounds of the gospel, lest others adventuring may be precipitated to ruin. Not that I should advise you to settle on Calvin's mount, on the hill of Arius, or on the hillock of Socinus, (these are all far too low,) but on the holy mount of God, revealed in his word. This, though high as the heavens, is safe for all to tread.

You object to the Calvinistic views of Trinity, and of calling Jesus the *eternal Son of God*, for reasons which have long since induced us to reject them. Yet, my dear sir, we confess we can see no material difference between your views and those of the Calvinists. What you call the WORD, they call the *eternal Son of God;* yet you both believe the Word of God and the Son of God to be the one, self-existent, and eternal God himself. We are led to conclude this of you, because frequently you apply the term *Eternal* to the *Word*—as " his eternal glory," "his eternal dignity," " co-eternal with God," " the eternal relation between the Saviour and God." We believe that whatever is eternal, is also self-existent and independent, and therefore God supreme. We cannot think that you believe in two eternal Gods, though some of your readers may draw this inference from some of your expressions. You speak of " the relation which the Saviour held to the God and Father of all, *anterior to his birth*"—" the relation existing between God and the Saviour, *prior to his becoming the Son of God*"—" the *eternal relation* between the Saviour and God." We have always thought that a relation implied more than one; and that if God from eternity had existed alone, there could have been no relation between him and non-entity. We view these expressions of yours as unguarded, and not designed by you to communicate what the language imports, as when you say, "God from eternity was manifest in and by the *Word*." It might be asked, To whom was he manifest from eternity, if he alone existed from eternity? Again, that you and Calvinists differ only in phraseology on this subject, while you believe the same things, appears in another particular. What they call the human nature of Christ, or the man Christ Jesus, you call the Son of God, Jesus, Christ, Messiah, Only Begotten. They believe that the human nature of Christ existed not till born of Mary; you believe and declare that " there was no Jesus, no Messiah, no Christ, no Son of God, no Only Begotten, before the reign of Augustus Cesar." Neither Calvinists nor Socinians should impeach your orthodoxy on this point. The Calvinists maintain that the eternal son of God, who was the very and eternal God himself, became man by taking to himself a reasonable soul and true body, being conceived by the power of the Holy Ghost in *the womb of the Virgin Mary*, of her substance, *and born of her.* Confession of Faith, Lar. Cat. Ques. 37 and 47, &c! You say, the *Word*, by whom all things were made, "became flesh and dwelt among us. He became a *child born* and a son of man."

You may deny that you ever affirmed the *Word* to be the only true God. Then we would humbly ask you, What was it? Was it an intelligent being or a mere name or relation? We think the query important. If it was an intelligent being, and "co-eternal with God," as you say, then it must be the eternal God himself, or

24

another eternal, distinct God. If it be neither of these, then it must have been an eternal, unintelligent name or relation; or, in your own language, it was *the sign or image of an idea,* which idea is God. Shall we think that the *Word,* which was God, and by which all things were made, and which was made flesh, was nothing but an unintelligent name, relation, or sign of the only true God? Can this be the Saviour of sinners? We dare not impute this absurdity to you, but we fear your unguarded speculations may cause the less informed to err.

Permit us, dear brother, to propose a few queries for your consideration, and we hope for our profit:—

1. When it is so frequently asserted of the Son of God that he came down from heaven; that he ascended up to heaven, where he was before; does not this language naturally convey the idea that he was there prior to his coming down, and consequently before the reign of Augustus Cesar?

2. What can be the meaning of John vi. 38? "Jesus says to them, I came down from heaven not to do mine own will, but the will of Him that sent me." Was this Jesus who spake the only true God? How could the only true God say, "I came *not to do mine own will, but the will of him that sent me?* No Christian can apply this to the only true God. Was this Jesus the person that never existed till the "reign of Augustus Cesar?" How, then, could he in truth say, I came down from heaven, where he was before? The text cannot apply to him. If he was not the only true God, nor the person that never was till Cesar's reign, it must be *the Word* whom we call the Son of the living God, God's own Son, his only begotten, his first begotten, brought forth before the world was; yet we agree with you, and the generality of all sects in the present day, that he was not eternally begotten, or eternal Son. We plainly suggest these objections to your scheme to elicit information.

3. How can John xvii. 5. be reconciled with your views? "Father, glorify you me with your own self, with the glory I had with you before the world was." This person could not, we think, be the only true God; for if he was, he prayed to himself, (v. 3.) Will Christians say that the only true God prayed to himself to be with himself, to be glorified with himself, and to restore to himself the glory he once had with himself, but which he had not now, (therefore changeable,) &c. Should we not consider a man deranged who should thus fervently pray to himself to be with himself, &c? We dare not impute this to the only true God, nor can we apply the text to the person who began his existence under Cesar's reign, for this person that prayed had a glory with the Father before the world was, and therefore must have then existed. If it cannot apply to the only true God, nor to the person who had no existence till Cesar's reign, to whom can it apply? Surely not to a mere name, or unintelligent effulgence, or relation.

4. Again—who was the person spoken of in 2d Cor. viii. 9? "For you know the grace of our Lord Jesus Christ, that though he was rich he became poor, that you through his poverty might be rich." It could not be the only true God, for he is unchangeable; nor could it be the Jesus or Christ, who existed not till Cesar's day, for he was never rich in any sense, and became poor! We ask, Who was he?

5. Who was the person mentioned Phil. ii. 6, 10? The whole passage plainly shows it was

not the only true God, nor the person who never existed before the christian era.

6. Who was the person that said, "A body have you prepared me, O God?"—the person that *took* flesh and blood? Heb. ii. 14, x. 5.

7. Is it any where said that *the* Word created or made any thing (*hup'autou*) by himself as the original cause? Is it not always said that all things were made (*di'autou*) by him as the instrumental cause? as Eph. iii. 9. God created all things (*dia*) by Jesus Christ. 1 Cor. viii. 6. "But to us there is but one God, the Father (*ex*) of whom are all things; and one Lord Jesus Christ, (*di'hou*) by whom are all things." Heb. i. 2. "God in these last days has spoken to us by his Son (*di'hou*) *by whom* he also made the worlds," the material worlds, Heb. xi. 3. Col. i. 16. "All things were created (*di'autou*) *by him* and for him." It is true in the beginning of this verse *en autou* is used, but in the same sense.— The Greek fathers of the second and third centuries, commenting on those texts above quoted, say that *hupo* means the original, or first cause, and that *dia* signifies the second, or instrumental cause. Thus Philo, Origen, Eusebius, and Cyril, who certainly better understood their language than we do. (Clarke on Trin. p. 91. 92.) Doctor Clarke also remarks that this was the constant and unanimous sense of the primitive church. If these observations be true, will it not follow undeniably, that the *Word* (*di'hou*) *by whom* all things were made, was not the only true God, but a person that existed with the only true God before creation began; not from eternity, else he must be the only true God; but long before the reign of Augustus Cesar?

We are not sticklers for names; we can grant to you, without any relinquishment of principle, that this person, the Word, never bore the name of Jesus, Christ, Messiah, or Son of God, till the reign of Augustus. But we cannot say with you that these names solely belong to him; for Joshua was called Jesus, Cyrus was called Messiah, or Christ, or Anointed (for the Hebrew is the same)—and Adam was called the Son of God. Heb. iv. 8. Isa. xlv. Luke iii. 38. But the person of Joshua existed long before he was called Jesus, or Saviour—and the person of Cyrus existed before he was called Messiah or Christ. This name he never bore till he was anointed and appointed by God to restore captive Israel. So we believe the intelligent person, the Word, or the Son of God, existed long before he was called Jesus, Christ, or Messiah.

Dear brother, we submit these thoughts to you and the public from the purest motives, which we have already stated. We did design to make a few remarks on your speculations on the relation of a word and idea. We think the application of this to God and the Word, is foreign from the truth and meaning of the spirit. But the short limits of our work forbid us to write more. With sentiments of high respect and brotherly love we bid you adieu. B. W. STONE, EDITOR.

To the Christian Messenger.

BROTHER STONE,—I WILL call you *brother* because you once told me that you could conscientiously and devoutly pray to the Lord Jesus Christ as though there was no other God in the universe than he. I then asked you of what import and consequence was all the long controversy you had waged with the Calvinists on the trinitarian questions. They did practically no more than pray to Jesus; and you could consistently and conscientiously do no less. Theoretically you differed, but practically you agreed. I think you told me that you were forced into this controversy, and that you regretted it. Some weak heads amongst my Baptist brethren have been scandalized at me because I called you *brother* Stone. What! say they, call an "*Arian, heretic*," a brother!! I know nothing of his Arianism, said I, nor of his Calvinism. I never seriously read one entire pamphlet of the whole controversy, and I fraternize with him as I do with the Calvinists.— Neither of their theories are worth one hour; and they who tell me that they supremely venerate, and unequivocally worship the King my Lord and Master, and are willing to obey him in all things, I call my brethren. But more than this, brother Stone, I have to say to you. Your enemies, and they are not a few, have, to a man, as far as I have heard them speak, said your christian character, your moral deportment, was unblemished. Would to Heaven that this could have been said of all who opposed you! I do not think it strange that, in running post haste out of Babylon, you should have, in some angles of your course, run past Jerusalem. Nay, verily, I have been astonished that you should have made so few aberrations in so many efforts.

But, brother Stone, I exceedingly regret that you have said and written so much on *two* topics, neither of which you, nor myself, nor any man living, can fully understand. One of these is the burthen of your late letter to me. You do not like my comment on John, ch. i. ver. 1st.— Well, then, just say so, and let it alone. I said in presenting it I was not about to contend for it, nor to maintain any theory upon the subject. My words are, " Nor would I dispute or contend for this as a theory or speculation with any body." Why, then, call me into the field? I have received many letters on the subject of that essay, not one of which confines itself to the things I have said, nor to the grand object I had in view, viz. to examine into the ideas attached to the *term* employed by the Holy Spirit to designate the relation existing between him that "*was made flesh*," and sent into the world, and him who sent him.

I have uniformly found that all writers for the trinity and against it, have much to say upon the *rationale* of the doctrine. Reason is either proscribed or enthroned. Those that one while proscribe her, at another appeal to her; and those who make her sovereign will not always do her homage. So that the controversy is from reason to Revelation and from Revelation to reason, as the parties are pressed. I will take the liberty of laying down a few positions on this subject, not for the sake of demonstrating them, but for the sake of deciding on a proper course of conduct.

1. The pretensions of the bible to a divine authority or origin, are to be examined by our reason alone. Its evidences are addressed to our reason, and by our reasoning powers the question is to be answered, "Is the bible of divine or human origin?" So soon as reason has decided this question, then

2. The truths of the bible are to be received as first principles, not to be tried by our reason, one by one, but to be received as new principles, from which we are to reason as from intuitive principles in any human science.

3. The terms found in the bible are to be interpreted and understood in the common acceptation, as reason or use suggests their meaning; but the things taught are to be received, not because we have proved them by our reason to be truths, but because God has taught them to us.

4. The strongest objections urged against the Trinitarians by their opponents are derived from what is called the unreasonableness, or the absurdity of three persons being but one God, and that each of these three is the Supreme God. Now as you know I am not at all disposed either to adopt the style nor to contend for the views of the Trinitarians, any more than I am the views of the Socinians or Unitarians of any grade: you will bear with me when I tell you that no man as a philosopher, or as a reasoner, can object to the Trinitarian hypothesis, even should it say that the Father, the Word, and the Spirit, are three distinct beings, and yet but one God. There is nothing unreasonable in it. I will, indeed, in one sense, say, that it is unreasonable there can be a God at all, or an *Eternal First Cause*; because in all the dominions of reason there is nothing could suggest the idea: and because it is contrary to all the facts before us in the whole world that any cause can be the cause of itself, or not the effect of some other cause. No man, from analogy, can reason farther than every cause is the effect of another, *ad infinitum.* Here reason shuts the door. Here analogy puts up her rule, and shuts her case of instruments. Now in this sense, the Unitarian and the Trinitarian are alike unphilosophic—alike unreasonable. But here is the sophism: the bible originates, or still keeps up the idea of a God—both the name and the idea. We see it is proved by every thing within and without us. The bible teaches us something concerning three beings, (I shall call them) the Father, the Word, and the Holy Spirit. It teaches us that there is but one God. From what the bible teaches A supposes that these three beings are each and together one God, the same in substance, equal in power and glory. B. says it is inconsistent—it is absurd. How can three persons or beings be one? How can one of these three be the Deity, and yet the three be no more than the Deity? C. says, This is not more unreasonable than that there should have been from all eternity one First Cause uncaused; and adds, Your error is this: you know nothing of the existence of spirits at all. All bodies you know any thing of occupy both time and place; consequently, it would be absurd to suppose that three beings whose modes of existence are such as to be governed by time and space, could be one being. But inasmuch as we do know nothing about the mode of existence of spirits, we cannot say that it would be incompatible with their nature, or modes of existence, that three might be one, and that one being might exist in three beings. Now, as no man can rationally oppose the Calvinistic hypothesis on principles of reason, so neither can he prove it to be correct by any analogy, or principle of reason whatsoever. Why, then, wage this warfare? We may disprove a theory by what the bible declares, but not by our reasoning on such topics. Why not, then, abide in the use of bible terms alone? [See Essay on Purity of Speech, No. 8. vol. 4.]— There is as much reason on the side of the Trinitarian as on the side of the Unitarian; and neither of them can, without a gross dereliction of their grand positions, accuse the other of being unreasonable in their reasoning or conclusions.

But I adopt neither system, and will fight for none. I believe that God so loved the world that he sent his only begotten Son: that Jesus was the Son of God, in the true, full, and proper import of these words; that the Holy Spirit is the Spirit of God, the Spirit of Christ, which was sent by the concurrence of the Father and the Son to attest and establish the truth, and remain a comforter, an advocate on earth, when Jesus entered the heavens. If any man's faith in this matter is stronger or greater than mine, I have no objection. I only request him not to despise my weakness, and I will not condemn his strength.

I am truly sorry to find that certain opinions, called Arian or Unitarian, or something else, are about becoming the sectarian badge of a people who have assumed the sacred name Christians; and that some peculiar views of atonement or reconciliation are likely to become characteristic of a people who have claimed the high character and dignified relation of "the Church of Christ." I do not say that such is yet the fact; but things are, in my opinion, looking that way; and if not suppressed in the bud, the name Christian will be as much a sectarian name, as Lutheran, Methodist, or Presbyterian.

Were I to contend for any of the speculative views found in the piece under consideration, I do not know but we might soon be found in the graveyards attached to the schools, digging up the bones of obsolete systems; or perhaps we might be trying our hands at the potter's wheel, making a new vessel; and rather than hazard this, I will decline for the present any thing more particular upon the subject, simply adding that your conclusion of the whole matter is admitted by me in a latitude as full as can be suggested by you, viz. "We believe the intelligent person, the Word, existed long before he was called Jesus Christ or Messiah."

Wishing you favor, mercy, and peace, from God our Father, and the Lord Jesus Christ, and that you may never set up a new sect I am yours in the Lord.   EDITOR.

Miscellaneous Letters.—No. I.

A HUNDRED letters, many of them of much consequence too, are on our files, and unless I should enlarge this work to double its present size, most of them must remain there until motheaten. I have concluded to attempt a sort of general answer in a series of letters called miscellaneous. The greatest inconvenience the reader may find in these letters, will be that he can seldom tell, when reading one period or paragraph, what he may expect in the next. If he have a taste for variety, this may compensate for the many disappointments and sudden vicissitudes he may in one single letter have to experience.—We proceed.

Common sense, No. I.—A Baptist preacher of considerable standing, a few weeks since, did "preach a sermon on *Eph. ii.* 10." The divinity he taught was—1. That man lost "good disposition" before he lost Eden, and that he must get a good disposition before Paradise can be regained. That regeneration consisted wholly and solely in getting a good disposition, and was a mere change of disposition. The parable of the sower was alleged as proof: and he concluded that a man would be judged and rewarded according to his disposition in the last judgment. That being created anew in Christ Jesus was simply to have a good disposition infused.—Now another Baptist preacher of still greater name and authority preaches thus: "Regeneration consists not in the creation nor infusion of new faculties, senses, perception, taste, *disposition,* or subjective light. But is a strong and lasting impression made on all our faculties by the almighty force of divine faithfulness and truth. It is an unshaken purpose and pursuit formed in the mind by a full view of the government of God as explained by Jesus Christ. It is supported by an abiding conviction that under his government it shall go well with the righteous and ill with the wicked. That infinite good may be obtained, and infinite evil escaped by a conformity to the laws and spirit of his government. If the infusion of a new and good disposition from the Holy Spirit was regeneration, then all laws and restraints imposed by the King would be as useless as to make laws requiring us to taste sweetness in honey, bitterness in gall, and sourness in vinegar: to eat when we are hungry, and to drink when we are thirsty. Those who make the infusion of a good disposition regeneration, have no need for self-denial in their system; for if a man have a disposition directly infused by the Holy spirit, to deny this good disposition would be a sin, so that all exhortation to self-denial would be exhortation to sin." So teach the good and well disposed doctors: and what is the practical influence? Ay that's the question. Common Sense says, there is no use in either theory, nor for any theory on the subject—for Christ says, "If you continue in my word then are you my disciples indeed, and you shall know the truth, and the truth shall make you free."

Elder John Secrest told me, at the meeting of the Mahoning association, Ohio, on the 27 ult. that he had immersed three hundred persons within the last three months. I asked him, *Into what* did he immerse them? he replied, he immersed them into the faith of Christ, for the remission of their sins. Many of them were the decendants of Quakers, and those who had formerly waited for "the baptism of the Holy Spirit" in the Quaker sense of those words— But brother Secrest had succeeded in convincing them that the *one baptism* was not that of Pentecost, nor that repeated in Cesaria, but an immersion into the faith of Jesus for the remission of their sins. He labors in the word and doctrine principally in the counties of Belmont and Monroe, state of Ohio. Thus while my friend Common Sense, and his two Baptist doctors, are speculating on what regeneration is, brother Secrest has, by the proclamation of repentance towards God and faith in the Lord Jesus Christ and immersion for the remission of sins, been the means of regenerating three hundred, in three months, in the proper import of the term. He thinks that a thousand persons have been immersed this season in the bounds of his labors, by himself and those laboring with him. Immense have been the crowds attending, and great the excitement produced by the simple proclamation of the gospel in the good old fashioned simplicity of unlettered and untaught eloquence.

The clergy, their love of titles, and human applause; the hireling system and all its springs; the missionary schemes, education societies, tract societies, with their endless retinue of offices and officers—and all those righteous projects, the life and soul of which seemed to be the mammon of unrighteousness, have been frequently noticed in this work. Because many have been enthusiastic and chimerical in all those projects, and have acted in direct opposition to many of the plainest precepts of the New Testament; others fold their arms and sit down in perfect apathy and say, We have washed our hands of all these crimes, we thank God we know better than others, and we will do less, we will give less, and labor less, and pray less than others; and while others are going to the other side of the globe to convert the Pagans, we will not go over the street, nor trouble ourselves or our neighbors about such matters. We believe that the christians must be all united at home before the world abroad can be converted, and therefore we will neither labor for the unity of christians at home nor the conversion of the world abroad—We will read our Bible at home and eat our own bread and wear our own apparel and be as independent of heaven and earth as we can.—This is Scylla, and that is Charybdis.

And you, Mr. Editor, are the cause of a good deal of this apathy and inactivity—Is it possible!! Did I ever teach that in avoiding one extreme, we must run into the other!! I do admit that I cannot sentimentally concur in almost any of the schemes of this day. Even the Bible Society and the Sunday school system, two of the best projects, and the most powerful moral engines in the world, are so clogged with sectarian appendages, and are so completely subordinated, in many instances, to sectarian purposes, that I can scarcely obtain my own approbation of any of their movements.

Jesus Christ belongs to no religious party. All the sects themselves declare that the Holy Spirit is not confined to them, that God respects them not. Every religious revival announced is said to have embraced all that believe in revivals. Presbyterians, Methodists, and Baptists, generally participate in all these excitements, because they believe in them. But the Seceders, Covenanters, and High Church folks never have any revivals among them, because they do not believe in them. Be this as it may, one thing is certain, that there is nothing special, indicating that God is a party in any sectarian scheme.

A query for the conscientious professors—*If God does not specially build up the cause of any party; but scatters his blessings upon them all, why should those who love God confine their affections, their labors, their efforts, their desires for the advancement of one party to the exclusion of all others?* I cannot do it. I must love, and labor for the benefit of all whom the Lord has received as far as I can judge.

All the good and virtuous in all sects belong to Jesus Christ, and if I belong to him they are my brethren. They cannot help being my brethren, and I cannot help loving them. Jesus the Lord cares not to what party the bad belong; neither do I.—They may be orthodox or heterodox, as they please, for aught I care—The Holy Spirit dwells in the heart of a christian Baptist, and a christian Paido-Baptist; but not because of the tail they have attached to their name; but because of the family name itself. Many, I hope, will stand on the right hand of the Judge in the great day, who cannot now walk on the same side of the street. Yes, they will feast at the same table who could not break bread together on earth. There sits John Calvin and John Wesley side by side in a close *tete-a-tete,* not far from where Michael and Gabriel are conversing, and their followers on earth biting and devouring one another! 'Tis a dream; but perhaps a true one—and for my part I am got so sick of all this partyism that henceforth, and forever, if the Lord will, I will never conduct myself towards any professor who walks piously, in such a way that I should feel ashamed to sit at his side, or at his feet in the King's own country.

Say, Mr. Editor, dont you love a good Baptist better than you do a good Presbyterian? Yes I do. But there is nothing christian in my predilections for my Baptist brother above my Presbyterian brother, provided they are equally good subjects of the King. As respects their christian character, they are equally amiable and equally entitled to my affection. If I love the Baptist brother better, then it is mere sectarian affection, or the affection I have for a near neighbor above a person who lives one hundred miles off.

Brother Thomas Bullock of Kentucky, suggested to me a good idea last winter concerning the present condition of the Baptist churches in that state. As respects the four churches and one pastor, or the monthly rotation, or " the horse mill plan," as some call it; that is, in plain Scotch, one preacher coming once-a-month to preach to one church in a regular round as many times as there are months in a year. Just as a blind horse when he has gone once round, begins a second tour in the same track. The preachers, as he judiciously observed, had been so long accustomed to going *round* in this way, that they could not now walk *straight* forward, and therefore never would make bishops of a particular flock. He thought they could do better at catching or gathering sheep in this circuitous way, than in feeding one flock; and suggested the following idea: Let every particular congregation elect one or more bishops who had never been spoiled by the preaching plan, and loose all the cords which bind these present preachers to four congregations, and let them go in circuits in rotation as often and as extensively as they could, and preach and teach; but let the congregations meet every Lord's day with their own bishops, and attend upon the ancient order of things; and when any of these circuit preachers made them a visit, let them exercise all the gifts they had, for the edification of the brotherhood and the conversion of all around; but by no means to interfere with the stated worship of the day. In this way the congregations would have as much, if not more, of the labors of all these public men, and their own enjoyments and edification would be greatly enhanced by their constant attention to all the ordinances of the Lord's house. Brother Bullock suggested this merely as a preparatory or preliminary step towards a full restoration of the ancient order of things, and not as a fixed system of procedure in all time coming. He would have the congregations to contribute weekly, and these contributions in the hands of the treasurers or deacons of the congregation, to be, at the discretion of the community, apportioned to such of the public brethren as visited them, according as they had need. This idea I think is a good one, and worthy the examination of the brethren.

The Mahoning Regular Baptist Association did one good work at their last meeting. They agreed to support one active, spiritually minded, and able brother, as a messenger of the churches, who is to labor every day, for one entire year, all things concurring, in the word and doctrine, amongst the churches in the Association. He is to proclaim the word to those without, and to teach those within to walk in the Lord. Brother Walter Scott, who is now in the field, accepted of the appointment; and few men on this continent understand the ancient order of things better than he. His whole soul is in the work, and there is great room for many such at home. It is to be hoped that all christians will turn their attention more to good works and to the conversion of those around them, and to the union of all disciples on primitive grounds, in order that the whole world may be brought under the dominion of the Root and Offspring of David. The religious communities of this country have long enough indulged the idea of converting other nations, and have squandered many thousands already, as well as sacrificed many useful lives in the chimerical project of converting foreign idolators, while millions at home demand more energies than all now employed to ameliorate their condition, and to accelerate the march of truth on its own high road throughout the earth. "Holy Father, may all that believe on me through the testimony of the apostles, be one—that the whole world may be converted and persuaded that you did send me to be the Saviour of the world!" So spoke the Lord Jesus. And who will not say, Amen!   EDITOR.

To Rev. S. M. Noel, D. D.

DEAR SIR:—I am obliged to request you to explain a small moral impropriety. The Minutes of the Franklin Association were published not more than two or three days after my first notice of your circular could have reached Frankfort. My first notice of it was published at Bethany on the 6th of August. The Franklin Association met the 4th of the same month. The August number could not have been received by you before the middle of August, about the time the Minutes were in press at Frankfort. How, then, could you have stated to the public, in a notice prefixed to said Minutes, that my *fruitless* assault on your circular had created a demand for it unprecedented and surprising, and it was implied that my assault had helped to sell some editions of your circular.

This needs some explanation from you. It is understood that it was through you, if not by you, this notice was prefixed to the Minutes. It is well known that my "assault" on your circular could not have been more than read by yourself and a few others in Frankfort when the Minutes were published. The question, then, is, How in *one*, or *two* days at most, my remarks could create a demand for your circular unprecedented and surprising, and contribute to sell *three* editions of it? This unprecedented and surprising fact, that two days at most after the arrival of my *first* notice of your circular, it should have created such an enormous demand as compelled you to announce the fact on the frontispiece of the Minutes, without leave or license from the Association, requires a word or two of explanation from yourself. That charity which hopes all things, induces me to hope that you will find some way of explaining this thing to divest it, at least, of any *moral* impropriety.
                                                EDITOR.

No. 4.]   NOVEMBER 5, 1827.
Review of Dr. Noel's Circular.—No. III.

I SHOULD much regret if my plainness in this review should incur the displeasure of my friend and brother, Dr. Noel. Had he not given such a direction to his circular as to impose it on me to notice it, I would have let it die a natural death, or if it preferred suicide I should not have disturbed its manes or its ashes. I hope the Doctor will remember that he first took up the tomahawk, (to speak in his own style) and that he fired twenty times at me from behind a tree, while I stood in the open field, and before I began to pick my flint. He built his ramparts, entrenched himself, and tried his cannon before he ever proclaimed hostilities. Nay, he placed the white flag, the flag of peace, at my side, and caused it to wave over my head, while his castles were building and his munitions of war were preparing. These hieroglyphics the Doctor will understand, and as for my other readers

it is not necessary that they should understand them.

I can still fraternize with the Doctor. I make it a rule to enumerate (if I could) how many great and glorious things there are in which we agree. Besides a great many things in the Doctor's creed, we agree in many other things of equal importance which he left out of it. For example, we agree in the hope and belief of the resurrection of the dead—and of a future state of happiness and misery, which capital points, we before saw, were not to be found in the Doctor's summary view of what the Bible teaches. Indeed, we agree in nine hundred and ninety-nine things in every thousand, and why should our difference in the thousandth have such a repulsive power as to burst through almost a thousand attractions. Nay, the Doctor will himself confess, and, were he dead, there are most unexceptionable witnesses to prove that he has repeatedly declared his hearty concurrence with me in almost every single point; that he would travel many miles every week to enjoy membership in such a church or christian society as I would construct on my views of the kingdom of Jesus. He has gone even farther than this. For he has declared to me, *viva voce*, that the time would come, and at no very distant day, when those views which I inculcated, would universally prevail amongst all Christians. And even *now*, in the present contest, the Doctor only advocates a creed because there are sects. If there were no heresies the Doctor would have no human creed. Indeed it would be difficult to find persons who agree in more incidents than Doctor Noel and myself. Why then should it be thought strange that we should examine the points of difference with so much plainness and honesty! I am sorry that the Doctor should have made even one digression from the straight forward course, and even that has something of virtue in it. The Doctor has but one failing, (and I wish that I had but one) and that leans to virtue's side. It is a weakness incident to Doctors of Divinity more than any other men. It is also a failing that carries its own punishment in its bosom. For when a man is desirous of always being on the popular side, it often gives him a great deal of uneasiness, and in some instances involves him in a very irksome suspense. But this failing I shall not now disclose, as it might appear invidious to expose the only failing of one who has obtained so good a degree and so much boldness in the faith.

After this round-about apology I resume the circular.—All Christians have faith and therefore must have a creed. The only question then is, Who shall be the author of this creed? The Holy Spirit, or the Philadelphia association? I opine that the former is the most fitting and capable author. And who says that the latter is? —No person will say so in *words*: it is only in *works* they say so. The making of a creed out of the inspired volume, or even the attempt to epitomize it, is, in effect, saying that, in the divine shape, or the shape which God has given the volume, it is not so well adapted as in the shape which the Westminster divines or the Philadelphia association have given it. Doctor Noel, and brother Doctor Miller of New-Jersey, represent the church as in the most lamentable condition without a "summary exhibition," an "epitome," or a "human creed;" for if the church had no other standard than the Bible, "every thing that wears the name of Christian" would find admittance. Yes! the Universalist, Socinian, Arian, Episcopalian, Presbyterian and

Methodist, would all be in the Baptist church, sitting around brother Noel, were it not for the admirable machinery of the creed, which equally keeps the Universalist and the Presbyterian aloof from the Doctor, and shuts the gates of the kingdom on earth equally against the "damnable" heretic, and the weak Methodist.—This is the omnipotent fact, and who can deny it?

I have said that Doctors Noel and Miller represent *the church* as in the most dangerous condition without a creed—liable to receive into her bosom "every thing under the name of Christian." What church? ——! *Into whose bosom?* ——! Not the church of Christ, my dear friends—For where is she?—Doctor Miller says, With us—Doctor Noel says, With us—and Dr. J. Owen says, With neither. The church in danger. Mark well the phrase. *The church in danger* means the *sect* in danger. The bosom of the church here means the bosom of the sect. Here now is a piece of the sophism, a small slice too, which our sagacious Doctors present on their spiritual servers to their guests; but remember they do not taste it themselves. Let us remove the vail, and then it reads, *the church* of Jesus Christ, that is the Baptist sect is in the most imminent danger of receiving into her bosom the Arian and Presbyterian unless she have a summary exhibition of what the scriptures teach; and *the church* of Jesus Christ, that is, the Presbyterian sect, is in the most imminent danger of receiving into her bosom the Baptist and the Universalist unless she have her summary exhibition of what the scriptures teach. And so the different churches, that is, *sects of Jesus Christ*, or *pieces of a divided Christ*, hand round the spiced and sweetened sophism to one another and to all their guests. I have said all Doctor Noel's letter, and all Doctor Miller's pamphlet is down right sophistry from first to last. I am now proving it by piece meal, and have, in this one instance, I opine, succeeded in stripping one pillar naked, that is the pillar called *the church*. When the plastering and white-washing is taken off this pillar, it is *sect*, and not *church*, within. And while the Doctors are white-washing and painting this pillar with the names church and church of Jesus Christ, it is in reality and fact sect and sect of Jesus Christ. The pillar reads thus— The Baptist sect of Jesus Christ has a divine warrant to draw up a summary exhibition of what the scriptures teach, and by this summary to exclude the Arian, Universalist, Methodist, and Presbyterian from the bosom of the Baptist sect; and the Presbyterian sect of Jesus Christ has a divine right or warrant to draw up her summary exhibition of what the scriptures teach, and by their summary to exclude from her bosom the Arian, Universalist, Baptist, and Methodist. So the naked truth is, that Jesus Christ has, while time endures, established and ordained and appointed sects to exist, make creeds and exclude one another; and calls each of them his church and people!! Now, Doctors, to work again—to your oars—for till time ends you must work in vain to establish the fact that Jesus Christ is on your side of the controversy.

Now, gentle reader, how do you think the Doctors will try to get out of this net. I will tell you: They will do as they have done. What is that? They will silently admit the fact, and retort. Well then, Mr. Editor, you have your creed too, you have your explanation, verbal, nuncupative, your meanings of scripture, your sermons; and you do by these what we more honestly do by our written creed. You have a creed too. You have your meaning of what the scriptures teach in another shape, and you make the same use of this as we do of our creed. Avaunt! Mr. Editor. Meet us here if you can. Yes, gentlemen, I will meet you in the face, and not meet you in the back, as, I opine, you have met your opponents. This is as palpable a sophism as the former. This pillar you have plastered and whitewashed again and again. We shall try what is inside of these pretty paintings and whitewashings.

To meet you in the face: You say I "have two creeds—the bible and my meaning of it." Now you say, "We have no more." We have the bible and our meaning of it. We are more honest than you. We give our meaning in writing. You keep yours in the evanescent form of sound. Here, then, gentlemen, I lay my hand upon your head. I have two creeds, you say. Well, then, according to the way, manner, reasoning, and argument, by which you establish this point, I will most certainly prove you have three creeds. I have the bible—that, you say, is one creed. True. I have also my meaning of the bible—that is, you say, another creed. Now, one and one make two. So, then, Mr. Christian Baptist, you have, by fair arithmetic, two creeds. For the sake of argument, *agreed.* You, then, dear doctors, have the bible—that is one creed. You have also the Westminster, or the Philadelphia—that is another creed. You have also the meaning of the Westminster— that is precisely the same as my meaning of the bible—this is another creed, if your logic be sound. Now it is just as certain that two and one make three, as that one and one make two. This is not that species of logic which enabled the graduate of Cambridge to prove that two ducks were three; but it is that species of logic by which Drs. Noel and Miller prove that their written creed and my meaning is just one and the same, or that I have two creeds, while I acknowledge the bible only. I will not let you go. You are as much bound by every law in creation to attach a meaning to the words in your Westminster and Philadelphia creeds, as I am to attach a meaning to the bible; and by every law in grammar, logic, and rhetoric, if my meaning of the bible is one creed different from it, so your meaning of the Westminster is a creed different from it. Here, then, I hold you. Now disentangle yourselves if you can. If you make an effort, Dr. Noel, I will turn Dr. Miller against you; for he will join me now. He will tell you there are seven sects of Presbyterians, at least six, who hold the same Westminster Confession, and will not commune with one another. And why will they not? Because they have different meanings attached to the same Westminster. What mean the words Covenanter, Relief, Burgher, Anti-Burgher, &c. &c., in Buck's Theological Dictionary—all Presbyterians, all holding the same creed, the Westminster, and differing in their meaning of it. Some of these have written out their testimony, shewing where they differ from others in their meaning of the creed; and it is a fact that they have as much need for a fourth creed or a meaning for their testimony, as I have, to say the least, for a second one. So you go. The Westminster explains the bible; the "*Testimony*" explains the Westminster; and then you have, in a case of difficulty, to shew how you understand the Testimony; and so forth, *ad infinitum.*

So, so, gentlemen, it all ends here. While you would place my "explanations" on the same footing with your written creed, you act as sophistically as when you use the word church instead of the word sect; for admitting I have my explanations, you have your bible, your Philadelphia, and your explanations. Such is the inside of your second main pillar. Remember the proof in fact. Count how many sorts of Presbyterians, Episcopalians, and Baptists there are, and talk no more of your little creed being a means of either uniting sects or christians. So much in proof that brother Noel's circular is all sophistry from first to last. I dislike mincing. Brother Clack is going to republish the circular. I could wish he would republish my review of it. Thus he might save me the trouble yet printing the Doctor's circular and my review in one pamphlet, and sending them hand in hand round the country. If the Doctor will say he will take the one half of the number I may print of his circular and my review, and use all his exertions to distribute them, I will publish the whole in one pamphlet, so soon as I shall have brought my review to a close.   EDITOR.

Remarks on Tassey's Vindication.

SIR:—IN this communication I proceed to close my remarks on Mr. Tassey's Vindication, &c. and, therefore, for this once, crave your indulgence to give it a place, with the former, in your interesting paper. Without further preface, I proceed to observe that Mr. Tassey not only appears to contradict himself, but also the express declaration of Holy Scripture; for he says, (p. 22.) speaking of the Mosaic and Christian dispensations, that "they are in substance and design the same, and are not to be regarded as, in any measure, opposed to each other." I presume it will be readily granted, that the former dispensation was by no means designed to oppose the latter, but the very reverse; for it was manifestly designed to prepare the way for it, and to introduce it with manifold advantage. But as certainly the latter was designed to supersede and annul the former, and therefore most certainly *in some measure* opposed to it. How, then, could they be in substance and design the same? Moreover, do they not essentially differ both in matter and form? Was not the former a dispensation of laws and institutes, moral, religious, and very many of them also typical, materially and formally differing from the laws and institutes of christianity. Compare the first christian church in Jerusalem, in all these respects, with the temple worship, and with the whole Mosaic constitution; how great, how striking, the dissimilarity! Where, then, I pray this substantial sameness? And as for the alleged sameness of design, how can any christian assert it? Was not the law added because of transgression—until the seed should come, to whom, or in relation to whom, the promise was made? Did not the law enter that the offence might abound? that sin by the commandment might become exceeding sinful? But was this the design of the gospel dispensation? Or was it intended for any of these purposes? Again, was the legal dispensation designed to give life, or to perfect the worshipers as pertaining to the conscience? But was it not the express design of the gospel dispensation to accomplish these all-important purposes? These things being so, who that believes the New Testament, can assert, that the design of both was the same. But we presently see what drove our otherwise much esteemed author into all these lamentable contradictions. It comes out plainly at the bottom of the page. He tells us that we are not " to regard the kingdom or church of Christ, as different in any of its essential

principles, from the church of God under the Old Testament times. In the spirituality of their nature and constitution they are the same. "Righteousness, peace, and joy in the Holy Ghost," were the grand constitutional principles of the kingdom of God from the commencement of the world; and faith in Jesus Christ, as the promised Messiah, was as necessary to constitute a man the true subject of this kingdom, in the days of Abraham, as it is at present. Nay, we are bold to affirm, that its regulations were the same, as far as made known to the children of God. But as the church of God was then in its non-age, and its laws were not as yet fully promulgated, so its advantages were not then equal to those now enjoyed; consequently the only differences that can be discovered, consist neither in its nature, its constitution, nor its laws; but in being now more immediately under the personal management of Jesus Christ himself, and in the clearer and more complete regulations it is now under, since the oracles of God were closed." If we leave out this, and the preceding paragraph, Mr. T's declarations and assertions, upon this branch of the subject, appear, for the most part, consistent and just. But how to reconcile this, and the preceding, with that sameness of religion, and of church, which he so strongly asserts, with what precedes and follows, and with the truth itself, appears utterly impossible, if language has any determinate meaning. For, after asserting, as above, that we are not to regard the two churches as different in essential principles; that is, in their nature, constitution, or laws; he goes on to assert, that "the great evil into which men have fallen on this subject consists in confounding the typical church of God with the *real*. For the typical church can never be regarded as the true church of God." If this be so, who has fallen more deeply into this evil than Mr. T.? For what can be more confounding than to assert the above sameness, in their nature, constitution and laws, the spirituality of their privileges, faith, &c.? And what more unintelligible, more confounding to common sense, than, after all this, to assert the essential difference of *typical* and *real* existing between them. "For the typical church can never be regarded as the true church of God." Yet we are not to regard them as *different in any of their essential* principles!!! Strange indeed! But, after all, what are we to understand by this mysterious sameness of the two churches, or kingdoms, under the Old and New Testaments? It cannot consist in the sameness of the subjects or members, for those of the former are all dead and gone. Nor in the laws and ordinances of divine worship, for these the apostle, and Mr. T. himself, declares to be abolished. Not in territorial and political regulations; for the latter, that is, the kingdom of Christ, is not like the former, of this world; nor yet in respect of moral regulations, for the subjects of the former were under certain restrictions in relation to their neighbors, and enjoyed certain liberties, such as polygamy, &c. which do not exist under the gospel dispensation. Neither were the qualifying terms of membership the same; for under the former, a person must be of the stock of Israel, or a proselyte to the faith and worship of the God of Israel; and if a male, to be circumcised, in order to membership under the theocracy; whereas, under the christocracy, no such thing is required or admitted.

Again, the faith and worship under the New Testament, differ essentially, i. e. both in matter and form, from what was required under the Old.

For we are commanded to believe that Jesus of Nazareth is the Christ, the Son of God, and Saviour of the world, whose blood cleanses from all sin; and to worship him accordingly, and to pray to the Father in his name. Not so under the Old. The terms of membership are also essentially different; under the New a confession of this faith, with baptism, is the term of admission. Not so under the Old. In a word, the New Testament church, constitution, or covenant, is established upon better promises than the Old. See *Heb.* viii. 6. 10. 11. 12. Therefore, neither in this respect, is it the same. These things being so, as Mr. T. in the sequel materially grants, and as every one must see that pays any due attention to the subject; how, then, can he, or any man of candor and common sense, boldly affirm that the revealed regulations under the former, were the same with those under the latter; and, that "the only differences that can be discovered, consist neither in its nature, its constitution, nor its laws," &c. But alas! all these contradictory and absurd inconsistencies, and a thousand more, if necessary, must be retained, rather than abandon a favorite dogma—namely, that baptism is come in the room of circumcision; consequently, that being born after the flesh confers membership in a spiritual kingdom. It is true, our author, in his elaborate and comprehensive treatise, says little directly upon baptism. He observes, (sect. 3. page 226,) when treating of the ordinances, that, "perhaps, of all the ordinances of religion which were instituted by the Redeemer, none have been more abused (viz. to the production of discord and disaffection) than baptism and the Lord's supper." But, while he labors much, and much to the purpose, to obviate the abuse, and vindicate the proper and legitimate use of the latter; he leaves the former out of view—except in so far as he argues against a sectarian use of it; though it must be confessed that in the order of institution it is the first—the first to be attended by every believer; faith as it were, stands upon its left hand, and salvation upon its right—it is the connecting medium between them. Why, then, should our author in his proposed representation of the different ordinances of religion as instituted by the authority of Christ, and practised by the primitive churches, have passed so slightly over this primary one; with briefly observing that "this ordinance was made the instrument of promoting faction and schism in the church at Corinth." Or why not rather in the preceding section, when ascertaining the proper materials of which a church of Christ ought to be composed, did he not fairly establish from scripture testimony, that it must consist of baptized believers? But, alas! such is the power of prejudice, that even our boasted author himself, notwithstanding his just and animated declamations against it, falls prostrate under its bewitching and bewildering influence! This lamentable prostration is not only apparent from the documents already adduced; but, if possible, still more evidently so by the partial and corrupt paraphrase of Eph. iv. 4, 5, 6. see page 148; not, indeed, formally quoted, but evidently adduced as an argument to prove the existence of a real and substantial union amongst christians, that should hold them united in spite of all corruption or seduction. In the above reference, the apostle's argument to induce christians, to keep the unity of the Spirit in the bond of peace, is truly catholic and forcible. For, says he, "there is one body and one Spirit, even as you are called in one hope of your calling, one Lord, one faith, one baptism, one God and Fa-

ther of all, above all, and through all, and in you all." No quotation could have been more pertinent and conclusive to Mr. T.'s purpose than this, had he fairly stated the subject; but this he has not done; for he declares above, that "the recognition of Jesus Christ was the only indispensable prerequisite in order to admission to the privileges of the children of God." Now this certainly is not true, unless by recognition he means baptism; for admission to the first and great privilege, the remission of sins, was so ordered in the gospel economy as to be only accessible through baptism. Hence, said Peter to his believing auditors, "repent and be baptized every one of you in the name of Jesus Christ, for the remission of sins;" &c. Likewise, said Ananias to believing Saul, "arise and be baptized and wash away your sins," &c. Likewise, the believing audience in the house of Cornelius, who were truly immersed in the Holy Spirit, were afterwards commanded to be immersed in water, that so they might be constitutionally admitted to the full enjoyment of all the privileges of the children of God. And Paul, in the connexion before us laboring to restore and preserve the unity of the church of Corinth, next to the unity of Christ. the one Lord who was crucified for them, (the belief of which constituted the unity of their faith) puts them in mind of the one baptism, by virtue of which they had all put on Christ; and therefore, of course, ought to wear his name, and not any other's; no, not even Paul's, who had not been crucified for them, and into whose name they had not been baptized. In like manner, in his most pathetic and earnest exhortation to the believing Ephesians to maintain the unity of the Spirit in the bond of peace, next to the one faith, urges upon them the consideration of the one baptism; by which they had all been immersed into one body; for says he, "there is one body and one Spirit, even as you are called into one hope of your calling, one faith, one Lord, one baptism, one God, and one Father of all," &c. Here we have the fundamental and real unity of the true church of God most distinctly and satisfactorily displayed—firmly established on a seven fold unity. "Thus Wisdom has builded her house; she has hewn out her seven pillars; but alas! Mr. T. with all his professed zeal for the sacred and inviolable prerogatives of Zion's King, and for the rights and privileges of his subjects, has, unhappily, through obstinate prejudice, and at the expense, too, of apparent self contradiction, attempted to bury the sixth of these seven in the apostolic order, under the rubbish and ruins of a party spirit—even that beautiful and highly interesting pillar upon which is inscribed the remission of the church's sins. "Oh, prejudice! Oh, bigotry! what have you done! You cease not to pervert the right ways of the Lord!" So says our author of M'Leod, p. 126, and so say we of him. "It is, (*indeed*,) of that love of system we complain, (*and that justly too*,) which grinds down and new-moulds every opposing passage of these holy records, until it is conceived to tally with our acknowledged creed; that blind and unconquerable love of party, which forces the oracles of heaven out of their natural and obvious meaning to support its unhallowed pretensions." p. 48. To these complaints and lamentations of our author we most heartily subscribe: and most sincerely wish, both for his sake and the truth's sake, and also for the brethren's sakes that are with him, that he had "first cast out the beam out of his own eye." Had he done so, he had not ground down and new modelled the passage under consideration as he has done, by adding to the word; thereby altering its obvious meaning, and making the apostle guilty of a kind of tautology; for he had previously said there is one body and one spirit; and finally destroyed one of his strong and palpable arguments; namely, the one baptism for the remission of sins, of which all from the beginning were made partakers, who believed in, and obeyed, the one Lord.—This, however, our author has paraphrased into "one baptism of the Spirit, enjoyed by all who are associated together, and thereby rendered one body with Christ." Now, pray, what does the apostle mean, if not this unity in one body with Christ, through the indwelling of his Spirit, when he says above, "There is one body and one Spirit?" Or is he so loose and verbose in his style, especially on a subject of such deep interest, that, in the course of a few words, he should repeat the same thing over again; and that, too, under the form of a distinct and additional argument? Far be it. The apostle is no such loose declaimer. Moreover it would be unreasonable to suppose that in the exhibition of the great fundamental and uniting topics of christianity, and for the express purpose, too, of enforcing and maintaining christian unity, the apostle would have omitted one of such leading importance, with which the present enjoyment of the remission of sins, and the promise of ultimate salvation stand so closely connected; and which, in the preceding epistles, both to the Romans, the Corinthians, and the Galatians, he had introduced, as indicative of the near and intimate relation of believers with Christ, and with each other in him. To the Romans he says, "Know you not, that as many of you as were baptized into Jesus Christ, were baptized into his death," &c. To the Corinthians, "By one Spirit are we all baptized into one body, and have been all made to drink into one Spirit." And to the Galatians "As many of you as have been baptized into Christ, have put on Christ; you are all one in Christ Jesus," &c.

But I see I have exceeded due bounds in this communication, and therefore must close it. Oh! presumption! Oh! prejudice! Oh! bigotry! what have ye done. Corrupting the word, changing the ordinances, or rejecting them; blinding the eyes, and steeling the heart; ye have led men away from the truth, and confirmed their apostacy. In the mean time, taking leave of our author and the subject, permit me to remind him, and through him, to admonish the public, in his own words, page 68, that "whatever receives not the sanction of heaven's authority, ought to be rejected as an unauthorised intruder into the service of Jehovah." Consequently, that infant sprinkling ought to be rejected; there being neither precept nor precedent for it of divine authority.

PHILALETHES.

Letters addressed to A. Campbell.—Letter II.
Bloomfield, Ky. June 1827.

BROTHER CAMPBELL—It is only by a free, unreserved correspondence either *viva voce* or by writing, that we can come to a proper understanding on subjects of a supposed difference. You are aware that it is foreign from my design to enter into a polemical combat. I wish by the help of the Lord, to lead you to a serious consideration of the importance of cultivating love and union with your brethren. From the many communications over different and anonymous signatures published in our paper, you see that many of our brethren are exceedingly opposed to what they suppose to be your sentiments. Have

they mistaken your real views? are they fighting against shadows? Do you indeed hold the sentiments and opinions which your brethren have charged upon you? I have no doubt you will answer in the negative; you will say they were mistaken. If so, what can be the cause of so many erroneous conceptions of your *real* views? Why is it that your brethren do not understand precisely what you mean? Can you ascribe it to the dullness of their intellection, to malignity of heart, or to an unjustifiable and illiberal prejudice? Surely not. Some who oppose your views are men of strong intellectual power—of fervent piety, and who are very justly esteemed your best friends. You remember a worthy bishop of Virginia, whom some time since you had occasion to praise; he is your friend; he loves you, but does not approve of your opinions. Hear what he says. Of Paulinus he speaks thus:—

"He wrote something last year in which he certainly went too far. He is now convinced (I am persuaded) and is guarded against our friend Campbell's chimeras."

Concerning yourself he remarks:—"What shall we do with Campbell? He is certainly wise, but not with the wisdom of God, at least not often. He seems to be misled by an ambition to be thought a reformer; but he will fail, or I shall miss my guess (as the Yankees say.) He may be as learned as Luther, or Calvin, or Melancthon, but they fell on other days than our friend Alexander. It is one thing to reform Popery, and another to reform the Reformation." And though he cannot approve of your opinions, "yet, after all," says he, "I can't throw him away as a good man, nor am I without hope of his veering about until he gets to the right point of the compass and his last days be his best days." Such is the opinion of this excellent bishop.—Consider what he says.

Our beloved "Paulinus" will not, though he much loves you, be found an advocate for your opinions. He is not disposed to rend the churches for the sake of establishing your constructions and interpretations of the only rule. In the western country you have friends, but who oppose your doctrine, perhaps because they misunderstand you. As a man, they love you; but as a teacher, you do not possess their confidence.

Now, brother Campbell, let me suggest to you the propriety and expediency of making out a summary of your faith. This is easily done. I can, on one half sheet of paper, give a summary view of my faith; or, if you choose, a synopsis of the leading and most prominent truths of the scriptures. By this means we can set down and compare your views with our own; and if any real difference exists, it will be seen at once. Will you be so kind as to let me hear from you on this subject. Believe me to be sincere, when I express for you my best wishes and prayers.

Yours, in very great haste,
SPENCER CLACK.

—

BETHANY, October 12, 1827.

BROTHER CLACK—I am fully aware of the purity of your motives, and of the excellency of the object of your address to me concerning "the importance of cultivating love and union with my brethren." I thank you for calling up the subject again to my recollection; and be assured every feeling of my heart, as a man, and as a christian, is on the side of love and union with my brethren. And if I would boast of any attainment I have made through the favor of

God, my boasting should be this—that I am willing to go the whole length taught and recommended by the holy apostles in maintaining the unity of the Spirit in the bond of peace. I feel myself strong on this point. I can go farther in bearing with the infirmities of the weak than ninety-nine in a hundred of my brethren will approve. As I said before, so say I again: If I thought there was a man upon this continent who would go farther than I to unite all christians in the bonds of love and christian union, I would travel on foot a hundred miles to see him.

What you say about "the many brethren who are opposed to my views," weighs not a feather in my estimation. I grant, indeed, that their concurrence in sentiment and co-operation with me would afford me much pleasure, and that I regret that there should be any to oppose, knowing, or walking in, the way of the Lord more perfectly. But what good cause does history record which has not had many opponents, both open and clandestine? And have not good men often opposed a good cause? Strong as the intellectual powers of some who oppose me are; fervent as their piety, and great as their erudition may be—(and I do not wish to derogate an iota from their merits)—I have the satisfaction to know that they have not studied the subjects on which they oppose me as I have done. They have either wanted the means, the opportunity, or the patience and perseverance necessary to such investigations. Of this I have the same proof which I would have when a professed linguist reads me an ode in Horace, or a passage in Pindar, that he had not studied it so well, or better, than I. A mechanic who inspects a clock or a watch, knows what sort of mechanical attainments its architect possessed, whether better or worse than his own. This is a very trite method of determining such matters; which are of little importance when decided. But yet it is a suitable reply to your remark. For if you intended to have caused me to doubt of any sentiments advanced by me because of these many avowed and clandestine opponents, I can assure you that, so far from this being the fact, if not one in a hundred of those who do concur in sentiment with me, did concur, I should be as firmly persuaded as I am: or, in other words, if my success had been ten times less than it has been, I should just be as certain as I am of the firmness and correctness of the ground on which I stand. And if you intended rather than myself, to make others doubt of my sentiments, (which a majority will likely say was the fact,) then I ask them, on whom you intended to operate. Of how much weight would be your remarks to a Baptist who firmly opposed infant sprinkling? You would tell him to consider how many good, and intelligent, and erudite christians, differed from him and opposed him; some in one way and some in another. He would say, if all the people in the state, or if an overwhelming majority of all the professors of christianity upon earth, should oppose me for opposing infant sprinkling, I would still say, and believe in my heart, that it is a human tradition. Think of this, brother Clack, and make use of stronger arguments in your next letter.

Your quotations from brother Bishop Semple's letter to Dr. Noel come next to be noticed. Without a single censorious remark on the means by which brother Noel obtained this morsel, or on his sending it to you for publication without the knowledge and consent of Bishop Semple; I say, passing by these and some other little things, which I hope not to be under the necessity of exposing, I proceed to remark, first. That as far

as respects Paulinus, he has since spoken for himself in the "Christian Baptist;" and as for my "chimeras," brother Semple has already been called upon for an explanation, which he cannot, consistently with his high standing, avoid presenting to the public.

I am sorry to see two sentences in this extract: Sorry, because of the regard and almost veneration I have for the author. The one is—"He is certainly wise, but not with the wisdom of God, at least not often." With what wisdom, if not the wisdom of God? Is it of the Devil? The other is, "He seems to be misled by an ambition to be thought a reformer." Where now that charity which thinks no evil? And where is the proof? But I push this matter no farther, waiting for brother Semple's explanations. I hope what Solomon says about him that separates chief friends, may not be applicable to either the tattler or the publisher of this garbled extract. I do hope that the cause I plead may never stand in need of such subterfuges or of such auxiliaries. I thank you upon the whole, brother Clack, for letting out so much of the secret. I am willing to gather honey from every flower. But my motto is,

"*Nullius addictus jurare in verba magistri.*"

"To reform the Reformation" is indeed a hard matter—and why? Because many think the *Reformation* was complete. But what man skilled in ecclesiastical history does not know that the reformers themselves were veering about from point to point till the day of their death, and that not one of them finished the work he had begun? The greatest moral calamity that has befallen the Protestants is this, that they imagined the Reformation was finished when Luther and Calvin died. The history of that Reformation, like that of Bonaparte, will never be fairly given. The Reformation was a mixture of ten grains in one cup, nine of which were political and one religious. The pope's chair is found in almost every sect. All synods and councils have need of it. And half or three-fourths of all our religious controversies is about who shall sit in the pope's chair. If the virtuous and good, along with the crafty and designing, join hands in opposing, it will be hard indeed to reform the Reformation. But it is not the less necessary on this account.

But so soon as brother Semple gives an account of my chimeras, I will shew, from good authority, that these chimeras have been favorites amongst the Baptists for ten centuries before the Reformation, and that every grand point for which I contend has been espoused and either directly or indirectly acknowledged by the church in the wilderness for nearly twelve hundred years. We shall have the imposing weight of *great names* on both sides.

What to think of your "suggestions about making out a summary of my faith," I know not. It looks about as queer as if I should say to you, Brother Clack, well now do burn your little half sheet summary when you have made it, and let not any infant see it. Your faith is *small*, if a summary view of it could be given on one half sheet. Half a quire would not give a summary of my faith. For my faith is as summarily comprehended in the New Testament as the wisest head in christendom could compendize it.

But what use have you for my summary? To compare your summary by mine, and to decide my christian fate according to the points of resemblance between your summary and mine.— You have no right to demand it of me, and I am under no moral, religious, or political obligation to give you such a summary statement; but if you wish to know for any useful and benevolent purpose my *belief* in any point or my *views* of any passage in scripture; or my *opinion* of any doubtful topic, I am at your command. It shall be given you.

I understand you published only a part of my first letter as yet in your paper. I do not think so well of this. I would rather see a little more justice and kindness amongst our modern professors, than a *new summary* for every new moon in the year. Your faithful and honest friend,

A. CAMPBELL.

Attempt at the Restoration of Ancient Order.

WE have promised our readers some historical notices of some churches which, in late years, have attempted to remove out of Babylon. We now endeavor to redeem this pledge.—The following sketches were drawn up by the churches themselves, in answer to a request from a church in New York, which published, in 1818, a circular to these societies in general, soliciting from them a statement of their views and practices, &c. We begin with the letter sent from New York, and will furnish a few of the narratives received in reply to it. We reserve our own remarks, approbatory and disapprobatory, until the documents are before our readers. Such information we deem of much importance to all who are desirous of understanding the will of the Great King. The faults and blemishes of those who have attempted a better order of things, are not without benefit to us who enquire after the ancient order of things. Many of these societies have progressed well, all things considered; and their attempts and efforts, however they may be disapprobated, are of more real importance to be known than the doings of Luther and Calvin, and other reformers from ancient popery.— The time must arrive, if there be any truth in prophecy, or any knowledge of it in the world, and that before many years too, when those who have been forward in reforming modern popery, will be as much esteemed as those who reformed ancient popery.　　ED. C. B.

The Church professing obedience to the faith of Jesus Christ, assembling together in N. York; To the Churches of Christ scattered over the earth, to whom this communication may come —Grace, mercy, and peace be multiplied from God the Father, by the Holy Spirit, through our Lord Jesus Christ.

Dearly Beloved,

THAT you may be better informed concerning those who thus address you, we have deemed it requisite to give the following brief sketch of our public worship—soliciting, at the same time, that wherein you may differ from us in any matter, faithfulness will dispose you to refer us to apostolic practice, plain and intelligible to the capacity of the plain and simple followers of the Lamb—as we have not much of this world's learning, and are disposed to admit that alone as obligatory, which can be clearly adduced from the New Testament, without the aid of sophistry or allusion to the practices of man. And we trust it may be given us from above, to receive with meekness whatever of this nature your love and concern for our welfare may dispose you to communicate.

The order, which we derive from the law of Christ, is as follows:

We require that all whom we receive into fellowship should believe in their heart, and confess with their mouth, that Jesus is the Christ; that he died for our sins, according to the scriptures; and that upon such confession, and such alone, they should be baptized.

We hold it to be the duty and privilege of the disciples of Jesus to come together into one place, on every first day of the week, rejoicing in the recollections which that day revives— whereon the Lord Jesus destroyed the power both of hell and death, by his resurrection from the dead, and gave sure hope to his people of being raised also. When thus assembled, we proceed to attend to all the ordinances which we can discover to be enjoined by the practice of the first churches, and the commandments of the Lord and his apostles.

1st. Our elders presiding, and the brethren all together, (having no fellowship in sacred things with those who confess and obey not the faith,) in obedience to the command, 1 *Tim.* ii. 1, &c.— we commence our public worship by kneeling down and offering the supplications, prayers, &c. directed in that passage—the elders by themselves, or one of the brethren selected by them as competent, speaking as the mouth of the body.

2d. One of the elders selects a suitable hymn or psalm, expressive of praise; in the singing of which all the members stand up and join.

3d. A portion of the word of God is read by one of the elders relative to the subject or institution of the Lord's Supper; upon which thanks are given, by one of the elders or brethren, for the bread;—and after the breaking of bread— thanks for the cup;—and after taking the cup a suitable hymn or psalm is sung.

4th. A passage relative to the fellowship or contribution for the poor saints is read; then prayer for suitable dispositions, and thanksgiving for ability and privilege to contribute in this way. The collection for the saints follows.

5th. Previous to reading the holy scriptures; prayer for the Holy Spirit to open the understanding of all present, to understand and receive the sacred word. The reading consists of a chapter in the Law, one in the Prophets, and one in the New Testament. After each, a pause is made to allow opportunity to any of the brethren to make remarks by way of illustration as the subject might require.

6th. Exhortation from the word of God, by the elders or brethren.

7th. Praise.

8th. Prayer and separate.

In the evening, the church assembles for worship; after which the elders in their turn, and some other of the brethren, approved by the church, declare the gospel to those without.

A love feast is also attended to—and a meeting on a week evening—but those not appearing to be of the same strict obligation with the duties of the Lord's day, are sometimes made to give way to circumstances.

The kiss of charity, the washing of the feet, and the entertainment of the disciples, being things the performance of which arises from special occasions exemplified in the New Testament, we deem of importance to be attended to on such occasions.

Discipline is also a duty which will sometimes fall to the lot of the disciples on the Lord's day.

It may be necessary to observe, that our elders labor at their respective callings, for their support, and are not burdensome to the church; but in case of need, or that the duties of their office render aid necessary, the church deem it their duty and privilege to communicate liberally to them, as "the laborer is worthy of his hire."

As to our intercourse with the world, we require strict uprightness in walk and in dealing, sobriety in spirit and behaviour—kindness towards all, even enemies—no evil speaking of any—but zeal for every good work—whether it respect the bodies or souls of men. In a word, that righteousness of character before all men, which the word enjoins as the evidence of being in Christ, and as the recommendation of his religion to mankind. We believe also, that according to the word of God, christians should be subject to "the powers that be" in every nation, unless where any of their commands might require a breach of the law of Christ. Consequently, that disciples should have no lot or part in any combinations for the overthrow or disturbance of governments—it being injurious to the cause of Jesus our Lord, that any of his people should suffer justly in this world as evil doers. 1 *Pet*.2.

In our relationship to each other as christians, we are all brethren, having no distinction in the church, except what gifts necessarily create—but we do not therefore seek to abolish, nor interfere with those earthly distinctions which our respective stations in the world may require, unless where, and so far as these might clash with the authority of the divine word.

We view it as our duty to be subject to, and to forbear each other, to please our brethren, and not wound their weak conscience; but to deny ourselves, and in all things seek the peace and comfort of the church, where such compliance would not countenance error. We esteem it also to be our duty to love our brethren in deed as well as in word; holding our substance (which we have as the stewards of God) in readiness to supply their necessities: showing by our willingness to contribute, that we walk by faith and not by sight, and are laying up our treasure where no moth can corrupt, nor thief break through and steal.

The questions and disputations that generally prevail among professing christians have no place among us: their reasonings and speculations occupy no part of our time. The knowledge of the simple truth, declared by the Lord Jesus and his apostles—and the practical godliness arising from that knowledge, are the things whereon we desire to bestow our attention.

It should not be omitted, that in all our measures and decisions, unanimity, and not majority, is deemed the scriptural rule.

There are scattered over this continent, a few small societies who have conformed in part to the simplicity of the apostolic faith and practice.— We also address to such a similar epistle, and should you favor us with your correspondence, we purpose, if the Lord will, to make known the result of this our communication, to all whom we shall have reason to esteem disciples of the Lord Jesus.

The date of your coming together—the number of members—whether you have elders and deacons—together with any additional information, will be very acceptable to the church that thus addresses you.

Now may He who was dead, and is alive, and lives—over all, God blessed forever, preserve you blameless—to Him be glory both now and for ever. Amen.

Approved and adopted by the church, and signed in their behalf, by

WILLIAM OVINGTON, } Elders.
HENRY ERRITT, }
JONATHAN HATFIELD, }
JAMES SAUNDERS, } Deacons.
BENJ. HENDRICKSON, }

New York, March 1, 1818.

The Church of Christ meeting in Morrison's Court, Glasgow, to their brethren the Church of Christ in New York.

DEARLY BELOVED,—Your epistle of March the 1st came duly to us, and our joy and gratitude to the Father of mercies, have been excited by this instance of a society of believers in Christ, meeting together among themselves, and separating from the world and from false professors, in order to walk according to the dictates of the kingdom of Zion, directed by his word and spirit in the exhibition of his kingdom. We are glad to observe also your zeal for ancient brotherly intercourse between churches holding the same faith and observing the same practices—an attainment too much neglected in our days. In apostolic times, a member of one christian church had access to fellowship in another, on the footing of his membership in the former alone. Thus Phebe is commended to the church at Rome, as being a member of the church at Cenchrea, Rom. xvi. 1, 2, and it appears that such recommendations were usual in those times. 2 *Cor.* iii. 1, 2, 3.

To maintain such brotherly intercourse, both in a church and between different churches, it is necessary to guard both against too much and too little forbearance; and especially in respect to the external order of the society. Accordingly, any shades of difference from your practices which are among us, we think should not affect or mar our relation as sister churches.

We, as well as you, require such as we receive into our fellowship to believe in their hearts, and confess with their mouths, that "Jesus is the Christ, the Son of God." We think the scriptural meaning of this expression includes the belief of the character of God manifest in the flesh, and of the all-perfect and all-efficacious atonement which he has made by shedding his blood: it includes also the belief of the promise, that whosoever believes the testimony of God respecting the efficacy of the atonement, shall be saved. The profession that Jesus is the Christ, includes also the acknowledgement of the dominion of the Redeemer, and the authority of his laws; that he is both "Lord and Christ." With regard to both faith and practice, we hold the meaning of a passage to be the word of God, rather than any form of speech. Hence, when a person professes to believe that "Jesus is the Christ," we satisfy ourselves that he understands and believes those words in the scriptural sense; for whilst we know that "no man can call Jesus Lord, but by the Spirit of God," we know also that many say to Jesus, "Lord, Lord," who have no part in his kingdom. The gospel contains the testimony of God respecting the Saviour and the salvation, the dignity of the Saviour's character and the efficacy and satisfactory nature of the atonement, and the completeness of the glorious redemption. It contains also the divine promise, that whosoever is illuminated to believe the divine testimony shall be saved, and is by this faith justified. Such as make a credible profession of this faith we baptize and receive into fellowship with the church.

On the first day of the week we count it our duty and privilege to meet, and joyfully commemorate the death of Christ as an atonement for sin, and his resurrection as the pledge of our justification, as that by virtue of which we are raised to the "newness of life," and as the sample and the earnest of our deliverance from the power of the grave at the last day. In these exercises we think it our duty to promote the glory of God and our mutual edification.

In our social observances on the Lord's day, we judge worshipping "in spirit and in truth," to be chiefly important, rather than any particular arrangement of observances, or any particular bodily exercises in them.

Except that we begin with praise and prayer, and interpose these exercises between the other observances, our general arrangement is taken from the words, Acts ii. "they continued in the apostles' doctrine and fellowship, and in the breaking of bread, and in prayers." In the forenoon we commence with praise and prayer, each twice; the first referring to the Lord's day, the second before reading the word. Then we read in the historical part of the Old Testament, from the beginning to the end of either. We read also in those books called Hagiographa, i. e. Job, and to the end of Canticles; and we read also in the historical part of the New Testament, i. e. from the beginning to the end of the Acts of the Apostles. We next sing and pray with a view to the exercise, and attend to mutual exhortation and instruction; and then conclude with prayer, praise, and the dismission. In the middle of the day, as many of the members as find it convenient meet to a temporal repast, where we think it right to enquire after each other's welfare, and to cultivate familiarity with each other. This is our love feast. In the afternoon we commence, as in the forenoon, with praise and prayer, each twice. Then we again attend to the apostles' doctrine by reading the prophets and apostles. We next praise and pray with a view to the collection or fellowship. We next attend to the Lord's supper, the observance being preceded by praise, and a reference to the institution, and thanksgiving preceding both the bread and the cup. After the supper a hymn is sung, and then (for some time past) prayer, and a discourse by one of the pastors or preachers, and conclude as in the forenoon. In the forenoon the members of the church sit generally apart from others; in the afternoon, almost universally so. And we are advancing more and more in this, whilst we still forbear on it. Such is our ordinary procedure; but we dont think it essential. Until lately the Lord's supper was our last observance, except praise and prayer. We stand at prayer and praise. In our "measures and decisions," the voice of the church is fairly taken, and the minority generally fall in with the majority. The difference generally arises from a misunderstanding, and is removed by explanation; or the difference may relate to a point not settled by the scriptures, and then it ought to be matter of forbearance. To exact a greater unanimity than this, leads, we think, to tyranny on one part and hypocrisy on the other, and to endless divisions of churches. Such is our mode, and we think it warranted by the word of God. But we do not blame you for commencing with prayer, though we think the words "first of all," 1 Tim. ii. 1. 1. and "first," 1 Tim. i. 16. mean "principally" and "principal," or chiefly and chief. And we read, "Enter into his gates and courts with praise." We will not blame you for kneeling at prayer, and we expect you will not blame us for standing at this exercise. We do not blame you for reading your warrant regularly before the Lord's supper and the collection; nor would we blame you though you should read a similar warrant regularly before prayers and praises, and the readings and exhortations; though we do not think this necessary. We expect you will not blame us

though we sometimes read these warrants, sometimes refer to them, and sometimes suppose them understood and admitted.

Such differences as subsist between us, we think, should not be grounds of separation nor matters of dispute among churches. "We must contend earnestly for the faith;" but unlearned questions, i. e. questions to which the word affords no decided answer, we must " avoid." If we do not avoid such disputes, they are sure to "engender strifes," and are the great cause of division, both among disciples and churches.

Regarding brotherly intercourse, and our conduct in the world both to men in general, and to rulers, your letter expresses our sentiments, and those of the churches with which we have fellowship.

Such churches as ours have existed in Scotland, at Edinburgh and Glasgow, from thirty to forty years. Of late (1812) a division took place on the question of small societies, without pastors, having a right to use the Lord's supper.— We took the affirmative of this question. We differ from some other Baptists also in receiving only baptized believers, whilst they plead for admitting all true believers to their fellowship. We differ from others who forbid the brotherly exhortations on the Lord's day in the public meetings of the church. Our members are about one hundred and eighty. Those of our sister church at Paisley about the same. There are besides a number of churches, as at Perth, London, Liverpool, &c. &c. and many societies without pastors, with whom we are in the habit of christian intercourse.

We are, on behalf of the church here, who wish you grace, mercy, and peace, in Christ Jesus, yours for the gospel's sake,

Glasgow, May 10, 1818.   JAMES WATT,
                                 JAMES BUCHAN.

Obituary Notice.

AFTER the first form of this number was in type, on Monday, the 22d ult. at nearly 11 o'clock A. M. after a tedious and painful illness of a consumptive character, which she bore with the utmost fortitude, patience, and resignation— departed this life, MRS. MARGARET CAMPBELL, consort of the editor of this paper, aged thirty-six years. The deceased was a christian in profession and practice, and did in her life and deportment for many years recommend the excellency of the christian profession to all her acquaintance; and during her long illness, and in her death, she did exhibit to her numerous connexions and friends, how tranquilly and cheerfully a christian can meet death and resign the spirit into the hands of a gracious and divine Redeemer. "I die," she said, "without an anxiety about any thing upon the earth, having committed all that interests me into the hands of my faithful and gracious Heavenly Father, and in the confident expectation of a glorious resurrection when the Lord Jesus appears unto the salvation of all who trust in him." Without an effort towards a eulogy or an encomium—without a single bias from the most endearing relation— we simply announce the above event for the information of a numerous acquaintance, widely extended, and as an apology for the delay of the present number beyond the usual time. Her dying address to her five surviving little daughters, we may, for their benefit and that of others, shortly lay before our readers in a subsequent number. "The Lord gave, and the Lord hath taken away. Blessed be the name of the Lord."
                                          EDITOR.

No. 5.]   December 3, 1827.

Attempt at the Restoration of Ancient Order.

July 31, 1818.

The Church of Christ assembling in Leith Walk, Edinburgh—to the Church of Christ in New York—Grace unto you, and peace from God the Father, and from the Lord Jesus Christ.

Dear Brethren,—We have been much refreshed, and edified, by the communication with which you have favored us. Convinced that the more general diffusion of the gospel of the kingdom must be accompanied with a greater degree of union among believers, and that that union can only be produced by renouncing our own wisdom, and keeping the ordinances as delivered by the apostles, 1 *Cor.* xi. 2.—We endeavor in all things to observe the instructions contained in the New Testament. We are, however, deeply sensible from what we observe in others, and still more from our own experience, that we are prone to be misled and blinded by prejudice, while professing a desire to do the will of God; and therefore we are happy to communicate with our brethren, that we may be mutually profitable to each other.

In compliance with your wish, we shall now proceed to give you a brief sketch of our history as a church, and inform you of the manner in which we conduct our worship. In most respects it agrees with your practice, and where it differs, we shall mention to you the reasons of our conduct.

It is about twenty years since we were first associated together. At that time, we observed the Lord's supper once a month; and although we had a pastor, we also procured a succession of preachers from a distance, whose discourses were more addressed to those who were without than to the church.

Our first step towards scriptural order, was our beginning to break bread every Lord's day. In examining this subject, we learned, that the churches of Christ, to the end of the world, ought in all things to be guided by the apostolic traditions.

The subject of mutual exhortation and discipline on the Lord's day was next agitated.— These had formerly been attended to at our weekly evening meeting, but we became convinced, that whatever is enjoined on the churches, should be observed on the first day of the week, as this is the only day on which the disciples are *commanded* to assemble, and on which the great body of the church are able to attend. About the same time, the question of baptism came under our consideration; and in consequence of many being baptized, and mutual exhortation and discipline on the Lord's day being introduced, a considerable number left us, who still continue to assemble as an Independent church. This took place about ten years ago, since which time we have observed our present order.

Our number is about two hundred and fifty. We have three elders and four deacons: we had four elders; but one of them, (brother Thompson) has for many years been desirous of preaching Christ in foreign lands, and has left us with this intention. He was commended to the Lord for the work by prayer, with fasting and laying on of hands. He sailed on the 12th instant from Liverpool for Buenos Ayres, as he considered the southern part of your continent to be more neglected than any other missionary field. We request your constant prayers on his behalf.

We meet at half past 10 o'clock on the Lord's day morning. After prayer by the presiding elder, (in which 1 *Tim.* ii. 1, 2. is particularly attended to,) any case of discipline which requires to be mentioned is laid before the church, the names of those who have applied for fellowship are also read, and the result of the conversation which the elders and two or more of the brethren have had with them, is stated. If the church be satisfied, they are baptized in the course of the week, and received next Lord's day. On their admission they are saluted with a kiss by the presiding elder, while the church stands up in token of approbation. We consider it necessary, not only to inquire into the views of the gospel which those who apply to the church entertain; but we endeavor to ascertain whether they are acting under its influence. We know from the testimony of God that the truth works effectually in all who believe; but we see many who make a scriptural profession of faith without bringing forth the fruits of righteousness, and consequently show that they are not standing in the true grace of God. Hence the necessity of inquiring into the conduct of men, since they have professed to know the truth. The example of scripture is clear on this subject. Paul's confession must have been unexceptionable; yet the disciples did not receive him till they heard the testimony of Barnabas respecting his conduct. The presiding elder then gives out a psalm or hymn, in singing which the brethren join, standing. A chapter is read from the Old Testament, and a corresponding one from the New. (We go regularly through the Old Testament in the morning, and through the New in the afternoon.) One of the brethren is called on by the elder to engage in prayer, and at the conclusion of this and all our prayers the church says *Amen.* Praise. The elder, after a few observations on the Lord's supper, gives thanks, or calls on one of the brethren to do so. The bread is then handed about by the deacons. In like manner the cup, after giving thanks. Praise. The contribution is made for the poor, and once a month an extraordinary collection for promoting the spread of the gospel. The brethren are invited to teach and to admonish each other. Praise. Prayer by one of the brethren. The church is called on to salute each other with a holy kiss, and separates.

We meet again at a quarter past two o'clock, after an interval of nearly an hour and a half. We begin with praise. A chapter in the Old and one in the New Testament are read. Prayer by one of the brethren. Praise. One or more of the elders teach. Prayer, praise, and separate at four o'clock.

We have a meeting at six in the evening; but this is not attended by all the brethren—some being engaged in instructing their families, others in teaching Sabbath schools, &c. After praise, reading a chapter, prayer, and praise, one of the elders preaches, and has particularly in view those that are without. On the third Lord's day of the month, we have in the evening a prayer meeting for the spread of the gospel, when any interesting intelligence which has been received is read.

On Wednesday evening we meet for an hour; when, after praise and prayer, one of the elders teaches. We conclude with prayer and praise. On Friday we do the same, only the time is occupied by the exhortations of the brethren.

Having thus, beloved, given you a full account of our order, we shall now make a few remarks on some points in which a slight difference appears to subsist between you and us. In doing so, we address you with all affection, and entreat

38

you to bear with us. We have all much to learn, and none of us imagine we have already attained, or are already perfect.

1st. We do not kneel in prayer, we stand both in prayer and singing. This does not arise from thinking that kneeling is unscriptural, but because our seats are not so constructed as to render it convenient, and we find both postures recognized in the word of God.

2d. We are not quite sure whether we understand you, when you say, "Having no fellowship in sacred things with those who confess and obey not the faith." We have no idea of a believer having fellowship in worship with an unbeliever. "How shall they call on him in whom they have not believed?" But we have known persons who entertain ideas on this subject which we judge to be unscriptural. Not only do they maintain that the church should sit together, (which we approve and practise,) but they entertain a dread of others seeming to join with them, of which we cannot perceive a trace in the word of God. Under the influence of this apprehension, some intimate to those who are present that they are not to stand up when the church prays or praises; others do not read the hymns lest any but the church should sing. There is not a shadow of any such thing in the apostolic history. We find prayer employed by the apostles in order to bring men to the knowledge of the truth, *Acts* xxvii. 35. xxviii. 8. and no apprehensions are ever expressed of unbelievers appearing to join in worship by putting themselves in the same posture with believers. Besides, where any number attend there generally are some disciples of Christ not connected with the church, and who consequently can, and do join in prayer and praise; and we know no reason why any man should forbid them. We know it has been said we might as well admit unbelievers to the Lord's supper as suffer them to stand up along with the church in prayer or praise. But by receiving them to break bread, we acknowledge them to be disciples, members of the body of Christ; whereas their placing themselves in the same posture with the church, implies no acknowledgment of them, on our part, as believers. On the whole, we think any attempt to prevent the hearers from assuming the same posture as the church, in any part of their worship, is unscriptural. It gives a false view of the encouragement given by Jesus to sinners, and while it has a show of faithfulness, it is calculated to foster a temper towards those who are without very different from what Christ has enjoined on his people. We do not know that your sentiments, beloved, differ from our own on this subject. If they do, we trust you will take our observations in good part, as we have known much evil result from the practice to which we have referred.

3d. We observe that you attend to a love-feast, but do not consider it "of the same strict obligation with the duties of the Lord's day." That any number of the church may eat and drink together according to circumstances, we are fully satisfied; but we see nothing like a love-feast in the New Testament, except the Lord's supper, 1 *Cor.* v. 8. The only passages on which what has been called a love-feast is founded, are, we believe, 2 *Peter* ii. 13. *Jude* 12. But if these refer to any feast observed by the churches, we see no reason to doubt that it is exclusively the Lord's supper: for we not only find no other feast enjoined on the churches, but we have positive evidence that it is improper on other occasions to eat and drink in the church. When the apostle reproves the Corinthians for satisfy-

2 Z

ing their hunger while professing to eat the Lord's supper, he says, Have you not houses to eat and drink in? 1 *Cor.* xi. 22. Had he appointed any thing like a modern love-feast, surely he would not have restricted their eating and drinking to their own houses. From comparing the various passages on this subject, we learn, that in partaking of the Lord's supper, we are not to satisfy our hunger, and that the place for doing so is our own houses, where we may exercise hospitality to our brethren, but that the church ought not to come together to eat and drink. We do not approve of holding any religious service as not being of "strict obligation." Every part of our worship is either commanded or not; if commanded, we are bound to obey; if not, it is in fact prohibited. As to the church meeting on week days, it is not enjoined; but social prayer, &c. is enjoined, and always proper when circumstances permit.

4th. As to washing the feet, it was a piece of hospitality which was general in the east; the neglect of it was an evidence of want of respect, *Luke* vii. 44. but we do not consider ourselves bound to observe this, more than any other civil custom, such as girding ourselves when about to engage in any work, *John* xiii. 4. If we compare the account of our Lord's washing his disciples' feet, as given by John, with the parallel passage in Luke, we shall find that it was intended as a reproof to his disciples, who, during supper, were disputing who should be greatest. The Lord said nothing at the time, but after supper rose and washed their feet, thus pointing out to them the way to true greatness in his kingdom. Compare *Luke* xxii. 24. 27. with *John* xiii. 5. 17. If washing our brother's feet were necessary for his comfort on any particular occasion, it would be our duty, just as it would be so to lay down our lives for the brethren, 1 *John* iii. 16. but as the latter is our duty only in peculiar circumstances, so we think is the former.

5th. The kiss of charity we consider to be very different. From the earliest ages a kiss has been the highest token of affection. It is not confined to any particular country, but being a natural expression of love, is universally practised. Customs may change as to the ordinary expressions of good will to an acquaintance; but if a son had been lost and was found, his father and mother would be impelled by nature to kiss him. The Lord does not interfere with civil customs, and in these his disciples ought not to affect singularity. As it is improper in believers to dress in a different manner from others, so when meeting on the street, they ought not to distinguish themselves by any peculiarity of address. But in the churches of the saints there is neither European nor Asiatic. Every distinction is lost in the character of disciples of Jesus, and to him alone all are to be subject. When he directs such a society to observe any thing, they are not at liberty to suppose that their obedience may be suspended on the local customs of the country in which they sojourn. Now the precept to salute one another with a holy kiss, is expressly given to the churches at Corinth and Thessalonica, 1 *Cor.* xvi. 20. 2 *Cor.* xiii. 12. 1 *Thess.* v. 26. But, this, it is supposed by some, is only to be done on "special occasions." We should be glad to know what these occasions are, for respecting them the scripture is silent. The commandment does not refer to the occasional meetings of individuals, for it is given to the churches, and includes all the brethren. If it be alleged, that although given to the church, it is to be observed by the brethren, not collectively,

39

but individually—we reply, this is the very argument adduced against mutual exhortation in the church; and those who do not practice salutation cannot, with any consistency, disapprove of the sentiments of those who affirm that the precepts to exhort each other do not refer to the church when assembled, but to our intercourse as individuals. We believe, however, the true reason of the prejudices of some disciples against salutation in the church, is, that it appears to them formal and unnatural. No doubt all the ordinances may degenerate into form; for instance, our meeting on every first day of the week, and proceeding in the same manner, may be nothing better than a form; we may draw near to God with our mouths, and honor him with our lips, while our hearts are far from him; and some have objected to the weekly observance of the Lord's supper on this very ground. It is certainly our duty to watch and pray against formality in our religious duties; but we do not see that we are more liable to become formal in obeying the commandment to salute each other, than in attending to the other ordinances. And is there any thing unnatural in the family of Christ, when they meet to commemorate his death and resurrection, expressing their mutual love by giving each other the highest token of affection? and why should it be thought a thing incredible that he should give such a commandment, who has said, By this shall all men know that you are my disciples if you have love one to another? who has described his people as brethren, as one body, as members one of another? The commandment to salute each other with a holy kiss, is five times repeated in the New Testament, and is delivered to the churches over the whole of the then known world, from Rome in the west, to Pontus and Cappadocia in the east.

6th. As to what you say of unanimity, and not majority, being the scriptural rule for the churches, we fully agree with you that the idea of voting in a church is improper. But you will observe that the New Testament lays down no rule on the subject of unanimity, and therefore we do not consider ourselves at liberty to do so. Unanimity is most desirable, but it may not be always attainable, and we should be sorry to insist on any thing which might tempt our brethren to hypocrisy. Some churches profess to hold the necessity of unanimity, and most consistently separate those who do not see exactly with the church, i.e. the majority. But this we hold to be unscriptural; and that while it is our duty to pray for unanimity, we are not entitled to add to the word of God by laying down a rule for the churches on this subject.

7th. There is one other point to which we would now, beloved, direct your attention. We do not know from your letter whether you are like-minded with us or not on the subject of forbearance, but we deem it highly important to be understood by all the disciples of Christ.

We are fully satisfied that only believers ought to be baptized. This is evident, First. From the precept given to the apostles, *Mark* xvi. 15, 16, which is as plain as any law of Moses. Second. From the uniformity of the apostolic practice as recorded in the New Testament, *Acts* ii. 42, viii. 12, 13, 36, 37, xviii. 8, &c. Third. From the explanation which is given of the import of the institution, by which it is necessarily restricted to believers, *Rom.* vi. *Col.* ii. &c. We are aware that error on this subject implies considerable darkness respecting the new covenant as distinguished from the old. We know also that the confounding of the two covenants lies at the

root of most of the corruptions of christianity. But notwithstanding this, we see many who are evidently taught of God, who adorn the doctrine of Jesus, and enjoy fellowship with the Father and with his Son, who have not been baptized, and that not from being ashamed to confess Christ, but from not understanding his will on that subject.

The question whether such persons should be received into the churches has been frequently agitated in this country. We have only once been put to the test by such an application being made, and we saw it to be our duty to receive the person, although unbaptized. Our reasons were these:—

1st. There is no example in the New Testament, of any disciple being refused fellowship with the churches of the saints, although various differences of sentiment prevailed. A church of Christ is a school for training up his disciples, and we conceive the only terms of admission are, that they give evidence of belonging to him. Hence we dare not refuse to receive a believer, although unbaptized.

2d. We are expressly commanded to receive those who are weak in the faith, *Rom.* xiv. 1. "to receive one another, as Christ also has received us to the glory of God," *Rom.* xv. 7. Now, a disciple who holds infant baptism is, in this respect, weak, yet he is in the faith; and, therefore, we think ourselves bound to receive him. We know it has been said, that the 14th and 15th chapters of the Romans refer to things in themselves indifferent, and that the precepts above quoted, respect only such matters; but those who argue thus, have not duly considered the subject. Meats and drinks are doubtless indifferent in themselves; but their introduction into religion is not a matter of indifference. The whole system of antichrist is founded on an attempt to introduce Jewish observances into the kingdom of Christ. The observance of days is spoken of in connexion with the precept to receive the weak believer, *Rom.* xiv. 5. and yet the apostle elsewhere declares, that the observance of days and times led him to fear that the Galatians had never received the truth, *Gal.* iv. 10, 11. We, therefore, understand the precepts, to receive him that is weak in the faith, in their plain and obvious meaning, and consider them as referring to any error into which a real disciple of Christ may fall. Of this we have a striking proof, 1 *Cor.* viii. where great ignorance on most important subjects, is declared to be compatible with true discipleship.

3d. We shall just refer to one more passage on this subject, *Phil.* iii. 15, 16. "Let us, therefore, as many as be perfect, be thus minded: and if, in any thing, you be otherwise minded, God shall reveal even this to you. Nevertheless, whereto we have already attained, let us walk by the same rule, let us mind the same thing." This appears conclusive on this question, and, therefore, while we pray that grace may be with all those who love our Lord Jesus Christ in sincerity, we cannot refuse to receive any of them who desire to observe the institutions on which we are agreed; and this we are convinced is the scripture way to unity of sentiment, which ought constantly to be the subject of our fervent prayers.

Such, beloved, are the observations which have occurred to us on the perusal of your letter. We regret that in consequence of the corruptions introduced into the kingdom of Jesus, it is necessary for his disciples to say so much about the external order of his churches. On this there ought to be no difference, and the time is approaching, when the existing differences shall be done away. It would have been far more agreeable to us, and we are assured also to you, to have written each other of the glory and dignity of the person of Immanuel; of the height, and depth, and breadth, and length, of his love; of the fulness of his atonement; of the freeness of his salvation; of the powerful obligations under which we are laid to live devoted to Him who purchased us with his blood. We should have preferred dwelling on the delight which we ought to feel in his service, the care we ought to take to adorn his doctrine, walking before our houses with a perfect heart, worshipping God in our families, manifesting our delight in the meeting with our brethren, and meditating on it at home—in short, whether we eat or drink, or whatsoever we do, doing all to the glory of God.

But we are very sensible, that it is necessary, diligently to search for the footsteps of Christ's flock in regard to his institutions; for they are all calculated to promote that holiness, without which no man shall see the Lord, and all the contrivances and commandments of men in religion turn us from the truth.

It is, however, highly important that we should be on our guard against the wiles of the devil. He is transformed into an angel of light, and, through the deceitfulness of our hearts, may divert our attention from that righteousness, and peace, and joy in the Holy Ghost, in which the kingdom of God consists; while we are zealously contending for those institutions, the real object of which is to promote every holy temper of mind.

In the course of our experience, we have seen not a few, who, while they *appeared* to be advancing in the knowledge of the nature of the kingdom of Christ, were evidently losing spirituality of mind, and becoming much less exemplary in their conduct than formerly. We have seen such make shipwreck of faith and a good conscience; while others, whose views they despised as being nearer Judaism than Christianity, have lived honorably, and died triumphing in the hope of eternal life through Christ.

Do we, therefore, account the ordinances of Jesus to be of little importance? Do we adopt the sentiments of those, who seem to think that the churches of Christ may do what seems good in their own eyes, according to their views of expediency? By no means, any more than we neglect the scriptures, because those who are unlearned and unstable, wrest them to their own destruction. But we wish to approve ourselves the servants of God, by the armor of righteousness on the right hand and on the left.

It is our earnest prayer for you, beloved brethren, that you may stand complete in all the will of God; that your light may so shine before men, that others, seeing your good works, may glorify our heavenly Father; that you may be blameless and harmless, the sons of God, without rebuke, in the midst of a crooked and perverse nation, shining among them as lights in the world.—Now the God of peace, that brought again from the dead our Lord Jesus, that Great Shepherd of the sheep, through the blood of the everlasting covenant, make you perfect in every good work to do his will, working in you that which is well-pleasing in his sight, through Jesus Christ; to whom be glory for ever and ever. Amen.

————

A Restoration of the Ancient Order of Things.
No. XXI.

Being an Extract from the Preface to a new selection of Psalms, Hymns, and Spiritual Songs, about to be issued from this press.

PSALM and hymn singing, like every other part of christian worship, has been corrupted by sectarianism. This demon, whose name is Legion, has possessed all our spirits, and given a wrong direction to almost all our religious actions. A consistent sectary not only contends for a few dry abstract opinions, nicknamed "articles of belief," or "essential points," but these he sings and prays with a zeal proportioned to the opposition made to them. How loud and how long does the Arminian sing his free grace, while he argues against the Calvinists' sovereign grace. And in what animating strains does the Calvinist sing of his imputed righteousness in the presence of the Arminian, who he supposes is seeking to be justified by his works. Annihilate these sects, and these hymns either die with them, or undergo a new modification. He that sings them in the spirit of the sect, pays homage to the idol of a party, but worships not the God of the whole earth. Were I asked for a good criterion of a sectarian spirit, I would answer, When a person derives more pleasure from the contemplation of a tenet because of the opposition made to it, than he would, did no such opposition exist; or when he is more opposed to a tenet because of the system to which it belongs, or the people who hold it, than on account of its own innate meaning and tendency, he acts the sectary, and not the christian: and so of all predilections and antipathies, when they are created, guided, or controlled by any thing extrinsic of the subject matter itself.

Our hymns are, for the most part, our creed in metre, while it appears in the prose form in our confessions. A methodistic sermon must be succeeded by a methodistic hymn, and a methodistic mode of singing it. And so of the Presbyterian. There is little or no difference in any sect in this one particular. Even the Quaker is not singular here; for as he has no regular sermon he has no regular song, hymn, nor prayer. Those who have many frames and great vicissitudes of feeling, sing and pray much about them, and those who are more speculative than practical, prefer exercises of intellect to those of the heart or affections.

The hymn book is as good an index to the brains and to the hearts of a people as the creed book; and scarce a "sermon is preached," which is not followed up by a corresponding hymn or song.

Does the preacher preach up Sinai instead of Calvary, Moses instead of Christ, to convince or convict his audience? Then he sings—

"Awak'd by Sinai's awful sound,
My soul in bonds of guilt I found,
    And knew not where to go;
O'erwhelm'd with sin, with anguish slain,
The sinner must be born again,
    Or sink to endless woe."

"When to the law I trembling fled,
It pour'd its curses on my head;
    I no relief could find.
This fearful truth increased my pain,
The sinner must be born again,
    O'erwhelm'd my tortur'd mind."

"Again did Sinai's thunder roll,
And guilt lay heavy on my soul,
    A vast unwieldy load!
Alas! I read and saw it plain,
The sinner must be born again,
    Or drink the wrath of God."

I know of nothing more anti-evangelical than the above verses; but they suit one of our law

41

convincing sermons, and the whole congregation must sing, suit or non-suit the one half of them. But to finish the climax, this exercise is called praising God.

But again—Does the preacher teach his congregation that the time and place when and where the sinner should be converted was decreed from all eternity? Then out of complaisance to the preacher, the congregation must *praise* the Lord by singing—

> " 'Twas fix'd in God's eternal mind
> When his dear sons should mercy find:
> From everlasting he decreed
> When every good should be conveyed."

> " Determin'd was the manner how
> We should be brought the Lord to know;
> Yea, he decreed the very place
> Where he would call us by his grace."

Is the absolute and unconditional perseverance of all the converted taught? Then, after sermon, all must sing—

> " Safe in the arms of Sovereign Love
> We ever shall remain,
> Nor shall the rage of earth or hell
> Make thy dear couusels vain."

> " Not one of all the chosen race
> But shall to heaven attain;
> Partake on earth the purpos'd grace,
> And then with Jesus reign."

But does the system teach that there are and must necessarily be cold and dark seasons in the experience of all christians, and that such only are true christians, who have their doubts, fears, glooms, and winters? Then the audience sings—

> " Dear Lord, if, indeed, I am thine,
> If thou art my sun and my song,
> Say why do I languish and pine,
> And why are my winters so long?
> O drive these dark clouds from my sky,
> Thy soul-cheering presence restore,
> Or take me unto thee on high,
> Where winter and clouds are no more."

Without being prolix or irksome in filing objections to all these specimens of hymn singing, I shall mention but two or three:—

1. They are *in toto* contrary to the spirit and genius of the christian religion.

2. They are unfit for any congregation, as but few in any one congregation can with regard to truth, apply them to themselves.

3. They are an essential part of the corrupt systems of this day, and a decisive characteristic of the grand apostacy. But a further developement of this subject we postpone to our next.

EDITOR.

Reply to Spencer Clack's 2d Letter.—Letter II.

BROTHER CLACK,—I feel constrained to tell you that there is a little too much management and apparent art in your correspondence with me. In the conclusion of your letter five, in two parts, you say—"I have, agreeably to your request, published your reply entire."—What the word "entire" means in Kentucky, you ought to know better than I; but in Virginia we never say we have a thing entire when we have just the half of it. Nor even if we had the whole of it in two slices we should not feel ourselves warranted in saying we had it entire. You published one-fourth of my reply in one paper, and another fourth in a second paper, and two-fourths of it are yet unpublished, you say you have "published my reply entire." This is one blemish in you, brother Clack. Are you afraid that your readers should have one of my letters entire at one time? If not, why give birth to the suspicion? And

why make them believe that they had my reply to your first letter "concluded," when, in fact, they had not more than the one half of it!! But you spent your energies in the last in dictating to me how I should have answered Elder Stone. Did I ask you for advice, brother Clack? Or did I choose you for my preceptor? When I sit for lessons I claim the right of choosing my instructor. And believe me, brother Clack, there are a hundred persons on this continent who would, in my judgment, be more eligible than you. Besides, I exceedingly reprobate your dictations regarding the course to be pursued in relation to Elder Stone, and "the Christians" with him. The policy of "fire brands, arrows, and death," is not the course that Paul persuades. However I cannot thank you for your advice, neither matter nor manner, inasmuch as it was not solicited.

An extract from Robinson Crusoe would have been of as much merit and utility in your last letter as the reported sermon detailed by some laugh-loving recorder, from the lips of some said-to-be Christian preacher. Why you should have made such a detail to me, unless to stir up the "odium theologicum," I know not. It is of a piece with your reported extracts from bishop Semple's letter to Doctor Noel—and designed to answer a similar purpose. This is another speck in you, brother Clack.

These hints, brief indeed, in comparison to what they might, and, perhaps, ought to be, will just suffice to show you that your policy is duly apprehended and appreciated. These impertinent items in your correspondence being thus noticed, I proceed to finish my reply to your second letter.

You asked for a summary exhibition of my faith in your second letter. This I did not think proper to give you in my last. And indeed I could not give you a more summary exhibition of my faith, than by presenting you with a New Testament. But seeing the acceptation of the word *entire* in Kentucky, I have been led to conclude that I might, in a similar acceptation of terms, give you a summary exhibition of at least a part of my faith. And as I wish to see what use you have for it, and being of a very accommodating disposition, I will, for once, draw up a summary, and consummate your happiness, by dedicating it to you.

A summary exhibition of the 49*th chapter of my faith.*

Credo, [I believe] that, In the beginning was the Word, and the Word was with God, and the word was God—this was in the beginning with God. All things were made by it, and without it not a single creature was made. In it was life, and the life was the light of men. And the light shone in darkness, and the darkness admitted it not.—That God has so loved the world as to give his only begotten Son, that whosoever believes on him may have eternal life. For God has sent his Son into the world, not to condemn the world, but that the world may be saved by him.—That Jesus Christ was born of the seed of David, with respect to the flesh; but was declared to be the Son of God, with respect to the Spirit of Holiness, by his resurrection from the dead—for he died for our sins, was buried and arose the third day, according to the scriptures, and commanded that glad tidings of great joy to all people should be published in his name—viz. That through faith in his name we are justified from all things, and being baptized for the remission of our sins, the Holy Spirit is given to us, and we having the Spirit of

42

God's Son sent into our hearts, cry, Abba, Father. And this is the will of him that sent him, that whosoever sees the Son and believes in him, shall have everlasting life, and Jesus will raise him up at the last day: for there shall be a resurrection of the just and of the unjust, and when the Son of man comes in his glory, all nations will be assembled before him, and he will separate them as a shepherd separates his sheep from his goats, and the righteous shall be received into everlasting life, and the wicked shall go away into everlasting punishment—for without holiness no man shall see the Lord:—and he gave himself for our sins, that he might purify to himself a chosen people, zealous of good works, and became the author of eternal salvation to all them who believe in, and obey him."

So ends this chapter of my creed, which is one of the most important chapters in it; and I can assure you that there is nothing in any other chapter at variance with this.

But I wait for your objections to my epitome.

Yours, &c.   A. CAMPBELL.

P. S.—Please inform the readers of your paper that I would advise them, if they wish to do themselves justice, not to depend too much upon your columns for obtaining a correct view of my sentiments; but to read the Christian Baptist for themselves, for a year or two before they decide upon my course.   A. C.

Review of Dr. Noel's Circular.—No. IV.

" BEFORE the adversaries of creeds can boast of having gained any thing in this controversy, it devolves upon them to do, what we apprehend cannot easily be done. They must exhibit some method, scriptural and practicable, of excluding corruption from the church without a creed." Thus speaks the Doctor's circular. When my criticisms upon the Doctor's use of the term creed, and his definition of it, upon the term church, and his application of it, are remembered, the thin veil which conceals the sophism in the above period is removed. But should any person inquire for any other exposure, I will answer thus: Many churches are commended in the New Testament for detecting and excluding corruptions and corruptors; for example, the church in Ephesus, A. D. 97, is thus addressed by Jesus Christ—" Thou hast *tried* them which say they are apostles and are not, and hast found them liars." They had also tried, detected, and " hated" the views and practices of the Nicolaitans. Now the question is, By what creed? Not by that ordained by Constantine; for this was not made till A. D. 325. Not by that of Dr. Luther; for that was published first A. D. 1529. Not by that of Dr. Calvin; for that appeared only in 1537. Not by that decreed at Westminster; for that was perfected A. D. 1640. Not by that made by Dr. Geo. Fox; for that was not known till A. D. 1655. Not by that adopted by the Philadelphia Association; for that was regenerated A. D. 1742. Not by that made by Dr. Erskine; for that was born A. D. 1733. Not by that finished by Dr. John Wesley; for that was not baptized till 1729. And most assuredly not by that made by Dr. Noel; for it is not yet finished, neither can be completed before the demise of the Doctor, unless he says he is as wise now as he ever can be. By what creed, then, did this church in Ephesus exclude these corruptions, if not by any human creed—it must have been by that creed which we have exclusively espoused—viz. the apostolic writings. If we have the same creed these churches had A. D. 97, we are as well furnished as they. But

how many corruptions have been kept out of the church by these human devices, such as Dr. Noel's creed? Are the corruptions excluded from the Baptist, Presbyterian, and Methodist church, and found only in the world among Jews, Turks, and Pagans? Are there not as many corruptions now in the churches as there were two centuries ago, before most of the present creeds were born? But as I aim at brevity, I will lay my hand at once upon the sophism of the sentence above quoted. The fact is, instead of excluding corruptions out of the church, creeds keep them in the church. I am sure of proving this to the Doctor's own satisfaction. Well, Dr. Noel, is not infant sprinkling a corruption in the church? Yes, as a baptist, I must say so. Could infant sprinkling, think you, Doctor, be gathered out of the apostolic writings? By no means. How did the protestants get into the practice of it? From the creed of the catholics. Have the protestants got this corruption in their creeds? Most certainly they have. Do you think, then, Doctor, that this corruption would have continued so long, even until now, had it not been for the creeds? I candidly avow, I do not think it would. I thank you, Doctor, for your honesty. Well, then, Doctor, I now say, Have not creeds kept this corruption in the church, and will not this corruption continue in the church so long as the Paido baptist sects retain their creeds? Yes, I must say, in my opinion, it will. Well, then, my dear sir, you must be convinced that creeds keep corruptions in the church just so long as the creed is in it, instead of keeping them out. I declare I forgot this point, when fixing my mind upon keeping corruptions out of the church. I know you did, Doctor, but I hope you will think more on this subject before you next write. For you must admit that if this corruption is kept in the church by a creed, every other corruption in the creed must be kept in the church until it excludes the creed. I think, Doctor, you are more than half convinced that when a church excludes a human creed, it excludes more corruption than the creed excludes.   EDITOR.

The Baptist Recorder.

SINCE writing the preceding articles, the Recorder of November 10th has been received. It has given the casting vote in the court of my understanding, as to its own character, and has declared itself to be conducted on the same partial, illiberal, and unfair principles, on which all those papers are conducted which advocate the cause of partyism, against the cause of catholicism or the cause of Christ. I say, such is the verdict which the last Recorder brings in the aforesaid court, on its own character.

The editors of that journal have tried every means of keeping up the present order of things against the ancient order of things exhibited in the Christian Baptist. Amongst these means, the following appear to be the principal:—

1. Never to investigate the merits of any one essay in the Christian Baptist.

2. To publish such excerpts from this work as were most likely to inflame the passions, and to arouse the prejudices of the readers of the Recorder.

3. To make a great display of opponents under various fictitious titles, and under this mask to attempt to render ridiculous any effort to restore the ancient order of things in the church.

4. To be very liberal in expressing strong doubts as to the piety, and great fears as to the orthodoxy of myself.

5. To pronounce encomiums on my talents, as if the impression made on the public was owing alone to my talent for writing and speaking, and not to what was written and spoken.

6. To represent me as in imminent danger of plunging into the vortex of Unitarianism, Arianism, or some tremendous error.

7. To pretend a great love for me, and a great desire to make me more useful, (to build up a sect, I suppose.)

8. To put me down by obtaining the opinions of men of some standing in the churches, and then to oppose the weight of names to the evidence of truth.

9. To publish letters full of apparent love and respect, and then to withhold and suppress my answers to them.

10. To blow the trumpet and sound a victory, before the battle was begun.

11. I was going to say something about the use of *falsehoods* in this cause; but I will refrain, and only make one allusion at present.

"We are of opinion," says the editor of the Recorder, "that Campbell has lost one hundred per cent. in. Kentucky, or more, within a year." A good argument truly. It is well it was only an opinion—and I am of the opinion that this opinion was formed from a mere wish that it were so, for it is grounded on no correct documents at all. The fact is, that the Christian Baptist is more generally read, and has more subscribers this year in Kentucky than it has ever had before. In Virginia, too, where it is represented as declining fast, it has gained, in the last two years, more than a hundred per cent. per annum. And for the last three months, since the commencement of the present volume, our regular increase has been about seventy new subscribers per month. Because I am not continually telling the folks of every few subscribers I have obtained, according to the manner of the Recorder, he took it into his head that "Campbell" had lost one hundred per cent. in Kentucky for one year. The fact is, both the increase of subscribers, and the hundreds of letters received from all parts of the Union, conspire in demonstrating that the good sense of this community will yet rise above the shackles and restraints imposed and imposing upon it by a creed taught, and a creed teaching priesthood.

I regret very much to see the manner of spirit of the editors of the Baptist Recorder. It is unbecoming this enlightened age. The time has been when it suited little spirits to shield themselves under mighty names, and to array great names against the evidences of reason and scripture. But we rejoice, that that time has passed away. How unbecoming, then, for the editor of a Baptist journal, with great apparent joy and with an air of triumph, to exclaim, "He and Campbell are fairly at issue!!" He alludes to Bishop Semple, of Virginia. Rejoice Kentucky! Rejoice Virginia! Bishop Semple and Campbell are at issue!!! Glorious news! Now we triumph! The victory is ours! Bishop Semple and Campbell are at issue!!! Mr. Clack, this will not cover your retreat—this will not secrete your cowardice from the discerning. They will ask you, Why did you fear to publish Campbell's reply to your letters? Why did you tell your readers that you had "concluded his reply," when you had not published the one half of his reply to your first letter? Some bold genius amongst your readers will, perhaps, say, What if Semple and Campbell are at issue—if Campbell and Paul are not at issue?

You finish the picture of human weakness,

when you tell your readers that Campbell is "growing popular among the New Lights." He must then decline amongst the *Old Lights*, Blue Lights, and No Lights. Yet, it would seem, if Elder Stone and his paper are of these New Lights, I am declining amongst them a hundred per cent. per month.

Such are the weapons, and such the mode of warfare of the editors of the Recorder. I have more important mattter to submit to my readers, and as the editors of that journal have fairly given up the publication of my replies, and have thus prevented their readers from any opportunity of judging for themselves, I shall neither trouble them, nor the public with any further notice of them. If they should, however, publish all my replies to Mr. Clack, up to the conclusion of this article, and if they have any thing better to say than, "He and Campbell are at issue," we will cheerfully present it to our readers. EDITOR.

A Letter, said to have been written by Bishop Semple, from Washington City, to somebody in Kentucky.

COLLEGE HILL, D. C., SEPT. 26, 1827.

DEAR BROTHER—THE Baptist Recorder reached me yesterday, in which mention is made of "Querens." Coming here two months ago, I have not seen a Christian Baptist since June or July—I think June. I do not therefore know what Querens says to me or of me. After receiving yours I inquired for a copy of the Christian Baptist, but was informed that nobody took it here, and I therefore am still uninformed as to Querens. The Recorder, however, says that he (Querens) has made a call upon me to point out Campbell's chimeras. In a social correspondence with yourself I used the expression chimeras in allusion to Mr. Campbell's extraordinary views of christianity. When I wrote, I did not calculate upon my letter's finding its way into the public prints. For its doing so you make an apology in your last to me. It was unnecessary; for although I did not expect my remarks to be published, I cared not who knew my opinions. If they are worth any thing their value cannot be better laid out than in sustaining truth against error. If they are of no value, they can of course hurt no body.

If, however, Querens thinks that I am bound to enter into a contest upon the many points in which I differ from my friend Campbell, I must beg leave to differ with him. Mr. Campbell's views are not new, at least, not many of them—Sandeman, Glass, the Haldanes, were master spirits upon this system many years ago. And they were effectually answered by Fuller and others. Mr. Campbell said in his answer to me, some time past, that Sandeman, as a writer, compared to Fuller and his compeers, was like a giant among dwarfs. It may be so, or, as Dr. Doubty says, it may not be so. I can say this, however, If Sandeman is a giant, he has been as completely beaten by the dwarf Fuller, as ever Goliath was by David. If I am called upon, then, to establish my assertions as to Mr. Campbell's views, I refer Querens, and all such, to Fuller's work against Sandeman, &c. I do not know a word in it that I would alter. On those on which brother Campbell differs from, or rather goes farther than these transatlantic writers, I am willing to adopt the defence of our principles, as they have been exhibited in the Recorder, so far as I have seen that defence, under different signatures. I do not say, by the by, that I may not, at some future day, attempt something further upon this subject. I am, however, from some

44

cause, not fond of controversy, and never have been. At my age, therefore, I should be rather afraid to embark upon so stormy an ocean. If, however, I should be induced to become a controversialist, I believe I should as soon enter the lists with my friend Campbell as any other, for three reasons—one is: on the points on which we differ, I am persuaded he is palpably on the wrong side, and it would not be a hard task to make it manifest. A second is, he is so much of a champion, that to be beaten by him would not be so discreditable as it might be with some other antagonists. A third is, I think him a generous combatant with one who wishes nothing but fair play. I believe, however, it is best to let Mr. Campbell's system confute itself by its effects. It has been practically tried somewhat in England, more in Scotland, and in the United States. What has been the result? To say the least, it has been found like many other schemes, more plausible in theory than in practice. They advance the sentiment that the scriptures are so plain that every person may comprehend them, and therefore require no comment, no confession of faith, no creed. Yet among themselves, they find it impossible to agree; and hence most of those who have left Scotland, &c. with these views, have so far relinquished them as to amalgamate with other denominations or have dwindled to nothing. When I think of Mr. Campbell's talents, conjoined with pleasant manners, and apparently a pious spirit, I am exceedingly grieved that he has been heretofore, and is likely to be hereafter, of so little advantage to the cause. I cannot but hope that he will be brought to a more scriptural and more rational course. If you think the above remarks will subserve the cause of truth, you are at liberty to furnish them for the Recorder, and let them take their chance.

Yours affectionately,   Ro. B. Semple.

To R. B. Semple, of Virginia.

Bishop Semple—Your kind wishes for me, and ardent desires that I may be brought to a more rational and scriptural course are most gratefully appreciated, and most sincerely reciprocated by your unworthy brother. I do, hereby, most sincerely claim your aid in putting me to rights.—You are the most competent person in Virginia for such an undertaking, for you see most clearly " that I am palpably on the wrong side on the points in which we differ." Whereas the editors of the Recorder are so palpably dull that they are continually complaining they cannot understand me, and therefore are, all the while, fighting against they know not what. All who are intimately acquainted with me, know that I am open to conviction. And I do most certainly assure you that there is nothing on earth so dear to me as the christian religion, and, therefore, to be wrong in any of my views of it, and consequently to teach others my errors, would be to me of all things the most grievous. Besides, my dear sir, it is not myself only that is endangered, but thousands besides; for, however you may be informed on this subject, and however you may think, this paper is very far from losing any thing of its influence in these United States. It is read in almost all the states in the Union, and is well received on the other side of the Atlantic. And I do know that in the mighty march of human inquiry, it will not do, for even you to decry any thing without showing the reason why. The time is past when great names silenced great arguments, and when the veto of a distinguished teacher silenced the most inquisitive searcher after truth. I am sensible, too, that you would

not wish to live in a community which had no more mind than to cease its inquiries, when you said, desist. I say, I am conscious that you will not adopt nor pursue a course which would be so incongruous with the spirit of the age, and so incompatible with the maxims of the holy men of both Testaments. You cannot but see the weakness of your correspondent and pupil, and of his coadjutors in Kentucky, in making such a struggle to get you to say something against me, that it might be proclaimed in Kentucky that "Bishop Semple is at issue with Campbell." I know that not only you, but all persons of discernment, cannot but regret that in the year of Grace 1827, any christians should be so much wedded to a system, and so opposed in any truth, as upon a failure to maintain the one and oppose the other, they should have to solicit the name of some influential friend to defend their own views, and disprove those of others, by the weight of his reputation.

Nor will it do for you to say that my views, or the cause which I advocate, has been already refuted by any other person. For this will not be satisfactory. To call me a Sandemanian, a Haldanian, a Glassite, an Arian, or a Unitarian, and to tell the world that the Sandemanians, Haldanians, &c. &c. have done so and so, and have been refuted by such and such a person, is too cheap a method of maintaining human traditions, and too weak to oppose reason and revelation. You might as well nickname me a Sabellian, an Anthropomorphist, a Gnostic, a Nicolaitan, or an Anabaptist, as to palm upon me any of the above systems. I do most unequivocally and sincerely renounce each and every one of these systems. He that imputes any of these systems to me, and ranks me amongst the supporters of them, reproaches me. I do not by this mean to say that there are not in each and in all these systems "many excellent things," as Bishop Semple himself once said of them: but when Bishop Semple asks himself how he would like to be called by any of these names, he will find an answer for me. This method of opposing me I know your better judgment will condemn, and on reflection you will see that it is injurious to your own reputation. The reflecting part of the community will say, Why not shew that Campbell is wrong, by the use of reason and scripture rather than by defaming him. Any one that is well read in those systems must know that the Christian Baptist advocates a cause, and an order of things which not one of them embraced. I repeat, you have only to apply the golden rule to yourself in this instance, and ask yourself how you would like an opponent to call you a Fullerite, a Hopkinsian, an Anabaptist, or something worse, in order to refute your sentiments when you cordially renounce the systems laid to your charge.

Nor will it suffice, brother Semple, for you to represent that the course which I advocate has been tried in Europe, in Scotland, England, and America, with bad success. You must either greatly misunderstand me, or you have got some history of religious sentiments and societies in Europe that I have never seen. If your remarks in this instance had been correct, they would be of the same weight and kind with those of the kings of Europe, who say to those who advocate civil liberty, "Look at the French Revolution, and desist;" or of the same weight and kind with that potentate at Rome, who has so often said to the Protestants, "Since you left the bosom of the mother church, you Protestants have in some places dwindled to nothing, in all places

45

you have divided and frittered into sects, and in *no place* for any length of time have you lived in harmony together." Consider how you would reply to him, and then you will find how easily I could find a reply to you, if your allusions had been founded on fact. But they are not, for the cause I advocate has never failed in any instance when it has been fairly and fully tried.

As you have more than once commended many excellent things in the Christian Baptist, and as you are now brought out, or dragged out to oppose me, it behooves you to discriminate the things which you disapprove from those you approve in the Christian Baptist. And now, brother Semple, I call upon you as a man, as a scholar, as a christian, and as a christian bishop, to come forward and make good your assertions against your "friend Campbell." My pages are open for you. You shall have line for line, period for period, page for page, with me. I pledge myself to address you and treat you as a gentleman and a christian ought to do. You will not find an insinuation nor a personality in all I may say of you. I wish to give you a fair specimen of that sort of discussion which I approve, and to shew what reason, demonstration, and scripture declaration can achieve with an able and an honorable opponent. There is no man in America I would rather have for an opponent, if I must have an opponent, than you. Come forward, then, brother Semple; choose the topics; one at a time; numerically arrange your arguments and proofs; make every thing plain and firm; and in good temper, spirit, and affection, shew me where I have erred; and if I cannot present reason, scripture, and good sense to support me, I will yield to your superior discernment, age, and experience, one by one, the points in which we differ. And as this work is generally bound in volumes, your essays, the antidote or the remedy, will descend with the poison to its future readers.

Your humble servant, under the King, my Lord and Master.   A. CAMPBELL.

Burke's opinion of Reformation.

"REFORMATION is one of those pieces which must be put at some distance in order to please. Its greatest favorers love it better in the abstract than in the substance. When any old prejudice of their own, or any interest that they value, is touched, they become scrupulous, they become captious, and every man has his separate exception. Some pluck out the black hairs, some the gray; one point must be given up to one; another point must be yielded to another; nothing is suffered to prevail upon its own principles: the whole is so frittered down, and disjointed, that scarcely a trace of the original scheme remains! Thus, between the resistance of power, and the unsystematical process of popularity, the undertaker and the undertaking are both exposed, and the poor reformer is hissed off the stage, both by friends and foes."

Farewell Address of Mrs. MARGARET CAMPBELL, *to her daughters, spoken to them in the immediate prospect of death.*

My DEARLY BELOVED CHILDREN,—It appears to be the will of our Heavenly Father to separate me from you by death. The only desire I have had to live for some time past was for the good of my family. For myself I could expect to enjoy nothing more on this earth than I have already enjoyed, and, therefore, for my own enjoyment, it is much better for me to be taken away than to continue with you. But I am reconciled to leave you, when I consider that if I continued with you I could not preserve you from evil. I might, indeed, advise you and instruct you; but if you hear not Moses and the prophets, Christ and the apostles, neither would you be persuaded by me. And as to natural evils, 'tis God alone who can defend you from these. You are all able to read the oracles of God, and these are your wisest and safest instructors in every thing. But I am reconciled to leave you from another consideration. I was left without a mother when I was younger than any of you; and when I reflect how kindly and how mercifully our Heavenly Father has dealt by me; how he watched over my childhood, and guarded my youth, and guided me until now, I am taught to commit you without a fear or an anxiety into his hands. The experience I have had of his abundant goodness towards me emboldens me to commend you to him. But you must remember that you can only enjoy his favor, and I can hope for his blessing upon you, only so far as you believe in, and obey him. I have said you can all read the holy scriptures. This is what I much desired to be able to say of the youngest of you, and it is with great pleasure I repeat it, You can all read that blessed book, from which I have derived more happiness than from any other source under the skies. The happiest circumstance in all my life I consider to be that which gave me a taste for reading and a desire for understanding the New Testament. This I have considered, and do now consider to be one of the greatest blessings which has resulted to me from my acquaintance with your father. Although I have had a religious education from my father, and was early taught the necessity and importance of religion, yet it was not until I became acquainted with the contents of this book, which you have seen me so often read, that I came to understand the character of God, and to enjoy a firm and unbounded confidence in all his promises. And now I tell you, my dear children, that all your comfort and happiness in this life, and in that to come, must be deduced from an intimate acquaintance with the Lord Jesus Christ. I have found his character, as delineated by Matthew, Mark, Luke, and John, in their testimonies, exceedingly precious; and the more familiarly I am acquainted with it the more confidence, love, peace, and joy, I have; and the more I desire to be with him. I say to you, then, with all the affection of a mother, and now about to leave you, I entreat you, as you love me, and your own lives, study and meditate upon the words and actions of the Lord Jesus Christ. Remember how kindly he has spoken to, and of, little children; and that there is no good thing which he will withhold from them who love him and walk uprightly.

With regard to your father, I need only, I trust, tell you that in obeying him, you obey God. For God has commanded you to honor him, and in honoring your father, you honor him that bade you so to do. It is my greatest joy in leaving you, that I leave you under the parental care of one who can instruct you in all the important concerns of life, and who I know will teach you to choose the good part, and to place your affections upon the only object supremely worthy of them. Consider him as your best earthly friend, and next to your Heavenly Father, your wisest and most competent instructor, guardian, and guide. While he is over you, or you under him, never commence, nor undertake, nor prosecute any important object without advising with him.

Make him your counsellor, and still remember the first commandment with a promise.

As to your conversation with one another, when it is not upon the ordinary business of life, let it be on subjects of importance, improving to your minds. I beseech you to avoid that light, foolish, and vain conversation about dress, and fashion, so common among females. Neither let the subject of apparel fill your hearts, nor dwell upon your tongues. You have never heard me do so. Let your apparel be sober, clean, and modest; but every thing vain and fantastic avoid. If persons wish to recommend themselves to the vain and the giddy, they will dress and adorn themselves to please such persons; but as I would deplore the idea of your either choosing or approving such companions, I would caution you, and entreat you to avoid the conversation, manners, and apparel, which would attract the attention of such persons—They are poor companions in sickness and death; they are no help-meets in the toils and sorrows of life, and therefore, we ought not to study to please them in the days of youth and health. I never desired to please such persons; if I had, my lot might have been, and, no doubt, would have been far different. No, my dear children, I chose the course which I now approve, and which, when leaving the world, I recommend to you. And I am sure you can never be more happy in any other course, than I have been in that which I recommend to you. Persons of discernment, men and women of good understanding, and of good education, will approve you; and it is amongst these, in the society of these, with such company, I wish you to live and die. I have often told you and instanced to you, when in health—the vain pursuits, and improfitable vanities of some females who have spent the prime and vigor of their lives in the servile pursuits of fashion, some of them have grown grey in the service, and where and what are they now! Let these be as beacons to you. I, therefore, entreat you neither to think of, nor pursue, nor talk, upon such subjects. Strive only to approve yourselves to God, and to commend yourselves to the discerning, the intelligent, the pious—Seek their society, consult their taste; and endeavor to make yourselves worthy of their esteem.

But there is one thing which is necessary to all goodness, which is essential to all virtue, godliness, and happiness; I mean, necessary to the daily and constant exhibition of every christian accomplishment, and that is, to keep in mind the words that Hagar uttered in her solitude, "Thou God seest me." You must know and feel, my dear children, that my affection for you, and my desires for your present and future happiness cannot be surpassed by any human being. The God that made me your mother, has, with his own finger, planted this in my breast, and his Holy Spirit has written it upon my heart. Love you I must, feel for you I must, and I once more say to you, Remember these words, and not the words only, but the truth contained in them— "Thou God seest me." This will be a guard against a thousand follies, and against every temptation.

I must, however, tell you that I have great confidence in the Lord, that you will remember and act upon, and according to the instructions given you. I feel grateful to you for your kind attention to me during my long illness: although it was your duty, still I must thank you for it; and I pray the Lord to bless, and, indeed, I know that he will bless you for it.

I cannot speak to you much more upon this subject; I have already, and upon various occasions, suggested to you other instructions, which I need not, as, indeed, I cannot, now repeat. As the Saviour, when last addressing his disciples, commanded and entreated them to love one another, so I beseech you to love one another. It is scarcely necessary, I hope, to exhort you to this; nevertheless, I will mention it to you, and beg of you, all your lives through, to love one another, and to seek to make one another happy by all the means in your power. But I must have done, and once more commend you to God and to the word of his grace; even to him who is able to edify you, and to give you an inheritance among all that are sanctified. That we may all meet together in the heavenly kingdom is my last prayer for you: and as you desire it, remember the words of him who is the way, the truth, and the life. Amen!

No. 6.]　　　JANUARY 7, 1828.

Ancient Gospel.—No. I.

Baptism.

IMMERSION in water into the name of the Father, Son, and Holy Spirit, the fruit of faith in the subject, is the most singular institution that ever appeared in the world. Although very common in practice, and trite in theory, although the subject of a good many volumes, and of many a conversation, it appears to me that this institution of divine origin, so singular in its nature, and so grand and significant in its design, is understood by comparatively very few. In my debate with Mr. Maccalla in Kentucky, 1823, on this topic, I contended that it was a divine institution designed for putting the legitimate subject of it in actual possession of the remission of his sins—That to every believing subject it did formally, and in fact, convey to him the forgiveness of sins. It was with much hesitation I presented this view of the subject at that time, because of its perfect novelty. I was then assured of its truth, and, I think, presented sufficient evidence of its certainty. But having thought still more closely upon the subject, and having been necessarily called to consider it more fully as an essential part of the christian religion, I am still better prepared to develope its import, and to establish its utility and value in the christian religion. I beg leave to call the attention of the reader to it under the idea of the BATH OF REGENERATION.

In the outer court of the Jewish Tabernacle there stood two important articles of furniture of most significant import. The brazen altar next the door, and the laver between the brazen altar and the sanctuary. In this laver, filled with water, the priests, after they had paid their devotion at the altar, as they came in, and before they approached the sanctuary, always washed themselves. This vessel was called in Greek, λουτηρ, and the water in it λουτρον, though sometimes the vessel that holds the water is called λουτρον—In English, the vessel was called laver, and the water in it loutron or bath. The bath of purification was the literal import of this vessel and its use. Paul, more than once, alludes to this usage in the tabernacle in his epistles, and once substitutes christian immersion in its place—that is, christian immersion stands in relation to the same place in the christian temple, or worship, that the laver, or bath of purification stood in the Jewish; viz. between the sacrifice of Christ and acceptable worship. In the Jewish symbols the figures stood thus: 1st. The brazen altar; 2d. The laver or bath; and 3d. The sanctuary. In the *antitupoi* or antitypes it stands thus: 1st. Faith in the sacrifice of Christ, the antitype of the altar; 2d. Immersion, or the bath of regeneration, the antitype of the *loutron* or bath of purification; and 3d, Prayer, praise, and vocal worship, the antitype of the priests approaching the holiest of all. Now all christians being made priests to God, and made to worship in the place where the Jewish priests stood, Jesus Christ having now, as our great High Priest, entered into the most holy place, he has "consecrated a way" for us christians: he has authorized us christians to draw nigh to that place where stood the priests under the law. Paul's exhortation to the Hebrews, taken in the whole context, chapter x. stands thus:

"Brethren, we believing Hebrews are authorized to approach much nigher to God, in our worship, than were the saints under the former economy. The people worshipped in the outer court, the priests officiated, at the same time, in the holy place—but we christians stand not in the outer court, but in the sanctuary. Since Jesus, as our great High Priest, passed into the heavens the true holy place, he has made it lawful for us, or "consecrated a way new and living for us" to approach as priests to the entrance of the true holy place, having had our hearts sprinkled from an evil conscience by faith in his sacrifice, and having had our bodies washed in clean water, in the bath of regeneration; we are now to draw near, with a true heart, in the full assurance of faith, and address Jehovah through the mediation of our great High Priest, in our prayers, praises, and thanksgivings." Such, I say, in general terms, is the import of Paul's exhortation to the Hebrews, based upon the fact that christian immersion stands in the place of the bath of purification in that most instructive system of types or figures, which God instituted to prepare the way of this new and perfect economy.

But Paul, in connecting the bath of regeneration* with the renewal of the Holy Spirit, goes no farther than the Lord Jesus himself when he said, except a man be born of water and of spirit, he cannot enter the kingdom of heaven.

Paul reasons well, for most certainly when a man is born of water there is the bath of regeneration. He is consistent with himself and with his Lord and Master. But it is not only for this that commendation is due the apostle, for he carries out this matter to its legitimate issue in Ephesians when he says, in the language of the Presbyterian translator Macknight, that the Lord Jesus gave himself for his bride, the church; and that she might be worthy of his affection, he had "cleansed her with a bath of water, and with the word."† Instead of the bath of regeneration and the renewal of the Holy Spirit of Titus, iii. he has it here "a bath of water and the word," because here he speaks without a figure and teaches the church, that it is by the word that the spirit of the living God renews the spirit of the children of God.

Christian reader, put these three sayings together in your mind and meditate upon them till next I address you, and I think I will be able to open to your view this wonderful and gracious institution of "christian immersion," which you never did understand, if you know no more about it than what the Paido-Baptists, the Old Baptists or the New Baptists, I mean the baptized Cal-

* As the Presbyterian Doctor Macknight, and many others, have rendered it, instead of "the washing of regeneration."

† Macknight, in his comment, substitutes baptism for the bath of water.

vinists and the baptized Arminians, have taught you. These sayings are found in Ephesians v. 26. Titus i. 5. and Hebrews x. 23. To these sayings of Paul I ought to have added, and you must add, the saying of Jesus to Nicodemus. They read thus in the new translation:

"Unless a man be born of water and the Spirit, he cannot enter the kingdom of God." "He cleansed the church with a bath of water and the word." "According to his mercy he saved us—through the bath of regeneration and the renewing of the Holy Spirit." "Therefore having our hearts sprinkled from an evil conscience, and our bodies washed with pure water, let us worship him."—Amen! I have not given the new translation as if the old differed from it in sense, for in all these instances it gives the same meaning, save that the new is clearer, and more forcible than the old.

Elder John Secrest told me on the 23d November in my own house, that since the Mahoning association last met, he had immersed with his own hands one hundred and ninety, thus lacking only ten of five hundred in about five months—for it is not more than about five months since he began to proclaim the gospel and christian immersion in its primitive simplicity and import.

What might be done if this matter was generally well understood, and ably proclaimed, I cannot conjecture—for my own part I know of no person who has so fairly and fully tested it as he.   EDITOR.

The Points at Issue.

WE argue that all christian sects are more or less apostatized from the institutions of the Saviour: that by all the obligations of the christian religion, they that fear and love the Lord are bound to return to the ancient order of things, in spirit and truth. Our opponents contend that the sects are not apostatized; or, if they admit that they are apostatized, they say the time is not yet come to return, but that they must await the millennium. Let this plea for a restoration of the ancient order of things embrace what topics it may, or let this controversy occupy what ground it may, this is the naked question at issue.

We have the concurrence of the wise and good in all parties, when we assert that the christian church is not now what it once was in its hale and undegenerate days; nor is it now what it will be in the glory of Christ's reign upon the earth, in the period called "the millennium." While many are content with merely affirming as above, we are not satisfied, neither can we be, without attempting something in a subserviency to this glorious Restoration. We wish all our readers never to lose sight of the points at issue. If creeds and systems, texts and textuaries, synods and councils, rites and ceremonies, come in review before us, let our readers remember that these are but a few of the items to be discussed in subserviency to the grand question.

Logic of the Ins and Outs, or of the Populars and Unpopulars.

I HAVE long since discovered that there are two systems of logic, or two modes of reasoning, that seem to be almost uniformly adopted by two classes in society, irrespective of their religious or political views. The *Ins* adopt one system, and the *Outs* another. By the *Ins* we understand those in authority with the people, and by the *Outs*, those not in authority with the people.

The former are the Populars, and the latter the Unpopulars. The logic of the *Ins* has in it the following rules:

1. Never submit any of those points essential to your good standing with the people, to the hazard of investigation. Remember you have something to lose, but nothing to gain.

2. When your system is attacked, always extol the wisdom, piety, or virtue of its founders; descant upon its antiquity, and enumerate its votaries.

3. Ridicule the pretensions and expose the arrogance of those who would dare to oppose names so revered, usages so ancient, and authorities so numerous.

4. If possible, as far as lies in your power, arraign the motives, and impeach the aims of your opposers.

5. Calumniate their characters, if you can, under any pretence, and defame them, but with apparent regret that you should be compelled to do so.

6. And lastly, when you are conscious that you cannot carry your point, represent your opponent as unworthy of your notice; give his system or his arguments the name of some obsolete heresy, and tell how it was blasted and refuted centuries ago.

The logic of the *Outs* is not so easily reduced to one system as that of the *Ins*. If in politics, one system is adopted; if in religion, another. But the general points of coincidence are—

1. To submit every thing to the test of reason; and if in religion, to revelation.

2. Neither to adopt nor to oppose any point because of the names of the persons who embrace or reject it.

3. Canvass the opinions and arguments of those who oppose, without invading their reputation, or attempting to injure it. When the cause of the *Outs* is a good one, such is the system of logic adopted. And even when it is not so good, there must be an apparent respect to the above decisions.

To make this matter still more intelligible and apparent we shall present a few remarks on

Moral Authority.

Political and moral authority, though different in some respects, are, in others, the same. The President of these United States is possessed of much political authority. So is the king of England. The popes of Rome have had very extensive political authority, and still have a good portion of it. They still possess a very great ecclesiastical authority; but this in church government is the same as political authority in the state. But besides this authority, and distinct from it, they are possessed of an authority over the minds of men affecting their understanding and consciences. This is purely what we mean by moral authority. The different sectarian teachers have each a certain amount of this authority over the minds of the religious community amongst whom they labor, and indirectly amongst others. Some of the sects know the value of this authority, and how to use it to the best advantage much better than others. Convert this moral authority over the people into arithmetical numbers, and some of the sects possess it in the ratio of ten, twenty, thirty, and forty millions of actual stock. In managing this stock there is a great diversity of talent exhibited. Some of them manage their capital stock so wisely as to make it count twenty-five per cent. per annum; while others, not so prudent in their affairs, cannot make it tell more than

eight or ten per cent. per annum. I see, or I think I see, through all the machinery of the involutions and evolutions of these sects, a constant attention to increase the capital stock; and some of them have blabbed out the secret too soon in anticipation of what was to be achieved through the immensity of their resources. The Mammoth Bank of these United States is not more formidable to the little county corporations, than is the moral authority, or the capital stock of influence, of the leading sects, to the small patrimony of the Sabbatarian or the Covenanter. But there is one thing which, above every thing else, is worthy of remark while on this topic, and I have felt and seen its truth very often exhibited. It is the ease, the uncommon ease, with which a person possessed of much moral authority can support any point against a person who rests his cause upon truth and evidence alone. A single assertion of such a person is worth at least ten good arguments of the disciple who has nothing but reason and the Bible to support him. A notable proof of this we gave in our last number. All the arguments in four volumes of this work in favor of the *restoration of the ancient order of things*, were set aside and proved to be erroneous by a single assertion from Mr. Spencer Clack of Kentucky, who announced that "*Semple and Campbell were at issue!!!*" Those, therefore, possessed of this most valuable property, are happily exempted from all the evils and hardships of those destitute folks who have to prove, double prove, and sometimes, treble prove a position, before they can expect even a polite hearing.

But in the production, increase, and exaltation of moral authority, I know of nothing which contributes so much as those *revivals*, so pompously announced by the actors. And here I beg leave to make a remark or two on

Revivals.

Some rumors and some symptoms exhibited not a hundred miles from Boston, within the last year, indicated that a *revival* was got up by some distinguished preacher or preachers for the sake of covering a defeat, or of carrying some favorite point. There was a great deal said in some of the eastern prints on this subject, to which we did not attend closely, as it was no way new or interesting to us, believing that such things were not very uncommon.* It seals the mission of a man to be "the instrument" of, or the great ac-

---

* The following is extracted from the "Western Christian (Methodist) Advocate," *verbatim et literatim*, Jan'y. 16, 1835. These *editorial* remarks show that the theory and practice of *getting up* revivals, (which the operators say, only result in the salvation of any one because the Holy Spirit moves the whole affair,) are improved by age. Such acknowledgements as follow were not made eight or ten years ago. I say convert as many as possible—thousands upon thousands by all lawful means, but use no trickery which will need to be sanctified bythe appellation "mysterious and sovereign movements of the Holy Spirit." —But I will let Mr. Morris speak for himself:—"If the ministers and members wish to build a new chapel, or enlarge an old one, let their unanimous prayer be, ' Lord revive thy work;' for when more people come to meeting than can be accommodated it will be a good time to circulate the subscription." " If they want to raise large contributions for any benevolent purpose, let the first step be to *get up* a good revival, for when the heart is warm with love, the money comes freely. If they desire to extend the circulation of religious periodicals, let them aim for a revival; for this increases the thirst for religious intelligence." Analysis.—1st, Objects.—To build—repair chapels—to raise large contributions—to get subscribers to the "Advocate." 2d, Means.—Convert men. How? "Pray for," "get up," and "aim at a revival." If any one says it is all mechanical, and the avowed object earthly, you readers of the Advocate must reply, "it is spiritual, and your objections are blasphemous." My limits forbid any thing farther.   PUBLISHER.

tor in, a *revival;* pretty much the same as miracles did the mission of the apostles. Many understand this topic full better than I do, and know how to gain one hundred per cent. per annum to their actual stock of moral authority.— Had it not been that some of the *dramatis personæ,* or the chief actors in these mighty movements and grand excitements, have afterwards fallen into some most scandalous crimes, and thereby have given a seal to their mission which annulled the former seal, I do not know to what extent the moral authority of some men might have been augmented. The fact of some having fallen into these notorious scandals, after having been the agents in great revivals; and another fact that revivals are often granted at the same time to the belligerents in the field, or to those who are engaged in giving one another over to Satan, or in some bitter opposition through strife and envy; I am at a loss to say whether we should not now have had many apostles and prophets, even more than they had in ancient times. But when we see a revival got up by two men, about the same time, in different parts of the country, who are opposing each other, and the one saying to the other, See how the Lord is blessing us;—(" but look how he has blessed and is still blessing us;") I say, when such is the fact, (as it is at this very time in some places to my knowledge,) revivals are divested of those miraculous powers which otherwise they would possess, and are incapable of being made seals or attestations to the mission of any of our textuaries.

I am fully convinced that there are *real* and *genuine revivals* of religion at different times and places, and that much good has resulted from them; but there are so many mock revivals, that any doctrine can be proved to be true by them, and any preacher can be proved to be sent by God by them, if a revival under his labors, or attendant on his doctrine, will be admitted as evidence.

I therefore judge of no doctrine or cause by the *revivals* that attend it. If I did, I cannot tell whether I should be a Cumberland Presbyterian, a Congregationalist, a common Presbyterian, a Baptist, of the Gillite, Fullerite—of the creed, or anti-creed school: whether I should be of the "Christian Church," or of the "Church of Christ" —a Methodist, a Calvinist, a Unitarian, or a Trinitarian; for they all, this year, have abounded in revivals. What says the Saviour and his apostles, what says the law and the testimony, THEREFORE, must turn the beam, or decide the point with me.

Those who consider all the revivals announced in the sectarian papers to be the work of the Holy Spirit, must either have a morbid conscience, or no conscience at all, if they refuse to unite in every act of social worship with those people amongst whom the Father, Son, and Holy Spirit vouchsafe to dwell. If God has thus gifted them all, and made no difference between the Baptist and the Paido-Baptist, the Methodist and the Calvinist, the "Christian Church" and the "Church of Christ," the old side and the new side Presbyterian; why, what are we that we should withstand God and oppose his Spirit and his work by declaring that we will commune with the Holy Spirit only when he pleases to meet us in our own quarters!!! I challenge all the believers in these revivals on this continent to present one good reason why all sects should not break down the middle walls of partition and unite in one holy communion, perfect and complete—if so be the Holy Spirit, *the Father,*

Son, and Holy Spirit makes no difference amongst them all! EDITOR.

Review of Dr. Noel's Circular.—No. V.

MAN being in a great measure a creature of experience, he is incessantly making experiments in order to better his condition. All the great systems now admired or extolled, in church or state, are the results of experiments. We are either ignorant of, or we have forgotten the movements, and changes, and experiments in society, that have given birth to the present order of things in the world. One system has gradually declined, and another arisen upon its ruins, just as men either felt disposed from information or passion, from inclination or aversion, to begin something new. As the mighty oak has sprung from the small acorn, as the majestic river can be traced to some small fountain, so most of the great systems have sprung from small beginnings, or can be traced to some feeble origin. In every thing but in the true religion man was left to learn by experiment. Unfortunately, however, the love of experiment, and constant attention to it on all other subjects, led some bold adventurers into the department of religion, and thus it became the subject of experiment, like the common concerns of worldly society. Forgetting that religion, in subject and form, was altogether supernatural, some attempted its accommodation, or, as it was called, its "improvement to circumstances." Now from this principle, however apprehended, felt, or expressed, has arisen every human system of religion now in christendom.

Even the man who contends for "a summary," or any other exhibition of supernatural truth, than that which the Bible presents, contends, in fact, for the very principle on which the "Mother of Harlots" took up house and prepared her bed for the kings of the earth. While Dr. Noel and a few kindred spirits who have, in contending for a creed, renounced the ancient sentiments of the Baptist society, are continually telling those who advocate the alone sufficiency and perfect adaptation of the Holy Oracles to all uses and ends connected with the individual or social happiness of man; I say, while he is associating us with what he calls New Lights, Arians, Universalists, and such like honorable company; we have ten better reasons for reminding him of the Romanists, the Protestants, and the Puritans; of telling him of all the horrid deeds of cruelty and murder attendant on the creed side of the controversy. For my part, I incomparably prefer to fraternize with all these blood guiltless heretics, than to have to fraternize with all the popes and inquisitors who have gorged themselves with blood of human sacrifice in order to sanctify their creed.

But to return to the question which was partially discussed in my last: It appears to me a little strange that Dr. Noel should impose a human creed upon a church to keep corruption out of it, and that I should oppose his imposition of a human creed upon a church for the same purpose, viz. to keep corruption out of it. This is just as strange as that Bishop Semple should have thought himself opposing me, and that he should have been represented by the *writing* editor of the Baptist Recorder as opposing me, as at issue with me, on the creed question; when, in fact, he does not express a syllable on the creed question in either of his letters from which I dissent. If language has any meaning, I understand Bishop Semple as keeping creeds in the light of servants, and forbidding them as masters—of making them mere vehicles to hand down to others our views of scripture; but not as standards to which all must submit on pain of excommunication. But *Deo volente*, I will make this matter as plain as the full moon, if Mr. Semple meet me as proposed.

Now I unfeignedly declare, that my chief and almost exclusive objections to a creed are the two following: 1st. That they do keep corruptions and heresies in the church; and 2dly, that they do lay unrighteous restraints upon the human mind. All the corruptions in the Romish church—all the corruptions in the Protestant or Episcopal church—all the corruptions in the Presbyterian church, are kept in them, locked up by the efficiency of their creeds from one generation to another. And in the second place, the minds of their youth are embargoed and restrained by the creed and her daughter, the catechism; so that the descendants of Papists and Protestants do not, and cannot keep pace with the advances and progress of light in the age in which we live. Thus I find the Catholic the same to day as before Luther was born. Although the world has made great advances for four hundred years, the Catholic youth is, in religious views and apprehensions, just the same that Frederick Credulitas was who lived in Germany, A. D. 1400. And among the Episcopalians, John Simplex, who is now an admirer of the 39 Articles, Liturgy and Homilies, has not one new idea above William Nomind, who flourished under the reign of Queen Elizabeth. Thus I find my neighbor George Stedfast, who got his child christened last "Sabbath day," has not advanced with the age one idea above Peter Bluesocks, who was nephew to John Knox, A. D. 1630. Now all this has been accomplished by a human creed, which has equally held fast the notions of a darker age, and shut out from the mind all the benefits and advances of this age in the knowledge of the Holy Scriptures. I say, then, that "creeds" are in my judgment, to be denounced as masters over our faith—as rules or standards: for instead of keeping corruption out, they lock it in, the church; and instead of helping the mind forward in the study of that book, the meaning of which was entirely lost two or three centuries ago, they do most undeniably prevent its illumination and emancipation. Say now, Dr. Noel, are not these the words of truth and soberness? Say not that you are almost persuaded to be a christian—I mean to be a christian like those who know no other creed than the sacred writings.

Are you afraid to trust the church to the Lord Jesus Christ and his book? or must you prop up his cause by your little creed, as though he and his covenant were not able to keep it from ruin? Are you desirous of thinking for the next generation? Can't you let them think and act for themselves, without, as far as in you lies, binding them fast to your dictations or dogmas, which you have long since known, from your frequent changes, to be very insecure. I pray you think of this.

I will likely get through with my exposition of your circular in my next, having already embraced in my remarks almost every prominent idea in it.   EDITOR.

Miscellaneous Letters.—No. II.

DEAR SIR—I WILL present you with some items for reflection.

Form of a Church Covenant founded upon the philosophy of Dr. Noel.

We, the undersigned, believing that we have progressed in the knowledge of good and wholesome doctrines, as far as mankind can or ought to attain, and not willing that either ourselves or our descendants in all time coming should ever think of going farther than we have already gone; do bind ourselves, our descendants, and successors, for ever, to hold fast the following doctrines, to wit:—

[Here follow the 21 Articles.]

Nota Bene.—We do, however, disclaim infallibility; and do expect that a time called "the Millennium" will arrive, when knowledge shall greatly increase; yet still, for reasons best known to ourselves, and especially for the sake of keeping corruption out, i. e. other opinions than our own; and not knowing how much other parties may have to yield before the Millennium be ushered in, we have deemed it expedient to resolve as above; and by these presents do bind ourselves, our children, and successors, for ever to think as above specified in the aforesaid articles. And, by divine aid, hope to remain immutable.

Signed, &c.

Another Form of a Church Covenant, based upon another system.

We, the undersigned, believing that the Millennium will not commence until all christians are united, and that all christians cannot be united so long as they are contending for different creeds of human inference, and that creeds do tend to perpetuate the parties which now exist; are resolved to pray for the Millennium. But, in the meantime, we bind ourselves and our brethren, from this time forth until the Millennium commences, to hold fast the following articles of belief.

Signed—

A third Form of a Church Covenant, founded on both the above premises, with some small additions.

We, the undersigned, to preserve unity of faith among ourselves, and to secure the purity of our communion, do declare that we will hold fast the Philadelphia Confession of Faith in name; and that when any person appears amongst us to oppose any of our views or practices, then, in that case, the said Confession of Faith shall be a living and powerful letter, able to save or to destroy. But in all other cases it shall be a dead letter; for no person, on admission into our communion, shall be asked any thing about it; nor will he hear any thing about it, so long as he behaves well; that is, patiently submits to our dictation. But should he become refractory or disobedient, then, in that case, we wish to have this little volume, as we have our munitions of war, ready for the day of combat, and fitted for the work of slaughter. We, therefore, pledge ourselves to one another and to all men, so to use and to hold the aforesaid creed—so long as creeds are in fashion, but no longer.

Signed—

Revivals.

Revivals are usually followed up by great declensions, and appear to be under the same law of nature which requires the animal system to come down as many degrees below par as it was elevated above par by extrinsic stimuli. Hence the cold season which follows the warm season is as melancholy as the former was joyous. We rejoice to know that there are some exceptions, but they are comparatively very few. Let him that thinks he stands firm take heed lest he fall.

Immersion.

The Dover Baptist Association in Virginia reported an addition of two thousand to its members by immersion during the last year. From the different accounts we have from all parts of the United States, from the different sects of Baptists; and from that sect called by themselves "the Christian Church," and by their opponents the New Lights, (a name, by the by, that several sects have worn out in days of yore)—I say, the aggregate amount of immersions in the United States alone, during the year just ended, cannot be less than between forty and fifty thousand. This is an immense inroad in one year upon the rite of baby sprinkling. The question of infant baptism is now generally discussed all over the land, and immense has been the result. Even some "Presbyterian ministers" during the last year have been obliged to go down, not *to*, but *into*, the water, to immerse some of their conscientious disciples. I said, five years ago, calculating the future from the past and the present, that fifty years would sweep from this continent, from north to south, this small item of the legacy of mother Babylon to her heirs at law. Seldom have we seen any estate so well managed, and so carefully husbanded as that of old grandmother Babylon. But really the children are becoming quite prodigal of this part of the inheritance. I rejoice in this event, and in the anticipation of many similar events, which, without any claims to remarkable foresight, I clearly perceive, not as a sectarian rejoices in the demolition of one party and in the exaltation of another; but because I know the human mind to be susceptible of being led farther and farther into light and liberty in proportion as it has been compelled by an increase of light to renounce any error. Revolutions rarely go back. And we have many proofs that so soon as a person is convinced of one error, he is more easily to be convinced of the second than of the first, and so on in a geometrical ratio. It is then in the gain of truth, and not of a party, that I rejoice; for there are many Paido-Baptists who, as men and as christians, we must love and esteem; not for their attachment to any human tradition, but from their general attachment to the gospel of Jesus Christ.

May favor, mercy, and peace, accompany all them who keep company with the apostles and prophets of the Saviour of men.   Editor.

A Restoration of the Ancient Order of Things.
No. XXII.

Psalms, hymns, and spiritual songs, embrace the praises of christians. Psalms are historic compositions, or poetic narratives. Hymns are odes of praise directly addressing the object of worship, and declaring his excellencies and glorious works. Spiritual songs are such compositions as declare the sentiments derived from the revelations of God, and such as are adapted to communicate to others the views and feelings which God's revelations suggest. Thus we define them. The reasons of this distribution are not obvious to all, nor is it needful to go into a labored criticism to establish them, as the end will be gained much better by an attention to the classification we have made in this new selection of psalms, hymns, and spiritual songs, than by any *critique* independent of such a specimen. Our hymn books are, in general, a collection of every thing under the sun in the form of religious rhyme. Not one in ten, or, perhaps, in twenty, of any selection, are usually sung by any individual from choice or approbation. And, indeed, the religious communities seem to be destitute of any fixed standard by which to judge of what is comely and suitable subject matter of social

praise. As was said, the greater part conceive they ought to sing every notion, speculation, or opinion, which they can imagine to be orthodox; not apprehending that the object of sacred song is to raise and exalt our spirits by divine contemplations to the sublime in the worship of our adorable God and Father, by admiring and extolling facts extrinsic of our conjectures or notions about them. But this is not all: every heretical or schismatical dogma is sung, as well as preached; and instead of *praising* God, we are often *scolding* men who differ from us. For even prayer has been abused to this end. Often have I seen a prayer to be dictated by the presence of some one in the congregation; and thus all the congregation were doing homage to the zeal of the preacher, who was praying in relation to some influential errorist as he conceived. I knew a preacher who got into a violent controversy with another, because of an insult he gave him in prayer. And not long since a preacher has been called to order by the legislature of the first state in the union in point of population, for an insult to the nation while praying as chaplain for the legislature. This spirit, which on many other occasions manifests itself in prayer, is equally at work in the department of religious praise. So that all our contests about religion get into our prayers and songs.

Let us analyze a few more specimens. There has been a controversy of long standing about faith. One hymn extols faith in the following words:—

"Faith—'tis a precious grace
    Where'er it is bestow'd!
It boasts of a celestial birth,
    And is the gift of God.

Jesus it owns a King,
    An all-atoning Priest;
It claims no merit of its own,
    But looks for all in Christ.

To him it leads the soul
    When filled with deep distress,
Flies to the fountain of his blood,
    And trusts his righteousness.

Since 'tis thy work alone,
    And that divinely free,
Lord, send the spirit of thy Son
    To work this faith in me."

Waving any discussion upon the propriety of singing praises to *faith* instead of the *Lord*, I proceed to observe that in singing the above verses we are boasting against those who are supposed to maintain that faith is not of a celestial birth, and not the gift of God. In the conclusion the singer is made to act a singular part; first to declare that he believes that Jesus is a King, an all-atoning Priest; that faith leads the soul to him, flies to the fountain of his blood, and trusts his righteousness; and yet, after having sung all this, he represents himself as destitute of such a faith as he has been singing, and prays for the spirit of Jesus Christ to *work* this faith in him! How the same person can sing the three first verses and the last one in this hymn I know not, unless they sing as a parrot speaks, without regard to the meaning. To convert the above sentiments into plain prose, it reads thus: "I believe that faith is a precious grace, the gift of God, of celestial origin. I believe that Jesus is King and an all-atoning Priest; that his righteousness is worthy of my trust, and his blood purifies me from sin. No, I dont believe this; but, Lord, send the Spirit of thy Son, who I believe works this grace in men's hearts; and as I dont yet believe, work this faith in me!"

52

"Come, Holy Spirit, heavenly dove,
    With all thy quick'ning powers;
Kindle a flame of sacred love,
    In these cold hearts of ours.

Look how we grovel here below,
    Fond of these trifling toys;
Our souls can neither fly, nor go,
    To reach eternal joys."

These verses, as well as the general scope of this song, are not accordant with the spirit of the christian religion. The Holy Spirit is always represented as the author of all goodness in us, and is not to be addressed by men as though they, without it, could say that Jesus is Lord, or, without it, breathe forth a spiritual desire. But here dead "cold hearts" are represented as panting after the Holy Spirit. But not only does the nature of the christian religion, which represents the Father as the terminating end of all christian worship, the Son as the only mediator between the Father and us, and the Holy Spirit as the immediate agent or author of all goodness in us. Not only, I say, does the nature of the religion itself, to those who understand it, teach the impropriety of direct addresses to the Holy Spirit; but this species of address is absolutely unauthorized by any prophet or apostle, by any oracle of God, commandment or precedent in the sacred books—for from the beginning of Genesis to the end of Revelation, no man, patriarch, Jew, nor christian; prophet, priest, nor apostle, ever did address the Holy Spirit directly in prayer or praise. They pray *for* the Holy Spirit, but never *to* it. Thus Paul desired that the love of the Father, the grace of the Lord Jesus, and the communion of the Holy Spirit, might be with the saints. This hymn, then, is not only contrary to the genius of the New Covenant: but uncommanded and unprecedented in the book of God. This I asserted to an association about ten years ago, which caused an old preacher to search the whole Bible through to disprove it. In something less than a year afterwards he wrote me he had found me in an error—for he had found an authority for this hymn. It was, he said, in the book of Canticles, where it says, "Awake, O North wind, and blow thou, South, upon my garden," &c. But the old gentleman has not, to this day, decided whether the Holy Spirit was in the North or in the South wind, and therefore, as yet, nothing has been adduced to show the assertion unfounded.   EDITOR.

Attempt at the Restoration of Ancient Order.

The Church of Christ at Tubermore, to the Church of Christ at New-York—Grace be to you, and peace from God our Father, and from our Lord Jesus Christ.

BELOVED BRETHREN—It was not from inattention, nor a want of impression of the importance of the subject of your communication, that we did not at first fully reply to you. The union of all who believe in the Lord Jesus, is a thing for which we are most deeply interested; and the almost total want of it among the churches of Christ, that we deem on the whole nearest to the model of the first churches, is a thing that causes to us the most unfeigned sorrow. If that brotherly intercourse, and earnest care for each other, that subsisted among the churches in the days of the apostles, is not now to be found among those who profess to follow their practice, as far as it was approved by Jesus, the causes ought to be sought out and removed. In our opinion the chief of those causes is not the difference of sentiment, great and greatly to be deplored as this is; but is owing to the exercise of an authority never conferred on the churches by the

Lord Jesus, to refuse or exclude, for difference of sentiment, any of those who give evidence that they have been bought by the blood of Jesus Christ. Not that we deem it a matter of slight importance that all the disciples of Christ should know and practice all his institutions; on the contrary, we hold this a matter of very great importance, for the attainment of which all the churches ought never to cease to plead with their Heavenly Father. Ignorance of any divine institution is an evil, and must be felt as such by a church as far as it exists in any of the body. But the question is, What is God's way of getting rid of this evil? We believe, from *Phil.* iii. 15, and numerous passages of scripture to which there is not room to refer in this letter, that it is by forbearance, affectionate instruction, and prayer. Many, on the contrary, have thought that the most effectual way to make a disciple receive an ordinance of Jesus, is to refuse him fellowship till he has complied. Notwithstanding all we have heard in favor of this plan, we still deem it the wisdom of man. Accordingly we have found that God has made foolish this wisdom. Long has it been tried without success; and of late in some parts of Ireland it has been carried so far, that some individuals can scarcely find a second to unite with them in constant fellowship. By permitting Satan to work them up to this phrenzy, it appears to us that God has affixed his seal of disapprobation on the sentiment in its lowest degree, and to lead soberminded christians, who have been led away by its plausibility, to examine more attentively the ground of their opinion.

You will observe, then, dear brethren, that we do not plead for forbearance as a useful scheme left to our own discretion, or justify it, as some have done, from that pleasing variety found among the works of God. Such language we hold in utter abhorrence. Variety in the works of creation is a beauty; but God is the author of that variety. Difference of sentiment upon every thing revealed by God is an evil, because it is the sinful ignorance of men. Can God command all his people to know his will, and shall it be a perfection to be variously ignorant of this? It detracts, then, considerably from the joy with which we should have received your letter, that we find no notice taken of this subject; but on the contrary, that you seem to make baptism a term of fellowship. The greater part of our number not only have been baptized, but we are convinced that views on this subject extensively affect other matters in scripture. But we all deem that the man who has been received by Jesus, ought not to be rejected by us; and that if he feed his people by his ordinances, it would be criminal in us, as far as lies in our power, to join in confederacy to starve the weakest of them. We think that the man who has been admitted to the fellowship of the general assembly and church of the first born, is undoubtedly worthy of a seat with us. Dear brethren, we know what has been objected to our views on this subject, and as we have not had time fully to reply to objections, we deem it unnecessary to state all the grounds of our opinion. We know that there is no command of Jesus but may be plausibly set aside. We entreat you to examine this subject, recollecting that if it be sinful to receive any that Christ has forbidden, it is also sinful to refuse any that he has invited. There is no safe side in error. That Jesus will not approve of refusing fellowship to any of his brethren known to be such, appears to us to have the irresistible light of self-evident truth.

53

With respect to the ordinances which you observe on the first day of the week, we agree with you in general; but with respect to the order of observing these ordinances, we find but little fixed in the New Testament. The only thing we can with any confidence say we have learned on this subject is, that, at whatever time a church meets to observe the institutions of the first day of the week, the Lord's supper ought to hold a distinguished place. But how often we should sing or pray, or whether we should pray or sing first, we find nothing fixed. Though we should have no objection with you to commence with prayer, yet we could not say that we considered ourselves bound to this order by 1 *Tim.* ii. 1. Prayer for our civil governors we consider an important duty; but the above passage does not appear to us to determine the time of it. *First of all* appears to us to refer to the order in which the apostle brought forward the subjects of exhortation. He had been speaking of his own deplorably wicked character, and, from the abounding mercy of God to him, he concludes that they ought not to despair of any man's salvation. Therefore, prayers, &c. ought to be made even for pagan and persecuting rulers; for the grace that saved Saul of Tarsus, was able to save the vilest of them. I exhort, then, first of all, that prayers, &c. The second thing he exhorted to was the deportment of women. From this he passed to the qualifications of bishops. This, dear brethren, is our view, which we do not obtrude upon you; but, as you have invited our faithfulness, we suggest to your consideration. Should we, at any time, perceive your view to be just, we shall most promptly adopt it. We conceive that whatever Christ has not fixed must be left free for ever, and that a church, though it may usually pursue the same order, has no right to bind itself to this, where Christ's authority is not interposed. In the house of God there is no discretionary authority, not in the least degree.

The order in which we observe the ordinances, on the first day of the week, is as follows:—Salutation, singing, reading the scriptures, prayer, singing, admission or exclusion, if necessary, the Lord's supper, singing, fellowship, exhortation, teaching, prayer, singing, prayer. But we do not consider ourselves bound to this order any further than we find it fixed in the scriptures. We have no meetings on any day but the first day of the week, nor any meetings but one on that day. We consider 1 *Cor.* xiv. 16. to warrant us to subjoin an *Amen* to the prayer. Your view of the kiss of charity does not satisfy the most of us. We think the limitation arbitrary, though some among ourselves have not yet observed it in any sense. The washing of feet we do not consider an ordinance, but the selection of one of the most humiliating offices, to inculcate the practice of all, when the brethren need them. It has not to us the least appearance of being enjoined to be observed in form. A love feast, as an ordinance, we consider as unscriptural. The passages that speak of it we view as referring to the Lord's supper. Is any feast so much a feast of love as this? Besides, we are forbid to eat in the church for the gratification of appetite. But what surprises us most, is the ground on which you hold it. You consider it not of strict obligation, and therefore sometimes omit it. We think this inconsistent with all your other views. If Christ has instituted a love feast, it must be strictly obligatory; and if he has not, you will have no praise from him in observing it in his name, though ever so seldom.

We see nothing to prevent the wealthy brethren from entertaining the church in their own houses, but we should beware of adding to the institutions of Christ.

We met as a church in May, 1807. There never was any schismatic separation from us. But on account of convenience, two churches have gone out from us; the one meeting at Maghralt, about four miles from us, the other at a country place called Cavindaisy, distant about six miles. The former of these did not get on well, and has returned to us. The latter continues to prosper, and lives in the utmost harmony and confidence with us Our number is about two hundred and fifty. We consider a presbytery an ordinance of God as soon as practicable, though we have now but one elder.

Dear brethren, we have observed with very great delight, the ardent spirit of love which your communication breathes towards the people of God, and your zeal for the increase of devotedness to the service of Christ. This, to us, is greater proof of growth in the divine life, than zeal, even for the purity of ordinances. Some of late make a great noise about the corruptions of other churches, and exert themselves much in vindicating scriptural order, who do not appear to have, in an equal degree, bowels of love to all the people of God, and concern for the salvation of sinners. The one ought to be done, but the other ought not to be left undone. We love to see christians fully awake, and waiting for the coming of their Lord. We love to see his servants girding themselves, and proposing to serve him with more exertion and alacrity. We love to see them looking to the coming of Jesus for the extension of their fame, instead of bandying compliments and mixing their own vanity with the service of their Master. These things, brethren, we think we behold in you, and therefore rejoice in you, right heartily. Come, then, dear brethren, and let us unite in making all things ready for his coming. Let our zeal extend to every part of his will. Let not any difference of sentiment alienate our hearts. Let us examine the scriptures more thoroughly, and more fervently pray to be directed fully into the way of God. Let not a word dropped by us be understood by you as suggested by unkindness.

While we take the liberty of stating our difference from others, we are fully convinced that we have much to learn, and that a full attainment to the order of the first churches would not necessarily imply great growth in grace, or in the knowledge of our Lord and Saviour Jesus Christ Our sheet is full. Great grace be upon you all.

Tubermore, May 6, 1819.

Signs of the Times.

LOTTERIES.—A SPLENDID lottery has just been drawn in Rhode Island for the express " benefit of the West Baptist Society of Providence." What must be the condition of that religion which is kept in repair by the same means as we use in repairing old bridges and old roads? Can there be a greater libel against duty and heaven than such proceedings? Religion maintained by gambling!—*Western Paper.*

Where is the spirit of Roger Williams now?—So the Baptists go in times of great prosperity. Brother Clack asked some time ago, " What need have the Baptists of Reformation?" Nay, indeed, they have more need of Lotteries!

The Columbian College needs a lottery or a religious fast, or the presence of some great spirit to help it to stand. Religion is made to aid the

54

masons and bricklayers, as much as the students of algebra; and all more than the students of the Bible, in the erection and support of such establishments as that of the Columbian College. Why not aid them all by a lottery? Because Congress will not grant it! A good reason, indeed—though not a commendable one.

Ed. C. B.

Dedications.

THE "new recruits" in Frankfort, Kentucky, have lately built one of the "neatest" houses (that is, the most tasteful) in the western country. This house was "begun and finished in four months," and "dedicated" on one Lord's day, by Doctor Noel. It was "chiefly" built by the new recruits, or first fruits of the late revival there!

The "Unitarians" have also been building fine meeting houses, and dedicating them, in the East, by their young recruits. The following item is taken from the Christian Herald, of December:

The following particulars of the dedication at Portland, has been furnished us by a friend who was present.

The services on the occasion were as follows:

1. Hymn, and reading of select portions of scripture, by Elder Samuel Rand, (the pastor of the church.)

2. The dedicatory prayer, by Elder Abner Jones, of Salem, Mass.

3. Sermon by Elder Moses How, of Portsmouth, N. H.

4. Concluding prayer, by Elder John Osborne, of Lee, N. H.

The house contains 112 pews on the lower floor, a gallery, large porch, steeple, and bell. The house is four story on one side, cellar and vestry.

The addition to the church, since the late revival, is one hundred and sixty-seven.

Why should there be so much ill-will existing between the subjects of these two revivals, seeing the Lord has moved them, by the same spirit, "to build and dedicate neat and commodious houses of worship?"

The Church of England, in England, without any revival, built this summer, sixty-nine complete churches, and have forty-eight on the way. Exchequer bills having been issued to the amount of fourteen millions of dollars for making "neat" churches.

It appears from a letter written to the editor of the Columbian Star, by our worthy friend Doctor Noel, that on the dedication day of this commodious and neat meeting house in Frankfort, the sacraments of baptism and the supper were both "administered," which gave a peculiar interest to the occasion." Now as the Unitarians in the East, who have had some awful and grand revivals lately, are like our Baptist Trinitarians in the West, much in the spirit of building and dedicating neat meeting houses, I shall do them all the favor of giving them a more elegant plan of dedications and consecrations—I am sorry that I had not published this before the late dedications, as it would have given a still more "peculiar interest to the occasion."

"St. Katharine Creed Church in the city of London, having been lately repaired, was suspended from all divine service till it was again consecrated; the formality of which being very extraordinary, may give us an idea of the superstition of this prelate. On Sunday, January 16, 1630,

bishop Laud came thither about nine in the morning, attended with several of the high commission, and some civilians. At his approach to the west door of the church, which was shut and guarded by halberdiers, some who were appointed for that purpose, cried with a loud voice, Open, open, ye everlasting doors, that the King of glory may come in; and presently the doors being opened, the bishop, with some doctors and principal men entered. As soon as they were come within the place, his lordship fell down upon his knees, and his eyes lifted up, and his arms spread abroad, said, This place is holy, the ground is holy: in the name of the Father, Son, and Holy Ghost, I pronounce it holy. Then walking up the middle aisle towards the chancel, he took up some of the dust, and threw it into the air several times. When he approached near the rail of the communion table, he bowed towards it five or six times, and returning, went round the church with his attendants in procession, saying first the hundredth and then the nineteenth psalm, as prescribed in the Roman pontificale. He then read several collects, in one of which he prays God to accept of that beautiful building; and concludes thus; We consecrate this church, and separate it to you as holy ground, not to be profaned any more to common use. In another he prays that all that should hereafter be buried within the circuit of this holy and sacred place, may rest in their sepulchres in peace, till Christ's coming to judgment, and may then rise to eternal life and happiness. After this, the bishop, sitting under cloth of state, in the aisle of the chancel, near the communion table, took a written book in his hand, and pronounced curses upon those who should thereafter profane that holy place by musters of soldiers, or keeping profane law courts, or carrying burdens through it; and at the end of every curse he bowed to the east, and said, Let all the people say Amen. When the curses were ended, which were about twenty, he pronounced a like number of blessings upon all who had any hand in framing and building that sacred and beautiful edifice, and on those who had given or should hereafter give, any chalices, plates, ornaments, or other utensils; and at the end of every blessing he bowed, to the east, and said, Let all the people say Amen. After this followed the sermon, and then the sacrament, which the bishop consecrated, and administered after the following manner:"

As he approached the altar, he made five or six low bows, and coming up to the side of it, where the bread and wine were covered, he bowed seven times; then, after reading many prayers, he came near the bread, and gently lifting up the corner of the napkin, beheld it, and immediately letting fall the napkin, retreated hastily a step or two, and made three low obeisances. His lordship then advanced, and having uncovered the bread, bowed three times as before; then laid his hand on the cup, which was full of wine, with a cover upon it, which having let go, he stepped back, and bowed three times towards it; then came near again, and lifting up the cover of the cup, looked into it, and seeing the wine, he let fall the cover again, retired back, and bowed as before. After which the elements were consecrated, and the bishop, having first received, gave it to some principal men in their surplices, hoods, and tippets; towards the conclusion, many prayers being said, the solemnity of the consecration ended."

Neal's History of the Puritans, vol. 2, p. 237.

Say, some of you orthodox, is there any need

of a reformation on this subject? If we have dedications, let us have them in decent style.

But alas, the day has come, that they who oppose such things are said not to be regenerated!!   Ed. C. B.

_____

.Nt. 7.]   February 4, 1828.

On the Influence of the Holy Spirit in the Salvation of Men.—By Paulinus.
No. I.

Whoever reads the sacred pages, with an enlightened and attentive mind, will discover that the operations of the Spirit of God are various and manifold. To this wonder-working Agent are ascribed creative energy—miraculous events —extraordinary qualifications—and sanctifying influences on the souls of men. It is only " parts of his ways" that we can undertake to speak of; or, indeed, of which we can have a conception. Those classes of divine operations, which appear more immediately to concern the salvation of men, are, the miraculous and the sanctifying. Of the first class of these operations, it is not my intention now to treat: and, indeed, any attempt of this sort, on my part, is amply and ably forestalled by a series of essays in the Christian Baptist, vol. 2. to which I would refer the reader for a luminous view of this part of the subject. The other class of divine operations, namely, those of a sanctifying nature, will furnish the subject for this undertaking; in the execution of which, it will be my aim to be short and plain.

The view which I wish to exhibit contains three points: First, the reality of a divine influence on the souls of men, in effecting the work of salvation; secondly, some of the principal effects produced by this operation; and, thirdly, the high practical import of this truth. To the first only I can attend in the present number.— And here I desire it may be observed, that I do not assume either Calvinian or Arminian ground, as being either of them exclusively necessary to this view. It is on scriptural ground that I propose to proceed: about any other term that may be used, I am not solicitous.

First, then, I lay down this position: that the influence of the Holy Spirit on the souls of men, in effecting the work of salvation, is a scriptural fact. That many have abused this sacred truth, by wild and fanciful imaginations, is readily conceded:—as what point of christian doctrine, indeed, has not been abused? But this, we contend, is no argument against the reality of the thing.

Let us endeavor to enter into this matter. And I begin with observing, that a persuasion of the necessity of an influence from the Divine Spirit, is a proper preparative for the more ready admission of that fact. Does this necessity then appear to exist? Let the scriptures of truth testify. " Without me, (said Jesus,)—or severed from me—you can do nothing:" John xv. 5. With this Paul accords; 2 *Cor.* ii. 5. " Not that we are sufficient of ourselves, to to think any thing as of ourselves; but our sufficiency is of God:" * and to this, the consciousness of every quickened soul responds: " Turn thou me, (is the language of all such,) and I shall be turned ;" *Jer.* xxx. 18. We might here enter into a view of that depravity of human nature, as represented in the scriptures, which appears to render it necessary that we should be visited with supernatural operations; but it is not deemed requisite to our present pur-

* This, it is true, refers originally to the ministry of the apostles; but it is a broad proposition, including general inability as to spiritual goodness.

pose. Suffice it to say, that our carnal minds are at enmity against God; and, therefore, need the changing efficacy of a divine influence; that we are naturally weak; and, therefore, have need to pray, " Strengthen you me according to your word." To what has been advanced, to shew the necessity of which we speak, I add the apostle's declaration, *Rom.* viii. 9. " If any one have not the Spirit of Christ, he is none of his."

We shall now come nearer to those evidences in favor of the point in hand, which are of a more direct nature. And in doing so, I shall be careful to distinguish between such passages of scripture as refer to miraculous operations, and such as regard those graces of the Spirit which *we* need as much as any in the time of primitive christianity could need them.

Many of the prayers of the inspired writers, (as Mr. Scott has justly remarked,) obviously imply the truth of our present position. David prays, " Take not your Holy Spirit from me," Psalm li. 11. Surely he considered himself favored by the influences of that Spirit. " Restore to me, (he adds,) the joy of your salvation; and uphold me with your free Spirit." He certainly believed a divine energy to be necessary to his support. Paul prayed for the Ephesian brethren to this effect: " That the God of our Lord Jesus Christ, the Father of Glory, may give to you the spirit of wisdom and revelation in the knowledge of him, (or for the acknowledgment of him;) the eyes of your understanding being enlightened; that you may know what is the hope of his calling," &c. *Eph.* i. 17. 18:— these are the blessings of salvation; not miraculous gifts. And again, " That he would grant you, according to the riches of his glory, to be strengthened with might, (or mightily strengthened,) by his Spirit in the inward man; that Christ may dwell in your hearts by faith," &c. ch. iii. 16. 17. These again are the things that accompany salvation: they are such as we now all need; and any argument brought to prove that they were peculiar to the season of miracles, would go as effectually to prove, that so likewise were faith, and hope, and love, and every christian grace peculiar to that season; and thus the very essence of christianity might be banished from the world! To the same effect is the apostle's prayer for the Colossians; i. 9. 10. 11. "That you might be filled with the knowledge of his will, in all wisdom and spiritual understanding," &c.—" Strengthened with all might, according to his glorious power," &c.—and so for the Romans; xv. 13: "Now the God of hope fill you with all joy and peace in believing; that you may abound in hope, through the power of the Holy Spirit." Other instances of the same sort might be adduced; but these are sufficient.

To the evidence arising from the prayers of the inspired writers, let us add some direct declarations—still cautiously regarding the difference between miraculous gifts and sanctifying operations. A few out of many must suffice :— " The love of God, (says Paul to the Romans) is shed abroad in our hearts, by the Holy Spirit which is given to us;" *Rom.* v. 5. Now, whether " the love of God" be taken here to mean a sense of God's love to us, or the exercise of our love to God—(for the phrase is ambiguous, and the better in this case for being so,) it will be allowed to be requisite that we possess it; and the Holy Spirit, as given to us, is the Agent to which it is ascribed. Again, chap. 8. ver. 9. " But you are not in the flesh, but in the Spirit; if so be that the Spirit of God dwell in you; or, because the Spirit of God dwells in you." This, verse 10, is termed "Christ in you;" and verse 11, it appears to be that Spirit which raised up Christ from the dead, and which is also to quicken the bodies of the saints. It must therefore be, not merely a holy spirit or temper in us; but truly and properly the Spirit of God. In verse 10 he affirms that " the Spirit itself bears witness with our spirit that we are the children of God." I shall not stop here to discuss the question, *How* the Spirit bears witness; whether directly and immediately, by suggesting a sense of our adoption; or mediately and indirectly, by producing that temper of heart which corresponds with the word of God, and enabling us thence to infer our adoption; or whether we ought not to admit both these views: it is enough, to our present purpose, that it is "the Spirit itself," as distinguished from our spirits, and from every other object. To the Galatians the same apostle says, chap. iv. 6. "God has sent forth the Spirit of his Son into your hearts, crying, Abba, Father." Allowing the Spirit of his Son here to mean, a spirit wrought in us, namely, the spirit of adoption, still it is expressly said to be sent forth from God; and of course must be the production of the Holy Spirit. The Ephesian brethren are represented as a part of that building, that "holy temple in the Lord," which is designed " for a habitation of God through the Spirit;" *Eph.* ii. 21. 22. We here remark, that God dwells in his church, in a manner in which he does *not* in the world; and that this inhabitation is through the Spirit: and this Spirit is said, *Rom.* viii. 26. "to help our infirmities," and "to make intercessions for us with groanings which cannot be uttered," or by inarticulate groanings.

These quotations appear to have reference to the case of believers; to their needs and their supplies. If believers must have the Divine Spirit to enable them to bring forth the fruits of righteousness, and prepare them for ultimate glory; then well might we opine that the unregenerate need the influences of that Spirit, to bring them into a gracious state: and this accordingly we find to be the fact. Christ assures Nicodemus, *John* iii. 7. that men "must be born again;" and this new birth is said, verse 8. to be " of the Spirit." The Spirit, then, of course, is necessary to the production of that change, without which there is no salvation. The Ephesians, in reference to their unbelieving, unregenerate state, are represented as having been "dead in trespasses and sins;" *Eph.* ii. 1.—in verse 5 the apostle includes himself, as in the same condition; and in both places ascribes to God the quickening (or life-giving) influence which they had experienced. In verse 10 the figure is changed; but the same idea is presented of a divine energy in their conversion to God: " For we are his workmanship, created in Christ Jesus to good works." I am aware, indeed, that the figures employed to express this important change, have often been abused; and that divine truth has thus been misrepresented by an extravagant zeal to establish some particular system: but surely there is an analogy which justifies the use of such figures; there is a strong meaning intended to be conveyed; a meaning which goes obviously to shew our natural alienation from God—our destitution of the principle of holiness—and the necessity of an influence from the Divine Spirit, to restore us to a meetness for the heavenly inheritance. Let one more particular reference suffice. In *Titus* iii. 5. salvation is ascribed, not to works of righteousness performed by us; but to divine mercy, " by the washing of regeneration and renewing of the Holy Spirit."

Comment here seems unnecessary, as I cannot conceive how language could more explicitly represent the agency of the Divine Spirit in the work of conversion.

I have mentioned above our natural alienation from God, and our destitution of the principle of holiness: and I here take occasion to repeat what I have before said—that this state of human nature, (which is so plainly held out in various parts of the sacred writings,) appears to be the ground of that necessity which exists, for a supernatural, regenerating influence from the Holy Spirit. But here it may possibly be objected that, allowing such to be the state of man, the Holy Spirit has so fitted the word of truth to our condition—has so adapted the means to the end, that no farther divine agency than what was employed in producing this word of truth, should be requisite in effecting the desired end. To such an argument I would reply, first, that a fair construction of the passages quoted, and of others that might be quoted, will not allow of such an idea: and secondly, that the fitness of the word to the condition of man, is no argument that regeneration and sanctification will follow, without a divine influence accompanying the truth:—no more, I say, a valid argument, in this case, than it would be to contend, that because seeds are adapted to vegetation, we may therefore expect a crop without the influence of sun or rain. That there is a happy, a beautiful adaptation of the word of truth to the condition of man, I readily admit; indeed it is one of my favorite ideas: this, however, does by no means supersede the necessity of a divine, spiritual influence, to give effect to the truth revealed.

But possibly it may be further suggested, that the same effects are, in many cases, ascribed to the word, which are also ascribed to the Spirit. This too is admitted; and I may add, the same effects are, in some instances, ascribed to the preacher, as the dispenser of the word. Thus, we are enlightened by the Spirit: "Open you my eyes, that I may behold wondrous things out of your law;"—and we are enlightened by the word: " The entrance of your word gives light." We are born again of the Spirit: "So is every one that is born of the Spirit;"—and we are born again by the word: "Being born again, not of corruptible seed, but of incorruptible, by the word of God," &c. We are sanctified by the Spirit: " But you are washed, but you are sanctified," &c. " by the Spirit of our God;"—and we are sanctified by the word: " Sanctify them through your truth: your word is truth." It belongs to God to open the eyes and to turn the sinner;—and Paul was sent to the Gentiles " to open their eyes, and to turn them from darkness to light." These instances are sufficient to illustrate the fact which has been admitted;—that the same effects are, in some instances, ascribed to the Holy Spirit—to the word of truth—and to the preacher or publisher of the gospel. It remains for us to see how this matter is to be understood.

Briefly, I remark, that the same things are ascribed to different objects, pretty much in the way in which the same effect is ascribed to the agent and to the instrument. My pen, the instrument, being adapted to the purpose of writing, forms these letters; and I, the agent, giving my pen direction, form these letters. The seed and the earth produce vegetation: the sun and the rain produce vegetation; and, in a certain sense, the man who sows the seeds and cultivates the earth, may be said to produce vegetation. I know, indeed, that such figures cannot adequately represent spiritual and moral objects. They are introduced only by way of illustration and I do by no means intend, by the use of them to reduce men to mere machines, or the operations of the Divine Spirit to mere physical energy. When Paul says to the Corinthians, "You are manifestly declared to be the epistle of Christ ministered by us, written not with ink, but with the Spirit of the Living God,"—there is a beautiful analogy which justifies the use of the figure; and we see in it the agency of Christ, the instrumentality of the preacher, and the influence of the Spirit. But he who should undertake to disprove the moral agency of man, would, it is presumed, pervert the truth by the abuse of a metaphor. If, however, on the other hand, one should be disposed to attribute to the efficiency of the instrument, what belongs to the efficiency of the agent, the apostle would certainly correct his error, by saying "Who then is Paul, and who is Apollos, but ministers by whom you believed even as the Lord gave to every man? I have planted, Apollos watered; but God gave the increase. So then, neither is he that plants any thing, neither he that waters; but God that gives the increase." 1 Cor. iii. 5, 6, 7.

The sum of these remarks on the effects ascribed to the Spirit and the word is this: that the word of truth is God's great instrument in effecting our salvation. By this, or with this, his spirit operates in the renewing and sanctifying of the soul; while under its influence, the soul itself becomes active in holy exercises: and thus, with Peter, we may say to believers, "You have purified your souls, in obeying the truth, through the Spirit." How God may otherwise work, I know not; though I would by no means "limit the Holy One of Israel," as to his designs or operations, in any respect whatever.

I now dismiss the first position—the reality of divine influence on the souls of men, in effecting the work of salvation. This was my leading object in the present undertaking. The other two points proposed will probably be treated on with more brevity: they must be reserved, however, for another number.   PAULINUS.
November, 1827.

[We make no remarks on the preceding communication until we have received Paulinus, No. II.]—Ed. C. B.

———

[Communicated by a correspondent in Georgia.]
An Extract from a Dialogue between a Baptist and a Baptist Clergyman.

Baptist. Well, sir, have you had time to examine those pamphlets I gave you?

Clergyman. I have examined them all, with the exception of the two last numbers.

B. What do you think of them?

C. I think some parts of them are good; but cannot agree as to that part respecting weekly communion.

B. By reading the seventh verse of the twentieth chapter of the Acts of the Apostles, I am led to think that the disciples mentioned there, met on the first day of the week, and that it was for the purpose of breaking bread that they met.

C. I have no doubt but that the first disciples broke bread each first day; but the disciples now, must be regulated in this, by time and circumstances.

B. If you depart from what you admit may have been the order of the first churches, how often now should the churches attend to the breaking of bread?

C. With the Baptists we think it proper to attend to it once a month.

B. But others think it also proper to break bread once in three months, some once in six months, and others only once in twelve months. But you think it proper to break bread once each month. Your convictions that it is proper does not arise from the word of God. For it is silent on breaking bread once each month. It arises, as already admitted, from the distance of time and change of circumstances since the first churches of Christ. Now are you sure that distance of time and change of circumstances will justify your departure from breaking bread each first day, to that of once each month. We have all to appear before the judgment seat of Christ to give an account of the actions done in this life. Now as it is his word that we are to be judged by, whether is it more safe to break bread at such a time as can at best have the appearance of being supported only by distance of time and change of circumstances, or attend to it each first day, having the first churches for our example, and of course supported by that word by which we are to be judged?

C. But some have thought that breaking bread so often might be the means of abusing this ordinance.

B. Yes, the men of this world have thought so, for they do abuse it if they attend to it so much as once in their lives. But I am sure that the saints will never abuse this ordinance willingly. For if they are saved only if they keep in memory what Paul at first received, and what first of all he delivered to the Corinthians, viz. that Christ died for our sins according to the scriptures, was buried, and rose again on the third day, according to the scriptures. If the saints are only saved by a remembrance of the death and resurrection of the Lord Jesus, then instead of their being alarmed at breaking bread as often as the first churches, they have cause to rejoice indeed, that they have the privilege of the same frequency as they; for if it tended to encourage and impress a remembrance of him who died for their sins, surely the same frequency is necessary to be observed by us so as to encourage and impress a remembrance of him who died for our sins. And if there is an aptness to forget these things, and we are only saved if we remember them, or, in scripture language, keep them in memory, how thankful ought we to be for this ordinance, each first day, which brings to our minds and memories Christ's dying for our sins, that we might not perish, but have everlasting life. Away, then, with monthly, quarterly, half yearly communions, as times fixed on by men, and not by God, periods which have been and still are opposed to the interests of the saints, and let the will of the Lord Jesus in his ordinance, as expressed by the example of the first churches, be our only rule, and by thus walking by his word, we will be justified whatever men may say. Whereas, depending on distance of time and change of circumstances, for justifying our departure from any part of the word of God, is at best but a sandy foundation. The mass of the great body called christians, practise and justify this departure; but we will esteem their applause but little, and the having had it will be but poor consolation to us, if we have been found opposing the truth when called upon to appear before the judgment seat of Christ.

———

Review of Dr. Noel's Circular.—No. VI.

I am not conscious of having passed by a single sentence in this honored circular, containing any thing in the form of an argument, which has not been embraced in the preceding essays on its contents. If, however, the author thinks otherwise, on his suggesting such a sentence to my notice, I will pay a more ceremonious regard to it. What now remains is to answer the Doctor's five triumphant questions, which he proposes as though the mere submission of them were to silence the whole race of believers in the all-sufficiency of the Holy Oracles.

"Let those," says the Doctor, "who oppose the use of creeds, answer these questions." Surely after this challenge we must expect to find some pith in them. We shall, with all due complaisance, attempt to answer them, in confident expectation that the Doctor will be as complaisant in turn, and answer me five questions in return.

Query 1st from Dr. Noel.—"Has the Head of the Church made no qualifications necessary for the admission of members into the church?" I answer, He has not made "a creed," nor an assent to it, in the popular sense of these words, a necessary qualification. But he has required just the same qualifications for admission into his church in Frankfort, which the twelve apostles required of the three thousand received in one day into the church in Jerusalem, A. D. 34.

Now, in return, I propose my first question to Dr. Noel. Seeing he has, for once, done homage to the authority of the Head of the Church, I ask, 1st. Has the Head of the Church made your own little creed, or an assent to it, a qualification necessary for admission into his church?

2d Query from Dr. Noel.—"Has he made no qualifications necessary for admission into office?" I answer, Paul's letters to Timothy and Titus very explicitly lay down certain qualifications for office; but amongst all the qualifications found in the volume, that of subscription to the Romish, Episcopal, Presbyterial, or even Dr. Noel's own summary, is not mentioned as any qualification to office.

In return I propose my 2d query for the Doctor. Has the Head of the Church any where referred to any other writings than the apostles', or has he in any of these writings commanded any epitome or summary exhibition to be drawn up or referred to in the admission of any person into office in his church?

3d Query from Dr. Noel.—"Has he established no tribunal on earth to judge of these qualifications?" We answer, Yes—namely, the Pope and his Cardinals at Rome—the Archbishop of Canterbury and his court in London—the Annual Assembly of the Church of Scotland in Edinburgh—and Dr. Noel's "called Presbytery," in Frankfort, Kentucky. These four tribunals, for the four quarters of the world, are established, and authorized, and by good ecclesiastical law appointed, to constitute the holy office of inquisition, when, in their judgment, the interests of religion may require it. These sacred tribunals are to judge of two things above all others: 1st. of the qualifications for office; and 2d. to decide who possesses them!

Our third query for Dr. Noel is—What punishment have these tribunals to inflict upon those destitute of these qualifications claiming these high offices?

Query 4th from Dr. Noel.—"Is an Arian, Socinian, or Universalist, qualified for either membership or office?" I answer, No. Because the apostles have so decreed. But I will amend the question in my 4th query to Dr. Noel, viz. Is an Arian, Socinian, Universalist, Catholic, Episcopalian, Presbyterian, or Methodist, qualified for either membership or office? But his 4th question is intimately connected with his 5th—namely:

Query 5th from Dr. Noel.—"Can it be said they are not without respect to a creed?" I answer, Without respect to such a creed as you espouse. (See my second No. on his circular, in which it will appear christian churches have a divine creed, and human churches have a human creed.) But I must also intimately connect my fifth query to my fourth as has the Doctor—and it is this:

5th Query for Dr. Noel.—Is not the Arian, Socinian, Universalist, Catholic, Episcopalian, Presbyterian, and Methodist, excluded from your church because they have a creed different from the sacred writings, which is the only creed I subscribe? If they had not some other creed than the bible, you surely could not exclude them. And here, Doctor, your five triumphant queries terminate. They are your "*five points;*" and *sharp* points they are, for they have pierced you through. For if you answer the above five queries as complaisantly as I have done yours, you must come to the conclusion that it was not for the want of a human creed, but because they had a human creed, that you exclude from your church the Arian, Socinian, Universalist, Presbyterian, Methodist, and Episcopalian.

To conclude a disquisition which already has far transcended its due merits, I will just state and briefly illustrate a single position of some importance in this controversy. It is this: These heretics, called Arians, Socinians, Universalists, Catholics, Protestants, &c. &c. are kept in existence and their numbers augmented by the reasonings of such philosophers as Dr. S. M. Noel. Destroy the Socinian's creed, and where will you find the Socinians? Let all his glosses, interpretations, and dogmas, be a dead letter, neither printed nor read, neither spoken nor heard, and where would the sect be in a generation or two? It would be so of all other sects. Consequently, these creeds keep up all these sects. Now each one contends for his creed as better than all others, and thus justifies himself to himself. But let him remember that this creed derives all its consequence and superiority in his own estimation, from a comparison of it with others. If there were none with which to compare it, its excellencies would be all invisible. If, instead of making inquisition for opinions; if, instead of condemning a person for his interpretations, glosses, or dogmas, we, as worshipping congregations, turned our attention to the behavior of others, and condemned professed disciples for their impiety, immorality, and indevotion—the church and the world would very soon exhibit a quite different aspect. If a man speak of any christian topic in any other language than did the apostles, hear him patiently. If he will force his opinions upon us in terms contrary to those furnished by the Holy Spirit, let us admonish him. But if he will not be admonished, and still aims at imposing his opinions or terms upon us, he then becomes what the new translation calls "a factionist:" and the common a "heretic;" and after a second admonition we are commanded to reject such a person. Not because of his opinions, even at last, but because of his dogmatical and faction-making spirit. If a man speaks of God our Father, and of Jesus Christ our Lord, in all the sentences and words of the Holy Oracles; if to this unexceptionable style he adds a holy, devout, moral, and unexceptionable life, the church of Jesus Christ has nothing more to inquire of him, or require from him. If he should be called a Socinian, a Universalist, a Presbyterian, or a Methodist, it matters not; if he speak in bible terms only, no man can justly impeach him, and by his works he must stand or fall in the estimation of all christians, as by these he must stand or fall in the day of the Lord Jesus. Now in this course it is easy to proceed without synod, or council, or creed. For if any man call Jesus Christ a " mere man," or a " mere creature," or an " eternal Son," and will insist upon our calling him so; we open the bible, and call for the express warrant. None can be produced. This being easily decided, the person is admonished; if he will still insist upon it, we admonish him a second time; and if still unreclaimed, we cast him out, not because his opinion differed from ours, but because he would lord it over our faith and conscience, and aimed at heading a faction. This most unquestionably is the meaning of all that is said upon this subject in the bible.

Now to test the correctness and utility of the course advised, we have only to consider how it would operate if universally adopted. Then if the result be obviously salutary on a general scale, no man can object to it either in principle or practice, if when only adopted by a few it does not do as much as if adopted by all. And this is precisely the logic and drift of all that the creed advocates, whether Catholic, Presbyterian, or Baptist, urge against our logic in this controversy. They say they must have a creed because other sects have a creed; and that although they should adopt the scriptures only, still sects would exist, and controversies would not universally cease. If there is any propriety in their logic, these sects or heresies, creeds and divisions, must, in defiance of the hopes of a Millennium, continue to destroy the peace and happiness of society for ever, or while time endures.

If Dr. Noel will clear up that "little moral impropriety," concerning which I spoke some two or three months ago; and if he will take up my reasonings in good earnest, piece by piece; or if he will agree to my publishing the whole of this Circular and this Review in one pamphlet, and if he will take and distribute the one half of the edition—I will still call him *Brother Noel*, and embrace him in the bosom of that charity which calls for nothing but the image of eternal truth stamped upon the heart, and reflected in the life, to arouse its energies, and to bound its fraternal activities.   EDITOR.

Attempt at the Restoration of Ancient Order.
The church professing obedience to the faith of Jesus Christ, assembling together in Manchester, to the church of Christ at New York.— Grace, mercy, and peace be multiplied to you, from God the Father, through Jesus Christ our Lord.

Dearly Beloved,
WITH one heart and one mind we unite in gratitude and praise to God our Saviour for the good news which your acceptable communication to the churches of Christ, scattered over the earth, brings to our ears; greatly rejoicing that you have been led, through the grace and mercy of God, to renounce the commandments of men— to separate from every religious connexion which walk not in all things according to the precepts and example of Christ and of his apostles; and to come together in one body for the observance of all the ordinances and institutions of our Lord and Master, continuing in the apostles' doctrine and fellowship, and breaking of bread and prayers. And upon every remembrance of you, we

cease not to pray for you, that you may be kept by the Spirit of Truth from the errors that abound in the world, and stedfast, immoveable, in the faith and hope of the gospel. We give praise to the God of all grace and mercy for your near approach in faith and practice to the first churches of Christ in Judea, and are persuaded you are desirous to walk in the footsteps of the flock. In the fullest conviction of this, we proceed to give you the required information.

In March, 1810, we first met in public for worship, only three in number, and continued till 1817 without any persons being appointed to discharge the duties of elders or deacons; notwithstanding, we observed, as our privilege and duty, all the ordinances of worship taught by the great Shepherd to his flock, as far as we knew them.

We are now thirty-three in number, several of our brethren having, from various causes, removed to other parts of England and Scotland, and three to America, viz. James Thornton, one of our first deacons, to Montreal; George and Elizabeth Flemming, (the latter one of our first deaconesses) to Baltimore.

The servants appointed, and still enjoyed, by the church, are one elder, one deacon, and one deaconess; to which will be added, from time to time, such persons as Jesus may give us for the edifying of his body, the church.

It is with unspeakable pleasure we observe such a general agreement between you and us in what relates to " The Faith," the influence of " Truth," working by love, as it appears in the life and conversation of those who believe it, and the order of worship enjoined upon such. And to avoid going over the subjects which you have so clearly and scripturally stated, we declare our entire agreement with you, except in the instances which will be particularly noticed: and as some of those relate to the order of our worship, we shall state the way in which we proceed.

1st. We meet three times on the Lord's day— in the afternoon separate from those who are not of our number. We commence by our elder, who presides, selecting a suitable hymn, in singing of which we all stand up and join.

2d. We all kneel down when our elder, or one of the brethren named by him, offers up prayers, supplications, &c. wherein brevity, and the scripture mode of expression, are preferred.

3d. A portion of scripture is read both from the Old and New Testament.

4th. Prayer, with a view to the fellowship, which follows.

5th. We greet each other with a holy kiss.

6th. After reading or repeating the words of the institution, we attend to the Lord's supper, by giving thanks for and then breaking the bread. We give thanks also for the cup, and we all drink of it in remembrance of the death of the Lord Jesus.

7th. A hymn suitable to the occasion is then sung.

8th. The brethren are requested to teach and admonish one another; but should they not be disposed, or time permit when we have concluded, our elder addresses the church, or those who are observing us, at the conclusion of which another hymn is sung—prayer is made—and we separate. This is our order in our several meetings on the Lord's day, with the exception of the fellowship, holy kiss, and the Lord's supper.

We meet twice in the week also for prayer, reading the scriptures, exhortation and teaching.

We proceed to remark on those things in which we seem to differ. You say, 1st. *In obedience to* the command, 1 *Tim.* ii. 1, &c. We also pray for kings; and all that are in authority; but we think the words, *first of all*, mark the beginning of Paul's exhortation to Timothy, and not the order of worship in the church. 5th. You say, After each chapter is read, a pause is made, &c. This is not regularly done among us, though sometimes remarks are made in illustration of any thing read which particularly demand it.— You say the observance of the kiss of charity rises from special occasions exemplified in the New Testament. *Acts* xx. 37, 38, informs us that (after Paul had given his last solemn charge to the elders of the church at Ephesus, verse 17, &c.) they all wept sore, and fell on Paul's neck and kissed him; sorrowing most of all that they should *see his face no more.* This, we think, cannot be an exemplification of the command given to the church at Rome, Corinth, &c. "Greet *you one another* with a holy kiss," no mention being then made of any special occasions. You, beloved brethren, will doubtless perceive the word *holy* marks the divine appointment of the kiss, and the word *charity* the design of it. So we attend to it, when assembled together, without regard to age or sex, as a solemn expression of mutual forgiveness, and of mutual love, for the truth's sake.

Our elder labors with his own hands, that he may live honestly and have to give to them that needs. But we are not sure that the faithful discharge of pastoral duties gives any right to elders to claim wages. *Theirs* is to be a crown of glory which fades not away, when the chief Shepherd shall appear; compare *Acts* xx. 34, 35, with 2 *Thess.* iii. 8, 12. To the twelve and the seventy disciples our Lord gave a right to wages, saying, "the laborer is worthy of his hire." Paul accordingly asks the Corinthians, "I only, and Barnabas, have not we power to forbear working?" 1 *Cor.* ix. 6, while he appears to blame them for suffering a man to take of them, 2 *Cor.* xi. 20. An individual going forth to preach the gospel to regions round about, by the appointment of the church, becomes his proper work, and we think him entitled to wages of those who send him. Other churches or individuals bringing him forward on his journey after a godly sort. 3 *Ep. John.*

In all the measures and decisions of a church, unanimity is preferable to majority, when it can be attained. Our church, however, is composed of "babes" as well as of those "who have their senses exercised by reason of use to discern between good and evil." And we do not defer our decisions until "Christ's little ones" can fully comprehend the reason upon which such decisions are made. They are left at liberty therefore to keep silence, as Paul directs. 1 *Cor.* xiv. 37, 38.

We attend to the Lord's supper in the afternoon, because all the examples we know of took place in the latter part of the day; for even the circumstance of time is not unworthy of notice in attending to an ordinance of commemoration, *Deut.* xvi. 6. compared with the institution, *Exodus* xii. 6. And we thereby cut off occasion from those who have, in this country, urged "an unnecessary deviation from their own professed rules," (viz. the apostolic examples,) against others who attend to this ordinance in the morning.

We have also a love feast on every Lord's day.

It is with great pleasure we read the reasons which induced you to write your epistle, to restore and promote the unity and prosperity of Christ's kingdom; and in order to lend our aid in this good cause, we have printed several hundred copies of your letter, which will probably bring you many communications from churches in Britain, various in their views of faith and order. And we pray that you may be preserved from receiving any thing contrary to the will of Christ, and that by manifestation of the truth you may commend it to the conscience of those to whose letters you reply.

We should be happy to hear from you at all times, anticipating much useful information and a mutual growth of affection from an increasing knowledge of each other.

Now, may he who is able to keep us from falling, preserve you blameless unto the second coming of our Lord and Saviour Jesus Christ, to whom be glory and honor now and evermore. Amen.

Approved and adopted by the church, and signed in their behalf, by

WILLIAM JACKSON, *Elder.*
BENJAMIN BEDDOME, *Deacon.*
Manchester, Sept. 13, 1818.

Ancient Gospel.—No. II.
Immersion.

"JESUS CHRIST came by water and by blood." At the water he was proved to be the Only Begotten by the voice of his Father, and the designation of the Holy Spirit. Through the water of Jordan he passed into the vineyard of the Lord of Hosts, and began to do the work the Father gave him to accomplish. On the cross, and from the shedding of his blood to the moment of his interment, divine attestations, numerous and diverse, marvellous and grand, were afforded; all declaring that he was sent by, and came forth from God. With much propriety, then, and with great force, too, it is said that "Jesus came by water and by blood." In the same laconic style, we may say, that immersion, I mean christian immersion, is the gospel in water, and that the Lord's supper is the gospel in bread and wine. These two ordinances of the glorious and mighty Lord fully exhibit the gospel in the most appropriate symbols. The preaching of the Lord and his apostles, we all agree was the gospel in words. The historic books of the New Testament are the gospel in fact. Immersion is the gospel in water—the Lord's supper is the gospel in bread and wine—and a pure heart and a holy life is the gospel in its effects. But I am now to show that christian immersion, as instituted by Jesus Christ, (not as corrupted by men,) is the gospel in water. The whole gospel is exhibited in this symbolic action. The subject declares his belief of the testimony which God has given concerning his only begotten Son, all summarily comprehended in this one sentence, Jesus is the Messiah, the Son of the only true God. But why recognize him in this character? Why submit to be immersed into this belief? Aye: that is the question. I say again, Why submit to be immersed into the faith of the Father, Son, and Holy Spirit, as an act of obedience to Jesus Christ? Tell me, ye mitred heads! ye learned Doctors of Divinity. Many reasons ye may give, perhaps, without giving the only one which gives deep interest to the ordinance. Shall I have to disclose the secret? We are immersed, then, that we may be christened! Very true, indeed: but how christened? Married to Jesus Christ, as some old-fashioned christians used to say. I will take it in your own terms, you sons of the English hierarchy; or in your terms, you sons of the Scotch hierarchy—"Married to Jesus Christ"— united to him by the New Covenant. Well, now, let us hear tne words of this matrimonial compact:—"I take you, O Woman, to be my lawful spouse; and I promise to provide for you all the days of your eternal life. I will succor you, defend you, support and comfort you forever. My name, my honors, and my fortune shall be yours. Your people shall be my people, and your God my God." In reply, she says: "I take you to be my Lord and master; my sovereign, husband; and I pledge myself, by putting myself under your control, to love and serve you faithfully all the days of my immortal existence." This is enough to constitute the parties one in law, in name, and in fortune. Shall we have now to prove that the sins of the church are washed away? I say, after reading the marriage covenant, one clause of which is in these identical words, "Your sins and your iniquities I will remember no more." I say, after reading this covenant, shall we hesitate to say, that the sins of the baptized are washed away? But, dismissing the obsolete style of the ancient founders of the modern hierarchies, let us turn over the leaves of the inspired volume.

And now I propose to do three things. 1st. To shew that the apostles addressed christians as having their sins remitted. 2d. That frequent allusions to baptism in the sacred epistles, represent it as an ablution. And in the third place I must shew that it is as plainly affirmed in the New Testament that God forgives men's sins in the act of immersion, as that he will raise the dead at the voice of the archangel, or as that Jesus Christ will come again to judge the world.

In the first place, then, let it be noticed that Paul affirms that the Gentile disciples of Christ (*Col.* ii. 13) had their sins forgiven: "And you being dead in your sins and the uncircumcision of your flesh, has he quickened, together with him, having forgiven you all trespasses." To the Hebrews he says, (chap. x. 17, 18,) "Where remission of sins is, no more offering for sin is needed." Therefore, inasmuch as no sin offerings are appointed for christians, remission of sins is enjoyed by them. This is necessary to make his argument conclusive. For the drift of that passage is to shew that one promise in the New Covenant secured the forgiveness of sins to all who embraced it; and that the fact of their sins having been forgiven, is the reason why there are no sin offerings under the New Testament.

To the same purpose the apostle speaks in all his epistles. Of the Lord Jesus, he says in general terms, "In him we have redemption through his blood; even the forgiveness of sins," &c. I do not wish to make a display of scriptural authorities where it is not necessary. This matter needs not to be proved to, but only to be remembered by, all intelligent christians. Suffice it, then, to remember that the ancient christians, both Gentiles and Jews, were taught to consider that their sins were forgiven them. Now here the inquisitive will ask, When, or at what time, were these sins forgiven? This we are not now to answer.

In the second place, we proceed to the allusions to immersion, which represent it as an ablution, or a washing away of sins.

Allusion 1st. *Cor.* vi. 11. "And such were some of you, but you are washed in the name of the Lord Jesus." We all admit that there is no public, outward, or symbolic washing in the name of the Lord Jesus, save christian immersion. To refer to it as a washing, indicates that it was an ablution.

Allusion 2d. *Eph.* v. 26. "That he might cleanse the church by a bath of water."

Allusion 3d. *Titus* iii. 5. "God has saved us by the bath of regeneration."

Allusion 4th. *Heb.* x. 22. "Our bodies are washed with clean water."

Allusion 5th. *2 Pet.* i. 9. "He has forgotten that he was purified from his old sins."

On this last quotation let me ask, What are the old sins or former sins except those committed before baptism. We affirm that no solution can be given to this question, except that which represents it as referring to immersion in the ancient sense. Four things are fairly implied in these words: 1. That the ancient disciples were taught to consider themselves as pardoned. 2. That there was a time when, and a certain act by, or in which their sins were forgiven. 3. That they were not unconscious of this act at the time when it was performed, for it was an action which could and should have been remembered; otherwise, how could any person be blamed for having forgotten that he had been purified from his old sins. And 4th, it is implied that these sins were those which had accumulated during a state previous to this purification. Let any person illustrate this matter to himself, by considering what is implied in telling a person, You have forgotten that you have been married.

Allusion 6th. 1 John ii. 12. "I write to you, little children, because your sins are forgiven you for his name's sake."

This last allusion few consider correctly; but, in my judgment, it is just equivalent to saying, I have written to you, exhorting you, little children; because you have been immersed into the name of the Lord Jesus. To these might be added other allusions, such as those sayings concerning apostates—"The sow that was washed has returned to its wallowing slough." Such were they who had tasted the good word of God and the powers of the world to come. Such were they who had made shipwreck of faith and a good conscience. But those less explicit allusions we consider unnecessary, as the above six allusions are more than sufficient for our purpose.

In the third place, I proceed to shew that we have the most explicit proof that God forgives sins for the name's sake of his Son, or when the name of Jesus Christ is named upon us in immersion:—that in, and by, the act of immersion, so soon as our bodies are put under water, at that very instant our former, or "old sins" are all washed away, provided only that we are true believers. This was the view and the expectation of every one who was immersed in the apostolic age; and it was a consciousness of having received this blessing that caused them to rejoice in the Lord, and, like the eunuch, to "go on their way rejoicing." When Jesus commanded reformation and forgiveness of sins to be announced in his name to all nations, he commanded men to receive immersion to the confirmation of this promise. Thus we find that when the gospel was announced on Pentecost, and when Peter opened the kingdom of heaven to the Jews, he commanded them to be immersed for the remission of sins. This is quite sufficient, if we had not another word on the subject. I say it is quite sufficient to shew that the forgiveness of sins and christian immersion were, in their first proclamations by the holy apostles inseparably connected together. Peter, to whom was committed the keys, opened the kingdom of heaven in this manner, and made repentance, or reformation, and immersion, equally necessary to forgiveness. In the common version it reads thus: "Repent and be baptized every one of you, for the remission of sins, and you shall receive the gift of the Holy Spirit." When any thing is done for any purpose, it is always understood that there is a necessary connexion betwixt that which is done, and the object in view. When a person is immersed for the remission of sins, it is just the same as if expressed, in order to obtain the remission of sins. But my limits are filled up, and I must interrupt my argument for the present, promising, all things concurring, to bring it to a legitimate or logical close in my next. In the mean time I have only to request my devout readers to remember one fact, which speaks volumes to all christendom. It is this: The first three thousand persons that were immersed after the ascension of Christ into heaven, were immersed *for the remission of their sins with the promise of the Holy Spirit.* I am bold, therefore, to affirm, that every one of them who, in the belief of what the apostle spoke, was immersed, did, in the very instant in which he was put under water, receive the forgiveness of his sins and the gift of the Holy Spirit. If so, then, who will not concur with me in saying that christian immersion is the gospel in water.

EDITOR.

CLINTON COUNTY, OHIO, OCTOBER 14, 1827.

BROTHER CAMPBELL,—A PERSON situated as you are, must submit to be assaulted on all sides, both by the wise and ignorant, and sometimes by persons of whom you have never heard, (which I apprehend is the case with myself.) Without further preface I shall proceed to inform you that I am one of that class of people called "Christians," and that I have for a number of years been received as a teacher or "preacher" among them. Ten years ago I believed in Jesus, and entered the field as a soldier under the banners of the King of Heaven. I earnestly desired the salvation of sinners, and could not enjoy comfort whilst I refused to invite them to come. I had from my infancy been taught that God by his Spirit, abstract from his word, did, in every age of the christian dispensation, call certain characters to preach the gospel; and that these characters, so called, acted under the same commission as the twelve apostles. This tradition, the feelings of my soul, and the opinion of those to whom I looked up as teachers in Israel, confirmed me in the belief that I was one of "the called by God." Accordingly, I went to work, and for about eighteen months labored in the word and doctrine, and some in tradition, (as I appropriated every thing said of the apostles to myself, and firmly believed myself an ambassador of Christ; that to me was committed the word of reconciliation, and that I had this treasure in an earthen vessel,) &c. At the end of this time an old brother ambassador took in hand to have me "ordained." Accordingly, inquiry was made of the church to which I belonged, if they had any objections to the measure. They made no objections: for in fact they believed the preachers had the hank all in their own hand; and accordingly I was "ordained" by three brethren, and believed myself then authorised to "administer" the ordinances of the Lord's house, throughout the whole realm, and that I was an elder of the church of Christ, though but a boy.

For a number of years I labored for the good of my fellow mortals, without in the least doubt-

ing the propriety of the ground I had assumed. I at length heard of A. Campbell, his debates with Walker and M'Calla; and somehow I conceived a strong dislike both for the man and the course he was pursuing, without knowing any thing certain of either. At length some numbers of the Christian Baptist fell in my way. I read them, and felt desirous to read more; and from that time (though not a subscriber) I have been a constant reader of the Christian Baptist. Yes, and this same Christian Baptist has stripped me of my "call," my ambassadorship, &c. and has taught me that the treasure which the apostles had in earthen vessels I have in the Bible; and, in a word, has left me simply a disciple and a laborer in the vineyard in common with all others, according to our several abilities. Your essays on "the ancient order of things," have carried such conviction to my mind that I am ashamed I never understood the matter before. But I, like you, can make "the mists of the river Nile," an apology for my former ignorance in this case; but I am glad they have "ascended the top of the mountains," and I am now, with some others, engaged in teaching the necessity of a return to Jerusalem: and while thus engaged I have occasionally to hear that Alexander Campbell has "denied the faith, and is worse than an infidel;" that he has denied the "operation of the Spirit," the "divine call to preach," &c. and that from men too who bear the christian name and are viewed as teachers in Israel. Notwithstanding this, my whole soul is awake to investigation, and I feel determined never to be chased from the field by the scoffs of the Rabbies and them who wish to do them homage.

I am much pleased with your remarks on the bishop's office, his call, qualifications, &c. but as it respects what is called "ordination," I am not prepared at present to say Amen to all you say. You admit that the seniors of the congregation did lay their hands on the bishops elect in case there was no bishop in the congregation, and when there was a bishop that he laid his hand on the bishop elect to manifest his concurrence with the choice of the people. What you may have learned from the "history of the world, or the pages of Jewish or Christian antiquity," on this subject, I know not; but for my soul I cannot find one word in the New Testament that proves to me that bishops were ordained by the laying on of the hands of any body. If there is such proof as the case requires in the New Testament, I wish to know it; and if not, I wish you to retract what you have said on the subject, for you are viewed by many as an oracle, and your wrong will become the wrong of thousands. I find in the New Testament that spiritual gifts were given by the laying on of hands; that the power of working miracles was conferred in the same way, and miracles were wrought by the same act. But I cannot find where a bishop was ordained by laying on of hands.

In answer to a certain question, you say that the work of an evangelist is preaching the gospel to those who have never heard it. Paul left Timothy in Macedonia on a certain occasion; he then wrote certain things to him that he might know how to behave himself in the house of God, which is the church of the living God; and both the epistles show that Timothy's business was chiefly among believers; and Paul concludes the whole matter by exhorting Timothy to do the work of an evangelist, and make full proof of his ministry. This consideration has induced me to request that you find both time and room for the proof of your assertion.

In your last number of the Christian Baptist you say, "The Mahoning Association did one good work at their last meeting: they agreed to support one active, spiritually minded, and able brother as a messenger of the churches, &c. Brother Walter Scott accepted of the appointment," &c. Now, brother Campbell, I confess I am at a loss to understand you; and as I consider the matter an important one, I wish information on the subject. No man under the heavens has said more against the divine right of associations, synods, councils, conferences, &c. than A. Campbell, and no man has spoken to better purpose on the subject. I now ask, If they have no divine right, by what authority did they act when they made the above appointment, and how are you justifiable in styling the person so appointed the Messenger of the Churches? A person that so ably advocates the restoration of a pure speech ought to be careful not to use the language of Ashdod. You know according to the best historical account we can get, that for more than a century after Christ the churches were perfectly independent of each other, neither were they joined together by association, confederacy, or any other bond than charity: and I know that I need not tell you that your association is an unscriptural institution, and how can an unscriptural association act according to the gospel? I would have thought it a good work if they had made their will, and voluntarily agreed to die, and appointed brother Scott to preach their funeral. But, to be serious, I see as great an incongruity between your messenger and the messengers of the churches mentioned in the New Testament, as you can see between the present order of preachers and a New Testament bishop. The messengers mentioned in 1st and 2d Corinthians were brethren appointed to travel with the apostles to carry the liberality of the Gentile churches to the poor saints at Jerusalem. Your messenger is appointed by the Association, in the name and likely by the authority, of the churches who compose the Association. But where do the churches find any account of the ancient churches sending messengers to such an assembly, with the power to act for them there? I am certain they do not find it in the New Testament.

There are seven messengers mentioned in the first chapter of Revelations, and, according to your view of their office, if it be proper to call it an office, they were men appointed to visit the old apostle in his banishment, and administer to his wants. This I have no doubt is the fact. But does not the circumstance of the Son of God walking in the midst of the seven candlesticks and holding the seven stars in his right hand, indicate that their business was something more than what you have stated? Is there not room for a strong presumption that they were men appointed, not only to administer to the wants of the apostle, but to teach that faith to others which the churches had professed, and that each church had one such messenger?

What I have written I submit without any apology to you as to a friend, a brother in Christ, and request the favor of a private answer to what I have written, as I have no desire to appear in public in my present unlettered situation, hoping that you will not cast my uncouth production to the moles and to the bats, without giving me a christian answer; and wishing you every blessing you desire for time and eternity, I subscribe myself your brother in the bonds of the gospel.

W.

To Mr. W.

Brother W.—I did, as you see, contrary to your desire, lay your letter to me of the 14th October, before my readers, because I believed it fraught with good sense, and because it gave me an opportunity of dilating upon one or two topics not sufficiently discussed in the previous volumes of this work. The first sentence in your letter which calls for my attention is this, "But for my soul I cannot find one word in the New Testament that proves to me that bishops were ordained by the laying on of the hands of any body." Let me ask you, Do you find from the New Testament that bishops were ordained at all? You will answer, Yes. I then ask, What was the sign, or token, or mode of ordination? To give you all the light I have on this subject from the volumes of holy writ, I will state a few biblical facts. 1st. Persons when appointed to an office, whether *viva voce;* by stretching forth the hand; or by lifting it up, are said to be ordained to that office. This, I presume, requires no proof. 2d. Persons have been elected to an office, and afterwards inaugurated, consecrated, or set apart, to that office; so that election to an office, and ordination or inauguration, are not always, nor necessarily, one and the same thing. This I also presume needs not a single quotation in proof. 3d. But in the third place, there was amongst the Jews, in all ages, a sign, token, or mode of ordination; and their sign, token, or mode of ordination was the laying on of hands. This I must attempt to prove whether it needs it or not:—

1. When the patriarchs blessed or devoted their children, they laid hands upon their head; as, for example, when Jacob blessed the sons of Joseph.

2. When any thing was devoted or consecrated to the Lord, hands were laid upon it, as upon the heads of the victims.

3. When persons were ordained or set apart to some sacred offices, hands were laid upon them; as, for example, when Moses laid his hands upon the head of Joshua to ordain him his successor; or when the congregation or the seniors of the congregation of Israel laid their hands upon the heads of the Levites. See *Numb.* viii. 10—18. *Numb.* xxvii. 18—23.

4. Hands were laid by the Saviour and his apostles upon the sick to impart cures; and thus the imposition of hands continued the sign of impartation and communication in the commencement of the christian era.

5. The Holy Spirit, or certain gifts of the Holy Spirit, were also imparted by the imposition of hands during the apostolic age.

6. And, in the last place, ordinations to office, or consecration to a particular service were signified, on some occasions at least, by the imposition of hands. Thus the prophets or teachers in the congregation which was in Antioch laid their hands upon Paul and Barnabas, and thereby set them apart to the work to which God had called them. So much for the general history of the laying on of hands.

Instances diverse from all these may be found in the Jewish and Christian scriptures, but these are the chief. From all which it is plain, that the laying on of hands, in a religious sense, was a very common act amongst patriarchs, Jews, and christians, whenever religion required it.— And although we are not told in so many words that bishops were inaugurated or ordained by the imposition of hands, yet it is fairly to be learned from the letters to Timothy taken in connexion with the above sacred usages. Paul tells Timothy who was, and who was not, eligible to the episcopal office—advises to let the persons be well proved first, and cautions him against laying hands hastily upon any one; which phrase, taken in connexion with the whole premises, can mean, I think, nothing else than the ordination of bishops and deacons. It is worthy of remark, in this place, that persons invested with no office at all were employed in ordaining, by laying on of hands, persons to office. Thus "the laity," as antichrist calls them, were the first persons who ordained or inaugurated into office in the annals of the religious world. See *Numbers* viii. 9—18. It is also worthy of notice that persons of inferior office laid hands upon those who were to officiate in a higher capacity than they who ordained them. See *Acts* xiii. 1, 2.

After these examples of the common people laying hands upon the Jewish clergy, (properly called clergy, for they were the Lord's lot or portion,) after the teachers in Antioch laid hands upon the apostles Paul and Barnabas to ordain them to an apostolic service—I say, after these instances by divine appointment too, there ought not to be much controversy upon the question, Who may lay hands upon those now appointed to office. To what has been said it may be added, that if the apostles ordained the seven servants of the Jerusalem congregation; and if, as the historian Luke tells us, Paul and Barnabas on their tour ordained elders or bishops in every congregation, the conclusion is unavoidable, in my judgment, that the sign or symbol of inauguration, devotion, or consecration was the same. From the time that the common people ordained the Levites, from the time that Moses laid his hands upon Joshua, to the time that Titus ordained bishops in Crete, and down to the death of John the Apostle, there is no ground on which, or from which, to conclude any thing else than that the sign of ordination was the laying on of hands. But as I am about to write on church discipline, I will not be farther tedious to you at present.

You next request some farther illustrations of the work of an evangelist. Timothy did more than the work of an evangelist while in Ephesus. To "proclaim the word," or gospel, is the primary idea in the work of an evangelist; but Paul commanded him not only to proclaim the word, but also to read, exhort, and teach in public, as well as to reprove, rebuke, and entreat, with all long suffering and gentleness. Timothy, so far as he proclaimed the word, performed the work of an evangelist; so far as he read, taught, exhorted, and kept good order in the assembly, he performed the work of a bishop; and so far as he or Titus planted churches and set things in order which were wanting, they acted the part of apostles. In various capacities these men acted; for Paul employed them as his agents in the work to which he was called. They who have required any persons to do the works assigned to Timothy and Titus, have forgotten that no men stand in the same relations to the apostles and to the churches as that in which they stood. The apostles for a time were bishops, deacons, evangelists, and every thing else which the churches required; so were some persons whom they appointed to assist them. But in process of time the apostles gave into the hands of others all their offices except that of planting churches, in which they continued as long as they lived. When they appointed deacons, they performed those duties no more; when they appointed bishops, they attended on that

work no longer in that place; when they appointed general agents, they gave over all their offices in that district to them. But now we have, in a well-regulated christian community, persons for every office, whose duty and work it is to attend on their ministry or service, whatever it may be.

The primitive churches had messengers, both male and female, employed by them as exigencies required. A messenger of a church does any work which the church would and could do in the place where the messenger acts. He must always *represent the congregation*. If he carry twenty dollars from the congregation in New York to that in Columbus—when he comes before the church in Columbus, he appears there to do that which the church which sent him would have done had they been there in their individual capacity. He can represent any thing which they have done, or declare their mind on any thing on which they have declared their mind to him; but he cannot represent them in any thing else. If a church sends a person to declare the glad tidings to a people ignorant of them, to carry their contributions to those in need, to protest against the misdeeds of any individual person or community, or to do any other act or deed which religion or humanity requires, the person or persons so sent act as the messengers or representatives of the church sending them, and are to be received and treated as the congregation deserves which sent them. That this is fully in the import of the messengers of the primitive church, neither reason nor revelation will permit me to doubt. But for farther illustrations on this topic, I must refer you to my essays, yet to appear, on the *Restoration of the Ancient Order of Things*.

As for associations, conferences, conventions, &c. presuming to act under the sanctions of a divine warrant, or claiming to be a court of Jesus Christ, to decide on any matters of conscience, or to do any act or deed interfering with, or in opposition to, the perfect independence of each individual congregation, or at all legislating for the churches in any district of country—it is altogether foreign to the letter and spirit—to the precepts and examples—to the law and to the testimony of the christian books. But that two churches or twenty may agree to meet at any given time or place to join together to worship God in all instituted acts of social worship; and if they think we can do any more good by co-operating in any public measure than they could in their individual capacity, I know of no law or rule of the Great King prohibiting such meetings or such attempts to do good, or to enjoy good. And moreover it may be said, that not only is there no law or precept prohibitory (which is of itself inadequate evidence or authority in favor of any practice) but the general scope of the apostolic doctrine on doing good, and enjoying good, sanctions all that was claimed by the Mahoning meeting, congregation, association, convention, or whatever it may be called. Their meeting was almost entirely occupied in acts of religious worship, or in public edification —and their concurring to support one person for one year as their messenger to proclaim the word, and to strengthen the things that were ready to die—to labor every day in the word and teaching—was as voluntary as would be the giving of counsel to those erring from the path of safety—and has no other divine warrant than the commandments and precepts, which say, " As you have opportunity do good to all men;" or "Let every man seek his neighbor's edifi cation;" or, "As every man has received a gift, so let him impart:" or "Whatsoever things are benevolent, pursue," &c. &c. These, and a few hundred such sayings scattered over the pages of twenty apostolic epistles, are still the authority, direct and indirect, authorizing the Mahoning meeting to seek to do good in that one specified way.

In the essays on church discipline and ecclesiastical proceedings, the first of which you will see in the present No. we hope to make all these matters and things plain and consistent with all the grand principles taught in the Bible, and argued in this work.

Being much entertained and gratified with the spirit and scope of your communication, I must solicit the favor of a letter from you at any time or on any topic which you may choose. In the mean time I subscribe myself your brother in the hope of immortality.   EDITOR.

A Year's Labor.

"He that sows plentifully shall reap plentifully."

ELDER JOHN SECREST, concerning whose success in announcing the gospel, some remarks have been made in a former number of this work, on New Year's day last addressed to me a few lines, from which I learned that during the last year he had travelled about three thousand miles and delivered about six hundred discourses, from one to three hours long; and notwithstanding these mighty exertions he said he enjoyed good health and spirits. He did not keep any account of the numbers immersed in the preceding part of the year; but during the last six months of the year he had, with his own hands, immersed five hundred and thirty persons. Let those who pretend to be called by God, specially and supernaturally, to preach, "Go and do likewise," and report progress to me at the close of the year.

Quarterly Meeting.

WALTER SCOTT, who is now doing the work of an evangelist in the Mahoning Baptist Association informs me, per letter of the 4th ult. that he had made an experiment in preaching the ancient gospel for the ten days preceding the date of his letter. He states the effects as having been immediate and astonishing. No less than thirty having been immersed in that time. He says, "After having announced the gospel in the terms of the apostles, I have awaked the lyre of Israel, and sung forth the high songs of salvation to all who believe and are baptized, declaring a just and a merited damnation to all who disobey God; piping forth the terrors of the Lord, and congregating the rebellious from Cain to Judas, and from him to the resurrection of the dead. A quarterly meeting is to be holden at Fairfield, Columbiana county, on the first Friday of February."

No. 8.]   MARCH 3, 1828.

Attempt at a Restoration of the Ancient Order.

To the Church of Christ in New York.

STEPHEN-STREET, DUBLIN.

BELOVED BRETHREN—Your desire of communicating with the various societies throughout the world, (united in the bonds and profession of the faith of God and his Son Jesus Christ,) for the purpose of paying obedience to the commands of his written word, is worthy of imitation, and calls for the cheerful correspondence of all that have in view the same object. Should the Lord ever restore those enviable days, when the multitude of his disciples were of one heart and

mind, it is probable he will employ such means as those now resorted to by you. Alas! to human sight those days appear to be far distant. For though, by a comparison of our times with those that immediately preceded us, it would appear that Christ's ordinances have been brought to light as though a copy of the laws of his kingdom had lately been discovered buried in the ruins and hidden under the rubbish of antiquity; yet does it seem that an adequate understanding of his laws is a discovery still wanted, and the spirit of interpretation rather to be desired than presumed. Whilst most disciples profess and lament this their ignorance, few are deficient in confidence: and in our impatience at the dulness of others, we all seem to forget the tardiness of our own progress. You will probably, in reply to your letter, receive communications from many bodies of disciples in this country, some of whom, though meeting in the same city, are well known to each other as brethren in Christ Jesus. Many of these different bodies were once united in association; but discussions having arisen among them, not concerning the principle of obedience to God's word and the apostolic authority, but concerning the meaning and force of certain precepts which perhaps for years were the subject of their doubts, they settled at length, each in the confidence of his own interpretation, and esteeming all difference to be disunion, they divided. On the contrary, we who now address you hold that difference is not necessarily disunion, and therefore it is that we deem disciples of this day deficient in the spirit of the apostolic practice. That the apostles demanded implicit obedience to all their precepts without exception, we doubt not; and all disobedience must have been esteemed equivalent to a rejection of the authority deputed to them by Christ. But we cannot perceive that every misconstruction of an apostle's precept amounts to such a rejection. The servant who knows not his master's will may be distinguished from the servant who knows and disregards it; it is difficult, in many instances, to ascertain the difference, but surely the maxim is acknowledged by the Lord himself, and was acted on by him towards his disciples. That errors can be imagined which the Lord would not have borne with, we deny not; but that he did bear with errors, even after the plainest declarations, is most manifest. We doubt not, brethren, that all blindness, as to apostolic precepts, is chargeable on the folly and slowness of our hearts. The same folly and slowness of heart prevented the apostles from receiving many truths at the mouth of Jesus; but as their folly and slowness of heart was not indicative of a rejection of Christ, so neither in these days do we apprehend that the folly and slowness of professors to receive many truths in the apostolic records, is in all cases indicative of a rejection of their authority; and as the Lord bore with the apostles, we see not but his example was recorded for our imitation.

In the apostolic days all mistakes concerning their precepts must speedily have been brought to an issue; for their own explanation was not hard to be obtained; and after reference to them it would soon appear who were disobedient and who acknowledged their authority. Moreover, the practice of the various churches being then recently instituted, derived immediately from the apostles, and recorded in every place where disciples associated, there was not equal room for mistake among them as in these days. Will any man assert, that now, after the lapse of centuries of darkness, during which time antichrist has perplexed the meaning, perverted the language, mimicked the institutions, and obliterated the customs of the first churches; during which time the records of the apostles have slept for near two thousand years, and the very language of those records become almost hieroglyphic, and open to the access only of the learned; will any man, we say, consider this, and assert that diversity of opinion argues in all cases the same spirit of disobedience now as formerly? Do they who carry the principle of uniformity to the utmost degree of non-forbearance, do they doubt that a criminal blindness of heart obscures yet from their eyes much of the Lord's will concerning his church? And do they conceive that their present attainments are the measure of universal progress, and the criterion of faithfulness among all God's people? Therefore it is, brethren, that we of Stephen-street, in this city, hold it to be very possible for a faithful disciple of Christ to deny or to acknowledge the doctrine of baptism—the kiss of charity—the washing of the saints' feet—the anointing of the sick, and many other things which the word of God mentions. And therefore our union as a body depends upon two things—a profession of faith in Jesus Christ as the Saviour of sinners without works; and a recognition of the principle that the apostles were authorized by Christ to order the practice of his household. Where the sentiments or conduct of a professor palpably militate against the former of these principles, he would be removed from among us; where palpably against the latter, he could not be admitted a member of our association. We doubt not but there may be, and are, many servants of God in associations which we deem to be constituted chiefly of unbelievers, and ordered by the establishments of human authority. With such professors of the faith we scruple not to converse as believers; joining with them in prayer, where believers should happen to meet for conversations on the scriptures; while they could form no part of our assembly, which has associated for the express purpose of studying and conforming with the apostolic precept. We have dwelt on this subject, brethren, at some length, because it is of the very last importance to the churches of God throughout the world. At the same time we confess that we hold these sentiments with fear and trembling, lest peradventure they be opposed to the will of God. And we are more particularly attentive to the arguments of those associations who differ in this matter from us, because they appear to be almost the only professors of a pure and unadulterated gospel, and because their walk in life is, with the exception of such instances as must have occurred occasionally in the first churches, becoming the doctrine which they profess.

The order of our worship wherein we do not deem preciseness to be matter of importance, is nearly the same as your own. We have as yet no elders, though we much lament the want of, and desire the supply of them. We are not fully agreed on the qualifications necessary for an elder. Some conceive that a man twice married is disqualified for the office; others, that an elder must have children, the well regulating of his family being, in their opinion, the criterion of his ability to rule in the household of Christ. Of the nature of the deacon's office we are very undecided in opinion. Many of us are baptized and many not. We do not understand that there was such an ordinance as a love feast among the first disciples, though we doubt not that their hospitality was much evinced in open-ing their houses to the brethren, and especially to the poor. Would that we were given to follow their example more affectionately than we are. Few, if any of us, hold the kiss of charity to be an ordinance, though many of us have great doubt on the subject. The washing of the saints' feet, we, for the most part, hold to be an expression synonymous with showing hospitality, and by no means a form or ordinance to be observed in any other sense. As to our intercourse with the world, and the other things wherein you have intimated to us your practice, it corresponds with our own sentiments. We cannot pass by one observation of your letter concerning the love feast without remark: " This (you say) not appearing to be of the same strict obligation, is made to give way to circumstances." We hold that every obligation is strict in the highest sense of the word, and that no one command is less obligatory on a disciple than another. Perhaps we have mistaken your meaning on this point; if so, you will not be offended at the remark. Indeed we trust and feel confident that you will receive these few observations as we have received yours, without any offence, but with affectionate consideration of your concern for the spiritual welfare of brethren. We must also make one other remark, which perhaps may show that we have also mistaken your meaning. We allude to the confession of one to be received into fellowship. We should require more than a confession that Jesus is the Christ; we are sure that every man calling himself a christian would make such a confession. We should therefore inquire, What such a person meant by that confession, and if we found that he meant no more than that Christ was the Son of God, we should not receive him; but if he appeared to be acquainted with the meaning of the word Christ, and with the nature of his great salvation, whereby forgiveness is revealed to the most deplorably guilty and spiritually wretched, through belief in his name alone, without works, or even the help of a good thought or intention to co-operate in the matter of salvation, we should receive him, and we should receive no man who held any other sentiment.

The church at present consists of about a hundred. We have been associated eight years.

And now, brethren, we commend you to the grace of God, who is able through his Holy Spirit to build you up, and keep that which we have committed to him, even the salvation of our souls to the last day, when we hope to meet you and to join with you in praising him where all obscurities will be removed, and where there will be no need of the sun, neither of the moon, for the glory of God shall enlighten us, and the Lamb shall be the light. Now to God the only wise, be glory through Jesus Christ for ever.

Signed in behalf of the church,

JOHN HOSKINS,
EDWARD COOKE.

June 24, 1818.

Ancient Gospel.—No. III.
Immersion.

1. THAT the apostles addressed christians as having their sins forgiven, was fully proved in our last. 2. That frequent allusions to baptism in the apostolic epistles represent it as an ablution or purification from sins, was demonstrated. And 3. That it is expressly said, and explicitly taught in the New Testament that God forgives men's sins in the act of immersion, was also attempted to be shown. In this we had advanced so far as to state that when Peter, to whom was commit-

ted the keys of the kingdom of heaven, opened that kingdom to the Jews on Pentecost, he opened it by an authoritative annunciation of the remission of sins through immersion into the faith of Jesus. When asked by thousands what they should do to escape the impending vengeance, and to obtain forgiveness for their transgressions, he said, "Reform," or, as in the common version, "repent and be immersed every one of you for the remission of your sins, and you shall receive the gift of the Holy Spirit." When he commanded them to be immersed in the name of the Lord, or by the authority of the Lord, into the name of the Lord, it was for some end, and that end or object was stated so explicitly as to authorize us to conclude our last essay with the declaration of one fact of immense meaning—viz. That the first three thousand persons that were immersed after the ascension of Jesus Christ into heaven were immersed for the remission of their sins. When any action is performed for any purpose the purpose is gained, provided that there is an established connexion between that which is done, and the purpose for which it is done. This must be the case always when infallible wisdom and perfect benevolence appoint the action and the end. The laws of grace are as sure in their operation, and as certain in their effects, as the laws of nature. When I put my finger into the fire, by a law of nature, it is burned: and just as certainly am I forgiven of all my trespasses, by a law of grace, when in faith I am immersed in water into the name of the Lord Jesus. This is the apostles' doctrine, and to all believers in revelation, this being proved, the above assertion is proved. To those who are aware of the use and importance of being explicit in the promulgation of law, or in the commencement of any institution, it will at once appear that had not christian immersion been designed primarily for the remission of sins, the apostles committed a most injurious error in giving birth to the idea, and in raising the expectation of an inquisitive audience to look for the remission of sins by or through immersion into the name of the Lord Jesus. Suppose, for example, when these three thousand were afterwards dispersed through the community, as many of them were to a great distance from Jerusalem, and that one or all of them had been asked, for what they had been immersed on the day of Pentecost; what answer could they have given but "for the remission of their sins?" If they believed either the words of Peter or their own experience they could not otherwise respond. Had not this been the true meaning of immersion, the apostles laid the foundation for universal imposition and deception, by thus commencing the administration of the reign of heaven. If ever any practice demanded circumspection in the institution and explanation of it, this one did; and if ever any person or persons were qualified so to do, these persons were. So that the inference is inevitable that the apostle meant what he expressed, and that in the act of immersion the remission of sins was bestowed.

That such was the universally received sense of immersion amongst the teachers and preachers of christianity, is most certain from express declaration and incident. For example: When Paul was immersed, it was declared and understood by the parties that all his previous sins were washed away in the act of immersion. The person sent to immerse him was sent expressly by heaven—Ananias said to him, "Arise and be immersed, and wash away your sins, calling upon the Lord." He obeyed and was im-

mersed, and his sins were washed away. Had any person met Paul and Ananias when on their way to the water, and asked Paul for what was he going to be immersed; what answer could he have given, if he believed the words of Ananias, other than, I am going to be immersed for the purpose of washing away my sins? Or had he been accosted on his return from the water, and requested to tell what benefit he had received through or by the immersion, what answer could he have given other than, I have washed away my sins? I argue, and who can argue otherwise? that whatever immersion was to Paul, it is the same to every person, man, woman and child; barbarian, Scythian; bondman or freeman, who has the same faith Paul had when Ananias immersed him.

What made the Eunuch go on his way rejoicing? Was it because he had some difficult texts explained? Or was it because he had some distant hope or remote prospect of enjoying pardon and acceptance after death, or after the lapse of certain years of travail and of trial? No, indeed; he had found what thousands before him had experienced, peace with God, from a conviction that his sins had been actually forgiven in the act of immersion. Indeed the preaching of all the apostles, as well as all their writings, embrace this as a fact never to be called into question. And it is impossible for us to understand many things which they have said upon other subjects unless we understand them aright upon this one. This is a beautiful and well-defined stripe which runs through the whole evangelical web. This authorized John the apostle when he wrote to the least child in the christian church, to say, Thy sins are forgiven thee—"I write to you, little children, because your sins have been forgiven you for or through his name." This authorized Peter to say, "Immersion does now save us; not the putting off the filth of the flesh in the water; but the answer of a good conscience, through the rising of Christ"—denoted in our rising with him in immersion. Hence, says Paul, "If, indeed, you are risen with Christ, (as you say you were both buried and raised with him)—if then you be risen with Christ, seek the things which are above, where Christ sits at the right hand of God."

Paul, in the sixth chapter of his letter to the Romans fitly illustrates the practical uses of this doctrine. He argues that as the disciples had died by sin, and were buried in water, in consequence of having died by sin; and as they had been raised to a new life out of the grave of water in which they had been interred, so they were as cleansed in conscience to live a new life. The argument for a new life is therefore drawn from the fact of a death by sin, of a burial and a resurrection with Christ, in this institution; and as "he that is dead is freed from sin," can sin no more, so he that is immersed is freed from the guilt and dominion of sin; because he is, after his metaphorical resurrection, in or under a new dominion. "Sin, says the apostle, shall not lord it over you, for you are not under law, but under favor."

Still it is possible for persons to sin under favor, and should they be deceived into transgression after they have been purified from their old sins, through confession, reformation, and petition, the blood of Christ will cleanse them from this also. The most effectual argument which Paul and John could urge upon christians to abstain from sin, was drawn from the love of God exhibited in the gift of his Son, and from the fact that they had been pardoned in baptism, and were under favor and not under a law which kept up a remembrance of sin. Some weak and erroneous philosophers have argued that to guard against a licentious tendency it is best not to make the forgiveness of sins a matter too cheap. They who found their plea either upon the cheapness or dearness of pardon, reason not as christians but as men who never knew the love of God. No heart that has felt the sovereign charms of that 'ove can from a sense of its forgiving favor be induced to guard less against every appearance of evil. But this is only by the way and not exactly in the path now before us.

Let us now look back. It has been shewn that the Apostle Paul taught that immersion was the bath of regeneration. Now if a person can be regenerated and not forgiven; if he can have a pure heart, and a guilty conscience at one and the same time—then is my reasoning erroneous, and my conclusions false. But if immersion is the bath of regeneration, and if a pure heart must have a good conscience, as Paul teaches, then is my reasoning correct, and my conclusions to be relied on. "The end of the commandment, or charge, or gospel, is, Love out of a pure heart, and a good conscience, and a faith unfeigned." This is the philosophy of Paul. But why reason to prove that for which we have a broad precept, an explicit promise, unequivocal precedents, and apostolic reasoning? Faith is not more evidently connected with immersion, than is immersion with the forgiveness of sins. In the ancient gospel, it was first a belief in Jesus; next immersion; then forgiveness; then peace with God; then joy in the Holy Spirit. Thus it stood in the order of nature; though the effects of pardon, peace, and joy, appeared in many instances to be simultaneous. But I must reserve something for another essay.　　　EDITOR.

KING AND QUEEN, 4TH JANUARY, 1828.
Brother Campbell,—

DEAR SIR,—AMIDST the numerous sources of pleasure and pain to the mind, the attainment of truth, seems so certainly to produce one or the other of these effects, as to become worthy of our pursuit upon all subjects particularly connected with our well-being. Many, and various circumstances tend, however, to increase or diminish our enjoyment from this source, and unavoidably, in many instances, our inquiries become productive, in temporal matters, of disappointment and unhappiness, and in spiritual concerns, the investigation of the natural and moral relation existing between other beings and ourselves, of the most acute sorrow. And we discover, that in proportion to the value or practical utility of any subject, to ourselves, or more remotely to others, or its pernicious operation upon us or them, will be the degree of enjoyment, or an opposite sensation, experienced in our own minds as the result of manifest truth on such subjects. Of all the subjects that have, at any time, engaged the studious care and researches of man, religion stands pre-eminent. The best form of civil government, and through such, the consequent amelioration of the present condition of the human family, is a subject, though old, still worthy the laborious study of the most comprehensive, philanthropic, and discerning mind;—the arts, sciences, and literature, exhibit subjects that require and merit the most profound attention of genius—ascending, intuitively and by the aid of science, amidst the starry hosts, and with a giant grasp seizing upon those objects far removed from common vision and ability, and embracing, with delight, those resistless principles that emanate from the mind of Jehovah for the government of the Universe, is a theme, inviting to the most exalted favorites of knowledge. But what are all these, and the result of that truth which they earnestly seek, when found, in comparison with the religion which Jesus of Nazareth has introduced into the world! By this, we are taught to know ourselves—to know God the maker of all—Jesus who saves us—our duty as individuals to our God, and those mutual, social relations that bind, and should ever endear us to each other, as members of a common family. This religion, unfolds to the eye of faith, scenes too remote, and could they be seen, too dazzling for the pleasure or discrimination of the natural eye. Though millions have explored, none but the Sun of Righteousness has illuminated the dreary valley and shadow of death—though millions have been bound by the narrow limits of the grave, till Christ came, none had burst the bars of death—though thousands had dreamed of future glory, none but Emanuel has brought immortality and life to light! All these inexpressibly valuable blessings, have been brought into being through the gospel of the blessed Saviour, which, in its own comprehensive and emphatic language, "is truth." If through the grace of God we have arrived at the knowledge of this principle, in reference to heavenly things, happy are we! Then may we with an apostle say, "Having been regenerated, not of corruptible seed, but of incorruptible, through the word of the living God which remains forever; all flesh is as grass, and all the glory of man as the flower of grass—the grass withers, and the flower of it falls down; but the word of the Lord endures forever."

The word of God, as a complete system, is most correctly designated by way of a peculiar characteristic, as truth; consequently, its numerous parts, as a revelation, are equally entitled to this distinction. The visions or prophecies—their accomplishment—and the teaching of Jesus and his apostles, are equally emanations from the divine mind—equally true, and adapted to all the designs of the author of truth. But among a multiplicity of subjects upon which the divine will has been expressed, some are more easy of conception, and some, when understood, more readily received than others. While some portions of the sacred record strike every enlightened mind with a unity of aspect, many other portions seem to convey, either no distinct meaning, or a variety of interpretations. Reasons are assignable for this diversity of conclusion from the same premises; but we believe that the former diversity of gifts and operations of the Spirit, or its present guidance, cannot fairly be included among the number. Natural differences between men; education; prejudices growing out of sectarianism; remaining darkness, from a want of a more perfect image of Jesus in the heart; and an apathy still indulged in relation to the existence of those causes, connected with an inordinate love of the world, are probably to be recognized among the reasons of that distraction and discordance of sentiment, that seriously disturb the proper harmony of the christian body.

Now it is with an eye to some of these differences of opinion, and to that unity of spirit and action, and for the diffusion of that truth which imparts peace to the mind of its recipients, which only, can bring about the happy period, when the lion and the lamb shall lie down together, that I now take the liberty of addressing you. Though I cannot say that I have read your works with unmingled emotions of pleasure, (there being a few points upon which I could desire to hear you farther, more explicitly,) yet, I feel grateful to the "giver of every good gift," so far as I am individually concerned, that the day in which I live should produce even one able advocate of that "order" of things, which I am induced most confidently to believe, both from the present state of man, especially the christian community, and the word of God, must again be restored. I feel no disposition to compliment you improperly as a man, whether good, bad, or great, for it would be a vain service; nor to flatter you, because that would be not only personally insulting to you, but highly inimical on my own part. My design is to bear testimony in the simplicity of candor, to the utility of those labors, which, I trust, at no very distant day, will be found to have been one of those tributary streams, that will make glad the city of God, when the children of the Great King will sit together in heavenly places, and in the solemnity, joy, and unity of spiritual devotion and intercourse, receive the droppings of the sanctuary.

Knowing your unwavering objections to questions of any kind, merely sectarian, and admitting your discretion to adhere to the plan that you consider best adapted to effect your designs, I shall not put you to the trouble of refusing an answer to an inquiry of that sort.

The understanding and proper application of the word of God, and the manifestation of a cheerful obedience thereto, seem to constitute the proper existence of the christian religion in the heart of man. And in proportion to the prevalence of these essentials will christianity be conspicuous or depressed. It is of great importance, then, that we understand the things written: otherwise our applications will be improper, and our obedience, rather the gratification of our own feelings, than the fulfilment of divine institutions.

Several questions of interest have occurred to me; but I shall propose only two at present.

What are we to understand from, and to what description of persons or character, are we to apply the language of the apostle in the seventh chapter of Romans?

Is the example of the Saviour, as given in the washing of feet, of literal obligation throughout all ages, upon all disciples; (See 1st Tim. v. 10.) or was it limited to those "sent," and confined to that age?

A word, in conclusion, to our baptist brethren: I feel confident that every one who has sought diligently the spirit of his Master, has contemplated, with pain, the schisms that mar the harmony of christians, and deform, in a great degree, the most lovely as well as the most glorious system the world ever saw, and with anxious desires not unfrequently implores the mercy of God in bestowing peace upon Israel. The language of scripture itself, sometimes affords a latitude of interpretation, that proves inimical in the hands of man, to the harmonious propagation of truth. As an instance of this sort, we need only direct your attention to the word *baptize*. Different acceptations of this term, lead into very different applications of water, and consequent doubt, in numerous instances, if nothing more, whether all those various actions should be considered as acts of obedience. And among those who dissent from the "one immersion," and contend for a wider range of application, it has become a matter of common inquiry by those who are not present when they have administered this ordinance, "What action was employed?" Now, though it be known what action *we* observe in the use of the ordinance, would it not still be better for us to drop, as far as possible, the use of the word which has created so much disturbance? The term immersion is of very ready expression and application, and seems to stand fairly justified by many of the most eminent Paido-baptist critics. It is highly probable that no very immediate effects of a favorable kind will be thus produced; yet time, and the approbation of God, if he should be pleased to confer it upon what seems to be a proper use of his word with proper motives, may ultimately contribute to bring about a union both in language and action. We can at least go on our way in "one faith, one Lord, one immersion," and endeavor, for the sake of the truth, of the approbation of our Master, and of that crown that awaits us, to obey him in all things.

AMOS.

Brother Amos,

DEAR SIR—THE passage in the "Epistle to the Romans," to which you refer, is one of no ordinary importance, and is thought very generally to be one of no very easy interpretation. I find the following interpretation to be the most in unison with the apostle's design, and to be liable to no serious objection. (See New Translation; 1st ed. p. 291.) Paul in his own person represents the Jew from the days of Abraham down to his own conversion. "Where there is no law reaching to the conscience, and taking cognizance of our thoughts, we must be ignorant of sin. For even strong desire I could not have known to be sin, unless the law had said, Thou shalt not covet." For without this knowledge sin was dead; that is, gave me no uneasiness; but under the restraints which the law imposed, it wrought effectually in me all strong desire. Now the fact is, that before the law was given in the days of Abraham, Isaac, and Jacob, I was alive without law, I never felt myself subject to death, for where no law is there is no transgression. But when the law was given, or when the commandment came from Mount Sinai, sin which was dead in that state, revived or came to life, and from the day of the entrance of the law death was inflicted upon us Jews in a way of which there was no example before the promulgation of law. For from the night in which the destroying angel passed through the houses of the Egyptians, until the law was promulged, not an Israelite died; but no sooner was the law given than every transgression and disobedience received a just recompense of reward—and all the way to Canaan death reigned through my transgression of positive law. So that the commandment which was to have been a rule and guide to the enjoyment of this life, I found to lead to death. "Besides is it obvious," says he, "that the law is *spiritual*, that is, has respect not only to the outward actions, but in some of its precepts reaches to the thoughts—but the people, of which I am one, to whom that law was given, were a fleshly people, enslaved to appetite.—Hence the conflict betwixt conscience and inclination. We, or I Paul, could not but approve the law in our minds; and yet we were by passion and appetite doing the things which we could not incline to do in our minds enlightened by law. So that it was not owing to any defect in the law, nor in my perceptions and approbation of it mentally, but in the inclinations and propensities to which a human being in this present state is unavoidably subjected—that I failed in finding happiness, peace, or comfort under the law.

In what wretched condition, then, were we Jews under this law; and do you ask how we are, or could be delivered from that state of sin and condemnation? I will tell you; through Jesus Christ our Lord, under whom we have no condemnation; for we are under him and not under law.

These are, my dear sir, but a few hints, paraphrastically, submitted rather as worthy of examination, than of hasty adoption. On this plan, however, I have no doubt, but every word and sentence in the seventh chapter of the Romans can be well and fully expounded. I have confounded the first person with the third on purpose to elicit inquiry and to make this view more forcible. And had I leisure and room to paraphrase the whole paragraph, and to argue the whole merits of it, I think it might be rendered more than plausible. But a hint to the wise is sufficient.

I must, being exceedingly embarrassed for time and room at present, refer you for an answer to your other query, to vol. 3, page 223.

I have heard many wicked professors of christianity justify themselves by what they called Paul's experience as a christian. Paul, said they, was like us—the evil that he hated he did, and the good that he loved he did not; and thus they flattered themselves their experience would lose nothing in this respect on a comparison with Paul's. Many, however, thus interpret the scripture to their own destruction. May you enjoy the clear and glorious light of life forever.

I had, in my haste, forgot to mention that your remarks on the use of the words *immerse* and *immersion*, in the practice of christians, when attending upon this sacred institution, are certainly worthy of the attention of all who wish the good of Zion. I have for a considerable time been wont to say on such occasions, "*I immerse thee into the name,*" &c. And, indeed, in speaking to an English audience, I would concur with you that we should always use such language as is explicit, intelligible, and conducive to harmony. Some other excellent hints in your letter I could wish were universally regarded.　　　EDITOR.

Letter to Bishop Semple.—No. I.
BETHANY, Va. Feb. 14, 1828.

Brother Semple,

DEAR SIR—THE love I bear to all good men constrains me to address you as a christian brother, although you may scarcely deem me worthy of such a compellation. But your being my christian brother depends not upon the will of the flesh, nor upon the will of man, but upon a higher and more exalted consideration. If you are a member of the family of God, (and few doubt it,) and if I should be recognized by the Great and Good Master as of the houschold of faith, our brotherhood is fixed as firm as the foundation of the earth, although it may not be indisputably evident to all who are acquainted with our standing upon the earth. But until I am proscribed by some new statute, I will claim my rights under an old statute of *the reign of grace* 49.

I love all christians, of whatever name; and if there is any diversity in my affection, it is predicated upon, or rather graduated by, the scale of their comparative conformity to the will of my Sovereign. I do profess, before heaven and earth, to be a christian. I will claim this title, and defend it by that course of behaviour which

I think my Master requires. This is the sole cause of my departure from the customs of my baptist brethren in those items, whenever they have departed from the customs of those elder brethren, the primitive christians. If I could have been satisfied in my conscience with that course which the populars pursue I would have greatly preferred it; but I cannot. For I remember that the Judge once taught, "Whosoever shall break one of the least of these commandments, and shall teach men so, shall be called the *least* in the kingdom of Heaven; but whosoever shall do and teach them, shall be called *great* in the kingdom of Heaven."

You and some of my other brethren represent my views as "chimeras." Well, then, I, and thousands say, Prove them to be such. Nay, you say, this is not necessary; it is enough to call them "chimeras." Such is the meaning of your conduct. Now, brother Semple, yourself and some two or three other men of high standing have confirmed me more in the truth and reality of my views than all my other opponents. And if you ask me, How? I am prepared to tell you. Many men of very slender parts, and as slender attainments, have opposed me. I soon found their weakness; but my victory over them I was sometimes afraid to attribute to my cause. I had no assurance from their failure that it was owing to the reality of the views I entertained, but perhaps owing to their incapacity. But when I have elicited the notice of some of our greatest and best men, and have heard them call my sentiments, in derision, by some obnoxious name —I say, when I have seen them willing to oppose me, and actually engaged in the opposition so far as to bespatter my reputation with foul and reproachful epithets; and when called to the proof, beg to be excused; I am constrained to feel myself panoplied with victorious truth, and to rejoice in its mighty power.

I do assure you, brother Semple, that I never felt more strong in the faith that the popular systems cannot be defended, than since I have seen you draw your sword, and before it was quite unsheathed, return it to its scabbard. Had you never lifted either your tongue or your pen against my "chimeras," I should not have known how invincible they appear; but, my dear sir, since I have seen the result, I am become as bold as a lion. Brother Brantley, of the "Star," has also set to his seal that I am "more than half right." He gave publicity to your two letters, and in the greatness of his admiration of the weight of your name, either forgot or feared to look into the argument of your two epistles. At all events, to this day he has not dared to let his readers see my address to you. He has been nibbling at some spirit or ghost, which he calls the "Spirit of the Reformers," and yet he dare not let the phantom shew its face in one corner of his imperial sheet. But under the light of a "Columbian Star," it is not to be expected that his vision can be so clear as those who enjoy the mid-day sun. Just think, brother Semple, how I must feel with these facts before me: neither the Presbyterian Luminary, Recorder, &c. neither the Baptist Recorder, Christian Secretary and Register, &c. not even "the Star that on Columbia shone," has yet dared to give to their readers my defence against their allegations, or to publish my defence against the charges to which they have given currency. Had they always been silent, I should never have thought my arguments so triumphant. But in their zeal to fight for their creeds, they showed that the fault was not in their volitions if I was not defeated. Their timidity, (for so I must call it until otherwise manifest,) has confirmed me in the truth and certainty of the sentiments exhibited in this work. Some may call this boasting, and thereby traduce "the manner of spirit" of which I am; but, my dear sir, I only express the genuine feelings and results which your conduct, and that of other great and good men have produced.

I would not, brother Semple, hurt your feelings for any personal consideration that would not affect my standing in the sight of Heaven. I do really feel tenderly for the awkward predicament in which the temerity of Dr. Noel placed you. He wanted your name, but deprecated your arguments against me. The former he coveted—but he trembled for the consequence of your attempt to argue the question at issue. He dragged you out. Your letters to him shew that you lacked confidence in yourself, as well as disliked to be made a mere accuser. I think your conduct here was rather imprudent than unchristian, especially as you knew what adroitness and good management distinguished the reputation of Dr. Noel. He knows as well how to economize his resources in argument, and to make as large a per cent. per annum, from a small capital, as any other Doctor of Divinity, Baptist or Paido-Baptist, in the fertile state of Kentucky. When brother Brantley, of the "Star" was giving me a lesson upon the manner of spirit of the reformers, he might have been so liberal and philanthropic as to have bestowed a word of admonition to the spirit of Aleph or of Dr. Noel, which most certainly was to have been expected: for in censuring the spirit of the reformers, he ought to have contrasted it with a few specimens of the excellent spirit of the opposers of reformation. But these little specks in our great and good men, like the spots in the sun, only serve to brighten their general character, and serve as foils to increase the lustre of their reputation.

But to return to the subject before us: Brother Semple, your charges and censures are, and were known both to yourself and your friends, to have some weight, and were intended to be a check to the progress of the sentiments inculcated in the Christian Baptist. You certainly consider them of much, or of considerable weight, when you were content merely to state them upon your personal credit. Your pretended friends, who drew them from you, thought so too. Now the question with me has been, What should I do? Shall I rebut these assertions, or shall I suffer the reputation of the wise and good to be every where urged as an *argumentum ad modestiam*, or as an argument to silence all farther inquiry and research. After much serious deliberation on this question, and after waiting for months to see what you would do of justice to me, yourself, and the cause; and having at length ascertained that you have, *sine die*, declined any other argumentation of the topics at issue than that contained in your two letters—I am resolved what to do.

I will tell you, then, that I am about to make as much as possible of what light you have thrown upon the controversy, by a most minute analysis of your two letters to Dr. Noel. Seeing you will vouchsafe us no other means of being set to rights and converted from the error of our way than these two letters, I am resolved to examine them, *ad unguem*, that I may see and exhibit all their logic and scriptural authority. This I shall do without a single reflection upon yourself as a man, a scholar, or a christian.

Nothing which I have yet seen can induce me to doubt of the ultimate triumph of the distinguishing sentiments expressed in this work. All wise and good men expect a millennium, or a period of great happiness upon earth. They all argue that greater light than that hitherto possessed will be universally enjoyed. They do not merely expect a universal subjugation of all nations, kindreds, and tongues, to the Lord Jesus: they do not merely expect a state of harmony, perfect peace and union among all the citizens of heaven; but they look for a vast accumulation of light and knowledge, religious, moral, and political. They do not, however, expect a new Bible or any new revelation of the Spirit, but only a more clear and comprehensive knowledge of the sacred writings which we now enjoy. This belief and expectation of all wise and good men, is unequivocally declarative of the conviction that the scriptures are not now generally understood, and that there are new discoveries of the true and genuine meaning of these sacred records yet to be made. The misfortune is, that while all sects and sectaries make similar acknowledgements, no one supposes that himself or his people have any advances to make. The Baptist thinks that all the world will be Baptists in the Millennium, and therefore supposes that the Paido-Baptist sects will make great advances in knowledge before they can come up to the light which he enjoys. The Presbyterian expects that all the world will be Presbyterians in the Millennium, and consequently that many advances by all the sects must be made in the science of church government. The Methodist supposes that in the Millennium all the world will be Methodists, and anticipates the day when one great conference of profound radicals will deliberate for the four quarters of the world. Thus it is that all hold fast their errors, never suspecting that they have any thing to cast away; and calculating that all others must come up to their standard if ever they enjoy the Millennial felicity. Thus every sect puts reformation and reformers from among them. Like some good hearers in our polite congregations, each suspects the parson means some lady or gentleman other than himself—and kindly and politely thanks the parson for his benevolence, and invites his neighbor to take a slice.

Amongst those who admit that they have some things which they ought not to have, there seems to be a reluctance to begin to cast any thing off, lest the other sects would gain, or themselves lose something thereby. Many cannot humble themselves so far as to admit that any thing they have held or taught has been wrong. And so it comes to pass, that if we are not getting farther from the commandments and institutions of the Lord and Saviour, we are not getting any nigher. The greatest paradox to my mind in my moral horizon is this: How any man can love our Lord and Saviour Jesus Christ supremely, (and if he does not he is to be *anathema maranatha*,) and yet be indifferent about knowing or doing any thing he has commanded. For my part I must confess that if my orbit has been eccentric—if my career hitherto has been marked with any eccentricities, the cause is, my fear of offending the great Lawgiver, and my desire to do his will. In this I am now, as I have been for years, immoveable; and although I should be opposed all the days of my life by some of the wise and good, as well as by the ignorant and evil, I must persevere. Always open to conviction, but never to be silenced by detraction, defamation, nor by the mere array of a confederation of great and illustrious names. I have been too long acquainted with great and good men to stand in awe of their decisions. I know too that many men can make good bargains, and purchase reputation at a very low price. None of these remarks, brother Semple, are, in my judgment, applicable to you, but they are to many whose influence may be felt by other great men. I have been just writing a preface to a series of letters to be addressed to yourself on the contents of your correspondence with Dr. Noel, so far as that correspondence is before the public. It is now public property, and as such I claim my right to a share in its benefits. I am always glad to hear from you, and any thing you may have to say by way of amendment, correction, or explanation, on this or any other epistle addressed to you in this work, I assure you it will give me great pleasure to insert it in full; and believe me to be, most unfeignedly, the devoted servant of the common Saviour, in hope of eternal life.

A. CAMPBELL.

Soliloquy.—No. I.

MEDITATION is a species of soliloquy, inasmuch as when we meditate or reflect, especially on serious subjects, we rather converse with ourselves. Some persons, when deeply engaged in meditation, talk aloud, and not unfrequently argue and debate with themselves. Thus I have, when alone, frequently found myself carrying on a dialogue betwixt myself and some personified opinion, virtue, vice, or opposing interest. Some of these soliloquys I could have wished to have had written down immediately on coming to a close, for in them I have sometimes had the best views of things, and heard the strongest arguments, *pro* and *con*, on some subject of importance. A few I have penned down, and may now and then submit one to the examination of my readers. The following brief soliloquy originated from a temptation to be on the strong side:—

How happy are they who sail with wind and tide down the stream of popular esteem, having the banks of the stream on which they are embarked lined with admiring crowds, waving their hats and bowing their heads in sign of approbation and admiration. How tranquilly they glide along. When the sun shines and all is calm, how easy and happy their voyage. When storms arise, they betake themselves to the shore, and find themselves safe and happy in the caresses of admiring thousands. How enviable they! Who would not desire and seek their happy lot. Contrast it with that of yonder small company in a little bark, toiling against wind and current, ascending the rapid stream of vulgar applause. How imperceptible their advances.—After whole nights and days of toilsome rowing, they appear not to have distanced the shadow of a man of tall stature. No cheers nor congratulations from the spectators who chance to cast an eye upon them from the bank, except now and then a solitary "God speed" from some obscure one perched upon some rock or island, who has himself been buffeted with hardships.

Such was the prospect before me while I viewed the landscape with the wrong end of the telescope next my eye; but all of a sudden I turned the other end, and strange indeed was the change in the scenery. I now could read the inscription on the colors of the descending barge and that on the ascending skiff. I could see all devoted to present happiness, and those

too who sought happiness in both worlds, on the side of those descending, but not one of the admirers of their course, nor of those embarked on that voyage, had yet died. I looked up the stream, and found, from the inscription and other hieroglyphics upon the skiff, that their destiny was not to any port on earth, and that their eye was fixed upon some invisible and distant good, of such charms as to make them sing and triumph at every pull they gave the oar. A small company of the living and all that had ever died looked upon them either with perfect complacency—with a wishful, or an envious eye. In presenting the two rival courses of the whole human race thus to the eye of my mind, I could better appreciate the wisdom and happiness which distinguish the respective courses of the sons of men. But am I not, said I, thus confounding my own reflections with a descriptive and symbolic representation of things addressed to the consideration of others? True, it appears so. But if I gain my end this way more readily, what is the difference?

O my soul, do you not know that every good intention of yours, and every good effort of yours, were it only to subdue one evil inclination, is witnessed with admiration by all the excellent that ever lived. Do you not remember that the Saviour said there is joy in heaven over one reforming sinner, and even too amongst the angels of God; and can you think that one good deed of yours is viewed with indifference by any of the exalted dignitaries of the heavens! When you make one righteous effort to promote goodness in yourself, or in any human being, know that every good man on earth approves your course, and is upon your side; yes, and all the spirits of the dead. The wicked spirits know that you are wise, and cannot but approve your way; and all the holy and happy from righteous Abel, look down upon you with delight, and congratulate you on every advance you can make in goodness. Stronger and more numerous are those upon your side than they that are on the side of your opposers—When you are tempted to consult your reputation and your worldly advancement amongst men, O reflect how little they can do for you, and how much against your happiness. Can they soothe your troubles, can they heal your wounds, can they remove your fears, or tranquilize your agitations? No, no—full well you might know, from your past experience, how little they can do for you. When they once smiled upon you and congratulated you, were not your acts foolish, and did not the very deeds for which they praised you give you pain? Have you not found yourself distressed beyond the reach of mortal power and earthborn remedies to relieve; and will you now, when God has smiled upon you, pay your homage to human adulation, and seek to please the proud and the vain who cannot bless you? No, my soul, you cannot thus sin against your own felicity. Will it not be more than a reward for all privations and affronts in the way of goodness and self-denied obedience, to reflect how all the good and wise in Heaven's estimation have toiled with you, and now approbate your progress; and when you struggle with allurements, they all with intense interest await the issue, and are ready to hail you with triumphant joy as victor. Be assured, then, in all your struggles in behalf of truth and goodness, that every just man upon earth, every happy spirit in the invisible world, every angel in heaven, and what is more than all, your Redeemer and your Heavenly Father, are all upon your side, and ready to put the incorruptible crown upon your head, and to greet you with a hearty welcome, saying, Well done, you good and faithful servant. Let these reflections cause you never to despond amidst difficulties; never to faint in adversity; never to yield to temptation; never to seek the praise of men at the risque of forfeiting the praise of God. Remember that that day hastens with every pulse, when you would rather have the smiles of your Lord and Saviour, when you would rather be approved by him, than to be hailed by an admiring world as the paragon of every worldly excellence, as the sovereign arbiter of all the crowns and thrones that mortals ever coveted. Think, O think, how many smiles attest your conquests, and how many eyes with sadness would behold your discomfiture in this glorious struggle.—Fired by these considerations, the weak side becomes the stronger, and it is easy to burst through all the restraints which worldly pride and worldly policy would throw as obstacles in your way. "Remember Lot's wife."

EDITOR.

A Restoration of the Ancient Order of Things. No. XXIII.

The Church.

"Let all things be done decently and in order," is a favorite saying, though seldom regarded with suitable respect by those who are wont to be charmed with the sound of the words. The two extremes in all associations, as respects government or rule, are despotism and anarchy. In some religious establishments there is, on the part of the rulers, an unrelenting and absolute tyranny, and on the part of the ruled, a passive servility, as if non-resistance and passive obedience were the cardinal virtues in a good sectarian. In other religious institutions there is, on the part of the rulers, no attribute of ecclesiastic authority, and on the part of the ruled there is the most licentious equality; which recognizes not either the letter or spirit of subordination. These doubtless are the extremes between which lies the temperate zone, or the "media tutissima via," the safe middle way.

But there are extremes not only in one department of congregational proceedings; but in all. Let us take an example from some popular measures;—Here in this hierarchy "the canaille" or mass of the community have nothing to say or do in the creation of their teachers or rulers. They are neither permitted to judge nor to decide upon their attainments before they are invested with the office of public instructors. But there, in yonder religious establishment, every man, woman, and child, is constituted into a competent tribunal, and made supreme judge of the attainments of the person, and feel themselves competent to invest him with the office of a religious instructor, without further ceremony than their own unanimity or majority. For instance, Here is a church of thirty members, ten males and twenty females. One of the ten is, by some of the twenty-nine, supposed to be qualified to become a preacher, or as they understand it, a public instructor. Now, of the nine males and twenty females, it so happens that there are six matrons who can read intelligibly the New Testament; and of the males there are about four of what might be called plain common sense, who can barely understand a piece of plain narrative composition. But among them, such as they are, they decide that A B is competent to be a public instructor, and then forthwith commission him to go into all the world, and preach the gospel to every creature. Now the question is, Are they to be condemned or justified who consider this man legitimately introduced into the world as a teacher of religion? Is any other society bound to credit his pretensions or to receive him bona fide as a legally authorized teacher of the Christian religion, and ruler in the christian church? Remember the question is not, Had the twenty females and the nine males, by and with his own consent, a right to create, appoint, and ordain him a ruler and teacher over themselves: but whether they have reason or revelation on their side, when they introduce him to all the world, as a regularly initiated minister, or ambassador, or teacher of and for Jesus Christ? That any society politically considered have a right to manage their own affairs as they please, is at once readily admitted; that any ecclesiastical community have a right to govern themselves by whatever laws they please, as far as the state jurisdiction extends, is also conceded; but that any society has any right to frame any regulations for its own government on christian principles is what we cannot so readily subscribe. But without being further tedious on the subject of extremes, having simply shown that we are prone to run into them on both hands, I will proceed to my object in this part of my series of essays on the ancient order of things.

As we have many volumes on church government and church discipline; and as the Episcopal, Presbyterian, and Independent, all have claimed a jus divinum, we cannot be expected to have much new on the subject, or to have little regard to the merits of the questions which they have with so much warmth debated. We wish however while we write, to forget all that we have ever read or heard on this subject, save what the apostolic writings contain upon such topics. And as we prefer perspicuity to all other attributes of good writing, we proceed to state—

1st. That as the church, or congregation, or assembly, (as it is expressed by all these names,) is repeatedly called a kingdom—the kingdom of God, and the kingdom of heaven, it is fairly to be presumed, from the terms themselves, that the government under which the church is placed, is an absolute monarchy. There cannot be a kingdom, unless there be a king. They are correlative terms, and the one necessarily supposes the existence of the other. But we are not left to inference; for it was not only foretold expressly that "the government would be upon his shoulders;" but he claims absolute dominion in express and unequivocal terms, and lays all his disciples under the strictest injunctions of unreserved submission. All authority in the Universe is given to him—"Therefore, kiss the Son."—"I have placed my king upon Mount Zion."—"He shall reign over the house of Israel, his people, forever." On this, as a first principle, I found all my views of what is commonly called church government. All the churches on earth that Christ has ever acknowledged as his, are so many communities constituting one kingdom, of which he is the head and sovereign.—The congregation or community in Rome, in Corinth, in Phillippi, in Ephesus, &c. &c. were so many distinct communities as respected their component members or individuals, but these were all under one and the same government, as the different counties or corporations in the state of Virginia are all component parts of the state, and under the same government. In every congregation or community of christians the persons that are appointed by the Great King to rule, act pretty much in the capacity of our civil magistrates; or, in other words, they have only to see that the laws are obeyed, but have no power nor right to legislate in any one instance, or for any one purpose. The constitution and laws of this kingdom are all of divine origin and authority, having emanated from the bosom, and having been promulged in the name of the Universal Lord.

There is no democracy nor aristocracy in the governmental arrangements of the church of Jesus Christ. The citizens are all volunteers when they enlist under the banners of the Great King, and so soon as they place themselves in the ranks they are bound to implicit obedience in all the institutes and laws of their sovereign. So that there is no putting the question to vote whether they shall obey any particular law or injunction. Their rulers or bishops have to give an account of their administration, and have only to see that the laws are known and obeyed, and hence proceed all the exhortations in the epistles to the communities addressed to submit to their rulers, as those who watch for their souls, and as those who must give an account of their administration.

This subject, it has appeared to me, is very little or very imperfectly understood in many congregations, and their meetings for church discipline are generally conducted in such a way as to divest every one in the assembly of every attribute of authority, and to place every one in the character of an interpreter of the law; and if not legislators, at least, they are all executors of it. But of this more hereafter.   EDITOR.

By a letter from brother Walter Scott, of the 10th ult. he informs me that his success in proclaiming the ancient gospel still increases. He and his associates have immersed in the first nine days of February, fifty-six persons—in three weeks, one hundred and one souls.   ED.

No. 9.]   APRIL 7, 1828.
On the Influence of the Holy Spirit in the Salvation of Men.—By PAULINUS.
No. II.
"Correct views of the office of the Holy Spirit in the salvation of men, are essential to our knowledge of the christian religion, as also to our enjoyment of it."— *Camp. Essays, C. B. vol. 2.*

IN my Essay, No. 1, I endeavored to lay before the reader a plain, concise, and scriptural view of this important subject, so far as it regards the *fact*, or the reality of a divine influence on the souls of men, in effecting the work of salvation. Deeply impressed with the persuasion that this is a matter of vital consequence, and earnestly hoping that my efforts may be acceptable to those who desire to form "correct views of the office of the Holy Spirit," I cheerfully resume the subject, and proceed to finish the task which I have assigned myself on this occasion.

Two points remain to be noticed; viz. "Some of the principal effects produced by this divine operation"—and "the high practical import of this truth."

The effects of divine influence are *manifold*—according to the manifold need of the sinful subjects of this blessed operation. Man, considered in a moral point of view, is *dark* in his understanding—*perverse* in his will—*unholy* in his affections—*impotent* in all his spiritual faculties—and *ignorant*, withal, as to the extent of his own wretchedness. This, it must be acknowledged, is not a comely picture; but a serious view of the state of men as delineated in the

Holy Scriptures, will convince us that the coloring is not too gloomy for a correct portrait. It would be easy to refer to those parts of the sacred volume which justify this representation; and easy to exemplify the representation to every enlightened mind by an appeal to facts. But this is not the leading object of our present attention; and this matter has been brought to view, by the way, for the purpose of introducing, in an appropriate manner, a notice of those operations and effects which are adapted to meet the case of fallen man. The evidence, however, of this representation will appear, at least *indirectly*, and by implication, from the effects which are ascribed to the influence of the "spirit of grace." These effects I state as being of the following nature; viz. *quickening* and *awakening*—*enlightening* and *convincing*—*converting*—*sanctifying*—and *strengthening*. Let us proceed to notice them accordingly.

The sinner is *ignorant* of the extent of his own wretchedness, and inattentive to his condition. The spirit of grace, then, is a quickening, awakening spirit. Paul testifies that the quickening influence of God had been experienced by the Ephesian converts, who were once "dead in sins:" *Eph.* ii. 1—5, and so of the Colossians; ii. 13. It is surely to this divine operation, attending the truth revealed, that we are to ascribe the awakening of a sinner to a sense of his condemned state; while "pierced to the heart," he anxiously inquires, "What must I do to be saved?"

We next remark, that the unconverted sinner is *dark* in his understanding; and (suitable to such a condition) the spirit of grace is a spirit of *illumination*. Conscious of this, David prays, "Open thou mine eyes, that I may behold wonderous things out of thy law;"—and Paul, for the Ephesians, that God might give them the spirit of wisdom and revelation in the knowledge of him;—the eyes of their understanding being enlightened, &c. By virtue of this illuminating influence, the mind is given to discover, through the word of truth, the insufficiency of man, and of man's righteousness—"the excellency of the knowledge of Christ Jesus," as "the way, the truth, and the life"—the necessity and beauty of that religion which is held out in the sacred volume.

The *perverseness* of the will is another unhappy trait in the character of the unregenerate; and the spirit of grace is a spirit of *conversion*, to give a new turn to the inclination and choice of the subject. Paul was sent to the Gentiles, "to turn them from the power of Satan to God." The Gentiles, then, needed to be turned, and so do *all*; for "all have gone out of the way, and there is none that doeth good, no, not one." But we have before seen that Paul was not the efficient cause of their conversion;—for "who is Paul? or who is Apollos?"—'twas God that gave the increase—the desired success to their ministrations. Hence, then, the changing of the perverse will, and turning it to God, is the effect of divine operation on the soul. And this comports with the prayer and the declaration of Ephraim, *Jer.* xxxi. 18, 19. "Turn thou me, and I shall be turned; for thou art the Lord my God. Surely after that I was turned, I repented," &c. May we not say, with propriety, it comports not only with Ephraim's case, but with that of every converted sinner?

Again we remark, that the unrenewed man is *unholy* in his passions or affections. His love and hatred—his joy and grief—his hopes and fears, are often excited by improper objects; never, as they should be, by those which have the highest claim to their exercise. Now, the spirit of grace is a *sanctifying* spirit—a spirit of *holiness*, to inspire his heart with new principles. Thus, christians are said to have "an unction (or anointing) from the Holy One,"—the Holy Spirit is promised to them that ask it of God;—the earnest of the Spirit is "given in our hearts;" and "the fruit of the Spirit is in all goodness, and righteousness, and truth." 1 *John*, ii. 20. *Luke* xi. 13. 2 *Cor.* i. 22. *Eph.* v. 9. The affections are now excited and exercised in a new manner. "The love of God" and hatred of sin —"joy in the Holy Spirit" and "godly sorrow" —"hope that maketh not ashamed" and "the fear of the Lord;"—these are the effects of this holy operation. And thus new modelled, the subject of divine grace answers to the apostle's description, 2 *Cor.* v. 17; "If any man be in Christ, he is a new creature: old things are passed away; behold, all things are become new."

Once more, let it be observed, that the unregenerate man is impotent in all his spiritual faculties, unable in his own strength, to achieve the victory over those formidable foes within and without, which he has to encounter. But the spirit of grace is a spirit of power; by which the favored subject is enabled effectually to wage the war, and finally to triumph. None are fully sensible of the need of the spirit, but they who are engaged in the conflict; and the more they know of themselves, the more they feel the need of this divine power. Hence Paul prayed for the Ephesian converts—"That he would grant you, according to the riches of his glory, to be strengthened with might, by his spirit in the inner man;" and for the Colossians, in like manner, that they might be "strengthened with all might, according to his glorious power." Though conscious of his own weakness, he felt persuaded that he "could do all things through Christ who strengthened him;" nor is he the only one who testifies, that, to them who have no might, the Lord increases strength." Testimonies to this effect, might be brought in abundance, from the Old Testament saints, as well as from the New;—testimonies which clearly evince that spiritual strength is the effect of an operation from God on the soul. Upon the whole (let me add) the effect of Divine influence on the soul, is, a correspondence of views, disposition, and desire, with the dictates of the word of truth—a responding of the heart to the voice of God in his word; and this too may be considered as (in general, the most abiding and substantial evidence of the work of God within us. The reader will excuse the repetition of several scripture quotations, which were introduced in my first number; and which it has been found requisite to bring forward in illustration of this part of our subject.

The importance of this truth, in a practical point of view, comes lastly to be considered. And here I remark, in the first place, that all scriptural truth is of practical import. I readily concur in the excellent sentiment, so frequently insisted on in the Christian Baptist, that the truths of our divine religion, as exhibited in the scriptures, are not mere abstract speculations, but practical principles; they are not dead branches, standing forth in their own nakedness, but living boughs, clothed with leaves and bearing fruit. This being the case, it follows that we are interested in the knowledge of all holy truth. But as I take it for granted, that there is a difference in the degrees of importance to be attached to th   n the system of revelation;

that some are of more vital consequence than others; as some parts of the human system are more necessary to life than others; so it will follow, that the more important any given truth, in its nature and effects, the more requisite will it be, that this truth be known and insisted on, in order to its practical bearing. Now, if what has been advanced, on the nature and effects of divine influence be correct, that truth at once commends itself to us, as of high importance to be known and insisted on. This argument, I must think, is to be admitted as a valid one, but as, to some minds, it may appear rather complex, I will condense the substance of it, and say, in a simple and short manner—that this truth (as we have seen) is inculcated in the Bible;—that, from the nature and effects of divine influence, it appears to be a truth of high importance; and therefore, that it is highly requisite we should hold it forth, in order to practical use.

This argument is intended merely to prove, that the truth under consideration is of high, practical effect, and the consequent propriety that it should be insisted on: it behooves us to shew, in some instances, wherein this appears to be the case. Two important points here present themselves to our notice. First, this truth is requisite to our own personal interest;—secondly, to the glory of divine grace.

It is requisite to our own personal interest. We are in a spiritual (or if you please, a moral) point of view, weak and needy creatures;—insufficient, with all the mere external means or aids afforded to us to accomplish the work of our salvation. Hence God has graciously promised to work in us: and the promises and declarations to this effect, and the fact that he does so, all go to prove our need of divine influence.

Now, if this be our case, surely we ought to know it—to be deeply persuaded that it is so,—that we may see and feel the necessity of applying "to the throne of grace, that we may obtain mercy and find grace to help in time of need." The prayer of faith is an appointed way for obtaining the necessary supply of strength from God: but if we believe that we really do not need this divine supply: or that God will not grant it; then the prayer of faith can have no place;—prayer, in this case, is rendered nugatory and absurd. Here, then, appears a highly important, practical use of the truth under consideration. This is a point of serious consequence, and I ask the reader's indulgence and attention a little further. If divine influence be not needed on man's part, nor to be given on God's part—then prayer for spiritual aid from God must be worse than useless—it must be improper;—prayer, in this respect, either for ourselves or for others. And if any public servant in the gospel should attempt to maintain the sentiment, then it is expected we shall no more hear him praying that God would touch the hearts of sinners—that he would awaken them—give them the grace of repentance, &c.

This truth is important (I add) to the glory of divine grace. This position follows from the above remarks, and a few words here will suffice. A due sense of our dependence, and of the kindness we have received, is necessary to excite our gratitude and praise; and God requires us gratefully to recognize his favor, in the various ways in which he has bestowed it upon us. But if we be persuaded that we do not need this favor, or that God does not grant it to us,—we may say, in this case, of praise, as of prayer, it cannot exist; and the gift of the Spirit's influence must then be dropped from the catalogue of divine favors, when the christian gratefully exclaims, " Bless the Lord, O my soul, and forget not all his benefits!" We have then another highly important, practical use of this truth, viz. as it is a memento to remind us of our obligation, and to excite our praise for that divine agency, without which we should have remained in our sins.

It is deemed unnecessary to enlarge on this point: but before I close this essay, my attention is demanded to a query which may here be brought forward: "Of what practical use is this subject, in teaching the unregenerate?"

In the specimens of public, apostolic preaching, with which we are furnished in the New Testament, there is, I readily acknowledge, but little appearance of a design to inculcate this truth on the minds of the impenitent and unbelieving. In direct addresses to the unconverted, it is admitted that this is not the leading object to be presented; and due reflection may enable us to account for it. God's methods of dealing with man are suited not only to man's nature, but to the nature of the case; and it must surely be owned, that to call upon the impenitent and unbelieving to repent and believe, is more appropriate, and better adapted to the end in view, than to set out with informing them that the influence of the Divine Spirit is requisite to awaken and convince them. True it is that such influence is requisite throughout the whole process of religion, but in this truth a careless sinner feels no interest, and until he shall become, in some measure, sensible of his situation, it will be either rejected, or admitted for the purpose of being abused. The more proper and scriptural method of dealing with the unawakened, appears to be—an exhibition of their state as sinners: of the method devised by Infinite Goodness for man's salvation; and the necessity of repentance towards God, and faith in our Lord Jesus Christ. In addressing sinners, then, in a careless, unawakened state, I am not prepared to say that the subject here treated on would be of any immediate, practical use: but as it forms one important branch of sacred truth, and frequently occurs in the general tenor of apostolic teaching; moreover, as every spiritual requisition involves the necessity of this divine agency, it surely ought to occupy a conspicuous place in our general exhibitions of the economy of divine grace. The awakened sinner, as well as the christian, will thus be furnished with a truth, which, as we have seen, is of deep interest, and of high practical importance.

The substance of the leading sentiment maintained in these two essays, is, that we are dependant on the influence of the Holy Spirit to render the word of truth effectual to our conversion and final salvation. I am not so sanguine as to imagine that every remark I have made is invulnerable to an attack: or that every quotation from scripture will certainly be found correctly applied, but the great object—the leading point, is, I humbly conceive, satisfactorily established; and this, I would hope, will meet with no opposition from the friends of divine truth.

PAULINUS.

P. S. I cannot consent to dismiss this essay, for the press, without dropping a few words further, to guard against any mistaken construction. Be it observed that I am not advocating any of the particular systems of the day; that I have said nothing about irresistible operations; that I am not here contending for a divine influence, of a mere physical nature, detached from revealed truth; though that, in some cases, may be a fact; and, though I believe that God, as a free, almighty agent, energizes more in some cases than in others, yet I admit that there dwells in the word of truth a living principle, which, when that word is received, has a never-failing tendency to bring forth the fruit of holiness in heart and life.

And now, if any part of these essays should be considered materially erroneous, they are open to animadversion. Divine truth is all I seek to establish.

Note.—I now feel disposed to lend my aid, ere long, in attempting to shake down the mighty Babel of high-toned spiritual authority, to which numbers in the religious world appear to be lamentably subjected. A little volume, which I have lately seen, puts forth claims, which ought to alarm and arouse every friend of the Bible and of religious liberty.   P.

[My reply to Paulinus is crowded out of the present number.]   ED. C. B.

———

[The following letter was published in the "Baptist Recorder" in November last. It was copied into the "Star" of December 1st, with some encomiums upon the writer. One which accompanied it was published and animadverted on in this work: but the following I did not publish at that time; and, for the sake of Mr. Semple, I hoped it would never appear in this work. When I proposed a discussion of the points at issue with him, I expected he would write something more pertinent and less objectionable; in which case, my intention was to suffer this piece to die a natural death. But as brother Semple will give us nothing better on the subject, it becomes our duty to be content with such things as we have.]   ED. C. B.

To Silas M. Noel.

COLLEGE HILL, D. C. SEPT. 3, 1827.

DEAR BROTHER.—You took the right ground. Creeds, are good servants, but bad masters. Give them too much authority, and they will tyrannize; but let them, as messengers, carry the digested opinions of one set of men to another, and of one generation to another, and their effect is excellent. The Baptists have been a divided people ever since my knowledge of them, owing (I think) to the want of a proper respect for established opinions, customs, and regulations, whether written or otherwise. Every "novice" thinks he has made discoveries overlooked by his ancients. In a few years he sees his error, that is, if he be honestly in pursuit of truth; and if he has not committed himself too far, he is ready to retrace his steps, and to acknowledge that there were much better reasons for his fathers' opinions and customs than he was aware of. Church government obviously is left by the Bible for the exercise of much discretion. It is the scaffold, and must be adapted to the house, and for this plain reason ought to go through modifications. What suits a country church may not suit a city, and vice versa; what was adapted to the Bereans, might not, and probably did not, comport with the habits of the Cretans. The church is a corporation having a perfect charter—the Bible. Its by-laws are properly subject to regulations; but those who act under the charter must be cautious not to violate its word or spirit by a stretch of power: but, on the other hand, must also not fold their hands and say, The charter is enough, and we want no regulations, no by-laws. To such we would say, the charter itself contemplates such regulations, and cannot be carried into effect without them. The Sandemanians, or Haldanians, pretend to find in the Bible an express warrant for every matter—for every measure; but when pressed, they have to resort to miserable subterfuges to prove various points of church government: and hence their frequent disagreement among themselves, and hence their constant resort to finding fault with the proceedings of others, rather than furnishing any plan of their own. The "Christian Baptist" has doubtless exhibited many valuable pieces and principles; but, taken as a whole, I am persuaded it has been more mischievous than any publication I have ever known. The ability of the editor, joined to the plausibility of his plans or doctrines, has succeeded in sowing the seeds of discord among brethren to an extent in many places alarming. In my address to him a year or two ago, I said if his principles prevailed a new sect started up. Such are my views; and my deliberate judgment tells me that there is much less ground for fellowship with such a sect, than with Presbyterians, Methodists, or even evangelical Episcopalians. In baptism, and the name Baptist, (though that they would change,) we agree, and in very few other matters. In our parts there have been a good many partial converts made, most of whom have retrograded on better acquaintance.

Grace, mercy, and peace.

R. B. Semple.

Reply.

Brother Semple,

Dear Sir—If you and I affix the same ideas to the terms *master* and *servant*, you are on my side of the creed question. The church you make master, and the creed the servant; whereas your friend Dr. Noel would make the creed master, and the church its humble servant.—When the creed says, Exclude A B because he believes not in the doctrine of absolute and unconditional reprobation or election, and the church obeys, you would say the creed was master, and the church servant; and then you would enter your protest against the usurper. But Dr. Noel could say to the church, "Well done, good and faithful servant." But suppose when the creed says, Exclude, the church says, "Nay—be silent, creed;" you would say the church acts master now, and keeps the creed in its proper place. You and I, therefore, are on the same side. I dont care if the church buys or brings forth a creed every year, and has as many servants as the wealthiest lord of the soil from the Ohio to the Euphrates, provided only she keeps them all as servants ought to be kept—from dictating to their masters. Had you said no more upon this subject than what you have said in the above comparison, I could find no cause to dissent from you; and if I am to interpret all you have said by this comparison, still we do not disagree. But there is an apparent discrepancy in the following words: "The baptists have been a divided people ever since my knowledge of them, owing (I think) to the want of a proper respect for established opinions, customs, and regulations, whether written or otherwise."—This sentence is somewhat ambiguous: "The Baptists have been, and still are, a divided people." This is a fact on which we shall not differ; but respecting the causes of this difference, perhaps we may.

On the supposition that you trace these divisions to the want of sufficient respect to a creed, then you have made a creed to mean, "estab-

lished opinions, customs, and regulations," Is this the servant? Surely if the "opinions, customs, and regulations" are established, they are, or must be, masters; and we must submit. To this I have no objections, provided the authority that establishes them be paramount to every other. But what right has one generation to establish "opinions, customs, and regulations" for another? And why should you and I submit to "the opinions, customs, and regulations" established by any human authority? If I must examine for myself, what shall I examine? The creed, or the bible? If I must not take the creed upon trust, but if you say I must go to the bible as well as to the creed, may I not as well go to the bible at first as at last? Say, brother Semple, may I not? Ought I not to go to the bible at first? If I take the creed at all, you will say, Take the creed in one hand, and the bible in the other. And of what use then is the creed? Why, say you, it will help you to understand the bible, or guide you in the examination of it. If so, then, I must make the creed a pair of spectacles instead of a staff, and wear it upon my nose instead of keeping it in my hand. If I must examine the bible through the creed, then the creed is my eyes; my artificial eyes, (for it cannot be my natural eyes)—my spectacles. If my spectacles are green glass, the bible is also green; if blue, the bible is blue; and as is the creed, so is the bible to me. I am a Calvinist, or an Arminian, or a Fullerite, according to my spectacles or my creed, my "established opinions, customs, and regulations."

Brother Semple, it comes to this—I say, the whole controversy comes to this—It is a plain case; it is all contained in one question: "Is every christian to examine for himself the book of God." Say Yea, or Nay. If you say Yea, you are a Protestant; the Catholic says Nay. If you say Yea, then it follows—yes, it follows, with power irresistible, that to a man whose duty it is to examine the scriptures, there can be no such a thing as "established opinions, customs, and regulations." For if established, why examine? I am a Protestant. I say Yea. And, therefore, I can never say to any man, When you open the bible, sir, you must pay a proper respect to "established opinions, customs, and regulations." I dare not say so. I say examine and judge for yourself. Pardon me, brother Semple, for saying, that I have never been able to discriminate between the logic of the "mother church" and that of all the daughters who argue for a due respect to "established opinions, customs, and regulations." This was her controversy with the heretics, Luther and Calvin.—They boldly said that her "established opinions, customs, and regulations" were not to be received nor regarded without examination, and that in examining them they disclaimed their being established. She complained and said, "that owing to a want of due respect to established opinions, customs, and regulations," they broke off from her jurisdiction, and divided among themselves.

But, my dear sir, I am led to suspect your logic from another consideration not yet stated.—You trace the divisions among the Baptists to a want of a due respect to "established opinions, customs, and regulations." The converse of which is, If the Baptists paid a due respect to "established opinions," &c. they would not be a divided people. Now it so happens that the Paido-Baptists are much more divided than the Baptists, and pay a much greater regard to "established opinions," &c. than the Baptists.—

How will your philosophy stand the test of experiment here? There are few religionists on earth who pay a much greater respect to "established opinions" than the Presbyterians. And have they not been a divided people ever since you knew them? In little more than a century they have split into five divisions, and erected *five distinct communions*. But, perhaps, you mean such a respect to "established opinions" as that shewn by the *mother church;* and here I must own you are right. For if the Baptists paid that due respect to "established opinions" which the Romanists do, they would be as united as the holy Catholic apostolic church. But any thing short of that due respect will cause them so be as divided as their Presbyterian neighbors. Except, then, you mean by the words "proper respect," such a respect as the Catholics shew, which precludes all examination of "established opinions," &c. your logic is, in my humble opinion, at variance with reason, as it is with matter of fact.

But, again. Perhaps we may agree at last on this very point. I do believe that all the divisions not only among the Baptists, but also among the Paido-Baptists, are to be traced to the want of a proper respect to "established opinions," &c. but these are the "opinions, customs and regulations" *established by the holy apostles.* If, then, brother Semple, you mean that the want of union among the Baptists is owing to a want of proper respect to the opinions, customs, and regulations established and ordained in the New Testament, I most cordially agree with you, and you and I are again on the same side. But I must cordially avow that I do not think that this was your meaning, and therefore would not flatter myself too far in the hope of your accordance with me on this topic. You mean the opinions, customs, and regulations established by our fathers; and I mean the opinions, &c. established by the apostles. We differ in the conclusion as much as in the premises. But as I do not want to pursue this point farther than necessary to test its claims upon our assent, I would dismiss it with a request to you to reconsider this matter; and if, in any respect, I have done injustice to your remarks, I request you to show it, and I promise to retract them upon conviction of my mistake.

What you say about *novices* is perhaps very just; and I give it my full and hearty approbation, with one small exception, and that is, that I do not give it so great a latitude as you do. You say "*every* novice." I am willing to make a few exceptions in favor of our young converts in the late revivals.

I am sorry, brother Semple, to find you in the next sentence in company with Cardinal Cajetan and Archbishop Laud. They just said and argued with you, as you have expressed it, viz.— "Church government obviously is left by the bible for the exercise of much discretion." The Erastians, too, in the Westminster Assembly contended for the truth of this position against the Independents and Presbyterians. These argued that there was a form of church government divinely established; whereas the Erastians said, "it was obviously left by the bible for the exercise of much discretion."

As far as my knowledge of ecclesiastical history extends, you are *solus* or singular in calling church government "*the scaffold*," and in making it "go through *modifications;*" or perhaps it may be owing to my want of discerning the propriety and beauty of these metaphors. However these matters may be, you are not singular in the fol-

3 E

lowing sentences; for Archbishop Laud agreed with the Erastians in this one sentence as you have expressed it—"What suits a country church may not suit a city, and *vice versa;*" and that form of government which "was adapted to the Bereans," who love to read the scriptures, most "probably did not comport with the habits of the Cretans." If you allow that the natural habits of the Cretans and the Bereans continued after their conversion, I would agree with you and other liberal writers upon the subject of church government, that that government which would keep in order the Cretans, who, as Paul said, "were always liars, evil beasts, and slow bellies," would be entirely unnecessary at Berea, where the noble folks lived, who searched the scriptures daily whether these things were so.

But, brother Semple, I do not condemn that sentiment you have uttered, when you say that "church government is obviously left by the bible for the exercise of much discretion," because Cajetan, Archbishop Laud, the Erastians, brother Brantley, and Dr. Noel have approved it. These all may agree on many points which are worthy of universal acceptation, and therefore I shall proceed to examine it in my next upon its own merits. In the mean time I beseech you not to identify my opposition to your views in this letter with an idea that I am not personally attached to yourself. In proportion to my esteem for you will be my opposition to those views which I conceive to be hostile to the bible and to the sentiments of those who Mr. Jones, in his Ecclesiastical History, considers the faithful witnesses against error. Adieu.

A. CAMPBELL.

<hr />

CANTON, OHIO, FEBRUARY 22, 1828.
Mr. Alexander Campbell:

VERY DEAR BROTHER—Though a personal stranger, I have this while past enjoyed a very useful acquaintance with your writings. I would be very much pleased if you could make it convenient to visit this place, as I desire to become more acquainted with you, for my own benefit. Not only a selfish motive, however, is it that I should wish a personal visit of you in this place; but also the great cause of christianity which you so ably advocate, prompts me to invite you to our neighborhood. You have, perhaps, heard of that co-operative society at Kendal, in this (Stark) county, which has been established on Robert Owen's principles, a year or two ago. To this society an emissary of infidelity, of considerable talents, Doctor Underhill, has been sent, and for two months or more, he has been indefatigably engaged preaching that sort of moral philosophy, which the "New Harmony Gazette" contains. He is going from place to place, and great numbers, I understand, are converted to his new doctrine. Though there is considerable alarm among the preachers about here, none but a Roman priest undertook to contradict him; with very little effect, however. Since that time the Deists and free thinkers of this place are getting quite bold, and even the apprentices in the workshops, and boys in the streets, begin to reason away, and rail at religion. I am ashamed for my brethren, the English preachers, who stand back when that man speaks, and only talk when he is not within hearing. Does not this show as if christianity could not be defended against its enemies, or that its priests were too lukewarm to undertake its defence? It grieves me the more, since Doctor Underhill has challenged, boldly, every one who would be willing to question his views, and has publicly called for opposition to his sentiments. I see well enough, that it is not easy for those who have yet so much of the leaven of the pharisees to defend their cause; and willingly I should step forward to show, at least, that there are some very good reasons why we christians still revere the bible as the revealed word of God. But what can I do? I feel myself, in every respect, especially in the knowledge of the English language, too weak for a debate in that language. I wish you would be willing to enter the list with this man. What do you say? Will you come?

That God, with his Holy Spirit, may guide you to do that which will best promote the kingdom of our Lord and Master, Jesus Christ, is the pray- of your poor fellow laborer in the vineyard of the Lord.   A.

—

Mr. A.——

DEAR BROTHER—Your favor of the 22d ultimo lies before me—I am always glad to co-operate with the household of faith in support of our common cause. As to this Doctor Underhill, he is too obscure to merit any attention from me on the Atheism or Deism of his philosophy. If I lived in the neighborhood with him, and should he throw himself in my way, I might find it my duty either to kill him, or to break a lance over his steel cap. But to go out of my way to meet such a gentleman would be rather incompatible with my views of propriety. If his great master, Mr. Robert Owen, will engage to debate the whole system of his moral and religious philosophy with me, if he will pledge himself to prove any position affirmative of his atheistical sentiments as they lie scattered over the pages of the New Harmony Gazette—if he will engage to do this coolly and dispassionately in a regular and systematic debate, to be moderated by a competent tribunal, I will engage to take the negative and disprove all his affirmative positions, in a public debate to be holden any place equi-distant from him and me. I think such a discussion is needed, and in the armor of the bible, I feel prepared to meet the sage philosopher of New Harmony at a proper time and place. But in the mean time I will not draw a bow, save against the king of the sceptics of the city of Mental Independence.

My dear sir, you are doubtless more than able to drive off to the wilderness this wild boar who lies under your hills and sheep folds, seeking whom he may devour.

Your neighboring clergy are true to the character the Saviour gave of such folks in his time—The hireling flees because he is a hireling, when the wolf comes; but the good shepherd endangers his life for the sheep. With every benevolent wish, I am your fellow-laborer in the Lord's vineyard.   A. CAMPBELL.

—

History of Churches, and other incidents connected with the Spirit of the Age.—Continued.

☞We intend commencing our Review of the History of Churches, already offered, in our next number.

Extract of a letter to the Editor of the Christian Baptist, dated
WEST PORT, KY, 28th Feb. 1828.

"In the counties of Fayette, Clark, Jessamine, Bourbon and Madison, there is a great revival of religion. There has been from the best information had, upwards of six hundred immersed into the name of the Father, Son, and Holy Spirit, in the course of three months. This revival

seems, too, to be under the preaching of the ancient gospel, by brothers J. Creath, W. Morton, J. Vardeman, George Boon, and J. Hewett. May the Lord's kingdom continue to increase!"

—

Extract of a Letter to the Editor, dated
"FAIRFIELD, COLUMBIANA Co. O.
Feb. 24th, 1828.

"We held a quarterly meeting at this place, from the 1st to the 4th of this month inclusive, and we declared to the people that the plan instituted by the Lord Jesus Christ and his apostles for the salvation of men, was accomplished in the exercise of faith in the Messiah, by repentance and baptism, or immersion; and that on these conditions they should receive the remission of their sins and the gift of the Holy Spirit, and that if they continued steadfast in the apostles' doctrine and fellowship, and breaking of bread, and in prayers, they should ultimately be saved.—Thus rehearsing the plain scripture doctrine held forth by the apostle Peter on the day of Pentecost. And the effects were very striking, and truly astonishing; for, in the short space of about three weeks, about forty persons have been immersed, and the church has seemed to be at peace."

—

Extract of a Letter, dated
"CLINTON Co., OHIO, 1828.

"We reside as a church, five miles east of Wilmington. Our meeting house is called *Antioch.* We commenced our march towards Jerusalem last spring, and we have been slowly progressing ever since. We have met with some opposition, but we still are moving on, and many of the people have a mind to work, notwithstanding the scoffs of the Tobiahs and the threats of the Sanballats. We feel awake to the imperious command of our Lord, Come out of her (Babylon) my people, that ye be not partakers of her plagues. The church met, and concluded she was not in gospel order, and that we search the New Testament to find that order and get into it; and we have come to the following conclusions: That the word *church*, when used in the New Testament, is with reference, in a general sense, to the whole congregation of believers habitually assembling at one place for the purpose of worshipping God; and that this term is used in the New Testament in this sense and no other; consequently when we hear of the methodist church, we say it is the language of Babylon, and so with the baptist church, &c. And also when we use the term church of Christ, or christian church, with reference to the widely dispersed congregations that bear that name in the United States, we convert the language of Canaan into the language of Babylon. In the second place we have agreed that the first day of the week is the only day set apart by divine appointment for the public worship of God. And 3d, that each congregation acting on the authority of the New Testament, has a right to a plurality of bishops or elders, and deacons. And 4th, that she has a right, acting with the New Testament in her hand, to judge of the qualifications of her officers, and to appoint or induct them into office, without calling for any form, bishop, or conference of elders, to assist in their ordination; and that the term *ordination*, in the New Testament sense of that word, never meant to lay hands on any body, but simply meant to appoint or set apart by a decree of the church. This far we have travelled together, at least all those who have felt themselves interested into our discussions. Further, some of us believe, from the New Testament, that it is the duty of the church to break bread every Lord's day, but the larger number think this discretionary with themselves, and have agreed, as a church, to have a general communion, so called; for we that believed in the weekly breaking of bread, had previously obtained liberty to go forward in it without hurting the feelings of those who did not see with us. Accordingly we commenced the third Lord's day of January last, and have observed it stedfastly ever since. We invite all those who really believe in our Lord the King, and whose conduct corresponds with that profession, to partake with us, irrespective of their private views or tenets, or their sectarian names; and those who have not been baptized, who bring forth the fruits of a Holy Spirit, are made welcome; and a spirit of brotherly love and forbearance, with a very small exception, has attended all our deliberations, and an earnest desire to know our Master's will that we may do it."

Extract of a Letter to the Editor, dated
"Nashville, Ten. January 10, 1828.

"Our church affairs go on smoothly and quietly thus far. We dont hear of as many things being said against us as at first. Whether our peaceable and inoffensive conduct towards our brethren, has put them to shame, or whether they have given us over as lost, is the cause of our present quietude, I cannot say. But whatever may be thought of our views, we have reason to hope our conduct is such as to afford no ground to others to speak evil, justly, of us—at least so far as I know. Those amongst us who have set out to do our Master's will, so far as we know it, with full purpose of heart, have no cause to repent in consequence of any departure from *Baptist* customs, or opinions, which has taken place. The breaking of bread, as a part of the worship of every Lord's day, does not, thus far, seem to lose any virtue in consequence of its frequency —but contrarywise. Nor have we discovered any evil in meeting early on the Lord's day morning, for the purpose of praying, and praising and blessing him for his continued mercies. Nor do we, as yet, find evil to grow out of any service we perform on that day, either in attending to the fellowship of the saints, the discipline of the church, or any thing else we are called upon to do. We have lately commenced our meetings on the Lord's day evening, for the purpose of reading the scriptures—commenting thereon, &c. when all speak, one by one, for our mutual instruction and edification. It is a kind of familiar conversation—from which I hope we may all derive much benefit.

"We have lately received a brother who had been excluded from a baptist church—not on account of misconduct: but because he would not, or could not conscientiously stay with those who retained disorderly persons amongst them. This is a new case in our days.

"Another novel and uncommon circumstance in these parts took place on last Lord's day. When the church had all broken bread, an unimmersed person, who was sitting on a separate seat, moved with the love of God through the heavenly institution, I suppose, came forward, and, without ceremony, broke off a part of the same loaf, and eat! No one forbade. And I do believe every member present experienced a glow of joy on the occasion. The wine was, then, first handed this same person, who drank thereof. And strange as it may appear, there were many of us who felt considerable solicitude

lest it should not be offered by the deacon. O that all God's children would put on Christ by being immersed into his death, and then walk as he has given commandment! What a glorious body would the christian church be!

"Can you ask us, why did we suffer this thing to take place?

"May the Lord bless you, and make you more and more useful in your day, and to your generation."

Sorrow for the Dead.

"The sorrow for the dead is the only sorrow from which we refuse to be divorced. Every other wound we seek to heal—every other affliction to forget: but this wound we consider it a duty to keep open—this affliction we cherish and brood over in solitude. Where is the mother that would willingly forget the infant that perished like a blossom from her arms, though every recollection is a pang? Where is the child that would willingly forget the most tender parents, though to remember be but to lament? Who, even in the hour of agony, would forget the friend over whom he mourns? Who, even when the tomb is closed upon the remains of her he most loved, and he feels his heart, as it were, crushed in the closing of its portal, would accept consolation that was to be bought by forgetfulness? No! the love which survives the tomb is one of the noblest attributes of the soul! If it has its woes, it has likewise its delights; and when the overwhelming burst of grief is calmed into the gentle tear of recollection; when the sudden anguish and the convulsive agony over the present ruins of all that we most loved, is softened away into pensive meditation on all that it was in the days of its loveliness—who would root out such a sorrow from the heart? Though it may sometimes throw a passing cloud even over the bright hour of gaiety, or spread a deeper sadness over the hour of gloom, yet who would exchange it even for the song of pleasure, or the burst of revelry? No! there is a voice from the tomb sweeter than song! There is a recollection of the dead, to which we turn even from the charms of the living. Oh the grave! the grave! It buries every error—covers every defect—extinguishes every resentment. From its peaceful bosom spring none but fond regrets and tender recollections. Who can look down upon the grave even of an enemy, and not feel a compunctious throb that ever he should have warred with the poor handful of earth that lies mouldering before him!"

"But the grave of those we loved—what a place for meditation! Then it is that we call up in long review the whole history of virtue and gentleness, and the thousand endearments lavished upon us almost unheeded in the daily intercourse of intimacy; then it is that we dwell upon the tenderness, the solemn, awful tenderness of the parting scene—the bed of death, with all its stifled griefs, its noiseless attendance, its mute, watchful assiduities—the last testimonies of expiring love—the feeble, fluttering thrilling, O how thrilling! pressure of the hand—the last fond look of the gazing eye, turning upon us, even from the threshold of existence—the faint, faltering accents, struggling in death to give one more assurance of affection!

"Aye, go to the grave of buried love and meditate! There settle the account with thy conscience for every past benefit unrequited—every past endearment unregarded, of that departed being who can never—never—return to be soothed by thy contrition!

"If thou art a child, and hast ever added a sorrow to the soul, or a furrow to the silvered brow of an affectionate parent—if thou art a husband, and hast ever caused the fond bosom that ventured its whole happiness in thy arms, to doubt one moment of thy kindness or thy truth—if thou art a friend, and hast ever wronged, in thought, or word, or deed, the spirit that generously confided in thee—if thou art a lover, and hast ever given one unmerited pang to that true heart that now lies cold and still beneath thy feet; then be sure that every unkind look, every ungracious word, every ungentle action, will come thronging back upon thy memory, and knocking dolefully at thy soul—then be sure that thou wilt lie down sorrowing and repentant on the grave, and utter the unheard groan, and pour the unavailing tear, more deep, more bitter, because unheard and unavailing.

"Then weave thy chaplet of flowers, and strew the beauties of nature about the grave; console thy broken spirit, if thou canst, with these tender, yet futile tributes of regret; but take warning by the bitterness of this thy contrite affliction over the dead, and be more faithful and affectionate in the discharge of thy duties to the living."—*W. Irving.*

Ancient Gospel.—No. IV.
Immersion.

In shunning one extreme, we are wont to run into the contrary. The Papists in former times made the mere act of immersion or of sprinkling, irrespective of the sentiments, faith, or feelings, of the subject, wash away all sins. They used the name of the "Father, Son, and Holy Ghost," or of "the Trinity," as they termed it, just as conjurors use the words of a charm. They supposed that the mere pronunciation of the names constituting "the Holy Trinity," together with two or three drops of water from the baptized finger of an ignorant priest, forgave all sins, whether "original or actual," and therefore contended, "no baptism, no salvation." Because they terminated in this abominable delusion and carried their notions to this immense extreme, the Protestants ran to an equal extreme on the other side of the equator of truth; and therefore gave to baptism, however administered, no connexion with the remission of sins. So much did they hate the errors of popery, that they did scarcely name "the forgiveness of sins" on the same day on which they "administered baptism." This is not the only instance in which the Protestants were driven entirely to neglect their duty, because the Catholics ran into some absurdity. Thus, as the Romanists laid so much stress upon fasting, as to make it almost more than "a sacrament," the Protestants will not fast at all, lest they should become Papists; and therefore, although they have some days called "fast days," they take good care to eat as abundantly on those holy days as upon other occasions.

Now, methinks we are not to be scared out of our duty or privilege because of the errors or follies of others. Nor do we lose sight of the forgiveness of our sins in immersion, because Papists have made a saviour of a mere ceremony. We connect faith with immersion as essential to forgiveness—and therefore, as was said of old, "According to your faith, so be it to you," so say we of immersion. He that goes down into the water to put on Christ, in the faith that the blood of Jesus cleanses from all sin, and that he has appointed immersion as the medium, and the act of ours, through and in which he actually and formally remits our sins, has when immersed the actual remission of his sins. So that he is dead by sin, buried with Jesus, and is born again, or raised to life again, a life new and divine, in and through the act of immersion. This we have seen in the preceding essays is the Bible import of the one immersion. In it we put on Christ, are buried with him, rise with him, have our sins remitted, enter upon a new life, receive the Holy Spirit, and begin to rejoice in the Lord.

Infidels and skeptics in general, as well as some weak minded christians, object to this doctrine because it is not complex or mysterious enough. It is too easy, too cheap, too simple to have such immense advantages attached thereto. What! say they, is a man to put on Christ, to be born again, to begin a new life, to rise with Christ to a heavenly inheritance, to have all his sins remitted, to receive the Holy Spirit, to be filled with joy and peace, through the mere act of a believing immersion in water into the name of the Father, Son and Holy Spirit. I say yea—most assuredly; and request the weak christian who objects to all this goodness and mercy, obtained so easily, so simply, so cheaply, to consider that it is just "thus and so," that God has always dealt with man in things natural and supernatural. Does not a man enjoy life itself and all its thousand joys, by the simple, cheap, and easy method of breathing atmospheric air? and is not this done with so much ease as never to interfere with eating, talking, sleeping, &c.? What so common and so accessible as the oxygen, which is the *pabula vitæ*, the very food of animal life. Are not all heaven's best blessings the cheapest, the most common, the most accessible of all others? And who from natural analogies can object to the communication of so many heavenly blessings through the medium of a believing immersion in water into the sacred name of the *Holies?* But is not this also analogous to every thing in the Bible? What, says the sceptic, can the Deity, so wise and benevolent, doom mankind to temporal, and, in some instances, to perpetual miseries, because Adam took a bite of an apple in Eden! Tell me, Mr. Sceptic, why should one drop of Prussic acid, or a simple inhalation of a few mouthfuls of mephitic gas, be able to deprive the strongest man on this continent of temporal or animal life for ever and ever! Tell me why a puncture from the point of a needle should deprive the wife of a beloved husband, and the children of a kind and useful parent for ever and ever:—tell me this, and I will tell you why the "eating of one apple," to speak in your own style, should entail so many calamities on the human race. You weak christians, who object to the import of immersion as here taught, remind me of Naaman, the Syrian, who you know was a leper. When told to dip in Jordan seven times and he should be healed of his leprosy, he replied as you—"Are not any of the streams of Damascus or of Egypt as good as the waters of Jordan?" Yes, says his servant, if the Lord had required you to do some great thing, would you not have done it? But he has offered his cure too cheap. It is too easy, too simple. Go, Naaman, and try, but go in faith. He went, he dipped himself in Jordan, and came up from its waters sound and cleansed. The divine appointment and faith gave all this efficacy to the waters of Jordan. Why then should it be thought incredible that the divine appointment should give such efficacy to believing immersion? But I have not yet done with the subject. I must resume it in my next, and shew why the Holy Spirit is promised through immersion.   EDITOR.

No. 10.]   May 5, 1828.

Remarks on the Essays of Paulinus.

The readers of the Christian Baptist are, and no doubt will feel themselves indebted to Paulinus for the very forcible, and elegant essays he has furnished on this subject. He has unquestionably thought very closely, examined the scriptures very fully, and has arranged and exhibited the testimonies in so methodical and forcible a manner, as to give the greatest and best possible effect to his sentiments on this theme. Few of the intelligent readers of this work will dissent from his conclusion of the whole matter, viz. p. 431—"The substance of the leading sentiment maintained in these two essays, is, that we are dependant on the influence of the Holy Spirit to render the word effectual to our conversion and final salvation. I am not so sanguine as to imagine that every remark I have made is invulnerable to an attack, or that every quotation from scripture will be found correctly applied; but the great object, the leading point is, I humbly conceive, satisfactorily established; and this, I would hope, will meet with no opposition from the friends of divine truth."

Although it might appear that some of the sentences extracted from different parts of the sacred volume, were not originally intended to prove the position which was before the mind of Paulinus, yet still the conclusions to which he has come will be very generally embraced as declarative of sentiments styled evangelical. The delicate point is very tenderly handled; and indeed it requires great caution lest this system be too much reprobated, in showing why the apostles did not contend for such a position, nor exhibit themselves in the descriptive and explanatory style, when preaching repentance and salvation to their auditors. Paulinus explains the reasons why they did not so preach to sinners, and very justly concludes that, "this was not the leading object to be presented."

There is one point which I should like to have seen occupy some place in the systems of this day with a reference to this subject, viz. As respects the actual possibility of salvation to those without the Bible—whether there is any advantage at all, as respects salvation, to those who have the Bible over those who have it not. Or is not a Virginian with the Bible, in exactly as hopeless a condition as a Hindoo without it, unless some special influence be exerted upon him? Or, for the sake of variety—can not, or does not, the Holy Spirit by its impressions or operations, make salvation as easy and as accessible to a Japanese without any written revelation as to a Virginian with all the sacred books?

We are apt, in interpreting the holy scriptures, to suppose that a hundred things said of "sinners," of "natural men," of "children of wrath," of "the dead," of "those without strength," were spoken of persons who were circumstanced as the inhabitants of the British Isles, or the citizens of the United States: never taking thought that there are essential differences between those without, and those under, the revelation of God. This single fact, clearly apprehended, is like applying the pruning hook to the vine: it lops off a great many quotations and applications of scripture which are thought to bear upon the sons and daughters, the brothers and sisters of christians, as if they were born in tribes, and nations, where the name of Jesus has not been heard.

I have long felt an unconquerable repugnance to that system of religion which destroys the use of the holy scriptures to unconverted or unregenerate men. The doctrine of physical and irresistible energies of God's Spirit upon unbelieving men, as absolutely and indispensably prerequisite to their deriving any religious benefit from all that is written on the sacred pages; from all that is spoken by christian tongues, from all prayer and supplication addressed to the Father of all; from all and every moral or religious means, is, in my view, at war with Moses and the prophets; with the Lord Jesus, and the apostles; with the whole Bible; with all rational analogies; with all the faculties yet belonging to the human race; with all and every thing, natural, moral, and religious, except the sheer inoperative dogma of some indoctrinated fatalist. I do therefore, with all my heart, soul, mind, and strength, oppose every proposition, position, and sentiment, which either grows out of, is connected with, or looks towards, the establishment of such a cold, lifeless, and inoperative system: believing it to be entirely unauthorized by the Holy Spirit, and that it is the most genuine wresting of the scriptures to the destruction of thousands, who are now, as they have been for centuries, standing all the day idle: some running into all manner of excess; and others looking with aching hearts for some irresistible wind, afflatus, or spirit, to carry them, not literally, but figuratively, as Elijah was taken, in a whirlwind to heaven.

I see some systems tinctured with this principle, which disavow it, and I have felt a good measure of it in all these theories about the Holy Spirit's operations upon unconverted men. If you, brother Paulinus, discard the doctrine of irresistible operations upon unbelievers, you are happily safe from the systems which I have been so long combating and endeavoring to expose in my various essays on the work of the Holy Spirit in the salvation of men. I have contended that the Spirit of God has done something which renders unbelief and unregeneracy a sin in all men who have access to the Bible; independent of any thing to be done; and I have taught that it will do something for those, who, from what it has done, are immersed into the faith of the gospel.

What it has done, has given strength to the weak, life to the dead, and reclaimed enemies to God—what it will do, is to beget a holy spirit and temper, to fill with peace and joy, and righteousness, those who believe. I will not therefore, with the speculative philosopher, make what the Spirit of God has already done of none effect, to make way for something yet to be done. Nor will I ascribe every thing to what the Spirit has done, in the inditing and confirming the testimony, to the exclusion of any influence upon the minds who, through faith, have been immersed for the remission of sins and this heavenly gift. Thus the Scriptures encourage all to activities. The whole world with whom this Spirit of God strives in the written word now as it once did in the mouths of the prophets and apostles, have no excuse for their infidelity or unregeneracy—and those who have put on the Lord Jesus are invited to abound in all the joys, consolations, and purifying influences of this Holy Spirit. Such is the operative system of supernatural truth—the scope of the practical principles of the Bible.

Those who have contended for physical and irresistible influences, have found themselves at variance with the manifest scope and bearing of a large portion of the apostolic addresses to their auditors. They, to prevent or to obviate the charge of making the word of God of none effect by their traditions, have invented a curious doctrine of "common operations," contradistinguished from the special; and, like the pious Mr. Baxter, have attempted to reconcile the jarring systems by making it possible for all gospel hearers to be saved and certain for some—possible for all who did not resist the common operations; and certain for all upon whom the irresistible or special operations were employed. This is a lame expedient. Their doctrine of common operations is as unscriptural, as their special operation in subversive of all praise or blame, of all virtue and vice, of all excellency in faith, or criminality in unbelief. The Bible doctrine requires not the aid of either system.

Let no man say that in explicitly opposing both systems, we argue that men are converted without the Holy Spirit. By no means. The Spirit of God works upon the human mind as well as dwells in it. It works by the record which God has given of his Son, as the spirit works by the body of a man—clothed with this record, it enlightens, convinces, and converts men. It is never once said to work in any other way upon the minds of men since it consummated the record. Even in convincing the world of sin, righteousness, and judgment, in the age of miracles, it did this in words concerning Jesus. When men hearken to the word, they hear the Spirit of God; when they will not hearken, they resist the Spirit of God. It makes every man who hears the word able to believe, by adapting its testimony to his capacity, so that his unbelief is wholly his own sin, owing to aversion, and not to incapacity.

Men are not made christians as Balaam's ass was made to speak, or the whale to vomit Jonah upon dry ground. Yet still they are enabled to believe by the Holy Spirit, and without its aid no man ever could have believed in Jesus, as God's own Son. In one sentence all men who hear the Spirit of God, (and every man born in these United States may hear this life giving Spirit,) have all natural inability removed, and faith is just as easy to them as it is to hear. Salvation, or the heavenly inheritance, "is of faith, that it might be by grace or favor," says an apostle. I rejoice to know that it is just as easy to believe and be saved as it is to hear or see. That the Spirit of the living God has made it so to every man, and so works upon all men who read or hear the record which God has given of his Son as to remove all natural incapacity out of the way, is just what makes the record of Jesus glad tidings of great joy to all people. And nothing less than the views above given make the gospel glad tidings of great joy to every body. There is not a phrase, word, or syllable in the New Testament that is in the least irreconcilable with this simple view of the Gospel. Where the Spirit of God is not heard, men are without strength, and cannot receive the things of the Spirit of God. Where it is heard, every person is empowered to believe. And if any man ask me why all do not believe, I will tell him, it is because all do not wish to believe: or if they say they wish to believe, I will tell him then, "They believe not because they are not of the sheep of Christ." And if he ask me who are the sheep of Christ, I will tell him, They who follow him: for the reason why disciples are called sheep, is because they hear and follow the Master's voice. But this matter will be further developed in the subsequent essay. And in the mean time I will only add, that while many agree with this view of the Gospel on one side,

they take a view of it on another side incompatible with the nature of grace or favor altogether, by representing the whole matter as dependant upon some *will* subduing operation as physical as the creation of light—without which it is all a dead letter.   EDITOR.

Ancient Gospel.—No. V.
Immersion.

THERE is a natural and a moral fitness of means to ends. In the vegetable and animal kingdoms there is a natural fitness existing between all the means employed in promoting all the changes of which vegetables and animals are susceptible. This is, however, owing to the Creator's own appointment. Why heat and moisture should contribute to vegetation—oxygen, food, and medicine, to animal heat and life, is, to us, very natural; yet it is owing entirely to the will of the creator that it is so. For he made the vegetable, the heat and the moisture; and the animal, the food and the medicine, for each other. The fitness which we discover in them we call natural, just because it appears invariably to exist. It is the law of nature, we say; yet this law of nature, when pushed back to its fountain, is only another name for the will and power of God.

In the moral empire, or the empire of mind, there is a moral fitness as well established, though, perhaps, not so clearly defined as that which is the object of sense. Intellectual light and love are as well adapted to mental health and vigor, as natural light and heat are to the animal and vegetable existences. There is natural and moral good, natural and moral evil, natural and moral beauty, natural and moral deformity, and natural and moral fitness. Kindness and beneficence are morally fitted to produce love;—forgiveness and generosity to overcome injuries, to destroy enmity, and to reconcile parties at variance.

Transgressions of law, whether natural or moral, are invariably productive of pain, though of different kinds. If I put my hand into the fire, corporal pain is not more certainly the consequence than that mental pain of guilt follows the infraction of moral law.

But were I thus to follow up the analogies in the natural and moral kingdoms, I might stray off from my present purpose altogether. It is sufficiently established that there is a moral as well as a natural fitness of means to ends.

Sometimes there is an apparent congruity or fitness between the means appointed by God and the end or object for which they are appointed, but at other times there is no discernible relation between them. The falling of the walls of Jericho upon the blowing of rams' horns; the anointing of a blind man's eyes with clay to recover his seeing; or the dipping of a leprous person in Jordan to remove a leprous affection, are all of the latter kind. But, perhaps, the amount of divine energy put forth in this way is no greater, though to us more extraordinary, than that employed in making a tulip grow, or a rose open and expand its leaves in obeisance to what we call a law of nature. I think it would not be more expensive on the treasury of divine power to rain loaves from heaven, than to give them to us in the ordinary way of twelve months vegetable and animal process. And, therefore, I can believe that it is as easy for God to forgive us our sins in the act of immersion as in any other way whatever.

But yet I have not arrived at the assigned point

to which I directed the expectation of my readers in my last.

Where there is a guilty conscience there is an impure heart. So teaches Paul: " To the unbelieving there is nothing pure; for even their mind and conscience is defiled." *In such a heart the Holy Spirit cannot dwell.* When God symbolically dwelt in the camp of Israel, every speck of filth must be removed even from the earth's surface. Before the Holy Spirit can be received, the heart must be purified; before the heart can be purified, guilt must be removed from the conscience; and before guilt can be removed from the conscience, there must be a sense, a feeling, or an assurance that sin is pardoned and transgression covered. For obtaining this there must be some appointed way—and that means or way is immersion into the name of the Father, Son, and Holy Spirit. So that, according to this order, it is incompatible, and therefore impossible, that the Holy Spirit can be received, or can dwell in any heart not purified from a guilty conscience. Hence it came to pass, that Peter said, " Be immersed for the remission of your sins, and you shall receive the gift of the Holy Spirit."

No man can have a holy spirit otherwise than as he possesses a spirit of love, of meekness, of humility; but this he cannot have unless he feel himself pardoned and accepted. Therefore the promise of such a gift wisely makes the reception of it posterior to the forgiveness of sins.— Hence in the moral fitness of things in the evangelical economy, baptism or immersion is made the first act of a christian's life, or rather the regenerating act itself; in which the person is properly born again—" born of water and spirit"—without which into the kingdom of Jesus he cannot enter. No prayers, songs of praise, no acts of devotion in the new economy, are enjoined on the *unbaptized.*

Catholics and protestants think so too, if they only knew it. They know that baptism, as they understand it, is prior to every other religious institute. They make it, in fact, *regeneration.* They suppose that by it the inconscious babe is born into the kingdom of heaven in some sense. They err not in making it, in the order of things, previous to every other act, but in separating it from faith in the subject. It is not more natural or necessary in the kingdom of nature, that blossoms should precede the ripe apple, than that, in the empire of salvation, baptism should precede the remission of sins and a holy spirit. For the Spirit of God is the spirit of holiness, and where there is a guilty conscience it cannot dwell.

If baptism be connected with the remission of sins, infants require it not; for they have no sins to be remitted. At least the Calvinists and Arminians teach this doctrine; for they say that "original sin" is all that is chargeable upon infants. This original *sin* is but one, and is always found in their dialect in the singular number. Now as christian baptism was always for the remission of *sins* in the plural number, in the primitive age, and never once said to be for the remission of *sin,* nor of original sin—infants, on the Calvinistic and Arminian hypothesis, need not be baptized: and in this I am both a Calvinist and an Arminian.

But I cannot, it seems, keep to the point. The question is, Why is the Holy Spirit promised as consequent upon immersion? I answer, 1st. Because forgiveness is through immersion; and because, in the 2nd place, the spirit of holiness cannot reside in any heart where sin is not absolved. This is an invariable law in the moral empire, over which the Lord Jesus reigns. The new constitution is based upon the fact that where remission of sins is there is no need for sacrifices; consequently I argue, that the reason why there are no sacrifices—no altars, priests, nor victims, under the reign of Jesus, is because remission of sins through immersion is enjoyed. And let it be noticed with great attention here, that God's dwelling in and among the people of the new reign, or his spirit ruling in their hearts, is based upon the fact that " the worshippers being once cleansed have no more conscience of sins." This admirably coalesces with the views exhibited in the previous essay, and indeed with all the essays upon the " Work of the Holy Spirit in the Salvation of Men," in the volumes of this work.

If men do not believe, and will not be immersed into the faith through what the Spirit of God has already done, there is not one promise in all the Book of God on which they can rely, or to which they can look as affording ground of expectation for the Spirit of God to dwell in their minds, or to aid them while in unbelief. Let him that says " Yea," tell us the promise.

EDITOR.

The Columbian Star.

MR. WM. T. BRANTLEY, Pastor of one of the richest and most flourishing Baptist churches in the United States—a church rich in annuities, neither dependant upon the head of the church nor any of its living members, for at least sixteen hundred dollars a year;—I say, Mr. Wm. T. Brantley, formerly of South Carolina, called to the pastoral office of said church, rich in good " deeds" and legacies, and editor of the "Columbian Star," has humbled himself so far as to notice this little periodical—which, with great good humor, he calls the "insolent," "pugnacious," and "insidious," "falsely called Christian Baptist." After having exactly in the letter and spirit of the Apostle Paul, honored me with a long retinue of epithets, full of christian charity—and declarative of a most benevolent and christian temper, he gives me over to Satan and the Arminian Expositors for good behavior.

I could have thanked him more if he had honored me less. But at the impulse of his strong affection for my person and labors, he oversteps the modesty of christian nature; and not only represents me as "self-willed," "merciless," "self-conceited," and "arrogant," but as insidiously aiming at the subversion of "the ancient order of things." So much for *Star*-light when the Sun shines. But for my joy he has promised me but one such friendly notice. Why but one, Mr. Brantley? If a proof of your condescension, it is too little to gain the reputation of being humble; which, perhaps, is not fashionable in the present order of things:—if a proof of your bravery, but once is too little to gain for you the reputation of a christian hero. But if "once only," lest your reputation for honesty and candor in a good cause should suffer, it would have been well for you to have thought twice before you promised "once only," lest this "once only" should prove too often for your good name.

The history of Mr. Brantley's course to the "falsely called Christian Baptist" is as follows: Some time in November last, if I remember right, he first introduces me to his readers through the medium of a false statement prefixed to the minutes of the Franklin Association. I call it a false representation, for so it was demonstrated, and the authors of it have not since vindicated themselves nor it, though called upon for an explanation in the third number of this present volume. I wrote a private letter to Mr. Brantley, complaining of this act of injustice; but he made no public amends for the falsehood published, and suffers his readers to remain under the false impression to this day.

Not willing to become "pugnacious" all at once, although he began to conjugate "*pugno, pugnas, pugnavi,*" I suffered him to pass without a word. By and by, in December, he gives me one or two thrusts, "*unguibus et pedibus,*" in his preface to Bishop Semple's two letters, but graciously promises to give me a column or two in his paper when I should demand it. The publication of these two letters following his kind introduction of me, were well designed and calculated to bias every reader of the "Star" against me. Still, though "self-conceited, self-willed, and arrogant" as I be, I did not notice these infractions of christian law, fully expecting and hoping, for the sake of christian character, that he would make a large amends, and so soon as my replies to Bishop Semple would appear he would permit his readers to hear with both ears and to examine both sides. But to my no little surprise, he next gives a dissertation upon "the Spirit of the Reformers," and castigates me over the shoulders of the *Reformer.* Still I could not give him up, nor lift my pen in self-defence, while I had his pledge—his public pledge, that he would do me justice. I concluded to write him, requesting him to redeem his pledge; and as he had published Bishop Semple's letters, I asked him to publish mine. This last letter he deigned not once only to answer, but in the "Star" of the 5th April he addresses me as "pugnacious, self-willed, self-conceited, insidious, arrogant," &c. &c.

The policy of this kind philippic is to represent me as fighting with the Baptists and Baptist Confession, and all the good, pious, and orthodox Baptist dignitaries, such as Dr. Noel and Mr. Brantley, and so forth—as exceedingly mad against the Baptists, the Confession, and the Doctors of Divinity, and those decent Rabbies who make out of the popular establishments two, three, and sometimes four thousand dollars a year.

No wonder they support the schemes that so well support them.

I could easily show that a Pharisee, a Sadducee, or an Epicurean Philosopher, or any Rabbi, with a good fat living, could have represented Paul the Apostle as "self-conceited, arrogant, self-willed, pugnacious," exceedingly mad against the little creed and the good and pious Jews who loved Moses and their own order of things. I say, I could show that, upon Mr. Brantley's plan, all this and much more could have been done with infinite ease; and the great majority would have been gulled with such a representation of things as easily eighteen centuries ago as at this day. But this is unnecessary for me. As Paul did appeal to his whole course in self-vindication, and as he ascribed to the dyspepsia, rather than to the head or the heart, the opposition of his opponents; so, for the sake of all parties, I do adopt and pursue the same course.

But if Mr. Brantley should ever condescend a second time to look down from his high and lofty seat in the great city of Philadelphia, upon the "arrogant and insidious Christian Baptist," I will ask him a query or two which he must feel himself bound to answer:—

1st. Why do you represent me in your first sentence as "selecting the brethren Semple, No-el," and yourself, for a wanton attack, when in fact you, and each of them, selected me, and tried, condemned, and denounced me, before I ever pointed a pen or opened my lips to publish a single word concerning any of you? Yourself and the brethren Semple and Noel, months before I noticed you, were making very free with my reputation. This is so notorious that it puts my charity to the torture to discover how you could innocently present me to your readers as the first to attack any of you. You made "the selection;" not I. But Mr. Brantley, you understand the logic of the *Ins* full as well as you understand the seventh chapter of the Romans. And I do not hereby question your orthodoxy in either. I want to see more honesty. We have enough of orthodoxy. Show me a little honesty in answering this pertinent request.

2d. Why do you not fulfil your promise made to me and the public in December last, of giving me an opportunity of vindicating myself from the vituperations you have given currency to—and why do you now append conditions to your promise which did not accompany it? I have fulfilled the only condition you attached to it, and will you plead with the Mother Church that an oath or promise made to a heretic is not binding?

3d. Why do you say there was a time when, as a writer, I professed to have "no fixed tenets?"

4th. Why do you affirm that, in opposing your little dead letter, called the Confession, (which, by the way, has not been the chief thing in my mind while opposing creeds,) I am casting off all cords? Is the little creed all the cords in the world?

5th. Why do you say that I "scatter my sentiments over a wide space (in the C. B.) to prevent their being compared and examined?" Do give the proof.

You make me a new promise instead of fulfilling an old one. You say if I "make out a synopsis of my sentiments you will publish it." If, in your logic and morals, the making of a new promise is equivalent to fulfilling a former one, I despair of inducing you to do me justice; and while you make yourself "the judge, jury, and witness," when I am worthy to appear in the "Columbian Star," I shall be content to suffer such acts of injustice as you have done or may do me, so long as it may please my good master to permit it to be so. I had once some hope that amongst the public and leading Rabbies of the day, I had found one who would not think himself degraded in serving the Saviour of the world. I will not yet say, "*Ab uno discite omnes.*"

                                        EDITOR.

A Restoration of the Ancient Order of Things.
No. XXIV.

Church Discipline, No I.—Third Letter to R. B. Semple.

Brother Semple,

DEAR SIR—You say that "church government is obviously left by the bible for the exercise of much discretion." How this can be I cannot conjecture. Whatever is left for the exercise of much discretion is obviously a discretionary thing. If, therefore, church government be a matter obviously of human discretion, I see not how any form of church government, though principally of human contrivance, such as the Papistical or Episcopalian, can be condemned.— Each of these forms takes something from the bible and much from human discretion. We may think that what their discretion adopts is very far from being discreet; but in condemning their taste, we cannot censure them as transgressors of law; for obviously where no law is there is no transgression. If there be no divine law enjoining any form of church government; if there be no divinely authorized platform exhibited in the bible, then why have the Baptists contended for the independent form, except they suppose that they have more discretion than their neighbors!

But what you may call "church government" may, perhaps, be entirely a matter of human discretion, such as fixing the time of day on which the church shall meet; also, the hour of adjournment; the place of meeting, whether in a stone, brick or wooden building; the shape and size of their house, and the seats and conveniences thereof. On these items the bible, indeed, says but little. Or, perhaps, brother Semple, under the terms "church government," you may place synods, councils, associations; the duties of moderators and clerks; rules of decorum and parliamentary proceedings in deliberative bodies; all of which some think as necessary to the well being of the church as "the scaffolding is to the house." If you embrace all these items, and other kindred ones, in your idea of church government, I perfectly agree with you in one part of your assertion, that the bible says little or nothing on such matters; but I do not say that they are all left to human discretion, and therefore I cannot flatter myself into the opinion that the synods and advisory councils of Presbyterians and Independents are innocent matters of human discretion!

You have, no doubt, brother Semple, often observed, and remarked to others, that a majority of the disputes in religion have originated from not defining the terms or using the same words as representatives of the same ideas. I have often said that the chief advantage which mathematical demonstration has above moral or philological proof, is owing to a greater precision in the terms used in the former, than in the latter species of reasoning. Many an angry and verbose controversy has been dissipated by the definition of a single term; and the angry disputants, after they had exhausted themselves, finally agreed that they misunderstood one another. When you say that "church government is obviously left by the bible for the exercise of much discretion," I am led to suspect that you attach a meaning to these terms quite different from that which I and many others attach to them. The reason I think so, is because I am puzzled to find a definition of them, that will accord with your assertion.

By "church government" I understand the government of the church; which the bible teaches is upon the shoulders of Immanuel. He placed the twelve apostles upon twelve thrones, and commanded the nations to obey them. I find, therefore, that the Lord Jesus is the governor, and the twelve apostles under him, sitting upon twelve thrones, constitute the government of the church of Jesus Christ. I know that synods and advisory councils have a right to govern voluntary associations, which owe their origin to the will of men; but in the church of Jesus the twelve apostles reign. Jesus, the king, the glorious and mighty Lord, gave them their authority. The church is a congregation of disciples meeting in one place, an assembly of regenerated persons who have agreed to walk together under the guidance of Jesus Christ. Hence they are to be governed by his laws. All the exhortations concerning temper, behavior, and discourse found in the apostolic writings, in all their addresses to the congregations after the day of Pentecost, constitute the government of the church, properly so called. When all the apostolic injunctions, such as those concerning the government of the thoughts, the tongue, and the hands of christians are regarded, then the church is under the government of the Lord. Laws moral and religious, i. e. laws governing men's moral and religious actions, are the only laws which Jesus deigns to enact. He legislates not upon matters of mere policy, or upon bricks, stones, and logs of timber. He says nothing about moderators, clerks, and parliamentary decorum: but upon moral and religious behavior he is incomparably sublime. He enacts nothing upon the confederation of churches, of delegate meetings, or any matter of temporal and worldly policy. Hence they strain out a gnat and swallow an elephant who complain there is no law authorizing the building of meeting houses, and yet find a warrant for a "state convention" or a religious convent, college or seminary of learning. The matter of church government which was discussed at Westminster was never mentioned by the Lord nor his apostles. When I hear Independents, Presbyterians and Episcopalians contending about their different forms of church government, I think of the three travellers contending about the color of the cameleon. One declared it was blue; another affirmed it was green; a third swore it was black; and yet when the creature was produced all saw "'.was white."

As some of the wisest philosophers of the present century have discarded what has been improperly called "moral philosophy" from the circle of sciences, because it has no foundation in nature; so methinks the subject of "church government" and the whole controversy about it, in the popular sense of these terms, might safely be sent back to the cloisters of the church of Rome, whence it came. Let the moral and religious government of the institutes and exhortations addressed to disciples in their individual and social capacities be regarded, and there is no need for one of your by-laws or borough regulations.

The decorum of a public assembly is well defined, both in the sacred oracles and in the good sense of all persons of reflection. And if disciples meet not "for doing business," but for edification, prayer and praise, or discipline, they will never need any other platform or rules of decorum, than the writings of Paul, Peter, James and John. But if you, brother Semple, will have the daughter attired like her mother; or if you wish any sect to become respectable in the eyes of those acquainted with the fashions in London and Rome, you must have sectarian colleges under the patronage of churches, and churches under the patronage of associations, and associations under the patronage of state conventions, and state conventions under the patronage of a constitution, creed, and book of discipline, called "church government." And the nigher these two latter approximate to the see of Canterbury, or that of Rome, the more useful and honorable will they appear in the estimation of such christians as are deemed orthodox in the District of Columbia.

I feel very conscious that the less you and other good christians say about "church government," in the popular sense, the better for its safety with the people, who have contended for something, they know not what, under this name. And just as certain am I, that if the laws governing moral and religious demeanor in the epistles are regarded, as they must be by all who are really taught by God, there will be found no need for our by-laws or regulations in the congregation of the faithful, not even in cases of discipline when transgressors present themselves.

Brother Semple, when I hear you call the church a "a corporation," the Bible "its charter," and the creed its "by-laws;" or, perhaps, you make the essay on discipline its by-laws: I say, when I hear a baptist bishop of such eminence, in the state of Virginia, in the reign of grace 1828, thus express himself, I feel almost constrained to take up my parable and sing—

"By Babel's streams we sat and wept,
"When Zion we thought on;
"In midst thereof we hang'd our harps
"The willow trees upon."

I hope to be still more explicit in my next.
Yours with all respect,   EDITOR.

Review of the History of Churches.—No. I.

WE have given the history or brief notices of the origin and progress of sundry churches or congregations, which, in Europe and America have attempted to move out of Babylon. To these we might have added many more, but a sufficient variety appears in the number given to afford a fair specimen. The history of another we have reserved for the last number of this volume. From the specimens given, several prominent features of characteristic importance appear pretty much alike in all:—

1st. Although in countries far remote from each other, and without the identifying influences of ecclesiastic jurisdiction, in the form of superintending judicatories, they appear to have agreed in making the scriptures the sole and all-sufficient rule of faith and manners—without the assistance of any creed or formula of human contrivance.

2d. In the next place, they appear to have drawn from the same source the same general views of the genius and design of the institution of a public weekly meeting of christians on the first day of the week.

3d. They all concur unanimously in the necessity and importance of the principal items of worship constituting the ancient order of things, such as the weekly commemoration of the death of Jesus and the resurrection; the contribution or fellowship for the necessity of saints; public and social prayer and praise, with the exercise of discipline when necessary; and, indeed, all the other public means of edification; such as public reading of the scriptures, teaching, preaching, and exhortation.

4th. They moreover give the same general representation of their regard for, as well as apprehension of, the nature and design of the true grace of God—and the indispensable need of a moral and pious life. But it has happened to some of them as it happened to those called Reformers from Popery. They disliked the Pope in Rome, but had no objections to a Pope in Geneva or at Wirtemberg. They disliked the incumbent rather than the incumbency; and each sect in setting up for itself, had either an effigy of the Pope's chair, or a few of the relics of an old one set up in their little *Sancta Sanctorum.* So some of those churches, in their honest and pious efforts towards a better order of things, inconsciously, no doubt, brought with them two misfortunes of very great injury both to themselves individually and to the progress of the more valuable and interesting parts of the Reformation. The first is the

catholic or textuary mode of interpreting scripture, and the second is not of much less deleterious influence, namely a too great regard to unity of opinion, or, as some would express it, unanimity of sentiments or views—an occurrence which, could it always be effected by any systematic course, neither presupposes the existence of moral goodness, nor necessarily contributes to its growth. Persons may be very unanimous in their views and efforts, and be no better than the projectors of the tower of Babel, whose misfortune it was that they were too much of one opinion. I trace every difficulty into which these virtuous communities fell, either to the textuary system and rules of interpretation, or to an unrighteous regard to similarity of sentiment. I say unrighteous regard, for when men make communion in religious worship dependent on uniformity of opinion, they make self-love, instead of the love of God, the bond of union, and elevate matters of mere speculation above the one faith, the one Lord, and the one immersion.

I am fully aware of the difficulties under which these christians withdrew from the popular establishments. They were sick of frivolous formalities, tired with the poor entertainment of insipid speculation and traditionary prescriptions, and desirous of understanding and living upon the Book of God. But they had lost the key of interpretation, or rather they withdrew from the popular establishments with much esteem for the bible, but with the textuary notions expounding it. They did not know or feel that when they commenced interpreting for themselves, they were only using the tools which they carried from the pulpits which they had forsaken. In many instances they only corrected a few opinions by their separation, and their reformed system left them as heady and high-minded and as cold-hearted towards the reign of heaven as before. The introduction of error, and the propagation of delusions are not the greatest evils chargeable upon the Mother of Harlots. She has done worse than even this. She has taken away the key of knowledge and rendered the oracles of God of none effect by her traditions.

A great deal has been said upon the evils arising from the mincing of the scriptures into texts, and the textuary plan of sermonizing: but as the queen of Sheba said when returning from her visit to king Solomon, "The half has not been told." There are not a few flowery and elegant sermonizers, as well as some scores of spiritualizers, who can make an ingenious sermon, and yet could not expound a single chapter in the whole volume, or give the meaning of the shortest epistle in the book. The reason is obvious: the art of making sermons and of expounding or understanding the contents of a book, are just as distinct as the art of managing vulgar fractions is from the whole science of mathematics, or the doctrine of magnitudes. Any person, by the help of a margin bible or a concordance, with the outlines of some system of theology in his cranium, can make as many sermons as there are verses in the bible, and deduce many doctrines and notions which never entered into the head or heart of any of the Jewish prophets or christian apostles. All this and much more he may do, and obtain the reputation of an eminent Divine, and yet could not tell the meaning or design of the first paragraph of the letter to the Hebrews. But this is not the worst evil resulting from this art. It gives birth to arbitrary and unreasonable rules of interpretation, which, so far as they obtain, perfectly disqualify the auditors from understanding any thing they read in the sacred volume. But this only by the way.

I do not offer these remarks as if they had been altogether elicited by the preceding letters; but because, in some of them, we see evident traces of the existence of these false premises in the minds of the communities which approved them. We are happy, indeed, in discovering in some of them a decided triumph over the narrow and illiberal principles which make a disagreement in what are called "doctrinal points," dismember a church; or exclude, as "unsound in the faith," the man whose head is too strong, or too weak, to assent to some far-fetched deductions of a more abstract or metaphysical reasoner. So far as this sentiment prevails, the way is opening to the return of the saints to the city of God. Had not this principle been recognized and acted upon in the primitive age, it would have been impossible for even the Apostles themselves to have united the believing Jews and Greeks in one religious community. It is as necessary now, if not more so, than in the apostolic age for the union of all who love the Lord Jesus in sincerity. Just what the more intelligent sectaries agree to constitute a christian in profession and practice, is all that they can reasonably demand of any applicant for admission into their communities. If they demand more or less, they sin against their own judgment, and sacrifice their good sense upon the altar of sectarianism. Admit this principle to be a correct one, and then when one point is settled the way is clear for the union of all christians. Let the question be discussed, What is necessary to constitute a disciple of Jesus Christ, both in profession and practice? and then who dare say that such should be excluded from the people of God? The man who would exclude such, will be hard puzzled and much perplexed to answer one interrogatory from the great Judge; namely, "Who has required this at your hands?"

EDITOR.

Mr. Robert Owen's Challenge.

SINCE the publication of my reply to a correspondent in Canton, Ohio, [Mr. A.] the following challenge from Mr. Owen to the clergy of New Orleans, reached us. It seems this challenge was published in several of the New Orleans papers.

TO THE CLERGY OF NEW ORLEANS.

'GENTLEMEN—I HAVE now finished a course of 'lectures in this city, the principles of which are 'in direct opposition to those which you have 'been taught it your duty to preach. It is of im- 'mense importance to the world that truth upon 'these momentous subjects should be now es- 'tablished upon a certain and sure foundation. 'You and I, and all our fellow men are deeply 'interested that there should be no further delay. 'With this view, without one hostile or unpleas- 'ant feeling on my part, I propose a friendly pub- 'lic discussion, the most open that the city of 'New Orleans will afford; or, if you prefer it, a 'more private meeting: when half a dozen friends 'of each party shall be present, in addition to 'half a dozen gentlemen whom you may associ- 'ate with you in the discussion. The time and 'place of meeting to be of your own appointment.

'I propose to prove, as I have already attempt- 'ed to do in my lectures, that all the religions of 'the world have been founded on the ignorance 'of mankind; that they are directly opposed to 'the never changing laws of our nature; that 'they have been and are the real source of vice, 'disunion and misery of every description; that

'they are now the only real bar to the formation 'of a society of virtue, of intelligence, of charity 'in its most extended sense, and of sincerity and 'kindness among the whole human family; and 'that they can be no longer maintained except 'through the ignorance of the mass of the peo- 'ple, and the tyranny of the few over that mass.

'With feelings of perfect good will to you, 'which extend also in perfect sincerity to all 'mankind, I subscribe myself your friend in a 'just cause. ROBERT OWEN."

Mrs. Herries, Chartres street,}
New Orleans, Jan. 28, 1820. }

'P. S.—If this proposal should be declined, I 'shall conclude, as I have long most conscien- 't.ously been compelled to do, that the principles 'which I advocate are unanswerable truths.

R. O.'

I have, from the first appearance of Mr. Owen in this country, considered his scheme of things, moral and political, as predicated either upon absolute Deism or Atheism. To decide which of the two, I was, for some time, in suspense. He has now come out full face against all religion, finding it at variance with his new theory of society. I have long wondered why none of the public teachers of christianity has appeared in defence of the last blest hope of mortal man.— This sceptical age and country is the proper soil, and the youth of this generation the proper elements for Mr. Owen's experiments. I have felt indignant at the aspect of things in reference to this libertine and lawless scheme. Mr. Owen, a gentleman of very respectable standing as a scholar and capitalist, of much apparent benevolence, travelling with the zeal of an apostle, through Europe and America; disseminating the most poisonous sentiments, as christians conceive; finding myriads in waiting to drink, as the thirsty ox swallows water, whatever he has to offer against the Bible and the hope of immortality, passes unchecked and almost unheeded by the myriads of advocates and teachers of the christian religion. If none but christian philosophers composed this society it might be well enough to let Mr. Owen and his scheme of things find their own level. But while a few of the seniors disdain to notice, or affect to disdain his scheme of things, it ought not to be forgotten that thousands are carried away as the chaff before the wind, by the apparently triumphant manner in which Mr. Owen moves along.

Impelled by these considerations and others connected with them, we feel it our duty to propose as follows:—

Mr. Owen says, in the challenge before us:— "I propose to prove, as I have already attempted to do in my lectures, that all the religions of the world have been founded on the ignorance of mankind; that they are directly opposed to the never changing laws of our nature; that they have been and are the real source of vice, disunion, and misery of every description; that they are now the only real bar to the formation of a society of virtue, of intelligence, of charity in its most extended sense, and of sincerity and kindness among the whole human family; and that they can be no longer maintained except through the ignorance of the mass of the people, and the tyranny of the few over that mass."

Now, be it known to Mr. Owen, and all whom it may concern, that I, relying on the author, the reasonableness, and the excellency of the christian religion, will engage to meet Mr. Owen at any time within one year from this date, at any place equi-distant from New Harmony and Bethany, such as Cincinnati, Ohio; or Lexington, Kentucky; and will then and there undertake to show that Mr. Owen is utterly incompetent to prove the positions he has assumed, in a public debate before all who may please to attend; to be moderated or controlled by a proper tribunal, and to be conducted in perfect good order from day to day, until the parties, or the moderators, or the congregation, or a majority of them are satisfied, as may afterwards be agreed upon. I propose, moreover, that a competent stenographer, perfectly disinterested, shall be employed to take down the speeches on the occasion; that for his trouble he shall have the exclusive right of printing and distributing said debate throughout the United States—and thus give all who feel desirous to hear or read, whether Mr. Owen, with all his arguments, benevolence, and sincerity, is able to do what he has proposed. After stating these prominent items, I leave every thing else open to negociation or private arrangement.

To quote the words of Mr. Owen—"With feelings of perfect good will to you, which extend also in perfect sincerity to all mankind, I subscribe myself your friend in a just cause."

ALEXANDER CAMPBELL.
Bethany, Va. April 25th, 1828.

Seed Time.

"Whatever a man sows that shall he also reap."

"HE that sows to the flesh shall of the flesh reap corruption; but he that sows to the Spirit shall of the Spirit reap life everlasting." Few persons seem to bear in mind that they are reaping every day what they have sown some days, months, or years before, even in their temporal enjoyments or sorrows. Still more plain it is to those who believe the words of the Great Teacher sent from God, that men will hereafter reap in the long, long harvest, what they have scattered in the seed time of their existence. Others also will reap, in some sense, the seeds which we are sowing, just as we are now reaping the seeds sown by our ancestors and predecessors. These facts suggest to us the necessity of great attention to our conduct. Ourselves here and hereafter, our children and our children's children, with their cotemporaries, may, and in many instances will, most assuredly reap what we are this day sowing. As we then regard our present and future happiness, that of our descendants, and that of all connected with them, we are admonished to take heed what we daily sow.

"To sow to the flesh," is to labor for fleshly or animal pleasures; or, taken in its worst sense, it is to labor for the gratification of our evil propensities, our corrupt passions and affections.—Such shall reap corruption. Remorse and its handmaid, Shame, must introduce them to the whole family of moral and physical agonies which terminate in the utter corruption of every sensual appetite and gratification. They reap rottenness and death, because they sowed the seeds thereof.

"To sow to the Spirit," is to devote our energies to the teachings of the Holy Spirit; to attend to the mental, more sublime, and heavenly objects of spiritual enjoyment, which are the objects of christian faith and hope; and to aim at the extension of these enjoyments by the introduction of others to a participation in them.

"To reap life everlasting," is to rise in bliss and exalted enjoyments, without any assignable point of termination. Such is the bright prospect of an eternal harvest to those engaged in sowing the precious seed which grows for an age, and ripens for ever.

In every sense, then, life is the seed time. To-day for to-morrow, this year for the next. And as we are reaping what others sowed, let us, as christians, and as wise men, sow not only for ourselves, but that generations yet unborn shall arise and call us blessed. I trust seed is this day scattering, which shall be reaped in the Millennium by all those engaged in introducing the ancient order of things. If, then, with the wisdom which comes from above, we go forth scattering the precious seeds of true bliss and real good, how happy for ourselves, and for all that are dear to us, in time and to eternity! But let none despair because he cannot sow and reap in the same day. Remember the patience of the husbandman—and imitate him in preparing for the golden harvest which will never end. EDITOR.

No. 11.]   JUNE 2, 1828.
To Bishop R. B. Semple.—Letter IV.

BROTHER SEMPLE,—You say that "the bible is the charter of the corporation called the church, and that this charter contemplates such regulations to be made by the church as answer to the by-laws of corporate bodies." This is precisely, as I understand your epistles and your language, your views of the system of church government. To express this idea fully, you allow that "the charter is not enough" for the government of the members of a church, but absolutely requires the church to make by-laws. And you aver that when the church is making "the by-laws" she is to take care only of one thing, that she "does not violate the word or spirit" of the charter. This, then, is a very luminous and clear view of your plan of church government. I am pleased with its clearness and intelligibility, though I have some formidable objections to such a representation of the matter. I must always commend perspicuity and precision in definitions, although the definition when given may be every way objectionable. That our readers may fully understand your definition, I will state the matter more fully; and, believe me, brother Semple, it will give me no little pleasure to receive from you either a retraction or counter exposition of the matter. When a legislature grants a charter to a bank, a borough, or a manufacturing company, it incorporates them into a separate, independent body, with full power to manage their own concerns; and they may appoint and must appoint either directors, a council, or managers, who have full power to make as many by-laws as they please for the government of their body, provided these by-laws are sanctioned by the charter; but the charter itself contains no particular or special laws for their government. It merely erects them into a body known in law, and grants them the privilege of legislation, and full power to enforce their own regulations and by-laws; that is, the same power which the legislature itself possesses.

The following are some of the more prominent objections to your plan of church government:—

1. I object to considering the bible merely as a charter granted by a legislature or civil government, because the bible does more than erect congregations, or constitute religious bodies invested with peculiar privileges. It gives them many laws for their general and particular beha-

vior. It authorizes the existence of congregations, or, as you call them, "corporate bodies," but it does more than any charter ever granted by any legislature ever did. It prescribes to the members in particular every requisite rule of behavior, for their thoughts, words, and actions. In fact it transcends any charter on earth in every respect: for if it was like other charters it ought to have left every thing, but the definition of the powers and privileges granted, to the management of the individuals incorporated. Now all the apostolic writings are filled with matter and laws entirely subversive of such a representation of the matter. The apostles taught christians a thousand times more than any charter teaches; and while the constitution of the christian church is laid down most fully in these writings, every important item of christian duty requiring the attention of christians, either in public or private capacity, is also laid down. In representing the bible, then, only as the charter of the church, injustice is done to it as great as I can conceive of. And the book is divested of all its utility as regulating the conduct of individuals. For you know, brother Semple, that charters regulate public bodies, and not individual persons; whereas almost the whole New Testament is engrossed with the regulations, and rules, and precepts which are to govern individuals. I am therefore constrained to differ essentially from you in this part of your plan of church government. But I hope, when you more maturely reflect upon this matter, you will differ from yourself as far as I differ from you; and indeed I must say, that I think you will agree with this view of the matter, and that your public lectures to congregations are at variance with your whole theory.

A second capital objection to your scheme of church government is, that it terminates in the same systems with those fashionable in Rome, Constantinople, and Edinburgh. In giving to the church the incorporated powers of legislation, even upon the subject of by-laws, the question is, Do the whole church, male and female, old and young—or do the rulers in the church make these laws? Or do you use the word church in the classic sense of presbyterians, or the New Testament sense of a single congregation? As a baptist, I suppose you use it in the latter sense. Well, then, the congregation in Washington city, for example, is chartered by the bible, and authorized to make its own by-laws or particular laws for the government of its members. The whole congregation must, then, make these laws, or their rulers. Now, to say nothing of the principles involved on either hypothesis, where do the sacred writings authorize or give directions for either? What command, law, or precedent, says, You may make your own by-laws or regulations? I must candidly say, I know of not one. If you know of any such, do, for the sake of the churches, declare it. The presbyterians and episcopalians, when pressed on this subject, have universally failed. The command, "Let all things be done decently and in order," has been oppressed until it has refused to carry one pound of by-laws. For "the decency and order" are declared in the volume. The 15th of the Acts absolutely refused to aid any of these councils unless they could say that their decisions were infallible and suggested by the Holy Spirit. But if you will have a church representative of churches, in the popular sense, then you are off the ground on which the baptists in former times always stood, and in union with the modern hierarchies.

But a third objection to this platform is, that if the charter authorizes a congregation to legislate in matters of faith or practice, it authorizes it to enforce, by proper sanctions, every act of disobedience or infraction of its by-laws. What then are the penalties? If no penalties, it all goes for nothing. And if the sanctions are enforced, then the decrees of the church are tantamount to the commandments of the Head of the Church. Divine institutes and human enactments are therefore at par   But I only glance at the incongruities of the scheme.

As I do not think you were aware of what was involved in this sentence, I will pursue it no farther and state no other objections to it until I learn that you are disposed to defend it. These three are, in my opinion, invincible.

What the Sandemanians or Haldanians say or do, it matters not to me. I defend them not. I am not answerable for their improprieties. I contend that the constitution of the church and its laws are found explicitly declared in the New Testament. And that in all matters of faith and christian practice it requires not one by-law to amend or adapt it to any christian society. And if you call the appointment of one bishop to four churches, a by-law, or the annual meeting of delegates to regulate the internal polity of congregations, or the system of text preaching, monthly communion, &c. &c. I say, if you call these by-laws, I protest against them as papistical and as anti-scriptural as any of the dogmas or sacraments of the Roman hierarchy.

I will finish my replies to your first letter in my next; and while I am discharging what to me appears an imperious duty, I beseech you, brother Semple, not to consider me in any other light than as faithfully and affectionately remonstrating against sentiments which I am convinced are of very injurious tendency and subversive of the grand characters of the divine volume. This I do without one unkind feeling for your person; and my reluctance to undertake this work was altogether owing to my high esteem for you as a good and great man, and a desire to have your co-operation in a cause which is triumphing and must be triumphant as certainly as the promises of God are all yea and amen in Jesus our Lord.

The public mind is aroused from its slumbers. The day is past when old usages and loose declamations can be passed current as the Oracles of God, or the decisions of reason. A thorough, a radical, a mighty revolution is not now to begin. It has actually commenced. And it is as vain to attempt to check its progress as to forbid the appearance of to morrow's dawn. The good and the wise do not wish to limit the expansion of the human mind; to retard the advancement of that happy period which you and I, and millions more, every day pray for. I would rather be found rolling the stumbling blocks out of the way when the King Eternal calls me home, than to be called from the chair of the most magnificent establishment which the East or the West ever saw.

O Lord! hasten thou the glorious day, when the light of thy philanthropy shall cheer the sons of men to earth's remotest bounds!

Truly your obedient servant,   EDITOR.

Ancient Gospel.—No. VI.
Immersion.

IN writing so much upon immersion under the head of the ancient gospel, I am not to be understood as identifying christian immersion with the ancient gospel. Immersion we have before said is the gospel in water; or the gospel exhibited in symbols the most significant and impressive. The truth to be believed is one thing, and the belief of the truth another. Both are prerequisites to immersion. The truth must be known and believed before we can be benefited by it. And one item of this truth is, that the blood of Jesus Christ, God's only Son, cleanses us from all sin. Yet God has made it accessible to us through water, as certainly as Jesus came by water and by blood. The virtue that cured all the blind, the halt and the maimed: the virtue that raised to life the dead, dwelt in the person of Jesus Christ; but something was necessary to elicit this virtue. The will of Jesus was the only absolute requisite. But he was pleased to institute certain media through which this virtue was to pass from him into the frame of the dead or the diseased. The media through which this virtue was communicated were various, but universally sensible. A word to the ear, a look to the eye, or a touch addressed to the sense of feeling, are equally sensible, and were occasionally employed in the impartation of divine restoratives to the sons and daughters of distress. As the electricity is drawn from the cloud at a certain moment of time, and by an established law in the material system; so the restoring virtue in the person of Jesus was elicited and communicated at a certain instant of time by a law in the spiritual system, as firmly established as any law of nature. So it is in the impartation of the blessings of salvation to the souls of men. There is an instant of time, and a medium through which the forgiveness of sins is imparted as well as the other blessings growing out of adoption into the family of God. This point is worthy of much investigation, and capable of the clearest demonstration. That there is a definite instant of time in which all former sins are absolved, is generally admitted; but that there is any sensible means ordained by which this blessing is conveyed, is not so generally apprehended. When Peter and John were addressed by the cripple at the beautiful gate of the temple, (*Acts* iii.) Peter said, "Silver and gold have I none, but such as I have give I you; in the name of Jesus the Nazarene, rise up and walk." The virtue which was reposed in the person of Peter was not imparted in the pronunciation of the words, "Silver and gold have I none," nor in the pronunciation of the words, "Such as I have I give thee;" but in saying, "In the name of Jesus the Nazarene, rise up and walk," and at the instant he took him by the hand, the healing virtue was communicated. But why select particular cases, when it was universally the case since the time when God put the rod of wonders into the hands of Moses, down to the imposition of the apostle's hands, that at a certain instant of time, and by sensible media, the powers called "supernatural" or "miraculous" were exhibited. Even the brazen serpent imparted no healing powers unless looked at by the stung Israelite. In respect to the remission of sins also in the religion of types, there was a definite moment, and an instituted way in which the conscience of a guilty Israelite was released. It would then be an anomaly in the history of the divine government, a defect to which there is nothing analogous in the natural or moral systems, should it have happened that there is no time fixed, nor sensible means appointed for the remission of sins in the new economy. Faith, indeed, is the grand medium through which forgiveness is accessible, but something more is necessary to the actual enjoyment of the blessing than a conviction that it is derived through the

blood of Jesus. Hence those who had obtained this belief were commanded to be immersed for the remission of their sins, or to arise and be immersed and wash away their sins, invoking the name of the Lord. The miracles wrought by Moses, by Jesus and the apostles, the sacrifices under the law, and the doctrine and commandments of the apostles, all concur in teaching us that there is a fixed time and instituted means in which all divine favors are communicated.

From the time when Moses was shown the glory of God, down to the close of the Jewish ages, it was known that the God of heaven was merciful and gracious, abundant in goodness and compassion. But until Peter the Apostle opened the kingdom of heaven, and announced the coronation of Jesus as Universal Lord, the means by which this mercy was exhibited in the actual remission of sins as communicated to, and enjoyed by, sinful men, was not clearly and fully developed. And one of the better promises on which the new economy is established, one of the superior excellencies of the New Covenant, is, that under it the forgiveness of sins is imparted, and the conscience perfected in and by means addressed to our senses, and of the easiest access to every believer of the philanthropy of God. So that the instant of time, and the means by which, the formal remission is granted, is an object of sense, and a proper subject of remembrance. Hence those who apostatized from the faith are said to have "forgotten that they were purified from their old or former sins;" i. e. sins committed before immersion. From which it is as clear as demonstration itself, that the forgiveness of sins was through some sensible means, or it could not have been a proper subject of remembrance.

But the documents which the scriptures afford for the demonstration of this most important fact, are as extensive as they are luminous and convincing. We shall attend to another illustration in the present essay. It is this: Jesus represents himself as the bridegroom; his people are compared to a bride; and their union is explained under the similitude of a marriage. Now, we know, that if the relation between christians and their Lord be at all analogous to that of a husband and wife, it must follow that something analogous to a marriage must be celebrated between them. This must be done at some definite period, and in some formal way. Hence persons are said to "put on Christ" as a woman puts on the name of her husband. We christians are said to be married to him; and in consequence of this marriage we are invested with an indefeasible right to all the honors, emoluments, and felicities originating from such an alliance. The property that christians derive from this alliance is thus described by the apostle Paul, "All things are yours, whether Paul, or Apollos, or Peter, or the world, or life, or death, or things present, or things to come; all are yours; and you are Christ's, and Christ is God's." Because ye are Christ's, we have all things. So reads the inventory of the christian's estate. Among these "all things," we can easily find the forgiveness of our sins. This, then, becomes ours when we become Christ's; and if we formally and actually become Christ's the moment we are immersed into his name, it is as clear as day that the moment a believer is immersed into the name of Christ, he obtains the forgiveness of his sins as actually and as formally as he puts him on in immersion. But as no woman is legally or in fact her husband's property, nor his property hers, until the marriage covenant is ratified and confirmed according to law; so no person can legally claim the blessings of pardon and acceptance who has not been according to law espoused to Jesus Christ. But so soon as the marriage is consummated, that moment the right is established and the blessings secured. And as nothing but a legal divorce can disannul the marriage covenant, so nothing but apostacy from Jesus Christ can alienate us from the rights and immunities guaranteed in immersion.

Some persons have thought that because they did not understand the import of christian immersion, at the time of their immersion, they ought to be immersed again in order to enjoy the blessings resulting from this institution; but as reasonably might a woman seek to be married a second, a third, or a fourth time to her husband, because at the expiration of the second, third, and fourth years after her marriage, she discovered new advantages and blessings resulting from her alliance with her husband, of which she was ignorant at the time of her marriage. It is true she may regret that she lived so long in that state without enjoying the privileges belonging to her; but her having the rites of matrimony celebrated ten times, or once for every new discovery she makes, would give her no better right to these enjoyments than she possessed through her first marriage. Nor will her repetition of the nuptial rites cause her to enjoy more fully the comforts of which she was deprived during the past years of her ignorance, than the mere consciousness that she now enjoys them. But of this more hereafter. We shall thank any of our intelligent readers for any objections they can offer to these essays on immersion so soon as we have brought them to a close.

EDITOR.

THE following extract of a letter from Col. J. Mason, of Kentucky, is published without his knowledge or consent. This is a liberty which I have sometimes taken when I thought the cause of truth could be promoted by either the information or the sentiment contained in any communication with which I have been favored, and especially when there is nothing in the communication, which ought to make the writer blush, either as a man or a christian. The writer is a gentleman of the first respectability both in church and state; and the information and sentiment contained in the extract cannot fail to be useful and interesting. If I have, in taking such liberties, ever given offence, I will confess my fault, and ask forgiveness, so soon as I am convicted of having done wrong. ED.

"MOUNT STERLING, KY. April 19, 1828.

"Dear Brother Campbell,

"YOUR interesting favor of the 4th April has been received, enclosing a prospectus for a new edition of the New Testament. I have no doubt, had I time to attend to it, I could obtain a number of subscribers. I shall, however, subscribe myself for ten copies, out of which I intend to present each of my children with one; for I am constrained to believe that the few copies of your first edition which have been scattered amongst us, together with the light issuing from the Christian Baptist, have been the instruments in the hands of God, of doing more good and producing happier times in Montgomery and Bath counties than was ever before witnessed. You are no doubt correct in your opinion of brother Smith: he certainly is in himself a host,

and the sectarian priesthood and their satellites have found it out, and are barking at him prodigiously; but the people are following him in crowds, and he is teaching them the ancient gospel with astonishing success. Indeed, sir, I am persuaded you would be amazed yourself were you present, and see with what adroitness he handles those arms which have been cleaned up and refitted in the Christian Baptist. The old and profane swearer, the long professed Deist, and many such as to all human appearance were given over to a hard heart and reprobate mind, have come forward and bowed to King Jesus.

"The second Lord's day in this month was our meeting. At Grassy Lick thirty-six were immersed and added to our church: on last Lord's day at Mount Sterling thirty-seven were immersed, and six others between the two days, which make seventy-nine in about eight days; amongst which are some of our most respectable citizens of the highest standing in civil society, particularly one of our most distinguished lawyers, who has long stood at the head of the bar, and an ornament to society.

"But I cannot deny myself the pleasure of telling you how much my soul is filled with joy at seeing a beloved brother according to the flesh, who unconscious of it himself, (till he heard brother Smith proclaiming the ancient gospel) has been a believer in the Lord Jesus Christ for more than twenty-six years; but because he could not tell what we have always been in the habit of calling a "christian experience," such as knowing the time and spot of ground when our souls were converted, things which the New Testament knows nothing about, he has been kept out of the fold of God ever since; till a few days ago he found that to believe in the Lord Jesus Christ and to obey his commands, was all that the Gospel required, he went down into the water, and told brother Smith he wished him to say he immersed, &c. instead of baptized, and, like the eunuch of old, is now going on his way rejoicing, as happy a man as can be found. His case is not the only one: but many within my knowledge, have been kept out of the church of God by our ignorant Doctors who profess to be teachers of religion, who in fact are no better than "blind leaders of the blind." It is true that when I joined the church and was baptized more than twenty years ago, in relating the exercise of my mind, or what we call "giving in our experience," (which was in accordance with the teaching I had received,) I was enabled to tell what was called "a good experience," and such a one as would bear the scrutiny of our ablest and most orthodox Doctors in Divinity; and, indeed, I got to believe myself that I could as easily tell a convert from one that was not, as I could distinguish black from white, and never was shaken in that opinion till I saw your Essay on Experimental Religion in the first volume of your Christian Baptist.

"O! my dear brother! what havoc has been made among the saints of God by the blindness, the ignorance, the superstition, and bigotry of the professed-to-be-Called and Sent—how many of God's dear children have been kept out of his fold, exposed to beasts of prey, and been wandering in darkness all their days, when they might have been ornaments in the house of God, and letting their light shine to all around."

Address to the Readers of the Christian Baptist.

THIS is one of the most momentous and eventful periods of the history of christianity since the commencement of our recollection of the

23

religious world, and, we think, from the commencement of the present century. All religious denominations are shaking. Christians in all parties are looking with inquisitive eyes into the sacred books, and examining the platforms of their respective schismatical establishments. Many run to and fro, and knowledge is increasing. What religious sect is not at this moment waking from its slumbers? Even the establishments of Rome, of England, of Scotland, fed and feasted as they are with political patronage, and bolstered up with their charming antiquity, are not likely long to retain their place in the veneration of their own children. The peaceful Quaker and the dogmatical Presbyterian, the zealous Methodist and the orthodox Baptist, together with the little hosts of more recent origin, are all on the tiptoe of expectation, and the cry of "Reform!" is now the loudest and longest which falls upon the ear from all the winds of heaven. Light mental, as light natural, is one of the most insinuating powers, and the most irresistible and rapid in its progress, we know any thing of. Its "swift-winged arrows" pierce the deep recesses of human hearts, and carry down the true images of things to the retina of the human soul. The bible, the fountain of religious light, is more generally distributed and more generally read now than at any former period. Even the measures often designed to uphold religious sects, are becoming battering rams to break down the walls of separation. Every day's report brings to our ears some new triumph of light over darkness—of truth over error—and of liberal minds over the enslaved and enslaving genius of sectarian despotism. The very efforts and measures of the abettors of sectarian schemes demonstrate not merely the imbecility of human skill when warring against the light of heaven, but open to the slowest apprehension the corruptions which have secretly crept into the bosom of every sect.

But of all the means which can be employed to promote peace on earth and good will among men, which have any influence to destroy sectarianism, or which are at all adapted to introduce the Millennium, there is none to compare with the simple proclamation of the ancient gospel. It was the proclamation of this which broke down judaism and paganism, at first, and amalgamated men of all religions in a holy brotherhood throughout the east and the west of the Roman empire. This was mighty through God to the subversion of all the strong holds of prejudice, error, and iniquity, which opposed the subjugation of the heathen to the obedience of faith. It was the substitution of human dogmas and speculations in room of this, which brought on the dark ages of papistical domination, and which to this day keeps up a sectarian spirit, and caters to the appetites of the demons of discord which have found resting places ready, swept, and garnished, in the inner temples of every religious sect. As all the religions existing in the days of the Cesars, in the countries where the ancient gospel was proclaimed, finally gave place to its purifying and associating influences, so all the sects now in christendom must give place to that holy spirit which the ancient gospel inspires. The proclamation of the ancient gospel from the data before us, from the experiments already made, proves its perfect adequacy to this important end, and shews itself to be perfectly adapted to reconcile men to God and to each other.

Of all the religious excitements which have been called Revivals, of which we have heard, there is nothing that it is exactly similar to the influences which attend the proclamation of the ancient gospel. I do not particularly refer to the great ingatherings mentioned in a former number, in Kentucky, amongst the friends and proclaimers of the ancient gospel and the ancient order of things, because I am not so well acquainted with all the circumstances attendant thereupon; but to what has been done in Ohio during the last few months, and what is still doing in sundry sections of that state. Many hundreds have received the ancient gospel within a few months, and have been immersed for the remission of sins, and have been filled with joy and peace in believing. Some of all religious parties embrace it and turn to the Lord, and it has wrought effectually in the hearts of all to produce the same benign and cheering influences.

I would not, however, test the true merits of any scheme solely by its effects on any partial experiments. Though this may be, and most generally is, the best proof of its true character. If we had always the fullest data which the nature of the case affords, submitted to our examination, we might then be fully able to decide upon the merits of any scheme by its actual success upon experiment. But this, from our limited information, is seldom, if ever, practicable. Reasoning, then, upon the nature of the means employed, in addition to the trials made, and sometimes in the absence of experiments, is necessary to the formation of right conclusions.—When, therefore, the obvious nature and tendency of any scheme, and the experiments made, concur in demonstrating its adaptation to the ends or objects in view, we are then in the possession of the best attainable means of deciding upon its real value.

The proclamation of the ancient gospel, we all know, was the grand scheme of Heaven to bring to nought all the false religion in the world. This is the highest commendation any thing can have. When God, the omniscient, and the all-wise, selects any means for any end, reason must humbly bow to it as the best in the universe. Now this is the fact, as all the intelligent declare. The proclamation of Christ crucified was both the wisdom and the power of God to salvation, and to bring to the dust all the boasted wisdom of Jew and Greek in ameliorating the moral condition of the world. It is now the only thing requisite to usher in the Millennium, or the reign of peace and good will among men. In other words, the clear apprehension and general diffusion of the ancient gospel, is all that is necessary, not to unite all sects; for this heaven designs not to do; but to grind to powder all sects and to destroy all sectarian feeling throughout the dominions of the Prince of righteousness and peace.

Do you not see, my christian readers, that in all Revivals, as they are called, the work of making christians is the all-engrossing work, and after the flame is extinct, (and sometimes it is extinguished by it,) then the struggle to make sectaries. The gospel makes the christian, and the schismatical theories make the sects. The preaching of the ancient gospel makes the christian: but the theory of Calvin or of Wesley makes the Presbyterian or the Methodist. In the language of one of our pious Presbyterian brothers, they must bring the new converts on "by degrees" to the spirit of the sect. Whatever real good is now done in the world is done by the simple narration of God's love of men, and all the mischief

94

is done by the dogmas of human speculation or the regulation of schismatical establishments. If the former is universally attended to and the latter abandoned, all christians would be one in name, in affection, in faith and hope.

Why, then, contend for shibboleths? Why fight about speculations and schismatical sentiments, when their tendency is, and must necessarily be, to procrastinate the approach of the events, for which we pray and ardently hope? 'Tis surpassing strange that we can believe ourselves sincere in praying for any thing which we are not using the means to obtain; nay, often using means to prevent. Should we see a nation preparing for war, and praying for peace, we would be led to suspect their sincerity. When then we see a people making new divisions and keeping up old ones, while praying for the Millennium or the triumph of love and harmony, we as naturally suspect that they are any thing but in earnest. I have called in vain for an exposition of one fact on the popular hypothesis. I wish to keep it before the public mind by frequent and various exhibitions of it. All sects that believe in revivals have them occasionally. The Lord is supposed to grant them. If then the Lord bestows these favors indiscriminately upon all the sects, does he not pour contempt upon all their little shibboleths by breaking through the cobweb fences when about to bestow his benefits? If the Lord makes no difference between the Presbyterian, the Methodist, and the Baptist, in these special interpositions, why should they keep up those schismatic walls when God overleaps them in his distributions? We must pause by again requesting some of our readers for a solution of this difficulty. EDITOR.

Review of the History of Churches.—No. II.

THE New Testament contains no liturgy, no congregational service, as did the Old Testament. In the writings of the great Jewish apostle Moses, there is a ritual, a liturgy, a tabernacle or temple service laid down; but no such thing is found in the apostolic epistles. This point seems not to have been so clearly apprehended by some of these churches as was necessary to their consistency and comfort. Finding all the public, religious and social services of the Jews so clearly and emphatically laid down in the Jewish scriptures, many have expected and looked in vain to find similar regulations in the christian scriptures. And yet could such a ritual be found, or a liturgy made out for christian congregations, it would be a discrepancy not to be reconciled to the genius of the book. Does any one ask, How this can be? I will attempt an answer: 1st. It was necessary, while the age of symbols lasted, that a worship, symbolic in its nature, and intended to adumbrate, or foreshadow, with prophetic accuracy, a new order of things, should be most minutely stated and most explicitly propounded by that infinite mind to which the things that be not are as real and present as the things which are, or do now exist; in order that the desired ends might be gained—that the salvation of the gospel might be thus introduced and fully confirmed. This alone rendered a liturgy or a divine service in the sanctuary necessary. But, in the second place, the Jewish age was the minority of the religious world. During that period there was not a full grown man. The patriarchal was the infancy or childhood; the Jewish, the youth; and the christian age, the manhood of the religious world. Let none think that this is an arbitrary disposition of the

3 G

ages or epochs in the religious world. There is the religious as well as the natural world, and both have their childhood, youth and manhood.* We have the authority of the Holy Spirit for considering the saints, during the Jewish age, in the same predicament as minors. In this state they were kept under a ritual or prescribed form of worship. A remark or two on the 4th chapter of the Galatians may be sufficient for our present purpose. "Now, I say," says Paul, "as long as the heir is a minor, he differs nothing from a bondman, although he be Lord of all. For he is under tutors and stewards until the time before appointed by his father. So also we, whilst we were minors, were in bondage under the elements of the world. But when the fulness of the time was come, God sent forth his Son, born of a woman, born under the law, that we might receive the adoption of sons. And because you are sons, God has sent forth the spirit of his Son into your hearts, crying Abba, Father."

Here the apostle asserts, First. That he and his brethren were, while under the law, in the state of minors. Second. While in that state they were in the condition of bondmen; kept under tutors and stewards, at whose command they must move obsequious. That the time appointed by the Father, in his Will and Testament, when this state of things should cease had actually arrived; and now they were raised from the rank of slaves to the standing of sons.

So soon as a person has terminated his nonage, or minority, and becomes a full grown man, he is no longer treated as a child or servant. He is allowed to have a judgment of his own, and to exercise it. This similitude the Apostle uses to represent the difference between the people of God under the old economy, and the people of God under the new. Under the latter they are permitted to exercise their reason, and to act from the principles infused into their minds from the development of the divine philanthropy. Hence the New Testament, after stating the ordinances and statutes of the kingdom of Jesus, prescribes no ritual or liturgy, but leaves the worshippers to act from that holy spirit which the gospel inspires. Being adopted into the family of God, they are to be treated as sons of God, and are to act as the children of God. Hence none of the circumstantials of the christian worship are laid down in the New Testament, as were all the circumstantials of the Jewish worship in the Old Testament. Take, for instance, the Lord's supper. The weekly and joint participation of the loaf and of the cup are clearly propounded and commanded, in commemoration of the Lord's death. But no rules are appended thereto regulating the sitting, standing, kneeling, or reclining of the members; no time of the day set apart; no particular form of a table or the furniture thereof; no arrangement of the seats; no

* I am now glancing at a subject on which I have long wished to write a series of essays. I promised them in the previous volumes of this work. I have always felt that my readers were badly prepared to receive many pieces presented in these volumes, because the premises which authorized them, at least in part, were not stated and not commonly adverted to. For the fact is, that since the reformation from Popery, the attention of christendom has been too generally engrossed in sectarian projects, and in making or defending new systems of the "Doctrines of Salvation," either to search into, or impartially learn, the oracles of God And owing to the methods and arts of interpretation which have been adopted from the Catholic church, the Protestant world, with a very few exceptions, has been quite disqualified for the task. These essays, so long promised, on the Patriarchal, Jewish, and Christian ages, we hope to be able to give in the next volume of this work.

29   95

collocation of the disciples; no prescriptions concerning the quantity of either element to be used, nor advices concerning what remains, &c. &c. All of these items would have merited attention under the old economy; but for the reasons assigned would be incompatible with the genius of the new. These or similar observations might be made concerning every item of the christian worship; but this sufficiently illustrates our meaning, and demonstrates the weakness of those who would lay down rules binding upon individuals, prescribing forms on these points which are left to the discretion of christians. Every attempt, therefore, on the part of any christian society to institute forms or models of the circumstantials, and to bind these upon individuals, or to require them in other societies before they can fraternize with them, is an attempt to judaize, or, what is the same thing in this connexion of ideas, to bring into bondage to the spirit of the elements of the world.

An attempt to find a liturgy in the New Testament, under the terms of "express precept or precedent for every thing," is what subjected those called Sandemanians and Haldanians to so much censure from many good men. How far they carried this attempt it matters not, or whether they deserved so much reproach on this account is not the question; the principle itself, if at all admitted, must lead to a stiff, unnatural, and formal profession of the christian religion, and to a spirit and temper not exactly in accordance with the spirit of adoption, and of high-born sons of God. Most of those congregations which commenced their career with a good share of this spirit, and with the expectation of finding as much precision in the New Testament in laying down express commands or precedents for every thing, as was exhibited during the non-age of the religious world, have since found their mistake, and have accordingly changed their course, and found a different spirit resulting from a change of sentiment on this important point. While they have found all the instituted acts of social worship and of the discipline of the church clearly laid down, they have found also that the absence of that minutia of prescription as to time, place, and circumstances, which characterized the Jewish age, has left it necessary for them to possess and exhibit a tolerant, forbearing, and condescending spirit, and to make love the bond of perfection.

In our next we hope to bring this review to a close.   EDITOR.

The Triumphs of Scepticism.

WHEN scepticism triumphs in the heart, the hope of immortality is banished. It crowns the tyrant death forever on his throne, and seals the conquests of the grave over the whole human race. It wraps the tomb in eternal darkness and suffers not one particle of the remains of the great, the wise and the good of all ages to see the light of eternity. But consigns by an irreversible doom all that was admired, loved and revered in man to perpetual annihilation. It identifies human existence with the vilest reptile and levels man to the grade of the meanest insect whose utility is yet undiscovered. Man's origin and his destiny are to its ken alike fortuitous, unimportant, and uninteresting. Having robbed him of every thing which could make him dear to himself and proud of his existence, it murders all his hopes of future being and future bliss. It cuts the cable, and casts away the golden anchor; it sets man adrift on the mighty, unfathom-

able and unexplored ocean of uncertainty, to become the sport of the wind and waves of animal passion and appetite, until at last in some tremendous gust, "he sinks to everlasting ruin." Say then, proud reasoner, of what utility is your philosophy—what your boast.

You boast that you have made man ignorant of his origin and a stranger to himself. You boast that you have deprived him of any real superiority over the bee, the bat or the beaver; that you have divested him of the highest inducements to a virtuous life by taking away the knowledge of God and the hope of heaven. You boast that you have made death forever triumphant not only over the body, but the intellectual dignity of man; and that you have buried his soul and body in the grave of an eternal sleep never to see the light of life again—O scepticism! is this your philosophy, is this your boasted victory over the bible! And for this extinguishment of light and life eternal what do you teach, and what bestow! you teach us to live according to our appetites, and do promise us that in your Millennium man shall live in a paradise of colonies almost as industrious, as independent, and as social as the bees. Well then do you preach with zeal, and exert your energies; for your heaven is worthy of your efforts, and the purity of your life is just adapted to the high hopes of eternal annihilation.

The Triumphs of Christianity.

A TRUE believer and practitioner of the christian religion, is completely and perfectly divested of a guilty conscience, and of the consequent fear of death. The very end and intention of God's being manifest in the flesh, in the person of Jesus our Saviour, was to deliver them who, through fear of death, were all their life time subject to slavery. Jesus has done this. He has abolished death and brought life and immortality to light. He has given strength to his disciples to vanquish death, and make them triumph over the grave—So that a living or a dying christian can with truth say, O death, where now thy sting! O grave where now thy victory! He conquered both, and by faith in him we conquer both. This is the greatest victory ever was obtained. To see a christian conquer him who had for ages conquered all, is the sublimest scene ever witnessed by human eyes. And this may be seen as often as we see a true christian die. I know that a perverted system of christianity inspires its votaries with the fear of death, because it makes doubts and fears, christian virtues. But this religion is not of God. His Son died that we might not fear to die, and he went down to the grave to show us the path up to life again, and thus to make us victorious over the king of tyrants, and the tyrant over kings. They understand not his religion who are not triumphant over those terrors of guilty man. The guilty only can fear, and the guilty are not acquainted with the character, mission, and achievements of Jesus our life. No one taught by God, can fear these horrors of the wicked. Jesus Christ made no covenant with death, he signed no articles of capitulation with the horrible destroyer. He took his armor away; he bound him in an invincible chain, and taught him only to open the door of immortality to all his friends.

A christian then must triumph and always rejoice. Our gloomy systems say, Rejoice not always, but afflict your souls: whereas the apostles say, Rejoice in the Lord always, and again, we say, rejoice. The gospel as defined by the angels of God, is, Glad Tidings of Great Joy; and who can believe glad tidings of great joy, and not rejoice? Deists, Atheists, and the whole host of sceptics may doubt, for this is their whole system; the wicked, the guilty, and the vile may fear, for this is the natural issue of their actions; but how a christian, knowing the Lord, believing the promises, and confiding in the achievements of the Saviour, can doubt or fear as respects death or the grave, is inconceivable. Thanks be to God who gives us the victory.

Some persons may doubt whether they are christians; and some may fear the pain of dying, as they would the tooth ache, or a dislocated joint: but that a christian should fear either death or the grave is out of character altogether. For this is the very drift, scope, and end of his religion. They who are under the influence of such fears and doubts, have much reason to fear and doubt whether ever they have known or believed the truth, the gospel of salvation. But a christian in fact, or one who deserves the name, is made to rejoice and triumph in the prospects of death and the grave. And why? Because his Lord has gone before him—because his rest, his home, his eternal friends and associates, his heaven, his God, all his joys are beyond the grave. Not to know this is to be ignorant of the favor of God, not to believe this is to doubt the philanthropy of God, not to rejoice in this is to reject the gospel, and to judge ourselves unworthy of eternal life. But the christian religion is not to be reproached because of the ignorance or unbelief of those who profess it. All rivers do not more naturally run down the declivities and wind their courses to the ocean, than the christian religion leads its followers to the sure, and certain, and triumphant hopes of immortality.   EDITOR.

The Columbian Star.

Mr. W. T. BRANTLEY, editor of this Columbian Star, gave us, some time since, his theoretic view of the "spirit of the reformers," and in his remarks upon the "pugnacious" Christian Baptist, he gave us a sample of the spirit of the opponents to reform. To assert in the wholesale, to dogmatize in the retail, to denounce investigation, and to extol the present "benevolent" schemes—appear to be the order of the day amongst all the great men who maintain that religious society is just, or very near, what it ought to be. I am not at present disposed to animadvert on the efforts, the temper, or style of those who are maintaining the schemes that maintain them. Perhaps gratitude, which is a fragrant virtue, obliges them to this course. But I complain of injustice, for which gratitude can make no reparation.

That the religious public may know the deportment of this same "Columbian Star" towards me, I will state a few facts. So soon as I commenced this work, I sent it on to the "Star," requesting an exchange. Six months revolved, but no star shone upon us. I wrote a second time, stating that I would pay the difference in the nominal value of the two papers; but no answer was received. After three months I wrote for the "Star" as any other subscriber, promising full compensation. But yet its conductors would not allow me a place on their list of subscribers. Elder Jehu Brown, of Ohio, to whom I related these facts, told me about the close of the first volume that he was "tired of the Star," and wished to discontinue it. I requested him not to discontinue it, but to order it to be sent in his name to Wellsburgh, Va. saying that I would take it out of the office and pay him for it. By

these means I got to read the Star for six months; but either because they found out the secret that I was a subscriber in the name of Jehu Brown, or for some other reason which was never assigned to me, they discontinued sending it. I got the "Star" no more. In 1826 I was favored with an interview with the Rev. O. B. Brown, in Washington city, who being one of the heads of departments, I supposed capable of explaining this mystery to me. But he could not. I complained to him, and on his engaging to have it forwarded to me regularly, I paid him for one year in advance, allowing the subscription price of the Christian Baptist in part pay. Before half of this year revolved, the "Star" again disappeared, and one ray of it I did not see till it arose in Philadelphia, in the latitude of my friend Brantley.

Hoping, as it had approximated towards my own latitude, I might be more readily cheered with its benignity, I made my prayer again for an exchange, but without obtaining a favorable answer. After waiting a few months I applied to Mr. Rhees, agent for this paper, in the city of Philadelphia, to ascertain why it did not come on; he wrote me in reply that friend Brantley, its present editor, some way hinted to him that there was a balance of one or two dollars per annum of difference in the nominal value of the papers, and that this balance must be paid to insure a regular exchange. I wrote to brother Rhees to stipulate the payment of difference, with a request to him to have it mailed himself that I might not again be disappointed. And owing to this arrangement, I have been able to read it regularly since.

So have the magnanimous editors and directors of the Columbian Star conducted themselves towards the Christian Baptist. This is only a little of the spirit of those who write essays on the spirit of the reformers. There is not a political paper in the union which we have solicited in exchange for the Christian Baptist, and some of them are at three and five dollars per annum, that would accept of the difference of price. But "the children of this world are in their generation wiser than the children of light." I complain not of paying the difference, (for I ask no favors from Stars;) but in this age of dissection of spirits, any facts throwing light upon men's souls cannot fail to be interesting. As the profits of the Columbian Star are sacred to missions in Philadelphia, it is likely that Mr. Brantley, wishes me to contribute to the cause in the way of an indirect tax.   EDITOR.

KENTUCKY, APRIL 15, 1828.
Campbellism.

THE following query was sent up to a small Association in this state for an answer:—

"What must a church do with her preacher who has embraced Campbellism?" To which the Association in her wisdom, replied, "As we know not what Campbellism is, we cannot tell her what to do."

A correspondent in Kentucky asks me, "What Campbellism is?" To which I answer: It is a nickname of reproach invented and adopted by those whose views, feelings, and desires are all sectarian; who cannot conceive of christianity in any other light than an *ism*. These *isms* are now the real reproaches of those who adopt them, as they are the intended reproaches of those who originate and apply them. He that gives them when they are disclaimed, violates the express law of Christ. He speaks evil against his brother, and is accounted as a railer or reviler, and placed along with haters of God and those who have no lot in the kingdom of heaven. They who adopt them out of choice disown the Christ and insult him; for they give the honor which is due to him alone to the creature of the Devil; for all slander and detractions are of the creation of the Devil. If christians were wholly cast into the mould of the Apostle's doctrine, they would feel themselves as much aggrieved and slandered in being called by any man's name, as they would in being called a thief, a fornicator, or a drunkard. And they who bestow such names are actuated either by the spirit of foolish jesting, or that vengeful spirit which would sacrifice the life as well as the reputation of those who deprive them of the means of self-aggrandizement at the expense of the intelligence, liberty, and true happiness of mankind. One uninspired man's name weighs as much as another's when put into the scales of the sanctuary, and where good information and moral character exist it is just as honorable: but no intelligent christian could be pleased to be named a Paulite, a Cephite, though either of these is a thousand times, ten thousand times more, honorable than a Calvinist or Lutheran. But neither Paul nor Peter would own that man as a consistent disciple of Christ who chooses to call himself by Paul, Apollos, or Cephas. I have always disclaimed every thing sectarian; and if the people of the different sects slander me or any of those who prefer the scriptures to any human creed, and the kingdom of Jesus the Messiah, to any sect; I say, if they slander us with the names and epithets which we disavow, they must answer to him who judges righteously. But for ourselves we protest against the name, the precepts, the feelings of any sect or schism in christendom.

Though some persons use such names without the intention of slander or reproach, and are not conscious of doing wrong, they ought to remember that in this way all sectarian names began to be approved. The time was that the terms Lutheran and Calvinist were a reproach. When these men died they became honorable, and are now gloried in. This was effected by the admirers of these men; first for the sake of distinction and to avoid circumlocution, and then with acquiescence, adopting the designation which their opposers gave them.

We wish all the friends of the ancient gospel and the ancient order of things, to remember that our motto is, and we hope ever will be, to call no man Master or Father, in the things pertaining to the kingdom of our Lord.

EDITOR.

Extracts of Letters, received by the last mail, stating the success of the ancient gospel in different parts of the country.

"Bishop Jeremiah Vardeman, of Kentucky, since the first of November last, till the first of May, immersed about five hundred and fifty persons."

"Bishop John Smith, of Montgomery co. Kentucky, from the first Lord's day in February, to the 20th of April, immersed three hundred and thirty-nine."

"Bishops Scott, Rigdon, and Bentley, in Ohio, within the last six months have immersed about eight hundred persons."

[We have heard a great deal said of the exertions and success of Bishop Morton; but correspondents have omitted to give the particulars.]

[Bishop Lane, of Washington county, Va. from whom I had a letter not many weeks ago, in his favor of the 16th April, received per last mail, says, "Since I last wrote you, I have immersed about sixty persons into the name of the Lord Jesus, for the remission of their sins."]

[A correspondent in May's Lick, Kentucky, under date of the 14th May, informs me that, "within a few months, about three hundred have been immersed into the name of the Father, Son, and Holy Spirit, on a profession of their faith that Jesus is the Messiah, the Son of God. These have been added to our church under the oversight of Bishop W. Warder. Great additions have been also made to other congregations in the same vicinity."]

No. 12.]   JULY 7, 1828.

To Bishop R. B. Semple.—Letter V.

Brother Semple,

You say, "The Christian Baptist has doubtless exhibited many valuable pieces and principles· but, taken as a whole, I am persuaded it has been more mischievous than any publication I have ever known." Almost all the Doctors of Divinity, of all denominations, Catholic and Protestant, with all the *great* men who are aspiring to a *good degree* in the modern faith, will heartily acquiesce with you in declaring that the Christian Baptist, taken as a whole, has been more mischievous [to them] than even the publications of Volney, Voltaire, and Paine. If such be the book, what shall we think of the author! To the kingdom of the clergy, and to the reign of ignorance and superstition, to false religion, and to all the aids and supports thereof; I have, brother Semple, always intended that my pen should be most mischievous. I was aware, too, that in advocating the cause of him who was to be as the refiner's fire to consume the dross, and as the fuller's soap to purify the filth of professors; I could not hope for an exemption from the fate of himself and his prime ministers. Him they accounted a public pest, a most mischief making spirit, and them they accounted pestilent fellows, and sowers of mischief among the people. It is enough for the disciple that he fare as his Lord. Some of the good people then, as now, joined with the priesthood in opposing him. When I hear Nathaniel, an Israelite indeed, in whom there was no guile, exclaim concerning him, "Can any good thing come out of Nazareth?" I am not so much alarmed to find brother Semple joining with W. L. M'Calla and such spirits in saying of the author and the work, that it is the most "mischievous" publication in the world.

But, brother Semple, what mischief has the Christian Baptist done? Tell me the christian on earth it has been mischievous to: tell me the sinner whom it has injured. If it has been so mischievous, so extensively mischievous, you can surely tell us of hundreds, if not of thousands, who have been injured by it. "Do then condescend to men of *low degree*," as Paul advises, and explain to us the nature, extent, and malignity of the mischief done, and then I will arise and make an effort to undo it. But how should I act, think you, when I receive one hundred letters for one like thine, asserting that it has done the most good, and been the most useful paper published in this country. How far a large majority of my readers may flatter me, I pretend not to say: but one thing I do say, that if only one tenth of my correspondents speak as they think, and as their own observation warrants, I shall have reason to thank the Lord while I live, that he gave me the heart to commence, and the ability to conduct this work as I have done. And if your charity will permit you to think that one so heterodox as I, can speak the truth at all, I would attempt to assure you that my anticipations of doing good by this work, have been outstripped a hundred fold. But this by the way.

I must say, however, that your assertion, if it could be documented by unequivocal facts, would be a justifiable reason for your reprobating the work. For I proceed upon the same principles of reasoning with yourself in editing this work. I feel conscious that some of the dogmas taught from the pulpits and the presses in this country, are more mischievous than the writings of Bolingbroke, Herbert, or Paine. Indeed I consider the doctrine of physical operations, and the textuary plan of preaching, to be mischievous beyond all my powers of expression. But I will not deal in assertions only. I will give the proof. First, with regard to the textuary mode of expounding scripture. Look at the ignorance and superstition of the baptist churches, to say nothing of the other sects; are there not many churches in Virginia, in which there are hundreds of members who cannot pray in public; who could not tell the contents, genius, or design of one epistle or section in the New Testament? I have found many congregations both in the East and West, in which not more than ten or a dozen persons seemed to have any taste for even reading or understanding the discourses of Jesus Christ or his Apostles; and if there were a hundred persons in the congregation, a large majority of these did not know their right hand from their left in the sacred writings, and could scarcely tell the names of the different epistles or writings in the two Testaments. I feel ashamed to avow, what I know to be fact, in nine tenths of the Baptist congregations in this country—and still worse is the condition of other sects. To say that I have found old men in the church that could not tell whether *Amos* wrote before or after the Christian era—or unable to find where in the bible the writings of any specified apostle or prophet lay, would be supposed an exaggeration almost insufferable. But I could wish that thousands could not be found of this standing. But only look over the faces of the members of many congregations who are polished in the ordinary attainments of this life, and who, you know, could not give the meaning of a single chapter of God's Book; and then, with me, can you not deplore the methods of teaching and the teachers of this age?

Again, look at the morality, to say nothing about the piety, of many called orthodox churches. I heard that you said of a certain church in Virginia, that so general was the crime of drunkenness amongst the members, that a majority could not be obtained to exclude one of the fraternity who had been beastly drunk on some public occasion. There were so many to sympathize and feel for him, and so many to form excuses for this "remaining corruption;" and because "he was not his own keeper," he ought to be forgiven, even before he had repented!! Again, consider the detractions, evil speakings, surmises; the breach of promises and covenants; the contracting of debts beyond the means to pay, and the many defrauds thus committed with impunity, blaming it too upon the times, and not upon the pride and vanity of the professors. I say, consider all the provisions made for the flesh, for the gratifications thereof, with all the kindred evils now countenanced, tolerated, and made matters of forbearance in the churches, and think how "mischievous" the systems and their supporters are to the myriads of professors in the present day.

Again, look at the tendency of the doctrines of special operations and miraculous conversions upon society at large, and especially upon the children of the members of churches, as far as your acquaintance extends. Not being so well acquainted in your vicinity as in many other parts of these States, I cannot say what opportunities you may have to judge of this matter. But I can say with truth, that not only the children of the members of the churches, but of the Bishops, are very generally (there are a few exceptions, and indeed but few,) the most hardened sinners and the most profligate in the country. It is almost proverbial that the "sons of preachers" are the greatest sinners in the congregations where they live, not whither they resort; for many of them are seldom seen, even within the doors of their fathers' meeting houses. O! brother Semple, if Paul were living amongst us, what would he say of our dogmas, and our bishops! If he proscribed from the bishop's office every man who had "not believing children," whose sons and whose daughters could be "accused of riotous living," or of "being unruly"—I say, if he were to act as he directed Timothy and Titus to act, what would become of nine-tenths of our bishops and congregations! Some of the bishops know full well that Paul would not tolerate them at all; and therefore they would rather be styled Doctor, or Rabbi, or Reverend, or any thing that would prevent a comparison of themselves or their families, or congregations, with the instructions given concerning bishops in the New Testament. Now I blame the proverbial profligacy and infidelity of the children of bishops and of members, upon the dogmas taught and the examples given by the teachers and their admirers. So long as a teacher makes the call of Saul to the apostolic office a pattern of conversion, and leads his children and hearers to expect something similar before they can be converted to God; so long will the present order of things continue to exist. I do, then, with these facts and documents before me, and volumes more which I could give, fearlessly assert that some dogmas, and the methods of teaching pursued, are doing more mischief than most of the infidel writers of the present day.

And when I see a good and wise man, like yourself, lured from the bishop's office, and severed from the flock, the oversight of which you had committed into your hands, and of which you are one day to give an account; I say, when I see one of your high attainments allured from all these sacred relations and this glorious responsibility, to help to build up a college in the city of Washington, which never did promise any spiritual good, and which the Lord Jesus never stood in need of, not even when he commenced with such fearful odds against him, from all the schools of philosophy in Greece and Rome: I again say, when I see you enticed to abandon your flock for this vain project, for the fashion of this world which passes away, I am at a loss to say what greater mischief can be done to the cause of the humble gospel, than the schemes and projects now in fashion are doing, and with the greater effect too, by the good words and fair speeches which make them go down so well with the good people.

The mischief I have done, namely, that of creating a distrust in the public mind of the divine call and infallibility of the public instructors, of making the laity read with more hopes of understanding the sacred writings; of showing the impropriety of shackling the human conscience, and fettering the human understanding by human creeds, and of placing in their true light some wild and abstract speculations of the scholastic theologies, of enlightening the religious mind on many items in which it was enveloped in ignorance and superstition, is nothing compared with one such occurrence. These, too, constitute the head and front of my offending. For as to the divisions and bickerings amongst members of churches charged upon me, they are as unreasonable as to charge the christian religion itself, its founder and his apostles, with all the divisions and persecutions which occurred in their day, which not themselves, but their enemies and opposers created. It is my opposers that create all the divisions and discords, which they afterwards unjustly charge upon me. I had hopes of finishing my replies to you in this number, but some things yet remain to be noticed. In the mean time I must close, wishing you health of mind and body.

Your sincere friend,   THE EDITOR.

Ancient Gospel.—No. VII.
Christian Immersion.

SOME say that we substitute water for the blood of Christ. This is so far from fact, that we give no efficacy to water, but through the blood of the Saviour. Had he not shed his blood, all the waters which once deluged the world would be unavailing. They who say that faith is necessary to salvation, include neither infants nor those who never heard of the Saviour, and argue that faith would be as unavailing as water, were it not for the blood of the Messiah. Yet they make faith necessary. Why then censure us for making immersion necessary to our enjoyment of forgiveness. We, like them, neither include infants nor those who hear not of the Saviour; and like them we make immersion nothing independent of the blood of the great sacrifice, and of faith in that blood. But we make immersion as necessary to forgiveness as they and we make faith, or as necessary to our being entitled to the blessings that are contained in the New Covenant, as they make sprinkling or immersion necessary to admission into the church. They will not (I mean Baptists and Paidobaptists) receive into the church unbaptized persons. We say that baptism or immersion is just as necessary to our obtaining the forgiveness of our sins, as they make it, to admission into the church. And if they will allow that there is a possibility of salvation without faith, baptism, or admission into the church, why should they object to our remarks upon immersion, which are not more exclusive than their own, seeing they can take so much latitude after laying so much emphasis upon faith, baptism, and admission into the church as to admit the possibility of salvation to infants, ideots, and pagans, remote from christian privileges. I now argue with them upon their own principles.

In fact, I say no more than the Lord Jesus said, "He that believes and is immersed shall be saved." And he spoke only of them to whom the gospel was preached. I make immersion just as necessary as they make faith, or as the Catholics and Protestants make sprinkling to admission into the church. The only difference is, that I give to immersion with faith the precise import which the New Testament gives it; and they give to immersion or sprinkling, without faith, a significance which it has not. I do earnestly contend that God, through the blood of Christ, forgives our sins through immersion—through the very act, and in the very instant; just as, they say, God receives infants into the covenant or church in the very act, and in the very instant they are sprinkled. Their opinion I have long since shown has no foundation in reason or revelation. We have shown that the truth, of which their views are a perversion, is that when a person believes in Jesus, and is immersed, he has obtained in fact and form, that which they ascribe to an unauthorized tradition. If they have become more ashamed of this human invention than formerly, and will not say of it all that their fathers have said, namely, that a babe in the act of sprinkling "was regenerated to God, and made an inheriter of the kingdom of glory;" if they have degraded this rite to a "mere ceremony;" and if some Baptists have made it mean no more than "making a profession;" they ought to remember that their ancestors did not do so.

We do most unequivocally connect immersion and the blessings of the New Covenant, as explained in our former essays. But we object to our objectors, the injustice they do us in representing us as ascribing to immersion the efficacy of Christ's blood; seeing we declare that it is through faith in his blood that we receive remission in the act of immersion. Hence faith and immersion are the media through which these blessings are conveyed to the minds of men as stated in our last. So that the actual enjoyment of forgiveness, acceptance, adoption, and the gift of the Holy Spirit, are by a gracious necessity, made consequent on a believing immersion into the name of the Lord Jesus. But this we presume was explicitly developed in our last essay.

With regard to the promise of the gift of the Holy Spirit mentioned in the second of the Acts, we beg the attention of our readers. The promise referred to in that discourse of Peter, was doubtless the promise quoted from Joel the Prophet, viz. "I will pour out of my Spirit upon all flesh; your sons and your daughters shall prophesy," &c. This promise of the gift of the Holy Spirit, he represents as fulfilled on Pentecost in himself and his associates, who had before known and trusted in the Messiah; and as proposed to the present audience when they should believe, and be immersed into the name of the Lord Jesus. This is what the apostle proposed to his inquiring audience when he said, "Be immersed every one of you into the name of the Lord Jesus for the remission of your sins; and you shall receive the gift of the Holy Spirit; for the promise of this gift is to you and to your children," &c. This gift of the Holy Spirit was precisely and definitely that which was promised by Joel, and not that which continued in the church after the age of spiritual or miraculous gifts expired. Peter, in the house of Cornelius witnessed the outpouring of it upon the Gentiles, when he was called to call them; thus proving the truth of his own words on Pentecost, when he said this gift was not only promised to the Jews and their children who received the Messiah, but also to such others (the Gentiles) as the Lord the God of the Jews and Gentiles should call. Hence the Gentiles spake with tongues, and glorified God before immersion; for this reason, that God designed to ground their plea, as well as their right, to christian immersion upon the fact that he had bestowed upon them the same gifts he had vouchsafed upon the Jews, and thus established their claims for admission into his family. If, then, we were to suppose that the gift of the Holy Spirit promised to the converts on Pentecost consequent upon their immersion for the remission of sins, was the same as that now expected, it might with propriety be said that the Gentiles were not to be immersed for the purpose of receiving the gift of the Holy Spirit, inasmuch as God bestowed it upon them previous to immersion. But when we understand the gift of the Holy Spirit promised on Pentecost and that bestowed on the first converts from among the Gentiles, as the words import in the New Testament usage, we are perfectly exempted from every difficulty and from any reasonable objection, in proposing to mankind indiscriminately the remission of sins and the Holy Spirit through faith and immersion. For so soon as any person, through faith and immersion, is adopted into the family of God, and becomes one of the sons of God, then he receives the Spirit of Christ: for as says Paul, " Because you are sons, God has sent forth the Spirit of his Son into your hearts, causing you to cry Abba, Father." This is the Holy Spirit, which all who are now immersed through faith in Christ's blood for the remission of sins, receive, as we explained in our fifth essay on this subject. It is in this sense only that the phrase " gift of the Holy Spirit" can now be understood. I have always contended for affixing the same ideas to the words used by the Apostles, which they affixed to them, and therefore would prefer, in this instance, to use the words Holy Spirit or Spirit of God, rather than the phrase gift of the Holy Spirit, being aware that this latter phrase is, in the New Testament, appropriated to what we now call "miraculous gifts," such as the gift of healing the sick, of speaking foreign languages, and of prophecy, &c. The phrases "Spirit of his Son," " Spirit of Christ," " Spirit of Holiness," "Spirit of God," "Spirit of Love," " the Spirit," "Holy Spirit," "fruit of the Spirit," and "a Holy Spirit," are never used as equivalent to the phrase "gift of the Holy Spirit." When, then, we mean not " spiritual gifts," but "the fruit of the Spirit," "the peace and joy in the Holy Spirit," "the Spirit of Christ," " the spirit of faith, of meekness, of truth, of a sound mind," we ought to use such terms as were by the Apostles used to express those ideas, and not those which by them always meant something else.*

The first disciples, when immersed into the name of the Lord Jesus for the remission of sins, obtained this blessing. Those on Pentecost obtained also the very gifts contained in the promise made by Joel; and also all those communications couched in the above expressions. For they not only possessed miraculous gifts, but were filled with peace and joy, with all the fruit of the Spirit of Holiness.

How gracious this institution! It gives to the convert a sensible pledge that God, through the blood of Christ, has washed away his sins, has adopted him into his family, and made him an heir of all things through Christ. Thus, having his heart sprinkled from an evil conscience, and his body washed with clean water, he becomes a habitation of God through the Holy Spirit.— Thus, according to the tenor of the New Testament, God dwells in him and he in God, by the Spirit which is imparted to him. Thus he is constituted a christian or a disciple of Jesus Christ.

We are now prepared to consider any objections made to these essays on immersion.
　　　　　　　　　　　　　　　　EDITOR.

* See Millennial Harbinger, vol. 5. p. 166.　PUBLISHER.

[From the New Harmony Gazette—May 14.]
Mr. Alexander Campbell,

SIR—IN the Christian Baptist of the 7th inst. published at Bethany, Brooke county, Va. there is a letter addressed to you by a correspondent, who signs himself A. in which he requests your aid and assistance to discuss some subjects of general interest relative to religion, with Dr. Underhill; and there is a letter from you in reply, declining to meet Dr. Underhill, but stating your readiness to engage with me in the examination of the whole religious and moral system which I advocate, and which you say appears scattered through the pages of the New Harmony Gazette.*

I have not the pleasure of a personal acquaintance with you or Dr. Underhill; but from the opinions expressed of the talents and good intentions of both, I have no doubt that if you had consented to meet the Doctor, and to engage in a public or private discussion on subjects so interesting to every human being, much truth would have been elicited, and that you would have separated with cordial friendly feelings, and with an increase of charity for each other and for all your fellow creatures.

As, however, you have declined the examination of these subjects with Dr. Underhill, and have expressed your desire to discuss them with me, upon certain conditions contained in your letter, I feel myself called upon to notice your proposals; and more particularly as my opinion coincides with yours, "that such a discussion is needed." The time is indeed come, when religion should be proved to be true or false, beneficial or injurious; in order that, if true and beneficial, it may become (as it well deserves to be made) the great business of life, or if it should be demonstrated to be founded in error and injurious, that it may be publicly known and acknowledged to be so.

The priesthood of all the sects in the world are, as it appears to me, as deeply interested to make this discovery as any portion of the human race.

An investigation, therefore, of a new character, upon these subjects, is become the one thing needful; an investigation that shall be entered into, not for the purpose of gaining a victory for any individuals, or for any sect or party in any country; but an investigation proceeding from a conviction that truth upon these matters is above all things to be desired, because of the benefits which it may be made to afford to mankind.

In fact, no object can be brought before the population of the world, of equal interest to a right decision upon these great questions.

Such a decision is required in the present advanced stage of human knowledge, as a foundation for an improved state of society. It cannot be effectually obtained by any two individuals, nor except by the agreement of numbers who feel interested for the happiness of their fellow beings.

Under this view of the subject, if the leading ministers of the religious sects in this western country will agree among themselves to enter with me and my friends into a friendly discussion upon these subjects either in Cincinnati or any other central place in the western country, this great object may be obtained.

From such a course it is impossible to say what extent of good may arise; and if you will engage to induce the leading ministers of religion in the western states and their friends to

* These letters have been republished in the last number but one of our Gazette.

meet me in that city or elsewhere, I will engage to muster those, who at present, are conscientiously opposed to all religions: and in that case, nothing on my part shall be wanting to infuse a genuine spirit of peace, good will, and charity, throughout the whole proceedings.

Our party would meet under such circumstances, solely with a desire to elicit truth, regardless of all personal considerations; and I hope that all would separate with a very improved knowledge of human nature, and in consequence, with real charity and affection for each other.

That, which the friends who think with me, wish to have discussed and decided, is—

1st. Whether all religions are, or are not opposed to facts?

2d. Whether all religions do or do not virtually destroy all charity, except for one sect, in thought, word and action?

3d. Whether religion does or does not render it necessary that the great mass of mankind, in all countries, should be kept in ignorance and poverty?

4th. Whether all religions do or do not require that infants and children should be taught to think that there is merit in believing that the doctrines of their own religion are true, and that all other religions are false; and that there is demerit in believing otherwise?

5th. Whether all religions do or do not teach that there is merit and demerit in loving and hating, liking and disliking, *according to their doctrines,* whether in unison with man's natural feelings or in opposition to them?

6th. Whether almost all bad passions, vices, and moral evils, do or do not emanate from the instructions given in infancy and childhood, that there is merit and demerit in belief and in liking and disliking?

7th. And lastly, whether mankind can be trained to become more happy, more intelligent, independent, charitable, and kind to each other, with or without religion?

I remain yours,
ROBERT OWEN.

To Robert Owen, Esq.

SIR,—ALTHOUGH I cannot agree with you, that christianity is yet to be proved true or false, I have no hesitation in saying that such a discussion is necessary, as I contemplated in my letter to Mr. A., a correspondent in Ohio, and as I have agreed to undertake in my acceptance of your challenge to the clergy. Had you seen my acceptance of your challenge, before you wrote the above epistle, it would have appeared to you, I think, unnecessary, to have made the proposals which I see in your letter before me. By this time you are, no doubt, informed that I have accepted your challenge in *ipsissimis verbis*, in the identical terms you proposed it in New Orleans. I take the negative of every position embraced in your challenge—And now I stand pledged to the public, to show that you cannot establish the positions which you have so repeatedly proposed, and attempted to do. I, as a logician, wish to have tangible positions definitely and unambiguously expressed, and I find those in your challenge are sufficiently so.

As to calling in a conference of all the clergy and such of your sceptical friends as you please, for the purpose of a sort of general confabulation, I have to remark, as this was no part of the challenge which I have accepted, I can say nothing about it. I may, indeed, remark that I have no objection to your assembling all your brethren sceptics, from Harmony to Lanark, if

any place could be found large enough to hold them. But as only one person can speak at once, to be understood and regarded, I see no good reason of calling such an assemblage—For my part, however, I can cordially agree to your assembling with you in the debate as many of your sceptical friends as you may think proper. For my own part, although always willing to receive counsel well intended, and ably tendered, I am of opinion that it is never to be solicited until we have some misgivings as to our own judgment, and feel our confidence in ourselves somewhat shaken.

When our debate is fairly brought to an issue, and published, by a faithful stenographer, every object is gained which could be gained from any discussion. I admit that all christendom is not pledged to the consequences of my argument with you; neither are all the sceptics on the continent obliged to yield to your fate in this discussion. All that can be promised from such a discussion, is, that all the arguments and gleanings of two persons, who have espoused the contrary sides in this momentous question, shall be fully exhibited; one of which has devoted all his energies to supplant the present order of society, and to introduce another—the other who has calmly and dispassionately, without any earthly emolument, office, or bribe, to prepossess him in favor of christianity, or to labor for its spread and prosperity. One of which, has felt so much assurance that all religion is false and injurious to society, as to embolden him to challenge the teachers of religion to maintain it if they can—the other, confident of its truth and divine excellence, impelled by its precepts, animated by its hopes, and emboldened by its promises, is willing to hazard every thing dear to him as a man, as a mortal, and an immortal being, in support of its truth, and in aid of its extension throughout the world.—Such a discussion cannot fail to be pleasing and profitable to all concerned, and the perusal of it, faithfully exhibited, cannot fail to be of some consequence to posterity. You will therefore please to remember, Mr. Owen, that I have accepted of your challenge, and all that remains, is to settle the preliminaries as soon as possible. I have, from a little experience in public discussions, no doubt, but that I shall be able to maintain perfect good humor throughout the whole; and I have reason to believe that your philosophy has improved your good nature so far as to make you an acceptable disputant.

Yours respectfully,
A. CAMPBELL.

Extract of a Letter from a Correspondent in Ohio to the Editor.

Constitution of a Congregation in Ohio.

"WINDHAM, May 27th, 1828, was constituted the Church of Christ in Windham, upon the declared and manifest faith and obedience of the ancient apostolic gospel, as delivered by the Apostle Peter to the Jews on the day of Pentecost, Acts ii. and afterwards by the same Apostle to the Gentiles, assembled in the house of Cornelius, Acts x. and by the Apostle Paul, to both Jews and Gentiles in Antioch in Pisidia, xiii. and as declared by all the Apostles in the apostolic writings: which writings, taken in their due connexion with the Old Testament, and the preceding books of the New, this church assumes as the only, and all-sufficient rule of faith and obedience; withal, assuming the New Testament as being as perfect a rule, directory, and formula for the faith, worship, discipline, and government of the New Testament church, and the particular duties of its members; as the Old Testament was, for the faith, worship, discipline, and government of the Old Testament church, and the particular duties of its members. Compare Mal. iv. 4. with Math. xxviii. 18—20. It is farther declared that this church, fully recognizing the constitutional unity of the body of Christ, and determined by the grace of God, in obedience to the apostolic doctrine, to maintain and promote this unity, both within itself, and with all the declared and obedient disciples of the Lord Jesus, extends its fellowship to all such as have obeyed the gospel according to the above scriptures, by immersion into the one faith once delivered to the saints, as the same is expressly declared in the portions above cited; and who continue to justify their profession of said faith by a life of practical holiness, (according to the law of Christ.) Under the profession of the faith and obedience specified and provided for, in the above declaration, the undernamed disciples, in obedience to the Great Head of the church, and for the performance of the duties which, under him, they owe to each other, and to all men, have unanimously agreed to form themselves into a church to be designated as above. Done in presence of Bishops Thomas Campbell and Marcus Bosworth, invited to preside and assist for said purpose. After the enrolment of the members, Reuben Ferguson, lately an exhorter and preacher of the Methodist order, was duly and unanimously chosen a Bishop of said church; and ordained by the imposition of the hands of the said bishops and others, elderly members of said church, or assisting with it, by request, upon the occasion."

Review of the History of Churches.—No. III.

WHILE all of the above churches manifest a scrupulous regard to the grand constitutional principles of the kingdom of Jesus Christ, they seem to differ from each other in their views of the ordinance of the Great King on the subject of naturalization. Some of them receive unnaturalized persons into his realm on the ground of forbearance. On this subject I write with great caution, for I know this question of forbearance has in it some perplexities of no easy solution, and is at least of as difficult solution as that concerning the amalgamation of the Jews and Gentiles in the christian church, decided by the apostles and elders in the city of Jerusalem. On the scriptural propriety of receiving unnaturalized or unimmersed persons into the kingdom into which the Saviour said none can enter but by being born of water and of Spirit, little can be said either from precept or example. For it is exceedingly plain, that from the day on which Peter opened the reign of the Messiah, on the ever memorable Pentecost, no man entered the realm but by being born of water. Jew and Gentile, Barbarian, Scythian, bond and free, could find but one gate into the empire of Immanuel, and with joy they enter in at this door. As yet there was no breach in the walls, no scaling ladders, no battering rams, to find an easier way. Jesus was yet recognized as the living way; and as he came by water and by blood, so he ordained that through faith in his blood and through water, the soldiers of the cross must follow him. There were even in those hale and undegenerate days, matters on which patience and endurance must be exercised; but they were all within the constituted realms. There was none without the gates demanding recognition from those within, on the

grounds of charity. But now the walls of this city of refuge, the ramparts of Zion have been broken through; and while the inhabitants of the city of God have gone out and trafficked with the world, the world has come in and trafficked with them. And now they sue for a treaty offensive and defensive. Well they urge their plea with an embassy of weeping mothers and screaming infants, and who is proof against such importunities? But the question of the greatest difficulty to decide, is, whether there should be any laws or rules adopted by the churches relating to the practice of receiving persons unimmersed in the assemblies of the saints. Whether on the ground of forbearance, as it is called, such persons as have been once sprinkled, or not at all, but who are satisfied with their sprinkling, or without any, are, on their solicitation, to be received into any particular congregation, and to be treated in all respects as those who have, by their own voluntary act and deed, been naturalized and constitutionally admitted into the kingdom. To make a law that such should be received, appears to me, after long and close deliberation, a usurpation of the legislative authority vested in the holy apostles, and of dangerous tendency in the administration of the Reign of Heaven. Again, to say that no weak brother, however honest in his professions, excellent in his deportment and amiable in his character, who cannot be convinced but that his infant sprinkling is christian baptism, and who solicits a participation with us in the festivities of Zion: I say, to say by a stern decree that none such shall on any account be received, appears to be illiberal, unkind, censorious, and opposite to that benevolence which is one of the primary virtues of christianity.

Yet some will urge that if such a person is very solicitous for the enjoyment of the benefits of the church, it is no very difficult or hazardous thing for him to be immersed on his own profession, and for the objects contemplated therein. And that if his love of the christian institution will not make him forbear with himself, or in other words, sacrifice his own partialities, we are not warranted, nor warrantable, in receiving him. Now, although I could feel myself at perfect liberty, in full accordance with the requirements of the Great King, to receive into the most cordial fellowship every one which I have reason to recognize as a disciple of Jesus Christ, with all his weaknesses, as I would call them; yet I could not, and dare not, say to all the members of a christian congregation, that they must do so too; and as I have no right to dispense with any of the institutions of Jesus Christ, I could not approve the adoption of a rule to receive such persons, which, in its direct tendency, aims at the abolition of one of the fundamental laws of the empire. Again, if we are to fritter down the christian institution to suit the prejudices and weaknesses of disciples, it would soon be divested of every prominent feature characteristic of its grand original. There are, indeed, many matters on which there is full scope given for the display of moderation, condescension, and forbearance, without infringing upon the constitutional provisions of the kingdom. We may shew all courtesy, kindness, and hospitality to strangers, but to invest them with the rights and immunities of citizens, without their voluntary submission to the constitutional requirements in order to naturalization, would neither be beneficial to them, nor safe to the empire. Christians were called a sect in the times of the apostles. They had their peculiarities then; and although there

3 H

were no sects tolerated amongst them, they were a sect as regarded all other religious communities. In divesting christianity of its sectarian character, we must not divest it of the peculiarities which made it a sect in its best days, and which will keep it a sect until all the kingdoms and religions in the world shall bow to our King.

I know that there is something called charity in the world, which is very much flattered; but when dissected, is a hideous thing. To please the taste of any body and every body, it will administer to all their requirements. If medicine or poison is sought after, with equal liberality it bestows on all. Like a too indulgent mother, it defeats itself. If it would be cruel to give a scorpion when a fish is asked, it is no better to give a scorpion when a scorpion is desired, especially if he who desires to obtain it sues for it through mistake. On the same principles, it is not charity, in its true import, to gratify the vitiated humor, or caprice, or prejudice, or weakness of every body. While we are willing to go more than half way, where it is optional with us to go at all, to meet the doubting and the weak, there are certain occurrences and circumstances which compel us not to move at all, and the same charity, properly so called, governs us in both cases. But here we do not argue the merits of this question at all; but only state the result of much examination and reflection on the subject.

We have stated our reasons long since why we do not consider either the holy kiss, or the washing of the saints' feet, ordinances of the church, or public acts, to be habitually and statedly practised. If christians are to salute one another with a holy kiss in the public assemblies, reason would say that it should be when they first see each other in the morning of the Lord's day, and not after they have shook hands and asked one another how they fare. To see them first salute one another in the usual way, and then afterwards introduce the holy kiss as a religious ordinance, and attend upon it with a stiff formality as such, is neither accordant with scripture nor reason. But of this we have said enough on a former occasion.

In the preceding page we gave, in lieu of the history of another church, the constituting of one among the new converts in the state of Ohio. We have had no room for remarks upon it in the present volume, and as every thing of importance in it has been so often canvassed in the preceding volumes, we do not think it so necessary to dilate on it at this time.   Editor.

Conclusion of Volume V.

"All things are full of labor" was no new discovery in the days of king Solomon. Yet all things are regularly and incessantly tending to certain ends and beginnings. The ceaseless changes in the face of nature, the varied year, are but the symbols of that spiritual and moral variety which characterize the world of minds; and every thing in the empire of thought is either beginning or ending some new condition or circumstance in the joys or sorrows of human beings. For all the rivers do not more certainly run into the ocean than all our actions tend to make us happy or miserable either in the present state or in the future. Men often do, but never should forget that all their actions, which are the result of their own volitions, have a tendency necessary and unavoidable to promote their own joy or sorrow. And as nothing is final on earth, but only tending to eternity, we ought to know and bear in mind that we can neither enjoy nor

suffer the full result of our conduct while in the first act, in the mere prelude of the great drama of human existence. Our own happiness or misery is so intimately connected with that of others, that few, if any, of our actions terminate wholly upon ourselves. The good or ill of human conduct is seldom or never individual in its character or termination. All these reflections ought to admonish us of our great responsibilities, and should teach us that there is nothing more unworthy of us as rational beings than to act without deliberation and proper motives. We are only so far rational as we act in subordination to truth; and nothing is truth, but what is real. All the actions which are prompted by mere appetite, animal passion, or caprice, are purely animal, and belong to us in common with other animals of inferior endowments. We only act the man when we act under the influence of motives drawn from the high relations in which we stand to the Creator and our fellow-immortals. Private and public good, mental and corporal, temporal and eternal, fill up the whole range of commendable actions. To lose sight of either, is folly—to keep the whole before our minds, is wisdom. Efforts designed and well directed to promote the more lasting enjoyments of rational beings, are of the highest order; and amongst the wise and good, are most highly appreciated. But it so happens, that, in consequence of the common blindness of men to their true interest, the imposing influence of present fascinations, and the consequent error thereby introduced into the mind, there is nothing more generally disparaged than those efforts which are intended to put men in the legitimate course to real enjoyment. Hence the opposition with which we have to conflict in attempting to direct the public in the acquisition of the true and lasting enjoyment of truth. For although truth is opposed to the happiness of no man, there are many to oppose truth. But they oppose it thro' mistake, imagining it to be at variance with their honor, interest, or something identified with their happiness. I have long thought that truth is recommended merely because it necessarily tends to happiness, and I do not know any thing in the volume of supernatural truth which is not in its very nature promotive of the true happiness of all who know and obey it. Being aware of this, and being assured that all error ends in misery, we have occupied ourselves now for five years in directing the public attention to what we have learned to be the most important truths bearing upon the actual condition of our cotemporaries. And in closing this fifth volume of our labors, we cannot refrain from reminding our readers that all their happiness consists in knowing and obeying truth. Error is the most unprofitable commodity in the whole universe—and the sooner it is detected, the better.

We oppose error because it opposes happiness. We are opposed by the same sort of characters who have always opposed reformation; and for the same reasons. There have been millions of the human family kept in vassalage, religious, moral, and political; and myriads have fattened upon them, merely through the influence of error. And now, even now, if error was detected, how many who are lording it over the consciences of men and rioting in insolent ease, would be divested of their influence and livings, and would sink down to their proper level in society. How many useful persons would arise and diffuse the blessings of light and liberty far and wide. But so long as the popular errors of the day are patronized and triumphant, both the proper development of the human mind and the enlargement of human happiness, must continue impracticable. And until men's ears are turned from theological fables to the oracles of God, we cannot expect better times or a greater augmentation of human enjoyment.

We intend continuing our exertions, with increased energy, in this cause; and hope never to be less deserving of public patronage than we have hitherto been.   Editor.

The true and only Standard.
Extract of a letter to the Editor.

"One thing, however, I was more than a little surprised at—to hear so many, and of so many, talking about the church coming out of Babylon, and the restoration of primitive christianity and order; and to see and hear of so little exertion made to bring it about; and even its warmest advocates stating that it would not do to emerge suddenly. It brought fresh into my mind a circumstance that transpired when I was a little boy, that I have often thought of when viewing the christian church receding from the right rule (the Scriptures) in measuring themselves by themselves: An old uncle of mine, who had use for a number of wooden pins, set me to sawing up tough rails into blocks for that purpose. He sawed off one as a measure for me to saw by, and went away. I commenced. I put the measure on for the first block. After starting the saw I threw down the measure, and held the block I was sawing with one hand till I cut it off; then made use of it to measure the next, and so on until I had sawed a great many. My uncle returned and told me I was spoiling his timber. I told him I did not know how that could be. Where is the measure I gave you? he said. I replied, I measured the first block by it, the next by the last one, and so on, and when I took a good look, I found I had about as many lengths as blocks. He recommended the propriety of hunting up the first block that he gave me, and requested me to preserve it as a measure."   N. P.

Passing Tidings.

One Methodist and two Universalist teachers, or "ministers," as they are called, in Ohio, of good standing and respectable attainments, have recently renounced their favorite isms, and have been immersed into the belief of the ancient gospel.   105.

END OF VOLUME V.

CHRISTIAN BAPTIST.

NO. I.—VOL. VI. BETHANY, BROOKE CO. VA., AUGUST 4, 1828.

Style no man on earth your Father: for he alone is your Father who is in heaven: and all ye are brethren. Assume not the title of Rabbi; for ye have only One Teacher; neither assume the title of Leader; for ye have only One Leader—the Messiah. *Messiah.*

PREFACE TO VOLUME VI.

The Fathers, the Moderns, the Populars, and the Heretics.

" Our Fathers, where are they? and the Prophets, do they live forever?"

At one time we speak of our remote ancestors as if they had been mere children in understanding in comparison of ourselves and our cotemporaries; at another, we represent their views and their authority as paramount to all our compeers. If their views were congenial with our own, then they were the wisest and the best of men; but if we differ far from them, then as duteous sons, we only wish they had been more wise and less superstitious. Thus their authority rises or sinks in our estimation, as they happen to coincide with our sentiments, or differ from us in their views. In all our comparisons we are wont to make ourselves the standard of perfection. If we at all admit that we are imperfect, we are sure to make our " failings lean to virtue's side;" and when compared with the faults we see in others, our frailties are to be attributed to circumstances beyond our control, and so completely eclipsed by the splendor of our virtues, as rather to represent the dark spots in the sun, or the shade in the picture, as necessary to the brilliancy of the whole.

But if we were to use that reason of which we boast, a little more, and submit less to the suggestions of self-love and self-admiration, we would not only think more humbly of ourselves, but we would do more justice to the merits of others. In that case neither the names nor the authority of our ancestors would be plead as a justification of our sentiments or practices, nor would their weaknesses be urged in extenuation of our own. They were men constitutionally like ourselves, and only circumstantially different. Whether they were wiser or better than ourselves or our coevals, depends not upon any constitutional superiority, but rather upon the superiority of their or our circumstances. Their opportunities may have been better or worse than ours, and all the difference of a moral or intellectual nature between them and us must be resolved into their or our superior attention and devotion to truth and goodness.

Many Doctors of the Church of Rome would have made first-rate Puritans; and many morose Dissenters would have made hierarchical tyrants in other times and other countries. Many in this age, whose illiberality and religious wrath are fully vented in bold invectives and ungenerous detractions, would, had they lived a few centuries ago, have found no gratification to their religious vengeance but in the racks and tortures of inquisitorial cruelty. They who are now sa-

ted with burning men's writings, would then have consumed their persons. Those too, who, in this century, are pleased to prove their faith and practice by an appeal to the fathers, would, in the days of Luther, have maintained the infallibility of the Pope and the sovereign arbitrements of clerical councils. And they who would now bind men's consciences to a covenant and creed framed by the fathers of modern traditions, would have argued in the days of John Huss and Jerome of Prague, that the Bible was not to be read by the ignorant laity.

While, in this age of invention, the winds and the waves, the rivers and the deserts, the mountains and the vallies are made to yield to scientific and mechanical skill; while the human mind is bursting through the shackles and restraints of a false philosophy, and developing the marvellous extent of its powers, it is not to be supposed strange and unaccountable that the moral and religious systems of antiquity should be submitted to the scrutiny of enlightened intellects, and that men of reflection and independence should dare to explore the creeds and the rubrics of ages of less light and more superstition. Truth has nothing to fear from investigation. It dreads not the light of science, nor shuns the scrutiny of the most prying inquiry.—Like one conscious of spotless innocence and uncontaminated purity, it challenges the fullest, the ablest, and the boldest examination. On the other hand, error, as if aware of its flimsy pretensions and of the thin veil which conceals its deformity, flies from the torch of reason, and dares not approach the tribunal of impartial inquiry. She hides herself in the fastnesses of remote antiquity, and garrisons herself in the fortifications erected by those she honors with the title of " the Fathers." When she dares to visit the temples of human resort, she attires herself in the attractions of popular applause, and piques herself upon the number, influence, and respectability of her admirers. But with all her blandishments, she is an impudent impostor, and is doomed to destruction with all her worshippers. But Truth, immortal Truth! the first-born of Heaven! by the indisputable rights of primogeniture, shall inherit all things, and leave her antagonist, Error, to languish forever in the everlasting shame and contempt of perfect and universal exposure.

To Truth eternal and immortal, the wise and good will pay all homage and respect. Upon no altar will they offer her as a victim; but at her shrine will sacrifice every thing. What, then, is Truth? Momentous question! She is *Reality* herself. 'Tis not merely the exact correspon-

1

dence of words with ideas. This is but *verbal* truth. 'Tis not the mere agreement of the terms of any proposition with logical arrangement.— This is *logical* truth. But it is the correspondence, the exact agreement of our ideas with things as they are. So that the representations of truth are the exact pictures of all the realities about which we are conversant, or in which we are interested. She leads to happiness all who obey her; but those that disdain her precepts destroy themselves forever.

But "the fathers" are often urged as decisive evidence, superseding the necessity of farther inquiry. All sects have their *fathers*, to whom they are wont to appeal. There is father Ireneus, Origen, Ambrose, Austin, Tertullian, Athanasius, of high repute amongst the more ancient sects. There is Father Calvin, Luther, Zuinglius, &c. &c. among the moderns. There is Father Wesley, Fletcher, Asbury, Coke, amongst the more recent. There are, too, Fathers Gill, Fuller, and Booth, amongst those who say they have no father on earth. Yea, even amongst these are already enrolled some whose graves are not yet green, and whose errors are not yet forgotten. Thus one of our *Stars* of the first magnitude, if we are to enumerate the square inches of its surface, has recently quoted in support of the popular schemes of ostentatious benevolence, Fathers Baldwin, Furman, and other Doctors, concerning whose standing in the unseen world we have as yet heard nothing. How long it may be before Drs. Holcomb, Rogers, and Allison are enrolled amongst the Fathers, we cannot guess; but from the spirit of some of our father-making writers already exhibited, it cannot be but a few days. But, methinks, those reputed wise and pious, who are yet with us, should here be admonished to take good heed to what schemes they lend their names and the weight of their influence. In this way they may see that good or evil of wide and long extent must result to posterity from the application of their reputation, however well or ill earned it may be, to those schemes which almost every month gives birth to. The good or ill that men do generally long survives them. The defects and weaknesses of great men are more frequently appealed to in justification of errors and mistakes, than their more wise and excellent actions. And such is the relaxing influence of the bad examples of men reputed great and good, that their admirers are much more wont to transcend their defects than their virtues. They are content with falling a little short of their excellences; and without much compunction, can go a little beyond their infirmities. One good example is worth a thousand lectures, but a bad one defeats the object of many admonitions.

"Our Fathers, where are they?"—Some of those looked up to as Fathers in Israel, were doubtless ignorant and evil men. And who in remote ages and countries can tell which of those men were real saints, and now in the presence of God? And before their names can sanction any thing, it ought to be ascertained whether God has approved of their views and behavior, and whether they have been rewarded with a place at his right hand; for would it not appear worse than ridiculous for us to quote as authority for any religious tenet or practice, men whose names are not found enrolled in the records of Heaven, but are now the associates of those who are reserved in chains of darkness until the judgment of the great day? The mere suspicion that such may be the unhappy fate of some canonized saints, forbids any appeal to the Fathers

as decisive of any question affecting the faith or practice of christians.

A few men in the United States, not more perhaps than half a dozen of Doctors of Divinity, have done more within forty years to divest the Baptists of their ancient simplicity and love for the Bible, than all the Doctors of modern Divinity among them will restore in one century. Scarce a relic of the ancient simplicity of the Waldenses, Albigenses, and those persecuted christians, from whom the Baptists in these United States are proud to reckon their descent, or to identify with themselves as fellow-professors of the same gospel and order of worship, now remains. These modern good, and wise, and leading men, being intoxicated with titles and worldly respectability, have co-operated to become imitators of their more respectable neighbors, the Presbyterians and Episcopalians. They have formed a young St. Giles for every old St. Giles amongst the Paidobaptists: and have actually got the whole machinery of the popular establishments in full employment to build up great meeting houses, parsonages, and colleges; to have a learned priesthood, tithes, and offerings; conventions, missionaries, tracts, and education societies, with all the "benevolent schemes" of the day. And those who will not say Amen to the whole paraphernalia, are heretics, unregenerated sinners, like myself. Their more fortunate and more respectable neighbors are pleased to see them follow up in the rear, for they want to see them of the same spirit with themselves, knowing full well that they can always keep them in the rear! Yes, they have the *money*, and the learning on their side, and this train of things going on for two centuries. When they wish to make a new levy for a new theological school, they can enforce their claims with a new argument Yes, they say, "See, brethren, all christendom is awaking from its slumbers to the importance of marshalling an army of effective clergymen. Even the Baptists are now convinced of their supineness and errors in former times in relation to their teachers, and now they are making great efforts to educate and support their clergy as they ought always to have done. Let us, then, advance in the even tenor of our way, stimulated, as we ought to be, by the exertions of those who have felt the force of our example, and feel it to be their duty to go and do likewise." So pleads a Paidobaptist; and what Baptist of the Old School would not blush in his presence! For my part, I feel no anxiety for the result. The children of the flesh will manifest themselves, and it is right that they who are of the world should speak of, and like, the world. But those who believe the good confession which the King of Martyrs confessed before Pontius Pilate, will delight to know and to teach that "Christ's kingdom is not of this world." And they do know that no carnal crowd of worshippers will be owned by him as a church of his. But some there are who would rather commune with orthodox Presbyterians and Episcopalians in building colleges, making clergymen, issuing tracts, raising funds for theological schools, and in the Lord's supper, than with such heretics as those who contend for carrying out the above good confession into practice.

In commencing the sixth volume of this work, I feel myself emboldened to say that my labors have not been in vain; and I do thank God that I have been enabled to persevere in one undeviating course, aiming at *the restoration of the ancient order of things*, and that he has given me so much success in my efforts, as to authorize me to

2

look forward with large expectations to a liberal harvest which is whitening all around. The number of my readers has regularly augmented from the first sheet until now, and every volume of this work has been commenced under an increased patronage. Many have solicited its enlargement, and numerous propositions have been made for changing its name, size, and terms of publication. Some of the reasons are weighty: but as we have not yet got through the items in our original proposals, we will continue it in its present form for at least the present volume. Our opponents are generally all silenced, and it is likely that those who are devoted to the present order of things will have, by this time, learned so much prudence, (if it can be learned,) as to allow us to proceed without opposition, except when and where they know we cannot hear them; and no doubt they are convinced that their own cause will best succeed when its merits are kept from investigation. EDITOR.

Essays on Man in his Primitive State, and under the Patriarchal, Jewish and Christian Dispensations.—No. I.

Primitive State.—No. 1.

"THE PROPER STUDY OF MANKIND IS MAN."

"KNOW thyself," was the wisest maxim of the wisest philosopher of the wisest pagan nation of antiquity. "Know thyself" is inculcated by all the prophets and apostles of all the ages of revelation. And while the wisest man of the wisest nation in theology taught as his first maxim, that "the fear of the Lord is the beginning of wisdom;" and while the Saviour of the world taught, that "it is eternal life to know the only true God, and his Son Jesus Christ whom he commissioned," both concur in inculcating the excellence, and in teaching the utility and importance of self-knowledge. Our *origin* necessarily engrosses the first chapter of self-knowledge; and here the bible begins. This volume, replete with all wisdom and knowledge requisite to the happiness of man during every period of his existence, in time and to eternity, wisely and kindly opens with the history of man's creation, and closes with his eternal destiny. To it we are indebted for every correct idea, for every just sentiment on this subject in all the volumes and in all the intellects on earth. Destroy it and all that has been deduced, borrowed or stolen from it, and man is not only a savage in disposition, but as rude and ignorant of his origin as the beasts that perish. This is an assertion made with full knowledge of all that is claimed by sceptics, and alleged by unbelievers, from the days of Celsus down to the era of *Mental Independence*. And the day is not far distant in which we trust this will be universally admitted.

Considering the bible, therefore, as the only oracle on this subject; viewing it as containing the whole sum total of all that mortal man can know of his origin, we shall only hear and attend to its representations of the origin of man. And first we shall attend to his creation:—After God Almighty had formed the heavens and the earth, and fitted the latter for the abode of that creature for whom it was made, he proceeded with singular deliberation to create this most august of all the creatures of his vast empire. When suns were to be lighted, and all the hosts of the heavens and the earth marshalled, he was pleased, without a preamble or a preface, to command them into being; but when man, the sovereign of this globe, was to be fashioned, he pauses, and retires within himself for a model, and makes his own image the grand archetype of man. He

builds his body from the elements of the earth. He gives him a soul or animal life in common with all the animals created; but he infuses into him from himself directly, without any intervention, a spirit, a pure intellectual principle. So that man stands erect, one being possessing body, soul and spirit. His body was as earthly as that of any other creature, only of more delicate and exquisite organization. His soul or animal life, which gives him all the passions, was like theirs, save that it was not the governing principle; but at the head of all, and above all, his intellect or spirit was enthroned, which placed him incomparably above every other inhabitant of the earth. Thus Adam stood a triune being, having a body, a soul, and a spirit, each of them perfect in every respect, and perfectly united and subordinated in one sublime constitution; the spirit enthroned in the head and as the head; the soul resident in the heart, and not only animating but energizing the whole body in perfect obsequiousness to the intellectual department.

By the way, we may observe, that the Jews, the Greeks, the Romans, as well as the English, have had three terms which they used as distinctly expressive of these three. These are the *body, soul* and *spirit*, of the English; the *corpus, anima* and *animus*, of the Latins; the *soma, psuche* and *nous*, of the Greeks; and the *nerep, nepesh* and *ruth*, of the Hebrews. These in each language are representatives of each other; and the most of the modern languages have the same distinctness of phraseology in marking each of the constituents of man. The body is the organic mass, animated and pervaded by the soul or animal life, which, as the scriptures say, is in the blood; and the spirit is that pure intellectual principle which acts immediately upon the soul and mediately upon the body. We know that in popular use, the terms *soul* and *spirit* are generally used as synonymous, and have been so in the practice of all languages; but when we wish to speak with the greatest perspicuity or emphasis, we distinguish these from one another. Thus Paul prays for the Thessalonians, that God would sanctify them wholly, their *body, soul* and *spirit*. The body and soul, in common usage, denote the whole man; but when we speak philosophically, we say, *body, soul* and *spirit*. Each of these has its respective attributes and powers. The spirit has the faculties we call the powers of understanding; the soul has its passions and affections; the body has its organs and their functions. In man reason and all intelligence belong to the spirit, together with volition in its primary character. All the passions and affections belong to the soul, and are identified with animal life; all the appetites and propensities strictly belong to the body. But so united are these constituents of man, that what one does the others do likewise. So that while we define thus, we know that in all the acts of the man there is such a combination of energies that the whole spirit, soul and body, move in perfect concert in all those acts which are properly called human. A hint or two of this sort, without an elaborate disquisition, illustration, or proof, we suppose necessary to a correct view of man; but to enter largely into this matter, would require a volume itself, and would not, perhaps, repay for either the trouble of writing or reading it.

The government belonged to the spirit; its ministers were the passions, and the whole body moved in subordination to these. So intimate were the soul and spirit in all their acts and movements, that they became perfectly identified with each other, and the one term became the

3

representative of both—as one family name represents both husband and wife. But while contemplating man in his first state, we must call in all the helps we have to conceive of him in accordance with his primitive dignity. As a perfect being, then, his reason, his passions, and his appetites existed in the most regular and harmonious connexion with each other. Their natural and necessary dependance was duly felt and acknowledged; and their subordination was founded in perfect reason.

Capable of deriving pleasure from a thousand sources in the material system by means of his senses, he was also qualified to enjoy the most intimate relation and acquaintance with the spiritual system by means of his intellectual faculties. Thus the pleasures and enjoyments of two worlds were made accessible to man in the state in which he was created.

Being thus constituted capable of enjoyments so numerous and multiform, he was the most perfect creature in the universe, as far as human knowledge extends. He was the *last*, and if we may judge by the regular gradation of all the works of creation, as narrated by Moses, he was the *best* work of God. But as he was endued not only with the powers of acquiring and accumulating enjoyment from two worlds, but with the faculties for communicating it, he was in his very nature social, and required co-ordinate beings for the gratification of his powers of communication. Hence from himself God created a co-ordinate being of the same endowments, but of still more delicate organization.

Kindred society became the consummation of human bliss, because necessary to fill up all man's capacities for enjoyment. A male and a female, possessed of one common nature, mutually dependent on each other for all the higher enjoyments of that nature; in their creation inseparably allied to each other; and in all their wants, desires, and enjoyments, reciprocal, finish the picture of primitive bliss in man's original state. Thus was man created and circumstanced; and after the intelligent, pure and happy pair were introduced to each other, God, their Creator, inducted them by his own hand into the garden of delights, which for them he had previously formed and beautified with all the exquisite charms which the combined influences of virgin heaven and earth were capable of producing. Then "the morning stars sang together, and all the sons of God shouted for joy." And here we shall leave them for the present.   EDITOR.

Remarks on Samuel xv. 22, 23.

"And Samuel said, Has the Lord as great delight in burnt offerings and sacrifices as in obeying the voice of the Lord? Behold to obey is better than sacrifice; and to hearken, than the fat of rams. For rebellion is as the sin of witchcraft, and stubbornness is as iniquity and idolatry: because you have rejected the word of the Lord, he has also rejected you from being king."

WHEN the mind is not in complete subjection to the authority of God, it is easy to find excuses to apologize for disobedience to the plainest injunctions. It is not easy to conceive a plainer command than that which was given to Saul with respect to the destruction of the Amalekites and all their possessions; yet he obeyed it only so far as it appeared reasonable to himself, and even attempted to cover his iniquity by a show of zeal for the institutions of religion. He conceived that he was not limited to exact and punctilious obedience; and that having performed what he considered the substance of his commission, he was at liberty to use his discretion in things of less importance. The part in which he failed

appeared to him so trifling, that, on meeting Samuel, he declared that he had "performed the commandment of the Lord." The trivial instances in which he departed from his instructions were not worth mentioning as an exception. He had paid due attention to what he looked upon as the fundamentals of his commission. He did not think that it was likely that he should be called to account for using his discretion as he had done, with respect to things of so little importance; and especially, as he had altogether consulted the interests of religion in the liberties he had taken. So far was he from seeing any criminality in the slight deviations which he had made from his instructions, that when Samuel charged him with disobeying the voice of the Lord, and laid before him the instances in which he had done so, he continued confidently to affirm that he had obeyed the commandment of the Lord; "yea, I have obeyed the voice of the Lord;" and notwithstanding the exceptions which he could not altogether conceal, he still pleaded that he had substantially fulfilled his commission. This was indeed a discriminating obedience, but it was not on that account the more acceptable to God, and although he had conceived that he had fulfilled the chief object of his mission, and that therefore small exceptions would be overlooked, we find that the Lord does not give him credit for fulfilling his instructions at all, but charges him with complete disobedience; "Because you have rejected the word of the Lord, he has also rejected you from being king." Temptation is never more dangerous than when it pretends to set aside obedience to certain divine injunctions for the sake of the general interests of religion. The covetousness of Saul and the Israelites was here cloaked by an apparent concern for the glory of God and gratitude for their victory. The command to destroy all the possessions of the Amalekites would appear unreasonable to human wisdom, and therefore they thought to evade it by destroying the most worthless of the property, and by consecrating the remainder to the service of God. If they did not exactly obey the word of the Lord, they considered that they had made a sufficient amends by devoting these costly sacrifices to his worship. But their carnal policy was utterly detestable in the estimation of God. "And Samuel said, Has the Lord as great delight in burnt offerings and sacrifices as in obeying the voice of the Lord? Behold to obey is better than sacrifice; and to hearken, than the fat of rams: for rebellion is as the sin of witchcraft, and stubbornness as iniquity and idolatry." The conduct of Saul and the Israelites on this occasion, cannot but remind us of those Christians who make the pretence of usefulness a justification of their conduct in not fully obeying the voice of the Lord. Some will not quit their connexion with anti-christian churches because, by giving up their stations, they would give up their usefulness. They have now an extensive field for labor, from which they would be excluded if they should give up their situation. "The chief thing is the salvation of sinners: we must sacrifice things of inferior moment to this great consideration." I would ask such persons how they can condemn Saul, and think to stand excused themselves? Is not their conduct rebellion against the Lord? Does it not charge him with giving commands inconsistent with the extensive propagation of the gospel, and exalt our wisdom above his? Has the Lord as much delight in our silly schemes of usefulness as he has in our obeying his voice? What should we think of a female who should allege, as a justification

4

of her infidelity to her husband, that, by this means, she provided for him and his family?—And is it not the same thing to disobey God under a pretence of serving him more effectually? At first view it might appear that, of all the servants of God, the persons I allude to were the most useful and successful propagators of the gospel, as they make this the ground of their disobedience. But in general we shall find it to be the reverse. They are usually toiling, and mourning the want of success throughout their lives. I beseech such persons to consider whether they are not deceiving themselves, and whether usefulness to their own temporal interest does not, as in the case of Saul, lie concealed under the pretext of usefulness to the cause of Christ. If worldly interests and honor were as much engaged to bring them out of their present situation as they are in holding them in it, I verily believe that the arguments of usefulness would appear in another light.—*Scripture Magazine.*

Z.

Extract of A Letter.

"Kentucky, June 25, 1828.

——"Your Christian Baptist of June has just come to hand, containing your expose of Bishop Semple's unwary sayings relative to the C. B. At the time those letters first appeared in the Star, the writer was sitting by the side of a white-headed and venerable Bishop, who, after the reading of those letters of Bishop Semple's, remarked that he regretted to hear such sentiments fall from the lips of any Baptist; especially from the pen of a man renowned for his wisdom, piety, and divinity; that he thought him very vulnerable, and that he expected you would wound him deeply, as your readers here think you have done. The writer has not those letters by him; but, as well as he recollects, the Bishop says that "there is much room left in the New Testament for conjecture upon the subject of church government." This is sound Episcopalian or Erastian divinity, but unsound Baptist divinity. This sentiment is more fully and clearly expressed by two learned Episcopalian or orthodox divines, Mosheim and Scott. The former is celebrated for his erudition, and for exhausting the vocabulary of his slander against the poor, defenceless, heretical, enthusiastic, and ungovernable Anabaptists; for whom he seems to heat his furnace sevenfold hotter than it was wont to be heated. The latter was renowned for his "deep-toned piety," and for adapting his divinity to the taste of doctrinal Calvinists and practical Arminians, two irreconcilable parties; *rara avis in terris*; an extraordinary talent. These Divines say that no form of " church government" can be proved to be exclusively of divine appointment. The Baptist Bishop has improved upon the Episcopalian Bishops, and says that "much room is left for conjecture." It was said long since that great men (Doctors of Divinity) are not always wise; neither do the aged understand judgment. "Therefore, said I, Hearken to me: I also will show mine opinion. Dead flies cause the ointment of the apothecary to send forth a stinking savor; so doth a *little folly* him that is in reputation for wisdom and honor." Notwithstanding this declaration, Dr. Scott, in his commentary upon the Ephesian Bishops, (*Acts.* xx.) says that Congregational episcopacy was that appointed by the Apostles, and that Catholic, English, and Methodistic episcopacy was introduced shortly afterwards, gradually and imperceptibly, by the superior age, experience, abilities, and services of the senior Bish-

ops. Mosheim speaks definitely of John's immersion, and calls immersion the primitive institution; and of faith being required before immersion in primitive times, and of bishops presiding over one congregation, who were remarkable for their simplicity in doctrine, inculcating faith, hope, love, and for their zeal and faithfulness; yet he practised sprinkling before faith, and was a dear and ardent lover of metropolitan and diocesan episcopacy. Dr. Scott studied and prayed two whole years upon the subject of baptism, during which time he sprinkled no infants, his concience was so tender; yet, with all his ample opportunities for research and investigation, and stores of ancient ecclesiastical literature, and his vast powers of comprehension, and his superabundant share of orthodoxy, he decrees that "*in the Jordan*," "*into the water*," can mean, (not does,) but *can* mean *at Jordan, at the water*, by a long charitable stretch of language, criticism, and divinity. He was also a satellite, revolving round metropolitan or city bishops, and ultimately lost all his tenderness and scruples of conscience about sprinkling babies. Doctor Semple, who has spent thirty-five or forty years of his useful and exemplary life in building up the Congregational and Independent form of Baptist " church government," in the republican state of Virginia, now, in his last days, throws his well-earned and dear-bought influence into the scale of latitudinarianism, by saying that " there is much room left for conjecture," and by calling the Christian Baptist " wild chimeras. All these, to say the least of them, are *dead flies* in the medicines of these physicians, and do now, and will continue to send forth a stinking savor.

" As this is an age of hard study and deep-toned divinity, and as thousands are now upon the big theological wheel, in the different sectarian factories, who will shortly be thrown upon the community, full of sweet-toned theology, we shall proffer a few themes for them to ruminate and write upon, in their devotional hours:—If there is nothing but "a charter of church government" in the New Testament, without any specific rule or bye-laws, are there any bye-laws upon any other subject? And if there be not, can there be any thing wrong in the religious world? Is not Shasterism and Mahometanism as right as any other *ism?* And are not their forms of " church government and bye-laws" as good as any ever made since the New Testament was finished? If the peace, order, government, and bye-laws of God's kingdom are left to conjecture, or are indefinite, does this idea not prove him deficient in wisdom and benevolence to legislate definitely? and does it not derogate from, and materially reflect upon his character, as the King eternal, immortal, and invisible?—What would the Americans think of a colossal and cedar-like politician, who would tell them that after electing, empowering, compensating, and sending their sages to Philadelphia to frame their constitution, to define and establish their laws—that now no person could divine whether oligarchy, aristocracy, monarchy, or democracy was the government of the United States? That great and good men had chosen and administered all four of these kinds of government, and that the government of England, France, Spain, and America, were all authorized by the constitution of the United States, and that they could all exist and all be administered at the same time by the Americans? Would he not either pity the ignorance or detest the dissimulation of the politician who would call a different opinion

" wild chimeras?" The publication of these sentiments is doubtless owing to Dr. Noel's political adroitness and insincerity, and not to Bishop Semple's well known prudence. If not, a man of Bishop Semple's dignity, generosity, and penetration, must have seen and lamented the folly of such management.

"Hoping that you may possess, and manifest, and cultivate that love which covers the blemishes of those who love our Lord Jesus Christ in sincerity, I subscribe myself your friend and brother.   "John Chrysostom."

Ancient Gospel.—No. VIII.

Faith and Reformation.

I have written seven essays under this head, on Immersion. I now proceed to Reformation. In the evangelical order, Faith is the first and capital item. But as we have said so much upon this item in the preceding volumes of this work, we thought it most expedient to call the attention of our readers to *Christian Immersion*, as exhibiting the gospel in water. Having exhibited the scriptural import and design of this christian institution in general terms, I feel at liberty to proceed to the other grand items associated therewith. And before we proceed to Reformation, we shall again call up the subject of Faith to the attention of our readers. As we have often said, no subject has been involved in greater mystery and darkness than the nature of faith. The labors of many commentators and of thousands of sermonizers have been employed to show that faith is something more than the mere belief of testimony, or something different from it. The people have been so often told what it is *not*, and what it *is*, that few of them know any thing certain about it. Before the age of metaphysical refinement, there was no difficulty in understanding this subject. Hence there is not an instance on record in the New Testament of any person inquiring of the Apostles what they meant when they proclaimed " reformation towards God and faith in the Lord Jesus Christ." This is a striking proof that their hearers understood the Apostles as using this word in the common acceptation of their times; as denoting *the persuasion of the truth, or the conviction of the certainty*, of what they proclaimed.— But to consider attentively the reason why so much stress or emphasis is laid upon faith or belief by our Lord and his Apostles, will do more than any definitions or descriptions, to render faith plain and intelligible to all.

And here let it be noted that the philanthropy of God, sometimes called his grace or his favor, must be known before it can reconcile, please, or comfort any human heart. This is the golden secret which unlocks all the bars of ignorance and superstition. I repeat it again—God's love of the world, his benevolence towards his ignorant, erring, and rebellious offspring, must be apprehended, known, and relied on, before any change in our views of his character, or of our conduct can be effected. And as the testimony given of the person, character, mission and work of Jesus Christ his Son, is that which developes this kindness, grace, favor, benignity, or philanthropy of God our Father, that testimony must be known, understood, or relied on, before it can operate upon our hearts, upon our understandings, wills, passions, appetites, and conduct.— Now as this testimony was first oral, then written; and as it is, and was from necessity oral or written, it cannot be known or acted upon as certain and sure, unless believed or relied upon as certain and true. This is just what renders

faith necessary, and it is just precisely that which prevents any living man from enjoying the favor of God in this life, or the blessings of the salvation of the gospel without faith. For if it could have been possible that men could have enjoyed the favor of God without knowing it, or known the favor of God without hearing of it, or heard the favor of God without a report or testimony concerning it—faith never would have been mentioned, required, or made a *sine qua non* to our enjoyment of salvation. For as Paul says about the law, we may say of faith: If there could have been a righteousness obtained by law, then faith would not have been preached; and if salvation could have been conferred without believing the report thereof, faith or belief had never been proclaimed to mortal man. But in no other way than by testimony, oral or written, could the love of God, through his Son, be known to men; and therefore in no other way than by believing the testimony, can the salvation of God be known or enjoyed in this life.— Now be it known to all men, that, so soon as any one is convinced, or knows certainly, that God will forgive sinners all offences, and accept of them through the mediation of Jesus Christ, upon their submission to the government of the Messiah, then that person has the faith or belief which the gospel proclaims; and upon the personal application of that individual for pardon and acceptance, then through immersion into the name of the Lord Jesus, remission of sins is granted. So that faith is understood when the necessity of it is understood and felt. Without it no man can know God; and, consequently, without it, no one can fear him, trust in him, love him, or please him. For he that comes to God or applies to him, must first know or " believe *that* he is, *what* he is, and that he is a *rewarder* of all who diligently seek him." Faith, therefore, is just to the mind what eating is to the body. The food must be discriminated before it can be eaten, and it must be eaten before it can contribute to the life of man. It is not the eating of it—we mean, the *action* of eating it; but the food, when eaten, that supports life So it is not the action of believing, but the truth which is believed, that renews the heart of man. Eating brings the food in contact with the organs of life; believing brings the truth in contact with the spirit of man. And as the food, when adapted to the human constitution, nourishes, invigorates, and animates it; so truth adapted to the mind of man, (as the gospel exactly and perfectly is) nourishes, invigorates, and imparts new life to the spirit of man. So that as man lives by eating bread, his soul lives by eating, or receiving, or believing the love and mercy of God. Faith then is just the belief or persuasion that the gospel is true: which persuasion comes by hearing, perceiving, or understanding what the Holy Spirit imparts or teaches concerning the Lord Jesus.

Hence the prophets and apostles say that the gospel or the truth concerning Jesus, converts the soul; for its admission renovates the moral character, and when apprehended as indubitable certainty, it must act and operate in reforming the life. And this leads to a remark or two upon *Repentance* or *Reformation*.

Repentance denotes a mere change of mind, generally accompanied with sorrow for the past; not necessarily, however, implying a reformation. But the term *Reformation* includes not merely a change of mind, but a change of life.

It is remarkable with what distinctness and precision the writers and speakers of the New

Testament use the terms μετανοεω and μεταμελομαι. They never use these terms as synonymous; though, in the king's translation, they are indiscriminately rendered by the term "repentance;" which, as all critics know, is not consistent with the true and distinct import of these terms. The former signifies such a change of mind as issues in a change of conduct; the latter includes nothing more than change of mind or sorrow for the past. Hence Paul, when speaking of his repentance for having written such a letter to the Corinthians as gave them so much sorrow; when the repentance of Judas for having betrayed the Lord; and when the repentance of the son in the parable, who at first refused to go and work in the vineyard, but afterwards repented and went—are spoken of, and in all similar places, *metamelomai* is used; but when a real reformation, resulting from a radical change of mind is spoken of, it is always *metanoeo* which is employed.— Therefore Dr. Campbell and other learned translators preferred reformation to the vague term repentance, as the proper representative in our language of the term used by the inspired writers when preaching or commanding that change of mind and behavior resulting from faith. Now this reformation of which we speak is the first fruit of believing, and hence the first act of reformation which was intended in the apostolic addresses to the Jews and Gentiles, was to be immersed in the name of the Lord Jesus. "Reform and be immersed every one of you in the name of the Lord Jesus for the remission of your sins." This, by a circumlocution, was equivalent to saying, 'Change your views of the person and character of the Messiah, and change your behavior towards him; put yourselves under his government and guidance, and obey him.' Or to the Gentiles, 'Change your views of the character of God and of his government towards you, and receive the Son as his Ambassador; and yield him the required homage by receiving his favor and honoring his institutions.' This is reformation towards God, and faith in the Lord Jesus Christ. An entire change of views, of feelings, and affections towards the Messiah, and an entire change of conduct, according to his gracious requirements, in submitting to him as our Teacher, Guide, Priest, King and Saviour, is the true import of that reformation enjoined by the ancient preachers of the Ancient Gospel. This is what we mean by "reformation," and not those movements of animal passion, those sudden panics of fear, or gusts of sorrow, which, like the repentance of Judas, frequently issue in no reformation of life, but leave the unhappy subjects of them in the same state of mind, and of the same character and deportment, as before. Let our readers bear in mind that such is our usage of this term, and let them apply it in this sense in its occurrences in the New Testament, and thereby test its importance.   EDITOR.

A Restoration of the Ancient Order of Things.
No. XXV.
On the Discipline of the Church.—No. II.

SUNDRY letters have been received on the subjects of associations, conferences, laying on of hands, family worship; all either objecting to some things advanced in this work, or seeking further expositions and elucidations of arguments already offered in this work on these subjects. These letters are too numerous and too long to be inserted in any reasonable time. We have therefore concluded to prosecute our inquiries on the order and discipline of the church, and intend meeting all these objections in the course of our essays as they may naturally occur. In the mean time we proceed to some matters of greater importance in the discipline of the church, and must solicit a due degree of patience on the part of our correspondents.

All matters of church discipline are either private injuries or public offences; sometimes designated "public and private offences," or "public and private trespasses." Private injuries, trespasses, or offences, are those which in the first instance directly affect individuals, and are known only to individuals. For a private injury or trespass, so soon as it is generally known, becomes a public offence. Now the object of the precepts in the New Testament concerning private trespasses, is to prevent their becoming public offences; and that by healing them when only felt and known by the parties;—the person injured and he that commits the trespass. The directions given by the Saviour in the eighteenth chapter of Matthew, section ix. page 48, New Translation, belong exclusively to this class of trespasses. Thus, according to this law, if A injure B, either by word or deed addressed to him alone, B, who is injured, privately tells A the injury he has received from him; and if, after expostulating with him, A confesses his fault and professes repentance, or if he explain the matter to the satisfaction of B, the affair ends, because the parties are reconciled to each other. But if neither acknowledgement, explanation, confession, nor repentance can be elicited, and B still feels himself aggrieved, he calls upon his brethren, D, E, and F, and in their presence states his grievance. They also hear what A has to offer. After having the case fairly before them, they are prepared to advise, expostulate, explain, and judge righteously. Now if A hears them, is convinced by them, and can be induced to make reparation either by word or deed for the trespass inflicted, or if they can effect a reconciliation between the parties, the matter terminates, and is divulged no farther. But if A cannot or will not hear or be persuaded by D, E, and F, but despise their interposition, expostulation, or advice, B must acquaint the congregation with the fact that A has trespassed against him. Then the congregation must inquire, not into the nature of the trespass, but whether he have taken the proper steps. He answers in the affirmative, and calls upon D, E, and F, for the proof. On the testimony of D, E, and F, every word is established or confirmed. The congregation being satisfied with the standing of D, E, and F, and having heard their testimony, proceed to admonish, expostulate with, and entreat A to make reparation to his brother B. If he is then persuaded and B is reconciled to him, the matter terminates, and both are retained; but if otherwise, and A will not hear nor regard, but despise the congregation, then he is to be excluded. It does not appear that the original quarrel, misunderstanding, or trespass is to be told to the whole congregation, and they made to sit together in judgement upon it. If this were so, there was no necessity for having any thing established upon the testimony of D, E, and F. Whereas the Saviour said that, by the testimony of two or three witnesses, every thing may be ascertained or established. Nothing would be ascertained or established if A and B were permitted now to disturb the congregation by a recital of the whole matter; for in this way, it is more likely to distract and injure the peace and harmony of the congregation, than to reconcile the parties. But if A complains of injustice in the case, then the congregation must appoint two or three others to hear and judge the matter; and upon their declaration to the congregation the matter terminates. But it does not appear, either from what the Lord enjoins in the passage before cited, or what Paul lays down in his first letter to the Corinthians, chapter vi. that the nature of the trespass is to be told. "When you have secular seats of judicature why do you make to sit on them those who are least esteemed in the church?" "Is there not *among you* a wise man, *not even one who shall be able to decide between his brethren?*"

The practice of telling all private scandals, trespasses, and offences, to the whole congregation, is replete with mischief. It often alienates members of the church from each other, and brings feuds and animosities into the congregation, and it is very seldom that a promiscuous congregation of men, women, and children can decide so unanimously or so wisely upon such cases, as two or three either called upon by the parties or appointed by the congregation. This moreover appears to be the true import of all the laws upon this subject in the New Testament. On the 18th chapter of Matthew the only question which can arise of any importance, is, whether B is to tell the original trespass to the whole congregation, or whether he is to tell the fact that A has injured him, and will not reform or make reparation. I think the original and the English version authorize the latter, viz. that he is to tell the congregation that A had trespassed against him, and would not hear D, E, and F. This is the immediate antecedent to the command, "*Tell the congregation.*" But on this I would not lay so much stress, as upon the other regulations and laws found in the volume concerning trespasses, and upon the necessary consequences arising from each method of procedure. Very often, indeed, the affair is of such a nature as ought not to be told, and could not be told in a public assembly of christians without violating some law or rule which the volume enjoins; and not unfrequently are whole congregations distracted by the injudicious, and, as we think, unscriptural practice, of telling the whole congregation a matter of which but few of them are able to form correct views. And such is the common weakness of the great majority of members of any community, that but few are able to judge profoundly in cases requiring the exercise of much deliberation. EDITOR.

The Bible Intelligible.

DEAR SIR—On Monday last I received your letter, and was much pleased to learn that you have determined to publish a translation of the New Testament, so divested of technical terms, as to destroy the only pretext, unintelligibility—which can be set up for clerical explanation. To aid you in such an all-important attempt would give me the sincerest pleasure; but I have reason to fear that my ability extends rather to the discovery than to the remedy of defects.

Some time ago an occurrence took place, which led me to reflect more closely on the subject of scriptural intelligibility than I had formerly done. For many years I had doubted the truth of the allegation that the scriptures were "a sealed book" till the seals were undone by clerical ingenuity; and I have now no doubt of the absurdity and gross impiety of the imputation. That God should send a message to mankind, on such an important subject as their eternal happiness, in language not intelligible to the most illiterate of them, is utterly incredible, and to impute such conduct to the Deity is manifest impiety. If, then, the scriptures do contain a divine communication, it follows of course, that the words chosen by the Revealing Spirit must be the fittest to convey the ideas which he meant to communicate, that could be selected, and such as he knew to be perfectly intelligible to those to whom he addressed them, so far as *he* intended them to be understood. This granted, we are certainly authorized to consider the words of Scripture as they stand in the connexion formed by the Spirit, as calculated to convey with perfect clearness and certainty, *all* the information which he designed to convey by them, and of course as insusceptible of additional clearness or certainty by any change of terms which man can devise. These remarks, however, I need not tell you apply only to the words in which the scriptures were originally written in Hebrew and Greek, for they alone are the choice of the Spirit. Of every translation the words are but the choice of man, and of course no sacrilege can be committed in the alteration of them. It is evidently then the duty of every translator to make himself as fully acquainted as possible with the two original tongues, that he may gain a distinct comprehension of the ideas which the Spirit has condescended to communicate to the human family, and then to select such words of the language into which he translates for the conveyance of the Spirit's ideas, as will place, in regard to intelligibility, the persons for whom the translation is made, on the same footing with those addressed directly by the Spirit's own words. This task performed, the words employed by the Spirit justly and clearly rendered, all, in my judgment, is done to render the scriptures intelligible to every rational creature, however illiterate, which can be done. For if the Spirit has seen fit to introduce either obscurity or ambiguity into the original, or his words correctly rendered leave either in a translation, it is not in the power of uninspired men to remove them. From their attempts all we can rationally expect, and all we have actually obtained, is a mass of dubious, conflicting, shall I say, impious conjecture in which no confidence can be reposed. But to be brief, whatever information the Spirit of God has designed, determined, and attempted, to communicate to the human family, he has employed for his purpose language perfectly intelligible to the most illiterate among them, and has actually accomplished his object. He has left no part of his communication dark or ambiguous, which he did not intend to leave in that state, as being most fit and proper in itself, and really necessary and useful to mankind. In no instance is the obscurity or ambiguity introduced into his intelligences to be ascribed to inadvertency, to negligence, to incapacity, but to design: and if designedly introduced, every attempt to remove either is not only vain, but excessively impious. My belief, however, is, that if we desire not more information, and of course attempt not to compel the words of the Spirit to give us more information than God intended to give us, we shall have little cause to complain either of obscurity or ambiguity; indeed, as to the latter, it is always used with much beauty and advantage; for in either sense of the ambiguous expression, the information it conveys will be found both true and important: and on the passages deemed by us obscure, the Spirit has no doubt conveyed clearly all the intelligence he meant to convey, or we stood in need of.

If in the preceding remarks there be truth, it evidently follows that all attempts to explain the scriptures, to remove from them either obscurity or ambiguity by translations, commentaries,

8

or any other means, are not only absurd, but detrimental and grossly impious: every such attempt being founded on the supposition that God has by inadvertency, incapacity, or design, sent to his perishing creatures an unintelligible message for their relief, but from which, as being incomprehensible by them, they can derive no benefit. To what purpose, then, are the countless legions of explanatory sermons, lectures, expositions, commentaries, annotations explanatory, or books of any name? Are they not all chargeable with the absurdity of undertaking to render that clearer which is already as clear as words can make it; nay, of rendering the meaning of the Spirit more clear and definite than he was himself able to do? yes, to outdo the Omniscient God? or to remove what he had inserted as irremovable? It appears, then, that the office of a translator is to exhibit the meaning of the original text neither more nor less clearly, neither more nor less definitely than the words employed by the Spirit conveyed it, and in such words and phrases in his own tongue as are in the most familiar use, and of course perfectly intelligible to the most illiterate ear. To effect such a translation of the New Testament will be no doubt a very difficult work, and will require the expulsion of an endless number of terms, either exceptionable as single terms, or as combined with others, which are to be found in our common translation. The causes which affect the familiarity, and of course intelligibility of words, are very various. Some of them I hinted at in my last letter; one, however, I presume I omitted, which has darkened numberless passages of the Book of Life—I mean technicalness, if such a word there be. When we translate, for example, διακονος, not servant the familiar, but minister the official or dignified term; πρεσβυτερος not aged man or aged christian, as its etymology imports, but Presbyter, an animal of which we literally know nothing.

For if such an officer did exist in the apostles' days, as we know nothing of the acts of which his office consisted, the naked name can convey no useful information to us, and therefore, without absolute necessity, ought not to appear in a translation. In like manner, when we translate επισκοπος, bishop, a foundling of unknown origin, a mere theological brat, of which the illiterate know nothing, instead of the familiar and well understood term *overseer;* with innumerable other terms, we utterly ruin the perspicuity of the sacred volume. Indeed the literal or etymological sense ought to be preferred in all cases in which metaphorical or official interpretation is not absolutely required. The literal meaning of ευαγγελιον is good news, glad tidings, terms, most unfortunately for perspicuity, changed into *gospel:* αγιος literally denotes, set apart, and with infinite advantage in my opinion would these two plain words occupy the place of every term by which either it or its derivatives are now translated. When we say a person is set apart, or has set himself for God's service, we immediately understand what is said to us; but when a person is styled a saint, or holy; a dictionary, a theological doctor, catechism, or sacred manual becomes necessary, before we know what sort of character is intended. Substitute delivered for justified, deliverance for justification, taken into God's family for adoption, and mark the influence of the change on perspicuity. The literal import of καθιστημι is to appoint in any way; but translate it ordain, and make that term denote the transaction now termed ordination, and the official authority now attached to it; and you have a transaction and institution conjured up, of which the faintest trace is not to be found in the word of God. Προιστημι literally signifies to stand before, lead the van, occupy the foremost place, and discharge its functions, implying, I presume, rather the authority of example, than command; in our translation, however, it is made to denote command only. Διαθηκη literally denotes disposition, arrangement, institution, terms which imply the agency of one individual or party only, and an action expressive of the will of only one person or party; yet we translate it covenant, a term which denotes a transaction of a very different character. Indeed it is impossible that a transaction such as the word covenant denotes in common use, could ever occur between God and any of his creatures, and when we attend to the transactions which did occur, as recorded either in the Old Testament or in the New, we discover none that justifies the use of that term. In all God's transactions with Adam, Noah, Abraham, Isaac, Jacob, not excepting Moses, we perceive neither more nor less than declarations on the part of the Deity of certain purposes which he had determined to execute either absolutely or conditionally: and what is the transaction at Sinai itself, but a declaration of the latter kind? After declaring on that ever-memorable occasion, what he had already done for the people assembled before him, as an aggregate body descended from Abraham, he proceeds to declare himself ready to become their political sovereign, to define the conditions on which he would consent to act as such, and specify the treatment which they were to expect on his assuming that character; namely, that if obedient to his orders, many political advantages and benefits would be conferred on them; if disobedient, many political evils would be inflicted. But what in the whole of this divine communication can be discovered that in any degree partakes of the essential properties of that transaction which we term in common language a covenant. The import of the term διαθηκη, when used to denote any transaction which relates to God, appears to be much more justly translated by declaration, or institution, than by covenant. But I must stop for the present.   A. S.

A Debate on the Evidences of Christianity.

It will be remembered that Mr. Robert Owen, of New Harmony, did, in the month of January last, challenge the clergy of New Orleans (as he had in effect the teachers of religion every where) to debate with him the truth of the christian religion. In his public discourses, as well as in the words of that challenge, he engages to prove that "*all the religions of the world have been founded on the ignorance of mankind; that they have been, and are, the real sources of vice, disunion, and misery of every description; that they are now the only bar to the formation of a society of virtue, of intelligence, of charity in its most extended sense and of sincerity and kindness among the whole human family; and that they can be no longer maintained except through the ignorance of the mass of the people, and the tyranny of the few over that mass.*" This challenge I have formally accepted, believing it to be my duty so to do in existing circumstances; and I stand pledged to prove, in a public discussion, that the above positions are every one untenable; that Mr. Owen *cannot* prove any one of them by any fair or legitimate process of reasoning whatsoever.

There are *four* grand positions assumed by Mr. Owen in the above challenge:—

9

"1. That all the religions of the world have been founded on the ignorance of mankind."

"2. That they have been, and are, the real sources of vice, disunion, and misery of every description."

"3. That they are *now* the only real bar to the formation of a society of virtue, intelligence, sincerity, and benevolence."

"4. That they can be no longer maintained except through the ignorance of the mass of the people, and the tyranny of the few over the mass."

To each of these I say, *Nay*; and am prepared to show that it is not in the power of any man living to prove one of them true, by any documents, facts, or just reasonings in the compass of human power or human knowledge.

Since my acceptance of the above challenge, I had the pleasure of a visit from Mr. Owen, on his way eastward; and, after an agreeable and desultory conversation on the premises, and various matters, we have agreed to meet, all things concurring, in the city of Cincinnati, on the SECOND MONDAY OF APRIL NEXT, in some large and commodious place in that city. Mr. Owen being on his way to Britain, and not contemplating his return to the United States as practicable before the beginning of winter next, requested the delay of the discussion to so remote a period. It is hoped that the season fixed upon will prove acceptable to the public in general, as it is to be expected that facilities of steam boat navigation, and the mildness of the weather at that season will be favorable to such as will feel interested to attend.

From the talents and acquisitions of Mr. Owen, we have no doubt but he will be as capable of defending his positions as any man living; and when we consider his superior opportunities from age, traveling, conversation, and extensive reading for many years, added to the almost entire devotion of his mind to his peculiar views during a period as long as we have lived, we should fear the result of such a discussion, were it not for the assurance we have and feel of the invincible, irrefragable, and triumphant evidences of that religion from which we derive all our high enjoyments on earth, and to which we look for every thing that disarms death of its terrors, and the grave of its victory over the human race.

A. CAMPBELL.

No. 2.]   SEPTEMBER 1, 1828.
Essays on Man in his Primitive State, and under the Patriarchal, Jewish and Christian Dispensations.—No. II.
Primitive State.—No. II.

IN the close of our former essay we left the progenitors of the human race in the full possession and enjoyment of paradisiacal bliss. Their Creator conversed with them *viva voce*, and they heard his voice without a tremor or a fear. They saw him, and were glad—they heard him, and rejoiced. All was calm and serene within—all was cheerful and joyous without. So rapid was their progress in this school, that Adam was soon able to give suitable names to all the animals around him; and when his acquaintance with language was thus tested by his Creator, not an imperfection or defect was found: for "whatsoever Adam called every living creature, that was the name thereof." His happiness consisted in the perfect subordination of his passions and appetites to reason, and of his reason to the character and will of his Creator. Conscious of the perfect approbation of his God, he had nothing to fear; and all his capacities for enjoyment being gratified, he had nothing to desire. In the full zenith of his enjoyment, he had not a wish uncrowned, nor a desire ungratified.

But some tenure of his enjoyment must be granted, and a test of his loyalty must be instituted. This is the reason, as it was the basis, of the promise and law promulged to him. How long he was to be possessed of this felicity was not yet defined, and on what terms he was to continue in friendly intercourse with his Creator had not yet been stated. This gave rise to the law under which he was placed. This arrangement reminded him of his origin, of his dependence, and accountability; as well as anticipated any inquiry respecting the tenure of his enjoyments, or his destiny. But the nature of the law and of the promise, or the design of the trial under which he was placed, is all that interests us in reference to our design.

However we may understand the terms or description of this arrangement, whether as literal or symbolic, one thing is obvious, and that is all and alone important to know, and that is the nature of the trial, viz. whether his spirit or his soul, his understanding, or his passions, shall control his actions. In one sentence, whether his spirit shall retain the sovereignty with which God had invested it, or his passions usurp the government. Reason was already enthroned, and had full command of all his passions, affections, and propensities; and so long as it continued at the helm, perfect subordination was to be expected and enjoyed. But if, by any means, his passions should gain the ascendant, and dethrone his reason, then disorder, confusion, and an awful reverse of circumstances, must inevitably ensue. Such was the nature of the trial. The law and promise promulged to him were predicated upon his nature and addressed to his reason, and could not fail to engage all his powers. The trial was made as easy as the nature of his relations to heaven and earth could admit, and was, therefore, the best possible test of his loyalty.

The temptation, artful as it may be supposed, was evidently addressed to the soul or passions of the woman, and of the same character was that offered to the man. It addressed the understanding through the medium of the passions; and thus the sad catastrophe was accomplished. Man fell through the triumph of passion. His reason was dethroned by the usurpation of passion, and the harmony and subordination before existing within were now destroyed. From being the son of reason, he became a child of passion, and the slave of appetite. Guilt, shame, fear, and all their horrible retinue, now invade his peace and overwhelm him in ruin and despair. There is no regaining his former standing; the controlling power is lost. In this miserable plight he was called to judgment, and the sentence was executed. Exiled from Eden, and from the approbation of heaven, he, by an act of mercy, is respited, and becomes a pensioner under a small annuity, until his physical energies should be worn out by the conflicts of reason and passion upon his animal life. This was the necessary result of his preternatural condition. So that by a law of nature death became necessary.

The change which now had taken place in Adam is difficult to be conceived of, as we can have but a very imperfect idea of his former moral and intellectual grandeur. But the best illustration we can conceive of, as it is the only analogical one we know any thing of, is a second fall of man, which sometimes takes place. When we have seen a person of what is now called

10

good moral character, and high intellectual endowments, by some sudden gust of passion, or by the ravage of some nervous disease, fall into a state of insanity, we have in his former and present character a partial representation of the nature and consequences of the fall of Adam. This we conceive to be, in many respects, a good analogical picture of the first fall of man, though we do not recollect of ever having heard it so used. Persons of good moral and intellectual standing, have fallen into fits and into habitual states of insanity, in which they neither morally nor intellectually exhibit a single trace of their former character. Yet these have all the faculties and powers which they once had, but in such a state of derangement as almost to obscure every spark of intellectual ability they once exhibited; and the balance being lost in the intellectual powers, actions foolish and wicked, mad and desperate, frequently characterize such unhappy beings. A restoration of such to reason and goodness is as great a change as that of a sinner from ignorance and wickedness to the knowledge, the fear and the love of God.

Ideots and madmen have sometimes, however, their lucid intervals, in which they seem to think and act like their former selves; but these are not often of long continuance. So fallen man seems, at times, in point of moral government and intellectual displays, to equal our highest conceptions of man's primitive standing: but these are often followed up by strong and long continued exhibitions of the triumphs of passions and prostration of reason and goodness.

But we may have better means of illustrating the nature of "the fall" when we contemplate man as he now appears as a fallen being. He is from his birth subjected to the control of appetite and passion. Adam begat a son in his own likeness, immediately after "the Fall." This child was born in the likeness of fallen Adam—not in the likeness of Adam in Eden. Its misfortune is, that it is now necessarily a child of appetite and passion before it can exercise reason at all. This gives a mastery to its passions, which no education, intellectual or moral, can perfectly subdue. The grand difference betwixt Adam in Eden and any of his sons, is comprehended in this one fact, viz. His reason first controlled his actions—passion first controls theirs. The appetites and passions of children govern all their actions for a time; we may say, for years, before reason at all developes itself. And what we call reason, is rather the shattered remains of reason, warped by passion and appetite, than that which is worthy of the name. Thus every child of Adam begins its career, impelled and prompted by its appetites and passions, for a long time unchecked by reason; and when reason at length appears, it is so weak and incapable of government, and so unaccustomed to control, that it is continually baffled by the fearful odds against it; and can never, by any effort of its own, gain the ascendancy.

But this is not all. The objects presented to the new born infant are so different from those which surrounded Adam in Eden, as of themselves, were there no other cause, to effect a wonderful change in its character and destiny. For an illustration, let us suppose that a prince and a princess, educated in the most courtly and magnificent style, surrounded with all the grandeur and majesty of an eastern palace, were immediately after their marriage to commit some crime worthy of imprisonment in some dreary dungeon; and while in this wretched confinement their first child is born, and confined to the scenery around it until it has arrived at manhood; what a difference in its views, feelings, and character, compared with the views, feelings, and character of its parents at its age; and is not this difference, of whatever nature and extent it may be, chiefly owing to the difference of objects or of scenery which surrounded it in prison, contrasted with those objects of contemplation which environed its parents from their birth to the moment of their imprisonment. This but imperfectly illustrates the essential difference in the circumstances of all human beings, compared with those of our progenitors in Eden. When we maturely reflect upon these two causes of human degradation, viz. The control of appetite and passion, and the sad reverse of circumstances surrounding the progeny of Adam, we shall find that in all their ramifications they are sufficient to constitute beings of a very different character from that which adorned our common father during his abode in Paradise.

Not prosecuting this inquiry any farther at present, we shall leave our readers engrossed in these reflections till our next.   Editor.

A Restoration of the Ancient Order of Things.
No. XXVI.
On the Discipline of the Church.—No. III.

In our last we wrote on the evangelical law relative to private offences. We are now to call the attention of our readers to public offences. And before opening the law and the testimony on the treatment of such offences, we will occupy the present number in treating of these offences in general.

Whatever action, or course of conduct, contrary either to the letter or spirit of either the moral or religious injunctions or restrictions delivered by the Saviour or his Apostles, is an offence against the gospel order and the author of it; and in proportion as such offences are known, either to the society or the world at large, are they more or less public; and, as such, to be examined, judged, and reprobated, according to the law of the Great King. After speaking in terms so general, it becomes expedient to descend to particulars. And here let it be noted that too little attention is paid to some infractions of the evangelical institution, and an extravagant emphasis laid upon others, as if they exclusively merited the attention of christian communities, and were the only actions to be inquired into according to scriptural authority. Such reasoners ought to be sent to the Apostle James to learn logic. He teaches that he that violates any one commandment, sins against the authority and will of the lawgiver, as well as he that transgresses all the laws of the empire. For he that said, "Do not commit adultery," said also, "Do not steal." Now if you commit no adultery, yet if you steal, you are a transgressor. So reasons James the Apostle. Now according to this logic, let us attend to some offences or public trespasses very commonly not submitted to discipline in this latitudinarian age. And in the first place, let us attend to detraction, slander, or evil speaking. I do not mean to confine my remarks to that species of slander of which civil laws take cognizance, nor to those gross detractions which the different codes of ecclesiastical law take notice of; but to what, in the judgement of the New Testament, is as really and as truly slander, detraction, and evil speaking, as those instances punished by law.

Every insinuation, inuendo, hint, allusion, or comparison, which is calculated or intended to diminish aught from the reputation or good name of any person; brother, or alien, is, in the discriminating morality and purity of the New Testament, accounted slander, detraction, or evil speaking. And here we may observe, that the terms evil speaking are generic, and include every word and sentence, the meaning or design of which is calculated to do injury to the reputation of others. *Slander* is a species of evil speaking, and imports false and foul imputations, or falsely ascribes to others reproachful actions incompatible with good character. Detraction simply derogates and defames, either by denying the merits of another, or subtracting from them. In this age and country evil speaking is as fashionable as lasciviousness was in Corinth. Our political papers at this time are rather vehicles of slander, than heralds of intelligence: and these feed and pamper a taste for slander and detraction, which is more likely to be the first trait of a national character, so soon as we can form one, than any other we can think of. I could wish that the same character was not likely to be merited by some of our religious prints, whose avowed object is to subserve the spread of evangelical principles and practices throughout the land. Where slander and detraction are the order of the day in the public walks of life, it is difficult to keep this great evil out of the church and from the fireside of christian circles.

Political and religious sects and parties, and the necessary rival interests to which they give rise, are the true causes of this awful deterioration of morals, both in church and state. Now if slander and detraction are as real infractions of the law of the great King as murder and theft, (and we must think they are,) it is difficult to decide whether any nation or any people are more rapidly degenerating than the good citizens of the American Republics. It is the more difficult to resist this contagion because of its almost universal prevalence, and few appear conscious either of the enormity of the evil, or of what constitutes it. Even "ministers of religion," as they are fashionably called, seem not to think that more than the tithe of their public sermons are religious slander or detraction. Nor is this sin confined to one sect either in church or state. Society is working itself into such a state as to make aspersions, defamations, and slander necessary to political health. And what is still worse, the "religious presses," controled by good and religious men, are giving countenance and encouragement to this pernicious custom. Insomuch that one-sided representations, inuendos, and detractions are supposed to be expedient for the maintainance of the popular plans and benevolent undertakings of the good men of the earth.

Men have their political and ecclesiastical idols; and these they worship not only with incessant adulations, but they offer them whole burnt offerings of the fame of their rivals. They seem to think no sacrifice is so acceptable to the idol of their party, as the good name of his competitor. The morning and the evening sacrifices of the Jews were not more regularly attended on in the tabernacles of Israel, than are the hecatombs of defamation and scandal in the temples of rival interests. No public nor private virtue can shield its possessor from the shafts of envy, and the calumnies of intrigue, should he be so unfortunate as to be nominated for any distinction amongst his peers. That moment his promotion is named, every restraint laid upon the tongue and the pen is withdrawn; and he stands a naked target upon a hill, to be pierced with the arrows of slander from every point in his horizon. He stands as a criminal upon a pillory, unprotected by law, unguarded by the sanctions of religion and morality. No man feels himself a sinner when he robs him of his good name, and as remorseless as the licensed hangman, he devotes him to destruction. So appears the state of things in the present crisis; yet but few seem to think that the evil is of much magnitude, or consider it in any other light than a tax which must be paid into the revenue of the Temple of Fame. And yet methinks the life and the public services of a Washington or a Moses, protracted to the age of a Methuselah, could not atone for the guilt contracted in the present campaign for a four years magistracy in these United States.

But whither am I straying from the subject before me! I only intended to observe, that so popular is the evil of which we complain, that it has become less offensive to our feelings, and we have become less conscious of its malignity; so that in religious, as well as in political society, it has become quite a matter of course, or a subject of easy endurance, if not of perfect forbearance. And even christians seem to feel little (if any) compunction when they are whispering, backbiting, evil surmizing, and suspicioning one against another. Judgments well informed and tender consciences recoil at the very thought of derogating from the good name of any one whom the law of love embraces as a fellow-christian. Christianity puts us upon quite a different course; it teaches us to esteem another better than ourselves; it extols that love which hides a multitude of sins, and ranks all detractions, slanders, and envy the root of this accursed fruit, amongst the works of the flesh, and associates the actors with Satan the accuser, and his kindred spirits bound over to the day of righteous retribution. Every thing incompatible with the most cordial affection, is incompatible with the relation subsisting in the church of Christ; the nearest and the dearest, as well as the most permanent relation known on earth. The second birth introduces all into one family, one brotherhood, one inheritance, one eternal relation, which neither time, nor distance, nor death itself can destroy. In this relation, the highest pleasure is to see all honorable, irreproachable, and of exalted purity. It prompts us to draw the vail of forgetfulness over the defects, and to hide the faults we see in our brethren. It constrains the whole brotherhood to take cognizance of the person who, by a hint, inuendo, or allusion, defames any one they have confided in, and honored as a christian brother. It constitutes the good name of each public property and can view in no other light than in that of a thief or a robber, the person who steals away a jot or tittle of the good character of any one of the sacred fraternity. Whenever this ceases to be the character of any religious society, they have fallen from their first love, and have lost the highest ornament which adorns christian character. And here let us pause for the present.　　　　　Editor.

———

The following Letter was written by a Christian in New-York, to a Christian in Georgia, without the least expectation of its ever finding its way into this work, or of being laid before the public; but it happened to fall into our hands, and after reading it, it seemed to breathe so much of the genuine christian spirit, that we thought it worthy of being preserved as a specimen of true devotion and of that christian affection which the love of the Sacred Oracles inspires. Both the writer and the person addressed are supremely attached the ancient order of things, and constant students of the Holy Scriptures. But it speaks for itself. EDITOR.

NEW-YORK, JANUARY 6, 1828.

DEAR BROTHER IN THE LORD,—I salute you, beloved, as a brother disciple; and would desire you to sit down by the road-side and commune together, and warm one another's hearts in talking over, with the greatest freedom, the wonderful, the super-astonishing subjects revealed in the Bible.

Here, brother, I have this precious book of Jehovah. Suppose we open it. But before we begin to read it, brother, dont our hearts respond to each other, and say, What an invaluable treasure we have in possessing this book—this book above all price! How insignificant all other books compared to this! We love and esteem it infinitely above every other book for its transcendant excellencies—for its antiquity—its sublimity. For example, "God said, Let there be light," and there was light," &c. Its history, the history of the world, from the creation to the consummation of all things. Its biography, the lives of prophets, kings, our blessed Saviour, and his apostles. If we want to read of crime and the end of this cursed fruit, we see it in the destruction of sinners by the flood, and of Sodom and Gomorrhah, &c. &c. Do we want to see pride humbled and humility exalted? we read it in the book of Esther—proud Haman degraded, and humble Mordecai exalted. Do we want to see God vindicating the cause of an oppressed people, who had been held in bondage by a cruel tyrant for centuries? we read here of the oppression and deliverance of the children of Israel out of Egypt, and the destruction of Pharaoh and his host in the Red Sea, &c. Do we want poetry full of sublime sentiment? let us read Job, Isaiah, the Psalms, and the lesser Prophets. Nothing can be compared to these poems in all the world. Do we want prophecies and their fulfilment? in what other book in the world shall we find this, but in this blessed Bible? Do we want to read of covenants or wills? we have them in this book—the Old Will or Covenant God made with the fleshly seed of Abraham, promising them the land of Canaan, and all other earthly blessings, on condition of their obedience, and sealing or ratifying this Will at Mount Sinai with the blood of beasts—hence the practice of sealing wills or covenants with *red* wax.

But our gracious God did not intend this should be his last Will and Testament for his prodigal children. Oh no! Our heavenly Father said (if we may so speak) in his benevolent, merciful, and compassionate heart, This Covenant will not do for my children, they will not, nor can they keep its requisitions; they will, according to this covenant, be all disinherited; they will remain prodigal; they will never return to my house; I shall never see my lost children; I cannot bear this; I must reclaim them; I must embrace them; I must make them happy under my roof. This Will or Covenant of mine must be defective; it embraces too few of my children; why, look! it only includes the family or fleshly children of Abraham; my Gentile children are all excluded. The ceremonies are too many, and too expensive and burdensome. Behold the inheritance I bequeath is too mean in its value and extent—too limited in its duration; and I perceive it has a clause in it that will kill every one of my children. Why I say in this Covenant, "Cursed is every one that continues not in all things written therein to do them," and "the soul that sins shall die." Why it is all defective, it will not answer the purpose; it will not bring back my children. I will therefore make a new covenant, which I am sure will bring them back. I will make a covenant that will include both my Jewish and Gentile children, all that will be reconciled in their minds to me. I will try to prove in the highest possible manner, that I love and pity them; that I desire above all things that they should return to my embrace as the only certain friend that can do them good, and not perish by the hand of their enemies. I will send my Son, my well beloved and only begotten Son, to the very place where they are to seek them, and to assure them of my love, and invite them to return to their Father's house; to forsake their wicked and unprofitable ways, and thoughts of me; that I will have mercy on them, and abundantly pardon all their sins and transgressions; that I will not upbraid them for any of their past conduct; but, on the contrary, embrace them most cordially, and rejoice over them as my beloved children, and bless them exceeding abundantly above all that they can desire. He, my Son, shall show them this my New Covenant, that includes every creature of them, no matter what their color or condition, or however far they have strayed, or drenched themselves in crimes; whoever of them believes this gracious proclamation of my Son and thereby becomes reconciled to me, shall inherit all the great provisions of this my Last Will and unalterable Covenant.

Why, my dear brother, give me your hand.— Let us embrace each other as redeemed sinners. Is it true? Is this wonderful good tidings true, that we have such a Covenant God and Father? Let us open this Covenant, for we have got it here in this blessed Bible, and in our own language. Blessed be our Heavenly Father for such a treasure to us his prodigal children. Dont it seem, brother, that " the trees clap their hands, the little hills skip, and the mountains leap for joy." All nature, animate, and inanimate, praises God for his goodness, and for his wonderful works to the children of men. But before we get up, brother, from our seats, to travel towards our Father's house, let us look a little into our Father's Will, and refresh our minds with some of the provisions and promises, and the love and mercy which appear to dwell in our Father's heart, expressed and made known in this blessed Will or Covenant. See, brother, this Covenant says we are all the children of God by belief in Jesus Christ, (his beloved Son, who came to seek and save us from our woe;) "and if children," it says further, (O wonderful love) "then heirs, heirs of God and joint heirs with his own peculiar Son." Did he rise from the dead? So says this Covenant, (see chap. xv. 1 Cor.) Shall all believers triumph over death and the grave? See, brother, in anticipation of this great event, the dead in Christ rising first, (before the living are changed or the wicked raised,) coming up out of the sea, and those out of the dry land, as they rise and ascend with their immortal and incorruptible bodies; the saints when alive on the earth will be changed too, in a moment, in the twinkling of an eye, and all ascend together, shouting and singing that triumphant song, "Oh Death, where is thy sting! On Grave, where is thy victory!" &c. 1 Cor. xv. And, my brother, dont you think, for this grand and glorious prospect overwhelms us with thoughts. I know you say, Yes, brother, my mind is full of thoughts of our future glory. Suppose we give vent, and let our thoughts flow a little, on this delightful subject. Dont you think, brother, our bodies and spirits will be made perfect, every faculty of soul and body fit to be a companion of a holy God, &c. our affections properly placed, undivided, our memories made so perfect as to retain all we see and hear, a storehouse of heavenly, holy, and wonderful knowledge, always accumulating through the countless ages of eternity; and on which faithful record we can at any time turn our eyes and read the past, though it may be millions of years back; so shall be never at a loss for a subject of God's goodness, love, mercy, wisdom, power, majesty, &c. and so our other faculties: our conceptions will be strong and clear, able to communicate our thoughts on any subject with ease, grace, and perspicuity—and so of our will. God's will, will be our will, perfectly so; so of our understanding, so of our reason, all perfect, &c. &c.

Brother, before we rise, let us consider a little more about our heavenly Father's Will. Let us look at the seal, and examine who are the witnesses. See what a long list of witnesses. Let us read their names: Enoch, Noah, Father Abraham, Isaac, and Jacob, Joseph, Moses, Joshua, David, Daniel, Isaiah, Jeremiah, Ezekiel, and all the Prophets, and John the Baptist, and all the Apostles; but time would fail us to read them all. But stop, here is a name in large capitals, JESUS CHRIST THE SON OF GOD. Wonderful! And look at this large red seal, which spreads before the names of all the witnesses.— It appears to be blood. Why, brother, it is blood. Perhaps the Covenant will inform us about this singular seal, that appears to ratify the whole Covenant. Let us look. Yes, read, brother, there it is (Heb. ix. 11. to end.) Hold, brother, that will do. No doubt this wonderful seal is explained in other parts of the Covenant more particularly. Look here, brother; while you were reading I cast my eye on another part of the Covenant. O wonderful! only to think of the compassion of our heavenly Father to us his prodigal children! his assuming our infirmities! that after giving us so many witnesses and ratifying this covenant with such a wonderful seal, he has confirmed the whole by an oath, (Heb. vi. from 13th verse,) it reads thus—" Wherein God, willing more abundantly to show to the heirs of promise the immutability of his counsel, confirmed it by an oath, that by two immutable things, in which it was impossible for God to lie, we might have strong consolation who have fled for refuge to lay hold on the hope set before us." Blessed and praised be God for such a glorious hope, full of immortality. Amen, you say, brother. Amen, say all the witnesses. Amen, say all the martyrs, all the church, all the angelic host, and at last we shall unite with all the redeemed around the throne, shouting and singing that blissful song, " To him that loved us, and washed us from our sins in his own blood, and made us kings and priests to his and our Father, forever and ever." Amen.

Let us now rise, brother, and travel on our journey. First, let us take good care of that blessed Covenant of our Father's, for we will want often to look into it to refresh our minds, and to know more perfectly our Father's will respecting us. Now that we have put it in a safe and convenient place, so that we can get it any moment we want to look into it, by day or by night, we will run with patience the race set before us, laying by every weight and the sin that doth most easily beset us, looking to Jesus, who has run the race before us. See him yonder, brother, seated at our Father's right hand, crowned with glory and honor, waiting to receive and crown us, and to set us down with himself in all his Father's glory. Come, brother, give me your hand, let us exceedingly reach ourselves forward, press along the mark for the prize of our high calling, that we may be crowned, not with such a perishable crown as a wreath of parsley or laurel; but with the ever-abiding crown of everlasting life, and never-ending happiness in our Father's house and presence.— While we are running this race, brother, let us take care that we run by the line marked out by the Judge. Let us be temperate in all things, and keep our bodies under, (our sinful lusts and passions,) thus running, brother, with our prize in full view, surrounded by a crowd of witnesses and our Judge looking at us.——   H.

Letter to the Editor.

Frankfort, Ky. May 31st, 1828.

Dear Sir—Being myself a student of the Scriptures and a seeker after truth, I have met with a difficulty of a very serious nature, which, if removable, I have thought you could remove; and doubting not your good disposition, I have determined to lay my case before you, and ask your aid. Christian or no christian, depends upon the answer; or rather I should say, upon a plain, clear and satisfactory reconcilement between the accounts of Matthew and Luke, of the origin, birth, and treatment of Jesus; and the conduct of " his parents," Joseph and Mary, until they were resettled in Nazareth. For, to me, very inconsistent are these accounts; and hence my difficulty, from which I have not been able to relieve myself, without supposing the accounts related to two persons who were born, or reported to have been born, at Bethlehem. You know the gospels too well to need a reference to the first and second chapters of the above named Evangelists for their respective histories.

Now you are possessed of the subject, permit me to tell you that I am unskilled in languages; I want no new translations; follow the obvious meaning of the words: and where they import facts, I shall admit the facts referred to, as they are represented:—if in nature, why in nature? if supernatural, then be they so; while I hold an adherence to fact an indispensable rule and condition of the exposition desired. There is no truth in narratives where the representation is different from the fact. Therefore, as a seeker after truth, I beg you, (supposing, for the cause you are engaged in, if not of courtesy, you will notice this letter,) attend to the facts of the two stories, and place them side by side, as you trace them step by step. I languish for conviction; and am willing, if it can come, it shall come from you. I shall lose no time in announcing it to you. Had I not known as one of your subscribers and otherwise, your readiness to engage in solutions of the kind proposed, I should not probably have taken this liberty with you, which may have an effect beyond the day.

Accept the respects of yours, &c. H. M.

—

Answer to the Above.

Dear Sir—I am always pleased to find a student of the bible inquiring after facts; for it is a volume of facts of the most interesting import ever presented to the human mind. These facts are stated with the most artless simplicity which can be conceived of, and are narrated in the style and manner of the ages in which they are said to have happened. Had the sacred historians been any thing else than what they pretended to be, they would have adopted any other course rather than that which they adopted. But, conscious of the irrefragable nature of the statements they give, they manifest, in no instance, the least solicitude about the credibility of their narrative. As though careless how their testimony would be received, they are at no pains to reconcile apparent incongruities, or to explain facts suitably to any particular design. They relate what they conceived necessary to be known in order to produce faith in their readers, and leave them to examine their histories without offering a bribe to their understanding, or a bias in favor of any darling scheme—well aware, as the fact proves, that the more strictly they are examined, the more impossible it will be to discredit their narration. But to the point in hand: Matthew and Luke do not, in any instance, contradict one another in the narratives to which you refer. They wrote in different parts of the world, and at dates more than twenty years apart, but do not record all the same facts nor all the same circumstances of the same facts which they record. [See my "Hints to Readers," New Translation, page 211.] This, you know, often happens among different witnesses on the most common-place topics, and in ten thousand cases where neither the court nor the jury ever suppose there is a real contradiction. First of all, Matthew gives the lineage of Jesus Christ from Joseph to Abraham. He begins with Abraham, descends through the line of Judah to David—from David through Solomon, down to the death of Josiah and the removal to Babylon; and thence through Jechonias, the youngest son of Josiah, till Joseph espoused Mary. Luke begins with Jesus and ascends through Eli, the father of Mary, up to Nathan, one of the sons of David; and thence through David ascends in the same line with Matthew, up to Abraham, and thence ascends higher than Matthew, even up to Adam. You know that David was the ancestor both of Solomon and Nathan; and as Luke gives the natural descent of Jesus by his mother from David, it behooved him to trace Eli, her father, up to David, through that branch of David's family in the line of Nathan. Whereas Matthew, intending only to show his legal descent by his reputed father Joseph, from David, he traces the ancestry of Joseph up to David through that branch of David's family descended from Solomon. Thus the lineage of Luke and Matthew differ from David down, but agree from David up. David was the ancestor of both Joseph and Mary, but by different sons. He was the ancestor of Joseph by Solomon's family, and he was the ancestor of Mary by Nathan's family. So far there is not the least contradiction. Luke mentions forty ancestors of Jesus by his mother, up to David. Matthew mentions twenty-six ancestors of Jesus from Joseph to David. In this there is no contradiction. You may have a hundred and forty ancestors by your father, up to Noah—and your wife may have two hundred ancestors, by her father, up to the same parent, without supposing any difficulty. In comparing these rolls of lineage with those found in 1st Chronicles, chapters xxiii. xxiv. xxv. and xxvi. you will find that, in the Jewish style, the word *father* often denotes *ancestor*, and the term *son* means sometimes no more than *descendant*, and the term *begot* only denotes the line of descent. This unfolds any difficulties that I know of in the registers of Matthew and Luke.

The most apparent contradiction in this department, on which some very ignorant sceptics have descanted with so much apparent triumph, is in Luke's calling Joseph a son of Eli, and in Matthew's calling him a son of Jacob. Now this, so far from being a contradiction, when fairly and fully understood, is rather a corroboration of the truth and honesty of the two historians—and, indeed, it tends to explain difficulties which have puzzled some commentators. This apparent contradiction and difficulty I solve as follows:—

1. According to the Jewish custom and law, when the head of a family had no male issue, whosoever married his daughter, especially his first born daughter or his only daughter, was enrolled as his son in the family registers, which were kept with great care by all the communities and tribes of the Jews. An instance of this sort, for illustration, I will just state. From the book of Ruth it appears that "the line from Salmon through Elimelech become extinct by the death of the two sons of Elimelech, whom I take to have been the eldest branch of Salmon's family. On this event the right of succession devolved on the next or second branch; but as the descendant of that branch declined to comply with the law of consanguinity, and chose to continue to be the head of a subordinate family bearing his own name, the right therefore devolved on Boaz, who appears to have been a grandson of Salmon, by the third son of Salmon; and by marrying the widow of Elimelech's son he gave up his claim of establishing a family to be called by his own name, and took the title of Son of Salmon. So in the case of Joram, and the succession of Ozias, it appears from 2 Chron xxi. that the Philistines and Arabians destroyed the family of Joram, so that he had not a son nor a daughter left, save only his youngest son Ochosias: and by 2 Chron. xxii. it appears that Ochosias being slain by Jehu, his mother Athaliah slew all the rest of the royal seed, save only Joas, whom Josabeth, the wife of the high priest Jodac, stole and kept concealed till he was seven years old. He was then made king, and reigned 40 years, and was succeeded by Amasias, [see 2 Chron. xxv.] who reigned 29 years; but a conspiracy being formed against him, Azarias *alias* Ozias [see 2 *Kings*, xv. 1.—2 *Chron.* xxii.] was made king in his stead, and called *Son of Joram*, the line through Ochosias, Joas, and Amasias, being then extinct or set aside." Here we see that a person is called the *Son of Salmon*, who was not his literal, but only his enrolled son; and another is called the *Son of Joram*, who was not his natural or literal, son, but only his *by law established*, or enrolled son. In this way the families and communities of the Jews were kept up.

2. Now Eli, the father of Mary, the mother of Jesus, having no male descendant, it was agreed in the espousals of his eldest daughter Mary—(for he had another daughter Mary, the wife of Cleopas, as it was not an uncommon thing among the Jews to have *two daughters* of the same name) to Joseph that he would renounce the idea of becoming the head of a subordinate family, and be enrolled as the *Son of Eli.*

3. His being enrolled as the *Son of Eli*, or as Luke expresses it, " by *law established the Son of Eli*," explains two items of some importance in the history. 1st. It was the occasion of Jesus being born in Bethlehem; and 2d. It was the cause why the children of Mary, the wife of Cleopas, viz, James, Joses, Simon, and Judas, were called the brothers of Jesus. When the decree of Cesar Augustus gave occasion for a general enrolment of the inhabitants of the land of Judea, it became necessary that Joseph should be placed upon the roll with Mary his

wife: and although it was not necessary that every woman should accompany her husband on such occasions, it was necessary on this occasion because of the transfer to be made in favor of the house of Eli, that Mary his daughter should be present, that it might be made in the most authentic manner, [See Ruth, ch. iv.] The decree of the emperor fixed the time, and the transfer to be made, obliged the attendance of Mary, though in such circumstances; and both together were the occasion of the Messiah being born in Bethlehem, according to the ancient prophecies. Again, when such a transfer was made the first born became the lineal descendant of the father of the family, and his children, though only cousins, were supposed to be nearer of kin than ordinary cousins, and were called *brothers*. This was the reason why the children of the other Mary, the wife of Cleopas, were called the brothers of Jesus. For in other cases the Jews used the term expressive of the relation we call *cousin*, as in the case of Elisabeth and Mary. Now all these circumstances taken together, show with what propriety Luke calls Joseph the *Son of Eli*, though the natural descendant of Jacob. It also accounts for the birth of Jesus at Bethlehem, and gives a suitable occasion why the cousins of Jesus were called his brothers. For the scrupulosity and care with which these matters were attended on, see Potter's Antiquities of Athens. These things premised, I proceed to state the facts concerning the nativity and childhood of the Messiah, gleaned from Matthew and Luke.

While Augustus Cesar was emperor of Rome, and Herod king of Judea, John the harbinger was born, son of Zacharias and Elisabeth. Before his birth an angel announced to Mary, the espoused wife of Joseph, the literal son of Jacob, and the by law established son of Eli, that she should bring forth a son miraculously conceived, of divine origin, and predicts his future destiny. Joseph and Mary at this time lived in Nazareth, a city of Galilee. In consequence of the decree of Augustus, and in fulfilment of the contract with Eli, Joseph and Mary went to Bethlehem the city of David to be enrolled. While there Jesus was born. That same night an angel of the Lord appeared to shepherds in the vicinity of Bethlehem and announced to them the birth of the Messiah in the city of David. When eight days old he was circumcised, and named Jesus. After the days of his mother's purification were accomplished he was taken up to Jerusalem by his parents, and the usual rites of dedication were attended on. While in the temple, Simeon, a just man, and Anna a prophetess, moved by a divine impulse, recognized him, eulogized his mother, and predicted his career.

About this time a star in the east appeared to a sect of eastern philosophers called the magians. They came to Jerusalem to inquire his birth place, and to do him homage. Herod and his courtiers are alarmed and consult for his life. The magians, led by the star, discover the place of his residence, enter and present their gifts. They return to their own country without acquainting Herod of his abode. Herod, incensed at the neglect of the magians, resolves on killing the child, and despatches those within the period he supposed of his age. Before this bloody decree is executed, Joseph is admonished to flee into Egypt, and by night departs thither. He continues with the child until Herod dies; returns to Judea, but is afraid to settle there, and by a divine monition retires to Nazareth.

Jesus passes his childhood there, and is not spoken of until he arrives at the age of twelve, at which time he is taken to Jerusalem, and on one of the great festivals is taken notice of by the Doctors, whom he astonishes by his uncommon wisdom and sagacity. Such are the facts as stated by Matthew and Luke. And as to incongruity or contradiction, I can see none. If any difficulties occur to you on these narratives, which I have not noticed, please state them definitely, and they shall receive due attention. I know of no other or greater than I have noticed.

Wishing you, and every student of the New Testament, all the revealed knowledge of the only true God, and his Son Jesus Christ, I subscribe myself your friend,   THE EDITOR.

An Appeal to the Uncharitable.

SO MUCH as has been plead for the rights and liberties of the free born sons of the free woman, even amongst the Baptists, who have gloried in the liberality and freedom of their church polity, there are frequent displays of intolerance and tyranny, which would not have been incompatible with the policy of the Old Mother of Bigotry and Proscription some few centuries ago. We are, however, glad to say, that these occurrences are comparatively very rare, and that we have only heard of two or three of recent date. These are not to be attributed so much to the genius of their ecclesiastical policy, as to the spirit and temper of unsanctified individuals who have crept in unawares. There is the peculiar genius of each ecclesiastical policy, as well as the peculiar genius of the individuals which adopt it. There are as good republicans under the monarchies of Europe as any in the United States, and some as staunch monarchists in these United States as there are in England or France. This is as true of the members of every ecclesiastic establishment, as of the citizens or subjects of the civil governments in the Old World and in the New. But there is no scheme of ecclesiastic policy under which tyranny and proscription appear so odious as under the Baptist system. There is light enough to exhibit its deformity, as the shade in the picture exhibits in stronger colors the beauties of the painting, so the light in the congregational economy seems to render more glaring the darkness of tyranny whenever it presents itself in the Baptist communities.

We have been often asked, What is a church to do when some of its members oppose any attempt towards a more exact conformity to the institutions of Jesus Christ? and, What is a church to do when other churches are threatening to declare non-fellowship with it for its attempts to obey more fully the apostolic traditions? To such questions the answer which Peter gave to the Sanhedrim seems to be always in season, viz. "Ought we not to obey God rather than men?" It is, however, expedient to avoid divisions, and to maintain peace, so long as it can be maintained without the sacrifice of truth. We must condescend to all christians, however weak, so far as allegiance to the Lord will permit. But the most zealous opposers of reform, and of a return to primitive usage, are said to be carnal, worldly, speculative and prayerless members of the respective communities. These are content with the forms of religion in any shape which does not pinch them too closely, or require a too great disconformity to the world. These, in all ages, have been the greatest opponents to a return to Jerusalem. They have married the Babylonish women, and prefer the latitudinarian principles and practices of the Chaldean idolatry to the strict and spiritual worship of the God of Israel. These have always been a dead weight on those who wish to worship God in spirit and in truth. Some of them will continue in Babylon all the days of their lives; for, like the Jews in the wilderness, they would rather return to Egypt, to the onions and flesh pots of Egyptian slavery, than eat the manna and proceed towards Canaan. These prayerless, speculative, worldly christians (forgive the abuse of the sacred name) are always zealous for the traditions of the elders, and are rigid in their contentions for the present state of things. But to please their taste you must be as latitudinarian as themselves, and prefer the friendship of the world to the honor which comes from God only. They will tell you they were converted under the present order of things, (and, indeed, they do tell the truth, for they look like it) and they can entertain you with a long recital of a work of grace upon their hearts. To this we have no objections, provided they could show a work of grace upon their lives. But so long as we have only *their word* for what they have felt, and *see* what they do, we are compelled to judge by the Saviour's prescription, which says, "By their fruits you shall know them." But all who have known the grace of God in their hearts, will show it in their lives; and it matters not, according to the above prescription, what men may have felt, or *say* they have felt, so long as their lives are not in subordination to the authority of the One Only Christian Lawgiver. We must say they are either self-deceived or gross hypocrites. For we hold it to be a self-evident position in the christian science, that *whosoever is born of God will keep his commandments*, and will, like Paul, desire to know the will of the Lord.

But to those *christians*, in any religious community, who seem unwilling to return to the Lord, or who are satisfied with their present circumstances, and somewhat disposed to proscribe all inquiry and investigation—I should think that an appeal such as the following, could not be made in vain, provided they have a spark of christian love, or even of Baptist liberality:—

Brethren, you profess to be *christians*. Like Isaac, the son of the free woman, the child of promise, you profess to be free born. This is a sacred and a solemn profession. The Lord your King, your Prophet, and your Priest, calls you his people, and requires your whole and undivided veneration and devotion. To honor and obey him you have solemnly vowed; and must either renounce your own profession or yield him unreserved submission. He has repeatedly taught you that you "cannot serve two masters." You cannot court honor, fame, or worldly respectability, and seek the honor which comes from God only. You cannot seek to please men, and at the same time be disciples and servants of the Lord Jesus. You cannot venerate the doctrines, traditions and commandments of men, and at the same time obey the commandments of your King. You must serve the Lord with your whole heart, or he will not own you at all. You must be content with his approbation, with the "Well done, good and faithful servant," or you will never obtain it.

Now we beseech you, for the sake of him who died for our sins, who opened to us the gates of immortality, that you put yourselves under his guidance. No obedience is acceptable to him but unreserved and universal obedience. He calls no religion his but that which governs all the actions of life. But if you cannot perceive, if you do not understand all his requirements as we do, we then ask your permission to allow us to obey him as far as we understand the meaning and scope of his requirements. We say we ask your permission, not as if our obedience was to be suspended upon, or measured by, your permission: for, whether or not, we must and will obey; but we desire you to permit this without uncharitably unchristianizing us, or attempting to lord it over our consciences. So long as you appear to us to love and venerate our King, we will love and honor you; we will bear with your mistakes and your misunderstandings, so long as they appear not to proceed from a perverse obliquity of will, but from a simple misapprehension of the will of our Lawgiver. We will not lord our views or our sentiments over you: we will not denounce you as either traitors or rebels against him that is crowned Lord of all, because you cannot walk as fast as we; nor will we submit to have our rights and liberties wrested from us; nor any lords to reign over our faith or obedience, but the Lord of all. Do then, brethren, allow us the rights and liberties we allow you. Your principles, your profession require this. As you would not permit others to become masters of your faith, nor dictators to your practice, assume not the character of masters nor dictators to us. So far as we are agreed in our apprehensions and sentiments, "let us walk by the same rule, let us mind the same thing;" and thus we will maintain unity and peace with all them of a pure heart. We will commune with you and welcome you to commune with us in all acts of religious worship, so long as you hold the head, and build upon the foundation of the Apostles and Prophets; and so long as you will allow us to worship him agreeably to our own consciousness of his will. We already agree in all the grand items of christian faith. We adore the same Lord God—we worship, confide in, and supremely love the same Saviour—we all partake of the same Holy Spirit. We believe the same glorious facts, and hope for the same blissful resurrection. Why, then, bite and devour, or consume one another. Let us, then, aim at union, harmony, and love; and by our mutual prayers and endeavors, we shall come to be one in all the items of christian worship, as we are now in the one body, the one spirit, the one hope, the one Lord, the one faith, the one immersion, the one God and Father of all. We entreat you, then, to extend to us that love and respect which you would require of us and all christians towards yourselves. We meet you then on holy ground, the ground on which the holy Apostles stood. We are for unity—for harmony—for peace. If discords and divisions must ensue, the blame shall not be ours. We will bear and forbear to the utmost limits which the constitution and laws of the kingdom of Jesus permit. We call Heaven and earth to witness that we will pursue peace with all our hearts; and that all which a conscience void of offence towards God and man can do, to prevent division, shall be done by us. But brethren, we trust that your love to him that gave himself for us, and your fear of offending him, will induce you more than any thing we can say, to seek the peace and prosperity of Zion, the city of our God.

EDITOR.

Bishop Beveridge's Resolutions concerning the Choice of a Wife.

"ALTHOUGH it be not necessary for me to resolve upon marrying, yet it may not be improper to resolve, in case I should, to follow these rules of duty:—First, in the choice of a wife; and secondly, in the affection that I ought to bear towards her. As for the first, I shall always endeavor to make choice of such a woman for my spouse, who has first made choice of Christ for a spouse to herself, that none may be made one flesh with me, who is not made one spirit with Christ my Saviour. For I look upon the image of Christ as the greatest mark of beauty I can behold in her; and the grace of God as the best portion I can receive with her. These are excellencies which, though not visible to our carnal eyes, are, nevertheless, agreeable to a spiritual heart, and such as all good and wise men cannot choose but be enamored with. For my own part, they seem to me such necessary qualifications, that my heart trembles at the thoughts of ever having a wife without them. What! shall I marry one that is already wedded to her sins? or have possession of her body only, when the Devil has possession of her soul? Shall such a one be united to me here, who shall be separated from me for ever hereafter? No: if ever it be my lot to enter into that state, I beg God that he would direct me in the choice of such a wife only, to lie in my bosom here, as may afterwards be admitted to rest in Abraham's bosom to all eternity;—such a one as will so live, and pray, and converse with me on earth, that we may both be entitled to sing, to rejoice, and be blessed together for ever in heaven. That this, therefore, may be my portion and my felicity, I firmly resolve never to set upon such a design before I have earnestly solicited the throne of grace, and begged of my Heavenly Father to honor me with the partnership of one of his beloved children; and shall afterwards be as careful and as cautious as I can, never to fix my affection upon any woman for a wife, until I am thoroughly convinced of the grounds I have to love her as a true christian. If I could be thus happy as to meet with a wife of these qualities and accomplishments, it would be impossible for me not to be hearty in loving, and sincere in my affections towards her, even although I had the greatest temptations to place them upon another; for how could I choose but love her, who has God for her father, the church for her mother, and Heaven for her portion—who loves God and is beloved by him; especially when I consider that thus to love her is not only my duty, but my happiness too?"

Religious News.

From the 22d March to the 22d June, a period of three months, Bishop John Secrest, immersed two hundred and twenty-two persons, about an equal number of males and females.

A correspondent informs me that Bishop Jeremiah Vardeman arrived in Cincinnati the Friday before the 4th Lord's day in June, and immediately after his arrival began to call upon the citizens to "reform and believe the gospel!" On the first Lord's day he immersed forty-one; on the second Lord's day he immersed forty-four; and on the third Lord's day from his arrival he immersed thirty-three; and had it not been for ill health, ten more would have been immersed the same day. Thus, in three weeks, one hundred and eighteen persons were immersed into the belief of the gospel, through the instrumentality of one individual proclaiming reformation towards God and faith in the Lord Jesus Christ. My correspondent farther informs me, that, amongst the persons immersed, were the descendants of all denominations in that place, except Jews, viz. Baptists, Methodists, Episcopalians, Presbyteri-

ans, Universalists, Catholics, Deists, Swedenborgians, &c. Also, that they were collected from almost all the grades and occupations in society doctors, lawyers, judges, clerks, auditors, merchants, mechanics and laborers.

A correspondent in Lincoln county, Ky., informs me in a letter dated the 8th ult. that between three and four hundred persons had been immersed in that and the adjoining counties within a few months before that time, under the labors of brethren Polson, Anderson, Sterman, and others. Another informs me that bishop G. G. Boon, since last fall, immersed about three hundred and fifty; and bishop Wm. Morton, three hundred at least. Bishop Jacob Creath, has immersed a great many.

Bishop John Smith, of Montgomery county, Ky., who labors abundantly in the proclamation of the ancient gospel, has immersed since the 20th of April, till the third Lord's day in July, two hundred and ninety-four persons. Thus, in a little more than five months, brother Smith has immersed six hundred and three persons " into the name of the Lord Jesus for the remission of sins."

We have received from our correspondents intelligence of very extensive additions to the numbers of the disciples in many other regions; but have not room for the details, nor are they sufficiently definite. May all these disciples remember, that as they have put on the Lord Jesus Christ, they are from every consideration, bound to walk in him, to submit to his government, and to glorify God with their spirits and their bodies, which are his. Amen!

Three Important Queries.

Which will be answered in our Essay on Church Discipline.

1. Is a church, or any member thereof, that lives in the neglect of the duties enjoined on them in the gospel of Jesus the Messiah; such as assembling themselves together on the first day of the week, commemorating the death and resurrection of our Lord, contributing to the necessities of the poor, worshipping God in their families, or training up their children in the nurture and admonition of the Lord, and when called upon in the assembly of the saints to pray, cannot or will not do it; capable of judging of the correctness or incorrectness of the doctrine of the gospel?

2. Is not any man or woman in disorder that has united himself or herself to a church or assembly of saints, to be whispering, back-biting, and defaming those persons and their doctrine or sentiments, that they never have seen, and know nothing about, and who will not read or hear what they have to say of those sentiments?

3. Are men or women, that have united themselves to a church or an assembly of saints, justified by the gospel of the Messiah, in omitting to attend on every first day of the week at the appointed place of worship, under pretence that they must go among their brethren in other churches, and that they are fulfilling their engagements to God in so doing?   H.

No. 3.]   October 6, 1828.

Review of the Fifth Letter to Bishop Semple.

Virginia, July 21, 1828.

Brother Campbell,—Dear Sir—It is presumed that your letters to Bishop Semple, in the Christian Baptist, though addressed to an individual, are rendered public property, by the vehicle in which they appear; and, of course, that no exception will be taken to the offering of some remarks from one not personally concerned in the

18

conflict. Your fifth letter now before me, has excited a particular interest in my feelings; and, without intending to take up the controversy in behalf of one who thinks proper to decline it in his own person, I wish only to offer some correction of the statement of a certain fact—and then some remarks on other parts of this letter.

The statement alluded to is this. In your last paragraph but one, you represent Bishop Semple as having been "lured from the bishop's office, and severed from the flock" of his own charge —"to help to build up a college in the city of Washington," &c. Now, I wish it understood, that I am no advocate for a college *at the expense of the interests of Zion:*—to be more explicit, I cannot think that any such institution has any just claim so to engage the attention and engross the labors of the public servants in the gospel, as to take them off from the business of advancing the interests of the King of Saints, in his own appointed way. In regard to this matter, I cannot help thinking of the parable of Jotham, as being applicable: "The trees went forth on a time to anoint a king over them; and they said to the olive tree, Reign you over us. But the olive tree said to them, Should I leave my fatness, wherewith by me they honor God and man, and go to be promoted over the trees?" (Judges, ch. ix.) Such (by the way) is my view of the matter; others must think for themselves. But, in brother Semple's case, there were circumstances (perhaps not generally known) which I think must present the matter to yourself and the public, in a light materially different from that in which it might otherwise appear. It is due to him that these circumstances should be mentioned; and your candor, I doubt not, will readily give the statement a place in the Christian Baptist.

For several years past, the family of brother Semple had been visited, season after season, successively, with sickness, long in its duration, and severe in its character;—death had again and again stepped over his threshold, and some of his children had been taken off in the bloom of life. His wife, several times severely attacked, found her health in a declining state, while he himself repeatedly shared in these afflicting visitations.

In this state of things, it seemed easy to be persuaded that the removal of his family was requisite to the restoration of his wife's health, and to the escape of his family from these frequently returning seasons of sickness. He had been, I believe, for some time meditating a removal, without any definite view as to *time* or *place,* when the request was urged on him to locate himself in Washington, and use his efforts and influence to resuscitate the college. And thus, prepared beforehand by the persuasion he had indulged, he accepted the invitation, and removed to Washington. The request he had received, no doubt, had its influence, as to the *particular time* of his removal, and the *particular place* of his location. And now, from these data, which I believe are fairly given, the candid may form their own judgment—whether to censure, excuse, or approve.

There remains much less room for my other remarks than I could wish: let me, however, offer a few hints.

My dear sir, there are some mortifying things in this letter. We may, indeed, as a people, deserve and need mortification; but these things are, I think, brought forward in a manner more mortifying than was requisite, even to the cause of reform. Bear with me if I say, that some of them appear to wear an aggravated aspect, and

seem to betray a spirit disposed to make the worst of the matter.

In noticing the *ignorance* of the churches, in regard to scriptural knowledge, I must think you have spoken in terms too degrading. At any rate, I may be allowed, in behalf of the churches in general, of my own acquaintance, to enter some exception—very considerable exception, to the sweeping censure with which this paragraph of your letter is so fully fraught. Allowing for the incapacity and the unimproved minds of many, I can say, with pleasure, that the range of your censure is abundantly too wide. Yet I admit, and I lament, that there is indeed great room for complaint, not only as to other sects, but as to the Baptists; and earnestly am I disposed to second every effort that may appear calculated to redress the evil. Though I am not such an enemy as yourself to *textuary* preaching, when the due connexion is regarded, I think that more general expounding is a happy means of extending scriptural knowledge; and that to excite among the churches a spirit for reading the sacred oracles, and for social discussions of their contents, would be a happier means still. Now, my dear sir, let me ask, could you not recommend and urge the necessity of all this—and with better effect than can be expected from these rigorous censures.

On the item of the *morality* of the churches, you bring an instance of one under the notice (as you had understood) of Bishop Semple himself, where the members were so corrupt that a majority could not be found to exclude a drunken member. Now, if this were a fact, I suppose you will think with me, that this was probably some very small church—a mere fragment; and certainly I shall think with you, that it greatly needed purgation and reformation; or that, persisting, it should be disowned by all sister churches having knowledge of it. But, is this case, I would ask, to be brought as authority for a sentence of proscription against the churches in general? Surely not. You know, sir, the case of the church at Corinth, in the golden days of primitive christianity; and you know that Paul reproved, rebuked, exhorted, and labored till a reformation was effected. This was doubtless as it should be: but we should not bring the case of this church to throw an odium on the morals of the christian churches in general. Now, on the supposition that some one preacher had designed to exhibit charges of immorality against the churches of that day, I put it to the candor of any one to say, whether he might not, according to your method of proceeding, have begun in a letter to Paul, by stating to this effect:—"I heard that you said of a certain church—that they were carnal!—that there were divisions amongst them —that they prostituted the Lord's supper to the purpose of common eating and drinking, &c.— and that a majority had not been found there, who were faithful enough to exclude a man who had taken his father's wife!"

But you bring forward a long list of prevailing evils, viz:—"detractions, evil speakings, surmises; the breach of promises and covenants, the contracting of debts, beyond the means to pay," &c. Alas! alas! I must own to my sorrow, that these evils, in a greater or less degree, are too often found amongst us; and pass, perhaps, too often without due notice. But, dear sir, what friend to Zion will think of opposing a reform of any such abuses? Bring the whole force of your talents and your best efforts to bear against them, and heartily do I wish you success!

The next matter, and the last I shall at present

notice, is, the effect which you ascribe to "the doctrines of special operations and miraculous conversions upon society at large, and especially upon the children of the members of churches." The children of church members, and particularly of the preachers, you represent as the most hardened sinners, and the most profligate of any in the country. Now though this is a painful and mortifying charge—because it is indeed too often found, that the children of professors, and of preachers, (as well as others,) are irreligious and immoral; and because it must be confessed that many of the Baptists have been deficient in moral and religious discipline; it is, nevertheless, a charge which, as far as my observation extends, will by no means apply in its full extent: so far from it, that the fact appears the very reverse. According to the best calculations I can make, the odds, in point of a regular, decorous, and moral deportment, is obviously in favor of the families of professors of religion. And as to the state of society at large, (though I would hope that we are not to be responsible for all the evils arising from human depravity)—as to the state of society, I say,—why, it is matter of triumph to the friends of evangelical truth and vital religion, to compare it with what it once was in these regions, when mere moral essays from the pulpit were the order of the day; when men were Christians of course, and mere reformation of manners, for the profligate, was deemed sufficient. Numbers of us are old enough to embrace in our minds the two stages and compare them together.

Still, however, I am ready to concede, that too little has been done amongst us, and that the best means have not been generally used to shed the influence of religion on the minds of the rising generation: though I do hope we are more awake to the importance of this matter than formerly. You ascribe the evil now under consideration to the doctrine of physical operations—special operations, and miraculous conversions. In regard to miraculous conversions (if I conceive rightly of the term) there may be, and probably there are some groundless and enthusiastic notions indulged, especially among the weaker and more uninformed; but we do not encourage such imaginations; and I believe there are but few, if any, who insist on the necessity of such conversions. And as to the nature or manner of divine influence,—more mysterious than the wind, to which it is compared, it seems to lie beyond our comprehension and I wish to be satisfied with understanding some of its blessed effects. But I will here take occasion to say, what I have long been persuaded of—that there appears to be amongst us something erroneous in the view which is sometimes taken of human inability and divine agency: both points, I have no doubt, are true, but both can be misconceived of, and misrepresented. Such a view, I mean, as leaves it to be inferred that the soul of man is dead in every sense,—even physically dead;* and therefore, that nothing, in the way of religion, is or can be expected of him, without the impulse of irresistible power. Such a view, I own, appears to me to be mischievous; and against such a view—and indeed against philosophising and theorizing, either in the calvinistic or arminian style, I am willing to record my testimony. Let me observe, however, that I think we are improving in this respect; and that we are learning to pay more attention to the various

* Yet this we know cannot be; because, in that case, man could have no mental capacity for the pursuit of even natural objects.

articles of scripture truth, in their own simplicity. May we be directed into all the truth, and help to build up Zion!

Yours in the gospel of love and peace,
PAULINUS.

Answer to Paulinus.

Brother Paulinus,

DEAR SIR—Your favor before me is cordially welcomed. So far as you are intent on extenuating the dereliction of his flock, or the abandonment of his charge, apparent in the migration of Bishop Semple to College Hill, you have my best wishes for your success. It would give me much pleasure to aid you in this generous effort. The reasons you assign for his removal are sufficient, in the estimation of a sensible community, to justify him in a change of residence, but not in a change of the nature of his charge. Had he migrated to another section of the country where he exercised, or intended to exercise the same religious functions he had so long exercised in King and Queen, either as a proclaimer of the gospel, or as an overseer of the saints, your excuses for him would have been convincing and conclusive; but I am sorry to say, that I cannot discover the logical acuteness of your reasoning to justify him in not only changing his residence, but the nature of his charge; you afford good reasons for the former; but arguments are yet wanting to justify the latter.

If my "censures" of the ignorance and apathy of our congregations are unfounded, they are not only "rigorous" but *unjust*. It gives me no pleasure to state the facts on which these censures are founded, much less " to make the worst of the matter." An appeal to facts, which at this time I do not much like to have to make, is the shortest method of determining the truth, or propriety of my remarks. I am happy to be assured upon your single testimony alone, that there are some exceptions, (and would to heaven that they were a thousand times more numerous than they be,) to the *universal* application of these remarks. I did not, however, you will recollect, go further than to say that there are many congregations most grossly ignorant of the christian scriptures— "that there are many" (not all) "congregations in Virginia as well as elsewhere, in which there are hundreds of members who cannot pray in public; who could not tell the contents, genius, or design of one epistle, or section in the New Testament." This is, in my judgment, and from my actual observation, the sober and unexaggerated fact. Indeed how could it be otherwise? Are there not some Baptist, as well as some other sorts of religious teachers, who can themselves scarcely read a chapter in the sacred volume? And to teach what the scriptures import, is not the business of many of our Baptist teachers. The gospel of the Holy Spirit, or the gospel of their own conversion, is with some the great burthen of their ministry. Any scrap of holy writ will answer their purpose as well as another, to declaim upon: and as an occasion for them to tell how bad they have been, and how good they are now. If a true history of the intellectual standing, or rather of the quantum of religious information of our religious assemblies, was published, I am persuaded it would shock the builders of colleges themselves, and would make the ears tingle of those who, like the "oyster man," have been so ingenious as to preach for twenty or thirty years without making any body the wiser in the holy writings. I know some churches in Virginia in which I am happy to think that it is otherwise; and you inform me of many within your acquaintance. But the exceptions are proportionally few when the great aggregate is viewed. But how any congregation which hears but twelve scraps of the sacred volume descanted on, in a whole year, and which has but one meeting in a month for social worship, can either be intelligent or devout, is to me incomprehensible. Indeed no individual, in my judgment, can be intelligent in the book of God, who is not a habitual and pious student of it; and no congregation can be intelligent in the oracles, which do not make the developement of them their weekly concern in the public assemblies, as well as their daily attention in their private devotions.

Had I made the character of a certain church in Virginia, mentioned in my 5th letter to Bishop Semple, charged with tolerating drunkenness, a reason of a sentence of proscription against the churches in general, I would not pretend to save myself from the condemnation implied in your remarks upon the morality of the churches. But as this was neither intended, nor in my judgment done, I will let the sharp sword of your reproof pierce whom it may, seeing it cannot reach me.

When you and I, my dear sir, speak of the influences of systems as exhibited in facts, we must be allowed to speak of them as the facts have presented themselves to our observation. That the children of professed christians are worse than the children of deists, atheists, or pagans, in the aggregate, is not asserted by any christian writer with whom I am acquainted. That there are some of the children of professors worse than some of the children of deists, atheists, or pagans, is not a disputable proposition. But that many of the children of professed christians and of the teachers of the christian religion, are amongst the most hardened sinners in the community, and sometimes worse than the descendants of those in the same communities in which they reside, has been frequently remarked; and I have said that, "*very generally*, the children of the teachers, as well as of the taught, are the most hardened sinners, and the most profligate in the country." This has accorded with my observation, both in Europe and in these United States. This I have heard often accounted for upon the validity of an old Scotch proverb, viz. "The nigher the kirk, the farther from God." But I have, in my letter alluded to, endeavored to account for it on other principles:—as the immediate result of the doctrines of physical energies, miraculous conversions, total inability, and effectual calling. It would be much more uncharitable to ascribe it to the laxness of discipline, or the neglect of the due exercise of parental authority, than to account for it upon the direct tendency of the system. If, however, the reverse is the fact, it precludes the necessity of thus accounting for it. I have very often found it so; others must decide according to their own observation.

But that the dogmas of physical energies and operations, total inability and irresistible calling, are in their very nature paralysing and deadening, rather than quickening, I have not only my own observation, but the nature and reason of things to demonstrate and confirm. Now that the whole design and tendency of the apostolic preaching and teaching, was to call forth all our activities, and to give immediate exercise to all our energies, is to me so palpable, that it is as axiomatic as almost any intuitive proposition in the doctrine of magnitudes.

But between you and me there is no controver-

sy here. If I have made matters worse than they appear to you to deserve, be assured it is because I have been more unfortunate than you, and have fallen upon states of society less worthy of admiration, and more worthy of censure, than has fallen to your more enviable lot. But all that is said in my letters to Bishop Semple, upon a very deliberate re-examination, is just as matters appear to me, and perfectly accordant in its legitimate acceptation to unsophisticated matter of fact. In much affection, yours as ever,
                                            Editor.

———

As we have given so many specimens of the spirit and temper of the opposers of our labors, we shall make room for one of our numerous friends to speak a word or two in our behalf and in the behalf of truth immortal and omnipotent
                                            Editor.

—

Louisiana, Parish of East Feliciana, July, 1828.

Brother Campbell,—I have taken the "Christian Baptist" since its commencement, and have read repeatedly all the numbers that have reached me, before I was disposed to decide on its merit. On my first reading I found (as I thought) some strong objections; which objections consisted in thinking that you indulged in too much of the spirit found in man; but, on a second and third reading, comparing your work with the New Testament, I am much relieved; for I find our Saviour and his apostles did, when mild and temperate means would not reclaim the wicked, use harsh ones. The inference is plain, that the followers of Christ may use the same means to effect the like consequences as did their Master. I think it is generally allowed by evangelical christians that apostolical examples are as binding as precepts. From a sense of duty to you, my strange, but beloved brother, I acknowledge freely before God and man, that your publication has been the greatest source of information that I ever enjoyed, except the Bible; and to me is worth more than all the commentaries and systems of divinity that I have any knowledge of. I bid you God speed while you confine yourself to the New Testament; for I view all mankind (or measurably so) in a state of insanity; and I find it one of the most difficult diseases among men to manage. I am a dealer in medicine. In some cases of mental derangement I use antispasmodics, amusements, plays, and other mild remedies, to divert the attention from folly and extravagance, so injurious to health. But in some cases they will have no effect; for I am obliged, for the good of my patients, to resort to blistering, opening painful issues, and in two or three cases, within a year or two, I have resorted to severe correction with a rod, which remedy succeeded well, after all the other means had failed: so that when I reflect on your sharp arrows, their rough beards, I condemn them not, believing there may be some constitutions that require them. But, my brother, remember that the right road is a straight and narrow way: for it is the King's highway: it is a holy way; having none of men's trash in it that you are laboring to clear it of: and be cautious that while you are clearing the road of thistles, you do not bring in thorns. Your adversaries first struck at you with much venom; but the sword of truth I see has wounded them, so that they have got behind the hedges, or the mountains, (for the King's way is guarded by the mighty fortifications of truth,) so that you need not dread their arrows; for the Lord is a sword and a shield to them that obey his commandments.

Let no man draw you into the craggy knobs of speculation, or boggy fields of theorising on the religion of our King: for Satan, Self & Co. have so nearly argued men out of their senses, that there is (as I conceive) but little of that simplicity of religion among christians that Christ and his apostles taught; yet I do rejoice in anticipating that the day is not far distant when all of my Father's children will return to his house and enjoy the sweet communion of his love, acknowledging one Lord, one faith, and one baptism. I believe that the seed, that will produce the long-prayed-for fruit, is germinating: and I believe the Christian Baptist one of the life-speaking leaves of that heavenly plant. May the Lord water it by a combination of all the lovers of truth! until the kingdoms of this world become the kingdoms of our Lord and Master. Your paper and the new translation have created great excitement here. Most of the professors of religion with us are Methodistic; some of them openly declare their approbation to a "*Restoration of the Ancient Order of Things,*" and seem desirous to get out of Babylon: while others say, "Lo, here! Lo, there!" So that from these, and other indications we see, that some of Mrs. Harlot's children, though educated in Mr. Pope's school, begin to doubt his right to rule over them always. Light seems to be advancing slowly in our region. Many of your correspondents complain of not understanding you. I think no man so blind as he who will not see. Dull as I am, I think I understand you perfectly; and I would propose a plan to others who appear so anxious to get an epitome of your faith; which is, to ask your opinion on any point or subject which they esteem as an important article of faith, as I have no doubt that you would comply.

I shall conclude my letter by observing, that as in ancient Rome it was regarded as the mark of a good citizen never to despair of the fortunes of the republic; so the good citizen of the world, the philosopher, and the christian, whatever may be the political, the scientific, and the religious aspect of their own times, will never despair of the fortunes of the human race; but will act upon the conviction, that prejudice, slavery, and corruption—ignorance, error, and speculative mysticism—irreligion, vice, and impiety—must gradually give way to truth, liberty, and virtue; to knowledge, good sense, and happiness: to piety, charity, and benevolence.

May your life be long extended for the good of mankind; and may your sun set in unclouded skies! Please to accept my best respects as a friend and brother, &c.   J. W.

Query from Old Virginia.

If I have received the truth in the love of it—have become a believer in Jesus Christ to the saving of my soul, and now desire to walk in obedience to him;—while another person, enjoying the same external opportunities and means continues to resist the truth and neglect religion;—am I to ascribe the difference in my favor, to my own more tractable disposition and improvement, or to a special divine influence? and would there not be room on the former solution for self-glorying?   Inquirer.

The Query Answered.

To make this matter as plain as possible, let us suppose that the privileges of the kingdom of Heaven are compared to a splendid supper, which is, indeed, the fact. The table is spread and covered with liberal collations of all that is desirable. A general invitation is given. Now for the *Query.*—If I have sat down at the table and refreshed myself by a liberal participation of the repast provided; while another person, who was as cordially invited as myself, perishes with hunger; am I to ascribe my enjoyment of the dainties to a more tractable disposition, or to some special call, invitation, or drawings, which were withholden from the others? And if I should answer not the latter but the former, would I not thereby be led to glory in myself? Very good; and if I should say not the former but the latter, will I not make the whole matter, terminate upon some absolute, unconditional, and uncontrolable determination; which, if not put forth in my favor, makes a general invitation no better than a pompous flourish of pretended humanity, and leaves all the world to starve with hunger as far as lies in them; not because there was not an abundance for them all, not because a generous invitation was withholden; but because a secret, non-descript special drawing was withholden. In this case will I not be led to glory in an imaginary stretch of sovereignty rather than in God's philanthropy; and will not my boast in God be as selfish as my boast in myself upon the former hypothesis? And query—Whether will boasting in myself, or in the special favor, be more injurious to the general good of all my fellows, or to the general character of the moral Governor of the world?

Under all these pressing difficulties, as puzzling as the Sadducean seven-sided embarrassment, I choose rather to say, that if I have sat down at the table and eaten abundantly of the provision, I bless the liberality of him that furnished the entertainment—and instead of blessing my hunger that made me willing to come without a cent in my pocket, I boast in the philanthropy of him who made me welcome; and when I see others standing off, instead of ascribing it to the want of a cordial and sincere welcome on the part of the founder of the feast; instead of glorying over them in my better fortune, or in my keener hunger; I only think that if they felt their hunger as much as I, and believed the sincerity of the invitation, they would regale themselves with the Lord's provisions and feel as grateful as myself. So that not knowing the philanthropy of God nor the Holy Scriptures, men proposed in former ages such questions as those. I therefore neither ascribe my participation of the salvation of God either to special calls or impulses, nor to my more tractable disposition; but to the philanthropy of God, and my greater need, or greater consciousness of my need of his goodness. I do not glory, then, in an attribute of the Deity, called his "sovereignty," nor in myself as possessing a better disposition, but in my Heavenly Father's philanthropy; and if I think of myself at all, I am glad that I felt so hungry, and so much in need as to come when called. There is in contemplation an Essay which will more fully develope this matter at some future day.   Editor.

Anno Domini 1637.

However it may be appreciated, we consider it no ordinary service we are about to render our readers, in laying before them the original preface published by king James' translators. We have been favored with one of the first impressions of the king's version, containing their preface and apology for the translation. We are indebted for this copy to the kindness of our venerable and much esteemed brother, *Sam-*

uel Harris, * lately from London, now a resident in Aurora, Ia. to whom we are also indebted for many invaluable hints and criticisms, both on this work and the New Translation, in his private correspondence. The first edition of the common version is a very great rarity, being now *one hundred and ninety-one years* old. This preface contains a mass of information of the first importance to all desirous of understanding the sacred writings. It would make more than one entire number of this work. We shall therefore divide it into such sections as will suit our convenience, and make such remarks at the end as may to us appear pertinent. Any thing and every thing which tends to break the spell which an ignorant and bewildered priesthood have thrown over this volume; every thing which can contribute to a more clear and comprehensive understanding of the volume, is, with us, of great moment. Such we believe to be the following. Let it speak for itself. We present it in its own orthography and punctuation.   EDITOR.

"The Holy Bible containing the Old Testament and the New; newly translated out of the original tongues, and with the former translations diligently compared and revised, by his Majesties special command. Appointed to be read in churches. Printed by Thomas Buck, and Roger Daniel, printers to the Universitie of Cambridge. 1637."

"The Translatours to the Reader.

"ZEAL to promote the common good, whether it be by devising any thing our selves, or revising that which hath been laboured by others, deserveth certainly much respect and esteem, but yet findeth but cold entertainment in the world. It is welcomed with suspicion in stead of love and with emulation in stead of thanks: and if there be any hole left for cavill to enter, (and cavill, if it do not finde an hole, will make one) it is sure to be misconstrued, and in danger to be condemned. This will easily be granted by as many as know story, or have any experience. For, was there ever any thing projected, that savoured any way of newnesse or renewing, but the same endured many a storm of gainsaying, or opposition?† A man would think that civility, wholesome laws, learning and eloquence, synods, and church-maintenance, (that we speak of no more things of this kinde) should be as safe as a sanctuarie, and out of shot, as they say, that no man would lift up his heel, no, nor dog-move his tongue against the motioners of them. For by the first, we are distinguished from brute beasts led with sensualitie. By the second, we are bridled and restrained from outragious behaviour, and from doing of injuries, whether by fraud or by violence: By the third, we are enabled to inform and reform others, by the light and feeling that we have attained to our selves: Briefly, by the fourth, being brought together to a parley face to face, we sooner compose our differences, then by writings, which are endless: And lastly, that the church be sufficiently provided for, is so agreeable to good reason and conscience, that those mothers are holden to be lesse cruel, that kill their children as soon as they are born, then those nursing fathers and mothers (wheresoever they be) that withdraw from them who hang upon their breasts (and upon whose breasts again themselves do hang to receive the spirituall and sincere milk of the word) livelyhood and support fit for their estates. Thus it is apparent, that these things which we speak of, are of

most necessarie use, and therefore that none either without absurditie can speak against them, or without note of wickedness can spurn against them.

Yet for that, the learned know that certain worthy men have been brought to untimely death for none other fault, but for seeking to reduce their countrey-men to good order and discipline: And in some common-weals it was made a capitall crime, once to motion the making of a new law for the abrogating of an old, though the same were most pernicious: And that certain, which would be counted pillars of the state, and patterns of vertue and prudence, could not be brought for a long time to give way to good letters and refined speech; but bare themselves as averse from them, as from rocks or boxes of poyson: And fourthly, that he was no babe, but a great Clerk, that gave forth (and in writing to remain to posteritie) in passion peradventure, but yet he gave forth, That he had not seen any profit to come by any synod or meeting of the Clergie, but rather the contrarie: And lastly, against Church-maintenance and allowance, in such sort as the ambassadours and messengers of the great King of kings should be furnished, it is not unknown what a fiction or fable (so it is esteemed, and for no better by the reporter himself, though superstitious) was devised: namely, That at such time as the professours and teachers of Christianitie in the Church of Rome, then a true church, were liberally endowed, a voice (forsooth) was heard from heaven, saying, Now is poyson poured down into the Church, &c. Thus not onely as oft as we speak, as one saith, but also as oft as we do any thing of note or consequence, we subject our selves to every ones censure, and happie is he that is least tossed upon tongues; for utterly to escape the snatch of them it is impossible.* If any man conceit, that this is the lot and portion of the meaner sort onely, and that Princes are priviledged by their high estate, he is deceived. *As the sword devoureth as well one as another*, as it is in *Samuel*; nay, as the great commander charged his souldiers in a certain battell, to strike at no part of the enemie, but at the face: And as the king of Syria commanded his chief captains *to fight with neither small nor great, save onely against the king of Israel*: so it is too true, that envie striketh most spitefully at the fairest, and at the chiefest. David was a worthy prince, and no man to be compared to him for his first deeds; and yet for as worthy an act as ever he did (even for bringing back the ark of God in solemnitie) he was scorned and scoffed at by his wife. Solomon was greater then David, though not in vertue, yet in power; and by his power and wisdome he built a temple to the Lord, such an one as was the glorie of the land of Israel, and the wonder of the whole world. But was that his magnificence liked of by all? We doubt of it. Otherwise, why do they lay it on his sonnes dish, and call unto him for easing of the burden? *Make*, say they, *the grievous servitude of thy father, and his sore yoke lighter.* Belike he had charged them with some levies, and troubled them with some carriages; hereupon they raise up a tragedie, and wish in their heart the temple had never been built. So hard a thing it is to please all, even when we please God best, and do seek to approve our selves to every ones conscience.

If we will descend to later times, we shall find many the like examples of such kinde or rather unkinde acceptance.† The first Romane

---

* He died in Cincinnati in 1833 full of years and wisdom and the Holy Spirit. "Blessed are the dead that die in the Lord."   PUBLISHER.

† Let the friends of the ancient order remember this.

* So we have proved, and we calculated upon it.

† Yes, to times still later: for now, two centuries since we have found no improvement in such matters.

emperour did never do a more pleasing deed to the learned, nor more profitable to posteritie, for conserving the record of times in true supputation, then when he corrected the Calendar, and ordered the yeare according to the course of the sunne: and yet this was imputed to him for noveltie, and arrogance, and procured to him great obloquie. So the first christened emperour (at the leastwise that openly professed the faith himself, and allowed others to do the like) for strengthening the empire at his great charges, and providing for the church, as he did, got for his labour the name *Pupillus*, as who would say a wastfull Prince, that had need of a guardian or overseer. So the best christened emperour, for the love that he bare unto peace, thereby to enrich both himself and his subjects, and because he did not seek warre but finde it, was judged to be no man at arms, (though, indeed, he excelled in feats of chivalrie, and shewed so much when he was provoked) and condemned for giving himself to his ease, and to his pleasure. To be short, the most learned emperour of former times (at the least, the greatest politician) what thanks had he for cutting off the superfluities of the laws, and digesting them into some order and method? This, that he hath been blotted by some to be an epitomist, that is, one that extinguished worthy whole volumes, to bring his abridgements into request. This is the measure that hath been rendered to excellent Princes in former times, *Cum bene facerent, male audire,* For their good deeds to be evil spoken of: Neither is there any likelyhood, that envie and malignitie died, and were buried with the ancient. No no, the reproof of Moses taketh hold of most ages, *You are risen up in your fathers stead, an increase of sinful men. What is that that hath been done? that which shall be done: and there is no new thing under the sunne,* saith the wise man: and S. Stephen, *As your fathers did, so do you.* This, and more to this purpose, his Majesty that now reigneth (and long and long may he reigne, and his off-spring for ever: *Himself and children, and children's children alwayes*) knew full well, according to the singular wisdome given unto him by God, and the rare learning and experience that he hath attained unto: namely, That whosoever attempteth any thing for the publick (especially if it pertain to religion, and to the opening and clearing of the word of God) the same setteth himself upon a stage to be glouted upon by every evil eye; yea, he casteth himself headlong upon pikes, to be gored by every sharp tongue. For he that medleth with men's religion in any part, medleth with their custome, nay, with their free-hold; and though they finde no content in that which they have, yet they cannot abide to hear of altering. Notwithstanding his royall heart was not daunted or discouraged for this or that colour, but stood resolute, *as a statue immovable, and an anvile, not easie to be beaten into plates,* as one saith; he knew who had chosen him to be a souldier, or rather a captain, and being assured that the course which he intended made much for the glorie of God, and the building up of his church, he would not suffer it to be broken off for whatsoever speeches or practises. It doth certainly belong unto kings, yea, it doth specially belong unto them, to have care of religion, yea, to know it aright, yea, to professe it zealously, yea, to promote it to the uttermost of their power. This is their glorie before all nations which mean well, and this will bring unto them a farre most excellent weight of glorie in the day of the Lord Jesus. For the scripture saith, not in vain, *Them that honour me, I will*

honour: neither was it a vain word that Eusebius delivered long ago, That piety towards God was the weapon, and the onely weapon that both preserved Constantines person, and avenged him of his enemies."*

Essays on Man in his primitive state, and under the Patriarchal, Jewish, and Christian Dispensations.—No. III.

Primitive State.—No. III.

Adam, by his fall, lost the image of God, and thereby ceased to be the object of his complacent affection and esteem. To love, delight in, and esteem, what God loves, delights in, and esteems; and to disapprobate what he disapprobates, constitutes man's moral likeness to God, and proves him to be in his image. God cannot but love those who are like him, and he cannot but dislike those who are unlike him. His benevolent regard towards man as his creature, even when fallen, may, and we are assured does continue, while he is susceptible of being reconciled to him: though he cannot love with complacent affection one of the species, until his moral image is restored.

Now man by his fall, did not lose his susceptibility of being restored to the image of God; nor did he incur eternal death by his original transgression. Had either of these been fact, his redemption had been impossible. Man cannot merit eternal death unless he sin against an economy which contains within it eternal life. And had God meant by the promise of death, in the economy under which Adam was first placed, what we understand by eternal death; his veracity required that Adam must go down to eternal ruin. But neither eternal life nor eternal death were proposed to Adam under that constitution; consequently the former could not be merited by obedience, nor the latter by disobedience. So far we proceed upon incontrovertible fact. It is true, indeed, that Adam by his fall was placed in such circumstances as it became possible for him to become liable to eternal ruin. But what we contend for here, is, that this was no part of the economy, nor contained either in the law or promises under which he was placed. He lost his glory. The dazzling splendor of his body vanished, and he was ashamed to look at himself; his understanding became bewildered: he lost the true idea of the similitude of God, as well as his moral image. But he neither lost the susceptibility of being restored to the image of God, nor did he actually incur eternal death. He was therefore still worthy of the divine benevolence, though unworthy of the divine complacency; or, in other words, there was still in man, in the species, as well as in the two progenitors, something which moved the divine benevolence, and which was worthy to move his compassion and kindness. This will not be the case, it cannot be the case, with those who fall from the economy under which we now live. For as eternal life is now promised, so is eternal death; and man can now render himself unworthy of even the divine benevolence, should he so sin against the divine philanthropy as to merit eternal death. But this is in anticipation of our subject.

To return to the fall of man, all speculations apart, the facts are these, man lost all his personal glory. The rays of glory which shone from the face of Moses, and the angelic beauty which appeared in the face of Stephen the protomartyr, were but resemblances of the pristine glory

* We cannot commend the servility and flattery in this incense to king James.

which, as the flame encompasses the burning wick, encompassed the persons of our illustrious progenitors. Man lost his mental excellence and beauty as he lost his corporeal. The moral image of God vanished; and the complacent favor of God departed with it. Such were the immediate consequences of his fall. But besides the guilt of sin, there is something called the power of it. It has a polluting influence. Remorse is not the only feeling of which we are conscious when we transgress. There is shame as well as remorse, and this arises from the pollution or defilement of sin.

One transgression necessarily leads to another, and the power of sin increases in an exact ratio with the overt acts. Let us look at some species of trangression. Take theft for example. The confirmed thief began by pilfering or purloining, perhaps, some trifle. He is much disturbed by this first act. In his own estimation he has fallen. He is conscious of the wrong he has done, and feels the guilt. But half the temptation which induced the first act will be sufficient to impel to a second; and half of the temptation which induced the second will induce to a third, and so on till he become a habitual thief. Now the power of sin increases in the same ratio as the need of temptation diminishes. The reason why half the temptation will induce to a second act is because the power of the first sin renders the second as much more easy to be committed, as the temptation is less than before. This dominion of sin is a most fearful thing. For such is the awful extent to which it triumphs, that persons who could hardly be tempted to the first sin of a certain species, such as theft, drunkenness, lying, uncleanness, can at last sin not only without any temptation, but even run into all excess with greediness.

A word or two on the *punishment* of sin, and we have the case fairly before us. For there is not only the guilt and the power of sin, but there is the *punishment* also. Remorse and shame are intimately allied to mental pain. Indeed a sense of God's disapprobation necessarily incurs that fear which torments the guilty. But all the mental pain which sinners feel in this mortal state, though it is sometimes intolerably great, is, in scripture, made but a figure, or a resemblance of that punishment which is inseparably annexed to it hereafter. But it is necessary here to observe that pain, *mental*, or, if you please, *moral*, just as necessarily follows the transgression of moral law, as corporeal pain follows the infraction of the laws of nature. If I thrust my finger into the fire, or swallow a mineral or a vegetable poison, pain as necessarily ensues as a stone gravitates to the centre. It is so in the spiritual system. When men violate any moral restraint which God has imposed on them, pain must be the consequence by an unavoidable law of the moral system. Men, indeed, may be morally besotted, conscience may be seared as flesh with a hot iron, until the unhappy transgressor become past feeling. But God can, and he has said that he will, make him feel hereafter. These hints on the guilt, power and punishment of sin, are, we deem, necessary to scriptural views of the divine economy towards man after his fall.

Had man actually lost the susceptibility of being renewed in the image of God, or had he actually incurred eternal death by his fall, it would have absolutely forbade any benevolent or merciful procedure towards him as a sinner. But again, if God had not set on foot a gracious institution adapted to the circumstances and condition of man, now fallen and degraded, he nev-

er could, by any device or act of his own, have been restored to the divine image and favor. These hints, which may be rendered very plain, constitute, in our judgment, the real import of the fall of man, and demonstrate the true basis of the divine economy under which fallen man has existed, under the Patriarchal, Jewish and Christian ages, or dispensations.

The *rationale* of the christian religion is founded upon the views which the scriptures give of the fall of man; and the reasonableness of it can be fairly and fully demonstrated on the premises now before us.

When we speak of man's losing the image of God, we include under this phrase his loss of a correct idea of God's image, as well as his conformity to it. And here we find the fountain of all the idolatry ever known on earth. It is almost, if not altogether, impossible for human beings to lose the idea of the existence of a first cause after it has been in any way communicated to the mind. But it is as easy to lose a correct idea of the moral image of God, as it is difficult to lose an idea of his existence. While fallen man retains an impression or a conviction of a first cause or of a divinity, and has no correct idea of his image, he will naturally assimilate his divinity to that object which most engages his imagination or his strongest desires. Hence the deification of heroes, animals, vegetables, vices, or the host of heaven, according to the ruling passion of the idolatrous nation, tribe or individual. These, however, are conclusions from various premises not now laid before our readers, which may afterwards require more attention. To conclude this essay:—Man lost by his fall his personal glory as above described; he lost a true idea of the image of his Creator; and the actual moral likeness he before had to him; with this he lost his favor also, and was thereby not only become obnoxious to all the punishment annexed to his original transgression; but was, as far as in him lay, utterly disqualified to regain either a true idea of God's moral character, conformity to him, or the enjoyment of his favor. Now the rational excellency of christianity is, that it adopts the only consistent means in the grasp of human comprehension to restore man to the image, favor and friendship of God. But of this more hereafter.   EDITOR.

A Restoration of the Ancient Order of Things.
No. XXVII.
On the Discipline of the Church.—No. IV.

OUR last essay under this head was rather to point out some of those moral evils which call for the discipline of the congregation, than to develope the procedure of the congregation in relation to public offences. We spoke of some aberrations from the law of Christ, very generally overlooked in the discipline of the church. We shall continue this subject in the present essay. We ought first to know the law of our King before we presume to execute it.

In our last we treated almost exclusively of *evil speaking* in its genuine import. Very nearly allied to this, and an evil almost as general, is that of breach of promises and covenants amongst the professors of the present day. This is an evil of very serious magnitude and of alarming extent among our cotemporaries. The foundation of this evil, will, we presume, be found in the cupidity, avarice or commercial spirit of this age and country. The propensity for contracting debts, and of risking largely on contingencies, and the want of a due estimate of the solemnity of a promise or covenant, constitute the root of this desolating evil. It has become almost fashionable in society to excuse delinquencies and to apologize for the breach of solemn engagements by attributing it to the hardness or unpropitiousness of what we call *the times*. Mankind are ever wont to blame their sins on any thing but themselves. There is no necessity for the disciples of him whose kingdom is not of this world, to incur such hazards or risk such responsibilities as the children of this world do, in their desires to amass treasures upon earth, or to follow in the train of pompous vanities which allure those whose eyes have never been raised from earth to heaven. The disposition thus to conform to the world, argues very forcibly that professors have not found that in Jesus Christ which fills their hearts; or which they found in him, who for his excellencies accounted all things but dregs that they might attain to that perfection in him which the resurrection of the dead will disclose. If we see a lady much abroad and seldom at home, we must conclude her happiness is not so much at home as abroad; or if we see a gentleman more attentive to other ladies than his wife, and more in their company, we are forced to conclude he finds not that in his wife which in his marriage covenant he professed to have found. In the same way we reason when we see a christian laboring to acquire those earth-born distinctions which exclusively engross the attention of the sons of earth. If we see him as eager in the chase as they, we suspect he has not found in his profession that which he professed to have found, when he made a formal surrender of himself to the Lord of life.

But lest we should stray from our subject, we must say that the whole system of speculation, of asking and giving securities, of incurring debts beyond the most obvious means to pay in any contingency which may be supposed, are just as opposite to the spirit and tendency of christianity as theft, lying, and slander. Hence no christian can be prosecuted at law in any such case, or, indeed, in any other case; but it behooves the congregation to examine his conduct whether he have been justly or unjustly prosecuted in the case. No man can be sued justly unless he have violated some law of Christ, or departed from the spirit and design of christianity. This is, at least, the case under the code of laws which govern our commercial intercourse in this country. But we do not suppose, nor teach, that only such cases of departure from the christian institution as become cases of prosecution, are to be inquired into, or remonstrated against, in a christian congregation. No, indeed; every appearance of this evil spirit is to be guarded against as a plague. No promise should be made, no covenant entered into, no obligation given, which is not to be held as sacred as a sacrament or an oath. When we hear of a christian compelled to pay his debts by law, or to atone for the breach of covenants by fines; when we see one asking securities to obtain money on which to speculate, or see him eagerly engaged in the pursuit of wealth or any earthly distinctions, we must consider his conduct as great a libel on christianity, as to see a college founded for the express purpose of aiding the cause of Christ, praying to the powers that be, to allow it the privilege of not paying its debts, or of departing from its own engagements with impunity.

Every christian's yea should be yes, and his no, no. Every christian's promise should be as inviolate as an oath, and all his engagements as sacred as his christian profession. It is only

when it is so, that persons will be cautious in entering into engagements, and punctual in living up to them. What a world of prevarication, double meanings, duplicity, circumvention, and lying, grow out of the latitudinarianism of these times. And when we trace all the bitterness, hard feelings, evil surmises, coldness of affection found in religious society, up to their proper source, we generally find they have originated either from the evils on which we descanted in our former essay, or from these of which we now treat. Punctuality in all engagements is an essential constituent of christian morality. "Owe no man any thing but love," and "Provide things honorable in the sight of all men," and "Let our brethren learn to practise useful trades for the necessary uses," and many other apostolic injunctions which naturally flow from the religion of our Lord, make it necessary that christian congregations should take these matters under their most serious consideration.

Nothing injures the cause of christianity, nor retards its progress more, than the immoralities of which we now speak. They are so visible, manifest, and so inimical to the political and temporal interests of society, that the children of this world, Deists, Atheists, and Sceptics of every name, are just as good judges of these questions, and can mark their progress and descant upon their effects with as much precision and fluency as Paul the Apostle could have done. They also pique themselves no little upon their superior attention to these matters. How lightly do they speak of the religion, the devotion, the praying, and religious gossiping of those who will not keep good faith, nor pay their debts, nor speak well of one another. This is the style in which they take off the edge of the reproofs and zeal of those who profess christianity. After all their boast, their morality is a matter of policy and self-interest. Yet it is a political advantage, highly beneficial to society, and therefore its tendency most commendable. But without this, a man's religion is vain. "For if a man does not know," says an Apostle, "how to bridle his own tongue, his religion is vain."

Every christian congregation has, therefore, the best of reasons, as well as the highest authority, to induce them to take this matter under cognizance, and to make every departure from the letter and spirit of christianity, in these respects, a matter of discipline. On the discipline of such offences we shall speak hereafter.

EDITOR.

Ancient Gospel—No. IX.

In the natural order of the evangelical economy, the items stand thus;—1. Faith; 2. Reformation; 3. Immersion; 4. Remission of sins; 5. Holy Spirit; and 6. Eternal Life. We do not teach that one of these precedes the other, as cause and effect; but that they are all naturally connected, and all, in this order, embraced in the glad tidings of salvation. In the apostolic age these items were presented in this order. The testimony of God, concerning Jesus of Nazareth, must first be believed before a person truly repents of his sin and forsakes it. Men are commanded with a reference to their conduct in one point of view, to reform and believe the gospel. Thus Paul proclaimed "reformation towards God and faith in the Lord Jesus Christ." But yet reformation, though sometimes first mentioned, is explained as resulting from faith or the accompaniment of it. Indeed the one is frequently used to the exclusion of the other, as supposed inseparable from it. Thus Peter proclaimed,

"Reform and be immersed for the remission of sins," and Paul said, "Believe and be saved." Both Matthew and Mark, in recording the commission, mention immersion; but Luke does not. He says Jesus commanded, "Reformation and forgiveness of sins to be proclaimed in his name, among all nations, beginning at Jerusalem." He therefore, by a metonymy, substitutes *forgiveness of sins*, for immersion, and *reformation* for faith, or else we must say he omits this part of the institution altogether;—which hypothesis is inadmissible. He that comes to God, must first believe that he exists, and that he is a rewarder of all who diligently seek him. This view of God induces reformation, which in its first exhibition where the scriptures are understood, immediately carries the subject to immersion. Remission of sins as inseparably accompanies immersion, as reformation accompanies faith. Then the Holy Spirit is bestowed, and the disciple is filled with the spirit of adoption, which inspires him with filial confidence in God. The gift of eternal life in anticipation, induces him to the cultivation of that holiness, without which, no man shall see the Lord, as well as fills him with abundant joy.

But while in reference to our ways of reasoning and thinking in this speculative age we represent matters thus, it must be remembered that persons may now, as they did formerly, believe, reform, be immersed, obtain pardon and the Holy Spirit in the period of time occupied in a single discourse, as the history in the Acts of the Apostles abundantly proves. Persons are said to reform the moment they turn to the Lord. The turning point is therefore fitly called *reformation.* Thus all the inhabitants of Lydda and Saron are said to have turned to the Lord, when Peter, in the name of Jesus, raised Eneas from a palsy which had confined him to his bed for eight years.

To derange this order in the reign of Favor, is an error of no ordinary magnitude. Yet it is a common error. The Presbyterian arrangement of the items is as follows, viz.—1st. Baptism; 2d. the Holy Spirit in effectual calling; 3d. Faith; 4th. Forgiveness of sins; 5th. Reformation. Some Regular Baptists arrange the items thus:—1st. the Holy Spirit; 2d. Faith; 3d. Repentance; 4th. Forgiveness of sins; 5th. Baptism. The Quaker has it the Holy Spirit throughout, and no immersion. Other Baptists have it—1st. Regeneration, or the Holy Spirit; 2d. Repentance; 3d. Faith; 4th. Forgiveness of sins; and 5th. Baptism. A very different tune is played upon the same notes when the arrangement of them is changed, and so different gospels are preached upon the different ordering of these items. Those who proclaim faith in the Lord Jesus Christ and reformation in order to immersion; and immersion in order to forgiveness and the Holy Spirit, proclaim the same gospel which the Apostles proclaimed.

"Into what were you immersed," is a question which must decide the character of a man's profession of the faith. His views of the gospel, his conscience towards God, as well as the motives which influence all his religious behavior, are decided according to the response of his heart to this question. And very different, indeed, would be the response of the heart of a primitive disciple from that of most of our modern sectaries, were they to give full utterance to their hearts on such a question. Would not the Episcopalian, the Presbyterian, the ordinary Baptist, whether Calvinistic or Arminian, and the Pentecostian converts give very different responses to

such a question!—Methinks they would. And just as discordant would be their general views of the gospel and of the christian religion, as their answers to the question, For what purpose were you immersed?

Were I then to *describe* the evangelical arrangement as I would describe the journey of the Israelites from Egypt to Canaan, I would proceed thus. And since I have mentioned the journey of old Israel, I will first tell their story in brief. First, Moses made a proclamation to them from the Almighty, and they believed it. Second, they changed their views of Egypt and began their march. They were, in the third place, immersed into Moses in the cloud and in the Red Sea. God then, in the fourth place, makes a covenant with them, or declares an institution through which they were to enjoy remission of sins; and, in the fifth place, promises to dwell among them and reign over them as their God and King. Thus they proceed towards Canaan, the type of the everlasting kingdom, with the promise of rest graciously tendered to them.

Now for the antitype. Jesus the Lord from heaven, makes a proclamation of mercy in his own person, and mediately through his Apostles, to all nations, in the name of the God and Father of all. Those that believe it, immediately turn to the Lord. This turning point is *reformation unto life* begun. The inward repentance and the outward reformation, which are coetaneous, are first constitutionally exhibited in the act of immersion into the name of the Lord Jesus for the remission of sins. The old sins are thus purified through faith in the blood of the Messiah, according to the divine appointment. The Holy Spirit is then given, for Jesus Christ is now glorified in heaven and upon earth. He is glorified in heaven, because God our Father has exalted him a Prince and a Saviour to his own throne; and he is, by every disciple who thus surrenders himself to his authority and guidance, glorified on earth,—and then he glorifies them whom he has thus justified, washed, and sanctified, by adopting them into the family of God, and honoring them with the most honorable title in creation, namely, *Sons of God.*

Now a conscience cast into this mould, I am certain, differs very much from a conscience cast into any systematic mould of human contrivance. For the gospel according to John Calvin, or the gospel according to John Wesley, or the gospel according to Martin Luther, or the gospel according to George Fox, are not exactly the same as the gospel according to Matthew, Luke, Paul, and Peter. The views, feelings, consciences, and practices of those who are immersed into each of these gospels, differ from each other as much as the vowels and consonants in the names of the founders of these gospels differ from one another. Some of them are the same, but others as far apart as A, B, C, and X, Y, Z.

Before I conclude these essays on the Ancient Gospel, I wish to present my readers with an essay on the spirit which it inspires, which I propose in my next number; and in the mean time, I conclude with remarking that we have one objection to the phrase "ancient gospel;" and that is, so far as it may tend to any thing like a rallying or discriminating badge amongst Christians. We know how easy it is to lay the foundation for names; and we know too that the world is ruled by names. If, then, the phrases "Ancient Gospel," or "Ancient Order of Things," should become a dividing discrimination among Christians, we must enter our protest against them in such acceptations. We now use them not for the discrimination of persons, but for the discrimination of truth from error, and of *primitive* from *modern* usages. As such we conceive them to be every way appropriate and just. And in so doing, we do no more than is usually done by those who define or describe the gospel which they preach. But the time will come when the terms glad tidings, christian, and congregation, without any epithet or adjunct, will be universally received as representing the same ideas as those attached to them in sacred scripture. For the speedy approach of that blissful era we labor and pray. We hope always to persevere in so doing, so long as the Lord sets before us an open door which no man can shut. May the gracious Lord ever patronize our efforts, and the efforts of all who labor for these sublime objects, and keep us and them from falling into error, either in sentiment or practice! Amen!

Scepticism.

THE editors of the New Harmony Gazette have very politely invited me to discuss with them in our respective papers the questions which are to be discussed between Mr. Owen and me, at Cincinnati, in April next. But inasmuch as we have a great variety of matter laid out for this volume of the Christian Baptist, and more, we fear, than can be crowded into it; and as the public will, in a few months, have their attention called to the merits of all these questions, we think it both unnecessary and inexpedient to introduce the subject to our readers, or add it to the series of topics and essays laid out for this volume.— Had this not been the fact, and, especially, had we not the pleasing anticipation of canvassing these sceptical whims and notions, and fine philosophy which finds no need nor room in the universe either for creator or creature, for heaven or hell, for angel or spirit, for moral good or moral evil, &c. &c. &c. which makes all our knowledge pass through our fingers, nose, tongue, eyes, and ears, and discards every thing not as gross as ignis fatuus or marsh miasmata, we should have gladly made all other arrangements subservient to an investigation of so much importance, and for which our friends in New Harmony are so well qualified. These fine topics on which this gay philosophy loves to dwell, will, we hope, be ceremoniously attended to, and fully discussed, when Mr. Owen attempts to prove his four grand positions in April next.

                                        EDITOR.

Miscellany.—No. I.

I HAVE found it utterly impossible to answer, in any formal way, either privately or publicly, the whole amount of sentimental letters which I have for the last six months received. To make public property of many of them would neither be expedient nor agreeable. Besides, the queries contained in some of them have been either formally or materially answered in the previous volumes. This I say, not to prevent my friends from writing me as usual, either on matters sentimental or otherwise, but to apologize for what they might interpret into neglect, and to tell them all at once, that my rules in all such cases are the following:—

1. To answer all letters of business as soon as possible after they arrive.

2. Such letters as are of a private character, and solicit information immediately affecting the duty or conscience of the correspondent, to be answered privately and as soon as possible.

3. All letters, the whole contents of which are for my own personal benefit, not to answer until I have leisure, and some of them in no other way than to thank my friends for them—and this I now do both with respect to the past, and in anticipation of the future.

4. All queries, anecdotes, historical sketches of the conduct of individuals—churches, associations, &c. &c. are to be published if I deem them useful, and if they have not been anticipated before.

5. All letters that I esteem of general use, or even sometimes of very high particular utility, I unceremoniously publish. I will thank any of my friends to suggest a more unexceptionable way. I will only add on this subject two remarks:—First, that I wish my friends and correspondents generally, to acquaint me of all facts and incidents either illustrative of the progress of truth, or of the opposition made to it, in their respective vicinities, and then to allow me to make such use of it as I think expedient. And, second, That all criticisms or remarks which are intended for my correction, and all sentimental communications are always welcome, and I trust will have all the influence upon my views and conduct which they deserve. These things premised, I proceed under this head to take notice of some items found on file in my long list of articles deferred.

"Some of our brethren are of opinion that it requires two or three preachers to be present to make the organization or constituting of a church *legal*; others think an agreement among the brethren sufficient, without the help of a solitary preacher.—What say you?" The latter most certainly is congenial with the letter and spirit of christianity, as contained in the New Testament, and also with the ancient genius of the Baptist constitution.

Where there is no law there is no transgression; and where is the law requiring one or ten preachers, overseers, or elders to be present to validate the constitution of a church or congregation? It may be agreeable to the brethren to have some other brethren of good repute present to witness their organization, and to testify that they have united to surrender themselves to the guidance of the Lord Jesus, and to keep his commandments as contained in the Apostles' teaching. This may be agreeable, and in some instances necessary, for the sake of the community in which they live; but never to make their organization as a christian congregation valid according to any law or requirement of the great king.

"What are the emerods mentioned 1 *Samuel*, ch. v. 6? See *Psalm* lxxviii. 66." He smote them with a disease in their hinder part analogous to the fistula ani in the modern nomenclature. Thompson translates *Deuteronomy* xxviii. 27. thus:—"The Lord smite thee with the Egyptian boil in thy seat, and with wild fire [even with wild fire, common version, "emerods,"] and with itching, so that thou canst not be cured." He also translates the verse in question thus:—"Still the hand of the Lord was heavy upon Azotus, and pressed them down. Leaks broke out in their vessels, and their country swarmed with mice, and in their city was a confusion of mortality." Also, the same word occurs 1 *Samuel*, vi. and 5. and is translated "*five golden stools;*" for these "stools" were a similitude of the plague among them called the 'emeroids.' This is all I know about those emerods.

"And these signs shall follow them who believe, or, as in the new version, these signs shall accompany them who believe. By my name they will expel demons; they will speak with new tongues; they will take up serpents, though they drink deadly poison, it shall not hurt them; upon sick persons they will lay their hands and they shall recover." *Query*—Do these promises apply to all believers, or to some?

How readest thou? Go back a little and read the connexion, verse 13, "Whereupon those came and told the rest, but they did not believe them. At length he appeared to the eleven when they were at table, and upbraided them for their incredulity and obstinacy, because they did not believe them who had seen him after his resurrection. Then he said to them, Go to all the world, proclaim the glad tidings to the whole creation. He who believes and is immersed, shall be saved; but he who disbelieves, shall be condemned." Now these signs, &c. Thus we see that this was spoken to the apostles, at that time upbraided for their incredulity. The commission and promises annexed were given to them, and the following sentences show how these promises were accomplished. Let us read them also—"So after the Lord had spoken to them, he was taken up to heaven and sat at the right hand of God; and they went forth and proclaimed the tidings every where, the Lord co-operating with them, and confirming the word with those concomitant signs" above mentioned. Thus when the whole context is read, the sneer of the sceptic, and the dubiety of the weak christian are without foundation. How many difficulties and objections might be overcome, if men would use the same common sense they exhibit on other occasions!!   EDITOR.

A good hint to our Teachers of Theology, both in Theological Schools and Pulpits: from the great Chalmers, author of the evidences of christianity.

"IN the popular religions of antiquity, we see scarcely a vestige of resemblance to that academical theism which is delivered in our schools, and figures away in the speculations of our moralists. The process of conversion among the first Christians was a very simple one. It consisted of an utter abandonment of their heathenism, and an entire submission to those new truths which came to them through the revelation of the gospel, and through it only. It was the pure theology of Christ and his apostles. That theology which struts in fancied demonstration from a professor's chair, formed no part of it. They listened as if they had all to learn; we listen as if it was our office to judge, and to give the message of God its due place and subordination among the principles which we had previously established. Now these principles were utterly unknown at the first publication of christianity. The Galatians, and Corinthians, and Thessalonians, and Philippians, had no conception of them. And yet, will any man say, that either Paul himself or those who lived under his immediate tuition, had not enough to make them accomplished christians, or that they fell short of our enlightened selves, in the wisdom which prepares for eternity, because they wanted our rational theology as a stepping-stone to that knowledge which came, in pure and immediate revelation from the Son of God. The gospel was enough for them, and it should be enough for us also. Every natural or assumed principle which offers to abridge its supremacy, or even so much as to share with it in authority and direction, should be instantly discarded. Every opinion in religion should be reduced to the question of—what readest thou? and the bible be acquiesced in, and submitted to, as the alone directory of our faith, where we can get the whole will of God for the salvation of men."

No. 4.]   NOVEMBER 3, 1828.

THE following epistle needs neither apology nor explanation. It speaks for itself. In the August number we introduced the writer of it to our readers, without asking permission. We have his permission for publishing two letters now received, to the serious consideration of which, we invite our readers.   EDITOR.

Remarks on the Bible.—No. I.

DEAR SIR—THE intelligibility, or perfect plainness of the sacred writings, just as they have been worded by the communicating Spirit, unaltered by the stupidity or craft of men, undarkened by the impertinent interference, and impious folly of arrogant and audacious mortals; presents a question of the utmost importance to the human family—a question which needs and merits the most dispassionate and thorough investigation. It was this impressive view of the subject, which made me rather regret the appearance of my hastily written and undigested letter in your August number of the Christian Baptist. It did no justice to this important subject. It contained scarcely a hint of what might and ought to have been presented to the consideration of a deeply interested world. It was intended to exhibit but a few hints on the subject of translation. And now it is not a regular and thorough inquiry which I propose. I mean only to offer a few remarks, calculated perhaps to throw some light on the subject, and to excite you and others to favor your fellow creatures with a discussion which may deserve their attention. On this subject my own belief is—

1. That God has graciously condescended to send into our ignorant, erroneous, and depraved world, a message, devised, worded, and digested by his unerring wisdom, for the avowed purpose of dispelling human ignorance, correcting human error, and removing human depravity; and in place of these pernicious sources of human guilt, degradation, and misery, of diffusing knowledge, truth, piety, and virtue through the human family, as the only means of rendering man truly noble, happy, and useful in this world or the next.

2. That the perfection of God's nature forbids us to imagine that he was not able to render his message perfectly intelligible to the most illiterate of his rational creatures: that for its communication he could not select such words and phrases as he knew to be perfectly intelligible to the most illiterate of them; such words and phrases as should neither need, nor be capable of receiving additional clearness from the ingenuity of man.

3. That the perfection of God's nature forbids us to imagine that any obscurity or ambiguity crept into his message, through the negligence, ignorance, or inadvertency of its author,—as often happens in human compositions. If then, obscurity or ambiguity occur in the sacred pages, it must be admitted that they were introduced not only with the perfect knowledge, but with the formal intention of the inspiring Spirit, when he suggested his words and phrases to his human agents.

4. The dignity and goodness of the divine character forbid us to imagine that God did send an unintelligible message to his perishing creatures. Such a message would have been not an act of divine compassion, but of unfeeling insult; not in fact a message, but a solemn mock-

ery. And can we believe that God, who knew with absolute certainty, every grade of intellect which he had ever bestowed, or would bestow, on his rational creatures; who could with as much ease frame an intelligible as an unintelligible message; who had declared that his message had been framed, and purposely sent to his miserable children for their relief; that it contained the only visible or revealed provision for their deliverance, which he had ever made or would make; and that if understood and complied with by them, it would infallibly effect their deliverance from all evil, and invest them immutably with all possible happiness and glory; can we, I say, believe that, notwithstanding all this knowledge, capacity, and express declaration, God did send, under the pretext of friendship, compassion, and tenderness, a message which was, in reality, only galling insult, and cruel disappointment? *Credat qui potest*—Let him believe who can.

5. The goodness of God is to us a certain assurance and pledge that he has neither introduced, nor suffered his inspired agents to introduce, into his message any obscurity or ambiguity, which was not necessary to limit with precision that quantity of information which he purposed to convey, and which was not actually requisite to promote the happiness of his creature man.— Knowing with absolute certainty the quantity and kind of information which our relief and comfort demanded, he selected and employed such words and phrases as were in his judgment fit and proper to convey in the clearest manner that quantity, and not one particle more. Hence it is, that concerning objects and events, susceptible in themselves of information greatly more extended, scripture gives us only a few hints, and that words and phrases do frequently occur, which convey to us *clearly* only a small portion of information, but which, under divine management, or by the use of other words or phrases in their stead, would have conveyed to us clearly a great deal more, perhaps all that even human curiosity would presume to ask.

God's nature then, alone, affords unquestionable assurance that he never sent to man an unintelligible message, nor one that required any other words than his own to render it plain: there are, however, other sources of evidence which it may be not improper to suggest:—

1. The character and condition of man, to whom God's message is addressed, require that, just as it is contained in sacred writ in the words of the communicating Spirit, unaltered by the impudence of human folly, it be perfectly intelligible, altogether fit to convey in the clearest manner possible, as much of his mind as he intended to reveal to man in this world. Man is by his constitution intelligent, and dependant on his knowledge of the objects revealed to him in sacred writ for the felicity of his mental part in time and through eternity. But though by nature intelligent and dependant on revelation for his mental happiness, yet man comes into this world, destitute, entirely destitute of the ideas communicated to him in the sacred pages, nor can he even by the most vigorous employment of his five senses, the only organs of information with which his Creator has deemed it proper to endow him, acquire them. And to this original poverty and incapacity we must add the awful and mortifying fact, that the human mind is every where on the subject of religion, over-run with error, laid prostrate and enchained by the most obstinate and pernicious prejudices and delusions, as well as enslaved by the most depraved inclinations, desires and practices. And to all this we must also add, that if the words of the message leave any where the Spirit's meaning obscure or ambiguous, by no human sagacity, ingenuity, or learning, can the obscurity or ambiguity be taken away. Mere conjecture about the Spirit's meaning, without the least certainty, is all that man can offer in this case.— Now, can any pious or reflecting man believe that an infinitely wise and compassionate God, the creator, owner and protector of his unhappy creatures, laboring under such intellectual and moral degeneracy as man incontestibly does, could transmit for his liberation and recovery a message that was not perfectly intelligible to every one of them on all points that necessarily concerned their recovery? I presume not.

2. The object to be accomplished by the message demands its perfect intelligibility. Man's spiritual recovery, which is the object of the message, requires, that on the subject of religion his ignorance be dispelled, his errors be corrected, his prejudices and delusions be chased away; that his conceptions of God, of spiritual and moral objects, be rectified; that, by the presence and influence of these rectified conceptions in his mind, his desires, affections and delights, be elevated to, and fixed on, proper objects, and his actions and pursuits of course be directed to their attainment; or in more popular style, that the seeds of piety and virtue be not only implanted, but nourished and brought to maturity in the human soul. Now can any human folly, inconceivably great as it is, imagine that such a stupendous change in the conceptions of the human mind, in the desires and affections of the heart, in the inclinations and propensities of the soul, in the pursuits and labors of the man, be effected by a string of words, of whose meaning the reformed has no distinct comprehension?— Surely not.

3. The account which God's message gives of itself in almost every page, establishes its claim to perfect intelligibility, beyond a doubt. It tells us that it makes the simple wise, enlightens the eyes, quickens the soul, directs the path, is a lamp to the feet, a light on the way, gives understanding to the simple; presents words that can save the soul, make wise to salvation, is a light shining in a dark world. Christ is styled a light to the Gentiles, the light of the world, &c. &c. Could these things be true, if the message destined to effect them was unintelligible to any of God's rational creatures? We think no man will say so.

4. God commands not a few, but every human creature, arrived at sufficient maturity, and in his right mind, to consult, to search, to study, to meditate the scriptures, because in them alone is that testimony concerning the Redeemer to be found that brings sinners to eternal life, and to hear what the Spirit says to the churches. But surely if the scriptures which we are commanded to consult, to search and meditate, and the declarations of the Spirit we are commanded to hear, be exhibited in words and phrases, that are unintelligible to us, God has commanded an impossible act, and threatened us with everlasting ruin, if we do not perform it. Is any prepared to defend this imputation?

5. Had the Spirit's message, just as it is presented in his own words, been considered by him as not intelligible, perfectly intelligible to all concerned, he would most certainly have qualified, appointed, and accredited in all ages expositors for the express purpose of rendering it intelligible: we do not find, however, that such agents were ever thought of. Neither in Egypt

nor in the wilderness did Moses ever employ an agent to explain any of his numerous addresses to the Israelites; nor did any of the subsequent rulers, priests, or prophets, employ such a character to explain any of their addresses to the same people afterwards. Certain it is that Christ employed no such character to explain any of his innumerable discourses, nor did his apostles after him. When Matthew, Mark, Luke and John published their memoirs, or proofs that Jesus of Nazareth was the Messiah; when the author of the Acts published his account of the manner and means by which the new or christian institution was introduced among Jews and Gentiles; when Paul, James, Peter, John, and Jude wrote their letters to the christian congregations, it is not so much as insinuated that such an agent was ever employed by any of them. They evidently acted as persons who were confident that every word which they had written or spoken was perfectly intelligible to all converted. With their several publications, addresses, or letters, they sent no expositors; nor among those to whom they were directed, did they nominate or appoint any. In short, scripture knows nothing of such an office, or of such an officer: nor in it is any human being commanded or authorized to attempt such a work, or offer such an insult to the all-wise God. With commands to proclaim or publish the Spirit's message, or good news, called the gospel, and to teach, instruct and exhort persons concerned by that proclamation to the christian faith, we meet in almost every page; but to proclaim or publish, to teach, instruct, or exhort, are acts very different from *explaining*, and need a very different qualification. To be able to read well, or to remember and pronounce distinctly what has been heard, is all the qualification, as to learning, which a preacher, proclaimer, or publisher, a teacher, instructer, or exhorter needs; but to explain, requires a knowledge of the subject not inferior to the original author. The residue will be found in the next letter.   A. S.

SEPTEMBER 27TH, 1828.

DEAR BROTHER CAMPBELL:—I HAVE read your letters addressed to Bishop Semple, with close attention, and find you have treated him with great respect. If I be not mistaken Bishop Semple complained in his letter to you of December, 1825, of the want of a *New Testament spirit* in the Christian Baptist. I am sorry to say that many of your readers think Bishop Semple has not shown that spirit towards you, or those who differed with him. When I read an extract from a letter of his, in the Recorder of June, 1827, my spirit was cast down, for I looked up to him as a father in the gospel. The course he had taken to give vent to his views, I did not approve; and the language he used, I was certain would injure his standing. "It is one thing to reform popery, and another to reform the reformation." I saw he left a door open for an attack from the Lutherans and Calvinists, for Bishop Semple will not admit that he is a Lutheran or Calvinist, or that the sect to which he belongs is the same with those reformers. His letters to Doctor Noel of the 3d and 26th of September, 1827, I was sorry to see, knowing the consequences that would follow, among those mighty regulars, or would-be popes, had they the power. In one of his letters he charges you with "sowing the seeds of discord among brethren, and that there is much less ground for fellowship with your principles, than with Presbyterians, Methodists, or even evangelical Episcopalians." In your fifth letter, you in a masterly and christian-like manner, refute this charge. ' You promise if he will explain to you the nature, extent and malignity of the mischief you have done, you will arise and make an effort to undo it.' Will Bishop Semple say as much? will he arise and undo all the mischief he has done by publishing these letters, and making use of sundry speeches? such as if the Baptist denomination were to adopt the sentiments of Paulinus and yourself, respecting the Old Testament, he would withdraw from the society, or words to that amount, and that he held no fellowship with your sentiments. Before the publication of these letters we were at peace among ourselves. What has followed? Resolutions of disapprobation from those churches which knew very little of your sentiments, against some of your readers, for expressing their views of the gospel and defending your principles from these fireside traducers. What has followed these resolutions? Discord and disunion amongst brethren. Who produced this disunion? not those who were willing that their brethren should enjoy their sentiments until they were better instructed, but these friends of Bishop S. who were unwilling that the friends of the ancient order of things should enjoy the rights of conscience without letters of proscription. Is this his New Testament spirit? When I read his letter of the 26th September, and your truly dignified appeal to him, to set you right, "inviting him to show you where you have erred, and if you could not present reason, scripture and good sense to support you, you would yield to his superior discernment, age and experience." I then expected to see his New Testament spirit. But it seems we must wait for the physical operations of that spirit, before he will show you "are palpably on the wrong side, although it would be no hard task to make it manifest." Did Bishop S. say these things with a belief they would pass as oracular, or with an intention to make them appear to every inquirer after truth? If I am to judge from his silence, you are mistaken in your opinion of "his not wishing to live in a community which had no more mind than to cease its inquiries, when he said desist." Should I be mistaken in Bishop S. I ask why he has not come forward agreeably to the request of Querens and make good his assertion? Why does he, as a shepherd, suffer you, (as many would make us believe a wolf in sheep's clothing) to destroy the sheep and the lambs? He may talk about his unwillingness to enter into controversy. If he was not prepared and willing to support his assertions, he ought to have kept silence, and not to have set all the bigots and diotrephan spirits, at war with the sheep and lambs. He knew there were many ready to seize upon any pretext to harass those who were hungering and thirsting for the bread and water of life. They had lived upon horns and bones and alcohol until their countenances and conversation indicated a perishing condition. The picture you have drawn of the state of the churches is undeniable. Thousands there are who never attempted to learn the contents of the book of God, and would rather go twenty miles to hear a man *preach* all the meanderings of his dark and foolish mind, than learn, at his own door, those sacred and divine lessons which are able to make him wise to salvation. This way of *preaching themselves* is the cause of the ignorance amongst us: to teach them the contents of the book of God, is considered an innovation in the church, and unprofitable to their souls. The teachers know how to keep the hold they have upon the consciences of the people, and the peo-

31

ple are flattered in their ignorance, that all is well, all is right with them; that none but those who are called and sent can understand the *mysteries* of the gospel, and all they have to do, is to listen to their teachers, and if their experience agree with the *preacher's*, they may rest assured they are the children of God. Thus ignorance and idleness are encouraged in the church.

I have read somewhere in the Christian Baptist, that Doctors of Divinity make deists—how this could be, I could not tell, until I heard of the arguments of one, when he was reasoned with on the evidences of the christian religion, in a manner which was unanswerable; he replied, that although the arguments were unanswerable, yet it was no proof of its being true; and to support him in this assertion, referred to your writings—that to your unprejudiced readers, your reasonings upon the ancient order of things were unanswerable, yet the Baptist Recorder and the Columbian Star, with those great Doctors of Divinity, considered you in error—therefore it was possible for a man to make error appear so plausible, that the human faculties cannot produce a clear and effectual refutation. If this be true, then error has the victory over truth, and deists have now such advocates as they desire. Is this the New Testament spirit? Among the number of teachers with us, there are a few who are advocates for a reformation. It appears they want courage to meet those regulars with their popish bulls, seasoned with what they call christian affection. To forsake the popular system is too great a cross, it would be attended with the loss of character, in the estimation of the populars. It would be as difficult a matter to get justice done them as to get their opponents to live upon the book of God, which is a thing impossible, so long as the present order of things continues.   THOMAS.

The Spirit of the Year of Grace, 1828; *and the Manners of Latitude* 37.

FAYETTE COUNTY, KY. September 8, 1828.

DEAR BROTHER CAMPBELL:—Judging from the specimens I have seen of the letters you receive, I dare say you have by this time become sufficiently accustomed to such as the following, to be able to read them without much wincing. Being myself sent as a messenger to the Elkhorn association which met on the second Saturday in last month, my attention was particularly caught by two of the letters read on this occasion, and being somewhat of a curious turn of mind, I felt a disposition to procure an extract from each, and accordingly obtained a loan of the aforesaid letters from the clerk, and as I sat on my seat at intervals extracted as follows:

Extract of a Letter from N. Elkhorn Church to Elkhorn Association.

"N. B. In as *mutch* as this association in committee at Town Fork, and in committee of the whole at Paris, agreed to a correspondence with the Licking brethren, and agreed to maintain the doctrine of grace as contained in the Bible, an set forth in the Philadelphia confession of faith, as the minutes of the association show, should not this association protest against *Armenianism* and *Cammelism and his new book*—as *Cammel* is against creeds and confessions, how can his sentiments be tolerated amongst us, and we be true to the above cited obligation."

Extract of a Letter from Mount Pleasant Church.

"Your object will be to consult the well being of society, to guard against heresy, and to study the dignity of the Baptist cause, by holding sa-

cred the doctrine of sovereign grace as revealed in the scriptures of the old and new Testament, and set forth in the Philadelphia confession, and as much as possible to hold original ground, and to guard against those churches that are throwing their creeds and confessions of faith, (as they cantingly call them) away. We as a church hold a particular atonement, and a special application of the same by the Holy Ghost in regeneration—we as a church profess not to understand what is meant by immersing into the name of the trinity, instead of baptizing by the authority or in the name of the Father, Son and Holy Ghost. The latter is our belief and no other. We hope the Lord will enable you promptly to oppose every false way."

This last church is under the pastoral care of Edmund Waller, of conflagration memory; which is enough to account for such a nondescript production. During preaching, on Sunday, from the weeping in the congregation it was manifest there were many persons present of a broken and contrite heart; and old brother Vardeman came down off the stage, and invited such as felt disposed to come up to be prayed for. Many of the preachers also came down and co-operated; but Edmund Waller, although in the midst of the people of his charge, retired to the most remote part of the stage, and sneered at what was going on, with as much contempt and apparent malignity as Satan need have done had he been there in person. I could but ask myself while contemplating the scenes before me, "how dwelleth the love of God in such a man?" It is said that the Turks hate all those who are not musselmen; more especially those that they are pleased to call "*Christian dogs;*" and so it seems there are those called Christians, who feel themselves at liberty to hate all such as they are pleased to call heretics. In the estimation of many among us, you are considered the arch-heretic, and did you live in other lands and other times, woe would be to you. I do rejoice, my brother, that the taper you have lighted up is not to be extinguished, or even obscured by the puny efforts of such. You have done much already in ridding the minds of many of those fetters which priestcraft and other crafts had fastened upon them—and so far as I understand your object, I do most heartily wish you God speed. Forgive my trespassing—I have a wish to send you the extracts, and having begun, I could not well stop short of what I have said. May the Lord in his great mercy grant that you may live to see your labors crowned with success, is the sincere prayer of your brother in gospel bonds.   W. C. T.

Preface of the King's Translators.
[Continued from page 483.]

BUT now what pietie without truth? what truth (what saving truth) without the word of God? what word of God (whereof we may be sure) without the scripture? The scriptures we are commanded to search, *John* 5. 39. *Isa.* 8. 20.— They are commended that searched and studied them, *Acts* 17. 11. and 8. 28. 29. They are reproved that are unskilfull in them, or slow to beleeve them, *Matth.* 22. 29. *Luke* 24. 25. They can make us wise unto salvation, 2. *Tim.* 3. 15. If we be ignorant, they will instruct us: if out of the way they will bring us home; if out of order, they will reform us: if in heaviness, comfort us; if dull, quicken us; if cold, enflame us. *Tolle, lege*; *Tolle lege*, Take up and reade, take up and reade the Scriptures, (for unto them was the direction) it was said unto S. *Augustine* by a supernaturall voice. *Whatsoever is in the Scriptures, beleeve me,* saith the same S. *Augustine, is high and divine; there is verily truth, and a doctrine most fit for the refreshing and renewing of mens mindes, and truly so tempered, that every one may draw from thence that which is sufficient for him, if he come to draw with a devout and pious minde, as true religion requireth.* Thus S. *Augustine,* and S. *Hierome, Ama Scripturas et amabit te sapientia,* &c. Love the Scriptures, and wisdom will love thee. And S. *Cyrill* against *Julian, Even boyes that are bred up in the Scriptures, become most religious,* &c. But what mention we three or foure uses of the Scripture, whereas whatsoever is to be beleeved or practised, or hoped for, is contained in them? or three or foure sentences of the Fathers, since whosoever is worthy the name of a Father, from Christs time downward, hath likewise written not onely of the riches, but also of the perfection of the Scripture? *I adore the fulnesse of the Scripture,* saith *Tertullian* against *Hermogenes.* And again, to *Apelles* an heretick of the like stamp, he saith, *I do not admit that which thou bringest in* (or concludest) *of thine own* (head or store, *de tuo*) without Scripture. So S. *Justin Martyr* before him, *We must know by all means* (saith he) *that it is not lawful* (or possible) *to learn* (any thing) *of God or of right pietie, save only out of the Prophets who teach us by divine inspiration.* So S. *Basil,* after *Tertullian, It is a manifest falling away from the faith, and a fault of presumption, either to reject any of those things that are written, or to bring in* (upon the head of them, εμειεχγειν) *any of these things that* are not written. We omit to cite to the same effect, S. *Cyrill* Bishop of *Jerusalem* in his 4 *Catechis,* S. *Hierome* against *Helvidius,* S. *Augustine* in his third book against the letters of *Petilian,* and in very many other places of his works. Also we forbear to descend to later Fathers, because we will not wearie the Reader. The Scriptures then being acknowledged to be so full and so perfect, how can we excuse ourselves of negligence, if we do not studie them? of curiositie, if we be not content with them? Men talk much of ειρεσιωνη, how many sweet and goodly things are had hanging on it; of the Philosophers stone, that it turneth copper into gold; of *Cornu-copia,* that it had all things necessarie for food in it; of *Panaces* the herb, that it was good for all diseases; of *Catholicon* the drug, that it is instead of all purges; of *Vulcans* armour, that it was an armour of proof against all thrusts, and all blows, &c. Well, that which they fastly or vainly attributed to these things for bodily good, we may justly and with full measure ascribe unto the Scripture for spirituall It is not onely an armour, but also a whole armourie of weapons, both offensive and defensive; whereby we may save our selves, and put the enemie to flight. It is not an herb, but a tree, or rather a whole paradise of trees of life, which bring forth fruit every month, and the fruit thereof is for meat, and the leaves for medicine. It is not a pot of *Manna,* or a cruse of oyl, which were for memory onely, or for a meals meat or two: but as it were, a showre of heavenly bread, sufficient for a whole host, be it never so great, and, as it were a whole cellar full of oyl vessels; whereby all our necessities may be provided for, and our debts discharged. In a word, it is a panary of wholesome feed, against fenowed traditions; a physicians shop (S. *Basil* calleth it) of preservatives against poysoned heresies; a product of profitable laws, against rebellious spirits, a treasury of most costly fuels, against beggarly rudiments; finally, a fountain of most pure water, springing up unto everlasting life. And what marvell? The originall thereof, being from heaven, not from earth; the author being God not man; the editer, the holy spirit, not the wit of the Apostles or prophets; the pen-men such as were sanctified from the wombe, and endued with a principall portion of Gods spirit; the matter verity, pietie, puritie, uprightness; the form, Gods word, Gods testimonie, Gods oracles, the word of truth, the word of salvation, &c. the effects, light of understanding, stablenesse of perswasion, repentance from dead works, newnesse of life, holiness, peace, joy in the holy Ghost; lastly, the end and reward of the studie thereof, fellowship with the saints, participation of the heavenly nature, fruition of an inheritance immortall, undefiled, and that never shall fade away: Happy is the man that delighteth in the Scripture, and thrice happy that meditateth in it day and night.

But how shall men meditate in that which they cannot understand? How shall they understand that which is kept close in an unknown tongue? as it is written *Except I know the power of the voice, I shall be to him that speaketh a Barbarian, and he that speaketh shall be a Barbarian to me.* The Apostle excepteth no tongue, not *Hebrew* the ancientest; not *Greek* the most copious, not *Latine* the finest. Nature taught a naturall man to confesse, That all of us, in those tongues which we do not understand, are plainly deaf: we may turn the deaf eare unto them. The *Scythian* counted the *Athenian,* whom he did not understand, barbarous: so the *Romane* did the *Syrian,* and the *Jew* (even S. *Hierome* himself calleth the *Hebrew* tongue barbarous, belike because it was strange to so many,) so the Emperour of *Constantinople* called the *Latine* tongue barbarous, though Pope *Nicolas* do storm at it: so the *Jews* long before *Christ,* called all other nations *Lognasim,* which is little better then barbarous. Therefore as one complaineth that always in the Senate of *Rome,* there was one or other that called for an interpreter: so lest the Church be driven to the like exigent, it is necessary to have translations in a readinesse.— Translation it is that openeth the window, to let in the light; that breaketh the shell, that we may eat the kernell: that puteth aside the curtain, that we may look into the most holy place; that removeth the cover of the well, that we may come by the water, even as *Jacob* rolled away the stone from the mouth of the well, by which means the flocks of *Laban* were watered. Indeed without translation into the vulgar tongue, the unlearned are but like children at *Jacobs* well, (which was deep) without a bucket or something to draw with: or as that person mentioned by *Esay,* to whom when a sealed book was delivered, with this notion, *Reade this I pray thee,* he was fain to make this answer, *I cannot, for it is sealed.*

While God would be known only in *Jacob,* and have his name great in *Israel,* and in none other place; while the dew lay on *Gideons* fleece only, and all the earth besides was drie; then for one and the same people, which shake off them the language of *Canaan* that is *Hebrew,* one and the same originall in *Hebrew* was sufficient, but when the fulnesse of time drew neare, that the Sunne of righteousnesse, the Sonne of God should come into the world, whom God ordained to be a reconciliation through faith in his bloud, not of the *Jew* onely, but also of the *Greek,* yea, of all them that were scattered abroad, then lo, it pleased the Lord to stirre up the spirit of a *Greek* Prince (*Greek* for descent and language) even of *Ptolomee Philadelph* king of Egypt, to procure the translating of the book of God out of Hebrew into Greek. This is the translation of the *Seventy* interpreters, commonly so called, which prepared the way for our Saviour among the Gentiles by written preaching, as S. *John Baptist* did among the *Jews* by vocall. For the *Grecians* being desirous of learning, were not wont to suffer books of worth to lie moulding in kings libraries, but had many of his servants, ready scribes to copy them out, and so they were dispersed and made common. Again, the *Greek* tongue was well known, and made familiar to most inhabitants in *Asia*, by reason of the conquests that there the *Grecians* had made, as also by the colonies, which thither they had sent. For the same causes also it was well understood in many places of *Europe*, yea, and of *Africk* too. Therefore the word of God being set forth in *Greek*, becometh hereby like a candle set upon a candlestick, which giveth light to all that are in the house, or like a proclamation sounded forth in the market-place, which most men presently take knowledge of; and therefore that language was fittest to retain the Scriptures, both for the preachers of the Gospel to appeal unto for witnesse, and for the learners also of those times to make search for triall by. It is certain, that that translation was not so sound and so perfect, but that it needed in many places correction; and who had been so sufficient for this work as the Apostles or Apostolike men? Yet it seemed good to the holy Ghost and to them, to take that which they found, (the same being for the greatest part true and sufficient) rather then by making a new, in that new world and green age of the Church, to expose themselves to many exceptions, and cavillations, as though they made a translation to serve their own turn; and therefore bear witnesse themselves, their witness not to be regarded. This may be supposed to be some cause, why the translation of the *Seventy* was allowed to pass for currant. Notwithstanding, though it was commended generally, yet it did not fully content the learned, no not of the *Jews*. For not long after *Christ*, *Aquila* fell in hand with a new translation, and after him a *Theodotion*, and after him *Symmachus*. yea, there was a fifth, and a sixth edition, the authors whereof were not known. These with the *Seventie* made up the *Hexapla*, and were worthily and to great purpose compiled together by *Origen*. Howbeit the edition of the *Seventie* went away with the credit, and therefore not onely was placed in the midst by *Origen* (for the worth and excellency thereof above the rest, as *Epiphanius* gathereth) but also was used by the *Greek* Fathers for the ground and foundation of their commentaries. Yea, *Epiphanius* above mentioned, doth attribute so much unto it, that he holdeth the authors thereof, not onely for interpreters, but also for Prophets in some respect; and *Justinian* the Emperour enjoyning the *Jews* his subjects to use especially the translation of the *Seventie*, rendereth this reason thereof, because they were, as it were enlightened with propheticall grace. Yet, for all that, as the *Egyptians* are said of the prophet to be men and not God, and their horses flesh and not spirit: so it is evident, (and S. *Hierome* affirmeth as much) that the *Seventie* were interpreters, they were not Prophets; they did many things well, as learned men, but yet as men they stumbled and fell, one while through oversight, another while through ignorance; yea, sometimes they may be noted to adde to the originall, and sometimes to take from it; which made the Apostles to leave them many times, when

they left the *Hebrew*, and to deliver the sense thereof according to the truth of the word, as the Spirit gave them utterance. This may suffice touching the *Greek* translations of the Old Testament.

There were also written a few hundred years after *Christ*, translations many into the *Latine* tongue; for this tongue also was very fit to convey the law and the gospel by, because in those times very many countreys of the West, yea of the South, East, and North, spake or understood *Latine* being made provinces to the *Romanes*. But now the *Latine* translations were too many to be all good: for they were infinite (*Latini interpretes nullo modo numerari possunt*, saith S. *Augustine*.) Again, they were not out of the *Hebrew* fountain (we speak of the *Latine* translations of the Old Testament) but out of the *Greek* stream; therefore the *Greek* being not altogether clear, the *Latine* derived from it must needs be muddy. This moved S. *Hierome*, a most learned Father, and the best linguist without controversie, of his age, or of any that went before him, to undertake the translating of the Old Testament out of the very fountains themselves; which he performed with that evidence of great learning, judgment, industry, and faithfulnesse that he hath for ever bound the Church unto him in a debt of special remembrance and thankfulnesse.

Essays on Man in his Primitive State, and under the Patriarchal, Jewish, and Christian Dispensations.—No. IV.

Primitive State.—No. IV.

ADAM, after his exile from Eden, begat a son in his own image, and after his own likeness. Naked, defenceless, and imbecile, the infant man commences his mortal career. The circumstances under which he makes his appearance upon the stage are incomparably more unpropitious than those amidst which his original progenitors made their entrance. Reason in its zenith, enthroned in the unpolluted temple of a sentient body, controlled all the actions of the animal nature of the illustrious progenitors. But the infant man feels the rod before he sees it. His delicate and unprotected body smarts beneath the very elements upon which he must live, and with which he must wage an interminable war while his heart is able to react. Upon the first invasion of the elastic fluid, his lungs heave, and with sighs and tears, the little sufferer begins his pilgrimage to the tomb. He feels before he reasons. He cries before he smiles. His first idea of ease, improperly denominated pleasure, is drawn from animal gratification. Thus his appetites and passions are first called into action by an unavoidable necessity. He remains, for months and years, almost a mere animal in all his impressions, feelings, desires, pains, and pleasures. The mind, by a wise accommodation to its companion, is not permitted to put forth its energies; the body is yet deficient in physical strength to sustain its activities. This law of our nature gives a fearful odds to all animal propensities in the future struggles between reason and passion. Hence the old complain of the sallies of youthful appetites, while the young lament the rigorous restraints of maturer years.

Were there no other difference between Adam in Eden and any of his natural descendants, than what arises out of his disparity in the commencement of life; this alone would constitute an immense dissimilarity between him and any

34

of his posterity. Adam, when he first opened his eyes, was in the zenith of his mental faculties; but twenty-one years of our time must pass in the turmoil of passion, appetite and reason before we can safely trust a human being to the keeping of his own reason.

As sensation first, and reflection afterwards, give man all his simple ideas or first views of things; so the symbols or types of all his ideas are the material objects around him. By comparing these objects with one another, by abstracting, classifying and compounding their qualities or properties he forms all the complex ideas of which he is possessed. So that all his simple ideas are the images of things which do exist, and he has not a single idea, the archetype or pattern of which is not to be met with, in the materials around him. His imagination may create a great many new forms, but the materials out of which it creates these new forms were originally presented him in the great magazine of nature. He may now fancy a tree, the roots of which are iron, the trunk and branches of which are brass, the leaves of which are silver, and the fruit of which is gold. But had he not obtained by sensation or observation the idea of a natural tree, he never could have imagined this unnatural one.

The inlets of all human knowledge are the five senses. Reflection upon the ideas thus acquired gives birth to new ones, akin, however, to those received by sensation. Imagination may now combine these ideas without any restraint but its own power. It may associate those ideas with, or without regard, to natural fitness, congruity, or consistency. It may create a Polyphemus or a Centaur; but it cannot create an idea perfectly new. As human skill and human power may new modify, but cannot create a particle of matter; so the imagination may vary or new modify the ideas acquired by sensation, but cannot create a new one. And here ends the chapter of all human science.

Revelation opens a new world, a new order of relations, and gives birth to new ideas, which, as the great apostle to the nations says, "The eye of man never saw, the ear of man never heard, nor the heart of man ever conceived." But this commences a new chapter in human knowledge. The first chapter contains all natural knowledge. The second, all supernatural. These things premised, we proceed to the consideration of the patriarchal age of the world.

However numerous the ages may be imagined, or however diversified in their character, yet as respects man's religious relations, they are scripturally distinguished into three. And these may be fitly styled the Patriarchal, the Jewish and the Christian. The Patriarchal continued from Adam to Moses; the Jewish, from Moses to the Messias; and the Christian from the Messias till now, and is never to be superseded by another. Religion is one and the same thing in all ages of the world as respects its distinguishing character and design. And a *good man* has been essentially the same sort of a being in all ages, and under all the instituted acts of religion which have ever been preached by divine authority. Faith, or confidence in God according to the developement of his character, has always been the basis and controling principle of all religious homage. A good man has ever been the man who paid a just regard to all the relations in which he stood to God and man. The principles of all true piety and humanity are as invariable as God himself. But the developement of the divine character, and of all our relations to

God and each other, has been progressive, and not consummated at once. Like the path of the just that shines more and more to the perfect day, has been the development of the character of God and the extent of human relations and obligations. Thus the patriarchal age was the star-light of the moral world; the Jewish age was the moon-light; the ministry of the harbinger the twilight; and the Christian age the sun-light of the moral world. If any object to this gradual and progressive exhibition of spiritual light: and impertinently ask why these things should so be; let him ask the heavens and the earth, why at one time the stars only are visible—at another the moon—and at another the sun. Let him ask the earth why there is first the tender germ; next the vigorous shoot; next the opening blossom; and by and by the mature fruit. Let him ask why God did not give us the milk and the honey as he gives the dew and the rain, or the baked loaves as he sends the hail and the snow. Let him ask rather why he has shown any kindness to a race of beings so ungrateful in their nature, and so desirous to exclude him from the honor of creating or of governing the universe of which we are a part. Of one thing we are certain, that the distribution of the globe into oceans and continents, into islands and lakes, into different latitudes and climates, into hills and vallies, mountains and plains; the year into seasons, and the moral world into ages or different economies, is all of the same character, founded upon the principles requisite to giving birth and perpetuity to the best possible system, both natural and moral; and of this we are equally certain, both when we can discover what we would call good and relevant reasons, and when we cannot.

The patriarchal age is distinguished by those institutions adapted to mankind in the infancy of the world. The religious institutions of this period found on record, are in exact conformity to the condition of society in its incipient stages, and confirm the pretensions of the volume which details them, to the antiquity and authenticity which it claims.

The Bible method of teaching is peculiarly its own. It does not begin nor proceed upon the principle of asserting any speculative truth to be believed, but communicates all its instruction either in relating facts or in explaining them. Creed-makers all begin with asserting the *Being* and perfections of God. Moses commences by telling us that "In the beginning God created the heavens and the earth." From what he has done, he leaves us to learn his character, and not from words or propositions concerning him.

The object we have in view with a reference to our condition and circumstances in descanting upon this and the succeeding age, requires us to ascertain two things, viz.—the actual amount of revelation enjoyed in this age, and the particular moral and religious institutions which belonged to it. This we can learn only from the narrative found in the book of Genesis; from the facts recorded in connexion with the memoirs of the illustrious personages which flourished in this age, amongst whom, the most considerable are Abel, Enoch, Noah, Shem, Abraham, Melchizedec, Isaac, Jacob, Joseph, and a few females connected with them. But this we must defer to a more convenient season.

EDITOR.

Ancient Gospel.—No. X.
I substitute the following Narrative for an Essay.

My father was a Scotch Presbyterian, and my mother was a regular Baptist—I was religiously brought up, and being taught the system of doctrine laid down in the confession of faith, I became a speculative Calvinist. My mother's views of baptism appeared the most scriptural, and although I always helped my father, when he and mother, of a winter evening, had their good natured fire side debates, yet still I gradually leaned more and more to my mother's side in my real sentiments. I finally became as firmly convinced of baptism as of Calvinism; and was a speculative calvinistic baptist, of the supralapsarian school. But as yet I had no real devotion, nor practical views of the Gospel. I went to meeting, sat as a judge upon every preacher who came amongst us, and when sermon was over, I had a little crowd around me listening to my criticisms and censures. I was very severe, and valued myself no little upon my quick discernment in all the doctrines of the day. So acute was my religious scent, that I could almost tell a man's whole system before he had spoken half a dozen of sentences. During these days of my vain and foolish behavior, a very practical calvinistic preacher came to our congregation, and so engagedly addressed us on justification by faith, in the imputed righteousness of Christ, that I saw a fitness and beauty in this scheme which wonderfully charmed me; I became quite religious, prayed twice each day in secret, and attended meeting with views and designs quite different from those which formerly actuated me—I had heard much upon faith, and was very precise in my definitions and disquisitions upon true and saving faith. I at length fancied I had obtained it, and had serious thoughts of joining the church. Baptism came up to my consideration again, and I concluded I ought to be baptized, for I perceived it to be a very plain duty: and a very commendable way of making a profession. I had fixed the day for making my profession, and had given in my experience to a baptist church. I was approved by the whole congregation, but the intended administrator taking sick, it was put off for another month. In the mean time a Mr. J. S. came round, who was accused of not being very orthodox, for he preached a gospel which some of his friends called the ancient gospel; and his enemies the water gospel. I went to hear him without any other object than to gratify my curiosity, and to be able to oppose this new heresy. But to my utter astonishment, in one hour and twenty minutes, I was as completely and entirely converted to this *ancient gospel*, or as some of the wits who cared for no gospel, called it, the *water gospel*. My whole views of God's character, philanthropy, and scheme of salvation were as radically changed as if I had heard nothing worthy of the name of gospel ever before. And strange as it may appear, I was immersed for the remission of my sins before I left the ground. I now saw for the first time in my life, that sinners were called to act upon the divine testimony alone—that they were not to wait for any change for the better to be discovered in themselves, nor any secret drawings, remarkable or sensible impressions, before they obeyed the commandment "to be baptized for the remission of sins." This command I saw to be binding upon all who feel any interest in the question " what shall I do to obtain pardon and peace with God?" The blood of Jesus I well knew, was the only sacrifice for sin, and was the only thing in the universe which could take away sin from the conscience, and present us without fault to God: but I now found that by this gracious institution we came to the blood

of Jesus, in God's own appointed way, and thus washed our robes and made them white, not red, in the blood of the Lamb. But my mind as the needle touched with the loadstone, always terminated upon the divine testimony and veracity, and the command, " to day if you will obey his voice, harden not your hearts," compelled me to take God upon his own word. I went to the river edge believing the promise of God, and that he could do this thing, even wash away my sins in the very act of immersion. Down into the water I went, and was immersed into the name of the Lord Jesus for the remission of my sins—and you may rest assured, for it is a fact, that I declare to you, I felt myself as fully relieved from the burthen of my former transgressions, as ever did a man to whom the Lord said, your sins are forgiven you: go and sin no more.—I had read about peace and joy before. I had thought I once understood these terms, and felt something worthy of the name; but I can assure you that all I ever knew of the import of these words before, was as unlike to my present feelings, as a marble statue is to a living man. Most assuredly, said I, and felt I, God is as good as his word, and I have found his promise yes and amen in Christ Jesus my Lord. But in all probability I would not have derived so much happiness from being buried with Christ by immersion into his name, had I not previously understood from the many declarations found in the sacred testimonies, that God's philanthropy embraced all those who were pleased to come to him in the appointed way, and had I not also been assured of two things; first, that the scriptures mean just what they say, and secondly, that they say, Be immersed for the remission of your sins—I went down to the very water just for this very purpose, in the honesty and simplicity of my heart, believing that it would be as God said, and according to my faith so has it been to me. And one thing more I well tell you, that " whereas I was blind now I see."

With regard to the Holy Spirit, which is also promised, I will tell you what I have since that time experienced—and you will please inform me whether you think I have received that promise. While I thought about religion before, and determined to act some day, I felt a considerable attachment to the distinctions found in society, growing out of wealth and popularity. I was strongly disposed to have as good a share of these as I could honestly obtain. I felt moreover a good deal of that sort of spirit which presumes upon the electing love of God, and so soon as I began to think I was a Christian, I saw in my secret devotions, as well as in my public exercises, a good degree of likeness to him who said, " I thank you, O Lord! that I am not like other men—I fast and pray, &c."—But now I am content with my lot, thank the Lord for what I have, and pray to him that I may be a good steward of what he has committed to me already: I feel the earth is the Lord's and the fulness thereof; and therefore, I hold every thing as a tenant at will of his landlord. I find it is more blessed to give than to receive—I know none of those little sectarian feelings which I once felt—I rejoice in the Lord, and in his people, and feel that every thing that affects his honor and glory, affects mine. I feel the same sort of interest in my Saviour's Kingdom, I used to feel in my father's character and estate—whatever added to either, I thought added to my fortune and fame: and now I feel that whatever advances the interest and reputation of the kingdom of my sovereign, adds to my individual gain and honor—I feel myself his, and him mine; and I would rather be the meanest soldier in his army, than the greatest potentate on earth—I do rejoice exceedingly in him all the day, and when I walk in the fields, or sit by the fire, my heart wanders after him; when travelling along the way, I sometimes speak out to him as if I were conversing with him: and the very idea that the eyes of the King of Kings are upon me, makes me bold in danger, and active in all the obedience of faith—I sometimes retire from the best company, to talk a few minutes to my Lord, and nothing is sweeter to my taste, than is an interview with Him who pardons my sins—takes me into his family, and promises to take me home to his own glorious abode by and by—I think no more about tenets or doctrines, but upon the love of God, the death of Jesus—his resurrection from the dead—his coming to judge the world, and the resurrection of the just. This is the spirit I have received and enjoyed since I put on the Lord. Now tell me is this the holy spirit promised?   BIBLICUS.

To the Editor of the Christian Baptist.

DEAR SIR,—I have got home to my friends and brethren, and found them all well. I find many of your opponents are preaching the very faith which once they condemned; and not only at home, but on my tour through Kentucky and Virginia, I find some of your opponents are deriving at least as much benefit from your writings as those who are your friends and open advocates. Some of the editors, too, who have opposed you, are now exhibiting your views on sundry subjects, for which a year or two ago you were very much censured by the Regular Baptists and some others. In a tavern in Maryland I picked up a "Columbian Star," and found, to my surprise, that brother Brantley had given your views of the baptism of the Holy Spirit, and under the editorial head, thereby showing that he had made them his own. In Kentucky, too, our brother Clack has come over wonderfully. He has given your views of the baptism of the Holy Spirit; and on sundry other topics he has appropriated your sentiments, and is detailing them in his paper—I mean those which were once reprobated by numbers in Kentucky. You will see in the last "Recorder," which I read to-day, that in one of brother Clack's late sermons, detailed under date of the 11th instant, he has given your views of the Keys given to Peter—of the Thrones on which the Apostles were placed—and indeed, substantially, your views on the Commencement of the Reign of the Messiah, as detailed in your Debate with M'Calla. I do not say that these views originated with you, but certainly they were once denominated *yours;* and I must confess I never learned them till I saw your writings. Brother Noel, since he has devoted himself to proclaiming the gospel and abandoned the contest about creeds, has been very successful. He made no converts by preaching up church covenants and creeds. I only regret to see so little candor amongst some of our brethren, who, unhappily for themselves and the public, took a stand too soon against what they called "your innovations"—I say, I regret to see them not give you credit either in their preaching or writings for views they as certainly learned from you as I received my name from my father. But still I rejoice to find that some of those who oppose you as an innovator, are making great innovations themselves. Persevere, brother. You are conquering, and will conquer. One of your most bigoted opposers said not long since, in a

public assembly, that, in travelling twenty-five hundred miles circuitously, he only found four Regular Baptist preachers which you had not corrupted. The Lord speed you, brother.   BARNABAS.

To Brother Barnabas.

DEAR SIR,—I HAVE seen many pieces published in several periodicals without giving me the least credit, which I well know were *borrowed* from my writings. But I gave myself no concern about it. I was glad to see them in the columns of those who have traduced me. In some instances I saw them neutralized by a preceding or succeeding paragraph, and by some crude mixtures of undisciplined minds. Many sentiments in this work are *original* to me. I dug them out of the mines of revealed truth. But how many more may have dug the same treasures out of the same mines, I know not. But one thing I know, that numbers who are now improving themselves and others by them, never dug them out themselves. But so long as they are held up to human view, I rejoice; and in this I will rejoice though all who publish them exhibit them as their own.

In much haste, yours in the hope of immortality.   EDITOR.

Ancient and Modern Bishops.

" LET none," says Dr. Mosheim, alluding to the first and second centuries, " confound the bishops of this primitive and golden period of the church, with those of whom we read in the following ages. For though they were both designated by the same name, yet they differed extremely, in many respects. A bishop, during the first and second centuries, was a person who had the care of one Christian assembly, which at that time, was, generally speaking, small enough to be contained in a private house. In this assembly he acted not so much with the authority of a master, as with the zeal and diligence of a faithful servant. The churches also, in those early times, were entirely independent; none of them subject to any foreign jurisdiction, but each one governed by its own rulers and its own laws. Nothing is more evident than the perfect equality that reigned among the primitive churches: nor does there ever appear, in the first century, the smallest trace of that association of provincial churches, from which *councils* and *metropolitans* derive their origin."—[*Ecc. Hist. vol. I. p.* 105—107.]

Constantine's Imperial way of Reconciling Bishops.

SOCRATES says, that the bishops having put into the emperor's hands written libels containing their complaints against each other, he threw them all together into the fire, advising them, according to the doctrine of Christ, to forgive one another as they themselves hoped to be forgiven. Sozomen says, that the bishops having made their complaints in person, the emperor bade them reduce them all into writing, and that on the day which he had appointed to consider them, he said, as he threw all the billets unopened into the fire, that it did not belong to him to decide the differences of christian bishops, and that the hearing of them must be deferred till the day of judgment.—*Life of Constantine*, book iii. ch. 10—14.

Character given Wickliffe by one of the Enemies of Reformation.

JONES says—As the clergy had hated and persecuted him with great violence during his life, they exulted with indecent joy at his disease and death, ascribing them to the immediate vengeance of Heaven for his heresy—"On the day of St. Thomas the Martyr, Arch bishop of Canterbury," says Walsingham, a contemporary historian, "that limb of the devil, enemy of the church, deceiver of the people, idol of heretics, mirror of hypocrites, author of schisms, sower of hatred, and inventer of lies, John Wickliffe, was, by the immediate judgment of God, suddenly struck with a palsy, which seized all the members of his body, when he was ready, as they say, to vomit forth his blasphemies against the blessed St. Thomas, in a sermon which he had prepared to preach that day."

No. 5.]   December 1, 1828.

Remarks on the Bible.—No. II.

Hence it is, that though Christ has entrusted the business of publishing, teaching, instructing, and exhorting, into the hands of uninspired men; nay, has made it the duty of every friend to his cause to perform these acts to the best of his ability, and full extent of his opportunity, with the single exception that females are not to teach in public assemblies; yet explanation, as being a work that requires the same degree of inspiration with original revelation, is never committed to or enjoined on, an uninspired man; for who can know the mind of the Spirit, but the Spirit himself, or those that are inspired by him?

On the Spirit's message being understood and complied with, depends its whole utility to man. Not understood, misunderstood, or neglected, it is no better than water poured on a rock. Can we then believe that God would send a message, which to be of any use to his creatures must be clearly understood by them, in words and phrases which they could not understand, or commit its interpretation to persons whom he had never qualified, appointed, or accredited for the purpose—that is, to uninspired men? Surely not.

Let it be observed further, that in every instance in which the words, arrangement, and connexion, preferred and adopted by the Spirit, have left his ideas in any degree uncertain, all the attempts made by uninspired men for nearly two thousand years, to explain and render them more certain, have entirely failed. Not one of these uncertain and obscure passages is at this day in the least clearer than it was when their abortive labors first began: nor will the total failure of these presumptuous attempts at all surprize us, if we call to mind an observation already made, that the obscurities and ambiguities that may be met with in sacred writ, were knowingly and intentionally introduced into it by its Divine Author, and that no adequate means have ever been provided by him for their removal: that is, the spiritual gift, which alone can enable man to remove them, has never since the days of the apostles been conferred on any mortal. Nay, for ever must they remain just as they are, unless God shall send an *inspired* expositor, furnished with *unquestionable* credentials of a divine commission for that purpose, to remove them. All that uninspired men, however sagacious, pious, and learned, can do in this superhuman undertaking, and certainly all they have done, is to exhibit an endless parade of discordant (often contradictory) conjectures, conceits, notions, opinions, suppositions, or by whatever name their dreams or reveries may be called, in which no confidence can be reposed, because in no instance does there exist the least certainty that any of their conjectures about the Spirit's meaning,

and what he really meant, are coincident. They to whom the words of the Spirit do not exhibit his meaning with clearness and certainty, have no standard by which they can try the opinions of others, and ascertain their agreement and disagreement with what the Spirit says. His faith, therefore, to whom the Spirit's own words do not clearly reveal his meaning, cannot rest on divine information, but on the words and information of fallible, erring man, and must partake of all its uncertainty. If the words of any writing do not clearly reveal its meaning to my mind, how can I determine whether another apprehends it? Impossible. I may deem his conjecture ingenious, plausible, probable, but certain I cannot pronounce it: for that would be to declare that it agreed with my own opinion, whereas in this case I have none. Indeed all we really mean when we pronounce other men's opinions true or false, correct or incorrect, is, that they agree or disagree with our own, our own conceptions being in all cases made the standard of our judgments respecting the truth or falsehood, the accuracy or inaccuracy of the conceptions of other men. The labor, therefore, of the countless host of commentators, lecturers, expositors, sermonizers, &c. who have vainly attempted and presumptuously pretended to render God's message plainer than he could, or at least chose to render it, to discover words fitter to express the Spirit's ideas than he could himself discover, deserves to be stigmatized not only as entirely useless, and grossly impious, but as excessively pernicious to ignorant incautious mortals. By the unhappy toil of these self conceited presumers to render God's message plainer than he thought fit, or deemed it necessary to render it, the world has been deluged with discourses and books, crammed with metaphysical jargon, airy speculation, doubtful disputation, jarring notions, discordant opinions, contradictory conjectures, and vain jangling, and the ignorant, unreflecting, unsuspecting multitude have, to their irreparable injury, had their veneration lessened, their affections alienated, and their attention diverted by these pernicious baubles from studying, or to use the Saviour's term, from searching the only volume on earth that contains one particle of certain information on the all-important subject of religion; their minds stuffed with error, prejudice, bigotry and delusion; their hearts corrupted with the vilest passions, and their lives degraded and embittered with all the jealousy, rancor, contempt, and contention, which a deluded and sectarian spirit can engender.

Let us mark the impiety of attempting to extort from the words of God's message more information than he has fitted them to impart, or of absurdly amusing ourselves in abortive trials to substitute words plainer than he has chosen to employ. Between man, and useless, perhaps, pernicious knowledge, God has kindly interposed *here* a profound silence, there a phraseology to us intelligible only to a certain degree: but regardless of Heaven's barring, human presumption has attempted to force its impious way into the uncommunicated secrets of the Almighty, and not contented with the quantity of information which God in his wisdom and goodness, has judged best for his miserable creatures, has charged him with ignorance, injustice, and illiberality: told him to his face, that either he did not know the quantity of information that man's condition required, and was justly due to him; or, if he knew it, that he was too illiberal to bestow it; and had thus compelled his creature to commit the atrocious impiety of attempting to increase his information whether his Creator would or would not. But insufficient information is not the only fault charged on the oracles of God—obscure diction is also imputed to them: and man, impudent and ungrateful man, has, in the plenitude of his self conceit, and profane folly, dared to imagine that he could select words and phrases fitter to convey the ideas of the Spirit in an intelligible manner, than he could. The question then is, Did God send his message so improperly worded, as to compel men, in order to derive from it all the benefit which God intended, to become grossly impious? We think not.

But whoever, with a mind void of prejudice, uncorrupted with the doctrines of the nursery, the family, the neighborhood, the church and its auxiliaries, repairs to the oracles of God for information, and contented to receive with humility and thankfulness the instruction there presented, will soon, from his own comfortable experience, be induced to vindicate the message sent him by his gracious Parent, from all charges of unnecessary deficiency of matter or diction: he will find it perfectly able to make him wise to salvation; and this is certainly all he can wish it to do.

But to terminate a discussion, already rendered through a desire of being understood, too long, let me ask, If the preceding remarks be just, that is, if the words chosen and employed by the Divine Spirit to communicate his thoughts to man, be the fittest that could be employed for that purpose; if they alone contain and offer certain information on the interesting subject of religion; if in them only, just as they have been arranged and connected by their all-wise author, unaltered, unmixed, undisturbed by the temerity of presumptuous mortals, be contained and presented to the human mind the good news called "The Gospel;" and if in the commentaries, lectures, expositions, sermons, tracts, treatises or discourses of men, no matter how sagacious, learned, and pious they may think themselves, or may in reality be, there are to be found, not the Spirit's message, denominated "The Gospel," but their own uninspired, crude, uncertain, and often discordant notions or conjectures about God's message; let me ask, I say, if it be not the most daring temerity, the most unpardonable arrogance and vanity, the very consummation of human impudence and vanity, to attempt to confound two things so entirely different as the Spirit's message contained and conveyed in his own well-chosen words, and men's miserable conjectures about that message; and to call the publication of these conjectures, either by written documents or verbal discourse, the preaching or publication of the gospel? Is it not to attempt to practise on the ignorant and unsuspecting the grossest imposition? Surely if the Spirit's own words alone contain and exhibit the gospel, reading or pronouncing from memory the Spirit's words, without the least alteration, mixture, or derangement, can only with truth be termed preaching or publishing the gospel: and surely they who impose on their deceived and deluded hearers or readers their own reveries about the gospel, for the gospel, cannot be held guiltless.

A— S—.

P. S.—*Query.* Did Paul and the other inspired men, when they spoke or wrote on the subject of religion, employ the words and phrases only in which the inspiring Spirit suggested his ideas to their minds, and thus strictly publish the Spirit's message, just as suggested to them, unmixed with any ideas or words of their own; or did they employ words invented by themselves, and of course publish in their own words only their own conceptions about what the Spirit had suggested to them? And if the inspired men published the Spirit's ideas only in the words suggested by the Spirit, by what authority do uninspired men publish what they fancy or imagine about the Spirit's message in their own words, and call their fancies the gospel?

Response.

The burthen of this query has occasioned considerable discussion amongst the more learned commentators and interpreters of sacred scripture. I cannot, however, discover any real difficulty in deciding the controversy, or in answering the query. In all matters purely supernatural, the communication was made in words. The ideas were suggested and expressed in words.— So that, as Paul says, "We speak spiritual things in spiritual words," or in words suggested by the Holy Spirit. But a very small portion of both Testaments are of this character. Communications purely supernatural occupy by far the least portion of the sacred books. In the historical books of both Testaments, and in the epistolary part of the New, there are many things presented to our minds which did not originate in heaven, or which did not pertain to heavenly things. In all such communications the writers were so guided, or had things so recalled to their memory, as to be able to give a faithful narrative.— The sentiment or sense of all passages purely moral or religious, is the result of divine teaching; and all matters pertaining to this life are of divine authority, though not supernatural either in their original communications or in the terms in which they are expressed. I presume the following criterion is both judicious, safe, and every way unexceptionable. Whatever information requiring nothing more than the memory of the writer, or whatever information on sensible objects is found in the sacred scriptures was neither supernatural in the matter nor manner of communication, unless the strengthening of the memory, or a new presentation of the things to the mind of the writer, may be called supernatural. The history of the Deluge, for instance, as written by Moses, is not of the same character as the institutions of the Jews' religion. The latter was purely supernatural—the former, an authentic account from tradition; in writing which, the historian was simply guided in the selection of the documents, and prevented from committing errors. The sense or sentiment of all the sacred books is of divine authority. The words and phrases were in all instances, except in communications purely supernatural, of the selection of the writer. Of this, more hereafter.

EDITOR.

Four Queries Answered.

Mr. Editor—Will you favor me with your thoughts on the following Questions:—

1. Did Christ commit, during the period of gifted men, the extension of his kingdom or multiplication of his subjects, to any besides these gifted men?

2. And to whom, after their death, did he consign it—to a few specially as now, or to the whole body of his subjects indiscriminately?

3. On what acts has Christ rested the multiplication of his subjects, and their confirmation in his service?

4. Does preaching the gospel consist in publishing it, as it is found in the Spirit's own words,

or in publishing discourses made by men about
it?   An Inquirer.

—

Answer to Query I. During the apostolic age
for the *establishment* of christianity, the Saviour
employed apostles, prophets, evangelists, pastors,
and teachers, all supernaturally endowed. To
these alone was the work of establishing or laying the foundation of his religion in the world
committed.

Answer to Query II. After their death, the
congregation of the saints was entrusted with
this work; that is, by the operation of parental
authority; by the proclaiming in word and deed
the excellency of the christian religion to all
men, in all the several relations;—by the simple proclamation of the gospel facts, with their
evidences, was the number of the saints to be
multiplied; and in their weekly meetings for
reading the apostolic writings and for observing
the ordinances composing the christian institution, the saints were to be edified.

Answer to Query III. Christ has rested the
multiplication of the faithful on the exertions of
the christian congregations. On their holding
forth in word and in their behavior the gospel
facts and their import, and not upon the exertions
of a certain class of individuals called Priests,
Clergy, Preachers, Teachers, or Bishops. The
giving up the conversion of the world into the
hands of a certain class, however designated,
chosen, and appointed, has been the greatest
check to the progress of christianity which it
has ever sustained.

Answer to Query IV. The preaching of the
gospel never did mean *making sermons or discourses about it,* no more than the cure of diseases has been effected by disquisitions upon
pathology or the nature of diseases and remedies; but in the proclamation of the great facts
found in the historical books of the New Testament, supported by such evidences and arguments as the apostolic testimonies contain and
afford.

Had I room for the demonstrations and proofs
from which these conclusions are drawn, which
would occupy at least an entire number of this
work, I would not despair of making the above
answers apparent and convincing to all honest
inquirers. But in the mean time I submit the
answers without the premises for examination
and reflection.   Editor.

———

A Restoration of the Ancient Order of Things.
No. XXVIII.

On the Discipline of the Church.—No. V.

They greatly mistake who expect to find a
liturgy, or a code of laws in the New Institution,
designed to govern christians either in their private or public relations and character. This may
be found in the Old Institution which the God of
Abraham set up amongst the children of the
flesh. The nation of the Jews affords both demonstration and proof that man cannot be governed or controlled either in piety or morality by
any extrinsic law, however excellent or spiritual.
The former institution was an institution of *law*
—the new an institution of *favor.* Christians are
not now, nor were they ever, under law, but under favor. Hence argues the Apostle:—"Sin
shall not lord it over you; for you are *not under
law,* but *under favor.*" A single monosyllable
represents the active principle, or law of subordination and of practical morality which it un-

folds. That monosyllable is love. "*Love is the
fulfilling of the whole law.*" The glad tidings of
the divine philanthropy is the instrument or medium of the inspiration of this principle. The
New Institution writes upon the heart, and not on
marble, the governing principle or laws of all religious and moral action. This truth recognized
and apprehended, solves the difficulty which has
puzzled so many minds, and so generally distracted religious society. Many christians have
read and rummaged the apostolic writings with
the spirit and expectations of a Jew in perusing
the writings of Moses—Jews in heart, but christians in profession. They have sought, but sought
in vain, for an express command or precedent for
matters as minute as the seams in the sacerdotal
robes, or the pins and pilasters of the tabernacle.

The remote or proximate causes of most errors
in disciplinary proceedings may be traced either
to the not perceiving that the distinguishing peculiarity of the New, or Christian Institution, is
this—that it aims at governing human action
without *letter,* and causes its votaries to "serve
in newness of spirit, and not in the oldness of the
letter;" or, to the not observing that the congregations which christianity forms are designed
rather as schools of moral excellence, than as
courts of inquiry possessed of judicial authority.

To look still farther into the genius of the New
Institution is yet prerequisite to just conclusions
on this subject. The New Institution, governing religious and moral action by a law or principle engraved upon the heart, proposes certain
acts of private and public edification and worship. These are stated in the apostolic writings,
and conformity to them is enjoined upon disciples from the new obligations which arise out of
the new law. The precepts found in the apostolic epistles and those found in the Pentateuch
or writings of Moses, have one differential attribute which cannot be too clearly presented here.
The precepts found in the apostolic epistles originated or were occasioned by the mistakes and
misdemeanors found in Jews and Pagans, recently converted to the christian faith. But the precepts or laws found in the Pentateuch were promulged before the people began to act at all, as
a part of the institution itself. Hence it was an
institution essentially of *law*—the New essentially an institution of *favor.* All the actions of
the former were prescribed by law; but subordination to the latter is implied in the gracious
promulgation itself.

The relation established between God and
Israel was a different relation from that established between God and christians. As all duties
and privileges arise from relations, if the relations
are different, the duties and privileges are different also. Now God made himself known to
Israel simply as their God and deliverer from
Egyptian bondage, and as their King in contradistinction from the kings of all other nations.
Upon this fact, as the grand premises, was the
Old Institution proclaimed. Thus it began:—
"I am the Lord your God who brought you out
of the house of bondage. Therefore you shall
acknowledge no other God besides me," &c.
But the premises upon which the New Institution proceeds are of a much more sublime and
exalted character. Relations more sublime than
national and temporal relations, enter into its
nature, and lay the foundation of the New
Economy. He is the God and King of christians
upon higher considerations—and more than simply their God and King—he is their Saviour and
Redeemer from worse than Egyptian bondage;

their leader and guide to a better inheritance than Canaan; and their Father by a new and glorious provision which the national compact at Mount Sinai knew nothing of.

The relation of Master and Servant is a very different relation from that of Father and Son. This is rather an illustration, than a full representation of the difference of relation in which Jews and Christians stand to the God of the whole earth. The relation of Creator and creature is the natural relation existing between God and all mankind. But besides this he has instituted political and gracious relations between himself and human beings. These flow from his own good will and pleasure, and, as such, will be acquiesced in by the wise and good. The natural and first relation in which mankind stand to each other is that of fellow-creatures; but besides this, a number of other natural, political, and gracious relations have been either necessarily or graciously called into existence—such as that of parent and child, husband and wife, and the whole table of consanguinity and affinity; besides all the political relations, and those found in the kingdom of Jesus Christ.

Now the relation between God and christians, or the relation which the New Institution developes, is the most gracious and desirable which can be conceived of; and therefore presents to the human mind the loftiest and most comprehensive principles which can excite to moral action. As in physics, so in ethics there are principles or powers more influential than others. But christianity discovers principles of action which no political, moral or religious relations hitherto known, could originate. These new relations, and these new principles of action, are stronger than death, more triumphant than the grave, and lasting as eternity. The discovery of a new, gracious, spiritual, and eternal relation, and correspondent principles of action, moral and religious, is the basis of that association called the christian church or congregation. It is called the Reign or Kingdom of Heaven, because of the high and sublime nature of the relations, principles, duties, and privileges which it developes. All the political, commercial, and temporal relations of what nature or kind soever, which human passions, interests, partialities, or antipathies have given rise to, are weak and transient as the spider's thread compared with these. Hence the superlative glory of the New Institution. The world knows it not. It knew not the founder, and it apprehends not the institution. The light shines in darkness, but the darkness reaches it not.

These premises merely stated, not illustrated, suggest the true reason why, in the discipline of the church, so much is to be done before a member is to be severed from her embraces. In the politico-ecclesiastical relations of schismatic corporations the ties of consociation are neither very binding, nor the relations very endearing. They are not much stronger than the purse-strings of the treasurer, nor more durable than the paper on which is written the shibboleth of their Magna Charta. Members may be, and often are, separated without a pang or a sorrow. There is none of that tenderness of reproof, of correction, of admonition, of dehortations, of persuasion, known in such confederations as that which the New Institution enjoins upon the citizens of Heaven.

The first effort which the genius of the New Institution enjoins with respect to offending brothers, is similar to that notable regulation concerning private trespasses, which, all who have read it, remember, aims at gaining the supposed aggressor or delinquent. Hence the most characteristic feature in all congregational proceedings in reference to those who sin, not so much against a brother as against Christ, is that condescending tenderness which aims at the conversion of the delinquent or transgressor. The dernier resort, when all means fail, is separation. This tender solicitude and earnestness to gain a brother who has fallen, is, in some cases, where the nature of the case does not forbid, extended even beyond exclusion. So that although public good, as well as that of the subject of censure, does require his exclusion; yet even then he is not to be treated as an enemy, but admonished as a brother. The lesson of all others the most difficult, and the most important to be learned on the subject of this essay, is that which the preceding considerations suggest, and that is briefly that every part of the proceedings in reference to an offending brother must be distinguished by every possible demonstration of sympathy and concern for his good standing and character in the sight of God and man: and that final seclusion from the congregation must not be attempted until admonition, reproof, and persuasion, have failed to effect a real change in his views and behavior. Though I neither hold Lord Chesterfield nor his writings in much esteem, yet I cannot but admire his happy use of the "*suaviter in modo*" and the "*fortiter in re*," so much commended in his letters. If the "*suaviter in modo*," or the sweetness or gracefulness in the manner of doing, could always accompany the "*fortiter in re*," or the firmness in the purpose, or in the thing to be done, it would be no less useful than ornamental even amongst christians in all their congregational proceedings relating to offenders.

EDITOR.

Preface of the King's Translators.
[Continued from page 494.]

Now though the church were thus furnished with Greek and Latin translations, even before the faith of Christ was generally embraced in the empire; (for the learned know, that even in S. Hieromes time, the consul of Rome and his wife were both Ethnicks, and about the same time the greatest part of the senate also) yet for all that the godly learned were not content to have the scriptures in the language which themselves understood, Greek and Latin, (as the good lepers were not content to fare well themselves) but also for the behoof and edifying of the unlearned which hungred and thirsted for righteousnesse, and had souls to be saved as well as they, they provided translations into the vulgar for their countrey-men: insomuch that most nations under heaven did shortly after their conversion, hear Christ speaking unto them in their mother tongue, not by the voice of their minister only, but also by the written word translated. If any doubt hereof, he may be satisfied with examples enow, if enow will serve the turn. First, S. Hierome saith, *Multarum gentium linguis Scriptura ante translata, docet falsa esse quæ addita sunt,* &c. that is, The Scripture being translated before in the languages of many nations, doth shew that those things that were added (by Lucian or Hesychius) are false. So S. Hierome in that place. The same Hierome elsewhere affirmeth that he, the time was, had set forth the translation of the *Seventie, suæ linguæ hominibus;* that is, for his countrey-men of Dalmatia. Which words not onely Erasmus doth understand to purport, that S. Hierome translated the Scripture into the Dalmatian tongue; but also Sixtus Senensis, and Alphonsus a Castro (that we speak of no more) men not to be excepted against by them of Rome, do ingenuously confesse as much. So S. Chrysostome that lived in S. Hieromes time, giveth evidence with him: The doctrine of S. John (saith he) did not in such sort (as the philosophers did) vanish away; but the Syrians, Egyptians, Indians, Persians, Ethiopians, and infinite other nations being barbarous people, translated it into their (mother) tongue, and have learned to be (true) philosophers, he meaneth christians. To this may be added Theodoret, as next unto him, both for antiquitie, and for learning. His words be these, Every country that is under the sunne, is full of these words, (of the Apostles and Prophets) and the Hebrew tongue (he meaneth the Scriptures in the Hebrew tongue) is turned not onely into the language of the Grecians, but also of the Romanes, and Egyptians, and Persians, and Indians, and Armenians, and Sautomatians, and briefly into all the languages that any nation useth. So he. In like manner, Upilas is reported by Paulus Diaconus and Isidore (and before them by Sozomen) to have translated the Scriptures into the Gothick tongue; John Bishop of Sivil by Vasseus, to have turned them into Arabick, about the yeare of our Lord 717. Beda by Cistertiensis, to have turned a great part of them into Saxon; Esnard by Trithemius, to have abridged the French Psalter, as Beda had done the Hebrew, about the yeare 800. King Alured by the said Cistertiensis, to have turned the Psalter into Saxon; Methodius by Aventinus (printed at Ingolstadt) to have turned the Scriptures into Sclavonian; Valdo, Bishop of Prising by Beutus Rhenanus, to have caused about that time, the Gospels to be translated into Dutch rhythme, yet extant in the library of Corbinian; Valdus, by divers to have turned them himself, or to have gotten them turned into French, about the yeare 1160; Charles the fifth of that name, surnamed The Wise, to have caused them to be turned into French, about 200 yeares after Valdus his time, of which translation there be many copies yet extant, as witnesseth Beroaldus. Much about that time, even in our King Richard the seconds dayes, John Trevisa translated them into English, and many English bibles in written hand are yet to be seen with divers, translated, as it is very probable, in that age. So the Syrian translation of the New Testament is in most learned mens libraries, of Widminstadius his setting forth; and the Psalter in Arabick is with many of Augustinus Nebiensis setting forth. So Postel affirmeth, that in his travel he saw the Gospels in the Ethiopian tongue: And Ambrose Thesius alledgeth the Psalter of the Indians, which he testifieth to have been set forth by Potken in Syrian characters. So that, to have the Scriptures in the mother tongue is not a quaint conceit lately taken up either by the L. Cromwell in England, or by the L. Radevil in Polonie, or by the L. Ungnadius in the emperours dominion, but hath been thought upon, and put in practise of old, even from the first times of the conversion of any nation; no doubt, because it was esteemed most profitable, to cause faith to grow in mens hearts the sooner; and to make them to be able to say with the words of the Psalm, As we have heard, so we have seen.

Now the church of Rome would seem at the length to bear a motherly affection towards her children, and to allow them the Scriptures in the mother tongue; but indeed it is a gift, not deserving to be called a gift, an unprofitable gift; they

must get a licence in writing before they may use them; and to get that, they must approve themselves to their confessour, that is, to be such as are, if not frozen in the dregs, yet sowred with the leaven of their superstition. Howbeit it seemed too much to Clement the eighth, that there should be any licence granted to have them in the vulgar tongue, and therefore he overruleth and frustrateth the grant of Pius the fourth. So much are they of aid of the light of the Scripture (*Lucifugæ Scripturarum*, as Tertullian speaketh) that they will not trust the people with it, no not as it is set forth by their own sworn men, no not with the licence of their Bishops and Inquisitours. Yea, so unwilling are they to communicate the Scriptures to the peoples understanding in any sort, that they are not ashamed to confesse, that we forced them to translate it into English against their wills. This seemeth to argue a bad cause, or a bad conscience, or both. Sure we are, that it is not he that hath good gold, that is afraid to bring it to the touch stone, but he that hath the counterfeit; neither is it the true man that shunneth the light, but the malefactour, lest his deeds should be reproved; neither is the plain-dealing merchant that is unwilling to have the weights, or the meteyard brought in place, but he that useth deceit. But we will let them alone for this fault, and return to translation.

Many mens mouthes have been open a good while (and yet are not stopped) with speeches about the translation so long in hand, or rather perusals of translations made before: and ask what may be the reason, what the necessitie of the employment: Hath the church been deceived, say they, all this while? Hath the sweet bread been mingled with leaven, her silver with drosse, her wine with water, her milk with lime? (*Lacte gypsum male miscetur*, saith S. Ireney.) We hoped that we had been in the right way, that we had had the oracles of God delivered unto us, and that though all the world had cause to be offended, and to complain, yet that we had none. Hath the nurse holden out the breast, and nothing but winde in it? Hath the bread been delivered by the Fathers of the Church, and the same proved to be *lapidosus*, as Seneca speaketh? What is to handle the word of God deceitfully, if this be not? Thus certain brethren. Also the adversaries of Judah and Jerusalem, like Sanballat in Nehemiah, mock, as we heare, both at the work and workmen, saying, *What do these weak Jews, &c. will they make the stones whole again out of the heaps of dust which are burnt? although they build, yet if a fox go up, he shall even break down their stony wall.* Was their translation good before? Why do they now mend it? Was it not good? Why then was it obtruded to the people? Yes, why did the Catholicks (meaning Papish Romanists) alwayes go in jeopardy, for refusing to go to heare it? Nay, if it must be translated into English, Catholicks are fittest to do it. They have learning, and they know when a thing is well, they can *manum de tabula*. We will answer them both briefly: And the former, being brethren, thus, with S. Hierome, *Damnamus veteres? Minime, sed post priorum studia in domo Domini quod possumus laboramus.* That is, Do we condemn the ancient? In no case: but after the endeavors of them that were before us, we take the best pains we can in the house of God. As if he said, Being provoked by the example of the learned that lived before my time, I have thought it my duty to assay whether my talent in the knowledge of the tongues, may be profitable in any measure to Gods church, lest I should seem to have labored in them in vain, and lest I should be thought to glory in men (although ancient) above that which was in them. Thus S. Hierome may be thought to speak.

And to the same effect say we, that we are so farre off from condemning any of their labours that travelled before us in this kinde, either in this lande or beyond sea, either in King Henries time, or K. Edwards (if there were any translation, or correction of a translation in his time) or Q. Elisabeth of ever renowned memorie, that we acknowledge them to have been raised up of God, for the building and furnishing of his church, and that they deserve to be had of us and of posterity in everlasting remembrance. The judgement of Aristotle is worthy and well known: If Timotheus had not been, we had not had much sweet musick: but if Phrynis (Timotheus his master) had not been, we had not had Timotheus. Therefore blessed be they, and most honored be their name, that break the ice, and give the onset upon that which helpeth forward to the saving of souls. Now what can be more available thereto, than to deliver Gods book unto Gods people in a tongue which they understand? Since of an hidden treasure, and of a fountain that is sealed, there is no profit, as Ptolemee Philadelph wrote to the Rabbins or masters of the Jews, as witnesseth Epiphanius: and as S. Augustine saith, *A man had rather be his dog, then with a stranger* (whose tongue is strange unto him.) Yet for all that, as nothing is begun and perfected at the same time, and the later thoughts are thought to be the wiser; so, if we building upon their foundation that went before us, and being holpen by their labours, do endeavor to make that better which they left so good; no man, we are sure, hath cause to mislike us; they, we perswade our selves, if they were alive, would thank us. The vintage of Abiezer, that strake the stroke: yet the gleaning of the grapes of Ephraim was not to be despised. See *Judges* viii. 2. Joash the king of Israel did not satisfie himself, till he had smitten the ground three times; and yet he offended the prophet, for giving over then. Aquila, of whom we spake before, translated the Bible as carefully, and as skilfully as he could, and yet he thought good to go over it again, and then it got the credit with the Jews, to be called κατ ακριζειμεν, that is, accurately done, as S. Hierome witnesseth. How many books of profane learning have been gone over again and again by the same translatours, by others? Of one and the same book of Aristotles Ethicks, there are extant not so few as six or seven several translations. Now if this cost may be bestowed upon the gourd, which affordeth us a little shade, and which to day flourisheth, but to morrow is cut down; what may we bestow, nay what ought we not to bestow upon the vine, the fruit whereof maketh glad the conscience of man, and the stemme whereof abideth for ever? And this is the word of God which we translate. *What is the chaff to the wheat? saith the Lord. Tanti vitreum, quanti verum margaritum* (saith Tertullian) if a toy of glasse be of that reckoning with us, how ought we to value the true pearl! Therefore let no mans eye be evil, because his Majesties is good; neither let any be grieved, that we have a Prince that seeketh the increase of the spirituall wealth of Israel; (let Sanballats and Tobiahs do so, which therefore bear their just reproof) but let us rather blesse God from the ground of our heart, for working this religious care in him, to have the translations of the bible maturely considered of and examined. For by this means it cometh to passe, that whatsoever is sound already (and all is sound for substance, in one or other of our editions, and the worst of ours farre better than their authentic vulgar) the same will shine as gold more brightly, being rubbed and polished; also, if any thing be halting or superfluous, or not so agreeable to the originall, the same may be corrected, and the truth set in place. And what can the King command to be done, that will bring more true honour than this? and wherein could they that have been set a work, approve their duty to the King, yea, their obedience to God, and love to his saints more, then by yeelding their service, and all that is within them, for the furnishing of the work? But besides all this, they were the principall motives of it, and therefore ought least to quarrell it. For the very historical truth is, that upon the importunate petitions of the Puritanes, at his Majesties coming to this crown, the conference at Hampton-court having been appointed for hearing their complaints: when by force of reason they were put from all other grounds, they had recourse at the last, to this shift, that they could not with good conscience subscribe to the communion book, since it maintained the bible as it was there translated, which was, as they said, a most corrupted translation. And although this was judged to be but a very poore and empty shift, yet ever hereupon did his Majestie begin to bethink himself of the good that might ensue by a new translation, and presently after gave order for this translation which is now presented unto thee. Thus much to satisfie our scrupulous brethren.

(TO BE CONTINUED.)

Essays on Man in his primitive state, and under the Patriarchal, Jewish, and Christian Dispensations.—No. V.

The Patriarchal Age.—No. I.

DURING the Patriarchal age of the world, there were sundry distinguished personages through whom divine communications were made. When sentence was pronounced upon the Serpent, his ultimate destination was threatened through a descendant of the woman whom he had seduced. This has been long understood to refer to some future controversy between a descendant of Eve, and the children of the wicked one; in which a son of Eve would finally vanquish the Arch-Apostate and his race. This threat of bruising the Serpent's head is supposed to be a gracious intimation of mercy to the human race. It was certainly a very dark and symbolic one, which could not without another communication, or revelation, intimate much consolation to man. Such as it was, it is the plainest object of faith and hope found in the annals of the world for 1656 years. It was about as clear an intimation of a Redeemer, as the translation of Enoch was of the resurrection of the just. But it is to be presumed that more light was communicated on this subject, than that found in the history of the antediluvian age. The first proof of this is of the same nature as that commonly called circumstantial evidence. That sacrifice was instituted, is to be inferred from the fact that Cain and Abel make their grand debut at the altar. Now had not the historian intended to acquaint the world with the death of Abel, in all probability there would not have been a single intimation on record, either of the institution, or the practice of sacrifice. As there was no public event accompanying the institution of sacrifice, there is no

43

mention of it; but as there was a public event connected with the practice of it, we have an incidental notice of it. Two things are worthy of notice here; the first, that the most significant institution in the antediluvian world, is to be learned incidentally; and the second, that the first controversy on earth began at the altar. There too, it shall end.

Another proof that more light on the subject of religion, and of the future destiny of man was communicated than is recorded in the narrative of the first 1656 years of the world, may be learned from the Apostle Jude. From oral tradition, or by some written tradition of undoubted authenticity, he says that Enoch prophesied.—Enoch the seventh in descent from Adam, said, "Behold the Lord comes with his holy myriads of heavenly messengers to pass sentence on all, and to convict all the ungodly among them of all the deeds of ungodliness which they have impiously committed, and of all the hard things which ungodly sinners have spoken against him." From this remarkable prophecy of an antediluvian prophet, which was certainly pronounced at least 145 years before Adam died, we may learn that during the lifetime of Adam the existence of myriads of holy messengers in another world was known; also, that the Lord would one day, judge and pass sentence on transgressors, as the moral governor of the world.

That there was also a religious regard paid to the seventh day, because the Lord set it apart as a commemoration of the accomplishment of the creation, is to be inferred from the original sanctification of the day from the calculation of time by weeks, as is found in the history of the Deluge, and from the manner in which the observance of it is enjoined upon the Jews—"Remember the Sabbath day," &c. This is the language of calling up an ancient institution, and not of introducing a new one.

That there was also a title assumed by those that feared God, which designated and distinguished them from those who disregarded his supremacy and moral government of the world, is apparent from some circumstances mentioned in the brief outlines of the antediluvian age. When Enos the son of Seth was born, we are told that men began to call themselves by the Lord, as in the margin of the king's translation of Genesis iv. 26. This distinction of sons of God seems to have obtained in the family and among the descendants of Seth; and while the posterity of Seth kept themselves separate from the descendants of Cain, there was a religious remnant upon earth. But so soon as the "sons of God," or the children of Seth, intermarried with "the daughters of men," or the descendants of Cain and the other progeny of Adam, an almost universal defection was the consequence, until Noah was left the sole proclaimer of righteousness in the world. Giants in crime and stature, of vigorous constitution and long life, quenched almost every spark of piety, and violated every moral restraint necessary to the existence of society. Thus a provision necessary for the multiplication and temporal prosperity of the human race, viz. great animal vigor and long life, fully demonstrated its incompatibility with the religious and moral interests of society. A change of the system became expedient, and the world was drowned with the exception of four pair of human beings. The first act of the great drama closes with the Deluge.

Four pair, instead of one, began to replenish the new world. After this baptism of the earth,

some gracious intimations, some benevolent promises are given. As a preservative against a similar deterioration, a great diminution of animal vigor, and curtailment of the life of man, take place. This is, however, gradual at first, until the inhabitants of the earth are considerably increased. To the immersed earth, emerging from its watery grave, it is promised that there shall be but *one immersion*—that this tremendous scene of awful and glorious import should never be reacted—*while time endures there shall be day and night, summer and winter, seed time and harvest.* An institution called the Institution of Day and Night is solemnly ratified; and a rainbow of peace embraces the immersed globe—symbols of high and glorious significance, as after times develope.

Shem is distinguished as the father of blessings to a future world. "Blessed be the Lord God of Shem!" Japheth, confined to narrower limits, has the promise of enlargement and of ultimate introduction to the family altar of Shem; while Canaan the son of Ham, for introducing the vices of the old world, is devoted to a long and grievous vassalage. Shem has Asia for his patrimony, and the God of the whole earth for his family God. So begins the second act of the great drama of human existence.

Sundry minor regulations distinguish this new chapter of the patriarchal age. A severe statute against murder, and a prohibition against the eating of blood, are of conspicuous notoriety. While animal food is conceded to man, a reservation of blood, in which is animal life, is connected with it. This reservation, although analogous to that proclaimed in Eden, is not merely, nor primarily, designed as a test of loyalty, but as a prevention of that barbarity which was likely to ensue, and which we see has ensued, from the eating of the bodies of other animals with their blood. It ought to be remembered by all the descendants of Noah, that *abstinence from blood* was enjoined upon them, and that it was no peculiarity of the Jewish age. God never gave man leave to eat it. He prohibited it under the Patriarchal, Jewish, and Christian ages.

In the days of Peleg, who, according to the vulgar computation, died three hundred and forty years after the flood,* the earth was divided amongst the sons of Noah. About this time, in order to prevent their dispersion, to consolidate their union, and to gain renown, an effort was made to build a city, and a tower which should reach up to heaven. At this time another check was given to the proficiency of men in wickedness. Their having one language afforded them facilities of cooperating in crime to an extent which seemed to threaten the continuation of the human race under the system adopted after the deluge. Human language was, by a divine and immediate interposition, confounded; and thus a natural necessity compels their forming smaller associations and dispersing all over the earth. This confusion of human speech was as necessary as was the deluge; and both events were interpositions of the most benevolent character, viewed in all their bearings upon the grand scale of events affecting the whole family of man.— The second grand act of the great drama of human existence closes with the confusion of language and the dispersion of the founders of all the Asiatic, African, and European nations.

About the year of the world 2000 Abraham was born. When he was seventy five years old, he was divinely called to leave his own country and

* The Septuagint makes it 870 years after the flood, and 3232 years after the Creation.

44

kindred and to become a pilgrim under a new series of divine revelations. But as this begins a new chapter in the patriarchal age, we shall reserve it for our next essay.

Before closing the present essay, there are a few things which deserve our particular attention. In the first place, all the antediluvian patriarchs, except Noah, were born before Adam died. So that all the information which Adam had acquired in nine hundred and thirty years, was communicated to all the patriarchs, or might have been communicated, from the lips of Adam. Noah was the only renowned personage of the antediluvian patriarchs who learned from Adam at second hand. But it is worthy of note that all the information which Adam possessed was no more than second hand to Noah. Multitudes who conversed with Adam conversed with Noah. Again, Abraham was more than fifty years old, according to the common version, when Noah died. So that Abraham might have had all the information which Adam possessed at third hand, and all that Noah possessed either from Noah himself, or from Shem. So that all the communications from heaven, as well as the history of the world, were transmitted through not more than three or four persons to Abraham.

Now as human language was confounded at this time, and all the nations of antiquity founded, the founders of these nations had all the knowledge of God which Adam, Noah, and Shem possessed. Hence all nations had either oral or written traditions containing divine communications.   EDITOR.

———

"TRUMBULL Co. OHIO, Nov. 28, 1828.

"BROTHER CAMPBELL,—I HAVE been pestered with a young Doctor, who is always showing his ingenuity in descanting upon *phrenology*, and in throwing out some cavils against the bible. I handed him your September number, in which was a letter to H. M., Frankfort, Kentucky, on one of those topics I had been talking with him a few days before. He returned me the number a few days ago, saying, that "if you could prove that Mary the Mother of Jesus, was the daughter of Eli, he would give up his objection to that part of the narrative of Matthew and Luke; but," said he, "I must have the proof from the bible, or I will not receive it; and," added he, "I am pretty sure he cannot give it from that source." Will you, dear brother, give me a private letter on this subject, if you think it unworthy of a place in the Christian Baptist.
Yours in the faith,   B.

———

Reply to Brother "B."

DR. MACKNIGHT points and translates *Luke* iii. 23, thus:—"And Jesus himself when he began his ministry was about thirty years of age, being (as was supposed the son of Joseph) the son of Heli." This is not, in sense, really different from the common reading—it is only plainer. But other critics, instead of rendering it "the supposed son of Joseph," have "the enrolled son of Joseph," or "the by law established son of Joseph." I lay no great emphasis upon the exclusive adoption of any one of these interpretations. That of Dr. Macknight is, upon the whole, the plainer, and as literal as any other. He very pertinently remarks upon this verse, that we have a parallel example in *Gen.* xxxvi. 2, where Aholibamah's pedigree is thus deduced: Aholibamah, the daughter of Anah, the daughter of Zibeon. "For since it appears from verses 24 and 25, that Anah was the son, not the daughter of Zibeon, it is undeniable that Moses

calls Aholibamah the daughter both of Anah and of Zibeon, as Luke calls Jesus the son both of Joseph and of Heli. And as Aholibamah is properly called the daughter of Zibeon because she was his grand daughter, so Jesus is fitly called the son of Heli because he was his grand son."

The exposition which I gave of this matter in the September number, is, I presume, not justly liable to a single exception. That Mary was the daughter of Eli, (or, as it is with the aspirate, Heli,) cannot be questioned: seeing the Jews, who had these genealogies, never denied it, but in fact the Talmudists themselves affirmed it: for they, although discrediting the pretensions of Jesus, called his mother "Heli's daughter." No other than Eli was ever said, by friend or foe, to be the father of Mary. Let those who affirm another parentage prove it. The thing was so notorious that the historian Luke does not think it worthy of a single remark.

It ought not to be overlooked that it was as necessary that the virgin mother of the Saviour of the world should be traced to David, as that any other prophecy given concerning the Messiah should be fulfilled. For in *Isaiah*, 7th chapter, it is said to the house of David that the virgin should bring forth a son. Now Luke the Evangelist very consistently traces Mary up to David by her father, and thus makes good the sign promised to the house of David, that the virgin should bring forth a son.

That Matthew aimed at no more than giving the ancestry of the husband of Mary, is incontrovertible from the close of his roll of lineage, and thus he showed his legal right to sit upon the throne of David. But that the Messiah was to be of the blood of David, was as necessary to the completion of the prophecies as that he should be the son of Abraham. Luke gives this detail in full from Eli up to David. So that the most perfect harmony is found in the two rolls of lineage.

To cavil at these narratives, because they are not explained by the writers, and to refuse to hear any other explanation from the history of those times than what is found in the sacred writings, indicates a very unhealthy state of mind. It is, in effect, saying, "I will not believe Matthew nor Luke because they have not explained the rolls of lineage which they have given, nor will I believe them if any other person should explain them, if they do not draw their explanation from Matthew and Luke, who I previously declared have not explained them." The rolls of lineage were as public amongst the Jews as our county or state records, and all the historian had to do was to get a copy. It was not for him to mutilate, garble, amend, nor explain them. They were authentic amongst the Jews and well understood by them; and inasmuch as no Jew ever did object to Jesus of Nazareth on the ground of any defect, incongruity, or contradiction found in his lineage from David and Abraham, or in the accounts of it given by their own historians, Matthew and Luke, it is preposterous in the extreme for the Gentile or foreigner to object against such documents, when all the first friends of Jesus, and many myriads of his foes afterwards, who had access to the documents, accredited them. I might as reasonably be called upon to prove that Isaac was the proper son of Abraham, or that Judah was the natural descendant of Jacob, as to prove that Jesus was the grand son of Heli, or that Mary was the daughter of Eli. The rolls of lineage were all of human keeping, and that was all-sufficient: for if the nation of the Jews agreed among themselves that Jesus was descended as foretold, it was all the world wanted; and to us Gentiles the Messiah has not suspended our faith in his pretensions upon a roll of lineage, but upon a chain of evidences comprehensive of miracles and prophecies, sublime, glorious, and supernatural, against which the gates of Hades have not yet prevailed, and against which we are infallibly assured they never shall prevail.

I hope the contemplated discussion in April next, to take place in Cincinnati, on Scepticism, Deism, and Atheism, will afford us a full opportunity of sending to the owls and to the bats, for their lucubrations, all those little squibs and puerile cavils, which either the follies of youth or the dotage of age have impiously invented and proclaimed.   EDITOR.

Baptist Associations.

I HAVE indulged the hope for some time past, that through the medium of the "Christian Baptist" there would have been elicited some remarks on the subject of "Baptist Associations," —particularly (if my recollection serves me) as there were several queries proposed with reference to the usefulness and scripturality of such assemblies, which appeared in your paper during the past year.

In my apprehension this subject (considering its wide spread influence) is one possessing much importance, upon the supposition that it is desirable for believers to escape from Babylon.

It would have been gratifying to me if some able writer had given it a clear elucidation; but having been disappointed in this, though I make no pretensions to those qualifications which are requisite to place the subject in its most proper form before the public, yet I solicit the privilege of presenting, through your useful paper, a few remarks, provided they should be considered by you as worthy of publicity.

It is well known that "Baptist Associations" exist. The plain simple question is, Are they authorized in the Bible? Perhaps the correct course to pursue in the investigation of this subject, will be to review those passages of the New Testament which the advocates of "associations" rely upon as competent authority to support their system—and as far as I have had an opportunity of knowing their sentiments, they are uniform in quoting the 15th chapter of Acts of Apostles as a sufficient warrant for representative assemblies, called associations—and for those assemblies to consult together, and propose for the benefit and adoption of their constituents as in their wisdom is deemed necessary for their spiritual welfare; but however secure the advocates for associations may feel while resting on this position of the heavenly word, I can but conclude, that a slight examination (even) of this testimony will leave their edifice without the least vestige of a foundation, from this passage of our Heavenly Father's Last Will. If so, it must rest on the vain support of worldly wisdom,—and its true name will then be (what Paul cautions his brethren against) an "institution merely human."

We will now attend to the record, which is, that the Apostles and Elders met together at Jerusalem to consult whether the believing Gentiles were bound to be circumcised and to keep the Law of Moses: the necessity of which was contended for by the Pharisees, and Teachers had proclaimed the same sentiments among the Gentiles. When the Apostles and Elders met, they were addressed by Peter, Paul, Barnabas, and James—and finally, together with the brethren, adopted the advice of James, communica-

ting the same to the believing Gentiles as follows: "It has seemed good to the Holy Spirit and to us to impose no further burthen upon you besides these necessary things, that you abstain from things offered to idols, and from blood, and from any thing strangled, and from fornication: from which you will do well to keep yourselves. Farewell."

In all this, where do we find the least feature of a "Baptist association?" Truly there is no resemblance. Some of the characters composing the assembly at Jerusalem were of a different order in the church from any that now live. The object for which they met together, was also different. This august assembly at Jerusalem, of which I speak, had an important question to determine, for which they were perfectly qualified, and their decision is a law of the Great King. Their decree had full force, and did then and forever settle and fix definitely the controversy submitted to their consideration. Can Baptist associations do such things now? The Jerusalem assembly had it in their power to say, "It seems good to the Holy Spirit and to us."— Will the same authority be assumed by any assembly in the present day? Will they arrogate to themselves the power exercised by the "apostles and brethren" at Jerusalem? I think not. Have they in truth any rules to make, or laws to establish in the kingdom of Jesus? but these two things particularly devolved upon the Apostles. And by unerring principles they fixed by divine authority (delegated to them only by the Great Head of the church) all the regulations by which Zion was to be governed, leaving no one subject to be determined by any association, synod, or presbytery on earth, whether promulgated as a law, or put forth under the more gilded appellation of recommendation. In fact, no "association" of which I have any knowledge, pretends to make regulations which are binding on their brethren; yet, in effect, obedience on their part, is almost, if not always, the result.— To be sure, they professedly leave the churches at liberty to adopt or reject their propositions. If this be so, what possible benefit is or can be secured to the churches, particularly when it is considered that Jesus has of himself, and by his ambassadors, clearly revealed the laws of his realm, (in all of which there is not one word about "Baptist associations") where exists the necessity of human aid? Although they assemble under the sanction of long-established usage, will it be said that thus says the King of Kings? Besides, the word of truth does not authorise representative congregations for any purpose— much less to sway a sceptre fraught with great evil— for these recommendations (as they term them) go forth, clothed in effect with princely authority. But again, as to the individuals who composed the august assembly at Jerusalem, they were in part the chosen ambassadors of Jesus, commissioned directly by him to go forth, clothed with miraculous powers, imbued with the Holy Spirit, for the philanthropic purpose of proclaiming to every nation under heaven the joyful tidings of a great salvation—also to set in order the kingdom, having received full authority to command, and to proclaim the Laws of their adored Master. Being faithful, they completely fulfilled the heavenly commission, leaving nothing to be adjudicated by any "association."

Your pen has truly delineated the evils of "Confessions of Faith," Presbyteries, Synods, &c. which are really the vain and valueless appendages of the popular religious systems of the present age. But if I am not greatly mistaken, you have not put forth one argument in this field of controversy which will not apply in all their pointed denunciations against Baptist associations.

I hope this subject will receive a full investigation, and I should be gratified to see any remarks calculated to bring christians to a just conclusion.

"A LOVER OF TRUTH."

Scripture Contradictions from various Sources.
OLDHAM COUNTY, KY.

I HAVE for a long time believed that faith comes by hearing, and hearing by the word of God, and just in proportion to the strength of the evidence, so is the faith. I firmly believe the christian religion to be true; but at the same time, I am not prepared to say that I understand all that is written. In reading the old and new scriptures, I find some difficulties that my limited reading does not enable me to reconcile, and the authors consulted have failed to give satisfaction. Will you therefore favor the public with an answer to a few queries, for more than myself are interested. 1st. Who is the author or writer of the five books of Moses? 2nd. What authority have we for believing that those five books were written by inspiration? 3d. If they are not the words of the Spirit under what obligation are we to believe every thing true that is written? and if they were written from the diction of the Spirit of God, how does it turn out that Ezra, in giving the total number of the children of Israel which had returned from Babylon, which, according to his statement, is forty two thousand three hundred and sixty, when in fact it is but twenty nine thousand eight hundred and eighteen persons? The same mistake is made by Nehemiah, chap. vii. verse 8.

4th. The four Evangelists in giving the History of the Resurrection of Christ, differ in the statement.

LUKE, XXIV. 1.	JOHN, XX. 1.
And very early in the morning, the first day of the week, they came to the sepulchre, at the rising of the sun.*	The first day of the week comes Mary Magdalene early, when it was yet dark, to the sepulchre and sees the stone taken away from the sepulchre.

The query then is this—How is it that these historians differ so widely, and yet both speak by the Holy Spirit? The one declares that it was at the rising of the sun, and the other says it was yet dark.

Answer to Query 1st.—Moses wrote the five Books, excepting some explanations and additions to the close of Deuteronomy by Ezra, the Scribe. In *Gen.* chap. xxxvi. verse 31, there is also a continuation of the Kings of Edom, from the same source.

Answer to Query 2.—They are quoted by the Saviour of the world and his Apostles, as of divine authority. And the Lord, by Malachi, the last of the Old Testament Prophets, enjoins them upon all Israel as of divine obligation till the Great Prophet should come. When this Prophet came, Moses and Elias came down from heaven to visit him, and to lay down their commission at his feet. On the subject of *inspiration* see page 499.

Answer to Query 3.—Both Ezra and Nehemiah gave a table of the number of "*the men*," which

* The querist has confounded Luke xxiv. 1, and Mark xvi. 2.   PUBLISHER.

amounts to about 30,000, but in the conclusion they state "*the whole congregation*" as amounting to 42,260. Take notice that both Ezra, chapter ii. verse 2, and Nehemiah, chapter vii. verse 7, emphatically distinguish the *men* of the people of Israel as given in the detail—but besides the men, in the conclusion they give the aggregate of all who accompanied them.

Answer to Query 4.—If you will examine these passages again, you will not find any difference. Luke says in the new version, at *day break*, and in the common version, "very early in the morning." John says in the common version, "*when it was yet dark.*" The same is said in the new version. "At the break of day" it is yet dark in Judea, and perhaps it is so in other countries. Matthew has it "*at the dawn of day.*" Mark says, "early in the morning about sunrise."—But in respect to the last reference he seems to have respect to what happened about sunrise.—And therefore some point it thus—"Early in the morning they came to the sepulchre." And about sunrise, and just as they were saying to one another "Who, &c.—upon looking up they see the stone removed."

"AND the children of Levi did according to the word of Moses, and there fell of the people that day, *about three thousand men.*" *Exo.* xxxii. 28. "Neither let us commit fornication as some of them committed, and fell in one day *three and twenty thousand.*" 1 *Cor.* x. 8.

Now I request you or some of your readers to reconcile these passages if you can; if not, to show which of them is the true one: for as they now stand, both cannot be true.

Please to let this small question have a place in your first number.   J.

Answer.—IF instead of bringing Exodus xxxii. 28, into comparison with 1 Corinthians x. 8, you had brought Numbers xxv. 9, you would not have found so much difficulty. Paul says, In *one day* there fell *twenty-three thousand*, and Moses says, In *all during the plague* there fell *twenty-four thousand*. No contradiction here. You did not refer to the proper passage. Some have with good reason supposed that twenty-three thousand died by the hand of God alone, and by the sword one thousand fell. It is evident that some were put to death by the sword. But as Paul speaks of *one day*, and Moses of the *whole plague*, there is no real difficulty in reconciling them.

EDITOR.

Intolerance and Heresy, properly so called.

SCORES of such occurrences as these mentioned below, have been received at this office within a few months. Those who love the dogmas of men more than the voice of the Bridegroom, will show them more veneration than the commandments of him who alone can bestow immortality. We have paid but little attention to the voice of sedition for some time, willing rather to obliterate than to perpetuate the recollection of such measures as must one day cover with shame the actors. O that men would hear that wisdom which comes from above! which is first pure, then peaceable, easy to be persuaded, full of good fruits, without partiality, and without hypocrisy.   EDITOR.

Three Baptist churches have excommunicated each one individual for having united with a congregation of disciples who take the New Testament as their only guide in all respects obeying the practice as recorded in the fortie verse of the second chapter of the Acts of the Apostles, on each first day of the week.

A Baptist association recommended to the churches connected with said association, not to countenance a certain individual who went from house to house, and elsewhere, proclaiming the good news of eternal life by Christ Jesus—because this individual had not conformed to their views of what they consider necessary, viz.—a licence to preach given by the church—and their recommendation in this particular, as it does in all others, was effectual to produce conformity throughout their Diocese (if I may so call it) as a Bull from the Pope would be where his authority is acknowledged.

At another meeting of the same association, they published, in connexion with their minutes, a circular letter as the product of the genius of two of their number, when in truth, it was taken from an old English publication.

Yours, affectionately in love of the truth.

A Good Omen.

LOUISA, VA.

THE advocates for the ancient order in this section, are beginning to call in question some of the popular schemes of the day. At the Goshen association, held at County-Line meeting house, 1st of the month, the propriety of the general association was called in question. And after a short but animated discussion, the Goshen association broke off from the General association!!! The conflict was between Uriah Higgason, the young man I mentioned in a former letter, and J. Fife, Luther Rice, and Billingsly, three popular preachers. Brother Higgason carried his point with ease by a large majority. He showed that money was the bond of union of that association, and that it was an unlawful amalgamation of the world and the church. This I think is a pretty good step in the cause of reform, and ought to be known throughout the union. I was pleased to see some of the populars in the minority for once. I hope they will learn to be more charitable to those whom they have so much opposed.

Three Questions answered by one emphatic No!

Quere.—Is a church or any member thereof, that lives in the neglect of the duties enjoined on them in the Gospel of Jesus the Messiah, such as assembling themselves together on the first day of the week, commemorating the death and resurrection of our Lord, contributing to the necessities of the poor, worshipping God in their families, or training up their children in the nurture and admonition of the Lord, and when called upon in the assembly of the Saints, to pray, cannot, or will not do it, capable of judging of the correctness or incorrectness of the doctrine of the Gospel?

Quere.—Is any man or woman, walking in truth, that has united himself to a church, or assembly of saints, to be whispering, backbiting, and defaming those persons and their doctrines or sentiments that he never has seen, knows nothing about them, nor will he read, or hear what they have to say of those doctrines?

Quere.—Are men or women that have united themselves to a church or an assembly of saints, justified from the Gospel of the Messiah, in omitting to attend on every first day of the week, at the appointed place of worship, under pretence that they must go among their brethren in other churches, and that they are fulfilling their engagements to God in so doing?

Extract from the Minutes of the Boon Creek Association of Baptists in Kentucky, for the present year.

"ON motion, The following remarks and resolution were adopted in answer to a request from several churches composing this association, for an amendment of her constitution, so as to make it more scriptural, or compatible with the word of God, viz. This association having taken into consideration the request of some of the churches for an amendment of her constitution, after mature deliberation, she is decidedly of opinion that the word of God does not authorise or prescribe any form of constitution for an association in our present organized state. (Our constitution we have caused to be printed in those minutes, for the inspection of the churches in making up their opinion to the next association;) but we do believe that the word of God authorises the assembling of saints together for his worship; we therefore recommend to the churches an abolition of the present constitution, and in lieu thereof, an adoption of this resolution:

Resolved, That we, the churches of Jesus Christ, believing the scriptures of the Old and New Testaments to be the word of God, and the only rule of faith and obedience given by the Great Head of the Church for its government, do agree to meet annually on every 3d Saturday, Lord's day, and Monday in September of each year, for the worship of God; and on such occasions voluntarily communicate the state of religion amongst us by letter and messengers."

This is a most excellent substitute for the annual advisory councils and legislative deliberations of a church representative of churches. Any number of christians who please to meet at any time or place for such purposes as the Boon Creek association contemplates, has all the authority which reason and Revelation make necessary to acceptable service. Instead of a judicial court of Inquiry, and of resolves, we have a meeting of fellow christians for prayer and praise and thanksgiving, for mutual exhortation and edification. It would be a happy era in the history of christianity if all ecclesiastical courts, whether papistical, episcopalian, presbyterian, independent, or any thing else would regenerate themselves into worshipping assemblies.

The Unbeliever's Creed.

"I believe that there is no God, but that matter is God, and God is matter; and that it is no matter whether there is any God or no. I believe also that the world was not made; that the world made itself; that it had no beginning; that it will last forever, world without end. I believe that a man is a beast, that the soul is the body, and the body is the soul; and that after death there is neither body nor soul. I believe there is no religion; that natural religion is the only religion; and that all religion is unnatural. I believe not in Moses; I believe in the first philosophy; I believe not the Evangelists; I believe in Chubb, Collins, Tolland, Tindal, Morgan, Mandeville, Woolston, Hobbes, Shaftsbury. I believe in lord Bolingbroke. I believe not in St. Paul. I believe not revelation; I believe in tradition; I believe in the Talmud; I believe in the Alcoran; I believe not in the Bible; I believe in Socrates; I believe Confucius; I believe in Sanconiathan; I believe in Mahomet; I believe not in Christ. Lastly, I believe in all unbelief."

No 6.]   January 5, 1829.

A Restoration of the Ancient Order of Things.
No. XXIX.

Discipline of the Church.—No. VI.

In the preceding essays under this head, we have paid some attention to the nature of private and public offences, and to some of the general principles which are to be regarded in our treatment of them. We have also had occasion to call up to the attention of our readers some prevailing defects in the morality of Christians, which are not generally taken cognizance of in any of the modern establishments. In our last we spoke of the deep solicitude for the restoration of a delinquent, and long continued forbearance which christians are to exhibit towards him, for his ultimate recovery from the snare of the wicked one. But, while recommending to the consideration of our brethren the christian propriety and expediency of exercising much long suffering towards transgressors, and all mildness in our efforts to reclaim them from the error of their way, we must imitate the conduct of one, who, while attempting to pull another out of the fire, has to use the greatest caution lest the flame seize his own garments. Jude says, "Have compassion indeed on some transgressors; but others save by fear, snatching them out of the fire; hating even the garment spotted by the flesh." There is to be no conformity to the obliquity of the transgressor to reclaim him. We are not to drink a little with the drunkard, nor to tattle a little with the tattler, nor to detract with the slanderer, in order to convert them from the error of their way. While we show all tenderness for their persons, and all solicitude for their complete and perpetual felicity, we are not to show the least partiality for their faults, or a disposition to diminish aught from the malignity of their trespasses. We ought to lay their sins before them in all their true colors, without extenuation or apology; while we beseech and entreat them to abandon every sinful and pernicious way. There is often too much care taken to diminish from, and make excuses for an immoral or unchristian act. Hence we cheapen offence in the eyes of those who were wont to regard it in a much more heinous point of view. To show all willingness to restore him that is overtaken in a fault, and at the same time to exhibit the most unmingled detestation of the fault, crime, or whatever it may be called, is just the point to be gained by all those who aspire to the character of perfect men in Christ Jesus.

Indeed there cannot be too much circumspection exercised over the conduct of all those with whom we fraternize in the kingdom of Jesus. Many of those in all countries who profess the christian religion, are extremely ignorant of the dignity of their profession, and they are too familiar with the low, mean, and demoralizing converse of the world. Many of them, too, are altogether uncultivated in their minds and manners, and so completely enchased in penury and ignorance, as to preclude the hope of much mental enlargement or improvement, except from the sheer influences of reading and hearing the oracles of God. Christianity can, and does, impart a real dignity and elevation to all who cordially embrace it. The poor and the unlettered become not only tolerable but agreeable members of the christian community; and while they are commanded to rejoice in that they are exalted, the rich and the learned in this world who rejoice in that they are made low, can most cordially congratulate them on their promotion to the rank of sons of God. But there must not be, for indeed there cannot be, any insolence, haughtiness, or superciliousness amongst those who are all made one in the kingdom of Jesus, arising from any of the relations which exist in the frame and government of this world. The virtuous, poor, and unlettered christian, who is walking in truth, is just as honorable and exalted in the estimation of all the inhabitants of the upper world, as those who, from circumstances beyond their creation, have ranked higher and been more adored by a mistaken and ill-judging world. Piety and pure morality constitute the only nobility in the kingdom of heaven.

It is, too, a happy circumstance in the original developement and exhibition of christianity, which must eternally echo the praise of its founder, that the scene of its perfecting purity is laid rather below, than at, or above mediocrity, as respects all earth-born distinction. While but a few of the rich, the learned, and the noble, were honored with a place amongst the heirs of immortality, the poor and the unlettered constituted not only the great mass of the army of the faithful; but all the captains, commanders, generals, and chiefs were of the most common class of society. So that the history and biography of the New Testament present the most astonishing spectacle ever seen before—the poorest and most illiterate of men, shining in wisdom and purity, which cast into an eternal shade the wisdom and morality of all the sages and moralists of the pagan world. It thus adapts itself to the great mass of society, and proves its superlative excellence in giving a moral polish and lustre to that great body of men which all other systems had proved ineffectual to renovate, to improve, or even to restrain.

Now this great improvement is not the effect of good laws, but of good examples. No system of policy, no code of laws could have at first effected it, or can effect it now. The living model of the glorious chief, the living example of his immediate disciples, and the example of the disciples in their associated capacity, give the first impulse. The continued watchfulness of the brotherhood and their affectionate regard for the welfare of one another, operate like the laws of attraction in the material system. But not only the happiness of the society, but also its usefulness in the world, depend chiefly upon this care and watchfulness of the members of the body, one over and for another. Nothing has ever given so much weight to the christian arguments as the congenial lives of those who profess them. On the other hand, nothing has defeated the all-subduing plea of speculative christianity (as it may be called) so much as the discordant lives of those who profess to believe it. Had it not been for this one drawback, christianity this day had known no limits on this side of the most distant home of man.

Now we must admit that in no age, the primitive age of christianity not excepted, have all who have professed it acted up to its requirements. Many have apostatized from its profession altogether, and many who have not acted so flagitiously as to exclude them from the name, have, even in the estimation of their own friends, forfeited the character of real believers. Paul wept over the lives of such professors, and deplored their profession as more inimical to the doctrine of the cross than the avowed hostility of the open enemies of christianity. The hardened sceptic (for such there are who hate the

49

light) rejoices over the flaws and blemishes of christians as the shamble fly over the putrid specks in the dead carcase. He feasts and fattens in his infidelity upon the moral corruptions of those who, in deeds, deny the Saviour. And as the heavenly messengers rejoice more over one sinner that reforms, than over ninety-nine just persons who need no reformation; so he rejoices more over one christian that apostatizes, than over the wickedness of ninety-nine profligates who never professed the faith. Now as a real christian would be the last in theory or in practice to afford him such a feast, so let every christian watch over his brethren, that none of them may either comfort the wicked or afflict the saints—that none of them may encourage the unbelieving, or cause the faithful to drop a tear over his fall.

So long as a man evidently desires to please Christ, whatever we may think of his opinions, we are to love him as a brother. But when he evidently departs from his law, and tramples upon the authority of the Great King, we must exclude him.

There are some who talk of forgiving their brethren when they transgress. This is a mode of expression which is to be used with great caution. When a brother trespasses against a brother, he that has received the injury may, and ought to forgive the injurious, when he acknowledges his fault. But when a man publicly offends against Christ, (for example, gets drunk,) his brethren cannot forgive him. There is no such power lodged in their hands. How then are they to be reconciled to him as a brother, and receive him as such? When they believe, or have reason to believe that God has forgiven him. But how is this to be ascertained? When any christian has been overtaken in a fault, repents of it, confesses it, and asks forgiveness for it, we have reason to believe that he is pardoned. "For if we confess our sins he is faithful and just to forgive us our sins; and the blood of Jesus Christ, his Son, cleanses us from all sin." Whenever, we have reason to believe that our Heavenly Father has forgiven our brother, we cannot avoid forgiving him, and receiving him, because God has received him. And if he has kindly and graciously received him, how much more we, who are also polluted, and in the same hazard of falling while in the body. This, then, is the rule and reason in all disciplinary proceedings against offenders:—When their penitence is so manifest as to authorize us to consider them as received into the kingdom of God, we must receive them into our favor, and treat them as though they had not transgressed. And here it may be observed, that the more frequently a brother transgresses, it will be the more difficult for us to know that he has repented; and it may be so often as to preclude, in ordinary cases, all hope of his restoration. But before there has been any fall, it is much easier to prevent than to restore; and therefore, in all christian congregations, prayer for one another, and watchfulness, with all love and tenderness, will, than all other means, do more to prevent faults and fallings in our brethren.   EDITOR.

———

Goochland, Va, August 22, 1828.
Brother Campbell,—As your correspondence is very extensive already I cannot ask you to notice any thing from me. But should it ever come in your way, I would be glad you would remove a difficulty that appears to me connected with the apostolic office. I will first state what I consider necessary to the qualifications of an apostle. And first—He must have seen the Lord, and received his commission from Christ immediately. I need not stop here to prove this. Paul's apostleship was called in question by some of the Galatians upon the ground that he had received his apostleship at second hand, and had not obtained it from the Lord, so they concluded. His answer is, "Am I not an apostle? Have I not seen the Lord?" Again he says, in writing to the Corinthians, "And last of all he was seen by me also." So that his *seeing* that Just One and *hearing* the voice of his mouth, was necessary to his being a witness of what he thus saw and heard. They could all say, "That which we have seen and heard, declare we to you." The second qualification regards their credentials, called by Paul the *signs of an apostle:* "Truly the signs of an apostle were wrought among you in all patience, in signs and wonders, and mighty deeds." Let me name them: Speaking with divers tongues, curing the lame, healing the sick, raising the dead, discerning of spirits, conferring these gifts upon others, &c. Thirdly, Inspiration.—Their word was to be received not as the word of men, but, as it is in truth, the word of God, (1 *Thess.* ii. 13.) and as that whereby we are to distinguish the spirit of truth from the spirit of error. And lastly, they had a power to settle the faith and order of all the churches, as models to future ages, to determine all controversies, and to exercise the rod of discipline upon all offenders, whether pastors or flock. *Acts* xv. 4. 1 *Cor.* v. 3—6. 2 *Cor.* x. 8. and xiii. 10. Well, now comes the difficulty. Can it be said of Barnabas, that he possessed all these qualifications? Try him by the first.—Again, had the apostles any power or authority given them to appoint successors? If they had none, how came they to appoint Matthias? Besides, if the first rule I have laid down be a correct one, then he had not his commission from the Lord in person. It will be said that they cast lots, and that the Lord, in making it to fall on Matthias, chose him. But does it not appear that they had not yet received the Spirit to guide them into all truth; and besides it was certain that the lot must fall on one or the other of the two they chose. Suppose then that either Matthias or Barnabas had been in Paul's place, and the Galatians had brought the charge against either, that they had received their commission from Peter and the other apostles at Jerusalem, and not from the Lord in person, I see not how either of them could have answered. And lastly, would there not be as many thrones as apostles in the kingdom of Christ, and instead of twelve be fourteen? or if there are to be only twelve, who shall we say occupies the seat—Matthias or Paul? Certainly from Paul have come forth many of the regulations of Christ's house. I have mentioned these things very briefly. They may perhaps not appear worthy of notice. They are, however, at your disposal. It has appeared to me that it is as great a presumption in our day for a man to claim the title of ambassador as it is that of apostle.

I remain affectionately yours,   F.

———

To Brother J. F.

I most cordially agree with you in the last sentence. Matthias kept the twelve thrones of the twelve apostles to the Jews' full to usher in the reign of the Messiah. If Matthias had not been elected, Peter, on Pentecost, could not have stood up with the eleven. From the twelve thrones, on that day, to the twelve tribes, were proclaimed the statutes and judgments of the new crowned King of heaven and earth. It was just as necessary that there should be twelve apostles on the day of Pentecost, in honor of the twelve tribes, as that there should have been seventy evangelists sent out to traverse Judea in honor of the seventy sons of Abraham who went down into Egypt, or of the seventy senators who aided Moses in the wilderness. Paul's call and mission to the Gentiles was an apostleship *sui generis*, of its own kind. Barnabas was sent out with him as an aid. He was also an apostle. Paul associates him with himself in this office. He asks the Corinthians, "Am I and Barnabas the only two apostles excluded from the immunities of the other apostles?" But they are not ranked amongst the original twelve. Matthias sat on Judas' throne. Paul's honors are not the honors of office. He labored more abundantly than they all. His crown is no ordinary crown. He will be venerated by the Gentile world, and his authority regarded while time endures. He is *our* apostle. He was not ashamed of us, and we have no right to be ashamed of him. A hint to the wise is better than a sermon to a fool.

Yours most affectionately,   EDITOR.

Essays on Man in his Primitive State and under the Patriarchal, Jewish and Christian Dispensations.—No. VI.

The Patriarchal Age.—No. II.

THE Fall of Adam, the Deluge, the Confusion of Human Speech, and the Dispersion of the Family of Man, at so early a period, over all the face of the earth, were, under the management and gracious government of the Most High, overruled to the general interests of the world, and made to contribute to the procurement of the greatest possible quantum of human bliss, on a scale which transcends the limits of time and space. The calling of Abraham is the next public and interesting fact in the annals of the Patriarchal Age. The defection of the world from the knowledge, and consequently from the love and fear of God, so essential to temporal felicity, rendered a more clear and full developement of the divine character absolutely necessary; and for this, as well as other very interesting purposes, it pleased the Possessor of heaven and earth to signalize Abraham, and to make him and his descendants the repository of his gracious purposes, and communication concerning the whole race of men.

The promises made to Abraham concerned his own progeny and the whole world. And because of the remarkable certainty with which Abraham believed or received them, he is distinguished as the most remarkable believer who had as yet lived upon the earth; insomuch that he is called the "Father of all who believe," in all nations and in all ages.

It might be interesting here to inquire what it was in the faith of Abraham that rendered it so illustrious, and made him the Father of so many nations? Something intimately connected with our own enjoyments depends upon our clear apprehension of this matter. Let us therefore take a brief view of the call of Abraham, the promises made to him, and his faith in them. The passage to which Paul alludes (Romans iv.) upon the faith of Abraham, is found in *Gen.* chapter xv. "After these things a word of the Lord came to Abraham in a vision, saying, Fear not, Abraham; I protect you. Your reward shall be exceedingly great. Whereupon Abraham said, O sovereign Lord, what will you give me, seeing I die childless, and the son of Masek my servant,

this Damascus Eliezer? Then Abraham said, Seeing you have not given me seed, this servant of mine is to be my heir. And immediately there came a voice of the Lord to him saying, He shall not be your heir; but one who shall spring from you shall be your heir. Then he led him out and said to him, Look up now to the heaven, and count the stars if you can number them. Then he said, So shall your seed be. And Abraham believed God, and it was counted to him for righteousness." So reads Genesis xv. in the Septuagint, which is not materially different from the common version.

Here we find the reason why Abraham became the father of all who believe. The promise made to him and believed so fully by him, is this—"So shall your seed be "—as innumerable as the stars of heaven. This faith in this promise was accounted to him for righteousness. So says Moses, and so says Paul; but so does not say John Calvin nor John Wesley. One says, his system says that it was Abraham's faith in a future Messiah which was accounted to him for righteousness; and the other says it was Abraham's obedience which made him righteous. I am not to argue the case with them. We shall let their ashes rest in peace. But as for this Moses and Paul, they teach us to consider that Abraham was distinguished, honored, and accounted righteous, through believing that his seed should be as numerous as the stars of the firmament. Some Nicodemus, methinks, says, How can this be? Let us endeavor to find out this mystery.

There was nothing more extraordinary ever believed by any man, than that he, an old man, ninety-nine years old, and his wife ninety, who had in her youth, and through all the years of parturition, been barren; should, by this woman, became the father of many nations, and have a progeny as innumerable as the countless myriads of the host of heaven. This was contrary to nature. When Abraham considered his own body as good as dead to these matters, and when he looked at the poor, wrinkled, shrivelled, and drooping old Sarah, and thought that they two, old and faded as they were, should become the parents of immense nations, it transcended all the powers of reason to believe it upon any other premises than the omnipotence and inviolate truth and faithfulness of God. To these he gave glory and rested assured that God would make good his promise. "Therefore," says that prince of commentators, Paul, "he staggered not at the promise of God by calling in question either his veracity or power, and was strong in faith, giving all the glory to God's power and truth. Therefore it was accounted to him (i. e. his belief in this promise) for righteousness." It brought him into a state of favor and acceptance with God. This faith was so unprecedented, so new, so simple, so strong, as to exalt Abraham to become not only the natural progenitor of nations, but also the covenant, instituted, or spiritual father of all believers in all ages and nations. His faith, then, becomes the model of "saving faith," or of that faith which terminates in the salvation of the whole man. For he that believes that God raised up the crucified, dead, and buried Jesus, and made him the Saviour of the world, believes in the same manner, i. e. rests upon the truth and power of God; and this belief of the promise of eternal life through a crucified Saviour, is just of the same kind as Abraham's faith —the object only different. And therefore all they of this faith are blessed with believing Abraham.

The distinguishing peculiarity of Abraham's belief was, that contrary to all evidence from the reason and nature of things, he embraced, with undoubting confidence, the promise: obviating all the arguments against his confidence, arising from nature and the common lot of men, by the power and faithfulness of God. Now he that believes that through the death and resurrection of Jesus Christ, God will pardon him, account him righteous, raise him up at the last day, and bestow on him eternal life, believes in the same manner (though the object be different) as Abraham did. For though in the reason and nature of things there is nothing to warrant such a confidence, yet the divine power and veracity are sufficient to overbalance all doubt and conjecture upon the question—How can this be?

When we talk of believing in the same manner, it is in accordance with common usage. For, in fact, there is but one manner of believing any thing; and that is, by receiving the testimony of another as true. Faith never can be more or less than the persuasion of the truth of narrative or of testimony, whether oral or written. The only distinction on this subject, which has any foundation in reason or revelation, is this— that the effect of believing is sometimes called faith, which, in this acceptation, is equivalent to confidence. For example, A. tells me that the ice on the Ohio river is strong enough to sustain my weight on the back of my horse. I believe his testimony, and my faith or confidence is such that I hazard my horse and my person on the ice. Faith, then, is sometimes used to denote the effect of believing. But still, when the grand question concerning faith comes to be discussed, there can be only one faith, and that is the belief of history, or the belief of testimony oral or written. Any operation of the mind detached from testimony, may be called perception, apprehension, memory, imagination, or what you please; but faith it cannot be. Any feeling of the mind may be called hope, fear, love, joy, peace, zeal, anger, or what you please; but faith it cannot be. A man might as reasonably talk of seeing without light, as of believing without testimony.

Now the true faith has, in all ages, been one and the same thing, in kind, if not in degree. The "true faith" has ever been the belief of all the revelation extant at that time. Hence Abel, Enoch, Noah, Abraham, Isaac, Jacob, Moses, &c. were all justified by believing the communications made to them. So Paul teaches, *Heb.* xi. Noah became heir of the righteousness which came through faith, by believing God's promise concerning the Deluge, and Abraham by believing, "So shall your seed be."

System-makers, to form a theory in the crucible of their invention, say, that "all were justified by believing the same thing." But this no man living is able to show. It is true, I contend, that the ground work of salvation by faith was either prospectively, or retrospectively the sacrifice of Christ. But not a person on earth believed that the Messiah would die as a sin-offering, or rise from the dead, from Eve to Mary Magdalene. Without believing this, now-a-days, none to whom it is reported can be saved. The patriarchs had visions and anticipations of a Messias; but so indistinct, that they who spoke most clearly, Peter tells us, were not able to understand them: for, although they sought diligently what the Spirit which spake in them could mean, they did not understand its communications. But to conclude this episode: The Father of the Faithful was accounted righteous through believing the promise made to him, and all his children will be ranked with him through believing the communications made to them. See *Rom.* iv. to the end.   EDITOR.

A Letter from Rev. A. Wright, to Mrs. Lane.

"MAHONING CREEK, June 17, 1828.

"MADAM—SINCE our interview at Mr. Bryan's, I have often thought of your case, which I consider as very singular. You are a professing member of the Presbyterian church; I therefore claim brotherhood with you, and deem it my duty to talk freely with you, and give you my reasons why I think your conduct strangely inconsistent. I shall state the facts, as far as my memory serves, from your own statement.

"Your parents were members of the Presbyterian church, and you were baptized in infancy. Your husband and son had left the communion of the Presbyterian church, and joined in connexion with the Baptist church. You have long had doubts that your baptism in infancy was not good or valid. After you arrived to the years of maturity you applied to the officers of the church for liberty to sit down at the Lord's table; and after examination, you were admitted. Thus you were in full communion with the Presbyterian church—First, as a child of believing parents, you were born a member of the visible church, and consequently had a right to all the privileges of the church; but in order to partake of the ordinance of the Lord's supper, it was necessary you should act as a free agent, and believe in him; or, in other words, that you should rely and rest on his obedience and death as the only ground of your hope for pardon and acceptance with God: and along with this, that your conduct, both in civil and religious life, should be according to the rule prescribed in his holy law. Now in a state of infancy, although you had a right to the ordinance of the Lord's supper as a privilege, yet you were under a natural incapacity of doing those things which are in the nature of things connected with it in the institution—"Do this in remembrance of me;" and therefore, in a state of infancy, this ordinance could be of no advantage to you. But it was otherwise with respect to the ordinance of baptism. It was a visible discriminating mark between you, as a church member, and the heathen world—the same as circumcision discriminated the visible church in Abraham's family from the heathen world which were around him. Being in full communion in the christian church, what more was necessary to your happiness as a church member, but a faithful discharge of every duty which you owed to God, to your neighbor, and to yourself. By some means, however, it came into your mind that you were not baptized, although the church was satisfied that you were. You became acquainted with Mr. Bentley. He took you under examination, and found you were a believer, and therefore had a right to baptism. He re-baptized you by dipping or plunging you under water. After this you had great joy and more spiritual comfort than ever you had before.

"This scene I consider as somewhat similar to what took place at Antioch in the early period of the christian church, *Acts* xv. 1. "Certain men which came down from Judea, taught the brethren, and said, Except you be circumcised after the manner of Moses, you cannot be saved." So in the present case, in the act of baptizing. Except you be plunged under the water by the person who administers, you cannot be baptized. To this I answer, Had the Lord Jesus Christ, who is infinite in wisdom and knowledge, seen it necessary to make plunging under water the mode in which it should be administered, he would have said so. When he commissioned his disciples to go into all nations, and preach the gospel, and baptize them in the name of the Father, and of the Son, and of the Holy Ghost, it is not to be doubted but he would have added, *By dipping them under water.* He did not say so; and therefore those who make dipping or plunging absolutely necessary to the right administration of the ordinance, are guilty of innovation. They add to God's institutions, and to him they must be accountable.

"Mr. Bentley's baptizing you, and your submitting to be baptized, was a superfluity in you both—you both did more than God required of you. You will both have to answer this question, "Who has required this at your hand?"

"Another item of your inconsistency is, you still wish to enjoy full communion in the Presbyterian church. I think that, all things considered, this looks like a wish to serve two masters; and Christ himself tells you that this you cannot do. I am a friend to occasional communion among Christians, but I consider your conduct as doing more—you annihilated your church membership through the medium of your parents, and submitted to a condition of church membership which God did not require you to do. This amounts to what is called "will-worship."

"After your second baptism you had more joy and peace of mind than you ever had before. As a friend who wishes you real happiness, I deem it my duty to urge you to enquire into the true ground of your joy upon that occasion. God says, "The heart is deceitful above all things, and desperately wicked." Here I observe that your joy was no conclusive evidence that your second baptism was right and approved by God. When Israel had made the golden calf in Horeb, they sung with joy and danced with gladness of heart; when, at the same time, God was highly displeased with them on account of their idolatry. He is the unchangeable God, who has said, "I will be glorified in all those persons who approach to me in the character of worshippers." If we do wrong, he is ready to forgive, but we must ask forgiveness in the name of Christ, and for his righteousness' sake; for it is only in Christ that all his promises are Yea and Amen. In all cases it should be our habitual concern to keep as much as possible out of the way of temptation to commit any sin, or neglect to perform any duty—to act habitually under this impression, "*Thou God seest me,*" and under every new occurrence we meet with, to put the interrogatory, "Lord, what wilt thou now have me to do?"

"That in all things, whether of civil or religious life, you may be careful to manifest the christian, is the sincere wish of your real friend,
ALEXR. WRIGHT.
"*Mrs. Lane.*"

—

Answer to the preceding.
MY DEAR SIR,—AFTER thanking you for your kindness in attending to my case, I have a few doubts which I beg you to resolve if compatible with your sense of propriety. "I was born," you say, "a member of the visible church." Then why should I have been baptized at all, for no person in the whole New Testament history, who was a member of the church, was ever baptized? Baptism was not for them in the church, as all the New Testament writers and many of our presbyterian doctors teach. If I was born a member of the church as any person is born a

member of the state, was this owing to my mother or my father, or to both? Must members of the church *be born again?* and if so, what use in being born a member of the church if I am to be born again before I can either understand or enter into the kingdom of heaven? If I was born a member of the church, I must have been born a worthy member of the church or an unworthy one: if an unworthy one, then there was no privilege in it: and if a worthy one, was not my salvation sure without regeneration or baptism? You say, in consequence of my "being born a member of the church, I had a right to all the privileges of the church; but in order to partake of the ordinance of the Lord's supper, it was necessary I should act as a free agent and believe in him." Then it was not necessary that I should act as a free agent and believe in order to being a member of the *true* church, or in order to being a worthy subject of baptism? Then I wish you to tell me of what value is a membership and a baptism destitute of faith and free agency?

"A natural incapacity," you say, kept me from the Lord's table, which could not keep me from baptism—because the one required "Do this in remembrance of me;" yet I had a right to do what I had a *natural incapacity* to do! Philip said, "If you believe, it is lawful for you to be baptized." Now does it not require as much natural capacity to *believe,* as to *remember the death of the Saviour?*

"If," you say, "the Saviour had intended to baptize by dipping, he would have said, Baptize them by dipping." Why did he not then say, Baptize them by sprinkling? But if our Doctors Macknight and Campbell are to be believed as good critics, would it not have been anomalous to read the commission as you would have it read in English—"Immerse them by sprinkling them in the name," &c. or, "Immerse them by immersing them." If *baptize* is Greek, it must mean something in English: and if a Greek word equally means two actions, as different as *sprinkling* and *dipping,* it was a very bad language for the wise and benevolent Saviour in which to communicate his will. I should be afraid to risk much upon a language in which two actions so different may be meant by one word. I am glad that you remind me of the question, "Who has required this at your hands?" Now this is just what I desire you to keep in mind in resolving my doubts.

But, my dear sir, you think my seeking for communion in your church and in the Baptist, is like serving two masters. Now, sir, I will thank you much to tell me what master the Presbyterian communicants serve, for the Baptists do profess to serve the Lord. If, then, I thought you had another master to serve, I should not have made such a request. If it be as inconsistent to seek communion in two churches as to serve two masters, in whose service are all sectarian preachers?

It seems I "annihilated my church membership received from my parents." Now if it can be annihilated by an act of a free agent, in obeying a command which was never given to parents, but to every one for himself, is it not a very weak and useless church membership which one rational act of a free agent annihilates!

I am obliged to you for the comparison you have made for me in bringing the Israelites dancing before the calf, to my recollection, as a counter part of, or an offset to, the peace and joy I informed you I experienced on my baptism. It may serve to keep me humble. But, my dear sir, if you compare my immersion into the name of the Lord Jesus for the remission of my sins, to the Israelites making a golden calf, I entreat you to tell me to what shall I compare the sprinkling of an infant? and when the question is asked you, "Who has required this at your hands?" tell me what answer you will make, and then I shall be able to decide who makes the calf. I will thank you, cordially, to explain these matters.

　　　　　Your friend,　　　CHARITY.

Preface of the King's Translators.

[Continued from page 503.]

Now to the later we answer, that we do not deny, nay we affirm and avow, that the very meanest translation of the Bible in English, set forth by men of our profession (for we have seen none of theirs of the whole Bible as yet) containeth the word of God, nay, it is the word of God, as the king's speech which he uttered in Parliament, being translated into French, Dutch, Italian and Latin, is still the king's speech, though it be not interpreted by every translation with the like grace, nor peradventure so fitly for phrase, nor so expressly for sense, every where. For it is confessed, that things are to take their denomination of the greater part; and a naturall man could say, *Verum ubi multa nitent in carmine, non ego paucis—Offendor maculis*, &c. A man may be counted a vertuous man, though he have made many slips in his life, (else there were none vertuous, for *in many things we offend all*) also a comely man and lovely, though he have some warts upon his hand; yea, not onely freckles upon his face, but also scarres. No cause therefore why the word translated should be denied to be the word, or forbidden to be currant, notwithstanding that some imperfections and blemishes may be noted in the setting forth of it. For whatever was perfect under the sunne, where apostles or apostolike men, that is men endued with an extraordinary measure of Gods spirit, and priviledged with the privilege of infallibility, had not their hand? The Romanists therefore in refusing to heare, and daring to burn the word translated, did no lesse then despite the Spirit of grace, from whom it originally proceeded, and whose sense and meaning, as well as mans weaknesse would enable, it did expresse. Judge by an example or two. *Plutarch* writeth, that after that *Rome* had been burnt by the *Galls*, they fell soon to build it again: but doing it in haste, they did not cast the streets, nor proportion the houses in such comely fashion, as had been most sightly and convenient: was Catiline therefore an honest man, or a good patriot, that sought to bring it to a combustion? or *Nero* a good Prince, that did indeed set it on fire? So, by the story of *Ezra* and the prophesie of *Haggai* it may be gathered, that the temple built by *Zerubbabel* after the return from *Babylon*, was by no means to be compared to the former built by *Solomon* (for they that remembered the former, wept when they considered the later) notwithstanding, might this later either have been abhorred and forsaken by the *Jews*, or profaned by the *Greeks*? The like we are to think of translations. The translation of the *Seventie* dissenteth from the Original in many places, neither doth it come neare it for perspicuity, gravity, majestie; yet which of the Apostles did condemn it? Condemn it? nay, they used it (as it is apparent, and as S. *Hierome* and most learned men do confesse) which they

would not have done, nor by their example of using it, so grace and commend it to the Church, if it had been unworthy the appellation and the name of the word of God. And whereas they urge for their second defence of their vilifying and abusing of the *English* bibles, or some pieces thereof, which they meet with, for that heretikes (forsooth) were the authors of the translations, (heretikes they call us by the same right that they call themselves catholikes, both being wrong) we marvel what divinity taught them so. We are sure Tertullian was of another mind: *Ex personis probamus fidem, an ex fide personas?* Do we try mens faith by their persons? we should try their persons by their faith. Also S. Augustine was of another minde: for he lighting upon certain rules made by Tychonius a Donatist, for the better understanding of the word, was not ashamed to make use of them, yea, to insert them into his own book, with giving commendation to them so farre forth as they were worthy to be commended, as is to be seen in S. Augustines third book De doctr. Christ. To be short, Origen, and the whole church of God for certain hundred yeares, were of another minde: for they were so farre from treading under foot (much more from burning) the translation of Aquila a Proselyte, that is, one that had turned Jew, of Symmachus and Theodotion both Ebionites, that is, most vile heretikes, that they joyned them together with the Hebrew original, and the translation of the Seventie (as hath been before signified out of Epiphanius) and set them forth openly to be considered of, and perused by all. But we weary the unlearned, who need not know so much, and trouble the learned, who know it already.

Yet before we end, we must answer a third cavil and objection of theirs against us, for altering and amending our translations so oft, wherein they deal hardly and strangely with us. For to whom ever was it imputed for a fault (by such as were wise) to go over that which he had done, and to amend it where he saw cause? S. Augustine was not afraid to exhort S. Hierome to a Palinodia or recantation: the same S. Augustine was not ashamed to retractate, we might say, revoke, many things that had passed him, and doth even glory that he seeth his infirmities. If we will be sonnes of the truth, we must consider what it speaketh, and trample upon our own credit, yea, and upon other mens too, if either be any way an hindrance to it. This to the cause. Then to the persons we say, That of all men they ought to be the most silent in this case. For what varieties have they, and what alterations have they made, not onely of their service-books, portesses, and breviaries, but also of their Latine translation? The service-book supposed to be made by S. Ambrose (*Officium Ambrosianum*) was a great while in speciall use and request: but Pope Hadrian calling a council with the aid of Charles the Emperour, abolished it, yea, burnt it, and commanded the service-book of S. Gregory universally to be used. Well, *Officium Gregorianum* gets by this means to be in credit, but doth it continue without change or altering? No, the very Romane service was of two fashions; the new fashion, and the old, (the one used in one church, the other in another) as is to be seen in Pamelius a Romanist, his preface before Micrologus. The same Pamelius reporteth out of Radulphus de Rivo, that about the yeare of our Lord 1277, Pope Nicolas the third removed out of the churches of Rome, the more ancient books (of service) and brought into use the missals of the Friars Minorites, and commanded them to be observed there; insomuch that about an hundred yeares after, when the above named Radulphus happened to be at Rome, he found all the books to be new, of the new stamp. Neither was there this chopping and changing in the more ancient times onely, but also of late; Pius Quintus himself confesseth, that every bishoprick almost had a peculiar kinde of service, most unlike to that which others had; which moved him to abolish all other breviaries, though never so ancient, and priviledged and published by Bishops in their dioceses, and to establish and ratifie that onely which was of his own setting forth, in the yeare 1568. Now, when the father of their church, who gladly would heal the sore of the daughter of his people softly and slightly, and make the best of it, findeth so great fault with them for their ods and jarring, we hope the children have no great cause to vaunt of their uniformity. But the difference that appeareth between our translations, and our often correcting of them, is the thing that we are specially charged with: let us see therefore whether they themselves be without fault this way, (if it is to be counted a fault, to correct) and whether they be fit men to throw stones at us: *O tandem major parcas insane minori:* they that are less sound themselves, ought not to object infirmities to others. If we should tell them that Valla, Stapulensis, Erasmus, and Vives, found fault with their vulgar translation, and consequently wished the same to be mended, or a new one to be made; they would answer peradventure, that we produced their enemies for witnesses against them; albeit, they were in no other sort enemies, then as S. Paul was to the Galatians, for telling them the truth: and it were to be wished that they had dared to tell it them plainer and oftener. But what will they say to this, that Pope Leo the tenth allowed Erasmus translation of the New Testament, so much different from the vulgar, by his apostolike letter and bull: That the same Leo exhorted Pagnin to translate the whole Bible, and have whatsoever charges was necessary for the work? Surely, as the apostle reasoneth to the Hebrews, that if the former Law and Testament had been sufficient, there had been no need of the later, so we may say, that if the old vulgar had been at all points allowable, to small purpose had labour and charges been undergone, about framing of a new. If they say, it was one Popes private opinions, and that he consulted onely himself; then we are able to go farther with them, and to averre, that more of their chief men of all sorts, even their own Trent champions, Paiva and Vega, and their own inquisitour Hieronymus ab Cleastro, and their own bishop Isidorus Clarius, and their own Cardinal Thomas a vio Caletan, do either make new translations themselves, or follow new ones of other mens making, or note the vulgar interpreter for halting, none of them fear to dissent from him, nor yet to except against him. And call they this an uniform tenour of text and judgement about the text, so many of their worthies disclaiming the now received conceit? Nay, we will yet come nearer the quick: does not their Paris edition differ from the Lovain, and Hentensius his from them both; and yet all of them allowed by authoritie? Nay, does not Sixtus Quintus confesse, that certain Catholicks (he meaneth certain of his own side) were in such a humour of translating the scriptures into Latine, that Satan taking occasion by them, though they thought of no such matter, did strive what he could, out of so uncertain and manifold a varietie of translations, so to mingle

all things, that nothing might seem to be left certain and firm in them? &c. Nay further, did not the same Sixtus ordain by an inviolable decree, and that with the counsel and consent of his Cardinals, that the Latine edition of the Old and New Testament, which the councel of Trent would have to be authentick, is the same without controversie which he then set forth, being diligently corrected and printed in the printing-house of Vatican? Thus Sixtus in his preface before his Bible. And yet Clement the eighth, his immediate successour to account of, published another edition of the Bible, containing in it infinite differences from that of Sixtus, (and many of them weighty and materiall) and yet this must be authentick by all means. What is it to have the faith of our glorious Lord Jesus Christ with yea and nay, if this be not? Again, what is sweet harmony and consent, if this be? Therefore, as Demaratus of Corinth advised a great king, before he talked of the dissensions among the Grecians, to compose his domestic broils (for at that time his queen and his sonne and heir were at deadly fuide with him) so all the while that our adversaries do make so many and so various editions themselves, and do jarre so much about the worth and authority of them, they can with no show of equity challenge us for changing and correcting.

(TO BE CONTINUED.)

No. 7.]   FEBRUARY 2, 1829.
To the Editor of the Christian Baptist.

MY DEAR BROTHER,—I beg leave to present to your readers some reflections concerning the present state of things as exhibited in the religious community, vulgarly styled "the Baptist church of Jesus Christ;" and if you think them worthy of a place in your periodical, please publish them.   A CONSTANT READER.

Time once was, when all that was necessary to ensure the kindest sympathies of their hearts, and to elicit all that could relieve the distressed, or comfort the afflicted, was to ascertain that the victim of the wrath of man, was suffering for conscience sake—for religion. It was immaterial what was his creed—to what sect he had chosen to attach himself was never inquired—if he owned the great head of the Church, and exhibited a desire to obey him, all was known that was desired, to call forth a brotherly greeting, and an offer of protection and friendship.

It never was said, with truth, of "the old Baptists," that they were persecutors. They felt it not to be their prerogative, to condemn any man for pursuing the honest dictates of his conscience. If they could not walk with those who walked in a disorderly manner, they would walk by themselves, but they would not persecute those they left. They had, themselves, been so often persecuted for their obedience to the truth, that they could not be so inconsistent, and so forgetful of their own protestations against all usurpation of the rights of conscience, as to punish, in any degree, those whom they had in their power, because they walked not with them.

If, at any time, they were charged with heresy or false teaching, they would reply firmly, but in the spirit of the truth; and by appeals to the word of truth, and their own peaceable and unblameable conduct put to silence the ignorance of foolish men. They knew that they were accountable to the great head of the Church for the course they pursued, and therefore, so far as they knew the way, they steadily kept it. If a sense of duty to their Master, at any time rendered it necessary for them to notice any one, who they thought was corrupting the simplicity of the Gospel—no low or cunning arts—no guile or subtilty were considered at all allowable.

They withstood them to the face if they were to be blamed; and he that was of a contrary part was ashamed on beholding their virtuous and blameless behavior. Arguing, too, from the general character of these holy men, they never were unwilling to take reproof when it was proper; nor did one of them ever think of crying out "slander"—when he was himself a delinquent.

The "old Baptists" were a plain and simple people. They aimed not after honors of this world. The honor which came from God was their delight. To be numbered among the great ones of the earth, to be in high esteem among men—to be popular as teachers of their religion, never entered their heads.

Their master was a plain, unostentatious man, and so poor that "he had not where to lay his head," and his disciples never thought that their whole business was to "Lay up to themselves treasures upon earth." In all their dealings, openness and sincerity were conspicuous; and any thing like policy in their religious concerns would have been looked upon "as the sin of witchcraft."

But how is the scene changed! How different the condition of the modern baptists! Let it only be understood that any one is alive to a due sense of the rights of conscience—that he is disposed freely and fearlessly to examine the truth for himself, and to question the prescriptions of the last fifty years; and every tongue is raised against him. Every obnoxious name that can be employed is heaped upon him; his piety is questioned—and it is directly said that "God has given him over to strong delusions that he may believe a lie, and be damned."

When arguments fail to convince him of his error, misrepresentation is resorted to. He is perhaps charged with having political designs—a design, probably, to subvert the government—he is a foreigner, an upstart, and is not to be compared as to age, sense, piety, or experience, to some other foreign monarchists, whose opinions are thought to be of vast consequence in settling the speculations of the day. Indeed, sir, these things are sometimes said of you.

Thus the "modern baptists" (for, Mr. Editor, the oldest baptists of the present day cannot in truth be called "the old baptists") have assumed a character altogether the reverse of that sustained by their predecessors. Instead of being the persecuted, they have become persecutors; and all who doubt their infallibility or that of their sentiments, are heretics.

I wonder that the folly of persecution on account of religious sentiments has not appeared to the most unreflecting. A catholic, for example, (and the spirit is the same in all) arraigns a heretic. He is obstinate, and will not, because he cannot, recant. As a heretic, he must be damned. But for the good of his soul, his body is killed. And thus under pretence of saving his soul the worst of it is, he dies a heretic; and, as a heretic, must be damned. It is, too, quite remarkable that any persons who have read the New Testament should have forgotten the advice Gamaliel gave the Jewish sanhedrim.

But, sir, there is one very astonishing feature in the character of some of the modern baptists, which ought not to be overlooked. It is, that those who say you slandered them, are, in the case alluded to, far from sinless. You recollect that in the remarks on your last tour, you said that very little attention was paid to the instruction of children—Indeed that they were almost uniformly neglected. I have seen but one remark, in writing, in contradiction of this; and that was from a certain doctor of divinity styling himself "Aleph."

In one of his essays in the Recorder, he declares you "slander" the baptists in so saying. Now, sir, if he had only recollected the remark of our Lord to the pharisees:—"Let him that is without sin cast the first stone," I can with difficulty persuade myself that *he* would have been so lost to all sense of propriety, and so destitute of any restraint from the authority of Christ, as to have said even a syllable on *that* subject.

I examine these matters with deep regret. But such are the "signs of the times" that the religious public ought to be awakened from its lethargy. Its leaders are crying "peace and safety," while they are in danger of "sudden destruction." The leaders of the people are persuading them, that they could not, without sin of the most heinous description, abandon a "plan or system" (for which there is not one word of authority in the book,) in favor of what they call "an undefined and undefinable something," while these very men have declared, as can be proved, that they would go many miles every Lord's day to enjoy this "undefined and undefinable something." The letter from the church at Frankfort intimates, that the baptists are "in the full tide of success, and have been abundantly blessed by God." This latter position is quite problematical. It is doubtful whether the blessing of God has had any thing to do with the excitement. It is quite probable that it is almost entirely the work of the preachers. They themselves allow that the word of God has had but little to do with the matter, and it is, therefore, on their own principles, certain that the Spirit of God has been quite as unconcerned in it; since they contend that "the Spirit accompanies the word."

Where therefore, the word is not used, the Spirit cannot be. In a letter to the editors of the Recorder, it is remarked that very little teaching from the word had been employed in the "Revival" at the Crossings. They who believe that the Spirit "accompanies" the word, ought certainly not to aim to convert people without the use of the word, especially if they wish them to be more than mere dupes.

All the boasting and puffing, too, that appear connected with the operations of the modern baptists is foreign from the character of "Baptists of the old stamp." A clergyman, now-a-days, can scarcely leave his home without announcing it in the newspapers; and if he should be successful in his assaults upon the passions of the people by his singing, shaking hands, and inflammatory harrangues, he sits down and gives an account of the "mighty work of the Lord," to some editor who will extol him to the skies as an able "defender of the faith." In return for this he does all he can to circulate his paper, and this gives rise to another puff. Thus the clergyman is certain of notoriety—of some sort. Their return to their homes is also duly announced by them to their Editors.

I cannot forbear, either to mention another circumstance indicative of the spirit of the modern baptists. Many of the "ministry" (as they call themselves,) are in the habit of abusing you and the Christian Baptist every time they "preach." And yet every one who reads the Christian Baptist may clearly see that they have obtained a great part of what they preach from it. It is, indeed, said of the Elkton clergyman, that two thirds of his *sermons* are sometimes made up of extracts from the Christian Baptist and that the other third is employed in abusing it. The editor of the Recorder, I perceive, notices the remarks of your correspondent " Barnabas," but he does not deny the truth of his allegations—He does not deny that his " sermon" on the kingdom was derived principally from the debate on baptism. Now, sir, it must be deemed ungenerous, to say the least of it, for a man to derive benefits from another, and then abuse him for it.

" It is lawful to learn even from an enemy." And surely candor requires that we should acknowledge our obligations—or if we cannot do this, at least be silent about it, and not deride the bridge which carries us across the stream.

If the religious communities could only understand, that it is just as possible for them to worship without clergymen, as for the political community to govern itself without kings; if it were only understood, that " the Church" is the light of the World; and that the plan on which their leaders now teach them, has necessarily a tendency to render them ignorant of the religion they profess;—if, too, they knew the benefits and privileges of the liberty wherewith Christ makes his sons free—I do think they would rise in all the majesty of their strength, and consign the clergy to that silence to which their ignorance justly entitles them.

To all the abuses of the christian religion already enumerated, I may add that the zeal now exhibited by the modern Baptists, is not such as was formerly in vogue.

If a preacher can get the people converted—and boast of the number he has baptized, he seems satisfied. He goes to a place, for instance, and makes a " revival "—(for I cannot but believe that there are some men who can make a " revival" just when they please.) The people crowd into the church, and for a time appear extremely zealous. After a while the preacher leaves them, and goes, " in the character of an Evangelist," into other parts; and wherever he goes he makes a stir. But just notice the desolations which follow him.

Apostacy, with awful strides, follows in his train, and, in many instances, the last state " of the people he has visited is worse than the first." It is more important, if possible, to set the disciples in order, than it is to make them. For without they obey their King, they had better not profess to be his disciples. All the religion of a social kind, however, of the modern Baptists, consists in *hearing* preaching; and that often but once in a month.

To keep the commandments of their King, is seldom thought of in their assemblies. They have, indeed, a " sacrament " once in a while; but the reading and studying of the Word, and mutual exhortation are altogether inadmissible. None but " the called and sent" must attempt to address their fellow sinners in public, even though the " laymen" of the church, be far more intelligent in the truth than their teachers. The people are not now " kings and priests" to God. The clergy occupy this character, and the people must sit and look on, while their leaders worship. In this, the modern Baptists have aped their more respectable neighbors, the Catholics and Presbyterians; so true is it, that "evil communications corrupt good manners."

I beg, Mr. Editor, to say, in conclusion, that if our religion is what it professes to be, it is the most important thing in the world. We should not, therefore, even for a moment, allow the thought, that so small a portion of our time alone, should be devoted to it. To provide things honest in the sight of all men, is a christian duty —but to labor for the gratification of our wishes, rather than of our wants, is to rob God of the time which ought to be devoted to him—his people of their demands upon us—and our fellow sinners of the light which God has commanded us to exhibit for their benefit.

In all these principles, they were evidently governed by the plainest dictates of the word of God, which they had for their only confession of faith.

The " signs of the times" indicate some wonderful revolution in the state of the world. This every candid and careful observer must see. To close our eyes, therefore, against it, is to act as the Ephesians did, when the uproar was raised by the teachings of Paul. May God grant that all who sincerely love the truth, may obey it with one heart; and may the happy period arrive, when the disciples shall walk together in the fear of God, and comfort of the Holy Spirit, and be multiplied.

Preface of the King's Translators.
[Continued from page 515.]

BUT it is high time to leave them and to shew in brief what we proposed to ourselves, and what course we held in this our perusall and survey of the bible. Truly (good Christian Reader) we never thought from the beginning, that we should need to make a new translation, nor yet to make a bad one a good one, (for then the imputation of Sixtus had been true in some sort, that our people had been fed with gall of dragons instead of wine, with wheat instead of milk) but to make a good one better, or out of many good ones, one principall good one, not justly to be excepted against; that hath been our endeavour, that our mark. To that purpose there were many chosen, that were greater in other mens eyes than in their own, and that sought the truth rather then their own praise. Again, they came or were thought to come to the work, not *exercendi causa,* (as one saith) but *exercitati,* that is, learned, not to learn; For the chief overseer and ϵϱγοδιαϰτης under his Majestie, to whom not onely we, but also our whole Church was much bound, knew by his wisdome, which thing also Nazianzen taught so long ago, that it is a preposterous order to teach first, and to learn after, yea, that το ϵν πιϑω ϰϵϱαμϵυ μανϑανϵιν, to learn and practise together, is neither commendable for the workman, nor safe for the work. Therefore such were thought upon, as could say modestly with S. Hierome, Et Hebræum sermonem ex parte didicimus, & in Latino pene ab ipsis incunabilis, &c. detriti sumus; both we have learned the Hebrew tongue in part, and in the Latine we have been exercised almost from our very cradle. Saint Hierome maketh no mention of the Greek tongue, wherein yet he did excell; because he translated not the Old Testament out of the Greek, but out of the Hebrew. And in what sort did these assemble? In the trust of their own knowledge, or of their sharpnesse of wit, or deepnesse of judgement, as it were in an arm of flesh? At no hand. They trusted in him that hath the key of David, opening and no man shutting, they prayed to the Lord the Father of our Lord, to the effect that S. Augustine did; O let thy scriptures be my pure delight, let me not be deceived in them, neither let me deceive by them. In this confidence, and with this devotion did they assemble together, not too many, lest one should trouble another; and yet many, lest many things haply might escape them. If you ask what they had before them, truly it was the Hebrew text of the Old Testament, the Greek of the New.—These are the two golden pipes, or rather conduits, where-through the olive-branches empty themselves into the gold. Saint Augustine calleth them precedent, or original tongues; S. Hierome, fountains. The same S. Hierome affirmeth, and Gratian hath not spared to put it into his decree, that as the credit of the old books (he meaneth of the Old Testament) is to be tried by the Hebrew volumes; so of the New by the Greek tongue, he meaneth by the originall Greek. If truth be to be tried by these tongues, then whence should a translation be made, but out of them? These tongues therefore, the Scriptures we say in those tongues, we set before us to translate, being the tongues wherein God was pleased to speak to his Church by his Prophets and Apostles. Neither did we run over the work with that posting hast that the Septuagint did, if that be true which is reported of them, that they finished it in seventie two days; neither were we barred or hindred from going over it again, having once done it, like S. Hierome, if that be true which himself reporteth, that he could no sooner write any thing, but presently it was caught from him, and published, and he could not have leave to mend it; neither, to be short, were we the first that fell in hand with translating the Scripture into English, and consequently destitute of former helps, as it is written of Origen, that he was the first in a manner, that put his hand to write commentaries upon the Scriptures, and therefore no marvell, if he overshot himself many times. None of these things: the work hath not been hudled up in seventie two dayes, but hath cost the workmen, as light as it seemeth, the pains of twice seven times seventie two dayes, and more. Matters of such weight and consequence are to be speeded with maturity; for in a businesse of moment a man feareth not the blame of convenient slacknesse. Neither did we think much to consult the translatours or commentatours, Chaldee, Hebrew, Syrian, Greek, or Latine, no nor the Spanish, French, Italian or Dutch, neither did we disdain to revise that which we had done, and to bring back to the anvil that which we had hammered; but having and using as great helps as were needfull, and fearing no reproach for slownesse, nor coveting praise for expedition, we have at the length, through the good hand of the Lord upon us, brought the work to that passe that you see.

Some peradventure would have no variety of senses to be set in the margine, lest the authority of the Scriptures for deciding of controversies by that shew of uncertainty, should somewhat be shaken. But we hold their judgment not to be so sound in this point. For though, whatsoever things are necessary, are manifest, as S. Chrysostome saith: and as S. Augustine, In those things that are plainly set down in the Scriptures, all such matters are found that concern faith, hope, and charity: Yet for all that it cannot be dissembled, that partly to exercise and whet our wits, partly to wean the curious from lothing of them for their everywhere plainnesse, partly also to stirre up our devotion to crave the assistance of God's Spirit by prayer; and lastly, that we might be forward to seek aid of our brethren by conference, and never scorn those that be not in all respects so complete as they should be, being to seek in many things ourselves, it hath pleased God in his divine providence, here and there to scatter words and sentences of that difficultie and doubtfulnesse, not in doctrinall points that concern salvation (for in such it hath been vouched that the Scriptures are plain) but in matters of lesse moment, that fearfulnesse would better beseem us than confidence, and if we will resolve, to resolve upon modesty with S. Augustine, (though not in this same case altogether, yet upon the same ground) *Melius est dubitare de occultis, quam litigare de incertis:* It is better to make doubt of those things which are secret, then to strive about those things that are uncertain. There be many words in the Scriptures which he never found there but once, (having neither brother nor neighbor, as the Hebrews speak) so that we cannot be holpen by conference of places. Again, there be many rare names of certain birds, beasts, and precious stones, &c. concerning which the Hebrews themselves are so divided among themselves for judgement, that they may seem to have defined this or that, rather because they would say something, then because they were sure of that which they said, as S. Hierome somewhere saith of the Septuagint. Now in such a case, doth not a margine do well to admonish the Reader to seek further, and not to conclude or dogmatize upon this or that peremptorily? For as it is a fault of incredulity, to doubt of those things that are evident; so to determine of such things as the Spirit of God hath left (even in the judgement of the judicious) questionable, can be no lesse then presumption. Therefore as Saint Augustine saith, that variety of translations is profitable for the finding out of the sense of the Scriptures: so diversitie of signification and sense in the margine, where the text is not so clear, must needs do good, yea, is necessary as we are perswaded. We know that *Sixtus Quintus* expressly forbiddeth, that any variety of readings of their vulgar edition, should be put in the margine (which though it be not altogether the same thing to that we have in hand, yet it looketh that way) but we think he hath not all of his own side his favourers, for this conceit. They that are wise had rather have their judgements at libertie in differences of readings, then to be captivated to one, when it may be the other. If they were sure that their high priest had all laws shut up in his breast, as Paul the second bragged, and that he were as free from errour by speciall priviledge, as the Dictatours of Rome were made by law inviolable, it were another matter; then his word were an oracle, his opinion a decision. But the eyes of the world are now open, God be thanked, and have been a great while, they finde that he is subject to the same affections and infirmities that others be; that his body is subject to wounds, and therefore so much as he proveth; not as much as he claimeth, they grant and embrace.

[TO BE CONTINUED.]

Doctor Noel vs. Creeds.

IT gives me pleasure to find that Dr. Noel has given as public and forcible a testimony against creeds, as he ever gave in their favor. He has laid his axe to the root of the tree, and asserted that the "Head of the Church has long since put an end to the business of legislation for the Church—But the following extract from a "circular" published in the Baptist Recorder, Dec. 13, 1828—fully asserts the Doctor's resentment against both creeds and creed makers.

"Now, be it known to all advocates of free or open communion, that we do most solemnly protest against all ecclesiastical attempts to prescribe terms of communion. The Head of the Church has vested no power in any community on earth, to make or modify laws or ordinances. To attempt it, is an impious invasion of his supreme royal prerogative. He has long since put an end to the business of legislation for the church. In the sovereign exercise of his power as King of kings, he has prescribed the terms and conditions on which his people shall have a place in his house and a seat at his table. It may be justly expected of his friends that they will receive his code entire, with gratitude and submission; that they will not arraign his wisdom, wound his majesty, and sully his glory, by ascribing imperfection to his plan. Before they approach the symbols of his broken body and shed blood, it becomes them to wear the simple attire of saints, not the gorgeous livery of the beast. If neither Moses nor the Elders of Israel could change a pin* of the Tabernacle, can those living under the new economy open up a new way to the Lord's table and be guiltless? The Spirit of inspiration points with unerring hand to one way, leading through the sacramental grave of Jesus. If others venture to bridge his grave, in order to reach the eucharistic banquet, let them see to it. We would have you to keep the ordinances as they were once delivered, carefully observing the order as well as the manner. To observe them in any other order or manner, impairs their sanctity and divests them of their sacred character."

Doctor Noel for "the entire Code."

I am as much pleased to find the Doctor advocating "the entire code" or ancient order of things, as to see him so nobly and boldly opposed to Creedism. I do not know, indeed, how he understands the entire code. But he says that Christians should submit with gratitude to be governed by the entire code—I wish some of the populars would shew us in what page, or chapter of the entire code, we shall find a law for monthly or quarterly breaking of bread, for Saturday meetings for business—for one bishop to four churches; for text preaching, &c. &c. &c. now in fashion among some Baptists of the *modern old* stamp!!

"We would have you," says he, "keep the ordinances as they were once delivered, carefully observing the order as well as the manner." This is all I contend for—Now, you bishops of the modern *old* stamp, tell us when was your order once delivered: and where!—? Your order of worship is to meet once a week, sing two or three hymns, hear one sermon on a text, such as some you will find in this number, and hear a prayer or two—In warm times you shake hands too, but in cold times you dispense with that also. Let us have the entire code!

The following *Constitution of a Church* lately fell into my hands.—Can any one find fault with it?—Ed.

See next No. page 527, Queries 9, 10, 11, 12, 13, and answers to them by the Editor.   Publisher.

"The Church at ——, believing that the Church of God in the Gospel, in its covenant, constitution, denomination, doctrine, laws, ordinances, offices, duties and privileges, is the only divinely established order of religious society

---

*The pins of the old tabernacle were not made of hickory. But, really, pins, pilasters, and skins of some modern tabernacles in good repute, are all of human contrivance. After what model are the Baptist tabernacles of the modern old stamp constructed?   Ed.

that now exists in the world; and that all others in reference to it, which differ or are distinguished from it, in any of these particulars are schismatic, and forbidden; disowns any other church covenant than the new covenant in the blood of Christ, or any other constitution or actual state of the church as of divine appointment than that which is built upon the foundation of the doctrine of the Apostles and Prophets, Jesus Christ himself being the chief corner stone.

She acknowledges no other bond of church union or principle of christian fellowship than faith in the Lord Jesus Christ, love, and obedience to him according to the Gospel, and love to his people.

She rejects all human inventions, and sectarian peculiarities, commandments of men in religion, and acknowledges no doctrine or ordinances but those that are revealed in the word of God, and which are manifested in the words and sentences, facts, statements and connexions in which they are made known in the fixed style of the Holy Spirit, regarding the word of God revealed to the Apostles and Evangelists in the New Testament, as the proper expounder and interpreter of what is written of Jesus Christ by Moses and the Prophets, and in the Psalms in the Old Testament.

She holds Christian fellowship in breaking of bread with all the saints of God who have made a profession of faith in the Lord Jesus Christ, and are orderly members of some church, and who hold fellowship with the Apostles and Evangelists in what they heard, saw, looked upon, and handled of the word of eternal life, and which they have declared and written 1 John i. 1, 4. and who consider themselves as directly under the authority of Jesus Christ as the one Lawgiver, and the author and finisher of their faith, and acknowledge the obligation and duty conscientiously to practice the ordinances and duties of the Gospel, as they are, or shall be, made known to them in the word of God: being confidently assured that schism is a sin, and that the Lord Jesus Christ has given no power or authority to any individual, or association of men, to compromise away, or to alter or modify any truth in doctrine, ordinance, or duty, to promote fellowship or union, and that christian union, through the word of the Apostles, by faith in Jesus Christ and the government of the perfect law of liberty, is the only one practicable for the glory of God, the happiness of the saints, and the conversion of the world as is evinced in the intercessory prayer of Jesus Christ, John xvii. 20, 21.

This church admits none to membership until after they have been immersed on a profession of their faith into the name of the Father, Son, and Holy Spirit.

Queries—Answered.

As queries are getting much in fashion, I have resolved to enter them numerically for easy reference; and shall, whenever a Query is received that is worthy of solution, distinguish it no other way than by adding it to the catalogue.

Query I.

What is it to be "born again?" *John* iii. 3.

Answer. The person who first used this figurative expression was the Saviour of the world. And he explained it in the same discourse, (*John* iii.) He represented it as being born of water, and of Spirit. Every one that is born of water and Spirit is born again. But if any one say, that being born of water, is a figure, we must say, that being born of Spirit, is also a figure.— We shall, then, hear Paul, Peter, John, and

James; and they are the only writers who use any words or phrases similar to these. Paul in his letter to Titus, (3d chap.) says: "He has saved us, not only by works, but through the washing of regeneration, and renewing of the Holy Spirit." This is being born of water and Spirit. The washing, or bath of regeneration, (or immersion) is contradistinguished from the *renewing* of the Holy Spirit. These are joined together, and let no man separate them. Peter says, "We are born again, or regenerated, not of corruptible, but of incorruptible seed, viz. through the word of the living God which remains for ever;" and this word, he adds, "is the gospel." And John says, "He that believes that Jesus is the Messiah, is begotten by God."— James, in speaking of begetting, says, "Of his own will he has impregnated us by the word of truth." This is the whole testimony upon this subject. I answer, then, every one who is immersed in the name of the Lord Jesus, and who is renewed in his heart by the Holy Spirit, is born again.

Query II.

How can we be assured that this work is accomplished in us?

Answer. Our immersion into the name of the Father, &c. is an act of which we are conscious at the time, and which we can remember; and our spirit is, when renewed by the Spirit of God, also conscious that we love the brethren and love God; and we are assured, as John teaches, that we have passed from death to life when we love the brethren.

Query III.

What foundation from scripture have we to believe that we may be assured of our salvation or that our sins are forgiven?

Answer. This is a question of great moment, and bears upon the preceding. I answer it thus: 1. *No person can forgive sins but God.* 2. Nothing can assure us that our sins are forgiven but the testimony of God. Now, unless we can have the testimony of God that our sins are forgiven, we can have no assurance that they are forgiven. 3. I assert that there is but one action ordained or commanded in the New Testament, to which God has promised or testified that he will forgive our sins. This action is christian immersion.* To him that believes and is immersed, God has testified or promised salvation, or the forgiveness of sins. He has promised pardon through immersion; and therefore he who believes and is immersed, has the testimony of God that his sins are forgiven. Paul was assured that his sins were forgiven when he came up out of the water—so were the three thousand on Pentecost— so were all who believed and were baptized in primitive times. Hence they rejoiced, were glad, and boasted in God. Hence says John, "I have written to you, little children, because your sins are forgiven you." This is the testimony of God. Hence said Paul, "forgive one another, as God, for Christ's sake, has forgiven you."

Query IV.

May we believe that a conviction of forgiveness of sins in this life, is often, or ever, an instantaneous operation of the spirit; so strong, and so clear, as not to be mistaken by the person so operated upon? Or is it more frequently a gradual work, by which the whole soul is drawn to God?

* This is spoken of the salvation of sinners. Immersion is the action for the pardon of sinners; prayer the exercise through which erring saints are forgiven.

                                        Publisher.

Answer. This question is in the language of scholastic theology. It is anticipated in the preceding question and answer; but we shall give it a distinct answer. Our convictions are very frequently the result of preconceived opinions. But our consciousness of forgiveness is not made to proceed from any inward impulses, voices, or operations, either instantaneous or gradual, but from a surer and more certain foundation—the testimony of God addressed to our ears. If operations, impulses, or feelings, were to be the basis of our conviction, it would be founding the most important of all knowledge upon the most uncertain of all foundations. "The heart of man is deceitful above all things;" and "He that trusts in his own heart, is a fool." But in the gospel our knowledge of forgiveness is made to depend upon the immutable and tangible promise of God. For example, I believe the testimony concerning Jesus of Nazareth in the apostolic import of it. I then feel myself commanded to be immersed for the forgiveness of my sins. I arise and obey. I then receive it, and am assured of it, because God cannot deceive. Thus I walk by faith—not by feeling. The belief of my forgiveness now rests upon the testimony of God; and my assurance of its truth and infallible certainty, produces in me the sense of forgiveness, peace, and joy in a holy spirit. Thus I have peace with God, which rules in my heart; constantly too, for he is faithful who has promised.

All the darkness, gloom, uncertainty, and conjecture, in the religious community upon this subject, are the genuine fruits of the popular teaching. And so long as the present theories and systems are in fashion, it will not, it cannot, be any better. But so soon as men are led to rely upon the testimony of God instead of their own conceits; so soon as they understand and believe the ancient gospel, they will begin to experience the joys and felicities which were the portion of those taught by the apostles. It is the ancient gospel which will break down all the superstition, schism, and sectarianism in this age. It is, as is daily proved to us, the most puissant weapon ever wielded; and, like a sharp two-edged sword, will cut to pieces all the sectarianism of christendom, and make infidelity stop its mouth and hang its head.

Query V.

Can we not be in a state of salvation without the conviction that our sins are forgiven?

Answer. "The state of salvation," is a curious phrase. "The state of matrimony" is equivalent to "the married state." The state of salvation is equivalent to the saved state. Now, "can we not be in a state of matrimony without the conviction that we are married?" I say, No —unless we have very bad memories, and no conjugal affection.

Schoolmen have bewildered christendom with their reveries upon "a state of salvation," and "a *salvable* state." "Like priest, like people," is a general truth, with but few exceptions; and, therefore, under the present darkness, it is possible for persons to be believers in Jesus Christ, and yet doubtful whether their sins are forgiven. But this is not the only difficulty. There are many who *conceit* that their sins are forgiven, without any just foundation. They *reason* themselves into this opinion. "I feel so and thus; but all who feel thus and so, have their sins forgiven; therefore I have forgiveness." In many instances the delusion is in opposite conclusions from the same premises. One fancies himself forgiven, and another doubts his forgiveness from the very same premises. But the ancient christians had not to gather the conviction of the pardon of their sins from *internal sensations or feelings;* but all their happy sensations arose from the conviction that they were forgiven. This was derived from the divine testimony, the only certain foundation on which any man can believe or know that his sins are forgiven.

Query VI.

Has true faith in Christ these two fruits inseparably attending it—dominion over sin, and constant peace from a sense of forgiveness?

Answer. As a sincere or unfeigned belief in Jesus Christ is *always* an *operative* principle, and impels to obedience, they who possess it are not under the dominion of sin, nor under a guilty conscience. Any belief that leaves its possessor under the guilt and dominion of sin, is a counterfeit—a dead faith, and worth nothing.

[The above six queries are from Essex, Va.—and are signed "SHELEMIAH."]

Query VII.

Is it, or is it not, through faith in the blood of Jesus Christ, that we receive the remission of our sins in the act of immersion?

Answer. I had thought that in my Essays on Immersion this point was fully settled. Every single blessing, and all blessings collectively, appertaining to salvation, flow to us from the sacrifice of Jesus the Son of God. The value and efficacy of his sacrifice is the very document itself which constitutes the burthen of the testimony. Belief of this testimony is what impels us into the water. Knowing that the efficacy of this blood is to be communicated to our consciences in the way which God has pleased to appoint, we "stagger not at the promise of God," but flee to the sacred ordinance which brings the blood of Jesus in contact with our consciences. Without knowing and believing this, immersion is as empty as a blasted nut. The shell is there, but the kernel is wanting. The simplicity of this gracious provision has staggered many. Can forgiveness, they say, be obtained so easily? Did they but reflect that the more easily and more sensibly it is obtained, the more agreeable it is to the nature of the divine favor, which *always makes the most needed blessings the most accessible.* Again, as to an equivalent on our part, either as to the procurement of the blessing or as to a return for it, it is all one what that should be. We have nothing, and could give nothing. Let the wisest man on earth presume to show any thought, word, or action, by which, through which, or on account of which, a person's sins are, or might be remitted, and I will undertake to show that there is more wisdom, i. e. fitness and propriety in making christian immersion that action, than any other.—But this always connected with faith in the blood of Jesus Christ, which blood is the only *consideration* in the universe worthy of the bestowment of such blessings upon the children of men.

[This query came from Lexington, Ky.]

Of four questions from Mount Vernon, Ky. we select one, the others being already answered in the previous volumes of this work:

Query VIII.

Is not baptism by sprinkling or pouring, a valid baptism, provided the candidate honestly believes either is the correct mode from having read the Testament?

Answer. Put the terms into English, and the question destroys itself. Is not immersion by sprinkling a real immersion!!! Or put it into Greek, and it commits suicide. Is not *baptism* by *rantism* real *baptism?* And no *honesty* in *thinking,* will convert one action into another, or

make one creature another. If I were honestly to think that the burning of a heretic was acceptable to God, my honesty in thought would not make the action acceptable.

Other Queries on hand will be disposed of in their turn.   EDITOR.

Essays on Man in his primitive state, and under the Patriarchal, Jewish, and Christian Dispensations.—No. VII.
The Patriarchal Age.—No. III.

As we are left to inference to learn the institution of sacrifice; we are made debtors to the same source of information for all our knowledge of the origin of the priesthood of the patriarchal age. It appears that as God raised up, by a special call and designation, the ancient prophets: in a similar way he originated and appointed the first priest of a public character. Under the necessity of circumstances, in the commencement of the human family, *natural* brothers and sisters entered into the marriage relation. From a similar necessity, each person who offered up a sacrifice, officiated at the altar. But in process of time arrangements, called *laws,* were made for the better accomplishment of all the high ends of society, both natural and religious. As the first intimation of sacrifice is made with a reference to the martyrdom of Abel, so the first intimation of a *public* priest, is made with a reference to Abraham's return from the slaughter of the kings. Then it was that Melchisedeck, king of Salem, and priest of the Most High God, carried out his bread and wine to the patriarch Abraham, blessed him, and received from him a tythe of the spoils of war. That this illustrious priest was *immediately called,* initiated, and ordained by God, is not only to be presumed from the circumstances of his appearance in the narrative of Moses, but it is to be learned from the comments of Paul in his letter to the Hebrews. There he assures us that Melchisedeck had neither predecessor, nor successor, in his office. He derived it not by a hereditary right from any ancestor; and his office was not, like that of Aaron, to be transmitted by descent to another. Hence it was of a dignity superior to that of Aaron, which was transferable, and, excepting in the case of Aaron, was as hereditary as a family name. Melchisedeck was, therefore, invested with the office by a special call; and was publicly recognized by, not only his cotemporaries in general, but by the Patriarch Abraham, as *the Priest of the Most High God.*

The Greek of Paul in the Hebrews is rather paraphrased, than translated by Thompson. But yet he gives the sense pretty well. He says, "Melchisedeck was, in the first place, by the interpretation of his name, king of righteousness; and, in the next place, he was actually king of Salem; that is, king of peace; of whose father and mother there is no mention, no account of descent, nor of the beginning of his days, nor the end of his life. But likened to the Son of God, he abides a priest continually." Paul's design, as the argument shews, was to exhibit the superiority in point of dignity, of the office of Melchisedeck to that of Aaron. Both priests, by a divine call and investiture, yet different in order or dignity. The glory of that of Melchisedeck was, that it was underived and incommunicable. Aaron's call and appointment, were equally divine, but his priesthood was to run through many persons; each of which was to derive it from, and to communicate it to, another like himself. Moreover, the office of Melchisedeck was more public than that of Aaron. One nation only claimed an interest in the office of Aaron. But the whole human race had an equal interest in that of Melchisedeck. The fact of the patriarch Abraham receiving the benediction from Melchisedeck, and of Levi and Aaron himself paying tithes to Melchisedeck in the person of Abraham, exhibited its superior excellency and glory. No period of time, no length of years, impaired the dignity or utility of the office of Melchisedeck. And the more illustrious fact that the glorious high priest of the christian profession was constituted according to the order of Melchisedeck, and not according to the order of Aaron, speaks still more distinctly of the superior eminence of the office of the king of Salem; who wears upon his head, not the diadem alone, but the mitre also. He wears the crown and stands before the altar.

That there was a law regulating the rights, honors, services, and immunities of Melchisedeck is also to be inferred, from the aphorism of Paul, who makes a change of the priesthood necessarily productive of a change also of the law. "For," says he, "the priesthood being changed, there is of necessity a change also in the law." This was true in the case of Melchisedeck and Aaron, or it was to no purpose to argue the necessity of it in the case of Aaron and Christ.

That priests were common in the patriarchal age, may be learned from the fact that all the nations of antiquity from the era of Melchisedeck, to that of Aaron, had priests. Joseph married the daughter of the priest of On. Moses married the daughter of the priest of Midian. The priests of Egypt were a numerous class in the days of the Pharaohs. Their land was not purchased by Pharaoh, and they had a portion assigned them by the king. Young men were chosen in Israel to officiate as priests before the order of Levi was set apart. All of which facts go to show that priests were appointed in all the ancient nations before the Aaronic order was instituted. Indeed we find not only Abel, but Noah, Abraham, Abimelech, Laban, Isaac, and Jacob officiating at the altar, and performing the office of priests in the patriarchal age. So that all the nations must have derived this office and custom from those favored with divine communications. Notwithstanding that the patriarchs all officiated at the altar, yet in the call and investiture of Melchisedeck, there was a peculiarity which elevated him above all others in that age. He appears to have been as far elevated in dignity above all who officiated at the altar, above all the patriarchs who offered victims, as Aaron was above all the priests of the house of Levi.

But we are not to view the office of the priesthood of the patriarchal age as exclusively restricted to the duties of the altar. Intercession and benediction were essential parts of the services which they rendered their cotemporaries. Thus Abraham intercedes for Sodom with a familiarity and a perseverance which could not have arisen from any other reason or cause than a consciousness that in consequence of a divine appointment he had more power with God than ordinary men. For the same reason Melchisedeck presumed to bless Abraham; and as Paul argues, beyond all contradiction the inferior is blessed by the superior. For this reason also the other patriarchs who were, like Isaac, the first born; or who, like Jacob, had bought the rights of primogeniture, acted as the priests of the family and blessed their offspring and households. It was the disparagement of this honour and privilege which made Esau appear so wicked in selling his birthright for a single mess of pottage.

A word or two more and we dismiss the priesthood of the patriarchal age. The origin of this divine institution is to be found in the fact that no sinful man can have access to God but through a Mediator. This lesson was taught in every age of the world; and no religious institution, divinely established, has appeared, in which the office of a Mediator was not the most prominent part. We see the first religious actions performed on earth were at the altar. But there never would have been priest, victim, nor intercessor, had it been compatible for a friendly correspondence to have subsisted on any other terms between the Holy One who inhabits eternity, and sinful mortals. No man ever could, ever did, or ever will, find access to God, and acceptance with him, but through a Mediator. No prayers, no intercessions, no religious services, can avail to any purpose, unless this necessity be known and regarded. It was pure benevolence on the part of Heaven which first disclosed the secret, originated the practice, and through it communicated blessings to men. It was from the plainness of this necessity that all the worshippers of God, in the first age of the world, so universally and so readily embraced this gracious provision; and from the pious fathers of all the nations it became as universal as the whole human race. Hence amongst all people, however rude and barbarous, however civilized and polished, we find mediators, altars, and sacrifices. This universal usage, as ancient as the remotest annals of the world, presents to the philosophic mind a stupendous monument in favor of supernatural revelation; which, like a rock in the midst of the ocean, proves that there is a bottom to the mighty deep, and that so firm as not to be shaken by winds or waves, how turbulent and boisterous soever. How vain, then, the expectation of the Deist, who, while he admits the truth of one God, expects to come into his presence without the intervention of sacrifice, altar, or priest. But of this more fully hereafter, when we come in contact with the Sceptics.   EDITOR.

Difference between Immersing in the name, and Immersing into the name of the Father, S n. and Holy Spirit; Being part of a Note in the Appendix to the second Edition of the New Translation.

"Now I am not desirous of diminishing the difference of meaning between immersing a person *in the name* of the Father, and *into the name* of the Father. They are quite different ideas. But it will be asked, Is this a correct translation? To which I answer most undoubtedly it is. For the preposition ις is that used in this place, and not εν. By what inadvertency the King's translators gave it *in* instead of *into* in this passage, and elsewhere gave it *into* when speaking of the same ordinance, I presume not to say. But they have been followed by most of the modern translators, and with them they translate it *into* in other places where it occurs, in relation to this institution: For example—1 *Cor.* xii. 13. For by one spirit we are all immersed into one body; *Rom.* vi. 3. Dont you know that so many of you as were immersed into Christ, were immersed into his death? *Gal.* iii. 27. As many of you as have been immersed into Christ, have put on Christ. Now for the same reason they ought to have rendered the following passages the same way. *Acts* viii. 16. Only they were immersed into the name of the Lord Jesus, xix. 3. Into what were you then immersed? When they heard this they were immersed into the name of the Lord Jesus. 1 *Cor.* 1, 13. Were you immersed into the name of Paul? Lest any should say, I had immersed into my own name. 1 *Cor.* x. 1. Our Fathers were all immersed into Moses in the cloud and in the sea. Now in all these places it is ις. The contrast between ις and ιν is clearly marked in the last quotation. They were immersed into Moses—not into the cloud, and into the sea, but in the cloud, and in the sea. To be immersed into Moses is one thing, and in the sea is another. To be immersed into the name of the Father, and in the name of the Father are just as distinct. "In the name" is equivalent to "by the authority of." In the name of the king, or commonwealth, is by the authority of the king or commonwealth. Now the question is, Did the Saviour mean that disciples were to be immersed by the authority of the Father, Son, and Holy Spirit? If by the authority of the Father, for what purpose were they immersed? The authority by which any action is done is one thing, and the object for which it is done is another. None who can discriminate, can think that it is one and the same thing to be immersed in the name of the Lord, and to be immersed into the name of the Lord Jesus. The former denotes the authority by which the action is performed—the latter the object for which it is performed. Persons are said to enter into matrimony, to enter into an alliance, to go into debt, to run into danger. Now to be immersed into the name of the Lord Jesus was a form of speech in ancient usage as familiar and significant as any of the preceding. And when we analyze these expressions, we find they all import that the persons are either under the obligations or influence of those things into which they are said to enter, or into which they are introduced. Hence those immersed into one body, were under the influences and obligations of that body. Those immersed into Moses, assumed Moses as their lawgiver, guide, and protecter, and risked every thing upon his authority, wisdom, power, and goodness. Those who were immersed into Christ, put him on, or acknowledged his authority and laws, and were governed by his will: and those who were immersed into the name of the Father, Son, and Holy Spirit, regarded the Father as the fountain of all authority—the Son as the only Saviour—and the Holy Spirit as the only advocate of the truth, and teacher of christianity. Hence such persons as were immersed into the name of the Father, acknowledged him as the only living and true God—Jesus Christ, as his only begotten Son, the Saviour of the world—and the Holy Spirit as the only successful advocate of the truth of christianity upon earth. Pagans, therefore, when immersed into the name of the Father, &c. renounced all the names that were worshipped by the Pagan world—all the saviours in which the Gentiles trusted; and all the inspiration and philosophy of which the heathen boasted. A woman, when she enters into matrimony, assumes the name of her husband, acknowledges him as her Lord and master, submits to his will, and looks to him for protection and support. Just so they who are immersed into the name of Christ, assume his name, acknowledge him as Lord and Master, and look to him for support and protection. This view of the matter made Paul thank God when the christians of Corinth were assuming different names, (one the name of Paul, and another the name of Apollos, &c.) that he had immersed few or none of them, lest the report should get abroad that he had immersed them into his own name.

"But as this criticism is already too long, we shall only add that it would be quite anomalous to suppose that the command in the commission to make disciples, immersing them into the name of the Father, Son, and Holy Spirit, means by the authority of. There is not one solitary example of the sort in all the oracles. Nothing is commanded to be done by the authority of the Father, Son, and Holy Spirit. In the antecedent economy the supreme authority was in the name of the Father. In the present economy the supreme authority is in the name of the Lord Jesus. But in no economy (for it is contrary to the genius of every economy) is the name of the Holy Spirit used as authoritative. Nothing was ever commanded to be done in the name, or by the authority of the Holy Spirit. When we speak of authority here, it is not the authority of a teacher, but the authority of a governor or lawgiver—a king or ruler. There is one sort of authority of which the Holy Spirit is possessed; and that is, to take the things of Christ and reveal them to us. His authority as a teacher we cheerfully submit to, but we speak here of the gubernatorial authority, the authority which a governor possesses. Invested with this authority, the Lord Jesus, in conjunction with his Father, sent the Holy Spirit to advocate his cause. The Father never gave the power of judging to the Holy Spirit. This he has given into the hands of the Lord Jesus. The Lord Messiah shall judge the world, and therefore by his authority all things are to be done in his kingdom. When Peter ordered the Gentiles to be immersed, he did it by the authority of the Lord Jesus. He says, "In the name of the Lord immerse them." Here it is, εν ονοματι, and not εις το ονομα. And it is by the authority of the Lord Jesus, or in the name of the Lord, that persons are to be immersed into the name of the Father, Son, and Holy Spirit. The great importance of the matters involved in this criticism will be a sufficient apology for the length of it. Indeed I scarcely know any criticism upon a single syllable, of so much importance, in all the range of my conceptions, as this one."

President Edwards, on Fulfilling Engagements and Paying Debts.

"Thou shalt not steal."—*Decalogue.*

——"They violate this command, in withholding what belongs to their neighbour, when they are not faithful in any business which they have undertaken to do for their neighbour. If their neighbour has hired them to labor for him for a certain time, and they be not careful well to husband the time; if they be hired to day's labor, and be not careful to improve the day, as they have reason to think he who hired them justly expected of them; or if they be hired to accomplish such a piece of work, and be not careful to do it well, but do it slightly, do it not as if it were for themselves, or as they would have others do for them, when they in like manner intrust them with any business of theirs; or if they be intrusted with any particular affair, which they undertake, but use not that care, contrivance, and diligence, to manage it so as will be to the advantage of him who intrusts them, and as they would manage it, or would insist that it should be managed, if the affair were their own; in all these cases they unjustly withhold what belongs to their neighbor.

"Another way in which men unjustly withhold what is their neighbor's, is in neglecting to pay their debts. Sometimes this happens because they run so far into debt that they cannot reasonably hope to be able to pay their debts; and this they do, either through pride and affectation of living above their circumstances, or through a grasping, covetous disposition, or some other corrupt principle. Sometimes they neglect to pay their debts from carelessness of spirit about it, little concerning themselves whether they are paid or not, taking no care to go to their creditor's, or to send to him; and if they see him from time to time, they say nothing about their debts. Sometimes they neglect to pay their debts because it would put them to some inconvenience. The reason why they do it not, is not because they cannot do it, but because they cannot do it so conveniently as they desire; and so they rather choose to put their creditor to inconvenience by being without what properly belongs to him, than to put themselves to inconvenience by being without what does not belong to them, and what they have no right to detain. In any of these cases, they unjustly usurp the property of their neighbor.

"Sometimes persons have that by them with which they could pay their debts if they would; but they want to lay out their money for something else, to buy gay clothing for their children, or to advance their estates, or for some such end. They have other designs in hand, which must fail if they pay their debts. When men thus withhold what is due, they unjustly usurp what is not their own. Sometimes they neglect to pay their debts, and their excuse for it is, that their creditor does not need it; that he has a plentiful estate, and can well bear to lie out of his money. But if the creditor be ever so rich, that gives no right to the debtor to withhold from him that which belongs to him. If it be due, it ought to be paid; for that is the very notion of its being due. It is no more lawful to withhold from a man what is his due, without his consent, because he is rich and able to do without it, than it is lawful to steal from a man because he is rich and able to bear the loss." [Wholesome doctrine.]

No. 8.]   MARCH 2, 1829.

Election.—No. I.

Our readers will recollect that in some of the previous volumes of this work we promised them a disquisition upon Election. Other matters pressing upon us we have delayed till now, and should probably have delayed still longer, had not a brother, much esteemed both on account of his clear and comprehensive views of the whole Institution of Heaven, and for his zeal and labors in the ancient gospel—made us a visit, and volunteered an essay or two on this subject. Our agreement in sentiment and views of the christian religion being so exact in all matters hitherto discussed, I fear not to answer for him on this subject. If any ambiguity should, in the apprehension of our numerous readers, still rest upon the subject, I promise to elucidate this topic at full length. In the mean time I give place to him, as other matters now engross my attention.   EDITOR.

"Migrati Coloni."

When the apostles preached the gospel they gave commandment to the discipled to retain it as it had been delivered to them, anathematizing man and angel who should dare to disorder, alter, or corrupt it. The whole New Testament was written either to establish or defend it, or to detach it from the corruptions of Jews and Gentiles, to whom it was either a stumbling block or an institution of manifest foolishness.

The Epistle to the Galatians is directed against the corruptions of the former, who, under the mask of an affected zeal for the law of Moses, eagerly desired, like some modern zealots, to superadd it as "a rule of life." But "if I or an angel," says the Apostle, "preach any thing else to you for gospel, let him be accursed," and he repeats the anathema. The four Evangelists, the great bulwarks of christianity, are for the purpose of supporting its reality on the principle of the conformity of its author's birth, life, offices, death, resurrection, and glorification to the predictions of the ancient oracles and the great power of God. The Acts are a history of its publication; and as there were not wanting among the Greeks those who sufficiently abhorred the resurrection, the reader will find this part of the gospel abundantly defended and illustrated in the 15th chapter of 1st Corinthians. Besides perverting and maiming the glad tidings, some would have circumscribed its entire influence to the Jewish nation, and "forbid it to be preached to the Gentiles."

The gospel proposes three things as the substance of the glad tidings to mankind—the remission of sins, the Holy Spirit, and eternal life; and the apostles every where, in conformity with their mission, plead for reformation towards God and faith in our Lord Jesus Christ, as the state of mind adapted to the reception of these inestimable blessings. In the proclamation of the gospel, therefore, these high matters were ordered thus—faith, reformation, baptism for the remission of sins, the Holy Spirit, and eternal life; but how this order has been deranged, some things added, some subtracted, and others changed, must be manifest to all who know, and, alas! who does not know this, that even now whole bodies of worshippers deny the resurrection of the body; some would, to this day, superadd the law as "a rule of life;" others deny the gift of a Holy Spirit; the Socinians totally object to the sacrifice; and almost all who do embrace it reject nevertheless the remission of sins in baptism, which the sacrifice has so greatly secured to all who believe and reform.

Some have substituted sprinkling, some the mourning bench, for the baptism of remission; and even those who most of all affect to be orthodox, publicly preach in direct contradiction to God's most universal commandment, that a man can neither believe nor repent; they publish that faith comes by the Spirit, and not by the word, "thus making the word of God of non-effect," and contradicting the apostles, who every where speak of the Spirit as a "Spirit of promise" to those who should receive the gospel. Others will immerse, but not for the remission of sins; and others preach the gospel maimed, disordered, changed, and corrupted, in connexion with a scholastic election, which not only retards the progress of the glad tidings, but opposes itself to christian election—to political election—to all rational ideas of election, and causes the entire gospel to stink in the estimation of all unprejudiced men.

The Apostles never preached election to unconverted people as the Calvinists do; and the disciples themselves were never spoken to on this matter as persons who had believed, because they were elect, but rather as those who were elected because they had believed—"formerly you were not a people, but now you are the people of God;" "you are an elect race;" "make your calling and election sure." After preaching the ancient gospel for a long time, I am finally convinced nothing, not even the grossest immorality, is so much opposed to its progress, as the scholastic election, which, indeed, is just the old fatalism of the Greeks and Romans.

Every election necessarily suggests to us six things—the elector or electors—the person or persons elected—the principle on which the election proceeds—the ends to be accomplished by it —when the election commenced, and when it shall cease. Let us peep at the scripture election, in this order; and, first, in regard to the elector. No one, I presume, will dispute that God is He. 2d. As for the person or persons elected, I would just observe, in accordance with the ancient oracles, that, although there were in the world previous to the days of Abraham, and even during the life of that patriarch, many who feared God and wrought righteousness; yet till then none but he ever worshipped the true God in the character of an elect person. Elect and election are words which do not occur in scripture with a reference to any who lived before Abraham; previously there were no elect head, no elect body, no elect principles, no ends to be accomplished by an elect institution; and therefore the scriptures speak of none of his contemporaries as they speak of Abraham: "Thou art the God who didst choose (i. e. elect) Abraham." This patriarch, therefore, is positively and scripturally the first elect person mentioned in the divine oracles; consequently the history of the doctrine of election commences with the fact of God's having chosen, for general and magnanimous purposes, this ancient worthy. But the choice of Abraham was accompanied with the following promise, which at once reflected the highest praise on God and honor on the patriarch: "In you and in your seed shall all the nations of the earth be blessed." Now the Apostle, in Galatians iii. says, "The seed is Christ." Substituting, therefore the definition for the term itself, then the promise would read, "In you and in Jesus Christ, or the Messiah, shall all the families of the earth be blessed." God here, then, has set forth two persons in which a man may certainly be blessed: for let it be attentively noticed that it is in Abraham and Christ, not out of them, that the blessing is to be obtained.— Christ and Abraham only are here represented as being strictly and primarily elect persons; for it is said of Christ, "Behold my elect." All other persons must be found in them before they are elect, and as a person can be related to Abraham and Christ only in one of two ways, i. e, by flesh or faith, it follows that if any one, from the patriarch's time to the present, would enjoy the blessing of an elect person or worshipper of the true God, he must be a child of Abraham. By one or both of these principles he must be a Jew or a Christian.   PHILIP.

Preface of the King's Translators.
[Continued from page 518.]

——"ANOTHER thing we think good to admonisn thee of (gentle reader) that we have not tied our selves to an uniformity of phrasing or to an identitie of words, as some peradventure would wish that we had done, because they observe, that some learned men somewhere, have been as exact as they could that way. Truly, that we might not vary from the sense of that which we had translated before, if the word signified the same thing in both places (for there be some words that be not of the same sense every where) we were especially carefull, and made a conscience according to our duty. But that we should express the same notion in the same particular word; as for example, if we translate the Hebrew or Greek word once by *purpose*, never to call it *intent*; if one where *journeying*, never *travelling*; if one where *think*, never *suppose*; if one where *pain*, never *ache*; if one where *joy*, never *gladnesse*, &c. Thus to mince the matter, we thought to savour more of curiosity then of wisdome, and that rather it would breed scorn in the Atheist, then bring profit to the godly reader. For is the kingdom of God become words or syllables? why should we be in bondage to them if we may be free? use one precisely, when we may use another no lesse fit, as commodiously? A godly Father in the primitive time showed himself greatly moved, that one of newfanglednesse called κρυββαλον, σκιμπους, though the difference be little or none; and another reporteth that he was abused for turning *cucurbita* (to which reading the people had been used) into *hedera*. Now if this happen in better times, and upon so small occasions, we might justly fear hard censure, if generally we should make verball and unnecessary changings. We might also be charged (by scoffers) with some unequall dealing towards a great number of good English words. For as it is written of a certain great philosopher, that he should say, that those logs were happy that were made images to be worshipped; for their fellows, as good as they, lay for blocks behind the fire; so if we should say, as it were, unto certain words, Stand up higher, have a place in the Bible alwayes; and to others of like quality, Get ye hence, be banished for ever; we might be taxed peradventure with S. James his words; namely, *To be partiall our selves, and judges of evil thoughts*. Add hereunto, that nicenesse in words was alwayes counted the next step to trifling, and so was to be curious about names too; also that we cannot follow a better pattern for elocution than God himself; therefore he using divers words, in his holy writ, and indifferently for one thing in nature: we, if we will not be superstitious, may use the same libertie in our English versions out of Hebrew and Greek, for that copie or store that he hath given us. Lastly, we have on the one side avoided the scrupulositie of the Puritanes, who leave the old ecclesiasticall words, and betake them to other, as when they put *washing* for *baptisme*, and *congregation* instead of *church*; as also on the other side, we have shunned the obscurity of the Papists, in their *azymes*, *tunike*, *rationall*, *holocausts*, *prepuce*, *pasche*, and a number of such like, whereof their late translation is full, and that of purpose to darken the sense; that since they must needs translate the Bible, yet by the language thereof, it may be kept from being understood. But we desire that the Scripture may speak like itself, as in the language of Canaan, that it may be understood even of the very vulgar.

Many other things we might give thee warning of (gentle reader) if we had not exceeded the measure of a preface already. It remaineth that we commend thee to God, and to the Spirit of his grace, which is able to build further than we can ask or think. He removeth the scales from our eyes, the vail from our hearts, opening our wits that we may understand his word, enlarging our hearts, yea correcting our affections, that we may love it above gold and silver, yea that we may love it to the end. Ye are brought unto fountains of living water which ye digged not; do not cast earth into them with the Philistines, neither preferre broken pits before them with the wicked Jews. Others have laboured, and you may enter into their labours. O receive not so great things in vain; O despise not so great salvation. Be not like swine to tread under foot so precious things, neither yet like dogs to tear and abuse holy things. Say not to our Saviour with the Gergesites, Depart out of our coasts; neither yet with Esau, sell your birthright for a messe of pottage. If light be come into the world, love not darknesse more then light: if food, if clothing be offered, go not naked, starve not yourselves. Remember the advice of Nazianzen, *It is a grievous thing* (or dangerous) *to neglect a great fair, and to seek to make markets afterwards:* also the encouragement of S. Chrysostome, *It is altogether impossible, that he that is sober (and watchful) should at any time be neglected:* lastly, the admonition and menacing of St. Augustine, *They that despise Gods will inviting them, shall feel Gods will taking vengeance of them.* It is a fearfull thing to fall into the hands of the living God; but a blessed thing it is, and will bring us to everlasting blessednesse in the end, when God speaketh unto us, to hearken; when he setteth his word before us, to read it; when he stretcheth out his hand and calleth, to answer, Here am I, here are we to do thy will, O God. The Lord work a care and conscience in us to know him and serve him, that we may be acknowledged of him at the appearing of our Lord Jesus Christ, to whom with the Holy Ghost, be all praise and thanksgiving. Amen.

Dialogue between the Editor of the Christian Baptist and Adelphos.

Adel.—And so, Mr. Editor, like the rest of your brethren, you report the revivals, but say nothing of the declensions: you tell of the conversions, but are mute concerning the apostacies! Is this fair play with the public?

Ed.—Have there been any remarkable apostacies? I have not seen nor heard it announced, and why should I be culpable in omitting to report that which has not been reported to me? Or do you expect that I must, like many others in the absence of news, manufacture a supply for the Athenian taste of the times?

Adel.—Apostacies! Yes! Your correspondents are certainly remiss or unfaithful if they do not inform you of them. I have heard of many in my late tour through Ohio and Kentucky. In one single day nine of the new converts in Cincinnati were thrown over the fence; and I can't enumerate how many twos, and threes, and fives, and sevens, I have met with in my travels, in the train of these great excitements. As Morgan says in his "Illustrations of Masonry"—(I mean Morgan *the martyr*)—"many of the initiated never revisit the Lodge:" so many of these converts mix immediately with the world, and indeed before they were well separated from it.

Ed.—This I am sorry to hear, for the sake of the apostates and for the sake of those who are spectators standing all the day idle. But still I hope these are but as a few grains of chaff in many bushels of wheat.

Adel.—Would to Heaven that were all! But I rather fear the real converts are like a few grains of wheat in many bushels of chaff! Indeed how can it be otherwise? What converted them? It was, I fear, neither the word nor Spirit of God. As for the word of God, they heard little or nothing of it and if the popular doctrine be true, that the Spirit accompanies the word, I am sure the Spirit could not convert them: for there was no word preached for it to accompany. And unless the Spirit accompanies the bible and makes it operate like a charm in

the sacred desk or by the fireside, unread or unheard, it was impossible for it to have any thing to do in most of these conversions. But there are other spirits besides the Spirit of God, which convert men, if I may believe either the bible or the Christian Baptist.

Ed.—You are certainly mistaken or misinformed about this matter. For I know many of the actors in these great excitements: and I know that they are men mighty and eloquent in the scriptures, and that they would not give a bean for any conversion not proceeding from the knowledge and belief of the gospel. I think some enemy has prejudiced your mind against this work and these workmen, and has exaggerated the apostacies. I was so doubtful of these conversions, that when I visited the Mahoning Association last August, I was asking every person who could inform me both of the means employed in the great conversions in that quarter, and also of the behavior of the converts. I was also particular in inquiring about the apostacies, and found that they were free from these exceptions, and that in about one thousand conversions in one year, in that district of country, not more than six or seven individuals had turned away from the holy commandment. But, indeed, the gospel was clearly and fully proclaimed with its evidences, its glorious and awful sanctions; and the disciples were as remarkable for their knowledge as for their zeal. Farther than this I cannot say from observation, for I have been pretty much confined at home during the past year.

Adel.—Of your Western Reserve preachers and people I know nothing. I heard, indeed, that their procedure was unlike any other that had ever happened in that country. But I must claim the right of affirming what I do know, and of declaring what I have seen. And I am assured that it was neither the word nor Spirit of God that converted many of those reported cases in the vicinities through which I have passed. Nay, did you not see it announced in the Baptist Recorder, that "very little teaching or preaching from the word was engaged in, in the great revivals about Georgetown and Frankfort, Ky." This is a speaking fact; and I am pretty well acquainted with the managements there. Singing, shaking of hands, and now and then an inflammatory exhortation taking hold of the animal frame, more than the intellectual man, did more than all that Paul, Apollos, or Cephas said, to bring them in scores into the water. Yes, I have known an Indian carried by a brother preacher from the Great Crossings to Frankfort, to be the proximate cause of many conversions.

Ed.—Stop, friend Adelphos. Have they got Indians yet in Kentucky? Tell me how can this be—An Indian the means of converting the citizens of Frankfort! You certainly proceed too fast. Like Nicodemus I must exclaim, How can this be?

Adel.—Indeed you are considered, Mr. Editor, very much like Nicodemus, by the regenerated. You are said to be as ignorant of the new birth as was the great Rabbi Nicodemus. I will explain this Indian affair, and by this means you may be instructed more perfectly in the new birth. There are a few domesticated Indians in the neighborhood of Georgetown, Ky., who are a training there for God and their countrymen. Some of these have been converted in the late revival; and our brother of Oakley, who has been the hero of two or three great revivals, in order to produce a good effect in Frankfort, had one of these Indians and a few of the finest and loudest singers of the new converts at the Great Crossings, conveyed to the seat of government. A *big* meeting was appointed. A brother J. A. Butler made a sermon. The Doctor *gave out a hymn.* A verse or two was sung. In this opportune moment, by preconcert or otherwise, the Indian arose—stretched out, *like Ethiopia*, his red hands to the good citizens of Frankfort. This set them all on fire. The flame was not extinguished from Friday evening till Monday morning. It was a glorious season! Singing, shaking of hands, and praying, with some appeals to the passions, were the order of the day, and of the *night* too, until the animal passions began to lag. Now, Mr. Editor, was this the ancient order of converting men to God? Or is this the way the kingdom of Jesus is to be built up in the world? If so, why not pursue this same course? Why are not our meeting houses built with "anxious seats" in them, and "big meetings" kept up, and all this shaking of hands, shouting, and singing, in continual operation? Or are there times for converting folks, and a time for not converting them? For my part I am conscious it is all a work of human contrivance and management from first to last. And I can tell a story about the commencement of it that must convince all. It was brother Nathan Hall, of Lexington, a good Presbyterian, that began the whole affair, as I will tell you.

Ed.—Stop, my friend, for a few moments, and tell me if you judge that all excitements and revivals are similar to that which you have been describing. For my part I must tell you that I do not think so. The magicians I know could work miracles in the eyes of the Egyptians as well as Moses. But still I contend that Moses wrought miracles by the finger of God.

Adel.—As you interrupted me, I need scarcely beg pardon for interrupting you. "The magicians could work miracles," you say. Well, that is just to my point. And so can our christian magicians work miracles too, and I have seen many of them.

Ed.—I will not dispute this point with you, for I must always yield to evidence. But remember Moses wrought miracles by the finger of God.

Adel.—Yes, but this is hardly to the point; and as you are a scripturean, you know that there were many magicians and one Moses. Jannes and Jambres, and many others of less fame, beguiled the Egyptians, and discredited the mission of Moses; and these revival making spirits were determined to discredit your pretensions to a Restorer. But I can make this matter plain if you will let me tell my story out about how this machine was put in motion. I was telling you that brother Hall of Lexington, and brother M'Farland of Paris,——

Ed.—Well, well, I can never infer a general principle or conclusion from a particular; for if I have not forgot all my logic, particulars are contained in generals, and can be inferred from them; but generals are not contained in particulars, and cannot be inferred from them. But without going into the detail, I must admit that your first position is a pretty plausible one—that many of those who fall away are neither converted by the word or Spirit of God.

Adel.—If you will not hear my recital now, will you hear a sermon which I heard preached for a specimen?

Ed.—If it bears upon the subject; for I wish to keep to one point at a time.

Adel.—It will bear upon the subject so far as to show what sort of a *word* it is which the Spirit must accompany, if it accompanies all, or most

of our called and missioned divines. My friend, the preacher is very zealous; and you might as well persuade some folks that Paul was not commissioned from Heaven, as that he is not. His text was, "*Paul's Shipwreck.*" His method was to show—

1. That the ship was the gospel, and exhibited its essential doctrines.

2. The escape of the mariners and prisoners denoted the salvation of the elect.

In the illustration of the first head he demonstrated the following particulars:—

1. The three masts denoted the three persons in one Divinity, because the three masts made but one ship.

2. The prow denoted the divinity of the Saviour, and the stern his humanity—their union, the union of the two natures.

3. The two seas meeting upon the ship, denoted the wrath of God and the malice of the Devil, concentrating upon the Saviour in his last scene.

4. The hinder part of the ship breaking, represented the weakness and death of the humanity of the Saviour.

5. Their throwing overboard the tackling of the ship, denoted saints renouncing all their own works.

In the demonstration of the second head, he showed—

1st. That the saints by taking hold of Christ, as the sailors and prisoners took hold of the plank and broken pieces of the ship, kept themselves from sinking under trials.

2d. Their swimming safe to land, denoted the sure and certain perseverance of all the saints.

3d. Their all getting safe to shore, proves the ultimate salvation of all the elect. And,

4th. Paul's behaviour during the scene of the shipwreck, denoted the use of gospel preachers, in aiding, directing, and encouraging the elect in the way of salvation.

Ed.—Is this fiction or reality?

Adel.—It is as true as preaching, and truer than the half of that.

Ed.—Have you neither added nor diminished?

Adel.—I have *diminished;* for he spiritualized many other occurrences which I cannot now recal.

Ed.—And how was it received by the hearers?

Adel.—It was well received; and the preacher praised, both for his profound knowledge of the spiritual sense of scripture, and extolled for his genuine orthodoxy.

Ed.—Well, I am sure none could be converted by such preaching.

Adel.—One would think so; but if you had heard them sigh and scream when he told of the lashings of the storm upon the dear Saviour, and of the breaking up of the stern, you would have thought they were well nigh converted.

Ed.—From such converts, and such conversions, may the good Lord deliver the church!

Adel.—From this prayer I cannot withhold my *Amen.* I have something more to add, but must defer it for the present.

Queries—Answered.

"Open Communion."

Query IX. Have you any objection to the Constitution of a Church, published in your last number? (page 519.)

Answer.—I have. I object to both matter and form. This Constitution or Covenant, besides other minor matters, is objectionable because it admits an *unimmersed* person to all the ordinances of the christian community or congregation, as an *occasional* member; and yet refuses to receive such as regular and constant members. I know of no scriptural authority for such a discrimination. It is arbitrary and unreasonable. If I can admit an unimmersed person once a-month for a year to all social ordinances, I can for life or good behaviour. When I say, *I can do so,* I mean that all precepts, precedents, and scriptural reasons, authorize such a course.

But I object to making it a rule, *in any case,* to receive unimmersed persons to church ordinances:—

1st. Because it is no where commanded.

2d. Because it is no where precedented in the New Testament.

3d. Because it necessarily corrupts the simplicity and uniformity of the whole genius of the New Institution.

4th. Because it not only deranges the order of the kingdom, but makes *void* one of the most important institutions ever given to man. It necessarily makes *immersion* of non-effect. For, with what consistency or propriety can a congregation hold up to the world either the authority or utility of an institution which they are in the habit of making as little of, as any human opinion?

5th. Because, in making a canon to dispense with a divine institution of momentous import, they who do so assume the very same *dispensing power* which issued in that tremendous apostacy which we and all christians are praying and laboring to destroy. If a christian community puts into its magna charta, covenant, or constitution, an assumption to dispense with an institution of the Great King, who can tell where this power of granting license to itself may terminate? For these five reasons I must object to the aforesaid Constitution, however much I respect the benevolence and intelligence of those who framed it.

Query X.

But will you not be considered uncharitable in so deciding?

Answer.—Yes. In the current use of the term I must be so considered. But if we are to be governed by the censures of our worse informed brethren, where is our courage? And besides, we will still be considered uncharitable by some, if we do not go the whole way with them in their superstitious or enthusiastic notions and practices. Go with the Presbyterian until he calls you charitable, and then the Methodist will exclaim against you; or go with the Methodist until he calls you charitable, and then the Presbyterian will exclaim, How uncharitable!

Query XI.

But do you not expect to sit down in heaven with all the christians of all sects, and why not sit down at the same table with them on earth?

Answer.—It is time enough to behave as they do in heaven when we meet there. I expect to meet with those whom we call Patriarchs, Jews, and Pagans, in heaven. But this is no reason why I should offer sacrifice like Abel or Abimelech; circumcise my children, like Reuben or Gad; or pray to the Great Spirit, as an Indian; because some of all these sort of people may be fellow-citizens in heaven. Perhaps I am too charitable now, for some. Be this as it may. I do expect to meet with some of "all nations, tribes, and tongues," in the heavenly country. But while on earth I must live and behave according to the order of things under which I am placed. If we are now to be governed by the manners and customs in heaven, why was any other than the heavenly order of society instituted on earth?— There will be neither bread, wine, nor water in heaven. Why, then, use them on earth? But if those who propose this query would reflect that all the parts of the christian institution are necessary to this present state, and only preparatory to the heavenly, by giving us a taste for the purity and joys of that state, they could not propose such a question.

Query XII.

What, then, will we do with all our Paidobaptist fellow disciples?

Answer.—Teach them the way of the Lord more perfectly; and tell them if they greatly desire our society, it can be had just on being born of water and Spirit, as the Lord told Nicodemus. Our society cannot be worth much if it is not worth one immersion.

Query XIII.

But do you not make schisms by so doing?

Answer.—No. He makes no schism who does no more than the Lord commands, and all know that christian immersion is a divine institution. It is he who makes a new institution, such as the sprinkling of an infant, and contends for it, that makes the schism. It was not he that obeyed the first commandment, but he that made the golden calf, who made confusion in Israel.

[These Queries, in substance and form, came per last mails from Kentucky and Indiana. If this matter is not plain enough, we have more ink and paper.]

Query XIV.

Do you really believe, that if a man can say simply that he believes in the truth of the scriptures, and that they are the word of God—that the salvation of that man is secured to him; or in other words, that a mere belief of that kind will entitle him to the approbation of "well done?" &c.

Answer.—To this query, in the fair import of the terms, I answer positively: No. It is only they "who keep his commandments, who shall have a right to enter into the heavenly city." Those whom the Judge of all will address with "well done," are those who have done well. No man, either at death, or in the final judgment, will be justified by believing the whole, or any part of scripture; believing it any way, historically, or in the popular style. Men are justified here by faith, and there by works: or in other words, by faith, they are introduced into a state of favor, so that their prayers may be heard, and their works accepted—But the justification here is of pure favor: it is God's own philanthropy which grants them acceptance through faith in his testimony.

No man, as the infidels object, will be condemned on the day of judgment for not believing —and no man will be justified for believing— It is here men are condemned for unbelief, and justified through belief—"I was hungry and you fed me," &c.—is the reason assigned for the justification of the righteous—"I was hungry and you did not feed me," &c. is the reason assigned for the condemnation of the wicked— We can reconcile Paul, and James, without a play on words, or without the labor of Luther. Few understand this matter scripturally. Calvinists have struck on Scylla—and Arminians have dashed on Charybdis. At least they have come well nigh breaking their prows—but nothing is more simple, nor more straight forward, than the ancient gospel—by a proclamation of mercy, all are brought into favor who receive the testimony of Jesus. The testimony believed assures them of forgiveness and acceptance through submission to Jesus—and being reconciled through faith to the divine character and government, they having been made accepted in the beloved—go to work, to fight, to run, to strive, to labor, for the crown—Paul did so: and he was not cast away—he did not make shipwreck of faith—he laid hold on the crown—and the Saviour has promised it to none but to him that conquers—This is the fact. And they are all dreamers and loungers who expect to receive the crown by believing any thing—We are able through the knowledge and favor of Jesus Christ our Lord, to wind up and settle this long controversy, if men will hear and be content with what the oracles of God and right reason say—But if they will have mysteries, and dreams, and notions for it, they may dream on till the Judge calls them to judgment.

Arise you sleepers: awake, stand up you loungers: embrace the proclamation of mercy, and the gift of eternal life through Jesus, and go to work and labor, as Jesus told you, for the food which endures to eternal life—be immersed for the remission of your past sins—get washed, you filthy and polluted transgressors, and get under the reign of favor, that your persons and your works may be accepted, and that the Lord may without equivocation or deceit say to you, Well done. Be assured he will not flatter you with "well done," unless you have done well.

Do you believe that Jesus is the Messiah, that he died for our sins, that he was buried, that he rose again, that he ascended on high, that he has commanded reformation and forgiveness of sins, to be proclaimed in his name among all nations—I say, do you believe these sacred historic facts? If you do believe them, or are assured of their truth, you have historic faith, you have the faith which Paul and the Apostles had, and proclaimed—Paul was no more than assured these facts were true; and if you are assured they are true, you have the same faith—Arise, and be immersed like Paul, and withhold not obedience; and your historic faith and obedience will stand the test of Heaven. You will receive the Holy Spirit too, for it is promised by him that cannot lie, through this faith—Schoolmen may ridicule your faith: but there is no other. I call upon them, one and all, to show or prove any other. They cannot. I admit many have a dead faith, they believe these facts, and do not obey the proclamation, and James told them 1800 years ago, that this faith cannot save them—it is like a breathless or spiritless corpse. All the sons of men cannot show that there is any other faith, than the belief of facts, either written in the form of history, or orally delivered. Angels, men, or demons cannot define any thing under the term faith, but the belief of facts, or of history, except they change it into confidence; while men are talking, and dreaming, and quarrelling about a metaphysical whim, wrought in the heart, do you arise and obey the captain of salvation. And my word—nay, the word of all the Apostles for it, and the Lord himself, you will find peace and joy, and eternal salvation, springing from the obedience of faith.

Query XV.

What is the state and condition of unconverted men, in other words, of all mankind, by nature?

Answer.—All mankind are not in the same state by nature—some are born in pagan lands, and some are born in Christian families. It is true they are all born naked, ignorant, helpless, and possessed of five senses, as well as of great mental and moral capacities. Some may become giants in intellect and crime, and others but pigmies in both. But I presume the querist meant something like what the Westminster metaphysicians meant, when making questions on the anvil of John System. If so, I answer they are not all born in one and the same state: for some are born to be saved, and some to be damned!!—Some are born holy and some unholy! But what do I say? I cannot keep this pen of mine from snorting at such curious hobgoblins. All persons are born children of wrath!—nay indeed, else they can never become vessels of wrath. All the Gentiles, Paul says, were in fact children of wrath, as in fact or nature, all the Jews were children of Abraham. Some of these children were seventy years old; mind this as you proceed. But scripture and experience both teach that all who live in Christendom, and who are unbelievers or disobedient are condemned. Not because they are the children of Adam and Eve, but because they have not believed the testimony of God—and consequently continue disobedient to the word of God. Farther than this, deponent says not.

Query XVI.

Is a sinner to be considered as possessed of that moral or spiritual power, by which he may by his own nature turn himself to God, repent, and savingly believe by virtue of the truth presented to him.

Answer. My soul travails, for the travailing mind which conceived such a question. It is awfully jumbled by system—*No sinner can turn himself to God by nature.* But let me put the question as I know the spirit of the querist would have it. Can men just as they are found, when they hear the gospel, believe? I answer boldly yes—just as easily as I can believe the well attested facts concerning the person and the achievements of General George Washington. I must hear the facts clearly stated and well authenticated, before I am able to believe them— The man who can believe one fact well attested, can believe any other fact equally well attested. A man who can carry fifty pounds in England, can carry fifty pounds in France. A man who can believe at all, can believe any thing well documented. The Saviour or his apostles never told any man they needed new powers to believe what he said. Indeed, if any person told me that I could not believe him, although I could believe others, I would at once suspect him to be intending to deceive me; for if I could not believe him, it must be because I prove him to be a liar. To suppose that men cannot believe the testimony concerning Jesus, is to suppose either that it is not plainly delivered, sufficiently proved, or in fact true. I know, indeed, that if the Holy Spirit had not helped us to the truth, or had not vouchsafed the proof, we could not have believed such lofty pretensions. But as the case is, he who does not believe is a wicked sinner; for he has all the power of believing bestowed upon him in the accumulation of evidence afforded. Millions have been tantalized by a *mock gospel* which places them as the fable placed Tantalus, standing in a stream, parched with thirst, and the water running to his chin, and so circumstanced that he could not taste it. There is a sleight of hand or a religious legerdemain in getting round this matter. To call any thing grace, or favor, or gospel, not adapted to man as it finds him, is the climax of misnomers. To bring the cup of bliss or of salvation to the lips of a dying sinner, and then tell him for his soul he cannot taste it, without some sovereign aid beyond human control, is to mock his misery and to torment him more and more. I boldly affirm then that all men to whom the gospel is proclaimed can believe it if they choose, except such as have sinned so long against the light as to have fallen into the slumber and blindness denounced against those who wilfully reject the counsel of heaven. THAT ONLY IS GOSPEL WHICH ALL CAN BELIEVE WHO WISH TO BELIEVE.

Query XVII.

Is a believer in Christ not actually in a pardoned state, before he is baptized.

Answer.—Is not a man clean before he is washed!! When there is only an imaginary or artificial line between Virginia and Pennsylvania, I cannot often tell with ease whether I am in Virginia or in Pennsylvania; but I can always tell when I am in Ohio, however near the line—for I have crossed the Ohio river.— And blessed be God! he has not drawn a mere artificial line between the plantations of nature and of grace. No man has any proof that he is pardoned until he is baptized—And if men are conscious that their sins are forgiven and that they are pardoned before they are immersed, I advise them not to go into the water for they have no need of it.

Query XVIII.

What should a church do with a member for marrying her deceased husband's brother?

Answer. Let her live with him. However repugnant it may be to our feelings or our customs, it is not condemnable from either Testament.— It was for having his brother's wife, in his brother's life time, which procured a rebuke to Herod from the first Baptist preacher. In ranking John among the baptists, I hope they will forgive me; for although John lived before the christian kingdom began, he was upon the whole, as good a christian as most of us Immerser preachers.

A Restoration of the Ancient Order of Things.
No. XXX.

On the Discipline of the Church.—No. VI.

WHILE on the subject of discipline, we wished to have been more methodical; but causes and circumstances too tedious to detail, have compelled us to break through our method, and to become immethodical. The subject of the present essay is forced upon us, from some incidents of recent and remote occurrence. A writer in the Religious Herald, under the name and character of *Herodion*, in December last, discusses the following question, "Does the expulsion of a member from an individual church of the baptist faith and order, exclude him from fellowship with the whole denomination?" If I correctly understand Herodion, he answers in the affirmative. The editor of the Religious Herald dissents from Herodion in this decision. The former will have the Association the sovereign arbiter—the latter would make his appeal to a coordinate or sister church. But to make out a case in point for illustrating this question, we shall introduce that of Titus Timothy.—Titus Timothy was a regular Baptist, but some how took it into his head that it was not right in a christian church to receive or retain slaveholders. The church to which he belonged, thought otherwise. And for his impertinence in advocating this matter and dissenting from his brethren, they excluded him. Now Titus found himself cast out of the church.

He did not like it, to be sure. But what could he do? He referred his case to Herodion. Herodion told him to "pray to God for redress, and to wait for a change of temper in his oppressors." He prayed and waited for a long time. No change took place in his favor. He went to my friend, the Religious Herald. He advised him to "appeal to a coordinate church." But thinking in the multitude of counsellors there was safety, he went back to Herodion. Herodion told him to "appeal to the Association." As Herodion was older and more experienced than his brother of the Herald, he took his advice and appealed to the Association. He made his appeal. But, alas! in vain! For the Association told him they had no power to overrule the decision of the church, for this would be to divest it of its independence. Titus was worse hurt than before: for now he found that the decision of the church was confirmed by the Association without seeming to take it into consideration; for by throwing him and his case out of doors, they indirectly confirmed the decision of the church. They retained it and excluded him. He went back to the Religious Herald— told over his case. His appeal to the Association was disapproved; and now, as the case stands, he is advised to call a council of helps from the neighboring churches. He does so. But the church which excluded him refuses to attend, or to admit of such interference. The council cannot act upon *exparte* testimony, and he is still excluded from the whole denomination. The two neighboring churches enter complaint at the next Association against the church for intolerance, and despite of an *advisory council*. The excluding church, by her delegates, protests against the conduct of the two neighboring churches for presuming to complain of her upon *exparte* testimony, and argues her independence. So the affair ends, and poor Titus Timothy is at his wit's end. He is excluded from the whole denomination for *thinking wrong*, or rather for uttering his thoughts.

But another case presents itself. Stephen Seektruth was a member of a church composed of eighteen members, six males and twelve females. He read the New Institution with great attention and unfeigned devotion. He was persuaded that the church was unsupported in her resolve to meet only once a month in her official capacity. He remonstrated, and, for insubordination to the brotherhood, was expelled. Four of the sisters were absent when the final vote was taken. Two of the brethren and five of the sisters voted for, and three of the brethren and three of the sisters voted against his exclusion. So that the voice of a single sister cast him out of the assembly. He appealed to the Associations, but they would not hear any individual. Consequently they confirmed the decision of the church, and Stephen was in fact excluded from the whole Baptist denomination by the vote of a woman! He was advised to call for helps from other churches, but they would not meet on the complaint of the injured: and the injurers would not submit to be arraigned before any such tribunal. Under the opprobrium of an excluded member he must live and die.

Sects and denominations require modes of government adapted to their genius. Romanists must have a pope in one man; the good old Episcopalians must have a king, and archbishops, and all the army of subalterns; the Presbyterians must have synods and a general assembly; and the good old English Baptists must have associations. Without these the denominations would be broken down, and might, perhaps, become christians of the old stamp. But each of these denominations require all the sectarian machinery to keep them in a thriving sectarian spirit. The Baptist system, we have always said and seen, is the most impotent of any of them. They have, in theory, sawed the horns off the Beast, and the Association is a hornless stag, with the same ferocious spirit which he had when the horns were on his head. If he is offended he makes a tremendous push with his brains, and bruises to death the obnoxious carcase which he would have gored clear through at a single push, if he had his horns. Herodion feels the want of horns, and would have the creature furnished with at least one artificial one, which he might occasionally use. My brother of the Herald would wish to feed the stag well, but would still be sawing off the horns: perhaps I may wrong him in so saying, for indeed he is very modest about it. But, for my part, I do not love even an image of the Beast. I have no objection to congregations meeting in hundreds, at stated times, to sing God's praise, and to unite their prayers and exhortations for the social good. But whenever they form a quorum, and call for the business of the churches, they are a popish calf, or *muley*, or a hornless stag, or something akin to the old grand Beast with seven heads and ten horns.

I cannot give my voice in favor of appeals to any tribunal, but to the congregation of which the offended is a member; neither to a council of churches specially called, nor to an association. The old book, written by the Apostles, has compelled me to hold this dogma fast. And I can, I know, show that it is superior to every other course. I will grant, however, that this plan will not suit a denomination or a sect; but it will suit the kingdom over which Immanuel reigns. And neither Herodion, nor any other brother of more or less experience, can support his scheme from the statute book of the Great King. But if he should think so, let him try, and I will try to make my assertion good. But I do pity such good old men. They have borne the burthen and heat of the day in maintaining a denominational scheme, and to suspect now that they have not fought in the ranks of the good old martyrs, is a terrible thought to an honest and Lord-loving and fearing spirit. My hopes are in the young men who are now entering the field. And I know some hundreds of them just now who are likely to die good soldiers of Jesus Christ. The friends of the ancient order would be too elated, perhaps, and its opposers would be too disconsolate, if they knew the forces now commencing and commenced their operations. I do not care for offending a coward. He will only fight when there is no danger. And a time-serving spirit I would rather see on the opposite side: for he will fight most stoutly for them who pay him best. We want men in the spirit and power of Elijah, who would tell a king Herod to his face that he was a transgressor. It cost the first Baptist his head, to be sure. But what of that? He will not want a head in the resurrection! O! for some Baptists of the good old stamp! Not the Kentucky old stamp of the Oakley school. But whither have I been driven? To the point: Every christian community must settle its own troubles. No appeal from one congregation to another. There is no need of it; for no intelligent christian congregation will ever cast out a person who could be an honor to any community. This much at present on this topic; but more hereafter.

Here a friend tells me I have mistaken the question; for Paul taught the Corinthians to appeal to a sister church. "See," says he, "1 *Cor.* ch. vii. where Paul says, 'Brethren, you greatly err: when any one troubles you, and when disputations arise among you, call for helps from the churches of Macedonia: let the disputers be brought face to face; and when the pleaders on each side have impleaded each other, then do you call for the votes of the brotherhood. If there is only one of a majority, cast him out; for as Moses says in the Law, "The majority is always right." But if any thinks that he is not fairly cast out, or that there is not a real majority against him, let him appeal to the whole Macedonian association, and let them judge the case. If the majority of the Macedonian association cast him or them out, then let them be stigmatized by all the associations in Greece. For I would have you, brethren, to mark out the heretics and the disturbers of the brethren, and therefore publish them in your Minutes, that all the churches on earth may be apprized of the ungodly.'"   EDITOR.

THE REV. G. T. CHAPMAN, D. D. of Lexington, Kentucky, has lately published a volume of "Sermons upon the Ministry, Worship, and Doctrines of the Protestant Episcopal Church, and other subjects" subservient thereto. I have only glanced as yet over the face of this work. The Protestant Episcopal Church, to our no little surprize, is proved to be the Holy Apostolic Church, gradually consummating herself through a long chain of Popes, perfecting herself in her match with King Harry and Miss Anne Boleyn—unchangeable in her doctrines and infallible in her "three orders of ministers." Our encomiast of the Church, has, as he says, shown that the holy rite of confirmation, and the use of precomposed prayers, is just according to the patterns of things in the heavens. In lieu of the High Priest, the Priests, and Levites, she has Bishops, Priests, and Deacons. And we are told one of the Doctor's Deacons lately said, on perusing this work, "Ministers may say what they please, but I'll be d——d if Chapman ain't wide enough awake for any of them!" This may be true of the Deacon and the Doctor, but we want to peruse the book a little more before we grant the holy rite of confirmation to the Doctor's book.

                                       EDITOR.

No. 9.]   APRIL 6, 1829.

Immersion, and not Sprinkling, another Presbyterian testifies.

WE feel peculiarly happy in laying before our readers the following critical disquisition from the pen of one of our most learned Presbyterians. Dr. Straith, of Virginia, from whose pen we have published in the November and December numbers of this volume, those excellent "Remarks upon the Bible," has, after a candid, impartial, and laborious investigation of the Greek and Hebrew scriptures, decided, in a very summary and forcible way, the Baptist controversy; and has unequivocally shown that immersion is the only baptism known, or enjoined in Holy Writ as a christian institution. Some other of our Presbyterian correspondents are fast advancing to the same issue. A testimony and criticism from a witness so learned and so honest as that of this venerable Scotsman is worth a volume of arguments from ordinary critics, and mere copyists. He has gone to the very fountain head of all correct information upon this subject, and the method on which the investigation has been conducted is the most natural, rational, and decisive that can be imagined. We would invite Doctor Wilson, of the "Pandect," and some of his kindred spirits, about to commence the "Paidobaptist," in Kentucky, to give Dr. Straith's disquisition a patient, and, if they could, an impartial examination. We should not have many such profane scoffs as Dr. Wilson's "much water scheme," if such men as he had either the talents or the honesty requisite to such an investigation as the following.

While we give all due respect to the talents and candor of Dr. Straith, and without doubt they are worthy of our unfeigned esteem, and while we must declare that he has, in our judgment, most triumphantly proved immersion to be the only baptism, our readers will see in the close of his remarks some difference in sentiment between him and myself on the import and design of the institution. As I was long of the same views with him on this subject, I can very cheerfully make all allowance for the diversity of sentiment which at present exists between him and me on this point. Indeed I know many brethren of the first talents and acquisitions, who do not agree with the views offered in the last volume of this work on this topic. I hear patiently all their strong reasons and proofs. As I claim forbearance, I can cheerfully exercise it with those differing on this subject. Although I feel no doubt of being able most irrefragably to establish the views already offered, this affords no reason why I should not hear and exhibit, as opportunity serves, the arguments of those differing from me.

The novelty of the views, as some of my brethren term it; or, as I, the antiquity of the views offered on this subject, being so far from the beaten track, have made some well-meaning persons afraid of the consequences likely to ensue from the adoption of them. And what calls forth the *odium theologicum* of such men as the editor of "The Pandect," is, that it cuts him off, and all other disobedient folks, from the hope of forgiveness. There are many who wish to have a system of religion which would promise them forgiveness without reformation. But there is a way of getting round all difficulties in argument by a new art first invented in Philadelphia—I think by somebody of *Star-light* erudition. It is by printing, or writing, or reporting any obnoxious sentiment with a note of admiration after it, and not a word of argument. Mr. Wilson has improved upon this a little; for he adds the words, "Look at this absurdity!!!" Pope Leo, or Cardinal Cajetan could have, by one such line, and three notes of admiration, answered all the writings of Luther, Calvin, Beza, and all the old Reformers. But let us hear Dr. Straith:

DEAR SIR—WHEN I come to reflect on the simplicity and fewness of the means, which God employs in the performance of all his own works, and on the simplicity and fewness of the means which he has rendered necessary for his creatures to use in the performance of theirs, I feel a moral certainty that the course pursued and the means employed by the learned world to ascertain the action, the subjects, and the uses of baptism, was not the course prescribed, nor the means appointed by God for the accomplishment of that object. So entirely devoid of analogy, so strikingly dissimilar are the means employed by men on this inquiry, and the means employed by God in all his operations, that I felt assured, even before I had discovered it, that a method of

deciding these interesting questions, incomparably more simple, short, plain, and certain, must exist. And to this conclusion the strongest confirmation was added, when I reflected on the ineffable care and concern of the Lord Jesus Christ, whose institution baptism is, for the tranquility, harmony, and happiness of his friends on earth, and on his perfect ability to relieve them from all the excessive labor, contention, and uncertainty, to which they have most unnecessarily and most perniciously exposed themselves for many ages. It is impossible to believe that the boundlessly kind and infinitely wise Redeemer would require, peremptorily require, his friends, learned and unlearned, without exception, to submit to, or rather perform an action, the ascertainment of which required such enormous labor, and such vast quantities of precious time, as have been expended most unprofitably and needlessly on this contested subject.

It was the impulse of this irresistible conviction that brought me to adopt the course which I have pursued; namely, First. To endeavour to gain a precise and distinct conception of the object in search of which I was about to set out; and secondly, to extricate that object from the immense mass of irrelative rubbish in which it has hitherto been involved. Scarcely had I formed this determination before I perceived that the object of my pursuit was nothing else than the action denoted by the words βαπτω and βαπτιζω, in the Greek language, at the time when the New Testament was written. For to me it appeared absolutely certain, that whatever was the action denoted by these words in the Greek tongue at that time, was the action which they were employed to denote in the New Testament; and, of course, the action in which baptism consists. And to this conclusion I was naturally led when I recollected, first, that the Greek language was the medium which the writers of the New Testament preferred and employed for the conveyance of their inspired message to mankind: secondly, that if they expected or wished to be understood by those who read their writings, it was absolutely necessary that they should use the words of the language in which they wrote in their usual acceptation, or declare their departure from it as soon as it occurred: for without one or other of these precautions, misunderstood they must inevitably have been: thirdly, that during a period of at least three hundred years before the New Testament was written a dialect of the Greek tongue had been springing up, which employed many of its words in senses in which they never occur in classical or native Greek, and that this dialect was principally in use among the Jews, and particularly in their religious writings and services: and lastly, that from the current use of Greek words in one or other of these dialects, which, for distinction's sake, may be called the Hellenistic or synagogal and classical dialects, the writers of the New Testament must have necessarily learned their use of all the Greek words which they employed, and of course, the meaning of βαπτιζω, (*baptizo*.)

The road was now plain, the course short, the object of pursuit full in view, and the certainty of seizing it unquestionable. Animated by this hope, I took up the Septuagint, (Holmesius and Boss's edition, Glasgow, 1822,) the great fountain of synagogal and New Testament idiom or use of words, and read every word of it, carefully noting every passage in which βαπτω, βαπτιζω, or any of their derivatives occur; and at the same time noting with equal care the Hebrew

72

terms which these words are employed to translate: and I now proceed to place the passages in which βαπτω, βαπτιζω, or any of their derivatives, are found, before you in the order of their occurrence. *Exod.* xii. 22. *Lev.* iv. 6, 17. ix. 9, xiv. 6, 16, 51. *Num.* xix. 18. *Deut.* xxxiii. 24. *Jos.* iii. 15. *Judg.* v. 30. *Ruth* ii. 14. 1 *Sam.* xiv. 27. *2 Kings* v. 14, viii. 15. *Job* ix. 31. *Isa.* xxi. 4. *Ezek.* xxiii. 15. *Dan.* iv. 30, v. 21. These are all the passages in which βαπτω, βαπτιζω, or any of their derivatives, is to be found: and I proceed to observe that *tebel* is the Hebrew term which βαπτω or βαπτιζω is commonly employed to translate. In Genesis, however, xxxvii. 31, this Hebrew word is translated loosely by μολυνω, but the sense evidently calls for βαπτω; for the unfeeling brothers no doubt dipped Joseph's dress in the blood of the kid which they slew for the purpose. In *Judges* v. 30, the Hebrew, or rather Chaldee term, is *tsebo*, dyed, immersed, wet. In *Isa.* xxi. 4, as in 2 *Kings* v. 14, the Greek word is βαπτιζω, the whole Greek expression και η ανομια με βαπτιζει, the Hebrew *peletsut botteni*, (trembling has suddenly seized me.) In *Dan.* iv. 30, v. 21, the Chaldaic term, as in *Judg.* v. 30, *tsebo*, and is translated in verse 12th by χοιταζομαι, and in verse 20th by αυλιζομαι. Note that verses 12th, 20th, 30th, Heb. and Greek, correspond to verses 15th, 23d, 33d, E. T.

Let me now observe, first, that βαπτω and βαπτιζω belong to the small class of words which denote only one idea or object, a circumstance of immense importance in this investigation, as it renders the meaning of these words absolutely certain, and determines beyond a possibility of doubt, the action which they are employed to denote wherever they occur, and entirely supersedes the necessity of consulting context, connected phraseology, a writer's scope, or any other means occasionally resorted to for the purpose of ascertaining, in particular cases, the precise meaning of words which may be used in more senses than one.

Second. That in all the passages in which they occur in the Septuagint and in classical Greek, so far as I am acquainted with it, or the best Greek dictionaries exhibit it, they denote, when used literally, the action which we call dipping; and allude, when employed metaphorically, to that action.

Third. That use in Hellenistic and classical Greek, is constantly resorted to and depended on to ascertain the meaning of every other Greek word in the New Testament; and why not be employed to determine the action denoted by βαπτιζω? Can human ingenuity discover a reason? Surely had not prejudice and interest interfered, no other method or means would have been devised. We should never have witnessed that frightful parade of irrelative argument and disgusting nonsense, which now insult us, and in which there is no fitness to decide the question. By usage alone in the language to which words belong, can their meaning be ascertained. But if usage be the only certain means by which the action denoted by βαπτιζω can be determined, and usage uniformly employ that word to denote the action of dipping, by what authority does any human being presume to assign it a different meaning, or make it denote a different action? Does not its meaning, fixed by unvarying use, rest insubvertible on the same immoveable foundation which supports and fixes the meaning of every other term in the book of God? And could the foundation on which the meaning of βαπτιζω rests be subverted, would not the foundation on which the meaning of every other term in scripture rests, sink with it, and the whole word of God become a chaos of hideous uncertainty?

4. That usage presents a method of determining the action, to which Christ requires all his friends to submit, that by that submission they may be discriminated from his enemies, which exhibits the strongest analogy to that which God always employs in the execution of his purposes, and manifests at the same time the peculiarly tender concern of the Redeemer for the peace and comfort of his disciples. It is simple, short, plain, certain, and easy, requiring only the labor necessary to ascertain the action which βαπτιζω denoted in the Greek tongue when the New Testament was written.

5. That usage constitutes the only species of evidence that suits the nature of the investigation. Every person knows, that if we would arrive at truth, we must employ such means and such evidence as comport with the nature of the subject which we investigate. For the solution of mathematical questions we must employ mathematical evidence: questions of fact require human testimony or the natural effects of an antecedent action; matters of probability depend on analogy; so questions of philology, or the meaning of words, must be determined by usage. Indeed all other methods are irrelative, fallacious, delusive and absurd.

——Usus
Quem penes arbitrium est, et jus, et norma loquendi.

6. Let it be remembered, too, that there is a natural fitness in actions, as well as in instruments to accomplish their respective ends, and that God never employs unfit means in the execution of any of his purposes. In the action, therefore, required by Christ, there must be a natural or intrinsic fitness to accomplish the ends for which he instituted it. These ends are, as we think, discrimination and representation; but of this more when we come to examine the uses of baptism. In the mean time we proceed to examine the comparative fitness of the actions of sprinkling, pouring, washing, and dipping, to answer baptismal purposes, taking it for granted at present that these purposes are the two just mentioned, discrimination and representation.

Presuming it then to be admitted that the uses of the baptismal action are, first, to discriminate friends from enemies; and, secondly, to furnish an image of the death, burial, and resurrection of the Saviour and of the person baptized, we pass on to the examination of the natural fitness of the actions of sprinkling, pouring, washing, and dipping, to accomplish these ends. With respect to these actions we observe, that they are not only dissimilar to the eye, but are performed for different reasons, and for different ends. We never sprinkle to accomplish the purpose for which we pour, dip, or wash: nor do we wash to effect the end for which we resort to sprinkling, dipping, or pouring: nor do we use dipping for the purposes of either. We sprinkle for the purpose of obtaining the effect of a fluid or other incoherent substance applied only in small quantity: we pour to obtain the effect of such a substance in large quantity and in a short time; we wash only on the supposition that the thing to be washed is filthy, and for the purpose of separating its filth from it; and for this end we employ friction more or less: we dip an object, not because it is dirty, nor for the purpose of removing any thing from it, but on the contrary with the view of incorporating something with it or attaching something to it, and in the process we use no friction. Hence the necessity of using distinct and never confounded terms to denote actions so dissimilar in their appearance, causes, and ends; and distinct terms are employed to denote them in all languages.

We admit that to accomplish the first purpose of baptism, discrimination, the actions of dipping, sprinkling, pouring, washing, have a like natural fitness; but the three latter are destitute of the adventitious fitness which belongs to dipping, hereafter to be noticed. As to the second purpose of the baptismal action, the furnishing of an image of the death, burial, and resurrection of the Redeemer and his friends, there manifestly exists no aptitude in either of them.

Moreover, sprinkling and pouring afford no indication or presumption of the state of the person claiming baptism, and washing furnishes a false one. The action of washing always presumes its subject to be filthy, and when morally or spiritually employed, certainly presumes that its subject is in a state of guilt and depravity; and also that the act about to be performed on him is able to deliver him from that wretched condition. Now we regard both these presumptions to be false and unscriptural. We think the scripture tells us very plainly, that faith in the blood of the Redeemer, without the aid of any other action performable by the sinner, removes his guilt, exempts him from punishment, and commences his regeneration. Now if this be true, the believer, when he claims baptism, and none but a believer is authorized to claim it, has no guilt to remove, his sins are already forgiven, his person exempted from punishment, and his soul delivered from the dominion of habitual depravity. The action of washing, therefore, is neither necessary, suitable, nor beneficial to him.

The actions, then, of sprinkling, pouring, washing, being manifestly unfit to answer the purposes of the baptismal institution, let us examine the pretensions of dipping. In the first place, the action of dipping, as it presumes its subject to be clean, necessarily implies that the candidate for baptism has had the guilt of his sins removed, his person exempted from punishment, and his soul delivered from habitual depravity by faith in the blood of the Redeemer; for by no other means could he acquire that purity, which dipping presupposes. Secondly, it presumes the baptismal action to have no power to remove guilt, release from punishment, enlighten the understanding, or rectify the feelings and affections of the heart; for all these are effected by faith in the divine message, and not by baptism. Thirdly, it presumes not the removal of any thing from the baptized person, but the attachment of something to him, namely, new social rights, moral qualities, and character. Fourthly, it furnishes the fittest image conceivable of the death, burial, and resurrection of the Saviour and his friends. Lastly, if what the New Testament seems to teach be true, that dipping never was employed by mankind as a religious action, till by God's express command it was used as such by John the Baptist, and attached to Christ's new institution as one of its discriminating features, it possesses the highest degree of adventitious as well as intrinsic fitness to answer both the ends of the baptismal institution.

If, then, God always employs the fittest means for the execution of his purposes, and there be in the action of dipping a manifestly superior fitness to answer all baptismal ends, can we forbear to consider its superior fitness as a strong ground of belief, that it was the action, which God preferred and prescribed for the accomplishment of those ends? But powerful as this evidence is, we regard its exhibition, when compared with usage, as only lighting a straw to aid the sun. Usage, decisive usage, stands in no need of such feeble assistance. It triumphs in its own invincible strength and derides all auxiliary support; and had not men rejected this short, plain, easy, and certain method, which God has graciously furnished them for determining the action that constitutes baptism, and resorted to means of decision which have no relation to the subject, no fitness to decide the question, and to which, in ascertaining the meaning of other terms, they never recur, the shadow of doubt could never have arisen respecting the action to which Christ requires all his friends, without exception, to submit.

I am with respect, &c. &c.
                                   Alex. Straith.
February 16, 1829.

Presbyterian Prospects and Wants.

Presbyterianism aims at high things, and will yet be on the throne in America if the Millennium does not soon arrive.

From the last *enumeration* of the Presbyterian Israel, and from the late *proclamation* of the Rt. Reverend Ezra Styles Ely, D. D. which appeared lately in "The Philadelphian," and which has been repromulged in "The Western *Luminary*" of concentrated light, it is fairly to be presumed that this learned and wealthy church expects, like Pharaoh's lean kine, to devour all the fat and well favored kine which will browze, some half a century hence, on all the hills from Maine to Florida, and from the splendid brass knocker, engraved "Rev. Ezra Styles Ely," to the Rocky Mountains.—I have not room for the whole report, else I would gladly give it. I will give a liberal extract from it, that it may be heard speaking for itself.   Ed. C. B.

"There are probably fifteen baptized members, who are pew holders, supporters of, and attendants on, public worship in our Presbyterian churches, for every communicant in our connexion; and if so, then our body in the United States contains 2,194,620 persons. If our denomination should be kept from disunion, and the blessing of God should be continued as it has been for the last twenty years, in 1848 there will be at least 5,000,000 of persons under the care of the General Assembly; for we have more than doubled in numbers in the last twenty years. At that time, to give every thousand people in our connexion one pastor, we shall need 5000 ministers. Of our present teachers 600 will probably decease before that time, leaving of the 1479 no more than 879. To these add the 1528 which may be gained in twenty years at the rate of our increase during the last ten years, and it will give us 2407, and will leave a deficiency of 2593 to make up the 5000: so that 2,593,000 of our people, or more than our present whole number, will then be without one man in a thousand to show to them their transgressions; if our increase of preachers shall not exceed that of any former period, in the proportion of about three to one. How wide is the field which is opening before us! Truly our portion of the harvest is great and the laborers are few. If we consider the relative strength of the Presbyterian church in the United States, every candid mind will be satisfied that we ought to perform more service in the building up of Zion than any other two denominations of christians in our country; for, of those to whom much is given, much will be required.

Two thirds of the colleges, theological seminaries, and other academic institutions in this country are under the control of Presbyterians. The Congregational churches of New England and the Presbyterian church together have the charge of more than three-fourths of all these fountains of literary influence.

Baptist and Methodist churches in the United States, contain not far from 1,500,000 people in each, but they are comparatively poor, and contain a larger proportion of slaves than other denominations.

Our ministers in the state of New York alone are 448; and all the Protestant Episcopal ministers of all grades in the United States do not exceed, according to their own estimation, 507.—In one synod, that of Albany, we have 206 ministers, and in the state of New York twenty-five presbyteries. In Pennsylvania we have 317 churches and 194 ministers. Four out of our sixteen synods contain 532 ministers.

The Congregational ministers, exclusive of about one hundred Arian or Socinian, or fence riding teachers, are estimated at 720, and their churches at 960.—The Methodist ministers, exclusive of their local exhorters, who correspond very much to our ruling elders, are 1465, and their members of classes 381,997. The Baptist church in the United States is estimated at 3723 congregations, 2577 ministers, and 238,654 baptized persons, which are, of course, all communicants. The proportion of non-communicating members in these two last named societies, is far less than the Presbyterian church.

Let our ministers and churches consider how much is expected from them by our blessed Lord, and act accordingly. Particularly let them decide whether every communicant ought not to form and express a purpose of contributing fifty cents, or a less sum annually, to the missionary operations of the General Assembly. The aid of others we *solicit;* but that of the communicants the Presbyterian church has a right to **CLAIM.**"

Remarks on the Preceding.

In the judgment of charity Dr. Ely counts *fifteen* disobedient to *one* obedient member in the Presbyterian church. Our *body* (with fifteen dead to one living member) says he, amounts to 2,194,620. Under the divine blessing, adds he, if the Lord keep us "from disunion," or from separating the *fifteen sixteenths* from the one sixteenth, from putting out the fifteen disobedient out of every sixteen members; in twenty years "our body" will amount, in these United States, to 5,000,000. That is, we shall, in twenty years, have 312,500 obedient disciples, and 4,687,500 disobedient disciples! What a dangerous church will this Presbyterian church yet be! Embracing, as she expects in twenty years, nearly one-third of all the carnal, worldly, and selfish sinners in the land, without one teacher to two thousand "transgressors," should she take it into her head to make a king or a "*long parliament,*" what could hinder her? If even the sixteenth should oppose the measure, there will be fifteen votes to one against it. A body of fifteen unsound or putrid members, for one sound and living member, must inevitably become a mass of corruption in twenty years exposure.

Richard M. Johnson, Esq. and such men, who will not, by act of congress, sanctify the First day of the week, or make a Jewish Sabbath of it, will have to seek some new country, if they wish to wear their heads. For my part, I would as lief live a door neighbor to the Spanish spiritual court of Inquisition, as live next door to a council of such spirits as the Editor of the Cincinnati "Pandect."

But this is not all. Dr. Ely says they have two thirds of all the colleges and fountains of learning and literary influence under their control. Yes, remember the word *control.* And two thirds of the money also. For, he says, the two great sects, the Methodists and Baptists, are "poor." The Presbyterian church with one third of all the sinners, two thirds of all the colleges, and two thirds of all the money, my friends, be assured, will one day, some twenty years hence, make you take off your hats and "stop your coaches." I do know it to be a fact, which all history and experience prove, that a society professing any religion, with the control of colleges, population and money, will be adored, if they have such a proportion of "baptized infidels" among them as gives to them a ponderosity of fifteen to one. I think as highly of Presbyterians as they deserve. I esteem many of their preachers and people as saints, who would not do such things. But what could or what can these do, under such a system, which, as Dr. Ely admits, gives influence to fifteen sixteenths of the whole membership, living in disobedience to Jesus Christ. I do not think that all his "communicants" are saints either. If the half of them were saints, we would have something to hope, from so much salt in so dead a carcase. But we have no good reason to think that more than a half of the communicants are real christians. If so, then on Dr. Ely's data, we would have thirty to one.

I never saw from a Protestant pen, so proud, so supercilious, so arrogant a display, as this same report of Dr. Ely! Numbers, literature, wealth, arrayed against poverty, "ignorance," and paucity. The Presbyterian sect is as two to one against all the sects in the country, by such a happy combination of literature, money, and numbers.

If I had not other data before my mind, and a different view of religious statistics, than Dr. Ely presents, I would really give up the contest and the ship, and sigh for the destiny of both church and state. But as things are, I do not despair. As a politician, then, we will now exhibit our data.

In less than one century the Baptists have risen from about five thousand members, and an influence not in the proportion of one to a hundred, to nearly three hundred thousand members, and an influence of more than one to ten of the whole population of the United States. This is a fact for which I can, when called upon, furnish the documents.

The Methodists have, in a little more than half a century, risen from nought to three hundred thousand members, and an influence of one to ten of the whole population. Without giving more than three of the proselytes of the gate to one of the actual members in the Baptist and Methodist societies, such is their real influence in the union. But I have no doubt that we are rather below, than up to the actual moral power of these two sects.

There is another sect, called "Christians"—by their enemies, "New Lights," which have, in little more than the quarter of a century, risen from nothing to fifteen hundred congregations, with a membership of one hundred and fifty thousand, and an influence equal to the one-

75

twentieth of the whole population. These are "poor and ignorant too." But let Dr. Ely know that these poor and ignorant folks have wrought all the wonders that have been of magnificent influence in the annals of the world. The spoke of the wheel which is now in the mud, will be nighest heaven by and by; and that which is "clean and dry" will soon descend. The rich become poor, and the poor become rich; and their children in the third generation generally change seats.

Now what shall we say of the Congregationalists, Episcopalians, Catholics, Quakers, and the swarms of little sects over the continent. Are the Presbyterians, like Moses' red, to devour them all! The influence of these minor sects is as one to ten; nay, perhaps, as two to ten of the whole population. And when you add that great sect of mere Mammonists to the whole, we shall find that if there were to be no Millennium, there is not so much to be feared from the prophecies of Dr. Ely. The Baptists, in a single state of the Union, have immersed more adults during the last year than all the infants which have been sprinkled by all the fifteen hundred Presbyterian preachers during the year in the whole United States. The Christian sect have, in two, or at most three states, made more proselytes during the last year, than the Presbyterians have made during two years. It is easier to carry fifteen infants to church to be "christened," than to make one proselyte.

Again, these poor and ignorant preachers, that never saw a college wall, would, in one year, cut and slash down more stubborn sinners with John Bunyan's Jerusalem blade, than a score of these nice fencers, who wear only a silver-handled dirk and a pocket-pistol. Dr. Ely and General Braddock may draw up their lines in great array; but take care of these fellows behind the trees! So much for the Doctor's prognostics—and so much for my religious politics.

For my part, as a christian, I must, in believing the apostles, look for the downfal of all the sects in a little time. I should not think it passing strange, both from the New Testament prophecies, and from the passing events of the day, if, before twice twenty years shall have run their rounds, Presbyterianism should be gathered to its fathers, and sleep in the sepulchre of the spiritual kings of Babylon, without the hope of a resurrection from the dead. Such an event is to my mind incomparably more probable than that in twenty years, this sect should control the government and establish itself by five millions of votes upon the throne of a new empire.

EDITOR.

THE following Report is rational, politic, and in the spirit of our constitution. It is one of the ablest state papers on the question, we have ever read. It cannot be resisted by good logic or sound policy. The preceding article we intended for a preface to it. And he must be blind who cannot see into the policy of these petitions after reading Dr. Ely's Report of the "wants," and "prospects," of the Presbyterian church.

EDITOR.

Transportation of the Mail on the Sabbath.

The senate proceeded to the consideration of the following report and resolution, presented by Mr. Johnson, with which the senate concurred:

The Committee to whom were referred the several petitions on the subject of mails, on the Sabbath, or first day of the week—Report,

That some respite is required from the ordinary vocations of life, is an established principle, sanctioned by the usages of all nations, whether Christian or Pagan. One day in seven has, also, been determined upon as the proportion of time; and in conformity with the wishes of a great majority of the citizens of this country, the first day of the week, commonly called Sunday, has been set apart to that object. The principle has received the sanction of the national legislature, so far as to admit a suspension of all public business on that day, except in cases of absolute necessity, or of great public utility. This principle the committee would not wish to disturb. If kept within its legitimate sphere of action, no injury can result from its observance. It should, however, be kept in mind, that the proper object of government is, to protect all persons in the enjoyment of their religious as well as civil rights: and not to determine for any, whether they shall esteem one day above another, or esteem all days alike holy.

We are aware that a variety of sentiment exists among the good citizens of this nation on the subject of the Sabbath day; and our government is designed for the protection of one as much as for another. The Jews, who, in this country are as free as christians, and entitled to the same protection from the laws, derive their obligation to keep the Sabbath day from the fourth commandment of their decalogue, and in conformity with that injunction, pay religious homage to the seventh day of the week, which we call Saturday. One denomination of christians among us, justly celebrated for their piety, and certainly as good citizens as any other class, agree with the Jews in the moral obligation of the Sabbath, and observe the same day. There are, also, many christians among us, who derive not their obligation to observe the Sabbath from the decalogue, but regard the Jewish Sabbath as abrogated. From the example of the apostles of Christ, they have chosen the first day of the week, instead of that day set apart in the decalogue, for their religious devotions. These have, generally, regarded the observance of the day as a devotional exercise, and would not more readily enforce it upon others, than they would enforce secret prayer or devout meditations. Urging the fact, that neither their Lord nor his disciples, though often censured by their accusers for a violation of the Sabbath, ever enjoined its observance, they regard it as a subject on which every person should be fully persuaded in his own mind, and not coerce others to act upon his persuasion. Many christians again differ from these professing to derive their obligation to observe the Sabbath from the fourth commandment of the Jewish decalogue, and bring the example of the apostles, who appear to have held their public meetings for worship on the first day of the week, as authority for so far changing the decalogue, as to substitute that day for the seventh. The Jewish government was a theocracy, which enforced religious observances; and though the Committee would hope that no portion of the citizens of our country would willingly introduce a system of religious coercion in our civil institutions, the example of other nations should admonish us to watch carefully against its earliest indication.

With these different religious views, the committee are of opinion that congress cannot interfere. It is not the legitimate province of the legislature to determine what religion is true, or what false. Our government is a civil, and not a religious institution. Our constitution recognizes in every person the right to choose his own religion, and to enjoy it freely, without molestation. Whatever may be the religious sentiments of citizens, and however variant, they are alike entitled to protection from the government, so long as they do not invade the rights of others.

The transportation of the mail on the first day of the week, it is believed, does not interfere with the rights of conscience. The petitioners for its discontinuance appear to be actuated by a religious zeal, which may be commendable if confined to its proper sphere; but they assume a position better suited to an ecclesiastical than to a civil institution. They appear, in many instances, to lay it down, as an axiom, that the practice is a violation of the law of God. Should congress, in their legislative capacity, adopt the sentiment, it would establish the principle, that the legislature is a proper tribunal to determine what are the laws of God. It would involve a legislative decision on a religious controversy, and on a point in which good citizens may honestly differ in opinion, without disturbing the peace of society, or endangering its liberties. If this principle is once introduced, it will be impossible to define its bounds. Among all the religious persecutions with which almost every page of modern history is stained, no victim ever suffered, but for the violation of what government denominated the law of God. To prevent a similar train of evils in this country, the constitution has wisely withheld from our government the power of defining the Divine Law. It is a right reserved to each citizen; and while he respects the rights of others, he cannot be held amenable to any human tribunal for his conclusions.

Extensive religious combinations to effect a political object are, in the opinion of the committee, always dangerous. This first effort of the kind, calls for the establishment of a principle, which, in the opinion of the committee, would lay the foundation for dangerous innovations upon the spirit of the constitution, and upon the religious rights of the citizens. If admitted, it may be justly apprehended, that the future measures of the government will be strongly marked, if not eventually controlled, by the same influence. All religious despotism commences by combination and influence; and when that influence begins to operate upon the political institutions of a country, the civil power soon bends under it; and the catastrophe of other nations furnishes an awful warning of the consequence.

Under the present regulations of the Post-Office Department, the rights of conscience are not invaded. Every agent enters voluntarily, and it is presumed conscientiously, into the discharge of his duties, without intermeddling with the conscience of another. Post-Offices are so regulated, as that but a small proportion of the first day of the week is required to be occupied in official business. In the transportation of the mail on that day, no one agent is employed many hours. Religious persons enter into the business without violating their own consciences, or imposing any restraints upon others. Passengers in the mail stages are free to rest during the first day of the week, or pursue their journeys at their own pleasure. While the mail is transported on Saturday, the Jew and the Sabbatarian may abstain from any agency in carrying it, from conscientious scruples. While it is transported on the first day of the week, another class may abstain, from the same religious scruples. The obligation of government is the same on both of these classes; and the committee can

discover no principle on which the claims of one should be more respected than those of the other, unless it should be admitted that the consciences of the minority are less sacred than those of the majority.

It is the opinion of the committee, that the subject should be regarded simply as a question of expediency, irrespective of its religious bearing. In this light, it has hitherto been considered. Congress have never legislated upon the subject. It rests, as it ever has done, in the legal discretion of the Postmaster General, under the repeated refusals of Congress to discontinue the Sabbath mails. His knowledge and judgment, in all the concerns of that department, will not be questioned. His intense labors and assiduity have resulted in the highest improvement of every branch of his department. It is practised only on the great leading mail routes, and such others as are necessary to maintain their connexions. To prevent this, would, in the opinion of the committee, be productive of immense injury, both in its commercial, political, and in its moral bearings.

The various departments of government require, frequently in peace, always in war, the speediest intercourse with the remotest parts of the country; and one important object of the mail establishment is, to furnish the greatest and most economical facilities for such intercourse. The delay of the mails, one whole day in seven, would require the employment of special expresses, at great expences, and sometimes with great uncertainty.

The commercial, manufacturing, and agricultural interests of the country are so intimately connected, as to require a constant and most expeditious correspondence betwixt all our seaports, and betwixt them and the most interior settlements. The delay of the mails during the Sunday, would give occasion to the employment of private expresses, to such an amount, that probably ten riders would be employed where one mail stage would be running on that day; thus diverting the revenue of that department into another channel, and sinking the establishment into a state of pusillanimity incompatible with the dignity of the government of which it is a department.

Passengers in the mail stages, if the mails are not permitted to proceed on Sunday, will be expected to spend that day at a tavern upon the road, generally, under circumstances not friendly to devotion, and at an expense which many are but poorly able to encounter. To obviate these difficulties, many will employ extra carriages for their conveyance, and become the bearers of correspondence, as more expeditious than the mail. The stage proprietors will themselves often furnish the travellers with those means of conveyance; so that the effect will ultimately be only to stop the mail, while the vehicle which conveys it will continue, and its passengers become the special messengers for conveying a considerable portion of what otherwise constitute the contents of the mail.

Nor can the committee discover where the system could consistently end. If the observance of a holiday becomes incorporated in our institutions, shall we not forbid the movement of an army; prohibit an assault in time of war; and lay an injunction upon our naval officers to lie in the wind, while upon the ocean, on that day? Consistency would seem to require it. Nor is it certain that we should stop here. If the principle is once established, that religion, or religious observances, shall be interwoven

3 s

with our legislative acts, we must pursue it to its ultimatum. We shall, if consistent, provide for the erection of edifices for the worship of the Creator, and for the support of christian ministers, if we believe such measures will promote the interests of Christianity. It is the settled conviction of the committee, that the only method of avoiding these consequences, with their attendant train of evils, is to adhere strictly to the spirit of the constitution, which regards the general government in no other light than that of a civil institution, wholly destitute of religious authority.

What other nations call religious toleration, we call religious rights. They are not exercised in virtue of governmental indulgence, but as rights, of which government cannot deprive any portion of citizens, however small. Despotic power may invade those rights, but justice still confirms them. Let the national legislature once perform an act which involves the decision of a religious controversy, and it will have passed its legitimate bounds. The precedent will then be established, and the foundation laid for that usurpation of the Divine prerogative in this country, which has been the desolating scourge to the fairest portions of the old world. Our Constitution recognises no other power than that of persuasion, for enforcing religious observances. Let the professors of christianity recommend their religion by deeds of benevolence—by christian meekness—by lives of temperance and holiness. Let them combine their efforts to instruct the ignorant—to relieve the widow and the orphan—to promulgate to the world the gospel of their Saviour, recommending its precepts by their habitual example; government will find its legitimate object in protecting them. It cannot oppose them, and they will not need its aid. Their moral influence will then do infinitely more to advance the true interests of religion, than any measure which they may call on Congress to enact.

The petitioners do not complain of any infringement upon their own rights. They enjoy all that christians ought to ask at the hand of any government—protection from all molestation in the exercise of their religious sentiments.

Resolved, That the committee be discharged from the further consideration of the subject.

Queries—Answered.
Query XIX.

WHAT does the Saviour mean in these words:—"He said to them, It is your privilege to know the secrets of the Reign of God; but to those without, every thing is veiled in parables, that they may not perceive what they look at, or understand what they hear?"

Answer. He just means what he says. The language is exceedingly plain, and just in the spirit of the original Greek. It is not the language at which some good minds revolt, but at the sense. They understand the language perfectly, but they do not approbate the sense. Let the following facts be noticed, and we shall be instructed from this passage and many similar ones:—1st. The Saviour concedes that those *without* could and would have understood him, if he had not used figures. He had not, then, so contemptible an opinion of human abilities, even in the most depraved state of morals, as some of our cotemporaries. His enemies *could* have understood him, (the Saviour being judge,) if he had not *veiled* his instructions in parables. 2d. We also learn that his disciples could not under-

stand him with all the *internal* aids they had from the Holy Spirit, unless the language was unveiled or the parables explained to them from his lips. This he did for them when apart; and having given them many lessons in secret, they improved so far as to be able to understand many of his parables delivered in mixed assemblies. These are two good lessons, which we learn incidentally from this and similar passages—worthy to be attended to, with a reference to the popular doctrines concerning human abilities, and *internal* aids. But this by the way.

But this does not reach the difficulty preying upon the mind of the querist. It seems to him that there is a partiality exhibited by the Saviour, incompatible with his professed philanthropy or love of the whole human race. This is by no means the fact. And it will appear so when we reflect upon the state of the case. Some persons in a future state will be beyond the reach of mercy—some are so in the present state. They have shut their eyes—alienated their hearts—seared their consciences—and most stubbornly resisted the Spirit of God. There is a certain crisis beyond which the moral disease becomes incurable, as well as the physical. Some men here survive this crisis for a period. In the physical disease they live hours and days after the crisis when all physicians know they are incurable. It is not true in physics, that "while there is life there is hope." For there is life where there is no hope. Neither is it true as the hymn sings—

"While the lamp holds out to burn,
"The vilest sinner may return."

Now many of the Jews in the days of Isaiah, of the Lord Jesus, and of the Apostle Paul, had survived this crisis. The Saviour treated them accordingly. And will he not be as merciful when he sits upon the throne of final judgment, as when he stood on earth, saying, "Come to me all ye weary and heavy burthened," &c. Most assuredly he will: yet he will condemn the wicked. Those persons, then, from whom he studiously veiled the gospel, were those whose characters he knew to be such as to exclude them from forgiveness and acceptance. This is a fact, and an *awful fact*—that, under the Reign of Favor, it is possible for men to become depraved, so wicked, so hardened, as to be beyond the reach of cure. Unless this fact be apprehended and regarded, there will occur many passages in both Testaments inexplicable, and there will appear many cases in our time unaccountable. But it may be remarked, while on this passage, that it was necessary for the Saviour, on many occasions, to conceal his meaning from his auditors under their present views and feelings towards him, else he would not have been permitted to finish his mission. Some, therefore, who through mistaken views, would have killed him at one time, would have been, in other circumstances, his friends and disciples. It is inferrible, therefore, that even some of them from whom at one time he was constrained to veil the doctrine of his Reign, at another time, and under other circumstances, were disposed to hear patiently, and did actually embrace him in all his pretensions.

Had Paul, for instance, at one time been amidst his auditors, it would have been necessary for him to have spoken to him in parables. And many of those who believed on Pentecost were of the same school and character.

Moreover, it was necessary for the Saviour to speak some parables, even to his disciples, without explaining them. They would not have kept the secret and it would have injured his cause. There were some secrets he dared not to confide in them all. Out of the twelve he permitted but three to be with him on the holy mount; and even these he had strictly to enjoin not to disclose what they there heard and saw while he was alive.

But still, although these are facts, and may be applied to the solution of some difficulties, the former exposition must not be lost sight of: for the apostles themselves so understood the matter and the ancient prophecies. Paul reminded the Antiochians, the Roman Jews, as well as the Corinthians and others, that there were some of his hearers who *could not* believe to life, because of their long resistance of the Holy Spirit. Many, too, who had made shipwreck of faith and a good conscience, and had apostatized from the faith, were, as Peter told some, reserved unto judgment, and doomed to destruction. One thing, however, may be affirmed with the utmost confidence, and in perfect conformity to the language of both Testaments, that neither, the Saviour while on earth, nor his apostles after him, in all they said and wrote, ever did veil the gospel, or shut the gates of mercy from any one who did, in the character of an humble and sincere penitent, sue for mercy.

Query XX.

Can you reconcile *Acts* ix. 23. with *Gal.* i. 17. 18. In the former Luke says, Paul went to Jerusalem from Damascus, immediately after his conversion; yet in the *Galatians*, Paul says, "After three years I went up to Jerusalem?"

Answer.—It does not appear, from Luke's account in the *Acts*, that Paul went immediately to Jerusalem. Luke gives no account of Paul's tour into Arabia. It appears from *Gal.* i. 17. that Paul from Damascus went into Arabia; continued there for some time, and *again* returned to Damascus; and then, after a long time, or "many days," when the Damascenes were determined to kill him, he was let down from the wall in a basket, and then went to Jerusalem, which was three years from his conversion. See my "Hints to Readers," new version, 2d ed. p. 27, No. 5. There is no real difficulty here.

Query XXI.

Is it consistent with the New Testament for the bishops or elders of churches to apply to the civil courts for license to marry?

Answer.—Marriage is a civil as well as a religious institution. It is, therefore, a proper subject of civil legislation. As the civil law has to do with estates, inheritances, widows, &c. it is necessary that it should pay some attention to the subject of marriage. To these regulations, where there is no contravention of the laws of the Great King, all his subjects will cheerfully submit. It is, therefore, the duty of all who celebrate the rites of matrimony, to do so according to law. But there is no compulsion on any person, bishop or other, to apply for such license if they do not like it. But such as are not legally authorized, ought not to desire to officiate.

Query XXII.

Ought not the Lord's supper to be celebrated at night? Was it not instituted at night? And is it not called a supper?

Answer.—It does not appear from any thing in the New Testament that the primitive churches, neither that at Jerusalem nor Corinth, had any particular hour or time in the twenty-four consecrated for this observance. Were we to seek for the precise hour in which it was instituted, and make its time of institution the hour of observance, we should have to observe it neither on the first day nor first night of the week. The first day of the week, among the Jews, began at the going down of the sun on our Saturday, and ended at the going down of the sun on our Sunday. So that the first night of the week with the Jews, is, with us, Saturday night. Again, it was on what we call Thursday night, that the supper was instituted. So that if we were to be fastidious about the time, and make the observance of it at night, because of the time of its institution, it ought to be on Thursday night.

But, say some, why call it a supper, if not observed at night? Yes, and carry this matter out legitimately, and I ask, Why call a small piece of bread and a sip of wine a supper? It ought to be a full meal, for the same reason it ought to be at night. Yet it was not a meal at its first institution, for it was instituted just after a supper had been eaten. We cannot, then, and be consistent with reason, make it an observance of the night, unless we in all other matters follow the same guide. The ancient supper and modern dinner correspond in point of importance in the usual meals of the day. But on this I lay no stress.

It is argued that Paul and the disciples at Troas ate the Lord's supper at night. But this cannot be legitimately made out; for they did not assemble till the first day of the week. The first night of the week was over before they came together. And if at the time that Paul broke bread for his own refreshment, it is supposed that the church eat the Lord's supper; it was then on the second day of the week on the current computation, and not on the first day or night, that the disciples at Troas broke bread.

The breaking of bread spoken of, after midnight, after the recovery of Eutychus, was most unquestionably a private refreshment. It reads in syntax thus:—"And Paul going up again, and he having broken bread, and he having eaten, he conversed a considerable time until day break." This refreshment was a natural and requisite one, preparatory to a journey, and occurred on our Monday morning, the second day of the week. There is, therefore, no grounds to presume that there was any such idea in the primitive church, as that they must eat the Lord's supper on the first night of the week.

Query XXIII.

Was ever the saying of the Lord accomplished which says, "As Jonah was three days and three nights in the whale's stomach, so will the Son of Man be three days and three nights in the bowels of the earth?"

Answer.—Not literally. For on the third day he rose from the dead. He spoke this as a sign to those who demanded a sign, in allusion to Jonah's interment in the whale. It was in the same style, though a little more figurative, that he said, "Destroy this temple, and in three days I will rebuild it." Repeatedly the Lord declared, "1 will rise the third day," so that it could not be in any other than in an allusive style to the case of Jonah he mentions the nights; and it is not improbable but that just in the same sense in which Jonah was three days and nights in the whale's stomach, was he interred in the earth. When he spake without figure or allusion, he always said he would rise on the third day.— Many say it was usual with the Jews to append the night to the day when it was not implied that the night was spent as the day; but such was their custom.

Query XXIV.

What mean these words, 1 *Cor.* xv. 29. "Else what shall they do who are baptized for the dead? If the dead rise not at all, why are they then baptized for the dead?"

Answer. The next verse gives the key of interpretation. "And why stand we in jeopardy every hour?" Why should I Paul hazard my life in attesting the resurrection of Jesus Christ, if I had not the most unequivocal proof of his resurrection? Through this medium contemplate the preceding words. Only first recollect that the word *immerse* is used frequently for sufferings. Jesus said, "I have an *immersion* to undergo, and how am I straitened till it be accomplished." I have to be immersed in an immense flood of sufferings. Also the phrase, "fallen asleep for Christ," is equivalent to dying for declaring faith in him. Now these criticisms regarded, and the elliptical verse 29, is plain and forcible—"If there be no resurrection from the dead, what shall they do who are immersed in afflictions and distress for believing and declaring that the dead will be raised? If the dead rise not at all, if they are not assured of their resurrection, why do they submit to be immersed in sorrows in the hope of a resurrection?"

[These queries came from Kentucky, New-York, Virginia, and Ohio.]

The Word of God.

So badly taught are many christians that they cannot think that any translation of the scriptures deserves the title of the Word of God except that of king James. The translators of the king's version did not themselves think so, as we have shown most conclusively by publishing their own preface—on which preface we have some remarks to make, at a more convenient time. But to the intelligent reader no remarks are necessary to show that they had very different ideas of their version, from those which this generation have formed. Have the French, the Spanish, the German, and all the nations of Europe, save the English, no Word of God? If king James' version is the only Word of God on earth, then all nations who speak any other language than the English, have no Revelation.

Much of the reasoning of both priests and people, on this subject, is as silly as that of an old lady who, for many years, has been deprived of her reason, from whom we heard the other day. She once had a sound judgment, and still has a retentive memory, though she has not been *compos mentis* one day in twenty years. Her husband was reading in the new version, the account of the cure of the blind man, (*Mark* viii. 24.) He came to these words: "I see men whom I can distinguish from trees only by their walking." In the king's version, "I see men as trees, walking." After reading these words he paused, and observed to the old lady, to elicit a reply, "How much better this, than the old version." "That is a good explanation," said she, "but it is not the scriptures, not the Word of God." So our good logicians reason.

I would thank some of those ignorant declaimers to tell us where the Word of God was before the reign of king James! Had they no divine book before this good king, in consequence of the Hampton Conference, summoned his wise men? Yes; they had version after version, each of which, in its turn, ceased to be the "Word of God" when a new one was given. This I say after the manner of these declaimers. Our good forefathers, two hundred and fifty years ago, read and preached from a different version, which they venerated in their day, as our compeers venerate James' Bible.—The English language has changed, and the original tongues are better understood now than then. The common version is, as many good and learned men have said, quite obsolete in its language, and in many places very defective in giving the ideas found in the original scriptures. Taken as a whole, it has outlived its day at least one century, and like a superannuated man, has failed to be as lucid and as communicative as in its prime.

There is no version in any language that does not clearly communicate the same great facts, and make the path of bliss a plain and easy found one; but there is an immense difference in the force, beauty, clearness, and intelligibility of the different versions now in use. And that king James' version needs a revision is just as plain to the learned and biblical student, as that the Scotch and English used in the sixteenth century, is not the language now spoken in these United States. And this may be made as plain to the common mind, as it is that the coat which suited the boy of twelve, will not suit the same person when forty years old. As the boy grows from his coat, so do we from the language of our ancestors.   EDITOR.

To the Readers of the Christian Baptist.

The Past, the Present, and the Future.

MY PATRONS AND FRIENDS,—It is full time that I should address you on the past, the present, and the future, as respects you, myself, and posterity.

With the exception of comparatively a few witnesses in the mountains and vallies of Europe, all christendom slept for one thousand years. Kings and priests made a golden goblet—filled it with medicated wine, of the most inebriating qualities—handed it to each other—and when they had freely indulged themselves, they handed it to their subjects, who all became intoxicated, and, like drunken sots, fell fast asleep! Luther arose and washed himself; and, like the angel that liberated Peter, he smote his brethren on the side until a number of them awoke. He led them out into the city, and left them in one of its streets. They were not as sagacious as Peter; for, instead of marching out, they took up a permanent abode in the great city, in whose prisons they had so long lain. This Reformation was too soon completed; and now for three centuries their descendants have done little else in the religious way than quarrel about it. We were born in the suburbs of the great city, and lived in its smoke during our nonage. But we have been awaked, and wish to awake our contemporaries.

For this purpose we blew the trumpet a few years ago. We feared and hoped. More were then awake, and many more have since awaked, than we dared at that time to have hoped. Thousands are now examining and searching into the foundations of all the present religious establishments. We have fared much better than we ever did anticipate. I expected to be honored with the appellation of heretic, schismatic, Arian, or some such title, from those who have the power of conferring honorary degrees. I can say that I set out with a single eye, and I have found the promised blessing. But more than I expected: for I have found able coadjutors, powerful friends, and a candid hearing. I have, as all who have read this work with candor will testify, given both sides. My ablest opponents have been permitted to speak all that they had to say in our pages. I have kept nothing back,

We have allowed and invited them to occupy our pages. The result has been that they have, to a man, declined the contest, and confirmed us more and more in the invincibility of truth. I knew their strength before they engaged in the conflict. They did not know mine. I do not speak of physical, or intellectual, or literary strength. In these respects many of them may be, and some of them, I know, are, my superiors. But I have studied the whole Bible, both Testaments, in a way which, I think, none of them have done. I studied their systems too. And I know there are two ways of studying the Oracles: one with, and one without, spectacles. There is a studying of them with no other design than to know, believe, teach, and practise them.

All men may be said to boast, who make pretensions to teach others. No man either writes or speaks as an instructer, who does not, in the very act, claim a right to the public ear. We claim that right, and acknowledge that we claim it. Whether this claim be well or ill-founded, whether it be mere conceit, or a zeal according to knowledge, our cotemporaries and posterity will decide. But whether it be enthusiasm, conceit, or right reason, impelling us, we candidly acknowledge that we claim the right of speaking what we do know, and of declaring what we do believe.

The present is a momentous crisis. All sects are shaking. The religious world is convulsed. Atheism has opened her batteries and unsheathed her sword. Scepticism is big with hopes. Catholic and protestant Popery are plodding and plotting for the supremacy. The little and the great Popes are on tiptoe. Saints are praying for the Millennium; myriads are laboring for its introduction. The bible and the creeds are at war. There is no truce. Such is the present, and such has been the past.

Our designs are, under the government of the great King, to contribute all our energies to the cause of real and unsophisticated christianity. We have never yet brought all our energies into the field. They have been too much distracted. We are now going forth into a new campaign—I have in all my public efforts, followed the openings of the way according to the directions of the great Captain.

With regard to the press, that most potent of all moral engines, we shall disclose our intentions.

It is, with the consent and concurrence of the friends of the ancient order of things, our intention to bring the Christian Baptist to a close in the next volume. We designed to have completed it with the present volume; but we cannot fill the outlines of our plan and prospectus in less than another. But we intend to publish the seventh volume in six months, or to finish it at the close of the present year. During which time we will issue a prospectus for a periodical of a more extensive range, and in some prominent items of a different character. Of these we shall, in due time, advise our friends.

And now we would inform all our readers that if any of them are unwilling to take the seventh volume to be issued before the first of January, 1830—they will please to inform us, either directly or through our agents, before the first of June next. Our limits in the present work are by far too confined for the public good, and we must have more room. I have no fears but the intended work will be patronised. There are so many already enlightened who know that it is their duty and their privilege to use their means and influence for the good of their own posterity, and mankind generally, that they cannot, as good stewards, withhold their support to this undertaking. I know they cannot. For the same gracious obligations that urge me to labor, urge them to add wings to my efforts. If they do not need my labors for themselves, that is no matter; they need them for their children, friends, neighbors, and they will have them. We christians are the Lord's people. He owns us, spirit, soul, body, and effects; and we owe all to him. And, I know, that we would rather hear him say to us, "Well done, good and faithful servants," than to have all the monarchs on earth bowing at our feet. Such is our profession, and I hope we will hold it fast to the end.

I have now disclosed my intentions for the future. I have no anxiety about them. If the Lord *will* I shall do as I have proposed. If otherwise, I shall be satisfied; and I doubt not, if he does not employ me in this work, he will employ a more suitable, bold, and active agent. For the earth is his, and the fulness thereof. I hope, through his favor, to acquit myself well, in whatever station he may place me. And I will ever bless his name that I would rather be a door keeper in his house, than reign over the greatest empire the sun surveys.   EDITOR.

Infallibility.

Extract from Doctor Chalmers Sermon on "the Doctrine of Christian Charity applied to the case of Religious Differences."

"IT is said of the Papists that they ascribe an infallibility to the Pope; so that if he were to say one thing, and the Bible another, his authority would carry it over the authority of God. And, think you, brethren, that there is no such Popery among you? You all have, or ought to have, bibles; and how often is it repeated there, "Hearken diligently to me?" Now, do you obey this requirement, by making the reading of your bibles a distinct and earnest exercise? Do you ever dare to bring your favorite minister to the tribunal of the word, or would you tremble at the presumption of such an attempt, so that the hearing of the word, carries a greater authority over your mind than the reading of the Word? Now this want of doing, this trembling at the very idea of a dissent from your minister, this indolent acquiescence in his doctrine, is just calling another man Master; it is putting the authority of man over the authority of God; it is throwing yourself into a prostrate attitude at the footstool of infallibility; it is not just kissing the toe of reverence, but it is the profound degradation of the mind, and of all its faculties; and without the name of Popery—that your bosoms, your souls may be infected with the deadly poison, and your consciences be weighed down by the oppressive shackles of Popery. And all this in the noon-day effulgence of a protestant country, where the bible, in your mother tongue, circulates among all your families; where it may be met with on almost every shelf, and is soliciting you to look to the wisdom that is inscribed on its pages."

Copy of the Indulgences, sold by the authority of Pope Leo, by Tetzel, which occasioned the Reformation.

"MAY our Lord Jesus Christ have mercy upon thee, and absolve thee by the merits of his most holy passion! And I, by the authority of his blessed Apostles Peter and Paul, and of the most holy Pope, granted and committed to me in these parts, do absolve thee, first from all ecclesiastical censures, in whatever manner they have been incurred, and then from all sins, transgressions, and excesses, how enormous soever they be, even from such as are reserved for the cognizance of the holy see, and as far as the keys of the holy church extend, I remit to thee all punishment which thou dost deserve in purgatory on their account; and I restore thee to the holy sacraments of the church, to the unity of the faithful, and to that innocence and purity which thou didst possess at baptism; so that when thou dost die, the gates of punishment shall be shut, and the gates of the paradise of delight shall be opened; and if thou shalt not die at present, this grace shall remain in full force when thou art at the point of death! In the name of the Father, and of the Son, and of the Holy Ghost."

No. 10.]   MAY 5, 1829.

Essays on Man in his Primitive state, and under the Patriarchal, Jewish, and Christian Dispensations.—No. VIII.

Patriarchal Age.—No. IV.

OUR last number adverted to the priesthood of the Patriarchal Age. An objection has been made to one sentence in the 6th No. It is to this sentence: "Not a person on earth believed that the Messiah would die a sin-offering, or rise from the dead, from Eve to Mary Magdalene." If we do not make good this assertion before we finish the Essays on the Jewish and Christian Dispensations, we shall eat it up. "Have patience with me, and I will pay you all." We proceed.

Before the Flood an idea got abroad into the world that some animals were clean and some unclean. This distribution of "birds and beasts" was as superhuman as the ordination of sacrifice. Noah made his selection according to it, and in the offering of sacrifices among the Patriarchs, from Noah to Moses, respect was paid to this distinction.

It is an idea which has generally obtained among the more learned antiquarians and which has some confirmation from ancient scripture, that the sacrifices of the godly were all consumed by fire from heaven—such of them, at least, as were of the burnt offering character. How such an idea obtained it would be hard to tell, unless from established fact. We do know most certainly that, in after times, some offerings were consumed by fire from heaven. And in the time of Abraham it appears that fire from heaven consumed some sacrifices. Abraham presented on one altar, at one time, "one heifer, a female goat, and a ram of three years old, a turtle dove, and a young pigeon." The former were all severed, and the birds laid on entire. After the sun set, "a smoking furnace and a burning lamp," or fire, from heaven fell upon these carcases and consumed them. To such offerings as these promises or covenants were usually appended. Thus after Noah had offered a similar sacrifice, God promised a continuation of the seasons without the intervention of a flood—and here to Abraham the promises concerning Canaan were confirmed.

Jacob, in confirmation of his vow, Gen. xxxv. 14, poured oil upon the stone which he had set up. And on another occasion "he set up a pillar in the place where God talked with him, even a pillar of stone; and he poured a drink offering thereon, and he poured oil thereon." Such were the positive acts of patriarchal worship of the sacrificial kind—sin-offerings, thank-offerings, vow or dedication-offerings.

Some sorts of ablutions or washings were also practised among the patriarchs before the Mosaic economy. Jacob, in order to prepare his family to offer sacrifice with him upon the altar, erected at Bethel, commands them to "change their garments" and "be clean," which, as the most learned critics have proved, is equivalent to "wash yourselves." All sorts of ancient writers, sacred and profane, viewed the deluge as a purification, or washing, or immersion of the earth. Philo the Jew, and Plato the Greek philosopher, give credit to this idea. It was so referred to by the Apostle Peter. And it is not improbable but the ablutions of the pagan world originated from this view of the deluge—sanctioned by the practice of the patriarchs.

It would appear also that the *proseuchæ* of which we read in the New Testament, or places of prayer built on hills or by brooks of water, in retired situations, may be traced back as far as the time of Abraham. (Gen. xxi. 35.) And Abraham planted a grove (or tree) in Beersheba, and there (or under it) he called on the name of the Lord, the everlasting God." From this custom unquestionably arose the corruptions of the pagan world in consecrating groves and high places to their gods. Such were the religious institutions, and such the venerable customs of the holy men of the Patriarchal Age.

In forming a correct view of the religious character of the ancient nations, it is necessary here to inquire how far the inhabitants of Persia, Assyria, Arabia, Canaan and Egypt, were affected or influenced by the religious institutions of this period: for these were the first nations whose institutions gave a character to all the nations of the world.

Abraham was the son of Shem by Arphaxad. The Persians were the descendants of Shem by Elam. The common parentage of Abraham and the Persians laid a foundation for some similarity in their religion. Abraham's ancestors dwelt in Chaldea, and at the time that God signalized Abraham, the Chaldeans began to apostatize from the service of the true God. Hence the expulsion of Abraham from among them. But Dr. Hyde and the most learned antiquarians presented documental proof that the Persians retained the true history of the Creation and the Antediluvian Age; and so attached were the Persians to the religion of Abraham, that the sacred book which contained their religion is called *Sohi Ibrahim*, i. e. the Book of Abraham. For a considerable time after Abraham's day they worshipped the God of Shem, for they did not know all the special communications to Abraham.

The Arabians, down to the time of Jethro, retained the knowledge of the true God. How long after we are not informed; but their religious institutions, as far as we have account, differed little from those practised by Abraham, with the exception of circumcision.

The Canaanites themselves, in Abraham's time, had not apostatized wholly from the religion of Shem. The king of Salem was priest of the most high God; and during Abraham's sojourning among them, they treated him with all respect as a prophet of the true God.

Even amongst the Philistines at Gerar, Abraham found a good and virtuous king, favored with the admonitions of the Almighty. This he little expected, for he was so prejudiced against those people, that, on entering their metropolis, he said, "Surely the fear of God is not in this place." But he was happily disappointed. For Abimelech, in his appeal to Heaven, says, "Lord, will you slay a virtuous nation?" And the Lord did not deny his plea, but heard and answered his request. There appears in the whole narrative no difference in the religious views or practice between Abraham and Abimelech the king of the nation.

The Egyptians, too, in the time of Abraham, were worshippers of the true God. In Upper Egypt they refused, as Plutarch informs us, to pay any taxes for the support of the idolatrous worship; asserting that they owned no mortal, dead or alive, to be a God. The incorruptible and eternal God they called *Cneph*, who they affirmed had no beginning, and never should have an end. In the first advances to mythology in Egypt, they represented God by the figure of a serpent, with the head of a hawk in the middle of a circle. We find no misunderstandings nor difference between Pharoah and Abraham, when the latter went down into Egypt. Indeed, with the exception of the Chaldeans, who were the oldest nation, and the first to introduce idol or image worship, we find a very general agreement in all the ancient nations respecting religious views and practice. And the only defection from the religion of Noah and Shem which we meet with in all antiquity, was that of the Chaldeans.

All the religious rites and usages of the Pagan nations down to the time of Homer, and still later, were very similar to the patriarchal institutions. They offered expiatory sacrifices, deprecations, vows, and ablutions; had altars, priests, and sacred groves; and made the same distinctions between clean and unclean victims. Homer talks of "hecatombs of bulls and goats," "lambs and goats without blemish." And not only the Greek, but the Roman poets, speak of the ablutions, purifications, and sacrifices of ancient times, in such a way as to leave no doubt but that they all came from the same origin.

                                    EDITOR.

Communication.

BROTHER CAMPBELL,—As society at large, both civil and religious, are engaged in examining the defects in their different constitutions, and the journals teeming with reformers and their essays on reformation, I took up the Christian Baptist with a determination of examining the foundation of the editor and his numerous correspondents—and can say that I have been fully compensated for the time I was engaged in this delightful work. The essays by the Editor are truly interesting, both scriptural and rational. Those on the Clergy, the Ancient Order of Things, and the Ancient Gospel, I opine are unanswerable. The Essay on the Primitive and Modern Christianity, signed by Philip, is superexcellent. He concluded by saying, "This induction may be pursued to greater length in some future paper." I searched through all the volumes expecting to meet with the author's promise, and found it not. I still flatter myself that ere long he will give us another essay upon this all-important subject.

In the fourth volume I read an excellent letter signed Paulinus, containing some very appropriate remarks upon the present order of things and a manifest desire for the restoration of the ancient order of things—such as the following: " I am greatly pleased with what appears to be your drift and aim, viz. to clear the religion of Jesus of all the adventitious lumber with which it has been encumbered, and bring back the christian church to its primitive simplicity and

beauty." The essay "on the Jewish Sabbath and the Christian Lord's day" is said to be superlatively excellent. He also speaks of the New Testament being an instrument, the most effectual, for sweeping off all the rubbish which has been gathered from the old ruins of former establishments to build withal on Christian grounds: " that the word of God is the instrument of our regeneration and sanctification, I have no doubt." "It is my wish (says the writer) not only to express my hearty approbation of your avowed hostility to certain abuses and follies prevalent in the religious world, but to lend any little aid in my power towards a correction of these evils. Among the objects here alluded to, let me just mention the adoption of creeds and confessions of faith—those fruitful sources of dissention, and stubborn barriers against the admission of divine light from the word of God, and the high pretensions of many among the clergy." The most interesting of all with the writer is, " Such a reformation in the church as shall restore, what you term the ancient order of things." In your opposition to error, he says, " I do not wish to see you abate one jot or tittle of the firmness with which you take your stand, or the keenness with which you make the attack. I would not wish you to cut off the points of your arrows whenever they are directed at error or folly." These independent and truly interesting sayings of Paulinus I am delighted with.

In his second epistle I find other excellent things. "Wherever the New Dispensation comes, it lays hold of every human creature, with the grasp of divine authority, while it presented the exhibition of divine mercy." " I think it is justly due to you to say, that you are an avowed friend to the Spirit's operations in the production of genuine religion." "I am no advocate for the formation of mere theories, nor for compiling abstract truths." " I have no disposition I assure you, to carry the fruits I may be enabled to gather from the tree of life (the Bible) to any distillery." " O for the time when divine truth, the whole divine truth, shall be relished as coming from God!" An answer to this aspiration, how important to the well being of the human family? and for the accomplishment of the vows of the writer? I think I discover in this epistle the writer's former opinions somewhat shaken.— Whether it was owing to your sweeping the houses of those distillers of alcohol, and the dust got into his eyes; that he was tippling there, or that he had been pressing the oil out of the bean, I am unable to determine. Upon reading the fifth volume my opinion is confirmed, there has been a lecture, caution, admonition, reproof, or rebuke given him from somewhere. Mark this: "He (that is Paulinus) wrote something last year in which he certainly went too far. He is now convinced (I am persuaded) and guarded against our friend Campbell's chimeras." After this appeared this excellent writer seems to have wanted confidence in all he undertook to write for the Christian Baptist. Notice the close of his "Essays on the Holy Spirit." Although he did not wish you to abate one jot or tittle of the firmness of your stand, nor the keenness of your attack, in your fifth letter to Bishop Semple, you must have had beards on your arrows, or he could not in justice to his own wishes have complained of the sharpness of your attack upon the ignorance, vice, and immorality of the professors of religion. Every one that has read the Essays of Paulinus no doubt expected to find him not only speaking those excellent things, but doing them! Whether this be the case or not, I cannot say positively. If he is

                                    83

the author of a series of essays published in the Religious Herald upon Reformation, signed Melancthon, his fourth essay authorizes me to say he is not. Notice the following recommendation. ☞ "I would respectfully suggest to the Baptist General Convention, at their ensuing meeting, the propriety of adopting a resolution that it is expedient we should be supplied with a set of suitable catechisms; that they nominate some person or persons for the purpose of compiling them; as also a committee of inspection, to whom may be confided the privilege of recommending the compilation to the use of our churches and our friends throughout the Union. The General Convention forms, in some sort, a centre of general union amongst us; and a recommendation from that body might have a powerful and happy influence, and could not be considered any usurpation of authority." This, it is true, is a little thing; but is intended to form the religious minds of our "little immortals." When we remember what a large tree grows from a little acorn, and when it is full grown in a good soil, that such is its attracting power that nothing flourishes within its reach, we then are admonished to attend to the seeds we sow, or in other words to attend to little things. Is this the way to clear the church of the "adventitious lumber with which it has been encumbered, and bring it back to its primitive simplicity and beauty?" Is this "clearing the religion of Jesus of those abuses and follies prevalent in the religious world?" Is this the way to "sweep off all the rubbish which has been gathered from the old ruins of former establishments to build withal on christian grounds?" Is this the instrument of God in regenerating and sanctifying these "little immortals?" Is this the aid he promised you to correct the evils, to wit, creeds and confessions of faith, "those fruitful sources of dissention and stubborn barriers against the admission of divine light from the word of God?" Is this his "hearty approbation of your hostility to certain abuses and follies prevalent in the religious world?" Is this the way to "reform the church and restore the ancient order of things?" Is this his "opposition to theories, or compiling abstract truths?" Is not this carrying our jugs to the distillery to get alcohol that our "little immortals" may tipple with us? When this little idol is completed, will this be the time when "divine truth, the whole of divine truth, shall be relished as coming from God?"

I am put to my wit's end to determine whether the writer of the above recommendation intends a reformation from, or restoration of, the "old ruins of former establishments!" What need can there be of the influence of the Holy Spirit, when it is admitted that these ecclesiastical bodies' recommendation will have "a powerful and happy influence in giving efficacy to these catechisms." Again, is this the way to correct the evils among the kingdom of the clergy, by soliciting resolutions of adoption to give energy to human productions, committees of inspections, and acknowledging their powerful and happy influence upon their recommendations? Again, what need is there for these catechisms, and recommendations of such powerful and happy influence, when it is admitted wherever the New Dispensation comes it lays hold of every human creature with the grasp of divine authority, while it presents the exhibition of divine mercy? Is not this an acknowledgment that the New Testament is not sufficient to instruct these "little immortals" in their duty to God? For my part, I think it is a deep reflection upon the

wisdom and philanthropy of Jesus Christ, in not giving to these "little immortals" what this writer has considered necessary for their religious education, and, I suppose, for their salvation. "O for the time when divine truth, the whole of divine truth, shall be relished as coming from God!"

I do not wish to be understood as finding fault with the essays of Paulinus, though I think his essays on the Holy Spirit are rather too much in the Calvinistic style. But with the recommendation of Melancthon, if he is the same writer, there is, to my judgment, a manifest inconsistency. As so much is said about the Holy Spirit's operations in this metaphysical day, I would, in a few words, give my views of what the New Testament teaches:—We must first hear, then believe and reform; then obey, that is, be immersed; then receive the regenerating Spirit, with all its heavenly blessings promised to the believing sons and daughters of Adam. This appears to be so plainly inculcated in the New Testament, that I am astonished that I so long remained ignorant of the gospel, when at the same time professed to be a teacher of it. And for this discovery I am indebted to you, brother editor. Let me conclude in the language of Paulinus, "that you may steer a straight forward course, alike unawed by custom, unprovoked by opposition, unseduced by novelty, is the prayer of yours in the gospel."

A LOVER OF THE WHOLE OF DIVINE TRUTH.

Profession and Principle, or Faith in Words and Faith in Works.

I HAVE often regretted to find the testimony of some eminent witness on one side of some important question—and his practice on the opposite side. This, indeed, is a very common occurrence; so common that we are more surprized to find a coincidence between the verbal profession and the actual conduct, than we are to find a discrepancy. Which of the two have the most influence, and which of the two ought to have the most influence, are two distinct questions. Mosheim, for example, in his compend of ecclesiastical history of the first centuries, gives a clear and forcible testimony against the present order of things, by showing its entire departure from the ancient order. He shows that the bishops, deacons, teaching, exhortation, prayers, praises, and, indeed, all the worship of the primitive church, were, in every grand point, dissimilar to the present. He unequivocally declares the "reformed churches" to be apostates in fact from the ancient order; and yet we find him among the Rabbins! What a pity!

A thousand Paidobaptists too, have declared against sprinkling—and still sprinkled infants! And myriads have remonstrated against popery, prelacy, and clerical intrigue; and yet were as full of the Pope as Queen Elizabeth! Whence is it, O Mammon, that you can make your votaries sing with so much sincerity—

" I see the better way, and I approve it too,
" Detest the worse, and still the worse pursue."

Intellect like conscience, is generally on the right side, and pravity, politics, and the flesh pot on the other. When intellect, conscience, and the stomach are on opposite sides, the latter is sure to be most obstreperous and intriguing. Hence the triumphs of the belly.

As I consider the decisions of the intellect to be the most impartial, it demands from me the greatest respect; though, indeed, I cannot but lament to find so many illustrious instances of the triumphs of the animal over the intellectual

84

man. I can find the greatest men now living in the religious world, substantially, and some of them most unequivocally, in their public attestations, on the side of the ancient order of things. It would astonish many were we to cull out the explicit and forcible attestations to the cause we advocate, from the distinguished men of the last and the present century; to see what agreement in views, both with respect to the ancient order of things, and the issue of the present contests. We do not say that every man who asserts some grand fundamental truth, sees its bearings; nor will we affirm that they are all, from appetite, avarice, or ambition, blinded against its connexion and authority. But one thing I will say, that I can find assertions and explicit declarations in the writings of such men as Dr. Adam Clarke, Thomas Scott, Messrs. Hall and Irving, and Dr. Chalmers, as, carry them out to their literal and legitimate issue, would subvert all the glittering schemes of the day, and leave in lieu of them all, nought but the ancient order of things!

The following extract from *Chalmer's Essay on the Evidence of Christianity*, is deserving of the attention and strict perusal of all the readers of this work:—

"What is the reason why there is so much more unanimity among critics and grammarians about the sense of any ancient author, than about the sense of the New Testament Because the one is made purely a question of criticism: the other has been complicated with the uncertain fancies of a daring and presumptuous theology. Could we only dismiss these fancies, sit down like a school boy to his task, and look upon the study of divinity as a mere work of translation, then we would expect the same unanimity among christians that we meet with among scholars and literati about the system of Epicurus or philosophy of Aristotle. But here lies the distinction betwixt the cases. When we make out, by a critical examination of the Greek of Aristotle, that such was his meaning, and such his philosophy, the result carries no authority with it, and our mind retains the congenial liberty of its own speculations. But if we make out by a critical examination of the Greek of St. Paul, that such is the theology of the New Testament, we are bound to submit to this theology; and our minds must surrender every opinion, however dear to them. It is quite in vain to talk of the mysteriousness of the subject, as being the cause of the want of unanimity among christians. It may be mysterious, in reference to our former conceptions. It may be mysterious in the utter impossibility of reconciling it with our own assumed fancies, and self-formed principles. It may be mysterious in the difficulty which we feel in comprehending the manner of the doctrine, when we ought to be satisfied with the authoritative revelation which has been made to us of its existence and its truth. But if we could only abandon all our former conceptions, if we felt that our business was to submit to the oracle of God, and that we are not called upon to effect a reconciliation betwixt a revealed doctrine of the bible, and an assumed or excogitated principle of our own; then, we are satisfied, that we would find the language of the Testament to have as much clear, and precise, and distinctive simplicity, as the language of any sage or philosopher that has come down to our time."

"Could we only get it reduced to a mere question of language, we should look at no distant period for the establishment of a pure and unanimous christianity in the world. But no.

While the mind and the reasoning of any philosopher are collected from his words, and these words tried as to their import and significancy upon the appropriate principles of criticism, the mind and the reasoning of the Spirit of God are not collected upon the same pure and competent principles of investigation. In order to know the mind of the Spirit, the communications of the Spirit, and the expression of these communications in written language, should be consulted. These are the only data upon which the inquiry should be instituted. But no. Instead of learning the designs and character of the Almighty from his own mouth, we sit in judgment upon them, and make our conjecture of what they should be, take the precedency of his revelations of what they are. We do him the same injustice that we do to an acquaintance, whose proceedings and whose intentions we venture to pronounce upon, while we refuse him a hearing, or turn away from the letter in which he explains himself. No wonder, then, at the want of unanimity among christians, so long as the question of "What thinkest thou" is made the principle of their creed, and, for the sake of criticism, they have committed themselves to the endless caprices of the human intellect. Let the principle of "what thinkest thou" be exploded, and that of "what readest thou" be substituted in its place. Let us take our lesson as the Almighty places it before us, and, instead of being the judge of his conduct, be satisfied with the safer and humbler office of being the interpreter of his language."——

"We must bring a free and unoccupied mind to the exercise. It must not be the pride or the obstinacy of self-formed opinions, or the haughty independence of him who thinks he has reached the manhood of his understanding. We must bring with us the docility of a child, if we want to gain the kingdom of heaven. It must not be a partial, but an entire and unexcepted obedience. There must be no garbling of that which is entire, no darkening of that which is luminous, no softening down of that which is authoritative or severe. The bible will allow of no compromise. It professes to be the directory of our faith, and claims a total ascendancy over the souls and the understandings of men. It will enter no composition with us or our natural principles. It challenges the whole mind as its due, and it appeals to the truth of heaven for the high authority of its sanction. "Whosoever adds to, or takes from the words of this book, is accursed," is the absolute language in which it delivers itself. This brings us to its terms. There is no way of escaping after this. We must bring every thought into the captivity of its obedience, and as closely as ever lawyer stuck to his documents or his extracts, must we abide by the rule and the doctrine which this authentic memorial of God sets before us."

"Now we hazard the assertion, that, with a number of professing christians, there is not this unexcepted submission of the understanding to the authority of the Bible; and that the authority of the Bible is often modified, and in some cases superseded, by the authority of other principles. One of these principles is, the reason of the thing. We do not know if this principle would be at all felt or appealed to by the earliest christians. They turned from dumb idols to serve the living and the true God. There was nothing in their antecedent theology which they could have any respect for: nothing which they could confront, or bring into competition with the doctrines of the New Testament. In these days, the truth as it is in Jesus came to the minds of its disciples, recommended by its novelty, by its grandeur, by the power and recency of its evidences; and, above all, by its vast and evident superiority over the fooleries of a degrading Paganism. It does not occur to us, that men in these circumstances would ever think of sitting in judgment over the mysteries of that sublime faith which had charmed them into an abandonment of their earlier religion. It rather strikes us that they would receive them passively; that, like scholars who had all to learn, they would take their lesson as they found it; that the information of their teachers would be enough for them; and that the restless tendency of the human mind to speculation, would for a time find ample enjoyment in the rich and splendid discoveries which broke like a flood of light upon the world. But we are in different circumstances. To us, these discoveries, rich and splendid as they are, have lost the freshness of novelty. The sun of righteousness, like the sun in the firmament, has become familiarized to us by possession. In a few ages, the human mind deserted its guidance, and rambled as much as ever in quest of new speculations. It is true that they took a juster and a loftier flight since the days of Heathenism. But it was only because they walked in the light of revelation. They borrowed of the New Testament without acknowledgement, and took its beauties and its truths to deck their own wretched fancies and self-constituted systems. In the process of time the delusion multiplied and extended. Schools were formed, and the way of the Divinity was as confidently theorized upon, as the processes of chymistry, or the economy of the heavens. Universities were endowed, and natural theology took its place in the circle of the sciences. Folios were written, and the respected luminaries of a former age poured their *a priori* and their *a posteriori* demonstrations on the world. Taste, and sentiment, and imagination, grew apace; and every raw untutored principle which poetry could clothe in prettiness, or over which the hand of genius could throw the graces of sensibility and elegance, was erected into a principle of the divine government, and made to preside over the councils of the Deity. In the mean time, the Bible, which ought to supersede all, was itself superseded. It was quite in vain to say that it was the only authentic record of an actual embassy which God had sent into the world. It was quite in vain to plead its testimonies, its miracles, and the unquestionable fulfilment of its prophecies. These mighty claims must be over, and be suspended, till we have settled—what? the reasonableness of its doctrines. We must bring the theology of God's ambassador to the bar of our self-formed theology. The Bible, instead of being admitted as the directory of our faith upon its external evidences, must be tried upon the merits of the work itself; and if our verdict be favorable, it must be brought in, not as a help to our ignorance, but as a corollary to our demonstrations. But is this ever done? Yes! by Dr. Samuel Clarke, and a whole host of followers and admirers. Their first step in the process of theological study, is to furnish their minds with the principles of natural theology. Christianity, before its external proofs are looked at or listened to, must be brought under the tribunal of those principles. All the difficulties which attach to the reason of the thing, or the fitness of the doctrines, must be formally discussed, and satisfactorily got over. A voice was heard from heaven, saying of Jesus Christ, "This is my beloved Son: hear ye him." The men of Galilee saw him ascend from the dead to the heaven which he now occupies. The men of Galilee gave their testimony; and it is a testimony which stood the fiery trial of persecution in a former age, and of sophistry in this. And yet, instead of hearing Jesus Christ as disciples, they sit in authority over him as judges. Instead of forming their divinity after the Bible, they try the Bible by their antecedent divinity; and this book, with all its mighty train of evidences, must drivel in their antichambers, till they have pronounced sentence of admission, when they have got its doctrines to agree with their own airy and unsubstantial speculations."

"We do not condemn the exercise of reason in matters of theology. It is the part of reason to form its conclusions, when it has data and evidences before it. But it is equally the part of reason to abstain from its conclusions, when these evidences are wanting. Reason can judge of the external evidences for christianity, because it can discern the merits of human testimony; and it can perceive the truth or the falsehood of such obvious credentials in the performance of a miracle, or the fulfilment of a prophecy. But reason is not entitled to sit in judgment over these internal evidences, which many a presumptuous theologian has attempted to derive from the reason of the thing, or from the agreement of the doctrine with the fancied character and attributes of the Deity. One of the most useful exercises of reason, is to ascertain its limits, and to keep within them, to abandon the field of conjecture, and to restrain itself within that safe and certain barrier which forms the boundary of human experience. However humiliating you may conceive it, it is this that lies at the bottom of Lord Bacon's philosophy, and it is to this that modern science is indebted for all her solidity and all her triumphs. Why does philosophy flourish in our days? Because her votaries have learned to abandon their own creative speculations, and to submit to evidences, let her conclusions be as painful and as unpalatable as they will. Now all that we want is to carry the same lesson and the same principle to theology. Our business is not to guess, but to learn. After we have established christianity to be an authentic message from God upon these historical grounds—when the reason and experience of man entitle him to form his conclusions—nothing remains for us, but an unconditional surrender of the mind to the subject of the message. We have a right to sit in judgment over the credentials of Heaven's Ambassador, but we have no right to sit in judgment over the information he gives us. We have no right either to refine or to modify that information, till we have accommodated it to our previous conceptions. It is very true, that if the truths which he delivered lay within the field of human observation, he brings himself under the tribunal of our antecedent knowledge. Were he to tell us, that the bodies of the planetary system moved in orbits which are purely circular, we would oppose to him the observations and measurements of astronomy. Were he to tell us, that in winter the sun never shone, and that in summer no cloud ever darkened the brilliancy of his career, we would oppose to him the certain remembrances, both of ourselves and of our whole neighborhood. Were he to tell us, that we were perfect men, because we were free from passion, and loved our neighbors as ourselves, we would oppose to him the history of our own lives, and the deeply-seated consciousness of our own infirmities. On all these subjects we can confront him; but when he brings truth from a quarter which no human eye ever explored, when he tells us the mind of the Deity, and brings before us the counsels of that invisible Being, whose arm is abroad upon all nations, and whose views reach to eternity, he is beyond the ken of eye or of telescope, and we must submit to him. We have no more right to sit in judgment over his information, than we have to sit in judgment over the information of any other visiter who lights upon our planet, from some distant and unknown part of the universe, and tells us what worlds roll in these remote tracts which are beyond the limits of our astronomy, and how the Divinity peoples them with his wonders. Any previous conceptions of ours are of no more value than the fooleries of an infant; and should we offer to resist or to modify upon the strength of our conceptions, we would be as unsound and as unphilosophical as ever schoolman was with his categories, or Cartesian with his whirlpools of ether."

"Let us go back to the first christians of the Gentile world. They turned from dumb idols to serve the living and the true God. They made a simple and entire transition from a state as bad, if not worse, than that of entire ignorance, to the christianity of the New Testament.— Their previous conceptions, instead of helping them, behoved to be utterly abandoned; nor was there that intermediate step which so many of us think to be necessary, and which we dignify with the name of the rational theology of nature. In these days, this rational theology was unheard of; nor have we the slightest reason to believe that they were ever initiated into its doctrines, before they were looked upon as fit to be taught the peculiarities of the gospel. They were translated at once from the absurdities of paganism to that christianity which has come down to us, in the records of evangelical history, and the epistles which their teachers addressed to them. They saw the miracles; they acquiesced in them, as satisfying credentials of an inspired teacher; they took the whole of their religion from his mouth; their faith came by hearing, and hearing by the words of a divine messenger. This was their process, and it ought to be ours. We do not see the miracles, but we see their reality through the medium of that clear and unsuspicious testimony which has been handed down to us. We should admit them as the credentials of an embassy from God. We should take the whole of our religion from the records of this embassy; and, renouncing the idolatry of our own self-formed conceptions, we should repair to that word, which was spoken to them that heard it, and transmitted to us by the instrumentality of written language. The question with them was, What hear you? The question with us is, What read you? They had their idols, and they turned away from them. We have our fancies, and we contend, that, in the face of an authoritative revelation from heaven, it is as glaring idolatry in us to adhere to these, as it would be were they spread upon canvass, or chiseled into material form by the hands of a statuary."

Election.—No. II.

THE election taught by the college men contemplates all the righteous, from Abel to the resurrection of the dead, as standing in the relation of elect persons to God; than which nothing can be more opposed to fact and scripture: for though Abel, Enoch, and Noah, were worshippers of the true God, they were not elect men; nay, though Melchisedeck himself, king of Salem, was at once priest of the Most High God, and the most illustrious type of Messiah; though he received tythes of Abraham, blessed him, and, as Paul informs us, was greater than he; yet neither Melchisedeck nor any of the numerous worshippers for whom he officiated in the quality of God's priest, did ever stand in the relation of elect worshippers in the scripture sense of the word elect. Abraham was the first elect man; and it remains for those who assert the contrary of this, to prove their proposition—a thing they never can do by scripture.

The elect institution reared upon the patriarch Abraham, and which has been made the deposite of covenants, laws, services, glory and promises, is quite distinct from the general righteousness of the world, whether that righteousness may have been derived from revelations made to men before the commencement of the elect institutions, or afterwards from traditions, or from an apprehension of God's existence derived from the face of nature, the currency of events, and the nature of human society among Gentiles, ancient and modern. I say the election is a *sui generis* institution, in which the worshiper does not, with the uncertainty of a Mahometan idolator, a Chinese or Japanese, ask the remission of sins; but in which this blessing is stable and certain, secured to him by the promise and oath of God, two immutable things, by which it was impossible for God to lie, that the man might have strong consolation, who has fled into this institution for refuge to lay hold of the hope set before him in the gospel; which is the second apartment of the elect building, as Judaism was the first,—"In *thee* shall all the families of the earth be blessed"—a promise made to no other institution.

In our last essay we ascertained two of the six things suggested to us by the term election, viz. that the living *God* was the *elector*, and that *Abraham* was the *first elect person;* and now if we ask when it began and when it shall end, I answer, first, that election will close at the end of the world—all the gracious purposes of the institution will be accomplished at that time—false religion and bad government—the domination of political and trading influences—and every thing which opposes itself to the religion and authority of this institution—shall have been put down; and angels and men shall behold this truth, that the God of Abraham is the true God, and Jesus the Messiah his Son; and that Mahomet and Confucius, Zoroaster, and Brahama, were self-created apostles.

As for the commencement of the election, if Abraham was the first elect person, as we see he was, it follows this must have been when God called that patriarch from his native country to be the head of the elect people: "Now the Lord had said to Abraham, Get you out of your country, and from your father's house to a land that I will show you, and I will make of you a great nation; and I will bless you, and make your *name great*, and *you shall be a blessing;* and I will bless them that bless you, and curse them that curse you; and *in you* shall all the families of the earth be blessed." *Gen.* xii. Here, then, is the commencement of that institution which is finally to triumph over imposition and falsehood.

It only remains for us to speak of the great and illustrious purposes for which God has set up this institution in the earth, and finally of the principle on which a man of any nation may be admitted to the privileges of it, viz. the remission of sins, &c. &c. First, then, in regard to the ends of the election, I say, it is the blessing of mankind—"In you shall all the families of the earth be blessed." This is God's declared purpose in regard to mankind by the institution called "the election;" consequently its purpose is not (like the election of Edwards, Calvin, and others,) to exclude, curse, and destroy; but to gather, to bless, and to save! "In you shall all the nations of the earth be blessed"—"I will make you a blessing." Abraham, Isaac, and Jacob, then, were not chosen by God for the mean partial purpose of being *dragged* into heaven, will or no will, on the principle of final perseverance; but for the general and benevolent purpose of saving mankind by an institution of which they were made the root or foundation.— While the pulpit of fatalism represents the God of heaven both partial and cruel, the scriptural election furnishes us with the fairest specimen of his peerless impartiality and philanthropy: the lineaments of the divine character is in nothing more effulgent than in the blessing of the nations on the principles of an election, because it represents the Most High as anticipating the alienations and apostacies of his self-willed and unhappy creatures, running into all the idolatries and consequent immoralities of Assyria, Persia, Greece, Rome, &c. &c. and then providing for their redemption from these things by this elect institution, in which he had deposited a correct theology and the principles of a pure morality to be preached to the world in the fulness of time, i. e. after the wisdom of this world, viz. philosophy, government, and idolatry had been sufficiently proved incompetent to the purification and elevation of the human family.

I am sure our Heavenly Father in all this has shown the wisdom and prudence of one who hides a piece of leaven in three measures of meal until the whole be leavened. He has treated the rebellious and refractory nation of the Jews as a woman would a bowl of meal set down by the fireside, with the leaven in it, and turned, and warmed, and tended, until the leavening process has commenced, in order that the whole mass may be more speedily and certainly transformed; yet, after all, it would scarcely work in us, so dead are we to heavenly things. Nevertheless the principles of this establishment, the church, must prevail—idolatry must be put down —the knowledge of God must cover the earth —the saints must obtain the government of the world—righteousness run down like a river, and peace like a flowing stream.

Having ascertained, in a summary way, the elector, the *person* elected, the ends of the election, the time when it began and when it shall end, I shall speak of the principle on which it proceeds, and also on the sovereignty of God, and where it obtains in our religion, in some subsequent numbers. I only observe here, that Calvinistic election exhibits the divine sovereignty in a point in which it by no means obtains in christianity. It is not exhibited in a capricious choice of this, that, and the other person, and passing by others, as Calvinism would and does have it; but in the justification of sinners of all nations on the principle of faith, as will appear by and by, an act of God's sovereignty, which was very displeasing to the Jews.

I shall close this paper with an observation or two for the reflection of the reader, until the appearance of the next number. First, then, it ought to be observed that scriptural election is managed entirely on the plan of political election, the ends thereof being the general welfare of the nations—"In you shall all the families of the earth be blessed."

Second. Whether a man can believe, i. e. imbibe the electing principle, is never answered in the Holy Scriptures—for this substantial reason, that, in it, it is never asked. This is an unlearned question of modern Divinity, (i. e. Devility, if such a word or thing there be,) and could be agitated only by fools and philosophers; all the world knowing that we must believe what is proved. Whether we will always act according to our rational and scriptural belief, is another question which the reader may answer by making an appeal to his own conscience. If we would, how many would immediately be baptized into Jesus Christ!   PHILIP.

The Pedobaptist.

THE "*Pedobaptist*," No. 1, has appeared; and, like every thing of the sort, will do good as well as evil. In its direct influence it is calculated to enslave the ignorant and unwary; in its indirect influence it will create suspicions in such as dare to presume to think, and in its efforts to lull the conscience of hereditary Paidobaptists, it will awaken doubts where there were none before. Whether as an earnest of its future harvest, I presume not to say; but so it came to pass, that one presbyterian, who I think had agreed to print the "Pedobaptist," was immersed just after the appearance of its first number. For on his going down into the water to be immersed, it was discovered that the first number of the "Pedobaptist" was in his hat. A dangerous place, indeed, to carry Paidobaptists. From this drop we might expect a shower. Indeed I would not be astonished if this work should make many Paidobaptists.

It gives up the point in the very first number; that is, it pretends to adduce no direct positive precept nor example for the sprinkling of an infant. It gives up the point in another way, which I am astonished has so long escaped the notice of the baptists. It does not even pretend to infer the rite from any one portion of scripture in either Testament. The "Pedobaptist" acts a sort of double sophist. He neither adduces command, precedent, example, nor inference for infant sprinkling from any one inspired writer. Infant sprinkling is but one rite, and as such, if proved by inference, it ought to be inferred from some one passage of scripture. But this has never been attempted, as far as I know by any Paidobaptist writer. Why, then, do they talk so much about inferring, and the validity of inference, you will ask, if they do not at least pretend to infer it? Because they despair of imposing it upon mankind in any other way than by inference; and few understand logic or the art of reasoning so well as to perceive that the whole must be in the premises. In this way I doubt not many honest Paidobaptists impose upon themselves. The sophism is this: Infant sprinkling is one rite, and ought to be all inferred from one passage of scripture. This they are conscious cannot be done, and therefore cut the rite into two; and then infer the infant from Moses, and the sprinkling from Paul; or they pretend to find an infant in Jesus' arms, and then find sprinkling in Isaiah; and by bringing the infant in Jesus arms, and the "sprinkling many nations" in Isaiah, they put these two together, and having glued them fast, there stands infant sprinkling upon two legs! one resting upon the Old Testament and the other upon the New.

Now, gentlemen, as you profess logic as well as divinity, I will try you here. It is conceded by you that you have neither command nor precedent for infant sprinkling: do, then, give me one passage of scripture in Old Testament or

New, and I will say you deserve more respect from us than all your predecessors. I only ask for one inference. Dont say you have a hundred. One will do. And I will stake all my pretensions to logic on this assertion, that you cannot produce one logical inference from the whole bible, Old and New Testament, in support of infant sprinkling.   EDITOR.

Paidobaptist Logic.

THE following extract from page 16, No. 1, of the *Pedobaptist*, is a beautiful sample of Paidobaptist Logic. Whether Paul would have placed this under the head of " science falsely so called," or of "old wives' fables," I leave to every reader:—

" Infants—where found.

Four places where infants are found, and two where they are not found.

" 1st. Infants of believers were found in the church *before* the coming of our Saviour.

" 2. Infants of believers are found in the Methodist, Presbyterian, Episcopalian, and other Pedobaptist churches, *since* the coming of our Saviour.

" 3. Infants were found in the Saviour's arms when he was on earth.

" 4. Infants are in heaven.

" Where Infants are not found.

" 1. They are not found in the land of Despair.

" 2. They are not found in the Baptist Church."

I will ask, Where Infants were not found?

1. They were not found in the garden of Eden.

2. They were not found in Noah's ark, " a type of" *something*.

3. They were not found in the Patriarchal Church, from Noah to Abraham.

4. They were not found subjects of *any rite* for 2000 years.

Where Infants were found.

1. They were found in the Jewish commonwealth.

2. They were found in the Ishmaelitish tribes.

3. They are found in the Mahometan church.

5. They are found in the Presbyterian church.

6. They were found in Sodom and Gomorrah.

Besides these places, they are found in a hundred other places, too tedious to mention. And what does this prove! It proves that because the infants of believers and unbelievers were found in the Jewish congregation, so they ought to be found in the christian church. Because they were found in Sodom and Gomorrah, therefore they ought to be found in Christian synagogues. Admirable logic!! We seriously request the Paidobaptist editor to insert Dr. Straith's critique found in this number, and to inform their readers that he is an impartial witness of their own party.

New Translations.

EVANS, in his Sketch of the Christian Sects, page 145, makes the following remarks on translations of the Scriptures:—

" Our English translation of the bible was made in the time and by the appointment of James the First. According to Fuller, the list of the translators amounted to forty-seven. This number was arranged under six divisions, and several parcels of the bible assigned them. Every one of the company was to translate the whole parcel; then they were to compare these together, and when any company had finished their part they were to communicate it to the other companies, so that nothing should pass without general consent. The names of the persons and places where they met together, with the portions of scripture assigned each company,

are to be found in Johnson's Historical Account of the several Translations of the Bible. These good and learned men entered on their work in the spring, 1607, and three years elapsed before the translation was finished.

" From the mutability of language, the variation of customs, and the progress of knowledge, several passages in the bible require to be newly translated, or to be materially corrected. Hence, in the present age, when biblical literature has been assiduously cultivated, different parts of the sacred volume have been translated by able hands. The substituting a new translation of the bible in the room of the one now in common use, has been much debated. Dr. Knox, in his ingenious essays, together with others, argues against it; whilst Dr. Newcome, the late Lord Primate of Ireland, the late Dr. Geddes, of the Catholic persuasion, and the late Rev. Gilbert Wakefield, contended strenuously for it. The correction of several passages, however, would deprive Deists of many of their objections, prevent christians from being misled into some absurd opinions, and be the means of making the scriptures more intelligible, and consequently more beneficial to the world.

" Dr. Alexander Geddes, at his decease, had got as far as the Psalms in the translation of the Old Testament. Dr. Newcome and Mr. Wakefield published entire translations of the New Testament. The Rev. Edmund Butcher, also, of Sidmouth, has laid before the public a Family Bible, in which many of the errors of the common translation are corrected, and notes added by way of illustration, whilst the text, broken down into daily lessons, is happily adapted to the purposes of family devotion."

A Restoration of the Ancient Order of Things. No. XXXI.
Discipline of the Church.—No. VIII.
Queries for the Christian Baptist—Continued.

Query 25.—SHOULD a member be excluded from a christian church, who only, once in a while, attends the meeting of the brethren; when, in other respects, his conduct is orderly?

Answer.—We are not aware of the importance of the question, unless we form a correct view of the nature of the christian institution.— Amongst some sects, and in some churches, they have agreed to meet once a fortnight, or once a month, and only require their members thus periodically to assemble. They censure those who depart from the covenant of the church, or those who do not assemble twelve or twenty-four times a year. But the Head and Founder of the christian religion disclaims both the covenant and practice of such assemblies. The covenant and the practice are in direct contravention of his authority and design. If, then, the whole church meets once a month, faithfully and fully according to the covenant, they are in a sort of mutiny against the Captain, or in a state of rebellion against the King. For they have neither his promises, blessing, nor presence, when they wittingly and cordially agree to neglect the weekly assembling of themselves together. They might as scripturally expect his countenance, blessing, and presence, should they agree to one annual or semi-annual meeting during their lives. The platform, as well as the practice, is antiscriptural. And I do not see why a church who agrees to meet once a month, should censure any member who will only visit them once a year. The same license for transgressing, which they claim for themselves, will equally tolerate him. But, I think, this matter is clearly proved in the preceding volumes of this work, if any thing is proved in it, viz. That the whole system of monthly meetings for business and to hear a text explained, is as foreign from the christian institutes as transubstantiation, consubstantiation, Christmas or Easter carnivals. Viewing, as I do, the custom of assembling monthly for business and preaching, to be a branch from the same root from which spring Lent, Easter, Christmas, Whitsunday, and Good Friday, I could not blame the delinquent more than the observer of this tradition of the fathers. But where an assembly, constituted upon the traditions of the apostles, agrees to meet every Lord's day, the person who willingly, for weeks, forsakes the assembling of the saints, is on the high road to apostacy. This Paul avows by his connecting with exhortation to perseverance, and dehortations against apostacy, his remonstrance against forsaking the assembling of themselves together. No person who detaches himself from a christian assembly for his ease or any worldly concern, can deserve the confidence of his brethren, any more than a wife who deserts the bed and board of her husband, or a child who, in his minority, deserts the table and fireside of his father and mother, can deserve the confidence and affection of those relatives they have forsaken. Nor can a church consistently regard and treat as brethren those who do not frequent their stated solemnities. Such absentees are to be dealt with as other offenders; and if reformation be not the result, they are as worthy of exclusion as other transgressors. Demas was as much of an apostate as Hymeneus and Philetus.

Few christians seem to appreciate the wisdom and benevolence of the Great Founder of the christian institution exhibited most impressively in this instance, in laying the disciples under the blissful necessity and obligation of keeping up a spirited social intercourse. The grand design of the christian institution is to draw us to a common centre, in approaching which we approximate towards each other in every step. Thus, with the great fountain of life and happiness in view, in soaring to it we are necessarily elevated together above earthly influences, and drawn together by ties and considerations which draw all hearts and hands to the throne of the Eternal. Now the christian institution is the most social thing under the heavens. But to substitute hearing the same sermon, subscribing the same covenant, and going to the same meeting place in lieu of the social institutions of the kingdom of heaven, is to substitute a spider's thread for a cable to retain a ship to her anchorage during a tempest. Nothing is more unlike the christian kingdom than the dry, cold formalities which appear in the inside of a Baptist or Presbyterian meeting house. The order within the walls is as near to the order of a country school, abating the ardor of youth, as it is to the order of that house over which the Son of God presides; "whose house are we, if we hold fast our begun confidence unshaken to the end."

Men depart as far from nature as they do from christianity in conforming to the regulations of the Geneva school. The doctrine is as cold as moonshine, and the initiated in their arrangements and order are like so many icicles hanging to the eaves of a house in a winter's morning, clear, cold, formal, in rank and file; but they will break rather than bend towards each other. A tree frog is generally the color of the timber, rail, or fence on which it it is found. So are the Baptists. They are, in these regions, generally the offspring, or converts from the Presbyterian

ranks, and they wear the same visage in their order, except with this small difference, that the Baptists build their meeting houses near ponds or rivers, while the Presbyterians build theirs on the tops of the hills.

But were christians to get into the spirit of the institution of the Great Philanthropist, they would have as much relish for the weekly meeting in honor of the resurrection of their chief, and in anticipation of their own, as the stranger has for the sweet word home. But so long as like the Jews they meet in memory of the reason assigned in the fourth commandment, or by an act of congress, they will have nothing to fire their zeal, kindle their love, animate their strains, or enlarge their hopes. And as demure and silent as Quakers, except when the parson, who has a plenary inspiration, is present, they will sit or stand, as the case may be, until they hear the sermon, and all the appurtenances thereto belonging. Now if such persons were to be translated into an old fashioned christian assembly, they would be as much astonished with the natural simplicity, affection, and piety of the worshippers, as a blind man would be on the recovery of his sight.

To return to the point—Were a member of a family to be missing from table ten times a week, or twice a day, would we not at last inquire for his health or cause of his absence, and visit him accordingly? Most certainly we would. Why not then exhibit the same concern for a member of Christ's family? Absence from the table always exhibits a want of appetite, or some more pressing call. On either hypothesis, when a member is missing, it deserves inquiry—and when the true cause is ascertained, it demands a suitable treatment. But that stiffness and formality which are now the mode, and the want of due regard to the nature, design, and authority of every part of the christian institution, lead us into a practice alike repugnant to reason and revelation.

Query 26.—Should the majority govern in all cases, or should unanimity be considered indispensable in all matters which come before the church?

Answer.—Carrying matters by a numerical force, or by a majority of votes, is very natural under popular governments. And as the Baptists have very generally been republicans in politics, they are republicans in ecclesiastics. And, indeed, in all matters of a temporal nature, there seems to be no other way of deciding. Yet it does not well consort with the genius of christianity to carry a point by a majority. Where the law and testimony are either silent or not very explicit upon any question, reason says that we ought not to be either positive or dictatorial. There are but some hints and allusions to be found in the New Testament on this subject. Perhaps the reason is, that the churches set in order by the apostles had not much occasion for the resolution of such queries. There was not so much left to their decision, as, in our superior sagacity, we have found necessary. As the government was on the shoulders of the Great King, the church had not so much to do with it as we moderns imagine. Some things, it is true, are left to the brethren; such as the reception of members, the selection of persons to offices, and the arrangements which are purely secular. The former in their nature require unanimity—the latter may dispense with a majority. In receiving a member, he must be received by all, for all are to love and treat him as a brother. In selecting a person to an office, such as the bishop's, deacon's, or that of a messenger, there is not the same necessity; yet a near approach to unanimity is absolutely necessary, and if attainable, is much to be preferred. But in matters purely secular, such as belong to the 'place of meeting, and all the prerequisites, circumstances, and adjuncts, there is not the same necessity for a full unanimity. To require a unanimity in all questions which we moderns bring into our churches, is to require an impossibility. But in secular affairs, in the primitive church, what we call a committee, or arbitrators, were chosen, and some of the questions which we submit to the brotherhood were submitted to the rulers or bishops. Take out of the church's business what the ancients referred to a committee, and what belonged to the bishops, there is not so much left to quarrel about. The overseers or rulers were only in such matters executors of the law of the sovereign authority. When a man was proved to be a drunkard, or a reviler, or a fornicator, it was not to be submitted to the vote of the brotherhood whether he ought to be expelled. When a man came forward, and was born of water, or immersed into the faith in the presence of a church, it was not to be decided by a vote whether he should be received into the society.' When a child is born into a family, it is not to be voted whether it shall be received into it. It is true that when a man is born into the kingdom of heaven, it may be necessary for him to apply, and to be received into some particular congregation, in which he is to be enrolled, and in fellowship with which he is to walk; and then he must be unanimously received. But it is worthy of remark that a large share of brotherly love, and the not laying an undue stress upon a perfect unanimity will be more productive of it than we are aware of; and the more it is sought after in a contrary spirit, the more difficult it will be to obtain. EDITOR.

For the Christian Baptist.

MR. EDITOR,—In your Essay No. VII. on the " Discipline of the Church," in the March number of the Christian Baptist, I discover that you have taken an improper view of the question which lately called forth a little discussion by "Herodion" and myself. He does, indeed, maintain the affirmative of the question, "Does the expulsion of a member from an individual church of the Baptist faith and order, exclude him from fellowship with the whole denomination?" and is, moreover, favorable to appeals, in some cases, to associations for the adjustment of differences: but, it was not from any thing said by me, that you received the impression that I approve of appeals to co-ordinate and sister churches. You probably received it from " Herodion" himself, who supposed that to be my alternative, if I rejected his opinion.

What I contend for is this, and if I am wrong, I am open to conviction, and shall be pleased to be corrected by those who are more experienced and better taught. If one congregation of professing, immersed believers, should take it into their head to exclude a brother, for any opinion or practice of his, derived from the scriptures, supported thereby, or not contradictory thereto,—such expulsion ought not to bring upon him the discountenance of other congregations or individuals. Let us suppose him expelled, merely because he believes that the proper exposition of scripture is by paragraphs, and not by texts,—that bread should be broken by disciples, not once a month or quarter, but on the first day of

each week, or that no covenant or by-laws are necessary in church government, but the New Testament alone. Shall he be frowned on as heretical and disorderly, by the whole community; or may he not with propriety be received into another congregation more liberal, or whose views of the gospel are more coincident with his own? This latter is the opinion maintained by me. The supposition that expulsions for such causes, are not to be apprehended, and could not produce the withdrawment of favor by other congregations, is contradicted by experience and facts, if report is true.

Notwithstanding these remarks in the following sentences,—"Herodion feels the want of horns, and would have the creature furnished with at least one which he might occasionally use. My brother of the Herald would wish to feed the stag well, but would still be sawing off the horns: perhaps I may wrong him in so saying, for indeed he is very modest about it; but, for my part, I do not love even an image of the beast." I say, notwithstanding these remarks, I am persuaded that, in relation to this subject, your opinions and my own are exactly the same. If not, I should be pleased to know what are yours.   RELIGIOUS HERALD.

Richmond, March 14, 1829.

Desultory Remarks.

BETHANY, APRIL 6, 1829.

TO-MORROW, *Deo volente*, I depart from home for Cincinnati, in the expectation of meeting there the Champion of Infidelity in two continents. I want something to complete the May number of this work, and finding my mind dissipated on a variety of concerns and topics, I cannot bring it to bear upon any one with any degree of energy. I this moment snatched my pen, determined to write something; and now that I have it in my fingers, I can find nothing to write. I have sometimes advised young public speakers when they began to excuse themselves for having nothing to say, to tell their audience how unprepared they were, and then to go into a detail of the reasons why they were destitute of any thing worthy of utterance or hearing. It occurs to me that the philosophy which authorises such a course in public speakers, on certain occasions, will equally apply to a writer for the public. And, perhaps, in going into such a detail a person may find something worthy of being heard or read. Now, to make an experiment, I have said that the reason why I cannot bring my mind to bear upon any topic, is, that the different excitements which a thousand little things unworthy of being told present, have exhausted all those energies of thought which lead into regular trains of reflection, and without which, no point can be carried which requires systematic ratiocination. But, like the needle touched with the magnet, which, though made to vibrate from point to point, settles to the pole; so my mind tends to the great question which engrosses life and death, time and eternity. And although I have not for months written any thing upon the sceptical system, it has not for a single hour during the day been absent from my thoughts. I have put myself upon the sceptical premises, and made myself, as far as I could, doubt with them. I have explored the different systems, ancient and modern, and have made their difficulties appear in my own eyes as large as life. Now I may tell my friends and the public, that, however I may manage this discussion, of one thing I am conscious, that I am much more radically and irrecoverably convinced of two things than I ever was before. The first is, that not one single good reason can be offered against the christian faith: and the other is, that sectarians and sectarianism are the greatest enemies to christianity in the world. Robert Owen, Esq. and all his disciples would be but like a swarm of grasshoppers amongst a a herd of cattle in a large meadow, were this monster beheaded. They might chirp and chirp, till the oxen tread them down or lick them up, but they never could devour an ox. Indeed a swarm of grasshoppers may make more noise than a herd of cattle, but where is their strength? So with these philosophers—they are ever and anon carping; but they never did, and never do, manfully attack one of its evidences.

But what I have now before me is this: the sectaries and the sceptics argue as though they had been trained in the same school. Their premises may differ and their conclusions, but their logic is the same. I am resolved, in the approaching contest, to do as the mariner in a storm—cast overboard not only the cargo, but even the tackling of the ship, rather than endanger the mooring of her in a safe haven. I cannot get ashore with so many bales of traditions, with the metaphysical subtilties of creeds, and the various human appendages of the popular establishments. These would be as fatal to the cause of the Bible, as a dead body would have been to Charon's boat. Indeed, I have more to fear from the objections which the sectaries have bestowed to the Deists, than I have from any other source of opposition. But I am under no necessity to try to pilot through the storm, the opinions, fancies, or by-laws of any sect. It is the religion of the Bible, and that alone, I am concerned to prove to be divine. It would be a vain and useless attempt to demonstrate that a religious establishment, set on foot by King James or King Henry, by John Knox, Charles Fox, or John Anybody, was the institution of Jesus Christ, or of divine authority.

I see some of the clerical order foresaw this as well as myself; and, like the editor of the "Pandect," they would rather christianity should be undefended, than their systems be endangered. I would apprize all such of my intentions, and my reasons for my intentions, if I were solicited with becoming temper.

But I do not think this a matter of ordinary importance; and therefore I start in the most confident expectation of that all-sustaining goodness and gracious assistance which have hitherto been bestowed upon me, and which have always been the strength and felicity of all them who have faithfully, sincerely, and benevolently asserted the Bible cause.

I rejoice to know and feel that I have the good wishes, the prayers, and the hopes of myriads of christians in all denominations. With such aids and such allies, I know that the truth must triumph over all the schemes of kings, priests, and sceptics.

But only see whither I am straying, and how far I have pursued the favorite point. Here sleep summons me to appear in her court, and to answer for my neglect of her authority. I will, therefore, go and compromise with my creditor, and get a furlough at some other time.

EDITOR.

No. 11.]   JUNE 1, 1829.

Debate on the Evidences of Christianity.

THE discussion between Mr. Owen and myself on the divine authority of the christian religion,

commenced in the city of Cincinnati, agreeably to previous arrangements, on the 13th of April last, and continued, with the intermission of one Lord's day, till the evening of the 21st. Dr. Wilson, in his usual politeness and liberality, having refused the citizens of Cincinnati the use of his meeting-house which they helped to rear, application was made to the Methodist society for the use of their largest meeting-house, which was readily and cheerfully granted. Seven very respectable citizens presided as Moderators over the meeting and the discussion. Three of these, namely, Rev. Timothy Flint, Col. Francis Carr, and Henry Starr, Esq. were chosen by Mr. Owen; and three were chosen by myself, namely, Judge Burnet, Col. Samuel W. Davies, and Major Daniel Gano. These six chose the Rev. Oliver M. Spencer. These, when met, selected from among themselves the Honorable Judge Burnet as Chairman, than whom no man was better qualified to preside. In the preliminary arrangements it was agreed that each of the disputants should speak alternately half an hour, and that Mr. Owen should lead the way as he had pledged himself to prove certain affirmative positions. A very large assemblage of citizens was convened. Some were present from the states of New-York, Pennsylvania, Virginia, Kentucky, Indiana, Tennessee, and Mississippi. The press at the opening of the discussion was very great, and many were forced to return to their homes in a day or two from the difficulty of getting seats. The discussion was heard by a very large and respectable congregation to its close. For good order, patient attention, and earnest solicitude to understand the subjects discussed, we presume no congregation ever excelled them since the publication of the gospel in Cesarea.

Mr. Charles H. Simms, a stenographer of good reputation, was employed by Mr. Owen and myself to report the discussion. In copying his abbreviation into long hand he is now employed. It does not become me to say much at this time on the merits of the discussion. The newspapers of Cincinnati have generally taken some notice of it. As far as they have gone they have, we presume, fairly echoed the opinions of the hearers in attendance. The Rev. Editor of the Western Monthly Review, being rather a facetious gentleman, and possessing a very fine romantic imagination, better adapted to writing novels and romances, than history or geography, has given a chivalrous air to the discussion; and, by mingling facts and fable, has, upon the whole, written a burlesque, rather than a sketch of the debate. This is his besetting sin, which he has hitherto combated in vain. It is seldom that a novelist can become a historian; and the author of "Francis Berrian" is as illy qualified to write a true history, as the author of "Waverley" was to do justice to Napoleon. He has his merits, however, and sorry would I be to detract from them. And if it be right to learn from an enemy, it is no less right to learn from a reviewer, even when, in a merry mood, he restrains reason and delivers up the reins to imagination. Upon the whole, I must thank him for the justice he has done me. I object to the manner rather than the matter of his critique.

I have an objection to saying much about this debate, as it is to be published immediately; yet the inquiries from all parts require me to say something. I prefer giving a sketch from some other pen than my own, and would cheerfully give that from the "Cincinnati Chronicle," because the fullest, and, upon the whole, the most satisfactory which I have seen, were it not that it is to myself too flattering. I have, on this account, hesitated about laying it before my numerous and far distant subscribers; but as I cannot find so full an account of it less exceptionable, and as I am entirely unacquainted with the writer of it, I have, upon the whole, concluded to risque the publication of it, wishing the reader to bear in mind that I think the complimentary part of it more than merited; and would rather the writer had decorated his details less with encomiums upon myself or acquisitions. But with this exception, we shall let it speak for itself:—

Messrs. Campbell and Owen.

The debate between these two individuals commenced in this city on Monday, the 13th instant, and continued for eight days successively. Seven Moderators were chosen, any three of whom were authorized to preside over the meetings. There was, each day of the debate, an audience of more than twelve hundred persons, many of whom were strangers, attracted to our city by the novelty and importance of the discussion. The arguments on both sides of the question have been regularly taken down by a stenographer, and will, we understand, be published.

We were not among those who anticipated any very beneficial results from this meeting, fearing that, as is too often the case in these personal interviews, the equanimity of temper would be disturbed, and the debate sink into acrimonious recrimination. Such, however, has not, we believe, been the case in the present instance—the christian forbearance of the one, and the philosophic complacency of the other, having, throughout the controversy, elicited from each, marked courtesy of deportment. The audience have listened with respectful attention, and we were not apprized of the occurrence of any incident, calculated to inspire a regret that the meeting has taken place. We have, however, reason for thinking, that if Mr. Owen had anticipated the acceptance of his challenge by so able an opponent as the one he has recently met, it never would have been given; and that if Mr. Campbell had been fully apprized of all the "circumstances" by which the philosopher of New Lanark is surrounded, the challenge would not have been accepted.

It is not, on this occasion, our intention to offer any particular analysis of this controversy, which is rendered the less necessary, by the prospect of an early publication of the entire argument.

It will be recollected that Mr. Owen proposed to prove that—all the religions of the world were founded in the ignorance of mankind—that they are opposed to the never changing laws of our nature—that they are the only source of vice, disunion and misery—and that they are the only bar to the formation of a society of virtue, of intelligence, and of charity in its most extended sense. To sustain these positions, Mr. Owen produced and read the following:

1. That a man at his birth is ignorant of every thing relative to his own organization, and that he has not been permitted to create the slightest part of any of his natural propensities, faculties, or qualities, physical or mental.

2. That no two infants at birth have yet been known to possess the same organization, while the physical, mental and moral differences between all infants, are formed without their knowledge or will.

3. That each individual is placed at his birth, without his knowledge or consent, within circumstances, which, acting upon his peculiar organization, impress the general character of those circumstances upon the infant child and man; yet the influence of those circumstances are to a certain degree modified by the peculiar natural organization of each individual.

4. That no infant has the power of deciding at what period of time or in what part of the world he shall be born, in what distinct religion he shall be trained or believe, or by what other circumstances he shall be surrounded from birth to death.

5. That each individual is so created that, when young, he may be made to receive impressions to produce either true or false ideas; and beneficial, or injurious habits; and to retain them with great tenacity.

6. That each individual is so created that he must believe according to the strongest impressions that can be made on his feelings and other faculties, while his belief in no case depends upon his will.

7. That each individual is so created that he must like that which is pleasant to him, or that which produces agreeable sensations on his individual organization; and he must dislike that which creates in him unpleasant or disagreeable sensations; whilst he cannot discover previous to experience, what those sensations shall be.

8. That each individual is so created that the sensations made upon his organization although pleasant and delightful at the commencement, and for some duration generally become, when continued beyond a certain period, without change, disagreeable and painful; while on the contrary, when too rapid changes of sensations are made on his organization, they dissipate, weaken, and otherwise injure his physical, intellectual and moral powers and enjoyments.

9. That the highest health, the greatest progressive improvement, and most permanent happiness of each individual, depends in a great degree upon the proper cultivation of all his physical, intellectual, and moral faculties and powers, from infancy to maturity; and upon all these parts of his natural being duly called into action at the proper period, and temperately exercised according to the strength and capacity of the individual.

10. That the individual is made to possess and acquire the worst character when his organization at birth has been compounded of the most inferior propensities, faculties, and qualities of our common nature; and when so organized, he has been placed from birth to death amidst the most vicious or worst circumstances.

11. That the individual is made to possess and acquire a medium character, when his original organization has been superior and when the circumstances which surrounded him from birth to death are of a character to produce superior impressions only, or when there is some mixture of good and bad qualities in the original organization, and when it had also been placed through life, in varied circumstances of good and evil. This last compound has been hitherto the common lot of mankind.

12. That the individual is made the most superior of his species, when his original organization has been compounded of the best propensities, of the best ingredients of which human nature is formed, and when the circumstances which surround him from birth to death are of a character to produce only superior impressions; or, in other words, when the circumstances in which he is placed, are all in unison with his nature.

How far these twelve "divine laws," or "gems," as Mr. Owen is pleased to call them, prove that all the religions of the world are founded in the ignorance of mankind, and are the cause of all the existing vice and misery, is for the reader to determine. The author of them seemed to consider their pertinency to the subject matter of debate so great that he read them, as we are informed, twelve times to the audience. They constituted, indeed the sum and substance of the philosopher's arguments, and interspersed with expressions of the rankest infidelity, and the most dangerous heresies in morals, they were repeated, from day to day, with fatiguing insipidity; and applied, without application, in every stage and condition of the debate. It will be perceived that these twelve "gems," which, until disinterred by the forty years' labor of their discoverer, had lain buried for two thousand years, are little more than the substance of certain lectures on the "Social System" of parallelograms, which have already been pronounced by Mr. Owen, in all the great cities from London to New-Orleans! That he has succeeded in impressing the truth upon a single one of his hearers, it would be hazarding too much to admit; and so far from having established, or even sustained, to any tolerable extent, the several positions in his challenge, we believe we are speaking the opinions of nine-tenths of his audience, when we say that a greater failure has seldom been witnessed on any occasion. All admit that the talent, the skill in debate, and the weight of proof were on the side of Mr. Campbell. Those who believed this philosopher of "circumstances" and "parallelograms" to be a great man, appeared to be sadly disappointed, many of those inclined to his theory of "social compacts" have relapsed into a state of sanity; while the disciples of infidelity have either been shaken in their faith, or provoked that their cause should have been so seriously injured by mismanagement and feebleness. So far as it regards the cause of truth, this discussion has been fortunate; but so far as respects the peculiar views of the challenger, unfortunate. We have already questioned the sincerity of Mr. Owen's expectation that his challenge would be accepted. The reason for giving it is obvious enough. His new system was falling into disrepute—his doctrines were beginning to pall upon the public ear—those who had been enchanted by his theories were disgusted with their practical results—and New Harmony was a striking, we can hardly say living memorial, of the egregious folly of his Utopian schemes. To sustain his character as a moral reformer, and gratify his ambition for notoriety, it became important to keep alive public interest upon the subject. The challenge was therefore given in New Orleans for effect, and was republished and perverted in its meaning, for a similar purpose in London. Mr. Owen's real or assumed enthusiasm on the subject of reforming the world, seems to be in no manner abated by his signal discomfiture at this meeting. We should not, indeed, be surprized to hear that he left our city exclaiming, to quote his own words, "My friends, in the day and hour when I disclaimed all connexion with the errors and prejudices of the old system—a day to be remembered with joy and gladness henceforward, through all ages, the dominion of faith ceased; its reign of terror, of disunion, of separation, and of irrationality, was broken to pieces like a potter's vessel. Now henceforth charity presides over the destinies of the world."

Mr. Campbell, after making an ineffectual effort for several days to confine his opponent to the points in dispute between them, set out to establish the truth of revelation, and to apply the precepts of christianity to the present condition and future hopes of mankind. In doing this he manifested an intimate acquaintance with the subject. He is undoubtedly a man of fine talents, and equally fine attainments. With an acute, vigorous mind, quick perceptions, and rapid powers of combination, he has sorely puzzled his antagonist, and at the same time both delighted and instructed his audience by his masterly defence of the truth, divine origin, and inestimable importance of christianity. That Mr. Campbell would bring forward any new facts upon this subject was not to be expected; but he has arranged, combined, and enforced those already existing, in a manner well calculated to carry, as we are informed it has in several instances, conviction to the doubting and sceptical mind.

We think that much the smaller number of his hearers were apprized of the overwhelming mass of evidence which exists in support of the authenticity of the scriptures. By this discussion, a spirit of inquiry has been set afloat, and the sources from whence this testimony has been drawn, and the mode of its application, pointed out. In this it is that we anticipated a result from the controversy more beneficial than was generally expected prior to its commencement. As it regards the reputation for talents, piety, and learning of Mr. Campbell, his friends have no cause to regret his present visit to our city. The same cannot, perhaps, be said of the infidel followers of Mr. Owen.

In conclusion, we may be permitted to say, that the signs of the times are greatly deceptive, if the "Twelve Fundamental Laws of Nature," by which Mr. Owen, with the aid of a few parallelograms, is to form an "entire new state of existence," are destined very speedily to supercede the divine laws of the Twelve Apostles.— We have no faith in the overthrow of the established order of society and the great system of christianity; even by the conjoint attacks of the New Lanark Philosopher, and Miss Fanny Wright. If the genius, the wit, the ridicule, and the argument of such men as Hume, and Voltaire, and Condorcet, and Gibbon, and Paine, have failed to arrest the mighty and wide-spreading march of the christian religion, it requires no small degree of credulity, to believe, that Robert Owen can ever be successful. As well might we anticipate, that the sun at his command would stand upon Gibeon, or the fiery comets be staid in their erratic wandering through the regions of infinite space.—*Cincinnati Chronicle.*

KING AND QUEEN, 12th April, 1829.

BROTHER CAMPBELL,—My last epistle was designed rather as a desultory exhibition of sentiments, than a perspicuous exposition of a point or two, as comprised among your writings for farther elucidation. These points however, were therein likewise hinted; and shall now, without unnecessary delay, be proposed. And the topic which engrosses attention, is your very broad assertion contained in the sixth number on the Patriarchal Age; and its most objectionable aspect reads thus: "System-makers, to form a theory in the crucible of their invention, say, "that all were justified by believing the same thing." But this no man living is able to show. It is true, I contend, that the groundwork of salvation by faith was either prospectively, or retrospectively, the sacrifice of Christ. But not a person on earth believed that the Messiah would die as a sin-offering, or rise from the dead, from Eve to Mary Magdalene."

In bringing this extremely important subject before your readers again, I am moved by several considerations; a few of which it may not be improper to premise. Accustomed then as I have been for some years past, to look upon the course of labors pursued by you as being highly calculated to promote the humble and faithful use of the scriptures to the great advantage of its readers and the disciples of Jesus, I conceive it to be the duty of every friend and brother in this good work, as their various circumstances may permit, to remark upon such steps taken by you, as are likely to alienate the affection of friends, or to strengthen the prejudices of enemies. This is my first consideration. Again: our being right upon the subject of faith is on all hands admitted to be of the last importance! Your view possesses, to the mass of your readers, much novelty; and lastly, for myself, I believe it to embrace much truth, but not the whole truth. This last consideration more particularly impels me to solicit your further attention, while I suggest a few difficulties and objections. It would be superfluous to multiply these to a great number, as I conceive that most of them are removed by the essay from which I have extracted the objectionable assertion; nor is it my design to give an elaborate letter upon faith, either saving or dead. But of the objections to your views: and first, as they come from others.—1. The gospel was preached to Abraham; therefore Abraham's faith comprehended the different parts of the New Testament dispensation: and for this conclusion we read the third chapter of Galatians and eighth verse; "And the scripture foreseeing that God would justify the heathen through faith, preached before the gospel to Abraham, saying, In thee shall all nations be blessed." Now we have here only to turn our attention to the import of the term gospel as used in the scriptures, to be convinced that it here signifies no more than the covenant of grace proposed to Abraham—the annunciation of glad tidings, good news to this old pilgrim and stranger as to what should afterwards result to the human family through his instrumentality. It is moreover to be remarked, that the gospel, as a divine institution, comprising a king, mediator, propitiatory sacrifice, laws, and imperious obligatory demands, must, in the nature of things, be a savor either of "life to life," or of "death to death;" in other words must claim the ascendancy over all other institutions, wherever preached. But again, Mark teaches that this system, as a rule of life and faith, was not proclaimed before the days of John the Immerser. See the beginning of Mark's Testimony.

2. The seed, concerning whom the promise was made to Abraham, is Christ; Abraham believed the promise, therefore he believed in Jesus the Messiah. "Now to Abraham and to his seed were the promises made. He (God) says not, and to seeds, as of many; but as of one, and to your seed, which is Christ," Gal. iii. 16. Let us for a moment turn our attention to a disclosure or two, which it pleased God to make to the father of the faithful, and it is probable we shall arrive at a different deduction from that just now proposed. The first intercourse recorded between God and Abraham, is presented in the twelfth chapter of Genesis, and the three first verses. This covenant and promise are brought again into notice by the Holy Spirit, in the writings of Luke in his seventh chapter of the Acts of the Apostles, and of Paul in the eleventh chapter of his epistle to the Hebrews; both

of whom interpret nationally. But it is in reference to the promise made in the 15th. ch. of *Gen.* "This shall not be your heir; but he that shall come out of your own bowels shall be your heir. And he brought him forth abroad, and said, Look now towards heaven, and tell the stars, if you be able to number them. And he said to him, So shall your seed be. And he believed in the Lord, and he counted it to him for righteousness."— And that comprised in the 17th ch. and 19th verse, that the Apostle Paul's interpretation, as above quoted, is considered conclusive. That the promise of the fifteenth chapter is national we need only read the connexion to perceive: and that the promise of Isaac, though typical of Christ, fixed the faith of Abraham in the veracity of God, upon the fruit of Sarah's womb, is most apparent. But the limited faith of Abraham, and Paul's interpretation—how are they to be reconciled?

First, then, as to Abraham: called, as he had been, most signally into the notice and favor of God, and confirmed by signs most awful in the reality of this state of things, he was prepared by grace to enter gradually into the reception of such things as his Maker might see fit to communicate to him. I said that he was prepared for a gradual reception of truth concerning the will of God. He is at first saluted with the promise of being made a great people: no great difficulty seeming to interpose here, he readily obeys God by taking up a strange pilgrimage to a strange land. But when his years had increased, and no uncommon multiplication of his seed taken place, his further exercise of faith is required and exhibited, but in close connexion with associated doubt; for he said, "Lord God, whereby shall I know that I shall inherit it?" Evidence was here, and subsequently afforded him, for his confirmation in faith in the promises of God. Though it be true, that without Christ, no promise would ever have saluted the ear of fallen man, yet it is equally true that the coming of this only true light into the world has been regularly gradated from the earliest or most obscure prophecy, down to the present day, and will, in all probability continue so till the arrival of millennial glory. And at no period has it been essential for any to exercise faith, beyond what God destined; the point of approbation, being constituted by the reception of God's testimony or declaration, concerning things present or to come, in reference to faith or practice. Abraham attained to the approbation of God upon this very principle, by believing all that God required him to believe, according to his own explanations, and doing all that was required at his hands according to God's direction.

But Paul says, "He saith not, And to seeds, as of many, but as of one, And to thy seed, which is Christ." We simply, and forcibly learn here from what the Apostle tells us, that God did not tell Abraham the particulars of this promise. That though he led his faithful heart into the reception of that economy without which Jesus could never have come, yet he gives us the assurance of confirmation, "that they without us should not be made perfect." The Apostle has no design to go farther than to remove the prejudices of his Galatian readers against the ancient foundation—true foundation of all the promises, by showing that even in the promises to Abraham, which had for time immemorial been looked upon as national, God meant, and actually promised more than met their eye, or had been ever realized by Israel as a people. And this conclusion seems to be confirmed by the evident addition of the words, "which is Christ;" words not uttered by the Lord God in any of his interviews with Abraham. It would be equally cogent reasoning, to argue that when Satan shall be bound, was to allow the moresublime displays of heavenly favor among men, that all who shall be found ultimately in heavenly felicity, must needs have comprehended the numerous particulars of millennium, or any other untried state. "They that have not the law, shall be a law to themselves." To whom much is given, God will look for corresponding fruits. One dispensation was made to succeed another, prophet succeeded prophet, till Christ came and opened, more clearly, the way of life, which even shines more and more brightly to the perfect day. It seems to me upon this point, that Paul neither means to teach that Abraham distinctly saw Christ by faith, nor yet that he rejected him by unbelief; but shows that in the rich promise of God to this eminent man, like many other parts of revelation, the fact that Jesus of Nazareth with the fullest of his blessings, were veiled from his observation, though certainly designed by the Almighty. To look upon the ark is not necessarily to be familiar with its inhabitants. So of God's promises and word at large.

3. Abraham is said to have seen the day of Christ and to have rejoiced; consequently he saw him by faith. *John* viii. 56.

No allusion can hence be traced, further than I have already gone. Christ here explains the promises before illustrated, as Paul did; and we arrive at the conclusion, to wit—What God, the Father, in the exercise of infinite wisdom, did not see fit to unfold, Christ, his Son, is now authorized to divulge and assert. And all this is not more wonderful than that "God is, in Christ, reconciling the world to himself;" an assertion gladly believed by thousands, while to millions it yet remains entirely hidden.

Thus I justify your view of the Abrahamic faith, as being, I conceive, entirely scriptural; and would refer the reader, for numerous additional illustrations, to the eleventh chapter of Hebrews, wherein it will particularly appear, that so far as the service of God is involved in faith, its design is, obedience to the Divine Being, who rewards us in proportion to this virtue, whether it has had its illustration in crediting the testimony concerning the creation; sacrifices for sin; the offering up of a child, or any other service required at our hands. Here I am compelled, for the present at least, to stop, and ask your regard to a difficulty still behind.

At the time when the promises, of which we have said so much, were made, but one other that seemed to refer to a deliverer, had ever been spoken, as we know of; and that leads to a *seed*. Should Abraham have heard of this, in the midst of that darkness and idolatry which surrounded him, it might readily have been forgotten, and even when darkly spoken to him again, so as not to be comprehended, could have had nothing enlightening to his mind, that he might impart to others; but when we come down to the days of Moses, and hear him saying, "The Lord your God will raise up to you a prophet from the midst of you, of your brethren, like to me; to him you shall hearken"—it seems to convey the impression that more light has come into the world;—and if nothing more, Moses himself must have looked to one who should succeed him in authority, and more abundantly endowed from on high. Whether the institution of the priestly office and the various typical sacrifices did not possess and impart light, pointing to the Great High Priest and sacrifice for sin, I submit to your consideration.

But the light continues to increase: consider the very striking predictions of Isaiah and others; especially the fifty-third chapter of this highly gifted prophet. Therein we find the character, reception, and sufferings of Messiah opened in the most sublime manner. And when we add to this the farther testimony of David upon the very obscure doctrine of the resurrection, as set forth in the sixteenth psalm—added to all which, the prophecy of Daniel, "and after three score and two weeks, shall Messiah be cut off, but not for himself," &c. we are unavoidably induced to believe that many, between the periods in which Eve and Mary Magdalene lived, believed that "*Messiah would die as a sin-offering*"—and some that he would *rise from the dead*.

I have been very brief upon this point, as I deemed a hint to be sufficient. Should you think with me, that your latitude has been too wide on this subject, or see fit to sustain your position, I trust that you will be enabled to look upon these productions properly.

I have for some time had it in contemplation to propose one or two other points, upon which objections have been raised, but have thus far been prevented. But, unless some other should call your attention to them, at some convenient season, I shall probably do it.

That you may be saved from every error, and richly prosper in accomplishing the great objects of your labors, is the sincere wish of your servant for Christ's sake.   Amos.

Reply to Amos.

Brother Amos—That the glad tidings were announced to Abraham, that in his seed all the families of the earth should one day be blessed, I rejoice to know. But whether Abraham, or any of the Patriarchs after him, apprehended the character of this seed, or the nature of the blessing in which all nations were to participate, I have much reason to doubt. When Abraham offered up his son Isaac upon the altar, it may be presumed, from what Paul says, that he saw *the day* of the resurrection: "Abraham rejoiced that he should see my day, and he did see it, and was glad," said the Messiah. He desired to see it; and in receiving his son Isaac from the dead, *in a figure*, he descried, as afar off, the resurrection of the antitype of Isaac. But all this, and much more to the same effect, found in the Prophets, is not sufficient to refute the assertion on which your remarks are predicated. That the sufferings of the Messiah and the glory to which he was destined, and the sufferings on account of Christ, and the glories to which they led, were literally and symbolically portrayed by many of the Prophets, I am happy to learn. But whether they who uttered these predictions, or they who read them, understood the import of them, is just the question. Peter authorizes me to think they did not understand them; for, says he, "they searched diligently to know what people and what times and things these were, which the spirit which was in them meant." Now if they who uttered the voice of the Spirit did not understand that voice, what reason have we to believe that their hearers understood it? But take, for example, a parallel case. No event was more clearly or frequently foretold, than the calling of the Gentiles into the family of God. David and Isaiah describe it in the plainest language, and in the most striking symbols. Yet, not one of the Apostles, until long after Pentecost, apprehended it. So universal was the mistake, or rather so perfect was the secret, that Paul says, "it was a secret hid from ages and generations," which none of the ancients understood—"that the Gentiles should be fellow-citizens with the saints" or Jewish converts, and members of the family of God. Now the argument is, if an event as clearly and fully predicted as any of the gospel facts was not understood by the Apostles during the lifetime of the Messiah, nor by any of the intelligent converts, highly gifted by the Holy Spirit, until the conversion of Cornelius, what good reason have we to conclude that because the sacrifice of Christ and his resurrection from the dead were clearly predicated, they were more distinctly understood, or more fully comprehended! But the fact that not one of his disciples expected his resurrection, nor knew why he died, is the fullest proof that can be offered in confirmation of the assertion. And have we not reason to think that during the lifetime of the Messiah there was as much knowledge of his mission and its object, as at any former period of the history of the nation. But when I write on the Jewish Age and Religion, it will become my duty to make these matters more plain.

In the mean time I could wish that all my readers would keep in mind that where there is no testimony there can be no belief. And where neither testimony nor the evidence of sense assures us of any fact, event, or existence, there may be opinions, but there can be neither faith nor knowledge. And in all matters of opinion the utmost liberty ought to be conceded.

That the Messiah was anticipated and expected to be a Prophet, a Priest, and a King, I may believe; but that the nature and design of these offices were understood as we christians understand them, by any of those who lived under the letter or law, evidence to my mind, at least, is wanting.　　　　　　　　　　　EDITOR.

The Three Kingdoms.

THE Jewish people were often called "the kingdom of God," because God was in a peculiar sense their King. For certain purposes he selected them, distinguished them, and took them under his own immediate protection. He gave them laws, ordinances, and customs, which had both a specific and general influence, and were preparatory to a new and better order of society. The new order of society which arises out of the belief of the gospel, is often called "the reign or kingdom of Heaven." In this kingdom the subjects enjoy more exalted blessings, and stand in new and heavenly relations unknown before the coming of the Messiah.— There is also the "kingdom of heaven, or glory," properly so called. This is the residence of angels, the abode of the saints, and the mansions of glory. The gates of admission into these three kingdoms are different—Flesh, Faith, and Works. To be born of the flesh, or to be a descendant of Abraham, introduced a child into the first kingdom of God. To be born of water and spirit, through faith in Jesus Christ, brings men and women into the second kingdom. But neither flesh, faith, nor water, without good works, will introduce a man or woman into the third kingdom. The nature of these three kingdoms, the privileges enjoyed by the subjects, and the terms of admission, are very imperfectly understood in the present day. These kingdoms are unhappily confounded in the minds of many. Hence we find that what is affirmed of the nature, subjects, and terms of admission of one, is frequently applied to another. This is one of the roots of popery, and all the hierarchies in christendom have sprung from it.

The nature of the kingdom of God amongst the Jews is very different from the nature of the kingdom of God amongst the christians, and both are different from the kingdom of glory.— The subjects are just as different. Under the first they were carnal; all the descendants of Jacob, without regard to regeneration, were lawful subjects of the first kingdom. None can be subjects of the second unless born again; and flesh and blood cannot inherit the third and ultimate kingdom.

I have discovered that the objections offered against the scriptural design and import of christian immersion, are based upon a misapprehension of the nature and privileges of these three kingdoms. Under the first there were various ablutions, purgations, and sin-offerings, which never perfected the conscience; but which, for the time being, served as symbols or types of a real purgation which would be enjoyed under the Reign of Heaven, or second kingdom.— These sacrifices did not cleanse the worshippers, else, as Paul reasons, the worshippers, once cleansed, would have no more consciousness of sins. Under the christian economy a real remission of sins is constantly enjoyed by all the subjects or citizens, and, as Paul argues, where remission of sins is enjoyed no more sacrifice for sin is needed. Now if the Jews by faith foresaw through the symbols the shedding of Christ's blood, the question is, Why could they not by faith in his sacrifice enjoy, as well as we, the remission of sins? The sacrifice of Christ, viewed prospectively, was as efficacious as when viewed retrospectively, to effect the cleasing of the conscience. And could they not, through one sacrifice, have more clearly understood the design of Christ's sacrifice, than by so many sacrifices. But it is a provision in the constitution of the christian kingdom which greatly distinguishes it from the Jewish, "that the sins and iniquities of the citizens shall be remembered no more." No daily, weekly, nor annual remembrances of sins under the reign of favor. This, faith in the sacrifice of Christ discovers, and submission to his institution puts us into the actual possession of that remission which never was enjoyed before.

Now, as Paul teaches, under the Constitution of the New Kingdom, remission of sins is a natural birthright. Hence every one, so soon as he enters the second or christian kingdom, or is born of water and spirit, is pardoned and accepted. So that those who are born into the kingdom of heaven, or christian kingdom, have peace with God, and sin cannot lord it over them; for they are not under law, but under favor.

But many say, "What will become of our Paidobaptist brethren, and millions more, if these things be so?" This is a stale objection which has been urged against every reformation in religion from the days of John Huss down to this century. I will, however, answer the interrogatory. They cannot enjoy the blessings of the second kingdom; in other words, they cannot have or enjoy that light, peace, liberty, and love, which are the national privileges of all who intelligently enter the kingdom of favor.

But the objector means, *Can* they enter into the third kingdom, or kingdom of glory? I am prepared to say that my opinion is, and it is but an opinion, that infants, idiots, and some Jews and Pagans may, without either faith or baptism, be brought into the third kingdom, merely in consequence of the sacrifice of Christ; and I doubt not but many Paidobaptists of all sects will be admitted into the kingdom of glory.—

Indeed all they who obey Jesus Christ, through faith in his blood, according to their knowledge, I am of opinion will be introduced into that kingdom. But when we talk of the forgiveness of sins which comes to christians through immersion, we have no regard to any other than the second kingdom, or the kingdom of favor. I repeat it again—there are three kingdoms: the Kingdom of Law, the Kingdom of Favor, and the Kingdom of Glory; each has a different constitution, different subjects, privileges, and terms of admission. And who is so blind, in the christian kingdom, as not to see that more is necessary to eternal salvation or to admission into the everlasting kingdom, than either faith, regeneration, or immersion? A man can enter into the second kingdom by being born of water and the spirit; but he cannot enter into the third and ultimate kingdom through faith, immersion, or regeneration. Hence says the Judge, Come you blessed of my Father, and inherit the kingdom of glory. Because you believed? No. Because you were immersed? No. Because you were born again by the Holy Spirit? No—but because I know your good works, your piety, and humanity. I was hungry, and you fed me, &c.

The plain state of the case is this:—The blood of Abraham brought a man into the kingdom of law, and gave him an inheritance in Canaan. Being born not of blood, but through water and the Spirit of God, brings a person into the kingdom of favor; which is righteousness, peace, joy, and a holy spirit, with a future inheritance in prospect. But if the justified draw back, or the washed return to the mire, or if faith die and bring forth no fruits—into the kingdom of glory he cannot enter. Hence good works through faith, or springing from faith in Jesus, give a right to enter into the holy city—and this is a right springing from grace or favor:—"Blessed are they who keep his commandments that they may have a right to the tree of life and enter through the gates into the city." This right, as observed, springs from a constitution of favor. And while men are saved by grace, or brought into the second kingdom, (for all in it are said to be saved in the New Testament style) by favor, they cannot enter the heavenly kingdom, but by patient continuance in well doing. So stands the decree of the Lord Almighty as I understand the Oracles.

Those who desire the enjoyment of remission of sins, peace with God, and abundance of joy, can obtain them through submission to an institution of pure favor, as already defined. But when we speak of admission into the everlasting kingdom, we must have a due respect to those grand and fundamental principles so clearly propounded in the New Institution. We must discriminate between the kingdom of favor, and the kingdom of glory.

This is in anticipation of my essays on the Jewish and Christian Dispensations, and I am compelled to divulge so much of the views which I have to lay before my readers under more appropriate heads, and as the results of premises not yet developed: I say, I am compelled to cross the Jordan, and to pull a cluster of the grapes to show those who are halting between two opinions, that there is good fruit in the land to which I invite them. The following narrative will shed more light on the three kingdoms:—

The Narrative of Simeon.

WHILE musing upon the three kingdoms, I fancied myself in the kingdom of glory after the final judgment. Amongst my companions in that happy kingdom, I was introduced to one Simeon, a Jew, who had been converted to christianity eight years after the resurrection of Jesus Christ. While in conversation on the wonders of redemption, Simeon gave us the following narrative. "I have been," said he, "a subject of these three kingdoms, and now I discern not only the true nature and design of each, but I am enraptured in contemplating the manifold wisdom developed in their respective constitutions. I was, when born of the flesh, born a citizen of the commonwealth of Israel. I was circumcised and made partaker of all the privileges of the first or prefatory kingdom of God. I distinctly remember all my views and feelings under that economy. When I waited at the altar and worshipped in the sanctuary, my conscience was often troubled, and its momentary pacifications were like the occasional appearances of the sun in a dark and cloudy day. If I felt peace at the altar, so soon as I mingled with my fellow-citizens, I contracted pollution, and my sin was ever before me; my iniquities took such hold upon me, that, at times, I could not lift up my eyes. Hopes and fears, joys and sorrows, alternated in my bosom. The thunders of Sinai and the flashing vengeance that destroyed in a moment thousands of my nation, often occurred to me. I prayed with fear and trembling. I expected a Redeemer, but knew not the nature of his redemption. But finally I believed that Jesus of Nazareth was he. I saw that his institution differed from that of Moses, as the sun excelled a star. I apprehended the reign of favor, and gladly became a citizen of the second kingdom. I was born of water and of the Spirit, and obtained a remission of sins, of which I had never formed an idea under the kingdom of law. The sacrifice of Jesus, and the divine testimony or assurance which I had from God our Father, in the proclamation of mercy, cured my conscience and implanted new life within me. I felt myself in a new kingdom, in a kingdom of favor. Sin did not now lord it over me as before, and my heart beat in unison with the favor which superabounded; so that, in comparison of the former kingdom, my sun always shone in a bright and cloudless sky. If, in one thought, I felt myself seduced from the path of life, with the quickness of a glance of the mind, I remembered that Jesus died, and that I had died and been buried with him in his sacred institution. This always cured my conscience and gladdened my heart. I ran the race and finished my course. I slept in Jesus; and, lo! I awoke at the sound of the trumpet, and all my deeds came into remembrance, not one of them was forgotten by God. I was found worthy through conformity to that favor which brought me into the fold of God, to approach the tree of life. I have tasted its fruit and feel myself imm____ ___ _____ contrast between the kingdom of la___ ___ the kingdom of favor prepared me to relish and to enjoy the contrast between the kingdom of favor and the kingdom of glory. And when I tell the wondrous story of nature and grace to those my companions who have come from the East and the West, from the North and the South, without circumcision or the proclamation of mercy through the gospel, their devotion in hearing and mine in telling, their joy in me, and my joy in them, swell our strains and raise our bliss to degrees ineffable and full of glory. I have been thrice born—once of the flesh, once of water and spirit, and once from the grave. Each birth brought me into a congenial society. My fellow-citizens always resembled my nativity. I was surrounded once with the children of the flesh, then with those born from above, and now with those born from the ashes of the grave." While proceeding to narrate some things I never before heard, my transports aroused me, but could not fancy again.   EDITOR.

Essays on Man in his Primitive State and under the Patriarchal, Jewish, and Christian Dispensations—No. IX.

Jewish Age.—No. I

As THE first religious economy was patriarchal, because adapted to families in an unassociated capacity; so the second was national, because adapted to families in an associated or national capacity. The first required but the existence of a single family for the enjoyment of all its institutions and privileges: the second required many families living together in close neighborhood and under one and the same civil government. Thus we find in the preliminaries to the Sinaitic institution, that it was proposed to constitute a religious nation a kingdom of priests, a holy people, upon a certain basis. To the preliminaries, as proposed by Moses, the people assented, and on their consent was issued the constitution. This was written by the King in his own handwriting upon two tables of stone. This was the supreme law of their social, religious, and moral relations. And all their other laws and institutions were but the developement and application of its principles to religion and politics.

Abraham was called at a time when idolatry began to appear in Chaldea, and when families began to have each a family god. When his descendants became numerous, and large enough to become a nation, and the nations had each its own god, it pleased the Ruler of the Universe to exhibit himself as the God of a nation. Hence originated the theocracy. Here it is necessary to suggest a few general principles of much importance in understanding the varieties which have appeared in the divine government. From the Fall of Man the Governor of the World withdrew from all personal intimacies with the race. He no longer conversed with man face to face as he was wont to do in Eden. The recollections of the Divinity became more and more faint as Adam advanced in years; and the traditionary information communicated to his descendants became less vivid and impressive in every generation. All new communications from the Creator were through symbols, by messengers, or rather through things already known. Things entirely unknown can only be communicated to the mind by things already known. This axiom is at the basis of all revelations, and explains many otherwise inexplicable incidents in the divine communications to man. The natural symbols and the artificial names of things became, from a necessity of nature, the only means through which God could make himself known to man. This, too, has been the invariable rule and measure of all the discoveries which God has made of himself, his purposes, and will. Hence the spangled heavens, all the elements of nature, the earth, and the sea, with all their inhabitants; the relations, customs, and usages existing among men, have all been so many types or letters in the great alphabet which constitutes the vocabulary of divine revelation to man. He has even personated himself by his own creatures, and spoken to man through human institutions. Hence he has been called a Sun, Light, Father, Husband, Man of War, General c. Hosts, a Lord of Battles, King, Prince, Master, &c. &c. He has been spoken of as having eyes, ears, mouth, hands, feet, &c. &c. He has been represented as sitting, standing, walking, hasting, awaking. He has been compared to a unicorn, lion, rock, mountain, &c. &c. He has made himself known in his character, perfections, purposes, and will, by things already known to man. This is the grand secret, which, when disclosed, removes many difficulties and objections, and sets in a clear light the genius of the Jewish age of the religious world.

Now when God became the king of one nation, it was only doing what, on a more extensive scale, and with more various and powerful effects, he had done in calling himself a Father. Both were designed to make himself known through human relations and institutions. One type, symbol, or name, is altogether incompetent to develope the wonderful and incomprehensible God. But his wisdom and goodness are most apparent in making himself known in those relations and to those extents which are best adapted to human wants and imperfections. And the perfection of these discoveries consists in their being exactly suited to the different ages of the world and stages of human improvement. At the time when he chose one nation and made himself known to all the earth as its King and God, no other name, type, or symbol, was so well adapted to this benevolent purpose, as those selected. For when Israel was brought out of Egypt all the nations had their gods; and these gods were esteemed and admired according to the strength, skill, prowess, and prosperity of the nation over which they were supposed to preside. Hence that God was the most adorable in human eyes whose people were most conspicuous.

Wars and battles were the offspring of the spirit of those ages contemporaneous with the first five hundred years of the Jewish history, and with the ages immediately preceding. Hence the idea was, that the nation most powerful in war had the greatest and most adorable God. Now as the Most High (a title borrowed from this very age) always took the world as it was at every period in which he chose to develope himself anew, or his purposes, he chose to appear as the Lord of Hosts, or God of Armies. And to make his name known through all the earth, he took one nation under his auspices, and appeared as their Sovereign and the Commander in Chief of all their Armies. Hence the splendid and easy bought victories of the Israelites. One could chase a hundred, and ten put a thousand to flight. This explains the deliverance out of Egypt, and how the Lord permitted Pharaoh's heart to be hardened—for the purpose of making his name known through all the earth. Pharaoh and his court knew not the God of Abraham, Isaac, and Jacob, and impiously asked, "Who is the Lord, that I should obey him?" But Moses made him know, and tremble, and bow. By the time when the Jews were settled in Canaan, the world was taught to fear the God of Israel, the Lord of Hosts; and so it came to pass that all the true and consistent knowledge of God upon the earth, amongst all nations, was derived directly or indirectly from the Jewish people.

But we must not think that only one purpose was gained, or one object was exclusively in view in any of these great movements of the Governor of the World. This is contrary to the general analogy of the material and spiritual systems. By the annual and diurnal revolutions of the earth, although by the former the seasons of the year, and by the latter day and night seem to be the chief objects, there are a thousand ends gained in conjunction with one principal one. So in this grand economy, many, very many illustrious ends were gained besides the capital one just mentioned. For, as in the vegetable kingdom we have a succession of stages in the growth of plants; as in the animal kingdom we have a succession of stages in the growth of animals; so in the kingdom of God there is a similar progression of light, knowledge, life, and bliss. We have in the vegetable kingdom the period of germinating, the period of blossoming, and the period of ripening the fruit. So we have infancy, childhood, youth, and manhood, in our own species. Each period calls for special influences and a peculiar treatment. So it is in the kingdom of God. It had its infancy, its childhood, and its manhood. In each stage it was diversely exhibited. The Patriarchal, Jewish, and Christian Ages were adapted to these.

Again, we are not to consider the special temporal favors bestowed upon the Jews as indicative that the divine benevolence was exclusively confined to one nation to the exclusion of all the earth besides. As well might we say that the husbandman who cultivates his garden despises or neglects his farm, or that he exclusively loved that part of the soil which he encloses with a peculiar fence. Other circumstances and considerations require these specialities. The general good of the human race, and the blessing of all nations in a son of Abraham, were the ultimate and gracious ends in view in all these peculiar arrangements. This promise and guarantee was made to Abraham before the times of these ages or dispensations. So that the calling of the Jews and their erection into a nation under the special government of God, were but means necessary to that reign of favor under which we now live.

These general and prefatory hints we thought expedient to suggest as preliminary to our essays on the Jewish economy. There is one lesson of more than ordinary importance, which all who have not attended to it ought to learn, not only with reference to our object in these essays, but with reference to many others—and that is, *that things unknown can only be taught through things already known.*   EDITOR.

Religious Controversy.

THE following remarks on " Religious Controversy," from the Pandect, are rational and worthy of a perusal.—ED. C. B.

It is much to be desired that correct views should obtain in the church and in the world relative to controversy on matters of religion. If we rightly scan the signs of the times, there is a special necessity for making this subject prominent at the present day. A fair moral estimate of the true nature and legitimate ends of controversy is we believe of less and less frequent occurrence. Persons of amiable and pacific tempers are apt to be offended with the very term. The argumentative discussion of any topic of religion is unhappily associated in their minds with the encounter of angry passions—with bitterness and evil speaking—with an entire dereliction of the charities and courtesies of both christian and civil intercourse. And candor compels us to admit that too much occasion has been given in all ages for connecting these repulsive attributes with religious debates of every kind. But they are by no means its inseparable

adjuncts. And no plea for the necessity of controversy ought to be construed as a plea for its common evils. We know not why the truest spirit of meekness and kindness towards the person of an opponent may not be coupled with the utmost force of reasoning in the defence of opinion. Yet in the minds of many these ideas appear to be wholly incompatible with each other; and to say of a tract, a treatise, a sermon, a book, it is controversial in its object or complexion, is at once to fix an indelible odium upon it. No matter how clear and luminous its exposition of error, or its defence of truth—no matter how engaging or conciliating its spirit—still it is controversy, hated controversy—and wormwood and coals of juniper and firebrands and arrows—all rush into the imagination as through an open door, and forbid it the least favor.

This surely is not calling things by their right names, nor judging righteous judgment. What is the scope of religious controversy, but the vindication of religious truth? Is not this truth liable to be denied, distorted, corrupted, or frittered away? Is it not often entangled with specious errors, and charged with false consequences? Are its friends required to stand silent by, and see its dearest interests jeopardised, without coming forward to its defence? Is there any alternative left them but to enter the lists, and to endeavor to show truth triumphant? By this we do not intend to advocate the belligerent spirit of controversy: however polemical or warlike may be our terms. But as to the thing itself, we see not but controversy is as inevitable as error, and as harmless as its refutation. If there *are* fundamental truths in the gospel, and these truths are liable to be assailed, they must be defended; and if they are continually assailed, they must be continually defended.

For this we unquestionably have the high authority both of scripture precepts and example. Mention is made of some " whose mouths must be stopped;" and " gainsayers are to be put to silence." And it ought to abate very considerably our aversion to *every* form of controversy when we find several of the Epistles written with the express design of confuting certain errors which had sprung up in the church, and were making head against the Apostles' doctrine. If inspired men stand foremost in the ranks of controvertists, it is a sickly or sinful sighing for peace, that keeps us not in the back ground merely, but off from the ground altogether.

Now we have yet to learn that the day in which we live is so happily distinguished above former periods as to absolve us from the necessity of controversy. Are errors less rife over the whole length and breadth of our land at this moment than in the times of our fathers? Is there a more general and cordial yielding to the pure principles of religion and morality? Are the advocates of the unadulterate doctrines of the gospel listened to and reported of with more candor? Does the weekly press teem with a more hopeful issue, and send out through its thousand channels a better influence over the bosom of society? Are the prejudices naturally engendered by sectarian divisions, melting away, and the hearts of good men panting to break through party pales and flow together? Are the smaller points of difference more frequently viewed as small than ever before, while all the true holders of the one Head are rallying round the central points of union?

If these auspicious omens were indeed visible, we might begin to think of discharging ourselves from this duty. But we do not see them.

On the contrary, we see what we are taught in prophecy to expect, growing indications of a more powerful spirit of error. With more real liberality than formerly, we believe there is also more false. There is a disposition to relax the rigor of truth. And here, if we mistake not, bedded in fragrant flower of lovely charity, lies the baneful cankerworm—an aversion to controversy. It is, in many cases, we are persuaded, the product of a spurious catholicism, which would bid us embrace error as well as truth—which would blind our eyes to the everlasting and indestructible distinction between them.

But we have wandered into a longer dissertation than we intended, though well aware, that much, very much, remains to be said on the subject, in order to present it in all its bearings. At present our aim has been to intimate that a dislike of all controversy, in every form, is exceedingly unreasonable, inasmuch as a wholesale reprobation of it is very apt to be connected with an indifference to truth which has a bad aspect.

Dangerous Attempt.

SOME persons think that it was a dangerous attempt, on my part, to discuss with the champion of infidelity the evidences of christianity. They did not know what we could do with a man who denied the bible, and were afraid that his cavils and objections would be unanswerable, and thus the discussion would more likely make sceptics of christians, than christians of sceptics. Bad enough, indeed, if we christians are not able to produce a reason, or many good reasons, for our faith! A handsome compliment, truly, they present to the christian community, who insinuate that they believe without reason, and cannot tell why! From such christians christianity has more to fear than from infidels. I trust the late debate will show that the reason is all on our side, and the sophistry all on that of our opponents. And I rejoice to know, from various sources, that some infidels were converted to christianity from the late debate, but no christians were converted to infidelity. Our great complaint against Mr. Owen was, that he would not reason, and that while sceptics boasted of reason, they had little or none to show.　　　　EDITOR.

"The Pedobaptist."

I HAVE not seen but the first and second numbers of this work. In the second I observe in the first article which I read, and the only one I have leisure at this time to read, that so hard pressed is the editor or some of its writers, on the meaning of the word *bapto*, that he is forced to affirm that the lexicons or Greek dictionaries are not to be depended on, inasmuch as there is none of them more than five hundred years old. So, then all the scriptures are of doubtful import, as far as dictionaries are concerned, for none of the Greek dictionaries can explain a single word in them, because they are only five hundred years old. How then does Doctor N. arrive at the meaning of them? Never before did I see the Paidoes so hard put to it to keep up the little golden idol. A prop under each arm, and one from the chin and spine, will not keep Dagon on his feet. I advise to prop it all round, and then to tie it and the props together with a golden chain.　　　　EDITOR.

Query—for the C. B.

WHY did Paul thank God that he had immersed none but Crispus and Gaius?

Answer.—Paul did not do so. He thanked God that he immersed none of the Corinthians but a few individuals. And the reason was, "Lest any one should say he had immersed into his own name," and thus afforded them some pretext for calling themselves after Paul. Paul was inveighing against christians calling themselves by the names of human leaders, and was thankful in this instance that he had afforded no pretext for any of the schismatics in Corinth to call themselves after his name.　　　ED.

No. 12.]　　　JULY 6, 1829.
Paulinus, to the Editor of the Christian Baptist.
MAY, 1829.

DEAR SIR,—A correspondent, who appears under the signature of "A Lover of the whole of Divine Truth," in the last number of the Christian Baptist, has labored to make it appear that "Paulinus" in your periodical, is at variance with "Melancthon" in the "Religious Herald;"—in other words, that the writer with these different signatures is inconsistent with himself; and, indeed, that "Paulinus," at one period of his correspondence with you, is not altogether consistent with "Paulinus" at another period.

Giving this writer all due credit for his sagacity—and especially for smelling the wonderful secret that "there has been a lecture, caution, admonition, reproof, or rebuke, given from somewhere;"—(some people have the faculty of smelling out what never existed)—I must beg your indulgence to say a little in reference to this communication; much I have no desire to say, and I hope it may not be necessary.

In the first letter of "Paulinus," your correspondent finds many things highly to commend, and none, as far as I observe, to censure. Very well! In the second epistle, too, he is pleased to say, he finds "other excellent things." But here he begins to suspect that "Paulinus" is wavering; and further onward he becomes confirmed in the opinion that there was a desertion of the sentiments with which "Paulinus" commenced the correspondence; or some inconsistency with the professions and declarations which he had made.

To a person, sir, who thinks, that because a man has expressed himself to be highly pleased with the sentiments and operations of another, to a certain extent, he must therefore approve *in toto*;—to him who may consider it proper, implicitly to deliver himself up, to go, *pari passu*, with another, and even run before him;—to such a person I own I may have appeared wavering and inconsistent; but from the decision of any such person, I must appeal to those who are capable of exercising more candor.

As it regards the inconsistency of "Paulinus" with himself, in his correspondence in the Christian Baptist, I do not feel concern enough, on this point, to trouble you, or your readers, or myself, with a review in detail of the quotations and remarks of this writer. If any of your readers should be so far interested in the matter as to examine for themselves, I refer them to the correspondence itself:—particularly to the first letter of "Paulinus," vol. 4, p. 266, and the answer, p. 268,—to the second letter, vol. 4, 306; and to Paulinus' note to the editor, vol. 5, p. 377. Let any intelligent person, without the colored spectacles of this writer, attentively read this correspondence, and then say whether the labor of this "Lover of the whole of Divine Truth," be not, thus far, lost labor.

It is of much more consequence to consider the charge of inconsistency between "Paulinus" in the Christian Baptist, and "Melancthon" in the Religious Herald. Of much more consequence, I say, not on my own account, but because it involves a matter which I deem of great importance to the rising generation;—I mean, the moral and religious culture of the minds of children.

What now is the lamentable inconsistency complained of? Let us see: and let me endeavor to condense: for I begin to apprehend I shall occupy more room than may be desirable.

"Melancthon," in his fourth essay, treating on the religious instruction of children, recommends, for early childhood, the use of plain and simple catechisms, adapted to the capacity of children: and that we might be supplied with these means of instruction, and have them more generally adopted amongst us, he undertook to suggest to the Baptist General Convention, the propriety of taking certain steps, for the purpose of effecting this object.

And behold, here is the offence!—and here is the inconsistency of "Paulinus" and "Melancthon!" If you ask, How? (as well you may)—I answer, thus; viz. "Paulinus" had expressed much pleasure in your apparent aim, "to clear the religion of Jesus of all the adventitious lumber with which it has been encumbered, and bring back the christian church to its primitive simplicity and beauty." He had also expressed his hearty approbation of "your opposition to the errors and follies, too prevalent in the religious world." Moreover, he had spoken of the most effectual way "for sweeping off all that rubbish which has been gathered from the old ruins of former establishments, to build withal on christian grounds;—alluding to the arguments for christian institutions, drawn from the abrogated ceremonies of the Old Testament. All this "Paulinus" had said: and now, lo! "Melancthon" recommends the use of plain and simple catechisms, as a help in the mode of instructing children! What is the conclusion?—Ergo, "Paulinus" and "Melancthon" are inconsistent." But this logic (please to observe) takes for granted what will not be allowed; viz. that well adapted catechisms are to be considered as adventitious lumber—as errors and follies—as rubbish, gathered from the ruins of former establishments. That this mode of instruction has been abused, "Melancthon" readily allows: but when your correspondent proves the propositions just mentioned;—when he proves that to instruct children in this way is error and folly, and that all catechisms are lumber and rubbish, I can, by the same arguments (and a fortiori) prove the same thing, with regard to all religious periodicals and publications, essays, &c. intended to instruct full grown learners. I say, I can do this more forcibly: because, if persons who are fully capable of reading the Bible for themselves, need human aid, in deriving instruction from that sacred source, then much more do children need such aid, who cannot read for themselves.

But "Paulinus" had declared his persuasion, that "the word of God is the instrument of our regeneration and sanctification:" and this writer asks, if a catechism is such an instrument for "these little immortals?" I answer, divine truth is God's instrument for doing good to the souls of men, whether it be held forth altogether in the express words of scripture or not; and whether viva voce or written. And if your correspondent is sure of the contrary, why does he attempt to teach by long lectures and by printed publications?

"Is this the way (asks our critical censor) to reform the church and restore the ancient order of things?" I answer, every well-adapted method ought to be used, for effecting a reformation where it is needed: and while the apostle enjoins on parents the duty of bringing up their children "in the nurture and admonition of the Lord," can your correspondent, by his sagacity, discover the precise method which we are directed to pursue?—or has the inspired writer left the modus operandi to christian prudence?

Let us hearken again. "Is this the aid he promised to correct the evils, to wit, creeds and confessions of faith, those fruitful sources of dissention," &c. And does your correspondent consider the mode of instructing children by a plain and simple catechism, the same thing with adopting creeds and confessions of faith, as standards (instead of the scriptures) by which to try the members of the church? If so, I may take the liberty to say, I differ with him; and very likely, so will most of your readers.

"Is this," (says he, in the same strain of fancied triumph)—"Is this his opposition to theories, or compiling abstract truths?"—A short quotation from Paulinus' second letter will suffice for the answer:—"not as mere abstract truths, but as having their adjuncts;—not as naked theories, but as practical lessons." Surely, sir, this writer uses terms without duly considering their import.

This method of proceeding, he conceives, is "carrying our jugs to the distillery to get alcohol, that our little immortals may tipple with us."— Your correspondent may enjoy the benefit of this happy application of the figure: but he (it seems) is a teacher in Israel, and doubtless wishes the people to attend his lectures.—Query;—to whose distillery then will they carry their jugs!

"What need can there be (he asks) of the influence of the Holy Spirit, when it is admitted that these ecclesiastical bodies' recommendation will have a powerful and happy influence?" It is enough to say here, that the writer ought to have resisted the temptation which led him to this ill-judged attempt at being witty.

But here comes the most serious charge. He thinks it "a deep reflection upon the wisdom and philanthropy of Jesus Christ, in not giving to these "little immortals" what Melancthon considers necessary for their religious education." He means, I presume, that it is a deep reflection, &c. to say that Christ has not given, &c. Now, sir, I believe that the holy scriptures contain all truth necessary to make us wise to salvation. But I believe also, that God designs we should aid one another in the economy of grace, as well as in that of nature; and particularly that the strong should assist the weak. And if this writer thinks differently, I ask again, why does he attempt to teach even grown folks by long lectures?

Your correspondent could stretch out his hand to pull down, but he has done nothing, in this case, to build up. Suffer me here to quote a passage from "Melancthon." "If, for a certain stage of childhood, a better method can be devised, in any regular or systematic manner to impart instruction, let some of the friends of these little immortals present it to our notice," &c. See Essays on Reformation, No. 4. Now, sir, I do think it is but the part of candor and good nature to admit, that "Melancthon" has shown a disposition to help forward in a most desirable object—and a disposition to do it in the most eligible manner. And deeply conscious of the importance of the object, he has invited the "friends of these little immortals" to lend their aid And what has this "Lover of the whole of Divine Truth" done, in compliance with this friendly invitation?—Let your readers judge.—I have already far transcended my proposed limits, and will only add—when next your correspondent attempts to write for the benefit of the public, I hope he may not amuse himself at the expense of a serious subject.

With every good wish I am, yours in the gospel of Christ,   Paulinus.

—

It would afford me no little pleasure—themselves and their mutual friends much happiness—the cause of truth some service—and Satan no little disappointment—could "Paulinus" and the "Lover of the whole of Divine Truth" agree to co-operate in the restoration of the ancient gospel and the ancient order of things. If they will agree to refer all difficult questions about expediencies, and about matters of mere abstract opinion, to the verdict of the grand jury of twelve Apostles; and should the twelve refuse, one and all, to decide the question, then to refer it to the General Convention of the Saints at their first anniversary of the resurrection of the dead, I will vouch for their most cordial agreement in sentiment, and zealous co-operation in effort in all things affecting the honor of the Saviour, the harmony of the saints, and the conversion of the world. But should they get into a warm controversy about baby catechisms, and long lectures about the capital *I* and the little *u*, I will predict that the leader *in* such a controversy will shed tears for it; and should he win the day on earth, he will lose it in heaven. What a pity that a modern *Paul* and a junior *Timothy* could not, like the good old Paul and Timothy, be fellow-laborers in God's vineyard!   Editor.

—

Virginia, March 20, 1829.

Dear Sir—When I wrote the observations that appeared in your monthly publication of November and December, concerning the intelligibility of sacred writ, I thought I had expressed my conceptions on that subject so guardedly as to preclude even a possibility of being misunderstood; with respect to that hope, however, I find I was mistaken. Some imagine that the condition of the creature's mind, to which, I had asserted, God had adapted his message, was its natural condition, unperverted by education, error, or prejudice; uncorrupted by evil inclinations, habits, or dispositions; and not its state as it actually exists when God's message visits it, perverted and corrupted by all these. This construction of my words, however, is certainly unauthorized by them, and the inference which some draw from their distinction is unsupported. God from all eternity knew, with absolute certainty, not only the quantity of intellect which he had determined to bestow on each of his rational creatures at their birth; but the actual condition of their minds, as produced by error, prejudice, habit, inclination, or disposition, when his message should be made to visit them: and to the then existing condition of the most illiterate, prejudiced, and depraved of them, is the clearness of his message evidently adapted. Hence it is, that, in his message to sinners, no allowance is made for the ignorance, illiterature, error, prejudice, or depravity of any of them.—God manifestly considers his message as sufficiently clear to his rational creature man in every condition in which it can visit him, and threatens, of course, to inflict the severest punishment upon him if he neglect, pervert, or reject it.—

Now, had not the message been deemed sufficiently clear and certain to every sinner when it reached him, justice could not have approved such severity, nor God threatened to inflict it—for this plain reason, that an unintelligible message is no message.

To terminate the strife, let me observe that if the bible be an unintelligible volume, either God or man has made it such; and, of course, unfitted it to answer the end for which it was sent into the world—to enlighten it; and let those who make this charge say on whom this heavy censure falls; if on God, he cannot be that merciful and kind being which he says he is; and if on man it is high time that they undo the darkness which they have spread over the face of God's message to a perishing world. Nor let it be said that God, unable or unwilling to qualify the first publishers for rendering his message plain, has been driven to the necessity of raising up a succession of uninspired, and, of course, unqualified men, to remedy his original failure.

I now proceed to offer a few observations, calculated in my judgment, to evince that in every instance in which the Divine Spirit has judged it proper (for he never acts inconsiderately or inadvertently) to conceal his mind from man by the use of obscure or ambiguous language, no uninspired man can defeat his design, or make his mind more fully or clearly known than he has condescended to do. This fact is explicitly declared in Paul's first letter to the christian society at Corinth, ii. 11. and the declaration ought to have repressed the impious attempts of presumptuous mortals to pry into the secrets of the Almighty. But as it seems there are men, and, still more wonderful, Christian Doctors, too, who pay little regard to divine authority, we invite them to attend to a fact that occurs daily, and to the abortive labor of many hundred years, for instruction on this important subject.

The fact to which we allude, is, that when a fellow creature employs, either designedly or inadvertently, obscure or ambiguous language in the enunciation of his thoughts, it is impossible for any other human being to determine with certainty his meaning: conjecture concerning it is all that can be reached. If, then, the use of obscure or ambiguous phraseology be resorted to by men with absolute certainty that the veil which they thus spread over their thoughts will prove impenetrable, and for ever defy the sagacity of their fellow men to pierce it, how ridiculous is it to imagine that the obscure or ambiguous phraseology *purposely* introduced by the Divine Spirit into his message, can be removed by human sagacity.

But in case this fact, like God's explicit declaration, should fail to work conviction and check the daring impiety of rash mortals, let the abortive labor of innumerable learned commentators, expositors, sermonizers, &c. who have most assiduously cultivated this barren field, at length dash the vain hopes of self-conceited men. Where, we ask, is the obscure or ambiguous word, phrase, or passage, to be found in the whole book of God, which is clearer or more certain now than it was seventeen hundred years ago? Conjecture, mere conjecture about the Spirit's meaning is, in every instance, in which his own words do not clearly announce it, all that has been, or indeed could have been advanced on the subject. And will any christian suffer himself to be so excessively deluded as to build his faith and rear his everlasting hopes on such a wretched foundation as human conjecture? No—the faith of a christian can fix on no other foundation than the clear and explicit declaration of a God who can neither lie nor be mistaken. Oh! human vanity! how long wilt thou obtrude thy disgusting visage upon us? How long wilt thou select the most obscure and ambiguous passages of God's word to exhibit thy self-conceit, and make an ignorant multitude gape, stare, marvel at, and talk about thy matchless skill in making darkness light?

Here it may not be improper to notice a fallacy which the learned as well as the unlearned are wont to practice upon themselves. It is not uncommon to hear people, who acknowledge that the words employed by the divine Spirit do not with certainty suggest his meaning to their minds, declare that by the aid of a commentator or other expounder, they can discover the Spirit's meaning clearly. We ask, How can this be? Have the words employed by the Spirit, or any of the inferior helps with which he has furnished us, undergone a change? Have they acquired a greater degree of fitness to reveal the Spirit's mind to us than they had before the commentator was consulted? We presume not. What then has happened? Just this—The commentator's notion has been substituted and mistaken for the Spirit's meaning. The deluded enquirer, pleased with an ingenious suggestion of his favorite commentator, admits it to be the real meaning of the Spirit, and henceforth employs it as a standard by which he tries the notions of others and his own. But it is plain that during this whole process of self-deception the Spirit's meaning is as little known to the enquirer, after he has got his commentator's aid as it was before; and instead of the Spirit's meaning, he has got only his commentator's notion—for it is not the Spirit's, but the commentator's words that suggest the meaning which he adopts.

But it may be asked, Has the Divine Spirit furnished no other means of ascertaining the meaning of his message than the words and phrases in which it is written? We answer, He has: even all the means that can be safely used to ascertain the meaning of any human speech or writing. Beside the words and phrases which the Spirit has selected to express his mind, he has given us the aid of context, connected phraseology, related passages, scope or purpose, and subject, recorded facts, antecedent institutions, previous and subsequent declaration of the divine mind, the state of morality and theology, and even the controversies that existed when any passage, to us obscure, was written. To all these, as to means furnished by the Spirit himself, and furnished to all alike, who have a bible in their hands, or its contents within their hearing, and which require, in order to obtain from them all the aid they can afford, not human learning, but common sense and scripture information. To all these, I say, we may occasionally resort, even where no doubt is entertained concerning the genuineness of the present text. And where the original text is suspected of having undergone any alteration, God has given us the benefit of ancient manuscripts, ancient translations, and even quotations of ancient date, by a diligent and cautious comparison of which, accidental alterations may be detected, and the original reading be restored. And here we admit human learning to be of real use, but here only. Now, though God has furnished the devout student of his word with all these inferior helps, yet the occasions are very few, we presume, on which he will find it necessary to use any of them. God's message being intended and constructed for the salvation of multitudes who have not leisure to peruse such subordinate aids, must be sufficient to answer his purpose without their use: nor can we believe that God meant that the illiterate should depend on the conjectural and of course uncertain information of the learned and ingenious, obtained from these inferior sources,—for this would compel the illiterate to depend on human sagacity, and not divine declaration; to build their faith on the suggestions of men, and not on the informations of God.   Yours, &c.
                                        ALEXANDER STRAITH.

The Bible.—No. III.

Dear Sir,—As closely connected with the consummate folly of attempting to remove the *intentional* obscurities and ambiguities of the Divine Spirit from his message, we mention the impious practice of attempting to make us more fully acquainted with events recorded—with minerals, animals, vegetables, and places; with manners, customs, and usages; in short, with any thing mentioned in sacred writ—than God has thought fit to do. What immense labor has been performed, what vast quantities of precious time have been spent, absolutely wasted, in vain attempts to furnish information; for example, respecting the formation of this planet and its inhabitants; its appearance when newly formed; the situation and extent of the place called the garden of Eden; its rivers and trees; the qualities of the tree called in scripture the tree of good and evil; the time man lived before he sinned; the animal by which Eve was deceived; the change produced by the prohibited fruit on the intellectual, moral, and physical constitution of our first parents; the duration of man's probationary state, and his destiny, had he continued to live in innocence; the change produced on our earth by Adam's transgression, and by the flood that succeeded it; and ten thousand other scriptural objects and occurrences in addition to what God has thought proper to give us. But, alas! this has proved to us another barren field, which learned presumption and folly have labored long and hard to change; the blasting curse, however, still adheres to it. Not one particle of *certain* information, additional to what God has condescended to furnish us, has been procured by the researches of man. Conjectures, often wild and extravagant, often puerile and ridiculous, generally variant, and even contradictory, but always *uncertain*, fill up the whole mass of pretended information which vain dreamers have affected to add to God's intelligence. Nor is this total failure of human labor a matter either of wonder or regret. Surely had God considered *more* information than he has furnished concerning any object mentioned in his word, to be either useful or necessary to man, his goodness affords the most ample assurance that he would have communicated it and given it absolute certainty. We ought, therefore, to regard the quantity of certain information concerning the objects mentioned in sacred writ which God has there vouchsafed to impart to us, as that quantity precisely which he knew to be fittest and safest for us, and, with it, it is our wisdom, our duty, and our interest, to be satisfied. To covet more is impious—to aim at more is downright rebellion. From the conjectures, notions, and dreams of self-conceited men, we can obtain no benefit; from them, however, we may derive much harm. Let us therefore reject and despise them as at least superfluous, if not pernicious, and cleave to the information of our all-wise Creator, as all that is necessary to make us truly wise and happy. Indeed it is astonishing that men should covet and laboriously strive to acquire notions, in the truth and certainty of which they know that they can repose no confidence, and which, of course, must remain useless lumber in their minds!

There is another current practice, which, as it offers to the Deity, if possible, still grosser insult, merits severer condemnation. It is the practice of attempting, by human researches and discoveries, to render God's declarations more credible than his veracity can render them. Many who seem but little disposed to believe the occurrence of events, or the existence of objects mentioned in scripture, merely because God has declared their existence, are ready, if any trace of the declared occurrence, or any specimen of the asserted object be now found, where the scripture says the occurrence did take place, or the object, whether animal, vegetable, mineral, custom, manner, usage, or place did exist—to admit that God has at least once told the truth, and deserves credit. This is truly horrible! Divine testimony accounted unworthy of belief till confirmed by human discovery! What insult here to that veracity, which, when it stamps its declarations with the seal of truth, suffers no other testimony, no other evidence to approach it. Vision itself creates not that certainty which divine veracity begets —which divine declaration affords. Away then with all confirmative discoveries, all confirmative arguments or reasonings of man, with respect to any matter concerning which God has made an explicit declaration! And let it be remembered also that one explicit declaration establishes the truth and certainty of what is declared, as effectually as if the declaration were to be repeated ten thousand times. And this, by the bye, manifests and condemns the impiety of the practice of attempting to render any explicit declaration of sacred writ more credible, by resorting to other passages in which the same declaration may be found.　　　　A. S.

TROY, MIAMI COUNTY, OHIO, June 8, 1829.

MR. EDITOR—Here is a glass of cordial to revive your spirits: it is presented merely as a compliment; and as treats are becoming quite unfashionable among the more temperate, I shall not think it impolite in you not to accept it.

Yesterday I attended a Methodist camp meeting, where I was again reminded (as I have often been within two years past) of a remark your father, Thomas Campbell, made to me nearly three years since; it was substantially this—"If you attend the ministry of a Presbyterian, you will hear many good things; if you hear a Methodist, many glorious truths will be uttered; should the preacher be an Episcopalian, he may edify you; a Baptist preacher will say many things that are said in the Bible; the Universalian is not entirely ignorant of the gospel; the Unitarian's sermon is true in part; and the like may be said of every sect in christendom; but among all these sects, without exception, nearly one-half you hear is false, or, to say the least, doubtful; that is to say, it is not to be found in the scriptures."

Among the many good and bad, true and false declarations, which were made from the stand yesterday, the following is one, or several in one. To which class does it belong?—

Presiding Elder, James Finley, upon the first of three heads, into which he divided this text, "For our light affliction, which is but for a moment, works for us a far more exceeding and eternal weight of glory," announced, with much warmth, "That he must, in justice to the cause of truth, warn his congregation to beware of the doctrines propagated by one Campbell, of the Baptist church, who denies the agency of the Holy Spirit in the conversion of a sinner, and opposes the divinity of our Lord Jesus Christ. Every thing pertaining to the new birth, regeneration, and pardon of sin, he resolves into baptism, and this into immersion!! He makes immersion the earnest of the inheritance. One of that class of preachers, when baptizing some persons in the Miami, near Dayton, not long ago, said to them, 'The time is coming when you will look down from Heaven upon this place, and rejoice that you here received the earnest of your inheritance,' meaning that baptism was the earnest! One of them came to Sandusky, and told the christian Indians and others at that place, that he had been at considerable pains in coming a long distance for the purpose of preaching the gospel to them, and requested an audience, with which the Indians very politely favored him. He commenced by telling them that he had a message of salvation for them; and, in the course of his lecture, informed them that this salvation was to be obtained only by being immersed; that the water would wash away all their sins, and they would be pardoned and justified immediately. After a consultation, as is the custom of the Indians in such cases, they made him the following reply: 'We thank you for the interest you have taken in our own welfare, and for all your trouble in coming so far to instruct us poor ignorant Indians. You have said some very good things, which we know by experience to be true; but you have said some things which we do not understand.* We do not understand how the water can wash away our sins. I have washed my body all over in the Mississippi, in the Missouri, in the Wabash, and in the great lake, many a time, but it did not wash away my sins. All my sins remained just as they were, until the blood of Christ was applied by the Spirit of God; then they were all taken away at once. The water could not wash away my sins, because it went no deeper than the skin, and my sins were not on my skin, but in my heart; nothing could get at them, but the Spirit of God; and if it *could* get at them, nothing but the Spirit of God could break them down and destroy them."

"Such preachers are ignorant of the gospel themselves. They have no experience of the love of God shed abroad in their hearts by the Holy Spirit. Would God call such a person to preach the glad tidings of salvation to lost sinners?"

The above is an abridgement of Elder Finley's observations on this part of the first head of his text. I think that in several sentences I have his own language *verbatim;* I should have given his own words throughout could I have recollected them. I have not intentionally added one thought, but have omitted several for brevity's sake, which were not essential to the design of the extract, or necessary to screen myself from the charge of misrepresentation.

After the discourse, I called on Mr. Finley as politely as one of my little etiquette could well do, and modestly asked him for a written extract of that part of the discourse, for the use of Mr. Campbell and the public. I informed him that I had resolved to make report of his representation of Mr. Campbell's doctrine as well as my memory and the imperfect notes I had taken would en-

* This same Elder Finley was the Missionary at Sandusky.

able me; [not knowing what was coming, my notes were not commenced in time;] but wishing not to misrepresent Mr. Finley in the least, I wished to have it from his hand in the very terms that he would wish to come under your review. The only satisfaction he gave me was this,—"I have heard his preachers say those very things, and I have seen them in his writings. B—— preaches the same things, and he says he got them from Campbell!!!" I repeated my request, accompanied with such reasons as candor and christian charity would suggest; but he turned from me, observing, "I am no controversialist." Every body, however, in these parts knows that there is not a greater controversialist (if this be not an abuse of the term) in the country than he, when his antagonist is not present.

M.

Remarks.

I think it is ten to one, in the doctrine of chances, whether Elder Finley ever struck upon the meaning of the Apostle Paul in the text, if he brought me out in the sermon. Paul's light afflictions which wrought out for him and his associates an eternal glory, were neither the toothache, rheumatism, pleurisy, jaundice, nor fever of any grade. Neither were they the little or great difficulties, pains, mortifications, prosecutions or persecutions, to which some are liable in the pursuit of wealth or fame. But that I am one of those light afflictions which was working out for Mr. Finley so much future glory, is one of the rarest things which my last mail laid upon the table. But the greatest curiosity is yet untold. How could Elder Finley think in lightly afflicting me he could promote his own glory! I should have expected more good sense from him than to change the theme of suffering light afflictions into a scene of creating light afflictions for one that never afflicted him to the burthen of a moschetto in his whole life.

But to get a little closer to Mr. Finley, I would seriously ask whether himself or the Indians so far perverted my language as to represent me as placing pardon, regeneration or the eternal inheritance, in water, or in mere immersion in water. Suppose he should tell the good people of Ohio, that through prayer "pardon and acceptance with God were obtained;" what would he think, or say of me, should I invent or publish an Indian colloquy, representing him, or some of his brethren, as stating that air or wind exhaled in a particular manner, caused guilt to be removed from the conscience, and effected a good understanding betwixt a sinner and the Sovereign of the Universe! Or suppose that he should have taught that good works, such as feeding the hungry, and clothing the naked, were some way necessary to admission into the everlasting kingdom; would he be pleased with me should I represent him as teaching that a certain quantity of corn and wool, or cash, was necessary to admission into heaven! Or suppose that he taught that men were pardoned, justified, and saved through faith, would he say that I did him justice if I held him up to ridicule in a public assembly for teaching that one single thought or act of the mind cancelled all guilt and brought a man into the enjoyment of the smiles of Heaven! Or suppose that he taught that the Holy Spirit regenerated an unbeliever or made him a christian in an instant of time, independent of a preacher or a written revelation! Or that the Spirit physically operated upon the human mind anterior to faith and made man able and willing to believe, could he say that I acted the part of a

christian if I held him up to scorn for teaching that men were as passive in being born again, as the trees in spring are in being covered with foliage and blossoms, or as the mill wheel is in performing its revolutions! Most certainly he would complain of me. Well, now, what if I should tell brother Finley that there is "one text" in a little book which he loves very much, which says, "All things you would that men should do to you, do you even so to them," and ask him to make a sermon upon it?

But now let me discourse familiarly with my friend Finley. Well, Mr. Finley, what is faith? Do you not define it an act of the mind? And what is prayer but words or sounds addressed to the Deity, expressive of the feelings or desires of the heart? And what is repentance but sorrow for the past? And what is reformation but a ceasing to do evil and a learning to do well? And what is the Lord's supper but eating bread and drinking wine in commemoration of the Lord's death? And what is baptism but immersion in water, or, as you may perhaps think, sprinkling a person into water? Well, now, what efficacy is there in any one of these elements or acts more than in any other elements or acts, but which the divine appointment communicates?

Your Indians, and a Syrian Indian who had the leprosy in the days of Elijah the Prophet, seem to have been methodistical logicians of the same school. They both laughed at the stupidity of a Jewish Prophet for thinking or saying that the water in Jordan had any such efficacy as to cure the leprosy of soul or body, or that it was any better than the waters of the Mississippi or the Lake of the Woods. No doubt they were very merry at the weakness of the old believer, and satirized his enthusiasm. However, the event proved, as you may remember, that the Indians of that day were all sophists: for God had given such efficacy by his own mere appointment to the water in Jordan as made it omnipotent to cure. Such efficacy, too, once had the waters of Siloam when God presided over them! And such efficacy old Paul found in the waters of Damascus after he had believed in the blood of Jesus. He washed his sins away at the command of a messenger of the Lord. Without faith, however, neither the waters of Jordan, Damascus, or Siloam, could possess such virtue. And if you have not this faith, we only ask you neither to mock nor defame those who are so credulous as to believe that he who once turned water into wine, is able to forgive us our sins through water, if we cheerfully receive him as our Prophet, Priest, and King, and submit to his institutions.

If you can only understand how men are born of the Spirit, and cannot understand how they are born of water too, I only request you to allow them who understand both, and have experienced both, to explain themselves. And when you hear Indians saying that sins are not in the skin, but in the blood or flesh of the heart, tell them that sin is not located in flesh, blood, or bones, and that no material application is ever taught, as in its own nature, qualified to absorb, wash away, or deface such moral impurities. But tell them that the blood of Jesus alone can cleanse the conscience from guilt. But, at the same time, there must be some act, medium, or means; some channel in and through which this blood can be felt, apprehended, or communicated. And moreover it will do them no harm to tell them that one Peter, who had the keys of the reign and kingdom of heaven, once proclaimed to all who asked what they should do—that they should reform and be immersed for the remission of their sins, and God would grant them the Holy Spirit. Tell them, So the New Institution reads, and that God does neither mock, insult, nor mislead the understanding of the fallen creatures of his love.—And if any one deride you, tell him that he may deride the whole scheme of redemption, and laugh at the mission and sacrifice of Jesus Christ as unworthy of God and unnecessary for men—but tell him if he laugh now, he will mourn and weep by and by. Tell him that the Messiah said, with the most solemn asseverations too, that unless a man was born of water and of the Spirit he could not enter into the kingdom of God.

I have no preachers, Mr. Finley; and I acknowledge no man as a servant of Jesus Christ who is content to take my conclusions, or John Wesley's *ipse dixit*, for any thing appertaining to the salvation of men. They must not be the servants of men who profess to be the servants of Jesus Christ. I trust they who proclaim reformation towards God, faith in Jesus Christ, and immersion for the remission of sins, know something of the love of God in their hearts and of the Holy Spirit, notwithstanding you have pronounced them destitute of both. As to our comparative ignorance I am not a judge. Though you were as wise as Solomon and as intelligent as Paul, you ought to have compassion on us poor ignorant disciples, and teach us the way of the Lord more perfectly. But I cannot conclude these remarks without calling upon Mr. Finley for the proof that I "oppose the divinity of Jesus Christ; deny the agency of the Holy Spirit in the conversion of a sinner; resolve every thing pertaining to the new birth, regeneration, and pardon of sin, into immersion, and make it the earnest of the inheritance." While I publish this calumny of yours to every state in the Union, I will give you an opportunity of explaining yourself to all who read these remarks, if you have any thing to offer in extenuation of this most illiberal and unfounded charge. You should know, reverend sir, that your *say so* is not like an oracle from heaven. We are not bound to believe you without evidence. Produce the evidence and we will try it. That I understand the gospel in quite a different light from the coloring you may give it, I doubt not. But you are not infallible; and when I choose a Pope, I will certainly have one better instructed, and more learned than you, to dictate to me what I must believe on peril of condemnation. No Methodist teacher, that I know of, has gone so far in the downward path of detraction as you, Mr. Finley; and I shall be sorry if your illiberal and unfounded calumnies should in the least mar that good understanding which now exists between me and many of the methodistic brotherhood, who are well disposed to call no man Master or Father on earth in the kingdom of Jesus.　　EDITOR.

Debates, Tumults, the Two Seeds, &c.

So GREAT has been the accumulation of essays, queries, and reports, for the last two months, that I find it impossible to lay any reasonable proportion of them before our readers in the present number. I have therefore resolved not to attempt it, and postpone them indefinitely. As I propose bringing this work to a close in the next volume, and as there are several subjects only commenced and on the way in the previous pages I must occupy a considerable proportion of the next volume in completing them. When this work is finished, I have proposed to publish an-

other as *sui generis* as this has been. This work has been but the pioneer—like the voice of one crying in the wilderness—a mere answer to a question proposed nearly three thousand years ago—"*Watchman, what of the night?*"

As was said of the Israelites, so we say of the generations of men now coming upon the stage: One shall chase a hundred, and ten shall put a thousand to flight. The present generation will dissipate the mists and exhalations of many generations; and the next will nearly, if not completely, vanquish the host of darkness and error. The period of antichrist is nigh its end: and the prophecies as well as the signs of the times clearly indicate the speedy dissolution of the present ecclesiastical heavens and earth. I have been astonished to see labors of friends and foes of the restoration all tending to one happy result. Those who advocate primitive christianity, and those who advocate the modern sectarian establishments, are both accelerating the march of truth, and securing the triumphs of light over darkness. Like the "*Paidobaptist*" of Danville, every new number diminishes the ranks of the Paidoes, and fills up that of the Baptist; so the struggles of the sectaries wound themselves, and strengthen the arms of the sons of the kingdom, without any such intention on their part. Hence all things work together for good to them who love the ancient gospel.

A correspondent from Ireland informed me per last mail, that six Episcopalian and six Roman Catholic divines recently debated fourteen days in Londonderry, on the points at issue betwixt Protestants and Catholics. In 1827, a debate took place in the city of Dublin between Messrs. Pope and M'Guire, the former a Protestant, the latter a Catholic. Both these controversies terminated in favor of Protestantism, and to the more intelligent part of the community in favor of New Testamentism.

A debate of two days continuance took place in Cumberland county, Kentucky, in April last, between Elder Stumper, a Presiding Elder in the Methodist Church, and Elder W. G. Jourdane, of the Christian Church, on this proposition—"*Jesus Christ is the very and eternal God.*" The former affirmed, and the latter denied. This is a question which, of all others, I conceive the most unsuitable for a public discussion. If men could debate such a question upon their knees, it would be scarcely admissible then. It is an "untaught question," a scholastic one in its form and terms, and tends to perpetuate a controversy and a peculiar style of speaking, which the sooner it could be forgotten the better for both saint and sinner. I have learned that during this controversy the correctness of Dr. George Campbell's translation of John iii. 13, was called in question; and as this affects the character of the new version which we have lately published, I will give Dr. Campbell's note. The phrase is, "*Whose abode is heaven.*" Chapter i. 18, has a similar expression—"*Who is in the bosom of the Father.*" Both are intended to denote what is habitual and characteristic of the person, rather than what obtains at a particular instant. By the phrase, "Who is in the bosom of the Father," is meant, not only who is the special object of the Father's love, but who is admitted to his most secret counsels. By the phrase "Whose abode is heaven," is meant whose home, whose residence is there.

I cannot approve of any one of the sermons, debates, or essays, with which the public ear is assailed, and public eye addressed, so repeatedly upon this question. From the days of Arius down to this day, it has ever been on the stage; and much mischief, but no real good, has resulted from the discussion. If the language of the holy apostles, the scripture names, phrases, and epithets will not suffice, in vain will the learned umber and scholastic jargon of the barbarous ages, be sought after to give satisfaction. If the time spent in arguing about the rank and honors of the Saviour of the world, were employed in the praises of God and the Lamb, we would have less *wordy*, but more holy and happy christians. There are many questions which may be debated with much propriety and profit, but they are practical, and lay at the foundation of the human establishments which have supplanted the institution of Jesus Christ.

Besides these debates, others have been threatened, and challenges proclaimed. Religious court martials have been erected, and modern "star chambers" have been opened. About the seat of government, in Kentucky, a religious court of inquiry has been established; and before some preachers are admitted into the sacred desks of the high priests of that vicinity, they must be interrogated on the *five points* of the Synod of Dort. If the preacher says *shibboleth*, loud and broad, proclamation is issued that all may do him reverence; but if he falters, or squeaks out *sibboleth*, he is proscribed and devoted to the pelting and pitiless storms of proscription. These are partial results of the great revivals at the Great Crossings and Frankfort.— Some of the most gifted men in Kentucky have been, as we have heard, proscribed already.

Particularism, under the auspices of my friend of Oakly and the new theological school, and the doctrine of the "*Two Seeds*," is rather looking up on the banks of the Licking. Elder Parker, of Illinois has been translated to Kentucky through the efficacy of his faith in the "two seeds."— He founds election on the natural birth, by a discovery which eluded the eagle eye of Calvin and Beza and all the Jansenists of Rome. He found that Cain was literally begotten by the Devil, and Seth by the Almighty, through the instrumentality of Adam. And so it has been ever since. The Devil is the literal father of all the *non-elect*, and the Almighty of the elect.— Hence the sons of Seth were literally the sons of God, and the daughters of Cain were really the daughters of the Devil; and so each after death must necessarily return to their respective parents.

Friend Parker has reduced the " five points" to two. His first is, that "God never created a set of beings, neither *directly* nor *indirectly*, that

he suffered to be taken from him and made the subjects of his eternal wrath and indignation." The wicked are therefore indirectly created by the Devil. Mr. Parker has literally taught this doctrine. This is the best argument against catechisms Illinois has yet produced. Mr. Parker cannot, dare not, ask any child, "Who made you?" for the good reason that neither he nor the child knows whether God or the Devil made it!! —Thus the friends of the creeds and catechisms are likely to help us much. His second point is, that "God, as God, in no case possesses more love and mercy than power and wisdom." This is sublimated fatalism. This new creed has great simplicity about it, though its inventor has made it so shameful in his different theories of generation and regeneration, that my nerves have never been strong enough to read it all through. There is a mystery in all cases of *twins*, which my friend Daniel Parker has not fully solved.— He admits, it is true, that the Devil begat Esau, and the Almighty begat Jacob, but fails very much in his exposition of the *modus operandi.* The struggling of the unborn infant comes in to his relief, but does not help him quite through. But his theory makes Jesus the Saviour no more the Son of God, than Jacob the brother of Esau.

I threw this pamphlet aside about a year ago, and never intended to open it again; but recent information that the Particulars in Kentucky were placing this modern Daniel along side of Silas and John, and about to have a theological school for teaching the *marrow of modern divinity,* in which one of the three was to act the *Principal,* I took it up to see if it had mellowed by time: but it smells as rancid as ever—and I cannot now read it all.

In Essex county, Virginia, several attempts of the "star chamber" stamp, have been recently made against a very intelligent and pious brother, who has rendered himself obnoxious to some little high priests in his vicinity, by his boldness in the faith of the ancient gospel; but some of the more sagacious ones began to see that their commands and threats were likely to have the same effect with those of the venerable Fathers of the Sanhedrim, who gave an injunction to Peter and John in old times to speak no more in their name, and they have desisted. I might fill a pamphlet with this case; but if they will reform, I will not hand their names to posterity. All these things are working together to open the eyes of all who can be made to see, and to hasten on the triumph of the ancient gospel and the ancient order of things over the sectarianism of the age.　　　　　　　　EDITOR.

108

END OF VOLUME VI.

CHRISTIAN BAPTIST.

NO. I.—VOL. VII. BETHANY, BROOKE CO. VA., AUGUST 3, 1829.

Style no man on earth your Father: for he alone is your Father who is in heaven: and all ye are brethren. Assume not the title of Rabbi; for ye have only One Teacher; neither assume the title of Leader; for ye have only One Leader— the Messiah. *Messiah.*

PREFACE TO VOLUME VII.

THIS is the fourth day of July, the day on which this nation was born, and the day on which Thomas Jefferson and John Adams died. On this day I wrote the preface to the first volume of the Christian Baptist, and it is the day on which I write the preface to the seventh and last volume of this work. On this day the Materialists of the Old World founded the city, and proclaimed the era, of *Mental Independence.* Like the French decree which abolished the christian times and seasons, this new epoch of the Free Inquirers is like to die before its own progenitors.

Every year, natural and political, teems with new and unexpected events. On the thirteenth of April last the king of Great Britain signed the law of emancipation, which broke to pieces the Protestant yoke of proscription, so long fastened on the necks of the Catholic worshippers of the image of St. Peter; and on the same day *Robert Owen,* Esq. and myself commenced a discussion which we have some reason to expect will emancipate some hundreds of the *Free Thinkers* from the chains of their own philosophic *necessity.* How absurd it is to claim the honors of *free thinkers* and *free inquirers* in a world where *circumstances* alone are free from human control, and where free agency and "free will" are aliens from the commonwealth of reason and philosophy, and exiles from the land of New Harmony and the city of *free* inquirers!

The weak heads and the strong heads are likely to become parties in the new war. The strong heads are on the side of the world, the flesh, and the grave: while the weak heads are thinking about heaven, future bliss, and a glorious immortality. The strong heads are pronouncing eulogies upon reason and common sense; while the weak heads are only following the former, and practising the latter. But this pen of mine is too soft in the point, and needs to be mended. We shall therefore apply it to the knife, as the philosopher would say; or, as the man of common sense, we shall apply the knife to it.

I have sharpened my pen; but while it is so well pointed I must not touch the free inquirers. Sharp instruments are for hard substances, and therefore we shall proceed to the word *rights.* This word, physically, politically, and morally considered, has had many a sermon preached on it. Some argue that a man has a *right* to be born black—another has a right to be born white. One has a right to be a *nobleman* without a *noble* sentiment, a *noble* idea, or a *noble* action. Another contends that he has a right to get drunk when he pleases; and some aver that any class of citizens has a right to go to perdition just in whatever way they please, either under

the decent garb of hypocrisy, or in the rough homespun of profanity and vice.

It would be endless to enumerate all the various sorts of the *rights of men,* for which there are many pleaders; or to show by what sophisms men wish to make their own interests *natural* and *unalienable rights,* and to vindicate with sword and faggot that every thing is right which gives them advantage over others. The Pope has a right to the keys—the King, to the crown; the Bishop, to his tithes—and the Free Inquirer to have no wife, or two, or three, as he pleases. Liberty, too, (what a sweet word!) has her different sects of worshippers and admirers. The King has liberty to sway the sceptre; the High Priest liberty to wear the mitre; the Sceptic liberty to laugh at superstition, and to pity the weak heads; and the Free Inquirer has a liberty to repudiate his wife after the honey moon. But it is right that I should keep to the *rights of man,* as I have proposed to wear out one pen upon them; and it is wrong that I should indulge in this liberty of roaming from theme to theme, as my fancy wanders over the wide fields of speculation.

By glancing at the natural rights of men, I may, perchance, hit upon some of the natural rights of christians.

Whatever the natural rights of men are, they belong to all men naturally; consequently the natural rights of men are equal rights. For whatever belongs to all men naturally, must equally belong to all. To give to others what belongs to them, is a duty we owe them; to withhold from them what belongs to them, is a sin. There can be no favor, donation, or gift, in conferring natural rights upon others; for natural rights cannot be conferred; they belong to man merely because he exists. Now if it be duty to give to others what belongs to them, it is our duty not to invade the rights of others, but to protect and guarantee them.

Whatever a man has received from his Creator it is right for him to preserve. He owes it to Heaven and himself. He is bound by the relation in which he stands to the *donor,* and by the laws of his own constitution to preserve it. And, in the second place, whatever a man has acquired by the consent of the society in which he lives, he has a right to possess and maintain. The former is the principle or basis of natural rights; the latter is the principle or basis of political rights. The former are invariably the same; the latter vary according to circumstances. Man has received certain animal and intellectual endowments. These he has an undeived right, as respects human society, to possess and retain. To preserve life, to pursue happiness, or to seek food and entertainment for mind and body, is the right and the duty of all men.

Dependence is the lot of the infant man. The new-born infant is necessarily dependant on its parent for support and protection. From dependance naturally arises obligation. Hence gratitude and obedience, or subjection, originate from our circumstances and from nature. Children are not naturally free. They are, and must be, under restraint. This restraint must continue while necessary. The period of its continuance is called minority. Minors are not to decide when this period terminates. This is a question for fathers and seniors to determine. Whenever this restraint is taken off, then liberty of action becomes the right of all who are released. All persons, then, who are of full age, are equally free. Of these we say that liberty is a natural, inherent, and unalienable right. To preserve life, to form a character, to acquire property, are the equal rights of all. To defend life, reputation, and property, is the common and inherent right of all.

Infants have rights as well as adults. These rights are to be regarded. Society owes them certain duties. But if society owes them any thing, it is because of natural rights which they possess. For where a person has no right there is no duty to be performed towards him. Where there is no debt there can be no payment. Sustenance, protection and education, are the claims of children. Parents owe them all these, or rather society owes them. The reason is, society were once infants, received this sustenance, protection and education from previous society, and can only pay those debts by recognizing and attending to those rights in others, circumstanced as they once were.

But the first society were adults, all equally free, independent and happy; and the rights of infants descending from this first society, were suggested by natural relation and by the law of the Creator. The passions and the feelings of the first parents were the natural and unbribed advocates of the rights of infants. From this general view of the natural, inherent and unalienable rights of man, and of infants, we wish to argue the necessity of political society providing for the education of every infant born within its precincts. But this only by the way.

Religious society is the object of our present concern. Christian society is composed of infants, or minors, and adults. These, when admitted into the kingdom or commonwealth over which Jesus Christ presides, have certain natural, inherent and inalienable rights. Amongst these are the preservation and enjoyment of christian life, the acquisition and enjoyment of christian reputation, and the pursuit and application of christian wealth. These are the inalienable rights of christians. They are all born equally free and equally independent of foreign agency. They are equally the sons and daughters of the Lord Almighty, have an equal and undivided share in the eternal inheritance, and are mutually dependent on each other for christian health and prosperity. They are under all the same reciprocal duties and obligations. No citizen of this kingdom is under more obligation than another to seek its good and promote its prosperity. They may have different talents and opportunities, but the obligation is equal upon all to make the same efforts, and contribute to the same extent, according to their means. There is no principle in the kingdom which obliges one citizen to spend

three hundred and sixty-five days in one year, and another to spend only ten days in promoting the interest of the kingdom. In the kingdoms of this world men are taxed according to their property. The law does not take all from one, and a little or a part from another. The proportion is equal, and the obligation to payment is equal. So in the empire of truth and life: the demands upon each citizen are the same. If a tenth be required from one, a tenth is required from all: if nothing be required from one, nothing is required from all. Men may volunteer in any cause beyond the requisitions of government; but never beyond the wants of society. Volunteers have their own rewards. But if it be my duty or my privilege to spend aught, time, learning, or money, in the service of the Great King, it is the duty and privilege of every one proportionately to spend time, learning or money.

No law but that of love, suggests the principle; and no rule but that of the first disciples, regulates the practice of christians in these particulars. But the rights of christians are just as clear and are as inferrible as the rights of man from the same stock of common sense, enlightened by religion; and he that is blind to the rights of christians, is so from choice, and not from necessity.

I now commence a volume which I hope will bring this work to a natural close. I wish to close it, not because it is irksome to me to continue it—not because its readers are decreasing—not because there is less need for the press than formerly—not because my opponents have gained any advantage over me—not because I have run short of matter. No: it is with pleasure I write; and my readers have increased with every volume. I have got a new reader or subscriber for every day since I commenced this publication, now six years. All my readers see that my opponents have dwindled to nothing. Numbers of them are converted to the very sentiments which they opposed before they understood them. But there is need for much yet to be said and written, both on the present, past and future order of things, and we have much to say. But of this again.

Because of the hurry and despatch necessary to complete the Debate now in press, I cannot issue this volume in the same regular proportions I contemplated, namely, two numbers per month. I intend still, however, to furnish it in six months, and soon to issue the plan and conditions of that work in contemplation. I have devoted my energies to this cause, and will, God willing, prosecute it with perseverance. The prospects of emancipating myriads from the dominion of prejudice and tradition—of restoring a pure speech to the people of God—of expediting their progress from Babylon to Jerusalem—of contributing efficiently to the arrival of the Millennium—have brightened with every volume of this work. To the King eternal, immortal and invisible, the only wise God our Saviour, we live and die. To him we consecrate the talents, information, means, and every influence he has given us, and, we trust, the day will come when all shall see, acknowledge and confess that our labors in the Lord are not in vain.   EDITOR.
July 4, 1829.

Religious Bequests, &c.

"The love of money is the root of all evil." So said an infallible teacher. I believe it in the fullest sense of the word. The day of judgment will, I think, disclose a secret which will astonish millions. It is this—that all sectarian-

2

ism and sectarian zeal spring from the love of money. I am not now about to show how this can be. But I will say that *legacies* for *ecclesiastical* purposes are very ill devised expedients for promoting peace on earth and good will among men. They are often roots of bitterness, springing up as pestilential as the deadly nightshade, and frequently more deleterious than the open assaults of the foes to the christian faith. I doubt not but the well-intended legacy of Mr. Paulding, of Kentucky, has already done more harm, and been productive of more rancor, strife and ill will, than the wisest appropriation of it will efface in a hundred years. And if it could be the means of making a hundred preachers of *particular sectarianism,* how much would mankind be the better of it? If each one of its beneficiaries should inherit the spirit of our good brother, who would shut the doors of his synagogue against every one who advocates the all-sufficiency and alone-sufficiency of the sacred writings of the apostles and prophets for the teaching, discipline, and edification of the church, what would Kentucky and the world gain from such appropriations of money? If it must operate to rivet men in the antiquated prejudices of dark ages, to secure the rising generation from the liberal spirit of christianity—I say it had better be tied up in a bag and attached to an upper millstone, and cast into the sea.

Some of the terms in the following communication I object to, particularly the term *predestination.* I object to this appropriation of it. Although I cannot find in the holy oracles any countenance for the dogma of Calvinian predestination, yet I am taught that God predestinated the Gentiles to the adoption of sons through Jesus Christ and all the saints to everlasting life. Words, then, which are in scripture appropriated to express the mind and will of God, I do not like to see abused to any sectarian purpose, or treated with disrespect, because others have misapplied them. We should discriminate between the terms and their appropriation of them, lest when opposing a peculiar and an appropriated sense of them, we may be suspected as opposing them in their legitimate acceptation. The same may be said on this much talked of, and very imperfectly understood subject, called " the operations of the Holy Spirit."

But is it so, that any congregation in Kentucky has decreed that no person except he be just five feet ten inches high, and wears green spectacles, shall preach within their brick walls!! Tell it not in Spain! publish it not in Rome! lest the Inquisitors rejoice, lest the Cardinals of the Holy See triumph! I will not believe that the congregation in Frankfort will decree that neither myself nor any one who proclaims the ancient gospel, or advocates the ancient order of things, shall enter their pavilion. No, I will not believe until I see the decree signed in the proper handwriting of the Bishop and all the members. I must see the autograph itself. I proclaimed in the Bishop's own house, at his own fireside, to a congregation, and repeatedly to the private circle of his friends and neighbors my most obnoxious principles. And I doubt not were I in Frankfort again, the gates of the new church would open to me of their own accord. And if they did not, who would gain or lose by holding the keys!! I hope yet to proclaim the ancient gospel even in Frankfort.

This singular intimation concerning the proscription of the brethren Creaths, (I will name them out in full, for they are men whose talents, information, zeal and piety, and actual services

to the saints and to the public indiscriminately, are of the highest order of which Kentucky can boast,) I must think is some way or other exaggerated. If it be not, it is as ridiculous as a motion that was made some few days ago by a foster child of a celebrated *Rake* respecting myself; " I move," said he, " that this congregation declare *non-fellowship* with Alexander Campbell." And the poignancy of the wit was, that Alexander Campbell rarely travels to the mountains of Pennsylvania, and never asked the mover for any sort of fellowship or hospitality, civil, political, or religious. I view such a motion pretty much in the same light as I would the motion of a musselman who would have it decreed in a mosque that I should never be the Dey of Algiers. For the honor of the fraternity in which this motion was made, I must state that the mover was laughed out of his motion.   EDITOR.

MR. EDITOR,—SEEING you request that information should be unceremoniously communicated to you from the different sections of the country, I have determined on making the following communication, and leaving it discretionary with you to publish it or not.

The matters involved in it I consider important to this vicinity, however unimportant they may appear to others. I will first premise a few things: it will be remembered by your readers that you have assailed human creeds, which are nothing more than religious politics—the strong fortification of clerical power, tyranny, and domination—the rallying and central point of all who prefer the traditions of the fathers to the traditions of the twelve Apostles. You have also done much towards the *dethronement* of the clergy, and much towards the *enthronement* of the twelve ambassadors: and, as you stated in your letter to Bishop Semple, this constitutes the front of your offending. This is the sum and substance of your heresies: you have denied the operations of the kingdom of clergy, and therefore they are unwearied in their efforts to prove that you deny the operation of God's Spirit.— This charge is preferred against you because you maintain that the Apostles first exhibited the gospel testimony; they heard and believed it— then were immersed for the remission of their sins—then were sealed, cheered, and blessed with the gift of the Holy Spirit. In support of this position I refer your readers to the apostolic congregations themselves. First, the Jerusalem congregation—Acts ii. 38. 39. 2. The Samaritan congregation—Acts viii. 15. 17. 3. The Corinthian congregation—Acts xviii. 8. Many of the Corinthians hearing, believed and were immersed. 4. The Ephesian congregation—Acts xix. 6. Eph. i. 13. Not to mention the many thousands who believed before the Spirit was given, when they saw our Saviour's miracles, these instances are sufficient to show that the Spirit was given to the apostolic churches after faith and immersion. Let him that saith to the contrary produce the proof. All who preach as the apostles did are charged with denying the operation of the Spirit. If the apostles were now upon earth, and were to preach as they formerly did, would they not be charged with denying the operations of the Spirit. They never preached the Spirit to the idolatrous Gentiles, nor mentioned him until after faith and immersion; see Acts xix. 6. Paul preached to the Jews and Gentiles that Christ ought to have suffered, and to have risen from the dead. This was preaching Christ and him crucified, and was saying no-

3

thing but what Moses and the prophets had said before him.

We have become so accustomed to the slanders of the clergy, that when we hear you and your friends charged with denying the operations of the Spirit, we understand that you deny their operations; that the Spirit is in them, and through them, and that they have the keys to open and to shut. All who continue stedfast in the apostles' doctrine (among whom are some of our ablest men) are subject to the same slanders, and to worse treatment than you were when through this country, without having the same means of defending themselves; for I do not recollect that any Baptist congregation shut their doors against you when in this country; yet our good brother Noel (as he is styled by the Baptist Recorder) and his church in Frankfort, contrived to shut their doors against the Messrs. Cs., who went to fill up Mr. Morton's appointments, who was hindered by indisposition; and it appears that neither this good brother, nor the church, nor any individual of it, is willing to have the honor of this noble deed; for they now skulk off by saying, "The church" (the wood or stone house I suppose) "passed a resolution three years ago, that neither Mr. Campbell nor any of his friends should preach in their house." Thus it seems that they are good predestinarians, as they ordained this act before it came to pass. This is their story; but the current belief is, that after you proved too hard for our good Doctor on the creed question, that he then decreed you should not preach in his house; and last winter, when it was rumored that Mr. Morton was expected in Frankfort, a second decree was passed in his favor; and when he heard last May that the two Messrs. Cs. were to accompany Mr. Morton, that he and his secretary of state, and some of the ruling spirits in secret conclave, passed a third decree in their favor. He predestinated in his own mind that the Great Crossing Church should shut their doors against the Messrs. Cs.; but the Johnsons and other principal members proved themselves not to be predestinarians in this case, and consequently the decree did not pass. Our "good brother" decreed that the donation of Mr. Paulding for the education of indigent and religious young men, should be fixed upon the Philadelphia confession of opinions, as the *Will* is said to have been in his handwriting. But this decree was not like that of the Medes and Persians, unalterable.

The indefatigable diligence and the luminous and eloquent orations of Doctor William Richardson, and the determined opposition of others, frustrated this wise purpose. There was also a decree passed by this and other good particular predestinarian brethren, that the first donation of said Paulding, made to our good brother Noel, amounting to four thousand five or seven hundred dollars, should be appropriated exclusively to the benefit of the particulars or predestinarian Baptists, after they heard that said Paulding determined that the donation should be built upon the terms of general union between the Elkhorn and Licking associations, one article of which says, that "preaching that Christ tasted death for every man, shall be no bar to communion." This Particular or Licking association grew out of an individual dispute, and when one of the parties was defeated they took shelter under the cool and secure covert of predestinarianism, and charged the other party with Arminianism. Notwithstanding, the Baptist education society, at their last meeting in Versailles, in June, by and with the consent and instruction of the donor, determined that the college should be erected on the terms of general union or liberal principles; it is feared by many that it will, through intrigue and management, prove to be nothing more than a hot-bed of predestinarianism, and that every man who prefers a divine creed (the New Testament) to the Philadelphia confession of opinions, will be excluded from the benefit of this liberal donation. When the donation was about to be made, it was supposed that our good brother decreed that the Transylvania University should have the benefit of that money, as he used the president of that institution in procuring and securing the donation, and as it was permanently located, possessed of competent and liberal-minded Baptist instructors, and meriting, as it does, the support and confidence of the western Baptists, and the community at large; but when he discovered that this institution, with its manager, could not be wielded to answer predestinarian and sectarian purposes, it was then decreed that a rival college should be built in Georgetown, a soil and atmosphere happily adapted to the culture of such predestination as terminates in a moderate and liberal inquisition.

As a proof of the liberality, christianity and the orthodox catholicism of this eminently pious people, they have under the administration and auspices of its present chief, appointed a standing committee (inquisition) whose pious business shall be to examine heretics, before they are executed or burnt, or delivered over to Satan to buffet their flesh for the good of their souls; or before they are admitted to behold the greater and lesser mysteries of predestination and effectual calling of the Spirit, exclusive and independent of the Bible, which is a revelation unrevealed to mankind. After "sovereign grace" falls upon and is made known to the elect, and after the Spirit has regenerated them, without any regard to the gospel or his wise and efficacious appointments, he then infuses spiritual life into the lampblack and paper. This almanack, newspaper, this dead letter, this sealed book is unsealed, and this unrevealed revelation is revealed a second time, to the elect only, and they are slowly and regularly initiated into the five sublime degrees of Dort and Westminster, and into all the chivalrous exploits of knight-errantry and Calvinism. There are certain great fundamental points (idols) which the chief of this congregation said the other day in his speech, (after he was defeated by Doctor Richardson, in his attempt to have all the young men initiated into these sublime mysteries,) he was not very anxious to have deposited in the Philadelphia oracles, provided he could move them about as the Jews did the tabernacle of Moloch, or the Pagans did the image that fell down from Jupiter, by which the craft said they had their wealth. As the priests sold these little silver shrines or images, to those worshippers who lived at a distance, and who could not conveniently come to Ephesus, to worship in the temple of Diana; so doctors of divinity and other priests and craftsmen, sell out an explanation of these mysteries of grace, to those who cannot comprehend a revelation unrevealed, and by this trade they also have their wealth and power—two powerful stimulants to diligence and persecution. All who refuse to subscribe to, or to be initiated into these mysteries of sovereign grace, which can neither be begged nor bought for any but those who were chosen from eternity—for the rest there is no revelation, no operations of the Spirit, no grace, no atonement, no Saviour, no possibility of salvation from the wrath of this Sovereign, who puts his feet upon their necks, and then damns them for not rising up.—All who deny this, deny the operations of the Spirit.

They have been publicly challenged, as I have been informed, in different places, and by different persons, to prove their charge of denying the operation of the Spirit, yet they will not do it, but continue to repeat the slander, and expect to ride down and over these persecuted men, and refuse to publish their meetings for them, and shut their doors against them upon this slander. When I say 'they,' I mean the good doctor and the old party of particulars, who were defeated by the elder C. twenty years ago; because it is now generally understood that this party is under his command, notwithstanding he professes to belong to the united Baptists, and to be for and against creeds alternately, just as it suits his purpose, as you have shown from his own circular etters. He secretly charged the Messrs. Cs., upon mere suspicion, with furnishing the materials for the dialogue relative to the Indians being carried to Frankfort; and when they publicly denied it, after hearing of it accidentally, he never attempted to prove their guilt, nor to counteract the slander, nor to make the least concession nor reparation for the injury they had sustained in their reputation, among the people of the Great Crossing, who were much displeased with that dialogue. I wish it distinctly understood, that I do not involve any of his friends in these statements, as he tells them you abuse and persecute them, and as he involves all who are friendly to you in your sins. " This proverb shall no more be used in Israel, The fathers have eaten sour grapes and the children's teeth are set on edge: The soul that sins shall die. The father shall not die for the sins of the son, nor the son for the sins of the father. The soul that sins shall die for his own sins"—so says Ezekiel, and so says your reader.   R. T. P.

To the Religious Public.

The following Queries, for the purpose of promoting a genuine scriptural reformation amongst the sincere professors of christianity, are respectfully submitted to their consideration.

1. Is not the christian community in a sectarian condition, existing in separate communities, alienated from each other?

2. Is not such a condition the native and necessary result of corruption; that is, of the introduction of human opinions into the constitution, faith, or worship of christian societies?

3. Is not such a state of corruption and division anti-natural, anti-rational, anti-christian?

4. Is it not the common duty and interest of all concerned, especially of the teachers, to put an end to this destructive anti-scriptural condition?

5. Can this be accomplished by continuing to proceed as hitherto; that is, by maintaining and defending each his favorite system of opinion and practice?

6. If not, how is it to be attempted and accomplished, but by returning to the original standard and platform of christianity, expressly exhibited on the sacred page of New Testament scripture?

7. Would not a strict and faithful adherence to this, by preaching and teaching precisely what the Apostles preached and taught, for the faith and obedience of the primitive disciples, be absolutely, and to all intents and purposes, sufficient for producing all the benign and blissful intentions of the christian institution?

8. Do not all these intentions terminate in producing the faith and obedience, that justifies and sanctifies the believing and obedient subject?

9. Is not every thing necessary for the justification and sanctification of the believing and obedient, expressly taught and enjoined by the Apostles in the execution of their commission for the conversion and salvation of the nations; and fully recorded in the New Testament?

10. If so, what more is necessary, but that we expressly teach, believe, and obey what we find expressly recorded for these purposes? And would not our so doing happily terminate our unhappy, scandalous, and destructive divisions?

N. B. The two following queries are subjoined for the sake of a clear definition of the leading and comprehensive terms, viz. *faith* and *obedience*—which comprehend the whole of the christian religion:—

11. Are not law and obedience, testimony and faith, relative terms, so that neither of the latter can exist without the former; that is, where there is no law, there can be no obedience; where there is no testimony, there can be no faith?

12. Again, is not testimony necessarily confined to facts, and law to authority, so that without the latter the former cannot be? that is, where there are no facts, there can be no testimony—no authority—no law. Wherefore, in every case, faith must necessarily consist in the belief of facts; and obedience in a practical compliance with the expressed will or dictate of authority.

N. B. By facts is here meant some things said or done.

Conclusion.

Upon the whole, these things being so, it necessarily follows, that christianity, being entirely a divine institution, there can be nothing human in it; consequently it has nothing to do with the doctrines and commandments of men: but simply and solely with the belief and obedience of the expressly recorded testimony and will of God, contained in the Holy Scriptures—and enjoined by the authority of the christian community.

Reflections.

The affirmative of each of the above propositions being, as we presume, evidently true, they most certainly demand the prompt and immediate attention of all the serious professors of christianity, of every name. The awful denunciations and providential indications of the divine displeasure against the present anti-christian state of christendom loudly call for reformation,—the personal and social happiness of all concerned, and the conversion of the unbelieving part of mankind equally demand it. Nevertheless, we are not authorized to expect, that any party, as such, will be induced by the above considerations, or by any other that can possibly be suggested, spontaneously and heartily to engage in the work of self-reformation. The sincere and upright in heart, however, ought not to be discouraged at the inattention and obstinacy of their brethren; for had this been the case in times past, no reformation had ever been effected. It becomes, therefore, the immediate duty and privilege of all that perceive and feel the necessity of the proposed reformation, to exert themselves by every scriptural means to promote it.—Seeing the pernicious nature, and anti-scriptural effects of the present corruptions of christianity, both upon professors and non-professors, in producing alienations amongst the former, in direct opposition to the law of Christ; and in casting almost insuperable obstacles in the way of the conversion of the latter;—the serious and upright, of all parties, must feel conscientiously

5

bound to endeavor, to the utmost of their power to effect a genuine and radical reformation; which, we presume, can only be effected by a sincere conformity to the original exhibition of our holy religion,—the divinely authorized rule and standard of faith and practice.—To such, therefore, we appeal; and for the consideration of such alone, we have respectfully submitted the above queries.

"Now I beseech you, brethren, by the name of our Lord Jesus Christ, that you *all* speak the same thing, and that there be no divisions among you, but that you be perfectly joined together in the same mind and in the same judgment."—Paul, 1 Cor. i. 10.

"Jesus lifted up his eyes to heaven, and said, Father, I pray for them who shall believe on me through the word of my Apostles: that they may all be one; as you, Father, are in me, and I in you, that they also may be one in us: that the world may believe that you have sent me; that the world may know that you have sent me; and have loved them as you have loved me."—John xvii.

"In vain do they worship me, teaching for doctrines the commandments of men."—*Christ.*

"From the days of your fathers you are gone away from mine ordinances, and have not kept them. Return to me, and I will return to you, says the Lord of hosts."—Mal. iii. 7.

"Come out of her, my people, that you be not partakers of her sins, and that you receive not of her plagues."—Rev. xviii. 4.

"He that testifies these things says, Surely I come quickly. Amen. Even so come, Lord Jesus." THOMAS CAMPBELL.

Essays on Man in his Primitive State and under the Patriarchal, Jewish, and Christian Dispensations.—No. X.

Jewish Age.—No. II.

THE first essay on this head was merely preparatory, or at most, introductory to the creation of the Jewish people into a national form. One important reason was assigned for taking this people into a peculiar relation to the Governor of the Universe. In pursuance of an original promise, now 430 years old, the God of Abraham, Isaac, and Jacob, assumes the peculiar relation of the God and King of the people who went down into Egypt. He made himself known to the most enlightened nation and court of that age, as Lord of lords, and as above all gods, venerated on earth. Moses, his ambassador to the court of Pharaoh, acts in a manner worthy of his sovereign, and makes the Proud Pharaoh and his courtiers own the supremacy of the God of Israel. The nation was brought out in heavenly style, with a strong and mighty arm. Pharaoh, his princes, and his mighty army were drowned; and Israel about two millions strong, having six hundred thousand warriors, encamped on yonder side the Red Sea. But not a bow was bent, not a sword was drawn, on the part of the sons of Jacob. They stood still and saw the salvation of God.

But so soon as they were entirely out of the precincts of the Egyptians it became necessary to give them a national existence, or to constitute them into a kingdom. Hitherto they were an unorganized assembly, under the conduct of the ambassador of the Sovereign of the Universe—Moses was their leader. But so soon as they reached Horeb, the purposes of the Almighty were disclosed to them. They are informed of the grounds on which they are to stand, and the preliminaries of a new relation are proposed to them, accompanied with many ample and sublime signals of the presence of God. They see and hear what they never heard nor saw before. They are prepared to accept of whatever the Lord was pleased to appoint.

In taking them thus by the hand, and in signalizing this people, it became necessary for the ends proposed, that they should be placed in the most enviable circumstances. It was necessary that they should exhibit a picture of the greatest earthly happiness.

The first thing necessary to this was a good constitution—this was therefore the first thing proposed. Although their King had a right to impose upon them as his creatures, such a one as he pleased, without asking their consent, or giving them a single vote in the whole transaction, he proposes to the whole people *en masse*, by his own ambassador, whether or not they would adopt or accept such an instrument from him. The articles of negotiation, entrusted to Moses, containing the original preliminaries, read thus: The Lord said to Moses, "*Thus* shall you say to the house of Jacob, and tell the children of Israel? You have seen what I did to the Egyptians, and how I bore you as on eagles wings and brought you to myself. Now, therefore, if you will obey my voice indeed, and keep my institutions (or covenant,) then you shall be a peculiar treasure to me, above all people: for all the earth is mine. And you shall be to me a kingdom of priests and a holy nation. These are the words which you shall speak to the children of Israel." Now, as Moses could not speak *viva voce* to the whole 600,000 militia, he called the seniors together, rehearsed the stipulations to them, and they to the people. Finally, *all the people answered and said*, "All that the Lord has spoken we will do." And Moses returned the words of the people to the Lord.

Constitutions in old times were called *covenants*, because both parties, the governors and the governed, stipulated and agreed to the items; and the whole transaction was confirmed over dead bodies. But an error obtained all over christendom from an inadvertence of the teachers of religion and morals, to a peculiarity in this transaction. The error is this, that the government and the people are two parties, and that each has its own interests; that all national compacts are but articles of agreement between those who have a *divine right* to govern, and those who have a *divine right* to be governed. The propagators of this error may have innocently fallen into it from not noticing that the first constitution which was ever written emanated from him who stood in a relation towards the governed in which no other being stood, or ever could stand—he was their Creator, and they were his creatures. Besides, in this transaction, there were really two parties of a nature and of a relation essentially different, and yet the happiness of one party only was sought by the arrangement. These peculiarities never did occur in any other case. Now to place the governors in the character of creators, and the governed in the character of creatures, has been the erroneous practice of all the (so called) Christian nations of the old world. It never occurred to any nation until long since the art of printing was discovered, that there could not be two parties in a nation having interests as different as Creator and creatures: nor that neither the dignity nor happiness of a nation could comport with the idea that the interest of the governors was different from that of the governed. It is scarcely yet sufficiently known, even in this country, where the science of government is better understood than in any other upon earth, that there never can be amongst an intelligent people, two parties in forming a constitution; or that there is any other interest to be consulted than that of the people. But it cannot be too distinctly stated, nor can it be too well known, that all the miseries of the old world, all the political degradations, privations and exclusions of monarchical christendom, grew out of the error which I am now combating; and for which some religious people of this country still have a religious hankering. The king of Israel was the Lord of Hosts. The WHOLE EARTH IS MINE, said he, when he condedescended to become the king of Israel. Yet he set us an example in this instance never to be forgotten. He gave a vote to every man on the muster-roll of Israel, in adopting the magna charta or constitution under which he would live. This single fact is worth all the arguments in the world against the right of suffrage, as being a natural right.

There are few people who are aware of the influence which a superstitious view of this constitution has had upon forming the present governments of Europe and Asia. We cannot now sufficiently trace the formative influence which the first written document, and the most public document on earth, has had in constituting the kingdoms of the earth. But we can see in the most despotic governments in the east and in the west of the old Roman empire, evident traces of the mistake just now noticed: and that superstition has converted this mistake into an engine of fearful influence upon the present happiness of men. Every thing now in Europe, called a "constitution," is neither more nor less than a league, or articles of agreement between the governors and the governed. The government promises not to cut the heads off the people, so long as they will allow the government to take out of their labors just as much as they want for their use and behoof. This compact is ridiculously called "a constitution," though as unlike it as a full-blooded Turk is to Paul the Apostle.

But to return to Mount Sinai. The preliminaries were *una voce*, without a dissenting voice agreed to. The constitution was pronounced by the living God, in words audible, and distinctly heard by about two millions of people. It was *written* also by the finger of God upon two blocks of marble. This constitution was perfectly *political*. Few seem to appreciate its real character. Many insipid volumes have been written upon it, both since and before Durham wrote a quarto volume on the Ten Commandments. Some have called it the Moral Law, and made it the law of the whole spiritual kingdom; affirming that Adam was created under it, and that even the angels were under it as a rule of life; nay, that it is now, and ever will be, the law of the whole spiritual world. Yes, indeed, though it speaks of fathers, mothers, wives and children, houses, lands, slaves and cattle; murder, theft and adultery; yet it is the moral code of the universe.

I remember well when I was about to be cut off from a Baptist association for affirming that this covenant or constitution at Sinai was not the Moral Law of the whole universe, nor the peculiar rule of life to christians. Another shade of darkness, and one degree more of political power on the side of three or four very illiterate, bigoted and consequential Regular Baptists, would have made a John Huss or a Jerome of Prague of me. But there was not quite darkness nor power enough, and therefore I am yet controlling

this feather which makes the mould for those characters you now read.

But I have said it was a *political* constitution, though religion and morality are delineated in it. Now "strike, but hear me!" It reads thus:*

"I am the Lord your God who have brought you out of the land of Egypt, out of the house of servants."

Table I.

Article 1. You shall have no other gods besides me.

Art. 2. You shall not make for yourselves an idol, nor the likeness of any thing, which is in the heaven above, or in the earth below, or in the waters under the earth: you shall not worship them; nor serve them; for I, the Lord your God am a zealous God, retributing to them who hate me the sins of fathers upon children to the third and fourth generation; but showing mercy for thousands [of generations] to them who love me and keep my commandments.

Art. 3. You shall not take the name of the Lord your God in vain; for the Lord your God will not hold him guiltless who takes his name in vain.

Art. 4. Remember the day of the sabbaths to hallow it. Six days labor and do all your works; but on the seventh day are sabbaths to the Lord your God; on it you shall not do any work, you nor your son, nor your daughter, nor your man servant, nor your maid servant, nor your ox, nor your ass, nor any of your cattle, nor the stranger who sojourns with you; for in six days the Lord made the heaven and the earth and the sea and all that are in them, and rested on the seventh day: therefore the Lord blessed the seventh day and hallowed it.

Table II.

Article 1. Honor your father and your mother that it may be well with you, and that you may live long in that good land which the Lord your God gives you.

Art. 2. You shall not commit adultery.

Art. 3. You shall not steal.

Art. 4. You shall not commit murder.

Art. 5. You shall not bear false witness against your neighbor.

Art. 6. You shall not covet your neighbor's wife; you shall not covet your neighbor's house, nor his field, nor his man servant, nor his maid servant, nor his ox, nor his ass, nor any of his cattle, nor any thing belonging to your neighbor.

Now let the following matters be attended to:

1. The stipulation or grand preliminary of this whole procedure was to make them a religious, wise, powerful and happy nation.

2. All the people were allowed to vote the adoption of this constitution.

3. The only qualification for this right of suffrage was implied in *being brought out of the land of Egypt, and from the house of bondage.* And the whole people, whether what we now call *regenerate* or *unregenerate*, alike adopted this constitution and submitted to it as their charter of national incorporation.

4. Protection, prosperity, and national renown were promised on the part of the government; and submission to him, honor and respect, admiration and homage, as the rightful sovereign, were agreed to by the people.

5. Idolatry, under this constitution, was treason, and this the first article declares. The second and third articles guard against the least approximation to mental treason. The fourth article of the first table institutes the revenue of

* This is a translation of the Septuagint taken from Thomson's bible.   PUBLISHER.

7

time which results to the king, not merely as such, but because he was their God also. As their king, he required other appropriations of time and property, but this he constitutionally requires, as due to himself as Creator, and essential to their national prosperity. Every day, it is true, was due to him, but this was to be formally sanctified or set apart to him in commemoration of his works of creation in general, and of his particular interposition on their behalf.

As a *nation*, therefore, the whole people were in guarantee of their political rights and advantages, most scrupulously to regard these four articles of the first table. The homage required in these four articles was such homage as a whole nation could yield—and such as could secure to them, according to stipulation, the friendship, protection and support of a governor, against whom there could be no successful opposition in the upper, nether or middle world.

6. All the social relations, rights and privileges of the confederates, or of the individuals, composing this nation, were defined and secured in the six articles of the second table. To be religious and moral was the policy of this nation, and hence religion and morality were the *politics* of the commonwealth of Israel.

A constitution is a law. But it is the supreme law or the general principles which authorize all the other laws and regulations of a people. That all the laws afterwards promulged to the Jews by their king, were accordant in their nature and obligations to the spirit of this constitution, needs not a single argument to prove. But that this was the covenant or constitution (for the latter term is the modern one corresponding with the obsolete term covenant, in both Hebrew and Greek originals) of the nation, and distinguished from all other laws, is evident from the seven following facts:

1. The preamble to it evidently declares that upon these principles Israel became a nation.

2. Because God pronounced these articles aloud, and no other were ever promulged by him, *viva voce*, to the Jewish people.

3. Because *he wrote* them with his own finger on two tables of stone.

4. Because the two stones were ever afterwards called the *two tables of the covenant* or constitution.

5. Because a chest was made and placed in the sanctuary in which these tables were deposited, and this chest was called the *ark or chest of the constitution.*

6. Because when the constitution of the second or new kingdom was foretold by Jeremiah, and developed by Paul, it was contrasted with this one.

And 7. Because the breach of no other law could dissolve or impair their national existence or character—but so soon as the nation departed from the articles of this constitution, God ceased to protect them, and gave them up to their enemies. But here we shall pause for the present.
EDITOR.

Extract from Appendix.

FROM the whole scope of Mr. Owen's discussion, and most unequivocally from his appendix, it appears that his whole scheme of things is founded upon one fundamental position. This position is;—MAN IS NOT A FREE AGENT. That *no man forms his own character but that every man's character is formed for him*, is one of his consequences from this position—Another is, *that merit and demerit, praise and blame, reward and punishment belong not to man, nor, in truth, to*

any being in the Universe. Such is the soul or life of his whole system.

He declaimed much against metaphysics in his speeches and in his writings—But I now make my appeal to the learned world, and ask;—Is there in the whole science of metaphysics more abtruse speculations or questions than those constituting and proceeding from the above positions?—If there be such a thing as the *quintessence* of metaphysics—I say, it is the question about *free agency* in all its sublimated ramifications.—But this only by the way.

Men of the most gigantic talents have fatigued themselves in writing octavos, quartos and folios upon the doctrines of liberty and necessity—From the learned folio of Peter Sterry down to the unanswerable octavo of President Edwards, there has been written a wagon load of learned lumber on this very question.—Before a popular assembly, and to the great majority of readers the plan of *reductio ad absurdum* appears to us the shortest way of settling these wordy disputes—And, therefore, we generally preferred this argument while on the stage of discussion, whenever Mr. Owen presented these metaphysical dogmas. That there is no moral difference on Mr. Owen's hypothesis between the actions of a machine and those of King Solomon, Sir Isaac Newton, and the apostle Paul; that a man, a fish, an oyster, a tree, a watch, are equally voluntary agents, alike praiseworthy, blameworthy, virtuous, vicious, good or evil, was repeatedly shown during the discussion. The tree that cools us with its shade, that refreshes us with its fruit, and that kills us by its fall, is neither praiseworthy nor blameworthy. So the patricide, the matricide, the homicide, and the philanthropic, the affectionate, kind, and benevolent son, daughter, brother, neighbor, are alike praiseworthy, alike blameworthy—in truth, neither to be praised nor blamed at all. All the feeling which Mr. Owen professes to have for such evil doers is *pity*—He may pity the child that kills his father, as he pities the widow which the wickedness of a son has made. He pities too the religious man as a deluded being—and, indeed, I cannot see why he may not equally pity every thing that exists, and be as much grieved for the virtues as the vices of men—I think his metaphysics which places the idiot, the madman, the philosopher and the sage upon the same footing with each other, and with all things animal, vegetable, and mineral, excludes pity altogether and divests man of all feelings as well as of all free agency.

Whenever the idea of merit and demerit is exiled from earth the idea of pity must follow it. No body pities a tree because the wind has torn a branch from it. No body pities the lion who kills himself in pursuit of a lamb; nor the hawk that breaks its head in the pursuit of a chicken. We pity suffering innocence—But take away the idea of innocence and we destroy all pity. Destroy merit and demerit, and we have no use for the word *innocence*; and then we can have no suffering innocence, and so no pity.

But the idea of a Philanthropist is just as inadmissible upon Mr. Owen's principles as that of praise or blame. Now Mr. Owen professes to be a *philanthropist*, that is, a lover of men. But is love a reasonable or an unreasonable thing? If reasonable, Mr. Owen cannot, upon his own principles, be truly a philanthropist. For what reason can induce him to spend his days in benefiting men more than crows or squirrels, more than in cultivating *hellebore* or *hemlock*? A lump of animated matter, of vegetable matter, wheth-

8

er in the form of a biped, a quadruped, or a tulip, is matter still, and as necessary in its figure, properties, and powers as it is in being material. There is nothing in man, upon his principles, amiable more than in a goose.—The goose which furnished this quill, and on whose coat I slept last night, and on whose carcase I feasted last Christmas, was a benefactor of man, and a philanthropist, upon Mr. Owen's theory, as worthy of praise as himself, because as reasonable and as unreasonable. If the size, figure, and animal qualities of man prompt Mr. Owen to be a philanthropist, he ought for as good reasons, to devote his life to the care of horses and elephants. If longevity, an erect position, and a peculiar organization make man worthy of so much love from him, the goose who lives longer, the tree which grows taller, and the crocodile which is as curiously organized as man, equally merit his labors of love. To say that he is a philanthropist because he belongs to the race of men, is to place philanthropy upon the same foundation with those animal affections which pervade most species of the quadrupeds and bipeds for their own. This is an unreasonable philanthropy and unworthy of the name. There cannot be a *philosophic philanthropist* upon any principle which divests man of merit and demerit, of praise and blame, of reward and punishment; upon any principle which excludes from the human mind the idea of a God and a future state. Men who deny these may call themselves philanthropists, they may labor for the good of men, but they are no more philanthropists than the bee which makes honey, nor the sheep which yields its fleece. They do not bestow their labors nor their coats on man from a love to him. Other motives prompt their actions. So Mr. Owen may spend time, money, and personal toils on what appears to be philanthropic objects;—but these may be demonstrated to proceed from vanity, by a much more convincing logic than can be employed to shew that they proceed from the love of man, properly so called.

For my part if I were compelled to give up the doctrine of immortality, or could be induced to think that man differed from other animals merely in so far as he differed from them in the organization of one hundred and fifty pounds of matter, I would think it just as reasonable and philosophic that I should spend my life in raising and teaching dogs and horses, and improving their condition, as in training men and improving their circumstances.

The materialist, or philosophic necessarian, who says that the earth is an immense prison, and the laws of nature so many jailors, and all mankind prisoners bound in chains which cannot be dissolved; or, to speak without a figure, who says that the actions of all men are as unavoidable as the ebbing and flowing of the sea, or the waxing and waning of the moon, can never rationally be a *reformer*. For what could he reform? He could not pretend to reform *nature*, nor any of its laws. On Mr. Owen's principles the present state of the world is perfectly natural and unavoidable. Nature in the regular operation of causes and effect has issued in his trinity of evils—Religion, matrimony, and private property. Now if nature has gone wrong, and man without *free agency* has landed in religion, matrimony, and private property, how unphilosophic is the philosopher of *circumstances*, who would preach up the necessity of a change in society when he cannot change necessity!!

It is a climax in the eloquence of absurdity which Mr. Owen is aspiring after. He preaches

that all things are just as they must be. The uncontrolable laws of nature have issued in the present system of things; and yet he would have us to make things what they ought not to be; that is, he would have us to abolish religion, matrimony and private property, which his own eternal and unchanging laws of nature, in their necessary and uncontrolable operations have originated and established. On Mr. Owen's theory all things are natural and unavoidable. It is mother nature working by her own laws, and yet he would make us all matricides!!! If Mr. Owen is not stranded here there is not a shoal in the universe.

From all eternity, according to Mr. Owen's scheme, the particles of matter have been in incessant agitation, working themselves up into ten thousand times ten thousand forms. A few of them at one time produced a Nimrod, a Pharaoh, a Moses, a Cyrus, a Nebuchadnezzar, an Alexander, a Julius Cæsar, a Buonaparte, a Paul, a Robert Owen, and a few such manufacturers of human character. Not one of them could help being born, nor being such characters, nor producing such effects on society. Blind and omnipotent Nature cast them forth as she does so much lava from the crater of a volcano.—She tied them fast in adamantine chains of inexorable fate and gave them no more liberty to act than the Peak of Teneriffe has to emigrate to New Harmony. Yet strange, surpassing strange, as it is, this singular piece of animated matter called Robert Owen, which required old Nature in her laboratory six thousand years to produce, would now teach us to rebel and become seditious against the queen of fate; and would have us claim and take the liberty from nature of forming human beings to our own mind, and of changing the powers of nature; in fact, of binding her fast in our own cords, so that we shall abolish religion, matrimony, and private property; put the old queen Nature into jail at New Harmony and never let her out upon a parole of honor, so long as grass grows and water runs.

Mr. Owen is, without knowing it, or intending it, the greatest advocate of *free agency* I have ever known; for he would have the present generation to adopt such arrangements and so to new modify the circumstances that surround us as to prevent the goddess Nature from having it in her power ever to make another religious animal, another wedding, or to use the words *mine or thine*. And yet the chorus of his new music is, that we have no more liberty to act than Gibraltar has to perch itself upon the cupola of the State House of Ohio.—Such a philosopher is my good natured friend Robert Owen.   EDITOR.

———

A writer of very respectable talent in the Western Review has undertaken to prove that language is a human invention, and that the ideas of a God, Altar, and priest, are also human inventions, contrary to some positions taken in my debate with Mr. Owen. Whether the writer is a bumpologist, craniologist, or a phrenologist—a believer in *rebus spiritualibus*, or in *rebus naturalibus* I am not quite so certain. But so soon as he has got through, and we have got a little leisure, we intend to try his logic, if he will only have the goodness to tell us to what school he belongs, or in what country the flowers grow inscribed with the name of their king. If this would be too serious a demand upon his courtesy, if he will only give us the vowels and consonants by which he is designated from any other of the species, this would save me the hazard of breaking two or three lances on the steel cap of some veteran bumpologist, or of wounding some innocent theorist who spends his time in gathering flowers for the female admirers of nature.

EDITOR.

No. 2.]   SEPTEMBER 7, 1829.

James Madison, D. D.

SOME men by their high standing in society, give great emphasis to all that they say or do. The same things said by persons in more obscure stations, would not have half the weight which they sometimes accidentally acquire from official dignity. The following expose of many sentiments for which I have been called a heretic, coming from a man who was in his days, and died in the office, of Bishop of the whole state of Virginia, will, to the minds of many, afford much more evidence of truth than if I had said them. Truth, however, is truth, whether a child or a philosopher affirms it.

I have not met in any one extract so many of the sentiments advanced in this work: nor have I seen so unexceptionable an exposition of my "peculiar views" from any pen; nor did I know, till yesterday, that any man in the United States had spoken so much good sense on these subjects, in the year 1786, as appears in the following extract. I wish Bishop Semple, Mr. Brantly of the Star, Dr. Noel, and some few others of the leaders of the day, to read the extract with more than ordinary attention.   ED. C. B.

Extract of a Sermon delivered by James Madison, D. D. President of the University of William and Mary, and Professor of Moral and Natural Philosophy, before the Protestant Episcopal Church, in the state of Virginia, May 26th, 1786.

The text is, "God is a spirit, and they that worship him must worship him in spirit and in truth." *John iv. 24.*

THE object of this sermon is to urge the necessity of christian union, and the injurious tendency of creeds, &c. in originating and promoting dissentions and feuds among christians.

Permit me, then, to make some observations upon the means most likely to forward such an event. This I attempt with readiness, however imperfect the observations may appear, not only because it is, in my mind, of great importance that we should particularly attend to those means at this period, but also because the same means which would most effectually promote the ends just spoken of, will be the best guides to us at a time when we are forming, as it were, anew our own religious society; for without attention to them, we shall deprive ourselves of the inestimable privilege of worshipping God in spirit and in truth.

Fortunately for christians, those means are altogether of the negative kind. They depend upon the rejection, not the adoption of those human systems of belief, or rules of faith, which have often usurped the place of christianity itself. They only require christians to revert to the gospel, and to abandon every other directory of conscience. I will then venture earnestly to recommend to all christians to reject every system as the fallible production of human contrivance, which shall dictate articles of faith; and adopt the gospel alone as their guide. Am I not sufficiently warranted, my brethren, in this recommendation? I trust there is scarce any one amongst us who will object to a recommendation of this nature whether we attend to the fallibility, the ignorance, the prejudice of men, or to the truth, wisdom and perfection of the Author of our divine religion.

I will take the liberty to advance a general proposition, the evidence of which, I persuade myself, may be established by the most incontestible proofs. The proposition is, indeed, simple and plain: it is, "that those christian societies will ever be found to have formed their union upon principles the wisest and the best, which impose the fewest restraints upon the minds of their members, making the scriptures alone, and not human articles or confessions of belief, the sole rule of faith and conduct."

It is much to be lamented that the venerable reformers, when they burst asunder the cords of popish tyranny, ever departed from the simplicity of this scripture plan; and that, instead of adhering to it, they thought theological systems the only means of preserving uniformity of opinion, or of evincing the purity of their faith. The experience of more than two centuries has proved how far they are capable of producing either effect. On the other hand, the consequences which such institutions have been productive of, have been more or less severely felt in every part of the Protestant world, from the Diet of Augsburgh to the present time.

They have in former, as well as in later ages, caused a religion, designed to unite men as brethren in the sacred bonds of charity and benevolence, too often to disseminate amongst them jealousies, animosities, and rancorous hatred. They have nursed the demon of intolerance; nay, aided by the civil power, they have led martyrs to the stake, and have offered up, as holy sacrifices to the God of mercy, christians who had the guilt to prefer what they esteemed the doctrine of Christ to the commandments of men. Even in America, the effects which they have produced on the minds of christians, have been seen written in blood. But thanks be to God, those days are past! May such never revisit the earth! So long, however, as we can trace within those human systems of belief, principles oppressive to christians and injurious to the cause of our holy religion, it matters not in how small a degree, I shall esteem it my duty to raise a warning, though perhaps, a feeble voice against them.

It is a maxim self-evident to every one, and which was held sacred by the fathers of Protestantism, "that the scriptures contain all things necessary to salvation, and are the sole ground of the faith of a christian." This maxim, the basis of reformation, and which is acceded to by all Protestants, is alone sufficient, independent of what experience has taught, to induce every Protestant church to reject all systems of belief, unless conceived in the terms of scripture, not only as unwarrantable, and in the highest degree oppressive to the rights of private judgment, but as presumptuous, and as casting an unworthy reflection on the scriptures themselves. Yet many pious and worthy christians are apt to suppose that such systems of faith are necessary for the maintenance of true religion, or, for preventing that disorder which arises from a diversity of opinions. But do such christians reflect sufficiently upon the example which our Lord himself and his apostles have placed before us? Did they, for this or any other purpose, prescribe or recommend summaries of faith? On the contrary, did not our Saviour constantly enjoin upon his followers to *search the scriptures themselves?* Do we not find that the Bereans were commended for their conduct in not receiving even the *doctrine of the inspired apostles*, until they had first searched the scriptures to see whether these things were so or not? Does not

St. Paul expressly say, that "other foundation can no man lay than that is laid, which is Jesus Christ?" Does he not every where recommend to christians the duty of examining the grounds of their faith, "to prove all things, and to hold fast that which is good?" And St. John, does he not exhort us to "believe not every spirit, but to try the spirits whether they be of God?" Now, if summaries of faith had been necessary for the prosperity of our religion, can we suppose that Christ and his apostles would have neglected, not only to leave such as must have been most proper to maintain the true faith; but that, by their precepts as well as conduct, they would rather have taught us the duty of avoiding them? No, my brethren, we may be assured that Christ and his apostles did not esteem any other summary necessary than the gospel itself; and that whatever is essential either as to faith or practice, is there expressed with that clearness which a revelation from heaven required. We are directed there to search and to judge for ourselves; for religion, to be profitable to the individual and acceptable to God, must be the result of free inquiry and the determination of reason. This right of free inquiry, and of judging for ourselves, is a right natural and unalienable. It is the glory of our nature, the truest source of joy and triumph to an American, and constantly to recur to it, the indispensable duty of a christian. For should we neglect this duty, where then would be all manly rational belief, where the sincere practice of piety and virtue, where the surest guide to moral and religious conduct? In their stead, a mean credulity would prevail; hypocrisy would usurp the place of true devotion; religion and morality would degenerate into superstition and sanguinary zeal. To suppose then, that the gospel would authorize a deprivation of this right, or that such deprivation is necessary to its support and progress, is to cast an unworthy reflection upon the gospel itself; it is to suppose, that a religion which utterly disclaims all dominion over the faith and consciences of men, which is the most friendly to the essential rights of mankind, and which, indeed, cannot exist where they are invaded, still requires to be supported by their destruction.

Besides, the very attempt, in matters dark and disputable, to prevent diversity of opinion, is vain and fruitless. It has existed and must ever exist among all christians even those of the same society, so long as human nature continues the same. The God of nature has for wise purposes bestowed upon different men, different degrees of reason and understanding; so that if they think at all, they must necessarily think differently upon those dark, mysterious subjects, which, however, are often reduced into the form of articles of faith. Nor can such difference cease, until the same precise portion of intellect be imparted to every individual of the human race. To attempt then to prevent diversity of opinions upon such subjects, is to oppose the very laws of nature, and consequently vain and fruitless.

But, in truth, that diversity of opinion, which most churches have been so sedulous to prevent, is neither any disgrace to a christian society, nor incompatible with its peace and good government; unless it be disgraceful to men that they are men, and unless the christian dispensation is incompatible with the nature of man. On the contrary, such diversity may be considered as most favorable to the progress of christian knowledge, and should also be equally favorable to christian peace, by teaching us, that dark and disputable points instead of being made articles of faith,

and standards of orthodoxy, should rather be considered as trials of our christian temper, and occasions to exercise mutual charity; or that those things alone should be held as essentials, which our Lord and Master has fully and clearly expressed, and which, therefore, cannot require the supposed improvements and additions of men. So long as men agree in these essentials, or fundamental articles of our religion, in those great and important truths and duties, which are so clearly expressed, that every sincere inquirer must readily apprehend them, where is the necessity, or reasonableness of compelling men to be of one mind, as to other matters of infinitely inferior moment, and which we may suppose, were designedly less clearly expressed? That christian unity, so strongly recommended to us as the bond of perfection, does not consist in uniformity of opinion upon abstruse, metaphysical subjects, but upon the great fundamentals of our religion, and in the unanimity of affections, love, peace and charity, which is enjoined on the brethren in Christ Jesus, who all walk by the same rule, and acknowledge one and the same Lord.

But still it may be thought, that theological systems, or seminaries of faith are necessary to exclude from the bosom of a church, men whose principles might endanger its very existence. But does experience, or do just observations upon human conduct justify such a belief? He will not be retarded in the accomplishment of his designs, or in the gratification of an avaracious appetite, though nineteen, twenty, or thirty thousand articles were presented to him. Trust me, articles will never prove a barrier to the advances of a secret enemy, or exclude from any church men of vicious principles, or no principles. Whom then will they be most likely to exclude? I answer with regret—Men of stubborn virtue, men of principle and conscience, men of that rigid tough integrity, which cannot be shaped and twisted to suit the system of the day, men who will not prefer the dictates and decisions of fallible mortals, to the infallible word of God.

I conceive, moreover, that no christian church hath a right to impose upon its members, human systems of belief, as necessary terms of communion. For what, I beseech you, do we understand by a christian church? According to the most general acceptation "every christian church is a voluntary society of men agreeing to profess the faith of Christ and stipulating to live according to the rules of the gospel." From this definition, we find the distinctive terms of union, or the fundamental laws of such a society, is to embrace the scriptures alone, as the rule of worship, faith, and conduct. Consequently every act of church government, which contravenes this fundamental law, is from its very nature void.

How then shall it be pretended, that other terms of communion may be prescribed to the members of a christian church? But all human systems, imposed as articles of belief, must be held as introductory of other terms. It follows then that every christian church, so far as it introduces such terms, is to be considered as having departed from its essential characteristic, and consequently to have exceeded its right as a church. This conclusion is the more incontrovertible, as it coincides with the maxim before mentioned, I should say with that christian axiom "That the scriptures contain all things necessary to salvation, and are the sole ground of the faith of a Christian."—What then, it may be asked, shall not a church prescribe to itself, terms of communion, shall it not have its particular confessions or articles of belief, provided they be agreeable to the word of God? How many Protestant churches have been built on this foundation of sand, unable to resist the winds and the tempests which beat against them? The condition is inadmissible. For who shall determine with certainty, that those terms are agreeable to the word of God? How is it possible, that all the members of a church should be sufficiently assured of this important point? Or is private judgment to be entirely annihilated; if so, to what end, did the benign Author of our being grant reason to man? Is the conscientious Christian to forget, that it is his duty to search the scriptures themselves, or are those human expositions to usurp the place of the word of God? But let us in the spirit of charity admit, that every church supposes, or firmly believes its articles or rules of faith to be agreeable to the word of God. What then is the consequence? The difference between them is surely a proof, that infallibility is not the attribute of all of them. Truth, like the Eternal, is one. In which church then shall we find it? I will presume to say in none of them. He who would search for the truth must search for it in the scriptures alone.

Let us then abandon all those systems, which to say the least can only involve us in error. Our venerable forefathers erred, or why a reformation? Their descendants will err. Nor shall the resurrection of true christianity be seen amongst men, until it shall appear in the white garment of the gospel alone.

Light is dawning in old Virginia.
The following is from the Religious Herald of Richmond.

"*Church rules.*—Under the control of bigotry we might be compelled to withhold our support from every thing not designed to advance the interest of our own denomination; and governed by interest we might suffer to pass, unmolested, what we consider evils, countenanced and maintained among the Baptists themselves. But we owe no allegiance either to bigotry or interest.* [*This is like a servant of the Messiah.]

"It is stated that cases have occurred in several portions of our commonwealth within the last year or two, in which individuals of unexceptionable morals and acknowledged piety, have been expelled from churches merely on account of difference of opinion, in some matters in church discipline; but not affecting the faith of the gospel, or necessarily connected with experimental and practical religion.—For our part we feel it our duty to say, that the longer we live we are the more convinced of the justice and expediency of liberality in all matters, and especially in those of religion. From religious tests, professed or understood (and they are oftener understood than professed) have arisen a large portion of the dissensions and wrangles and persecutions that have distracted the church and cursed mankind.—Human theories have been substituted for revealed truths and injunctions, and all who are conscientious enough to oppose them, have been denounced as heretics. What extravagance in Religion, as in Philosophy, has not found its advocates and supporters? Eminent men have denied the existence of matter, and others equally eminent, have opposed the doctrine of the connexion of cause and effect. Some have contended that the descendants of Adam are sinners by a Divine constitution; others by propagation—souls descending from pa-

rents to offspring by natural generation. One has asserted the identity and volition of our whole race with Adam in the first transgression; another, that moral character is transferred from one account to another, precisely as pecuniary transactions are; and a third, that in virtue of the death of Christ we are born with a corrupt nature only, but without guilt or exposure to punishment, original guilt being thus cancelled. Indeed almost every man has his own particular theory, as touching matters of opinion concerning human depravity, while that which the christian feels authorized and required to believe is, that by one man sin *entered* into the world, and death by sin, and so death passed upon all men, for that all have sinned, *Rom.* v. 12; and so in relation to other matters in religion: the faith of the gospel is one and its experience is one; and theories and conjectures and opinions, may be as numerous as the race of men. But some of our brethren are of opinion that no creed or Confession of Faith is necessary but the bible, and that they are in fact injurious—that the exclusive system of rules by which a church should be governed are those contained in the New Testament, that the instructions and edification of believers are better promoted by expositions of chapters or sections of the scriptures than by sermons founded on isolated texts—that the same Elder cannot preside over several churches at the same time, although he may visit as many as is convenient or practicable—that the Lord's supper was celebrated by the early disciples, the first day of every week, and should be now:—because worthy brethren of sound moral and religious principles and lives, entertain opinions like these, shall they be declared disorderly and heretical, and expelled from fellowship!!

"Now we know a number of such brethren, who are retained in churches tenacious of doctrine and order, without a word said, or a hard thought cherished; and these churches act wisely and correctly. Let us suppose that such opinions are not required by the scriptures, does it follow that they are improper, or if they are, that they are so to such an extent as to merit censure and excision! But it would be difficult to show that the opinions above mentioned are improper and contrary to the word of God. And while, on the one hand, we deprecate the looseness of government and extent of charity which considers confusion to be order, and all sentiments proper, if sincere; on the other hand, we would watch with a jealous eye that rigour of discipline which demands unanimity of opinion in every particular, at the expense of pains and penalties, and those of the highest class allowed by the civil government under which we live. It is scarcely to be doubted that there are many persons, in other respects worthy of esteem, whose principles and habits would lead them, had they the power, to establish religion by law, and to renew all the terrors of excommunication, torture, confiscation, the inquisitorial tribunal sanctified by prayer, and the *auto-da-fe*.* [*Like apples of gold in pictures of silver.] Thanks to God, we remain as yet free from the dominion of his Holiness the Pope, and are yet unthreatened by the glittering of the sword and the thunder of cannon; but unless our civil and religious liberties are guarded with a watchful eye, we may have, at some future period, to face the bayonet, or to go to the stake.* [*An important truth.]

"We hope that kind demeanor, and good feelings will be cherished in churches in which such differences may exist. It is not our wish to wound the sensibilities of our brethren; nor would we set up ourselves as umpires of contending parties, but moderation and forbearance are respectfully and affectionately recommended. Let brethren who, without reproach as to morals, standing, and the faith of the gospel, have been discountenanced, be restored and be declared to be restored, to all former confidence and affection. If such differences as those referred to be inconsistent with harmonious union, let the separation be friendly. What good object is gained by strife? "Seeing you are brethren, why do you wrong one to another? Grieve not the Holy Spirit of God whereby you are sealed to the day of redemption. Let all bitterness, and wrath, and anger, and clamor, and evil speaking, be put away from you, with all malice. And be you kind one to another, tender-hearted, forgiving one another, even as God, for Christ's sake, has forgiven you. Him that is weak in the faith receive ye, but not to doubtful disputations. For one believes that he may eat all things; another who is weak eats herbs.—Let not him that eats despise him that eats not; and let not him that eats not judge him that eats, for God has received him."—*Eph.* iv. 30. 32.—*Rom.* xiv. 1. 3.—*Acts* viii. 26."

" We are decidedly of the opinion that expulsions, or any other harsh measures, in cases like those to which we refer, are calculated to promote the object they are intended to impede. Persecutions always injure the persecutors, and benefit the persecuted. If severity in these cases were right, it would be *impolitic,* but its *righteousness* may be seriously called in question."

Queries.

Query 1.—Does the parable of the Talents apply to Saints or Sinners, as recorded in the 25th chapter of Matthew?

Answer.—To neither as such. It is intended to represent the administration of the Reign of favor during the absence from earth of the King. The persons to whom the management of the affairs of this kingdom was committed during the time from the departure of the King till his second coming, were compared to the public servants or stewards of a prince or nobleman. To each of these public servants certain trusts were committed, and the management of these trusts was to be the subject of inquiry when the Prince returned.—The stewards, according to their capacity for management, had more or less committed to their management. To one was committed a very large trust, to another a less one, and to a third a very small one. The same fidelity and diligence were exhibited by persons of very different capacities and trust. Hence he that had gained five and he that gained two talents were equally praiseworthy, for as the *ratio* of increase was the same, so the diligence and fidelity were the same; and the reward was equal. Now had the steward who had the least trust, only one talent, managed it so as to have gained one he would have been as commendable as he that had gained five. But the error was that he thought himself disparaged, conceived himself neglected, and formed a very unfavorable opinion of the King. This paralyzed all his energies, and he did nothing. His evil eye was the cause of his apathy, and instead of going to work he set himself to frame excuses for himself. As is very natural for persons of this character, he threw the blame upon his Ma-

ker, and vainly expected to justify himself by criminating the administration of the King. The parable very forcibly demonstrates the consolatory and animating maxim of Paul—viz: "It is always accepted according to what a man has, and not according to what he has not." The widow and her two mites exhibits just the contrast of the man and the one talent, and unequivocally teaches all disciples that it is equally in the power of all to obtain the greatest eminence in the Kingdom of Jesus, whatever their earthly means or opportunities may be. This parable has been grossly misapplied when turned to the advantage of unconverted men.

Query 2.—Is an unmarried person or a youth who has never been married, eligible to the office of bishop or overseer?

Answer.—If Paul be admitted a competent witness in the case, he is not. A stripling married or unmarried, is not eligible. A person of middle age if recently converted, is not eligible. And a man who has had no experience in domestic management is illy qualified to manage the family of God. But Paul says a bishop or overseer must be blameless, and as very intimately connected therewith, " he must be the husband of one wife." That elderly persons were most eligible is evident from his adding, "having believing children," of good behaviour too, "not accused of riot, nor unruly." We have very good reason to believe that if the apostle's qualifications were all literally observed in selecting such persons only as possess these qualifications to the discharge of the duties of this office, it would be much better with the christian communities; and that the evils which are supposed to flow from the want of bishops of some sort, are much more imaginary than real.

The Scriptures.—No. I.

THE next impious practice, which as well on account of its general adoption amongst people who profess religion, as its pernicious tendency, claims attention, is that of resorting in pursuit of *religious* information, to other means of instruction, than those with which God has himself furnished us in his own word. To evince the folly and impiety of this evil device, I offer the following remarks:—

1. God has declared expressly, that the writings which he has himself furnished us, and just as he has furnished them, unaltered by the tongue or pen of man, unmixed, undiluted with a single human conception, do contain all the information which our salvation needs. His Holy Spirit tells us positively, that the holy scriptures are, *as worded by him,* sufficient to make us wise to salvation: that his word implanted in our minds, can save them; nay, that even the hearing of his word, can save both ourselves and our families; and that by belief of the scriptures the deliverance of lost sinners is rendered absolutely sure. It is then certain, that in order to insure the salvation of our souls, we stand in no need of any other information than that which the sacred pages, untouched by man, afford.

2. Sacred writ contains all the correct and certain information on the subject of religion, which the world ever enjoyed or will obtain. Nay more, its words selected and consecrated by the Spirit have not only been the only vehicles of his mind to man, but in all ages, have also been the only guardians and preservers of what they did convey. No sooner did remote antiquity abandon the phraseology of the Spirit, and employ words of their own devising, to express their religious notions, than with their new

terms they introduced new and erroneous conceptions of God and divine things, and sunk into idolatry every where. And by the same cause a similar effect has been produced oftener than once in after times. No sooner did the Jewish clergy cease after the captivity, to employ in their religious instructions and services, the words used in their sacred books, and invented terms, fitter as they no doubt thought, to express their religious conceptions, than with their new religious language, they brought into vogue doctrines, rules, institutions and practices, unknown and unsanctioned by the word of God. And by a like departure in their religious instructions and services from the words employed by the Holy Spirit in the New Testament have christian teachers introduced into the world a multiplicity of notions, institutions, rules and practices wholly unauthorized by sacred writ. So invariably true is it, that if we would with absolute certainty secure the sense or ideas of a writer or speaker, we must retain his words.

3. But if the only certain means of securing the ideas or sense of an author be to retain his language, it follows, that if we would certainly secure to our minds the ideas which the Spirit of God has communicated to us in sacred writ, we must resort to the very words which he has employed in sacred writ to convey them. For there, and then, alone can we infallibly find them. When men attempt to express the Spirit's ideas by words of their own selecting, we have no certainty that their attempts have been successful. On the contrary we are certain that complete success never attended the enterprize. Into every performance of the kind error more or less has never failed to insinuate itself; and certainly this danger, from which no human language is free, ought of itself to be sufficient to deter us from resorting in a matter of such infinite importance as the eternal happiness of our souls to these sources of religious information, from which we are as liable to inhale ruinous error as saving truth. And here let me add as a general truth, that there exists no other method of guarding any message from misrepresentation, but that of selecting and prescribing the very words which the person charged with its publication, is to employ for that purpose.

4. God's information, as conveyed in his own words, unaltered by man, is alone safe, alone certain, alone entirely exempt from error. As just hinted, the notions, opinions, harangues and compositions of men, not excepting their religious notions, opinions, harangues and compositions of every name, are all fraught with error, mistake, misconception and misrepresentation. In God's declarations alone are unmixed truth and infallible certainty to be found. What inducement, then, can any rational being have, what reason or apology can he devise for his conduct, when he abandons even for a single moment the sure unerring information of his God, and devotes his time and attention to hearing, reading, studying, searching, and consulting sources of information which he knows to be replete with danger, from which he is certain he is liable to imbibe error, suck in falsehood, and deceive, mislead, and ruin his soul eternally?

5. When we prefer human to divine means of information, of which vile preference we are incontestably guilty, when we lay down our bibles and take up the written compositions or listen to the religious harangues of men, we grossly insult our Divine Teacher—we tell him flatly, that he is not as capable to teach, inform and instruct us as our uninspired fellow-creatures, and therefore we abandon his offered means of instruction and resort to theirs. For surely no reason can be assigned for closing our bibles and giving our eyes, our ears, our time and attention to the means of information offered by fellow-mortals, but that we expect during the same time to receive more information and greater benefit, from the latter than we do from the former! And is not God insulted, grossly insulted, by such an expectation?

6. Again, when we resort to human means of instruction, we in effect make the Spirit of God a liar. As already observed, God has declared the information which he has provided for us, sufficient, without alteration, for the salvation of our souls. Do we not, then, when we abandon that information more or less, and resort to that which our fellow-creatures offer, tell our Divine Teacher that we have no confidence in the declarations which he has published concerning the sufficiency of his message to save our souls, at least before it has been altered, modified, and largely mixed with what is human? We in reality deny its sufficiency.

7. God has not only not commanded us to resort to any other means of acquiring religious information, than that which he has provided for us in his word; but he has peremptorily forbidden us to resort to any other teacher than himself, which is manifestly equivalent to forbidding us to seek religious instruction from any other source than the bible.

8. In innumerable passages of his word God commands his creatures to read, search, meditate, remember, and converse about the contents of his message; and to these commands the pious have yielded prompt obedience in all ages. Like David, they have day and night read, studied and meditated the information sent them by their God; but nowhere are we told that they ever applied for religious instruction either to uninspired men, or uninspired books. There is no such precedent on the divine record. Indeed, till the fatal Jewish Apostacy, which occurred not long after the Captivity, there is strong ground to believe that no uninspired man ever dared to set himself up as a religious teacher, in the modern sense of that term. It was then, for the first time, that uninspired men arrogated to themselves the titles, honors, functions, and homage due to an inspired instructer, and the lamentable result of this impious innovation is well known.

Let me now ask, if God's information, believed, but not altered, be, in his judgment, sufficient so to enlighten our understandings, purify our affections, elevate our desires, and rectify our conduct, as to render us fit to become members of his family and subjects of his kingdom, why resort to other or additional means? Can we expect to derive ampler or clearer information from human discourses and human writings, than we can obtain from the unadulterated instructions of the Divine Spirit? Can we imagine that a small fragment, a few words, torn from their connexion with the rest of God's message, and wrought up into, or diffused through, such a huge mass of human notions and human words, as require an hour to utter them, and which so dilute and obscure the fragment, that not a trace of it can be discerned, can by such violent separation and such immense dilution, be rendered more fit to convey the Spirit's meaning, inform the human mind, or impress the human heart, than it was when it occupied its original place in God's book, and its primitive concentration? Truly, we cannot believe it. If either the principal objects, concerning which sacred writ professes to give information, be the existence and attributes of God, the dignity, office and character of the Redeemer, the character and office of the Spirit, the nature, character, condition, prospects and duty of man, and the means provided by God for man's extrication from his present ruined state, and elevation to a state of moral perfection and complete happiness: I say if these be the great objects concerning which the bible treats, can any rational being be so senseless as to suppose that he can, by any ingenuity of his, render God's information concerning these things, fitter to answer its purpose than he has made it? Is it not mere waste of time, then, is it not worse, is it not contempt of God, to resort to tracts, (silly stories,) to pamphlets, sermons, lectures, commentaries, expositions, to the neglect of God's own information on these infinitely important subjects? Depraved, indeed, must that taste be which prefers the muddy, filthy stream, to the clear unpolluted fountain!

It was my intention to mention at least a few of the many sad evils which have been produced by the impious innovation now the subject of censure; but one must suffice at this time. It is the tendency of this innovation to bring *God's information* into disrepute, and alienate the affections of men from it, and so keep them ignorant of it. This is the natural effect of the imposition practiced on an ignorant and credulous world by an artful and interested clergy. By them mankind have been long taught to believe that God's information, at least before it is acted on by their metamorphosing powers, before it is completely new-modelled, before it is perfectly saturated with their ingenious notions, before its arrangement and connexion formed by the Divine Spirit, have been thoroughly subverted, and its plain phraseology also the choice of its all-wise author the Spirit, has been compelled to give place to their gaudy, pompous diction, is fit for no human purpose, can convey no instruction that can be depended on; in short, is entirely unfit to save a human soul. They must break the bread of life ere it can be chewed, swallowed, digested, or a particle of nourishment obtained from it. Is it any wonder that creatures, justly alarmed about their perishing souls, should, under such persuasion, pay little respect to God's word, expect little benefit from it, and flatter, caress, and fairly idolize a set of men, from whose ingenuity and eloquence they are taught to expect the deliverance of their endangered souls?

A. Straith, M. D.

Virginia, July 20, 1829.

Brother Campbell,

Dear Sir:—The divided state of the worshipers of God has been a source of much unhappiness to me for many years. I do cordially believe it is owing to the presumption of the teachers making *their opinions a bond of union.* And every attempt to perpetuate this state of things is at war with the spirit of the gospel. In every sect there is a set of *opinions*, which is the life-blood of the sect, and made paramount to the word of God. A dissent from these opinions invariably produces a breach of fellowship in that sect; of course there cannot be any improvement or correction of any error without the consent of the leading teachers. This is not to be expected while they have full sway over the consciences of their disciples; for they have the power of stopping the mouth of every dissenter in their congregations. One popular teacher often sways the sceptre over thousands. My opposition to this state of things brought me into collision with some of my brethren. When I read brother Melancthon's recommendation to an ecclesiastical body, I felt mortified, believing, as I now do, it will only tend to perpetuate the spirit of sectarianism, which every lover of truth ought to banish from the earth. This is my apology for my letter to you in your May number.

I see in your last number "*Paulinus again.*" I wish to say a few things, and I am done with this subject, without new matter should be introduced.

The Baptist, in this section of country, I am satisfied is nearer the christian church than any other denomination I know of here. If they would exercise more liberality, pay a greater attention to the character and conduct of the New Testament christians, and the manner of their instruction, it would soon place them, in my estimation, upon the ancient order of things. It is truly pleasing to me to find of late a growing spirit of liberality flowing from the press, and I do hope ere long to hear it from the pulpit. There is great room for reformation *here*. Brother Melancthon promised in his next essay to go *there*. We shall watch him closely.

I do not love the spirit of the capital *I*, and the little *u*, and I hope brother Paulinus does not. "Charity vaunteth not itself, is not puffed up." "I am less than the least of all saints."—Paul.

Again, his letter contains not that simplicity for which he is noted. This may be owing to a conviction of the difficulty of supporting his recommendation from revelation—*pari passu, modus operandi, fortiori, ergo.* Many of your readers do not know what these words mean. Were it not for a *Latin* dictionary, he would have been a barbarian to me. "Except you utter by the tongue words easy to be understood, how shall it be known what is spoken, for you speak into the air?" "Therefore, if I know not the meaning of the voice, I shall be to him that speaks a barbarian, and he that speaks a barbarian to me." "In the church I had rather speak five words with my understanding, that by my voice I might teach others also, than ten thousand words in an unknown tongue."—Paul.

What the magnet is to the needle on the compass, this world is to the spirit of a man. Speaking of me, "From such a one I must appeal to those of more candor," says brother Paulinus. When the ancient order of things was attended to, we hear nothing of appealing to brethren's opinions. This brings to mind a stratagem of two travellers, who were without money, to procure them a drink of alcohol. They caught a frog just before they reached an inn, which they agreed to call a mouse. One was to go on before the other and ask the keeper of the inn if that was not a mouse. He replied, "No—it is a frog." The traveller proposed a wager of a pint of whiskey that it was a mouse, and would leave it to the first man that passed by. The inn-keeper agreed to it. Up comes the other traveller. "What is this?" said the inn-keeper. "It is a mouse," replied the traveller. "A mouse! No, sir, it is a frog." "You are mistaken, my friend," replied the traveller; "it is a mouse." Thus, the inn-keeper, contrary to the evidence of his own senses, was made to pay the wager. In ancient times, in all matters of difficulty, "What say the scriptures" was the watch-word, and not to the candor of erring mortals. "He that sows to the flesh, shall of the flesh reap corruption; but he that sows to the spirit, shall of the spirit reap life everlasting."—Paul.

Again brother Paulinus measures my corn by his bushel, because he goes an equal pace with others. *Pari passu*, I go with you, and even run before you. "We dare not make ourselves of the number, or compare ourselves with some that commend themselves: but they measuring themselves by themselves, and comparing themselves among themselves, are not wise." "We know no man after the flesh; *ergo*, if any be in Christ Jesus, he is a new creature." "But we have a measure to reach even to you," &c. "Charity thinks no evil."—Paul.

Again—"If persons who are fully capable of reading the bible for themselves need human aid in deriving instruction from that sacred source, then much more do children need such aid that cannot read for themselves." Brother Paulinus is an excellent portrait painter, and by his pencil has drawn his miniature of the subject in controversy. The burthen of his argument is this: If old children that can read the scriptures for themselves, need lectures—then little children that cannot read, much more need catechisms! "From a child you have known the holy scriptures, which are able to make you wise to salvation."—Paul. If brother Paulinus' catechisms are purely historic they cannot do this, and are as innocent as breath. If he aims at the salvation of these little immortals, catechisms will prove injurious to them, as much so, as any Catholic manual, creed, rubric, or formula. They will dogmatize. *Fortiori*. "If I will prove catechisms," &c. If catechisms cannot quicken and convert the souls of these little ones that cannot read, then they are RUBBISH. If they can read let them read the scriptures; and brother Paulinus says "they contain all truth necessary to make us wise to salvation; and that wherever they come, they lay hold of every human being with the grasp of divine authority, while they present the exhibition of divine mercy. What a pity men are not satisfied with God's way of saving sinners, but must hew out cisterns of their own which hold no water. This was Israel's error of old."*

I have never considered them clothed with ecclesiastical authority as those catechisms have sought to be, and thereby obtaining "a powerful influence amongst us. The keeping alive a sectarian spirit, and the opinions of brethren as a bond of union, is supplanting the word of God (and what I opposed) by acknowledging and soliciting the powerful influence of the kingdom of the clergy, which was one of the evils which brother Paulinus wished to aid you in correcting. "I stretched out my hand to pull down," &c. If my attention to the education of my children, teaching them at my family altar, the contents of the New Testament, and exhorting my brethren to do the same, is doing nothing, this charge is correct, *God has commanded teaching and exhortation.* Brother Paulinus appears to prefer his catechisms. I have nothing to build up. If dissecting the word of God to get materials to build up catechisms, is what he means, I must beg to be excused in not lending a hand to this work. This is to keep up the old divisions, if not to make new ones, and I maintain that they have a vicious tendency in keeping back the salvation of the world.

Your advice is so reasonable, I cannot doubt that brother Paulinus will cheerfully comply before long; nor can I see how any man can refuse to comply with such a course, unless he has prospects of sitting in the *chair*, and thereby to lord it over the consciences of his brethren. This advice followed up by all sects, would soon restore the purity and simplicity of the gospel of Messiah, bring about the millennian state of the church, and banish from the earth party spirit in the holy religion of Jesus Christ. All sects that are honest acknowledge errors are among them. Could they but once see error is no advantage to men, angels or devils, saint or sinner, every honest man in pursuit of truth, would cast it away from him as *folly* and *rubbish*, and inquire, "What say the scriptures?" and if they are silent, leave it to the first general convention of the anniversary of the saints at the resurrection of the dead. May the minds of all your readers be directed to this important point, is the constant prayer of

A LOVER OF THE WHOLE OF DIVINE TRUTH.

Sermons to Young Preachers.—No. I.

MY YOUNG FRIENDS,—You are so much accustomed to preach from texts that I shall have to take one when I preach to you. My text at this time will be found in the first book of kings, xviii. 38. *"And they cried aloud and cut themselves after their manner, with knives and lancets till the blood gushed out upon them."* I intend no allusion to those reverend gentlemen who officiated in the temple of Baal, as analogous to you, save one; and that I will specify in its proper place. You know, I presume, my young friends, that the term *prophet* means not primarily to foretel future events. This is an *appropriated* sense of the term. There have been hundreds of prophets who have never foretold any thing except that all men will die. The interpreters of oracles were called *prophets* as well as the *poets* by the Greeks and Romans. Extemporaneous speakers on all subjects, especially upon religious matters, were called *prophets*. He that *interpreted*, as well as he that *predicted*, was, in the scripture sense, called a prophet. You, my young friends, perhaps, had better assume the name of *prophets*, than that of *elders, bishops*, or *ministers*. You are sometimes heralds, or criers, or preachers, and all these three are comprehended in the term *prophet*. You sometimes *interpret*, and an interpreter is a prophet. I therefore *move* that all young preachers who have no certain dwelling place; no special charge; who are not overseers, nor strictly called evangelists, be denominated *prophets*. When you proclaim the gospel, interpret ancient oracles, and speak extemporaneously, you are truly prophets. Now, having found a suitable name for you, I proceed to show you the bearing of my text.

All superstitions, false oracles, and false gods have had prophets. Every thing has been counterfeited except a rogue, a villain, and Lycurgus' iron money. You must know we have had counterfeit gold, silver, and brass coins. We have had counterfeit bank bills, and the world has been filled with counterfeit gods, oracles, and priests. Counterfeiters seldom deal in brass, or in small bank bills. They are mean villains who counterfeit cheap articles. High minded rogues have counterfeited the most precious metals, and bank bills of the highest denominations. Hence it came to pass that gods, priests, and oracles have had the largest stock, at all times, in the counterfeit markets. But in all these things I have no allusion to you. For I am speaking to my young friends, who are desirous, sincerely desirous, of promoting glory to the heavens, peace on earth, and good will among men. Baal, however, you may remember, had four hundred and fifty prophets

---

* I ask brother Paulinus to look and see who it was that first advised Israel of old to make cisterns of their own. 2 Kings, ch. xviii.

for one Elijah. But the point to which I allude, and which I wish you to consider, is that they appear to have been very *sincere* and very *vociferous*. The doctrine which I deduce from my text is therefore this, *that persons may be so sincere as to wear out their lungs, and so zealous as to spill their blood in the cause of error—" They cried aloud and cut themselves with knives."* And you may cry aloud and spill your blood sincerely and zealously without proving that your doctrine is true. I do not know that loud talking and blood letting will prove any opinion, theorem, or proposition to be true.

From these desultory remarks I come now to the application of my sermon. And although I dare not boast of my eloquent exordium, nor logical distribution, if I can only make a good application, I will be pleased with myself, and that, be assured, is the main point. For many a preacher pleases his congregation, who fails to please himself. And now for the application—

Young orators, in the pulpit and at the bar, are more in need of an instructor than children at school, or students at college. For if they begin wrong, and contract a bad habit, they seldom can cure it. Their ideas will only run in a certain channel. Often have I seen a preacher try to get his mind abroach until he began to snuff the breeze like a whale snorting in the North Atlantic Ocean. It is more easy to bring a seventy-four gun ship into action in a gale of wind, than to get the mind to bear upon the text, until the nostrils catch the corner of a volume of air, and sneeze it out like a leviathan in the deep. I have seen other preachers who can strike fire no other way than by the friction of their hands, and an occasional clap, resembling a peal of distant thunder. In this holy paroxysm of clapping, rubbing, sneezing, and roaring, the mind is fairly on the way, and the tongue in full gallop, which, like a race horse, runs the swifter the less weight it carries. The farther from nature the nearer the skies, some preachers seem to think. But so it is whenever they acquire this habit it is almost incurable. They can neither speak to God nor man in the pulpit to purpose, as they think, unless when, like the boiler of a steam boat, they are almost ready to burst. This is one extreme. There are various degrees marked on the scale before we arrive at this dreadful heat. There is a certain pitch of voice which at least is ten degrees above a natural key. To this most preachers have to come before their ideas get adrift. Their inspiration is kindled from the noise they create. I have seen children cry who began quite moderately, but when they heard the melody of their own voice their cries rose in a few seconds to screams. No person can tell how much is to be ascribed to these factitious influences in giving play to the imagination and wings to our ideas. Some people have to milk all their sermons from their watch chains—and others from the buttons on their coats.

Now all these habits are no more according to reason, than were the screams and cuts of the prophets of Baal. And as for religion I hope none of my young friends think there is any of it in a watch chain, or a button, or in mere vociferations.

Some preachers seem to think that suicide is equivalent to martyrdom; in other words that it is a good cause in which they die who burst their lungs in long, and loud, and vehement declamations. I doubt not but that hundreds kill themselves or shorten their days by an unmeaning and unnecessary straining of their lungs.

I do intend, my young friends, to devote a few

sermons to yourselves, and I wish I could put them in a corner of the Christian Baptist which none could find but yourselves. I am conscious you need a few sermons to convert you from customs and habits as injurious to yourselves to your health, usefulness, and improvement, as intemperance is to the well-being of the soul, body, and estate of the worshipper of Bacchus.

I do think that nature, when followed, is a better teacher of eloquence than Longinus, or all the Grecian and Roman models.—Mimics never can excel, except in being mimics. There is more true gracefulness and dignity in a speech pronounced in the natural tone of our own voice, and in the natural key, than in all the studied mimicry of mere actors, whether stage or pulpit actors, and which is the more numerous we will not be able to decide till after the census of 1830. But above all others, these prophets of Baal are the worst models for young preachers; and I trust none of you, my friends, will, from this time forth, ever follow so scandalous an example. EDITOR.

A Restoration of the Ancient order of Things. No. XXXII.

Official Names and Titles.

THE religious theatre of public actors is crowded. To find suitable names to designate them all would be a desideratum. We have Ministers, Divines, Clergymen, Elders, Bishops, Preachers, Teachers, Priests, Deans, Prebendaries, Deacons, Arch-Bishops, Arch-Deacons, Cardinals, Popes, Friars, Priors, Abbots, Local Preachers, Circuit Preachers, Presiding Elders, Missionaries, Class Leaders, Licentiates, *cum multis aliis*. I do not know what to do with them all. I would call them all by scriptural names if I could find them. But it is very difficult to find scriptural names for unscriptural things.

I have rummaged the inspired books to find some scriptural names for them all, or some general names, under which, with some sort of affinity, we might hope to class them. But this is also a difficult task. I find the following are the nearest approach I can make: Deacons, Bishops, Preachers, Evangelists, Antichrists. This last term is a sort of *summum, genus* for a large majority of them. The term *preacher* will hardly apply to any of them, in its scriptural import. Christian *mothers* who make known to their children the glad tidings, or the facts concerning the Saviour, are the most worthy of this name of any persons now on earth. Evangelists will not strictly apply to any, in its primitive usage. Though the *printers* of the history of Jesus Christ, and those who proclaim the ancient gospel, in the capacity of public speakers, may, of all others, deserve to inherit this name with the most reasonable pretensions. *Elders* will apply to old men, only, whether they are official or unofficial members of society. *Overseers* or *Bishops* will apply to all, and to none but those who have the presidency or oversight of one congregation. *Deacons*, to those males who are the public servants of the whole congregation. *Deaconesses*, to those female public servants, who officiate amongst the females. *Teacher*, is a generic term which will apply to all men in the capacity of public instructers. As for the others, I cannot classify them. The word *antichrist* covers a goodly number of them: and it is not worth the labor to tell which of them may escape the enrollment. They who have more leisure may amuse themselves with such speculations.

The officers of the christian congregations found in the *New Institution* were *overseers* and *public servants*, or *bishops* and *deacons*.—Every well ordered congregation was supplied with these. They had one, or more, male and female deacons, who served the congregations in performing such service or ministry to the male and female members of their respective communities, as circumstances required; but all these official duties were confined to one single congregation. Such a thing as a bishop, over two, three, or four congregations, was as unknown, unheard of, and unthought of in the primitive and ancient order of things in the christian communities, as a husband with two, three, or four living wives. There is just as much reason and scripture for one pope and twelve cardinals, as for one bishop and four congregations.

A *bitter sweet* or a *sweet bitter* is not more incongruous than a *young elder*, or to see a young stripling addressed as an elder. It is not long since I saw, in a newspaper, such an annunciation as this: "Elder A. B. will preach at such a place at such an hour." But the satire was, that *elder* A. B. was not *twenty-three* years old. Another equally incongruous was, that "bishop W. T. will lecture in the court house on the first Sunday of July." The humor was that *Bishop* W. T. had no diocess, nor cure, nor see, nor congregation, nor oversight on this side of the moon. Now what shall we do with these anomalies? I answer, call no man a *bishop* or overseer, who has not a flock or an oversight; call no man a *deacon* who is not the public servant of a community; call those who proclaim the ancient gospel *evangelists*.

This, upon the whole, is the least exceptionable name for them. It does in its etymology, just express the proclamation of the glad tidings; and if it did not import any thing more, it cannot now. The ancients called those who wrote as well as those who spoke the facts constituting the gospel history, by this name. Besides, the office of evangelist, as a proclaimer of the gospel, was always contingent. He was needed only in some places, and at some times, and was not a permanent officer of the christian church. His office now answers to that of the prophets of old. The prophets as extemporaneous and occasional teachers became necessary. When, then, any congregation has a brother well qualified to proclaim the gospel, and when there is, in the vicinity, a people in need of such a service, let the person so sent by them, be called an evangelist. Perhaps the present distress requires such persons as much as any former period. But when christian congregations cover the country, and walk in the instituted order of the new constitution, such persons will not be necessary, any more than a standing army in time of peace.

But when we speak of the armies of the sects, how shall we denominate them? Let us call them all teachers of their respective tenets; such as teacher of Methodism, teacher of Presbyterianism; or Independent teachers, Baptist teachers, Methodist teachers, &c. This is not at all disrespectful nor incongruous. In addressing letters, or in publishing the names and offices of persons, in order to save time, paper, and ink, let us use the following abbreviations: Bp. for bishop, Dn. for Deacon, Et. for Evangelist.

Distinctions of this sort are only necessary for discrimination from persons of similar names in the same vicinities. There is a great love in the American people for titles. So strong is this passion that many retain the title of an office, which, perhaps, they only filled a year or two, all their lives. How many captains, majors, colonels, generals, esquires have we who have become obsolete. Christians cannot, consistently with their profession, desire the official name without the *work*. If a man, says Paul, desire the office of a bishop, he desires a *good work*. The work then and not the name or title engrosses the ambition of the christian.

In the common intercourse of life, it is requisite that we give all their dues. Even where honor is due, the debt ought to be paid. Paul thought it no incongruity with the christian apostleship to call a Pagan governor "*Most noble Felix.*" This very term, Luke, the amiable physician, and evangelist, applies to a christian brother of high political standing, "*most excellent Theophilus.*" We ought to address all men wearing official titles, when we address them publicly, by the titles which designate their standing among men. There is a squeamishness of conscience, or a fastidiousness of taste, which some men, and some sectaries exhibit about giving any official names or titles to men of high rank or standing. This proceeds more from pride than from humility, and more from the intimation of some eccentric genius than from the examples of either patriarchs, prophets, saints, or martyrs in the age of God's Revelations. Let us then endeavor to call things by their proper names; and render to all men their dues.   Editor.

New Harmony Gazette, now the Free Enquirer, of New York.

It would seem, if any reliance could be reposed upon the testimony of those who reject testimony as a source of certain information, that the materialists, once of New Harmony, now of New York, are carrying all before them. These philosophers have silenced all the cannon of all the christian batteries of New York, themselves being judges, and have even pitched a bomb into our camp, a distance of four hundred miles. These good reasoners came hither to build up a social system in the back woods. They founded the city of Mental Independence, and proclaimed a new era, on the Wabash somewhere. But finding themselves and their converts too social, so that love itself burned into jealousy; and mine and thine no longer designated wife or husband; becoming in fact too social and too much in the community spirit, they found it expedient for these and other good reasons, to turn their mortal souls and dying minds to pull down that fell demon, religion: for the traces of it, still remaining, though scarcely legible, on some of the good hearts of some of the good citizens of New Harmony, made some of the folks willing to have some interest in their wives and children, and therefore religion became inimical to the social system. Those who loved their wives and offspring, fled from the city; and of the rest, some who had no wives nor husbands resolved to form a league offensive and defensive against religion.—Hence the New Harmony Gazette renounces "Harmony," in word and deed, in time and space, and freely inquires, in New York, whether man or woman ought to form a more intimate compact than that existing between Miss Frances, Mr. R. D. O. and Mr. Jennings, as coeditors of free inquiries. They have swords and lances now to pierce the hearts and kill the souls of all who love religion; and have devoted their whole souls to the cause of no religion.

But, to come to the point at once, these new era folks have agreed to write down religion; and so, have made that the all-engrossing theme in every number of their Free Enquirer. One of these three editors, in the 8th of July number, gave me a sort of an indirect challenge. It will be time enough for him to offer the terms when he has seen how it fared with his father at Cincinnati; or perhaps he is determined to wage war at all events and at all risques. Now I must tell my friend R. D. Owen that I have examined all the principles which have issued from the new school as proposed by Robert Owen, Esq. in our late discussion, and I have read and examined most of the principles of the old school of sceptics, and I heard all that forty years' experience, reading, and observation could array in vindication of them without any other emotion than that of wonder, why men, claiming to be governed by so much reason, could be so much the dupes of imagination, and hold principles antipodes to reason, knowledge, and experience. I now know as certainly as I know that I have physical strength to lift fifty-six pounds avoirdupois, that I can demonstrate that every system of scepticism is at variance with all reason, knowledge, and human experience; and that the sceptics, one and all, are as surely infatuated as ever was an idealist, who imagined there was not a particle of matter in the universe. This much I did not say before I put on my armor, but this much I now say, that I have put it off, and laugh as you please, gentlemen, unless you repent and believe the gospel, you will as surely perish as you die. I know all you can say against the bible, gentlemen, the priests, and corruptions of christianity, and it weighs no more in the scales of reason than the logic of the old woman in the Highlands of Scotland, who ridiculed the idea of the sphericity of the earth, by alleging that the hills in Jura were ocular evidence 'that the world was not round.' But so soon as any sceptic of learning and writing talent, such as I believe some of the editors of the Free Enquirer are, shall have deliberately read through our discussion, and if he shall then be willing to attack any one of the evidences on which we have made the truth of christianity to rest, I will then show, in my periodical, that he cannot undermine, sap, weaken, or impair a single pillar in the citadel of supernatural truth.—Every position that I have taken in this discussion, belonging to the logical defence of christianity, I will defend against every opposition whatever. That I can do so I profess to be as certain as that I can raise my arm or wield a goose quill.　　　　　EDITOR.

No. 3.]　　　OCTOBER 5, 1829.

DAYTON, August 25, 1829.

DEAR BROTHER CAMPBELL:—I HASTEN to inform you of the result of our meeting in this place, on Saturday and Sunday last. There were ten or twelve preachers here, all of whom were either partially or altogether reformed, as far as reformation now goes. The congregation was very large, and on Sunday looked extremely interesting, assembled in one of the finest groves our country affords. After three sermons on Saturday, in the evening, in the presence of many hundreds, in the meeting house, our public teachers rehearsed, one by one, accounts of the congregations with which they were respectively connected, informing us of their progress in grace and reformation; of their order, duties, relations and prospects; and all concurred in acknowledging but one law book, from whose decision they never attempt to appeal. This was one of the most interesting exercises in which I ever participated, or ever witnessed. Its influence was visible upon all the brethren. With each other they were immediately acquainted, and mutual confidence and a reciprocation of christian feeling, were the consequences. At ten the next morning I immersed William R. Cole, Esq.* of Wilmington, with whom you are acquainted, and three others. After some of the brethren had labored in word and doctrine, two or three hundred feasted at the King's table upon bread and wine; all of them having previously had their hearts sprinkled from an evil conscience, and their bodies washed with pure water. I believe we had no sectarianism among us. Not a discordant note was heard in the house or among the trees. Brother Rains was with us. Our exercises were resumed and terminated pleasantly in the evening. Upon the whole, I believe, such a meeting is rarely held.

Week before last, I attended Todd's Fork Association, where I received encouraging news from Indiana. We had a very interesting meeting. It was resolved with but one dissentient vote, that the association request the churches to consider this question, " *Shall we dissolve our association, and as a substitute, hold an annual meeting for worship and acquaintance?*" and disclose the result of their deliberations at their next session.

By a letter from your father, which I have seen, I learn that the gospel is very successful with you.† Remember me to him.

Yours in Christ,　　　　D. S. BURNET.

For the Christian Baptist.

BESIDE the unfounded imputation of want of plainness, which its pretended advocates, the clergy, have brought against God's address to perishing sinners, and out of which, false as the imputation is, they have extracted more gold than was ever dug from the mines of Peru, and more homage than was ever paid to crowned heads from Nimrod to the present hour: besides impious and vain attempts to remove from the divine message, such obscurities or silence as the communicating Spirit has thought proper to introduce into his original phraseology; or has suffered, in the course of his all-wise providence, to creep into the sacred pages; and, of course, to force the divine oracles to impart *more* information than God intended or fitted them to convey: besides a vast mass of dubious tales which a presumptuous priesthood have either incorporated with or stuck to the divine text, a mass entirely conjectural, and totally useless: besides

---

* I cordially congratulate brother Cole on his entrance into the kingdom of the Messiah. Two or three years since I thought of him as the King once said of every discreet young scribe, " Indeed you are not far from the kingdom of God." Brother Cole is not the only respectable member of the bar who has recently bowed to the sceptre of the mighty Lord. Father Campbell, a few weeks since, immersed four members of the bar of high standing, in Somerset County, Pennsylvania, together with several other persons of the same place, of much influence in society. Several Methodist preachers have also lately obeyed the ancient gospel. One and a brother exhorter was immersed in the primitive faith by brother Philips of Steubenville, Ohio, and one by myself who called to spend an evening with me, on his way through Virginia to Ohio. When lawyers and preachers thus come into the kingdom, it is not only a striking proof of the power of the truth, but matter of great joy, as by their influence and example others may be induced to come into the fold of God.—ED. C. B.

† We have much reason to be thankful for the success attendant upon the proclamation of the ancient gospel every where. Although I devote but little of my time, except the first day of every week, to the oral teaching and preaching of Jesus Christ, I have had the pleasure of immersing more than thirty disciples in my own immediate neighborhood, within a few months back, into the faith of the apostolic gospel.—ED.

19

gross insults offered to the God of truth by audacious attempts to augment the credibility of his
information by human researches or the exhibition of repeated declarations: besides, I say,
these atrocious wrongs done to divine intelligence, our heavenly visitant has just cause to
complain aloud of another gross indignity offered to her hallowed person, by the rude hands
of ungodly men. By them her fair celestial robe
has been torn into fragments; the integrity of her
sacred form has been violated; her graceful limbs
have been dislocated or broken to pieces; and
her very bones, stripped of their natural covering and made bare, have been deprived of every
original tie. Upon her beautiful form every daring anatomist, learned, and unlearned, has exercised his dissecting knife; and, after mangling
it into such slices as suited his perverted taste,
locked them together again, in such ludicrous
combinations as best comported with his wayward fancy. By this barbarous treatment the
loveliness of her heavenly image has been destroyed, her power to captivate the human heart
annihilated, and her graceful form distorted and
disfigured by artificial and unnatural deformities; so that, instead of a visage possessed of
irresistible charms, she is compelled to exhibit
a mangled carcase, a haggard skeleton of naked
bones hung together by human wires. Christian reader, there is no misrepresentation, there
is no exaggeration here: there is but a faint outline of the indignity offered to God's gracious
message, by a self-created order of men, who have
had the address to procure to themselves unlimited human confidence, with the title, the honor,
and the sanctity of God's lot.

But to use plain language, the outrage committed on the order, connexion, beauty and power of the divine message, by profane sinners who
have broken it into chapters, frittered it into
verses, ground it into catechisms, and after flay-
ing, picking, and completely disjointing it, have
sent it forth in the true skeleton guise of confessions and creeds, calls aloud for the severest reprobation of every real friend of Jesus Christ.
Shall it be asked, Is not God's intelligence a
most hallowed object? Has it not come from the
sovereign Lord of all? What mortal, then, will
dare to alter, or derange or displace even a jot or
tittle found therein? Does not God know infinitely better than man the arrangement, both in
respect to time, words, and matter, which it is
proper for him to adopt, and which the benefit of
his creature man requires him to observe? Is it
then within the daring effrontery of miserable
sinners to impugn, to deny this knowledge?
Will they tell the infinitely wise God to his face,
that he knows not how to arrange and connect
the materials of his communication to the best
advantage, nor how to render them as beneficial
to the human race as they might be made, or as
that race could themselves render them; and
that therefore, his arrangement, connexion and
diction must be changed, and the whole message
new-modelled? Is there nothing horrible, nothing awfully profane in this impudent interference? Surely we ought to remember that all
God's ways are perfect, and that to his work nothing can be added, or change performed on it,
without manifest impairment of its fitness to answer its purpose. And we ought, also to remember that God is a great economist, a very summary agent, who accomplishes in an instant by a
single exertion of his will, simultaneously, many objects; and that nowhere is this truth more
illustriously displayed, than in the operations of
sacred writ on the human mind. By every new

idea which God conveys into the soul of man,
he not only enlightens the understanding but
electrifies his heart. By him light and heat are
imparted together. He does not as human teachers usually do, first propose in technical forms
and language, cold as polar ice, rules of action,
and then discharge red hot bullets, glowing motives, to drive the enlightened into motion. God's
precepts and motives as they stand in scriptural
array come simultaneously on the conscience
with all the light, authority and power of a God.
On the whole soul they act at once. At the same
instant do they inform the mind and move the
heart. But by the chilling, ludicrous operations
of the frittering, crumbling, dislocating, distort-
ing and new-modelling system, is God's message completely divested of this ineffable power.
By its malign influence, the fitness of God's word
to direct the understanding, and impress and impel the heart at once, or in other words to excite
such feelings and emotions there, as the ideas
presented in the divine message, are calculated
to excite, is entirely destroyed; and no doubt, to
this paralyzing process, to this impious, uncommanded, unauthorized interference of daring sinners with the order, arrangement and connexion
in which God has judged it most proper and useful
to send his instruction to perishing men, is its astonishing inefficacy to be ascribed. Did mankind do as the Saviour not only recommends,
but peremptorily enjoins, and as David and other
pious men constantly did; did they diligently and
attentively read God's message just as it appears
in sacred writ, unmixed, unaltered by man, and
seriously reflect or meditate on its infinitely important information, it is impossible that the human
mind could remain in that listless, careless, cold,
unmoved state in which we generally behold it,
even among those who loudly boast religion.
But when God's address to sinners is stript of all
the power and energy, of all the beauty and loveliness which it possesses, when presented to them
unaltered, underanged, unadulterated, undiluted; and is exhibited in the form of a string of
metaphysical questions or abstract propositions,
is it any wonder that its energy should evaporate
during the process of such an enfeebling transformation, and that the mortal torpor, so alarming
to reflecting observers, should ensue?

But the gross impiety and enfeebling effect of
this daring interference with God's word, are but
two of the many sad evils, which this unhallowed practice has produced. Of these evils, however, I shall at present take no notice.

                                             A. Straith.

Religious History of Dr. A. Straith.
Written by himself at the request of the Editor.—Pub.

Dear Sir:—An outline of my religious history
is this. About thirty years ago I determined to
carry into effect a purpose, which had been occasionally visiting my mind from my boyhood, of
investigating the two important questions, *Has
God indeed spoken to the human family; and if he
has, what has he said?* Upon forming this resolution, I determined to consult none of those productions called evidences of christianity, no sermons, no commentaries, no bodies of divinity,
&c. but the volume alone which purported itself,
and was generally admitted, to be a divine communication. This volume I consulted in the
original Hebrew and Greek. After it was perceived, that I was seriously disposed, I was induced by my Presbyterian acquaintances, to
unite myself to that society, and after some time,
though I had never seen the inside of a theological school, and knew nothing of the drilling of a

preacher, I was induced to accept a *licence* to preach, which I continued to do for two or three years as it suited me, but without fee or reward. At last I found the arbitrary spirit of my party did not suit the independence of my mind, nor their views quadrate with the views that were daily opening to my inquiries; and, on the 20th day of April, 1811, I sent the Presbytery the following note. "It is my desire and request, after much deliberation, and for a variety of reasons not necessary to be stated in detail, that the Presbytery enter on their records a minute, purporting my voluntary separation:—it being my intention as soon as opportunity may present, to unite with that body of christians known in the United States by the denomination of Independents; their principles of association being more congenial to my sentiments than any other."—The result of this movement was a bitter and unrelenting persecution, attended with the excitement of such prejudices, and outpourings of abuse, that I resolved to suspend my endeavors to communicate what little I knew, or thought I knew, of the divine message, and since that time I have seldom heard those foolish and unprofitable harangues called sermons. On the 9th instant, however, at Harper's ferry, I heard one from a Presbyterian orator, two thirds of which consisted of circumstances, which if they did exist, were certainly considered by the Holy Spirit too insignificant to merit his notice, and a considerable portion of it, of matters that related to the orator's dear self; so that, these superfluities being deducted, the residue was pretty nearly reduced to the diction of the Holy Spirit. On the same day I exhibited to a large collection of people the evidences which had satisfied me that immersion was the action enjoined by Christ on all his followers, and accordingly submitted to it. I have been requested to suffer the address to be published, and perhaps after some consideration I may consent to it.

I neglected to annex the Presbytery's entry. "Therefore Dr. Straith is no longer considered under the care of this Presbytery."

I am, with respect, your ob't. serv't.
ALEX. STRAITH.

Essays on Man in his Primitive State, and under the Patriarchal, Jewish, and Christian Dispensations.—No. XI.

Jewish Age—No. III.

NEXT to the *constitution* or natural compact at Sinai was the institution of the symbolic worship. The Jewish religion is a wonderful display of Divine wisdom, goodness, and condescension to the wants and circumstances of mankind. No infidel ever understood it, no man can understand it and doubt the Divine truth of christianity. To lay down a diagram in figures, which should one thousand five hundred years afterwards, and not before, be read and understood, by millions of human beings as plain as a literal description could be, containing a whole volume in the compass of a single sheet, exhibits such an insight into futurity, as no human being ever did, or ever could possess. Suppose that some person were to pretend to be divinely inspired and commissioned, and, in the mean time, would afford to the living indubitable proofs of his mission by a stupendous display of Almighty power, but designing to have the same credit with posterity a thousand years hence, that he has with the living, how would he most likely obtain that credit? The evidences, which, when *living*, he presents, he cannot present when dead. Let

him, however, leave behind him any work which when examined shall be found to contain a knowledge of future events and developements, which no human being could possess, this knowledge being as supernatural as a power which could lift the mountains, must afford equal proof to all who examine it, as the miraculous display of physical energy. Could any man have written in symbols, or laid down a diagram in figures and numbers presenting a full description of America before Columbus discovered it, and a history of all the changes which have taken place since its discovery till the present year; I say, could such a work have been executed and deposited in the archives of the Spanish government, well attested as the genuine work of a Spanish prophet, who had died at any time, say a hundred years, before Christopher Columbus was born, no person could rationally doubt the inspiration of the author, nor the certainty of the yet future and unaccomplished part of it. Such a work is the symbolic worship of the Jews' religion in all its prominent characteristics and import, in reference to the institution of Jesus Christ.

On the doctrine of chances it would be more than two billions to one that any fifty incidents could all happen in any one character to live a thousand years after the incidents detailed were recorded. Now, more than one hundred distinct incidents are found in the Jews' religion and history detailed concerning the Messiah, all of which exactly met in him, and were circumstantially completed in him. This is an argument in proof of the mission of Moses and of Christ, against which the gates of scepticism cannot prevail.—Whatever proves the mission of Moses proves the mission of Christ; and whatever proves the mission of Christ proves the mission of Moses. This is a happy arrangement, which is in accordance with the whole Divine scheme of things.

If a pretended chemist should, in testing or explaining the affinities of certain elementary principles, mingle and combine such simples as have no chemical affinity, it would not prove the whole doctrine of chemistry a whimsical or imaginary science. Or should a pedagogue, when instructing infants in the powers of vowels and consonants, form unnatural combinations in syllabication, it would not prove that the powers of letters and the import of words were unintelligible and indeterminate. Neither does the foolish and whimsical interpretation of types and symbols prove that all symbols and types are arbitrary, unmeaning, unintelligible, and undefinable things. Yet in this way some reason. Because some young novices, and some old visionaries, have made types where there were none, and misapplied those that were; therefore, say they, the whole system of types and symbols is unmeaning and unintelligible.

It is well for man that *faith* and not *reason* is the principle, on which all revealed religion is founded. For although some sceptics scowl at the idea of faith, and extol the superiority of reason, as a guide, yet the truth is, that faith is incomparably a more safe guide, than reason. Not one in a thousand reasons infallibly or even correctly. Numerous as are the falsehoods believed, they do not bear the proportion of one to ten to the errors committed in reasoning. And were a man to make reason his sole guide, even in the common affairs of this life, and reject all faith in human testimony, he would be in proportion as he lived conformably to his reason, the greatest errorist in his day. Hence it was that the Grecian and Roman philosophers erred more extravagantly, and ran into wilder extremes in religion, than the tribes which implicitly followed tradition, or acted upon the principles of faith. Not a husbandman in ten, who attempts to strike out a new course in agriculture, but miscarries oftener than he succeeds. And so precarious are the best reasoners upon the plough and the shuttle, that nothing is relied upon but experiment. Not a husbandman in ten can rely upon his own judgment or reason in deciding the pretensions of a new plough, or of a new mode of cultivation, until experience has taught him its merits or its defects. Hence, experience is continually correcting the errors of reason. Hence an ounce of experience is worth a pound of reason in the common business of life. They then, who believe, or in other words, rely upon the experience of others in human affairs, err less frequently, and much less fatally, than they who rejecting faith, or the experience of others, set sail upon the ocean of speculation and reason. The wise man rests upon experience, until he is able to prove by reason, or by his own experiments, that his ancestors have erred. If every generation was to reject the experience and instructions of the past, there would soon be a rapid retrogression in the improvements of society. But, without being tedious, they use reason best, who pay a good regard to those who have lived before them, and never dare to rely on their own reasonings, any farther than they have proved them by experiment. He that drinks water to extinguish the burning sensations occasioned by swallowing vitriol, though he reasons plausibly, does not reason more discordantly with fact, than the majority of reasoners who reason themselves into universal doubt. If then, in the material world, and with reference to the common business of life, men more frequently err in implicitly following their own reason, than in following the experience related to them by others, how much dependence ought to be placed upon sheer reason, in the things pertaining to the invisible and future world. But there is one tremendous consequence attached to the errors of reason in things pertaining to the spiritual and eternal world, that is not necessarily attendant on errors pertaining to temporal affairs. Experiments may, generally do, and almost universally might, divorce us from these errors.—But if experience of our mistakes in religious faith, or in rejecting faith altogether and adopting reason, is to be the means, the sole means of detecting them, deplorable beyond the powers of expression will be the detection of our own sophistry.

But whither have I strayed from my purpose? Out of the abundance of the heart the mouth speaks, and the pen writes; and as I have been preparing some documents of this sort for the appendix of the Debate in press, I find that when I write for the Christian Baptist, my pen will wander off into a much frequented path. To return, then, to the symbolic worship:—

There is a most ingenious and instructive symbolizing or adumbrating of the christian history or facts in the whole history of the Jewish people. Their history, as well as their worship, seems to have been designed for figures or types of the Kingdom of the Messiah.

Joseph was sold into Egypt by his own brethren. He was sold, too, for thirty pieces of silver. His own good conduct and the Divine wisdom bestowed upon him, after a few years degradation, sorrow, and suffering, placed him upon the throne, or made him viceroy of Egypt. He forgave his brothers and provided an inheritance for them. Israel went down into Egypt;—Moses

was finally raised up to bring them out;—and then a new scene of things commences. Now he must be blind indeed, who cannot see in the decree that exposed Moses, in his exaltation, Divine call, and mission, in his leading Israel through the Red Sea, in the mediation at Mount Sinai, in the peregrinations through the wilderness, and in a hundred incidents of this history, an exact coincidence with the facts recorded by Matthew, Mark, Luke, and John, concerning the Messiah. But these historic incidents though evidently figurative, and made to have a prospective reference to the incidents in the evangelical narrations, do not rank among those symbolic institutions, whose primary design was to prefigure the Messiah and his redemption. Such were the instituted acts of worship belonging to the tabernacle.

Sacrifice is as old as the fall of man, or at least was instituted immediately afterwards, and continued in practice among all those favored with divine revelations, till the sacrifice of the Messiah, when it legitimately ceased. All sacrifices since offered have been unauthorized by God. He accepted one sacrifice which forever perfects the believers as to sacrifices. This divine institution has spread all over the world. No nation of antiquity, and, perhaps, not a tribe now on earth is without some vestiges of it. It was an institution that human reason never could have originated. The idea that the blood or life of any animal could be acceptable to the Creator of the world has no archetype, model, or analogy, in the sensible or visible creation to originate it. The ancients confirmed all their covenants over the bodies of slain animals. But this practice seems to have originated from the sacrifices, which were offered at the times when God commanded them in confirmation of any promise, which he gave to any of the human family. Thus the patriarchs confirmed their covenants, and from them the custom obtained of confirming all covenants with blood. Hence the seals of all the articles of stipulation of solemn import were seals of blood. And when this custom was laid aside, and wafers instead of victims became the seals of written contracts, they were colored red, as the symbol of the seals of blood.

Among the ancients, the gradations in the obligation and solemnity of all agreements were, first, a mere verbal promise without witness; second, a verbal promise before witnesses; third, an oath; and fourth, a victim slain. Thus when the national constitution of Israel was consummated, Moses, after he had audibly spoken the whole items and conditions, had, by divine appointment, animals slain, and the blood was scattered over the parchment and the people. So the highest pledge or assurance of God's love ever given to mortal man, greater than promise, oath, or even human sacrifice, is the blood of Jesus, by which the new institution has been ratified. But after these generals, we may come to particulars in the symbolic worship at another day.

EDITOR.

Extract of a Letter from a Christian Brother at Brookfield, N. S. to his friend at Eastport, Me. dated July 18, 1829.

"When the experience of professors is soothed by flattery, and moved by the breath of words, 'tis feverish, impetuous and unstable; like the furious tide it ebbs and flows, rises, and falls as circumstances change. But sacred, divine, immutable truth, the blessed source of fortitude and faith in the christian's soul, holds firm empire, and like the steady pole star, never from its fixed and faithful point declines. Hence the apostle, " We walk *by faith*, not by *sight*." Sense is governed by what *appears;* faith by what *God says*. Sense looks inwards and rests on happy *impulses;* faith looks outward on the sure word of *prophecy*. Sense has her anchor cast in the midst of *frames changeable as the wind*. Faith has her anchor cast within the veil, whither the forerunner is entered, and is both *sure* and *steadfast*, and secures effectually from being tossed to and fro amidst storms of trouble and dark seasons of desertion. Sense judges by what is felt. Faith forms its judgment, not by the things which are seen, but by the things that are not seen, calling the things which are not as though they were. Sense says, now I am in the favor of God, for I *feel* it, now he is my God, for I *find him so*. (How so?) I feel nearness to him in prayer, I feel lively in duty with warm affections; these are my *assurances* and *demonstrations* of his love, and I am full of comfort. But what is the result when these are not enjoyed? These, depended on as the soul's sunshine, and lost, contrary inferences are drawn. Now I am not in the favor of God, for I *do not feel it*. Now he is not my God, for I do not find him so; I am dead and stupid in prayer, &c. &c. Thus, frames, feelings, and impulses, produce no solid ground of comfort. When these are enjoyed, the dependent thinks himself a christian; and when not enjoyed he thinks himself a cast-away;—changing his thoughts of his state as his feelings do, like the wind; and varying his comforts like the weather.

What an unsettled state of mind a professor is in, who has no way to judge of himself but by these changeable things! What doubting, trouble, and perplexity ensue from depending on sense and frames for comfort! But when comfort springs from the right source, it is pure and solid, and joy and peace abound because of the word of his grace.

" He that believes—He that believes not."

The extent of a moral obligation is not to be determined by man's limited disposition to obey or comply. That notwithstanding the decisive tone assumed by the sacred writers on the necessity of divine influence, how unconscious they seem of any thing like embarrassment and perplexity; when they exhort men to duty, they are not only free in the utmost degree from all metaphysical explanations and distinctions, but use plain, confident and energetic assertions of the obligations of men to repent and believe. On faith their statements are simple and intelligible, being a spiritual perception and cordial reception of divine truth. The object to which they direct its operations is the gospel; and such a statement the gospel affords as is adapted to impress such a conviction of guilt and wretchedness, as will compel the anxious mind to an immediate and cordial reception of the message of mercy, which, by the sacredness of its subject-matter, communicates a holy influence to the mind that receives it. This cordial and spiritual reception or belief, is regarded by the sacred writers not as a merciful *succedaneum* adapted to the impotence of our nature, for the more rigid obedience which the law demands; but as the instituted method of becoming personally interested in the divine favor, and of final salvation. Such a *pistis* or faith, such a *peithomai* or divine persuasion, in consequence of the peculiar sacredness of its object, forms the only principle of acceptable obedience. It is *that* faith which "purifies the heart and works by love." While it leads the mind which possesses it to an entire renunciation of all meritorious claims derived rather from itself, or its influence or grace received, and to an exclusive, undivided reliance on the *perfect atonement* of the Lord Jesus Christ, as able to save to the uttermost; and thus the believer has *one* object to *look to* and *live by*—Christ, the all in all. For me, Eternal Spirit, may truth's effulgence my path illumine. May I by your celestial guidance led, fix deep in my own heart your sacred testimony, and in my life its holy influence transcribe. O help me to note how all the parts of truth agree in one fair, one finished, one harmonious whole; which, in all its gradations and beautiful connexions, begins, proceeds, and ends, in love Divine! And may the blessing of the Lord go with you, and in all things keep you free of the fell venom and malignant tendency of error, which strikes at the root of truth—pollutes the heart, and is as a cup full of delicious ruin. May you go forth in " the fulness of the blessing of the gospel." The more that you are a man of *one book*, humble, and counting yourself " less than the least," the more will you enjoy primitive simplicity, and thus more acceptable to God, whatever you may be to the world; and as a minister of Christ, study to approve yourself to him who will not forget your work of faith and labor of love."

I am, yours, affectionately,   J. B.

The Moral Law and the Christian Baptist.

WE did not intend so soon to return to the idle bravado of this publication; but our attention has been so forcibly arrested by its extravagant paradox respecting the moral law, that we consider it due to our readers to justify our former strictures, and to lift up the warning voice to them, by exhibiting the sentiments of Mr. Alexander Campbell, on the subject of the moral law. 1 As he never appears to write or think in a serious mood, it may be possible that he has thrown out the odd fancy to which we now refer, as a sort of rhetorical banter, or that he merely intends to try an experiment, and to ascertain how far he can lead his blind admirers upon the implicit faith which his authority alone challenges. He boasts of the number and of the attainments of his readers and partizans; but he should remember, that there is as much of ignorance and illiterature among his advocates, as among his opponents. 2 Who are the Baptists that have been converted to his new creed?— They are such as were previously Arminians, or Sandemanians, such as never stood firm on the basis of truth, such as were ready to take up with the first leader of discontent and faction, such as always opposed united effort in promoting the spread of the gospel, and the advancement of education, and those who through ignorance, become an easy prey to greedy error. 3 Of course there are many who read Mr. Campbell, and who fall in with his views in part, who are not included in the above description, they not yet being thoroughly indoctrinated. It is thorough converts to which we refer.

Among his other pre-eminent qualifications, it would appear that Mr. Campbell is an *antinomian*. 4 The following extract will show that he is one *anti-nomos—against the law*. These are his very words :—

"But to return to Mount Sinai. The preliminaries were, *una voce*, without a dissenting voice, agreed to. The constitution was pronounced by the living God, in words audible, and distinctly heard by about two millions of people. It was written also by the finger of God upon two blocks of marble. This constitution was perfectly political. Few seem to appreciate its real character. Many insipid volumes have been written upon it, both since and before Durham wrote a quarto volume on the Ten Commandments. Some have called it the *moral law*, and made it the law of the whole spiritual kingdom; affirming that Adam was created under it, and that even the angels were under it as a rule of life; nay, that it is now, and ever will be the law of the whole spiritual world. Yes, indeed, though it speaks of fathers, mothers, wives, and children, houses, lands, slaves, and cattle, murder, theft, and adultery; yet it is the moral code of the universe." '

"I remember well when I was about to be cut off from a Baptist Association for affirming that this Covenant or Constitution at Sinai was not the Moral Law of the whole universe, nor the peculiar rule of life to christians. Another shade of darkness, and one degree more of political power on the side of three or four very illiterate, bigoted and consequential regular Baptists, would have made a John Huss or a Jerome of Prague of me. But there was not quite darkness nor power enough, and therefore I am yet controlling this feather which makes the mould for those characters you now read."

Here we perceive that the law uttered from the mouth of God himself, ratified by the most awful interposition of the divine presence, and recognized and expounded by our blessed Saviour, is nothing more than a secular policy, a worldly constitution. See how extremes meet! Excessive Arminianism and Antinomianism are more nearly allied than at first we should imagine. Was the holy law given at Sinai nothing more than a form of government? 5 Was that tremendous covenant nothing more than a sort of treaty upon which the people were to coalesce? Were the Israelites not a nation before this time? What were they in Egypt? What were they during their sojourn in the wilderness? 6 Did ever any system of secular policy teach the love of God and the love of our neighbor? 7 The history of the world cannot produce an instance. Mr. Campbell is surely thinking of the coming debates of the Virginia Convention, of which it is understood he is to be a member. Perhaps he is already preparing his speeches. He is maturing the whole doctrine of Constitutions, and means to bring in Moses as the first Exemplar. 8 The fable of the river fish which played off into the sea, and was soon overmatched, one might suppose, would offer a seasonable hint to him. 9
—*Columbian Star.*

Note 1. I never wrote nor spoke one word against any "moral law." Define *your* moral law, Mr. Brantly; and then call bible *things* by bible *names.*

2. I will not rank among my advocates any so ignorant of the Old and New Institution, as the writer of these remarks, though ever so well skilled in the traditions of the elders, or in the dogmas of Egyptian theology.

3. Who told you, Mr. Brantly, that such were my converts? Do you know them all? or are you the judge of all hearts?

4. Yes; call me antinomian, then arminian, then heretic, then socinian, then deist, and the work is done. The ninth commandment says, in my Bible, "You shall not bear false testimony against your neighbor." How does it read in your "moral law," Mr. Brantly?

5. Every law that the Most High promulged,

was nothing more than a form of government. Did he ever promulge a law which was not to *govern* men individually or collectively?

6. This gentleman appears as ignorant of the Jewish history, as of the genius of their religion. It was only *three months* after their departure from Egypt, until this constitution was ratified and carried into effect.

7. Yes; God's constitution and secular policy did it. The "royal constitution, or royal law," governing Israel, and that of the Lord Messiah, governing the New Kingdom, made piety and morality the best policy. But Mr. Brantly will have something else to be better worldly policy for a nation than piety and morality; and thinks that the Governor of the world is like himself.

8. This is pitiful indeed! What convincing logic! What does it prove?—that I am doing what he says? No: for I have never written one sentence on the subject. What then does it prove?—that my views are erroneous? No. What then? that Mr. Brantly has the jaundice? Yes.

9. And that is what Mr. Brantly fears. I wish that he would keep in shallow water, only let it be clear.

I can find leisure only to remark, that I am sorry to witness such a spirit breathed from a "teacher in Israel" as that in the "Star" of the 29th August. If I thought Mr. Brantly was as ignorant of the constitution of the theocracy, and as negligent a reader of the essay to which he alludes, as these cynical remarks import, he and his readers would merit my sympathy rather than my censure. But I cannot think that there is such an ignorance or such a negligence. I must, in spite of all my charities, impute these invidious remarks to the spirit of this world. I am sorry to find Mr. Brantly so entirely unacquainted with me, and with the cause I advocate; and worse than all, that he has so little regard for the Author of the Christian Religion. It is of no consequence that I call him to an account, or enter into a discussion with him: for he will not argue a single point with me. He will occasionally aim a poisoned arrow at me; or he will *ad captandum vulgus*, to inveigle those who do not read, and will not read for themselves, occasionally throw out such slanders and insinuations as those above quoted. I will not now analyze them. They speak for themselves. My readers will please again read the essay from which he has taken his text.

If I do not, before my essays on the Jewish and Christian Dispensations are closed make it manifest to the impartial, that these preachers of the law, neither understand what they say, nor whereof they affirm, then I will assent to be governed by the doctrines and commandments of men; and for the sake of an honorable editorship and a rich congregation, agree to preach whatever the prejudices of the age require.
														Editor C. B.
September 17, 1829.

Election.—No. III.

The following sentence is found in our last essay: "Having ascertained in a summary way, the elector, the person first elected, the ends of the election, the time when it began, and when it shall terminate, I shall speak of the principle on which it proceeds," &c. Let us then speak of the principle on which a person might, at any time, be admitted into the elect institution, or church of God and Christ.

1. This election divides itself into two great

departments, the Jewish and Christian churches, the first receiving its members on the gross, limited, and partial principle of the flesh, i. e. relationship to Abraham by the line of Isaac and Jacob. The second, admitting its members on the exalting, universal, and impartial principle of faith in Jesus Christ.

2. The election of individuals to church privileges in the first of these principles, viz: Fleshly relationship, can be justified only by the fact, that in the infancy of the world, the rudeness of the age, &c. rendered the introduction of the higher and more refining principle of faith, if not impossible, at least altogether impolitic, in regard to the ends to be accomplished by the institution.

I need not observe that the change of principle from *flesh* to *faith* occurred at the coming of our Lord Jesus Christ, and that many of the Jews, who stood in the first apartment of the election, failed to be received into the second for want of the proper principle of faith in Jesus. But the limited nature of family descent, the extent of belief as the first principle of Christianity, the degradation of the infidel Jews, and the elevation of the believing Gentiles, are all set forth by the apostle, in the following beautiful allegory, in his letter to the Roman disciples: "Now if some of the branches were broken off, and you, who are a wild olive, are engrafted instead of them, and are become a joint partaker of the root and fatness of the olive, boast not against the branches, for if you boast against them you bear not the root but the root you."

You may say, however, the branches were broken off, that I might be grafted in.

"True—by *unbelief* they were broken off, and you, by *faith*, stand; be not high minded, but fear—For if God spared not the natural branches, perhaps neither will he spare you. Behold then, the goodness and severity of God: towards them who fell, severity; but towards you, goodness, if you continue in his goodness; otherwise, you also shall be cut off; and even they, if they abide not in unbelief, shall be grafted in, for God is able to graft them in. For if you were cut off from the olive, by nature wild, and contrary to nature were grafted into the good olive, how much rather shall those who are the natural branches be grafted into their own olive?"

The Magna Charta of the whole elect institution are the covenants made by God with Abraham; from the superior and inferior branches of which are derived what the apostle, in *Heb.* viii. calls the new and old, the first and second, the inferior and better; or, in other words, the Jewish and Christian, covenants, i. e. the law and the gospel—the one enjoyed by the Jews on the footing of *flesh*, the other by men of all nations on *faith*. It is thus the apostle, by a metonymy of principle and privilege, styles the law *flesh*, and the gospel *faith*. The infancy and rudeness of the age of law, is indicated by the apostle in the following metaphor: "So the law was our *school master* until Christ." Again allegorically— "Now I say, as long as the *heir* is a minor he differs nothing from a bondman, although he be lord of all; for he is under tutors and stewards, until the time before appointed by his father." The grossness of fleshly relationship and the spirituality of faith, together with the substitution of the last for the first of these principles, is thoroughly enforced upon the Galatians, in the allegory of Sarah and Hagar: "Cast out (says the scripture) the bond maid and her son; for the son of the bond maid shall not inherit with the son of the free woman. Well then, brethren, we

3 Z

(christians) are not the children of the bond maid, but of the free woman:" i. e. not of flesh but of faith. It must be manifest, therefore, from what has been written, that the entire election has been managed, first and last, upon these two principles, and that the one half now superseded the other.

I shall close this paper with two or three remarks upon *faith* and family *relationship*: It is on this limited and partial principle of birth or blood, that the old world has obtained its chiefs, judges, dictators, kings, sultans, emperors, priests, &c. and the consequence has been that an alarming proportion of such officers has proved the worst of tyrants and knaves. The fact is, that, in the old world, a man may, by family connexion, become the heir both of religious and civil offices, to which neither his talents nor character at all entitle him. Yet this was just the principle on which the Jews obtained their kings and priests; nay, it was the principle, also, on which they were introduced into the church. Their priests, therefore, were most corrupt. Nadab and Abihu were slain of the Lord, and the two sons of Eli also perished in their immorality and presumption. The arrogance of Rehoboam issued in the dismemberment of the kingdom; and but few of his successors were famous for piety. Religion flowing from family pride went on apace until the appearing of John and Jesus, the first of whom told the people not (now) to say "We have Abraham for our father;" and the last that they must be "born *again*," if they would enter into the reign of the Messiah; not that the new birth and faith are the same thing, for they are not. The new birth is a thing proposed to the believer in Jesus—Nicodemus believed, and to him it was said, "You must be born again." i. e. of water and Spirit. Preachers are very apt to mistake here, and to tell the unbelieving man that he must be born again; but it is a fact that no unbelieving man can be born again. The scriptures expressly assert that "to those only who received him he gave the power of *becoming* the sons of God, even to those who believe upon his name; who are born not of blood, nor of flesh, nor of the will of man, but of God;" i. e. by water and Spirit—the way which he wills his children to be born to him on the principle of faith. The apostle defines faith, in general, to be "the confidence of things hoped for, the evidence of things not seen;" of course christian faith, in particular, must be an assent to the evidence of the existence of the Messiah, though we do not see him, and a confident reliance on him as one who means what he says, and who will perform what he has promised. Thus true belief engages both the head and heart of a man. "He that comes to God must not only believe that he exists, but that he is a rewarder of those who diligently seek him." This definition is illustrated in the 11th chapter of Hebrews, by the faith of Abel, Enoch, Abraham, Isaac, Jacob, Sarah, Moses, and his parents, Gideon, Barak, Samson, David, Samuel, and the prophets. But as Cain believed in the existence of God, without exercising any confidence in him as a rewarder of his worshippers; so, many now have only the one half of true faith, and believe that Christ exists, without having the least confidence in either him, his words, or his institutions. Hence they wont be baptized, they wont be born again, neither-ought they, until they can trust his words. Sinners, look to the history of his faithfulness.

I would observe that the teachers of christianity ought never to go out of the Bible for a defi-

38   25

nition of faith. In regard to the origin of faith, I would just observe, that, like our affections, it is not dependent upon the will, but upon evidence. Other powers of the mind, as recollection, imagination, &c. are dependent on the will in their exercise, while the *will* itself is solely under the direction of that law which governs all animated nature: viz. the desire of happiness.

Man is possessed of other powers of acquiring knowledge besides the power of believing; for he is a creature of sense and reason, as well as of morality: but while for the propagation and education of mankind, God has laid hold of appetite, passion, reason, &c., rather than faith; yet it must be granted that we cannot see how our gracious Father, in bestowing upon our fallen family a system of morals, should make the practice of it to proceed upon any other principle than that of belief. Faith and sense act with supreme power among mankind, and are the two most universal principles of our nature.— They are very closely allied to each other; and it is not easy to say where the one begins and the other ends. Had the Divine Father predicated our salvation upon a fine imagination, a strong memory, a piercing intellect; military, philosophic, and literary talent; upon high birth, or even good morals; then we should have seen coming up to the christian altar our Homers, Virgils, and Miltons; our Lockes and Newtons; our Washingtons, Alexanders, &c., and men might have complained. But so long as it is written, "He who believes and is baptized shall be saved," no one who has ears to hear, and feet to carry him to the water, has the least ground of complaint. The principle, then, on which christian election proceeds, is faith, a power of action in human nature alike distinguished for its utility, purity and universality.   PHILIP.

Election.—No. IV.

WE now come to speak of the sovereignty of God, and the point of our religion at which it appears.

In order to arrive at our conclusions with effect, I would observe that the following phrases are used in scripture to mean the same thing: "justification from sin," "righteousness of God," "righteousness of faith," "forgiveness of sins," "remission of sins." If the reader will bear these phrases in mind, I shall show him shortly how the same sentiment comes to be varied into five different expressions by the scripture's writers.

Meanwhile, let us peep at the history of the remission of sins among the Jews. The Jewish religion was exceedingly comforting to the man of God in this respect; much more so, indeed, than modern christianity; for if a man sinned, the Lord had appointed five different sorts of animals, as the mediums of remission. These were calves, lambs, kids, turtle doves and young pigeons, any of which the man of God could carry to the altar, and by confession at the sanctuary obtain forgiveness of the God of Israel.

If a man feared God, he would have been very poor who could not muster a pair of young pigeons. But if he could not, the Lord had appointed what was styled "the poor man's offering." If, says the law, "he (the sinner) be not able to bring two turtle doves, or two young pigeons, then he that sinned shall bring for his offering the tenth part of an ephah of fine flour for a sin offering; he shall put no oil upon it, neither frankincense; for it is a sin offering." Again—"Then the priest shall make an atonement for him as touching the sin that he hath

sinned in one of these (sins specified in the beginning of the chapter,) and it shall be forgiven him." *Lev.* ch. v. As rich and poor were liable to commit sin, these different animal offerings were evidently appointed with a reference to the different degrees of wealth among the worshippers—while the very poor and destitute were permitted to present what we have seen was called "the poor man's offering," stript of every·article, of oil, wine, and frankincense, which could render it expensive. Thus our heavenly Father, in giving a law, made all possible provision for the comfort of the worshipper, by instituting the above means of forgiveness.

In christianity the institution for forgiveness is baptism, which is not to be repeated, a real superiority over the law remission: the Lord Jesus, by his precious blood, sanctifying in this way the believer once for all (his life.) "Be baptized every one of you, in the name, (i. e. by the authority) of Jesus Christ for the forgiveness of your sins. Thus the symbol of remission in the true religion is changed from animal *blood* to *water*; while the blood of Christ, between them, like the sun at the equator, reaches to the ends of the earth, and forms the real cause of pardon to all who ever shall be forgiven, from Abel to the resurrection of the dead.

Now, I say, it is just here that the sovereignty of God appears in christianity in forgiving sins of men in the institution of baptism, upon the principle of faith in the blood of Christ, as the great and efficacious offering for all. And now we shall see how the same sentiment came to be expressed in five different ways by the scriptures, while the phrase "forgivness of sins" was the expression used among the vulgar of the Jewish nation. The doctors and teachers of law, more affected and technical, varied from the civil style, for the more learned and juridical expressions, "justification from sins," "remission of sins." The Doctors, then, in speaking of the officers at the Temple, pronounced them "justified," and again they said they were constituted "righteous" according to law, i. e. in offering they had done just what the letter of the law demanded; for had they not done so, the Lord ordered that every such person should be cut off from among the people.

Now, the Apostle being a Jew, and infinitely skilled by his education in the *technia* of the Jewish lawyers, adopts their own phrases in discoursing with them on the subject of forgiveness, e. g. he says in the synagogue of Antioch in Pisidia, "Be it known to you, therefore, men and brethren, that through this man is preached to you the forgiveness of sins; and by him all that believe are justified from all things from which you could not be justified by the law of Moses." And as the lawyers made use of the word "righteousness" in reference to remission, or to describe a person whose sins had been forgiven: so the Apostle, speaking of the baptized believer whose sins had been forgiven, and was justified in the language of the law, calls this the righteousness of God; because it was a righteousness granted by God; and the righteousness of faith, because it was on the principle of faith in the Son of God, that any one was allowed to approach baptism. I pertinaciously keep baptism in view in this matter, both because the scriptures make it the institution of forgiveness, and because it is altogether unusual both in law and religion, either to forgive or condemn on account of a latent principle. Faith is not justification; forgiveness or remission is justification; and faith is the principle, and the only principle too, on which remission can be obtained. Now both faith in Jesus, and baptism for remission, were novelties to the Jews; and it was in the promulgation of these things that they took offence; and God's sovereignty is exerted in the changing of the righteousness by law for the righteousness by faith, and in offering the last not to Jews only, but to Gentiles also, and in degrading the former from their ancient standing for not embracing the good message of favor.

When we consider the display of God's sovereignty in the introduction of christianity, it appears both immense and absolute: absolute, because he consulted no one among men or angels; immense, because it swept away at one stroke all that the world of both Jews and Gentiles accounted holy and venerable. The law was a ponderous and imposing establishment. Its theology and morality distinguished it from, and rendered it superior, infinitely superior to, all the systems of the Gentiles.

The sanctuary and its inestimable furniture, the altar, the priesthood, and the services, consisting of offerings, sacrifices, washings, meat and drink offerings, &c. their tithes, feasts, fasts, synagogues, and books of law, with their psalters and book of prophecies, that these, all these, founded upon divine authority, most flattering to the senses, and handed down to them from the most remote antiquity, should be abandoned for the sake of Christ and the remission of sins, with the other remote advantages held out by christianity, was what the Jews could not contemplate but with amazement mingled with abhorrence. Yet did the Divine Father, in his absolute and uncontrolled sovereignty, command all the Jews every where to do this, and to do it too on pain of incurring his highest displeasure: but the same sovereignty which withdrew authority from the law of Moses, denounced at the same time the superstition of the whole world besides, and ordered all men every where to repent and believe the gospel; and here it is that the sovereignty of God appears in our religion in all its sublimity. What! denounce the religion of the world, and introduce a new one!! Yes, all, all was condemned and withdrawn, and the aspirant after immortality left with nothing before him to save and encourage him in the thorny road through which he followed his Master, but the flesh and blood of Jesus Christ; every thing now called for spirit instead of letter, and love instead of law, until righteousness should be established in the earth, and christianity became the religion of the world.

This exhibition of the divine sovereignty, gave birth to many questions between the Jews and Christians, the management and settlement of which devolved chiefly on the Apostles. Of these questions, the following are a few: the christian method of remission made them ask, "What profit there was in circumcision," i. e. the law of Moses? and the admission of the Gentiles to this remission on the same footing with the Jews, made them enquire, "What advantage then has the Jew?" These two questions are answered by the Apostle, in the 3d chap. of his epistle to the Romans. The third question, was levelled at the very vitals of christianity itself; for the remission being granted on the principle of faith, and consequently by a favor, and neither by works of law, or righteousness, which men had done. The Jews, from an ignorance of human nature, and the true character of God, mistook the tendency of the Apostolic doctrine, and ask thirdly, whether christianity was not essentially this, "Let us sin that favor may abound?" In reply, the Apostle shows that it was by faith and favor, that both Abraham and David were saved, and that law had originally issued in the death of the first of men, and in all who came from his loins while the law of Moses which they all knew was good only for showing how severe and universally sin had taken hold of mankind.

The casting off of the infidel Jews, gave occasion finally to the question—Whether God had not departed from his former character and violated his promise to Abraham? This question is answered in the famous ninth chapter of the same Epistle, a portion of Holy Scripture which some Sectaries have most shamefully abused, but which I hope this view of the matter will ultimately redeem from their partial and limited systems—Here the Apostle shows them that they considered it no more infringement of the divine character when for popular purposes, he preferred their fathers, Isaac and Jacob, to Ishmael and Esau; and raised to the throne of Egypt Pharoah by whom he wished to make his power known, and who on account of his own bad character, should have been damned long before he was either drowned, or even made monarch of the land of Ham; but both Ishmael and Esau and Pharoah, and even they themselves, when cast off were treated by God in the only way their abominable character merited; and therefore, God dealt with them as the potter does with a dishonorable vessel; he dashed and would dash them in pieces.—Moreover, the Apostle lets them know that the blessings of christianity, were never held out or promised indiscriminately to Abraham's seed, but only to so many of them as believed Justification from sin is a blessing, which, indeed, it were folly to offer to an unbelieving man, whether Jew or Gentile.

Having given the reader a clue to the question of God's Sovereignty, I shall now review some Scriptures which have been quoted as opposing the doctrine of the Christian Baptist, against the partial pickings of sectarianism.

1. It is said, Romans viii. "Whom he foreknew, he also predestinated to be conformed to the image of his Son, that he might be the first born among many brethren.—Moreover, whom he did predestinate, them he also called: and whom he called, them he also justified; and whom he justified, them he also glorified."—Now what is this, but that God, as may be seen from fact and from the ancient writings of the prophets, foreknew, that the Jews and Gentiles, indiscriminately, would believe on his Son, and for that, had predestinated or appointed them to share in his honors; he therefore, in the fullness of time, called them; remitted their sins, and glorified them as his only worshippers, by making to rest upon them, the Spirit of God and of Glory.

But it is said: "Well then, he has mercy on whom he will have mercy, and whom he will, he hardens." This is true—and blessed be his holy name, that he will, if the scriptures mean what they say, have mercy on all who believe, not of the Jews only, but of the Gentiles also; and the unbelieving wretch who will not accept of pardon on the gospel plan, ought to be hardened and heated seven times in a furnace of fire; Romans ix. The ancient idolaters were hardened, and the case of the modern Jews illustrates this verse. Again it is said, Eph. 1st chapter, "According as he has elected us in him, before the foundation of the world." This is also very

27

true, and means just what it says; but, observe, that it is one thing to elect us in him, and quite another to elect us to be in him. It would be one thing to elect a Jacksonite, and another to elect a man to be a Jacksonite; the one would be to make him a Jacksonite, and the other to elect a Jacksonite to some other matter; but there it was "Before the foundation of the world." We many times determine who shall fill certain offices, so soon as we have succeeded in the election of a superior officer. Many Jacksonites were marked out for offices long before the general was inaugurated; and so the disciples of the Messiah, were chosen to love and purity, before the foundation of the world—while the disciples of Mahomet, Confucius, and others have been appointed to no such distinction.

But again, "No man can come to me unless the Father draw him." How common is this form of speech, even among ourselves! Who has brought you here, and what has drawn you here, are phrases which are current every where, and yet, who ever thinks that the charm or power by which one person is drawn after another is a physical one. The power of drawing is moral, not physical, and so the Saviour, in the 5th John, says that no man could come to him, unless the Father draw him, because the political mob which he addressed, had followed him, from the gross and animal reason of having got their bellies filled the night before with the loaves and fishes; paying no regard to the divine power which wrought the miracle, "Verily, I say to you, you followed me not because you saw the miracle, (Father in the miracle,) but because you did eat of the loaves and were filled."

PHILIP.

No. 4.]   NOVEMBER 2, 1829.

KING AND QUEEN, VA., May 10, 1829.
Mr. EDITOR:—IN your remarks on the 16th Query, in the Christian Baptist, of March last, you say, "Millions have been tantalized by a *mock-gospel*, which places them as the fable placed Tantalus, standing in a stream, parched with thirst, and the water running to his chin, and so circumstanced that he could not taste it." There is a sleight of hand, or a religious legerdemain, in getting round this matter. In your answer to the 19th Query, in the Christian Baptist of April last, you have, I think, though I dare say without intention on your part, (as I believe the remarks on the 16th Query, were especially intended for the populars,) given us a key to unlock the mystery contained in the sleight of hand business quoted above. The query reads thus: "What does the Saviour mean in these words: 'He said to them, It is your privilege to know the secrets of the reign of God, but to those without, every thing is veiled in parables, that they may not perceive what they look at, or understand what they hear.'" Now you say "he means just what he says. The language is exceedingly plain," &c. And I think so too; and now for the key to unlock the sleight of hand, &c. You say, and I suppose you mean what you say, &c. You say then, "Some persons in a future state will be beyond the reach of mercy; some are in the present; they have shut their eyes, alienated their hearts, seared their consciences, and most stubbornly resisted the Spirit of God. There is a certain crisis beyond which the moral disease becomes incurable, as well as the physical. Some men have survived this crisis for a period. In the physical disease they live hours and days

when all physicians know they are incurable. It is not true in physics, that "while there is life there is hope;" for there is life when there is no hope. Neither is it true as the hymn sings:

"While the lamp holds out to burn,
The vilest sinner may return."

Now many of the Jews, in the days of Joshua, of the Lord Jesus, and of the apostle Paul, had survived this crisis. The Saviour treated them accordingly; and will he not be as merciful when he sits upon the throne of final judgment, as when he stood on earth, saying, "Come to me, all you weary and heavy burthened?" &c.— Most assuredly he will, yet he will condemn the wicked. Those persons then, from whom he studiously veiled the gospel, were those characters he knew to be such as to exclude them from forgiveness and repentance. This is a fact, and an *awful fact*, that under the Reign of Favor, it is possible for men to become so depraved, so wicked, so hardened, as to be beyond the reach of cure. Unless this fact be apprehended and regarded, there will occur many passages in both Testaments inexplicable;" and I think so too, Mr. Editor, and thought so too, before I saw your remarks on the 16th Query, and I think the remarks on the 19th Query afford a key, as I said before, to unlock this mysterious sleight of hand! Now the scriptures tell us that man is born into the world as a wild ass's colt; yet vain man would be wise! But the apostle tells us, "For after that *in the wisdom of God*, the world by wisdom *knew not God*, it pleased God *by the foolishness of preaching*, to save them that *believe*." Now from *your remarks*, it appears that there were at different periods of the world, men living, from whose hearts the gospel or grace of God, was *studiously veiled*, while you admit it may be so, at the present time. Now as none of our *popular preachers* do certainly know, whether there may not be some of this class of persons among the congregations to whom they preach, from whose hearts the Lord *studiously veils* the gospel, how would you have them to preach? Would you have them to tell a lie? and say, that each and every one of you can, by reading the sacred scriptures, become partakers of the divine nature? When the Lord may have seen fit to suffer a part of them to fulfil that promise, which says, "Behold, you despisers, and wonder and perish, for I work a work *in your day*, which you shall not believe, though *a man declare it* to you!" Now if it ever pleased God, by the foolishness of preaching, to save those that believe, I have no doubt but it pleases him yet. For the gospel is preached by living witnesses, having the Spirit of Christ, who stand as in Christ's stead, for the purpose of *turning the minds of men*, towards these things which are able, through divine grace, to make them (from whom the gospel is not veiled) wise to salvation; namely, the word of God and prayer. One thing I do know, that the *populars* about here, (unless they be hypocrites,) think so, for they labor night and day; and they preach the ancient gospel too, which I heard before I heard of you, Mr. Editor! They preach as they always have done, saying, "The time is fulfilled, the kingdom of heaven is at hand, repent you, and *believe* the gospel." They say too, "Ho! every one that thirsts, come you to the waters." And they say, too, "Come to me all you weary and heavy laden, and I will give you rest." That "The Spirit and the bride say come, and let him that hears say come, and let him that is athirst come, and whosoever *will*, let him come, and take the water of life freely." They warn people, too, saying, "Take heed lest this come upon you."

" Behold, you despisers! and wonder and perish! for I work a work *in your day*, which you shall not believe, though *a man* declare it to you!" Now, this is the way the *populars* preach about here. I do not know how they preach in your part of the world. Now the Lord Jesus veils the ancient gospel which they preach now, just as he used to do, from whom he pleased. According to the command, it is the duty of all men to seek the Lord, for all have sinned. But God has mercy on whom he* will have mercy, (as you have shown in your remarks in your answer to the 19th Query, quoted above.) A man, therefore, cannot believe† to the saving of his soul, unless God give him the power; for they that thus believe are blessed.‡

Be pleased to give this a place in your paper, and thereby oblige a subscriber, who is

A Constant Reader.

—

Reply to the above.

Upon reviewing the sixteenth and nineteenth queries referred to, it appears that the writer of the foregoing animadversions must have read these queries with a captious intention,—with a jaundiced eye. The sixteenth query explicitly states the exception which is amplified and illustrated in the nineteenth. Under the sixteenth query, p. 530, it is affirmed, "that all men, to whom the gospel is proclaimed, can believe it, if they choose; except such as have sinned so long against the light, as to have fallen into the slumber and blindness denounced against those who wilfully reject the counsel of heaven." Now, the above quotations from the answer to the nineteenth query, page 538, are expressly confined to such characters. "Those persons, then, from whom he studiously veiled the gospel, were those, whose characters he knew to be such, as to exclude them from repentance and forgiveness." But how, in the name of common sense, does the exclusion of such characters, by the righteous judgment of God, from a participation of the blessings of the gospel, furnish a key for the relief of the popular preachers from the religious legerdemain, or sleight of hand business, alleged against them? Does it necessarily follow as a universal truth, that, because some men have so sinned as to render themselves incapable of reformation by the belief and obedience of the gospel, that all, to whom it comes, labor under the same incapacity? Or, does it necessarily follow, that because some have so abused the divine goodness as to render it inconsistent with the immaculate dignity of the divine character to admit them to a participation of the blessings of salvation; that all to whom the gospel comes must be considered precisely in the same condition? Surely no. And if not, how does it go to relieve the populars from the impeachment of tantalizing mankind with a mock gospel, while they indiscriminately assert the entire incapacity of all, to whom the word of salvation is sent, to believe and obey it? While they assert, that without something more than either the preacher or hearer can do, the gospel can neither be believed nor obeyed; consequently, that it can only minister condemnation, for "he that believes not shall be damned." Did Peter or Paul so preach the gospel either to Jews or Gentiles? Let the populars produce the specimen, and they will stand exonerated. But

our correspondent seems mightily concerned for the character of the popular preachers. He alleges their ignorance of the characters of their hearers; and gravely asks, "How would you have them to preach? Would you have them to tell lies? and say, that each and every one of you can," &c. Surely no. We would not have them tell lies; nay, we would not have them even to hazard such a thing; and, therefore, would have them to preach just as did the apostles. When Paul preached to the Antiochians, *Acts* xiii. we may justly consider him as ignorant of the personal characters of his hearers, as any of our modern populars can be; and yet he did not tell them that they were incapable of believing; nor yet, "that every one of them could, by reading the sacred scriptures, become partakers of the divine nature." Instead of this, he preached to them Jesus and the resurrection, and through faith in him the remission of sins, with certification, "that whosoever believes in him, is justified from all things." And concludes by warning them to beware, lest that which was spoken by the prophets should come upon them; saying, "Behold, you despisers, and wonder and perish," &c. Let our modern preachers go and do likewise; and they will neither risk preaching lies; nor yet expose themselves to the just censure of tantalizing their hearers with a mock gospel, as they are in the habit of doing; when, after laboring with apparent fervor to convince and persuade their hearers, as Paul did in the passage above cited, they gravely conclude, by assuring them, that after all that can be said or done on both sides, it will be all lost labor without the intervention of a supernatural influence, over which neither preacher nor hearer has any control; so did not Paul nor any of the apostles. Nor have we a single petition for such an influence on record in the apostolic writings; neither as offered up by the apostles, nor by the churches at their request, in behalf of the success of the gospel in the conversion of sinners.

It seems to have been the happiness of our correspondent to have heard the ancient gospel before he ever heard of the editor of the Christian Baptist. This will not be thought strange, since the said gospel was in the world seventeen hundred years before said editor was born. But the query is, Did he hear it from the populars? If we believe his own account of their character and preaching, we should think not. He styles them "living witnesses, who stand as in Christ's stead." Who preach, saying, "The kingdom of heaven is at hand; repent you, and believe the gospel." According to these characteristics, we should first conclude that they are false witnesses, because they never witnessed one single item of what they preach, if so be it is contained in the bible; for this plain reason, they were born too late. We should next conclude them shameless pretenders, if they assume to be in Christ's stead, either to the church, or to the world; for none ever occupied this place but the apostles, who had power on earth to forgive sins, and to settle for ever all the affairs of his kingdom in this world. And lastly, as to the subject of their preaching, (if our informant be correct,) that "the kingdom of heaven is at hand," they belong not to the gospel dispensation at all, but to the preparatory dispensation of John the Baptist; for this was his text,—the subject of his introductory ministration. That the Baptist's gospel was really gospel; that is, good news, in its day, no one will question; also, that it is more ancient, than what we, at this day, call the ancient gospel, will be readily granted; but what

* If God, peradventure, will give them repentance to the acknowledging of the truth.
† It pleased God by the foolishness of preaching, to save them that believe.
‡ So, then, they that are of faith, are blessed, with faithful Abraham.

is this to the purpose? The ancient gospel, of which we speak, began to be preached on the day of Pentecost, Acts, chap. ii. It announced the coronation of the King and the commencement of his kingdom by the Holy Spirit sent down from heaven; with the remission of sins, through baptism, to every believing penitent sinner, thenceforth to the end of time, that should take the benefit of the institution, divinely appointed for that purpose. The successive publication of this pure apostolic gospel is what we plead for, without any additions, or intermixture of human opinions. If our correspondent and his populars be in the full possession of this blissful, ancient, apostolic gospel, we should rejoice to know it: but from the spirit and tenor of the above communication, we have our doubts that it is far otherwise. For as already stated in the close of the reply to the sixteenth query, "that only is gospel, which all can believe who wish to believe." Or, in other words, that only is good news to all, which presents a good adapted to the capacity, the condition, and reception of all that choose to receive it. And such most evidently, is the apostolic gospel.

T. W. *alias* Thos. Campbell.*

Query.

Did Christ die in our law room and stead, according to the popular preaching?

Answer.—This is one of the many ignorant, unprofitable, vain questions, so strongly reprobated by the Apostle in his letters to Timothy and Titus; "whereof come envy, strife, railings, evil surmisings, perverse disputings of men of corrupt minds," &c. "rather than godly edification which is in faith."

As an advocate for a genuine scriptural reformation by the re-exhibition of the ancient apostolic gospel and law of Christ, once delivered to the saints, I feel imperiously bound to protest against all such impertinent and unprofitable questions, as have no direct tendency to godly edification, of which there are thousands in this speculative, contentious age. For this purpose I would humbly suggest to all who desire to promote and enjoy this desirable reformation, to meet all religious queries with a direct appeal to the Bible; viz. What does the Bible say? Does it afford any direct and explicit information upon the subject? If so, well. Let it be so. But, if not, we have nothing to do with it. Let it pass as an untaught, unprofitable question, with which we have no concern. By so doing, we shall continue in the Apostles' doctrine; for so they teach.

But if this should not at all times satisfy the querist, we may next for his sake, reasonably appeal to common sense, by inquiring what good, what utility will result from the solution of the question, provided it could be solved with certainty? Would it increase our faith, our hope, our love to God or man? Our piety, temperance, justice, benevolence? Would it make us more devout, more humane, more humble, more pure, more spiritual? In short, would it advance our moral or religious character? If not, why spend time, why exhaust our mental energy in vain speculation? By proceeding thus, we shall avoid those vain janglings and strifes of words, whereof comes envy, &c. so vehemently and repeatedly prohibited by the Apostle. Of this sort is the above query. The gothic barbarism of its form, the awkward abstrusity of its import, consign it to the dark era of monastic ignorance, of scho-

* A Correspondent now at Bethany, to whom was referred the above letter in the absence of the Editor.

lastic jargon; the bible knows nothing about it; it shocks all common sense. A thousand such questions are not worth a drink of water. The bible furnishes a direct answer, in proper terms, to every important question that can be proposed concerning the death of Christ, either by Jew or Gentile. The apostle to the believing Galatians, tells them collectively, that "he gave himself for our sins, that he might deliver us from this present evil world, according to the will of our God and Father." To the Jews among them he declares, that "God sent forth his Son, born of a woman, born under the law; that he might buy off those who were under law;"—under the curse; and, that this was accomplished by the manner of his death; for it is written, "Accursed is every one that hangs on a tree." To the believing Corinthians—that "he died for our sins according to the scriptures." To the believing Cretans—that "he gave himself for us to redeem us from all unrighteousness," &c. &c. What need, then, for the above artificial barbarous question, except to support some abstruse speculative theory? If we want to know why Christ died—why on a cross—for what—for whom—the effects of his death, &c. the bible affords direct pertinent answers to all those interesting questions; and this should suffice. Why should we desire to be vainly wise above what is written?   T. W.

The following letter from Richmond, Virginia, is from an intelligent and amiable brother, who was called home to the king's own country in August last.   Editor.

"Richmond, June 12, 1829.

"*Mr. Campbell,*

"Dear Sir—Your views of the christian religion, as given by one who styles himself "A Lover of Truth," in a communication to the Constitutional Whig, so entirely correspond with mine, that I cannot withhold my mite of encouragement in the dissemination of your opinions. They are based upon the Rock of Ages, and the gates of hell shall not prevail against them, nor all the arts of priestcraft subvert them. We are yet in that state of the church represented in Revelations by the beast and his image. The time is coming, however, when the Angel of the Covenant shall preach the everlasting gospel.

"Sectarianism is, indeed, the greatest enemy to christianity. The Spirit of Christ never made a sectarian. Come from what source he may, he is none of Christ's. The apparent good that is done by sectarians in spreading the gospel, arises rather from party emulation, than the love of our Master. Sectarianism has been, is now, and ever will be, so long as the monster lives, a great obstacle to the progress of christianity.— Does this need illustration? Send forth, as missionaries, to a heathen people, a Romish priest, an Episcopal clergyman, a Presbyterian, a Baptist, and a Methodist. Each in the pomp and circumstance of his peculiar tenets, styling himself the ambassador of Christ, teaches the christian religion—all in different forms, and none adhering simply to the Book which all profess to follow. What is the conclusion of these poor heathen, forming a judgment, as all ignorant people do, from the sight?—any other, methinks, than that these ambassadors are sent by one Master for one and the same purpose. And reasoning to prove it would be in vain. Every christian knows that this is a stumbling block to unbelievers, even in christian countries, where the people are comparatively enlightened. The mischiefs of sectarianism are not confined to its effects on the heathen. This monster still tyrannizes in our land of liberty and gospel light, and thousands are kept from the Redeemer by the shaking of his many heads. In this country sects are free, while sectarians are slaves to the prejudices and dogmas of their sect.

"Where is the love of Christ, that when one would not sacrifice a cassock or a wax light, and another would not give a little more water, to save these souls from perishing; lest the pope, the archbishop, the presbytery, or what not, of temporal lordlings, should anathematize? Here the civil law, as it should do, tolerates all religions: but it does not follow that God will bless idolatry, will-worship, or any departure from the purity and simplicity of his instituted worship. We want missionaries to preach the gospel to our doctors of divinity, right reverend, and reverend clergy, and fashionable—very fashionable laity.

"Sectarians will do some good by uniting on the Bible Society, if they do not counteract it by their sectarian Bible Classes.

"Persevere to the end. You are in a good cause, and the Lord will own and bless your efforts.

"One that loves you for your work's sake,
"A Disciple of Christ."

Louisa, August 22, 1829.

Brother Campbell—You will be much surprised, no doubt, to hear of the rebaptism that has lately taken place in this neighborhood, (Louisa county.) In the summer of 1827 sundry persons were immersed into the name of the Father, Son, and Holy Spirit, by brother James M. Bagley. As some of those persons lived in the vicinity of the Fork church, Louisa county, it became a matter of question by said church, whether they should be received into their fellowship.

They finally agreed to refer the matter to the last association. This, however, was not done. One of those persons (a colored man) wishing to join the Fork church, could not be admitted, it seems, because he had been baptized in the "new way," as they said; that is, because the preacher said, "I *immerse* thee *into* the name," &c. instead of "I *baptize* thee *in* the name," &c. They determined, therefore, to hear his experience over again, and to baptize him in the old way. On the first Sunday in June, he told his experience to their satisfaction, and on the last Saturday in July he was rebaptized by the Rev. Timothy T. Swift!! after being disappointed several times; and the poor negro exclaimed, as he came out of the water, " I an't no Campbellite now"!!* Is not this a new thing under the sun? And was it not taking the name of the Lord in vain in the most solemn manner? When we consider all the circumstances of this case— that the preacher who immersed this Ethiopian, in 1827, was regularly ordained according to the Baptist order, and a member at that time of a regular Baptist church; a man of intelligence

* He should have said, I, having been baptized into my own experience, and agreeably to the commandment of Mr. Swift, I am a Swiftite now. As Mr. Swift is, perhaps, the first protestant on earth who has ever committed such a deed, I think it due to him and to posterity, that he should have the honor of it—therefore, to distinguish this *ism* from all others, I move that it shall be called Swiftism. In the vocabulary for the next theological dictionary Wallerism will be found to denote the burning of the holy scriptures; and Swiftism the rebaptism of immersion into baptism, and of *into* into *in*. If men can thus profane the most sacred institutions in obedience to their own antipathies and envy, what "ark of the covenant" can save the sanctuary of the Lord from the desolating abominations of the Roman eagles?—Ed. C. B.

and of exemplary character—I say, when all these things are considered, should we not weep over the ignorance, and prejudice, and bigotry of many in this enlightened age? I am almost ashamed for the Baptists to make this communication. But it is our duty to expose every false way.   N. H.

The following documents are worthy of an attentive perusal. A very amiable young physician, of good education, and of a clear, discriminating mind, who lately embraced the ancient gospel, is addressed in the following letter from an Episcopalian minister, from whose cathedral he had strayed into the fold of Christ. The parties are both known to myself, and the circumstances relative to his immersion. This letter was written to him by the reverend Episcopal teacher on hearing of his having rode off some hundred miles to be immersed for the remission of his sins. His reply to his former pastor, contains so much good sense and christian independence, that I could wish it to be read by every Episcopalian in the United States. This young disciple, was formerly very taciturn when addressed by his pastor on religious topics, which will explain one allusion in his reply.

Ed. C. B.

July 9th, 1829.

My dear young Friend,—You will not, I trust, take it amiss if I express to you the surprize and regret with which I heard from your father, of the change in your religious sentiments. But my design in troubling you with this, is not a controversial one. I merely wish to set before your excellent judgment a few reasons for questioning the propriety of your course, even supposing that your conclusion were a right one.

You are the eldest of a numerous family; I believe I may add, the best endowed both by nature and by education, and engaged in a highly respectable profession. That you should be looked up to in a great degree by your brothers and sisters, and peculiarly cherished by your parents, is, under these circumstances, a very rational consequence. That you are so, is a fact with which you must be perfectly acquainted. I do not myself know any young man, therefore, to whose opinions a more ready and favorable attention might have been expected to be paid by his immediate connexions, and certainly none who could have calculated more fully on being allowed, after due consultation, to have his own way.

In the honor due to our father and mother, I am sure you will agree that a sacred regard to their feelings and their principles must, of necessity, be included; and that a son, who is at once warmly beloved and greatly respected by them, is the last who could, with any piety or justice, act without regard to either, or show, by any decision of his, the slightest contempt of their opinions. But in abandoning the church of your father, in which you had taken your place as a member in full communion, at your parents' request, and in doing this without one word of previous communication with them—without one attempt to debate the propriety of the measure with those towards whom the word of God directs every reasonable manifestation of gratitude and kind consideration—without a single exhibition of any anxiety to prepare them for the change, or of solicitude to lighten the blow about to be inflicted on their comfort and joy in their eldest and favorite child. Have you done as you would, one day, wish your son to do by you?

Have you acted according to the spirit of the gospel? Have you not been led by your zeal to do a positive evil, at least in the mode pursued to secure your object? And are you sure that your course has produced to others the hundreth part of the pleasure, that it has inflicted pain, on those whose love for you is probably greater than that of the whole united world besides?

I trust you will pardon the frankness of this expostulation. I am a father, and therefore may presume that I can estimate the misery of a parent who sees and mourns over the estrangement of a darling son, much more correctly than you can *yet* do. God grant that you may never experience the terrible reality of such a visitation. But beholding, as I did, the grief of your father; hearing him say that he had passed a sleepless and a wretched night in consequence of your conduct in this matter, and observing the tears of strong emotion which his manhood could not restrain while he spoke, I could easily conjecture the state of your mother's mind, and thought it a duty to intrude myself no longer as a pastor, but as a christian friend, to ask you whether you are not bound in conscience and in principle, to acknowledge your error in taking such a step without consulting them? Whether you are not bound by the precepts of Christ Jesus to reconcile yourself to your parents by every acknowledgment consistent with truth?

I do not mean at all to impeach the soundness of your religious views. My sincere desire is to have you unmolested and entirely free, even from any unwelcome solicitation on that subject. But I do beseech you not to suffer this breach between you and your parents to remain unclosed for want of a speedy and thorough effort to heal it. In the mode of your procedure, you have been exceedingly to blame, because this mode was a plain declaration of want of confidence, want of kindness, want of reverence, want of filial submission. I confine myself to this single point, believing it a plain one, and in the hope that, however your light may exceed mine in the other doctrines of christianity, we shall agree in the practical application of the moral law: "Honor your father and your mother, that your days may be long in the land which the Lord your God gives you."

May the good spirit of the Most High direct and bless you.

Your affectionate friend, &c.   J.

—

Reply to the above—Letter 1.
July 15th, 1829.

My dear Friend,—As it would be highly inconsistent with my profession to take amiss any friendly attempt to convince me of a supposed error, I am very far from doing so in regard to that which you have made. On the contrary, I have to thank you for endeavoring to convince me that I was at fault in not consulting my parents upon my choice of religion, although my own heart as yet acquits me. As I cannot, however, exonerate myself from the charge before others, without declaring the motives which prompted me to that choice, it becomes necessary for me to offer to you an apology for preferring Christianity to Episcopalianism. An apology for becoming a Christian!—and to a professed minister of the gospel! This is strange—but circumstances require it!

As old Mr. Wrenshall set forth in a petition which he wrote for a tailor, that "he had been born and bred a tailor; and, notwithstanding all the vicissitudes of human life, was a tailor still,"

so, I suppose, it happened with me, that I was born and bred an Episcopalian; but, more mutable than the tailor, I am not an Episcopalian still. At least as soon as I knew my right hand from my left, I found myself an Episcopalian—I don't know how—perhaps by hereditary descent; and full, too, of sectarian prejudice, derived probably from the same source from which the children of Papists derive their Babylonish propensities. I was bred an Episcopalian, as far as compulsory attendance on Episcopalian ceremonies could constitute me one, and lived, until my sixteenth year, without religion and without God in the world.

About this time a beloved Christian brother (not an Episcopalian) directed my thoughts and affections, in some degree, towards the Lord Jesus, as the Rose of Sharon that had no thorn; and the occasional reading of the scriptures, and a more particular attention to prayer and to sermons was the consequence. After some time, being taught to consider the Episcopal church as my spiritual mother, and supposing (like any other silly child) that she was the handsomest and best in the world, I introduced myself, at my father's request and yours, to what I then considered her privileges. And although I believed in the doctrine of the scriptures, and wished to obey it, yet, having no certain testimony in my heart or life that my sins were forgiven—that I was born of water and Spirit, and united to Christ, (and I could not have this testimony because Episcopacy had already carefully deprived me of the only one the scriptures have appointed, and that, too, at a time when, on account of infancy, I was unable to agree to, or resist, the measure,) the Lord's supper was to me rather a punishment, than a comfort, because I did not realize my title to it; and yet I was unwilling to disobey what I knew was a command of God, and my conscience was sometimes quieted with the Episcopalian or Pharisaical reflection, that I also had gone through all the preliminary ceremonies of the church, and had therefore as good a right to her ordinances as any other Episcopalian. Still no motive had so strong an influence over my conduct in this matter, as the fear of disobeying my earthly parent.

The fear of the Lord, however, soon began to sink deeper into my soul, and I made stronger efforts to get rid of the burden of sin—but in vain; and my life afterwards was compounded of long seasons of torpid religious despondency, "that frost of the soul, that binds up all its powers, and congeals life in perpetual sterility;" a species of hopeless carelessness, if I may so speak, alternated with transient glimpses of the happiness which religion would have afforded me if I had possessed it in its purity.

"When I was a child I thought as a child, I acted as a child; but when I became a man I put away childish things"—that is to say, when I began to look about me, I became weaned from my spiritual mother, because I perceived that she was neither so well favored nor so good as I was taught to believe. And it seemed to me that a simple rule of judgment would apply. As it would be unwise to consider a lady identical with the house she lived in, the garments she wore, the professions she made, or to judge of her by these, it would be equally so to esteem a church to consist in a meeting-house, a liturgy, or a profession, or by these to estimate her real character. A church is composed of members, and by their conduct the purity of the church (i. e. their purity) must be decided.

After musing on these things and reading in

the Book of God, as I reclined on the verdant carpet of nature, beneath the luxuriant foilage of a spreading tree, I insensibly fell into a reverie. I beheld at a distance an elegant mansion, whose gothic minarets and battlements broke against the light, and whose lofty towers raised themselves towards the clouds. Presently a lady, with her train-bearer, descended from the building and entered into a magnificent carriage, in waiting at the door, and attended by a retinue of servants, which then rapidly approached me, and halted near the place where I was. The lady immediately alighted and came towards me. Her person seemed to be adorned with the gorgeous trappings of fashion; her step was slow and measured; and the striking affectation of her manners could only have been acquired in what I was accustomed to hear called the highest and politest circles. She thus addressed me: "My son, why have you forsaken my house? Why have you not appeared with me on the appointed days, to render praises to my spouse and seek his face? Is not Christ my spouse? Do I not enjoy his smiles? Behold I am rich, and increased with goods, and have need of nothing. My servants are many: they are clothed in silk and fine linen; I reward them liberally, and they praise me, for I am pure and holy." So you did teach me, I replied, that you were the spouse of Christ; and in him who is altogether lovely, my soul delighted; therefore did I seek his face with you; but I perceived that he hid his face from you, and that I could not gain his smiles. You gave me a little book that I might praise him and call to him by reading therein; but he told me that out of the abundance of my heart my mouth must speak, and not out of the abundance of your little book. Nay, your own speech betrays you. Say you, "I am pure and holy?" and does not your little book testify of you that you are a "miserable sinner?" that you have "no health in you?" and that the "burden of your sins is intolerable?" And truly you seem to mourn grievously for your iniquities. Would not sackcloth and ashes become your situation better than this gorgeous apparel? And I beheld also that hatred and enmity, revilings, drunkenness, profanity, and every evil prevailed in the conduct of most of your children. O! you daughter of Babylon! if he whom you call your spouse, had sanctified you, would not your children be holy? You did profess to appear before God one day in the week, while not only then, but during the whole week, your actions showed that your heart was far from him. Therefore, did I refuse to take any longer your counsel, but resolved to follow the directions of him who could not deceive me. My Lord smiled upon me, and in his presence my soul takes delight: therefore do I rejoice in the God of my salvation, who "never leaves me nor forsakes me." Perceiving that pride curled her lip into an insulting smile of incredulity, I added, "You know not that you are wretched and miserable, and poor, and blind, and naked." Repent of your wickedness, therefore, and obey Christ. I now observed anger sparkling in her eyes; and her servants, emulous of each other, began to raise their voices in her eulogy, and withal occasioned such a din that it awoke me.

I could not deny that the Episcopalians, and the Presbyterians, and other sects had faith; but I perceived that it was Episcopalian, Presbyterian, and sectarian faith, producing nothing but Episcopalian, Presbyterian, and sectarian works; that each would boast in his own scheme and hate his neighbor. I therefore concluded it was high

time for me to apply to a teacher sent from God, and to take the holy scriptures as my guide. Believing that my Heavenly Father meant what he said, and that in every thing essential to salvation his words were plain, I threw behind me all sectarianism, and took up the bible. And I took it up with the resolution that what I discovered to be my Father's will, I would endeavor to perform: and if the idea of consulting any human being about the propriety of doing what I believed to be the command of God, had ever entered my thoughts, it would have done so only to be discarded as a suggestion of Satan.

Considering the Christian church as it was first formed by the Apostles, and the ancient gospel as preached by Peter on the day of Pentecost, I perceived that faith in Jesus, as the Son of God and Saviour of sinners, was the first duty; the second, repentance; and the third, baptism for the remission of sins and the gift of the Holy Spirit; and the fourth, that we should walk in newness of life.

Having been all my life dwelling upon the two first principles of the doctrine of Christ, i. e. repentance from dead works and faith towards God, (and, as far as my observation extends, this little primer constitutes the entire library of most sectarians, and the consequence is, that very few of them ever learn to read,) it became necessary for me now to think of baptism. I need not detail the progress of that examination which forced me to conclude that infant sprinkling was not baptism. Suffice it to say, that both in the Septuagint and New Testament, I found that the words βαπτω and βαπτιζω signify to immerse, or dip; and that to translate them thus would make complete sense and harmony of the passage in which they occur; whereas, to introduce the idea of sprinkling, would frequently make absolute nonsense of scripture, (ex. gra. Rom. vi. 3, 4, 5. Coloss. ii. 12, &c.) I also found that faith and repentance were absolute prerequisites for christian baptism, if we wished it to be of any benefit to us, and that the word of God commanded me to be baptized for the remission of my sins and the gift of the Holy Spirit. Coming to this conclusion, therefore, I could not conceive that I was bound, by any principle, to consult my parents, or any body else, about the propriety of fulfilling this duty, any more than Abraham was to consult his wife Sarah about the propriety of sacrificing Isaac in obedience to the command of God.

Besides this, my father's "feelings and principles" in religion, which you say, are worthy of "sacred regard," I knew to be strictly and exclusively Episcopalian; and, as such, I considered them unworthy of that regard. For I do not accustom myself to pay "sacred regard" to any thing which I do not believe sacred and holy; and I cannot admit without reservation, a principle that sanctifies the "feelings and principles" of all parents from those who cause their children to pass through the fire to Moloch, or set them beneath the wheels of the image of Juggernaut, to those who bring them up in papal superstition, or impiously presume to "sprinkle them into Christ's death," (as their traditions would make the scriptures say,) while the parents themselves, at the very time, though they may go to church, and the children, as soon as they are able, show by their works of unrighteousness whose children the word of God declares them to be.

I might, indeed, have gone as Lot went to his sons-in-law, and said, "Up, get you out of this place!" but I would have "seemed as one that mocked to them;" and I feared to rouse in my father those violent passions which it seems Episcopalianism has no power to subdue, and by announcing my intention to enlist them in the use of every means against its fulfilment; thus giving occasion to sin, and finally obliging me to commit a positive act of disobedience.

And taking another view of the matter: religion never was the subject of conversation between me and my father, and I never perceived him to be interested in it. As long as I remained quiet in that net which human ingenuity and the prejudice of education had thrown around him and his forefathers, and in which I was retained from my infancy; as long as I "went to church," as the phrase is, all was well. My being a christian seemed to be a secondary consideration, or rather no consideration at all. I know not how he could expect me to consult him in a matter in which I never saw him interested, and about which he never conversed with me.

Obeying the command, therefore, without consulting man, I received, to use the words of the Presbyterian Confession of Faith, and the declaration of the 27th Article in Episcopacy, "the sign and seal of the covenant of grace, of regeneration, of the remission of sins, and of giving up to God through Jesus Christ, to walk in newness of life." And, oh! that all poor sinners might experience with me that the promises of God are "yea and amen;" that he will bless them who trust in him; that he is able to forgive sin; that the yoke of Christ is easy and his burden light: and that the Holy Spirit is indeed "a Comforter." "Why should the children of a King go mourning all their days?" Why not lay their sins at the feet of Jesus, and flounder no more in the slough of Despond, but wash in the laver that stands between the tabernacle and the altar, that, as kings and priests, they may serve the Lord in the beauty of holiness. "Praise the Lord, O my soul! and all that is within me praise his holy name. Praise the Lord, O my soul! and forget not all his benefits: who forgives all your sin, and heals all your infirmities. Who saves your life from destruction, and crowns you with mercy and loving kindness."

To conclude the matter, I have thus escaped quietly from these Episcopalian and Presbyterian nets; and my father is displeased. How much greater you may judge would his displeasure have been, if my deliverance had been accomplished in defiance of his efforts to prevent it. I rejoice in the liberty and light of the gospel, and in communion with the church of Christ, where we are all brethren, and where we enjoy all that blessedness that is promised to those whom men revile, and slander, and persecute. Unfortunate sectarians! the world does not hate or persecute you; for the world loves its own. I am happy; but my father is angry. And this is strange—that he should mourn for me—that my joy has become his sorrow, and my happiness his displeasure. Do his Episcopalian "feelings and principles" teach him to show his affection for his children by rejoicing when they are in darkness and distress, and have the "spirit of bondage continually to fear," and can enjoy no comfort in religion, no confidence towards God, no certainty of remission of sins, no power to walk in newness of life; and to mourn when they are joyful in the God of their salvation; when they have received the spirit of adoption, and rejoice in the glorious liberty of the children of God?

The free and plain manner in which I have declared my motives, may, perhaps give occasion to offence and misconstruction. My wish has

not been to offend, but to speak the truth; and that I may not be misconstrued, I will observe that my observations have not been directed against any individual, but against that principle of parental dictation in religious matters which my father claims as his right. This may do among Episcopalians, who, from the Bishop to the sexton, seem to me to delight in doing all things " by authority" of men. But I am not amenable to their rules. I call no man master, for I think I have but one master, even Christ; and that to his own master every one must stand or fall. My affection for my parents is unabated. To my heavenly Father my first obedience and love is due, and in heavenly things he alone should be consulted. To my earthly parents my obedience in things not interfering with rights of conscience, and abundant gratitude is due; since they labored for my comfort in temporal things, and incurred expense, and bestowed opportunities of education on me, more than I deserved or duty required of them. In making changes in my situation as it regards earthly things, therefore, their "feelings and principles" I would consult, and consider that I can only show my gratitude for their kindness by rendering to them that assistance in all things which the Lord will enable me to afford, and paying to them that respect which, as my earthly parents, they are entitled to receive. You seem to think that my mother regrets my happiness more than my father. You are in error. She rejoices in it. One presents the picture of " Affection conquered by Pride;" the other, " Pride conquered by affection." I think I have acted in this matter exactly as I would be done by, and that I could not set a better example to my brothers and sisters, than that of consulting and obeying God rather than man.

As to your insinuation that a desire to please others influenced me, I can only deny it. The person you allude to never advised me to receive baptism, or to leave the Episcopal church, though he had ample opportunity to do so. It gives him pleasure, indeed, to behold—nay, " there is joy in heaven over one sinner that repents." Why do you and my father mourn upon such an occasion? This denial, however, I suppose will not avail with my father; and I can only say, that against blindness of prejudice, violence of passion, and obstinacy of unbelief, I will not condescend to defend either him or myself in any other way than by simply declaring that such stories are slanderous and false.

Finally, lest any thing I have said should cause the church of Christ to be misrepresented, I will observe, that for many years, in different parts of Europe, a few of the sheep of Christ, in various sects, have recognized their Master's voice, and refused to listen to the voice of a stranger: from some congregations, two or three—from others, eight or ten, separated themselves, and resolved to take the scriptures as their guide. All these appear to have fallen on the same plan, without any knowledge of each other, i. e. the plan formed by the Apostles. And this "wild fire," as you like to call it, (in contradistinction, I suppose, to the glimmering taper of Episcopacy,) is now making its way in America. In many districts Babylon's bells are tolling, and many of the clergy have been released from the bondage of sectarianism, and are now preaching the ancient gospel; while others are terrified because the hope of their gains is in danger of being lost." We have the same God, the same Saviour, the same Spirit, the same Bible, the same faith, that the people of God scattered among the sects, have. All are admitted among us who profess faith in Christ as the Son of God and Saviour of sinners, and have the seal of remission of sins through his precious blood; and every one is immediately expelled and delivered over to Satan, whose behavior does not correspond to this profession. Nor can a disorderly person be long undiscovered; for, as under the reign of Jesus the blind see, and the deaf hear; so also do the dumb speak, (of which miracle you yourself will acknowledge me to be a living example;) and being thus possessed of all our faculties, we keep a watchful eye over our own conduct and that of our brethren. We have also the same liturgy and confession of faith which the church had in the days of the Apostles; and we can only say to the sects, "Show us your faith by your liturgy and your confessions of faith, and we will show you our faith by our works."

I might speak more fully upon many points, but as the interruptions of business have already detained me, and the letter has extended beyond ordinary limits, I will close by observing that your knowledge of "this way" is very limited. You merely seem to know that "it is every where spoken against." And now do not reason, religion, and prudence concur in saying to you, do not speak or act ignorantly; "for, if it be of God you cannot overthrow it, lest haply you be found to fight against God?"

That the purity and simplicity of the ancient gospel may cease to be foolishness to men, and that the elected by God may be enabled to walk worthy of their high vocation, is my prayer to him who is able and willing to save all who come to him through Christ our Lord.

DISCIPULUS.

Essay on the Eighth day.

"As EVERY thing belonging to the New Dispensation was prefigured and shadowed forth under the Old, so we shall find that different typical intimations were given of this change of the day of weekly rest. The eighth day is particularly distinguished throughout the Old Testament. Circumcision was to be administered to children on the eighth day. The first born of cattle which belonged to the Lord, were not to be received till the eighth day of their age. On the eighth day, and not before, they were accepted in sacrifice. On the eighth day the consecration of Aaron and his sons was completed, and he entered on his office as priest.—The cleansing of the leprosy, which was typical of cleansing from sin, took place, after various ceremonies, on the eighth day. The same was the case as to those who had issues, and also respecting the cleansing of the Nazarites. On the feast of tabernacles, the eighth day was a Sabbath, and was called the great day of the feast. On the first day of this feast thirteen bullocks were offered; on the other six days the number of bullocks was decreased by one each day; so that, on the seventh day, there were only seven bullocks offered. But on the eighth day the number was reduced to one bullock, after which these sacrifices were ended. At the dedication of the temple, when it was completed or perfected, the ark of the covenant being placed in it, Solomon kept the feast seven days, and all Israel with him; and, on the eighth day, they made a solemn assembly. Ezekiel, in his vision of the city and temple and land, towards the end of his prophecies, says, "Seven days shall they purge the altar, and purify it, and they shall consecrate themselves; and when these days are expired, it shall be, that upon the eighth day, and so forward, the priest shall make your offerings upon the altar, and your peace offerings, and I will accept you, says the Lord." Now let the correspondence of the spirit with the letter be observed.

"On the eighth day, when Jesus rose from the dead, those who were dead in their sins, and the uncircumcision of their flesh, were quickened together with him in whom they are circumcised. On that day he was received as the first born from the dead. On the eighth day he was accepted as a sacrifice. On the eighth day, when he was "consecrated for ever more," he entered on his office as a priest; for while on earth he was not a priest. On the eighth day he cleansed his people from sin. On the eighth day, having by one sacrifice for ever perfected those that are sanctified, he made an end of sin offering. On the eighth day, the temple of his body being raised up, and perfected through sufferings, his disciples, on that day, hold solemn assemblies. And upon the eighth day, and so forward, he, as that priest who having consecrated himself for evermore, entered into the holiest of all, and who "ever lives to make intercession" for his people, stands at the altar, as the Apostle John beheld him, having a golden censer with much incense, which he offers with the prayers of all saints, upon the golden altar which is before the throne."—*Haldane's Evidences.*

Moses.

"MOSES at his birth, was saved from the general slaughter of the infants of the Israelites which took place by a tyrant's command, and was afterwards compelled to flee into a foreign country to save his life. Moses, accredited by the signs and miracles which he was enabled to perform—the meekest of men—and the most distinguished prophet, whom the Lord knew face to face, was the deliverer of his people from Egyptian bondage. He was the lawgiver of Israel. He was their leader in their journey through the wilderness to the promised land; and above all, the mediator of that covenant which God made with them. When receiving the law, he fasted forty days and forty nights; and when he descended from the mountain, his face shone with the reflected glory of God. In these, and in many other respects, Moses resembled and prefigured Jesus Christ, with whom also his parents were compelled to flee into a foreign land, to escape from a tyrant's slaughter of the infants in the place where he was born; who was meek and lowly, but approved by signs and miracles which God did by him. He is the great deliverer of his people from the bondage of sin and Satan. He is their lawgiver—the mediator of the new covenant made with the house of Israel—the leader and captain of their salvation, leading them through the wilderness of this world, in which they are pilgrims and strangers, to the promised land of rest, which Canaan prefigured. In entering upon his work, he fasted forty days and forty nights. When he was on the holy mount, "his face did shine as the sun." Jesus Christ was that prophet whom Moses foretold God was to raise up like to him. "Moses verily was faithful in all his house as a servant, for a testimony of those things which were spoken after, but Christ as a son over his own house." "Let us search," says one, "all the records of universal history, and see if we can find a man who was so like to Moses as Christ, or so like to Christ as Moses. If we cannot find such a one, then we have found him of whom Moses in the law and the prophets did write, Jesus of Nazareth, the Son of God."

"One thing further respecting Moses may be remarked. On account of his sinning against God, he was not permitted to enter the promised land, of which he was exceedingly desirous, and he earnestly besought the Lord on this account. The sentence, however, remained unchanged, and he was commanded to say no more on that matter. It was necessary that his death, as the mediator of that first covenant, should intervene before Israel could enter the land of promise, otherwise an important part of the typical resemblance between him and the Lord Jesus, as the mediator of the new covenant, could not have been exhibited. Through sin Moses forfeited this privilege; and, on account of sin, the death of their mediator is necessary, in order that the people of God may be put in possession of their eternal inheritance. From this part of the history of Moses, christians may derive a very useful lesson respecting the refusal of God to comply with his earnest prayer on this subject. In reference to spiritual things, they cannot be too importunate. It is the will of God, even their sanctification, and in this respect they may ask what they will and it shall be done to them. But as to temporal matters, they are very bad judges of what is best for them. And were many of their petitions on that head to be granted, it would prove their ruin, or the granting them would be contrary to some of the great but unknown purposes of God. Moses, although he wrote of Christ, was not fully aware of the correspondence, in all its circumstances, of the part he was acting with the history of the Messiah, which was intended "for a testimony to the things which were to be spoken after," otherwise he would not have urged this request as he did."—*Haldane's Evidences.*

No. 5.]   December 7, 1829.

Sermons to Young Preachers.—No. II.

Some men speak merely for the sake of speaking. It is their object to speak. Others speak for the sake of some point to be gained. Their object is to gain that point. Now the difference between this class of speakers and the other is immense, and distinguishes every period which is uttered. The orator who speaks for the sake of speaking, has himself continually placed before his mind. Like a person looking into a mirror, he sees only his own image reflected. This he admires, and his every effort is to appear to advantage. The admiration of men is courted; and every sentence which is uttered, is spoken with a reference to this end. Hence such orators weigh and estimate all their sentences as happy, or the reverse, as they may tend to advance their own reputation as speakers. Every fine comparison, parable, or allusion—every fine trope or figure which they employ, is valued because of its tendency to exalt the speaker in the esteem of his hearers. Such speakers are easily distinguished by the discriminating part of their audience. There is a stiffness, a formality, a squinting in their public addresses, which no veil can conceal from those of sound vision. I do not allude only to those coarse or fine apologies which we so often hear from public speakers with regard to their unpreparedness, indisposition, and all the unpropitious circumstances under which they appear. These too much resemble the lady in the play—

"Who, in hopes of contradiction, oft would say,
"Methinks I look so wretchedly to-day!"

The meaning of all such apologies is, or appears to be—'If I have done so well under all these disadvantages, how well do you think I could have done, if I had enjoyed all the benefits from which I have been excluded?'

But he who speaks for some great, or good, or interesting object, loses himself in the subject; forgets almost his own identity, and sees or feels nothing but that for which he speaks. His object is in his heart and before his eyes continually. From it he derives his inspiration, his zeal, his eloquence. When a speaker has an object to gain, which his understanding, his conscience, his heart approves—'tis then, and then only he can be truly eloquent.

The fear of man is destroyed by the love of man. That fear of man which brings a snare, which restrains equally the powers of reason and the wings of imagination, can only be effectually overcome by having some object at heart suggested by the love of man. When a man feels his subject, he forgets himself. 'Tis then, and then only, he speaks to the heart, and speaks with effect. The understanding is, and must be addressed, that the heart may be taken. For unless the heart or the affections of men are elevated to the admiration and love of God, and fixed upon him, all religion is a name, a pretence, vain, and useless.

The great end and object of all who teach or preach Jesus to men, should be to gain the hearts of men to him. Not to gain popularity for themselves, but to woo men to Christ. This effort can be most successfully made when we are hearty in the cause, and sincerely, from the heart, speak to the understandings and hearts of men. All, then, who love the praise of men more than the favor of God, are defective, radically defective in those qualifications requisite to the service of the Great King.

But I am now attending to the manner, rather than to the matter, of the addresses of young prophets. In my last sermon to young preachers, I directed their thoughts to the influence of bad habits, and the danger of beginning wrong. Nothing is more disgusting to persons of good judgment than affectation. But to affect an awkward and disgusting original or model, makes affectation doubly disgusting. There is nothing more pleasing than the artless simplicity which sincerity produces. We love nature more than art. While we sometimes admire the skill of the artist, we, nevertheless, more admire and are pleased with the work of nature. So the unaffected orator never fails to reach our hearts or to touch our sensibilities sooner, and with more effect, than the imitator.

In the art of speaking, the great secret is first to form clear conceptions of the subject to be spoken; and then to select such terms as exactly express our conceptions. To do this naturally, is the consummation of the art of speaking. All men can speak intelligibly, and many men fluently, upon the subjects with which they are every day conversant. And if we would make others feel, we must feel ourselves. It has been said by them of old time, He that would make his audience weep, must himself weep. But the man who strives to make others weep, will fail in producing the effect desired by it, unless he is more than an ordinary mimic. But when a speaker is compelled to drop a tear without intending it, then he may expect a corresponding feeling in the bosoms of his audience. These are the lessons which experience and meditation teach.

But in all this we speak after the manner of

men. The man who would gain the skies, must stretch his wings thitherward; and he that would effectually preach Christ, must do it *sincerely*. There is more meaning in this word *sincerely*, than is apparent in its common usage. By it I here mean without any thing foreign to the simplicity, humility, zeal, and love which he himself taught.

I heard here, in Richmond, the other evening, a sermon of the good old John Calvin stamp. I saw old John sparkling in the eyes of my erudite textuary, while he was making Paul and the amiable John the Apostle say what they never meant. But I have respect here to the manner. There was a zeal or a warmth depicted in the countenance of our preacher which seemed unnatural, because it came from a system and not from Christ. He seemed angry when he rose—angry, I presume, because any one could be so impertinent as to think differently from him. He proved nothing to me, save that he had never been initiated into the Temple of Solomon, or had tasted of the waters of Siloam. He only wanted the surplice, the cravat, and the manuscript of our chaplain, who furnished us with the Lord's prayer in writing every morning, to give him a prelatic appearance. There is something very venerable in the English aspect of the Right Reverend Bishop Moore, who was our first chaplain to the Convention. The old gentleman looked like he had got his full share of the good things of this life;—but really when I saw him pull his prayer out of his pocket every morning, and put on his spectacles, and finish his manuscript by reading the Lord's prayer, I could not but sigh for the stubbornness of forms and ceremonies, which are the only things that can pass from one age to another without acquiring or imparting a single ray of the light accumulated either by reading, reflection or conversation. I would offer no indignity to the Bishop of Virginia, for he deserves well for his fine appearance and devout reading of the confessions and petitions prescribed by Queen Elizabeth; save that the spirit of innovation has substituted the word President of these United States in lieu of His Majesty the King of Great Britain. For this courteous change in our favor, we republicans are ever grateful to the Bishop. These prayers have another merit which I ought not to pass unnoticed, because it is a rare virtue in a Right Reverend Bishop's prayers. They are "without money and without price." This is peculiarly acceptable to us republicans; for we have not much faith in mercenary prayers, nor much disposition to make the people pay for prayers for our benefit. For we argue that if any political assembly have a right to make the people pay for a chaplain to minister for them, they have a right to make the people pay for prayers in every pulpit in the state made in their behalf.

But to return to our young prophets. We would exhort them to choose such a subject as will make them forget themselves when they rise to address a public assembly, and then they cannot fail to be interesting, especially if they speak naturally, without that violence to reason and common sense, of which we complained in our former address to them.

EDITOR.

To Dr. A. Straith.

DEAR SIR—Your letters in the "Christian Baptist" have attracted my attention, and have excited a deep interest in the subject treated on. They appear to me to be the result of deep inves-

tigation into the oracles of God, and manifest a spirit of freedom that every devout disciple of the Saviour ought to possess. A time serving spirit to a few of the popular leaders of the various sects, is the greatest barrier to the admission of divine light from the word of God that exists at this day.

There can be no doubt upon the mind of any man, who is not under the influence of a sectarian spirit, that the metaphysical jargon handed down from the pulpits once in four weeks, and impiously called "the gospel of Jesus Christ," has a vicious tendency in keeping back the salvation of the world.

The word of God is wrested to serve the purpose of every sect in christendom. Hence the members of these sects imbibe a sectarian spirit; and when this spirit is raised, and they get their hearers to fall in love with their systems of religion, they call it "the pouring out the Spirit of God."

It is a question with me, whether those who impiously ascribe to the Holy Spirit what are the effect of their own spirits, know what the "outpouring of the spirit" properly means.

I heard a teacher, a good man, take a text— "You are saved by grace." His whole sermon was upon the word grace. Some of his hearers had been taught that it meant nothing more nor less than favor. This good man professes to be specially called and sent by God to preach the gospel of Christ—and he gave it eighteen different meanings. If he really was called and sent by God to preach the gospel, he certainly had the right, if speaking by the Spirit, to give it five hundred meanings, and we dare not dispute one of them, or complain. But this rebellious heart of mine disbelieves what he says; for he cannot produce one particle of evidence to support his pretensions to his call. I therefore conclude that all such are deceived, and are impostors, either intentionally or unintentionally. There appears but a shade's difference between a man who says he is specially called by God, and sent to preach the gospel, and his "Holiness," who professes to be the successor of Peter. One makes any thing and every thing of the word of God, so that his hearers cannot understand what is its meaning. The other keeps the word from his hearers, save that which falls from his lips. And neither of them can speak infallibly, and say they heard the audible voice of God calling them by name, and work a miracle to prove it to be true. Thus they stand upon an equal footing.

It is a lamentable fact, that there are many professors of the christian religion who cannot tell the reason why this or that epistle was written to the congregations, as they have read them. I heard an old teacher advise his hearers to read the scriptures; and to prove the necessity of it, related the following story;—He said, an individual who had attended preaching, was asked where was the text? He replied it was in the New Testament, in the book of Job. Another was asked, on another occasion, where was the preacher's text? He said it was in the New Testament, in the book of Nicodemus. If I rightly understood him, they were professors of religion that could read!!!

I am sorry to say, that there are many families whose whole religion appears to consist in going to a meeting house once in four weeks, to hear a text divided and subdivided, and return home as well contented as if they were "standing perfect and complete in all the will of God." If they can only get their passions wrought up to a certain pitch, and led to believe by this they are

37

christians, that is all and all with them. Hence a warm declamation, whether it contains one syllable of revelation or not, is more admired than reading the scriptures. The inspired penmen, in their epistles, commanded that the communications of the Holy Spirit should be read in their congregations, (not preach from them.) Eph. iii. 4. Colossians iv. 16. 1 Thess. v. 27. Rev. i. 3. But this would be too easy a way of making men wise to salvation, therefore it cannot be done by the populars. They must sermonize it, and make the word of God speak like a barbarian. Alas! alas! when will men cease to pervert the right ways of the Lord, and teach their hearers the word of God by reading for them and with them!

If their hearers are never allowed to inquire of them what they are to understand by this or that part of the word of God, how can they ever get out of the Babylonish orthography? If they mount the rostrum to display their talents like a play-actor, and will not teach the people, but continue to sermonize it from a scrap of revelation, the people will find it difficult indeed to know the word of God, so long as they are led to believe this is all God requires.

In reading over your letters, it appears you are not as explicit upon the foregoing subject as I could wish to see you. Your opposition to the preaching priesthood may have led you to neglect teaching and exhortation. It appears to me these duties are clearly revealed, and they are an important part of the office of a Bishop. "He must be apt to teach." Exhortation is enjoined on all that have this gift, and are necessary to the edification of the congregations at this day. Your having renounced sectarianism, every word you write will be closely scrutinized to render your arguments fallacious. I wish to see you throw around you such bulwarks as shall prove imperishable to all who know and love the truth, and impregnable to all who are disposed to pervert it; and as you appear to have drank so deep into the mind of the communicating Spirit, I do hope you will not cease to communicate to us your views of the excellency of the knowledge of Christ Jesus our Lord, until men shall be contented with God's way of saving the world.

Yours in hope of immortality,
A LOVER OF THE WHOLE OF DIVINE TRUTH.

To A. Straith, M. D., of Virginia.

DEAR SIR,—Having a few leisure moments, I have concluded to address you by letter, through the medium of the "Christian Baptist," edited by Bishop Alexander Campbell of your state. The subject of this address is your communication to brother Campbell, commencing at page 581 of the Christian Baptist, vol. 7th, issued on Monday the 7th inst. In this communication you have boldly and fearlessly entered the dominions of the kingdom of the clergy; and from reason, analogy, and good sense, shown that it is not only inconsistent with the spirit and genius of the christian religion, as established by Jesus Christ, the great head of the church, and the stay and support of christians in all ages of the world; but that it is "impious" to resort to any other means of religious instruction "than those with which God himself furnished us in his own word." That "God has declared expressly that the writings which he has himself furnished us, and just as he has furnished them, unaltered by the tongue or pen of man, unmixed, undiluted with a single human conception, do contain all the information which our salvation needs." And after exhibiting all the means provided by God for the extri-

cation from his present ruined state, concerning which the Bible treats, and showing him how God designs that he may be elevated to complete happiness, you ask, "Is it not mere waste of time, then? Is it not worse? Is it not contempt of God, to resort to tracts, (silly stories,) to pamphlets, sermons, lectures, commentaries, expositions, to the neglect of God's own information on these infinitely important subjects?" This is now to inform you, sir, that your sentiments, as contained in the last Christian Baptist, and just referred to, have created considerable excitement in these regions, and objections and answers thereto have already found their way into the sacred desk. Since these objections and answers to your views have been thus publicly promulged, they have, like your sentiments, become public property, and equally to yours, subject to animadversion, by yourself, or any who may choose to wield the pen upon the subject. It is argued with great zeal and ingenuity by one, whom I believe to be as pious and useful as any man that this state produces, that your views are directly calculated, not only to overturn and subvert the kingdom of the clergy in its popular sense, but to destroy every thing like teaching, preaching, lecturing, exhortation, reading pamphlets, sermons, commentaries, or expositions of the oracles of God. That although we have been commanded to raise our offspring in the nurture and admonition of the Lord; that when we surround the family altar, we are only authorized to read to our children and servants the words of holy writ, without being permitted to make one single comment, by the way of explanation or illustration, no matter how illiterate or ignorant our hearers may be. That your views are rightly calculated to keep miserable and wretched all those millions of the human race, both in civil and pagan nations, that have not the power of reading within themselves. That, destroy the gospel ministry, carry your views to their legitimate issue, and in less than one hundred years this mighty globe will become paganized. Under the prevalence of your views, it is asked, Where would be the utility of the disciples ever meeting, except alone, for the commemoration of the supper, as instituted by our Lord Jesus Christ himself? A further meeting in the house of God, by the disciples of the Lord Jesus Christ, even to read, would be unnecessary and unscriptural; yes, "impious," as this act of reading could be performed at home by all able to read? Here I beg to remark that I, as well as many others who read the Christian Baptist, understand your views very differently from your highly respectable opponent. From your arguments I draw the conclusion emphatically, that you are not opposed to suitable religious instruction, when due and faithful regard is paid to the word of God by the instructed; and that your arguments are plainly and clearly designed to guard men from receiving religious instruction alone from tracts, silly stories, pamphlets, sermons, lectures, commentaries, and expositions, to the entire exclusion and neglect of God's word. This I understand and agree with you to be "impious." And this seems to afford a reason to your opponents to believe that you are wholly opposed to all and every means of religious instruction in christendom, except the simple reading of the Bible. For my views of an apostolic church, permit me, my good sir, to refer you to an extract from the "Scripture Magazine," printed at Edinburgh in 1809, and republished in the "Christian Baptist," vol. iii. page 244.

Should this communication meet your eye, and you feel disposed (as I hope you will) to give us another essay explanatory of the subjects herein alluded to, you will certainly confer a lasting favor on an unknown friend and brother in Christ, as well as on many admirers among us of your writings.   BENGELIUS.

Letter II. to Bishop J., by DISCIPULUS.

SIR—It is some time since I received a letter from you respecting the change in my religious sentiments, in which you charged me with having committed a fault because I did not follow my feelings, or the feelings of others, in preference to my faith. In my reply, I showed that such a course of conduct, even if it were not contrary to the precepts of christianity, would, in the circumstances in which I was placed, have been neither necessary nor expedient. The free exposition of my motives which I thought proper to give you, might, I feared, give occasion to offence; but I am very happy to find it otherwise, and that, in this matter, you yourself have acted upon your faith rather than your feelings.

To that communication I did not expect, nor have I received, an answer. And now you may think it strange that I should reply to your silence. But even although you should consider it an intrusion, I cannot forbear addressing you for two reasons—that I may express to you, as I now do, my approbation of the manner in which I understand you have acted since you received my letter, together with my sincere acknowledgements for the kindness and prudence which marked your conduct; and that I may set before you a general view of the foundation on which we build, the materials used, and a sketch of the manner in which we think the house of God should be constructed.

Unwilling to put a piece of new cloth upon an old garment, or new wine into old bottles, we do not seek to reform sectarianism, but to *restore christianity.* Turning away from Babylon, the mother of harlots and abominations of the earth, we also pass by "her popes, monks, and friars, with all their trumpery," the piles of hay, straw, and stubble, that have been so industriously built up by the various sects which have sprung from her, of whom the Church of England is the eldest born, and to whose polluted fountain she is indebted for the purity of her hierarchy, and come at once to the true foundation, the apostles and prophets, Jesus Christ himself being the chief corner stone. Considering the scriptures as the only rule of faith and practice, and believing that they mean what they say, just as we do; taking literal expressions literally, and figurative ones figuratively, we reject every human system; treating with contempt the verbose attempts at explanation, and the unlawful inferences of those theologians, "who darken counsel by words without knowledge." Indeed, we are very good Episcopalians in this respect, if we may believe the witness which one of your own prelates has borne in our behalf. This I will now take the liberty to lay before you, as it may not probably be so unacceptable as the observations of one so unaccustomed to write as I am:—

[For the testimony here alluded to, see Christian Baptist, page 578.]

Such are our views; and thus must the Saviour and the apostles live and reign when that happy period arrives in which the nations shall cease to be deceived. But now, while sectarians have been indulging in all the intolerance of party zeal, and amusing themselves with the boasted purity of certain articles of religion, they have often trusted their salvation to a mere assent to the correctness of particular forms and doctrines. While seeking to defend their standards, they have forgotten to defend themselves; and clothed with their own garments of ——, immorality and irreligion have mingled with their ranks, piercing them through their armor (for it is not divine) and binding them in chains of slavery, until the whole land is polluted, and it is hard to distinguish friend from foe.

We, however, who, by the blessing of God, live in peace under the reign of heaven, do not erect any standard but the Bible, nor do we receive those who merely assent to its truth, but those only who are willing to do what it commands. If any wish to enter the kingdom of God upon earth, we tell them to apply to "Peter, who will tell them words whereby they may effect their object." For to Peter the keys were given, and on the day of Pentecost the door was opened by him. "What shall we do?" said the people who believed his words and were pricked in their hearts. "Repent and be immersed every one of you for the remission of sins, and you shall receive the gift of the Holy Spirit," was the reply of Peter. The Apostles arrange the gospel thus:—1st. Faith. 2d. Repentance. 3d. Immersion. 4th. Remission of Sins. 5th. The Holy Spirit. And 6th. Eternal Life. But sectarians have broken up the regular arrangement; and some put the Holy Spirit first; others Immersion; many change this into sprinkling, and others throw it away altogether. And in this very way you will find most of the sects have started up, and hewn out to themselves "broken cisterns that can hold no water."

Those who enter the kingdom of heaven are born of water and spirit. After faith and repentance, they are immersed *into* the name of the Father, Son, and Holy Spirit, and receive through the blood of Christ (of which the water is the symbol) remission of past sins, and also a spirit of holiness, which teaches them to love God, his word, and his people; and having their hearts sprinkled from an evil conscience, and their bodies washed with pure water, they trust in God that sin shall no longer have dominion over them, and rejoice in the liberty of his children. Taught of God to love one another, they know that they have passed from death to life, and the peace of God, which passes all understanding, keeps their hearts and minds through Jesus Christ. Being perfect in the Captain of their Salvation, and having the breast-plate of faith and love, and for a helmet the hope of salvation, they are devoted to the service of him who has loved them, and given himself for them. Knowing their own weakness and the temptations of the enemy, they watch, and endeavor to avoid sin; and if, trusting to their own strength, they are overtaken in a fault, upon confessing they are assured of forgiveness, knowing that they have an advocate with the Father—Jesus Christ the Just One.

It is of lively stones we think the church of God should be composed, and not of dull and lifeless ones, which cannot be animated by sprinkling, consecration, or confirmation, any more than they can be sanctified by the crafty hands of a Master in Free Masonry. Nor do we believe they are to be called the *laity,* a name with which they have been insulted by those who wish to raise themselves by lowering their fellows. God does not call his people the *laity,* but saints, children of God, kings and priests, a holy nation, redeemed and precious.

The proper order of God's house we believe to

be plainly showed in the New Testament. Considering that there is no distinction among us, except that which diversity of gifts occasions, we think that he that is the greatest among us should be our servant, and that we are " all brethren." We meet every first day of the week to break bread, as was the practice of the first churches for three hundred years. Not being gagged by human law, we know that we are permitted and commanded to speak one by one in the congregation, to exhort, comfort, and edify one another. We meet without pastors, as did the church of Corinth and those of Crete before Titus was sent thither to ordain such; and whenever persons are found among us having the specified qualifications, we appoint them to the offices of bishops and deacons. We know that the churches in the time of the apostles were independent of each other. So are they now. Each had its own bishop, who had no authority in any other than his own congregation. So it is with us; and in all things we endeavor to follow the pattern showed us in the New Testament, having the apostles restored to us as *universal bishops*; for though dead, they yet speak.

This imperfect outline I have given, that one whose talents and acquirements I have always regarded with surprise and admiration, may be undeceived with regard to us; and not without the faint hope that the simplicity of the gospel, as it is in Jesus, may even make an impression upon one whose gifts and energies, if properly directed, might break down the strongest holds of Satan, and be instrumental in bringing peace and righteousness to a deluded and blinded people. Be not deceived: think not that a more frequent administration of the Lord's supper will plant spiritual life in those who have not their sins forgiven.* Think not that preaching will save those who will not believe and obey the gospel. Not one of your hearers would say before God that his sins were forgiven, or that he had received the spirit of adoption into his family. Death has not lost its sting to them, nor the grave its victory over them. Those that have been for a number of years in the church, do not know the names even of the books of the New Testament, much less what is inculcated in them. And can you continue to waste your life, your time, and your gifts upon those who are unmoved by entreaty, not governed by the scriptures, uninfluenced by eloquence, without humility, without love for each other, lovers of the world? It is better to serve in the kingdom of heaven than to reign over such a people. But I forbear. May God grant that the simplicity of the gospel may not be foolishness to you, and that you may at least give these things an unprejudiced consideration.

Of one thing we are assured, that we have a lamp to our path which gives both heat and light. You may call it wild fire; but—not like the ignis fatuus which flits through the swamp of sectarianism and leads men into pools and ditches —it will consume the rank weeds and shapeless and unseemly reptiles: it will lick up the stagnant pools, and the beams of the Sun of Righteousness will enter, that the purified soil may bring forth fruit to the comfort of man and the glory of God.   Yours, &c.

                                        Disciplus.

* We have been informed that the Rev. Bishop has recently attended to the ordinance of the Lord's supper more frequently than formerly, and that he enjoins it upon his flock as a duty to break bread every first day of the week.
                                        Editor.

To the Editor of the Christian Baptist.

Respected Sir,—As the grand object of your periodical, titled the "Christian Baptist," is, as I understand it, the restoration of the ancient gospel and discipline, or order of things (as you term it) as the same was published and inculcated by the apostles, those divinely qualified and authorized teachers and founders of the christian religion, I take the liberty of suggesting to you, and, with your permission, to your numerous readers, the imperious, and indispensable necessity of a strict and undeviating practical use of the holy scriptures in the inculcation of every item of faith and obedience. It may, perhaps, be thought strange, that, at such an advanced period in the progress of this work, and after all that has been urged in behalf of the all sufficiency and alone sufficiency, perfection, and excellence of the holy scriptures, for every purpose of religion and morality, a constant and attentive reader should think it expedient to suggest or add any thing to excite the friends and advocates of the desired restoration to a strict practical use of the holy scriptures in preaching and teaching. However this may be, the writer of this, who is also a constant reader of your valuable paper, and a zealous advocate for the proposed restoration, feels deeply impressed with the urgent necessity of a much more strict and universal compliance with the above proposition. And, indeed, till this strict and appropriate use of the holy scriptures become the established and universal practice of the advocates of the proposed restoration, it appears impossible to conceive how it ever can be effected. What is it, that at first, and hitherto, has corrupted the purity, and broken the unity, of the christian profession? *Was* it not, and *is* it not, the teaching of human opinions in human propositions; that is, in words suggested by human wisdom, instead of divine declarations in divine terms, chosen and suggested by the revealing Spirit? So did not the apostles. See 1 Cor. ii. 9—13. &c.

Now if this departure from the apostolic doctrine at first corrupted the christian religion, produced divisions, and continues them; how shall they ever be remedied, but by ceasing from the noxious cause that produced and continues them? Is it possible? Surely no. It is asked if this be the case, what shall be done? Must preaching and teaching cease in order to restore and rectify the church, that it may resume and enjoy its original constitutional unity and purity? By no means. The christian religion was introduced, promoted, and maintained by preaching and teaching. Human agency was employed in propagating as well as in corrupting the christian religion, and will be again employed in its restoration. All that is necessary, in the mean time, is to make the proper distinction respecting the subject matter of preaching and teaching. The primitive preachers and teachers were duly qualified, instructed, and authorized to preach the gospel and teach the law of Christ. Compare *Matt.* xxviii. 19, 20. *Mark* xvi. 15, 16. with *Luke* xxiv. 44—49. and *Acts* i. 1—9. &c. The propagation and establishment of the christian religion in the world was the immediate, direct, and proper effect of the above commission and instructions, by the personal ministry of the apostles:—the production of the New Testament—the complete and permanent record of their preaching and teaching, that is, of what they preached and taught—was the next and permanent effect of said commission, &c.— Wherefore, being thus furnished with a faithful and authentic record of what they preached and taught by divine authority, for the conversion and salvation of the world, let us go and preach and teach the same things—the same identical propositions. We are not left to our own wisdom or discretion as to what we should declare in the name of the Lord, more than they;—though we don't receive it in the same manner, that is, immediately from the Holy Spirit, as they did; but, at second hand, from them that first received it: nevertheless if we really receive it as they have delivered it to us, and so declare it to others, it will do us and them the same good as it did to those who received it immediately, at first hand. See 1 *John* i. 1, 2, 3. ii. 24, 25. &c.

Now this only limits us in our preaching and teaching as were the apostles. Their preaching was limited to the gospel, which, as we learn from their practice—from the records of their sermons, was Jesus Christ, and him crucified; and their teaching was limited to all the things whatsoever Christ commanded them; so that, in this respect, we have no more reason to complain of restriction than they had. They were limited to what was given them by the Holy Spirit, and just so are we, according to our profession, to what the Spirit has given us by their ministry; for we profess to be followers of them, as they also were of Christ—to preach and teach the very self-same things that they preached and taught; that is, the ancient gospel and order of things established by the apostles; and these, not in the words that man's wisdom teaches, but which the Holy Spirit teaches us by their ministry; and surely he knows best what words and phrases will best convey his meaning. But upon the sacred importance of holding fast the form of sound words, selected by the Holy Spirit, for revealing to us spiritual things, Dr. Straith's Essays in the previous Nos. of this volume, may suffice. What we here insist upon, is, the moral necessity of the constant, strict, and undeviating use of the language of the holy scriptures upon every item of divine truth, that whether we preach or teach, it may be in the words of the Holy Spirit; that by so doing we may neither corrupt the truth nor cause divisions. Compare 1 *Cor.* i. 10. and ii. 12, 13. with 2 *Cor.* ii. 17. and iv. 1, 2, &c. We say, "the moral necessity," for we are bound both by our profession, and by the divine authority, to a strict and undeviating adherence to the letter of the divine testimony; professing, as we do, to preach and teach neither more nor less than the apostles' doctrine, originally delivered to the churches; and acting under the high responsibility of the divine injunction of "holding fast the faithful word as we have been taught,"—"the form of sound words" used by the apostles,—"that we all speak the same thing, that there be no divisions amongst us; but that we may be perfectly joined together in the same mind, and in the same judgment." Now, therefore, as professed restorers, as healers of the breaches, as faithful disciples, and followers of the apostles, we must, upon principles of fidelity and self-consistency, feel ourselves morally bound, by those high considerations to a strict and undeviating adherence to the letter of the divine testimony upon every article of faith and duty.

It may be still objected, however, that if thus restricted, there is an end to all preaching and teaching. All that can be morally and consistently done henceforth, is to read the apostolic writings, for the edification of saints, for the conversion of sinners, for the restoration of the an-

cient gospel and order of things, &c. The writer of this thinks otherwise. He thinks, however, that the present views and forms of preaching and teaching are derived from unscriptural models—that they are generally founded in ignorance and error—in ignorance of the very nature and design of the christian religion, which is love—love to God, love to Christ, love to one another, love to all mankind—the love of all moral excellence, the abhorrence of all moral evil. In ignorance also of the provision which the Heavenly Father has made by his Son Jesus Christ, and by his holy apostles and prophets in the holy scriptures, for all those divine and blissful purposes. Let this threefold ignorance, the ignorance of the nature, and of the design, of the christian religion; and of the provision made in the holy scriptures for carrying it into effect and supporting it:—I say, let the ignorance of these three things be once fairly removed, and the erroneous specimens of public teaching, so universally prevalent, will soon disappear.— Fairly understanding the divine character and intention, in connexion with the actual condition and character of mankind, as delineated on the sacred page, we will clearly perceive, that the Divine Author has made adequate provision for carrying into effect his benign and gracious intention; that he has adapted the means to the end; so that all that now remains to be done is a judicious exhibition of the provision he has already made;—to give every one his portion of meat in due season. This discovery, I say, will go very far, indeed, to correct the present erroneous and unscriptural manner of preaching and teaching.

It will be clearly perceived that the exhibition of the ancient gospel and law of Christ, in the very terms in which we find them recorded in the sacred volume, presents every necessary instruction, calculated to produce the above effects; as also to maintain and increase them. Let us take, for example, Peter's sermon on the day of Pentecost, *Acts* ii. He first gives us a scriptural account of the wonderful phenomena of that ever-memorable day;—he next introduces the grand subject of the gospel; viz. Christ, and him crucified, and now highly exalted by the right hand of God, made both Lord and Messiah. His propositions and proofs had the desired effect to convince three thousand of the audience of their sin and danger; and having answered their anxious and important inquiry, he proceeded "with many other words to testify and exhort, saying, Save yourselves from this untoward generation." Now, in this specimen of apostolic preaching, after an appropriate introduction originating in the peculiarity of his circumstances, having clearly stated the gospel with the proofs, and distinctly informed his audience how they might become partakers of the benefit—viz. of remission of sins, and the gift of the Holy Spirit, the apostle continues to testify and exhort, with many other words not recorded, that his hearers might be excited to save themselves, by a prompt compliance with his gracious and saving proposal, from the judgments about to come upon that unbelieving and impenitent generation. Thus, like Paul upon a certain occasion, he might have continued his speech till midnight, for the excitement of his hearers, without adding a new proposition to his premises, or so much as attempting to explain one of those he had advanced. Moreover, it is equally certain, that his audience believing the propositions recorded, and yielding the obedience of faith, as directed, were instantly made partakers of the promised salvation, as appears from what immediately follows, being all filled with righteousness, peace, and joy, by the Holy Spirit, as we see in the close of the chapter. Now, it is just as certain, that the belief of the same propositions, connected with the obedience required, will introduce the believing and obedient subjects into the actual enjoyment of the same blissful privileges that they enjoyed who first believed and obeyed.

These things being so, what then should hinder us from taking the same course, from following the recorded examples both of the primitive preachers and hearers of the ancient gospel, first delivered to the apostles, to be by them published to the nations, without a single exception of man or woman, with a special certification by the Divine Author, that whosoever believed it, and was baptized, should be saved. Are we not in possession of the whole doctrine of Christ,—of all that the apostles and prophets have left recorded concerning him? yea, of every proposition? Are we not also aware of the circumstances in which we are placed?—of the character of the generation with which we have to do? If not, we are but illy prepared to assume the office of teachers. But if we are, let us act rationally and faithfully, as did the apostles—Rationally, by introducing ourselves to the attention of our hearers, with an appropriate introduction adapted to their character and circumstances, as did the apostle Peter both in the courts of the temple, and in the house of Cornelius. Compare *Acts* iii. 11. 12. with ch. x. 25—35. Both rationally and faithfully, as did the apostles upon every occasion, by holding forth such particular statements concerning Christ, as the immediate condition of their hearers seemed to demand, (see 1. *Cor.* iii. 1. 2. 3. &c.) and in the very terms in which they received them from the Holy Spirit, (see 1. *Cor.* ii. 9—13;) and lastly, by every pertinent and impressive argument testifying and exhorting to a prompt obedience of the truth. Compare *Acts* ii. 40. with chapter xiii. 40. 41. Thus uniting faithfulness with zeal and intelligence, we shall have the goodly assurance, that our labor shall not be in vain in the Lord. We shall neither corrupt the word nor offend the brethren;—produce new divisions, nor keep up old ones, by substituting our guesses and glosses, our comments and paraphrases, for the diction of the Holy Spirit; while we faithfully, with the apostles, teach the things of God in the very terms in which they received them, and in which they have delivered them to us.

Let it not be supposed, while we thus speak, that we are altogether unacquainted with the apparent difficulties that have originated upon the subject of translation, some alleging that if we will thus strictly confine ourselves to the diction of the Holy Spirit, we must speak the very words of the Hebrew and Greek originals, for these only are the very words of the Holy Spirit. Formidable as this objection or difficulty may appear, there is nothing in it; it is a mere bugbear. In the beginning, on the day of Pentecost, in the very first instance, the revealing Spirit spoke in almost all the languages of the then known world; so that the strangers then dwelling at Jerusalem out of every nation under heaven, heard the apostles speak, in their proper languages, the wonderful works of God. Also, the commission was, "Go you into all the world, preach the gospel to every creature," &c. Therefore, the gospel, and the New Testament that contains it, was to be the common property of all nations. And although the autographs of the New Testament, the gospel of Matthew only excepted, were all found in the Greek, this can afford no relevant objection against the just and pure exhibition of the communications or dictates of the Divine Spirit in the languages of the nations, seeing that from the beginning they were actually published in all nations and were to be their common property,—the vehicle of the common salvation. Besides, the current translations, or copies of the holy scriptures in the various living languages, may be compared with, and corrected by, the most perfect copies of the Hebrew and Greek originals; they may also be compared with each other. So that upon the whole, while we allow the possibility of a fair translation in connection with the truth of the above allegations, which cannot be denied, we feel ourselves perfectly at ease upon this subject. It has never been supposed that a fair translation of any author, ever destroyed its authority; or that such a translation of the bible into any language, was not the word of God. Neither have the different sects originated in the mere difference of translations; but in the different expositions, theological comments, and forced interpretations of certain passages of holy scripture.

In dismissing this subject, let it not be thought that the writer means to detract any thing from the authenticity or authority of the gospel by Matthew, by the above exception. The genuineness and purity of that gospel being as satisfactorily established by the proper authorities, as that of any of the others. If, then, upon the whole, the professed advocates for the restoration of the ancient gospel and order of things, would act consistently with their profession, they would studiously and conscientiously avoid inculcating their own opinions upon divine subjects; and also the use of a factitious, systematic, technical phraseology, in their religious communications; confining themselves to a scriptural purity of speech, and to the inculcation of scripture doctrine in the terms in which it is recorded; avoiding the dangerous and unauthorized practice of theological explanation, that fertile source of corruption and error. In short, if the advocates of a genuine, radical, scriptural reformation would justify their profession, and prove successful, they must labor to evince the abundant and complete sufficiency of the holy scriptures for the formation and perfection of christian character, independent of the learned labors of the paraphrast or commentator. It must be fully understood and evinced that the belief and obedience of the gospel perfects the conscience, gives peace and joy, gratitude and gladness to the heart, (see *Acts* ii. 41—47;) and that the obedience of the law of Christ perfects the character,—secures the practice of every virtue, and prohibits the indulgence of any vice. In a word, that the simple exhibition, reception, and obedience of the gospel and law of Christ, in the very terms of the record, without explanation, comment, or paraphrase, are abundantly sufficient to make the christian disciple perfect, thoroughly furnished to all good works. This being clearly demonstrated, as a thing most clearly demonstrable, what remains to the faithful and intelligent friend and advocate of the ancient gospel and order of things, but that he zealously and constantly call the attention of his hearers to that which is written for their instruction in righteousness; always bearing in mind, and clearly evincing, that christianity is a practical doctrine, the design of which is to stamp or form a character, that shall be happy in itself, pleasing to God, and acceptable to men;—*Rom.* xiv. 16

—19;—that shall, at least, be such, as men may have no just reason to except against. That the formative principles of this character being knowledge, faith, and love; namely, the knowledge of the only true God, and of Jesus Christ, whom he has sent, and of the actual condition of mankind to whom, and for whose sake, he sent him;—together with the end and design of his coming, what he has done, is doing, and will do for his people, and the means he has ordained for their coming to the complete enjoyment of all this; every item of which is most expressly and explicitly declared upon the sacred page; so that he that runs may read it: as are likewise the items of that faith and love, which reconciles us to God and man, and renders us acceptable to both; see *Titus* iii. 1—8. Wherefore, the genuine advocate of the desired restoration will thus find himself sufficiently occupied without dealing in human opinions, either his own or any one's else, whether of ancient or modern date. He will find his materials made ready to his hand by the holy apostles and prophets; so that his sole and sufficient business will be to hand them out, to hold them forth as occasion requires, to give every one his portion of meat in due season; earnestly laboring with all persuasion, like Peter on Pentecost, (*Acts* xxi. 10.) and Paul with the Corinthians, (2d *Epis.* v. 10. 11. 20,) to prevail upon men to receive it. Thus will every scribe well instructed for the kingdom of heaven, in bringing forth out of his treasures, of the Old and New Testaments, things new and old, find himself sufficiently employed, without racking his invention, or pillaging the labors of the learned, to procure and prepare materials for the entertainment, not the edification, of his hearers.

To conclude, respected sir, this much too lengthy address, for which, I hope, the importance of the subject will apologize—I would beg leave to assure you, that all your labors, and those of your most zealous co-operants, will be measurably lost, nay, must eventually fail, unless those who professedly labor in the good cause, confine themselves to the inculcation of scripture doctrine in scripture terms; abstaining from all sectarian controversies, ancient or modern, and from inculcating any thing as matter of christian faith or duty, not expressly contained on the sacred page, and enjoined by the authority of the Saviour and his Apostles upon the christian community.

Yours very respectfully,   T. W.

To the Editor of the Christian Baptist.

RESPECTED SIR,—In your number of October last, we have the third and fourth, and we suppose the last, of Philip's Essays on Election, the first of which appeared in the March number, wherein you inform your readers, "that in some of the previous volumes of this work, you promised them a disquisition upon Election." This promise the writer does not remember to have met with, though a constant reader of your monthly publication; if he had, he thinks, from the deep felt interest he takes in the grand object of the work, he would have challenged it. But why promise your numerous readers a disquisition on Election only? Many of them, no doubt, would be equally gratified with a disquisition on Reprobation, on Eternal Justification, on Original Sin, on Imputed Righteousness, on the Extent of the Atonement, on Consubstantiation, on the Spirits in Prison, &c. &c. and on many other such interesting topics; for, it may well be presumed, that a goodly number of your numerous readers feel much interested in the above, and such like sub-jects. But what then? Shall we, &c. &c. We acknowledge, however, the force of the old adage: "It is hard to live in Rome, and strive with the Pope." Perhaps not much easier to leave Rome, and bring nothing of the Pope along with us. Indeed, it appears rather wonderful, that in so many volumes of a living work, a work of an almost universal controversy, expositive of the various and manifold corruptions of the antichristian world, there should be so little notice taken of those distinguishing sectarian topics, that have inflamed and distracted the professing people for the last three hundred years. Yet, considering the scope and intention of the work, we regret to see any notice taken of those topics, at all, except to denounce them as antiscriptural, antichristian, unprofitable, and vain, having no other tendency than to gender strifes. The restoration of pure primitive christianity in principle and practice, can never be accomplished by disquisitions, however learned and scriptural, upon those controversial subjects.

The christian religion, properly so called, is holy and divine, pure and heavenly, altogether of God, nothing human in it. It was introduced and established by a ministry that spoke and acted under the immediate influence and direction of the Holy Spirit. The belief and obedience required on the part of the teachers, and yielded on the part of the disciples, were to the dictates of the Holy Spirit; not to the dictates or decisions of men. Consequently it is of no importance to the christian how men decide upon any scriptural topic, or to what conclusion they may come; except it be so declared, and can be so read, upon the sacred page, it cannot enter into the christian religion;—can constitute no article of the christian faith or obedience, for the Lord not having taught or enjoined it by the ministry of his attested servants, it, therefore, cannot be inculcated with a "Thus saith the Lord."

We know it is urged, and will be readily granted, that there may be, and really are, many logical deductions, or inferential truths, upon moral and religious subjects, not expressly declared in the sacred volume. But what then? they cannot be binding upon disciples as such; first, because the Lord has not expressly declared and enjoined them; therefore, has not rendered the belief or obedience of these truths necessary to constitute an accepted disciple; second, because he has expressly declared and enjoined other propositions or truths, the belief and obedience of which render the person an approved and accepted disciple; see *Rom.* xiv. 16—19. Such is the facility, the simplicity, and excellence of the christian religion, blessed be the gracious Author! that the belief of a few fundamental propositions, virtually includes, and practically infers, a pious, virtuous, christian "character, acceptable to God, and approved of men;" *Rom.* xiv. 17, 18. Nay, so clear, so full and explicit is the exhibition of the christian religion in the New Testament, that the belief and obedience of certain distinct propositions, precisely specified, perfects the conscience and character, or justifies and sanctifies the believing and obedient, independent of every thing that may be thenceforth acquired. So complete is this exhibition, in clear, distinct, formal propositions, that a religious property or privilege, or a moral virtue cannot be named, that the believing and obedient do not possess. This is demonstrable. Only let all the attributes, absolute and relative, be ascribed to God, to Christ, to the Spirit, that are distinctly ascribed to each in the holy scriptures, and all that love, worship, and

43

obedience duly rendered, which we find therein expressly required and ascribed: and then say, what will be wanting to complete the character;—to render it, in this life, more happy in itself, more pleasing to God, or more acceptable to men? We are sure you cannot. That item or attribute of piety or virtue, not expressly contained in the holy scriptures, is yet without name. Take, for instance, only the brief account of the church of Jerusalem, which we have in the first six chapters of the Acts; from the day of Pentecost till the martyrdom of Stephen;—a space, we may reasonably suppose, not exceeding two years—the first two years of the christian dispensation or economy. Paul was not yet converted, the gospel was not yet preached to the Gentiles—no dispute yet about election—the term is not so much as to be found in the portion alluded to; nor any thing yet occurring that should tend to introduce it; yet, most assuredly, the gospel was fully preached and enjoyed, and its blissful effects abundantly manifested. Can the fondest partisan, the most zealous stickler, either for the Calvinistic or Arminian hypothesis, point to a society of his connexion, even the best instructed, the most privileged, that can compare with the primitive church above mentioned,—that can equal it in the fruits of righteousness. Its creed was Christ the Messiah, the Son of God, the Lord of all; Christ and him crucified, and highly exalted, a Prince and Saviour, to give forth repentance to Israel, and remission of sins through faith in his blood, by baptism, with the promised gift of the Holy Spirit and eternal life. Its law was gratitude, piety, and love, the law of the New Covenant in the heart; and its fruits were fruits of beneficence, liberal and abundant. Say, what were the deficiencies of this church in piety, temperance, justice, charity, benevolence, or beneficence? Yet neither the Epistle to the Romans, nor the disputes that occasioned it, were in existence; nor indeed any other part of the New Testament. The church of Jerusalem, during this period of its history, was only in possession of that exhibition of the gospel, with the concomitant events recorded in the portion referred to: yet even this, duly considered, will be found to contain doctrine sufficient to produce all the effects above specified; and if so, how much more abundantly are we provided for, who have not only their portion, but the respective portions of all the churches under heaven, addressed by the apostles in their epistles, and in their other subsequent writings. Thus superabundantly furnished with all the documents of faith and obedience, divinely provided for the whole christian community under heaven, we cannot surely be deficient, in any respect, either for our present or future happiness; and, if not fully satisfied, as well provided for, we must, indeed be hard to satisfy. These things being so, and having as reformers, nay, more, as restorers, assumed these premises, what have we to do with the results of theological controversies? Have we yet to wait for the discoveries of the 29th year of the 19th century, to perfect our creed? Or have we to go farther than the record itself, to know what we should believe concerning the divine election, more than any other item of revealed truth? Surely no. And if we have nothing to do with the results of such controversies, what can we have to do with the controversies themselves? The ground that we have assumed, the stand that we have taken, blessed be God! puts us beyond the reach of all such controversies. The principles

or propositions of our faith and obedience were established beyond contradiction, 1800 years ago. The christian community, then existing, was put in complete possession of every item of faith and obedience that the Lord required; the authentic documents of which have come down to us. The whole of our duty, then, as christians, now is, to hold fast in profession, and reduce to practice, what is therein declared and enjoined, after the goodly example of the primitive churches. Thus contending earnestly for the faith once delivered to the saints, and conforming to the apostolic injunctions, after their approved example, we also shall stand approved. But for the achievement of all this, we have only to look into the New Testament, and not to any later production; no, not even though it bore date in the first year of the second century.

Some however may allege, as we know they do, that, although all things necessary to faith and holiness are fully recorded, yet we are liable to mistake the meaning, to differ about the sense of some things in the sacred writings. Grant this, and what follows—that the scriptures are not a certain, sufficient, and infallible guide in matters of faith and holiness? What then shall we do? Who is authorized to supply the deficiency? Where is the infallible expositor? None, none. Our concession, then, must be limited to things not affecting faith and holiness; we mean, the belief and obedience of the gospel and law of Christ; or if it respect any item of the revealed salvation, or the knowledge of any thing intimately connected with it, it must be further limited to mere verbal ignorance, to matters of grammatical exposition; but what has this to do with theological exposition, or with the well known subjects of sectarian controversy? Certainly nothing definitive; though such controversialists sometimes seek to avail themselves of verbal criticism. Nevertheless, doing common justice to the sacred diction, according to the established rules of grammatic exposition, no undue advantage can be taken unfavorable to truth, otherwise the language of the holy scripture has no certain meaning; consequently, we have no revelation at all. Upon the whole, this indefinite allegation is a mere cavil, a mere scarecrow, one of the last shifts of a desperate and dying cause. The faith and obedience of the christians of the second century, were not paralyzed with it, who willingly and joyfully suffered all things for the truth's sake.

We, then, as advocates for a genuine radical reform, even for the restoration of the ancient gospel, and order of things established by the apostles, insist upon it, that we have nothing to do with sectarian controversies; with the theological contentions of the present or former ages; with any thing of the kind that happened since the apostles' days. They have settled all the theological, not, indeed, all the verbal controversies, that we are concerned with: and have assured us, that, if what they heard, and saw, and handled, and contemplated, and from the beginning delivered to the churches concerning the eternal life, which from the Father was manifested to them; yea, that if that which we have heard from them from the beginning, shall remain in us, we also shall continue in the Son, and in the Father, and have the promise of eternal life. So John the apostle, in his first epistle general, informs all the christians under heaven; and surely this should satisfy us. It is, then, nowise incumbent upon us to intermeddle with the contending brethren, neither for their sakes nor ours, for it can neither do them nor us any good.

It can be of no service to them, for they will not allow us a decisive umpirage to bring their tedious, improfitable, perplexing disputes to a final issue: nor can it be of any service to us to investigate their matters, in order to ascertain who is in the right; for if their conclusions, whether right or wrong, be not found in our premises, be not contained in that which was heard from the beginning, " even as they delivered them to us, who were eye witnesses and ministers of the word;" we say, if their conclusions be not found in these our premises, we know nothing about them. They enter not into our christianity; they affect not our faith nor obedience. All that we have to do with the multiplied and multiplying contentions of a sectarian age, is, for our own part, to avoid them, as subversive of the benign and blissful intention of the gospel, which is godly edification in faith, love, and peace; whereas the end of these controversies is contention, strife, envy, evil surmisings, backbitings, persecutions, and every evil work, as the scriptures and woful experience amply testify. In addition to this cautious and conscientious avoidance of those hurtful and divisive controversies, our incumbent duty is to bear a faithful scriptural testimony against them; not, indeed, distinctively, or as belonging to this or the other sect, but *in cumulo*, as constituting sectarianism, without any respect to their intrinsic or comparative merit or demerit. Thus proceeds the Apostle in his epistles to Timothy and Titus. In brief, then, and in simplicity, let us testify against sectarianism itself, without condescending to notice in particular any of the *isms* that compose it. The very moment we depart from this rule, we become a sect. I might also add, the very moment we preach or teach our own opinions, as matters of christian faith or duty, that moment we become sectarians; for this is the very essence, the *sine qua non* of sectarianism, without which there could be no sect. The writer of this most seriously declares, for his own part, that were not the all-sufficiency of the holy scriptures, without comment or paraphrase, clearly demonstrable; so that the inculcation of their express and explicit declarations were alone sufficient to make the christian wise to salvation, thoroughly furnished to all good works; he would have either continued with his quondam brethren, of the Westminster school, or joined with some of the modern creed-reforming parties: for, by no means would he have committed himself to the capricious and whimsical extemporaneous effusions of every one, who might have confidence enough to open his mouth in public. If we are to be entertained and edified with human opinions of divine truth, let us, by all means, have the opinions of the learned, of the deep thinking, and judicious; among these also let us have our choice. All have certainly a right to choose where there is a variety, and that we may always expect to find in the religious world, while the fashionable opinion is indulged, that every man has a right to entertain the public with his own opinions upon religious subjects. I dont mean a civil, but a religious right; for civil society, as such, can take no cognizance of religious matters. However, while this assumed right is conceded by the religious world, we shall never want a variety of religions; for what is it, but granting to every one that pleases, the right of making a religion out of the Bible to suit his own fancy, and of teaching it to as many as will receive it, and thus becoming the head of a new party? While, then, the religious world justify this mode of proceeding, sects cannot fail to increase: for, as before observed, this is the productive principle of sectarianism. But I perceive I have exceeded all due bounds. My apology is the prodigious extent, and ruinous tendency of the sectarian evil here opposed; and especially as affecting the desired reformation in the hands of many, who, while they profess to advocate the all-sufficiency and alone-sufficiency of the holy scriptures, to the rejection of every thing of human invention or authority, are but making a new start, to run the old race over again, by preaching every man his own opinions, reviving the old controversies, or producing new ones; thus sowing the seeds of new parties, and hardening the old, they prevent the success of those that are honestly and consistently contending for the truth, and zealously laboring to promote it. Let such remember, that, in thus really building again, the things they have professedly destroyed, they make themselves transgressors; and, like the people in the days of Nehemiah, who would be thought to be builders in the Lord's house, they are enemies in disguise, and will be considered as such by the true builders. Farewell.

Yours very respectfully,   T. W.

November 14.

P. S.—It appears, sir, by your number of September last, that you intend a series of sermons to young preachers, of which, in said number, you have favored us with the first. According to custom you begin at the outside, which, for humanity's sake, appears to need the dressing you have given it. We hope your labor may not be in vain; and that, as you proceed, at least before you finish, you will pay a justly apportionate attention to the inside; for it would appear lost labor, if not ridiculous, to be at much pains and cost to fit out vessels for sea which were to carry nothing but sails and ballast. Perhaps a solid and judicious answer to the following queries might be of some service to the good cause in which you labor, as well as to those whom you professedly intend to serve by the proposed sermons:—

Quere 1. When should a young person think himself qualified to become a preacher? At what age? With what attainments?

2. Should he be able to read his Bible grammatically—that is, distinctly and intelligibly, with proper emphasis, and without miscalling?

3. Should he know the names and order of the books in the Old and New Testaments, and to which volume they respectively belong?

4. Should he have carefully and devoutly read both volumes of the holy scriptures, so as to apprehend the precise design of each, and their respective bearings upon the christian community?

5. How many weeks or months should pass, after his having publicly made a scriptural profession of christianity, before he begins to prophesy? And is such a profession previously necessary?

6. Should he be an approved member of a christian church, and have its approbation, both as to his age and talents; as a person of considerable standing, of established character, of sound comprehensive scriptural knowledge, duly acquainted with the actual condition and character of the religious world? &c.

7. Or may every person whose zeal, or self-conceit may prompt him, become a prophet, without any respect to the qualifications above specified, or any at all; and say what he pleases in the name of the Lord, without respect to any authority, divine or human? And have the churches of the saints no cognizance of such characters—no defence against them?

45

Extracts from Haldane's " Evidence and Authority of Divine Revelation."

The Land of Canaan.

"The land of Canaan was a type of the heavenly country. It was the inheritance given to Abraham by promise to himself and his posterity. As his descendants after the flesh inherited the one; so his spiritual seed shall inherit the other. Canaan was the land of rest, after the toils and dangers of the wilderness. To make it a fit inheritance, and an emblem of that inheritance "which is incorruptible and undefiled, and which fades not away," it was cleared of the ungodly inhabitants. No spot could have been selected as so fit a representation of that better country. It is called in scripture "the pleasant land," "the glory of all lands," "a land flowing with milk and honey." "A sight of this territory," says a late traveller, "can alone convey any adequate idea of its surprising produce. It is truly the Eden of the East, rejoicing in the abundance of its wealth. Under a wise and beneficent government, the produce of the Holy Land would exceed all calculation. Its perennial harvest; the salubrity of its air; its limpid springs, its rivers, lakes, and matchless plains; its hills and vales; all these, added to the serenity of its climate, prove this land to be indeed "a field which the Lord has blessed." God has given it of the dew of heaven and the fatness of the earth, and plenty of corn and wine."

Nation of Israel.

" The nation of Israel, after the flesh, chosen by God, and separated from all the rest of the world, shadowed forth in its many institutions and privileges, the person, offices, and sacrifice of the Redeemer. And it represented that nation of Israel after the Spirit, with its ultimate inheritance in a future state—that nation which was chosen in Christ before the foundation of the world, consisting of believers who are the subjects of Messiah's kingdom, which he has set up, while all the rest of the world, whether called Christians, Mahometans, Pagans, or by whatever other name, belong to the kingdom of Satan, the god of this world, and are his bond slaves. Jesus brings forth his people as he brought forth Israel of old out of this house of bondage. They are baptized unto his name, as that typical nation was baptized unto Moses in the cloud and in the sea. They are called to commemorate their spiritual deliverance from bondage as Israel was commanded to commemorate their deliverance from Egypt, and to believe in the promises of God respecting the heavenly Canaan, of which the earthly Canaan was a type. He makes with them a new covenant, of which he himself is the surety and mediator. He gives them a law by which they are to conduct themselves, and institutions of worship. He guides them through this wilderness by his word and spirit, as he directed Israel after the flesh by the pillar of fire and cloud. He supplies them with food during their pilgrimage, giving them spiritually to eat his flesh and drink his blood, of which the manna and the rock that was smitten were types. He heals their wounds which they receive from sin and Satan, whom he will bruise under their feet shortly. He makes them more than conquerors over their spiritual enemies. And when their wanderings in this wilderness world are finished, conducts them, like Israel at Jordan, safely through death, and puts them in possession of the promised land and the New Jerusalem."

The Tribe of Judah.

"The tribe of Judah was first in offering its gifts at the Tabernacle, as well as in the order of encampment of the tribes. In the journies of Israel, it was appointed to march foremost. Moses denominated it the *lawgiver*. David declared that God had chosen Judah to be the *ruler*. The royalty was granted to Judah in the person of David, and his descendants; and this tribe communicated its name to the remains of all the other tribes. Jerusalem, the chief city of Judah, was the capital of the whole nation, and there the temple was built, to which all the other tribes resorted to worship; where alone the sacrifices were offered, and all the services which prefigured the Messiah were performed. Even during the captivity in Babylon, the tribe of Judah continued a distinct people, and had with it one of its own princes, who lived in a degree of royal splendor. Afterwards, when under the dominion of the Persians, the Greeks, and the Romans, it continued to have senators, magistrates, and princes of its own, who governed according to its own laws. But above all, the theocracy or government of God, under which Judah was placed, continued without interruption till Shiloh came, allowed by Jews and Christians to be a name for the Messiah, to whom the gathering of the nations was to be. Soon after his coming, the government of Judah was finally subverted, and their temple and capital destroyed. The Jews were expelled from Judea, and it became utterly impossible for them to attend to the observances of the law which was then abrogated. Here then we have a most remarkable prediction of the coming of the Messiah. Jacob, uttering by the spirit of God, particular and minute predictions, respecting each of his twelve sons, which were all afterwards verified, singles out one of them, declares his pre-eminence over his brethren, and that he should be invested with power, and continue to enjoy it, till one should descend from him, to whom the gathering of the nations was to be. And all this verified through the whole intervening period, was fully accomplished at the distance of about 1690 years."

No. 6.]   JANUARY 4, 1830.

Remarks on a Circular Letter, found in the Minutes of the Mount Pleasant Baptist Association, for 1829.

It has long been a custom to repudiate, by opprobious names, a sentiment or a doctrine which cannot be refuted by argument. Men who can refute by argument, have never been accustomed to use the weapons of calumny and detraction. A Mr. Rogers, in the state of Missouri, converted the circular letter of the Mount Pleasant Baptist Association into a vehicle of slander and personal abuse. The custom of addressing circulars from and in the name of associations, originated from a desire to address the brethren once a year on some evangelical topic, calculated to enlighten the understanding, to purify and cheer the hearts of the brotherhood. But behold, this letter is a little acrimonious anathema upon some sentences, torn from their connexion in the Christian Baptist, and tortured and gibbeted by the evil genius of sectarian jealousy until they appear as much to disadvantage as an Indian victim painted for massacre. I am clothed in the mantle of *Sandemanianism* and led forth as a heretic of the deepest atrocity, to an *auto de fe*, because I have asserted and proved that faith is only the belief of the testimony of God, and that, when

God commanded all men to believe and reform, he did not command that which is impossible for them to do.

The writer of this letter casts his eyes over Fuller's Strictures on *Sandemanianism*, and Buck's Theological Dictionary on the article of *Sandemanianism*, and there thinks he sees all the *"doctrines"* found in the Christian Baptist, in miniature or in full life in those sketches. The term *Sandemanianism* is, I suppose, an opprobrious name in his country, that will answer my heterodoxy. I will not kill thee, said the Quaker, but I will call thee *mad dog*. Thus the work is done. It does not, however, succeed so well in this country as in Old England, the native place of the erudite gentleman. For the people of these United States are a little more inquisitive, and are wont to inquire, What has he done? What, say they, do we know of Sandeman or of Glass? Will their names condemn a sentiment to hell or exalt it to heaven! Now I would inform the same disciple who nicknames my remarks, *Sandemanianism*, that he is much more of a *Sandemanian* than I am. But this will neither, I hope, condemn his sentiments to heterodoxy, nor justify them as righteous. But it is a fact, if he be a good hypercalvinistic Baptist, or if he be a believer in physical and accompanying special influences producing faith. This I have shown in the Christian Baptist to be an essential part of *Sandemanianism*;—not from Buck or Fuller, but from Sandeman's letters on Theron and Aspasio. I disclaim *Sandemanianism* as much as I do any system in christendom; but I agree with Sandeman in making faith no more than the belief of the truth, and I agree with the Roman Catholics in the belief of the resurrection of the dead. But I differ from Sandeman in making this belief the effect of physical influence, and I disagree with the Catholics in the doctrine of Purgatory.

But I would inform this Son of the church militant, that I would not give a grain of wheat for any faith that does not purify the heart, work by love and overcome the world. And if he could speak with the tongue of an angel, and write with the pen of an apostle, and exhibit no more regard to truth and christian love than this circular evinces; I would not give a farthing for his faith, though he may think with Fuller, that he was regenerated before he believed the Gospel.

As I have seen this letter nearly four hundred miles from home, I cannot write an elaborate criticism upon it; but I will inform those into whose hands it may fall, that it is a most unfaithful and unchristian representation of my views. All the scriptures quoted in it, I believe in their plain, literal, and obvious import. For example, I believe and I know, that "God who fills all things in all places, did fill the Gentiles who were dead in trespasses and in sins, with the gifts of the Holy Spirit;" yea, that, "us who were dead in trespasses and sins, he has raised up together, and has set us down together, with the Jews who believed in the heavenly places by Jesus Christ," and this he has done for us out of pure favor. I believe that it is the Spirit that quickens; the flesh profits nothing; "that the wicked will not seek after God—God is not in all their thoughts." "And God saw that the wickedness of man was great in the earth, and that every imagination of the thoughts of his heart was only evil continually." "There is none righteous, no, not one; there is none that understands—there is none that seeks after God—they are all gone out of the way—they are to-

gether become unprofitable—there is none that does good, not one—there is no fear of God before their eyes." All these sayings I believe most sincerely, in the connexion in which they stand in the volume. I say, these and every other sentence of scripture found in the circular letter, I most sincerely believe in the connexions in which they stand; and in the fullest and most literal sense the words will bear, according to any legitimate rules of interpretation. But if the gentleman has any private interpretation of these words, or any appropriated sense of them, either borrowed, or invented by himself, I beg leave to dissent from such appropriations and private interpretations. I will also inform the worthy gentleman, that the name Calvinism is worth no more in heaven than the name Sandemanianism, or Fullerism. But I rejoice to know that the gospel does not need to be put into any of these distilleries to make it either intelligible or healthful. It is glad tidings of great joy to all people. It demands of no man what he has not to pay. It calls for no powers which he has not: it enjoins no duty which he cannot perform. It is adapted to men just as they are, and therefore it is a scheme of pure favor—of divine love and mercy. No man can complain and say, that it only tantalizes him by offering him what he cannot receive—by requiring what he cannot perform—by presenting what he cannot accept. Such a scheme would not be glad tidings to all people. It would be only good news to the qualified, to the regenerated, to them who are made able to receive it. Such a gospel did not Paul preach; and he that preaches a gospel which is not adapted to unconverted sinners, preaches another gospel—a gospel of his own, or some other person's invention.

I do hope that every man who feels any interest in examining any thing I have written, or may write, on the great questions which divide the religious world, will put himself to the trouble to examine it in my own words, and in the connexions in which they are placed, and not in the garbled extracts which party spirit and the spirit of this world please to present them. I protest against having the *Christian Baptist* treated no better than these gentlemen treat the apostolic writings. The apostles are dead, and must submit to the textuaries, to be handled as the textuaries please. The Calvinists and the Arminians tear them limb from limb, and make Paul say just what they please. The Universalists and the Quakers, the Socinians and the Arians are very adroit in making the sacred writers affirm or deny what they please. But I cannot conscientiously submit to have my writings treated no better than these popular sermon makers treat the holy scriptures. Those, then, who feel any interest in understanding what I teach, will do me and themselves the justice of examining, in my own words, my own statements. One scripture says, "*There is no God;*" another says, "*I could wish myself to be accursed from Christ;*" another says, "*Worship the Beast;*" and another says, "*Go and do likewise.*" Put these together, and what does the Bible teach!! It will teach any thing men please to make it teach, only let them have one liberty—and that is, of quoting it just as they please. Yet if treated according to the only fair and just rules of interpretation, it will only teach one and the same thing to every reader.

The editor of the *Utica Register*, New York, has given some weeks since, as I have lately seen in a paper forwarded to me to Richmond, from Rochester, what he is pleased to call doubtless " a fair summary of the sentiments and doctrines taught by Alexander Campbell." I would seriously ask this gentleman if he ever read one volume which he wrote, and whether he has examined for himself the whole of my writings. If he have not, I ask how, in the name of truth and righteousness, could he solemnly affirm a most libellous caricature of my sentiments on one or two topics, to be a *fair summary* of my sentiments!!! If this gentleman would look back into history only a few centuries, he could find many brief summaries, which he would doubtless call blasphemous libels on his own sentiments; nay, he would find as ugly things said of Baptist sentiments and practices as he can now say of mine. And if he would read the history of the apostles, he would find that one of the " fair summaries" given by some of his contemporaries, was that Paul taught that Moses ought not to be regarded, and that men should " do evil that good might come." No doubt but Paul had said something which gave rise to, or afforded a pretext for such summaries; and so may I have said or written something which ungodly men may have perverted to such an extent. I therefore call upon this *Utica Register* either to make good his *allegata*, or eat up his libel.   EDITOR.

Ancient Baptisms.

SACRED history is, of all reading, the most instructive, entertaining, and profitable. It presents God and man to our view in such a way as engrosses all the energies of our minds, and all the feelings of our hearts. We think and we feel at the same moment. All true history is profitable to all attentive readers. It is the best substitute for personal acquaintance. It brings to light and developes that most wonderful and interesting of all themes, the human heart. But in this the sacred writings claim, as they deserve, all precedence. The hidden springs of human action, and the great attractives of human passion, are there laid open and pictured out by a master painter. Reality, and not shadows, pass before us in every character which these writings portray. No portrait so approaches real life as these characters exhibit man, both good and bad, to human meditation; but sketches only are given of the most brilliant and eminent characters. But these sketches present, in the most instructive attitudes, the great characters which God selected for human admiration.

Events are but the results of human action, or of divine interposition; and those great events which the Mosaic history records, are, of all others, the most instructive, if we except the eventful history of the New Testament. But there is one peculiarity in the characters and events recorded in the Mosaic history which I wish to notice here, because it proves the authenticity of the sacred volumes, while it greatly illuminates the pages of the apostolic writings. I allude to their emblematic reference. No pencil but that guided by an eye which penetrates all futurity, could have in ten thousand instances painted out the christian institution, with all its influences, moral and religious, ages before its author was born—Adam the first, and Adam the second—the Fall, and the Resurrection of man—Hagar and Sarah—Ishmael and Isaac—Jacob and Esau—Elijah and John—Moses, Aaron, Joshua, and Jesus—circumcision and baptism—the passover and the Lord's supper—and a hundred other allusions, symbols, and emblems, need only be mentioned to revive the remembrance of the exact adaptation of Jewish and patriarchal history to the developement of the divine philanthropy in the christian scriptures.

To this subject the apostles only occasionally glance. I will only allude at present to two instances:—The first preacher, not only of the New Testament, but of the Old, was what some now call a *Baptist.* I allude to *Noah* and *John.* Noah preached *reformation* or *drowning* to the Antediluvians. John preached *reformation* or *burning* to his cotemporaries. Noah was saved by water, and the old world was baptized in water without a resurrection, because it would not reform. The earth was buried and rose again before a rainbow of peace spanned hill or valley. After the resurrection of the earth Noah was born of water. The waters which drowned the sinners saved the righteous Noah, and made him the father of a new world. The heavenly proclamation believed brought him into the ark, and God's promise brought him out. After his baptism, or second birth, God promised him life, and enlarged his privileges. Water translated him from the old world into the new; and while it purified the earth for him, it fitted him for the earth. But he was born of promise too. His faith in the resurrection of the earth sustained him in entering, and while immured in the ark; and when born of water his faith in God's promise gave him a lively hope that there should never be a second baptism of the earth, nor an entire withdrawal of the influences of heaven from the earth. So after Noah was born of water, he was begotten again to a lively hope by the promise of God.

All this and more Peter saw in this event, when he was inspired to say, " The antitype of this water, *immersion,* does now *save us* christians." As water saved Noah, so baptism saves us. He had faith in the resurrection of the earth; and we have faith in the resurrection of Jesus. He believed God's promise of bringing him out of the water, and we his promise of raising us from the dead. We leave our sins where Noah's baptism left the ungodly. They were buried and Noah saved. As Noah entered a new world by being born of water and the promise, so we enter the kingdom of heaven by being born of water and the Spirit. As life and temporal blessings were promised Noah after his second birth, so eternal life and spiritual blessings are promised us after we are born of water and the Spirit. As no one entered into the second world who was born in the first world, unless those born again; so Jesus said, " Except a man be born of water and Spirit, he cannot enter into the kingdom of God."

The baptism of the Israelites is the next event of this sort to which we now allude. This is found in the 14th and 15th chapters of Exodus. Faith in God's promise had brought the Israelites from their houses and their homes into one assembly, on the coast of the Red Sea. Faith in the divine call and mission of Moses, had induced them to put themselves under his conduct and guidance. But notwithstanding this faith, they could not leave the land of their nativity and get on the way to Canaan until they were baptized into Moses and born of water as Noah was. Hence they could not cross the Red Sea in ships. They must descend into the bottom of the Red Sea before they could ascend into the relation of the saved people. The cloud covered them also. " They were all baptized into Moses in the cloud and in the sea." So says a high authority—Paul the apostle to the Gentiles. But the water which saved Israel drowned the Egyptians. Faith led the Jews under the guidance of Moses into the Red Sea; but rage, and envy, and resentment led Pharaoh and his hosts in the pursuit. Passion, however, did not bring the Egyptians out; but faith placed Israel on yonder side. So soon as they were born of the water and of the cloud—so soon as they came up out of the Red Sea, God promised to feed them and lead them. The heavens then dropped down manna upon them, and they eat the bread of heaven. Now, these things, says Paul, happened to them as *types*—as figures—and they are written for our admonition, upon whom the ends of the world have come. The christian institutions were thus pictured out to us by the pencil of Omniscience ages before the founder of our religion was born. We should not have ventured to trace these analogies had not the apostles Peter and Paul directed us. Following their guidance, we cannot but see that the *one baptism* of christians is an institution of so great moment as to have had two resemblances of it in the two most extraordinary events in Jewish and Patriarchal history—the one baptism of the fathers of the once baptized earth, and the one baptism of the once baptized fathers of the Jewish people. How interesting, then, this sacred institution! How important is it for christians to know its meaning well, and to teach it accurately to others. We shall find it, on examination, to be the most gracious institution, and the most instructive, with which any age of the world has been favored.

EDITOR.

For the Christian Baptist.

BROTHER BRANTLY:—I HAVE read, with regret, your remarks copied from the "Star" of the 29th August last, in the October number of the "Christian Baptist;" in which you say, "We consider it due to our readers to justify our former strictures, and to lift up the warning voice to them, by exhibiting the sentiments of Mr. Alexander Campbell on the subject of the moral law."

It is not my object to defend brother Campbell's views of the "moral law," because I am sure he is able to defend himself; yet I am far from thinking that there are not hundreds, besides him, that are more than "stout enough" for you upon that subject. If you feel it your duty to "lift up the warning voice" against brother Campbell because he may have denied the existence of any such a law in the bible, you must surely plead that your obligations to defend scholastic divinity are greater than those you acknowledge under the oracles of God. And if you say that there is such a law as the "moral law" in God's revealed word, do tell us, brother Brantly, where it is to be found; give us book, chapter and verse. "Come and help us." But 1 have said that it was not my intention to defend brother Campbell on this subject.

I should not have taken up my pen to address a D. D. if it were not in self-defence. I acknowledge myself one of the avowed friends of brother Campbell and the cause which he advocates in the "Christian Baptist;" viz. "the restoration of the ancient order of things." And I am much mortified at seeing such a charge as you have made in your strictures against the christian character and standing of those brethren who are avowedly united with brother Campbell in defence of primitive christianity. Your charge is thus stated:—

"Who are the Baptists that have been converted to his new creed? They are such as were previously Arminians, or Sandemanians—such as never stood firm on the basis of truth—such

as were ready to take up with the first leader of discontent and faction—such as always opposed united effort in promoting the spread of the gospel, and the advancement of education, and those, who, through ignorance, become an easy prey to greedy error."

You have here made seven charges or allegations in your bill. "*Affirmanti incumbit probatio;*" consequently you must either make good your allegations, or else defeated you are, and must pay the cost. Is not the "*norma disputandi*" the same in Pennsylvania as in Kentucky? I presume it is. I now call upon you, as a brother in Christ, to establish your charges if you can; for I am bold to say that there is not one word of truth in all that you have said about them, as far as *I* know or have learned, and I know many of them well. Who told you, brother Brantly, that those Baptists were "Sandemanians or Arminians," and that they were "ready to take up with the first leader of discontent and faction?" What a pity, brother, that you have made such assertions, when you must have known, that, for your life, you could not establish one of them as true. Are these the fruits of your "moral law" of which you are so tenacious? If they be, we need not trouble ourselves much about opposing it, for you yourself will shortly put it to death. *God's* law forbids bearing false testimony against any man; and that you have done so against many in this instance, is as certain as that two and two make four.

Again you say, in speaking of those whose religious sentiments correspond with brother Campbell's, that "they are such as never stood firm on the basis of truth." What do you define to be "the firm basis?" for you have not told us. All the friends of brother Campbell, with whom I am acquainted, believe that Jesus Christ is the Son of God, the Saviour of the world; and brother John says, 1st Epistle, chapter v. "Whosoever believes that Jesus is the Christ, is begotten by God." Have you not *again* slandered your brethren, who love the Lord Jesus and look for his second appearing? 'Tis a thousand pities that you should have so little regard for your standing both as a man and a christian. You have sinned against God, and I beseech you to repent in sackcloth and ashes.

You should never have appeared in public as an accuser of brethren, of whom, perhaps, you knew nothing, except through their enemies, who are most likely to misrepresent them. You have not only endeavored to pour contempt upon them, but to destroy their character as christians. You represent them as extremely ignorant; in which, however, you have assertion only to bear you out; and if *assertion only* is considered good proof, you have and can prove your allegations as well as any other *Star* on this terrestrial globe.

You have attempted to act the part of a critic in your strictures of the 29th August; but if I do not convince every candid reader that you are equally ignorant with brother Campbell's friends, before I bid you adieu, I shall be much disappointed. And in order to fulfil this promise, I shall beg leave to offer a few remarks on a sermon which I had the honor of hearing you deliver on the fourth Lord's day in September last in the city of Philadelphia, in your new meeting house. Your text was the 19th verse of the 5th chapter of I. Thessalonians; "Quench not the Spirit."— Your first position was, that there was "no Holy Spirit except through the word of God;" but before five minutes had gone by, you declared that you did not "wish to be understood to say, that

God did not regenerate sinners *without* the word." In this you displayed logic worse, if possible, than a schoolboy of the age of fifteen; for you say that "there is no Holy Spirit except through the word of God," and that " the Spirit, independent of the word, regenerates the sinner." Then God regenerates sinners *without* his own word, and, of course, without the Holy Spirit. ,What a display of biblical acquirements! *Query*—Judging from this illustration, is its author much superior to those ignoramuses, who you say " never stood firm on the basis of truth?" Your whole sermon from the above text was made up of the Spirit and its influences. You and brother Paul, who gave the exhortation, do not agree; for in exhorting his son Timothy, he says, "Preach the *word;* be instant in season and out of season." Brother Brantly preaches the Spirit, stripped of the word, *ergo*, " out of season," and not the " word in season!" After a discourse of at least one hour's length on the subject, you prayed to the Holy Spirit to come down and do his work among the people. Tell me, brother Brantly, I beseech you, in what part of the sacred oracles you are authorized to pray to the Holy Spirit, for we, the readers of the bible; are totally ignorant of any such authority? If you know of any, I pray you to point us to it; and if you should be unable to find it in the scriptures, perhaps by a reference to some of your popular creeds, you may find it. In John's gospel, 16th chap. 13th verse, thus says the Lord, " And whatsoever you shall ask in my name, that will I do, that the Father may be glorified in the Son. If you shall ask any thing in my name, I will do it. If you love me, keep my commandments. And I will pray the Father, and he shall give you another Comforter, that he may abide with you forever, even the Spirit of truth." Again, xvi. 7. " It is expedient for you that I go away; for if I go not away, the Comforter will not come to you; but if I depart, I will send him to you." Thus speaks the great King of Saints. Is not this " the firm basis of truth" in regard to the *office* of the Spirit? Yes, I am persuaded it is.

Now, brother Brantly, upon what principle of reason, or scripture, can you sustain the prayer made by you as above? Was there ever a similar one in God's oracles, either in the Old or New Testament? Surely they who pay you two thousand dollars annually will be poorly remunerated if they wait till the Spirit obeys your *illegal* request, and, divested of the all-conquering *word*, *regenerates them.* What! pray to the Holy Spirit to come down and do his work among the people! Can it be possible that any man may fail seeing that you have displayed a great ignorance of the scriptures! Now, I think it will appear by and by, that you are equally ignorant with those Baptists who have, through ignorance, joined brother Campbell in the cause of truth. In the case above quoted the Lord Jesus prayed to the Father, or promised to do so, that he would send the Comforter; and again he promised, in an after discourse, upon the same topic, to send the Comforter himself. Think you that he understood the office of the Holy Spirit? If *he* did, it is self-evident that you do not; for, according to his own word, the Comforter is controlled by the *Father and the Son;* but according to your word, the Spirit may come or do as *he* pleases! I have never understood from my Bible that it was proper to pray to the Holy Spirit for any thing.

Again, let us hear the Lord Jesus once more, in the 14th chapter and 26th verse of John. "But the Comforter, which is the Holy Spirit, whom the Father will send *in my name,* he shall teach you all things," &c. &c. I have given you at least three quotations from the Lord Jesus hostile to what is contained in your prayer. And by the mouth of two or three witnesses every word shall be established. And that being the case, it must appear evident that the weight of testimony is against you.

Your prayer being ended, you then sang to the Holy Spirit, as follows:—

" Come, Holy Spirit, Heav'nly Dove,
		With all thy quick'ning powers!
	Kindle a flame of sacred love
		In these cold hearts of ours."

In the singing this hymn, which is very ingeniously adapted to your sermon and prayer, you have very unfortunately fallen into two errors. First—you are singing to the Holy Spirit, as you prayed to it, without any example from any one of the old saints, either in the Old or New Testament, and without the possibility of ever receiving an answer to your prayer. The second error into which you have fallen, is this: you acknowledge your church to be the church of Christ: and if the church of Christ, its members of course have the spirit of Christ. Hear brother Paul, *Gal.* iv. 6. "Because you are sons, God has sent forth the spirit of his Son into your hearts, crying, Abba, Father;" and having the Spirit, "*a flame of sacred love*" had long since been kindled in their "*cold hearts,*" and yet you request in your song that the Holy Spirit would come and kindle that which had long since been set on fire! This is fine logic, brother Brantly! Why, sir, I should blush for any of our backwoods Baptists were such logic displayed before me by them.

Do you not think, brother Brantly, that you had better read your creed less and Bible more, before you undertake another stricture upon the character of those ignorant and factious Baptists, of whom you have said so many hard things? You must know, sir, that we closely adhere to God's word, and delight in *such* ignorance and faction. That we have never opposed united effort in promoting the spread of the gospel; but that we have long since opposed "*education*" such as yours, for I perceive that you have drawn largely from the distilleries of scholastic divinity.

Before I bid you adieu, I beg you never again to offer such an insult to the *word* of God as you did in your sermon. The time has been, when the unwarrantable dissections of an ungodly and supercilious priesthood were endured without a murmur; but remember that that Virgin of the Skies which heretofore has borne with their sacrilegious innovations, is now appearing in her heavenly power and majesty; and what she has gently suffered she will endure no more; but being "living and effectual, and more cutting than any two-edged sword," she will *pierce* "even to the parting both of animal life and spirit, and the joints also and marrow;" and thus satiate her vengeance in their destruction, if they reform not.					A Western Baptist.

The Happy New Year.

Paternus had been accustomed to call together his descendants to celebrate the anniversary of his birth, which happened to be on the first day of the year. On these occasions he was wont to recite to his children and grand children the most interesting incidents of his life, and to deduce such moral lessons as the occasions suggested and the exigencies of the times required. He was now entering upon his eightieth year, and the wife of his youth had more than completed her seventy-sixth. He had assembled the eight families of his sons and daughters, and two families of his grand-sons, a-mounting in all to seventy-five souls, and all residents of the county in which he lived. The old mansion of his grandfather and the large dining hall, the scene of this happy new year, was filled with the prattling objects of his parental solicitude and affection. The affectionate greetings of the little cousins, uncles, and aunts, and the little exploits of the young talkers and walkers imparted much gaiety and cheerfulness to the scene. After they had all refreshed themselves with the liberal collations which the season afforded, and had retired from the festive table, they were arranged, according to seniority, around the cheerful fire, which a fierce north wind had made most comfortable. Meanwhile the prattling of the little ones had been lulled to repose, and all who had not capacity for rational entertainment were found at rest in the arms of sleep. Paternus sat in the old fashioned armed chair, in which his own grand father had sat, and the fondest object of his youthful affection, and the comfort of his old age, sat by his side, in the very chair on which she had often sung to repose her first born son. Thus placed, they all sang a hymn of thanksgiving, after which the old patriarch with a clear and tremulous voice, thus began:

"Kind and indulgent Heaven has once more brought us all together under the roof of our ancestors, and surrounded us with his guardian arms, and with favors more than we can tell. I have yesterday completed my seventy-ninth year, hallowed be his name! and yet continue to enjoy both health of body and vigor of mind. But my withered face and hoary locks admonish me that soon I must go the way of all the earth and sleep with my good forefathers. I am glad to see my children and my grand-children all around me on this my birth day; and now that I am permitted to see and salute so many of the objects of my dearest affection, I wish to make this opportunity an occasion of inculcating one lesson upon all of you, which I have often suggested to you before, but now from new considerations and more mature reflections. But to do this with the most advantage, I will give you the history of our family for three generations, which is as far back as I am able to trace it. This I have often purposed to do, and have occasionally given to some of you some sketches of it, but have never done it fully, nor even partially, to all of you. I do this not to gratify your pride, nor to inflame your worldly ambition; for in our history there is nothing, or very little, adapted to cherish the former or augment the latter. 'Tis true that both my father and my grandfather attained to the distinction of a good name, and left to me the rich inheritance of an unspotted integrity, which I have endeavored to transmit unimpaired to you. They were respected in their day for their virtues; and their industry and christian morality obtained a patrimony which afforded themselves a competence, and gave to their children a good and useful, though not a learned education. I had two brothers and one sister who shared my father's inheritance with me; and I, being the eldest, inherited this farm and the old mansion, which, for the same reason, my father inherited from my grandfather, who obtained it by his own industry and some little aids which a distant relative extended to him. Our family has, indeed, become numerous. My sister left behind her eleven children, and my two brothers have to-

gether more descendants than I have. But it is neither the number, wealth, nor political respectability of our family on which I have any desire to expatiate; but the moral virtue and christian excellence of many of your relatives which I desire to lay before you for the purpose which I have supremely in view. Of my grand father's family seven brothers and three sisters lived and died members of the kingdom of Jesus Christ. My grandmother was reputed to be the most eminent christian in her vicinity in her day, and is said to have been a sort of mother to the whole church in Hellensborough on the banks of the Humber. My grand father was proverbially a just and pious man, and some of you have seen and known both my father and mother. Their virtues are known, and, I trust, appreciated by the elder branches of my family, and are yet alive in the memory of many of our neighbors in this vicinity. Sixty-three persons of our family, including my grandfather and grandmother, my own father and mother, uncles, aunts, and cousins, are enrolled in the church books of our parish, as having lived and died members of the family of God; and there are yet living, including those here present, of our family, eighty-five persons professing godliness. But why, you will ask me, do I make these enumerations and go into these details? I will answer you. It is to open to your view the instrument and source of all this good, from which I am to draw my moral, and which I am about to present to you all as my new year's gift —and, perhaps, my last new year's gift to my dear offspring. All the christian excellence and christian happiness possessed and enjoyed in our family can be traced to the mother of my grand father, and through her to another disciple of our glorious Master and Redeemer. The history of my great grand mother is briefly this:—Her father was a wild and profligate character, whose vices brought him immaturely to the grave at the age of twenty-seven. Her mother pined away and died heart-broken and disconsolate, leaving behind her two daughters, my great grand mother and her sister, the former aged two years, and the latter four, when they lost their mother. A kind and amiable christian lady, Mrs. Richardson, daughter of the pious and learned William Tindal, took my great grandmother, when two years old, into her own family, and brought her up, when a proud and unfeeling aunt, Mrs. Stockton, refused the trouble. Her sister fell into the hands of another aunt, who had no more religion, but a little more humanity, and a good deal more natural affection than Mrs. Stockton. She brought her up after her own heart and example: and having married an officer in the army, she accompanied him to the Indies, where, in a few years, she died. Concerning her descendants I have no information.

"To return to Mrs. Richardson. This amiable lady, like Job, "the case which she knew not she sought out." She spent the greater part of her time in ministering to the saints, and in acts of christian sympathy and tenderness. Tradition has informed me that she was one of the most diligent matrons in her day in educating her family in the knowledge of the sacred scriptures. Her husband was a barrister of some note, but not a christian himself, he left the management of his daughters entirely to his wife.— She is said to have read the scriptures to her children, accompanied with her prayers, in her own closet; and so soon as they could understand the meaning of the most familiar language, she imbued their minds with the knowledge of God and his Son Jesus Christ. She was wont to interrogate them on the subjects which she read to them; and so soon as they could read, she induced them, by every sort of allurement, to read and commit to memory many passages of the evangelical history and of the devotional part of the Old and New Testaments. She brought up my great grand-mother as one of her own children, and it is said that she did not know that Mrs. Richardson was not her own mother until she was in her sixteenth year. She is, moreover, said to have shed many tears of sorrow when she heard, for the first time, that she whom she had always called *mother* was not her mother, but her benefactress. Mrs. Richardson said to her, 'Mary, Do you not love Jesus Christ?' 'I do,' she replied. 'Why do you love him?' she next asked her.— 'Because I believe that he loved me and died for me,' she rejoined. 'Well, then, was it not I who made you acquainted with him, who first taught you who he was, and what he had done for you; and if you have been *born again,* as I trust you are, I am your *mother in the Lord;* and although not your natural parent in the flesh, I am your mother in a relation and sense dearer than nature knows, and more durable than time itself. Weep not, my dear Mary; I am your mother, you are my daughter in the Lord; and I trust that as I have hitherto been to you a mother, I will so continue, and that you shall always be my daughter.' Thus speaking, she fell upon her neck, and embracing her, said, 'The Lord bless you, my daughter, and keep you from evil, and make you a mother to many as I have been to you!'' This prayer, said the venerable Paternus, while the tears were rolling down the furrows of his wrinkled face—this prayer has been answered as certainly as I live; for this very Mary was in her nineteenth year married to him who was the progenitor of all those families of which I have told you, and from whom we are all descended. I can trace our history no farther back, and I am glad that so far I can trace it with perfect certainty, through channels the most authentic.—Behold, then, the source of all our nobility, of all that has given respectability to our family, and religion and happiness to so many now living, and so many already dead. I have now, my dear children, told you the history of our family, and I hope you will each of you preserve it with as much fidelity and accuracy, and transmit it to your families with as much precision as I now give it to you.

"But now for the moral. You will, no doubt, have seen that all the good, religious and moral, which our family has enjoyed, has been instrumentally derived to us from the piety of Mrs. Richardson. Had my great grand-mother fallen into the hands of her who took charge of her sister, how different in all human probability, would have been our lot at this day! 'Tis true she was but the instrument in the hand of our Heavenly Father; but he always works by means; and what a scheme of benevolence is that which honors and rewards the *instrument* as though it had been the *author* of so much good! And such most certainly is the scheme of divine philanthropy. Now let me present this matter to you in another light. If it be true, as it most unquestionably is, that all human beings will be rewarded according to their works, how great will be the reward of those who, like the christian matron, the benefactress of our family, have originated a cumulative system, which, as the current of time advances, transmits in deeper and wider channels its blessings and its bounties to men? How long must this stream flow before the actual result can be computed and de-

cided? Perhaps a thousand years may be completed before her good works have ceased to follow her! And if you transmit these blissful influences, precepts, and examples, which have descended by a sort of inheritance to you—I say, if you hand down the cup of bliss to your offspring uncorrupted, I am sure many more will drink of it. But as yet we have not considered the influence which acts collaterally upon our contemporaries. We have only considered those which descend in the direct lines of succession. I cannot form any estimate of the good that has passed from my progenitors to their associates in life. I have heard much, and know a good deal, of what happiness has accrued to other families, and to the neighborhoods with which they conversed. They were lights in their day and salt to the generation in which they lived; but I am without sufficient data to conclude, or form a correct idea, of how much was achieved by them to the glory of God and the good of men. When the book of God's remembrance is opened I know much will appear to their praise, and honor, and glory, at the coming of our Lord Jesus Christ.

"There is another light in which this subject is to be viewed. You are not to think that she who originated this wide diffusive scheme of benevolence is the only individual who is to be rewarded for all that has grown out of it, or is yet growing out of it. God's rewards are not so few, nor his favor so parsimonious, as that he can distinguish but a few of his faithful servants. He can afford to reward the originator of a scheme of benevolence for all the good it produces, and each one of the continuators, as though he had no fellow-servant assisting in the cause. Were it otherwise, the twelve apostles would have all the rewards for all the temporal and eternal good which christianity has produced, or is capable of producing. Each and every one of the faithful laborers in the Lord's vineyard will receive a reward for all the good he does and produces, although he had no predecessor nor successor in the work.

"But if, and I know no reason why it should not be so—I say, but if the negligent and the indifferent are to be charged with evil which they might have prevented, and condemned for not having done the good in their power, how cumulative, too, is the system of iniquity, and how awful the condemnation of them who instituted a course or system of sinning, which has increased and is increasing with every revolution of time. The apostles of infidelity, the propagators of error and of schemes of immorality, diffusive and operative in their nature, are as worthy of condemnation for the remote, as well as for the proximate evil effects of their respective systems. And upon the same principles of remunerating justice, the originator and the coadjutor, the continuator and his abettor, will each receive a recompense according to his deeds. Thus it is that we are not like isolated beings, each one acting for himself alone, as angels do; but the condition of this department of the universe, of the human family, is, that we are all standing together in a peculiar chain or concatenation of causes and effects, of parents and children, mutually dependent on, and responsible to one another, and to our common parent, the Creator and Judge of All. It is a department of the universe *sui generis,* of its own sort, and can be understood correctly only when the parts are viewed in relation to the whole, and the whole in relation to the parts. But the bible is the best, for it is the only expositor of the whole, and he that is not governed by it in his reasonings, as well as in his conduct, has ever proved himself to be a fool. But I feel disposed to hear in return your views on all that I have suggested, and will yield to you when I have expressed one, and the most ardent wish of my heart, and that is, that you may transmit to your posterity every christian quality you have inherited from your ancestors; that you may not only yourselves enjoy the blessings of the salvation of God, but that you may hand them down with your names to the remotest times, ever remembering that the mercy of God is upon them that fear him to many generations, even to thousands of them that love him and keep his commandments."

After singing the ninetieth psalm, the venerable Paternus knelt down and prayed with them all, recounting the mercies of God through many years, and commending his children, grand children, and great-grand children to the God of his fathers, with a fervor and affection that none of the adults present can ever forget.

If you think this incident worthy of reading, I may furnish you with another, of a similar character, on some future occasion.

EDITOR.

Richmond, Dec. 14, 1829.

Extract of a letter to the editor of the Christian Baptist, dated,

"LONDONDERRY, Nov. 5th, 1829.

"VERY DEAR BROTHER—Although personally a stranger to you, I have enjoyed an acquaintance with your writings for a length of time. From them I have received great advantages. Many opinions which I formerly held very strenuously, I found, upon examination, were unfounded; and many truths, of which I was ignorant, have been brought before my mind through the instrumentality of that ably edited periodical, the Christian Baptist. Many of my friends in this your native land have reason to bless God that ever they saw it; and although their prejudices were against you at first, they yielded to the evidence of all-powerful truth. Many of *us* (for I class myself among them) were so prejudiced, that when we read a few pages of the Christian Baptist we resolved on reading no more, conceiving your sentiments to be heterodox, &c. &c. thus condemning you unheard. When we gave you a hearing, however, we found that your sentiments were in general accordance with the revelation of the King of kings and Lord of lords.

"I, in common with my brethren, am greatly pleased with your Essays on the Clergy, the Work of the Holy Spirit, the Ancient Order of Things, &c. &c. Whilst, however, we agree with you in the main, and consider you a zealous, fearless, and able champion of truth, we cannot assent to all that you have written. You know that faith depends upon evidence, and that your motto is, "Prove all things: hold fast that which is good." Now, my dear brother, as a professed disciple of Christ and a student of his word, I would open my mind to you, and hope you will consider and answer the following:—

"1. Would not your arguments against missionaries to the heathen militate equally against the proclamation of the gospel in these lands; and could not the same evidence be produced in heathen lands for its authenticity, as in Britain or America?

"2. You consider it right for an approved brother to act as a messenger of the churches, and you consider him as the representative of the church. Now could not an individual represent a church in heathen lands as well as in those parts of Ireland where there is no christian church?

"Is it right for any individual to deprive himself of an opportunity of meeting with a church on the Lord's day, for the purpose of preaching the gospel to the world? And are there any means in operation for the conversion of the heathen upon the plan you think scriptural?

"4. In your essays upon immersion, you say that Peter on the Pentecost proclaimed 'reformation and immersion as equally necessary to forgiveness. Faith is not more evidently connected with immersion than is immersion with the forgiveness of sins.' In essay 5th, 'Where there is a guilty conscience there is an impure heart; in such a heart the Holy Spirit cannot dwell. Without immersion nothing can be done acceptably,' &c. Now if this be true, how can any individual be a believer, enjoy peace, the pardon of his sins, have the Holy Spirit, and ultimately arrive at heaven, and yet unimmersed?

"5. You say, 'No acts of devotion are enjoined on the unbaptized.' How can you, then, join them in prayer, praise, the Lord's supper, &c. upon this hypothesis, no matter how excellent their christian character may be?

"6. I think you are very inconsistent with yourself in admitting unimmersed persons into the church, seeing you lay so much stress upon immersion. If immersion be necessary to forgiveness of sins, as you endeavor to prove, can remission of sins be enjoyed without it? And if not, why admit the unimmersed into that kingdom concerning which the Saviour said, "Except a man be born of water and of the Spirit, he cannot enter into the kingdom of God?"

"7. I am decidedly hostile to the admission of unimmersed believers into the church, finding neither precept nor precedent for it in the sacred record, and considering with you that it would be dangerous to the empire of Emanuel.

"8. How inconsistent your Review of the History of Churches, No. 3. vol. 5, page 379,—I mean how inconsistent the latter part of the first paragraph with the former part of it and the second paragraph, and with the views of this subject contained in your debate with M'Calla.

"9. You call those weak-headed Baptists who blame you for calling that creature named Stone a brother. I must class myself among those weak heads; for I cannot conceive how any man can be a christian and worship a created intelligence, no matter how exalted. 'Neither theories are worth an hour.'—What! not worth an hour's reflection to consider whether we are worshipping God or one of his creatures? Oh! think of this. If Christ be not God, it is idolatry to worship him. If he were not God, he could not have made an atonement for sin. His obedience would have been circumscribed by his own individuality. How, then, can we call them christians or brethren, who would degrade him to the rank of a mere creature? The best kind of Arianism I consider as bad as the worst Socinianism. Both strike at the root of christianity. Besides, I consider your answer to Mr. Stone very uncandid. Why did you not vindicate that unanswerable dissertation upon *John* i. 1.? If it be right to make assertions, it is right to defend them; or if you consider speculation upon the incomprehensible Jehovah wrong, why did you attack the Trinitarians at all? and is it not of infinitely greater consequence to vindicate what you term 'the proper divinity of the Saviour,' against the Arians and Unitarians (these worst of all sects) than to prune the redundancies of the Calvinists?

"10. Your friends in Ireland would feel very much obliged by your writing an essay on the divinity of Christ, not in the language of Ashdod, but in language consonant with that of the Holy Oracles. We would wish you to express clearly your views of his character, so that we may have more gags to stop the mouths of some little creatures even in this country, who are 'striving to undo your influence by the charge of Arianism, Socinianism, and other obnoxious *isms*.'

"Thus, my dear brother, have I opened my mind to you. I think it necessary to say, that in general I approve of your Essays on Immersion; but I cannot account for the above-mentioned inconsistency. Your Remarks on Missionaries I also approve of; but wish my mind to be satisfied about what I have stated. Your works are read by a good many in the north of Ireland.— Would to God they were generally diffused, that the community might be no longer duped by a race of creatures calling themselves ambassadors of Christ. We see the dawn of that day when the inhabitants of Ireland shall be emancipated from religious slavery and surrender themselves to the guidance of the great and mighty Lord.— Oh! that all the saints would exert themselves in their Master's cause. There is scarcely an individual in Ireland to proclaim the ancient gospel, save those who have received a college education. And I verily believe that the gospel preached by the generality of such characters is not more ancient than John Calvin or John Wesley.

"Since I wrote my last to you, a church of Christ, near Dungannon, ordained two of their brethren to the office of overseers. These are unlettered men, but possess the qualifications mentioned in Timothy and Titus. The Baptist churches in Ireland are increasing a little. In America you are a century before us. All the churches with which I am acquainted request me to present their Christian salutation to you. They also send their love to all those congregations in the New World who worship Christ as the God of the Universe, regard his sacrifice as the sole basis of a sinner's hope, and walk in all the ordinances and commandments of the Lord blameless. Praying that your body, soul, and spirit may be preserved blameless until the King Eternal calls you home; and having no reason either for publishing or concealing my name, I remain, with much affection, your brother in the hope of glory, W. T.

"P. S.—I am well pleased with your New Testament, and generally with your Preface and Appendix. We are very anxious to see your Debate with Mr. Owen. He has got a great hackling in the Irish prints. All parties in Ireland rejoice in your triumph over him."

Extract of a Letter to the Editor, dated
"Cincinnati, December 14, 1829."

"Dear Brother Campbell—For some years past I have occasionally heard Campbellism spoken of as a very heterodox and dangerous thing; but feeling myself tolerably well established in the orthodox creed, I did not trouble myself much about it until within a short time. A few months since there were many in these parts who manifested an increasing desire to investigate the New Testament on the subject of religion, and endeavor, if possible, to understand what was meant by what is called the "Ancient Gospel." My wife was one who soon became entangled with "Campbellism," (as the good brethren called it,) and much engaged in what

she conceived to be the ancient order; and tried to teach myself and others, almost night and day, the way of the Lord more perfectly. This ancient order I could not understand, believing that the Baptist order was the most ancient, as they were in the habit of baptizing, (not rantizing.) I concluded, however, to pay some attention to the subject, although I had been a professed Baptist for about thirteen years. So soon as I began to reflect and examine whether there was a "more excellent way," I found a mountain of prejudices in my mind which must be broken down and levelled to the earth. I found, too, all of my opinions; and, in addition to these, there were the "Articles of Faith and Practice" to be laid aside, which you know the Baptists look upon as almost or quite sound.— Horrible thing! With these conflicting sentiments, I at length concluded to lay aside all— Campbellism, Calvinism, and all other *isms*, and take the New Testament as my creed, rule of faith and practice.

"The word of the Great King appears to be simple and plain, and that he meant just what he told the people—so plain, that "the wayfaring man, though a fool, need not err therein." The simplicity of the gospel is the glory of it: and I think that thousands would have embraced it, who are now infidels, had not our clergy shrouded it in such dark mysticism that they themselves cannot understand it. Now is it possible that the great God, in making his last revelation to man, on the reception or rejection of which depends his salvation or condemnation, should make it in unintelligible language which they could not understand, or have any just conception of? I think not. The world appears to be in an awful state. Darkness covers the earth, and gross darkness the minds of the people. Prejudice and bigotry seem to pervade the minds of the christian world. Professors are wedded to their creeds, and preconceived opinions; and it is like taking off a right arm, or plucking out a right eye, for them to lay them all aside as they would an old worn out garment, which had become entirely useless, and embrace the truth as it is in Jesus.

"I have said much more than I at first intended, but I will observe further, that I have come to this conclusion, that the gospel is plain and simple, and is yet the power of God to every one that believes it; to the Jew first, and also to the Greek. That our brethren are in darkness as it respects the simplicity of the gospel, and its superiority over the inventions of men, and yet they know it not. That it is high time for a general reformation, and that it ought to begin among the professed followers of our Lord and Saviour Jesus Christ. But while I deplore the present state of things, I rejoice that a glorious reformation has commenced, and that there are many who dare to be singular, and preach the ancient gospel; that its light is spreading like fire in a dry stubble; and although it will meet with opposition and persecution, I am confident that it will prevail and spread until all shall believe in one Lord, one faith, one baptism; that opposers might as well attempt to stop the sun in its course, or pluck the moon from its orbit, as to stop the spreading of this glorious light, emanating, as it does, from the gospel of the blessed God. And while I feel thus confident of the present and ultimate success of the truth, I feel to groan and lament over the prejudices of our dear brethren, who cannot, (at present) enter with enraptured delight into these views. They cannot, I say, because they will not seriously and impartially investigate the subject. So soon as they consent to do this, they will, they must embrace them. I would say, then, Go on, combat every opposition by the word of eternal truth! and while you have opposers on every hand, there are here and there one who feels disposed to encourage your heart and strengthen your hands in the good work. As such I would, for this time, subscribe myself

An INQUIRER FOR TRUTH.

No 7.]   FEBRUARY 1, 1830.
To Bengelius.

DEAR SIR,—THAT my papers published in the Christian Baptist, if noticed at all, would—among a self-created order of proud, overbearing usurpers, whose predecessors had, for many ages, been accustomed to lord it over the understandings, consciences and purses of their fellow-men, not less than the present race—produce such effects as you mention, was precisely what I calculated on. That, like the approvers and defenders of all existing customs, practices, or systems by which they profit, no matter how false, unjust, and oppressive they may be, they should, as Demetrius and his workmen formerly did when their craft was in danger, raise a hideous clamor, and, instead of coming forth as honest men and real lovers of truth, attempt to demonstrate the falsehood of my assertions by showing their inconsistency with God's word and human reason, they should, by imputing to them a multitude of frightful, but wholly imaginary consequences, labor to deter their bigoted followers from receiving the truth, is no unexpected occurrence, it being the course and the means which interested impostors have adopted in all ages to maintain their influence. When my essays shall be completed, and the system of religious instruction which I think the Spirit of God has proposed and enjoined in the New Testament, shall be, according to the best of my weak judgment, unfolded, all I shall claim for it is a fair and full trial of its efficiency. Should it prove wretchedly abortive like the present, or paganize the world, as its dreaming opposers predict, cast it out; but if, on a fair trial, it should christianize the world in a much higher degree than the present has done, it will no doubt receive to itself a continuance. At any rate let neither friend nor foe censure and condemn it before it is known. All I have yet attempted is mere assault on a few of the out-works of the clerical castle; against the citadel itself not a shot has been fired—and as to the new edifice, not even the foundation stone has been laid. Did ever mortal man act so foolishly as to proceed to erect a new building on the very site on which an old one stood, before he had pulled down the old fabric and cleared away its rubbish? About preaching, teaching, and exhorting, in the scriptural use and sense of these terms, I have certainly said nothing, at least condemnatory.— What place they are destined to occupy in the system of religious instruction which I intend to propose, and propose merely because I believe it to be the system proposed and enjoined by the great Teacher and Ruler of the church on earth, for into it not one peg of mine shall enter, unless it enter inadvertently, will be seen when my views are exhibited. Till then let fuss and foolish clamor cease.

But if, in the mean time, the tenants of the old castle be disposed to defend their out-posts, I blame them not. A craft which poured annually so many millions into the clerical purse is not likely to be given up without a struggle; let them, however, confine the means which they employ to the defence which they undertake.

I have asserted that in my judgment it is an act of gross impiety, of great disrespect to God, to presume to alter in any manner, or by any means, the order, connection, or diction of his instructive message; that the act sets our wisdom above the wisdom of God, and tells that omniscient and all-wise Being, to his face, that his message has not been as well contrived and clearly worded as it might have been, or as we can still render it: in short, that we can ameliorate God's best effort to serve us.

I have asserted that all that is necessary to render God's message as plain and instructive as he ever intended it to be, or our salvation required it to be, is a correct and perfectly intelligible translation, that is, a translation devoid of all unintelligible words.

I have asserted that unless a person understand the scriptures perfectly himself, he cannot possibly determine whether the explanations and meanings proposed by others, be correct or not; and that, of course, if he receives such explanations as divine information, he deceives himself, and builds his faith on a human, and not on a divine foundation; on the notions of men about the meaning of scripture, and not on scripture itself. It much concerns, therefore, those who are in the practice of proposing their own explanations or notions about the meaning of scripture, instead of proposing God's own word to either children, servants, or others, to see that their children, servants, and others be not made to build their eternal hopes on the fallacious apprehensions of men, instead of the infallible declarations of God. What! Is the language of men fitter to convey information clearly than the language of God?—Truly I cannot believe it.

As to the inferences drawn from my papers, if they really be such as you state, they can, with truth, be considered only as the ravings of men who have bid adieu to common sense. To obey the positive commands of their Redeemer, and to perform, in a social manner, every action which he has commanded to be so performed, as well as the commemorative supper, and none else, is not only of great use, but of indispensable use to the followers of their Redeemer. We are told that the primitive christians persevered in the apostles' doctrine, (and where, pray, is it to be found? In the inspired written oracles of God, or in the blundering compositions of men?) and in the performance of an action termed *koinonia*, and in prayers, as well as in the breaking of bread: and in other places that they met for mutual edification. But where is the command to listen to the harangues of uninspired, fallible, blundering clergymen?

I am engaged at present in instituting a comparison between the instrument of instruction sent by God to a perishing world, and the clerical inventions, which have bred so much dissension, wasted so much time, and cost more than man's residence in this life would sell for.

A. STRAITH.

Extract of a Letter to the Editor, dated
BLUFFDALE, GREEN Co. ILLINOIS, Dec. 5, 1829.
"My opinion is not of sufficient importance to render any one vain, but such as it is, it is warmly in favor of the Christian Baptist. I know of no work in our country so well conducted, and, what will be far more gratifying to your feelings, none that is doing half the good in this state that it is. "Campbellism," and "Campbellites,"

have become very common terms in Illinois, and they are not unfrequently pronounced with a bitterness that reminds me of the "Christian Dog" of the Turks. Is hostility to pure, unde-filed religion found nowhere except among Infi-dels? It is not; nor is persecution confined to the walls of the inquisition. Public opinion on the subject of religion is however, rapidly under-going a change: inquiry is abroad, and the time has gone by when religious sentiments are to be adopted merely because they are prescribed by men of high sounding titles. In bringing about this revolution, the fearless numbers of the Chris-tian Baptist have been chiefly instrumental, and I deeply regret that you have felt so much of the persecuting spirit of the middle ages assailing you from almost every section where your work circulates:—but go on; and may you not desist till primitive religion is every where restored. How deeply every sincere christian must regret to hear the boast that a "christian party in poli-tics shall be established." Even in this state religion is too often made an electioneering hob-by. We have not yet arrived at the "Free grace candidates," and "Unconditional election can-didates," of good old orthodox New England; but we are making some advances towards it. A powerful effort is making at the eastward, to direct and control religion in this state. Ten thousand dollars are raising to establish a college here, and for the support of its faculty. You have seen the speech of Rev. Mr. Ellis, to his employers, in which he so feelingly makes known our profound ignorance, and the deplorable state of our morals. He represents us as but little above the *zero* of absolute heathenism; as elect-ing to the office of lieutenant governor, a cler-gyman who solicited our suffrages with "a Bible in one hand, and a bucket of whiskey in the other." This, he tells us, is literally true. Pity that no man should have known it except Mr. Ellis. With the lieutenant governor and Mr. Ellis both, I happen to be acquainted. Of the former, even his political enemies acknowledge him to be an amiable and pious man. Of the latter, more hereafter. Several missionaries have recently been sent here, and more are promised. How kind, how generous, and how benevolent in the eastern people to make us the magnificent present of ten thousand dollars! How great must be the love to *us* that could have induced them to pass by the tens of thousands in their own section, who are suffering poverty, and "all the ills that flesh is heir to," and to whom this dona-tion would have been like a well of cold water to travellers perishing in the desert! The num-ber of paupers in New England and New-York are as four hundred to one, compared with those of Illinois; this, too, when the relative population of these sections are taken into account. A large majority of the eastern people are compelled to toil incessantly and practise the severest economy to support life on their barren soil. I do not speak unadvisedly when I say that the necessaries of life can be procured in this state in as great abundance by two days' labor in seven, as they can in New-England by six. This is a land of plenty, where want is unknown, and where almost every table is bountifully spread. The great mass of the eastern population feel the reverse of all this; they toil like a western slave, and if their labor is remitted for but a single day;

"*Non aliter quam qui adverso vix flumine lembum*
"*Remigiis subigit: brachia forte remisit,*
"*Atque illum in praeceps prono rapit alveus amni.*"

"To this class of people, to whom a barrel

of flour, or of pork, is of more value than six would be to an Illinois farmer—to this class, their missionaries inform us, we are indebted for a large portion of this magnificent donation. What obligations are we not under to make good use of this donation, wrung, drop by drop, as it has been, from hands barely removed from breaking the bread of charity! But I will pursue this subject no farther, and nothing was more remote from my intentions when I commenced writing, than touching upon it at all.

"I have seen but one copy of your Testament. I set up a large portion of the night in examining it. I think it much truer to the spirit of the original than any other version that I have seen. I have not the presumption to criticise, but you will pardon me for thinking that a passage in John (Evangelist) is not conformable to the Greek of the common copy. Perhaps I shall only dis-play my own ignorance. In *John*, chap. ii. ver. 4, Τι εμοι και σοι γυναι; I should have translated, "Woman, what is that to you and me?"

To Mr. T. W.

King and Queen, December 18, 1829.

Sir,—While I acknowledge the oversight, for it was an oversight, that a solution of the nine teenth query, published in the Christian Baptist of April last, had been partially given in the latter part of the remarks made on the sixteenth query published in the Christian Baptist of March last; yet I cannot agree with you in opinion in your very positive declarations made in reply to "A Constant Reader," published in November last. In speaking of our popular preachers, (so called in the Christian Baptist) you say—"He styles them living witnesses, who stand as in Christ's stead. Who preach, saying, The king-dom of heaven is at hand; repent and believe the gospel. According to these characteristics, we should first conclude, that they are false wit-nesses; because they never witnessed one single item of what they preach, if so be it is contained in the Bible; for this plain reason, they were born too late." Alas! alas! has "the fine gold become dim?" Now, sir, going much farther back than seventeen hundred years, before the editor of the Christian Baptist was born, I would ask you whether, as an individual, you ever wit-nessed this item, which is contained in the Bible? "They that wait upon the Lord, shall renew their strength; they shall mount up as eagles; they shall run and not be weary; walk and not faint." Again, "To you that fear my name, shall the Sun of Righteousness arise with healing in his wings." And again, coming down to a more recent day; "My yoke is easy and my burden is light." If Mr. T. W. has never wit-nessed these items, by having the witness in his own breast, I fear that he is, at best, nothing more than a nominal christian. Believe me, there is a difference between belief and knowledge. He that comes to God must believe, that he is, &c. but there is such a thing as knowing him; and not only believing that he is; but of knowing it too. I know, said Job, that my Redeemer lives, &c. Our populars profess to have witnessed those items with many others; having witnessed, in their own persons, the truth contained in them, they stand, being living witnesses, declaring to the church and to the world, that they are such. If any man have not the spirit of Christ, he is none of his! If, then, a man have the spirit of Christ and preach the gospel, he stands as in Christ's stead—God moving in him, both to will and to do, of his good pleasure. Should Mr.

56

T. W. have left Bethany, the Editor of the Christian Baptist will please publish the above, (indeed, in any event, I ask of the Editor this favor) and thereby oblige a subscriber who is

"A Constant Reader."

Reply to "A Constant Reader."

Dear Sir,—It so happened, that, in the course of my peregrinations, I arrived at Bethany just as your *critique* upon my reply to your communication of May 10th, 1829, was put to press. Not finding the editor at home, as I expected, I take the liberty of correcting the mistake which elicited your criticisms upon said reply. The mistake is simply this: You confound receiving testimony with giving testimony:—"having the witness in one's self," with being one's self the witness; than which no two things can be more distinct. The original and only proper witnesses bore testimony to that which from the beginning "they had heard," had seen, had contemplated, had handled, of the word of life; all which things being external—the proper objects of sense, and consequently of testimony-bearing, the apostles were competent to declare in the character of witnesses. Not so the witness or testimony of which John speaks, general epistle, v. 10. and of which the quotations which you make, as intending the internal experimental efficacy of the truth upon the heart, speak; for this is purely matter of experience. Now, although a man's testimony may be justly credited concerning his feelings, concerning the effects of the word upon his mind; yet it would be an abuse of language—an outrage upon common sense, to call him a witness of the things that passed in his own mind; and still more so, to style him, on this account, a witness of facts, of which he possessed not one item of the certainty of the apostolic evidence, (see said epistle, chap. i. 1. 2. 3.;) but, on the contrary, merely became conscious of the blissful effects of the truth believed through the persuasive evidence of the apostolic testimony above cited.

You justly say, "There is a difference between belief and knowledge," and I believe you: and had you believed yourself in so saying, it would have saved both you and me some trouble;—you the trouble of striving to defend the unfounded and presumptuous pretensions of the "populars," and of laboring to prove me and others destitute of the genuine and blissful effects of the truth believed, by supposing us ignorant of the internal evidence, because we refuse to assume the apostolic character—and me the trouble of endeavoring to rectify those mistakes.

Now, my dear sir, as you assert with earnestness, that there is a difference between faith and knowledge, let me ask you upon which of these do you say,—do the populars say,—they found their testimony, when they style themselves,—when you style them—living witnesses? If they are such in the true apostolic sense, they can justly claim apostolic certainty—they can justly say, "That which was from the beginning, which we have seen," &c. and prove the truth of their testimony as the apostles did. In this way they will ask no favors; they will make no unreasonable demands upon our faith. But every body knows, the populars claim no such certainty; they pretend to no such proofs; they differ nothing from the weakest of their brethren in these respects. They have received and learned all at second hand, upon the testimony of others; and like others, in so far as they have believed the truth, they have felt its influence;

and, like others, they can testify what they feel, and this is all they know; and all the rest is faith: and between knowledge and faith you declare there is a difference—and so do I. I, therefore, boldly affirm, that these, so called, "living witnesses," never witnessed one item of what they preach, in so far as it is contained in the bible; and this for the plain reason before assigned—"they were born too late." They may, however, preach their own experiences, and these may correspond with what is written; and, in so far be to themselves a matter of fact evidence of the truth believed; but, of which truth they themselves have been first persuaded, upon the evidence of the divine testimony, and is therefore neither designed to produce faith in themselves nor in any body else—not in themselves, for it is the effect of faith—"He that believes has the witness in himself." Not in others, for they have it not. This witness or evidence of the truth of the divine testimony, is the property only of him that believes, (*John* v. 10.) consequently, has nothing to do with the unbeliever, nor he with it. Nor is this given to be preached for the conviction and conversion of sinners; Christ, and him crucified, is to be preached for these purposes: but this internal evidence is for the comfort and support of the believer.

Again, though the witness or testimony which the believer possesses, is to him divine, being the result of his belief in the divine testimony; yet his declaration of it, being that of an uninspired man, cannot produce a divine faith, his testimony being merely human: whereas, every thing that is necessary to be taught or believed for the salvation and perfection of the believing and obedient subject, was published, confirmed, and recorded in the divine oracles seventeen hundred years ago.

By this time, sir, I hope you see the striking difference between having a witness, and being a witness;—of having a thing duly certified to me, and my duly certifying the same thing to others. Let us apply this to the subject under consideration. I, for instance, have been convinced of the truth of the gospel testimony by the divine evidence, as exhibited in the holy scriptures, and consequently have the witness in myself according to *John* v. 16. the truth of the gospel being thus first duly certified to me. I now feel disposed to become a preacher for the purpose of bringing others to enjoy, with me, the same happy privilege, of which I feel conscious in myself; of the truth of which I also thus feel able to bear a certain testimony.

Shall I now reverse the order of things, substitute my testimony instead of the apostles', preach my happy feelings instead of the gospel, or attempt to prove the truth of it by its effects upon my heart? and thus attempt to convince others that Jesus is the Christ, the Son of God, the Saviour, because I feel so happy since I believed in him, and seek to persuade them to believe by promising them like happiness? Now if I preach my own experience, and bear testimony as a living witness, I must confine myself to what I thus feel and know. And even suppose this were sufficient to prove the truth of the gospel, and recommend the Saviour, who knows whether I tell the truth, or be a deceiver? or whether I may not be under the power of delusion myself? Ought I not rather, if I mean to be useful, to lay hold on the divine testimony that convinced myself; namely, that of the holy apostles and prophets, with all their arguments and demonstrations, urging these home upon the understandings and hearts of the people, according to the scriptures—being fully persuaded that, if they hear not Moses and the Prophets, Christ and the Apostles, they would not be persuaded though one rose from the dead. These things duly considered, no reasonable person, I presume, could hesitate a moment which of these courses to take; whether to avail himself of the testimony of the primary witnesses as confirmed by God, with all its evidence and authority; or make use of his own experience,—the witness in himself, to accomplish his object. Nor is it supposable, these things duly considered, that there can remain any difficulty to discern between having a witness in one's self, and being one's self the witness of the same thing. Twelve men, eye and ear witnesses to any fact, may be able to produce a certainty in one's mind, which certainty, the person thus duly certified, may not be able to produce in the mind of another by his own testimony of the fact, and effect of his conviction, without referring to, and producing the primary and proper witnesses, that convinced himself. Nor, indeed, in the very nature of things can we conceive how it could possibly be otherwise; he being in the mean time no witness at all to the truth of the things which produced the conviction and its effects in himself. I therefore hope my good friend, the "Constant Reader," will, upon due consideration, feel convinced of the justice and propriety of my former conclusions, respecting the pretensions of his "living witnesses."   T. W.

Bethany, January 29, 1830.

The Times.

OUR files are full of invectives, slanders, falsehoods, caricatures, &c. &c. accumulated during the last four months, and laid up for my inspection. There are from the orthodox supporters of the fashions of the religious age, in opposition to our efforts. In glancing over a few of them, and only a few of them as yet, I discover that the adversary, called in Hebrew, Satan, is exceeding wroth. I hope it is because his time is short! No person ever was more misrepresented, or more diversely and incongruously characterized than the humble editor of the Christian Baptist. After the reasoning and reasonable opponents had generally gone to repose, a new set of scribblers, for whom I can find no generic name comprehending either their characters or productions, have awakened as from wine, and have raised a frightful and dolorous cry of every note and key against the Restoration. Antinomianism, Arminianism, Calvinism, Arianism, Deism, and every other *ism*, are ascribed to me from some one or other of this new race of belligerents. "The church is in danger," and "damnable heresy" is the chorus of every verse in these new lamentations of these weeping prophets. They are not *dumb* dogs: but they bark at something which they cannot bite. I cannot honor them all with due attention, and shall not now select any one of them; but I have one word for all of them—Can your cause be defended, gentlemen? If so, defend it. Show your scriptural authority, show your strong reasons, show your unanswerable proofs. There is no danger you can apprehend from me, if you have scripture or reason on your side. I will not hurt a hair upon your head, nor endanger a penny in your pocket, if you have reasons an ounce weight—if you have a "Thus says the Lord" for it. I will help you if help is in me; and if you build upon the One Foundation, upon the apostles and prophets, I will love you, pray for you, write for you, when you fight for my

Lord. I will aid and abet, I will counsel and assist, I will hold up the arms or carry water for every one who stands up for the King. I cannot oppose you, only as you oppose him. I say, I *cannot*. I have vowed to serve the King to the end of the war, or as long as he gives me a post in the Army of the Faith. You cannot affright me while I remember the deeds of the worthies, nor the impotence of the King's enemies—while I remember the words of him who commands us to fight, to be valiant for the truth, and who holds out crowns to all the victors. Could Noah, Daniel, Elijah, John, Peter, Paul, be terrified by an army of epithets, when they could not be moved from their purpose by all the vengeance of the King's enemies? Lord inspire all thy servants with a courage and boldness like theirs!! Fear not the loaves and the fishes; if you serve the Lord your bread and your water shall be secure. The Lord will not, for he cannot lie. But let me ask you for your proofs—for your thus says the Lord. I bow to this authority. Let my tongue cleave to the roof of my mouth, and my right hand forget its cunning, if either shall be wittingly employed against the truth. I have for a few months past had many interviews with the leaders of the people. I have heard them, reasoned with them, and have canvassed their opinions. They of the present order, they of the sects, of the different streets of the great city, deepened my convictions that all sects have drunk of the wine of the cup of the mother of abominations. They are not yet sobered. They have taken upon implicit faith, the cup out of her hands. When asked for the *why* they do this, and the *wherefore* they teach that, they show that they are led not by the apostles, but by great modern names. They have their Fuller or their Gill, or their Chrysostom or their Jerome, or their Wesley or their Calvin. They have not studied the Oracle with their own eyes, nor heard it with their own ears. They can string texts as the Romanists sort beads of the same color upon the same necklace. They have been taught to quote them thus, and thus to apply them. Hence each sectary gives you the same texts differently assorted. Some preach Calvinism and others Arminianism from the same text. Truly, we are yet in the smoke of Babylon. Lord, turn the people to a pure speech!! "They have itching ears; they have heaped to themselves teachers, after their own taste; and they have turned the people's ears from the truth to fables." These are the signs of the times, and is not this "a perilous age?"

I speak what I do know, and I testify what I have seen. And now shall I hold my peace, and suffer the taunts of the captivators? Shall I not rather lift up my voice like a trumpet, and show Israel their sins and their errors. And this will we do, if the Lord permit.

"For Zion's sake I will not rest, and for Jerusalem's sake I will not hold my peace until the righteousness thereof go forth as brightness, and the salvation thereof as a lamp that burns, and the Gentiles your righteousness and all kings your glory."—The spirit that breathes in these words is that spirit with which I hope ever to be inspired. And when I look around me on the ignorance, stupidity, superstition, enthusiasm, and immoralities of many who have assumed the christian name, I feel myself called and impelled to exert every nerve, and to put forth every energy in this holy enterprize. "Like people like priest," is an old and a true adage. Great has been the success of those who have preached and taught the schismatical dogmas of the times in which we live. The distracted and alienated state of the religious world is more than sufficient proof of the unhallowed influences which are abroad in the earth. Many spirits, indeed, have gone forth into the world. The paper walls of opinions which separate the fractions of the professing world, though inscribed with the essential doctrines of salvation, are, when pasted over and over again, but mere religious phantoms of mystic imaginations. On these topics it is not now my task to dilate; but to say that while this is the order of the day, I will feel it my duty, as I shall answer to the King in his own person, to essay to overturn, to overturn, to overturn, until moths and worms shall have fattened upon the fruits of metaphysical mysteries registered in the forms of creeds, rubrics, and commentaries. Men may ridicule, may taunt, may laugh or cry, as the whim, the interest or the prejudice of the day may move them; but so long as 'tis written, "It is better to obey God rather than man," I will, relying on the once traduced and persecuted, but now triumphant King of saints, continue in the course which I have commenced. To him I owe a debt which I can never repay; but the homage of a grateful heart is, in his sight, more acceptable than the most costly incense, than the richest oblations which the earth affords.

Avaunt! then, you who laugh at every one who dares question your divinity. Your power, your influence, though great over the mass of your admirers, is not omnipotent. Greater and mightier still is the truth, and will prevail. You make void the revelation of mercy by your traditions, God will make void your power over the people. Tell me not that you can prove your doctrines from the bible—The Romanist can prove his *Ave Maria*, and his purgatory after death, from the bible too. The bible will prove any thing if bribed by your rules of interpretation. You can prove the *jus divinum*, the divine right of synods, conferences, and associations, as St. James, of the English throne, could prove the *jus divinum* of his family to reign forever over the British Isles. You can prove that creeds are necessary to unite the church, or divide christians; that one man ought to be the archbishop of four churches, or of the commonwealth of Virginia, as it may happen to suit your education. You can prove semi-annual sacraments, and all the religious idols of the age—the holy enterprizes which Messrs. Beecher, Ely, and Brantly eulogize as having fallen down from heaven since the ascent of John from Patmos.— You can pipe and the people will dance; you may sing mournful songs and the people will cry: for as many of them as have been baptized into your systems have put you on.

But say not this is egotism, and that your course is pointed out by the Star of Bethlehem. If you say so, prove it—not by the traditions of the elders, but by the apostles, and then I will help you. Till then, however, as long as life endures, I shall pray—Lord teach my hands to war, and my fingers to fight with the weapons of truth and goodness; from love, good will, and a zeal according to knowledge.   EDITOR.

Dear Brother,

IF I can judge from the signs of the times, you have chosen a very appropriate title to your new periodical, (Millennial Harbinger.) The rights of men, both natural and acquired, are better understood at this day among us than they ever were since my memory. The rights of conscience, too, seem to be better understood. Those who have so long lorded it over the consciences of men are obliged to resort to underhand measures to keep in subjection the free-born sons of God: yes, they are compelled to make use of some tools to work with, lest the cloven foot should be too visible. There are in several of our congregations one or two individuals who are willing to engage in the antichristian work of suppressing the rights of conscience, and preventing all improvement, or approach to the happy millennial state. The standing of these individuals in christian society, or their success for popularity, depends principally upon the service they render to the popular *preachers*. If they can keep the people tied down to the dogmas of their teachers, they may calculate on being honored with a *seat in the Association!* These men are of great value with the priesthood—caressed, and honored with many honors. This makes them as tyrannical and dogmatical as the Jewish Sanhedrim. I cannot discover any difference in their spirits. Some have gone so far as to pass resolutions to prohibit those who are advocates for the Ancient Gospel from the privilege of proclaiming the gospel in their meeting houses, to the people, that they might be saved!!! The priesthood who have so long kept the people in darkness, are apprehensive they will lose their influence over their congregations. Some of them are lazy men, and depend upon their flocks for the fleece to support them. They are obliged to keep a watch out lest the people learn too fast, and there would be no need of their sermonizing to them. This is one of the reasons why the populars will not come out with the whole armor of God, like christian soldiers, and confute your views of the gospel, which they pretend to say are errors of a serious nature. They find it easier to keep the people's conscience under their control by their silence, than if they were to reason the points at issue with you.— This is the principal cause of their aversion to controversy.

The light that we have enjoyed from the Christian Baptist has produced a shaking among the dry bones. I do hope the breath of life will soon enter into them. They seem to want an acquaintance with the testimony of Jesus, which is the spirit of prophecy—sinews and flesh, (courage and knowledge,) to enable them to stand up together. I find it a more difficult task to get some sectarians to attend to the ancient apostolic gospel, than those that are without. The spirit imparted by the teachers of some of the sects seems to be both dumb and deaf. Except when these teachers speak, then there is a kind of enchantment, which makes them halloo and squall as if the spirit of the sons of Sceva was in the neighborhood.* How different are the effects of the spirit of the gospel! It was "good tidings, which should prove matter of great joy to all the people." But this hallooing and squalling, then shouting and rejoicing, all at the same time, by the same individual, savors of hypocrisy. Some seem to think there is no religion unless they strike fire and set every thing on fire around them. This is an evil much to be lamented, and savors too much of Samson's trick, when he tied his three hundred foxes, and put firebrands to them. No good came from it.— They burnt up the "Philistines' corn, with the vineyards and olives," and they in return "burnt

---

*Reader, do not think I am opposed to teaching and exhorting men and women to believe and obey the gospel. Very far from it. I am only opposing an enthusiastic manner of teaching the word of God, which is a serious injury to the improvement of a believer.

up his wife and her father." It appears from the language of some, that those who can make the loudest noise are the most pious men and women, though they cannot tell us the contents or genius of one epistle or chapter in the New Testament, nor never were known to read one chapter. I was at a meeting where one of those noisy men was. (He refused to let a brother Baptist commune with him because he was an advocate for the Ancient Gospel. No other fault or charge could be laid against him.) After his communion was over, he strained every nerve to make the people halloo. *Quere*—Is there no sin in opposing a man in the discharge of his duty to God, when he has become a regular, orderly, naturalized subject of his kingdom? It is the opinion of some that this devout man to *his own spirit,* (which he labors to make the people believe is the Spirit of God,) has been instrumental in putting out more members of the church than he ever was in getting in! He is ever and anon making discoveries to his hearers, and not one of them have made any improvement from him, but that of prejudice and bigotry against the ancient apostolic gospel. If the conduct of such men proceeds from ignorance, they have a claim upon our pity, and should have an interest in our prayers. But if they know better, and act thus, they are not fit for teachers; and we dare not say such are good conscientious men. What makes our charity fail with such, they will not examine impartially the religious views of others; they make no improvement, nor will they suffer others to do so if they can prevent it.— This is the true cause of some having charged the "Christian Baptist" with being "more mischievous than any publication ever known."

I find that the intelligent part of the christian congregations are persuaded [they say so] that sectarianism is a curse to the peace of christian societies, and a barrier to their union. I find in the debates of the Virginia Convention, that the wisest and best politicians admit that there is a species of property in that state a curse to them, and they have spent nearly two months laboring to entail that curse upon their posterity!!! I cannot discover any difference in the spirit of the sectaries and the worldly politicians; neither appear to act from principle, but from policy. I always understood honesty was the best policy. When we hear men acknowledge that such an evil does exist among them, und yet reproach and condemn those who are truly desirous of aiding them to free themselves from the curse, how can we reconcile such a course of conduct? Is not this the very same spirit that moved the Jewish Sanhedrim to persecute, condemn, and put to death the Messiah and his apostles? And may we not truly say to those sectaries, You know not what manner of spirit you are of?

These sectarians call themselves the Church of Christ. Is not this one of those "unlearned sayings and unsound words which gender strife?" that is, the title Baptist, Presbyterian, Episcopalian, or Methodist Church. Can any unprejudiced man calmly sit down and examine into the state of the congregation of worshippers, the manner in which the gospel is taught them, and the claims their teachers set up over them, and not feel like the Prophet Jeremiah? ch. ix. 1—8. The prayers of all truly pious and benevolent men will (if not now) sooner or later be offered up for the blessing of God upon the labors of those who are trying to destroy the spirit of sectarianism, and introduce the primitive state of the church, which all good men desire to see   EPAPHRAS.

To the Editor of the Christian Baptist.

DEAR BROTHER,—I have read your book on the subject of immersion, until I find that you arrive at the following conclusion concerning this ordinance, viz.—That faith and immersion are equally necessary to the forgiveness of sins; or that the blood of Christ is the cause, and immersion the agent or medium through which the effect comes, or, in other words, that, under the administration of the Spirit, sin is not forgiven until this ordinance is complied with;—that no acceptable worship, prior to it, can be rendered; or that immersion stands between the sacrifice of Christ and all acceptable worship. Although I admire your zeal and talents as a defender of the truth, and have, on many occasions been much edified by your writings, yet I must differ from you on this subject. I do not do this hastily, but after mature examination of that only standard, the word of God, on this subject, and from which I am brought to this conclusion— That Jehovah, in all ages and at all times, under all dispensations, appointed but one way of redeeming guilty man, to wit, the sacrifice of his own Son. He, though pointed out in various manners, was to all, by faith, the only sovereign relief. Abel, and all the descendants of Adam down to John the Baptist, were directed to look forward to the blood of Christ which was to be shed, and the Bible gives the assurance that whoever understood this subject and cordially believed God's testimony concerning it, had their sins pardoned, and all who shall live upon the earth from the day of the resurrection until the last trumpet shall sound to call the dead to life and the living to immortality, who shall believe God's testimony concerning this fact, shall receive the remission of all their sins, peace with God, and the hope of eternal glory. This all without the performance of any work, or without the loss of a moment of time.

The wisdom of God is wonderful in this, that the same remedy stood good to all men, during various dispensations, proving itself effectual to all who should receive it, in accordance with the different methods by which God was pleased to make it known. Abraham believed God, and it was counted to him for righteousness, and just by the same means the Roman and the Galatian believers were saved, and had their sins pardoned, without any kind of works evangelical or Levitical. The terms always run thus, "That God so loved the world that he sent his only begotten Son, that whosoever believes on him should not perish, but have eternal life." *John* iii. 16. and the following statements to the same effect, viz. *Rom.* iii. 21, 22, 25, 28, 30. and iv. 5. and v. 1. *Gal.* ii. 16—21. and 1 *John* v. 1. The apostle, in the above statements, clearly declares that the gospel or good news taught by himself and his fellows, when believed with the heart, gave to all who received it immediate peace, without a moment's delay, or a single work of any kind.

But, it may be asked, why did Peter connect immersion with faith, (or reformation,) when preaching to the Jews on Pentecost, in order to the forgiveness of sins? I answer, that had Peter considered immersion indispensable, and that sins could not be taken away without it, in this or any other statement delivered to men in order to their forgiveness, it would have been criminal in any of the apostles, at any time while preaching, to have left their audience without it. If forgiveness and all acceptable worship depend on obedience to this, then surely the way to be saved must always have included it. But if acceptance and the forgiveness of sins hung on this thing, how, I would ask, did this same apostle, in his next address to these same Jews, omit including it in his statement? *Acts* iii. 19. Verily if immersion were indispensable to the blotting out of sins, and all acceptable worship, then the first preachers of the glad tidings were deficient in not mentioning it in a great majority of their statements delivered for the salvation of guilty men. See *Acts* xiii. 38, 39. yet Paul in this, and Peter to the Gentiles, *Acts* x. 43. scruple not to declare the forgiveness of sins through faith in Jesus alone. If it be true that immersion, or any other ordinance, is the agent, or absolute medium, by which the blood of Christ is to purify the conscience, or wash away sin, surely such an agent or medium is of the utmost importance to the sons of men. If it be true that there is no way of escape without it, then nothing in heaven or on earth can be of more value to the sinner. If the atonement, in this way, can alone cure me, then, to me this and the atonement are of equal value. Suppose, for example, I owed you a million of dollars, and was unable to pay you one, and that you were generous enough to forgive me all; but in one way, and by an unalterable rule which you had adopted for yourself in all cases, that, in order to my relief, I must wait on, and obtain the consent of a third person —would not the consent and concurrence of the third person be equally valuable to me as yours? I think it would, equally so. Think you then that God would have, or has placed the way of salvation in such a plight as in its effects to the sons of men be dependent on the action of the man himself, much less on the action of another? Think you, would not the apostle Paul have called such another gospel? or think you that he would be any better pleased with having immersion a partner with the blood of Christ than he would circumcision in this great work? *Gal.* i. 6—9, and ii. 15, 18. Make immersion the pivot on which justification turns, and, with one sweep, you unjustify the larger portion of the Old and New Testament worthies. If my safety rests on this, that of all men does the same. I must then look for the same evidence that all others are saved by attending to this ordinance. But on examination I find that I have no testimony in favor of the Old Testament saints. Abraham with Lazarus in his bosom, and on the other side of this new set up gulf the cloud of witnesses must be shut out. Peter, James, John, Jude, Andrew, &c. gives me no confidence for them on this score; and the one hundred and twenty who waited for the Spirit at Jerusalem, give no evidence of their safety in this way. O! no, my friend, the salvation of God stands on better ground than this! It is placed on a Rock which man cannot touch, which no ordinance or any dispensation can add to, or take from, no matter however divinely appointed. God has declared this fact to the sons of men: That he gave his only beloved Son; that this Son was born of a woman; that he was every way qualified to be a ransom for sin; that he was put to death; that he was buried; that he rose from the dead; and all this in accordance with what the holy prophets said since the world began. The facts presented here to the sinner, believed and understood, never failed, and never will fail, to give the man or the woman who thus receives it, immediate peace without, and distinct from, any subsequent act whatever. *Rom.* v. 1, 2. Until then, I humbly conceive there is no right to immersion, or the privilege to any other ordinance belonging to the kingdom of Christ. But it may be said that he cannot worship acceptably until he attends to this. To which I answer, He can. If justified by faith he has peace with God, and access to him also. *Rom.* v. 2. *Acts* ix. 6. " Lord, what wilt thou have me to do?" Then, and not till then, will his prayer come up as a memorial before God, who will answer, " Go to Damascus: it shall be told thee; or send for Peter," &c. *Acts* x. 4. Then will he be qualified to learn " the ways of the Lord more perfectly:" having first been taught or discipled in the facts concerning the Lord Jesus Christ, he is prepared to attend to immersion and to all other things which the Lord has commanded. Having had his heart " sprinkled from an evil conscience," he is ready to have his " body washed with pure water;" or, like Paul, to " arise and be immersed and wash away his sins, and call on the name of the Lord," and more and more to purify his heart in obeying the truth; for all the laws of the kingdom of Jesus are qualified to do this, and to keep alive in the believing mind the facts by which at first his deliverance came, with all its purifying influences.

You say in your book that the testimony of the apostles concerning Jesus, is the gospel in *word*, and that immersion is the gospel in *water*. And does it, according to this, take the two gospels to save the sinner? or does it take the first and one half of the last? or does it take one half of each to make one whole saving gospel? What do the words of the apostles amount to? To this: they represent a saving fact, which brings the mind of man to the Lord Jesus, the knowledge of whom is eternal life. Immersion does the same: the Lord's supper does the same. But words which convey the fact, the water which represents the fact, the bread and wine which show forth the fact—these are all shadows, figures, or representations. None of them, nor are they jointly, the *substance*. Christ is the only one in heaven or on earth that can save the guilty.

After all this, obedience to all the commandments of the Lord is absolutely necessary to the safety of the believer. They all promote his happiness, joy, and peace; they increase his faith, his hope, and love; by them he becomes partaker of the divine nature; and by them he escapes the pollutions of the world. The first of these is immersion. To this time things stood as a matter between God and himself, but he now looks abroad in the light which God has shone upon his mind, and relatively he sees that he has to enter into company with the family of God upon the earth; and his first step is to be immersed, professing in words first and in figure, the truth by which he was made free; the hopes engendered by this truth of life and immortality, his connexion with Christ and his people in the victory obtained in the truth figured in this ordinance; his putting off the old and putting on the new man; and from henceforth to walk in newness of life Zionward, in the hope of immortality and eternal glory.

Yours in christian love,   C. F.
Baltimore, Jan. 23, 1830.

P. S. With regard to acceptable worship before immersion, see *Acts* iii. 8, 9, ix. 6—11. and x. 4—46.

——

Reply to C. F.

DEAR BROTHER,—WHAT portion of the human family may attain to the resurrection of the just, I presume not to say. How many Antediluvians, Patriarchs, and Jews—how many of the Pagan nations, before or since the Christian era—how many infants, idiots, and deaf and dumb persons—the testimony of God says not. But the intervention of the Mediator, the "obedience to death" of the Messiah, whether with faith or without it, whether with circumcision, baptism, or the law, or without them, is declared to be the ground and reason which will render their salvation possible.

Many confound the salvation to be revealed at the final consummation, with the enjoyment of the present salvation which primarily consists in a deliverance from the guilt, pollution, and dominion of sin, and which salvation has been, under the Reign of the Messiah, proclaimed through faith and immersion. In this way "baptism does now save us," so Peter declares. Hence Jesus said, "He that believes and is immersed shall be saved." Few seem to believe Jesus. I must, however, call me weak or credulous, or what you please, believe him. And he that pretends to know better than the Lord, or to separate what Jesus has joined together, presumes farther than I dare follow him.

You say that all, "from Abel down to John the Baptist, who cordially believed the testimony of God," &c. had their sins pardoned. Do you mean they had their sins pardoned while on earth, and through faith? This is necessary to your hypothesis. Now I must confess that I know of no scripture, from Abel to John the Baptist which teaches any such thing. Not an instance do I know of the pardon of sin by faith only. Without "shedding of blood," without attendance upon the altar, without obedience to the appointed means of pardon, "there was no remission." We know that neither animal blood nor the element of water, *per se*, could take away sin. But under the former economy blood was necessary to forgiveness; and under the new economy water is necessary—faith is the principle of action in both—and they are the means, not "agents," through which God imparted remission.

You seem to be aware that your conclusion is at variance with Peter's address on Pentecost, and then endeavor to show that Peter was not always consistent with himself; or, which is the same thing, that in his other addresses he did not speak in the same manner. This mode of reasoning may be employed, and has been employed, times without number, to explain not only immersion, but water baptism, entirely away. But yet you would be able to refute all objections made against Philip for not mentioning baptism to the Eunuch, or against Luke the historian for not recording it, by showing that although Luke did not always relate all that was said, he did it frequently enough to show the usual mode of address.

But after all, Peter was not so inconsistent with himself in the discourses to which you refer. In *Acts* iii. 19. he does not proclaim forgiveness as attendant on faith, but on an act called turning to God, or conversion. In the new version it reads, "Reform, therefore, and turn to God, that so your sins may be blotted out; that seasons of refreshment may come from the presence of the Lord," &c. And in the king's version, "Repent and be converted that your sins may be blotted out." So that in both versions the blotting out of sins is not connected simply with faith, but with an act called turning to God, or conversion. Have you, my dear brother, ever adverted to the import of the participle in the commission, *Matt.* xxviii. Disciple, or convert the nations, immersing them. I need not tell you that this is the exact translation. Let me

ask you, then, does not the active participle always, when connected with the imperative mood, express the manner in which the thing commanded is to be performed. Cleanse the room, washing it; clean the floor, sweeping it; cultivate the field, ploughing it; sustain the hungry, feeding them; furnish the soldiers, arming them; convert the nations, baptizing them—are exactly the same forms of speech. No person, I presume, will controvert this. If so, then no man could be called a disciple or a convert—no man could be said to be discipled or converted until he was immersed. Whatever inward change might have taken place, still the person was not, in the estimation of those who acted under the commission, converted until he was immersed. That was the act by which the command given to convert the nations was to be obeyed. Like or dislike the import of this sentence, it must unquestionably be admitted by all scholars and persons of plain common sense, to be the unsophisticated meaning of it. So that *Acts* iii. 19. is just equivalent, when the terms are understood, to *Acts* ii. 38. So is *Acts* x. 43. "To him give all the prophets witness, that, through his name, whosoever believes in him, shall receive remission of sins." Remission is here affirmed to come some way through his name. It was the pronouncing of the name of Jesus upon the cripple, *Acts* iii. which, together with his faith, gave him perfect soundness. It was not simply his faith, but the pronouncing of this name upon him. So Luke teaches. Peter said, "Yea, his name and the faith which is in him, has given him this perfect soundness in the presence of you all."

In the same style Peter spoke to Cornelius' household. Yet in neither of these instances does Peter speak fully, or the historian does not give all that he said—"With many other words" (than those recorded) "did he testify and exhort on Pentecost, saying, Save yourselves from this untoward generation." And in the house of Cornelius, while he was yet speaking, in the midst of his discourse, did the Holy Spirit fall on all the hearers.

I might, were it necessary, show that in no one instance in the New Testament, is remission connected with faith alone. Have you considered why, when both Mark and Matthew mention baptism, Luke does not, though he, as well as they, records the commission? He substitutes the effect of faith and the effect of immersion for them both; and instead of saying Jesus commanded "faith and baptism to be proclaimed," expresses himself thus: "He commanded reformation and forgiveness of sins to be proclaimed to all nations." Nothing can be more plainly taught in the New Testament than that the actual remission of sins is now connected with immersion.

But system will not permit us to hearken to the apostles. Yes, you, yourself, though a century before most of your cotemporaries in the knowledge of christianity, ask me, How can this be, and such a system be true! You speak in glowing terms of making immersion equal in importance "with the atonement." Don't you make faith of equal importance with the atonement? Nay, you make the paper and ink, or the words of a living speaker—the vowels and consonants of the English alphabet, of equal value with the atonement!! Your remarks stop not short of this, my brother, startle at it as you may. And your concern about the Old Testament saints and the Paidobaptist saints, reminds me of the concern exhibited for the salvation of the whole Roman Catholic Church before the Reformation, when the priests beset Luther.

The super-excellency of christianity is, that it makes the conscience perfect. The Jews, and the Gentiles too, many of them at least, were saved without any distinct knowledge of the sacrifice of Jesus. And I have much reason to think that infants dying will be citizens of the kingdom of glory, without, in this life, knowing, or believing any thing of the sacrifice of Christ, of faith, or immersion. And I doubt not but such Paidobaptists as simply mistake the meaning and design of the christian institution, who nevertheless are, as far as they know, obedient disciples of Jesus, will be admitted into the kingdom of glory. But what has this to do with our obedience who are better instructed? If we profess to know our Master's will, or profess to know it better than others, and do it not, shall we compare ourselves to Jews, Pagans, Paidobaptists, infants, and all other uninstructed persons? To do so would be to prove ourselves hypocrites.

I have carefully considered all that you have advanced, and many other communications to the same effect; and instead of weakening my assurance that the act by which we put on Christ, the act by which we come to Christ, the act by which we confess Christ, the act by which we become disciples of Christ, the act by which we come into the kingdom of Christ, the act by which we are married to Christ, the act by which we receive the pardon of our past sins, the act by which we come into the actual enjoyment of the salvation of Christ in this present life—is the act of immersion into the name of Christ: which act presupposes faith in him. The principle on which I find yourself and most of the more evangelical brethren object to this, is not because the whole current of the New Testament allusions do not run in this channel; it is not because many of the most literal addresses and expositions of the apostles do not, in the most obvious construction, teach this; but because it is incompatible with the received notions of salvation by faith or salvation by grace. To this, therefore, I shall briefly attend.

Now I do not think there lives a man who will, or who can, with more cheerfulness, with more cordiality, with more unequivocal sincerity, affirm his belief or his conviction, or, if you please, his assurance that "salvation is by faith that it might be by grace," or pure favor, than myself. But many have been indoctrinated into a faith and a grace of another character than that which the apostles proclaimed.

Can we not say that men live by breathing, by eating, by motion; and that they live by air, by food, by exercise? Is there any contradiction in all this? Is it incompatible with the idea of living by breathing, that men must eat, must drink, must sleep? Is it incompatible with the idea of almsgiving that the beneficiary must receive the alms tendered? If from pure mercy A. gives bread to the hungry, does it destroy the idea of mercy that they must use their hands and their teeth before they can receive nourishment from it? According to the ideas of grace which some entertain, if God does not, by irresistible force, moral or physical, snatch men to heaven in a whirlwind, or by some almighty influence which requires them to be as passive as a stone, they are not saved by grace at all. And, indeed, many so live, that, if saved, they must be saved as Elijah was translated to heaven, by pure physical energy. This they call grace. And as for faith, it is something wrought in the heart supernaturally, like the creation of Eve out of a rib taken out of the side of Adam. They fall into a dead sleep, and while they are dead God creates faith in them. This being wholly God's creature, they call it the faith of God's elect, or grace. Yet methinks I could suggest to these speculators upon free grace ideas still more gracious. Would it not be more in accordance with their views of grace to have saved men without imposing upon them the necessity of self-denial, repentance, reformation, or regeneration? Would there not be more grace in saving men without either faith, reformation, baptism, or self-denial of any sort?

My dear sir, you will at once perceive, that while I contend that salvation is of grace, proceeding from the pure, unbought, and unsolicited philanthropy of God, exhibited in the mission and gift of his Son, the only begotten, I do not suppose it to be in reason, nor according to scripture, incompatible with the idea of pure favor, that we must receive the salvation, or that we cannot be saved. And as to grace, if we must receive it by any act at all, it matters not what that act be, if it is one which is in the compass of our faculties—whether by looking with the eye, hearing with the ear, believing with the heart, speaking with the tongue, or walking with the feet. I believe it was of grace that the blind man was healed, though he walked to Siloam and washed in the pool before the power of Jesus touched his eye.

To graft religion upon a natural principle was exceeding gracious; but I cannot see the grace in grafting it upon a supernatural principle.—Now it is grafted upon a natural principle that it might be by grace.

But here I have a query for those who talk so much about salvation through grace, which I would be glad to see them answer. Whether would there be more grace apparent in grafting salvation upon a natural principle, or in grafting it upon a supernatural principle? Suppose that the easiest act that a man can perform is believing; that the most natural, common, and universal principle of action is faith; and that God had adapted his salvation to this most common and natural of all principles of action—would this be more accordant with our ideas of favor, than if, after having finished the whole work of redemption, and consummated the whole scheme, it was not adapted to any capacity, or faculty of mind and body which belonged to man; but that, in order to embrace it, he must be created anew, or endowed with new capacities, faculties, and powers, before he can see it, touch it, taste it, or possess it? I say, I wish some of these declaimers upon something they call grace, would humble themselves so much as to answer this question.

If, however, they will not answer this question, I know they will concur with me in saying that salvation must be received before it can be enjoyed. What then is the action by which it is received? Whatever it may be, it cannot deprive the salvation of the attribute of grace. It is faith, say they, by which we receive the salvation. Then faith ceases to be a principle of action, if it be the action itself. But "faith, works" and is not itself the work. Faith can receive a promise or a truth, and then the promise or the truth becomes the principle of action. Now if there was a promise that I should be pardoned the moment I believe that promise, then I might have a pardon through faith. But if the promise of pardon is connected with any other action than believing, then it is only when

I perform that action that I can be assured of pardon. Pardon is ascribed to the blood of Christ as the worthy cause; but it is connected with, because promised through, certain actions. Suppose a Christian, one who has put on Christ, should commit some sin. How is he to be pardoned? By faith simply? No—he must confess it, and ask for pardon. Pardon, then, follows confession and prayer. So the Apostle John teaches. Now, when a disciple who sins, confesses his fault and obtains forgiveness, does the fact of his confession, or his prayer destroy the nature of grace, or render faith of no value? If, then, God has promised pardon to christians for particular sins through confession and prayer, why should it be thought incompatible that he would require "confession to salvation," or baptism, as a means of bestowing remission of all past sins on coming into the kingdom of the Messiah? If he will not through faith without confession forgive a christian a known transgression, why suppose that he would forgive all past sins prior to believing simply through faith!

Our Saviour taught his disciples that, when they asked for forgiveness for themselves, if they did not forgive one another, neither would their heavenly Father forgive them. If, then, conditions of forgiveness are appended to faith in one case, why object to baptism as a condition of remission in another! And surely if neither our confession nor our prayer, nor our forgiving those who trespass against us, precludes the idea of grace, nor impairs the value of faith in obtaining remission, baptism can impair neither the one nor the other, when proclaimed for the remission of sins.

Nay, it is an act of grace to appoint some act of ours as a medium of remission, that we might have the assurance of forgiveness, and know when we are forgiven. With how much satisfaction and joy can we arise from our knees, assured that we have, through confession and prayer, obtained forgiveness. It heightens the grace by making us sensible when we need it, and when we receive it. No wonder the eunuch went on his way rejoicing after he was immersed. We do not, then, make water prayer, confession, and faith, saviours—Jesus is our Saviour. 'Tis he forgives our sins. And these are the means through which, by faith, we are forgiven.

But I have wearied you in laboring a subject which is too plain to require much argumentation. Nothing but the obliquities of a metaphysical theology could have created any doubt upon this subject. If, on further examination, you are not satisfied, please write again.

With all affection, I remain
Yours in our common Lord, Editor.

No. 8.]   March 1, 1830.
Sermons to Young Preachers.—No. III.

Young preachers are not always young men. I once heard a man say, that, though an *old man*, he was a *young preacher*. This was certainly true. For he had been converted, he said, but very recently; and it required no great penetration to see that he had not even learned how ignorant of the scriptures he was, and how incompatible it was for him to presume to teach what he could scarcely read. Yet this man produced more noise, or, as some would call it, more *effect*, than the most experienced and erudite Doctor could have done. The people were so accustomed to such warm-hearted and divinely inspired proclaimers, they thought even his blunders were graces of the Holy Spirit, and his flights of unmeaning declamation were the inspirations

of Infinite Wisdom. Whenever a person is considered as a legate of the skies, he has gained the day. Whenever a preacher appears before a congregation as one specially called by God and sent, he has but little trouble in gaining the implicit audience of the people. How dare they reject the message of God, and what need have they to examine the truth of one acting under the commission of the Omniscient? Would God send a liar, a deceiver, one unacquainted with his will, one unaccomplished for the task? No, most assuredly. He never did, he never will, call, commission, and send one incompetent agent. And therefore all his proclaimers had an authority which it was impious to oppose. But mind, they could all prove their mission not by words, assertions, or protestations, but by works as supernatural as their doctrine.

Neither young nor old proclaimers can, with either reason or scripture to sustain them, make such pretensions now. If, then, we would appear credible, or worthy of the audience of the people, we must appear before them, not under the assumption or pretension of ambassadors from heaven, or as God's special ministers; but as the pious, and humble and devout students of the Bible; as persons who have believed the gospel ourselves, and upon such grounds and reasons as will not make us ashamed to give a reason of the hope which we entertain.

No disciple, old or young, can, with any consistency of character, refuse to tell the reasons why he believes in, and loves the Lord Jesus. But all who either tell or proclaim in a pulpit, or on a chair, their own convictions and feelings, doubts, fears, and hopes, preach themselves or their feelings, instead of Jesus-Christ. I presume a pious Mussulman could narrate his feelings, doubts, extacies, and joys in "the Prophet Mahomet." But he who could expect to convert others to any faith by such a course, calculates very largely upon the ignorance and weakness of his audience.

All evidences are addressed to the higher and more noble faculties of man. The understanding, and not the passions, is addressed; and therefore an appeal to the latter, before the former is enlightened, is as unphilosophic as it is unscriptural. As the helm guides the ship, and the bridle the horse, so reason is the governing principle in man. Now in preaching Jesus, arguments are to be used—and these are found in the testimony of God. To declare that testimony, and to adduce the evidences which support it, is to proclaim the gospel. To perceive that testimony and to feel its force, is therefore the first and the indispensable qualification for a proclaimer of the gospel—to be able to discover it to others, to hold it up to the eye of the mind, and to recommend it in its fulness and force, is the second.

To *make a sermon*, and to *proclaim the gospel*, are two things which are as different as logic and gospel. To make a sermon is the art of logic applied to any theme, whether law, medicine, or general science. To write or speak a sermon, is an art which requires much study, a general education, or else an extraordinary genius and much reading. The theme for a sermon may be any topic in any science or art in the whole circle. "*And Balaam rose in the morning and saddled his ass*" is a text, or theme, on which a very logical sermon may be spoken. "*Remember Lot's wife*" is another suitable theme; so is "*God is a Spirit.*" Each of the proverbs of Solomon, each period in the Bible, each sentence in any book, may be a text on which, by the art of logic, a man may build a sermon. One theme may be more instructive than another, more pleasing and more suitable to the genius or taste of the speaker and his audience; but by the art of logic a grammarian and logician may make a good sermon on any topic. Statesmen make *speeches*, and Divines make *sermons;* but there is no difference in the art, and often very little difference in the theme. To make a sermon, and to make a speech, is just one and the same thing; the difference is in the topic on which the sermon or the speech is made. I have heard Lawyers make as good *sermons* as Divines; and Divines make as good *speeches* as Lawyers. Sometimes "Ministers" *read* their sermons; and we had one Judge in the Virginia Convention who read his speeches. The word *sermon* is the Roman name of a speech; and the word *speech* is the English name of a sermon. There is one difference. The tone of voice which a lawyer, or a statesman, or a literary lecturer uses, is not generally the same tone which a Divine uses. There is the sacred and the common tone. The same ideas communicated by a Lawyer and a "Minister" differ not only in the place where they are spoken, the pulpit and the bar; but in the tones, semitones, and the gestures which accompany them. The Preacher supposes that, as his subject is sacred he ought to have a sacred tone; and the Lawyer who knows his theme is common, conceives that a common tone will be suitable enough.

To make a sermon is as much the work of art as to make a speech at the bar, or in the forum. No man can make a good one without much study, training, and general reading. Hence Colleges and Theological Schools are necessary, to make sermonizers. Men may talk, declaim, or exhort in public, without much art, or logic, or learning; but to make a good sermon on religion or politics, on physics or metaphysics, requires much learning and many years training. The course of education is too limited and the term of attendance on schools and colleges is too short, especially in these United States, to make many good sermonizers. Men of extraordinary genius in some six or seven years, may make a neat, logical, chaste, and classical oration. But in general, and for ordinary minds, it requires ten of the best years of a man's life, from fourteen to twenty-four, or say from infancy to twenty-one. But it must be noted that a sermon may be logical, ingenious, forcible, and classically correct, and yet not eloquent; and it may be eloquent without much logic, grammar, or science. Logan was always eloquent—Dugald Stuart never. The latter was too profound a scholar, too acute a metaphysician, too great a critic to be eloquent; the former had the feelings of a man and the imagination of a poet, without the fetters of philosophy.

A man, to be truly eloquent, must follow natural feeling, and must be born with an imagination, with a fancy, and with an ardor of feeling which never can be acquired, but which may be repressed at school.

But a sermon-maker, without education, and without much training, is, to persons of discernment, one of the most disgusting performers, and one of the most useless speakers we can imagine. Hence of all drones, political, economical, or ecclesiastical, I know of none more deserving of neglect, and I know of none more likely to obtain it, than those drivelling, prosing, and illiterate sermonizers. But to make sermons is a business, a trade, or calling by itself. To proclaim or preach Jesus, is a work of another kind. Of this in my next. EDITOR.

Essays on Man in his Primitive State, and under the Patriarchal, Jewish, and Christian Dispensations.—No. XII.
Jewish age.—No. IV.

THE Jewish religion as instituted by Moses, as recorded by Moses in the five books, has not a single promise, nor a single curse, which looks beyond time. Whatever previous or subsequent revelations may have taught—whatever the Patriarchs before Moses, or the Prophets after him, may have taught, one thing to me, at least, is certain—that Moses, in originating or instituting the Jews' religion, taught nothing concerning a future state—not a word concerning eternal salvation, or future and eternal punishment in the Jewish religion. This being a truth not to be resisted, (and if it can, direct me to the chapter and verse)—I say, this being granted, then it must follow that the design of the Jewish religion and the design of the Christian are not the same. The former looked exclusively to this present world; the latter primarily, and almost exclusively, looks to the next.

Long life, health, and abundance of corn, wine, and oil—rivers of milk and honey, were the blessings which it promised; and to the disobedient, wasting and famine, and bitter destruction in their persons, families, flocks, herds, and property, were the curses which it proposed. A happy nation, enjoying abundance of all earthly good; victorious and triumphant in war, and secure under the auspices of the Almighty from all foreign invasion, was the tendency and the consummation of that peculiar constitution under which Israel lived. "How goodly are thy tents, O Jacob! and thy dwellings, O Israel!" The moral effect and meaning, and unquestionably the great design of this peculiar institution, is very appositely expressed in the following lines;

"With Israel's God who can compare?
Or who, like Israel, happy are?
O people saved by the Lord,
He is thy shield and great reward!

Upheld by everlasting arms,
Thou art secure from foes and harms;
In vain their plots, and false their boasts—
Thy refuge is the Lord of hosts!"

While they kept the law, or lived agreeably to their institution, they exhibited to all the world the peculiar happiness of living under the institutions and protection of the Almighty. And when they transgressed the law, or departed from the divine institutions, the visitations of Heaven, the judgments and calamities which befel them, taught the world the awful consequences of departing from the living God.

By the oracles deposited in their sanctuary, by the institutions of their religion, by their prosperity and security when obedient, and by the calamities which befel them as individuals, families, and as a nation when disobedient, the knowledge of the one only living and true God was preserved in the world—his mercy and his justice—his goodness and his truth were rendered most conspicuous.

They read these records and consider the history of this people—they study this institution and examine this religion with very little profit, who do not view it thus. To think that the law of Moses, or the institution from Mount Sinai—to think that the whole or any part of this economy had for its object the eternal salvation of the people under it, is not only to think without reason and contrary to authority, but it is to confound the whole oracles of God, and to make christianity a mere continuation of the principle of law amended and improved.

There were saints before Moses, cotemporary

with Moses, and after Moses, in the other nations, under the constitution given to Noah and his descendants after the flood. Salvation was accessible to the nations who held fast the traditions derived from the family of Noah, as it was to the Jews, who most exactly complied with all the national institutions. As reasonably might we conclude that all who fell in the wilderness through unbelief of God's promise concerning Canaan, or for any of the misdemeanors of which they were guilty, including both Moses and Aaron, are not to partake in the resurrection of the just, never to enter the New and Heavenly Jerusalem, as to think that all of them who were without the commonwealth of Israel and not included in the covenant with Abraham and with Israel, were forever cut off from the everlasting kingdom of glory.

Melchisedec was as illustrious a saint as ever Aaron was, and of a much more illustrious office. The children of Edom and of the surrounding nations long retained the knowledge of God among them, and even down to the days of John the Harbinger, there were men of other nations who feared the God of heaven, many besides the eastern magi who looked for the coming of the Just One.

Submission to the institution of Moses was not " essential," as some would have it, to the salvation of the world, neither was circumcision the door of salvation to the human race. But this only by the way.

We are warranted in saying that the enjoyment of eternal salvation was not derived to the Jews from any thing in their religion but what was prospective in it; and that it was not instituted for that purpose. There was a righteousness of law inseparably connected under that economy with the greatest temporal felicity; and there was a want of the righteousness of works which superinduced the greatest earthly calamities. But now "a righteousness without law has been manifested, attested by the law and the prophets"—a righteousness upon a new principle, and tending to another inheritance. Under the old constitution, though a man might be blameless, still he could not relish nor enjoy the blessings of the life promised under the new institution, unless born again, unless possessed of a righteousness not revealed but only attested by the law and the prophets. Yes, he might enjoy the life promised in the old constitution, and he might possess the righteousness required by the law, as Paul boasted he once did; but except born of water and of the Spirit—unless he saw, discerned, and relished the kingdom of heaven and the righteousness and life thereof, into that kingdom he could not enter. Had Moses himself lived in the time of Nicodemus, and had they both come to the Messiah at one and the same time, he would have told them both what he told this ruler of the Jews. To Moses the lawgiver, he would have said, 'Moses, unless you are born again, you cannot discern the kingdom of God—and unless you are born of water and of Spirit, you cannot enter into it.'

The life promised in the law and the righteousness required under the law, were just as dissimilar to the life promised by Jesus, and the righteousness now revealed, as the flesh is to the Spirit, or a kingdom of this world is to the kingdom of glory. "The life and immortality" of the gospel were no part of the Jewish economy; and neither of them was developed in that economy. Jesus brought life and immortality to light; and what was contained or portrayed in the symbols has been manifested to us, and realized by us.

" The law made no one perfect." It only superinduced "a better hope by which we draw near to God."

To contemplate the Jewish constitution and kingdom in this light, in the light which Paul throws upon it in his letter to the Hebrews, will do much to unveil Moses, and to present the unveiled face of Jesus to the eyes of his disciples, will do very much to save us from the influence of ancient and modern judaizers, from those teachers who are always " desiring to be teachers of the law, understanding not what they say, nor whereof they affirm;" who are compounding Jewish and Christian institutions, and endeavoring to place men under the law as a rule of life to guide them to heaven, which was only designed to guide men in the pursuit and enjoyment of a rational and felicitous life upon earth. The Jews had the egg whence came life to the nations; but now since the life has come, they have but the shell. In their symbols the gospel was contained; but now that the Messiah has come and brought life and immortality to light, there is to us Gentiles in the law of Moses neither promise of the life that now is nor of that which is to come. As many as are of the works of the law are under the curse. But Christ is the end of the law for righteousness to every one that believes on him. EDITOR.

To the editor of the Christian Baptist.

DEAR BROTHER CAMPBELL: Being born of very humble parentage, I was compelled, from circumstances over which I had no control, to live for the first twenty years of my life, in some measure secluded from the social circle; and up to this time I have not been able to overcome the habits thus acquired in my early life, from which cause I have been deprived of much of the information which might have been received from you in the social and private circle during your stay in this city; and hence, know but little of your views and feelings, except what has been derived from your writings and public discourses. But the pleasure and the profit, derived from these sources will never, I am certain, this side the grave be fully expressed. I must be permitted to say, however, that I have received more instruction and satisfaction, on religious subjects from these sources, than from all others, the Bible only excepted.

But not to weary you with an unprofitable introduction to the main object of this letter, let me proceed to state that a part of your discourse on the 15th ch. of the 1st epistle to the Corinthians was not so clear to my mind as I could wish. I think I heard you say that "there was not a single individual in the church of Corinth who did not verily believe that Jesus was raised from the dead—that this was an axiomatic truth, admitted by them all," or words to that effect.

Now, you know that "these books were designed to be read and understood by persons of the humblest capacity, as well as by those of the most exalted genius; readers of the most limited education, as well as those of the most liberal attainments, were equally embraced in the views of the writers. If particular attention was paid to any class of readers, it was doubtless to the poor who have not the means of a refined education." New Version, page 11. Now, being such a one myself, and feeling that I had a right to read and understand for myself as well as I can, let me proceed to say that I had taken a different view of the subject in that portion of the good book referred to above, from the one given by yourself. Without consulting any human teacher whatever. I had taken up the idea that there were some persons in the church who actually denied the resurrection of the Lord Jesus. The reasons why I thus concluded are—1st. He lays before them the evidence, or the proof of the fact that he was risen. If they all believe it, why prove it? Surely this was unnecessary. But, 2d. He asks, "how say some among you, that there is no resurrection?" and adds, "for if there be no resurrection of the dead, neither has Christ been raised." From which I had concluded that there were persons "among" the brethren (but not therefore brethren) who had adopted the Saducean sentiment that there was "no resurrection, nor angel, nor spirit," which sentiment, having a paralyzing influence, and being opposed to fact, (the fact on which christianity hangs) the Apostle here meets and destroys, by showing, first, that Christ was raised from the dead by the glory of the Father, and thus at once refutes the sentiment that there was no resurrection; and 2d, that Christ was raised as the first fruits, and a certain pledge that "those that sleep in Jesus, God will bring with him."

Now, with this one exception, I fully concurred with you in your remarks on that chapter, and I shall continue to rejoice that I was permitted to hear you on that occasion; and as truth is my object, I have no doubt but you will feel pleasure in putting me right if I have a mistaken view of the subject, or misunderstood you on that occasion.

But before I lay aside the pen I will take this opportunity and the liberty to express the pleasure which I felt in reading, among other things, the "Sermons to Young Preachers," and the hope that you will follow up the subject until your readers are well informed as to their duty on that subject. And may I here be permitted to make an inquiry predicated upon the circumstances by which I am surrounded. Some years ago, when my soul was liberated from the bondage of sin and fear of death, I was so enamoured with the glories of Jesus and his cause, that I wished all persons to partake with me the joys of salvation; and I felt it my duty and privilege to say "come;" but did not believe that the terms preacher, teacher, minister, &c. ought to be applied to me, and hence thought that I was a nondescript in religion. The textuary system was tried, but the Christian Baptist came to hand and soon exploded that; and your own teachings in person have convinced me that I knew so little about the scriptures, that I am almost ready to sit down and never again say in public, "God now commands all men every where to reform."

Now, my inquiry is this, What shall I do in this matter? If I know myself, I love the truth so dearly, that I contemplate with horror the idea of erring and thereby teaching others to err; and at the same time it is written, "Let every one according as he has received a spiritual gift, minister it to one another, as good stewards of the manifold favor of God. If any one speak, let him speak as the oracles of God require." Sacred writings, page 432. To this last item I do most cheerfully subscribe, and am willing to do all I can to induce others to do likewise. On this subject, also, let me hear from you; and believe me to be, in the mean time, your unworthy but affectionate brother, in the hope of a glorious resurrection and blessed immortality.

                                        THOMAS.
                        —
                  Reply to Thomas.

DEAR BROTHER—That Jesus rose from the dead, was not denied by any member of the church in Corinth. The Saducean part of that congregation either denied or doubted the literal resurrection of the bodies of the saints. "Some of you say there is no resurrection of the dead:" and you ask, "Suppose there were a resurrection of the dead, with what sort of a body will they come to life again?" These are the two questions which called forth this admirable section of the first letter to the Corinthians; an analysis of which I shall one day, if the Lord permit, present in the Millennial Harbinger. The Saducean hypothesis had not been fully abandoned by some of this sect converted to the christian faith. After the renunciation of their former schemes and conversion to the Lord, it seems true in their example, as in that of many others, that old associations of ideas and old prejudices got for a time the ascendancy over their new faith, and their former philosophic doubts returned with all their perplexing influences:— "How shall the dead be raised? and (if raised) with what body do they come?"

At present suffice it to say, that Paul reminds them of their convictions when he came to Corinth; declares what he proclaimed; enumerates the facts alleged; asserts their cordial reception of these facts, and assures them of complete and eternal salvation if they retained these facts in their memories. He hastens to the resurrection of Jesus, repeats the evidences he had submitted to them, and from the certainty and assurance with which they had received and accredited the fact of Christ's resurrection, he reduces to an absurdity their doubts concerning the resurrection of the saints.

"So we proclaimed and so you believed," said he, when he had repeated what he formerly had announced. Now mark the consequences which will result from your denial of the resurrection of the just;—

1. You will deny your own faith; for if there be no resurrection of the dead, then neither has Christ been raised!—contrary to your own belief!

2. Again, if there be no resurrection of the dead, false is our proclamation, and your faith in it is also false. Not false *was your faith*, but false *is your faith* in our proclamation!

3. Besides, we have not only proclaimed what is false in itself, but we are false witnesses as respects God; for we have declared against God that he did, what, on this hypothesis, he never did—raise up Jesus from the dead. And recollect the corollary is, if the dead rise not, Christ has not been raised.

4. Farther, if Christ be not raised, your faith in him would be *useless*. Your sins have not been washed away.

5. In the fifth place, all the martyrs, all who have died on account of their testifying the resurrection of Jesus, have perished—have thrown their lives away for nothing, and are gone forever.

6. And we, too, who have not yet died, but are in jeopardy of our lives every day in making this proclamation, are leading the most miserable lives for no purpose but for deceiving and seducing men, in proclaiming and attesting the resurrection of Jesus and of the dead. These and other absurd consequences must result from your questioning the resurrection of the dead.

You will then, my brother, perceive that Paul reasons from the fact of Christ's resurrection as from an axiom, a first principle, which no one in the congregation of Corinth for a moment questioned. So clear was their perception, and so deep was their conviction of this truth, that Paul does no more than remind them of it, and of the evidences on which it rested, and argues from it as from some self-evident principle.

The next item in your letter will be attended to in my fourth sermon to young preachers. The third you will find in this number. The desire which you feel is the most natural and the most commendable in the world—for if the heavenly messengers in the presence of God rejoice more over one reforming sinner than over ninety and nine just persons who need no reformation, who are running the christian race in the prescribed course; if a father rejoices more over one returning prodigal than over all his sons and daughters which are virtuously walking in his commandments—surely we cannot but feel most solicitous to be the means, the humble instruments, of turning sinners from the error of their way, and of saving men from death. It is, therefore, the most natural desire in the heart of every christian to be instrumental in bringing others into the fold of God, and in making them happy under the peaceful and benign reign of the Prince of Peace. To see men professing godliness, and remiss in their activities, and cold in their zeal for the conversion of sinners, is one of the greatest incongruities which I can conceive, and one of the most unequivocal symptoms of a *form* of godliness without the power. "I would you were either cold or hot. But because you are lukewarm, and neither cold nor hot, I will spue you out of my mouth."

In all christian affection, and in the kingdom of Jesus,   Yours,   EDITOR.

Bishop Semple.

I HAD the pleasure of an interview with the venerable Bishop Semple, on my way from Richmond, as well as with most of my former acquaintance, friends and brethren, in the counties of Louisa, Hanover, King William, King and Queen, Essex, Caroline, and Spottsylvania. My interview with none of the Bishops was so interesting as that with Bishop Semple. From the collision into which we had fallen through Dr. Noel's instrumentality, and from the notoriety of the differences existing, as detailed in the preceding volumes of this work, our meeting derived additional interest.—While I was lecturing in Upper Essex meeting-house, the Bishop arrived nearly two hours before I had finished my address. After an interchange of the most friendly salutations, we repaired together to enjoy the christian hospitalities of our common friend and brother Bishop Henley. Many guests accompanied us, and we had quite a little congregation around the social, and I might add, the christian fireside.

After the Bishop and myself had felt the cheering influences of the fire, and the inspiring influences of our mutual friends and acquaintance, we got into a four hours' very agreeable fireside discussion of many matters and things pertaining to the christian institution. Not a word was said, nor an allusion made to what had formerly transpired between us, or was written in this work. All was as though it had never been. And after comparing the grounds and reasons of our respective views and courses in the christian profession, and after we had united in prayer and praise, we reposed together upon the same couch, until the eyelids of the morning opened upon us, and bade us look to Heaven. We arose. And after we had dressed, and the family and guests had assembled, we repaired to a pond, on which the ice was about an inch thick,

not more than one fourth of a mile from the house; and there, while the sun was lifting his golden locks over the tops of the trees and the little congregation standing round the pool, I immersed a disciple from King William into the christian faith, as they were wont to do before Antichrist was born! We returned to the house, united in worship, breakfasted; and after some friendly conversation, we prepared to depart, each one his own way. Bishop Semple and I, after expressing for each other our mutual good wishes, bade each other adieu, he proceeding to King and Queen, and I to Caroline.

It would be unbecoming for me, and it is a task for which I was never well qualified, to give any account of the topics, arguments, and discussions which filled up the hours we were together. There were a goodly number of very intelligent brethren and sisters present who could do this much better than I. What I admired most of all was the good temper and christian courtesy of this venerable disciple, who, although unable to rise above all his early associations and the long received opinions which a long course of reading and teaching had riveted upon his mind, yet he did not lose sight of the meekness and mildness, the candor and complaisance which the religion of Jesus teaches, and without which, though a man's head were as clear as an angel's intellect, his religion is vain.

There is certainly a very great advance in the knowledge of the christian scriptures in most of those counties within the last five years. I was not a little surprized to mark the vast progress of some elderly persons who had been stationary, as they now say, for many years before. The liberality and inquisitiveness which now are manifest every where, indicate that nothing can stand which is not founded upon the oracles of God. A few years more will wither up the systems of human device, and dry up the fountains of error which so long have afflicted the church with barrenness, and which have reduced christianity to a lifeless skeleton, alike impotent to reform the world and to console those who have sought for happiness in the kingdom of Jesus.

EDITOR.

New Periodicals.

THIS country is likely to become one of the most intelligent in the world. The increase of readers, writers, and periodicals, is astonishing. When this work was about one year old, or, perhaps, before it was a year old, a Presbyterian paper published that itself was the only religious paper in seven states and three territories. In Kentucky alone there are the Christian Messenger, the Baptist Recorder, the Christian Examiner, the Baptist Chronicle, the Western Luminary, and the Paidobaptist, said to be defunct, but to be succeeded by the Presbyterian Advocate. How many more I know not. There is no doubt but they will all do good. The Paidobaptist, I have understood, though intending to build up "*babyism*" in the form of sprinkling infant faces—a rite the most unmeaning in all the world, Jewish, Christian, or Pagan, has helped in some instances to pull it down. The person who was to have published it, then a Presbyterian, after the appearance of the first number was himself inclined to renounce paidobaptism as they call it—did renounce it—was immersed, and is now the editor of the Christian Examiner. The "Paidobaptist" did certainly expose the weakness of the cause it plead, the most ably of any print in the backwoods—so much so that one year seems to have been enough for it. The Baptist Recorder, I learn, though I have seen but one number of it in six months, holds on the even tenor of its way. It, now and then, I hear, from those who read it, gives me "a mortal wound." But I have been so often "mortally wounded" that I cannot die except by my own hands. Whether it was too weak or too strong for the zeal of my opponents, I know not; but they have got up the Baptist Chronicle. This goes hand in hand with the Western Luminary in advocating creeds and councils of human mechanism, and in publishing such calumnies against me as that from the pen of Randolph Stone, noticed in the first number of the Millennial Harbinger. The Baptist Chronicle will not fail for ingenuity and tact, as the Editor, Uriel Chambers, Esq. is both a Baptist, a lawyer, and a christian—one, however, of the Georgetown school. He wrote me a long letter which I have heard he has published in the Baptist Recorder; but I never saw it in print, and I have little recollection of its contents, for I read it in great haste immediately before my departure for Richmond, and resolved to publish it on my return; but he would not wait for that, and gave it himself. I have an answer to it on file, sent me from the West, containing an exposition of facts and documents, and reasonings, which would nearly fill half of this number.— I cannot think of bestowing so much importance upon such a trifle, as to publish either of them, unless it should become necessary from some cause I yet cannot see. One thing I will say, that, if published, it will not be very savory to my friend Mr. Chambers; and I do not like to publish what would appear a retaliatory act upon him, unless other causes call it forth. I have already exposed so many tricks of my restive opponents, that it seems a work of supererogation—like throwing water on a drowned mouse; to be killing a third time those who are twice dead.

The "Church Advocate," edited in Vincennes, by elder Daniel Parker, author of the *two seeds*, or modernized Manichean doctrine of two principles changed from the Persian to the American philosophy, is engaged in slandering me with his usual dexterity in the good work of defamation. He boasts of great intimacy with Dr. Noel, and says he found a cordial welcome into his pulpit in Frankfort. This pulpit, it is said, is consecrated after the manner of the sanctum sanctorum of the Jews.

I did not till lately know that such was the fact, if it be, and that any church in Kentucky had refused to let any one into their house, who affirmed that the scriptures of the apostles were a perfect rule of life, intelligible, suitable, and able to furnish every one who loved them to every good word and work. No, I did not believe, and like Thomas, I cannot believe upon almost any testimony, that Dr. Noel, or any church of which he is a member, will, by a solemn resolution, declare that any one of good moral and religious character who teaches that Jesus Christ has come in the flesh, is the Son of God, and that he died for our sins, was buried, and rose again, ascended into heaven, and is the Judge of all men, and who teaches that the scriptures are a divine revelation, clear, intelligible, and perfect; even should he oppose the Doctor's own creed book, would be refused to speak in any house, public or private, which might be convenient. Rumors to this effect, it is true, I have heard some time ago; but that such a step has actually been taken, I want stronger proof than is now before my mind to believe. I cannot reconcile this to all I know of the Doctor, nor of the intelligence of Frankfort.

Mr. Parker resolves every thing into his philosophic scheme of predestination, and he that denies his work of the Holy Spirit, or his call to the ministry, he represents in his last number as having committed the unpardonable sin. Reader, brace your nerves, and read what follows from his fourth number!

"If so be, that denying the office and work of the Spirit in experimental religion, and call to, and work of the ministry, should be that sin against the Holy Ghost, (which appears to me to be the fact,) then with awful sensation of feelings, we know the fate of those who are thus engaged. We need not pray for them; the Lord will not hear on their behalf; their doom is filled, and their conscience seared. You cannot bring conviction to their minds—and to say that we do not deny the office or work of the Spirit, and yet contend that the Spirit and Word are one, or that there is no spirit but what is in the Word, is making the matter worse. It is not only denying the work of God, as a Spirit, but also lying before God, for the purpose of covering a blasphemous sin."

Surely this is a wonderful age, an eventful time! We may expect to hear soon that the Earth is as flat as a trencher, and that the Sun is a ball of fire whirling round it; that language has any meaning, or that Revelation is any blessing to man, may soon be denied. Every one who opposes the dreams of Daniel Parker about his call to the ministry, is not to be prayed for!!! This is the fair meaning of the text and context.   EDITOR.

———

No. 9.]   APRIL 5, 1830.

Essays on Man in his Primitive State, and under the Patriarchal, Jewish, and Christian Dispensations.—No. XIII.

Jewish Age.—No. V.

AFTER the Jewish religion was introduced and established by Moses, there were no persons set apart to teach it or to preach it. Its genius being adapted to one nation only, and for temporary and national purposes, it looked not for proselytes beyond the commonwealth of Israel: hence it had no preachers, no proclaimers whose business it was to make proselytes. Congregations were not to assemble to hear discourses, nor was there a single missionary to go out of the precincts of the land of promise to make converts to the institutes of Moses. This is a fact of much importance, and ought to be well understood by the judaizers of this age, who are now making proselytes from among christian disciples to the law of Moses as *a rule of life.* No person was enjoined to take any steps to extend that religion beyond the *children of the flesh of Abraham.* Such as wished to become citizens of the commonwealth, and wished to be incorporated with the congregation, might, on their own application and request, be circumcised and added to the nation as *proselytes.* But no proselyting institution was set up by the author of that economy, nor was such a spirit cherished among the people. The priests were to officiate at the altar, to read the law, and to take care of the sacred edifice and of the autograph of the law and the constitution; so that if any difficulty should arise among the people, they were to go to the priest for the original and to seek the law at his mouth.

How, then, was this religion to be perpetuated?

By the instrumentality of parental authority and instruction. Fathers and mothers were to teach the religion to their children. This was the statute of Moses, (Deut. iv. 9.) "Teach them your sons, and your sons' sons," chap. vi. 6. "And these words which I command you this day, shall be in your heart; and you shall teach them diligently to your children, and shall talk of them when you sit in your house, and when you walk by the way, and when you lie down, and when you rise up; and you shall bind them for a sign upon your hand, and they shall be as frontlets between your eyes. And you shall write them upon the posts of your house and on your gates." In this way was the religion of Moses to be perpetuated and inculcated.

David, in the 78th Psalm, gives us the whole law concerning the Jews' religion. "Attend, my people, to my law; incline your ear to the words of my mouth. I will open my mouth with parables, I will utter dark sayings of old;—such as we have heard and known, which our fathers have related to us. They were not hid from their children; one generation told another the praises of the Lord, his acts of power, and the wonders which he has done. Thus he raised up a testimony in Jacob, and *established* a law in Israel, *which he commanded our fathers to make known to their children:* that the succeeding generation, the children to be born, might know it and rise and *tell the same to their children: that they might put their trust in God,* and not forget the works of God, but seek diligently his commandments, that they might not be like their fathers, a perverse and rebellious generation, a generation which set not their hearts aright, and whose spirit was not stedfast with God."

Parents were divinely instituted teachers of the Jews' religion. To their instrumentality was referred the continuance and the influence of this institution. The confidence in God of children was made dependent exclusively upon parental authority. No sermons nor sermonizers were known in the world for more than four thousand years of its history. The religion which God gave the Jews was written in a book. That book was copied, and read, committed to memory, and taught by all the people. It was supposed sufficiently plain and intelligible to all the people; and as the religion was designed for one nation only, it was not their duty to promulgate it abroad.

I have been censured for teaching that the promises of this religion looked to the present life and not beyond it: for saying that its motives of obedience were drawn from temporal objects. But as I have Moses with me here, I care not for such objections. I will ask them who complain to respond to Moses, and not to me. Moses exhorts to obedience in the following strains. (*Deut.* vi. 3.) "Hear, therefore, O Israel, and observe to do it, that it may be well with thee, and that you may increase mightily, as the Lord God of your fathers promised you, in the land that flows with milk and honey." (vi. 12.) "If you keep these statutes, the Lord your God will keep *his covenant* with you, and *the mercy* which he promised your fathers." What is the *covenant,* and the *mercy?* It is this;—"He will love you, and bless you, and multiply you: he will also bless the fruit of your womb, and the fruit of your land; your corn, and your wine, and your oil, the increase of your kine, and the flocks of your sheep, in the land which he sware to your fathers to give you. You shall be blessed above all people; there shall not be *male* or female barren among you, or among your cattle.

And the Lord will take away from you all sickness, and will put none of the evil diseases of Egypt upon you, but will inflict them upon all who hate you." This is the whole tenor of the *covenant and the mercy* promised the Jews in that institution. The threats and penalties were the reverse of these blessings. Now, why is it, let me ask, that this religion, that this institution, is confounded with christianity? Why is it that it is made a rule of life, a model for christian imitation? Does not christianity propose more sublime objects of holy enterprize? Does it not furnish stronger motives, better arguments for obedience and a rule of life of higher and purer morality?

But my present business is with the means of its propagation and the nature of the institution as contradistinguished from the Reign of Heaven. The prophets of after times, besides their exhortations to compliance with the statutes and judgments from Horeb, gave various new revelations concerning the destinies, the future destinies of Israel and the Gentiles. They added nothing to the institution, gave no new laws, offered no comments, and made no amendments to the institution. They remonstrated against apostacy, preached reformation, and intimated judgments and calamities upon the disobedient and rebellious.

There is a distinction of much importance to understanding aright both Testaments, which we wish here to suggest. The prophets *under* an economy, and the prophets *of* an economy are quite different characters as respects their mission and their duties. Moses was the only prophet of the economy; Isaiah, Daniel, and others prophesied under that economy, or while it was yet standing. The prophets under that economy interfered not with any item of the institution—they added nothing—they took away nothing—they warned the people of Israel of the calamities which would come upon them if they reformed not. They showed Israel their transgressions and sins against their own law, but were neither commentators nor interpreters of either the constitution or laws of Israel. They also spoke the fates and destinies of other nations, and foretold the fortunes of the Jews and Gentiles to the latest times. But as well might one call Agabus a prophet of the New Testament, because he prophesied under this new economy, as call Daniel, Ezekiel, or Malachi prophets of the Jewish economy, because they were Jews, and lived while that economy was yet standing. The Scribes or Doctors of the Law among the Jews were first employed to write off copies of the law; from this they were called *scribes.* Some of them, from repeated writings of the law, became more skilful in it than others, and in process of time began to add their notes, glosses, and interpretations, and were looked up to as Doctors of the Law. These Doctors soon obtained credit with the people, and their opinions and interpretations were venerated; so that as the Doctors increased, the people became more ignorant, and the traditions of the Senior Doctors became of tantamount and ultimately of paramount authority and veneration to the text itself. But as interpreters and expounders of the law, they had no more divine authority than Adam Clarke or Thomas Scott had to undertake their ponderous and voluminous commentaries.

They were no part of the means appointed by Moses for the perpetuation of the knowledge and meaning of the law. They were an excrescence upon his institution. It only required to be read, and parents were as competent to be instructors of their offspring in the whole institution of Moses, as the most learned and skilful scribe in the family of Levi or commonwealth of Israel. Copies only were wanting, and scribes were as necessary then as printers now. But whenever the scribes became "Doctors of the Law," the people became ignorant of the laws: and so it has come to pass in every country that, in proportion as the teachers of religion have been multiplied, in the same proportion has ignorance of the sacred writings abounded. It is with learning as with wealth. A few cannot be immensely wealthy, but the many must be poor. One palace, and a thousand cabins—a few "nobles," and a "numerous rabble," constitute those societies where there are patented and privileged classes. So it is in learning sacred and common. A few trained and privileged teachers of religion have always produced an ignorant "laity." Nothing can prevent this but the illumination of the public mind upon one point—the plainness and intelligibility of the New Institution—and that men of common education, by strict attention, may be able to understand the christian facts, and teach their meaning to their own households as usefully as any one of the privileged classes.

I have much to say upon this subject which I have not yet said; but for the present, these remarks, suggested by examining the method of perpetuating the Jews' religion, must suffice. We have seen that no order of teachers, nor expositors, sermonizers, textuaries, commentators, nor public instructers, other than readers of the law, and parents were ordained by divine authority in the former institutions, whether Jewish or Patriarchal. To conclude. The Messiah said all this in one sentence:—"The law and the prophets," (the writings of Moses and the writings of the prophets, all inspired,) "were your instructers till John the Immerser" began to proclaim the acceptable year of the Lord, and to introduce a new economy, called emphatically the Reign of Heaven.

The priesthood was the symbolic gospel, or the gospel under a veil in the Jewish institution. This part of the institution Paul does ample justice to in his letter to the Hebrews. They, their service, and the house in which they officiated, were the patterns of things in the heavens; but never intended to be the patterns or models of christian teachers, congregations, and meeting houses, as some have foolishly supposed. EDITOR.

Sermons to Young Preachers.—No. IV.

IT is owing to want of observation and reflection, that many grow up to manhood without any fixed principles, without any certain knowledge of men or things. We are obliged from the law of our creation at first to take every thing upon trust. This is the fate of childhood, and some never rise above it.

The world, many think, is too old, and men have reflected so deeply on all subjects that there is nothing to be originated, and little advance to be made in any department of thought. This is a great mistake. The last four hundred years have done more, by new discoveries and inventions, to improve human circumstances, than the twelve hundred years before. There is scarcely any thing of which it can be said, This is altogether new. New combinations, and new associations of ideas, and new discoveries, are, however, incessantly obtruding themselves upon the world. Ten years now almost count a hundred in improvement, and the seventy or eighty years of man's life teem with as many

new and unexpected events, as we have reason to think distinguished the seven and eight hundred years of the antediluvians.

But in religion the most important of all objects of thought, there is nothing new, or at least there are no new discoveries to be made. All that we can discover is, how far men have corrupted christianity; and to me the greatest wonder is, that a book so small, so simple, so perspicuous, so plain, as the New Testament, on which so many ship loads of books have been written, could have been so little understood, even by those who teach it for a lifetime.

The first thing which a young preacher ought to consider in respect of any particular congregation which he is about to address, and, indeed, old preachers had better also attend to it, is, to ascertain the stature of the mind, or the amount of information which his audience may be supposed to possess. What foundation he has to build upon, is the first question as respects the audience, which a prudent speaker proposes to himself. And here it may be noted, and it is at all times worthy of note, how much is taken for granted by almost every preacher. It is almost universally taken for granted that the audience believe that there is a God, a Saviour, a judgment, a heaven, a hell. I do not recollect that I have heard any preacher address any congregation, who did not presume thus much upon the previous instruction of his congregation. There is more in this than I am able to unfold in half a dozen of essays of the dimensions of this paper. A few remarks I am, however, constrained to make upon this presumption.

How, let me first ask, how is it that all preachers presume this much? The principal answer, if not the only one which can be given, is this—That in the early education of all persons born in a christian land, these fundamental truths are planted in the minds of all. All some way know, all have some perception of those first and most fundamental truths. Hence it was that I once asserted that I did not know that the ten thousand preachers in these United States had, in ten years, converted any one individual, *out and out*, as some would express it. The ground was fallowed, was ploughed once before their share ever touched it. Mothers, fathers, uncles, aunts, or some other benevolent being, nurse, guardian, schoolmaster, or other, had planted these seeds before the preacher ever addressed them from his sacred tub. He only harrowed the ground which they had fallowed. If he convicted his audience of guilt, it was because he had revived their early convictions: and their incongruous actions, their departure from their own concessions, and their suppressing the light which they had, were the arguments which he found available to convict them.

'Tis because missionaries to pagan lands have not the ground thus fallowed for them, that so poor a harvest rewards their toils. I might ask some curious questions here were it in my way; such as, Why could not those who broke up the soil, who fallowed the field, have harrowed it? Or why could not those who first planted these fundamental truths in the infant mind, have also planted all the other truths of the gospel, had they been as well instructed in them, themselves? Why, in one word, could they who instructed the infants in the knowledge of those first truths, have made them equally well acquainted with all the gospel facts? Nay, let me go a little farther and ask, What in reason, in scripture, or in experience, hinders, or could hinder them being christians themselves, to finish the converting of their children, as well as the preachers. They do much the greater part who forward the work thus far. Has the Lord promised to honor the preacher more than the parent? The time will come, nor far distant is the day, when it will be acknowledged that the most puissant converting army that ever entered the field, is that composed of fathers, mothers, nurses, and schoolmasters. Whenever this secret is fully developed, then will there be a mighty breaking in upon the ranks of the adversary.

It is always expensive keeping up a regular army, and not the best policy in times of peace. It is better to arm all the young men in the country. 'Tis better to have 600,000 militia well *armed*, than to have some ten or twenty thousand "*regulars*"—under pay too!

I know from a little experience, and from some observation, as well as from what the Acts of the Apostles teach, that the most efficient system, ever yet adopted, was that of the founder of the christian institution of making every man and woman in the ranks *a preacher* in the ancient import of that term. Every church on his plan, was a theological school—every christian a missionary; and every day's behavior, a sermon, either in word or deed.

But I am setting a bad example to young preachers. I am straying from my text. We must have preachers to introduce a better order of things. Preachers have become as necessary as prophets were in the worst times of the Jewish history. In prosperous times they needed no prophets. Had not Baal had them in hundreds, there would have been no need for Elijah, and Obadiah, and other kindred spirits. How shall we preach profitably to them unless we first form a correct view of the actual improvement, or of the real condition of our congregation?

To begin to prove the being and perfections of God to a people who confess, acknowledge, and believe that he exists; and that his excellencies are perfect and unsearchable, appears very inconsiderate. To begin to proclaim that all men will die, and to prove it by argument, would not be more unnecessary and superfluous, than to proclaim that there will be a judgment—that there is a Saviour, and a future state of bliss and woe, to them who doubt not any of these fundamentals. It is necessary to proclaim *reformation* to such a people who, with all these acknowledgments, are serving diverse lusts and passions, living in malice and envy, hated and hating one another. Indeed, the more I think upon this subject, the more similarity I discover between the circumstances of the people now, as respects Christianity, and the circumstances of those as respects Judaism, in the time of John the harbinger, whom he addressed. I, therefore, think, that there is more propriety in imitating John, than at first view appears. He addressed a people acknowledging all the cardinal truths of Judaism, and we address a people acknowledging all the great cardinal facts and truths of Christianity. He proclaimed reformation; so ought we.

Were Paul on earth now, he would proclaim reformation. He would from the acknowledgments, and from the behavior of our cotemporaries, denounce the judgments of God upon them if they reformed not. He would show them that sects, opinions, speculations, and doctrines, were not the religion of Jesus Christ, and if they reformed not, into the kingdom of glory they could not enter.

He would also denounce the unrighteous works of Christians—their envy—their pride, and covetousness. He would find occasion to take the advice he gave to Timothy, to reprove and rebuke with all authority. He would show us that the denunciations of Jesus, in some of the seven letters to the Asiatic churches, were applicable to us. That the candlestick had actually been removed, and that darkness, gross darkness covers the minds of almost all the people. Like Greece and Rome in their glory, we have our *enlightened* legislators; but yet, in the affairs of the kingdom of heaven, it is dark as night, in many, in most portions of the self-ycleped reformed churches of this age.

I hesitate not to say, that there is an alarming ignorance of the scripture, even amongst the most enlightened teachers of christianity so called. I seldom read a passage in a newspaper, in which I do not see two perversions for one right application of the scriptures. It is an awful time of darkness among the popular teachers of religion. I know what invidiousness there is in this assertion; I know how many tongues and pens it will move against me; but I cannot, I dare not conceal this conviction. I can take the most celebrated periodicals of the day, and bring proof upon proof, and adduce argument after argument to establish this assertion.

But to you, young preachers, I would say, you must, if you would be useful, take John for a model—you must proclaim reformation—you must take the acknowledgments and practices of your congregations, as topics from which to urge reformation. You must endeavor to introduce that state of things which will make every man and woman in the christian ranks a preacher in word and deed. This is a prominent part of the reformation now needed; and it will be then, and not till then, when all the citizens of the kingdom of Heaven are *citizen soldiers*, that the armies of the aliens can be completely routed.

But to give you a specimen of such addresses as those which in our time would be in accordance with the genius of John's preaching, and in reference to the public assemblies of this our age, and country, would be a desideratum to me: but such I find difficult to do on paper and in the compass of a few pages. However, something of this sort will be attempted in my next sermon to you.

In the meantime recollect that every thing depends upon your accurate knowledge of the scriptures of the Old and New Testament, and upon your forming just conceptions of the human mind, and the prejudices and prepossessions of your cotemporaries. You must know yourselves, your bibles, and the prejudices of your auditors, if you would be a successful champion in the ranks of the faithful, in the armies of the living God.   EDITOR.

The Bible.—No. IV.

DEAR SIR—It is very possible that there have been in use among the people called Christians, for upwards of seventeen centuries, two instruments of religious instruction, very different in their origin, character, tendency, and effects. Of these one has been devised, digested, fitted for its purpose, and transmitted to his perishing creature man, by an unerring and compassionate God. In this divine instrument there is no mistake, no misconception, no misrepresentation, no inconsistency, nothing false, nothing fictitious. In it truth, and nothing but truth, is to be found. While engaged in searching its divine contents, the honest inquirer is in no danger of imbibing error, or of swallowing falsehood. Here no poison is mixed with his spiritual food, nothing which can conduct his soul to hell, while sincerely seeking here his way to heaven. And this incomparable instrument of religious instruction is no other than revelation, just as it has been arranged and worded by its unerring author, the Holy Spirit, untouched, unaltered, unmixed, uncorrupted by any debasing intermixture of human conjectures, fictions, and conceits.

The other instrument is a human contrivance, most likely first devised and introduced among Christians by the heathen orators and Jewish priests, who at a very early period embraced the religion of Christ and corrupted it. It consists generally of some portion, more or less, of revealed truth, mixed up in a huge mass of human fables, conjectures, opinions, and fancies. In this horrid jumble of divine and human conceptions, the discordant elements are blended together in almost every possible proportion. Nor are its external forms less various than the proportions of its ingredients; sometimes it assumes the form and title of sermons, speeches, discourses, orations, arguments, lectures, commentaries, expositions, paraphrases, economies, catechisms, creeds, confessions, and whole bodies of new-fangled divinity, &c. Sometimes it appears in the shape of a pamphlet, or tract of scarcely ten pages, and anon in a folio of a thousand, and in every intermediate magnitude. But, perhaps, the most astonishing fact in its astonishing history, is, that it should, however little impregnated with divine truth, or however much crammed with human falsehood, nonsense and reverie, be termed by its inventors and patrons, God's Word, and the Gospel of Jesus Christ; and be almost universally preferred to that Word and Gospel, by a deluded, credulous, and unthinking multitude, who greedily devour the pernicious fiction, and defend it with all the fury of an excited bigot.

After this general view of the nature, origin, tendency, and effects of these two instruments of religious instruction, we proceed to inquire more particularly whether that provided and sent us by God, and just as he has sent it, or that fabricated by men, and made up of the materials just mentioned, be best entitled to our confidence and employment.

First, then, God's instrument of instruction is the *only* one that can be relied on as perfectly fit for its purpose. In it we are sure that there is no deficiency to be found. Its order, its connexion, its diction, its quantity, its perspicuity, are all the work of an unerring God, and therefore must be the fittest for its intended purpose possible. Its declarations are all true, whether yet accomplished or unaccomplished. Its declarations are clear, just, and beneficent. Its motives are the most interesting and powerful that the boundless wisdom of a God could make them. Its counsels, admonitions, reproofs, and threatenings, are full of wisdom, utility, and kindness—and its examples and histories are peculiarly impressive and instructive. In short, like its divine Author, it is in all respects perfect, and therefore no change can possibly be made on it without destroying, in proportion to the magnitude of that change, its fitness to accomplish its most benevolent and important purpose, to enlighten the mind, regenerate the heart, and rectify the external conduct of mankind.

2. God's instrument of instruction is alone safe. When we resort to any human composition, written or spoken, for religious information, we are in constant and imminent danger of imbibing more or less of that soul-destroying error from which no human production is exempt. But

when we consult God's word, we are absolutely certain that we can meet with nothing dangerous there—nothing to mislead or deceive us—nothing untrue—no insidious mixture of truth and falsehood—nothing pregnant with evil tendency—no mortal poison blended with our spiritual food.

3. God's instrument of instruction is alone authorized. For the employment of any other we have neither precedent nor command within the Book of God. During the patriarchal ages we hear of no uninspired teachers, nor means of religious instruction, but the inspired declaration of an unerring and omniscient God. During the Mosaic institution, before its gross corruption after the Captivity, God employed none but his own inspired teachers, nor means of religious information but his own inspired word. The prophets who addressed the people in the name of Jehovah, delivered his messages in the very words in which they were communicated to them by the Inspiring Spirit: and the Priests and Levites, who were constituted the national instructors, in conformity to God's express command, (see *Deut.* xxxi. 11, 28.) read for their instruction the written law in the hearing of all Israel. Josiah pursues the same prescribed mode of instruction, 2 *Kings* xxiii. 3. and Ezra follows in his steps, *Nehem.* viii. 3, 8. translating the original Hebrew, which few of his hearers understood, into Chaldee, which from their long residence at Babylon, had become in a manner their vernacular tongue; and we find the same mode of instruction still in use among the Jews, and among christians even in the time of Christ and his Apostles, (*Acts* xv. 21. xiii. 15. *Ephes.* iii. 4. *Col.* iv. 16. 1 *Thess.* v. 27. *Rev.* i. 3.) although after the Captivity, uninspired men had arrogated to themselves the honor, functions, and authority of God's inspired instructors, and employed their own crude, pernicious and unauthorized institutions and notions for the edification of the people, a fatal innovation to the Jewish nation. For their uninspired teachers, presuming to comment on, and explain the passages of scripture that related to the Messiah's person, character, and kingdom, mistook their meaning, deceived and misled the ignorant multitude, and by inducing them to form false notions of his character and office, led them to reject him when he appeared among them, (from this awful fact, let commentators, expositors, explainers—in short, intermeddlers with God's word, of every name, receive warning, and learn modesty and wisdom.) Nor under his new institution did God intrust the religious instruction of his perishing creatures to any but men rendered infallible by the gifts of his spirit, till he had caused an inspired system of religious information to be committed to writing, and so rendered permanent, uniform, and transmissible to all parts of the world and to all generations of men: a device by which, as we shall soon see, the continuance of immediately inspired instructors became unnecessary. As, then, we have no precedent to authorize us to employ any other instrument of religious instruction than that which God has himself directly furnished us; so we have no command. He whom God commissions to teach, speaks or relates God's own words, not man's—*John* iii. 34. and men are every where commanded to read, meditate, and search the scriptures, hear what the Spirit says to them, and earnestly desire the unadulterated milk of God's word; but no where, to the best of my knowledge, are they commanded to listen to the speeches or read the writings of uninspired mortals, in order to gain religious knowledge. This seems to be en-

tirely a human invention, and a most dangerous one.

4. God's instrument secures to inspired instruction both perpetuity and uniformity. By this glorious contrivance the instruction offered to God's ignorant creatures is, in respect of certainty and substance, the same in all places, and at all times. To past generations it has spoken the same inspired language and presented the same inspired ideas which it addresses and exhibits to the present race, and to future generations it will present no variation. Like its unchangeable author, it is the same to-day, yesterday, and forever. Here the never changing nature of God shines forth in all its unclouded majesty. How unlike that discordant and ever changing instrument of religious instruction invented by men.

5. It displays the uniformity of the divine conduct towards all God's rational offspring. The great Common Parent has not allowed to one portion of his human family all the certainty of inspired instruction, and the advantages of inspired instructors, and to another all the uncertainty of uninspired harangues, and all the danger which necessarily attends the employment of uninspired teachers. No, he feeds the first rational production of his wisdom, power, and goodness upon earth, with the same inspired intellectual food, which he provides, prepares, and presents to the last men of the race, and to every intermediate member. He commands not his children to sit down at tables so different, and partake of nourishment so very dissimilar as inspired and uninspired instruction is. But with the same inspired knowledge of himself, the only true God, and of Jesus Christ, his glorious commissioner to our guilty and ruined race, he uniformly offers to feed and feast, delight and ravish every member of it. In his instrument of instruction are no different conflicting, confounding, separating, and dividing creeds, confessions, formulas of worship, or terms of communion; no different catechisms, sermons, commentaries, expositions, or blotted bodies of human divinity; no different marks externally imposed on Christ's property, nor different elements required in the constitution of a christian. These motley, incongruous, discordant inventions, are left to decorate and commend the instrument of religious instruction contrived by bungling man.

6. It qualifies, or rather puts it in the power of the *saints* to execute the office, and discharge the great and difficult trust devolved on them. *Dan.* vii. 18, 22. *Eph.* iv. 12. 2 *Tim.* ii. 2. From these passages it is manifest that the saints are charged with the work or labor, called the service, and the building up of the body of Christ, language which figuratively denotes the further instruction of converts already made, and the augmentation of their number. Now who are the *saints* and faithful men, on whom this great, important, and honorable labor is devolved? Are they not the human beings, who, through the operation of the Divine Word and Spirit on their minds, have set themselves apart to the service of their God?— And is not every believer *one* of this happy and honorable number? Is not every believer equally a member of this blessed society? equally entitled to all its privileges, and equally bound to perform all its duties? Has Christ made odious and offensive distinctions among his friends? Is not each dear and acceptable to him in proportion to the zeal which he manifests in his Master's service? Is Christ's family the theatre of a senseless and unjust favoritism? Has he conferred any privilege, or imposed any duty on one

believer, which he has not conferred and imposed on all? (I speak now of ordinary believers, not of inspired or gifted men, whose offices were arranged according to the gifts which they had received, and by which they were immediately and infallibly qualified for the performance of the several extraordinary functions which the prosperity of the christian community in its infant state required.) But if the privileges and duties of all uninspired believers be the same in kind, then it follows as a necessary consequence, that a share proportioned to ability and opportunity of the work called the service, and the edification of the body of Christ, is assigned to every believer, &c. &c.   PHILALETHES.

THE following instructions from a father to a son, I committed to memory when a child.— Whether owing to early prejudices, or to more mature reflections I will not say; but I have always thought it, and do still think it, one of the best pieces of the kind I have ever read. Finding it of some use to myself even in riper years, I have, for the sake of others, thought it deserved to be snatched from forgetfulness, and to have a chance of living at least another generation. If it will prove as instructive to youth as I think it did to me, I will require no apology to either parents or children for presenting it in the last volume of this work. Though I was compelled to commit it to memory, as I was many fine pieces of prose and verse, I have found it a pleasing theme of reflection; and, indeed, many pieces which cost me some tears at school, have many a time since furnished me both instruction and joy at the recollection of them. This in prose, and Gray's Elegy in verse, were, I think now, as I thought then, the two best selections out of some hundred which a father, solicitous for my improvement, made a part of my task at school. For in those days it was usual to commit and recite some of the finest pieces of prose and verse as a regular part of education, during the whole course of academic instruction.   Ed. C. B.

The Instructions of Paternus to his Son.

PATERNUS lived about two hundred years ago; he had but one son, whom he educated himself in his own house. As they were sitting together in the garden, when the child was ten years old, Paternus thus spoke to him:

The little time you have been in the world, my child, you have spent wholly with me; and my love and tenderness to you, have made you look upon me as your only friend and benefactor, and the cause of all the comfort and pleasure that you enjoy. Your heart I know would be ready to break with grief if you thought this would be the last day that I should live with you.

My child, you think yourself very happy because you have hold of my hand; but you are now in the hands and under the tender care of a much greater father and friend than I am, whose love to you far exceeds mine, and from whom you receive such blessings as no mortal can give.

That God whom you have seen me daily worship; whom I daily call upon to bless both you and me, and all mankind; whose wonderous acts are recorded in those scriptures which you constantly read; that God who created the heavens and the earth; who brought a flood upon the old world; who saved Noah in the ark; who was the God of Abraham, Isaac, and Jacob; whom Job blessed and praised in the greatest afflictions; who delivered the Israelites out of the hands of the Egyptians; who was the protector of righteous Joseph, Moses, Joshua, and holy Daniel; who sent so many prophets into the world; who sent his Son Jesus Christ to redeem mankind; this God, who has done all these great things; who has created so many millions of men, who lived and died before you were born, with whom the spirits of good men that are departed this life now live, whom infinite numbers of angels now worship in heaven; this great God, who is the creator of worlds, of angels, and of men, is your loving Father and friend, your good creator and nourisher, from whom, and not from me, you received your being ten years ago, at the time that I planted that little tender elm which you there see.

I myself am not half the age of this shady oak under which we sit; many of our fathers have sat under its boughs, we have all of us called it ours in our turn, though it stands, and drops its masters as it drops its leaves.

You see, my son, this wide and large firmament over our heads, where the Sun and Moon, and all the stars appear in their turns. If you were to be carried up to any of these bodies, at this distance from us, you would still discover others as much above you, as the stars that you see here are above the earth: were you to go up or down, east or west, north or south, you would find the same height, without any top, and the same depth, without any bottom. And yet, my child, so great is God, that all these bodies added together, are but as a grain of sand in his sight; and yet *you* are as much the care of this great God, and Father of all worlds, and all spirits, as if he had no son but you, or as if there were no creature for him to love and protect but you alone. He numbers the hairs of your head, watches over you sleeping and waking, and has preserved you from a thousand dangers, which neither you nor I know any thing of.

How poor my power is, and how little I am able to do for you, you have often seen. Your late sickness has shown you how little I could do for you in that state; and the frequent pains in your head are plain proofs, that I have no power to remove them. I can bring you food and medicines, but have no power to turn them into your relief and nourishment; it is God alone that can do this for you. Therefore, my child, fear, worship, and love God; your eyes, indeed, cannot yet see him, but every thing you see, are so many marks of his power and presence, and he is nearer to you, than any thing you can perceive. Take him for your Lord, and Father, and Friend; look up to him as the fountain and cause of all the good that you have received, through my hands; and reverence me only as the bearer and messenger of God's good things to you; and he that blessed my father before I was born, will bless you when I am dead.

Your youth and tender mind are only yet acquainted with my family, and therefore you think there is no happiness out of it. But, my child, you belong to a much greater family than mine; you are a younger member of this Almighty Father of all nations, who has created infinite orders of angels, and numberless generations of men, to be fellow-members of one and the same society in Heaven. You do well to reverence and obey my authority, because God has given me power over you, to bring you up in his fear, and to do for you as the Holy Fathers, recorded in scripture, did for their children, who are now in rest and peace with God.

I shall, in a short time die, and leave you to God, and yourself; and I trust in God that I shall go to his Son Jesus Christ, and live among Patriarchs and Prophets, Saints and Martyrs, where I shall hope for your arrival at the same place.

Therefore, my child, meditate upon these great things, and your soul will soon grow great and noble, by so meditating upon them. Let your thoughts often leave these gardens, these fields and farms, to contemplate upon God and Heaven, and upon Angels and the spirits of good men living in light and glory.

As you have been used to look to me in all your doings, and have been afraid to do anything, unless you first knew my will; so let it now be a rule of your life, to look up to God in all your actions, to do every thing in his fear, and to abstain from every thing that is not according to his will. Keep him always in your mind, teach your thoughts to reverence him in every place, for there is no place where he is not.

God keeps a book of remembrance, wherein all the actions of all men are written: your name is there my child, and when you die, this book will be laid open before men and angels; and accordingly as your actions shall be there found, you will either be received to the happiness of these holy men who have died before you, or be turned away amongst wicked spirits, that are never to see God any more. Never forget this book, my son, for it is written, it must be opened, you must see it, and you must be tried by it; strive therefore to fill it with your good deeds, that the hand-writing of God may not appear against you.

God, my child, is all love, and wisdom, and goodness; and every thing that he has made, and every action that he does, is the effect of them all; therefore you cannot please God, but so far as you strive to walk in love, wisdom and goodness. As all wisdom, love, and goodness, proceed from God; so nothing but love, wisdom, and goodness, lead to God. When you love that which God loves, you act with him, you join yourself to him, and when you love what he dislikes, then you oppose him and separate yourself from him. This is the true and right way; think what God loves, and do you love it with all your heart.

First of all, my child, worship and adore God with humility; think of him magnificently, speak of him reverently, magnify his providence, adore his power, frequent his service, and pray to him constantly and ardently.

Next to this, love your neighbor, which is all mankind, with such tenderness and affection as you love yourself. Think how God loves all mankind, how merciful he is to them, how tender he is of them, how carefully he preserves them, and then strive to love the world as God loves it. God would have all men to be happy, therefore do you desire, and will the same. All men are great instances of divine love, therefore let all men instance your love.

But above all, my son, mark this, never do any thing through strife, or envy, or emulation, or vainglory; never do any thing in order to excel other people, but in order to praise God, and because it is his will that you should do every thing in the best manner you can; for if it be once a pleasure to you to excel other people, it will, by degrees, be a pleasure to you not to see other people so good as yourself. Banish, therefore, every thought of self-pride, and self-distinction, and accustom yourself to rejoice in all the excellencies and perfections of your fellow-creatures; and be as glad to see any of their good actions as your own. For as God is as well pleased with their well doings, as with yours; so you ought to desire that every thing that is wise, and holy, and good, may be performed in as high a manner, by other people, as by yourself. Let this, therefore, be your only motive and spur to all good actions, honest industry and business, to do every thing in as perfect a manner as you can, for this only reason, because it is pleasing to God, who desires your perfection, and writes all your actions in a book.

When I am dead, my son, you will be master of all my estate, which will be a great deal more than the necessities of one family require.— Therefore as you are to be charitable to the souls of men, and to wish them the same happiness with yourself in Heaven; so be charitable to their bodies; endeavor to make them as happy as you can upon earth. As God has created all things for the common good of all men; so let that part of them, which is fallen to your share, be employed as God would have all to be employed for the common good of all. Do good, my son, first of all to those that most deserve it; but remember to do good to all. The greatest sinners receive daily instances of God's goodness towards them; he nourishes and preserves them, that they may repent and return to him; do you, therefore, imitate God, and think no man too bad to receive your relief and kindness, when you see that he wants it.

I am teaching you Latin and Greek, that at proper times you may look into the history of past ages, and learn the methods of God's providence over the world. That, reading the writings of the ancient sages, you may see how wisdom and virtue have been the praise of great men of all ages, and fortify your mind by their wise sayings.

Let truth and plainness, therefore, be the only ornament of your language, and study nothing but how to think of all things, as they deserve, to choose every thing that is best, to live according to reason and order, and to act, in every part of your life, in conformity to the will of God. Study how to fill your heart full of love to God, and love to your neighbor. As true religion teaches us to be governed by right reason; so it loves and requires great plainness and simplicity of life. Therefore avoid all superfluous show of finery and equipage; don't consider what your estate can afford, but what right reason requires. Let your dress be sober, clean, and modest: not to set off the beauty of your person, but to declare the sobriety of your mind, that your outward garment may resemble the inward plainness and simplicity of your heart. For it is highly reasonable, that you should be one man, all of a piece, and appear outwardly such as you are inwardly.

As to your meat and drink, in them observe the highest rules of christian temperance and sobriety; consider your body only as the servant of your soul; and only so nourish it, as it may best perform an humble and obedient service to the latter.

But, my son, observe this as a most principal thing, of which I shall remind you as long as I live with you. Hate and despise all human glory, for it is nothing else but human folly: it is the greatest snare and the greatest betrayer that you can possibly admit into your heart. Love humility in all its instances—practise it in all its parts, for it is the noblest state of the soul of man—it will set your heart and affections right towards God, and fill you with every temper that is tender and affectionate towards him. Let every day, therefore, be a day of humility—condes-

cend to all the weaknesses and infirmities of your fellow creatures—cover their frailties—love their excellencies—encourage their virtues—relieve their wants—rejoice in their prosperity—compassionate their distress—receive their friendship—overlook their unkindness, and condescend to do the lowest offices to the lowest of mankind. Aspire after nothing but your own improvement and perfection, and have no ambition but to do every thing in so reasonable and religious a manner, that you may be glad that God is everywhere present, and observes all your actions.

The greatest trial of humility is an humble behavior towards your equals in age, estate, and condition of life. Therefore, be careful of all the motions of your heart towards these people; let all your behavior towards them be governed by unfeigned love. Have no desire to put any of your equals below you, nor any anger at those that would put themselves above you. If they are proud they are ill of a very bad distemper; let them, therefore, have your tender pity, and perhaps your meekness may prove an occasion of their cure. But if your humility should do them no good, it will, however, be the greatest good that you can do to yourself.

Remember that there is but one man in the world with whom you are to have perpetual contention, and be always striving to excel him, and he is, yourself.

The time of practising these precepts, my child, will soon be over with you; the world will soon slip through your hands, or rather you will soon slip through it: it seems but the other day since I received these instructions from my dear father, that I am now leaving with you: and the God that gave me ears to hear, and a heart to receive what my father said to me, will, I hope, give you grace to love and follow the same instructions.

Thus did Paternus educate his son.

Sermons to Young Preachers.—No. V.

The following conclusion of an address to a mixed congregation of religious sectaries, may afford you some idea of what was intended in my last by proclaiming reformation to a people, and arguing with them on their own concessions:—

Conclusion of an Address from Ecclesiastes.

"You acknowledge that God the Almighty, the Omnipresent, the Omniscient, created you, preserves you, and sent his Son to save you; and yet you fear not his omnipotence, regard not his omnipresence, and think to conceal yourselves from his all-seeing eye! He preserves you, and where is your gratitude—where your affection for him? Do you not owe him every thing, and will you not give him even the homage of a grateful heart? And you say he sent his Son to save you, and will you reject the message of his love, and refuse submission to him that died for your sins, and called you to honor and immortality?

Can you think he created you for no purpose, with no design, and that he feels no interest in you? Why, then, has he built the universe for you? Why does he make his sun to shine upon you, and send you the rain and dew of heaven?

And what regard to him do you show? How many thoughts do you give him every day—how much of your affection does he share? Has he given you eyes to see every thing but his wonderful displays of himself—ears to hear every thing but his voice—a tongue to speak every thing but his praise—and a heart to feel every thing but his love? Which of your appetites and passions, and evil habits are restrained by the fear of him? What energies of your nature are called forth by your veneration and love for him? With what fear does his frown, his indignation fill you? And with what love and ardent desire do his promises inspire you?

You acknowledge the Bible to be his oracle to men. How do you regard it? Do you represent it to be obscure, unintelligible, a barren and dead letter? What an insult to its author! what a reproach to his wisdom, goodness, and mercy! Do you read it, do you search for its meaning as for hidden treasure? Are the words and works of men sought after, read, and valued more than the volumes of God's authorship? Will you not be ashamed and afraid to see him, when you reflect that you have not read, nor studied, nor regarded the message which he sent you; that you honored any, and almost every author more than him; and that while he displayed the greatest regard for you, you showed the least to him? How can you think of appearing in his presence, having thus insulted his spirit of wisdom and revelation? Surely he has called, and you have refused; he has stretched out his hand, and you would not regard. Will he not laugh at your calamity, and mock when your fear comes? How vain and fruitless to implore his mercy then, when you disdain it now; to ask for pardon then, when you refuse it now; to sue for favor then, when you reject it now!

You have contended for correct opinions and sound doctrines, but what sort of lives are you leading? You have been zealous for what you call the "glory of God," when it was, in fact, and when stripped of its disguise, the glory of your own opinions and forms. What avails your sound opinions, and what your barren and unfruitful lives? Have you considered that you are not your own, but that you are God's property? What revenue of praise does he reap from you, and what good have men received from you? While contending for the opinions of men, do you not feel that there is no life in them; that they are cold and lifeless as moonshine; that they neither warm, nor cheer, nor purify your hearts; that they are but the shadows of truth, and that in feeding upon them, you only feed upon the wind? Have you ever felt the power of the love of God? have you ever breathed in an atmosphere perfumed with the fragrance of his grace, while contending for your speculative abstractions? Does not experience teach you that you seek the living among the dead, when you visit the sepulchres of the sectaries, when you look for salvation in and through their speculations? These opinions for which we now contend, are the ghosts of departed philosophers, who could not find peace in their lifetime, and now cannot rest in their graves.

Will you not, then, eat the bread of God, and drink the water of life, by coming to Jesus and receiving him as the Son of the living God and the Saviour of men? Has he not taught you that none can reveal the Father but himself; that none can know the Father but he to whom he reveals him? Why then will you not come to him and learn from him, seeing that he has told you that he alone can teach you—that he alone can reveal the Father to you? 'Tis vain for you to go to Moses, to those who preceded him; and it is still more vain for you to go to those who have succeeded the apostles, and who have endeavored to supplant them by new theories, to "know the living God and his son Jesus Christ, which is eternal life," as he has taught you.

Do you not acknowledge Jesus to be the Great Prophet, the great high Priest, and the Almighty King of his own kingdom? If he be the Great Prophet, why not be taught by him? Moses would have rejoiced to have lived under him, and yet you would rather be under Moses or Calvin than under this Great Prophet. May he not say, "If I be your Prophet, where is my honor? Do you sit at my feet? Do you hearken to my voice? Do you take your lessons from my instructions? Do you think that I speak less clearly, less intelligibly, less forcibly, less authoritatively, than your compeers?" Yes, were you to be asked these questions, what answers could you give?

You say he is your High Priest. Have you reposed confidence in his sin-offering? have you fled to him as your intercessor? have you been reconciled to God through him? If not, call him not your High Priest, for he is not. By one offering of himself he has perfected the conscience of all them who obey him. If by him you are not reconciled to God's government, to others he may be a High Priest, but to you he is not. Had you come to him as your High Priest, you would have found peace with God, and you would have rejoiced in him as your shield and hiding place.

But you say he is the King eternal, immortal, and invisible, and he is your King. Then you obey him; then you must submit to his government. But have you vowed allegiance to him? When and where? when did you make the vow? when did you enlist? when did you say, "Your God shall be my God, and your people shall be my people?" Tell me when did you make this vow? And tell me, did he receive you into his kingdom? If so, surely you must wear the livery of your master, and bow to the ensign which your King has raised.

"If I be your King," may he not say, "where is my reverence and where is my fear? Are my commands obeyed—are my instructions regarded? Do you expect me to promote and honor you in my kingdom without any proof of your loyalty? Who has ever done so? Who has rewarded cowards, traitors, and neutrals, except with chastisement? Call me not Lord, Master, nor King, unless you regard and honor me as such."

No, my friends, unless you act consistently with your convictions and concessions, better, infinitely better, you had made none. You only treasure up wrath against the day of wrath and revelation of the righteous judgment of God. You had better remember that the King has declared that he that knew his Master's will, and prepared not himself, shall be beaten with many stripes. And, adds he, "Bring out these mine enemies, who would not that I should reign over them, and slay them before my face."

But you must obey or perish. This is his decree. You say that God is the God of truth; that he cannot lie; that heaven and earth may pass away, but his word can never pass away. Tell me who has proved that God has ever failed to honor his own word? What promise or what threat has he uttered which he has not made good? None, none. Individuals, families, cities, nations, a whole world perished when he threatened it. Remember the fall of Adam, the curse inflicted upon man and upon woman, upon the old world, upon the sons of Ham, upon the cities of Sodom, Gomorrah, Babylon, Nineveh, Jerusalem—upon the Canaanites, the Egyptians, the Chaldeans, the Medes, the Romans, the Jews, upon the antichristian nations of Europe. And he that said, "In the day you eat thereof, dying you shall die;" who said, "Yet one hundred and twenty years, and the whole world shall be drowned," has said, that "he who hears the

77

gospel and disbelieves it—that he who knows not God, and obeys not the gospel, shall be punished with everlasting destruction from the presence of the Lord and from the glory of his power." Do you believe this, and acknowledge that God cannot lie, and will you promise yourselves impunity in your disobedience!

And are you not *disobedient* to the gospel? What, do you ask, "Can a person *disobey* the gospel?" If the gospel be all *promise* and no command, then you cannot disobey it. We never talk of *obedience*, but when there is a *command*. And certainly nothing can be more unequivocal than that God "*commands* all men every where to *reform;*" that the "*obedience of faith,*" and "obeying the gospel" are common expressions in the apostolic writings. Yes, certainly, you have read that God commands all men every where to reform; and he that has not obeyed this command, has not obeyed the gospel, and is a rebel.

It is not the ten commandments, but the *new* commandment which will condemn you. Yes, this is *his* commandment, that we should believe on his Son Jesus Christ; and the condemnation now is, that you obey not him whom God commissioned, but "that you love darkness rather *than light.*"

To command men to reform is a proclamation of mercy—yes, it is the gospel. For who proclaims reformation without forgiveness? It is not God. When he commands reformation, it implies forgiveness—when he says "*reform*" it is "that your sins may be blotted out"—it is "that times of refreshing from the presence of the Lord, may come upon you"—it is "that he may send Jesus a second time to your salvation, to raise you from the dead, and to induct you into eternal life."

And again, I ask, are you not disobedient to the gospel? Have you reformed? Have you turned to the Lord? And what is the proof of it? Nay, rather, what is the first act thereof? Have you put on Christ? In one sentence, have you been immersed into the name of the Father, and of the Son, and of the Holy Spirit? Have you, or have you not? If you have not, you have not obeyed the first commandment of the Great King. For that reads, "*Reform and be immersed for the remission of your sins.*"

Now what is your excuse?—*Ignorance* you cannot plead, for you have the oracle. *Inability* you cannot plead, for here is water; *pollution* can be no excuse, for the clean need no washing. Would you make your sins a reason why you should continue to sin?—your former disobedience a reason why you should always disobey? —your want of disposition a reason for continued indisposition? Would you disobey to-day, because you disobeyed yesterday; and will you promise to be more docile, and more obedient *to-morrow*, than you are *to-day?* Will the Lord be more gracious to-morrow, than to-day; and will it be more easy for you to shake off the dominion of sin when it has longer reigned over you, than it is at this instant?

If you did not say, you believe in the divine mission of Jesus, that he is the Son of God, the Saviour of *sinners*, I should not thus address you. But this you confess. And this is the very reason why your sin is so grievous. Because you say, "*We see*, therefore your sin remains."

Tell me not that you want a better heart, better feelings, and more assurance of God's favor, before you obey. This is all a deception, a delusion How could a disobedient heart become better by continuing disobedient? How could

you expect better feelings while rebelling against Jesus! How can you expect any more assurance of the divine favor, while you trample under foot the pledges of his love, which he has given. Nothing can cure your heart, nothing can produce better feelings, nothing can increase your assurance of the divine favor, but your obedience. Humble yourselves, and God will exalt you. Take Christ's yoke upon you, and *he will give you rest.* But if you will not kiss the Lord, if you will not bow to his sceptre, if you will not submit to his guidance; and yet feel happy, and find peace, and have good feelings, and a new heart in so doing; though all men should flatter you, there is one who will tell you that it is all delusion, strong delusion, for you to feel peace of mind, while you refuse to obey the gospel, and to come into the kingdom of Jesus through the washing of regeneration, and renewal of the Holy Spirit.   ECCLESIASTES.

Bible Society.

"The American Bible Society now have 16 steam and 12 hand presses at work; and are able to complete 1000 full copies, of the Bible every day. They have about 300,000 Bibles and Testaments now ready for distribution."

No. 10.]   MAY 3, 1830.

Essays on Man in his Primitive State, and under the Patriarchal, Jewish and Christian Dispensations.—No. XIV.

Jewish Age.—No. VI.

The Ministry of John.

THE ministry of *John the Harbinger* was in the conclusion of the Jewish age. He and the Messiah were born while the Temple was yet standing. Once in the end of the *world*, or in the end of the *age*, did the Messiah appear, says Paul, to put away sin by the sacrifice of himself. We are, then, to consider both John and Jesus as born, living and dying under the Jewish age.— Few regard this as a fact, though a fact of great importance it assuredly is. Malachi, the last of the Jewish prophets, taught the Jews to expect John or Elijah before the coming of the great and terrible day of the Lord upon the Jewish nation.

During the ministry of John, neither he, nor the Saviour, nor his apostles, nor the seventy disciples, went to proclaim out of the commonwealth of Israel. The proselyting era did not commence while the Messiah lived, for the reasons assigned in my last. Jesus once visited Samaria, and was made known to some of the Samaritans as the Messiah; but it was not until after his resurrection that he ordered the glad tidings of his reign to be promulged through Samaria. Nay, indeed, he forbade it: "Enter not a Samaritan city," gave he in charge to his attendants and heralds.

The reign of God was announced, and the glad tidings of the coming reign were proclaimed first and exclusively to the Jews, that among them a people might be prepared for the Lord. Hence the lost sheep of the house of Israel first and exclusively engrossed the attention and the labors of the original heralds of an eternal salvation.

Not only was the character of the author of the christian institution revealed, but also the genius and character of his kingdom opened to many, taught in parables, and literally developed by Jesus in his own lifetime to the apostles, and to many in Judea who expected salvation to Israel,

The Jewish age terminated with the burial of Jesus. It began with the paschal lamb which the Jews killed in Egypt and eat the night before they marched. Fifty days after they ate that passover, their institution was proclaimed from Mount Sinai; that was, so to speak, the *first Pentecost*. Jesus ate the last passover of divine authority; he died at the time Israel crossed the Red Sea; he kept the last sabbath of the Jewish law in the grave; he arose the day the manna first fell on Israel; and on the day of Pentecost, the day on which the Lord spoke to Israel from Mount Sinai, the fiftieth from the passover, on the same day did the Holy Spirit, from Mount Zion in the city of Jerusalem, first announce the New Institution.

The Jewish age and Jesus died at the same moment. Their sabbath and he slept in the same tomb; and during the forty days from his resurrection to his ascension, and thence to Pentecost, there was a period, a full period between the Jewish and the Christian age. He suffered no one to speak to the unbelieving during this period. He would not let his apostles open their lips until he was crowned in heaven. "Tarry in Jerusalem," said he, "until you be endued with power from on high."

These are the grand landmarks in the progress of God's revelations. These are the distinct chapters of the great volume of events which ought to be regarded as of primary importance in understanding God's book. "Jesus then was a minister of the circumcision to confirm the promises made by God to the fathers" of the Jewish nation; and John appeared in the conclusion of the Jewish age to prepare the way of the Lord.

These facts in the sacred history, clearly and unequivocally taught, do throw much light upon the testimony of the Evangelists. Those who confound and jumble every thing to make a system of their own, can never understand these sacred writings. Some make christianity as old as the creation, and teach that Moses was in reality as much a christian as Paul or John.

There is infancy, childhood, and manhood in religion, as well as in human life. There is starlight, moonlight, twilight, and sunlight in religion, in the moral, as in the natural world. And he that objects against this economy might as well object that we are infants before we are men, or that Spring must precede Summer, and seed time harvest.

But to the conclusion of the Jewish age. John took the Jews as he found them. He argued with them on, and from, their own acknowledgements. He pretended to a mission from God, which was confirmed by the manner of his birth, and the peculiarities of his life, and by the descent of the Holy Spirit upon Jesus as soon as John immersed him. He averred that he was "The voice of one crying in the wilderness," as spoke Isaiah. He remonstrated against the defection of the Jews—taught and practiced a more strict righteousness and devotion than any of his cotemporaries of the Jews, and commanded an entire reformation of manners.

To his preaching of reformation, an immersion of reformers for the remission of sins committed under the law, was added. Multitudes flocked to him, confessed their sins against God under the economy of Moses, and were immersed, confessing their sins, and reforming from them. He proclaimed that the Messiah was soon to appear; nay, that he stood among them, though they knew him not, and that they should believe in him who was to come after him.

His immersion differed from that instituted by Jesus in the four following respects:—

1. He immersed in the name or by the authority of God, and not in the name or by the authority of the Lord. No act in religion, from the beginning of the world until Pentecost, was ever done by any other name or authority, than the simple name of God. By the authority of Jesus or the Messiah, no act had ever been performed until in his own person he appeared in Judea, and until he declared that authority was given him and commanded no man to perform any act by his authority.

2. He immersed *into* no name. That he did not immerse *into* the name of Jesus as the Messiah, as the Lord, is obvious from the following considerations;—

It is manifest from the narrative, that John immersed some persons, if not many, before he immersed Jesus. Now, in whatever manner, and in whatever name John immersed, he uniformly immersed. His immersion was the same during his whole life. But it has been said that he immersed some persons before he immersed Jesus: now these he could not immerse *into* the name of Jesus because *he did not know him* when he first began to baptize. His words are, "As for me, I knew him not; but to the end that he may be discovered to Israel, I am come immersing in water. For my part, I should not have known him, had not HE who sent me to immerse in water told me, Upon whomsoever you shall see the Spirit descending and remaining, the same is he who immerses in the Holy Spirit. Having therefore seen, I testify that he is the Son of God." But the Spirit did not descend on Jesus till after his immersion; consequently John immersed others before he knew the Messiah.

Again, he did not immerse into the name of the Holy Spirit, because the Spirit was not yet given; for Jesus was not yet glorified; and those who were immersed by John had not heard any thing of the Holy Spirit. [See *Acts* xix. 1—8.] The Son and the Holy Spirit not being yet revealed, he could not immerse into either the name of the Son or of the Holy Spirit.

The Jews at this time had but the knowledge of God common to the nation, and it was therefore simply by the authority of the God of Abraham the Jews were immersed; and as they had always professed that name, there was neither need for, nor propriety in, their being immersed into that name.

3. But in the the third place he did not immerse into the christian faith. All the Jews believed that a Messiah would come; this was the common expectation of all the commonwealth of Israel. But it is one thing to believe that a Messiah was to come, and soon to come; and another thing to believe that any particular person and character was he.

It is one thing to believe that some person killed A B, and another thing to believe that C D killed A B. The former faith would not now injure any person though a whole jury possessed it; but the latter faith imperils the life of C D. So a belief that some person was to be the Saviour and Redeemer of Israel was one thing, and to believe that Jesus the Nazarene was that person, was another, and produced very different feelings and behavior.

To believe that Jesus is the Lord of all, that he died as a sin offering, and that he arose from the dead, was impossible to any of John's cotemporaries. For Jesus was not made Lord, as Peter imparted on Pentecost, until he ascended into heaven. He must first be a servant before he could be king. He must suffer before he could be made perfect as the Captain of Salvation. He must first be humbled, before he could be glorified. That he was to die for our sins, and to rise from the dead, neither John nor any of John's disciples knew or believed. For long after John had died, and after Jesus had taught his followers farther than John led them, when he talked of his resurrection they could not understand him: and after he rose from the dead and appeared to the women, this testimony appeared to the wisest of the Apostles as idle tales, and they believed them not. It is useless to reason farther to show that the disciples of John had not the faith which christians after Pentecost had; consequently, could not be baptized into a faith which they did not possess.

In the fourth place, John's immersion brought no man into the kingdom of heaven. The reason is obvious: no person could come into a kingdom which was not set up. I need not, to the readers of this work, at this late period, be at much pains to illustrate this point. All who have read the new translation must know that the Reign of Jesus is called the Reign of Heaven, and the institution which he has set up on earth is called the Kingdom of Heaven. This kingdom and reign was the burthen of John's proclamation, and of the Saviour's preaching and teaching. John and the Messiah, during their personal ministry, only said it was approaching, or near at hand, and soon to appear. It was impossible that the kingdom could be set up on earth until the King was placed upon his throne. This could not be until Jesus was exalted. It was after his humiliation unto death that his Father highly exalted him. Then he began his reign. Then he sent down the Holy Spirit; for the Spirit was not given until Jesus was glorified. John's preaching and baptism only prepared the people and brought them nigh to the kingdom. It introduced no man into it. John's disciples entered not in by virtue of John's immersion. Every man, Jew and Gentile, who came into the kingdom, must be born of water and of the Spirit.

But the fact that Jesus was not exalted until he rose from the dead; that he did not commence to reign until he was prepared by sufferings; that his kingdom was not begun until he was crowned Lord of all, is sufficient to establish the truth of the proposition that John's immersion brought no man into the kingdom of heaven; for that kingdom had not, in John's time, come. Christian immersion, then, differs from John's in four great and important particulars:—First, in the name, or by the authority, by which it is done. Second, into the name, into which it is done. Third, the faith upon which it is done; and fourth, the kingdom or institution into which it introduces us.

John's immersion was by the authority of the God of Abraham, or the God of the Jews as he once chose to be called. It was, as christians would say, performed by the command and authority of the Father, in his own name: whereas, after Jesus had received all authority in heaven and earth, he instituted an immersion to be performed by his authority as Lord, and as Christ.

John immersed into no name, but only that they should believe on him that was to come after him. But Jesus commanded his disciples to be immersed into the name of the Father, and of the Son, and of the Holy Spirit.

The faith and reformation upon which John immersed, would not entitle any person to christian immersion. No man, by the authority of Jesus Christ, would be authorized to immerse any man professing to believe that the Messiah would soon appear, or that the reign of heaven was soon to commence. Nor would such fruits of reformation as John required, which was an exact conformity to the institution of Moses, be required now. A righteousness, and a reformation, and fruits of reformation, proceeding from loftier principles, and from more extensive relations, and issuing in a purer and more heavenly morality, is required now. For this purpose we require a disciple to believe and confess that Jesus is the Messiah, has died as a sin-offering, has risen from the dead, and is now exalted to be a Prince and a Saviour to give reformation to Israel and forgiveness of sins.

The state in which John's immersion left his disciples, was a state of preparation for the kingdom of heaven, which at first must be gradually developed and progressively exhibited to the world. But the state in which christian immersion leaves the disciples of Jesus, is the kingdom of heaven—a state of righteousness, peace, joy, and possessed of the holy spirit of adoption into the family of God. They are pardoned, justified, glorified, with the title, rank, and spirit of sons and daughters of the Lord God Almighty.

Such are the prominent points of dissimilarity between the immersion of John and that of the New Institution. Hence we never read of any person being exempted from christian immersion because of his having been immersed by John. But though all Judea and Jerusalem turned out, and were immersed in the Jordan confessing their sins, and receiving absolution from John; yet when the reign of heaven was commenced on pentecost, of all the myriads immersed into John's immersion, not one refused, or was exempted from christian immersion. We read, however, of the immersion of some of John's disciples into Jesus Christ, who had been immersed. See *Acts* xix. I know to what tortures the passage has been subjected by such cold, cloudy, and sickening commentators as John Gill. But no man can, with any regard to the grammar of language, or the import of the most definite words, make Luke say that when these twelve men heard Paul declare the design of John's immersion, they were not baptized *into* the name of the Lord Jesus.

Nothing but the bewildering influence of some phantasy, of some blind adoration, of some favorite speculation, could so far becloud any man's mind, as to make him suppose for a moment that these twelve persons were not at that time *immersed into* the name of the Lord Jesus. Luke says, literally, "Hearing this, or upon hearing this they were immersed into the name of the Lord Jesus." Then, after they were immersed into the name of the Lord Jesus, Paul laid his hands upon them, and the Holy Spirit fell upon them. Nothing can more fully exhibit the pernicious influence of favorite dogmas, than to see how many of the Baptists have been Gillized or Fullerized into the notion that these twelve men were not baptized into the name of the Lord Jesus when they heard Paul expound to them the design and meaning of John's immersion.

But for the present we dismiss this subject. Having thus briefly glanced at a few of the prominent items of the Jewish age, the distinguishing features of that dispensation in its origin, progress, and termination, we shall in the present work proceed to glance at the prominent characteristics of the christian age, in doing which, by way of contrast, still additional light will be thrown upon the Jewish institution. EDITOR.

Elder John Leland,

—*A name intimately connected with the prosperity and success of* Baptist principles *and* practice *in the New-England states, and indeed throughout the Union.* This old disciple, though tottering on the brink of the grave, has stepped forward and sounded the alarm. We are not informed as to the age of brother Leland—he states, that " it has been more than fifty-five years since I began to preach; in doing which I have travelled 80,000 miles, preached 10,000 times, and baptized 1458 persons, a good portion of whom professed to be seals of my ministry."—*Baptist Recorder.*

Come, brother Clack, and you Baptists of the *modern old stamp*, come, hear the testimony of this aged servant of the Lord. Nay, start not; they are "Baptist principles" proclaimed by Elder Leland in his "*blow at the root,*" thirty years ago. Hear him!

" I presume there are a thousand different creeds in the christian world; they cannot all be right, they may all be wrong. If we consider that all men are fallible, liable to error, it will not be illiberal to say, that some imperfection is to be found in all of them. I question whether there now is, or ever was, a body of men, or an individual, who should coolly compose a creed of faith, or in short a constitution of government or code of laws, but, upon examining the same once a year, would not annually see cause to alter some parts thereof. Such is the school that men are in, such the theatre on which they act, so many the objects that pass before them, that he who says he never alters his mind, evidently declares that he is either very weak or stubborn. Shall *human creeds*, then, mixed at least with imperfection, be made a standard to measure the conscience by, which is God's vicegerent in the human breast?"—p. 9.

" Those who call themselves christians have but a contemptible opinion of Christ, if they call in question the sufficiency of the New Testament, to govern the churches in all places, at all times, and in all cases. If he was infallible, infinitely wise, and universally good, his laws must be tantamount to the exigencies of his disciples in every circumstance; but if this is called in question, let his followers live up to all the rules which he has given, and see if there is any want. It is observable that those who live the most according to the New Testament, make the least complaint of its deficiency. After all, if it still is maintained, that there is a deficiency in the New Testament, who is to supply that deficiency? Not ecclesiastical officers; for they are not to be lords over God's heritage. Not civil rulers; for in their official capacity they have nothing to do with religion. Let those who attempt it, remember one text: " If any man shall *add* to the words of this book, God shall add to him the plagues therein written."—p. 12.

What becomes now, of your pitiful cry of " new fangled notions," " modern heresy," and " Campbellism," raised to excite the prejudices of our brethren against us, and to prevent investigation? O what a " heretic," " deceiver," " restorationist," and " Campbellite," this old brother Leland has been for fifty years! These *old* " Baptist principles" are " of the most pernicious tendency," says Spencer. Away with him!! such men are too contemptible " to be reasoned with," responds Silas.—EDITOR.

For the Christian Baptist.

DEAR BROTHER CAMPBELL—YOUR short visit among us, the discourses and conversations we had the pleasure of hearing from you, have produced a spirit of inquiry into the christian religion, among several of those who heretofore thought little or nothing about it. Your readers generally were edified, some of your opponents have become more liberal, and some who will not see remain blind.

A certain writer informs us that " prejudice is a rash and premature judgment, made up without evidence, has neither eyes nor ears;" and it follows of course, notwithstanding what they say, or whereof they affirm, there are a few of those characters among us, and but few. They give sufficient evidence to whom they belong, or whose descendants they are. They are ever and anon telling us of a spiritual religion, separate from that revealed to us in the New Testament. When I hear them relating this religion in their sermons, which is as certain as they take a text to preach to the people, I wish some kind messenger would whisper in their ears the first title of the old mother recorded in the 17th chapter of Revelations, in large capitals, MYSTERY. These true sons of MYSTERY often talk of shutting the doors of their meeting houses against all those that are of opinion that testimony alone produces faith, and that, upon our being immersed into this faith, remission of sins and the Holy Spirit are enjoyed, according to the promise made on the day of Pentecost. These men make great confession of sins in their prayers, (there is need for it,) and yet try to make the people believe they are infallible—that there are no errors among them. One of these sons of the bondwoman, I have been informed, publicly declared that the Baptist church was as pure in doctrine as in the days of the apostles, or ever would be; and therefore he did not want to hear what you had to say about the ancient gospel. Could you but once hear this man, you would pity the people that he feeds with his enigmatical sermons. He will neither read nor hear what you have to say, but condemns you without evidence. When I see men act so rigidly with their brethren, when they are themselves so far from the path of duty, my mind is forcibly drawn to what is called the Sermon of the Messiah on the Mount: "Judge not, that you be not judged; for with what judgment you judge, you shall be judged; and with what measure you mete, it shall be measured to you again." How awful will it be for some sectarians to appear before the bar of God! Little do they think the Holy Spirit has decreed their fate: " they that practise such things shall not inherit the kingdom of God."

The foregoing subject is too unpleasant to dwell upon. I am happy to inform you there are not more than two such characters in any one congregation that I am acquainted with.—The greater portion of them are convinced there is great room for improvement; many are waiting to take up the line of march from Babylon to Jerusalem; their only fear is, that you are mistaken in the road that leads from the one to the other, or that you have gone past Jerusalem. This makes them examine all your communications carefully—more so than any other writings of this day. In your January number a note under the correspondence of " An Inquirer for Truth," is thought by some to admit too much. This writer says he " found that we need not look for the operation of any other spirit than that which he found to be nigh him, even in his mouth and in his heart, that is, the word of faith which the apostles preach;" that is, they understand him that there is no need of any influence but the written word alone. Your being absent when this number was published, they doubt whether this is your opinion, and would be pleased to hear you more fully upon that point.

Your discourse on Matthew xi. was so interesting, and some of your hearers rather dull of hearing, they are anxious for you to give them an essay or two upon the subject of conversion, including your views of what is called regeneration by Jesus Christ and the Apostle Paul.

Your Essay upon Sacred History is truly interesting. Some of your readers, who are no sectarians, and will not unite with any of them under the present order of things, have requested of me to state their difficulties to you, and request you to attend to them. They say, as they read of none others that were immersed from the time the children of Israel came up out of the sea, until the days of John the Baptist, what evidence have you now to immerse the descendants of those who were immersed by the apostles. As all the children of Israel were immersed in the cloud and in the sea, and none of their descendants afterwards, until the beginning of the gospel, so they think immersion ceased with the apostles. They earnestly beg you would examine this matter, and give them the evidence upon which your mind is made up. They are resolved to follow no man any farther than he follows Christ; nothing but matters of fact govern them in their religious views—and, I hope, in their conduct.

We have heard some complaining that they would not baptize, as you do, upon a profession of Jesus Christ—no, not for the world. This led me to think of some of their baptizings upon a christian's experience, as they erroneously call it. In the year 1811 there were in this section of country great numbers added by immersion to two churches in our county. I have counted up the white male members that were received with all their sifting system. Out of fifty-eight men that were immersed, soon forty apostatized. Eighteen, including those that died members of the church, with those now living, are all I can find that stood to their profession; and if they were to put out of their churches all those sectarian spirits that the Holy Spirit has classed with murderers and drunkards, and says, "Such shall not inherit the kingdom of God," there would be very few except the friends of the ancient order of things. Such is the superiority of their system over that of Jesus Christ and his apostles. Should this statement be denied, I am prepared to give the evidence.

Yours in hope of immortality, JASON.

Reply to Jason.

DEAR BROTHER,—There is one new topic in your letter, and but one which requires a remark from me at this time. And that is, why are the descendants of christian parents to be immersed now, seeing that the descendants of the Jews were not immersed? This question presumes that there is more than an analogy between the Jewish and Christian immersion—that the latter is, in fact, a continuation of the former. This is not taught in the sacred scriptures. But supposing the analogy the most exact in the introduction of the two institutions, it will not follow from any necessity that the two institutions are in other respects analogous. For instance, the Old Institution was national, and based upon family blood. But not so the Christian. It takes

not the whole of any man's family, from any necessity or provision in the Constitution. It is based, not upon flesh, but upon faith: and therefore, every citizen must be born again of water and spirit before admitted into the kingdom of Jesus. He is not a citizen until born of the water. If all the children of the flesh were counted for the seed now, as formerly under the old economy, then some plea more plausible might be urged for dispensing with the converting or proselyting institution. But as every one must be born again before admitted into the Kingdom of Heaven, and as every one must be justified and washed before adopted into the family of God, christian immersion must remain a unit in the Christian Institution until all are brought home. For as in the beginning, so shall there be to the end of the Christian Institution, one Lord, one faith, one immersion. As to the note to which you refer in the January number, additional light will be thrown upon that subject in an essay upon the voice of God in the third number of the Millennial Harbinger.

In all affection yours, EDITOR.

No. 11.] JUNE 7, 1830.

ARCADIA, RUSH CO. IA., March 15, 1830.
Dear Brother,

A GENERAL conspiracy is forming among the "Orthodox Calvinistic Baptists" in Indiana, the object of which is to put a stop to the alarming spread of those principles contained in the Christian Baptist, and advocated by all who earnestly pray for a "restoration of the ancient order of things;" which they, however, have seen proper to honor with the name of "damnable heresies." I have had the honor of being ranked among the first victims of this conspiracy. I have been immolated on the altar of party prejudice and sectarian jealousy. I have passed through the furnace of clerical indignation, "heated seven times hotter than it was wont to be heated." But the smell of fire has not passed on my garments.— Clothed with the panoply of faith, with the volume of unerring *wisdom* in my hand, I would be ashamed to fear a host of sectarians who have no stronger armor, either offensive or defensive, than their *creed*.

Nearly four years ago I had the presumption to oppose the doctrine of creeds, &c. in a public assembly, for which I received repeated rebukes from the dominant clergy, who, however, made no attempt to oppugn the arguments I advanced in favor of my position. The three years immediately succeeding this, passed with my saying little or nothing on this or any other of the religious questions which, during that period, were agitated; my time being entirely engrossed by studies of a different nature.

After spending some time at Cincinnati, I returned to my former residence in Rush county, and being more at leisure I determined to give the scriptures a careful, and if possible, an impartial examination. I did so, without favor or affection to any party. The effect was a thorough conviction of the truth of the following propositions, viz.—

1. Faith is nothing more nor less than a conviction of the truth of any position from evidence.

2. That faith in Jesus Christ is nothing more than a belief of the facts recorded of him by the Evangelists, to wit: that Jesus of Nazareth was the promised Messiah, and that he gave impregnable proof of his divine mission by his miraculous birth, by the numerous miracles which

he wrought while living, and by his death, resurrection, and ascension.

3. The evangelical writings, containing the facts relative to the mighty works which were done by Christ and his apostles, together with the corroborating testimony of the prophecies, form altogether a phalanx of evidence sufficient to convince any reasonable mind that "Jesus is the Christ."

4. I became convinced that the popular doctrine of a partial atonement, and unconditional election and reprobation, were alike antichristian and unscriptural.

These opinions I at all times expressed freely, not a little to the annoyance of my Calvinistic friends. At length, after considerable threatening, the following resolution was adopted by the church on Clifty for my special benefit:—

"*Resolved*, That we will not fellowship the doctrines propagated by Alexander Campbell, of Bethany, Virginia."

I entered my protest against this resolution, as I conceived it was intended to condemn a man without giving him an opportunity of defence. But I soon learned I was to share the same fate. The heresies of Campbellism (as they pleased to call it) were charged home on me. I claimed the right of defence, but was informed it was a crime which did not admit of a defence. I next denied the charge of being the disciple or follower of any man, and required the proof of it. I was again told that no evidence was necessary. Thus you see I was charged without truth, tried without a hearing, and condemned without evidence; and thus, in due form, delivered over to Satan as an incorrigible heretic. Several more of this church are destined shortly to share my fate. Bishop John P. Thompson, and about forty members of Little Flat Rock Church, have been arrested for denying the traditions of the fathers, and will no doubt be formally excommunicated.

Notwithstanding these sorry attempts of the clergy to patch the worn out veil of ignorance which has long covered the eyes of the people, light is dawning apace. Truth is omnipotent and must prevail.

I shall make a defence of my *principles* before a candid public, the substance of which I would send you for publication in the Harbinger, if it would not be too much a repetition of what you have already said on those subjects in your essays published in the Christian Baptist.

The above facts I consider as public property.

Yours in the bonds of christian love,

R. T. BROWN.

—

Remarks on the above.

WHAT means this intolerant spirit? I ask again, What is the meaning of it? Is every man who acknowledges in word and deed the supreme authority of Jesus of Nazareth as Lord Messiah—who has vowed allegiance to him—who is of good report as respects good works, to be sacrificed upon the altar of opinion—because his opinion upon some speculation, fact, or doctrine, differs from mine? Because, while he admits that Jesus died for our sins, he will not dogmatize upon the nature, extent and every attribute of "the atonement"—is he to be deemed unfit for the kingdom of heaven? Admitting "an election of favor," is he to be given over to Satan because of some opinion about the conditionality or unconditionality of that election?—In one word, are we to understand that an exact agreement in opinion, a perfect uniformity is contended for as a bond of union? If so, let our

Baptist brethren say so. Let them declare to the world, that

" Tenth, or ten thousandth, breaks the chain alike;"

That a disagreement in the tenth opinion, or in the ten thousandth opinion, breaks the bond of union. If this be the decree, let it be published and translated into all languages—let it be known and read by all men. If, again, a perfect uniformity be not decreed, but a partial uniformity, let it be proclaimed in how many opinions an agreement must be obtained; then we shall know who are, and who are not, to be treated as heathen men and publicans.

Who makes divisions now? The man who sets up his private judgments as the standard of truth, and compels submission to them; or the man who will bear with a brother who thinks in some things differently from him?

No man can, with either reason or fact on his side, accuse me of making divisions among christians. I declare non-fellowship with no man who owns the Lord in word and deed. Such is a christian. He that denies the Lord in word or deed is not a christian. A Jew or a Gentile he may be, a Pharisee or a Sadducee he may be, but a *Christian* he cannot be! If a man confess the Lord Jesus, or acknowledge him as the only Saviour sent by God; if he vow allegiance to him, and submit to his government, I will recognize him as a christian and treat him as such. If a man cause divisions and offences by setting up his own decisions, his private judgment, we must consider him as a *factionist*, and as such he must be excluded—not for his difference in opinions, but because he makes his opinion an idol, and demands homage to it.

There are some *preachers* in the East and in the West—some self-conceited, opinionative dogmatizers, who are determined to rend the Baptist communities into fractions by their intolerance. They wish, moreover, to blame it upon us. As well might they blame the sun for its light and heat, as blame us for creating divisions. When we shall have cut off from the church any person or persons because of a difference of opinion, then they may say, with reason, we cause divisions. Till then it is gratuitous. They are the heretics, not we. Yes, they are the heresiarchs, and will be so regarded by all the intelligent on earth, and by all in heaven. EDITOR.

—

MILLERSBURG, March 16, 1830.

DEAR BROTHER:—NOT long since I addressed you a letter, in which I expressed my decided approbation of your *Christian Baptist*, and of the manner in which you, as an editor, had conducted that paper. My reason for so doing was simply because, in the general, I most highly approved of your course, so far as I could understand it, from a constant perusal of all you had written, from your debate with Walker down to the time of my writing that letter. I approved of your writings because I saw, generally, a clearness and candor in them, rarely to be met with in these dogmatical days.

I also saw, as I thought, a foundation laid for a general union of all christians who believed Jesus to be the Christ, the Son of the living God, were baptized into his name, and bore the peaceable fruits of righteousness.

I supposed that when a pure speech was restored to Zion, sectarian technicalities would die a natural death. I judged that when high-sounding titles were no more, and the crown of glory had fallen from the heads of the proud usurpers of the throne of the King of Saints, that the free-born sons of God would flow together as tributary streams to the ocean.

I had hoped that, through your influence, thousands would be taught the pure language of Canaan; and that, of course, those angry bickerings would cease to afflict the christian world, as they have done for the last fifteen hundred years. And I do think, that, taking into view what you have written upon the various subjects that have occupied your attention, you ought to have been the last man in the world who would have used the scriptures in any other than their most natural import. You have contended, and justly too, that the word of God should stand erect in its connexion, unmutilated by the cunning artifice of designing men; and that its most natural import is truth. And yet, after all, from expressions occasionally found in your writings I am fearful lest my high hopes of your usefulness should be blasted.

In a paragraph said to be written by you, and published in a Cincinnati paper, you say, "It is necessary to believe, as a cardinal point, that Jesus Christ is God manifested in the flesh, the Messiah of God;" that "you cannot fraternize with those who deny the Lord that bought them;" &c.

Far be it from *me* to fraternize with such: but who are they? Those who confess him to be the Son of God, who speak of him in scripture language, or those who speak of him in language not known in holy writ? The meaning of the article under consideration, if I understand it, is simply this: "Trinitarian brethren, in answer to whom I write this letter, dismiss your fears; I'm no Unitarian; I believe Jesus Christ to be the Supreme God; and that it is essential to salvation to believe this doctrine; I cannot, therefore, fraternize with Mr. Flint, or any other man who denies this *cardinal point*—who denies the Lord that bought him." If this be not the plain meaning of that letter, I confess I know not what it means. Will you please to tell me in your answer whether or not this is your meaning; whether or not you are disposed to exclude from your fellowship those who, though they heartily believe all that the scriptures say concerning Christ, as they understand them, do nevertheless reject the doctrine that Christ is God Supreme?

In the first number of the Millennial Harbinger, you say, that, "from the demonstrations of the Spirit, the ancients were enabled to call *Jesus* King Eternal, immortal, and invisible." (Should you not have added, "the only wise God?" then you would have been understood.) In volume vii. No. 8, of the Christian Baptist, you say, "The King Eternal, Immortal, and Invisible, died for our sins," &c. Now if you will show me the scripture that says the ancients were enabled, or ever did call Jesus King Eternal, Immortal, Invisible; or says that the King Immortal and Invisible, died for our sins, I will yield the point. And I now pledge myself to you, so soon as you prove that the King Eternal, Immortal, and Invisible, died for our sins, I will prove to you and to the world, that the only wise God died upon the Roman cross!!

That Jesus is any where called King Eternal, Immortal, and Invisible, I do deny.

This very language, if we are to understand the scriptures in their most natural import, is used to show us that there is a King Eternal, Immortal, and Invisible, who only has immortality, dwelling in the light; whom no man has seen or can see; who is the God and Father of

our Lord Jesus Christ. But how could such language be applied to Christ? He was seen by Cephas—then by the twelve—after that he was seen by above five hundred brethren—and last of all he was seen by Paul. How, then, can he be that Invisible God whom no man has ever seen, or can see?

Jesus is our great High Priest, who is passed into the heavens to appear in the presence of God for us; and it is said, on the best authority, that, to him every knee shall bow, and every tongue confess that he is Lord, to the glory of God the Father. And to this my heart responds, Amen!

I am fully aware that you do not like to insert or answer such communications as this. And although you may think my criticisms little things; yet as sure as I write, these little things are identifying you with the belligerents and sectarians of the day; and so far as you are concerned, will give tone to the reformation in which you are a principal actor, and ultimately exclude from fellowship those who cannot use the same language. I had never troubled you with this scrap, but for the love I have for you and for that cause with whose interests you stand so closely connected. No man probably in America has as much in his power as you. The eyes of thousands are upon you. You certainly occupy a most responsible station; and I had fondly hoped (But alas! I hoped in vain) that no unscriptural expression would ever have dropped form your pen. And now, my dear brother, I declare to you, that I am neither a Unitarian, nor Trinitarian, but a lover of a pure speech, and an humble advocate for a restoration of the ancient order of things. In conclusion, I beseech you not to pass this communication silently by. An answer to it is called for loudly and speedily. I am well persuaded that in this communication I express the wishes of hundreds of your warmest friends and supporters, of whom I am one, though I have thus written.   I. I****.

Reply to Brother I****.

DEAR BROTHER,—As a lover of a pure speech, to a lover of a pure speech, I am always bound to offer an explanation or an apology. I have not written a piece for any Cincinnati paper since my debate with Mr. Owen. In the next place, I cannot find in number 8, vol. 7, nor even in the first number of the Millennial Harbinger, the phrases in the identical words, nor even in the same connexion of idea which you have quoted. It is true, in the first number of the Harbinger I assert (not, however, in the form of a quotation, nor of a direct and exclusive appropriation of the words,) that Jesus Christ is now attested as the King Eternal, Immortal, and Invisible; or rather, that "the ancient christians were enabled to call Jesus Lord of All—the King Eternal, Immortal, and Invisible, from the demonstrations of the Holy Spirit confirming the testimony, without any other aid than the power of God exhibited in attestation of the testimony." That he is Lord of All, the Immortal King, of whose government there shall be no end; and although the invisible, yet the real Governor of the whole Universe, I am taught to believe, and do believe.

But it is one thing to say that the ancient christians believed, or that I, or any christian, believes that Jesus is the Lord of All; that he is the King of kings, the Lord of lords; that he is now immortal or incorruptible; that he is to reign for ever an Eternal King, of whose government there shall be no end; and another to affirm that the verse which you cite is applied to Jesus. That is what I have not affirmed. But one thing is certain, that the Father has placed his Son upon the throne of the Universe—has made him Lord and Messiah, and has given him all the names, titles, and honors which belong to the Governor of the Universe; because he has, by inheritance, obtained a more excellent name than any creature. There is no one sentence which says that Jesus is the Great Prophet, the Eternal High Priest, and the Universal King. Yet that he is the Great Prophet of whom Moses spoke— "a Priest forever"—and Lord of All, is incontrovertibly plain;—equally plain that he is now the King Eternal, Immortal, and Invisible.

I have so often and so explicitly spoken upon this subject—so repeatedly declared that we ought to confine ourselves to bible terms and phrases in speaking upon all subjects which have occasioned divisions and strifes, that I cannot suppose that any person could imagine that I have any peculiar or appropriated sense which I wish to impose, in any form, upon the religious communities. I do apply to the Father, to the Son, and to the Holy Spirit, every attribute, name, title, and work, ascribed to them by the writers of the New Institution, and will never agree that a peculiar or an appropriated sense shall be affixed to this language and made a term of communion. Nor will I agree that the deductions of any man's reason shall stand at par with the plain and definite declarations of the Holy Spirit; much less in opposition to, and subversive of, the testimony the direct and unequivocal testimony which God has given of his Son.

There is, I must add, a morbid sensibility in the minds of many upon this theme. The Trinitarian, Arian, and Unitarian dogmata have been so much debated in Kentucky, that the greatest alarm is produced in the minds of one of the belligerents if a single ambiguous expression or allusion bearing for or against one or other party, happens to fall from the lips or pens of any one advocating the ancient order of things. This is a rickety conscience—a morbid sensibility. A healthy conscience and a sound mind are equally jealous of every part and every item of the Christian Institution, and is as zealous for speaking, thinking and acting agreeably to the utmost minutia of the divine will, as in the greater and weightier matters of the eternal salvation.

I have no sectarian technicalities, because I have no sect in my heart, except that originally called the "christian sect." This I love, and its technicalities I admire. I intend, however, to propose a plan in the next number of the Harbinger, which will, if carried out, terminate the controversy, and prevent the existence of a Unitarian, Arian, and Trinitarian. Till that is adopted, or something like it, sects and all their consequences will be unavoidable.

In the mean time I can assure you and all my readers, that I will never aid or abet, knowingly or willingly, any sectarian scheme, theory, or practice, though called by its fabricators the essential or capital doctrine of christianity. The original institution of Jesus Christ, unmingled with Judaism and Pagan philosophy, is that, and that only, to which I stand pledged. Hoping that such is your determination, I subscribe myself yours under the reign of favor.   EDITOR.

A Dialogue between A and B, the one a member of Silver Creek Association, and the other of Lost River Association.

A.—GOOD morning, brother B; I am glad to see you—I have had a wish to see you, and have some plain talk with you ever since your last Association.

B.—Good morning to you, brother A; I suppose I may venture to call you brother, as I cannot believe every member of your Association is a heretic, and my long acquaintance forbids the idea that you have been led astray. I have always taken you to be a man of stability and very sound in the faith.

A.—That is just to my hand—you have gone right into what I aimed to be at—has not your Association voted to drop correspondence with ours?

B.—Yes, indeed, she has done that very thing.

A.—Can you tell the reason why?

B.—I do not know that I can; but reports say that your Association has been corrupted, or led astray by a Mr. Alexander Campbell, and has become heterodox in faith.

A.—I call for proof of the fact. I do not know that the Silver Creek Association has ever been charged with any such thing.

B.—I suppose no formal charge has ever been exhibited against your Association; but it is a common talk in our neighborhood, that the Silver Creek people are Campbellites; and it is said they have admitted Dunkers to their communion table, which you know is contrary to the rules and regulations of all regular Baptist churches, and therefore insufferable.

A.—Did you ever hear that the Silver Creek Association had admitted Dunkers to the Lord's Table?

B.—As an act of the Association, I never heard that it had been done.

A.—In what then has Alexander Campbell led us astray?

B.—I do not think I am able to satisfy you in that either; but I suppose you are aware that it is said by many, that Alexander Campbell is an Arian or Socinian, by some a Sandemanian, and by others a Deist in disguise; and many, very many of every sect and denomination of christians, speak of him as a most dangerous heretic and desperately wicked bad man.

A.—Unless you have sufficient testimony of what you have related, I should say it is evil speaking—yes, mere slander.

B.—As to that, I have to confess that I have not sufficient proof, but it does appear to me that Campbell has done abundance of harm, and I am seriously alarmed at the rapid spread of heresy, and am much afraid that he has been, and will be the cause of schisms and divisions in all the churches, and ultimately will do the cause he professes to advocate a great injury.

A.—You may have just cause of alarm; but I hold you to the point. If I understand you rightly, you do not know, neither have you ever heard of any charge of heresy, or any thing like it, being preferred against the Silver Creek Association.

B.—I know of no such thing, neither have I ever heard of any charge of any sort being preferred against your Association.

A.—Well now, brother B, is it not astonishing? Just consider the matter seriously—no solid proof that the man, who is accused of leading us astray, is himself in error; and admitting that to be the case, it remains to be proved, that the Silver Creek Association are followers of him. But our Association has never been legally charged with any thing like it; yet strange to tell, a large majority of your Association voted to reject us; or which is the same, to drop correspondence with us. Now, I would ask, in the name of common sense, why so much hurry? we ought always to remember, that one false step in the beginning, is apt to do abundance of mischief. The course she has taken, to say the least of it, is imprudent and unscriptural; for if we had been charged with being heterodox in faith, and that charge had been substantiated, then, and in that case, in order to follow Scripture direction, a first and second admonition should have preceded rejection; but you rejected us without any charge in a legal way, and consequently, no fair discussion or chance of defence on our part; without proof, or even a charge, of our being guilty of any kind of disorderly conduct, or of any departure from the faith. Now, my dear brother, what have you to say in vindication of the course your Association has taken? have you treated us like brethren? does it appear as if you had any desire to reclaim us, or to heal the wound? or has it not more the aspect of the proceedings of a court of Inquisition? Does it not virtually say, Cut them off—away with them—cast them out of the synagogue? why? because the disorder is catching, the disease is contagious—the faith of our own society, and not only ours, but the craft of all the sects is in danger of being overturned.

B.—Stop, brother A, you seem to be getting too warm on the subject; and you know that is not the best way to settle matters. I assure you that I shall not attempt to vindicate the conduct of our Association, any further in what she has done. I confess I was not pleased with it myself—to me it seems to discover something of the spirit of persecution in it; but I hope you, as you say you take the scriptures for your sole guide, will in this case let your moderation be known to all men, and by christian forbearance, and in the spirit of meekness your Association will treat with ours in a christian-like, faithful, and tender manner; and by that means she may be brought to see that the course she has taken is, at least, censurable—that she will, at her next meeting, reconsider the matter, and that the wound will yet be healed without loss of life or reputation.

A.—I should be glad; yes, indeed, I should rejoice to see peace restored, and union and love abound among us; but I fear that a reconciliation will not be so easily effected; because there are some of our preachers, and many of our people, who have come into the opinion that the creeds and confessions of faith, adopted by the many different sects of professed christians, are, and have for a long time been, the prime cause of schisms and divisions among christians; and since the hasty vote of your Association, they have become more established in that opinion, and much more warm in the cause; and some seem to be determined to preach them down if possible; but that you may not misunderstand me, you will please take notice, we do not so much condemn the doctrines set forth in the creed—we would not say that the doctrine contained in the Baptist Confession of Faith is absolutely unscriptural, but do contend that it is unreasonable, and we think unscriptural, to make abstruse metaphysical questions articles of faith for weak believers to subscribe to; or otherwise be kept out of the church. We insist upon it, that it should suffice for all to subscribe to the plain, simple truths of the gospel, taking the whole of the scriptures as the revealed word of God, and the sole rule of faith and manners; and any thing therein contained appearing vague, ambiguous, or of uncertain signification, or very mysterious, admitting of a fair debate, in that case, difference of opinion should not break fellowship, but should agree to think and let

think, bear and forbear, as we unhesitatingly affirm, that it is the unalienable right of every individual to think for himself. I would say more, but time fails, and I must desist, but hope to see you again shortly. Farewell.

[The publication of the above Dialogue in a Western paper, occasioned the writer of it to be excluded from the church. Such is the intolerance of the populars!   Ed. C. B.

Essays on Man in his Primitive State, and under the Patriarchal, Jewish, and Christian Dispensations.—No. XV.

Christian Age.—No. I.

This is the consummation of the Ages. Types, symbols, prophecies, and promises have their completion here. The law by Moses came; the favor and the reality by Jesus Christ. A righteousness without law, and eternal life are its new and joyful developements. Faith, first honored in the person of Abraham, is now made the principle on which the enjoyment of the new salvation turns. "You shall call his name Jesus, for he shall save his people from their sins." This was the novelty of this salvation. Of all the Saviours and Messiahs which God sent to Israel, not one came to save that people from their sins. From their temporal enemies, from the power of them which hated them, they were their redeemers. But now, once, in the end of the ages, has a Redeemer, a Saviour, come to redeem and save men from the guilt, pollution and dominion of sin.

The supe lative excellency of this economy consists in the clear discovery it affords of the character of God, his gracious purposes to be developed at the Resurrection, and the immediate and perfect pardon of all sin, which at once perfects the conscience and begets that peace of God which passes all understanding. On this so much has been said in the preceding volumes, and as we have arrived so near the close of this work, only a few general views, rather inferential from the premises so amply laid, than from any new topics, shall be submitted in two essays.

It has been somewhere said that the priesthood of every divine economy was to the whole system what the heart is to the human system. It gives life and energy to it. It is the vital office. So the office of a High-Priest was the active and operative principle in every dispensation.

All Priests have been a sort of Mediators, and the High-Priest the great Mediator of the institution under which he officiated. To present sacrifices and oblations—thank-offerings and peace-offerings—to make reconciliation for sins—was at least one half of his official duties. The other pertained to intercessions and benedictions.—Every High Priest taken from among men is ordained for men in things pertaining to God, to offer both gifts and sacrifices for sins.

To perfect the conscience as respects sin; to reconcile to the divine government; and to produce a perfect reconciliation among men, is the great object of the High Priesthood of the Christian Economy. "Glory to God in the highest! peace on earth! and good will among men!" —are the tendencies of the Christian Institution.

The experience of all christians—nay, of all men who ever had the consciousness of sins, who ever felt the pangs of a guilty conscience, will attest the truth, I am about to utter. It will vouch for the truth of this assertion, viz. that to be assured of the pardon of sin—to feel ourselves justified in the sight of God, is the reign of heaven in the heart—the very essence of happiness, from which, as from a fountain of living water, springs up eternal joy. This is the peace of God which passes all understanding, ruling and reigning in the heart. This is, then, just wherein christianity, rightly understood, has the excellency over Judaism, and every other institution, human or divine, which the ear of man has ever heard.

To speak in the figurative style with Paul in his letter to the Hebrews:—The Holy Spirit signified by and in the Jewish Institution, that the way into the holiest was not laid open while the tabernacle had a standing upon earth. This figurative representation was for the time being; according to which gifts and sacrifices were offered which could not make him who performed that service perfect as pertains to the conscience; they being imposed for meats and drinks, and diverse immersions, and rules of conduct respecting the flesh until the time of the Reformation. But now Christ being come a High Priest of the future and eternal good things, has entered into the holies—having by his own blood, once for all, procured everlasting redemption. If the former sacrifices cleansed the flesh, how much more will the sacrifice of Christ purify the conscience from dead works, to serve in a new spirit the living God? He having offered one sacrifice for sins to last forever, sat down at the right hand of God, waiting till his enemies are made his footstool. For by one offering he has made perfect forever them who are sanctified. Having, then a great High Priest over the house of God, let us approach with a true heart in the full assurance of faith, having our hearts sprinkled from an evil conscience, and our bodies washed with pure water.

In this way the Apostle directs us to the superlative character of the New Institution as respects its purifying influence upon the conscience. The first and most distinguishing character of the New Institution is the ample provision which it makes for taking away sin from its damnatory and polluting power over the conscience. It authorizes all its subjects to say, from experience, "Blessed is the man to whom the Lord imputes not sin!" This blessedness is theirs who have intelligently submitted to the government of Jesus.

Something that was wanting in every previous dispensation is supplied in this—a rational and certain pledge of the forgiveness of all sins.— True, the Jewish Economy made provision for the transgressors; but how the blood of bulls and goats could take away sin in any sense, was a mystery of that Economy. No developement was made until God said, "In sacrifice and burnt offerings and offerings for sin according to the law, I have no pleasure." To do his *will* Jesus came. The New Constitution, so often dilated on in these volumes, contains the distinguishing privileges of this economy. "Their sins and their iniquities I will remember no more," stands forth to view as the constitutional privilege of all christians. An act of oblivion on the past, and a promise that sin shall not lord it over them in future, are the pledges which in baptism are given to all who come to Jesus. I could wish that this excellency of the New Institution was held up to the eye of this generation as was the brazen serpent to the eyes of Israel in the wilderness. It is not known—I say, comparatively it is a secret to this age. The confessions and prayers for pardon echoing every

Lord's day from ten thousand pulpits on this continent; the mournful and long details of past sins offered up with every morning and evening sacrifice upon the family altars of the worshipping families, more resemble a Jewish sacrifice or sin offering than the incense of purified hearts warmed and cheered with the forgiving love of God. "The worshippers once cleansed should have no more consciousness of sins." But in their prayers and confessions there is a remembrance of past sins every morning and every Lord's day. This is proof positive flowing from the hearts and lips of professors, that they are either ignorant of, or unbelieving in, the Christian Institution. They feel not the blessedness of the man to whom God imputes not sin. If they do, their lips utter the words of deceit and guile. They profess to feel and to desire that which they neither feel nor desire.

To open these prison doors, to release these captives, to introduce them to the golden day of christianity, to proclaim to them the jubilee of heaven, to declare the acceptable year of the Lord, has been a primary object in all the essays I have written upon the Ages.

To this purpose I again call their attention to the distinguishing character of the Reign of God. "It is not," says Paul, "meat and drink, but righteousness, and peace, and joy in a holy spirit." This is a summary view of the Kingdom or rather the Reign of God. The reign of these principles *within men* is, what the Lord himself affirmed, the discriminating criterion of his reign. The reign of God comes not with observation, with external signs and evidences, as does the reign of a worldly prince. It comes with no external pomp. It is within men. And it is the dominion of righteousness, peace, and joy, terminating in a holy spirit—issuing in that spirit and temper conforming to the Spirit of God. The alliance of King Righteousness, King Peace, and King Joy, produces the happiest heart under heaven. Melchisedeck, the type of our High Priest, was King of Righteousness and Prince of Peace. Our King of Righteousness and Prince of Peace was anointed with the oil of joy, with the Unction of the Holy One, above all who ever sat upon a throne—above all God's Messiahs. His dominion, his rule and reign, is, therefore, the reign of these principles—righteousness, peace, and joy. To be under the sway of these is to be holy, and that is to be happy. To feel ourselves righteous in the presence of God, to feel ourselves pardoned and accepted, naturally produces peace with God, and that naturally fills with joy. Being made righteous through faith, we have peace with God through our Lord Jesus Christ, and we rejoice in hope of the glory of God. This is the whole philosophy of the Reign of Heaven. But it is not only the effects produced by the Reign of Favor, to which we look in fixing our attention upon it. There is the Kingdom and there is the Reign. The Kingdom is the effect of the Reign, as it is simply that embraced under it. But there is an activity, an agency in these principles, which may be called a Reign in strict conformity with the liberties of human speech. We say of some they are under the reign of pride, or cupidity, or ambition, under the reign of whatever principle seems to control their actions. Avarice and ambition are as dominant principles controlling the actions of men as ever was an eastern despot; nay, more dominant and tyrannical than a Turkish Sultan. It is no departure from analogy, no abuse of speech, to say, that a man is under the reign of righteousness, when he is righteous in character and loves righteousness;—to say, that he is under the reign of peace, when the peace of God triumphs in his heart, and he cultivates peace with all men; to say that he is under the dominion of joy, when he rejoices always and is habitually employed in thanksgivings. These all conspire in purifying the heart. These all, like fires operating upon precious metals, purge the dross. Hence the result of the combined operation of these principles is a holy spirit or temper of mind, and this is the Canaan of bliss into which all the believing enter. This is the land of promise, and whether rich or poor, whether learned, or unlearned, all who enter these precincts feel themselves happy and triumphant in the Lord. Hence it was ordained that one sacrifice should make an end of sin-offerings—should at once, and forever, perfect them thus separated from the world; and that the first act of mercy in the new reign of God would be an act of oblivion, a cancelment of all guilt, an ablution from all sin, an ample and perfect remission from all former transgressions. *" Where remission of these is, no more sacrifice, confession, or prayer for pardon is needed."* Hence it came to pass, that when the proclamation of the Reign of God was first made, reformation and remission of sins, or faith and immersion went hand in hand. Every baptized person, not a hypocrite, was pardoned, and after being born of the water and the Spirit, they came into a new kingdom—felt new relations and partook of a joy before unknown. The first strong impulse which the mind of the converted felt, was a sense of the pardoning love of God through the sacrifice of Jesus. This, like the touch of the magnet, turned the affections towards the skies. Risen with Christ, not only from the grave in which they had buried their guilt and their fears, but risen in their hopes of heaven and aspirations after glory everlasting, their affections were placed on things above, and not on the things on earth. This was the strong hold which christianity took on the hearts and affections of the converted. This drew a clear, legible, sensible, memorable line between their former state and the state of favor and reconciliation to God in which they found themselves after they had obeyed the gospel.

To the strength of this conviction, to the vividness and force of this impression upon their putting on Christ, is attributable the great difference between the first converts to Jesus Christ, and the converts to the various creeds and sects now so numerous. There is something so impotent in an assent to mere opinions in joining a sect, in becoming a Baptist, Methodist, or Presbyterian, that it makes no sensible difference in the affections towards heaven, and therefore fails to purify and elevate the heart, and to reform and decorate the character of the proselyted. The first converts to christianity in the converting act in the assurance of remission, were made strong in the Lord and able to deny themselves, filled with joy and peace. Of them it could be said, "Whom having not seen, you love; on whom not now looking, but believing, you rejoice with joy unspeakable and full of glory." But, I ask, Is this true of all or of a majority, or of a respectable minority of them who are converted to a sect? If I may judge from long observation, one such christian is almost a prodigy in a city, in a county, or large district of country. The reason is our forms of christianity want something which the gospel, as proclaimed and exhibited by the Apostles, presented to the apprehension of the converted. Ours is a shadow—theirs was the substance.

Ours is opinion—theirs was fact. Ours is the distant hope of future pardon—theirs the reward of their faith, the salvation of their souls. This they all received in Baptism. "Receiving," said Peter, "the reward of your faith, the salvation of your soul." They were pardoned and felt it—we feel it not. They had an assurance of it, which we have not. This is the true philosophy of the difference between the ancient or true gospel, and the modern—between the first converts and the present converts. Indeed, few profess to believe the same gospel. Many of the preachers laugh at receiving the forgiveness of sins through the obedience of faith—through immersion. They ridicule it; they nickname it, like Mr. Brantly, "Baptismal Regeneration;" they hold it up to derision. How, then, can those, led by them, experience any great felicity from that which their spiritual guides ridicule!! They cannot. The popular immersion is no better than a Jewish ablution. It is a mere *rite*, a *ceremony*, an *ordinance*, or any thing but a pledge of our pardon and acceptance with God, or the means of our entering into the kingdom of God. The popular preachers preach another gospel and another baptism. Theirs is the gospel of the Holy Spirit and the baptism of the Holy Spirit. Theirs is a speculative gospel about spiritual operations—cold and inoperative. If ever it flames, it is by a friction of the hands, or by a vigorous operation of the lungs, the bellows of life. As Samson's strength lay in his hair, so the strength of the popular gospel of speculative influences lies in the vociferations of the proclaimers.

The ancients never strove to produce good feelings by describing them; they were better taught than to make such an effort. They called the attention of men to that which would make them feel, and good feelings followed as a matter of course. I will now assert it, and I shall leave it to philosophers and historians to disprove it if they can, that he who is immersed for the remission of his sins, in the full belief that he will receive remission in the act, will enjoy more of the life and joy of christianity, and not be half so likely to apostatize as he that is immersed for any other purpose, I care not what it be. This I have proved by observation—I was going to say, by experience too. And to this chiefly is to be attributed the superior attainments in righteousness, peace, joy, and a holy spirit of the first converts, compared with the moderns. It is not the withholding of God's Spirit, but it is our immuring ourselves in the cells of anchorites, our burying ourselves under the traditions of the fathers, our explaining away the testimony of God, and our substituting the meteors of a moonless night for the radiance of the risen day, which has given such a pale and ghastly hue, such a wan and livid aspect to the christians of the new schools, of the modern brands, of the new mints of modern orthodoxy. May the Lord deliver us from the ghosts and spectres of an untoward generation!   Editor.

No. 12.]   July 5, 1830.

Essays on Man in his Primitive State and under the Patriarchal, Jewish, and Christian Dispensations.—No. XVI.

Christian Age.—No. II.

Paul to the Galatians asserts one of the distinguishing features of the Christian Age to which we have formerly adverted. It is a characteristic of the Reign of Favor, to which much attention ought to be paid. When the people of God were minors, says he, we were kept in bondage under the elements of the world. As a son who is an heir, during his minority differs nothing from a servant, though he be lord of all, but is kept under tutors and stewards until the time fixed upon for manhood, or full age: even so we were treated under the law. But now, in the wisdom of our Heavenly Father, the fulness of time being come for the enlargement of the people of God, we are raised to the relation of sons of God. This is the new and high relation into which christianity elevates its subjects, the reason of which is suggested by the great apostle to be this;—that God made his Son a servant to buy off those who were held in bondage; that, as he became a servant, so we might be made sons. Hence, as our nature was adopted by God's Son, so the sons of men are adopted into the family of God.

As young men arrive at the full age of manhood they are emancipated from the government of mere precepts, and put under the government of principles. Here is the secret. The Jews were under a government of precepts—we are under a government of principles. Hence all was laid down to them in broad and plain commandments; and the book which contained their worship was a ritual, a manual of religious and moral duties, accurately defined to the utmost conceivable minutia; insomuch that nothing was left to discretion—nothing to principle.

There is nothing like this in the New Institution. We have no ritual, liturgy, nor manual. The New Constitution and Law of Love does no more than institute the converting act, the Lord's supper, and the Lord's day. Immersion, or the converting act, by which persons are brought into the kingdom of principles and introduced into the rank of sons, is not so much an ordinance in the kingdom as that which brings us into it. The Lord's supper, a weekly commemoration of the great sacrifice, and the day of the resurrection of Jesus, though positive institutions, are not presented to christians accompanied with directions for the mode of celebration, as were any of the former institutions under the Jewish Age. There were more directions about the celebration of the Passover and the observance of the Sabbath, than is to be found in the whole New Institution. Nay, indeed, there is nothing of that sort in the christian economy. No mode of eating the supper, no mode of observing the Lord's day is suggested in the apostolic writings. In this christians are left to the discretion of full grown men to the government of principle. All things are to be done decently and in order; but the modes of decency and order in the celebration of these christian institutions are no where pointed out.

Sometimes the apostles notice glaring aberrations from this order and decency, and this is the reason of those remarks which we find in the epistles noticing any egregious departure from that order and decency which become the elevated rank and dignity of sons of God. But even then no code of laws, no enumeration of ceremonies, no forms of observance are suggested. There is nothing in the christian economy of the nature of ceremony—nothing for the sake of form. There is a principle in every thing instituted. And all the principles of obedience, all the principles of action, how numerous soever we may suppose them, are reducible to one great principle, sometimes called the new commandment. Now, says Paul, "the end or object of the commandment is love out of a pure heart, out of a good conscience, and from faith unfeigned." The Christian Institution creates in the heart of man this love. It gives it birth and

being. It is a love of a higher order, of a sublimer genius, than any former age or economy could produce. The love for God which Judaism implanted and matured, was love for a benefactor, a preserver, or, if you please, a Creator; but love for a Redeemer, for a Saviour, is of a loftier birth and character. Love for one who has redeemed from everlasting death, who bestows immortality, is a love which none could feel who did not understand the doctrine of life and immortality.

The dominion of love is the dominion of favor, and its service the easiest conceivable. Hence the liberty and perfect freedom felt in slavery to Jesus Christ. All who serve any favorite principle feel themselves free. The man who toils harder than any menial bondman ever did, provided he toil in the service of some grateful principle, (avarice, or ambition, for example,) feels perfect liberty. Liberty is all in the mind. Hence the slaves of Jesus, or the slaves of love, are the veriest freemen in the world. This is the grandeur of the christian scheme, that it sets men in love with such principles and such a person; that it makes virtue and goodness almost as necessary as the Pagans' fate, and yet as free and easy as the action of the heart or the labor of the lungs.

There is no serving from memory in the service of love. The Jews required a good memory rather than a good judgment. Children act from memory before they act from judgment. Hence the memory is strong and the judgment weak in youth. In manhood the judgment is strong and the memory becomes weaker. In the religious minority of the world the religious acted from memory rather than from judgment or pure principle. Let no man infer that I exclude principle from the saints of former ages, in the vulgar acceptation of that term. I mean no such thing. But the principles of christianity, the principles of action which the love of God developed in the mission of Jesus, and the glory to be revealed in us at the resurrection, are so transcendant as to eclipse every thing like principle flowing from love or gratitude to a creator, or benefactor, or guardian as the God of Israel was revealed to the Jews. Their outward services, their yoke of bondage, the elements of the world under which they groaned, are clear monuments of the slavery of the letter, and of the want of what we here call principles. I said, the service of love is not the service of memory. Love is a master whose power is felt without recollection. Omnipresent and omnipotent too in moral influence. It is the moral principle of gravity in the moral universe, and, like the physical attraction, controls every thing.

The christian scheme is the wisdom and power of God in producing this principle. When created its aliment is the will of God. On the sincere milk of the word it feeds. This nourishes and strengthens it. To its government the new man ts subjected. Hence the obedience of faith is also the obedience of love. There requires no precepts nor commands, with a penalty, other than that the enjoyment of this love of God and his favor necessarily requires conformity. Hence all the exhortations to religious and moral observances are drawn from the love of God to us.

This is the great principle of the New Institution; although the two great commandments of the law required the love of the whole heart to God and benevolence equal to self-love, it did not afford the strength nor the motive to call them forth. Hence it was a condemnatory precept, rather than a quickening principle. But now the love of God, shed abroad in the heart by the Holy Spirit, excites to an activity, and imparts an energy which the law could not do.

But that which calls for our notice here, is that God now deals with us as sons, and not as servants—not as sons who are minors, but as sons who are of full age. Hence the suggestions in the form of general principles in preference to a ritual prescribing every act in mode and form to perfect exactitude as under the law.

There was another consideration in the law requiring an exactness in the forms of worship, which does not exist under the Reign of Favor. The genius of the Jewish Age was figurative, prophetic, or symbolical. Many of the observances of that economy were types or figures of the good things which we enjoy; and that there might be a true representation of these things for the confirmation of the faith, and enlargement of the views of those who are now called into the kingdom, it behoved that nothing should be left to the discretion of man. Every thing must be done according to the pattern exhibited in the law. So that when these two considerations are duly regarded, we shall find two good reasons why the christian economy should differ so materially from the Jewish. The former was delivered to persons retained in the condition of minors, and it always treated them as such. The latter is addressed to persons in the rank of sons who have passed their minority, and it treats them as such.

Not regarding this difference between the Old and New Constitution is a chief cause why many have turned the New Testament into a sort of ritual or liturgy, and have sought from it a command or a precedent for every thing, even to the manner of eating the Lord's supper. Hence it has come to pass, that some societies which have taken it for their only guide in all religious observances and actions, having regarded it as the Jews did the book of Leviticus, have reduced christianity to a frigid and lifeless skeleton, wanting the splendor and earthly attractions of the Jewish worship. They have frittered away into small fractions; and in many instances societies of this sort have become extinct. They were laboring to find in the Christian Scriptures what they contained not; and not finding an exact agreement in those things which they deemed of much importance to scriptural order, they degenerated in their piety and zeal, and languished away into a barren and improfitable profession.

We must have either a good share of worldly splendor to keep alive a show of religious affection in public assemblies; or wanting these worldly and carnal attractions, we must feel and we must exhibit that love of God and that pure devotion to Jesus Christ springing from a lively sense of the pardoning love of God. Without one or other of these attractions religious communities will languish and pine away, and die like a consumptive patient. Religious and worldly pride combined have made what the world calls flourishing churches; but they have been rather synagogues of Satan than temples of the Holy Spirit.

There is an objection, and one of much apparent, but not of real weight against the prominent idea in the preceding remarks upon this alleged feature of the Christian Institution. It is the following:—If Christians are not under an economy of precepts and precedents, but under an economy of principles in which much is left to the discretion or to the natural tendency of principles, will it not follow that christian societies may have different practices and a different order, according to their views of decency and order, and yet be alike acceptable to the King and alike acceptable to the world? This is partially a true and partially a false conclusion, and therefore requires examination.

It is not alleged by me that there are no divinely instituted acts of christian worship nor ordinances in the christian church; nay, the contrary I have undeviatingly affirmed. These are a part, an essential part of the Institution of Favor. It is not discretionary with disciples whether they shall or shall not enter the kingdom without obtaining the remission of their sins by immersion; whether christian societies shall regard the first day of the week to the Lord; whether they shall show forth the Lord's death at the Lord's table till he come to raise the dead; whether they shall continue in the fellowship for the saints and the Lord's poor; whether they shall sing psalms, hymns, and spiritual songs; unite in social prayers, and in reading the sacred writings in their regular meetings. These are the traditions of the Holy Apostles who were commanded to teach the disciples to observe all things which the King in his own person had commanded them. But they are not in these observances bound by a prescribed form. There is no law, command, nor precept, prescribing the form of immersion, the place where, nor the manner in which the subject shall be disposed of in the act. There is no mode of observing the Lord's day—no law upon that subject. There is no prescription concerning the time of meeting in the congregation; whether they shall first do this, and then that; or whether they shall eat the Lord's supper standing, sitting, kneeling, or reclining; whether prayer and singing shall always succeed or accompany each other; whether all shall pronounce the same words after the speaker, or only say Amen after his thanksgivings. In brief, there are no distinctions of this sort in the Institution. With regard to moral injunctions the great principle called the golden rule is a fair sample. Exhortations and admonitions concerning morals, found in the Epistles, grew out of the occasion, or were suggested by the inadvertencies of the disciples. But had these Epistles never been written, or only a part of them, the Christian Institution would have been perfect and entire, wanting nothing. The gospel—yes, the gospel, the proclamation of God's philanthropy, as it was uttered by the apostles on Pentecost, or in any one of their converting discourses, would have been, and still is, alone sufficient to produce those principles in the heart which issue in all holiness and in all morality.

It is then true, that different communities might, in following up their own sense of propriety, attend upon some of the institutions of the christian worship in the christian assemblies differently, and yet be equally acceptable to God and profitable to men. But the great principles of christian morality never can legitimately issue in a different practice no more than the great law of attraction can produce antagonist results or opposing effects at the same time and in the same place. I would also add, that a hearty and unreserved submission to the authority of Jesus Christ, will generally, and, perhaps, universally, issue in a uniformity of practice as respects even those discretionary matters which we have seen to result from the fact of our being treated as men rather than as children.

EDITOR.

The Beaver Anathema.

CONCERNING those four churches, said to belong to the Mahoning Association which are represented in the Beaver Minutes as having left their former connexion, because of "damnable heresy," I solicited information from brother Walter Scott, who has been the active agent of one of the most important revolutions and conversions in the present day, as far as has come to my ears. He favored me with the following hasty sketch which will throw some light upon the Beaver anathema.   ED. C. B.

—

NEW LISBON, April 9th, 1830.

BROTHER CAMPBELL,—THE following are the particulars which I have learnt and know of the four churches.

Youngstown Church.—About eight or nine years ago there was a revival within the bounds of the church; the acting minister was brother Woodsworth, a regular baptist. There was a great stir, and many were baptized in the name of our Lord Jesus Christ. Mr. West, I believe, then lived in Nelson; but some of the members conceiving a partiality for him, he was elected Minister of the Youngstown Church to the rejection and dismissal of brother Woodsworth, the successful laborer. Affairs began to put on a different aspect immediately—the church declined from that day—conversions stopped, and after the lapse of some years the meeting was embroiled in family quarrels—Mr. West himself being grossly implicated.

When I called about two years ago, I found the church in a state of entire prostration. For four years they had not eaten the Lord's Supper; all was delinquency—a perfect web of wickedness, the like of which I never had seen. It was an involved labyrinth of personal and family quarrels.

For about three weeks I strove to disentangle the sincere hearted, but in vain. Strife is like the lettings out of water—what is spilt is lost. When the threads and filaments of a quarrel have forced themselves like waves over the whole body ecclesiastic, that body should be dissolved.

We accordingly looked upon this institution to be entirely lost, and began to preach the ancient gospel—the word of the Lord is a hammer and a fire. All hearts were immediately broken or burnt; and of that sinful people there have been immersed nearly one hundred and fifty individuals. These have become a church, and are walking in the commandments and ordinances of the Lord blameless, as I hope. The scriptures are their sole authority, and they have three bishops bold in the Lord Jesus, and five deacons.

All those who could not, should not, or would not join the young converts, to the amount of about sixteen, styled themselves the Church of Youngstown, and went to the Beaver Association to aid in the framing of that enormous bull which has excommunicated our name from the list of the Baptist Associations in the United States. Be it observed, however, that nothing said here is to be construed evilly in regard to the sixteen members—I believe them to be misguided christians. They are eleven, or at most sixteen—the disciples we baptized are about one hundred and fifty.

Palmyra Church. About a year after I had been in Youngstown, I went to Palmyra, in company with brother Hayden, a faithful laborer in Jesus Christ. Here too all was worse than decay—'twas ruin all. The Methodist class was a desolation strewed over the town—a race of backsliders. I talked with many of them, and their quondam class leader was the first person who was immersed—a man who had maintained his purity amid the general delinquency—he stood like Lot in Sodom. The Baptist meeting, like Sardis, engrossed a few names, and but a few who had not defiled themselves; but as at Youngstown, so here also, the church was filled with creeds, swellings, and personal and family quarrels.

We forthwith read the gospel from the sacred page, and exhorted to obedience, whereupon many believing were baptized in the name of our Lord Jesus Christ. We afterwards separated the young converts, and informed the old folks that so many of them as choosed to embrace the new institution, would be admitted with all pleasure; nearly all of them united, and the church now includes about one hundred names.

They break bread every first day, have the scriptures for their sole authority, the settlement of their differences is attended to promptly, (*Matt.* xviii.) and not deferred till a monthly meeting—they have none—they are very lively, and have overseers and servants.

But here again, as at Youngstown, fifteen, or at most twenty, although I suppose only eleven went off, betook themselves to their old ways of creeds, monthly meetings, &c.—called themselves Palmyra Church, of course, and joined the Beaver Association.

Achor Church. This used to be a flourishing church. The causes of its decay are more easily conjectured than detailed. Mr. Winters used to visit it about two years ago, and aided in the ejectment of some of its best and liveliest members who have since been associated as a church in St. Clair township—since that occurred, Judge Brown, a pillar in the Achor Church, has deceased, and the remaining members have been laboring by means of divers ministers to resuscitate matters. I was told that Mr. West preached there last Lord's day, and baptized one convert. I visited the church about two years ago, but felt so much hurt by their indelicate behavior that I would not preach, and retired from their meeting house—since that I have heard but little about them.

Salem Church. In one place where I was baptizing, just as I raised the baptized person up out of the water, I saw a great stick hanging or rather shaking over my head. On another occasion I was interrupted by a person with a sword cane—at one place they set loose my mare in the night, and at Noblestown in the midst of six Presbyterian congregations the sectarian population cut off all the hair from her tail; but in no place did I ever experience such deceitful treatment as at Salem. According to my appointment I visited this church soon after I began to ride. The brethren received me with seeming courtesy, and I began to speak. The ancient gospel had set straight in my mind things which were formerly crooked. I felt my soul enlarged; the Lord had opened my eyes, and filled my mouth with arguments. I was all transported with the gospel—its novelty, its power, its point, its glory. Accordingly I rushed upon the sinful people like an armed man—forty-one were immersed in ten days, and all seemed to rejoice with me in the victory; but we had to wait until monthly meeting before we could propose the young converts for admission. As this was two or three weeks in the future, those who were secretly or openly opposed to the proceedings had abundance of time to put into requisition all the little arts which they supposed would be necessary to keep out so many of the young converts as they thought unconverted: so many of God's children as they thought had not been born aright the second time. The meeting came round and none of them were admitted, yet they were many of them their own children, and nearly all of them related either immediately or remotely with the members of the church.

Creeds, confessions, and experiences, were *sine qua nons* with a few of the old folks, and particularly, with one woman, so that we separated without doing any thing but disgusting the new converts; but I had to leave the place for five weeks, there being revivals in New Lisbon, Warren, Braceville, and Windham, all at the same time. In my absence twenty-one of the converts were cajoled into the church; the rest have since been formed into a meeting three miles south of Salem, and are likely to do well. At my return to Salem I was requested to be absent for a little, until things became settled, and finally had word sent not to return. Thus a people who would have plucked out their own eyes, and given them to me, did all of a sudden turn round and separate me from their own relations and townsmen, whom under God, I had been the means of bringing back to the Lord, and to righteousness. I never spoke to all the converts again.

WALTER SCOTT.

Mr. Brantly's Views of Reformation and of New Versions.

" By "the present order of things" we understand Mr. Campbell to mean the prevailing order and doctrine of our Baptist churches, and the existing forms of ecclesiastical government. The doctrinal views most prevalent in the churches of our persuasion, in the United States, may be summarily expressed in the annexed sentences. The sufficiency of the Scriptures in their present version, for knowledge and practice, is strenuously asserted. The total depravation and corruption of human nature, is invariably admitted. The dependence of salvation upon election, and not upon man's will, is a tenet generally held with much decision and firmness. The sufferings and death of Christ are believed to be the foundation of that atonement, or propitiation, or pacification, upon which the salvation of all the elect is insured. It is believed amongst us that there is a Holy Spirit of promise, by which christians are sealed after they may have come to the exercise of faith; that this same Spirit presides over, and produces every instance of regeneration which occurs in the world; and that he ordinarily employs the Word of God as the instrumental action in regeneration. Immersion in the name of the Trinity, is regarded as nothing more than the figure, the symbol of salvation. It is not a moral purification, but the answer of a good conscience. To the question, Do you believe with all your heart, Baptism answers, Yes. It is a most significant answer. The constitution and government of our churches are such as to provide for the perfect independence of every church or congregation, and to make it a religious commonwealth in itself, having authority and jurisdiction over its own affairs, and not answerable for its acts to any Presbytery, Synod, or other ecclesiastical tribunal. The duty of extending the gospel by missions, is generally admitted. The value of extensive learning to the ministry, but not its indispensable necessity, is commonly recognized. The duty of believers to maintain a holy life is universally allowed; and the claims to the character of christians disallowed to all

those who lead unholy lives. The efficacy of faithful prayer in obtaining the blessing of Heaven, is confidently believed.

" This is a concise view of that "order of things" to which we are attached, not merely because it is old, but because it is true. The "inefficiency" of which we complain, does not originate in any defect of our system, but in its defective use and application. That which is true in Mr. Campbell's system, is not new; and that which is new, is not true. " The order of things" under which people live, may be good, whilst their practice is bad; and, unless we have had erroneous information, Mr. Campbell himself is an instance in point to prove that a man may have a good deportment under an " order of things" which we consider radically bad.

" The reformation which we should be pleased to see, and to which we endeavor to make these pages subservient, consists barely in one article; and that is, the more exact conformity of christian practice, to that "present order of things" which has been briefly sketched above. It is not new systems that we need—it is new hearts. There is no necessity to attempt the amendment of the law; but the amendment of morals is highly requisite. "The present order of things" is not to be blamed; but they are to be blamed who charge the faults of their conduct to wrong systems, instead of charging them to their wrong hearts. Revolutionists, either in civil or religious matters, are often to be suspected. In their harsh attempts to repair the building, they frequently subvert the very foundation. In their amputations and excisions, they cut off the vital parts, and thus destroy the very life of the body. As they act under a plausible pretext, they can take advantage of public credulity, and proceed to almost every extravagance. Another misery with religious revolutionists, is, that they never know when and where to stop. We may consent to go with them as far as the old version will authorize; but when we shall have arrived at a limit, they can easily substitute a new version, and by the help of this can raise us over mountains of difficulty. Wesley found predestination and election so strongly blended with the common version of the New Testament, that he applied himself to the task of making a new translation. The Unitarians, finding the old version rather a dead weight upon them, constructed a new dress for the Testament, from which the more offensive features of the ancient readings were carefully expunged. And now Mr. Campbell has a version, the fabric of which was not woven by himself, but collected in fragments and stitched together. Some of these patches he has borrowed from his old Scottish name-sake, Dr. George Campbell, a very different man from himself; some from Macknight, some from Doddridge, and we know not from how many more. It is obvious that, as the great and good men named above, made out their respective versions to suit their own views of Scripture, there can be very little uniformity in a book composed of such various materials. Why is it that all innovators become tired of the old version and seek new ones? Some, who were not innovators, have made new translations of the Bible, or parts thereof; but none of the leaders of innovation so far as we know, have remained contented with the old-fashioned Book in its present dress."—*Col. Star.*

It gives me pleasure always to acknowledge a favor, and to give a person credit for all that he is worth. I thank Mr. Brantly for this notice.

What he has written in the above remarks he prefaces thus:—

REFORMATION.—The last number of the Millennial Harbinger contains the following sentence at page 81, which seems designed for our attention:—

"*The Rule of Life of the Columbian Star.*—I know not why it is that Mr. Brantly is so much attached to the present order of things, while complaining so much of its inefficiency, and why he should at one time talk as if friendly to a reformation, and at another exhort his readers to keep in the good old way, alluding to the way of their grandfathers, or ancestors for two or three generations. A little light on this subject would be acceptable. We would thank him to say whether any reformation in the system of things is necessary; and, if any, in how many particulars his reformation would consist."

I must give him credit for possessing a great degree of art—yes, of *art*. It is not the art displayed on one occasion, but on many occasions, which I admire. We admire art, although exhibited against honesty and candor; and while admiring, we only regret that it is not displayed on the side of truth and goodness. In a very artful manner this gentleman substitutes a string of opinions, and calls them *the present order of things*, and thus evades the whole subject presented to him in the paragraph he cites.

This is certainly a new order of things which consists in the *doctrinal views* most prevalent in the churches of our persuasion. It is the first time that I have heard a number of abstractions, purely sentimental, called *an order of things*. I will define what I mean by the phrase *order of things* in the connexion in which this phrase appeared. The present order of things amongst the Regular Baptists is this:—A person applies for baptism. He is called before the church, at its Saturday monthly meeting. He is interrogated respecting his conversion. He relates all that he has felt and thought, more or less, since the time of the commencement of a "*work of grace*" upon his heart. After being examined to the satisfaction of the church, the question is put—"Ought the candidate to be baptized?" If the church, or a majority of them *present*, give a verdict in his favor, he may then be immersed. He is then immersed *in the name of the Trinity* on a suitable occasion, and joins the church. This church of which he is a member meets statedly once a month in its church capacity. After meeting on the Lord's day, and talking over the affairs of the neighborhood out of doors for a while, the preacher calls them into the house, either by going into the pulpit or giving out a hymn. They sing a few stanzas of a hymn or song, the precentor or the choir, as the case may be, standing, and the congregation sitting. This ended, the preacher prays *for the people*, and for a sermon, sometimes *for a text*, and for the conversion of the converted. Then comes the sermon, homily, or discourse, explanatory of some word, phrase, or verse found somewhere in the Old or New Testament. Sometimes it is the saying of an angel, a good man; sometimes the saying of a wicked man, and sometimes the saying of the *****. [I must here declare that I did positively hear a sermon delivered before an Association from the words of a demoniac or person possessed of a demon.] The sermon ended, a prayer is made for a blessing upon the seed sown, or the doctrine delivered; a song is sung, and the benediction is pronounced.—Home they go.

I will say nothing about the order of things in the families of those who have been worshipping God in worshipping a *preacher*, or in sitting once a month under the allegories and comments of a person who, five times in seven, cannot tell the nominative case to a verb, or the antecedent to a relative. I never did disdain, nor did I ever cast a disdainful look upon a brother because he was illiterate. Nay, so far from it, I have generally encouraged them "to improve their gifts." But I cannot compliment any illiterate man for assuming the office of an interpreter, or expositor of Scripture. Men may proclaim Jesus, and exhibit the reasons why they believe on him; they may preach Christ successfully without English, Latin, or Greek, just in the language of the nursery; but to hear such a man expounding texts or explaining scripture, is a burlesque on the pulpit and a satire upon the age. Yet a large proportion of our preachers, are not content with being preachers; however illiterate, they must make sermons, and become pulpit commentators.

Once a quarter, often once in six months, there is a *sacrament*. The table is spread, and bread and wine placed upon it. The preacher breaks the bread into crumbs, talking all the while about the eucharist; and after prayer the deacons carry it round upon plates. *None of the disciples break the loaf.* The consecrated hands of the pastor alone is privileged thus to handle it. Then a cup is carried round by the deacons, whose sole office it is to wait upon the pastor to help to serve the tables.

The sacrament being over, all things continue as they were; the people dress and mount their horses, walk, or ride in carriages, as it happens, once a month, to hear a text explained, and often as much to see their relatives, neighbors, and friends, as to hear the sermon. Their children are generally left to the Lord to be converted; for if embraced in the atonement or the election of the party, they are "insured."

But now and then a missionary, a Sunday school agent, a temperance preacher, or a tract eulogizer, makes them a visit. He tells a good story of the scheme, and inculcates liberality. He inspires the people with his spirit. If he is on the tract expedition he gets up a society. A president, directors, and a treasurer are wanting. This serves to gratify the pride of some of the wealthier sort. It also serves for a theme of conversation, discussion, and religious talk on Sunday. By the time they have worn out, or got tired of this religious plaything, (for religion has its toys,) a *temperate* preacher announces temperance as the order of the day. This is a good work, and there must be some other society, other than the church of God, created upon a new bond of union, and upon a new principle of co-operation. Officers for this are wanting, and a new knighthood is formed. If the rich in the neighborhood were all taken into the first order of dignitaries, rather than take into this new communion the virtuous poor, they conclude to double or treble title some of the order of St. Dominic. They will confer the ribbon or the garter upon dignitaries of the Tract or some other fraternity. The people become temperate, and the question has been decided that this is a good institution. Then comes the training of "pious youths for the gospel ministry," and the importance of education is discussed. An education society is wanting, and pious youths, who want to rise to the dignity of pastors, are sought after. Many are found, but few can be qualified for the want of money! The missionary cause and its agents come always before us. The poor pagan cannot be saved without the gospel, though Mr. Brantly admits they may be regenerated without the word of God! And what shall I more say? for time would fail me to tell of Gideon, Barak, and Samson—to tell of the Sunday School Union—of things domestic and foreign—of the cessation of Sunday mails, and of all the benevolent enterprizes of the age. These generally are a part of the present order of things. This I give as a sample, and it is but a sample of the present order of things among the Baptists.

In the mean time the people are not instructed in the Holy Writings; they are ignorant I say comparatively, and generally they are ignorant of the message of God to the world. The consequence of this ignorance is a deadness and coldness in the whole profession. The love of the world and the honor that comes from man leave little room in the affections for the love of God and the joys of his salvation. Light cheers, quickens, animates. The light of salvation gives life. But the dead, and the obdurate, and the disconsolate, are under the dominion of darkness.

By the fruits of the popular order of things I judge of its character. I well know the history of the Baptist churches, as well as of many of the Paidobaptist. I will not write a history of one of them at this time; but I may yet give the history of a few for a sample if Mr. Brantly will affirm that I have not given a fair outline of the present order of things. I do not say that every church in the Baptist connexion is exactly represented in the preceding outline; but one thing I will say, that more than the nine-tenths of them in half the states of the union where I have formed an acquaintance with them, are fairly represented in this hasty sketch. In lieu of this order of things, Mr. Brantly gives us a list of their opinions, and all the reformation he wants is to see them acting up to these opinions. Now I do know many individuals living up to these opinions, as far as one can live up to opinions so contradictory to each other, and I know of none professing the christian name less to be envied than they. I presume Mr. Brantly lives up to these opinions, and what are the effects of them upon his mind and behavior, and upon his church? I leave those best acquainted to answer this question. But read the Star! Behold the system! Behold the man! I dare say that Mr. Brantly is as good a man as the system can produce.

I will not now repeat what has been so often said in the preceding volumes upon the items of opinion in Mr. Brantly's present order of things. I confess that with many of these opinions I agree as I do with Mr. Locke or Mr. Reed in their philosophy, or with Sir Isaac Newton in his *Principia*. And viewed in the light of Mr. Brantly's optics, they are as inefficient to reform the world, as the doctrine of Sir Isaac was to change the transit of a star or the orbit of a comet. I do not, indeed, understand what Mr. Brantly means in some expressions—such as, "coming into the exercise of faith"—"the total depravation of human nature"—"the death of Christ, the foundation of pacification"—"the Spirit's ordinarily employing the word of God as the instrumental action in regeneration"—"immersion, the figure or symbol of salvation"—Past salvation or future salvation, as respects the moment of immersion?—Say? "The Baptist church, a religious commonwealth"—"the efficacy of faithful prayer."

There is such a new-fangledness and awkwardness in this phraseology—such an unintelligibility about it, that it requires for me a commentator. I know it will puzzle even Mr. Brantly to explain some of these *tertium quid* phrases. Suppose the following questions were asked him Where was faith before the exercise of faith? How does a person come into the exercise of any principle? Does "total" mean entire and perfect? Has it any parts or degrees? Can the most impious wretch be any thing more than totally depraved? Is the newborn infant as depraved as the vilest sinner that lives? Does atonement mean God's pacification to us, or our pacification to him? Is the death of Christ an atonement of God to us, or our atonement or reconciliation to God? Is not God reconciling us to himself by the sacrifice of his Son for our sins? Can there be two seeds of the same plant—two seeds of the same animal—two instrumental actions or means of regeneration? Can there be an ordinary instrumental action of regeneration, and an extraordinary instrumental action of regeneration? Does not the Apostle Peter declare that the word of God is the incorruptible seed of regeneration? What new seed is this which you have found, Mr. Brantly?

My dear sir, permit me to assure you that there needs no witness to depose that you have drunk too deeply into human systems. The Oracle of God you have seen through the glasses of a system, which have given a new and strange hue to the whole volume. Pull off your glasses and read with the naked eye and see what a different colored volume it is!

What means "immersion in the name of the Trinity?" Is there any act—was there ever any act instituted as a figure of what we had formerly received, of any gift or favor bestowed upon us? Is faithful prayer and "the prayer of faith" equivalent? What means the answer of a good conscience through a symbol?" Explain, if you please. Your correspondent (Mr. Clopton) talks about "high-sounding words of vanity." I would thank him or you to show that these are not unintelligible sounds, words without ideas, which neither yourself nor one of your readers can explain. So much for your "order of things," or new order of expressions.

There is one great truth, and I will always pick up a truth as I would a diamond out of the mud—I say there is one great truth in your second section. It is this: "That which is true in Mr. Campbell's system is not new, and that which is new is not true." I know there is an ambiguity in this sentence. But in its common meaning it is most true. Suppose it had read, That which is true in religion is not new, that which is new in religion is not true, I would have said a hearty Amen. The fault I have found with the popular schemes of religion is well expressed by Mr. Brantly in this antithesis. They are all too new for me. I have said, as every reader of these volumes knows, that nothing in religion is worth a thought which is not as old as the New Testament. Has Mr. Brantly agreed with me at last—what is new in religion is not true!! This was my starting point in the year 1810. It is found minutely detailed in the first and second volumes of this work. I am all for the old things—not Mr. Brantly's old things, some of which are not older than the fortieth year of Andrew Fuller. Old things may become new, however. Many of the positions of Luther and Calvin were called new, and were new, at the era of the Reformation; but yet they were as old as the era of Christianity itself.

Some new things in "my system" may be true. Many things said about the modes of preaching and teaching are as new as the practices, and therefore may be true; for both that which is opposed and that which opposes are of recent date. But this is a mere criticism on the phraseology. What Mr. Brantly means is true. I understand him to mean that all new things in religion are false, and that whatever is true is as old as the religion. I request all my readers to bear this concession of my most inexorable opponent in long remembrance.

Bad hearts are next complained of. "It is not new systems, but new hearts that we need." True it may be of many, and, for aught I know, of many of the popular preachers. But I go upon this principle, that the heart is not to be cured by a charm, nor to be purified by false notions. Therefore, I contend for the ancient gospel—the gospel found in the New Testament, because it is the wisdom of God and the power of God to purify the heart. Neither Calvinism, Fullerism, Arminianism, nor any human system can purify the heart; for very wicked men have been indoctrinated into all these systems. None, however, believe and obey the gospel whose hearts are not purified; for God purifies the hearts of men by believing the gospel. This is the reason faith purifies the heart, for it brings the truth of God into the heart.

Then comes Wesley's, the Unitarian's, and some other versions of the New Testament. Then comes the denunciation against the New Version—the wholesale denunciation. Who can stand before envy? Let me here say, and let me be put to the proof, that there is no important item for which I contend that I cannot prove from the worst version I ever saw. I will take the common version and meet Mr. Brantly on any one item he chooses to select—Baptism for the remission of sins, if he pleases. Yes, the common version will sustain, ably sustain me in every point; and I will predict, that, upon this point and many others, Mr. Brantly will call upon the aid of new versions before I call for help. I look upon all that is said on the subject of the New Version by Mr. Brantly as most illiberal, uncalled for, and insupportable. It exhibits a rancor and a spirit of denunciation more becoming his Holiness than a Protestant. I am always prepared to defend not only the New Version which I have published, but the necessity of new versions for the confirmation of the faith and the enlargement of the views of christians. There is not a commentator in christendom that has not given as much of a new version as I have done. Not one catholic or protestant who has not attempted to correct a thousand times the version on which he wrote. Nay, Mr. Brantly must be a *rara avis in terris simillima nigroque cycno* (in plain English a black swan,) if he has not in his pulpit harangues often attempted to improve the version. But these remarks were intended to prejudice those who have not examined the version both against the publisher and the work. I am an innovator and the version is an innovation. I am glad that in these volumes will be found the preface to the king's version, a very scarce document in this day. From that preface, written by the publisher of the king's version, it will appear that all Mr. Brantly has said, in spirit and substance, was said by the opposers of the present version.— The common version was introduced by *authority* in defiance of all objections. Is not this a fact, Mr. Brantly? Was it not more objected to than the reading of the New Version? Surely he is not so ignorant of the history of the versions of the bible as not to know that not one

was ever introduced without much opposition. Mr. Brantly takes the same ground to oppose myself and the version I have published on which the Catholics stood in all their opposition to all the new translations. They said all the *innovators* wanted new versions.* Wickliffe (*we* call) the first reformer [the Catholics call him the heretical innovator, John Wickliffe] published a translation just to suit his own views. This was the first English bible. An innovator he was, and the bible he published was an innovation upon the Church of Rome.

Tyndal, A. D. 1526, another innovator and heretic, published an English version of the New Testament. The bishops of England condemned it; King Harry proscribed it; the bishops bought up and burned all they could find; the laity would read it, and the king and the clergy had their hands full to keep the people in the dark. In ten years five editions were sold in Holland. The king proposed a new translation, but the bishops opposed it; and in spite of both, the people got to understand the scriptures better than their teachers. The same version, dressed up a little, and called "Thomas Matthews' Testament," when recommended by archbishop Cranmer, took with the clergy; and when they found the people would have it, they said it was a good version, and took off all restraints against the reading of it.

Luther and Beza—indeed, all the *innovators,* now called *reformers,* either gave new versions, or aided in giving them. So that the Catholics and Mr. Brantly have good reason to lament that all innovators gave new versions. [See the History of the Bible, vol. 2.] Well may he ask, "Why is it that all innovators become tired of the old version and seek new ones?" All reformers hitherto have had occasion to lament that the people, either through imperfect translations, or through the want of translations, were kept under the dominion of the clergy!

Had I made a version myself it might have been said, with more plausibility, I was tired of the old one. I chose rather to collect a version already made by men, that Mr. Brantly called "great and good." His commendation of them, however, goes not very far with me. But those who look to him for instruction will please remember that Mr. Brantly calls the authors of the New Version *great and good men.* But see what sort of men are great and good in Mr. Brantly's calendar; such as make a translation "to suit their own views." "These great and good men," says he, "made out their respective versions to suit their own views." So did the king's translators—so did Beza. They pleased the king, the court, and the bishops of England. But it is *gratuitous* to say that Drs. Campbell, Macknight, and Doddridge made a version to suit their own views; for none of them strove to sustain their own sect farther than their prejudices directed them, and two of them, (Campbell and Macknight) rose as far above the sectarian feeling as any translators in ancient and modern times. Dr. George Campbell was a very different man from Mr. Brantly and A. Campbell, it is true. But that cannot be helped; and I know not why any two men, born at different periods, and educated in different schools, are to be blamed for not being item per item the same.

I think I have not passed over a single item worthy of a remark in this Mr. Brantly's *present*

* So early as A. D. 1160, Peter Waldus, an innovator and heretic, attempted a translation of the Four Gospels into the French language. We call him a great and good man.

order of things. As I have thanked him for this notice he has taken of me, I will thank him twice if he will be as liberal to his readers as I have been to mine. Let them once hear me in his paper as I have let mine hear him, *in extenso.*

I am not afraid (because I have nothing to lose) to permit my readers to hear all that can be said against my views and my deeds. This has always been my course. This hasty sketch appears in this paper to make room for Mr. Clopton's No. 2, in the fourth number of the Harbinger. The cause I plead cannot be defeated by its enemies: retard it they may. They cannot make a *sect* of us as we shall show. We have more to fear from our friends than from our enemies. Let them act with christian prudence and in a christian spirit, then their efforts cannot fail.

EDITOR.

Concluding Remarks.
Part of the Editor's History.

To the co-operation of a few friends, under the divine government, is to be ascribed the success which has accompanied this first effort to restore a pure speech to the people of God—to restore the ancient order of things in the christian kingdom—to emancipate the conscience from the dominion of human authority in matters of religion, and to lay a foundation, an imperishable foundation, for the union of all christians, and for their co-operation in spreading the glorious gospel throughout the world. I had but very humble hopes, I can assure the public, the day I wrote the first essay or the preface for this work, that I could at all succeed in gaining a patient hearing. But I have been entirely disappointed. The success attendant on this effort has produced a hope which once I dared not entertain, that a blissful revolution can be effected. It has actually begun, and such a one as cannot fail to produce a state of society far surpassing in the fruits of righteousness, and peace, and joy, any result of any former religious revolution, since the great apostacy from christian institutions.

Having been educated as Presbyterian clergymen generally are, and looking forward to the ministry as both an honorable and useful calling, all my expectations and prospects in future life were, at the age of twenty-one, identified with the office of the ministry. But scarcely had I begun to make sermons, when I discovered that the religion of the New Testament was one thing, and that of any sect which I knew was another. I could not proceed. An unsuccessful effort by my father to reform the presbytery and synod to which he belonged, made me despair of reformation. I gave it up as a hopeless effort: but did not give up speaking in public assemblies upon the great articles of christian faith and practice. In the hope, the humble hope, of erecting a single congregation with which I could enjoy the social institutions, I labored. I had not the remotest idea of being able to do more than this; and, therefore, I betook myself to the occupation of a farmer, and for a number of years attended to this profession as a means of subsistence, and labored every Lord's day to separate the truth from the traditions of men, and to persuade men to give up their fables for the truth—with but little success I labored.

When pressed by some of the most influential Baptists in the cities of New York and Philadelphia, in the year 1816, to settle in one of those cities, I declined the friendly offers and kind persuasions of both deacon Withington of New York and deacon Shields of Philadelphia, alledging that I could not take the charge of any

church in those cities, because I did not think they would submit to the government of Jesus Christ, or to the primitive order of things. They asked me what that order was? I gave them my views. To which neither of them objected.— Deacon Withington alluded to Mr. M'Clay's church in that city as practising in part that order; and said that for himself he preferred it. I replied that however well disposed he might be towards it, I could not think that many of the members of that church would (Mr. Williams' it was then,) and rather than produce divisions among them, or adopt the order of things then fashionable in that city, I would live and die in the backwoods. The same or similar remarks were made to deacon Shields in Philadelphia.

Such were my views and feelings at that time, and so slight were the hopes which I entertained of seeing the least impression made upon the kingdom of the clergy. But my own mind labored under the pernicious influence of scholastic divinity, and the Calvinian metaphysics; and although I greatly desired to stand perfect and complete in the knowledge of the will of God, and my conscience could bow to nothing but the authority of the King Eternal, yet a full emancipation from the traditions of the elders I had not experienced. This was as gradual as the approaches of spring.

In the year 1820, when solicited to meet Mr. Walker on the subject of baptism, I hesitated for about six months whether it were lawful thus to defend the truth. I was written to three times before I gained my own consent. I did not like controversy so well as many have since thought I did; and I was doubtful of the effects it might have upon society. These difficulties were, however overcome, and we met. It was not until after I discovered the effects of that discussion that I began to hope that something might be done to rouse this generation from its supineness and spiritual lethargy. About two years afterwards I conceived the plan of this work, and thought I should make the experiment. I did so, and the effects are now before the public.

Little is done, it is true, compared with what is yet to be done; but that little is a great deal compared with the opposition made, and the shortness of the time in which it has been done. He that sails against both wind and tide sails slowly, and if he advance at all it must be by great exertion of the mariners. The storm now rages more than at any former period; but the current is more favorable. The winds of doctrine are raging upon the great sea; but they are continually shifting, and though we may be tossed and driven sometimes out of our course, the vessel is good, the Pilot the most skilful, so we cannot fear to reach the desired haven.

Many apologies ought to be made for the execution of the prospectus of this work. Things changed so much from our expectations that we were compelled to change with them. Our series of essays upon more topics were much shorter, and longer between, than was contemplated. The publication of two debates, and of two editions of the New Testament, unexpected when we issued our proposals, distracted our attentions, and so increased my labors, that more was done than could be done well. The compositions for this work were almost universally written in the despatch of ordinary letter writing, the half of an essay being often in type, or in the press, before the other half of it was conceived or written. During the last two months we have issued three numbers of the Millennial Harbinger, and this is the sixth number of this work, in nearly the same period. Besides we have written scores of long letters. These things ought not to have been so, but a willingness to do all that the most unremitting attentions could do, and the demands upon our services in various departments having been so urgent, we were compelled to undertake too much. We hope to avoid these excesses of labor in future, and to rally and concentrate our energies upon one work.

Many subjects introduced into this work have not been fully and systematically discussed. General views have been submitted, rather than full developements and defences. Not a single topic has received that finish, or that elucidation which it is in the compass of our means to bestow upon it. I have thought if life should be prolonged, and an opportunity offer, that I would one day revise this work, and have a second edition of it published, with such emendations as experience and observation might suggest.*

I have commenced a new work, and taken a new name for it on various accounts. Hating sects and sectarian names, I resolved to prevent the name of Christian Baptists from being fixed

* I do not recollect having seen this sentence until now, when half of the work is stereotyped; and I certainly never heard the editor express this determination. However, it is not very remarkable that we should arrive at the same judgment in reference to the revision and republication of a work which has done so much good.—PUBLISHER.

4 I

upon us, to do which efforts were making. It is true, men's tongues are their own, and they may use them as they please; but I am resolved to give them no just occasion for nicknaming advocates for the ancient order of things. My sheet admonishes me that I must close, and as usual on such occasions, I ought to return thanks to all those who have aided in the circulation of this work and patronized it, were it not that I cannot consider it as a favor done to me. Those who write for a subsistence should feel grateful to those who sustain them; but the patrons of this work, its real friends, were actuated by other considerations, than personal respect for me; and as it was not to sustain an individual, but to promote the truth, they bestowed their patronage, I can only say that the God of truth has blessed them, and will bless them, having acted sincerely in this matter. To him I commend them, and to him to whom I owe my being, and all that I call mine, to whom I have vowed allegiance never to be recalled, to him I will now and forever ascribe praise for the good which he has made me to enjoy, and for the good, if any, he has enabled me to do to others. I have found myself blessed in this undertaking—my heart has been enlarged, and no reader of the Christian Baptist, I think, will ever derive more advantage from it, than I have from the writing and conducting of it. To Jesus Christ my Lord be everlasting praise.   EDITOR.

97

END OF VOLUME VII.